HISTORICAL STATISTICS OF CANADA

SECOND EDITION

F. H. LEACY
EDITOR

M. C. URQUHART
EDITOR
AND
K. A. H. BUCKLEY
ASSISTANT EDITOR
FIRST EDITION

Published by Statistics Canada
in joint sponsorship with the
Social Science Federation of Canada

Statistics Canada   Statistique Canada

A wide range of socio-economic data
Statistics Canada, the nation's central statistical agency, provides social and economic data and analysis used for planning, evaluation, research and decision-making. Information produced and disseminated by the agency describes most of the characteristics, conditions and activities of Canadians. Data are provided in a variety of forms and special tabulations are available.

The agency also offers consultative services that assist users to locate statistics and to employ them as effectively as possible.

How to obtain more information
Statistics Canada's advisory services are available at regional reference centres across Canada. Inquiries about this publication, or about any other of Statistics Canada's programs and services, should be directed to the regional office nearest you.

The following symbols are used in this edition:
— nil or zero
.. not available (this symbol was not used in the first edition)
e estimate
r revised
x figure not given for reasons of confidentiality

Statistics Canada should be credited when reproducing or quoting any part of this document

© Minister of Supply and Services Canada 1983

Available in Canada through

Authorized Bookstore Agents
and other bookstores

or by mail from

Canadian Government Publishing Centre
Supply and Services Canada
Ottawa, Canada, K1A 0S9

Catalogue No. CS11-516E   Canada: $60.00
ISBN 0-660-11259-0   Other countries: $72.00

Price subject to change without notice

Statistics and History

As the current Chief Statistician of Canada, it is my pleasure to be able to comment on this historical document, which was started well before my tenure.

In the press of rapidly changing current events, and with the need and desire to provide statistical services relevant to those events, it is essential to sustain an historical perspective. This volume, a joint product of the Social Science Federation of Canada and Statistics Canada, contributes to that perspective.

Just as current statistical information provides the foundation and matrix for identification of current societal issues, for policy formulation and for program monitoring, so also does historical statistics help portray the realities of Canadian history.

In this volume, one can trace the historical conditions of Canadians respecting inflation, housing, employment, health, education, balance of payments — all matters of current relevance.

This volume also displays the many changing complexities and difficulties of statistical measurement of social, economic, institutional and environmental phenomena. Concepts, definitions, design, methods, and processing procedures must be evolved over time, but with balanced attention to consistency among statistical series and to continuity over time.

I want to express my appreciation to all those who contributed to this work — some are further identified in the following foreward and preface. In particular, Professor M.C. Urquhart deserves unique thanks for his persistence in the production of this work.

Martin B. Wilk

FOREWORD

This volume, like its predecessor, contains a wide range of economic, social and political data and a considerable amount of material descriptive of the data for the period from Confederation to the mid-1970s. The justification for the preparation of such a compendium has been amply demonstrated by the breadth of circulation and use of the original edition. This edition, like the earlier volume, is the result of a wide collaboration involving many persons from the academic community and from the public service.

The sponsors, on this occasion, have been the Social Science Federation of Canada and Statistics Canada. The Social Science Federation appointed a Steering Committee to set broad policy with respect to content and to arrange for the appointment of section authors and their advisors; it also paid half of the salary of the chief officer of the project, Mr. Leacy. Statistics Canada provided all other financial and material support of the project, including support of its staff, provision of office space, and processing of material to an advanced state in what is ordinarily considered the publication process. Statistics Canada, of course, also provided much help with the data themselves through its subject matter divisions.

It is impossible to acknowledge individually the contributions of the host of people who helped in the project in one way or another—we can make only a general although most genuine expression of gratitude to them for their part in the undertaking. However, a special acknowledgement must be made of the debt of the project to Mr. Frank Leacy and Mr. D.A. Worton.

Mr. Leacy's contribution has been indispensable. He was in effect the chief executive officer of the project, with full responsibility for co-ordinating and aiding the work of the section chiefs, for arranging for much of the substantive work on the tables to be done in Statistics Canada and other parts of the public service, and for guiding the preparation of the text through a considerable part of the publishing process. But his work went far beyond this. It is in the nature of such a project that some parts of the project stall or lag. In such circumstances, Mr. Leacy did much of the preparation of text and of materials in the tables himself. He wrote the texts for four of the sections and redrafted those for two others. He did the major part of the preparation of the tables for five sections and prepared at least some tables in most other sections. Without his effort there would not have been a volume. We owe him our special gratitude.

Mr. D.A. Worton, Assistant Chief Statistician, Statistics Canada, made the arrangements for the support of the project in Statistics Canada, for collaboration in these arrangements with the Social Science Federation and for publication and also provided general encouragement and support for the project from the beginning. His understanding of the problems encountered in carrying out the project, his work on the time-consuming task of changing arrangements in Statistics Canada as parts of the project beyond his control were delayed, and his facilitation of work within Statistics Canada itself have made all of us greatly indebted to him.

Finally, acknowledgement should be made of the contribution of those who participated in the preparation of the first volume. Much of the material of that volume is reproduced in the new edition. Since a list of participants in the preparation of the first volume is reproduced in this new edition, it is not necessary to name them here. However, we take the occasion to acknowledge Kenneth Buckley's outstanding contribution to both volumes through his work as assistant editor of the first edition and as author of three of its sections.

M.C. Urquhart
Chairman, Steering Committee
Historical Statistics Project

March 26, 1979

Postscript

After the above foreword was written, at the time of completion of the section manuscripts, it turned out the publication process took longer than anticipated. The camera-ready copy needed extensive tidying up and correction in its format and these tasks took longer than expected. These matters led to a regrettably long delay in publication date. The project is most indebted to Miss Frances O'Malley of Statistics Canada for her heroic efforts in revising the form of the camera-ready copy and in arranging for the translations and to Mr. Lorne Rowebottom, Mr. Jeffrey Holmes and Mr. Tim. C. Davis of Statistics Canada for taking in hand the publication arrangements in 1982 and carrying them through with dispatch.

Most regrettably Mr. Leacy has not lived to see the results of his labours in published form. His death occurred shortly after he had completed his work on the project in 1979. This volume then becomes a memorial to him.

M.C.U.

June 30, 1982

PREFACE TO SECOND EDITION

The purpose of the present volume is to bring up-to-date the material from the first edition of *Historical Statistics of Canada,* which was published by the Macmillan Company of Canada, Toronto, in 1965. In the course of preparing the present edition, it became apparent that a substantial number of new series and important revisions of older series had become available since 1960, the last date of most of the series in the original volume. Thus the present edition is both an updating and a revision of the first edition.

The first and second editions are similar with respect to the self-contained nature of the text and tables. In most cases there is a sufficient description of the content of the individual series to enable the reader to use them without reference to the numerous basic sources. The contents of the editions are also alike, the only exceptions being now more distinctly identified sections on Vital Statistics and Health; Social Security; Minerals; and Energy.

A few series which terminated prior to 1960 have not been reproduced in the present volume and lengthy lists of earlier source material have also been dropped. In such cases, the necessary references have been provided to locate the source material in the first edition.

The organization of textual material in the new edition follows closely that of the first, providing information on each section's contents, the principal sources of material, and general explanatory notes regarding the statistics. The majority of the series in the present volume end in 1975, although a few series have been updated to 1976 or 1977.

Brief history of the second edition

The project to revise the first edition was initiated in 1974, under the joint sponsorship of the Social Science Federation of Canada (formerly the Social Science Research Council of Canada) and Statistics Canada. A Policy Steering Committee was formed, consisting of the following members:

M.C. Urquhart, Queen's University, (Chairman);
Yves Dubé, Laval University;
D.G.G. Kerr, University of Western Ontario;
Gilles Paquet, Carleton University;
A.M. Sinclair, Dalhousie University;
D.A. Worton, Statistics Canada;
John Banks, Social Science Research Council of Canada (Secretary).

Subsequently, Mr. Jan Loubser of the Social Science Federation replaced Mr. John Banks on the Steering Committee and Mr. Frank H. Leacy was appointed editor and co-ordinator of the project. Office space, facilities and staff were provided by Statistics Canada which also took responsibility for proofreading, typesetting and preparation of the final copy.

The section chiefs were appointed by the Steering Committee and they in turn chose panel members to assist in the determination of content specifications. The work on actually obtaining and compiling the statistics was overseen by the co-ordinator through the various subject-matter divisions of Statistics Canada, other government departments and agencies, or various outside sources.

Sincere thanks for hard work, patience and persistence to all those who participated in the production of this volume.

CONTENTS

Contents

Second Edition

SECTION CHIEFS AND PANEL MEMBERS

The affiliation of the section chiefs, panel members and others who helped directly in the preparation of the volume is that at the time that the main work of preparing the material was done. Some of those listed will have a different affiliation at the time the volume appears.

Section A: Population and Migration

Section Chief:

K.G. BASAVARAJAPPA.   Director, Population Estimates and Projections Division, Statistics Canada.

Acknowledgments:

J. HENRIPIN.   Department of Demography, University of Montreal.
BALI RAM.   Census Characteristics Division, Statistics Canada.
A. ROMANIUC.   Director. Census Characteristics Division, Statistics Canada.

Section B: Vital Statistics and Health

Section Chief:

R.D. FRASER.   Department of Economics, Queen's University.

Panel members:

GERARD BELANGER.   Department of Economics, Laval University.
J.B. DAVIS.   Assistant Director, Health Division, Statistics Canada
ROBERT EVANS.   Department of Economics, University of British Columbia.
W.A. MENNIE.   Director, Health Economics and Statistics Division, Health and Welfare Canada.

Section C: Social Security

Section Chief:

T. RUSSELL ROBINSON.   Health and Welfare Canada.

Panel members:

EDWARD PAZDZIOR.   Health and Welfare Canada.
WILLIAM T. STANBURY.   Faculty of Commerce and Business Administration, University of British Columbia.
KAREN L. TRAVERSY.   Health and Welfare Canada.
CHARLES B. WALKER.   Health and Welfare Canada.

Section D: the Labour Force

Section Chief:

FRANK T. DENTON.   Department of Economics, McMaster University.

Panel members:

PETER HICKS.   Director, Labour Force Survey Division, Statistics Canada.
T. MARVIN MCINNIS.   Department of Economics, Queen's University.
JOHN VANDERKAMP.   Department of Economics, University of Guelph.

Section E: Wages and Working Conditions

Section Chief:

NOAH M. MELTZ.   Centre for Industrial Relations, University of Toronto.

Section F: Gross National Product and the Capital Stock

Section Chief:

R.B. CROZIER.   Economic Council of Canada, Ottawa.

Panel members:

BARBARA CLIFT.   Gross National Product Division, Statistics Canada.
P. KOUMANAKOS.   Construction Division, Statistics Canada.
B. MCCORMICK.   Input-Output Division, Statistics Canada.
M.C. URQUHART.   Department of Economics, Queen's University.
H. WASLANDER.   Economic Council of Canada.

Section G: The Balance of International Payments, International Investment Position and Foreign Trade

Section Chief:

B.W. WILKINSON.   Department of Economics, University of Alberta.

Panel members:

ROBERT ANKLI.   Department of Economics, University of Guelph.
E.B. CARTY.   Balance of Payments Division, Statistics Canada.
S.F. KALISKI.   Department of Economics, Queen's University.
CLARKE LEITH.   Department of Economics, University of Western Ontario.
D.K. MCALISTER.   Director, Balance of Payments Division, Statistics Canada.
J.D. RANDALL.   Director, Financial Flows Division, Statistics Canada.
J. RYTEN.   Director General, General Statistics Branch, Statistics Canada.

Section H: Government Finance

Section Chief:

RICHARD M. BIRD.   Institute for Policy Analysis, University of Toronto.

Panel members:

D.A.L. AULD.   Department of Economics, University of Guelph.
GILLES PAQUET.   Department of Political Science, Carleton University.
DAVID B. PERRY.   Canadian Tax Foundation, Toronto.
J.B. SMITH.   Director, Public Finance Division, Statistics Canada.

Special Acknowledgment:

D.J. BAILEY.   Labour Division, Statistics Canada.

Panel members:

RUSSELL BELL.   Canadian Labour Congress, Ottawa.
JEAN-FRANCOIS GOUTRAM.   Department of Economics, Laval University.
CECIL HARPER.   Labour Canada.

Section J: Banking and Finance

Section Chief:

JOHN CHANT.   Department of Economics, Carleton University.

Panel members:

DAVID BOND.   Consumer and Corporate Affairs Canada.
JOHN GRANT.   Wood Gundy Limited, Toronto.
W.A. McKAY.   Chief, Department of Banking and Financial Analysis, Bank of Canada.
J.L. MIGNE.   Department of Economics, Laval University.
J.D. RANDALL.   Director, Financial Flows Division, Statistics Canada.
RON SHEARER.   Department of Economics, University of British Columbia.

Special Acknowledgments:

POLLY KIMBER.   Department of Banking and Financial Analysis, Bank of Canada.
STUART McLEOD.   Business Finance Division, Statistics Canada.
GORDON THIESSEN.   Chief, Department of Banking and Financial Analysis, Bank of Canada.

Section K: Price Indexes

Section Chief:

A.D. HOLMES.   formerly Director, Prices Division, Statistics Canada.

Panel members:

A. ASIMAKOPOLIS.   Department of Economics, McGill University.
MARCEL DAGENAIS.   Department of Economics, University of Montreal.
ANTHEA FOSTER.   Prices Division, Statistics Canada.

Section L: Lands and Forests

Section Chief:

B.S. OSBORNE.   Department of Geography, Queen's University.

Section M: Agriculture

Section Chief:

G.I. TRANT.   Agriculture Canada.

Panel members:

R.H. CAMPBELL.   Agriculture Division, Statistics Canada.
I.F. FURNISS.   Economics Branch, Agriculture Canada.
L.R. RIGAUX.   Department of Economics, University of Manitoba.
J-P. WAMPACH.   Department of Economics, Laval University.

Section N: Fisheries

Section Chief:

NORMAN MORSE.   Department of Economics, Dalhousie University.

Panel members:

PARZIVAL COPES.   Department of Economics, Simon Fraser University.
D.A. MacLEAN.   Fisheries and Marine Service, Fisheries and Environment Canada, Halifax.

Section P: Mining

Section Chief:

G.D. QUIRIN.   Faculty of Management Studies, University of Toronto.

Section Q: Energy and Electric Power

Section Chief:

G.D. QUIRIN.   Faculty of Management Studies, University of Toronto.

Panel members:

PAUL BRADLEY.   Department of Economics, University of British Columbia.
JOSEPH DeBANNE.   Department of Business Administration, University of Ottawa.

Section R: Manufactures

Section Chief:

JOHN A. SAWYER.   Institute for Policy Analysis, University of Toronto.

Acknowledgments:

A.D. AMERY.   Dupont of Canada, Toronto.
D.G. CAMPBELL.   Manufacturing and Primary Industries Division, Statistics Canada.
D.G. MARTIN.   Dominion Foundries and Steel, Hamilton.
HARLEY POTTER.   Manufacturing and Primary Industries Division, Statistics Canada.

Section S: Construction and Housing

Section Chief:

MARION STEELE.   Department of Economics, University of Guelph.

Panel members:

CYRIL HODGINS.   Caneco, Ottawa.
J.G. LORANGER.   Department of Economics, University of Montreal.
A.S. STUKEL.   Central Mortgage and Housing Corporation.
DON TRAQUAIR.   Director, Business Statistics Integration Group, Statistics Canada.
H. WASLANDER.   Economic Council of Canada.

Section T: Transportation and Communication

There was no section chief for this chapter. The work of preparing text and tables was done in the Transportation and Communications Division of Statistics Canada, under the Director, G.E. Clarey. The officers principally responsible for both text and tables were Miss June Forgie and Mr. Murray McRae of that division. Advice in the early stages of the work was given by John Baldwin, Department of Economics, Queen's University.

Section V: Internal Trade

Section Chief:

M.S. MOYER. Faculty of Administrative Studies, York University.

Panel members:

HAROLD SHAFFER. Ottawa.

GERRY SNYDER. Associate Director, Merchandising and Services Division, Statistics Canada.

DAVID VAN LUVEN. Merchandising and Services Division, Statistics Canada.

Acknowledgments:

The following members of the Merchandising and Services Division, Statistics Canada, made important contributions to the preparation of this section: John Cline, Morris Griese, Ben Marios, Shalom Perel, Ronald Tanner, Marcel Tremblay and Ed Yablonski.

Section W: Education

Section Chief:

M. WISENTHAL. Director General, Institutions and Public Finance Branch, Statistics Canada.

Panel members:

CLIFF CONWAY. formerly Director of Education, Province of British Columbia.

YVON FORTIN. Education, Science and Culture Division, Statistics Canada.

J.E. REID. Department of Education, Province of Alberta.

Acknowledgments:

A. ALEXANDER. Education, Science and Culture Division, Statistics Canada.

Z. ZSIGMOND. Education, Science and Culture Division, Statistics Canada.

Section Y: Politics and Government

Section Chief:

J.L. ROY. Centre for French-Canadian Studies, McGill University.

Panel members:

G.R. BLANCHET. External Affairs Canada.

JEAN P. GABOURY. Department of Political Science, University of Ottawa.

PAUL PROSS. Department of Political Science, Dalhousie University.

Special Acknowledgments:

W.N. HUNT. Information Division, Statistics Canada.

ANDRE MARCIL. Information Division, Statistics Canada.

Section Z: Justice

Section Chief:

PAUL REED. Assistant Director, Justice Statistics Division, Statistics Canada.

Panel members:

MARIE-ANDREE BERTRAND. Centre of Criminology, University of Montreal.

EZZAT FATTAH. Centre of Criminology, Simon Fraser University.

JAMES GIFFEN. Department of Sociology, University of Toronto.

Acknowledgment:

JAMES McLAUGHLIN. Justice Statistics Division, Statistics Canada.

SECTION CHIEFS AND PANEL MEMBERS

Listed here are the section chiefs and others who contributed to the First Edition of Historical Statistics of Canada and whose work was of great value to those who prepared this subsequent volume.

Section A: Population and Migration

Section Chief:

K.A.H. BUCKLEY. Department of Economics and Political Science, University of Saskatchewan.

Panel members:

A.H. LeNeveu. Chief, Analysis Immigration and Citizenship Statistics Section, Census Division, Dominion Bureau of Statistics.

J.P. Delisle. Chief, Statistics Section, Administrative Services, Department of Citizenship and Immigration.

Mrs. Helen Buckley. Centre of Community Studies, University of Saskatchewan.

Section B: Vital Statistics, Health and Welfare

Section Chief:

Jacques Henripin. Department of Economics, University of Montreal.

Panel members:

Gordon H. Josie. Principal Research Officer, Research and Statistics Division, Department of National Health and Welfare.

Joseph W. Willard. Deputy Minister, Department of National Health and Welfare.

F.F. Harris. Director, Health and Welfare Division, Dominion Bureau of Statistics.

Yves Martin. Faculty of Social Sciences, Laval University.

Section C: The Labour Force

Section Chief:

K.A.H. Buckley. Department of Economics and Political Science, University of Saskatchewan.

Panel members:

W.A. Nesbitt. Chief, Processing and Analysis Section, Special Surveys Division, Dominion Bureau of Statistics.

A.H. LeNeveu. Chief, Analysis Immigration and Citizenship Statistics Section, Census Division, Dominion Bureau of Statistics.

G.V. Haythorne. Deputy Minister, Department of Labour, Ottawa.

Section D: Wages and Working Conditions

Section Chief:

Douglas Hartle. Department of Political Economy, University of Toronto.

Panel members:

C.H. Curtis. Department of Political and Economic Science, Queen's University.

J.C. Weldon. Department of Economics and Political Science, McGill University.

Section E: National Income and the Capital Stock

Section Chief:

M.C. Urquhart. Department of Political and Economic Science, Queen's University.

Panel member:

Simon Goldberg. Assistant Dominion Statistician, Dominion Bureau of Statistics.

Acknowledgement:

H.J. Adler. Assistant Director, National Income and Balance of Payments Division, Dominion Bureau of Statistics.

Section F: The Balance of International Payments, International Indebtedness and Foreign Trade

Section Chief:

Herbert Marshall. Dominion Statistician, Retired.

Panel members:

F.A. Knox. Department of Political and Economic Science, Queen's University.

George Watts. Research Department, Bank of Canada.

C.D. Blyth. Director, National Income and Balance of Payments Division, Dominion Bureau of Statistics.

A.E. Safarian. Department of Economics and Political Science, University of Saskatchewan.

Section G: Government Finance

Section Chief:

J.H. Perry. Director, Canadian Tax Foundation, Toronto.

Panel members:

J. Lowther. Commissioner of Finance, City of Ottawa.

G.A. Wagdin. Director, Public Finance and Transportation Division, Dominion Bureau of Statistics.

J. Howes. Secretary, Metropolitan Study Committee, Vancouver, British Columbia.

H.R. Balls. Comptroller of the Treasury, Department of Finance, Ottawa.

Acknowledgement:

Miss E.R. Cram.   Chief, Public Finance Section, Dominion Bureau of Statistics.

Section H: Banking and Finance

Section Chief:

E.P. Neufeld.   Department of Political Economy, University of Toronto.

Acknowledgement:

P.A.T. Campbell.

Section J: Price Indexes

Section Chief:

A. Asimakopulos.   Department of Economics and Political Science, McGill University.

Panel members:

J. Weldon.   Department of Economics and Political Science, McGill University.

L.E. Rowebottom.   Assistant to the Dominion Statistician, Dominion Bureau of Statistics.

W.C. Hood.   Department of Political Economy, University of Toronto.

Acknowledgements:

F. Curry.   Chief, Retail Prices Section, Prices Division, Dominion Bureau of Statistics.

K. Wallace.   Chief, Wholesale Prices Section, Prices Division, Dominion Bureau of Statistics.

Miss B.J. Emery.   National Accounts and Balance of Payments Division, Dominion Bureau of Statistics.

Section K: Lands and Forests

Section Chief:

G.K. Goundrey.   Department of Political Economy, University of Alberta.

Panel members:

Vernon Fowke.   Department of Economics and Political Science, University of Saskatchewan.

A.L. Best.   Department of Forestry, Ottawa.

Section L: Agriculture

Section Chief:

D.L. MacFarlane.   Macdonald College, McGill University.

Panel members:

J.W. Channon.   Grain Division, Department of Trade and Commerce, Ottawa.

J.A. Dawson.   Economics Division, Department of Agriculture, Ottawa.

R.S. Ellis.   Chief, Census of Agriculture Section, Census Division, Dominion Bureau of Statistics.

W.F. Ewert.   Chief, Livestock and Animal Products Section, Agriculture Division, Dominion Bureau of Statistics.

A.D. Holmes.   Director, Prices Division, Dominion Bureau of Statistics.

C.V. Parker.   Director, Agriculture Division, Dominion Bureau of Statistics.

W.D. Porter.   Assistant Director, Agriculture Division, Dominion Bureau of Statistics.

J.B. Rutherford.   Assistant Director, Economics Service, Department of Fisheries, Ottawa.

Section M: Fisheries

Section Chief:

H.S. Gordon.   Department of Economics, Carleton University.

Panel members:

W.C. MacKenzie.   Director, Economics Service, Department of Fisheries, Ottawa.

J.B. Rutherford.   Assistant Director, Economics Service, Department of Fisheries, Ottawa.

R.E. Johnson.   Chief, Fisheries Section, Dominion Bureau of Statistics.

Acknowledgement:

D.A. MacLean.   Economics Service, Department of Fisheries.

Section N: Minerals and Fuel

Section Chief:

John Davis.   British Columbia Electric Company Limited, Vancouver, British Columbia.

Panel members:

A.R. Deir.   Chief, Mineral Statistics Section, Dominion Bureau of Statistics.

W.K. Buck.   Chief, Mineral Resources Division, Mines and Technical Surveys Department, Ottawa.

R.D. Howland.   Commissioner, Royal Commission on Energy.

C.L. O'Brian.   Chairman, Dominion Coal Board.

L.S. Evans.   Chief, Communications, Distribution and Transmission Section, Dominion Bureau of Statistics.

Section P: Electric Power

Section Chief:

John Davis.   British Columbia Electric Company Limited, Vancouver, British Columbia.

Panel members:

R.D. Howland.   Commissioner, Royal Commission on Energy.

C.L. O'Brian.   Chairman, Dominion Coal Board.

R.L. Borden.   Chief, Communications, Distribution and Transmission Section, Dominion Bureau of Statistics.

S.A. Wagdin.   Director, Public Finance and Transportation Division, Dominion Bureau of Statistics.

Section Q: Manufactures

Section Chief:

Arthur J.R. Smith.   Director of Research, Private Planning Association of Canada, Montreal.

Panel members:

T. Vout.   Economist, Prime Minister's Office.

V.R. Berlinguette.   Assistant to Director, and Chief, Manufactures Section, Industry and Merchandising Division, Dominion Bureau of Statistics.

D.H. Fullerton.   President, Fullerton, MacKenzie and Associates Limited, Investment Consultants.

John Dales.   Department of Political Economy, University of Toronto.

A. Cohen.   Assistant Director, Industry and Merchandising Division, Dominion Bureau of Statistics.

Section R: Construction and Housing

Section Chief:

K.A.H. BUCKLEY. Department of Economics and Political Science, University of Saskatchewan.

Panel members:

MRS. HELEN BUCKLEY. Centre of Community Studies, University of Saskatchewan.

ALBERT GORACZ. Economist, Central Mortgage and Housing Corporation.

DEREK KNIGHT. Surpervisor, Economic Research Department, Central Mortgage and Housing Corporation.

D.A. TRAQUAIR. Business Finance Division, Dominion Bureau of Statistics.

Section S: Transportation and Communication

Section Chief:

J.L. MCDOUGALL. School of Business, Queen's University.

Panel members:

JOHN STENASON. Director of Economic Research, Canadian Pacific Railway Co.

R.A. BANDEEN. Senior Staff Officer, Planning, Department of Research and Development, Canadian National Railways.

G.A. RICHARDSON. Chief, Transportation and Public Utilities Section, Dominion Bureau of Statistics.

C.S. CARTER. Chief Statistician, Bell Telephone Company of Canada.

A.W. CURRIE. Department of Political Economy, University of Toronto.

K.W. STUDNICKI-GIZBERT. Chief, Economics Division, Air Transport Board, Ottawa.

A.L. BROWN. Chief, Transportation Section, Dominion Bureau of Statistics.

ADAM JAWORSKI. Economic Policy and Research Branch, Department of Transport.

N.M. GRIFFITH. Comptroller, Post Office Department, Ottawa.

Section T: Internal Trade and Service

Section Chief:

M.C. URQUHART. Department of Political and Economic Science, Queen's University.

Acknowledgements:

J.C. BRIERLEY. Merchandising Section, Retail Trade, Dominion Bureau of Statistics.

G. SNYDER. Merchandising Section, Retail Trade, Dominion Bureau of Statistics.

Section V: Education

Section Chief:

R.W.B. JACKSON. Director, Department of Educational Research, Ontario College of Education, University of Toronto.

Panel members:

CHARLES BILODEAU. Department of Education, Quebec.

OSWALD HALL. Department of Political Economy, University of Toronto.

C.E. HENDRY. School of Social Work, University of Toronto.

E.F. SHEFFIELD. Canadian Universities Foundation.

F.E. WHITWORTH. Education Division, Dominion Bureau of Statistics.

Acknowledgements:

WILLARD BREHAUT. Department of Educational Research, Ontario College of Education, University of Toronto.

N. LESEELLEUR. Education Division, Dominion Bureau of Statistics.

R.D. MITCHENER. Education Division, Dominion Bureau of Statistics.

Section W: Politics and Government

Section Chief:

NORMAN WARD. Department of Economics and Political Science, University of Saskatchewan.

Acknowledgements:

CHARLES DUNLOP. Department of Economics and Political Science, University of Saskatchewan.

J.E. HODGETTS. Department of Political and Economic Science, Queen's University.

HOWARD SCARROW. University of Michigan.

Section Y: Justice

Section Chief:

NICOLAS ZAY. Director of Research, School of Social Work, University of Montreal.

Panel members:

W.A. MAGILL. Chief, Judicial Section, Dominion Bureau of Statistics.

P.J. GIFFEN. Department of Political Economy, University of Toronto.

B.R. BLISHEN. Department of Anthropology and Sociology, University of British Columbia.

STUART RYAN. Faculty of Law, Queen's University.

Special Acknowledgement:

W.A. MAGILL. Chief, Judicial Section, Dominion Bureau of Statistics.

Section A: Population and Migration

K.G. Basavarajappa and Bali Ram, *Statistics Canada*

The statistics in this section are mainly from two sources. Series A1-349 are from censuses, or derived from censuses, published by Statistics Canada or its predecessors. Series A350-416 are from the official records of the Department of Employment and Immigration or its predecessors.

The statistics are presented in four main divisions: population (series A1-247), from censuses of Canada; household and family statistics (series A248-259), from censuses of Canada; interprovincial and international migration (series A260-349), derived from censuses of Canada; and immigration (series A350-416), from annual immigration statistics.

Except for series A15-66, A185-259 and A385-416, which have been newly introduced, all other series are updates of those presented by Kenneth Buckley in the first edition of *Historical Statistics of Canada*. Many of the series presented by Buckley could not be updated in this section because the necessary data have not been available during more recent years.

The discussions of concepts, definitions and limitations of some of the series presented by Buckley have not been repeated here. The reader is referred to them in appropriate notes accompanying the following series.

It should be noted that the references and the notes provided for each series are integral parts of the series themselves. More details about the differences in concepts and definitions which affect the comparability of the series can only be obtained from the original sources. The main purpose here is to present some selected series and their sources. It should also be mentioned that, because of space limitations in many cases, data are available in greater detail in the original sources.

Population (Series A1-247)

A1. Estimated population of Canada, 1867 to 1977

SOURCE: for 1867 to 1920, first edition of *Historical Statistics of Canada*, (for details of methods used and their limitations see p. 3); for 1921 to 1971, Statistics Canada, *Population by Sex and Age, 1921-1971*, revised annual estimates of population, Canada and the provinces, (Catalogue 91-512); for 1972 to 1977, Statistics Canada, *Estimates of Population for Canada and the Provinces, June 1, 1977*, (Catalogue 91-201). (Note that the 1977 figure is a revised intercensal estimate.)

A2-14. Population of Canada, by province, census dates, 1851 to 1976

SOURCE: for 1851 to 1951, Statistics Canada (formerly Dominion Bureau of Statistics), *Census of Canada, 1951*, vol. X, table 1; for 1956, Census of Canada, 1956, vol. I, table 1; for 1961 *Census of Canada, 1961*,, Vol. I, part 1, table 12, (Catalogue 92-536); for 1966, *Census of Canada, 1966*, vol. I, table 14, (Catalogue 92-608); for 1971, *Census of Canada, 1971*, vol. I, part 2, table 14, (Catalogue 92-716);

for 1976, *Census of Canada, 1976*, vol. II, table 11, (Catalogue 92-824).

For a brief discussion of possible under-enumeration in earlier censuses, 1851, 1861 and 1871, see first edition of this volume, pp. 3-4. For completeness of enumeration in censuses of 1961 to 1976, see series A15-53 below.

A15-53. Estimates of undercoverage of population by selected characteristics, Canada, 1961 to 1976

SOURCE: for 1961, I.P. Fellegi, 'Coverage Check of the 1961 Census of Population', Technical Memorandum (Census Evaluation Series) No. 2, Ottawa, Statistics Canada, 1968 (Mimeographed); for 1966, R.C. Muirhead, 'Reverse Record Check', Census Evaluation Program 1966, Ottawa, Statistics Canada, 1969 (Mimeographed); for 1971, G.J. Brackstone and J.F. Gosselin, '1971 Evaluation Project, MP-1: 1971 Reverse Record Check' and Result Memorandum CDN 71-E-23E (Parts 1 and 2), Ottawa, Statistics Canada, 1974 (Mimeographed); for 1976, G. Théroux and J.F. Gosselin, '1976 Census Parametric Evaluation Project, Reverse Record Check', Ottawa, Statistics Canada, CSMD, 1978 (Mimeographed).

Completeness of enumeration

Although the extent of coverage at earlier censuses is not known with any precision, since 1961 it has been studied by a procedure termed 'reverse record check'. The method essentially consists of taking a sample of persons from a complete list of all persons living in Canada on the census day, and verifying whether they had been enumerated at the census. Based on the results of this verification, the estimates of net under- or over-enumeration have been derived. Although a complete list of persons has never been available in Canada, an approximation to it has been constructed. For instance, in 1966, the approximate list was constructed as follows: all persons enumerated in the 1961 Census; immigrants during 1 June 1961 to 31 May 1966; registered births during 1 June 1961 to 31 May 1966; and all persons missed by the 1961 Census but detected by the 1961 Census Evaluation Program.

A sample of persons was then selected from each of the above frames for verification of enumeration. A tracing operation was then mounted and eventually all the selected persons in the sample were classified as belonging to one of the following five mutually exclusive categories: (i) enumerated in 1966; (ii) missed; (iii) dead; (iv) emigrated; and (v) tracing failed.

The dead and emigrated do not constitute the population that should have been enumerated in 1966. By assuming that the tracing failed category is not a special group but is distributed according to (i) to (iv) categories in the same way as those traced (an assumption which is most probably incorrect), the percentage of under-enumeration was calculated as $100 [ii/(ii+i)]$. Although the assumption that the tracing failed category is not a special group is most probably incorrect, the percentage of undercoverage obtained may not be significantly affected because the tracing failed group amounted to only about 3 per cent in 1961, 2.8 per cent in 1966, 4.4 per cent in 1971 and 4.8 per cent in 1976.

Following the procedure described above, the completeness of enumeration has been examined in Canadian censuses since 1961. Estimates of net under-enumeration thus obtained are presented according to selected characteristics in series A15-53.

A54-66. Population density per square mile, Canada and provinces, 1871 to 1976

SOURCE: for 1871 to 1941, *Census of Canada, 1941*, vol. II, table 5; for 1951, *Census of Canada, 1951*, vol. I, table 2; for 1956, *Census of Canada, 1956*, vol. I, table 2; for 1961, *Census of Canada, 1961*, vol. I, part 1, table 2, (Catalogue 92-540); for 1966, *Census of Canada, 1966*, vol. I, table 2, (Catalogue 92-601); for 1971, *Census of Canada, 1971*, special bulletin, table 1, (Catalogue 98-701; for 1976, *Census of Canada, 1976*, vol. VIII, table 1, (Catalogue 92-831).

A67-69. Population, rural and urban, census dates, 1871 to 1976

SOURCE: (basis 1941 rural and urban definition) for 1871 to 1956, *Census of Canada, 1951*, vol. I, table 13 and first edition of this volume, p. 14; for 1961, *Census of Canada, 1961*, vol. I, part 1, Introduction, (Catalogue 92-535); for 1966, *Census of Canada, 1966*, vol. I, Introduction, (Catalogue 92-607); for 1971, *Census of Canada, 1971*, (unpublished tabulation produced by Census Characteristics Division of Statistics Canada) (Basis 1976 rural and urban definition); for 1976, *Census of Canada, 1976*, vol. I, table 7, (Catalogue 92-807).

Definitions of rural and urban used in Canadian censuses are:

1871 to 1941
Urban: population living in incorporated villages, towns and cities regardless of size.
Rural: includes all the remaining population.

1951
Urban: all persons living in cities, towns and villages of 1,000 and over whether incorporated or not, plus the urban fringes of census metropolitan areas.
Rural: includes all the remaining population.

1956
Urban: population living in cities, towns and villages of 1,000 and over whether incorporated or not, plus the urban fringe of census metropolitan areas, plus the urban fringe of major urban areas (cities with a population of 25,000 to 50,000).
Rural: includes all the remaining population.

1961 to 1971
Urban: (1) population of incorporated cities, towns and villages with a population of 1,000 and over, plus (2) unincorporated places of 1,000 and over having a population density of at least 1,000 per square mile, plus (3) built-up fringes of (1) and (2) having a minimum population of 1,000 and a density of at least 1,000 per square mile.
Rural: includes all the remaining population.

1976
Urban: population living in an area having a population

concentration of 1,000 or more and a population density of at least 1,000 per square mile.
Rural: includes all the remaining population.

A70-74. Population in incorporated centres of 1,000 persons and over, by size groups, census dates, 1871 to 1976

SOURCE: for places 5,000 and over in 1871 and 1881, *Census of Canada, 1921*, vol. I, table 12; for 1891, *Census of Canada, 1951*, vol. X, table 4; for 1901 to 1956, *Census of Canada, 1956*, Bulletin 3-2, table 2, and *Census of Canada, 1941*, vol. I, table 7; for 1961, *Census of Canada, 1961*, vol. I, part 1, (Catalogue 92-535); for 1966, *Census of Canada, 1966*, vol. I, (Catalogue 92-607); for 1971 and 1976 *Census of Canada, 1971*, and *Census of Canada, 1976*, (unpublished tabulations by Census Characteristics Division of Statistics Canada).

A75-77. Rural population, farm and non-farm, census dates, 1931 to 1976

SOURCE: for figures based upon the 1941 definition, *Census of Canada, 1951*, vol. X, table 9; for 1951 definition, *Census of Canada, 1951*, vol. X, table 8; for 1956 definition, *Census of Canada, 1956*, Bulletin 3-2, table 11; for 1961 and 1966, *Census of Canada, 1966*, vol. I, table 13, (Catalogue 92-608); for 1971, *Census of Canada, 1971*, vol. I, part 2, table 18 (Catalogue 92-717) *Census of Canada, 1976*, vol. I, table 7, (Catalogue 92-807).

Definitions of rural farm and non-farm populations are as follows: population living in dwellings located on a census-farm in areas designated as rural are termed 'rural farm population' and all remaining rural residents as 'rural non-farm population'. For definition of rural see note to series A67-69.

A78-93. Population, by age and sex, census dates, 1851 to 1976

SOURCE: for 1851 to 1871, Nathan Keyfitz, *The Growth of Canadian Population*, table 3, p. 50; for 1881 and 1891, *Census of Canada, 1941*, vol. I, table 12; for 1901 to 1951, *Census of Canada, 1951*, vol. I, table 19; for 1956, *Census of Canada, 1956*, Bulletin 1-9, table 16; for 1961, *Census of Canada, 1961*, vol. I, part 2, table 20, (Catalogue 92-542); for 1966, *Census of Canada, 1966*, vol. I, table 20, (Catalogue 92-610); for 1971, *Census of Canada, 1971*, vol. I, part 2, table 7, (Catalogue 92-715); for 1976, *Census of Canada, 1976*, vol. VIII, table 1, (Catalogue 92-835).

Persons whose ages were not stated have been assigned to various age groups by two methods. Prior to 1941 the total 'age not stated' in each census was prorated on the basis of the distribution of the remaining population. See *Census of Canada, 1931*, vol. I, table 8, p. 387, for the numbers so distributed from 1851 to 1931 and pp. 197-198 for a discussion of some of their attributes. Beginning with the 1941 Census the method used to distribute 'age not stated' has been much more precise. The unstated ages were assigned before any tabulations were made on the basis of all other relevant information available in the census schedules. During 1971 and 1976, such assignment was made by the computer.

For a discussion of accuracy of reporting age in 1941 and in previous censuses, and for totals of 'age not stated' in each census from 1881 to 1941, see *Census of Canada, 1941,* vol. I, pp. 120-127.

In 1951 and 1956, maximum use was made of other information from the census schedule, as well as the laws of probability, in estimating a value for each 'not given' case. (See *Census of Canada, 1951,* vol. I, Population: General Characteristics, p. xvii; *Census of Canada, 1956,* vol. I, Population: General Characteristics, Households and Families, p. xviii.)

Since 1961, the assignment for the unstated ages has been made by the computer. The computer was also programmed to check for internal consistency. The procedure used other relevant data on the person, *Census of Canada, 1961,* Administrative Report of the 1961 Census of Canada, vol. VII, part 2, pp. 101-102, (Catalogue 99-537).

It should be noted that in the 1971 and 1976 censuses, age was derived from the information on the date (month and year) of birth, whereas in the previous censuses, respondents were asked to state their age in completed years as of their last birthday before the census date. The tendency toward 'age heaping' at certain specific ages may be of far less significance in the 1971 and 1976 censuses than in the earlier censuses.

A94-109. Population, by age and sex, urban and rural, census dates, 1921 to 1976

SOURCE: for 1921, *Census of Canada, 1921,* vol. II, table 7; for 1931, *Census of Canada, 1931,* vol. III, table 1; for 1941, *Census of Canada, 1941,* vol. II, table 21; for 1951, *Census of Canada, 1951,* vol. I, table 21; for 1956, *Census of Canada, 1956,* Bulletin 1-9, table 17; for 1961, *Census of Canada, 1961,* vol. I, part 2, table 21, (Catalogue 92-542); for 1966, *Census of Canada, 1966,* vol. I, table 20, (Catalogue 92-610); for 1971, *Census of Canada, 1971,* vol. I, part 2, table 8, (Catalogue 92-715); for 1976, *Census of Canada, 1976,* vol. II, table 12, (Catalogue 92-823).

In 1921 and 1931, persons whose ages were not stated have been distributed by age. For details see p. 6. Of the first edition of this volume. For treatment of such persons after 1941, see note to series A78-93.

A110-124. Population, by marital status and sex, census dates, 1871 to 1976

SOURCE: for population, all ages, *Census of Canada, 1941,* vol. I, table 18; for population 15 years and over for 1891 to 1931, *Census of Canada, 1941,* vol. I, table 20; for 1941 and 1951, *Census of Canada, 1951,* vol. X, table 17; for 1956, *Census of Canada, 1956,* Bulletin 1-12, table 28; for 1961, *Census of Canada, 1961,* vol. I, part 2, table 30, (Catalogue 92-514); for 1966, *Census of Canada, 1966,* vol. I, table 34, (Catalogue 92-613); for 1971, *Census of Canada, 1971,* vol. I, part 4, table 1, (Catalogue 92-730); for 1976, *Census of Canada, 1976,* vol. II, table 17, (Catalogue 92-824).

Prior to 1951, with the exception of 1901, persons whose marital status was not stated have been distributed on a *pro rata* basis. During 1951 to 1956 such persons have been assigned to the various categories on the basis of supplementary information. During 1971 and 1976, for persons who did not report their marital status, this was imputed, by the computer, on the basis of various other relevant supplementary information.

A125-163. Origins of the population, census dates, 1871 to 1971

SOURCE: for 1871 to 1921, *Canada Year Book, 1948-49,* p. 154; for 1931 to 1951, *Canada Year Book, 1957-58,* p. 137; for 1961, *Census of Canada, 1961,* vol. I, part 2, table 34, (Catalogue 92-545); for 1971, *Census of Canada, 1971,* vol. I, part 3, table 1, (Catalogue 92-723).

For a brief discussion of comparability of concepts, definitions and figures relating to origin and for relevant references see Kenneth Buckley, "Population and Migration", in the *Historical Statistics of Canada,* first edition, p. 6, and W.B. Hurd, *Ethnic Origin and Nativity of the Canadian People,* 1941 Census Monograph, Statistics Canada, Ottawa, Queen's Printer (restricted).

A164-184. Principal religious denominations of the population, census dates, 1871 to 1971

SOURCE: for 1871 to 1921, *Canada Year Book, 1948-49,* p. 155; for 1931 to 1951, *Canada Year Book, 1957-58,* p. 137; for 1961, *Census of Canada, 1961,* vol. I, part 2, table 41, (Catalogue 92-546); for 1971, *Census of Canada, 1971,* vol. I, part 3, table 9, (Catalogue 92-724).

A185-237. Mother tongues of the population, census years, 1931 to 1976

SOURCE: for 1931, *Census of Canada, 1931,* vol. I, table 28; for 1941 to 1961, *Census of Canada, 1961,* vol. I, part 2, table 63, (Catalogue 92-549); for 1971, *Census of Canada, 1971,* vol. I, part 3, table 17, (Catalogue 92-725); for 1976, *Census of Canada, 1976,* vol. II, table 1, (Catalogue 92-821).

A238-247. Number of children ever born per 1,000 ever married women, 15 years of age and over, total, rural and urban, Canada, 1941, 1961 and 1971

SOURCE: for 1941, *Census of Canada, 1941,* vol. I, tables 74 and 75; for 1961, *Census of Canada, 1961,* vol. IV, table H1, (Catalogue 98-508); for 1971, *Census of Canada, 1971,* vol. I, part 2, table 24, (Catalogue 92-718).

In order to collect data on fertility, a question on the 'number of children ever born' was asked to 'ever married' (currently married, widowed, divorced and separated) women 15 years of age and older in the 1941, 1961 and 1971 censuses. These statistics as shown in these series include children born of the present marriage, previous marriage, or before marriage and children who died after birth, but do not include stillbirths, adopted children and stepchildren.

Household and Family Statistics (Series A248-259)

A248-253. Number of households and average number of persons per household, Canada, 1881 to 1976

SOURCE: for 1881 to 1921, *Census of Canada, 1921,* vol. III, tables 1 and 2; for 1931, *Census of Canada, 1931,* vol. V, tables 47 and 48; for 1941, *Census of Canada, 1941,* vol. V, table 4; for 1951, *Census of Canada, 1951,* vol. III, table 4; for 1956, *Census of Canada, 1956,* vol. I, table 34; for 1961,

Census of Canada, 1961, vol. II, part 1, table 2, (Catalogue 93-510); for 1966, *Census of Canada, 1966,* vol. II, table 9, (Catalogue 93-603); for 1971, *Census of Canada, 1971,* vol. II, part 1, table 1, (Catalogue 93-702); for 1976, *Census of Canada, 1976,* vol. III, table 16, (Catalogue 93-805).

The changes in definitions of 'household', briefly discussed below, should be taken into account when statistics from one census are compared with those from another. Prior to 1951, a 'household' referred to all persons living together in a housekeeping unit regardless of blood or marriage relationship, and it might consist of one person only. Since 1951, the household was defined as a person or a group of persons who occupy one dwelling. It usually consists of a family group, with or without lodgers, employees, etc. However, it may consist of two or more families sharing a dwelling, of a group of unrelated persons or of one person living alone. A household occupying a 'private dwelling' is termed a 'private household' and that occupying a 'collective dwelling', a 'collective household'. (See *Census of Canada, 1951,* vol. III, pp. xxii-xxiii; *Census of Canada, 1961,* vol. II, part 1, pp. xiv-xv; Statistics Canada, *Dictionary of the 1971 Census Terms,* (Catalogue 12-540), pp. 9-11.)

A dwelling is a structurally separate set of living quarters with a private entrance from outside the building or from a common hallway or stairway inside the building. A dwelling is either 'private' or 'collective'. A 'private dwelling' refers to a dwelling in which one person, a family, or other small group of individuals may reside, such as a single house or apartment. A 'collective dwelling' refers to a dwelling in which a large number of persons are likely to reside. Included are hotels, motels, hospitals, staff residences, institutions, military camps, work camps, all jails and missions, etc. (See *Census of Canada, 1961,* vol. II, part 1, pp. xiv-xv; Statistics Canada, *Dictionary of the 1971 Census Terms,* (Catalogue 12-540), pp. 36-37.)

A254-259. Number of families and average number of persons per family, Canada, 1881 to 1976

SOURCE: for 1881, *Census of Canada, 1880-81,* vol. I, table 1; for 1891, *Census of Canada, 1890-91,* vol. I, table 2; for 1901, *Census of Canada, 1901,* vol. I, table 2; for 1911, *Census of Canada, 1911,* vol. I, table 2; for 1921, *Census of Canada, 1921,* vol. III, table 16; for 1931, *Census of Canada, 1931,* vol. IV, table 86; for 1941, *Census of Canada, 1941,* vol. V, table 4; for 1951, *Census of Canada, 1951,* vol. III, table 127; for 1956, *Census of Canada, 1956,* vol. I, table 44; for 1961, *Census of Canada, 1961,* vol. II, part 1, table 44, (Catalogue 93-514); for 1966, *Census of Canada, 1966,* vol. II, table 53, (Catalogue 93-609); for 1971, *Census of Canada, 1971,* vol. II, part 2, table 2, (Catalogue 93-714); for 1976, *Census of Canada, 1976,* vol. IV, table 7, (Catalogue 93-822), and *Census of Canada, 1976,* vol. III, table 27, (Catalogue 93-807).

Changes in the definition of family, briefly discussed below, should be taken into account when statistics from one census are compared with those from another.

Prior to the 1921 Census, no distinction was made between the household, indicating a group of people in the same housekeeping unit, and the family. In that year, a distinction was made between the 'census family', which comprised the household, and the 'private family', which was composed of parents, children, and natural dependents (for example, uncles, nieces, mothers-in-law, etc.). In many cases, the census family and the private family represented the same group of persons, just as today the family and the household are frequently one and the same group of persons. In 1921, individuals maintaining their own households were enumerated as one-person families. In 1931, the terms 'census family' and 'private family' were replaced by the simpler terms 'household' and 'family' respectively, but otherwise little change from the 1921 Census was made, and families of one person were still accepted. In 1941, however, the following significant changes were made in the census definitions of 'family' and 'children in families': (a) a one-person household no longer constituted a family; (b) relatives of the head, not part of the immediate family (for example, uncles, nieces, brothers, etc.), were not included as family members, whether or not they were dependent upon the head, in other words, the family was strictly a husband and wife with or without children or a parent-child relationship; and (c) children in the family were restricted to unmarried sons and daughters of the head living at home and the statistics regarding age, schooling, and occupations of children were shown only for children under 25 years of age, whereas in former censuses this information was either not given or was shown for all children living at home. These changes in definition have more sharply delineated the concept of family, so that all families fit into one of several categories, the most important by far being the so-called 'normal family', which consists of husband and wife living together with or without children. (See Statistics Canada, *Census of Canada, 1941,* vol. I, Ottawa, pp. 430-431.)

The 1941 definition of the 'family' was retained in 1951.

Since 1956, a distinction has been made between the 'census family' and the 'economic family'. A 'census family' consists of a husband and wife (with or without children who have never been married, regardless of age) or a parent with one or more children never married, living in the same dwelling. A family may consist also of a man or woman living with a guardianship child or ward under 21 years for whom no pay was received. In contrast, an 'economic family' is defined as a group of two or more persons living together and related to each other by blood, marriage or adoption. 'Economic family' is a broader concept and includes within its definition a larger group of persons than does the 'census family'. For example, a widowed mother living with her married son and daughter-in-law would be treated as a non-family person under the definition of a census family, but would be counted as a member of the economic family. (See Statistics Canada, *Dictionary of the 1971 Census Terms,* (Catalogue 12-540), pp. 6-7.)

Interprovincial and International Migration (Series A260-349)

A260-269. Population, Canadian, other British and foreign-born, by sex, census dates, 1871 to 1971

SOURCE: for totals from 1871 to 1951, *Census of Canada, 1951,* vol. I, table 44; for sex breakdown in 1911, Statistics Canada, unpublished data, folio CXL; for sex breakdown in 1921, 1931, 1941, *Census of Canada, 1941,* vol. I, table 7, p. 177; for sex breakdown in 1951, *Census of Canada, 1951,* vol. I, table 45; for 1961, *Census of Canada, 1961,* vol. I, part 2, table 50, (Catalogue 92-547); for 1971, *Census of Canada, 1971,* vol. I, part 4, table 25, (Catalogue 92-737).

The following note on the treatment of 'place of birth not stated' applies to series A133-142 and to the three tables which follow. In 1871, although there were 84,247 persons, mostly Indians in British Columbia and the Northwest Territories for whom the 'place of birth was unknown', they have not been included among 'Canadian-born'. In later censuses, Indians have been included among 'Canadian-born'.

In 1871, 1881 and 1891 there were 1,828, 6,334 and 3,491 persons respectively for whom the 'place of birth' was not known (see *Canada Year Book, 1910*, p. 2). As the Canadian, other British and foreign-born cannot be distinguished, they have been included in the 'Canadian born' in series A134-136.

Beginning with the 1901 Census, the totals of 'birthplace not stated' have been distinguished according to major components and have been included in Canadian, other British or foreign-born (see *Canada Year Book, 1913*, p. 73; *Canada Year Book, 1943-44*, p. 114; *Census of Canada, 1931*, vol. I, p. 215). The 'not stated' for the foreign-born are included with 'other foreign-born' in the census figures until 1931. In 1941 a small number (945) are not assigned to any category (see footnote 3 to series A260-269).

Since 1951, the 'not stated' have been assigned to countries before tabulation. In 1971, such assignment was made by the computer (see the respective administrative reports of censuses).

Persons who were born at sea have been classified among 'other' under either 'British possessions' or 'British Commonwealth' (see *Canada Year Book, 1950*, p. 162 and *Census of Canada, 1931*, vol. I, table 1, p. 214, for the relevant footnotes).

A270-281. Population, by birthplace and sex, rural and urban, census dates, 1921 to 1971

SOURCE: for 1921, *Census of Canada, 1921*, vol. I, table 7, p. 177; for 1931, *Census of Canada, 1931*, vol. iv, table 5; for 1941, *Census of Canada, 1941* vol. II, table 42; for 1951, *Census of Canada, 1951*, vol. I, table 46; for 1961, *Census of Canada, 1961*, vol. I, part 2, table 50, (Catalogue 92-547); for 1971, *Census of Canada, 1971*, vol. I, part 4, table 25, (Catalogue 92-737).

A282-296. Population, Canadian, other British and foreign-born, by age and sex, census dates, 1911 to 1971

SOURCE: for sex and age distribution in 1911, Statistics Canada, unpublished data, folio CXL; for 1921, *Census of Canada, 1921*, vol. II, table 10; for 1931, *Census of Canada, 1931*, vol. III, table 23; for 1941, *Census of Canada, 1941*, vol. III, table 18; for 1951, *Census of Canada, 1951*, vol. II, table 10; for 1961, *Census of Canada, 1961*, vol. I, part 3, table 89, (Catalogue 92-555); for 1971, *Census of Canada, 1971*, vol. I, part 4, table 25, (Catalogue 92-737).

A297-326. Country of birth of the other British-born and the foreign-born population, census dates, 1871 to 1971

SOURCE: for 1871 to 1951, *Census of Canada, 1951*, vol. I, table 44; for 1961, *Census of Canada, 1961*, vol. I, part 2, table 48, (Catalogue 92-547); for 1971 and for more details, see *Census of Canada, 1971*, vol. I, part 3, tables 33 and 34, (Catalogue 92-727).

A327-338. Province of residence and province of birth of native-born internal migrants in Canada, census dates, 1871 to 1971

SOURCE: for 1871 to 1941, Buckley, "Historical Estimates of Internal Migration", *Canadian Political Science Association, Conference on Statistics, 1960, Papers* (Toronto, University of Toronto Press, 1962) table 1, pp. 6-7; for 1951, *Census of Canada, 1951*, vol. II, tables 10 and 11; for 1961, *Census of Canada, 1961*, vol. I, part 3, tables 89 and 90, (Catalogue 92-555); for 1971, *Census of Canada, 1971*, vol. I, part 4, table 26, (Catalogue 92-737) and vol. I, part 3, table 34, (Catalogue 92-727).

For treatment of persons whose place of birth is not stated during 1871 to 1941 see Buckley, "Historical Estimates of Internal Migration", pp. 1-17.

For the purpose of series A327-338, any Canadian-born person not living in the province of his or her birth is termed a native-born internal migrant. *Panel A* shows the number of persons living in each province who were born in another province. *Panel B* shows the number of persons not living in the province of birth, by the province in which they were born.

A339-349. Changes in the population through natural increase and migration, by province, by intercensal intervals, 1931 to 1976

SOURCE: for 1931-41 and 1941-51, *Canada Year Book, 1957-58*, Chapter III, table 3, p. 120; for 1951-56 and 1956-61, *Canada Year Book, 1966*, Chapter IV, table 3, p. 179; for 1961-66 and 1966-71, *Canada Year Book, 1973*, Chapter 5, table 5.5, p. 209; for 1971-76, the figures have been calculated using the enumerated populations in the 1971 and 1976 censuses and the unpublished annual reports on vital statistics. The figures are preliminary and are subject to change. For birth statistics, Statistics Canada, *Vital Statistics*, vol. I, (Catalogue 84-204) ; For death Statistics, Statistics Canada, *Vital Statistics*, vol.III, (Catalogue 84-206).

Immigration (Series A350-416)

A350. Immigrant arrivals in Canada, 1852 to 1977

SOURCE: for 1852 to 1976, Department of Manpower and Immigration, *1976 Immigration Statistics*, table 2, p. 4, Ottawa, 1977; for 1977, Employment and Immigration Canada, *Immigration 1977, Quarterly Statistics, Fourth Quarter*, table 2, p. 7.

For a discussion of the history of collection of immigration statistics, their conceptual consistency and their reliability, see Kenneth Buckley, "Population and Migration", in the *Historical Statistics of Canada*, first edition, pp. 10-11.

A351-368. Immigration to Canada by intended occupations and dependents, 1953 to 1976

SOURCE: for 1953 to 1960, first edition of *Historical Statistics of Canada* p. 23; for 1961 to 1976, Department of Manpower and Immigration, *Immigration Statistics*, 1961 to 1976.

For distribution of immigration to Canada by intended occupations and dependents for 1932 to 1952, according to an older classification, and for distribution of immigration to Canada by occupational groups, sex of adults, children, from overseas and the U.S., and from overseas, for 1904 to 1951, see first edition of this volume, pp. 11-12 and 23-25.

A369-384. Immigration to Canada by age, sex and marital status, 1933 to 1976

SOURCE: for 1933 to 1960, first edition of this volume, p. 26; for 1961 to 1976, Department of Manpower and Immigration, *Immigration Statistics,* 1961 to 1976. Greater details on age and marital status may be found in this annual publication.

A385-416. Immigration to Canada by country of last permanent residence, 1956 to 1976

SOURCE: for 1956 to 1976, Department of Manpower and Immigration, *Immigration Statistics,* 1956 to 1976. Only a selected number of countries are presented in this volume. The source publication provides greater detail.

Series A1. Estimated population of Canada, 1867 to 1977
(thousands)

Year[1,2]	Total population	Year[1,2]	Total population	Year[1,2]	Total population	Year[1,2]	Total population		Total population
	1		1		1		1		1
		1955	15,698	1930	10,208	1905	6,002	1880	4,255
		1954	15,287	1929	10,029	1904	5,827	1879	4,185
		1953	14,845	1928	9,835	1903	5,651	1878	4,120
1977	23,258[3]	1952	14,459	1927	9,637	1902[1]	5,494	1877	4,064
1976	22,993[3]	1951	14,009	1926	9,451	1901	5,371	1876	4,009
1975	22,697	1950	13,712	1925	9,294	1900	5,301	1875	3,954
1974	22,364	1949[2]	13,447	1924	9,143	1899	5,235	1874	3,895
1973	22,043	1948	12,823	1923	9,010	1898	5,175	1873	3,826
1972	21,802	1947	12,551	1922	8,919	1897	5,122	1872	3,754
1971	21,568	1946	12,292	1921	8,788	1896	5,074	1871	3,689
1970	21,297	1945	12,072	1920	8,556	1895	5,026	1870	3,625
1969	21,001	1944	11,946	1919	8,311	1894	4,979	1869	3,565
1968	20,701	1943	11,795	1918	8,148	1893	4,931	1868	3,511
1967	20,378	1942	11,654	1917	8,060	1892	4,883	1867	3,463
1966	20,015	1941	11,507	1916	8,001	1891	4,833		
1965	19,644	1940	11,381	1915	7,981	1890	4,779		
1964	19,291	1939	11,267	1914	7,879	1889	4,729		
1963	18,931	1938	11,152	1913	7,632	1888	4,678		
1962	18,583	1937	11,045	1912	7,389	1887	4,626		
1961	18,238	1936	10,950	1911	7,207	1886	4,580		
1960	17,870	1935	10,845	1910	6,988	1885	4,537		
1959	17,483	1934	10,741	1909	6,800	1884	4,487		
1958	17,080	1933	10,633	1908	6,625	1883	4,430		
1957	16,610	1932	10,510	1907	6,411	1882	4,375		
1956	16,081	1931	10,377	1906	6,097	1881	4,325		

[1] From 1867 to 1901 the figures apply to 1 April; from 1902 to 1977 the figures apply to 1 June. For census dates see series A2–14.
[2] The population of Newfoundland is included beginning in 1949.

[3] The figure for 1976 is the final census figure and the figure for 1977 is the revised intercensal estimate.

Series A2-14. Population of Canada, by province, census dates, 1851 to 1976

Year	Canada	Newfoundland	Prince Edward Island	Nova Scotia	New Brunswick	Quebec	Ontario	Manitoba	Saskatchewan	Alberta	British Columbia	Yukon Territory	Northwest Territories
	2	3	4	5	6	7	8	9	10	11	12	13	14
1976	22,992,604	557,725	118,229	828,571	677,250	6,234,445	8,264,465	1,021,506	921,323	1,838,037	2,466,608	21,836	42,609
1971	21,568,311	522,104	111,641	788,960	634,557	6,027,764	7,703,106	988,247	926,242	1,627,874	2,184,621	18,388	34,807
1966	20,014,880	493,396	108,535	756,039	616,788	5,780,845	6,960,870	963,066	955,344	1,463,203	1,873,674	14,382	28,738
1961	18,238,247	457,853	104,629	737,007	597,936	5,259,211	6,236,092	921,686	925,181	1,331,944	1,629,082	14,628	22,998
1956	16,080,791	415,074	99,285	694,717	554,616	4,628,378	5,404,933	850,040	880,665	1,123,116	1,398,464	12,190	19,313
1951	14,009,429	361,416	98,429	642,584	515,697	4,055,681	4,597,542	776,541	831,728	939,501	1,165,210	9,096	16,004
1941	11,506,655	—	95,047	577,962	457,401	3,331,882	3,787,655	729,744	895,992	796,169	817,861	4,914	12,028
1931	10,376,786	—	88,038	512,846	408,219	2,874,662	3,431,683	700,139	921,785	731,605	694,263	4,230	9,316
1921	8,787,949[1]	—	88,615	523,837	387,876	2,360,510	2,933,662	610,118	757,510	588,454	524,582	4,157	8,143
1911	7,206,643	—	93,728	492,338	351,889	2,005,776	2,527,292	461,394	492,432	374,295	392,480	8,512	6,507
1901	5,371,315	—	103,259	459,574	331,120	1,648,898	2,182,947	255,211	91,279	73,022	178,657	27,219	20,129
1891	4,833,239	—	109,078	450,396	321,263	1,488,535	2,114,321	152,506	—[2]	—[2]	98,173	—	98,967
1881	4,324,810	—	108,891	440,572	321,233	1,359,027	1,926,922	62,260	—	—	49,459	—	56,446
1871	3,689,257	—	94,021	387,800	285,594	1,191,516	1,620,851	25,228	—	—	36,247	—	48,000
1861	3,229,633	—	80,857	330,857	252,047	1,111,566	1,396,091	—[2]	—	—	51,524[3]	—	6,691[3]
1851	2,436,297	—	62,678[4]	276,854	193,800	890,261	952,004	—	—	—	55,000[3]	—	5,700[3]

[1] Includes 485 members of the Royal Canadian Navy whose province of residence is not known.
[2] Included with Northwest Territories.
[3] For the discussion of the ambiguities and under-enumeration contained in these figures consult the notes to series A2–14 in original volume. For completeness of enumeration in censuses of 1961 and later years, see notes to series A15–53.
[4] 1848 figure.

Series A15-53. Estimates of undercoverage of population by selected characteristics, Canada, 1961 to 1976

Series no.	Characteristics	1961	1966	1971	1976
	Region				
15	Atlantic	5.2	1.98	1.66	1.30
16	Quebec	2.1	2.95	2.10	2.95
17	Ontario	3.0	2.65	1.68	1.52
18	Prairies	4.0	2.24	1.75	1.34
19	British Columbia	4.1	2.84	2.89	3.13
20	Total	3.3	2.62	1.93	2.04
	Age group[1]				
	Both sexes				
21	0-4	—	2.96	1.99	2.00
22	5-14	2.1	1.53	0.90	1.20
23	15-19	—	3.57	2.60	1.99
24	20-24	—	7.76	4.49	5.31
25	25-39	6.0	2.73	2.50	2.61
26	40-59	1.5	1.67	1.40	1.17
27	60+	3.0	1.97	1.22	1.02
28	Total	3.3	2.62	1.93	2.04
	Males				
29	0-4	—	2.30	1.73	2.53
30	5-14	—	1.44	0.93	1.14
31	15-19	—	3.77	2.71	1.93
32	20-24	—	9.79	4.97	5.99
33	25-39	—	3.23	3.38	3.47
34	40-59	—	2.27	1.90	1.70
35	60+	—	1.72	1.37	1.43
36	Total	—	2.90	2.27	2.46
	Females				
37	0-4	—	3.68	2.25	2.07
38	5-14	—	1.63	0.87	1.26
39	15-19	—	3.35	2.49	2.05
40	20-24	—	5.60	4.01	4.62
41	25-39	—	2.22	1.58	1.73
42	40-59	—	1.09	0.90	0.65
43	60+	—	2.37	1.10	0.68
44	Total	—	2.35	1.59	1.61
	Marital status				
45	Single	—	—	2.36	2.62
46	Married	—	—	1.45	1.20
47	Widowed	—	—	1.42	2.48
48	Divorced	—	—	5.47	9.28
	Residence				
49	Census metropolitan area	—	—	1.84	—
50	Urban	—	—	1.95	—
51	Rural	—	—	1.84	—
	Mother tongue				
52	English	—	—	—	1.55
53	French and other	—	—	—	—[2]

[1] For 1961 only, figures correspond to age groups 5-14, 15-34, 35-54, 55+ and 5+ years respectively. For other years they are as given.

[2] Consists of French, 2.76 per cent and other, 3.01 per cent.

Series A54-66. Population density[1] per square mile, Canada and provinces, 1871 to 1976

Year	Newfound-land	Prince Edward Island	Nova Scotia	New Brunswick	Quebec	Ontario	Manitoba	Saskat-chewan	Alberta	British Columbia	Yukon Territory	Northwest Territories	Canada[2]
	54	55	56	57	58	59	60	61	62	63	64	65	66
1976	3.89	54.51	40.61	24.51	11.89	23.33	4.83	4.19	7.46	7.15	0.11	0.03	6.46
1971	3.64	51.08	38.67	22.96	11.50	21.75	4.67	4.21	6.61	6.34	0.09	0.03	6.06
1966	3.45	49.70	37.06	22.16	11.04	20.23	4.55	4.34	5.88	5.22	0.07	0.02	5.62
1961	3.20	47.91	36.12	21.48	10.04	18.12	4.35	4.20	5.35	4.53	0.07	0.02	5.12
1956	2.90	45.46	33.49	20.19	8.84	16.19	4.01	4.00	4.51	3.89	0.06	0.02	4.53
1951	2.44	45.07	30.98	18.77	7.14	12.66	3.53	3.50	3.78	3.24	0.04	0.01	3.88
1941	—	43.52	27.86	16.65	6.36	10.43	3.32	3.77	3.20	2.28	0.02	0.01	3.32
1931	—	40.31	24.72	14.73	5.49	9.45	3.19	3.87	2.94	1.93	0.02	0.01	2.99
1921	—	40.57	25.25	14.00	4.51[3]	8.08	2.78	3.18	2.37	1.46	0.02	0.01	2.53
1911	—	42.92	23.74	12.70	3.83	6.96	2.10	2.07	1.50	1.09	0.04	0.01	2.08
1901[4]	—	47.28	22.16	11.95	3.15	6.01	1.16	0.38	0.29	0.50	0.13	0.02	1.55
1891	—	49.94	21.71	11.69	2.84	5.82	0.69	—[5]	—[5]	0.27	—[5]	0.08	1.39
1881	—	49.86	21.24	11.69	2.59	5.30	0.28	—[5]	—[5]	0.14	—[5]	0.04	1.25
1871	—	43.05	18.70	10.40	2.27	4.46	0.11	—[5]	—[5]	0.10	—[5]	0.04	1.06

[1] Density of population in years previous to 1941 are based on 1941 areas.

[2] Canada total includes Newfoundland from 1951 on only.

[3] Northwest River Arm and Rigolet on Hamilton Inlet, population deducted from Quebec as these parts were awarded to Newfoundland by decision of the Judicial Committee of the Privy Council, 1 March 1927.

[4] The population of Ontario, Quebec, Manitoba and Northwest Territories in 1901 is not adjusted according to the provisions of the Boundaries Extension Act, 1912.

[5] Included with Northwest Territories.

Series A67-69. Population, rural and urban, census dates, 1871 to 1976

Year	Total population	1941 definition[1]	
		Urban	Rural
	67	**68**	**69**
1976	22,992,605	17,366,970[2]	5,625,635[2]
1971	21,568,310	14,114,970	7,453,340
1966	20,014,880	12,625,784	7,389,096
1961	18,238,247	11,068,848	7,169,399
1956	16,080,791	9,286,126	6,794,665
1951[3]	14,009,429	7,941,222	6,068,207
1941	11,506,655	6,252,416	5,254,239
1931	10,376,786	5,572,058	4,804,728
1921	8,787,949	4,352,122	4,435,827
1911	7,206,643	3,272,947	3,933,696
1901	5,371,315	2,014,222	3,357,093
1891	4,833,239	1,537,098	3,296,141
1881	4,324,810	1,109,507	3,215,303
1871	3,689,257	722,343	2,966,914

[1] For urban, rural figures for censuses of 1901 to 1956, based on 1956 definition, see note to series A15–19 in original volume.

[2] Based on the definition of the 1976 Census. For all definitions, see notes to this table.

[3] Includes Newfoundland beginning in 1951. The total population of Newfoundland in 1951 is distributed as follows: basis 1941 definition, urban, 104,377; rural, 257,039; total, 361,416.

Series A70-74. Population in incorporated centres of 1,000 persons and over, by size groups, census dates, 1871 to 1976

Year	Total	100,000 persons and over	30,000–99,999 persons	5,000–29,999 persons	1,000–4,999 persons
	70	**71**	**72**	**73**	**74**
1976	20,832,787	8,287,145	4,349,816	4,842,849	3,352,977
1971	13,663,160	5,767,205	3,045,306	3,314,026	1,536,623
1966	12,180,538	4,847,632	2,592,121	3,285,665	1,455,120
1961	10,631,641	4,154,341	2,206,106	2,898,528	1,372,666
1956	8,842,206	3,661,994	1,394,055	2,511,245	1,274,912
1951[1]	7,511,539	3,260,939	1,147,888	1,947,128	1,155,584
1941	5,853,603	2,645,133	928,367	1,370,375	909,728
1931	5,160,901	2,328,175	696,680	1,305,304	830,742
1921	3,977,064	1,658,697	495,566	1,057,965	764,836
1911	3,007,576	1,080,960	488,748	782,771	655,097
1901	1,867,260	475,770	343,266	503,187	545,037
1891[2]	1,440,605	397,865	224,760	390,670	427,310
1881[2]	—[3]	140,747	220,922	298,371	—[3]
1871[2]	—[3]	107,225	115,791	228,354	—[3]

[1] Includes Newfoundland beginning in 1951.

[2] Not including the Yukon Territory and the Northwest Territories. There were no centres of 1,000 persons and over in the Yukon Territory and the Northwest Territories in earlier census years.

[3] Centres of 1,000–4,999 were estimated as follows: 1881, 316,000; 1871, 196,000. See note to series A20–24 in original volume.

Series A75-77. Rural population, farm and non-farm, census dates, 1931 to 1976

Year	Total rural	Non-farm	Farm
	75	**76**	**77**
		1976 definition	
1976	5,625,635	4,591,070	1,034,560
		1971 definition	
1971	5,157,525	3,737,730	1,419,795
		1966 definition	
1966	5,288,121	3,374,407	1,913,714
		1961 definition	
1961	5,537,857	3,465,072	2,072,785
		1956 definition	
1956[1]	5,365,936	2,734,349	2,631,587
1951	5,191,792	2,422,506	2,769,286
		1951 definition[2]	
1951	5,375,328	2,559,633	2,815,695
1941	5,236,164	2,123,396	3,112,768
1931	4,907,833	1,670,116	3,237,717
		1941 definition[2]	
1951	5,789,686	2,955,815	2,833,871
1941	5,239,094	2,122,172	3,116,922

[1] Includes the Yukon Territory, the Northwest Territories and Newfoundland in 1956 and later years.

[2] Excludes the Yukon Territory, the Northwest Territories and Newfoundland.

Series A78-93. Population, by age and sex, census dates, 1851 to 1976[1]

(thousands)

Year[2]	Sex	Total population (78)	Under 5 years (79)	5-9 years (80)	10-14 years (81)	15-19 years (82)	20-24 years (83)	25-29 years (84)	30-34 years (85)	35-39 years (86)	40-44 years (87)	45-49 years (88)	50-54 years (89)	55-59 years (90)	60-64 years (91)	65-69 years (92)	70 years and over (93)
1976	Both sexes	22,993	1,732	1,888	2,276	2,345	2,134	1,993	1,627	1,329	1,268	1,253	1,220	1,019	905	721	1,282
	Male	11,450	889	967	1,165	1,196	1,066	1,000	823	671	644	630	596	492	436	339	537
	Female	11,543	843	921	1,112	1,149	1,068	993	805	657	625	622	624	527	470	382	745
1971	Both sexes	21,568	1,816	2,254	2,311	2,114	1,889	1,584	1,305	1,264	1,263	1,239	1,053	955	777	620	1,124
	Male	10,795	930	1,152	1,181	1,074	942	801	661	645	641	613	519	472	382	296	486
	Female	10,773	887	1,102	1,129	1,040	948	783	645	619	622	626	534	482	395	324	639
1966	Both sexes	20,015	2,197	2,301	2,094	1,838	1,461	1,242	1,242	1,286	1,257	1,090	988	816	663	532	1,008
	Male	10,054	1,129	1,173	1,071	929	727	619	630	650	625	543	498	413	330	255	462
	Female	9,961	1,069	1,128	1,022	909	734	622	611	636	632	547	490	403	333	277	546
1961	Both sexes	18,238	2,256	2,080	1,856	1,433	1,184	1,209	1,272	1,271	1,119	1,015	863	706	584	487	904
	Male	9,219	1,154	1,064	948	729	587	614	644	631	560	516	443	362	293	240	434
	Female	9,019	1,102	1,016	908	704	597	595	627	640	559	500	420	344	291	247	470
1956	Both sexes	16,081	1,984	1,807	1,435	1,162	1,129	1,198	1,216	1,114	1,025	879	733	629	525	464	780
	Male	8,152	1,012	920	732	587	567	606	603	556	523	456	382	322	266	238	385
	Female	7,929	972	887	703	576	562	592	614	559	503	423	351	307	259	227	395
1951	Both sexes	14,009	1,722	1,398	1,131	1,058	1,089	1,131	1,043	999	869	745	663	571	506	433	653
	Male	7,089	879	714	575	532	538	553	513	504	446	388	340	293	264	228	323
	Female	6,921	843	684	556	526	551	578	530	496	423	357	322	278	242	205	330
1941	Both sexes	11,507	1,052	1,046	1,101	1,120	1,032	967	844	760	677	635	592	507	407	308	460
	Male	5,901	534	529	556	565	518	488	432	396	349	333	316	275	219	163	228
	Female	5,606	518	517	545	555	514	479	412	363	328	303	276	232	189	145	232
1931	Both sexes	10,377	1,075	1,133	1,074	1,040	912	787	709	689	646	586	489	367	295	231	345
	Male	5,375	543	573	543	526	464	410	368	359	348	322	268	199	157	121	174
	Female	5,002	531	560	531	514	448	376	341	329	298	264	221	168	138	110	171
1921	Both sexes	8,788	1,059	1,050	914	805	713	688	655	634	529	436	363	281	240	172	248
	Male	4,530	534	529	462	405	352	349	344	343	287	238	196	149	127	91	124
	Female	4,258	525	521	452	400	361	340	310	291	241	199	167	133	113	82	124
1911	Both sexes	7,207	890	785	702	686	712	663	559	471	392	333	287	214	179	132	204
	Male	3,822	450	396	356	355	390	374	313	260	215	180	154	114	95	68	103
	Female	3,385	440	389	346	331	322	289	246	211	177	153	133	100	84	64	101
1901	Both sexes	5,371	646	618	583	557	515	430	369	336	294	242	206	162	142	106	165
	Male	2,752	326	313	297	283	260	220	192	176	155	127	107	83	74	55	84
	Female	2,620	320	306	285	275	255	209	177	160	139	115	99	79	69	52	81
1891	Both sexes	4,833	611	592	554	521	482	395	326	275	235	198	173	131	121	85	135
	Male	2,460	309	300	282	262	242	199	167	142	121	102	89	68	63	45	70
	Female	2,373	302	292	272	259	240	196	158	132	114	96	84	64	58	40	65
1881	Both sexes	4,325	599	562	513	483	436	337	265	232	196	171	143	112	98	69	109
	Male	2,189	304	284	262	240	215	168	134	117	100	88	73	58	53	37	57
	Female	2,136	295	278	251	243	221	169	132	115	97	83	70	54	46	32	52
1871	Both sexes	3,689	541	519	476	408	351	282	223	188	158	139	113	90	69	56	79
	Male	1,869	276	264	243	202	172	138	111	94	81	72	60	48	38	31	43
	Female	1,820	265	255	233	206	179	144	112	94	77	67	53	42	31	25	36
1861	Both sexes	3,230	543	429	399	374	304	254	200	161	136	110	89	71	58	42	56
	Male	1,660	277	218	203	187	154	129	103	84	72	59	48	38	32	24	30
	Female	1,570	266	211	196	187	150	125	97	77	64	51	41	33	26	18	26
1851	Both sexes	2,436	451	346	298	277	223	184	145	118	101	81	64	49	35	23	42
	Male	1,250	233	173	152	136	112	93	75	62	54	43	35	27	19	13	22
	Female	1,186	218	173	146	141	111	91	70	56	47	38	29	22	16	10	20

1 Components may not add to totals due to rounding.
2 Includes Newfoundland beginning in 1951.

Series A94-109. Population, by age and sex, urban and rural, census dates, 1921 to 1976

(thousands)

Year[1,2] Locale and sex	Total	0-4 years	5-9 years	10-14 years	15-19 years	20-24 years	25-29 years	30-34 years	35-39 years	40-44 years	45-49 years	50-54 years	55-59 years	60-64 years	65-69 years	70 years and over
	94	95	96	97	98	99	100	101	102	103	104	105	106	107	108	109
1976 Urban male	8,529	641	691	828	871	833	780	628	512	492	482	451	364	318	244	392
female	8,838	609	661	794	858	861	781	624	510	487	487	488	407	366	302	603
Rural non-farm male	2,364	211	226	264	248	188	193	167	131	118	112	108	96	93	80	128
female	2,227	201	213	249	227	179	187	154	118	106	103	105	97	89	72	127
Farm male	557	36	50	72	77	45	28	27	28	33	37	37	31	24	14	16
female	478	34	50	68	64	28	25	27	29	31	33	31	23	15	9	14
1971 Urban male	8,105	688	837	849	778	746	643	521	505	498	470	387	348	277	210	348
female	8,306	656	801	817	775	781	634	512	489	491	492	413	375	307	253	509
Rural non-farm male	1,929	188	230	228	196	144	126	108	103	98	94	85	82	72	64	112
female	1,809	179	219	216	180	134	121	101	92	88	89	82	77	67	58	108
Farm male	762	54	86	104	101	52	32	31	38	45	49	47	43	33	22	26
female	658	51	82	97	85	33	29	32	38	43	45	39	31	21	13	21
1966 Urban male	7,283	807	824	736	647	553	482	488	498	473	399	360	293	230	175	317
female	7,444	764	797	707	658	589	491	479	496	490	416	372	304	251	210	420
Rural non-farm male	1,748	221	223	200	163	112	98	99	98	92	83	78	69	58	51	103
female	1,627	209	213	189	151	103	95	89	88	85	77	70	61	54	48	94
Farm male	1,024	122	126	135	119	62	40	44	53	60	61	60	52	42	29	42
female	890	116	118	126	100	42	36	43	52	57	54	48	38	28	19	32
1961 Urban male	6,291	780	696	609	461	411	452	476	460	397	361	306	245	195	158	284
female	6,409	745	667	588	477	453	451	473	478	411	367	309	250	212	181	347
Rural non-farm male	1,807	252	230	200	147	109	103	100	109	98	88	76	63	55	50	104
female	1,658	241	218	191	132	101	89	90	101	88	77	64	54	50	46	89
Farm male	1,120	122	137	139	121	67	49	55	62	65	66	61	54	43	32	47
female	953	116	130	129	94	42	42	51	60	60	56	48	40	29	21	34
1956 Urban male	5,299	644	569	435	344	374	426	426	384	357	307	254	211	172	152	242
female	5,416	621	551	423	365	410	437	450	402	362	303	250	218	184	162	281
Rural non-farm male	1,442	196	175	134	110	104	103	100	91	83	72	59	51	43	42	79
female	1,293	187	170	129	100	86	89	90	81	70	57	46	43	39	37	68
Farm male	1,411	172	175	163	132	89	76	77	81	82	77	69	61	50	43	63
female	1,220	164	166	151	111	66	66	74	76	71	63	55	47	36	28	47
1951 Urban male	4,222	504	389	301	289	330	358	328	320	281	242	213	181	163	137	187
female	4,406	484	376	296	317	382	401	359	336	287	240	218	188	164	138	218
Rural non-farm male	1,339	188	148	113	100	99	100	94	91	78	65	56	48	45	43	71
female	1,214	180	142	111	91	88	95	89	80	64	51	46	41	38	36	62
Farm male	1,527	187	176	161	144	109	94	91	93	86	81	72	64	57	48	65
female	1,301	179	167	149	117	81	83	82	80	72	66	58	49	39	31	49

Series A94-109. Population, by age and sex, urban and rural, census dates, 1921 to 1976 (concluded)

(thousands)

Year[1][2] Locale and sex	Total	0-4 years	5-9 years	10-14 years	15-19 years	20-24 years	25-29 years	30-34 years	35-39 years	40-44 years	45-49 years	50-54 years	55-59 years	60-64 years	65-69 years	70 years and over
	94	95	96	97	98	99	100	101	102	103	104	105	106	107	108	109
1941 Urban																
male	3,079	250	248	270	284	275	272	241	221	195	186	176	149	116	83	115
female	3,174	242	244	270	303	315	297	254	221	200	184	168	139	113	86	138
Rural																
male	2,822	284	281	286	281	243	217	190	176	154	147	140	126	102	80	114
female	2,432	276	273	274	252	200	182	158	142	128	119	108	93	75	59	94
1931 Urban																
male	2,773	260	278	265	257	236	221	205	202	196	179	146	104	79	59	82
female	2,801	255	275	266	286	274	231	207	200	181	158	132	97	79	63	96
Rural																
male	2,602	283	294	278	268	228	189	163	157	152	143	121	96	78	62	91
female	2,201	276	286	266	229	173	145	133	129	117	105	90	71	58	47	75
1921 Urban																
male	2,147	238	241	207	179	164	175	178	177	147	118	95	70	58	40	53
female	2,205	235	242	211	203	203	196	178	164	135	109	91	70	61	42	61
Rural																
male	2,383	295	288	254	224	187	173	165	165	140	118	100	78	68	50	71
female	2,054	289	278	241	196	157	143	132	126	106	90	76	62	52	39	62

1 Includes Newfoundland for 1951 and later years.
2 Except for figures of 1921, 1931 and 1941 which are based on 1941 rural, urban definition, the figures for all other years are based on definitions adopted in respective censuses.

Series A110-124. Population, by marital status and sex, census dates, 1871 to 1976

Year	Total			Single			Married[1]			Widowed			Divorced		
	Both sexes	Male	Female	Both sexes	Male	Female	Both sexes	Male	Female	Both sexes	Male	Female	Both sexes	Male	Female
	110	111	112	113	114	115	116	117	118	119	120	121	122	123	124

Population, 15 years and over

Year	110	111	112	113	114	115	116	117	118	119	120	121	122	123	124
1976	17,096,430	8,429,515	8,666,915	4,776,420	2,646,580	2,129,840	10,973,905	5,474,235	5,499,670	1,043,565	189,665	853,900	302,535	119,035	183,505
1971	15,187,410	7,531,890	7,655,525	4,290,675	2,377,650	1,913,030	9,777,600	4,888,760	4,888,845	944,020	191,125	752,895	175,115	74,355	100,755
1966	13,423,123	6,681,497	6,741,626	3,764,833	2,100,917	1,663,916	8,723,217	4,359,554	4,363,663	870,297	195,647	674,650	64,776	25,379	39,397
1961	12,046,325	6,052,802	5,993,523	3,191,206	1,811,473	1,379,733	8,024,304	4,019,725	4,004,579	778,223	199,507	578,716	52,592	22,097	30,495
1956	10,855,581	5,488,060	5,367,521	2,960,929	1,691,761	1,269,168	7,146,673	3,586,641	3,560,032	711,211	194,722	516,489	36,768	14,936	21,832
1951[2]	9,758,712	4,920,815	4,837,897	2,821,788	1,579,351	1,242,437	6,261,578	3,141,754	3,119,824	643,348	186,595	456,753	31,998	13,115	18,883
1941	8,308,104	4,281,237	4,026,867	3,032,324	1,703,795	1,328,529	4,736,585	2,400,100	2,336,485	525,163	170,773	354,390	14,032	6,569	7,463
1931	7,095,010	3,715,527	3,379,483	2,671,820	1,522,491	1,149,329	3,978,012	2,039,918	1,938,094	437,731	149,063	288,668	7,447	4,055	3,392
1921	5,764,598	3,004,173	2,760,425	2,062,520	1,177,952	884,568	3,337,535	1,702,526	1,635,009	357,132	120,020	237,112	7,411	3,675	3,736
1911	4,830,093	2,619,817	2,210,276	1,952,341	1,182,167	770,174	2,602,295	1,345,386	1,256,909	271,031	90,121	180,910	4,426	2,143	2,283
1901[3]	—	—	—	—	—	—	—	—	—	—	—	—	—	—	—
1891	3,075,749	1,569,502	1,506,247	1,295,937	710,576	585,361	1,588,023	796,149	791,874	191,789	62,777	129,012	—	—	—

Population, all ages

Year	110	111	112	113	114	115	116	117	118	119	120	121	122	123	124
1901	5,371,315	2,751,708	2,619,607	3,312,593	1,748,582	1,564,011	1,833,043	928,952	904,091	225,018	73,837	151,181	661	337	324
1891	4,833,239	2,460,471	2,372,768	3,053,392	1,601,541	1,451,851	1,588,055	796,153	791,902	191,792	62,777	129,015	—	—	—
1881	4,324,810	2,188,854	2,135,956	2,784,396	1,447,415	1,336,981	1,380,084	690,544	689,540	160,330	50,895	109,435	—	—	—
1871[4]	3,689,257	1,869,264	1,819,993	2,366,876	1,226,347	1,140,529	1,119,659	560,075	559,584	118,475	37,874	80,601	—	—	—

[1] In all years, 'married' includes all married persons whether or not they are living together except in 1911 and 1921, when 'permanently separated' were included with 'divorced'.
[2] Includes Newfoundland for 1951 and later years.
[3] Classification by age and marital status not available for 1901.
[4] Total includes total population of British Columbia and Northwest Territories for which marital status not available.

Series A125-163. Origins of the population, census dates, 1871 to 1971

Series no.	Origin[1]	1871	1881	1901	1911	1921	1931	1941	1951	1961	1971
125	British	2,110,502	2,548,514	3,063,195	3,999,081	4,868,738	5,381,071	5,715,904	6,709,685	7,996,669	9,624,115
126	English	706,369	881,301	1,260,899	1,871,268	2,545,358	2,741,419	2,968,402	3,630,344	4,195,175	—
127	Irish	846,414	957,403	988,721	1,074,738	1,107,803	1,230,808	1,267,702	1,439,635	1,753,351	—
128	Scottish	549,946	699,863	800,154	1,027,015	1,173,625	1,346,350	1,403,974	1,547,470	1,902,302	—
129	Other	7,773	9,947	13,421	26,060	41,952	62,494	75,826	92,236	145,841	—
130	Other European	1,322,813	1,598,386	2,107,327	3,006,502	3,699,846	4,753,242	5,526,964	6,872,889	9,657,195	11,139,800
131	French	1,082,940	1,298,929	1,649,371	2,061,719	2,452,743	2,927,990	3,483,038	4,319,167	5,540,346	6,180,120
132	Austrian	—	—	10,947[2]	44,036	107,671	48,639	37,715	32,231	106,535	42,120
133	Belgian	—	—	2,994	9,664	20,234	27,585	29,711	35,148	61,382	51,135
134	Czech and Slovak	—	—	—	—	8,840	30,401	42,912	63,959	73,061	81,870
135	Danish	—[3]	—[3]	—[3]	—[3]	21,124	34,118	37,439	42,671	85,473	75,725
136	Finnish	—	—	2,502	15,500	21,494	43,885	41,683	43,745	59,436	59,215
137	German	202,991	254,319	310,501	403,417	294,635	473,544	464,682	619,995	1,049,599	1,317,200
138	Greek	39	—	291	3,614	5,740	9,444	11,692	13,966	56,475	124,475
139	Hungarian	—	—	1,549[4]	11,648	13,181	40,582	54,598	60,460	126,220	131,890
140	Icelandic	—[3]	—[3]	—[3]	—[3]	15,876	19,382	21,050	23,307	30,623	27,905
141	Italian	1,035	1,849	10,834	45,963	66,769	98,173	112,625	152,245	450,351	730,820
142	Jewish	125	667	16,131	76,199	126,196	156,726	170,241	181,670	173,344	296,945
143	Lithuanian	—	—	—	—	1,970	5,876	7,789	16,224	27,629	24,535
144	Netherlander	29,662	30,412	33,845	55,961	117,505	148,962	212,863	264,267	429,679	425,945
145	Norwegian	—[3]	—[3]	—[3]	—[3]	68,856	93,243	100,718	119,266	148,681	179,290
146	Polish	—	—	6,285	33,652	53,403	145,503	167,485	219,845	323,517	316,430
147	Romanian	—	—	354[5]	5,883	13,470	29,056	24,689	23,601	43,805	27,375
148	Russian	607[6]	1,227[6]	19,825	44,376	100,064	88,148	83,708	91,279	119,168	64,475
149	Scandinavian[7]	1,623	5,223	31,042	112,682	167,359	228,049	244,603	283,024	386,534	384,795
150	Swedish	—[3]	—[3]	—[3]	—[3]	61,503	81,306	85,396	97,780	121,757	101,870
151	Ukrainian	—	—	5,682	75,432	106,721	225,113	305,929[8]	395,043	473,337	580,660
152	Yugoslavic	—	—	—	—	3,906	16,174	21,214	21,404	68,587	104,955
153	Other	3,791	5,760	5,174	6,756	17,945	9,392	9,787	35,616	88,190	194,850

Series A125-163. Origins of the population, census dates, 1871 to 1971 (concluded)

Series no.	Origin[1]	1871	1881	1901	1911	1921	1931	1941	1951	1961	1971
154	Asiatic	4	4,383	23,731	43,213	65,914	84,548	74,064	72,827	121,753	285,540
155	Chinese	–	4,383	17,312	27,831	39,587	46,519	34,627	32,528	58,197	118,815
156	Japanese	–	–	4,738	9,067	15,868	23,342	23,149	21,663	29,157	37,260
157	Other	4	–	1,681	6,315	10,459	14,687	16,288	18,636	34,399	129,460
158	Other origins	52,442	173,527	177,062	157,847	153,451	157,925	189,723	354,028	462,630	518,850
159	Native Indian and Inuit (Eskimo)	23,037	108,547	127,941	105,611	113,724	128,890	125,521	165,607	220,121	312,760
160	Negro	21,496	21,394	17,437	16,994	18,291	19,456	22,174	18,020	32,127	34,445
161	Other	348	2,780	145	18,310	187	681	36,753[9]	170,401	210,382	171,645[10]
162	Not stated	7,561	40,806	31,539	16,932	21,249	8,898	5,275			
163	Total	3,485,761	4,324,810	5,371,315	7,206,643	8,787,949	10,376,786	11,506,655	14,009,429	18,238,247	21,568,310

[1] The data for 1871 refer only to the four original provinces of Canada. The data for 1951 and later years include Newfoundland.
[2] Includes Bohemian, Bukovinian and Slavic.
[3] Included under Scandinavian.
[4] Includes Lithuanian and Moravian.
[5] Includes Bulgarian.
[6] Includes Finnish and Polish.
[7] Since 1921 Scandinavian has been divided into Danish, Icelandic, Norwegian and Swedish.
[8] Includes Bukovinian, Galician and Ruthenian.
[9] Includes 35,416 Métis.
[10] Origin 'not stated' cases in 1971 were computer assigned.

Series A164-184. Principal religious denominations of the population, census dates, 1871 to 1971

Year	Anglican	Baptist	Congregationalist	Evangelical Church	Greek Orthodox[1]	Jehovah's Witnesses	Jewish	Lutheran	Mennonite[2]	Methodist	Mormon
	164	165	166	167	168	169	170	171	172	173	174
1971	2,543,180	667,245	–[3]	–[4]	316,605	174,805	276,025	715,740	181,800	–[3]	66,635
1961	2,409,068	593,553	–[4]	27,079	239,766	68,018	254,368	662,744	152,452	–[4]	50,016
1951	2,060,720	519,585	–[4]	50,900	172,271	34,596	204,836	444,923	125,938	–[4]	32,888
1941	1,754,368	484,465	–[4]	37,064	139,845	7,007	168,585	401,836	111,554	–[4]	25,238
1931	1,639,075	443,944	694[5]	22,239	102,529	13,582	155,766	394,920	88,837	–[4]	22,041
1921	1,407,780	421,730	30,730	13,905	169,832	6,689	125,197	286,458	58,797	1,159,246	19,622
1911	1,043,017	382,720	34,054	10,595	88,507	938	74,564	229,864	44,625	1,079,993	15,971
1901	681,494	318,005	28,293	10,193	15,630	101	16,401	92,524	31,797	916,886	6,891
1891	646,059	303,839	28,157	–	–	–	6,414	63,982	–	847,765	–
1881	574,818	296,525	26,900	–	–	–	2,393	46,350	–	742,981	–
1871	501,269	243,714	21,829	4,701	18	–	1,115	37,935	–	578,161	534

Year	Pentecostal	Presbyterian	Roman Catholic	Salvation Army	Ukrainian (Greek) Catholic	United Church of Canada	Other	Not stated	No religion	Total
	175	176	177	178	179	180	181	182	183	184
1971	220,390	872,335[6]	9,974,895	119,665	227,730[7]	3,768,800	1,617,270		929,580	21,568,310
1961	143,877	818,558[6]	8,342,826	92,054	189,653[7]	3,664,008	598,225		94,763	18,238,247
1951	95,131	781,747[6]	6,069,496	70,275	190,831[7]	2,867,271	322,017		59,679	14,009,429
1941	57,742	830,597[6]	4,806,431	33,609	185,948[7]	2,208,658	243,466	17,159	19,161	11,506,655
1931	26,349	872,428[6]	4,102,960	30,773	186,879[7]	2,021,065	250,245	16,042	21,155	10,376,786
1921	7,003	1,409,406	3,389,626	24,733	–	8,728	235,897	19,259	21,819	8,787,949
1911	513	1,116,071	2,833,041	18,834	–	–	201,784	32,490	26,893	7,206,643
1901	–	842,531	2,229,600	10,308	–	–	127,540	43,222	6,193	5,371,315
1891	–	755,326	1,992,017	13,949	–	–	95,464	80,267	–[3]	4,833,239
1881	–	676,165	1,791,982	–	–	–	79,927	86,769	3,486	4,324,810
1871	–	574,577	1,532,471	–	–	–	66,080	126,853[8]	5,198	3,689,257

[1] Greek Orthodox and Greek Catholic combined under the term 'Greek Church' in 1921 and prior years.
[2] Includes Hutterite. Mennonites were included with Baptists in 1871 and 1881; in 1891 they were included with 'other'.
[3] Included with 'Other' and 'Not stated'.
[4] Included in the 'United Church of Canada'.
[5] The figure for 1931 under "Congregationalist" is the number of that denomination not included in "United Church of Canada".
[6] The figures for 1931 and later years opposite 'Presbyterian' are the numbers of that denomination not included in the 'United Church of Canada'.
[7] Includes 'Other Greek Catholics'.
[8] Includes 109,475 population in Manitoba, British Columbia and the Northwest Territories who were largely Indian and hence likely pagan.

Series A185-237. Mother tongues of the population, census years, 1931 to 1976

Series no.		1931[1]	1941[1]	1951	1961	1971	1976
185	English	5,914,402	6,448,190	8,280,809	10,660,534	12,973,810	14,122,770
186	French	2,832,298	3,354,753	4,068,850	5,123,151	5,793,650	5,887,205
187	Armenian	..	..	..	..	..	10,335
188	Baltic languages	..	..	28,110	42,889	43,385	34,185
189	Estonian	..	..	8,784	13,830	14,520	11,975
190	Lettish	..	..	7,019	14,062	14,140	11,150
191	Lithuanian	5,506	6,910	12,307	14,997	14,725	11,065
192	Bulgarian	2,661	..	..	..	..	1,500
193	Celtic languages	..	..	..	..	24,360	10,060
194	Gaelic	..	7,533	13,974	32,708	21,200	1,620
195	Welsh	..	..	..	3,040	3,160	2,055
196	Others	..	..	..	..	—[2]	6.385
197	Chinese and Japanese	69,281	55,859	45,878	66,955	111,745	148,085
198	Chinese	..	33,500	28,289	49,099	94,855	132,560
199	Japanese	..	22,359	17,589	17,856	16,890	15,525
200	Croatian, Serbian, etc.	..	..	..	..	74,190	77,575
201	Croatian					20,860	20,390
202	Serbian	10,521	14,863	11,031	28,886	5,225	3,855
203	Slovenian	..	..	..	..	6,415	4,785
204	Yugoslav, n.e s.[3]	..	..	..	..	41,690	48,535
205	Czech and Slovak	..	..	..	51,423	45,150	34,950
206	Czech	..	..	..	8,877	27,780	22,035
207	Slovak	25,099	37,604	45,516	42,546	17,370	12,915
208	Dutch	26,532	53,215	87,935	170,177	144,925	114,760
209	Finnish	39,965	37,331	31,771	44,785	36,725	28,470
210	Flemish	18,048	14,557	12,623	14,304	14,240	7,790
211	German	362,011	322,228	329,302	563,713	561,085	476,715
212	Greek	7,346	8,747	8,036	40,455	104,455	91,530
213	Native Indian and Inuit	..	130,929	144,787	166,531	179,820	133,005
214	Native Indian	..	..	..	..	164,525	117,105
215	Inuit (Eskimo)	..	..	..	..	15,295	15,900
216	Indo-Pakistan	..	..	1,731	4,505	32,555	58,415
217	Iranian	..	..	..	..	..	1,455
218	Italian	85,520	80,260	92,244	339,626	538,360	484,050
219	Magyar (Hungarian)	37,959	46,287	42,402	85,939	86,835	69,300
220	Polish	118,599	128,711	129,238	161,720	134,780	99,845
221	Portugese	..	..	150	18,213	86,925	126,535
222	Romanian	18,115	16,402	10,105	10,165	11,300	8,755
223	Russian	50,759	52,431	39,223	42,903	31,745	23,485
224	Scandinavian	159,854	143,917	106,848	116,714	84,335	59,410
225	Danish	21,453	18,776	15,714	35,035	27,395	21,315
226	Icelandic	16,034	15,510	11,207	8,993	7,860	5,030
227	Norwegian	64,125	60,084	43,831	40,054	27,405	18,070
228	Swedish	58,242	49,547	36,096	32,632	21,680	15,000
229	Semitic languages	..	..	..	..	28,550	37,100
230	Spanish	1,472	1,030	1,516	6,720	23,815	44,135
231	Syrian and Arabic	9,226	8,111	5,475	12,999	28,550	..
232	Turkish	..	..	..	..	..	2,595
233	Ukrainian	252,802	313,273	352,323	361,496	309,855	282,060
234	Yiddish	149,520	129,806	103,593	82,448	49,890	23,435
235	Other[4]	179,290	61,231	29,933	17,976	41,835	48,065
236	Not stated	—	—	—	—	—	445,020
237	Total	10,376,786	11,506,655	14,009,429	18,238,247	21,568,310	22,992,605

[1] Excludes Newfoundland.
[2] Included with Gaelic.

[3] Not elsewhere stated, includes a number of other Yugoslav languages.
[4] Includes mother tongue not stated prior to 1951.

Series A238-247. Number of children ever born per 1,000 ever married women, 15 years of age and over, total, rural and urban, Canada, 1941, 1961 and 1971

Year	15–19	20–24	25–29	30–34	35–39	40–44	45–54	55–64	65+	Total
	238	**239**	**240**	**241**	**242**	**243**	**244**	**245**	**246**	**247**
Total										
1971	634	910	1,706	2,621	3,158	3,348	3,257	3,049	3,565	2,775
1961	735	1,327	2,178	2,775	3,102	3,231	3,130	3,506	4,038	2,987
1941[1]	529	1,003	1,640	2,425	3,206	3,795	4,167	4,398	4,818	3,341
Rural										
1971	758	1,239	2,196	3,265	3,974	4,259	4,177	3,930	4,466	3,567
1961	842	1,646	2,720	3,493	3,979	4,233	4,201	4,512	4,897	3,835
1941[1]	1,100		2,497		4,260		4,936	5,010	..	..
Urban										
1971	592	832	1,583	2,448	2,936	3,098	2,990	2,784	3,320	2,558
1961	682	1,212	1,991	2,528	2,792	2,850	2,719	3,102	3,698	2,671
1941[1]	795		1,698		2,943		3,637	3,965	..	..

[1] Excludes Newfoundland. Figures include women for whom number of children ever born was not stated.

Series A248-253. Number of households and average number of persons per household, Canada, 1881 to 1976

Year[1]	Total		Urban		Rural	
	Number	Average	Number	Average	Number	Average
	248	**249**	**250**	**251**	**252**	**253**
1976	7,166,095	3.1	5,613,045	3.0	1,553,050	3.5
1971	6,041,302	3.5	4,743,279	3.4	1,298,023	3.9
1966	5,180,473	3.7	3,941,459	3.6	1,239,014	4.1
1961	4,554,736	3.9	3,280,682	3.7	1,274,054	4.2
1956	3,923,646	3.9	2,701,234	3.8	1,222,412	4.2
1951	3,409,284	4.0	2,155,028	3.9	1,254,256	4.2
1941[2]	2,575,744	4.3	1,416,893	4.2	1,158,851	4.5
1931	2,252,729	4.4	1,240,715	4.3	1,012,014	4.6
1921	1,897,227	4.6	958,371	4.5	938,856	4.7
1911	1,482,980	4.8	..	..	..	..
1901	1,058,386	5.0	..	..	..	..
1891	900,080	5.3	..	..	..	..
1881	800,410	5.3	..	..	..	..

[1] Includes private and collective households from 1881 to 1921 and private households only from 1931 to 1976.
[2] Excludes Newfoundland, the Yukon Territory and the Northwest Territories in 1941 and earlier years.

Series A254-259. Number of families and average number of persons per family, Canada, 1881 to 1976

Year	Total		Urban		Rural	
	Number	Average	Number	Average	Number	Average
	254	**255**	**256**	**257**	**258**	**259**
1976	5,727,895	3.5	4,372,090	3.4	1,355,805	3.7
1971	5,070,682	3.7	3,923,380	3.6	1,147,305	4.1
1966	4,526,266	3.9	3,413,178	3.8	1,113,088	4.3
1961	4,147,444	3.9	2,985,055	3.7	1,162,389	4.3
1956	3,711,500	3.8	2,583,568	3.6	1,127,912	4.3
1951	3,287,384	3.7	2,123,540	3.5	1,163,844	4.1
1941[1]	2,525,299	3.9	1,437,415	3.7	1,087,884	4.3
1931[1]	2,419,360	3.9	1,333,579	3.7	1,085,781	4.1
1921[1]	2,001,512	4.3	1,023,736	4.0	977,776	4.6
1911[2]	1,488,353	..	..	..	..	..
1901	1,070,747	..	..	..	..	..
1891	921,643	..	..	..	..	..
1881	812,136	..	..	..	..	..

[1] Excludes Newfoundland, the Yukon Territory and the Northwest Territories.
[2] Excludes Newfoundland only in 1911 and earlier years.

Series A260-269. Population, Canadian, other British and foreign-born, by sex, census dates, 1871 to 1971

Year	Total population	Canadian-born			Other British-born[1]			Foreign-born		
		Total	Male	Female	Total	Male	Female	Total	Male	Female
	260	261	262	263	264	265	266	267	268	269
1971	21,568,310	18,272,780	9,147,060	9,125,720	1,103,145	521,595	581,550	2,192,390	1,135,475	1,056,910
1961	18,238,247	15,393,984	7,746,249	7,647,735	1,017,602	490,681	526,921	1,826,661	981,963	844,698
1951	14,009,429	11,949,518[2]	6,001,035[2]	5,948,483[2]	933,049	462,640	470,409	1,126,862	625,198	501,664
1941	11,506,655[3]	9,487,808	4,794,439	4,693,369	1,003,769	527,423	476,346	1,014,133	577,906	436,227
1931	10,376,786	8,069,261	4,076,001	3,993,260	1,184,830	631,411	553,419	1,122,695	667,129	455,566
1921	8,787,949	6,832,224	3,443,109	3,389,115	1,065,448	567,068	498,380	890,277	519,466	370,811
1911	7,206,643	5,619,682	2,849,442	2,770,240	834,229	501,626	332,603	752,732	470,927	281,805
1901	5,371,315	4,671,815	–	–	421,051	–	–	278,449	–	–
1891	4,833,239	4,189,368	–	–	490,573	–	–	153,298	–	–
1881	4,324,810	3,721,826	–	–	478,615	–	–	124,369	–	–
1871	3,689,257[4]	3,010,803	–	–	498,953	–	–	95,254	–	–

[1] Other British-born covers England and Wales, Northern Ireland, Scotland, the Lesser Isles and Other British Commonwealth (1951 Census). For breakdown, see series A170-176. Previous to 1951, the item "Other British-born" includes also Newfoundland and the Republic of Ireland. From 1951, the Republic of Ireland is included in "Foreign-born".

[2] Includes Newfoundland in 1951 and later years.

[3] Total population in 1941 includes 945 'birthplace not stated'.

[4] Total population in 1871 includes 84,247 population, largely Indians, in British Columbia and the Northwest Territories for whom birthplace is unknown. For discussion of 'not stated' in all years see the note to this table.

Series A270-281. Population, by birthplace and sex, rural and urban,[1] census dates, 1921 to 1971

Year	Canadian-born[2]				Other British-born[2]				Foreign-born			
	Rural		Urban		Rural		Urban		Rural		Urban	
	Male	Female	Male	Female	Male	Female	Male	Female	Male	Female	Male	Female
	270	271	272	273	274	275	276	277	278	279	280	281
1971	2,469,625	2,258,470	6,677,430	6,867,255	57,935	59,430	463,660	522,125	155,625	130,375	979,855	926,535
1961	2,634,927	2,373,216	5,111,322	5,274,519	78,622	73,478	412,059	453,443	214,031	163,583	767,932	681,115
1951	2,526,344	2,257,036	3,474,691	3,691,447	99,783	86,526	362,857	383,883	240,484	171,003	384,714	330,661
1941[3]	2,358,768	2,097,622	2,435,671	2,595,747	175,604	138,372	351,819	337,974	287,014	196,442	290,892	239,785
1931	2,047,970	1,829,124	2,028,031	2,164,136	220,574	159,927	410,837	393,492	333,477	211,916	333,652	243,650
1921	1,879,938	1,704,725	1,563,171	1,684,390	212,083	157,986	354,985	340,394	291,420	192,080	228,046	178,731

[1] 1941 and all previous years are based on 1941 definition of urban, rural, etc., 1951 and later years are based on the definitions in respective censuses. See note to series A67-69.

[2] In 1951 and later years, 'Canadian-born' includes Newfoundland. In other years, Newfoundland is under "Other British-born".

[3] Excludes 945 whose birthplace is not stated; rural, 417; urban, 528; males, 768; females, 177.

Series A282-296. Population, Canadian, other British and foreign-born, by age and sex, census dates, 1911 to 1971
(thousands)

Year	All ages			Under 15 years			15–24 years			25–64 years			65 years and over		
	Both sexes	Male	Female	Both sexes	Male	Female	Both sexes	Male	Female	Both sexes	Male	Female	Both sexes	Male	Female
	282	283	284	285	286	287	288	289	290	291	292	293	294	295	296
Canadian-born															
1971	18,273	9,147	9,126	6,096	3,118	2,978	3,593	1,816	1,777	7,477	3,729	3,748	1,108	485	623
1961	15,394	7,746	7,648	5,923	3,027	2,896	2,365	1,191	1,174	6,255	3,130	3,124	851	398	453
1951[1]	11,950	6,001	5,948	4,154	2,118	2,036	2,046	1,019	1,027	5,058	2,528	2,530	691	336	355
1941[2]	9,488	4,794	4,693	3,149	1,594	1,555	2,016	1,014	1,002	3,794	1,925	1,869	529	261	268
1931[3]	8,069	4,076	3,993	3,129	1,580	1,548	1,662	834	828	2,854	1,448	1,406	422	211	211
1921[3]	6,833	3,443	3,389	2,834	1,429	1,405	1,177	583	594	2,490	1,264	1,226	312	157	155
1911[3]	5,620	2,849	2,770	2,130	1,074	1,056	1,068	537	531	2,165	1,109	1,057	240	119	121
Other British and foreign-born															
1971	3,296	1,657	1,638	283	146	137	406	202	204	1,971	1,011	959	636	298	338
1961	2,844	1,473	1,372	269	139	130	251	125	126	1,784	932	852	540	276	264
1951	2,060	1,088	972	96	50	46	101	50	50	1,468	772	696	395	215	180
1941[2]	2,018	1,105	913	50	25	25	136	69	67	1,593	882	712	239	130	109
1931[3]	2,308	1,299	1,009	152	78	74	289	155	134	1,711	982	729	154	83	71
1921[3]	1,956	1,087	869	185	95	91	336	171	165	1,326	763	563	107	57	50
1911[3]	1,587	973	614	241	124	117	318	200	118	913	582	332	94	50	44

[1] 1951 and later years include Newfoundland. Prior to 1951 persons born in Newfoundland are included under heading "Other British and foreign-born".

[2] Not including some portion of the 768 males and 177 females whose place of birth was not stated.

[3] All ages includes 'age not stated'.

Series A297-326. Country of birth of other British-born and the foreign-born population, census dates, 1871 to 1971

Year	Total all countries[1]	Other British-born						United States	Europe	
		England and Wales	Scotland	Northern Ireland[2]	Lesser Isles	Newfound-land	Other British Common-wealth		Total	Republic of Ireland[2]
	297	298	299	300	301	302	303	304	305	306
1971	3,295,535	–	–	–	–	–[3]	170,105	309,640	1,684,515	38,490
1961	2,844,263	662,102	244,052	61,588	1,973	–[3]	47,887	283,908	1,468,058	30,889
1951	2,059,911	627,551	226,343	56,685	1,903	–[3]	20,567	282,010	801,618	24,110
1941	2,017,902	635,221	234,824	86,126	3,954	25,837	17,807	312,473	653,705	–
1931	2,307,525	746,212	279,765	107,544	5,421	26,410	19,478	344,574	714,462	–
1921	1,955,725	700,442	226,481	93,301	4,807	23,103	17,226	374,022	459,325	–
1911	1,586,961	519,401	169,391	92,874	2,860	15,469	14,526	303,680	404,941	–
1901	699,500	203,803	83,631	101,629	956	12,432	3,771	127,899	125,549	–
1891	643,871	219,688	107,594	149,184	1,269	9,336	3,502	80,915	53,841	–
1881	602,984	169,504	115,062	185,526	814	4,596	3,113	77,753	39,161	–
1871	594,207	147,081	125,450	223,212	852	–[3]	2,358	64,613	28,699	–

Year	Europe									
	Scandinavia	France	Belgium	Netherlands	Germany	Austria and Hungary	Czecho-slovakia	Switzerland	Italy	Greece
	307	308	309	310	311	312	313	314	315	316
1971	60,210	51,655	25,770	133,525	211,060	108,945	43,100	13,895	385,755	78,780
1961	74,616	36,103	28,253	135,033	189,131	143,092	35,743	11,381	258,071	38,017
1951	64,522	15,650	17,251	41,457	42,693	70,527	29,546	6,414	57,789	8,594
1941	72,473	13,795	14,773	9,923	28,479	82,526	25,564	5,505	40,432	5,871
1931	90,042	16,756	17,033	10,736	39,163	65,914	22,835	6,076	42,578	5,579
1921	64,795	19,247	13,276	5,827	25,266	65,028	4,322	3,479	35,531	3,769
1911	61,240	17,619	7,975	3,808	39,577	78,088	1,689	–	34,739	2,640
1901	18,388	7,944	2,280	385	27,300	28,407	–	1,211	6,854	213
1891	7,827	5,381	–	–	27,752	–	–	–	2,795	–
1881	2,076	4,389	–	–	25,328	–	–	–	777	–
1871	588	2,908	–	–	24,162	102	–	–	218	–

Year	Europe						Asia			Other countries
	U.S.S.R.	Poland	Finland	Romania	Yugoslavia	Other	China	Japan	Other	
	317	318	319	320	321	322	323	324	325	326
1971	160,120	160,040	24,930	24,405	78,285	85,550	57,150	9,485	52,795	78,800
1961	186,653	171,467	29,467	27,011	50,826	22,305	36,724	6,797	14,240	16,934
1951	188,292	164,474	22,035	19,733	20,912	7,619	24,166	6,239	6,740	6,089
1941	124,402	155,400	24,387	28,454	17,416	4,305	29,095	9,462	5,886	3,512
1931	133,869	171,169	30,354	40,322	17,110	4,926	42,037	12,261	6,310	3,051
1921	112,412	65,304	12,156	22,779	1,946	4,188	36,924	11,650	5,062	3,294
1911	89,984	31,373	10,987	18,271	–	6,951	27,083	8,425	5,438	3,165
1901	31,231		–	1,066	–	270	17,043	4,674	1,863	1,421
1891	9,222	695	–	–	–	169	9,129	–	–	9,413
1881	6,376		–	–	–	215	–	–	–	7,455
1871	,416		–	–	–	305	–	–	–	1,942

[1] The totals for all countries in 1901, 1911 and 1921 include 14,829, 19,708 and 88, respectively, "Other British-born' whose countries of birth are unknown.

[2] Prior to 1951, the Republic of Ireland is included with Northern Ireland.

[3] Included with Canadian-born.

Series A327-338. Province of residence and province of birth of native-born internal migrants in Canada, census dates, 1871 to 1971

(thousands of persons)

Year	Total[1]	Newfoundland	Prince Edward Island	Nova Scotia	New Brunswick	Quebec	Ontario	Manitoba	Saskatchewan	Alberta	British Columbia	Yukon Territory and Northwest Territories
	327	328	329	330	331	332	333	334	335	336	337	338
Panel A: Migrants by province of residence												
1971	2,470.0	16.8	13.1	90.3	72.0	256.3	785.8	135.0	105.7	342.5	631.8	20.9
1961	1,892.1	9.8	8.0	74.1	56.3	223.2	577.6	118.8	111.0	255.1	445.1	13.0
1951	1,382.4	4.1	5.6	52.7	26.1	161.0	410.0	97.3	107.0	161.0	349.3	8.2
1941	916.7	—	2.8	24.1	25.3	109.5	218.0	87.8	125.0	124.3	197.3	2.5
1931	783.5	—	2.5	15.8	23.6	79.4	145.4	89.2	160.0	125.0	140.7	2.0
1921	684.1	—	2.0	16.1	20.4	46.2	108.4	95.6	169.0	119.1	106.1	1.2
1911	537.3	—	1.7	11.7	13.5	28.8	77.5	92.4	140.1	86.4	83.1	2.0
1901	298.1	—	2.5	11.2	12.7	25.2	71.6	81.1	41.8		39.8	12.2
1891	210.1	—	3.3	8.7	12.2	19.3	68.6	57.4	20.6[2]		20.2	—[2]
1881	130.2	—	4.1	6.9	12.3	13.2	57.9	31.0	2.1		2.8	—
1871	67.8	—	—	4.0	7.9	8.8	47.2	—	—		—	—
Panel B: Migrants by province of birth												
1971	2,470.0	97.5	43.8	212.6	179.0	347.7	420.3	309.2	473.7	256.9	114.2	15.0
1961	1,892.1	56.0	36.5	155.1	136.7	268.4	361.9	245.5	365.9	177.4	82.8	6.0
1951	1,382.4	44.1	27.1	99.0	90.2	185.8	307.5	188.7	268.5	121.1	47.9	2.5
1941	916.7	—	18.6	55.7	51.7	158.1	288.1	122.1	135.9	65.6	19.9	1.0
1931	783.5	—	17.0	52.3	42.9	154.2	315.7	89.7	59.9	36.5	14.5	.7
1921	684.1	—	17.3	43.0	33.3	145.2	330.2	60.0	27.2	17.1	10.1	.7
1911	537.3	—	14.0	32.3	26.0	113.1	296.6	38.3	6.3	4.8	3.4	2.5
1901	298.1	—	9.1	18.9	16.6	85.5	143.3	10.9	12.4[2]		1.2	—[2]
1891	210.1	—	6.7	18.5	13.7	75.1	88.6	5.8	1.3		.5	—
1881	130.2	—	5.8	14.4	10.6	58.7	32.3	1.6	6.6		.1	—
1871	67.8	—	—	9.5	7.2	43.3	7.5	—	.4		—	—

[1] Series A327 may not be the exact sum of series A328-338, as a result of rounding.

[2] Data for the Yukon Territory and the Northwest Territories are included with Saskatchewan and Alberta for this and earlier years.

Series A339-349. Changes in the population through natural increase and migration, by province, by intercensal intervals, 1931 to 1976

Intercensal interval	Population change	Canada[1]	Newfound-land[2]	Prince Edward Island	Nova Scotia	New Bruns-wick	Quebec	Ontario	Manitoba	Saskat-chewan	Alberta	British Columbia
		339	340	341	342	343	344	345	346	347	348	349
1971-76	Natural increase	931,016	41,832	4,519	32,142	32,920	225,905	325,615	44,869	38,148	95,852	82,832
	Net migration	+493,279	-6,212	+2,066	+7,468	+9,765	-19,225	+235,745	-11,614	-43,068	+114,308	+199,158
1966-71	Natural increase	1,089,387	49,096	5,207	37,418	35,233	288,727	373,072	49,260	50,867	105,293	88,494
	Net migration	+464,044	-20,388	-2,101	-4,497	-17,464	-41,808	+369,164	-24,079	-79,969	+59,378	+222,453
1961-66	Natural increase	1,517,893	59,577	8,506	59,526	53,229	457,717	487,852	70,340	75,691	134,607	104,103
	Net migration	+258,740	-24,034	-4,600	-40,494	-34,377	+63,917	+236,926	-28,960	-45,528	-3,348	+140,489
1956-61	Natural increase	1,674,987	59,145	8,662	65,160	59,687	521,673	523,107	76,006	86,294	144,234	125,585
	Net migration	+482,469	-16,366	-3,318	-22,870	-16,367	+109,160	+308,052	-4,360	-41,778	+64,594	+105,033
1951-56	Natural increase	1,473,211	51,851	8,959	63,133	59,774	476,627	430,386	73,684	86,030	120,961	98,206
	Net migration	+598,151	+1,807	-8,103	-11,000	-20,855	+96,070	+377,005	-185	-37,093	+62,654	+135,048
1941-51	Natural increase	1,972,394	—	15,802	103,512	99,904	736,058	505,034	107,510	135,106	150,303	116,527
	Net migration	+168,964	—	-12,420	-38,890	-41,608	-12,259	+304,853	-60,713	-199,370	-6,971	+230,822
1931-41	Natural increase	1,221,787	—	9,681	57,268	59,359	459,211	278,488	78,083	131,752	106,405	41,100
	Net migration	-91,918	—	-2,672	+7,848	-10,177	-1,991	+77,484	-48,478	-157,545	-41,841	+82,498

[1] Includes the Yukon Territory and the Northwest Territories.   [2] Newfoundland is included for 1951 and later years.

Series A350. Immigrant arrivals in Canada, 1852 to 1977

Year	Number 350	Year	Number 350	Year	Number 350	Year	Number 350	Year	Number 350
		1950	73,912	1920	138,824	1890	75,067	1860	6,276
		1949	95,217	1919	107,698	1889	91,600	1859	6,300
		1948	125,414	1918	41,845	1888	88,766	1858	12,339
1977	114,914	1947	64,127	1917	72,910	1887	84,526	1857	33,854
1976	149,429	1946	71,719	1916	55,914	1886	69,152	1856	22,544
1975	187,881	1945	22,722	1915	36,665	1885	79,169	1855	25,296
1974	218,465	1944	12,801	1914	150,484	1884	103,824	1854	37,263
1973	184,200	1943	8,504	1913	400,870	1883	133,624	1853	29,464
1972	122,006	1942	7,576	1912	375,756	1882	112,458	1852	29,307
1971	121,900	1941	9,329	1911	331,288	1881	47,991		
1970	147,713	1940	11,324	1910	286,839	1880	38,505		
1969	161,531	1939	16,994	1909	173,694	1879	40,492		
1968	183,974	1938	17,244	1908	143,326	1878	29,807		
1967	222,876	1937	15,101	1907	272,409	1877	27,082		
1966	194,743	1936	11,643	1906	211,653	1876	25,633		
1965	146,758	1935	11,277	1905	141,465	1875	27,382		
1964	112,606	1934	12,476	1904	131,252	1874	39,373		
1963	93,151	1933	14,382	1903	138,660	1873	50,050		
1962	74,586	1932	20,591	1902	89,102	1872	36,578		
1961	71,689	1931	27,530	1901	55,747	1871	27,773		
1960	104,111	1930	104,806	1900	41,681	1870	24,706		
1959	106,928	1929	164,993	1899	44,543	1869	18,630		
1958	124,851	1928	166,783	1898	31,900	1868	12,765		
1957	282,164	1927	158,886	1897	21,716	1867	10,666		
1956	164,857	1926	135,982	1896	16,835	1866	11,427		
1955	109,946	1925	84,907	1895	18,790	1865	18,958		
1954	154,227	1924	124,164	1894	20,829	1864	24,779		
1953	168,868	1923	133,729	1893	29,633	1863	21,000		
1952	164,498	1922	64,224	1892	30,996	1862	18,294		
1951	194,391	1921	91,728	1891	82,165	1861	13,589		

Series A351-368. Immigration to Canada by intended occupations and dependents, 1953 to 1976

Year	Total immigration	Workers													Dependents[10]			
		Total	Managerial[1]	Professional[2]	Clerical	Transport and communication	Commercial and financial[3]	Service[4]	Agriculture[5]	Logging, fishing and trapping[6]	Mining[7]	Manufacturing, mechanical and construction[8]	Labourers[9]	Others and not stated	Total	Spouse	Children	Other[11]
	351	352	353	354	355	356	357	358	359	360	361	362	363	364	365	366	367	368
								From overseas and the United States										
1976	149,429	61,461	5,655	14,378	9,345	784	2,632	5,774	1,162	60	103	16,578	915	4,075	87,968	25,330	42,197	20,441
1975	187,881	81,189	5,763	19,821	11,803	1,055	3,294	7,198	1,511	171	178	24,696	1,183	4,516	106,692	30,175	56,722	19,795
1974	218,465	106,083	6,445	21,599	15,660	1,315	4,119	10,739	2,637	293	233	34,620	1,787	6,636	112,382	32,470	61,008	18,904
1973	184,200	92,228	5,464	19,112	13,422	1,261	3,657	11,917	3,068	211	173	26,396	2,734	4,813	91,972	27,530	44,149	20,293
1972	122,006	59,432	4,368	15,262	8,549	795	2,460	6,575	2,127	93	144	15,389	1,184	2,486	62,574	21,749	30,977	9,848
1971	121,900	61,282	3,464	16,307	9,909	740	2,486	6,387	2,160	87	237	16,166	1,324	2,015	60,618	21,333	29,684	9,601
1970	147,713	77,723	3,095	22,412	12,143	843	3,030	7,852	2,129	111	272	22,006	1,614	2,216	69,990	25,361	34,493	10,136
1969	161,531	84,349	2,566	26,883	12,222	932	3,287	9,060	2,283	132	389	23,443	2,018	1,134	77,182	27,389	38,754	11,039
1968	183,974	95,446	2,385	29,250	12,651	1,257	3,195	9,235	3,164	114	496	30,926	2,681	92	88,528	32,091	44,925	11,512
1967	222,876	119,539	3,023	30,853	16,609	1,894	3,358	10,716	3,203	324	380	38,761	8,792	1,626	103,337	37,894	56,417	9,026
1966	194,743	99,210	2,292	23,637	13,235	1,809	3,306	8,681	3,153	260	334	34,047	7,593	863	95,533	34,216	53,895	7,422
1965	146,758	74,195	1,728	16,654	9,919	1,203	2,660	7,587	2,362	187	230	24,167	7,112	386	72,563	25,809	40,315	6,439
1964	112,606	56,190	1,212	11,965	7,931	768	1,999	6,420	2,234	73	114	17,476	5,737	261	56,416	21,023	29,819	5,574
1963	93,151	45,866	1,159	9,640	6,186	652	1,496	6,099	2,398	66	130	14,415	3,559	66	47,285	19,305	23,226	4,754
1962	74,586	36,748	1,093	8,218	4,898	489	1,214	5,853	1,923	78	100	9,685	3,145	52	37,838	15,674	18,137	4,027
1961	71,689	34,809	896	6,696	4,232	574	1,241	6,557	2,341	65	90	8,076	3,982	59	36,880	15,882	17,315	3,683
1960	104,111	53,573	825	7,436	5,860	1,223	2,152	8,763	5,321	188	479	13,551	7,482	293	50,538	20,654	24,626	5,258
1959	106,928	53,551	837	6,947	5,459	999	2,107	9,740	4,965	123	248	12,792	8,940	394	53,377	21,223	26,133	6,021
1958	124,851	63,078	944	7,553	6,745	1,229	2,229	11,501	5,071	169	344	17,476	9,388	429	61,773	24,795	30,444	6,534
1957	282,164	151,511	1,216	16,040	16,829	5,254	6,559	17,574	10,838	827	1,866	54,376	19,471	661	130,653	52,533	70,673	7,447
1956	164,857	91,039	996	9,343	9,492	2,255	3,823	13,800	7,500	505	1,144	29,264	12,482	435	73,818	30,547	38,461	4,810
1955	109,946	57,987	1,404	7,159	5,775	1,190	2,146	9,588	7,036	260	254	15,117	7,687	371	51,959	21,637	25,397	4,925
1954	154,227	84,376	1,633	8,350	6,775	1,938	2,735	11,974	10,920	335	428	25,699	13,011	578	69,851	28,897	35,503	5,451
1953	168,868	91,133	1,176	8,845	6,339	1,855	3,185	13,766	17,250	415	464	26,492	10,380	966	77,735	31,343	41,253	5,139
								From overseas										
1976	132,114	54,452	4,386	11,705	8,637	677	2,364	5,396	1,053	49	93	15,646	851	3,903	77,662	22,126	36,882	18,654
1975	167,726	73,009	4,284	16,376	10,873	932	2,984	6,834	1,371	128	164	23,545	1,117	4,401	94,717	26,574	50,311	17,832
1974	191,924	94,658	4,673	17,100	14,293	1,141	3,542	10,095	2,373	193	216	32,951	1,658	6,423	97,266	27,980	53,092	16,194
1973	158,958	81,735	3,949	14,704	12,145	1,080	3,133	11,134	2,850	148	152	25,182	2,578	4,680	77,223	27,649	36,873	17,701
1972	99,388	49,728	2,907	11,081	7,452	604	1,938	5,846	1,960	60	131	14,203	1,089	2,427	49,660	17,097	24,535	8,028
1971	97,534	50,648	1,977	11,479	8,610	595	1,893	5,738	1,939	57	209	14,949	1,235	1,967	46,886	16,378	22,851	7,657
1970	123,289	66,261	1,901	17,020	10,562	707	2,336	7,138	1,891	74	250	20,704	1,509	2,169	57,028	20,488	28,094	8,446
1969	138,746	74,129	1,610	21,645	10,816	831	2,691	8,516	2,075	106	379	22,413	1,939	1,108	64,617	22,958	32,282	9,377
1968	163,552	85,906	1,589	24,186	11,381	1,153	2,688	8,773	2,889	98	470	29,977	2,613	89	77,646	28,325	39,119	10,202
1967	203,838	111,273	2,061	26,899	15,440	1,759	2,965	10,342	3,015	289	358	37,830	8,716	1,599	92,565	34,380	50,402	7,783
1966	177,229	91,802	1,319	20,422	12,146	1,698	2,921	8,254	3,007	219	318	33,140	7,514	844	85,427	30,883	48,322	6,222

Series A351-368. Immigration to Canada by intended occupations and dependents, 1953 to 1976 (concluded)

Year	Total immigration	Workers													Dependents[10]			
		Total	Mana-gerial[1]	Profes-sional[2]	Clerical	Trans-port and communi-cation	Com-mercial and finan-cial[3]	Service[4]	Agri-culture[5]	Logging, fishing and trapping[6]	Mining[7]	Manu-facturing, mechanical and construction[8]	Labour-ers[9]	Others and not stated	Total	Spouse	Children	Other[11]
	351	352	353	354	355	356	357	358	359	360	361	362	363	364	365	366	367	368
								From overseas (concluded)										
1965	131,615	67,760	841	13,960	8,939	1,100	2,286	7,225	2,223	148	216	23,408	7,049	365	63,855	23,094	35,446	5,315
1964	100,041	51,269	557	9,935	7,228	683	1,728	6,137	2,066	57	104	16,852	5,699	223	48,772	18,565	25,701	4,506
1963	81,415	41,656	551	7,894	5,710	580	1,238	5,861	2,166	45	113	13,938	3,524	36	39,759	16,591	19,464	3,704
1962	62,943	32,603	467	6,575	4,418	417	949	5,585	1,691	52	88	9,213	3,114	34	30,340	12,979	14,302	3,059
1961	60,173	30,607	274	5,153	3,772	469	922	6,255	2,069	47	75	7,615	3,918	38	29,566	13,243	13,541	2,782
1960	92,864	49,192	275	5,808	5,360	1,129	1,778	8,414	5,095	157	463	13,011	7,417	285	43,672	18,081	21,131	4,460
1959	95,590	49,370	305	5,502	4,998	916	1,670	9,416	4,764	91	236	12,214	8,875	383	46,220	18,562	22,424	5,234
1958	114,005	58,862	379	6,277	6,249	1,096	1,859	11,174	4,898	140	322	16,726	9,334	408	55,143	22,274	27,061	5,808
1957	271,156	147,181	617	14,886	16,365	5,125	6,137	17,245	10,702	747	1,815	53,526	19,382	634	123,975	49,910	67,227	6,838
1956	155,080	87,189	441	8,322	9,027	2,157	3,411	13,508	7,351	429	1,113	28,650	12,368	412	67,891	28,171	35,481	4,239
1955	99,554	53,803	486	6,037	5,334	1,083	1,771	9,312	6,846	194	235	14,572	7,613	320	45,751	19,053	22,361	4,337
1954	144,117	80,205	811	7,269	6,331	1,831	2,355	11,735	10,709	277	390	25,095	12,924	478	63,912	26,417	32,694	4,801
1953	159,489	87,129	704	7,664	5,943	1,749	2,739	13,566	17,037	379	432	25,791	10,312	813	72,360	29,041	38,836	4,483

1 Managerial and administrative.
2 Natural sciences, engineering, mathematics, social sciences and related, religion, teaching, medicine and health, artistic, literary, performing arts.
3 Also referred to as "Sales".
4 Service, sports and recreation.
5 Referred to also as farming, horticultural and animal husbandry.

6 Fishing, hunting, trapping, forestry and logging.
7 Mining and quarrying including gas and oil.
8 Processing, machining, fabricating, assembling and repairing, and construction.
9 Material-handling, other crafts and equipment-operating.
10 Referred to also as "non-workers".
11 Includes fiancé, fiancée, students (18 years and over) and others.

Series A369-384. Immigration to Canada by age, sex and marital status, 1933 to 1976

Year	All ages		0-14 years		15-19 years				20-39 years				40 years and over			
	Male	Female	Male	Female	Male		Female		Male		Female		Male		Female	
					Married	Other[1]	Married	Other[1]	Married	Other[1]	Married	Other[1]	Married	Other[1]	Married	Other[1]
	369	370	371	372	373	374	375	376	377	378	379	380	381	382	383	384
1976	72,605	76,824	19,678	18,441	96	5,602	1,433	4,918	20,266	14,314	25,592	10,161	10,924	1,725	9,501	6,778
1975	92,683	95,198	26,178	24,944	88	6,571	1,721	6,139	26,485	20,041	32,198	13,319	11,412	1,908	9,725	7,152
1974	111,122	107,343	27,950	26,141	54	7,194	1,604	6,846	31,134	29,594	35,269	20,164	13,033	2,163	10,222	7,097
1973	94,768	89,432	20,112	19,022	70	6,802	1,656	6,115	25,109	30,577	27,702	20,141	10,254	1,844	8,146	6,650
1972	60,070	61,936	14,056	13,563	68	4,133	1,359	4,127	17,320	16,799	20,165	12,555	6,517	1,177	5,481	4,686
1971	60,445	61,455	13,752	12,756	74	3,914	1,365	3,847	17,147	17,919	20,069	13,579	6,426	1,213	5,317	4,522
1970	74,257	73,456	16,050	15,160	80	4,748	1,593	4,279	22,116	22,875	24,311	17,385	7,088	1,300	5,814	4,914
1969	80,007	81,524	18,079	16,987	75	5,422	1,542	4,798	23,291	23,766	26,578	19,549	7,973	1,401	6,618	5,452
1968	93,503	90,471	20,986	19,544	84	6,682	1,601	5,307	25,993	28,286	29,625	19,451	9,681	1,791	8,384	6,559
1967	115,158	107,718	26,601	25,100	104	7,276	2,005	6,148	33,343	34,081	35,824	23,336	11,960	1,793	9,363	5,942
1966	100,349	94,394	25,395	24,041	95	6,973	1,839	5,806	28,587	26,495	31,187	17,606	11,145	1,659	8,750	5,165
1965	74,707	72,051	18,977	17,848	76	5,813	1,482	4,670	20,200	19,793	22,793	13,544	8,477	1,371	6,884	4,830
1964	55,825	56,781	13,986	13,162	51	4,412	1,193	3,654	15,112	14,504	17,856	11,002	6,615	1,145	5,579	4,335
1963	45,163	47,988	10,718	10,330	52	3,540	1,013	3,089	12,684	12,109	15,054	10,220	5,022	1,038	4,435	3,847
1962	34,546	40,040	8,449	8,043	31	2,868	877	2,613	9,204	9,027	12,112	9,072	4,108	859	3,863	3,460
1961	32,106	39,583	8,144	7,581	35	2,575	1,007	2,386	8,205	8,287	12,144	9,019	4,018	842	3,922	3,524
1960	51,018	53,093	11,625	11,105	36	4,145	998	3,403	12,812	15,505	16,330	11,924	5,881	1,014	5,301	4,032
1959	51,476	55,452	12,531	11,675	46	4,387	934	3,685	12,560	14,413	16,615	12,552	6,490	1,049	5,742	4,249
1958	60,630	64,221	14,599	13,584	56	5,136	1,072	4,412	14,934	17,576	19,704	14,503	7,196	1,133	6,518	4,428
1957	154,226	127,938	34,337	32,049	129	10,753	1,665	7,382	47,314	44,901	48,227	21,374	14,595	2,197	11,323	5,918
1956	89,541	75,316	18,879	17,334	62	7,208	1,019	4,735	24,508	29,182	25,947	15,059	8,221	1,481	6,934	4,288
1955	56,828	53,118	12,334	11,292	46	4,456	698	3,254	14,290	18,504	17,571	11,157	5,935	1,263	5,574	3,572
1954	84,531	69,696	17,222	15,876	68	6,407	673	4,159	22,563	27,669	23,835	13,856	9,093	1,509	7,382	3,915
1953	91,422	77,446	19,901	18,420	60	7,294	628	5,030	24,128	27,188	25,799	14,558	11,037	1,814	8,581	4,430
1952	89,849	74,649	20,743	18,912	41	6,093	456	3,983	23,334	25,359	26,010	11,952	12,066	2,213	8,818	4,518
1951	120,166	74,225	20,700	18,774	52	8,796	600	3,820	33,453	39,593	27,293	9,952	14,541	3,031	9,135	4,651
1950	40,987	32,925	8,421	7,668	24	3,520	276	1,876	9,749	11,631	10,113	4,897	6,269	1,373	4,841	3,254
1949	51,162	44,055	10,214	9,595	16	3,739	372	2,820	12,720	14,910	13,671	7,125	7,864	1.699	6,367	4,105
1948	67,090	58,324	11,862	11,211	23	4,323	343	3,919	16,043	22,536	16,293	13,387	9,771	2,532	7,959	5,212
1947	33,435	30,692	5,162	4,907	18	1,600	369	1,949	8,536	11,646	8,326	6,910	5,245	1,228	4,467	3,764
1946	20,483	51,236	9,998	9,466	14	793	3,504	1,121	4,191	2,336	30,466	2,656	2,489	662	2,487	1,536
1945	7,701	15,021	3,237	3,019	6	443	804	657	1,421	983	7,715	1,196	1,268	343	951	679
1944	4,494	8,307	1,907	1,749	4	338	329	554	681	483	3,539	841	828	253	722	573
1943	3,290	5,214	995	917	3	365	160	445	581	424	1,654	847	700	222	654	537
1942	3,208	4,368	784	746	4	356	99	371	526	636	1,347	728	656	246	581	496
1941	4,791	4,538	810	816	1	453	92	455	785	1,704	1,302	794	762	276	624	455
1940	5,371	5,953	1,221	1,176	2	375	89	444	914	1,348	1,687	827	1,101	410	1,010	720
1939	7,681	9,313	2,284	2,027	3	812	96	758	1,417	1,191	2,851	1,154	1,566	408	1,399	1,028
1938	7,416	9,828	2,682	2,457	3	807	133	829	1,375	1,063	3,043	1,258	1,160	326	1,239	869
1937	6,300	8,801	2,255	2,248	3	602	106	632	1,126	995	2,849	1,085	1,012	307	1,076	805
1936	4,818	6,825	1,846	1,735	—	383	74	436	784	735	2,269	913	815	255	814	584
1935	4,656	6,621	1,886	1,762	2	338	79	414	645	754	2,160	853	767	264	696	657
1934	5,159	7,317	1,911	1,953	3	391	80	414	748	923	2,496	982	862	321	772	620
1933	6,191	8,191	2,234	2,157	2	407	106	474	995	1,061	2,645	1,126	1,116	376	961	722

[1] Includes single, widowed, divorced and separated.

Series A385-416. Immigration to Canada by country of last permanent residence, 1956 to 1976

Year	Europe										
	Total	Britain	France	Federal Republic of Germany	Greece	Italy	Netherlands	Portugal	Switzerland	Yugoslavia	Other countries
	385	386	387	388	389	390	391	392	393	394	395
1976	49,908	21,548	3,251	2,672	2,487	4,530	1,359	5,344	1,192	1,741	5,784
1975	72,898	34,978	3,891	3,469	4,062	5,078	1,448	8,547	1,272	2,932	7,221
1974	88,694	38,456	4,232	3,619	5,632	5,226	2,103	16,333	1,336	3,200	8,557
1973	71,883	26,973	3,586	2,564	5,833	5,468	1,898	13,483	953	2,873	8,252
1972	51,293	18,197	2,742	2,025	4,016	4,608	1,471	8,737	778	2,047	6,672
1971	52,031	15,451	2,966	2,275	4,769	5,790	1,301	9,157	1,024	2,997	6,301
1970	75,609	26,497	4,410	4,193	6,327	8,533	1,916	7,902	2,098	5,672	8,061
1969	88,363	31,977	5,549	5,880	6,937	10,383	2,494	7,182	2,307	4,053	11,601
1968	120,702	37,889	8,184	8,966	7,739	19,774	3,264	7,738	3,529	4,660	18,959
1967	159,979	62,420	10,122	11,779	10,650	30,055	4,401	9,500	3,738	2,089	15,225
1966	148,410	63,291	7,872	9,263	7,174	31,625	3,749	7,930	2,982	1,502	13,022
1965	108,285	39,857	5,225	8,927	5,642	26,398	2,619	5,734	2,169	1,230	10,484
1964	82,798	29,279	4,542	5,992	4,391	19,297	2,029	5,309	1,446	1,187	9,326
1963	69,069	24,603	3,569	6,744	4,759	14,427	1,728	4,000	999	781	7,459
1962	53,790	15,603	2,674	5,548	3,741	13,641	1,555	2,928	802	862	6,436
1961	52,132	11,870	2,330	6,231	3,766	14,161	1,787	2,762	805	852	7,568
1960	82,922	19,585	2,944	10,774	4,856	20,681	5,429	5,023	1,048	881	11,701
1959	84,517	18,222	2,153	10,423	4,867	25,655	5,243	4,080	855	958	12,061
1958	102,279	24,777	2,727	13,888	5,190	27,043	7,420	1,938	1,024	984	17,288
1957	257,540	108,989	5,869	28,430	5,460	27,740	11,934	4,423	1,800	1,048	61,847
1956	145,554	50,390	3,809	26,061	4,986	27,739	7,792	1,697	1,514	453	21,113

Year	Africa				Asia						
	Total	Egypt	Republic of South Africa	Other countries	Total	China[1]	Hong Kong	India	Israel	Lebanon	Pakistan[2]
	396	397	398	399	400	401	402	403	404	405	406
1976	7,752	728	1,611	5,413	44,328	833	10,725	6,733	1,201	7,161	2,173
1975	9,867	892	1,567	7,408	47,382	903	11,132	10,144	1,527	1,506	2,165
1974	10,450	928	1,154	8,368	50,566	379	12,704	12,868	1,090	1,762	2,315
1973	8,307	905	766	6,636	43,193	60	14,662	9,203	984	1,325	2,285
1972	8,308	606	440	7,262	23,325	25	6,297	5,049	620	996	1,190
1971	2,841	730	729	1,382	22,171	47	5,009	5,313	600	928	968
1970	2,863	913	646	1,304	21,170	5,377	—[5]	5,670	818	1,206	1,010
1969	3,297	1,429	599	1,269	23,319	8,272	—[5]	5,395	863	1,196	1,005
1968	5,204	1,915	924	2,365	21,686	8,382	—[5]	3,229	1,497	1,682	627
1967	4,608	1,728	1,366	1,514	20,740	6,409	—[5]	3,966	2,345	1,096	648
1966	3,661	1,854	892	915	13,835	4,094	—[5]	2,233	1,488	889	566
1965	3,196	1,378	545	1,273	11,215	197	4,155	2,241	822	602	423
1964	3,874	1,855	417	1,602	6,121	184	2,490	1,154	871	347	282
1963	2,431	1,476	296	659	3,553	179	1,008	737	688	456	121
1962	2,171	1,322	340	509	2,593	244	426	529	558	303	55
1961	1,088	31	531	526	2,706	118	710	568	652	293	72
1960	833	58	503	272	4,002	183	1,146	505	1,532	283	83
1959	843	120	287	436	5,368	519	2,018	585	1,490	377	62
1958	1,355	116	367	872	4,223	894	1,752	325	531	312	62
1957	2,970	421	464	2,085	3,244	856	866	186	482	401	83
1956	1,079	194	342	543	3,537	1,516	615	254	309	454	50

Series 385-416. Immigration to Canada by country of last permanent residence, 1956 to 1976 (concluded)

Year	Asia		Australasia	North and Central America			Caribbean	South America	Other countries n.e.s.[4]	Grand total
	Philippines[3]	Other countries		Total	United States	Other countries				
	407	**408**	**409**	**410**	**411**	**412**	**413**	**414**	**415**	**416**
1976	5,939	9,563	1,886	18,671	17,315	1,356	14,842	10,628	1,414	149,429
1975	7,364	12,641	2,174	21,665	20,155	1,510	17,973	13,270	2,652	187,881
1974	9,564	9,884	2,594	27,932	26,541	1,391	23,885	12,528	1,816	218,465
1973	6,757	7,917	2,671	26,383	25,242	1,141	19,563	11,057	1,143	184,200
1972	3,946	5,202	2,143	23,483	22,618	865	8,353	4,309	792	122,006
1971	4,180	5,126	2,902	25,002	24,366	636	11,017	5,058	878	121,900
1970	3,240	3,849	4,385	25,135	24,424	711	12,660	4,943	948	147,713
1969	3,001	3,587	4,411	23,378	22,785	593	13,315	4,767	681	161,531
1968	2,678	3,591	4,815	20,796	20,422	374	7,755	2,693	323	183,974
1967	2,994	3,282	6,168	19,460	19,038	422	8,582	3,090	249	222,876
1966	2,639	1,926	4,057	17,738	17,514	224	4,133	2,604	305	194,743
1965	1,502	1,273	2,711	15,348	15,143	205	3,215	2,471	317	146,758
1964	—	793	2,303	12,751	12,565	186	2,281	2,257	221	112,606
1963	—	364	1,692	11,904	11,736	168	2,443	1,779	280	93,151
1962	—	478	1,384	11,826	11,643	183	1,659	1,103	60	74,586
1961	—	293	1,432	11,663	11,516	147	1,307	1,301	60	71,689
1960	—	270	1,657	11,449	11,247	202	1,340	1,823	85	104,111
1959	—	317	1,512	11,498	11,338	160	1,369	1,750	71	106,928
1958	—	347	2,344	11,005	10,846	159	1,360	2,168	117	124,851
1957	—	370	3,345	11,180	11,008	172	1,414	2,376	95	282,164
1956	—	339	1,924	9,883	9,777	106	1,245	1,551	84	164,857

[1] Includes Hong Kong for 1966 to 1970.
[2] Before 1973, Bangladesh was a part of Pakistan.
[3] Before 1964, Philippines was included with other countries (Asia).
[4] 'n.e.s.' — not elsewhere specified.
[5] Included with China.

Section B: Vital Statistics and Health

R.D. Fraser, *Queen's University*

Statistics in the tables of Section B are in two divisions. Series B1-81 contain data on vital statistics and series B82-543 on health. Data on social welfare, formerly contained in this section, are presented separately in Section C.

The principal sources for vital statistics (series B1-81) are: Statistics Canada, *Vital Statistics*, 1921 to 1970, (Ottawa, Queen's Printer); Statistics Canada, *Vital Statistics*, vol. I, *Births;* vol. II, *Marriages and Divorces;* vol. III, *Deaths;* all three volumes published annually since 1971 (Ottawa, Queen's Printer). Additional sources on historical series are given in the first edition of *Historical Statistics of Canada*, p. 30.

The principal sources for health (series B82-543) are: Department of National Health and Welfare, *Canada Health Manpower Inventory,* annual (Ottawa, Department of National Health and Welfare); Statistics Canada, *Hospital Statistics,* vols. I-VII, (Ottawa, Queen's Printer); Statistics Canada, *Mental Health Statistics,* vols. I-III, annual (Ottawa, Queen's Printer); Department of National Health and Welfare, *National Health Expenditures in Canada, 1960-1973,* updated every two years (Ottawa, Department of National Health and Welfare).

Vital Statistics (Series B1-81)

General note

Data for the Yukon Territory and the Northwest Territories are included in all tables unless otherwise noted.

Data for Newfoundland, which entered Confederation in 1949, are included in all historical tables unless otherwise specified. Available figures prior to 1949 were extracted from the appropriate provincial reports. Similarly, 1921 to 1925 data for Quebec, which entered the vital statistics system in 1926, have been extracted from the reports of the provincial health department.

Population figures for 1921, 1931, 1941, 1951, 1956, 1961, 1966 and 1971, are those of the census at 1 June; for 1926, 1936 and 1946, for the provinces of Manitoba, Saskatchewan and Alberta, the figures are those of the quinquennial censuses of 1 June; for all other years they are estimates as of 1 June.

Causes of death are classified according to the appropriate revision of the International Statistical Classification of Diseases, Injuries and Causes of Death and since 1969 they have been classified according to the 8th (1965) Revision which was put into effect on 1 January 1969. Tables on causes of death use the International Intermediate "A" List of 150 categories, unless otherwise specified; those for perinatal deaths use the International "P" List.

Prior to 1959 the following definitions of 'live birth' and 'stillbirth' were incorporated in the vital statistics legislation of the provinces.

'Live birth' means the birth of a foetus which, after complete separation from the mother, shows any sign of life.
'Stillbirth' means the birth of a foetus, after at least 28 weeks' pregnancy, which, after complete separation from the mother, does not show any sign of life.

Subsequently, the above definitions were revised to conform to new definitions of 'live birth' and 'foetal death' recommended by the World Health Organization. At the same time the compulsory registration of stillbirths was extended to 20 weeks' gestation. Following are the new definitions adopted by each province, with minor modification of the stillbirth definition in one province.

'Live birth' means the complete expulsion or extraction from its mother, irrespective of the duration of pregnancy, of a product of conception in which after such expulsion or extraction, there is breathing, beating of the heart, pulsation of the umbilical cord, or unmistakable movement of voluntary muscle, whether or not the umbilical cord has been cut or the placenta is attached.

'Stillbirth' means the complete expulsion or extraction from its mother, after at least 20 weeks' pregnancy, of a product of conception in which, after such expulsion or extraction, there is no breathing, beating of the heart, pulsation of the umbilical cord, or unmistakable movement of voluntary muscle.

Following is the month and year in which the new definitions were implemented: Nova Scotia, March 1959; Manitoba, August 1959; Alberta, January 1960 and January 1963; Quebec and Saskatchewan, January 1961; Ontario, December 1961; New Brunswick, January 1962; British Columbia, July 1962; Prince Edward Island, January 1964.

Hospital: an institution operated for the regular accommodation of in-patients in which medical or obstetrical care is provided and which is recognized as a hospital by a federal agency or by the provincial government in which the hospital is located, or by a municipality duly authorized under the laws of that province. The term 'hospital' includes institutions for tuberculosis and mental diseases, but excludes institutions which provide custodial or domiciliary care only.

Since 1944 births and stillbirths have been classified according to the residence of the mother; deaths by the residence of the deceased; marriages by the place in which the marriage was solemnized. Prior to 1944 all events were classified by place of occurrence. Except for marriages, events occurring in the United States to Canadian residents are included and events occurring in Canada to United States residents are excluded.

Definitions

Population: de jure (resident) population as enumerated in census years or estimated for intercensal years.

Births: unless otherwise indicated, infants born alive (excluding stillbirths).

Stillbirths: unless otherwise indicated, foetal deaths of 28 or more weeks' gestation.

Deaths: unless otherwise indicated, exclude stillbirths. Types of deaths are as follows: infant, deaths under one year of age; neonatal, deaths under 28 days of age; post-neonatal, deaths between 28 days and one year of age; maternal, deaths due to delivery and complications of pregnancy, childbirth and the puerperium (categories 630-678 International List); perinatal, foetal deaths of 28 or more weeks' gestation plus infant deaths under seven days of age.

Natural increase: excess of births over deaths.

Crude rates: birth, marriage, death and natural increase rates per 1,000 population.

Total births: live births and stillbirths.

Age: completed ages in years, months, etc. Average age is the arithmetic mean and median age is the age above and below which half of the total events occur.

B1-14. Live births, crude birth rate, age-specific fertility rates, gross reproduction rate and percentage of births in hospital, Canada, 1921 to 1974

SOURCE: for 1921 to 1974, Statistics Canada, *Vital Statistics,* vol. I, *Births,* (Catalogue 82-204).

B1. The criteria adopted for defining live births and stillbirths were changed in 1955. Before this date a live birth was defined as the birth of a child who breathes after the body of the foetus is outside the body of the mother. Since 1955, following the definition of the World Health Organization, a live birth is the complete expulsion from its mother of a product of conception which, after such separation, breathes or shows any other evidence of life. See above for the dates when the provinces implemented these new definitions.

B2-3. Illegitimate births are births for which parents reported themselves as not having been married to each other at the time of birth or registration. In the case of Ontario, since 1949, they are births for which the marital status of the mother was reported as single.

B5-11. The age-specific fertility rates are the annual number of births to women in a specified age group per 1,000 female population in that age group.

B12. The total fertility rate is the sum of the fertility rates of women at each year of age. This sum represents the number of children that a thousand women would have throughout their lifetime, assuming no mortality, if they experienced at each age the fertility observed during the year for which the age-specific fertility rates have been calculated.

B13. The gross reproduction rate is similar to the total fertility rate except that only female children are considered. It represents the number of daughters a cohort of a thousand women would have during their lives under the same hypotheses as for the total fertility rate.

B15-22. Total number of deaths, crude and standardized death rates by sex, natural increase and rate, Canada, 1921 to 1974

SOURCE: for 1921 to 1974, Statistics Canada, *Vital Statistics,* vol. III, *Deaths,* (Catalogue 84-206).

B19-20. Standardized death rates are death rates corrected for differences in age composition. See definitions above.

B23-34. Average age-specific death rates, both sexes, Canada, for five-year periods, 1921 to 1974

SOURCE: same as series B15-22. Death rates by age groups are published annually, for the current year and for each province.

B35-50. Average annual number of deaths and death rates for leading causes of death, Canada, for five-year periods, 1921 to 1974

SOURCE: same as in series B15-22. Number of deaths and death rates by cause and sex are published annually for the current year for each province on the basis of the intermediate international list of causes of deaths. They are also published for Canada by sex and age groups.

Comparison of rates between years should be made with caution. The system of classification of deaths by cause has to change from time to time to be consistent with current medical knowledge and terminology and discontinuities are introduced into the time trends of death rates for certain causes of death.

B51-58. Stillbirths and rate, infant deaths and rate by sex, neonatal death rate and maternal mortality rate, Canada, 1921 to 1974

SOURCE: same as series B1-14 and B15-22. In the same publications, these data are also given for each province; for the current year, infant deaths are given by sex and month of death for selected causes of death, and by sex and age for selected causes of death. Neonatal deaths and rates are also given for selected causes of death, as well as maternal mortality.

B51-52. Since 1955, stillbirths are defined as the birth of a foetus, after at least 28 weeks of pregnancy, which, after complete separation from the mother, does not show any sign of life. Prior to this date a stillbirth was defined as the birth of a foetus, after at least 28 weeks of pregnancy, which after complete separation from the mother, does not breathe (see general note). The registration of stillbirths is probably less complete than for live births and the criteria for defining a stillbirth are more or less subject to medical practice.

B53-57. Neonatal deaths are included in infant deaths. Neonatal deaths until 1950 included deaths under one calendar month; since 1951, they include deaths under 28 days.

B59-64. Average annual infant death rates for selected causes, Canada, for five-year periods, 1931 to 1970, and single years, 1971 to 1975

SOURCE: same as series B15-22. Numbers and rates of infant deaths by cause are published annually for the current year and for each province.

The same caution as the one given for series B35-50 would apply here, probably with greater emphasis on the lack of comparability of rates between periods, particularly for immaturity.

B65-74. Life expectancy by sex, at selected ages, Canada, census years, 1871 to 1971

SOURCE: same as series B15-22.

The life expectancy at a specified age is the average number of years to be lived by members of a hypothetical cohort of individuals, assumed to be subject throughout the remainder of their lives to the age-specific mortality rates observed in a given time period. Figures for 1871, 1881 and 1921 are interpolated from original figures which were not given for the ages appearing in our table. They are to be interpreted with caution because of difficulties in registration of deaths in these early years.

B75-81. Number of marriages and rate, average age at marriage for brides and bridegrooms, number of divorces and rate, net family formation, Canada, 1921 to 1974

SOURCE: *Vital Statistics*, vol. I, *Births*, (Catalogue 84-205). In this publication, these series are also given for each province. Source of net family formation: for 1951 to 1975, Central Mortgage and Housing Corporation, *Canadian Housing Statistics;* for 1921 to 1950, O.J. Firestone, *Canada's Economic Development 1867-1953*, pp. 240 and 241.

Net family formation is the number of marriages, plus married female immigrants, less deaths of married persons, less married female emigrants, less divorces. Marriages, married female immigrants and deaths of married persons and divorces are obtained from registration statistics; married female emigrants are assumed to be one-fifth of the total number of emigrants (see O.J. Firestone, *Residential Real Estate in Canada*, (Toronto, 1951), pp. 436-437).

Health (Series B82-543)

General note

The framework within which the data on the health care sector are presented follows as closely as was deemed possible to that of 'inputs', 'production processes' and 'outputs'. Data on physicians, dentists and nurses are presented first. In the case of the number of physicians, the series has been redeveloped starting with the year 1951. In addition, data on the immigration of physicians to Canada and the emigration of physicians to the United States has been included, starting with the years 1946 and 1950, respectively.

Presented in the second and principal part of the data on health is information on hospitals in Canada. These data provide an indication of inputs, production processes, and outputs. It should be noted that these data series represent a major rebuilding of the historical information on hospitals in Canada. The basic classification system has been changed from that of the 'type of service', as was used in the first edition of *Historical Statistics of Canada*, to that of 'type of ownership' and then, within type of ownership, type of service.

The three categories of type of ownership are public, private, and federal hospitals. A public hospital is 'one which is not operated for profit, accepts all patients regardless of their ability to pay, and is recognized as a public hospital by the province in which it is located', Statistics Canada, *Hospital Statistics, 1956*, vol. 1, (p. 10). Private hospitals are those set up with restrictions on admissions; usually they are established for profit and accept paying patients only. Federal hospitals are those set up and operated by departments of the federal government for the care of special groups of patients. Included are such facilities as internment camp hospitals, military hospitals, veterans

homes, quarantine hospitals, Indian hospitals, military camp hospitals, and health and occupational centres.

Within type of ownership, hospitals are classified by type of service. There are four principal types: general, including paediatric; allied special; mental; tuberculosis.

When hospitals offer more than one type of service, the predominant type is applied to the entire hospital with one exception: if an institution contains a 'general' unit, it will be classed as general. 'Allied special' category includes: chronic, communicable disease, convalescent, maternity, orthopaedic hospitals and unclassified hospitals. Almost all mental and tuberculosis beds are in public hospitals. The great majority of 'general beds' are also in public hospitals but a significant amount are in federal hospitals. 'Allied special' beds is the only category where there is a significant proportion of beds in private hospitals (approximately 20 per cent).

Data on public and private mental hospitals include psychiatric units. These are units, within a hospital or sanatorium, which are organized for the treatment of patients with psychiatric disorders. Treatment in these units is generally more intensive and shorter than in mental hospitals.

These newly reconstructed historical data for the years 1932 to 1975 are presented in 15 tables each one of which, to the extent the availability of data permitted, involves the classification of hospitals by type of ownership and within that, by type of service. Data for the grand total of all hospitals and that for all hospitals of a given type of ownership are also presented.

For historical data describing the hospital sector prior to 1932, the reader is referred to the provincial data on hospitals in Ontario for the period 1900 to 1935 and that on hospitals in Quebec for quinquennial years 1885 to 1930, as presented in series B182-194 and series B195-215, respectively, in the original *Historical Statistics of Canada*.

Data on expenditures on health care by type of expenditure completes the presentation of evidence on the inputs.

Selected data on the growth of enrolment in non-profit health insurance plans supplement the data on the nature of the hospital system.

The last group of data provide some evidence on the nature of the 'outputs' of the health care sector. Included in this group are data on annual rates of notifiable diseases and on hospital morbidity by major diagnosis.

B82-92. Number of physicians, dentists and nurses, population per physician, dentist and nurse, number of graduates of medical and dental schools and nursing programs, immigration and emigration of physicians, Canada, 1871 to 1975

B82-84. Physicians and graduates.

SOURCE: for 1968 to 1974, computer tapes purchased from Sales Management Systems, Don Mills, Ontario, and provincial sources of data on interns and residents in 1973 and 1974; for 1962 to 1967, Department of National Health and Welfare, *Review of Health Services in Canada*, 1973 and 1974; for 1951 to 1961, S. Judek, *Medical Manpower in Canada*, (Ottawa, Queen's Printer, 1964); for 1901 to 1950, Department of National Health and Welfare, *Survey of Physicians in Canada*, 1954, pp. 10 and 18; for the years 1881 and 1891, *Census of Canada, 1921*, vol. IV, p. 6; for 1871, *Census of Canada, 1871*, vol. II, p. 341.

Figures on physicians for 1943 to 1950 are based on individual records of Canadian doctors kept by the Department of National Health and Welfare; for other years, they are census figures. In the *Survey of Physicians,* the distribution of physicians is given by province, sex, age groups, nature of major work and urban concentration. The records of the Department of National Health and Welfare are checked periodically by surveys; six were made between 1943 and 1954. Much more detailed data are now available for recent years from the Department of National Health and Welfare, and the computer tapes mentioned above. For example, as of 31 December 1974, there were in Canada 1,643 interns, 4,546 residents, 15,565 specialists, and 15,543 general or family practitioners; there were 33,467 registered physicians and 3,830 not registered; there were 24,896 physicians in fee practice and 6,212 not in fee practice, excluding interns and residents.

In particular, other data on physicians, from 1968 and for each year after that, appear in the annual *Canada Health Manpower Inventory.* Included, for example, in the 1973 inventory, are the number of active physicians by province; physicians to population ratios, from 1963; number of general practitioners and specialists by province; number of graduates of Canadian medical schools and year of graduation for 1961 to 1972; number of Canadian graduates and graduates of foreign universities, by specialty and province of practice, 1971 and 1972.

The *Canada Health Manpower Inventory* series also contain data on dentists, nurses and other health personnel. This publication is intended to present much of the available basic data on all categories of health manpower. Furthermore, detailed data for registered nurses, physicians and surgeons, radiological technicians, and physiotherapists and for eleven occupational groups associated with hospitals are presented in the four-volume series, *Health Manpower,* (Catalogues 83-220 and 83-223 to 83-225), and in the eleven-volume series, *Health Manpower in Hospitals,* (Catalogues 83-508 through 83-518).

For graduates of Canadian medical schools, for 1951 to 1974, see Association of Canadian Medical Colleges, *Forum,* vol. 7, no. 5 (September-October, 1974).

B85-86. Immigrant physicians and emigrants to the United States.

SOURCE: for immigrant physicians, for 1962 and 1975, Department of Manpower and Immigration; for 1946 to 1961, S. Judek, *Medical Manpower in Canada,* table 2-6, (Ottawa, Queen's Printer, 1964); for physicians emigrating to the United States, for 1972 to 1974, Department of National Health and Welfare, Health Manpower Directorate; for 1953 to 1971, R. Stevens and J. Vermeulen, *Foreign Trained Physicians and American Medicine,* Department of Health, Education and Welfare Publication No. (NIH) 73-325, table A5, (Washington, United States Department of Health, Education and Welfare, June, 1972); for 1950 to 1952, S. Judek, *Medical Manpower in Canada.*

Data on emigration of physicians to other countries are not available but are not thought to be significant compared to emigration to the United States.

B87-89. Dentists and graduates.

SOURCE: for 1961 to 1974, Bureau of Dental Statistics, Canadian Dental Association; for number of dentists, 1947 to 1960. "Statistical Data re Dentists"; for other years, *Census of Canada, 1941,* vol. VII, p. 32; *Census of Canada, 1931,* vol. VII, p. 72; *Census of Canada, 1921,* vol. IV, p. 6; *Census*

of Canada, 1871, vol. II, p. 337; for number of graduates, *Canadian Dental Students Register.*

In the publications of the Canadian Dental Association, data are presented on distribution of dentists by province, sex, specialty, on deaths, retirements, additions, relocations of dentists, on distribution of students by province and university, and on average cost for a four-year course.

B90-92. Nurses and graduates.

SOURCE: for graduates from initial Canadian nursing programs for 1950 to 1974 and for nurses for 1961 to 1973, Canadian Nurses Association, *Countdown;* for nurses for 1951 to 1959, *Facts and Figures About Nursing;* for 1941 to 1950, *Information on Nurses and Nursing;* for other years, *Census of Canada, 1931,* vol. VII, p. 72; *Census of Canada, 1921,* vol. IV, p. 6. Other data on distribution by province, sex, major field, institutions, students and nurse migrations are given in *Facts and Figures About Nursing.*

B93-503. **Number of hospitals operating and reporting, rated bed capacity, number of patient days, number of separations, percentage occupancy, and average length of stay, total paid hours of employees, number of full-time and part-time personnel, number of graduate nurses, costs per patient day and operating expenditures and revenues by type of ownership and by service, Canada, 1932 to 1975**

SOURCE: special tabulations and historical tables prepared by Statistics Canada at the beginning of the 1960s; annual listing of hospitals; and annual publications on hospitals, mental institutions, and tuberculosis facilities. Most of these figures are published, albeit sometimes in another form, in the following publications of Statistics Canada: *List of Canadian Hospitals and Related Institutions and Facilities,* (Catalogue 83-201); *Hospital Statistics,* six volumes on beds, services, personnel, balance sheets, revenues, and expenditures, (Catalogues 83-210 through 83-215); *Mental Health Statistics,* three volumes, on admissions and separations, on facilities, services and finances, and on patients, (Catalogues 83-204, 83-205, and 83-208); *Tuberculosis Statistics,* two volumes on morbidity and mortality and on facilities, services, and finances, (Catalogues 83-206 and 83-207). Both provincial data and much more detailed data on patient characteristics, manpower, and facilities are provided in these publications.

The figures for rated bed capacity, number of patient days, number of separations, percentage occupancy, and average length of stay refer to adults and children.

B93-140. Number of operating and reporting hospitals by type of ownership and service. From 1932 to 1955, federal hospitals reported irregularly and since many small base hospitals opened and closed during and after the wars, there were large variations in the numbers reporting.

B141-188. Rated bed capacity in reporting hospitals. Rated bed capacity is defined as the number of beds which the hospital is designed to accommodate on the basis of established standards of floor area per bed as at 31 December of the reporting year. It is, therefore, a theoretical number, representing the number of beds that could be placed on a given hospital structure if a standard number of square feet were allowed for each bed. This number may be equal to, or be greater or less than the actual number of beds in regular use (referred to as beds set up)....It is not possible to ascertain to what extent standards have been scrupulously applied (by province or hospitals) but it is known that their application is becoming more general (see *Hospital Statistics, 1956*, p. 9).

It must be pointed out that, except for most recent years, data on bed capacity were collected for beds set up and not for rate capacity. Moreover, beds set up were usually over-estimated. In these conditions, the Statistics Canada esti-mates of rated bed capacity should be interpreted cautiously.

B189-236. Number of patient days in reporting hospi-tals. A patient-day is defined as the period of service to an in-patient between the census-taking hours on two succes-sive days; the day of admission is counted as a patient-day but the day of separation is not.

B237-260. Number of separations in reporting hospi-tals. In general and allied special hospitals, a separation is defined as the number of discharges and deaths of in-pa-tients. In tuberculosis sanatoria, it is defined as the number of direct discharges on or against medical advice, discharges to continue treatment, reviews out, discharges for discipli-nary reasons, and transfers out and deaths. In mental health institutions, a separation is defined as the number of deaths, discharges and transfers out.

B261-284. Percentage occupancy in reporting hospi-tals. Percentage occupancy is defined as the number of ac-tual patient-days recorded during the year expressed as a percentage of the potential patient-days in that year based either on rated bed capacity or actual beds set up.

B285-297. Average length of stay of separated patients in reporting hospitals. Average length of stay is defined as the mean number of days' stay in hospital from the date of admission of patients separated during the reporting year.

B298-303. Total paid hours of all employees in report-ing public hospitals.

B304-351. Total personnel (full- and part-time) in reporting hospitals. The figures are for personnel employed on 31 December of the reporting year and include: all nurs-ing staff, all paid medical staff, interns and residents, pro-fessional and technical staff, and all other staff.

B352-399. Total full-time personnel in reporting hos-pitals. Personnel are as defined in series B304-351 and in-clude persons employed on a full-time basis, that is, reg-ularly employed throughout the hospital's full work week.

B400-431. Total part-time personnel in reporting hos-pitals. Personnel are as defined in series B304-351 and in-clude persons employed on a part-time basis, that is, reg-ularly employed on selected days or partial days in the hospital's work week.

B432-455. Number of graduate nurses (full- and part-time) in reporting hospitals. Graduate nurses are persons who have graduated from a recognized formal nursing edu-cational program. These nurses can be registered according to appropriate provincial legislation, or non- registered.

B456-460. Operating expenditure per patient-day in reporting public hospitals. Included in expenditures are the costs on an accrual basis, of operating and maintaining the hospital during the year, per patient-day.

B461-475. Operating expenditures of reporting public hospitals by salary and non-salary expenditures. Operating

expense is defined as the cost, on an accrual basis, of oper-ating and maintaining the hospital during the year, regard-less of the amounts of disbursements made during the year.

Salary expenditures include the gross salaries and wages earned during the year by all hospital personnel except those engaged in special research projects, ambulance ser-vice, and ancillary operations, whether or not actually paid during the year. Gross salaries and wages comprise the following:

(1) Salaries, wages and other remuneration earned by paid personnel, including special allowances paid and per-quisites supplied to such personnel; also any earned fees or other remuneration, perquisites, and special allowances to physicians for services rendered to the hospital.

(2) The value of contributed services of regular staff members working without pay, and of perquisites supplied to such personnel, calculated on the basis of salary scales for similar services in the community and supported by reg-ular payroll records.

The distribution of the gross salary or wages of an em-ployee working in more than one department of a hospital, including allowances for student nurses and interns, nor-mally are made proportionately to the numbers of paid hours of work done by the employee in each of the several departments; however, if the employee received separate remuneration for services in each department, these amounts are charged to the departments concerned.

Non-salary expenditures are the difference between oper-ating expense and salary expense.

B476-499. Operating expenditures of public general and allied special hospitals by selected services.

Nursing services consist of: nursing administration, nurs-ing units, newborn nursery, delivery room, operating room, emergency unit and central supply services.

Special services consist of: organized out-patient depart-ment, special clinics, electrocardiogram[1], electroencephalo-gram[1], radioisotope services[1], pharmacy, physical medicine and rehabilitation, special research projects, and other services[2].

Laboratory consists of laboratory services.

Radiology consists of radiology services.

Educational services consist of: medical education, nurs-ing education, laboratory technologist training, radiology technician training, and other student training services.

General services[3] consist of: general administration, medi-cal records and medical library, dietary, laundry, linen ser-vice and housekeeping[4], plant operation and hospital secur-ity and plant maintenance[4], and other services.

From 1959 to 1973, "Other" did not exist. Prior to 1959, "Other" consisted of those gross salaries and wages which were not distributed to any of the departments.

B500-503. Operating revenue of reporting mental in-stitutions by source. Operating revenue is defined as income that accrues during the year for the purpose of operation and maintenance of the hospital.

B504-513. Health expenditures, Canada, 1926 to 1975

SOURCE: for 1960 to 1973, Department of National Health and Welfare, *National Health Expenditures in Canada, 1960-1973*, tables 1, 12, 37, 42 and 47, and their basic data; for 1957 to 1959, Department of National Health and Wel-fare, *Expenditures on Personal Health Care in the Prov-inces of Canada, 1957-69*; for 1953 to 1956, Department of

National Health and Welfare, *Expenditures on Personal Health Care in Canada, 1953-1961,* tables 1, 5, 12, 16, 20 and 25; for 1926 to 1952, *Royal Commission on Health Services 1964,* vol. 1 (Ottawa: Queen's Printer, 1964), table 11-1, pp. 426-427.

B514-516. Estimated enrolment in non-profit medical insurance plans, Canada, at 31 December, 1937 to 1975

SOURCE: for 1961 to 1968, data are summarized in the annual series, *Health and Welfare Services in Canada,* comparable with the annual series contained in the *Canada Year Book,* and in more detail in *Survey of Voluntary Health Insurance in Canada,* an annual series prepared by the Canadian Health Insurance Association; for 1954, 1959 and 1960, unpublished compilation, Department of National Health and Welfare, Research and Statistics Division; for 1955 to 1958, annual issues of *Voluntary Hospital and Medical Insurance in Canada;* for 1937 to 1953, Department of National Health and Welfare, *Voluntary Medical Care Insurance, A Study of Non-Profit Plans in Canada,* pp. 29, 47, 187. Public medical care insurance plans had supplanted most of the voluntary sector by 1970.

The material relating to enrolment has been assembled in co-operation with the non-profit plans. The first plan was introduced in 1937, in Ontario. A comprehensive plan is one which provides a wide range of benefits, including payments for each of the following services: physicians' calls in office, home and hospitals consultations; surgical operations and procedures; confinements; anaesthesia; X-ray, laboratory and other diagnostic procedures. A limited plan is one which provides only a limited selection of these benefits such as surgical and obstetrical care, with or without medical (non-surgical) care in hospital (see Department of National Health and Welfare, *Voluntary Medical Care Insurance,* p. 24).

The figures give the number of persons covered. In addition to enrolments in non-profit plans which are covered in the data of series B514-516 there were private plans carried, in the main, with insurance companies. In 1968 the number in such private plans, reported in the annual series *Survey of Voluntary Health Insurance in Canada* was 5,303,000 persons. A total of 4,870,000 were enrolled in comprehensive plans covering both surgical and medical care, and another 433,000 in limited plans comprising 'major medical' or 'extended' health benefits. A small proportion of the 433,000 would be duplicated in the 5,303,000 count.

Provincial data on the enrolment in government insurance plans for hospital services and medical care separately are available from Health and Welfare Canada for census years, 1941 to 1961, and on an annual basis from 1968.

B517-525. Annual rates of notifiable diseases, Canada, 1926 to 1975

SOURCE: Statistics Canada, *Annual Report of Notifiable Diseases,* (Catalogue 82-201), especially the 1969 edition which contains historical data for the years 1921 to 1969.

These rates are based on reports to their respective provincial governments of local medical officers of health on notifiable diseases reported to them. Each provincial officer of health consolidates these reports and submits them to Statistics Canada. The reporting of notifiable diseases on a national level was affected by provincial differences in lists of reportable diseases, variations between provinces concerning exact international categories associated with each reportable disease and the proportion of cases reported by physicians.

There is evidence that the number of cases reported is far from being complete. In the national survey on sickness conducted in Canada during 1950 and 1951, the number of persons reporting illness as commencing during the survey year for the same diseases as those reported here is much greater. The ratio of the number of cases reported in the survey is as follows: measles, 13.8 per cent; whooping cough, 10.9 per cent; chickenpox, 17.3 per cent; mumps, 13.9 per cent; German measles, 17.1 per cent (see Lossing, 'Reporting of Notifiable Diseases', pp. 444-448; also, *Canadian Sickness Survey, 1950-51,* no. 10, table 7). At least the figures in the table presented here may represent the evolution of each disease. But in the paper quoted above, the author says that reporting is probably more incomplete during epidemic periods than during periods of lesser incidence. It should be noted that revised figures and analysis of the principal findings of the Canadian Sickness Survey have been assembled in *Illness and Health Care, 1950-51,* (Catalogue 82-518), a joint study of Statistics Canada and the Department of National Health and Welfare.

B526-543. Separations and days of stay by major diagnosis, 1967 to 1975

SOURCE: Statistics Canada, *Hospital Morbidity,* (Catalogue 82-206); *Hospital Morbidity, Canadian Diagnostic List,* (Catalogue 82-209); and *Hospital Morbidity, Historical Summary, Canada, 1964, 1966 and 1968,* (Catalogue 82-532).

This information on hospital morbidity, like that on annual rates of notifiable diseases, provides some indication of the health care needs toward which the manpower and facilities of the health care sector are being directed. Care must be exercised in interpreting changes from 1967 and 1968 to 1969 and later years since the former data are classified according to the 7th Revision of the International Classification of Diseases Adapted (ICDA) and the latter according to the 8th Revision of the ICDA. Similar information for males and females taken separately and for the 188 diagnostic subcategories of the 8th ICDA, namely the Canadian List, are also available. Selected data are available back to 1960.

Detailed information on patients treated, medical services rendered, and rates and costs per patient by diagnostic group has been assembled for the province of Saskatchewan in 1971 and is presented in *Medical Services and Associated Diagnosis, Saskatchewan, 1971,* (Catalogue 82-533), a joint publication of Statistics Canada and the Saskatchewan Medical Care Insurance Commission.

With regard to the numbers of actual services rendered, some data are available in Statistics Canada publications, *Surgical Procedures and Treatments,* (Catalogue 82-208), and *Surgical Procedures and Treatments, 1968,* (Catalogue 82-529).

Footnotes

[1] In some instances these services may be provided by other departments.

[2] Includes ambulance service and office of the medical staff.

[3] Definitions or components of departments for all years are based

on information given for 1973, in the "Hospital Statistics" publications. Differences in organization have resulted in changes in department names and components. Because of this it was necessary to extract components and to recombine them in order to be comparable with information given in 1973. It was decided to list, for the years in which department names and components were changed, 1973 department names and their historical components, in order to give a better understanding of how the figures were arrived at. Prior to 1969 an expense under the name of

"Other Non-Departmental Expenses", which is now included in "General Services" under "General Administration" and "Plant Operation, Hospital Security and Plant Maintenance", was listed separately under "General Services". This expense was also called "Other Revenue Fund Expense".

[4] These are separate departments but have been combined for purposes of consistence with tabular presentations.

Series B1-14. Live births, crude birth rate, age-specific fertility rates, gross reproduction rate and percentage of births in hospital, Canada, 1921 to 1974
(all fertility rates based on live births per thousand women for the specified group)

Year	Live births			Crude birth rate[3]	Fertility rates by age of mother[1]							Total fertility rate[1]	Net reproduction rate (per thousand women)[1]	Percentage of births occurring in hospital[4]
	Total number	Number illegitimate[2]	Percentage illegitimate[2]		15–19 years	20–24 years	25–29 years	30–34 years	35–39 years	40–44 years	45–49 years			
	1	2	3	4	5	6	7	8	9	10	11	12	13	14
1974	350,650	..	..	15.4	35.3	113.1	131.1	66.4	23.0	5.5	0.4	1,875	886	99.7
1973	343,373	31,005	9.0	15.5	37.2	117.7	131.6	67.1	25.7	6.4	0.4	1,931	909	99.6
1972	347,319	31,257	9.0	15.9	38.5	119.8	137.1	72.1	28.9	7.8	0.6	2,024	953	99.6
1971	362,187	32,693	9.0	16.8	40.1	134.4	142.0	77.3	33.6	9.4	0.6	2,187	1,029	99.6
1970	371,988	35,588	9.6	17.5	42.8	143.3	147.2	81.8	39.0	11.3	0.9	2,331	1,099	99.6
1969	369,647	34,041	9.2	17.6	42.2	147.7	149.8	85.0	42.6	12.5	1.1	2,405	1,136	99.5
1968	364,310	32,629	9.0	17.6	43.0	152.6	148.7	86.3	44.8	13.8	1.4	2,453	1,150	99.5
1967	370,894	30,915	8.3	18.2	45.2	161.4	152.6	91.8	50.9	15.9	1.5	2,597	1,224	99.4
1966	387,710	29,391	7.6	19.4	48.2	169.1	163.5	103.3	57.5	19.1	1.7	2,812	1,322	99.2
1965	418,595	28,078	6.7	21.3	49.3	188.6	181.9	119.4	65.9	22.0	2.0	3,145	1,476	99.0
1964	452,915	26,556	5.9	23.5	50.2	212.8	203.1	134.9	72.0	25.1	2.1	3,502	1,644	98.7
1963	465,767	24,458	5.3	24.6	53.1	226.0	210.6	140.3	75.8	25.9	2.1	3,669	1,718	98.3
1962	469,693	22,443	4.8	25.3	55.0	231.6	214.6	143.1	77.1	27.6	2.1	3,756	1,759	97.8
1961	475,700	21,490	4.5	26.1	58.2	233.6	219.2	144.9	81.1	28.5	2.4	3,840	1,795	96.9
1960	478,551	20,413	4.3	26.8	59.8	233.5	224.4	146.2	84.2	28.5	2.4	3,895	1,893	94.6
1959	479,275	20,221	4.2	27.4	60.4	233.8	226.7	147.7	87.3	28.5	2.7	3,935	1,915	93.1
1958	470,118	19,027	4.0	27.5	59.2	226.5	223.3	147.9	87.6	28.9	2.7	3,880	1,886	91.7
1957	469,093	18,629	4.0	28.2	60.2	227.1	224.1	149.4	90.7	30.7	2.8	3,925	1,907	90.2
1956	450,739	17,510	3.9	28.0	55.9	222.2	220.1	150.3	89.6	30.8	2.9	3,858	1,874	88.4
1955	442,937	17,034	3.8	28.2	54.2	218.3	215.1	153.8	89.8	32.3	2.9	3,831	1,863	86.5
1954	436,198	16,947	3.9	28.5	54.3	217.4	213.2	156.5	88.5	32.4	3.2	3,828	1,861	84.6
1953	417,884	16,064	3.8	28.1	52.0	208.2	208.4	153.2	88.1	31.2	2.9	3,721	1,812	83.4
1952	403,559	15,174	3.8	27.9	50.4	201.0	205.2	150.7	87.4	30.7	2.8	3,641	1,763	81.4
1951	381,092	14,537	3.8	27.2	48.1	188.7	198.8	144.5	86.5	30.9	3.1	3,503	1,701	79.1
1950	372,009	14,510	3.9	27.1	46.0	181.3	200.6	141.3	87.9	30.8	3.0	3,455	1,678	76.0
1949	367,092	14,390	3.9	27.3	45.2	181.5	201.2	139.7	88.8	31.5	3.2	3,456	1,678	74.3
1948	359,860	15,302	4.3	27.3	43.2	181.1	197.6	141.4	89.0	32.6	3.3	3,441	1,676	72.3
1947	372,589	14,912	4.0	28.9	42.6	189.1	206.4	150.5	93.1	34.1	3.3	3,595	1,753	71.0
1946	343,504	14,102	4.1	27.2	36.5	169.6	191.4	146.0	93.1	34.5	3.8	3,374	1,640	67.6
1945	300,587	13,394	4.5	24.3	31.6	143.3	166.8	134.3	90.3	33.5	3.7	3,018	1,462	63.2
1944	293,967	12,409	4.2	24.0	31.3	143.3	168.7	134.1	88.1	33.0	3.4	3,010	1,457	61.0
1943	292,943	11,944	4.1	24.2	32.1	146.8	175.4	131.9	86.5	31.9	3.5	3,041	1,478	54.7
1942	281,569	11,531	4.1	23.5	32.0	145.1	168.7	128.0	83.0	32.3	3.6	2,964	1,434	53.7
1941	263,993	10,430	4.0	22.4	30.7	138.4	159.8	122.3	80.0	31.6	3.7	2,832	1,377	48.9
1940	252,577	9,822	3.9	21.6	29.3	130.3	152.6	122.8	81.7	32.7	3.7	2,766	1,348	45.3
1939	237,991	9,346	3.9	20.6	27.2	119.7	144.0	120.4	83.0	32.6	3.9	2,654	1,294	41.7
1938	237,091	9,452	4.0	20.7	26.9	121.2	145.3	123.9	84.8	34.0	4.1	2,701	1,314	39.4
1937	227,869	8,843	3.9	20.1	25.6	113.6	142.2	123.4	85.3	34.7	4.2	2,646	1,286	36.4
1936	227,980	8,917	3.9	20.3	25.7	112.1	144.3	126.5	90.0	36.3	4.4	2,696	1,310	34.5
1935	228,396	8,527	3.7	20.5	26.5	112.5	148.5	128.6	92.6	37.3	4.9	2,755	1,346	32.3
1934	228,296	8,321	3.6	20.7	26.2	113.1	151.2	133.1	93.0	39.2	4.9	2,803	1,368	30.0
1933	229,791	8,644	3.8	21.0	27.4	117.8	155.6	132.8	94.9	39.3	5.1	2,864	1,394	28.5
1932	242,698	8,655	3.6	22.5	28.7	129.6	168.3	140.6	100.5	43.7	5.5	3,084	1,499	27.5
1931	247,205	8,543	3.5	23.2	29.9	137.1	175.1	145.3	103.1	44.0	5.5	3,200	1,555	26.8
1930	250,335	8,255	3.3	23.9	30.5	143.0	176.0	148.0	106.7	46.6	5.5	3,282	1,599	26.6
1929	242,226	7,670	3.2	23.5	30.3	139.9	172.5	144.2	104.8	46.2	5.4	3,217	1,565	24.5
1928	243,616	7,436	3.1	24.1	30.2	140.3	172.8	149.9	111.0	48.8	5.9	3,294	1,604	21.5
1927	241,149	6,865	2.8	24.3	29.6	140.0	173.6	151.2	113.8	49.4	6.2	3,319	1,609	19.3
1926	240,015	6,307	2.6	24.7	29.0	139.9	177.4	153.8	114.6	50.7	6.0	3,357	1,628	17.8
1925	249,365	4,201[5]	2.6[5]	26.1	–	–	–	–	–	–	–	–	–	–
1924	251,351	3,848[5]	2.3[5]	26.7	–	–	–	–	–	–	–	–	–	–
1923	247,404[6]	3,556[5]	2.2[5]	26.7[3]	–	–	–	–	–	–	–	–	–	–
1922	259,825[6]	3,515[5]	2.1[5]	28.3[3]	–	–	–	–	–	–	–	–	–	–
1921	264,879[6]	3,334[5]	2.0[5]	29.3[3]	–	–	–	–	–	–	–	–	–	–

[1] Data for the Yukon Territory and the Northwest Territories not available prior to 1950; Newfoundland excluded throughout.

[2] Excludes the Yukon Territory and the Northwest Territories prior to 1950.

[3] Number of live births per thousand population; excludes the Yukon Territory and the Northwest Territories, 1921 to 1923.

[4] Excluding the province of Newfoundland; excludes the Yukon Territory and the Northwest Territories, 1926 to 1949.

[5] Excluding the province of Quebec, 1921 to 1925; excluding Newfoundland, 1921.

[6] Excludes the Yukon Territory and the Northwest Territories.

Series B15-22. Total number of deaths, crude and standardized death rates by sex, natural increase and rate, Canada, 1921 to 1974
(all rates are per thousand population)

Year	Total number of deaths	Crude death rates			Standardized death rates[1]		Natural increase	
		Male[1]	Female[1]	Both sexes	Male	Female	Number	Rate
	15	16	17	18	19	20	21	22
1974	166,794	8.6	6.2	7.4	8.4	5.0	178,851	8.0
1973	164,039	8.6	6.2	7.4	8.5	5.1	179,334	8.1
1972	162,413	8.7	6.2	7.4	8.6	5.2	184,906	8.5
1971	157,272	8.5	6.1	7.3	8.4	5.2	204,915	9.5
1970	155,961	8.5	6.1	7.3	8.5	5.4	216,027	10.1
1969	154,477	8.6	6.1	7.4	8.6	5.5	215,170	10.3
1968	153,196	8.6	6.2	7.4	8.7	5.6	211,114	10.2
1967	150,283	8.6	6.1	7.4	8.7	5.6	220,611	10.8
1966	149,863	8.7	6.2	7.5	8.8	5.7	237,847	11.9
1965	148,939	8.8	6.3	7.6	8.8	5.9	269,656	13.7
1964	145,850	8.8	6.3	7.6	8.8	5.9	307,065	15.9
1963	147,367	9.0	6.5	7.8	9.0	6.2	318,400	16.8
1962	143,699	8.9	6.5	7.7	8.9	6.2	325,994	17.6
1961	140,985	9.0	6.5	7.7	9.0	6.3	334,715	18.4
1960	139,693	9.0	6.6	7.8	9.1	6.4	338,858	19.0
1959	139,913	9.2	6.8	8.0	9.3	6.7	339,362	19.4
1958	135,201	9.1	6.7	7.9	9.3	6.6	334,917	19.6
1957	136,579	9.5	6.9	8.2	9.6	6.9	332,514	20.0
1956	131,961	9.4	7.0	8.2	9.4	7.0	318,778	19.8
1955	128,476	9.4	6.9	8.2	9.4	6.9	314,461	20.0
1954	124,855	9.3	7.0	8.2	9.3	7.0	311,343	20.3
1953	127,791	9.8	7.4	8.6	9.8	7.5	290,093	19.5
1952	126,385	10.0	7.5	8.7	9.9	7.6	277,174	19.2
1951	125,823	10.1	7.8	9.0	10.0	8.0	255,269	18.2
1950	124,220	10.1	7.9	9.1	10.1	8.1	247,789	18.0
1949	124,567	10.3	8.1	9.3	10.3	8.3	242,525	18.0
1948	122,974	10.4	8.3	9.3	10.4	8.5	236,886	18.0
1947	121,503	10.4	8.3	9.4	10.6	8.7	251,086	19.5
1946	118,785	10.3	8.4	9.4	10.7	9.0	224,719	17.8
1945	117,325	10.3	8.5	9.5	10.9	9.2	183,262	14.8
1944	120,393	10.5	8.9	9.8	11.3	9.7	173,574	14.2
1943	122,640	10.9	9.2	10.1	11.8	10.1	170,303	14.1
1942	117,110	10.6	8.8	9.8	11.6	9.8	164,459	13.7
1941	118,797	10.8	9.1	10.1	12.0	10.3	145,196	12.3
1940	114,717	10.5	9.0	9.8	11.8	10.2	137,860	11.8
1939	112,729	10.4	9.0	9.7	11.8	10.4	125,262	10.9
1938	110,647	10.3	8.9	9.7	11.8	10.4	126,444	11.0
1937	118,019	10.9	9.7	10.4	12.7	11.4	109,850	9.7
1936	111,111	10.2	9.3	9.9	12.0	11.0	116,869	10.4
1935	109,724	10.2	9.2	9.9	12.1	11.0	118,672	10.6
1934	105,277	10.0	8.9	9.5	11.9	10.8	123,019	11.2
1933	105,603	10.0	9.2	9.7	12.0	11.2	124,188	11.3
1932	108,161	10.3	9.5	10.0	12.5	11.6	134,537	12.5
1931	108,446	10.5	9.6	10.2	12.7	11.7	138,759	13.0
1930	113,283	11.2	10.2	10.8	13.5	12.4	137,052	13.1
1929	117,622	11.8	10.8	11.4	14.3	13.3	124,604	12.1
1928	113,176	11.6	10.6	11.2	14.0	13.0	130,440	12.9
1927	109,104	11.4	10.4	11.0	13.8	12.7	132,045	13.3
1926	111,055	11.9	10.9	11.4	14.3	13.4	128,960	13.3
1925	102,528	10.3	9.5	10.7	12.5	11.7	146,837	15.4
1924	102,820	10.3	9.6	10.9	12.6	11.9	148,531	15.8
1923	108,858[2]	11.0	10.4	11.8[2]	13.5	12.9	138,546[2]	14.9[2]
1922	106,068[2]	11.0	10.3	11.6[2]	13.4	12.6	153,757[2]	16.7[2]
1921	104,531[2]	10.9	10.2	11.6[2]	13.3	12.4	160,348[2]	17.7[2]

[1] Excluding the province of Quebec for 1921 to 1925, Newfoundland for 1921 to 1948 and the Yukon Territory and the Northwest Territories for 1921 to 1949.

[2] Excluding the Yukon Territory and the Northwest Territories.

Series B23-34. Average age-specific death rates, both sexes, Canada, for five-year periods, 1921 to 1974
(per thousand population)

Period[1]	All ages	0 years	1–4 years	5–14 years	15–24 years	25–34 years	35–44 years	45–54 years	55–64 years	65–74 years	75–84 years	85 years and over
	23	24	25	26	27	28	29	30	31	32	33	34
1974	7.4	15.0	0.8	0.4	1.2	1.1	2.2	5.7	13.6	31.6	74.1	177.5
1973	7.4	15.5	0.8	0.4	1.2	1.1	2.3	5.6	13.9	31.1	75.0	179.0
1972	7.4	17.1	0.9	0.4	1.2	1.2	2.3	5.6	13.7	32.1	75.4	178.8
1971	7.3	17.5	0.8	0.4	1.1	1.1	2.3	5.6	13.5	31.3	75.4	177.3
1966–70	7.4	20.8	0.9	0.5	1.0	1.2	2.3	5.7	14.2	33.0	78.6	187.9
1961–65	7.7	25.9	1.1	0.5	1.0	1.2	2.3	5.9	14.7	34.7	84.0	196.8
1960	7.8	28.3	1.2	0.5	1.0	1.2	2.3	6.0	15.0	35.5	86.8	207.4
1959	8.0	29.6	1.2	0.6	1.0	1.3	2.3	6.0	15.2	36.7	89.1	211.3
1956–60	8.0	31.3	1.3	0.5	1.0	1.3	2.3	6.1	15.4	36.2	88.7	208.7
1951–55	8.5	37.5	1.7	0.7	1.1	1.5	2.6	6.6	15.9	36.9	90.6	213.1
1946–50[1]	9.3	49.0	2.4	0.9	1.5	1.8	3.2	7.2	16.7	39.3	93.6	213.5
1941–45	9.8	61.0	3.6	1.2	1.9	2.4	3.8	7.7	17.3	41.1	102.0	233.0
1936–40	9.8	70.8	5.0	1.5	2.2	2.9	4.4	8.0	17.7	42.2	103.2	227.5
1931–35	9.8	80.7	5.5	1.5	2.5	3.4	4.7	8.2	17.7	42.1	103.2	225.2
1926–30	11.1		26.7	2.2	3.3	4.0	5.5	8.7	18.3	44.7	109.6	255.1
1921–25[1]	10.3		23.5	2.2	3.1	3.9	5.2	8.2	17.6	43.2	105.7	243.5

[1] Excluding Quebec, 1921 to 1925; Newfoundland, 1921 to 1948; and the Yukon Territory and the Northwest Territories, 1921 to 1949.

Series B35-50. Average annual number of deaths and death rates for leading causes of death, Canada, for five-year periods, 1921 to 1974
(all rates are per 100,000 population)

Period[1]	Cardiovascular renal diseases, 330–4, 400–68, 592–4[1]		Cancer, 140–205[1]		Accidents, 800–962[1]		Tuberculosis, 001–019[1]		Diseases of early infancy,[2] 760–76[1]		Influenza, bronchitis and pneumonia,[2] 480–3, 490–3, 500–2, 763[1]		Gastritis, duodenitis, enteritis and colitis, 543, 571, 572[1]		Communicable diseases,[3] 055, 056, 085, 050, 040, 041[1]	
	Number	Rate	Number	Rate	Number	Rate	Number	Rate	Number	Rate	Number	Rate	Number	Rate	Number	Rate
	35	36	37	38	39	40	41	42	43	44	45	46	47	48	49	50
1974	82,651	368.2	33,751	150.4	12,945	57.7	330	1.5	—	—	7,171	31.9	686	3.1	29	0.1
1973	80,849	365.9	33,069	149.7	13,167	59.6	408	1.8	—	—	7,352	33.3	716	3.2	18	0.1
1972	80,372	368.3	32,265	147.9	12,825	58.8	453	2.1	—	—	7,592	34.8	747	3.4	4	—
1971	78,395	363.5	31,036	143.9	12,031	55.8	447	2.1	—	—	7,393	34.3	685	3.2	25	0.1
1966–70	77,103	372.9	28,718	138.9	11,526	55.7	602	2.9	—	—	7,601	36.8	702	3.4	49	0.2
1961–65	73,653	388.9	24,987	131.9	10,304	54.4	735	3.9	—	—	7,205	38.0	835	4.4	111	0.6
1960	70,754	395.9	23,181	129.7	9,403	52.6	823	4.6	7,085	39.6	7,223	40.4	974	5.5	149	0.8
1959	70,152	401.3	22,243	127.2	9,439	54.0	959	5.5	7,453	42.6	8,227	47.1	995	5.7	145	0.8
1956–60	68,083	399.9	21,895	128.6	9,385	55.1	1,050	6.2	7,527	44.2	7,652	44.9	964	5.7	195	1.1
1951–55	61,522	414.0	19,120	128.7	8,531	57.4	2,175	14.6	7,355	49.5	6,816	45.9	1,152	7.8	376	2.5
1946–50[4]	53,466	413.0	16,737	129.3	7,624	58.9	4,803	37.1	7,543	58.3	7,159	55.3	1,840	14.2	639	4.9
1941–45	47,498	403.3	14,521	123.3	7,139	60.6	5,898	50.1	6,740	57.2	8,139	69.1	2,261	19.2	1,145	9.7
1936–40	37,617	337.6	12,682	113.8	6,225	55.9	6,265	56.2	6,708	60.2	10,864	97.5	2,690	24.1	1,733	15.6
1931–35	31,559	297.5	10,699	100.9	5,555	52.4	6,950	65.5	7,900	74.5	10,674	100.6	3,757	35.4	1,888	17.8
1926–30	26,818	273.1	8,638	88.0	5,772	58.8	7,884	80.3	9,597	97.7	13,138	133.8	5,387	54.9	3,436	35.0
1921–25	20,008	221.9	6,848	75.9	4,643	51.5	7,671	85.1	10,009[5]	111.0[5]	12,772	141.1	6,514	72.2	4,251	47.1

[1] Numbers refer to categories of the International Statistical Classification of Diseases, Injuries and Causes of Death (Seventh Revision), although these may not be strictly comparable over the period for some diseases.
[2] Pneumonia of the newborn included in both 'diseases of early infancy' and 'influenza, bronchitis and pneumonia' for all years (except for the province of Quebec, 1921 to 1925).
[3] Includes diphtheria, whooping cough, measles, scarlet fever, typhoid fever.
[4] Newfoundland included in 1949 and following years. The Yukon Territory and the Northwest Territories included in 1950 and following years.
[5] Excludes pneumonia of the newborn for the province of Quebec.

Series B51-58. Stillbirths and rate, infant deaths and rate by sex, neonatal death rate and maternal mortality rate, Canada, 1921 to 1974
(all rates are per thousand live births)

Year	Stillbirths[1]		Infant deaths (under one year of age)				Neonatal death rate[3]	Maternal mortality
				Infant death rates				
	Number	Rate	Number	Male[2]	Female[2]	Both sexes		
	51	**52**	**53**	**54**	**55**	**56**	**57**	**58**
1974	2,766	8.0	5,192	17	13	15	10	0.1
1973	2,866	8.3	5,339	17	14	16	11	0.1
1972	3,046	8.8	5,938	19	15	17	12	0.2
1971	3,396	9.4	6,356	20	15	18	12	0.2
1970	3,687	9.9	7,001	21	16	19	14	0.2
1969	3,694	10.0	7,149	22	17	19	14	0.2
1968	3,926	10.8	7,583	23	19	21	15	0.3
1967	4,248	11.5	8,151	24	20	22	15	0.2
1966	**4,429**	11.4	8,960	26	20	23	16	0.4
1965	4,847	11.6	9,862	26	21	24	16	0.3
1964	5,520	12.2	11,169	28	21	25	17	0.3
1963	5,732	12.3	12,270	30	23	26	18	0.4
1962	5,882	12.5	12,941	31	24	28	19	0.4
1961	6,019	12.7	12,940	31	24	27	18	0.5
1960	6,471	13.5	13,077	31	24	27	18	0.4
1959	6,560[1]	13.7[1]	13,595	32	25	28	18	0.5
1958	6,726	14.3	14,178	34	26	30	19	0.6
1957	6,837	14.6	14,517	34	27	31	20	0.5
1956	**6,976**	15.5	14,399	35	29	32	20	0.6
1955	6,918	15.6	13,884	35	27	31	19	0.8
1954	7,231	16.6	13,934	36	28	32	19	0.7
1953	6,991	16.7	14,859	40	31	36	21	0.8
1952	7,277	18.0	15,408	43	34	38	23	0.9
1951	7,023	18.4	14,673	43	34	39	23	1.1
1950	7,192	19.3	15,441	46	37	42	24	1.1
1949	7,285	19.8	15,935	48[2]	38[2]	43	24[3]	1.5
1948	7,071	19.6	15,965	49	39	44	26	1.5
1947	7,646	20.5	17,229	52	40	46	27	1.6
1946	7,368	21.4	16,407	53	42	48	27	1.8
1945	6,884	22.9	15,779	57	47	52	29	2.3
1944	6,895	23.5	16,541	62	50	56	30	2.8
1943	6,988	23.9	16,117	61	49	55	30	2.9
1942	7,319	26.0	15,585	61	49	55	28	3.1
1941	7,091	26.9	16,117	68	53	61	31	3.6
1940	6,810	27.0	14,542	64	51	58	30	4.0
1939	6,515	27.4	14,607	69	53	61	31	4.3
1938	6,595	27.8	15,233	71	57	64	32	4.3
1937	6,433	28.2	17,628	86	68	77	34	4.9
1936	6,531	28.6	15,442	75	60	68	34	5.6
1935	6,594	28.9	16,549	81	63	72	35	4.9
1934	6,613	29.0	16,603	81	64	73	36	5.3
1933	6,988	30.4	17,022	83	65	74	37	5.0
1932	7,396	30.5	18,098	83	66	75	38	5.0
1931	7,778	31.5	21,269	96	76	86	42	5.1
1930	7,847	31.3	22,677	100	81	91	43	5.8
1929	7,720	31.9	22,501	103	82	93	44[3]	5.7
1928	7,673	31.5	21,979	100	80	90	44	5.6
1927	7,464	31.0	22,784	105	84	95	45	5.5
1926	7,245	30.2	24,377	113[2]	90[2]	102	48	5.6[4]
1925	8,176	32.8	23,128	87[2]	70[2]	93	41[3]	4.9[4]
1924	8,401	33.4	23,602	86	71	94	42	5.3[4]
1923	8,425	34.1	25,571[4]	98	77	103[4]	44	5.0[4]
1922	8,536	32.9	26,399[4]	97	76	102[4]	44	5.1[4]
1921	9,089	34.3	27,051[4]	98	77	102[4]	43	4.7[4]

[1] See the note to series B51-52 for definition of stillbirth in text. Beginning in 1959, some provinces reduced the gestation period to 20 weeks and broadened the definition of 'life' by giving specific criteria. Excludes the Yukon Territory and the Northwest Territories in 1921 to 1926.

[2] Quebec is excluded for 1921 to 1925; Newfoundland for 1921 to 1926; and the Yukon Territory and the Northwest Territories for 1921 to 1949.

[3] See the note to series B53-57 in text for definiton. Quebec is excluded for 1921 to 1925; Newfoundland for 1921 to 1929; and the Yukon Territory and the Northwest Territories for 1921 to 1949.

[4] Excludes the Yukon Territory and the Northwest Territories.

Series B59-64. Average annual infant death rates for selected causes, Canada, for five-year periods, 1931 to 1974

(average annual rates per 100,000 live births)

Period[1]	Imma-turity[2]	Congenital malfor-mations and birth injuries, 750-61[3]	Bronchitis and pneumonia, 490-3, 500-2, 763[3]	Diarrhoea and enteritis, 571.0, 572.2, 572.3, 573,764[3]	Asphyxia and atelec-tasis, 762[3]	Commu-nicable diseases[4]
	59	60	61	62	63	64
1974	—	498	96	26	109	14
1973	—	523	113	29	124	15
1972	—	583	139	29	123	17
1971	—	584	157	25	148	19
1966-70	—	627	213	38	213	26
1961-65	—	712	328	81	292	..
1960	1,079	698	412	119	318	57
1959	1,107	740	406	129	320	64
1956-60	1,140	773	447	136	339	76
1951-55	1,159	865	522	211	332	143
1946-50[1]	1,163	989	628	433	—	245
1941-45	1,167	1,092	780	625	—	449
1936-40	1,436	980	826	793	—	681
1931-35	1,647	1,002	864	1,227	—	743

[1] Newfoundland included for 1949 and following years. The Yukon Territory and the Northwest Territories included for 1950 and following years.

[2] Due to changes in classification, not strictly comparable over the period; includes all deaths involving immaturity either as the underlying cause or as a complication.

[3] Numbers refer to categories of the International Statistical Classification of Diseases, Injuries and Causes of Death (Seventh Revision), although these may not be strictly comparable over the period for some diseases.

[4] Includes measles, scarlet fever, whooping cough, diphtheria, influenza, erysipelas, acute poliomyelitis, cerebrospinal meningitis, tuberculosis and syphilis.

Series B65-74. Life expectancy by sex, at selected ages, Canada, census years, 1871 to 1971

Year	At birth		At age 20		At age 40		At age 60		At age 80	
	Male	Female	Male	Female	Male	Female	Male	Female	Male	Female
	65	66	67	68	69	70	71	72	73	74
1971	69.34	76.36	51.71	58.18	33.22	38.99	16.95	21.39	6.41	7.88
1966	68.75	75.18	51.50	57.37	33.01	38.15	16.81	20.58	6.36	7.26
1961	68.35	74.17	51.51	56.65	32.96	37.45	16.73	19.90	6.14	6.90
1956	67.61	72.92	51.19	55.80	32.74	36.69	16.54	19.34	5.89	6.75
1951	66.33	70.83	50.76	54.41	32.45	35.63	16.49	18.64	5.84	6.38
1941	62.96	66.30	49.57	51.76	31.87	33.99	16.06	17.62	5.54	6.03
1931	60.00	62.10	49.05	49.76	31.98	33.02	16.29	17.15	5.61	5.92
1921[1]	—	—	49.1	49.2	32.2	33.0	16.6	17.1	6.0	6.1
1881[2]	—	—	48.0	47.8	33.2	33.8	18.0	19.0	6.9	7.5
1871[2]	—	—	47.9	47.3	33.4	33.6	18.2	18.2	6.8	6.5

[1] Includes all provinces except Quebec.   [2] Includes Ontario, Quebec, Nova Scotia and New Brunswick.

Series B75-81. Number of marriages and rate, average age at marriage for brides and bridegrooms, number of divorces and rate, net family formation, Canada, 1921 to 1974

Year	Marriages		Average age at marriage (years)[1]		Divorces[2]		Net family formation[2] (thousands of families)
	Number	Rate per thousand population	Brides	Bridegrooms	Number	Rate per hundred thousand population	
	75	76	77	78	79	80	81
1974	198,824	8.9	24.7	27.4	45,019	200.6	111
1973	199,064	9.0	24.8	27.3	36,704	166.1	111
1972	200,470	9.2	24.7	27.1	32,389	148.4	105
1971	191,324	8.9	24.8	27.3	29,685	137.6	100
1970	188,428	8.8	24.9	27.3	29,775	139.8	103
1969	182,183	8.7	24.9	27.3	26,093	124.2	103
1968	171,766	8.3	24.4	26.8	11,343	54.8	111
1967	165,879	8.1	24.4	26.8	11,165	54.8	117
1966	155,596	7.8	24.4	27.0	10,239	51.2	101
1965	145,519	7.4	24.5	27.2	8,974	45.7	81
1964	138,135	7.2	24.5	27.3	8,623	44.7	69
1963	131,111	6.9	24.6	27.5	7,686	40.6	60
1962	129,381	7.0	24.6	27.5	6,768	36.4	58
1961	128,475	7.0	24.7	27.7	6,563	36.0	67
1960	130,338	7.3	24.7	27.7	6,980	39.1	67
1959	132,474	7.6	24.8	27.7	6,543	37.4	67
1958	131,525	7.7	24.8	27.8	6,279	36.8	71
1957	133,186	8.0	24.9	27.8	6,688	40.3	103
1956	132,713	8.3	25.0	27.9	6,002	37.4	84
1955	128,029	8.2	25.1	28.0	6,053	38.6	74
1954	128,629	8.4	25.2	28.1	5,923	38.8	86
1953	131,034	8.8	25.3	28.2	6,160	41.6	91
1952	128,474	8.9	25.3	28.3	5,650	39.1	90
1951	128,408	9.2	25.3	28.3	5,270	37.7	93
1950	125,083	9.1	25.3	28.5	5,386	39.3	71
1949	124,087	9.2	25.4[1]	28.7[1]	6,052	45.1	74
1948	126,118	9.6	25.4[1]	28.6[1]	6,978	54.5	79[2]
1947	130,400	10.1	25.3	28.6	8,213	65.6	72
1946	137,398	10.9	25.3	28.6	7,757	63.2	104
1945	111,376	9.0	25.5	29.0	5,101	42.3	50
1944	104,656	8.5	25.6	29.2	3,827	32.1	48
1943	113,827	9.4	25.4	29.0	3,398	28.9	55
1942	130,786	10.9	25.2	29.0	3,091	26.6	72
1941	124,644	10.6	25.1	28.9	2,462	21.4	68
1940	125,797	10.8	25.2	28.9	2,416	21.3	70
1939	106,266	9.2	25.1	29.0	2,073	18.4	54
1938	90,709	7.9	25.3	29.3	2,228	20.0	39
1937	89,983	7.9	25.2	29.3	1,833	16.6	39
1936	82,941	7.4	25.0	29.1	1,570	14.4	32
1935	78,908	7.1	25.0	29.0	1,431	13.2	30
1934	75,034	6.8	24.9	29.1	1,123	10.5	28
1933	65,516	6.0	24.9	29.2	931	8.8	20
1932	64,141	5.9	24.9	29.2	1,007	9.6	19
1931	68,239	6.4	24.9	29.2	700	6.8	29
1930	73,341	7.0	25.0	29.2	875	8.6	39
1929	78,977	7.7	24.9	29.1	817	8.2	48
1928	76,009	7.5	25.0	29.3	790	8.0	47
1927	71,071	7.2	25.1	29.3	748	7.8	44
1926	68,378	7.0	25.1	29.3	608	6.4	38
1925	66,378	6.9	25.3[1]	29.8[1]	550	5.9	31
1924	66,573	7.1	25.2	29.7	540	5.9	29
1923	67,820[3]	7.3[3]	25.3	29.7	505	5.6	25
1922	65,861[3]	7.2[3]	25.4	29.9	543	6.1	20
1921	71,254[3]	7.9[3]	25.5	29.9	558	6.4	37

[1] Excluding the province of Quebec for 1921 to 1925; Newfoundland for 1921 to 1948; and the Yukon Territory and the Northwest Territories for 1921 to 1949.

[2] Excluding Newfoundland for 1921 to 1948. For the definition of net family formation, see the text.

[3] Excluding the Yukon Territory and the Northwest Territories.

Series B82-92. Number of physicians, dentists and nurses, population per physician, dentist and nurse, number of graduates of medical and dental schools, Canada, 1871 to 1975

Year	Physicians[1]		Graduates of Canadian medical schools[4]	Number of immigrant physicians	Emigrant number of physicians[5]	Dentists[6]		Graduates of Canadian dental schools[8]	Nurses[9]		Graduates from initial Canadian nursing programs
	Number[2]	Population per physician[3]				Number[7]	Population per dentist[3]		Number[10]	Population per nurse[3]	
	82	83	84	85	86	87	88	89	90	91	92
1975	39,104	585	1,548	806	286	8,930	2,563	436	177,182	129	9,778
1974	37,297	605	1,562	1,090	222	8,679	2,600	448	168,530	134	9,899
1973	35,923	619	1,332	1,170	274	8,325	2,671	401	162,976	136	9,594
1972	34,508	636	1,280	988	439	7,981	2,749	398	156,630	140	10,083
1971	32,942	659	1,152	987	474	7,664	2,833	363	148,767	146	10,058
1970	31,166	689	1,070	1,113	240	7,413	2,873	344	141,173	151	8,625
1969	29,659	714	1,016	1,347	236	7,156	2,935	339	134,184	157	8,359
1968	28,209	740	1,016	1,277	314	6,932	2,986	306	126,712	163	7,891
1967	27,544	747	923	1,213	449	6,713	3,036	307	117,614	173	7,522
1966	26,528	763	888	995	393	6,532	3,064	296	109,513	182	7,387
1965	25,481	779	835	792	380	6,396	3,071	290	104,349	189	7,360
1964	24,847	785	787	668	440	6,218	3,102	253	88,558	220	7,261
1963	24,082	795	818	687	467	6,103	3,102	260	80,670	237	6,935
1962	23,248	808	817	530	280	5,999	3,098	225	76,183	246	6,394
1961	21,290	857	834	445	287	5,906	3,088	174	70,647	258	6,188
1960	20,517	879	863	441	245	5,780	3,018	215	68,502	255	5,483
1959	19,800	893	859	439	210	5,753	2,963	193	64,666	264	5,710
1958	19,096	905	828	394	218	5,564	2,981	203	60,864	273	5,244
1957	18,523	920	893	635	256	5,481	2,934	186	59,419	271	5,034
1956	17,871	928	816	415	151	5,416	2,898	168	54,518	288	4,866
1955	17,221	934	894	333	128	5,354	2,855	174	50,131	305	4,995
1954	16,431	955	896	311	116	5,298	2,802	172	47,775[11]	303[11]	5,055
1953	15,829	960	825	402	130	5,215	2,773	178	43,880	321	4,753
1952	15,135	968	783	293	186	5,071	2,763	215	43,924	311	4,434
1951	14,325	976	858	166	173	4,912	2,792	295	41,088	325	4,349
1950	—	—	791	68	260	4,627	2,906	306	41,159	318	4,068
1949	13,873	969	679	78	—	4,549[11]	2,819[11]	180	38,292	335	—
1948	13,373[11]	959[11]	632	95	—	4,601	2,728	99	37,917	331	—
1947	13,263[12]	945[12]	567	81	—	4,602	2,671	149	34,929	352	—
1946	—	—	513	56	—	—	—	102	33,348	362	—
1945	—	—	769	—	—	—	—	116	31,389	381	—
1944	—	—	523	—	—	—	—	140	31,087	379	—
1943	11,620	1,014	496	—	—	—	—	166	29,595	394	—
1942	—	—	539	—	—	—	—	120	27,853	413	—
1941	11,873	968	562	—	—	4,210[12]	2,729[12]	97	25,826	441	—
1940	—	—	606	—	—	—	—	117	—	—	—
1939	—	—	—	—	—	—	—	115	—	—	—
1931	10,020	1,034	482	—	—	4,039	2,566	—	20,462[12]	506[12]	—
1921	8,706	1,008	406	—	—	3,158	2,779	—	21,385[13]	410[13]	—
1911	7,411	970	351	—	—	2,183	3,294	—	5,600	1,284	—
1901	5,442	978	—	—	—	1,310	4,064	—	280	19,014	—
1891	4,448	1,065	—	—	—	753	6,290	—	—	—	—
1881	3,507	1,217	—	—	—	510	8,369	—	—	—	—
1871[14]	2,792	1,249	—	—	—	319	10,928	—	—	—	—

[1] Active civilian; census figures for 1941 and earlier years.
[2] As of September for 1949 and 1948; July for 1947; March for 1943; June for other years up to 1967; 31 December for 1968 to 1975.
[3] Based on census data and Statistics Canada intercensal estimates of population; for dentists, 1947 to 1975, and nurses, 1941 to 1970, population is for June of previous year and from 1971 to 1975 it is 31 December of the same year.
[4] Number of schools producing graduates increased from eight in 1911 to nine in 1925; 10 in 1951; 11 in 1954; 12 in 1957 and to 16 in 1970.
[5] Physicians emigrating to the United States; fiscal year data.
[6] Registered dentists for 1947 to 1975; census figures for 1941 and earlier years; includes active service personnel for 1941 and later years.

[7] As of January for 1947 to 1968; June for 1969 to 1973; and 31 December for 1974 to 1975.
[8] Schools producing graduates totalled five prior to 1961, but had reached 10 in number by 1972.
[9] Registered nurses for 1941 to 1975; census figures for 1931 (graduate nurses) and earlier years ('nurses').
[10] As of January for 1941 to 1973; June for earlier years; and 31 December for 1974 to 1975.
[11] Excludes Newfoundland for this and earlier years.
[12] Excludes the Yukon Territory and the Northwest Territories for this and earlier years.
[13] Includes nurses-in-training.
[14] Provinces of Nova Scotia, New Brunswick, Quebec and Ontario.

Series B93-140. Operating and reporting hospitals, by type and service, Canada, 1932 to 1975

Year	Public											
	All hospitals		Total general and allied special		General, including paediatric		Allied special		Mental		Tuberculosis	
	Operating	Reporting	Operating	Reporting	Operating	Reporting	Operating	Reporting	Operating	Reporting	Operating	Reporting
	93	94	95	96	97	98	99	100	101	102	103	104
1975	1,163	1,154	1,043	1,041	865	864	178	177	114	107	6	6
1974	1,158	1,148	1,043	1,040	868	866	175	174	108	102	7	6
1973	1,171	1,162	1,049	1,047	868	866	181	181	110	104	12	11
1972	1,175	1,168	1,051	1,049	870	869	181	180	111	106	13	13
1971	1,176	1,174	1,043	1,043	867	867	176	176	110	108	23	23
1970	1,173	1,170	1,039	1,038	866	865	173	173	107	105	27	27
1969[3]	1,180	1,176	1,040	1,038	871	869	169	169	108	106	32	32
1968	1,181	1,179	1,043	1,043	881	881	162	162	104	102	34	34
1967	1,173	1,169	1,036	1,035	874	873	162	162	100	97	37	37
1966	1,164	1,162	1,027	1,027	869	869	158	158	99	97	38	38
1965	1,149	1,147	1,011	1,009	852	850	159	159	96	96	42	42
1964	1,129	1,126	996	996	845	845	151	151	91	88	42	42
1963	1,098	1,090	976	975	838	838	138	137	83	76	39	39
1962	1,086	1,071	964	956	832	830	132	126	79	72	43	43
1961	1,076	1,068	946	946	856	856	90	90	80	72	50	50
1960[4]	1,059	1,044	936	925	852	844	84	81	70	67	53	52
1959	1,085	1,059	963	940	855	846	108	94	69	69	53	50
1958	1,080	1,044	957	922	848	833	109	89	71	71	52	51
1957	1,046	1,020	920	894	833	820	87	74	72	72	54	54
1956	1,035	998	909	872	821	796	88	76	71	71	55	55
1955	1,028	983	896	858	808	781	88	77	74	70	58	55
1954	1,008	946	870	817	794	762	76	55	76	73	62	56
1953[7]	990	939	855	810	782	751	73	59	73	69	62	60
1952	924	899	795	777	730	721	65	56	67	66	62	56
1951[10]	905	879	780	778	—	707	—	71	63	44	62	57
1950	892	834	770	741	—	692	—	49	62	39	60	54
1949	859	809	743	719	—	617	—	102	59	38	57	52
1948	785	774	688	678	—	588	—	90	55	55	42	41
1947	769	752	669	653	—	567	—	86	56	55	44	44
1946	718	695	618	595	—	514	—	81	56	56	44	44
1945	711	681	617	587	—	507	—	80	54	54	40	40
1944	702[e]	680	608	586	—	509	—	77	54	54	40	40
1943	689	687	596	594	512	512	84	82	54	54	39	39
1942	688	684	597	594	511	511	86	83	54	54	37	36
1941	691[e]	685	598	592	507	507	91	85	54	54	39	39
1940	700[e]	680	607	587	500	500	107	87	54	54	39	39
1939	699	680	607	588	497	497	110	91	53	53	39	39
1938	700[e]	700	610	610	496[e]	496	114	114	51	51	39	39
1937[13]	673[e]	673	584	584	480	480	104	104	51	51	38	38
1936	661[e]	661	573	573	474	474	99	99	51	51	37	37
1935	658	658	572	572	470	470	102	102	50	50	36	36
1934	652	651	568	568	463	463	105	105	50	49	34	34
1933	658	656	572	571	467	466	105	105	52	51	34	34
1932	643	633	555	547	470	462	85	85	54	52	34	34

Series B93-140. Operating and reporting hospitals, by type and service, Canada, 1932 to 1975 (continued)

Year	Private											
	All hospitals		Total general and allied special		General		Allied special		Mental		Tuberculosis	
	Operating	Reporting	Operating	Reporting	Operating	Reporting	Operating	Reporting	Operating	Reporting	Operating	Reporting
	105	106	107	108	109	110	111	112	113	114	115	116
1975	101	100	90	89	9	9	81	80	11	11	—	—
1974	111	107	99	95	11	10	88	85	12	12	—	—
1973	115	113	103	101	12	11	91	90	12	12	—	—
1972[2]	124	120	112	108	15	12	97	96	12	12	—	—
1971	137	132	125	120	24	21	101	99	12	12	—	—
1970	148	144	136	132	35	31	101	101	12	12	—	—
1969[3]	156	151	144	139	41	37	103	102	12	12	—	—
1968	164	159	153	148	44	41	109	107	11	11	—	—
1967	173	169	165	161	52	49	113	112	8	8	—	—
1966	181	177	172	168	52	50	120	118	9	9	—	—
1965	197	195	187	185	62	60	125	125	9	9	1	1
1964	207	205	197	196	65	64	132	132	9	9	1	—
1963	209	204	199	96	70	68	129	128	9	8	1	—
1962	215	197	206	190	68	57	138	133	8	7	1	—
1961	214	159	204	152	86	59	118	93	9	7	1	—
1960[4]	200	158	192	152	85	62	107	90	7	6	1	—
1959	336	237	331	232	93	68	238	164	5	5	—	—
1958	269	210	264	205	81	55	183	150	5	5	—	—
1957[5]	314	237	309	232	86	63	223	169	5	5	—	—
1956	271	209	266	204	84	65	182	139	4	4	1	1
1955	280	180	275	175	98	55	177	120	4	4	1	1
1954	266	172	263	169	—	62	—	107	2	2	1	1
1953[7]	241[8]	148[8]	236[8]	143[8]	—	52[8]	—	91[8]	4	4	1	1
1952	250	194	243	187	—	61	—	126	6	6	1	1
1951	—	225	—	220	—	—	—	—	5	4	1	1
1950	235	229	230	225	—	—	—	—	4	3	1	1
1949	255	198	251	194	—	—	—	—	3	3	1	1
1948	236	212	233	209	—	—	—	—	2	2	1	1
1947	228	215	225	212	—	—	—	—	2	2	1	1
1946	255	238	252	235	—	—	—	—	2	2	1	1
1945	255	238	251	234	—	—	—	—	3	3	1	1
1944	271	271	267	267	—	—	—	—	3	3	1	1
1943	269	267	265	263	—	—	—	—	3	3	1	1
1942	291	291	287	287	—	—	—	—	3	3	1	1
1941	327	327	322	322	—	—	—	—	4	4	1	1
1940	298	297	293	292	—	—	—	—	4	4	1	1
1939	281	281	276	276	—	—	—	—	4	4	1	1
1938	272	272	267	267	—	—	—	—	4	4	1	1
1937[13]	248	246	243	241	—	—	—	—	4	4	1	1
1936	264	264	259	259	—	—	—	—	4	4	1	1
1935	272	272	267	267	—	—	—	—	4	4	1	1
1934	269	269	261	261	—	—	—	—	6	6	2	2
1933[14]	238	238	230	230	—	—	—	—	6	6	2	2
1932	218	214	212	208	—	—	—	—	4	4	2	2

Series B93-140. Operating and reporting hospitals, by type and service, Canada, 1932 to 1975 (continued)

Year	Federal											
	All hospitals[1]		Total general and allied special[1]		General[1]		Allied special[1]		Mental		Tuberculosis	
	Operating	Reporting	Operating	Reporting	Operating	Reporting	Operating	Reporting	Operating	Reporting	Operating	Reporting
	117	**118**	**119**	**120**	**121**	**122**	**123**	**124**	**125**	**126**	**127**	**128**
1975	107	94	107	94	26	24	81	70	–	–	–	–
1974	99	90	99	90	26	24	73	66	–	–	–	–
1973	100	94	100	94	27	25	73	69	–	–	–	–
1972	97	91	97	91	26	25	71	66	–	–	–	–
1971	94	90	94	90	26	26	68	64	–	–	–	–
1970	87	82	87	82	26	25	61	57	–	–	–	–
1969	77	71	77	71	25	25	52	46	–	–	–	–
1968	74	71	73	70	25	24	48	46	–	–	1	1
1967	77	74	76	73	28	28	48	45	–	–	1	1
1966	76	73	74	71	27	27	47	44	–	–	2	2
1965	87	86	85	84	41	41	44	43	–	–	2	2
1964	78	78	76	76	32	32	44	44	–	–	2	2
1963	77	74	75	72	35	35	40	37	–	–	2	2
1962	84	70	80	66	37	36	43	30	–	–	4	4
1961	85	74	80	69	76	66	4	3	–	–	5	5
1960	94	79	86	71	82	69	4	2	2	2	6	6
1959	60	54	53	47	44	44	9	3	2	2	5	5
1958	51	49	44	42	35	33	9	9	2	2	5	5
1957	52	50	44	42	35	33	9	9	2	2	6	6
1956	62	52	54	44	45	35	9	9	2	2	6	6
1955	62	53	55	46	46	37	9	9	–[6]	–[6]	7	7
1954	61	53	51	44	41	37	10	7	2	2	8	7
1953[7]	57	56	46	46	–	40	–	6	2	2	9	8
1952[9]	59	52	47	42	–	40	–	2	2	2	10	8
1951	–	88	–	78	–	67	–	11	2	2	10	8
1950	85	77	73	67	–	54	–	13	2	2	10	8
1949	94	85	81	76	–	57	–	19	2	2	11	7
1948	82	74	68	66	–	44	–	22	2	2	12	6
1947	83	74	71	66	–	45	–	21	2	2	10	6
1946	78	73	70	66	–	43	–	23	2	2	6	5
1945	136	21[11]	130	15[11]	–	–	–	–	2	2	4	4
1944	98	17[11]	93	13[11]	–	10[11]	–	3[11]	2	2	3	2
1943	17	17[11]	13	13[11]	–	7[11]	–	6[11]	2	2	3	2
1942	16	16[11]	13	13[11]	–	7[11]	–	6[11]	2	2	2	1
1941	21	21[11]	18	18[11]	–	–	–	–	2	2	2	1
1940	194	194	191	191	–	–	–	–	2	2	1	1
1939[12]	127	84	124	81	–	–	–	–	2	2	1	1
1938	34	32	32	30	–	–	–	–	2	2	–	–
1937	34	32	32	30	–	–	–	–	2	2	–	–
1936	34	32	32	30	–	–	–	–	2	2	–	–
1935	34	33	32	31	–	–	–	–	2	2	–	–
1934	34	32	32	30	–	–	–	–	2	2	–	–
1933	34	32	32	30	–	–	–	–	2	2	–	–
1932	35	35	33	33	–	–	–	–	2	2	–	–

Series B93-140. Operating and reporting hospitals, by type and service, Canada, 1932 to 1975 (concluded)

Year	Total											
	All hospitals		Total general and allied special		General, including paediatric		Allied special		Mental		Tuberculosis	
	Operating	Reporting	Operating	Reporting	Operating	Reporting	Operating	Reporting	Operating	Reporting	Operating	Reporting
	129	130	131	132	133	134	135	136	137	138	139	140
1975	1,371	1,348	1,240	1,224	900	897	340	327	125	118	6	6
1974	1,368	1,345	1,241	1,225	905	900	336	325	120	114	7	6
1973	1,386	1,369	1,252	1,242	907	902	345	340	122	116	12	11
1972	1,396	1,379	1,260	1,248	911	906	349	342	123	118	13	13
1971	1,407	1,396	1,262	1,253	917	914	345	339	122	120	23	23
1970	1,408	1,396	1,262	1,252	927	921	335	331	119	117	27	27
1969	1,413	1,398	1,261	1,248	937	931	324	317	120	118	32	32
1968	1,419	1,409	1,269	1,261	950	946	319	315	115	113	35	35
1967	1,423	1,412	1,277	1,269	954	950	323	319	108	105	38	38
1966	1,421	1,412	1,273	1,266	948	946	325	320	108	106	40	40
1965	1,433	1,428	1,283	1,278	955	951	328	327	105	105	45	45
1964	1,414	1,409	1,269	1,268	942	941	327	327	100	97	45	44
1963	1,384	1,368	1,250	1,243	943	941	307	302	92	84	42	41
1962	1,385	1,338	1,250	1,212	937	923	313	289	87	79	48	47
1961	1,375	1,301	1,230	1,167	1,018	981	212	186	89	79	56	55
1960	1,353	1,281	1,214	1,148	1,019	975	195	173	79	75	60	58
1959	1,481	1,350	1,347	1,219	992	958	355	261	76	76	58	55
1958	1,400	1,303	1,265	1,169	964	921	301	248	78	78	57	56
1957	1,412	1,307	1,273	1,168	954	916	319	252	79	79	60	60
1956	1,368	1,259	1,229	1,120	950	896	279	224	77	77	62	62
1955	1,370	1,216	1,226	1,079	952	873	274	206	78	74	66	63
1954	1,335	1,173	1,184	1,032	–	863	–	169	80	77	71	64
1953[7]	1,288	1,143	1,137	999	–	842	–	157	79	75	72	69
1952[9]	1,233	1,145	1,085	1,006	–	822	–	184	75	72	73	67
1951	–	1,192	–	1,076	–	–	–	–	70	50	–	66
1950	1,212	1,140	1,073	1,033	–	–	–	–	68	44	71	63
1949	1,208	1,092	1,075	989	–	–	–	–	64	43	69	60
1948	1,103	1,060	989	953	–	–	–	–	59	59	55	48
1947	1,080	1,041	965	931	–	–	–	–	60	59	55	51
1946	1,051	1,006	940	896	–	–	–	–	60	60	51	50
1945	1,102	940	998	836	–	–	–	–	59	59	45	45
1944	1,071	968	968	866	–	–	–	–	59	59	44	43
1943	972	971	870	870	–	–	–	–	59	59	43	42
1942	993	991	894	894	–	–	–	–	59	59	40	38
1941	1,034	1,033	932	932	–	–	–	–	60	60	42	41
1940	1,171	1,171	1,070	1,070	–	–	–	–	60	60	41	41
1939[12]	1,107	1,045	1,007	945	–	–	–	–	59	59	41	41
1938	1,006	1,004	909	907	–	–	–	–	57	57	40	40
1937	955	951	859	855	–	–	–	–	57	57	39	39
1936	959	957	864	862	–	–	–	–	57	57	38	38
1935	964	964	871	870	–	–	–	–	56	56	37	37
1934	955	955	861	859	–	–	–	–	58	57	36	36
1933	930	926	834	831	–	–	–	–	60	59	36	36
1932	896	882	800	788	–	–	–	–	60	58	36	36

[1] Federal hospitals include such facilities as aid stations and base hospitals. This fact could explain in part the irregular fluctuations of operating and reporting hospitals.
[2] Private hospitals decreased due to provincial government concern about duplication of services.
[3] Reorganized hospital classification structure.
[4] Reclassification of hospitals resulted in 36 hospitals being reclassified to related institutions (nursing stations, homes for the aged, etc.)
[5] The increase in private hospitals is mainly due to an increase of 30 private hospitals in Quebec. However, 56 of Quebec's private hospitals did not report.
[6] The two mental hospitals were differently classified for this year only.

[7] Introduction of Newfoundland into national statistics.
[8] Only 39 of 101 private hospitals in Quebec reported; only 60 per cent of overall reported data for private hospitals.
[9] Reclassification of federal hospitals to avoid overlap with tuberculosis report; drop in Department of National Defence hospitals from 40 down to 8.
[10] Includes 23 incurables in public hospitals.
[11] Includes only Indian health services hospitals of Department of National Health and Welfare.
[12] Expansion of federal government hospitals for Department of National Defence from 9 to 67 hospitals.
[13] Tuberculosis is a separate report.
[14] Forty-three new private hospitals opened while 19 closed.

Series B141-188. Rated bed capacity in reporting hospitals, Canada, 1932 to 1975

Year	Public											
	All hospitals		Total general and allied special		General, including paediatric		Allied special		Mental		Tuberculosis	
	Reporting	Rated bed capacity	Reporting	Rated bed capacity	Reporting	Rated bed capacity	Reporting	Rated bed capacity	Reporting	Rated bed capacity	Reporting	Rated bed capacity
	141	142	143	144	145	146	147	148	149	150	151	152
1975	1,154	197,601	1,041	151,761	864	128,509	177	23,252	107	45,489	6	351
1974	1,148	194,827	1,040	147,113	866	126,419	174	20,694	102	47,278	6	436
1973	1,162	194,652	1,047	142,011	866	120,988	181	21,023	104	51,644	11	997
1972	1,168	195,140	1,049	140,704	869	120,356	180	20,348	106	53,018	13	1,418
1971	1,174	197,224	1,043	138,280	867	118,470	176	19,810	108	56,084	23	2,860
1970	1,170	198,405	1,038	135,867	865	115,961	173	19,151	105	59,237	27	3,301
1969	1,176	197,244	1,038	132,293	869	114,022	169	18,271	106	61,232	32	3,719
1968	1,179	197,319	1,043	129,856	881	111,886	162	17,970	102	63,355	34	4,108
1967	1,169	194,189	1,035	126,082	873	108,403	162	17,679	97	63,652	37	4,455
1966	1,162	191,681	1,027	122,315	869	105,501	158	16,814	97	64,535	38	4,831
1965	1,147	187,780	1,009	116,981	850	110,562	159	16,419	96	65,249	42	5,550
1964	1,126	184,896	996	114,545	845	98,825	151	15,720	88	64,368	42	5,983
1963	1,090	179,633	975	111,105	838	95,029	137	16,076	76	60,497	39	8,031
1962	1,071	175,880	956	101,558	830	88,320	126	13,238	72	67,446	43	9,254
1961	1,068	177,269	946	100,506	856	88,625	90	11,881	72	66,606	50	10,157
1960	1,044	168,863	925	96,594	844	85,427	81	11,167	67	61,662	52	10,607
1959	1,059	167,719	940	97,610	846	83,916	94	13,694	69	59,022	50	11,087
1958	1,044	162,334	922	93,271	833	80,123	89	13,148	71	57,032	51	12,031
1957	1,020	155,728	894	88,158	820	77,372	74	10,786	72	54,367	54	13,203
1956	998	154,593	872	86,018	796	75,384	76	10,634	71	54,994	55	13,581
1955	983	150,392	858	82,330	781	71,699	77	10,631	70	54,327	55	13,735
1954	946	141,406	817	75,478	762	66,081	55	9,397	73	51,986	56	13,942
1953[2]	939	134,663	810	70,223	751	62,102	59	8,121	69	49,290	60	15,150
1952	899	128,103	777	68,033	721	59,816	56	8,217	66	46,417	56	13,653
1951	879	126,775	778	68,674	707	58,732	71	9,942	44	44,205	57	13,896
1950	834	118,404	741	61,415	692	56,172	49[3]	5,243[3]	39	43,250	54	13,739
1949	809	112,906	719	57,885	617	52,310	102	5,575	38	42,395	52	12,626
1948	774	110,611	678	55,899	588	50,909	90	4,990	55	44,277	41	10,435
1947	752	108,726	653	54,075	567	49,139	86	4,936	55	43,789	44	10,862
1946	695	107,385	595	53,068	514	47,561	81	5,507	56	44,176	44	10,141
1945	681	105,060	587	51,670	507	46,169	80	5,501	54	43,678	40	9,712
1944	680	102,443	586	51,593	509	46,452	77	5,141	54	41,044	40	9,806
1943	687	101,046	594	50,544	512	44,749	82	5,795	54	40,912	39	9,590
1942	684	98,883	594	49,559	511	43,620	83	5,939	54	40,571	36	8,753
1941	685	97,525	592	50,070	507	44,130	85	5,940	54	38,800	39	8,655
1940	680	96,199	587	49,238	500	43,305	87	5,933	54	38,421	39	8,540
1939	680	95,423	588	48,414	497	42,318	91	6,096	53	38,276	39	8,733
1938	700	95,297	610	50,074	496	40,998	114	9,076	51	37,527	39	7,696
1937	–	–	584	48,345	480	39,711	104	8,634	51	36,654	–	–
1936	661	91,366	573	47,657	474	39,847	99	7,810	51	36,237	37	7,472
1935	658	79,122	572	46,879	470	38,927	102	7,952	50	24,839	36	7,404
1934	651	86,938	568	45,936	463	38,069	105	7,867	49	33,759	34	7,243
1933	656	84,512	571	45,027	466	37,608	105	7,419	51	32,255	34	7,230
1932	633	77,808	547	38,685	462	35,054	85	3,631	52	31,973	34	7,150

Series B141-188. Rated bed capacity in reporting hospitals, Canada, 1932 to 1975 (continued)

Year	Private											
	All hospitals		Total general and allied special		General		Allied special		Mental		Tuberculosis	
	Reporting	Rated bed capacity	Reporting	Rated bed capacity	Reporting	Rated bed capacity	Reporting	Rated bed capacity	Reporting	Rated bed capacity	Reporting	Rated bed capacity
	153	154	155	156	157	158	159	160	161	162	163	164
1975	100	4,814	89	3,882	9	346	80	3,536	11	932	—	—
1974	107	4,833	95	3,831	10	361	85	3,470	12	1,002	—	—
1973	113	5,052	101	4,054	11	437	90	3,617	12	998	—	—
1972	120	5,802	108	4,833	12	446	96	4,387	12	969	—	—
1971	132	5,907	120	4,973	21	658	99	4,315	12	934	—	—
1970	144	6,125	132	5,189	31	953	101	4,196	12	936	—	—
1969	151	6,065	139	5,094	37	1,044	102	4,050	12	971	—	—
1968	159	6,226	148	5,356	41	1,420	107	3,936	11	870	—	—
1967	169	6,410	161	5,634	49	1,651	112	3,983	8	776	—	—
1966	177	6,391	168	5,688	50	1,718	118	3,970	9	703	—	—
1965	195	6,657	185	5,953	60	1,918	125	4,035	9	679	1	25
1964	205	6,295	196	5,661	64	2,027	132	3,634	9	634	—	—
1963	204	6,199	196	5,607	68	2,084	128	3,523	8	592	—	—
1962	197	5,515	190	5,050	57	1,585	133[1]	3,465[1]	7	465	—	—
1961	159	4,397	152	3,932	59	1,515	93	2,417	7	465	—	—
1960	158	4,067	152	3,652	62	1,488	90	2,164	6	415	—	—
1959	237	5,823	232	5,417	68	1,636	164	3,781	5	406	—	—
1958	210	5,114	205	4,721	55	1,211	150	3,510	5	393	—	—
1957	237	5,364	232	4,883	63	1,470	169	3,413	5	481	—	—
1956	209	4,581	204	4,138	65	1,335	139	2,803	4	428	1	15
1955	180	3,977	175	3,525	55	1,067	120	2,458	4	431	1	21
1954	172	3,781	169	3,465	62	1,180	107	2,285	2	295	1	21
1953[2]	148	3,341	143	2,891	52	836	91	2,055	4	435	1	15
1952	194	3,922	187	3,351	61	1,112	126	2,239	6	559	1	12
1951	225	4,429	220	3,997	—	—	—	—	4	420	1	12
1950	229	4,398	225	3,955	—	—	—	—	3	431	1	12
1949	198	3,568	194	3,225	—	—	—	—	3	331	1	12
1948	212	3,645	209	3,350	—	—	—	—	2	280	1	15
1947	215	3,537	212	3,259	—	—	—	—	2	266	1	12
1946	238	3,608	235	3,356	—	—	—	—	2	240	1	12
1945	238	3,678	234	3,380	—	—	—	—	3	286	1	12
1944	271	4,977	267	4,579	—	—	—	—	3	386	1	12
1943	267	4,636	263	4,251	—	—	—	—	3	373	1	12
1942	291	4,000	287	3,761	—	—	—	—	3	223	1	16
1941	327	4,503	322	3,957	—	—	—	—	4	530	1	16
1940	297	3,738	292	3,480	—	—	—	—	4	242	1	16
1939	281	3,493	276	3,234	—	—	—	—	4	243	1	16
1938	272	3,017	267	2,704	—	—	—	—	4	297	1	16
1937	—	—	241	2,811	—	—	—	—	4	297	—	—
1936	—	—	259	2,860	—	—	—	—	4	295	—	—
1935	—	—	267	2,818	—	—	—	—	4	295	—	—
1934	—	—	261	2,919	—	—	—	—	6	306	—	—
1933	—	—	230	2,740	—	—	—	—	6	344	—	—
1932	214	2,267	208	1,895	—	—	—	—	4	306	2	66

Series B141-188. Rated bed capacity in reporting hospitals, Canada, 1932 to 1975 (continued)

Year	Federal											
	All hospitals		Total general and allied special		General		Allied special		Mental		Tuberculosis	
	Reporting	Rated bed capacity	Reporting	Rated bed capacity	Reporting	Rated bed capacity	Reporting	Rated bed capacity	Reporting	Rated bed capacity	Reporting	Rated bed capacity
	165	166	167	168	169	170	171	172	173	174	175	176
1975	94	5,930	94	5,930	24	4,476	70	1,454	–	–	–	–
1974	90	5,946	90	5,946	24	4,576	66	1,370	–	–	–	–
1973	94	7,406	94	7,406	25	6,012	69	1,394	–	–	–	–
1972	91	7,422	91	7,422	25	6,053	66	1,369	–	–	–	–
1971	90	7,843	90	7,843	26	6,461	64	1,382	–	–	–	–
1970	82	7,754	82	7,754	25	6,388	57	1,308	–	–	–	–
1969	71	8,037	71	8,037	25	6,773	46	1,264	–	–	–	–
1968	71	8,323	70	8,173	24	6,868	46	1,305	–	–	1	150
1967	74	8,804	73	8,654	28	7,374	45	1,280	–	–	1	150
1966	73	9,125	71	8,788	27	7,348	44	1,440	–	–	2	337
1965	86	11,333	84	10,996	41	9,554	43	1,442	–	–	2	337
1964	78	11,455	76	11,113	32	9,665	44	1,448	–	–	2	342
1963	74	11,816	72	11,181	35	9,693	37	1,488	–	–	2	635
1962	70	11,621	66	10,659	36	9,332	30	1,327	–	–	4	962
1961	74	11,273	69	10,091	66	8,702	3	1,389	–	–	5	1,182
1960	79	13,309	71	10,583	69	10,404	2	179	2	1,371	6	1,355
1959	54	11,986	47	9,709	44	9,523	3	186	2	1,354	5	923
1958	49	13,820	42	11,458	33	10,886	9	572	2	1,375	5	987
1957	50	14,130	42	11,586	33	11,072	9	514	2	1,471	6	1,073
1956	52	15,200	44	11,793	35	11,137	9	656	2	2,325	6	1,082
1955	53	13,485	46	12,211	37	11,390	9	821	–	–	7	1,274
1954	53	14,686	44	12,004	37	11,696	7	308	2	1,471	7	1,211
1953[2]	56	14,236	46	11,549	40	11,241	6	308	2	1,471	8	1,216
1952	52	14,007	42	11,326	40	11,092	2	234	2	1,471	8	1,210
1951	88	14,746	78	11,992	67	10,919	11	1,073	2	1,471	8	1,283
1950	77	14,414	67	11,826	54	10,365	13	1,461	2	1,398	8	1,190
1949	85	14,436	76	12,071	57	10,089	19	1,982	2	1,329	7	1,036
1948	74	13,484	66	11,410	44	9,448	22	1,962	2	1,125	6	949
1947	74	13,250	66	11,237	45	9,319	21	1,918	2	1,125	6	888
1946	73	13,533	66	11,748	43	9,454	23	2,294	2	1,207	5	578
1945	21[4]	2,016[4]	15[4]	485[4]	–[4]	–[4]	–[4]	–[4]	2	1,160	4	371
1944	17[4]	1,603[4]	13[4]	235[4]	10[4]	196[4]	3[4]	39[4]	2	1,070	2	298
1943	17[4]	1,468[4]	13[4]	167[4]	7[4]	101[4]	6[4]	66[4]	2	989	2	312
1942	16[4]	1,432[4]	13[4]	139[4]	7[4]	97[4]	6[4]	42[4]	2	968	1	325
1941	21[4]	1,513[4]	18[4]	492[4]	–	–	–	–	2	785	1	236
1940	194	10,337	191	9,554	–	–	–	–	2	751	1	32
1939	84	3,881	–	–	–	–	–	–	2	747	–	–
1938	32	3,398	30	2,575	–	–	–	–	2	823	–	–
1937	32	3,418	30	2,571	–	–	–	–	2	847	–	–
1936	32	3,393	30	2,551	–	–	–	–	2	842	–	–
1935	33	3,418	31	2,565	–	–	–	–	2	853	–	–
1934	32	2,222	30	1,369	–	–	–	–	2	853	–	–
1933	32	2,538	30	1,563	–	–	–	–	2	975	–	–
1932	35	3,427	33	2,477	–	–	–	–	2	950	–	–

Series B141-188. Rated bed capacity in reporting hospitals, Canada, 1932 to 1975 (concluded)

Year	Total											
	All hospitals		Total general and allied special		General, including paediatric		Allied special		Mental		Tuberculosis	
	Reporting	Rated bed capacity	Reporting	Rated bed capacity	Reporting	Rated bed capacity	Reporting	Rated bed capacity	Reporting	Rated bed capacity	Reporting	Rated bed capacity
	177	178	179	180	181	182	183	184	185	186	187	188
1975	1,348	208,345	1,224	161,573	897	133,331	327	28,242	118	46,421	6	351
1974	1,345	205,606	1,225	156,890	900	131,356	325	25,534	114	48,280	6	436
1973	1,369	207,110	1,242	153,471	902	127,437	340	26,034	116	52,642	11	997
1972	1,379	208,364	1,248	152,959	906	126,855	342	26,104	118	53,987	13	1,418
1971	1,396	210,974	1,253	151,096	914	125,589	339	25,507	120	57,018	23	2,860
1970	1,396	212,284	1,252	148,810	921	123,302	331	24,655	117	60,173	27	3,301
1969	1,398	211,346	1,248	145,424	931	121,839	317	23,585	118	62,203	32	3,719
1968	1,409	211,868	1,261	143,385	946	120,174	315	23,211	113	64,225	35	4,258
1967	1,412	209,403	1,269	140,370	950	117,428	319	22,942	105	64,428	38	4,605
1966	1,412	207,197	1,266	136,791	946	114,567	320	22,224	106	65,238	40	5,168
1965	1,428	205,770	1,278	133,930	951	112,034	327	21,896	105	65,928	45	5,912
1964	1,409	202,646	1,268	131,319	941	110,517	327	20,802	97	65,002	44	6,325
1963	1,368	197,648	1,243	127,893	941	106,806	302	21,087	84	61,089	41	8,666
1962	1,338	193,016	1,212	121,131	923	102,916	289	18,215	79	61,669	47	10,216
1961	1,301	192,939	1,167	114,529	981	98,842	186	15,687	79	67,071	55	11,339
1960	1,281	186,239	1,148	110,829	975	97,319	173	13,510	75	63,448	58	11,962
1959	1,350	185,528	1,219	112,736	958	95,075	261	17,661	76	60,782	55	12,010
1958	1,303	181,268	1,169	109,450	921	92,220	248	17,230	78	58,800	56	13,018
1957	1,307	175,222	1,168	104,627	916	89,914	252	14,713	79	56,319	60	14,276
1956	1,259	174,374	1,120	101,949	896	87,856	224	14,093	77	57,747	62	14,678
1955	1,216	167,786	1,079	98,066	873	84,156	206	13,910	74	54,758	63	14,962
1954	1,173	159,873	1,032	90,947	863	78,957	169	11,990	77	53,752	64	15,174
1953[2]	1,143	152,240	999	84,663	842	74,179	157	10,484	75	31,196	69	16,381
1952	1,145	146,032	1,006	82,710	822	72,020	184	10,690	72	48,447	67	14,875
1951	1,192	145,950	1,076	84,663	–	–	–	–	50	46,096	66	15,191
1950	1,140	137,216	1,033	77,196	–	–	–	–	44	45,079	63	14,941
1949	1,092	130,910	989	73,181	–	–	–	–	43	44,055	60	13,674
1948	1,060	127,740	953	70,659	–	–	–	–	59	45,682	48	11,399
1947	1,041	125,513	931	68,571	–	–	–	–	59	45,180	51	11,762
1946	1,006	124,526	896	68,172	–	–	–	–	60	45,623	50	10,731
1945	940	110,754	836	55,535	–	–	–	–	59	45,124	45	10,095
1944	968	109,023	866	56,407	–	–	–	–	59	42,500	43	10,116
1943	971	107,150	870	54,962	–	–	–	–	59	42,274	42	9,914
1942	991	104,315	894	53,459	–	–	–	–	59	41,762	38	9,094
1941	1,033	103,541	932	54,519	–	–	–	–	60	40,115	41	8,907
1940	1,171	110,274	1,070	62,272	–	–	–	–	60	39,414	41	8,588
1939	1,045	102,797	–	–	–	–	–	–	59	39,266	–	–
1938	1,004	101,712	907	55,353	–	–	–	–	57	38,647	40	7,712
1937	–	–	855	53,727	–	–	–	–	57	37,798	–	–
1936	–	–	862	53,068	–	–	–	–	57	37,374	–	–
1935	–	–	870	52,262	–	–	–	–	56	25,987	–	–
1934	–	–	859	50,224	–	–	–	–	57	34,918	–	–
1933	–	–	831	49,330	–	–	–	–	59	33,574	–	–
1932	882	83,502	788	43,057	–	–	–	–	58	33,229	36	7,216

[1] Includes 45 nursing homes temporarily approved by the Ontario Hospital Services Commision.
[2] Introduction of Newfoundland in national statistics.

[3] Red Cross hospitals previously under allied special are now under general.
[4] Includes only Indian health services.

Series B189-236. Patient-days (adult and children) in reporting hospitals, Canada, 1932 to 1975

Year	Public											
	All hospitals		Total general and allied special		General, including paediatric		Allied special		Mental		Tuberculosis	
	Reporting	Patient-days	Reporting	Patient-days	Reporting	Patient-days	Reporting	Patient-days	Reporting	Patient-days	Reporting	Patient-days
	189	190	191	192	193	194	195	196	197	198	199	200
1975	1,152	57,714,669	1,039	42,844,899	864	35,270,191	175	7,574,708	107	14,761,013	6	108,757
1974	1,145	57,419,029	1,037	41,758,504	865	34,980,581	172	6,777,923	102	15,547,115	6	113,410
1973	1,160	58,113,361	1,045	40,757,455	866	33,955,357	179	6,802,098	104	17,118,841	11	237,065
1972	1,168	58,749,541	1,049	40,521,589	869	33,896,615	180	6,624,974	106	17,928,613	13	299,339
1971	1,174	60,699,274	1,041	40,907,324	866	34,419,661	175	6,487,663	108	19,253,011	23	538,939
1970	1,169	60,833,453	1,037	40,040,656	864	33,722,833	173	6,317,823	105	20,112,599	27	680,198
1969	1,176	60,991,492	1,038	38,952,938	869	32,970,953	169	5,981,985	106	21,164,148	32	874,406
1968	1,177	60,853,147	1,041	38,312,318	879	32,402,654	162	5,909,664	102	21,533,497	34	1,007,332
1967	1,169	60,433,503	1,035	36,789,118	873	31,059,926	162	5,729,192	97	22,494,813	37	1,149,572
1966	1,162	60,651,671	1,027	35,905,717	869	30,576,544	158	5,329,173	96	23,535,843	38	1,210,111
1965	1,146	60,820,573	1,009	34,925,891	850	29,812,073	159	5,113,818	95	24,489,579	42	1,405,103
1964	1,126	60,643,663	996	33,995,691	845	29,241,414	151	4,754,277	88	25,059,761	42	1,588,211
1963	1,090	59,081,702	975	33,175,509	838	28,228,633	137	4,946,876	76	23,942,344	39	1,963,849
1962	1,071	57,588,508	956	31,595,855	830	27,344,396	126	4,251,459	72	23,626,910	43	2,365,743
1961	1,048	57,165,360	926	29,900,834	841	26,160,051	85	3,740,783	72	24,646,914	50	2,617,612
1960	1,044	56,158,350	925	28,980,106	844	25,257,143	81	3,722,963	67	24,199,750	52	2,978,494
1959	1,055	55,589,740	936	28,668,039	842	24,333,060	94	4,334,979	69	23,789,871	50	3,131,830
1958	1,044	54,626,077	922	27,270,087	833	23,267,730	89	4,002,357	71	23,942,562	51	3,413,428
1957	1,020	53,075,144	894	25,794,298	820	22,441,322	74	3,352,976	72	23,393,648	54	3,887,198
1956	998	52,365,312	872	24,855,330	796	21,712,949	76	3,142,381	71	23,269,402	55	4,240,580
1955	983	50,878,276	858	23,655,377	781	20,429,995	77	3,225,382	70	22,824,487	55	4,398,412
1954	–	–	817	21,978,256	762	19,033,664	55	2,944,592	–	–	55	4,765,751
1953[2]	–	–	810	20,813,371	–	18,322,787	–	2,490,584	–	–	56	5,160,391
1952	–	–	–	20,186,443	–	17,568,587	–	2,617,851	–	–	56	4,808,365
1951	–	–	–	19,798,448	–	16,979,902	–	2,818,546	–	–	57	4,640,217
1950	–	–	–	17,373,569	–	16,071,732	–	1,311,837	–	–	52	4,670,008
1949	–	–	–	16,477,607	–	15,287,681	–	1,189,926	–	–	–	–
1948	–	–	–	15,821,293	–	14,566,514	–	1,254,779	–	–	–	–
1947	–	–	–	15,160,110	–	14,105,789	–	1,054,321	–	–	–	–
1946	–	–	–	14,827,360	–	13,538,987	–	1,288,373	–	–	–	–
1945	–	–	–	13,963,042	–	12,831,712	–	1,131,330	–	–	–	–
1944	–	–	–	13,298,090	–	12,141,957	–	1,156,133	–	–	–	–
1943	–	–	–	12,803,262	–	11,504,971	–	1,298,291	–	–	–	–
1942	–	–	–	12,170,518	–	10,861,154	–	1,309,364	–	–	–	–
1941	–	–	–	11,869,005	–	10,690,776	–	1,178,229	–	–	–	–
1940	–	–	–	11,504,063	–	10,294,961	–	1,209,102	–	–	–	–
1939	–	–	–	10,539,552	–	9,561,688	–	977,864	–	–	–	–
1938	–	–	–	12,003,676	–	9,841,206	–	2,162,470	–	–	–	–
1937	–	–	–	11,772,578	–	9,769,999	–	2,002,579	–	–	–	–
1936	–	–	–	11,726,871	–	9,921,146	–	1,805,725	–	–	–	2,483,249
1935	–	–	–	11,320,303	–	9,389,166	–	1,931,137	–	–	–	2,472,029
1934	–	–	–	10,471,459	–	8,639,491	–	1,831,968	–	–	–	2,420,671
1933	–	–	–	9,790,240	–	8,155,883	–	1,634,357	–	–	–	2,378,388
1932	–	–	547	8,782,933	462	8,155,836	85	627,097	–	–	34	2,225,202

Series B189-236. Patient-days (adult and children) in reporting hospitals, Canada, 1932 to 1975 (continued)

Year	Private											
	All hospitals		Total general and allied special		General		Allied special		Mental		Tuberculosis	
	Reporting	Patient-days	Reporting	Patient-days	Reporting	Patient-days	Reporting	Patient-days	Reporting	Patient-days	Reporting	Patient-days
	201	202	203	204	205	206	207	208	209	210	211	212
1975	100	1,620,345	89	1,294,006	9	97,514	80	1,196,492	11	326,339	–	–
1974	107	1,626,752	95	1,275,330	10	104,706	85	1,170,624	12	351,422	–	–
1973	113	1,718,088	101	1,366,707	11	130,375	90	1,236,332	12	351,381	–	–
1972	120	1,995,263	108	1,654,821	12	135,903	96	1,518,918	12	340,442	–	–
1971	132	2,017,174	120	1,682,035	21	195,577	99	1,486,458	12	335,139	–	–
1970	144	2,019,447	132	1,682,711	31	277,639	101	1,405,072	12	336,736	–	–
1969	149	1,968,910	137	1,630,310	37	297,223	100	1,333,087	12	338,600	–	–
1968	159	2,084,553	148	1,801,019	41	436,411	107	1,364,608	11	283,534	–	–
1967	169	2,115,757	161	1,850,800	49	514,490	112	1,336,310	8	264,957	–	–
1966	177	2,125,315	168	1,863,928	50	526,196	118	1,337,732	9	261,387	–	–
1965	195	2,091,349	185	1,838,378	60	579,308	125	1,259,070	9	252,731	1	240
1964	205	2,058,944	196	1,812,849	64	595,392	132	1,217,457	9	246,095	–	–
1963	204	1,950,040	196	1,739,519	68	593,112	128	1,146,407	8	210,521	–	–
1962	197	1,686,009	190	1,529,280	57	444,949	133[1]	1,084,331[1]	7	156,729	–	–
1961	149	1,218,732	142	1,063,264	55	372,105	87	691,159	7	155,468	–	–
1960	158	1,142,692	152	998,192	62	365,304	90	632,888	6	144,500	–	–
1959	237	1,730,726	232	1,599,417	68	435,220	164	1,164,197	5	131,309	–	–
1958	210	1,565,515	205	1,443,585	55	305,254	150	1,138,331	5	121,930	–	–
1957	237	1,560,262	232	1,410,249	–	–	–	–	5	150,013	–	–
1956	208	1,375,292	204	1,229,214	–	–	–	–	4	146,078	–	–
1955	179	1,080,788	175	935,189	–	–	–	–	4	145,599	–	–
1954	–	–	169	922,813	–	–	–	–	–	–	–	–
1953	–	–	143	793,135	–	–	–	–	–	–	–	–
1952	–	–	187	908,247	–	–	–	–	–	–	–	–
1951	–	–	220	983,079	–	–	–	–	–	–	–	–
1950	–	–	225	930,117	–	–	–	–	–	–	–	–
1949	–	–	194	877,054	–	–	–	–	–	–	–	–
1948	–	–	209	827,230	–	–	–	–	–	–	–	–
1947	–	–	212	828,071	–	–	–	–	–	–	–	–
1946	–	–	235	762,931	–	–	–	–	–	–	–	–
1945	–	–	234	825,882	–	–	–	–	–	–	–	–
1944	–	–	267	800,417	–	–	–	–	–	–	–	–
1943	–	–	263	748,789	–	–	–	–	–	–	–	–
1942	–	–	287	713,166	–	–	–	–	–	–	–	–
1941	–	–	322	686,135	–	–	–	–	–	–	–	–
1940	–	–	292	610,386	–	–	–	–	–	–	–	–
1939	–	–	276	519,909	–	–	–	–	–	–	–	–
1938	–	–	–	369,377	–	–	–	–	–	–	–	–
1937	–	–	–	374,897	–	–	–	–	–	–	–	–
1936	–	–	–	363,960	–	–	–	–	–	–	–	–
1935	–	–	–	358,171	–	–	–	–	–	–	–	–
1934	–	–	–	323,115	–	–	–	–	–	–	–	–
1933	–	–	–	317,950	–	–	–	–	–	–	–	–
1932	–	–	207	512,443	128	214,678	79	297,765	–	–	2	11,629

Series B189-236. Patient-days (adult and children) in reporting hospitals, Canada, 1932 to 1975 (continued)

Year	Federal											
	All hospitals		Total general and allied special		General		Allied special		Mental		Tuberculosis	
	Reporting	Patient-days	Reporting	Patient-days	Reporting	Patient-days	Reporting	Patient-days	Reporting	Patient-days	Reporting	Patient-days
	213	214	215	216	217	218	219	220	221	222	223	224
1975	91	1,395,112	91	1,395,112	24	1,019,155	67	375,957	–	–	–	–
1974	90	1,415,746	90	1,415,746	24	1,055,444	66	360,302	–	–	–	–
1973	92	1,870,100	92	1,870,100	25	1,504,650	67	365,450	–	–	–	–
1972	91	1,941,716	91	1,941,716	25	1,575,984	66	365,732	–	–	–	–
1971	86	2,038,086	86	2,038,086	26	1,689,559	60	348,527	–	–	–	–
1970	79	2,102,469	79	2,102,469	25	1,746,326	54	356,143	–	–	–	–
1969	70	2,045,088	70	2,045,088	24	1,678,487	46	366,601	–	–	–	–
1968	71	2,245,651	70	2,211,680	24	1,842,410	46	369,270	–	–	1	33,971
1967	74	2,405,168	73	2,368,488	28	1,999,863	45	368,625	–	–	1	36,680
1966	73	2,500,090	71	2,419,658	27	2,001,436	44	418,222	–	–	2	80,432
1965	86	3,026,928	84	2,934,565	41	2,518,519	43	416,046	–	–	2	92,363
1964	78	3,076,666	76	2,986,588	32	2,565,428	44	421,160	–	–	2	90,078
1963	74	3,135,279	72	2,969,108	35	2,549,217	37	419,891	–	–	2	166,171
1962	70	3,157,489	66	2,876,724	36	2,487,147	30	389,577	–	–	4	280,765
1961	73	3,048,117	68	2,705,092	65	2,270,859	3	434,233	–	–	5	343,025
1960	78	3,623,490	71	2,826,555	69	2,772,428	2	54,127	2	420,262	6	376,673
1959	54	3,333,479	47	2,595,051	44	2,542,048	3	53,003	2	451,036	5	287,392
1958	49	3,949,189	42	3,191,128	33	3,093,621	9	97,507	2	460,263	5	297,798
1957	50	4,065,591	42	3,277,518	–	–	–	–	2	468,437	6	319,636
1956	52	4,225,856	44	3,416,810	–	–	–	–	2	469,730	6	339,316
1955	53	3,866,729	46	3,516,646	–	–	–	–	–	–	7	350,083
1954	53	3,979,441	–	–	–	–	–	–	–	–	7	399,077
1953	56	3,866,658	–	–	–	–	–	–	–	–	8	401,397
1952	52	3,258,982	–	–	–	–	–	–	–	–	8	407,328
1951	51[3]	3,715,232	–	–	–	–	–	–	–	–	8	384,664
1950	57[3]	3,587,201	–	–	–	–	–	–	–	–	8	395,237
1949	85	3,748,700	–	–	–	–	–	–	–	–	7	316,531
1948	74	3,372,047	–	–	–	–	–	–	–	–	6	214,022
1947	74	3,470,505	–	–	–	–	–	–	–	–	6	232,893
1946	–	–	–	–	–	–	–	–	–	–	5	124,068
1945	–	–	–	–	–	–	–	–	–	–	–	–
1944	–	–	–	–	–	–	–	–	–	–	–	–
1943	–	–	–	–	–	–	–	–	–	–	–	–
1942	–	–	–	–	–	–	–	–	–	–	–	–
1941	–	–	–	–	–	–	–	–	–	–	–	–
1940	–	–	–	–	–	–	–	–	–	–	–	–
1939	–	–	–	–	–	–	–	–	–	–	–	–
1938	–	–	–	–	–	–	–	–	–	–	–	–
1937	–	–	–	–	–	–	–	–	–	–	–	–
1936	–	–	–	–	–	–	–	–	–	–	–	–
1935	–	–	–	–	–	–	–	–	–	–	–	–
1934	–	–	–	–	–	–	–	–	–	–	–	–
1933	–	–	–	–	–	–	–	–	–	–	–	–
1932	–	–	35	731,394	–	–	–	–	–	–	–	–

Series B189-236. Patient-days (adult and children) in reporting hospitals, Canada, 1932 to 1975 (concluded)

Year	Total											
	All hospitals		Total general and allied special		General, including paediatric		Allied special		Mental		Tuberculosis	
	Reporting	Patient-days	Reporting	Patient-days	Reporting	Patient-days	Reporting	Patient-days	Reporting	Patient-days	Reporting	Patient-days
	225	226	227	228	229	230	231	232	233	234	235	236
1975	1,343	60,730,126	1,219	45,534,017	897	36,386,860	322	9,147,157	118	15,087,352	6	108,757
1974	1,342	60,461,527	1,222	44,449,580	899	36,140,731	323	8,308,849	114	15,898,537	6	113,410
1973	1,365	61,701,549	1,238	43,994,262	902	35,590,382	336	8,403,880	116	17,470,222	11	237,065
1972	1,379	62,686,520	1,248	44,118,126	906	35,608,502	342	8,509,624	118	18,269,055	13	299,339
1971	1,392	64,746,534	1,247	44,619,445	913	36,296,797	334	8,322,648	120	19,588,150	23	538,939
1970	1,392	64,955,369	1,248	43,825,836	920	35,746,798	328	8,079,038	117	20,449,335	27	680,198
1969	1,395	65,005,490	1,245	42,628,336	930	34,946,663	315	7,681,673	118	21,502,748	32	874,406
1968	1,407	65,183,351	1,259	42,325,017	944	34,681,475	315	7,643,542	113	21,817,031	35	1,041,303
1967	1,412	64,954,428	1,269	41,008,406	950	33,574,279	319	7,434,127	105	22,759,770	38	1,186,252
1966	1,412	65,277,076	1,266	40,189,303	946	33,104,176	320	7,085,127	105	23,797,230	40	1,290,543
1965	1,427	65,938,850	1,278	39,698,834	951	32,909,900	327	6,788,934	104	24,742,310	45	1,497,706
1964	1,409	65,779,273	1,268	38,795,128	941	32,402,234	327	6,392,894	97	25,305,856	44	1,678,289
1963	1,368	64,167,021	1,243	37,884,136	941	31,370,962	302	6,513,174	84	24,152,865	41	2,130,020
1962	1,338	62,432,006	1,212	36,001,859	923	30,290,778	289	5,361,844	79	23,783,639	47	2,646,508
1961	1,270	61,432,209	1,136	33,669,190	961	28,803,015	175	4,866,175	79	24,802,382	55	2,960,637
1960	1,280	60,924,532	1,148	32,804,853	975	28,394,875	173	4,409,978	75	24,764,512	57	3,355,167
1959	1,346	60,653,945	1,215	32,862,507	954	27,320,502	261	5,542,005	76	24,372,216	55	3,419,222
1958	1,303	60,140,781	1,169	31,904,800	921	26,666,605	248	5,238,195	78	24,524,755	56	3,711,226
1957	1,307	58,232,560	1,168	30,013,628	—	—	—	—	79	24,012,098	—	4,206,834
1956	1,258	51,496,730	1,120	29,031,624	—	—	—	—	77	23,885,210	—	4,579,896
1955	1,208	55,825,793	1,071	28,107,212	—	—	—	—	74	23,644,000	—	—
1954	—	—	1,021	26,481,433	—	—	—	—	—	23,006,000	—	—
1953	—	—	—	—	—	—	—	—	—	22,081,000	—	—
1952	—	—	—	—	—	—	—	—	—	21,060,000	—	—
1951	—	—	—	—	—	—	—	—	—	20,299,000	—	—
1950	—	—	—	—	—	—	—	—	—	19,797,000	—	—
1949	—	—	—	—	—	—	—	—	—	19,292,000	—	—
1948	—	—	—	—	—	—	—	—	—	18,706,000	—	—
1947	—	—	—	—	—	—	—	—	—	18,286,000	—	—
1946	—	—	—	—	—	—	—	—	—	18,025,000	—	—
1945	—	—	—	—	—	—	—	—	—	17,642,000	—	—
1944	—	—	—	—	—	—	—	—	—	17,384,000	—	—
1943	—	—	—	—	—	—	—	—	—	17,044,000	—	—
1942	—	—	—	—	—	—	—	—	—	16,865,000	—	—
1941	—	—	—	—	—	—	—	—	—	16,525,000	—	—
1940	—	—	—	—	—	—	—	—	—	16,104,000	—	—
1939	—	—	—	—	—	—	—	—	—	15,786,000	—	—
1938	—	—	—	—	—	—	—	—	—	15,758,000	—	—
1937	—	—	—	—	—	—	—	—	—	15,036,000	—	—
1936	—	—	—	—	—	—	—	—	—	14,362,000	—	—
1935	—	—	—	—	—	—	—	—	—	13,889,000	—	—
1934	—	—	—	—	—	—	—	—	—	13,250,000	—	—
1933	—	—	—	—	—	—	—	—	—	—	—	—
1932	—	—	—	10,026,770	—	—	—	—	—	—	—	—

[1] Includes 45 nursing homes temporarily approved as hospitals by the Ontario Hospital Services Commision.
[2] Introduction of Newfoundland into national statistics.

[3] Excludes Department of National Defence hospitals as they did not report patient-days.

Series B237-260. Number of separations (adult and children) in reporting hospitals, Canada, 1932 to 1975

Year	Public						Private					
	All hospitals	Total general and allied special	General, including paediatric	Allied special	Mental	Tuber-culosis	All hospitals	Total general and allied special	General	Allied special	Mental	Tuber-culosis
	237	238	239	240	241	242	243	244	245	246	247	248
1975	3,760,800	3,701,473	3,616,839	84,634	58,009	1,318	27,249	24,962	12,383	12,579	2,287	—
1974	3,762,657	3,703,264	3,619,381	83,883	58,169	1,224	29,628	255,524	12,874	12,650	4,104	—
1973	3,719,819	3,652,620	3,564,442	93,178	59,840[1]	2,359[1]	31,327	27,565	15,385	12,180	3,762[1]	—
1972	3,653,966	3,596,310	3,499,243	97,067	54,486[1]	3,170[1]	32,564	28,793	15,001	13,792	3,771[1]	—
1971	3,615,851	3,556,442	3,461,739	94,703	54,019[1]	5,390[1]	38,701	34,674	20,578	14,096	4,027[1]	—
1970	3,493,713	3,427,442	3,335,048	92,394	59,927[1]	6,344[1]	42,818	39,303	25,396	13,907	3,515[1]	—
1969	3,350,586	3,284,851	3,198,308	86,543	57,981[1]	7,754[1]	44,653	41,136	27,853	16,283	3,517[1]	—
1968	3,274,596	3,206,417	3,124,259	82,158	60,279[1]	7,900[1]	64,044	60,631	44,223	16,408	3,413[1]	—
1967	3,150,108	3,084,105	2,997,482	86,623	57,076[1]	8,927[1]	72,015	68,694	52,147	16,547	3,321[1]	—
1966	3,105,767	3,041,970	2,967,992	73,978	54,645[1]	9,152[1]	77,573	72,743	54,789	17,954	4,830[1]	—
1965	3.051,747	2,988,795	2,904,327	84,468	52,713[1]	10,239	87,651	83,161	66,667	16,494	4,490	—
1964	3,000,754	2,944,922	2,865,800	79,122	45,178	10,654	89,982	86,257	69,500	16,757	3,725	—
1963	2,908,089	2,856,519	2,768,623	87,896	40,307	11,261	92,558	88,632	72,310	16,322	3,926	—
1962	2,799,746	2,748,154	2,670,239	77,915	39,046	12,546	77,263	73,473	54,295	19,178	3,790	—
1961	2,706,936	2,657,984	2,598,283	59,701	34,883	14,069	66,021	62,766	49,127	13,639[2]	3,255	—
1960	2,621,708	2,580,625	2,526,379	54,246	27,506	13,577	72,990	70,059	51,256	18,803	2,931	—
1959	2,528,282	2,488,900	2,436,572	52,328	25,605	13,777	76,661	73,907	53,078	20,829	2,754	—
1958	2,442,470	2,399,524	2,363,529	35,995	26,172	16,774	—	62,097	—	—	2,609	—
1957	—	2,316,558	2,282,564	33,994	—	18,937	—	60,092	—	—	—	—
1956	—	2,217,559	2,182,307	35,252	—	17,499	—	59,521	—	—	—	—
1955	—	2,083,345	2,042,774	40,571	—	17,152	—	63,413	—	—	—	—
1954	—	1,913,995	1,880,864	33,131	—	—	—	43,361	—	—	—	—
1953[5]	—	1,846,841	1,810,069	36,772	—	—	—	38,052	—	—	—	—
1952	—	1,758,978	1,722,451	36,527	—	—	—	45,060	—	—	—	—
1951	—	1,677,895	1,624,715	53,180	—	—	—	51,100	—	—	—	—
1950	—	1,583,813	1,535,292	48,521	—	—	—	54,267	—	—	—	—
1949	—	1,523,712	1,461,711	62,001	—	—	—	60,852	—	—	—	—
1948	—	1,423,958	1,371,625	52,333	—	—	—	47,038	—	—	—	—
1947	—	1,347,225	1,297,813	49,412	—	—	—	46,691	—	—	—	—
1946	—	1,254,655	1,202,143	52,512	—	—	—	44,029	—	—	—	—
1945	—	1,139,916	1,094,669	45,247	—	—	—	38,379	—	—	—	—
1944	—	1,069,688	1,021,339	48,349	—	—	—	40,080	—	—	—	—
1943	—	1,005,822	954,351	51,471	—	—	—	39,630	—	—	—	—
1942	—	937,702	885,738	51,964	—	—	—	37,196	—	—	—	—
1941	—	890,187	841,274	48,913	—	—	—	36,494	—	—	—	—
1940	—	839,713	795,093	44,620	—	—	—	33,702	—	—	—	—
1939	—	760,542	719,685	40,857	—	—	—	29,103	—	—	—	—
1938	—	765,962	723,156	42,806	—	—	—	25,609	—	—	—	—
1937	—	740,574	699,657	40,917	—	—	—	29,844	—	—	—	—
1936	—	698,995	659,568	39,427	—	14,007	—	29,428	—	—	—	—
1935	—	645,023	609,501	35,522	—	13,133	—	24,617	—	—	—	—
1934	—	592,045	557,324	34,721	—	13,006	—	20,494	—	—	—	—
1933	—	550,559	521,421	29,138	—	11,171	—	19,949	—	—	—	—
1932	—	—	—	—	—	11,942[3]	—	21,154[3]	18,103[3]	3,051[3]	—	66[3]

Series B237-260. Number of separations (adult and children) in reporting hospitals, Canada, 1932 to 1975 (concluded)

Year	Federal						Total					
	All hospitals	Total general and allied special	General	Allied special	Mental	Tuber-culosis	All hospitals	Total general and allied special	General, including paediatric	Allied special	Mental	Tuber-culosis
	249	250	251	252	253	254	255	256	257	258	259	260
1975	51,765	51,765	47,130	4,635	–	–	3,839,814	3,778,200	3,676,352	101,848	60,296	1,318
1974	49,813	49,813	46,184	3,629	–	–	3,842,098	3,778,601	3,678,439	100,162	62,273	1,224
1973	58,090	58,090	54,511	3,579	–	–	3,817,654	3,743,275	3,634,338	108,937	72,020	2,359
1972	60,838	60,838	57,045	3,793	–	–	3,747,368	3,685,941	3,571,289	114,652	58,257	3,170
1971	64,759	64,759	60,985	3,774	–	–	3,776,522	3,655,875	3,543,302	112,573	58,046	5,390
1970	63,410	63,410	59,990	3,420	–	–	3,599,941	3,530,155	3,420,434	109,721	63,442	6,344
1969	63,588	63,588	61,086	2,502	–	–	3,458,827	3,389,575	3,287,247	105,328	61,498	7,754
1968	60,480	60,480	57,590	2,890	–	–	3,399,120	3,327,528	3,226,072	101,456	63,692	7,900
1967	69,151	67,744	65,082	2,662	–	1,407[1]	3,291,274	3,220,543	3,114,711	105,832	60,397	10,334
1966	71,453	70,849	67,820	3,029	–	1,604[1]	3,254,793	3,185,562	3,090,601	94,961	59,475	9,756
1965	89,409	87,493	84,643	2,850	–	1,916[1]	3,228,807	3,159,449	3,055,637	103,812	57,203	12,155
1964	85,831	85,527	82,559	2,968	–	304	3,176,567	3,116,706	3,017,859	98,847	48,903	10,958
1963	87,206	86,764	83,496	3,268	–	442	3,087,853	3,031,915	2,924,429	107,486	44,235	11,703
1962	86,970	86,238	–	–	–	732	2,963,979	2,907,865	–	–	42,836	13,278
1961	76,514	75,488	–	–	–	1,026	2,831,442	2,778,209	–	–	38,138	15,095
1960	81,597	81,833	81,524	309	–	764	2,776,295	2,732,517	2,659,159	73,358	30,437	14,341
1959	79,631	78,712	78,354	358	274	645	2,684,574	2,641,519	2,568,004	73,515	28,633	14,442
1958	–	76,488	–	–	–	1,050	2,584,714	2,538,109	–	–	28,781	17,824
1957	–	77,927	–	–	–	1,102	2,513,681	2,454,577	–	–	39,065	20,039
1956	–	82,829	–	–	–	1,046	2,415,111	2,359,909	–	–	36,657	18,545
1955	–	85,208	–	–	–	1,145	2,282,006	2,231,866	–	–	31,853	18,297
1954	–	83,475	–	–	–	–	2,091,167	2,040,831	–	–	28,803	21,533[3,4]
1953[5]	–	79,835	–	–	–	–	2,004,055	1,964,728	–	–	21,213	18,114
1952	–	71,458	–	–	–	–	1,914,354	1,875,496	–	–	21,284	17,574[3,4]
1951	–	57,931	–	–	–	–	1,820,334	1,786,926	–	–	17,804	15,604[3,4]
1950	–	56,428	–	–	–	–	1,726,642	1,694,508	–	–	16,472	15,622[3,4]
1949	–	73,997	–	–	–	–	1,689,989	1,658,561	–	–	15,611	15,817[3,4]
1948	–	61,895	–	–	–	–	1,563,135	1,532,891	–	–	14,156	16,088[3,4]
1947	–	61,908	–	–	–	–	1,483,207	1,455,824	–	–	12,966	14,417[3,4]
1946	–	–	–	–	–	–	–	–	–	–	13,715	14,23[3,4]
1945	–	–	–	–	–	–	–	–	–	–	12,995	12,897[3,4]
1944	–	–	–	–	–	–	–	–	–	–	12,221	11,868[3,4]
1943	–	–	–	–	–	–	–	–	–	–	10,937	12,353[3,4]
1942	–	–	–	–	–	–	–	–	–	–	10,771	12,054[3,4]
1941	–	–	–	–	–	–	–	–	–	–	9,958	11,877[3,4]
1940	–	30,087[6]	–	–	–	–	–	903,500[6]	–	–	10,262	11,230[3,4]
1939	–	17,729[6]	–	–	–	–	–	807,374[6]	–	–	13,416	10,155[3,4]
1938	–	14,760[6]	–	–	–	–	–	806,331[6]	–	–	10,369	9,423[3,4]
1937	–	12,826[6]	–	–	–	–	–	783,244[6]	–	–	10,124	8,268[3,4]
1936	–	–	–	–	–	–	–	–	–	–	10,246	–
1935	–	–	–	–	–	–	–	–	–	–	9,518	–
1934	–	–	–	–	–	–	–	–	–	–	8,630	–
1933	–	13,801[6]	–	–	–	–	–	584,309[6]	–	–	8,081	–
1932	–	14,214[6]	–	–	–	–	–	–	–	–	7,870	–

[1] Figures are for operating hospitals and institutions, and include estimates.
[2] Certain maternity hospitals included in 1960 data were deleted in 1961, contributing to the drop in separations.
[3] Includes newborn separations.
[4] Includes tuberculosis annexes.
[5] Introduction of Newfoundland in national statistics.
[6] Includes Federal Tuberculosis Sanatoria statistics.

Series B261-284. Percentage occupancy (adult and children) in reporting hospitals by type, Canada, 1932 to 1975

Year	Public						Private					
	All hospitals	Total general and allied special	General, including paediatric	Allied special	Mental	Tuberculosis	All hospitals	Total general and allied special	General	Allied special	Mental	Tuberculosis
	261	262	263	264	265	266	267	268	269	270	271	272
1975	80.0	77.3	75.2	89.3	88.9	84.9	92.2	91.3	77.2	92.7	95.9	—
1974	80.7	77.8	75.8	89.7	90.1	71.3	92.2	91.2	79.5	92.4	96.1	—
1973	81.8[1]	78.6[1]	76.9[1]	88.6[1]	90.8[1]	65.1	93.2[1]	92.8[1]	81.7[1]	93.6[1]	96.5	—
1972	82.5[1]	78.7	77.2[1]	89.2[1]	92.6[1]	57.7	94.2[1]	93.2	83.5[1]	94.9[1]	96.0	—
1971	84.3[1]	81.3	79.6[1]	89.7[1]	94.1[1]	51.6	93.6[1]	92.7	81.4[1]	94.4[1]	98.3	—
1970	84.3[1]	80.9	79.7[1]	90.4[1]	93.0[1]	55.8	90.9[1]	89.2	79.8[1]	91.7[1]	98.6	—
1969	84.7[1]	80.7	79.2[1]	89.7[1]	94.7[1]	64.4	88.9[1]	89.5	78.0[1]	90.2[1]	95.5	—
1968	86.4[1]	81.2	79.7	91.0[1]	93.2	64.2	91.7[1]	91.1	84.0	95.0[1]	91.6	—
1967	86.0[1]	80.2	78.7	89.7[1]	98.1	70.7	90.4[1]	89.6	85.4	93.0[1]	93.5	—
1966	88.4[1]	81.4	80.4	87.8[1]	100.0	68.4	90.0[1]	89.3	85.6	91.1[1]	101.9	—
1965	90.8[1]	82.3	81.4	86.3[1]	102.8	69.4	86.4[1]	87.3	82.8	85.5[1]	102.0	2.6
1964	89.9[1]	81.1	80.8	82.6	106.4	72.2	89.6[1]	86.4	80.3	91.4	106.2	—
1963	80.7[1]	81.8	81.4	84.3	108.4	67.0	86.2[1]	83.8	78.0	88.7	97.5	—
1962	77.6[1]	82.3	81.6	86.8	105.8	70.0	65.7[1]	63.3	76.9	85.7[2]	92.3	—
1961	86.7[1]	83.1	82.3	89.4	101.4	70.6	76.0[1]	78.5	71.5	82.9	91.6	—
1960	91.1[1]	82.0	80.8	91.1	107.2	76.7	65.3[1]	76.8	67.1	79.9	95.1	—
1959	91.2[1]	80.4	79.4	86.7	110.4	77.4	81.4[1]	80.1	72.9	82.2	88.6	—
1958	92.2[1]	80.1	79.6	83.4	115.0	77.7	80.0[1]	83.9	69.1	88.9	85.0	—
1957	93.7[1]	80.2	79.5[1]	85.2[1]	119.1[1]	80.6[1]	80.0[1]	74.8	—	—	89.2	—
1956	92.7[1]	78.9	78.9[1]	81.0[1]	115.5[1]	85.5[1]	82.5[1]	76.7	—	—	93.5	—
1955	92.7[1]	78.7	78.1[1]	83.1[1]	115.1[1]	87.6[1]	74.9[1]	72.7[1]	—	—	92.6	—
1954	—	79.8	78.9[1]	85.9[1]	—	91.8[1]	—	73.0[1]	—	—	—	—
1953[3]	—	81.2	80.8[1]	84.0[1]	—	93.2[1]	—	75.4[1]	—	—	—	—
1952	—	81.1	80.5[1]	87.3[1]	—	91.7[1]	—	74.3[1]	—	—	—	—
1951	—	79.0	79.2[1]	77.7[1]	—	91.5[1]	—	67.4[1]	—	—	—	—
1950	—	78.8	78.4[1]	68.5[1]	—	93.1[1]	—	64.4[1]	—	—	—	—
1949	—	79.1	80.1[1]	58.5[1]	—	—	—	74.5[1]	—	—	—	—
1948	—	78.2	78.4[1]	68.9[1]	—	—	—	67.7[1]	—	—	—	—
1947	—	77.9	78.6[1]	58.5[1]	—	—	—	69.6[1]	—	—	—	—
1946	—	77.5	77.7[1]	63.0[1]	—	—	—	62.3[1]	—	—	—	—
1945	—	74.9	76.1[1]	61.1[1]	—	—	—	67.0[1]	—	—	—	—
1944	—	71.6	75.9[1]	66.0[1]	—	—	—	47.9[1]	—	—	—	—
1943	—	70.6	71.9[1]	66.0[1]	—	—	—	48.3[1]	—	—	—	—
1942	—	69.6[1]	70.1[1]	65.3[1]	—	—	—	52.0[1]	—	—	—	—
1941	—	69.4[1]	70.3[1]	62.3[1]	—	—	—	47.5[1]	—	—	—	—
1940	—	68.2[1]	69.2[1]	61.0[1]	—	—	—	48.1[1]	—	—	—	—
1939	—	64.5[1]	66.6[1]	49.6[1]	—	—	—	44.0[1]	—	—	—	—
1938	—	65.7[1]	65.8[1]	65.3[1]	—	—	—	37.4[1]	—	—	—	—
1937	—	66.7[1]	67.4[1]	63.6[1]	—	—	—	36.5[1]	—	—	—	—
1936	—	67.4[1]	68.2[1]	63.3[1]	—	91.1[1]	—	34.9[1]	—	—	—	—
1935	—	66.2[1]	66.1[1]	66.6[1]	—	91.5[1]	—	34.8[1]	—	—	—	—
1934	—	63.7[1]	62.9[1]	67.7[1]	—	91.5[1]	—	30.3[1]	—	—	—	—
1933	—	57.9[1]	56.8[1]	64.3[1]	—	90.1[1]	—	31.8[1]	—	—	—	—
1932	—	62.7[1]	62.9[1]	59.7[1]	—	85.2[1]	—	74.1[1]	44.7[1]	140.7[1]	—	48.3[1]

Series B261-284. Percentage occupancy (adult and children) in reporting hospitals by type, Canada, 1932 to 1975 (concluded)

Year	Federal						Total					
	All hospitals	Total general and allied special	General	Allied special	Mental	Tuber-culosis	All hospitals	Total general and allied special	General, including paediatric	Allied special	Mental	Tuber-culosis
	273	274	275	276	277	278	279	280	281	282	283	284
1975	64.5	64.5	62.4	70.8	–	–	79.9	77.2	74.8	88.7	89.0	84.9
1974	65.2	65.2	63.2	72.1	–	–	80.6	77.6	75.4	89.2	90.2	71.3
1973	69.2[1]	69.5[1]	68.6[1]	71.8[1]	–	–	81.6[1]	78.8[1]	76.5	–	90.9	65.1
1972	71.5[1]	71.3	71.3[1]	72.2[1]	–	–	82.4[1]	78.8	76.9	–	92.7	57.7
1971	70.9[1]	71.4	71.3[1]	69.1[1]	–	–	84.1[1]	–	79.2	–	94.1	51.6
1970	74.9[1]	74.5	74.9[1]	74.6[1]	–	–	84.2[1]	–	79.4	–	93.1	55.8
1969	69.7[1]	74.3	73.5[1]	79.5[1]	–	–	84.3[1]	–	78.6	–	94.7	64.4
1968	73.9[1]	73.9	73.3	77.5[1]	–	61.9	86.1[1]	81.8	79.4	–	93.0	66.4
1967	74.9[1]	75.1	74.3	78.9[1]	–	67.0	85.7[1]	80.2	78.5	–	96.9	70.6
1966	75.1[1]	75.4	74.6	79.6[1]	–	65.4	87.8[1]	81.3	80.1	–	100.0	68.2
1965	73.2[1]	73.1[1]	72.2[1]	79.0[1]	–	75.1	89.7[1]	81.7	80.7	–	102.8	69.4
1964	73.6[1]	73.4	72.5	79.5	–	71.9	88.9[1]	80.6	80.1	83.6	106.4	72.2
1963	72.3[1]	72.8	72.1	77.3	–	71.7	90.8[1]	81.1	80.5	84.3	108.3	67.4
1962	74.4[1]	73.9[1]	73.0	80.3	–	80.0	87.1[1]	80.6	80.6	80.6	105.7	71.0
1961	74.1[1]	73.5[1]	71.5	85.6	–	79.5	85.7[1]	83.2	81.2	88.1	101.3	71.5
1960	74.6[1]	73.3[1]	72.8	82.6	–	75.9	89.3[1]	89.4	79.7	89.2	107.1	76.6
1959	76.2[1]	75.1[1]	73.1	78.1	85.4	85.3	89.9[1]	89.5	78.7	85.6	109.9	78.0
1958	78.3	76.8[1]	77.9	46.7	82.7	82.5	–	90.9	79.2	83.3	114.8	78.1
1957	78.8[1]	77.5[1]	–	–	87.2	81.6[1]	92.1[1]	79.8[1]	–	–	118.0[1]	80.6[1]
1956	76.2[1]	79.4[1]	–	–	55.4	85.9[1]	91.0[1]	79.3[1]	–	–	112.9[1]	85.5[1]
1955	78.6[1]	78.9[1]	–	–	–	75.3[1]	91.1[1]	78.5[1]	–	–	115.0[1]	86.6[1]
1954	74.2[1]	81.7[1]	–	–	–	90.3[1]	–	79.8[1]	–	–	116.0	89.6[1]
1953[3]	74.4[1]	75.9[1]	–	–	–	90.4[1]	–	44.8[1]	–	–	118.0	93.3[1]
1952	63.7[1]	78.6	–	–	–	92.0[1]	–	44.5[1]	–	–	118.0	92.0[1]
1951	69.0	–	–	–	–	90.8[1]	–	77.0[1]	–	–	121.0	90.8[1]
1950	–	–	–	–	–	91.0[1]	–	–	–	–	120.0	92.0[1]
1949	71.1[1]	–	–	–	–	83.7	–	–	–	–	120.0	–
1948	68.5[1]	–	–	–	–	61.8	–	–	–	–	112.0	–
1947	71.8[1]	–	–	–	–	71.8	–	–	–	–	111.0	–
1946	–	–	–	–	–	58.8	–	–	–	–	109.0	–
1945	–	–	–	–	–	–	–	–	–	107.0	–	–
1944	–	–	–	–	–	–	–	–	–	112.0	–	–
1943	–	–	–	–	–	–	–	–	–	110.0	–	–
1942	–	–	–	–	–	–	–	–	–	111.0	–	–
1941	–	–	–	–	–	–	–	–	–	113.0	–	–
1940	–	–	–	–	–	–	–	–	–	112.0	–	–
1939	–	–	–	–	–	–	–	–	–	110.0	–	–
1938	–	–	–	–	–	–	–	–	–	112.0	–	–
1937	–	–	–	–	–	–	–	–	–	109.0	–	–
1936	–	–	–	–	–	–	–	–	–	105.0	–	–
1935	–	–	–	–	–	–	–	–	–	106.0	–	–
1934	–	–	–	–	–	–	–	–	–	104.0	–	–
1933	–	–	–	–	–	–	–	–	–	–	–	–
1932	–	64.1	–	–	–	–	–	63.3	–	–	–	–

[1] These figures were computed figures using the following formula:

$$\text{percentage occupancy} = \frac{\text{Patient–days}}{\text{Rated bed capacity}} \times \frac{100}{365}$$

[2] Contains 45 nursing homes temporarily approved as hospitals by the Ontario Hospital Services Commission.

[3] Introduction of Newfoundland into national statistics.

Note: In most cases, it was not known if the same number of hospitals reported both 'Patient-days' and 'Rated bed capacity'.

Series B285-297. Average length of stay of separated patients (adult and children) in reporting hospitals, Canada, 1939 to 1975

Year	Public			Private			Federal			Total			
	Total general and allied special	General, including paediatric	Allied special	Total general and allied special	General,	Allied special	Total general and allied special	General	Allied special	Total general and allied special[1]	General, including paediatric[1]	Allied special[1]	Tuberculosis
	285	286	287	288	289	290	291	292	293	294	295	296	297
1975	11.2	9.5	43.2	46.4	7.9	84.2	29.1	23.2	87.7	11.5	11.7	42.0	—
1974	11.0	9.5	41.0	45.3	8.0	83.2	30.5	24.7	104.3	11.4	9.6	45.1	—
1973	10.8	9.4	64.7[1]	42.0	8.6[1]	85.2[1]	32.1	28.0[1]	92.9[1]	11.3	9.7	42.0	—
1972	11.1	9.6	64.8	46.5	8.9[1]	88.0[1]	33.7	29.2[1]	100.4[1]	11.8[2]	10.0	68.7	—
1971	11.3	9.9	64.0	39.6	9.5[1]	83.5[1]	33.8	28.2[1]	99.0[1]	12.0[2]	10.2	67.6	—
1970	11.5	10.0	63.0	36.9	10.8[1]	84.7[1]	34.7	29.9[1]	118.3[1]	12.1[2]	10.4	67.5	—
1969	11.7	10.2	63.0	33.9	10.6[1]	82.7[1]	39.1	34.4[1]	152.7[1]	12.4	10.7	67.8	—
1968	11.7	10.3	63.7[1]	25.3	10.0	66.5[1]	37.2	33.6	109.7[1]	12.3	10.7	65.5	—
1967	11.5	10.3	56.2[1]	23.2	9.7	65.0[1]	36.9	32.1	153.3[1]	12.3	10.7	60.0	—
1966	11.7	10.2	70.2[1]	22.2	9.4	61.0[1]	36.1	32.2	123.8[1]	12.5	10.7	70.2	—
1965	11.6	10.3	55.7[1]	19.2	8.8	56.0[1]	37.0	33.0	155.6[1]	12.4	10.8	58.5	—
1964	11.5	10.2	58.6[1]	17.7	8.5	53.0[1]	37.4	34.2	—	12.4	—	—	—
1963	11.5	10.2	52.3[1]	18.8	8.3	57.1[1]	37.1	32.8	—	12.3	—	—	224.0
1962	11.3	10.2	47.0[1]	20.4	8.4	—	33.8	—	—	12.0	—	—	220.0
1961	11.1	10.0	52.9[1]	17.0	8.5	—	32.6	—	—	11.6	—	—	241.0
1960	11.1	9.9	—	—	—	—	—	—	—	—	—	—	264.0
1959	11.2	9.8	—	—	—	—	—	—	—	—	—	—	284.0
1958	10.9	9.8	—	18.8	—	—	44.3	—	—	—	—	—	300.0
1957	10.7	9.8	—	18.5	—	—	44.4	—	—	—	—	—	310.0
1956	11.0	10.0	—	16.6	—	—	41.9	—	—	—	—	—	327.0
1955	10.9	9.9	—	15.6	—	—	44.7	—	—	—	—	—	362.0
1954	11.1	10.1	—	15.5	—	—	46.0	—	—	—	—	—	372.0
1953[3]	10.9	10.0	—	18.5	—	—	41.2	—	—	—	—	—	362.0
1952	10.7	10.0	—	12.8	—	—	—	—	—	—	—	—	337.0
1951	10.5	9.9[1]	30.7[1]	17.4	—	—	—	—	—	—	—	—	301.0
1950	10.6	10.0[1]	20.0	14.6	—	—	—	—	—	—	—	—	331.0
1949	10.3	10.1[1]	15.0[1]	15.4	—	—	—	—	—	—	—	—	312.0
1948	10.5	10.2[1]	19.1[1]	16.9	—	—	—	—	—	—	—	—	290.0
1947	10.6	10.3[1]	18.4[1]	17.0	—	—	—	—	—	—	—	—	298.0
1946	11.1	10.8[1]	19.8[1]	16.6	—	—	—	—	—	—	—	—	287.0
1945	11.4	11.0[1]	19.9[1]	20.5	—	—	—	—	—	—	—	—	316.0
1944	11.6	11.2[1]	20.4[1]	19.0	—	—	—	—	—	—	—	—	320.0
1943	12.0	11.5[1]	21.1[1]	17.9	—	—	—	—	—	—	—	—	322.0
1942	12.5	12.0[1]	21.1[1]	18.2	—	—	—	—	—	—	—	—	317.0
1941	12.7	12.3[1]	20.9[1]	17.9	—	—	—	—	—	—	—	—	322.0
1940	13.4	12.7[1]	27.3[1]	17.3	—	—	—	—	—	—	—	—	326.0
1939	13.4	12.9[1]	24.3[1]	18.4	—	—	—	—	—	—	—	—	311.0

[1] Computed figures less the average days of stay equal: Total days of stay of separations divided by the total number of separations. Note: In some cases, it was not known if the number of institutions reporting days of stay equaled the number of institutions reporting the number of separations.

[2] Includes newborn.
[3] Introduction of Newfoundland into national statistics.

Series B298-303. Total paid hours of all employees in reporting public hospitals, Canada, 1952 to 1975

Year[1]	All hospitals	Total general allied special	General, including paediatric	Allied special	Mental	Tuberculosis
	298	299	300	301	302	303
1975	—	606,196,208	546,795,156	59,401,052	—	1,264,369
1974	—	578,928,425	524,934,926	53,993,499	—	1,404,748
1973[2]	—	559,389,824	504,958,348	54,431,476	—	2,286,499
1972[2]	—	549,320,194	496,184,366	53,135,828	—	2,991,634
1971[2]	—	543,277,761	491,398,141	51,879,620	—	4,989,907 [3]
1970[2]	—	532,616,165	481,859,350	50,756,815	—	5,994,543
1969[2]	—	518,188,197	469,630,411	48,557,786	—	6,329,063 [4]
1968	—	535,013,720	487,837,184	47,176,536	—	7,415,533 [5]
1967	—	507,971,393	463,267,730	44,703,663	—	7,732,913 [4]
1966	—	474,579,958	433,880,678	40,699,280	—	7,941,014 [4]
1965	—	452,911,188	414,311,582	38,599,606	—	9,043,004 [5]
1964	—	430,623,206	395,211,686	35,414,520	—	10,568,084
1963	—	402,766,473	369,734,039	33,032,434	—	—
1962	—	372,582,253	347,292,208	25,290,045	—	—
1961	—	337,780,494	315,488,375	22,292,119	—	—
1960	—	322,335,695	300,954,076	21,381,669	—	—
1959	—	297,385,866	275,275,357	22,110,509	—	—
1958	—	270,966,769	254,043,027	16,923,742	—	—
1957	—	255,349,953	—	—	—	—
1956	—	240,561,408	—	—	—	—
1955	—	232,987,928	—	—	—	—
1954	—	200,025,060	—	—	—	—
1953[6]	—	185,994,344	—	—	—	—
1952	—	169,004,255	—	—	—	—

[1] No data available prior to 1952.
[2] Excludes medical staff.
[3] Includes paid hours for general services provided for Alberta School Hospital facilities.

[4] Does not include Alberta and British Columbia.
[5] Does not include Alberta.
[6] Incorporation of Newfoundland into national statistics.

Series B304-351. Total personnel (full- and part-time) in reporting hospitals, Canada, 1932 to 1975

Year	Public											
	All hospitals		Total general and allied special		General, including paediatric		Allied special		Mental		Tuberculosis	
	Number reporting	Personnel	Number reporting	Personnel	Number reporting	Personnel	Number reporting	Personnel	Number reporting	Personnel	Number reporting	Personnel
	304	305	306	307	308	309	310	311	312	313	314	315
1975	–	–	1,041	348,971	864	314,794	177	34,177	–	–	–	386
1974	–	–	1,038	332,114	865	301,290	173	30,824	–	–	–	645
1973	–	–	1,044	315,569	863	284,290	181	31,279	–	–	–	1,195
1972	–	–	1,047	309,642	868	280,211	179	29,431	–	–	–	1,631
1971	–	–	1,039	302,371	864	274,267	175	28,104	–	–	–	2,592
1970	–	–	1,036	295,105	863	267,699	173	27,406	–	–	–	3,320
1969	–	–	1,030	290,626	867	264,111	163	26,515	–	–	–	3,945
1968	–	–	1,042	285,692	880	259,711	162	25,981	–	–	–	4,324
1967	–	–	1,034	273,018	873	248,317	161	24,701	–	–	–	4,773
1966	–	–	1,027	255,523	869	233,207	158	22,316	–	–	–	4,587
1965	–	–	1,009	238,424	850	217,435	159	20,989	–	–	–	5,035
1964	–	–	994	224,540	844	205,502	150	19,038	–	–	–	–
1963	–	–	949	208,421	821	191,018	128	17,403	–	–	–	–
1962	–	–	919	193,335	809	181,115	110	12,220	–	–	–	7,357
1961	–	–	914	179,847	834	167,604	80	12,243	–	–	–	7,352
1960	–	–	923	172,880	842	161,179	81	11,701	–	–	–	7,923
1959	–	–	932	158,137	841	146,413	91	11,724	–	–	–	7,786
1958	–	–	920	143,885	832	134,342	88	9,543	–	–	–	8,144
1957	–	–	894	133,287	820	125,297	74	7,990	–	–	–	8,711
1956	–	–	870	122,122	–	–	–	–	–	–	–	8,982
1955	–	–	856	114,553	–	–	–	–	–	–	–	9,163
1954	–	–	817	102,495	–	–	–	–	–	–	–	9,598
1953[1]	–	–	807	95,051	–	–	–	–	–	–	–	10,005
1952	–	–	775	86,198	–	–	–	–	–	–	–	9,350
1951	–	–	778	83,405	707	76,921	71	6,484	–	–	–	8,168
1950	–	–	741	75,998	692	72,089	49	3,909	–	–	–	7,913
1949	–	–	719	70,662	617	66,528	102	4,134	–	–	–	6,708
1948	–	–	678	64,065	588	60,560	90	3,505	–	–	–	6,183
1947	–	–	653	60,695	567	57,248	86	3,447	–	–	–	5,771
1946	–	–	595	55,222	514	51,852	81	3,370	–	–	–	5,346
1945	–	–	587	49,166	507	46,179	80	2,987	–	–	–	4,934
1944	–	–	586	47,302	509	44,204	77	3,098	–	–	–	4,403
1943	–	–	592	44,364	510	41,149	82	3,215	–	–	–	4,456
1942	–	–	594	42,041	511	38,861	83	3,180	–	–	–	4,326
1941	–	–	592	40,868	507	37,928	85	2,940	–	–	–	4,406
1940	–	–	587	38,963	500	36,104	87	2,859	–	–	–	4,453
1939	–	–	587	36,335	497	33,754	90	2,581	–	–	–	4,557
1938	–	–	610	36,823	496	32,872	114	3,951	–	–	–	3,548
1937	–	–	584	34,465	480	30,622	104	3,843	–	–	–	–
1936	–	–	568	33,424	474	30,192	94	3,232	–	–	34	3,427
1935	–	–	572	31,350	470	28,348	102	3,002	–	–	36	3,367
1934	–	–	568	30,569	463	27,195	105	3,374	–	–	34	3,263
1933	–	–	571	29,330	466	26,266	105	3,064	–	–	32	3,148
1932	–	–	417	27,662	461	25,902	44	1,760	–	–	34	3,229

Series B304-351. Total personnel (full- and part-time) in reporting hospitals, Canada, 1932 to 1975 (continued)

Year	Private											
	All hospitals		Total general and allied special		General		Allied special		Mental		Tuberculosis	
	Number reporting	Personnel	Number reporting	Personnel	Number reporting	Personnel	Number reporting	Personnel	Number reporting	Personnel	Number reporting	Personnel
	316	317	318	319	320	321	322	323	324	325	326	327
1975	–	–	64	4,486	9	782	55	3,704	–	–	–	–
1974	–	–	68	4,392	10	724	53	3,668	–	–	–	–
1973	–	–	74	4,571	11	891	63	3,680	–	–	–	–
1972	–	–	107	5,518	12	904	95	4,614	–	–	–	–
1971	–	–	118	5,521	20	1,101	98	4,420	–	–	–	–
1970	–	–	132	5,664	31	1,598	101	4,066	–	–	–	–
1969	–	–	136	5,503	37	1,717	99	3,786	–	–	–	–
1968	–	–	148	5,976	41	2,446	107	3,530	–	–	–	–
1967	–	–	161	6,114	49	2,674	112	3,440	–	–	–	–
1966	–	–	165	5,849	49	2,691	116	3,158	–	–	–	–
1965	–	–	185	6,124	60	2,948	125	3,176	–	–	–	–
1964	–	–	189	5,472	64	2,893	125	2,579	–	–	–	–
1963	–	–	141	4,368	66	2,685	75	1,683	–	–	–	–
1962	–	–	107	3,161	47	1,858	60	1,303	–	–	–	–
1961	–	–	139	3,376	53	1,753	86	1,623	–	–	–	–
1960	–	–	142	3,104	–	–	–	–	–	–	–	–
1959	–	–	200	4,410	–	–	–	–	–	–	–	–
1958	–	–	201	3,663	–	–	–	–	–	–	–	–
1957	–	–	211	3,568	–	–	–	–	–	–	–	–
1956	–	–	199	2,954	–	–	–	–	–	–	–	–
1955	–	–	172	2,373	–	–	–	–	–	–	–	–
1954	–	–	167	2,345	–	–	–	–	–	–	–	–
1953[1]	–	–	143	1,853	–	–	–	–	–	–	–	–
1952	–	–	187	2,090	–	–	–	–	–	–	–	–
1951	–	–	220	2,538	–	–	–	–	–	–	–	–
1850	–	–	225	2,459	–	–	–	–	–	–	–	–
1949	–	–	194	2,071	–	–	–	–	–	–	–	–
1948	–	–	209	1,996	–	–	–	–	–	–	–	–
1947	–	–	212	1,924	–	–	–	–	–	–	–	–
1946	–	–	235	1,858	–	–	–	–	–	–	1	8
1945	–	–	234	1,735	–	–	–	–	–	–	1	8
1944	–	–	267	1,865	–	–	–	–	–	–	1	8
1943	–	–	263	1,800	–	–	–	–	–	–	1	8
1942	–	–	287	1,736	–	–	–	–	–	–	1	8
1941	–	–	322	1,762	–	–	–	–	–	–	1	9
1940	–	–	292	1,550	–	–	–	–	–	–	1	9
1939	–	–	276	1,485	–	–	–	–	–	–	1	10
1938	–	–	267	1,229	–	–	–	–	–	–	1	9
1937	–	–	241	1,523	–	–	–	–	–	–	–	–
1936	–	–	259	1,442	–	–	–	–	–	–	–	–
1935	–	–	267	1,472	–	–	–	–	–	–	–	–
1934	–	–	261	1,404	–	–	–	–	–	–	–	–
1933	–	–	238	1,225	–	–	–	–	–	–	–	–
1932	–	–	208	1,026	128	750	80	276	–	–	2	37

Series B304-351. Total personnel (full- and part-time) in reporting hospitals, Canada, 1932 to 1975 (continued)

Year	Federal											
	All hospitals		Total general and allied special		General		Allied special		Mental		Tuberculosis	
	Number reporting	Personnel	Number reporting	Personnel	Number reporting	Personnel	Number reporting	Personnel	Number reporting	Personnel	Number reporting	Personnel
	328	329	330	331	332	333	334	335	336	337	338	339
1975	–	8,559	94	8,559	24	6,841	70	1,718	–	–	–	–
1974	–	8,494	88	8,494	23	6,909	65	1,585	–	–	–	–
1973	–	–	93	10,095	25	8,492	68	1,603	–	–	–	–
1972	–	–	91	10,146	25	8,575	66	1,571	–	–	–	–
1971	–	–	88	10,634	26	9,107	62	1,527	–	–	–	–
1970	–	–	81	10,330	24	8,840	57	1,490	–	–	–	–
1969	–	–	70	10,578	25	9,140	45	1,438	–	–	–	–
1968	–	11,173	70	11,083	24	9,613	46	1,470	–	–	–	90
1967	–	11,800	72	11,705	27	10,319	45	1,386	–	–	–	95
1966	–	11,697	71	11,407	27	9,942	44	1,465	–	–	–	290
1965	–	14,102	81	13,772	40	12,317	41	1,455	–	–	–	330
1964	–	–	76	13,413	32	11,984	44	1,429	–	–	–	–
1963	–	–	69	13,257	35	11,821	34	1,436	–	–	–	–
1962	–	11,391	31	10,264	30	9,056	1	1,208	–	–	–	1,127
1961	–	13,856	66	12,544	63	11,143	3	1,401	–	–	–	1,312
1960	–	–	71	12,831	69	12,670	2	161	–	–	–	1,292
1959	–	–	47	11,630	44	11,475	3	155	–	–	–	813
1958	–	–	–	12,095	–	–	–	–	–	–	–	746
1957	–	–	–	11,571	–	–	–	–	–	–	–	753
1956	–	–	–	11,441	–	–	–	–	–	–	–	757
1955	–	–	–	10,805	–	–	–	–	–	–	–	746
1954	–	–	–	10,187	–	–	–	–	–	–	–	1,266
1953[1]	–	–	–	10,007	–	–	–	–	–	–	–	1,467
1952	–	–	42	9,659	–	–	–	–	–	–	–	1,409
1951	–	–	78	11,704	–	–	–	–	–	–	–	1,335
1950	–	–	67	10,476	–	–	–	–	–	–	–	–
1949	–	–	76	10,823	–	–	–	–	–	–	–	–
1948	–	–	66	10,412	–	–	–	–	–	–	–	–
1947	–	–	–	9,309	–	–	–	–	–	–	–	–
1946	–	–	–	–	–	–	–	–	–	–	–	–
1945	–	–	–	–	–	–	–	–	–	–	–	–
1944	–	–	–	–	–	–	–	–	–	–	–	–
1943	–	–	–	–	–	–	–	–	–	–	–	–
1942	–	–	–	–	–	–	–	–	–	–	–	–
1941	–	–	–	–	–	–	–	–	–	–	–	–
1940	–	–	–	–	–	–	–	–	–	–	–	–
1939	–	–	–	–	–	–	–	–	–	–	–	–
1938	–	–	–	–	–	–	–	–	–	–	–	–
1937	–	–	–	–	–	–	–	–	–	–	–	–
1936	–	–	–	–	–	–	–	–	–	–	–	–
1935	–	–	–	–	–	–	–	–	–	–	–	–
1934	–	–	–	–	–	–	–	–	–	–	–	–
1933	–	–	32	1,009	–	–	–	–	–	–	–	–
1932	–	–	35	1,109	–	–	–	–	–	–	–	–

Series B304-351. Total personnel (full- and part-time) in reporting hospitals, Canada, 1932 to 1975 (concluded)

Year	Total											
	All hospitals		Total general and allied special		General, including paediatric		Allied special		Mental		Tuberculosis	
	Number reporting	Personnel	Number reporting	Personnel	Number reporting	Personnel	Number reporting	Personnel	Number reporting	Personnel	Number reporting	Personnel
	340	341	342	343	344	345	346	347	348	349	350	351
1975	—	413,984	1,199	362,016	897	322,417	302	39,599	—	51,582	—	386
1974	—	398,459	1,194	345,000	898	308,923	291	36,077	—	52,814	—	645
1973	—	384,281	1,211	330,235	899	293,693	312	36,542	—	52,851	—	1,195
1972	—	377,719	1,245	325,306	905	289,690	340	35,616	—	50,782	—	1,631
1971	—	373,360	1,245	318,526	910	284,475	335	34,051	—	52,242	—	2,582
1970	—	365,792	1,249	311,099	918	278,137	331	32,962	—	51,373	—	3,320
1969	—	361,483	1,236	306,707	929	274,968	307	31,739	—	50,831	—	3,945
1968	—	356,096	1,260	302,751	945	271,770	315	30,981	—	48,931	—	4,414
1967	—	342,036	1,267	290,837	949	261,310	318	29,527	—	46,331	—	4,868
1966	—	319,780	1,263	272,779	945	245,840	318	26,939	—	42,124	—	4,877
1965	—	304,430	1,275	258,320	950	232,700	325	25,620	—	40,745	—	5,365
1964	—	287,564	1,259	243,425	940	220,379	319	23,046	—	37,565	—	5,674
1963	—	268,641	1,159	226,046	922	205,524	237	20,522	—	34,676	—	7,919
1962	—	246,106	1,057	206,760	886	192,029	171	14,731	—	30,862	—	8,484
1961	—	234,578	1,119	195,767	950	180,500	169	16,267	—	30,147	—	8,664
1960	—	226,284	—	188,815	—	—	—	—	—	28,254	—	9,215
1959	—	209,812	—	174,177	—	—	—	—	—	27,036	—	8,599
1958	—	194,229	—	159,643	—	—	—	—	—	25,696	—	8,890
1957	—	181,808	—	148,426	—	—	—	—	—	23,918	—	9,464
1956	—	167,714	—	136,517	—	—	—	—	—	21,458	—	9,739
1955	—	156,936	—	127,731	—	—	—	—	—	19,296	—	9,909
1954	—	145,130	—	115,027	—	—	—	—	—	19,329	—	10,864
1953[1]	—	138,867	—	109,911	—	—	—	—	—	17,484	—	11,472
1952	—	124,583	—	97,947	—	—	—	—	—	15,877	—	10,759
1951	—	121,678	—	97,647	—	—	—	—	—	14,528	—	9,503
1950	—	—	—	88,933	—	—	—	—	—	13,579	—	—
1949	—	—	—	83,556	—	—	—	—	—	12,933	—	—
1948	—	—	—	76,473	—	—	—	—	—	12,124	—	—
1947	—	—	—	71,928	—	—	—	—	—	11,481	—	—
1946	—	—	—	—	—	—	—	—	—	10,346	—	—
1945	—	—	—	—	—	—	—	—	—	9,938	—	—
1944	—	—	—	—	—	—	—	—	—	9,007	—	—
1943	—	—	—	—	—	—	—	—	—	8,866	—	—
1942	—	—	—	—	—	—	—	—	—	8,533	—	—
1941	—	—	—	—	—	—	—	—	—	8,563	—	—
1940	—	—	—	—	—	—	—	—	58	8,814	—	—
1939	—	—	—	—	—	—	—	—	59	8,590	—	—
1938	—	—	—	—	—	—	—	—	57	8,515	—	—
1937	—	—	—	—	—	—	—	—	57	8,175	—	—
1936	—	—	—	—	—	—	—	—	57	7,538	—	—
1935	—	—	—	—	—	—	—	—	56	7,017	—	—
1934	—	—	—	—	—	—	—	—	56	6,915	—	—
1933	—	—	—	—	—	—	—	—	58	6,632	—	—
1932	—	—	—	29,797	—	—	—	—	56	6,605	—	—

[1] Entry of Newfoundland into national statistics.

Series B352-399. Total full-time personnel in reporting hospitals, Canada, 1951 to 1975

Year	Public											
	All hospitals		Total general and allied special		General, including paediatric		Allied special		Mental		Tuberculosis	
	Number reporting	Personnel	Number reporting	Personnel	Number reporting	Personnel	Number reporting	Personnel	Number reporting	Personnel	Number reporting	Personnel
	352	**353**	**354**	**355**	**356**	**357**	**358**	**359**	**360**	**361**	**362**	**363**
1975	–	–	1,041	282,646	864	256,300	177	26,346	–	–	–	358
1974	–	–	1,038	271,776	865	247,864	173	23,912	–	–	–	608
1973	–	–	1,044	262,152	863	237,826	181	24,326	–	–	–	1,011
1972	–	–	1,047	261,900	868	238,087	179	23,813	–	–	–	1,469
1971	–	–	1,039	259,006	864	235,634	175	23,372	–	–	–	2,245
1970	–	–	1,036	255,294	863	232,273	173	23,021	–	–	–	2,922
1969	–	–	1,030	251,862	867	229,341	163	22,521	–	–	–	3,455
1968	–	–	1,042	248,434	880	226,649	162	21,785	–	–	–	3,811
1967	–	–	1,034	238,546	873	217,753	161	20,793	–	–	–	4,255
1966	–	–	1,027	225,271	869	206,314	158	18,957	–	–	–	4,079
1965	–	–	1,009	212,795	850	194,596	159	18,199	–	–	–	4,576
1964	–	–	994	201,371	884	184,827	110	16,544	–	–	–	–
1963	–	–	949	187,999	821	172,708	128	15,291	–	–	–	–
1962	–	–	919	173,966	809	163,437	110	10,529	–	–	–	–
1961	–	–	914	162,805	834	152,133	80	10,672	–	–	–	–
1960	–	–	923	155,992	842	145,947	81	10,045	–	–	–	–
1959	–	–	932	142,870	841	132,482	91	10,388	–	–	–	–
1958	–	–	920	131,920	832	123,234	88	8,686	–	–	–	–
1957	–	–	894	122,024	820	114,790	74	7,234	–	–	–	–
1956	–	–	870	112,838	–	–	–	–	–	–	–	–
1955	–	–	856	106,677	–	–	–	–	–	–	–	–
1954	–	–	817	95,471	–	–	–	–	–	–	–	–
1953[1]	–	–	807	88,804	–	–	–	–	–	–	–	–
1952	–	–	775	80,948	–	–	–	–	–	–	–	–
1951	–	–	–	–	–	–	–	–	–	–	–	–

Series B352-399. Total full-time personnel in reporting hospitals, Canada, 1951 to 1975 (continued)

Year	All hospitals		Private										
			Total general and allied special		General		Allied special		Mental		Tuberculosis	
	Number reporting	Personnel	Number reporting	Personnel	Number reporting	Personnel	Number reporting	Personnel	Number reporting	Personnel	Number reporting	Personnel
	364	365	366	367	368	369	370	371	372	373	374	375
1975	—	3,643	64	2,599	9	547	55	2,052	—	—	—	—
1974	—	3,698	68	2,624	10	523	58	2,101	—	—	—	—
1973	—	—	74	2,793	11	617	63	2,176	—	—	—	—
1972	—	—	107	3,505	12	656	95	2,849	—	—	—	—
1971	—	—	118	3,664	20	792	98	2,872	—	—	—	—
1970	—	—	132	4,006	31	1,262	101	2,744	—	—	—	—
1969	—	—	136	3,870	37	1,359	99	2,511	—	—	—	—
1968	—	—	148	4,481	41	2,026	107	2,455	—	—	—	—
1967	—	—	161	4,580	49	2,160	112	2,420	—	—	—	—
1966	—	—	165	4,466	49	2,191	116	2,275	—	—	—	—
1965	—	—	185	4,804	60	2,415	125	2,389	—	—	—	—
1964	—	—	189	4,339	64	2,380	125	1,959	—	—	—	—
1963	—	—	141	3,566	66	2,259	75	1,307	—	—	—	—
1962	—	—	107	2,559	47	1,543	60	1,016	—	—	—	—
1961	—	—	139	2,658	53	1,432	86	1,226	—	—	—	—
1960	—	—	142	2,482	—	—	—	—	—	—	—	—
1959	—	—	200	3,532	—	—	—	—	—	—	—	—
1958	—	—	201	3,066	—	—	—	—	—	—	—	—
1957	—	—	211	2,908	—	—	—	—	—	—	—	—
1956	—	—	199	2,444	—	—	—	—	—	—	—	—
1955	—	—	172	1,896	—	—	—	—	—	—	—	—
1954	—	—	167	1,911	—	—	—	—	—	—	—	—
1953[1]	—	—	143	1,498	—	—	—	—	—	—	—	—
1952	—	—	—	—	—	—	—	—	—	—	—	—
1951	—	—	—	—	—	—	—	—	—	—	—	—

Series B352-399. Total full-time personnel in reporting hospitals, Canada, 1951 to 1975 (continued)

Year	Federal											
	All hospitals		Total general and allied special		General		Allied special		Mental		Tuberculosis	
	Number reporting	Personnel	Number reporting	Personnel	Number reporting	Personnel	Number reporting	Personnel	Number reporting	Personnel	Number reporting	Personnel
	376	377	378	379	380	381	382	383	384	385	386	387
1975	94	8,083	94	8,083	24	6,495	70	1,588	–	–	–	–
1974	88	7,938	88	7,938	23	6,475	65	1,463	–	–	–	–
1973	93	–	93	9,671	25	8,169	68	1,502	–	–	–	–
1972	91	–	91	9,731	25	8,286	66	1,445	–	–	–	–
1971	88	–	88	10,231	26	8,823	62	1,408	–	–	–	–
1970	81	–	81	10,004	24	8,651	57	1,353	–	–	–	–
1969	70	–	70	10,262	25	8,881	45	1,381	–	–	–	–
1968	–	–	70	10,727	25	9,296	46	1,431	–	–	–	–
1967	–	–	72	11,279	28	9,928	45	1,351	–	–	–	–
1966	–	–	71	11,147	27	9,711	44	1,436	–	–	–	–
1965	–	–	81	13,363	40	11,933	41	1,430	–	–	–	–
1964	–	–	76	12,920	32	11,508	44	1,412	–	–	–	–
1963	–	–	69	12,754	35	11,337	34	1,417	–	–	–	–
1962	–	–	31	9,696	30	8,488	1	1,208	–	–	–	–
1961	–	–	66	11,802	63	10,415	3	1,387	–	–	–	–
1960	–	–	71	12,117	69	11,960	2	157	–	–	–	–
1959	–	–	47	11,131	44	10,983	3	148	–	–	–	–
1958	–	–	–	–	–	–	–	–	–	–	–	–
1957	–	–	–	–	–	–	–	–	–	–	–	–
1956	–	–	–	–	–	–	–	–	–	–	–	–
1955	–	–	–	–	–	–	–	–	–	–	–	–
1954	–	–	–	–	–	–	–	–	–	–	–	–
1953[1]	–	–	–	–	–	–	–	–	–	–	–	–
1952	–	–	–	–	–	–	–	–	–	–	–	–
1951	–	–	–	–	–	–	–	–	–	–	–	–

Series B352-399. Total full-time personnel in reporting hospitals, Canada, 1951 to 1975 (concluded)

Year	Total											
	All hospitals		Total general and allied special		General, including paediatric		Allied special		Mental		Tuberculosis	
	Number reporting	Personnel	Number reporting	Personnel	Number reporting	Personnel	Number reporting	Personnel	Number reporting	Personnel	Number reporting	Personnel
	388	389	390	391	392	393	394	395	396	397	398	399
1975	—	339,581	1,199	293,328	897	263,342	302	29,986	—	45,895	—	358
1974	—	329,931	1,194	282,338	898	254,862	296	27,476	—	46,985	—	608
1973	—	323,578	1,211	274,616	899	246,612	312	28,004	—	47,951	—	1,011
1972	—	323,413	1,245	275,136	905	247,029	340	28,107	—	46,808	—	1,469
1971	—	323,280	1,245	272,901	910	245,249	335	27,652	—	48,134	—	2,245
1970	—	319,835	1,249	269,304	918	242,186	331	27,118	—	47,609	—	2,922
1969	—	316,641	1,236	265,994	929	239,581	307	26,413	—	47,192	—	3,455
1968	—	—	1,260	263,642	945	237,971	315	25,671	—	45,741	—	—
1967	—	—	1,267	254,405	949	229,841	318	24,564	—	43,613	—	—
1966	—	—	1,263	240,884	945	218,216	318	22,668	—	39,910	—	—
1965	—	—	1,275	230,962	950	208,944	325	22,018	—	38,716	—	—
1964	—	259,674	1,259	218,630	940	198,715	319	19,915	—	35,849	—	5,195
1963	—	244,730	1,159	204,319	922	186,304	237	18,015	—	33,081	—	7,330
1962	—	—	1,057	186,221	886	173,468	171	12,753	—	30,862	—	—
1961	—	—	1,119	177,265	950	163,980	169	13,285	—	29,019	—	—
1960	—	—	—	160,546	—	—	—	—	—	27,182	—	—
1959	—	—	—	157,533	—	—	—	—	—	26,005	—	—
1958	—	—	—	—	—	—	—	—	—	24,773	—	—
1957	—	—	—	—	—	—	—	—	—	23,095	—	—
1956	—	—	—	—	—	—	—	—	—	20,598	—	—
1955	—	—	—	—	—	—	—	—	—	18,543	—	—
1954	—	—	—	—	—	—	—	—	—	18,561	—	—
1953[1]	—	—	—	—	—	—	—	—	—	16,870	—	—
1952	—	—	—	—	—	—	—	—	—	—	—	—
1951	—	—	—	—	—	—	—	—	—	—	—	—

[1] Entry of Newfoundland into national statistics.

Series B400-431. Total part-time personnel employed by reporting hospitals, Canada, 1947 to 1975

Year	Public								Private					
	Total general and allied special		General, including paediatric		Allied special		Tuberculosis		Total general and allied special		General		Allied special	
	Number reporting	Personnel	Number reporting	Personnel	Number reporting	Personnel	Number reporting	Personnel	Number reporting	Personnel	Number reporting	Personnel	Number reporting	Personnel
	400	401	402	403	404	405	406	407	408	409	410	411	412	413
1975	1,017	66,325	845	58,494	172	7,831	··	28	61	1,887	6	235	55	1,652
1974	1,004	60,338	844	53,426	160	6,912	··	37	65	1,768	7	201	58	1,567
1973	1,044	53,417	863	46,464	181	6,953	—	184	74	1,778	11	274	63	1,504
1972	1,047	47,742	868	42,124	179	5,618	—	162	107	2,013	12	248	95	1,765
1971	1,039	43,365	864	38,633	175	4,732	—	347	118	1,857	20	309	98	1,548
1970	1,036	39,811	863	35,426	173	4,385	—	398	132	1,658	31	336	101	1,322
1969	1,030	38,764	867	34,770	163	3,994	—	490	136	1,633	37	358	99	1,275
1968	1,042	37,258	880	33,062	162	4,196	—	513	148	1,495	41	420	107	1,075
1967	1,034	34,472	873	30,564	161	3,908	—	518	161	1,534	49	514	112	1,020
1966	1,027	30,252	869	26,893	158	3,359	—	508	165	1,383	49	500	116	883
1965	1,009	25,629	850	22,839	159	2,790	—	459	185	1,320	60	533	125	787
1964	994	23,169	844	20,675	150	2,494	—	—	189	1,133	64	513	125	620
1963	949	20,422	821	18,310	128	2,112	—	—	141	802	66	426	75	376
1962	919	19,369	809	17,678	110	1,691	—	—	107	602	47	315	60	287
1961	914	17,042	834	15,471	80	1,571	—	—	139	718	53	321	86	397
1960	923	16,888	842	15,232	81	1,656	—	—	142	622	—	—	—	—
1959	932	15,267	841	13,931	91	1,336	—	—	200	878	—	—	—	—
1958	920	11,965	832	11,108	88	857	—	—	201	597	—	—	—	—
1957	894	11,263	820	10,507	74	756	—	—	211	660	—	—	—	—
1956	870	9,284	—	—	—	—	—	—	199	510	—	—	—	—
1955	856	7,876	—	—	—	—	—	—	172	477	—	—	—	—
1954	817	7,024	—	—	—	—	—	—	167	434	—	—	—	—
1953¹	807	6,247	—	—	—	—	—	—	143	355	—	—	—	—
1952	775	5,250	—	—	—	—	—	—	—	—	—	—	—	—
1951	—	—	—	—	—	—	—	—	—	—	—	—	—	—
1950	—	—	—	—	—	—	—	—	—	—	—	—	—	—
1949	—	—	—	—	—	—	—	—	—	—	—	—	—	—
1948	—	—	—	—	—	—	—	—	—	—	—	—	—	—
1947	—	—	—	—	—	—	—	—	—	—	—	—	—	—

Series B400–431. Total part-time personnel employed by reporting hospitals, Canada, 1947 to 1975 (concluded)

Year	Federal — Total general and allied special, Number reporting (414)	Personnel (415)	General, Number reporting (416)	Personnel (417)	Allied special, Number reporting (418)	Personnel (419)	All hospitals, Number reporting (420)	Personnel (421)	Total² — Total general and allied special, Number reporting (422)	Personnel (423)	General including paediatric, Number reporting (424)	Personnel (425)	Allied special, Number reporting (426)	Personnel (427)	Mental, Number reporting (428)	Personnel (429)	Tuberculosis, Number reporting (430)	Personnel (431)
1975	46	476	19	346	27	130	..	74,403	1,124	68,688	870	59,075	254	9,613	..	5,687	..	28
1974	43	556	19	434	24	122	..	68,528	1,112	62,662	870	54,061	242	8,601	..	5,829	..	37
1973	93	424	25	323	68	101	—	60,703	1,211	55,619	899	47,061	312	8,558	—	4,900	—	184
1972	91	415	25	289	66	126	—	54,306	1,245	50,170	405	42,661	340	7,509	—	3,974	—	162
1971	88	403	26	284	62	119	—	50,080	1,245	45,625	910	39,226	335	6,399	—	4,108	—	347
1970	81	326	24	189	57	137	—	45,957	1,249	41,795	918	35,951	331	5,844	—	3,764	—	398
1969	70	316	25	259	45	57	—	44,842	1,236	40,713	929	35,387	307	5,326	—	3,639	—	490
1968	70	356	25	317	46	39	—	—	1,260	39,109	945	33,799	315	5,310	—	3,190	—	—
1967	72	426	28	391	45	35	—	—	1,267	36,432	949	31,469	318	4,963	—	2,718	—	—
1966	71	260	27	231	44	29	—	—	1,263	31,895	945	27,624	318	4,271	—	2,214	—	—
1965	81	409	40	384	41	25	—	—	1,275	27,358	950	23,756	325	3,602	—	2,029	—	—
1964	76	493	32	476	44	17	—	26,990	1,259	24,795	940	21,664	319	3,131	—	1,716	—	479
1963	69	503	35	484	34	19	—	23,911	1,159	21,727	922	19,220	237	2,507	—	1,595	—	589
1962	31	568	30	568	1	—	—	—	1,057	20,539	886	18,561	171	1,978	—	—	—	—
1961	66	742	63	728	3	14	—	—	1,119	18,502	950	16,520	169	1,982	—	1,128	—	—
1960	71	714	69	710	2	4	—	—	—	18,224	—	—	—	—	—	1,072	—	—
1959	47	499	44	492	3	7	—	—	—	16,644	—	—	—	—	—	1,031	—	—
1958	—	—	—	—	—	—	—	—	—	—	—	—	—	—	—	923	—	—
1957	—	—	—	—	—	—	—	—	—	—	—	—	—	—	—	823	—	—
1956	—	—	—	—	—	—	—	—	—	—	—	—	—	—	—	860	—	—
1955	—	—	—	—	—	—	—	—	—	—	—	—	—	—	—	753	—	—
1954	—	—	—	—	—	—	—	—	—	—	—	—	—	—	—	768	—	—
1953[1]	—	—	—	—	—	—	—	—	—	—	—	—	—	—	—	614	—	—
1952	—	—	—	—	—	—	—	—	—	—	—	—	—	—	—	—	—	—
1951	—	—	—	—	—	—	—	—	—	—	—	—	—	—	—	—	—	—
1950	—	—	—	—	—	—	—	—	—	—	—	—	—	—	—	—	—	—
1949	—	—	—	—	—	—	—	—	—	—	—	—	—	—	—	—	—	—
1948	—	—	—	—	—	—	—	—	—	—	—	—	—	—	—	280	—	—
1947	—	—	—	—	—	—	—	—	—	—	—	—	—	—	—	113	—	—

[1] Introduction of Newfoundland into national statistics.

² Total available in some cases, but no breakdown between public, private and federal.

Series B432-455. Total number of graduate nurses[1] (full- and part-time) in reporting hospitals, Canada, 1932 to 1975

Year	Public						Private					
	All hospitals	Total general and allied special	General, including paediatric	Allied special	Mental	Tuber-culosis	All hospitals	Total general and allied special	General	Allied special	Mental	Tuber-culosis
	432	433	434	435	436	437	438	439	440	441	442	443
1975	–	92,446	86,371	6,075	–	66	–	993	227	766	–	–
1974	–	87,897	82,275	5,622	–	102	–	973	180	793	–	–
1973	–	83,038	77,449	5,589	–	190	–	1,026	250	776	–	–
1972	–	79,511	74,179	5,332	–	244	–	1,025	257	768	–	–
1971	–	75,849	70,747	5,102	–	407	–	1,062	317	745	–	–
1970	–	75,018	67,198	7,820	–	507	–	1,162	457	705	–	–
1969	–	69,490	64,762	4,728	–	590	–	1,106	475	631	–	–
1968	–	67,349	62,804	4,545	–	660	–	1,348	731	617	–	–
1967	–	62,983	58,670	4,314	–	666	–	1,517	854	663	–	–
1966	–	58,036	53,726	4,310	–	635	–	1,288	813	475	–	–
1965	–	53,240	49,811	3,429	–	702	–	1,340	933	407	–	–
1964	–	49,415	46,433	2,982	–	–	–	1,230	880	350	–	–
1963	–	44,982	42,402	2,584	–	–	–	1,172	896	276	–	–
1962	–	41,204	39,350	1,854	–	–	–	–	–	–	–	–
1961	–	37,929	36,157	1,772	–	–	–	834	542	292	–	–
1960	–	36,856	35,254	1,602	–	–	–	775	–	–	–	–
1959	–	34,096	32,558	1,538	–	–	–	1,079	–	–	–	–
1958	–	30,061	28,884	1,177	–	–	–	881	–	–	–	–
1957	–	27,585	26,562	1,023	–	–	–	916	–	–	–	–
1956	–	25,204	–	–	–	1,221	–	793	–	–	–	–
1955	–	23,674	–	–	–	1,248	–	665	–	–	–	–
1954	–	21,472	–	–	–	1,280	–	620	–	–	–	–
1953[2]	–	19,471	–	–	–	1,348	–	468	–	–	–	–
1952	–	17,299	–	–	–	1,280	–	583	–	–	–	–
1951	–	16,143	15,115	1,028	–	1,151	–	682	–	–	–	–
1950	–	14,923	14,137	786	–	1,111	–	735	–	–	–	–
1949	–	13,585	12,673	912	–	976	–	658	–	–	–	–
1948	–	12,220	11,456	764	–	921	–	649	–	–	–	–
1947	–	11,488	10,796	692	–	914	–	630	–	–	–	–
1946	–	10,386	9,682	704	–	820	–	573	–	–	–	1
1945	–	9,202	8,536	666	–	770	–	554	–	–	–	1
1944	–	8,923	8,266	657	–	760	–	627	–	–	–	1
1943	–	8,679	7,952	727	–	792	–	614	–	–	–	6
1942	–	8,142	7,427	715	–	828	–	584	–	–	–	6
1941	–	7,835	7,227	608	–	860	–	591	–	–	–	6
1940	–	7,486	6,612	874	–	851	–	–	–	–	–	6
1939	–	7,263	6,562	701	–	861	–	511	–	–	–	7
1938	–	7,205	6,436	769	–	–	–	459	–	–	–	–
1937	–	6,742	5,946	796	–	–	–	485	–	–	–	–
1936	–	6,442	5,761	681	–	662	–	457	–	–	–	–
1935	–	5,893	5,248	645	–	610	–	454	–	–	–	–
1934	–	5,368	4,766	602	–	564	–	426	–	–	–	–
1933	–	4,580	4,112	468	–	517	–	365	–	–	–	–
1932	–	4,231	3,900	331	–	484	–	289	222	67	–	5

Series B432-455. Total number of graduate nurses[1] (full- and part-time) in reporting hospitals, Canada, 1932 to 1975 (concluded)

Year	Federal						Total					
	All hospitals	Total general and allied special	General	Allied special	Mental	Tuber-culosis	All hospitals	Total general and allied special	General, including paediatric	Allied special	Mental	Tuber-culosis
	444	445	446	447	448	449	450	451	452	453	454	455
1975	1,643	1,643	1,408	235	–	–	–	95,082	88,006	7,076	7,751	–
1974	1,563	1,563	1,355	208	–	–	–	90,433	83,810	6,623	7,635	–
1973	1,897	1,897	1,701	196	–	–	–	85,961	79,400	6,561	7,994	–
1972	1,968	1,968	1,769	199	–	–	–	82,504	76,205	6,299	7,540	–
1971	2,019	2,019	1,822	197	–	–	–	78,930	72,886	6,044	7,766	–
1970	1,958	1,958	1,765	193	–	–	–	78,138	69,420	8,718	7,549	–
1969	1,914	1,914	1,727	187	–	–	–	72,510	66,964	5,546	7,037	–
1968	–	2,050	1,793	257	–	–	–	70,747	65,328	5,419	6,000	–
1967	–	2,282	2,039	243	–	–	–	66,782	61,563	5,220	5,859	–
1966	–	2,119	1,890	229	–	–	–	61,443	56,429	5,014	5,294	–
1965	–	2,389	2,169	220	–	–	–	56,969	52,913	4,056	4,897	–
1964	–	2,336	2,130	206	–	–	–	52,981	49,343	3,538	4,563	–
1963	–	2,241	2,041	200	–	–	53,914	48,395	45,339	3,060	4,345	1,174
1962	–	1,458	1,326	132	–	–	–	–	–	–	3,902	1,206
1961	–	1,985	1,801	184	–	–	45,908	40,748	38,500	2,248	4,001	1,159
1960	–	2,092	2,067	25	–	–	44,872	39,723	–	–	3,945	1,204
1959	–	1,886	1,863	23	–	–	41,961	37,061	–	–	3,790	1,110
1958	–	2,162	–	–	–	–	36,934	32,223	–	–	3,513	1,198
1957	–	2,180	–	–	–	–	35,214	30,681	–	–	3,280	1,252
1956	–	2,002	–	–	–	112	32,394	27,999	–	–	3,062	1,333
1955	–	2,030	–	–	–	106	30,419	26,369	–	–	2,696	1,354
1954	–	1,965	–	–	–	188	28,253	24,057	–	–	2,728	1,468
1953[2]	–	1,933	–	–	–	200	25,830	21,872	–	–	2,410	1,548
1952	–	1,754	–	–	–	176	23,569	19,636	–	–	2,477	1,456
1951	–	1,986	–	–	–	–	–	18,811	–	–	2,492	–
1950	–	1,834	–	–	–	–	–	17,492	–	–	1,957	–
1949	–	1,873	–	–	–	–	–	16,116	–	–	1,429	–
1948	–	1,528	–	–	–	–	–	14,397	–	–	1,268	–
1947	–	–	–	–	–	–	–	–	–	–	1,131	–
1946	–	–	–	–	–	–	–	–	–	–	855	–
1945	–	–	–	–	–	–	–	–	–	–	886	–
1944	–	–	–	–	–	–	–	–	–	–	935	–
1943	–	–	–	–	–	–	–	–	–	–	969	–
1942	–	–	–	–	–	–	–	–	–	–	985	–
1941	–	–	–	–	–	–	–	–	–	–	1,135	–
1940	–	–	–	–	–	–	–	–	–	–	1,147	–
1939	–	–	–	–	–	–	–	–	–	–	1,140	–
1938	–	–	–	–	–	–	–	–	–	–	1,128	–
1937	–	–	–	–	–	–	–	–	–	–	1,091	–
1936	–	–	–	–	–	–	–	–	–	–	1,032	–
1935	–	170	–	–	–	–	–	6,517	–	–	838	–
1934	–	170	–	–	–	–	–	5,964	–	–	938	–
1933	–	184	–	–	–	–	–	5,129	–	–	772	–
1932	–	201	–	–	–	–	–	4,721	–	–	598	–

[1] Includes psychiatric, registered and non-registered nurses.

[2] Introduction of Newfoundland into national statistics.

Series B456-460. Reporting public hospitals, operating expenditure per patient-day, Canada, 1942 to 1975[1]

Year	Total general and allied special	General	Allied special	Mental	Tuberculosis
	456	**457**	**458**	**459**	**460**
1975	109.98	121.82	54.84	46.59	79.70
1974	92.45	101.20	47.26	38.61	65.34
1973	77.09	84.09	41.02	31.57	48.07
1972	68.52	75.31	37.35	27.52	44.95
1971	61.58	66.61	33.36	22.49[2]	41.56
1970	56.24	60.72	31.90	19.93[2]	35.85
1969	50.69	54.30	28.53	16.67[2]	30.77
1968	45.01	48.44	25.73	14.34[2]	27.19
1967	40.38	43.40	23.16	12.23[2]	23.41
1966	36.06	38.56	21.19	9.92	21.76
1965	31.92	34.05	18.70	8.33	18.72
1964	29.18	31.00	17.26	7.10	16.67
1963	26.87	28.58	15.77	6.69	15.64
1962	24.82	26.36	13.68	6.01	14.02
1961	23.10	24.34	13.00	5.37	12.77
1960	21.32	22.75	10.96	4.94	10.76
1959	18.88	20.45	8.56	5.31	10.23
1958	17.84	19.05	8.95	4.08	9.57
1957	16.11	17.36	7.37	3.70	8.84
1956	14.91	15.95	6.81	3.34	7.90
1955	14.05	15.21	6.30	2.97	7.42
1954	12.85	13.78	6.62	2.92	—
1953[3]	11.95	12.79	5.96	2.70	—
1952	13.09	11.67	—	2.53	—
1951	9.60	9.05	6.40	2.40	—
1950	8.54	8.13	7.03	2.23	—
1949	7.85	8.00	6.51	1.94	—
1948	7.04	7.20	5.48	1.77	—
1947	6.14	6.28	4.82	1.45	—
1946	5.16	5.27	4.10	1.20	—
1945	4.73	4.81	3.74	1.05	—
1944	4.50	—	—	1.01	—
1943	4.08	—	—	.96	—
1942	4.06	—	—	.92	—

[1] Figures published in the form of a historical series in "Hospital Statistics", 1975 and 1958, published by Statistics Canada.
[2] Excludes Newfoundland from 1967 to 1971.
[3] Introduction of Newfoundland into national statistics.

Series B461–475. Operating expenditures of reporting public hospitals, by salary and non-salary expenditures, Canada, 1943 to 1975
(thousands of dollars)

Year	Total operating expense					Salary					Non-salary				
	Total general and allied special	General including paediatric	Allied special	Mental	Tuberculosis	Total general and allied special	General including paediatric	Allied special	Mental	Tuberculosis	Total general and allied special	General including paediatric	Allied special	Mental	Tuberculosis
	461	462	463	464	465	466	467	468	469	470	471	472	473	474	475
1975	4,712,385	4,296,933	415,452	681,899	8,265	3,306,929	3,011,789	295,140	524,950	6,100	1,405,456	1,285,144	120,312	156,949	2,165
1974	3,860,724	3,540,335	320,389	593,098	7,410	2,703,430	2,473,341	230,089	453,336	5,525	1,157,295	1,066,995	90,300	139,762	1,885
1973	3,121,287	2,853,972	267,315	523,855	10,545[1]	2,175,796	1,982,172	193,724	410,041	7,740[1]	945,491	871,901	73,591	117,182	2,805[1]
1972	2,779,371	2,537,646	241,724	470,250	13,455	1,946,682	1,770,656	176,025	363,607	10,049	832,689	766,990	65,699	109,359	3,406
1971	2,509,232	2,292,804	216,427	435,643[2]	20,854	1,764,014	1,606,594	157,420	335,855	15,530	745,218	686,211	59,007	102,154	5,324
1970	2,244,333	2,047,676	196,657	400,730[2]	24,493	1,584,555	1,440,475	144,079	307,622	18,449	659,778	607,200	52,578	95,347	6,044
1969	1,961,026	1,790,378	170,647	352,168[2]	26,908	1,378,887	1,255,604	123,282	267,131	19,665	582,139	534,774	47,365	87,243	7,242
1968	1,718,990	1,573,595	145,395	309,402[2]	27,514	1,150,711	1,048,687	102,024	232,482	18,953	568,279	524,908	43,371	78,957	8,560
1967	1,475,438	1,348,443	126,995	274,942	26,916	984,378	895,601	88,778	200,369	18,320	491,060	452,843	38,217	76,529	8,595
1966	1,275,200	1,167,521	107,679	241,199	26,230	836,060	762,681	73,380	171,935	17,426	439,140	404,841	34,299	72,238	8,803
1965	1,107,348	1,016,743	90,606	201,881[3]	26,307	720,529	658,601	61,928	141,129	17,398	386,819	358,141	28,678	63,760	8,908
1964	983,568	906,346	77,223	177,363	26,477	634,359	582,405	51,954	122,078	17,424	349,209	323,941	25,269	55,558	9,054
1963	872,250	804,239	68,012	159,726	30,661	556,363	511,534	44,829	106,846	20,027	315,888	292,704	23,183	52,880	10,634
1962	769,164	717,537	51,626	141,645	33,115	502,528	468,216	34,312	94,099	21,961	266,636	249,321	17,315	47,546	11,154
1961	677,551	635,226	42,324	132,206[4]	30,034	438,292	410,739	27,553	86,352[4]	19,052	239,258	224,487	14,771	45,854[4]	10,942
1960	592,842	555,814	37,029	116,585	31,900	376,897	353,129	23,768	76,498	20,504	215,945	202,684	13,260	41,274	12,384
1959	509,846	477,736	32,110	89,923	29,607	316,606	296,642	19,964	59,820	18,685	193,239	181,094	12,146	30,848	12,010
1958	444,161	416,026	28,134	96,327[5]	30,410	281,787	264,468	17,319	61,560	19,049	162,374	151,559	10,815	36,149[5]	12,506
1957	393,401	369,947	23,454	85,302[6]	32,190	245,123	230,788	14,335	53,735[6]	19,950	148,278	139,159	9,120	32,852[6]	13,400
1956	347,356	326,745	20,611	76,942	32,003	213,280	200,945	12,335	47,494	19,800	134,076	125,800	8,276	31,367	13,695
1955	309,722	290,394	19,328	68,048	31,133	190,468	178,721	11,747	42,172	18,875	119,254	111,673	7,581	27,720	13,770
1954	273,604	255,349	18,256	64,087	31,180	167,768	156,835	10,933	38,617	17,152	105,836	98,513	7,323	26,854	14,028
1953[7]	235,513	221,085	14,427	57,229[8]	32,204[4]	141,799	133,348	8,452	34,459	17,119	93,713	87,738	5,975	23,935[8]	15,085
1952	204,041	191,721	12,321	59,925[9]	29,184	111,765	105,182	6,583	29,888	14,275	92,276	86,538	5,738	30,933	14,909
1951	196,203	182,332	13,872	57,078[10]	26,815	101,099	94,220	6,879	26,288[10]	12,245	95,105	88,112	6,992	31,585[10]	14,570
1950	162,714	155,252	7,462	48,453	22,893	82,646	79,025	3,621	22,614	10,639	80,068	76,227	3,841	26,530	12,254
1949	146,867	138,636	8,231	39,413	19,166	72,975	69,060	3,915	20,460	9,191	73,892	69,576	4,316	19,722	9,975
1948	125,005	119,187	5,818	34,879	17,043	60,219	57,728	2,491	17,876	7,999	64,786	61,459	3,327	17,936	9,044
1947	106,792	101,390	5,402	27,757	14,223	51,167	48,847	2,320	14,859	6,706	55,759	52,543	3,216	13,844	7,517
1946	84,503	79,816	4,687	27,316	11,483	39,904	37,805	2,098	14,359	5,311	44,599	42,011	2,589	12,957	6,172
1945	74,059	70,189	3,870	22,951	10,189	34,539	32,753	1,786	11,238	4,697	39,520	37,436	2,084	11,713	5,396
1944	68,940	64,680	4,260	21,878	—	31,114	29,203	1,911	9,922	—	37,826	35,477	2,348	11,956	—
1943	59,403	—	—	19,199	—	25,963	—	—	8,929	—	33,440	—	—	10,208	—

1 Excludes Newfoundland, New Brunswick, Ontario, Manitoba and Alberta.
2 Estimations for British Columbia.
3 Does not include depreciation.
4 Estimations for Quebec.
5 Salaries increased by 15% on the average.
6 Excludes Quebec.
7 Introduction of Newfoundland into National Statistics.
8 Decrease from 1952 partially due to large non-maintenance expenditure in Ontario in 1952 for which there is not a comparable expenditure in 1953.
9 Depreciation not specifically mentioned.
10 Newfoundland included.

Series B476-499. Operating expenditures of public general and allied special hospitals by selected services, Canada, 1943 to 1975

(thousands of dollars)

Year	Total[1]			Nursing services			Special services[2]			Laboratory		
	Total general and allied special	General, including paediatric	Allied special	Total general and allied special	General, including paediatric	Allied special	Total general and allied special	General, including paediatric	Allied special	Total general and allied special	General, including paediatric	Allied special
	476	477	478	479	480	481	482	483	484	485	486	487
1975	4,712,385	4,296,933	415,452	1,574,871	1,429,215	145,656	318,405	280,787	37,618	304,717	296,001	8,717
1974	3,860,724	3,540,335	320,389	1,259,744	1,145,910	113,835	269,213	240,254	28,959	250,590	243,653	6,937
1973	3,121,287	2,853,972	267,315	1,047,044	946,284	100,760	201,603	177,610	23,994	206,846	200,570	6,276
1972	2,779,371	2,537,646	241,724	930,433	840,863	89,570	161,572	139,750	21,822	180,312	174,784	5,528
1971	2,509,732	2,292,804	216,427	858,061	775,223	82,837	138,914	119,629	19,285	164,032	158,880	5,153
1970	2,224,433	2,047,676	196,657	762,723	687,266	75,458	120,331	102,804	17,526	140,658	136,199	4,459
1969	1,961,026	1,790,378	170,647	661,962	596,910	65,052	99,392	84,760	14,632	119,565	115,822	3,742
1968	1,718,990	1,573,595	145,395	584,320	528,152	56,169	69,006	57,565	11,441	112,969	109,928	3,041
1967	1,475,438	1,348,443	126,995	487,654	440,782	46,873	56,574	46,774	9,800	91,492	89,154	2,338
1966	1,275,200	1,167,521	107,679	411,761	373,218	38,543	46,509	38,265	8,244	74,110	72,202	1,907
1965	1,107,348	1,016,743	90,606	353,382	320,915	32,467	38,226	32,208	6,019	62,945	61,424	1,521
1964	983,568	906,346	77,223	309,902	282,848	27,054	31,620	26,635	4,985	52,512	51,101	1,411
1963	872,250	804,239	68,012	268,665	246,446	22,219	27,662	23,122	4,540	44,136	43,002	1,134
1962	711,079	661,357	49,722	233,675[4]	216,316[4]	17,360[4]	21,571[4]	18,411[4]	3,160[4]	37,772	36,937	835
1961	677,551	635,226	42,324	205,293	191,442	13,851	16,691	14,124	2,567	32,093	31,403	690
1960	545,083	503,947	41,136	177,421	165,158	12,263	12,095[5]	9,840[5]	2,255[5]	26,560	26,011	548
1959	509,846	477,736	32,110	149,817	139,741	10,076	13,774[5]	12,415[5]	1,359[5]	20,996	20,584	412
1958	444,161	416,026	28,134	123,419[6]	116,171[6]	7,247[6]	12,670	11,716	954	17,296	16,971	326
1957	393,401	369,947	23,454	105,282[6]	99,325[6]	5,956[6]	9,710	9,032	679	14,390	14,190	200
1956	347,356	326,745	20,611	91,545[6]	86,921[6]	4,624[6]	8,493	7,948	545	12,016	11,848	168
1955	309,722	290,394	19,328	78,791[6]	71,620[6]	7,171[6]	6,904	6,444	461	10,005	9,803	202
1954	273,604	255,349	18,256	62,910[6]	58,288[6]	4,622[6]	5,328	4,269	1,059	7,845	7,610	235
1953[8]	235,513	221,085	14,427	46,623[6]	43,672[6]	2,950[6]	4,792	3,169	1,623	6,109	5,996	112
1952	204,041	191,721	12,321	–	–	–	–	–	–	–	–	–
1951	196,203	182,332	13,872	–	–	–	–	–	–	–	–	–
1950	162,714	155,252	7,462	–	–	–	–	–	–	–	–	–
1949	146,867	138,636	8,231	–	–	–	–	–	–	–	–	–
1948	125,005	119,187	5,818	–	–	–	–	–	–	–	–	–
1947	106,792	101,390	5,402	–	–	–	–	–	–	–	–	–
1946[9]	84,503	79,816	4,687	–	–	–	–	–	–	–	–	–
1945[9]	74,059	70,189	3,870	–	–	–	–	–	–	–	–	–
1944[9]	68,940	64,680	4,260	–	–	–	–	–	–	–	–	–
1943[10]	59,403	–	–	–	–	–	–	–	–	–	–	–

Series B476-499. Operating expenditures of public general and allied special hospitals by selected services, Canada, 1943 to 1975 (concluded)

(thousands of dollars)

Year	Radiology			Administrative and supportive			Education			Other[3]		
	Total general and allied special	General, including paediatric	Allied special	Total general and allied special	General, including paediatric	Allied special	Total general and allied special	General, including paediatric	Allied special	Total general and allied special	General, including paediatric	Allied special
	488	489	490	491	492	493	494	495	496	497	498	499
1975	188,186	179,072	9,113	1,840,632	1,652,818	187,813	144,219	140,838	3,381	—	—	—
1974	159,801	152,912	6,889	1,506,353	1,364,323	141,980	118,988	116,601	2,387	—	—	—
1973	137,694	131,917	5,777	1,222,875	1,103,766	119,109	119,456	117,261	2,194	—	—	—
1972	124,715	119,165	5,550	1,059,046	954,845	104,202	120,856	118,575	2,282	—	—	—
1971	118,906	114,021	4,886	959,940	865,402	94,538	118,343	115,890	2,452	—	—	—
1970	104,611	100,354	4,257	862,468	777,312	85,156	116,116	113,336	2,779	—	—	—
1969	92,050	88,335	3,715	762,586	687,936	74,650	102,969	100,545	2,425	—	—	—
1968	84,383	80,905	3,478	677,937	569,336	108,601	86,031	84,001	2,030	—	—	—
1967	69,182	66,813	2,369	597,426	539,650	57,776	76,006	74,057	1,949	—	—	—
1966	58,202	56,430	1,772	523,807	472,602	51,205	64,091	62,574	1,516	—	—	—
1965	50,484	48,928	1,556	471,614	427,807	43,807	54,020	52,577	1,443	—	—	—
1964	44,349	43,012	1,337	427,263	388,920	38,343	49,537	48,307	1,230	—	—	—
1963	38,868	37,820	1,048	388,250	357,913	30,337	43,678	42,340	1,339	—	—	—
1962	34,146	33,195	951	348,347	321,547	26,800	35,568	34,952	617	—	—	—
1961	29,880	29,122	758	313,767	290,578	23,189	31,693	31,211	483	—	—	—
1960	27,185	26,486	699	277,006	251,982	25,024	24,816	24,469	347	—	—	—
1959	21,622	21,130	492	244,429	226,176	18,352	18,198	17,999	199	—	—	—
1958	18,852	18,533	319	218,681	202,494	16,187	10,524[7]	10,475[7]	48[7]	20,723	17,669	3,054
1957	16,206	16,083	124	196,667	183,171	13,496	8,806[7]	8,701[7]	104[7]	23,818	20,748	3,070
1956	14,358	14,252	106	176,951	165,085	11,866	7,116[7]	7,083[7]	33[7]	21,302	18,116	3,187
1955	12,039	11,930	109	157,468	146,285	11,183	6,321[7]	6,257[7]	64[7]	25,789	21,931	3,858
1954	10,029	9,897	132	135,702	124,950	10,753	5,153[7]	5,050[7]	102[7]	35,305	29,173	6,132
1953[8]	8,529	8,453	76	117,189	108,995	8,193	4,297[7]	4,251[7]	46[7]	34,617	32,177	2,441
1952	—	—	—	—	—	—	—	—	—	—	—	—
1951	—	—	—	—	—	—	—	—	—	—	—	—
1950	—	—	—	—	—	—	—	—	—	—	—	—
1949	—	—	—	—	—	—	—	—	—	—	—	—
1948	—	—	—	—	—	—	—	—	—	—	—	—
1947	—	—	—	—	—	—	—	—	—	—	—	—
1946	—	—	—	—	—	—	—	—	—	—	—	—
1945	—	—	—	—	—	—	—	—	—	—	—	—
1944	—	—	—	—	—	—	—	—	—	—	—	—
1943	—	—	—	—	—	—	—	—	—	—	—	—

[1] In all years, expenses for drug, medical and surgical supplies are included in the 'Total' figures only.
[2] Excluding laboratory and radiology.
[3] Other consists of undistributed gross salaries and wages.
[4] Figures here consist of gross salaries and wages only.
[5] Includes, during these two years, 'Other supplemental services', which in later years is included in education.
[6] Does not contain nursing administration. This figure is combined with 'General Administration' and is included in 'Administration and Support'.

[7] These figures consist of 'School of Nursing' only. In 1959 the other two categories of education were introduced. (See definitions)
[8] Introduction of Newfoundland into national statistics.
[9] Available for 'Acute Disease Hospitals' which now include Public General and Allied Special hospitals.
[10] Available for 'Acute Disease Hospitals' which include Tuberculosis Hospitals, Mental Institutions as well as Public General and Allied Special Hospitals.

Series B500-503. Operating revenue of reporting mental institutions by source, Canada, 1933 to 1975
(dollars)

Year	Government	Patient revenue[1]	Other[1]	Total	Year	Government	Patient revenue[1]	Other[1]	Total
	500	**501**	**502**	**503**		**500**	**501**	**502**	**503**
1975	656,286,000	9,160,000	15,726,000	681,172,000	1950	41,253,952	4,516,725	2,353,797	48,124,474
1974	570,606,000	9,862,000	12,408,000	592,876,000	1949[4]	32,589,945	4,646,384	2,139,978	39,376,307
1973[2]	505,324,000	8,656,000	10,505,000	524,485,000	1948	28,766,403	4,203,697	2,089,087	35,059,187
1972[2]	452,481,000	8,843,000	8,816,000	470,140,000	1947	22,591,216	3,380,693	1,642,476	27,614,385
1971[2]	419,108,000	10,422,000	7,684,000	437,214,000	1946	22,203,060	3,259,516	1,515,840	26,978,416
1970[2]	381,431,000	9,135,000	5,528,000	396,094,000	1945	18,414,131	3,017,471	1,201,965	22,633,567
1969[2]	328,958,000	9,536,000	5,376,000	343,870,000	1944	17,468,554	3,139,441	1,255,781	21,863,776
1968[2]	289,976,000	9,960,000	4,936,000	304,872,000	1943	15,476,261	2,625,219	1,113,956	19,215,436
1967[2]	258,109,000	9,711,000	4,972,000	272,792,000	1942	15,069,935	2,347,508	1,119,712	18,537,155
1966[2]	217,975,000	9,221,000	4,159,000	231,355,000	1941	16,031,626	2,064,222	988,302	19,084,150
1965[2]	187,209,000	8,434,000	3,949,000	199,592,000	1940	14,037,916	2,062,418	3,445,240	19,545,574
1964[2]	162,438,000	8,990,000	3,964,000	175,392,000	1939	13,138,352	1,986,521	1,498,895	16,623,768
1963[2]	145,179,000	6,353,000	4,254,000	155,786,000	1938	12,671,623	2,094,696	1,020,382	15,786,701
1962[2]	129,945,000	5,226,000	4,659,000	139,830,000	1937	10,934,608	2,225,054	891,866	14,051,528
1961[2]	123,324,000	4,701,000	2,278,000	130,303,000	1936	10,064,049	1,974,131	2,262,772	14,300,952
1960[2]	110,282,000	4,383,000	2,034,000	116,700,000	1935	8,346,897	1,418,700	1,175,200	10,940,797
1959[2,3]	81,007,000	3,807,000	5,831,000	90,645,000	1934	10,080,689	1,884,538	1,755,331	13,720,558
1958[2]	87,098,000	8,268,000	1,083,000	96,449,000	1933	8,069,032	2,394,263	931,790	11,395,085
1957[2]	76,013,000	8,072,000	1,650,000	85,735,000					
1956	67,186,000	8,875,000	1,784,000	77,845,000					
1955	57,697,466	9,108,957	1,217,182	68,023,605					
1954	52,035,029	9,374,214	1,575,005	62,984,248					
1953	46,867,524	9,021,163	1,814,405	57,703,092					
1952	50,857,972	7,205,951	1,919,123	59,983,046					
1951	47,976,192	5,286,288	2,657,842	55,920,322					

[1] Variations in data over the years could be explained by changes in definitions of "patient revenue" and "other revenue".
[2] Does not include private or federal institutions.

[3] Does not include Quebec.
[4] Introduction of Newfoundland into national statistics.

Series B504-513. Health expenditures, Canada, 1926 to 1975
(thousands of dollars)

Year	Hospitals	Physicians	Dentists	Subtotal	Perscribed drugs	Subtotal	Other drugs and appliances	Other personal health care	Other health expenses	Total
	504	505	506	507	508	509	510	511	512	513
1975	5,533,707	1,900,483	592,304	8,026,494	573,715	8,600,209	703,303	969,549	1,476,180	11,749,241
1974	4,579,041	1,647,025	482,115	6,708,181	498,026	7,206,207	611,232	791,280	1,303,569	9,912,288
1973	3,803,610	1,471,971	418,294	5,693,875	466,929	6,160,804	556,756	652,430	1,085,665	8,455,655
1972	3,384,801	1,375,127	350,141	5,110,069	421,074	5,531,143	499,986	564,878	969,584	7,565,591
1971	3,095,367	1,239,775	311,229	4,646,371	402,498	5,048,869	462,544	500,080	936,333	6,947,826
1970	2,775,391	1,031,555	264,820	4,071,766	368,663	4,440,429	410,715	424,090	805,791	6,081,025
1969	2,456,687	901,435	241,038	3,599,160	331,835	3,930,995	360,217	371,677	728,735	5,391,624
1968	2,179,906	788,089	212,157	3,180,152	297,288	3,477,440	327,547	330,789	678,406	4,814,182
1967	1,880,699	686,189	187,166	2,754,054	265,478	3,019,532	298,272	291,509	635,534	4,244,847
1966	1,637,647	605,200	176,402	2,419,249	231,954	2,651,203	265,831	260,987	592,835	3,770,856
1965	1,434,274	545,056	160,062	2,139,392	211,540	2,350,932	243,008	235,365	532,788	3,362,093
1964	1,273,380	495,657	147,824	1,916,861	178,584	2,095,445	218,180	218,393	485,214	3,017,232
1963	1,150,306	453,395	136,946	1,740,647	161,734	1,902,381	205,366	193,906	467,821	2,769,474
1962	1,031,749	406,075	121,491	1,559,315	144,431	1,703,746	191,429	181,826	456,184	2,533,185
1961	930,568	388,305	116,729	1,435,602	135,841	1,571,443	184,621	168,820	423,899	2,348,783
1960	834,932	355,014	109,644	1,299,590	132,602	1,432,192	177,828	159,834	385,222	2,155,076
1959	735,626	325,689	98,966	1,160,281	130,188	—	—	—	—	1,290,469
1958	640,608	301,337	90,505	1,032,450	112,439	—	—	—	—	1,144,889
1957	587,370	271,795	85,008	944,173	103,230	—	—	—	—	1,047,403
1956	541,455	240,100	81,500	863,055	71,849	—	—	—	—	934,904
1955	480,058	206,500	68,600	755,158	59,503	—	—	—	—	814,661
1954	446,824	188,600	66,400	701,824	52,108	—	—	—	—	753,932
1953	404,019	176,600	60,500	641,119	48,818	—	—	—	—	689,937
1952	356,500	168,000	56,000	580,500	46,200	—	—	—	—	626,700
1951	326,400	153,000	51,000	530,400	42,900	—	—	—	—	573,300
1950	283,300	135,000	46,500	464,800	37,800	—	—	—	—	502,600
1949	247,100	117,000	43,000	407,100	34,600	—	—	—	—	441,700
1948	215,000	101,400	40,000	356,400	32,400	—	—	—	—	388,800
1947	186,700	91,000	38,800	316,500	28,900	—	—	—	—	345,400
1946	150,700	86,700	36,300	273,700	26,800	—	—	—	—	300,500
1945	129,500	76,200	29,500	235,200	23,200	—	—	—	—	258,400
1944	115,300	66,000	25,500	206,800	—	—	—	—	—	—
1943	102,200	68,600	23,100	193,900	—	—	—	—	—	—
1942	93,100	68,900	21,200	183,200	—	—	—	—	—	—
1941	89,200	66,700	21,900	177,800	—	—	—	—	—	—
1940	89,700	62,800	19,000	171,500	—	—	—	—	—	—
1939	81,400	57,100	16,700	155,200	—	—	—	—	—	—
1938	76,000	54,800	15,100	145,900	—	—	—	—	—	—
1937	75,500	50,100	13,400	139,000	—	—	—	—	—	—
1936	68,100	44,500	13,200	125,800	—	—	—	—	—	—
1935	61,300	43,800	11,100	116,200	—	—	—	—	—	—
1934	55,300	36,700	11,400	103,400	—	—	—	—	—	—
1933	55,000	37,900	13,800	106,700	—	—	—	—	—	—
1932	58,000	45,900	19,100	123,000	—	—	—	—	—	—
1931	58,000	63,600	21,400	143,000	—	—	—	—	—	—
1930	57,000	71,100	23,300	151,400	—	—	—	—	—	—
1929	56,000	77,500	23,300	156,800	—	—	—	—	—	—
1928	54,000	74,100	22,300	150,400	—	—	—	—	—	—
1927	52,000	69,200	20,800	142,000	—	—	—	—	—	—
1926	17,600	64,600	19,500	101,700	—	—	—	—	—	—

Series B514-516. Estimated enrolment in non-profit[1] medical insurance plans, Canada, at 31 December, 1937 to 1975

(number of persons)

Year	Total	Comprehensive plans	Limited plans	Year	Total	Comprehensive plans	Limited plans
	514	**515**	**516**		**514**	**515**	**516**
1975	—	—	—	1955[3]	3,143,000	1,695,000	1,448,000
1974	—	—	—	1954	2,688,000	—	—
1973	—	—	—	1953	2,353,000	1,105,000	1,249,000
1972	—	—	—	1952	1,948,000	930,000	1,019,000
1971	—	—	—	1951	1,569,000	735,000	834,000
1970	1,142,000	1,132,000	10,000	1950	1,240,000	562,000	678,000
1969	1,982,000	1,910,000	72,000	1949	888,000	411,000	478,000
1968	8,281,000	5,603,000	2,678,000	1948	632,000	332,000	300,000
1967	8,962,000	6,802,000	2,160,000	1947	417,000	237,000	180,000
1966	8,883,000	6,630,000	2,253,000	1946	167,000	154,000	13,000
1965	7,809,000	6,541,000	1,268,000	1945	112,000	—	—
1964	7,389,000	6,506,000	883,000	1944	75,000	—	—
1963	6,682,000	5,303,000	1,379,000	1943	50,000	—	—
1962	6,023,000	5,555,000	468,000	1942	41,000	—	—
1961	5,684,000	5,370,000	314,000	1941	35,000	—	—
1960[2]	5,201,000	5,075,000	126,000	1940	25,000	—	—
1959	4,861,000	3,146,000	1,715,000	1939	13,000	—	—
1958	4,446,000	2,730,000	1,717,000	1938	4,000	—	—
1957	4,154,000	2,353,000	1,801,000	1937	1,000	—	—
1956	3,601,000	2,006,000	1,595,000				

[1] "Non-profit" plans include: (a) plans operated or sponsored by medical associations; (b) plans operated by Blue Cross-type agencies; and (c) independent plans, such as those sponsered or operated by co-operatives and labour unions.

[2] Beginning in 1960, the term "comprehensive" is defined as comprising surgical and medical benefits, and the term "limited" as comprising major medical (i.e., so-called catastrophic) coverage and/or extended benefits. Some duplication of coverage occurs in the "total" count.

[3] Includes Newfoundland beginning in 1955. The Yukon Territory and the Northwest Territories excluded throughout.

Series B517-525. Annual rates of notifiable diseases, Canada, 1926 to 1975
(per 100,000 population)

Year[1]	Chickenpox[2] 052[4]	Diphtheria 032[4]	Measles[3] 055[4]	Mumps[2] 072[4]	Pertussis (Whooping cough) 033[4]	Poliomyelitis (all types) 040-043[4]	Scarlet fever and streptococal sore throat 034[4]	Tuberculosis 010-019[4]	Typhoid and paratyphoid fever 001-002[4]
	517	518	519	520	521	522	523	524	525
1975	..	0.5	57.9	..	14.9	—[5]	94.9	13.5	0.8
1974	..	0.8	53.7	..	7.0	—[5]	90.3	14.9	0.8
1973	..	0.8	49.4	..	4.5	—[5]	71.8	16.1	0.7
1972	..	0.3	14.4	..	5.9	—	56.0	17.9	0.7
1971	..	0.3	34.4	..	13.8	—	50.0	18.2	0.6
1970	..	0.2	135.8	..	9.8	—	48.8	18.3	0.3
1969[6]	..	0.2	64.2	..	5.9	—	53.0	21.1	0.6
1968	..	0.3	..	..	12.1	—	64.6	22.3	0.4
1967	..	0.2	..	..	24.3	—	98.3	22.5	0.6
1966	..	0.2	..	..	22.8	—	100.9	22.5	0.6
1965	..	0.3	..	..	12.6	—	69.2	24.5	0.8
1964	..	0.1	..	..	25.1	0.1	55.0	23.5	1.0
1963	..	0.4	..	..	32.4	0.6	52.4	30.1	0.8
1962	..	0.4	..	..	43.5	0.5	55.1	33.8	1.5
1961	..	0.5	..	..	30.0	1.0	71.6	32.7	1.5
1960	..	0.3	..	..	33.6	5.1	119.1	35.5	1.9
1959	..	0.2	..	..	41.5	10.8	133.9	37.6	3.1
1958	..	0.4	..	..	40.7	1.9	65.2	42.3	1.8
1957	—	0.9	—	—	45.0	1.6	52.5	46.2	1.7
1956	—	0.8	336.1	—	53.0	3.8	72.7	52.3	2.8
1955	214.5	0.9	363.3	173.5	87.3	6.5	59.7	58.6	2.4
1954	247.3	1.4	241.5	176.3	76.0	15.7	86.0	63.0	3.1
1953	320.2	0.9	390.5	244.9	63.3	59.8	107.8	65.7	3.1
1952	317.9	1.3	389.2	266.3	59.0	33.0	145.4	70.0	3.5
1951	333.5	1.8	438.3	251.6	63.6	18.2	110.4	77.8	4.0
1950[1]	260.1	3.1	406.6	319.0	89.0	6.8	71.9	87.0	5.2
1949	346.2	6.1	447.4	187.8	60.7	18.6	71.2	94.8	5.8
1948	326.3	7.0	515.7	192.2	55.3	9.1	63.5	93.9	4.4
1947	258.9	12.4	315.0	257.5	82.4	18.3	63.2	105.7	5.6
1946	237.3	20.7	550.4	212.4	62.5	20.6	80.5	119.1	7.5
1945	262.5	23.1	223.8	169.2	101.1	3.2	105.5	113.9	7.3
1944	297.6	27.0	463.7	166.1	103.8	6.1	181.1	125.3	10.4
1943	258.6	23.8	513.5	410.1	162.0	2.8	163.4	104.5	9.8
1942	265.7	25.4	225.6	449.8	158.0	5.9	185.2	100.6	9.8
1941	242.5	24.9	705.4	199.6	144.9	16.4	153.9	88.0	13.5
1940	288.3	20.5	403.5	118.8	174.9	1.7	128.0	86.6	13.8
1939	225.1	25.8	395.3	51.9	159.8	3.2	140.5	88.4	11.7
1938	242.3	33.0	236.4	75.4	143.7	5.2	154.9	81.0	16.5
1937	220.1	26.7	520.5	130.9	157.7	35.4	156.5	77.4	20.5
1936	232.6	18.6	509.6	272.1	148.7	8.9	198.5	79.2	16.7
1935	255.2	18.5	767.6	209.1	166.1	3.4	167.3	81.0	18.2
1934	218.7	21.1	271.4	78.9	181.6	4.8	154.0	76.3	21.7
1933	219.8	22.4	127.8	108.9	137.7	2.4	97.1	79.6	22.0
1932	170.5	37.3	510.7	118.3	114.9	9.1	93.8	84.2	23.6
1931	185.8	57.1	247.6	107.7	88.5	12.9	125.8	69.4	28.4
1930[1]	199.7	78.8	211.9	92.8	115.2	10.1	173.1	64.4	22.1
1929	180.7	90.6	424.3	121.4	106.1	7.7	161.5	57.6	19.0
1928	165.3	90.2	284.9	245.8	68.3	8.1	151.3	56.9	23.1
1927	143.5	89.1	295.2	—	70.2	6.4	162.5	55.4	85.1
1926	139.5	76.7	421.6	—	74.5	1.2	152.3	59.7	19.6

[1] Newfoundland is included since 1950 and Prince Edward Island since 1930.
[2] Not reportable since 1958.
[3] Not reportable for the years 1958 to 1968.
[4] Numbers refer to categories of the International Statistical Classification of Diseases, Injuries and Causes of Death (Seventh Revision).

[5] Less than 0.05 cases per 100,000 population.
[6] Seventh edition of the International Classification used until 1968; 8th edition used from 1969 on.

Series B526-543. Number of separations, days of stay and percentages, by chapter, in Canada, 1967 to 1975

Year		Total	Infective and parasitic diseases	Neoplasms	Endocrine, nutritional and metabolic diseases	Diseases of the blood and blood-forming organs	Mental disorders	Diseases of the nervous system and sense organs	Diseases of the circulatory system	Diseases of the respiratory system	Diseases of the digestive system	Diseases of the genito-urinary system	Complications of pregnancy, childbirth, puerperium	Diseases of skin and subcutaneous tissue	Diseases of the musculo-skeletal system and connective tissue	Congenital anomalies	Symptoms and ill-defined conditions	Accidents, poisonings and violence (nature)	Supplementary classifications
		526	527	528	529	530	531	532	533	534	535	536	537	538	539	540	541	542	543
1975	Separations	3,677,274	103,619	220,616	71,850	24,833	150,498	157,521	379,311	442,840	421,261	342,831	503,960	60,776	162,936	42,807	154,213	345,100	92,302
	Days of stay	40,924,511	895,976	3,547,653	1,187,648	279,656	2,744,451	2,714,380	8,829,057	3,158,413	3,802,297	2,415,835	2,620,946	547,424	2,277,231	455,377	1,039,100	3,681,198	727,869
	% of separations	100.0	2.8	6.0	2.0	0.7	4.1	4.3	10.3	12.0	11.5	9.3	13.7	1.6	4.4	1.2	4.2	9.4	2.5
	% of days of stay	100.0	2.2	8.7	2.9	0.7	6.7	6.6	21.6	7.7	9.3	5.9	6.4	1.3	5.6	1.1	2.5	9.0	1.8
1974	Separations	3,714,932	109,705	217,703	72,620	25,457	152,070	155,536	377,599	465,330	433,921	349,811	496,633	62,561	162,111	42,659	148,675	348,359	94,182
	Days of stay	41,841,489	988,814	3,549,667	1,239,800	282,491	2,745,663	2,825,919	8,935,200	3,270,714	4,012,848	2,502,367	2,610,689	566,100	2,302,668	468,668	997,484	3,811,124	731,273
	% of separations	100.0	2.9	5.9	2.0	0.7	4.1	4.2	10.2	12.5	11.7	9.4	13.4	1.7	4.4	1.1	4.0	9.4	2.5
	% of days of stay	100.0	2.4	8.5	3.0	0.7	6.6	6.7	21.4	7.8	9.6	6.0	6.2	1.3	5.5	1.1	2.4	9.1	1.7
1973	Separations	3,693,552	109,290	208,912	73,899	26,400	148,566	155,060	365,357	470,106	447,856	350,154	490,342	64,099	159,730	43,310	139,597	347,512	93,362
	Days of stay	41,590,230	1,024,269	3,510,643	1,286,225	291,571	2,573,827	2,688,680	8,519,504	3,366,261	4,200,378	2,618,091	2,642,880	582,168	2,312,438	501,084	947,927	3,794,184	730,100
	% of separations	100.0	3.0	5.7	2.0	0.7	4.0	4.2	9.9	12.7	12.1	9.5	13.3	1.7	4.3	1.2	3.8	9.4	2.5
	% of days of stay	100.0	2.5	8.4	3.1	0.7	6.2	6.5	20.5	8.1	10.1	6.3	6.3	1.4	5.6	1.2	2.3	9.1	1.7
1972	Separations	3,634,706	103,625	205,792	71,816	26,933	138,313	150,391	357,075	496,376	446,240	343,711	492,108	61,522	151,930	41,077	127,024	340,271	80,502
	Days of stay	42,027,231	962,656	3,573,087	1,302,848	293,593	2,465,048	2,742,162	8,673,825	3,608,302	4,301,969	2,709,948	2,709,499	575,278	2,306,056	513,010	873,615	3,753,193	663,141
	% of separations	100.0	2.9	5.7	2.0	0.7	3.8	4.1	9.8	13.7	12.3	9.5	13.5	1.7	4.2	1.1	3.5	9.4	2.2
	% of days of stay	100.0	2.3	8.5	3.1	0.7	5.9	6.5	20.6	8.6	10.2	6.5	6.4	1.4	5.5	1.2	2.1	8.9	1.6
1971	Separations	3,568,887	106,704	196,164	71,527	28,042	131,231	147,733	344,994	503,424	434,614	336,218	505,788	63,475	143,897	40,512	117,000	328,559	69,005
	Days of stay	41,228,313	1,013,510	3,494,342	1,295,179	307,597	2,366,826	2,779,363	8,137,623	3,522,124	4,291,892	2,753,185	2,810,376	600,357	2,231,508	551,762	804,781	3,672,537	595,351
	% of separations	100.0	3.0	5.5	2.0	0.8	3.7	4.1	9.7	14.1	12.2	9.4	14.2	1.8	4.0	1.1	3.3	9.2	2.1
	% of days of stay	100.0	2.5	8.5	3.1	0.7	5.7	6.7	19.7	8.5	10.4	6.7	6.8	1.5	5.4	1.3	2.0	8.9	1.4
1970	Separations	3,449,323	109,150	188,588	70,013	28,293	124,606	138,568	324,210	517,401	412,655	328,768	504,101	64,690	133,209	36,622	99,224	318,221	51,004
	Days of stay	40,357,019	1,021,614	3,384,090	1,271,358	315,102	2,163,380	2,453,761	7,616,093	3,706,599	4,231,096	2,726,073	2,853,997	681,630	2,103,705	493,275	726,565	3,571,273	1,037,408
	% of separations	100.0	3.2	5.5	2.0	0.8	3.6	4.0	9.4	15.0	12.0	9.5	14.6	1.9	3.9	1.1	2.9	9.2	1.6
	% of days of stay	100.0	2.5	8.4	3.2	0.8	5.4	6.1	18.9	9.2	10.5	6.8	7.1	1.7	5.2	1.2	1.8	8.8	0.3
1969	Separations	3,308,647	95,389	179,678	69,137	27,866	112,837	131,497	314,163	513,564	398,523	308,266	490,452	64,741	124,132	37,318	94,712	309,732	36,640
	Days of stay	39,320,982	924,741	3,306,060	1,275,512	324,922	2,040,588	2,146,575	7,698,341	3,647,704	4,188,272	2,661,562	2,815,188	631,240	2,064,617	509,348	705,087	3,481,967	899,258
	% of separations	100.0	2.9	5.4	2.1	0.8	3.4	4.0	9.5	15.5	12.0	9.3	14.8	2.0	3.8	1.1	2.9	9.4	1.1
	% of days of stay	100.0	2.4	8.4	3.2	0.8	5.2	5.5	19.6	9.3	10.6	6.8	7.2	1.6	5.3	1.3	1.8	8.8	2.3
1968[1]	Separations	3,245,540	40,436	188,105	98,515	19,209	106,745	170,783	275,890	505,278	444,683	290,025	488,581	56,198	123,871	33,991	91,495	294,979	16,635
	Days of stay	37,289,823	571,315	3,216,740	1,528,364	274,270	1,947,631	3,822,164	5,358,414	3,339,221	4,519,147	2,544,666	2,832,547	559,621	2,108,396	483,244	674,036	3,263,513	245,839
	% of separations	100.0	1.2	5.8	3.0	0.6	3.3	5.3	8.5	15.6	13.7	8.9	15.0	1.7	3.8	1.0	2.8	9.1	1.0
	% of days of stay	100.0	1.5	8.6	4.1	0.7	5.2	10.2	14.4	9.0	12.1	6.8	7.6	1.5	5.7	1.3	1.8	8.8	1.1
1967[1]	Separations	3,180,209	44,444	186,461	94,052	18,221	98,611	163,972	270,213	486,429	438,312	278,100	496,956	57,620	116,268	32,732	85,545	287,875	19,006
	Days of stay	35,486,000	617,042	3,290,775	1,395,890	264,432	1,683,755	3,035,198	5,027,102	3,157,676	4,453,557	2,486,164	2,878,669	561,737	1,919,454	450,101	618,218	3,108,108	523,759
	% of separations	100.0	1.4	5.9	3.0	0.6	3.1	5.2	8.5	15.3	13.8	8.7	15.6	1.8	3.6	1.0	2.7	9.0	0.8
	% of days of stay	100.0	1.7	9.3	3.9	0.7	4.7	8.6	14.2	8.9	12.6	7.0	8.1	1.6	5.4	1.3	1.7	8.8	1.5

[1] ICDA 7th classification used for 1967 and 1968.

Section C: Social Security

T. Russell Robinson, *Health and Welfare Canada*

The statistics in this section are in six main divisions: federal income security programs (series C1-195); federal and provincial income insurance programs (series C196-286); cost-shared federal-provincial income security programs (series C287-442); federal and provincial social service programs (series C443-507); provincial-municipal income security programs (series C508-559); government expenditures on social security by broad program areas (series C560-599).

The conceptual framework for the above arrangement is described first, followed by a brief historical review of the development of various programs and concluding with detailed statistical source references.

The Conceptual Framework

The growth of government activity, particularly in the sphere of social policy, has come to be identified with the concept of the welfare state. It is important, therefore, to attempt to describe in some detail the changes in the size of social security (or social welfare) expenditures in Canada. The first step is to define what is meant by social security expenditures.[1] Unfortunately, there is no common definition and those advanced by different public or private agencies vary greatly in the scope of public expenditures which they include. There is, then, an element of arbitrariness in what shall be defined as expenditures on social security programs and activities. Even with a precise definition, it may not be possible to obtain data on all the expenditures which fall within the purview of the conceptual framework indicated by the definition.

For purposes of this section a broad concept of social security expenditures has been adopted. It has been defined as the sum of the publicly financed and publicly or privately administered[2] programs of three general types: income maintenance (which includes both income insurance and income security programs); social welfare services; and health care services (see Section B). The purposes of such programs and expenditures are: to maintain the income of individuals or families in the face of involuntary loss of earnings due to a wide variety of contingencies of life; to provide a variety of income assistance to those unable to earn an adequate income; to provide a variety of supportive and developmental personal services which may amount to income support in kind, or be ancillary to income transfers; and to finance and/or provide curative or preventive medical care.

Unlike the very broad definition offered in *Income Security and Social Services*, the present definition does not include "...urban redevelopment and the development of depressed regions and other programmes"[3], except where the expenditures on such activities are effectively a substitute for direct income maintenance programs and related services. The definition adopted, however, is similar to that utilized by the International Labour Organization and the International Social Security Association.

This definition does not include private (or voluntary) expenditures on social security. In fact, the term social security is sometimes taken to imply that such expenditures

and activities are collective in nature and involuntarily financed through the tax system or via earmarked contributions to public plans. Private expenditures (on individual pension plans or for drugs and other forms of health care not covered in public programs) do contribute to social security objectives, but they are largely individual in nature or involve much smaller groups[4] of contributors and beneficiaries than those programs operated by one or more of the various levels of government.

Income maintenance expenditures take the form of cash payments made by governments (or related agencies) directly to individuals or families, and may be grouped into two main categories, income insurance and income security. Income insurance programs are publicly administered and are financed largely from contributions required of employers and employees.[5] The current programs are designed to protect individuals and families against a loss of income due to involuntary unemployment (Unemployment Insurance), work-related accidents (Workmen's Compensation) and retirement (Canada and Quebec Pension Plans).[6] They are insurance programs in the sense that benefit levels are at least partially a function of the level of contributions and/or previous earnings. Also, the risks are widely shared among potential beneficiaries.

Income security expenditures are incorporated in a large number of cost-shared programs and also those programs financed and delivered by individual levels of government. Some take the form of payments to eligible persons which are unchanged with respect to income level or demonstrated need. The most important examples are family and youth allowances, and Old Age Security (OAS) pensions. Other income security expenditures depend upon the indicated need of the recipient as assessed by income, needs or means tests. The Canada Assistance Plan is by far the largest program of this type in which the federal and provincial governments share the cost of providing social assistance payments, as well as services, to persons in need.

The second major component of public social security expenditures, social welfare services, involves expenditures on programs which provide tangible and intangible services, or transfers in kind, rather than direct cash payments. Tangible services would include, for example, child welfare expenditures which go to provide the child with food, shelter, clothing, school supplies and other basic needs in lieu of a cash payment. Intangible services would include, for example, the counselling services of social workers, vocational rehabilitation programs and adoption services.

The third major component, health care services, includes programs providing hospital and medical care as well as public health clinics and other preventative health measures. Conceptually, public expenditures for the provision of health care services can be included in a comprehensive definition of social security expenditures. As already mentioned, this is in conformity with the practice of several international organizations. Data on health care services, other than total public expenditures given below, can be found in Section B.

In most cases, expenditures and caseload, beneficiary or

recipient data are provided on a provincial basis. With respect to federal-provincial cost-shared programs, the federal portion of expenditure figures given for Quebec is the amount of revenue received by the province of Quebec in lieu of direct contributions under the relevant cost-sharing arrangement.[7]

Historical Development

In the early days of settlement in Canada, it was common practice for settlers to receive assistance, in the form of land grants, basic food requirements, clothing and working equipment, from both public and private sources, within Canada and abroad, in order to establish themselves in their new homeland. Care for the sick and the needy was essentially a local responsibility. During periods characterized by large flows of immigration, many people were held at immigration centres because of sickness and contagious disease. Initial legislation to provide welfare aid by the provincial governments was directed toward support for families left destitute due to illness, death or desertion. The British North America Act indicated that welfare was primarily the responsibility of provincial and local governments except for the indigenous and immigrant populations for whom the federal government assumed primary responsibility.

One of the earliest forms of income security provided to workers and their families by provincial governments was financial aid as authorized under workmen's compensation legislation, and took the form of pensions and payments during periods of disability. Financing was based on contributions from employers. The earliest provincial workmen's compensation legislation was introduced in 1908 by Quebec and Ontario and was progressively implemented by all provinces. Provincial legislation to provide allowances to mothers in single parent families was initially introduced during World War I and was also extended to all provinces. In 1927, the federal government introduced legislation providing for old age pensions paid on a cost-shared basis by the provincial governments. Extensive legislation to cover services and basic financial support was also developed in all provinces in the field of child welfare.

Due to the major economic depression which Canada shared with other nations during the 1930s, the federal government was thrown into a major role as a provider of basic financial support to many families who were left destitute. These circumstances also made apparent the need for federal involvement in the development of income maintenance and welfare service programs across the nation.

In 1940, the federal government secured agreement of the provinces to amend the British North America Act to permit it to introduce a nationwide program of unemployment insurance, funded through employer and employee contributions. The program became fully operational in 1942. The federal government passed legislation in 1944 to introduce family allowances, for each child up to 16 years of age, funded from general revenue and in 1948, it introduced several federal grants under orders-in-council to support the development of provincial health services. In 1952, the federal government introduced old age security, a program of universal pensions paid by the federal government to all qualified residents 70 years of age and over. This program replaced former provincial cost-sharing of old age pension programs. Provincial old age assistance was also introduced in 1952 to provide financial support for people aged 65 to

69 on a cost-sharing basis with the federal government. Two years later, in 1954, legislation was passed to permit the federal government to finance allowances for totally disabled adults of working age on a cost-sharing basis with the provinces.

Unemployment assistance was introduced by the federal government in 1956. This provincially administered, cost-shared program provided for basic financial support for unemployed persons and their dependents and also for persons considered unemployable. Support of public health services was significantly extended through the introduction of a universal hospital insurance program proclaimed in 1959. By 1961, agreements had been signed between the federal government and all provincial governments. A schooling allowance for children 16 and 17 years of age was introduced by Quebec in 1961 and was extended to all other provinces by the federal Youth Allowances Act of 1964.

In 1966, the federal government introduced much new legislation to extend the role of government in the field of social security. The Canada and Quebec Pension Plans provided for contributory pensions for working persons aged 65 and over on retirement, based on their accumulated annual contributions. In addition, in the event of death prior to retirement, the plans provided for survivors' benefits to wives and orphan children and, in the event of disability that removed the worker from the labour force, a disability pension which likewise covered wives and dependent children. Complementary legislation, the Canada Assistance Plan, was passed to permit cost-sharing by the federal government of provincial programs of social assistance, social services and work activity and agreements were signed with each of the provinces over the subsequent two years. To maintain the income of elderly persons, including those who could not benefit from the Canada Pension Plan, the federal government also introduced a Guaranteed Income Supplement to the Old Age Security Program for pensioners with little or no other income.

The federal government, in 1968, introduced full-time manpower training allowances to workers needing additional skills to obtain employment, and direct income support to refugee immigrants unable to obtain immediate employment. In 1972, a new Unemployment Insurance Act was introduced with virtually universal coverage and substantially increased benefits which were extended to include coverage of maternity and sickness.

These pieces of legislation have been revised periodically to increase both contributions and benefits. Automatic indexation of income security benefits, to adjust for inflation has been provided for in recent federal legislation and regulations. The principle of supplementing the incomes of persons who are employed, but whose incomes are low in relation to their family responsibilities, has in some cases taken the form of adjustments to existing programs to permit the retention of part of their earnings without full corresponding loss of benefits. In other cases, new programs such as tax credits have been introduced in several provinces.

In 1974, the new federal Family Allowance Act was introduced in all provinces to provide for a significantly increased benefit per child but to be included in income subject to taxation. Special provincial adjustments to the federal Family Allowance Program have been developed by Quebec and Alberta, while both Quebec and Prince Edward Island have their own child allowances, which supplement the federal payments.

The extent and variety of changes in the social security

system in Canada since the early 1960s have made presentation of relevant historical statistics necessarily complex. Considerable care should be exercised in the use of such data.

Statistical Sources

The references for Social Security (series C1-599) are from two main sources: the published documents of the Government of Canada, the Gouvernement du Québec and several private sources; and the unpublished reports of the governments of Canada and Quebec. The sources are listed numerically and the source references for each table are shown by the pertinent numerical reference.

Published source documents

1. *Annual Report of the Department of Citizenship and Immigration*, Queen's Printer, Ottawa.

2. *Economic Review*, prepared by the Department of Finance, (Catalogue F1-21), Department of Supply and Services, Ottawa.

3. *Annual Report of the Department of Indian Affairs and Northern Development*, Department of Supply and Services, Ottawa.

4. *Labour Gazette*, published monthly by the Department of Labour.

5. *Annual Report of the Department of Manpower and Immigration*, (Catalogue MP-1), Department of Supply and Services, Ottawa.

6. *Annual Report of the Department of National Health and Welfare*, (Catalogue H1-3), Department of Supply and Services, Ottawa.

7. *Annual Report of the Administration of the Canada Pension Plan*, published by the Department of National Health and Welfare.

8. *Annual Report of the Administration of the Canada Assistance Plan*, published by the Department of National Health and Welfare.

9. *Chronology of Social Welfare and Related Legislation*, fiscal years 1908-1976, published by the Department of National Health and Welfare.

10. *Canada Year Book*, (Catalogue 11-202), Statistics Canada.

11. *Local Government Finance*, (Catalogue 68-203), Statistics Canada.

12. *System of National Accounts - National Income and Expenditure Accounts*, (Catalogue 13-201), Statistics Canada.

13. *Provincial Government Finance*, (Catalogue 68-206), Statistics Canada.

14. *Social Security, National Programs*, 1946-1975, (Catalogue 86-201), Statistics Canada.

15. *Statistical Report on the Operation of the Unemployment Insurance Act*, (Catalogue 73-001); and *Benefit Periods Established and Terminated Under the Unemployment Insurance Act*, (Catalogue 73-201), Statistics Canada.

16. *Estimates - Government of Canada*, Department of Supply and Services, (Catalogue BT-21).

17. *Public Accounts of Canada*, Department of Supply and Services, (Catalogue P51-1).

18. *Annuaire du Québec*, Bureau de la statistique du Québec, Québec.

19. *Rapport Statistique Annuelle, Régie des Rentes du Québec*, Bureau de la statistique du Québec, Québec.

20. *The National Finances*, Canadian Tax Foundation, Toronto.

21. *Financing Education, Health and Welfare*, Twenty-first colloquium, 1968, Canadian Tax Foundation, Toronto.

Unpublished source documents[8]

22. "Monthly Program Statistics, Income Maintenance Branch," Department of National Health and Welfare, 1946-1976.

23. "Annual Report of Family Allowances," prepared annually, 1946-1976, Department of National Health and Welfare.

24. "Report on the Administration of the Youth Allowances Act," prepared annually from 1964 to 1974, Department of National Health and Welfare.

25. Contributions to Quebec provided by the Department of Finance under the Federal-Provincial Fiscal Revision Act, 1964, and the Established Programs (Interim Arrangements Act) in lieu of cost-sharing arrangements. Information passed to National Health and Welfare annually by the Federal Department of Finance.

26. "Annual Report of Old Age Security," prepared annually since 1952, Department of National Health and Welfare.

27. Department of Manpower and Immigration, Manpower Training Allowances Rate Structure, special statistical tables made available to National Health and Welfare.

28. War Veterans Allowances Statistics, special statistical tabulations prepared by the Department of Veterans Affairs, 1977.

29. Veterans, Disability and Dependent Pensions Statistics, special statistics tabulations prepared by the Department of Veterans Affairs, 1977.

30. "Canada Pension Plan Statistical Bulletin," published quarterly, 1969-1976, Department of National Health and Welfare.

31. "Quebec Pension Board Statistical Bulletin," published quarterly, 1967-1976, Quebec.

32. Unemployment Insurance, Net Payments by Province, special tabulations prepared by province, 1941-1976, Statistics Canada, 1977.

33. Workmen's Compensation, Provincial and National Statistics, compiled annually by the Accident Compensation Division, Federal Department of Labour, 1915-1976.

34. "Canada's Health and Welfare", published 1955-1971, by the Research and Statistics Directorate, Department of National Health and Welfare.

35. "Annual Report on the Administration of Allowances for Blind Persons in Canada," published annually, 1952-1975, Department of National Health and Welfare.

36. "Annual Report on the Administration of Allowances for Disabled Persons in Canada," published annually, 1955-1975, Department of National Health and Welfare.

37. "Annual Financial Reports," 1927-1948, federal Department of Finance.

38. "Annual Report of the Vocational Rehabilitation of Disabled Persons," published annually by the Department of Labour, 1962-1966; the Department of Manpower and Immigration, 1967-1973; and the Department of National Health and Welfare, 1973-1976.

39. Provincial annual, quarterly and monthly reports of welfare, various titles, appropriate provincial governments.

40. "Historical Review of Financial Statistics of Governments in Canada," 1952-1962, Statistics Canada.

Notes to tables

This section provides a summary introduction to describe the programs represented in the accompanying tables. Because rate structures of benefits changed frequently, it has not been possible to incorporate tables of changes in rate structures. However, such tables are referred to in the sources, which are presented (by number) immediately following each set of table headings. The full table headings are not repeated since they are all for Canada and provinces, and contain information about beneficiaries and amounts received, in adjacent tables.

Federal Income Security Programs (Series C1-195)

C1-65. Family and youth allowances

SOURCE: 16, 17, 22, 23, 24, 25, 34.

The Family Allowance Act, proclaimed in 1945, provided for direct payments to families with established residence providing support of children under 16 years of age. In 1961, the Family Assistance Act extended coverage to children of first year immigrants and the Schooling Allowances Act of Quebec extended coverage to children 16 and 17 years of age attending school. Similar benefits were extended to this age group in 1964 by the federal government for all other provinces under the Youth Allowances Act. In 1973 the Family Allowance Act was revised to cover all resident children up to 18 years of age living at home and monthly benefits were increased to $20.00 per child as of 1 January 1974. Family assistance payments for Canada are found in series C562. For information on the historical rate structure see source 14, pp. 209-217.

C66-117. Old Age Security and Guaranteed Income Supplement

SOURCE: 16, 17, 23, 26, 34.

In 1952 the Old Age Security Act was introduced to replace the Old Age Pension Act, a cost-shared federal-provincial program. Old Age Security provided a basic monthly income of $40.00 to all persons 70 years of age and over who qualified on the basis of residence in Canada. In 1966 the program was modified to reduce the age of eligibility annually by one year down to the age of 65 in 1970. In 1966, provision was also made for adding an income-tested

Guaranteed Income Supplement (GIS) for all OAS beneficiaries with little or no taxable income. In October 1975 the Spouses Allowance Act was introduced; this program provides OAS/GIS level benefits to spouses aged 60 to 64 years who qualify on an income-tested basis. For information on the historical rate structure, see source 14, pp. 254-261.

C118-143. Manpower Training

SOURCE: 5, 12, 16, 17, 27.

In 1967, the federal government introduced the Canada Manpower Training Program. Manpower training allowances were intended to provide a basic income to unemployed persons during their period of institutional training to acquire skills to permit them to re-enter the labour force. For the historical rate structure of allowances, see source 27. The program also provides direct payments to firms providing on-the-job training in industry. Expenditures for Canada for the Canada Manpower Industrial Training Program are found in series C560-571.

Since 1957 the federal government has also provided financial aid to refugee immigrants during their initial period of adjustment to living in Canada. National expenditure figures are reported in series C567.

C144-156. Social Assistance Payments to Registered Indians

SOURCE: 10, 14 (pp. 695-698), 16, 17.

Since 1948, the federal government has undertaken to provide direct financial aid to registered or status Indians in need to maintain themselves. These payments are currently provided through the Department of Indian Affairs and Northern Development and are administered by Indian band councils, by officials of the Department of Indian Affairs and Northern Development and by provincial welfare departments.

C157-195. War Veterans Allowances and Veterans Disability Pensions

SOURCE: 16, 17, 28, 29.

After World War I, under the War Veterans Pension Act of 1919, the federal government undertook to provide pensions to persons previously in the armed services and who suffered from demonstrated residual disability resulting from any war-related activity. In 1930, the federal government introduced the program of War Veterans Allowances for veterans who were unable to maintain themselves on an independent basis. For information on the historical rate structure, see sources 9, 10, 34.

In all the above programs the value of benefits has been improved over time either through amendments to the legislation or more recently for the family allowances, old age security and guaranteed income supplement programs, through indexing of benefits in accordance with the Consumer Price Index. See sources 1, 3, 5, 6, 9, 10, 14, 34.

Federal and Provincial Income Insurance Programs (Series C196-286)

C196-247. Canada and Quebec Pension Plans

SOURCE: 7, 9, 10, 14, 16, 17, 18, 19, 30, 31, 34.

The Canada and Quebec Pension Plans were introduced in 1966 to provide income protection to contributors in accordance with years of contributions and level of contributory earnings. Benefits include retirement pensions after age 65, survivors and death benefits to families of contributors who die before age 65 and disability benefits to contributors who become unable to work because of disability. The programs have been funded by contributions of 1.8 per cent of earnings from employers and 1.8 per cent from employees, up to the level of maximum pensionable earnings. In order to obtain total payments under the Canada and Quebec Pension Plans it is necessary to add the figures in series C209-221 and C235-247. For historical rates of payments under these programs see source 14, pp. 149-156.

C248-273.   Unemployment Insurance

SOURCE: 9, 10, 14, 15, 16, 17, 20, 32, 34.

The Unemployment Insurance Act, through an amendment to the BNA Act, was proclaimed by the federal government in 1941. The act provided unemployment benefits to persons employed in industry but excluded certain groups such as teachers and the public service. In 1972, the revised act extended coverage to almost all employees in the labour force; benefits were extended to provide income protection against sickness and temporary disability, for maternity leave, for fishermen and for retiring employees during an initial period of retirement. The program is funded by contributions from employers and employees with supplementary contributions from federal general revenues to cover periods of continuing high unemployment on a regional basis. In order to obtain total payments under the Unemployment Insurance program it is necessary to add the figures in series C248-260 and C261-273. For information on the historical rate structure see source 14, pp. 98-106.

C274-286.   Workmen's Compensation

SOURCE: 4, 9, 13, 33, 34, 407.

Workmen's compensation programs, funded by contributions from employers, have operated under provincial legislation since World War I. The programs provide for medical benefits as well as disability benefits and pensions to injured workmen or their survivors. Included here are the income maintenance aspects, that is, cash payments to direct beneficiaries. The cost of services, or goods in kind, are not included here but are included under expenditures for health care services. For information on the historical rates structure, see sources 4, 9, 10.

Under all three programs above, coverage of benefits has been extended and benefits have increased through the years. In recent years, the Canada and Quebec Pension Plans have indexed benefits in accordance with increases in the Consumer Price Index, while all these plans have increased the maximum levels of earnings that are 'insured'. See sources 4, 7, 9, 10, 14, 34.

Federal-Provincial Cost-Shared Income Security Programs (Series C287-442)

C287-312.   Old Age Pensions

SOURCE: 6, 9, 10, 12, 13, 14, 17, 39, 40.

The Old Age Pension Act of 1927 represented the first

time that the federal and provincial governments undertook to share the costs of a national program of income security. In 1928 there was 50 per cent sharing in the monthly payment of a pension of $20.00 to needy persons, 70 years of age and over. In 1933, the federal share was increased to 75 per cent. Payments continued under the program until 1951 at which time the program was replaced by the Old Age Security program which is federally administered and financed. For information on the historical rate structure, see sources 6, 9, 10, 14 (pp. 290-293), 39.

C313-338.   Old Age Assistance

SOURCE: 6, 8, 9, 10, 13, 14, 16, 17, 18, 34, 39, 40.

In 1952 the Old Age Assistance Act was introduced. This program provided monthly payments to persons 65 to 69 years of age who were in need, and the benefits were cost-shared equally by the federal and provincial governments. The program was withdrawn in 1970 when eligibility for OAS was reduced to the age of 65. For information on the historical rate structure see source 14, pp. 290-293.

C339-364.   Blind Persons Allowances

SOURCE: 6, 8, 9, 10, 13, 14, 16, 17, 18, 25, 34, 35, 39, 40.

Cost-shared pensions for the blind were introduced under the Blind Pensions Act in 1937 with rates parallel to the old age pension. Payments under this program continued up until 1951 at which time the Blind Persons Allowances Act was introduced with higher rates of benefits, with an equal sharing of costs by the federal and provincial governments. For information on the historical rate structure, see source 14, pp. 295-297.

C365-390.   Disabled Persons Allowances

SOURCE: 6, 8, 9, 10, 13, 14, 16, 17, 18, 25, 34, 36, 40.

In 1954, the Disabled Persons Allowance Act was introduced, providing a monthly benefit of $65.00 to persons 18 to 64 years of age who were unable to work because of disability. This program was cost-shared equally by the federal and provincial governments. For information on the historical rate structure, see source 14, pp. 298-301.

C391-416.   Unemployment Assistance

SOURCE: 6, 8, 9, 10, 14, 16, 17, 18, 25, 34, 39, 40.

In 1955, the Unemployment Assistance Act was introduced, providing benefits to families and single individuals in need. The act was administered by the provinces with 50 per cent cost-sharing of payments by the federal government. While directed primarily to the employables, the Unemployment Assistance Program was empowered to provide financial assistance to unemployables cared for in public institutions and to provide supplementary assistance on the basis of need to persons under the three programs above, namely Old Age Assistance, Blind Persons Allowances and Disabled Persons Allowances. For information on the historical rate structure, see sources 6, 9, 10, 34, 39.

C417-442.   Canada Assistance Plan

SOURCE: 6, 9, 10, 12, 13, 14, 16, 17, 18, 25, 34, 39.

The integration of federal-provincial cost-sharing activities was undertaken in 1966 through the introduction of the Canada Assistance Plan. Under this legislation, financial assistance to families and individuals was calculated on the basis of need in essentially the same manner as for the Unemployment Assistance Program. The act also provided for cost-sharing the delivery of social services and work activity projects with the provinces. Cost-sharing continued on an equal basis as with unemployment assistance.

Since the introduction of the Canada Assistance Plan, it has been general policy of provincial governments to discontinue categorical programs (Old Age Assistance, Blind Persons Allowances and Disabled Persons Allowances) in favour of the general social assistance program under the Canada Assistance Plan. There has also been a similar phasing out of the financial assistance provided under the Unemployment Assistance Program. Social assistance rates are adjusted in various provinces, from time to time, either to compensate for inflation or to improve the benefit structure generally. Eligibility rules, benefit structures, and administrative aspects of programs often vary from province to province. For information on the historical rate structure, see sources 6, 8, 10, 14, 18, 34, 39.

Federal and Provincial Cost-Shared Social and Related Services Programs (Series C443-507)

C443-481. Canada Assistance Plan, Homes for Special Care, Child Welfare and Other Welfare

SOURCE: 8, 9, 12, 25.

Under the Canada Assistance Plan, the federal government shares with the provinces the cost of maintaining persons in institutions, such as homes for the aged, homes for unmarried mothers, youth hostels, etc. They also share in administering child welfare services such as protective services, adoption and child care, and provision of a wide range of social welfare services in the community, such as counselling, rehabilitation and work activity projects. The Canada Assistance Plan also cost-shares in the provision of non-insured health services. The costs of these latter services are included under health care services in Section B of this publication.

C482-494. Vocational Rehabilitation of Disabled Persons

SOURCE: 1, 5, 6, 8, 9, 10, 14, 38.

Under the Vocational Rehabilitation of Disabled Persons Act, the federal government cost-shares with the provinces in the expenses of providing an integrated program of social, vocational and medical services, to aid the disabled individual to become re-employable and re-established in a job.

C495-507. Social Services for Registered Indians

SOURCE: 1, 3, 10, 16, 17, 34.

Under the Indian Act the federal government provides a wide range of social welfare services to registered or status Indians. These include child welfare, institutional care for the aged and disabled, rehabilitation services for the disabled and work opportunity programs.

Also included are expenditures for the Canada Manpower

Trainee Travel Program which provides special services to workers by paying transportation charges to bring trainees to the manpower training centres and by providing counselling to workers with special difficulties in obtaining suitable employment opportunities. National expenditures for this service are reported in series C587. See source 5.

Provincial-Municipal Income Security Programs (Series C508-559)

C508-533. Mothers Allowances, 1926 to 1966

SOURCE: 6, 9, 10, 34, 39.

Commencing during World War I, some provinces introduced mothers allowances legislation to provide income support to single-parent mothers with dependent children. The programs, which were funded by the province and the municipalities, were eventually available in all provinces. Some provinces discontinued funding these programs after the introduction of the Unemployment Assistance Act in 1955. Others later transferred their caseloads to the Canada Assistance Plan. For information on historical rate structures, see sources 6, 9, 10, 34, 39.

C534-559. Other Provincial-Municipal Income Security Expenditures not Federally Shared

SOURCE: 2, 6, 7, 8, 9, 10, 11, 12, 13, 34, 39.

This area of expenditures has not been well defined historically on a statistical basis. It has therefore been necessary to restrict our presentation to combined figures for all other programs. These were derived by subtracting the total cost-shareable expenditures of federal-provincial welfare programs from the total provincial welfare expenditures (excluding Workmen's Compensation 1971-1976) as compiled by Statistics Canada in *Provincial Government Finance*, (Catalogue 68-206). The residual represents provincial and municipal welfare expenditures which were not federally shareable, thus they exclude expenditures for mothers allowances (series C534-546). The lower part of the table, series C547-559, includes mothers allowances from 1951 to 1966, that is, prior to the inception of the Canada Assistance Plan.

There are four main components to these provincial-municipal expenditures which need to be identified. Provincial welfare payments (mothers allowances) and provincial administration expenses represent the broadest categories. Under federal-provincial cost-sharing arrangements, the federal government has not shared fully in *all* costs. Thus the federal government has not fully shared in all welfare administration expenditures of the provincial governments; and capital expenditures on development of welfare facilities have also been traditionally excluded from federal cost-sharing except for a small part of capital and maintenance expenditures allowed for under the Canada Assistance Plan and under federal-provincial arrangements for sharing in the costs of construction of day care services.

Child welfare services, for example, represent an area of provincial welfare in which there was no federal sharing during the period prior to the introduction of the Canada Assistance Plan in 1966. At present, there is no federal sharing in the provincial tax rebates and credits allowed to tax filers on rent and other housing costs and to farmers on their capital costs. It is not possible to allocate these expenditures precisely on an historical basis but their relative importance has increased substantially (to over one-half billion dollars) in recent years.

Government Expenditure on Social Security by Broad Program Areas (Series C560-599.)

This section summarizes the statistical information given in the first five sections of this chapter in order to estimate the total amount of public expenditures at all levels of government on social security programs, broadly defined.

C560-571. Federal Income Security Program Expenditures

This table is composed of the national totals drawn from Federal Income Security Program Expenditures, with the addition of three programs: Family Assistance, Canada Manpower Industrial Training Program and Aid to Refugee Immigrants. These are federal programs for which a provincial breakdown of expenditures was not available.

C572-576. Federal and Provincial Income Insurance Expenditures

This table summarizes total federal and total provincial transfer payments under the Income Insurance programs.

C577-582. Federal-Provincial Shareable Expenditures of Direct Financial Assistance to Persons

Federal and provincial total shared expenditures on cost-shared programs which provide direct financial assistance to persons, that is, the income maintenance aspect of programs, are summarized in this table.

C583-590. Social Services Expenditures under Federal and Federal-provincial Shareable Welfare Services Programs.

This table provides an estimate of total expenditures for social service programs paid for by the federal government or by federal and provincial governments jointly. It includes the three main service areas funded under the Canada Assistance Plan; Vocational Rehabilitation of Disabled Persons Act (also federal-provincially cost-shared); federal services

to registered Indians; Canada manpower mobility grants to assist the unemployed to relocate where employment can be found; and a subtotal for other expenditures made by the federal government in the field of social security, for example, National Welfare Grants Program (for research and demonstration projects), New Horizons and family planning.

C591-599. Summary of all Government Expenditures on Social Security by Broad Program Areas.

This table provides estimates of total annual expenditures by all levels of government on social security, broadly defined. The components for the first part of this table are found in the preceding summary tables[9]. Included in the grand total of social security expenditures are administrative expenditures for welfare programs as well as total expenditures on health care services. Health care expenditures are given in detail in Section B of this volume.

Footnotes

[1] For most of the programs for which information has been obtained, both expenditure data and caseload, beneficiary, or recipient counts have been provided.

[2] For example, in a number of provinces child welfare programs are administered by private, non-profit agencies such as Children's Aid Societies.

[3] 'Income Security and Social Services,' Ottawa, Privy Council Office, 1969, p. 8.

[4] Examples of such private collective activities are group life insurance, dental, and pension plans.

[5] Public service employee pension plans are not included in this category. They would be included in 'Private Expenditures on Social Security' as they are analogous to employee/employer financed plans in private industry.

[6] The Canada and Quebec Pension Plans also provide for disability, survivor's and death benefits while the Unemployment Insurance Program provides some sickness and maternity benefits.

[7] See the Established Programs (Interim Arrangements) Act and, for a brief explanation, "General Payments to Other Governments", Chapter 10, 'The National Finances,' (Toronto, The Canadian Tax Foundation, 1977), pp. 134-147.

[8] For further information concerning the National Health and Welfare documentation on unpublished sources, inquiries should be directed to the Welfare Information Systems Branch, Department of National Health and Welfare, Brooke Claxton Building, Tunney's Pasture, Ottawa, Ontario. K1A 0K9.

[9] Provincial and municipal expenditures on income maintenance and welfare services programs not cost-shareable with the federal government were reported in C534-559. Those totals are also carried forward to the above table.

Series C1-13. Family Allowances,[1] average number of children under allowances,[2] for Canada and by province, fiscal years ending 31 March, 1947 to 1976

Year	Canada	New-found-land[3]	Prince Edward Island	Nova Scotia	New Bruns-wick	Quebec	Ontario	Manitoba	Saskat-chewan	Alberta	British Columbia	Yukon Terri-tory[4]	North-west Terri-tories[4]
	1	2	3	4	5	6	7	8	9	10	11	12	13
1976	7,320,493	226,154	41,252	276,395	237,154	1,968,706	2,561,532	326,265	306,405	604,101	742,920	7,822	19,256
1975	7,311,436	225,991	41,255	277,930	235,894	1,980,611	2,561,059	326,785	306,965	594,868	738,429	7,554	18,418
1974[1]	6,768,279	211,531	37,750	256,045	217,227	1,840,685	2,426,877	305,201	283,307	549,199	616,887	6,388	17,182
1973	6,767,000	208,710	37,038	251,620	213,010	1,844,900	2,397,200	308,270	283,620	546,050	653,460	23,031[4]	
1972	6,809,400	209,510	37,541	254,550	215,590	1,893,500	2,383,900	304,240	297,990	545,690	645,160	21,642	
1971	6,844,200	209,280	37,820	256,450	217,430	1,937,200	2,365,800	306,650	307,230	545,350	638,420	22,551	
1970	6,867,700	210,770	38,298	259,000	221,170	1,980,600	2,345,200	309,630	317,220	536,700	629,850	19,189	
1969	6,887,000	210,870	38,866	262,040	225,500	2,009,300	2,330,900	312,380	324,700	533,620	620,680	18,228	
1968	6,892,300	210,450	39,200	263,960	228,910	2,028,100	2,321,000	313,750	328,760	528,410	612,210	17,548	
1967	6,877,000	210,410	39,454	266,180	231,500	2,038,900	2,300,000	316,940	331,730	526,390	598,650	16,878	
1966	6,843,700	210,400	39,986	268,600	234,810	2,041,200	2,266,600	322,990	334,220	526,260	582,000	16,609	
1965	6,780,500	209,580	40,430	270,880	236,280	2,028,200	2,230,000	322,760	334,920	523,530	567,790	16,220	
1964	6,697,800	208,410	40,532	271,210	238,060	2,009,100	2,190,900	320,770	332,600	514,580	555,860	15,817	
1963	6,617,600	206,090	40,281	271,720	239,690	1,988,500	2,155,400	317,610	330,480	504,690	545,730	17,471	
1962	6,491,000	203,410	39,594	269,030	238,420	1,959,400	2,103,600	312,560	328,230	488,430	532,020	16,232	
1961	6,317,800	199,010	38,599	264,280	234,420	1,917,400	2,035,000	304,970	322,770	469,640	516,500	15,209	
1960	6,134,100	194,460	37,920	260,420	231,270	1,872,700	1,961,700	296,870	317,250	448,950	498,440	14,153	
1959	5,933,900	189,790	37,264	256,090	226,850	1,821,500	1,881,900	289,030	310,840	428,310	479,450	12,928	
1958	5,682,400	184,160	36,550	251,310	221,310	1,757,000	1,779,700	280,090	302,270	404,970	453,570	11,843	
1957	5,480,000	178,610	36,206	246,630	217,000	1,703,500	1,698,200	275,230	297,520	388,480	427,440	11,243	
1956	5,282,700	172,770	36,040	241,840	213,060	1,652,000	1,618,900	269,270	293,990	372,270	401,600	10,957	
1955	5,064,100	166,780	35,683	236,000	208,190	1,595,400	1,534,400	259,360	287,060	352,210	378,520	10,401	
1954	4,840,800	160,440	35,279	230,370	203,600	1,534,900	1,449,000	249,560	277,600	331,830	358,380	9,788	
1953	4,633,700	154,270	34,938	225,000	198,640	1,480,900	1,367,700	240,270	270,680	312,810	339,050	9,419	
1952	4,454,000	148,310	34,528	220,420	193,330	1,430,600	1,298,100	232,270	266,780	298,780	321,870	9,004	
1951	4,294,500	142,440	34,094	216,420	190,760	1,381,400	1,237,300	225,250	264,140	287,240	306,880	8,593	
1950[3]	4,116,200	134,820	33,166	211,270	185,770	1,326,600	1,174,100	216,850	260,300	274,620	290,680	8,065	
1949	3,823,400	—	32,268	204,740	178,750	1,281,300	1,118,900	210,050	258,580	259,930	271,460	7,536	
1948	3,704,900	—	31,715	199,940	172,390	1,247,200	1,078,000	206,070	257,750	252,620	252,330	6,664	
1947	3,429,600	—	30,736	187,260	161,500	1,170,900	976,240	193,070	250,400	236,220	218,810	4,601	

[1] The 1944 Family Allowances Act was revised in January 1974. In accordance with this new act, the number of children in-pay includes children formerly covered under Youth Allowances and Family Assistance programs.
[2] There is a separate account for each child in a special care facility and for each child cared for in a foster family.
[3] Newfoundland is included beginning in 1950.
[4] Separate figures for the Yukon Territory and the Northwest Territories were not available before 1974.

Series C14-26. Family Allowances,[1] average number of families receiving allowances,[2] for Canada and by province, fiscal years ending 31 March, 1947 to 1976

Year	Canada	New-found-land[3]	Prince Edward Island	Nova Scotia	New Bruns-wick	Quebec	Ontario	Manitoba	Saskat-chewan	Alberta	British Columbia	Yukon Terri-tory[4]	North-west Terri-tories[4]
	14	15	16	17	18	19	20	21	22	23	24	25	26
1976	3,476,940	90,333	17,337	126,455	104,682	945,946	1,250,250	151,254	135,238	279,552	364,878	3,641	7,375
1975	3,400,544	87,788	16,829	124,308	101,122	928,276	1,226,900	148,913	132,630	269,292	355,805	3,448	6,953
1974[1]	3,178,700	82,699	15,551	116,208	93,532	879,409	1,142,304	139,352	125,430	250,672	323,892	3,203	6,506
1973	3,086,000	79,799	15,049	112,460	90,027	855,750	1,110,000	137,040	123,360	242,910	310,350	9,233[4]	
1972	3,047,900	77,669	14,700	111,030	88,522	848,350	1,097,500	134,460	124,590	239,320	302,880	8,802	
1971	3,001,400	75,534	14,463	109,450	86,807	839,630	1,078,000	133,390	126,510	234,810	294,530	8,209	
1970	2,960,300	74,516	14,343	108,160	86,033	834,540	1,058,100	132,420	129,880	229,410	285,320	7,580	
1969	2,914,600	73,010	14,284	107,250	85,502	823,860	1,039,600	131,780	131,210	223,970	277,030	7,071	
1968	2,863,800	71,229	14,165	105,970	83,685	812,240	1,019,900	130,990	131,140	218,590	269,250	6,689	
1967	2,813,700	70,016	14,085	105,010	82,884	799,860	997,840	131,330	131,160	214,770	260,310	6,447	
1966	2,766,800	68,993	14,133	104,880	82,810	787,410	973,570	132,790	131,420	213,111	251,310	6,338	
1965	2,730,900	68,042	14,313	105,610	82,680	774,540	957,210	133,450	131,460	212,130	245,200	6,240	
1964	2,697,100	67,215	14,419	105,840	82,925	760,700	944,740	133,010	131,130	209,990	241,020	6,142	
1963	2,667,900	66,249	14,327	106,140	83,285	746,540	935,090	132,760	131,700	207,040	238,250	6,482	
1962	2,630,100	65,168	14,099	105,450	82,941	732,240	922,610	131,740	132,090	202,350	235,300	6,120	
1961	2,580,700	63,881	13,797	104,450	81,947	715,030	904,790	129,890	131,630	197,080	232,380	5,796	

Series C14-26. Family Allowances,[1] average number of families receiving allowances,[2] for Canada and by province, fiscal years ending 31 March, 1947 to 1976 (concluded)

Year	Canada	New-found-land[3]	Prince Edward Island	Nova Scotia	New Bruns-wick	Quebec	Ontario	Manitoba	Saskat-chewan	Alberta	British Columbia	Yukon Terri-tory[4]	North-west Terri-tories[4]
	14	15	16	17	18	19	20	21	22	23	24	25	26
1960	2,525,500	62,809	13,612	103,700	81,292	697,030	883,370	127,970	130,940	191,100	228,210	5,460	
1959	2,457,800	61,605	13,379	102,330	80,114	677,840	855,970	125,840	129,260	184,300	221,960	5,218	
1958	2,366,900	60,318	13,198	100,730	78,543	654,130	816,810	123,111	127,070	175,900	212,100	4,935	
1957	2,297,500	58,995	13,146	99,433	77,519	634,180	787,690	122,210	126,750	170,390	202,370	4,792	
1956	2,233,100	57,494	13,195	98,324	76,808	616,190	760,500	120,980	127,080	165,170	192,680	4,714	
1955	2,159,600	55,983	13,191	96,576	75,714	596,930	729,700	118,030	125,550	158,700	184,720	4,523	
1954	2,081,700	54,510	13,207	94,987	74,913	575,670	698,080	114,860	122,460	151,161	177,570	4,307	
1953	2,006,400	53,166	13,245	93,630	73,985	554,750	667,000	111,990	120,000	143,950	170,480	4,213	
1952	1,940,100	52,051	13,303	92,433	72,850	534,580	640,080	109,500	118,840	138,490	163,890	4,070	
1951	1,885,000	51,118	13,307	91,571	72,781	517,870	616,410	107,190	118,160	133,880	158,720	3,958	
1950[3]	1,818,100	49,417	13,104	90,108	71,736	498,870	590,710	103,950	116,280	127,890	152,300	3,721	
1949	1,702,100	—	12,863	88,063	69,665	479,410	566,280	101,230	115,220	122,040	143,930	3,448	
1948	1,638,500	—	12,570	86,005	67,244	460,570	544,190	99,154	114,310	117,800	133,640	3,051	
1947	1,477,600	—	12,097	79,034	61,388	419,610	480,270	91,622	109,000	108,250	114,370	2,030	

[1] The 1944 Family Allowances Act was revised in January 1974. In accordance with this new act, the number of children in-pay includes children formerly covered under Youth Allowances and Family Assistance programs.
[2] There is a separate account for each child in a special care facility and for each child cared for in a foster family.
[3] Newfoundland is included beginning in 1950.
[4] Separate figures for the Yukon Territory and the Northwest Territories were not available before 1974.

Series C27-39. Family Allowances,[1] federal payments,[2] for Canada and by province, fiscal years ending 31 March, 1946 to 1976

(thousands of dollars)

Year	Canada	New-found-land[3]	Prince Edward Island	Nova Scotia	New Bruns-wick	Quebec	Ontario	Manitoba	Saskat-chewan	Alberta	British Columbia	Yukon Terri-tory[4]	North-west Terri-tories[4]
	27	28	29	30	31	32	33	34	35	36	37	38	39
1976	1,957,500	60,200	11,000	73,600	63,300	528,200	685,800	87,100	81,600	160,700	198,700	2,100	5,200
1975	1,824,082	55,970	10,196	68,828	58,755	496,632	637,404	81,332	76,165	148,094	184,145	1,899	4,663
1974[1]	946,246	29,301	5,408	35,965	30,352	257,930	330,836	42,259	40,031	76,644	94,171	3,348[4]	
1973	548,623	16,906	3,062	20,718	17,517	152,650	190,324	24,434	23,570	44,157	53,405	1,882	
1972	554,407	16,946	3,080	20,892	17,687	156,176	191,377	24,748	24,266	44,345	53,086	1,804	
1971	557,878	16,943	3,092	21,016	17,810	159,084	191,450	24,978	24,997	44,296	52,514	1,699	
1970	560,050	17,048	3,121	21,145	18,071	161,788	190,540	25,165	25,937	44,001	51,646	1,586	
1969	560,186	17,047	3,160	21,307	18,399	163,502	189,231	25,332	26,471	43,554	50,686	1,497	
1968	558,774	16,983	3,179	21,411	18,596	164,637	187,636	25,433	26,711	42,991	49,774	1,425	
1967	555,795	16,960	3,190	21,508	18,752	165,096	185,309	25,651	26,871	42,564	48,526	1,367	
1966	551,735	16,945	3,232	21,637	18,983	164,972	182,378	25,926	26,988	42,346	47,007	1,322	
1965	545,775	16,871	3,266	21,776	19,069	163,888	179,056	25,927	26,891	41,996	45,745	1,289	
1964	538,312	16,747	3,274	21,791	19,198	162,172	175,545	25,727	26,650	41,228	44,712	1,268	
1963	531,566	16,562	3,260	21,839	19,341	160,299	172,711	25,524	26,540	40,316	43,834	1,341	
1962	520,781	16,337	3,205	21,624	19,223	157,713	168,442	25,065	26,313	38,928	42,687	1,244	
1961	506,192	15,960	3,124	21,242	18,878	154,185	162,611	24,385	25,849	37,365	41,433	1,160	
1960	491,214	15,566	3,063	20,933	18,589	150,463	156,682	23,731	25,364	35,766	39,984	1,075	
1959	474,787	15,163	2,994	20,560	18,202	146,278	150,186	23,092	24,789	34,123	38,409	990	
1958	437,887	14,131	2,824	19,400	17,075	136,081	136,706	21,521	23,242	31,030	34,969	907	
1957	397,518	12,881	2,641	17,973	15,779	124,368	122,539	19,889	21,645	27,953	31,029	819	
1956	382,535	12,415	2,622	17,597	15,452	120,390	116,604	19,419	21,401	26,753	29,097	786	
1955	366,466	11,968	2,591	17,148	15,073	116,057	110,492	18,705	20,895	25,391	27,406	740	
1954	350,114	11,498	2,558	16,716	14,701	111,441	104,410	17,980	20,245	23,958	25,904	703	
1953	334,198	11,039	2,523	16,297	14,288	107,084	98,304	17,284	19,723	22,576	24,400	681	
1952	320,458	10,614	2,496	15,950	13,893	102,884	93,207	16,703	19,424	21,573	23,064	650	
1951	309,465	10,224	2,467	15,660	13,708	99,558	89,035	16,236	19,237	20,762	21,953	625	
1950[3]	297,514	9,747	2,411	15,292	13,375	95,902	84,941	15,669	18,954	19,822	20,814	588	
1949	270,910	—	2,295	14,515	12,462	89,304	80,151	15,016	18,527	18,695	19,348	595	
1948	263,165	—	2,256	14,208	12,087	87,157	77,329	14,798	18,561	18,182	18,012	574	
1947	245,141	—	2,192	13,358	11,394	82,390	70,326	14,007	18,120	17,159	15,722	471	
1946	172,632	—	1,619	9,519	8,112	57,962	49,208	9,896	13,195	12,262	10,693	166	

[1] The 1944 Family Allowances Act was revised in January 1974. In accordance with this new act, the number of children in-pay includes children formerly covered under Youth Allowances and Family Assistance programs.
[2] There is a separate account for each child in a special care facility and for each child cared for in a foster family.
[3] Newfoundland is included beginning in 1950.
[4] Separate figures for the Yukon Territory and the Northwest Territories were not available before 1974.

Series C40-52. Youth Allowances[1] and Quebec Schooling Allowances,[2] children under allowances, for Canada and by province, fiscal years ending 31 March, 1965 to 1974

Year	Canada	New-found-land	Prince Edward Island	Nova Scotia	New Bruns-wick	Quebec	Ontario	Manitoba	Saskat-chewan	Alberta	British Columbia	Yukon Terri-tory	North-west Terri-tories
	40	41	42	43	44	45	46	47	48	49	50	51	52
1974[3,4]	698,055	17,029	3,788	26,995	24,334	186,722	249,337	31,523	31,423	55,089	70,682	428	705
1973	709,739	18,405	3,908	27,605	23,626	196,025	248,745	31,972	32,874	56,015	69,518	407	639
1972	717,372	18,876	3,953	28,010	23,790	201,119	248,194	32,702	34,132	56,263	69,352	418	563
1971	705,193	18,682	3,848	27,716	23,449	196,233	245,042	32,812	34,094	54,743	67,632	402	540
1970	671,530	18,046	3,765	26,584	22,368	187,054	233,271	31,484	33,347	51,264	63,554	314	479
1969	642,681	17,206	3,543	25,025	21,659	180,296	222,576	30,331	32,155	48,663	60,502	296	429
1968	606,250	16,024	3,380	23,673	20,840	171,685	208,575	28,833	30,510	45,129	56,939	280	382
1967	573,815	15,684	3,470	23,130	20,077	161,694	194,095	27,909	29,804	43,103	54,291	244	314
1966	550,310	15,121	3,593	23,148	20,072	145,516	190,706	28,078	29,699	42,058	51,770	259	290
1965[5]	537,195	13,798	3,435	23,549	20,079	139,158	187,713	28,123	29,253	41,451	50,139	262	235

[1] Commenced operations in all provinces except Quebec in 1964 with a $10 monthly benefit for all youths 16 and 17 years of age attending school.
[2] Commenced operations in Quebec in 1961 with a $10 monthly benefit for all youths 16 and 17 years of age attending school. (Payments represent contributions to Quebec under the Federal-Provincial Fiscal Revision Act, 1964, and the Established Programs (Interim Arrangements) Act).
[3] Both Youth Allowances and Quebec Schooling Allowance programs were terminated 31 December 1973. As of January 1974, payments to families with youths 16 and 17 were made under the authority of the new Family Allowances Act of 1973.
[4] Nine-month period ending 31 December 1973.
[5] Seven-month period ending 31 December 1965.

Series C53-65. Youth Allowances[1] and Quebec Schooling Allowances,[2] federal payments, for Canada and by province, fiscal years ending 31 March, 1965 to 1974
(thousands of dollars)

Year	Canada	New-found-land	Prince Edward Island	Nova Scotia	New Bruns-wick	Quebec	Ontario	Manitoba	Saskat-chewan	Alberta	British Columbia	Yukon Terri-tory	North-west Terri-tories
	53	54	55	56	57	58	59	60	61	62	63	64	65
1974[3,4]	65,418	1,551	353	2,537	2,173	18,354	23,193	2,882	2,932	5,072	6,269	38	64
1973	82,790	2,063	450	3,205	2,741	23,582	28,778	3,699	3,802	6,426	7,925	45	74
1972	82,654	2,117	452	3,256	2,746	23,000	28,856	3,800	3,941	6,447	7,922	48	69
1971	80,420	2,061	441	3,173	2,676	22,400	28,054	3,722	3,916	6,217	7,656	41	61
1970	76,502	1,967	422	3,003	2,561	21,400	26,653	3,602	3,783	5,823	7,195	39	52
1969	73,257	1,865	401	2,834	2,486	20,800	25,343	3,475	3,633	5,498	6,837	34	50
1968	68,927	1,747	392	2,698	2,361	19,500	23,763	3,294	3,487	5,148	6,462	29	45
1967	66,033	1,687	398	2,654	2,300	18,637	22,492	3,243	3,435	4,961	6,159	28	39
1966	63,975	1,592	395	2,692	2,311	17,506	21,978	3,249	3,415	4,837	5,934	30	34
1965[5]	36,411	882	231	1,591	1,353	9,541	12,652	1,916	1,990	2,807	3,415	16	17

[1] Commenced operations in all provinces except Quebec in 1964 with a $10 monthly benefit for all youths 16 and 17 years of age attending school.
[2] Commenced operations in Quebec in 1961 with a $10 monthly benefit for all youths 16 and 17 years of age attending school. (Payments represent contributions to Quebec under the Federal-Provincial Fiscal Revision Act, 1964, and the Established Programs (Interim Arrangements) Act).
[3] Both Youth Allowances and Quebec Schooling Allowance programs were terminated 31 December 1973. As of January 1974, payments to families with youths 16 and 17 were made under the authority of the new Family Allowances Act of 1973.
[4] Nine-month period ending 31 December 1973.
[5] Seven-month period ending 31 December 1965.

Series C66-78. Old Age Security, average number of recipients of pensions, for Canada and by province, fiscal years ending 31 March, 1953 to 1976

Year	Canada	New-found-land	Prince Edward Island	Nova Scotia	New Bruns-wick	Quebec	Ontario	Manitoba	Saskat-chewan	Alberta	British Columbia	Yukon Terri-tory[1]	North-west Terri-tories[1]
	66	67	68	69	70	71	72	73	74	75	76	77	78
1976	1,936,200	35,903	13,118	78,602	59,674	472,190	709,640	104,120	100,870	131,490	229,004	533	1,002
1975	1,887,800	34,858	12,958	76,821	58,267	458,060	692,630	102,140	99,535	128,220	222,850	534	959
1974	1,838,000	33,879	12,783	75,286	56,975	442,970	675,200	100,150	98,201	124,750	216,319	529	913
1973	1,791,400	33,076	12,561	73,806	55,642	429,980	659,420	98,238	96,758	121,250	209,300	511	882
1972	1,745,500	32,464	12,361	72,501	54,557	416,690	642,960	96,409	94,579	118,060	203,590	502	848
1971	1,701,500	31,915	12,334	71,041	53,637	403,150	626,910	94,627	93,085	115,030	198,450	468	815
1970	1,560,900	29,640	11,671	66,040	49,940	364,440	575,050	88,005	86,839	104,850	183,200	430	745
1969	1,406,800	26,710	10,780	60,901	45,632	322,640	518,090	80,332	79,677	94,130	166,860	382	665
1968	1,273,600	24,129	9,908	56,063	41,781	286,670	470,520	73,556	73,053	85,035	151,990	344	583
1967	1,143,800	21,876	9,086	51,393	38,047	253,590	417,800	67,338	67,905	76,860	139,100	305	513
1966[2]	1,028,800	19,215	8,236	46,489	34,309	223,550	374,340	61,580	62,846	69,469	127,710	235	499
1965	985,320	18,707	7,899	44,823	33,043	211,780	357,630	59,375	61,100	66,612	123,650		700[1]
1964	963,130	18,319	7,716	44,065	32,344	205,600	348,740	58,203	60,283	65,108	122,080		671
1963	941,980	17,994	7,631	43,273	31,738	200,020	340,920	57,284	59,260	63,677	119,510		670
1962	919,070	17,583	7,562	42,399	31,171	194,360	332,510	56,065	58,092	61,954	116,730		642
1961	894,810	17,199	7,435	41,561	30,561	188,600	324,410	54,504	56,528	59,844	113,550		613
1960	869,810	16,859	7,247	40,682	29,903	182,640	315,750	52,915	54,690	57,447	110,270		618
1959	845,840	16,703	7,225	40,310	29,448	177,760	307,870	51,386	52,859	54,993	106,670		613
1958	816,610	16,403	7,102	39,447	28,697	172,180	298,430	49,167	50,488	52,196	101,920		592
1957	788,460	16,129	6,985	38,735	28,036	166,320	289,140	47,447	48,377	49,595	97,132		566
1956	761,670	15,841	6,868	38,131	27,453	161,060	280,370	45,624	46,301	46,993	92,473		551
1955	734,080	15,536	6,761	37,605	26,836	155,990	270,810	43,772	43,950	44,378	87,937		506
1954	704,550	15,081	6,642	36,701	26,128	150,500	261,280	41,683	41,689	41,747	82,644		458
1953	671,240	14,547	6,529	35,747	25,386	145,160	249,510	39,501	39,370	38,189	76,318		447

[1] Prior to 1966 recipients for the Yukon Territory and the Northwest Territories were combined.

[2] Commencing in 1966 the age of eligibility for Old Age Security was decreased annually by one year of age to 65 years in 1970.

Series C79-91. Old Age Security, federal payments, for Canada and by province, fiscal years ending 31 March, 1952 to 1976
(thousands of dollars)

Year	Canada	New-found-land	Prince Edward Island	Nova Scotia	New Bruns-wick	Quebec	Ontario	Manitoba	Saskat-chewan	Alberta	British Columbia	Yukon Terri-tory[1]	North-west Terri-tories[1]
	79	80	81	82	83	84	85	86	87	88	89	90	91
1976	2,975,562	55,470	19,879	120,928	91,782	727,954	1,087,498	159,905	154,703	202,982	351,963	887	1,613
1975	2,607,724	48,306	17,938	106,378	81,686	630,827	958,094	141,724	137,010	175,915	307,630	747	1,471
1974	2,274,424	41,993	15,862	93,330	71,083	546,609	834,159	123,827	122,983	154,272	268,522	640	1,145
1973	1,781,532	33,147	12,412	73,924	56,704	429,326	653,404	97,398	93,159	122,426	208,217	516	898
1972	1,679,946	31,223	11,926	69,532	53,038	398,359	620,867	92,335	91,905	112,846	195,971	480	813
1971	1,627,219	30,633	11,810	67,995	51,591	384,223	602,581	90,135	89,122	107,639	190,241	456	793
1970	1,467,057	27,962	10,992	62,651	47,287	342,436	540,908	82,432	82,051	96,819	172,401	407	708
1969	1,296,849	24,899	10,023	56,489	42,465	297,932	475,409	73,990	73,806	86,675	154,192	354	615
1968	1,153,284	23,972	9,542	52,784	39,419	267,445	412,802	66,781	66,153	77,574	135,849	343	619
1967	1,033,408	19,707	8,207	46,533	34,358	228,797	377,628	60,767	61,479	69,525	125,662	282	463
1966[2]	927,299	17,586	7,447	42,049	30,995	201,031	337,195	55,495	56,755	62,794	115,293	255	406
1965	885,294	16,811	7,119	40,400	29,781	189,682	321,065	53,360	55,063	60,053	111,327		633[1]
1964	808,391	15,377	6,493	37,064	27,248	171,997	292,547	48,875	50,752	54,835	102,639		565
1963	734,382	14,014	5,963	33,817	24,858	155,360	265,742	44,617	46,335	49,787	93,363		524
1962	625,108	11,948	5,152	28,896	21,291	131,711	226,065	38,085	39,621	42,276	79,622		440
1961	592,413	11,355	4,944	27,610	20,350	124,322	214,626	36,089	37,573	39,688	75,451		405
1960	574,887	11,131	4,823	27,013	19,906	120,319	208,616	35,047	36,311	38,153	73,156		412
1959	559,280	11,013	4,810	26,780	19,584	116,993	203,257	34,030	35,100	36,535	70,769		409
1958	473,859	9,881	3,750	23,008	16,748	99,490	172,804	28,562	29,420	30,443	59,408		344
1957	379,111	7,738	3,371	18,706	13,528	79,651	138,793	22,842	23,335	23,942	46,924		281
1956	366,038	7,597	3,314	18,402	13,239	77,018	134,623	21,946	22,324	22,671	44,635		268
1955	353,205	7,460	3,262	18,150	12,946	74,725	130,296	21,051	21,203	21,418	42,450		245
1954	338,971	7,243	3,204	17,702	12,607	72,033	125,775	20,053	20,111	20,138	39,880		226
1953	323,142	6,996	3,156	17,259	12,255	69,570	120,083	19,020	19,037	18,745	36,803		218
1952	76,067	1,697	755	4,124	2,935	16,580	28,195	4,457	4,399	4,333	8,543		48

[1] Prior to 1966 recipients for the Yukon Territory and the Northwest Territories were combined.

[2] Commencing in 1966 the age of eligibility for Old Age Security was decreased annually by one year of age to 65 years in 1970.

Series C92-104. Guaranteed Income Supplement to the Old Age Security Program,[1] average number of recipients, for Canada and by province, fiscal years ending 31 March, 1967 to 1976

Year	Canada	New-found-land	Prince Edward Island	Nova Scotia	New Bruns-wick	Quebec	Ontario	Manitoba	Saskat-chewan	Alberta	British Columbia	Yukon Terri-tory	North-west Terri-tories
	92	93	94	95	96	97	98	99	100	101	102	103	104
1976	1,069,800	29,141	9,717	52,061	39,378	291,150	332,920	61,326	56,641	74,951	121,440	294	741
1975	1,070,500	28,986	9,802	51,805	39,367	285,190	336,690	61,964	58,276	74,625	122,740	298	731
1974	1,065,200	28,646	9,847	51,427	39,018	280,110	335,630	62,429	59,642	75,985	121,370	326	753
1973	1,015,900	27,901	9,703	49,902	37,933	267,780	318,860	59,576	58,423	72,217	112,510	317	740
1972	967,620	27,312	9,469	48,469	36,712	254,490	302,720	56,784	55,905	68,540	106,190	306	732
1971	823,920	25,114	8,541	42,192	32,203	226,300	251,800	47,867	45,301	57,853	85,832	253	674
1970	788,000	23,549	8,347	40,455	30,959	214,030	242,280	46,801	42,797	55,023	82,899	235	623
1969	743,960	21,627	7,913	38,950	29,035	195,540	232,370	44,419	40,879	51,318	81,127	234	544
1968	703,550	20,004	7,421	37,028	27,533	178,210	224,480	42,407	39,503	48,289	77,974	228	472
1967	505,240	18,037	6,444	30,613	21,937	136,306	128,639	35,633	33,132	36,526	57,922	26	25

[1] The Guaranteed Income Supplement was introduced in 1966 to provide additional income to Old Age Security pensioners with limited or no income.

Commencing in 1966 the age of eligibility for Old Age Security was decreased annually by one year of age to 65 years in 1970.

Series C105-117. Guaranteed Income Supplement to the Old Age Security Program,[1] federal payments, for Canada and by province, fiscal years ending 31 March, 1967 to 1976
(thousands of dollars)

Year	Canada	New-found-land	Prince Edward Island	Nova Scotia	New Bruns-wick	Quebec	Ontario	Manitoba	Saskat-chewan	Alberta	British Columbia	Yukon Terri-tory	North-west Terri-tories
	105	106	107	108	109	110	111	112	113	114	115	116	117
1976	923,413	28,048	9,073	46,629	35,304	261,998	275,027	51,823	48,394	64,525	101,451	311	831
1975	836,750	24,761	7,998	41,952	31,180	233,086	248,668	47,526	46,054	60,924	93,688	296	617
1974	760,068	22,216	7,261	38,121	28,471	209,418	229,819	44,416	41,213	54,777	83,405	293	658
1973	742,813	21,327	7,251	36,756	27,298	198,702	227,989	43,870	45,786	51,410	81,521	274	629
1972	526,060	15,960	5,278	27,585	20,170	145,392	155,043	31,158	30,044	37,986	56,737	217	490
1971	280,005	9,077	2,925	14,943	11,138	80,259	78,524	16,379	15,595	22,266	28,528	101	269
1970	263,479	8,413	2,776	13,467	10,433	73,376	77,154	15,545	14,197	20,388	27,401	89	239
1969	244,470	7,379	2,564	12,768	9,555	66,182	75,202	14,370	13,099	17,271	25,784	82	215
1968	234,835	4,874	1,941	10,739	8,027	54,424	84,127	13,586	13,464	15,789	27,665	71	128
1967	39,597	1,520	522	2,465	1,796	10,968	9,761	2,731	2,546	2,864	4,422	1	2

[1] The Guaranteed Income Supplement was introduced in 1966 to provide additional income to Old Age Security pensioners with limited or no income.

Commencing in 1966 the age of eligibility for Old Age Security was decreased annually by one year of age to age 65 in 1970.

Series C118-130. Canada Manpower Training Program, number of clients enrolled in institutional or industrial training, for Canada and by province, fiscal years ending 31 March, 1967 to 1976

Year	Canada	New-found-land	Prince Edward Island	Nova Scotia	New Bruns-wick	Quebec	Ontario	Manitoba	Saskat-chewan	Alberta	British Colum-bia[1]	Yukon Terri-tory	North-west Terri-tories
	118	119	120	121	122	123	124	125	126	127	128	129	130
1976	274,573	11,731	3,434	15,307	13,088	91,647	68,145	8,410	9,126	21,439	30,722	516	1,008
1975	291,573	10,302	3,229	13,987	11,392	113,478	67,936	8,166	7,909	17,062	36,904	679	529
1974	319,726	10,502	2,274	15,752	12,817	144,249	62,428	9,675	8,696	16,554	36,779[1]	—	—
1973	352,831	11,388	2,411	16,948	13,704	155,973	74,447	11,394	10,287	19,303	36,976	—	—
1972	352,200	12,138	2,560	18,064	14,651	142,846	81,803	12,176	11,168	20,454	36,340	—	—
1971	344,846	10,635	2,264	16,030	12,898	161,740	70,161	10,766	10,033	17,790	32,529	—	—
1970	304,899	8,981	1,909	13,578	10,892	135,657	70,527	11,449	10,874	18,712	22,320	—	—
1969	301,200	10,310	2,220	15,552	12,550	98,652	101,216	13,498	12,821	22,061	12,320	—	—
1968	183,540	3,775	832	5,765	4,706	68,748	69,049	6,120	5,968	9,820	8,757	—	—
1967	..	..	..	..	..	..	..	..	..	..	..	..	..

[1] British Columbia includes the Yukon Territory and the Northwest Territories from 1968 to 1974.

Series C131-143. Canada Manpower Training Allowance expenditures, for Canada and by province, fiscal years ending 31 March, 1967 to 1976

(thousands of dollars)

Year	Canada	New-found-land	Prince Edward Island	Nova Scotia	New Bruns-wick	Quebec	Ontario	Manitoba	Saskat-chewan	Alberta	British Columbia	Yukon Terri-tory	North-west Terri-tories
	131	132	133	134	135	136	137	138	139	140	141	142	143
1976	186,272	8,192	2,307	10,802	8,460	49,949	59,891	7,172	6,204	14,294	17,784	470	747
1975	148,715	6,908	1,999	7,828	6,733	43,349	45,174	6,241	5,137	10,037	14,521	393	396
1974	147,735	7,278	2,012	8,036	7,023	45,282	42,558	6,157	5,538	10,225	12,971	343	312
1973	146,167	6,645	2,186	8,066	7,232	46,313	43,217	5,673	5,256	9,414	11,542	293	330
1972	161,333	6,471	2,333	9,522	8,046	55,950	45,316	5,936	5,589	9,927	11,697	286	259
1971	156,563	5,892	2,334	9,995	6,571	55,705	45,043	5,900	5,402	9,518	9,892	165	145
1970	131,150	5,101	2,099	9,978	4,348	46,864	38,761	5,195	3,857	8,002	6,781	109	54
1969	108,300	3,562	1,320	6,645	3,051	35,867	38,008	4,632	3,461	6,570	5,123	27	35
1968	55,878	2,059	565	2,594	1,032	13,031	25,200	2,534	1,834	4,148	2,878	3	—
1967	52,344	2,129	40	3,019	585	5,440	30,985	4,412	2,627	1,913	1,026	167	1

Series C144-156. Registered Indians, federal social assistance payments, for Canada and by province,[1] fiscal years ending 31 March, 1968 to 1976

(thousands of dollars)

Year	Canada[2]	New-found-land	Prince Edward Island	Nova Scotia	New Bruns-wick	Quebec	Ontario	Manitoba	Saskat-chewan	Alberta	British Colum-bia[3]	Yukon Terri-tory	North-west Terri-tories[4]
	144	145	146	147	148	149	150	151	152	153	154	155	156
1976	82,276[4]	–	–	–	–	–	–	–	–	–	–	–	–
1975	64,104	–	319	2,236	1,821	5,529	6,702	12,165	12,139	10,554	11,929	710	–
1974	52,958	–	256	1,799	1,458	3,886	4,876	9,806	10,736	9,006	10,437	698	–
1973	46,164	–	225	1,580	1,281	3,497	4,293	7,793	9,579	7,309	9,866	741	–
1972	42,285	–	231	1,633	1,312	3,779	4,132	7,077	8,514	6,230	8,884	493	–
1971	34,509	–	134	965	774	2,660	3,736	5,445	7,576	4,982	8,237[3]	–	–
1970	24,776	–	104	730	592	2,437	2,465	3,929	5,546	3,774	5,199	–	–
1969	21,808	–	95	668	545	2,153	2,437	3,197	5,128	2,787	4,797	–	–
1968	17,725	–	92	645	525	1,577	1,800	2,613	4,775	1,925	3,773	–	–

[1] Maritime caseload provincially distributed in accordance with provincial population.
[2] To obtain full social security payments to registered Indians, add figures from series C495-507.
[3] British Columbia includes the Yukon Territory from 1968 to 1971.
[4] Services are provided directly by the territorial government.

Series C157-169. War Veterans Allowance recipients, for Canada and by province, fiscal years ending 31 March, 1954 to 1976[1]

Year	Canada[2]	New-found-land	Prince Edward Island	Nova Scotia	New Bruns-wick	Quebec	Ontario	Manitoba	Saskat-chewan	Alberta	British Columbia	Yukon Terri-tory	North-west Terri-tories
	157	158	159	160	161	162	163	164	165	166	167	168	169
1976	89,371	4,947	1,366	8,248	5,640	11,354	29,773	4,719	3,496	6,005	13,128	–	–
1975	87,501	4,877	1,268	7,883	5,419	11,076	29,296	4,696	3,356	5,855	13,108	–	–
1974	85,238	4,685	1,195	7,716	5,203	10,638	28,568	4,599	3,301	5,625	13,063	–	–
1973	78,484	4,281	1,076	7,078	4,911	9,744	26,128	4,255	2,955	5,071	12,333	–	–
1972	78,514	4,088	1,069	7,004	4,795	9,818	26,274	4,211	2,970	5,137	12,460	–	–
1971	83,955	3,791	1,109	7,201	4,920	10,481	28,539	4,772	3,189	5,382	13,889	–	–
1970	84,530	3,445	1,086	7,222	4,868	10,689	28,916	4,873	3,221	5,404	14,138	–	–
1969	85,495	3,198	1,120	7,165	4,728	10,667	29,478	5,123	3,244	5,547	14,560	–	–
1968	85,505	2,900	1,114	7,010	4,602	10,505	29,894	5,141	3,232	5,619	14,841	–	–
1967	87,763	2,633	1,089	6,957	4,507	10,634	31,173	5,393	3,376	5,899	15,422	–	–
1966	87,153	2,540	1,098	6,713	4,324	10,421	31,174	5,394	3,418	5,964	15,439	–	–
1965	85,294	2,391	1,047	6,376	4,161	10,036	30,907	5,361	3,379	5,839	15,257	–	–
1964	83,007	2,252	1,027	6,081	3,985	9,746	30,084	5,317	3,352	5,684	15,021	–	–
1963	80,365	2,053	986	5,668	3,841	9,366	29,250	5,182	3,386	5,492	14,761	–	–
1962	76,011	1,744	927	5,219	3,586	8,803	27,757	5,033	3,285	5,203	14,176	–	–
1961	69,546[2]	1,604	862	4,783	3,376	8,142	25,108	4,684	3,007	4,817	13,022	–	–
1960	67,858	1,543	858	4,651	3,227	7,926	24,602	4,623	3,019	4,688	12,721	–	–
1959	64,653	1,435	834	4,369	3,004	7,472	23,498	4,519	2,926	4,366	12,230	–	–
1958	59,949	1,330	768	3,990	2,796	6,896	21,701	4,231	2,741	4,079	11,417	–	–
1957	53,590	1,140	685	3,486	2,423	6,167	19,213	3,843	2,434	3,499	10,700	–	–
1956	50,564	1,035	638	3,255	2,275	5,708	18,018	3,624	2,295	3,248	10,468	–	–
1955	44,418	911	571	2,708	2,024	4,855	15,760	3,221	2,024	2,778	9,566	–	–
1954	41,487	789	526	2,474	1,857	4,439	14,776	2,974	1,853	2,573	9,226	–	–

[1] Provincial data are not available from 1931 to 1953. Canada totals for these years are: 1931, 2,219; 1932, 3,825; 1933, 4,867; 1934, 5,837; 1935, 7,186; 1936, 8,820; 1937, 11,306; 1938, 13,244; 1939, 20,010; 1940, 23,211; 1941, 24,024; 1942, 24,360; 1943, 24,192; 1944, 25,125; 1945, 26,427; 1946, 28,312; 1947, 30,532; 1948, 28,357; 1949, 30,283; 1950, 33,324; 1951, 38,600; 1952, 37,959; 1953, 39,793.

[2] From 1961 to 1976, the Canada figures include recipients residing outside Canada: 1961, 141; 1962, 278; 1963, 380; 1964, 458; 1965, 540; 1966, 668; 1967, 680; 1968, 647; 1969, 665; 1970, 668; 1971, 682; 1972, 688; 1973, 652; 1974, 645; 1975, 667; 1976, 695.

Series C170-182. War Veterans Allowances, payments for Canada and by province, fiscal years ending 31 March, 1954 to 1976[1]

(thousands of dollars)

Year	Canada[2]	New-found-land	Prince Edward Island	Nova Scotia	New Bruns-wick	Quebec	Ontario	Manitoba	Saskat-chewan	Alberta	British Columbia	Yukon Terri-tory	North-west Terri-tories
	170	**171**	**172**	**173**	**174**	**175**	**176**	**177**	**178**	**179**	**180**	**181**	**182**
1976	172,702	11,982	3,460	19,431	14,418	23,084	52,216	7,453	6,625	11,085	21,330	—	—
1975	141,781	9,650	2,647	15,543	11,554	19,139	43,263	6,141	5,403	9,098	18,032	—	—
1974	111,765	7,804	2,010	12,404	8,824	14,826	33,818	4,972	4,232	7,060	14,795	—	—
1973	86,664	6,006	1,521	9,755	6,955	11,465	25,934	3,877	3,217	5,327	11,707	—	—
1972	77,220	5,270	1,382	8,898	6,330	10,450	22,641	3,344	2,840	4,797	10,374	—	—
1971	88,912	4,816	1,415	9,165	6,396	11,407	27,971	4,580	3,391	5,443	13,547	—	—
1970	92,038	4,473	1,417	9,443	6,479	12,017	29,180	4,858	3,507	5,642	14,230	—	—
1969	95,500	4,198	1,502	9,569	6,384	12,341	30,486	5,294	3,686	6,058	15,175	—	—
1968	98,401	3,936	1,574	9,545	6,396	12,505	32,181	5,499	3,641	6,298	16,039	—	—
1967	103,629	3,637	1,513	9,430	6,207	13,080	35,200	6,021	3,990	6,777	16,976	—	—
1966	99,902	3,553	1,481	8,913	5,862	12,508	34,128	5,846	3,851	6,717	16,306	—	—
1965	92,846	3,173	1,352	7,946	5,284	11,428	32,852	5,491	3,657	6,288	14,833	—	—
1964	83,207	2,754	1,223	6,923	4,643	10,185	29,099	4,990	3,320	5,667	13,979	—	—
1963	81,782	2,274	1,194	6,645	4,538	9,912	28,921	4,969	3,460	5,603	14,075	—	—
1962	75,290	2,153	1,092	5,880	4,126	9,023	26,522	4,735	3,268	5,135	13,115	—	—
1961	58,428[2]	1,753	876	4,674	3,330	7,077	20,232	3,680	2,512	3,973	10,226	—	—
1960	57,304	1,720	860	4,300	3,211	6,880	19,797	3,713	2,580	3,842	10,401	—	—
1959	54,871	1,591	878	4,280	3,018	6,535	18,999	3,602	2,469	3,676	9,823	—	—
1958	47,990	1,392	720	3,647	2,639	5,719	16,576	3,235	2,206	3,216	8,640	—	—
1957	40,975	1,155	619	3,012	2,228	4,917	14,133	2,818	1,856	2,682	7,555	—	—
1956	38,648	1,082	580	2,821	2,126	4,610	13,271	2,640	1,739	2,513	7,266	—	—
1955	28,246	780	424	2,073	1,508	3,079	9,612	1,909	1,316	1,675	5,870	—	—
1954	26,847	687	397	1,949	1,393	2,883	9,005	1,841	1,213	1,595	5,884	—	—

[1] Provincial data are not available from 1931 to 1953. Canada totals for these years are *(thousands of dollars)*: 1931, 318; 1932, 1,040; 1933, 1,389; 1934, 1,646; 1935, 2,017; 1936, 2,531; 1937, 3,179; 1938, 3,899; 1939, 5,308; 1940, 7,028; 1941, 7,334; 1942, 7,140; 1943, 6,820; 1944, 6,880; 1945, 9,216; 1946, 10,093; 1947, 11,804; 1948, 14,370; 1949, 19,741; 1950, 20,018; 1951, 22,923; 1952, 23,545; 1953, 27,115.

[2] From 1961 to 1976, the Canada figures include expenditures made to recipients outside Canada *(thousands of dollars)*: 1961, 95; 1962, 241; 1963, 351; 1964, 424; 1965, 542; 1966, 737; 1967, 798; 1968, 787; 1969, 807; 1970, 792; 1971, 781; 1972, 894; 1973, 900; 1974, 1,020; 1975, 1,311; 1976, 1,617.

Series C183-195. Veteran disability and dependent pensioners, payments for Canada and by province, fiscal years ending 31 March, 1953 to 1976[1]

(thousands of dollars)

Year	Canada[2]	New-found-land	Prince Edward Island	Nova Scotia	New Bruns-wick	Quebec	Ontario	Manitoba	Saskat-chewan	Alberta	British Columbia	Yukon Terri-tory	North-west Terri-tories
	183	**184**	**185**	**186**	**187**	**188**	**189**	**190**	**191**	**192**	**193**	**194**	**195**
1976	346,554	4,535	4,326	23,339	14,424	37,322	115,934	26,661	14,230	24,412	57,345	—	—
1975	332,568	4,281	4,051	22,271	13,676	35,612	111,595	25,538	13,630	23,063	55,075	—	—
1974	290,526	3,724	3,485	19,118	11,796	31,003	97,985	22,081	11,937	19,949	48,092	—	—
1973	241,005	3,020	2,812	15,635	9,731	25,639	81,460	18,401	9,881	16,441	39,545	—	—
1972	231,377	2,808	2,648	14,877	9,220	24,753	78,547	17,627	9,432	15,763	37,643	—	—
1971	212,922	2,613	2,427	13,611	8,395	22,632	72,595	16,204	8,656	14,470	34,504	—	—
1970	218,554	2,644	2,469	13,920	8,544	23,230	74,654	16,652	8,960	14,925	35,074	—	—
1969	223,321	2,724	2,546	14,023	8,708	24,004	76,796	17,149	9,155	15,296	35,749	—	—
1968	205,599	2,364	2,302	12,787	7,853	22,099	70,826	15,829	8,470	14,061	32,686	—	—
1967	195,910	2,311	2,194	12,164	7,561	21,097	67,646	15,122	8,110	13,438	30,636	—	—
1966	185,560	2,171	2,078	11,522	7,162	19,963	64,351	14,193	7,755	12,672	28,646	—	—
1965	180,327	2,110	2,001	11,107	6,851	19,400	62,662	13,883	7,519	12,315	27,532	—	—
1964	173,190	1,957	1,836	10,199	6,355	17,853	57,793	12,797	6,909	11,360	25.247	—	—
1963	175,926	1,231	1,935	10,202	6,508	17,942	59,127	13,193	7,036	11,610	25,330	—	—
1962	177,893	1,245	1,957	10,316	6,581	17,965	60,144	13,340	7,293	11,739	25,435	—	—
1961	150,717	1,055	1,507	8,740	5,425	15,220	51,109	11,302	6,178	9,795	21,549	—	—
1960	149,678	1,048	1,497	8,530	5,388	15,115	50,904	11,224	6,136	9,728	21,401	—	—
1959	150,745	1,055	1,507	8,591	5,426	15,073	51,418	11,304	6,180	9,646	21,554	—	—
1958	145,603	1,019	1,456	8,153	5,241	14,558	49,810	11,064	6,114	9,317	20,673	—	—
1957	130,326	912	1,303	7,297	4,691	12,900	44,976	10,034	5,473	8,209	18,373	—	—
1956	128,793	902	1,288	7,211	4,636	12,749	44,439	9,916	5,408	8,115	18,159	—	—
1955	128,775	734	1,249	7,134	4,958	13,663	46,114	10,534	5,808	9,079	18,363	—	—
1954	127,580	727	1,238	7,068	4,912	13,536	45,686	10,436	5,754	8,994	18,193	—	—
1953	127,029	800	1,245	7,406	4,713	12,576	45,654	10,213	5,640	8,333	18,305	—	—

[1] Provincial data are not available from 1946 to 1952. Canada totals for these years are *(thousands of dollars)*: 1946, 59,466; 1947, 70,761; 1948, 77,093; 1949, 102,951; 1950, 96,091; 1951, 95,577; 1952, 103,703.

[2] From 1953 to 1976, the Canada figures include expenditures made to recipients outside Canada *(thousands of dollars)*: 1953, 12,144; 1954, 11,036; 1955, 11,139; 1956, 15,970; 1957, 16,158; 1958, 18,198; 1959, 18,991; 1960, 18,707; 1961, 18,837; 1962, 21,878; 1963, 21,812; 1964, 20,884; 1965, 14,947; 1966, 15,047; 1967, 15,631; 1968, 16,322; 1969, 17,171; 1970, 17,482; 1971, 16,815; 1972, 18,059; 1973, 18,440; 1974, 21,356; 1975, 23,776; 1976, 24,026.

Series C196-208. Canada and Quebec Pension Plans, annual average number of retirement beneficiaries, for Canada and by province, fiscal years ending 31 March, 1967 to 1975

Year	Canada	New-found-land	Prince Edward Island	Nova Scotia	New Bruns-wick	Quebec[1]	Ontario	Manitoba	Saskat-chewan	Alberta	British Columbia	Yukon Terri-tory	North-west Terri-tories
	196	197	198	199	200	201	202	203	204	205	206	207	208
1975	489,682	5,882	2,490	17,659	12,868	104,295	197,591	28,741	23,743	35,012	61,177	152	72
1974	408,539	4,888	2,014	14,488	10,683	90,440	164,346	23,432	19,256	28,552	50,247	129	64
1973	337,659	4,014	1,616	11,980	8,821	74,535	136,962	19,411	15,633	23,417	41,106	107	57
1972	280,488	3,378	1,325	9,860	7,453	63,025	113,916	16,053	12,639	19,142	33,566	86	45
1971	220,230	2,825	990	7,667	5,755	49,291	89,972	12,801	9,849	14,661	26,314	64	41
1970	146,695	1,915	685	5,118	3,830	32,182	60,907	8,697	6,559	9,424	17,323	31	24
1969	73,367[2]	1,043	338	2,620	1,832	15,283	31,557	4,266	3,147	4,581	8,212	22	—
1968	24,140	389	108	892	561	4,521	11,534	1,400	910	1,414	2,405	4	2
1967	4,586	54	20	134	99	1,119	2,181	209	136	205	427	2	—

[1] Includes recipients under the Canada Pension Plan, to Quebec residents: 1967, 8; 1968, 56; 1969, 202; 1970, 426; 1971, 662; 1972, 860; 1973, 1,020; 1974, 1,253; 1975, 1,375.

[2] Includes 466 persons not identified by province of residence.

Series C209-221. Canada and Quebec Pension Plans,[1] payments to retirement beneficiaries, for Canada and by province, fiscal years ending 31 March, 1967 to 1976[2]
(thousands of dollars)

Year	Canada	New-found-land	Prince Edward Island	Nova Scotia	New Bruns-wick	Quebec[3]	Ontario	Manitoba	Saskat-chewan	Alberta	British Columbia	Yukon Terri-tory	North-west Terri-tories
	209	210	211	212	213	214	215	216	217	218	219	220	221
1976p	428,149	4,068	1,596	13,582	9,389	116,230	167,303	22,282	16,493	27,477	49,509	157	63
1975	237,253	2,397	932	7,977	5,601	49,500	101,236	13,402	9,741	16,266	30,078	85	38
1974	158,648	1,591	614	5,304	3,719	33,812	67,744	8,756	6,478	10,802	19,743	61	25
1973	112,416	1,120	431	3,745	2,424	24,101	48,570	6,104	4,648	7,505	13,706	45	20
1972	81,796	843	284	2,678	1,961	17,853	35,094	4,528	3,310	5,292	9,912	30	13
1971	51,262	565	177	1,655	1,230	10,471	22,442	2,945	2,180	3,281	6,286	18	11
1970	21,789	242	74	705	526	3,928	10,030	1,253	979	1,382	2,659	7	4
1969	6,459	72	23	210	142	1,090	3,192	336	275	388	727	2	1
1968	1,070[4]	..	..	..	..	..	..	..	..	..	..	..	..
1967	51[4]	..	..	..	..	..	..	..	..	..	..	..	..

[1] To obtain total payments under the Canada and Quebec Pension Plans, combine the figures in series C209-221 and C235-247.
[2] Data on payments by Quebec Pension Plan are on a calendar year basis.

[3] Includes payments under the Canada Pension Plan to Quebec residents *(thousands of dollars)*: 1969, 21; 1970, 77; 1971, 175; 1972, 279; 1973, 373; 1974, 531; 1975, 727; 1976, 1,033.
[4] Payments of retirement pensions commenced in January 1967 but Canada Pension Plan data by province were not available until the fiscal year 1968-69.

Series C222-234. Canada and Quebec Pension Plans, annual average number of survivors and disability pensions beneficiaries,[1] for Canada and by province, fiscal years ending 31 March, 1967 to 1975

Year	Canada	New-found-land	Prince Edward Island	Nova Scotia	New Bruns-wick	Quebec[2]	Ontario	Manitoba	Saskat-chewan	Alberta	British Columbia	Yukon Terri-tory	North-west Terri-tories
	222	223	224	225	226	227	228	229	230	231	232	233	234
1975	331,890	7,519	2,041	18,855	11,235	88,301	124,952	14,274	13,043	20,694	30,531	222	226
1974	281,531	6,381	1,707	15,777	9,672	75,652	105,330	12,128	11,308	17,566	25,637	176	197
1973	225,853	4,981	1,329	12,728	7,806	59,912	84,728	9,926	9,287	14,312	20,559	132	153
1972	168,035	3,427	927	8,885	5,670	46,861	61,612	7,356	7,076	10,646	15,399	98	78
1971	111,256	2,182	610	4,961	3,594	31,671	40,535	5,006	4,986	7,321	10,286	63	43
1970	62,493[3]	1,100	344	2,703	2,136	17,712	22,870	2,823	2,606	4,269	5,876	35	19
1969	22,780[3]	411	114	1,118	824	7,345	7,565	942	800	1,488	2,047	21	—
1968	232	14	—	19	9	70	50	12	12	30	16	—	—
1967	—	—	—	—	—	—	—	—	—	—	—	—	—

[1] There is a minimum of three years contributions to be eligible for survivors benefits and five years contributions to be eligible for disability pensions.

[2] Includes recipients under the Canada Pension Plan, to Quebec residents: 1968, 5; 1969, 138; 1970, 350; 1971, 667; 1972, 964; 1973, 1,307; 1974, 1,519; 1975, 1,375.

[3] Includes 105 persons not identified by province of residence.

Series C235-247. Canada and Quebec Pension Plans,[1] federal and provincial payments to survivors and disability pensions beneficiaries,[2] for Canada and by province, fiscal years ending 31 March, 1969 to 1976[3]
(thousands of dollars)

Year	Canada	New-found-land	Prince Edward Island	Nova Scotia	New Bruns-wick	Quebec[4]	Ontario	Manitoba	Saskat-chewan	Alberta	British Columbia	Yukon Terri-tory	North-west Terri-tories
	235	236	237	238	239	240	241	242	243	244	245	246	247
1976p	425,868[4]	7,448	1,904	19,812	11,238	152,499	146,508	15,927	12,924	21,798	35,382	233	195
1975	292,717	5,418	1,394	14,758	8,427	89,087	109,072	11,751	9,947	16,288	26,244	177	154
1974	219,359	4,033	1,024	11,096	6,311	67,759	80,966	8,800	7,563	12,130	19,433	123	121
1973	153,133	2,999	776	8,719	4,807	35,834	62,578	6,912	6,039	9,414	14,859	91	102
1972	107,765	1,962	508	5,987	3,271	26,538	42,625	4,822	4,474	6,790	10,659	70	58
1971	66,126	1,100	311	2,821	1,931	16,139	26,406	3,172	3,046	4,425	6,689	53	34
1970	38,671	551	174	1,574	1,146	8,901	15,916	1,901	1,777	2,679	4,004	31	12
1969	12,544	200	56	619	426	2,544	5,249	636	504	934	1,360	10	8

[1] To obtain total payments under the Canada and Quebec Pension Plans, combine the figures in series C209-221 and C235-247.

[2] There is a minimum of three years contributions to be eligible for survivors benefits and five years contributions to be eligible for disability pensions.

[3] Data on payments by Quebec Pension Plan are on a calendar year basis.

[4] Includes payments under the Canada Pension Plan to Quebec residents *(thousands of dollars)*: 1969, 76; 1970, 208; 1971, 389; 1972, 605; 1973, 881; 1974, 1,111; 1975, 1,243; 1976, 1,515.

Series C248-260. Unemployment Insurance, net payments to direct unemployment beneficiaries,[1] for Canada and by province, fiscal years ending 31 March, 1942 to 1976
(thousands of dollars)

Year	Canada[2]	New-found-land	Prince Edward Island	Nova Scotia	New Bruns-wick	Quebec	Ontario	Manitoba	Saskat-chewan	Alberta	British Columbia	Yukon Terri-tory[3]	North-west Terri-tories[3]
	248	249	250	251	252	253	254	255	256	257	258	259	260
1976	3,002,349	170,030	30,537	135,756	169,628	1,156,362	801,827	55,151	42,039	61,823	366,667	7,107	2,687
1975	2,892,489	150,593	23,174	114,828	143,844	1,006,185	886,305	45,993	41,320	68,705	402,363	5,480	2,363
1974	1,924,739	106,747	15,677	81,568	98,633	684,433	537,188	40,369	40,869	53,496	258,997	3,738	2,429
1973	1,850,157	83,899	12,450	72,057	84,029	589,019	552,464	57,607	50,254	88,788	253,624	3,215	2,161
1972[4]	1,764,167	64,835	9,267	64,883	66,408	540,019	567,521	61,264	48,366	105,388	235,773	–	–
1971	890,594	30,578	5,094	37,049	33,160	263,388	301,094	40,364	24,071	50,909	104,802	–	–
1970	695,222	25,347	4,199	26,514	25,217	212,077	229,642	25,091	21,515	33,820	91,800	–	–
1969	498,992	23,870	3,887	23,343	22,107	164,347	152,503	17,652	16,263	19,928	55,091	–	–
1968	438,128	20,526	3,695	19,540	19,784	145,463	133,116	16,094	11,864	17,206	50,840	–	–
1967	352,645	19,664	3,163	18,152	17,388	111,971	108,051	11,538	8,810	13,196	40,714	–	–
1966	295,301	17,568	2,953	16,376	16,201	94,493	82,291	11,481	8,631	11,771	33,535	–	–
1965	312,110	18,019	3,096	16,517	16,570	101,593	86,234	13,243	9,487	15,033	32,317	–	–
1964	344,390	17,911	3,013	18,225	16,732	110,480	99,506	14,951	10,046	18,839	34,686	–	–
1963	394,163	19,493	3,349	20,069	19,268	124,865	114,319	18,227	12,209	22,139	40,224	–	–
1962	409,208	19,256	3,320	21,790	19,616	121,728	122,745	20,361	13,889	22,438	44,065	–	–
1961	493,971	19,951	3,316	24,150	22,575	149,958	156,597	21,846	15,211	25,485	54,881	–	–
1960	481,837	18,413	3,397	22,038	21,295	153,348	155,481	18,326	13,614	23,706	52,220	–	–
1959	406,097	15,249	2,918	20,146	19,417	133,140	127,190	14,964	11,534	18,278	43,261	–	–
1958	492,901	18,188	2,966	22,613	23,134	158,367	154,605	18,719	12,695	21,794	59,822	–	–
1957	305,076	12,144	1,880	13,716	16,204	98,263	94,238	12,248	8,345	13,660	34,379	–	–
1956	210,330	8,485	1,395	9,933	11,131	73,109	60,161	10,093	7,261	9,332	19,430	–	–
1955	228,865	7,232	1,240	11,001	10,308	76,208	71,098	10,823	7,450	11,374	22,131	–	–
1954	240,722	6,893	1,182	10,878	10,446	79,658	79,895	10,159	5,273	10,917	25,420	–	–
1953	157,779	4,654	945	8,611	8,110	56,581	41,339	7,088	3,343	6,475	20,633	–	–
1952	118,112	2,619	615	5,402	5,105	39,584	36,342	5,541	2,427	4,057	16,419	–	–
1951	75,996	1,225	534	4,085	3,051	25,239	19,403	4,351	2,596	3,553	11,960	–	–
1950	98,994	294	541	5,884	4,935	35,623	25,122	5,293	2,932	4,053	14,318	–	–
1949	69,351	20	459	4,495	3,602	23,428	17,558	3,478	2,020	2,325	11,966	–	–
1948	40,268	–	305	3,424	1,697	12,598	10,044	2,499	1,478	1,592	6,633	–	–
1947	32,039	–	223	3,337	1,126	9,695	8,748	2,159	1,060	1,394	4,297	–	–
1946	51,085	–	193	2,666	1,088	18,973	16,383	2,507	965	1,524	6,785	–	–
1945	14,576	–	57	715	152	6,606	3,510	964	319	664	1,589	–	–
1944	3,277	–	12	163	43	1,561	471	255	130	278	364	–	–
1943	941	–	6	45	38	410	144	101	48	71	78	–	–
1942	353	–	–	–	–	–	–	–	–	–	–	–	–

[1] To obtain total payments to beneficiaries under the Unemployment Insurance Program, combine the figures in series C248-260 and C261-273.
[2] Includes the following amounts which were paid to claimants residing outside Canada *(thousands of dollars)*: 1971, 84; 1972, 443; 1973, 590; 1974, 595; 1975, 1,336; 1976, 2,735.
[3] Included in other provinces in 1972 and earlier years.
[4] In July 1971, a new Unemployment Insurance Act was proclaimed with greatly extended coverage and benefits.

Series C261-273. Unemployment Insurance, net payments to direct beneficiaries of special benefits,[1] for Canada and by province, fiscal years ending 31 March, 1972 to 1976
(thousands of dollars)

Year	Canada[2]	New-found-land	Prince Edward Island	Nova Scotia	New Bruns-wick	Quebec	Ontario	Manitoba	Saskat-chewan	Alberta	British Columbia	Yukon Terri-tory	North-west Terri-tories
	261	262	263	264	265	266	267	268	269	270	271	272	273
1976	339,897	12,977	1,445	17,666	11,516	89,731	119,023	14,563	9,576	24,767	38,039	238	356
1975[3]	251,533	8,466	3,055	14,129	8,016	67,334	88,253	10,881	6,517	16,299	28,174	183	226
1974	194,474	7,587	2,318	11,398	6,285	51,145	68,858	7,975	4,922	12,214	21,421	163	188
1973	154,057	6,696	1,907	9,511	5,020	41,664	52,234	7,131	3,889	8,866	16,895	106	138
1972	107,636	5,661	1,943	7,909	4,324	27,139	35,681	4,098	2,076	5,225	13,580	–	–

[1] To obtain total payments to beneficiaries under the Unemployment Insurance Program, combine the figures in series C248-260 and C261-273.
[2] Includes payments to claimants residing outside Canada.
[3] In 1975 there were 277,248 claimants of special benefits under the Unemployment Insurance Act of which 169,817 were for sickness benefits, 69,895 for maternity benefits and 37,536 for fishermen and retirement benefits.

Series C274-286. Workmen's Compensation, payments of cash compensation to direct beneficiaries,[1] for Canada and by province,[2] calendar years ending 31 December, 1915 to 1975

(thousands of dollars)

Year	Canada	New-found-land	Prince Edward Island	Nova Scotia	New Bruns-wick	Quebec	Ontario	Manitoba	Saskat-chewan	Alberta	British Columbia	Yukon Terri-tory	North-west Terri-tories
	274	275	276	277	278	279	280	281	282	283	284	285	286
1975[3]	537,416	4,997	820	13,960	8,765	140,173	222,500	12,842	15,231	45,049	73,079	–	–
1974	419,365	4,299	895	13,850	7,356	102,439	173,690	10,550	13,192	35,616	57,477	–	–
1973	331,716	4,022	800	10,988	6,028	75,637	148,814	9,036	11,613	23,821	40,957	–	–
1972	280,509	3,647	550	10,675	8,763	65,771	116,303	8,551	9,136	22,114	34,999	–	–
1971	237,990	2,233	496	9,309	6,034	57,572	98,174	6,867	7,353	18,162	31,790	–	–
1970	229,787	2,233	418	6,887	6,980	52,283	102,221	6,638	5,189	16,545	30,393	–	–
1969	203,135	1,816	360	6,677	5,846	46,471	80,641	5,863	5,314	14,307	35,840	–	–
1968	177,378	1,981	300	6,366	5,856	46,999	68,763	5,162	4,369	12,048	25,534	–	–
1967	162,756	1,835	286	6,048	5,460	39,990	63,648	4,888	4,239	12,141	24,221	–	–
1966	156,424	1,545	286	5,453	6,342	38,247	61,466	4,488	4,159	10,802	23,636	–	–
1965	142,111	1,278	286	4,826	5,340	38,672	52,672	2,870	5,441	10,053	20,673	–	–
1964	119,618	1,202	595	4,323	4,882	25,800	46,392	3,481	5,197	9,093	18,653	–	–
1963	111,651	1,112	509	4,178	3,417	24,966	43,000	3,124	4,900	8,545	17,900	–	–
1962	104,523	1,094	364	3,935	2,992	22,359	41,005	3,089	4,699	7,807	17,179	–	–
1961	94,181	1,084	161	3,804	2,514	20,717	34,916	2,894	4,510	7,135	16,446	–	–
1960	91,616	992	132	3,745	2,382	19,235	35,227	2,985	3,800	6,674	16,444	–	–
1959	85,235	789	130	3,553	2,238	17,171	33,032	2,542	3,659	6,512	15,609	–	–
1958	80,028	663	91	4,130	1,587	16,928	30,408	2,179	3,279	6,021	14,742	–	–
1957	76,632	717	171	3,324	1,436	16,183	28,309	1,995	3,266	5,941	15,288	–	2
1956	69,562	766	158	3,558	1,494	13,863	24,823	1,805	2,801	5,514	14,778	–	2
1955	62,157	572	99	3,015	1,262	12,173	22,293	1,669	2,495	4,715	13,864	–	–
1954	58,227	484	90	2,928	1,082	11,101	21,771	1,600	2,239	4,432	12,500	–	–
1953	57,285	601	50	2,723	1,157	12,536	20,726	1,512	1,871	4,235	11,874	–	–
1952	55,985	356	66	1,358	929	12,338	22,048	2,115	2,375	1,497	12,902	–	–
1951	48,640	189	62	1,298	1,288	10,938	18,914	1,641	1,700	1,159	11,451	–	–
1950	43,845	..	44	1,317	1,188	9,241	15,318	1,683	1,805	1,085	12,165	–	–
1949	40,905	..	13	1,098	1,140	9,343	14,309	1,672	1,589	976	10,765	–	–
1948	45,260	–	–	1,055	1,248	9,208	19,428	1,684	1,577	858	10,202	–	–
1947	40,058	–	–	1,704	1,313	8,913	15,025	1,439	1,551	721	9,391	–	–
1946	36,679	–	–	1,181	1,120	8,596	14,143	1,415	1,176	635	8,414	–	–
1945	32,007	–	–	1,243	1,060	7,738	11,246	1,353	801	518	8,048	–	–
1944	32,258	–	–	2,693	1,193	7,012	10,597	1,379	853	498	8,032	–	–
1943	29,477	–	–	2,898	697	6,462	9,197	1,386	677	816	7,344	–	–
1942	24,865	–	–	1,730	569	5,500	8,959	938	539	609	6,021	–	–
1941	21,404	–	–	1,286	648	4,731	8,127	1,041	472	498	4,602	–	–
1940	17,236	–	–	1,285	432	4,302	5,876	830	372	447	3,693	–	–
1939	14,957	–	–	1,392	369	3,144	5,058	737	389	464	3,404	–	–
1938	15,901	–	–	1,976	328	3,480	5,310	785	370	469	3,183	–	–
1937	16,720	–	–	1,190	459	5,743	4,878	688	350	447	2,966	–	–
1936	14,141	–	–	1,161	445	3,917	4,585	702	358	436	2,536	–	–
1935	12,266	–	–	954	376	3,396	4,276	572	245	353	2,092	–	–
1934	10,063	–	–	795	359	2,579	3,658	562	208	312	1,591	–	–
1933	8,629	–	–	571	315	2,238	3,031	456	225	291	1,502	–	–
1932	11,449	–	–	688	244	3,048	4,308	637	256	407	1,860	–	–
1931	14,242	–	–	951	330	3,997	4,961	670	309	453	2,572	–	–
1930	16,225	–	–	950	410	3,792	6,087	953	131[4]	498	3,404	–	–
1929	16,339	–	–	936	484	3,230	6,627	966	–	507	3,589	–	–
1928	11,865	–	–	1,076	465	210[5]	5,901	858	–	457	2,898	–	–
1927	10,150	–	–	1,052	405	–	5,022	645	–	372	2,654	–	–
1926	9,497	–	–	876	358	–	4,833	650	–	298	2,481	–	–
1925	9,077	–	–	639	424	–	4,690	592	–	313	2,419	–	–
1924	9,712	–	–	874	484	–	5,287	517	–	241	2,309	–	–
1923	9,790	–	–	809	429	–	5,385	686	–	323	2,158	–	–
1922	8,675	–	–	577	374	–	5,000	692	–	265	1,767	–	–
1921	9,420	–	–	706	455	–	5,526	708	–	254	1,771	–	–
1920	10,711	–	–	1,135	398	–	7,077	391	–	–	1,710	–	–
1919	6,117	–	–	629	–	–	3,807	286	–	–	1,395	–	–
1918	5,870	–	–	827	–	–	3,515	304	–	–	1,224	–	–
1917	4,307	–	–	503	–	–	2,911	290[6]	–	–	603	–	–
1916	2,005	–	–	–	–	–	2,005	–	–	–	–	–	–
1915	893	–	–	–	–	–	893	–	–	–	–	–	–

[1] Includes temporary disability benefits, pension payments and survivors benefits.
[2] These programs were introduced in different years in different provinces under provincial legislation.

[3] In 1975, total compensation payments included $333,272,000 for temporary disability and $204,144,000 for pensions.
[4] Six-month period ending 31 December 1930.
[5] Four-month period ending 31 December 1928.
[6] Ten-month period ending 31 December 1917.

Series C287-299. Old Age Pensions,[1] number of recipients, for Canada and by province, at 31 March, 1928 to 1951

Year	Canada	New-found-land	Prince Edward Island	Nova Scotia	New Bruns-wick	Quebec	Ontario	Manitoba	Saskat-chewan	Alberta	British Columbia	Yukon Terri-tory	North-west Terri-tories
	287	288	289	290	291	292	293	294	295	296	297	298	299
1951[2]	302,173	11,394	3,136	20,808	16,681	73,564	91,509	17,573	17,409	17,990	31,983	100	26
1950	282,584	10,296	2,976	19,966	16,231	69,017	85,100	16,868	16,566	16,445	28,988	108	23
1949	251,865	–	2,688	18,450	15,412	64,366	78,413	16,110	15,785	14,988	25,633	–	20
1948	229,158	–	2,417	16,984	14,524	59,204	70,765	15,026	14,806	13,792	21,621	–	19
1947	209,029	–	2,112	15,403	13,360	54,489	65,085	13,583	14,204	12,738	18,039	–	16
1946	196,941	–	1,980	14,771	12,663	51,567	60,831	12,981	13,398	12,098	16,637	–	15
1945	187,512	–	1,884	14,032	12,269	49,289	58,113	12,324	12,827	11,418	15,344	–	12
1944	181,384	–	1,888	13,838	11,843	47,153	56,156	12,188	12,755	11,071	14,481	–	11
1943	183,601	–	1,904	14,080	11,818	47,045	57,692	12,498	13,074	11,134	14,348	–	8
1942	185,922	–	1,952	14,285	11,779	47,338	59,232	12,701	13,211	10,952	14,464	–	8
1941	185,946	–	1,987	14,454	11,747	48,000	59,224	12,727	13,111	10,746	13,942	–	8
1940	186,035	–	2,007	14,502	11,815	48,797	59,717	12,560	12,567	10,677	13,386	–	7
1939	181,514	–	1,891	14,221	11,564	47,939	58,858	12,227	12,227	10,175	12,504	–	7
1938	175,673	–	1,811	13,827	11,142	46,490	57,530	11,800	11,775	9,726	11,563	–	9
1937	146,524	–	1,768	13,456	9,803	22,620	55,950	11,559	11,436	9,100	10,824	–	8
1936	108,415	–	1,659	13,044	–	–	54,040	10,862	10,706	8,086	10,011	–	7
1935	101,051	–	1,439	12,241	–	–	50,771	10,229	10,137	7,151	9,076	–	7
1934	86,873	–	1,258	6,509	–	–	46,281	9,236	9,203	6,286	8,095	–	5
1933	71,705	–	–	–	–	–	42,853	8,280	8,195	5,244	7,128	–	5
1932	67,006	–	–	–	–	–	41,300	7,190	7,643	4,382	6,486	–	5
1931	57,930	–	–	–	–	–	37,334	5,834	5,913	3,287	5,557	–	5
1930	42,553	–	–	–	–	–	26,370	5,104	4,482	2,017	4,576	–	4
1929	10,588	–	–	–	–	–	–	3,953	2,768	–	3,867	–	–
1928	2,712	–	–	–	–	–	–	–	–	–	2,712	–	–

[1] The program was introduced in 1927 and terminated in December 1951 when the Old Age Security Program was introduced.

[2] For month of December 1951.

Series C300-312. Old Age Pensions,[1] total federal-provincial cost-shared payments to pensioners, for Canada and by province, fiscal years ending 31 March, 1928 to 1952

(thousands of dollars)

Year	Canada	New-found-land	Prince Edward Island	Nova Scotia	New Bruns-wick	Quebec	Ontario	Manitoba	Saskat-chewan	Alberta	British Columbia	Yukon Terri-tory	North-west Terri-tories
	300	301	302	303	304	305	306	307	308	309	310	311	312
1952[2]	102,939	4,127	993	6,708	5,538	25,437	31,048	6,128	6,021	6,120	10,783	32	12
1951	132,357	5,092	1,260	8,763	7,236	32,639	40,087	7,980	7,732	7,835	13,669	49	15
1950	119,536	2,972	1,153	8,076	6,779	29,772	37,152	7,439	7,141	6,911	12,096	32	13
1949	85,643	–	791	6,212	5,280	21,699	27,056	5,503	5,487	5,120	8,485	–	11
1948	75,971	–	639	5,259	4,845	19,619	24,000	4,969	5,116	4,621	6,895	–	8
1947	58,440	–	468	4,124	3,532	15,289	18,515	3,769	4,113	3,599	5,024	–	5
1946	55,055	–	429	3,885	3,332	14,431	17,507	3,579	3,871	3,368	4,648	–	5
1945	52,671	–	416	3,744	3,188	13,848	16,388	3,840	3,727	3,201	4,315	–	4
1944	42,928	–	359	2,849	2,311	11,380	13,748	2,671	3,136	2,751	3,721	–	3
1943	38,481	–	279	2,597	2,141	9,399	12,845	2,791	2,724	2,445	3,257	–	3
1942	38,041	–	267	2,583	2,080	9,016	13,031	2,784	2,679	2,396	3,204	–	3
1941	38,536	–	271	2,588	2,069	9,600	13,085	2,809	2,632	2,371	3,108	–	3
1940	38,775	–	259	2,551	2,040	10,344	13,027	2,749	2,525	2,316	2,960	–	3
1939	37,711	–	238	2,489	1,920	10,183	12,821	2,656	2,428	2,211	2,761	–	3
1938	38,033	–	223	2,449	1,779	11,181	12,703	2,663	2,344	2,081	2,608	–	3
1937	28,199	–	216	2,353	1,157	3,127	12,196	2,563	2,275	1,879	2,431	–	3
1936	22,352	–	197	2,215	–	–	11,569	2,396	2,111	1,632	2,231	–	3
1935	19,923	–	172	1,973	–	–	10,230	2,208	1,940	1,428	1,971	–	3
1934	16,419	–	99	92	–	–	9,448	2,021	1,771	1,245	1,739	–	1
1933[1]	15,351	–	–	–	–	–	9,104	1,816	1,756	1,104	1,568	–	1
1932	13,376	–	–	–	–	–	8,053	1,504	1,580	860	1,377	–	1
1931	7,544	–	–	–	–	–	4,689	871	781	427	775	–	1
1930	3,074	–	–	–	–	–	712	854	666	126	716	–	–
1929	1,666	–	–	–	–	–	–	484	382	–	798	–	–
1928	262	–	–	–	–	–	–	–	–	–	262	–	–

[1] The program was introduced in 1927 and terminated in December 1951 when the Old Age Security Program was introduced. The original program authorized the federal government to cost-share 50 per cent of expenditures on pensions to old age persons. In 1933 the federal share was increased to 75 per cent of the total cost.

[2] Nine-month period ending 31 December 1951.

Series C313-325. Old Age Assistance,[1] number of recipients of assistance, for Canada and by province, at 31 March, 1952 to 1970

Year	Canada	New-found-land	Prince Edward Island	Nova Scotia	New Bruns-wick	Quebec	Ontario	Manitoba	Saskat-chewan	Alberta	British Columbia	Yukon Terri-tory	North-west Terri-tories
	313	314	315	316	317	318	319	320	321	322	323	324	325
1970	4,818	374	50	524	448	2,115	258	255	68	264	430	4	28
1969	6,147	–	–	786	822	2,871	4	658	–	13	949	4	40
1968	24,922	844	206	1,879	1,957	12,839	1,340	1,647	39	1,710	2,377	9	75
1967	58,363	3,110	712	3,134	3,033	22,817	13,279	2,956	1,496	3,617	4,074	15	120
1966	84,959	4,080	988	4,423	4,200	31,971	19,991	4,241	3,975	5,453	5,478	26	133
1965	107,354	5,088	1,229	5,574	5,356	39,239	26,049	5,520	5,463	6,810	6,829	38	159
1964	105,241	5,081	1,130	5,509	5,447	38,206	25,197	5,436	5,549	6,644	6,864	31	147
1963	103,159	5,187	1,039	5,421	5,491	37,086	23,925	5,448	5,866	6,479	7,039	40	138
1962	98,944	5,184	897	5,248	5,421	34,615	22,868	5,082	5,760	6,494	7,189	46	140
1961	100,184	5,342	801	5,395	5,555	35,441	22,736	5,098	5,727	6,584	7,322	48	135
1960	98,773	5,377	750	5,477	5,682	34,312	22,544	4,998	5,726	6,336	7,391	52	128
1959	97,836	5,378	756	5,485	5,795	34,134	22,381	4,836	5,537	6,096	7,276	38	124
1958	92,484	5,119	659	5,219	5,724	32,318	21,077	4,474	5,129	5,715	6,906	41	103
1957	89,907	4,893	580	4,950	5,624	31,031	20,744	4,560	4,963	5,400	7,029	31	102
1956	93,023	4,848	600	5,081	5,891	32,227	21,731	4,652	4,925	5,521	7,441	20	86
1955	94,625	5,073	612	5,178	5,808	32,882	22,061	4,847	4,853	5,341	7,868	12	90
1954	93,273	5,124	594	5,173	5,756	32,391	21,587	4,838	4,584	5,014	8,144	4	64
1953	87,675	5,037	551	4,789	5,371	30,490	20,401	4,400	4,206	4,688	7,685	–	57
1952	41,601	–	305	2,271	3,237	12,267	12,697	1,239	2,497	2,954	4,134	–	–

[1] Under the Old Age Assistance Act 1951, the federal government contributed 50 per cent of payments by the provinces for assistance to persons aged 65 and over but who were not eligible for Old Age Security. The program ended in January 1970 when the eligible age for Old Age Security was lowered to 65.

Series C326-338. Old Age Assistance,[1] total federal-provincial cost-shared payments to recipients, for Canada and by province, fiscal years ending 31 March, 1952 to 1970
(thousands of dollars)

Year	Canada	New-found-land	Prince Edward Island	Nova Scotia	New Bruns-wick	Quebec	Ontario	Manitoba	Saskat-chewan	Alberta	British Columbia	Yukon Terri-tory	North-west Terri-tories
	326	327	328	329	330	331	332	333	334	335	336	337	338
1970	1,688	–	–	382	444	–	–	302	–	–	538	2	20
1969	13,282	378	36	1,226	1,366	6,394	284	1,090	–	752	1,688	6	62
1968	36,000	1,970	412	2,178	2,280	18,100	2,732	2,078	592	2,512	3,042	12	92
1967	63,980	3,352	780	3,334	3,240	24,480	14,478	3,224	2,262	4,184	4,504	18	124
1966	85,842	4,242	996	4,376	4,324	31,882	20,012	4,376	4,196	5,592	5,672	28	148
1965	90,018	4,442	1,018	4,642	4,606	33,178	20,930	4,658	4,588	5,802	5,982	172	
1964	78,416	3,890	790	4,168	4,242	27,720	18,270	4,212	4,302	5,120	5,564	138	
1963	76,358	3,974	750	4,016	4,132	27,588	16,916	4,004	4,442	5,048	5,350	140	
1962	61,622	3,346	498	3,138	3,520	21,792	13,806	3,304	3,524	4,002	4,568	32	92
1961	61,314	3,416	434	3,216	3,494	21,954	13,260	3,202	3,540	4,018	4,666	32	86
1960	60,696	3,472	410	3,238	3,578	21,376	13,216	3,162	3,514	3,910	4,708	30	80
1959	60,414	3,430	384	3,224	3,658	21,186	13,414	3,146	3,528	3,754	4,584	26	80
1958	49,922	2,598	284	2,636	3,120	17,406	11,300	2,594	2,870	3,078	3,958	20	58
1957	40,798	2,034	196	2,052	2,552	14,318	9,356	2,132	2,320	2,440	3,340	14	46
1956	41,836	1,754	200	2,094	2,606	14,714	9,838	2,224	2,300	2,480	3,576	6	42
1955	41,738	1,798	198	2,126	2,576	14,786	9,718	2,240	2,180	2,330	3,746	4	38
1954	40,576	1,792	172	2,058	2,496	14,374	9,452	2,224	2,036	2,214	3,726	2	28
1953	38,258	1,668	132	1,786	2,228	13,856	9,174	2,072	1,994	1,936	3,404	–	8
1952	4,554	–	14	192	332	1,380	1,346	214	266	288	526	–	–

[1] Under the Old Age Assistance Act 1951, the federal government contributed 50 per cent of payments by the provinces for assistance to persons aged 65 and over but who were not eligible for Old Age Security. The program ended in January 1970 when the eligible age for Old Age Security was lowered to 65.

Series C339-351. Blind Persons Allowances,[1] number of direct recipients of allowances, for Canada and by province, at 31 March, 1953 to 1975

Year	Canada	New-found-land	Prince Edward Island	Nova Scotia	New Bruns-wick	Quebec	Ontario	Manitoba	Saskat-chewan	Alberta	British Columbia	Yukon Terri-tory	North-west Terri-tories
	339	340	341	342	343	344	345	346	347	348	349	350	351
1975	1,560	222	46	373	358	247	50	89	27	141	–	–	7
1974	1,814	273	48	398	341	312	81	122	32	161	31	2	13
1973	2,557	310	47	435	364	480	99	134	36	190	429	4	29
1972	2,916	352	46	474	397	636	152	147	43	209	429	5	26
1971	4,015	374	50	511	424	1,554	183	169	54	234	432	4	26
1970	4,818	374	50	524	448	2,115	258	255	68	264	430	4	28
1969	5,267	401	63	577	491	2,242	330	276	99	315	439	4	30
1968	5,808	417	69	636	536	2,424	435	292	131	376	451	6	33
1967	7,582	438	67	682	589	2,560	1,710	325	272	412	484	5	38
1966	8,149	445	72	714	626	2,712	1,820	364	366	448	532	6	44
1965	8,586	460	71	750	679	2,843	1,906	401	391	475	556	5	49
1964	8,581	436	79	775	679	2,855	1,902	383	406	465	551	4	46
1963	8,634	429	83	792	701	2,891	1,877	379	422	463	547	4	46
1962	8,573	429	80	771	697	2,901	1,846	378	406	454	563	3	45
1961	8,642	422	81	786	696	2,949	1,845	380	409	461	568	3	42
1960	8,671	418	85	773	706	3,012	1,847	396	397	459	541	3	34
1959	8,747	407	87	787	724	3,056	1,833	409	417	464	530	5	28
1958	8,400	376	96	745	715	2,956	1,720	392	412	451	505	5	27
1957	8,256	370	90	714	719	2,918	1,713	402	399	418	482	6	25
1956	8,230	353	96	726	717	2,905	1,719	411	389	415	475	6	18
1955	8,122	338	95	706	706	2,866	1,731	405	374	409	474	2	16
1954	8,214	336	90	718	731	2,949	1,710	411	366	400	488	2	13
1953	8,332	336	79	722	750	3,041	1,751	430	342	383	485	2	11

[1] The program was phased out, in 1966 and subsequent years, as social assistance recipients were transferred to provincial programs under the Canada Assistance Plan.

Series C352-364. Blind Persons Allowances,[1] total federal-provincial cost-shared payments to direct recipients, for Canada and by province, fiscal years ending 31 March, 1952 to 1975
(thousands of dollars)

Year	Canada	New-found-land	Prince Edward Island	Nova Scotia	New Bruns-wick	Quebec	Ontario	Manitoba	Saskat-chewan	Alberta	British Columbia	Yukon Terri-tory	North-west Terri-tories
	352	353	354	355	356	357	358	359	360	361	362	363	364
1975	2,069	288	61	504	475	347	36	109	35	201	–	–	13
1974	2,713	386	64	548	463	507	55	141	44	231	240	4	30
1973	3,448	435	64	590	501	707	73	166	50	261	557	6	38
1972	3,925	476	63	649	543	897	147	194	57	292	568	6	34
1971	5,720	495	66	679	579	2,457	163	259	78	329	572	5	38
1970	6,603	524	75	740	629	2,896	272	349	103	385	585	5	40
1969	7,198	555	81	810	690	3,084	357	374	134	459	602	7	46
1968	7,921	570	91	881	744	3,292	519	401	221	516	632	8	46
1967	10,210	584	92	932	816	3,455	2,163	452	409	568	673	8	56
1966	10,947	608	95	975	877	3,682	2,306	503	496	615	717	8	65
1965	11,249	601	102	1,020	914	3,786	2,358	518	512	624	744	5	65
1964	9,976	494	94	938	836	3,286	2,091	461	492	556	671	4	54
1963	9,764	495	94	900	820	3,326	1,985	428	481	543	639	4	47
1962	8,260	418	80	772	698	2,824	1,673	377	387	445	541	3	41
1961	8,324	406	80	762	683	2,914	1,682	374	392	442	538	3	38
1960	8,396	401	84	758	698	2,988	1,679	390	391	448	526	4	30
1959	8,470	400	87	754	715	3,002	1,734	397	406	447	498	5	25
1958	7,151	305	75	626	621	2,530	1,471	340	352	377	428	5	22
1957	5,919	265	63	516	517	2,094	1,227	295	284	302	339	4	15
1956	5,837	252	65	510	517	2,072	1,220	291	270	291	334	3	13
1955	5,772	240	61	496	513	2,058	1,215	290	265	280	342	2	10
1954	5,828	244	56	502	527	2,116	1,204	296	252	271	350	1	9
1953	5,970	236	53	508	548	2,208	1,265	307	247	268	326	1	3
1952[2]	1,443	56	13	128	138	544	286	72	61	68	76	–	–

[1] The program was phased out, in 1966 and subsequent years, as social assistance recipients were transferred to provincial programs under the Canada Assistance Plan.

[2] Three-month period ending 31 March 1952.

Series C365-377. Disabled Persons Allowances,[1] number of direct recipients of allowances, for Canada and by province, at 31 March, 1955 to 1975

Year	Canada	New-found-land	Prince Edward Island	Nova Scotia	New Bruns-wick	Quebec	Ontario	Manitoba	Saskat-chewan	Alberta	British Columbia	Yukon Terri-tory	North-west Terri-tories
	365	366	367	368	369	370	371	372	373	374	375	376	377
1975	3,902	13	4	113	2,006	387	84	154	29	1,100	–	–	12
1974	4,369	16	4	183	1,743	556	168	220	46	1,198	216	3	16
1973	8,213	28	5	280	1,824	1,472	233	267	59	1,281	2,722	5	37
1972	9,468	32	7	359	1,972	2,340	310	330	75	1,388	2,618	5	32
1971	18,608	43	28	494	2,068	10,876	445	463	91	1,479	2,580	6	35
1970	25,739	49	38	591	2,215	16,327	901	1,331	119	1,596	2,533	5	34
1969	30,663	82	54	3,371	2,292	17,506	1,436	1,428	170	1,810	2,480	3	31
1968	34,438	1,393	78	3,482	2,265	18,649	2,401	1,498	272	1,925	2,445	3	27
1967	53,863	1,873	814	3,522	2,266	19,273	19,800	1,547	390	1,931	2,422	2	23
1966	54,191	1,817	788	3,474	2,320	19,603	18,406	1,566	1,871	1,933	2,385	2	26
1965	53,106	1,746	797	3,329	2,263	20,171	17,222	1,538	1,780	1,874	2,336	3	47
1964	51,671	1,586	801	3,108	2,141	20,753	15,938	1,518	1,657	1,815	2,319	3	32
1963	50,621	1,436	795	2,919	2,060	21,347	14,886	1,520	1,602	1,780	2,248	4	24
1962	50,029	1,292	780	2,776	2,000	22,528	13,762	1,447	1,502	1,762	2,156	5	19
1961	50,650	1,220	752	2,704	1,963	24,009	13,307	1,415	1,449	1,790	2,017	4	20
1960	49,889	1,128	650	2,484	1,874	25,103	12,354	1,376	1,337	1,702	1,866	3	12
1959	48,040	980	596	2,184	1,734	25,352	11,469	1,230	1,248	1,648	1,585	2	12
1958	41,840	822	460	1,790	1,474	22,929	9,412	1,028	1,146	1,492	1,281	–	6
1957	31,835	720	345	1,465	1,262	15,856	8,065	819	988	1,245	1,067	–	3
1956	26,027	606	292	1,172	947	12,128	7,501	738	788	1,150	705	–	–
1955	7,166	–	–	285	177	–	6,623	45	36	–	–	–	–

[1] The program was phased out, in 1966 and subsequent years, as social assistance recipients were transferred to provincial programs under the Canada Assistance Plan.

Series C378-390. Disabled Persons Allowances,[1] total federal-provincial cost-shared payments to direct recipients, for Canada and by province, fiscal years ending 31 March, 1955 to 1975
(thousands of dollars)

Year	Canada	New-found-land	Prince Edward Island	Nova Scotia	New Bruns-wick	Quebec	Ontario	Manitoba	Saskat-chewan	Alberta	British Columbia	Yukon Terri-tory	North-west Terri-tories
	378	379	380	381	382	383	384	385	386	387	388	389	390
1975	3,483	9	4	105	1,737	365	79	153	26	991	–	2	12
1974	5,378	14	4	203	1,582	877	143	198	41	1,076	1,211	4	24
1973	7,588	21	5	259	1,675	1,610	198	242	53	1,159	2,330	5	32
1972	8,580	24	10	339	1,802	2,173	277	316	58	1,256	2,287	5	32
1971	19,418	34	26	446	1,915	12,280	428	566	79	1,356	2,253	5	31
1970	23,790	44	35	764	2,012	14,986	849	1,218	115	1,503	2,232	3	29
1969	28,680	924	37	3,072	2,045	15,904	1,371	1,292	162	1,643	2,199	3	29
1968	30,713	931	354	3,128	2,032	16,585	2,194	1,343	259	1,690	2,173	3	22
1967	47,124	1,667	738	3,168	2,084	17,071	16,755	1,375	380	1,718	2,144	2	22
1966	47,602	1,608	700	3,048	2,061	17,643	15,647	1,377	1,650	1,704	2,123	2	39
1965	46,731	1,501	720	2,893	1,975	18,181	14,756	1,360	1,570	1,660	2,075	2	37
1964	40,413	1,174	621	2,460	1,720	16,163	12,366	1,231	1,338	1,455	1,859	5	21
1963	39,269	1,066	624	2,228	1,582	17,156	11,074	1,155	1,262	1,395	1,707	5	16
1962	32,867	827	518	1,817	1,337	14,922	9,006	956	979	1,117	1,371	4	13
1961	32,772	778	461	1,696	1,267	15,992	8,327	911	928	1,112	1,285	2	12
1960	32,102	697	396	1,519	1,193	16,615	7,717	866	866	1,073	1,149	2	8
1959	30,661	604	338	1,325	1,105	16,725	6,972	762	811	1,032	980	–	6
1958	22,183	412	226	914	809	12,098	5,048	547	634	794	698	–	3
1957	14,335	326	131	581	564	7,187	3,706	386	444	553	456	–	–
1956	11,330	239	113	509	437	5,124	3,424	345	326	582	231	–	–
1955[2]	839	–	–	24	16	–	778	16	4	–	–	–	–

[1] The program was phased out, in 1966 and subsequent years, as social assistance recipients were transferred to provincial programs under the Canada Assistance Plan.

[2] Three-month period ending 31 March 1955.

Series C391-403. Unemployment Assistance,[1] number of recipients of direct financial assistance, for Canada and by province, at 31 March, 1956 to 1966

Year	Canada	New-found-land	Prince Edward Island	Nova Scotia	New Bruns-wick	Quebec	Ontario	Manitoba	Saskat-chewan	Alberta	British Columbia	Yukon Terri-tory	North-west Terri-tories
	391	392	393	394	395	396	397	398	399	400	401	402	403
1966	789,694	58,046	2,741	25,770	27,474	275,580	163,326	44,115	37,572	62,069	91,417	288	1,296
1965	717,030	63,906	2,631	26,556	24,552	247,389	130,987	31,514	39,200	60,352	88,839	334	770
1964	727,961	65,443	3,004	28,079	32,342	239,614	138,890	31,542	41,914	53,837	91,787	299	1,210
1963	760,466	66,068	3,236	28,146	42,653	266,355	136,003	32,127	43,798	47,494	93,356	294	936
1962	684,348	62,948	2,494	26,072	34,769	237,891	120,793	30,790	44,291	35,220	88,499	250	331
1961	562,720	51,985	2,395	23,338	30,567	175,165	111,235	27,113	27,286	26,388	86,702	244	302
1960	322,553	52,505	2,258	11,093	9,077	63,946	83,762	20,165	18,920	17,636	42,870	147	174
1959	297,760	58,257	1,418	9,209	7,589	55,145	79,385	16,065	15,507	15,824	39,103	101	157
1958	182,054	45,799	1,724	5,083	5,800	—	61,623	12,785	12,873	11,845	24,522	—	—
1957	123,445	39,489	1,532	—	3,797	—	37,379	9,836	10,123	—	21,289	—	—
1956	86,234	38,641	1,596	—	3,843	—	—	10,905	10,464	—	20,785	—	—

[1] The program was phased out, in 1966 and subsequent years, as social assistance recipients were transferred to provincial programs under the Canada Assistance Plan.

Series C404-416. Unemployment Assistance,[1] total federal-provincial cost-shared payments of direct financial assistance, for Canada and by province, fiscal years ending 31 March, 1956 to 1975
(thousands of dollars)

Year	Canada	New-found-land	Prince Edward Island	Nova Scotia	New Bruns-wick	Quebec	Ontario	Manitoba	Saskat-chewan	Alberta	British Columbia	Yukon Terri-tory	North-west Terri-tories
	404	405	406	407	408	409	410	411	412	413	414	415	416
1975	126	—	—	—	—	80	—	—	—	40	—	—	6
1974	1,288	—	—	—	—	278	—	—	—	56	—	—	954
1973	2,676	—	—	—	—	550	—	—	—	98	—	—	2,028
1972	2,148	—	—	—	—	—	—	—	—	128	—	—	2,020
1971	28,258	—	—	—	—	26,692	428	—	—	184	—	16	938
1970	29,280	—	—	—	—	27,818	836	—	—	212	—	174	240
1969	33,564	—	20	104	—	31,400	1,306	—	—	356	—	170	208
1968	88,140	—	1,332	46	260	75,200	3,480	634	—	3,254	3,612	184	138
1967	286,542	19,896	1,210	6,742	4,046	66,576	85,846	14,790	15,014	27,714	44,400	168	140
1966	203,414	8,956	806	3,734	3,482	49,148	55,176	11,204	8,778	22,074	39,788	140	130
1965	215,106	9,408	562	3,726	2,828	82,032	42,102	10,798	9,172	18,424	35,716	144	194
1964	214,740	9,024	800	3,582	3,850	78,878	48,978	11,548	9,282	15,960	32,526	118	194
1963	192,948	8,606	388	3,170	3,214	67,158	47,588	9,248	9,116	12,404	31,880	90	86
1962	175,798	8,128	348	3,486	3,054	64,678	37,482	8,570	9,050	8,924	31,930	80	68
1961	119,216	6,826	310	3,708	2,990	34,310	29,092	7,102	4,454	5,836	24,484	64	40
1960	76,404	7,062	244	1,438	720	15,298	23,340	5,740	3,648	4,188	14,610	66	50
1959	61,696	6,538	194	896	548	10,466	20,336	4,138	2,984	3,650	11,900	14	32
1958	21,626	3,576	146	152	188	—	7,290	2,170	1,626	820	5,658	—	—
1957	11,524	3,124	108	—	66	—	1,264	1,338	1,026	—	4,600	—	—
1956	7,666	2,350	110	—	38	—	—	986	740	—	3,442	—	—

[1] The program was phased out, in 1966 and subsequent years, as social assistance recipients were transferred to provincial programs under the Canada Assistance Plan.

Series C417-429. Canada Assistance Plan, number of recipients, including dependents of direct financial assistance, for Canada and by province,[1] at 31 March, 1971 to 1976

Year	Canada	New-found-land	Prince Edward Island	Nova Scotia	New Bruns-wick	Quebec[2]	Ontario	Manitoba	Saskat-chewan	Alberta	British Columbia	Yukon Terri-tory	North-west Terri-tories[3]
	417	418	419	420	421	422	423	424	425	426	427	428	429
1976	1,322,918	61,009	8,812	54,160	52,521	428,713	367,943	57,574	43,490	78,220	162,076	8,400	
1975	1,280,441	63,127	8,401	52,358	55,604	416,558	336,415	56,616	45,332	77,970	162,349	5,711	
1974	1,208,629	63,250	7,291	47,597	51,879	395,820	317,283	60,681	44,405	80,609	137,192	2,622	
1973	1,221,413	70,912	7,238	52,864	58,575	406,452	307,880	70,427	56,728	85,456	103,989	892	—
1972	1,379,257	80,574	15,913	52,278	61,717	462,571	333,584	78,544	69,604	88,983	134,198	1,291	—
1971	1,460,064	91,852	10,552	45,593	65,756	489,073	364,046	75,763	68,338	93,960	154,851	280	—

[1] Provincial data not available prior to 1971.
[2] Formula used to obtain Quebec figures was calculated by multiplying the number of cases by the average number of recipients (for example, March $1976 = 202,730 \times 2.117 = 428,713$).

[3] The Northwest Territories introduced the plan in the fiscal year 1973-74.

Series C430-442. Canada Assistance Plan, federal-provincial cost-shared payments of direct financial assistance, for Canada and by province, fiscal years ending 31 March, 1969 to 1976
(thousands of dollars)

Year	Canada[1]	New-found-land	Prince Edward Island	Nova Scotia	New Bruns-wick	Quebec	Ontario	Manitoba	Saskat-chewan	Alberta	British Columbia	Yukon Terri-tory[2]	North-west Terri-tories[2]
	430	431	432	433	434	435	436	437	438	439	440	441	442
1976	1,605,430	47,080	6,274	48,158	78,836	520,708	483,790	51,170	44,024	105,250	215,802	306	4,032
1975	1,374,850	45,846	5,722	39,798	55,644	427,826	411,706	46,524	42,106	88,856	203,878	482	6,462
1974	1,079,386	33,526	3,868	35,608	42,656	368,908	311,242	42,732	47,696	77,004	115,242	430	474
1973	1,027,206	40,024	3,758	27,686	34,756	367,380	280,468	45,668	40,202	80,336	106,564	364	..
1972	987,148	41,090	3,404	27,454	28,988	336,540	296,398	47,280	36,790	65,980	103,092	132	..
1971	782,132	35,328	3,182	20,338	22,056	236,446	232,624	41,574	29,650	61,056	99,622	256	..
1970	580,270	33,069	2,583	18,600	13,357	180,800	171,771	28,997	21,269	47,567	61,950	306	..
1969	521,900	35,191	2,033	12,920	12,805	168,250	155,184	20,164	19,249	40,945	55,160	..	..

[1] Provincial data not available for 1967 and 1968. Canada totals were *(thousands of dollars)*: 1967, 20,992 and 1968, 440,054.

[2] The Yukon Territory introduced the plan in the fiscal year 1969-70 and the Northwest Territories in 1973-74.

Series C443-455. Federal-provincial cost-shared payments under the Canada Assistance Plan, for homes for special care, for Canada and by province, fiscal years ending 31 March, 1970 to 1976
(thousands of dollars)

Year	Canada[1]	New-found-land	Prince Edward Island	Nova Scotia	New Bruns-wick	Quebec[2]	Ontario	Manitoba	Saskat-chewan	Alberta	British Columbia	Yukon Terri-tory[3]	North-west Terri-tories[3]
	443	**444**	**445**	**446**	**447**	**448**	**449**	**450**	**451**	**452**	**453**	**454**	**455**
1976	668,104	15,112	7,000	17,004	6,596	331,582	132,086	13,662	25,392	36,898	80,326	580	1,866
1975	364,098	10,500	6,346	11,934	2,658	239,306	29,692	9,602	13,792	8,230	28,858	532	2,648
1974	277,200	8,310	4,694	9,950	4,180	180,560	19,284	13,572	11,332	5,988	17,836	394	1,100
1973	283,276	5,374	3,832	9,850	6,058	154,228	68,182	12,016	7,194	6,422	9,680	440	—
1972	265,172	4,270	3,794	7,828	4,278	149,140	62,956	11,036	6,050	4,754	11,066	..	—
1971	207,020	2,878	3,470	6,938	3,846	107,240	59,428	2,166	5,722	3,470	11,562	300	—
1970	92,952	2,686	3,068	7,010	3,630	23,800	36,892	284	4,898	2,348	8,336	—	—

[1] Provincial data not available for 1968 and 1969. Canada totals were *(thousands of dollars)*: 1968, 81,300 and 1969, 91,364.
[2] Estimated payments made to Quebec under the Established Programs (Interim Arrangements) Act through the Department of Finance.
[3] The Yukon Territory introduced the plan in the fiscal year 1970-71 and the Northwest Territories in 1973-74.

Series C456-468. Federal-provincial cost-shared payments under the Canada Assistance Plan, for child welfare, for Canada and by province, fiscal years ending 31 March, 1970 to 1976
(thousands of dollars)

Year	Canada[1]	New-found-land	Prince Edward Island	Nova Scotia	New Bruns-wick	Quebec[2]	Ontario	Manitoba	Saskat-chewan	Alberta	British Columbia	Yukon Terri-tory[3]	North-west Terri-tories[3]
	456	**457**	**458**	**459**	**460**	**461**	**462**	**463**	**464**	**465**	**466**	**467**	**468**
1976	124,850	2,902	468	5,130	2,138	44,262	28,358	10,818	4,130	14,394	11,788	184	278
1975	124,462	2,272	452	3,214	1,886	44,620	31,408	8,794	3,968	10,752	16,648	12	436
1974	112,400	2,036	518	3,718	1,868	44,450	29,768	6,230	2,706	8,272	12,098	428	308
1973	89,430	1,642	426	2,760	1,718	26,702	33,938	4,220	2,654	7,502	7,698	170	—
1972	82,470	1,690	368	3,260	2,236	26,700	26,808	4,426	2,206	6,728	7,964	84	—
1971	80,668	1,416	394	2,442	1,908	25,404	27,684	3,954	1,962	6,962	8,034	508	—
1970	114,508	1,342	384	2,242	2,020	67,600	22,856	3,552	2,020	6,316	6,176	—	—

[1] Provincial data not available for 1968 and 1969. Canada totals were *(thousands of dollars)*: 1968, 76,200 and 1969, 79,034.
[2] Estimated payments made to Quebec under the Established Programs (Interim Arrangements) Act through the Department of Finance.
[3] The Yukon Territory introduced the plan in the fiscal year 1970-71 and the Northwest Territories in 1973-74.

Series C469-481. Federal-provincial cost-shared payments under the Canada Assistance Plan, for other welfare services and work activity, for Canada and by province, fiscal years ending 31 March, 1970 to 1976
(thousands of dollars)

Year	Canada[1]	New-found-land	Prince Edward Island	Nova Scotia	New Bruns-wick	Quebec[2]	Ontario	Manitoba	Saskat-chewan	Alberta	British Columbia	Yukon Terri-tory[3]	North-west Terri-tories[3]
	469	**470**	**471**	**472**	**473**	**474**	**475**	**476**	**477**	**478**	**479**	**480**	**481**
1976	306,006	4,432	2,342	10,628	10,132	65,406	108,318	15,476	7,564	25,484	54,102	1,654	468
1975	203,138	3,358	1,376	6,760	8,006	58,128	67,084	11,650	6,228	13,690	23,912	454	2,492
1974	159,164	3,334	1,078	5,570	9,360	43,082	51,646	10,078	5,408	13,652	14,824	314	818
1973	114,970	2,484	680	3,486	1,384	38,000	35,816	7,372	4,822	10,810	9,802	314	—
1972	96,226	1,626	458	4,660	3,254	28,630	33,464	6,130	2,380	7,268	8,254	102	—
1971	80,788	1,382	188	3,310	—	21,000	30,606	5,510	1,686	6,088	10,646	372	—
1970	62,710	956	174	2,126	1,598	19,000	20,638	3,382	4,284	4,896	5,656	—	—

[1] Provincial data not available for 1968 and 1969. Canada totals were *(thousands of dollars)*: 1968, 54,000 and 1969, 59,784.
[2] Estimated payments made to Quebec under the Established Programs (Interim Arrangements) Act through the Department of Finance.
[3] The Yukon Territory introduced the plan in the fiscal year 1970-71 and the Northwest Territories in 1973-74.

Series C482-494. Vocational rehabilitation of disabled persons, federal-provincial cost-shared payments for clients, for Canada and by province, fiscal years ending 31 March, 1963 to 1976
(thousands of dollars)

Year	Canada	New-found-land	Prince Edward Island	Nova Scotia	New Bruns-wick	Quebec[1]	Ontario	Manitoba	Saskat-chewan	Alberta	British Columbia	Yukon Terri-tory	North-west Terri-tories
	482	483	484	485	486	487	488	489	490	491	492	493	494
1976	41,222	398	210	1,778	514	—	23,192	3,500	3,624	5,582	2,044	274	105
1975	24,000	320	134	988	794	—	14,092	1,192	1,680	4,678	100	—	22
1974	19,986	124	92	200	174	—	13,176	1,712	1,614	2,162	732	—	—
1973	14,900	138	38	558	424	—	8,484	1,308	1,572	1,716	662	—	—
1972	13,000	94	28	460	148	—	7,476	1,832	1,444	1,008	500	—	—
1971	10,518	88	34	530	292	—	5,468	1,424	1,252	1,020	410	—	—
1970	10,026	90	34	410	322	—	4,514	2,190	1,356	628	484	—	—
1969	7,800	58	22	208	192	—	4,044	1,080	1,374	488	354	—	—
1968	4,900	34	22	132	128	—	2,790	940	526	122	208	—	—
1967	2,050	30	16	80	140	—	912	280	346	74	172	—	—
1966	1,688	32	14	70	124	—	614	342	342	58	90	—	—
1965	1,284	26	14	60	108	—	418	268	254	84	54	—	—
1964	1,034	16	8	56	110	—	278	226	238	68	34	—	—
1963	668	22	6	48	104	—	152	168	96	44	28	—	—

[1] The Vocational Rehabilitation of Disabled Persons Act 1961, authorized the federal government to share on a 50/50 basis with the provinces in providing a comprehensive program for the vocational rehabilitation of disabled persons. Initially administered by the Department of Labour, the program was transferred to the Department of Manpower and Immigration in 1967 and to the Department of National Health and Welfare in 1973. Agreements have been signed with all provinces except Quebec.

Series C495-507. Registered Indians, federal payments for social services,[1] for Canada and by province, fiscal years ending 31 March, 1968 to 1975
(thousands of dollars)

Year	Canada	New-found-land	Prince Edward Island[2]	Nova Scotia[2]	New Bruns-wick[2]	Quebec	Ontario	Manitoba	Saskat-chewan	Alberta	British Columbia	Yukon Terri-tory	North-west Terri-tories
	495	496	497	498	499	500	501	502	503	504	505	506	507
1975	16,595	—	47	336	273	897	2,849	2,465	1,630	2,763	4,708	625	..
1974	14,545	—	30	209	170	1,001	2,223	2,118	1,188	2,866	4,247	493	..
1973	13,188	—	32	224	181	579	1,796	1,573	1,268	1,915	5,184	436	..
1972	10,944	—	32	223	179	578	1,821	1,570	1,204	1,355	3,606	376	..
1971	12,911	—	29	210	169	763	1,537	1,114	1,032	960	7,097	..	..
1970	9,018	—	24	168	136	475	1,507	737	923	692	4,356	..	..
1969	7,537	—	23	164	134	290	1,323	541	696	559	3,807	..	..
1968	6,172	—	63	440	359	203	1,210	458	586	395	2,458	..	..

[1] Care of adults, child care, rehabilitation and other welfare services.

[2] Regional payments allocated in accordance with provincial populations.

Series C508-520. Mothers Allowances,[1] number of families receiving allowances, for Canada and by province, fiscal years ending 31 March, 1926 to 1966

Year	Canada	New-found-land	Prince Edward Island	Nova Scotia	New Bruns-wick	Quebec	Ontario	Manitoba	Saskat-chewan	Alberta	British Columbia	Yukon Terri-tory	North-west Terri-tories
	508	**509**	**510**	**511**	**512**	**513**	**514**	**515**	**516**	**517**	**518**	**519**	**520**
1966	46,216	5,733	370	3,361	2,222	15,816	13,621	2,256	2,380	457	—	—	—
1965	44,389	5,382	314	3,436	2,284	15,785	12,073	1,975	2,461	679	—	—	—
1964	46,235	5,172	314	3,331	2,254	19,222	10,700	1,845	2,466	931	—	—	—
1963	45,247	4,836	293	2,760	2,165	19,531	10,182	1,811	2,459	1,210	—	—	—
1962	45,472	4,498	269	2,754	2,119	19,842	10,359	1,638	2,382	1,611	—	—	—
1961	45,918	4,211	256	2,658	2,212	20,309	10,149	1,350	2,316	2,457	—	—	—
1960	49,937	4,024	267	2,210	2,213	25,778	9,722	1,209	2,242	2,272	—	—	—
1959	45,451	3,770	276	2,196	2,235	22,403	9,433	823	2,222	2,093	—	—	—
1958	40,478	..	266	2,131	2,213	21,766	8,580	1,121	2,279	1,879	243	—	—
1957	36,960	..	238	2,107	2,151	19,397	7,418	1,128	2,390	1,847	284	—	—
1956	37,809	386	285	2,065	2,022	19,944	7,266	1,188	2,521	1,809	323	—	—
1955	40,580	3,152	237	2,077	2,087	20,024	7,292	1,202	2,397	1,719	393	—	—
1954	39,569	3,031	261	2,313	2,096	19,403	7,059	1,099	2,272	1,609	426	—	—
1953	39,038	3,017	256	2,405	2,066	18,250	7,621	1,005	2,424	1,524	470	—	—
1952	37,612	3,267	225	1,996	1,848	17,032	7,748	932	2,573	1,488	503	—	—
1951	37,155	3,129	230	2,043	1,814	16,915	7,382	880	2,690	1,503	569	—	—
1950	33,115	—	170	1,918	1,788	16,434	7,304	786	2,610	1,462	643	—	—
1949	31,194	—	—	1,725	1,611	15,714	6,815	701	2,555	1,392	681	—	—
1948	32,669	—	—	1,938	1,526	15,321	7,817	708	2,986	1,622	751	—	—
1947	29,540	—	—	1,787	1,396	14,312	6,587	685	2,349	1,561	863	—	—
1946	28,388	—	—	1,615	1,207	13,685	6,687	613	2,117	1,559	905	—	—
1945	27,818	—	—	1,441	918	13,057	7,083	600	2,078	1,701	940	—	—
1944	28,289	—	—	1,365	—	11,973	9,176	643	2,222	1,830	1,080	—	—
1943	26,584	—	—	..	—	—	20,932	..	2,468	1,990	1,194	—	—
1942	33,192	—	—	1,227	—	—	24,715	873	2,734	2,091	1,552	—	—
1941	36,271	—	—	1,221	—	—	27,203	946	2,958	2,246	1,697	—	—
1940	38,705	—	—	1,258	—	—	29,353	1,016	3,054	2,262	1,762	—	—
1939	23,409	—	—	1,291	—	—	13,937	1,055	3,071	2,304	1,751	—	—
1938	23,034	—	—	1,295	—	—	13,644	1,079	3,007	2,317	1,692	—	—
1937	22,101	—	—	1,260	—	—	12,856	1,141	2,958	2,319	1,567	—	—
1936	20,068	—	—	1,222	—	—	11,189	1,140	2,944	2,088	1,485	—	—
1935	16,272	—	—	1,239	—	—	7,875	1,110	2,826	1,812	1,410	—	—
1934	16,172	—	—	1,168	—	—	8,144	1,092	2,608	1,724	1,436	—	—
1933	15,589	—	—	1,158	—	—	7,653	1,078	2,511	1,675	1,514	—	—
1932	15,014	—	—	1,108	—	—	7,418	1,070	2,372	1,499	1,547	—	—
1931	12,980	—	—	1,030	—	—	7,157	1,042	2,183	—	1,568	—	—
1930	12,305	—	—	—	—	—	6,712	1,055	1,800	1,270	1,468	—	—
1929	11,151	—	—	—	—	—	6,411	1,062	1,214	1,094	1,370	—	—
1928	9,205	—	—	—	—	—	5,976	967	—	1,029	1,233	—	—
1927	8,463	—	—	—	—	—	5,540	855	—	968	1,100	—	—
1926	7,933	—	—	—	—	—	5,215	825	—	907	986	—	—

[1] The Mothers Allowances programs were introduced in different years in different provinces and originally the cost was borne entirely by the provinces. At the introduction of federal-provincial cost-shared programs under the Canada Assistance Plan, in 1966 and subsequent years, the Mothers Allowances programs were phased out.

Series C521-533. Mothers Allowances,[1] total provincial-municipal cost-shared payments to families, for Canada and by province, fiscal years ending 31 March, 1926 to 1966
(thousands of dollars)

Year	Canada	New-found-land	Prince Edward Island	Nova Scotia	New Bruns-wick	Quebec	Ontario	Manitoba	Saskat-chewan	Alberta	British Columbia	Yukon Terri-tory	North-west Terri-tories
	521	522	523	524	525	526	527	528	529	530	531	532	533
1966	61,776	5,660	255	2,659	2,046	20,882	22,530	3,397	3,844	503	—	—	—
1965	56,074	5,343	247	2,684	2,089	21,068	17,044	3,047	3,811	741	—	—	—
1964	55,426	5,101	212	2,533	2,031	22,539	15,554	2,777	3,669	1,010	—	—	—
1963	50,642	4,688	141	2,312	1,347	20,743	13,914	2,577	3,513	1,407	—	—	—
1962	48,105	4,309	131	2,259	1,356	19,480	13,650	2,361	2,680	1,879	—	—	—
1961	46,245	4,061	124	2,166	1,399	19,314	12,878	2,073	1,957	2,273	—	—	—
1960	44,885	3,225	131	1,920	1,378	20,156	12,140	1,900	1,950	2,085	—	—	—
1959	41,477	2,859	129	1,888	1,365	18,991	11,033	1,325	2,030	1,857	—	—	—
1958	33,237	2,355	89	1,577	1,336	14,612	8,947	1,092	1,573	1,513	143	—	—
1957	24,146	1,820	79	1,554	1,304	8,275	6,985	1,148	1,482	1,339	160	—	—
1956	23,015	1,418	79	1,525	1,250	7,825	6,761	1,149	1,508	1,315	185	—	—
1955	22,512	1,324	73	1,505	1,302	7,956	6,545	1,132	1,252	1,198	225	—	—
1954	21,437	1,228	66	1,445	1,274	7,621	6,219	1,007	1,217	1,113	247	—	—
1953	21,332	1,217	65	1,406	1,225	7,483	6,431	866	1,329	1,049	261	—	—
1952	18,188	1,262	60	1,390	859	5,503	6,038	783	1,111	896	286	—	—
1951	17,531	1,113	52	1,387	854	5,624	5,546	680	1,107	836	332	—	—
1950	15,897	—	27	1,377	844	5,455	5,346	606	1,083	792	367	—	—
1949	14,298	—	—	1,119	760	5,239	4,535	536	1,069	651	389	—	—
1948	12,805	—	—	1,005	681	5,138	3,485	384	1,026	644	442	—	—
1947	12,011	—	—	920	599	4,766	3,376	373	895	593	489	—	—
1946	11,740	—	—	847	488	4,664	3,451	354	868	569	499	—	—
1945	11,011	—	—	735	385	4,186	3,634	320	652	571	528	—	—
1944	10,056	—	—	631	—	3,698	3,751	319	520	555	582	—	—
1943	6,328	—	—	513	—	..	3,736	336	514	562	667	—	—
1942	9,643	—	—	443	—	2,707	4,319	368	459	595	752	—	—
1941	9,700	—	—	418	—	2,304	4,666	406	489	619	798	—	—
1940	9,506	—	—	418	—	1,970	4,741	431	501	634	811	—	—
1939	9,131	—	—	425	—	1,350	5,017	428	498	623	790	—	—
1938	8,460	—	—	413	—	910	4,852	427	496	614	748	—	—
1937	7,159	—	—	389	—	—	4,583	446	482	576	683	—	—
1936	6,355	—	—	364	—	—	3,947	445	474	508	617	—	—
1935	3,807	—	—	413	—	—	1,380	441	475	508	590	—	—
1934	5,361	—	—	356	—	—	3,026	439	456	462	622	—	—
1933	5,230	—	—	358	—	—	2,802	433	417	440	780	—	—
1932	5,188	—	—	342	—	—	2,690	472	403	439	842	—	—
1931	5,177	—	—	331	—	—	2,582	466	502	480	816	—	—
1930	4,925	—	—	311	—	—	2,377	485	525	467	760	—	—
1929	4,437	—	—	—	—	—	2,306	558	499	397	677	—	—
1928	4,112	—	—	—	—	—	2,190	531	398	365	628	—	—
1927	3,719	—	—	—	—	—	2,008	414	335	349	613	—	—
1926	3,433	—	—	—	—	—	1,877	402	322	314	518	—	—

[1] The Mothers Allowances programs were introduced in different years in different provinces and originally the cost was borne entirely by the provinces. At the introduction of federal-provincial cost-shared programs under the Canada Assistance Plan, in 1966 and subsequent years, the Mothers Allowances programs were phased out.

Series C534-546. Other provincial-municipal cost-shared expenditures on income security, for Canada and by province, fiscal years ending 31 March, 1961 to 1976
(thousands of dollars)

Year	Canada	New-found-land	Prince Edward Island	Nova Scotia	New Bruns-wick	Quebec	Ontario	Manitoba	Saskat-chewan	Alberta	British Columbia	Yukon Terri-tory	North-west Terri-tories
	534	535	536	537	538	539	540	541	542	543	544	545	546
1976	1,228,798	3,830	1,212	18,756	16,423	160,711	748,613	92,218	62,974	56,019	62,346	3,535	2,161
1975	1,276,083	2,248	3,953	16,404	19,332	152,754	689,670	58,595	54,034	148,028	129,296	1,769	–
1974	886,304	3,633	1,579	17,779	1,620	119,370	464,499	52,043	20,048	79,474	122,786	680	2,793
1973	406,851	2,267	1,218	6,643	3,948	94,373	182,659	11,092	19,246	25,389	57,953	558	1,505
1972	267,563	1,551	838	444	3,051	115,464	62,497	3,916	12,685	24,535	41,100	1,408	74
1971	245,463	2,195	1,270	5,914	3,498	124,222	46,193	3,699	10,144	13,995	33,048	10	1,275
1970	277,653	2,675	809	2,981	2,074	116,984	50,836	1,184	3,779	17,297	76,860	678	1,496
1969	457,039	7,352	4,827	10,715	5,494	212,434	112,711	13,597	16,550	24,732	47,947	680	–
1968	280,867	7,517	3,160	9,757	1,751	97,223	82,311	9,957	15,349	33,254	20,097	431	60
1967	266,088	1,828	4,318	7,066	5,495	123,441	54,819	8,301	16,292	23,706	20,556	266	–
1966	209,279	834	1,954	3,448	2,252	101,779	47,211	4,477	9,509	18,700	18,905	210	–
1965	153,850	291	727	3,010	2,121	55,018	46,436	4,591	8,414	17,113	16,103	26	–
1964	120,337	527	390	2,210	1,237	48,647	24,539	1,334	8,109	15,557	17,574	213	–
1963	107,649	–	643	1,559	1,576	49,018	13,750	5,765	6,120	16,309	12,669	187	53
1962	115,901	–	533	938	832	47,378	20,963	5,219	3,838	15,116	21,038	46	–
1961	121,947	253	405	38	–	57,465	22,076	3,795	7,076	12,566	18,211	62	–

Series C547-559. Provincial-municipal cost-shared social security program expenditures, for Canada and by province, fiscal years ending 31 March, 1951 to 1976
(thousands of dollars)

Year	Canada	New-found-land	Prince Edward Island	Nova Scotia	New Bruns-wick	Quebec	Ontario	Manitoba	Saskat-chewan	Alberta	British Columbia	Yukon Terri-tory	North-west Terri-tories
	547	548	549	550	551	552	553	554	555	556	557	558	559
1976	1,228,798	3,830	1,212	18,756	16,423	160,711	748,613	92,218	62,974	56,019	62,436	3,535	2,161
1975	1,276,083	2,248	3,953	16,404	19,332	152,754	689,670	58,595	54,034	148,028	129,296	1,769	–
1974	886,304	3,633	1,579	17,779	1,620	119,370	464,499	52,043	20,048	79,474	122,786	680	2,793
1973	406,851	2,267	1,218	6,643	3,948	94,373	182,659	11,092	19,246	25,389	57,953	558	1,505
1972	267,563	1,551	838	444	3,051	115,464	62,497	3,916	12,685	24,535	41,100	1,408	74
1971	245,463	2,195	1,270	5,914	3,498	124,222	46,193	3,699	10,144	13,995	33,048	10	1,275
1970	277,653	2,675	809	2,981	2,074	116,984	50,836	1,184	3,779	17,297	76,860	678	1,496
1969	457,039	7,352	4,827	10,715	5,494	212,434	112,711	13,597	16,550	24,732	47,947	680	–
1968	280,867	7,517	3,160	9,757	1,751	97,223	82,311	9,957	15,349	33,254	20,097	431	60
1967	266,088	1,828	4,318	7,066	5,495	123,441	54,819	8,301	16,292	23,706	20,556	266	–
1966	271,055	6,494	2,209	6,107	4,298	122,661	69,741	7,874	13,353	19,203	18,905	210	–
1965	209,924	5,634	974	5,694	4,210	76,086	63,480	7,638	12,225	17,854	16,103	26	–
1964	175,763	5,628	602	4,743	3,268	71,186	40,093	4,111	11,778	16,567	17,574	213	–
1963	158,291	4,688	784	3,871	2,923	69,761	27,664	8,342	9,633	17,716	12,669	187	53
1962	164,006	4,309	664	3,197	2,188	66,858	34,613	7,580	6,518	16,995	21,038	46	–
1961	168,192	4,314	529	2,204	1,399	76,779	34,954	5,868	9,033	14,839	18,211	62	–
1960	44,885	3,225	131	1,920	1,378	20,156	12,140	1,900	1,950	2,085	–	–	–
1959	41,477	2,859	129	1,888	1,365	18,991	11,033	1,325	2,030	1,857	–	–	–
1958	33,237	2,355	89	1,577	1,336	14,612	8,947	1,092	1,573	1,513	143	–	–
1957	24,146	1,820	79	1,554	1,304	8,275	6,985	1,148	1,482	1,339	160	–	–
1956	23,015	1,418	79	1,525	1,250	7,825	6,761	1,149	1,508	1,315	185	–	–
1955	22,512	1,324	73	1,505	1,302	7,956	6,545	1,132	1,252	1,198	225	–	–
1954	21,437	1,228	66	1,445	1,274	7,621	6,219	1,007	1,217	1,113	247	–	–
1953	21,332	1,217	65	1,406	1,225	7,483	6,431	866	1,329	1,049	261	–	–
1952	18,188	1,262	60	1,390	859	5,503	6,038	783	1,111	896	286	–	–
1951	17,531	1,113	52	1,387	854	5,624	5,546	680	1,107	836	332	–	–

Series C560-571. Federal income security programs expenditures for Canada, fiscal years ending 31 March, 1961 to 1976

(thousands of dollars)

Year	Family Allowances	Youth Allowances	Family Assistance	Old Age Security[1]	Guaranteed Income Supplement	Canada Manpower Allowances	Canada Manpower Industrial Training	Aid to Refugee Immigrants	Registered Indians	War Veterans Allowances	Veteran Disability and Dependent Pensions	Total expenditures
	560	561	562	563	564	565	566	567	568	569	570	571
1976	1,957,500	–	–	2,975,562	923,413	186,272	48,705	1,200	82,276	172,702	346,553	6,694,183
1975	1,824,082	–	–	2,607,724	836,750	148,715	37,288	6,000	64,104	141,781	332,569	5,999,013
1974	946,246	65,418	2,418	2,274,424	760,068	147,735	42,604	2,000	52,958	111,765	290,526	4,696,162
1973	548,623	82,790	2,057	1,781,532	742,813	146,167	51,750	3,000	46,164	86,664	241,006	3,732,566
1972	554,407	82,654	2,180	1,679,295	526,060	161,333	7,993	2,000	42,285	77,220	231,377	3,366,804
1971	557,878	80,420	2,717	1,627,219	280,005	156,563	6,402	2,000	34,509	88,912	212,920	3,049,545
1970	560,050	76,502	2,857	1,467,057	263,479	131,150	7,785	2,000	24,776	92,038	218,555	2,846,249
1969	560,186	73,257	3,468	1,296,849	244,470	108,300	4,467	5,000	21,808	95,500	223,321	2,636,626
1968	558,774	68,927	4,212	1,153,284	234,835	55,878	1,114	4,000	17,725	98,401	205,599	2,402,749
1967	555,795	66,033	3,757	1,033,408	39,597	52,344	900	2,000	–	103,629	195,910	2,053,373
1966	551,735	63,975	2,770	927,299	–	–	–	1,000	–	99,902	185,559	1,832,240
1965	545,775	36,411	2,073	885,294	–	–	–	2,000	–	92,846	180,326	1,744,725
1964	538,312	–	1,500	808,391	–	–	–	2,000	–	83,207	173,189	1,606,599
1963	531,566	–	1,200	734,382	–	–	–	2,000	–	81,782	175,925	1,526,855
1962	520,781	–	1,100	625,108	–	–	–	1,000	–	75,290	177,894	1,401,173
1961	506,192	–	1,300	592,413	–	–	–	2,000	–	58,428	150,718	1,311,051

[1] Under the Old Age Assistance Act 1951, the federal government contributed 50 per cent of payments by the provinces for assistance to persons age 65 and over who were not eligible for Old Age Security. The program ended in January 1970 when the eligible age for Old Age Security was lowered to 65.

Series C572-576. National expenditures, federal and provincial income insurance programs, fiscal years ending 31 March, 1961 to 1976[1]

(thousands of dollars)

Year	Canada and Quebec Retirement Pensions[2]	Canada and Quebec Special Pension Benefits[3,4]	Unemployment Insurance	Workmen's Compensation	Total expenditures
	572	573	574	575	576
1976	428,149	425,868[4]	3,342,247	537,416	4,733,680
1975	237,253	292,717	3,144,022	419,365	4,093,357
1974	158,648	219,359	2,119,213	331,716	2,828,936
1973	112,416	153,133	2,004,212	280,509	2,550,270
1972	81,796	107,765	1,871,802	237,990	2,299,353
1971	51,262	66,126	890,594	229,787	1,237,769
1970	21,789	38,671	695,222	203,135	958,817
1969	6,459	12,544	498,992	177,378	695,373
1968	1,070	–	438,129	162,756	601,955
1967	51	–	352,645	156,424	509,120
1966	–	–	295,301	142,111	437,412
1965	–	–	312,110	119,618	431,728
1964	–	–	344,390	111,651	456,041
1963	–	–	394,163	104,523	498,686
1962	–	–	409,208	94,181	503,389
1961	–	–	493,971	91,616	585,587

[1] Data on payments by Quebec Pension Plan and Workmen's Compensation are on a calendar year basis.
[2] Includes the following amounts for the Quebec Pension Plan *(thousands of dollars)*: 1967, 200; 1968, 1,100; 1969, 3,900; 1970, 10,000; 1971, 17,600; 1972, 23,700; 1973, 33,300; 1974, 48,800.
[3] Survivors, death and disability benefits.
[4] Includes the following amounts for the Quebec Pension Plan *(thousands of dollars)*: 1968, 2,400; 1969, 8,600; 1970, 25,700; 1971, 25,900; 1972, 35,000; 1973, 66,600; 1974, 87,800.

Series C577-582. Federal-provincial shareable expenditures of direct financial assistance to persons in Canada, fiscal years ending 31 March, 1961 to 1976
(thousands of dollars)

Year	Blindness Allowances	Old Age Assistance	Disability Allowances	Unemployment Assistance	Canada Assistance Plan	Total federal-provincial cost-shared direct assistance to persons
	577	578	579	580	581	582
1976	–	–	–	–	1,605,430	1,605,430
1975	2,069	–	3,483	126	1,374,850	1,380,528
1974	2,713	–	5,378	1,288	1,079,386	1,088,765
1973	3,448	–	7,588	2,676	1,027,206	1,040,918
1972	3,925	–	8,580	2,148	987,148	1,001,801
1971	5,720	–	19,418	28,258	782,132	835,528
1970	6,603	1,688	23,790	29,280	580,270	641,631
1969	7,198	13,282	28,680	33,564	521,900	604,624
1968	7,921	36,000	30,713	88,140	440,054	602,828
1967	10,210	63,980	47,124	286,542	20,992	428,848
1966	10,947	85,842	47,602	203,414	–	347,805
1965	11,249	90,018	46,731	215,106	–	363,104
1964	9,976	78,416	40,413	214,740	–	343,545
1963	9,764	76,358	39,269	192,948	–	318,339
1962	8,260	61,622	32,867	175,798	–	278,547
1961	8,324	61,314	32,772	119,216	–	221,626

Series C583-590. Social services expenditures,[1] under federal and federal-provincial shareable welfare services programs, excluding health, fiscal years ending 31 March, 1963 to 1976
(thousands of dollars)

Year	Canada Assistance Plan			Vocational rehabilitation of disabled persons	Federal services to Indians	Canada manpower trainee travel	Other federal welfare services[2]	Total expenditures
	Homes for special care	Child welfare	Other welfare services					
	583	584	585	586	587	588	589	590
1976	668,104	124,850	306,006	41,222	18,000 e	5,087	14,879	1,324,498 [3]
1975	364,098	124,462	203,138	24,000	16,595	3,316	12,559	864,364 [3]
1974	277,200	112,400	159,164	19,986	14,545	2,622	11,417	597,334
1973	283,276	89,430	114,970	14,900	13,188	2,150	5,050	522,964
1972	265,172	82,470	96,226	13,000	10,944	1,800	3,349	472,961
1971	207,020	80,668	80,788	10,518	12,911	1,300	2,444	395,649
1970	92,952	114,506	62,710	10,026	9,018	900	1,924	292,036
1969	91,364	79,034	59,784	7,800	7,537	750	1,999	248,268
1968	81,300	76,200	54,000	4,900	6,172	540	1,889	225,001
1967	–	–	–	2,050	–	–	1,278	3,328
1966	–	–	–	1,688	–	–	1,132	2,820
1965	–	–	–	1,284	–	–	635	1,919
1964	–	–	–	1,034	–	–	343	1,377
1963	–	–	–	668	–	–	157	825

[1] Excludes federal-provincial expenditures for homes for special care under Unemployment Assistance which are included with social assistance payments (series C404–416).
[2] National Welfare Grants, New Horizons and Family Planning.

[3] Includes expenditures under special agreements for cost-sharing of nursing home care for Ontario, Manitoba and Alberta, and for treatment of young offenders for Ontario and New Brunswick. This amounted to $116,196,000 in 1975 and $146,350,000 in 1976.

Series C591-599. Summary of all government expenditures on social security by broad program areas, for Canada, fiscal years ending 31 March, 1961 to 1976

(thousands of dollars)

Year	Federal Income Security Programs[1] (series C571)	Federal and Provincial Income Insurance Programs[1] (series C576)	Federal-provincial cost-shared payments of financial aid to persons[1] (series C582)	Federal and Provincial Social Services Programs[1] (series C590)	Provincial-municipal Welfare Programs, not shareable with the federal government[2] (series C547)	Social security administration, excluding health[3]	Social security all governments, excluding health (sum of series C591-596)	Health programs all governments[2]	Total social security expenditures all governments, including health[2] (series C597 plus C598)
	591	592	593	594	595	596	597	598	599
1976	6,694,183	4,733,680	1,605,430	1,324,498	1,228,798	431,900	16,018,489	8,864,638	24,883,127
1975	5,999,013	4,093,357	1,380,528	864,364	1,276,083	382,200	13,995,545	7,120,049	21,115,594
1974	4,696,162	2,828,936	1,088,765	597,334	886,304	344,800	10,442,301	6,266,637	16,708,938
1973	3,732,566	2,550,270	1,040,918	522,964	406,851	285,700	8,539,269	5,548,988	14,088,257
1972	3,366,804	2,299,353	1,001,801	472,961	267,563	205,400	7,613,882	4,855,654	12,469,536
1971	3,049,545	1,237,769	835,528	395,649	245,463	189,400	5,953,354	4,404,570	10,357,924
1970	2,846,249	958,817	641,631	292,036	277,653	149,500	5,165,886	3,554,000	8,719,886
1969	2,636,626	695,373	604,624	248,268	457,039	131,600[3]	4,773,530	2,846,754	7,620,284
1968	2,402,749	601,955	602,828	225,001	280,867	122,190	4,235,590	2,428,828	6,664,418
1967	2,053,373	509,120	428,848	3,328	266,088	102,649	3,363,406	2,017,514	5,380,920
1966	1,832,240	437,412	347,805	2,820	271,055	102,338	2,993,670	1,680,904	4,674,574
1965	1,744,725	431,728	363,104	1,919	209,924	84,923	2,836,323	1,541,933	4,378,256
1964	1,606,599	456,041	343,545	1,377	175,763	79,950	2,663,275	1,333,751	3,997,026
1963	1,526,855	498,686	318,339	825	158,291	73,818	2,576,814	1,247,245	3,824,059
1962	1,401,173	503,389	278,547	—	164,006	68,634	2,415,749	1,125,668	3,541,417
1961	1,311,051	585,587	221,626	—	168,192	67,772	2,354,228	933,753	3,287,981

[1] Excluding administration.
[2] Including administration.
[3] Prior to 1970 data are estimated.

Section D: The Labour Force

Frank T. Denton, *McMaster University*

This section provides series relating to the labour force, employment, unemployment and job vacancies. For the most part, the series are obtained from publications of Statistics Canada, formerly the Dominion Bureau of Statistics. Some of the older series are directly from census tabulations while others are derived from such tabulations but incorporate adjustments to improve the consistency of the series through time. Many of the series of more recent vintage are derived from the Labour Force Survey. Also included are series from the Statistics Canada Employment Survey, the Statistics Canada Job Vacancy Survey, the set of Help-Wanted Indexes developed in the Department of Finance and taken over subsequently by Statistics Canada, and a few other series.

The actual numbers compiled for many of the tables have been taken from a variety of places, including published and unpublished tables and worksheets. In many cases it would be difficult to list exact locations to which a user might refer and we shall not attempt to do this. Instead, we shall refer to the sources in a general way, for example, particular series from the Labour Force Survey will be identified as from that source, but not as coming from particular tables in particular publications. The following general notes on the basic sources may be helpful.

Decennial Censuses

The decennial censuses provide figures for the working population going back into the latter part of the 19th century. Such figures are presented in the first table of this section. A problem with the 'raw' census figures is that definitions and measurement procedures were not the same from one census to another. A major break occurred in 1951. From that time on, the census used a 'labour force' concept roughly in line with the concept used in the Labour Force Survey, while in earlier censuses a 'gainfully occupied' concept was used. In addition, the definitions of industries and occupations have not remained constant in successive censuses. Estimates on a consistent labour force basis have been constructed by Frank T. Denton and Sylvia Ostry, by age and sex, back to 1921; by sex, back to 1901; and in total, back to 1851. R. Marvin McInnis has constructed series of male and female employment, by industry and by province, back to 1911, and by occupation, back to 1891, on as consistent bases as data permitted.

The Labour Force Survey

The Labour Force Survey is a sample survey of Canadian households which provides a wide range of data relating to the labour force, employment and unemployment. The only exclusions from the survey are members of the armed services, inmates of institutions, Indians on reserves and residents of the Yukon Territory and the Northwest Territories. The survey was initiated in November 1945 and carried out roughly at quarterly intervals until November 1952. Since that time it has been a monthly survey. The definitions of employment and unemployment were formally constant from the inception of the survey until 1960 when a decision was made to transfer persons on temporary layoff from the employed to the unemployed category. Prior to that change, the official employment and unemployment series were labelled 'persons with jobs' and 'persons without jobs and seeking work'. After the change, the official series became 'employed' (defined as the old 'persons with jobs' series, less temporary layoffs) and 'unemployed' (the old 'persons without jobs and seeking work' series, plus temporary layoffs). Starting in January 1976, the survey was modified substantially as a result of the introduction of a new questionnaire and a new set of operational definitions. However, all of the series in this section are based on pre-1976 data and are not affected by the latter changes. The series, in most cases, are thus consistent with the definitions instituted in 1960. In 1957, Statistics Canada published estimates for the period 1921 to 1945, based on various related series, and according with the 'persons with jobs' and 'persons without jobs and seeking work' definitions then in effect. They are presented here also. Inasmuch as these pre-1946 estimates were not revised to allow for the change in the treatment of temporary layoffs, some Labour Force Survey series for 1946 to 1960 are shown also on the unrevised basis, in order to provide some continuity of the earlier series into the post-war period.

The Employment Survey

The Employment Survey is a monthly mail survey of industrial and business establishments having more than a certain minimum number of employees. The survey provides information on employment, payrolls, average earnings and hours of work. Employment indexes are calculated by relating current employment in the establishments covered, to employment for the same set of establishments in a specified base year. At the present time, establishments with 20 or more employees are included in the survey. In earlier times, the cut-off point was 15. The survey covers all industries except agriculture, fishing and trapping, education and related services, health and welfare services, religious organizations, private households, and public administration and defence. Different base years have been used at different times. Also, there have been changes in the industrial classification system used. In this section, two sets of indexes are shown, for major industry groups and for provinces. One set is based on the 1960 Standard Industrial Classification system (S.I.C.), with 1961 = 100, and the other on the 1948 S.I.C., with 1949 = 100. The first set covers the period 1957 to 1975; the second covers the period 1921 to 1962, thus providing an overlap with the first set.

Job Vacancy Statistics

The Job Vacancy Survey is a sample survey of employers, conducted in part by mail and in part by interview. All sectors are covered except agriculture, fishing and trapping, domestic service and the armed services. The survey is conducted twice a month and results are published regularly at quarterly intervals. Published series for the years 1971 to 1975 are reproduced in this section, by geographic region.

Series of longer duration are the Help-Wanted Indexes developed in the federal Department of Finance and taken over and maintained subsequently by Statistics Canada. These series extend back to 1962 and are reproduced here for the period 1962 to 1975. The Help-Wanted Indexes are based on help-wanted advertising space in selected daily newspapers across the country.

Vacancy series, going back further in time, were available from the records of the National Employment Service (NES). These series relate only to vacancies of which the NES was notified. The NES series themselves are not shown here. However, synthetic estimates for the entire period 1951 to 1975 have been constructed by Frank T. Denton, Christine H. Feaver and A. Leslie Robb, based on a combination of Job Vacancy Survey data, Help-Wanted Indexes, and NES vacancy series. These are provided here for the period 1951 to 1975.

References

The following list of basic references, relating to the data sources discussed above, may be consulted for more detailed descriptions of sources, methods and definitions: *Historical Statistics of Canada*, Section C: The Labour Force, (especially the notes relating to the census series), Kenneth Buckley; *Census of Canada*, decennial censuses from 1911 to 1971, Statistics Canada; *Historical Estimates of the Canadian Labour Force*, 1961 Census Monograph, Frank T. Denton and Sylvia Ostry, Statistics Canada, 1967, (Catalogue 99-549); *The Growth of Manpower in Canada*, 1961 Census Monograph, Frank T. Denton, Statistics Canada, 1970, (Catalogue 99-556); *Notes to Accompany Tables of Working Population by Industry and Occupation Group*, R. Marvin McInnis, mimeographed, Queen's University, 1976; *The Labour Force*, Statistics Canada, (Catalogue 71-001); *Canadian Labour Force Survey, Methodology*, 1965, Statistics Canada, (Catalogue 71-504); *Canadian Labour Force Estimates, 1931-1945*, Statistics Canada, (Reference Paper No. 23, revised 1957); *Employment, Earnings and Hours*, (formerly *Employment and Payrolls*), Statistics Canada, (Catalogue 72-002); *Annual Report on Job Vacancies*, Statistics Canada, (Catalogue 71-203); *Canadian Job Vacancy Survey: Technical Appendix, 1972*, Statistics Canada, (Catalogue 71-521); 'The Canadian Help-Wanted Index', appendix A, *Economic Review, April 1973*, Department of Finance; *Patterns of Unemployment Behaviour in Canada*, Frank T. Denton, Christine H. Feaver and A. Leslie Robb, Economic Council of Canada, Discussion Paper No. 36, 1975 (construction of synthetic job vacancy series is described on pages 45-49).

D1-7. Population of working age and either gainfully occupied or labour force, in non-agricultural and agricultural pursuits, census years, 1881 to 1971 (gainfully occupied 1881 to 1941, labour force 1951 to 1971)

SOURCE: for 1971, *Census*, 1971; for 1961, *Census*, 1961; for 1881 to 1951, reproductions of series C1-7, with minor rounding of percentages, from *Historical Statistics of Canada*, which are taken from *Census*, 1951, vol. IV, tables I, II and IV; *Census*, 1921, vol. IV, tables III and VI.

Series D1-7, for 1881 to 1941, are based on the gainfully occupied concept employed in Canada up to, and including, the 1941 Census. For 1951 to 1971 they are based on the labour force concept. For discussion and comparison of

these concepts, see Buckley's notes and also Denton and Ostry, *Historical Estimates of the Canadian Labour Force.*

D8-85. Work force, by industrial category and sex, census years, 1911 to 1971 (gainfully occupied 1911 to 1941, labour force 1951 to 1971)

SOURCE: *Notes to Accompany Tables of Working Population by Industry and Occupation Group*, R. Marvin McInnis, Queen's University.

These series are based on published and unpublished census data, using a standard industrial classification system developed by McInnis in order to achieve approximate consistency of industry definitions through time. The figures have been provided by him in the form of mimeographed tables for reproduction here. They are from a larger set of historical series to be included in a forthcoming monograph by McInnis.

The following general notes are edited versions of ones provided by McInnis. These notes apply to the occupational series D86-106 and the provincial series D512-521, as well as to the industrial series D8-85.

1. Figures for Canada are exclusive of the Yukon Territory and the Northwest Territories, as currently defined.

2. Data for 1891 to 1941 are for 'gainful workers'. For 1951 to 1971, they adhere to the 'labour force' concept. The differences in the totals are generally small but some industry and occupation groups are particularly sensitive to the concept selected.

3. The age coverage is left at that of the census of each year. From 1891 through 1931 this was the working population over 10 years of age. In 1941 and 1951 this was raised to 14 years of age and in 1961 and 1971 it was 15 years of age. Before 1941 the number of gainful workers 10-14 years of age was small and heavily concentrated in agriculture. Age coverage is the principal reason that the totals shown in earlier years do not agree with those published in the original edition of *Historical Statistics of Canada*.

4. The 1911 total differs from that in the published census of that year by a small amount. The unpublished data used for the industry tables of that year had never been fully and explicitly reconciled. The difference is only 1,514 workers. It differed in direction so that the tables for female workers were in disagreement by 1,808. Half of that was female unpaid family workers in agriculture which were excluded by definition from the published 1911 Census tables.

5. The figures for 1921 and 1951 exclude Indians living on reserves, in line with the published censuses of those years. The McInnis monograph, from which these tables have been extracted, includes 1921 and 1951 estimates of Indian fishermen and trappers. Hence the totals shown here agree with the published censuses rather than the McInnis monograph.

The following notes provided by McInnis relate specifically to the industrial series D8-85.

The industry classification used in these series is a condensation of a classification developed by McInnis and reported on in greater detail in a forthcoming monograph. McInnis' groupings identify 50 industry categories into which the work force can be grouped with a high degree of definitional consistency over all of the censuses from 1911 through 1971. They incorporate features of both the 1951 and 1961 S.I.C. but lean somewhat toward the latter. The figures for 1921 are the most subject to possible definitional inconsistencies. The 1911 figures are entirely drawn from unpublished tabulations and fit quite consistently into the classification scheme. Unfortunately, 1911 is the earliest census year for which the 'occupational' statistics could satisfactorily be reorganized to get a consistently-defined, detailed industrial categorization.

Owing to limitations of space the 50 industries of McInnis' classification have been further grouped into the condensation provided here. The groupings were selected to fit as closely as possible the categories used in the historical statistical tables of a number of other major countries and by the United Nations.

Attention might be drawn to a few noticeable problems. 'Fishing and trapping' is downwardly biased in 1921 and 1951 by the exclusion of native Indians on reserves. For the years from 1931 onward 'Other and unspecified manufacturing' consists of miscellaneous manufacturing industries while in 1911 and 1921 it includes a relatively large number of workers who were listed in census tables as working in just 'Manufacturing, type unspecified'. 'Other transport' excludes Post Office employees who are grouped with 'Government'. The number of workers with 'Industry unspecified', which had shrunk to a small fraction of the total labour force in 1951 and 1961, rose to an alarming 8 per cent in 1971. Statistics Canada is not yet able to offer an explanation of this.

The 1961 S.I.C. numbers included in each group of industries are as follows:

Agriculture: 001, 003, 006, 011, 013, 015, 017, 019, 021 less own account veterinarians;
Forestry: 031, 039;
Fishing and trapping: 041, 045, 047;
Coal mining: 061;
Other mining: 051-059, 063, 065, 071, 073, 077, 079, 083, 087, 092, 094, 096, 098, 099;
Food, beverages and tobacco manufacturing: 101-153;
Leather and rubber products: 161, 163, 169, 172, 174, 175, 179;
Textiles and clothing: 183, 193, 197, 201, 211-218, 221, 223, 229, 231, 239, 242-249, 395, 878;
Wood products, paper and publishing: 251, 252, 254, 256, 258, 259, 261, 264, 266, 268, 271-274, 286-289;
Metal products, machinery and transport equipment: 291, 292, 294-298, 301-309, 311, 315, 316, 318, 321, 323-329, 331, 332, 334-339;
Chemical, petroleum and non-metallic mineral products: 341, 343, 345, 347, 348, 351-357, 359, 365, 369, 371-379;
Other and unspecified manufacturing: 381-385, 393, 397, 399;
Electricity and gas: 572, 574;
Construction: 404, 406, 409, 421, 516;
Railway transport: 506, 545;
Other transport: 501, 502, 504, 505, 507-509, 512, 515, 517, 519, 524, 527, 543, 544;
Retail and wholesale trade: all groups of same title in 1961;
Finance, insurance and real estate: 702, 704, 731, 735, 737;
Education: 801, 803, 805, 807, 809;
Health and welfare services: 821, 823, 825, 827, 828, plus own account veterinarians from 021;
Food and lodging: 875, 876;
Personal and recreational services: 851, 853, 859, 872-874, 877, 879, 893;
Other services: 831, 861, 862, 864, 866, 869, 871, 891, 894, 896, 897, 899;
Government: 548, 576, 579, 902, 909, 931, 951, 991;
Industry unspecified: 999.

D86-106. Work force, by occupation and sex, census years, 1891 to 1961(gainfully occupied 1891 to 1941, labour force 1951 and 1961)

SOURCE: same as series D8-85.

The general notes provided in the description of series D8-85 apply here also. In addition, McInnis has provided the following specific notes relating to the occupational series D86-106.

1. Only the broadest sort of occupational breakdown is used here but the intention is to make it a more purely 'occupational' classification than was presented in the original edition of *Historical Statistics of Canada*, in which tables tended to have a heavy industrial orientation.

2. The earliest that this broad categorization could be carried back was 1891. Before that the census data for occupations are much less amenable to systematic grouping. Among other things they do not distinguish the sex of workers in any but a few occupations.

3. The occupational classes adhere very closely to those used in the 1961 Census. The 'operatives' grouping is purely a residual and consists of all workers not grouped with one of the five other classes.

4. The category 'Owners and managers' includes business proprietors and salaried managerial personnel. Independent or 'own-account' craftsmen such as tailors, dressmakers and blacksmiths are counted as 'operatives' rather than 'owners and managers'.

The sharp jump in the 'owners and managers' group between 1901 and 1911 might lead to suspicions that, in the 1891 and 1901 censuses, large numbers of persons who should have been grouped with that class were hidden in other categories. A careful examination of the data suggests that this is not the case. Indeed there are several instances of particular occupations where the managerial content may be *overstated* in 1891 and 1901, for example, 'government officials'. The increase in 'owners and managers' between 1901 and 1911 was widely distributed across the industry structure but especially large gains are found in the construction industry, where the number of builders and contractors increased sevenfold, and in wholesale and retail trade, where the number of merchants increased by almost 30,000. In manufacturing, there appears to have been a large increase in the number of small enterprises. What was happening seems to have been partly an increase in the number of business units, and partly an upgrading of independent craftsmen and working proprietors of craft shops to become owners and managers of businesses with employees. Before 1911 the 'owners and managers' group did not include the operators of many small firms such as cheesemakers, millers, furniture makers, butchers, draymen and liverymen.

Between 1921 and 1931 there was a sizable fall in the number of 'owners and managers'. This was heavily concentrated in two industries. In construction, the number of builders and contractors declined markedly as a consequence of the particularly depressed condition of the industry. In urban and other transport, the reduction in the numbers of 'owners and managers' was due to a long-run shift associated with the disappearance of local livery stables and carters, as automobiles and motor trucks increasingly substituted for horse-drawn carriages.

From 1941 to 1951 the number of 'owners and managers' again increased dramatically due to the rise of middle management. By far the greater part of the increase came in paid managers rather than business proprietors. Again the change was widely diffused across the industry structure and a close examination revealed no basis for suspecting that the change may have been largely definitional.

5. 'Professional occupations' agree as consistently as possible with the 1961 Census definition. Lawyers, physicians, engineers and other recognized professionals in independent practice are included here rather than with 'owners and managers'.

One possible anomaly should be noted. In 1911 only nuns who were active as teachers were evidently treated as gainfully employed. In 1901, although the record is not perfectly clear, it appears that all nuns were included.

In the earlier years some accountants who would now be treated as professional workers were probably grouped with clerical occupations.

6. The 'Clerical and sales workers' category is consistent with the clerical and sales occupation division of the 1961 Census. It is fairly narrowly defined and leaves out several occupations that might be regarded as white collar, sales-type occupations, for example, bartenders, waiters, recreation and amusement attendants, and radio announcers. On the other hand the grouping does include service station attendants, who are more akin to blue collar 'operatives'.

7. 'Operatives' refers mainly to skilled and semi-skilled craftsmen but is essentially a catch-all that includes everything not in the other occupational classes. All farm workers are grouped separately, as are persons who are explicitly designated common or unskilled labourers. In accordance with recent census practice, unskilled workers in fishing, forestry and mining are grouped with 'operatives' rather than 'labourers'.

8. 'Farmers and farm workers' include farm operators, paid farm labourers and unpaid family workers. The last of these categories has been highly sensitive to census procedure and has varied widely from census to census.

In 1891 unpaid family workers ('farmers' sons') comprised one-third of the agricultural work force. Of the 241,000 'farmers' sons', some 61,000 were under 15 years of age. Without question, a very comprehensive definition of gainful occupation in agriculture was followed in 1891. Between 1891 and 1901, when the numbers of farmers and hired farm workers rose by about 5 per cent, the number of 'farmers' sons' declined by 23 per cent. The major part of the decline occurred in the group under 16 years of age. 'Farmers' sons' were not counted with the gainfully occupied if they were attending school. In this connection, footnote 9 of series C8-35 in the original *Historical Statistics of Canada* is wrong in stating that the figure "includes all farmers' sons 14 years and over, whether or not reported in gainful occupation". That may have been true in earlier census years but it was explicitly not the case in 1901.

The relative number of unpaid family workers in agriculture fell to an unusually low level in 1911, when they accounted for only 11 per cent of all agricultural workers. This was noted by George V. Haythorne in his book, *Labour in Canadian Agriculture*, which offered a fanciful explanation of the phenomenon. It is quite clearly a definitional matter. While the number of paid farm labourers rose over the 1901 to 1911 decade there does not appear to have been a simple transfer from unpaid to paid classification. The ratio of both paid and unpaid farm labour to the number of farm operators in 1911 was only two-thirds of what it was in either 1901 or 1921. The figures presented here include some female unpaid farm workers who were simply dropped from the published 1911 Census tables.

The number of unpaid family workers in agriculture rose again in 1921 as the census treatment of 'farmers' sons' and increasingly now, daughters, again became more comprehensive. A significant number of unpaid agricultural workers under 15 years of age reappears and the proportion of the total male population 15-24 years that was classed by the census as unpaid farm workers almost doubled from what it had been a decade earlier. The ranks of the unpaid agricultural workers were smaller in 1931, mirroring the unemployment in the non-agricultural sector, and the numbers remained high in 1941. However, there is little indication of any consequential change owing to definitional alteration after 1921.

The 1951 Census and the shift to the labour force concept brought new problems. The entire agricultural labour force declined sharply and male unpaid family workers fell even more. The change in concept, however, admitted many more females to the status of unpaid agricultural labour. Between 1951 and 1961, with the same labour force concept, the number of female unpaid family workers in agriculture increased dramatically. The trend has continued, possibly reinforced by the shift to self-enumeration, so that by 1971, about a quarter of Canada's agricultural labour force consisted of unpaid females.

Over the long term it would seem that the numbers have come full circle. In 1891, the agricultural work force was inflated by the large numbers of children reported as gainfully occupied. In the early years of the century the farm work force included a much smaller number of unpaid family workers. The number rose again and has continued high as farmers' wives have replaced farmers' sons. The effect upon the total measured work force is far from insignificant. In their estimates of the Canadian labour force, Denton and Ostry included an adjustment for female unpaid family workers in agriculture. There exists no series, however, that attempt to correct for the changing definitional treatment of males.

9. 'Labourers' are rather narrowly defined and exclude unskilled workers in fishing, forestry and mining, as well as agricultural labourers, paid and unpaid. This is in line with the 1961 Census treatment. Furthermore, there has been no attempt to add into the category unskilled workers with specific occupational titles who would most likely have been classed as labourers in the earlier censuses. Thus the decline in the relative size of this occupational group is probably overstated.

Prior to 1931 it was generally the practice not to label female workers as 'labourers', although that does not seem to have been the case in the unpublished 1911 tabulations from which these figures are drawn. In 1921 there were, by definition, virtually no female 'labourers'. The numbers were very small in 1891 and 1901 also, although it is less certain that the problem was a definitional one in those years. No euphemistically titled female occupation could be found in the census tables that might be suspected of sheltering the missing female labourers.

D107-122.   Population, labour force and labour force participation rates, by age and sex, census years, 1921 to 1961, and by sex, 1901 and 1911

SOURCE: *Historical Estimates of the Canadian Labour Force*, 1961 Census Monograph, Statistics Canada, (Catalogue 99-549).

The series for 1951 and 1961 are based on Labour Force Survey estimates, adjusted to include the armed services, the Yukon Territory and Northwest Territories, and Indians on reserves. For 1941 and earlier, census data were adjusted to convert from a gainfully occupied to a labour force basis. The adjustments were based on conversion ratios derived for 1951. Estimates were made of what the gainfully occupied figures would have been, had the 1951 Census used the gainfully occupied concept, rather than the labour force concept. Ratios of 1951 labour force (based on the survey) to estimated census gainfully occupied were then used to adjust the pre-1951 Census figures. This was done by age and sex, back to 1921. Estimates for 1911 and 1921 were also constructed, but the absence of age detail for the recorded census gainfully occupied made it necessary to use a different approach, and made it possible only to provide estimates by sex, and not age and sex. The 1921 participation rates were reweighted, using the 1901 and 1911 population age distributions. This was done both on the labour force basis and on the gainfully occupied basis. The ratios of reweighted labour force to reweighted gainfully occupied were then used to adjust the recorded 1901 and 1911 Census gainfully occupied figures.

More detailed information about the methods used in constructing the series is provided in the source publications, along with additional tabular detail.

D123.   Total labour force, census years, 1851 to 1961

SOURCE: same as series D107-122.

The figures for 1901 to 1961 are totals of the components estimated by the procedures described in connection with series D107-122. For 1881 and 1891, the estimates are based on adjustments of recorded census counts of the gainfully occupied. The 1891 count was adjusted by applying the 1901 ratio of labour force to gainfully occupied, separately for each sex, and combining the results. The 1881 count was then adjusted on the basis of the 1891 ratio for both sexes combined.

The estimates for the earlier dates were obtained by a different method, there being no acceptable census gainfully occupied totals to work with for the period before 1881. (The actual figures for the gainfully occupied, from the 1871 Census, were not used because of incompleteness of coverage and doubts as to their accuracy.) Ratios of labour force to population, for individual age-sex groups, were constructed on the basis of data for 1921; the earliest date for which the necessary age-sex detail was available. These ratios were applied to the actual census population figures in each age-sex group and the results summed over all groups. In this way, a preliminary labour force series was constructed for each census year in the period 1851 to 1881. This series was then used as an index to project backwards the 1881 benchmark total, obtained previously, to 1871, 1861 and 1851.

D124-133.   Labour force and main components, non-institutional population and armed services, 14 years of age and over, 1 June of each year, 1921 to 1960

SOURCE: for 1946 to 1960, *The Labour Force*, Statistics Canada, (Catalogue 71-001), and the Department of National Defence; for 1921 to 1945, *Canadian Labour Force Estimates, 1931-1945*, Statistics Canada, (Reference Paper No. 23, revised 1957).

These series are reproductions of series C47-55, in Urquhart and Buckley, *Historical Statistics of Canada*, with the addition of a single series for the total labour force, inclusive of the armed services. The series are regarded as pertaining to 1 June of each year but in practice, for 1946 to 1960, data were used from the Labour Force Survey, with the reference week closest to 1 June.

The 1921 to 1945 series are estimates based on various data. Census enumerations of the total gainfully occupied in 1921, 1931 and 1941, and of the unemployed in 1931 and 1941, were adjusted to conform with the labour force concept used in the survey. Estimates for years in between these dates were obtained by interpolation, based on related series. In the case of persons without jobs and seeking work, no 1921 benchmark existed and the pre-1931 estimates were derived by backward projection from 1931. The persons with jobs and persons without jobs and seeking work series conform to the Labour Force Survey definitions in effect prior to the change in 1960. Persons on temporary layoff up to 30 days are thus counted as having jobs. These numbers are reported by Buckley in Section C of *Historical Statistics of Canada*, for 1946 to 1960, based on Labour Force Survey estimates, as follows: 1946, 18; 1947, less than 10 (actual figure not available); 1948, 16; 1949, less than 10; 1950, 13; 1951, 13; 1952, 19; 1953, 12; 1954, 10; 1955, 11; 1956, less than 10; 1957, 13; 1958, 19; 1959, 21; 1960, 20.

More detailed information on the methods used in constructing the 1921 to 1945 series can be found in *Canadian Labour Force Estimates, 1931-1945*. Additional information about the Labour Force Survey methodology, underlying the 1946 to 1960 series, can be found in *The Labour Force* and *Canadian Labour Force Survey, Methodology*.

D134-145. Labour force and main components, non-institutional population and armed services, 14 years of age and over, annual averages, 1946 to 1975

SOURCE: *The Labour Force*, Statistics Canada, (Catalogue 71-001), and the Department of National Defence.

The definitions of civilian labour force, employed, and unemployed are those used by the survey prior to the changes in 1976. From 1953 on, the averages are based on 12 monthly surveys per year; prior to 1953, they are based on four surveys per year, roughly at quarterly intervals. Newfoundland is excluded before 1950 and the Yukon Territory and Northwest Territories are excluded in all years. Also excluded in all years are Indians living on reserves. For additional information about the Labour Force Survey methodology, see *The Labour Force* and *Canadian Labour Force Survey, Methodology*.

Series D134, 135 and 137, which involve the armed services, were furnished from Labour Force Survey files but are based on data from the Department of National Defence. The total non-institutional population and labour force are obtained by adding the armed services to the civilian non-institutional population and labour force.

D146-159. Civilian labour force and main components, civilian non-institutional population, 14 years of age and over, by sex, annual averages, 1946 to 1975

SOURCE: *The Labour Force,* Statistics Canada, (Catalogue 71-001).

See the note to series D134-145.

D160-174. Civilian labour force, by age and sex, annual averages, 1946 to 1975

SOURCE: same as series D146-159.

See the note to series D134-145.

D175-189. Civilian employment, by age and sex, annual averages, 1946 to 1975

SOURCE: same as series D146-159

See the note to series D134-145.

D190-204. Unemployment, by age and sex, annual averages, 1946 to 1975

SOURCE: same as series D146-159.

See the note to series D134-145.

D205-222. Civilian labour force participation rates, by age and sex, annual averages, 1946 to 1975

SOURCE: same as series D146-159.

The participation rates are obtained by expressing labour force figures as percentages of corresponding non-institutional population figures. See the note to series D134-145.

D223-235. Unemployment rates, by age and sex, annual averages, 1946 to 1975

SOURCE: same as series D146-159.

The unemployment rates are obtained by expressing unemployment figures as percentages of corresponding civilian labour force figures. See the note to series D134-145.

D236-259. Civilian employment in agriculture and non-agricultural industries, by class of worker and sex, annual averages, 1946 to 1975

SOURCE: same as series D146-159.

See the note to series D134-145.

D260-265. Civilian persons with jobs in non-agricultural industries, by class of worker and sex, 1 June of each year, 1931 to 1958

SOURCE: for 1946 to 1958, *The Labour Force,* Statistics Canada, (Catalogue 71-001); for 1931 to 1945, *Canadian Labour Force Estimates, 1931-1945,* Statistics Canada, (Reference Paper No. 23, revised 1957).

See the note to series D124-133.

D266-289. Civilian employment, by industry (1948 S.I.C.**), both sexes and males, annual averages, 1946 to 1964**

SOURCE: same as series D146-159.

These series are based on the 1948 Standard Industrial Classification system. See the note to series D134-145.

D290-317. Civilian employment, by industry (1960 S.I.C.**), both sexes and males, annual averages, 1961 to 1975**

SOURCE: same as series D146-159.

These series are based on the 1960 Standard Industrial Classification system. The availability of figures for 1961 to 1964 provides an overlap with series D266-289, which extend back to 1946 but are on the 1948 S.I.C. basis. See the note to series D134-145.

D318-328. Civilian persons with paid-worker jobs, by industry (1948 S.I.C.**), 1 June of each year, 1931 to 1960**

SOURCE: for 1946 to 1960, *The Labour Force,* Statistics Canada, (Catalogue 71-001); for 1931 to 1945, *Canadian Labour Force Estimates, 1931-1945,* Statistics Canada, (Reference Paper No. 23, revised 1957).

See the note to series D124-133.

D329-340. Civilian employed paid workers, by industry (1948 S.I.C.**), annual averages, 1946 to 1964**

SOURCE: same as series D146-159.

These series are based on the 1948 Standard Industrial Classification system. See the note to series D134-145.

D341-354. Civilian employed paid workers, by industry (1960 S.I.C.**), annual averages, 1961 to 1975**

SOURCE: same as series D146-159.

These series are based on the 1960 Standard Industrial Classification system. The availability of figures for 1961 to 1964 provides an overlap with series D329-340, which extend back to 1946 but are on the 1948 S.I.C. basis. See the note to series D134-145.

D355-382. Civilian employment, by occupation and sex (1951 classification system), both sexes and males, annual averages, 1948 to 1960

SOURCE: same as series D146-159.

These series are based on the occupational classification system established for the 1951 Census. See the note to series D134-145.

D383-412. Civilian employment, by occupation (1961 classification system), both sexes and males, annual averages, 1961 to 1973

SOURCE: same as series D146-159.

These series are based on the occupational classification system established for the 1961 Census. The availability of figures for 1961 to 1964 provides an overlap with series D355-382, which extend back to 1948 but are based on the 1951 classification system. See the note to series D134-145.

D413-430.   Female civilian labour force, by age and marital status, annual averages, 1966 to 1975

SOURCE: same as series D146-159.

See the note to series D134-145.

D431-448.   Female civilian labour force participation rates, by age and marital status, annual averages, 1959 to 1975

SOURCE: same as series D146-159.

The participation rates are obtained by expressing labour force figures as percentages of corresponding non-institutional population figures. The 1959 to 1963 rates for the 'married' and 'other' categories incorporate minor adjustments to take account of subsequent data revisions. (Based on an observed revision of 0.1 per cent in 1964, the 1959 to 1963 rates were all adjusted downward by this amount.) See the note to series D134-145.

D449-454.   Civilian employment, by full-time and part-time status and by sex, annual averages, 1953 to 1975

SOURCE: same as series D146-159.

'Full-time' employment includes all persons who worked 35 hours or more during a survey reference week, plus those who had a job and did not work, or worked less than 35 hours, but said they usually work 35 hours. 'Part-time' employment includes those who worked less than 35 hours, or who had a job and did not work, and said they usually work less than 35 hours. See the note to series D134-145.

D455-462.   Unemployment, by type of job sought (full-time or part-time) and by length of time unemployed, annual averages, 1953 to 1975

SOURCE: same as series D146-159.

See the note to series D134-145. See also the note to series D449-454 for the definitions of 'part-time' and 'full-time' employment.

D463-469.   Civilian labour force, by region, annual averages, 1946 to 1975

SOURCE: same as series D146-159.

Newfoundland is included in the Canada total and Atlantic region series starting in 1950. Newfoundland is also shown separately, series D469, so that the Canada total and Atlantic region series can be adjusted to exclude that province, for purposes of comparability with the 1946 to 1949 figures. See the note to series D134-145.

D470-476.   Civilian employment, by region, annual averages, 1946 to 1975

SOURCE: same as series D146-159.

See the note to series D134-145. See also the note to series D463-469, regarding Newfoundland.

D477-483.   Unemployment, by region, annual averages, 1946 to 1975

SOURCE: same as series D146-159.

See the note to series D134-145. See also the note to series D463-469, regarding Newfoundland.

D484-490.   Civilian labour force participation rates, by region, annual averages, 1946 to 1975

SOURCE: same as series D146-159.

The participation rates are obtained by expressing labour force figures as percentages of corresponding non-institutional population figures. See the note to series D134-145. See also the note to series D463-469, regarding Newfoundland.

D491-497.   Unemployment rates, by region, annual averages, 1946 to 1975

SOURCE: same as series D146-159.

The unemployment rates are obtained by expressing unemployment figures as percentages of corresponding civilian labour force figures. See the note to series D134-145. See also the note to series D463-469, regarding Newfoundland.

D498-504.   Total labour force growth and its components, intercensal decades, 1851 to 1961

SOURCE: *The Growth of Manpower in Canada*, 1961 Census Monograph, Statistics Canada, (Catalogue 99-556); *Historical Estimates of the Canadian Labour Force*, 1961 Census Monograph, Statistics Canada, (Catalogue 99-549).

The components of labour force growth for each decade of the period 1851 to 1961 were based on historical population data, immigration data, and labour force participation rates. For the decades since 1921, the labour force contents of immigration and emigration were estimated and then the difference between the two was subtracted from total labour force growth, to arrive at an estimate of the domestic supply component. For decades before 1921, the labour force content of natural increase was estimated first, using age-sex distributions of natural increases calculated by Nathan Keyfitz, ("The Growth of Canadian Population", *Population Studies*, vol. IV, No. 1, June 1950), together with the 1921 labour force participation rates estimated by Denton and Ostry. This provided the basis for estimation of the domestic supply component. The contribution of net immigration to labour force growth was then estimated as the difference between total labour force growth and the domestic supply component. More detailed information about the methods and sources of basic data can be found in *The Growth of Manpower in Canada*. With regard to the total labour force estimates for 1851 to 1961, from which the total labour force growth series was calculated, see the notes to series D107-122 and D123.

D505-511.   Civilian labour force growth and its components, quinquennial periods, 1946 to 1966

SOURCE: *The Growth of Manpower in Canada*, 1961 Census Monograph, Statistics Canada, (Catalogue 99-556).

The total civilian labour force series is based on Labour

Force Survey data. The 1946 labour force total was adjusted, to include an estimate for Newfoundland, and both the 1946 and 1951 totals were then adjusted further, to allow for the effects of differences in the frequency and timing of the survey on the annual averages for those years. (The survey was conducted more or less on a quarterly basis before November 1952, but on a monthly basis since then.) The calculation of the components of growth involved the estimation of the labour force contents of immigration and emigration by the application of participation rates to the numbers of immigrants and emigrants in various age-sex groups. The total contributions of immigration and emigration were then calculated and their difference, the contribution of net immigration, was subtracted from total labour force growth to obtain an estimate of the domestic supply component. Additional information on methods and basic data sources can be found in *The Growth of Manpower in Canada.*

D512-521. Total work force, by province and sex, census years, 1911 to 1971

SOURCE: same as series D8-85.

These series were compiled by R. Marvin McInnis, based on published and unpublished census data. See the notes to series D8-85 and D86-106.

D522-527. Job vacancies and help-wanted indexes, by region, annual averages, 1951 to 1975

SOURCE: *Annual Report on Job Vacancies*, Statistics Canada, (Catalogue 71-203); *Canadian Job Vacancy Survey: Technical Appendix*, Statistics Canada, (Catalogue 71-521); "The Canadian Help-Wanted Index", appendix A, *Economic Review, April 1973*, Department of Finance; *Patterns of Unemployment Behaviour in Canada*, Frank T. Denton, Christine H. Feaver and A. Leslie Robb.

Three sets of annual series are presented here. The first set, labelled 'job vacancies', is extracted from the Statistics Canada Job Vacancy Survey. These series refer to 'full-time' vacancies and vacancies for 'casual, part-time, seasonal and temporary' jobs are excluded. For additional information about the survey, see the source material from Statistics Canada.

The second set of series are 'help-wanted indexes'. These were developed in the federal Department of Finance and later taken over, for regular calculation and publication, by Statistics Canada. The indexes were modelled after the index developed for the United States by the U.S. National Industrial Conference Board. The Canadian indexes are based on counts of columns in the classified advertising sections of selected daily newspapers in larger Canadian cities.

Data were collected on a monthly basis. (Microfilmed newspapers were used to gather data as far back as January 1962.) The data for different cities are weighted, using population weights from the 1971 Census. The index base year is also 1971. For more information, see the source publication, from the Department of Finance.

The third set of series is a synthetic set constructed by Denton, Feaver and Robb, using data from three sources: the Job Vacancy Survey, the Help-Wanted Indexes, and the series of unfilled vacancies of the National Employment Service (NES). Job Vacancy Survey series (all categories, full-time and other combined), for the 36-month period December 1970 to November 1973, were used to establish average benchmark levels and seasonal patterns for the synthetic series. The Help-Wanted Indexes were used to project from these levels, forward to 1975 and backward to 1962. The synthetic series were then taken back from 1962 to 1951 on the basis of the NES series. All of the initial calculations were monthly, although only annual averages are presented here. The original series for 1951 to 1973 are from Denton, Feaver and Robb, *Patterns of Unemployment Behaviour in Canada,* and a detailed description of methods is provided there. The series were extended to 1974 and 1975 by the authors of that study, for presentation here.

D528-539. Employment indexes, by industry, annual averages, 1921 to 1975

SOURCE: *Employment, Earnings and Hours,* Statistics Canada, (Catalogue 72-002).

These indexes are from the Statistics Canada Employment Survey, a monthly survey of industrial and business establishments with more than a certain minimum number of employees. The survey covers all employment sectors except agriculture, fishing and trapping, education and related services, health and welfare services, religious organizations, private households, and public administration and defence. Two sets of indexes are presented. One is based on the 1960 Standard Industrial Classification system and has 1961 as its base year. This series is provided for the period 1957 to 1975. The other set is based on the 1948 Standard Industrial Classification system and has 1949 as its base year. This latter set is provided for the period 1921 to 1962. There is thus a six-year period of overlap of the two sets. For further information see the source publication.

D540-550. Industrial composite employment indexes, by province, annual averages, 1921 to 1975

SOURCE: same as series D528-539.

See the note to series D528-539.

Series D1-7. Population of working age and either gainfully occupied or labour force, in non-agricultural and agricultural pursuits, census years, 1881 to 1971 (gainfully occupied 1881 to 1941, labour force 1951 to 1971)

Year	Population of working age[1]	Number of persons engaged in				Per cent of total in	
		All occupations		Non-agricultural pursuits	Agricultural pursuits	Non-agricultural pursuits	Agricultural pursuits
		Number[2]	Per cent of population of working age				
	1	2	3	4	5	6	7
1971	15,157,615[3]	8,607,820[3]	56.7	8,126,650	481,170	94.4	5.6
1961	12,023,211[3]	6,458,156[3]	53.7	5,817,427	640,729	90.1	9.9
1951	9,949,737[4]	5,286,153[4]	53.1	4,455,712	830,441	84.3	15.7
1941	8,205,766[4,6]	4,195,951[4,6]	49.3	3,112,135	1,083,816	74.2	25.8
1941	8,520,350[4,7]	4,510,535[4,7]	52.9	3,426,719	1,083,816	76.0	24.0
1931	7,298,447[4]	3,921,833[4]	53.7	2,794,151	1,127,682	71.3	28.8
1921	5,928,687[4]	3,164,348[4,5]	53.4	2,129,065	1,035,283	67.3	32.7
1911	4,955,585[4]	2,723,634[8]	55.0	1,789,899	933,735	65.7	34.3
1911	5,514,388[8]	2,723,634[8]	49.4	—	—	—	—
1901	4,063,943[8]	1,782,832[5,8]	43.9	1,065,972	716,860	59.8	40.2
1891	3,611,882[8]	1,606,369[8,9]	44.5	871,162	735,207	54.2	45.8
1881	3,162,122[8]	1,377,585[8,9]	43.6	715,319	662,266	51.9	48.1

[1] Excludes the Yukon Territory and the Northwest Territories for all years. Includes Newfoundland for 1951 and later years.

[2] Indians on reserves are excluded in gainfully occupied and labour force data, but are included in population.

[3] Age 15 and over.

[4] Age 14 and over.

[5] Gainfully occupied data exclude Indians engaged in fishing and trapping.

[6] Excludes persons on active service.

[7] Includes persons on active service.

[8] Gainfully occupied data are for persons 10 years of age and over in 1911 and all previous censuses. Population in 1911 is shown, first, for 14 years and over; second, for 10 years and over. Prior to 1911 population is for 10 years and over.

[9] Gainfully occupied data exclude nomadic Indians.

Series D8-85. Work force, by industrial category and sex, census years, 1911 to 1971 (gainfully occupied 1911 to 1941, labour force 1951 to 1971)

Year	Total work force[1]			Agriculture			Forestry			Fishing and trapping		
	Total	Males	Females	Total	Males	Females	Total	Males	Females	Total	Males	Females
	8	9	10	11	12	13	14	15	16	17	18	19
1971[2]	8,626,925	5,665,715	2,961,210	481,190	369,625	111,565	74,380	71,025	3,355	25,435	24,540	900
1961[2]	6,458,156	4,694,294	1,763,862	639,221	560,525	78,696	108,497	106,305	2,192	34,576	34,088	488
1951[3,4]	5,286,153	4,121,832	1,164,321	827,030	791,931	35,099	129,832	127,488	2,344	50,583	50,178	405
1941[3,5]	4,195,951	3,363,111	832,840	1,082,074	1,062,928	19,146	93,792	93,313	479	50,902	50,533	369
1931[6]	3,927,230	3,261,371	665,859	1,128,154	1,103,899	24,255	49,952	49,709	243	47,782	47,274	508
1921[4,6]	3,173,169	2,683,019	490,150	1,041,618	1,023,706	17,912	40,026	40,019	7	34,088	33,693	395
1911[6]	2,725,148	2,358,519	366,629	931,602	914,784	16,818	42,917	42,901	16	34,885	34,619	266

Year	Coal mining			Other mining			Food, beverage and tobacco manufacturing			Leather and rubber products		
	Total	Males	Females	Total	Males	Females	Total	Males	Females	Total	Males	Females
	20	21	22	23	24	25	26	27	28	29	30	31
1971[2]	8,805	8,610	195	130,230	121,060	9,170	251,375	183,325	68,045	53,170	34,000	19,160
1961[2]	12,473	12,355	118	107,227	102,563	4,664	227,965	174,019	53,946	52,009	33,592	18,417
1951[3,4]	24,338	24,125	213	79,510	77,395	2,115	182,083	142,316	39,767	53,762	36,589	17,173
1941[3,5]	29,142	29,064	78	63,898	63,392	506	109,112	87,979	21,133	46,232	32,392	13,840
1931[6]	31,496	31,423	73	40,467	40,185	282	103,733	86,040	17,693	38,997	29,155	9,842
1921[4,6]	30,754	30,690	64	20,992	20,853	139	61,340	49,986	11,354	29,615	22,588	7,027
1911[6]	27,518	27,508	10	30,371	30,662	69	53,174	44,750	8,424	24,821	20,721	4,100

Year	Textiles and clothing			Wood products, paper and publishing			Metal products, machinery and transport equipment			Chemical, petroleum and non-metallic mineral products		
	Total	Males	Females	Total	Males	Females	Total	Males	Females	Total	Males	Females
	32	33	34	35	36	37	38	39	40	41	42	43
1971[2]	181,800	76,585	105,220	372,070	309,560	62,505	611,895	519,765	92,125	154,295	125,955	28,350
1961[2]	178,479	82,474	96,005	320,386	275,774	44,612	446,125	392,002	54,123	133,413	110,332	23,081
1951[3,4]	201,969	97,749	104,220	298,569	262,328	36,241	439,305	390,661	48,644	100,176	83,618	16,558
1941[3,5]	159,298	76,294	83,004	178,816	160,327	18,489	340,321	309,763	30,558	60,521	51,670	8,851
1931[6]	120,926	59,189	61,737	152,846	138,239	14,607	189,828	178,517	11,311	43,175	38,833	4,342
1921[4,6]	98,625	40,293	58,332	129,232	118,990	10,242	139,059	132,808	6,251	27,163	24,233	2,930
1911[6]	102,484	34,976	67,508	107,098	99,200	7,898	113,438	111,490	1,948	20,045	18,608	1,437

Year	Other and unspecified manufacturing			Electricity and gas			Construction			Railway transport		
	Total	Males	Females	Total	Males	Females	Total	Males	Females	Total	Males	Females
	44	45	46	47	48	49	50	51	52	53	54	55
1971[2]	82,725	53,445	29,285	74,105	63,725	10,380	568,285	541,080	27,205	117,530	109,760	7,775
1961[2]	50,308	34,618	15,690	62,426	54,382	8,044	465,963	454,453	11,510	147,573	139,334	8,239
1951[3,4]	37,714	25,205	12,509	47,802	42,750	5,052	350,896	344,889	6,007	170,956	162,835	8,121
1941[3,5]	22,694	16,672	6,022	23,089	21,134	1,955	220,221	218,732	1,489	127,445	123,514	3,931
1931[6]	15,950	13,055	2,895	22,482	20,730	1,752	249,999	248,423	1,576	140,863	135,838	5,025
1921[4,6]	45,419	35,665	9,754	10,443	9,824	619	182,133	181,555	578	134,551	129,248	5,303
1911[6]	52,645	43,627	9,018	10,587	10,350	237	199,182	198,933	249	97,947	96,748	1,199

Series D8-85. Work force, by industrial category and sex, census years, 1911 to 1971 (gainfully occupied 1911 to 1941, labour force 1951 to 1971) (concluded)

Year	Other transport			Retail and wholesale trade			Finance, insurance and real estate			Education		
	Total	Males	Females	Total	Males	Females	Total	Males	Females	Total	Males	Females
	56	**57**	**58**	**59**	**60**	**61**	**62**	**63**	**64**	**65**	**66**	**67**
1971[2]	379,250	301,030	78,225	1,269,290	803,100	466,190	358,060	173,825	184,235	569,485	253,560	315,925
1961[2]	305,559	250,530	55,029	990,598	689,423	301,175	228,811	124,260	104,551	266,394	102,766	163,628
1951[3,4]	231,751	191,110	40,641	745,904	534,792	211,112	143,995	80,027	63,968	152,817	56,634	96,183
1941[3,5]	139,145	123,321	15,824	496,150	384,046	112,104	89,680	61,311	28,369	110,946	35,872	75,074
1936[6]	136,737	119,109	17,628	425,159	339,765	85,394	92,340	67,375	24,965	100,781	29,490	71,291
1921[4,6]	114,623	98,792	15,831	327,879	266,544	61,335	61,425	46,207	15,218	77,946	20,915	57,031
1911[6]	83,343	77,728	5,615	259,859	209,731	50,128	36,853	33,289	3,564	47,479	12,666	34,813

Year	Health and welfare services			Food and lodging			Personal and recreational services			Other services		
	Total	Males	Females	Total	Males	Females	Total	Males	Females	Total	Males	Females
	68	**69**	**70**	**71**	**72**	**73**	**74**	**75**	**76**	**77**	**78**	**79**
1971[2]	513,090	127,790	385,300	331,500	141,450	190,055	253,555	104,730	148,820	373,750	237,810	135,940
1961[2]	308,432	83,833	224,599	238,094	104,980	133,114	234,889	84,957	149,932	210,597	137,681	72,916
1951[3,4]	173,948	54,147	119,801	155,452	79,177	76,275	187,113	69,960	117,153	114,809	77,421	37,388
1941[3,5]	91,812	27,998	63,814	120,320	58,312	62,008	263,395	59,955	203,440	91,315	61,886	29,429
1936[6]	79,382	26,518	52,864	107,057	58,291	48,766	236,870	69,505	167,365	86,187	63,977	22,210
1921[4,6]	70,465	22,745	47,720	58,076	35,192	22,884	142,243	42,030	100,213	62,888	56,310	6,578
1911[6]	34,466	13,813	20,653	56,330	34,005	22,325	138,314	38,753	99,561	53,416	47,184	6,232

Year	Government			Industry unspecified		
	Total	Males	Females	Total	Males	Females
	80	**81**	**82**	**83**	**84**	**85**
1971[2]	709,705	529,665	180,045	681,940	380,700	301,240
1961[2]	529,968	432,788	97,180	158,173	116,260	41,913
1951[3,4]	318,284	263,964	54,320	67,557	54,545	13,012
1941[3,5]	139,636	111,634	28,002	45,995	41,069	4,926
1936[6]	116,817	101,303	15,514	169,250	165,529	3,721
1921[4,6]	97,574	84,991	12,583	134,992	115,142	19,850
1911[6]	78,243	74,157	4,086	87,771	87,316	455

[1] Excludes the Yukon Territory and the Northwest Territories. Includes Newfoundland for 1951 and later years.
[2] Age 15 and over in 1961 and 1971.
[3] Age 14 and over in 1941 and 1951.
[4] Indians on reserves engaged in fishing and trapping were excluded from the 1921 and 1951 Censuses.
[5] Excludes persons on active service.
[6] Age 10 and over in 1911, 1921 and 1931.

Series D86-106. Work force, by occupation and sex, census years, 1891 to 1961 (gainfully occupied 1891 to 1941, labour force 1951 and 1961)

Year	Total, all occupations[1]			Owners and managers			Professional occupations			Clerical and sales workers		
	Total	Males	Females	Total	Males	Females	Total	Males	Females	Total	Males	Females
	86	87	88	89	90	91	92	93	94	95	96	97
1961[2]	6,305,630	4,582,476	1,723,154	540,214	482,547	57,667	628,911	356,578	272,333	1,244,871	588,040	656,831
1951[3,4]	5,218,596	4,067,287	1,151,309	423,100	384,810	38,290	379,803	213,127	166,676	851,698	428,062	423,636
1941[3,5]	4,195,951	3,363,111	832,840	227,111	212,460	14,651	278,972	150,379	128,593	518,354	308,342	210,012
1931[6]	3,927,230	3,281,371	665,859	221,079	211,221	9,858	233,572	116,565	117,007	465,248	302,474	162,774
1921[4,6]	3,173,169	2,683,019	490,150	264,245	253,825	10,420	173,222	80,249	92,973	389,886	262,023	127,863
1911[6]	2,725,148	2,358,519	366,629	219,008	207,923	11,085	84,153	49,817	34,336	226,448	175,434	51,014
1901[6]	1,782,621	1,544,050	238,571	84,040	81,004	3,036	82,590	42,389	40,201	111,041	91,402	19,639
1891[6]	1,607,945	1,411,936	196,009	78,639	74,668	3,971	52,893	33,184	19,709	84,474	75,944	8,530

Year	Operatives			Farmers and farm workers			Labourers		
	Total	Males	Females	Total	Males	Females	Total	Males	Females
	98	99	100	101	102	103	104	105	106
1961[2]	2,928,840	2,289,322	639,518	647,792	571,930	75,862	315,002	294,059	20,943
1951[3,4]	2,383,620	1,914,407	469,213	829,169	796,614	32,555	351,206	330,267	20,939
1941[3,5]	1,824,767	1,375,879	448,888	1,080,806	1,061,896	18,910	265,941	254,155	11,786
1931[6]	1,423,341	1,082,959	340,382	1,127,149	1,103,027	24,122	456,841	445,125	11,716
1921[4,6]	996,020	755,448	240,572	1,040,787	1,022,906	17,881	309,009	308,568	441
1911[6]	933,577	689,890	243,687	929,847	913,067	16,780	332,115	322,388	9,727
1901[6]	663,755	498,102	165,653	715,528	706,627	8,901	125,667	124,526	1,141
1891[6]	543,560	392,911	150,649	734,122	722,021	12,101	114,257	113,208	1,049

[1] Excludes the Yukon Territory and the Northwest Territories. Includes Newfoundland for 1951 and later years.
[2] Age 15 and over in 1961.
[3] Age 14 and over in 1951 and 1941.

[4] Indians on reserves engaged in fishing and trapping were excluded from the 1951 and 1921 Censuses.
[5] Excludes persons on active service.
[6] Age 10 and over in 1931 and earlier years.

Series D107-122. Population, labour force and labour force participation rates, by age and sex, census years, 1921 to 1961, and by sex, 1901 and 1911

Year[1]	Men							Women							Both sexes	
	10–13	14–19	20–24	25–34	35–64	65+	Total	10–13	14–19	20–24	25–34	35–64	65+	Total	Total 10+	Total 14+
	107	108	109	110	111	112	113	114	115	116	117	118	119	120	121	122
1961[1]																
Population ('000)	–	869	567	1,221	2,716	633	6,006	–	837	580	1,192	2,682	671	5,962	–	11,968
Labour force ('000)	–	353	535	1,202	2,588	194	4,872	–	265	294	348	801	41	1,749	–	6,621
Participation rates (%)	–	40.6	94.4	98.4	95.3	30.6	81.1	–	31.7	50.7	29.2	29.9	6.1	29.3	–	55.3
1951[1]																
Population ('000)	–	613	517	1,028	2,155	522	4,835	–	611	535	1,080	2,059	507	4,792	–	9,627
Labour force ('000)	–	329	487	1,010	2,047	206	4,079	–	206	261	274	407	23	1,171	–	5,250
Participation rates (%)	–	53.7	94.2	98.2	95.0	39.5	84.4	–	33.7	48.8	25.4	19.8	4.5	24.4	–	54.5
1941																
Population ('000)	–	672	513	911	1,864	378	4,338	–	661	512	886	1,674	364	4,097	–	8,435
Labour force ('000)	–	367	475	899	1,791	181	3,713	–	177	240	247	254	21	939	–	4,652
Participation rates (%)	–	54.6	92.6	98.7	96.1	47.9	85.6	–	26.8	46.9	27.9	15.2	5.8	22.9	–	55.2
1931																
Population ('000)	431	627	459	771	1,633	285	4,206[2]	423	616	445	713	1,406	272	3,875[2]	8,081	7,227
Labour force ('000)	5	360	431	760	1,579	161	3,296[2]	1	163	211	174	186	17	752[2]	4,048	4,042
Participation rates (%)	1.2	57.4	93.9	98.6	96.7	56.5	78.4[2]	0.2	26.5	47.4	24.4	13.2	6.2	19.4[2]	50.1	55.9
1921																
Population ('000)	371	488	349	687	1,323	208	3,426[2]	364	483	359	647	1,133	198	3,184[2]	6,610	5,875
Labour force ('000)	8	334	329	673	1,282	124	2,750[2]	1	143	143	126	136	13	562[2]	3,312	3,303
Participation rates (%)	2.2	68.4	94.3	98.0	96.9	59.6	80.3[2]	0.3	29.6	39.8	19.5	12.0	6.6	17.7[2]	50.1	56.2
1911																
Population ('000)	–	–	–	–	–	–	2,913	–	–	–	–	–	–	2,521	5,434	4,874
Labour force ('000)	–	–	–	–	–	–	2,390	–	–	–	–	–	–	419	2,809	2,799
Participation rates (%)	–	–	–	–	–	–	82.0	–	–	–	–	–	–	16.6	51.7	57.4
1901																
Population ('000)	–	–	–	–	–	–	2,066	–	–	–	–	–	–	1,957	4,023	3,558
Labour force ('000)	–	–	–	–	–	–	1,618	–	–	–	–	–	–	281	1,899	1,885
Participation rates (%)	–	–	–	–	–	–	78.3	–	–	–	–	–	–	14.4	47.2	53.0

[1] Excludes Newfoundland in all years.

[2] Total men and total women include age 10–13 in 1931 and 1921 only.

Series D123. Total labour force, census years, 1851 to 1961[1]
(thousands)

Year	Labour force	Year	Labour force	Year	Labour force	Year	Labour force
	123		123		123		123
1961	6,741	1931	4,048	1901	1,899	1871	1,201
1951	5,355	1921	3,312	1891	1,732	1861	1,053
1941	4,652	1911	2,809	1881	1,474	1851	762

[1] Includes Newfoundland in 1961 and 1951. Includes residents of the Yukon Territory and the Northwest Territories, Indians on reserves and members of the armed services. Includes labour force age 10 and over from 1851 to 1931, but age 14 and over from 1941 to 1961.

Series D124-133. Labour force and main components, non-institutional population and armed forces, 14 years of age and over, 1 June of each year, 1921 to 1960[1,2]
(thousands)

Year	Non-institutional population	Armed services	Civilian non-institutional population	Total labour force	Civilian labour force					Persons not in the labour force
					Total	Persons with jobs			Persons without jobs and seeking work	
						Total	In non-agricultural industries	In agriculture		
	124	125	126	127	128	129	130	131	132	133
1960	11,879	120	11,759	6,511	6,391	5,992	5,317	675	399	5,368
1959	11,651	120	11,531	6,306	6,186	5,852	5,128	724	334	5,345
1958	11,452	119	11,333	6,239	6,120	5,750	5,011	739	370	5,213
1957	11,183	117	11,066	6,087	5,970	5,774	5,002	772	196	5,096
1956	10,888	117	10,771	5,855	5,738	5,572	4,753	819	166	5,033
1955	10,689	118	10,571	5,703	5,585	5,371	4,498	873	214	4,986
1954	10,475	113	10,362	5,589	5,476	5,255	4,362	893	221	4,886
1953	10,231	104	10,127	5,490	5,386	5,271	4,373	898	115	4,741
1952	10,028	95	9,933	5,439	5,344	5,239	4,312	927	105	4,589
1951	9,764	68	9,696	5,304	5,236	5,155	4,164	991	81	4,460
1950[2]	9,657	47	9,610	5,245	5,198	5,056	3,990	1,066	142	4,412
1949	9,296	42	9,254	5,134	5,092	4,991	3,877	1,114	101	4,162
1948	9,158	35	9,123	5,070	5,035	4,954	3,768	1,186	81	4,088
1947	9,030	37	8,993	4,991	4,954	4,862	3,690	1,172	92	4,039
1946	8,981	213	8,768	5,075	4,862	4,738	3,467	1,271	124	3,906
1945[1]	8,784	736	8,048	5,256	4,520	4,447	3,303	1,144	73	3,528
1944	8,699	779	7,920	5,327	4,548	4,485	3,349	1,136	63	3,372
1943	8,587	716	7,871	5,283	4,567	4,491	3,373	1,118	76	3,304
1942	8,477	392	8,085	4,961	4,569	4,434	3,295	1,139	135	3,516
1941	8,352	296	8,056	4,762	4,466	4,271	3,047	1,224	195	3,590
1940	8,247	107	8,140	4,714	4,607	4,184	2,840	1,344	423	3,533
1939	8,131	9	8,122	4,658	4,649	4,120	2,741	1,379	529	3,473
1938	8,004	7	7,997	4,595	4,588	4,066	2,707	1,359	522	3,409
1937	7,876	6	7,870	4,532	4,526	4,115	2,776	1,339	411	3,344
1936	7,754	6	7,748	4,472	4,466	3,895	2,576	1,319	571	3,282
1935	7,626	5	7,621	4,407	4,402	3,777	2,479	1,298	625	3,219
1934	7,496	5	7,491	4,343	4,338	3,707	2,430	1,277	631	3,153
1933	7,371	5	7,366	4,280	4,275	3,449	2,192	1,257	826	3,091
1932	7,245	5	7,240	4,216	4,211	3,470	2,233	1,237	741	3,029
1931	7,121	5	7,116	4,156	4,151	3,670	2,454	1,216	481	2,965
1930	6,978	6	6,972	4,066	4,060	3,689	2,451	1,238	371	2,912
1929	6,825	5	6,820	3,969	3,964	3,848	2,541	1,307	116	2,856
1928	6,660	5	6,655	3,866	3,861	3,796	2,491	1,305	65	2,794
1927	6,491	5	6,486	3,762	3,757	3,690	2,406	1,284	67	2,729
1926	6,331	5	6,326	3,663	3,658	3,550	2,299	1,251	108	2,668
1925	6,206	4	6,202	3,584	3,580	3,423	2,203	1,220	157	2,622
1924	6,082	4	6,078	3,506	3,502	3,344	2,138	1,206	158	2,576
1923	5,973	4	5,969	3,437	3,433	3,323	2,110	1,213	110	2,536
1922	5,893	5	5,888	3,385	3,380	3,230	2,038	1,192	150	2,508
1921	5,785	5	5,780	3,318	3,313	3,121	1,956	1,165	192	2,467

[1] From 1946 on, the figures apply to the survey week ending closest to 1 June. For 1921 to 1945 the figures apply to 1 June.

[2] Includes Newfoundland beginning in 1950. Excludes the Yukon Territory, the Northwest Territories and Indians on reserves.

Series D134-145. Labour force and main components, non-institutional population and armed forces, 14 years of age and over, annual averages, 1946 to 1975[1]
(thousands)

Year	Non-institutional population	Armed services	Civilian non-institutional population	Total labour force	Civilian labour force	Employed (civilian)			Unemployed			Persons not in the labour force
						Total	Agriculture	Non-agricultural industries	Total	Persons without jobs and seeking work	Persons on temporary layoff	
	134	135	136	137	138	139	140	141	142	143	144	145
1975	17,099	80	17,019	10,095	10,015	9,308	479	8,828	707	658	49	7,005
1974	16,643	81	16,562	9,743	9,662	9,137	473	8,664	525	493	32	6,900
1973	16,207	82	16,125	9,361	9,279	8,759	467	8,292	520	492	28	6,846
1972	15,831	84	15,747	8,975	8,891	8,329	481	7,848	562	532	30	6,856
1971	15,476	88	15,388	8,719	8,631	8,079	510	7,569	552	523	30	6,757
1970	15,108	92	15,016	8,466	8,374	7,879	511	7,368	495	458	36	6,642
1969	14,735	97	14,638	8,259	8,162	7,780	535	7,245	382	356	26	6,475
1968	14,364	100	14,264	8,019	7,919	7,537	546	6,992	382	356	26	6,344
1967	13,980	106	13,874	7,800	7,694	7,379	559	6,820	315	290	25	6,179
1966	13,581	106	13,475	7,526	7,420	7,152	544	6,609	267	247	20	6,055
1965	13,240	112	13,128	7,253	7,141	6,862	594	6,268	280	262	18	5,986
1964	12,936	119	12,817	7,052	6,933	6,609	630	5,979	324	305	19	5,884
1963	12,659	123	12,536	6,871	6,748	6,375	649	5,726	374	352	21	5,787
1962	12,406	126	12,280	6,741	6,615	6,225	660	5,565	390	368	23	5,665
1961	12,174	121	12,053	6,642	6,521	6,055	681	5,374	466	438	28	5,531
1960	11,950	119	11,831	6,530	6,411	5,965	683	5,282	446	416	30	5,420
1959	11,725	120	11,605	6,362	6,242	5,870	700	5,170	372	349	23	5,363
1958	11,508	120	11,388	6,257	6,137	5,706	718	4,988	432	404	27	5,250
1957	11,241	118	11,123	6,126	6,008	5,731	748	4,983	278	257	21	5,115
1956	10,924	117	10,807	5,899	5,782	5,585	777	4,808	197	180	17	5,025
1955	10,714	117	10,597	5,727	5,610	5,364	819	4,546	245	232	14	4,987
1954	10,505	114	10,391	5,607	5,493	5,243	878	4,365	250	235	15	4,898
1953	10,270	106	10,164	5,503	5,397	5,235	858	4,377	162	137	25	4,767
1952	10,054	98	9,956	5,422	5,324	5,169	891	4,278	155	—	—	4,632
1951	9,809	77	9,732	5,300	5,223	5,097	939	4,158	126	—	—	4,509
1950[1]	9,668	53	9,615	5,216	5,163	4,976	1,018	3,958	186	—	—	4,453
1949	9,312	44	9,268	5,099	5,055	4,913	1,077	3,837	141	—	—	4,213
1948	9,177	36	9,141	5,024	4,988	4,875	1,096	3,779	114	—	—	4,153
1947	9,042	35	9,007	4,977	4,942	4,832	1,122	3,711	110	—	—	4,065
1946	8,907	128	8,779	4,957	4,829	4,666	1,186	3,480	163	—	—	3,950

[1] Includes Newfoundland beginning in 1950. Excludes the Yukon Territory, the Northwest Territories and Indians on reserves.

Series D146-159. Civilian labour force and main components, civilian non-institutional population, 14 years of age and over, by sex, annual averages, 1946 to 1975[1]
(thousands)

Year	Civilian non-institutional population		Labour force		Employed						Unemployed		Persons not in the labour force	
					Total		Agriculture		Non-agricultural industries					
	Males	Females	Males	Females	Males	Females	Males	Females	Males	Females	Males	Females	Males	Females
	146	147	148	149	150	151	152	153	154	155	156	157	158	159
1975	8,418	8,601	6,499	3,515	6,016	3,291	398	81	5,618	3,210	483	224	1,919	5,086
1974	8,194	8,368	6,338	3,324	5,976	3,161	397	76	5,579	3,085	361	163	1,856	5,043
1973	7,978	8,146	6,127	3,152	5,767	2,992	397	70	5,371	2,921	360	160	1,851	4,995
1972	7,795	7,952	5,938	2,953	5,533	2,796	406	75	5,127	2,721	405	157	1,857	4,999
1971	7,622	7,766	5,800	2,831	5,392	2,687	440	70	4,953	2,616	408	144	1,822	4,935
1970	7,441	7,575	5,684	2,690	5,310	2,569	442	69	4,867	2,500	374	121	1,757	4,885
1969	7,255	7,383	5,560	2,602	5,272	2,508	460	75	4,812	2,434	288	94	1,695	4,780
1968	7,070	7,194	5,443	2,476	5,146	2,391	476	70	4,670	2,321	297	85	1,626	4,718
1967	6,876	6,997	5,329	2,365	5,083	2,296	486	72	4,597	2,223	246	70	1,547	4,632
1966	6,678	6,796	5,193	2,227	4,983	2,169	476	67	4,507	2,102	209	58	1,486	4,570
1965	6,505	6,623	5,065	2,076	4,842	2,020	522	72	4,320	1,948	224	56	1,440	4,547
1964	6,351	6,466	4,961	1,972	4,698	1,911	561	69	4,136	1,843	264	61	1,390	4,494
1963	6,215	6,320	4,879	1,870	4,567	1,808	580	68	3,987	1,739	312	62	1,337	4,451
1962	6,094	6,186	4,819	1,797	4,488	1,737	598	62	3,890	1,675	331	60	1,276	4,389
1961	5,991	6,061	4,782	1,739	4,381	1,674	622	59	3,758	1,615	401	65	1,209	4,322

Series D146-159. Civilian labour force and main components, civilian non-institutional population, 14 years of age and over, by sex, annual averages, 1946 to 1975[1] (concluded)
(thousands)

Year	Civilian non-institutional population		Labour force		Employed						Unemployed		Persons not in the labour force	
					Total		Agriculture		Non-agricultural industries					
	Males	Females	Males	Females	Males	Females	Males	Females	Males	Females	Males	Females	Males	Females
	146	**147**	**148**	**149**	**150**	**151**	**152**	**153**	**154**	**155**	**156**	**157**	**158**	**159**
1960	5,890	5,942	4,754	1,657	4,368	1,597	632	50	3,736	1,546	386	60	1,136	4,285
1959	5,785	5,820	4,687	1,554	4,363	1,507	651	49	3,712	1,458	325	47	1,098	4,266
1958	5,684	5,703	4,641	1,496	4,263	1,442	666	52	3,598	1,390	377	54	1,044	4,207
1957	5,559	5,564	4,573	1,435	4,329	1,402	709	39	3,620	1,363	244	33	986	4,129
1956	5,398	5,409	4,437	1,346	4,266	1,320	737	40	3,528	1,280	171	26	961	4,064
1955	5,290	5,306	4,341	1,269	4,128	1,236	783	35	3,345	1,201	213	33	949	4,038
1954	5,188	5,203	4,263	1,231	4,044	1,199	839	39	3,205	1,160	218	32	925	3,973
1953	5,075	5,089	4,206	1,191	4,063	1,172	816	42	3,248	1,129	143	19	869	3,898
1952	4,971	4,985	4,144	1,180	4,015	1,154	826	65	3,188	1,090	129	26	827	3,805
1951	4,857	4,874	4,076	1,147	3,974	1,123	867	72	3,107	1,051	103	24	781	3,728
1950[1]	4,822	4,793	4,050	1,112	3,891	1,085	940	78	2,951	1,007	159	27	772	3,681
1949	4,661	4,606	3,969	1,086	3,847	1,066	974	103	2,873	963	122	20	693	3,520
1948	4,611	4,530	3,923	1,066	3,828	1,047	974	122	2,854	925	95	19	689	3,465
1947	4,548	4,459	3,869	1,074	3,777	1,056	977	145	2,800	911	92	18	680	3,385
1946	4,400	4,379	3,746	1,082	3,609	1,057	1,030	156	2,579	901	137	26	653	3,297

[1] Includes Newfoundland beginning in 1950. Excludes the Yukon Territory, the Northwest Territories and Indians on reserves.

Series D160-174. Civilian labour force, by age and sex, annual averages, 1946 to 1975[1]
(thousands)

Year	14-19			20-24			25-44			45-64			65 and over		
	Total	Males	Females	Total	Males	Females	Total	Males	Females	Total	Males	Females	Total	Males	Females
	160	**161**	**162**	**163**	**164**	**165**	**166**	**167**	**168**	**169**	**170**	**171**	**172**	**173**	**174**
1975	1,148	658	489	1,618	940	677	4,386	2,900	1,485	2,682	1,863	819	181	137	44
1974	1,131	646	485	1,545	907	638	4,158	2,806	1,352	2,649	1,840	809	178	137	41
1973	1,041	597	444	1,477	864	614	3,962	2,711	1,251	2,620	1,818	802	179	138	41
1972	952	545	407	1,407	827	580	3,807	2,636	1,171	2,546	1,791	756	179	139	39
1971	895	509	386	1,353	795	558	3,671	2,576	1,096	2,520	1,773	747	191	146	45
1970	861	492	369	1,286	760	526	3,558	2,521	1,038	2,462	1,748	715	206	163	43
1969	840	470	369	1,240	731	509	3,465	2,472	993	2,406	1,720	686	212	167	46
1968	834	471	363	1,164	690	475	3,356	2,432	924	2,347	1,681	666	218	170	48
1967	816	460	357	1,090	657	433	3,281	2,390	891	2,290	1,652	638	217	170	46
1966	778	435	343	1,019	620	399	3,188	2,346	842	2,212	1,613	598	224	179	45
1965	738	420	318	935	578	357	3,107	2,314	793	2,139	1,576	563	222	177	45
1964	700	398	301	878	547	331	3,064	2,297	767	2,068	1,541	526	224	178	46
1963	672	386	286	833	519	314	3,021	2,288	734	2,006	1,512	494	216	174	42
1962	648	367	280	800	499	300	2,999	2,286	713	1,944	1,480	464	225	186	39
1961	630	353	278	786	499	287	2,984	2,286	698	1,892	1,456	437	229	189	40
1960	627	359	268	777	498	279	2,951	2,277	674	1,826	1,428	398	230	192	37
1959	603	350	253	763	495	268	2,893	2,257	636	1,755	1,391	364	228	194	34
1958	591	349	242	767	496	271	2,848	2,237	611	1,699	1,360	339	232	199	33
1957	587	348	239	751	489	262	2,791	2,200	590	1,640	1,328	312	239	208	31
1956	568	333	235	736	476	260	2,687	2,138	548	1,561	1,285	276	231	204	27
1955	548	327	222	729	475	254	2,618	2,095	523	1,501	1,254	247	213	190	23
1954	551	330	221	727	472	255	2,549	2,045	503	1,454	1,224	230	213	191	21
1953	545	332	213	730	473	257	2,488	2,001	487	1,420	1,205	214	215	195	20
1952	542	333	209	726	470	256	2,440	1,958	482	1,394	1,182	212	222	201	21
1951	555	342	213	725	469	255	2,364	1,907	457	1,358	1,158	201	222	201	21
1950[1]	559	352	207	735	480	255	2,307	1,869	438	1,331	1,140	191	230	209	21
1949	574	358	216	727	479	248	2,229	1,802	427	1,294	1,120	174	232	210	22
1948	566	360	206	723	478	245	2,180	1,768	413	1,288	1,109	179	231	208	23
1947	605	377	229	717	471	246	2,136	1,730	406	1,257	1,089	168	228	203	25
1946	614	376	237	694	434	260	2,053	1,652	401	1,242	1,079	163	226	205	21

[1] Includes Newfoundland beginning in 1950. Excludes the Yukon Territory, the Northwest Territories and Indians on reserves.

Series D175-189. Civilian employment, by age and sex, annual averages, 1946 to 1975[1]
(thousands)

Year	14-19			20-24			25-44			45-64			65 and over		
	Total	Males	Females	Total	Males	Females	Total	Males	Females	Total	Males	Females	Total	Males	Females
	175	**176**	**177**	**178**	**179**	**180**	**181**	**182**	**183**	**184**	**185**	**186**	**187**	**188**	**189**
1975	977	552	424	1,443	821	622	4,158	2,743	1,415	2,555	1,768	787	175	132	44
1974	1,000	564	436	1,417	821	596	3,992	2,692	1,301	2,556	1,768	788	172	131	40
1973	916	520	396	1,351	777	574	3,798	2,596	1,202	2,521	1,742	779	172	132	40
1972	822	462	360	1,273	732	542	3,626	2,503	1,123	2,435	1,703	732	173	134	39
1971	764	426	337	1,229	705	524	3,499	2,443	1,056	2,404	1,679	725	182	138	44
1970	744	418	327	1,179	680	499	3,402	2,396	1,006	2,356	1,660	696	198	156	42
1969	749	412	336	1,166	676	490	3,345	2,377	968	2,319	1,648	670	202	158	44
1968	744	410	333	1,092	637	455	3,232	2,329	903	2,261	1,609	652	209	162	48
1967	740	410	331	1,036	617	419	3,179	2,305	873	2,216	1,589	627	208	162	46
1966	714	393	321	976	587	389	3,104	2,278	826	2,144	1,555	589	215	171	44
1965	673	377	296	892	546	346	3,014	2,236	778	2,070	1,515	555	212	168	44
1964	628	349	279	824	504	320	2,954	2,202	752	1,987	1,471	516	216	171	45
1963	596	332	264	770	469	300	2,889	2,170	718	1,913	1,430	484	207	166	41
1962	573	314	259	739	450	289	2,854	2,158	696	1,845	1,390	455	215	176	38
1961	548	294	253	715	439	275	2,799	2,120	680	1,776	1,349	427	217	178	39
1960	545	300	245	705	437	268	2,777	2,120	657	1,719	1,329	390	220	183	37
1959	536	300	236	701	443	258	2,748	2,126	622	1,668	1,310	358	217	184	34
1958	515	290	224	693	433	260	2,677	2,082	595	1,600	1,269	331	221	188	33
1957	537	309	228	703	449	254	2,681	2,102	580	1,579	1,271	308	230	199	31
1956	531	306	225	704	449	255	2,610	2,070	540	1,516	1,243	273	224	198	27
1955	504	294	210	689	441	248	2,523	2,010	513	1,444	1,202	242	205	182	23
1954	506	297	210	684	436	248	2,450	1,957	493	1,398	1,171	227	205	184	21
1953	515	309	207	702	450	252	2,425	1,944	481	1,384	1,172	212	209	189	20
1952	512	312	200	699	449	250	2,382	1,908	474	1,360	1,151	209	217	196	21
1951	526	322	204	702	453	250	2,321	1,871	450	1,331	1,132	199	217	196	21
1950[1]	523	326	197	700	451	249	2,240	1,809	430	1,292	1,104	188	222	201	21
1949	541	333	208	700	457	243	2,178	1,757	421	1,267	1,095	172	227	205	22
1948	540	339	201	701	461	241	2,143	1,737	406	1,265	1,089	177	226	204	22
1947	583	361	222	694	453	241	2,097	1,697	401	1,236	1,069	167	223	198	25
1946	584	355	229	660	408	253	1,991	1,599	393	1,212	1,050	162	219	198	21

[1] Includes Newfoundland beginning in 1950. Excludes the Yukon Territory, the Northwest Territories and Indians on reserves.

Series D190-204. Unemployment, by age and sex, annual averages, 1946 to 1975[1]
(thousands)

Year	14-19			20-24			25-44			45-64			65 and over		
	Total	Males	Females	Total	Males	Females	Total	Males	Females	Total	Males	Females	Total	Males	Females
	190	**191**	**192**	**193**	**194**	**195**	**196**	**197**	**198**	**199**	**200**	**201**	**202**	**203**	**204**
1975	172	106	66	175	119	58	228	158	70	127	95	32	—	—	—
1974	130	82	49	128	86	42	166	115	51	93	73	20	—	—	—
1973	125	77	48	126	86	40	164	115	49	99	76	23	—	—	—
1972	129	83	46	134	96	38	181	133	48	111	88	24	—	—	—
1971	131	83	48	125	90	34	172	133	39	116	94	22	—	—	—
1970	117	74	42	107	80	27	157	125	32	106	88	19	—	—	—
1969	91	58	33	74	55	19	120	95	25	87	72	15	10	—	—
1968	90	60	30	73	53	20	124	103	21	86	73	13	—	—	—
1967	76	50	26	54	40	14	103	85	18	74	63	11	—	—	—
1966	64	42	22	43	33	10	84	68	16	68	59	—	—	—	—
1965	65	43	22	44	33	11	93	78	15	70	61	—	—	—	—
1964	72	49	23	54	43	11	110	94	15	81	70	11	—	—	—
1963	77	54	22	63	50	13	133	117	16	93	82	11	—	—	—
1962	75	53	22	61	50	11	145	128	17	100	90	—	10	—	—
1961	83	58	24	71	59	12	185	166	18	116	106	10	12	11	—
1960	82	59	23	72	61	11	174	157	17	107	99	—	10	—	—
1959	67	50	17	62	52	10	145	131	14	86	81	—	11	10	—
1958	76	58	18	74	63	11	171	155	16	100	92	—	11	10	—
1957	50	39	11	48	40	—	110	99	11	61	57	—	—	—	—
1956	36	27	—	32	27	—	77	68	—	45	42	—	—	—	—
1955	45	33	11	41	34	—	95	85	10	57	53	—	—	—	—
1954	45	33	12	43	36	—	99	89	10	56	53	—	—	—	—
1953	30	24	—	28	23	—	63	57	—	36	34	—	—	—	—
1952	30	21	—	28	22	—	58	50	—	34	31	—	—	—	—
1951	29	20	—	22	17	—	43	36	—	28	26	—	—	—	—
1950[1]	36	26	10	36	29	—	67	60	—	40	37	—	—	—	—
1949	33	25	—	26	21	—	51	45	—	27	25	—	—	—	—
1948	27	21	—	22	18	—	37	31	—	23	21	—	—	—	—
1947	22	16	—	23	18	—	39	34	—	21	19	—	—	—	—
1946	30	22	—	34	26	—	62	54	—	30	29	—	—	—	—

[1] Includes Newfoundland beginning in 1950. Excludes the Yukon Territory,
the Northwest Territories and Indians on reserves.

Series D205-222. Civilian labour force participation rates, by age and sex, annual averages, 1946 to 1975[1]
(per cent)

Year	14-19			20-24			25-44		
	Total	Males	Females	Total	Males	Females	Total	Males	Females
	205	206	207	208	209	210	211	212	213
1975	41.7	46.6	36.5	75.2	85.5	64.4	73.1	96.8	49.4
1974	41.6	46.3	36.7	74.7	86.1	63.0	71.7	97.0	46.6
1973	39.1	43.7	34.2	74.0	85.3	62.5	70.6	96.8	44.5
1972	36.5	40.8	32.0	72.4	84.0	60.5	69.7	96.8	42.8
1971	35.1	39.0	31.1	71.8	83.4	59.9	68.7	96.7	40.9
1970	34.6	38.6	30.4	71.0	83.2	58.5	68.0	96.7	39.6
1969	34.6	37.9	31.1	71.8	84.2	59.3	67.6	96.9	38.5
1968	35.3	39.1	31.3	71.4	84.4	58.4	66.6	97.1	36.4
1967	35.5	39.4	31.6	71.3	86.0	56.6	66.3	97.3	35.7
1966	35.0	38.6	31.4	71.5	87.4	55.6	65.6	97.6	34.3
1965	34.5	38.7	30.2	69.8	87.6	52.6	64.7	97.6	32.6
1964	34.2	38.3	29.9	69.2	88.2	51.0	64.3	97.7	31.7
1963	34.6	39.2	29.9	68.8	88.7	50.3	63.7	97.7	30.5
1962	35.4	39.6	30.9	68.6	88.6	49.7	63.3	97.7	29.7
1961	36.2	40.3	32.3	68.9	90.7	48.7	63.0	97.7	29.2
1960	37.7	42.8	32.6	68.9	91.2	47.9	62.7	97.8	28.3
1959	37.9	43.6	32.1	68.1	91.0	46.5	62.0	97.8	27.0
1958	38.9	45.6	32.1	68.9	91.7	47.4	61.6	97.8	26.2
1957	40.4	47.8	33.1	68.4	91.4	46.5	61.4	97.7	25.7
1956	41.0	48.1	33.9	68.7	91.7	47.1	60.7	97.6	24.5
1955	40.7	48.6	32.9	68.5	92.2	46.3	60.2	97.6	23.8
1954	41.9	50.2	33.6	68.6	92.0	46.6	59.8	97.3	23.3
1953	42.4	51.7	33.2	69.3	92.9	47.2	59.8	97.6	23.1
1952	42.9	52.8	33.1	69.2	92.9	47.1	60.0	97.9	23.4
1951	44.7	55.3	34.2	69.3	93.4	46.9	59.8	97.9	22.8
1950[1]	44.4	55.9	33.0	69.0	93.0	46.4	59.6	97.4	22.4
1949	46.7	58.1	35.2	69.2	93.6	46.1	60.3	98.0	23.0
1948	45.6	57.9	33.3	68.3	92.1	45.4	60.2	98.0	22.8
1947	48.4	60.2	36.7	67.5	90.6	45.3	60.2	97.4	22.9
1946	49.1	60.5	37.7	67.4	88.9	48.0	59.9	97.1	23.2

Year	45-64			65 and over			All ages		
	Total	Males	Females	Total	Males	Females	Total	Males	Females
	214	215	216	217	218	219	220	221	222
1975	62.0	87.9	37.2	10.1	17.4	4.4	58.8	77.2	40.9
1974	62.4	88.3	37.4	10.2	17.8	4.2	58.3	77.3	39.7
1973	62.9	88.9	37.8	10.6	18.3	4.4	57.5	76.8	38.7
1972	62.3	89.2	36.3	10.9	18.7	4.3	56.5	76.2	37.1
1971	62.9	90.0	36.7	11.9	20.0	5.1	56.1	76.1	36.5
1970	62.9	90.6	36.0	13.1	22.7	5.0	55.8	76.4	35.5
1969	63.0	91.1	35.5	13.8	23.6	5.5	55.8	76.6	35.2
1968	63.0	91.1	35.5	14.5	24.4	5.9	55.5	77.0	34.4
1967	63.2	91.7	35.0	14.7	24.7	5.9	55.5	77.5	33.8
1966	62.8	91.8	33.9	15.5	26.4	5.9	55.1	77.8	32.8
1965	62.4	91.8	32.9	15.6	26.3	6.0	54.4	77.9	31.3
1964	61.9	91.8	31.6	16.1	26.8	6.3	54.1	78.1	30.5
1963	61.4	91.9	30.5	15.7	26.4	5.9	53.8	78.5	29.6
1962	60.9	91.7	29.4	16.7	28.5	5.6	53.9	79.1	29.0
1961	60.7	92.2	28.5	17.3	29.3	5.9	54.1	79.8	28.7
1960	60.2	92.5	26.7	17.7	30.3	5.6	54.2	80.7	27.9
1959	59.4	92.3	25.1	17.9	31.0	5.2	53.8	81.0	26.7
1958	59.0	92.4	24.1	18.5	32.1	5.2	53.9	81.7	26.2
1957	58.6	92.6	22.8	19.5	34.1	5.0	54.0	82.3	25.8
1956	57.4	92.0	20.8	19.2	34.0	4.5	53.5	82.2	24.9
1955	56.3	91.7	19.0	18.2	32.3	3.9	52.9	82.1	23.9
1954	55.6	91.3	18.1	18.6	33.2	3.7	52.9	82.2	23.7
1953	55.6	91.8	17.2	19.4	34.8	3.6	53.1	82.9	23.4
1952	55.8	91.9	17.5	20.5	36.7	3.9	53.5	83.4	23.7
1951	55.6	92.1	17.0	21.2	37.9	4.1	53.7	83.9	23.5
1950[1]	55.3	91.9	16.4	22.7	40.4	4.2	53.7	84.0	23.2
1949	55.5	92.9	15.5	24.2	42.9	4.7	54.5	85.2	23.6
1948	56.1	93.0	16.2	24.9	44.0	5.1	54.6	85.1	23.5
1947	55.6	92.8	15.5	25.7	44.9	5.7	54.9	85.1	24.1
1946	55.9	93.4	15.3	26.6	47.5	5.0	55.0	85.1	24.7

[1] Includes Newfoundland beginning in 1950. Excludes the Yukon Territory, the Northwest Territories and Indians on reserves.

Series D223-235. Unemployment rates, by age and sex, annual averages, 1946 to 1975[1]
(per cent)

Year	14-19		20-24		25-44		45-64		65 and over		Total	Total	
	Males	Females	Males	Females	Males	Females	Males	Females	Males	Females		Males	Females
	223	224	225	226	227	228	229	230	231	232	233	234	235
1975	16.1	13.5	12.7	8.3	5.4	4.7	5.1	3.9	–	–	7.1	7.4	6.4
1974	12.7	10.1	9.5	6.6	4.1	3.8	4.0	2.5	–	–	5.4	5.7	4.9
1973	12.9	10.8	10.0	6.5	4.2	3.9	4.2	2.9	–	–	5.6	5.9	5.1
1972	15.2	11.3	11.6	6.6	5.0	4.1	4.9	3.2	–	–	6.3	6.8	5.3
1971	16.3	12.4	11.3	6.1	5.2	3.6	5.3	2.9	–	–	6.4	7.0	5.1
1970	15.0	11.4	10.5	5.1	5.0	3.1	5.0	2.7	–	–	5.9	6.6	4.5
1969	12.3	8.9	7.5	3.7	3.8	2.5	4.2	2.2	–	–	4.7	5.2	3.6
1968	12.7	8.3	7.7	4.2	4.2	2.3	4.3	2.0	–	–	4.8	5.5	3.4
1967	10.9	7.3	6.1	3.2	3.6	2.0	3.8	1.7	–	–	4.1	4.6	3.0
1966	9.7	6.4	5.3	2.5	2.9	1.9	3.7	–	–	–	3.6	4.0	2.6
1965	10.2	6.9	5.7	3.1	3.4	1.9	3.9	–	–	–	3.9	4.4	2.7
1964	12.3	7.6	7.9	3.3	4.1	2.0	4.5	2.1	–	–	4.7	5.3	3.1
1963	14.0	7.7	9.6	4.1	5.1	2.2	5.4	2.2	–	–	5.5	6.4	3.3
1962	14.4	7.9	10.0	3.7	5.6	2.4	6.1	–	–	–	5.9	6.9	3.3
1961	16.4	8.6	11.8	4.2	7.3	2.6	7.3	2.3	5.8	–	7.1	8.4	3.7
1960	16.4	8.6	12.2	3.9	6.9	2.5	6.9	–	–	–	7.0	8.1	3.6
1959	14.3	6.7	10.5	3.7	5.8	2.2	5.8	–	5.2	–	6.0	6.9	3.0
1958	16.6	7.4	12.7	4.1	6.9	2.6	6.8	–	5.0	–	7.0	8.1	3.6
1957	11.2	4.6	8.2	–	4.5	1.9	4.3	–	–	–	4.6	5.3	2.3
1956	8.1	–	5.7	–	3.2	–	3.3	–	–	–	3.4	3.9	1.9
1955	10.1	5.0	7.2	–	4.1	1.9	4.2	–	–	–	4.4	4.9	2.6
1954	10.0	5.4	7.6	–	4.4	2.0	4.3	–	–	–	4.6	5.1	2.6
1953	7.2	–	4.9	–	2.8	–	2.8	–	–	–	3.0	3.4	1.6
1952	6.3	–	4.7	–	2.6	–	2.6	–	–	–	2.9	3.1	2.2
1951	5.8	–	3.6	–	1.9	–	2.2	–	–	–	2.4	2.5	2.1
1950[1]	7.4	4.8	6.0	–	3.2	–	3.2	–	–	–	3.6	3.9	2.4
1949	7.0	–	4.4	–	2.5	–	2.2	–	–	–	2.8	3.1	1.8
1948	5.8	–	3.8	–	1.8	–	1.9	–	–	–	2.3	2.4	1.8
1947	4.2	–	3.8	–	2.0	–	1.7	–	–	–	2.2	2.4	1.7
1946	5.9	–	6.0	–	3.3	–	2.7	–	–	–	3.4	3.7	2.5

[1] Includes Newfoundland beginning in 1950. Excludes the Yukon Territory, the Northwest Territories and Indians on reserves.

Series D236-259. Civilian employment in agriculture and non-agricultural industries, by class of worker and sex, annual averages, 1946 to 1975[1]
(thousands)

Year	Agriculture											
	Paid workers			Own account workers			Employers			Unpaid family workers		
	Total	Males	Females	Total	Males	Females	Total	Males	Females	Total	Males	Females
	236	237	238	239	240	241	242	243	244	245	246	247
1975	110	87	23	224	217	–	46	45	–	100	50	50
1974	99	80	18	225	219	–	46	45	–	103	52	50
1973	96	77	19	226	221	–	44	43	–	100	56	44
1972	99	80	19	228	222	–	45	43	–	110	60	49
1971	102	86	16	243	238	–	48	46	–	118	69	48
1970	99	84	15	252	247	–	44	43	–	116	69	47
1969	96	80	15	270	265	–	44	43	–	125	72	53
1968	99	84	14	273	268	–	46	44	–	128	79	49
1967	99	84	15	291	286	–	47	45	–	122	72	50
1966	98	85	13	285	279	–	50	48	–	110	65	45
1965	105	92	13	307	302	–	55	54	–	126	75	51
1964	99	88	11	336	330	–	61	59	–	134	85	49
1963	103	94	10	341	334	–	64	63	–	141	89	51
1962	110	98	11	352	347	–	62	61	–	137	92	45
1961	112	101	11	370	365	–	66	64	–	133	92	41

Series D236-259. Civilian employment in agriculture and non-agricultural industries, by class of worker and sex, annual averages, 1946 to 1975[1] (concluded)
(thousands)

Year	Agriculture *(continued)*											
	Paid workers			Own account workers			Employers			Unpaid family workers		
	Total	Males	Females	Total	Males	Females	Total	Males	Females	Total	Males	Females
	236	237	238	239	240	241	242	243	244	245	246	247
1960	112	102	10	379	375	—	66	64	—	127	92	35
1959	111	103	—	392	386	—	64	62	—	133	101	32
1958	99	90	10	408	402	—	64	62	—	147	112	35
1957	97	89	—	434	429	—	65	63	—	152	128	24
1956	103	94	—	448	444	—	66	65	—	160	134	27
1955	106	98	—	475	470	—	68	67	—	170	149	21
1954	121	111	10	496	491	—	76	76	—	185	163	23
1953	113	102	11	477	473	—	75	74	—	193	167	27
1952	111	103	—	477	470	—	80	79	—	223	175	48
1951	100	91	—	554	547	—	42	41	—	243	188	55
1950[1]	111	104	—	582	574	—	47	46	—	279	217	63
1949	143	129	14	592	585	—	70	69	—	273	192	80
1948	133	123	11	599	588	11	70	69	—	295	195	100
1947	120	107	12	603	590	13	61	60	—	338	220	118
1946	147	134	13	618	607	11	62	60	—	360	229	131

Year	Non-agricultural											
	Paid workers			Own account workers			Employers			Unpaid family workers		
	Total	Males	Females	Total	Males	Females	Total	Males	Females	Total	Males	Females
	248	249	250	251	252	253	254	255	256	257	258	259
1975	8,162	5,107	3,055	288	221	68	314	278	35	64	11	52
1974	8,006	5,079	2,927	292	220	73	302	271	32	63	—	54
1973	7,661	4,896	2,765	279	209	71	284	255	29	67	11	56
1972	7,211	4,650	2,561	270	200	70	301	266	35	66	11	56
1971	6,927	4,475	2,453	275	202	73	295	265	31	71	12	60
1970	6,740	4,399	2,341	271	199	72	288	258	30	69	12	57
1969	6,625	4,343	2,282	261	193	68	293	265	27	66	10	56
1968	6,391	4,216	2,175	252	186	65	282	256	26	67	12	55
1967	6,206	4,137	2,069	262	189	73	288	259	28	64	12	53
1966	5,999	4,040	1,959	255	191	65	294	268	26	60	—	52
1965	5,655	3,857	1,798	253	184	69	295	268	27	65	10	54
1964	5,368	3,667	1,700	248	188	60	297	271	26	66	10	56
1963	5,138	3,522	1,615	243	193	51	286	263	23	59	—	50
1962	4,980	3,428	1,552	245	192	52	283	259	24	57	10	47
1961	4,799	3,304	1,495	237	186	51	281	258	23	56	10	46
1960	4,732	3,296	1,436	231	184	47	269	245	23	51	10	41
1959	4,624	3,270	1,354	220	178	42	275	254	21	51	—	42
1958	4,461	3,173	1,287	217	174	42	260	241	19	51	10	41
1957	4,442	3,179	1,263	233	193	40	253	236	18	54	12	42
1956	4,286	3,094	1,193	226	191	34	246	229	16	51	14	37
1955	4,027	2,914	1,113	229	195	34	234	217	17	56	19	37
1954	3,840	2,766	1,075	246	211	35	223	208	15	56	20	36
1953	3,842	2,800	1,042	248	212	35	230	215	15	58	22	36
1952	3,755	2,753	1,002	237	203	34	229	213	16	58	19	38
1951	3,623	2,660	963	349	302	47	135	128	—	52	17	35
1950[1]	3,411	2,495	916	361	308	52	133	127	—	53	21	32
1949	3,298	2,422	875	335	290	46	151	144	—	53	18	35
1948	3,234	2,399	835	338	288	50	155	147	—	52	21	32
1947	3,156	2,338	818	348	297	51	153	145	—	55	20	34
1946	2,990	2,171	819	301	256	44	149	139	—	41	13	28

[1] Includes Newfoundland beginning in 1950. Excludes the Yukon Territory, the Northwest Territories and Indians on reserves.

Series D260-265. Civilian persons with jobs in non-agricultural industries, by class of worker and sex, 1 June of each year, 1931 to 1958[1]
(thousands)

Year	Total persons with jobs		Paid workers		Other than paid workers	
	Males	Females	Males	Females	Males	Females
	260	**261**	**262**	**263**	**264**	**265**
1958	3,633	1,378	3,214	1,279	419	99
1957	3,643	1,359	3,186	1,264	457	95
1956	3,494	1,259	3,049	1,170	445	89
1955	3,307	1,191	2,880	1,097	427	94
1954	3,216	1,146	2,768	1,057	448	89
1953	3,249	1,124	2,803	1,039	446	85
1952	3,218	1,094	2,789	1,006	429	88
1951	3,101	1,063	2,653	972	448	91
1950[1]	2,971	1,019	2,501	928	470	91
1949	2,910	967	2,446	880	464	87
1948	2,854	914	2,399	826	455	88
1947	2,792	898	2,332	807	460	91
1946	2,578	889	2,178	808	400	81
1945	2,110	1,193	2,014	923	96	270
1944	2,150	1,199	2,041	935	109	264
1943	2,189	1,184	2,085	849	104	335
1942	2,421	874	2,090	711	331	163
1941	2,247	800	1,883	683	364	117
1940	2,107	733	1,595	602	512	131
1939	2,055	686	1,504	575	551	111
1938	2,030	677	1,500	575	530	102
1937	2,088	688	1,531	577	557	111
1936	1,920	656	1,432	562	488	94
1935	1,843	636	1,380	561	463	75
1934	1,806	624	1,374	557	432	67
1933	1,608	584	1,182	535	426	49
1932	1,647	586	1,291	557	356	29
1931	1,844	610	1,512	516	332	94

[1] Includes Newfoundland beginning in 1950. Excludes the Yukon Territory, the Northwest Territories and Indians on reserves.

Series D266-289. Civilian employment by industry (1948 S.I.C.), both sexes and males, annual averages, 1946 to 1964[1]

(thousands)

Year	Total employed		Agriculture		Forestry		Fishing and trapping		Mining, quarrying and oil wells		Manufacturing	
	Total	Males	Total	Males	Total	Males	Total	Males	Total	Males	Total	Males
	266	**267**	**268**	**269**	**270**	**271**	**272**	**273**	**274**	**275**	**276**	**277**
1964	6,595	4,696	624	555	82	81	26	26	87	83	1,702	1,347
1963	6,364	4,567	641	574	81	80	25	25	72	68	1,614	1,278
1962	6,217	4,487	653	591	74	73	23	23	81	78	1,567	1,245
1961	6,048	4,378	674	616	86	85	18	17	79	76	1,515	1,201
1960	5,955	4,362	675	625	97	96	17	17	93	89	1,470	1,168
1959	5,856	4,353	692	644	94	93	15	15	88	84	1,494	1,193
1958	5,695	4,256	712	660	85	84	16	16	107	104	1,459	1,169
1957	5,725	4,325	744	706	105	104	21	20	118	114	1,492	1,190
1956	5,585	4,265	776	736	118	117	20	20	117	113	1,435	1,141
1955	5,364	4,128	819	783	113	112	22	21	109	106	1,373	1,093
1954	5,243	4,044	878	839	91	90	24	23	102	100	1,326	1,057
1953	5,235	4,063	858	816	83	82	26	26	91	89	1,384	1,102
1952	5,159	4,005	886	823	97	95	28	28	92	90	1,333	1,064
1951	5,097	3,974	939	867	115	114	30	30	79	78	1,350	1,077
1950[1]	4,976	3,891	1,018	940	82	81	39	38	75	74	1,316	1,043
1949	4,913	3,847	1,077	974	69	68	26	26	84	83	1,303	1,041
1948	4,875	3,828	1,096	974	97	96	22	22	74	73	1,268	1,026
1947	4,832	3,777	1,122	977	94	93	23	23	69	68	1,264	1,019
1946	4,666	3,609	1,186	1,030	84	83	27	27	74	72	1,214	964

Year	Construction		Transportation, storage and communication		Public utilities		Trade		Finance, insurance and real estate		Service	
	Total	Males	Total	Males	Total	Males	Total	Males	Total	Males	Total	Males
	278	**279**	**280**	**281**	**282**	**283**	**284**	**285**	**286**	**287**	**288**	**289**
1964	449	434	451	389	77	69	1,067	717	264	146	1,768	851
1963	450	437	455	388	85	76	1,019	688	254	135	1,669	819
1962	429	416	446	383	82	73	1,002	677	248	134	1,615	795
1961	406	394	432	370	77	69	982	667	239	130	1,541	753
1960	418	407	442	379	73	65	981	668	226	119	1,463	728
1959	442	430	445	381	75	66	946	647	216	117	1,348	683
1958	427	416	429	366	78	70	913	628	211	115	1,257	629
1957	438	427	438	372	73	66	899	618	206	112	1,192	597
1956	412	403	433	373	67	60	882	614	194	106	1,131	582
1955	368	362	403	347	62	56	844	590	178	100	1,073	558
1954	334	327	397	340	61	56	828	578	169	94	1,034	540
1953	347	340	423	369	58	53	816	571	165	92	984	525
1952	338	331	421	367	58	53	785	537	162	91	959	526
1951	348	341	398	344	51	46	718	487	154	87	916	503
1950[1]	331	326	376	328	46	42	644	436	142	78	908	506
1949	317	312	364	319	45	41	647	441	144	82	840	462
1948	286	281	371	332	41	37	649	446	140	81	832	461
1947	251	246	373	332	38	34	637	435	131	77	831	473
1946	224	220	344	303	33	29	573	377	124	74	784	431

[1] Includes Newfoundland beginning in 1950. Excludes the Yukon Territory, the Northwest Territories and Indians on reserves.

Series D290-317. Civilian employment, by industry (1960 S.I.C.), both sexes and males, annual averages, 1961 to 1975[1]

(thousands)

Year	Total employed		Agriculture		Forestry		Fishing and trapping		Mining and quarrying		Manufacturing		Construction	
	Total	Males	Total	Males	Total	Males	Total	Males	Total	Males	Total	Males	Total	Males
	290	**291**	**292**	**293**	**294**	**295**	**296**	**297**	**298**	**299**	**300**	**301**	**302**	**303**
1975	9,308	6,016	479	398	72	69	23	22	132	122	1,951	1,478	605	569
1974	9,137	5,976	473	397	82	79	24	24	127	120	2,024	1,534	598	566
1973	8,759	5,767	467	397	80	78	25	24	123	116	1,968	1,500	549	522
1972	8,329	5,533	481	406	71	69	22	22	124	117	1,857	1,420	501	477
1971	8,079	5,392	510	440	72	70	22	22	129	122	1,795	1,381	495	471
1970	7,879	5,310	511	442	72	71	20	20	125	119	1,790	1,397	471	451
1969	7,780	5,272	535	460	80	79	21	21	116	109	1,819	1,409	482	460
1968	7,537	5,146	546	476	80	78	24	24	117	112	1,754	1,369	470	450
1967	7,379	5,083	559	486	79	78	25	25	114	108	1,756	1,362	475	457
1966	7,152	4,983	544	476	76	74	26	26	121	116	1,744	1,361	499	482
1965	6,862	4,842	594	522	77	75	23	22	134	130	1,636	1,287	463	447
1964	6,609	4,698	630	561	82	81	26	26	87	84	1,650	1,294	410	396
1963	6,375	4,567	649	580	80	80	25	25	72	69	1,552	1,218	406	393
1962	6,225	4,488	660	598	74	73	23	23	81	78	1,502	1,186	393	381
1961	6,055	4,381	681	622	86	85	18	17	80	76	1,452	1,144	376	365

Year	Transportation, communication and other utilities		Transportation, storage and communication		Public utilities		Trade		Finance, insurance and real estate		Community, business and personal service		Public administration	
	Total	Males	Total	Males	Total	Males	Total	Males	Total	Males	Total	Males	Total	Males
	304	**305**	**306**	**307**	**308**	**309**	**310**	**311**	**312**	**313**	**314**	**315**	**316**	**317**
1975	806	666	702	576	104	90	1,633	1,013	460	201	2,508	1,034	639	444
1974	790	655	694	572	96	83	1,575	985	446	202	2,386	979	613	436
1973	773	644	674	556	99	88	1,498	940	410	187	2,284	936	582	423
1972	730	618	637	536	93	83	1,410	899	385	185	2,194	908	553	412
1971	702	595	615	519	87	76	1,330	859	385	185	2,118	863	520	384
1970	692	585	603	509	89	76	1,320	863	365	184	2,025	814	486	364
1969	693	583	600	502	93	81	1,292	845	350	179	1,918	774	474	353
1968	673	568	582	489	90	79	1,260	827	327	166	1,830	728	458	347
1967	659	563	580	492	80	71	1,224	818	312	164	1,732	684	443	338
1966	620	530	543	462	77	68	1,180	793	302	158	1,622	643	419	324
1965	617	529	540	460	77	69	1,145	772	280	152	1,489	590	403	316
1964	591	508	522	447	69	61	1,105	753	264	146	1,386	556	377	293
1963	597	509	521	442	76	67	1,062	730	254	135	1,306	535	371	293
1962	588	504	513	438	75	66	1,049	722	248	134	1,244	509	362	280
1961	563	482	492	420	71	63	1,025	710	239	130	1,178	473	356	276

[1] Includes Newfoundland. Excludes the Yukon Territory, the Northwest Territories and Indians on reserves.

Series D318-328. Civilian persons with paid-worker jobs, by industry (1948 S.I.C.), 1 June of each year, 1931 to 1960[1]

(thousands)

Year[1,2]	Agriculture	Forestry	Fishing and trapping	Mining, quarrying and oil wells	Manu-facturing	Con-struction	Trans-portation, storage and communi-cation	Public utilities	Trade	Finance, insurance and real estate	Service
	318	319	320	321	322	323	324	325	326	327	328
1960	112	62	—	93	1,414	364	417	74	783	209	1,352
1959	124	53	—	84	1,437	375	407	77	723	200	1,211
1958	102	62	—	114	1,401	393	407	76	725	191	1,116
1957	88	89	12	116	1,413	387	407	75	705	184	1,062
1956	107	71	11	109	1,347	355	403	67	682	176	998
1955	124	69	—	107	1,297	302	368	59	649	165	952
1954	125	49	—	104	1,281	277	371	59	630	158	888
1953	109	61	—	91	1,319	299	382	54	629	141	859
1952	105	63	13	95	1,282	289	385	59	607	149	853
1951	111	70	—	85	1,270	279	356	46	538	144	828
1950[1]	124	47	11	74	1,222	267	343	44	479	134	808
1949	153	47	—	83	1,212	271	329	45	470	130	733
1948	142	51	—	73	1,166	226	329	39	469	122	743
1947	123	47	—	74	1,199	182	333	39	436	115	707
1946	157	31	—	72	1,144	184	308	34	419	111	674
1945[2]	—		58	52	1,196	113	305	29	389	102	693
1944	—		63	60	1,263	110	292	27	364	97	700
1943	—		62	68	1,250	149	276	26	337	92	674
1942	—		81	81	1,131	144	262	25	344	89	644
1941	—		87	89	904	170	247	26	346	80	617
1940	—		59	84	712	126	219	24	309	82	582
1939	—		56	82	627	127	206	22	302	82	575
1938	—		55	79	632	134	204	23	296	82	570
1937	—		65	80	657	139	212	21	289	82	563
1936	—		58	70	592	132	207	21	280	82	552
1935	—		60	64	579	125	194	21	262	82	554
1934	—		49	58	560	165	193	20	254	83	549
1933	—		31	52	481	81	190	21	237	83	541
1932	—		31	55	528	118	208	23	254	83	548
1931	—		40	60	605	154	246	24	269	83	547

[1] Includes Newfoundland beginning in 1950. Excludes the Yukon Territory, the Northwest Territories and Indians on reserves.

[2] From 1946 on, figures apply to the survey week ending closest to 1 June. For 1931 to 1945 the figures apply to 1 June.

Series D329-340. Civilian employed paid workers, by industry (1948 S.I.C.), annual averages, 1946 to 1964[1]
(thousands)

Year	Total employed paid workers	Agricul-ture	Forestry	Fishing and trapping	Mining, quarrying and oil wells	Manufac-turing	Construc-tion	Transpor-tation, storage and commu-nication	Public utilities	Trade	Finance, insurance and real estate	Service
	329	330	331	332	333	334	335	336	337	338	339	340
1964	5,458	98	71	10	85	1,622	373	418	77	865	246	1,596
1963	5,234	101	69	–	70	1,535	377	421	84	825	235	1,509
1962	5,085	108	62	–	79	1,484	355	414	82	806	228	1,459
1961	4,909	111	75	–	77	1,434	336	399	77	783	220	1,390
1960	4,837	110	84	–	91	1,399	352	410	73	786	208	1,319
1959	4,724	109	81	–	85	1,424	372	412	75	751	200	1,209
1958	4,551	97	75	–	105	1,389	363	399	78	724	195	1,120
1957	4,535	96	90	–	116	1,417	371	406	73	711	190	1,057
1956	4,388	102	100	–	116	1,364	348	401	67	699	178	1,007
1955	4,133	106	91	–	108	1,306	305	372	62	659	165	952
1954	3,961	121	67	–	100	1,255	274	363	60	647	156	911
1953	3,955	113	61	–	90	1,307	288	384	58	635	150	864
1952	3,853	108	72	–	90	1,258	275	387	58	607	149	840
1951	3,722	100	85	–	78	1,266	278	360	51	553	142	803
1950[1]	3,522	111	65	10	74	1,219	261	342	46	480	131	786
1949	3,440	143	53	–	83	1,206	249	325	45	479	130	723
1948	3,367	133	76	–	73	1,170	220	332	40	481	123	714
1947	3,275	120	67	–	67	1,167	183	333	37	470	118	710
1946	3,137	147	67	10	70	1,119	167	311	33	424	112	678

[1] Includes Newfoundland beginning in 1950. Excludes the Yukon Territory, the Northwest Territories and Indians on reserves.

Series D341-354. Civilian employed paid workers, by industry (1960 S.I.C.), annual averages, 1961 to 1975[1]
(thousands)

Year	Total employed paid workers	Agricul-ture	Forestry	Fishing and trapping	Mining and quarrying	Manufac-turing	Construc-tion	Transpor-tation, communi-cation and other utilities	Transpor-tation, storage and communi-cation	Public utilities	Trade	Finance, insurance and real estate	Commu-nity, business and personal service	Public adminis-tration
	341	342	343	344	345	346	347	348	349	350	351	352	353	354
1975	8,272	110	65	–	130	1,915	499	761	658	103	1,424	439	2,282	639
1974	8,105	99	73	–	125	1,986	490	745	650	96	1,375	424	2,167	613
1973	7,757	96	72	–	121	1,928	452	731	633	98	1,295	392	2,078	582
1972	7,310	99	64	–	122	1,816	415	688	596	92	1,205	363	1,977	553
1971	7,029	102	65	–	126	1,757	412	664	578	86	1,119	363	1,894	520
1970	6,839	99	64	–	124	1,751	389	660	572	88	1,105	345	1,809	486
1969	6,720	96	71	–	114	1,781	396	656	563	93	1,078	329	1,718	474
1968	6,490	99	70	–	116	1,711	390	639	549	90	1,057	306	1,635	458
1967	6,305	99	71	–	112	1,716	396	625	545	79	1,010	293	1,532	443
1966	6,096	98	68	–	120	1,702	418	584	507	77	970	279	1,430	419
1965	5,760	105	66	–	132	1,590	385	582	505	76	931	260	1,298	403
1964	5,466	99	70	10	86	1,596	334	556	488	68	886	247	1,204	377
1963	5,241	103	68	–	70	1,504	333	562	487	76	850	236	1,133	371
1962	5,089	110	62	–	80	1,451	321	557	482	75	834	228	1,077	362
1961	4,911	112	75	–	78	1,406	307	529	458	71	805	220	1,016	356

[1] Excludes the Yukon Territory, the Northwest Territories and Indians on reserves.

Series D355-382. Civilian employment, by occupation and sex (1951 classification system), both sexes and males, annual averages, 1948 to 1960

(thousands)

Year[1,2]	Managerial		Professional		Clerical		Transportation		Communication		Commercial		Financial	
	Total	Males	Total	Males	Total	Males	Total	Males	Total	Males	Total	Males	Total	Males
	355	**356**	**357**	**358**	**359**	**360**	**361**	**362**	**363**	**364**	**365**	**366**	**367**	**368**
1960	505	449	598	344	752	285	—	374	93	55	· 432	258	—	56
1959	534	478	562	334	722	276	—	356	89	54	418	253	—	52
1958	494	441	510	315	699	260	—	376	85	49	395	241	—	50
1957	509	460	490	298	695	271	—	358	86	45	397	236	—	48
1956	452	410	423	261	664	263	—	373	77	41	366	226	—	45
1955	443	397	416	256	619	253	—	352	82	44	363	220	—	39
1954	476	436	377	235	602	248	—	333	82	45	340	202	—	37
1953	496	454	386	229	569	239	—	343	83	44	340	205	—	29
1952	459	410	346	223	595	262	—	344	75	41	349	200	—	35
1951	422	376	343	222	577	250	—	333	69	39	328	191	—	32
1950[2]	410	359	340	223	554	249	—	328	70	38	326	202	—	22
1949	375	333	305	195	513	224	—	343	66	39	333	195	—	27
1948[3]	254	225	287	187	505	223	—	335	63	39	397	269	—	32

Year[1,2]	Service		Agricultural		Fishing, logging and trapping		Mining		Manufacturing and mechanical trades[4]		Construction		Labourers and unskilled workers[5]	
	Total	Males	Total	Males	Total	Males	Total	Males	Total	Males	Total	Males	Total	Males
	369	**370**	**371**	**372**	**373**	**374**	**375**	**376**	**377**	**378**	**379**	**380**	**381**	**382**
1960	619	271	682	637	—	77	—	60	1,050	871	—	328	—	337
1959	564	251	729	684	—	68	—	52	1,014	833	—	337	—	333
1958	552	247	746	690	—	75	—	71	1,005	831	—	336	—	334
1957	519	234	782	743	—	105	—	72	1,018	830	—	345	—	331
1956	503	232	830	788	—	96	—	67	963	781	—	343	—	345
1955	470	217	880	844	—	94	—	69	921	758	—	304	—	297
1954	461	215	901	866	—	79	—	66	904	734	—	288	—	290
1953	430	207	903	853	—	79	—	60	921	746	—	315	—	294
1952	435	215	933	846	—	101	—	63	907	736	—	316	—	267
1951	400	196	998	899	—	109	—	60	911	725	—	323	—	238
1950[2]	416	214	1,071	978	—	101	—	54	909	725	—	343	—	108
1949	371	184	1,122	990	—	72	—	61	886	719	—	347	—	163
1948[3]	376	191	1,183	1,025	—	76	—	60	911	754	—	259	—	205

[1] Figures apply to the survey week ending closest to 1 June.
[2] Newfoundland included beginning in 1950. Excludes the Yukon Territory, the Northwest Territories and Indians on reserves.
[3] Figures are also available in the source for August 1947. No earlier figures are available.

[4] Includes stationary engineers and occupations associated with electric power production.
[5] Excludes labourers in agriculture, fishing, logging, trapping and mining.

Series D383-412. Civilian employment, by occupation (1961 classification system), both sexes and males, annual averages, 1961 to 1973[1]

(thousands)

Year	Total employed		Managerial		Professional and technical		Clerical		Communication		Farmers and farm workers		Loggers and related workers		Fishermen, trappers and hunters	
	Total	Males	Total	Males	Total	Males	Total	Males	Total	Males	Total	Males	Total	Males	Total	Males
	383	**384**	**385**	**386**	**387**	**388**	**389**	**390**	**391**	**392**	**393**	**394**	**395**	**396**	**397**	**398**
1973	8,759	5,767	823	698	1,265	744	1,388	370	71	34	488	422	54	54	25	25
1972	8,329	5,533	817	700	1,180	695	1,279	358	70	35	488	418	45	45	22	22
1971	8,079	5,392	789	683	1,142	673	1,217	339	70	36	513	447	43	43	22	22
1970	7,879	5,310	786	685	1,070	620	1,168	339	65	31	513	449	46	46	21	21
1969	7,780	5,272	748	657	1,038	602	1,152	348	63	30	534	464	51	51	21	21
1968	7,537	5,146	714	624	980	564	1,100	344	69	33	548	482	54	54	25	24
1967	7,379	5,083	693	607	917	522	1,038	334	65	29	564	496	57	57	26	26
1966	7,152	4,983	669	591	876	496	1,007	343	63	29	552	487	53	53	27	27
1965	6,862	4,842	637	560	782	450	919	320	60	28	599	531	53	53	23	23
1964	6,609	4,698	609	536	702	407	884	324	56	27	632	566	62	62	25	24
1963	6,375	4,567	589	524	674	402	857	311	57	24	655	588	58	58	24	24
1962	6,225	4,488	581	516	659	385	830	310	56	25	662	602	54	54	21	21
1961	6,055	4,381	560	498	598	347	805	303	57	24	684	627	82[2]	82[2]	_[2]	_[2]

Year	Miners, quarrymen and related workers		Sales		Service and recreation		Transportation and communication		Transportation		Craftsmen, production process		Labourers and unskilled workers	
	Total	Males	Total	Males	Total	Males	Total	Males	Total	Males	Total	Males	Total	Males
	399	**400**	**401**	**402**	**403**	**404**	**405**	**406**	**407**	**408**	**409**	**410**	**411**	**412**
1973	53	52	625	378	1,068	453	462	415	391	382	2,206	1,874	300	281
1972	53	53	583	357	1,010	413	445	401	375	366	2,054	1,748	352	321
1971	57	56	573	350	996	397	431	389	361	353	1,945	1,670	350	322
1970	58	58	558	347	967	388	418	377	353	345	1,954	1,685	319	296
1969	56	56	530	325	937	376	415	376	352	346	1,981	1,700	318	297
1968	58	58	516	316	908	369	413	372	344	339	1,910	1,647	312	292
1967	58	58	501	309	874	356	412	372	347	342	1,924	1,652	315	294
1966	63	63	480	300	813	331	403	365	340	336	1,864	1,603	345	324
1965	76	76	482	306	793	328	432	395	372	366	1,730	1,484	335	316
1964	49	49	491	318	772	325	429	394	372	367	1,628	1,383	327	310
1963	41	41	462	299	708	299	412	376	355	352	1,585	1,353	308	292
1962	46	46	454	293	676	294	407	372	351	347	1,536	1,312	298	281
1961	48	48	446	287	658	278	409	372	352	348	1,464	1,250	302	289

[1] Excludes the Yukon Territory, the Northwest Territories and Indians on reserves.

[2] Combined loggers and related workers and fishermen, trappers and hunters in 1961.

Series D413-430. Female civilian labour force, by age and marital status, annual averages, 1966 to 1975[1]
(thousands)

Year	All ages			14-24			25-34		
	Total	Married	Other[2]	Total	Married	Other[2]	Total	Married	Other[2]
	413	**414**	**415**	**416**	**417**	**418**	**419**	**420**	**421**
1975	3,515	2,029	1,486	1,167	341	826	864	617	248
1974	3,324	1,899	1,426	1,123	321	801	764	543	221
1973	3,152	1,792	1,360	1,058	303	755	705	503	202
1972	2,953	1,681	1,272	987	282	705	643	460	183
1971	2,831	1,604	1,227	944	272	671	580	418	162
1970	2,690	1,525	1,165	894	249	646	532	386	145
1969	2,602	1,451	1,152	878	244	635	502	355	147
1968	2,476	1,355	1,121	838	222	616	452	315	137
1967	2,365	1,260	1,106	790	188	602	424	298	126
1966	2,227	1,160	1,067	742	162	580	394	271	123

Year	35-44			45-54			55 and over		
	Total	Married	Other[2]	Total	Married	Other[2]	Total	Married	Other[2]
	422	**423**	**424**	**425**	**426**	**427**	**428**	**429**	**430**
1975	621	495	126	540	403	137	323	173	150
1974	588	471	117	532	394	138	318	169	148
1973	546	434	112	519	383	137	324	168	155
1972	528	416	112	490	364	126	305	159	146
1971	515	406	109	478	350	128	313	157	157
1970	506	404	102	464	337	128	294	149	144
1969	491	390	101	439	317	122	292	145	148
1968	471	370	101	437	315	122	277	132	145
1967	468	358	110	422	291	130	263	125	138
1966	448	341	106	390	269	121	253	116	137

[1] Excludes the Yukon Territory, the Northwest Territories and Indians on reserves.

[2] Includes single, widowed, separated and divorced.

Series D431-448. Female civilian labour force participation rates, by age and marital status, annual averages, 1959 to 1975[1]
(per cent)

Year	All ages			14-24			25-34		
	Total	Married	Other[2]	Total	Married	Other[2]	Total	Married	Other[2]
	431	**432**	**433**	**434**	**435**	**436**	**437**	**438**	**439**
1975	40.9	38.4	44.7	48.7	52.1	47.5	49.9	43.5	79.2
1974	39.7	36.7	44.7	48.1	50.2	47.3	46.5	39.9	78.4
1973	38.7	35.5	43.8	46.4	48.5	45.6	45.2	38.6	79.2
1972	37.1	33.9	42.4	44.3	45.7	43.8	43.2	36.7	78.2
1971	36.5	33.0	42.2	43.4	45.1	42.7	40.7	34.4	77.5
1970	35.5	32.0	41.4	42.3	42.5	42.3	39.0	32.8	77.5
1969	35.2	31.2	42.2	42.9	43.5	42.8	38.2	31.4	80.3
1968	34.4	29.6	42.7	42.5	41.0	43.0	35.6	28.7	79.7
1967	33.8	28.3	43.4	41.7	36.2	43.8	34.4	27.6	81.3
1966	32.8	26.8	43.3	41.0	33.5	43.7	32.8	25.8	80.9
1965	31.3	25.2	42.4	—	—	—	—	—	—
1964	30.5	24.1	42.1	—	—	—	—	—	—
1963	29.6	22.5	42.4	—	—	—	—	—	—
1962	29.1	21.5	43.2	—	—	—	—	—	—
1961	28.8	20.7	43.8	—	—	—	—	—	—
1960	28.0	19.1	44.5	—	—	—	—	—	—
1959	26.7	17.9	43.4	—	—	—	—	—	—

Series D431-448. Female civilian labour force participation rates, by age and marital status, annual averages, 1959 to 1975[1] (concluded)
(per cent)

Year	35-44			45-54			55 and over		
	Total	Married	Other[2]	Total	Married	Other[2]	Total	Married	Other[2]
	440	**441**	**442**	**443**	**444**	**445**	**446**	**447**	**448**
1975	48.8	45.1	72.4	43.5	39.3	64.0	16.4	16.0	17.0
1974	46.7	43.1	71.3	43.4	38.8	65.4	16.7	15.9	17.7
1973	43.7	39.8	70.4	42.9	38.1	66.8	17.5	16.5	18.7
1972	42.2	38.1	70.4	41.2	36.5	65.6	17.0	15.9	18.2
1971	41.1	36.9	70.3	41.0	36.0	66.0	17.9	16.3	20.1
1970	40.2	36.3	69.9	40.6	35.6	65.3	17.3	15.9	19.0
1969	38.9	34.8	71.6	39.3	33.9	66.7	17.8	16.0	20.1
1968	37.2	32.8	73.2	40.1	34.8	66.3	17.4	14.8	20.7
1967	37.0	32.1	73.8	39.7	33.3	69.5	17.0	14.5	20.2
1966	35.7	30.6	75.7	37.8	31.5	67.6	16.9	14.0	20.5
1965	-	-	-	-	-	-	-	-	-
1964	-	-	-	-	-	-	-	-	-
1963	-	-	-	-	-	-	-	-	-
1962	-	-	-	-	-	-	-	-	-
1961	-	-	-	-	-	-	-	-	-
1960	-	-	-	-	-	-	-	-	-
1959	-	-	-	-	-	-	-	-	-

[1] Excludes the Yukon Territory, the Northwest Territories and Indians on reserves.

[2] Includes single, widowed, separated and divorced.

Series D449-454. Civilian employment, by full-time and part-time status and by sex, annual averages, 1953 to 1975[1]
(thousands)

Year	Full-time			Part-time		
	Total	Males	Females	Total	Males	Females
	449	**450**	**451**	**452**	**453**	**454**
1975	8,072	5,626	2,446	1,236	390	845
1974	7,972	5,608	2,364	1,166	368	797
1973	7,675	5,419	2,256	1,084	348	736
1972	7,291	5,190	2,101	1,038	343	695
1971	7,067	5,047	2,020	1,012	345	667
1970	6,908	4,978	1,931	971	332	639
1969	6,880	4,979	1,901	900	293	607
1968	6,708	4,879	1,829	829	267	562
1967	6,634	4,844	1,791	745	239	505
1966	6,475	4,772	1,703	678	212	466
1965	6,205	4,631	1,573	657	210	446
1964	6,012	4,501	1,511	597	197	400
1963	5,842	4,391	1,452	532	176	356
1962	5,728	4,318	1,410	497	170	327
1961	5,578	4,220	1,358	476	161	316
1960	5,565	4,234	1,331	400	134	266
1959	5,503	4,238	1,265	367	125	242
1958	5,356	4,142	1,214	349	121	228
1957	5,442	4,231	1,211	289	98	191
1956	5,342	4,186	1,156	243	79	164
1955	5,139	4,049	1,091	225	80	145
1954	5,035	3,970	1,065	208	74	134
1953	5,038	3,991	1,047	197	72	125

[1] Excludes the Yukon Territory, the Northwest Territories and Indians on reserves.

Series D455-462. Unemployment, by type of job sought (full-time or part-time) and by length of time unemployed, annual averages, 1953 to 1975[1]
(thousands)

Year	Persons seeking full-time work	Persons seeking part-time work	Persons on temporary layoff up to 30 days	Total persons seeking work	Persons seeking less than 1 month	Persons seeking 1-3 months	Persons seeking 4-6 months	Persons seeking more than 6 months
	455	456	457	458	459	460	461	462
1975	612	45	49	658	157	256	144	101
1974	459	34	32	493	130	190	100	72
1973	464	28	28	492	125	184	103	81
1972	499	34	30	532	126	196	109	101
1971	494	29	30	523	116	188	106	113
1970	429	30	36	458	120	174	87	77
1969	333	23	26	356	104	134	60	58
1968	333	23	26	356	106	140	61	48
1967	274	16	25	290	100	114	45	32
1966	232	15	20	247	83	100	38	26
1965	246	16	18	262	85	98	43	36
1964	289	16	19	305	93	113	54	45
1963	336	17	21	352	95	133	70	55
1962	349	19	23	368	95	138	71	64
1961	412	26	28	438	98	162	100	78
1960	397	19	30	416	108	166	89	54
1959	333	16	23	349	90	133	73	52
1958	387	17	27	404	98	158	93	55
1957	242	15	21	257	87	112	41	17
1956	166	14	17	180	61	74	30	16
1955	217	15	14	232	67	91	44	31
1954	221	14	15	235	70	94	46	26
1953	124	13	25	137	51	55	21	10

[1] Excludes the Yukon Territory, the Northwest Territories and Indians on reserves.

Series D463-469. Civilian labour force, by region, annual averages, 1946 to 1975[1]
(thousands)

Year	Canada total[2]	Atlantic region[2]	Quebec	Ontario	Prairie region	British Columbia	Newfoundland
	463	464	465	466	467	468	469
1975	10,015	802	2,701	3,810	1,582	1,120	192
1974	9,662	777	2,618	3,671	1,537	1,060	185
1973	9,279	742	2,542	3,509	1,484	1,002	180
1972	8,891	698	2,426	3,381	1,436	950	165
1971	8,631	676	2,394	3,249	1,401	911	158
1970	8,374	658	2,328	3,130	1,380	878	148
1969	8,162	654	2,290	3,032	1,351	836	146
1968	7,919	643	2,227	2,934	1,318	797	144
1967	7,694	635	2,196	2,834	1,268	762	143
1966	7,420	626	2,116	2,719	1,248	710	139
1965	7,141	611	2,022	2,614	1,228	666	133
1964	6,933	588	1,951	2,556	1,199	639	126
1963	6,748	577	1,904	2,476	1,181	610	126
1962	6,615	578	1,852	2,422	1,175	590	117
1961	6,521	571	1,820	2,401	1,154	575	113

Series D463-469. Civilian labour force, by region, annual averages, 1946 to 1975[1] (concluded)
(thousands)

Year	Canada total[2]	Atlantic region[2]	Quebec	Ontario	Prairie region	British Columbia	Newfoundland
	463	464	465	466	467	468	469
1960	6,411	550	1,803	2,377	1,115	565	111
1959	6,242	541	1,758	2,301	1,084	556	111
1958	6,137	535	1,735	2,264	1,055	548	108
1957	6,008	537	1,678	2,238	1,019	536	111
1956	5,782	520	1,615	2,147	998	503	107
1955	5,610	511	1,591	2,059	969	480	104
1954	5,493	501	1,562	2,022	949	461	100
1953	5,397	506	1,538	1,948	956	449	102
1952	5,324	502	1,504	1,908	964	446	101
1951	5,223	513	1,462	1,870	948	431	102
1950[2]	5,086	524	1,433	1,826	874	429	105
1949	5,083	455	1,423	1,815	953	437	—
1948	4,988	426	1,385	1,776	968	433	—
1947	4,942	428	1,358	1,759	971	427	—
1946	4,829	415	1,337	1,702	969	407	—

[1] Excludes the Yukon Territory, the Northwest Territories and Indians on reserves.　　　[2] Includes Newfoundland beginning in 1950. First surveyed October 1949.

Series D470-476. Civilian employment, by region, annual averages, 1946 to 1975[1]
(thousands)

Year	Canada total[2]	Atlantic region[2]	Quebec	Ontario	Prairie region	British Columbia	Newfoundland
	470	471	472	473	474	475	476
1975	9,308	710	2,462	3,581	1,528	1,027	158
1974	9,137	702	2,427	3,519	1,494	996	155
1973	8,759	676	2,353	3,366	1,426	937	157
1972	8,329	635	2,225	3,218	1,372	879	145
1971	8,079	618	2,197	3,079	1,338	847	139
1970	7,879	609	2,144	2,996	1,320	810	133
1969	7,780	605	2,132	2,936	1,312	795	131
1968	7,537	596	2,082	2,830	1,280	750	130
1967	7,379	593	2,080	2,745	1,238	723	131
1966	7,152	586	2,016	2,651	1,222	678	127
1965	6,862	566	1,912	2,548	1,196	639	119
1964	6,609	542	1,827	2,473	1,162	605	112
1963	6,375	522	1,762	2,382	1,138	571	108
1962	6,225	516	1,713	2,317	1,129	551	97
1961	6,055	507	1,652	2,269	1,100	527	91
1960	5,965	492	1,639	2,249	1,069	516	91
1959	5,870	482	1,620	2,198	1,049	521	89
1958	5,706	469	1,582	2,142	1,013	501	88
1957	5,731	492	1,576	2,161	992	509	101
1956	5,585	489	1,535	2,096	976	489	101
1955	5,364	478	1,493	1,993	939	462	100
1954	5,243	468	1,470	1,945	925	437	98
1953	5,235	478	1,480	1,907	938	432	94
1952	5,169	479	1,448	1,867	947	429	95
1951	5,097	491	1,420	1,838	933	416	95
1950[2]	4,976	483	1,370	1,782	931	411	91
1949	4,913	406	1,376	1,774	935	422	—
1948	4,875	407	1,351	1,745	953	418	—
1947	4,832	408	1,324	1,729	957	415	—
1946	4,666	392	1,283	1,654	947	390	—

[1] Excludes the Yukon Territory, the Northwest Territories and Indians on reserves.　　　[2] Includes Newfoundland beginning in 1950. First surveyed October 1949.

Series D477-483. Unemployment, by region, annual averages, 1946 to 1975[1]
(thousands)

Year	Canada total[2]	Atlantic region[2]	Quebec	Ontario	Prairie region	British Columbia	Newfoundland
	477	478	479	480	481	482	483
1975	707	93	239	228	54	93	35
1974	525	75	190	152	43	64	29
1973	520	66	189	142	58	65	23
1972	562	63	201	162	64	72	20
1971	552	58	197	170	63	64	18
1970	495	50	183	134	61	67	16
1969	382	49	158	95	39	42	15
1968	382	47	145	104	39	47	14
1967	315	42	116	89	29	39	12
1966	267	40	100	69	26	32	11
1965	280	45	109	66	31	28	15
1964	324	46	124	83	37	34	13
1963	374	55	142	94	44	39	19
1962	390	62	139	105	46	39	20
1961	466	64	168	132	53	49	22
1960	446	59	164	128	47	48	20
1959	372	59	138	103	35	36	22
1958	432	67	153	122	43	47	20
1957	278	45	101	77	27	27	10
1956	197	31	80	51	22	14	—[3]
1955	245	33	98	66	30	18	—[3]
1954	250	33	92	77	24	24	—[3]
1953	162	28	58	41	18	18	—[3]
1952	155	23	56	42	18	17	—[3]
1951	126	22	42	32	15	15	—[3]
1950[2]	186	41	63	44	20	19	—[3]
1949	141	20	48	41	18	15	—[3]
1948	114	19	34	31	15	15	—[3]
1947	110	20	34	31	14	12	—[3]
1946	163	23	54	48	21	16	—[3]

[1] Excludes the Yukon Territory, the Northwest Territories and Indians on reserves.

[2] Includes Newfoundland beginning in 1950. First surveyed October 1949.

[3] Less than 10,000.

Series D484-490. Civilian labour force participation rates, by region, annual averages, 1946 to 1975[1]
(per cent)

Year	Canada total[2]	Atlantic region[2]	Quebec	Ontario	Prairie region	British Columbia	Newfoundland
	484	485	486	487	488	489	490
1975	58.8	51.9	57.2	61.3	59.3	60.2	49.4
1974	58.3	51.6	56.7	60.7	59.2	59.3	48.7
1973	57.5	50.5	56.2	59.7	58.4	58.4	48.5
1972	56.5	48.6	54.7	59.1	57.5	57.5	45.7
1971	56.1	48.1	54.9	58.3	57.0	57.2	44.9
1970	55.8	47.5	54.3	58.0	57.1	57.3	42.9
1969	55.8	48.1	54.5	58.0	56.9	56.7	43.2
1968	55.5	48.2	54.3	57.7	56.8	56.0	43.6
1967	55.5	48.5	54.9	57.6	55.8	55.8	44.3
1966	55.1	48.6	54.3	57.2	55.7	54.9	44.3
1965	54.4	48.1	53.2	56.7	55.5	53.8	43.3
1964	54.1	47.0	52.6	57.0	55.1	53.6	42.0
1963	53.8	46.8	52.6	56.5	55.0	52.8	43.0
1962	53.9	47.8	52.5	56.3	55.7	52.3	41.2
1961	54.1	48.1	52.8	56.7	55.6	51.8	41.1

Series D484-490. Civilian labour force participation rates, by region, annual averages, 1946 to 1975[1] (concluded)

(per cent)

Year	Canada total[2]	Atlantic region[2]	Quebec	Ontario	Prairie region	British Columbia	Newfoundland
	484	485	486	487	488	489	490
1960	54.2	47.1	53.6	57.0	54.7	51.7	41.1
1959	53.8	47.0	53.5	56.2	54.2	51.7	41.7
1958	53.9	47.0	54.0	56.4	53.8	51.5	41.4
1957	54.0	47.7	53.6	57.2	52.9	51.9	43.2
1956	53.5	46.6	53.1	56.9	52.4	51.5	42.5
1955	52.9	46.4	53.5	55.7	51.4	50.9	42.1
1954	52.9	46.0	53.7	55.9	51.0	50.4	41.2
1953	53.1	46.9	54.1	55.2	52.2	50.6	43.0
1952	53.5	47.1	54.0	55.4	53.6	51.6	43.6
1951	53.7	48.6	53.8	55.8	53.6	51.0	45.1
1950[2]	53.7	49.3	53.6	55.5	54.1	51.4	46.3
1949	54.5	51.1	54.1	56.0	54.8	53.0	—
1948	54.6	51.2	53.5	55.7	56.1	53.5	—
1947	54.9	51.6	53.3	56.1	56.9	54.3	—
1946	55.0	51.2	53.6	55.8	58.0	54.1	—

[1] Excludes the Yukon Territory, the Northwest Territories and Indians on reserves.

[2] Includes Newfoundland beginning in 1950. First surveyed October 1949.

Series D491-497. Unemployment rates, by region, annual averages, 1946 to 1975[1]

(per cent)

Year	Canada total[2]	Atlantic region[2]	Quebec	Ontario	Prairie region	British Columbia	Newfoundland
	491	492	493	494	495	496	497
1975	7.1	11.6	8.8	6.0	3.4	8.3	18.2
1974	5.4	9.7	7.3	4.1	2.8	6.0	15.7
1973	5.6	8.9	7.4	4.0	3.9	6.5	12.8
1972	6.3	9.0	8.3	4.8	4.5	7.6	12.1
1971	6.4	8.6	8.2	5.2	4.5	7.0	11.4
1970	5.9	7.6	7.9	4.3	4.4	7.6	10.8
1969	4.7	7.5	6.9	3.1	2.9	5.0	10.3
1968	4.8	7.3	6.5	3.5	3.0	5.9	9.7
1967	4.1	6.6	5.3	3.1	2.3	5.1	8.4
1966	3.6	6.4	4.7	2.5	2.1	4.5	7.9
1965	3.9	7.4	5.4	2.5	2.5	4.2	11.3
1964	4.7	7.8	6.4	3.2	3.1	5.3	10.3
1963	5.5	9.5	7.5	3.8	3.7	6.4	15.1
1962	5.9	10.7	7.5	4.3	3.9	6.6	17.1
1961	7.1	11.2	9.2	5.5	4.6	8.5	19.5
1960	7.0	10.7	9.1	5.4	4.2	8.5	18.0
1959	6.0	10.9	7.8	4.5	3.2	6.5	19.8
1958	7.0	12.5	8.8	5.4	4.1	8.6	18.5
1957	4.6	8.4	6.0	3.4	2.6	5.0	9.0
1956	3.4	6.0	5.0	2.4	2.2	2.8	—[3]
1955	4.4	6.5	6.2	3.2	3.1	3.8	—[3]
1954	4.6	6.6	5.9	3.8	2.5	5.2	—[3]
1953	3.0	5.5	3.8	2.1	1.9	4.0	—[3]
1952	2.9	4.6	3.7	2.2	1.9	3.8	—[3]
1951	2.4	4.3	2.9	1.7	1.6	3.5	—[3]
1950[2]	3.6	7.8	4.4	2.4	2.3	4.4	—[3]
1949	2.8	4.4	3.4	2.3	1.9	3.4	—[3]
1948	2.3	4.5	2.5	1.7	1.5	3.5	—[3]
1947	2.2	4.7	2.5	1.8	1.4	2.8	—[3]
1946	3.4	5.5	4.0	2.8	2.2	3.9	—[3]

[1] Excludes the Yukon Territory, the Northwest Territories and Indians on reserves.

[2] Includes Newfoundland beginning in 1950. First surveyed October 1949.
[3] Less than 10,000.

Series D498-504. Total labour force growth and its components, intercensal decades, 1851 to 1961
(thousands)

Decade	Labour force at beginning of decade	Labour force at end of decade	Total increase	Domestic supply component of increase	Contribution of gross immigration	Contribution of gross emigration	Contribution of net immigration
	498	**499**	**500**	**501**	**502**	**503**	**504**
1951-1961[1]	5,355	6,741	1,386	838	767	-305[2] -219[3]	462[2] 548[3]
1941-1951	4,652	5,250	598	557	262	-221	41
1931-1941	4,048	4,652	604	693	55	-144	-89
1921-1931	3,312	4,048	736	694	657	-615	42
1911-1921	2,809	3,312	503	440	—	—	63
1901-1911	1,899	2,809	910	343	—	—	567
1891-1901	1,732	1,899	167	329	—	—	-162
1881-1891	1,474	1,732	258	324	—	—	-66
1871-1881	1,201	1,474	273	316	—	—	-43
1861-1871	1,053	1,201	148	262	—	—	-114
1851-1861	762	1,053	291	211	—	—	80

[1] Includes Newfoundland in 1951-61.
[2] Based on residual estimate of emigration.
[3] Based on estimate derived from immigration statistics of other countries.

Series D505-511. Civilian labour force growth and its components, quinquennial periods, 1946 to 1966
(thousands)

Period	Labour force at beginning of each period	Labour force at end of each period	Total increase	Domestic supply component of increase	Contribution of gross immigration	Contribution of gross emigration	Contribution of net immigration
	505	**506**	**507**	**508**	**509**	**510**	**511**
1961-66	6,521	7,420	899	784	260	-145	115
1956-61	5,782	6,521	739	501	367	-129	238
1951-56	5,200	5,782	582	272	399	-89	310
1946-51	4,920	5,200	280	204	235	-159	76

Series D512-521. Total work force, by province and sex, census years, 1911 to 1971[1]

Year	Newfoundland	Prince Edward Island	Nova Scotia	New Brunswick	Quebec	Ontario	Manitoba	Saskatchewan	Alberta	British Columbia
	512	513	514	515	516	517	518	519	520	521
Both sexes										
1971	147,975	43,040	286,462	223,445	2,169,119	3,354,333	413,910	371,052	688,235	910,069
1961	112,310	34,148	236,819	178,355	1,768,119	2,393,015	342,642	325,589	489,511	577,648
1951[1]	106,540	34,125	220,806	169,038	1,471,840	1,884,941	298,501	302,112	353,898	444,352
1941	–	31,201	190,973	146,815	1,188,655	1,455,055	265,537	315,846	288,015	313,854
1931	–	32,166	181,087	140,005	1,025,709	1,346,214	270,672	338,911	286,203	306,263
1921	–	31,106	185,556	132,808	785,591	1,118,519	216,643	266,975	216,244	219,727
1911	–	31,972	173,421	119,919	653,535	991,166	178,460	208,606	161,701	206,368
Males										
1971	107,170	28,635	195,475	151,575	1,447,364	2,151,754	268,042	249,709	450,500	602,352
1961	88,702	26,068	178,559	132,549	1,289,425	1,700,567	246,198	248,479	361,961	421,786
1951[1]	89,460	28,156	178,087	134,953	1,130,194	1,439,966	232,296	251,077	291,269	346,374
1941	–	26,088	153,941	119,341	928,464	1,140,105	215,705	273,122	247,622	258,723
1931	–	27,818	153,151	117,933	823,287	1,096,726	225,764	301,435	252,742	262,515
1921	–	27,052	156,777	112,944	646,440	923,413	184,961	242,116	195,102	194,214
1911	–	27,965	148,935	103,278	552,178	835,742	155,954	195,241	149,684	189,542
Females										
1971	40,805	14,405	90,987	71,870	721,755	1,202,579	145,868	121,343	237,735	307,717
1961	23,608	8,080	58,260	45,806	478,694	692,448	96,444	77,110	127,550	155,862
1951[1]	17,080	5,969	42,719	34,085	341,646	444,975	66,205	51,035	62,629	97,978
1941	–	5,113	37,032	27,474	260,191	314,950	49,832	42,724	40,393	55,131
1931	–	4,348	27,936	22,072	202,422	249,488	44,908	37,476	33,461	43,748
1921	–	4,054	28,779	19,864	139,151	195,106	31,682	24,859	21,142	25,513
1911	–	4,007	24,486	16,641	101,357	155,424	22,506	13,365	12,017	16,826

[1] Includes Newfoundland for 1951 and later years. Excludes the Yukon Territory and the Northwest Territories. For age coverage, see series D86-106.

Series D522-527. Job vacancies and help-wanted indexes, by region, annual averages, 1951 to 1975

Year	Canada total	Atlantic region	Quebec	Ontario	Prairie region	British Columbia
	522	523	524	525	526	527
Job vacancies (full-time)						
1975	56,600	4,100	14,200	19,900	14,400	4,000
1974	91,500	5,700	20,100	36,000	21,300	8,500
1973	78,000	5,600	20,600	30,200	13,100	8,500
1972	58,300	4,500	14,700	23,700	10,400	5,000
1971	32,600	3,400	6,600	13,100	5,600	3,800
Help-wanted indexes (1971 = 100)						
1975	191	243	216	144	223	183
1974	231	272	218	213	261	266
1973	173	157	152	185	177	200
1972	134	120	123	145	137	136
1971	100	100	100	100	100	100
1970	95	90	92	104	90	90
1969	116	111	108	125	112	119
1968	95	122	91	96	95	86
1967	108	139	117	99	118	80
1966	124	164	137	120	116	90
1965	113	157	127	108	98	84
1964	92	111	110	81	83	65
1963	76	97	95	65	69	48
1962	72	100	97	55	61	49

Year	Canada total	Atlantic region	Quebec	Ontario	Prairie region	British Columbia
	522	523	524	525	526	527
Synthetic estimates of job vacancies						
1975	87,800	10,200	27,900	24,200	17,400	8,200
1974	108,400	11,200	27,800	36,500	20,600	12,300
1973	80,300	6,400	19,100	32,100	13,800	9,000
1972	62,000	4,900	15,400	24,900	10,800	6,100
1971	45,800	4,100	12,500	17,000	7,800	4,500
1970	43,500	3,700	11,600	17,200	6,900	4,100
1969	53,600	4,600	13,500	21,100	8,800	5,500
1968	44,300	5,100	11,500	16,400	7,500	3,800
1967	50,100	5,700	14,800	16,600	9,300	3,700
1966	57,400	6,800	17,100	20,400	9,000	4,100
1965	52,100	6,500	16,100	18,100	7,600	3,800
1964	41,700	4,500	13,900	13,900	6,400	3,000
1963	34,100	3,900	11,800	10,900	5,300	2,200
1962	32,500	4,000	12,100	9,400	4,800	2,300
1961	23,800	3,300	7,400	6,700	4,600	2,000
1960	23,200	3,400	7,200	5,800	4,900	1,900
1959	24,400	3,200	7,400	6,300	5,300	2,100
1958	19,100	2,700	5,200	5,000	4,500	1,700
1957	29,600	4,100	9,600	6,900	6,300	2,700
1956	44,800	5,300	16,400	11,300	8,000	3,800
1955	30,100	4,500	11,400	6,800	4,600	2,900
1954	22,900	4,100	7,500	5,100	4,200	2,000
1953	32,200	4,600	11,500	7,800	5,800	2,400
1952	34,100	5,800	12,000	7,300	6,400	2,700
1951	45,100	5,400	18,300	11,100	7,800	2,500

Series D528-539. Employment indexes, by industry, annual averages, 1921 to 1975

Year	Industrial composite	Forestry	Mining	Manufacturing			Con-struction	Transpor-tation, communi-cation and other utilities	Trade		Finance, insurance and real estate	Service
				Total	Durable goods	Non-durable goods			Wholesale	Retail		
	528	529	530	531	532	533	534	535	536	537	538	539

Based on the 1960 Standard Industrial Classification (1961 = 100)

Year	528	529	530	531	532	533	534	535	536	537	538	539
1975	141.1	76.0	114.1	126.3	139.8	115.5	117.1	125.8	157.1	174.6	175.0	231.9
1974	142.8	87.4	115.5	133.8	149.4	121.1	117.1	124.6	154.6	171.7	167.3	224.0
1973	135.9	86.4	111.4	129.9	144.1	118.4	109.9	118.0	143.8	161.5	157.1	206.1
1972	129.9	76.3	110.4	123.7	134.9	114.7	109.7	116.0	135.1	152.2	148.7	193.5
1971	127.8	79.4	114.9	121.6	131.4	113.7	115.5	114.6	132.8	144.3	145.9	186.5
1970	127.1	84.2	115.7	122.8	132.8	114.7	113.9	112.6	132.8	142.8	143.6	178.5
1969	126.9	88.7	107.9	125.2	136.7	115.9	119.1	111.9	129.0	140.7	138.8	171.8
1968	122.7	91.1	109.8	122.1	131.7	114.1	119.4	109.5	122.5	133.2	131.4	157.9
1967	122.6	102.3	109.1	123.2	133.9	114.5	122.5	111.0	121.1	128.4	126.0	153.4
1966	120.7	106.2	107.0	123.5	134.7	114.4	128.9	107.5	117.5	124.6	120.5	139.1
1965	114.3	104.1	105.1	117.2	126.0	110.1	118.4	104.8	110.8	116.2	116.6	125.9
1964	108.2	102.8	98.8	111.1	116.7	106.6	104.1	101.8	105.4	109.6	111.9	114.7
1963	104.4	96.9	97.9	106.1	109.5	103.4	100.0	100.7	102.4	104.4	107.6	106.1
1962	102.2	99.5	99.4	103.8	105.9	102.1	101.1	99.7	101.1	101.7	103.2	101.7
1961	100.0	100.0	100.0	100.0	100.0	100.0	100.0	100.0	100.0	100.0	100.0	100.0
1960	100.7	114.0	103.5	100.6	101.6	99.9	105.9	100.3	102.6	98.5	96.6	96.8
1959	102.2	107.8	108.0	102.0	104.2	100.3	112.1	104.7	100.7	96.9	95.7	95.2
1958	100.4	102.4	102.8	100.1	101.8	98.8	109.4	104.5	99.0	93.8	93.8	92.6
1957	100.0	129.8	112.7	105.5	111.9	101.4	125.0	106.4	100.4	93.4	90.4	91.8

Based on the 1948 Standard Industrial Classification (1949 = 100)

Year	528	529	530	531	532	533	534	535	536	537	538	539
1962	121.4	70.9	116.4	113.3	117.0	110.2	124.3	108.4	139.5	141.3	170.1	156.5
1961	118.1	71.6	116.5	108.9	110.6	107.5	121.7	108.6	136.1	138.7	163.1	148.9
1960	118.7	84.0	120.1	109.5	112.6	106.8	125.7	111.1	136.1	137.1	156.7	143.2
1959	119.7	78.9	123.4	111.1	115.5	107.3	130.3	114.3	134.8	135.6	153.2	139.3
1958	117.9	75.9	123.5	109.8	114.8	105.6	126.2	115.5	131.8	131.6	149.3	135.1
1957	122.6	99.3	127.2	115.8	125.3	107.6	135.7	120.4	133.2	131.0	145.0	131.9
1956	120.7	113.2	122.7	115.8	126.4	106.6	131.8	118.3	128.0	125.4	137.1	125.1
1955	112.9	102.9	113.7	109.8	117.4	103.2	115.0	110.8	120.7	117.7	132.1	115.0
1954	109.9	96.3	110.4	107.3	114.2	101.4	110.6	109.0	117.0	113.7	128.0	111.7
1953	113.1	98.3	110.8	113.0	123.5	103.9	118.1	111.2	116.1	111.6	122.4	108.8
1952	111.9	119.5	116.9	109.9	118.0	102.8	123.1	110.9	113.7	108.5	122.1	107.0
1951	109.1	140.3	111.0	108.1	113.2	103.5	110.7	106.8	108.7	106.8	116.1	103.3
1950	102.1	104.8	106.0	101.4	101.7	101.1	103.1	100.2	103.0	103.8	105.9	101.0
1949	100.0	100.0	100.0	100.0	100.0	100.0	100.0	100.0	100.0	100.0	100.0	100.0
1948	99.7	138.4	97.2	100.1	101.2	99.3	95.4	99.0	96.2	96.3	96.0	99.1
1947	95.7	149.6	88.6	97.2	98.6	96.7	85.6	95.4	90.9	89.9	91.5	94.6
1946	88.2	129.9	86.9	91.0	90.2	92.5	69.5	89.3	82.6	83.4	85.3	88.3
1945	88.8	119.7	82.3	100.0	108.8	92.9	53.8	86.0	74.8	76.5	77.4	81.1
1944	92.5	104.4	86.5	110.6	129.8	94.0	51.9	82.6	68.8	72.3	75.0	79.6
1943	93.0	87.3	88.7	111.5	133.8	91.9	69.4	79.5	63.4	68.7	73.4	74.8
1942	87.9	95.1	95.9	101.6	113.3	91.6	70.2	74.6	63.7	69.3	72.9	70.5
1941	77.4	91.0	99.0	82.6	85.0	80.8	68.6	70.1	65.0	69.3	69.5	66.1
1940	64.7	82.2	95.8	65.1	58.5	69.6	47.1	62.2	62.2	64.3	67.3	57.9
1939	60.1	59.3	93.7	56.3	46.5	62.3	62.0	59.8	60.2	62.3	67.8	56.8
1938	59.0	71.1	89.2	55.6	48.1	63.4	57.4	59.1		59.8	..	55.8
1937	60.2	94.2	87.7	57.3	50.7	64.6	52.3	60.2		59.5	..	53.8
1936	54.7	69.0	78.2	51.8	43.4	60.4	42.6	60.6		57.4	..	51.4
1935	52.5	63.2	70.6	48.6	40.0	57.4	51.3	57.6		55.0	..	48.8
1934	50.6	62.1	63.4	45.2	35.4	54.9	59.5	57.0		53.1	..	47.6
1933	44.0	33.1	55.8	40.5	30.0	50.6	37.2	56.5		50.5	..	44.1
1932	46.2	21.2	56.8	42.3	33.1	51.1	43.7	60.4		52.3	..	46.9
1931	54.1	29.9	61.7	47.8	42.3	53.2	71.1	69.9		55.7	..	51.5
1930	59.8	53.8	67.4	54.6	51.5	58.2	68.5	77.9		57.6	..	54.4
1929	62.8	62.6	68.8	58.7	58.7	59.5	64.3	82.6		56.9	..	53.8
1928	58.9	57.0	65.5	55.1	..	..	54.3	79.9		52.3	..	48.8
1927	55.2	54.4	61.3	51.8	..	..	52.2	75.4		48.4	..	43.9
1926	52.6	49.5	57.0	49.9	..	..	45.1	73.3		44.7	..	41.1
1925	49.4	52.5	57.1	46.6	..	..	37.8	69.6		42.9	..	39.4
1924	49.3	58.1	60.3	46.2	..	..	32.8	72.2		41.7	..	38.7
1923	50.5	56.9	60.8	48.4	..	..	34.5	70.8		41.5	..	36.3
1922	47.0	42.4	56.9	44.3	..	..	32.7	69.1		40.9	..	33.8
1921	46.9	51.3	56.1	44.0	..	..	30.3	66.5		41.8	..	34.6

Series D540-550. Industrial composite employment indexes, by province, annual averages, 1921 to 1975

Year	Canada	Newfoundland	Prince Edward Island	Nova Scotia	New Brunswick	Quebec	Ontario	Manitoba	Saskatchewan	Alberta	British Columbia
	540	541	542	543	544	545	546	547	548	549	550
Based on the 1960 Standard Industrial Classification (1961 = 100)											
1975	141.1	135.5	149.9	128.9	136.1	128.5	144.2	130.1	137.0	169.6	161.3
1974	142.8	139.5	152.0	130.2	134.4	129.9	147.5	128.4	130.0	163.1	167.2
1973	135.9	131.3	144.4	123.0	126.8	124.6	141.2	119.9	120.3	150.8	157.4
1972	129.9	126.5	140.6	116.7	122.7	120.1	134.2	117.6	116.8	143.7	148.4
1971	127.8	125.9	139.4	113.7	122.9	118.7	132.1	117.2	114.4	139.6	144.5
1970	127.1	121.8	134.0	114.3	119.2	119.3	131.6	117.7	113.2	138.2	139.3
1969	126.9	120.0	130.6	117.8	119.1	119.9	131.0	118.0	118.1	136.7	137.5
1968	122.7	119.3	131.9	114.3	116.5	117.7	126.1	115.6	119.5	128.7	128.8
1967	122.6	121.7	124.9	113.3	116.5	119.4	125.1	115.0	119.5	126.2	128.7
1966	120.7	126.3	124.3	113.0	115.2	118.1	123.3	111.2	116.5	120.5	126.1
1965	114.3	118.0	112.2	108.6	109.7	112.9	116.5	106.1	110.4	112.6	118.2
1964	108.2	107.6	105.9	103.6	104.6	107.5	110.1	103.4	105.1	106.1	109.4
1963	104.4	102.0	101.8	101.1	100.6	103.0	105.4	101.6	102.4	102.3	104.9
1962	102.2	100.1	105.3	100.4	99.8	101.7	103.0	100.4	100.7	102.0	102.1
1961	100.0	100.0	100.0	100.0	100.0	100.0	100.0	100.0	100.0	100.0	100.0
1960	100.7	97.3	95.8	104.6	101.2	99.7	100.9	101.9	103.4	98.2	102.8
1959	102.2	96.8	98.1	106.4	99.9	100.1	103.1	103.8	107.3	100.5	103.5
1958	100.4	94.6	89.1	106.6	96.5	98.7	101.1	100.2	105.7	97.8	103.3
1957	100.0	101.3	89.7	112.8	101.4	102.1	105.7	103.4	104.8	100.0	112.5
Based on the 1948 Standard Industrial Classification (1949 = 100)											
1962	121.4	133.2	135.8	94.4	103.8	121.6	123.0	111.1	124.6	158.1	115.7
1961	118.1	131.7	130.7	94.0	103.9	118.3	118.7	110.0	123.1	154.2	112.3
1960	118.7	129.7	128.5	95.5	103.4	118.6	119.2	111.0	126.0	153.3	114.7
1959	119.7	125.8	126.3	96.3	101.7	118.5	121.3	112.2	130.0	155.0	115.1
1958	117.9	122.6	114.9	95.5	98.0	117.0	119.6	108.7	126.6	150.5	114.7
1957	122.6	130.1	115.2	100.2	103.8	121.5	124.3	110.9	125.3	152.2	123.9
1956	120.7	136.9	117.4	101.7	110.1	120.1	121.4	108.6	121.1	148.5	121.5
1955	112.9	131.1	114.2	97.1	103.5	112.5	113.5	105.2	117.0	133.0	111.9
1954	109.9	128.0	109.9	97.6	98.0	109.2	110.6	104.7	118.0	128.0	106.3
1953	113.1	140.4	115.5	101.0	100.8	112.4	114.5	107.0	116.2	128.5	108.4
1952	111.9	130.2	123.2	104.0	109.5	113.4	112.0	106.0	111.4	120.8	106.7
1951	109.1	111.7	112.6	100.3	109.0	109.2	110.4	103.9	106.0	112.4	106.1
1950	102.1	—	110.3	95.6	102.6	100.5	102.7	100.8	100.8	104.5	100.8
1949	100.0	—	100.0	100.0	100.0	100.0	100.0	100.0	100.0	100.0	100.0
1948	99.7	—	102.6	99.6	105.2	101.2	98.9	97.2	99.5	93.7	101.3
1947	95.7	—	93.3	92.1	104.3	97.8	94.7	93.6	97.2	88.1	97.1
1946	88.2	—	87.2	95.4	98.1	90.4	86.8	89.6	92.2	82.6	83.6
1945	88.8	—	81.9	101.5	98.6	92.8	86.7	85.3	86.4	76.3	87.5
1944	92.5	—	85.9	105.0	98.4	99.1	89.5	85.8	85.5	77.6	92.5
1943	93.0	—	74.7	106.8	95.0	100.9	90.0	83.1	81.5	74.3	94.5
1942	87.9	—	70.8	103.3	89.8	94.1	87.0	80.0	78.1	70.9	82.2
1941	77.4	—	75.7	90.0	82.1	80.3	77.9	74.1	76.1	65.5	67.9
1940	64.7	—	67.2	71.4	67.4	67.4	64.2	63.4	70.1	57.4	58.0
1939	60.1	—	64.1	66.8	59.6	64.6	57.3	59.7	71.4	55.1	55.8
1938	59.0	—	59.9	66.0	62.4	62.5	57.1	58.4	70.2	52.0	54.1
1937	60.2	—	—	68.1	—	61.7	59.2	—	—	—	55.4
1936	54.7	—	—	—	—	53.8	53.5	—	—	—	52.5
1935	52.5	—	—	—	—	51.0	51.8	—	—	—	50.7
1934	50.6	—	—	—	—	49.0	50.8	—	—	—	46.9
1933	44.0	—	—	—	—	43.8	42.2	—	—	—	40.5
1932	46.2	—	—	—	—	45.7	44.4	—	—	—	41.7
1931	54.1	—	—	—	—	53.9	50.7	—	—	—	49.6
1930	59.8	—	—	—	—	58.9	57.4	—	—	—	56.0
1929	62.8	—	—	—	—	60.6	61.7	—	—	—	57.9
1928	58.9	—	—	—	—	57.9	56.9	—	—	—	55.2
1927	55.2	—	—	—	—	55.6	52.9	—	—	—	52.5
1926	52.6	—	—	—	—	53.1	49.9	—	—	—	52.0
1925	49.4	—	—	—	—	49.0	47.5	—	—	—	48.6
1924	49.3	—	—	—	—	48.8	47.9	—	—	—	46.4
1923	50.5	—	—	—	—	48.5	49.9	—	—	—	45.3
1922	47.0	—	—	—	—	43.5	46.5	—	—	—	43.0
1921	46.9	—	—	—	—	43.9	45.2	—	—	—	42.1

Section E: Wages and Working Conditions

Noah M. Meltz, *University of Toronto*

The statistics of this section are in eight parts as follows: labour income (series E1-40); employment, earnings and hours of work (series E41-135); employer labour cost (series E136-151); unemployment insurance (series E152-171); employment service (series E172-174); labour unions and strikes and lockouts (series E175-197); index numbers of wage rates, wage rates and salaries (series E198-375); workmen's compensation (series E376-389).

The following notes for series E1-171 were prepared by Mr. Don Bailey of Statistics Canada while those for series E172-389 were prepared by the author. The latter notes combined new material with an updating of the notes prepared for the first edition of *Historical Statistics of Canada* by Professor Douglas C. Hartle.

While a few new series have been added, several series have been dropped either because the particular surveys were discontinued or because the series had been developed by Professor Hartle for the first edition and those series could not be extended.

The main sources of data for this section are the following federal government publications: Department of Labour, *Wage Rates, Salaries and Hours of Labour,* an annual publication since 1920 which has appeared under a variety of titles beginning with *Wages and Hours of Labour in Canada,* 1920, Report No. 1. Other publications of the Department of Labour are: *Labour Organizations in Canada,* annual from 1911 to 1973 then biennial for 1974-1975 and 1975-1976; *The Labour Gazette,* monthly since September 1900; *Strikes and Lockouts in Canada,* reviewed annually in *The Labour Gazette* until 1946, as a supplement to *The Labour Gazette,* 1947 to 1951, and as a separate document since 1952.

The following publications of Statistics Canada (until 1972 known as the Dominion Bureau of Statistics) were used: *Labour Income, 1926-1958,* 1960; *Estimates of Labour Income,* (Catalogue 72-005); *General Review of the Manufacturing Industries of Canada,* (Catalogue 31-201), years 1957, 1958, 1959, 1960 and 1961; *Manufacturing Industries of Canada; National and Provincial Areas,* (Catalogue 31-203), 1962 to 1975; *Review of Employment and Payrolls,* annual, 1939 to 1970; *Employment, Earnings and Hours,* (Catalogue 72-002); *Review of Man-hours and Hourly Earnings,* (Catalogue 72-202), annual, 1939 to 1970; *Labour Costs in Canada,* (Catalogue 72-610 to 72-618), selected years; *The Labour Force,* (Catalogue 71-001); *Benefit Periods Established and Terminated Under the Unemployment Insurance Act,* (Catalogue 73-201), annual 1942 to 1971; *Statistical Report on the Operation of the Unemployment Insurance Act,* (Catalogue 73-001); *Earnings and Hours of Work in Manufacturing,* annual reports, 1946 to 1969.

Other publications used are: Department of Health and Welfare, *Government Expenditures and Related Data on Health and Social Welfare, 1947 to 1953,* 2nd edition, and *1947 to 1959,* 3rd edition (Ottawa: Queen's Printer, 1955 and 1961); Economics and Research Branch, Canada Department of Labour: *Union Growth in Canada 1921-1967,* 1970; and *Union Growth in Canada in the Sixties,* 1976 (by J.K. Eaton).

Labour Income (Series E1-40)

General note

The labour income estimates are industrial and geographic breakdowns of wages, salaries and supplementary labour income which form part of the gross national product estimates. The estimates for most industries are based on the data obtained in the census of industry annual surveys and other Statistics Canada surveys. As would be expected the estimates are probably less reliable for such sectors as service, agriculture and trade, and more recent estimates are probably more reliable than estimates for prewar years. Sources and methods are discussed in the source document and in *National Income and Expenditure Accounts,* 1926-1974, Vol. 3, (Catalogue 13-549E), pp. 120-130.

Supplementary labour income includes expenditures by employers on labour account that can be regarded as payment for labour services. It includes employers' contributions to pension funds, employee welfare funds, unemployment insurance and workmen's compensation. Employer contributions to medical aid and hospitalization are excluded.

E1-13.   Wages, salaries and supplementary labour income, by province, 1926 to 1975

SOURCE: for 1947 to 1975, *Estimates of Labour Income;* for 1926 to 1946, *Labour Income, 1926-1958.*

E14-29.   Wages, salaries and supplementary labour income, by industry, 1926 to 1975

SOURCE: same as series E1-13.

E30-40.   Annual wages and salaries in manufacturing, by province, 1926 to 1975

SOURCE: same as series E1-13.

This table supplements series E1-13 and E14-29 by providing a provincial breakdown, excluding supplementary labour income.

Employment, Earnings and Hours of Work (Series E41-135)

General note

Statistics Canada produces, on a continuing basis, a large number of establishment derived series on employment, earnings and hours of work. This basic information is classified in a wide range of ways including industrial, regional, provincial and city breakdowns. The more important series

from a variety of sources are presented here but many series have been omitted because of space limitations.

There are three basic surveys conducted by Statistics
Canada from which the following series are derived: first,
the census of industry surveys which have been conducted
annually since 1917 and which, as the title implies, collect
data from all establishments in the industry regardless of
size. One of the more important of these surveys is the census of manufacturers which is the responsibility of the
Manufacturing and Primary Industries Division.

Results of the census of manufacturers were published up
to 1961, in the *General Review of Manufacturing Industries*. Since 1962, data from this survey have been published
annually in *Manufacturing Industries of Canada, National
and Provincial Areas*.

Prior to 1925, the number of production workers was
computed as the sum of the numbers recorded each month
divided by 12, whether or not the establishment was operating 12 months. Beginning with the statistics for 1925, in
seasonal industries the average was computed by dividing
the sum of the production workers on the 15th of each
month by the number of months in operation. This change
in method increased the apparent number of employees in
groups containing seasonal industries and in the overall total. In 1931 the old method of computing the average number of production workers was again adopted.

Second, the survey of employment, payrolls and man-
hours, which covers business establishments having 20 or
more employees, has collected employment data from business establishments since 1921; payroll data since 1941 and
man-hours data since 1945. The conduct of the survey is
the responsibility of the Employment, Payrolls and Labour
Income Section of the Labour Division.

Up to December 1970, data on employment and average
weekly wages and salaries were published in the monthly
publication *Employment and Payrolls,* and man-hours and
hourly earnings were published in the monthly publication
Man-hours and Hourly Earnings. Commencing with January 1971, these were consolidated in a single monthly publication entitled *Employment, Earnings and Hours*.

A basic limitation of this survey is the somewhat restricted industrial and establishment coverage. Some industries such as agriculture and fishing and trapping are not
covered at all. Others such as services are only partially
covered (government and health services for example are
surveyed by other divisions of Statistics Canada).

The coverage within the industries that come within the
purview of the survey is uneven. The monthly survey as
noted covers larger firms only, that is, firms having 20 or
more employees in any month of the year (prior to January
1971, firms with 15 or more employees were covered). However all establishments of a multi-unit company are included if the company had 20 or more employees in total.
Because of this limitation, in industries where a large proportion of total employment is in a large number of small
establishments (such as trade and service), coverage is substantially less than in highly concentrated industries such
as mining.

Third, for many years, an annual survey of hours and
earnings in manufacturing was conducted as a supplement
to the monthly survey of employment, payrolls and man-
hours. This annual survey was discontinued in 1969.

**E41-48.   Annual earnings in manufacturing
industries, production and other workers, by sex,
Canada, 1905, 1910 and 1917 to 1975**

SOURCE: for 1962 to 1975, *Manufacturing Industries of
Canada, National and Provincial Areas;* for 1948 to 1961,
General Review of the Manufacturing Industries; for 1905,
1910, 1917 to 1947 inclusive, the data were supplied directly
by the Central Research and Development Staff, Statistics
Canada.

Beginning in 1961, statistics of the manufacturing industries cover their total activity, including non-manufacturing
activity. Data for employees other than manufacturing production and related workers of both sexes reflect this
change and accordingly from 1961 on are not strictly comparable with data for earlier years.

**E49-59.   Average weekly wages and salaries,
industrial composite, by province, 1939 to 1975**

SOURCE: for 1971 to 1975, the monthly publication *Employment, Earnings and Hours;* for the period 1939 to 1970,
Annual Review of Employment and Payrolls.

**E60-68.   Average annual, weekly and hourly
earnings, male and female wage earners,
manufacturing industries, Canada, 1934 to 1969**

SOURCE: for 1946 to 1969, *Earnings and Hours of Work in
Manufacturing;* for 1934 to 1945, *General Review of the
Manufacturing Industries of Canada*.

Data are not available after 1969 since the annual survey
of earnings and hours of men and women working in manufacturing establishments was discontinued.

From 1934 to 1945 inclusive, all data refer to one week in
the month of highest employment of all establishments covered by the annual census of manufacturers. In 1946 and
1947 the weekly and hourly data apply to the last week in
the month of November; since 1947 they refer to the last
week in October.

In 1969 the survey included all manufacturing establishments employing 20 or more persons in any month of the
year representing approximately 90 per cent of the total
number of employees working in the manufacturing industries of Canada.

Wage earners are defined as production and ancillary
workers, including working foremen, route-drivers, shipping,
delivery and maintenance staffs and related employees.
Earnings comprise gross pay for the week, before deductions for taxes, unemployment insurance contributions and
so forth. Gross pay includes salaries, straight-time wages,
piecework and commission earnings, regularly-paid incentive, cost-of-living and other bonuses, overtime earnings and
payments to persons absent with pay in the survey week.
Supplementary labour costs are not included (see descriptive notes in *Earnings and Hours of Work in Manufacturing, 1969, p. 40*).

The annual earnings data was calculated separately from
the census of manufacturers and was discontinued in 1959.
For a description of the method of calculating annual earnings for males and females separately, see pages 84 and 85
of *General Review of Manufacturing Industries of Canada,
1957*.

E69-77. Average annual, weekly and hourly earnings, male and female salaried employees, manufacturing industries, Canada, 1946 to 1969.

SOURCE: for 1946 to 1969, *Earnings and Hours of Work in Manufacturing;* for 1934 to 1945, *General Review of the Manufacturing Industries of Canada,* 1958, table 35, p. 82.

See notes to series E60-68.

Salaried employees comprise executive, administrative, supervisory and professional personnel and travelling salesmen directly responsible to the administration as well as general office and clerical workers in the office and plant, for whom statistics are segregated.

E78-85. Averages of weekly wages of hourly rated wage earners, selected industry groups, Canada, 1945 to 1970

SOURCE: for 1945 to 1970, *Review of Man-hours and Hourly Earnings.*

From 1945 to 1970, separate earnings data were collected and published for hourly paid workers in respect of whom records of hours were maintained. Commencing in 1971 earnings were published only for all wage earners including those for whom hours were not collected.

Weekly wage data are averages of wages paid for the last pay period in each month. Wages are gross earnings and include payments for overtime work, incentive bonuses and cost-of-living bonuses (if paid on a regular basis). They do not include payments made by employers to pension plans or social insurance schemes, such as unemployment insurance, on behalf of employees.

E86-103. Annual averages of weekly wages and salaries, selected industry groups and composite, Canada, 1939 to 1975

SOURCE: for 1971 to 1975, *Employment, Earnings and Hours;* for 1939 to 1970, *Annual Review of Employment and Payrolls.*

E104-119. Average weekly wages and salaries, by major groups of manufacturing, 1939 to 1975

SOURCE: for 1971 to 1975, *Employment, Earnings and Hours;* for 1939 to 1970, *Review of Man-hours and Hourly Earnings.*

E120-127. Annual averages of hourly earnings of hourly rated wage earners, selected industry groups, Canada, 1945 to 1970

SOURCE: for 1945 to 1970, *Review of Man-hours and Hourly Earnings.* See E78-85 regarding termination of series in 1970.

E128-135. Average weekly hours of hourly rated wage earners, selected industry groups, Canada, 1945 to 1970.

SOURCE: same as series E120-127.

Employer Labour Cost (Series E136-151)

General note

A survey program to measure the cost to employers of the total compensation package was initiated by Statistics Canada in co-operation with the federal Department of Labour in 1967 (the Department of Labour dropped out of the program following the 1972 survey).

The initial survey was restricted to manufacturing. In subsequent years coverage was rotated on an individual industry basis to mines, quarries and oil wells in 1969 (and 1972), finance, insurance and real estate in 1970, trade in 1972, education in 1974, and services to business management in 1975. In 1976 the first all industry survey was carried out.

The Survey of Employer Labour Costs of 1977 obtained information from a sample of employers concerning the following items: pay for time worked (regular work and overtime, shift work, etc.); paid absence (vacation, paid holidays, sick leave, etc.); miscellaneous direct payments (severance pay, etc.); employer contributions or payments to social insurance, welfare and benefit plans (Unemployment Insurance, Workmen's Compensation, private pension plans, group life and health plans, etc.). The most recent survey covers reporting units with 20 or more employees in all industries except agriculture, fishing and trapping. Results of this survey are published in *Labour Costs in Canada, All Industries, 1976,* (Catalogue 72-618). Additional detailed information is contained in the technical notes found at the end of this publication.

E136-151. Estimated labour costs, selected industries, selected years, 1968 to 1976

SOURCE: *Labour Costs in Canada,* for the industries and years specified, Statistics Canada, (Catalogues 72-506, 72-510, 72-511, 72-610, 72-613, 72-615 to 72-618).

The following detailed comments relate to the handling of certain items in series E136-151. Prior to 1976 commission and incentive bonuses were not identified as separate items in manufacturing; transportation and communication; finance, insurance and real estate; trade and education or in the case of mines, quarries and oil wells and services to business management were included in 'other pay for time worked'. Part-time casual wage earners were excluded from trade and part-time and casual teaching staff were excluded from education; employment agencies and security services were excluded from services to business management; provincial medicare was included in taxable benefits in manufacturing (1976), in mines, quarries and oil wells (1972, 1976), in transportation, communication and other utilities (1976), in finance, insurance and real estate (1976), in trade (1972, 1976), in education (1974, 1976), and in services to business management (1975, 1976); provincial medicare was also included in life and health plans in all the industries specified up to and including 1971.

As noted above the first all industry sample survey was taken in 1976. Data are based on the calendar year, thus the survey of manufacturing published in 1977 related to the calendar year 1976.

Unemployment Insurance (Series E152-171)

General note

A federal unemployment insurance scheme went into effect in July 1941. Since that time there have been extensive changes in coverage and in the provisions governing the payment of unemployment insurance benefits.

In assessing the statistics relating to coverage, claimants, beneficiaries and benefit paid presented in series E152-165 and E166-171, it must be kept in mind that these are byproducts of administrative operations. As such, while some series, for example benefit data, are influenced to a considerable extent by economic conditions, changes in the Unemployment Insurance Act, regulations and operational practices may also introduce sudden and often sharp discontinuities in the series presented.

The main changes in coverage were those related to changes in the wage ceiling as applied to salaried workers (wage earners from the inception of the act were insured regardless of earnings level), and extension of coverage to additional industries. Thus the wage ceiling was raised through successive increases from an initial level of $2,000 to $7,800 in 1968 and in the revision of the act in 1971, coverage became virtually universal regardless of earnings. Major extensions of coverage took place with the inclusion of lumbering and logging in 1950, fishing in 1957 and as noted, coverage was extended to all industries in 1971.

Some of the more important changes relating to qualifying for benefit and amount of benefit paid included reduction of the waiting period in 1952, easing conditions for requalifying for a second benefit period in 1955, elimination of restrictions on eligibility of married women to obtain benefit in 1957; benefit rates substantially increased in 1955 and duration of benefit increased in 1957 and 1971.

E152-165. Number of persons insured with unemployment insurance commission, by industry, at book renewal periods, 1942 to 1974

SOURCE: for 1972 to 1974 inclusive, number of paid workers employed and unemployed at 1 June in each of these years, as reported in *The Labour Force;* for 1942 to 1971, *Benefit Periods Established and Terminated Under the Unemployment Insurance Act.*

As noted above, there have been sharp changes in the data due to extensions of industry coverage and upward adjustments in the wage ceiling. These are described in the annual issues of *Benefit Periods Established and Terminated Under the Unemployment Insurance Act.*

The estimates of insured persons by industry are based on a 10 per cent sample of unemployment insurance book renewals. No industry breakdown is available for 1972 to 1974.

E166-171. Unemployment insurance, insured population and beneficiary and claimant data, 1942 to 1976

SOURCE: for all years, *Statistical Report on the Operation of the Unemployment Insurance Act.* (Estimates of insured population as published in this report were obtained by compiling annual averages of paid workers, employed and unemployed, reported in the monthly publication, *The Labour Force*).

As noted at the beginning of this section the series in this

table must be interpreted with extreme caution because they reflect changes in administrative procedures, as well as economic conditions. The estimates of the insured population in series E152-165 do not equal estimates of the insured population in series E166-171. The former relates to a point of time and the latter to an annual average.

Employment Service (Series E172-174)

General note

Various provinces had employment services prior to 1919. These provided facilities, through local offices, for the listing of vacancies by employers and for applications for work by persons seeking jobs. The Employment Offices Coordination Act of 1918 made provision for federal government participation in the employment service with the Department of Labour being charged with the responsibility. The employment service was a joint dominion-provincial operation from 1919 until July 1941, with the federal government acting largely as a co-ordinating agency. With the establishment of national unemployment insurance, the employment service became mainly a national responsibility and has been operated nationally since 1 August 1941.

Until 1940, measures concerning unemployment, involving as they did civil rights, were the responsibility of the provinces. An amendment to the British North America Act in 1940 permitted the federal government to undertake an unemployment insurance operation. A federal unemployment insurance scheme went into effect on 1 July 1941 under the Unemployment Insurance Act of 1940.

The National Employment Service was separated from the unemployment insurance commission in 1965 and became an operating part of the Department of Labour. In 1966, both the unemployment insurance commission and the National Employment Service were transferred from the Department of Labour to the new Department of Manpower and Immigration and the National Employment Service offices were changed to become Canada Manpower Centres. In 1977, the department was renamed the Canada Employment and Immigration Commission and the centres became Canada Employment Centres.

E172-174. Monthly averages of applications, vacancies and placements by federal employment offices in regular and casual work, 1919 to 1975

SOURCE: prior to July 1941, data from the Dominion-Provincial Employment Service published regularly in *The Labour Gazette* beginning with the issue for July 1919. From 1 July 1941 to 31 December 1960 the data are from monthly issues of *The Labour Gazette* and are based on returns made by the unemployment insurance commission on form 751. The data continued to be published in *The Labour Gazette* up to the April 1977 issue, with the last data relating to January 1977. The figures from 1961 were prepared by Mrs. M. F. Leslie of Manpower and Immigration.

These series should be interpreted with extreme caution, for they are a byproduct of administrative procedures and may reflect changes in those procedures as well as in underlying conditions. In particular it should be borne in mind that the applications and vacancy statistics are probably affected by prevailing employment conditions. With persistent and widespread unemployment, employers have ample applicants for jobs and may not register their vacancies with an employment agency. Similarly, under these conditions workers who are not entitled to unemployment benefits may not apply for jobs with the employment agency after repeated disappointments. The revisions in the Unemployment Insurance Act in 1971 which greatly extended the coverage has considerably reduced the number of persons who are not entitled to unemployment benefits.

Vacancies include the vacancies for casual placements except for the period 1 January 1968 to 31 May 1974. Placements also include casual as well as regular placements except for the period 1 January 1968 to 31 May 1974 when casual placements are excluded. The annual reports of the Department of Manpower and Immigration for 1970-71 to 1973-74 indicate a monthly average of casual placements of over 23,000. When this figure is added to those of both columns 173 and 174, the sharp reduction after 1968 in both vacancies notified and placements is moderated and is consistent in the general direction of change with information from other sources on vacancies, particularly Statistics Canada's *Quarterly Report on Job Vacancies,* (second Quarter 1977, pp. 20-21). For a discussion of the differences between Statistics Canada's Job Vacancy Survey and the figures from the Department of Manpower and Immigration see: Noah M. Meltz, 'Information Requirements for Government Programs Directed toward the Labour Market', a study prepared for the Economic Council of Canada, 1975. For earlier historical series see F. T. Denton, C. H. Feaver and A. L. Robb, 'Patterns of Unemployment Behaviour in Canada', a study prepared for the Economic Council of Canada, Discussion Paper No. 36, 1975.

From April 1943 to 27 March 1952 placements included 'transfers in' only. The definition of a placement was changed on 28 March 1952. Subsequent to that date placements included 'transfers out' (confirmed transfers between local Canada Manpower Centres in which one centre refers an applicant to a vacancy registered at another centre).

The substantial increases in the series in 1942 arose because of compulsory registrations of workers and vacancies during the war. See *The Labour Gazette,* May 1942, p. 551, June 1942, p. 675 and September 1942, p. 1018.

Labour Unions and Strikes and Lockouts (Series E175-197)

General note

The statistics of union membership and strikes and lockouts have been collected by the federal Department of Labour established in 1900 under the Conciliation Act, 1900. Included in its chief duties were the administration of certain provisions of the Conciliation Act 'designed to aid in prevention and settlement of labour disputes' and 'the collection and classification of statistical and other information relative to the conditions of labour' (*Canada Year Book,* 1920, p. 525). The department collected data on strikes and lockouts from the beginning; it was only in 1911 that the information it gathered on union membership was sufficiently complete to permit publication of a total.

For the long-term patterns in the development of the labour movement in Canada see: Economics and Research Branch, Canada Department of Labour, *Union Growth in Canada, 1921-1967,* Ottawa, Information Canada, 1970; and

J. K. Eaton, *Union Growth in Canada in the Sixties,* Economics and Research Branch, Department of Labour, Ottawa, Information Canada, 1976.

An alternative source of data on union organization is contained in the Statistics Canada publication *Corporations and Labour Unions Returns Act,* report for 1974, Part II-Labour Unions, (Catalogue 71-202). This report includes the following in its forward:

The Corporations and Labour Unions Returns Act, Chapter 26, 10-11 Elizabeth II, was passed by Parliament in April, 1962 and is administered by the Chief Statistician of Canada under the authority of the Minister of Industry, Trade and Commerce. The purpose of the Act is to collect financial and other information on the affairs of certain corporations and labour unions carrying on activities in Canada. Such information was considered necessary to evaluate the extent and effects of non-resident ownership and control of corporations in Canada and the extent and effects of the association of Canadians with international labour unions. The legislation applies to every labour union in Canada having a local in Canada and 100 or more members resident in Canada.

The first report was released in July 1965 covering fiscal periods of corporations and labour unions ending in 1962. The union data in this and later reports differ from that published by Labour Canada in its *Labour Organizations in Canada* for two reasons. First, there are differences in the coverage of unions under the act and second, the reporting under the Corporations and Labour Unions Returns Act varies according to the fiscal periods of individual unions.

E175-177. Union membership in Canada, in total and as a percentage of non-agricultural paid workers and union members with international affiliation, 1911 to 1975

SOURCE: for series E175-177, Labour Canada, *Labour Organizations in Canada, 1976-1977;* for series E175 and E177, 1911 to 1960, from estimates prepared for the first volume by Dr. J. T. Montague; 1961 to 1975, prepared by Mr. B. Fortin of Labour Canada from information contained in the annual reports. The percentage of non-agricultural paid workers in E176 was calculated using estimates of the actual number of non-agricultural paid workers in January of each year as provided by Statistics Canada's monthly Labour Force Survey. The figures for 1971 to 1975 are revised estimates which are not the same as the figures published in the annual reports for 1971 to 1975.

Until 1959 no specific definition of a trade union had been adopted by the department for statistical purposes so that the coverage probably was not entirely consistent from year to year. However, because the vast majority of union members belonged to trade organizations which posed no definitional problems, the marginal cases were not of great numerical importance and probably do not affect the trend significantly.

A substantial part of the increase in union membership from the mid-1960s was due to the inclusion of public sector employee groups, particularly government employee associations and teachers' associations. The large increase in 1967 resulted from the formation of the Public Service Alliance of Canada. The detailed footnotes to series E178-189 show when the major groups were included in the union statistics.

E178-189. Union membership by congress affiliation, 1942 to 1975

SOURCE: Labour Canada, *Labour Organization in Canada*, for the years to which the data apply except for 1971 to 1975 where revised figures have been provided by Mr. Bernard Fortin of Labour Canada.

The international affiliations of Canadian unions in the period covered were with either the American Federation of Labor (AFL) or with the Congress of Industrial Organizations (CIO), both having their membership mainly in the United States.

From 1942 to 1947 inclusive, the split in membership between 'other' unaffiliated international unions, series E187, and 'unaffiliated national, regional and local unions', series E189, was not given in the reports. In each of these years the total membership of the 'other' unaffiliated membership was determined from the data given in the table entitled 'International Unions; Number of Branches and Membership' in the annual reports, *Labour Organization in Canada*. This total was then subtracted from the item 'Unaffiliated National and International Unions'. This residual, together with the items giving the membership in national, regional or local unions, is given in the table as 'Unaffiliated National, Regional and Local Unions'.

Similarly, from 1942 to 1947, inclusive, the splits in membership between TLC only, series E179, and TLC/AFL, series E180, or CCL only, series E182, and CCL/CIO, series E183, were not given in the annual reports cited above. The membership of TLC only was determined by summing the membership of: international unions affiliated with TLC in Canada but unaffiliated in the United States; TLC national union affiliate; TLC local and federal unions. The same procedure was used to determine the membership of unions affiliated with CCL only.

This table could possibly be pushed back to earlier years using the data available in the annual reports, but the changing forms of the report make this procedure much more precarious for the years prior to 1942.

See the note to series E175-177 for a discussion of the basic data problem. The definitional problem is largely confined to the data included in series E189.

Since 1968 there has been over a fourfold growth in the category 'Other congresses and unaffiliated national, regional and local unions'. The main source of this increase has been the unaffiliated national and regional unions which grew from 77,489 persons in 1968 to 471,909 in 1977. This category largely comprises public sector employees, teachers, civil servants and nurses. The major changes are indicated in the footnotes to the table. Independent local organizations have actually decreased from 50,927 in 1968 to 40,239 in 1975. In 1975 there were a total of 60,633 in the two other congresses. These were the 20,352 member CCU (Confederation of Canadian Unions) founded in 1969 and the 40,275 member CSD (Centrale des syndicats démocratiques) founded in 1972 by breakaway units of the CNTU.

E190-197. Number of strikes and lockouts, employers and workers involved and time loss, Canada, 1901 to 1975

SOURCE: series E190-195 and E197 are from Labour Canada, *Strikes and Lockouts in Canada*, 1976 and 1977, table 1, pp. 5-6. Series E196 was calculated by dividing series E194 by series E193. Series E195 was calculated by dividing series E194 by the average annual number of non-agricultural paid workers obtained by Statistics Canada's

Monthly Labour Force Survey. Series E197 was calculated by dividing the time loss in man working days (series E194) by the product of the number of non-agricultural paid workers times 252. The figure 252 was calculated as 52 weeks of 5 days each less 8 statutory holidays. In 1975 the figure 250 was used by assuming there were 10 statutory holidays.

Since 1964 data are based on strikes or lockouts which amount to 10 or more man-days as long as the duration was at least half a man-day. From 1958 to 1963 the data were based on strikes or lockouts involving six or more workers and lasting at least one working day, and strikes and lockouts lasting less than one day or involving fewer than six workers but exceeding a total of nine man-days. The basis for inclusion in the series prior to 1958 was unspecified. The figures from 1961 were provided by Mr. Ed Walker of Labour Canada.

The total number of workers involved includes the reported total number on strike or locked out, even if those on strike did not belong to the union. Workers laid off as the result of a work stoppage are not included. Where the number of workers involved varied in the course of the stoppage, the maximum number is used in tabulating annual totals. The total number of workers shown may include the same workers more than once, if they were involved in more than one work stoppage during the year.

Since 1956 the number of employees (series E192) has been deleted because in some cases, for example, the 'employer' is a builders' exchange that comprises a multitude of individual contractors. Series E195 and E196 have also been dropped because the former was unreliable and the latter was difficult to interpret.

Political strikes are included where the objective is to influence government policies affecting pay, working conditions or other labour related matters.

See the 'Explanatory Notes', pp. 91-93 of *Strikes and Lockouts in Canada*, 1976, for additional details and concepts.

Index Numbers of Wage Rates, Wage Rates and Salaries (Series D198-375)

General note

All the published data in the tables contained in this division were taken from annual wage reports of the Department of Labour. While the Department of Labour collected some data on wages and hours beginning in 1900, parts of which were published from time to time in *The Labour Gazette*, it was only in 1921 that publication of a series of regular annual reports on wages and hours began. Prior to 1950 these reports were published as supplements to *The Labour Gazette;* beginning with 1950 they have been published as separate documents. These reports are entitled *Wage Rates, Salaries and Hours of Work*. Until 1973 a single report was issued. From 1974 there was a series of separate reports for a number of major communities across Canada. From 1975, a separate report presenting information on a national basis was added to the series.

The early wage reports were based on information obtained from trade unions, collective agreements, departmental field representatives and *The Labour Gazette* field representatives throughout Canada as well as from an annual mail survey of employers. With the expansion of the survey of employers over the years the information obtained from employers has supplanted information obtained from other sources.

The following summary of the technical notes of the present survey is taken from *Wage Rates, Salaries and Hours of Labour,* Canada, October 1976.

The survey, covering all establishments in Canada with 20 or more employees, is conducted by means of a reporting form which is mailed to employers. The form includes, for each occupation surveyed, a short description of the work characteristically performed.

These occupational descriptions are based on the Canadian Classification and Dictionary of Occupations, commonly referred to as the CCDO, which was developed and published by the Canada Department of Manpower and Immigration in collaboration with Statistics Canada in 1971.

The occupational descriptions included in the reporting schedules are designed to help employers identify the specific jobs for which wage information is requested. The descriptions are not to be construed as 'standards' for jobs in any particular establishment or industry, as the specific duties and work loads involved in some occupations may vary slightly from plant to plant, as well as from industry to industry.

The most important criteria used in selecting the occupations to be surveyed are the following: numerical importance, prevalence throughout the industry or community, importance in the production process, and capability of clear definition.

Employers are asked to submit returns on the basis of 'establishment' rather than for 'company' or 'enterprise', as many companies are of a multiple-unit type having one or more branches in different localities. Moreover, because of the variety of products made by some companies, all branches of the company may not come under the same industrial classification, as defined by Statistics Canada's *Standard Industrial Classification Manual.*

All major industrial areas are covered by this survey with the exception of agriculture, fishing, hunting, trapping and construction. Only the logging industry is covered in the forestry division.

The wage statistics generally apply to the last normal pay period preceding 1 October in the survey year. The term 'normal pay period' means a pay period in which there were no strikes, unusual layoffs or other abnormal conditions. Wage changes occurring on or after 1 October are not included, even where such changes are made retroactive.

For an average to be published for an occupation, the rates must apply to at least five employees in three establishments, or to 10 or more employees in two establishments, provided that more than 20 per cent of the total number of employees is reported by both establishments. Further to these criteria, the median, deciles and quartiles are not published unless the rates apply to at least 10 employees or more.

These criteria are applied for two reasons: to avoid revealing the rates paid by any one establishment; and to ensure a reasonable degree of representativeness of the data.

Some important features of the wage data are described below:

(1) The most common type of time rate for non-office employees is an hourly rate under which the employee is paid a fixed amount for each hour worked. Consequently, in cases where hourly rates are requested on the survey forms, and daily, weekly or monthly rates are reported, the reported rates are converted to an hourly basis. However, daily, weekly or monthly rates are sometimes shown for occupations in industries in which such methods of wage payment are common. When monthly rates are converted to weekly rates, or vice versa, a conversion factor of 4 weeks per month is used. When weekly rates are converted to hourly rates, the weekly rate (exclusive of overtime or other premiums) is divided by the standard weekly hours of work as reported. All rates include cost-of-living bonus payments where applicable.

(2) The most common types of straight-time earnings are those based on piece-work or various production or incentive bonus systems; other types are based on commission or mileage.

Overtime premium rates are not included in the wage figures published. Also excluded are shift differentials, non-production bonuses (except cost-of-living allowance payments), shares in company profits and the monetary value of fringe benefits such as group insurance, sick benefits, uniforms, etc. The rates are derived from the employee's wage before deductions are made for taxes, unemployment insurance contributions, pension payments, etc.

The rates published in this report are those applying to fully qualified employees in the occupations surveyed. Rates for beginners, learners, apprentices, improvers, foremen and lead hands are not included, although rates for helpers, which are sometimes requested on the reporting forms, are shown separately.

Rates for part-time employees working less than half the standard hours are not included.

Data for this section since 1960 were provided by Mr. Wayne Baxter of Labour Canada.

E198-208   Index numbers of average wage rates for selected main industries, 1901 to 1965

SOURCE: for 1961 to 1965, *Wage Rates, Salaries and Hours of Labour,* 1965, Report No. 48; pp. 26-27; for 1959 and 1960, Report No. 43, p. 26; for 1910 to 1958, Report No. 42, p. 26.

For a description of the construction of the indexes and their coverage see especially Reports Nos. 1, 3, 19, 24, 26, 36, 42, 43 and 48.

The method of constructing the indexes had one common element throughout the period. The first step was always to obtain a measure of the change in a rate for an occupation within an industry for each region. The occupational rate was in each case specific to the industry and the occupations were selected to be representative of all occupations in the industry. These measures of change of rate for an occupation within an industry were then averaged for all localities to give a countrywide average. The countrywide averages for all the occupations within an industry were then averaged to give a measure of the change for the industry as a whole on a contrywide basis.

A detailed discussion of the basis used to calculate the averages is contained in the 1960 edition of *Historical Statistics of Canada,* pp. 69-70 as well as in the notes to the reports cited above.

The series ends in 1965 since the use of the Standard

Industrial Classification of 1960 prevented linking the particular industry groups beyond this point; see notes to series E209-219. Series E198-208 are based on 1949 = 100 while series E209-219 are based on 1961 = 100.

E209-219. Index numbers of average wage rates, for selected main industries, 1961 to 1972

SOURCE: for 1968 to 1972,*Wage Rates, Salaries and Hours of Labour,* 1972, Report No. 55; for 1963 to 1967, Report No. 50; for 1962, Report No. 49. For a description of the construction of the indexes and their coverage, see Reports Nos. 49 and 55.

Four major changes were introduced in the 1966 survey:

(1) The classification of industries was changed from the 1948 to the 1960 Standard Industrial Classification. Complete details on this classification appear in the *Standard Industrial Classification Manual,* (Catalogue 12-501.) The changes in the industrial presentation of the information caused by the introduction of the 1960 Standard Industrial Classification are summarized in the 'Technical Notes' of *Wage Rates, Salaries and Hours of Labour,* Report No. 49, October 1966. The allocation of reporting units or establishments to individual classifications was also reviewed.

(2) A revised basis of geographic classification was introduced. As a result, the number of communities for which information is published was increased from 52 to 58.

(3) The index number series was revised to include the use of 1961 as base year and the selection of new occupational and geographical weights.

In addition to the above, a new series of data for the construction industry was introduced in the 1966 report. The figures shown are, with the exception of those for the province of Quebec, rates of pay and hours of work specified in collective agreements in effect at 1 October 1970. The figures for the communities in the province of Quebec are those established under the Collective Agreement Decrees Act, administered by the Building Trades Parity Committees in the province. The data was made available to the Canada Department of Labour by the various provincial labour departments or other provincial government agencies.

The series of index numbers for selected main industries was discontinued after 1972. This is due mainly to technical difficulties brought about by the conversion of the occupational titles and the duties of each occupation covered in the survey from the American Dictionary of Occupational Titles to the Canadian Classification and Dictionary of Occupations.

E220-247. Index numbers of average wage rates for industry groups and selected components in manufacturing, Canada, 1939 to 1972

SOURCE: for 1961 to 1972 on a 1961 = 100 base, see Labour Canada, *Wage Rates, Salaries and Hours of Labour,* Report No. 55; for earlier years, see *Wage Rates and Hours of Labour:* annual reports as follows for indexes on the base 1949 = 100: 1965 to 1961, No. 48; 1960 and 1959, No. 43; 1958 to 1954, No. 41; 1953 to 1949, No. 36. Indexes on the base 1939 = 100: 1953, No. 36; 1952 to 1949, No. 35; 1948 to 1941, No. 31; 1940 to 1939, No. 26.

See the discussion of series E198-208. From 1939 on indexes for a much larger number of industry groups were published. The 1949-based series end in 1965 since the use of the Standard Industrial Classification of 1960 prevented linking the particular industry group beyond this point.

E248-267. Hourly wage rates in selected building trades, by city, 1901 to 1974

SOURCE: Department of Labour, *Wage Rates, Salaries and Hours of Labour,* annual reports as follows: 1974 to 1947, Nos. 57-30; 1946 to 1942, No. 29; 1941 to 1929, No. 25; 1928 to 1920, No. 14 1919 to 1901, No. 1.

Rates are given here for four occupations in five major Canadian cities. Comparable data for other occupations and cities also have been published. It is believed that these series for the building trades are among the most consistent series which have been published in the annual wage reports. In 1973 the survey introduced new titles and definitions of occupations based on the CCDO. The department believes that for traditional occupations such as those in this series and for occupations which cut across industries, the change in definitions has not significantly altered the comparability of the results. It should be noted, however, that there is a possibility that in some cases the data for 1973 and subsequent years may not be entirely comparable.

The published wage rates for each occupation represent the 'prevailing' rates in the particular city. Up to 1965 these data were obtained from a field survey conducted by the Industrial Relations Branch of the Department of Labour for the administration of the Fair Wages and Hours of Labour Act. Since 1966 the data on the construction industry, with the exception of Quebec, have been based on rates of pay and hours of work specified in collective agreements in effect at 1 October of each year. The figures shown are, with the exception of those for the province of Quebec, rates of pay and hours of work specified in collective agreements in effect at 1 October 1966. The figures for the communities in the province of Quebec are those established under the Collective Agreement Decrees Act, administered by the Building Trades Parity Committees in the province. The data were made available to the Canada Department of Labour by the various provincial labour departments or other provincial government agencies. The rates are 'deemed to be generally accepted as current for competent workmen in each trade or classification employed in the location indicated', and in nearly all cases are union rates.

The rates published for this and all other industries in the annual wage reports do not include overtime earnings, shift differentials, non-production bonuses (except cost-of-living bonus payments), shares in company profits and the monetary value of such fringe benefits as group insurance, sick benefits, uniforms, etc. The rates are derived from the employee's wage before deductions are made for taxes, unemployment insurance contributions, pension payments, etc. The rates are intended to apply to fully qualified workers in their occupations. Unless otherwise stated, the rates apply to male workers only. Where women and men are reported in an occupation, separate rates are shown for them. Rates for beginners, learners, apprentices, foremen and lead hands, are not included, although rates for helpers are sometimes shown separately. The rates for part-time employees working less than half the standard hours are not included.

E268-279.   Hourly wage rates in selected occupations in the pulp and paper industry, for Canada and by region, 1911 to 1920 and 1943 to 1974

SOURCE: for 1943 to 1974, Department of Labour, *Wage Rates, Salaries and Hours of Labour*, Reports Nos. 26-57; for 1911 to 1920, No. 1.

Wage rates were published for the years 1920 to 1941 but they are not included here because of difficulties in deriving a consistent time series.

E280-295.   Hourly wage rates for selected occupations in the motor-vehicle industry, 1943 to 1974

SOURCE: for all years, Department of Labour, *Wage Rates, Salaries and Hours of Labour*, Reports Nos. 26-57.

The wage rates are weighted average rates prepared by the Department of Labour. Until 1958 all of the reporting establishments were located in Ontario. Prior to 1945 the industry was called the automobile industry. It is now defined to include 'establishments primarily engaged in manufacturing or assembling complete motor vehicles such as passenger automobiles, commercial cars and buses, trucks, and special purpose motor vehicles' (see Report No. 55, p. 163). Consistent data are not available prior to 1943.

E296-325.   Average hourly wage rates for selected maintenance and service occupations, by city, 1956 to 1975

SOURCE: for all years, Department of Labour, *Wage Rates, Salaries and Hours of Labour,* Reports Nos. 39-58.

The wage and salary data published on a community basis are derived from survey returns for establishments having 15 or more employees in the community up to 1965 and 20 or more employees from 1966 onward. Where no information is published for an occupation, insufficient data are available to meet the criteria for publishing an average or range of wage rates for an occupation (see Report No. 47, Technical Notes, for description of the publication criteria applied to the results of the survey).

E326-375.   Average weekly salaries for selected office occupations, by city, 1956 to 1975

SOURCE: same as series E296-325.

See the note to series E296-325.

Workmen's Compensation (Series E376-389)

General note

Workmen's compensation is under provincial jurisdiction. The data, therefore, are obtained from reports of the various provincial workmen's compensation boards. Data since 1960 were provided by Mr. Jim Wong of Labour Canada.

E376-386.   Industrial accidents, fatal and non-fatal, reported by provincial workmen's compensation boards, by province, 1928 to 1974

SOURCE: federal Department of Labour, and its publication, *The Labour Gazette* and 'Work-Injury Experience and Cost in Canadian Industry' (annual). The data were published first in the March issue, 1931, and annually in the issues for the same months until 1945, in the April issues of 1946 to 1952, in the June issue, 1953, and in May issues, 1954 to 1965. Subsequent revised data are shown in the following issues: July 1966; August 1967; and July of 1968, 1969, 1970 and 1971. The 1963, 1967 and 1969 figures were subsequantly revised slightly because of changes in particular provincial data. Data from 1970 to 1974 were provided by the Department of Labour with the totals shown in *The Labour Gazette,* December 1977, p. 553.

The principal limitation of these series is that they do not include accidents of workers not covered by workmen's compensation. For a number of provinces accidents which required 'medical aid only' were not reported in the early years; only accidents which required compensation were included. The source document provides details on the number of fatal accidents and the number that involved permanent disabilities.

E387-389.   Provincial expenditures for workmen's compensation, 1921 to 1975

SOURCE: data for series E389 for the years 1921 to 1943 are from an unpublished table supplied by the federal Department of National Health and Welfare, Research Division, and are based on information provided by the National Income Section of Statistics Canada. For years 1947 to 1952 the data are from the federal Department of National Health and Welfare, Research Division, *Government Expenditures and Related Data on Health and Social Welfare, 1947-1953,* table 9, p. 21 (second edition). For the years 1953 to 1958 the data are from the third edition of this report which covers the years 1947 to 1959, appendix 10. Data were not available for 1959 to 1961 inclusive. From 1962 the data were provided by Labour Canada. For 1967 to 1975 see *The Labour Gazette,* December 1977, p. 555.

The data give totals for all provinces. Prior to 1947 only the 'total' expenditures, and then only for some years, were available.

Series E1-13. Wages, salaries and supplementary labour income, by province, 1926 to 1975
(millions of dollars)

Year	Canada	Newfound-land	Prince Edward Island	Nova Scotia	New Brunswick	Quebec	Ontario	Manitoba	Saskat-chewan	Alberta	British Columbia	Yukon Territory and Northwest Territories	Foreign countries
	1	2	3	4	5	6	7	8	9	10	11	12	13
1975	93,562	1,422	262	2,476	2,032	23,567	38,554	3,888	2,709	7,384	10,953	282	33
1974	80,086	1,208	215	2,125	1,657	20,258	33,619	3,270	2,165	5,873	9,431	237	28
1973	66,757	967	183	1,759	1,357	16,741	28,536	2,695	1,743	4,796	7,765	189	26
1972	57,570	807	148	1,503	1,151	14,469	24,888	2,339	1,494	4,114	6,474	158	25
1971	51,528	745	134	1,310	1,038	13,019	22,304	2,103	1,326	3,694	5,699	134	22
1970	46,706	673	119	1,195	926	11,965	20,182	1,936	1,231	3,351	4,976	131	21
1969	43,065	610	107	1,102	854	11,149	18,447	1,815	1,203	3,043	4,604	105	26
1968	38,444	552	94	968	758	10,189	16,374	1,646	1,130	2,623	4,009	86	15
1967	35,303	496	87	881	708	9,624	14,809	1,486	1,049	2,354	3,723	73	13
1966	31,878	461	77	801	649	8,685	13,433	1,312	944	2,083	3,354	67	12
1965	28,201	408	68	718	570	7,721	11,840	1,194	844	1,843	2,929	57	9
1964	25,367	361	61	660	516	6,975	10,660	1,104	759	1,641	2,562	59	9
1963	23,262	334	57	616	474	6,343	9,774	1,046	709	1,522	2,324	56	7
1962	21,816	306	56	591	446	5,935	9,130	995	677	1,449	2,172	52	7
1961	20,399	297	53	561	423	5,472	8,518	944	655	1,370	2,051	49	6
1960	19,582	271	46	540	405	5,154	8,225	924	645	1,298	2,016	53	5
1959	18,596	248	43	507	379	4,827	7,853	889	627	1,238	1,929	51	5
1958	17,435	230	38	481	351	4,542	7,385	819	587	1,140	1,812	45	5
1957	16,988	237	37	474	345	4,431	7,162	790	554	1,074	1,833	46	5
1956	15,696	221	36	445	335	4,090	6,568	743	518	1,025	1,663	48	4
1955	13,930	196	33	407	302	3,626	5,862	669	459	861	1,479	33	3
1954	13,043	181	30	397	285	3,448	5,452	638	451	793	1,337	28	3
1953	12,714	173	30	388	283	3,367	5,317	631	417	768	1,312	25	3
1952	11,768	151	28	373	270	3,127	4,958	579	355	655	1,248	22	2
1951	10,538	137	25	334	263	2,807	4,447	524	323	569	1,089	18	2
1950	8,998	117	23	296	218	2,372	3,771	464	282	505	948	—	2
1949	8,349	115	21	288	208	2,229	3,483	437	266	452	848	—	2
1948	7,754	—	20	275	207	2,127	3,246	409	247	403	819	—	1
1947	6,662	—	18	256	183	1,835	2,772	350	225	339	683	—	1
1946	5,487	—	16	232	153	1,493	2,257	291	204	289	550	—	2
1945	5,037	—	15	223	135	1,406	2,082	256	176	244	499	—	1
1944	4,998	—	14	226	126	1,411	2,081	242	163	233	501	—	1
1943	4,812	—	12	210	117	1,369	2,028	218	144	208	505	—	1
1942	4,282	—	9	183	104	1,197	1,834	206	132	185	431	—	1
1941	3,608	—	9	147	89	980	1,569	187	124	171	332	—	—
1940	2,959	—	9	122	77	778	1,272	158	112	147	284	—	—
1939	2,601	—	9	107	70	683	1,103	143	101	133	252	—	—
1938	2,515	—	8	102	68	667	1,061	137	97	128	247	—	—
1937	2,538	—	8	101	68	673	1,064	145	103	131	245	—	—
1936	2,241	—	7	88	59	594	936	132	94	117	214	—	—
1935	2,079	—	7	80	55	550	865	126	90	110	196	—	—
1934	1,939	—	6	74	51	512	804	121	86	104	181	—	—
1933	1,788	—	6	67	47	472	739	114	81	97	165	—	—
1932	1,975	—	7	74	52	519	814	129	92	108	180	—	—
1931	2,408	—	8	90	64	632	989	160	114	132	219	—	—
1930	2,786	—	9	106	75	727	1,141	189	134	154	251	—	—
1929	2,940	—	10	114	81	762	1,202	201	143	164	263	—	—
1928	2,715	—	9	108	76	699	1,107	188	134	153	241	—	—
1927	2,506	—	8	102	72	640	1,021	175	124	142	222	—	—
1926	2,366	—	8	100	69	598	962	166	119	135	209	—	—

Series E14-29. Wages, salaries and supplementary labour income, by industry, 1926 to 1975
(millions of dollars)

Year	Agri-culture	Forest-ry	Fishing and trapping	Mines, quarries and oil wells	Manufac-turing	Con-struc-tion	Transpor-tation	Storage	Commu-nication	Electric power, gas and water utilities	Whole-sale trade	Retail trade	Finance, insur-ance and real estate	Public adminis-tration	Commu-nity, business and personal service	Total
	14	15	16	17	18	19	20	21	22	23	24	25	26	27	28	29
1975	696	988	69	2,437	21,617	8,584	5,873	231	2,520	1,404	5,276	7,226	5,642	8,559	22,440	93,562
1974	566	970	74	2,062	19,509	7,083	5,098	200	2,165	1,211	4,482	6,139	4,786	7,026	18,715	80,086
1973	500	795	81	1,643	16,599	5,845	4,223	173	1,738	1,005	3,739	5,121	4,023	5,658	15,614	66,757
1972	412	626	60	1,395	14,478	4,765	3,714	158	1,536	852	3,247	4,447	3,269	4,971	13,640	57,570
1971	392	586	52	1,328	13,087	4,367	3,354	144	1,356	803	2,870	3,931	2,771	4,340	12,147	51,528
1970	371	521	52	1,233	12,298	3,570	3,078	133	1,242	839	2,642	3,626	2,552	3,746	10,803	46,706
1969	347	521	48	1,049	11,754	3,371	2,872	123	1,128	744	2,387	3,363	2,360	3,405	9,593	43,065
1968	337	476	48	993	10,765	3,023	2,670	114	1,012	690	2,096	3,007	2,060	2,924	8,229	38,444
1967	319	483	42	912	10,083	2,944	2,516	106	931	632	1,920	2,753	1,842	2,582	7,238	35,303
1966	291	444	45	817	9,388	2,788	2,247	98	825	564	1,762	2,501	1,661	2,301	6,146	31,878
1965	282	406	41	743	8,363	2,336	2,065	88	738	511	1,570	2,287	1,490	2,003	5,278	28,201
1964	252	379	38	661	7,569	1,954	1,884	81	664	465	1,442	2,103	1,330	1,843	4,702	25,367
1963	250	343	33	631	6,939	1,750	1,764	74	633	435	1,347	1,937	1,202	1,706	4,218	23,262
1962	253	336	33	621	6,503	1,663	1,699	67	589	401	1,231	1,828	1,112	1,621	3,859	21,816
1961	252	317	28	593	6,086	1,541	1,669	68	561	379	1,106	1,726	1,037	1,519	3,517	20,399
1960	245	363	27	590	6,010	1,538	1,619	66	533	360	1,055	1,662	968	1,421	3,125	19,582
1959	227	325	26	578	5,816	1,498	1,614	63	504	344	982	1,596	911	1,319	2,793	18,596
1958	217	310	25	560	5,501	1,406	1,523	61	484	317	909	1,488	867	1,248	2,519	17,435
1957	206	384	24	562	5,508	1,471	1,532	56	454	283	860	1,424	822	1,132	2,270	16,988
1956	199	425	23	521	5,207	1,325	1,460	52	402	244	766	1,309	729	1,021	2,013	15,696
1955	186	377	22	447	4,705	1,047	1,313	48	357	218	671	1,191	652	930	1,766	13,930
1954	182	355	21	418	4,424	984	1,235	44	327	210	609	1,128	603	878	1,625	13,043
1953	186	400	20	352	4,469	1,036	1,268	41	299	199	560	1,062	553	791	1,478	12,714
1952	186	357	19	414	4,107	983	1,176	37	271	181	504	985	512	714	1,322	11,768
1951	178	430	18	361	3,694	769	1,061	33	246	161	425	909	461	626	1,166	10,538
1950	163	295	17	300	3,131	663	898	28	216	142	366	799	403	537	1,040	8,998
1949	152	218	14	277	2,921	614	880	27	196	131	341	731	366	503	978	8,349
1948	148	276	15	243	2,773	565	837	25	170	108	307	638	337	437	875	7,754
1947	147	271	12	199	2,398	450	711	23	148	82	269	538	300	380	734	6,662
1946	120	234	15	179	1,836	293	555	20	111	68	292	457	219	442	646	5,487
1945	109	177	14	163	1,933	189	518	20	91	54	248	392	180	397	552	5,037
1944	107	151	12	170	2,115	165	501	19	82	50	225	359	166	372	504	4,998
1943	103	134	11	168	2,074	225	457	16	74	48	203	329	154	350	466	4,812
1942	95	112	9	169	1,756	228	384	14	69	46	196	313	144	310	437	4,282
1941	86	98	7	165	1,315	194	336	13	64	42	185	305	132	258	408	3,608
1940	83	85	5	148	954	131	286	11	60	39	157	260	120	250	370	2,959
1939	78	62	4	139	765	104	267	10	59	39	141	228	119	234	352	2,601
1938	77	45	4	131	732	107	261	8	57	37	132	224	118	237	345	2,515
1937	76	73	4	132	749	108	259	9	56	36	137	231	116	218	334	2,538
1936	71	50	4	107	635	81	244	9	51	33	124	204	113	203	312	2,241
1935	67	40	4	90	580	68	229	8	50	33	115	188	106	197	304	2,079
1934	62	34	4	79	521	53	219	8	47	32	106	179	105	195	295	1,939
1933	59	25	3	63	451	51	213	8	47	32	103	161	109	175	288	1,788
1932	61	23	3	63	490	83	239	7	50	35	113	174	114	197	323	1,975
1931	78	31	4	77	608	155	290	7	58	38	129	211	126	217	379	2,408
1930	100	53	6	97	723	191	337	8	62	40	144	250	139	216	420	2,786
1929	113	69	7	107	804	232	362	8	60	36	139	247	142	197	417	2,940
1928	113	65	7	100	745	187	353	6	56	35	129	224	128	182	385	2,715
1927	112	61	7	88	683	158	338	6	53	35	121	203	112	170	359	2,506
1926	112	59	7	81	643	155	319	5	50	32	114	181	103	158	347	2,366

Series E30-40.   Annual wages and salaries in manufacturing, by province, 1926 to 1975
(millions of dollars)

Year	Total Canada[1,2]	Newfoundland	Prince Edward Island	Nova Scotia	New Brunswick	Quebec	Ontario	Manitoba	Saskatchewan	Alberta	British Columbia
	30	31	32	33	34	35	36	37	38	39	40
1975	19,257	133	17	365	306	5,393	9,745	555	198	742	1,803
1974	17,757	129	18	318	264	4,866	9,147	481	168	614	1,752
1973	15,416	103	13	272	218	4,219	8,042	403	139	504	1,503
1972	13,581	79	12	231	194	3,808	7,076	352	119	439	1,271
1971	12,293	74	10	191	176	3,506	6,412	315	105	390	1,114
1970	11,589	74	11	176	161	3,350	6,060	300	100	364	991
1969	11,088	67	10	169	152	3,237	5,786	284	97	343	943
1968	10,157	59	8	153	137	2,998	5,303	258	92	300	848
1967	9,530	56	8	146	125	2,821	4,966	249	86	280	792
1966	8,890	52	7	143	113	2,600	4,674	225	80	248	747
1965	7,997	43	7	130	102	2,350	4,192	204	71	222	675
1964	7,239	41	6	120	95	2,164	3,749	189	66	205	603
1963	6,640	39	5	109	90	2,000	3,410	178	61	193	554
1962	6,232	38	5	105	85	1,924	3,147	171	59	184	514
1961	5,829	37	4	96	79	1,815	2,924	164	56	172	481
1960	5,759	33	4	93	75	1,803	2,892	156	55	169	479
1959	5,591	31	4	88	68	1,717	2,858	156	51	162	456
1958	5,291	30	3	87	69	1,638	2,687	144	48	149	441
1957	5,305	33	3	92	64	1,638	2,705	142	44	145	439
1956	5,023	31	3	84	65	1,549	2,564	135	40	127	425
1955	4,548	29	3	77	61	1,407	2,317	122	38	112	382
1954	4,276	31	3	73	59	1,343	2,168	116	37	102	344
1953	4,326	27	3	77	64	1,352	2,226	121	36	97	323
1952	3,976	26	3	77	60	1,241	2,034	112	33	86	304
1951	3,573	23	2	64	57	1,110	1,833	100	28	72	284
1950	3,022	21	3	59	51	928	1,537	97	25	63	238
1949	2,824	20	2	59	49	882	1,419	94	24	59	216
1948	2,689	—	2	58	50	844	1,349	89	23	55	219
1947	2,329	—	2	51	44	743	1,156	77	22	47	187
1946	1,770	—	2	44	34	575	859	62	18	36	140
1945	1,869	—	2	52	33	615	894	61	17	33	162
1944	2,053	—	2	61	33	676	985	63	18	34	181
1943	2,013	—	1	56	31	667	968	55	17	30	188
1942	1,704	—	1	42	27	543	852	52	13	24	150
1941	1,281	—	1	28	22	399	669	41	10	21	90
1940	933	—	1	22	18	281	485	32	9	17	68
1939	747	—	1	17	14	227	382	29	7	15	55
1938	715	—	1	16	13	216	367	28	7	14	53
1937	732	—	1	17	15	220	377	28	7	14	53
1936	620	—	1	14	12	185	319	25	6	12	46
1935	567	—	1	13	11	167	292	24	6	12	41
1934	510	—	1	12	11	154	258	21	6	11	36
1933	442	—	1	10	9	136	223	19	5	10	29
1932	479	—	1	11	10	143	243	23	6	11	31
1931	595	—	1	14	12	178	299	29	7	14	41
1930	707	—	1	17	14	208	356	33	9	16	53
1929	787	—	1	17	15	228	412	32	9	15	58
1928	730	—	1	15	14	211	378	31	8	15	57
1927	669	—	1	13	14	197	342	28	7	13	54
1926	631	—	1	13	14	183	323	26	6	12	53

[1] Includes Yukon Territory, Northwest Territories and Canadian residents abroad.

[2] Preliminary data, 1971 to 1975.

Series E41-48. Annual earnings in manufacturing industries, production and other workers, by sex, Canada, 1905, 1910 and 1917 to 1975

Year	Production workers				Supervisory and office employees			
	Number of males (thousands)	Number of females (thousands)	Total Earnings (millions of dollars)	Average annual earnings (dollars)	Number of males (thousands)	Number of females (thousands)	Total earnings (millions of dollars)	Average annual earnings (dollars)
	41	42	43	44	45	46	47	48
Based on the 1960 Standard Industrial Classification								
1975	997.6	294.5	12,672.2	9,962	342.3	127.2	6,488.5	13,820
1974	995.6	305.2	11,637.1	8,946	354.4	130.8	5,920.0	12,201
1973	976.4	299.5	10,060.0	7,884	349.9	125.2	5,160.0	10,861
1972	931.2	281.9	8,763.1	7,224	344.7	118.3	4,651.5	10,046
1971	901.0	266.8	7,819.0	6,695	344.7	115.9	4,310.8	9,359
1970	901.1	265.9	7,232.3	6,197	352.2	117.7	4,131.5	8,791
1969	918.5	271.4	6,921.5	5,817	360.4	125.0	3,926.8	8,089
1968	896.6	263.6	6,278.4	5,411	358.4	123.7	3,627.1	7,523
1967	907.8	260.8	5,869.1	5,022	362.1	122.1	3,385.1	6,991
1966	912.0	261.0	5,575.2	4,753	354.4	118.7	3,120.7	6,597
1965	870.4	245.5	5,012.3	4,492	341.5	112.9	2,810.6	6,185
1964	822.8	234.7	4,513.6	4,268	326.3	107.5	2,567.3	5,919
1963	780.2	223.3	4,095.9	4,081	317.9	104.0	2,399.4	5,687
1962	757.3	217.1	3,834.5	3,935	311.0	104.2	2,261.7	5,448
1961	729.4	210.0	3,532.9	3,761	311.1	102.1	2,168.7	5,249
1960	764.7	206.9	3,565.2	3,669	219.9	84.0	1,585.3	5,217
1959	779.0	209.9	3,517.5	3,557	215.5	83.3	1,512.3	5,062
1958	764.9	207.6	3,306.0	3,400	217.0	84.2	1,458.6	4,842
1957	819.5	215.8	3,391.8	3,276	220.3	85.3	1,386.2	4,536
Based on the 1948 Standard Industrial Classification								
1959	786.0	211.9	3,543.5	3,551	220.9	85.2	1,529.6	4,998
1958	772.3	209.4	3,333.2	3,395	221.9	86.0	1,469.3	4,773
1957	827.3	217.8	3,416.2	3,269	226.3	87.6	1,403.4	4,471
1956	831.3	220.4	3,298.7	3,136	216.3	85.0	1,272.0	4,222
1955	796.7	214.3	2,995.3	2,963	206.9	80.6	1,147.1	3,990
1954	780.0	209.1	2,821.6	2,853	199.8	79.2	1,075.1	3,854
1953	828.4	224.9	2,940.3	2,792	195.8	78.4	1,016.7	3,707
1952	810.1	215.3	2,713.7	2,647	188.2	74.8	923.9	3,513
1951	792.4	218.2	2,459.6	2,434	176.9	70.9	816.7	3,296
1950	736.5	215.8	2,078.6	2,183	164.5	66.6	692.6	2,998
1949	732.5	217.2	1,963.5	2,067	157.5	64.0	628.4	2,836
1948	738.7	218.8	1,876.8	1,960	141.0	57.2	532.6	2,687
1947	721.4	219.2	1,610.6	1,712	135.2	55.9	474.4	2,482
1946	662.2	214.4	1,329.2	1,516	126.9	54.0	410.7	2,305
1945	679.8	248.0	1,426.9	1,538	128.3	62.0	416.9	2,192
1944	743.6	285.6	1,610.4	1,565	126.4	65.4	416.6	2,172
1943	761.8	285.0	1,597.4	1,526	128.3	64.3	387.6	2,013
1942	731.3	242.5	1,347.0	1,383	122.9	53.9	334.2	1,890
1941	626.2	175.4	977.9	1,220	117.1	41.6	285.9	1,801
1940	491.0	135.0	678.9	1,084	104.2	31.5	241.4	1,779
1939	415.2	117.8	519.7	975	98.1	26.6	217.6	1,746
1938	408.9	112.2	498.0	956	95.2	25.3	207.2	1,720
1937	426.9	117.3	525.4	965	91.0	24.7	195.8	1,692
1936	379.8	110.0	438.7	896	81.3	23.0	172.9	1,659
1935	353.7	104.9	398.9	870	76.1	21.7	160.2	1,638
1934	326.5	101.1	355.0	830	71.8	20.1	148.5	1,615
1933	287.2	94.7	296.9	777	67.7	18.7	139.0	1,608
1932	288.7	93.0	322.2	844	68.1	18.7	151.1	1,739
1931	337.5	99.5	415.2	950	71.0	20.2	171.9	1,884
1930	416.6	113.2	527.4	995	64.1	20.5	169.9	2,008
1929	454.5	122.9	601.5	1,041	67.7	21.1	175.4	1,976
1928	427.6	119.3	558.3	1,021	64.3	19.8	162.8	1,936
1927	400.0	114.2	511.1	994	60.4	18.0	151.3	1,930
1926	374.0	109.6	483.2	999	58.2	17.1	142.2	1,890
1925		451.4	436.4	967		71.3	133.4	1,872
1924		422.4	411.0	973		70.5	131.5	1,864
1923		437.3	420.2	961		73.8	137.2	1,857
1922		386.5	363.8	941		71.9	130.6	1,816
1921		371.3	370.9	999		70.5	130.8	1,854
1920		499.1	544.3	1,090		77.4	140.0	1,810
1919		496.3	456.9	920		75.6	113.1	1,497
1918		520.7	453.2	870		64.8	95.2	1,470
1917		523.5	397.8	760		62.5	82.2	1,317
1910		465.0	194.0	417		42.9	42.7	994
1905		347.7	130.4	375		35.0	29.6	846

Series E49-59. Average weekly wages and salaries, industrial composite, by province, 1939 to 1975
(dollars)

Year	Canada	Newfound-land	Prince Edward Island	Nova Scotia	New Brunswick	Quebec	Ontario	Manitoba	Saskat-chewan	Alberta	British Columbia
	49	50	51	52	53	54	55	56	57	58	59

Based on the 1960 Standard Industrial Classification

Year	Canada	Newfound-land	Prince Edward Island	Nova Scotia	New Brunswick	Quebec	Ontario	Manitoba	Saskat-chewan	Alberta	British Columbia
1975	203.34	196.44	149.84	172.40	182.40	199.22	204.85	186.10	188.31	207.39	229.97
1974	178.09	168.48	126.92	149.98	154.58	172.89	181.43	162.71	160.99	178.72	200.55
1973	160.46	149.09	111.17	134.44	133.97	154.30	165.61	144.76	142.28	161.12	178.22
1972	149.22	134.60	101.02	123.20	125.08	142.86	154.92	135.59	133.18	149.94	165.08
1971	137.64	123.79	89.97	112.82	113.32	132.04	143.04	123.84	121.71	138.78	152.50
1970	126.82	117.70	83.82	104.21	104.01	122.38	131.52	115.88	114.87	128.15	137.97
1969	117.63	106.00	80.87	94.51	96.80	114.24	121.55	107.67	107.90	117.95	129.35
1968	109.88	99.15	72.41	88.19	89.55	107.92	113.52	100.46	102.11	108.02	120.76
1967	102.83	90.92	70.58	82.64	85.25	101.16	105.86	91.95	95.77	100.86	114.50
1966	96.34	84.68	64.18	77.04	79.21	94.83	99.40	84.45	89.11	94.87	107.42
1965	91.01	80.22	62.48	73.43	74.76	88.62	94.41	82.28	84.90	89.88	100.71
1964	86.51	77.42	60.49	70.14	71.01	84.46	89.82	79.02	81.27	85.82	94.11
1963	83.27	74.89	58.70	68.03	68.28	80.99	86.22	77.56	79.32	83.61	90.10
1962	80.54	72.49	55.95	65.43	65.59	78.23	83.65	75.62	77.08	80.99	87.10
1961	78.24	71.06	54.91	63.72	63.62	75.67	81.30	73.66	74.38	80.29	84.99
1960	75.76	67.43	53.24	62.49	62.62	73.01	78.74	71.77	72.33	76.75	82.85
1959	73.40	61.55	50.80	59.99	60.42	70.65	76.48	70.14	70.34	74.43	79.92
1958	70.35	59.94	47.84	58.19	58.20	67.80	73.21	66.91	68.37	72.11	75.63
1957	67.90	59.96	47.68	56.25	57.31	65.22	70.63	63.74	65.56	69.17	73.62

Based on the 1948 Standard Industrial Classification

Year	Canada	Newfound-land	Prince Edward Island	Nova Scotia	New Brunswick	Quebec	Ontario	Manitoba	Saskat-chewan	Alberta	British Columbia
1961	78.11	71.41	57.03	63.98	63.55	75.33	81.14	73.45	74.19	80.45	85.20
1960	75.83	67.91	55.00	62.65	62.66	73.00	78.71	71.71	72.13	77.83	82.97
1959	73.47	63.68	54.75	60.17	60.39	70.56	76.39	70.16	70.13	75.63	80.09
1958	70.43	62.36	51.15	58.33	58.14	67.69	73.20	66.85	68.14	72.88	75.88
1957	67.93	61.99	50.68	56.36	57.33	65.18	70.56	63.73	65.26	69.62	73.80
1956	64.44	57.57	47.50	52.90	55.10	61.86	66.86	60.88	61.66	66.93	70.15
1955	61.05	54.32	45.76	50.83	52.17	58.62	63.55	58.30	58.02	62.30	66.00
1954	59.04	54.30	44.41	49.56	50.49	56.58	61.36	56.34	56.21	60.19	64.42
1953	57.53	55.74	44.56	48.61	49.09	54.74	59.66	55.05	54.77	59.04	63.61
1952	54.41	51.00	40.08	45.88	46.04	51.66	56.36	51.73	50.90	54.90	59.46
1951	50.04	44.51	37.52	42.51	43.02	47.37	51.69	48.37	46.68	50.37	52.93
1950	45.08	40.10	34.44	39.40	38.76	42.89	46.58	43.84	42.86	45.61	47.70
1949	42.96	..	33.56	37.65	38.08	41.19	44.36	42.68	41.50	44.40	45.65
1948	40.06	..	31.77	35.97	36.21	38.46	41.26	39.93	38.76	41.48	42.47
1947	36.19	..	29.14	32.60	33.35	34.74	37.16	36.15	35.35	37.19	38.67
1946	32.48	..	27.12	30.80	30.09	31.37	32.59	33.34	32.15	34.02	35.25
1945	32.04	..	26.09	31.57	28.94	30.88	32.55	32.03	30.83	33.33	34.72
1944	31.85	..	25.81	31.84	28.17	30.32	32.79	31.07	30.09	32.95	34.53
1943	30.79	..	24.00	29.30	26.61	29.16	31.81	29.92	28.86	31.53	34.37
1942	28.62	..	22.13	26.16	24.31	26.83	29.83	28.77	27.50	29.57	31.23
1941	26.65	..	21.06	23.44	22.72	24.96	28.02	27.48	26.31	27.28	28.81
1940	24.94	..	20.86	22.89	21.23	23.14	25.97	26.33	26.00	26.13	27.24
1939	23.44	..	19.79	21.42	20.21	21.26	24.45	25.69	24.18	25.39	26.01

Series E60-68. Average annual, weekly and hourly earnings, male and female wage-earners, manufacturing industries, Canada, 1934 to 1969
(dollars)

Year	Wage-earners (both sexes)			Male wage-earners			Female wage-earners		
	Annual	Weekly	Hourly	Annual	Weekly	Hourly	Annual	Weekly	Hourly
	60	**61**	**62**	**63**	**64**	**65**	**66**	**67**	**68**
1969	–	116.11	2.86	–	129.17	3.12	–	72.39	1.92
1968	–	108.19	2.64	–	120.34	2.88	–	66.26	1.74
1967	–	100.27	2.45	–	111.60	2.67	–	62.99	1.63
1966	–	94.52	2.29	–	105.45	2.50	–	58.01	1.51
1965	–	89.39	2.14	–	99.50	2.33	–	54.88	1.41
1964	–	84.37	2.02	–	94.08	2.21	–	51.45	1.33
1963	–	80.79	1.94	–	90.04	2.13	–	49.31	1.27
1962			Survey on earnings and hours of work in manufacturing was not conducted in 1962.						
1961			Survey on earnings and hours of work in manufacturing was not conducted in 1961.						
1960	–	72.39	1.77	–	80.34	1.93	–	43.96	1.14
1959	3,551	71.35	1.72	3,929	79.20	1.88	2,149	43.36	1.11
1958	3,396	67.85	1.65	3,749	75.03	1.80	2,092	41.90	1.08
1957	3,269	65.31	1.61	3,609	72.21	1.75	1,974	39.49	1.05
1956	3,136	63.97	1.53	3,458	70.67	1.66	1,923	39.29	1.00
1955	2,963	60.53	1.44	3,267	66.86	1.57	1,833	37.52	.95
1954	2,853	57.99	1.40	3,145	63.98	1.51	1,764	35.90	.93
1953	2,792	56.75	1.36	3,082	62.71	1.47	1,723	35.07	.91
1952	2,647	55.17	1.30	2,915	60.85	1.40	1,638	34.17	.86
1951	2,434	51.32	1.22	2,693	56.46	1.31	1,492	31.27	.82
1950	2,183	45.94	1.06	2,419	50.93	1.14	1,376	29.00	.72
1949	2,067	42.61	.98	2,291	47.33	1.07	1,315	27.18	.68
1948	1,960	41.25	.95	2,175	45.73	1.02	1,233	25.91	.65
1947	1,713	37.19	.85	1,909	41.35	.92	1,067	23.11	.58
1946	1,516	32.38	.74	1,702	36.23	.81	943	20.08	.50
1945	1,538	30.98	.67	1,739	35.04	.74	984	19.84	.47
1944	1,564	31.05	.65	1,761	34.95	.71	1,051	20.89	.48
1943	1,525	29.87	.61	1,726	33.80	.67	987	19.33	.43
1942	1,383	28.18	.56	1,558	31.75	.62	854	17.41	.37
1941	1,220	24.95	.49	1,355	27.72	.54	736	15.05	.32
1940	1,084	22.35	.45	1,202	24.82	.49	655	13.52	.27
1939	975	20.14	.43	1,076	22.23	.46	619	12.78	.28
1938	956	19.49	.42	1,055	21.49	.45	594	12.10	.27
1937	965	–	–	–	–	–	–	–	–
1936	896	18.96	.39	995	20.92	.42[1]	577	12.20	.26[1]
1935	870	18.50	.38	966	20.41	.41[1]	570	12.04	.26[1]
1934	830	18.30	.37	930	20.31	.41[1]	539	11.80	.25[1]

[1] Estimated on the basis of hours worked by female workers in 1938 and 1939 as compared with those worked by male workers in these years.

Series E69-77. Average annual, weekly and hourly earnings, male and female salaried employees, manufacturing industries, Canada, 1946 to 1969
(dollars)

Year	Salaried employees (both sexes)			Male salaried employees			Female salaried employees		
	Annual	Weekly	Hourly	Annual	Weekly	Hourly	Annual	Weekly	Hourly
	69	**70**	**71**	**72**	**73**	**74**	**75**	**76**	**77**
1969	–	156.12	–	–	178.60	–	–	92.86	–
1968	–	142.06	–	–	163.56	–	–	83.56	–
1967	–	136.11	–	–	155.92	–	–	80.29	–
1966	–	128.79	–	–	147.95	–	–	75.26	–
1965	–	120.30	–	–	139.01	–	–	69.35	–
1964	–	115.59	–	–	133.64	–	–	66.51	–
1963	–	111.40	–	–	128.67	–	–	64.24	–
1962			Survey on earnings and hours of work in manufacturing was not conducted in 1962.						
1961			Survey on earnings and hours of work in manufacturing was not conducted in 1961.						
1960	–	100.47	–	–	116.41	–	–	57.98	–
1959	4,998	97.10	2.52	5,817	112.78	2.90	2,874	55.73	1.48
1958	4,773	93.74	2.43	5,549	108.34	2.79	2,769	54.07	1.44
1957	4,471	89.92	2.33	5,205	104.63	2.68	2,576	51.84	1.38
1956	4,222	85.23	2.19	4,918	99.05	2.51	2,449	49.31	1.30
1955	3,990	80.57	2.06	4,636	93.50	2.36	2,332	47.02	1.24
1954	3,854	77.81	2.00	4,499	90.99	2.31	2,227	45.00	1.19
1953	3,707	73.87	1.89	4,327	86.43	2.19	2,159	43.13	1.14
1952	3,513	70.75	1.80	3,985	82.60	2.07	2,323	41.26	1.09
1951	3,296	65.98	1.67	3,852	77.55	1.94	1,907	38.42	1.01
1950	2,998	58.74	1.48	3,507	69.35	1.73	1,739	34.38	.90
1949	2,836	54.85	1.37	3,317	65.37	1.60	1,655	32.62	.85
1948	2,687	52.91	1.31	3,147	63.47	1.54	1,551	31.26	.81
1947	2,484	49.78	1.23	2,933	60.21	1.46	1,396	28.68	.74
1946	2,270	43.85	1.07	2,680	53.21	1.27	1,305	25.91	.66

Series E78-85. Averages of weekly wages of hourly rated wage-earners, selected industry groups, Canada, 1945 to 1970
(dollars)

Year	Mining			Manufacturing			Construction	Service
	All	Metal	Coal	All	Durable goods	Non-durable goods		
	78	**79**	**80**	**81**	**82**	**83**	**84**	**85**

Based on the 1960 Standard Industrial Classification

Year	All	Metal	Coal	All	Durable goods	Non-durable goods	Construction	Service
1970	152.10	154.68	130.37	119.69	130.75	108.92	165.04	..
1969	135.94	137.68	108.58	111.72	121.76	101.64	147.68	..
1968	128.28	131.55	97.66	104.00	113.83	94.34	134.84	..
1967	119.09	122.79	90.68	96.84	105.32	88.37	128.76	..
1966	109.77	112.21	85.61	91.65	100.31	82.92	118.06	..
1965	102.92	105.19	80.78	86.94	96.16	77.92	105.11	..
1964	97.43	99.48	80.84	82.96	91.60	74.97	95.96	..
1963	93.87	96.22	79.25	79.51	87.83	72.02	90.76	..
1962	90.98	93.92	73.86	76.75	84.68	69.77	86.89	..
1961	88.82	92.32	70.65	74.45	81.99	68.02	84.22	..
1960	87.00	90.17	69.82	72.14	79.35	65.82	84.24	..
1959	84.56	87.24	67.20	70.33	77.32	64.04	79.37	..
1958	80.81	83.72	67.43	66.91	73.11	61.33	77.95	..
1957	78.94	81.68	63.17	64.94	70.71	59.28	77.93	..
1956	73.92	77.27	61.04	62.40	67.45	56.74	67.77	35.94
1955	69.68	73.07	58.88	59.45	64.35	54.30	60.49	34.62
1954	67.14	71.27	57.02	57.43	62.13	52.36	59.85	34.03
1953	65.69	69.75	56.93	56.25	61.55	50.51	60.26	32.93
1952	63.20	66.11	57.78	53.83	58.49	48.65	54.99	31.52
1951	58.06	60.02	54.04	49.29	53.38	45.03	47.86	29.62
1950	52.46	54.93	49.49	44.03	47.74	40.57	42.13	28.09
1949	50.22	52.75	48.37	41.74	45.28	38.18	40.18	26.92
1948	48.02	49.93	47.80	38.96	42.24	35.70	36.89	24.87
1947	41.83	44.49	41.37	34.47	37.71	31.39	33.25	22.70
1946	37.53	39.60	37.98	30.15	33.00	26.92	29.53	20.08
1945	37.40	38.85	38.23	30.47	34.04	26.57	28.59	18.92

Series E86-103. Annual averages of weekly wages and salaries, selected industry groups and composite, Canada, 1939 to 1975

(dollars)

Year	Forestry (chiefly logging)	Mining All	Mining Metal	Mining Coal	Manufacturing All	Manufacturing Durable goods	Manufacturing Non-durable goods	Construction	Transportation, storage and communication All	Steam rail	Storage	Communication All	Communication Telephones	Public utility operation	Trade	Finance, insurance and real estate	Service	Industrial composite
	86	87	88	89	90	91	92	93	94	95	96	97	98	99	100	101	102	103
Based on the 1960 Standard Industrial Classification																		
1975	249.58	280.44	278.68	254.01	213.43	227.11	199.98	290.95	233.98	244.20	217.89	212.89	228.73	277.00	159.06	193.12	143.68	203.34
1974	219.64	238.97	238.08	223.69	185.62	198.39	172.86	250.30	204.39	216.16	185.58	185.14	196.88	239.28	139.92	172.25	126.08	178.09
1973	197.04	211.42	209.20	189.35	167.48	180.41	154.71	225.45	181.89	177.82	164.37	170.00	179.02	212.43	126.49	154.44	114.53	160.46
1972	172.92	190.29	187.88	165.60	156.10	168.09	144.64	209.90	167.94	171.89	150.40	160.97	167.92	197.34	117.58	140.79	107.32	149.22
1971	155.53	177.00	176.78	145.86	143.99	155.33	133.28	188.26	154.14	154.65	141.11	148.11	152.33	180.60	108.45	129.59	98.57	137.64
1970	137.60	164.70	165.26	135.75	132.75	142.87	123.27	167.15	142.35	146.03	129.19	135.21	139.21	165.61	100.50	120.52	90.65	126.82
1969	133.60	148.93	147.89	112.75	122.97	132.13	114.21	150.68	131.03	135.05	116.44	127.46	126.15	149.55	93.81	113.83	84.23	117.64
1968	122.04	139.16	140.00	101.20	114.42	123.30	106.19	137.59	122.70	125.43	107.39	117.91	116.12	141.23	86.93	106.21	78.99	109.90
1967	113.64	129.81	129.77	93.75	106.54	114.04	96.46	130.93	113.20	115.00	98.01	108.28	106.43	129.76	81.24	99.02	75.39	102.83
1966	104.79	119.51	119.45	88.38	100.16	107.82	92.93	120.21	103.55	102.01	92.64	99.34	97.48	119.88	76.89	93.04	70.25	96.34
1965	96.71	111.53	111.52	83.46	94.78	102.97	87.24	108.40	98.84	102.19	86.32	95.02	95.63	111.31	73.49	88.29	65.76	91.01
1964	92.13	105.73	105.07	82.72	90.42	97.96	83.79	98.47	93.68	95.77	82.74	90.28	91.04	106.06	71.07	81.88	62.30	86.51
1963	87.02	101.96	101.71	80.73	86.90	94.16	80.69	93.59	90.10	92.77	79.86	86.73	88.22	102.23	68.80	77.63	60.44	83.27
1962	82.15	98.53	99.05	75.70	84.00	90.97	78.16	89.36	86.44	89.29	76.39	83.10	85.51	97.60	66.53	75.35	59.31	80.54
1961	79.02	95.57	97.15	72.44	81.55	88.22	76.17	86.93	82.47	86.27	74.44	80.32	81.43	94.79	64.54	72.82	57.87	78.24
1960	73.85	93.19	94.45	71.67	78.88	85.17	73.73	86.90	79.68	82.82	71.48	75.15	76.40	92.43	62.93	69.57	54.86	75.76
1959	70.18	90.41	91.97	69.13	76.51	82.74	71.27	82.28	76.93	81.14	68.49	71.76	72.34	88.92	60.91	67.41	52.21	73.40
1958	70.55	86.14	87.32	69.51	73.10	78.76	68.34	80.54	72.84	75.49	65.97	68.31	67.80	84.73	58.45	65.20	50.18	70.35
1957	69.03	83.58	84.90	65.57	70.27	75.54	65.49	79.47	69.52	72.72	62.54	64.18	62.74	79.50	56.07	62.32	48.04	67.90
Based on the 1948 Standard Industrial Classification																		
1961	80.43	95.90	—	—	80.73	87.08	75.25	82.57	88.86	—	—	—	—	—	—	76.37	57.23	78.11
1960	74.85	93.80	—	—	79.19	84.20	72.86	80.46	82.32	—	—	—	—	—	—	70.83	53.08	75.83
1959	71.63	90.76	—	—	75.84	81.67	70.52	76.55	79.65	—	—	—	—	—	—	68.82	50.27	73.47
1958	71.74	86.60	—	—	72.67	77.93	67.67	74.54	74.72	—	—	—	—	—	—	66.40	48.23	70.43
1957	69.38	83.89	—	—	69.94	74.81	65.08	73.63	71.20	—	—	—	—	—	—	63.36	45.77	67.93
1956	65.40	78.01	80.32	62.02	66.71	71.42	61.91	68.58	67.29	69.32	59.92	61.23	60.05	74.39	54.64	60.29	42.93	64.44
1955	60.62	73.53	76.28	60.20	63.48	68.01	59.04	62.11	64.56	66.59	57.18	59.58	58.68	70.80	52.42	56.79	40.71	61.05
1954	59.89	70.67	74.15	58.48	61.15	65.56	56.87	61.15	62.76	65.27	55.66	56.56	56.02	67.87	50.73	53.93	38.91	59.04
1953	58.26	68.91	72.43	58.35	59.29	63.93	54.52	60.88	61.24	64.51	55.34	53.92	53.27	65.45	48.51	51.86	37.12	57.53
1952	55.84	65.79	68.37	58.73	56.36	60.65	52.07	55.82	56.81	58.96	51.53	50.15	49.55	62.00	46.08	49.35	34.23	54.41
1951	49.13	60.33	62.74	54.71	51.68	55.31	48.14	48.79	54.14	58.03	47.73	45.78	45.29	56.48	43.08	46.48	31.81	50.04
1950	42.44	54.27	57.02	50.48	46.49	49.76	43.54	43.42	49.34	52.64	43.28	42.48	42.06	51.44	39.02	44.09	29.64	45.08
1949	40.62	51.49	54.41	48.92	43.97	47.14	41.18	41.28	48.39	52.37	42.01	39.59	39.39	48.14	36.97	42.22	28.05	42.96
1948	39.11	48.77	51.12	47.81	40.67	43.46	38.20	37.99	45.51	49.44	39.32	36.69	36.59	45.16	34.38	40.08	25.87	40.06
1947	35.42	43.03	46.25	41.61	36.34	38.96	34.08	34.85	41.23	44.63	35.55	33.73	33.63	41.05	31.29	38.34	23.48	36.19
1946	29.03	39.21	41.63	39.03	32.27	34.66	30.27	31.62	37.53	40.06	33.95	32.44	32.57	38.17	28.45	36.11	21.90	32.48
1945	26.90	38.61	41.03	38.20	32.46	35.58	29.24	30.66	36.05	38.45	32.95	31.53	31.62	36.91	26.85	34.77	20.71	32.04
1944	26.54	38.05	40.68	36.95	32.49	35.71	28.55	30.63	34.62	36.06	31.99	31.27	31.37	37.01	26.21	33.61	20.25	31.85
1943	24.78	36.09	39.70	33.18	31.39	34.44	27.28	30.83	33.15	34.55	32.10	29.59	29.64	35.70	25.24	32.48	19.42	30.79
1942	20.70	34.81	38.61	31.11	28.99	32.14	25.52	27.29	31.70	33.21	30.61	28.26	28.21	34.16	24.07	31.46	18.21	28.62
1941	19.18	32.64	36.58	27.68	26.73	29.28	24.31	23.78	30.34	31.64	29.92	27.96	27.85	31.88	22.81	30.00	17.43	26.65
1940	17.30	30.24	34.60	24.34	24.48	26.72	23.09	22.71	29.72	30.85	29.45	28.20	28.13	30.20	22.53	29.70	16.74	24.94
1939	17.37	28.69	33.50	22.16	22.79	24.28	21.82	18.83	28.68	30.17	26.64	28.55	28.53	29.53	21.83	29.59	16.33	23.44

Series E104-119. Average weekly wages and salaries, by major groups of manufacturing, 1939 to 1975
(dollars)

Year	Non-durable manufacturing								Durable manufacturing							
	Food and beverage	Rubber products	Leather products	Textile products	Clothing	Paper and allied industries	Petroleum and coal products	Chemicals and chemical products	Wood products	Furniture and fixtures	Primary metal industries	Metal fabricating industries	Machinery (excluding electrical)	Transportation equipment	Electrical products	Non-metallic mineral products
	104	105	106	107	108	109	110	111	112	113	114	115	116	117	118	119
	Based on the 1960 Standard Industrial Classification															
1975	198.27	214.46	139.15	175.41	132.59	250.56	314.09	234.61	208.91	171.02	253.01	221.07	229.51	243.80	211.89	234.72
1974	168.71	184.73	120.26	150.76	114.45	218.43	271.91	204.88	179.92	148.19	221.75	192.24	202.73	219.36	182.78	202.85
1973	150.92	171.89	107.83	135.65	102.03	192.35	244.41	186.27	161.18	134.13	218.47	174.85	185.25	201.39	163.28	184.52
1972	139.64	160.78	100.90	127.88	96.17	180.46	224.66	173.94	146.63	126.38	186.07	163.68	178.02	186.07	153.95	170.57
1971	127.68	146.27	94.52	118.52	88.23	166.78	206.23	160.98	132.82	117.61	170.90	151.55	166.53	170.09	145.06	156.34
1970	118.26	136.95	86.42	110.03	80.76	152.76	192.41	149.97	118.92	107.86	159.29	140.30	153.09	155.61	134.59	141.68
1969	108.56	127.96	80.36	102.05	75.29	143.17	179.23	139.23	111.07	100.47	145.92	128.89	140.59	145.10	125.33	131.58
1968	100.89	116.05	75.54	95.29	70.21	133.15	168.20	129.49	104.03	93.01	137.40	119.72	129.16	135.76	116.93	121.35
1967	94.44	109.16	70.20	88.62	64.68	125.35	156.20	121.70	95.79	87.14	128.59	111.45	120.33	123.10	107.90	112.96
1966	87.25	102.91	66.41	82.58	60.96	118.69	148.40	114.71	88.05	81.37	120.47	105.81	114.15	117.80	103.53	106.68
1965	83.08	97.19	62.64	76.86	57.51	109.68	135.11	108.45	83.13	77.35	115.17	100.09	107.62	115.43	99.00	100.00
1964	79.53	93.27	60.27	73.59	55.53	105.31	130.81	105.03	78.51	73.96	109.78	95.59	103.09	109.43	94.89	96.06
1963	76.53	88.78	57.45	70.25	53.40	101.63	127.50	101.18	75.27	71.07	106.66	92.26	98.59	105.21	91.26	91.96
1962	74.08	86.73	55.61	68.02	51.43	98.28	123.70	97.96	72.27	69.04	103.98	90.24	94.80	99.36	89.42	88.84
1961	72.56	83.54	54.12	65.96	50.15	95.69	119.35	94.39	70.62	67.12	101.09	87.39	91.63	94.87	87.72	85.55
1960	70.57	80.31	51.66	64.01	48.27	91.86	115.39	90.63	68.97	64.50	96.62	84.84	88.21	91.51	84.41	81.99
1959	68.91	79.49	50.45	61.88	47.46	88.30	111.32	86.44	65.82	62.95	94.11	82.30	85.57	88.98	81.25	80.03
1958	65.73	74.67	49.01	59.27	45.80	84.79	104.62	82.99	63.70	60.44	89.04	78.53	80.20	83.92	78.22	77.28
1957	62.60	71.50	47.56	56.85	43.96	82.89	101.18	79.06	60.64	57.99	85.75	75.57	76.83	79.22	74.89	73.87
	Based on the 1948 Standard Industrial Classification															
1961	71.18	83.24	54.48	64.35	50.26	95.21	117.46	94.92	69.71	67.59	..	..	87.48	91.90	87.85	84.59
1960	69.25	79.98	52.11	62.36	48.41	91.57	115.74	90.92	67.64	65.10	..	..	84.90	88.71	84.64	81.05
1959	67.78	79.12	50.75	60.53	47.37	88.16	111.56	86.70	64.80	63.23	..	..	82.35	80.05	81.42	79.01
1958	64.75	74.27	49.32	58.11	45.84	82.77	104.31	83.41	62.64	60.82	..	..	78.09	81.47	78.30	76.32
1957	61.73	71.13	47.78	55.89	44.14	82.77	101.24	79.29	59.80	58.49	..	..	75.46	77.28	75.22	72.94
1956	58.48	68.43	45.54	53.48	43.18	79.37	94.53	73.99	57.67	56.06	..	..	73.03	74.09	72.27	69.52
1955	56.29	65.05	43.76	51.92	41.46	75.03	89.68	69.98	56.06	53.83	..	..	69.02	70.95	68.26	66.44
1954	54.39	62.47	41.72	50.02	40.64	72.18	85.87	66.88	54.17	51.80	..	..	66.56	68.88	66.18	63.88
1953	52.41	61.09	40.96	48.25	40.25	69.51	82.72	64.13	52.57	50.27	..	..	64.69	67.65	63.42	61.37
1952	50.20	57.77	39.50	46.48	38.60	66.85	78.72	61.07	50.05	47.50	..	..	61.05	63.09	61.11	58.03
1951	46.71	53.77	35.93	43.02	35.97	62.89	69.20	56.08	46.02	43.72	..	..	56.37	58.23	55.91	53.39
1950	42.59	47.68	33.57	39.96	33.79	55.12	61.55	50.22	41.48	40.21	..	..	50.22	53.33	50.25	48.19
1949	40.40	44.89	32.54	37.84	32.25	51.81	55.77	47.61	39.23	38.33	..	..	47.07	50.36	47.79	45.12
1948	37.45	42.60	30.12	33.78	29.87	49.10	51.99	44.23	35.90	34.91	..	..	43.68	46.67	43.26	41.54
1947	33.45	38.45	27.76	29.24	27.16	43.64	45.59	39.51	32.68	31.40	..	..	39.68	42.43	37.71	36.53
1946	29.97	32.61	25.18	25.87	24.72	37.37	41.78	34.96	29.12	27.90	..	..	35.23	38.08	33.20	31.35
1945	28.76	32.46	24.18	24.58	23.58	34.13	41.73	33.84	27.94	26.86	..	..	35.75	40.46	33.52	30.85
1944	28.04	32.39	23.46	24.03	22.90	33.20	39.57	32.07	26.63	26.45	..	..	35.89	37.62	32.66	31.13
1943	27.25	29.90	22.30	22.91	21.55	32.09	39.41	30.69	25.56	25.13	..	..	35.23	36.37	31.86	29.82
1942	25.67	27.59	20.51	21.37	20.10	31.45	37.94	28.55	23.92	23.89	..	..	33.11	34.35	30.59	27.75
1941	23.82	25.76	18.85	20.40	19.20	30.64	36.93	28.05	22.16	22.51	..	..	30.90	32.52	27.50	26.20
1940	23.42	22.96	17.36	19.17	17.98	28.91	36.01	28.69	20.59	20.34	..	..	27.73	30.48	25.43	24.64
1939	22.76	21.45	16.75	18.00	17.15	26.82	35.31	28.14	19.32	18.92	..	..	25.39	26.73	24.38	23.17

Series E120-127. Annual averages of hourly earnings of hourly rated wage-earners, selected industry groups, Canada, 1945 to 1970
(dollars)

Year	Mining			Manufacturing			Construction	Service
	All	Metal	Coal	All	Durable goods	Non-durable goods		
	120	121	122	123	124	125	126	127
Based on the 1960 Standard Industrial Classification								
1970	3.71	3.84	3.09	3.01	3.25	2.77	4.21	..
1969	3.28	3.38	2.59	2.79	3.00	2.57	3.71	..
1968	3.07	3.20	2.34	2.58	2.79	2.37	3.33	..
1967	2.84	2.98	2.13	2.40	2.58	2.22	3.12	..
1966	2.60	2.70	2.02	2.25	2.43	2.06	2.80	..
1965	2.43	2.52	1.96	2.12	2.30	1.93	2.53	..
1964	2.31	2.39	1.92	2.02	2.20	1.85	2.34	..
1963	2.24	2.32	1.86	1.95	2.12	1.79	2.23	..
1962	2.18	2.26	1.83	1.88	2.05	1.73	2.14	..
1961	2.13	2.21	1.77	1.83	2.00	1.69	2.06	..
1960	2.09	2.18	1.75	1.79	1.95	1.64	2.03	..
1959	2.05	2.13	1.74	1.73	1.88	1.58	1.93	..
1958	1.95	2.03	1.73	1.66	1.81	1.53	1.86	..
1957	1.87	1.94	1.60	1.61	1.74	1.47	1.84	..
Based on the 1948 Standard Industrial Classification								
1961	2.13	2.20	1.77	1.83	1.99	1.68	1.98	1.07
1960	2.09	2.17	1.75	1.78	1.94	1.64	1.94	1.04
1959	2.04	2.13	1.74	1.72	1.87	1.53	1.84	1.00
1958	1.90	2.03	1.73	1.66	1.80	1.53	1.78	.97
1957	1.88	1.95	1.62	1.61	1.73	1.47	1.76	.94
1956	1.73	1.80	1.50	1.52	1.64	1.39	1.65	.89
1955	1.61	1.66	1.48	1.45	1.56	1.33	1.52	.86
1954	1.58	1.62	1.48	1.41	1.52	1.30	1.48	.83
1953	1.54	1.57	1.50	1.36	1.48	1.23	1.44	.79
1952	1.48	1.49	1.50	1.30	1.41	1.18	1.32	.74
1951	1.35	1.36	1.37	1.18	1.27	1.08	1.19	.70
1950	1.22	1.22	1.30	1.04	1.13	.96	1.06	.66
1949	1.18	1.16	1.28	.99	1.07	.91	1.01	.64
1948	1.12	1.11	1.25	.92	.99	.85	.94	.59
1947	.99	1.00	1.11	.81	.88	.74	.85	.53
1946	.88	.88	.97	.71	.77	.64	.77	.47
1945	.85	.85	.94	.69	.76	.61	.74	.43

Series E128-135. Average weekly hours of hourly rated wage-earners, selected industry groups, Canada, 1945 to 1970
(hours)

Year	Mining			Manufacturing			Construction	Service
	All	Metal	Coal	All	Durable goods	Non-durable goods		
	128	129	130	131	132	133	134	135
Based on the 1960 Standard Industrial Classification								
1970	41.0	40.3	42.1	39.7	40.2	39.3	39.2	..
1969	41.4	40.7	41.9	40.0	40.6	39.5	39.8	..
1968	41.8	41.2	41.8	40.3	40.9	39.7	40.5	..
1967	41.9	41.3	42.6	40.3	40.8	39.8	41.3	..
1966	42.2	41.5	42.5	40.8	41.3	40.3	42.2	..
1965	42.4	41.8	41.3	41.1	41.7	40.4	41.5	..
1964	42.2	41.7	42.2	41.0	41.6	40.5	41.0	..
1963	42.0	41.5	42.6	40.8	41.4	40.3	40.8	..
1962	41.7	41.5	40.3	40.7	41.3	40.3	40.7	..
1961	41.8	41.8	39.8	40.6	40.9	40.3	40.9	..
1960	41.6	41.4	39.9	40.4	40.7	40.1	41.6	..
1959	41.3	41.2	38.6	40.7	41.0	40.4	41.1	..
1958	41.4	41.3	39.0	40.2	40.3	40.1	41.9	..
1957	42.3	42.2	39.5	40.4	40.6	40.3	42.4	..

Series E128-135. Average weekly hours of hourly rated wage-earners, selected industry groups, Canada, 1945 to 1970 (concluded)
(hours)

Year	Mining			Manufacturing			Construction	Service
	All	Metal	Coal	All	Durable goods	Non-durable goods		
	128	129	130	131	132	133	134	135
Based on the 1948 Standard Industrial Classification								
1961	41.8	42.2	39.3	40.6	40.9	40.3	40.3	38.7
1960	41.7	41.9	39.0	40.4	40.7	40.1	40.4	39.1
1959	41.5	41.7	38.6	40.7	41.0	40.4	40.2	39.4
1958	41.5	41.8	39.7	40.2	40.3	40.1	40.7	39.5
1957	42.3	42.9	39.7	40.4	40.5	40.2	41.2	39.8
1956	42.8	43.0	40.8	41.0	41.1	40.7	41.1	40.2
1955	43.2	44.1	39.7	41.0	41.2	40.8	39.9	40.4
1954	42.6	44.1	38.5	40.7	40.9	40.4	40.3	40.9
1953	42.6	44.4	37.9	41.3	41.7	40.9	41.7	41.9
1952	42.7	44.4	38.6	41.5	41.6	41.3	41.5	42.6
1951	43.1	44.1	39.3	41.7	41.9	41.5	40.3	42.5
1950	43.0	45.1	38.1	42.3	42.4	42.3	39.9	42.5
1949	42.7	45.4	37.7	42.2	42.4	42.0	39.7	42.2
1948	42.8	44.9	38.3	42.3	42.5	42.1	39.2	42.3
1947	42.3	44.4	37.2	42.5	42.8	42.3	39.3	42.5
1946	42.7	44.9	39.2	42.7	42.8	41.8	38.4	43.1
1945	43.9	45.7	40.8	44.1	44.5	43.7	38.9	43.8

Series E136-151. Estimated labour costs, selected industries, selected years, 1968 to 1976
(dollars per employee)

	Manufacturing			Mines, quarries and oil wells			Transportation, communication and other utilities	
	1976	1971	1968	1976	1972	1969	1976	1970
	136	137	138	139	140	141	142	143
Pay for time worked								
Basic pay for regular work	10,498	6,595	5,251	12,868	8,097	6,448	11,888	6,593
Commissions, incentive bonuses	239	–	–	308	–	–	60	–
Overtime, straight-time pay	365	247	230	705	317	338	461	234
Overtime, premium pay	187	119	115	360	157	169	257	108
Shift work, premium pay	66	44	33	102	51	34	39	31
Other pay for time worked	36	18	6	104	308	260	106	18
Total	*11,391*	*7,023*	*5,635*	*14,446*	*8,930*	*7,249*	*12,812*	*6,984*
Paid absence								
Paid holidays	472	264	186	562	305	205	517	262
Vacation pay	698	397	289	977	557	409	855	413
Sick leave pay	68	31	23	113	37	26	145	85
Personal or other leave	14	6	3	23	5	4	66	18
Total	*1,252*	*698*	*501*	*1,675*	*904*	*644*	*1,583*	*778*
Miscellaneous direct payments								
Bonuses (Christmas, year-end)	68	38	40	66	45	34	34	11
Severance pay	17	14	12	14	17	31	13	15
Taxable benefits	153	45	24	206	111	32	140	30
Other payments	35	6	7	13	17	52	108	12
Total	*273*	*103*	*83*	*299*	*190*	*149*	*295*	*68*
Total (gross payroll)	*12,915*	*7,823*	*6,218*	*16,420*	*10,025*	*8,042*	*14,690*	*7,831*
Employer contributions to employee welfare and benefit plans								
Workmen's compensation	223	76	58	611	215	199	166	56
Unemployment insurance	177	58	47	200	76	57	186	47
Canada or Quebec Pension Plan	133	84	74	139	93	91	132	81
Private pension plans	378	210	170	610	278	160	1,079	384
Life and health plans	258	200	153	314	163	131	269	119
Supplementary unemployment benefits and other plans or funds	26	30	9	100	46	22	9	5
Total	*1,196*	*657*	*511*	*1,974*	*871*	*660*	*1,842*	*692*
Total compensation	*14,110*	*8,480*	*6,729*	*18,394*	*10,896*	*8,702*	*16,532*	*8,523*

Series E136-151. Estimated labour costs, selected industries, selected years, 1968 to 1976 (concluded)
(dollars per employee)

	Finance, insurance and real estate		Trade		Education, libraries and museums		Services to business management	
	1976	1970	1976	1972	1976	1974	1976	1975
	144	**145**	**146**	**147**	**148**	**149**	**150**	**151**
Pay for time worked								
Basic pay for regular work	8,909	5,623	9,970	6,712	12,729	9,917	11,885	10,045
Commissions, incentive bonuses	849	–	671	–	–	–	565	–
Overtime, straight-time pay	95	50	111	120	37	24	295	234
Overtime, premium pay	45	21	55	49	17	12	86	82
Shift work, premium pay	5	2	13	6	8	4	27	14
Other pay for time worked	6	9	5	5	30	7	25	252
Total	*9,909*	*5,705*	*10,824*	*6,893*	*12,821*	*9,964*	*12,883*	*10,627*
Paid absence								
Paid holidays	382	211	413	248	643	127	508	421
Vacation pay	513	286	547	332	837	162	760	565
Sick leave pay	200	59	71	56	186	48	263	102
Personal or other leave	14	4	15	4	20	12	34	17
Total	*1,109*	*560*	*1,046*	*639*	*1,686*	*349*	*1,564*	*1,105*
Miscellaneous direct payments								
Bonuses (Christmas, year-end)	48	47	110	133	–	4	208	262
Severance pay	26	35	18	14	8	10	42	20
Taxable benefits	95	19	111	77	61	60	167	117
Other payments	2	2	12	4	50	22	4	11
Total	*171*	*103*	*252*	*228*	*119*	*97*	*421*	*410*
Total (gross payroll)	*11,188*	*6,370*	*12,122*	*7,759*	*14,626*	*10,410*	*14,868*	*12,142*
Employer contributions to employee welfare and benefit plans								
Workmen's compensation	15	2	104	46	29	16	84	50
Unemployment insurance	159	44	165	64	177	101	182	152
Canada or Quebec Pension Plan	121	75	128	83	131	100	132	110
Private pension plans	364	249	235	119	428	500	386	285
Life and health plans	141	82	165	80	113	67	183	130
Supplementary unemployment benefits and other plans or funds	15	4	31	13	2	3	86	9
Total	*812*	*456*	*828*	*405*	*880*	*786*	*1,054*	*735*
Total compensation	*12,003*	*6,826*	*12,950*	*8,164*	*15,506*	*11,196*	*15,922*	*12,876*

Series E152-165. Number of persons insured with unemployment insurance commission, by industry, at book renewal periods, 1942 to 1974

(thousands)

Year[1]	Total	Agriculture	Forestry and logging[2]	Fishing, hunting and trapping	Mining, quarrying and oil wells	Manufacturing	Construction	Transportation, storage and communication	Public[3] utility operation	Trade	Finance, insurance and real estate	Service and public administration	Unspecified	Claimants[4]
	152	153	154	155	156	157	158	159	160	161	162	163	164	165
						Based on the 1970 Standard Industrial Classification								
1974	8,579.0	..	..	..	..	..	..	..	..	..	..	..	..	..
1973	8,239.0	..	..	..	..	..	..	..	..	..	..	..	..	..
1972	7,807.0	..	..	..	..	..	..	..	..	..	..	..	..	..
1971	5,340.8	30.0	49.9	14.8	124.1	1,591.4	329.9	502.4	..	961.9	259.3	839.2	638.1 [5]	..
						Based on the 1960 Standard Industrial Classification								
1970	5,399.6	49.6	59.5	15.0	133.1	1,735.9	362.0	537.2	..	1,033.2	279.6	891.5	303.0	..
1969	5,300.0	45.1	63.4	15.5	128.6	1,786.2	377.2	592.2	..	1,000.0	276.1	870.9	145.0	..
1968	4,812.0	44.8	72.6	19.5	117.6	1,680.1	374.5	491.0	..	923.0	229.5	812.9	46.5	..
1967	4,734.8	24.3	78.8	23.5	116.4	1,704.2	384.9	519.7	..	869.8	214.3	769.2	29.6	..
1966	4,487.4	13.1	80.9	25.8	102.8	1,628.8	377.4	474.6	..	830.8	206.6	709.7	37.0	..
1965	4,256.6	11.2	75.5	21.5	105.5	1,536.3	335.4	437.6	..	768.6	193.9	647.4	123.7	..
1964	4,169.8	13.8	82.2	27.9	104.4	1,432.0	330.3	423.0	..	760.7	182.8	657.0	155.7	..
1963	4,113.4	11.4	45.2	15.9	100.7	1,366.7	269.4	443.9	..	703.8	177.6	575.5	18.8	384.6
1962	4,084.1	10.4	44.2	8.8	93.4	1,344.3	261.4	453.3	..	690.9	171.5	558.4	16.8	430.8
1961	4,021.4	9.6	49.8	17.6	100.6	1,255.6	251.8	419.3	..	688.9	167.0	533.8	11.7	515.5
						Based on the 1948 Standard Industrial Classification								
1960	4,109.6	9.9	59.9	7.6	102.6	1,286.6	275.5	371.6	47.0	703.8	161.8	548.9	16.4	518.1
1959	4,072.9	9.6	63.0	6.7	104.4	1,295.7	317.1	371.1	48.2	699.3	156.3	538.7	20.0	442.9
1958	4,055.1	7.4	69.2	8.0	109.7	1,288.4	325.1	390.4	47.1	681.7	153.2	525.7	11.2	438.0
1957	3,807.3	7.5	81.0	10.8	102.6	1,286.3	318.3	384.5	45.0	643.0	141.7	478.4	16.0	292.3
1956	3,726.3	6.4	125.5	.7	104.8	1,218.9	378.2	336.0	39.8	608.1	130.9	476.5	32.4	268.1
1955	3,256.9	4.1	76.3	.3	98.6	1,184.5	270.9	319.7	40.9	566.3	124.0	412.4	14.5	144.3
1954	3,231.1	2.7	55.2	.1	95.3	1,143.5	182.0	328.3	36.8	522.3	117.7	345.5	22.0	379.9
1953	3,150.7	2.2	73.2	.3	90.9	1,180.7	199.9	343.9	34.3	494.6	111.0	348.2	8.9	262.6
1952	3,090.2	2.1	97.1	.4	101.2	1,123.3	185.1	345.9	34.2	485.9	107.0	341.0	28.4	238.7
1951	3,007.9	2.2	107.8	.4	93.0	1,161.1	172.4	320.8	38.2	487.3	105.1	325.8	7.0	186.7
1950	2,618.6	1.7	39.5	.6	81.7	986.7	142.5	294.9	31.8	423.8	84.8	291.1	11.7	227.8
1949	2,610.2	1.4	11.9	.6	79.8	1,000.8	143.5	251.0	30.9	444.4	82.8	296.6	25.0	241.7
1948	2,298.3	1.9	14.8	.8	72.8	981.0	124.3	235.6	23.6	390.7	75.7	254.5	9.8	113.1
						Based on the 1941 Census classification of industries								
1947	2,280.2	1.5	13.4	.2	72.3	996.7	117.4	218.3	23.8	392.5	70.2	256.2	5.7	112.0
1946	2,128.7	1.5	2.3 [2]	— [2]	71.0	924.3	93.3	222.9	19.5	346.1	68.9	237.2	141.9	—
1945	2,198.8	1.5	1.0	—	68.2	1,143.1	69.5	200.4	20.3	332.8	65.4	266.1	30.6	—
1944	2,209.9	1.4	.5	—	78.0	1,191.3	67.1	178.2	19.2	313.4	63.9	253.9	43.0	—
1943	1,997.7	1.1	.2	—	70.4	1,064.4	104.9	167.7	14.1	274.5	59.3	219.4	21.8	—
1942	2,438.9	2.3	3.8	—	92.5	1,235.1	160.7	206.4	21.4	361.4	67.5	287.8	—	—

[1] The data for 1942 relate to 31 August. From 1943 to 1954 inclusive, the data apply to 1 April. From 1955 to 1971 inclusive, with the exception of 1957, when the data relate to 1 May, for subsequent years the data apply to 1 June. From 1972 on, data are annual averages.

[2] From 1942 to 1946 forestry and logging, series E154, includes fishing, hunting and trapping, series E155.

[3] Public utility operation included with transportation beginning in 1961.

[4] Claimants, 1964 to 1974, industry attachment not identified.

[5] Unspecified 1971, mainly claimants.

Series E166-171. Unemployment insurance, insured population and beneficiary and claimant data, 1942 to 1976

(thousands)

Year	Insured population (annual average)	Initial and renewal claims (yearly total)	Claimants (annual average)	Benefi- ciaries[1] (annual average)	Weeks compen- sated (yearly total)	Net benefits paid (yearly total) (dollars)
	166	167	168	169	170	171
1976	9,249	2,678	1,006	701	36,190	3,342,247
1975	8,951	2,857	1,049	617[2]	37,327	3,144,022
1974	8,617	2,410	828	..	28,461	2,119,213
1973	8,264	2,238	828	..	29,537	2,004,212
1972	7,845	2,470	804	..	30,461	1,871,802
1971[3]	5,439	2,371	604	..	22,634	890,594
1970	5,426	2,261	540	385	19,817	695,222
1969	5,367	1,855	410	308	15,735	498,992
1968	5,028	1,928	423	313	16,488	438,128
1967	4,753	1,817	367	268	13,852	352,645
1966	4,535	1,548	315	234	12,041	295,301
1965	4,338	1,628	322	254	12,718	312,110
1964	4,260	1,860	357	282	14,017	344,390
1963	4,157	2,038	402	324	16,122	394,163
1962	4,062	2,192	414	340	16,928	409,208
1961	4,043	2,461	487	416	20,735	493,971
1960	4,134	2,700	518.2	430.0	21,601	481,836
1959	4,114	2,428	454.2	384.8	19,170	406,097
1958	4,108	2,781	551.5	459.8	23,152	492,901
1957	3,987	2,373	380.2	295.0	14,572	305,076
1956	3,750	1,625	272.3	218.1	11,177	210,330
1955	3,436	1,930	319.1	261.0	12,389	229,124
1954	3,294	2,102	356.8	270.0	13,124	241,113
1953	3,197	1,680	251.7	168.6	8,718	157,779
1952	3,129	1,391	219.4	139.5	7,257	118,810
1951	3,046	1,144	167.3	100.1	5,222	76,669
1950[4]	2,743	1,150	188.0	127.9	6,988	99,057
1949	2,591	934	149.3	130.3	5,148	65,351
1948	2,436	649	94.7	92.2	3,390	40,268
1947	2,314	443	71.3	70.1	2,756	32,039
1946	2,168	489	97.8	101.3	4,245	51,085
1945	2,148	296	41.1	31.7	1,224	14,576
1944	—	91	10.5	8.6	283	3,277
1943	—	37	—	2.8	85	941
1942	—	27	—	1.4	30	353

[1] Series discontinued in 1970.
[2] Average for the last eight months.
[3] New Unemployment Insurance Commission Act, June 1971. Coverage was extended in January 1972.
[4] Claims data on supplementary (now called seasonal) benefit included as of March 1950. The period during which these benefits were paid varied. In the winter of 1957-58 these benefits were paid in the period 1 December 1957 to 30 June 1958. In subsequent years the dates were 1 December to mid-May.

Series E172-174. Monthly averages of applications, vacancies and placements, by federal employment offices in regular and casual work, 1919 to 1975

Year	Applications	Vacancies	Placements	Year	Applications	Vacancies	Placements
	172	173	174		172	173	174
1975	372,142	117,609	89,013	1945	209,749	201,771	124,465
1974	353,320	141,691[1]	100,417[2]	1944	207,107	227,397	144,993
1973	331,921	128,771[1]	90,767[2]	1943	224,135	253,050	162,002
1972	313,514	111,976[1]	83,216[2]	1942	128,677	115,153	74,635
1971	281,113	89,500[1]	66,751[2]	1941	69,288	45,975	42,314
1970	309,058	74,028[1]	53,497[2]	1940	74,050	42,656	39,592
1969	293,736	89,380[1]	62,231[2]	1939	65,664	33,533	32,073
1968	273,223	84,020[1]	59,141[2]	1938	65,222	33,437	31,858
1967	307,923	119,651	89,295	1937	59,352	34,866	32,461
1966	311,982	128,684	97,194	1936	56,671	29,615	27,621
1965	325,509	136,225	104,810	1935	54,702	31,381	29,483
1964	338,714	130,065	103,423	1934	60,364	35,649	33,841
1963	336,914	120,497	98,176	1933	56,185	30,807	29,341
1962	362,344	129,597	111,313	1932	54,369	30,502	29,351
1961	352,622	108,804	93,322	1931	68,846	40,532	39,292
1960	346,167	94,077	79,858	1930	51,082	32,169	30,723
1959	315,961	97,986	82,173	1929	45,894	35,669	33,197
1958	316,949	82,887	70,011	1928	49,791	42,202	39,194
1957	304,455	93,295	73,142	1927	46,156	37,798	34,564
1956	249,348	118,802	87,248	1926	45,206	38,078	34,180
1955	249,235	102,748	79,465	1925	46,420	37,254	34,402
1954	247,499	90,693	71,799	1924	43,281	34,339	30,511
1953	227,940	107,430	82,784	1923	49,098	45,082	38,546
1952	203,848	109,073	81,709	1922	45,690	39,157	32,793
1951	180,390	110,964	76,520	1921	45,369	35,966	29,646
1950	173,048	97,027	65,900	1920	48,501	47,413	37,320
1949	149,220	85,557	57,015	1919[3]	39,922	41,186	30,387
1948	138,052	98,799	59,362				
1947	135,769	128,065	64,154				
1946	163,225	158,544	71,618				

[1] Vacancies include the vacancies for casual placements except for the period 1 January 1968 to 31 May 1974.

[2] Placements include casual as well as regular placements except for the period 1 January 1968 to 31 May 1974 when casual placements are excluded.

[3] Averages of final 10 months of 1919.

Series E175-177. Union membership in Canada, in total, as a percentage of non-agricultural paid workers, and union members with international affiliation, 1911 to 1975
(thousands)

Year	Total union membership	Percentage of non-agricultural paid workers in union	Membership in unions with international affiliation	Year	Total union membership	Percentage of non-agricultural paid workers in union	Membership in unions with international affiliation
	175	176	177		175	176	177
1975	2,876	36.8	1,479	1940	362	16.3	227
1974	2,726	35.7	1,450	1939	359	17.3	217
1973	2,610	36.3	1,443	1938	382	18.4	231
1972	2,371	34.4	1,412	1937	384	18.2	218
1971	2,211	33.6	1,351	1936	323	16.2	175
1970	2,173	33.6	1,359	1935	281	14.5	144
1969	2,075	32.5	1,346	1934	281	14.6	161
1968	2,010	33.1	1,345	1933	286	16.7	168
1967	1,921	32.3	1,273	1932	283	15.3	176
1966	1,736	30.7	1,220	1931	311	15.3	216
1965	1,589	29.7	1,125	1930	322	13.1	231
1964	1,493	29.4	1,062	1929	320	12.6	230
1963	1,449	29.8	1,032	1928	301	12.1	211
1962	1,423	30.2	1,025	1927	290	12.1	204
1961	1,447	31.6	1,040	1926	275	12.0	203
1960	1,459	32.3	1,052	1925	271	12.3	200
1959	1,459[2]	33.3	1,056	1924	261	12.2	202
1958	1,454	34.2	1,062	1923	278	13.2	204
1957	1,386	32.4	991	1922	277	13.6	206
1956	1,352	33.3	948	1921	313	16.0	223
1955	1,268	33.7	894	1920	374	—	267
1954	1,268	33.8	905	1919	378	—	260
1953	1,220	33.0	851	1918	249	—	201
1952	1,146	30.2	796	1917	205	—	165
1951	1,029[3]	28.4	726	1916	160	—	129
1950	—	—	—	1915	143	—	115
1949	1,006[1]	29.5	713	1914	166	—	141
1948	978	30.3	675	1913	176	—	150
1947	912	29.1	621	1912	160	—	136
1946	832	27.9	573	1911	133	—	119
1945	711	24.2	471				
1944	724	24.3	468				
1943	665	22.7	425				
1942	578	20.6	379				
1941	462	18.0	288				

[1] Includes Newfoundland for the first time.
[2] Approximately 23,000 members added as a result of change in coverage.

[3] Data for 1949 and earlier years apply to 31 December. From 1951 the figures relate to 1 January.

Series E178-189. Union membership by congress affiliation, 1942 to 1975

Year	Canadian Labour Congress			Canadian Congress of Labour			American Federation of Labor only	Congress of Industrial Organizations only	Unaffiliated international unions		Confederation of National Trade Unions	Other congresses and unaffiliated national, regional and local unions[1]
	CLC total	CLC only	CLC/ AFL-CIO	CCL total	CCL only	CCL/CIO			Railway brotherhoods	Other		
	178	179	180	181	182	183	184	185	186	187	188	189
1975	2,052,604	814,588[2,3]	1,238,016[2]	–	–	–	869		84,963		176,824	569,202[3,4]
1974	1,962,207	751,297[5]	1,210,910	–	–	–	556		79,339		169,764	520,077
1973	1,806,205	580,917[6]	1,225,288	–	–	–	619		90,216		211,249[7]	482,679[6,7,8]
1972	1,722,319	538,324	1,183,995[9]	–	–	–	616		96,071		217,578	351,543[9,10]
1971	1,691,530	508,346	1,183,184	–	–	–	537		95,938		226,100	217,138
1970	1,632,253	521,332	1,110,921	–	–	–	549		104,095		207,372[11]	228,838[12]
1969	1,588,651	481,790[13]	1,106,861[13]	–	–	–	604		111,111		207,983	166,267[14]
1968	1,571,514	349,265[15]	1,222,249	–	–	–	678[15]		107,833[15]		201,292	128,416
1967	1,450,619	330,218[16]	1,120,401	–	–	–	15,005		122,899		197,787	134,337
1966	1,282,039	212,031	1,070,008	–	–	–	16,389		118,832		188,401[17]	130,179
1965	1,181,147	198,399	982,748	–	–	–	17,555		118,022		150,053	121,978
1964	1,106,020	197,072	908,948	–	–	–	31,282		109,144		121,540	125,187
1963	1,079,909	197,687	822,222	–	–	–	30,507		106,315		110,577	121,873
1962	1,049,145	188,517[18]	860,628	–	–	–	33,137		118,575		102,186	119,740[18]
1961	1,070,837	196,609[19]	874,228	–	–	–	34,170		116,559[19]		98,457[20]	126,919[20]
1960	1,122,831	234,083[21]	888,748	–	–	–	33,117		9,857	66,434	101,942[22]	124,978
1959	1,153,756	256,646	897,110	–	–	–	18,699[23]		9,808	70,994	97,092	108,227
1958	1,144,120	237,054[24]	907,066[23,25]	–	–	–	18,432		9,608[25]	79,970	104,255	97,615[24]
1957	1,070,129	203,643[26]	866,486[27]	–	–	–	1,184		33,594[23]	81,205	99,372	100,701

Year	Trades and labour congress											
	TLC total	TLC only	TLC/AFL									
1956[28]	640,271	111,467	528,804[29]	377,926	86,836	291,090[29]	1,050[30]		43,877	81,122	101,169	106,237
1955	600,791	107,260	493,531	361,271	96,361	264,910	9,290	2,500	40,307	58,627	99,801	95,620
1954	596,004	100,212	495,792	360,782	92,590	268,192	9,748	2,430	40,922	62,127	100,312	95,586
1953	558,722	97,450	461,272	352,538	101,737	250,801	10,524	3,000	41,751	61,935	104,486	86,758
1952	522,965	91,999	430,966	330,778	102,256	228,522	9,555	2,000	41,385	62,592	89,013	87,833
1951	470,926	80,953	389,973	312,532	107,587	204,945	11,307	1,500[31]	40,459	50,205[31]	86,184	55,408
1950[32]	–	–	–	–	–	–			–	–	–	–
1949	459,068	104,265	354,803	301,729	98,461	203,268[31,33]	13,996	27,475[31]	41,363	25,303[33]	80,089	56,616
1948	439,029	105,782	333,247	338,627	93,771	244,856	9,367	3,777	41,126	2,351	93,370	49,947
1947	403,003	104,590	298,413	329,058	97,100	231,958	6,274	2,174	39,627	2,326	91,026	38,636
1946	356,121	93,582	262,539	314,025	92,912[34]	221,113	9,513	1,680	37,731	2,247	70,367	40,013
1945	312,391	87,687	224,704	244,750	93,268	151,482	6,227	163	37,273	2,669	68,205	39,439
1944	284,732	52,886	231,846	272,146	99,687	172,459	9,516	159	36,147	1,924	74,624	44,940
1943	249,450	39,324	210,126	245,812	105,514	140,298	11,459	3,877	34,590	1,330	68,576	49,439
1942	230,290	32,634	197,656	200,089	84,942	115,147	6,622	2,400	32,984	607	54,556	50,832

[1] Includes the Canadian Council of Unions established in 1969 and the Centrale des syndicats démocratiques established in 1972.

[2] In September 1974 most of the Canadian members of the United Paperworkers International Union (AFL-CIO/CLC) formed a separate entity, the Canadian Paperworkers Union affiliated only with the CLC, with 56,000 members. Ten locals with 3,250 members remained with the international union.

[3] Four provincial government employee associations with 88,171 members ceased to be independents and affiliated with the CLC: the Manitoba Government Employees Association; the Nova Scotia Government Employees Association; the Civil Service Association of Ontario and the Saskatchewan Government Employees Association.

[4] Five independent teacher associations with 38,696 members and two independent nurses associations with 17,484 members are included for the first time in the 1974-1975 report, *Labour Organizations in Canada*. The associations are: The Manitoba Teachers' Society; New Brunswick Teachers' Federation; Northwest Territories Teachers' Association; Quebec Provincial Association of Protestant Teachers; Saskatchewan Teachers' Federation; Nurses Staff Association of Nova Scotia and the Ontario Nurses Association.

[5] Includes for the first time the Newfoundland Association of Public Employees (CLC) with 9,529 members and the Prince Edward Island Public Service Association (CLC) with 2,672 members.

[6] At the end of 1972 the United Electrical, Radio and Machine Workers of America (UE) and the United Fishermen and Allied Workers Union affiliated with the CLC after having been independent unions. Their combined total was approximately 27,000 members.

[7] In 1972 three federations withdrew from the CNTU and are included with other congresses and independent unions: the Fédération Canadienne des travailleurs du textile, 8,372 members and the Fédération nationale de l'industrie du vêtement, 7,886 members, both joined the

Centre des syndicats démocratiques (CSD); and the Syndicat des fonctionnaires provinciaux du Québec, 30,009 members also became independent.

[8] Seven independent teachers associations are included for the first time with a combined membership of 95,779: Alberta Teachers' Association; Newfoundland Teachers' Association; Nova Scotia Teachers' Association; Ontario English Catholic Teachers' Association; Ontario French Teachers' Association; Ontario Secondary School Teachers' Federation; and the Prince Edward Island Teachers' Federation. Also included was the Provincial Staff Nurses' Council, Manitoba, with 2,800 members.

[9] In early 1972 the 11,000 member International Union of District 50 (Ind.) merged with the United Steelworkers (CLC/AFL-CIO).

[10] The following three groups were included as independent unions in 1973 with a combined membership of 78,602: Corporations des enseignants du Québec (Ind.); Alberta Association of Registered Nurses (Ind..) and the Registered Nurses' Association of British Columbia (Ind.).

[11] Includes for the first time the Fédération nationale des enseignants Québécois (CNTU) with 4,500 members.

[12] Includes for the first time independent government employee associations in Alberta, Manitoba, Nova Scotia and Ontario with 58,825 members and the New Brunswick Association of Registered Nurses with 1,814 members.

[13] In 1968 the United Automobile Workers with 113,000 members disaffiliated from the AFL-CIO becoming CLC only.

[14] The New Brunswick Public Employees Association with 4,811 members is included for the first time.

[15] The International Union of Mine, Mill and Smelter Workers, with 13,000 members, merged with the United Steelworkers (CLC/AFL-CIO). The Seafarers' International Union of Canada (AFL-CIO) with 7,500 members reaffiliated with CLC. Membership in the SIU had dropped from 13,500 in 1967 to 7,500 in 1968.

[16] The Public Service Alliance of Canada (PSAC) with 92,835 members affiliated with the CLC on 1 January 1967. Only the Canadian Railway Mail

Clerks' Federation, 616 members in 1966, had previously been included in union membership figures.

17 The Syndicat des fonctionnaires provinciaux du Québec (CNTU) with 25,835 members is included for the first time.

18 Two groups disaffiliated from the CLC to become independent unions: the Amalgamated Lithographers of America, 3,402 members; and the Saskatchewan Civil Service Association, 6,865 members.

19 The International Brotherhood of Teamsters with 40,000 members was expelled from the CLC.

20 In early 1960 the Municipal and School Employees' Federation withdrew from the CNTU but about half the locals chose to remain. Approximately 3,200 left and formed the Centre professionnel des employés de corporations municipales et scolaires (Ind.).

21 Three groups withdrew from the CLC in 1959: the 6,500 member National Unemployment Insurance Commission Association, the 8,500 member Civil Service Association of Alberta and the 1,200 member Newfoundland Government Employees Association. These groups were dropped from the list of union members until 1967, 1970 and 1974 respectively.

22 In 1960 the Canadian and Catholic Federation of Labour changed its name to the Confederation of National Trade Unions (CNTU).

23 Operating Engineers (15,000 members) and Technical Engineers (1,000 members) were expelled from CLC but retained affiliation with AFL-CIO.

24 Amalgamated Civil Servants of Canada (11,000 members) left CLC and joined with CSAO to form CSA of C (independent).

25 Brotherhood of Railroad Trainmen joined CLC/AFL-CIO in 1957.

26 British Columbia Teachers' Federation (8,000 members) left CLC and were dropped from the survey.

27 Brotherhood of Locomotive Firemen joined CLC and AFL-CIO in the United States.

28 On 1 May 1956 the TLC and CCL were merged to form CLC. One big union agreed to affiliate members gradually with CLC.

29 These figures represent TLC/AFL-CIO and CCL/AFL-CIO. The first convention of the merged AFL-CIO was held in December 1955.

30 In 45th Report, *Labour Organization in Canada*, shown in Table 2, p. 15, as affiliated with AFL only as of 1 January 1956. Because AFL had, at that time, merged with CIO, membership shifted to AFL-CIO affiliation.

31 The International Union of Mine, Mill and Smelter Workers, with about 25,000 members, was expelled from the CCL in 1949 and from the CIO in 1950.

32 Data for 1950 not published because of change in dating. For 1949 and earlier years data refer to 31 December; subsequently to 1 January.

33 The United Electrical Radio and Machine Workers of America, with a membership of about 25,000, was expelled from the CIO in the United States and from the CCL in Canada in 1949.

34 In December 1946 the United Mine Workers of America which had been unaffiliated with respect to its United States membership, and affiliated with the CCL with respect to its Canadian membership, became affiliated with the AFL. The union withdrew from the AFL in December 1947. The data do not take this change in United States affiliation into account.

Series E190-197. Number of strikes and lockouts, employers and workers involved and time loss, Canada, 1901 to 1975

Year	Number beginning during the year	Strikes and lockouts in existence during year, all industries						
		Number of strikes and lockouts	Number of employers	Number of workers involved	Time loss			
					In man working days	Average days per non-agricultural paid worker	Average days per worker involved	Per cent of estimated working time
	190	191	192	193	194	195	196	197
1975	1,103	1,171	—	506,443	10,908,810	1.34	21.54	.53
1974	1,173	1,218	—	580,912	9,221,890	1.15	15.87	.46
1973	677	724	—	348,470	5,776,080	.75	16.58	.30
1972	556	598	—	706,474	7,753,530	1.08	10.97	.45
1971	547	569	—	239,631	2,866,570	.41	11.96	.16
1970	503	542	—	261,706	6,559,560	.97	24.98	.39
1969	566	595	—	306,799	7,757,880	1.17	25.26	.46
1968	559	582	—	223,562	5,082,732	.80	22.73	.32
1967	498	522	—	252,018	3,974,760	.64	15.77	.27
1966	582	617	—	411,459	5,178,170	.68	12.58	.34
1965	478	501	—	171,870	2,349,870	.42	13.96	.17
1964	327	343	—	100,535	1,580,550	.29	15.72	.11
1963	318	332	—	83,428	917,140	.18	10.99	.07
1962	290	311	—	74,332	1,417,900	.28	19.07	.11
1961	272	287	—	97,959	1,336,080	.28	13.63	.11
1960	268	274	—	49,408	738,700	.16	14.95	.06
1959	203	218	—	100,127	2,286,900	.49	22.08	.19
1958	253	262	—	112,397	2,872,340	.63	25.55	.24
1957	242	249	—	91,409	1,634,880	.37	17.89	.14
1956	221	229	437	88,680	1,246,000	.29	14.05	.11
1955	149	159	386	60,090	1,875,400	.47	31.21	.18
1954	156	174	872	62,250	1,475,200	.39	23.70	.15
1953	167	174	384	55,988	1,324,720	.34	23.66	.13
1952	216	222	518	120,818	2,879,960	.77	23.84	.29
1951	257	259	646	102,870	901,740	.25	8.77	.08
1950	158	161	345	192,153	1,389,040	.40	7.23	.13
1949	132	137	542	51,437	1,063,670	.32	20.68	.11
1948	147	154	674	42,820	885,790	.27	20.68	.09
1947	232	236	1,173	104,120	2,397,340	.77	23.02	.26
1946	225	228	1,299	139,474	4,516,390	1.49	32.38	.50
1945	196	197	418	96,068	1,457,420	.49	15.17	.17
1944	195	199	400	75,290	490,139	.16	6.51	.06
1943	401	402	651	218,404	1,041,198	.35	4.77	.12
1942	352	354	492	113,916	450,202	.16	3.95	.05
1941	229	231	658	87,091	433,914	.17	4.98	.06
1940	166	168	894	60,619	266,318	.12	4.39	.04
1939	120	122	243	41,038	224,588	.11	5.47	.04
1938	142	147	614	20,395	148,678	.08	7.29	.02
1937	274	278	630	71,905	886,393	.44	12.33	.15
1936	155	156	709	34,812	276,997	.15	7.96	.05
1935	120	120	719	33,269	288,703	.16	8.68	.05
1934	189	191	1,100	45,800	574,519	.33	12.54	.11
1933	122	125	617	26,558	317,547	.20	11.96	.07
1932	111	116	497	23,390	255,000	.15	10.90	.05
1931	86	88	266	10,738	204,238	.10	19.02	.04

Series E190-197. Number of strikes and lockouts, employers and workers involved and time loss, Canada, 1901 to 1975 (concluded)

Year	Number beginning during the year	Strikes and lockouts in existence during year, all industries						
		Number of strikes and lockouts	Number of employers	Number of workers involved	Time loss			
					In man working days	Average days per non-agricultural paid worker	Average days per worker involved	Per cent of estimated working time
	190	191	192	193	194	195	196	197
1930	67	67	338	13,768	91,797	.04	6.67	.01
1929	88	90	263	12,946	152,080	.07	11.75	.02
1928	96	98	548	17,581	224,212	.11	12.75	.04
1927	72	74	480	22,299	152,570	.08	6.84	.03
1926	75	77	512	23,834	266,601	.14	11.19	.05
1925	86	87	497	28,949	1,193,281	.69	41.22	.23
1924	64	70	435	34,310	1,295,054	.76	37.75	.26
1923	77	86	450	34,261	671,750	.39	19.61	.13
1922	89	104	732	43,775	1,528,661	.95	34.92	.32
1921	159	168	1,208	28,257	1,048,914	.66	37.12	.22
1920	310	322	1,374	60,327	799,524	.42	13.25	.14
1919	332	336	1,967	148,915	3,400,942	1.79	22.84	.60
1918	228	230	782	79,743	647,942	–	–	–
1917	158	160	758	50,255	1,123,515	–	–	–
1916	118	120	332	26,538	236,814	–	–	–
1915	62	63	120	11,395	95,042	–	–	–
1914	58	63	261	9,717	490,850	–	–	–
1913	143	152	1,077	40,519	1,036,254	–	–	–
1912	179	181	1,321	42,860	1,135,786	–	–	–
1911	99	100	533	29,285	1,821,084	–	–	–
1910	94	101	1,233	22,203	731,324	–	–	–
1909	88	90	372	18,114	880,663	–	–	–
1908	72	76	179	26,071	703,571	–	–	–
1907	183	188	950	34,060	520,142	–	–	–
1906	149	150	965	23,382	378,276	–	–	–
1905	95	96	332	12,513	246,138	–	–	–
1904	103	103	591	11,420	192,890	–	–	–
1903	171	175	1,124	38,408	858,959	–	–	–
1902	124	125	532	12,709	203,301	–	–	–
1901	97	99	285	24,089	737,808	–	–	–

Series E198-208. Index numbers of average wage rates for selected main industries, 1901 to 1965
(1949 = 100)

Year	General index	Logging	Coal mining	Metal mining	Manufacturing			Con- struction	Railways	Telephones	Personal service
					All manu- facturing	Durable goods	Non-durable goods				
	198	199	200	201	202	203	204	205	206	207	208
1965	210.1	239.0	166.7	195.0	207.0	207.8	206.0	235.2	201.3	212.3	195.4
1964	199.8	219.6	157.4	188.0	197.2	197.6	196.8	223.6	193.8	206.5	182.2
1963	192.5	208.2	155.6	182.0	190.5	190.6	190.4	214.1	185.9	200.2	171.1
1962	185.9	199.4	161.1	177.2	184.5	184.7	184.3	206.2	180.5	195.3	162.2
1961	180.0	190.8	154.5	173.9	179.5	180.3	178.7	196.3	176.5	188.0	158.8
1960	175.5	184.3	148.2	169.4	175.0	176.6	173.2	192.6	166.4	178.0	156.8
1959[1]	168.9	176.2	147.3	164.3	168.9	170.8	167.0	180.7	165.7	–	146.1
1959[2]	169.5	176.5	147.8	165.5	169.9	172.1	167.7	180.7	165.7	178.7	144.9
1958	162.5	172.0	147.6	160.8	164.2	166.1	162.2	171.0	153.3	169.4	143.5
1957	156.5	168.4	137.4	156.2	158.6	160.7	156.3	160.7	153.3	165.9	138.9
1956	148.7	160.8	123.6	150.8	149.8	151.2	148.3	150.7	146.8	157.6	136.1
1955	141.7	138.2	122.8	140.3	142.2	143.7	140.7	145.4	137.8	152.8	132.3
1954	137.9	138.0	123.5	136.7	138.5	140.0	136.9	140.0	137.8	147.6	128.6
1953	133.6	135.5	124.0	132.3	134.6	136.3	132.8	136.2	137.2	136.6	123.3
1952	127.7	133.3	124.0	130.1	128.4	130.2	126.5	128.6	136.8	128.4	117.6
1951	119.1	109.6	111.1	121.6	120.3	121.7	118.8	118.6	121.9	115.7	110.6
1950	105.5	97.0	102.8	106.8	106.1	106.6	105.6	104.8	105.1	104.8	102.9
1949	100.0	100.0	100.0	100.0	100.0	100.0	100.0	100.0	100.0	100.0	100.0
1948	95.7	101.2	98.4	95.7	94.5	94.7	94.4	95.7	100.0	92.7	92.7
1947	84.9	90.2	85.0	87.2	84.1	84.9	83.5	84.1	83.6	87.3	87.4
1946	75.9	77.4	74.8	75.1	74.1	74.5	73.8	78.1	82.0	82.6	75.6
1945	69.3	70.9	74.6	70.9	67.2	68.2	66.5	71.2	73.7	82.9	69.4
1944	67.4	67.6	74.5	69.2	64.9	65.6	64.4	70.4	73.7	80.8	66.1
1943	65.3	66.2	63.6	68.1	62.8	63.6	62.1	69.3	73.7	80.5	65.3
1942	59.9	58.2	57.7	65.7	57.6	57.7	57.5	64.4	67.5	73.9	59.7
1941	55.3	52.7	55.8	62.1	52.9	52.0	53.6	60.6	64.3	70.2	56.7

Series E198-208. Index numbers of average wage rates for selected main industries, 1901 to 1965 (concluded)
(1949 = 100)

Year	General index	Logging	Coal mining	Metal mining	Manufacturing			Con-struction	Railways	Telephones	Personal service
					All manu-facturing	Durable goods	Non-durable goods				
	198	199	200	201	202	203	204	205	206	207	208
1940	50.8	48.5	52.1	56.9	47.9	46.6	48.8	56.7	58.8	66.9	54.1
1939	48.9	46.3	51.0	55.3	45.9	45.1	46.5	54.3	58.8	66.0	51.3
1938	48.7	47.1	51.0	55.1	45.5	–	–	53.9	58.8	65.8	51.1
1937	47.3	43.4	48.8	54.8	44.1	–	–	52.6	56.4	65.0	50.4
1936	44.0	37.4	48.5	52.5	40.9	–	–	51.1	52.9	61.9	49.8
1935	43.2	33.8	48.4	51.2	39.9	–	–	50.8	52.9	61.4	49.5
1934	42.0	30.4	47.6	50.3	39.1	–	–	49.2	51.8	61.8	49.3
1933	41.6	26.5	47.3	49.0	38.0	–	–	50.2	51.7	58.0	49.7
1932	43.8	31.0	48.0	49.6	39.9	–	–	56.7	52.9	58.5	50.8
1931	47.2	37.7	49.5	51.2	42.7	–	–	62.3	57.3	62.7	52.1
1930	48.8	45.1	49.5	51.9	43.8	–	–	64.7	58.8	62.5	52.3
1929	48.5	45.7	49.4	51.9	43.8	–	–	62.9	58.8	62.2	52.2
1928	47.7	45.8	49.4	51.5	43.5	–	–	59.0	57.1	61.5	52.1
1927	47.1	45.2	49.1	51.6	43.2	–	–	57.0	57.1	60.3	51.7
1926	46.1	44.2	49.0	51.5	42.6	–	–	54.8	53.6	59.2	51.2
1925	45.8	44.0	49.0	51.6	42.4	–	–	54.2	53.6	58.8	50.8
1924	46.3	49.0	56.2	50.9	42.8	–	–	54.0	53.6	58.7	51.2
1923	45.7	43.2	57.8	50.8	42.5	–	–	52.9	53.6	58.5	51.1
1922	44.5	36.8	57.8	48.7	40.9	–	–	51.7	53.1	57.6	50.4
1921	47.7	47.3	60.9	52.7	43.8	–	–	54.2	56.3	60.6	49.9
1920	52.3	65.9	57.8	56.9	47.0	–	–	57.5	63.6	60.9	45.2
1919	44.0	58.9	49.9	48.9	39.0	–	–	47.1	52.9	–	38.5
1918	37.4	51.0	46.1	48.7	31.8	–	–	40.1	45.4	–	33.6
1917	31.9	44.3	38.2	44.9	27.7	–	–	35.0	35.8	–	29.1
1916	27.8	33.8	32.6	40.5	24.9	–	–	32.6	30.4	–	26.0
1915	26.0	28.3	29.9	36.6	23.0	–	–	32.2	29.3	–	24.4
1914	25.8	29.7	29.8	36.2	22.3	–	–	32.1	29.0	–	25.2
1913	25.5	31.8	29.2	36.1	21.7	–	–	31.8	28.8	–	24.1
1912	24.8	31.3	28.8	36.7	21.0	–	–	30.5	28.1	–	–
1911	24.0	30.3	28.5	34.9	20.7	–	–	28.7	27.6	–	–
1910	24.4	29.6	27.5	34.6	–	–	–	27.6	25.9	–	–
1909	23.6	28.6	27.8	35.0	–	–	–	26.4	24.9	–	–
1908	23.2	27.1	27.7	34.6	–	–	–	25.9	24.8	–	–
1907	22.6	27.9	27.3	34.1	–	–	–	25.5	23.3	–	–
1906	21.9	27.5	25.5	34.6	–	–	–	24.4	22.9	–	–
1905	21.1	26.4	25.2	32.5	–	–	–	23.2	21.4	–	–
1904	20.7	25.3	24.9	32.1	–	–	–	22.2	22.1	–	–
1903	20.2	24.9	24.9	32.9	–	–	–	21.4	21.6	–	–
1902	19.6	24.3	24.5	34.1	–	–	–	20.5	20.7	–	–
1901	18.6	23.8	24.2	33.8	–	–	–	19.2	19.8	–	–

[1] Expanded survey coverage.   [2] 1958 survey coverage.

Series E209-219. Index numbers of average wage rates for selected main industries, 1961 to 1972
(1961 = 100)

Year	General index	Logging	Mining	Manufacturing			Con-struction	Trans-portation, communi-cation and other utilities	Trade	Service	Local government
				All manu-facturing	Durable goods	Non-durable goods					
	209	210	211	212	213	214	215	216	217	218	219
1972	197.4	226.1	190.1	190.8	190.1	191.5	239.9	196.6	195.7	191.7	217.2
1971	182.3	212.3	169.9	176.3	175.7	176.9	223.7	183.8	178.9	178.0	200.2
1970	167.8	192.8	159.4	162.9	162.3	163.2	195.5	166.2	166.1	166.4	183.3
1969	155.1	179.8	146.2	151.2	149.7	152.5	167.0	154.9	155.2	154.0	163.4
1968	143.8	162.5	138.9	140.6	139.7	141.4	154.9	143.4	144.5	141.8	146.7
1967	133.4	156.0	130.2	130.5	130.0	131.0	142.0	132.8	132.5	133.9	136.9
1966	124.0	140.2	122.7	121.6	121.2	121.9	129.8	122.3	123.9	125.5	124.6
1965	116.5	126.4	113.3	115.0	114.4	115.5	119.8	114.3	116.9	118.4	118.1
1964	110.9	117.5	109.6	109.7	108.9	110.5	113.9	109.8	111.0	111.7	111.5
1963	107.0	110.1	107.0	106.0	105.1	106.7	109.1	106.0	107.9	106.6	107.4
1962	103.1	103.9	104.0	102.7	102.1	103.3	105.0	103.1	103.5	101.9	103.3
1961	100.0	100.0	100.0	100.0	100.0	100.0	100.0	100.0	100.0	100.0	100.0

Series E220-247. Index numbers of average wage rates for industry groups and selected components in manufacturing, Canada, 1939 to 1972

| Year | Food and beverages | | | Tobacco, cigars and cigarettes | Rubber products | Leather products | Textile products (except clothing) | | | Clothing (textile and fur) | | |
| | All | Slaughtering and meat packing | Breweries | | | | All | Cotton yarn and cloth | Synthetic and silk textiles | All | Men's and boys' suits and overcoats | Women's and misses' coats and suits |
	220	221	222	223	224	225	226	227	228	229	230	231
						Base 1961 = 100						
1972	197.2	187.5	203.1	215.2	190.1	192.0	196.4	—	194.9	179.3	186.1	165.6
1971	183.0	173.2	185.2	206.1	173.9	177.3	178.1	—	175.5	165.5	170.0	153.9
1970	168.7	160.1	164.5	188.9	161.5	166.2	169.0	—	166.7	152.2	156.7	141.6
1969	158.1	148.5	154.0	169.0	151.5	158.5	155.0	154.6	152.7	145.0	150.3	135.4
1968	145.2	137.9	135.6	156.4	140.4	147.5	143.4	142.0	144.3	135.7	137.9	128.2
1967	132.9	132.2	126.4	140.8	128.7	137.4	136.1	136.7	136.8	124.4	127.2	115.9
1966	121.1	111.9	120.2	133.4	120.5	127.5	125.9	128.2	124.3	118.7	123.1	108.3
1965	115.0	110.5	113.7	127.7	115.2	120.3	116.0	116.6	116.2	115.6	117.6	111.2
1964	109.9	106.4	109.5	123.5	109.4	114.5	111.9	112.6	112.1	110.7	110.0	110.8
1963	105.9	104.4	105.3	118.9	106.1	108.5	106.4	106.2	106.8	107.6	107.3	107.8
1962	102.7	102.7	101.8	105.6	102.0	104.3	104.5	104.4	104.7	102.5	101.2	103.3
1961	100.0	100.0	100.0	100.0	100.0	100.0	100.0	100.0	100.0	100.0	100.0	100.0
						Base 1949 = 100						
1965	208.0	204.7	247.4	260.8	191.3	198.1	189.8	192.3	185.9	187.0	201.1	169.6
1964	198.8	197.7	238.1	248.7	180.1	189.4	183.5	185.6	180.7	177.7	189.6	164.2
1963	191.4	193.8	228.9	240.5	177.0	180.2	174.7	175.1	172.6	172.9	186.9	162.9
1962	185.9	192.7	221.7	216.6	169.1	173.7	170.6	171.9	166.7	164.8	174.4	156.7
1961	181.3	187.3	217.7	207.1	167.0	167.3	163.1	164.8	157.0	161.5	169.0	151.1
1960	176.4	181.6	207.8	198.0	164.3	164.0	157.6	160.2	151.1	156.2	161.3	149.5
1959[1]	170.5	176.5	198.1	193.3	159.7	159.4	150.3	150.3	145.1	152.5	155.2	150.8
1959[2]	170.8	178.8	198.1	193.3	160.2	161.6	151.3	151.0	145.4	153.4	155.8	148.7
1958	164.8	169.7	188.1	184.4	153.2	155.2	146.4	145.8	140.3	149.1	153.1	138.8
1957	156.7	161.4	181.3	174.6	150.4	151.5	141.6	143.0	133.8	144.0	148.3	135.6
1956	147.9	151.2	168.6	164.8	145.0	143.8	135.7	138.6	128.1	136.4	143.4	126.7
1955	140.3	144.2	157.9	160.3	139.6	134.5	131.0	131.5	125.3	129.7	133.3	125.2
1954	135.5	138.5	152.9	155.0	138.1	133.1	129.5	129.5	125.4	126.8	130.8	119.5
1953	131.2	136.3	148.1	152.0	134.9	129.9	128.1	128.7	124.3	124.9	130.0	110.9
1952	125.1	129.6	131.9	141.0	127.4	123.2	125.0	127.5	120.1	119.6	124.9	110.8
1951	117.5	125.4	117.7	135.1	124.3	115.3	117.6	117.1	115.7	112.8	116.9	101.0
1950	104.6	106.1	105.2	109.6	105.4	103.7	106.7	106.1	107.7	103.5	104.0	98.4
1949	100.0	100.0	100.0	100.0	100.0	100.0	100.0	100.0	100.0	100.0	100.0	100.0
						Base 1939 = 100						
1952	—	299.0	267.4	351.0	277.0	279.0	—	312.4	305.7	—	257.3	226.9
1951	—	289.4	236.5	340.8	269.3	260.8	—	288.1	294.2	—	241.5	204.2
1950	—	245.2	210.4	281.8	228.8	235.4	—	262.0	256.2	—	216.0	203.8
1949	—	231.3	199.7	253.9	217.6	228.1	—	248.6	248.4	—	207.0	210.8
1948	—	217.0	182.9	232.2	213.7	219.3	—	230.6	218.2	—	214.8	206.3
1947	—	189.1	160.7	186.4	190.1	198.5	—	189.0	186.8	—	203.0	186.2
1946	—	165.4	148.4	156.9	167.7	167.5	—	161.6	164.7	—	182.1	176.2
1945	—	141.0	127.9	140.5	143.4	153.5	—	148.7	148.9	—	164.1	152.7
1944	—	137.3	123.5	140.3	139.8	145.4	—	139.1	147.0	—	151.9	137.5
1943	—	135.1	121.9	131.5	134.4	142.9	—	136.6	141.3	—	146.6	134.5
1942	—	119.0	117.1	120.4	127.1	134.8	—	128.1	129.0	—	129.8	131.8
1941	—	112.7	113.3	113.0	117.1	122.5	—	123.8	122.9	—	117.9	126.9
1940	—	103.2	103.9	102.8	102.1	105.9	—	109.6	106.8	—	107.2	101.7
1939	—	100.0	100.0	100.0	100.0	100.0	—	100.0	100.0	—	100.0	100.0

Series E220-247. Index numbers of average wage rates for industry groups and selected components in manufacturing, Canada, 1939 to 1972 (concluded)

Year	Wood products	Paper products			Printing and publishing	Primary metal	Metal fabricating	Machinery	Transportation equipment			Brass and copper products	Electrical apparatus and supplies	Clay products	Petroleum refining and products	Chemical products
		All	Newsprint	Boxes and containers					All	Motor vehicles	Aircraft and parts					
	232	233	234	235	236	237	238	239	240	241	242	243	244	245	246	247
Base 1961 = 100																
1972	211.2	191.5	183.6	186.4	186.1	182.8	190.9	187.2	193.5	202.9	190.5	..	170.4	..	188.8	191.8
1971	191.4	177.2	169.0	174.0	169.7	165.8	176.8	173.0	179.5	189.1	174.3	..	163.4	..	175.4	179.9
1970	174.5	162.0	155.8	160.5	156.6	154.5	162.7	163.3	164.2	170.7	162.3	..	151.0	..	162.0	166.7
1969	161.2	150.9	144.6	151.4	145.9	135.1	151.9	151.8	152.8	156.0	154.0	..	141.7	..	146.2	152.6
1968	149.3	139.9	135.0	139.6	136.4	128.5	140.4	140.5	142.1	145.4	142.0	..	133.8	..	139.3	140.9
1967	137.3	132.4	128.0	128.8	127.5	123.1	131.2	131.0	131.7	134.6	129.7	..	123.4	..	131.4	131.1
1966	127.4	122.4	118.8	120.3	121.5	116.5	125.0	122.7	122.5	126.7	121.6	..	112.3	..	123.1	121.9
1965	119.5	113.9	110.0	114.1	117.0	114.8	115.7	114.9	115.4	118.7	116.1	..	105.9	..	112.6	113.2
1964	113.2	107.7	104.9	108.2	111.8	109.3	109.3	109.5	109.6	111.3	110.0	..	102.7	..	109.8	109.3
1963	107.4	105.3	104.1	105.8	107.5	105.9	104.9	107.4	106.0	106.8	105.7	..	99.2	..	106.8	106.0
1962	103.4	103.3	103.3	103.1	105.1	103.6	101.7	103.1	102.7	102.1	103.6	..	98.2	..	103.6	101.8
1961	100.0	100.0	100.0	100.0	100.0	100.0	100.0	100.0	100.0	100.0	100.0	..	100.0	..	100.0	100.0
Base 1949 = 100																
1965	200.0	219.7	213.8	207.2	218.9		213.1		211.1	210.4	224.1	..	200.7	..	221.2	220.1
1964	189.0	207.2	203.8	195.4	209.1		203.1		199.4	196.5	210.2	..	194.2	..	217.0	212.5
1963	180.2	203.7	201.6	191.4	201.2		198.6		191.4	188.2	203.0	..	187.5	..	209.6	207.1
1962	173.0	201.0	199.5	186.8	195.2		192.7		185.1	179.9	198.1	..	180.3	..	203.2	199.7
1961	168.8	194.8	193.3	181.9	186.9		187.9		179.8	176.2	192.7	..	176.2	..	196.1	195.7
1960	165.8	187.2	186.1	177.5	181.3		182.9		176.3	170.6	188.8	184.4	172.3	183.7	194.3	189.0
1959[1]	160.0	178.7	177.4	169.4	173.7		176.0		171.9	163.9	182.7	177.6	166.5	177.0	185.2	182.1
1959[2]	161.3	179.1	177.4	171.0	174.2		176.6		172.8	164.1	182.8	179.1	170.9	178.0	185.2	183.0
1958	155.6	175.4	173.4	167.3	166.3		170.9		165.1	156.6	178.4	175.3	166.2	173.5	178.4	177.3
1957	152.6	171.6	170.8	158.3	159.5		165.2		158.8	152.6	169.9	166.0	160.2	170.7	176.1	169.4
1956	142.9	162.7	162.7	149.3	152.5		156.4		149.9	142.7	163.6	153.7	149.9	161.0	164.0	160.2
1955	136.4	151.7	151.8	142.0	146.9		148.0		142.3	134.1	158.3	149.4	142.8	149.2	154.0	150.3
1954	132.6	145.5	144.4	138.2	142.8		143.3		140.0	130.0	154.2	145.4	139.5	144.7	147.5	146.2
1953	131.4	138.4	138.5	131.0	137.3		139.9		134.5	129.8	141.8	142.9	134.6	138.6	143.4	139.6
1952	128.4	129.9	128.8	126.2	130.0		133.7		128.3	125.7	133.9	132.2	130.1	126.1	137.6	133.1
1951	120.5	126.3	126.5	116.6	117.2		124.8		118.6	116.0	119.1	123.6	122.1	121.4	124.9	121.5
1950	107.1	105.6	105.3	102.3	108.1		107.3		104.9	105.2	105.8	109.9	106.1	105.7	107.2	107.9
1949	100.0	100.0	100.0	100.0	100.0		100.0		100.0	100.0	100.0	100.0	100.0	100.0	100.0	100.0
Base 1939 = 100																
1952	307.8	—	224.7	275.7	227.6	—	—		—	207.6	227.7	—	298.5	—	—	—
1951	293.2	—	220.4	259.7	204.9	—	—		—	191.9	212.1	—	281.6	—	—	—
1950	257.6	—	183.5	234.8	188.1	—	—		—	174.3	192.9	—	253.0	—	—	—
1949	238.8	—	175.6	223.4	173.9	—	—		—	165.9	181.8	—	239.6	—	—	—
1948	226.2	—	174.3	202.3	158.2	—	—		—	163.1	173.3	—	225.6	—	—	—
1947	205.2	—	158.4	175.8	138.9	—	—		—	151.1	162.9	—	195.5	—	—	—
1946	178.3	—	137.3	151.6	127.3	—	—		—	140.4	154.6	—	169.1	—	—	—
1945	156.1	—	120.9	138.5	118.5	—	—		—	130.3	148.7	—	156.8	—	—	—
1944	148.2	—	119.6	133.1	116.3	—	—		—	126.3	138.7	—	154.1	—	—	—
1943	142.9	—	115.4	128.9	113.7	—	—		—	122.7	134.0	—	149.2	—	—	—
1942	131.0	—	109.6	123.9	110.0	—	—		—	115.8	122.7	—	133.7	—	—	—
1941	117.7	—	107.7	115.5	105.8	—	—		—	108.6	109.5	—	123.2	—	—	—
1940	104.4	—	103.7	102.9	101.7	—	—		—	100.6	99.0	—	105.6	—	—	—
1939	100.0	—	100.0	100.0	100.0	—	—		—	100.0	100.0	—	100.0	—	—	—

[1] Expanded survey coverage.   [2] 1958 survey coverage.

Series E248-267. Hourly wage rates in selected building trades, by city, 1901 to 1974
(dollars)

Year	Halifax				Montreal				Toronto			
	Carpenter	Electrician	Plumber	Labourer	Carpenter	Electrician	Plumber	Labourer	Carpenter	Electrician	Plumber	Labourer
	248	249	250	251	252	253	254	255	256	257	258	259
1974	5.81	6.53	6.50	5.05	6.30	6.54	6.54	5.39	–	8.90	8.44	6.15
1973	5.31	5.98	5.26	4.55	5.80	6.24	6.24	4.89	7.55	8.39	7.89	5.80
1972	4.65	5.41	5.26	3.90	5.29	5.73	5.73	4.38	6.98	7.80	7.49	5.20
1971	4.10	4.97	4.86	3.35	5.04	5.48	5.48	4.13	6.32	7.00	6.81	4.55
1970	3.70	3.88	4.46	2.95	4.84	5.28	5.28	3.93	5.40	6.20	6.15	3.90
1969	3.35	3.78	4.26	2.60	4.37	4.80	4.80	3.87	4.75	5.40	5.37	3.50
1968	3.05	3.48	3.65	2.35	4.14	4.55	4.55	3.32	4.15	4.70	4.67	3.10
1967	2.80	3.08	3.25	2.15	3.89	4.25	4.25	3.12	3.90	4.40	4.37	2.95
1966	2.54	2.78	2.86	1.91	3.39	3.65	3.35	2.95	3.68	4.40	4.16	2.70
1965	2.42	2.65	2.72	1.81	2.91	3.20	3.25	2.26	3.38	4.10	4.00	2.40
1964	2.32	2.53	2.60	1.73	2.73	3.00	3.05	2.11	3.30	3.88	3.69	2.35
1963	2.22	2.43	2.46	1.65	2.60	2.70	2.87	2.00	3.25	3.78	3.59	2.25
1962	2.15	2.35	2.42	1.58	2.55	2.70	2.82	1.95	3.10	3.68	3.56	2.15
1961	2.02	2.35	2.21	1.45	2.35	2.55	2.62	1.75	2.95	3.60	3.51	2.00
1960	2.02	2.27	2.21	1.45	2.35	2.45	2.62	1.75	2.90	3.40	3.41	2.00
1959	1.95	2.06	2.11	1.41	2.20	2.35	2.47	1.60	2.80	3.30	3.14	1.80
1958	1.91	2.01	2.02	1.37	2.10	2.20	2.32	1.50	2.50	3.00	2.79	1.70
1957	1.84	1.94	1.93	1.33	2.00	2.00	2.22	1.40	2.50	2.80	2.44	1.55
1956	1.77	1.87	1.86	1.26	1.90	2.00	2.12	1.30	2.40	2.65	2.44	1.45
1955	1.69	1.79	1.78	1.18	1.90	2.00	2.12	1.30	2.30	2.50	2.35	1.30
1954	1.61	1.71	1.70	1.10	1.80	1.90	2.00	1.25	2.25	2.43	2.35	1.25
1953	1.56	1.66	1.65	1.10	1.80	1.85	2.00	1.25	2.20	2.33	2.30	1.20
1952	1.48	1.58	1.55	1.06	1.70	1.80	1.79	1.15	2.10	2.20	2.15	1.10
1951	1.33	1.43	1.40	.91	1.55	1.65	1.70	1.00	2.00	2.15	2.00	1.10
1950	1.23	1.33	1.30	.81	1.40	1.50	1.58	.85	1.75	1.85	1.85	.95
1949	1.23	1.33	1.30	.81	1.25	1.35	1.55	.80	1.60	1.75	1.75	.95
1948	1.23	1.33	1.30	.75	1.25	1.35	1.45	.80	1.50	1.65	1.60	.85
1947	1.11	1.23	1.19	.64	1.06	1.11	1.15	.67	1.35	1.45	1.48	.78[1]
1946	1.05	1.17	1.13	.60	1.06	1.11	1.11	.67	1.20	1.35	1.30	.67
1945	.95	1.06	1.03	.52	.96	1.01	1.01	.61	1.11	1.21	1.17	.67
1944	.95	1.06	1.03	.53[1]	.95	1.00	1.00	.60	1.07	1.17	1.17	.66
1943	.85	1.05	1.03	.53[1]	.95	1.00	1.00	.60	1.05	1.16[1]	1.16	.62
1942	.80	1.00	.95	.43[1]	.86	.92	1.00	.51	1.03	1.15	1.15	.62
1941	.80	1.00	.95	.38[1]	.81	.87	.90	.46	1.00	1.10	1.10	.45[1]
1940	.70	.95	.95	.35[1]	.77	.83	.85	.44	.95	1.10	1.00	.45[1]
1939	.70	.85	.85	.35[1]	.70	.75	.75	.40	.90	1.00	1.00	.43[1]
1938	.65	.85	.85	.35[1]	.70	.75	.75	.40	.95	1.00	1.00	.43[1]
1937	.60	.80	.75	.35[1]	.70	.75	.75	.40	.85	1.00	.90	.43[1]
1936	.60	.80	.75	.35[1]	.65[1]	.68[1]	.70[1]	.38[1]	.80	1.00	.90	.50
1935	.58[1]	.80	.75	.35[1]	.65[1]	.68[1]	.70[1]	.35[1]	.80	1.00	.90	.50
1934	.55	.80	.75	.35[1]	.45[1]	.58[1]	.63[1]	.28[1]	.70[1]	.93[1]	.85	.45[1]
1933	.55	.80	.78[1]	.35[1]	.48[1]	.65	.63[1]	.28[1]	.70[1]	1.00	.85	.43[1]
1932	.68	.85	.85	.38[1]	.68[1]	.75	.75	.35	.90	1.00	1.00	.40[1]
1931	.73	1.00	1.00	.38[1]	.70[1]	.83[1]	.90	.35	1.10	1.25	1.25	.50[1]
1930	.73	.90	.90	.40[1]	.80[1]	.83[1]	.90	.40[1]	1.10	1.25	1.25	.53[1]
1929	.73	.80	.85	.40	.83[1]	.75[1]	.85	.38[1]	1.00	1.15	1.25	.53[1]
1928	.66	.70	.70	.35	.73[1]	.70[1]	.85	.35[1]	1.00	1.00	1.13	.53[1]
1927	.60	.60	.65	.35	.70[1]	.70[1]	.73[1]	.35[1]	.90	.90	1.00	.50[1]
1926	.57	.60	.60	.30[1]	.70[1]	.65[1]	.75[1]	.35[1]	.85[1]	.80	1.00	.50[1]
1925	.57	.60	.60	.33[1]	.70[1]	.65[1]	.73[1]	.35[1]	.85[1]	.80	1.00	.50[1]
1924	.57	.60	.60	.33[1]	.70[1]	.68[1]	.70[1]	.38[1]	.85[1]	.80	1.00	.53[1]
1923	.57	.60	.60	.33[1]	.66[1]	.68[1]	.70[1]	.40[1]	.88[1]	.80	.90	.53[1]
1922	.57	.60	.60	.33[1]	.58[1]	.58[1]	.70[1]	.33[1]	.80[1]	.80	.90	.53[1]
1921	.66	.70	.70	.38[1]	.65[1]	.63[1]	.70[1]	.35[1]	.90	.88	.90	.55[1]
1920	.66	.70	.70	.43[1]	.68	.73[1]	.75[1]	.45	.90	.88	.90	.60[1]
1919	.66	.70	.70	.45	.60	.70	.55	.40	.73[1]	.75	.70[1]	.50
1918	.50	.50	.55	.40	.50	.45[1]	.43	.35	.63[1]	.68	.65	.45
1917	.40	.38	.40	.25	.50	.43[1]	.43	.30	.55	.55[1]	.50	.40
1916	.40	.38	.40	.25	.45	.40	.43	.30	.45	.48[1]	.48	.35
1915	.40	.38	.40	.25	.45	.40	.43	.30	.45	.40	.45	.30
1914	.35	.35	.39	.25	.45	.40	.43	.30	.45	.40	.45	.30
1913	.35	.35	.35	.25	.42	.35	.40	.30	.45	.40	.45	.30
1912	.34[1]	.30	.35	.22	.40	.30	.38	.28	.40	.40	.40	.28
1911	.30	.26[1]	.30	.20	.35	.28	.35	.25	.37	.40	.40	.28
1910	.30	.26[1]	.30	.20	.30	.28	.35	.22	.35	.35	.40	.28
1909	.27	.25	.25	.20	.29[1]	.28	.33	.22	.33	.33	.40	.25
1908	.26[1]	.25	.25	.20	.28	.28	.32	.22	.33	.33	.38	.25
1907	.26[1]	.20[1]	.25	.17	.28	.25	.32	.20	.33	.33	.38	.25
1906	.25	.19[1]	.25	.17	.28	.22	.30	.20	.33	.33	.38	25
1905	.25	.20[1]	.22	.17	.28	.22	.25	.20	.33	.28	.35	.25
1904	.24[1]	.19[1]	.22	.17	.23	.22	.25	.20	.30	.25	.33	.25
1903	.24[1]	.20	.22	.15	.23	.20	.25	.18	.30	.25	.32	.25
1902	.22	.19	.22	.15	.20	.20	.25	.18	.30	.25	.30	.25
1901	.22	.15	.22	.14	.18	.17	.19	.15	.25	.23[1]	.28	.23

Series E248-267. Hourly wage rates in selected building trades, by city, 1901 to 1974 (continued)
(dollars)

Year	Winnipeg Carpenter	Electrician	Plumber	Labourer	Vancouver Carpenter	Electrician	Plumber	Labourer
	260	261	262	263	264	265	266	267
1974	6.40	7.05	7.20	5.00	7.97	8.62	8.34	6.71
1973	5.85	6.50	6.65	4.60	7.00	7.78	7.49	5.54
1972	5.40	5.80	6.05	4.15	6.68	7.46	7.27	5.24
1971	5.00	5.00	5.50	3.75	6.06	6.80	6.50	4.79
1970	4.60	4.80	5.00	3.35	5.50	6.35	6.20	4.07
1969	4.10	4.40	4.40	3.00	4.88	5.45	5.34	4.07
1968	3.75	4.05	3.76	2.65	4.38	5.20	4.18	3.69
1967	3.35	3.70	3.57	2.40	4.14	4.75	3.99	3.24
1966	3.05	3.40	3.39	2.10	3.69	4.34	3.81	2.94
1965	2.80	3.00	3.25	1.95	3.49	3.97	3.59	2.67
1964	2.60	3.00	3.10	1.65	3.34	3.80	3.47	2.47
1963	2.60	2.90	2.95	1.65	3.14	3.53	3.39	2.37
1962	2.60	2.80	2.90	1.65	3.02	3.43	3.24	2.19
1961	2.50	2.80	2.80	1.65	2.92	3.26	3.14	2.19
1960	2.50	2.75	2.80	1.65	2.92	3.26	3.14	2.19
1959	2.40	2.65	2.70	1.55	2.80	3.10	2.90	2.07
1958	2.30	2.55	2.60	1.45	2.68	3.10	2.90	1.95
1957	2.15	2.35	2.40	1.30	2.44	2.81	2.70	1.81
1956	2.05	2.20	2.25	1.20	2.25	2.42	2.55	1.66
1955	2.10	2.10	2.15	1.10	2.22	2.42	2.35	1.63
1954	1.90	1.90	2.00	1.05	2.22	2.38	2.35	1.60
1953	1.90	1.90	2.00	1.05	2.17	2.30	2.25	1.55
1952	1.80	1.90	1.90	.95	2.00	2.10	2.10	1.50
1951	1.65	1.65	1.75	.88	2.00	1.95	2.10	1.40
1950	1.50	1.50	1.65	.80	1.68	1.78	1.75	1.20
1949	1.40	1.40	1.55	.75	1.60	1.70	1.70	1.00
1948	1.35	1.35	1.50	.75	1.55	1.70	1.65	1.00
1947	1.25	1.25	1.35	.70	1.40	1.50	1.50	.90
1946	1.15	1.15	1.25	.63	1.25	1.35	1.35	.80
1945	1.05	1.05	1.15	.63	1.12	1.19	1.19	.71
1944	1.00	1.03	1.10	.59[1]	1.12	1.19	1.19	.73[1]
1943	1.00	1.03	1.10	.53[1]	1.12	1.17[1]	1.19	.68[1]
1942	1.00	.95	1.10	.48[1]	.99	1.09[1]	1.13	.59
1941	.95	.95	1.05	.48[1]	.86[1]	.98[1]	1.13	.50[1]
1940	.85	.85	.95	.47[1]	.83[1]	.93[1]	1.00	.48[1]
1939	.85	.85	.95	.43[1]	.83[1]	.88[1]	1.00	.48[1]
1938	.85	.85	.95	.43	.83[1]	.88[1]	1.00	.48[1]
1937	.85	.85	.95	.43	.76[1]	.88[1]	1.00	.48[1]
1936	.75	.85	.90	.40[1]	.71[1]	.88[1]	1.00	.48[1]
1935	.75	.85	.90	.40[1]	.71[1]	.88[1]	1.00	.48[1]
1934	.75	.88[1]	.90	.40[1]	.75[1]	.88[1]	.88[1]	.43[1]
1933	.75	.95[1]	1.00	.38[1]	.76[1]	.88[1]	.95[1]	.43[1]
1932	1.00	1.00	1.15	.45[1]	.88	1.00	1.00	.45[1]
1931	1.00	1.00	1.15	.45[1]	1.00	1.09[1]	1.13	.50
1930	1.10	1.10	1.25	.46[1]	1.00	1.09[1]	1.25	.56[1]
1929	1.10	1.10	1.20	.46[1]	1.00	1.13	1.19	.50
1928	1.05	1.00	1.13	.45[1]	1.00	1.00	1.13	.56[1]
1927	1.00	1.00	1.13	.45[1]	.94	1.00	1.13	.56[1]
1926	1.00	1.00	1.13	.45[1]	.94	.95[1]	1.05	.51[1]
1925	.85	.85	1.00	.43[1]	.88	.88[1]	1.00	.51[1]
1924	.85	.85	1.00	.45[1]	.84[1]	.88[1]	1.00	.51[1]
1923	.85	.81[1]	.95[1]	.45[1]	.81	.88[1]	1.00	.51[1]
1922	.85	.81[1]	.90	.45[1]	.81	.83[1]	.95[1]	.48[1]
1921	.90	.90	1.00	.53[1]	.81	.83[1]	.90	.56[1]
1920	1.00	.93	1.00	.58[1]	.89[1]	1.00	1.00	.63[1]
1919	.75	.75	.80	.50	.75	.75	.78	.55[1]
1918	.60	.70	.65	.38[1]	.70	.75	.75	.47
1917	.55	.65	.59[1]	.35	.51[1]	.63	.63	.31
1916	.50	.65	.55	.30	.45	.62	.56	.31
1915	.48[1]	.65	.55	.28	.45	.63	.63	.31
1914	.48[1]	.45	.55	.28	.53	.63	.63	.37
1913	.48[1]	.45	.55	.28	.53	.63	.63	.44
1912	.48[1]	.45	.55	.28	.52[1]	.63	.63	.44
1911	.45	.40	.50	.28	.50	.50	.63	.44
1910	.45	.40	.50	.25	.50	.50	.63	.44
1909	.45	.40	.50	.25	.44	.50	.50	.38
1908	.38[1]	.35	.48[1]	.25	.44	.50	.50	.35
1907	.38[1]	.35	.48[1]	.25	.44	.44	.50	.35
1906	.36[1]	.35[1]	.43[1]	.25	.44	.44	.50	.35

Series E248-267. Hourly wage rates in selected building trades, by city, 1901 to 1974 (concluded)
(dollars)

Year	Winnipeg				Vancouver			
	Carpenter	Electrician	Plumber	Labourer	Carpenter	Electrician	Plumber	Labourer
	260	**261**	**262**	**263**	**264**	**265**	**266**	**267**
1905	.35	.30	.40	.25	.44	.44	.50	.35
1904	.35	.30	.40	.25	.40	.44	.50	.35
1903	.35	.28	.40	.25	.40	.39	.50	.35
1902	.28	.23	.40	.22	.33	.39	.40	.30
1901	.25	.23	.40	.20	.33	.33	.34	.25

[1] A range of hourly wage rates for this occupation was published. To conserve space the arithmetic mean of the two items of the range was computed and rounded where applicable.

Series E268-279. Hourly wage rates in selected occupations in the pulp and paper industry, for Canada and by region, 1911 to 1920 and 1943 to 1974
(dollars)

Year	Canada		New Brunswick		Nova Scotia		Quebec		Ontario		British Columbia	
	Machine[1] tender (newsprint)	Millwright (maintenance)	Machine[1] tender (newsprint)	Millwright (maintenance)	Machine[1] tender (newsprint)	Millwright (maintenance)	Machine[1] tender (newsprint)	Millwright (maintenance)	Machine[1] tender (newsprint)	Millwright (maintenance)	Machine[1] tender (newsprint)	Millwright (maintenance)
	268	**269**	**270**	**271**	**272**	**273**	**274**	**275**	**276**	**277**	**278**	**279**
1974	–	6.31	–	5.96	–	6.17	–	5.75	–	6.12	–	7.50
1973	6.89	5.33	7.59	4.82	7.47	5.28	6.38	4.93	6.89	5.23	8.35	6.15
1972	6.58	5.06	6.80	4.65	–	4.91	6.35	4.75	6.49	4.92	7.36	5.67
1971	6.01	4.64	–	4.19	–	4.52	5.78	4.41	5.98	4.54	6.86	5.25
1970	5.63	4.18	–	3.82	–	4.00	5.50	4.04	5.68	4.18	6.25	4.64
1969	5.21	3.89	–	3.57	–	3.79	5.06	3.69	5.30	3.84	5.45	4.34
1968	4.97	3.59	–	3.26	–	3.50	4.97	3.44	4.94	3.60	4.96	3.96
1967	4.73	3.40	–	3.09	–	3.26	4.62	3.20	4.79	3.41	5.05	3.92
1966	4.48	3.15	–	2.89	–	3.01	4.34	2.97	4.52	3.14	4.89	3.70
1965	4.17	2.88	–	2.73	–	2.71	3.97	2.72	4.27	2.92	4.73	3.39
1964	4.00	2.73	–	2.54	–	–	3.84	2.57	4.03	2.75	4.63	3.26
1963	3.95	2.67	–	2.50	–	–	3.81	2.57	4.00	2.72	4.57	3.02
1962	3.94	2.63	–	2.47	–	–	3.83	2.54	4.00	2.66	4.24	2.86
1961	3.85	2.55	–	2.42	–	–	3.77	2.47	3.88	2.58	4.04	2.71
1960	3.73	2.44	–	2.31	–	–	3.60	2.35	3.80	2.49	4.03	2.70
1959	3.58	2.34	–	2.33	–	–	3.49	2.26	3.62	2.35	3.76	2.56
1958	3.52	2.33	–	2.28	–	–	3.45	2.27	3.54	2.33	3.68	2.53
1957	3.48	2.26	–	2.24	–	–	3.48	2.22	3.46	2.30	3.38	2.24
1956	3.31	2.15	–	2.15	–	–	3.30	2.10	3.25	2.19	3.32	2.23
1955	3.16	1.99	–	2.01	–	–	3.16	1.90	3.11	2.05	3.16	2.17
1954	2.99	1.92	–	1.92	–	–	3.00	1.84	2.92	1.97	3.00	2.06
1953	2.88	1.82	–	1.81	–	–	2.84	1.74	2.92	1.87	2.97	1.93
1952	2.69	1.67	–	1.64	–	–	2.60	1.58	2.74	1.78	2.82	1.91
1951	2.65	1.63	–	1.66	–	–	2.58	1.57	2.70	1.69	2.75	1.81
1950	2.24	1.36	–	1.38	–	–	2.21	1.31	2.20	1.40	2.41	1.48
1949	2.16	1.26	–	1.26	–	–	2.15	1.21	2.14	1.32	2.16	1.41
1948	2.15	1.25	–	1.25	–	–	2.14	1.18	2.08	1.32	2.32	1.42
1947	1.99	1.10	–	1.09	–	–	1.98	1.06	1.93	1.17	2.15	1.27
1946	1.79	.96	–	–	–	–	1.79	.91	1.74	1.03	1.93[2]	1.12[2]
1945	1.65	.82	–	–	–	–	1.63	.77	1.63	.91	1.75[2]	.96[2]
1944	1.63	.77	–	–	–	–	1.58	.71	1.62	.89	1.75[3]	.89[3]
1943	1.59	.76	–	–	–	–	1.54	.71	1.64	.89	1.73[3]	.92[3]
1920	–	–	–	–	.50	–	–	–	.54	–	–	–
1919	–	–	–	–	.43	–	.39	–	.45	–	–	–
1918	–	–	–	–	.28	–	.32	–	.382	–	–	–
1917	–	–	–	–	.25	–	.29	–	.255	–	–	–
1916	–	–	–	–	.23	–	.25	–	.215	–	–	–
1915	–	–	–	–	.22	–	.23	–	.16	–	–	–
1914	–	–	–	–	.22	–	.22	–	.19	–	–	–
1913	–	–	–	–	.22	–	.22	–	.19	–	–	–
1912	–	–	–	–	–	–	.22	–	–	–	–	–
1911	–	–	–	–	–	–	.22	–	–	–	–	–

[1] From 1959 to 1972, machine tender retitled machine tender, Fourdrinier. From 1973 on, machine tender, Fourdrinier retitled Fourdrinier-machine operator.

[2] Figures are for Manitoba and British Columbia.

[3] Figures are for the Western provinces.

Series E280-295. Hourly wage rates for selected occupations in the motor vehicle industry, 1943 to 1974
(dollars)

Year	Assemblers[1]				Machine operators[2]				Painters and enamellers[3]				Body trimmers[4]			
	Industry	Quebec	Ontario	British Columbia	Industry	Quebec	Ontario	British Columbia	Industry	Quebec	Ontario	British Columbia	Industry	Quebec	Ontario	British Columbia
	280	281	282	283	284	285	286	287	288	289	290	291	292	293	294	295
1974	5.35	5.35	—	—	5.68	5.68	—	—	5.45	4.63	5.60	—	—	—	—	—
1973	4.85	4.53	4.92	4.15	4.91	3.79	5.18	4.39	4.82	4.26	4.98	4.07	5.05	—	5.07	—
1972	4.42	4.00	4.46	4.20	4.50	—	4.52	4.13	4.54	4.22	4.59	4.58	4.40	—	4.57	—
1971	4.08	3.95	4.14	3.74	4.05	—	4.11	4.02	4.23	4.11	4.27	4.25	4.12	3.91	4.26	—
1970	3.66	3.63	3.72	3.63	3.71	—	3.99	—	3.77	3.58	3.82	3.78	3.69	3.18	3.82	—
1969	3.38	3.34	3.43	3.27	3.40	—	3.52	3.20	3.43	3.20	3.49	3.47	3.32	3.04	3.39	—
1968	3.17	3.18	3.19	3.02	3.16	—	3.24	—	3.25	3.14	3.27	3.10	3.16	2.83	3.23	—
1967	2.92	2.93	2.97	3.03	2.92	—	3.01	—	3.02	2.92	3.04	3.11	2.94	2.61	3.02	—
1966	2.75	2.08	2.81	2.88	2.78	—	2.83	—	2.82	2.21	2.87	2.89	2.77	2.00	2.86	—
1965	2.61	1.50	2.66	2.51	2.63	1.91	2.67	—	2.67	1.86	2.70	2.59	2.68	—	2.70	2.52
1964	2.47	1.84	2.48	2.42	2.47	—	2.48	—	2.52	—	2.54	2.54	2.51	—	2.54	—
1963	2.37	1.48	2.38	2.43	2.34	—	2.39	—	2.40	1.38	2.43	2.52	2.39	—	2.44	—
1962	2.26	1.51	2.27	2.46	2.22	—	2.26	2.50	2.31	—	2.33	2.51	2.28	—	2.34	—
1961	2.20	1.90	2.21	2.41	2.15	1.66	2.19	2.48	2.26	1.86	2.28	2.46	2.28	—	2.28	—
1960	2.12	1.89	2.14	2.40	2.07	1.69	2.11	2.46	2.18	1.88	2.20	2.39	2.18	—	2.19	—
1959	2.06	1.49	2.06	2.10	2.01	—	2.03	2.30	2.11	—	2.12	—	2.04	—	2.06	—
			Ontario				Ontario				Ontario				Ontario	
1958[5]			1.98				1.95				2.03				2.03	
1957			1.94				1.87				2.00				1.96	
1956			1.80				1.74				1.88				1.86	
1955			1.68				1.69				1.80				1.75	
1954			1.63				1.66				1.73				1.70	
1953			1.65				1.64				1.73				1.63	
1952			1.60				1.61				1.66				1.61	
1951			1.49				1.42				1.58				1.47	
1950			1.35				1.34				1.37				1.35	
1949			1.27				1.29				1.30				1.31	
1948			1.26				1.28				1.27				1.27	
1947			1.15				1.20				1.19				1.21	
1946			1.07				1.10				1.11				1.12	
1945			1.01				.97				1.06				.95	
1944			.99				.96				1.00				.97	
1943			.94				.95				.98				.96	

[1] From 1973 on 'Assemblers' retitled 'Automotive' assembler.
[2] From 1973 on, 'Machine operators' retitled 'Machine-tool operator, production'.
[3] In 1951, 'Painters and enamellers' retitled 'Painter, spray'; in 1973 'Painter, spray' retitled 'Spray painter, rough'.

[4] From 1943 to 1951, 'Body trimmers' titled 'Trimmers', in 1973 'Body trimmers' retitled 'Cutter and installer, seat cover'.
[5] Up to and including 1958 all of the reporting establishments were located in Ontario.

Series E296-325. Average hourly wage rates for selected maintenance and service occupations,[1] by city, 1956 to 1975

(dollars)

Year	Halifax[2]						Montreal					
	Carpenter, maintenance	Tool and die maker	Millwright, maintenance	Labourer, non-production	Stationary engineer, first class (service)	Stationary engineer, fourth class (service)	Carpenter, maintenance	Tool and die maker	Millwright, maintenance	Labourer, non-production	Stationary engineer, first class (service)	Stationary engineer, fourth class (service)
	296	297	298	299	300	301	302	303	304	305	306	307
1975	5.52	5.51	5.55	4.32	7.13	4.99	5.43	5.80	5.79	4.34	6.32	4.72
1974	4.80	5.03	5.25	3.55	6.68	4.16	4.76	5.16	5.08	3.73	5.54	4.23
1973	4.32	—	4.49	3.08	5.16	3.76	4.38	4.54	4.51	3.34	4.72	3.62
1972	4.03	—	4.37	2.80	5.18	3.19	3.94	4.12	4.09	2.97	4.50	3.40
1971	3.40	—	4.05	2.60	4.95	3.17	3.64	3.82	3.85	2.76	4.34	3.28
1970	3.01	—	3.91	2.35	4.60	2.79	3.50	3.67	3.55	2.58	4.09	2.98
1969	2.86	—	3.67	2.18	3.98	2.63	3.16	3.48	3.38	2.38	3.82	2.71
1968	2.68	2.97	—	1.96	3.56	2.39	2.97	3.25	3.19	2.24	3.67	2.56
1967	2.55	2.84	—	1.88	3.56	2.39	2.79	3.01	2.90	2.06	3.51	2.43
1966	2.40	2.61	2.52	1.71	3.16	2.22	2.56	2.76	2.64	1.89	3.15	2.26
1965	2.23	2.55	2.55	1.68	3.29	2.23	2.37	2.62	2.46	1.73	2.85	2.10
1964	2.09	2.37	2.21	1.61	—	1.95	2.26	2.51	2.40	1.67	2.80	1.97
1963	2.09	2.26	—	1.54	2.75	2.01	2.19	2.47	2.35	1.64	2.69	1.93
1962	2.03	2.26	2.39	1.50	2.76	1.92	2.16	2.39	2.29	1.57	2.61	1.88
1961	1.89	2.18	—	1.38	2.71	1.93	2.10	2.35	2.19	1.52	2.54	1.82
1960	1.83	2.16	—	1.34	—	—	2.02	2.29	2.10	1.46	2.37	1.75
1959	1.63	—	—	1.39	—	—	1.95	2.24	2.06	1.44	2.38	1.75
1958	1.57	—	—	1.29	—	—	1.86	2.14	2.02	1.43	—	—
1957	—	—	—	1.28	—	—	1.83	2.05	1.91	1.40	—	—
1956	—	—	—	1.18	—	—	—	—	—	1.31	—	—

Year	Toronto						Winnipeg					
	308	309	310	311	312	313	314	315	316	317	318	319
1975	5.91	6.40	6.27	4.53	7.65	5.34	5.47	5.93	6.10	4.53	7.77	5.24
1974	5.12	5.77	5.47	3.94	6.78	4.72	4.81	4.93	4.88	3.90	6.95	4.35
1973	4.50	4.97	4.99	3.78	5.84	4.12	4.38	4.55	4.46	3.38	5.78	3.82
1972	4.32	4.61	4.69	3.18	5.43	3.84	4.09	4.12	4.32	3.07	5.58	3.46
1971	3.84	4.33	4.43	2.94	5.04	3.55	3.88	3.77	4.03	2.94	4.99	3.23
1970	3.59	4.06	3.98	2.68	4.70	3.26	3.43	3.54	3.70	2.60	4.90	2.97
1969	3.40	3.94	3.65	2.53	4.34	3.01	3.27	3.21	3.35	2.41	4.20	2.68
1968	3.07	3.50	3.41	2.38	4.07	2.78	2.94	2.96	3.18	2.24	3.70	2.48
1967	2.90	3.23	3.09	2.20	3.84	2.58	2.85	2.71	3.01	2.02	3.60	2.36
1966	2.66	3.07	2.83	2.03	3.39	2.40	2.63	2.41	2.69	1.78	3.26	2.19
1965	2.47	2.89	2.67	1.94	3.16	2.29	2.44	2.33	2.57	1.77	2.90	2.03
1964	2.40	2.70	2.54	1.80	3.19	2.14	2.39	2.35	2.45	1.74	2.81	2.04
1963	2.33	2.59	2.41	1.78	2.81	2.08	2.32	2.22	2.34	1.70	2.69	2.01
1962	2.27	2.47	2.34	1.71	2.70	2.03	2.24	2.16	2.17	1.68	2.67	1.86
1961	2.23	2.35	2.29	1.66	2.67	1.94	2.18	2.15	2.14	1.60	2.60	1.84
1960	2.16	2.34	2.21	1.59	2.62	1.92	2.07	2.10	2.03	1.53	2.41	1.66
1959	1.99	2.23	2.15	1.57	2.40	1.89	1.98	2.02	1.96	1.45	2.41	1.60
1958	1.97	2.22	2.09	1.57	—	—	1.88	1.84	1.92	1.44	—	—
1957	1.91	2.15	1.97	1.54	—	—	1.76	—	1.66	1.32	—	—
1956	—	—	—	1.45	—	—	—	—	—	1.30	—	—

Series E296-325. Average hourly wage rates for selected maintenance and service occupations,[1] by city, 1956 to 1975 (concluded)
(dollars)

	Carpenter, maintenance	Tool and die maker	Millwright, maintenance	Labourer, non-production	Stationary engineer, first class (service)	Stationary engineer, fourth class (service)
	320	**321**	**322**	**323**	**324**	**325**
1975	7.44	7.66	7.52	5.67	8.65	7.08
1974	6.17	6.55	6.74	4.48	7.45	6.04
1973	5.51	5.79	5.80	4.03	6.17	5.12
1972	4.90	5.13	5.26	3.71	5.29	4.67
1971	4.55	4.63	4.80	3.36	4.93	4.33
1970	4.11	4.26	4.29	3.14	4.90	3.87
1969	3.71	4.09	3.95	2.98	4.10	3.48
1968	3.50	3.69	3.77	2.78	3.84	3.14
1967	3.25	3.35	3.56	2.58	3.88	2.97
1966	3.06	3.12	3.24	2.39	—	2.78
1965	2.88	2.98	3.04	2.24	3.24	2.65
1964	2.72	2.85	2.87	2.13	3.08	2.46
1963	2.60	2.74	2.64	2.03	—	2.33
1962	2.52	2.64	2.57	1.97	2.81	2.28
1961	2.44	2.58	2.48	1.94	2.65	2.20
1960	2.41	2.67	2.45	1.90	2.67	2.27
1959	2.40	2.57	2.34	1.80	2.64	2.23
1958	2.24	—	2.20	1.77	—	—
1957	2.12	2.32	2.19	1.71	—	—
1956	—	—	—	1.61	—	—

[1] From 1956 to 1959 inclusive, only data for those establishments reporting in the manufacturing sector were included in the published figures. From 1960 to current year, most major industry groups are included.
[2] Includes Dartmouth from 1974.

Series E326-375. Average weekly salaries for selected office occupations,[1] by city, 1956 to 1975
(dollars)

Year	Junior general office clerk Male	Female	Senior general office clerk Male	Female	Draughtsman Junior	Senior	Female typist Junior	Senior	Senior bookkeeper Male	Female
	326	**327**	**328**	**329**	**330**	**331**	**332**	**333**	**334**	**335**
1975	124	117	196	171	178	251	116	132	204	169
1974	113	104	178	161	156	223	102	122	185	147
1973	89	86	152	139	142	203	85	102	152	125
1972	85	80	154	132	134	183	80	97	144	110
1971	76	72	138	119	114	164	73	87	140	103
1970	73	68	127	104	100	163	72	81	126	100
1969	69	63	127	98	94	154	64	75	111	90
1968	63	56	111	89	86	135	58	70	113	87
1967	59	53	103	74	80	125	55	65	109	77
1966	56	49	106	69	73	118	51	58	101	75
1965	52	45	101	64	71	111	48	54	99	69
1964	48	43	94	65	67	105	46	52	89	65
1963	46	41	90	58	68	102	45	50	91	67
1962	45	41	86	54	62	98	45	50	85	64
1961	45	40	85	48	65	94	44	47	84	60
1960	43	36	85	50	54	96	40	46	78	59
1959	39	36	76	—	—	86	39	44	—	54
1958	—	34	—	—	—	—	36	—	69	52
1957	40	36	71	—	—	—	—	—	—	48
1956	41	35	70	45	—	—	39	—	66	45

Series E326-375. Average weekly salaries for selected office occupations,[1] by city, 1956 to 1975 (continued)
(dollars)

Year	Montreal									
	Junior general office clerk		Senior general office clerk		Draughtsman		Female typist		Senior bookkeeper	
	Male	Female	Male	Female	Junior	Senior	Junior	Senior	Male	Female
	336	**337**	**338**	**339**	**340**	**341**	**342**	**343**	**344**	**345**
1975	125	120	212	176	162	268	118	133	224	183
1974	112	105	189	158	152	246	106	125	219	161
1973	100	93	167	141	135	215	92	107	170	142
1972	92	85	159	132	120	194	82	100	157	128
1971	87	78	149	121	115	185	79	93	145	122
1970	81	75	142	116	115	175	76	89	142	115
1969	76	70	134	107	108	164	70	83	133	109
1968	71	65	124	101	94	157	66	79	130	103
1967	68	61	120	94	89	148	62	74	127	98
1966	61	56	110	87	81	138	59	70	117	93
1965	57	53	108	82	76	135	55	66	111	87
1964	54	50	103	79	75	126	52	63	107	84
1963	52	47	99	76	73	122	49	60	104	80
1962	53	46	97	74	72	119	48	58	98	77
1961	51	45	94	71	70	114	47	56	96	75
1960	49	43	91	70	69	110	46	55	94	72
1959	49	44	93	71	64	106	47	55	89	72
1958	47	43	87	69	–	–	46	54	84	70
1957	45	41	82	66	–	–	44	51	79	65
1956	43	38	78	63	–	–	41	49	76	62

Year	Toronto									
	Junior general office clerk		Senior general office clerk		Draughtsman		Female typist		Senior bookkeeper	
	Male	Female	Male	Female	Junior	Senior	Junior	Senior	Male	Female
	346	**347**	**348**	**349**	**350**	**351**	**352**	**353**	**354**	**355**
1975	134	130	216	185	179	289	132	147	233	190
1974	124	114	195	163	157	262	115	131	203	169
1973	109	98	174	145	142	226	100	116	182	148
1972	98	90	167	132	135	205	90	105	168	136
1971	94	85	153	122	126	193	84	98	162	124
1970	88	81	144	116	116	186	81	94	149	119
1969	83	75	135	109	111	171	75	87	140	110
1968	76	69	124	101	100	157	70	81	136	105
1967	73	65	119	93	90	148	65	76	126	99
1966	67	61	114	89	85	141	61	73	120	93
1965	64	57	108	84	81	130	58	68	113	87
1964	60	54	103	80	77	122	55	65	108	82
1963	57	52	99	78	74	114	52	63	106	80
1962	55	50	96	74	73	112	51	60	103	77
1961	54	49	94	73	70	108	50	59	99	75
1960	55	48	92	71	65	106	48	58	95	73
1959	54	48	91	69	63	101	49	56	90	70
1958	53	47	92	67	–	–	47	54	83	68
1957	51	44	85	65	–	–	45	51	78	63
1956	47	42	81	61	–	–	42	48	76	61

Series E326-375. Average weekly salaries for selected office occupations, by city, 1956 to 1975 (concluded)
(dollars)

Year	Winnipeg									
	Junior general office clerk		Senior general office clerk		Draughtsman		Female typist		Senior bookkeeper	
	Male	Female	Male	Female	Junior	Senior	Junior	Senior	Male	Female
	356	357	358	359	360	361	362	363	364	365
1975	125	119	204	177	159	277	122	143	208	155
1974	108	101	189	160	142	245	103	121	168	135
1973	88	90	160	139	124	208	90	104	163	123
1972	86	81	157	126	120	193	82	97	153	112
1971	82	76	145	116	108	184	77	90	138	106
1970	74	69	138	108	100	170	70	85	129	99
1969	70	64	128	100	93	166	66	79	125	89
1968	65	60	114	92	83	151	60	71	119	86
1967	61	55	110	88	81	139	57	67	108	81
1966	56	51	105	83	73	122	53	63	105	78
1965	54	49	98	76	70	113	50	59	97	73
1964	49	45	94	71	68	108	47	56	92	69
1963	47	44	88	68	68	102	45	55	90	68
1962	46	42	85	65	64	101	44	52	86	67
1961	47	41	82	64	64	107	44	51	84	66
1960	46	40	81	60	61	98	42	49	82	64
1959	47	39	83	57	58	90	40	47	84	61
1958	44	37	82	57	—	—	38	46	84	61
1957	42	35	77	52	—	—	36	44	79	61
1956	41	34	75	47	—	—	35	41	73	55

Year	Vancouver									
	Junior general office clerk		Senior general office clerk		Draughtsman		Female typist		Senior bookkeeper	
	Male	Female	Male	Female	Junior	Senior	Junior	Senior	Male	Female
	366	367	368	369	370	371	372	373	374	375
1975	161	143	241	194	204	297	142	157	255	210
1974	138	128	213	174	167	261	131	138	219	181
1973	110	105	179	149	151	225	102	114	189	148
1972	99	93	177	132	141	205	89	104	176	132
1971	93	86	167	125	131	186	83	98	161	123
1970	86	80	153	115	120	176	79	92	150	114
1969	79	73	139	106	112	162	71	84	142	106
1968	73	66	130	100	103	159	66	77	138	103
1967	68	62	126	90	98	148	62	73	130	96
1966	65	58	120	85	90	141	58	69	123	90
1965	68	56	117	80	92	136	55	66	119	86
1964	61	60	111	83	88	130	52	64	109	83
1963	52	52	102	73	80	119	49	60	105	81
1962	51	50	102	72	77	115	48	59	102	79
1961	55	50	99	73	76	113	48	58	99	76
1960	53	49	97	70	75	111	48	57	99	73
1959	59	45	101	69	64	106	46	55	98	72
1958	58	43	92	67	—	—	44	52	87	68
1957	54	39	86	57	—	—	42	49	80	63
1956	47	37	81	56	—	—	40	45	75	59

[1] From 1956 to 1959 inclusive, only data for those establishments reporting in the manufacturing sector were included in the published figures. From 1960 to current year, most major industry groups are included.

[2] Includes Dartmouth from 1974.

Series E376-386. Industrial accidents, fatal and non-fatal, reported by provincial workmen's compensation boards, by province, 1928 to 1975

(number)

Year	Total	Newfound-land	Prince Edward Island	Nova Scotia	New Brunswick	Quebec	Ontario	Manitoba	Saskat-chewan	Alberta	British Columbia[1]
	376	377	378	379	380	381	382	383	384	385	386
1975	985,317	11,990	2,830	30,620	27,005	283,855	367,937	36,174	29,622	83,494	111,790
1974	1,047,033	14,334	2,991	32,718	27,575	279,639	427,680	35.668	28,547	83,069	114,812
1973	985,680	13,915	2,885	30,230	25,607	255,140	420,708	32,036	24,869	72,549	107,741
1972	860,485	12,098	2,694	28,702	24,011	188,373	384,679	30,844	26,943	65,624	96,517
1971	793,533	11,206	2,273	26,529	24,756	189,455	333,864	29,898	22,483	62,993	90,076
1970	793,697	10,802	2,307	25,565	24,347	182,365	348,324	30,587	24,274	60,918	84,208
1969	795,429	10,077	2,158	24,884	23,753	178,278	354,249	31,521	25,228	62,298	82,983
1968	762,027	11,836	2,202	25,614	23,289	17,570	340,594	29,447	26,302	56,673	75,500
1967	782,070	11,747	2,367	25,885	24,745	172,679	352,232	29,760	27,294	57,690	77,671
1966	781,884	11,711	2,319	25,552	24,434	171,011	354,296	28,954	26,507	56,306	80,794
1965	741,764	10,225	2,393	23,988	23,633	162,070	331,405	26,768	24,916	54,777	81,589
1964	672,690	8,900	2,274	21,680	21,605	143,969	293,126	25,897	24,063	55,277	75,899
1963	603,871	10,152	2,244	20,058	18,747	122,248	262,787	24,099	21,562	52,044	69,930
1962	573,306	9,642	1,826	19,177	19,167	115,243	250,192	22,589	21,210	49,566	64,694
1961	539,092	8,864	1,809	16,248	16,764	99,502	239,890	21,837	22,302	48,883	62,993
1960	542,657	10,498	1,791	17,879	19,311	100,704	240,469	22,071	22,032	46,471	61,431
1959	547,058	9,385	1,861	17,462	13,587	99,258	252,504	18,588	21,800	48,277	64,336
1958	511,544	8,179	1,468	15,797	13,385	95,868	228,539	18,588	20,699	45,912	63,109
1957	563,299	8,658	1,393	17,623	14,711	110,401	248,492	18,414	20,803	46,933	75,871
1956	553,387	10,855	1,469	18,890	16,482	106,004	232,291	18,342	20,195	49,594	79,265
1955	496,396	9,913	1,420	17,902	15,032	95,257	208,814	17,332	17,282	43,432	70,012
1954	463,943	9,233	1,151	17,287	12,946	87,011	193,588	16,827	18,363	40,452	67,085
1953	480,269	9,732	1,005	16,855	12,928	93,306	201,976	17,346	16,218	41,965	68,938
1952	476,313	9,675	882	17,724	14,267	97,177	195,206	17,246	14,579	39,520	70,037
1951	447,011	6,228[2]	860	17,573	15,177	95,930	176,563	17,212	13,676	35,804	67,988
1950	415,170	—	686	16,697	15,023	86,246	163,723	16,513	11,441	33,337	71,504
1949	412,343	—	219[3]	17,055	13,794	85,040	166,632	17,125	10,830	32,396	69,252
1948	417,396	—	—	17,519	15,115	93,028	161,733	16,753	10,627	28,557	74,064
1947	371,245	—	—	16,445	14,693	96,135	117,192	15,746	10,152	25,864	75,018
1946	351,524	—	—	17,507	13,275	90,900	122,523	14,795	9,509	23,068	59,947
1945	310,141	—	—	16,537	11,193	82,724	103,693	13,477	7,509	19,154	55,854
1944	322,067	—	—	16,725	11,365	84,308	109,506	13,630	6,784	19,286	60,463
1943	349,291	—	—	16,931	11,355	90,564	121,237	13,948	6,921	19,700	68,635
1942	348,795	—	—	17,778	11,535	96,888	117,886	13,787	6,766	18,680	65,475
1941	295,582	—	—	15,804	11,295	82,568	102,290	13,378	6,823	16,928	46,496
1940	233,804	—	—	13,948	10,940	65,704	72,292	11,202	6,249	14,982	38,487
1939	180,979	—	—	11,823	8,126	53,651	53,110	9,401	5,260	11,832	27,776
1938	183,103	—	—	11,408	7,834	58,335	52,272	9,331	4,508	11,928	27,487
1937	212,022	—	—	11,953	11,521	70,081	62,042	9,153	4,296	11,313	31,663
1936	150,363	—	—	10,246	8,957	39,502	54,147	9,299	4,642	9,198	14,372
1935	140,451	—	—	8,971	7,251	35,163	52,128	8,237	3,597	11,058	14,046
1934	125,454	—	—	8,063	7,858	31,557	48,573	6,578	3,223	9,608	9,994
1933	95,966	—	—	5,168	6,683	26,723	33,163	5,505	2,390	8,160	8,174
1932	111,331	—	—	5,024	4,386	30,643	34,758	5,695	2,817	8,974	19,034
1931	117,625	—	—	6,349	5,841	25,921[4]	45,239	6,671	3,969	10,049	13,586
1930	134,098	—	—	8,812	5,624	19,850	58,343	8,310	2,639[5]	12,607	17,913
1929	155,086	—	—	9,474	7,507	21,377	71,291	10,449	—	14,899	20,089
1928	123,030	—	—	7,669	6,699	2,625[6]	65,468	9,591	—	13,400	17,578

[1] Cases of 'medical aid only' not included from 1928 to 1931 and in 1934 and 1936.
[2] From 1 April 1951.
[3] From 1 July 1949.
[4] Cases of 'medical aid only' included after 1 September 1931.
[5] From 1 July 1930.
[6] From 1 September 1928.

Series E387-389. Provincial expenditures for workmen's compensation, 1921 to 1975
(thousands of dollars)

Year[1]	Total cash benefits and medical aid and hospitalization	Cash benefits[2]	Medical aid and hospitalization[3]	Year[1]	Total cash benefits and medical aid and hospitalization	Cash benefits[2]	Medical aid and hospitalization[3]
	387	388	389		387	388	389
1975	668,447	513,684	154,763	1955	85,867	62,157	23,710
1974	526,280	410,491	115,789	1954	79,997	58,227	21,770
1973	418,531	324,828	93,703	1953	76,550	57,285	19,265
1972	361,650	278,088	83,561	1952	74,080	55,985	18,095
1971	314,438	236,749	77,689	1951	64,268	48,640	15,628
1970	304,513	229,029	75,484	1950	57,592	43,845	13,747
1969	272,719	205,246	67,473	1949[1]	53,857	40,905	12,952
1968	233,793	172,021	61,772	1948	57,117	45,260	11,857
1967	216,446	159,102	57,344	1947	49,271	40,058	9,213
1966	208,062	154,694	53,368	1946	—	—	—
1965	178,731	131,011	47,720	1943	—	—	32,515
1964	158,658	116,535	42,123	1941	—	—	25,579
1963	145,508	108,054	37,455	1939	—	—	18,782
1962	137,847	102,983	34,864	1937	—	—	20,155
1961	..	..	..				
				1933	—	—	11,788
1960	..	..	..	1930	—	—	17,544
1959	..	..	..	1926	—	—	11,034
1958	112,448	80,028	32,420	1921	—	—	10,400
1957	106,225	76,632	29,593				
1956	95,720	69,562	26,158				

[1] Newfoundland included in 1949 and subsequent years.
[2] Includes both compensation for lost earnings and capitalized value of pensions for permanent, partial or total disabilities, but not including funds set in reserve.

[3] Medical aid includes hospitalization, rehabilitation service, funeral and related expenses. Medical aid payments are for both disabling and medical treatment injuries.

Section F: Gross National Product, the Capital Stock, and Productivity

Robert B. Crozier, *Conference Board of Canada*

The statistical data of this section are in five subsections. They contain data on national income and expenditure and related aggregates from 1926 to 1976 in series F1-152; on income produced, by industry, from 1919 to 1926 and on gross capital formation from 1901 to 1930 in series F153-182; on the stock of tangible capital from 1926 onwards in series F183-220 and on inventory book values in series F221-224; on real gross domestic product by industry in series F225-240; and on indexes of labour productivity in series F241-294.

The arrangement of this section differs somewhat from that of most of the other sections in that the first two tables on national income and gross national product, on the one hand, and gross national expenditure, on the other, for the period 1926 to 1976, are not immediately followed by data on national income or income produced for the period preceding 1926. The reason for the different arrangement is that all the data in series F1-152 are articulated in the sense that each set of series is consistent with, or can be easily reconciled with, the other data of the subsection. Therefore, these data form a logical group.

The following official publications were used as sources of material: Statistics Canada, *National Income and Expenditure Accounts, Volume 1, the Annual Estimates 1926-1974,* (Catalogue 13-531); *National Income and Expenditure Accounts, Volume 3, A Guide to the National Income and Expenditure Accounts: Definitions, Concepts, Sources and Methods,* (Catalogue 13-549), hereafter referred to as *Volume 3; Fixed Capital Flows and Stocks, 1926-1973,* (Catalogue 13-211) and subsequent volumes in the same series; *Indexes of Real Domestic Product by Industry of Origin, 1935-1961,* (Catalogue 61-505) and *Indexes of Real Domestic Product by Industry, 1961-1969,* (Catalogue 61-510), plus subsequent volumes in the same series; and *Aggregate Productivity Measures,* (Catalogue 14-201) plus *Indexes of Output per Person Employed and per Man-Hour in Canada, Commercial Non-Agricultural Industries, 1947-1963,* (Catalogue 14-501) and subsequent updates to these publications.

Two privately available sources were used: K.A.H. Buckley, *Capital Formation in Canada, 1896-1930,* (Toronto, University of Toronto Press, 1951); and some unpublished material provided directly by Statistics Canada from an unpublished private memorandum by D.H. Jones.

General Note

In contrast with other sections of this volume, detailed descriptions of the concepts and methods of estimation for most of the data of this section are found in a small number of readily accessible sources. A lengthy description of such concepts and methods for the data of the national accounts for 1926 to 1974 is found in Statistics Canada, *Volume 3.* Likewise, descriptions of concepts and methods used in the capital formation estimates can be found in Statistics Canada publication, *Private and Public Investment in Canada, 1946-57,* and the report of the Department of Trade and Commerce, *Private and Public Investment in Canada, 1926-51.* In addition, much of the comment on the development of estimates of construction expenditures, given in Section S, Construction and Housing, in this volume, applies to all fixed capital formation. The material on the capital stock and the explanation of concepts and methods (with the exception of inventory stocks) come from various issues of the Statistics Canada report, *Fixed Capital Flows and Stocks, 1926-73* (Catalogue 13-211). Because of the accessibility of this limited number of sources and of the general familiarity of users with the concepts of the national accounts, the general description of concepts is made relatively short. Descriptions of the content of the various individual series are given, however, in sufficient detail for general use of the material.

The source volumes were used extensively for the descriptions given here, without explicit acknowledgment in each instance. Substantial parts of this text have been reproduced or paraphrased from them.

Since national income estimation draws on nearly the whole range of economic statistics, many segments of other sections of this volume are related closely to the data of this section. These data include: the distribution of labour income by industry and by province, Section E; detail of the current account balance of payments which appears in Section G; the implicit price deflators obtained in the conversion of gross national expenditure in current dollars to constant dollars, Section K; income in agriculture, Section M; capital formation in manufacturing by main groups, Section R; and some of the detail of construction expenditure, in Section S. Of the foregoing data, the industrial distribution of labour income and the implicit price deflators are taken from the *National Accounts* and hence are consistent with the totals of the national accounts. The remainder were modified slightly for national accounts purposes. There are also other data, in several sections, related to but not explicitly adjusted to concepts and methods used in preparing the national accounts.

The data of this section are, with one exception, national totals, whether the particular series is a component of some larger aggregate or a grand total. For example, each component of gross national product in series F1-13, as well as each of the aggregates for national income and for gross national product, is a total for all Canada. The exception is series F91-102 which gives personal income by province.

In all data of this section Newfoundland is included from 1949 onward.

Revisions for the period 1962 to 1976 are incorporated in series F1-152. They were released in December 1977, in *National Income and Expenditure Accounts, 1962-1976,* (Catalogue 13-201).

National Income and Expenditure and Related Aggregates, 1926 to 1976 (Series F1-152)

General Note

The first estimates of national income of Canada, prepared by scholars in Great Britain, predate World War I. The history of the official preparation of national income estimates in Canada begins in 1919, with the publication of estimates for 1911 and 1918, prepared by R.H. Coats, Dominion Statistician, even though they appeared in a private publication, the *Monetary Times Annual*, 3 January 1919. Thereafter at intervals, estimates of national income, with limited component detail, were published by the Dominion Bureau of Statistics until World War II. In the meantime, D.C. McGregor in 1934, the Bank of Nova Scotia in 1935 and later years, and the research staff of the Rowell-Sirois Royal Commission on Dominion- Provincial Relations in 1939 and 1940 also published historical estimates.

The development of a comprehensive set of national accounts by the Dominion Bureau of Statistics, with all the now familiar detail, began at the end of Word War II. The estimates in elaborated form were eventually carried back to 1926 with the use of concepts, methods and additional raw material that rendered the earlier estimates obsolete. The earlier work was useful, however, in having resulted in the preparation and preservation of many data that were of great value for the revised estimates. A description of the historical background and of the uses and applications of the national accounts in Canada is given in, *Volume 3*, pp. 21-29.

Gross national product is defined as the value of the unduplicated total of all goods and services produced in a given period by Canadian residents. It can also be regarded as a money measure of the income and other costs generated in the production of these goods and services. Gross national product is 'gross' because it is a measurement of output before any allowance is made for capital consumption, the using up of capital in the form of depreciation, obsolescence, fire loss and the like during the period for which output is measured. The basic measurement is made in terms of the prices at which these goods and services are valued in the market in the period in which they are produced, though for some purposes measurement is made in constant dollars, the dollars of some base period. The period of measurement for all the data given here is a year. Statistics Canada also publishes quarterly data which are available as far back as 1947.

National income is the total of all income paid to or accruing to Canadian residents for the services of factors of production owned by them. In it, property income is a net measurement after making provision for capital consumption. The addition to national income of indirect taxes less subsidies and of capital consumption allowances and miscellaneous valuation adjustments yields a total containing all the charges against gross national product as defined. In conformity with common practice, gross national product in Canada is calculated as the sum of the three foregoing items.

Gross national expenditure at market prices is also a measure of the value of all goods and services produced by Canadian residents in a given period, but it is arrived at by tracing and adding together all final sales of the national output to final purchasers, making allowance for any unsold economic production which takes the form of additions to inventory stocks. Conceptually it is exactly equal in size to gross national product.

Canadian residents are defined as both individuals and institutions such as government agencies, corporations, and non-profit institutions which are normally resident in Canada. Canadian tourists and commercial travellers travelling abroad and members of the Canadian diplomatic service or official missions and of the armed forces abroad are treated as Canadian residents. Their counterparts from other countries, temporarily in Canada, are not treated as Canadian residents.

Underlying the derivation of gross national product and expenditure is a vast network of transactions which reflects the flows of income and expenditure taking place among different parts or sectors of the economy. In the organizing framework of the national accounts, the economy is viewed as consisting of four separate groups of transactors or sectors. These are: persons, governments, businesses, and non-residents; each representing a class of transacting unit which is separately distinguishable from other groups of transactors on the basis of the particular role or function which each group occupies in the operation of the economy. The personal or household sector is essentially concerned with the transactions of members of the community in their capacity as final consumers. The government sector is focused around the transactions of the public authorities (all levels of government) as they relate to taxation and public expenditures. The business sector encompasses that group of transactors who produce goods and services for sale at a price which is calculated to cover costs and yield a profit (this profit-motivated group of transactors produces the bulk of the nation's output). All three of these sectors or group of transactors are motivated and behave in ways which are relatively homogeneous within groups but are essentially quite different between groups. This principle of homogeneity of transacting groups from the standpoint of motivation and behavior is the basic idea behind the division of the economy into separate sectors.

The fourth sector, the non-residents sector, groups together the transactions taking place between Canada and the rest of the world. In this particular instance, the principle of grouping together transactors in accordance with the similarity of their economic behavior and motivation cannot be followed. This is because the transactors involved are in reality the business, personal and government sectors of the national economy and the economies of the rest of the world. The motivation and behavior of these sectors are different, regardless of whether the transactions take place internally or with the rest of the world. The treatment of setting up a separate sector to show transactions with non-residents simply meets the practical test of facilitating the analysis of economic inter-relationships in these accounts.

The transactions of each one of these four sectors of the economy can be broken down into an income and outlay account, and a capital finance (saving and investment) account. These accounts can, in turn, be recombined and consolidated to yield the gross national product, the gross national expenditure, and the capital finance account for the economy as a whole. The complete system of sector accounts is not given in the tables in this section, but the personal income and outlay account is shown, as well as the revenue and expenditure transactions of the government sector. In addition, a consolidated capital finance account for the economy as a whole is shown. For a fuller description of the logic of the sector accounts, see Statistics Canada, *Volume 3*, Chapter 4.

There are two basic types of transactions distinguished in these accounts, transactions which take the form of requited payments involving a two-way exchange between transactors, in which there is compensation, and transactions which take the form of unrequited payments involving a unilateral transfer in which there is no compensation.

Requited payments fall into three classes: payments for goods and services received (for example, personal expenditure on consumer goods and services); payments to factors of production (such as, wages and salaries, profits and rents); and payments in exchange for financial assets (for example, lending involving the acquisition of bonds and mortgages, or direct purchases of equity stocks). Transactions of the last class, financial assets, appear in the national accounts only in the capital finance accounts, as consolidated net lending or borrowing.

Unrequited transactions, or 'transfer payments', are divided into two classes: current transfers, involving a redistribution of incomes earned in the course of current production (for example, welfare-type transfers from governments to persons, or tax transfers from persons and businesses to governments); and capital transfers. Almost all transfer payments in these accounts are 'current' transfers. However, one class of transactions, migrants' funds and inheritances (both receipts and payments), are defined as capital transfers since they are more closely identified with transfers of accumulated wealth than with transfers of current income from productive activity.

Only requited payments in the form of payments to factors of production or payments for goods and services enter into the gross national product and expenditure. Such requited transactions measure, on the one hand, the incomes generated in the course of current production and, on the other hand, the sale of this production to final users. Unrequited payments in the form of current transfers simply represent a redistribution of the incomes earned in current production and do not add to the total of the national income.

Attention is drawn to a few of the conventions followed in the construction of the national accounts.

First, the personal sector covers consumers and savers, in addition to individuals and families, in their capacity as income receivers; private non-commercial institutions and private pension funds. Private non-commercial institutions are bodies whose service charges are not expected to cover expenses and include universities, labour unions, professional organizations, fraternal societies and charitable institutions. These institutions are, in effect, treated as associations of individuals. Their operating expenditures are included with personal expenditure, their investment income is included with investment income of persons, and gifts to them from government and business are treated as transfer payments to persons. In the following notes, the word 'persons' is to be interpreted as meaning the 'personal sector' as described in this paragraph.

Second, personal insurance with all insurance companies, in their strictly insurance operations, is regarded as having two aspects. The contribution to output of various types of insurance services purchased by persons (life, accident, theft, personal property, casualty and automobile) cannot be measured by simply taking the premiums for such insurance as equal to the value of the insurance service, since the premiums include moneys to be disbursed in the form of claims either in the same year or in future years. Since the premiums paid and the claims received constitute to a large extent simply a redistribution of income within the persons and unincorporated business sector, both premiums and claims are ignored in these accounts. The value of the service of the institutions which facilitate this process of redistribution is measured by their administrative expenses, that is, premiums minus claims, which are included in personal expenditure on consumer goods and services.

Life insurance companies and fraternal societies have, however, an additional characteristic which must be considered in their treatment in the accounts. These institutions not only redistribute income of persons; they also perform a saving function on behalf of persons. The personal savings accumulated in the life insurance group give rise to investment income which accrues on behalf of individuals. In order not to omit this investment income from the income of this sector, life insurance companies are treated as 'associations of individuals' insofar as their investment function is concerned. Their investment income is included in the 'interest, dividends, and miscellaneous investment income' of the personal sector. The administrative expenses of life insurance companies include the investment expenses of these companies, that is, a 'fee' which persons pay to the insurance companies for the management of their investments.

Third, banks and similar institutions render services to persons without specific charge. They recover the cost of these services from the excess of interest received on their own loans and investments, over payments of deposit interest. An imputed amount equal to the value of these services is included in both personal income and national income and expenditure. Deposit interest paid to persons is also included as a part of personal and national income. In this aspect of their operations, banks are treated somewhat like associations of individuals.

Fourth, in common with the practice of nearly all countries which have a highly developed market economy, the measurement of gross national product and expenditures covers mainly provision of goods and services through transactions in markets. But there are exceptions. Income in kind of farmers and of employees in non-farm sectors is included in both income and expenditure. Imputed income and expenditure on owner-occupied homes and imputed capital consumption allowances on them are also included. The current operation of these owner-occupied buildings is regarded as taking place in the business sector, however, and all capital consumption allowances are allocated to it. While owner-occupied residential construction is included with business gross fixed capital formation, government building construction is included with government capital formation.

Fifth, the operation of extra-budgetary government funds, such as those of the Unemployment Insurance Commission, Workmen's Compensation and the Canada and Quebec Pension Plans, are consolidated in the government account.

Finally, government enterprises that operate mainly on a commercial basis, meeting their operating expenditures from the sale of goods and services, are included with the business sector and only net profits and interest on advances or loans to them are credited to government receipts. Their capital expenditure is also classified as business gross fixed capital formation.

The raw material for constructing the national accounts is drawn from a major part of all economic statistics. Much of it appears in other sections of this volume. The source material becomes progressively better from earlier to later years, less improvisation in its use is needed and the final estimates become correspondingly more accurate.

Five main categories of estimating techniques are used,

either separately or in combination. First, a substantial part of the final data is obtained more or less in the form required from annual surveys or reports frequently covering the whole period, or, in other cases, only the later years. Relatively little manipulation of the data is required to obtain the final estimates. Second, some of the data are available in fairly full coverage in the form desired for benchmark years. Interpolation or extrapolation to other years is made by use of related but less complete data. Third, the estimates may be built up by combining data on quantities of goods and services with their prices in unit value or index form to obtain a value estimate. In some cases, the price and quantity data are those actually desired; in others, particularly for price series, data for closely related items are used. Fourth, some of the income data, particularly for unincorporated business, are estimated by construction of synthetic operating accounts, income being obtained by subtracting expenses from gross income. Fifth, certain incomes are obtained by their calculation as a percentage of some larger total.

The general method used in the preparation of the labour income estimates consists of calculating the payments made on the labour account by the various industrial groups and summing the results. In recent years, by far the greater portion of the estimate is based on monthly and annual sample or full-coverage surveys conducted by Statistics Canada, the decennial and quinquennial censuses of Canada, and published statements of governments. In areas where the annual coverage is incomplete, the problems of estimation are more difficult, and greater reliance must be placed on directly related data. In such cases, benchmark estimates are developed from the decennial censuses of population, agriculture and distribution, and interpolation or projection techniques are employed to obtain estimates for intercensal years using indexes of aggregate earnings, employment and wage rates from various sources. In a number of cases, methods of estimation have had to be devised from indirect evidence, but such instances are few and, in the aggregate, quite small.

In recent years, a major new source of information has become available in the labour income field. This consists of the tabulation of total wages and salaries from 'T4' forms submitted by employers with respect to employees' earnings, undertaken by the Department of National Revenue in connection with the administration of the Canada Pension Plan. This information has been available on a regular basis since 1966. The coverage is very comprehensive and closely approximates the total of wages and salaries as required for national accounting purposes. This new information has revealed that the estimates prepared by Statistics Canada on the industry-by-industry basis were somewhat understated and since 1966 this material has served to provide a control for the total labour income estimate. The data for all years from 1947 to 1966 have also been adjusted to compensate for this undercoverage.

The value of board and lodging (income in kind) received by employees is estimated separately for industries where they are important. In agriculture, census benchmark data are adjusted to arrive at estimates for intercensal years in accordance with changes in employment and farm living costs. In forestry, income in kind is estimated, from 1944 on, on the basis of data from annual surveys. The 1944 benchmark is projected back to other years on the basis of an index combining food prices and employment in logging. In other groups, such as water transport, hospitals, religious institutions and domestic service, similar techniques are

employed. Income in kind consumed by farm proprietors is not a part of the labour income estimates but is included with accrued net income of farm operators from farm production. Food and clothing supplied to the Canadian forces are a form of employee income, but are included under military pay and allowances.

Supplementary labour income, that is, employers' contributions to pensions, social insurance and welfare funds on behalf of employees are also estimated separately by industry. For the period 1926 to 1960, contributions to pension and welfare funds in manufacturing, electric power, trade, mining and telephone industries were based on a survey made in 1944 and projected to other years on the trend of total wages and salaries in each industry. Figures for pension contributions after 1946 and for welfare contributions after 1954 were obtained from *Taxation Statistics,* published by the Department of National Revenue. In steam railways, insurance, banking, and federal and provincial governments, the estimates of employer contributions were made available through correspondence, through annual surveys, or from publications of the agencies concerned. For municipal governments, estimates for the years 1938 to 1944 were based on an analysis of financial statements of a number of larger cities, and since 1945, on questionnaires collected by Statistics Canada.

For the period since 1960, employers' contributions to pension funds, except those to the Canada and Quebec Pension Plans, are derived from Statistics Canada's *Trusteed Pension Plans, Financial Statistics,* (Catalogue 74-201), supplemented by data from annual surveys conducted by Statistics Canada. Employers' contributions to the Canada and Quebec Pension Plans are obtained from the tabulation by the Department of National Revenue of employers' taxation reports. Employers' contributions to welfare funds for the 1961 to 1964 period are derived by industry, mainly from *Taxation Statistics* supplemented by data obtained from annual surveys conducted by Statistics Canada, with projections to date based on the movement of wages and salaries.

Employers' contributions to the Unemployment Insurance Fund are obtained from data supplied by the Unemployment Insurance Commission. Employers' contributions to Workmen's Compensation Funds are obtained from the reports of the Workmen's Compensation Board in each province.

The estimates of corporation profits are based essentially on data compiled from the financial statements of corporations filed with the Department of National Revenue under the Income Tax Act, or, in the years since 1964, on tabulations of corporation financial data undertaken by Statistics Canada in collaboration with the Department of National Revenue under the Corporations and Labour Unions Returns Act.

During the period 1944 to 1964 inclusive, the Department of National Revenue compiled corporation financial statistics from the 'T2' income tax returns filed by corporations under the Income Tax Act. These statistics were published in the Department of National Revenue annual report, *Taxation Statistics,* and constituted the basic source of the data on corporation profits entering the national accounts for the period 1944 to 1964. For the period prior to 1944, a special sample study of corporation financial statistics was undertaken within the Department of National Revenue, drawing upon income tax records. The results of this sample study have provided the basic source of information on corporation profits for the period 1926 to 1944.

The Corporations and Labour Union Returns Act, passed in 1962, created an additional requirement to those imposed by the Income Tax Act for the reporting of financial data by a substantial number of corporations in Canada. This involved considerable duplication of the tabulations of corporation financial data already being carried out by the Department of National Revenue. In order to prevent this duplication, legislation was passed that enabled a joint statistical operation to be undertaken. An amendment to the Corporations and Labour Unions Returns Act in 1965 relieved corporations from filing financial statements under the Income Tax Act. At the same time, access to corporation income tax returns was made available to the Chief Statistician of Canada.

Commencing in 1965, Statistics Canada began publication of *Corporation Financial Statistics,* (Catalogue 61-207), and *Corporation Taxation Statistics,* (Catalogue 61-208), which in combination replace and extend the annual information on corporation statistics previously available in the Department of National Revenue reports. These two publications now constitute the basic source of information for estimating corporation profits as entered in the national income and expenditure accounts. All of the profits estimated since 1965 are based on these sources.

Interest and miscellaneous investment income is divided between that received by or accruing to persons on the one hand and governments on the other. Income of this kind received by corporations is reflected in profits. Investment income of farm operators and most other unincorporated business, from outside their own businesses, is included with personal investment income. Dividends received from Canadian corporations are not included since corporate profits are calculated before dividend payments.

Basic sources of data for estimating investment income received and paid by businesses and government are found, for all years, in *Taxation Statistics* and the corporate sample study (see above); in reports of the Superintendent of Insurance for Canada for federally registered insurance companies, loan and trust companies, and fraternal and mutual benefit societies; in the reports required of provincially-registered loan and trust companies and fraternal societies, particularly in Ontario and Quebec; in material on credit unions, assembled by the federal Department of Agriculture; in federal and provincial public accounts and departmental and agency reports. In addition, the Central Mortgage and Housing Corporation, in operation since the end of World War II, has collected much information on mortgages, housing and housing rentals.

Personal investment income is in most cases calculated for each of its various categories as a residual. First, estimates of total net interest and like payments are made. Then that portion paid to business and government is calculated. The remainder is then assigned to the personal sector.

The calculation of net farm income of unincorporated farmers from farm production is described in Section M. Adjustments for national income purposes are explained in the notes to series F6 of this section.

Net income of non-farm unincorporated business consists of the earnings of working proprietors from their own businesses. Such businesses are 'unincorporated' as distinct from the corporate form of organization. The estimates represent a mixture of labour and investment income that cannot be segregated on anything but an arbitrary basis. To the extent that working proprietors supply their own labour, they earn wages and salaries: to the extent that they

supply their own capital, they earn profits, interest and rents. These elements are inextricably mixed in the estimates of the net income field. The net rental income of persons is also included here in order to consolidate all forms of income from non-farm unincorporated business activity in a single category.

The methods of estimating net unincorporated business income can be classified broadly into four main groups: the synthetic operating account method wherein estimates of gross income are obtained and brought to a net basis by subtracting expenses; the ratio method wherein estimates of gross income are obtained and brought to a net basis by the application of a ratio of 'net to gross income' based on survey or income tax data; direct enquiry; projection from benchmark data. In a number of the industrial groups, a combination of two or more methods is required to complete the series back to 1926. To a considerable extent, information in the net income field is of a fragmentary nature and for this reason a number of the estimates are in some degree arbitrary.

The estimates themselves can be grouped under three broad headings: net professional income, net income of other unincorporated non-farm businesses and net rental income of persons.

Net professional income includes independent professional practitioners such as doctors, dentists, lawyers and engineers. In general, the estimates for the more recent years are obtained by multiplying average net income by the number of independent practitioners. For the earlier years, the estimates are projected on related data.

An example may serve to illustrate the methods used in this area. From 1957, the average net income of independent doctors is obtained from *Earnings of Physicians in Canada* which was first published in that year by the Department of National Health and Welfare. For the years 1947 to 1956, average net income is obtained from *Taxation Statistics.* Average net income for the years 1939, and 1944 to 1946, is obtained from the Survey of Incomes in the Medical Profession in Canada, conducted by Statistics Canada in 1939, 1944, 1945 and 1946. For the years 1938, and 1940 to 1944, average net income is estimated on the basis of dentists' average gross income obtained from *Survey of Incomes in the Profession of Dentistry, 1941-44* and adjusted for expenses by the ratio of 'net to gross income' obtained from the survey of the medical profession.

The number of active independent doctors in Canada is obtained, for the years 1941 to 1956, from surveys carried out by the Department of National Health and Welfare since 1946, linked to a census benchmark for the 1951 Census, and extrapolated to the years 1941 to 1945, on the trend of medical graduates from universities. For the years 1938 to 1941 the number is obtained on the basis of the decennial censuses of 1931 and 1941. The figures are adjusted to exclude salaried doctors and doctors in the Canadian forces.

The non-professional unincorporated business group covers a heterogeneous range of industries. Little actual information on net unincorporated income in these industries is available for many of the years covered by this report. For the most part, the estimates rest upon directly related material but in a number of cases indirect information is used.

Rental figures are reflected on both the income and expenditure sides of the national accounts. On the income side, net rental income of persons and unincorporated businesses, including imputations for owner-occupied dwellings, are consolidated with and shown as part of 'net income of non-farm unincorporated business, including rent'. Net rental income of corporations is implicitly included in corporation profits. The facility and space expenses deducted in arriving at residential net rents are included implicitly in the other components of gross national product. On the expenditure side, gross rents on residential tenant-occupied dwellings and an estimate of gross imputed rents on owner-occupied dwellings are explicitly included in personal expenditure on consumer goods and services. Non-residential rents, which are business expenses, are reflected in the price of products sold and therefore in the gross national expenditure.

The calculation of the net rent estimates of persons and unincorporated businesses is divided into three parts: non-farm rents, residential; non-farm rents, non-residential; farm rents, both residential and non-residential.

Of these three classes, the first is the most important in size and is also the one for which statistical coverage is the most satisfactory. Residential non-farm rents, including garages, are divided into rents paid on tenant-occupied dwellings and rents imputed on owner-occupied dwellings. The steps used in both cases are similar and can be outlined as follows:

Gross paid rents

Less: expenses of facilities supplied by landlords and included in paid rent;

Equals: gross space rent paid by tenant occupants;

Plus: gross space rent imputed to owner occupants;

Equals: gross paid and imputed rent for space;

Less: space expenses for tenant and owner-occupied dwellings: repair and maintenance, municipal property taxes, depreciation, insurance premiums and mortgage interest;

Equals: net paid and imputed rents;

Less: net rents paid to non-personal sectors;

Equals: net rent paid and imputed, received by individuals.

The basic data sources from which these estimates are calculated vary considerably but they include information from Central Mortgage and Housing Corporation, the Construction Division of Statistics Canada, reports of the Superintendent of Insurance and family expenditure surveys conducted by Statistics Canada.

Imputed returns for services provided without direct charge by banks and other financial institutions are made from their operating expenses.

Indirect taxes and subsidies are from the public accounts and department and agency reports, all available annually.

Depreciation allowances were obtained directly from annual data for private incorporated business and government enterprises and, less directly, for the remaining part. Information on corporate depreciation as it applies to the stock of business plant and equipment (non- residential construction and machinery and equipment) is obtained essentially from the same sources as the estimates of corporation profits which were discussed earlier in this section. For the years prior to 1944, the results of a special corporation sample study were used. For the years from 1944 to the mid-1960s, the estimates are based on information from *Taxation Statistics* up to that time. For the more recent years, the figures are based for the most part on corporate depreciation as published in *Corporation Financial Statistics,*

(Catalogue 61-207), and *Corporation Taxation Statistics,* (Catalogue 61-208). Other sources of information include *Financial Institutions, Financial Statistics,* (Catalogue 61-006), and *Industrial Corporations, Financial Statistics,* (Catalogue 61-003).

While most of the basic data is available from the above-noted sources, in some instances additional sources were drawn on. In the case of banks, the estimates are based on published reports of the chartered banks; estimates of depreciation on real estate holdings and equipment owned by insurance companies are based on reports of the Superintendent of Insurance; and depreciation on co-operatives is derived from information from the Department of Agriculture.

Information on depreciation in the persons and unincorporated business sector comes from a variety of sources. The replacement cost estimates of capital consumption in agriculture are calculated by the Agriculture Division of Statistics Canada and form an item of expense in the synthetic operating account from which estimates of farm net income are derived. The replacement cost estimates of capital consumption on housing are based on estimates of fixed reproducible capital at market value made by the Construction Division of Statistics Canada. The historical cost estimates for other unincorporated businesses, including independent professional practitioners, are built up industry by industry, using data obtained from tabulations of the Department of National Revenue. The claim portion of business and residential insurance, the largest part of the miscellaneous valuation adjustments, is based on information from reports of the Superintendent of Insurance.

Methods similar to those used in calculating incomes are used on the expenditure side. Government expenditure comes from public accounts and department and agency reports. The estimation of private construction expenditure is dealt with in Section S; gross expenditure on machinery and equipment, the other component of business gross fixed capital formation, is obtained by methods very similar to those used for construction. The estimation of exports and imports is described in Section G.

The estimates of personal expenditure on consumer goods and services are calculated under three broad categories: personal expenditures on commodities or goods, personal expenditures on services and net personal expenditures abroad.

The method of estimating consumer spending on goods involves a number of procedures in which basic primary data on total retail sales are adjusted and supplemented by data from other sources, to build up an estimate of total consumer outlays for goods consistent with the concepts and definitions of these accounts. For the period since 1947, benchmark values of total retail sales are first established from the censuses of merchandising and services for the years 1951, 1961 and 1966. To these totals are added estimates of the value of commodities purchased by individuals through non-retail trade outlets. The totals thus obtained are then broken down into appropriate trade groupings: shoe stores, furniture and appliance stores, hardware stores, clothing stores, grocery and combination stores and so forth. The sales of each one of these trade groupings are then adjusted where necessary to remove non-personal commodity purchases at retail, for example, business purchases of new passenger cars, commercial vehicles, auto parts, and oil, gas and grease, which should not be included in personal expenditure; and to remove receipts for services sold at retail, which should not be included in personal expenditures on goods. In addition, a deduction is made to adjust for the trade-in value of used goods. Further adjustments are made to remove the sales of commodities which are only partially or inadequately reflected in retail sales in order that more complete estimates can be derived independently and added back, for example, sales of alcoholic beverages and tobacco.

Each of the major trade groups derived as above is in turn broken down into various commodity groupings: food and non-alcoholic beverages, men's and boys' clothing, footwear and repair, household appliances, furniture and carpets, books, newspapers and magazines, drugs and sundries, and so forth. In the majority of cases, except where independent commodity estimates are made, these trade groups are broken down into their commodity components using the commodity distribution of retail trade establishment sales from the 1951, 1961 and 1966 censuses, together with data from a retail commodity survey taken in 1968. The commodity distribution of sales made through non-retail outlets is also based on census data and on annual surveys.

For the non-census years, annual estimates of consumer spending on goods are derived essentially by taking the census benchmark figures of sales for each trade group as estimated above, and interpolating or projecting the figures using the movement of sales of equivalent kind-of-business groupings found in the annual retail trade publications published by Statistics Canada. A large amount of annual information on retail sales is available from these sources. Matching this annual information to the census benchmark trade groups and then carrying the benchmark estimates forward, or interpolating, on the basis of the change in the relevant annual series, provides the principal means of deriving annual estimates of consumer spending on goods by major retail trade groups. For the non-retail trade groups, census benchmark estimates are interpolated or projected to non-census years on the basis of data from a variety of sources: surveys of wholesale and service trade, annual surveys of direct selling and surveys of vending machine sales.

The annual estimates of consumer spending on goods by major trade groups calculated as above are then broken down to yield sales by major commodity groups. For the most part, these breakdowns are based on information from the regular annual retail trade surveys, combined with census estimates of the commodity detail of sales of goods.

Personal expenditure on services includes the value of services rendered directly to individuals as distinct from those rendered to business or to government. For many classes of services, a preponderant proportion of total revenue is represented by sales to individuals and the presence of business services is not an important source of error. In those classes where sales to business or government form an important part of total revenue, for example, air transportation, telephone service, data as to the amount of such sales are not always available and arbitrary allowances must be made.

For certain classes of services, annual surveys, or published reports of Statistics Canada and other agencies give information regarding personal expenditure. Other groups depend upon the decennial censuses and the 1966 Census of Merchandising and Services, with projections to other years being made on directly related series. In some cases, benchmark estimates are taken from census data but projections must be made on indirect evidence regarding trends. In a considerable number of cases, the estimates are explicitly articulated with calculations on the income side.

As already noted, services of private non-commercial institutions (universities, charitable institutions and so on) are measured by the expenses of these institutions rather than by the fees paid by individuals. Services of insurance companies are also measured by their expenses.

An adjustment for net personal expenditures abroad is necessary to include, in personal expenditure, the expenditures of Canadian residents in foreign countries and to exclude the expenditures of non-residents in Canada. The adjustment covers net expenditures of members of the Canadian forces, as well as net tourist expenditures. To the extent that gifts in kind sent abroad do not appear in retail sales, for example, Red Cross parcels, an estimate of their value is also added. An arbitrary adjustment is made to Canadian tourist expenditures abroad to exclude expenditures chargeable to business expense accounts. The basic data are obtained from the Balance of Payments Division, Statistics Canada.

Inventory holdings consist of non-farm business inventories plus inventories held on farms and grain in commercial channels. Estimates of annual book values of non-farm business inventories for the majority of industries are available, for current years, from annual censuses or sample surveys carried out by the Manufacturing and Primary Industries Division, the Merchandising and Services Division and the Business Finance Division of Statistics Canada. When these data are inflated to full coverage for the relevant industries, by the use of inventory-to-production or inventory-to-sales ratios, they account for between 80 and 90 per cent of total inventory book values. Estimates for the remaining industries are based on data from a range of other sources including special tabulations in Statistics Canada, summaries of taxation statistics by the Department of National Revenue and the published annual reports of companies. For earlier years, mainly before 1944, sources include a special corporation sample study analysis of the records and reports of the Industry Statistics Branch of Statistics Canada and projections from annual and decennial census data.

In general, before 1947, year-end holdings of inventory are reported on a fiscal year-end basis. Since 1947, data are available for the manufacturing industry which permit adjustment to a calendar year basis. New sample surveys, introduced to cover the years from 1954 onward, for wholesale and retail trade permit more comprehensive coverage of these groups on a calendar year basis.

For inventories held on farms and grain in commercial channels, comprehensive figures on the quantities of physical stocks are available from the Agriculture Division of Statistics Canada. These are valued at appropriate prices, as indicated below, and the value of the physical change is calculated directly. The value of the physical change in inventories of field crops on farms is computed on the basis of annual changes in physical quantities valued at average annual prices for the years 1926 to 1946 inclusive. From 1947 on, use is made of the sum of the physical change in each of the four quarters of the year, valued at quarterly average prices. The physical change in livestock and poultry held on farms is valued for all years on the basis of an average of three price quotations obtained from regular surveys, namely, December, June and December. The sum of the field crop, livestock and poultry estimates provides the total estimate of farm inventory change.

In the case of inventories of grain in commercial channels held by private dealers, the value of the physical change is calculated on the basis of average annual prices 1926 to 1946 and average quarterly prices from 1947.

National Income and Expenditure and Related Aggregates (Series F1-152)

F1-13. National income and gross national product, by components, 1926 to 1976

SOURCE: for 1971 to 1976, *National Income and Expenditure Accounts, 1962-1977*, (Catalogue 13-201); for 1926 to 1970, Statistics Canada, *National Income and Expenditure Accounts, Volume 1, The Annual Estimates, 1926-1974*, (Catalogue 13-531).

For methods of estimation, see the general note to series F1-152.

F1. Wages and salaries cover all of the earnings from employment of Canadian residents paid for work performed, including payments in kind such as free board and lodging. Also included are such payments as commissions, directors' fees, tips and bonuses, and taxable allowances such as cost-of-living allowances and allowances in respect of holidays and sick leave. The estimates do not include earnings from self-employment or partnership, income from independent professional practice, income of farmers from farming operations, or military pay and allowances. Wages and salaries are estimated before tax deductions and before contributions of employees to unemployment insurance, pensions and other social insurance schemes. Bonuses, commissions and retroactive wage increases are included in the period in which they are paid because of statistical difficulties of allocating these items to the period in which they were earned.

Supplementary labour income consists of other expenditures by employers on labour account that can be regarded as payment for employees' services. Included here are employers' contributions to pension funds, employee welfare funds, unemployment insurance and workmen's compensation.

F2. Military pay and allowances consist of payments to members of the Canadian forces in Canada and overseas and are treated as compensation for services rendered. Under this heading are included military pay, various types of allowances and employer contributions to the Canadian Armed Forces Pension Fund. War service gratuities and all post-discharge re-establishment benefits are excluded and treated as transfer payments. Prior to 1966, the estimated value of food and clothing issued in kind is also included. Since 1966, the amounts involved have been small.

F3. The estimates of corporation profits before taxes used in the national accounts are closely based on business accounting practice as reflected in business 'book profits'. However, a number of adjustments are needed to convert data drawn from business accounting records to a basis compatible with national accounts concepts and definitions. For the most part, these adjustments relate to the treatment of items which are charged as operating expenses by business but which are not regarded as a charge against production as measured by the national income. Thus, depletion charges, which are treated as an operating expense on the books of business, are added back to net profits in these accounts. Discoveries of new natural resources are not capitalized in the accounts (they are not counted as a part of gross fixed capital formation) and the exhaustion of natural resources is not therefore regarded as a charge against national income. Provincial mining and logging taxes, which

are treated as an operating expense by business, are also added back to profits in these estimates. They are defined in the accounts as direct taxes. Similarly, appropriations for losses of chartered banks are added back to profits and national income since they are not considered a charge against current production. Bad debts owed by persons to corporations and written off on company books are treated in these accounts as a transfer payment from corporations to persons. An adjustment is therefore made to add back to net profits the amounts applicable. Charitable contributions made by corporations, also deducted as an expense by business, are added back on the grounds that they are not a direct cost of production but merely a distribution of earnings and, therefore, a transfer payment. All capital gains or losses of corporations are excluded, since these have no counterpart in current productive activity.

Mining development and exploration costs, which involve the acquisition of durable tangible assets, and construction and drilling costs, are included in the accounts as gross fixed capital formation. In some cases such costs are treated by business as current operating expenses and where this occurs the amounts must be added back to profits in the accounts. In other instances, costs such as geological and geophysical survey costs, which are not regarded as gross fixed capital formation in the accounts, are charged to capital account by business. In such cases, profits as reported by business must be reduced by these amounts before inclusion in the national income.

A variety of other adjustments are made to business book profits. All profit figures are adjusted from a fiscal to calendar year basis, insofar as this is possible. The profits of incorporated co-operatives are included as a part of corporation profits in these estimates. In addition, corporate losses are deducted from estimated total profits in order to bring the figures to a 'profits less losses' basis. It should be noted also that business accounting records include in book profits the dividends received from other Canadian corporations. An adjustment is therefore necessary to eliminate the double counting which this involves. Profits of government business enterprises are not included here but are included in series F5.

The profits of corporations as given in series F3 reflect income from interest on their holdings of the public debt and from consumer financing. Since these payments are treated as transfer payments, they must be eliminated in arriving at a total of national income. For the way in which this adjustment is made, see the note to series F5.

F4. Dividends paid to non-residents are deducted here in order to eliminate from corporate profits, and the national income, the earnings of non-resident factors of production. This deduction is required because the national income is defined to include only the earnings of Canadian factors of production. In principle, *all* earnings of non-residents, both distributed and undistributed earnings, should be eliminated from the national income. In practice, because of statistical problems, only that portion of profits which is actually distributed to non-residents, that is dividends, is eliminated. The undistributed profits of corporations which accrue to foreign owners are thus included as a part of the national income of Canada.

F5. Interest and miscellaneous investment income consists of the interest income of persons, and government investment income. These items are measured before deduction of direct taxes and cover the earnings of Canadian residents only. The component also includes a major adjustment needed to eliminate from the national income all interest on the public debt as well as the transfer portion of interest on consumer debt.

Interest income of persons includes the interest received by or accruing to persons (includes individuals, private noncommercial institutions, estates and trust funds); the interest income of life insurance companies, fraternal and mutual benefit societies and trusteed pension plans, accruing on behalf of persons; and small amounts of miscellaneous income. Interest paid to corporations and government business enterprises is automatically included in the profits of these institutions and is not counted here. Interest paid to government is included in government investment income.

Interest income of persons is thus made up of the following items: Canadian bond and mortgage interest received by or accruing to persons; paid and imputed interest on deposits with chartered banks and similar financial institutions, received by or accruing to persons; investment income received on behalf of persons by life insurance companies, fraternal and mutual benefit societies and trusteed pension plans (all of which are treated as associations of individuals for this purpose); interest and dividends received by persons from non-residents; and some smaller categories of income, namely, royalties received by persons, the interest credited to persons from federal government annuities accounts and the profits and interest of mutual non-life insurance companies.

Government investment income includes the profits of government business enterprises, royalties, interest on government loans and advances, interest on publicly held funds such as government pension and social insurance funds, and imputed interest. Profits of government business enterprises consist of profits, less losses, of those government agencies which conduct their activities on an essentially commercial basis, setting a price for their services which is calculated to cover costs. Included here are profits of the Canadian National Railways and other Crown corporations, and provincial and local public utilities such as hydroelectric systems, telephone systems, transit systems and so forth. The profits of the federal Post Office Department are included here, its gross expenditures being offset against its gross revenues to arrive at an estimate of profits. Interest on government loans and advances includes interest on loans to government agencies, such as various public utilities and interest on loans to foreign and domestic governments.

Interest on the public debt is made up of two parts. One part is paid to Canadian residents and is regarded as a transfer payment rather than as a payment to a factor of production for a productive service, and which is therefore excluded from the national income. In this instance, an explicit deduction is made in the interest and miscellaneous investment income component to exclude from the national income that portion of the interest received by Canadian residents. Not all interest on the public debt received by Canadians accrues to persons and governments but the full adjustment is nevertheless made in this component of the accounts. If it were statistically possible to identify the amounts, corporation profits as well as the interest income of persons and governments would each be reduced by their relevant share of the debt interest received.

The other portion requires special treatment. Such interest payments represent a direct claim by non-residents on the pool of goods and services produced domestically. Accordingly, an explicit subtraction is made to reduce the national income, an adjustment which reflects the charge against domestic production which must be paid to non-residents. This adjustment is balanced on the expenditure side of the accounts by an entry under 'Imports of goods and services'.

Part of the interest on consumer debt is also treated as a transfer payment and is excluded from the national income by an explicit deduction in the interest and miscellaneous investment income component. All consumer outlay is regarded as current consumption in these accounts, except outlay on housing which is regarded as capital expenditure. Since consumer goods, except housing, cannot give rise to investment income, it is necessary to exclude interest on the debt which finances such goods. The administrative expenses which are incurred in rendering services to borrowers are, however, included in personal expenditure and also in the gross national product.

F6. Accrued net income of farm operators from farm production includes the net income that could properly be attributed to unincorporated farm operators for their own contribution of labour and entrepreneurial inputs, for labour provided by unpaid family workers and for the services of farm capital, land, structures and equipment owned by farm operators, except housing. It covers sales of farm products, *plus* the imputed value of farm output consumed by the farmer and his family, *plus* the value of the physical change in farm inventory, *less* farm operating expenses and capital consumption allowances on farm buildings and equipment. Farm production includes the sale of logs cut from forests on farm lots and income from fur farming. It excludes, however, other forms of income of farmers such as net rental or interest receipts and imputed net rent of owner-occupied houses. These are included in series F5 and F7. It also excludes transfer payments such as payments under the Prairie Farm Assistance Act since these are not in exchange for goods or services and are therefore excluded from national income. Since the national income attempts to measure earnings arising out of current production rather than cash receipts, the accrued earnings of farm operators arising out of the operations of the Canadian Wheat Board are included as is the accrued income represented by inventories held on the farm.

The estimates given here do not include profits of incorporated farms, which are treated like any corporation, wages and income in kind paid hired labour, rent paid others for farm lands, buildings and other facilities and rents on housing. Also excluded is any outside income such as property income from ownership of outside property or labour income for services provided to others outside the operator's own farm.

The total given here, therefore, is much less than gross domestic product originating on farms, series F56, even after allowing for the fact that capital consumption allowances are included in the latter. Nor is it a measure of income available to farmers because it excludes rental income and other receipts of outside income.

F7. Net income of non-farm unincorporated business consists of the earnings of working proprietors from their own businesses. Such businesses are 'unincorporated' as distinct from the corporate form of organization. The estimates cover a heterogeneous range of industries which includes unincorporated retail stores, unincorporated operators in construction and in transportation and communication, unincorporated manufacturing establishments and many types of unincorporated service establishments. It also includes the net income of independent professional practitioners such as doctors, dentists, lawyers and engineers.

As in the case of accrued net income of farm operators from farm production, net income of non-farm unincorporated business represents a mixture of both labour income and investment income which cannot be segregated on anything but an arbitrary basis. To the extent that working proprietors supply their own labour, they earn wages and salaries; to the extent that they supply their own capital, they earn profits, interest and rents. These elements are inextricably mixed in the estimates of the net income field.

Net rental income of persons acting in a landlord capacity is included in these estimates. Such rental income covers net rents, either paid or imputed, received from the ownership of residential property, and also net paid rents from the ownership of non-residential property. In each case, the *net* rent received by persons is equivalent to gross rents received *less* landlord expenses such as heating costs, property taxes, capital consumption allowances, mortgage interest, insurance and repairs. The inclusion of net rental income of persons in this component of the national income consolidates all forms of income from non-farm unincorporated business activity in a single category.

F8. Inventory valuation adjustment is to correct for the fact that corporation profits and the net income of those non-farm unincorporated businesses that deal in commodities contain an element of capital gain or loss which arises from the method by which business firms record the value of their inventories. Production in the national income and expenditure accounts must be measured at the current market prices of the period in question. This means that net investment, or disinvestment, in inventories, represented by the change in inventories from one period to the next, should be valued at the average prices of the period in question. However, the principles of inventory valuation used in business accounting are usually quite different from those required for the accounts. In periods of rising prices, changes in recorded business inventory book values will frequently include an element of capital gain which simply reflects the fact that beginning-of-period inventories and withdrawals have been recorded at original cost, while purchases and end-of-period inventories are recorded at a higher price. In other words, the recorded money value of the 'book change' in inventories will have increased by more than the physical change in inventories valued at current, or replacement cost, prices.

In these circumstances, corporation profits and net incomes of non-farm unincorporated businesses included in national income will contain an element of capital gain, stock appreciation, which is not related to the measurement of current production and which is not consistent with the way in which other flows and transactions in the national accounts system are valued. The inventory valuation adjustment is thus designed to remove from the national income any such capital gains, or losses, resulting from the inventory accounting procedures of business firms.

The method of carrying out the inventory valuation adjustment is described in detail in *Volume 3*, Chapter 7. The adjustment represents the difference between the 'change in book values' as recorded on the books of business firms and the 'value of physical change', valued at the prices prevailing in the current period.

F9. Net national income at factor cost is the sum of all factor remunerations received by or accruing to Canadian residents from the contributions of services of the factors to production. It is the sum of the entries in series F1-8.

F10. Indirect taxes represent a part of the market price of goods and services which is not received by factors of production. They are, therefore, not included in the national income but must be added to factor costs to arrive at total costs entering into market prices. Business accounting procedures provide a guide as to whether a tax is to be regarded as direct or indirect. Thus, all taxes which represent a business cost and which are likely to be partly or fully reflected in final or market prices paid by the purchaser, such as sales and excise taxes, import duties, and property taxes, are taken as indirect. Such taxes make up a part of the producers' costs but they do not form a part of the income of the factors of production. In effect, they are taxes on expenditure, not on income. Taxes which are levied directly on the net incomes of the factors of production, whether of individuals or corporations, are regarded as direct taxes.

Indirect taxes include: customs import duties, federal excise duties and excise (sales) taxes, and miscellaneous small other federal indirect taxes; provincial government amusement taxes, corporation taxes (not on profits), gasoline and retail sales taxes, revenue from licences, permits and fees, the business share of motor-vehicle licences and permits, miscellaneous taxes on natural resources and small amounts of other miscellaneous indirect taxes; municipal real and personal property taxes, retail sales taxes, and miscellaneous other indirect taxes and licences, permits and fees.

Subsidies represent amounts contributed by governments toward current costs of production. For this reason, they must be deducted from factor costs to arrive at gross national product at market prices. The larger part of the subsidy figure consists of federal production and consumption subsidies. There are a variety of purposes, some of them inter-related, behind the payment of subsidies. Producer subsidies are usually made to encourage certain types of economic production (Emergency Gold Mines Assistance), to assist producers in areas of special difficulty (railway subsidies under the National Transportation Act), to protect the producer against a decline in the price of his product (Canadian Dairy Commission payments), or to support activities which are regarded as socially desirable (broadcasting activities of the Canadian Broadcasting Corporation). Consumer subsidies are usually paid in order that the consumer may benefit from lower prices, as in the case of many of the subsidies paid on agricultural products during World War II.

F11. Capital consumption allowances represent the using up or 'consumption' of capital through the depreciation, wear, tear and obsolescence associated with the processes of economic production. Since productive assets in the form of capital goods such as machinery and equipment and buildings are for the most part highly durable products, this 'using up' of productive assets, or loss in value, is a gradual process occurring over periods of time often covering many years. Businesses therefore customarily charge to each year's operating expenses a 'depreciation charge' or 'capital consumption cost' designed to cover the cost of the wearing out of capital assets which has occurred during the accounting period in question. Thus, depreciation or capital consumption charges represent business costs which are implicitly included in the market price of goods and services sold to final users.

In these accounts there are three major types of productive assets for which depreciation charges are calculated: business plant and equipment, housing, and government fixed assets. Depreciation on business plant and equipment is quantitatively the most important of the three sets of estimates. The estimates of depreciation in this area, except for agriculture, are based on the original cost of the assets. In the case of housing and government fixed assets, the estimates of depreciation are based on replacement cost and not original cost.

Charges for the depletion of exhaustible natural resources are not included in the consumption of fixed capital in these accounts, even through they are charged by business as operating costs. The discovery of such natural resources is not regarded as gross fixed capital formation.

The definition of gross fixed capital formation for the national accounts is framed in terms of the tangibility and durability of the goods in question. Certain durable items such as furniture, office equipment, tools and so forth are sometimes not capitalized by business but are charged as a current operating expense. In order to include depreciation on all durable equipment defined as fixed capital in these accounts, these *capital outlays charged to current expense* are included in capital consumption allowances in the gross national product. In other words, the assumption is made that these items are all used up in the year in which they are purchased.

Included under the category of miscellaneous valuation adjustments are two adjustments which are needed to bring information based on business accounting records into conformity with the definitions employed in the national income and expenditure accounts, or to maintain balance between the income and expenditure side of the accounts. The first of these adjustments concerns *non-capital outlays charged to capital account* by business. In some instances, non-tangible items such as brokerage fees on the purchase and sale of stocks and bonds are capitalized by business. In keeping with the tangibility criterion used in the accounts, such items are excluded from gross fixed capital formation on the expenditure side. In order to keep the accounts in balance, however, a negative adjustment must be made on the income side to offset the overstatement of business net income inherent in the income figures.

The second adjustment relates to the *claim portion of business and residential insurance* paid out to compensate for fire and other types of losses. These are treated in the accounts as a form of capital consumption and an explicit entry is made to account for them.

F12. Residual error of estimate is an allowance for inaccuracies of the statistical estimates of series F1-11. Conceptually, gross national product and gross national expenditure should be exactly equal. In the calculations, owing to shortcomings in the accuracy of estimates of the components of gross national product and gross national expenditure, the components of each do not add to exactly the same totals. The totals are made equal by adding half the difference to the lower unadjusted total and subtracting half the difference from the higher unadjusted total. Thus, series F13 is made equal in absolute value to series F32.

F13. Gross national product at market prices is the sum of series F9-13.

F14-32. Gross national expenditure, by components, 1926 to 1976

SOURCE: same as series F1-13.

The items of series F14-30 are components of total gross expenditure by Canadian residents on final goods and services and on inventories. In this 'sum of expenditures' approach, the measurement of economic production is arrived at by tracing the disposition of final output through the various channels in which it is used. Series F29, exports of goods and services, is the value of goods and services sold to residents of other countries. Because of the fact that sales to final purchasers, both domestic and foreign, ordinarily include elements of imports of goods and services, foreign production, as well as of national production, and because it is not feasible to eliminate imports separately from each of the individual expenditure categories, the deduction to eliminate imports of goods and services is made in total as a single adjustment in series F30. Gross national expenditure at market prices is the total of gross expenditure on goods and services measured at the prices that are actually paid in the market.

F14. Personal expenditure on consumer goods and services is the largest single component of gross national expenditure. Around 60 per cent of the nation's total production is purchased in final markets for consumer use. Such outlays include personal expenditure for durable goods, such as automobiles, and household appliances and furniture; expenditure for semi-durable goods, such as clothing and footwear; expenditure for non-durable goods, such as food, alcoholic beverages and tobacco; expenditure for a wide variety of services, covering such outlays as gross rents, including the rental value of owner-occupied housing, recreation, railway, air and urban transportation costs, laundry, cleaning and personal care service costs.

Free board and lodging and other income in kind for which an imputation is made are also included in personal expenditure, as if persons received income equal to the value of such goods and services and then purchased these items. Purchases of houses are regarded as business gross fixed capital formation but an imputed space rent on owner-occupied houses is included in both rental income of persons and in personal expenditure. The operating costs of private non-commercial institutions which provide their services to the community collectively, and which are treated as 'associations of individuals' in these accounts, are also included in personal expenditure. In addition, the operating costs and profits, premiums less claims, of life insurance companies are included to reflect the value of the services rendered by such companies. The estimates also cover expenditures of Canadian residents temporarily abroad, that is, tourists and members of the Canadian forces; these expenditures are offset by a negative entry under imports of goods and services, so that gross national expenditure as a whole is not affected, as no Canadian production is involved. To avoid double counting, an adjustment is made to the total estimate of personal expenditure to deduct expenditures of foreign residents temporarily in Canada, since this expenditure is already included as a positive entry in exports of goods and services. The value of used goods sold to persons is excluded from these estimates but the dealer's commission and other factor incomes generated by the transaction are included as current production, to maintain balance with the income side.

F15. Government current expenditure on goods and services consists of the current, non-capital outlays for goods and services of the federal, provincial and local governments, including locally administered elementary and secondary school systems and government administered hospital care services. It does not include government purchases on capital account, gross fixed capital formation, or inventories, or any of the activities of government business enterprises. The outlays cover all current purchases of goods and services for general operating expenses of government departments and agencies, including wages and salaries of government employees, office supplies, and maintenance and repair costs. The estimates also include defence expenditures. An imputation for the capital consumption or depreciation of government fixed assets is included here.

It needs to be emphasized that these expenditures relate to government current purchases of goods and services only. They do not include such current expenditures of government as transfer payments to persons, interest on the public debt, subsidies to producers, capital assistance to producers, or transfers to non-residents. These latter items, together with government gross fixed capital formation, must be added to government current expenditure on goods and services to arrive at figures of total government spending for all purposes.

F16. This series is the sum of series F17-24, gross fixed capital formation by government and gross fixed capital formation by business. Gross fixed capital formation is defined to include outlays on durable tangible assets with a lifetime use of one year or more. Only new construction, both residential and non-residential, and new machinery and equipment are included. Outlays on used buildings and second-hand machinery and equipment are excluded, since such goods do not represent a part of the nation's current production. They have been counted in gross national expenditure in the period in which they were produced. An exception relates to imports of used machinery and equipment which are included in gross fixed capital formation and are deducted as an import of goods and services, leaving gross national expenditure unaffected.

Outlays for land, mineral deposits and timber tracts are also excluded from gross fixed capital formation since such assets do not represent current production of goods and services. However, capital costs involved in the preparation of sites, land improvements, mining development and exploration costs, involving the acquisition of tangible assets, and construction and drilling costs are included in gross fixed capital formation. Such costs represent stages in the process through which natural resources are discovered, developed and brought into use. The value of the resources themselves is not capitalized in these accounts.

Replacements and major alterations of capital installations are included as part of gross fixed capital formation but ordinary repairs and maintenance expenses are not. Also included are various associated expenses which are capitalized along with the cost of the fixed assets acquired, such as architectural, legal and engineering fees. Outlays on construction works which are to be used primarily for military purposes, and purchases of military equipment are not included in the estimates of gross fixed capital formation.

The estimates of fixed capital formation in these accounts are on a 'gross' basis, before any deduction to allow for the depreciation or capital consumption of existing assets. The calculation of 'net' fixed capital formation is not possible on the basis of the estimates of depreciation as presently prepared, since the bulk of the depreciation figures are calculated on an original cost rather than a replacement cost basis of valuation.

F17-20. Government gross fixed capital formation consists mainly of construction-type expenditures, series F19: for schools, hospitals, waterworks, sewerage systems, roads, harbours, airports and various other capital installations. It also includes outlays for machinery and equipment, series F20, and a small amount of housing, series F18. Federal, provincial and local levels of government are included but the investment spending of government business enterprises is not covered here. The decision to capitalize government investment spending in this revised set of accounts was made on the basis that such assets add to the country's stock of capital and yield a flow of economic services over a period of years into the future. The gradual 'using up' of government fixed capital is reflected in the imputation which is made for depreciation on government assets in the accounts.

F21-24. Business gross fixed capital formation consists of outlays for residential construction, series F22, outlays for non-residential construction, series F23, and outlays for new machinery and equipment, series F24. Outlays for residential construction cover all expenditures for new housing except a small amount shown with government capital formation. The estimates include single units, multiple units and apartment dwellings, as well as garages and major improvements and alterations. The term 'business' is defined here to include individual home-owners who are treated in the accounts as businessmen renting to themselves. All personal purchases of housing for owner use are therefore included in these estimates, as well as commercial-type construction undertaken for rent.

Business gross fixed capital outlays for non-residential construction and machinery and equipment cover investment in all forms of productive assets by business which are used to produce a future flow of goods and services. Included here are all plant and equipment expenditures of corporations, unincorporated business enterprises, including farm operators, and government business enterprises, for example, buildings of all kinds, engineering construction such as railway road beds, dams, power transmission lines, oil pipelines, industrial machinery, generating turbines, transportation equipment, office and store equipment, furniture, small tools and like items. The capital outlays of non-commercial institutions include universities, churches, and charitable and welfare agencies.

F25-28. The value of the physical change in inventories held by businesses and governments must be included in the gross national expenditure in order to allow for that portion of current production which has not yet been sold (a positive change in inventories) or to eliminate that portion of previous years' production which is included in sales of the current year (a negative change in inventories). The change in the value of inventories relevant to gross national expenditure should reflect the change in physical volume valued at the average market prices of the period. This change is referred to as the value of the physical change in inventories. Because the value of inventories reported by businessmen reflects 'book values' based on accounting procedures which are not consistent with national accounts requirements, an inventory valuation adjustment must be made to produce an appropriate figure. This inventory valuation adjustment is described in the earlier discussion of national income and gross national product.

There are three main types of inventories for which estimates of the value of physical change are computed: government inventories, series F26; business non-farm inventories, series F27; and farm inventories and grain in commercial channels, series F28. The latter are also a part of total business inventories. Government inventory holdings are a relatively small and insignificant part of total inventory holdings and exercise little leverage in the total change in inventory stocks. They include inventories held by government commodity agencies such as the Agricultural Commodities Stabilization Board, the Canadian Dairy Commission and some uranium stocks.

Business non-farm inventory stocks represent by far the largest part of total inventory holdings in the economy. They include all inventories of raw materials, goods-in-process, and finished products held by corporations, non-farm unincorporated businesses, and government business enterprises. By industry, the major part of non-farm business inventory stocks is held in manufacturing and in wholesale and retail trade.

Farm inventories and grain in commercial channels consists mainly of grain and livestock held on farms and grain in the hands of the Canadian Wheat Board. This category also includes some grain inventories held privately by commercial dealers. It may be noted that in the case of grain and livestock inventories held on farms, and grain held by the Canadian Wheat Board, the value of the physical change in inventories, and the corresponding estimates of net income on the income side, is computed directly, and no inventory valuation adjustment is necessary.

The inventory valuation adjustment in these accounts applies only to business non-farm inventory stocks and grain in the hands of private dealers, areas where the primary data entering into the accounts on the income side are based on book values.

Due to space limitations, the box heading in the table where series F28 appears, has been condensed to read 'Farm'. The full heading should read 'Farm and grain in commercial channels'.

F29-30. Because a part of Canada's current production of goods and services is sold to non-residents, it is necessary to add the value of exports of goods and services to arrive at a final accounting of current production through final sales, series F29. Conversely, because sales to persons, governments, business and non-residents, as enumerated in series F14-29, include goods and services produced by non-residents, that is, imports of goods and services, series F30, it is necessary to subtract these in order to arrive at a correct summation of the value of Canadian output.

Exports of goods and services, series F29, as defined in the accounts include current receipts from exports of merchandise, freight and shippimg credits earned on Canadian account, travel expenditures of non-residents in Canada, interest and dividends received from abroad, gold production available for export, and other current earnings, including receipts from business services rendered to non-residents. Imports of goods and services, series F30, include current payments for imports of merchandise, freight and shipping charges incurred by Canada on foreign account, travel expenditures of Canadians abroad, interest and dividends paid to non-residents, and other current payments, including payments for business services rendered by non-residents. Entries corresponding to the interest and dividend payments to and receipts from non-residents are made on the income side of the accounts in keeping with the concept of 'national' production expressed in the gross national product and expenditure measurements.

The figures of exports and imports of goods and services appearing in the gross national expenditure table are those published by Statistics Canada in *The Canadian Balance of International Payments,* (Catalogue 67-201), subject to certain modifications and adjustments in the earlier years. The relationship between transactions in goods and services and the current account of the balance of payments is described in *Volume 3,* pp. 244-249. Basically, current account receipts and current account payments as per the balance of payments reflect, in addition to exports and imports of goods and services, current transfers and transfers of inheritances and migrants' funds. Current transfers such as personal and institutional remittances and pensions paid to or received from abroad are not included with exports and imports of goods and services in gross national expenditure since they are not considered to represent current earnings of Canadian or foreign factors of production. Inheritances and migrants' funds paid to or received from abroad are transfers of a capital nature and for this reason do not appear in the gross national expenditure.

Until fairly recently the links between balance of payments data and the national income and expenditure accounts were not fully articulated in the balance of payments reports. Users of historical balance of payments reports will find it necessary to make a number of adjustments to move to the national accounts basis of presentation shown here. In recent balance of payments publications, however, the figures are fully reconciled.

In some earlier years in the balance of payments reports there appears in both current receipts and current payments an entry for mutual aid to NATO countries. These entries have to be eliminated for use in the national income and expenditure accounts since the amounts represent provision of goods and services which have already been counted as Canadian production in government defence expenditure for goods and services, either in the current period or in some previous period. The adjustments are self-cancelling since they reduce both exports of goods and services and imports of goods and services by identical amounts, and gross national expenditure is not affected.

In earlier years, and particularly in the war and early post-war period, a number of special adjustments have been made to the basic balance of payments data for national income and expenditure accounts purposes. These and other aspects of transactions with non-residents are described more fully in *Volume 3,* Chapter 8. A complete reconciliation between the national accounts presentation and the balance of payments presentation is given in table 60 of *National Income and Expenditure Accounts, 1962-1976.*

F31. Residual error of estimate is an adjustment for inaccuracies and imperfections in the basic statistics required to bring the gross national product and gross national expenditure into arithmetical balance. (See note to series F12).

F33-55. Gross national expenditure in constant (1971) dollars, by components, 1926 to 1976

SOURCE: same as series F1-13.

The data of series F33-45 differ from those of series F14-32 only in that these expenditures are measured in constant (1971) dollars rather than current dollars and that there are adjusting entries, described below, not present in series

F14-32. The content of each of the series given here is the same, therefore, as that given under the same heading in series F14-32.

In principle, the conversion of the current value figures to constant dollar estimates involves the breakdown of changes in current value estimates into the price and quantity constituents. This is accomplished by constructing appropriate price indexes which are then used to 'deflate' the value data and to reveal the underlying change in physical volume.

The estimation of constant dollar expenditure from current dollar expenditure was done in two steps, common to all the main categories given here with the exception of inventories. First, the individual subcomponents of the expenditure categories of series F14-32 were deflated in rather fine detail by, for the most part, Laspeyres-type price indexes. For example, 140 subcomponents of personal expenditure on consumer goods and services were deflated separately; government and business gross capital formation were deflated in considerable but somewhat less detail. Exports and imports were deflated in fine detail, about 35 subcomponents each, using mainly unit value price indexes for the period up to 1961, and specially constructed price deflators based on specific pricing procedures in the more recent period.

Once the deflation of the subcomponent detail was completed, the second step was to add all of this deflated subcomponent detail to derive the constant dollar aggregates given here.

The procedure used for converting the value of the physical change in inventories into constant dollar estimates is somewhat different. For farm inventories and grain in commercial channels, the constant dollar series is derived by valuing, in prices relevant to the base period chosen, the physical quantities of stocks. Data on prices, physical quantities of grain stocks held in inventory, and numbers of poultry and livestock are obtained from the Agriculture Division of Statistics Canada. The procedures in this area are therefore quite straightforward.

The procedure for the conversion of non-farm inventories differs from the above because detail on physical quantities is not available. The information given consists of current dollar book values only, from which it is necessary to remove the effect of price changes relevant to the base period. The first step is to estimate the book values of inventory stocks. This process is carried out in considerable detail for a large number of industry groups. The second step is to construct a weighted price index for deflating industry book values. This step involves knowledge of the commodity composition of inventory book values, the change in the price of these commodities and the time period over which the stocks have been acquired based on the rate of turnover of inventory holdings. The third step involves calculating the constant dollar book values in terms of base-period prices. The final step is to calculate the year-to-year change in the physical volume of inventories expressed as the change in these constant dollar book values.

The grand total of gross national expenditure in constant dollars is the sum of all the components measured in constant dollars plus the adjusting entries.

When constant dollar estimates are put on a new time reference base, such as 1971 in the present series, the entire constant dollar series from 1926 is not reweighted on the basis of 1971 prices. Although 1971 is the current time reference base for the entire span of years, five different sets of price weights are incorporated in the series, covering five different time segments. The results are linked together mechanically at the overlap years. The five weight bases reflect the prices of 1935 to 1939 for the period 1926 to 1947; 1949 for the period 1947-56; 1957 for the period 1956 to 1961; 1961 for the period 1961 to 1971; and 1971 for the period 1971 to 1975. The retention of the early price weights in the rebased constant dollar series is required in order that the price-weight base will best reflect the patterns of relative prices in the period for which it is used.

As a result of the mechanical linking process, constant dollar gross national expenditure and its components retain the same year-to-year volume movements as was shown in each original series. However, the linking process gives rise to adjusting entries, as the individually linked components will not add exactly to the gross national expenditure totals which are independently linked. These adjusting entries are primarily a function of differences in the structure of the price-weight base at the year of overlap.

Implicit price deflators may be obtained for each component, for each subtotal and for gross national expenditure by dividing each series in current dollars by the corresponding series in constant dollars. These implicit price indexes are given in Section K. It should be noted that in effect the implicit deflators are currently weighted Paasche-type indexes at the aggregate level but in corporate fixed weighting of the Laspeyres type of index at the detailed subcomponent level.

A full description of the deflation procedure is given in the basic reference document, *Volume 3*, Chapter 9.

F56-75. Gross domestic product at factor cost, by industry, 1926 to 1976

SOURCE: same as series F1-13.

Gross domestic product at factor cost measures the value of production arising within the geographical boundaries of Canada irrespective of whether the factors of production involved are resident or non-resident. It differs from gross national product at market prices in two ways: first, it includes net income earned by and paid to non-residents but originating in Canada (see adjustment series F73); second, it excludes indirect taxes less subsidies (see adjustment series F72). The adjustments required to move from gross domestic product at factor cost to gross national product at market prices are shown in series F72-74.

Gross domestic product at factor cost, by industry, shows the industrial origin of economic production. In effect, it reveals the 'value' added by each industry to the value of the country's total production. For the assembly and analysis of industrial statistics, the domestic product concept is preferable to the national product concept since it deals with production originating within the country's geographical boundaries, and also avoids the statistical problem of having to allocate net interest and dividends paid to non-residents by industrial origin. In addition, the 'factor cost' concept is more appropriate for this purpose than the 'market price' concept, since indirect taxes levied by governments with respect to purchases and sales of goods and services bear much more heavily on some industries than on others. The relative share of an industry's contribution to production in terms of factor use is therefore more clearly depicted if indirect taxes less subsidies are excluded from the calculations.

The contribution to production of each industry, that is, the net value added, is the sum of factor payments originating in the industry. These are wages, salaries, supplementary labour income, profits and other forms of investment income, net rents, net income of unincorporated business enterprises and the capital consumption allowances in the industry.

To produce an industrial classification of gross domestic product according to 'type of activity' involved, the unit of classification should in principle be an operating entity which engages in only one type of economic activity. For statistical purposes, the smallest unit that is a separate operating entity capable of reporting all elements of basic industrial statistics is the 'establishment'. The establishment is usually engaged in only one major kind of activity and since it is the smallest statistical unit capable of collecting all the essential elements of industrial statistics, it is the preferred unit of classification in the industrial distribution. Some establishments, however, are rather complex and engage in a number of activities. In such cases, the establishment is assigned wholly to the industry of its principal activity and its total output is included in the measure of output for that industry.

In the industrial distribution of gross domestic product, the largest single component (wages, salaries and supplementary labour income) is classified industrially on the basis of establishment data. Net income of non-farm unincorporated business is partly on an establishment basis and accrued net income of farm operators from farm production is on an activity basis which is not too far removed from the concept of the establishment. Other major elements of gross domestic product which cannot be obtained by establishment are corporation profits, corporate capital consumption allowances and some elements of investment income. In these cases, the data are not reported by individual establishments, but by the company, which may include one or more establishments. The unit of classification must necessarily be based on this broader statistical entity.

The industrial classification of gross domestic product groups together all operating units, for example, establishments or companies, according to whether they are engaged in the same or a similar kind of economic activity. In effect, it shows the way in which the gross domestic product is produced by principal type of economic activity. In this context, the industrial grouping does not depend upon whether the activity is carried on by a government agency or by a business enterprise, or whether on a profit or non-profit basis. An industry is defined for this purpose simply as a group of establishments or operating units whose activities have sufficient common characteristics that they may be usefully grouped together for analytical purposes.

Thus, in series F56, agriculture includes not only establishments engaged in commercial farming activity, but also experimental farms operated by federal or provincial governments, university farms and institutional farms operated in connection with penitentiaries or religious orders. Forestry, series F57, includes establishments engaged in forestry patrol, fire inspection, fire fighting, forest nurseries, reforestation and other forestry services, whether conducted by government organizations or commercial enterprises. Fishing, series F58, includes establishments engaged in operating fish hatcheries and fishery inspection and protection services, whether operated by government departments or not. Transportation, series F62, includes government services incidental to air transport such as establishments engaged in the operation and maintenance of civil airports; government services incidental to water transport, such as the establishments engaged in the operation and maintenance of piers, docks, wharves and associated facilities; and government establishments providing services associated

with the operation and maintenance of highways, bridges and tunnels. The community, business and personal service industry, series F70, includes all government establishments engaged in education and in the delivery of hospital and medical care services. The service industry includes, in addition to the activities noted above, theatres and other entertainment, professional services, domestic services, barber shops, hotels, cleaning and laundering and the like.

Because so much of the economic activity which is related to the operations of 'general government' is reallocated and assigned to its related industrial group in the industrial distribution, the 'public administration and defence' industry, series F69, provides a very much truncated view of the full range of government activity. It includes only those establishments of government which clearly do not belong in any other branch of economic activity but which are essentially concerned with general administration, the internal service agencies of the public service, and defence, for example, the enactment of legislation, law enforcement and administration, the collection of public revenues and controlling the disbursement of public funds. Defence services maintained primarily for the protection of the state are in the same general category. The industrial classification of an establishment is thus not dependent on whether it is owned privately or publicly, or on whether it is organized on a commercial or a non-commercial basis. The classification system is based essentially on the concept of type of activity.

The industrial distribution of wages, salaries and supplementary labour income is given in Section E. Labour income by industry for the period 1919 to 1926 is given in series F166-178. The industrial distribution of investment income and of income of unincorporated business, including farm income, may be found in tables 30 and 31, respectively, in *National Income and Expenditure Accounts, 1962-1976*.

All imputed income must be allocated to the appropriate industry of origin in the industrial classification of gross domestic product. Thus, imputed net rents, and capital comsumption allowances, of owner-occupied housing are classified to the finance, insurance and real estate industry. Farm products consumed directly in farm households are assigned to gross domestic product originating in agriculture. Food and lodging provided to employees in lieu of wages is allocated to the industry in which the particular 'income in kind' originates. Depreciation on government fixed assets is allocated largely to three main industrial groups: public administration and defence (general government assets); community, business and personal service (primarily schools and hospitals); and electric power, gas, and water utilities (municipal water systems). All imputed banking services rendered without charge to persons and governments is shown as originating in finance, insurance and real estate.

A basic question on origin of economic production is raised in the case of leased equipment and rented property. If a real estate operator, for example, rents a building to a group of retail establishments, present practices call for showing the net rents and capital consumption allowances originating in the real estate, or owning industry. A case can be made that since renting is simply an alternative way of obtaining capital equipment for use in the production process, the net rental income from such capital and the associated capital consumption allowances should, in principle, be treated as originating in the using industry. As a practical matter, because it is not ordinarily possible for the using industry to report data on capital consumption allowances and net rents, the production and income associated with leased equipment and rented property are at present assigned to the industry owning the assets.

F76-90. Personal income and its disposition, 1926 to 1976

SOURCE: same as series F1-13.

Personal income includes all factor incomes of persons such as wages and salaries and net incomes of unincorporated businesses; interest, dividends and various types of investment income of persons (including investment income accumulated on behalf of persons by life insurance companies, private pension funds and similar institutions); and all transfer payments received by persons from governments (such as old age pensions, mothers' and dependents' allowances, and unemployment insurance benefits) as well as transfers from corporations and non-residents. 'Persons' and the 'personal sector' are defined to include private pension plans and private non-commercial institutions such as universities, labour unions, professional organizations, fraternal societies and charitable institutions.

While the national income includes all earnings of the various factors of production arising from the current production of goods and services, personal income includes only the part of the national income which is paid out to persons. It also includes large amounts of income of a transfer payment nature which is not included in the national income. The relationship between the national income and personal income is shown in series F76-81. All earnings not paid out to persons, series F80, are deducted from the national income to arrive at personal income. Such earnings include the undistributed earnings of corporations and government business enterprises, the direct taxes of corporations and government business enterprises, government investment income and the inventory valuation adjustment. At the same time, income received by persons in the form of current transfer payments from the government and other sectors are added back, series F77 and F78. The resulting figure is the total of personal income, series F81.

F76. National income is described in the general note to series F1-152 and in the notes to series F1-8.

F77. Transfer payments shown here are mainly transfer payments to persons from government, such as family allowances, old age pensions, pensions to the blind, mothers' allowances, veterans' pensions and gratuities, unemployment insurance benefits, workmen's compensation benefits, pensions to government employees and government grants to the non-profit institutions, such as operating and capital grants to charitable organizations and universities. Also included in this series are current transfers from non-residents, mainly personal and institutional remittances and pensions received from non-residents, and a small amount of capital assistance to persons from government. Current transfers to persons from corporations, in the form of charitable contributions and bad debts, are not included here since they are already incorporated in the national income.

F78. Interest on the public debt includes the entire amount of interest paid by all levels of government. That part which is received by non-residents is offset by the explicit subtraction made in series F5 and described earlier in these notes. The transfer portion of interest on consumer debt paid by persons to corporations is included here to

compensate for its omission in the national income as described in series F5. The amount is subtracted in series F89 in arriving at personal saving.

F79. This is the sum of series F76-78.

F80. Earnings not paid out to persons include the undistributed earnings of corporations and government business enterprises, the direct taxes of corporations, government investment income and the inventory valuation adjustment.

F81. Personal income is a mixed concept. It consists essentially of that part of national income paid out to persons plus transfer payments from other sectors. However, it includes some income that is not received by persons in the accounting period in which it is entered. For example, it includes the interest earnings of life insurance companies. (See the general note to series F1-152.)

F82. Personal direct taxes consist of personal income taxes, succession duties and estate taxes, and employer and employee contributions to social insurance and government pension funds. The latter category includes contributions to unemployment insurance, workmen's compensation, non-trusteed public service pensions, industrial vacation claims, and the Canada and Quebec pension plans. Other current transfers from persons to the government consist of hospital and medical care premiums, the personal share of motor vehicle licenses and permits, miscellaneous licences and permits such as hunting and fishing permits and marriage licenses, and various fines and penalties.

F83. Personal disposable income is essentially that income available for discretionary disposal, after payment of direct taxes and other current transfers.

F84. Personal expenditure on consumer goods and services consists of personal expenditures on durable goods, semi-durable goods, non-durable goods, and services. For general note, see series F14.

F85. Personal expenditure on consumer durable goods includes outlays on new and used automobiles, home furnishings and furniture, stoves and ranges, other appliances, radios and television sets, sporting goods, household tools and garden equipment and like items. The values of trade-ins are subtracted.

F86. Personal expenditure on consumer semi-durable goods consists of outlays on men's and boys' clothing, women's and children's clothing, footwear and repairs, household textiles, glassware and tableware, books and magazines, and jewellery, watches and repairs.

F87. Personal expenditure on non-durable consumer goods consists of outlays for food and beverages, tobacco, electricity and gas, non-durable household supplies, drugs and sundries, gasoline, oil and grease, and toilet articles and cosmetics.

F88. Personal expenditure on services consists of such things as laundry and dry-cleaning service; expenditure on food in restaurants and hotels; gross space rent of tenants; imputed net residential rents of owner-occupied dwellings; telephone; domestic service; moving expenses; janitor service; rental of furniture and appliances; bridge, tunnel and ferry tolls; fares for taxis, railway, electric railway and bus, steamship and plane travel; personal health outlay expenses for medical, dental, osteopathic, chiropractic, nursing and hospital care, not covered under government administered insurance schemes; death expenses; expenditures on beauty parlours and barber shops; outlays for recreational, educational, religious and charitable activities; financial and legal services; hotel services; net expenditure abroad and miscellaneous services.

For a more detailed breakdown of consumer expenditures, see *National Income and Expenditure Accounts, 1962-1976*, table 53.

F89. Current transfers to corporations and non-residents consist of the transfer portion of interest on consumer debt paid to corporations and personal and institutional remittances paid to non-residents. These amounts are subtracted here since they are not available for personal saving.

F90. Personal saving is the residual amount left over after deducting personal expenditure on consumer goods and services, direct personal tax payments and various other current transfers from the total of personal income. Because the personal saving figure is calculated residually, it reflects the net effect of any errors occurring in the component estimates of income, consumer spending, and transfers to the government and other sectors. The error factor in this estimate is therefore likely to be greater than the error factor in any of the component estimates associated with it.

If the personal saving figure were to be disaggregated, it would be seen to consist of many elements of saving by persons and households such as the accumulation of bank balances, purchases of stocks and bonds, the repayment of mortgages, the net retirement of bank and finance company loans, accumulations in life insurance and pension funds, changes in farm inventories and inventories of other unincorporated businesses and many other forms of savings.

F91-102.   Personal income, by province, 1926 to 1976

SOURCE: same as series F1-13.

Personal income of each province and 'foreign countries' is that part of total personal income of Canadian residents, given in series F81, received by or accruing to persons in the province. (See the general note to series F1-152 for the definition of a person.)

The part of personal income assigned to 'foreign countries', series F102, consists of the income of Canadians temporarily abroad, such as those in the diplomatic service and members of the Canadian forces abroad.

F103-120.   Government revenue, expenditure and surplus or deficit, by component, all governments, 1926 to 1976

SOURCE: same as series F1-13.

The consolidated government revenues and expenditures presented here cover a very broad range of activities carried out directly by various levels of government or by their agencies. The essential characteristic of these government activities is that they are non-commercial in nature. They represent activities undertaken by the society on a collective basis and financed for the most part out of taxation or government borrowing. The activities of government business enterprises operating for a profit are not included here. Such enterprises are considered to be a part of the business sector since their method of operation and their motivations are similar to those of private business enterprises.

In general, the government sector as defined here covers

three main groups of activity for which the public authorities carry the primary responsibility. First, the departmental activities of the three levels of government (federal, provincial and local) ordinarily included in the so-called 'budgetary' transactions of governments. Second, the transactions of many government administered social insurance and trust funds, such as the Unemployment Insurance Fund, the Old Age Security Fund, Workmen's Compensation Funds, the Canada and Quebec pension plans, and various government employee pension funds, ordinarily regarded as 'extra-budgetary' transactions of governments. Third, the transactions of various government agencies, commissions and boards which are financed out of public funds, receiving all or most of their income from government grants. The revenues and expenditures of the Post Office Department are excluded from the departmental activities of government since this agency is treated in the national accounts as a government business enterprise.

The 'extra-budgetary' transactions of the social insurance and trust funds now comprise a substantial part of the total income and outlay of the public sector.

In addition, the activities of government agencies, commissions and boards which operate on an essentially non-commercial basis and which carry out various functions delegated to them by the public authorities are included here. These comprise such federal agencies as Atomic Energy of Canada Limited, the National Research Council, the National Capital Commission, and the National Film Board; such provincial agencies as hospital and health services commissions; and various municipal boards and agencies, including school boards and municipal waterworks authorities.

Certain other activities of government, however, have quite different characteristics in that they involve the production of goods and services for sale on the open market at a price to the consumer which is intended to compensate wholly or largely for their costs or to yield a profit. Such agencies are classified as government business enterprises. The activities of these enterprises are of a commercial or industrial nature. Examples of such agencies are the provincial hydro commissions, provincial telephone companies and federal transportation companies. The distinguishing feature of a government business enterprise in contrast to a general government operation is that its motivation and behaviour essentially parallels that of a private business enterprise. Its revenues are derived mainly from the sale of goods and services, it usually aims to be self-sustaining and it generally maintains control over its transactions in the form of a profit and loss statement. The revenue and expenditure transactions of such entities are not included here but their remitted profits are consolidated with government investment.

Since 1961 the revenue and expenditure transactions of public hospitals, which were treated as part of the personal sector prior to 1961, have been included with the 'non-commercial' government sector. These transactions are consolidated with the revenue and expenditure figures in the table. The transactions of all government administered medical care plans are also included. In addition, all of the activities in the field of education coming under locally administered elementary and secondary school systems, and provincially operated community colleges are included. Municipal waterworks are also regarded as a part of the 'general government' sector and their activities are consolidated with the transactions shown in this table.

Government capital outlays, government gross fixed capital formation and investment in inventories, are capitalized and treated as a part of the economy's gross capital formation in physical assets. They form a part of total government expenditure for all purposes. An imputed depreciation or capital consumption allowance is entered in the accounts of the government sector to record the using up of the fixed capital portion of these assets.

A more complete description of the government sector as presented in this table will be found in *Volume 3, Chapter 6.*

F103. Personal direct taxes are described in the note to series F82. More detail, by level of government, is given in table 44 of *National Income and Expenditure Accounts, 1962-1976.*

F104. Corporation direct taxes are taxes on corporation income (profits) by the federal and provincial governments. They include the non-refundable part of federal excess profits taxes, the special provincial taxes on mining and logging profits and the part of the federal profits tax earmarked for the old age security fund. They exclude, in addition to the refundable part of excess profits taxes, profits taxes later adjusted by renegotiation of war contracts. Corporation profits taxes are given on an accrual basis here. Table 21, of the source volume mentioned above, gives the amounts actually collected and the adjustment for accruals separately, and table 45 of the same volume gives further detail by level of government.

Due to space limitations, the box heading in series F104 has been condensed by eliminating the word 'enterprise'. The full heading should read 'Corporate and government business enterprise'.

F105. Direct taxes on non-residents, withholding taxes, are federal taxes representing amounts of income withheld from payment and remitted to the federal government on earnings of non-residents. The taxes apply on interest, dividends, rents, royalties and other forms of income payable to non-residents.

F106. Indirect taxes are described in the note to series F10. Detail by type and level of government may be found in table 46 of the above mentioned source volume.

F107. Other current transfers to government from persons are described in the note to series F82. Details by type and level of government may be found in table 47 of the above mentioned source volume.

F108. Government investment income is described in the note to series F5. Details by type and level of government may be found in table 48 of the above mentioned source volume.

F109. Total government revenue is the sum of series F103-108.

F110. Government current expenditure on goods and services is described in the note to series F15. Details by type and level of government may be found in table 49 of the above mentioned source volume.

F111. Government transfer payments to persons do not measure currently produced goods and services, but represent simply a redistribution of income already earned and counted. They are unilateral transactions in which there is no compensation. Included here are such federal government payments to persons as family and youth allowances, unemployment benefits, old age security benefits, veterans' disability pensions, pensions paid to government employees,

various scholarships and research grants, grants to private non-commercial institutions and adult occupational training payments. At the provincial and local levels, these transfer payments include such items as social welfare payments, for example, direct relief, old age and blind pensions, and mothers' and disabled persons' allowances; workmen's compensation benefits; grants to post-secondary educational institutions; and grants to other private non-commercial institutions and associations. Pensions paid out under the Canada and Quebec pension plans also form a part of the total of government transfer payments to persons.

A detailed breakdown of government transfers to persons, by level of government and by type of payment, is provided in table 50 of the above mentioned source volume.

F112. Government subsidy payments are described in the note to series F10. Details by type and level of government may be found in table 51 of the above mentioned source volume.

F113. Capital assistance covers grants to industry for plant expansion and improvement or to encourage new construction. Specific examples of such payments are grants under programs of the Department of Regional Economic Expansion, grants toward the construction of fishing vessels, the $500 winter house-building bonus and grants to foster the technical capability of Canadian industry.

F114. Current transfers to non-residents consist of federal pensions and other benefits paid abroad, such as old age security benefits, public service pensions, veterans' pensions, and official payments for international assistance.

F115. Interest on the public debt consists of all interest paid or accruing to Canadian residents and non-residents on the outstanding debt of the various levels of government. The figures are shown on a gross basis and do not reflect any netting out to take account of receipts of interest on government loans and advances to its own or other agencies.

F116. Total government current expenditure is the sum of series F110-115. It may be noted that the grand total of government expenditure for all purposes may be obtained by adding together series F116, total current expenditure, and series F119, total government gross capital formation, that is, capital expenditure. The difference between this grand total of all expenditures and the grand total of revenues, series F109, plus depreciation allowances, series F118, is equal to the government surplus (+) or deficit (-) position, series F120.

F117. Government saving is the difference between government current revenues, series F109, and government current expenditures, series F116.

F118. Government capital consumption allowances are described in the note to series F11.

F119. Government gross capital formation, that is, capital expenditure, is described in the note to series F17-20.

F120. The government surplus (+) or deficit (-) on transactions related to the national accounts is the residual obtained by subtracting total government expenditures, both current and capital, from total government revenues including capital consumption allowances. The figure is a measure of the government sector's net lending to (if positive) or net borrowing from (if negative) other sectors. It shows whether the government sector has been a net contributor to, or a net demander of, funds for the finance of investment.

F121-134. Finance of saving and investment, 1926 to 1976

SOURCE: same as series F1-13.

This table is designed to show total gross fixed capital formation in the economy and the sources from which these capital outlays were financed. In effect, the right hand side of the table shows the demand for saving required to finance investment; and the left hand side of the table shows the sources from which this saving was provided, in the form of national saving by persons, business and governments, and in the form of saving provided by non-residents, that is, net borrowing by Canada from abroad.

F121. This total is the sum of series F122-127.

F122. Personal saving is described in the note to series F90.

F123. The adjustment on grain transactions is essentially an allocation of earnings arising out of the operations of the Canadian Wheat Board and, in earlier years, the Canadian Cooperative Wheat Producers, to place the earnings of farmers arising out of these operations on an accrual basis.

F124. Government saving is described in the note to series F117.

F125. Undistributed profits of corporations and government business enterprises consist of the amount of earnings retained after payment of taxes, distribution of dividends to Canadian residents and to abroad, payment of various transfer payments and, in the case of government business enterprises, after profits remitted to governments.

F126. The inventory valuation adjustment is described in the note to series F8.

F127. Capital assistance is described in the note to series F113.

F128. Capital consumption allowances are described in the note to series F11.

F129. The surplus (-) or deficit (+) of Canada on current transactions with non-residents is simply a measure of the degree to which Canada has been required to draw upon foreign resources from abroad to help finance its capital investment program. In this table, a positive sign (+) means that Canada has drawn upon foreign resources or foreign savings, that is, has incurred a deficit on transactions in goods and services with non-residents. A negative sign (-) means that Canada has run a surplus on transactions in goods and services with non-residents and has thereby contributed to the savings resource requirements of the rest of the world. The net figures shown here are equal to the difference between exports of goods and services and imports of goods and services, series F29 and F30, plus or minus a small amount of net current transfers paid to or received from abroad. The full reconciliation with series F29 and F30 may be obtained from table 60 of *National Income and Expenditure Accounts, 1962-1976*.

F130. The residual error of estimate is described in the note to series F12 and F31.

F131. This total is the sum of the subtotal series F121 plus series F128-130 inclusive. It is also equal to the sum of series F132-134.

F132. Gross fixed capital formation is described in the notes to series F16 and F17-24.

F133. Value of physical change in inventories is described in the notes to series F25-28.

F134. The residual error of estimate is described in the note to series F12 and F31.

F135-152. Gross fixed capital formation, by industry, 1926 to 1976

SOURCE: same as series F1-13.

The industrial breakdown of gross fixed capital formation is based on the industrial classification of capital expenditures set out in the regular series of Statistics Canada reports, *Private and Public Investment in Canada, Outlook*, (Catalogue 61-205), and similar reports for earlier years from Statistics Canada and the Department of Industry, Trade and Commerce. The basis of classification is the Standard Industrial Classification in which the establishment is the key unit of reporting. The classification by industry refers to the industry of ownership.

A number of adjustments are required to move from the private and public investment figures which form the basic source data to the figures given here on the national accounts basis or presentation. *Volume 3*, provides a summary view of these adjustments, on pages 231 and 233.

F135. Total gross fixed capital formation in current dollars is the sum of series F136, business gross fixed capital formation, and series F148, government gross fixed capital formation.

F136. This series covers business outlays for non-residential construction, machinery and equipment, and housing. It corresponds to series F21 discussed earlier. The reader is referred to the notes to series F21-24 for a more complete description of concepts and coverage.

F137-147. This group of series shows the industrial breakdown of business outlays for plant and equipment and for housing. The housing estimates, except for a small amount of government housing, are included with finance, insurance and real estate.

F137. Excludes investment of government experimental farms. Also excludes government-owned fish hatcheries and fishing inspection and protection services.

F142. Includes air, railway and water transport services; motor transport; urban transit systems; pipelines; grain elevators; toll highways and bridges; and warehousing.

F143. Includes broadcasting, and telephone and telegraph services.

F145. Includes wholesale and retail trade.

F146. Includes capital outlays by banks, insurance, trust and loan companies, real estate establishments primarily engaged in owning and operating real estate, or in developing and improving real estate. Estimates for residential housing are included in this industry, except for residential housing by government.

F147. Includes investment by laundries and dry cleaners, motion picture theatres, hotels and other commercial services. In recent years this last category has reflected an increase in the leasing of machinery and equipment.

F148. This series covers government outlays for non-residential construction, machinery and equipment, and a small amount of housing. It corresponds to series F17-20 discussed earlier.

F149. Includes investment by municipal water systems which are treated as a part of general government and are not included with series F144.

F150. Includes investment in residential construction by the federal government.

F151. Communication and community service has been reduced to only community service since the year 1959 with the transfer of the Canadian Broadcasting Corporation from government to the business sector in the national accounts classification system. It now contains only investment by hospitals and provincial and municipal schools.

F152. Includes estimates of gross fixed capital investment by federal, provincial and municipal government departments.

Income Produced and Capital Formation before 1926 (Series F153-182)

General note

Many of the sources of data for national income used for the period from 1926 onward were also available for earlier years. For example, fairly comprehensive data on annual production in agriculture began in 1908. Fisheries production was available annually, in improved form, from 1911. The annual census of manufactures and of electrical stations began in 1917, mineral production was available from 1886, the census of mining from 1920 and collection of employment data began in 1921. Many of the data on banks, insurance and other financial companies; on railways, telegraphs and telephones; and on governments, were available annually as were the data on foreign trade. During this period, improved annual data on wage rates and prices were emerging. A census of manufacturing was taken with each decennial census until 1911 and 'postal' censuses for 1905 and 1915. An incomplete census of trade was taken for 1923.

In addition, some material was available for Ontario from an annual census of manufactures from 1900 to 1914.

These data form much of the basis for the estimates of national income from 1919 to 1926 and the estimates of capital formation from 1901 to 1930 given in this subsection.

F153-165. Net domestic income, by industry, 1919 to 1926

SOURCE: *Estimates of Net Domestic Income at Factor Cost and Labour Income by Industry, 1919-1926*, (a private, unpublished, mimeographed memorandum prepared by D.H. Jones, of Statistics Canada).

These estimates of net domestic income, 1919 to 1926, correspond to those appearing for gross domestic product, by industry, in series F56-75 for 1926 to 1976, with the exception that the latter measures product at factor costs plus capital consumption allowances and miscellaneous valuation adjustments while the former includes only factor incomes. The difference between the two totals in 1926, the year of

overlap, is equal to the capital consumption allowances and adjustments.

The concepts of the two sets of series are identical but methods of measurement are quite different. Estimates of national income and related aggregates, prepared by Statistics Canada before it began publication of the national accounts at the end of World War II had been ' ...derived for the most part by subtracting estimates of materials and services used and depreciation from the value of gross output, industry by industry, using for this purpose a fairly extensive body of economic statistics collected annually or decennially by the Dominion Bureau of Statistics', see source, p. 2. The worksheets underlying the earlier estimates provided the main basis for the estimates given here. Unpublished revisions of the original data were used and in a few cases the data were traced back to the primary sources. The data were rearranged and adjusted to fit the later concepts and industry classification.

The levels of the estimates were adjusted, industry by industry, by linking them with the official series at 1926. As a check, estimates of net domestic income were extended to 1927, 1928 and 1929, excluding agriculture, public administration and defence. The estimates of the projected series were 99.2 per cent of the sum of the same components of the official series in 1927, 99.2 per cent in 1928 and 99.6 per cent in 1929. Agriculture, public administration and defence were calculated by exactly the same methods for 1919 to 1926 as for the later official series.

The relation of the industry groups given here to those of series F56-75 is apparent from the headings. Two points need attention. No inventory valuation adjustment has been made for wholesale and retail trade; the net imputed rent of government buildings is included with finance, insurance and real estate and not with service.

F166-178. Labour income, by industry, 1919 to 1926

SOURCE: same as series F153-165.

Wages and salaries were estimated for 1919 to 1925, insofar as possible, by methods identical to those used from 1926 onward, (see the general note to series F1-152). Wages in construction were based on the value of construction and its implied labour content from material in Buckley, *Capital Formation in Canada, 1896-1930*. The resulting estimates were then adjusted upwards to take account of supplementary labour income, industry by industry, in the proportion that it had to wages and salaries in 1926.

A check made by comparing the change in labour income as derived from earnings of wage earners in the 1921 and 1931 censuses with that obtained from the national income data between the two periods suggested, on the basis of reasonable assumptions, that the estimating techniques were quite good.

F179-182. Gross domestic capital formation, by quinquennial periods, 1901 to 1930

SOURCE: Buckley, *Capital Formation in Canada, 1896 to 1930.*

Conceptually, Buckley's estimates cover the same items as in the national accounts from 1926 onward and in series F135-152. Government fixed capital formation is included as well as private capital formation. All commercial vehicles and 20 per cent of outlay on passenger automobiles are included as belonging to government or business capital formation. Housing is included but consumer durables are not. The estimate of inventory investment is the value of the physical change in inventories.

Buckley's estimates of fixed capital formation were built up, in the main, from annual flows of construction materials and machinery and equipment. Imports are added to production and exports are subtracted to estimate the flows. The derivation of the construction estimates is described in Section S. The values of flows of machinery and equipment at producers' prices were adjusted for taxes, freight and mark-ups.

The main sources of the machinery and equipment data were annual reports of external trade, the federal censuses of manufactures for 1900, 1905, 1910, 1915 and annually from 1917 to 1930 and the Ontario census of manufactures for 1900 to 1914. In addition, annual direct estimates of outlay on railway rolling stock, for the whole period, were calculated from railway and government accounts; on ship-building from shipping reports of the Department of National Revenue; on motor vehicle sales from registration of motor vehicles for 1904 to 1916. Freight costs were estimated by data provided by Statistics Canada as far back as 1913, or before that, from estimates in Viner, *Canada's Balance*, (see Section G). Sales and excise taxes were calculated by applying rates of tax to the values at producers' prices, including import duties, and mark-up margins from material provided by Statistics Canada. The data for 1926 to 1930 are mainly from estimates in *Public Investment and Capital Formation*, which were based on the same methods, (see Section S).

Investment in inventories was calculated from various official annual data for livestock on farms from 1907, grain on farms from 1909 and grain in commercial channels from 1910; for earlier years some data were obtained from censuses and some were estimated on the basis of production. Manufacturing inventories were obtained from Statistics Canada for the postal census of 1915 and the annual census of manufactures. For 1900, 1905 and 1910 they were taken as 50 per cent of the working capital, the ratio being based on the 1915 data. Trade inventories were estimated as a constant proportion of the sum of exports and imports, the proportion being based on the same ratios that existed in 1925 to 1930. All trade inventory investment in 1901 to 1925 and manufacturing investment in 1901 to 1915 were estimated by the five-year periods given here. Price indexes used for deflating inventory investment in livestock and grain were mainly based on official sources. For manufacturing and trade, the wholesale price index of Statistics Canada, *Prices and Price Indexes*, was used, (see Section K).

The years 1926 to 1930 are given to provide an overlap with the official data.

The source also contains annual estimates of the flow of five categories of machinery and equipment at producers' prices and quinquennial estimates of capital formation for the same categories.

Stock of Business and Social Capital at Mid-year, and Inventories at Year-end, (Series F183-224)

General note

The concept of capital used here corresponds very closely to that underlying the estimates of fixed capital formation given in earlier tables of this section. The estimates cover fixed tangible capital stocks with the capacity to produce goods and services into the future and that have themselves been produced by human effort. They do not include gifts of nature such as the value of natural resources, land, forest stands, mineral and oil deposits and the like, or intangible assets such as goodwill and the accumulated training, skills and knowledge of people. Residential housing is included in capital but other consumer durables are not. Inventories in the usual sense of the term are not included.

Gross capital is valued at its monetary cost. Most of the estimates reproduced here are valued at cost expressed in terms of constant (1971) dollars. Thus, they provide a means of measuring the growth or decline in the real gross physical stock of fixed capital assets. In addition, estimates of 'industry' capital are also provided here in terms of their original cost at the time of purchase. In these estimates, each item of capital in the stock is measured in the prices that prevailed at the time it was actually produced.

The net capital stock is measured by subtraction from the gross stock of an estimate of the service capacity of the gross stock which has been used up in depreciation, obsolescence, fire destruction and other damage. For the estimates of the net capital stock in constant dollars, depreciation and the like are measured in constant dollars, just as the gross stock was. For the estimates of the net capital stock at original cost, the depreciation and like items are valued in prices of the years in which the capital was produced.

Industry capital covers a slightly different part of the economy than that covered in the national accounts by business gross fixed capital formation in non-residential construction and machinery and equipment. The latter includes churches, universities and other non-commercial institutions; in the capital stock figures, these institutions are covered in social capital. Government business enterprises, however, remain in the industry group.

In the calculation of the size of the capital stock, the 'perpetual inventory' method was used. The estimation of capital stock in any one year requires a knowledge of the length of life of capital goods and the amount of gross capital formation in them for each year before the date for which the stock is being measured, as far back as the average length of life of the capital. The gross stock, at the required date, is then estimated as the sum of capital formation in these preceding years. For example, if the length of life of a capital item is 10 years and if the gross stock at the end of 1969 were to be measured, it would be obtained by adding together gross capital formation for the item from 1960 to 1969. The estimation of the gross capital stock at the end of 1970 would be obtained by subtracting from the 1969 year-end stock the gross capital formation in 1960 and adding to it that in 1970.

The net capital stock is obtained by accumulating the annual capital consumption of the capital goods still covered in the gross stock and by subtracting this accumulated amount from the gross stock. This involves calculating depreciation and like costs on a straight-line basis over the life of the capital good. A capital good with a 10-year life would be depreciated at 10 per cent per year.

When the capital formation, on which the stock estimates are based, was first estimated in current dollars, it was calculated in constant dollars by deflation of the current dollar estimates of capital formation by an index of the cost per unit of the capital formed. Similarly, for the constant dollar net capital formation estimates, it was necessary to adjust the depreciation on the capital item to the constant dollar basis.

The above methods of calculating the capital stock require estimates of capital formation of the length of life of capital goods and of the movements of prices (costs) of the capital goods. In some instances, for long-lived capital, it was necessary to go back as far as 1870 to obtain the 1926 stock estimate.

Capital formation was obtained by somewhat different methods for 1926 to 1975 and for the period before 1926. For 1926 to 1945, the capital formation estimates were, with slight modification, taken from Department of Trade and Commerce, *Private and Public Investment in Canada, 1926-1951;* for 1945 to 1975, they are based on the reports of actual expenditure obtained in the preparation of the annual report, *Private and Public Investment in Canada, Outlook.* (See Section S for a discussion of the construction component obtained in these two sources.) For the period prior to 1926, the main source for capital formation estimates was Buckley's, *Capital Formation in Canada, 1896-1930* (see Section S); and some rough estimates for this earlier period from other data. The capital formation estimates, and their accumulation, were in fairly fine detail for 1926 to 1975; they were in much broader aggregates for the preceding period.

Detail on the length of life of capital goods was obtained, mainly, from studies by engineers and accountants in Canada, the United States and the United Kingdom in the 1930s, to determine appropriate depreciation allowances for income tax purposes. The results were available in bulletins published by internal revenue services. Greatest use was made of Bulletin F prepared in the United States. Few provisions were made for changing the length of life of specific types of capital. An exception was in urban transport systems where the change from streetcars to buses resulted in a shorter life for equipment.

Price indexes came from a variety of sources. Some were based on indexes used for deflating capital expenditure in the national accounts, from 1926 onward; some were from United States indexes, adjusted for duties, transportation and the like; some were constructed from data on material prices and indexes on wages. In some cases before 1926, Buckley's implicit price index of construction costs and wholesale indexes of prices for machinery were used.

The data for earlier years, on which capital formation and price indexes were based, were frequently sketchy. Fortunately, the seriousness of this shortcoming is mitigated by the fact that when capital formation is growing rapidly, the capital stock is largely made up of capital formed in the years immediately preceding its date of measurement.

F183-192. Industry gross and net capital stock, in 1971 prices, by structure and machinery and equipment, mid-year, 1926 to 1975

SOURCE: for 1972 to 1975, Statistics Canada, *Fixed Capital Flows and Stocks, 1972-1976*, (Catalogue 13-211); for 1970 and 1971, same title, 1970-1974; for 1926 to 1969, same title, 1926-1973.

F183-187. See general note for a description of the industry gross stock estimates in constant (1971) dollars. Series F187, capital items charged to operating expenses, consists of certain durable items such as furniture, office

equipment, tools and so forth, which are sometimes not capitalized by business but are charged off as a current operating expense. To ensure the inclusion of these items in the capital stock, they are added here.

F188-192. See general note for a description of the industry net stock estimates in constant (1971) dollars. For series F192, see note to series F187.

F193-202. Industry gross and net capital stock, at original cost, by structure and machinery and equipment, mid-year, 1926 to 1975

SOURCE: same as series F183-192.

F193-197. See general note for a description of industry gross stock estimates at original cost. For series F197, see note to series F187.

F198-202. See general note for a description of industry net stock estimates at original cost. For series F202, see note to series F187.

F203-209. Gross stock of social capital, in 1971 prices, public and private, by type, mid-year, 1926 to 1975

SOURCE: for 1972 to 1975, Statistics Canada, *Fixed Capital Flows and Stocks, 1972-1976*, (Catalogue 13-211); for 1970 and 1971, same title, 1970-1974; for 1926 to 1969, same title, 1926-1973; housing estimates for all years were obtained from the Construction Division, Statistics Canada.

F203-206. Government social capital consists of schools, hospitals, waterworks, sewerage systems, bridges, roads, harbours, airports and various other publicly financed capital installations. See general note for a description of gross stock in constant (1971) dollars.

F207-208. Privately owned social capital consists of housing, universities, churches and various types of privately financed institutional capital of a non-commercial nature. Estimates were not available for the gross stock of housing expressed in constant (1971) dollars, the basic source material being collected on a net basis only.

F209. The sum of gross stock of government and privately owned social capital in constant (1971) dollars is available only for machinery and equipment. The construction component is not available because gross stock of housing cannot be estimated at the present time. For the net stock of housing, see series F215.

F210-220. Net stock of social capital, in 1971 prices, public and private, by type, mid-year, 1926 to 1975

SOURCE: same as series F203-209.

F210-213. See note to series F203-206. The difference between these two groups of series is that the one is on a gross basis, the other on a net basis.

F214-217. See note to series F207-208. The difference between these two groups of series is that one is on a gross basis, the other on a net basis. In addition, estimates of privately owned housing stocks are included here on a net basis.

F218-220. The sum of net stocks of government and privately owned social capital in constant (1971) dollars.

F221-224. Non-farm business inventories, year-end book value estimates, 1925 to 1976

SOURCE: National Accounts Branch, Statistics Canada.

Real Domestic Product, by Industry, (Series F225-240)

General note

This system of indexes shows the industrial composition of changes in the physical volume of output. Its principal feature is that it portrays the pattern of industry advances or declines, behind the increases or declines in total real output. This permits the contribution of each industry to be measured against the total change in real output.

The system of real output by industry indexes was originally developed in conjunction with the constant dollar estimates (deflation) of gross national expenditure, to provide an independent check on the results of the deflation procedure. This supplements and extends the measurement of the change in real output with information on its industrial composition. A description of these constant (1971) dollar estimates, derived by deflating the gross national expenditure with price indexes, is provided in the notes to series F33-55.

The indexes of real domestic product by industry are built around the concept of gross domestic product at factor cost. This aggregate provides the principal link from the national income and expenditure accounts to the real output indexes. Thus, gross national product or expenditure at market prices in current value can be converted to gross domestic product by subtracting indirect taxes less subsidies, to convert to a 'factor cost' concept, and adding back net interest and dividends paid abroad, to convert to a 'domestic' concept. The relationship is shown explicitly in the reconciliation between series F71 and F75.

In the indexes shown here, the data for gross domestic product at factor cost are expressed in terms of constant (1971) base-year prices so that changes in the physical volume of real output, in total and by industry, may be measured. In effect, these indexes of real domestic product are simply an extension of the index of industrial production (which includes only manufacturing, mining, quarrying and oil wells, and electric power, gas and water utilities) to cover the entire Canadian economy.

It may be noted that series F56-71 in this section provide data on the *value* of gross domestic product at factor cost by industry, that is, net value added by industry, in current dollar terms. However, the industrial classification employed in series F56-71 is not identical to that used in connection with the indexes of real domestic product by industry, for reasons which have to do with the nature of the primary data. In the former case, the classification is based on a mixture of company and establishment information, with profits, investment income, and capital consumption allowances classified on a company basis and most other components classified on an establishment basis. By contrast, the basic unit of classification employed throughout the indexes of real domestic product by industry is the establishment, the primary data being available in this form. Thus, the industry classifications in series F56-71 are not fully compatible with the system of industry classifications underlying the real domestic product by industry. The principal differences in the two sets of industry classifications concern the relationship between manufacturing and forestry, mining, and wholesale trade. For example, a manufacturing company whose profits, investment income and capital consumption allowances would be classified to manufacturing in series F60, might well have establishments producing output in forestry (pulp and paper manufacturing companies with their own forestry operations) or in mining (smelting and refinery companies with their own mining or oil and gas operations), or in wholesale trade (manufacturers' sales branches). In the real domestic product by industry indexes, the output of these manufacturing companies would be classified in four places: manufacturing, forestry, mining and wholesale trade. The user should be aware of this problem if industry information in series F56-71 is used in conjunction with industry information provided by the real domestic product indexes.

The indexes of real domestic product by industry are derived by a process of 'double deflation', deflating each industry's gross output and subtracting from it the deflated value of each industry's material inputs.

F225-240. Real domestic product, by industry, 1935 to 1976

SOURCE: for 1961 to 1976, Statistics Canada publications, *Indexes of Real Domestic Product by Industry*, (Catalogue 61-005), *Indexes of Real Domestic Product by Industry, 1961-1969*, (Catalogue 61-510), and *Real Domestic Product by Industry, 1971-1976*, (Catalogue 61-213); for 1935 to 1960, Statistics Canada, *Indexes of Real Domestic Product by Industry of Origin, 1935-61*, (Catalogue 61-505), which contain a full description of concepts, sources and methods.

Indexes of Labour Productivity and Unit Labour Cost, (Series F241-294)

General note

The measures of productivity given in these six tables relate output to labour input only, that is, output per person (column five in each table), or output per man-hour (column six in each table). It should be emphasized, however, that changes in output per unit of labour input cannot be attributed directly and solely to labour. The measures reflect not only changes in the skill and effort of the labour force, but also the contribution of other productive resources and the effectiveness with which all are combined and organized for production. In other words, changes in technology, capital investment, capacity utilization, work-flow, managerial skills and labour-management relations all have a bearing on movements in the 'labour productivity' series.

The unit labour cost series (column nine in each table) measure the relationship of labour compensation to real output, that is, labour cost per unit of output. This makes explicit the relationship between productivity and 'average wage rates' as expressed broadly in the series 'Compensation per man-hour'.

F242, 251, 260, 269, 278 and 287. Persons employed denote all persons engaged in the production of output, including paid and own-account workers, working employers and unpaid family workers.

F243, 252, 261, 270, 279 and 288. Man-hours worked are the sum of man-hours spent at the place of employment by persons employed and therefore differ from a measure of 'man-hours paid' by excluding time used on vacation, holiday, illness, accident and other authorized leave.

F244, 253, 262, 271, 280 and 289. Labour compensation is a measure of the value of labour services engaged in the production process. It includes all payments in cash or in kind by domestic producers to persons employed as remuneration for work, including wages, salaries and supplementary labour income of paid workers plus an imputed labour income for self-employed workers. Statistics of labour compensation represent the most comprehensive labour cost data available for all industries at the present time since they include both cash payments and supplements, and cover all persons employed for gain.

F245, 254, 263, 272, 281 and 290. Column five, 'Output per person', is calculated by dividing the indexes of column one, 'Output', by the indexes of column two, 'Persons employed'.

F246, 255, 264, 273, 282 and 291. Column six, 'Output per man-hour', is calculated by dividing the indexes of column one, 'Output', by the indexes of column three, 'Man-hours'.

F247, 256, 265, 274, 283 and 292. Column seven, 'Compensation per person', is calculated by dividing the indexes of column four, 'Labour compensation', by the indexes of column two, 'Persons employed'.

F248, 257, 266, 275, 284 and 293. Column eight, 'Compensation per man-hour', is calculated by dividing the indexes of column four, 'Labour compensation', by the indexes of column three, 'Man-hours'.

F249, 258, 267, 276, 285 and 294. Column nine, 'Unit labour cost', is calculated by dividing the indexes of column four, 'Labour compensation', by the indexes of column one, 'Output'. It may also be calculated by dividing the indexes of column eight, 'Compensation per man-hour', by the indexes of column six, 'Output per man-hour'.

F241-249.   Indexes of labour productivity and unit labour cost, in all commercial industries, 1946 to 1976

SOURCE: for all years, Statistics Canada, *Aggregate Productivity Measures*, (Catalogue 14-201); additional information on sources and methods is given in an earlier Statistics Canada report, *Indexes of Output per Person Employed and per Man-hour in Canada, Commercial Non-agricultural Industries, 1947-63*, (Catalogue 14-501).

All commercial industries consist of agriculture, manufacturing, all other commercial goods- producing industries and all commercial service-producing industries.

F250-258.   Indexes of labour productivity and unit labour cost, in commercial goods-producing industries, 1946 to 1976

SOURCE: same as series F241-249.

Commercial goods-producing industries include agriculture, manufacturing, forestry, fishing and trapping, mines (including milling), quarries and oil wells, construction, and electric power and gas distribution.

F259-267.   Indexes of labour productivity and unit labour cost, in commercial non-agricultural goods-producing industries, 1946 to 1976

SOURCE: same as series F241-249.

Commercial non-agricultural goods-producing industries are the same as that described for series F250-258, with agriculture omitted.

F268-276.   Indexes of labour productivity and unit labour cost, in agriculture, 1946 to 1976

SOURCE: same as series F241-249.

Agricultural indexes are shown separately in these series.

F277-285.   Indexes of labour productivity and unit labour cost, in commercial service-producing industries, 1946 to 1976

SOURCE: same as series F241-249.

Commercial service-producing industries include transportation, communication and other utilities (except highway and bridge maintenance and electric power, gas and water utilities); wholesale and retail trade; finance, insurance and real estate; offices of physicians and dentists; other commercial health services; motion picture and recreational services; services to business management; and personal (except private households) and miscellaneous services.

F286-294.   Indexes of labour productivity and unit labour cost, in manufacturing, 1946 to 1976

SOURCE: same as series F241-249.

Manufacturing output, by major groups, is shown in Section R. The concept of output used for each of these industrial groups is constant price gross domestic product at factor cost, by industry (real domestic product by industry), and is the summation of constant price output indexes for individual industries. The weights used to aggregate the industry measures are each industry's share of gross domestic product in the base year. A more complete description of the concepts, sources and methods of the output indexes is found in *Indexes of Real Domestic Product by Industry*, (Catalogues 61-506 and 61-510).

Series F1-13. National income and gross national product, by components, 1926 to 1976
(millions of dollars)

Year	Wages, salaries, and supplementary labour income	Military pay and allowances	Corporation profits before taxes	Deduct: dividends paid to non-residents	Interest and miscellaneous investment income	Accrued net income of farm operators from farm production	Net income of non-farm unincorporated business, including rent	Inventory valuation adjustment	Net national income at factor cost	Indirect taxes less subsidies	Capital consumption allowances and miscellaneous valuation adjustments	Residual error of estimate	Gross national product at market prices
	1	2	3	4	5	6	7	8	9	10	11	12	13
1976	107,922	1,453	19,985	-1,719	11,175	3,317	8,438	-2,064	148,507	21,520	20,738	266	191,031
1975	93,289	1,336	19,663	-1,835	8,661	3,944	7,669	-2,938	129,789	17,584	18,270	-300	165,343
1974	80,086	1,203	20,062	-1,645	7,632	3,859	6,901	-4,244	113,854	18,257	16,046	-629	147,528
1973	66,757	1,092	15,417	-1,277	5,359	3,009	6,656	-2,362	94,651	15,598	13,355	-44	123,560
1972	57,570	979	10,799	-1,031	4,577	1,662	6,170	-1,032	79,694	13,876	11,474	190	105,234
1971	51,528	908	8,681	-1,079	3,906	1,576	5,928	-665	70,783	12,276	10,500	891	94,450
1970	46,706	914	7,699	-952	3,428	1,211	5,424	-195	64,235	11,299	9,806	345	85,685
1969	43,065	884	8,294	-854	3,082	1,435	5,187	-576	60,517	10,722	9,019	-443	79,815
1968	38,444	874	7,742	-835	2,623	1,321	4,778	-341	54,606	9,662	8,308	10	72,586
1967	35,303	857	6,823	-874	2,362	1,239	4,355	-327	49,738	8,852	7,786	33	66,409
1966	31,878	751	6,714	-850	2,070	1,950	4,116	-335	46,294	8,030	7,322	182	61,828
1965	28,201	677	6,318	-828	1,891	1,389	3,893	-322	41,219	7,284	6,655	206	55,364
1964	25,367	667	5,841	-787	1,724	1,307	3,705	-144	37,680	6,441	6,108	51	50,280
1963	23,262	670	4,932	-652	1,563	1,562	3,576	-213	34,700	5,714	5,603	-39	45,978
1962	21,816	652	4,450	-621	1,416	1,377	3,380	-100	32,370	5,446	5,236	-125	42,927
1961	20,399	610	4,066	-622	1,284	826	3,261	-41	29,783	4,838	4,883	142	39,646
1960	19,582	559	3,870	-495	1,129	1,026	3,192	-26	28,837	4,587	4,739	196	38,359
1959	18,596	553	3,966	-527	1,062	1,008	3,207	-108	27,757	4,401	4,461	227	36,846
1958	17,435	547	3,669	-486	1,063	1,116	3,133	-41	26,436	4,036	4,135	170	34,777
1957	16,988	531	3,554	-505	977	908	2,962	-59	25,356	3,975	4,159	23	33,513
1956	15,696	475	3,928	-450	869	1,283	2,827	-245	24,383	3,731	3,814	130	32,058
1955	13,930	439	3,485	-396	764	1,120	2,748	-182	21,908	3,321	3,337	-38	28,528
1954	13,043	408	2,755	-339	628	918	2,498	87	19,998	3,042	2,930	-52	25,918
1953	12,714	348	2,985	-328	583	1,462	2,359	2	20,125	2,994	2,634	80	25,833
1952	11,768	305	3,071	-346	523	1,878	2,155	114	19,468	2,799	2,333	-12	24,588
1951	10,538	232	3,144	-379	463	1,868	1,976	-643	17,199	2,548	2,098	-205	21,640
1950	8,998	154	2,608	-412	396	1,301	1,882	-374	14,553	2,065	1,876	-3	18,491
1949	8,349	128	2,009	-326	291	1,211	1,773	-112	13,323	1,878	1,644	-45	16,800
1948	7,754	95	2,041	-257	243	1,360	1,604	-506	12,334	1,832	1,449	-106	15,509
1947	6,662	92	1,854	-255	194	1,100	1,506	-571	10,582	1,678	1,227	-14	13,473
1946	5,487	340	1,474	-205	170	1,031	1,320	-254	9,363	1,371	1,071	80	11,885
1945	5,037	1,117	1,244	-138	227	890	1,166	-37	9,506	1,084	1,042	231	11,863
1944	4,998	1,068	1,234	-153	220	1,073	1,065	-52	9,453	1,167	1,077	151	11,848
1943	4,812	910	1,281	-156	227	707	980	-83	8,678	1,170	1,099	106	11,053
1942	4,282	641	1,305	-170	185	917	939	-122	7,977	1,133	1,091	64	10,265
1941	3,608	386	1,119	-168	148	454	815	-156	6,206	1,090	934	52	8,282
1940	2,959	193	849	-182	115	473	699	-121	4,985	859	786	83	6,713
1939	2,601	32	698	-177	80	362	632	-56	4,172	759	671	19	5,621
1938	2,515	9	509	-175	68	353	596	67	3,942	661	639	30	5,272
1937	2,538	9	598	-166	94	280	564	-87	3,830	727	624	60	5,241
1936	2,241	9	475	-161	85	199	502	-36	3,314	680	575	65	4,634
1935	2,079	9	357	-120	94	218	434	-20	3,051	601	550	99	4,301
1934	1,939	8	295	-104	74	167	392	-39	2,732	591	536	110	3,969
1933	1,788	8	171	-98	55	66	360	-22	2,328	547	532	85	3,492
1932	1,975	8	32	-130	77	104	422	109	2,597	552	578	87	3,814
1931	2,408	8	163	-150	88	94	548	172	3,331	578	649	135	4,693
1930	2,786	8	321	-177	135	343	688	239	4,343	619	719	39	5,720
1929	2,940	8	554	-158	160	393	770	-15	4,652	711	726	50	6,139
1928	2,715	7	548	-115	143	633	746	1	4,678	707	676	-11	6,050
1927	2,506	7	474	-106	109	600	691	29	4,310	653	618	-20	5,561
1926	2,366	7	420	-95	94	607	641	46	4,086	627	572	-139	5,146

Series F14-32. Gross national expenditure, by components, 1926 to 1976

(*millions of dollars*)

Year	Personal expenditure on consumer goods and services	Government current expenditure on goods and services	Gross fixed capital formation										Value of physical change in inventories				Exports of goods and services	Imports of goods and services	Residual error of estimate	Gross national expenditure at market prices
			Total	Government				Business				Total	Government	Business					
				Total	Residential construction	Non-residential construction	Machinery and equipment	Total	Residential construction	Non-residential construction	Machinery and equipment			Non-farm	Farm				
	14	15	16	17	18	19	20	21	22	23	24	25	26	27	28	29	30	31	32
1976	110,886	38,325	44,895	6,318	26	5,334	958	38,577	12,321	12,105	14,151	1,563	41	1,049	473	45,601	-49,973	-266	191,031
1975	96,955	33,380	40,044	6,323	25	5,374	924	33,721	9,232	11,691	12,798	-239	31	-511	241	40,452	-45,589	300	165,343
1974	83,388	27,816	34,260	5,462	23	4,650	789	28,798	8,776	9,128	10,844	3,451	26	3,730	-305	38,992	-41,009	630	147,528
1973	71,278	23,037	27,848	4,305	24	3,697	584	23,543	7,387	7,327	8,829	1,588	-15	1,484	119	30,718	-30,954	45	123,560
1972	62,208	20,291	23,051	3,968	24	3,475	469	19,083	5,820	6,205	7,058	544	16	801	-273	24,580	-25,250	-190	105,234
1971	55,616	18,368	20,800	3,754	18	3,310	426	17,046	4,816	5,952	6,278	392	-40	406	26	22,181	-22,016	-891	94,450
1970	50,327	16,630	18,015	3,173	15	2,823	335	14,842	3,500	5,385	5,957	105	-13	255	-137	21,167	-20,214	-345	85,685
1969	47,492	14,241	17,232	3,055	14	2,706	335	14,177	3,845	4,772	5,560	1,467	6	969	492	18,761	-19,821	443	79,815
1968	43,704	12,684	15,754	2,983	15	2,591	377	12,771	3,253	4,553	4,965	745	30	479	236	16,719	-17,010	-10	72,586
1967	39,972	11,153	15,628	2,954	13	2,584	357	12,674	2,809	4,548	5,317	260	28	218	14	14,663	-15,234	-33	66,409
1966	36,890	9,748	15,361	2,841	13	2,469	359	12,520	2,605	4,664	5,251	1,225	1	1,026	198	13,045	-14,259	-182	61,828
1965	33,947	8,358	13,179	2,440	8	2,149	283	10,739	2,634	3,840	4,265	1,244	-10	1,233	21	11,182	-12,341	-205	55,364
1964	31,389	7,593	11,205	2,023	7	1,769	247	9,182	2,382	3,298	3,502	553	-55	718	-110	10,503	-10,913	-50	50,280
1963	29,225	6,982	9,556	1,985	7	1,758	220	7,571	1,959	2,760	2,852	669	-12	387	294	9,068	-9,561	39	45,978
1962	27,452	6,608	8,885	1,903	9	1,683	211	6,982	1,854	2,568	2,560	667	-3	429	241	8,234	-9,045	126	42,927
1961	25,930	6,206	8,392	1,674	9	1,479	186	6,718	1,789	2,611	2,318	116	8	518	-410	7,624	-8,480	-142	39,646
1960	25,479	5,281	8,473	1,560	5	1,416	139	6,913	1,794	2,594	2,525	409	-49	342	116	7,004	-8,092	-195	38,359
1959	24,390	4,976	8,647	1,508	6	1,366	136	7,139	2,133	2,598	2,408	414	62	385	-33	6,674	-8,028	-227	36,846
1958	22,845	4,854	8,535	1,397	2	1,258	137	7,138	2,089	2,808	2,241	-296	29	-238	-87	6,329	-7,321	-169	34,777
1957	21,492	4,573	8,689	1,327	2	1,209	116	7,362	1,669	3,099	2,594	170	-21	268	-77	6,379	-7,767	-23	33,513
1956	20,090	4,426	8,000	1,144	2	1,037	105	6,856	1,825	2,588	2,443	985	-6	750	241	6,350	-7,664	-129	32,058
1955	18,388	4,036	6,422	948	3	856	89	5,474	1,785	1,863	1,826	285	1	112	172	5,749	-6,390	38	28,528
1954	16,934	3,825	5,714	873	2	778	93	4,841	1,412	1,679	1,750	-202	-8	-113	-81	5,137	-5,543	53	25,918
1953	16,181	3,824	5,733	782	2	702	78	4,951	1,252	1,745	1,954	600	-27	416	211	5,380	-5,806	-79	25,833
1952	15,162	3,620	5,096	779	2	705	72	4,317	946	1,574	1,797	499	68	64	367	5,568	-5,369	12	24,588
1951	13,857	2,811	4,424	640	2	572	66	3,784	834	1,303	1,647	871	-20	564	327	5,052	-5,580	205	21,640
1950	12,482	1,928	3,862	521	2	459	60	3,341	953	1,051	1,337	549	-24	399	174	4,158	-4,492	4	18,491
1949	11,365	1,722	3,439	456	3	398	55	2,983	795	933	1,255	78	27	150	-99	4,004	-3,853	45	16,800
1948	10,370	1,454	3,057	424	2	354	68	2,633	659	830	1,144	97	-32	85	44	4,055	-3,630	106	15,509
1947	9,362	1,343	2,350	304	2	253	49	2,046	455	610	981	343	-71	437	-23	3,661	-3,601	15	13,473
1946	8,012	1,655	1,682	237	2	191	44	1,445	416	451	578	195	-138	360	-27	3,281	-2,861	-79	11,885
1945	6,972	3,576	1,230	157	2	119	36	1,073	360	263	450	-340	-29	148	-459	3,561	-2,906	-230	11,863
1944	6,260	4,929	964	87	2	71	14	877	246	259	372	-134	11	-10	-135	3,541	-3,562	-150	11,848
1943	5,783	4,093	902	93	2	76	15	809	148	314	347	-142	38	-28	-208	3,429	-2,906	-106	11,053
1942	5,466	3,622	1,055	86	2	70	14	969	128	333	508	145	10	-202	337	2,347	-2,306	-64	10,265
1941	5,089	1,576	1,096	101	2	84	15	995	155	290	550	85	-3	130	-42	2,456	-1,969	-51	8,282
1940	4,464	1,048	833	92	—	79	13	741	123	211	407	264	9	87	168	1,795	-1,609	-82	6,713
1939	3,972	566	687	148	—	124	24	539	121	165	253	282	—	101	181	1,437	-1,305	-18	5,621
1938	3,884	534	717	161	—	136	25	556	110	172	274	57	—	-21	78	1,343	-1,233	-30	5,272
1937	3,878	471	755	177	—	154	23	578	108	189	281	9	—	113	-104	1,575	-1,388	-59	5,241
1936	3,542	450	531	117	—	99	18	414	85	150	179	-72	—	68	-140	1,413	-1,165	-65	4,634
1935	3,331	442	458	122	—	105	17	336	74	118	144	39	—	34	5	1,129	-1,000	-98	4,301
1934	3,174	418	380	105	—	92	13	275	67	92	116	32	—	19	13	1,004	-930	-109	3,969
1933	2,974	392	299	86	—	74	12	213	53	78	82	-91	—	-68	-23	813	-810	-85	3,492
1932	3,182	472	432	125	—	108	17	307	76	123	108	-100	—	-127	27	793	-878	-87	3,814
1931	3,759	515	809	183	—	160	23	626	160	267	199	-95	—	-54	-41	951	-1,112	-134	4,693
1930	4,336	502	1,150	228	—	200	28	922	187	383	352	77	—	41	36	1,272	-1,579	-38	5,720
1929	4,583	469	1,361	183	—	160	23	1,178	245	492	441	52	—	146	-94	1,617	-1,894	-49	6,139
1928	4,272	412	1,195	157	—	136	21	1,038	248	416	374	159	—	126	33	1,757	-1,757	12	6,050
1927	3,868	404	994	135	—	117	18	859	229	303	327	253	—	163	90	1,602	-1,580	20	5,561
1926	3,508	390	814	106	—	92	14	708	205	242	261	135	—	154	-19	1,633	-1,473	139	5,146

Series F33-55. Gross national expenditure in constant (1971) dollars, by components, 1926 to 1976
(millions of dollars)

Year	Personal expendi-ture on consumer goods and services	Govern-ment current expendi-ture on goods and services	Gross fixed capital formation												Adjusting entry
			Total	Government					Business					
				Total	Residen-tial construc-tion	Non-resi-dential construc-tion	Machinery and equipment	Adjusting entry	Total	Residen-tial construc-tion	Non-resi-dential construc-tion	Machinery and equipment	Adjusting entry	
	33	34	35	36	37	38	39	40	41	42	43	44	45	46
1976	75,251	21,689	27,397	3,860	14	3,163	683	—	23,537	6,564	7,422	9,551	—	—
1975	70,645	21,399	26,661	4,127	15	3,421	691	—	22,534	5,503	7,822	9,209	—	—
1974	67,160	20,584	25,694	3,957	15	3,291	651	—	21,737	5,935	6,898	8,904	—	—
1973	63,879	19,795	24,384	3,751	20	3,194	537	—	20,633	5,966	6,411	8,256	—	—
1972	59,841	18,930	21,955	3,772	23	3,294	455	—	18,183	5,432	5,869	6,882	—	—
1971	55,616	18,368	20,800	3,754	18	3,310	426	—	17,046	4,816	5,952	6,278	—	—
1970	51,526	17,650	18,904	3,329	17	2,976	345	-9	15,581	3,718	5,715	6,118	30	-6
1969	50,353	15,993	18,850	3,350	14	2,982	359	-5	15,501	4,175	5,327	5,982	17	-1
1968	48,138	15,429	17,964	3,430	18	2,998	410	4	14,537	3,702	5,360	5,481	-6	-3
1967	45,863	14,343	17,942	3,403	14	2,994	391	4	14,543	3,229	5,405	5,865	44	-4
1966	43,778	13,388	18,015	3,307	16	2,895	391	5	14,716	3,168	5,774	5,755	19	-8
1965	41,606	12,253	16,259	3,003	11	2,686	314	-8	13,261	3,413	5,042	4,826	-20	-5
1964	39,218	11,637	14,549	2,652	11	2,370	277	-6	11,898	3,264	4,565	4,116	-47	-1
1963	36,992	11,070	12,841	2,682	11	2,436	249	-14	10,167	2,794	3,928	3,488	-43	-8
1962	35,272	10,911	12,278	2,664	14	2,419	245	-14	9,625	2,704	3,756	3,218	-53	-11
1961	33,761	10,494	11,748	2,378	13	2,161	216	-12	9,378	2,602	3,835	3,009	-68	-8
1960	33,392	9,218	11,790	2,142	8	1,984	165	-15	9,676	2,631	3,796	3,299	-50	-28
1959	32,264	8,999	12,191	2,090	9	1,934	163	-16	10,139	3,190	3,837	3,190	-78	-38
1958	30,562	9,074	12,126	1,942	3	1,785	165	-11	10,235	3,120	4,170	3,035	-90	-51
1957	29,504	8,807	12,262	1,751	3	1,618	143	-13	10,582	2,485	4,585	3,570	-58	-71
1956	28,440	8,956	11,446	1,425	3	1,296	133	-7	10,107	2,794	3,823	3,540	-50	-86
1955	26,456	8,736	9,678	1,308	3	1,190	121	-6	8,431	2,776	2,891	2,809	-45	-61
1954	24,375	8,549	8,858	1,296	3	1,170	128	-5	7,609	2,237	2,671	2,737	-36	-47
1953	23,512	8,890	8,861	1,162	3	1,055	110	-6	7,760	1,967	2,738	3,093	-38	-61
1952	21,984	8,624	7,892	1,090	3	989	102	-4	6,850	1,499	2,491	2,896	-36	-48
1951	20,546	7,000	7,068	915	3	821	96	-5	6,201	1,346	2,182	2,704	-31	-48
1950	20,394	5,367	7,042	884	3	787	99	-5	6,211	1,773	1,990	2,478	-30	-53
1949	19,138	4,982	6,553	806	4	710	95	-3	5,797	1,552	1,817	2,458	-30	-50
1948	18,099	4,504	6,103	779	3	655	125	-4	5,367	1,342	1,669	2,384	-28	-43
1947	18,546	4,747	5,316	627	3	526	100	-2	4,731	1,085	1,370	2,300	-24	-42
1946	17,324	6,302	4,207	537	3	435	100	-1	3,697	1,118	1,131	1,512	-64	-27
1945	15,592	13,326	3,182	368	3	285	83	-3	2,839	1,033	699	1,189	-82	-25
1944	14,160	19,379	2,486	200	3	168	30	-1	2,324	713	692	962	-43	-38
1943	13,210	16,878	2,371	219	3	183	34	-1	2,183	447	850	887	-1	-31
1942	12,831	15,421	2,923	214	6	177	34	-3	2,756	410	946	1,376	24	-47
1941	12,512	7,367	3,206	271	6	229	36	—	2,980	528	889	1,553	10	-45
1940	11,717	5,095	2,619	263	—	227	36	—	2,387	463	682	1,240	2	-31
1939	10,915	2,891	2,295	433	—	364	70	-1	1,850	483	551	836	-20	12
1938	10,613	2,720	2,371	460	—	387	73	—	1,896	442	567	897	-10	15
1937	10,766	2,423	2,483	504	—	438	68	-2	1,959	426	611	928	-6	20
1936	10,133	2,397	1,870	351	—	294	58	-1	1,509	361	523	635	-10	10
1935	9,693	2,382	1,645	378	—	323	55	—	1,247	320	422	517	-12	20
1934	9,284	2,282	1,379	327	—	285	43	-1	1,032	291	335	422	-16	20
1933	8,827	2,162	1,094	268	—	229	40	-1	807	237	286	296	-12	19
1932	9,054	2,568	1,532	378	—	323	55	—	1,131	324	442	380	-15	23
1931	9,822	2,647	2,762	530	—	459	73	-2	2,215	627	918	700	-30	17
1930	10,326	2,505	3,722	631	—	547	85	-1	3,085	681	1,216	1,200	-12	6
1929	10,778	2,287	4,254	494	—	430	68	-4	3,794	868	1,500	1,444	-18	-34
1928	10,148	2,034	3,845	436	—	373	64	-1	3,444	922	1,310	1,250	-38	-35
1927	9,265	2,012	3,235	378	—	326	51	1	2,885	873	975	1,088	-51	-28
1926	8,295	1,924	2,619	294	—	256	40	-2	2,348	783	780	840	-55	-23

**Series F33-55. Gross national expenditure in constant (1971) dollars,
by components, 1926 to 1976 (concluded)**

(millions of dollars)

Year	Value of physical change in inventories				Exports of goods and services	Imports of goods and services	Residual error of estimate	Adjusting entry	Gross national expenditure in constant (1971) dollars
	Total	Government	Business						
			Non-farm	Farm and grain in commercial channels					
	47	48	49	50	51	52	53	54	55
1976	788	22	743	223	26,225	-32,166	-135	—	119,249
1975	-252	16	-344	76	23,993	-29,684	243	—	113,005
1974	2,642	18	2,729	-105	25,620	-30,538	516	—	111,678
1973	1,346	-16	1,359	3	26,156	-27,824	76	—	107,812
1972	515	15	835	-335	23,655	-24,489	-159	—	100,248
1971	392	-40	406	26	22,181	-22,016	-891	—	94,450
1970	84	-19	228	-125	21,223	-20,588	-341	-68	88,390
1969	1,518	-1	1,043	476	19,462	-20,727	491	285	86,225
1968	771	20	615	136	17,727	-18,284	-6	125	81,864
1967	253	15	225	13	15,770	-16,805	-31	9	77,344
1966	1,385	-8	1,165	228	14,315	-15,989	-215	167	74,844
1965	1,441	-20	1,452	9	12,606	-14,140	-256	212	69,981
1964	655	-66	865	-144	12,058	-12,595	-64	152	65,610
1963	764	-18	481	301	10,631	-11,125	54	260	61,487
1962	756	-3	527	232	9,744	-10,769	175	108	58,475
1961	251	4	629	-382	9,374	-10,559	-196	-132	54,741
1960	523	-52	419	156	8,717	-10,347	-271	209	53,231
1959	468	55	474	-61	8,360	-10,357	-317	129	51,737
1958	-280	24	-278	-26	8,047	-9,386	-239	-60	49,844
1957	249	-25	329	-55	8,075	-10,096	-31	-52	48,718
1956	1,144	-11	930	225	8,002	-10,215	-187	13	47,599
1955	410	-3	194	219	7,442	-8,799	61	-93	43,891
1954	-238	-12	-157	-69	6,917	-7,761	86	-680	40,106
1953	752	-34	568	218	7,185	-8,151	-124	-320	40,605
1952	481	72	100	309	7,260	-7,527	20	-117	38,617
1951	1,025	-27	760	292	6,513	-7,277	333	242	35,450
1950	789	-32	611	210	5,956	-6,469	10	673	33,762
1949	215	28	231	-44	5,997	-5,939	83	359	31,388
1948	109	-40	108	41	6,375	-5,781	211	611	30,231
1947	672	-106	799	-21	6,170	-6,411	39	419	29,498
1946	420	-415	847	-12	6,208	-5,711	-184	-274	28,292
1945	-122	-59	317	-380	7,402	-6,173	-537	-3,599	29,071
1944	-70	17	9	-96	7,600	-7,760	-360	-5,699	29,736
1943	-45	65	78	-188	7,874	-6,553	-263	-4,868	28,604
1942	-21	14	-454	419	5,663	-5,500	-166	-3,654	27,497
1941	245	-11	325	-69	6,329	-5,122	-138	-1,205	23,194
1940	573	17	239	317	4,817	-4,423	-235	114	20,277
1939	604	-4	288	320	4,225	-3,964	-55	863	17,774
1938	154	-4	-55	213	3,836	-3,708	-89	648	16,545
1937	246	-4	317	-67	4,248	-3,971	-177	392	16,410
1936	2	-4	202	-196	4,158	-3,596	-200	148	14,912
1935	152	-4	112	44	3,459	-3,174	-310	432	14,279
1934	81	-4	52	33	3,137	-2,957	-350	389	13,245
1933	-236	-4	-202	-30	2,774	-2,775	-276	241	11,811
1932	-306	-4	-397	95	2,748	-2,921	-277	256	12,654
1931	-253	-4	-164	-85	2,967	-3,403	-391	-33	14,118
1930	221	-4	80	145	3,319	-4,248	-98	427	16,174
1929	311	-4	386	-71	3,817	-4,670	-129	246	16,894
1928	390	-4	294	100	4,055	-4,274	29	604	16,831
1927	533	-4	423	114	3,577	-3,804	50	555	15,423
1926	399	-4	391	12	3,563	-3,443	362	367	14,086

Series F56-75. Gross domestic product at factor cost, by industry, 1926 to 1976
(millions of dollars)

Year	Agriculture	Forestry	Fishing and trapping	Mines, quarries and oil wells	Manufac-turing	Construc-tion	Transpor-tation	Storage	Communi-cation	Electric power, gas and water utilities
	56	57	58	59	60	61	62	63	64	65
1976	5,905	1,300	291	7,170	36,032	12,681	9,328	400	4,230	5,037
1975	6,147	1,092	198	6,157	32,035	11,729	8,023	352	3,738	4,071
1974	5,780	1,212	202	5,864	30,147	9,675	7,132	310	3,339	3,554
1973	4,602	937	225	4,713	25,129	7,748	6,078	255	2,938	3,007
1972	2,967	640	158	3,160	21,384	6,236	5,437	223	2,689	2,652
1971	2,791	608	135	2,840	19,013	5,687	4,892	225	2,285	2,385
1970	2,472	622	132	3,040	17,606	4,748	4,434	187	2,105	2,198
1969	2,607	612	119	2,677	17,294	4,522	4,144	158	1,929	1,980
1968	2,423	570	125	2,679	15,909	4,060	3,875	160	1,670	1,813
1967	2,259	546	111	2,394	14,663	3,954	3,635	168	1,552	1,639
1966	2,886	513	116	2,203	14,023	3,726	3,399	157	1,384	1,489
1965	2,258	499	105	2,067	12,751	3,124	3,078	116	1,265	1,357
1964	2,083	460	103	1,872	11,896	2,575	2,868	116	1,154	1,248
1963	2,297	403	84	1,647	10,777	2,323	2,652	107	1,042	1,162
1962	2,076	422	82	1,518	10,007	2,202	2,501	91	977	1,086
1961	1,498	388	74	1,398	9,182	2,090	2,449	94	899	1,036
1960	1,690	438	72	1,382	9,020	2,043	2,358	92	841	963
1959	1,634	404	73	1,327	8,834	2,076	2,361	90	773	891
1958	1,718	380	81	1,167	8,330	2,061	2,147	87	706	835
1957	1,480	454	65	1,239	8,413	2,085	2,214	81	656	780
1956	1,839	514	74	1,219	8,192	1,860	2,180	84	599	691
1955	1,648	486	64	1,080	7,301	1,519	1,903	73	533	597
1954	1,438	448	68	889	6,785	1,417	1,654	68	475	555
1953	1,971	467	62	726	6,889	1,476	1,703	74	428	504
1952	2,358	408	69	804	6,538	1,301	1,582	59	396	453
1951	2,322	488	74	814	5,803	1,015	1,473	51	353	410
1950	1,707	385	75	651	4,913	976	1,225	43	290	378
1949	1,577	274	62	540	4,522	882	1,124	40	251	335
1948	1,700	312	63	510	4,095	764	1,113	40	229	298
1947	1,416	302	49	434	3,461	617	998	33	209	265
1946	1,305	268	82	364	2,812	439	857	29	170	224
1945	1,144	208	77	323	2,954	310	874	31	152	216
1944	1,320	166	64	316	3,164	246	860	26	141	219
1943	949	155	59	362	3,187	301			1,206	
1942	1,147	131	51	386	2,875	305			1,065	
1941	670	114	42	391	2,208	262			896	
1940	682	100	29	363	1,608	187			722	
1939	570	76	25	333	1,247	155			646	
1938	559	54	23	302	1,161	154			593	
1937	486	81	25	328	1,156	153			591	
1936	403	55	25	270	972	117			552	
1935	424	44	23	213	865	98			506	
1934	373	38	21	183	771	81			488	
1933	276	30	17	133	629	73			435	
1932	326	27	16	109	711	113			472	
1931	343	40	20	143	948	205			565	
1930	629	61	30	183	1,231	253			662	
1929	699	78	39	218	1,328	293			725	
1928	929	72	41	189	1,241	242			733	
1927	883	69	39	168	1,135	210			660	
1926	884	66	41	154	1,050	204			626	

Series F56-75. Gross domestic product at factor cost, by industry, 1926 to 1976 (concluded)
(millions of dollars)

Year	Wholesale trade	Retail trade	Finance, insurance and real estate	Public adminis- tration and defence	Community, business and personal service	Gross domestic product at factor cost	Indirect taxes less subsidies	Net income paid to non- residents	Residual error of estimate	Gross national product at market prices
	66	67	68	69	70	71	72	73	74	75
1976	8,848	11,741	20,767	13,508	35,346	172,584	21,520	-3,339	266	191,031
1975	7,751	10,440	17,313	11,707	29,973	150,726	17,584	-2,667	-300	165,343
1974	6,945	8,669	14,462	9,762	25,202	132,255	18,257	-2,355	-629	147,528
1973	5,504	7,386	12,288	7,938	21,082	109,830	15,598	-1,824	-44	123,560
1972	4,803	6,507	10,723	6,979	18,161	92,719	13,876	-1,551	190	105,234
1971	4,195	5,674	9,666	6,152	16,319	82,867	12,276	-1,584	891	94,450
1970	3,965	5,383	8,497	5,530	14,508	75,427	11,299	-1,386	345	85,685
1969	3,581	4,991	8,067	5,077	13,020	70,778	10,722	-1,242	-443	79,815
1968	3,109	4,592	7,395	4,497	11,288	64,165	9,662	-1,251	10	72,586
1967	2,960	4,205	6,515	4,095	10,097	58,793	8,852	-1,269	33	66,409
1966	2,746	3,820	5,917	3,671	8,714	54,764	8,030	-1,148	182	61,828
1965	2,394	3,529	5,606	3,233	7,512	48,894	7,284	-1,020	206	55,364
1964	2,246	3,350	5,000	2,996	6,729	44,696	6,441	-908	51	50,280
1963	2,015	3,101	4,676	2,828	6,036	41,150	5,714	-847	-39	45,978
1962	1,877	2,923	4,420	2,686	5,509	38,377	5,446	-771	-125	42,927
1961	1,708	2,774	4,195	2,511	5,092	35,388	4,838	-722	142	39,646
1960	1,645	2,722	3,974	2,348	4,604	34,192	4,587	-616	196	38,359
1959	1,590	2,639	3,771	2,215	4,149	32,827	4,401	-609	227	36,846
1958	1,470	2,513	3,697	2,114	3,790	31,096	4,036	-525	170	34,777
1957	1,451	2,408	3,308	1,969	3,475	30,078	3,975	-563	23	33,513
1956	1,339	2,233	2,903	1,789	3,142	28,658	3,731	-461	130	32,058
1955	1,130	2,077	2,819	1,624	2,776	25,630	3,321	-385	-38	28,528
1954	1,004	1,875	2,528	1,519	2,544	23,267	3,042	-339	-52	25,918
1953	973	1,829	2,251	1,362	2,345	23,060	2,994	-301	80	25,833
1952	989	1,779	2,017	1,232	2,140	22,125	2,799	-324	-12	24,588
1951	762	1,377	1,766	1,059	1,921	19,688	2,548	-391	-205	21,640
1950	700	1,365	1,557	859	1,730	16,854	2,065	-425	-3	18,491
1949	664	1,296	1,316	788	1,651	15,322	1,878	-355	-45	16,800
1948	577	1,075	1,159	675	1,481	14,091	1,832	-308	-106	15,509
1947	476	978	1,035	595	1,263	12,131	1,678	-322	-14	13,473
1946	468	918	832	885	1,063	10,716	1,371	-282	80	11,885
1945	384	785	755	1,611	924	10,748	1,084	-200	231	11,863
1944	371	726	743	1,536	852	10,750	1,167	-220	151	11,848
1943	304	641	689	1,354	799	10,006	1,170	-229	106	11,053
1942	302	585	673	1,041	739	9,300	1,133	-232	64	10,265
1941	281	533	579	728	686	7,390	1,090	-250	52	8,282
1940	232	443	548	520	611	6,045	859	-274	83	6,713
1939	197	406	537	339	571	5,102	759	-259	19	5,621
1938	207	413	493	316	557	4,832	661	-251	30	5,272
1937	179	387	470	295	539	4,690	727	-236	60	5,241
1936	164	351	457	273	495	4,134	680	-245	65	4,634
1935	152	320	427	264	478	3,814	601	-213	99	4,301
1934	131	283	403	259	454	3,485	591	-217	110	3,969
1933	122	253	445	238	440	3,091	547	-231	85	3,492
1932	151	299	459	261	496	3,440	552	-265	87	3,814
1931	187	395	515	281	620	4,262	578	-282	135	4,693
1930	267	476	578	279	702	5,351	619	-289	39	5,720
1929	197	476	607	260	719	5,639	711	-261	50	6,139
1928	195	453	575	240	673	5,583	707	-229	-11	6,050
1927	187	409	532	226	626	5,144	653	-216	-20	5,561
1926	164	370	497	214	596	4,866	627	-208	-139	5,146

Series F76-90. Personal income and its disposition, 1926 to 1976
(millions of dollars)

Year	Net national income at factor cost	Transfer payments	Interest on the public debt and on consumer debt	Total	Earnings not paid out to persons	Personal income	Personal direct taxes and other current transfers from persons	Personal disposable income	Personal expenditure on consumer goods and services					Current transfers to corporations and non-residents	Personal saving
									Total	Durable goods	Semi-durable goods	Non-durable goods	Services		
	76	77	78	79	80	81	82	83	84	85	86	87	88	89	90
1976	148,507	19,933	9,909	178,349	-23,006	155,343	-29,833	125,510	-110,886	-17,021	-14,176	-33,967	-45,722	-2,064	12,560
1975	129,789	17,531	8,154	155,474	-19,269	136,205	-25,209	110,996	-96,995	-15,320	-12,428	-30,422	-38,825	-1,862	12,139
1974	113,854	14,180	6,942	134,976	-18,109	116,867	-22,322	94,545	-83,338	-13,139	-11,184	-26,218	-32,847	-1,751	9,406
1973	94,651	11,472	5,774	111,897	-14,065	97,832	-18,113	79,719	-71,278	-11,481	-9,059	-22,302	-28,436	-1,211	7,230
1972	79,694	10,137	4,836	94,667	-10,900	83,767	-15,667	68,100	-62,208	-9,440	-7,962	-19,432	-25,374	-877	5,015
1971	70,783	8,437	4,270	83,490	-9,398	74,092	-14,149	59,943	-55,616	-7,883	-7,133	-17,521	-23,079	-818	3,509
1970	64,235	7,102	3,891	75,228	-8,595	66,633	-12,624	54,009	-50,327	-6,799	-6,645	-16,186	-20,697	-810	2,872
1969	60,517	6,260	3,293	70,070	-8,266	61,804	-10,893	50,911	-47,492	-6,975	-6,426	-15,073	-19,018	-689	2,730
1968	54,606	5,572	2,757	62,935	-7,258	55,677	-8,857	46,820	-43,704	-6,494	-5,953	-14,019	-17,238	-477	2,639
1967	49,738	4,765	2,358	56,861	-6,282	50,579	-7,456	43,123	-39,972	-5,915	-5,539	-13,219	-15,299	-415	2,736
1966	46,294	3,855	2,101	52,250	-6,156	46,094	-6,193	39,901	-36,890	-5,490	-5,054	-12,364	-13,982	-349	2,662
1965	41,219	3,529	1,883	46,631	-5,560	41,071	-4,808	36,263	-33,947	-5,085	-4,671	-11,526	-12,665	-315	2,001
1964	37,680	3,270	1,721	42,671	-5,389	37,282	-4,233	33,049	-31,389	-4,560	-4,388	-10,798	-11,643	-277	1,383
1963	34,700	3,056	1,581	39,337	-4,508	34,829	-3,661	31,168	-29,225	-4,127	-4,086	-10,213	-10,799	-252	1,691
1962	32,370	2,983	1,458	36,811	-4,023	32,788	-3,448	29,340	-27,452	-3,729	-3,892	-9,691	-10,140	-241	1,647
1961	29,783	2,777	1,314	33,874	-3,770	30,104	-3,200	26,904	-25,930	-3,365	-3,698	-9,220	-9,647	-229	745
1960	28,837	3,129	1,216	33,182	-3,587	29,595	-3,028	26,567	-25,479	-3,236	-3,577	-9,002	-9,664	-221	867
1959	27,757	2,762	1,133	31,652	-3,544	28,108	-2,668	25,440	-24,390	-3,176	-3,501	-8,651	-9,062	-206	844
1958	26,436	2,645	926	30,007	-3,356	26,651	-2,338	24,313	-22,845	-2,898	-3,346	-8,241	-8,360	-190	1,278
1957	25,356	2,098	862	28,316	-3,146	25,170	-2,456	22,714	-21,492	-2,775	-3,183	-7,832	-7,702	-175	1,047
1956	24,383	1,786	805	26,974	-3,443	23,531	-2,224	21,307	-20,090	-2,731	-3,075	-7,234	-7,050	-166	1,051
1955	21,908	1,747	739	24,394	-3,129	21,265	-1,934	19,331	-18,388	-2,440	-2,834	-6,691	-6,423	-146	797
1954	19,998	1,650	715	22,363	-2,646	19,717	-1,849	17,868	-16,934	-2,070	-2,657	-6,312	-5,895	-130	804
1953	20,125	1,474	678	22,277	-2,727	19,550	-1,832	17,718	-16,181	-2,116	-2,634	-6,004	-5,427	-114	1,423
1952	19,468	1,367	696	21,531	-2,939	18,592	-1,670	16,922	-15,162	-1,867	-2,518	-5,836	-4,941	-95	1,665
1951	17,199	1,044	647	18,890	-2,099	16,791	-1,356	15,435	-13,857	-1,651	-2,338	-5,497	-4,371	-82	1,496
1950	14,553	1,040	573	16,166	-1,904	14,262	-977	13,285	-12,482	-1,576	-2,162	-4,896	-3,848	-65	738
1949	13,323	961	593	14,877	-1,481	13,396	-1,013	12,383	-11,365	-1,258	-2,071	-4,545	-3,491	-53	965
1948	12,334	875	574	13,783	-1,191	12,592	-1,033	11,559	-10,370	-987	-1,946	-4,375	-3,062	-51	1,138
1947	10,582	851	570	12,003	-1,077	10,926	-962	9,964	-9,362	-911	-1,779	-3,871	-2,801	-58	544
1946	9,363	1,128	561	11,052	-1,165	9,887	-937	8,950	-8,012	-495	-1,278	-3,636	-2,603	-45	893
1945	9,506	578	517	10,601	-1,309	9,292	-938	8,354	-6,972	-225	-1,102	-3,225	-2,420	-31	1,351
1944	9,453	275	427	10,155	-1,139	9,016	-965	8,051	-6,260	-196	-987	-2,905	-2,172	-31	1,760
1943	8,678	222	376	9,276	-1,093	8,183	-821	7,362	-5,783	-177	-916	-2,750	-1,940	-36	1,543
1942	7,977	232	317	8,526	-1,004	7,522	-604	6,918	-5,466	-262	-903	-2,435	-1,866	-31	1,421
1941	6,206	202	299	6,707	-770	5,937	-360	5,577	-5,089	-402	-813	-2,179	-1,695	-33	455
1940	4,985	217	281	5,483	-511	4,972	-174	4,798	-4,464	-381	-669	-1,884	-1,530	-34	300
1939	4,172	240	282	4,694	-344	4,350	-143	4,207	-3,972	-330	-531	-1,717	-1,394	-33	202
1938	3,942	237	273	4,452	-326	4,126	-145	3,981	-3,884	-326	-494	-1,695	-1,369	-34	63
1937	3,830	251	280	4,361	-291	4,070	-144	3,926	-3,878	-345	-541	-1,676	-1,316	-31	17
1936	3,314	237	283	3,834	-232	3,602	-121	3,481	-3,542	-284	-491	-1,531	-1,236	-26	-87
1935	3,051	233	285	3,569	-171	3,398	-104	3,294	-3,331	-249	-449	-1,461	-1,172	-22	-59
1934	2,732	233	289	3,254	-79	3,175	-85	3,090	-3,174	-220	-418	-1,432	-1,104	-22	-106
1933	2,328	193	287	2,808	32	2,840	-88	2,752	-2,974	-161	-363	-1,350	-1,100	-20	-242
1932	2,597	170	280	3,047	16	3,063	-85	2,978	-3,182	-177	-400	-1,410	-1,195	-21	-225
1931	3,331	156	258	3,745	-76	3,669	-87	3,582	-3,759	-259	-504	-1,563	-1,433	-28	-205
1930	4,343	125	250	4,718	-326	4,392	-98	4,294	-4,336	-328	-614	-1,793	-1,601	-45	-87
1929	4,652	107	241	5,000	-335	4,665	-93	4,572	-4,583	-389	-706	-1,852	-1,636	-50	-61
1928	4,678	102	236	5,016	-416	4,600	-79	4,521	-4,272	-351	-662	-1,699	-1,560	-49	200
1927	4,310	92	239	4,641	-360	4,281	-77	4,204	-3,868	-296	-566	-1,522	-1,484	-47	289
1926	4,086	91	236	4,413	-356	4,057	-69	3,988	-3,508	-266	-489	-1,334	-1,419	-47	433

Series F91-102. Personal income, by province, 1926 to 1976
(millions of dollars)

Year	New-found-land	Prince Edward Island	Nova Scotia	New Bruns-wick	Quebec	Ontario	Manitoba	Saskat-chewan	Alberta	British Columbia	Yukon Territory and Northwest Territories	Foreign countries
	91	92	93	94	95	96	97	98	99	100	101	102
1976	2,582	547	4,416	3,460	39,204	60,959	6,473	6,199	12,783	18,187	398	135
1975	2,259	493	3,894	3,080	33,801	53,902	5,865	5,660	10,991	15,787	346	127
1974	1,903	400	3,375	2,539	28,980	47,060	4,985	4,519	9,019	13,687	293	107
1973	1,526	355	2,850	2,105	24,067	39,884	4,244	3,673	7,471	11,331	235	91
1972	1,301	287	2,436	1,810	20,823	34,822	3,564	2,767	6,267	9,417	193	80
1971	1,143	243	2,100	1,576	18,369	30,966	3,192	2,555	5,534	8,182	158	74
1970	1,025	229	1,895	1,412	16,682	27,974	2,857	2,133	4,953	7,245	148	80
1969	923	205	1,766	1,295	15,565	25,629	2,704	2,269	4,589	6,645	122	92
1968	837	189	1,580	1,183	14,193	22,844	2,523	2,187	4,111	5,837	104	89
1967	755	168	1,446	1,067	13,175	20,553	2,280	1,932	3,665	5,348	90	100
1966	680	151	1,302	979	11,880	18,655	2,039	2,047	3,374	4,817	80	90
1965	604	137	1,181	880	10,685	16,537	1,892	1,789	2,941	4,271	69	85
1964	531	128	1,108	809	9,742	15,030	1,775	1,539	2,652	3,822	70	76
1963	493	116	1,043	751	8,933	13,976	1,647	1,686	2,535	3,509	67	73
1962	462	114	995	707	8,446	13,098	1,611	1,529	2,411	3,279	62	74
1961	440	102	946	671	7,828	12,187	1,436	1,084	2,199	3,091	59	61
1960	412	97	920	664	7,422	11,923	1,492	1,352	2,134	3,058	63	58
1959	383	96	874	626	7,005	11,406	1,419	1,200	2,039	2,948	61	51
1958	361	83	820	585	6,655	10,802	1,352	1,156	1,958	2,786	59	34
1957	350	77	785	556	6,363	10,211	1,223	1,037	1,749	2,728	59	32
1956	325	85	732	534	5,840	9,320	1,206	1,205	1,719	2,482	59	24
1955	292	67	683	489	5,296	8,525	1,073	1,058	1,475	2,242	43	22
1954	272	69	664	468	5,029	7,930	1,002	824	1,346	2,050	39	24
1953	256	65	637	447	4,862	7,681	1,012	1,138	1,417	1,976	34	25
1952	229	78	604	438	4,558	7,207	1,006	1,213	1,344	1,863	31	21
1951	209	64	533	415	4,085	6,521	938	1,069	1,250	1,665	26	16
1950	186	55	494	374	3,547	5,638	810	722	955	1,477	—	4
1949	175	52	467	351	3,292	5,199	780	802	929	1,344	—	5
1948	—	49	441	337	3,158	4,851	776	787	917	1,270	—	6
1947	—	45	428	305	2,755	4,235	655	643	765	1,091	—	4
1946	—	44	420	289	2,378	3,805	602	644	696	949	—	60
1945	—	41	387	254	2,213	3,722	524	538	570	859	—	184
1944	—	36	367	226	2,111	3,568	503	658	588	808	—	151
1943	—	33	338	210	2,008	3,354	459	433	456	777	—	115
1942	—	28	290	182	1,781	3,016	428	548	512	662	—	75
1941	—	23	232	151	1,489	2,529	350	274	329	521	—	39
1940	—	22	193	129	1,229	2,057	291	279	315	441	—	16
1939	—	21	166	111	1,096	1,773	256	268	267	392	—	—
1938	—	19	161	105	1,049	1,693	244	200	275	380	—	—
1937	—	20	161	108	1,048	1,679	276	150	258	370	—	—
1936	—	17	142	96	939	1,490	216	178	194	330	—	—
1935	—	16	130	86	868	1,419	200	183	190	306	—	—
1934	—	13	119	79	822	1,329	198	148	186	281	—	—
1933	—	12	110	73	743	1,200	178	118	148	258	—	—
1932	—	13	113	77	797	1,271	197	149	173	273	—	—
1931	—	16	138	97	965	1,554	225	147	202	325	—	—
1930	—	20	163	114	1,112	1,802	292	238	274	377	—	—
1929	—	24	172	121	1,175	1,896	307	273	294	403	—	—
1928	—	22	167	118	1,092	1,770	323	404	329	375	—	—
1927	—	22	154	110	1,002	1,647	273	377	354	342	—	—
1926	—	21	150	110	946	1,553	297	359	297	324	—	—

Series F103-120. Government revenue, expenditure and surplus or deficit, by component, all governments, 1926 to 1976

(millions of dollars)

Year	Direct taxes — Persons	Direct taxes — Corporate and government business	Direct taxes — Non-residents	Indirect taxes	Other current transfers from persons	Investment income	Total	Current expenditure on goods and services	Transfer payments to persons	Subsidies	Capital assistance	Current transfers to non-residents	Interest on the public debt	Total	Saving (total revenue less total expenditure)	Add: capital consumption allowances	Deduct: gross capital formation	Equals: surplus (+) or deficit (-)
	103	104	105	106	107	108	109	110	111	112	113	114	115	116	117	118	119	120
1976	28,353	7,113	504	24,864	1,480	8,357	70,671	38,325	19,483	3,344	564	542	8,101	70,359	312	2,825	6,359	-3,222
1975	24,070	7,486	465	21,442	1,139	7,112	61,714	33,380	17,080	3,858	486	592	6,538	61,934	-220	2,525	6,354	-4,049
1974	21,197	7,051	430	20,876	1,125	5,916	56,595	27,816	13,880	2,619	326	407	5,425	50,473	6,122	2,161	5,488	2,795
1973	17,041	5,080	322	16,686	1,072	4,386	44,587	23,037	11,198	1,088	326	318	4,788	40,755	3,832	1,710	4,290	1,252
1972	14,631	3,920	287	14,760	1,036	3,690	38,324	20,291	9,918	884	245	279	4,137	35,754	2,570	1,495	3,984	81
1971	13,042	3,346	278	13,048	1,107	3,180	34,001	18,368	8,255	772	225	249	3,622	31,491	2,510	1,334	3,714	130
1970	11,547	3,070	269	12,055	1,077	2,705	30,723	16,630	6,985	756	123	244	3,250	27,988	2,735	1,231	3,160	806
1969	10,055	3,221	234	11,423	838	2,257	28,028	14,241	6,161	701	110	185	2,767	24,165	3,863	1,113	3,061	1,915
1968	8,244	2,852	209	10,303	613	1,765	23,986	12,684	5,473	641	100	170	2,391	21,459	2,527	988	3,013	502
1967	7,009	2,396	218	9,489	447	1,495	21,054	11,153	4,667	637	91	217	2,081	18,846	2,208	922	2,982	148
1966	5,792	2,355	204	8,669	401	1,241	18,662	9,748	3,750	639	65	195	1,862	16,259	2,403	864	2,842	425
1965	4,431	2,197	167	7,741	377	1,080	15,993	8,358	3,423	457	92	119	1,675	14,124	1,869	768	2,430	207
1964	3,917	2,100	140	6,877	316	978	14,328	7,593	3,175	436	92	95	1,546	12,937	1,391	676	1,968	99
1963	3,387	1,891	127	6,115	274	885	12,679	6,982	2,979	401	77	89	1,431	11,959	720	629	1,973	-624
1962	3,180	1,753	125	5,807	268	784	11,917	6,608	2,912	361	41	59	1,316	11,297	620	574	1,900	-706
1961	2,944	1,649	116	5,159	256	710	10,834	6,206	2,709	321	21	77	1,184	10,518	316	531	1,682	-835
1960	2,794	1,588	79	4,901	234	649	10,245	5,281	3,090	314	17	74	1,093	9,869	376	465	1,511	-670
1959	2,444	1,615	74	4,651	224	604	9,612	4,976	2,721	250	22	85	1,023	9,077	535	434	1,570	-601
1958	2,214	1,350	48	4,186	124	542	8,464	4,854	2,605	150	18	67	826	8,520	-56	404	1,426	-1,078
1957	2,350	1,378	83	4,095	106	490	8,502	4,573	2,052	120	29	52	774	7,600	902	385	1,306	-19
1956	2,127	1,443	69	3,858	97	537	8,131	4,426	1,746	127	27	42	718	7,086	1,045	365	1,138	272
1955	1,855	1,310	67	3,407	79	420	7,138	4,036	1,719	86	8	36	664	6,549	589	320	949	-40
1954	1,776	1,115	58	3,131	73	373	6,526	3,825	1,626	89	13	23	650	6,226	300	293	865	-272
1953	1,748	1,244	54	3,107	84	378	6,615	3,824	1,449	113	14	37	620	6,057	558	280	755	83
1952	1,588	1,403	55	2,901	82	368	6,397	3,620	1,343	102	14	28	651	5,758	639	265	847	57
1951	1,279	1,431	56	2,677	77	285	5,805	2,811	1,024	129	13	21	609	4,607	1,198	248	620	826
1950	915	993	54	2,129	62	280	4,433	1,928	1,023	64	10	14	544	3,583	850	201	497	554
1949	956	723	47	1,955	57	242	3,980	1,722	942	77	13	15	572	3,341	639	187	483	343
1948	986	687	41	1,907	47	261	3,929	1,454	857	75	10	32	558	2,986	943	171	392	722
1947	927	702	35	1,855	35	261	3,815	1,343	834	177	6	46	559	2,965	850	146	233	763
1946	906	654	29	1,607	31	263	3,490	1,655	1,102	236	1	104	554	3,652	-162	124	99	-137
1945	909	599	29	1,346	29	310	3,222	3,576	542	262	2	7	512	4,901	-1,679	116	128	-1,691
1944	938	598	27	1,434	27	273	3,297	4,929	255	267	1	7	423	5,882	-2,585	115	98	-2,568
1943	792	640	27	1,381	29	259	3,128	4,093	207	211	2	7	371	4,891	-1,763	113	131	-1,781
1942	579	629	29	1,226	25	184	2,672	3,622	218	93	1	6	310	4,250	-1,578	108	96	-1,566
1941	332	510	24	1,164	28	140	2,198	1,576	191	74	1	6	291	2,139	59	101	98	62
1940	149	327	13	912	25	104	1,530	1,048	204	53	3	7	273	1,588	-58	92	101	-67
1939	121	115	10	742	22	64	1,074	566	226	-17	—	7	275	1,057	17	88	148	-43
1938	124	94	10	723	21	49	1,021	534	224	62	—	7	266	1,093	-72	85	161	-148
1937	125	101	10	737	19	66	1,058	471	235	10	—	7	273	996	62	83	177	-32
1936	100	83	9	694	21	72	979	450	222	14	—	7	277	970	9	75	117	-33
1935	86	65	7	624	18	50	850	442	219	23	—	7	280	971	-121	72	122	-171
1934	67	52	6	599	18	41	783	418	219	8	—	7	284	936	-153	70	105	-188
1933	70	37	5	555	17	82	712	392	180	8	—	7	283	870	-158	68	86	-176
1932	67	32	—	561	18	74	698	472	159	9	—	7	275	922	-224	70	125	-279
1931	72	33	—	596	15	75	735	515	140	18	—	7	253	933	-198	70	183	-311
1930	81	40	—	626	17	45	809	502	111	7	—	7	244	871	-62	69	228	-221
1929	75	48	—	716	18	76	933	469	92	5	—	7	235	808	125	69	183	11
1928	62	45	—	712	17	82	918	412	86	5	—	7	231	741	177	64	157	84
1927	62	38	—	656	15	74	845	404	76	3	—	7	234	724	121	61	135	47
1926	54	34	—	629	15	75	807	390	74	2	—	7	231	704	103	60	106	57

Series F121-134. Finance of saving and investment, 1926 to 1976
(millions of dollars)

Year	Finance										Total	Disposition		
		Saving						Capital consumption allowances	Surplus(−) or deficit(+) of Canada on current transactions with non-residents	Residual error of estimate		Gross fixed capital formation	Value of physical change in inventories	Residual error of estimate
	Total	Persons and unincorporated business		Government	Corporate and government business enterprises									
		Personal saving	Adjustment on grain transactions		Undistributed profits	Inventory valuation adjustment	Capital assistance							
	121	122	123	124	125	126	127	128	129	130	131	132	133	134
1976	20,800	12,560	33	312	9,567	−2,064	392	20,738	4,388	266	46,192	44,895	1,563	−266
1975	16,883	12,139	−114	−220	7,723	−2,938	293	18,270	5,252	−300	40,105	40,044	−239	300
1974	20,925	9,406	500	6,122	8,886	−4,244	255	16,046	1,999	−629	38,341	34,260	3,451	630
1973	15,928	7,230	13	3,832	6,948	−2,362	267	13,355	242	−44	29,481	27,848	1,588	45
1972	11,074	5,015	−49	2,570	4,371	−1,032	199	11,474	667	190	23,405	23,051	544	−190
1971	9,094	3,509	65	2,510	3,472	−665	203	10,500	−184	891	20,301	20,800	392	−891
1970	8,540	2,872	92	2,735	2,923	−195	113	9,806	−916	345	17,775	18,015	105	−345
1969	9,487	2,730	11	3,863	3,353	−576	106	9,019	1,079	−443	19,142	17,232	1,467	443
1968	7,903	2,639	−260	2,527	3,242	−341	96	8,308	268	10	16,489	15,754	745	−10
1967	7,421	2,736	−95	2,208	2,813	−327	86	7,786	615	33	15,855	15,628	260	−33
1966	7,668	2,662	156	2,403	2,739	−335	43	7,322	1,232	182	16,404	15,361	1,225	−182
1965	6,222	2,001	−40	1,869	2,645	−322	69	6,655	1,135	206	14,218	13,179	1,244	−205
1964	5,157	1,383	116	1,391	2,339	−144	72	6,108	392	51	11,708	11,205	553	−50
1963	4,213	1,691	135	720	1,810	−213	70	5,603	487	−39	10,264	9,556	669	39
1962	3,788	1,647	4	620	1,582	−100	35	5,236	779	−125	9,678	8,885	667	126
1961	2,485	745	27	316	1,425	−41	13	4,883	856	142	8,366	8,392	116	−142
1960	2,601	867	3	376	1,373	−26	8	4,739	1,151	196	8,687	8,473	409	−195
1959	2,715	844	−12	535	1,445	−108	11	4,461	1,431	227	8,834	8,647	414	−227
1958	2,690	1,278	−6	−56	1,511	−41	4	4,135	1,075	170	8,070	8,535	−296	−169
1957	3,236	1,047	−9	902	1,346	−59	9	4,159	1,418	23	8,836	8,689	170	−23
1956	3,572	1,051	28	1,045	1,680	−245	13	3,814	1,340	130	8,856	8,000	985	−129
1955	2,789	797	50	589	1,531	−182	4	3,337	657	−38	6,745	6,422	285	38
1954	2,273	804	−18	300	1,089	87	11	2,930	414	−52	5,565	5,714	−202	53
1953	3,097	1,423	−33	558	1,136	2	11	2,634	443	80	6,254	5,733	600	−79
1952	3,482	1,665	45	639	1,009	114	10	2,333	−196	−12	5,607	5,096	499	12
1951	3,088	1,496	−5	1,198	1,031	−643	11	2,098	519	−205	5,500	4,424	871	205
1950	2,227	738	136	850	869	−374	8	1,876	315	−3	4,415	3,862	549	4
1949	2,131	965	−110	639	738	−112	11	1,644	−168	−45	3,562	3,439	78	45
1948	2,334	1,138	−100	943	849	−506	10	1,449	−417	−106	3,260	3,057	97	106
1947	1,514	544	34	850	651	−571	6	1,227	−19	−14	2,708	2,350	343	15
1946	980	893	22	−162	480	−254	1	1,071	−333	80	1,798	1,682	195	−79
1945	74	1,351	70	−1,679	367	−37	2	1,042	−687	231	660	1,230	−340	−230
1944	−556	1,760	−22	−2,585	342	−52	1	1,077	8	151	680	964	−134	−150
1943	−24	1,543	−50	−1,763	327	−83	2	1,099	−527	106	654	902	−142	−106
1942	35	1,421	−47	−1,578	360	−122	1	1,091	−54	64	1,136	1,055	145	−64
1941	635	455	—	59	276	−156	1	934	−491	52	1,130	1,096	85	−51
1940	325	300	33	−58	168	−121	3	786	−179	83	1,015	833	264	−82
1939	384	202	−50	17	271	−56	—	671	−123	19	951	687	282	−18
1938	174	63	5	−72	111	67	—	639	−99	30	744	717	57	−30
1937	203	17	−7	62	218	−87	—	624	−182	60	705	755	9	−59
1936	−1	−87	−27	9	140	−36	—	575	−245	65	394	531	−72	−65
1935	−124	−59	−4	−121	80	−20	—	550	−126	99	399	458	39	−98
1934	−273	−106	−21	−153	46	−39	—	536	−70	110	303	380	32	−109
1933	−496	−242	−29	−158	−45	−22	—	532	2	85	123	299	−91	−85
1932	−517	−225	−11	−224	−166	109	—	578	97	87	245	432	−100	−87
1931	−379	−205	−23	−198	−125	172	—	649	175	135	580	809	−95	−134
1930	92	−87	4	−62	−2	239	—	719	339	39	1,189	1,150	77	−38
1929	275	−61	1	125	225	−15	—	726	313	50	1,364	1,361	52	−49
1928	666	200	16	177	272	1	—	676	35	−11	1,366	1,195	159	12
1927	658	289	−7	121	226	29	—	618	11	−20	1,267	994	253	20
1926	783	433	12	103	189	46	—	572	−128	−139	1,088	814	135	139

Series F135-152. Gross fixed capital formation, by industry, 1926 to 1976

(millions of dollars)

Year	Total	Business Total	Agriculture, fishing and trapping	Forestry	Mines, quarries and oil wells	Manufacturing	Construction	Transportation and storage	Communication	Electric power, gas and water utilities	Trade	Finance, insurance and real estate	Community, business, personal services	Government Total	Water systems	Real estate	Communication, community services	Public administration
	135	136	137	138	139	140	141	142	143	144	145	146	147	148	149	150	151	152
1976	44,895	38,577	2,837	187	3,397	5,260	759	1,679	2,041	4,416	1,009	14,526	2,466	6,318	314	26	1,143	4,835
1975	40,044	33,721	2,403	196	2,563	5,232	568	1,906	1,857	4,139	932	11,175	2,750	6,323	246	25	1,176	4,876
1974	34,260	28,798	1,920	244	1,983	4,652	467	1,547	1,629	2,919	961	10,450	2,026	5,462	211	23	1,098	4,130
1973	27,848	23,543	1,569	179	1,662	3,498	404	1,513	1,169	2,401	783	8,724	1,641	4,305	140	24	888	3,253
1972	23,051	19,083	1,208	117	1,604	2,820	346	1,248	991	1,923	643	6,786	1,397	3,968	124	24	893	2,927
1971	20,800	17,046	930	94	1,749	2,839	307	1,128	909	1,887	502	5,477	1,224	3,754	100	18	995	2,641
1970	18,015	14,842	821	90	1,341	3,076	274	1,018	799	1,755	534	4,114	1,020	3,173	82	15	922	2,154
1969	17,232	14,177	958	106	1,171	2,484	264	972	739	1,533	495	4,428	1,027	3,055	70	14	921	2,050
1968	15,754	12,771	1,002	77	1,070	2,114	254	950	662	1,463	495	3,799	885	2,983	84	15	994	1,890
1967	15,628	12,674	1,096	86	1,046	2,452	244	1,010	627	1,358	527	3,362	866	2,954	89	13	929	1,923
1966	15,361	12,520	1,024	92	1,026	2,832	249	923	589	1,251	453	3,130	951	2,841	102	13	825	1,901
1965	13,179	10,739	905	96	716	2,253	263	767	464	1,014	379	3,113	769	2,440	111	8	673	1,648
1964	11,205	9,182	816	88	701	1,750	197	678	430	819	354	2,773	576	2,023	68	7	512	1,436
1963	9,556	7,571	745	60	583	1,287	135	527	435	696	325	2,270	508	1,985	62	7	659	1,257
1962	8,885	6,982	647	54	563	1,203	109	449	384	651	306	2,190	426	1,903	64	9	639	1,191
1961	8,392	6,718	561	50	535	1,017	136	609	341	626	295	2,138	410	1,674	74	9	424	1,167
1960	8,473	6,913	592	54	397	1,118	130	672	379	595	370	2,108	498	1,560	85	5	279	1,191
1959	8,647	7,139	581	48	339	1,075	145	713	323	663	350	2,439	463	1,508	92	6	263	1,147
1958	8,535	7,138	500	33	339	1,034	157	921	332	758	344	2,294	426	1,397	80	2	250	1,065
1957	8,689	7,362	461	48	601	1,393	158	967	307	866	356	1,826	379	1,327	73	2	250	1,002
1956	8,000	6,856	515	76	536	1,305	200	687	247	690	309	1,965	326	1,144	71	2	227	844
1955	6,422	5,474	458	63	332	882	174	359	214	460	317	1,902	313	948	50	3	219	676
1954	5,714	4,841	437	46	275	768	97	415	188	461	358	1,532	264	873	59	2	176	636
1953	5,733	4,951	601	34	249	903	91	454	164	536	319	1,342	258	782	49	2	155	576
1952	5,096	4,317	588	39	201	907	73	396	139	564	185	1,007	218	779	45	2	156	576
1951	4,424	3,784	564	58	160	731	66	275	123	461	225	913	208	640	35	2	134	469
1950	3,862	3,341	472	34	111	466	71	214	110	408	228	1,022	205	521	—	2	108	411
1949	3,439	2,983	436	26	94	509	55	206	116	347	188	835	171	456	—	3	88	365
1948	3,057	2,633	347	28	68	549	59	198	107	247	159	699	172	424	—	2	59	363
1947	2,350	2,046	277	33	41	521	52	188	86	132	119	479	118	304	—	2	35	267
1946	1,682	1,445	184	13	26	333	33	126	47	76	83	437	87	237	—	2	28	207
1945	1,230	1,073	126	12	15	275	31	78	23	34	42	373	64	157	—	2	16	139
1944	964	877	101	14	16	206	19	160	13	21	38	254	35	87	—	2	9	76
1943	902	809	59	6	15	272	23	195	10	38	13	153	25	93	—	2	8	83
1942	1,055	969	90	7	21	440	25	86	20	79	35	135	31	86	—	2	7	77
1941	1,096	995	110	7	31	426	17	71	22	64	32	163	52	101	—	2	8	91
1940	833	741	99	6	29	274	12	73	21	37	35	131	24	92	—	—	8	84
1939	687	539	77	5	31	98	11	62	23	35	30	130	37	148	—	—	17	131
1938	717	556	80	5	34	115	9	76	20	39	34	117	27	161	—	—	15	146
1937	755	578	77	5	33	140	12	85	21	35	28	115	27	177	—	—	13	164
1936	531	414	56	4	31	83	7	55	15	23	19	91	30	117	—	—	11	106
1935	458	336	44	3	31	67	7	32	15	26	15	80	16	122	—	—	9	113
1934	380	275	40	3	11	50	2	27	13	22	18	73	16	105	—	—	6	99
1933	299	213	23	2	9	42	2	20	14	20	10	59	12	86	—	—	10	76
1932	432	307	32	2	7	47	4	31	18	46	17	85	18	125	—	—	20	105
1931	809	626	40	4	22	95	11	109	31	81	25	173	35	183	—	—	29	154
1930	1,150	922	90	6	45	163	28	156	43	96	43	203	49	228	—	—	41	187
1929	1,361	1,178	127	7	46	224	32	219	45	80	68	268	62	183	—	—	36	147
1928	1,195	1,038	142	7	32	215	25	146	34	66	50	265	56	157	—	—	31	126
1927	994	859	114	6	18	179	15	126	28	50	27	246	50	135	—	—	27	108
1926	814	708	94	6	17	129	14	102	26	46	24	215	35	106	—	—	22	84

Series F153-165. Net domestic income, by industry, 1919 to 1926
(millions of dollars)

Year	Total net domestic income	Agri-culture	Forestry	Fishing, hunting and trapping	Mining, quarrying and oil wells	Manufac-turing	Con-struction	Trans-portation, commu-nication and public utilities	Whole-sale trade	Retail trade	Finance, insurance and real estate	Public adminis-tration and defence	Service
	153	154	155	156	157	158	159	160	161	162	163	164	165
1926	4,337	795	64	33	139	929	201	551	155	358	381	165	566
1925	4,139	896	59	31	122	829	175	496	136	326	364	163	542
1924	3,641	574	64	29	104	769	165	477	122	297	355	155	530
1923	3,829	699	57	30	109	821	181	488	117	312	341	157	517
1922	3,589	643	48	32	108	725	187	460	114	299	322	156	495
1921	3,454	561	37	22	92	723	179	441	108	314	305	164	508
1920	4,541	924	69	38	135	1,142	245	468	146	360	277	175	562
1919	3,958	783	53	35	99	1,032	165	413	144	280	238	222	494

Series F166-178. Labour income, by industry, 1919 to 1926
(millions of dollars)

Year	Total labour income	Agri-culture	Forestry	Fishing, hunting and trapping	Mining, quarrying and oil wells	Manufac-turing	Con-struction	Trans-portation, commu-nication and public utilities	Whole-sale trade	Retail trade	Finance, insurance and real estate	Public adminis-tration and defence	Service
	166	167	168	169	170	171	172	173	174	175	176	177	178
1926	2,373	112	59	7	81	643	155	406	114	181	103	165	347
1925	2,236	108	54	6	74	586	156	380	106	169	97	163	337
1924	2,194	104	59	5	72	559	156	390	104	161	92	155	337
1923	2,191	103	53	5	80	573	152	395	101	160	88	157	324
1922	2,028	94	44	6	66	508	137	383	95	154	84	156	301
1921	2,091	106	34	5	71	516	133	392	100	166	90	164	314
1920	2,602	132	64	6	78	704	197	436	133	225	91	175	361
1919	2,181	110	49	7	54	586	123	349	113	119	77	222	300

Series F179-182. Gross domestic capital formation, by quinquennial periods, 1901 to 1930
(millions of dollars)

Period	Gross domestic capital formation	Construction	Machinery and equipment	Inventories
	179	180	181	182
1926-30	5,831	3,109	2,097	625
1921-25	3,641	2,271	1,211	159
1916-20	4,033	2,122	1,322	589
1911-15	3,279	2,007	912	360
1906-10	2,287	1,439	586	262
1901-05	1,283	681	380	222

Series F183-192. Industry gross and net capital stock in 1971 prices, by structure and machinery and equipment, mid-year, 1926 to 1975
(millions of dollars)

Year	Gross stock					Net stock				
	Total	Construction		Machinery and equipment	Capital items charged to operating expenses	Total	Construction		Machinery and equipment	Capital items charged to operating expenses
		Building	Engineering				Building	Engineering		
	183	184	185	186	187	188	189	190	191	192
1975	225,426.4	53,640.0	73,322.0	96,357.4	2,107.0	145,739.8	36,272.8	50,682.2	57,674.6	1,110.2
1974	212,847.2	50,824.0	69,840.4	90,193.0	1,989.8	137,318.8	34,282.0	48,399.9	53,599.0	1,037.9
1973	201,185.0	48,228.5	66,666.6	84,419.8	1,870.1	129,695.3	32,467.2	46,406.5	49,851.9	969.7
1972	190,755.8	46,068.3	63,594.2	79,302.6	1,790.7	123,256.8	31,040.4	44,485.0	46,809.5	921.9
1971	181,434.2	44,212.7	60,484.5	74,979.9	1,757.1	117,670.6	29,865.6	42,411.2	44,495.5	898.3
1970	172,675.6	42,450.4	57,511.3	71,011.9	1,702.0	112,175.8	28,710.5	40,238.8	42,360.9	865.6
1969	164,548.3	40,768.9	55,060.4	67,097.9	1,621.1	106,875.9	27,571.6	38,305.9	40,165.5	832.9
1968	157,060.4	39,167.6	52,908.3	63,450.3	1,534.2	101,839.5	26,485.2	36,465.3	38,075.1	813.9
1967	149,635.0	37,525.4	50,850.4	59,834.3	1,424.9	96,498.4	25,292.2	34,583.4	35,846.6	776.2
1966	141,787.2	35,616.4	48,811.1	56,067.1	1,292.6	90,469.8	23,757.1	32,720.2	33,290.4	702.1
1965	134,514.0	33,690.9	46,840.9	52,798.6	1,183.6	84,824.9	22,196.1	30,959.6	31,042.5	626.7
1964	128,445.6	32,137.5	44,969.5	50,219.3	1,119.3	80,325.0	20,955.0	29,379.5	29,417.5	573.0
1963	123,529.7	30,964.7	43,279.2	48,208.4	1,077.4	76,849.4	19,955.2	28,030.0	28,319.7	544.5
1962	119,425.0	29,985.9	41,846.9	46,518.9	1,073.3	74,068.4	19,071.8	26,893.8	27,567.4	535.4
1961	115,229.1	29,022.2	40,307.2	44,798.1	1,101.6	71,422.7	18,228.9	25,691.5	26,962.3	540.0
1960	110,674.8	28,029.9	38,688.2	42,853.5	1,103.2	68,623.5	17,388.9	24,442.6	26,245.9	546.1
1959	105,934.2	26,989.7	37,066.9	40,803.6	1,074.0	65,598.8	16,524.1	23,188.1	25,342.6	544.0
1958	101,078.2	26,069.8	35,071.7	38,870.6	1,066.1	62,322.3	15,737.4	21,583.0	24,449.7	552.2
1957	95,596.9	25,204.5	32,612.3	36,733.4	1,046.7	58,193.6	14,892.6	19,534.1	23,223.6	543.3
1956	89,735.8	24,251.0	30,269.4	34,221.0	994.4	53,629.7	13,947.6	17,597.3	21,579.2	505.6
1955	84,794.6	23,347.7	28,560.5	31,936.7	949.7	50,141.9	13,178.2	16,276.7	20,202.8	484.2
1954	80,723.6	22,578.4	27,258.7	29,969.3	917.2	47,553.9	12,563.0	15,359.2	19,151.5	480.2
1953	76,526.1	21,879.5	26,002.0	27,765.5	879.1	44,691.0	11,935.5	14,456.4	17,836.6	462.5
1952	72,276.0	21,282.7	24,678.9	25,473.4	841.0	41,565.1	11,382.7	13,473.4	16,275.3	433.7
1951	68,389.1	20,717.0	23,486.1	23,384.2	801.8	38,727.5	10,893.2	12,642.7	14,783.7	407.9
1950	65,073.8	20,203.5	22,499.8	21,518.5	852.0	36,310.1	10,435.1	12,018.1	13,453.9	403.0
1949	62,194.7	19,797.6	21,591.5	19,850.1	955.5	34,125.1	10,057.7	11,451.2	12,191.2	425.0
1948	59,370.9	19,338.6	20,823.7	18,189.5	1,019.1	31,998.0	9,687.9	10,991.1	10,855.8	463.2
1947	56,867.8	18,851.3	20,259.8	16,606.4	1,150.3	30,088.0	9,320.3	10,712.2	9,538.4	517.1
1946	55,165.4	18,447.5	19,863.3	15,483.5	1,371.1	28,830.3	9,023.8	10,587.8	8,599.6	619.1
1945	54,250.3	18,192.9	19,622.4	14,943.7	1,491.3	28,338.1	8,904.3	10,600.7	8,148.7	684.4
1944	53,553.3	18,090.6	19,530.6	14,528.1	1,404.0	28,171.9	8,952.3	10,734.7	7,772.9	712.0
1943	52,884.0	18,065.5	19,404.3	14,180.5	1,233.7	28,022.5	9,045.0	10,813.8	7,410.6	753.1
1942	52,129.1	17,932.2	19,187.6	14,013.3	996.0	27,626.8	9,012.7	10,788.7	7,144.0	681.4
1941	51,128.7	17,661.6	18,989.2	13,803.9	674.0	26,913.5	8,855.6	10,765.8	6,814.8	477.3
1940	50,292.8	17,394.7	18,877.6	13,646.5	374.0	26,329.7	8,755.7	10,800.4	6,532.0	241.6
1939	50,059.7	17,220.3	18,946.2	13,659.0	234.2	26,227.8	8,776.0	10,880.4	6,443.6	127.8
1938	50,136.4	17,126.0	19,062.9	13,738.2	209.3	26,353.2	8,855.1	10,961.0	6,418.1	119.0
1937	50,006.1	17,002.2	19,059.7	13,763.8	180.4	26,377.9	8,906.9	11,017.3	6,352.4	101.3
1936	49,907.9	16,856.5	18,958.0	13,920.5	172.9	26,525.7	8,965.5	11,078.7	6,394.3	87.2
1935	50,164.8	16,764.4	18,803.0	14,397.2	200.2	26,965.7	9,094.4	11,168.2	6,618.8	84.3
1934	50,661.6	16,724.6	18,664.7	15,025.8	246.5	27,633.4	9,275.7	11,301.8	6,962.2	93.7
1933	51,290.0	16,719.1	18,561.5	15,710.4	299.0	28,524.2	9,484.9	11,486.7	7,432.0	120.6
1932	51,868.9	16,711.7	18,406.4	16,402.5	348.3	29,426.6	9,692.7	11,618.7	7,957.5	157.7
1931	51,811.0	16,604.1	18,019.3	16,813.2	374.4	29,850.6	9,818.5	11,492.2	8,352.1	187.8
1930	50,748.6	16,313.6	17,387.6	16,680.9	366.5	29,468.1	9,791.6	11,078.0	8,404.1	194.4
1929	48,988.0	15,787.7	16,649.9	16,201.9	348.8	28,380.3	9,544.9	10,536.5	8,114.1	184.8
1928	47,251.8	15,163.4	15,953.2	15,799.6	335.6	27,150.9	9,181.5	10,029.3	7,767.7	172.4
1927	45,985.9	14,643.5	15,440.6	15,588.2	313.6	26,319.6	8,909.3	9,697.4	7,552.5	160.4
1926	45,084.2	14,264.5	15,046.8	15,482.5	290.4	25,936.7	8,776.5	9,502.1	7,505.2	152.9

Series F193-202. Industry gross and net capital stock, at original cost, by structure and machinery and equipment, mid-year, 1926 to 1975
(millions of dollars)

Year	Gross stock					Net stock				
	Total	Construction		Machinery and equipment	Capital items charged to operating expenses	Total	Construction		Machinery and equipment	Capital items charged to operating expenses
		Building	Engineering				Building	Engineering		
	193	194	195	196	197	198	199	200	201	202
1975	190,390.7	42,130.7	56,186.3	89,701.6	2,372.1	134,791.1	31,739.2	43,647.7	58,081.4	1,322.8
1974	171,001.0	37,957.4	50,668.8	80,292.6	2,082.2	119,965.1	28,358.1	39,196.7	51,280.6	1,129.7
1973	155,058.8	34,488.5	46,252.0	72,466.6	1,851.7	108,171.2	25,600.4	35,758.7	45,827.8	984.3
1972	142,266.6	31,849.8	42,455.7	66,245.0	1,716.1	99,232.6	23,608.1	32,862.2	41,859.9	902.4
1971	131,438.1	29,699.3	38,939.9	61,145.8	1,653.1	91,908.6	22,049.4	30,158.7	38,843.8	856.7
1970	121,577.4	27,739.6	35,707.5	56,550.6	1,579.7	85,190.9	20,617.4	27,639.7	36,127.1	806.7
1969	112,585.9	25,941.8	32,967.2	52,193.3	1,483.6	79,079.8	19,299.3	25,511.7	33,504.7	764.1
1968	104,463.9	24,306.4	30,542.9	48,231.3	1,383.3	73,590.4	18,123.2	23,611.9	31,112.3	743.0
1967	96,505.0	22,666.4	28,236.5	44,344.0	1,258.1	67,998.1	16,906.1	21,763.6	28,624.5	703.9
1966	88,258.1	20,815.6	26,047.4	40,294.8	1,100.3	61,848.1	15,437.7	19,999.1	25,791.2	620.1
1965	80,779.6	19,058.1	24,065.4	36,698.9	957.2	56,220.3	14,035.2	18,411.4	23,248.1	525.6
1964	74,679.6	17,677.4	22,329.0	33,812.6	860.6	51,830.4	12,968.6	17,053.2	21,353.4	455.2
1963	69,717.9	16,570.5	20,832.5	31,518.6	796.3	48,446.1	12,118.9	15,914.9	19,999.0	413.3
1962	65,515.4	15,597.4	19,543.7	29,606.7	767.6	45,707.9	11,371.6	14,954.2	18,990.3	391.8
1961	61,505.5	14,663.5	18,244.2	27,834.7	763.1	43,152.2	10,657.1	13,968.5	18,144.2	382.4
1960	57,413.2	13,738.1	16,937.1	25,998.2	739.8	40,506.4	9,938.1	12,954.6	17,238.3	375.4
1959	53,248.9	12,811.6	15,654.3	24,086.6	696.4	37,693.6	9,203.9	11,939.1	16,187.6	363.0
1958	49,073.2	11,963.0	14,167.7	22,275.5	667.0	34,735.4	8,524.0	10,701.5	15,153.8	356.1
1957	44,480.0	11,101.3	12,413.7	20,332.7	632.3	31,211.5	7,797.0	9,177.6	13,899.9	337.0
1956	39,743.2	10,174.0	10,769.4	18,218.6	581.2	27,453.9	6,999.9	7,736.5	12,416.8	300.7
1955	35,913.5	9,364.5	9,587.5	16,422.6	538.9	24,571.4	6,335.4	6,731.5	11,225.3	279.2
1954	32,844.2	8,686.1	8,718.4	14,936.4	503.3	22,389.6	5,789.5	6,020.3	10,309.3	270.5
1953	29,704.6	8,017.7	7,885.2	13,340.5	461.2	20,052.2	5,229.9	5,328.1	9,240.9	253.3
1952	26,554.3	7,406.2	7,031.2	11,702.1	414.8	17,584.9	4,715.2	4,599.4	8,043.6	226.7
1951	23,734.6	6,852.7	6,310.6	10,206.4	364.9	15,353.9	4,256.6	3,993.8	6,905.5	198.0
1950	21,420.3	6,368.2	5,766.9	8,931.3	353.9	13,519.6	3,856.0	3,554.0	5,931.2	178.4
1949	19,540.4	5,979.1	5,302.9	7,883.5	374.9	12,009.4	3,543.2	3,183.2	5,108.6	174.4
1948	17,859.7	5,606.0	4,918.6	6,946.9	388.2	10,642.8	3,248.0	2,882.2	4,334.0	178.6
1947	16,490.1	5,263.2	4,646.3	6,148.2	432.4	9,516.1	2,979.9	2,685.6	3,657.7	192.9
1946	15,612.2	4,997.2	4,473.7	5,628.2	513.1	8,822.1	2,782.5	2,584.2	3,225.0	230.4
1945	15,124.4	4,822.7	4,371.4	5,378.5	551.8	8,512.1	2,677.7	2,549.6	3,028.0	256.8
1944	14,710.5	4,719.5	4,316.4	5,163.1	511.5	8,319.4	2,644.5	2,558.0	2,851.9	265.0
1943	14,286.8	4,639.8	4,248.1	4,955.9	443.0	8,128.5	2,629.2	2,548.7	2,675.4	275.2
1942	13,818.9	4,519.8	4,153.0	4,797.4	348.7	7,849.1	2,569.3	2,509.6	2,527.9	242.3
1941	13,269.9	4,362.1	4,067.3	4,614.5	226.0	7,469.1	2,472.9	2,478.5	2,355.2	162.5
1940	12,827.5	4,234.2	4,007.3	4,467.9	118.1	7,174.3	2,409.8	2,470.3	2,216.3	77.9
1939	12,605.3	4,152.6	3,980.4	4,402.9	69.4	7,073.0	2,393.3	2,477.2	2,163.6	38.9
1938	12,476.2	4,093.9	3,961.7	4,360.3	60.3	7,050.7	2,396.7	2,484.8	2,134.0	35.2
1937	12,296.4	4,023.6	3,929.7	4,294.1	49.0	6,994.0	2,389.1	2,487.7	2,088.8	28.4
1936	12,164.3	3,953.9	3,888.0	4,277.7	44.7	6,985.0	2,384.3	2,493.2	2,084.9	22.6
1935	12,163.7	3,907.5	3,842.4	4,362.7	51.1	7,079.3	2,404.7	2,506.1	2,147.2	21.3
1934	12,230.4	3,877.6	3,804.7	4,483.9	64.2	7,241.9	2,440.7	2,529.9	2,247.5	23.8
1933	12,331.4	3,856.5	3,776.8	4,617.7	80.4	7,467.1	2,483.9	2,565.4	2,386.5	31.3
1932	12,411.3	3,834.4	3,736.9	4,743.9	96.1	7,695.9	2,525.5	2,589.2	2,539.4	41.8
1931	12,311.1	3,782.3	3,640.7	4,783.0	105.1	7,789.9	2,539.9	2,555.2	2,646.2	51.6
1930	11,923.6	3,671.0	3,477.5	4,669.8	105.3	7,631.7	2,498.1	2,439.6	2,638.9	55.1
1929	11,291.9	3,476.7	3,278.5	4,435.0	101.7	7,219.0	2,373.4	2,284.9	2,507.5	53.2
1928	10,643.3	3,249.4	3,091.4	4,203.3	99.2	6,750.6	2,210.8	2,137.8	2,351.9	50.1
1927	10,146.4	3,065.5	2,956.4	4,030.8	93.7	6,412.2	2,086.4	2,038.7	2,239.7	47.4
1926	9,766.0	2,933.5	2,848.4	3,896.2	87.9	6,199.6	2,011.2	1,970.9	2,171.4	46.1

Series F203-209. Gross stock of social capital in 1971 prices, public and private, by type, mid-year, 1926 to 1975
(millions of dollars)

Year	Government social capital				Privately owned social capital				Total social capital		
	Total	Construction		Machinery and equipment	Total¹	Construction		Institutional machinery and equipment	Total¹	Con-struction¹	Machinery and equipment
		Building	Engineering			Housing¹	Institutional				
	203	204	205	206			207	208			209
1975	59,615.8	12,927.5	42,644.2	4,044.1	–	–	23,795.0	3,009.2	–	–	7,053.3
1974	56,795.4	12,316.5	40,776.6	3,702.3	–	–	23,001.2	2,856.7	–	–	6,559.0
1973	54,206.8	11,799.9	38,981.2	3,425.7	–	–	22,279.4	2,703.1	–	–	6,128.8
1972	51,719.7	11,327.3	37,175.3	3,217.1	–	–	21,516.1	2,544.2	–	–	5,761.3
1971	49,300.9	10,868.2	35,391.1	3,041.6	–	–	20,539.8	2,364.3	–	–	5,405.9
1970	47,181.4	10,441.8	33,848.3	2,891.3	–	–	19,436.9	2,174.4	–	–	5,065.7
1969	45,329.0	10,068.5	32,504.1	2,756.4	–	–	18,286.7	1,986.7	–	–	4,563.1
1968	43,528.8	9,715.0	31,205.6	2,608.2	–	–	17,005.0	1,787.0	–	–	4,395.2
1967	41,686.2	9,334.5	29,899.0	2,452.7	–	–	15,702.5	1,582.1	–	–	4,034.8
1966	39,768.6	8,938.4	28,536.5	2,293.7	–	–	14,490.1	1,394.6	–	–	3,688.3
1965	37,943.2	8,560.1	27,206.9	2,176.2	–	–	13,387.3	1,234.8	–	–	3,411.0
1964	36,276.6	8,251.2	25,906.5	2,118.9	–	–	12,491.4	1,101.4	–	–	3,220.3
1963	34,811.1	8,015.7	24,661.8	2,133.6	–	–	11,633.2	984.5	–	–	3,118.1
1962	33,449.4	7,767.8	23,488.9	2,192.7	–	–	10,687.5	873.9	–	–	3,066.6
1961	32,003.2	7,467.1	22,294.3	2,241.8	–	–	9,877.2	777.1	–	–	3,018.9
1960	30,498.4	7,151.1	21,085.7	2,261.6	–	–	9,214.8	696.4	–	–	2,958.0
1959	28,964.0	6,822.2	19,925.8	2,216.0	–	–	8,574.9	626.8	–	–	2,842.8
1958	27,489.6	6,500.6	18,854.2	2,134.8	–	–	7,957.5	563.8	–	–	2,698.6
1957	26,108.7	6,173.2	17,872.6	2,062.9	–	–	7,388.1	505.4	–	–	2,568.3
1956	24,818.2	5,787.8	17,030.9	1,999.5	–	–	6,878.9	455.8	–	–	2,455.3
1955	23,689.5	5,429.4	16,317.8	1,942.3	–	–	6,386.6	408.9	–	–	2,351.2
1954	22,646.9	5,123.5	15,643.1	1,880.3	–	–	5,925.7	362.1	–	–	2,242.4
1953	21,563.0	4,796.8	14,965.2	1,801.0	–	–	5,530.4	320.9	–	–	2,121.9
1952	20,426.1	4,420.4	14,287.2	1,718.5	–	–	5,167.2	285.5	–	–	2,004.0
1951	19,446.5	4,101.9	13,683.9	1,660.7	–	–	4,839.0	253.6	–	–	1,914.3
1950	18,715.3	3,917.4	13,165.4	1,632.5	–	–	4,535.5	228.0	–	–	1,860.5
1949	18,077.9	3,785.0	12,684.6	1,608.3	–	–	4,239.4	204.2	–	–	1,812.5
1948	17,445.5	3,667.6	12,217.7	1,560.2	–	–	3,986.1	179.7	–	–	1,739.9
1947	16,854.4	3,575.5	11,774.8	1,504.1	–	–	3,802.4	162.0	–	–	1,666.1
1946	16,367.9	3,511.2	11,398.2	1,458.5	–	–	3,655.7	152.9	–	–	1,611.4
1945	15,952.8	3,420.0	11,127.2	1,405.6	–	–	3,540.6	149.4	–	–	1,555.0
1944	15,418.1	3,222.4	10,858.1	1,337.6	–	–	3,472.1	151.5	–	–	1,489.1
1943	14,426.7	2,811.5	10,393.6	1,221.6	–	–	3,431.8	155.8	–	–	1,377.4
1942	13,257.3	2,231.9	9,954.9	1,070.5	–	–	3,403.4	160.7	–	–	1,231.2
1941	12,301.6	1,704.1	9,676.1	921.4	–	–	3,376.7	164.9	–	–	1,086.3
1940	11,584.5	1,349.7	9,431.5	803.3	–	–	3,346.1	167.9	–	–	971.2
1939	11,127.8	1,197.5	9,183.6	746.7	–	–	3,297.2	169.0	–	–	915.7
1938	10,753.3	1,155.0	8,881.7	716.6	–	–	3,234.5	169.2	–	–	885.8
1937	10,337.2	1,123.5	8,526.9	686.8	–	–	3,180.0	170.8	–	–	857.6
1936	9,978.2	1,097.9	8,212.9	667.4	–	–	3,134.2	173.2	–	–	840.6
1935	9,685.5	1,071.8	7,949.5	664.2	–	–	3,096.9	175.4	–	–	839.6
1934	9,416.8	1,046.1	7,689.7	681.0	–	–	3,066.9	177.9	–	–	858.9
1933	9,222.4	1,023.6	7,488.5	710.3	–	–	3,034.9	180.4	–	–	890.7
1932	9,014.4	996.5	7,289.0	728.9	–	–	2,975.5	180.6	–	–	909.5
1931	8,672.2	953.5	6,993.4	725.3	–	–	2,868.1	175.3	–	–	900.6
1930	8,197.0	892.3	6,599.0	705.7	–	–	2,726.6	165.7	–	–	871.4
1929	7,740.3	836.4	6,220.0	683.9	–	–	2,589.4	157.2	–	–	841.1
1928	7,372.0	798.5	5,900.2	673.3	–	–	2,474.0	151.4	–	–	824.7
1927	7,045.9	769.2	5,608.4	668.3	–	–	2,367.2	146.5	–	–	814.8
1926	6,775.2	748.0	5,367.6	659.6	–	–	2,273.1	142.1	–	–	801.7

¹ Only the net stock of housing was available, as given in series F215. It was based on replies to a special question in the 1941 Census. The gross stock could not be estimated because of the lack of a benchmark. Hence the 'total' columns above must remain blank at the present time.

Series F210-220. Net stock of social capital in 1971 prices, public and private, by type, mid-year, 1926 to 1975

(millions of dollars)

Year	Government social capital				Privately owned social capital				Total social capital		
	Total	Construction		Machinery and equipment	Total	Construction		Institutional machinery and equipment	Total	Construction	Machinery and equipment
		Building	Engineering			Housing	Institutional				
	210	211	212	213	214	215	216	217	218	219	220
1975	40,765.9	8,539.5	29,719.7	2,506.7	88,965.1	69,570.8	17,569.0	1,825.3	129,731.0	125,399.0	4,332.0
1974	38,892.9	8,151.9	28,473.5	2,267.5	85,480.9	66,567.7	17,147.1	1,766.1	124,373.8	120,340.2	4,033.6
1973	37,204.1	7,847.5	27,298.9	2,057.7	81,603.4	63,133.7	16,765.2	1,704.5	118,807.5	115,045.3	3,762.2
1972	35,579.9	7,579.0	26,105.5	1,895.4	77,726.4	59,775.6	16,315.9	1,634.9	113,306.3	109,776.0	3,530.3
1971	33,963.8	7,316.4	24,871.4	1,776.0	74,023.9	56,832.7	15,649.6	1,541.6	107,987.7	104,670.1	3,317.6
1970	32,541.9	7,078.4	23,764.6	1,698.9	70,743.0	54,450.0	14,857.0	1,436.0	103,284.9	100,150.0	3,134.9
1969	31,254.9	6,885.0	22,729.9	1,640.0	66,196.6	52,183.7	14,012.9	1,326.3	97,451.5	95,811.5	2,966.3
1968	29,942.8	6,703.6	21,689.1	1,550.1	64,159.0	49,941.3	13,021.9	1,195.8	94,101.8	91,355.9	2,745.9
1967	28,603.2	6,493.6	20,666.4	1,443.2	61,155.3	48,117.9	11,983.3	1,054.1	89,758.5	87,261.2	2,497.3
1966	27,206.5	6,259.8	19,616.6	1,330.1	58,445.2	46,525.6	10,997.5	922.1	85,651.7	83,399.5	2,252.2
1965	25,862.7	6,024.0	18,610.0	1,228.7	55,715.2	44,833.1	10,071.2	810.9	81,577.9	79,538.3	2,039.6
1964	24,631.1	5,834.4	17,640.6	1,156.1	53,095.5	43,066.3	9,306.1	723.1	77,726.6	75,847.4	1,879.2
1963	23,526.6	5,706.5	16,712.9	1,107.2	50,730.6	41,521.1	8,565.3	644.2	74,257.2	72,505.8	1,751.4
1962	22,483.0	5,572.0	15,836.8	1,074.2	48,477.4	40,175.1	7,733.9	568.4	70,960.4	69,317.8	1,642.6
1961	21,393.2	5,392.1	14,955.2	1,045.9	46,424.9	38,884.7	7,034.0	506.2	67,818.1	66,266.0	1,552.1
1960	20,281.9	5,197.9	14,051.5	1,032.5	44,510.5	37,569.2	6,484.2	457.1	64,792.4	63,302.8	1,489.6
1959	19,178.3	4,988.1	13,165.8	1,024.4	42,301.1	35,927.4	5,957.6	416.1	61,479.3	60,038.9	1,440.5
1958	18,145.3	4,777.6	12,357.3	1,010.4	39,765.3	33,937.3	5,448.2	379.8	57,910.6	56,520.4	1,390.2
1957	17,188.6	4,554.6	11,628.6	1,005.4	37,468.7	32,143.4	4,979.4	345.9	54,657.3	53,306.0	1,351.3
1956	16,310.9	4,273.2	11,028.7	1,009.0	35,312.1	30,425.3	4,569.5	317.3	51,623.0	50,296.7	1,326.3
1955	15,578.5	4,012.8	10,549.3	1,016.4	32,950.8	28,487.9	4,174.2	288.7	48,529.3	47,224.2	1,305.1
1954	14,913.4	3,797.1	10,098.3	1,018.0	30,833.4	26,769.5	3,806.6	257.3	45,746.8	44,471.5	1,275.3
1953	14,191.7	3,557.7	9,634.6	999.4	29,126.4	25,395.9	3,502.8	227.7	43,318.1	42,091.0	1,227.1
1952	13,402.6	3,263.3	9,169.5	969.8	27,749.3	24,323.7	3,225.4	200.2	41,151.9	39,981.9	1,170.0
1951	12,753.5	3,019.8	8,777.3	956.4	26,656.4	23,508.5	2,975.3	172.6	39,409.9	38,280.9	1,129.0
1950	12,317.4	2,906.4	8,446.8	964.2	25,426.1	22,533.9	2,745.2	147.0	37,743.5	36,632.3	1,111.2
1949	11,958.0	2,844.4	8,139.6	974.0	24,074.8	21,433.6	2,518.6	122.6	36,032.8	34,936.2	1,096.6
1948	11,616.3	2,796.2	7,854.2	965.9	22,943.3	20,516.7	2,328.8	97.8	34,559.6	33,495.9	1,063.7
1947	11,319.2	2,772.3	7,595.5	951.4	22,088.1	19,804.6	2,204.9	78.6	33,407.3	32,377.3	1,030.0
1946	11,117.9	2,775.4	7,397.9	944.6	21,361.3	19,177.8	2,116.5	67.0	32,479.2	31,467.6	1,011.6
1945	10,971.7	2,749.3	7,299.8	922.6	20,696.4	18,578.5	2,057.6	60.3	31,668.1	30,685.2	982.9
1944	10,690.4	2,613.1	7,196.3	881.0	20,283.2	18,179.3	2,044.0	59.9	30,973.6	30,032.7	940.9
1943	9,943.3	2,258.2	6,893.0	792.1	20,137.0	18,017.1	2,057.3	62.6	30,080.3	29,225.6	854.7
1942	8,994.6	1,725.8	6,603.1	665.7	20,107.2	17,958.6	2,081.6	67.0	29,101.8	28,369.1	732.7
1941	8,233.3	1,234.0	6,459.6	539.7	20,055.3	17,877.7	2,105.8	71.8	28,288.6	27,677.1	611.5
1940	7,698.1	905.8	6,351.0	441.3	–	–	2,123.7	76.3	–	–	517.6
1939	7,409.6	774.4	6,234.3	400.9	–	–	2,120.9	79.0	–	–	479.9
1938	7,196.5	751.5	6,057.7	387.3	–	–	2,104.9	80.2	–	–	467.5
1937	6,942.1	738.2	5,829.5	374.4	–	–	2,099.1	82.5	–	–	456.9
1936	6,732.6	729.5	5,637.7	365.4	–	–	2,101.9	86.0	–	–	451.4
1935	6,568.2	720.2	5,489.0	359.0	–	–	2,113.7	90.5	–	–	449.5
1934	6,400.5	710.5	5,332.9	357.1	–	–	2,133.7	95.9	–	–	453.0
1933	6,287.7	704.0	5,220.9	362.8	–	–	2,151.5	101.3	–	–	464.1
1932	6,163.6	693.7	5,101.8	368.1	–	–	2,140.7	104.1	–	–	472.2
1931	5,919.0	666.6	4,889.2	363.2	–	–	2,080.8	101.5	–	–	464.7
1930	5,550.6	619.8	4,584.8	346.0	–	–	1,985.1	94.5	–	–	440.5
1929	5,200.6	577.5	4,294.2	328.9	–	–	1,890.5	87.4	–	–	416.3
1928	4,938.4	551.6	4,066.3	320.5	–	–	1,813.2	82.8	–	–	403.3
1927	4,721.6	532.6	3,871.1	317.9	–	–	1,741.1	79.1	–	–	397.0
1926	4,566.2	521.4	3,724.0	320.8	–	–	1,678.6	76.5	–	–	397.3

Series F221-224. Non-farm business inventories, year-end book value estimates, 1925 to 1976
(millions of dollars)

Year	Current dollars		Constant (1971) dollars		Year	Current dollars		Constant (1971) dollars	
	Total non-farm	Manufacturing	Total non-farm	Manufacturing		Total non-farm	Manufacturing	Total non-farm	Manufacturing
	221	**222**	**223**	**224**		**221**	**222**	**223**	**224**
1976	38,234	18,558	24,207	11,311	1950	5,495	2,752	7,910	3,783
					1949	4,723	2,413	7,299	3,620
1975	35,144	17,161	23,464	11,058	1948	4,459	2,348	7,068	3,589
1974	32,664	16,210	23,808	11,454	1947	3,859	2,111	6,960	3,654
1973	24,672	11,883	21,079	10,054	1946	2,867	1,596	6,161	3,342
1972	20,868	9,821	19,720	9,323					
1971	19,045	9,084	18,885	9,048	1945	2,249	1,352	5,314	3,084
					1944	2,074	1,229	4,997	2,829
1970	17,973	8,756	18,479	8,953	1943	2,024	1,186	4,988	2,772
1969	17,522	8,603	18,251	8,982	1942	1,940	1,033	4,910	2,471
1968	15,976	7,777	17,208	8,432	1941	2,037	1,059	5,364	2,660
1967	15,155	7,496	16,593	8,179					
1966	14,613	7,238	16,368	8,057	1940	1,747	893	5,039	2,426
					1939	1,537	753	4,800	2,199
1965	13,252	6,488	15,203	7,370	1938	1,386	707	4,512	2,151
1964	11,697	5,775	13,751	6,679	1937	1,463	725	4,567	2,093
1963	10,834	5,312	12,886	6,169	1936	1,263	618	4,250	1,919
1962	10,235	5,048	12,405	5,968					
1961	9,705	4,817	11,878	5,751	1935	1,161	577	4,048	1,861
					1934	1,107	564	3,936	1,830
1960	9,150	4,504	11,249	5,410	1933	1,051	540	3,884	1,821
1959	8,781	4,352	10,830	5,252	1932	1,100	564	4,086	1,973
1958	8,289	4,136	10,356	5,061	1931	1,331	676	4,483	2,128
1957	8,485	4,260	10,634	5,226					
1956	8,158	4,128	10,305	5,081	1930	1,564	805	4,647	2,271
					1929	1,716	835	4,567	2,056
1955	7,163	3,592	9,375	4,548	1928	1,559	793	4,181	1,936
1954	6,871	3,457	9,181	4,522	1927	1,435	721	3,887	1,758
1953	7,071	3,604	9,338	4,672	1926	1,304	673	3,464	1,604
1952	6,652	3,431	8,770	4,453					
1951	6,698	3,456	8,670	4,353	1925	1,191	646	3,073	1,475

Series F225–240. Real domestic product, by industry, 1935 to 1976
(1971 = 100)

Year	Real domestic product	Agriculture	Forestry	Fishing and trapping	Mines (including milling), quarries and oil wells	Manufacturing industries	Construction industry	Transportation, storage and communications	Electric power, gas and water utilities	Trade	Wholesale trade	Retail trade	Finance, insurance and real estate	Community, business and personal service industries	Public administration and defence	Index of industrial production
	225	226	227	228	229	230	231	232	233	234	235	236	237	238	239	240
1971 weights[1]	100.000	3.238	0.804	0.177	3.779	22.869	7.022	19.479	2.635	11.777	4.928	6.850	11.517	19.314	7.389	29.283[2]
1976	126.4	109.3	105.4	98.0	103.1	123.1	119.6	132.0	142.0	138.0	133.3	141.4	132.3	127.3	123.0	122.2
1975	120.4	103.0	97.8	85.8	100.9	116.2	116.0	125.4	130.5	132.5	130.8	133.7	125.9	121.1	119.4	115.5
1974	119.3	89.5	112.1	90.2	114.0	123.4	110.3	123.6	130.1	129.5	130.2	129.1	120.9	115.8	113.9	122.8
1973	114.1	96.9	113.7	101.6	117.8	119.1	106.1	117.2	120.3	119.8	120.1	119.7	114.0	109.8	109.7	119.0
1972	105.9	88.7	105.7	95.7	104.4	107.7	103.0	107.8	111.1	109.9	109.5	110.2	105.3	104.8	104.2	107.6
1971	100.0	100.0	100.0	100.0	100.0	100.0	100.0	100.0	100.0	100.0	100.0	100.0	100.0	100.0	100.0	100.0
1970	94.4	89.0	103.3	105.4	98.7	94.5	90.9	94.2	93.3	93.2	93.9	92.6	94.6	95.5	95.2	94.9
1969	92.2	90.6	102.4	102.6	86.9	95.8	92.5	89.0	85.4	91.7	92.7	91.0	92.4	91.6	91.6	93.6
1968	86.9	85.2	94.4	115.6	86.2	89.1	90.1	82.8	78.2	87.1	87.7	86.6	86.7	85.7	89.1	87.6
1967	82.3	78.9	90.1	102.0	79.9	83.9	87.1	77.9	72.6	83.7	84.5	83.1	81.7	81.4	86.8	82.3
1966	79.5	96.7	88.3	107.5	74.1	81.5	88.5	73.1	67.9	80.2	81.8	79.1	78.8	75.0	82.7	79.2
1965	74.5	85.3	85.7	96.9	70.5	75.8	81.5	69.2	62.4	75.6	76.2	75.0	75.5	69.7	80.0	73.8
1964	69.4	82.8	78.0	99.1	67.0	69.5	73.7	64.4	58.0	69.8	69.4	70.1	71.9	64.9	78.7	68.0
1963	65.0	91.5	71.6	96.8	62.2	63.4	67.8	59.1	53.5	64.9	62.9	66.2	67.5	60.5	77.5	62.3
1962	61.6	81.6	68.8	97.3	59.6	59.4	66.5	55.5	50.5	61.8	59.2	63.5	65.1	56.7	76.7	58.6
1961	57.5	66.8	65.5	90.3	55.7	54.4	63.3	53.1	47.9	58.0	55.4	59.8	62.7	53.4	74.6	54.0
1960	56.4	77.1	68.4	85.8	54.3	52.3	61.4	49.8	45.3	56.6	53.9	58.5	60.4	51.7	73.5	51.9
1959	55.1	73.7	59.7	88.5	54.2	51.4	62.5	48.4	41.8	56.5	54.3	58.1	58.2	49.7	72.4	50.8
1958	52.4	76.1	52.8	98.6	47.9	47.9	65.7	44.8	37.0	53.0	49.3	55.4	55.7	47.1	71.5	46.8
1957	51.5	68.6	59.7	88.4	47.2	48.8	63.5	46.4	33.8	51.8	48.4	54.0	54.1	45.4	68.2	47.1
1956	51.3	81.6	65.6	93.4	43.0	48.9	58.4	46.2	31.5	51.8	48.9	53.6	50.5	44.0	66.4	46.3
1955	47.2	76.8	62.1	88.4	37.0	44.7	51.9	41.4	28.4	47.5	44.3	49.6	49.0	41.5	65.4	41.9
1954	42.8	62.2	58.7	94.0	31.3	40.8	46.7	36.5	25.3	42.6	39.2	44.8	47.2	40.5	63.3	37.8
1953	43.4	81.0	56.6	86.7	28.2	41.7	45.5	37.4	23.3	42.1	38.9	44.2	44.8	39.7	60.3	37.8
1952	41.7	88.6	59.3	85.0	25.9	38.9	40.6	36.9	22.2	39.5	36.8	41.2	43.0	38.3	57.0	35.2
1951	38.7	72.4	64.7	93.2	24.3	37.5	35.8	35.0	20.6	37.0	34.6	38.6	41.2	36.6	49.8	33.8
1950	35.9	63.4	54.4	91.1	21.6	34.5	35.5	31.9	18.2	36.6	32.0	39.5	38.2	35.0	44.6	30.9
1949	33.6	58.0	45.7	83.8	19.7	32.4	32.9	30.9	16.3	34.1	30.8	36.2	36.2	33.9	41.8	28.8
1948	32.6	61.6	54.4	73.4	17.7	31.5	29.3	30.8	15.5	32.7	30.0	34.5	33.9	32.5	38.6	27.8
1947	31.5	59.6	54.3	67.8	15.4	30.2	26.2	30.3	14.7	33.2	29.8	35.3	31.8	31.5	38.8	26.4
1946	30.2	63.5	47.2	72.9	14.7	27.6	22.5	28.0	13.2	30.5	27.6	32.3	29.5	30.2	52.2	24.6
1945	32.6	55.0	42.8	73.4	15.2	30.0	18.0	30.5	12.6	26.4	26.8	26.4	27.3	27.6	129.5	26.0
1944	34.6	73.2	39.8	65.7	15.7	34.3	17.6	30.9	12.9	24.8	26.8	23.9	26.1	26.1	143.2	29.2
1943	33.3	59.4	38.4	67.7	17.5	33.6	21.5	30.3	12.8	23.4	25.5	22.5	25.3	25.2	130.2	29.0
1942	31.9	95.3	37.3	67.0	19.5	31.1	22.3	27.1	12.0	22.9	24.6	22.2	24.4	24.4	98.4	27.3
1941	27.1	61.8	37.9	70.2	19.9	25.5	20.9	24.0	10.7	22.2	22.8	22.1	23.3	24.0	66.8	23.1
1940	23.2	74.1	38.2	66.8	19.0	19.5	16.1	19.6	9.4	19.9	18.9	20.6	22.2	22.4	43.8	18.4
1939	20.2	73.6	32.5	65.6	17.8	15.8	14.2	16.0	8.5	18.2	16.5	19.3	21.9	21.2	25.8	15.4
1938	19.0	63.6	26.0	63.2	16.5	14.6	13.9	15.0	8.0	17.4	15.4	18.6	21.6	20.9	23.6	14.3
1937	19.0	49.6	39.8	61.9	15.7	15.9	14.7	15.3	8.0	17.8	15.8	19.1	21.9	20.8	21.6	15.1
1936	17.6	49.3	30.5	63.6	13.4	13.9	12.3	14.4	7.4	16.5	14.7	17.7	22.0	19.6	20.5	13.2
1935	16.7	55.1	27.0	60.6	12.0	12.6	11.0	13.4	7.0	15.4	13.4	16.7	21.1	18.9	20.1	11.9

[1] 1971 gross domestic product.

[2] Includes mining, manufacturing and electric power, gas and water utilities.

Series F241-249. Indexes of labour productivity and unit labour cost, in all commercial industries, 1946 to 1976
(1971 = 100)

Year	Output	Persons employed	Man-hours	Labour compensation	Output per person	Output per man-hour	Compensation per person	Conpensation per man-hour	Unit labour cost
	241	242	243	244	245	246	247	248	249
1976	128.9	116.7	113.5	203.8	110.4	113.5	174.6	179.5	158.1
1975	122.2	115.1	112.6	177.9	106.2	108.5	154.6	157.9	145.5
1974	121.7	113.9	112.3	154.4	106.9	108.4	135.6	137.5	126.8
1973	116.0	108.4	107.6	129.6	107.0	107.8	119.5	120.4	111.7
1972	106.6	103.3	102.5	111.1	103.2	104.0	107.6	108.4	104.2
1971	100.0	100.0	100.0	100.0	100.0	100.0	100.0	100.0	100.0
1970	94.1	98.3	99.0	91.5	95.7	95.1	93.1	92.4	97.2
1969	92.3	98.4	100.0	85.5	93.8	92.3	87.0	85.5	92.7
1968	86.7	95.4	97.9	77.2	90.9	88.6	80.9	78.8	89.0
1967	82.1	95.3	99.0	72.4	86.2	82.9	76.0	73.2	88.2
1966	79.8	93.6	97.7	66.3	85.3	81.6	70.8	67.8	83.0
1965	74.6	90.5	95.7	59.2	82.4	77.9	65.4	61.9	79.4
1964	69.3	86.8	92.6	53.6	79.8	74.9	61.7	57.9	77.3
1963	64.6	83.9	90.0	49.6	77.0	71.8	59.1	55.1	76.7
1962	61.1	82.1	88.7	46.8	74.4	68.9	57.1	52.8	76.7
1961	57.0	80.1	86.6	44.4	71.1	65.8	55.4	51.3	77.9
1960	55.8	79.9	87.4	43.1	69.8	63.9	54.0	49.4	77.3
1959	54.6	80.2	88.3	41.2	68.1	61.9	51.4	46.7	75.5
1958	51.9	78.9	87.0	39.2	65.8	59.6	49.7	45.0	75.5
1957	51.1	81.3	90.3	38.9	62.9	56.6	47.8	43.0	76.1
1956	51.0	80.3	90.0	36.1	63.7	56.7	45.1	40.1	70.8
1955	46.8	77.0	86.8	32.2	60.8	53.9	41.8	37.1	68.7
1954	42.1	76.1	86.5	30.2	55.3	48.7	39.7	34.9	71.8
1953	43.0	76.7	87.5	30.1	56.1	49.1	39.2	34.3	69.9
1952	41.3	76.3	87.1	28.1	54.1	47.4	36.9	32.3	68.1
1951	38.5	75.7	86.9	25.9	50.9	44.3	34.2	29.8	67.3
1950	35.7	73.8	85.3	22.2	48.4	41.8	30.1	26.0	62.3
1949	33.3	74.0	87.3	20.3	45.0	38.2	27.5	23.3	61.1
1948	32.5	73.0	86.8	19.3	44.5	37.4	26.4	22.2	59.3
1947	31.3	71.8	85.4	17.3	43.6	36.7	24.1	20.2	55.2
1946	29.4	68.7	83.6	13.9	42.8	35.2	20.2	16.6	47.1

Series F250-258. Indexes of labour productivity and unit labour cost, in commercial goods-producing industries, 1946 to 1976
(1971 = 100)

Year	Output	Persons employed	Man-hours	Labour compensation	Output per person	Output per man-hour	Compensation per person	Compensation per man-hour	Unit labour cost
	250	251	252	253	254	255	256	257	258
1976	120.3	107.2	105.3	197.9	112.2	114.2	184.6	187.9	164.5
1975	114.1	106.5	105.1	173.5	107.1	108.6	162.8	165.1	152.0
1974	117.6	107.8	106.9	153.2	109.1	110.1	142.0	143.3	130.2
1973	114.9	105.1	104.6	129.2	109.3	109.8	122.9	123.5	112.5
1972	105.2	101.1	100.4	109.2	104.1	104.8	108.1	108.8	103.8
1971	100.0	100.0	100.0	100.0	100.0	100.0	100.0	100.0	100.0
1970	94.2	99.6	100.2	91.9	94.6	94.0	92.3	91.7	97.6
1969	93.4	102.1	103.4	87.6	91.5	90.4	85.8	84.7	93.7
1968	88.0	101.0	103.0	80.1	87.0	85.4	79.3	77.8	91.1
1967	82.8	102.1	104.8	75.9	81.2	79.0	74.4	72.4	91.7
1966	82.1	101.7	105.4	70.5	80.7	77.9	69.4	66.9	85.9
1965	76.0	99.8	104.0	62.9	76.2	73.1	63.0	60.4	82.7
1964	70.2	96.9	101.8	56.8	72.5	69.0	58.6	55.8	80.9
1963	65.7	94.3	99.6	52.4	69.7	66.0	55.6	52.6	79.8
1962	61.8	93.2	99.1	49.8	66.3	62.3	53.4	50.3	80.6
1961	56.5	91.8	97.4	47.2	61.6	58.0	51.4	48.4	83.5

Series F250-258. Indexes of labour productivity and unit labour cost, in commercial goods-producing industries, 1946 to 1976 (concluded)
(1971 = 100)

Year	Output	Persons employed	Man-hours	Labour compensation	Output per person	Output per man-hour	Compensation per person	Compensation per man-hour	Unit labour cost
	250	251	252	253	254	255	256	257	258
1960	55.9	93.0	99.9	46.8	60.2	56.0	50.4	46.9	83.7
1959	54.7	94.5	102.1	45.1	57.9	53.6	47.7	44.2	82.5
1958	52.2	93.9	101.6	43.4	55.6	51.4	46.2	42.7	83.1
1957	51.4	99.3	108.0	44.1	51.8	47.6	44.4	40.8	85.8
1956	51.9	99.9	110.3	41.6	52.0	47.1	41.7	37.7	80.1
1955	47.3	97.6	108.2	37.1	48.5	43.7	38.0	34.3	78.4
1954	41.8	97.6	109.0	34.9	42.8	38.3	35.7	32.0	83.5
1953	43.7	99.6	111.6	35.6	43.9	39.2	35.7	31.9	81.3
1952	42.1	100.1	111.5	33.8	42.1	37.8	33.8	30.3	80.4
1951	38.8	101.0	113.2	31.6	38.4	34.3	31.3	27.9	81.5
1950	35.4	99.2	111.7	26.7	35.7	31.7	26.9	23.9	75.4
1949	32.7	100.5	115.2	23.7	32.5	28.4	23.6	20.6	72.7
1948	32.1	99.8	115.3	23.0	32.2	27.8	23.1	20.0	71.7
1947	30.5	99.4	114.8	20.9	30.7	26.6	21.1	18.2	68.5
1946	28.8	96.8	115.1	15.6	29.8	25.0	16.1	13.6	54.2

Series F259-267. Indexes of labour productivity and unit labour cost, in non-agricultural goods-producing industries, 1946 to 1976
(1971 = 100)

Year	Output	Persons employed	Man-hours	Labour compensation	Output per person	Output per man-hour	Compensation per person	Compensation per man-hour	Unit labour cost
	259	260	261	262	263	264	265	266	267
1976	119.4	109.6	108.7	196.7	109.0	109.9	179.5	181.1	164.7
1975	114.6	107.7	106.6	175.2	106.4	107.5	162.6	164.3	152.9
1974	118.8	110.1	109.7	154.3	108.0	108.4	140.2	140.7	129.8
1973	115.1	107.2	107.1	129.6	107.4	107.4	121.0	121.0	112.6
1972	106.1	102.1	101.9	109.9	104.0	104.2	107.6	107.8	103.5
1971	100.0	100.0	100.0	100.0	100.0	100.0	100.0	100.0	100.0
1970	94.7	99.4	100.3	91.5	95.2	94.4	92.0	91.2	96.7
1969	93.7	101.5	102.8	86.6	92.3	91.2	85.3	84.3	92.4
1968	88.2	99.8	101.9	79.0	88.4	86.5	79.1	77.4	89.5
1967	83.2	100.4	102.9	74.6	82.8	80.8	74.3	72.5	89.7
1966	80.8	100.7	104.1	69.5	80.2	77.6	69.1	66.8	86.1
1965	75.2	96.2	100.0	61.5	78.1	75.2	63.9	61.5	81.8
1964	69.1	91.2	94.6	54.9	75.7	73.0	60.2	58.0	79.5
1963	63.3	87.3	90.2	50.3	72.6	70.2	57.6	55.8	79.4
1962	60.0	85.4	88.4	47.6	70.2	67.8	55.8	53.8	79.4
1961	55.6	82.8	84.8	44.7	67.1	65.6	53.9	52.7	80.4
1960	53.6	84.3	87.1	44.3	63.6	61.6	52.6	50.9	82.6
1959	52.7	85.4	88.8	42.8	61.7	59.3	50.1	48.2	81.2
1958	49.5	83.8	86.8	40.4	59.1	57.0	48.2	46.6	81.6
1957	49.6	88.9	92.3	41.1	55.7	53.7	46.3	44.6	83.0
1956	48.5	88.3	92.6	38.8	54.9	52.4	43.9	41.9	80.0
1955	43.8	83.7	87.6	34.2	52.3	50.0	40.9	39.1	78.2
1954	39.4	81.2	85.1	32.3	48.6	46.4	39.8	38.0	81.9
1953	39.2	84.5	90.2	32.8	46.4	43.5	38.8	36.3	83.6
1952	36.4	83.6	89.1	30.6	43.5	40.8	36.6	34.3	84.0
1951	34.7	82.8	88.9	27.8	41.9	39.0	33.6	31.3	80.2
1950	32.0	77.3	83.4	23.2	41.4	38.4	30.0	27.8	72.5
1949	29.6	75.9	82.3	21.4	39.0	36.0	29.3	26.1	72.4
1948	28.5	74.6	82.2	20.4	38.2	34.7	27.3	24.8	71.6
1947	26.9	73.0	80.4	17.7	36.9	33.5	24.2	22.0	65.6
1946	24.5	67.2	74.5	13.4	36.5	32.9	20.0	18.0	54.8

Series F268-276. Indexes of labour productivity and unit labour cost, in agriculture, 1946 to 1976
(1971 = 100)

Year	Output	Persons employed	Man-hours	Labour compensation	Output per person	Output per man-hour	Compensation per person	Compensation per man-hour	Unit labour cost
	268	269	270	271	272	273	274	275	276
1976	100.4	91.8	93.6	192.6	109.3	107.3	209.7	205.8	191.9
1975	89.2	94.1	96.5	164.0	94.8	92.4	174.4	169.9	183.9
1974	80.6	92.9	94.6	143.1	86.8	85.2	154.1	151.3	177.6
1973	90.2	91.5	92.9	129.5	98.6	97.1	141.5	139.4	143.5
1972	87.9	94.3	92.8	101.8	93.2	94.7	108.0	109.7	115.8
1971	100.0	100.0	100.0	100.0	100.0	100.0	100.0	100.0	100.0
1970	89.0	100.2	99.9	96.8	88.9	89.2	96.6	97.0	108.7
1969	90.6	104.9	105.5	99.9	86.3	85.9	95.2	94.7	110.3
1968	85.2	106.9	106.8	95.0	79.7	79.8	88.9	89.0	111.5
1967	78.9	109.7	111.6	92.1	72.0	70.7	83.9	82.5	116.6
1966	96.7	106.5	110.0	83.0	90.7	87.9	77.9	75.4	85.8
1965	85.3	116.5	118.4	80.3	73.2	72.1	68.9	67.8	94.1
1964	82.8	123.6	127.1	80.3	67.0	65.2	65.0	63.2	97.0
1963	91.5	127.3	132.9	78.9	71.9	68.9	62.0	59.4	86.3
1962	81.6	129.5	136.8	77.2	63.0	59.6	59.6	56.4	94.7
1961	66.8	133.6	142.2	78.8	50.0	47.0	59.0	55.4	117.9
1960	77.1	133.8	145.1	78.6	57.6	53.1	58.8	54.2	102.0
1959	73.7	137.2	149.3	74.7	53.7	49.3	54.5	50.0	101.4
1958	76.1	141.1	154.0	81.0	53.9	49.4	57.4	52.6	106.5
1957	68.6	147.5	163.6	81.5	46.5	41.9	55.3	49.8	118.8
1956	81.6	153.8	172.7	77.0	53.0	47.2	50.1	44.6	94.4
1955	76.8	162.3	180.9	73.0	47.3	42.5	44.9	40.3	95.0
1954	62.2	174.0	193.5	66.8	35.8	32.2	38.4	34.5	107.3
1953	81.0	170.1	187.2	70.1	47.6	43.3	41.2	37.4	86.5
1952	88.6	176.6	190.6	74.5	50.2	46.5	42.2	39.1	84.1
1951	72.4	186.1	198.9	79.3	38.9	36.4	42.6	39.9	109.6
1950	63.4	201.8	211.8	70.0	31.4	29.9	34.7	33.1	110.4
1949	58.0	215.5	231.3	52.5	26.9	25.1	24.4	22.7	90.5
1948	61.6	217.3	232.6	55.8	28.3	26.5	25.7	24.0	90.6
1947	59.6	222.4	236.2	61.6	26.8	25.2	27.7	26.1	103.4
1946	63.5	235.1	258.6	43.1	27.0	24.6	18.3	16.7	67.9

Series F277-285. Indexes of labour productivity and unit labour cost, in commercial service-producing industries, 1946 to 1976
(1971 = 100)

Year	Output	Persons employed	Man-hours	Labour compensation	Output per person	Output per man-hour	Compensation per person	Compensation per man-hour	Unit labour cost
	277	278	279	280	281	282	283	284	285
1976	134.4	123.3	119.5	211.5	109.0	112.5	171.6	177.1	157.4
1975	127.1	119.2	116.7	184.0	106.6	108.9	154.4	157.7	144.8
1974	123.0	116.2	114.5	156.4	105.8	107.4	134.6	136.6	127.2
1973	115.5	109.2	108.5	129.8	105.7	106.4	118.9	119.6	112.4
1972	107.2	104.2	103.5	113.3	102.9	103.5	108.7	109.4	105.6
1971	100.0	100.0	100.0	100.0	100.0	100.0	100.0	100.0	100.0
1970	94.0	97.8	98.4	91.0	96.1	95.5	93.1	92.5	96.8
1969	91.0	95.5	97.3	83.4	95.3	93.5	87.3	85.6	91.6
1968	85.5	90.7	93.3	74.0	94.3	91.6	81.6	79.3	86.6
1967	81.4	89.6	93.7	68.7	90.9	86.8	76.7	73.3	84.4
1966	77.3	86.5	90.6	61.7	89.4	85.3	71.4	68.2	79.9
1965	73.1	82.4	87.9	55.4	88.7	83.1	67.2	63.0	75.8
1964	68.2	77.9	83.8	50.2	87.6	81.4	64.4	59.8	73.5
1963	63.5	74.6	80.7	46.6	85.0	78.6	62.4	57.7	73.4
1962	60.5	72.1	78.6	43.7	83.9	77.0	60.6	55.6	72.2
1961	57.5	69.6	76.1	41.5	82.6	75.6	59.6	54.5	72.1

Series F277-285. Indexes of labour productivity and unit labour cost, in commercial service-producing industries, 1946 to 1976 (concluded)
(1971 = 100)

Year	Output	Persons employed	Man-hours	Labour compensation	Output per person	Output per man-hour	Compensation per person	Compensation per man-hour	Unit labour cost
	277	278	279	280	281	282	283	284	285
1960	55.4	68.1	75.2	39.2	81.3	73.7	57.6	52.2	70.8
1959	54.1	67.1	74.7	37.1	80.6	72.5	55.3	49.7	68.5
1958	51.0	65.2	72.7	34.7	78.3	70.2	53.3	47.8	68.1
1957	50.4	64.9	72.9	33.4	77.7	69.2	51.4	45.8	66.2
1956	49.2	61.8	69.8	30.3	79.7	70.5	49.1	43.4	61.6
1955	45.7	58.1	65.6	27.0	78.6	69.7	46.5	41.2	59.1
1954	42.2	56.4	64.1	25.3	74.8	65.7	44.9	39.5	60.1
1953	41.6	55.6	63.4	24.3	74.9	65.7	43.6	38.3	58.2
1952	39.9	54.3	62.8	22.1	73.5	63.6	40.8	35.3	55.5
1951	37.8	52.2	60.7	19.9	72.4	62.3	38.1	32.8	52.6
1950	35.8	50.3	59.0	17.5	71.2	60.7	34.9	29.8	49.0
1949	34.0	49.5	59.3	16.7	68.7	57.3	33.9	28.2	49.3
1948	32.7	48.2	58.2	15.3	67.9	56.3	31.8	26.3	46.8
1947	32.1	46.2	55.9	13.5	69.4	57.4	29.1	24.1	41.9
1946	29.8	42.6	52.0	12.0	70.0	57.3	28.1	23.0	40.2

Series F286-294. Indexes of labour productivity and unit labour cost, in manufacturing, 1946 to 1976
(1971 = 100)

Year	Output	Persons employed	Man-hours	Labour compensation	Output per person	Output per man-hour	Compensation per person	Compensation per man-hour	Unit labour cost
	286	287	288	289	290	291	292	293	294
1976	120.0	108.2	107.2	188.7	110.9	112.0	174.4	176.0	157.2
1975	114.2	106.7	105.0	164.9	107.1	108.8	154.5	157.0	144.3
1974	120.1	109.5	108.7	148.9	109.6	110.4	136.0	137.0	124.0
1973	116.1	107.4	107.0	126.8	108.1	108.6	118.1	118.6	109.2
1972	106.9	102.9	102.5	110.6	103.9	104.3	107.5	107.9	103.4
1971	100.0	100.0	100.0	100.0	100.0	100.0	100.0	100.0	100.0
1970	94.5	100.6	101.2	94.0	94.0	93.4	93.5	92.9	99.5
1969	95.8	102.9	104.1	89.9	93.1	92.0	87.3	86.4	93.8
1968	89.1	101.0	102.5	82.4	88.2	86.9	81.6	80.4	92.5
1967	83.9	101.7	103.1	77.2	82.6	81.4	75.9	74.9	92.0
1966	81.6	101.3	103.4	71.9	80.5	78.9	71.0	69.6	88.2
1965	75.8	96.7	99.4	64.1	78.4	76.3	66.3	64.5	84.6
1964	69.5	92.0	94.6	58.1	75.5	73.4	63.2	61.4	83.7
1963	63.5	88.0	90.1	53.3	72.1	70.4	60.6	59.2	84.0
1962	59.4	85.8	87.6	50.1	69.2	67.8	58.3	57.1	84.2
1961	54.5	83.6	84.4	46.9	65.1	64.5	56.1	55.5	86.0
1960	52.3	84.3	85.6	46.3	62.1	61.1	54.9	54.1	88.4
1959	51.5	85.1	87.1	44.8	60.5	59.1	52.6	51.4	87.0
1958	47.9	84.2	85.6	42.4	56.9	56.0	50.4	49.5	88.4
1957	48.8	88.7	90.1	42.4	55.1	54.2	47.9	47.1	86.9
1956	49.0	88.3	90.9	40.1	55.4	53.8	45.5	44.1	82.0
1955	44.8	84.7	86.6	36.3	52.8	51.7	42.8	41.9	81.0
1954	40.8	82.7	84.2	34.2	49.3	48.5	41.3	40.6	83.7
1953	41.7	86.6	89.8	34.5	48.2	46.5	39.8	38.4	82.7
1952	38.9	84.1	86.7	31.7	46.3	44.9	37.7	36.6	81.5
1951	37.5	82.1	85.8	28.6	45.7	43.7	34.8	33.3	76.2
1950	34.5	77.4	82.1	24.2	44.6	42.0	31.3	29.5	70.1
1949	32.4	76.6	82.1	22.6	42.3	39.5	28.5	27.5	69.8
1948	31.5	75.4	82.3	21.5	41.7	38.2	28.4	26.1	68.2
1947	30.2	73.9	80.2	18.5	40.8	37.6	25.1	23.1	61.4
1946	27.6	69.0	75.9	14.2	40.0	36.4	20.6	18.8	51.6

Section G:

The Balance of International Payments, International Investment Position and Foreign Trade

B.W. Wilkinson, *University of Alberta*

The statistics presented in this section are in three major divisions. The first of these, series G1-151, cover private and official estimates of the balance of payments on current and capital account from 1900 to 1975. This subsection is itself divided into three parts: series G1-56 contain the estimates of the balance of payments of Professors Jacob Viner and Frank Knox for the period 1900 to 1926; series G57-83 contain the official estimates of the balance of payments, current account, prepared by Statistics Canada (formerly Dominion Bureau of Statistics) for the period 1926 to 1975; series G84-152 contain the official estimates of the balance of payments, capital account for 1926 to 1975.

The second major division consists of series G152-380 covering estimates of the Canadian international investment position and the extent of foreign-ownership and/or control in the Canadian economy for the period 1900 to 1975. It has two main parts. The first one consists of a few private estimates and the official Statistics Canada estimates of Canadian foreign indebtedness and Canadian claims on foreign assets. The second one provides detail on foreign direct investment in Canada according to the Corporation and Labour Union Returns Act for the years 1968 to 1975.

The third major division, series G381-487, presents statistics on foreign trade, export and import price indexes, and import duties for the years 1968 to 1975.

The major sources are the following: Jacob Viner, *Canada's Balance of International Indebtedness, 1900-1913*, (Cambridge: Harvard University Press, 1924), hereafter referred to as *Canada's Balance;* Frank A. Knox, "Canadian Capital Movements and the Canadian Balance of International Payments, 1900-1934", in Herbert Marshall, Frank A. Southard and Kenneth W. Taylor, *Canadian American Industry,*(New Haven: Yale University Press and Toronto, Ryerson Press, 1936), hereafter referred to as "Excursus"; Frank A. Knox, *Dominion Monetary Policy, 1929-1934*, a report prepared for the Royal Commission on Dominion-Provincial Relations (Ottawa, mimeographed, 1939), hereafter *Dominion Monetary Policy;* Statistics Canada, *The Canadian Balance of International Payments, A Study of Methods and Results,* (Ottawa, King's Printer, 1939), hereafter *Red Book;* Statistics Canada, *The Canadian Balance of International Payments, 1926 to 1948,* (Ottawa, King's Printer, 1949), hereafter *Blue Book;* Statistics Canada, "The Canadian Balance of International Payments and International Investment Position: A Description of Sources and Methods" (forthcoming), hereafter "Sources and Methods"; Statistics Canada, *The Canadian Balance of International Payments,* (Catalogue 67-201); Statistics Canada, *Canada's International Investment Position, 1926 to 1967,* (Catalogue 67-202) and subsequent issues; Statistiscs Canada, *Corporations and Labour Unions Returns Act, Part I: Corporations,* 1968 and subsequent annual issues; hereafter CALURA; Statistics Canada, *Trade of Canada, Volume I, Summary and Analytical Tables,* calendar years 1966-1968, (Catalogue 65-201), and other years; Statistics Canada, *The 1971-based Price and Volume Indexes of Canada's Internal Trade,* (Catalogue 65-001), December 1976; J.D. Randall, "A Brief Guide to Statistics Related to Foreign Ownership in Canada", *Canadian Statistical Review,* (January 1974), pp. 4-7 and 14-16; and M.C. Urquhart, *Historical Statistics of Canada,* (Toronto: The Macmillan Company of Canada Ltd., 1965), hereafter *HSC I*; Statistics Canada, Canadian Socio-Economic Information Management System, hereafter CANSIM.

The material in the following is taken verbatim, or in paraphrased form, from these above sources, without any further specific reference.

Canadian Balance of International Payments (Series G1-151)

General note

The balance of payments is a systematic record of all transactions between residents of Canada and residents of other countries over a year, or one quarter of a year. (The historical series presented here are confined to annual data.) The main divisions in it are the current account, the capital account and net official monetary movements. The current account is presently subdivided into trade in merchandise, trade in services and transfer items. Services, in turn, consist of travel, interest and dividends, freight and shipping, and other service transactions. Transfer items include inheritances and migrants' funds, personal and institutional remittances and official contributions. Withholding taxes, although of a somewhat different nature (to be clarified below), are included under service items and tranfers. The capital account has two major sections, long-term flows and short-term flows, with numerous subdivisions in each of these. The sum of the net balance of the current account, the capital account and the allocation of special drawing rights, is reflected in net official monetary movements.

The balance of payments data in this section cover the period 1900 to the mid-1970s, but they are presented in three distinct periods because comparability cannot be maintained between the different periods. Indeed, there are elements of incomparability within a single period.

In the earliest years for which balance of payments statements are reported here, 1900 to 1926, lack of recorded data for many of the items made extensive reliance on estimates necessary and indirect methods by the researchers, Viner and Knox. These methods are indicated more fully in the various Statistics Canada publications, in *HSC I*, Section F, pp. 142-146, and in Knox, "Excursus", and Viner, *Canada's Balance*. Other estimates of Canada's balance of payments back to 1868 were made by Penelope Hartland in her "Canadian Balance of Payments since 1868" in *Trends in the American Economy in the Nineteenth Century*, Studies in Income and Wealth, Vol. 24, Princeton, Princeton University Press, 1960. New measures are currently being produced by Professor Allister Sinclair of Dalhousie University.

A brief summary of the evolution of balance of payments methods within Statistics Canada up to the years shortly after World War II is found in *HSC I*, pp. 146-153, and also in Statistics Canada, "Sources and Methods", Section 1.33. Developments of more recent years are found in "Sources and Methods", and a very quick outline of them is given in the remainder of this section.

With the termination of exchange control late in 1951, extensive use of questionnaires to obtain the desired information was re-instituted. There were some difficulties in obtaining statistics on short-term items such as accounts receivable and payable, and it was during this early period that the practice of treating the balancing item 'errors and omissions' as a short-term capital flow was instituted.

Other discontinuities occurred during the post-war period, owing to the desire to break out and isolate new developments of importance such as the program of export credits and of international money market transactions. Additional changes, carried consistently back through the series, included the presentation in the balance of payments of taxes withheld on payments to non-residents, the elimination of entries with respect to mutual aid to NATO countries, and changes in 1963 in the handling of international financial agencies and Canada's official monetary reserves.

Other discontinuities could not be wholly eliminated. Pension receipts could not be isolated until 1952, and for earlier years remained with the series for services. Additional adjustments in the coverage of official international reserves introduced in 1970 led to a small discontinuity at the end of 1960, and a change in 1973 in the treatment of foreign currency operations of the Canadian chartered banks could be carried back only to 1964. The change in 1973 in the conceptual treatment of gold was carried back to the second quarter of 1968 when the two-tiered market for gold was introduced. Marked discontinuities exist between 1970 and 1971 in a number of current account series. These reflect the culmination in 1975 of a long process of evaluation and development of basic series. Revisions were made to incorporate conceptual and statistical changes arising from the reconciliation of merchandise trade and other balance of payments current account statistics with the United States. At the same time, adjustments were introduced to eliminate from merchandise trade with overseas countries transportation costs which under Canadian conventions were already included in the freight and shipping charges. The union with Newfoundland and the changes in area classifications also introduced discontinuities ("Sources and Methods", Section 1.13).

Balance of payments data are linked with the national income and expenditure accounts and with the financial flow accounts. Detailed descriptions of the relationships between the balance of payments and the national income and expenditure accounts may be found in Statistics Canada, *National Income and Expenditure Accounts, Volume 3, A Guide to the National Income and Expenditure Accounts: Definitions, Concepts, Sources and Methods*, (Catalogue 13-549), Chapters 3, 8 and 12. Linkages with the financial flow accounts together with details on the re-arrangement of capital flows and official monetary movements, as they appear in the balance of payments so as to conform to the standard classifications employed for all sectors of the financial flows, may be found in Statistics Canada, "Sources and Methods", Appendix 3.

Reports by Canada to the International Monetary Fund (IMF), and Organization for Economic Co-operation and Development (OECD),conform insofar as possible to international standards adopted by these institutions; see Statistics Canada, "Sources and Methods", Appendix 6, for a discussion of the main variations between the statistics normally published in Canada and the standards provided in the IMF *Balance of Payments Manual*.

G1-17.   Canadian balance of international payments, between Canada and all countries, current account, 1900 to 1913

SOURCE: Viner, *Canada's Balance*, table II, p. 31; table III, p. 32; table XXVI, p. 95; table XXIX, pp. 102-103; table XXX, p. 105; table XXXI, p. 106.

Details of Viner's methodology relevant to these series are to be found in the source document and in *HSC I*, pp. 143-145.

G18-33.   Canadian balance of international payments, between Canada and all countries, capital account, 1900 to 1913

SOURCE: Viner, *Canada's Balance*, table XXV, p. 94; table XXXVIII, p. 126; table XLI, p. 134; table XLIII, p. 138; table XLIV, p. 139.

Details of Viner's methodology relevant to these series are to be found in the source document and in *HSC I*, p. 145.

G34-46.   Canadian balance of international payments, between Canada and all countries, current account, 1900 to 1926

SOURCE: for series G34-45, Knox, *Monetary Policy*, Appendix; series G46, calculated by Herbert Marshall from Knox's data; also see Knox, "Excursus".

Details of Knox's methodology may be found in the source material and are summarized in *HSC I*, p. 145.

G47-56.   Canadian balance of international payments, between Canada and all countries, capital account, 1900 to 1926

SOURCE: same as series G34-46.

Details of Knox's methodology may be found in the source material and they are summarized in *HSC I*, pp. 145-146.

G57-83. Canadian balance of international payments, all countries, current account, 1926 to 1975, and by major areas 1946 to 1975

SOURCE: for all countries, the United States and the United Kingdom: Statistics Canada, *The Balance of Payments, 1975 and subsequent years*, (Catalogue 67-201), table 2; for all other country relationships, CANSIM, numbers as indicated in *The Balance of Payments*, table 36.

G57 and 70. Commodity trade. Statistics based on customs data are tabulated on a 'statistical month' rather than a calendar month. For example, motor vehicle trade with the United States for any calendar month actually refers to shipments from the 26th of the previous month to the 25th of the current month. Again, because of reporting time lags, statistics on electricity, trade and exports of petroleum and natural gas via pipeline for one calendar month are reported in trade statistics in the following month. Adjustments are made where possible to correct the timing of these data in the balance of payments series.

Trade flows in the balance of payments exclude 'Special transactions, non-trade'. Even before 1960 when this new category was first established in the commodity trade statistics, its components were removed from the commodity totals when arriving at the values of merchandise trade in the balance of payments. However, up to that date, the treatment of the various import and export items in the series was not uniform. This weakness was rectified with the introduction of the new category. Items in this subdivision include settlers' effects, private donations and gifts, identifiable commodity shipments by tourists, current coin, imports and exports by foreign and domestic diplomats and armed services personnel, temporary shipments for exhibition or competition, film processing abroad, and gold and gold products shipments. Gold has been added back to merchandise trade since 1968, and is not excluded for balance of payments purposes from the merchandise account as are the other 'Special transactions, non-trade'. For more detail of the changes introduced in 1960, see Statistics Canada, *Review of Foreign Trade, Calendar Year 1959*, (Catalogue 65-205), Chapter IV.

The *Trade of Canada* statistics exclude entirely several specific types of merchandise transactions. These are temporary exports or imports (other than contractors' equipment, items for exhibition, etc.), ships of British construction and registry imported for use in Canada, and ships and aircraft (until 1966) purchased abroad for use as international carriers but not used to carry goods between points in Canada, and goods exported or imported on a lease or rental basis. Also excluded from merchandise trade figures are bunker supplies and ships' stores sold to foreign vessels or aircraft in Canada, or purchased abroad by Canadian vessels or aircraft, although these items are covered in the balance of payments series for freight and shipping, or, in the case of military vessels and aircraft, for 'other' services (government).

Commencing with 1964, trade statistics have been tabulated on a 'general trade' basis, that is, according to when they crossed the national boundary. Until then, since 1917 for imports and 1920 for exports, statistics were collected on a 'special trade' basis, that is, measured at the 'customs frontier', the point at which imports leave, or exports enter, customs supervision. The statistics in series G57 and 70 back to 1951 and 1946 respectively, however, are on the general trade basis. Until 1962, when temporary surcharges

were levied and some inducement existed to leave merchandise in customs warehouses until the surcharges were removed, there was little difference between the two series. For details see Statistics Canada, *Review of Foreign Trade, Calendar Years 1960-1963*, (Catalogue 65-205), Chapter IV.

From 1940 to 1949, when Newfoundland entered Confederation, Canadian exports to and imports from Newfoundland were not included in the commodity trade figures used for balance of payments purposes. The only item entered in the current account from Canada-Newfoundland transactions during this period was the surplus of United States dollars earned by Newfoundland. This was included under miscellaneous receipts (from the United States) in the Canadian balance of payments. Since 1949, Newfoundland transactions with other nations have been included in the appropriate parts of the balance of payments.

Exports are classified to the country to which they are consigned at the time the goods leave Canada, that is, to the furthest known destination. Imports are generally classified to the country from which goods are consigned to Canada. However, since July 1946, goods originating in Caribbean, Central or South American countries yet consigned to Canada from the United States have been classified to the country of origin in *Trade of Canada* statistics. For balance of payments purposes, adjustments have been made, beginning in 1971, to reverse this procedure and show such imports as coming from the United States.

Most exports are valued at 'f.o.b. (free on board) place of lading', that is, at the point of production. But for grain, oilseeds and iron ore, valuation is f.o.b. Vancouver or St. Lawrence ports. Most imports are valued at the 'selling price f.o.b. point of shipment' reported by importers. Thus, inland freight from the point of consignment to the foreign point of exit, transportation, insurance, handling charges and duties are excluded. For shipments valued under $50,000, or transactions between affiliated companies (other than automotive imports from the United States), the value recorded is the 'fair market value' determined according to the Customs Act. It is generally the wholesale value at which equivalent items could be sold for domestic consumption in the country of origin, less any excise, purchase or sales taxes by the exporting country on domestic sales. All goods are normally valued at their full value, but in the case of repair and improvement trade, only the value added of the repair work is counted.

A valuation problem exists with respect to commodity exports up to 1968, the year when Statistics Canada began requiring exporters to indicate in what currency they were denominating their exports. Prior to that time, it was often not clear to those tabulating the export documents whether exporters were using Canadian or United States dollars. This problem became evident in the early 1960s when the depreciation of the Canadian dollar occurred and the trade series did not behave as was expected, if all shipments abroad had been reported in Canadian currency. The effect of exporters using United States currency on their reports and the statisticians interpreting the numbers as though they were in Canadian dollars meant that when the Canadian dollar was worth more than one American dollar, as in the 1950s, Canadian exports were overstated, and when the Canadian dollar was worth less than one American dollar, Canadian sales abroad were understated. The magnitudes of the annual errors that may exist in the statistics until 1968 are unknown. Unofficial estimates vary from very small to perhaps several hundred million dollars annually.

Adjustments to *Trade of Canada* statistics for balance of

payments purposes for the years 1946 to 1975 are discussed under series G443-472. For adjustments covering earlier years, see the discussion in *HSC I,* under F57 and F64, pp. 146-147.

G58. Gold production available for export. Until 1968, the convention was that new gold produced and sold to the monetary authorities was treated as a current account receipt and the offsetting entry was to augment the nation's official international reserves. But in March 1968, the governors of the central banks of the members of the international Gold Pool (which had been formed to stabilize the price of gold) ceased sales of gold to the pool and created two separate markets for gold: an official one in which the gold price remained at U.S. $35 an ounce, and a free market in which the price would move in response to market pressures. As the free market price of gold rose well above the official price, Canadian producers found it increasingly advantageous to sell their production on the open market and forego assistance from the government under the Emergency Gold Mining Assistance Act. From the second quarter of 1968, sales and purchases of non-monetary gold between Canadians and non-residents were included with other commodity transactions, while resident holdings of gold in Canada, apart from those of the Exchange Fund Account, were no longer considered a foreign asset. Hence, series G58 is blank from 1969 onward. And even though the international arrangement of March 1968 was terminated in November 1973, the same method of handling gold transactions in the balance of payments has been continued.

G59 and 71. Travel. Receipts and payments on travel account include all expenses incidental to travel in Canada by non-residents and travel abroad by residents of Canada respectively. These include international fare costs (Canadian payments to foreign carriers and Canadian carrier receipts from foreign travellers), plus outlays on lodging, food, entertainment, local transportation, gifts and goods to be exported or imported for the personal use of the travellers.

The international travel series used in Canada are basically of a 'frontier-check' type, involving collection at the border of numbers of border crossings together with some information on lengths of stay. Expenditure surveys carried out mainly by questionnaires, but supported occasionally by more intensive 'auto-exit' surveys, are then used to derive a variety of averages which are applied to particular segments of travel. The Canada-United States components of the estimates are derived from a co-operative effort of the statistical authorities in Canada and the United States, with each country assuming responsibility for those elements which it can most effectively and economically produce.

G60 and 72. Interest and dividends. Interest receipts include interest on bonds and debentures held directly by residents of Canada, interest on intergovernmental loans and advances, and earnings on Canada's net official monetary assets. But they do *not* include any interest on export credits, bank deposits, treasury bills and other short-term claims on non-residents, and revenues from non-residents of Canadian banks and insurance companies.

Interest payments comprise, primarily, payments on bonds and debentures held by non-residents. Excluded are interest on bank deposits, treasury bills, commercial and finance paper and other short-term claims on residents of Canada, interest on bank loans, mortgages, and on all other forms of long-term debt apart from bonds and debentures, as well as net revenues in Canada of foreign insurance companies and the net expenses abroad of Canadian banks,

rentals and other payments on foreign investments such as estates, trusts, management and safekeeping accounts, and other items under the administration of Canadian financial intermediaries. All these excluded items are recorded under the 'miscellaneous income' component of series G62 and 76, 'other service receipts and payments'.

No allowance is made in the balance of payments for interest foregone under the concessionary rates applicable to the 'soft' development loan program, nor is any entry recorded for deferrals of interest under the terms of the 1946 loan to the United Kingdom under the United Kingdom Financing Agreement Act.

Dividend receipts are those actually remitted to Canadian shareholders of foreign corporations as well as the profits, both distributed and undistributed, of unincorporated branches abroad of Canadian companies, except banks and insurance companies which are recorded as miscellaneous income under 'other service receipts and payments'. Dividend payments are those remitted to foreign shareholders of Canadian corporations plus the distributed and undistributed profits of unincorporated branches of foreign companies, except insurance companies. An entry offsetting the undistributed portion of branch profits is made under direct investment in the capital account. The undistributed profits of all other foreign operations in Canada or Canadian operations abroad are excluded entirely from dividend payments and receipts and from official balance of payments data. Thus, an inconsistency exists between the way undistributed profits of branches and separately incorporated direct investment establishments are handled.

Stock dividends paid by wholly owned subsidiaries to their parent companies are shown as investment income (dividends) in the current account with an offsetting entry under direct investment in the capital account.

All amounts, whether receipts or payments, are recorded net after deduction of any applicable withholding taxes.

For details on special problems and early sources of information for the series up to 1960, see *HSC I,* pp. 145 and 147-149, and references cited there. For a discussion of contemporary methodology and sources, see Statistics Canada, "Sources and Methods", Section 2.15.

G61 and 73. Freight and shipping. Receipts in this account arise from Canadian-operated carriers transporting exports (both inland and beyond the borders of Canada) and foreign-owned goods both in transit in Canada and between foreign ports, and from the expenditure in Canada of foreign carriers (other than airlines). Payments arise from the transportation by non-resident carriers of imports to Canada (including inland freight charges in other countries) and of Canadian commodities (in particular oil and natural gas) in transit through the United States or in Canada, expenditures abroad by Canadian carriers (other than airlines), and payments made to non-residents for chartering vessels. The account does not, however, include passenger fares, for these are in the travel account. International airline expenditures and railway expenditures such as rental for freight cars are included with other service transactions, series G62 and 74.

For detailed notes on the measurement of these items, see Statistics Canada, "Sources and Methods", Section 2.21.

G62 and 74. Other service receipts and other service payments. These accounts include three broad groups: government transactions not included elsewhere, miscellaneous items and business services, and related transactions.

The receipts side of government transactions include the estimated costs of foreign governmental diplomatic, military and commercial representation in Canada, international postal revenues and taxes (apart from withholding taxes), military and civilian pensions paid to residents of Canada by foreign governments prior to 1952, some expenditures related to Canadian aid abroad such as the outlays of foreign students in Canada financed under aid programs, and amounts paid to Canadian teachers and experts serving abroad which were not spent there, and settlements received by Canada in the post-war period on account of military relief supplied to European countries at the end of World War II.

Payments with respect to government transactions include costs of Canadian diplomatic, military and commercial representation abroad, international postal payments, and assessments for Canada's memberships in international organizations such as the United Nations, Organization for Economic Co-operation and Development (OECD), North Atlantic Treaty Organization (NATO), Food and Agriculture Organization (FAO), International Civil Aviation Organization (ICAO), etc.

Miscellaneous income comprises all those transfers of earnings on investment not included under series G60 and 72, 'Interest and dividends'. Hence, on the revenue side it covers net revenues resulting from the transactions of Canadian chartered banks with non-residents, interest on private non-bank holdings of foreign exchange and other short-term claims abroad, interest on export credits either financed by or guaranteed directly or indirectly by the Government of Canada, and net revenues of Canadian insurance companies from insurance operations abroad. Payments cover net expenses paid to non-residents by head offices and Canadian branches of Canadian chartered banks, interest on long-term debt such as intercompany and bank loans, mortgages, etc. and on short-term debt such as intercompany and bank loans, money market instruments, income remitted to non-residents on assets in management (including real estate), safe custody and agency accounts, including estates and trusts, and net revenues of foreign insurance companies from operations in Canada. From 1940 to 1949, any current account surpluses Newfoundland earned in United States dollars were also included here.

Business service receipts and payments relate to management and administrative services, consulting and other professional services, insurance premiums and other insurance transactions, scientific research and product development, commissions, advertising and sales promotion, royalties, patents, copyrights, trademarks, equipment rentals, franchises and other similar rights, film rental payments, special tooling and other automotive payments, receipts and payments of Canadian railways and airlines abroad and of foreign railways and airlines in Canada, and some other services. The tabulating in this account of local expenditures of international air carriers is not consistent with the classification of corresponding expenditures of ocean and lake carriers in freight and shipping. But the practice arose during World War II when U.S. operations in Newfoundland and Labrador became important and it was difficult to separate such expenditures from other military receipts.

Business service items also comprise other receipts and payments such as commissions to agents, net earnings in the United States of Canadian resident commuters, other insurance transactions, and a host of miscellaneous services relating to union operations, telecommunications, transportation of migrants, miscellaneous engineering and consulting services, magazine and other such subscriptions, professional society membership fees, payments to foreign correspondents, and education by correspondence and in foreign schools. But by far the largest components of business services, at least on the payments side, are those between branches, subsidiaries and their foreign head offices. For the detailed results of a special survey on business service transactions for 1973, and licensing agreements for 1972, see Statistics Canada, *The Canadian Balance of International Payments, 1973-1974*, (Catalogue 67-201), pp. 63-78.

Mutual aid to NATO countries was shown as a separate item from 1950 through 1967. It involved mainly transfers of military equipment, provision of aircraft training in Canada, and contributions toward the NATO military budget for infrastructure represented by fixed defence installations used by the armed forces of more than one country of the alliance.

Two entries were normally made for this aid: the credit, or export, item was a measure of the real resources provided, whereas the debit item was the transfer itself. On security considerations, no bilateral or quarterly detail was published. By the mid-1960s, the amounts involved had become relatively small, and a growing proportion was duplicated in current estimates of Canadian military expenditures abroad. On the basis of these considerations, the two series were eliminated from balance of payments statistics, but continued to be made available annually in the form of a footnote.

In 1970, a restructuring of 'other service receipts' and 'other service payments' was undertaken and transfers were separated from service transactions. Accordingly, personal and institutional remittances, which in earlier presentations were included under 'all other transactions', were segregated and carried back to 1926 on an annual basis. But receipts of pensions for 1926 to 1951 were included with other service transactions, although from 1952 onward they are tabulated with personal and institutional remittances.

Information on sources and methods of gathering the data for these series is to be found in "Sources and Methods", Section 2.23.

G65 and 78. Inheritances and migrants' funds. These are primarily the transfer of accumulations of capital. But if they were entered in the capital account, where their offsetting entries would normally be found, the capital account would then not reflect any net acquisition or disposition of international claims, as there should be.

For immigrants to Canada, the measure used, insofar as possible, is the total of cash and similar claims brought with them at the time of migration, plus the amounts they intend to transfer later. Since notes and specie will likely appear in due course under various banking transactions, the balancing entry under inheritances and migrants' funds is necessary to explain the financial change. There will be some cases where holdings abroad of immigrants' unregistered securities or real estate will not be picked up as inflows at the time of immigration. Subsequently, therefore, their disposition and the resulting transfer of funds to Canada will show up as an increase in Canadian holdings of foreign exchange, that is, as a capital inflow.

Estimates of immigrants' funds data are, in general, much superior to those for emigrants. The former are based upon data provided by immigrants at the time of entry into Canada while the latter are based upon a per capita figure applied to the number of emigrants. See "Sources and Methods", Section 2.30.

Personal and household effects are classified as non-trade

transactions and do not enter into the balance of payments under transfers.

G66 and 79. Personal and institutional remittances. These series cover most private transfers other than inheritances and migrants' funds, and government transfers other than official contributions. Examples of receipts are pensions paid by the U.S. and U.K. governments to Canadian residents (since 1952), indemnification and restitution payments by the Government of Germany, estate taxes received by Canada, gifts, alimony, and institutional remittances for relief, charitable, religious, educational or research purposes. Examples of payments are pensions by governments in Canada to non-residents, remittances similar to those described under receipts, and support for relatives abroad. The series do not cover gifts in kind which are non-trade transactions excluded from the balance of payments.

G67 and 75. Withholding tax. The balance of payments series have historically been constructed on a net basis, or after deduction, of taxes withheld. However, explicit series covering withholding taxes received by the Government of Canada on account of non-residents were introduced in the current account with the report for the first quarter of 1972, at which time, the series back to the introduction in Canada in 1933 of withholding taxes on payments to non- residents, were provided to establish historical continuity. The entries appear on the receipt side among transfers, and on the payments side among imports of services. The data are derived from the financial records of the Government of Canada, adjusted to take account of remittance and accounting lags.

G80. Official contributions. While the institutional arrangements for Canada's official contributions have varied over the years, the activities are now largely concentrated in the Canadian International Development Agency (CIDA). They currently include such programs as international development assistance, international food aid, grants to international organizations for multilateral assistance programs, contributions for overseas projects of Canadian non-governmental organizations and contributions to Canadian firms for feasibility and related studies to establish or expand operations in developing countries. The work of the International Development Research Centre established in 1970 with funding from CIDA is included here too. The administrative costs of these two organizations are not counted among the official contributions. The goods and services provided as part of this aid, such as exports and outlays by educational trainees in Canada, are in turn recorded on the receipt side in the current account.

Country classification used in series G57-83 is as follows: the European Economic Community (EEC) includes, from 1973, Belgium, Denmark, Federal Republic of Germany, France, Ireland, Italy, Luxembourg, and the Netherlands. The United Kingdom is also a member of the EEC, but is shown separately.

'Other OECD' countries include, from 1973, Australia, Austria, Finland, Greece, Iceland, New Zealand, Norway, Portugal, Spain, Sweden, Switzerland and Turkey. Japan, although a member of the OECD, is shown separately.

'Other OECD Europe' comprises, from 1946 to 1972, Austria, Belgium and Luxembourg, Denmark (with Greenland), Federal Republic of Germany, Finland (from January 1969), France, Greece, Italy, Netherlands, Norway, Portugal, Spain, Sweden, Switzerland and Turkey.

'Other sterling area' comprises, from 1946 to 1972, the

Commonwealth countries, United Kingdom dependencies, Burma (from 1948 to 1966), Iceland, Iraq (until 1959), Ireland, Jordan (from 1950), Kuwait, Libya (from 1952 to 1971), Rhodesia (until 1965), Republic of South Africa and People's Republic of Yemen.

'Other non-residents', from 1973 to 1975, and 'All other non-residents', from 1946 to 1977, cover all countries in Africa, Asia, Oceania, Central and South America (not otherwise included in the sterling area), as well as Sino-Soviet countries, international financial agencies and all other countries not specified above. International financial agencies consist of the International Bank for Reconstruction and Development, the International Monetary Fund, International Finance Corporation, the International Development Corporation and corresponding institutions.

From 1971, merchandise trade with Puerto Rico and the U.S. Virgin Islands is included with the United States. From 1973, all other current transactions with these areas are included with the United States.

G84 - 115. Canadian balance of international payments, all countries, capital account, 1927 to 1975, and by major areas, 1946 to 1975

SOURCE: for all countries and the U.S. and U.K., Statistics Canada, *The Canadian Balance of International Payments, 1975*, (Catalogue 67-201), table 2; for other country relationships, CANSIM numbers as in *The Balance of Payments*, table 36.

A description of development of the methodology used to collect and tabulate the data up to 1960 is found in *HSC I*, pp. 151-153. For information on recent changes or adjustments in data gathering techniques and an evaluation of the reliability of the series, see Statistics Canada, "Sources and Methods", Part III. All subsequent discussion of the meaning of individual series and the components of them is also taken from this same source unless specific reference is made to other sources.

Many of the series in this section are largely self-explanatory in their titles so that, unlike the discussion of the current account, not all series will be separately defined.

G84 and 85. Direct investment in Canada and abroad. These items cover flows of capital leading to changes in net capital invested by controlling groups of non-residents in direct investment enterprises in Canada, and of Canadian residents in direct investment enterprises abroad.

Direct investment means investment motivated by the desire to create or expand some kind of permanent interest in a particular enterprise. It normally implies, if not the actual exercise of control, a degree of potential control. Enterprises in which there is direct investment are classified as 'direct investment enterprises'. This classification is normally assigned when the proportion of voting stock held by an associated group of non-residents exceeds a certain level (generally 50 per cent). 'Direct investment enterprises' need not be incorporated and therefore include branch operations of non-resident companies in Canada and branches of Canadian companies abroad.

Transactions recorded under direct investment are restricted to those of a long-term character with principal owners only, rather than with all residents of the controlling country. Estimates do not reflect the large sums of undistributed earnings of incorporated companies. Only the retained earnings of unincorporated foreign branches in

Canada are included under dividends declared in the current account and again as direct investment inflows in the capital account. The former amounts omitted from the accounts are much larger in magnitude than the latter sums. The series also include stock dividends paid to parent companies by wholly owned subsidiaries.

The direct investment category covers foreign investment in realty companies but excludes real estate held directly by non-residents which is classified under series G97, 'Other long-term capital transactions'. In addition, companies established to make portfolio investments in Canada, even though perhaps largely foreign-owned and controlled, are counted as portfolio investments, not direct investments, because their holdings are widely diversified and not for controlling or entrepreneurial purposes. Again, Canadian-owned firms essentially controlled by foreigners via processes other than investment, such as licensing, franchises, supply contracts, etc. are not counted with foreign direct investment.

The definition of long-term as opposed to short-term capital is based on the probable behaviour of the capital flows rather than its strict form. Hence, what may be in the form of a short-term capital flow may nevertheless be included with direct investment if it is believed that it will essentially be a long-term loan of working capital. To illustrate, working capital lent by a parent abroad to a domestic subsidiary, although perhaps in the form of a demand obligation or open-account claim, if intended or expected to be outstanding for more than one year, would be classified as a long-term obligation.

G86-89. Portfolio transactions in Canadian securities.

These series cover international movements of capital relating to new issues, trading and retirements of portfolio holdings of long-term Canadian securities. An exception occurred from 1963 through 1973 with regard to Government of Canada direct issues with an original term of over one year for which 'buy-back' transactions under sale and repurchase agreements were treated as short-term money market transactions. In the latter part of the period, few such transactions were reported, and the distinction was abandoned. Other exclusions, apart from those transactions more appropriately classified as direct investment, are transactions in mortgages or export finance paper. Transactions in the securities of Canadian companies counted for statistical purposes as non-residents of Canada (for example, foreign business corporations) are treated as transactions in foreign securities.

Values used in the series are net amounts received by, or paid on account of, residents of Canada.

In 1954 and continuing through 1964, a group of special Canadian diversified management investment companies, controlled by residents of the United States, were established to provide a medium for portfolio investment in Canada attractive to United States investors. They were treated in the Canadian balance of payments statistics as non-resident companies, representing, collectively, United States portfolio investors. For a discussion of them, see Statistics Canada, *The Canadian Balance of International Payments 1963, 1964 and 1965 and International Investment Position*, (Catalogue 67-201), pp. 44-47, and *Canada's International Investment Position 1926-1967*, (Catalogue 67-202), table IV.

G90-92. Portfolio transactions in foreign securities.

These series cover international movements of capital relating to new issues, trading and retirements of portfolio holdings of long-term foreign securities. Items excluded from the series are similar to those excluded from series G86-89, with the addition of official holdings of medium-term, non-marketable United States government securities acquired under the Columbia River Treaty arrangements, or securities held as part of Canada's official holdings of foreign exchange.

G93 and 94. Loans and subscriptions of the Government of Canada.

These series cover extensions and repayments of credit to non-residents by the Government of Canada (except post-war credits directly related to the financing of specific exports) and the provision of capital by the Government of Canada to international investment agencies such as the International Bank for Reconstruction and Development. Details of the government loans made since 1942 are found in Statistics Canada, "Sources and Methods", Section 3.40.

For repayment information see the same publication, Section 3.44.

G95. Columbia River Treaty.

This series covers receipts from the United States of payments under the Columbia River Treaty, including related investment and disinvestment by the Government of Canada in medium-term non-marketable United States government securities.

G96. Export credits directly or indirectly at the risk of the Government of Canada.

The series covers all medium-term and long-term export credits extended by Canada directly or indirectly at the risk of the Government of Canada, whether financed by public or private sources. The main agencies involved in this series are the Export Development Corporation and the Canadian Wheat Board.

G97. Other long-term capital transactions.

This series covers such items as medium- and long-term borrowing from foreign banks and other unrelated entities; loans by agencies of foreign governments to Canadian corporations generally associated with long-term commodity supply contracts or the financing of Canadian imports; movements of capital between branches and head offices of insurance companies; purchases by non-residents of, and repayments to them on mortgages on, Canadian real estate; transfers of capital from abroad for administration by Canadian trust companies and the repatriation of such capital; loans in Canadian dollars to non-residents by the head offices and Canadian branches of Canadian chartered banks, and their repayment; international transactions in real estate; and, commencing in 1972, allowances for the initial deferral and subsequent transfer to Canada after migration, of capital of immigrants. Also, in the period immediately following the termination of exchange restrictions in Canada in 1951, an estimate was included for the liquidation and transfer from Canada to the credit of emigrants, of capital they had not previously been permitted to take with them. Also, until 1962, the series covered medium- and long-term export credits extended directly or indirectly at risk of the Government of Canada. (These are now shown under series G96.)

G99 and 100. Resident holdings of foreign currencies.

The first of these series covers changes in net (spot) foreign currency positions, or net claims, with non-residents and net transactions in foreign treasury bills and any other foreign paper of the head offices and branches in Canada of the chartered banks. It was introduced in the second quarter of 1973, retroactively to 1964. The second series covers other resident holdings of foreign currencies abroad as well as gold- gold-denominated claims on non-residents held by offices and branches in Canada of Canadian chartered banks. Although these gold claims are not 'non-bank' holdings, they are included in series G100 instead of series G99 so as to preserve the consistency of the latter series with those published regularly by the Bank of Canada which, after the introduction of banking guidelines in 1968, excluded gold bullion and gold-based claims. Series G100 also includes non-bank and non-monetary authorities holdings of foreign treasury bills and other foreign short-term funds.

For additional information on these series prior to 1964 when they first began to be published separately, see "Sources and Methods", Sections 3.601, 3.602 and 3.611.

G101. Non-resident holdings of Canadian dollar deposits. This series comprises changes in two items: Canadian dollar deposits of non-residents with Canadian banks and other deposit-accepting institutions, and net Canadian dollar liabilities of the head offices and branches in Canada of Canadian chartered banks to their branches, agencies and subsidiaries abroad. Canadian dollars accepted from abroad by the Bank of Canada are counted here too, as are some of the changes in 'money employed' accounts (these are securities the Bank of Canada sets aside, the interest from which is used to compensate the party leaving a balance with the bank).

G102. Non-resident holdings of Government of Canada demand liabilities. These are largely notes that bear no interest payable on demand to international investment agencies. They usually represent parts of Canadian capital subscriptions and advances to the agencies which have not yet been utilized. (The Canadian subscriptions and advances are themselves a component of series G93.)

G103-106. Non-resident holdings of Canadian treasury bills, commercial paper, finance company paper and other short-term paper. These instruments comprise the main ones in the Canadian short-term money market which began, essentially, in 1954 when the Bank of Canada set up special facilities to encourage trading in treasury bills.

G107. Non-resident holdings of other Canadian finance companies. These are obligations not covered explicitly elsewhere. They are primarily bank borrowings abroad by finance companies and the funds to them by parent companies through open-end intercompany accounts.

G108. Other short-term capital transactions. This series consists of such items as foreign accounts receivable and payable (including intercompany accounts), short-term loans and similar claims and the 'net errors and omissions' which embodies all unidentified transactions (that is, the balancing item) in the Canadian balance of payments. For change in treatment of net errors and omissions, see Statistics Canada, *Quarterly Estimates of the Canadian Balance of International Payments,* First Quarter, 1978, (Catalogue 67-001). The main identifiable component in this series is tied in with 'leads and lags' or the differences in timing between the provision of goods and services and the financial statement for them. The 'net errors and omissions' component has usually been attributed to transactions with the United States. See "Sources and Methods", Section 3.82.

G111. Balance settled by exchange transfers. In the balance of payments, certain movements of capital are allocated by country or area on the basis of the residence of the foreign creditor or debtor rather than that of the foreign party to the transactions. To bring each bilateral statement into balance, it is necessary to record the relevant multilateral settlements. A negative figure in the account indicates the extent to which the account in which it appears has been settled by transfers in Canada's favour, while a positive figure in another account indicates the application of these receipts. Settlements occur between bilateral sectors but cancel out as a whole and consequently do not appear in the statement between Canada and all countries.

G112. Allocation of special drawing rights (SDR). Member countries of the International Monetary Fund (IMF) participating in the Special Drawing Account receive supplements to their reserves in the form of SDRs. These are reserve assets created by the IMF to increase the total level of world reserves. A liability is created for a country when it accepts the allocation, and its official international reserves are correspondingly increased. The liability is of an unusual nature in that repayment of it would be necessitated only if the entire SDR arrangement was terminated.

G113-115. Net official monetary movements. In February 1970, changes were made in Canada's international reserve reporting to the format shown in series G113-115. The new series were extended back to 1961. Series G113 now includes changes in convertible foreign currency holdings of the Exchange Fund Account, the Receiver General for Canada and the Bank of Canada, gold, SDRs, and Canada's reserve position in the IMF. Adjustments to values are made to eliminate the effects on the Canadian dollar values arising from changes in exchange parities between the Canadian dollar and foreign currencies (including SDRs). These do not appear as flows in the balance of payments.

No distinction is made in practice or for statistical purposes in Canada with respect to the types or terms of United States government securities in which Canada's official international reserves are employed.

For many years, gold holdings were valued at their realizable value, that is, after allowance for the potential cost of moving them to other financial centres for sale. In 1972, this practice was discontinued, and gold was valued at its then newly established price of U.S. $38 per ounce rather than U.S. $34.90 as previously. In October 1973, it was raised to U.S. $42.22 per ounce. But neither these adjustments nor subsequent ones have been reflected in the flows recorded in series G113.

Canada's reserve position in the IMF, its SDRs and its monetary gold holdings have been designated in SDRs, whose value was linked to a 'basket' of 16 currencies since July 1974.

Official monetary liabilities cover transactions related to the level of Canada's official international reserves, such as the use of IMF credit, foreign exchange deposit liabilities of the Bank of Canada to non-residents and the reported use of central bank reciprocal credit facilities. However, long-term debt issues placed abroad specifically to enlarge Canada's official international reserves are not included as official monetary liabilities.

G116-151. Canadian balance of international payments, all countries and by major areas, capital account, 1938 to 1945

SOURCE: Statistics Canada, *Blue Book,* pp. 168-170, and *HSC I,* series F104-145, with amendments as in footnote 2 of series G116-151.

For discussion of methodology, see the write-up under series F91-103 of *HSC I,* pp. 151-153.

Canadian International Investment Position (Series G152-380)

General note

The international investment position shows Canada's situation as both a creditor and debtor. Changes in this position stem both from capital flows recorded in the balance of payments and from numerous additional factors. The most important of these other factors is undistributed earnings, primarily of Canadian subsidiaries of foreign corporations in Canada, but also, to a much lesser extent, of foreign subsidiaries of Canadian corporations abroad. Such earnings in the early 1970s equalled or exceeded all new net capital inflows as a contributor to Canada's rising international indebtedness. Other items affecting Canada's net international investment position include undistributed earnings on portfolio investment, revaluation of assets and liabilities (including the write-off of exploration and development expenses), untransferred inheritances and capital of migrants insofar as it has not been allowed for in capital flows, reclassifications and similar accounting adjustments.

The absolute and relative importance of foreign capital to Canada's economic development is unique among advanced nations and accordingly deserves some comment. By the end of 1974, Canada's gross liabilities had reached $72.8 billion, while assets amounted to $37.5 billion, so that net international indebtedness was $35.3 billion, or 8.8 times greater than its post-World War II low of $4.0 billion in 1949.

Although foreign capital has frequently been an important source of financing for Canadian development, it is sometimes overlooked that since 1926, the year when the balance of payments was first tabulated on a reasonably consistent basis, Canada has had a current account surplus in 21 of the 50 years. That is, excluding undistributed earnings and the other adjustments to the balance of payments necessary to arrive at the annual balance of international indebtedness, Canada has been a net lender 42 per cent of the years since 1925. If the entire period 1900-1974 is considered, Canada has a current account surplus in 26 years, or 35 per cent of the time.

Until the end of World War II in 1945, the statistics on Canada's international investment position were not revised to a basis comparable with current methodology, with the exception of 1926, 1930, 1933 and 1939. Hence, a gap of 15 years exists for this period. Unrevised statistics for years omitted up to 1937 are to be found in the *Red Book,* but similar data do not exist for 1938 to 1944.

The periods of most rapid increase in foreign capital invested in Canada were from 1907 until 1913, when the annual average expansion was 13.6 per cent. The pace slackened thereafter and during the depression of the 1930s foreign capital invested in Canada actually declined. Not until 1949 did the magnitude of such investment once again

exceed what it had been in 1930. The pace of such investment quickened again in the 1950s when annual increases averaged 9.9 per cent for the decade. The early 1960s saw a drop in the size of annual increases, but in the late 1960s and even more so in the 1970s, these increases again began to reach a rate approaching, and on occasion exceeding, that of the 1950s (see series G190).

In the early portion of the 20th century, the United Kingdom was the major supplier of capital, mostly in the form of bonds. But even during these years, the yearly rate of increase of capital invested by the United States (with the exception of 1908 and 1909) exceeded that by the United Kingdom and it was increasingly in the form of direct investment. Consequently, by 1922, total investment in Canada by the United States exceeded that by the United Kingdom and has done so ever since. In the early 1970s the magnitude of U.S. investment in Canada was over 8.5 times greater than that by the United Kingdom. Investment by the United Kingdom in Canada diminished absolutely during World War II and through 1948 as the British sold off Canadian government and railway bonds (series G199). The United Kingdom negotiated loans in 1942 and 1946 to assist them in financing their war effort and post-war readjustment (series G338). Canada's *net* liabilities to the U.K. reached a low of $0.2 billion in 1947-1949, rose to a high of $2.0 billion for 1960-1962, diminished again to a low of $0.1 billion in 1969, and rose subsequently in 1973 to $1.5 billion (series G182).

Canada's total liabilities to the United States rose from $3.5 million in 1926 to $49.9 billion in 1974, with over 70 per cent of this expansion occurring after 1960. Concurrently, Canadian investment in the United States also grew, and amounted to $8.4 billion by 1974. Canada's net indebtedness to the United States, exclusive of net official monetary assets and short-term payables and receivables which are not classified geographically, totalled $41.4 billion in 1974 (series G159, 174 and 181).

Canada is also, on balance, a net debtor to the nations of the world other than the United States and the United Kingdom, although until 1955 she was a very small net creditor of them. The growth in liabilities since 1970 has been the result of a large influx of direct investment and portfolio capital, with the latter mainly in provincial and municipal government bonds. Over the same period, the advance in assets has been mainly due to Canadian direct investment, export credits and the reduction in net foreign liabilities of the Canadian chartered banks to this group of countries.

As net foreign investment in Canada has expanded, foreign ownership and control, especially of the manufacturing, petroleum and natural gas and mining and smelting industries, has enlarged considerably. Since 1951 for mining and smelting (including petroleum and natural gas until 1954) and 1952 for manufacturing, foreign control has exceeded domestic control. Foreign control of manufacturing and petroleum and natural gas has been quite stable at around 60 per cent and 75 per cent respectively since the early 1960s. For mining and smelting, it rose fairly steadily until 1971. Thereafter, some sizable shifts in the classification of control reduced the proportion to a level prevailing in the mid-1950s of about 56 to 57 per cent. Concomitantly, the importance of foreigners in other sectors such as railways and utilities has remained small and is less than in the period up to 1951 (series G291-294).

Canadian short-term assets abroad have been growing

steadily since the early 1960s, and beginning in 1970 exceeded long-term assets in value (compare the sum of series G158, 163 and 164 with series G157), although the effect of the treatment of errors and omissions should be noted (see series G164 and 178). Short-term liabilities, however, although growing modestly, have become a significantly smaller proportion of total liabilities. If net official monetary reserves are included, short-term assets exceed short-term liabilities for all years since 1926. Even if net official monetary reserves are excluded, this is still true for all years since 1967.

A number of general comments to assist the reader in interpreting the statistics follow. For greater detail on methodology and sources of particular series, the reader is referred to the Statistics Canada publication, "Sources and Methods".

Valuation

All common and preferred stocks held in Canada by non-residents are included at book values as shown in the balance sheets of the issuing or debtor companies. Book value is net worth including both earned and capital surpluses, but less deficits which may exist. The resulting value is the total of the assets less specific reserves such as those for deferred taxes, depreciation and depletion and less other liabilities which the company may have. In effect, it is a measure of the equity of the shareholders in the depreciated value of the assets.

Bonds and debentures are valued at par. All long-term liabilities in foreign currencies are expressed in Canadian dollars at the rate of $1.00 U.S. = $1.00 Canadian where denominated in United States dollars ($\div 1 = \$4.86$ Canadian for pre-World War II sterling debt), and at exchange rates current at the time of issue for all other currencies. Thus, totals are free of the sporadic changes they would undergo if converted at current rates of exchange. The securities appear in statistics of indebtedness without change in value through their lives. Changes in the amounts outstanding accordingly reflect alterations in holdings due to such factors as new issues, retirements or trading in outstanding securities.

These valuation methods may affect the statistics in a variety of ways. Several examples may be useful. First, the actual market value of corporate shares may be greater or less than book values. Hence, Canada's net foreign indebtedness may at times be somewhat understated or overstated in current terms. Second, depending upon whether long-term interest rates at the time of issuance are above or below those at the date of the published estimates, market values of bonds and debentures will be above or below, respectively, those shown in the accounts. Third, if the Canadian dollar remains below parity with the U.S. dollar, then the Canadian dollar value of long-term liabilities expressed in U.S. currency will be understated. The opposite would be true if the Canadian dollar should rise above parity with the U.S. dollar.

In contrast to estimates of Canada's foreign liabilities, Canadian investments abroad have been calculated in terms of Canadian dollars generally at rates of exchange prevailing at the date to which the estimate relates. This is because of the necessity of expressing a wide variety of foreign investments in common terms. As in the case of foreign investments in Canada, the basis of valuing Canadian direct investments abroad is the book value derived from the balance sheets of the issuing companies abroad. Canadian portfolio investments abroad, also, have been calculated at book values in the case of those stocks of foreign companies whose values could be ascertained. Holdings of foreign bonds are carried at the nominal par values converted from foreign currencies to Canadian dollars at current exchange rates.

Residency

The same concept of residency is used when measuring Canada's international investment position, as for the national accounts in general, (see Section F). It is particularly worth noting that where Canadian companies are nothing more than legal intermediaries in the ownership of assets in another country by persons or corporations resident outside Canada, such investments are, insofar as possible, excluded from statistics of Canada's international investment position.

Ownership and control

To obtain measures of the relative importance of foreign ownership and control for Canadian industry, estimates of the magnitude of Canadian-owned investment have to be made in a form as comparable as possible to the numbers on foreign ownership and control. Problems arise, however, because while estimates of foreign investment are based largely on the ownership of the capital structure reflected on consolidated balance sheets of enterprises classified according to the principal activity pursued, the primary source available for estimating the comparable aggregate capital values of Canadian industries are the summations of unconsolidated balance sheets of companies found in the Statistics Canada publication, *Corporation Financial Statistics*, (Catalogue 61-207) and its predecessor series in *Taxation Statistics*, published by National Revenue Canada. These are classified according to the principal activity of the individual company rather than of the enterprise of which it may form part. Additional problems of comparability arise from variations in accounting practices and in reporting dates, and from the inclusion or exclusion in the two sets of aggregates of non-corporate enterprises, Crown corporations, and foreign branches and subsidiaries.

The concepts of control and ownership need to be distinguished. As indicated under the discussion for series G84 and 85, an enterprise is deemed to be foreign controlled if at least 50 per cent of its voting stock is known to be held by one investor outside Canada. But if effective control is held with less than 50 per cent of the voting stock, then the enterprise is classified as controlled by the group holding the controlling block of stock. For other details on the definition of control see series G84 and 85.

Foreign ownership includes both direct and portfolio capital invested in an enterprise. Depending upon whether the control of an enterprise rests abroad or in Canada, the enterprise's total book value will be shown as under foreign or Canadian control respectively. But the value of any minority holding of such a concern, will be classified in the foreign and domestic ownership statistics according to the country holding this interest. Hence, the value of foreign ownership may exceed or fall short of foreign-controlled investment.

In all tables showing a country of ownership subdivision of investment, some investments designated as held by residents of the United States and the United Kingdom may include items held for residents of other nations.

G152-187. Canada's balance of international indebtedness, selected year ends, 1926 to 1974

SOURCE; Statistics Canada, *Canada's International Investment Position*, (Catalogue 67-202), table 1.

Not all series will be mentioned individually, but working definitions of concepts are provided where it is deemed useful to do so.

G152 and 166. Direct investment. Direct investment abroad is the book value of long-term investment abroad owned by the controlling or principal shareholders resident in Canada. While investments by Canadian chartered banks via wholly owned foreign subsidiaries engaged in providing trust services or in holding real estate are considered as direct investment, their investments in foreign banking operations are covered under 'Other Canadian short-term holdings of foreign exchange', and their investments in foreign real estate *not* held through separate corporations were not covered anywhere in Canada's external assets until 1974 when they were included in 'miscellaneous investment'.

The equity of non-residents in Canadian investment abroad through ownership in Canadian companies is reflected in a separate series, G171, in Canada's external liabilities, 'Equity of non-residents in Canadian assets abroad'.

Direct investment in Canada is the book value of long-term investment in Canada by *all* residents of the country in which control is considered to lie. This differs from direct investment as used in the balance of payments which covers only flows from controlling, affiliated, or principal owners.

The capital flows altering the value of foreign direct investment in Canada are primarily those shown in the balance of payments under 'Foreign direct investment in Canada'. But on occasion, other flows recorded under portfolio transactions, other long-term capital transactions and Canadian direct investment abroad affect the totals. By far the most important item not recorded in the balance of payments but influencing the direct investment figures is retained earnings of foreign-controlled Canadian corporations. (See "Sources and Methods", Sections 4.3 to 4.5.)

G153, 167 and 168. Portfolio investment. Portfolio investment abroad is the book value of the holdings by residents of Canada of portfolio investments in foreign securities. Foreign securities are defined to include holdings by Canadian residents in Canadian companies whose activities and assets are wholly situated outside Canada. But foreign securities retained by Canadian insurance companies as a consequence of their activities abroad are not included. Such assets are deemed to be, essentially, the property of the foreign policyholders. There are difficulties, however, with attempting to distinguish between holdings of foreign securities from funds supplied by Canadian policyholders and those from funds supplied by foreign policyholders. Hence, when foreign companies have been asked to supply figures for holdings by residents of Canada, holdings of Canadian insurance companies have been expressly excluded. To this extent, then, Canadian assets abroad are understated.

Portfolio investment in Canada covers investment in corporations by non-residents, other than investments in direct investment enterprises from the countries in which control of them is deemed to lie. Government bond liabilities includes foreign investment in bonds of the Government of Canada, provinces and municipalities, including all the funded debt guaranteed by them with the sole exception of railways, which are treated differently. (See series G249-290.)

G154 and 169. Miscellaneous investment. This

is a residual category. Canadian investments abroad include all long-term Canadian investment abroad other than direct investment, portfolio investment in stocks and bonds, Government of Canada credits, and Government of Canada subscriptions to international investment agencies. A large element in the category consists of medium- and long-term export credits extended by Canada directly or indirectly at the risk of the Government of Canada, whether financed by public or private sources. Other items include real estate held abroad by Canadians, Canadian claims on foreign estates and trusts, deferred receivables, and equity of Canadian members in international trade unions.

Miscellaneous foreign investments in Canada include Canadian securities, real estate, mortgages, and other assets held or administered for non-residents by trustees, agents nominees, private investment companies, etc.

Miscellaneous investments are separated from 'Other portfolio investment' because measures of them are less exact and because no industrial distribution is feasible.

G155. Government of Canada credits. These include most of the Government of Canada's long-term investments abroad including loans to foreign governments and holdings of United States government medium-term non-marketable securities acquired under the Columbia River Treaty arrangements, except those described under series G154 above and some holdings at the end of 1966 and 1967 of bonds of the International Bank for Reconstruction and Development acquired in order to lower Canada's official holdings of United States dollars, which were treated as portfolio investments.

G156. Government of Canada subscriptions to international investment agencies. These are discussed under series G93 and 94.

G158 and 173. Private short-term holdings of foreign exchange and non-resident holdings of Canadian dollars. The first of these series shows net foreign currency claims of the Canadian chartered banks on non-residents, together with deposits of residents with banks abroad and foreign treasury bills held by residents (apart from those of the Canadian banking system and the official monetary authorities). The second consists of Canadian dollar deposits of non-residents with financial institutions in Canada, Government of Canada demand liabilities, and holdings by non-residents of Government of Canada treasury bills. These series differ from 'Short-term receivables and payables n.e.s.' in that the estimates of them are more precise and can be identified by geographical distribution.

G163. Net official monetary assets. These comprise the convertible foreign currency holdings of the Exchange Fund Account, the Receiver General for Canada and the Bank of Canada, official holdings of monetary gold, SDRs, and Canada's reserve position in the International Monetary Fund, less any associated liabilities of a short-term nature.

G164 and 178. Short-term receivables n.e.s., and short-term payables n.e.s. Short-term receivables cover estimated short-term claims of Canadians on non-residents apart from those represented by net official monetary assets and other Canadian short-term holdings of foreign exchange. (See "Sources and Methods", Sections 4.2-29.) The series represent the projection of a benchmark estimate constructed for the year 1956. Until that time, no estimate for these claims had been included in the measure of Canada's international investment position. A benchmark for the end of 1956 having been established, series were constructed back to the end of 1945 and the benchmark has been projected forward from 1956. See Statistics Canada publication, *Canadian External Short-term Assets and Liabilities, 1945-1957,*(Catalogue 67-504). Essentially, the year-end estimates are projected on the basis of the identified flows in series G108. The balance of errors and omissions is a component of this series. This balance was reflected as a liability until the end of 1966 but since the beginning of 1967 it has been included in the asset series for short-term receivables n.e.s.

Short-term payables n.e.s. consists of holdings by non-residents of the short-term paper of sales finance and consumer loan companies, bank borrowings abroad by such companies, advances to them from parent companies abroad, holdings by non-residents of Canadian short-term commercial paper, holdings by non-residents of other short-term paper, and all other short-term payables to non-residents.

G171. Equity of non-residents in Canadian assets abroad. The value of Canadian assets abroad includes the equity of non-residents in them via their ownership in Canadian enterprises. Hence, an estimate of this non-resident interest must be included with Canadian liabilities to offset, as closely as possible, the overstatement of Canadian assets abroad. This series must then be taken together with the other series for foreign investment in Canada in order to arrive at totals for foreign long-term investment in Canadian enterprises.

G172. Official SDR liabilities. This series represents the value of allocations to Canada by the International Monetary Fund of SDRs. Since it is the general practice in these indebtedness statistics to value Canada's external long-term liabilities at the exchange rates applicable when they were created, the same procedure is followed here, despite the close relationship existing between the long-term liability and the holding of SDRs in Canada's short-term external assets.

G180. Net indebtedness. This series equals series G179 less series G165, or the sum of series G184-187.

G188-202. Estimates of foreign capital invested in Canada, selected year ends, 1900 to 1974

SOURCE: Statistics Canada, *Canada's International Investment Position,*(Catalogue 67-202), table II in the 1926 to 1967 publication and table 10 in subsequent publications for 1926 to 1974; Knox, "Excursus", table A, p. 299 for 1913 to 1926; and Viner, *Canada's Balance,* p. 139 and reproduced in Knox, "Excursus", table A, for 1900 to 1913.

Statistics for 1926 and subsequent years which have not been footnoted are the official estimates compiled by Statistics Canada.

G203-226. Foreign long-term investment in Canada, all countries and by major areas, by type of investment, selected year ends, 1926 to 1974

SOURCE: Statistics Canada, *Canada's International Investment Position,* (Catalogue 67-202), table V in the 1926 to 1967 publication and table 13 in subsequent publications.

Data sought and tabulated for Canada's international investment position are generally on a Canadian consolidated basis, closely approximating the enterprise, but excluding that part of the enterprise extending outside Canada. Enterprises are defined broadly as firms or aggregations of firms under common ownership and financial control. But enterprise statistics have not yet been highly developed and no satisfactory and widely accepted standard industrial classification exists for them. For this reason, the data on industries are still organized on the early classification system based upon the chief material components employed, but influenced by the character of the information available and the principal industrial activities of the corporate units from which the data are obtained. Use of this classification preserves the historical continuity of the investment position statistics back to 1926.

As a result of using the enterprise as the statistical unit, and consequently for Canadian consolidations of data inputs, all investment in Canada of a corporation, together with its subsidiaries, is normally attributed to their principal activity. Also, a company established to provide facilities for a particular enterprise is normally classified with it. Thus, for example, a railway subsidiary set up by a mining company primarily to provide transportation of its output, is included with 'other mining and smelting' investment. Again, companies established in connection with the lease-back of service station properties are shown with 'petroleum and natural gas', not with merchandising. In fact, the 'petroleum and natural gas industries' category includes a wide variety of activities such as exploration and development, refining, pipelines, wholesale and retail distribution, and some petrochemicals. The data for 1930, 1945, 1951 and all years since 1953 have followed this classification system for the petroleum and natural gas sector rather than distributing the activities among the other relevant categories of manufacturing, mining, utilities and merchandising.

A few other noteworthy characteristics of the industry subdivisions of data are as follows. 'Mining and smelting' refers only to native ores so that the smelting of alumina, for example, is included with manufacturing. The 'railway' category includes investments in rolling stock, production and maintenance, ships, airlines, trucking, hotels, telegraphs and so forth. It also includes foreign investment in the funded debt of the Canadian National Railways and of provincial railways. This procedure has its roots deep in Canadian history, and is in contrast with the fact that foreign investment in the debt of other public enterprises guaranteed by provinces and municipalities is normally included with investment in government securities. 'Other enterprises' covers a wide variety of activities such as logging, engineering services, construction, film distribution, entertainment, advertising, hotel operation, cartage, shipping agents, stevedoring, geophysical services and so on.

G227-243. Foreign direct investment in Canada, all countries and by major areas, by industry, selected year ends, 1926 to 1974

SOURCE: Statistics Canada, *Canada's International Investment Position,* (Catalogue 67-202), table VI in the 1926 to 1967 publication and table 16 in subsequent publications.

G244-248. Contributors to change in book value of foreign direct investment in Canada, 1946 to 1974

SOURCE: Statistics Canada, *Canada's International Invest-ment Position*, (Catalogue 67-202), table VIII in the 1926 to 1967 publication and table 15 in subsequent publications.

Net capital inflow for direct investment corresponds to series G84.

G249-290. Ownership and control of capital employed in selected Canadian industries, selected year ends, 1926 to 1973

SOURCE: Statistics Canada, *Canada's International Invest-ment Position*, (Catalogue 67-202), table XVI in the 1926 to 1967 publication and table 26 in subsequent publications.

The figures in this table are subject to important statisti-cal qualifications described under the note "Estimated Val-ues of Total Capital and Resident-owned Capital in Some Areas of National Wealth" in Statistics Canada, *The Cana-dian Balance of International Payments, 1960 and Inter-national Investment Position*, (Catalogue 67-201), pp. 62-63. In particular it may be noted that in these series foreign investment in debentures associated with public enterprises in other utilities is shown in the other utilities category rather than with government. See also under the general discussion of series G341-380 how these data compare with CALURA data.

G291-302. Foreign control of selected Canadian industries, selected year ends, 1926 to 1973

SOURCE: Statistics Canada, *Canada's International Invest-ment Position*, (Catalogue 67-202), table XVIII in the 1926 to 1967 publication and table 28 in subsequent publications.

G303-317. Control of manufacturing, petroleum and natural gas and mining, year ends, 1954 to 1973

SOURCE: Statistics Canada, *Canada's International Invest-ment Position*, (Catalogue 67-202), table XX in the 1926 to 1967 publication and table 30 in subsequent publications.

G318-340. Canadian long-term investment abroad, all countries and by major areas, by type and industry, selected year ends, 1926 to 1974

SOURCE: Statistics Canada, *Canada's International Invest-ment Position*, (Catalogue 67-202), tables XXIII and XXIV in the 1926 and 1967 publication and tables 2 and 3 in sub-sequent publications.

Corporations and Labour Unions Returns Act (Series G341-380)

General note

The Corporations and Labour Unions Returns Act (CA-LURA) was approved by Parliament in April 1962. This act, administered by Statistics Canada, calls for the gathering and tabulation of financial and other data on large corpora-tions having annual gross revenues in excess of $500,000 or assets in excess of $250,000, as well as any labour union having a local and at least 100 members in Canada. (Only the corporate data is relevant for this section.)

The first annual report under this act was published in 1965 covering data commencing in 1962. Since that date the annual report has been extended both in terms of the num-ber of corporations covered and the data provided on their activities. Information obtained under the authority of other Government of Canada statutes is also included, if relevant, in the reports. One example of this is information on government business enterprises. For additional informa-tion on the history and coverage, see Statistics Canada, *Corporations and Labour Unions Returns Act, Report for 1975, Part I*, (Catalogue 61-210), "Statistical Notes and Definitions". The annual reports contain a large number of other detailed series on the affairs of foreign corporations in Canada in addition to those covered here. Because foreign ownership and control of Canadian corporations has long been an important issue in Canada, the focus here is on various measures of the importance of foreign control. The remainder of this section discusses the concepts involved and differences from the foreign investment series included in series G152-340.

Control

In the CALURA data, in the absence of conclusive evidence to the contrary, a corporation is considered to be foreign controlled if 50 per cent or more of its voting rights are known to be held outside Canada or are held by one or more Canadian corporations that are themselves foreign controlled. The country of control of a Canadian corpora-tion is ascribed to that foreign country in which the major-ity of the voting rights are held or where the majority of the voting rights of its Canadian parent company or compa-nies are held. The control is assigned to Canada, however, in those instances where the holding of over 50 per cent of the voting rights is distributed among non-associated share-holders in two or more different countries, and where the voting rights held in Canada constitute the largest single holding reported by any country.

In contrast to the international investment series under G152-340 where the degree of control is measured by the capital employed in Canada (long-term debt plus net worth), in the CALURA data the extent of control is mea-sured by the number of corporations, assets, equity, sales and profits.

Although the CALURA data has been gathered since 1962, the series on control commences only in 1968. The CALURA reports provide detail on a 34 industry breakdown, but lim-itations of space require that only an aggregated eight in-dustry subdivision be presented here. Finally, whereas the series included give only dollar values or absolute numbers, the CALURA reports also provide percentages for those who desire them.

Reporting unit

The CALURA series are based on individual corporation returns whereas the international investment series deal with Canada-consolidated statements for enterprises. The latter concept eliminates certain intercorporate items between Canadian parent companies and their subsidiaries in Canada which will be retained in the CALURA material. That is, the CALURA statistics may reflect organizational changes arising from amalgamation, mergers, takeovers, etc., which might not have been reflected in statistics reported at the enterprise level. Also, the CALURA series uses the cor-poration as the unit for industrial classification, whereas the enterprise (the family of related companies) is used in the international investment series. Differences in industry sta-tistics between the two series will be particularly acute in fine industry breakdowns because of diversified conglomerate enterprises, and in areas where enterprises reflect large-scale vertical integration. But at the highly-aggregated level of presentation being used in the following tables, the differences will not be as great. Differences will arise as well between the two series because the CALURA data exempt smaller corporations.

For additional details comparing and contrasting CALURA with other foreign investment series, see Statistics Canada, *The Canadian Balance of International Payments, 1963, 1964 and 1965 and International Investment Position,* (Catalogue 67-201), pp.81-84; and J.D. Randall, "A Brief Guide to Statistics Related to Foreign Ownership in Canada", in the *Canadian Statistical Review, January 1974* (Catalogue 11-003), pp. 4-7 and 14-16.

G341-348. Country of control of corporations, by eight major industry groups, (number of corporations), 1968 to 1975

SOURCE: for 1968 to 1969, the annual CALURA reports for those years, table 2; for 1970 to 1975, the annual CALURA reports, table 3.

G349-356. Country of control of corporations, by eight major industry groups, (assets), 1968 to 1975

SOURCE: same as series G341-348.

In this report, assets identified separately are cash, marketable securities, accounts receivable, inventories, fixed assets, investments in affiliated corporations and other assets. The amounts tabulated are those shown on the balance sheets of corporations after deducting allowance for doubtful accounts, amortization, depletion and depreciation.

G357-364. Country of control of corporations, by eight major industry groups, (equity), 1968 to 1975

SOURCE: same as series G341-348.

Equity represents the shareholders' interest in the net assets of the corporation and generally include the total amount of all issued and paid-up shared capital, earnings retained in the business, and other surplus accounts such as contributed and capital surplus.

G365-372. Country of control of corporations, by eight major industry groups, (sales), 1968 to 1975

SOURCE: same as series G341-348.

For corporations in the non-financial industries, the figure tabulated as sales is gross revenues from non-financial operations.

G373-380. Country of control of corporations, by eight major industry groups, (profits), 1968 to 1975

SOURCE: same as series G341-348.

Profits comprise net earnings from operations, investment income and net capital gains. The profits are tabulated after deducting allowances for amortization, depletion and depreciation but before income tax provisions or declaration of dividends.

Foreign Trade (Series G381-487)

General note

For notes on trade statistics up to 1960, see *HSC I,* Foreign Trade, (series F242-350), pp. 154- 155. Also see the preceding comments under series G57 and 70 in this volume with regard to trade valuation, classification and other relevant topics. In this edition of the *Historical Statistics of Canada,* all trade figures have been adjusted to exclude 'special transactions, non-trade' back to 1926, whereas figures before 1926 still include special transactions. In *HSC I,* 'special transactions, non-trade' were excluded only for 1959 and 1960.

G381-385. Foreign trade, domestic exports, total exports, total imports and balance of trade, declared values, Canada and all countries, 1868 to 1975

SOURCE: for 1868 to 1965, Statistics Canada, *Trade of Canada, Volume I, Summary and Analytical Tables,* calendar years, 1966 to 1968, (Catalogue 65-201), tables 1 and 2; for 1966 to 1975: Statistics Canada, External Trade Division, data files. Current reference publications are Statistics Canada, *Exports, Merchandise Trade,* (Catalogue 65-202); and *Imports, Merchandise Trade,* (Catalogue 65-203).

G386-388. Foreign trade, indexes of import and export prices and the terms of trade, 1869 to 1975

SOURCE: for 1869 to 1960, see notes in *HSC I* relating to series F357-359, and references cited there; for 1961 to 1975, Statistics Canada, External Trade Division, data files. Data are also available from CANSIM for the years 1968 to date.

Details on the indexes used up to 1960 are in *HSC I,* under series F298-315, pp. 156-157 and references cited there.

For 1961 to 1975, the price indexes, like those for earlier years, are Laspeyres type. That is, prices are weighted by the base year quantities, which, for 1968 to 1975, are those of 1971. For 1961 to 1967, 1948-based indexes have been linked to the 1971-based series. Although not presented in this volume, import and export price indexes are also available now on a current-weighted Paasche type basis. For more information, see Statistics Canada, *Summary of External Trade,* (Catalogue 65-001), 1976.

SOURCE: Statistics Canada, *Trade of Canada, Volume I, Summary and Analytical Tables, 1966-1968,* (Catalogue 65-201), table 5.

G396-400. Foreign trade, imports, excluding gold, by origin, major areas, 1886 to 1946

SOURCE: same as series G389-395.

G401-407. Foreign trade, domestic exports, excluding gold, by destination, major areas, 1946 to 1975

SOURCE: for U.S. and U.K., 1946 to 1965, Statistics Canada,

Trade of Canada, Volume I, Summary and Analytical Tables, 1966-1968, table 5; for other country groupings, same publication, table 9, and also the same publication for earlier years; for 1966 to 1975, Statistics Canada, External Trade Division, data files.

G408-414. Foreign trade, imports, excluding gold, by origin, major areas, 1946 to 1975

SOURCE: for U.S. and U.K. 1946 to 1975, same as series G401-407; for other country groupings, same publication, table 10, and also the same publication for earlier years; for 1966 to 1975, same as series G401-407.

G415-428. Foreign trade, domestic exports, excluding coin and bullion, by main commodity sections, current values, 1946 to 1975

SOURCE: for 1946 to 1965, Statistics Canada, *Trade of Canada, Volume I, Summary and Analytical Tables, 1966-1968,* table 8, and the same publication for earlier years; for 1966 to 1976, Statistics Canada, External Trade Division, data files.

G429-442. Foreign trade, imports, excluding coin and bullion, by main commodity sections, current values, 1946 to 1975

SOURCE: same as series G415-428.

G443-458. Adjustments to trade of Canada exports for balance of payments use, 1946 to 1975
G459-472. Adjustments to trade of Canada imports for balance of payments use, 1946 to 1975

SOURCE: Statistics Canada, "Sources and Methods", tables II-1 and II-2.

The basic *Trade of Canada* series are now constructed to reflect transfer (transactions) prices for trade of automotive vehicles. To the extent possible, adjustments are made regarding other commodities to put them on a tranfer price basis for use in the balance of payments. Other adjustments are made to place trade statistics on a basis consistent with other elements of the balance of payments in terms of coverage, valuation and timing. The adjustments include the following:

G444 and 460. Non-monetary gold. Since the end of the first quarter of 1968, non-monetary gold, which has been recorded under 'special transactions, non-trade', had been added to commodity exports and imports in the balance of payments.

G445. Wheat. For balance of payments purposes, a series for the value of wheat exports is calculated by applying to the record of wheat clearances of the Board of Grain Commissioners the unit values derived from the *Trade of Canada* series. This resulting series is thought to be better in terms of coverage, timing and information on ultimate destination of Canadian-owned wheat held from time to time outside Canada.

G446. Energy. Additions were made to exports in the early 1960s for natural gas exported by pipeline which

had not been recorded in the trade series. Also, since exports by pipeline of petroleum and natural gas are published in *Trade of Canada* with a lag of one month, balance of payments adjustments made in 1973 and carried back to the beginning of 1968 assigned such energy exports to the appropriate quarter.

G447 and 461. Automotive products. Deductions are made from both exports and imports for special tooling and other automotive charges recorded on trade documents as these charges are already included among service transactions. Also, export adjustments in 1967 through mid-1969, and import adjustments in 1967 and 1968, included deductions to reduce the reported values to a transfer price basis.

G448-G450 and G462-464. Ships, civil aircraft and defence goods. Additions are made to the balance of payments for both exports and imports of items not recorded in *Trade of Canada,* such as ships of British construction and registry for use in Canada or, until 1966, of aircraft to be used for international travel. Also, rather than recording ships, aircraft and some military equipment in the balance of payments just when deliveries are made, progress payments in connection with their construction are recorded instead. This is done because the items are often quite large, production extends over a considerable period and, on occasion, documentation lags behind delivery. The procedure eliminates the need to have any additional series in the capital account to cover progress payments made on undelivered equipment, or in the current account to cover purchases delivered outside Canada, such as deliveries to the armed forces abroad.

G451. Tourist purchases. A rather arbitrary deduction is made in the balance of payments for goods counted in recorded exports but actually purchased by tourists and already included in Canada's travel receipts.

G452 and 468. Warehousing. The adjustments represent estimates of the difference in value of goods moving across the customs frontier and goods moving across the national frontier for the years prior to 1955, the earliest year for which the trade data were adjusted to reflect the change to the 'general trade' basis mentioned earlier.

G453 and 469. Newfoundland. Exports and imports of goods between Canada and Newfoundland which appeared in trade series after 1939, until Newfoundland joined Canada in 1949, were deducted from the series for balance of payments purposes. This means that from 1940 onward, Newfoundland was treated, for balance of payments purposes, as though it were a part of Canada, even though it did not become so politically until 1949.

G454. War supplies. Payments by the United States government for war supplies and metals exported by Canada to them under the Hyde Park agreement were not initially recorded in the basic trade data, but rather in a special merchandise account. Hence, they had to be added to commodity exports for balance of payments purposes.

G455. UNRRA cash purchases. Foreign contributions used for the purchase of Canadian goods were recorded as special receipts in the merchandise account and not in the primary trade data. Therefore, like war supplies, the amounts had to be added to exports for balance of payments purposes.

G456 and 470. Other adjustments. These cover a range of items such as additions to exports in the late 1940s and 1950s to adjust the value of uranium exports recorded in the primary trade data at nominal values (for security reasons); deductions in the mid-1950s to lower to the amounts actually received from the United Kingdom, the values for exports of beef, which were recorded in the trade statistics at substantially higher support prices paid to the producers by the Canadian government; retroactive price adjustments; and adjustments relating to reporting lags. Since 1971, major revisions have been made to remove from export and import totals the value of transportation costs already covered in the freight and shipping series, and to reflect necessary changes as identified by the United States-Canada Trade Statistics Committee. For exports, the most important of these is an addition for shipments on which statistical documents were not received by Statistics Canada; and for imports, the most significant change is a deduction from imports to lower customs values to transactions values.

465. Advertising. An arbitrary deduction is made for imports of advertising materials. Part of this material is travel promotion literature which does not involve direct outlays by Canada, and part is included in payments for advertising services.

G466. Official valuations. An arbitrary deduction is made from the value of imports with respect to valuations for customs duty purposes which are higher than the actual amounts paid for goods; the amount is a notional one, not well founded.

G467. Foreign exchange rates spread. A deduction was made during the period of fixed exchange rates under exchange control to reduce the values recorded on import documents by the amount of the spread between the official buying and selling rates which constituted a domestic rather than an international cost.

G473-487. Foreign trade, imports, by free, dutiable, and duty collected, 1868 to 1975

SOURCE: for 1868 to 1918, Statistics Canada, *Trade of Canada, Volume I, Summary and Analytical Tables, 1939*; for 1919 to 1965, *Trade of Canada, Volume I, Summary and Analytical Tables, 1966-1968*, tables 2,3 and 4; for 1966 to 1975, External Trade Division, data files.

Series G1-17. Canadian balance of international payments, between Canada and all countries, current account, 1900 to 1913
(millions of dollars)

Year	Current receipts								Current payments								Current account balance
	Merchandise exports[1]	Exports of gold coin and bullion	Travel	Interest and dividends	Freight and shipping	Insurance receipts	All other current receipts[2]	Total current receipts	Merchandise imports[1]	Imports of gold coin and bullion	Travel	Interest and dividends	Freight and shipping	Insurance payments[3]	All other current payments[2]	Total current payments	
	1	2	3	4	5	6	7	8	9	10	11	12	13	14	15	16	17
1913	458.8	12.6	30.5	8.7	9.2	4.0	51.9	575.7	664.1	30.1	37.2	137.2	28.6	6.4	86.3	990.0	-414.3
1912	361.9	13.8	29.4	8.7	7.3	3.6	54.2	479.0	640.2	11.0	33.0	117.5	28.5	6.4	77.6	914.2	-435.2
1911	295.9	5.7	26.2	8.6	5.9	3.3	56.7	402.3	501.6	32.6	28.6	101.5	23.1	4.9	64.7	757.0	-354.7
1910	294.6	2.0	24.7	9.6	5.9	3.0	54.2	394.2	436.7	13.7	25.0	92.1	18.8	3.9	54.6	644.8	-250.6
1909	287.3	1.4	19.6	8.3	5.8	2.8	46.5	371.6	353.7	8.2	19.6	83.9	15.4	4.2	46.6	531.5	-159.9
1908	264.0	4.1	19.2	4.6	5.3	2.5	38.2	337.9	286.8	25.8	18.1	75.9	14.1	3.1	45.8	469.6	-131.7
1907	252.6	18.7	16.2	5.5	5.1	2.3	41.3	341.7	369.6	22.9	15.8	56.6	15.5	3.2	40.8	524.5	-182.8
1906	252.3	15.4	16.8	6.0	5.1	2.0	36.7	334.3	309.1	20.5	15.4	51.7	14.6	4.7	30.0	445.9	-111.6
1905	221.6	7.5	13.3	5.3	4.5	2.0	31.5	285.7	262.1	7.1	11.4	47.4	12.6	4.7	23.4	368.7	-83.0
1904	195.6	2.5	12.8	4.5	3.9	1.6	23.9	244.8	246.4	10.4	8.9	43.0	11.4	+3.2	18.9	335.8	-91.0
1903	226.5	0.3	10.5	5.2	4.5	1.5	24.7	273.2	253.9	11.4	7.4	40.7	10.8	3.1	15.1	342.4	-69.2
1902	215.3	0.6	11.0	5.0	4.3	1.2	20.9	258.4	206.8	6.0	7.5	39.4	9.9	4.3	11.9	285.8	-27.4
1901	199.5	5.7	8.0	3.9	4.0	0.9	12.1	234.1	187.8	4.9	6.4	37.4	9.6	0.7	8.7	255.4	-21.3
1900	181.2	3.7	7.1	4.0	3.6	0.7	10.2	210.5	181.6	7.7	5.9	36.0	9.2	0.5	7.1	247.0	-36.5

1 Trade of Canada figures with certain valuation, coverage and timing adjustments appropriate for balance of payments.

2 Includes capital of immigrants and emigrants and non-commercial remittances.

3 Excess of claims receipts over premium payments shown as a plus sign.

Series G18-33. Canadian balance of international payments, between Canada and all countries, capital account, 1899 to 1913
(millions of dollars)

Year	Investments by Canadian banks in		Miscellaneous Canadian investments abroad	Total Canadian capital moving abroad	British and foreign capital										Totals net	
					Securities			Miscellaneous			Total				Net capital movement	Errors and omissions
	Foreign securities	Banking abroad			By Britain	By United States	By other countries	By Britain	By United States	By other countries	By Britain	By United States	By other countries	All countries		
	18	19	20	21	22	23	24	25	26	27	28	29	30	31	32	33
1913	1.5	12.3	5.0	18.8	359.9	85.1	18.3	15.8	49.9	17.7	375.7	135.0	36.0	546.7	+527.9	+113.6
1912	2.6	7.8[1]	5.0	0.2[1]	194.6	34.6	5.0	20.2	47.1	19.6	214.8	81.7	24.6	321.1	+321.3	-113.9
1911	3.6	5.1[1]	5.0	3.5	222.1	21.1	0.4	22.3	55.1	27.4	244.4	76.1	27.8	348.4	+344.9	-9.8
1910	6.3	37.2[1]	5.0	25.9[1]	188.5	6.1	6.8	30.0	66.5	15.3	218.4	72.7	22.1	313.2	+339.1	+88.5
1909	3.9	25.7	4.0	33.6	187.5	20.4	1.1	25.2	15.8	3.4	212.7	36.2	4.5	253.4	+219.8	+59.9
1908	1.5	87.0	4.0	92.5	156.5	12.3	4.5	24.9	20.5	3.4	181.4	32.7	8.0	222.1	+129.6	-2.1
1907	0.3	26.2[1]	4.0	21.8[1]	41.0	10.3	0.4	24.2	15.7	3.4	65.3	26.0	3.8	95.1	+116.9	-65.9
1906	1.2	16.7[1]	3.0	12.5[1]	46.7	12.1	3.8	21.8	17.5	3.4	68.5	29.5	7.3	105.3	+117.8	+6.2
1905	0.6	12.2	3.0	15.8	54.5	14.8	0.3	21.9	17.7	3.4	76.4	32.4	3.7	112.5	+96.7	+13.7
1904	0.3	17.9	3.0	21.2	23.9	6.5	3.2	5.6	19.3	3.4	29.5	25.8	6.6	61.9	+40.7	-50.3
1903	1.0	20.7[1]	3.0	16.7[1]	23.7	3.5	0.3	5.2	18.6	3.4	28.9	22.1	3.7	54.7	+71.4	+2.2
1902	3.3	2.0[1]	2.0	3.3	6.6	5.6	3.6	5.3	17.8	3.4	11.9	23.3	7.1	42.3	+39.0	+11.6
1901	4.3	22.4	2.0	28.7	10.0	1.0	0.3	5.0	17.3	3.4	15.1	18.3	3.7	37.1	+8.4	-12.9
1900	7.2	12.1[1]	2.0	2.9[1]	5.1	1.0	0.3	5.0	16.9	3.4	10.1	17.9	3.7	31.7	+34.6	-1.9
1899[2]	—	—	—	100.0	—	—	—	—	—	—	1,040.0	150.0	10.0	1,200.0	—	—

1 Capital withdrawals from abroad.

Series G34-46. Canadian balance of international payments, between Canada and all countries, current account, 1900 to 1926

(millions of dollars)

Year	Current receipts						Current payments					Net balance	
	Merchandise exports[1]	Gold trade balance	Travel	Interest and dividends	All other current receipts	Total current receipts (excluding gold)	Merchandise imports[1]	Travel	Interest and dividends	All other current payments	Total current payments	Net balance including all gold	Net balance excluding all gold
	34	35	36	37	38	39	40	41	42	43	44	45	46
1926	1,266.5	+38.0	182.2	45.3	167.5	1,661.5	989.1	79.1	263.4	156.7	1,488.3	+211.2	+173.2
1925	1,241.1	+19.9	170.4	40.2	140.2	1,591.9	872.4	69.7	250.7	145.8	1,338.6	+273.2	+253.3
1924	1,032.6	+7.0	149.4	40.3	131.3	1,353.6	789.9	68.3	242.3	122.6	1,223.1	+137.5	+130.5
1923	1,003.9	+80.3	130.7	40.5	135.3	1,310.4	885.1	61.8	254.0	139.7	1,340.6	+50.1	-30.2
1922	884.1	-46.0	110.5	39.9	116.9	1,151.4	744.6	56.8	230.3	121.1	1,152.8	-47.4	-1.4
1921	800.4	+42.0	98.2	47.3	124.7	1,070.6	827.8	57.5	234.3	150.2	1,269.8	-157.2	-199.2
1920	1,267.1	+35.0	91.4	46.8	159.9	1,565.2	1,428.7	62.5	212.9	219.5	1,923.6	-323.4	-358.4
1919	1,261.7	+13.9	75.9	39.6	122.0	1,499.2	951.4	52.4	211.5	247.5	1,462.8	+50.3	+36.4
1918	1,209.4	+16.0	66.8	32.4	108.6	1,417.2	922.4	34.7	214.0	343.9	1,515.0	-81.8	-97.8
1917	1,555.2	-0.9	55.1	28.3	110.7	1,749.3	996.5	31.5	204.1	340.3	1,572.4	+176.0	+176.9
1916	1,072.4	+11.6	45.8	23.6	114.5	1,256.3	762.4	29.3	190.5	262.8	1,245.0	+22.9	+11.3
1915	613.9	-14.6	37.2	13.1	91.0	755.2	447.2	29.2	173.3	148.2	797.9	-57.3	-42.7
1914	369.1	+23.0	34.8	16.6	73.2	493.7	470.8	41.8	180.9	111.4	804.9	-288.2	-311.2
1913	442.9	-4.8	30.5	8.7	65.1	547.2	654.9	37.2	137.2	121.3	950.6	-408.2	-403.4
1912	351.7	+12.8	29.4	8.7	65.1	454.9	626.0	33.0	117.5	112.5	889.0	-421.3	-434.1
1911	284.1	-19.4	26.2	8.6	65.9	384.8	506.3	28.6	101.5	92.7	729.1	-363.7	-344.3
1910	280.8	-6.1	24.7	9.6	63.1	378.2	429.0	25.0	92.1	77.3	623.4	-251.3	-245.2
1909	269.0	-1.1	19.6	8.3	55.2	352.1	339.6	19.6	83.9	66.2	509.3	-158.3	-157.2
1908	249.3	-13.9	19.2	4.6	46.0	319.1	282.6	18.1	75.9	63.0	439.6	-134.4	-120.5
1907	253.8	+3.8	16.2	5.5	48.7	324.2	363.0	15.8	56.6	59.5	494.9	-166.9	-170.7
1906	254.0	+6.1	16.8	6.0	43.8	320.6	312.3	15.4	51.7	49.3	428.7	-102.0	-108.1
1905	205.2	+14.0	13.3	5.3	38.0	261.8	263.6	11.4	47.4	40.7	363.1	-87.3	-101.3
1904	176.1	+7.9	12.8	4.5	29.4	222.8	249.2	8.9	43.0	27.1	328.2	-97.5	-105.4
1903	201.9	+6.5	10.5	5.2	30.7	248.3	251.8	7.4	40.7	29.0	328.9	-74.1	-80.6
1902	190.4	+11.6	11.0	5.0	26.4	232.8	203.4	7.5	39.4	26.1	276.4	-32.0	-43.6
1901	170.2	+23.2	8.0	3.9	17.0	199.1	182.6	6.4	37.4	19.0	245.4	-23.1	-46.3
1900	156.0	+16.0	7.1	4.0	14.5	181.6	176.5	5.9	36.0	15.8	234.2	-36.6	-52.6

[1] Trade of Canada figures with certain valuation, coverage and timing adjustments appropriate for balance of payments.

Series G47-56. Canadian balance of international payments, between Canada and all countries, capital account, 1900 to 1926

(millions of dollars)

Year	New issues Canadian securities	Retirement of Canadian securities	Net movement(+) inward net retirement (−)[1]	Net sales of outstanding securities (estimated)	Dominion Government dealing with other governments, war finance	Net change in external assets of Canadian banks	Other capital movements net	Total net movement of capital	Balance on current account	Balancing item; errors or omissions
	47	48	49	50	51	52	53	54	55	56
1926	326.2	165.9	+161.0	-135.0	+2.3	-51.8	+26.3	+2.8	+211.2	-214.0
1925	239.8	231.4	+13.0	-80.0	+1.9	-92.8	+14.6	-143.3	+273.2	-129.9
1924	280.6	146.2	+143.0	-50.0	+20.7	-15.7	-0.4	+97.6	+137.5	-235.1
1923	156.3	51.0	+109.6	-40.0	+63.8	-12.7	+9.0	+129.7	+50.1	-179.8
1922	292.6	80.4	+210.3	-20.0	+46.8	+27.0	-0.1	+264.1	-47.4	-216.7
1921	246.3	113.9	+123.6	-40.0	+27.9	+144.4	+26.1	+282.0	-157.2	-124.8
1920	221.5	61.0	+153.7	-55.0	+31.0	+42.4	+13.5	+185.6	-323.4	+137.8
1919	239.4	216.2	+25.1	-40.0	-25.6	-21.7	+30.9	-31.3	+50.3	-19.0
1918	56.4	66.5	-12.8	-10.0	-119.3	-28.5	+6.3	-164.3	-81.8	+246.1
1917	196.2	68.7	+126.9	-10.0	-113.1	+10.8	+12.4	+27.0	+176.0	-203.0
1916	315.0	56.3	+254.2	-8.0	-52.6	-129.4	+8.2	+72.4	+22.9	-95.3
1915	236.7	54.0	+179.0	-5.0	+60.4	-113.4	+0.4	+121.4	-57.3	-64.1
1914	197.1	4.5	+298.1	-3.0	+24.3	+21.2	+1.2	+341.8	-288.2	-53.6
1913	—	—	+463.2	—	—	-15.9	+78.5	+525.8	-408.2	-117.6
1912	—	—	+236.1	—	—	+8.4	+80.0	+324.5	-421.3	+96.8
1911	—	—	+255.5	—	—	+8.7	+87.9	+352.1	-363.7	+11.6
1910	—	—	+202.0	—	—	+33.5	+106.2	+341.7	-251.3	-90.4
1909	—	—	+209.0	—	—	-31.8	+40.4	+217.6	-158.3	-59.3
1908	—	—	+173.3	—	—	-99.0	+44.8	+119.1	-134.4	+15.3
1907	—	—	+51.7	—	—	+25.9	+39.4	+117.0	-166.9	+49.9
1906	—	—	+62.6	—	—	+13.3	+39.7	+115.6	-102.0	-13.6
1905	—	—	+69.5	—	—	-10.4	+40.0	+99.1	-87.3	-11.8
1904	—	—	+33.6	—	—	-23.4	+25.3	+35.5	-97.5	+62.0
1903	—	—	+27.5	—	—	+20.4	+24.2	+72.1	-74.1	+2.0
1902	—	—	+15.8	—	—	-2.0	+24.5	+38.3	-32.0	-6.3
1901	—	—	+11.3	—	—	-24.5	+23.8	+10.6	-23.1	+12.5
1900	—	—	+6.4	—	—	+12.1	+23.4	+41.9	-36.6	-5.3

[1] For the years 1914 to 1926, complete new issues and retirement figures are not available; some small net amounts are included in series G49, thus explaining the apparent arithmetical errors in these columns during those years.

Series G57-83. Canadian balance of international payments, all countries, current account, 1926 to 1975, and by major areas, 1946 to 1975
(millions of dollars)

Year	Current receipts												
	Merchandise exports[1]		Service transactions					Total goods and service receipts[3,4]	Transfers				Total current receipts[5]
		Gold production available for export[2]	Travel	Interest and dividends	Freight and shipping	Other service receipts[3]	Total service receipts		Inheritances and immigrants' funds	Personal and institutional remittances[3]	Withholding tax	Total transfer receipts	
	57	58	59	60	61	62	63	64	65	66	67	68	69
1975	33,347	—	1,815	826	1,767	2,278	6,686	40,033	664	268	465	1,397	41,430
1974	32,591	—	1,694	880	1,812	1,927	6,313	38,904	702	223	430	1,355	40,259
1973	25,461	—	1,446	790	1,501	1,527	5,264	30,725	516	210	322	1,048	31,773
1972	20,129	—	1,230	665	1,241	1,315	4,451	24,580	443	173	287	903	25,483
1971	17,877	—	1,246	558	1,184	1,316	4,304	22,181	432	160	278	870	23,051
1970	16,921	—	1,206	528	1,126	1,386	4,246	21,167	389	107	269	765	21,932
1969	15,035	—	1,047	451	935	1,262	3,695	18,730	366	95	234	695	19,425
1968	13,720	33	953	353	891	840	3,070	16,790	370	95	209	674	17,464
1967	11,338	112	1,318	295	830	770	3,325	14,663	329	93	218	640	15,303
1966	10,326	127	840	318	758	676	2,719	13,045	268	83	204	555	13,600
1965	8,745	138	747	322	668	562	2,437	11,182	216	83	167	466	11,648
1964	8,238	145	662	332	644	482	2,265	10,503	169	75	140	384	10,887
1963	7,082	154	609	230	563	430	1,986	9,068	151	70	127	348	9,416
1962	6,387	155	562	202	509	419	1,847	8,234	124	65	125	314	8,548
1961	5,889	162	482	213	486	392	1,735	7,624	104	60	116	280	7,904
1960	5,392	162	420	171	442	395	1,590	6,982	102	52	79	233	7,215
1959	5,151	148	391	180	420	364	1,503	6,654	109	50	74	233	6,887
1958	4,890	157	349	167	401	346	1,420	6,310	97	45	48	190	6,500
1957	4,894	144	363	153	445	367	1,472	6,366	124	39	83	246	6,612
1956	4,837	147	337	142	457	417	1,500	6,337	99	39	69	207	6,544
1955	4,332	155	328	161	398	363	1,405	5,737	86	36	67	189	5,926
1954	3,934	155	305	147	313	271	1,191	5,125	89	34	58	181	5,306
1953	4,152	144	302	164	318	288	1,216	5,368	91	34	54	179	5,547
1952	4,339	150	275	152	383	257	1,217	5,556	85	32	55	172	5,728
1951	3,950	150	274	115	351	212	1,102	5,052	77	18	56	151	5,203
1950	3,139	163	275	94	284	203	1,019	4,158	57	15	54	126	4,284
1949	2,989	139	285	83	303	205	1,015	4,004	68	17	47	132	4,136
1948	3,030	119	279	70	336	211	1,015	4,045	84	18	41	143	4,188
1947	2,723	99	251	64	322	203	939	3,662	69	17	35	121	3,783
1946	2,393	96	221	70	311	183	881	3,274	65	26	29	120	3,394
1945	3,474	96	165	80	340	247	928	4,402	19	36	29	84	4,486
1944	3,590	110	119	71	322	325	947	4,537	11	20	27	58	4,595
1943	3,050	142	88	59	288	422	999	4,049	8	15	27	50	4,099
1942	2,515	184	81	67	221	294	847	3,362	11	14	29	54	3,416
1941	1,732	204	111	60	185	155	715	2,447	15	11	24	50	2,497
1940	1,202	203	104	52	138	50	547	1,749	24	13	13	50	1,799
1939	906	184	149	57	102	39	531	1,437	10	14	10	34	1,471
1938	844	161	149	66	95	28	499	1,343	5	13	10	28	1,371
1937	1,041	145	166	76	112	35	534	1,575	3	16	10	29	1,604
1936	954	132	142	75	80	30	459	1,413	2	15	9	26	1,439
1935	732	119	117	64	68	29	397	1,129	2	14	7	23	1,152
1934	648	114	106	57	52	27	356	1,004	2	14	6	22	1,026
1933	532	82	89	38	44	28	281	813	3	13	5	21	834
1932	495	70	114	37	38	39	298	793	4	11	—	15	808
1931	601	57	153	48	54	38	350	951	5	16	—	21	972
1930	880	39	180	59	70	44	392	1,272	11	14	—	25	1,297
1929	1,178	37	198	61	92	51	439	1,617	14	15	—	29	1,646
1928	1,341	40	177	46	96	57	416	1,757	15	16	—	31	1,788
1927	1,215	32	163	41	97	54	387	1,602	15	16	—	31	1,633
1926	1,272	30	152	32	96	51	361	1,633	15	17	—	32	1,665

Series G57-83. Canadian balance of international payments, all countries, current account, 1926 to 1975, and by major areas, 1946 to 1975 (continued)
(millions of dollars)

Year	Current receipts												
	Merchandise exports[1]	Service transactions						Total goods and service receipts[3,4]	Transfers				Total current receipts[5]
		Gold production available for export[2]	Travel	Interest and dividends	Freight and shipping	Other service receipts[3]	Total service receipts		Inheritances and immigrants' funds	Personal and institutional remittances[3]	Withholding tax	Total transfer receipts	
	57	58	59	60	61	62	63	64	65	66	67	68	69
United States[6]													
1975	21,927	—	1,337	488	845	927	3,597	25,524	112	191	—	303	25,827
1974	21,650	—	1,328	533	892	924	3,677	25,327	143	153	—	296	25,623
1973	17,333	—	1,160	459	788	769	3,176	20,509	124	142	—	266	20,775
1972	14,107	—	1,023	385	690	696	2,794	16,901	168	119	—	287	17,188
1971	12,161	—	1,092	363	640	646	2,741	14,902	181	110	—	291	15,193
1970	10,959	—	1,054	336	590	776	2,756	13,715	165	66	—	231	13,946
1969	10,599	—	934	260	523	743	2,460	13,059	155	54	—	209	13,268
1968	9,258	33	866	231	467	573	2,170	11,428	137	54	—	191	11,619
1967	7,277	112	1,164	176	425	491	2,368	9,645	105	57	—	162	9,807
1966	6,249	127	730	194	411	429	1,891	8,140	106	55	—	161	8,301
1965	4,993	138	660	204	337	353	1,692	6,685	91	56	—	147	6,832
1964	4,396	145	590	190	301	308	1,534	5,930	77	51	—	128	6,058
1963	3,970	154	549	155	279	295	1,432	5,402	65	47	—	112	5,514
1962	3,767	155	512	120	259	301	1,347	5,114	61	44	—	105	5,219
1961	3,213	162	435	112	230	298	1,237	4,450	51	38	—	89	4,539
1960	3,040	162	375	98	220	308	1,163	4,203	50	34	—	84	4,287
1959	3,191	148	351	97	228	287	1,111	4,302	52	32	—	84	4,386
1958	2,911	157	309	99	206	257	1,028	3,939	47	31	—	78	4,017
1957	2,931	144	325	94	222	284	1,069	4,000	47	26	—	73	4,073
1956	2,854	147	309	80	223	332	1,091	3,945	45	26	—	71	4,016
1955	2,598	155	303	81	203	293	1,035	3,633	45	25	—	70	3,703
1954	2,360	155	283	70	169	210	887	3,247	42	25	—	67	3,314
1953	2,458	144	282	101	164	229	920	3,378	41	25	—	66	3,444
1952	2,346	150	257	88	174	204	873	3,219	38	24	—	62	3,281
1951	2,326	150	258	57	164	158	787	3,113	32	14	—	46	3,159
1950	2,046	163	260	53	157	146	779	2,825	31	11	—	42	2,867
1949	1,521	139	267	40	126	145	717	2,238	18	13	—	31	2,269
1948	1,508	119	267	37	131	153	707	2,215	18	14	—	32	2,247
1947	1,061	99	241	36	104	140	620	1,681	18	13	—	31	1,712
1946	948	96	216	47	101	130	590	1,538	19	10	—	29	1,567
United Kingdom[6]													
1975	1,861	—	129	35	174	447	785	2,646	145	24	—	169	2,815
1974	1,993	—	94	45	190	342	671	2,664	135	20	—	155	2,819
1973	1,583	—	82	45	149	278	554	2,137	90	17	—	107	2,244
1972	1,355	—	57	26	126	220	429	1,784	71	16	—	87	1,871
1971	1,379	—	42	27	120	298	487	1,866	55	14	—	69	1,935
1970	1,507	—	44	29	125	282	480	1,987	68	12	—	80	2,067
1969	1,120	—	29	46	108	245	428	1,548	78	12	—	90	1,638
1968	1,240	—	23	16	124	128	291	1,531	77	12	—	89	1,620
1967	1,199	—	40	36	127	110	313	1,512	81	15	—	96	1,608
1966	1,133	—	39	32	121	101	293	1,426	81	12	—	93	1,519
1965	1,184	—	34	44	132	97	307	1,491	55	12	—	67	1,558
1964	1,219	—	33	80	130	92	335	1,554	46	10	—	56	1,610
1963	1,017	—	28	31	105	67	231	1,248	43	10	—	53	1,301
1962	924	—	22	28	98	57	205	1,129	28	9	—	37	1,166
1961	924	—	21	37	100	45	203	1,127	25	9	—	34	1,161
1960	924	—	20	32	93	46	191	1,115	26	7	—	33	1,148
1959	782	—	18	35	80	37	170	952	26	8	—	34	986
1958	766	—	18	32	84	38	172	938	17	7	—	24	962
1957	734	—	18	10	95	37	160	894	40	7	—	47	941
1956	818	—	14	14	98	43	169	987	24	7	—	31	1,018
1955	772	—	13	39	97	36	185	957	20	6	—	26	983
1954	660	—	13	34	73	32	152	812	19	6	—	25	837
1953	656	—	12	26	79	33	150	806	18	6	—	24	830
1952	727	—	10	29	105	31	175	902	20	6	—	26	928
1951	636	—	8	30	91	43	172	808	14	—	—	14	822
1950	469	—	7	6	61	35	109	578	12	—	—	12	590
1949	701	—	11	9	89	49	158	859	38	—	—	38	897
1948	703	—	9	9	105	44	167	870	52	—	—	52	922
1947	749	—	7	8	114	42	171	920	47	—	—	47	967
1946	626	—	3	7	107	52	169	795	45	—	—	45	840

Series G57-83. Canadian balance of international payments, all countries, current account, 1926 to 1975, and by major areas, 1946 to 1975 (continued)

(millions of dollars)

Year	Merchandise exports[1]	Gold production available for export[2]	Travel	Interest and dividends	Freight and shipping	Other service receipts[3]	Total service receipts	Total goods and service receipts[3,4]	Inheritances and immigrants' funds	Personal and institutional remittances[3]	Withholding tax	Total transfer receipts	Total current receipts[5]
	57	58	59	60	61	62	63	64	65	66	67	68	69
European Economic Community[7]													
1975	2,296	—	122	63	190	197	572	2,868	97	44	—	141	3,009
1974	2,108	—	102	64	187	153	506	2,614	85	41	—	126	2,740
1973	1,564	—	84	40	148	138	410	1,974	54	42	—	96	2,070
Japan[7]													
1975	2,102	—	34	7	150	50	241	2,343	32	1	—	33	2,376
1974	2,223	—	20	9	154	49	232	2,455	3	1	—	4	2,459
1973	1,789	—	18	11	116	36	181	1,970	5	1	—	6	1,976
Other Organization for Economic Co-operation and Development[7]													
1975	897	—	65	15	98	88	266	1,163	38	4	—	42	1,205
1974	1,106	—	52	23	115	74	264	1,370	36	4	—	40	1,410
1973	762	—	34	22	86	66	208	970	30	4	—	34	1,004
Other non-resident[3]													
1975	4,264	—	128	218	310	569	1,225	5,489	240	4	—	244	5,733
1974	3,511	—	98	206	274	385	963	4,474	300	4	—	304	4,778
1973	2,430	—	68	213	214	240	735	3,165	213	4	—	217	3,382
Other sterling area[7]													
1972	643	—	33	83	88	125	329	972	106	4	—	110	1,082
1971	695	—	24	86	88	87	285	980	84	5	—	89	1,069
1970	785	—	23	65	77	75	240	1,025	68	1	—	69	1,094
1969	619	—	17	84	55	53	209	828	68	2	—	70	898
1968	618	—	13	65	56	33	167	785	66	2	—	68	853
1967	642	—	18	53	58	40	169	811	61	1	—	62	873
1966	576	—	12	54	43	28	137	713	24	1	—	25	738
1965	531	—	9	46	44	20	119	650	21	1	—	22	672
1964	515	—	11	41	44	14	110	625	13	—	—	13	638
1963	409	—	8	26	33	12	79	488	12	—	—	12	500
1962	338	—	8	33	29	9	79	417	8	—	—	8	425
1961	331	—	7	43	27	10	87	418	6	—	—	6	424
1960	340	—	6	20	31	8	65	405	6	—	—	6	411
1959	289	—	6	28	26	8	68	357	7	—	—	7	364
1958	299	—	6	13	24	7	50	349	13	—	—	13	362
1957	246	—	5	22	27	7	61	307	8	—	—	8	315
1956	256	—	4	21	29	9	63	319	5	—	—	5	324
1955	254	—	4	21	27	8	60	314	4	—	—	4	318
1954	206	—	3	17	18	7	45	251	4	—	—	4	255
1953	251	—	3	13	18	7	41	292	4	—	—	4	296
1952	293	—	3	8	20	5	36	329	3	—	—	3	332
1951	265	—	3	4	23	3	33	298	3	—	—	3	301
1950	201	—	3	8	18	3	32	233	1	—	—	1	234
1949	300	—	2	4	30	3	39	339	1	—	—	1	340
1948	293	—	1	4	34	4	43	336	2	—	—	2	338
1947	366	—	1	6	39	3	49	415	1	—	—	1	416
1946	269	—	1	2	34	3	40	309	—	—	—	—	309

Series G57-83. Canadian balance of international payments, all countries, current account, 1926 to 1975, and by major areas, 1946 to 1975 (continued)
(millions of dollars)

Year	Merchan-dise exports[1]	Current receipts								Transfers				Total current receipts[5]
		Gold production available for export[2]	Travel	Interest and dividends	Freight and shipping	Other service receipts[3]	Total service receipts	Total goods and service receipts[3,4]	Inheri-tances and immi-grants' funds	Personal and institu-tional remit-tances[3]	With-holding tax	Total transfer receipts	
	57	58	59	60	61	62	63	64	65	66	67	68	69

Organization for Economic Co-operation and Development (Europe)[7]

1972	1,493	—	79	29	163	115	386	1,879	49	30	—	79	1,958
1971	1,527	—	54	28	172	126	380	1,907	46	28	—	74	1,981
1970	1,619	—	53	40	164	119	376	1,995	40	27	—	67	2,062
1969	1,211	—	40	29	115	107	291	1,502	36	22	—	58	1,560
1968	1,053	—	32	10	104	58	204	1,257	45	25	—	70	1,327
1967	909	—	58	8	89	68	223	1,132	58	18	—	76	1,208
1966	893	—	36	9	76	57	178	1,071	40	13	—	53	1,124
1965	840	—	27	11	82	49	169	1,009	35	13	—	48	1,057
1964	749	—	17	8	76	35	136	885	21	13	—	34	919
1963	662	—	16	8	68	33	125	787	21	12	—	33	820
1962	622	—	14	11	62	31	118	740	19	11	—	30	770
1961	618	—	13	12	67	26	118	736	15	11	—	26	762
1960	591	—	13	12	57	22	104	695	15	10	—	25	720
1959	448	—	11	11	49	22	93	541	16	9	—	25	566
1958	522	—	11	13	46	30	100	622	14	6	—	20	642
1957	502	—	10	12	54	27	103	605	22	5	—	27	632
1956	456	—	6	12	61	21	100	556	18	4	—	22	578
1955	365	—	5	13	39	16	73	438	13	4	—	17	455
1954	335	—	4	12	29	13	58	393	20	2	—	22	415
1953	355	—	4	13	30	8	55	410	22	2	—	24	434
1952	450	—	4	13	43	8	68	518	20	2	—	22	540
1951	340	—	4	14	40	5	63	403	22	—	—	22	425
1950	185	—	4	14	24	12	54	239	11	—	—	11	250
1949	232	—	4	14	28	4	50	282	8	—	—	8	290
1948	275	—	2	6	32	4	44	319	8	—	—	8	327
1947	320	—	1	2	38	7	48	368	2	—	—	2	370
1946	296	—	1	2	45	4	52	348	1	—	—	1	349

All other non-residents[7]

1972	2,531	—	38	142	174	159	513	3,044	49	4	—	53	3,097
1971	2,115	—	34	54	164	159	411	2,526	66	3	—	69	2,595
1970	2,051	—	32	58	170	134	394	2,445	48	1	—	49	2,494
1969	1,486	—	27	32	134	114	307	1,793	29	5	—	34	1,827
1968	1,551	—	19	31	140	48	238	1,789	45	2	—	47	1,836
1967	1,311	—	38	22	131	61	252	1,563	24	2	—	26	1,589
1966	1,475	—	23	29	107	61	220	1,695	17	2	—	19	1,714
1965	1,197	—	17	17	73	43	150	1,347	14	1	—	15	1,362
1964	1,359	—	11	13	93	33	150	1,509	12	1	—	13	1,522
1963	1,024	—	8	10	78	23	119	1,143	10	1	—	11	1,154
1962	736	—	6	10	61	21	98	834	8	1	—	9	843
1961	803	—	6	9	62	13	90	893	7	2	—	9	902
1960	497	—	6	9	41	11	67	564	5	1	—	6	570
1959	441	—	5	9	37	10	61	502	8	1	—	9	511
1958	392	—	5	10	41	14	70	462	6	1	—	7	469
1957	481	—	5	15	47	12	79	560	7	1	—	8	568
1956	453	—	4	15	46	12	77	530	7	2	—	9	539
1955	343	—	3	7	32	10	52	395	4	1	—	5	400
1954	373	—	2	14	24	9	49	422	4	1	—	5	427
1953	432	—	1	11	27	11	50	482	6	1	—	7	489
1952	523	—	1	14	41	9	65	588	4	—	—	4	592
1951	383	—	1	10	33	7	51	434	6	—	—	6	440
1950	238	—	1	13	24	11	49	287	2	—	—	2	289
1949	235	—	1	16	30	8	55	290	3	—	—	3	293
1948	251	—	—	14	34	10	58	309	4	—	—	4	313
1947	227	—	1	12	27	15	55	282	1	—	—	1	283
1946	254	—	—	12	24	10	46	300	—	—	—	—	300

Series G57-83. Canadian balance of international payments, all countries, current account, 1926 to 1975, and by major areas, 1946 to 1975 (continued)

(millions of dollars)

Year	Merchandise imports[1]	Service transactions — Travel	Service transactions — Interest and dividends	Service transactions — Freight and shipping	Service transactions — Other service payments	Service transactions — Withholding tax	Service transactions — Total service payments	Total goods and service payments[4]	Transfers — Inheritances and emigrants' funds	Transfers — Personal and institutional remittances	Transfers — Official contributions	Transfers — Total transfer payments	Total current payments[5]	Current account balance
	70	71	72	73	74	75	76	77	78	79	80	81	82	83
1975	33,986	2,542	2,796	2,137	3,478	465	11,418	45,404	179	299	513	991	46,395	-4,965
1974	30,893	1,978	2,409	2,047	3,202	430	10,066	40,959	168	292	332	792	41,751	-1,492
1973	22,726	1,742	2,050	1,587	2,554	322	8,255	30,981	159	284	253	696	31,677	+96
1972	18,272	1,464	1,713	1,315	2,199	287	6,978	25,250	162	230	227	619	25,869	-386
1971	15,314	1,448	1,699	1,196	2,081	278	6,702	22,016	185	218	201	604	22,620	+431
1970	13,869	1,422	1,550	1,106	1,998	269	6,345	20,214	199	212	201	612	20,826	+1,106
1969	14,071	1,261	1,366	996	1,862	234	5,719	19,790	204	204	144	552	20,342	-917
1968	12,249	982	1,259	931	1,441	209	4,822	17,071	209	148	133	490	17,561	-97
1967	10,772	895	1,211	861	1,277	218	4,462	15,234	213	173	182	568	15,802	-499
1966	10,102	900	1,140	823	1,090	204	4,157	14,259	198	139	166	503	14,762	-1,162
1965	8,627	796	1,086	761	904	167	3,714	12,341	211	133	93	437	12,778	-1,130
1964	7,537	712	1,010	679	835	140	3,376	10,913	201	128	69	398	11,311	-424
1963	6,579	585	860	648	762	127	2,982	9,561	185	126	65	376	9,937	-521
1962	6,203	605	783	595	734	125	2,842	9,045	175	122	36	333	9,378	-830
1961	5,716	642	764	568	674	116	2,764	8,480	176	120	56	352	8,832	-928
1960	5,540	627	656	533	654	79	2,549	8,089	184	114	61	359	8,448	-1,233
1959	5,572	598	671	525	588	74	2,456	8,028	165	109	72	346	8,374	-1,487
1958	5,066	542	614	460	592	48	2,256	7,322	159	103	53	315	7,637	-1,137
1957	5,488	525	594	515	561	83	2,278	7,766	157	100	40	297	8,063	-1,451
1956	5,565	498	524	502	506	69	2,099	7,664	131	91	30	252	7,916	-1,372
1955	4,543	449	473	415	443	67	1,847	6,390	116	83	24	223	6,613	-687
1954	3,916	389	424	356	400	58	1,627	5,543	99	77	11	187	5,730	-424
1953	4,212	365	406	374	395	54	1,594	5,806	96	68	25	189	5,995	-448
1952	3,854	341	413	375	332	55	1,516	5,370	94	61	16	171	5,541	+187
1951	4,101	280	452	354	337	56	1,479	5,580	70	56	9	135	5,715	-512
1950	3,132	226	475	301	304	54	1,360	4,492	61	45	5	111	4,603	-319
1949	2,696	193	390	253	274	47	1,157	3,853	59	41	6	106	3,959	+177
1948	2,598	134	325	279	243	41	1,022	3,620	50	44	23	117	3,737	+451
1947	2,535	167	337	278	240	35	1,057	3,592	49	55	38	142	3,734	+49
1946	1,822	135	312	219	337	29	1,032	2,854	35	45	97	177	3,031	+363
1945	1,442	83	251	222	862	29	1,447	2,889	17	33	858	908	3,797	+689
1944	1,398	58	264	252	1,533	27	2,134	3,532	9	34	960	1,003	4,535	+60
1943	1,579	36	261	294	650	27	1,268	2,847	6	38	518	562	3,409	+690
1942	1,406	26	270	228	315	29	868	2,274	4	30	1,002	1,036	3,310	+106
1941	1,264	21	286	167	198	24	696	1,960	5	31	—	36	1,996	+501
1940	1,006	43	313	132	99	13	600	1,606	9	33	—	42	1,648	+151
1939	713	81	306	119	76	10	592	1,305	5	33	—	38	1,343	+128
1938	649	86	307	105	76	10	584	1,233	5	34	—	39	1,272	+99
1937	776	87	302	137	76	10	612	1,388	5	31	—	36	1,424	+180
1936	612	75	311	97	61	9	553	1,165	3	27	—	30	1,195	+244
1935	526	64	270	82	51	7	474	1,000	3	24	—	27	1,027	+125
1934	484	50	268	79	43	6	446	930	4	24	—	28	958	+68
1933	368	44	264	66	63	5	442	810	3	23	—	26	836	-2
1932	398	49	302	66	63	—	480	878	3	23	—	26	904	-96
1931	580	71	330	79	52	—	532	1,112	4	30	—	34	1,146	-174
1930	973	92	348	103	63	—	606	1,579	9	46	—	55	1,634	-337
1929	1,272	108	322	130	62	—	622	1,894	12	51	—	63	1,957	-311
1928	1,209	98	275	116	59	—	548	1,757	12	51	—	63	1,820	-32
1927	1,057	100	257	109	57	—	523	1,580	14	49	—	63	1,643	-10
1926	973	99	240	105	56	—	500	1,473	16	49	—	65	1,538	+127

Series G57-83. Canadian balance of international payments, all countries, current account, 1926 to 1975, and by major areas, 1946 to 1975 (continued)

(millions of dollars)

Year	Merchandise imports[1]	Current payments						Total goods and service payments[4]	Transfers				Total current payments[5]	Current account balance
		Service transactions							Inheritances and emigrants' funds	Personal and institutional remittances	Official contributions	Total transfer payments		
		Travel	Interest and dividends	Freight and shipping	Other service payments	Withholding tax	Total service payments							
	70	71	72	73	74	75	76	77	78	79	80	81	82	83

United States[6]

1975	23,049	1,587	2,313	1,066	2,305	—	7,271	30,320	85	89	—	174	30,494	-4,667
1974	20,632	1,196	2,009	988	2,134	—	6,327	26,959	83	97	—	180	27,139	-1,516
1973	16,091	1,073	1,692	816	1,770	—	5,351	21,442	84	80	—	164	21,606	-831
1972	12,594	919	1,423	697	1,540	—	4,579	17,173	88	64	—	152	17,325	-137
1971	10,716	898	1,444	605	1,454	—	4,401	15,117	105	57	—	162	15,279	-86
1970	9,838	898	1,306	587	1,313	—	4,104	13,942	114	55	—	169	14,111	-165
1969	10,127	862	1,143	562	1,242	—	3,809	13,936	127	50	—	177	14,113	-845
1968	8,869	684	1,074	561	984	—	3,303	12,172	145	49	—	194	12,366	-747
1967	7,846	627	1,058	522	893	—	3,100	10,946	156	47	—	203	11,149	-1,342
1966	7,242	628	985	530	756	—	2,899	10,141	145	45	—	190	10,331	-2,030
1965	6,034	548	906	465	615	—	2,534	8,568	160	41	—	201	8,769	-1,937
1964	5,204	481	850	399	561	—	2,291	7,495	157	41	—	198	7,693	-1,635
1963	4,458	388	727	378	521	—	2,014	6,472	152	38	—	190	6,662	-1,148
1962	4,205	419	656	353	500	—	1,928	6,133	139	39	—	178	6,311	-1,092
1961	3,828	459	630	333	457	—	1,879	5,707	136	37	—	173	5,880	-1,341
1960	3,713	462	535	324	435	—	1,756	5,469	142	35	—	177	5,646	-1,359
1959	3,727	448	547	326	403	—	1,724	5,451	123	33	—	156	5,607	-1,221
1958	3,443	413	502	294	396	—	1,605	5,048	104	32	—	136	5,184	-1,167
1957	3,878	403	485	351	380	—	1,619	5,497	124	31	—	155	5,652	-1,579
1956	4,021	391	428	351	337	—	1,507	5,528	108	30	—	138	5,666	-1,650
1955	3,283	363	382	287	299	—	1,331	4,614	90	28	—	118	4,732	-1,029
1954	2,800	320	346	261	282	—	1,209	4,009	78	27	—	105	4,114	-800
1953	3,048	307	335	296	261	—	1,199	4,247	78	26	—	104	4,351	-907
1952	2,819	294	342	302	253	—	1,191	4,010	77	24	—	101	4,111	-830
1951	2,846	246	382	276	275	—	1,179	4,025	55	24	—	79	4,104	-945
1950	2,096	193	411	240	250	—	1,094	3,190	47	15	—	62	3,252	-385
1949	1,899	165	325	193	232	—	915	2,814	44	12	—	56	2,870	-601
1948	1,797	113	267	213	198	—	791	2,588	37	15	—	52	2,640	-393
1947	1,951	152	274	221	191	—	838	2,789	37	20	—	57	2,846	-1,134
1946	1,378	130	250	169	200	—	749	2,127	31	16	—	47	2,174	-607

United Kingdom[6]

1975	1,224	242	124	259	269	—	894	2,118	44	37	—	81	2,199	+616
1974	1,171	211	117	281	262	—	871	2,042	40	34	—	74	2,116	+703
1973	996	194	106	165	200	—	665	1,661	38	32	—	70	1,731	+513
1972	972	174	100	121	167	—	562	1,534	37	32	—	69	1,603	+268
1971	877	180	101	114	144	—	539	1,416	43	32	—	75	1,491	+444
1970	734	156	93	113	158	—	520	1,254	49	32	—	81	1,335	+732
1969	809	145	104	107	135	—	491	1,300	40	34	—	74	1,374	+264
1968	723	103	94	94	111	—	402	1,125	38	32	—	70	1,195	+425
1967	651	88	90	104	100	—	382	1,033	31	32	—	63	1,096	+512
1966	664	94	93	89	94	—	370	1,034	30	30	—	60	1,094	+425
1965	624	89	114	86	83	—	372	996	30	27	—	57	1,053	+505
1964	584	80	104	89	95	—	368	952	24	29	—	53	1,005	+605
1963	521	70	82	94	74	—	320	841	15	28	—	43	884	+417
1962	578	71	85	88	74	—	318	896	18	27	—	45	941	+225
1961	593	71	87	93	73	—	324	917	23	26	—	49	966	+195
1960	611	70	83	89	72	—	314	925	25	26	3	54	979	+169
1959	618	62	90	85	65	—	302	920	26	24	—	50	970	+16
1958	537	52	76	70	73	—	271	808	34	23	—	57	865	+97
1957	520	47	78	69	64	—	258	778	20	23	—	43	821	+120
1956	493	46	73	59	58	—	236	729	16	20	—	36	765	+253
1955	406	40	71	49	47	—	207	613	19	19	—	38	651	+332
1954	391	35	62	39	48	—	184	575	15	18	—	33	608	+229
1953	463	31	58	42	77	—	208	671	13	14	—	27	698	+132
1952	352	27	58	42	36	—	163	515	12	14	—	26	541	+387
1951	417	20	59	43	50	—	172	589	10	—	—	10	599	+223
1950	399	19	54	36	48	—	157	556	10	—	—	10	566	+24
1949	300	17	55	32	37	—	141	441	10	—	—	10	451	+446
1948	287	12	50	34	46	—	142	429	7	—	—	7	436	+486
1947	182	9	53	32	50	—	144	326	8	—	—	8	334	+633
1946	138	3	54	32	110	—	199	337	3	—	—	3	340	+500

Series G57-83. Canadian balance of international payments, all countries, current account, 1926 to 1975, and by major areas, 1946 to 1975 (continued)

(millions of dollars)

Year	Merchandise imports[1]	Travel	Interest and dividends	Freight and shipping	Other service payments	Withholding tax	Total service payments	Total goods and service payments[4]	Inheritances and emigrants' funds	Personal and institutional remittances	Official contributions	Total transfer payments	Total current payments[5]	Current account balance
	70	71	72	73	74	75	76	77	78	79	80	81	82	83
European Economic Community[7]														
1975	2,047	249	200	145	331	—	925	2,972	15	30	—	45	3,017	-8
1974	1,895	195	198	138	322	—	853	2,748	13	28	—	41	2,789	-49
1973	1,451	168	187	119	243	—	717	2,168	11	27	—	38	2,206	-136
Japan[7]														
1975	1,191	11	15	104	45	—	175	1,366	—	2	—	2	1,368	+1,008
1974	1,414	5	13	102	48	—	168	1,582	—	2	—	2	1,584	+875
1973	996	6	12	67	30	—	115	1,111	—	2	—	2	1,113	+863
Other Organization for Economic Co-operation and Development[7]														
1975	1,187	161	59	211	272	—	703	1,890	9	22	—	31	1,921	-716
1974	1,154	129	55	205	232	—	621	1,775	8	20	—	28	1,803	-393
1973	864	120	39	139	155	—	453	1,317	8	20	—	28	1,345	-341
Other non-resident[7]														
1975	5,288	292	85	352	256	—	985	6,273	26	119	513	658	6,931	-1,198
1974	4,627	242	17	333	204	—	796	5,423	24	111	332	467	5,890	-1,112
1973	2,328	181	14	281	156	—	632	2,960	18	123	253	394	3,354	+28
Other sterling area[7]														
1972	763	67	9	70	63	—	209	972	10	21	112	143	1,115	-33
1971	616	70	8	77	54	—	209	825	10	22	105	137	962	+107
1970	627	66	6	83	46	—	201	828	9	20	112	141	969	+125
1969	586	52	5	25	35	—	117	703	6	18	87	111	814	+84
1968	458	41	6	15	46	—	108	566	6	5	83	94	660	+193
1967	434	43	1	12	37	—	93	527	5	4	156	165	692	+181
1966	449	29	1	11	29	—	70	519	4	4	142	150	669	+69
1965	385	27	2	11	28	—	68	453	4	4	73	81	534	+138
1964	417	23	1	7	25	—	56	473	5	1	58	64	537	+101
1963	418	21	1	5	23	—	50	468	4	2	57	63	531	-31
1962	326	21	1	5	20	—	47	373	4	2	29	35	408	+17
1961	298	21	1	4	18	—	44	342	4	2	49	55	397	+27
1960	284	14	1	4	18	—	37	321	3	2	42	47	368	+43
1959	263	13	1	3	16	—	33	296	3	1	64	68	364	—
1958	212	11	1	3	15	—	30	242	3	1	49	53	295	+67
1957	239	11	1	2	17	—	31	270	2	1	38	41	311	+4
1956	222	8	1	3	12	—	24	246	1	1	28	30	276	+48
1955	211	8	1	3	11	—	23	234	1	1	22	24	258	+60
1954	183	7	—	3	9	—	19	202	1	—	8	9	211	+44
1953	172	6	—	6	9	—	21	193	1	1	18	20	213	+83
1952	185	5	—	5	6	—	16	201	1	—	15	16	217	+115
1951	310	5	—	5	4	—	14	324	1	—	—	1	325	-24
1950	244	5	—	3	4	—	12	256	1	—	—	1	257	-23
1949	187	4	1	5	6	—	16	203	2	—	—	2	205	+135
1948	192	4	1	7	4	—	16	208	1	—	—	1	209	+129
1947	160	3	1	5	5	—	14	174	—	—	—	—	174	+242
1946	129	1	1	6	3	—	11	140	—	—	5	5	145	+164

Series G57-83. Canadian balance of international payments, all countries, current account, 1926 to 1975, and by major areas, 1946 to 1975 (continued)

(millions of dollars)

Year	Merchandise imports[1]	Service transactions						Total goods and service payments[4]	Transfers				Total current payments[5]	Current account balance
		Travel	Interest and dividends	Freight and shipping	Other service payments	Withholding tax	Total service payments		Inheritances and emigrants' funds	Personal and institutional remittances	Official contributions	Total transfer payments		
	70	71	72	73	74	75	76	77	78	79	80	81	82	83

Organization for Economic Co-operation and Development (Europe)[7]

	70	71	72	73	74	75	76	77	78	79	80	81	82	83
1972	1,642	230	180	196	281	—	887	2,529	14	41	2	57	2,586	-628
1971	1,327	226	142	200	271	—	839	2,166	14	37	7	58	2,224	-243
1970	1,196	207	141	184	299	—	831	2,027	15	36	2	53	2,080	-18
1969	1,171	153	111	170	300	—	734	1,905	17	36	3	56	1,961	-401
1968	982	121	82	151	217	—	571	1,553	11	37	2	50	1,603	-276
1967	843	105	58	119	186	—	468	1,311	12	36	2	50	1,361	-153
1966	821	120	58	92	160	—	430	1,251	13	35	1	49	1,300	-176
1965	707	106	61	159	137	—	463	1,170	13	35	1	49	1,219	-162
1964	558	105	52	146	119	—	422	980	11	34	1	46	1,026	-107
1963	474	86	48	137	121	—	392	866	11	33	2	46	912	-92
1962	454	75	39	124	117	—	355	809	11	32	—	43	852	-82
1961	416	72	44	114	101	—	331	747	11	33	1	45	792	-30
1960	371	65	35	99	111	—	310	681	11	31	4	46	727	-7
1959	364	60	31	95	89	—	275	639	11	31	1	43	682	-116
1958	302	52	33	79	94	—	258	560	13	29	1	43	603	+39
1957	287	48	28	80	83	—	239	526	10	27	1	38	564	+68
1956	306	41	20	75	87	—	223	529	4	23	1	28	557	+21
1955	188	32	17	64	75	—	188	376	4	20	1	25	401	+54
1954	159	23	14	42	47	—	126	285	4	19	1	24	309	+106
1953	158	18	11	23	37	—	89	247	3	15	—	18	265	+169
1952	134	13	11	19	23	—	66	200	3	13	1	17	217	+323
1951	156	8	9	21	9	—	47	203	3	—	5	8	211	+214
1950	92	8	8	14	10	—	40	132	2	—	2	4	136	+114
1949	72	6	7	16	8	—	37	109	2	—	1	3	112	+178
1948	62	4	5	15	9	—	33	95	1	—	13	14	109	+218
1947	53	2	7	14	11	—	34	87	2	—	7	9	96	+274
1946	32	1	5	9	38	—	53	85	1	—	34	35	120	+229

Series G57-83. Canadian balance of international payments, all countries, current account, 1926 to 1975, and by major areas, 1946 to 1975 (concluded)

(millions of dollars)

Year	Merchan-dise imports[1]	Service transactions						Total goods and service pay-ments[4]	Transfers				Total current pay-ments[5]	Current account balance
		Travel	Interest and dividends	Freight and shipping	Other service payments	With-holding tax	Total service payments		Inheri-tances and emi-grants' funds	Personal and institu-tional remit-tances	Official contri-butions	Total transfer payments		
	70	**71**	**72**	**73**	**74**	**75**	**76**	**77**	**78**	**79**	**80**	**81**	**82**	**83**
						All other non-residents[7]								
1972	2,301	74	1	231	148	—	454	2,755	13	72	113	198	2,953	+144
1971	1,778	74	4	200	158	—	436	2,214	13	70	89	172	2,386	+209
1970	1,474	95	4	139	182	—	420	1,894	12	69	87	168	2,062	+432
1969	1,378	49	3	132	150	—	334	1,712	14	66	54	134	1,846	-19
1968	1,217	33	3	110	83	—	229	1,446	9	25	48	82	1,528	+308
1967	998	32	4	104	61	—	201	1,199	9	54	24	87	1,286	+303
1966	926	29	3	101	51	—	184	1,110	6	25	23	54	1,164	+550
1965	877	26	3	40	41	—	110	987	4	26	19	49	1,036	+326
1964	774	23	3	38	35	—	99	873	4	23	10	37	910	+612
1963	708	20	2	34	23	—	79	787	3	25	6	34	821	+333
1962	640	19	2	25	23	—	69	709	3	22	7	32	741	+102
1961	581	19	2	24	25	—	70	651	2	22	6	30	681	+221
1960	561	16	2	17	18	—	53	614	3	20	12	35	649	-79
1959	600	15	2	16	15	—	48	648	2	20	7	29	677	-166
1958	572	14	2	14	14	—	44	616	5	18	3	26	642	-173
1957	564	16	2	13	17	—	48	612	1	18	1	20	632	-64
1956	523	12	2	14	12	—	40	563	2	17	1	20	583	-44
1955	455	6	2	12	11	—	31	486	2	15	1	18	504	-104
1954	383	4	2	11	14	—	31	414	1	13	2	16	430	-3
1953	371	3	2	7	11	—	23	394	1	12	7	20	414	+75
1952	364	2	2	7	14	—	25	389	1	10	—	11	400	+192
1951	372	1	2	9	31	—	43	415	1	—	4	5	420	+20
1950	301	1	2	8	22	—	33	334	1	—	3	4	338	-49
1949	238	1	2	7	20	—	30	268	1	—	5	6	274	+19
1948	260	1	2	10	15	—	28	288	4	—	10	14	302	+11
1947	189	1	2	6	18	—	27	216	2	—	31	33	249	+34
1946	145	—	2	3	15	—	20	165	—	—	58	58	223	+77

[1] Trade of Canada figures with certain valuation, coverage and timing adjustments appropriate for balance of payments.

[2] Gold production available for export is by convention, included in the account with the United States.

[3] Receipts of pensions are included with other service transactions from 1926 to 1951; from 1952 these are included with personal and institutional remittances.

[4] As used in the national income and expenditure accounts, except for the years 1940 through 1948 when there were special adjustments relating to the treatment of official contributions and of Newfoundland.

[5] Includes tax withheld on service payments and income distributions to non-residents. Regional distribution is not available.

[6] For details for years 1926 to 1945 see first edition of *Historical Statistics of Canada*, series F57-71.

[7] In addition to the United States and the United Kingdom, the geographical dissection introduced in 1973 consists of the European Economic Community, Japan, other Organization for Economic Co-operation and Development and all other countries; the former categories of the Organization for Economic Co-operation and Development, Europe and other sterling area were discontinued.

Series G84-115. Canadian balance of international payments, all countries, capital account,[11] 1927 to 1975, and by major areas, 1946 to 1975

(millions of dollars)

Year	Direct investment[1] In Canada	Direct investment[1] Abroad	Portfolio transactions – Canadian securities – Out-standing bonds[2]	Canadian securities – Out-standing stocks	Canadian securities – New issues	Canadian securities – Retire-ments	Foreign securities – Out-standing issues	Foreign securities – New issues	Foreign securities – Retire-ments	Loans and subscriptions – Government of Canada – Advances	Repay-ments	Columbia River Treaty	Export credit directly or indirectly at risk of the Government of Canada	Other long-term capital trans-actions	Balance of capital movements in long-term forms
	84	85	86	87	88	89	90	91	92	93	94	95	96	97	98
All countries[10]															
1975	630	-650	302	5	5,150	-691	18	-69	12	-378	40	—	-397	134	+4,106
1974	725	-775	41	-112	2,423	-626	73	-39	12	-350	38	—	-588	49	+871
1973	750	-785	29	-24	1,324	-737	109	-61	21	-269	43	1	-198	182	+385
1972	620	-400	292	-59	1,722	-603	278	-65	31	-249	37	1	-246	230	+1,588
1971	925	-230	-96	-142	1,191	-845	252	-68	12	-190	36	24	-230	25	+664
1970	905	-315	-40	-145	1,230	-552	93	-34	11	-145	36	31	-129	61	+1,007
1969	720	-370	2	53	2,089	-440	112	-47	37	-89	22	32	-12	228	+2,337
1968	590	-225	-70	114	1,917	-431	-420	-77	30	-78	5	88	29	197	+1,669
1967	691	-125	-57	12	1,307	-357	-382	-65	15	-38	34	44	107	229	+1,415
1966	790	-5	-104	-136	1,465	-499	-361	-57	17	-35	24	32	-41	138	+1,228
1965	535	-125	55	-274	1,240	-390	-53	-57	25	-14	10	32	-187	36	+833
1964	270	-95	77	-98	1,100	-382	-31	-31	10	-10	10	54	-164	40	+750
1963	280	-135	39	-170	984	-404	40	-39	21	-18	25	—	-72	86	+637
1962	505	-105	64	-115	729	-319	-68	-17	20	-22	129	—	-63	-50	+688
1961	560	-80	61	39	548	-301	-6	-38	9	-8	38	—	:	108	+930
1960	670	-50	3	51	448	-266	-19	-18	18	-11	32	—	:	71	+929
1959	570	-85	92	110	709	-258	-32	-13	11	-1	34	—	:	42	+1,179
1958	430	-40	—	88	688	-158	11	-17	7	-34	64	—	:	114	+1,153
1957	545	-80	-45	142	800	-134	19	-25	7	-1	50	—	:	42	+1,320
1956	650	-105	11	187	667	-141	15	-18	—	-4	69	—	:	159	+1,490
1955	445	-85	-165	137	166	-185	26	-48	17	—	69	—	:	37	+414
1954	425	-90	-66	129	333	-205	7	-33	2	—	72	—	:	25	+599
1953	450	-70	-52	21	335	-146	21	-23	1	—	87	—	:	25	+649
1952	360	-85	-168	73	323	-89	11	-22	—	—	56	—	:	-4	+455
1951	320	-30	38	—	411	-184	15	-3	3	—	68	—	:	28	+666
1950	225	35	329	:	210	-284	70	-2	8	-50	74	—	:	-5	+610
1949	94	13	8	:	105	-147	22	-4	2	-126	18	—	:	-14	-29
1948	71	15	3	:	150	-114	-7	-3	2	-142	80	—	:	-12	+43
1947	61	6	-13	:	95	-364	-1	-3	7	-598	111	—	:	-24	-721
1946	40	-14	194	:	218	-539	25	-4	13	-783	132	—	:	3	-715
1945	:	:	245	9	95	-226	98	-2	:	-314	64	—	—	-15	-46
1944	:	:	163	7	92	-200	43	-1	:	-1	57	—	—	78	+224
1943	:	:	221	1	154	-324	45	-1	:	-9	18	—	—	-420	-315
1942	:	:	123	—	22	-372	25	-1	:	-700	—	—	—	116	-787
1941	:	:	11	-2	12	-236	18	-1	3	—	—	—	—	248	+53
1940	:	:	-28	-1	15	-191	21	-2	2	—	—	—	—	82	-102
1939	-29	-24	38	14	161	-251	30	-7	:	—	—	—	—	-36	-104
1938	-4	-29	-3	29	99	-151	-1	-6	:	—	—	—	—	-29	-95
1937	-21	-43	-7	-5	102	-170	6	-9	:	—	—	—	—	-10	-157
1936	-27	-35	8	:	113	-270	:	:	:	—	—	—	—	-26	-237
1935	-14	-30	51	:	117	-257	:	:	:	—	—	—	—	-18	-151
1934	-6	-39	9	:	111	-169	:	:	:	—	—	—	—	3	-91
1933	-31	-28	51	:	138	-166	:	:	:	—	—	—	—	-1	-37
1932	-4	-24	40	:	104	-107	25	:	:	—	—	—	—	-1	+33
1931	31	-21	-10	:	238	-208	30	:	:	—	—	—	—	27	+87
1930	64	-27	—	:	418	-110	47	-3	:	—	—	—	—	3	+392
1929	38	-20	35	:	351	-150	-10	-1	:	—	—	—	—	-31	+212
1928	40	-19	20	:	227	-200	-112	-24	:	—	—	1	—	-27	-94
1927	49	-14	-40	:	328	-160	-83	-35	:	—	4	—	—	-35	+14

Series G84-115. Canadian balance of international payments, all countries, capital account,[11] 1927 to 1975, and by major areas, 1946 to 1975 (continued)

(millions of dollars)

Year	Direct investment[1] In Canada	Direct investment Abroad	Portfolio transactions — Canadian securities — Outstanding bonds[2]	Outstanding stocks	New issues	Retirements	Foreign securities — Outstanding issues	New issues	Retirements	Loans and subscriptions — Government of Canada — Advances	Repayments	Columbia River Treaty	Export credit directly or indirectly at risk of the Government of Canada	Other long-term capital transactions	Balance of capital movements in long-term forms
	84	85	86	87	88	89	90	91	92	93	94	95	96	97	98

United States[12]

Year	84	85	86	87	88	89	90	91	92	93	94	95	96	97	98
1975	535	-324	38	-12	3,453	-531	18	-26	8	—	—	—	-3	223	+3,379
1974	615	-482	16	-68	1,816	-504	71	-8	8	—	—	—	-45	153	+1,572
1973	423	-453	-29	21	990	-428	91	-8	11	—	—	1	-7	307	+919
1972	457	-149	-5	-145	1,007	-458	253	-15	19	—	—	1	-6	101	+1,059
1971	599	-122	-74	-39	891	-649	263	-26	6	—	—	24	—	4	+877
1970	628	-258	-71	-79	1,027	-395	75	-20	6	—	—	31	1	44	+989
1969	564	-287	-27	2	1,502	-382	112	-30	7	—	—	32	3	173	+1,669
1968	354	-108	-67	104	1,391	-376	-402	-46	16	—	—	88	8	189	+1,151
1967	575	-72	-63	77	1,239	-301	-355	-38	8	—	—	44	7	196	+1,317
1966	718	87	-72	-95	1,409	-456	-344	-33	6	—	—	32	25	116	+1,393
1965	421	-24	21	-195	1,200	-330	-49	-28	5	—	—	32	—	21	+1,074
1964	188	-35	38	-52	1,040	-300	-26	-20	5	—	—	54	9	42	+943
1963	220	-36	35	-99	930	-315	42	-34	17	—	—	—	7	76	+843
1962	328	6	84	-11	690	-247	-59	-13	17	—	—	—	-33	-82	+680
1961	366	-25	74	122	489	-220	7	-19	5	—	—	—	..	154	+953
1960	461	-18	-9	56	382	-214	5	-13	12	—	—	—	..	84	+746
1959	428	-10	18	75	624	-212	-34	-8	5	—	—	—	..	41	+927
1958	304	—	-10	70	611	-132	10	-13	4	—	—	—	..	106	+950
1957	403	-35	-70	10	724	-106	16	-15	4	—	—	—	..	32	+963
1956	465	-68	-35	68	602	-134	6	-13	—	—	—	—	..	143	+1,034
1955	317	-63	-159	91	127	-169	32	-8	2	—	—	—	..	39	+209
1954	305	-53	-87	87	300	-186	6	-3	1	—	—	—	..	25	+395
1953	357	-35	-85	5	322	-132	20	-19	1	—	—	—	..	6	+440
1952	323	-49	-172	67	322	-75	8	-7	—	—	—	—	..	-30	+387
1951	276	-5	20	..	404	-159	18	-3	2	—	—	—	..	7	+560
1950	202	41	362	..	210	-263	68	-2	7	—	—	—	..	—	+625
1949	84	16	25	..	105	-136	19	-4	1	—	—	—	..	6	+116
1948	61	15	5	..	150	-96	-9	-3	1	—	—	—	..	2	+126
1947	58	6	-3	..	95	-313	-2	-3	3	—	—	—	..	1	-158
1946	38	-7	241	..	218	-460	21	-4	6	—	—	—	..	-4	+49

Series G84-115. Canadian balance of international payments, all countries, capital account,[11] 1927 to 1975, and by major areas, 1946 to 1975 (continued)

(millions of dollars)

United Kingdom[12]

Year	Direct investment[1] In Canada	Direct investment[1] Abroad	Portfolio transactions — Canadian securities				Portfolio transactions — Foreign securities			Loans and subscriptions – Government of Canada		Columbia River Treaty	Export credit directly or indirectly at risk of the Government of Canada	Other long-term capital transactions	Balance of capital movements in long-term forms
			Outstanding bonds[2]	Outstanding stocks	New issues	Retirements	Outstanding issues	New issues	Retirements	Advances	Repayments				
	84	85	86	87	88	89	90	91	92	93	94	95	96	97	98
1975	-56	-13	142	-19	143	-34	7	-19	—	—	22	—	-20	14	+167
1974	-1	-43	9	-58	21	-19	-9	-2	—	—	22	—	-18	33	-65
1973	133	-122	26	-58	14	-45	-7	-3	1	—	22	—	-10	10	-39
1972	-9	-29	43	-41	47	-45	9	-17	1	—	21	—	-36	87	+30
1971	81	-13	-13	-98	81	-50	-5	-1	1	—	21	—	-7	90	+87
1970	32	12	8	-43	123	-13	4	—	—	—	21	—	—	64	+208
1969	14	-7	20	6	33	-14	2	—	—	—	20	—	—	-3	+71
1968	83	9	15	-41	56	-31	-10	—	—	—	—	—	—	-16	+65
1967	12	20	-3	-56	41	-20	-27	—	—	—	19	—	—	-1	-15
1966	-10	-22	-12	-25	36	-16	-6	—	1	—	19	—	—	-5	-40
1965	46	-38	-3	-50	15	-23	-1	—	—	—	—	—	—	-5	-59
1964	55	-3	-1	-27	22	-39	-8	—	—	—	—	—	—	4	+3
1963	38	-40	-5	-55	18	-40	-2	—	—	—	18	—	—	-12	-80
1962	62	-21	—	-65	18	-37	-2	—	—	—	17	—	—	19	-8
1961	125	-16	-12	-61	24	-41	-11	-2	1	—	17	—	::	5	+28
1960	117	-15	-13	-17	27	-27	-3	—	—	—	17	—	::	-4	+82
1959	88	-44	4	7	45	-30	2	—	—	—	16	—	::	14	+102
1958	94	-5	3	5	41	-16	2	—	1	—	46	—	::	-2	+169
1957	73	3	—	87	59	-21	2	-1	1	—	30	—	::	8	+241
1956	101	-5	11	72	35	-2	4	-1	1	—	45	—	::	2	+263
1955	79	-2	-2	28	15	-11	-10	-2	—	—	45	—	::	-1	+139
1954	85	-17	—	21	20	-12	2	-1	—	—	45	—	::	-1	+142
1953	52	-5	20	7	7	-8	2	—	—	—	64	—	::	21	+160
1952	24	-3	3	-6	1	-9	3	—	—	—	37	—	::	23	+73
1951	34	-2	-16	::	7	-24	—	—	1	—	48	—	::	22	+70
1950	20	-4	-35	::	—	-19	1	—	1	-50	51	—	::	-4	-39
1949	13	-3	-16	::	—	-10	2	—	1	-120	5	—	::	-8	-136
1948	10	-2	-4	::	—	-14	2	—	1	-52	64	—	::	5	+5
1947	3	-3	-11	::	—	-42	3	—	1	-423	104	—	::	-5	-373
1946	2	-10	-48	::	—	-77	1	—	5	-540	127	—	::	7	-533

Series G84-115. Canadian balance of international payments, all countries, capital account,[11] 1927 to 1975, and by major areas, 1946 to 1975 (continued)

(millions of dollars)

	Direct investment[1]		Portfolio transactions							Loans and subscriptions — Government of Canada		Columbia River Treaty	Export credit directly or indirectly at risk of the Government of Canada	Other long-term capital transactions	Balance of capital movements in long-term forms
	In Canada	Abroad	Canadian securities				Foreign securities								
Year			Outstanding bonds[2]	Outstanding stocks	New issues	Retirements	Outstanding issues	New issues	Retirements	Advances	Repayments				
	84	85	86	87	88	89	90	91	92	93	94	95	96	97	98
European Economic Community[13]															
1975	90	-72	31	19	654	-50	-3	—	14	—	16	—	-26	-38	+635
1974	10	-53	23	13	88	-51	-1	—	—	—	15	—	-22	-50	-28
1973	41	-33	1	31	217	-142	-1	-2	3	—	15	—	-11	-2	+117
Japan[13]															
1975	-6	-12	—	-6	—	—	-1	—	—	—	—	—	-1	-3	-29
1974	4	-12	—	-7	—	-5	13	—	—	—	—	—	—	-2	-9
1973	61	3	5	-5	15	-13	5	-2	2	—	—	—	—	-6	+67
Other Organization for Economic Co-operation and Development[13]															
1975	47	9	19	12	436	-33	-1	—	—	—	—	—	-3	-15	+471
1974	70	27	15	9	59	-34	-1	-1	—	-5	—	—	-47	5	+103
1973	80	-13	4	21	82	-101	—	—	—	-5	—	—	-23	-37	+7
Other non-resident[13]															
1975	20	-238	72	11	464	-43	-2	-24	—	-378	2	—	-344	-47	-507
1974	27	-212	-22	-1	439	-13	—	-29	4	-350	1	—	-456	-90	-702
1973	12	-167	22	-34	6	-8	21	-48	4	-264	6	—	-147	-89	-686
Other sterling area[13]															
1972	3	-95	5	3	3	-7	8	-5	1	-108	—	—	-3	-13	-209
1971	-1	-75	1	-1	1	-1	3	—	1	-113	—	—	-27	-56	-268
1970	-2	-15	1	-1	2	—	3	—	—	-106	—	—	-19	-1	-135
1969	54	-22	1	—	—	—	—	-7	—	-53	—	—	-22	2	-47
1968	18	-60	4	—	—	—	-1	-4	2	-44	3	—	-28	2	-109
1967	21	-54	3	—	—	—	-1	—	2	-22	13	—	-29	3	-64
1966	9	-46	—	—	—	—	—	—	1	-11	3	—	-20	-4	-68
1965	3	-42	—	—	1	—	-2	-5	2	-1	8	—	-17	-10	-63
1964	4	-35	—	—	—	—	—	-4	1	-2	8	—	-17	-7	-52
1963	-11	-13	—	—	—	—	-1	—	1	-10	5	—	4	4	-29
1962	-4	-41	—	—	—	—	—	—	—	—	5	—	-4	-2	-44
1961	9	-20	—	-3	—	—	—	-13	1	—	5	—	...	-2	-23
1960	5	-3	—	—	—	—	—	-1	—	—	—	—	...	+1	+1
1959	-1	-9	—	—	—	—	—	—	1	—	—	—	...	—	-9
1958	4	-12	—	—	—	—	—	—	—	-34	—	—	...	4	-38
1957	4	-26	—	—	—	—	—	—	—	—	—	—	...	—	-22
1956	1	-25	—	—	—	—	—	—	—	—	—	—	...	—	-24
1955	-2	-10	—	—	—	—	—	-19	1	—	—	—	...	1	-30
1954	—	-7	—	—	—	-4	—	—	1	—	—	—	...	-2	-12
1953	—	-20	—	—	—	-3	—	—	1	—	—	—	...	-1	-23
1952	-1	-17	—	—	—	—	—	—	—	—	—	—	...	—	-18
1951	—	-4	—	—	—	—	—	—	—	—	—	—	...	—	-4
1950	...	...	...	...	...	...	...	...	...	...	...	...	...	...	...
1949	...	...	...	...	...	...	...	...	...	...	...	...	...	...	...
1948	...	...	...	...	...	...	...	...	...	...	...	...	...	...	...
1947	...	...	...	...	...	...	...	...	...	...	...	...	...	...	...
1946	...	...	...	...	...	...	...	...	...	...	...	...	...	...	...

Series G84-115. Canadian balance of international payments, all countries, capital account,[11] 1927 to 1975, and by major areas, 1946 to 1975 (continued)

(millions of dollars)

Year	Direct investment[1] In Canada	Direct investment[1] Abroad	Canadian securities Outstanding bonds[2]	Canadian securities Outstanding stocks	Canadian securities New issues	Canadian securities Retirements	Foreign securities Outstanding issues	Foreign securities New issues	Foreign securities Retirements	Loans and subscriptions – Government of Canada Advances	Loans and subscriptions – Government of Canada Repayments	Columbia River Treaty	Export credit directly or indirectly at risk of the Government of Canada	Other long-term capital transactions	Balance of capital movements in long-term forms
	84	85	86	87	88	89	90	91	92	93	94	95	96	97	98
						Other Organization for Economic Co-operation and Development[13]									
1972	148	-39	137	108	592	-63	5	-1	8	—	15	—	-28	51	+933
1971	176	-8	-11	-11	213	-135	-3	—	—	—	15	—	-31	34	+239
1970	215	-60	20	-26	64	-138	10	—	—	—	15	—	-11	-49	+40
1969	75	-34	6	28	539	-14	—	—	—	—	2	—	-5	60	+657
1968	83	-57	-22	51	465	-19	-8	-5	3	—	2	—	2	28	+523
1967	64	-28	-3	-9	27	-36	1	—	1	—	2	—	-7	71	+83
1966	59	-22	-2	-16	20	-27	-11	—	1	—	2	—	—	29	+33
1965	66	-17	31	-29	24	-29	-1	—	—	—	2	—	-4	16	+59
1964	27	-18	42	-19	20	-31	3	—	—	—	2	—	1	-3	+23
1963	37	-33	6	-16	22	-42	—	—	—	—	2	—	1	19	-4
1962	111	-29	-20	-39	21	-35	-9	—	—	—	107	—	1	3	+111
1961	57	-1	-1	-19	20	-19	-2	—	—	—	15	—	...	-4	+46
1960	86	-16	25	12	38	-23	-1	—	—	—	15	—	...	-3	+133
1959	55	-6	66	28	40	-16	-6	—	—	—	18	—	...	-13	+172
1958	30	-6	17	13	26	-10	-1	-5	—	—	18	—	...	12	+99
1957	63	-3	30	45	16	-7	1	—	—	—	18	—	...	-10	+148
1956	82	1	38	47	30	-4	4	—	—	—	18	—	...	-5	+211
1955	50	—	-2	18	21	-4	4	—	—	—	15	—	...	—	+102
1954	35	-3	-3	17	12	-2	—	—	—	—	20	—	...	2	+78
1953	40	1	16	9	3	-1	—	—	—	—	18	—	...	-2	+83
1952	12	1	-3	12	—	-5	—	—	—	—	16	—	...	3	+36
1951	10	-6	34	—	—	-1	—	—	—	—	13	—	...	-1	+49
1950	3	-3	2	—	—	-2	—	—	—	—	16	—	...	-1	+15
1949	-3	-2	-1	—	—	-1	—	—	—	-62	11	—	...	-8	-4
1948	—	—	-1	—	—	4	—	—	—	-113	16	—	...	-5	-56
1947	—	—	—	—	—	-9	—	—	—	183	2	—	...	-10	-130
1946	—	—	1	—	—	-2	—	—	—	—	—	—	...	—	-184

Series G84-115. Canadian balance of international payments, all countries, capital account,[11] 1927 to 1975, and by major areas, 1946 to 1975 (continued)

(millions of dollars)

Year	Direct investment[1] In Canada	Abroad	Portfolio transactions — Canadian securities — Outstanding bonds[2]	Outstanding stocks	New issues	Retirements	Foreign securities — Outstanding issues	New issues	Retirements	Loans and subscriptions — Government of Canada — Advances	Repayments	Columbia River Treaty	Export credit directly or indirectly at risk of the Government of Canada	Other long-term capital transactions	Balance of capital movements in long-term forms
	84	85	86	87	88	89	90	91	92	93	94	95	96	97	98
All other non-residents[13]															
1972	21	-88	112	16	73	-30	3	-27	4	-141	1	—	-173	4	-225
1971	70	-12	1	7	5	-10	-6	-41	4	-77	—	—	-165	-47	-271
1970	32	6	2	4	14	-6	1	-14	5	-39	—	—	-100	—	-95
1969	13	-20	2	17	15	-30	-2	-10	30	-36	—	—	12	-4	-13
1968	52	-9	—	—	5	-5	—	-22	9	-34	—	—	47	-4	+39
1967	19	9	9	—	—	—	—	-27	4	-16	—	—	136	-40	+94
1966	14	-2	-18	—	—	—	—	-24	8	-24	—	—	-46	2	-90
1965	-1	-4	6	—	18	-8	—	-24	18	-13	—	—	-166	14	-178
1964	-4	-4	-2	—	14	-12	—	-7	4	-8	—	—	-156	4	-167
1963	-4	-13	3	—	—	-7	1	-5	3	-8	—	—	-76	-1	-93
1962	8	-20	—	—	—	—	2	-4	2	-22	—	—	-27	10	-51
1961	3	-18	—	—	15	-21	—	-4	3	-8	1	—	..	-45	-74
1960	1	2	—	—	1	-2	-20	-4	5	-11	—	—	..	-5	-33
1959	—	-16	4	—	—	—	—	-5	4	—	—	—	..	-6	-13
1958	-2	-17	-10	—	10	—	—	-4	2	-1	2	—	..	-12	-27
1957	2	-9	-5	—	1	—	—	-4	2	-1	2	—	..	—	-10
1956	1	-8	-3	—	—	-1	—	-5	—	-4	6	—	..	20	+6
1955	1	-10	-2	—	3	-1	—	-19	15	—	9	—	..	-2	-6
1954	-1	-10	24	4	1	-1	-1	-29	—	—	7	—	..	1	-4
1953	-1	-17	-3	—	3	-2	-1	-4	—	—	5	—	..	—	-11
1952	2	-17	4	—	—	—	—	-15	—	—	3	—	..	—	-23
1951	—	-13	—	—	—	—	-3	—	—	—	7	—	..	—	-9
1950	—	1	—	—	—	—	1	—	—	-6	7	—	..	—	+9
1949	—	2	—	—	—	—	1	—	—	-28	2	—	..	-4	-5
1948	—	2	3	—	—	—	—	—	—	-62	5	—	..	-9	-32
1947	—	3	1	—	—	—	—	—	3	-60	5	—	..	-10	-60
1946	—	3	—	—	—	—	3	—	2	—	5	—	..	—	-47

Series G84-115. Canadian balance of international payments, all countries, capital account,[11] 1927 to 1975, and by major areas, 1946 to 1975 (continued)

(millions of dollars)

All countries[10]

Year	Chartered bank net holdings of foreign currency position with non-residents (99)	Non-bank net holdings of foreign currencies abroad (100)	Dollar deposits (101)	Government demand liabilities (102)	Treasury bills (103)	Commercial paper[5,6,7] (104)	Finance company short-term paper[5,7] (105)	Other short-term paper[6] (106)	Other finance company obligations[5,7] (107)	Other short-term transactions[5,8] (108)	Balance of capital movements in short-term forms (109)	Total net capital balance (110)	Balance settled by exchange transfers (111)	Allocation of special drawing rights (112)	Official international reserves (113)	Official monetary liabilities (114)	Net official monetary movements[4,9] (115)
1975	488	-236	557	-4	37	41	217	147	-92	-700	+455	+4,561	—	—	-404	—	-404
1974	-1,354	1,590	597	45	77	53	94	-70	158	-545	+645	+1,516	—	—	24	—	24
1973	-343	-176	143	155	-24	9	-23	166	7	-862	-948	-563	—	—	-467	—	-467
1972	637	-189	139	27	22	-113	-50	-18	-30	-1,408	-983	+605	—	117	336	—	336
1971	1,405	-551	95	50	-3	41	-39	75	-25	-1,366	-318	+346	—	119	896	—	896
1970	-122	-32	26	-7	-79	71	203	36	-109	-570	-583	+424	—	133	1,662	1	1,663
1969	-506	-928	52	-34	20	42	177	-1	116	-293	-1,355	+982	—	—	65	—	65
1968	-488	39	72	21	48	2	-132	-2	24	-807	-1,223	+446	—	—	350	-1	349
1967	-384	22	24	-4	4	-11	-64	24	35	-542	-896	+519	—	—	17	3	20
1966	-467	-53	11	5	-15	16	-1	-12	154	-63	-425	+803	—	—	-360	1	-359
1965	426	-11	31	2	12	-15	-162	25	209	-62	+455	+1,288	—	—	158	—	158
1964	-303	-26	28	—	-16	-11	196	—	52	118	+38	+788	—	—	297	67	364
1963	-259		43	1	-27	-23	93	:	35	166	+29	+666	—	—	56	89	145
1962	92		-10	-4	4	:	:	:	119	95	+296	+984	—	—	307	-153	154
1961	142		33	-2	-58	:	:	:	95	80	+290	+1,220	—	—	296	-4	292
1960	-60		79	-12	56	:	:	:	59	143	+265	+1,194	—	—	:	:	-39
1959	-119		10	-8	14	:	:	:	68	332	+297	+1,476	—	—	:	:	-11
1958	-58		39	45	21	:	:	:	24	22	+93	+1,246	—	—	:	:	109
1957	-274		-15	-5	-18	:	:	:	4	329	+26	+1,346	—	—	:	:	—
1956	-216		-30	-8	3	:	:	:	64	109	-70	+1,420	—	—	:	:	48
1955	91		60	-9	29	:	:	:	23	35	+229	+643	—	—	:	:	-44
1954	-75		27	-15	8	:	:	:	10	-6	-239	+548	—	—	:	:	124
1953	-80		-22	-11	-2	:	:	:	-2	-122	+410	+410	—	—	:	:	-38
1952	-165		-66	33	1	:	:	:	35	-405	-605	-150	—	—	:	:	37
1951	-14		-190	25	2	:	:	:	:	112	-98	+568	—	—	:	:	56
1950	11		235	-4	-3	:	:	:	:	192	+431	+1,041	—	—	:	:	722
1949	-2		33	8	8	:	:	:	:	-59	-20	-49	—	—	:	:	128
1948	-2		-21	—	—	:	:	:	:	21	+41	+41	—	—	:	:	492
1947	-8		-26	—	—	:	:	:	:	5	+4	-717	—	—	:	:	-668
1946	-15		71	—	—	:	:	:	:	5	+86	-629	—	—	:	:	-266
1945	:		35	—	—	:	:	:	:	-10	+25	-21	—	—	:	:	668
1944	:		22	—	—	:	:	:	:	-32	-10	+214	—	—	:	:	274
1943	:		37	—	1	:	:	:	:	-48	-11	-326	—	—	:	:	364
1942	:		15	—	1	:	:	:	:	-8	+7	-780	—	—	:	:	-674
1941	:		-9	—	:	:	:	:	:	-23	+14	+67	—	—	:	:	568
1940	3		-84	—	1	:	:	:	:	35	-46	-148	—	—	:	:	3
1939	4		:	—	:	:	:	:	:	8	+13	-91	—	—	:	:	37
1938	6		:	—	:	:	:	:	:	7	+13	-82	—	—	:	:	17
1937	-7		:	—	:	:	:	:	:	-11	-17	-174	—	—	:	:	6
1936	8		:	—	:	:	:	:	:	-10	-2	-239	—	—	:	:	5
1935	4		:	—	:	:	:	:	:	28	+32	-119	—	—	:	:	6
1934	-19		:	—	:	:	:	:	:	46	+27	-64	—	—	:	:	4
1933	24		:	—	:	:	:	:	:	9	+33	-4	—	—	:	:	-6
1932	38		:	—	:	:	:	:	:	22	+60	+93	—	—	:	:	-3
1931	53		:	—	:	:	:	:	:	1	+54	+141	—	—	:	:	-33
1930	-25		:	—	:	:	:	:	:	6	-19	+373	—	—	:	:	36
1929	88		:	—	:	:	:	:	:	-26	+62	+274	—	—	:	:	-37
1928	87		:	—	:	:	:	:	:	-10	+77	-17	—	—	:	:	-49
1927	16		:	—	:	:	:	:	:	-13	+3	+17	—	—	:	:	7

Series G84-115. Canadian balance of international payments, all countries, capital account,[11] 1927 to 1975, and by major areas, 1946 to 1975 (continued)

(millions of dollars)

Year	Resident holdings of foreign currencies[3,4]		Non-resident holdings of Canadian:							Short-term capital flows					Net official monetary movements[4,9]		
	Chartered bank net foreign currency position with non-residents	Non-bank holdings of foreign currencies abroad	Dollar deposits	Government demand liabilities	Treasury bills	Commercial paper[5,6,7]	Finance company paper[5,7]	Other short-term paper[6] obligations[5,7]	Other finance company obligations[5,7]	Other short-term capital transactions[5,8]	Balance of capital movements in short-term forms	Total net capital balance	Balance settled by exchange transfers	Allocation of special drawing rights	Official international reserves	Official monetary liabilities	Net official monetary movements
	99	100	101	102	103	104	105	106	107	108	109	110	111	112	113	114	115
1975	1,484	-92	78	—	2	41	237	153	-92	-557	+1,254	+4,633	-534	—	-568	—	-568
1974	1,073	172	165	—	9	42	73	-108	148	-684	+890	+2,462	-1,111	—	-165	—	-165
1973	-271	-250	50	—	2	1	-22	167	4	-765	-1,084	-165	+567	—	-429	—	-429
1972	262	-89	8	—	-1	-113	-52	-17	-30	-1,624	-1,656	-597	+1,025	—	291	—	291
1971	1,526	106	26	—	—	37	36	76	-21	-1,267	+519	1,396	-250	—	1,060	—	1,060
							United States[12]										
1970	55	49	44	—	-4	69	128	35	-105	-611	-340	+649	+968	—	1,452	—	1,452
1969	-477	-146	31	—	3	44	190	2	113	-218	-458	+1,211	-578	—	-212	—	-212
1968	-464	-20	24	—	-3	1	-62	10	22	-931	-1,423	-272	+1,500	—	483	-2	481
1967	-197	-69	3	—	-4	-4	-67	7	32	-467	-766	+551	+771	—	-20	—	-20
1966	-517	20	17	-1	-1	3	-33	-1	152	-112	-473	+920	+626	—	-484	—	-484
1965	-519	-20	5	-2	7	-15	-208	13	205	-103	-637	+437	+1,543	—	43	—	43
1964	310	-11	34	-2	-16	-11	196	—	52	141	+693	+1,636	+27	—	28	—	28
1963	-247		31	-1	-23	-23	93	:	35	118	-17	+826	+378	—	56	—	56
1962	140		18	-9	18	:	:	:	121	103	+391	+1,071	+554	—	536	-3	533
1961	127		54	-9	-68	:	:	:	100	158	+362	+1,315	+257	—	231	—	231
1960	-26		1	-13	71	:	:	:	59	136	+228	+974	-346	—	:	:	-39
1959	-135		9	-8	7	:	:	:	64	448	+385	+1,312	-158	—	:	:	-67
1958	-44		27	45	10	:	:	:	26	31	+95	+1,045	+230	—	:	:	108
1957	-284		-7	—	-2	:	:	:	4	268	-21	+942	+533	—	:	:	-104
1956	-216		-24	—	-24	:	:	:	59	62	-143	+891	+793	—	:	:	34
1955	25		42	—	24	:	:	:	23	43	+157	+366	+621	—	:	:	-42
1954	-42		14	—	6	:	:	:	11	-5	-16	+379	+542	—	:	:	121
1953	-63		-1	—	—	:	:	:	-3	-174	-241	+199	+666	—	:	:	-42
1952	-140		-37	—	—	:	:	:	35	-351	-493	-106	+1,016	—	:	:	80
1951	-30		-53	—	—	:	:	:		79	-4	+556	+428	—	:	:	39
1950	26		88	—	—	:	:	:	:	207	+321	+946	+133	—	:	:	694
1949	1		-8	—	—	:	:	:	:	-45	-52	+64	+671	—	:	:	134
1948	—		-14	—	—	:	:	:	:	-1	-15	+111	+778	—	:	:	496
1947	-10		-3	—	—	:	:	:	:	8	-5	-163	+554	—	:	:	-743
1946	-15		27	—	—	:	:	:	:	28	+40	+89	+267	—	:	:	-251

Series G84-115. Canadian balance of international payments, all countries, capital account,[11] 1927 to 1975, and by major areas, 1946 to 1975 (continued)

(millions of dollars)

Year	Resident holdings of foreign currencies[3,4] — Chartered bank net foreign currency position with non-residents	Non-bank holdings of foreign currencies abroad	Non-resident holdings of Canadian: Dollar deposits	Government demand liabilities	Treasury bills	Commercial paper[5,6,7]	Finance company paper[5,7]	Other short-term paper[6] obligations	Other finance company[5,7]	Other short-term capital transactions[5,8]	Balance of capital movements in short-term forms	Total net capital balance	Balance settled by exchange transfers	Allocation of special drawing rights	Official international reserves	Official monetary liabilities	Net official monetary movements
	99	100	101	102	103	104	105	106	107	108	109	110	111	112	113	114	115
1975	-504	-114	93	—	15	—	-1	9	1	4	-497	-330	-285	—	1	..	1
1974	-1,986	1,386	11	—	4	—	1	1	9	11	-563	-628	-75	—	..	..	-1
1973	376	100	-15	—	-1	-1	—	-1	3	-31	431	392	-906	—	-1	—	-1
1972	471	-91	21	—	1	1	—	—	—	91	493	523	-792	—	-1	—	-1
1971	445	-648	10	—	-1	—	-14	-1	1	-31	-237	-150	-296	—	-2	—	-2
1970	-108	-64	-31	—	-3	1	14	1	2	-15	-203	5	-820	—	-83	—	-83
1969	-546	-756	33	—	1	—	-12	-2	3	-16	-1,295	-1,224	+938	—	-22	—	-22
1968	-401	62	4	—	-1	—	-34	-9	-1	-24	-404	-339	+23	—	109	—	109
1967	-337	93	-8	—	2	-11	25	11	3	-44	-266	-253	-253	—	-22	—	-22
1966	75	-65	4	—	1	13	13	—	1	79	121	81	-485	—	21	—	21
1965	536	13	16	—	-1	—	7	1	4	-24	552	493	-1,052	—	-54	—	-54
1964	-579	-2	-11	—	1	—	—	—	—	-40	-631	-628	+78	—	55	—	55
1963		-5	1	—	—	-1	—	..	—	-12	-17	-97	-320	—	-1	—	-1
1962		-37	-12	—	-1	—	—	..	—	-28	-77	-85	-142	—	-1	-1	-2
1961		18	4	—	-3	-3	..	..	—	2	+21	+49	-242	—	2	—	2
1960	-43		13	—	-4	..	..	..	—	13	-21	+61	-230	—	..	..	..
1959	18		3	—	-12	..	..	..	—	-21	-12	+90	-109	—	..	..	-3
1958	9		-4	—	8	..	..	..	—	-20	-25	+144	-240	—	..	..	1
1957	12		-5	..	-12	..	..	..	..	15	+10	+251	-372	—	..	..	-1
1956	6		-7	..	22	..	..	..	..	9	+30	+293	-547	—	..	..	-1
1955	63		6	..	3	..	..	..	..	-51	+21	+160	-494	—	..	..	-2
1954	-32		9	..	1	..	..	..	..	—	-22	+120	-346	—	..	..	3
1953	-14		-12	..	—	..	..	..	..	32	+6	+166	-294	—	..	..	4
1952	-26		-13	..	-3	..	..	..	..	-60	-102	-29	-401	—	..	..	-43
1951	16		-141	..	3	..	..	..	..	40	-82	-12	-194	—	..	..	17
1950	-15		116	..	—	..	..	..	..	-21	+80	+41	-14	—	..	..	28
1949	-3		62	..	—	..	..	..	..	-16	+43	-93	-494	—	..	..	-6
1948	-2		-20	..	—	..	..	..	..	20	-2	+3	-622	—	..	..	-4
1947	2		-4	..	—	..	..	..	..	19	+17	-356	-518	—	..	..	1
1946	—		32	..	—	..	..	..	..	-6	+26	-507	-173	—	..	..	-16

United Kingdom[12]

Series G84-115. Canadian balance of international payments, all countries, capital account,[11] 1927 to 1975, and by major areas, 1946 to 1975 (continued)

(millions of dollars)

Year	99	100	101	102	103	104	105	106	107	108	109	110	111	112	113	114	115
	Resident holdings of foreign currencies[3,4]		Non-resident holdings of Canadian:							Short-term capital flows					Net official monetary movements[4,9]		
	Chartered bank net foreign currency position with non-residents	Non-bank holdings of foreign currencies abroad	Dollar deposits	Government demand liabilities	Treasury bills	Commercial paper[5,6,7]	Finance company paper[5,7]	Other short-term paper[6]	Other finance company obligations[5,7]	Other short-term transactions[5,8]	Balance of capital movements in short-term forms	Total net capital balance	Balance settled by exchange transfers	Allocation of special drawing rights	Official international reserves	Official monetary liabilities	Net official monetary movements
European Economic Community[13]																	
1975	39	-20	64	—	-4	—	-19	-15	-1	-79	-35	+600	-579	—	3	—	3
1974	-95	39	55	—	10	11	20	34	1	123	+198	+170	-121	—	1	—	1
1973	82	-44	28	—	—	—	-1	—	—	36	+101	+218	-81	—	—	—	—
Japan[13]																	
1975	30	-6	3	—	—	—	—	—	—	-32	-5	-34	-974	—	—	—	—
1974	-63	-1	-5	—	—	—	—	—	—	17	-52	-61	-814	—	—	—	—
1973	15	16	8	—	—	—	—	—	—	10	+49	+116	-979	—	—	—	—
Other Organization for Economic Co-operation and Development[13]																	
1975	226	-4	10	—	—	—	—	—	—	8	+240	+711	+4	—	-1	—	-1
1974	791	-6	47	—	—	—	—	3	—	4	+839	+942	-549	—	—	—	—
1973	61	2	-5	—	—	—	—	—	—	-3	+55	+62	+279	—	—	—	—
Other non-resident[13]																	
1975	-787	—	309	-4	24	—	—	—	—	-44	-502	-1,009	+2,368	—	161	—	161
1974	-1,074	—	324	45	54	9	—	—	—	-16	-667	-1,369	+2,670	—	189	—	189
1973	-606	—	77	155	-26	—	—	—	—	-109	-500	-1,186	+1,120	—	-38	—	-38
Other sterling area[13]																	
1972	-321	—	14	—	-4	—	—	—	—	20	-291	-500	+533	—	—	—	—
1971	-351	—	11	—	-4	—	—	—	—	-18	-362	-630	+523	—	—	—	—
1970	-249	—	-4	—	—	—	—	—	—	-11	-256	-391	+266	—	—	—	—
1969	-63	—	-17	—	—	—	—	—	—	-11	-91	-138	+54	—	—	—	—
1968	178	—	19	—	2	—	—	—	—	7	+206	-37	-290	—	—	—	—
1967	80	—	17	—	8	—	—	—	—	-7	+98	+34	-215	—	—	—	—
1966	22	—	3	—	—	—	—	—	—	-10	+15	-53	-16	—	—	—	—
1965	46	-1	-2	—	—	—	—	—	—	4	+47	-16	-122	—	—	—	—
1964	11	1	5	—	—	—	—	—	—	-22	-5	-57	-44	—	—	—	—
1963	1		5	—	—	—	—	—	—	8	+14	-15	+46	—	—	—	—
1962	-13		-2	—	—	—	—	—	—	-6	-21	-65	+48	—	—	—	—
1961	—		3	—	—	—	—	—	—	2	+5	-18	-9	—	—	—	—
1960	7	—	-3	—	—	—	—	—	—	-16	-12	-11	-32	—	—	—	—
1959	-3		-10	—	—	—	—	—	—	-19	-32	-41	+41	—	—	—	—
1958	-8		5	—	—	—	—	—	—	4	+1	-37	-30	—	—	—	—
1957	—		-2	—	—	—	—	—	—	10	+8	-14	+10	—	—	—	—
1956	-5		-2	—	—	—	—	—	—	-7	-14	-38	-10	—	—	—	—
1955	6		3	—	—	..	..	..	..	-3	+6	-24	-36	—	—	—	—
1954	-1		-5	—	—	..	..	..	..	—	-6	-18	-26	—	—	—	—
1953	-2		-4	—	—	..	..	..	..	—	-6	-29	-54	—	—	—	—
1952	1		-9	—	—	..	..	..	..	—	-8	-26	-89	—	—	—	—
1951	—		10	—	—	..	..	..	..	—	+10	+6	+18	—	—	—	—
1950	..		..	—	..	..	..	..	..	—		..	..	—	..	..	..
1949	..		..	—	..	..	..	..	..	—		..	..	—	..	..	..
1948	..		..	—	..	..	..	..	..	—		..	..	—	..	..	..
1947	..		..	—	..	..	..	..	..	—		..	..	—	..	..	..

Series G84-115. Canadian balance of international payments, all countries, capital account,[11] 1927 to 1975, and by major areas, 1946 to 1975 (continued)

(millions of dollars)

Year	Resident holdings of foreign currencies[3,4]		Non-resident holdings of Canadian:							Short-term capital flows					Net official monetary movements[4,9]		
	Chartered bank net holdings of foreign currency position with non-residents	Non-bank holdings of foreign currencies abroad	Dollar deposits	Government demand liabilities	Treasury bills	Commercial paper[5,6,7]	Finance company short-term paper[5,7]	Other short-term paper[6]	Other finance company obligations[5,7]	Other short-term capital transactions[5,8]	Balance of capital movements in short-term forms	Total net capital balance	Balance settled by exchange transfers	Allocation of special drawing rights	Official international reserves	Official monetary liabilities	Net official monetary movements
	99	100	101	102	103	104	105	106	107	108	109	110	111	112	113	114	115
1972	145	-3	57	—	—	-1	2	—	-5	41	+241	1,174	-546	—	—	—	—
1971	-64	-3	30	—	—	1	-61	-2	-5	-24	-128	+111	+133	—	1	-1	1
1970	-256	-17	2	—	-5	-1	61	-1	-6	17	-205	-165	+183	—	—	—	—
1969	58	-39	-1	—	5	-2	-1	-1	—	-43	-24	+633	-230	—	-1	-1	-2
1968	183	2	17	—	-1	1	-36	-3	3	48	+214	+737	-462	—	2	2	2
1967	64	-1	9	—	1	4	-16	6	—	-15	+52	+135	+24	—	-3	3	6
1966	6	-7	-5	—	—	—	4	—	1	-35	-48	-15	+192	—	3	1	1
1965	181	-4	8	—	-1	—	2	—	—	35	+221	+280	-117	—	—	1	1
1964	21	-14	1	—	-1	—	—	—	—	33	+40	+63	+49	—	1	4	5
1963			6	—	1	—	—	...	-2	-7	-5	-9	+104	—	1	3	3
1962	-5		-10	—	-21	...	—	...	-2	6	-27	+84	-2	—	—	—	—
1961	-2		8	—	12	...	...	...	-5	-17	-4	+42	-14	—	2	2	2
1960			20	—	-13	...	...	...	4	22	+29	+162	-155	—	...	...	...
1959	1		-3	—	13	...	...	...	4	64	-49	+123	-7	—	...	...	...
1958	1		2	—	2	...	...	...	-2	1	+4	+103	-142	—	...	...	...
1957	-1		2	—	-6	...	...	...	—	40	+35	+183	-251	—	...	...	...
1956	-1		-2	...	5	...	...	...	5	36	+43	+254	-275	—	...	...	...
1955	-5		9	...	2	...	...	...	—	52	+58	+160	-214	—	...	...	...
1954	-1		3	...	1	...	...	...	-1	4	+6	+84	-190	—	...	...	...
1953			3	...	—	...	...	...	—	11	+15	+98	-267	—	...	...	...
1952			-7	...	2	...	...	...	—	20	+15	+51	-374	—	...	...	...
1951			-10	...	-1	...	...	...	...	—	-11	+38	-252	—	...	...	...
1950			25	...	-3	...	...	...	...	-1	+21	+36	-150	—	...	...	...
1949			-20	...	8	...	...	...	...	3	-9	-13	-165	—	...	...	...
1948			10	...	—	...	...	...	...	—	+10	-46	-172	—	...	...	...
1947			-20	...	—	...	...	...	...	—	-20	-150	-124	—	...	...	...
1946			13	...	1	...	...	...	...	—	+13	-171	-58	—	...	...	...

Other Organization for Economic Co-operation and Development (Europe)[13]

Series G84-115. Canadian balance of international payments, all countries, capital account,[11] 1927 to 1975, and by major areas, 1946 to 1975 (concluded)

(millions of dollars)

Column descriptions (series numbers 99–115):

- **Resident holdings of foreign currencies[3,4]** — 99: Chartered bank net foreign currency position with non-residents; 100: Non-bank holdings of foreign currencies abroad
- **Non-resident holdings of Canadian:** — 101: Dollar deposits; 102: Government demand liabilities; 103: Treasury bills; 104: Commercial paper[5,6,7]; 105: Finance company paper[5,7]; 106: Other short-term paper[6]; 107: Other finance company obligations[5,7]
- **Short-term capital flows** — 108: Other short-term capital transactions[5,8]; 109: Balance of capital movements in short-term forms; 110: Total net capital balance; 111: Balance settled by exchange transfers; 112: Allocation of special drawing rights
- **Net official monetary movements[4,9]** — 113: Official international reserves; 114: Official monetary liabilities; 115: Net official monetary movements

Other non-residents[13]

Year	99	100	101	102	103	104	105	106	107	108	109	110	111	112	113	114	115
1972	80	-6	39	27	26	—	—	—	—	64	+230	+5	-220	117	46	—	46
1971	-151	-6	18	50	2	3	—	—	—	-26	-110	-381	-110	119	-163	—	-163
1970	436	—	7	-7	-67	2	—	—	—	50	+421	+326	-597	133	293	1	294
1969	522	13	6	-34	11	—	—	—	—	-5	+513	+500	-184	—	297	—	297
1968	16	-5	8	21	51	—	-6	—	—	93	+184	+223	-771	—	-239	-1	-240
1967	6	-1	3	-4	-3	—	15	—	—	-9	-14	+80	-327	—	56	—	56
1966	-41	-1	-8	6	-15	—	—	-11	—	15	-40	-130	-317	—	103	—	103
1965	182	1	4	4	7	—	37	11	—	26	+272	+94	-252	—	168	—	168
1964	-66	—	-1	2	—	—	—	—	—	6	-59	-226	-110	—	213	63	276
1963		-3		2	-4	..	..	..	..	59	+54	-39	-208	—	—	86	86
1962		-2	-4	5	7	..	..	..	..	20	+30	-21	-458	—	-228	-149	-377
1961		-1	-36	7	1	..	..	..	..	-65	-94	-168	+8	—	61	—	61
1960		2	48	1	2	..	..	..	..	-12	+41	+8	+71	..	..	..	—
1959		—	11	—	6	..	..	..	..	-12	+5	-8	+233	..	..	..	59
1958		2	9	—	1	..	..	..	..	6	+18	-9	+182	..	..	..	—
1957		-1	-3	—	2	..	..	..	..	-4	-6	-16	+80	..	..	..	—
1956		—	5	—	—	..	..	..	..	9	+14	+20	+39	..	..	..	15
1955		2	6	-9	—	..	..	..	..	-6	-13	-19	+123	..	..	..	—
1954		1	-8	-15	-2	..	..	..	..	-5	-13	-17	+20	..	..	..	—
1953		-1	4	-11	2	..	..	..	..	9	-13	-24	-51	..	..	..	—
1952		—		-5		..	..	..	..	-14	-17	-40	-152	..	..	..	—
1951		—		-8		..	..	..	..	-7	-11	-20	—	..	..	..	—
1950		—	6	-4	—	..	..	..	..	7	+9	+18	+31	..	..	..	—
1949		—	-1	—	—	..	..	..	..	-1	-2	-7	-12	..	..	..	—
1948		—	3	—	—	..	..	..	..	2	+5	-27	+16	..	..	..	—
1947		—	1	33	—	..	..	..	..	-22	+12	-48	+88	..	..	..	74
1946		—	-1	25	—	..	..	..	..	-17	+7	-40	-36	..	..	..	1

1 Excludes undistributed profits, (except undistributed after-tax earnings of branches of foreign firms as well as stock dividends by wholly-owned subsidiaries to their parents). Also excludes investment in commercial real estate.

2 Includes common and preferred stocks from 1927 to 1936 and from 1946 to 1951.

3 Bank balances and other short-term funds abroad (excluding official reserves).

4 Canada's official monetary movements were revised from 1961 in accordance with the definition as detailed in the press statement of the Minister of Finance dated 3 February, 1970. All "convertible" currency deposits are, as of 1961, included with the official international reserves.

5 Canadian commercial and finance company paper and other finance company obligations included with other short-term capital transactions until 1951.

6 Other short-term paper included with Canadian commercial paper for 1963.

7 Other Canadian finance company obligations include Canadian commercial and finance company paper between 1952 and 1962.

8 Includes balancing item representing difference between recorded measures of current, capital and reserve movements and embodies all unidentified transactions.

9 For years 1926 to 1939 includes only monetary gold movements and from its establishment in 1935, holdings of foreign currencies by the Bank of Canada.

10 Series F91-103 in the first edition of Historical Statistics of Canada are the definitive series for the period 1927 to 1937. Figures shown here for these years are simply reconstructions to provide a continuous series from 1927 to 1975. Some users may prefer the previously published series for these years.

11 A minus sign in accounts for capital movements indicates an outflow of capital from Canada and represents an increase in holdings of assets abroad or a reduction in liabilities to non-residents.

12 For subdivision of the capital account into United Kingdom, United States and other countries for the years 1927 to 1937, see series F91-103 in the first edition of Historical Statistics of Canada. For the years 1938 to 1945, see following table in this volume.

13 In addition to the United States and United Kingdom, the geographical dissection introduced in 1973 consists of the European Economic Community, Japan, other Organization for Economic Co-operation and Development and all other countries; the former categories of Organization for Economic Co-operation and Development, Europe and other sterling area were discontinued.

Series G116-151. Canadian balance of international payments, all countries and by major areas, capital account, 1938 to 1945

(millions of dollars)

Year	New issues of Canadian securities	Retirement of Canadian securities	Net new issues or net retirements	Net sales of outstanding securities	Canadian government loans to other countries[1] War loans	Canadian government loans to other countries[1] Post-war loans	Change in reserves of gold and United States dollars increase (-)	Change in sterling balances increase (-)	Other capital movements	Net movement of capital	Current account balance[2]	Balancing item
	116	117	118	119	120	121	122	123	124	125	126	127

All countries

Year	116	117	118	119	120	121	122	123	124	125	126	127
1945	+91	-211	-120	+351	+64	-105	-667	-1	-215[1]	-693	+688	+5
1944	+92	-200	-108	+198	+57	—	-278	+4	+79	-48	+58	-10
1943	+146	-322	-176	+272	+18	—	-364		-427	-677	+688	-11
1942	—	-351	-351	+148	-700	—	-144	+818	+123	-106	+99	+7
1941	—	-229	-229	+38	—	—	+160	-728	+262	-497	+491	+6
1940	—	-191	-191	+5	—	—	+79	-82	+1	-188	+149	+39
1939	+155	-251	-96	+82	—	—	..	..	-122	-136	+126	+10
1938	+89	-151	-62	+29	—	—	..	..	-73	-106	+100	+6

Year	Redemption of securities	Net purchase of securities	Other capital (net)	Repatriation of securities	War loans to United Kingdom	Investment in fixed production assets	Change in sterling balances decrease (+)	Special payments and adjustments	Net capital movements	Special receipts of convertible exchange[3]	Balancing item[4]	Total[2]
	128	129	130	131	132	133	134	135	136	137	138	139

United Kingdom and other Commonwealth countries[5]

Year	Private transactions 128	129	130	Capital debit or credits (+) official transactions 131	132	133	134	135	136	137	138	139
1945	-31	-41	-16	-1	+64	—	-1	-324[6]	-350	-33	+1	-382
1945	-32	-27	+61	-2	+57	-2	+4	-57	+2	-55	+8	-45
1943	-10	-26	-33	-4	+18	-205	—	-306[7]	-566	-143	-4	-713
1942	-30	-8	-13	-296	-700	+58	+818	-74	-245	-23	-1	-269
1941	-10	-36	-4	-188	—	+157	-728	—	-809	—	+4	-805
1940	-13	-28	-54	-137	—	+100	-82	—	-214	-248	+43	-419
1939	-45	-5	+42	-75	—	—	—	—	-83	-2	—[4]	—
1938	-21	-12	-26	—	—	—	—	—	-59	—	—[4]	—

Year	New issues of Canadian securities	Retirement of Canadian securities	Net new issues (+) or net retirements (-)	Net sales (+) or net purchases (-) of outstanding securities Canadian securities	Net sales (+) or net purchases (-) of outstanding securities Foreign securities	Net change in reserves of gold and United States dollars decline (+) or increase (-)	Export credits and interim advances	Other capital movements and adjusting entries (net)	Net capital movements above	Special receipts of convertible exchange[3]	Balancing item[4]	Total[2]
	140	141	142	143	144	145	146	147	148	149	150	151

Non-Commonwealth countries

Year	140	141	142	143	144	145	146	147	148	149	150	151
1945	+91	-179	-88	+296	+96	-667	-105	+125	-343	+33	+4	-306
1944	+92	-166	-74	+183	+42	-278	—	+77	-50	+55	-18	-13
1943	+146	-308	-162	+254	+44	-364	—	+117	-111	+143	-7	+25
1942	—	-25	-25[8]	+132	+24	-144	—	+152	+139	+23	+8	+170
1941	—	-31	-31[8]	+46	+28	+160	—	+109	+312	—	+2	+314
1940	—	-41	-41	+15	+18	+79	—	-45	+26	+248	-4	+270
1939	+155	-131	+24	+69	+18	—[9]	—	-164	-53	+2	—[4]	—
1938	+38	-79	-41	+48	-7	—[9]	—	-47	-47	—	—[4]	—

[1] Excluding interim advances to sterling area in 1945 of $209 million which is included in 'Other capital movements'.

[2] The current account balances shown here differ from those shown in series F71 and F116 in the original volume of Historical Statistics of Canada. Mutual aid and 1942 contributions as well as United Nations Relief and Rehabilitation Association, military and other official relief (series F114, 115, 127 and 140 to 142 in the original volume), which were previously treated as capital account items, have now been treated as transfer payments, thereby reducing the current account balances. Correspondingly, the capital account balances, series G139 and 151, are also reduced from the balances shown under series F130 and F145.

[3] This represents gold and United States dollars received from the United Kingdom in part settlement of her deficiency with Canada, and used in turn to settle part of Canada's deficiency with the United States.

[4] Reflecting multilateral settlements up to the introduction of exchange control and thereafter, errors and omissions.

[5] Transactions with the sterling area are covered from 1940 to 1945.

[6] Includes $209 million interim advances, most of which were cancelled in the 1946 financial settlement with the United Kingdom.

[7] Including $190 million repayment of working capital.

[8] Excluding refunding issues.

[9] Available data included in other capital movements.

Series G152–187. Canada's balance of international indebtedness, selected year ends, 1926 to 1974
(billions of dollars)

Year	Direct invest-ment	Portfolio invest-ment	Miscel-laneous invest-ment	Govern-ment of Canada credits	Govern-ment of Canada subscrip-tions to inter-national financial agencies	Total Canadian long-term invest-ments abroad	Private short-term holdings of foreign exchange	Assets in U.S.	Assets in U.K.	Assets in other countries	Sub-total[1]	Net official monetary assets	Short-term receiv-ables n.e.s.	Gross assets
	152	153	154	155	156	157	158	159	160	161	162	163	164	165
1974	9.3	3.9	2.9	2.1	0.6	18.8	2.7	8.4	4.6	8.5	21.5	5.8	10.2	37.5
1973	7.8	3.7	2.2	1.8	0.5	16.0	2.9	8.4	3.9	6.6	18.9	5.8	8.4	33.1
1972	6.7	3.3	1.8	1.7	0.4	13.9	2.3	7.2	4.0	5.0	16.2	6.0	7.2	29.4
1971	6.5	3.0	1.4	1.6	0.3	12.8	2.7	7.1	4.4	4.0	15.5	5.6	5.5	26.6
1970	6.2	2.8	1.0	1.5	0.3	11.8	3.6	8.6	4.1	2.6	15.3	4.7	3.8	23.9
1969	5.2	3.0	0.8	1.4	0.2	10.7	3.6	8.6	4.1	1.5	14.2	3.3	3.2	20.8
1968	4.6	2.9	0.8	1.4	0.2	9.9	2.2	7.5	2.8	1.8	12.1	3.3	2.9	18.2
1967	4.0	2.6	0.8	1.4	0.2	9.0	1.7	6.4	2.3	2.0	10.7	2.9	1.9	15.5
1966	3.7	2.2	0.8	1.4	0.2	8.3	1.4	5.7	2.2	1.8	9.7	2.9	1.3	13.9
1965	3.5	1.9	0.6	1.5	0.1	7.6	0.8	4.8	2.2	1.5	8.5	3.3	1.2	12.9
1964	3.3	1.8	0.5	1.5	0.1	7.2	1.2	4.2	2.6	1.6	8.4	3.1	1.0	12.5
1963	3.1	1.7	0.3[4]	1.3	0.1	6.4	0.8[4]	4.1[4]	1.9[4]	1.2[4]	7.2	2.8	0.9[4]	10.9
1962	2.8	1.6	0.2	1.3	0.1	6.1	1.8	4.0	1.6	1.5	7.1	2.6	0.5	10.1
1961	2.6	1.4	0.1	1.4	0.1	5.7	1.1[4]	3.8	1.5	1.4	6.7	2.4[4]	0.5	9.6
1960	2.5	1.3	—	1.5	0.1	5.3	1.2	3.7	1.5	1.3	6.5	2.0	0.5	8.9
1959	2.3	1.2	—	1.5	0.1	5.0	1.0	3.3	1.4	1.3	6.0	1.9	0.5	8.5
1958	2.1	1.1	-0.1	1.5	0.1	4.8	1.0	3.1	1.4	1.3	5.8	2.0	0.5	8.2
1957	2.1	1.1	-0.1	1.6	0.1	4.7	0.9	3.0	1.4	1.2	5.6	1.9	0.4	7.9
1956	1.9	1.0	—	1.6	0.1	4.5	0.6	2.6	1.4	1.1	5.1	2.0	0.4	7.5
1955	1.7	1.0	-0.1	1.6	0.1	4.4	0.4	2.3	1.4	1.1	4.8	2.0	0.3	7.1
1954	1.6	0.9	-0.1	1.7	0.1	4.3	0.5	2.2	1.5	1.0	4.7	2.0	0.3	6.9
1953	1.5	0.9	-0.1	1.8	0.1	4.1	0.4	2.0	1.5	1.1	4.6	1.9	0.2	6.6
1952	1.3	0.8	-0.1	1.9	0.1	4.0	0.3	1.8	1.5	1.1	4.4	1.9	0.3	6.4
1951	1.2	0.6	-0.1	1.9	0.1	3.7	0.1	1.4	1.5	1.0	3.9	1.9	0.2	6.0
1950	1.0	0.6	—	2.0	0.1	3.7	0.1	1.2	1.6	0.9	3.7	2.0	0.2	5.9
1949	0.9	0.6	—	2.0	0.1	3.7	0.1	1.3	1.6	0.9	3.8	1.3	0.2	5.3
1948	0.8	0.6	—	1.9	0.1	3.4	0.1	1.0	1.5	1.0	3.5	1.1	0.1	4.7
1947	0.8	0.6	—	1.8	0.1	3.3	0.1	1.0	1.5	1.0	3.5	0.6	0.2	4.1
1946	0.8	0.6	—	1.4	—	2.7	0.1	0.9	1.2	0.7	2.8	1.3	0.1	4.2
1945	0.7	0.6	—	0.7	—	2.0	0.1	1.0	0.7	0.5	2.2	1.7	0.1	4.0
1939	0.7	0.7	—	—	—	1.4	—	0.9	0.1	0.4	1.4	0.5	..	1.9[6]
1933	0.4	0.9	—	—	—	1.3	—	0.8	—	0.6	1.4	—	..	1.4[6]
1930	0.4	0.8	—	—	—	1.3	—	0.9	0.1	0.5	1.5	—	..	1.5[6]
1926	0.4	0.5	—	—	—	0.9	—	0.7	0.1	0.5	1.3	—	..	1.3[6]

Series G152-187. Canada's balance of international indebtedness, selected year ends, 1926 to 1974 (continued)
(billions of dollars)

Year							Canada's liabilities							
	Direct invest-ment	Govern-ment bonds	Other portfolio invest-ment	Miscel-laneous invest-ment	Total non-resident long-term invest-ment in Canada	Equity of non-residents in Canadian assets abroad	Official SDR liabil-ities	Non-resident holdings of Canadian dollars	Geographical distribution				Short-term payables n.e.s.	Gross liabil-ities
									Liabil-ities to U.S.	Liabil-ities to U.K.	Liabil-ities to other countries[2]	Sub-total[3]		
	166	**167**	**168**	**169**	**170**	**171**	**172**	**173**	**174**	**175**	**176**	**177**	**178**	**179**
1974	36.2	11.4	9.1	3.5	60.2	3.4	0.4	2.1	49.8	5.8	10.4	66.0	6.8	72.8
1973	32.8	9.9	8.6	3.3	54.6	3.1	0.4	1.3	44.9	5.4	9.1	59.4	5.3	64.7
1972	29.6	9.4	7.8	3.2	50.0	2.6	0.4	1.1	41.1	4.9	8.1	54.1	4.8	58.9
1971	27.9	8.1	7.1	3.1	46.2	3.0	0.3	1.0	39.1	4.7	6.7	50.5	4.6	55.1
1970	26.4	7.9	6.9	2.9	44.0	2.7	0.1	0.8	37.4	4.3	6.0	47.7	4.3	52.1
1969	24.4	7.8	6.8	2.7	41.6	2.3	—	0.9	35.2	4.2	5.4	44.7	4.0	48.8
1968	22.5	6.8	6.1	2.6	38.0	2.0	—	0.8	32.4	4.0	4.4	40.7	3.7	44.4
1967	20.7	5.8	5.8	2.4	34.7	1.8	—	0.7	29.7	3.8	3.6	37.1	3.6	40.8
1966	19.0	5.2	5.7	2.3	32.1	1.6	—	0.6	27.4	3.8	3.2	34.4	3.6	37.9
1965	17.4	5.0	5.1	2.2	29.6	1.6	—	0.6	25.1	3.7	3.1	31.9	3.4	35.3
1964	16.0[4]	4.7	4.8	2.1	27.5	1.5	—	0.6	23.2[4]	3.6	2.8	29.6	3.3[5]	32.9
1963	15.5	4.2	4.7	1.8	26.2	1.4	—	0.6	22.1	3.5	2.6	28.2	2.3	30.5
1962	14.7	3.7	4.7	1.8	24.9	1.3	—	0.6	20.6	3.6	2.6	26.8	2.0	28.8
1961	13.7	3.4	4.7	1.7	23.6	1.2	—	0.6	19.3	3.5	2.5	25.4	1.9	27.3
1960	12.9	3.3	4.6	1.4	22.2	1.1	—	0.6	18.0	3.5	2.4	24.0	1.6	25.6
1959	11.9	3.1	4.6	1.3	20.9	1.0	—	0.5	17.0	3.4	2.1	22.4	1.4	23.8
1958	10.9	2.6	4.4	1.1	19.0	0.9	—	0.5	15.5	3.2	1.7	20.4	1.1	21.5
1957	10.1	2.3	4.1	0.9	17.5	0.8	—	0.4	14.1	3.1	1.5	18.7	1.0	19.6
1956	8.9	2.1	3.8	0.8	15.6	0.8	—	0.4	12.6	2.9	1.3	16.8	0.7	17.5
1955	7.7	1.9	3.3	0.6	13.5	0.7	—	0.4	11.1	2.5	1.0	14.6	0.5	15.2
1954	6.8	2.1	3.2	0.6	12.6	0.6	—	0.4	10.3	2.3	0.9	13.6	0.4	14.0
1953	6.0	2.1	2.9	0.5	11.5	0.6	—	0.4	9.5	2.2	0.7	12.4	0.4	12.7
1952	5.2	2.0	2.7	0.4	10.4	0.4	—	0.4	8.5	2.0	0.7	11.2	0.5	11.7
1951	4.5	2.1	2.5	0.3	9.5	0.4	—	0.5	7.9	1.9	0.5	10.3	0.9	11.3
1950	4.0	2.0	2.4	0.3	8.7	0.3	—	0.6	7.1	2.0	0.5	9.6	0.8	10.4
1949	3.6	1.8	2.3	0.3	8.0	0.3	—	0.4	6.4	1.8	0.5	8.7	0.6	9.3
1948	3.3	1.6	2.3	0.3	7.5	0.3	—	0.4	6.0	1.7	0.5	8.2	0.6	8.8
1947	3.0	1.5	2.4	0.3	7.2	0.3	—	0.4	5.7	1.7	0.5	7.9	0.6	8.5
1946	2.8	1.6	2.5	0.3	7.2	0.3	—	0.4	5.7	1.7	0.4	7.8	0.6	8.4
1945	2.7	1.7	2.4	0.3	7.1	0.2	—	0.3	5.4	1.8	0.4	7.6	0.6	8.2
1939	2.3	1.7	2.6	0.3	6.9	0.2	—	0.3	4.5	2.6	0.3	7.4	..	7.4[6]
1933	2.4	1.7	3.0	0.3	7.4	..	..	..	4.7	2.8	0.2	7.7	..	7.7[6]
1930	2.4	1.7	3.2	0.3	7.6	..	..	..	4.9	2.9	0.2	8.0	..	8.0[6]
1926	1.8	1.4	2.5	0.3	6.0	..	..	..	3.5	2.7	0.2	6.4	..	6.4[6]

Series G152-187. Canada's balance of international indebtedness, selected year ends, 1926 to 1974 (concluded)
(billions of dollars)

Year	Canada's international indebtedness							
	Net indebt- edness	Geographical distribution				Net liabilities not distributed geographically		
		Net liabil- ities to U.S.	Net liabil- ities to U.K.	Net liabil- ities to other countries	Sub- total	Net official monetary assets	Net short- term liabil- ities	Sub- total
	180	181	182	183	184	185	186	187
1974	35.3	41.4	1.2	1.9	44.5	-5.8	-3.4	-9.2
1973	31.6	36.5	1.5	2.5	40.5	-5.8	-3.1	-8.9
1972	29.5	33.9	0.9	3.1	37.9	-6.0	-2.4	-8.4
1971	28.5	32.0	0.3	2.7	35.0	-5.6	-0.9	-6.5
1970	28.2	28.9	0.2	3.3	32.4	-4.7	0.5	-4.2
1969	28.0	26.6	0.1	3.8	30.5	-3.3	0.9	-2.4
1968	26.2	24.9	1.2	2.6	28.7	-3.3	0.8	-2.5
1967	25.3	23.4	1.5	1.6	26.5	-2.9	1.8	-1.1
1966	24.0	21.7	1.6	1.4	24.7	-2.9	2.3	-0.6
1965	22.4	20.3	1.6	1.6	23.5	-3.3	2.2	-1.1
1964	20.4	19.0	1.1	1.2	21.3	-3.1	2.2	-0.9
1963	19.6	18.0[4]	1.6[4]	1.4[4]	21.0	-2.8	1.4	-1.4
1962	18.7	16.7	2.0	1.1	19.8	-2.6	1.6	-1.0
1961	17.7	15.5	2.0	1.1	18.6	-2.4	1.4	-1.0
1960	16.6	14.3	2.0	1.1	17.4	-2.0	1.1	-0.9
1959	15.3	13.6	1.9	0.8	16.3	-1.9	1.0	-0.9
1958	13.3	12.4	1.8	0.4	14.6	-2.0	0.6	-1.4
1957	11.8	11.1	1.6	0.3	13.0	-1.9	0.6	-1.3
1956	10.1	10.1	1.4	0.2	11.7	-2.0	0.3	-1.7
1955	8.0	8.7	1.1	-0.1	9.7	-2.0	0.2	-1.8
1954	7.0	8.2	0.8	-0.2	8.8	-2.0	0.1	-1.9
1953	6.1	7.5	0.7	-0.3	7.9	-1.9	0.1	-1.8
1952	5.3	6.7	0.5	-0.3	6.9	-1.9	0.3	-1.6
1951	5.3	6.5	0.4	-0.5	6.4	-1.9	0.7	-1.2
1950	4.5	5.9	0.4	-0.4	5.9	-2.0	0.6	-1.4
1949	4.0	5.1	0.2	-0.4	4.9	-1.3	0.4	-0.9
1948	4.1	5.0	0.2	-0.5	4.7	-1.1	0.5	-0.6
1947	4.3	4.7	0.2	-0.5	4.4	-0.6	0.4	-0.2
1946	4.2	4.8	0.5	-0.3	5.0	-1.3	0.4	-0.9
1945	4.2	4.4	1.1	-0.1	5.4	-1.7	0.4	-1.3
1939	5.5[7]	3.6	2.5	-0.1	6.0	-0.5	..	..
1933	6.3[7]	3.9	2.8	-0.4	6.3	—	..	..
1930	6.5[7]	4.0	2.8	-0.3	6.5	—	..	..
1926	5.1[7]	2.8	2.6	-0.3	5.1	—	..	..

[1] Excludes net official monetary assets and short-term receivables not distributed geographically.
[2] Includes international financial agencies.
[3] Excludes short-term payables not distributed geographically.
[4] New series not strictly comparable with earlier series.

[5] At the end of 1964, about $450 million previously classified as long-term investment was shown as part of short-term finance company obligations.
[6] Excludes short-term receivables and payables.
[7] Net external assets of the chartered banks in Canada amounted to $370 million in 1926, $180 million in 1930 and $91 million in 1933.

Series G188-202. Estimates of foreign capital invested in Canada, selected year ends, 1900 to 1974
(millions of dollars)

Year	Total non-resident investment			Percentage of total non-resident investment			Investment by residents of the United States			Investment by residents of the United Kingdom			Investment by residents of other countries		
	Direct	Port-folio[1]	Total	United States	United Kingdom	Other countries	Direct	Port-folio[1]	Total	Direct	Port-folio[1]	Total	Direct	Port-folio[1]	Total
	188	189	190	191	192	193	194	195	196	197	198	199	200	201	202
1974	36,237	23,952	60,189	77	9	14	28,996	17,679	46,675	3,525	1,805	5,330	3,716	4,468	8,184
1973	32,805	21,805	54,610	77	9	14	26,113	16,037	42,150	3,151	1,841	4,992	3,541	3,927	7,468
1972	29,605	20,409	50,014	77	9	14	23,679	15,020	38,699	2,821	1,728	4,549	3,105	3,661	6,766
1971	27,918	18,332	46,250	79	9	12	22,443	13,895	36,338	2,715	1,606	4,321	2,760	2,831	5,591
1970	26,358	17,679	44,037	79	9	12	21,403	13,511	34,914	2,503	1,518	4,021	2,452	2,650	5,102
1969	24,424	17,178	41,602	80	9	11	19,959	13,086	33,045	2,426	1,399	3,825	2,039	2,693	4,732
1968	22,534	15,445	37,979	80	10	10	18,510	11,999	30,509	2,310	1,396	3,706	1,714	2,050	3,764
1967	20,699	14,003	34,702	81	10	9	17,000	11,030	28,030	2,152	1,424	3,576	1,547	1,549	3,096
1966	19,008	13,082	32,090	80	11	9	15,570	10,153	25,723	2,046	1,472	3,518	1,392	1,457	2,849
1965	17,356	12,247	29,603	79	12	9	14,059	9,330	23,389	2,033	1,479	3,512	1,264	1,438	2,702
1964	15,961	11,513	27,474	78	13	9	12,959	8,599	21,558	1,933	1,527	3,460	1,069	1,387	2,456
1963	15,502	10,703	26,205	78	13	9	12,785	7,752	20,537	1,761	1,587	3,348	956	1,364	2,320
1962	14,660	10,230	24,890	77	14	9	12,006	7,149	19,155	1,706	1,693	3,399	948	1,388	2,336
1961	13,737	9,872	23,609	76	14	10	11,284	6,717	18,001	1,613	1,768	3,381	840	1,387	2,227
1960	12,872	9,342	22,214	75	15	10	10,549	6,169	16,718	1,535	1,824	3,359	788	1,349	2,137
1959	11,906	8,951	20,857	76	15	9	9,912	5,914	15,826	1,384	1,815	3,199	610	1,222	1,832
1958	10,880	8,130	19,010	76	16	8	9,045	5,396	14,441	1,296	1,792	3,088	539	942	1,481
1957	10,129	7,335	17,464	76	17	7	8,472	4,792	13,264	1,163	1,754	2,917	494	789	1,283
1956	8,868	6,759	15,627	76	17	7	7,392	4,418	11,810	1,048	1,650	2,698	428	691	1,119
1955	7,728	5,799	13,527	76	18	6	6,513	3,782	10,295	890	1,494	2,384	325	523	848
1954	6,764	5,833	12,597	77	17	6	5,787	3,897	9,684	759	1,446	2,205	218	490	708
1953	6,003	5,458	11,461	77	18	5	5,206	3,664	8,870	612	1,396	2,008	185	398	583
1952	5,218	5,167	10,385	77	18	5	4,530	3,467	7,997	544	1,342	1,886	144	358	502
1951	4,520	4,957	9,477	76	19	5	3,896	3,363	7,259	497	1,281	1,778	127	313	440
1950	3,975	4,689	8,664	76	20	4	3,426	3,123	6,549	468	1,282	1,750	81	284	365
1949	3,586	4,377	7,963	74	22	4	3,095	2,811	5,906	428	1,289	1,717	63	277	340
1948	3,270	4,239	7,509	74	22	4	2,807	2,760	5,567	400	1,210	1,610	63	269	332
1947	2,986	4,205	7,191	72	23	5	2,548	2,653	5,201	372	1,275	1,647	66	277	343
1946	2,826	4,355	7,181	72	23	5	2,428	2,730	5,158	335	1,335	1,670	63	290	353
1945	2,713	4,379	7,092	70	25	5	2,304	2,686	4,990	348	1,402	1,750	61	291	352
1939	2,296	4,617	6,913	60	36	4	1,881	2,270	4,151	366	2,110	2,476	49	237	286
1933	2,352	5,013	7,365	61	36	3	1,933	2,559	4,492	376	2,307	2,683	43	147	190
1930	2,427	5,187	7,614	61	36	3	1,993	2,667	4,660	392	2,374	2,766	42	146	188
1926	1,782	4,221	6,003	53	44	3	1,403	1,793	3,196	336	2,301	2,637	43	127	170
1926[2]	—	—	5,966	58	40	2	—	—	3,465	—	—	2,355	—	—	146
1925[2]	—	—	5,714	56	41	3	—	—	3,219	—	—	2,346	—	—	149
1924[2]	—	—	5,616	55	42	3	—	—	3,094	—	—	2,372	—	—	150
1923[2]	—	—	5,414	52	46	3	—	—	2,794	—	—	2,471	—	—	149
1922[2]	—	—	5,207	50	47	3	—	—	2,593	—	—	2,464	—	—	150
1921[2]	—	—	4,906	46	51	3	—	—	2,260	—	—	2,494	—	—	152
1920[2]	—	—	4,870	44	53	3	—	—	2,128	—	—	2,577	—	—	165
1919[2]	—	—	4,637	39	57	4	—	—	1,818	—	—	2,645	—	—	174
1918[2]	—	—	4,536	36	60	4	—	—	1,630	—	—	2,729	—	—	177
1917[2]	—	—	4,493	35	61	4	—	—	1,577	—	—	2,739	—	—	177
1916[2]	—	—	4,323	30	66	4	—	—	1,307	—	—	2,840	—	—	176
1915[2]	—	—	4,017	27	69	4	—	—	1,070	—	—	2,772	—	—	175
1914[2]	—	—	3,837	23	72	5	—	—	881	—	—	2,778	—	—	178
1913[2]	—	—	3,529	22	73	5	—	—	780	—	—	2,569	—	—	180
1913[3]	—	—	3,746	21	75	5	—	—	780	—	—	2,793	—	—	173
1912[3]	—	—	3,199	20	76	4	—	—	645	—	—	2,417	—	—	137
1911[3]	—	—	2,878	20	77	4	—	—	563	—	—	2,203	—	—	112
1910[3]	—	—	2,529	19	77	3	—	—	487	—	—	1,958	—	—	84
1909[3]	—	—	2,216	19	78	3	—	—	414	—	—	1,740	—	—	62
1908[3]	—	—	1,963	19	78	3	—	—	378	—	—	1,527	—	—	58
1907[3]	—	—	1,741	20	77	3	—	—	345	—	—	1,346	—	—	50
1906[3]	—	—	1,646	19	78	3	—	—	319	—	—	1,280	—	—	46
1905[3]	—	—	1,540	19	79	2	—	—	290	—	—	1,212	—	—	38
1904[3]	—	—	1,428	18	80	2	—	—	258	—	—	1,135	—	—	35
1903[3]	—	—	1,366	17	81	2	—	—	232	—	—	1,106	—	—	28
1902[3]	—	—	1,311	16	82	2	—	—	209	—	—	1,077	—	—	25
1901[3]	—	—	1,269	15	84	1	—	—	186	—	—	1,065	—	—	18
1900[3]	—	—	1,232	14	85	1	—	—	168	—	—	1,050	—	—	14

[1] Including miscellaneous investments.
[2] Estimated by F.A. Knox, 'Excursus', Table A, p. 299.
[3] Estimated by Jacob Viner, *Canada's Balance*.

Series G203-226. Foreign long-term investment in Canada, all countries and by major areas, by type of investment, selected year ends, 1926 to 1974

(millions of dollars)

Year	Government securities				Manufacturing									
	Government of Canada	Provincial	Municipal	Total government	Vegetable products	Animal products	Textiles	Wood and paper products	Iron and products	Non-ferrous metals	Non-metallic minerals[1]	Chemicals and allied products	Miscellaneous manufactures	Total manufacturing
	203	204	205	206	207	208	209	210	211	212	213	214	215	216
	Owned by all non-residents													
1974	550	9.281	1,588	11.419	1,875	388	402	3,540	4.958	2.069	789	2.364	323	16.708
1973	639	7.926	1,348	9.913	1,632	346	336	3.272	4.421	1.967	721	2.064	280	15.039
1972	666	7.234	1,497	9.397	1.471	288	303	3.170	4.024	1.776	610	1.874	255	13.771
1971	577	6.068	1,445	8.090	1.359	294	277	3.141	3.681	1.622	510	1.808	269	12.961
1970	603	5.806	1,529	7.938	1.265	274	250	2.882	3.482	1.724	486	1.692	261	12.316
1969	758	5.432	1,572	7.762	1.146	273	237	2.654	3.344	1.649	484	1.612	240	11.639
1968	779	4.552	1,491	6.822	1.063	249	210	2.416	2.965	1.569	420	1.544	195	10.631
1967	556	3.819	1,438	5.813	989	239	195	2.296	2.726	1.576	389	1.436	171	10.017
1966	649	3.171	1.333	5.153	911	228	180	2.195	2.445	1.428	358	1,378	156	9.279
1965	880	2.828	1.253	4.961	889	198	166	1.907	2.226	1.301	311	1.232	150	8.380
1964	897	2.564	1.221	4.682	830	169	150	1.722	1.970	1.191	319	1.095	134	7.580
1963	899	2.217	1.091	4.207	833	161	146	1.549	1.810	1.213	319	943	123	7.097
1962	788	1.862	1.087	3.737	787	149	142	1.464	1.742	1.211	310	810	116	6.731
1961	657	1.743	1.038	3.438	749	145	148	1.410	1.647	1.185	286	768	108	6.446
1960	611	1.632	1.026	3.269	720	132	141	1.315	1.580	1.155	276	698	98	6.115
1959	612	1.585	915	3.112	664	128	140	1.211	1.451	1.153	227	660	92	5.726
1958	564	1.276	781	2.621	608	114	135	1.200	1.312	1.103	207	617	85	5.381
1957	501	1.165	660	2.326	577	108	128	1.166	1.198	1.031	179	582	82	5.051
1956	502	1.081	552	2.135	524	103	128	1.081	1.083	895	170	527	68	4.579
1955	529	888	452	1,869	483	103	122	968	894[2]	783	136	477	59[2]	4.025
1954	659	964	433	2.056	443	97	120	939	722	727	126	430	117	3.721
1953	744	930	413	2.087	424	89	115	840	699	694	111	366	93	3.431
1952	858	816	354	2.028	380	83	117	772	623	599	538	339	87	3.538
1951	1.013	771	319	2.103	366	74	117	718	530	463	80	297	70	2.715
1950	1.141	565	256	1.962	338	71	111	658	505	385	364	263	62	2.757
1949	975	534	246	1.755	320	67	98	638	443	344	324	249	59	2.542
1948	823	528	248	1.599	320	58	96	562	407	321	275	229	52	2.320
1947	713	551	264	1.528	290	62	88	505	361	293	185	203	45	2.032
1946	750	594	267	1.611	272	59	84	481	332	277	167	186	40	1.898
1945	726	624	312	1.662	268	61	83	455	319	274	57	169	37	1.723
1939	823	536	344	1.703	206	56	59	451	232	146	135	137	23	1.445
1933	752	572	394	1.718	209	53	48	496	210	118	135	130	23	1.422
1930	682	592	432	1.706	208	50	49	586	262	125	24	122	33	1.459
1926	638	422	374	1.434	150	27	40	390	265	94	116	79	37	1.198

Series G203-226. Foreign long-term investment in Canada, all countries and by major areas, by type of investment, selected year ends, 1926 to 1974 (continued)
(millions of dollars)

Year	Government securities				Manufacturing									
	Government of Canada	Provincial	Municipal	Total government	Vegetable products	Animal products	Textiles	Wood and paper products	Iron and products	Non-ferrous metals	Non-metallic minerals[1]	Chemicals and allied products	Miscellaneous products	Total manufacturing
	203	204	205	206	207	208	209	210	211	212	213	214	215	216
Owned in United States														
1974	303	7.026	1.189	8.518	1.496	345	304	2.733	4.582	1.834	423	1.969	310	13.996
1973	339	6,156	1.024	7.519	1.314	313	258	2.544	4.100	1.727	376	1.685	270	12.587
1972	449	5.571	1.176	7.196	1.182	256	232	2.513	3.670	1.564	348	1.513	246	11.524
1971	342	5.057	1.265	6.664	1.084	260	206	2.464	3.374	1.434	320	1.431	260	10.833
1970	368	4.921	1,346	6.635	1.027	244	177	2.354	3.162	1.538	308	1,341	254	10.405
1969	419	4.664	1,414	6.497	962	239	174	2.198	3.045	1.429	307	1.296	232	9.882
1968	446	4.151	1.425	6.022	866	223	155	2.037	2.636	1.371	283	1.272	186	9.029
1967	395	3.672	1.393	5.460	802	215	142	1.994	2.398	1.317	262	1.186	165	8.481
1966	486	3.056	1.290	4.832	734	205	129	1.891	2.124	1.188	234	1.133	150	7.788
1965	675	2.729	1.210	4.614	713	180	118	1.632	1.906	1.075	183	997	143	6.947
1964	690	2.470	1.176	4.336	652	153	101	1.441	1.661	970	181	853	127	6.139
1963	695	2.127	1.047	3.869	653	147	98	1.329	1.501	996	172	717[2]	116	5.729
1962	576	1.768	1.043	3.387	620	135	92	1.242	1.425	992	162	584	109	5.361
1961	416	1.641	992	3.049	586	132	93	1.207	1.339	973	158	553	101	5.142
1960	382	1.544	977	2.903	551	118	84	1.116	1.286	928	151	492	92	4.818
1959	383	1.509	872	2.764	509	115	79	1.026	1.172	928	142	473	86	4.530
1958	396	1.207	741	2.344	469	102	73	1.021	1.038	879	129	444	79	4.234
1957	342	1.099	620	2.061	440	96	71	986	971	813	111	418	76	3.982
1956	340	1.021	511	1.872	401	91	70	911	891	700	109	371	62	3.606
1955	393	836	411	1.640	365	91	65	798	769[2]	616	87	329	53[2]	3.173
1954	515	914	393	1.822	338	84	62	774	668	571	91	294	79	2.961
1953	608	886	376	1.870	323	78	59	682	649	543	78	276	66	2.754
1952	737	782	316	1.835	284	72	61	620	580	480	499	259	60	2.915
1951	887	732	279	1.898	277	64	61	568	492	367	60	227	57	2.173
1950	1.009	525	212	1.746	252	61	57	529	463	316	329	200	54	2.261
1949	844	492	198	1.534	242	57	52	514	417	277	297	191	53	2.100
1948	775	494	198	1.467	241	51	47	493	382	257	245	173	48	1.937
1947	665	515	207	1.387	211	48	43	444	339	231	166	153	42	1.677
1946	701	554	183	1.438	201	46	42	413	311	214	151	140	37	1.555
1945	682	574	194	1.450	199	47	41	383	297	209	48	124	34	1.382
1939	567	473	181	1.221	135	49	26	371	205	137	120	94	23	1.160
1933	451	493	248	1.192	133	48	23	429	183	111	130	92	23	1.172
1930	440	517	248	1.205	123	44	26	489	233	118	19	89	33	1.174
1926	382	342	185	909	82	22	22	321	220	86	112	61	27	953

Series G203-226. Foreign long-term investment in Canada, all countries and by major areas, by type of investment, selected year ends, 1926 to 1974 (continued)
(millions of dollars)

Year	Government securities				Manufacturing									
	Govern-ment of Canada	Provin-cial	Municipal	Total govern-ment	Vegetable products	Animal products	Textiles	Wood and paper products	Iron and products	Non-ferrous metals	Non-metallic minerals[1]	Chemicals and allied products	Miscel-laneous products	Total manu-facturing
	203	204	205	206	207	208	209	210	211	212	213	214	215	216
					Owned in United Kingdom									
1974	53	274	44	371	181	10	75	276	221	120	119	274	3	1.279
1973	77	256	31	364	159	11	65	213	208	132	92	221	3	1.104
1972	43	256	46	345	151	13	65	184	181	127	95	218	3	1.037
1971	44	242	48	334	150	11	58	229	153	108	62	255	3	1.029
1970	37	219	50	306	142	9	58	225	166	102	58	243	3	1.006
1969	35	130	25	190	138	13	51	226	173	120	62	233	4	1.020
1968	23	132	27	182	165	12	49	223	215	128	43	211	4	1.050
1967	12	90	29	131	164	10	48	235	210	194	37	192	5	1.095
1966	7	73	28	108	157	10	47	246	200	188	38	192	5	1.083
1965	10	62	28	100	151	8	44	234	205	182	50	187	6	1.067
1964	21	60	30	111	153	6	47	243	203	182	49	182	6	1.071
1963	34	58	29	121	155	7	46	180	203	184	66	181	6	1.028
1962	48	60	29	137	136	7	48	188	209	183	66	183	6	1.026
1961	50	67	30	147	136	7	53	174	209	177	54	176	6	992
1960	48	47	32	127	137	8	55	167	201	188	55	169	5	985
1959	60	48	33	141	131	7	59	159	194	192	45	153	5	945
1958	65	47	33	145	124	6	60	155	202	195	40	146	5	933
1957	64	47	34	145	125	6	55	160	168	192	34	142	5	887
1956	72	45	35	152	109	6	56	153	153	175	31	137	4	824
1955	67	39	35	141	106	6	55	155	103[2]	153	32	132	4[2]	746
1954	71	38	35	144	96	6	55	151	37	146	27	121	37	676
1953	79	36	35	150	93	5	53	147	37	142	27	77	26	607
1952	68	32	36	136	88	5	52	142	31	113	33	68	26	558
1951	70	38	38	146	80	5	52	140	28	91	20	60	12	488
1950	82	39	42	163	80	5	50	121	34	65	31	53	7	446
1949	84	41	46	171	74	5	42	118	17	64	24	49	5	398
1948	—	33	48	81	75	3	45	61	17	63	29	46	3	342
1947	—	35	55	90	73	5	41	54	15	61	18	40	2	309
1946	—	37	78	115	65	4	38	62	13	62	14	37	2	297
1945	—	45	112	157	66	6	38	64	12	64	8	36	2	296
1939	238	58	157	453	69	5	30	74	19	7	14	39	—	257
1933	291	74	144	509	75	4	24	64	22	6	5	37	—	237
1930	235	69	182	486	84	5	22	95	24	6	5	32	—	273
1926	250	73	187	510	67	3	18	68	40	7	4	17	10	234

Series G203-226. Foreign long-term investment in Canada, all countries and by major areas, by type of investment, selected year ends, 1926 to 1974 (continued)

(millions of dollars)

| Year | Government securities | | | | Manufacturing | | | | | | | | | |
	Government of Canada	Provincial	Municipal	Total government	Vegetable products	Animal products	Textiles	Wood and paper products	Iron and products	Non-ferrous metals	Non-metallic minerals[1]	Chemicals and allied products	Miscellaneous products	Total manufacturing
	203	204	205	206	207	208	209	210	211	212	213	214	215	216

Owned in all other countries

Year	203	204	205	206	207	208	209	210	211	212	213	214	215	216
1974	194	1.981	355	2.530	198	33	23	531	155	115	247	121	10	1.433
1973	223	1.514	293	2.030	159	22	13	515	113	108	253	158	7	1.348
1972	174	1.407	275	1.856	138	19	6	473	173	85	167	143	6	1.210
1971	191	769	132	1.092	125	23	13	448	154	80	128	122	6	1.099
1970	198	666	133	997	96	21	15	303	154	84	120	108	4	905
1969	304	638	133	1.075	46	21	12	230	126	100	115	83	4	737
1968	310	269	39	618	32	14	6	156	114	70	94	61	5	552
1967	149	57	16	222	23	14	5	67	118	65	90	58	1	441
1966	156	42	15	213	20	13	4	58	121	52	86	53	1	408
1965	195	37	15	247	25	10	4	41	115	44	78	49	1	366
1964	186	34	15	235	25	10	2	38	106	39	89	60	1	370
1963	170	32	15	217	25	7	2	40	106	33	81	45	1	340
1962	164	34	15	213	31	7	2	34	108	36	82	43	1	344
1961	191	35	16	242	27	6	2	29	99	35	74	39	1	312
1960	181	41	17	239	32	6	2	32	93	39	70	37	1	312
1959	169	28	10	207	24	6	2	26	85	33	40	34	1	251
1958	103	22	7	132	15	6	2	24	72	29	38	27	1	214
1957	95	19	6	120	12	6	2	20	59	26	34	22	1	182
1956	90	15	6	111	14	6	2	17	39	20	30	19	2	149
1955	69	13	6	88	12	6	2	15	22	14	17	16	2	106
1954	73	12	5	90	9	7	3	14	17	10	8	15	1	84
1953	57	8	2	67	8	6	3	11	13	9	6	13	1	70
1952	53	2	2	57	8	6	4	10	12	6	6	12	1	65
1951	56	1	2	59	9	5	4	10	10	5	—	10	1	54
1950	50	1	2	53	6	5	4	8	8	4	4	10	1	50
1949	47	1	2	50	4	5	4	6	9	3	3	9	1	44
1948	48	1	2	51	4	4	4	8	8	1	1	10	1	41
1947	48	1	2	51	6	9	4	7	7	1	1	10	1	46
1946	49	3	6	58	6	9	4	6	8	1	2	9	1	46
1945	44	5	6	55	3	8	4	8	10	1	1	9	1	45
1939	18	5	6	29	2	2	3	6	8	2	1	4	—	28
1933	10	5	2	17	1	1	1	3	5	1	—	1	—	13
1930	7	6	2	15	1	1	1	2	5	1	—	1	—	12
1926	6	7	2	15	1	2	—	1	5	1	—	1	—	11

Series G203-226. Foreign long-term investment in Canada, all countries and by major areas, by type of investment, selected year ends, 1926 to 1974 (continued)

(millions of dollars)

Year	Petroleum and natural gas[1]	Mining and smelting[1]	Utilities			Merchandising[1]	Financial	Other enterprises	Miscellaneous investment	Total investment
			Railways	Other (excluding pipelines and public enterprise)[1]	Total utilities					
	217	218	219	220	221	222	223	224	225	226

Owned by all non-residents

Year	217	218	219	220	221	222	223	224	225	226
1974	10.088	5.122	916	1.955	2.871	2.638	6.480	1.416	3.447	60.189
1973	9.517	4.611	883	1.845	2.728	2.360	5.893	1.275	3.274	54.610
1972	8.537	4.278	899	1.604	2.503	2.065	5.197	1.103	3.163	50.014
1971	8.067	4.072	894	1.478	2.372	1.989	4.654	970	3.075	46.250
1970	7.594	3.865	957	1.327	2.284	1.857	4.355	939	2.889	44.037
1969	7.165	3.695	987	1.142	2.129	1.762	3.968	820	2.662	41.602
1968	6.450	3.553	977	998	1.975	1.582	3.729	673	2.564	37.979
1967	6.009	3.150	1.018	812	1.830	1.432	3.415	605	2.431	34.702
1966	5.719	2.872	1.055	758	1.813	1.297	3.134	559	2.264	32.090
1965	5.268	2.558	1.040	667	1.707	1.197	2.876	485	2.171	29.603
1964	4.854	2.442	1.105	605	1.710	1.092	2.650	407	2.057	27.474
1963	4.749	2.322	1.174	591	1.765	1.017	2.914	363	1.771	26.205
1962	4.384	2.297	1.270	691	1.961	973	2.688	366	1.753	24.890
1961	4.029	2.094	1.366	656	2.022	920	2.616	348	1.696	23.609
1960	3.727[2]	1.977	1.406	743	2.149	872	2.380	297	1.428	22.214
1959	3.455	1.783	1.405	739	2.144	878	2.190	284	1.285	20.857
1958	3.187	1.657	1.413	712	2.125	784	1.938	254	1.063[2]	19.010
1957	2.849	1.570	1.396	661	2.057	715	1.782	235	879	17.464
1956	2.275	1.402	1.412	628	2.040	683	1.488	207	818	15.627
1955	1.854	1.190	1.349	574	1.923	616	1.231	178	641	13.527
1954	1.488	1.049	1.413	570	1.983	571	1.014	154	561	12.597
1953	1.252	823	1.424	559	1.983[2]	493	774	151	467	11.461
1952	—	1.076	1.429	639	2.068	447	648	133	447[2]	10.385
1951	693	586	1.436	524	1.960	377	595	120	328	9.477
1950	—	631	1.446	547	1.993	330	573	98	320	8.664
1949	—	494	1.445	494	1.939	300	548	83	302	7.963
1948	—	424	1.504	468	1.972	277	541	78	298	7.509
1947	—	396	1.586	473	2.059	262	553	71	290	7.191
1946	—	386	1.583	557	2.140	238	557	69	282	7.181
1945	160	356	1.599	493	2.092	220	525	70	284	7.092
1939	—	329	1.871	549	2.420	189	473	69	285	6.913
1933	—	339	2.245	625	2.870	191	480	75	270	7.365
1930	150	311	2.244	634	2.878	190	543	82	295	7.614
1926	—	219	1.938	395	2.333	150	344	65	260	6.003

Series G203-226. Foreign long-term investment in Canada, all countries and by major areas, by type of investment, selected year ends, 1926 to 1974 (continued)
(millions of dollars)

| Year | Petro-leum and natural gas[1] | Mining and smelting[1] | Utilities | | | Merchan-dising[1] | Financial | Other enter-prises | Miscel-laneous invest-ment | Total invest-ment |
			Railways	Other (excluding pipelines and public enterprise)[1]	Total utilities					
	217	218	219	220	221	222	223	224	225	226

Owned in United States

Year	217	218	219	220	221	222	223	224	225	226
1974	7.986	4.095	501	1.765	2.266	1.995	4.320	1.117	2.382	46.675
1973	7.596	3.774	436	1.627	2.063	1.777	3.746	964	2.124	42.150
1972	6.824	3.552	414	1.429	1.843	1.529	3.298	860	2.073	38.699
1971	6.525	3.360	398	1.298	1.696	1.486	2.990	764	2.020	36.338
1970	6.179	3.163	427	1.174	1.601	1.375	2.848	764	1.944	34.914
1969	5.859	3.054	450	1.007	1.457	1.277	2.580	677	1.762	33.045
1968	5.296	3.002	425	894	1.319	1.121	2.462	548	1.710	30.509
1967	4.905	2.656	440	750	1.190	1.007	2.241	500	1.590	28.030
1966	4.656	2.464	427	703	1.130	913	2.040	463	1.437	25.723
1965	4.223	2.197	399	620	1.019	821	1.817	396	1.355	23.389
1964	4.016	2.085	440	554	994	738	1.673	327	1.250	21.558
1963	3.975	2.028	456	506	962	700	2.054	295	925	20.537
1962	3.662	1.998	472	557	1.029	674	1.872	300	872	19.155
1961	3.444	1.821	506	513	1.019	629	1.775	282	840	18.001
1960	3.184[2]	1.701	479	551	1.030	608	1.587	234	653	16.718
1959	3.108	1.513	472	544	1.016	612	1.471	225	587	15.826
1958	2.866	1.386	489	523	1.012	549	1.314	200	536	14.441
1957	2.570	1.307	489	471	960	508	1.202	185	489	13.264
1956	2.063	1.155	531	460	991	496	983	170	474	11.810
1955	1.716	1.001	554	433	987	448	816	147	367	10.295
1954	1.426	893	621	470	1.091	412	649	128	302	9.684
1953	1.205	725	624	470	1.094	353	482	130	257	8.870
1952	—	976	644	550	1.194	317	395	116	249[2]	7.997
1951	682	497	656	439	1.095	260	353	106	195	7.259
1950	—	549	675	448	1.123	230	362	88	190	6.549
1949	—	416	664	399	1.063	211	338	74	170	5.906
1948	—	347	718	372	1.090	194	297	72	163	5.567
1947	—	324	724	372	1.096	185	312	65	155	5.201
1946	—	311	717	441	1.158	173	321	62	140	5.158
1945	152	277	720	374	1.094	158	285	62	130	4.990
1939	—	251	588	432	1.020	129	201	64	105	4.151
1933	—	261	831	524	1.355	131	221	70	90	4.492
1930	147	234	832	522	1.354	125	251	76	94	4.660
1926	—	165	510	290	800	99	125	60	85	3.196

Series G203-226. Foreign long-term investment in Canada, all countries and by major areas, by type of investment, selected year ends, 1926 to 1974 (continued)

(millions of dollars)

Year	Petroleum and natural gas[1]	Mining and smelting[1]	Utilities			Merchandising[1]	Financial	Other enterprises	Miscellaneous investment	Total investment
			Railways	Other (excluding pipelines and public enterprise)[1]	Total utilities					
	217	218	219	220	221	222	223	224	225	226

Owned in United Kingdom

Year	217	218	219	220	221	222	223	224	225	226
1974	956	364	316	89	405	382	1.255	158	160	5.330
1973	865	251	337	119	456	345	1.231	156	220	4.992
1972	771	237	358	98	456	332	1.034	127	210	4.549
1971	705	233	364	95	459	311	919	111	220	4.321
1970	613	250	388	84	472	312	803	89	170	4.021
1969	556	253	396	82	478	350	738	80	160	3.825
1968	549	218	410	71	481	323	651	74	178	3.706
1967	554	215	422	36	458	308	555	69	191	3.576
1966	542	209	467	29	496	289	524	67	200	3.518
1965	543	199	476	24	500	281	567	61	194	3.512
1964	451	210	500	24	524	271	561	58	203	3.460
1963	392	162	555	54	609	260	514	46	216	3.348
1962	355	184	618	78	696	241	487	45	228	3.399
1961	296	148	699	76	775	238	512	50	223	3.381
1960	270[2]	152	755	125	880	214	469	51	211	3.359
1959	162	160	783	125	908	225	413	45	200	3.199
1958	134	171	794	115	909	197	360	41	198	3.088
1957	108	162	784	112	896	174	332	36	177	2.917
1956	72	156	757	97	854	159	284	29	168	2.698
1955	31	122	690	86	776	145	241	25	157	2.384
1954	17	104	691	65	756	136	213	22	137	2.205
1953	14	59	702	57	759	120	167	16	116	2.008
1952	—	61	699	55	754	112	139	12	114[2]	1.886
1951	7	58	704	56	760	102	142	10	65	1.778
1950	—	55	707	69	776	90	147	8	65	1.750
1949	—	54	716	66	782	83	155	7	67	1.717
1948	—	56	724	69	793	76	188	5	69	1.610
1947	—	52	792	72	864	71	186	5	70	1.647
1946	—	56	795	85	880	60	182	5	75	1.670
1945	7	60	806	90	896	57	186	6	85	1.750
1939	—	61	1.216	89	1.305	55	221	4	120	2.476
1933	—	72	1.354	88	1.442	56	213	4	150	2.683
1930	3	72	1.352	100	1.452	61	243	5	171	2.766
1926	—	51	1.371	97	1.468	49	176	4	145	2.637

Series G203-226. Foreign long-term investment in Canada, all countries and by major areas, by type of investment, selected year ends, 1926 to 1974 (concluded)
(millions of dollars)

| Year | Petroleum and natural gas[1] | Mining and smelting[1] | Utilities | | | Merchandising[1] | Financial | Other enterprises | Miscellaneous investment | Total investment |
			Railways	Other (excluding pipelines and public enterprise)[1]	Total utilities					
	217	218	219	220	221	222	223	224	225	226

Owned in all other countries

Year	217	218	219	220	221	222	223	224	225	226
1974	1.146	663	99	101	200	261	905	141	905	8.184
1973	1.056	586	110	99	209	238	916	155	930	7.468
1972	942	489	127	77	204	204	865	116	880	6.766
1971	837	479	132	85	217	192	745	95	835	5.591
1970	802	452	142	69	211	170	704	86	775	5.102
1969	750	388	141	53	194	135	650	63	740	4.732
1968	605	333	142	33	175	138	616	51	676	3.764
1967	550	279	156	26	182	117	619	36	650	3.096
1966	521	199	161	26	187	95	570	29	627	2.849
1965	502	162	165	23	188	95	492	28	622	2.702
1964	387	147	165	27	192	83	416	22	604	2.456
1963	382	132	163	31	194	57	346	22	630	2.320
1962	367	115	180	56	236	58	329	21	653	2.336
1961	289	125	161	67	228	53	329	16	633	2.227
1960	273[2]	124	172	67	239	50	324	12	564	2.137
1959	185	110	150	70	220	41	306	14	498	1.832
1958	187	100	130	74	204	38	264	13	329[2]	1.481
1957	171	101	123	78	201	33	248	14	213	1.283
1956	140	91	124	71	195	28	221	8	176	1.119
1955	107	67	105	55	160	23	174	6	117	848
1954	45	52	101	35	136	23	152	4	122	708
1953	33	39	98	32	130	20	125	5	94	583
1952	—	39	86	34	120	18	114	5	84[2]	502
1951	4	31	76	29	105	15	100	4	68	440
1950	—	27	64	30	94	10	64	2	65	365
1949	—	24	65	29	94	6	55	2	65	340
1948	—	21	62	27	89	7	56	1	66	332
1947	—	20	70	29	99	6	55	1	65	343
1946	—	19	71	31	102	5	54	2	67	353
1945	1	19	73	29	102	5	54	2	69	352
1939	—	17	67	28	95	5	51	1	60	286
1933	—	6	60	13	73	4	46	1	30	190
1930	—	5	60	12	72	4	49	1	30	188
1926	—	3	57	8	65	2	43	1	30	170

[1] New series not strictly comparable with earlier series except for the years 1930, 1945 and 1951. Refer to the general note for series G203-226 on the treatment of the petroleum and natural gas industry.

[2] New series not strictly comparable with earlier series.

Series G227-243. Foreign direct investment[1] in Canada, all countries and by major areas, by industry, selected year ends, 1926 to 1974

(millions of dollars)

| Year | Manufacturing | | | | | | | | | | Petroleum and natural gas[2] | Mining and smelting[2] | Utilities[2] | Merchandising[2] | Financial | Other enterprises | Total direct investment |
| | Vegetable products | Animal products | Textiles | Wood and paper products | Iron and products | Non-ferrous metals | Non-metallic minerals[2] | Chemicals and allied products | Miscellaneous manufactures | Total manufacturing | | | | | | | |
	227	228	229	230	231	232	233	234	235	236	237	238	239	240	241	242	243
	Owned by all non-residents																
1974	1,748	365	383	2,775	4,709	1,555	661	2,300	300	14,796	8,934	4,032	512	2,375	4,309	1,279	36,237
1973	1,499	325	315	2,560	4,220	1,408	623	2,001	258	13,209	8,397	3,621	542	2,116	3,844	1,076	32,805
1972	1,345	275	284	2,495	3,775	1,278	498	1,821	234	12,005	7,523	3,302	545	1,841	3,470	919	29,605
1971	1,241	281	253	2,310	3,450	1,119	423	1,746	245	11,068	7,137	3,488	445	1,850	3,127	803	27,918
1970	1,140	260	221	2,030	3,247	1,615	412	1,611	231	10,767	6,574	3,231	442	1,699	2,845	800	26,358
1969	1,039	262	205	1,808	3,091	1,492	411	1,530	204	10,042	6,103	3,077	412	1,560	2,535	695	24,424
1968	958	232	183	1,694	2,715	1,427	350	1,462	183	9,204	5,643	2,931	423	1,408	2,360	565	22,534
1967	899	223	167	1,618	2,469	1,369	314	1,373	167	8,599	5,269	2,547	344	1,252	2,170	518	20,699
1966	822	212	155	1,534	2,181	1,234	282	1,316	154	7,890	5,012	2,279	318	1,132	1,889	488	19,008
1965	793	188	141	1,423	2,008	1,118	261	1,175	148	7,255	4,600	2,017	301	1,061	1,694	428	17,356
1964	740	160	130	1,307	1,793	1,014	271	1,045	131	6,591	4,251	1,888	301	968	1,600	362	15,961[3]
1963	745	153	128	1,190	1,647	1,036	273	916	121	6,209	4,158	1,736	300	898	1,874	327	15,502
1962	691	140	124	1,098	1,584	1,022	265	780	115	5,819	3,901	1,686	294	859	1,769	332	14,660
1961	648	135	122	1,064	1,504	1,020	249	741	106	5,589	3,534	1,549	289	804	1,660	312	13,737
1960	637	122	118	1,033	1,441	983	240	671	97	5,342	3,313	1,439	285	757	1,464	272	12,872
1959	578	119	117	951	1,345	977	198	637	89	5,011	3,082	1,223	282	761	1,289	258	11,906
1958	521	105	115	945	1,205	926	174	595	82	4,668	2,816	1,116	287	684	1,073	236	10,880
1957	492	98	108	924	1,089	867	157	561	80	4,376	2,559	1,044	286	621	1,026	217	10,129
1956	441	91	105	847	978	728	143	507	66	3,906	2,144	908	292	605	818	195	8,868
1955	397	91	98	784	805[3]	624	122	456	57	3,434	1,754	811	320	538	706	165	7,728
1954	373	84	92	763	638	570	111	411	114	3,156	1,384	671	319	501	590	143	6,764
1953	351	77	85	682	617	541	99[3]	317	91	2,860	1,164	580	320	434	504	141	6,003
1952	315	73	87	610	548	486	494[2]	295	85	2,993	..	850	404	431	417	123	5,218
1951	291	66	86	564	467	375	74[3]	257	68	2,248	641	419	361	361	378	112	4,520
1950	268	64	80	538	442	322	327	230	60	2,331	..	476	399	313	364	92	3,975
1949	250	61	70	529	387	280	294	218	57	2,146	..	349	397	281	336	77	3,586
1948	248	53	70	462	354	257	244	200	50	1,938	..	294	368	260	339	71	3,270
1947	223	50	64	418	318	230	158	176	43	1,680	..	272	367	247	356	64	2,986
1946	206	45	58	383	288	214	142	160	38	1,534	..	264	385	225	358	60	2,826
1945	200	47	56	348	277	211	43[3]	144	33	1,359	141	237	375	202	339	60	2,713
1939	157	50	39	319	193	136	115	111	22	1,142	..	228	415	168	284	59	2,296
1933	163	48	32	349	167	110	126	106	21	1,122	142	238	455	165	311	61	2,352
1930	165	42	33	378	203	116	203[3]	102	31	1,090	..	217	450	160	304	64	2,427
1926	124	21	29	295	184	85	112	69	25	944	..	169	275	134	209	51	1,782

Series G227-243. Foreign direct investment[1] in Canada, all countries and by major areas, by industry, selected year ends, 1926 to 1974 (continued)

(millions of dollars)

Owned in United States

| Year | Manufacturing | | | | | | | | | | Petroleum and natural gas[2] | Mining and smelting[2] | Utilities[2] | Merchandising[2] | Financial | Other enterprises | Total direct investment |
| | Vegetable products | Animal products | Textiles | Wood and paper products | Iron and products | Non-ferrous metals | Non-metallic minerals[2] | Chemicals and allied products | Miscellaneous manufactures | Total manufacturing | | | | | | | |
	227	228	229	230	231	232	233	234	235	236	237	238	239	240	241	242	243
1974	1,395	328	292	2,071	4,416	1,374	353	1,915	288	12,432	7,146	3,397	474	1,861	2,669	1,017	28,996
1973	1,206	296	242	1,935	3,957	1,252	309	1,633	249	11,079	6,746	3,149	469	1,649	2,216	805	26,113
1972	1,079	247	219	1,936	3,532	1,146	279	1,470	226	10,134	6,037	2,909	463	1,432	1,999	705	23,679
1971	988	250	191	1,844	3,242	1,007	250	1,379	238	9,389	5,761	3,057	356	1,397	1,857	626	22,443
1970	917	233	157	1,643	3,025	1,506	250	1,275	225	9,231	5,290	2,851	366	1,261	1,755	649	21,403
1969	868	230	149	1,500	2,881	1,398	250	1,227	197	8,700	4,968	2,754	347	1,105	1,523	562	19,959
1968	781	214	133	1,435	2,469	1,338	225	1,203	177	7,975	4,615	2,669	359	964	1,479	449	18,510
1967	723	206	119	1,408	2,221	1,255	205	1,138	162	7,437	4,290	2,323	316	841	1,371	422	17,000
1966	656	196	108	1,328	1,942	1,132	175	1,084	148	6,769	4,062	2,107	297	759	1,176	400	15,570
1965	628	174	97	1,227	1,763	1,027	159	950	142	6,167	3,653	1,875	280	696	1,043	345	14,059
1964	576	148	90	1,094	1,556	924	153	811	126	5,478	3,521	1,747	276	623	1,027	287	12,959[3]
1963	581	141	88	1,035	1,400	950	146	699	115	5,155	3,489	1,645	251	587	1,393	265	12,785
1962	539	129	82	950	1,326	939	136	565	109	4,775	3,277	1,595	238	565	1,287	269	12,006
1961	504	125	78	939	1,248	931	140	538	100	4,603	3,060	1,451	228	520	1,171	251	11,284
1960	488	111	72	886	1,198	890	134	478	91	4,348	2,885[3]	1,348	224	501	1,028	215	10,549
1959	442	108	68	822	1,095	892	127	460	83	4,097	2,836	1,146	217	505	904	207	9,912
1958	403	95	63	819	961	845	110	434	76	3,806	2,598	1,030	216	458	750	187	9,045
1957	375	89	62	798	896	789	101	405	75	3,590	2,380	971	215	423	719	174	8,472
1956	339	83	58	726	816	663	91	358	61	3,195	1,978	857	223	428	551	160	7,392
1955	302	83	53	659	706[3]	585	79	316	52[3]	2,835	1,637	781	270	377	475	138	6,513
1954	279	76	47	642	606	543	82	281	77	2,633	1,344	650	298	348	396	118	5,787
1953	261	70	43	560	591	519	72	266	65	2,447	1,130	561	298	301	347	122	5,206
1952	230	66	46	499	528	473	469	250	59	2,620	..	825	382	306	289	108	4,530
1951	214	60	46	454	451	362	59	219	56	1,921	636	397	341	249	253	99	3,896
1950	193	58	42	446	420	311	307	194	53	2,024	..	453	379	219	267	84	3,426
1949	182	55	38	441	378	270	279	185	52	1,880	..	331	375	199	241	69	3,095
1948	179	49	35	427	346	250	229	167	47	1,729	..	275	347	183	208	65	2,807
1947	155	46	32	383	312	225	152	147	41	1,493	..	254	345	175	222	59	2,548
1946	146	42	29	350	283	208	138	134	36	1,366	..	245	366	165	232	54	2,428
1945	140	44	28	316	272	203	39	118	31	1,191	144	215	358	147	198	54	2,304
1939	96	47	20	281	188	130	112	88	22	984	..	198	399	119	126	55	1,881
1933	97	45	17	313	163	107	124	89	21	976	141	211	427	117	144	58	1,933
1930	94	38	20	334	199	113	17	86	31	932	..	191	423	109	136	61	1,993
1926	69	18	18	256	180	83	109	60	25	818	..	141	249	89	58	48	1,403

Series G227-243. Foreign direct investment[1] in Canada, all countries and by major areas, by industry, selected year ends, 1926 to 1974 (continued)

(millions of dollars)

Year	Vegetable products	Animal products	Textiles	Wood and paper products	Manufacturing Iron and products	Non-ferrous metals	Non-metallic minerals[2]	Chemicals and allied products	Miscellaneous manufactures	Total manufacturing	Petroleum and natural gas[2]	Mining and smelting[2]	Utilities[2]	Merchandising[2]	Financial	Other enterprises	Total direct investment
	227	228	229	230	231	232	233	234	235	236	237	238	239	240	241	242	243

Owned in United Kingdom

Year	227	228	229	230	231	232	233	234	235	236	237	238	239	240	241	242	243
1974	169	7	69	235	191	100	70	271	3	1,115	728	277	6	288	971	140	3,525
1973	146	8	60	165	190	78	70	217	2	936	665	169	43	252	954	132	3,151
1972	142	10	60	139	171	73	57	214	2	868	602	162	53	235	787	114	2,821
1971	140	9	55	144	143	57	48	249	2	847	597	160	52	294	666	99	2,715
1970	132	7	54	167	146	52	45	233	3	839	536	155	52	298	543	80	2,503
1969	130	13	49	176	153	48	48	225	4	846	470	154	56	338	487	75	2,426
1968	157	11	47	173	200	44	32	206	4	874	471	136	56	317	386	70	2,310
1967	157	10	46	181	193	71	22	186	4	870	477	123	21	304	293	64	2,152
1966	152	9	45	190	179	64	22	186	5	852	476	111	14	283	248	62	2,046
1965	145	8	42	184	186	58	25	183	5	836	488	100	14	274	262	59	2,033
1964	146	6	39	193	185	59	31	178	4	841	391	104	14	265	262	56	1,933
1963	148	7	39	133	187	62	48	176	5	805	335	63	33	255	227	43	1,761
1962	129	6	41	133	190	60	49	177	5	790	298	67	38	236	234	43	1,706
1961	123	6	43	115	191	65	37	170	5	755	234	62	38	231	246	47	1,613
1960	124	6	45	138	185	65	38	162	5	768	208[3]	66	40	208	198	47	1,535
1959	117	6	49	127	180	64	34	150	5	732	116	68	40	219	168	41	1,384
1958	108	5	51	125	186	63	30	143	5	716	90	77	41	191	142	39	1,296
1957	110	5	46	125	147	61	26	139	4	663	64	68	37	167	131	33	1,163
1956	95	4	47	120	134	49	23	135	4	611	56	48	39	151	115	28	1,048
1955	91	4	45	124	87[3]	27	26	129	4[3]	537	23	26	33	139	109	23	890
1954	90	4	44	120	23	19	21	119	37	477	7	17	16	131	90	21	759
1953	86	3	41	121	21	15	22	42	26	377	9	15	16	115	65	15	612
1952	82	3	39	111	15	8	25	36	26	345	..	18	16	107	47	11	544
1951	74	3	38	109	14	10	15	30	12	305	4	18	16	97	48	9	497
1950	74	3	36	92	20	9	19	28	7	288	..	19	16	84	54	7	468
1949	68	3	30	88	7	8	15	26	5	250	..	17	17	76	61	7	428
1948	69	2	33	32	7	7	15	25	3	193	..	19	18	70	95	5	400
1947	68	3	30	33	5	5	6	21	2	173	..	18	18	67	92	4	372
1946	60	2	27	31	4	6	4	19	2	155	..	19	16	55	85	5	335
1945	60	3	26	30	4	8	4	19	2	156	—	22	16	51	98	5	348
1939	61	2	18	38	4	6	3	21	—	153	..	29	15	46	120	3	366
1933	66	2	15	36	3	3	2	16	—	143	..	26	26	45	133	3	376
1930	71	3	13	44	3	3	3	15	—	155	1	25	27	48	133	3	392
1926	55	2	11	39	3	2	3	8	—	123	..	27	26	43	114	3	336

Series G227-243. Foreign direct investment¹ in Canada, all countries and by major areas, by industry, selected year ends, 1926 to 1974 (concluded)

(millions of dollars)

Owned in all other countries

Year	Vegetable products	Animal products	Textiles	Wood and paper products	Iron and products	Non-ferrous metals	Non-metallic minerals²	Chemicals and allied products	Miscellaneous manufactures	Total manufacturing	Petroleum and natural gas²	Mining and smelting²	Utilities²	Merchandising²	Financial	Other enterprises	Total direct investment
	227	228	229	230	231	232	233	234	235	236	237	238	239	240	241	242	243
1974	184	30	22	469	102	81	238	114	9	1,249	1,060	358	32	226	669	122	3,716
1973	147	21	13	460	73	78	244	151	7	1,194	986	303	30	215	674	139	3,541
1972	124	18	5	420	72	59	162	137	6	1,003	884	231	29	174	684	100	3,105
1971	113	22	7	322	65	55	125	118	5	832	779	271	37	159	604	78	2,760
1970	91	20	10	220	76	57	117	103	3	697	748	225	24	140	547	71	2,452
1969	41	19	7	132	57	46	113	78	3	496	665	169	9	117	525	58	2,039
1968	20	7	3	86	46	45	93	53	2	355	557	126	8	127	495	46	1,714
1967	19	7	2	29	55	43	87	49	1	292	502	101	7	107	506	32	1,547
1966	14	7	2	16	60	38	85	46	1	269	474	61	7	90	465	26	1,392
1965	20	6	2	12	59	33	77	42	1	252	459	42	7	91	389	24	1,264
1964	18	6	1	20	52	31	87	56	1	272	339	37	11	80	311	19	1,069
1963	16	5	1	22	60	24	79	41	1	249	334	28	16	56	254	19	956
1962	23	5	1	15	68	23	80	38	1	254	326	24	18	58	248	20	948
1961	21	4	1	10	65	24	72	33	1	231	240	36	23	53	243	14	840
1960	25	5	1	9	58	28	68	31	1	226	220³	25³	21	48	238	10	788
1959	19	5	—	2	70	21	37	27	1	182	130	9	25	37	217	10	610
1958	10	5	1	1	58	18	34	18	1	146	128	9	30	35	181	10	539
1957	7	4	—	1	46	17	30	17	1	123	115	5	34	31	176	10	494
1956	7	4	—	1	28	16	29	14	1	100	110	3	30	26	152	7	428
1955	4	4	—	1	12	12	17	11	1	62	94	4	17	22	122	4	325
1954	4	4	1	1	9	8	8	11	—	46	33	4	5	22	104	4	218
1953	4	4	1	1	5	7	5	9	—	36	25	4	6	18	92	4	185
1952	3	4	2	1	5	5	—	9	—	28	...	7	6	18	81	4	144
1951	3	3	2	—	2	3	—	8	—	22	1	4	4	15	77	4	127
1950	1	3	2	—	2	2	1	8	—	19	...	4	4	10	43	1	81
1949	—	3	2	—	2	2	—	7	—	16	...	1	5	6	34	1	63
1948	—	2	2	3	1	—	—	8	—	16	...	—	3	7	36	1	63
1947	—	1	2	2	1	—	—	8	—	14	...	—	4	5	42	1	66
1946	—	1	2	2	1	—	—	7	—	13	...	—	3	5	41	1	63
1945	—	1	2	2	1	—	—	7	—	12	...	1	1	4	43	1	61
1939	—	1	1	—	1	—	—	2	—	5	...	1	1	3	38	1	49
1933	—	1	—	—	1	—	—	1	—	3	...	1	2	3	34	—	43
1930	—	1	1	—	1	—	—	1	—	3	...	1	—	3	35	—	42
1926	—	1	1	—	1	—	—	1	—	3	...	1	—	2	37	—	43

¹ Direct investment covers investment in branches, subsidiaries and controlled companies.
² Refer to general note for series G203-226 on treatment of the petroleum and natural gas industry.
³ New series not strictly comparable with earlier series. See general note referred to in footnote 2.

Series G244-248. Contributors to change in book value of foreign direct investment in Canada, 1946 to 1974
(millions of dollars)

Year	Net capital inflow for direct investment	Net increase in undistributed earnings	Other factors[1]	Net increase in book value	Book value at year end
	244	**245**	**246**	**247**	**248**
1974	725	2.800	-93	3.432	36.237
1973	750	2.280	170	3.200	32.805
1972	620	1.650	-583	1.687	29.605
1971	925	1.335	-700	1.560	27.918
1970	905	830	199	1.934	26.358
1969	720	1.045	125	1.890	24.424
1968	590	810	435	1.835	22.534
1967	691	845	155	1.691	20.699
1966	790	640	222	1.652	19.008
1965	535	735	125	1.395	17.356
1964	270	480	-291[2]	459	15.961[3]
1963	280	435	127	842	15.502
1962	505	325	93	923	14.660
1961	560	240	65	865	13.737
1960	670	280	16	966	12,872
1959	570	350	106	1.026	11.906
1958	430	235	86	751	10.880
1957	545	425	291	1.261	10.129
1956	650	400	90	1.140	8.868
1955	445	335	184	964	7.728
1954	425	280	56	761	6.764
1953	450	305	30	785	6.003
1952	360	295	43	698	5.218
1951	320	190	35	545	4.520
1950	225	150	14	389	3.975
1949	94	155	67	316	3.586
1948	71	160	53	284	3.270
1947	61	125	-26	160	2.986
1946	40	120	-47	113	2.826

[1] New issues, retirements, borrowing, investment abroad, etc., affecting the total value of foreign direct investment in Canada, and other factors including revaluations, reclassifications and similar accounting adjustments.

[2] See "About the figures — Foreign Direct and Short-term investment in Canada, 1964, Discontinuities" in *The Canadian balance of international payments 1963, 1964 and 1965 and International Investment Position.* (Catalogue 67-201) p.65.

[3] New series not strictly comparable with earlier series.

Series G249-290. Ownership and control of capital employed in selected Canadian industries, selected year ends, 1926 to 1973

(billions of dollars)

Year	Total capital employed[1]							Resident-owned capital						
	Manufacturing	Petroleum and natural gas[2]	Other mining and smelting	Railways	Other utilities	Merchandising and construction[3]	Total capital employed	Manufacturing[4]	Petroleum and natural gas	Other mining and smelting	Railways	Other utilities[5]	Merchandising and construction	Total resident-owned capital
	249	250	251	252	253	254	255	256	257	258	259	260	261	262
1973	31.1	16.4	8.4	6.1	28.5	25.3	115.8	14.5	6.9	3.8	5.2	23.2	23.0	76.6
1972	28.4	15.0	7.7	6.0	25.9	22.0	104.9	13.3	6.4	3.4	5.1	21.0	19.9	69.2
1971	26.7	13.6	7.2	6.0	23.6	20.9	98.0	12.7	5.6	3.1	5.1	19.2	18.9	64.6
1970	25.0	12.4	6.5	5.9	21.4	19.7	90.9	11.7	4.8	2.7	5.0	17.3	17.8	59.2
1969	23.5	11.4	6.2	5.7	19.8	18.6	85.2	10.9	4.2	2.5	4.8	16.1	16.8	55.3
1968	21.7	10.4	5.9	5.6	17.8	16.1	77.5	10.3	4.0	2.3	4.6	14.4	14.5	50.1
1967	20.5	9.7	5.2	5.5	16.2	14.4	71.6	9.8	3.7	2.0	4.5	13.2	13.0	46.3
1966	18.7	9.1	4.8	5.4	14.9	12.9	65.7	8.8	3.3	2.0	4.3	12.2	11.6	42.3
1965	16.7	8.3	4.4	5.3	13.4	12.0	60.0	7.8	3.1	1.8	4.2	11.1	10.8	38.8
1964	14.8	7.9	4.1	5.3	12.3	10.9	55.3	6.8	3.0	1.7	4.2	10.2	9.9	35.8
1963	13.7	7.6	3.8	5.3	11.3	10.1	51.8	6.2	2.8	1.5	4.1	9.8	9.0	33.5
1962	13.1	6.9	3.6	5.4	10.6	9.5	49.2	6.0	2.5	1.3	4.1	9.2	8.5	31.8
1961	12.7	6.4	3.4	5.4	10.3	9.4	47.6	5.9	2.4	1.3	4.0	9.0	8.5	31.1
1960	12.2	6.1	3.3	5.3	9.2	9.4	45.6	5.8	2.3	1.3	3.9	7.9	8.5	29.9
1959	11.7	5.6	3.1	5.2	8.5	9.5	43.6	5.7	2.2	1.3	3.8	7.3	8.6	28.8
1958	11.0	5.1	2.9	4.9	8.0	8.5	40.5	5.4	2.0	1.3	3.5	6.9	7.7	26.7
1957	10.7	4.5	2.8	4.6	7.3	7.7	37.6	5.4	1.6	1.3	3.2	6.3	7.0	24.8
1956	10.0	3.5	2.5	4.3	6.4	7.3	34.0	5.2	1.2	1.1	2.9	5.5	6.6	22.6
1955	8.9	3.0	2.1	4.2	5.8	6.6	30.4	4.7	1.1	0.9	2.8	5.0	6.0	20.5
1954	8.3	2.5	1.9	4.1	5.3	6.1	28.2	4.4	1.0	0.8	2.7	4.6	5.5	19.0
1954	9.3	—	3.0	4.1	5.6	6.2	28.2	4.8	—	1.3	2.7	4.7	5.6	19.1
1953	8.6	—	2.5	3.9	5.1	5.6	25.7	4.5	—	1.1	2.5	4.3	5.0	17.4
1952	7.8	—	2.0	3.8	4.3	5.1	23.0	4.1	—	0.9	2.4	3.6	4.6	15.6
1951	7.3	—	1.6	3.6	3.8	4.5	20.8	4.1	—	0.8	2.2	3.1	4.1	14.3
1948	5.7	—	1.1	3.4	2.6	3.2	16.0	3.3	—	0.7	1.9	2.1	2.9	10.9
1939	3.5	—	0.8	3.4	2.1	2.1	11.9	2.0	—	0.5	1.5	1.5	1.9	7.4
1930	3.9	—	0.8	4.0	1.7	2.5	12.9	2.3	—	0.5	1.7	1.1	2.3	7.9
1926	3.1	—	0.6	3.5	1.3	2.1	10.6	1.9	—	0.4	1.6	0.9	1.9	6.7

Year	Non-resident-owned capital							United States-owned investment						
	Manufacturing	Petroleum and natural gas	Other mining and smelting	Railways	Other utilities	Merchandising and construction	Total non-resident-owned capital	Manufacturing[4]	Petroleum and natural gas	Other mining and smelting	Railways	Other utilities[5]	Merchandising and construction	Total United States-owned investments
	263	264	265	266	267	268	269	270	271	272	273	274	275	276
1973	16.6	9.5	4.6	0.9	5.2	2.4	39.2	13.7	7.6	3.8	0.4	4.4	1.8	31.8
1972	15.0	8.5	4.3	0.9	4.9	2.1	35.7	12.5	6.8	3.6	0.4	4.2	1.5	29.0
1971	14.0	8.1	4.1	0.9	4.4	2.0	33.5	11.7	6.5	3.4	0.4	3.9	1.5	27.3
1970	13.3	7.6	3.9	1.0	4.1	1.9	31.8	11.3	6.2	3.2	0.4	3.7	1.4	26.1
1969	12.5	7.2	3.7	1.0	3.7	1.8	29.9	10.6	5.9	3.1	0.5	3.4	1.3	24.7
1968	11.4	6.5	3.6	1.0	3.4	1.6	27.4	9.7	5.3	3.0	0.4	3.2	1.1	22.7
1967	10.7	6.0	3.1	1.0	3.0	1.4	25.3	9.0	4.9	2.7	0.4	2.9	1.0	21.0
1966	9.8	5.7	2.9	1.0	2.6	1.3	23.4	8.3	4.7	2.5	0.4	2.5	0.9	19.3
1965	8.9	5.3	2.6	1.0	2.3	1.2	21.2	7.3	4.2	2.2	0.4	2.2	0.8	17.2
1964	8.0	4.9	2.4	1.1	2.1	1.1	19.6	6.5	4.0	2.1	0.4	2.0	0.7	15.8
1963	7.5	4.7	2.3	1.2	1.5	1.0	18.3	6.0	4.0	2.0	0.5	1.4	0.7	14.6
1962	7.1	4.4	2.3	1.3	1.3	1.0	17.4	5.7	3.7	2.0	0.5	1.2	0.7	13.6
1961	6.8	4.0	2.1	1.4	1.3	0.9	16.5	5.4	3.4	1.8	0.5	1.1	0.6	12.9
1960	6.4	3.7	2.0	1.4	1.3	0.9	15.7	5.1	3.2[6]	1.7	0.5	1.1	0.6	12.1
1959	6.0	3.5	1.8	1.4	1.2	0.9	14.8	4.8	3.1	1.5	0.5	1.0	0.6	11.5
1958	5.6	3.2	1.7	1.4	1.1	0.8	13.8	4.4	2.9	1.4	0.5	0.9	0.5	10.7
1957	5.3	2.8	1.6	1.4	1.0	0.7	12.9	4.2	2.6	1.3	0.5	0.8	0.5	9.9
1956	4.8	2.3	1.4	1.4	0.9	0.7	11.5	3.8	2.1	1.2	0.5	0.7	0.5	8.7
1955	4.2	1.9	1.2	1.3	0.7	0.6	9.9	3.3	1.7	1.0	0.6	0.6	0.4	7.6
1954	3.9	1.5	1.0	1.4	0.7	0.6	9.1	3.1	1.4	0.9	0.6	0.6	0.4	7.1
1954	4.5	—	1.7	1.4	0.9	0.6	9.1	3.6	—	1.6	0.6	0.8	0.4	7.0
1953	4.1	—	1.4	1.4	0.8	0.6	8.3	3.4	—	1.3	0.6	0.7	0.4	6.4
1952	3.7	—	1.1	1.4	0.7	0.5	7.4	3.0	—	1.0	0.6	0.7	0.3	5.6

Series G249-290. Ownership and control of capital employed in selected Canadian industries, selected year ends, 1926 to 1973 (concluded)

(billions of dollars)

Year	Non-resident-owned capital (concluded)							United States-owned investment (concluded)						
	Manufac-turing	Petroleum and natural gas	Other mining and smelting	Railways	Other utilities	Merchan-dising and construc-tion	Total non-resident-owned capital	Manufac-turing[4]	Petroleum and natural gas	Other mining and smelting	Railways	Other utilities[5]	Merchan-dising and construc-tion	Total United States-owned invest-ments
	263	264	265	266	267	268	269	270	271	272	273	274	275	276
1951	3.2	—	0.8	1.4	0.7	0.4	6.5	2.7	—	0.7	0.6	0.6	0.3	4.9
1948	2.4	—	0.4	1.5	0.5	0.3	5.1	2.0	—	0.4	0.7	0.4	0.2	3.7
1939	1.5	—	0.3	1.9	0.6	0.2	4.5	1.2	—	0.2	0.6	0.5	0.1	2.6
1930	1.6	—	0.3	2.3	0.6	0.2	5.0	1.3	—	0.3	0.8	0.5	0.1	3.0
1926	1.2	—	0.2	1.9	0.4	0.2	3.9	0.9	—	0.2	0.5	0.3	0.1	2.0

Year	Canadian and foreign investments in enterprises controlled outside Canada							Canadian and foreign investment in enterprises controlled in the United States						
	Manufac-turing	Petroleum and natural gas	Other mining and smelting	Railways	Other utilities	Merchan-dising and construc-tion	Total Canadian and foreign invest-ment in enterprises controlled outside Canada	Manufac-turing[4]	Petroleum and natural gas	Other mining and smelting	Railways	Other utilities[5]	Merchan-dising and construc-tion	Total Canadian and foreign invest-ment in enterprises controlled in the United States
	277	278	279	280	281	282	283	284	285	286	287	288	289	290
1973	18.2	12.4	4.7	0.1	2.1	2.6	40.1	13.6	9.6	3.8	0.1	1.2	1.9	30.1
1972	16.6	11.2	4.4	0.1	2.0	2.4	36.7	12.5	8.6	3.6	0.1	1.2	1.7	27.6
1971	15.5	10.5	5.1	0.1	1.7	2.5	35.4	11.7	8.3	4.3	0.1	1.0	1.6	26.9
1970	15.2	9.4	4.6	0.1	1.4	2.3	33.0	11.7	7.5	3.9	0.1	0.8	1.5	25.5
1969	14.1	8.5	4.3	0.1	1.2	2.0	30.2	11.1	6.8	3.7	0.1	0.8	1.3	23.7
1968	12.6	7.8	4.0	0.1	0.9	1.9	27.2	10.1	6.3	3.4	0.1	0.8	1.1	21.8
1967	11.8	7.2	3.4	0.1	0.8	1.6	24.9	9.4	5.8	2.9	0.1	0.7	1.0	19.9
1966	10.7	6.7	3.0	0.1	0.6	1.5	22.6	8.5	5.4	2.6	0.1	0.6	0.9	18.0
1965	9.8	6.1	2.6	0.1	0.5	1.4	20.5	7.7	4.8	2.3	0.1	0.5	0.8	16.2
1964	8.9	5.7	2.4	0.1	0.5	1.3	18.9	6.8	4.7	2.1	0.1	0.5	0.7	15.0
1963	8.2	5.5	2.2	0.1	0.5	1.2	17.7	6.3	4.6	2.0	0.1	0.4	0.7	14.1
1962	7.8	5.1	2.1	0.1	0.5	1.1	16.7	5.9	4.3	1.9	0.1	0.4	0.6	13.2
1961	7.5	4.7	2.0	0.1	0.5	1.1	15.7	5.7	4.0	1.8	0.1	0.4	0.6	12.6
1960	7.2	4.4	2.0	0.1	0.5	1.0	15.2	5.4	3.9[6]	1.7	0.1	0.4	0.6	12.0
1959	6.7	4.1	1.9	0.1	0.5	0.8	14.0	5.1	3.7	1.6	0.1	0.4	0.6	11.5
1958	6.3	3.8	1.8	0.1	0.4	0.7	13.1	4.8	3.5	1.5	0.1	0.3	0.5	10.7
1957	5.9	3.4	1.7	0.1	0.4	0.7	12.2	4.6	3.1	1.5	0.1	0.3	0.5	10.0
1956	5.2	2.8	1.4	0.1	0.4	0.6	10.5	4.1	2.6	1.3	0.1	0.3	0.5	8.8
1955	4.6	2.3	1.2	0.1	0.4	0.6	9.3	3.7	2.2	1.1	0.1	0.4	0.4	7.9
1954	4.3	1.7	1.0	0.1	0.4	0.5	8.0	3.4	1.7	0.9	0.1	0.4	0.4	6.9
1954	5.0	—	1.7	0.1	0.7	0.5	8.0	4.2	—	1.6	0.1	0.6	0.4	6.9
1953	4.5	—	1.4	0.1	0.6	0.5	7.1	3.8	—	1.4	0.1	0.5	0.4	6.2
1952	4.0	—	1.1	0.1	0.5	0.5	6.2	3.4	—	1.1	0.1	0.5	0.3	5.4
1951	3.5	—	0.8	0.1	0.8	0.4	5.6	3.0	—	0.8	0.1	0.8	0.3	5.0
1948	2.5	—	0.4	0.1	0.6	0.3	3.9	2.2	—	0.4	0.1	0.6	0.2	3.5
1939	1.3	—	0.3	0.1	0.6	0.2	2.5	1.1	—	0.3	0.1	0.6	0.1	2.2
1930	1.4	—	0.3	0.1	0.5	0.2	2.5	1.2	—	0.3	0.1	0.5	0.1	2.2
1926	1.1	—	0.2	0.1	0.3	0.1	1.8	0.9	—	0.2	0.1	0.2	0.1	1.5

[1] Estimated from *Taxation Statistics* and other sources.

[2] Petroleum and natural gas industry not available separately before 1954.

[3] Estimates of total capital employed in merchandising are founded on less satisfactory data than for other series and must be regarded as illustrating broad relative magnitudes only. Corporations engaged in the construction industry are included in the post-war period.

[4] What have been classified as "other enterprises" in earlier series, such as G242, have been included with manufacturing.

[5] Some funded debt of governments and municipalities relevant to "other utilities" has been included in this latter series.

[6] New series not strictly comparable to earlier series.

Series G291-302. Foreign control of selected Canadian industries, selected year ends, 1926 to 1973
(per cent)

Year	Percentage of total control by all non-residents						Percentage of total control by United States residents					
	Manufac-turing	Petroleum and natural gas[1]	Other mining and smelting	Railways	Other utilities	Total (including merchan-dising not shown separately)[2]	Manufac-turing	Petroleum and natural gas[1]	Other mining and smelting	Railways	Other utilities	Total (including merchan-dising not shown separately)[2]
	291	292	293	294	295	296	297	298	299	300	301	302
1973	59	76	56	2	7	35	44	59	45	2	4	26
1972	59	75	57[3]	2	8	35	44	58	47[3]	2	5	26
1971	58	77	71	2	7	36	44	61	59	2	4	27
1970	61	76	70	2	7	36	47	61	59	2	4	28
1969	60	74	70	2	6	36	47	60	59	2	4	28
1968	58	75	68	2	5	35	46	61	58	2	4	28
1967	58	74	65	2	5	35	46	60	56	2	4	28
1966	57	74	62	2	4	34	45	59	53	2	4	27
1965	59	73	60	2	4	34	46	58	52	2	4	27
1964	60	72	59	2	4	34	46	60	51	2	4	27
1963	60	72	59	2	4	34	46	61	52	2	4	27
1962	60	74	58	2	4	34	45	63	52	2	4	27
1961	59	72	59	2	5	33	45	63	52	2	4	26
1960	59	73	61	2	5	33	44	64[4]	53	2	4	26
1959	57	73	61	2	5	32	44	67	53	2	4	26
1958	57	73	60	2	5	32	44	67	51	2	4	26
1957	56	76	61	2	5	32	43	70	52	2	4	27
1956	52	80	58	2	6	31	41	73	52	2	4	26
1955	52	79	57	2	8	30	42	73	55	2	6	26
1954[4]	51	69	51	2	8	28	41	67	49	2	7	24
1954	54	—	57	2	11	28	45	—	54	2	11	24
1953	52	—	57	2	11	28	44	—	55	2	11	24
1952	51	—	56	2	11[3]	27	44	—	53	2	11[3]	24
1951	48	—	53	2	20	27	42	—	51	2	20	24
1948	43	—	40	3	24	25	39	—	37	3	24	22
1939	38	—	42	3	26	21	32	—	38	3	26	19
1930	36	—	47	3	29	20	31	—	42	3	29	18
1926	35	—	38	3	20	17	30	—	32	3	20	15

[1] Petroleum and natural gas industry not available separately before 1954. For treatment see *The Canadian balance of international payments, 1957 and International Investment Position*, (Catalogue 67-201), page 33.
[2] Corporations engaged in the construction industry are included in the post-war period.
[3] Ratio altered significantly through unusually large reclassifications between foreign- and Canadian-controlled companies.
[4] New series not strictly comparable with earlier series.

Series G303-317. Control of manufacturing, petroleum and natural gas and mining, year ends, 1954 to 1973
(millions of dollars)

Year	Total capital employed	Total capital employed in enterprises controlled outside Canada	Total capital employed in enterprises controlled in United States	Per cent of total capital controlled outside Canada	Per cent of total capital controlled in United States	Total capital employed	Total capital employed in enterprises controlled outside Canada	Total capital employed in enterprises controlled in United States	Per cent of total capital controlled outside Canada	Per cent of total capital controlled in United States	Total capital employed	Total capital employed in enterprises controlled outside Canada	Total capital employed in enterprises controlled in United States	Per cent of total capital controlled outside Canada	Per cent of total capital controlled in United States
	303	304	305	306	307	308	309	310	311	312	313	314	315	316	317
	Beverages					*Rubber*					*Textiles*				
1973	1,199	343	—	29	—	564	559	—	99	—	1,317	396	277	30	21
1972	991	337	—	34	—	494	489	—	99	—	1,194	326	245	27	20
1971	903	328	—	36	—	452	448	—	99	—	1,154	302	229	26	20
1970	807	322	—	40	—	387	381	—	99	—	1,029	270	193	26	19
1969	721	256	—	36	—	381	375	—	99	—	964	250	179	26	19
1968	675	135	—	20	—	362	358	—	99	—	908	215	154	24	17
1967	615	127	—	21	—	325	320	—	99	—	868	191	132	22	15
1966	583	110	—	19	—	287	285	—	99	—	824	176	118	21	14
1965	571	108	—	19	—	258	257	—	99	—	746	164	108	22	15
1964	563	98	—	17	—	228	217	—	95	—	714	149	100	21	14
1963	571	101	—	18	—	216	208	—	96	—	702	146	97	21	14
1962	550	78	—	14	—	210	206	—	98	—	639	138	90	22	14
1961	522	75	—	14	—	211	209	—	99	—	614	138	85	23	14
1960	497	73	—	15	—	221	217	—	98	—	588	128	76	22	13
1959	456	62	—	13	—	203	198	—	98	—	622	143	88	23	14
1958	435	60	—	14	—	184	180	—	98	—	605	122	66	20	11
1957	418	57	—	13	—	177	172	—	97	—	609	115	65	19	11
1956	383	49	—	13	—	160	155	—	97	—	588	111	61	19	10
1955	385	52	—	14	—	139	136	—	98	—	594	106	57	18	10
1954	330	66	—	20	—	134	125	—	93	—	605	100	50	16	8
	Pulp and paper					*Agricultural machinery*[1]					*Automobiles and parts*				
1973	4,714	2,364	1,602	50	34	264	170	..	64	..	2,092	2,010	..	96	..
1972	4,499	2,422	1,677	54	37	267	153	—	57	—	1,835	1,765	..	96	..
1971	4,380	2,362	1,688	54	39	239	139	—	58	—	1,646	1,589	..	97	..
1970	3,950	2,108	1,505	53	38	232	128	—	55	—	1,536	1,496	..	97	..
1969	3,701	1,876	1,365	51	37	265	143	—	54	—	1,484	1,452	..	98	..
1968	3,462	1,721	1,341	50	39	254	118	—	47	—	1,231	1,194	..	97	..
1967	3,367	1,677	1,316	50	39	280	110	—	39	—	1,059	1,018	..	96	..
1966	3,217	1,572	1,202	49	37	267	103	—	38	—	953	919	..	96	..
1965	2,862	1,387	1,016	48	35	193	104	—	54	—	815	784	..	96	..
1964	2,582	1,259	913	49	35	207	115	—	56	—	696	668	..	96	..
1963	2,339	1,113	834	48	36	203	100	—	49	—	586	559	..	95	..
1962	2,282	1,061	784	46	34	187	99	—	53	—	495	472	..	95	..
1961	2,223	1,027	773	46	35	186	94	—	50	—	467	454	..	97	..
1960	2,079	1,048	763	51	37	191	97	—	51	—	440	427	..	97	..
1959	1,889	928	721	49	38	170	93	—	55	—	407	393	..	97	..
1958	1,700	938	731	55	43	201	91	—	45	—	382	369	369	97	97
1957	1,639	902	704	55	43	184	70	—	38	—	386	365	365	95	95
1956	1,617	876	685	54	42	169	58	—	34	—	375	356	356	95	95
1955	1,442	785	626	54	43	160	53	—	33	—	335	322	322	96	96
1954	1,433	810	648	56	45	155	54	—	35	—	292	277	277	95	95
	Transport equipment n.e.s.					*Primary iron and steel*					*Aluminum*[2]				
1973	655	385	232	59	35	1,893	47	..	3	..	944	..	..	..	..
1972	632	369	216	58	34	1,753	52	..	3	..	894	..	..	..	..
1971	628	372	235	59	37	1,687	11	11	1	1	836	..	..	..	..
1970	627	408	268	65	43	1,469	11	11	1	1	901	898	..	100	..
1969	556	394	234	71	42	1,321	19	19	1	1	911	907	..	100	..
1968	591	454	249	77	42	1,332	19	19	1	1	871	868	..	100	..
1967	593	448	283	76	48	1,261	120	18	9	1	941	938	..	100	..
1966	471	298	167	63	35	1,216	156	18	13	2	863	858	..	99	..
1965	374	251	132	67	35	1,156	166	15	14	1	842	840	..	100	..
1964	263	190	72	72	27	1,006	141	16	14	2	814	814	..	100	..
1963	264	208	95	79	36	868[3]	121	13[3]	14	2[3]	878	877	..	100	..
1962	243	185	67	76	28	938	200	92	21	10	..	..	..	..	..
1961	249	175	64	70	26	873	222	114	25	13	..	..	..	..	..
1960	275	201	75	73	27	781	219	103	28	14	—	—	—	—	—
1959	267	194	71	73	27	707	163	61	23	9	—	—	—	—	—
1958	275	192	69	70	25	615	153	51	25	8	—	—	—	—	—
1957	277	186	57	67	21	557	144	46	26	8	—	—	—	—	—
1956	268	165	53	62	20	549	38	38	7	7	—	—	—	—	—

Series G303-317. Control of manufacturing, petroleum and natural gas and mining, year ends, 1954 to 1973 (continued)

(millions of dollars)

Year	Total capital employed	Total capital employed in enterprises controlled outside Canada	Total capital employed in enterprises controlled in United States	Per cent of total capital controlled outside Canada	Per cent of total capital controlled in United States	Total capital employed	Total capital employed in enterprises controlled outside Canada	Total capital employed in enterprises controlled in United States	Per cent of total capital controlled outside Canada	Per cent of total capital controlled in United States	Total capital employed	Total capital employed in enterprises controlled outside Canada	Total capital employed in enterprises controlled in United States	Per cent of total capital controlled outside Canada	Per cent of total capital controlled in United States
	303	304	305	306	307	308	309	310	311	312	313	314	315	316	317
	Transport equipment n.e.s.					*Primary iron and steel*					*Aluminum[2]*				
1955	242	134	44	55	18	438	34	34	8	8	–	–	–	–	–
1954	245	89	51	36	21	390	25	25	6	6	–	–	–	–	–
	Electrical apparatus					*Chemicals*					*Other*				
1973	1,784	1,297	1,093	73	61	2,888	2,490	1,864	86	64	12,815	8,138	5,735	64	45
1972	1,634	1,216	1,038	74	63	2,590	2,270	1,692	88	65	11,600	7,230	5,124	62	44
1971	1,428	1,033	884	72	62	2,519	2,210	1,582	88	63	10,844	6,684	4,889	62	45
1970	1,434	1,043	904	73	63	2,585	2,090	1,498	81	58	10,048	6,010	4,374	60	44
1969	1,270	945	822	75	65	2,436	1,960	1,429	81	59	9,447	5,543	4,081	59	43
1968	1,160	906	791	78	68	2,405	1,941	1,449	81	60	8,464	4,694	3,470	55	41
1967	1,064	818	709	77	67	2,256	1,787	1,361	79	60	7,905	4,269	3,226	54	41
1966	984	753	654	77	67	2,071	1,668	1,284	81	62	6,936	3,826	2,877	55	41
1965	819	639	554	78	68	1,858	1,490	1,137	80	61	6,158	3,573	2,736	58	44
1964	741	569	492	77	67	1,657	1,354	999	82	60	5,362	3,340	2,447	62	45
1963	694	529	456	76	66	1,407[3]	1,135	820[3]	81	58[3]	4,959[3]	3,140	2,282	63	46
1962	669	512	439	77	66	1,351	1,014	697	75	52	5,525	3,834	2,903	69	52
1961	595	467	394	78	66	1,226	929	638	76	52	5,502	3,669	2,801	66	50
1960	558	444	365	80	66	1,119	845	570	76	51	5,498	3,491	2,631	63	48
1959	526	424	351	81	67	1,073	823	561	77	52	5,351	3,264	2,553	61	48
1958	504	399	328	79	65	993	738	506	74	51	5,100	3,022	2,390	59	47
1957	494	382	317	77	64	942	708	484	75	51	4,968	2,819	2,282	57	46
1956	470	361	296	77	63	823	627	426	75	51	4,574	2,372	1,957	52	43
1955	411	335	279	82	68	737	563	373	77	51	4,011	2,109	1,776	53	45
1954	402	309	261	77	65	654	500	341	76	52	3,663	1,895	1,581	52	43
	Total manufacturing[4]					*Petroleum and natural gas*					*Smelting and refining — non-ferrous native ores*				
1973	31,129	18,199	13,591	59	44	16,429	12,418	9,602	76	59	3,022	681	..	23	..
1972	28,383	16,629	12,457	59	44	14,963	11,161	8,624	75	58	2,814	811	..	29	..
1971	26,716	15,478	11,728	58	44	13,619	10,465	8,265	77	61	2,420	1,592	..	66	..
1970	25,005	15,165	11,738	61	47	12,355	9,388	7,480	76	61	2,138	1,427	..	67	..
1969	23,457	14,120	11,080	60	47	11,406	8,465	6,813	74	60	1,908	1,248	..	65	..
1968	21,715	12,623	10,084	58	46	10,425	7,776	6,320	75	61	1,827	1,175	..	64	..
1967	20,534	11,823	9,413	58	46	9,739	7,230	5,836	74	60	1,503	835	835	56	56
1966	18,672	10,724	8,475	57	45	9,051	6,734	5,380	74	59	1,336	697	697	52	52
1965	16,652	9,763	7,673	59	46	8,334	6,106	4,813	73	58	1,230	610	610	50	50
1964	14,833	8,913	6,838	60	46	7,887	5,678	4,719	72	60	1,175	580	580	49	49
1963	13,687	8,237	6,329	60	46	7,576	5,469	4,610	72	61	1,066	545	545	51	51
1962	13,089	7,799	5,900	60	45	6,922	5,126	4,334	74	63	1,042	536	536	51	51
1961	12,668	7,459	5,671	59	45	6,428	4,660	4,038	72	63	968	534	534	55	55
1960	12,247	7,190	5,372	59	44	6,054	4,430	3,857	73	64	936	601	601	64	64
1959	11,671	6,685	5,128	57	44	5,609	4,080	3,737	73	67	922	611	611	66	66
1958	10,994	6,264	4,821	57	44	5,138	3,753	3,456	73	67	880	573	573	65	65
1957	10,651	5,920	4,598	56	43	4,483	3,422	3,145	76	70	893	585	585	66	66
1956	9,976	5,168	4,118	52	41	3,524	2,831	2,571	80	73	844	586	586	69	69
1955	8,894	4,629	3,736	52	42	2,961	2,338	2,173	79	73	785	539	539	69	69
1954	8,303	4,250	3,447	51	41	2,484	1,721	1,671	69	67	715	392	392	55	55
	Other mining					*Total mining*					*Total manufacturing, petroleum and natural gas, and mining*				
1973	5,341	4,008	..	75	61	8,363	4,689	3,770	56	45	55,921	35,306	26,963	63	48
1972	4,902	3,615	..	74	61	7,716	4,426	3,622	57	47	51,062	32,216	24,703	63	48
1971	4,748	3,520	..	74	60	7,168	5,112	4,266	71	59	47,503	31,055	24,259	65	51
1970	4,409	3,166	..	72	59	6,547	4,593	3,894	70	59	43,907	29,146	23,112	67	53
1969	4,278	3,101	..	73	60	6,186	4,349	3,682	70	59	41,049	26,934	21,575	66	53
1968	4,038	2,799	..	69	57	5,865	3,974	3,378	68	58	38,005	24,373	19,782	64	52
1967	3,691	2,542	2,084	69	57	5,194	3,377	2,919	65	56	35,467	22,430	18,168	63	51
1966	3,488	2,301	1,886	66	54	4,824	2,998	2,583	62	53	32,547	20,456	16,438	63	51
1965	3,122	2,004	1,675	64	54	4,352	2,614	2,285	60	52	29,338	18,483	14,771	63	50
1964	2,928	1,841	1,515	63	52	4,103	2,421	2,095	59	51	26,823	17,012	13,652	63	51
1963	2,742	1,687	1,417	62	52	3,808	2,232	1,962	59	52	25,071	15,938	12,901	64	52
1962	2,595	1,574	1,353	61	52	3,637	2,110	1,889	58	52	23,648	15,035	12,123	63	51
1961	2,428	1,460	1,243	60	51	3,396	1,994	1,777	59	52	22,492	14,113	11,486	63	51

Series G303-317. Control of manufacturing, petroleum and natural gas and mining, year ends, 1954 to 1973 (concluded)
(millions of dollars)

Year	Total capital employed	Total capital employed in enterprises controlled outside Canada	Total capital employed in enterprises controlled in United States	Per cent of total capital controlled outside Canada	Per cent of total capital controlled in United States	Total capital employed	Total capital employed in enterprises controlled outside Canada	Total capital employed in enterprises controlled in United States	Per cent of total capital controlled outside Canada	Per cent of total capital controlled in United States	Total capital employed	Total capital employed in enterprises controlled outside Canada	Total capital employed in enterprises controlled in United States	Per cent of total capital controlled outside Canada	Per cent of total capital controlled in United States
	303	304	305	306	307	308	309	310	311	312	313	314	315	316	317
	Other mining					*Total mining*					*Total manufacturing, petroleum and natural gas, and mining*				
1960	2,355	1,422	1,149	60	49	3,291	2,023	1,750	61	53	21,592	13,643	10,979	63	51
1959	2,145	1,258	1,002	59	47	3,067	1,869	1,613	61	53	20,347	12,634	10,478	62	51
1958	2,066	1,204	922	59	45	2,946	1,777	1,495	60	51	19,078	11,794	9,772	62	51
1957	1,934	1,134	866	59	45	2,827	1,719	1,451	61	52	17,961	11,061	9,194	61	51
1956	1,609	837	683	52	42	2,453	1,423	1,269	58	52	15,953	9,422	7,958	59	50
1955	1,315	656	610	50	46	2,100	1,195	1,149	57	55	13,955	8,162	7,058	59	51
1954	1,148	560	526	49	46	1,863	952	918	51	49	12,650	6,923	6,036	55	48

[1] Includes enterprises also engaged in the manufacture of heavy equipment, which tends to overstate foreign-owned and controlled proportion of capital actually engaged in the manufacture of agricultural implements only.
[2] Aluminum industry not available separately prior to 1963; included with "other" manufacturing.

[3] New series not strictly comparable with earlier years.
[4] Includes some corporate debt guaranteed by provincial governments, which is shown as part of the liabilities of provincial governments to non-residents in series G204.

Series G318-340. Canadian long-term investment abroad,[1] all countries and by major areas, by type and industry, selected year ends, 1926 to 1974
(millions of dollars)

Year	Beverages	Non-ferrous metals	Wood and paper products	Iron and products	Chemicals and allied products	Other manufacturing	Total manufacturing	Merchandising	Mining and smelting	Petroleum and natural gas	Railways
	318	319	320	321	322	323	324	325	326	327	328
					Located in all countries						
1974	1,121	1,396	824	909	203	234	4,687	378	798	1,148	411
1973	1,064	1,031	727	771	153	173	3,919	376	621	863	414
1972	1,021	971	651	694	111	183	3,631	280	404	634	396
1971	974	908	536	656	121	250	3,445	273	393	547	328
1970	938	837	480	593	112	247	3,207	278	378	492	326
1969	952	695			1,401		3,048	276	376	428	318
1968	929	633			1,182		2,744	267	356	240	309
1967	902	590			954		2,446	262	324	200	306
1966	877	550			862		2,289	174	296	191	303
1965	826	502			783		2,111	155	253	242	302
1964					2,155				278	242	273
1963					1,995				274	255	279
1962					1,769				257	285	282
1961					1,566				243	280	278
1960					1,482				275	268	271
1959					1,342				258	259	271
1958					1,250					532	..
1957					1,198					522	..
1956					1,106					451	
1955					993					410	..
1954					935				133	228	273
1953					851					317	..
1952					765					163	..
1951					722					117	..
1950					..					..	..
1949					553					91	..
1948					..					..	..
1947					414					155	..
1946					..					..	..

Series G318-340. Canadian long-term investment abroad,[1] all countries and by major areas, by type and industry, selected year ends, 1926 to 1974 (continued)
(millions of dollars)

Year	Direct investment in branches, subsidiaries and controlled companies							Merchandising	Utilities		
	Manufacturing										
	Beverages	Non-ferrous metals	Wood and paper products	Iron and products	Chemicals and allied products	Other manufacturing	Total manufacturing		Mining and smelting	Petroleum and natural gas	Railways
	318	319	320	321	322	323	324	325	326	327	328

Located in all countries

Year	318	319	320	321	322	323	324	325	326	327	328
1945					337					138	..
1939					289					123	..
1930					..					..	..
1926					..					..	..

Year	Utilities		Financial	Other	Total direct investment	Portfolio investment in foreign securities			Miscellaneous investment[2]	Government of Canada credits[3]	Government of Canada subscriptions to international investment agencies	Total
	Other utilities	Total utilities				Stocks	Bonds	Total portfolio investment				
	329	330	331	332	333	334	335	336	337	338	339	340

Located in all countries

Year	329	330	331	332	333	334	335	336	337	338	339	340
1974	995	1,406	630	260	9,307	3,250	674	3,924	2,951	2,055	581	18,818
1973	853	1,267	530	234	7,810	3,055	639	3,694	2,191	1,839	485	16,019
1972	787	1,183	393	181	6,706	2,820	545	3,365	1,770	1,695	403	13,939
1971	955	1,283	406	191	6,538	2,490	520	3,010	1,368	1,565	319	12,800
1970	899	1,225	421	187	6,188	2,345	474	2,819	977	1,490	268	11,742
1969	267	585	313	185	5,211	2,517	459	2,976	789	1,444	239	10,659
1968	260	569	270	171	4,617	2,410	475	2,885	755	1,434	209	9,900
1967	125	431	206	161	4,030	2,094	472	2,566	762	1,406	180	8,944
1966	124	427	190	144	3,711	1,866	372	2,238	786	1,450	162	8,347
1965	105	407	165	136	3,469	1,617	280	1,897	659	1,495	138	7,658
1964	84	357	160	80	3,272	1,504	275	1,779	465	1,517	125	7,158
1963	77	356	134	68	3,082	1,426	266	1,692	264	1,285	117	6,440
1962	57	339	75	59	2,784	1,370	273	1,643	212	1,301	110	6,050
1961	97	375	65	67	2,596	1,167	276	1,443	108	1,424	99	5,670
1960	87	358	32	52	2,467	1,050	265	1,315	-18	1,462	85	5,311
1959	78	349	27	51	2,286	934	249	1,183	-20	1,495	65	5,009
1958	..	324	43		2,149	868	250	1,118	-54	1,528	66	4,807
1957	..	313	40		2,073	811	257	1,068	-53	1,560	67	4,715
1956	..	307	27		1,891	785	221	1,006	-48	1,587	66	4,502
1955	..	319	20		1,742	767	224	991	-52	1,635	65	4,381
1954	38	311	3	9	1,619	723	203	926	-53	1,705	63	4,260
1953	..	300	9		1,477	690	179	869	-55	1,778	63	4,132
1952	..	326	11		1,265	669[8]	161	830	-57	1,866	63	3,967
1951	..	321	6		1,166	467	142	609	-58	1,922	66	3,705
1950	..	..	..		990	..	..	598	16	1,990	69	3,663
1949	..	276	6		926	477	161	638	31	2,009	71	3,675
1948	..	..	..		788	..	..	605	37	1,878	65	3,373
1947	..	246	7		822	426	153	579	-10	1,816	65	3,272
1946	..	..	..		772	..	..	551	-8	1,362	32	2,709
1945	..	239	6		720	454	167	621	-8	707	—	2,040
1939	..	249	10		671[8]	511	208	719[8]	..	31	—	1,421
1930	..	..	..		443	..	..	789	..	31	—	1,263
1926	..	..	..		397	..	..	493	..	36	—	926

Series G318-340. Canadian long-term investment abroad,[1] all countries and by major areas, by type and industry, selected year ends, 1926 to 1974 (continued)
(millions of dollars)

Year	Direct investment in branches, subsidiaries and controlled companies							Merchandising	Utilities		Railways
	Manufacturing										
	Beverages	Non-ferrous metals	Wood and paper products	Iron and products	Chemicals and allied products	Other manufacturing	Total manufacturing		Mining and smelting	Petroleum and natural gas	
	318	319	320	321	322	323	324	325	326	327	328
Located in United States											
1974	728	757	621	254	130	168	2,658	179	345	968	411
1973	744	431	557	188	87	126	2,133	180	222	722	414
1972	794	400	523	192	60	124	2,093	125	67	556	396
1971	768	374	416	172	63	184	1,977	140	59	501	328
1970	751	341	366	160	64	188	1,870	145	51	453	326
1969	714	242		777			1,733	138	54	390	318
1968	715	192		629			1,536	138	40	203	309
1967	713	182		463			1,358	151	36	168	306
1966	695	189		389			1,273	120	47	168	303
1965	661	170		355			1,186	109	34	223	302
1964			1,252						36	224	273
1963			1,211						41	240	279
1962			1,092						33	271	282
1961			1,018						51	266	278
1960			971						53	254	271
1959			862						44	246	271
1958			833							302	..
1957			833							318	..
1956			804							301	..
1955			710							294	..
1954			686						39	222	273
1953			624							225	..
1952			566							95	..
1951			549							71	..
1950			..							..	..
1949			413							58	..
1948			..							..	..
1947			272							37	..
1946			..							..	..
1945			214							25	..
1939			176							21	..
1930			..							..	..
1926			..							..	..

Series G318-340. Canadian long-term investment abroad,[1] all countries and by major areas, by type and industry, selected year ends, 1926 to 1974 (continued)
(millions of dollars)

Year	Utilities — Other utilities	Utilities — Total utilities	Financial	Other	Total direct investment	Portfolio investment in foreign securities — Stocks	Portfolio investment in foreign securities — Bonds	Portfolio investment in foreign securities — Total portfolio investment	Miscellaneous investment[2]	Government of Canada credits[3]	Government of Canada subscriptions to international investment agencies	Total
	329	330	331	332	333	334	335	336	337	338	339	340

Located in United States

Year	329	330	331	332	333	334	335	336	337	338	339	340
1974	25	436	184	139	4,909	2,765	202	2,967	500	—	—	8,376
1973	13	427	132	108	3,924	2,640	203	2,843	365	—	—	7,132
1972	8	404	119	67	3,431	2,475	200	2,675	337	—	—	6,443
1971	137	465	166	91	3,399	2,185	217	2,402	277	—	—	6,078
1970	143	469	190	84	3,262	2,115	224	2,339	234	26	—	5,861
1969	121	439	155	70	2,979	2,155	214	2,369	216	58	—	5,622
1968	119	428	147	54	2,546	2,086	212	2,298	212	90	—	5,146
1967	10	316	115	46	2,190	1,779	188	1,967	189	123	—	4,469
1966	8	311	138	43	2,100	1,559	143	1,702	122	155	—	4,079
1965	11	313	129	47	2,041	1,309	99	1,408	69	187	—	3,705
1964	14	287	137	31	1,967	1,200	103	1,303	69	219	—	3,558
1963	17	296	111	23	1,922	1,116	101	1,217	63	—	—	3,202
1962	13	295	64	31	1,786	1,060	111	1,171	106	—	—	3,063
1961	13	291	57	41	1,724	916	119	1,035	62	—	—	2,821
1960	5	276	25	39	1,618	827	120	947	18	—	—	2,583
1959	3	274	23	40	1,489	734	111	845	15	—	—	2,349
1958	..	274	31		1,440	659	111	770	-6	—	—	2,204
1957	..	268	32		1,451	593	118	711	6	—	—	2,168
1956	..	267	22		1,394	569	84	653	-2	—	—	2,045
1955	..	274	15		1,293	539	89	628	14	—	—	1,935
1954	1	274	3	7	1,231	490	89	579	13	—	—	1,823
1953	..	263	7		1,119	469	95	564	12	—	—	1,695
1952	..	293	8		962	450[8]	86	536	10	—	—	1,508
1951	..	288	4		912	289	87	376	9	—	—	1,297
1950	..	..	..		..	..	..	..	8	—	—	..
1949	..	247	3		721	345	98	443	6	—	—	1,170
1948	..	..	..		..	..	..	..	6	—	—	..
1947	..	217	5		531	283	83	366	5	—	—	902
1946	..	..	..		..	..	..	..	5	—	—	..
1945	..	212	4		455	317	92	409	5	—	—	869
1939	..	211	4		412	380	121	501	..	—	—	913
1930	..	..	..		260	..	..	459	..	—	—	719
1926	..	..	..		250	..	..	195	..	—	—	445

Series G318–340. Canadian long-term investment abroad,[1] all countries and by major areas, by type and industry, selected year ends, 1926 to 1974 (continued)
(millions of dollars)

Year	Direct investment in branches, subsidiaries and controlled companies							Merchandising	Utilities		
	Manufacturing										
	Beverages	Non-ferrous metals	Wood and paper products	Iron and products	Chemicals and allied products	Other manufacturing	Total manufacturing		Mining and smelting	Petroleum and natural gas	Railways
	318	319	320	321	322	323	324	325	326	327	328
Located in United Kingdom											
1974	198	210	105	137	5	14	669	43	—	59	—
1973	181	199	93	117	4	15	609	57	1	33	—
1972	135	193	64	109	3	14	518	33	4	25	—
1971	132	191	59	107	3	12	504	38	2	12	—
1970	123	196	51	97	3	9	479	39	2	11	—
1969	177	152			155		484	50	3	9	—
1968	159	146			154		459	67	2	7	—
1967	146	145			136		427	49	1	6	—
1966	151	156			159		466	28	2	5	—
1965	133	144			146		423	24	1	2	—
1964					406				—	1	—
1963					367[8]				—	—	—
1962					327				—	—	—
1961					271				—	—	—
1960					240				—	—	—
1959					223				—	—	—
1958					196				—	—	—
1957					168				—	—	—
1956					135				—	—	—
1955					128				—	—	—
1954					118				—	—	—
1953					103				—	—	—
1952					80				—	—	—
1951					73				—	—	—
1950					..					..	..
1949					58					—	—
1948					..					..	..
1947					64					—	—
1946					..					..	..
1945					53					—	—
1939					53					—	—
1930					..					..	..
1926					..					..	..

Series G318-340. Canadian long-term investment abroad,[1] all countries and by major areas, by type and industry, selected year ends, 1926 to 1974 (continued)
(millions of dollars)

Year	Utilities Other utilities	Utilities Total utilities	Financial	Other	Total direct investment	Portfolio investment in foreign securities Stocks	Portfolio investment in foreign securities Bonds	Portfolio investment in foreign securities Total portfolio investment	Miscellaneous investment	Government of Canada credits[5]	Government of Canada subscriptions to international investment agencies	Total
	329	330	331	332	333	334	335	336	337	338	339	340

Located in United Kingdom

Year	329	330	331	332	333	334	335	336	337	338	339	340
1974	26	26	71	11	879	90	34	124	180	932	—	2,115
1973	14	14	69	14	797	75	35	110	158	954	—	2,019
1972	17	17	16	17	630	70	33	103	110	976	—	1,819
1971	10	10	13	11	590	65	20	85	78	997	—	1,750
1970	13	13	32	10	586	60	20	80	74	1,017	—	1,757
1969	12	12	31	6	595	60	20	80	50	1,038	—	1,763
1968	7	7	23	5	570	57	20	77	36	1,058	—	1,741
1967	5	5	22	5	515	52	15	67	54	1,040	—	1,676
1966	9	9	22	9	541	51	13	64	53	1,059	—	1,717
1965	10	10	13	9	482	53	15	68	55	1,078	—	1,683
1964	8	8	10	6	431	50	15	65	53	1,059	—	1,608
1963	9	9	11	5	392	48	16	64	49	1,039	—	1,544
1962	9[8]	9	2	6	344	47	16	63	32	1,057	—	1,496
1961	12	12	2	3	288	43	16	59	17	1,074	—	1,438
1960	14	14	2	1	257	26	16	42	18	1,092	—	1,409
1959	10	10	1	1	235	25	12	37	16	1,108	—	1,396
1958	3	3	1		200	27	14	41	17	1,125	—	1,383
1957	3	3	1		172	33	15	48	12	1,171	—	1,403
1956	3	3	1		139	30	16	46	12	1,179	—	1,376
1955	2	2	1		131	29	17	46	13	1,202	—	1,392
1954	1	1	—	—	119	17	13	31	15	1,247	—	1,412
1953	1	1		—	104	16	13	29	13	1,292	—	1,438
1952	1	1		—	81	17	14	31	13	1,357	—	1,482
1951	1	1		—	74	17	17	34	13	1,394	—	1,515
1950	..	..	..	..	..	..	..	..	13	1,442	—	..
1949	—	—	1		59	21	19	40	13	1,443	—	1,555
1948	..	..	..	..	..	..	..	..	12	1,319	—	..
1947	—	—	—		64	26	26	52	14	1,331	—	1,461
1946	..	..	..	..	..	..	..	..	16	1,021	—	..
1945	—	—	1		54	26	27	53	16	561	—	684
1939	—	—	6		59	22	21	43	..	—	—	102
1930	..	..	..	..	14	..	..	45	..	—	—	59
1926	..	..	..	..	7	..	..	45	..	—	—	52

Series G318-340. Canadian long-term investment abroad,[1] all countries and by major areas, by type and industry, selected year ends, 1926 to 1974 (continued)

(millions of dollars)

Year	Direct investment in branches, subsidiaries and controlled companies										
	Manufacturing							Merchandising	Utilities		
	Beverages	Non-ferrous metals	Wood and paper products	Iron and products	Chemicals and allied products	Other manufacturing	Total manufacturing		Mining and smelting	Petroleum and natural gas	Railways
	318	319	320	321	322	323	324	325	326	327	328
Located in other Commonwealth countries[6]											
1974	11	66	2	287	1	20	387	118	165	52	—
1973	9	67	3	267	2	17	365	110	146	61	—
1972	7	62	2	229	2	21	323	91	121	19	—
1971	8	60	3	198	2	19	290	69	142	10	—
1970	7	46	3	182	2	16	256	64	160	7	—
1969	6	40		186			232	60	165	7	—
1968	7	46		161			214	43	189	20	—
1967	5	36		149			190	47	173	18	—
1966	9	40		139			188	18	147	6	—
1965	10	40		131			181	12	137	5	—
1964				186					160	4	—
1963				149					162	1	—
1962				132					161	1	—
1961				95					145	—	—
1960				121					156	—	—
1959				120					152	1	—
1958				102						150	—
1957				93						131	—
1956				85						98	—
1955				83						72	—
1954				74					60	—	—
1953				73						54	—
1952				70						35	—
1951				61						20	—
1950				..						..	..
1949				51						19	—
1948				..						..	..
1947				47						30	..
1946				..						..	..
1945				34						28	—
1939				30						17	—
1930				..						..	..
1926				..						..	..

Series G318-340. Canadian long-term investment abroad,[1] all countries and by major areas, by type and industry, selected year ends, 1926 to 1974 (continued)
(millions of dollars)

Year	Utilities — Other utilities	Utilities — Total utilities	Financial	Other	Total direct investment	Portfolio investment in foreign securities — Stocks	Portfolio investment in foreign securities — Bonds	Portfolio investment in foreign securities — Total portfolio investment	Miscellaneous investment	Government of Canada credits	Government of Canada subscriptions to international investment agencies	Total
	329	330	331	332	333	334	335	336	337	338	339	340

Located in other Commonwealth countries[6]

Year	329	330	331	332	333	334	335	336	337	338	339	340
1974	308	308	137	87	1,254	30	44	74	..	605	—	1,933
1973	257	257	136	85	1,160	25	36	61	..	473	—	1,694
1972	219	219	116	76	965	20	31	51	..	465	—	1,481
1971	154	154	101	77	843	20	27	47	..	354	—	1,244
1970	105	105	117	82	791	15	23	38	..	243	—	1,072
1969	79	79	100	82	725	15	22	37	..	137	—	899
1968	68	68	84	82	700	14	24	38	..	78	—	816
1967	49	49	54	82	613	13	27	40	..	36	—	689
1966	54	54	24	68	505	15	29	44	..	27	—	576
1965	34	34	18	66	453	14	31	45	..	19	—	517
1964	26	26	11	39	426	13	32	45	..	25	—	496
1963	17	17	10	38	377	12	29	41	..	29	—	447
1962	16	16	6	20	336	12	31	43	..	25	—	404
1961	15	15	4	20	279	11	30	41	..	30	—	350
1960	10	10	3	9	299	10	18	28	..	35	—	362
1959	8	8	2	8	291	8	19	27	..	35	—	353
1958	7	7		7	266	8	21	29	..	34	—	329
1957	8	8	3		235	7	21	28	..	—	—	263
1956	8	8	—		191	7	21	28	..	—	—	219
1955	4	4	—		159	7	21	28	..	—	—	187
1954	4	4	—		138	6	7	13	..	—	—	151
1953	6	6	—		133	6	8	14	..	—	—	147
1952	7	7	—		112	6	8	14	..	—	—	126
1951	7	7	—		88	6	8	14	..	—	—	102
1950	..	..	..		..	..	..	..	..	—	—	..
1949	6	6	—		76	6	8	14	..	—	—	90
1948	..	..	..		..	..	..	..	..	—	—	..
1947	8	8	—		85	7	11	18	..	—	—	103
1946	..	..	..		..	..	..	..	..	—	—	..
1945	7	7	—		69	7	12	19	..	—	—	88
1939	7	7	—		54	7	15	22	..	—	—	76
1930	..	..	..		..	..	..	..	..	—	—	..
1926	..	..	..		..	..	..	..	..	—	—	..

Series G318-340. Canadian long-term investment abroad,[1] all countries and by major areas, by type and industry, selected year ends, 1926 to 1974 (continued)
(millions of dollars)

Year	Direct investment in branches, subsidiaries and controlled companies										
	Manufacturing							Merchandising	Utilities		Railways
	Beverages	Non-ferrous metals	Wood and paper products	Iron and products	Chemicals and allied products	Other manufacturing	Total manufacturing		Mining and smelting	Petroleum and natural gas	
	318	319	320	321	322	323	324	325	326	327	328

Located in all other countries[7]

Year	318	319	320	321	322	323	324	325	326	327	328
1974	184	363	96	231	67	32	973	38	288	69	—
1973	130	334	74	199	60	15	812	29	252	47	—
1972	85	316	62	164	46	24	697	31	212	34	—
1971	66	283	58	179	53	35	674	26	190	24	—
1970	57	254	60	154	43	34	602	30	165	21	—
1969	55	261		283			599	28	154	22	—
1968	48	249		238			535	19	125	10	—
1967	38	227		206			471	15	114	8	—
1966	22	165		175			362	8	100	12	—
1965	22	148		151			321	10	81	12	—
1964				311					82	13	—
1963				268					71	14	—
1962				218					63	13	—
1961				182					47	14	—
1960				150					66	14	
1959				137					62	12	—
1958				119						80	—
1957				104						73	—
1956				82						52	—
1955				72						44	—
1954				57					34	6	—
1953				51						38	—
1952				49						33	—
1951				39						26	—
1950				..						..	..
1949				31						14	—
1948				..						..	..
1947				31						88	—
1946				..						..	..
1945				36						85	—
1939				30						85	—
1930				..						..	..
1926				..						..	..

Series G318-340. Canadian long-term investment abroad,[1] all countries and by major areas, by type and industry, selected year ends, 1926 to 1974 (concluded)
(millions of dollars)

Year	Utilities — Other utilities	Utilities — Total utilities	Financial	Other	Total direct investment	Portfolio investment in foreign securities — Stocks	Portfolio investment in foreign securities — Bonds	Portfolio investment in foreign securities — Total portfolio investment	Miscellaneous investment[2]	Government of Canada credits	Government of Canada subscriptions to international investment agencies	Total
	329	330	331	332	333	334	335	336	337	338	339	340
					Located in all other countries[7]							
1974	636	636	238	23	2,265	365	394	759	2,271	518	581	6,394
1973	569	569	193	27	1,929	315	365	680	1,668	412	485	5,174
1972	543	543	142	21	1,680	255	281	536	1,323	254	403	4,196
1971	654	654	126	12	1,706	220	256	476	1,013	214	319	3,728
1970	638[8]	638	82	11	1,549	155	207	362	669	204	268	3,052
1969	55	55	27	27	912	287	203	490	523	211	239	2,375
1968	66	66	16	30	801	253	219	472	507	208	209	2,197
1967	61	61	15	28	712	250	242	492	519	207	180	2,110
1966	53	53	6	24	565	241	187	428	611	209	162	1,975
1965	50	50	5	14	493	241	135	376	535	211	138	1,753
1964	36	36	2	4	448	241	125	366	343	214	125	1,496
1963	34	34	2	2	391	250	120	370	152	217	117	1,247
1962	19[8]	19	3	2	318	251	115	366	74	219	110	1,087
1961	57	57	2	3	305	197	111	308	29	320	99	1,061
1960	58	58	2	3	293	187	111	298	-54	335	85	957
1959	57	57	1	2	271	167	107	274	-51	352	65	911
1958	40	40		4	243	174	104	278	-65	369	66	891
1957	34	34		4	215	178	103	281	-71	389	67	881
1956	29	29		4	167	179	100	279	-58	408	66	862
1955	39	39		4	159	192	97	289	-79	433	65	867
1954	32	32	—	2	131	210	93	303	-81	458	63	874
1953	30	30		2	121	199	63	262	-80	486	63	852
1952	25	25		3	110	196	53	249	-80	509	63	851
1951	25	25		2	92	155	30	185	-80	528	66	791
1950	..	..		..	..	..	..	..	-5	548	69	..
1949	23	23		2	70	105	36	141	12	566	71	860
1948	..	..		..	..	..	..	..	19	559	65	..
1947	21	21		2	142	110	33	143	-29	485	65	806
1946	..	..		..	..	..	..	..	-29	350	32	..
1945	20	20		1	142	104	36	140	-29	146	—	399
1939	31	31		—	146	102	51	153	—	31	—	330
1930	..	..		..	169[9]	105[9]	180[9]	285[9]	—	31[9]	—	485[9]
1926	..	..		..	140[9]	—	..	253[9]	—	36[9]	—	429[9]

[1] Figures include the equity of non-residents in assets abroad of Canadian companies (series G171), but exclude investment of insurance companies and banks held mainly against liabilities to non-residents.

[2] Negative amounts in miscellaneous investment arise from the application of reserves against government inactive assets and short positions of Canadian financial institutions.

[3] Includes United Nations bonds from 1962, which amounted to $4 million in 1974.

[4] Includes medium-term non-marketable United States government securities, acquired under the Columbia River Treaty arrangements from 1964 to 1970.

[5] Includes deferred interest on the United Kingdom 1946 loan agreement, starting from 1956 and amounting to $101 million in 1974.

[6] Includes investment in Newfoundland prior to 1949.

[7] Republic of South Africa and Rhodesia are included with all other countries since 1961 and 1967, respectively.

[8] New series not strictly comparable with earlier series.

[9] Includes investments in other Commonwealth countries.

Series G341-348. Country of control of corporations by eight major industry groups, 1968 to 1975
(number of corporations)

Year	Foreign			Canadian			Unclassified	Total
	United States	Others	Total	Private sector	Government business enterprise	Total		
	341	342	343	344	345	346	347	348

Agriculture, forestry and fishing

Year	341	342	343	344	345	346	347	348
1975	76	32	108	3,487	2	3,489	7,242	10,839
1974	72	36	108	3,076	—	3,076	6,569	9,753
1973	77	36	113	2,637	—	2,637	5,763	8,513
1972	67	33	100	2,126	1	2,127	5,398	7,625
1971	64	28	92	1,578	1	1,579	5,353	7,024
1970	59	27	86	1,420	—	1,420	5,131	6,637
1969	53	29	82	1,223	—	1,223	4,489	5,794
1968	48	28	76	963	—	963	4,354	5,393

Mining[1]

Year	341	342	343	344	345	346	347	348
1975	365	126	491	1,292	10	1,302	2,118	3,911
1974	372	127	499	1,303	8	1,311	2,131	3,941
1973	413	141	554	1,336	8	1,344	2,026	3,924
1972	397	146	543	1,204	7	1,211	1,967	3,721
1971	402	146	548	1,173	4	1,177	2,014	3,739
1970	360	163	523	1,220	4	1,224	2,026	3,773
1969	330	168	498	1,183	3	1,186	2,026	3,710
1968	286	181	467	1,070	3	1,073	2,123	3,663

Manufacturing[1]

Year	341	342	343	344	345	346	347	348
1975	1,894	543	2,437	10,608	24	10,632	14,404	27,473
1974	1,951	556	2,507	10,031	24	10,055	13,919	26,481
1973	1,896	499	2,395	8,869	29	8,898	12,925	24,218
1972	1,883	495	2,378	8,082	21	8,103	12,540	23,021
1971	1,873	462	2,335	7,471	19	7,490	12,133	21,958
1970	1,912	526	2,438	7,182	22	7,204	12,439	22,081
1969	1,835	506	2,341	6,895	23	6,918	11,826	21,085
1968	1,678	500	2,178	6,434	22	6,456	12,222	20,856

Construction

Year	341	342	343	344	345	346	347	348
1975	136	64	200	9,205	—	9,205	23,948	33,353
1974	138	60	198	8,084	—	8,084	21,484	29,766
1973	124	70	194	6,796	—	6,796	19,096	26,086
1972	114	62	176	5,652	—	5,652	17,170	22,998
1971	119	65	184	4,740	1	4,741	16,365	21,290
1970	116	67	183	4,362	1	4,363	15,428	19,974
1969	109	51	160	4,350	1	4,351	14,692	19,203
1968	100	46	146	3,960	1	3,961	13,587	17,694

Utilities

Year	341	342	343	344	345	346	347	348
1975	195	86	281	3,038	332	3,370	9,015	12,666
1974	203	88	291	2,732	324	3,056	8,597	11,944
1973	196	94	290	2,503	498	3,001	7,465	10,756
1972	195	75	270	2,141	519	2,660	6,901	9,831
1971	193	74	267	1,752	293	2,045	6,740	9,052
1970	189	81	270	1,575	291	1,866	6,689	8,825
1969	205	61	266	1,516	299	1,815	6,052	8,133
1968	173	62	235	1,396	295	1,691	5,630	7,556

Series G341-348. Country of control of corporations by eight major industry groups, 1968 to 1975 (concluded)
(number of corporations)

| Year | Foreign | | | Canadian | | | Unclassified | Total |
	United States	Others	Total	Private sector	Government business enterprise	Total		
	341	**342**	**343**	**344**	**345**	**346**	**347**	**348**
Wholesale trade								
1975	1,051	592	1,643	11,827	8	11,835	18,249	31,727
1974	1,070	611	1,681	10,935	8	10,943	17,659	30,283
1973	963	568	1,531	9,678	10	9,688	16,797	28,016
1972	961	534	1,495	8,562	8	8,570	16,507	26,572
1971	974	545	1,519	7,478	6	7,484	16,079	25,082
1970	946	524	1,470	7,132	2	7,134	16,240	24,844
1969	877	510	1,387	6,787	4	6,791	14,836	23,014
1968	748	492	1,240	6,261	4	6,265	14,251	21,756
Retail trade								
1975	279	78	357	12,635	13	12,648	33,877	46,882
1974	301	94	395	10,967	13	10,980	32,413	43,788
1973	303	87	390	9,313	14	9,327	30,227	39,944
1972	319	81	400	8,069	12	8,081	27,685	36,166
1971	319	73	392	6,330	12	6,342	27,095	33,829
1970	309	85	394	5,841	12	5,853	26,078	32,325
1969	288	62	350	5,353	12	5,365	24,762	30,477
1968	245	54	299	4,822	12	4,834	22,469	27,602
Services								
1975	458	127	585	9,046	10	9,056	39,148	48,789
1974	472	131	603	7,733	11	7,744	35,701	44,048
1973	453	131	584	6,541	20	6,561	31,395	38,540
1972	449	106	555	5,351	10	5,361	28,628	34,544
1971	451	86	537	4,197	2	4,199	26,049	30,785
1970	422	98	520	3,771	2	3,773	24,371	28,664
1969	365	98	463	3,472	2	3,474	22,823	26,760
1968	276	99	375	3,116	2	3,118	21,368	24,861
Total non-financial industries								
1975	4,454	1,648	6,102	61,138	399	61,537	148,001	215,640
1974	4,579	1,703	6,282	54,861	388	55,249	138,473	200,004
1973	4,425	1,626	6,051	47,673	579	48,252	125,694	179,997
1972	4,385	1,532	5,917	41,187	578	41,765	116,796	164,478
1971	4,395	1,479	5,874	34,719	338	35,057	111,828	152,759
1970	4,313	1,571	5,884	32,503	334	32,837	108,402	147,123
1969	4,062	1,485	5,547	30,779	344	31,123	101,506	138,176
1968	3,554	1,462	5,016	28,022	339	28,361	96,004	129,381

[1] A discontinuity exists between 1968 and 1969 as a result of a reclassification to the metal mining industry of several large integrated mining and smelting and refining companies, formerly classified to the primary metal industries. For details, see *Corporations and Labour Unions Returns Act: Report for 1969, Part 1*, pp.76-77.

Series G349-356. Country of control of corporations by eight major industry groups, 1968 to 1975 Assets
(in millions of dollars)

Year	Foreign			Canadian			Unclassified	Total
	United States	Others	Total	Private sector	Government business enterprise	Total		
	349	**350**	**351**	**352**	**353**	**354**	**355**	**356**

Agriculture, forestry and fishing

1975	169	118	286	2,127	x	x	x	3,115
1974	154	101	255	1,858	–	1,858	646	2,759
1973	142	93	235	1,427	–	1,427	563	2,225
1972	110	89	199	1,132	x	x	x	1,860
1971	146	73	219	985	x	x	x	1,734
1970	137	63	200	817	–	817	497	1,515
1969	137	70	207	703	–	703	430	1,340
1968	128	16	144	596	–	596	398	1,138

Mining[1]

1975	12,377	2,539	14,916	10,558	382	10,941	161	26,018
1974	11,173	2,317	13,490	9,128	252	9,380	169	23,038
1973	9,863	2,035	11,898	8,249	204	8,453	151	20,503
1972	9,067	1,827	10,894	6,969	190	7,159	164	18,216
1971	10,310	1,740	12,050	5,039	104	5,143	174	17,367
1970	8,905	1,749	10,654	4,346	97	4,443	184	15,281
1969	8,019	1,491	9,510	4,126	84	4,210	189	13,909
1968	5,918	1,315	7,233	3,717	72	3,789	178	11,200

Manufacturing[1]

1975	32,930	11,826	44,756	33,565	1,133	34,697	1,151	80,605
1974	30,082	10,541	40,623	30,282	1,009	31,292	1,099	73,013
1973	24,994	9,018	34,012	24,471	673	25,144	999	60,157
1972	22,239	7,983	30,222	21,649	456	22,105	1,018	53,346
1971	21,926	7,282	29,208	18,894	566	19,460	1,008	49,677
1970	20,986	7,105	28,091	17,623	558	18,180	1,053	47,325
1969	19,828	5,720	25,548	17,468	510	17,978	1,047	44,573
1968	19,826	5,387	25,213	16,224	450	16,674	1,093	42,980

Construction

1975	913	1,071	1,984	10,263	–	10,263	1,630	13,876
1974	752	951	1,703	8,865	–	8,865	1,456	12,024
1973	478	801	1,279	6,756	–	6,756	1,239	9,275
1972	471	734	1,205	5,778	–	5,778	1,169	8,151
1971	609	700	1,309	4,883	x	x	x	7,334
1970	497	568	1,065	4,427	x	x	x	6,590
1969	447	283	730	4,323	x	x	x	6,111
1968	464	299	763	3,596	x	x	x	5,290

Utilities

1975	4,656	405	5,061	21,944	37,824	59,768	649	65,478
1974	4,106	393	4,499	20,331	32,718	53,049	621	58,169
1973	4,176	1,226	5,402	16,418	29,356	45,774	507	51,682
1972	3,993	1,120	5,113	14,700	26,878	41,578	475	47,165
1971	3,210	935	4,145	13,921	24,577	38,498	487	43,131
1970	3,018	278	3,296	12,767	22,972	35,740	482	39,517
1969	2,548	231	2,779	12,195	21,345	33,540	427	36,746
1968	2,303	227	2,530	11,157	19,835	30,992	398	33,920

Wholesale trade

1975	3,702	3,232	6,934	14,557	2,158	16,716	1,307	24,957
1974	3,421	3,450	6,871	12,907	2,532	15,439	1,255	23,565
1973	2,693	2,923	5,616	10,134	1,080	11,214	1,130	17,960
1972	2,573	2,560	5,131	8,494	875	9,369	1,175	15,677
1971	2,147	2,493	4,640	7,294	991	8,285	1,151	14,076
1970	1,878	1,552	3,430	6,750	x	x	x	12,457
1969	1,803	1,277	3,080	6,291	1,145	7,436	1,128	11,644
1968	1,816	1,108	2,924	5,639	969	6,608	999	10,531

Retail trade

1975	2,602	789	3,391	10,340	347	10,688	2,460	16,539
1974	2,293	757	3,050	8,780	300	9,080	2,282	14,413
1973	1,475	739	2,214	7,190	259	7,449	2,026	11,687
1972	1,423	867	2,290	5,874	221	6,095	1,878	10,263
1971	1,327	714	2,041	5,046	201	5,247	1,875	9,163

Series G349-356. Country of control of corporations by eight major industry groups, 1968 to 1975 (concluded)
Assets *(in millions of dollars)*

Year	Foreign			Canadian			Unclassified	Total
	United States	Others	Total	Private sector	Government business enterprise	Total		
	349	**350**	**351**	**352**	**353**	**354**	**355**	**356**

Retail trade

Year	United States	Others	Total	Private sector	Government business enterprise	Total	Unclassified	Total
1970	1,196	688	1,884	4,446	180	4,626	1,779	8,288
1969	1,369	307	1,676	4,318	156	4,474	1,676	7,826
1968	1,156	288	1,444	3,930	156	4,086	1,495	7,025

Services

Year	United States	Others	Total	Private sector	Government business enterprise	Total	Unclassified	Total
1975	2,946	606	3,552	9,165	x	x	x	15,237
1974	2,915	685	3,601	7,637	102	7,739	2,220	13,559
1973	1,787	591	2,378	5,917	74	5,991	1,887	10,256
1972	1,483	418	1,901	5,011	x	x	x	8,716
1971	1,261	338	1,599	3,696	x	x	x	6,936
1970	1,114	321	1,435	3,240	x	x	x	6,221
1969	1,056	314	1,370	2,892	x	x	x	5,715
1968	738	243	981	2,502	x	x	x	4,784

Total non-financial industries

Year	United States	Others	Total	Private sector	Government business enterprise	Total	Unclassified	Total
1975	60,294	20,586	80,881	112,519	41,926	154,446	10,498	245,825
1974	54,897	19,195	74,092	99,789	36,913	136,702	9,747	220,541
1973	45,609	17,426	63,035	80,561	31,644	112,206	8,504	183,745
1972	41,358	15,598	56,954	69,607	28,657	98,265	8,176	163,394
1971	40,935	14,275	55,210	59,759	26,466	86,225	7,981	149,418
1970	37,731	12,324	50,055	54,416	24,922	79,339	7,800	137,193
1969	35,207	9,693	44,900	52,316	23,258	75,574	7,390	127,864
1968	32,349	8,883	41,232	47,361	21,501	68,862	6,774	116,868

[1] A discontinuity exists between 1968 and 1969 as a result of a reclassification to the metal mining industry of several large integrated mining and smelting and refining companies, formerly classified to the primary metal industries. For details, see *Corporations and Labour Unions Returns Act: Report for 1969*, Part 1, pp.76-77.
x means confidential.

Series G357-364. Country of control of corporations by eight major industry groups, 1968 to 1975
Equity *(in millions of dollars)*

Year	Foreign			Canadian			Unclassified	Total
	United States	Others	Total	Private sector	Government business enterprise	Total		
	357	**358**	**359**	**360**	**361**	**362**	**363**	**364**

Agriculture, forestry and fishing

Year	United States	Others	Total	Private sector	Government business enterprise	Total	Unclassified	Total
1975	72	66	138	663	x	x	x	969
1974	65	52	118	610	—	610	159	886
1973	61	52	113	495	—	495	136	743
1972	55	45	100	366	x	x	x	582
1971	98	47	145	349	x	x	x	614
1970	102	43	145	269	—	269	122	536
1969	98	45	143	238	—	238	107	488
1968	99	6	105	233	—	233	96	434

Mining[1]

Year	United States	Others	Total	Private sector	Government business enterprise	Total	Unclassified	Total
1975	6,434	1,143	7,577	5,564	264	5,827	13	13,417
1974	6,047	1,157	7,204	5,091	163	5,254	28	12,486
1973	5,695	1,198	6,893	4,853	132	4,985	53	11,931
1972	5,331	1,043	6,374	4,077	113	4,190	65	10,628
1971	6,322	991	7,313	3,136	59	3,195	79	10,587
1970	5,512	1,115	6,627	2,961	57	3,018	94	9,740
1969	4,930	907	5,837	2,871	57	2,928	94	8,859
1968	3,324	769	4,093	2,596	58	2,654	91	6,838

Series G357-364. Country of control of corporations by eight major industry groups, 1968 to 1975 (concluded)
Equity   *(in millions of dollars)*

Year	Foreign			Canadian			Unclassified	Total
	United States	Others	Total	Private sector	Government business enterprise	Total		
	357	**358**	**359**	**360**	**361**	**362**	**363**	**364**
Manufacturing[1]								
1975	16,735	5,181	21,916	13,591	173	13,764	320	36,000
1974	15,036	4,638	19,674	12,289	175	12,464	310	32,447
1973	13,537	4,187	17,724	10,375	97	10,472	309	28,505
1972	12,159	3,785	15,944	9,434	99	9,533	322	25,800
1971	11,917	3,473	15,390	8,279	211	8,490	327	24,207
1970	11,145	3,395	14,540	8,052	217	8,269	360	23,169
1969	10,665	2,901	13,566	8,167	198	8,365	352	22,283
1968	10,576	2,710	13,286	7,792	162	7,954	400	21,640
Construction								
1975	293	156	449	2,235	—	2,235	493	3,177
1974	269	143	412	1,758	—	1,758	435	2,605
1973	191	111	302	1,438	—	1,438	381	2,121
1972	175	111	286	1,252	—	1,252	363	1,901
1971	156	88	244	1,100	x	x	x	1,714
1970	112	73	185	1,028	x	x	x	1,569
1969	120	49	169	1,019	x	x	x	1,531
1968	94	64	158	927	x	x	x	1,396
Utilities								
1975	1,691	125	1,816	8,354	8,407	16,761	177	18,755
1974	1,553	120	1,673	7,595	7,936	15,530	178	17,382
1973	1,571	224	1,795	6,719	7,104	13,823	140	15,759
1972	1,501	183	1,684	6,251	6,731	12,982	140	14,806
1971	1,188	177	1,365	5,960	6,117	12,077	166	13,608
1970	1,074	95	1,169	5,550	5,823	11,373	164	12,705
1969	955	76	1,031	5,265	5,636	10,901	139	12,071
1968	874	74	948	5,046	5,297	10,343	113	11,404
Wholesale trade								
1975	1,311	776	2,087	4,741	37	4,777	422	7,286
1974	1,259	887	2,146	4,149	32	4,181	410	6,738
1973	1,066	832	1,898	3,382	29	3,411	367	5,676
1972	989	889	1,878	3,003	20	3,023	383	5,284
1971	757	815	1,572	2,673	80	2,753	388	4,714
1970	671	373	1,044	2,530	x	x	x	3,998
1969	609	273	882	2,358	-26	2,332	400	3,614
1968	566	237	803	2,145	2	2,147	358	3,308
Retail trade								
1975	1,155	231	1,387	3,323	230	3,553	818	5,758
1974	1,058	244	1,302	2,913	202	3,116	776	5,194
1973	715	261	976	2,732	175	2,907	701	4,584
1972	676	447	1,123	2,289	146	2,435	664	4,223
1971	676	344	1,020	2,039	138	2,177	692	3,889
1970	625	336	961	1,906	128	2,034	674	3,669
1969	726	187	913	1,683	95	1,778	628	3,319
1968	640	181	821	1,561	94	1,655	581	3,057
Services								
1975	1,095	208	1,302	2,809	x	x	x	4,842
1974	1,036	280	1,316	2,475	44	2,519	655	4,490
1973	554	214	768	2,004	16	2,020	587	3,377
1972	475	180	655	1,800	x	x	x	3,012
1971	417	173	590	1,199	x	x	x	2,299
1970	394	179	573	1,083	x	x	x	2,145
1969	418	142	560	1,014	x	x	x	2,034
1968	324	130	454	794	x	x	x	1,672
Total non-financial industries								
1975	28,787	7,886	36,673	41,278	9,128	50,407	3,124	90,204
1974	26,323	7,523	33,845	36,880	8,553	45,433	2,950	82,228
1973	23,388	7,080	30,468	31,999	7,553	39,552	2,676	72,697
1972	21,361	6,682	28,043	28,472	7,108	35,580	2,613	66,236
1971	21,531	6,110	27,641	24,736	6,603	31,337	2,653	61,633
1970	19,635	5,609	25,244	23,380	6,238	29,618	2,670	57,533
1969	18,521	4,580	23,101	22,615	5,958	28,573	2,525	54,199
1968	16,497	4,171	20,668	21,094	5,612	26,706	2,375	49,749

[1] A discontinuity exists between 1968 and 1969 as a result of a reclassification to the metal mining industry of several large integrated mining and smelting and refining companies, formerly classified to the primary metal industries. For details, see *Corporations and Labour Unions Returns Act: Report for 1969*, Part 1, pp.76–77.
x means confidential.

Series G365-372. Country of control of corporations by eight major industry groups, 1968 to 1975
Sales (in millions of dollars)

Year	Foreign			Canadian			Unclassified	Total
	United States	Others	Total	Private sector	Government business enterprise	Total		
	365	366	367	368	369	370	371	372

Agriculture, forestry and fishing

Year	United States	Others	Total	Private sector	Government business enterprise	Total	Unclassified	Total
1975	170	30	200	1,840	x	x	x	2,675
1974	153	25	178	1,729	—	1,729	604	2,512
1973	123	43	166	1,317	—	1,317	491	1,975
1972	93	22	115	926	x	x	x	1,472
1971	73	24	97	743	x	x	x	1,275
1970	56	28	84	635	—	635	420	1,139
1969	57	27	84	531	—	531	367	982
1968	58	16	74	443	—	443	341	858

Mining[1]

Year	United States	Others	Total	Private sector	Government business enterprise	Total	Unclassified	Total
1975	8,223	820	9,042	4,200	111	4,311	110	13,463
1974	6,958	817	7,774	4,121	74	4,195	102	12,072
1973	4,901	650	5,551	3,383	49	3,432	89	9,072
1972	3,622	428	4,050	2,150	40	2,190	86	6,326
1971	4,038	295	4,333	1,303	4	1,307	82	5,722
1970	3,863	405	4,268	1,351	24	1,375	88	5,731
1969	3,071	324	3,395	1,402	20	1,422	83	4,900
1968	2,189	278	2,467	1,341	27	1,368	89	3,924

Manufacturing[1]

Year	United States	Others	Total	Private sector	Government business enterprise	Total	Unclassified	Total
1975	48,730	12,031	60,761	41,889	571	42,460	2,046	105,267
1974	44,404	10,872	55,276	36,696	453	40,149	1,974	97,399
1973	35,652	8,312	43,964	31,066	287	31,353	1,761	77,079
1972	30,789	6,605	37,394	25,962	236	26,198	1,828	65,421
1971	27,851	5,681	33,532	23,073	298	23,371	1,817	58,719
1970	24,429	5,568	29,997	21,343	308	21,651	1,909	53,557
1969	24,519	4,665	29,184	21,164	326	21,490	1,894	52,568
1968	22,053	4,277	26,330	19,600	223	19,823	1,956	48,109

Construction

Year	United States	Others	Total	Private sector	Government business enterprise	Total	Unclassified	Total
1975	2,090	805	2,895	14,449	—	14,449	3,162	20,507
1974	1,312	627	1,939	11,920	—	11,920	2,905	16,764
1973	904	577	1,481	8,971	—	8,971	2,397	12,850
1972	979	474	1,453	7,515	—	7,515	2,261	11,228
1971	1,019	469	1,488	6,405	x	x	x	9,979
1970	885	372	1,257	5,848	x	x	x	9,112
1969	822	256	1,078	5,705	x	x	x	8,737
1968	676	263	939	5,557	x	x	x	8,300

Utilities

Year	United States	Others	Total	Private sector	Government business enterprise	Total	Unclassified	Total
1975	2,048	325	2,373	11,087	8,037	19,125	947	22,444
1974	1,697	298	1,996	9,560	7,081	16,641	903	19,539
1973	1,518	282	1,800	7,546	6,095	13,641	732	16,172
1972	1,330	191	1,521	6,662	5,439	12,101	700	14,321
1971	1,158	178	1,336	5,843	4,780	10,623	693	12,653
1970	1,170	177	1,347	5,238	4,376	9,614	687	11,649
1969	1,011	152	1,163	4,844	3,882	8,726	585	10,474
1968	901	151	1,052	4,357	3,552	7,909	517	9,478

Series G365-372. Country of control of corporations by eight major industry groups, 1968 to 1975 (concluded)
Sales   *(in millions of dollars)*

Year	Foreign			Canadian			Unclassified	Total
	United States	Others	Total	Private sector	Government business enterprise	Total		
	365	**366**	**367**	**368**	**369**	**370**	**371**	**372**

Wholesale trade

1975	8,391	6,894	15,284	33,992	2,861	36,853	2,366	54,503
1974	7,418	7,012	14,430	31,090	2,476	33,565	2,321	50,316
1973	5,701	5,119	10,820	23,106	1,058	24,164	2,072	37,055
1972	4,829	4,084	8,913	19,484	786	20,270	2,172	31,355
1971	4,178	3,653	7,830	16,538	491	17,029	2,188	27,048
1970	3,670	3,005	6,675	15,395	x	x	x	24,553
1969	3,401	2,380	5,781	14,815	341	15,156	2,162	23,099
1968	4,107	2,098	6,205	13,952	487	14,439	1,955	22,599

Retail trade

1975	6,319	2,001	8,320	29,281	2,126	31,407	5,516	45,243
1974	5,509	1,846	7,354	24,938	1,833	26,771	5,195	39,230
1973	3,840	1,508	5,348	19,941	1,607	21,548	4,426	31,322
1972	3,741	1,958	5,699	16,405	1,524	17,929	4,278	27,904
1971	3,495	1,787	5,282	13,610	1,267	14,877	4,304	24,463
1970	2,962	1,787	4,749	12,052	1,176	13,228	4,117	22,095
1969	3,225	679	3,904	11,603	1,145	12,748	3,846	20,498
1968	2,819	604	3,423	10,473	1,080	11,553	3,439	18,415

Services

1975	2,815	356	3,172	8,201	x	x	x	14,981
1974	2,525	309	2,834	6,387	126	6,513	3,123	12,470
1973	1,317	248	1,565	4,579	102	4,682	2,492	8,738
1972	1,204	201	1,405	3,889	x	x	x	7,705
1971	1,054	130	1,184	3,085	x	x	x	6,466
1970	980	130	1,110	2,654	x	x	x	5,810
1969	809	104	913	2,417	x	x	x	5,195
1968	646	104	750	2,135	x	x	x	4,574

Total non-financial industries

1975	78,785	23,263	102,047	144,939	13,837	158,776	18,260	279,084
1974	69,975	21,806	91,781	129,440	12,043	141,483	17,128	250,392
1973	53,957	16,738	70,695	99,908	9,199	109,107	14,461	194,264
1972	46,587	13,962	60,549	82,992	8,096	91,088	14,094	165,732
1971	42,867	12,216	55,081	70,600	6,852	77,452	13,789	146,324
1970	38,015	11,472	49,487	64,515	6,105	70,620	13,538	133,646
1969	36,915	8,587	45,502	62,481	5,717	68,198	12,753	126,453
1968	33,449	7,791	41,240	57,858	5,371	63,229	11,788	116,257

[1] A discontinuity exists between 1968 and 1969 as a result of a reclassification to the metal mining industry of several large integrated mining and smelting and refining companies, formerly classified to the primary metal industries. For details, see *Corporations and Labour Unions Returns Act: Report for 1969*, Part 1, pp.76–77.

x means confidential.

Series G373-380. Country of control of corporations by eight major industry groups, 1968 to 1975
Profits *(in millions of dollars)*

Year	Foreign			Canadian			Unclassified	Total
	United States	Others	Total	Private sector	Government business enterprise	Total		
	373	**374**	**375**	**376**	**377**	**378**	**379**	**380**

Agriculture, forestry and fishing

1975	9	16	25	72	x	x	x	131
1974	15	—	16	128	—	128	40	184
1973	12	4	16	154	—	154	38	209
1972	6	1	7	60	x	x	x	81
1971	5	4	9	42	x	x	x	58
1970	10	5	15	26	—	26	10	51
1969	5	6	11	30	—	30	13	54
1968	5	—	5	25	—	25	11	41

Mining[1]

1975	1,686	164	1,851	1,004	17	1,021	-6	2,866
1974	1,301	186	1,488	1,319	5	1,323	-9	2,802
1973	903	201	1,104	990	-6	984	-2	2,087
1972	347	70	417	399	-7	392	-12	797
1971	702	53	755	219	-2	217	-17	954
1970	804	109	913	337	-2	335	-14	1,234
1969	654	76	730	347	—	347	-14	1,063
1968	421	52	473	342	1	343	-8	808

Manufacturing[1]

1975	4,000	1,052	5,052	2,565	-57	2,508	66	7,626
1974	4,118	1,197	5,315	3,313	-13	3,300	82	8,697
1973	3,319	780	4,099	2,505	-15	2,490	81	6,670
1972	2,411	462	2,873	1,469	-10	1,458	29	4,361
1971	2,017	412	2,429	1,216	-6	1,210	36	3,675
1970	1,543	285	1,828	1,002	13	1,015	32	2,876
1969	1,991	294	2,285	1,298	4	1,302	44	3,631
1968	1,918	272	2,190	1,235	-8	1,227	50	3,467

Construction

1975	85	89	174	827	—	827	148	1,150
1974	67	42	108	543	—	543	138	789
1973	58	39	97	356	—	356	102	555
1972	60	32	92	259	—	259	47	396
1971	30	19	49	250	x	x	x	373
1970	25	8	33	140	x	x	x	230
1969	34	18	52	174	x	x	x	297
1968	25	15	40	197	x	x	x	304

Utilities

1975	343	21	364	1,411	165	1,576	28	1,968
1974	311	24	335	1,221	365	1,587	35	1,956
1973	341	52	393	970	298	1,268	31	1,693
1972	290	26	316	870	278	1,148	18	1,483
1971	240	18	258	835	122	957	27	1,242
1970	228	16	244	716	117	833	23	1,101
1969	143	16	159	674	88	762	20	941
1968	150	16	166	636	182	818	16	1,000

Series G373-380. Country of control of corporations by eight major industry groups, 1968 to 1975 (concluded)
Profits *(in millions of dollars)*

Year	Foreign			Canadian			Unclassified	Total
	United States	Others	Total	Private sector	Government business enterprise	Total		
	373	**374**	**375**	**376**	**377**	**378**	**379**	**380**

Wholesale trade

1975	381	127	508	1,179	5	1,184	95	1,787
1974	519	236	755	1,296	1	1,298	113	2,166
1973	316	138	454	896	2	898	86	1,438
1972	274	100	374	660	2	662	43	1,078
1971	183	101	284	505	69	574	63	921
1970	125	54	.179	366	x	x	x	613
1969	123	46	169	416	-26	390	66	625
1968	135	45	180	356	..	356	56	592

Retail trade

1975	228	23	251	787	866	1,652	193	2,096
1974	219	36	255	689	770	1,459	193	1,907
1973	137	24	161	556	691	1,247	146	1,553
1972	147	113	260	440	546	987	77	1,323
1971	129	26	155	309	552	861	107	1,122
1970	105	48	153	266	512	778	97	1,028
1969	134	20	154	228	388	616	102	872
1968	128	22	150	233	363	596	100	846

Services

1975	312	21	334	540	x	x	x	1,117
1974	340	131	471	432	45	477	169	1,118
1973	137	22	159	285	33	318	141	618
1972	127	9	136	215	x	x	x	460
1971	116	10	126	183	x	x	x	416
1970	98	16	114	133	x	x	x	333
1969	88	10	98	142	x	x	x	334
1968	82	11	93	116	x	x	x	298

Total non-financial industries

1975	7,045	1,513	8,558	8,384	1,048	9,432	751	18,741
1974	6,891	1,853	8,743	8,942	1,174	10,115	761	19,619
1973	5,223	1,260	6,483	6,713	1,003	7,716	623	14,823
1972	3,662	812	4,474	4,374	837	5,211	297	9,980
1971	3,421	643	4,064	3,560	735	4,295	403	8,761
1970	2,938	542	3,480	2,986	654	3,639	349	7,468
1969	3,172	486	3,658	3,309	453	3,762	397	7,817
1968	2,864	433	3,297	3,140	537	3,677	382	7,356

[1] A discontinuity exists between 1968 and 1969 as a result of a reclassification to the metal mining industry of several large integrated mining and smelting and refining companies, formerly classified to the primary metal industries. For details, see *Corporations and Labour Unions Returns Act: Report for 1969*, Part 1, pp.76-77.

x means confidential.

Series G381-385. Foreign trade, domestic exports, total exports, total imports and balance of trade, declared values, Canada and all countries, 1868 to 1975
(millions of dollars)

Year	Domestic exports	Re-exports	Total exports	Total imports	Balance of trade	Year	Domestic exports	Re-exports	Total exports	Total imports	Balance of trade
	381	**382**	**383**	**384**	**385**		**381**	**382**	**383**	**384**	**385**
1975	32,549	779	33,328	34,716	-1,388	1920	1,268	30	1,298	1,337	-39
1974	31,676	767	32,442	31,722	+720	1919[2]	1,236	54	1,288	940	+349
1973	24,838	583	25,421	23,325	+2,095	1919[2]	1,216	52	1,270	921	+349
1972	19,671	479	20,150	18,669	+1,481	1918	1,540	46	1,586	964	+623
1971	17,397	423	17,820	15,618	+2,202	1917	1,151	28	1,179	846	+333
1970	16,401	419	16,820	13,952	+2,868	1916	742	38	779	508	+271
1969	14,443	428	14,871	14,130	+741	1915	409	52	461	456	+5
1968	13,325	354	13,679	12,360	+1,319	1914	432	24	455	619	-164
1967	11,121	299	11,420	10,873	+547	1913	356	21	377	671	-294
1966	10,089	255	10,343	10,072	+271	1912	290	17	308	522	-215
1965	8,525	242	8,767	8,633	+134	1911	274	16	290	453	-163
1964	8,094	209	8,303	7,488	+816	1910	279	20	299	370	-72
1963	6,799	182	6,980	6,558	+422	1909	243	17	260	289	-27
1962	6,179	169	6,348	6,258	+90	1908	247	16	263	353	-89
1961	5,755	140	5,895	5,769	+127	1907	181	12	192	250	-58
1960	5,256	131	5,387	5,483	-96	1906	235	11	247	284	-37
1959	5,022	119	5,140	5,509	-369	1905	191	11	201	252	-50
1958	4,791	103	4,894	5,050	-156	1904	198	13	211	244	-33
1957	4,789	95	4,884	5,473	-589	1903	214	11	225	225	—
1956	4,760	73	4,834	5,547	-713	1902	196	14	210	197	+13
1955	4,258	69	4,328	4,568	-240	1901	177	17	195	178	+17
1954	3,860	66	3,926	3,967	-42	1900	169	14	183	173	+11
1953	4,097	55	4,152	4,248	-96	1899	137	18	155	149	+5
1952	4,282	55	4,337	3,916	+421	1898	145	15	160	126	+33
1951	3,897	49	3,946	4,005	-59	1897	124	11	134	107	+28
1950	3,104	39	3,143	3,125	+17	1896	110	7	116	105	+11
1949	2,975	29	3,004	2,714	+290	1895	103	6	109	101	+9
1948	3,052	34	3,087	2,618	+468	1894	104	12	116	109	+7
1947	2,753	37	2,790	2,543	+247	1893	105	9	114	115	-1
1946	2,272	27	2,299	1,841	+458	1892	99	13	112	115	-3
1945	3,167	48	3,214	1,514	+1,700	1891	89	9	97	112	-14
1944	3,358	41	3,398	1,730	+1,669	1890	85	9	94	112	-17
1943	2,897	25	2,923	1,686	+1,237	1889	80	7	87	109	-22
1942	2,292	20	2,312	1,505	+807	1888	81	9	90	101	-10
1941	1,570	18	1,588	1,274	+314	1887	81	9	90	105	-16
1940	1,171	14	1,185	1,023	+162	1886	78	7	85	96	-11
1939	922	11	933	736	+197	1885	79	8	87	100	-13
1938	835	11	846	665	+181	1884	80	9	89	106	-17
1937	994	15	1,009	798	+211	1883	88	10	97	122	-24
1936	935	13	947	628	+319	1882	94	8	102	111	-9
1935	722	13	735	547	+188	1881	84	13	97	90	+7
1934	646	7	653	510	+143	1880	73	13	86	70	+16
1933	526	6	532	397	+136	1879	62	8	71	79	-8
1932	487	8	495	445	+50	1878	68	11	79	90	-11
1931	583	12	595	619	-24	1877	68	7	75	94	-19
1930	868	19	887	996	-109	1876	72	7	80	93	-13
1929	1,146	26	1,172	1,288	-116	1875	70	7	77	117	-41
1928	1,333	24	1,358	1,211	+146	1874	77	11	87	123	-36
1927	1,205	20	1,225	1,078	+148	1873	77	9	86	125	-39
1926[1]	1,254	15	1,269	1,001	+269	1872	66	13	79	105	-26
1925	1,240	12	1,252	890	+361	1871	58	10	67	84	-17
1924	1,030	13	1,042	808	+234	1870	59	7	66	67	-1
1923	1,002	14	1,016	903	+113	1869	52	4	56	63	-7
1922	880	14	894	762	+132	1868	49	4	53	67	-14
1921	800	14	814	799	+15						

[1] In this edition, "special transactions, non-trade" have been excluded from 1926. In the previous edition, "special transactions, non-trade" were excluded only from 1959. See general note to series G381-503 in text.

[2] The data are for calendar years since 1919, for fiscal years ending 31 March of the year given from 1908 to 1919 and for fiscal years ending 30 June of the year given from 1868 to 1906. Both calendar and fiscal totals are shown for 1919. The totals for 1907 are for the nine months ending 31 March 1907. Should the user wish to derive trade data on a calendar year basis for years prior to 1919, he may refer to Dominion Bureau of Statistics, *Historical Monthly Statistics* (Catalogue 11-503), Tables 4.1 and 4.2.

Series G386-388. Foreign trade, indexes of import and export prices and the terms of trade, 1869 to 1975
(per cent)

Year[1,2]	Price indexes — Import	Price indexes — Export	Terms of trade[3]	Year[1,2]	Price indexes — Import	Price indexes — Export	Terms of trade[3]
	386	387	388		386	387	388
	(1971 = 100)[4]				*(1913 = 100)*		
1975	165.7	181.0	109.2	1926	131.2	147.0	112.0
1974	142.9	161.5	113.0				
1973	111.3	119.0	106.9	1925	139.2	151.7	109.0
1972	102.6	103.3	100.7	1924	141.7	139.6	98.5
1971	100.0	100.0	100.0	1923	147.6	136.8	92.7
				1922	135.3	137.8	101.8
1970	98.1	99.3	101.2	1921	160.6	164.8	102.6
1969	97.2	96.9	99.7				
1968	95.5	95.0	99.5	1920	220.2	229.7	104.3
1967	94.0	91.7	97.6	1919	179.9	205.1	114.0
1966	93.2	90.0	96.6	1918	166.4	195.9	117.7
				1917	143.3	178.1	124.3
1965	92.1	86.4	93.8	1916	114.7	125.4	109.3
1964	92.1	85.3	92.6				
1963	91.1	84.1	92.3	1915	92.7	111.2	120.0
1962	87.6	83.6	95.4	1914	92.7	103.4	111.5
1961	83.8	80.9	96.5	1913	100.0	100.0	100.0
	(1948 = 100)				*(1900 = 100)*		
1961	119.7	124.0	103.6	1915	103.1	122.5	118.8
				1914	112.9	116.9	103.5
1960	115.5	123.0	106.5	1913	110.0	122.5	111.4
1959	114.4	122.8	107.3	1912	107.2	120.7	112.6
1958	116.5	120.6	103.5	1911	110.5	123.7	111.9
1957	116.4	121.0	104.0				
1956	113.0	121.4	107.4	1910	109.3	124.8	114.2
				1909	108.6	123.5	113.7
1955	110.5	117.7	106.5	1908	117.0	124.2	106.2
1954	109.5	115.1	105.1	1907	113.8	118.5	104.1
1953	109.4	118.3	108.1	1906	107.7	113.4	105.3
1952	110.4	121.8	110.3				
1951	126.2	123.0	97.5	1905	102.7	105.3	102.5
				1904	103.1	108.7	105.3
1950	110.3	108.3	98.2	1903	100.7	107.6	106.8
1949	102.6	103.3	100.7	1902	98.0	104.3	106.4
1948	100.0	100.0	100.0	1901	101.0	102.5	101.5
1947	88.0	91.6	104.1				
1946	76.5	79.9	104.4	1900	100.0	100.0	100.0
				1899	89.6	95.4	106.5
1945	73.3[2]	70.9[2]	96.7[2]	1898	88.8	97.0	109.2
1944	72.8[2]	67.8[2]	92.9[2]	1897	83.8	90.9	108.5
1943	69.8[2]	61.0[2]	87.4[2]	1896	87.9	93.1	105.9
1942	63.4[2]	55.0[2]	86.8[2]				
1941	57.6[2]	51.9[2]	90.1[2]	1895	85.3	96.5	113.1
				1894	93.7	101.0	107.8
1940	53.0	49.9	94.2	1893	96.3	100.7	104.6
1939	47.2	45.1	95.6	1892	97.8	103.0	105.3
1938	47.2	47.1	99.8	1891	104.2	104.0	99.8
1937	50.8	53.4	105.1				
1936	46.3	45.8	98.9	1890	102.4	103.5	101.1
				1889	102.1	101.3	99.2
1935	45.5	43.4	95.4	1888	95.9	101.6	106.0
1934	46.4	42.6	91.8	1887	97.7	96.3	98.6
1933	43.7	39.9	91.3	1886	101.5	96.1	94.7
1932	45.6	40.3	88.4				
1931	46.6	44.8	96.1	1885	107.3	99.2	92.5
				1884	114.3	104.8	91.7
1930	55.1	54.0	98.0	1883	117.8	109.6	93.1
1929	63.0	64.4	102.2	1882	117.4	107.2	91.3
1928	64.7	65.4	101.1	1881	113.3	97.5	86.1
1927	65.7	67.6	102.9				
1926	68.9	70.2	101.9	1880	109.4	93.8	85.7
				1879	104.4	91.6	87.8
				1878	113.5	100.9	88.9
				1877	119.2	98.1	82.3
				1876	132.9	109.1	82.1
				1875	135.4	105.8	78.2
				1874	132.9	101.0	76.1
				1873	140.1	99.1	71.7
				1872	145.7	95.5	65.6
				1871	137.2	93.4	68.1
				1870	117.6	88.4	75.2
				1869	133.0	89.4	67.2

[1] The indexes are for calendar years for 1913 to 1960, for the data of base 1948 = 100 and base 1913 = 100. They are for fiscal years ending 31 March of the year given from 1908 to 1915 and for fiscal years ending 30 June of the year given from 1869 to 1907.

[2] Price indexes and terms of trade for war years are not subject to the usual interpretation. See references cited in the text.

[3] Export price as a percentage of import price.

[4] The data for 1968 to 1975 are on a 1971 base; the data for 1961 to 1967 were calculated on a 1948 base and linked to the 1971-based index at 1968.

Series G389-395. Foreign trade, exports, excluding gold, by destination, major areas, selected year ends, 1886 to 1946

(millions of dollars)

Year	Exports of Canadian produce					Exports of foreign produce (re-exports)	
	United States	United Kingdom	Other Commonwealth countries	Other countries	Total	Total Commonwealth countries	Total other countries
	389	**390**	**391**	**392**	**393**	**394**	**395**
1946	884	594	293	500	2,272	3	24
1945	1,193	948	503	522	3,167	14	34
1944	1,296	1,194	363	504	3,358	8	33
1943	1,147	988	353	410	2,897	10	15
1942	881	696	392	323	2,292	8	12
1941	599	623	203	145	1,570	5	13
1940	442	503	141	85	1,171	5	9
1939	380	328	98	116	922	1	10
1938	270	339	98	128	835	2	9
1937	359	402	99	134	994	2	13
1936	333	395	80	127	935	1	11
1935	260	303	71	88	722	1	12
1934	217	270	61	98	646	1	6
1933	166	210	41	109	526	1	5
1932	157	178	36	116	487	1	7
1931	237	170	46	130	583	2	10
1930	369	235	78	186	868	2	17
1929	488	290	102	267	1,146	2	24
1928	477	446	94	317	1,333	3	22
1927	462	409	85	249	1,205	3	18
1926[1]	452	459	90	254	1,254	2	13
1921[1,2]	542	313	91	243	1,189	2	19
1916	201	452	31	58	742	12	26
1911	104	132	17	21	274	5	11
1906[1]	84	127	11	14	235	6	5
1901	68	93	8	9	177	13	4
1896	38	63	4	5	110	4	2
1891	38	43	4	4	89	6	3
1886	34	37	3	4	78	5	2

[1] Figures from 1926 to 1946 are for calendar years. From 1911 to 1921 they are for fiscal years ending 31 March of the year given and prior to 1907, they are for fiscal years ending 30 June of the year given.

[2] Figures in this table, for 1921, are for the fiscal year ending 31 March; in series G381-395, they are for the calendar year.

G389-400. Foreign trade, imports excluding gold, by origin, major areas, selected year ends, 1886 to 1946

(millions of dollars)

Year	Imports for consumption from				Total imports	Year	Imports for consumption from				Total imports
	United States	United Kingdom	Other Commonwealth countries	Other countries			United States	United Kingdom	Other Commonwealth countries	Other countries	
	396	**397**	**398**	**399**	**400**		**396**	**397**	**398**	**399**	**400**
1946	1,387	137	136	181	1,841						
1945	1,183	100	130	101	1,514	1930	643	162	64	127	996
1944	1,435	94	108	92	1,730	1929	884	194	62	148	1,288
1943	1,410	101	103	72	1,686	1928	817	190	63	142	1,211
1942	1,209	118	112	66	1,505	1927	700	181	58	139	1,078
1941	912	138	140	84	1,274	1926[1]	663	163	50	124	1,001
1940	711	137	105	70	1,023	1921[1,2]	856	214	52	118	1,240
1939	485	112	74	65	736	1916	371	77	28	32	508
1938	414	118	66	66	665	1911	276	110	20	47	453
1937	482	146	89	81	798	1906[1]	169	69	15	31	284
1936	364	122	66	76	628	1901	107	43	4	24	178
1935	310	116	57	64	547	1896	54	33	2	17	105
1934	291	113	43	62	510	1891	52	42	2	15	112
1933	213	97	35	51	397	1886	43	39	2	12	96
1932	257	93	34	61	445						
1931	386	109	42	82	619						

[1] Figures from 1926 to 1960 are for calendar years. From 1911 to 1921 they are for fiscal years ending 31 March of the year given and prior to 1907, they are for fiscal years ending 30 June of the year given.

[2] Figures in this table, for 1921, are for the fiscal year ending 31 March; in series G381-395, they are for the calendar year.

Series G401-407. Foreign trade, domestic exports, excluding gold, by destination, major areas, 1946 to 1975
(millions of dollars)

Year	United States	United Kingdom	Japan	Other European Economic Community[1]	Other America[2]	Centrally-planned economies[3]	Other countries
	401	**402**	**403**	**404**	**405**	**406**	**407**
1975	21,074	1,795	2,130	2,347	1,583	1,049	2,571
1974	20,762	1,912	2,227	2,146	1,560	633	2,435
1973	16,671	1,588	1,807	1,552	909	692	1,620
1972	13,585	1,370	961	1,158	805	640	1,152
1971	11,683	1,380	829	1,129	734	397	1,244
1970	10,563	1,481	810	1,226	750	311	1,261
1969	10,211	1,096	625	873	589	160	890
1968	8,997	1,210	607	774	544	307	887
1967	7,088	1,169	572	709	482	275	825
1966	6,046	1,123	394	662	496	583	785
1965	4,840	1,174	316	626	433	418	717
1964	4,271	1,200	330	555	436	619	683
1963	3,766	1,007	296	475	357	316	582
1962	3,608	909	215	455	302	197	492
1961	3,107	909	232	466	308	247	487
1960	2,932	915	179	439	255	47	488
1959	3,083	786	140	314	238	40	421
1958	2,808	772	105	420	241	30	415
1957	2,847	721	139	401	291	31	359
1956	2,803	811	128	336	238	73	371
1955	2,548	768	91	261	216	12	363
1954	2,309	651	96	238	239	13	314
1953	2,413	663	118	259	249	2	392
1952	2,303	744	102	341	325	24	442
1951	2,296	630	73	252	260	3	382
1950	2,021	468	20	117	188	7	284
1949	1,505	702	6	141	191	20	411
1948	1,499	683	8	213	229	49	372
1947	1,030	747	—	230	285	74	387
1946	884	594	1	189	202	91	312

[1] Up to 1972, includes Belgium, France, West Germany (as well as East Germany up to and including 1952), Italy, Luxembourg, and the Netherlands. After 1973, the European Economic Community also includes Denmark and Ireland. The United Kingdom also joined the European Economic Community in 1973, but is counted separately.

[2] Includes all countries and territories of North and South America (other than the United States and Canada), including Greenland, Bermuda and Puerto Rico.

[3] Includes Albania, Bulgaria, Czechoslovakia, East Germany (included with West Germany up to and including 1952), Hungary, Poland, Romania, U.S.S.R., Yugoslavia and People's Republic of China. (Taiwan is included with the People's Republic of China up to and including 1952. From 1953 on, Taiwan is included with "other countries".)

Series G408-414. Foreign trade, imports, excluding gold, by origin, major areas, 1946 to 1975
(millions of dollars)

Year	United States	United Kingdom	Japan	Other European Economic Community[1]	Other America[2]	Centrally-planned economies[3]	Other countries
	408	**409**	**410**	**411**	**412**	**413**	**414**
1975	23,641	1,222	1,205	2,074	1,802	234	4,537
1974	21,387	1,126	1,430	1,920	2,015	259	3,585
1973	16,502	1,005	1,011	1,477	1,033	196	2,101
1972	12,878	949	1,071	1,215	788	158	1,610
1971	10,951	837	803	984	755	111	1,177
1970	9,917	738	582	849	691	94	1,081
1969	10,243	791	496	831	714	109	947
1968	9,051	696	360	698	682	105	769
1967	7,952	649	294	635	551	100	693
1966	7,204	672	270	613	523	88	701
1965	6,045	619	230	514	548	59	618
1964	5,164	574	174	406	581	39	549
1963	4,445	527	130	342	536	27	552
1962	4,300	563	125	335	474	23	437
1961	3,864	618	117	318	447	21	384
1960	3,687	589	110	293	420	19	364
1959	3,709	589	103	292	461	17	339
1958	3,460	519	70	237	457	16	292
1957	3,887	507	61	225	503	16	273
1956	4,031	476	61	215	468	16	279
1955	3,331	393	37·	143	409	8	246
1954	2,871	382	19	120	361	3	211
1953	3,115	445	13	113	342	6	213
1952	2,888	352	13	96	349	8	211
1951	2,752	415	13	115	360	8	342
1950	2,090	401	12	65	299	12	247
1949	1,915	302	6	53	259	10	170
1948	1,799	294	3	39	273	9	202
1947	1,952	184	—	26	202	6	172
1946	1,387	137	—	14	164	5	134

[1] Up to 1972, includes Belgium, France, West Germany (as well as East Germany up to and including 1952), Italy, Luxembourg, and the Netherlands. After 1973 the European Economic Community also includes Denmark and Ireland. The United Kingdom also joined the European Economic Community in 1973, but is counted separately.

[2] Includes all countries and territories of North and South America (other than the United States and Canada), including Greenland, Bermuda and Puerto Rico.

[3] Includes Albania, Bulgaria, Czechoslovakia, East Germany (included with West Germany up to and including 1952), Hungary, Poland, Romania, U.S.S.R., Yugoslavia and People's Republic of China. (Taiwan is included with the People's Republic of China up to and including 1952. From 1953 on, Taiwan is included with "other countries".)

Series G415-428. Foreign trade, domestic exports, excluding coin and bullion, by main commodity sections, current values, 1946 to 1975

(millions of dollars)

Year	Live animals		Food, feed, beverages, tobacco		Crude materials, inedible		Fabricated materials, inedible		End products, inedible		Special transactions, trade		Total	
	All countries	United States	All countries	United States	All countries	United States	All countries	United States	All countries	United States	All countries	United States	All countries	United States
	415	**416**	**417**	**418**	**419**	**420**	**421**	**422**	**423**	**424**	**425**	**426**	**427**	**428**
1975	83	66	4,064	852	7,966	5,230	9,884	6,527	10,473	8,339	79	60	32,549	21,074
1974	90	72	3,780	804	7,793	5,042	10,696	7,043	9,237	7,736	80	66	31,676	20,762
1973	145	118	3,013	862	5,025	2,734	8,224	5,720	8,387	7,198	45	40	24,838	16,671
1972	86	67	2,269	668	3,560	2,003	6,578	4,668	7,136	6,142	42	36	19,671	13,585
1971	67	56	2,045	600	3,264	1,735	5,797	3,912	6,193	5,355	31	25	17,397	11,683
1970	68	55	1,800	605	3,084	1,626	5,866	3,603	5,551	4,651	31	23	16,401	10,563
1969	54	46	1,410	556	2,463	1,371	5,163	3,573	5,318	4,637	35	27	14,443	10,211
1968	59	51	1,554	489	2,468	1,373	4,855	3,351	4,351	3,703	38	31	13,325	8,997
1967	42	35	1,602	430	2,108	1,186	4,229	2,822	3,116	2,598	22	18	11,121	7,088
1966	78	69	1,888	429	1,948	1,123	4,012	2,761	2,137	1,644	25	20	10,089	6,046
1965	79	72	1,630	409	1,764	1,012	3,729	2,482	1,300	847	24	18	8,525	4,840
1964	35	30	1,806	362	1,616	979	3,502	2,237	1,109	643	26	20	8,094	4,271
1963	42	38	1,420	333	1,426	881	3,107	2,069	779	425	25	19	6,799	3,766
1962	68	64	1,172	306	1,362	884	2,907	1,968	655	376	15	10	6,179	3,608
1961	67	61	1,198	298	1,195	695	2,777	1,761	506	284	12	9	5,755	3,107
1960[1]	41	39	947	288	1,115	677	2,729	1,698	410	221	14	9	5,256	2,932
1959	56	55	1,020	290	1,087	731	2,461	1,768	387	235	11	4	5,022	3,083
1958	102	100	1,032	318	963	652	2,247	1,555	435	178	13	5	4,791	2,808
1957	54	53	911	306	1,025	655	2,406	1,660	369	157	13	6	4,779	2,837
1956	13	11	1,083	312	873	556	2,442	1,756	326	152	9	2	4,746	2,788
1955	16	14	885	274	686	425	2,364	1,679	290	143	5	1	4,247	2,536
1954	19	19	963	326	502	297	2,031	1,472	332	184	2	–	3,849	2,298
1953	18	17	1,243	384	476	287	1,949	1,513	397	201	3	1	4,086	2,402
1952	6	6	1,319	392	467	278	2,034	1,427	439	187	5	–	4,269	2,290
1951	65	65	1,053	397	431	272	1,972	1,405	358	142	3	–	3,882	2,281
1950	85	84	815	287	333	222	1,595	1,312	265	106	2	1	3,094	2,011
1949	69	68	911	242	310	189	1,310	898	367	101	2	–	2,969	1,499
1948	88	85	840	201	309	208	1,391	901	415	97	4	–	3,046	1,493
1947	20	18	886	99	222	148	1,239	707	375	54	6	1	2,748	1,026
1946	23	18	817	151	184	120	896	547	342	41	3	–	2,265	878

[1] Totals for the years before 1960 may not agree with totals on other tables, because of a change in the classification system.

Series G429-442. Foreign trade, imports, excluding coin and bullion, by main commodity sections, current values, 1946 to 1975

(millions of dollars)

Year	Live animals		Food, feed, beverages, tobacco		Crude materials, inedible		Fabricated materials, inedible		End products, inedible		Special transactions, trade		Total	
	All countries	United States	All countries	United States	All countries	United States	All countries	United States	All countries	United States	All countries	United States	All countries	United States
	429	**430**	**431**	**432**	**433**	**434**	**435**	**436**	**437**	**438**	**439**	**440**	**441**	**442**
1975	75	64	2,607	1,256	5,086	1,432	5,944	4,044	20,679	16,578	325	266	34,715	23,641
1974	112	102	2,404	1,139	4,073	1,078	6,482	4,209	18,362	14,627	289	232	31,722	21,387
1973	137	131	1,844	861	2,018	780	4,282	2,824	14,797	11,714	247	192	23,325	16,502
1972	45	40	1,356	615	1,540	644	3,579	2,233	11,948	9,195	202	151	18,669	12,878
1971	39	36	1,118	504	1,322	577	3,140	1,981	9,832	7,733	167	120	15,618	10,951
1970	30	28	1,085	488	1,172	535	2,885	1,915	8,618	6,832	161	119	13,952	9,917
1969	19	17	1,044	508	1,085	452	2,905	1,912	8,885	7,207	192	148	14,130	10,243
1968	16	15	903	454	1,129	538	2,435	1,580	7,620	6,244	259	219	12,360	9,051
1967	22	21	833	418	1,025	510	2,254	1,479	6,465	5,283	274	241	10,873	7,952
1966	13	12	818	408	1,048	508	2,290	1,499	5,570	4,488	333	290	10,072	7,204
1965	11	10	759	375	1,006	491	2,114	1,350	4,476	3,578	266	241	8,633	6,045
1964	17	16	778	356	961	443	1,813	1,197	3,701	2,955	218	197	7,488	5,164
1963	10	9	770	358	897	384	1,571	1,037	3,172	2,533	137	124	6,558	4,445
1962	8	7	657	341	827	360	1,487	981	3,152	2,499	127	112	6,258	4,300
1961	7	6	622	320	764	336	1,396	943	2,880	2,178	101	80	5,769	3,864
1960[1]	7	7	575	289	745	326	1,344	922	2,718	2,066	94	76	5,483	3,687
1959	13	12	564	273	728	301	1,393	955	2,731	2,104	80	64	5,509	3,709
1958	6	5	561	263	690	292	1,313	943	2,402	1,893	79	65	5,050	3,460
1957	5	4	557	257	830	397	1,506	1,096	2,501	2,072	74	62	5,473	3,887
1956	5	5	524	252	826	402	1,528	1,096	2,590	2,215	74	62	5,547	4,031
1955	5	4	463	207	699	339	1,188	875	2,150	1,852	62	54	4,568	3,331
1954	4	3	454	197	601	310	1,013	748	1,819	1,544	77	69	3,967	2,871
1953	4	3	405	170	666	359	1,110	830	2,006	1,703	57	50	4,248	3,115
1952	4	3	403	165	712	407	1,037	787	1,690	1,462	71	63	3,916	2,888
1951	3	3	423	157	905	487	1,109	774	1,515	1,287	50	44	4,005	2,752
1950	2	2	382	124	745	457	825	574	1,146	912	24	20	3,125	2,090
1949	3	3	312	102	613	383	750	560	1,009	845	26	22	2,714	1,915
1948	3	3	279	75	685	426	741	527	880	749	30	19	2,618	1,798
1947	3	3	286	135	532	372	727	555	954	851	38	34	2,541	1,950
1946	3	3	260	123	410	283	499	378	643	577	23	21	1,838	1,384

[1] Totals for the years before 1960 may not agree with totals on other tables, because of a change in the classification system.

Series G443-458. Adjustments to trade of Canada exports for balance of payments use, 1946 to 1975
(millions of dollars)

Year	Trade of Canada exports (including re-exports)	Balance of payments adjustments														Total adjusted exports
		Non-mone-tary gold	Wheat	Energy	Auto-motive prod-ucts	Ships	Civil air-craft	Defence goods	Tourist pur-chases	Ware-housing	New-found-land	War supplies Ltd.	United Nations Relief and Rehabil-itation Associ-ation cash purchases	Other[1]	Total adjust-ments	
	443	444	445	446	447	448	449	450	451	452	453	454	455	456	457	458
1975	33,103	350	31	36	-78	60	–	–	-6	–	–	–	–	-149	244	33,347
1974	32,441	187	60	183	-132	74	–	–	-5	–	–	–	–	-217	150	32,591
1973	25,421	144	54	76	-86	-21	–	–	-5	–	–	–	–	-122	40	25,461
1972	20,150	173	11	28	-68	22	-7	-35	-5	–	–	–	–	-140	-21	20,129
1971	17,820	159	-4	19	-53	44	3	39	-4	–	–	–	–	-146	57	17,877
1970	16,819	156	5	15	-54	1	-4	-12	-5	–	–	–	–	–	102	16,921
1969	14,868	207	13	18	-112	1	-8	52	-4	–	–	–	–	–	167	15,035
1968	13,679	123	-4	5	-91	3	-20	29	-4	–	–	–	–	–	41	13,720
1967	11,420	–	-29	..	-57	1	6	2	-5	–	–	–	–	–	-82	11,338
1966	10,325	–	-10	..	..	–	22	-9	-3	–	–	–	–	1	1	10,326
1965	8,767	–	16	..	..	2	5	-42	-3	–	–	–	–	–	-22	8,745
1964	8,303	–	-29	5	..	3	–	-42	-2	–	–	–	–	–	-65	8,238
1963	6,990	–	33	17	..	2	–	42	-2	–	–	–	–	–	92	7,082
1962	6,357	–	6	18	..	–	–	7	-2	–	–	–	–	1	30	6,387
1961	5,903	–	-15	..	..	2	–	–	-2	–	–	–	–	1	-14	5,889
1960	5,390	–	-6	..	..	7	2	–	-2	–	–	–	–	1	2	5,392
1959	5,144	–	6	..	..	4	–	–	-3	–	–	–	–	–	7	5,151
1958	4,899	–	-2	..	..	–	–	-4	-2	–	–	–	–	-1	-9	4,890
1957	4,890	–	-6	..	..	7	–	5	-2	–	–	–	–	–	4	4,894
1956	4,839	–	-5	..	..	6	–	-1	-3	–	–	–	–	1	-2	4,837
1955	4,332	–	-2	..	..	–	–	5	-3	–	–	–	–	–	–	4,332
1954	3,926	–	-2	..	..	–	–	-14	-3	5	–	–	–	22	8	3,934
1953	4,152	–	-4	..	..	–	–	-8	-3	6	–	–	–	9	–	4,152
1952	4,337	–	-10	..	..	–	–	15	-4	14	–	–	–	-13	2	4,339
1951	3,946	–	-6	..	..	-1	–	9	-5	8	–	–	–	-1	4	3,950
1950	3,143	–	–	..	..	-5	–	–	-6	..	–	–	–	7	-4	3,139
1949	3,004	–	-4	..	..	-5	–	–	-3	..	-10	–	–	7	-15	2,989
1948	3,087	–	14	..	..	-16	–	–	-2	..	-57	–	–	4	-57	3,030
1947	2,790	–	-14	..	..	-4	–	–	-3	..	-57	13	–	-2	-67	2,723
1946	2,299	–	38	..	..	5	–	3	..	..	-38	55	33	-2	94	2,393

[1] Includes adjustments for freight and Canada-United States reconciliation n.e.s.; these amounts are (*in millions of dollars*): freight: 1975, -348; 1974, -351; 1973, -315; 1972, -253; 1971, -229; Canada-United States reconciliation n.e.s.: 1975, +198; 1974, +134; 1973, +189; 1972, +113; 1971, +83.

Series G459-472. Adjustments to trade of Canada imports for balance of payments use, 1946 to 1975
(millions of dollars)

Year	Trade of Canada imports	Balance of payments adjustments												Total adjusted imports
		Non-monetary gold	Auto-motive products	Ships	Civil aircraft	Defence goods	Adver-tising	Official valu-ations	Foreign exchange rates spread	Ware-housing	New-found-land	Other[1]	Total adjust-ments	
	459	**460**	**461**	**462**	**463**	**464**	**465**	**466**	**467**	**468**	**469**	**470**	**471**	**472**
1975	34,636	153	-38	—	-51	—	-11	-11	—	—	—	-692	-650	33,986
1974	31,692	172	-159	—	-80	—	-11	-10	—	—	—	-711	-799	30,893
1973	23,325	49	-93	—	48	—	-10	-9	—	—	—	-584	-599	22,726
1972	18,669	66	-84	—	9	—	-10	-7	—	—	—	-371	-397	18,272
1971	15,618	66	-80	—	-19	32	-9	-6	—	—	—	-288	-304	15,314
1970	13,952	14	-95	—	4	24	-16	-16	—	—	—	2	-83	13,869
1969	14,130	64	-83	—	-11	—	-14	-15	—	—	—	—	-59	14,071
1968	12,360	85	-147	—	-33	5	-10	-11	—	—	—	—	-111	12,249
1967	10,873	—	-129	—	29	-2	-10	-11	—	—	—	22	-101	10,772
1966	10,072	—	..	—	50	1	-10	-11	—	—	—	—	30	10,102
1965	8,633	—	..	2	10	3	-10	-11	—	—	—	—	-6	8,627
1964	7,488	—	..	3	27	39	-9	-11	—	—	—	—	49	7,537
1963	6,578	—	..	5	22	-5	-7	-11	—	—	—	-3	1	6,579
1962	6,294	—	..	8	6	-86	-8	-11	—	—	—	—	-91	6,203
1961	5,781	—	..	13	-22	-38	-9	-11	—	—	—	2	-65	5,716
1960	5,495	—	..	5	32	27	-9	-9	—	—	—	-1	45	5,540
1959	5,530	—	..	13	43	4	-9	-9	—	—	—	—	42	5,572
1958	5,060	—	..	24	1	—	-9	-9	—	—	—	-1	6	5,066
1957	5,488	—	..	10	11	—	-8	-12	—	—	—	-1	—	5,488
1956	5,566	—	..	16	5	-1	-8	-10	—	—	—	-3	-1	5,565
1955	4,578	—	..	15	—	-38	-7	-8	—	—	—	3	-35	4,543
1954	3,967	—	..	10	—	-54	-7	-7	—	3	—	4	-51	3,916
1953	4,248	—	..	8	3	-48	-6	-6	—	14	—	-1	-36	4,212
1952	3,916	—	..	—	3	-67	-5	-6	—	3	—	10	-62	3,854
1951	4,005	—	..	1	—	95	-5	-8	—	23	—	-10	96	4,101
1950	3,125	—	..	—	—	11	-5	-4	-11	15	—	1	7	3,132
1949	2,714	—	..	6	—	-2	-4	-3	-12	—	-1	-2	-18	2,696
1948	2,618	—	..	4	—	-9	-3	-3	-12	14	-11	—	-20	2,598
1947	2,543	—	..	—	—	-3	-2	..	-12	25	-9	-7	-8	2,535
1946	1,841	—	..	5	—	-6	-2	-5	-6	10	-9	-6	-19	1,822

[1] Includes adjustments for freight and Canada-United States reconciliation n.e.s.; these amounts are *(in millions of dollars)*: freight: 1975, -93; 1974, -91; 1973, -99; 1972, -78; 1971, -64; Canada-United States reconciliation n.e.s.: 1975, -599; 1974, -628; 1973, -485; 1972, -300; 1971, -240.

Series G473-487. Foreign trade, imports, by free, dutiable, and duty collected, 1868 to 1975
(thousands of dollars)

Year	Duty free imports			Dutiable imports			Duty collected[1]			Ratio of duty collected to dutiable imports			Ratio of duty collected to total imports		
	All countries	United Kingdom	United States	All countries	United Kingdom	United States	All countries	United Kingdom	United States	All countries	United Kingdom	United States	All countries	United Kingdom	United States
	473	474	475	476	477	478	479	480	481	482	483	484	485	486	487
1975	21,748,892	648,081	15,208,524	12,966,816	573,818	8,432,788	1,948,251	115,576	1,202,557	15.0	20.1	14.3	5.6	9.5	5.1
1974	18,713,668	589,551	12,999,944	13,008,456	536,787	8,386,770	1,923,819	106,383	1,182,218	14.8	19.8	14.1	6.1	9.4	5.5
1973	13,800,498	545,593	10,576,792	9,524,822	459,804	5,925,223	1,440,942	89,653	843,779	15.1	19.5	14.2	6.2	8.9	5.1
1972	10,651,093	498,915	8,260,392	8,018,334	450,552	4,617,787	1,242,560	85,987	682,451	15.5	19.1	14.8	6.7	9.1	5.3
1971	9,083,457	428,280	7,118,898	6,534,647	408,978	3,831,732	1,007,453	77,069	558,055	15.4	18.8	14.6	6.5	9.2	5.1
1970	8,042,307	371,330	6,325,106	5,909,596	366,933	3,591,939	898,987	67,784	517,688	15.2	18.5	14.4	6.4	9.2	5.2
1969	8,220,272	439,342	6,523,913	5,910,103	351,631	3,719,328	920,512	67,569	549,959	15.6	19.2	14.8	6.5	8.5	5.4
1968	7,336,429	415,678	5,766,930	5,023,758	280,415	3,283,634	814,927	54,547	506,197	16.2	19.5	15.4	6.6	7.8	5.6
1967	5,876,686	385,550	4,580,786	4,996,043	263,385	3,370,778	823,348	52,486	532,734	16.5	19.9	15.8	7.6	8.0	6.7
1966	5,105,957	388,808	3,818,755	4,966,049	283,667	3,385,703	816,825	56,443	534,956	16.5	19.9	15.8	8.1	8.4	7.4
1965	4,266,300	369,513	3,081,848	4,366,849	249,545	2,962,983	721,922	50,221	481,436	16.5	20.1	16.2	8.4	8.1	8.0
1964	3,452,804	350,518	2,335,344	4,034,903	223,478	2,828,941	677,113	44,048	472,433	16.8	19.7	16.7	9.0	7.7	9.1
1963	3,015,623	314,034	1,972,216	3,542,586	212,766	2,472,340	630,208	42,698	436,872	17.8	20.1	17.7	9.6	8.1	9.8
1962	2,777,494	298,930	1,840,822	3,480,282	264,132	2,458,717	669,498	53,075	461,348	19.2	20.1	18.8	10.7	9.4	10.7
1961	2,653,170	416,647	1,640,185	3,115,408	201,574	2,223,783	549,186	42,856	380,051	17.6	21.3	17.1	9.5	6.9	10.1
1960	2,434,112	382,586	1,490,533	3,048,583	206,346	2,196,092	539,507	43,554	376,677	17.7	21.1	17.2	9.7	7.4	10.2
1959	2,365,856	369,810	1,438,532	3,143,065	218,763	2,270,533	550,031	45,009	388,310	17.5	20.6	17.1	10.0	7.6	10.5
1958	2,097,778	305,359	1,272,469	2,952,714	213,146	2,187,678	517,027	44,292	370,108	17.5	20.8	16.9	10.2	8.5	10.7
1957	2,250,149	274,341	1,423,156	3,223,197	232,978	2,464,235	554,213	36,751	408,105	17.2	15.8	16.6	10.1	7.2	10.5
1956	2,254,435	255,861	1,453,821	3,292,516	220,510	2,577,573	577,654	34,805	431,067	17.5	15.8	16.7	10.4	7.3	10.7
1955	1,929,717	217,495	1,250,744	2,638,037	175,622	2,080,399	479,782	29,106	360,190	18.2	16.6	17.3	10.5	7.4	10.8
1954	1,655,833	210,805	1,063,923	2,311,568	171,424	1,807,356	417,578	28,052	312,790	18.1	16.4	17.3	10.5	7.3	10.9
1953	1,829,848	251,746	1,204,479	2,417,960	193,695	1,910,822	448,658	31,214	332,132	18.6	16.1	17.4	10.6	7.0	10.7
1952	1,753,536	194,722	1,187,125	2,162,882	156,819	1,700,503	393,805	25,810	285,948	18.2	16.5	16.8	10.1	7.3	9.9
1951	1,830,635	241,570	1,124,468	2,174,304	173,624	1,627,619	375,956	27,504	268,960	17.3	15.8	16.5	9.4	6.6	9.8
1950	1,503,697	249,669	910,525	1,621,534	151,142	1,179,006	276,532	25,091	192,601	17.1	16.6	16.3	8.8	6.3	9.2
1949	1,269,901	171,013	822,514	1,444,124	131,407	1,092,713	251,010	21,277	175,169	17.4	16.2	16.0	9.2	7.0	9.1
1948	1,236,073	158,748	744,415	1,382,203	134,787	1,054,092	242,804	23,104	165,286	17.6	17.1	15.7	9.3	7.9	9.2
1947	979,969	107,708	622,975	1,562,690	76,499	1,328,631	325,654	12,149	258,921	20.8	15.9	19.5	12.8	6.6	13.3
1946	762,333	85,828	465,045	1,078,934	51,595	922,341	229,156	9,018	178,649	21.2	17.5	19.4	12.4	6.6	12.9
1945	715,534	62,539	490,987	798,795	37,627	692,225	168,228	6,618	133,863	21.1	17.6	19.3	11.1	6.6	11.3
1944	844,791	53,024	647,652	884,752	41,282	787,732	177,853	6,715	147,331	20.1	16.3	18.7	10.3	7.1	10.3
1943	849,379	62,825	650,996	836,549	37,763	759,094	173,505	7,076	143,084	20.7	18.7	18.8	10.3	7.0	10.1
1942	790,156	79,640	578,372	715,019	38,766	631,019	154,046	9,365	120,014	21.5	24.2	19.0	10.2	7.9	9.9
1941	541,532	94,340	291,300	732,791	43,645	620,904	160,164	10,231	116,954	21.9	23.4	18.8	12.6	7.4	12.8
1940	439,973	82,615	255,367	582,935	54,371	455,181	139,194	13,490	92,408	23.9	24.8	20.3	13.6	9.8	13.0
1939	308,667	59,716	182,318	427,471	52,589	302,943	103,366	14,187	64,463	24.2	27.0	21.3	14.0	12.6	13.3
1938	285,841	63,310	160,056	379,095	54,908	253,954	92,297	..[2]	..[2]	24.3	..[2]	..[2]	13.9	..[2]	..[2]
1937	361,733	77,803	190,942	436,328	68,320	290,672	104,808	..	..	24.0	..	..	13.1	..	..
1936	277,494	63,830	141,348	350,904	58,163	222,560	87,775	..	..	25.0	..	..	14.0	..	..
1935	240,106	59,730	122,490	306,116	56,521	187,461	84,217	..	..	27.4	..	..	15.4	..	..
1934	214,260	52,401	117,392	295,566	60,595	173,566	83,891	..	..	28.4	..	..	16.5	..	..
1933	161,334	44,730	83,906	235,196	52,741	129,390	69,676	..	..	29.6	..	..	17.6	..	..
1932	156,741	29,500	93,665	288,425	63,624	163,151	86,573	..	..	30.0	..	..	19.4	..	..
1931	202,973	27,108	132,461	416,180	81,704	253,594	120,250	..	..	28.9	..	..	19.4	..	..
1930	348,991	41,362	239,740	647,230	120,311	403,333	161,395	..	..	24.9	..	..	16.2	..	..
1929	438,414	40,497	334,175	849,115	153,276	549,726	206,950	..	..	24.4	..	..	16.1	..	..
1928	423,212	36,905	324,723	788,271	152,782	492,056	192,266	..	..	24.4	..	..	15.9	..	..
1927	381,271	34,236	291,090	696,253	146,999	408,273	168,303	..	..	24.2	..	..	15.6	..	..
1926	358,197	28,413	282,236	642,448	135,021	380,788	155,166	..	..	24.2	..	..	15.5	..	..
1925	329,132	30,177	258,018	561,061	131,942	320,557	137,858	..	..	24.6	..	..	15.5	..	..
1924	279,232	25,258	224,255	528,912	123,634	300,218	123,163	..	..	23.3	..	..	15.2	..	..
1923	308,932	29,044	248,299	594,099	125,435	362,055	136,065	..	..	22.9	..	..	15.1	..	..
1922	249,079	22,678	195,416	513,331	114,181	314,493	132,172	..	..	25.7	..	..	17.3	..	..
1921	252,615	21,825	207,000	546,863	101,325	348,091	117,693	..	..	21.5	..	..	14.7	..	..
1920	446,074	52,320	350,388	890,847	179,168	570,848	203,029	..	..	22.8	..	..	15.2	..	..
1919	333,555	24,643	278,553	607,458	63,016	461,045	168,921	..	..	27.8	..	..	18.0	..	..
1918	421,191	23,277	363,596	542,342	58,047	429,299	116,577	..	..	21.5	..	..	12.1	..	..
1917	384,717	31,592	333,273	461,734	75,505	332,039	109,801	..	..	23.8	..	..	13.0	..	..
1916	218,835	25,395	171,414	289,367	52,009	199,467	78,683	..	..	27.2	..	..	15.5	..	..

Series G473-487. Foreign trade, imports, by free, dutiable, and duty collected, 1868 to 1975 (concluded)
(thousands of dollars)

Year	Duty free imports			Dutiable imports			Duty collected[1]			Ratio of duty collected to dutiable imports			Ratio of duty collected to total imports		
	All countries	United Kingdom	United States	All countries	United Kingdom	United States	All countries	United Kingdom	United States	All countries	United Kingdom	United States	All countries	United Kingdom	United States
	473	474	475	476	477	478	479	480	481	482	483	484	485	486	487
1915	176,164	22,147	128,484	279,792	68,010	168,658	76,567	..	..	27.4	..	..	16.8	..	..
1914	208,935	29,695	146,820	410,259	102,376	249,483	107,181	..	..	26.1	..	..	17.3	..	..
1913	229,600	30,687	160,557	441,607	108,056	276,330	115,064	..	..	26.1	..	..	17.1	..	..
1912	187,101	27,392	134,499	335,304	89,514	196,886	87,576	..	..	26.1	..	..	16.8	..	..
1911	170,001	25,423	122,757	282,724	84,512	153,067	73,312	..	..	25.9	..	..	16.2	..	..
1910	143,054	23,514	99,170	227,264	71,823	118,834	61,024	..	..	26.8	..	..	16.5	..	..
1909	113,580	18,463	79,848	175,014	52,220	90,585	48,060	..	..	27.5	..	..	16.7	..	..
1908	134,381	23,205	94,948	218,160	71,212	110,361	58,331	..	..	26.7	..	..	16.5	..	..
1907	98,160	15,665	70,117	152,066	48,751	78,969	40,290	..	..	26.5	..	..	16.1	..	..
1906	110,694	16,568	79,716	173,046	52,616	89,541	46,671	..	..	27.0	..	..	16.4	..	..
1905	101,035	15,243	73,981	150,929	45,100	78,797	42,024	..	..	27.8	..	..	16.7	..	..
1904	95,000	16,785	65,786	148,910	44,940	77,544	40,954	..	..	27.5	..	..	16.8	..	..
1903	88,299	16,583	60,533	136,796	42,210	68,538	37,110	..	..	27.1	..	..	16.5	..	..
1902	78,080	13,960	54,820	118,657	35,063	60,182	32,426	..	..	27.3	..	..	16.5	..	..
1901	71,961	11,119	53,778	105,970	31,702	53,600	29,107	..	..	27.5	..	..	16.4	..	..
1900	68,305	12,718	48,327	104,347	31,562	53,898	28,889	..	..	27.7	..	..	16.7	..	..
1899	59,989	9,445	44,035	89,433	27,522	44,472	25,734	..	..	28.8	..	..	17.2	..	..
1898	51,682	9,487	36,761	74,625	22,556	38,064	22,158	..	..	29.7	..	..	17.5	..	..
1897	40,397	9,184	26,541	66,221	20,217	30,483	19,892	..	..	30.0	..	..	18.7	..	..
1896	38,121	8,458	24,428	67,240	24,366	29,102	20,219	..	..	30.0	..	..	19.2	..	..
1895	42,118	7,747	24,383	58,558	23,312	25,796	17,887	..	..	30.5	..	..	17.8	..	..
1894	46,292	9,543	24,922	62,779	27,493	25,824	19,380	..	..	30.9	..	..	17.8	..	..
1893	45,297	10,660	23,778	69,874	31,869	28,562	21,162	..	..	30.3	..	..	18.4	..	..
1892	46,000	10,232	22,237	69,161	30,832	29,506	20,550	..	..	29.7	..	..	17.8	..	..
1891	36,998	10,571	22,243	74,536	31,448	29,790	23,416	..	..	31.4	..	..	21.0	..	..
1890	34,576	10,009	20,790	77,106	33,268	30,575	23,921	..	..	31.0	..	..	21.4	..	..
1889	34,623	10,031	21,047	74,475	32,220	28,982	23,742	..	..	31.9	..	..	21.8	..	..
1888	31,026	8,320	19,343	69,646	30,848	27,098	22,188	..	..	31.8	..	..	22.0	..	..
1887	26,987	8,975	14,225	78,121	35,766	30,571	22,438	..	..	28.7	..	..	21.3	..	..
1886	25,333	8,647	13,159	70,659	30,386	29,660	19,427	..	..	27.5	..	..	20.2	..	..
1885	26,486	9,329	14,345	73,270	30,702	31,232	19,121	..	..	26.1	..	..	19.2	..	..
1884	25,962	9,097	13,989	80,010	32,828	35,797	20,156	..	..	25.2	..	..	19.0	..	..
1883	30,273	10,947	16,495	91,588	40,732	38,652	23,163	..	..	25.3	..	..	19.0	..	..
1882	25,388	8,897	14,112	85,757	41,460	32,941	21,700	..	..	25.3	..	..	19.5	..	..
1881	18,868	7,025	10,706	71,621	35,860	25,632	18,493	..	..	25.8	..	..	20.4	..	..
1880	15,718	5,726	8,627	54,183	28,038	19,567	14,130	..	..	26.1	..	..	20.2	..	..
1879	23,276	3,892	18,367	55,427	27,076	23,803	12,935	..	..	23.3	..	..	16.4	..	..
1878	30,623	5,113	24,538	59,773	32,140	23,465	12,792	..	..	21.4	..	..	14.2	..	..
1877	33,210	6,415	25,865	60,917	32,917	23,511	12,544	..	..	20.6	..	..	13.3	..	..
1876	32,275	8,094	22,765	60,238	32,385	21,334	12,829	..	..	21.3	..	..	13.9	..	..
1875	39,270	11,059	26,618	78,139	48,950	22,313	15,354	..	..	19.6	..	..	13.1	..	..
1874	46,948	13,630	30,609	76,233	47,795	21,098	14,407	..	..	18.9	..	..	11.7	..	..
1873	53,311	20,554	28,510	71,198	47,443	16,679	12,998	..	..	18.3	..	..	10.4	..	..
1872	36,679	14,012	20,471	68,276	48,197	13,271	13,021	..	..	19.1	..	..	12.4	..	..
1871	24,120	8,683	13,100	60,094	39,816	14,085	11,808	..	..	19.6	..	..	14.0	..	..
1870	21,775	7,514	12,998	45,127	30,023	8,699	9,425	..	..	20.9	..	..	14.1	..	..
1869	22,086	7,013	13,704	41,069	28,484	7,794	8,285	..	..	20.2	..	..	13.1	..	..
1868	23,434	9,333	12,646	43,656	28,284	10,014	8,801	..	..	20.2	..	..	13.1	..	..

[1] Duty collected is the amount levied at the time imported goods are cleared through customs, exclusive of any subsequent adjustments or refunds. Refunds and drawbacks amount to approximately 10 per cent of gross collections in each fiscal year. Readers may refer to annual, *Report of Revenue Canada, Customs and Excise*, (of Supply and Services Canada, Catalogue RU 1-4), for amount of refunds and drawbacks in any given fiscal year.

[2] Not available prior to 1939.

Section H: Government Finance

Richard M. Bird, *University of Toronto*

The data contained in this section for the most part relate only to the revenues, expenditures and debt of the federal, provincial and municipal governments proper. The first part of the chapter contains information on the finances of the federal government from Confederation to 1975. The second part contains information on the finances of all governments for various years since 1933 to 1975. The final part of the chapter contains miscellaneous data relating to various aspects of governmental finance.

Most of the data for years before 1960 are identical to that contained in the original *Historical Statistics of Canada*. In order to establish conformity with more recent data, however, some revisions have been made to the earlier data, especially those for the 1950s. Where appropriate, such changes are noted in the detailed table notes that follow. In order to discuss adequately the very substantial changes that have taken place in governmental financial arrangements in Canada since 1960, it has been necessary to omit some of the material relevant to earlier years contained in the original edition. Readers who require more details on some aspects of the data from earlier years are therefore urged to consult the earlier volume.

The principal source used for the most recent data has been the collection of publications on government finance described as the Financial Management series of Statistics Canada. In addition, however, owing in part to the major revision which took place in this series in 1970, it has proved necessary to do a good deal of special work in order to present the series found in this section. Most of the necessary work was done at the Department of Finance and in Statistics Canada. These organizations were also responsible for most of the detailed notes to the tables in this section.

The principal published sources for the information included in this section are various official documents, particularly, for the most recent years, the various series produced by Statistics Canada's Public Finance Division, including *Federal Government Finance*, (Catalogue 68-211), *Provincial Government Finance*, (Catalogue 68-207), *Local Government Finance*, (Catalogue 68-204), and *Consolidated Government Finance*, (Catalogue 68-202). For earlier years various other publications of Statistics Canada, the public accounts of the federal and provincial governments, and the earlier studies of the Royal Commission on Dominion-Provincial Relations were particularly valuable. More detailed references may be found in the original *Historical Statistics of Canada*. In addition to these sources, readers interested in the public finances will find additional data of interest in the *Estimates* and *Budget Speeches* of the federal and provincial governments, in various publications of the Bank of Canada, and a particularly valuable secondary source in two publications of the Canadian Tax Foundation, the *National Finances* and *Provincial and Municipal Finances*.

General note

Readers who are not familiar with Canadian government financial statistics may be puzzled to find that many data relevant to this subject do not appear in this section. As explained below, this is due primarily to the particular way in which financial data are constructed in Canada. Most of the other relevant information will, however, be found elsewhere in this volume, particularly in the sections on the national accounts, on employment, on price deflators, and on health and welfare. Indeed, almost every section of this book contains some reference in one way or another to the government finances. Readers interested in any particular aspect of this subject are therefore urged to consult the index. (Although some attention was paid to the possibility of including in this section information on changing tax rates over time, it was found to be too complex to undertake here. Readers interested in this subject are referred to the publications of the Canadian Tax Foundation cited earlier.)

A particular problem should be called to the attention of readers who may wish to use data from this section in conjunction with data from other sections. Most data presented in this section are on a fiscal year basis. For the federal and provincial governments in recent years the fiscal year has normally ended at the end of March (that is, including the first quarter of the following year). For municipalities, however, the fiscal year is normally identical to the calendar year. A more detailed account of the varied fiscal years of the different governments in the period since Confederation may be found in the original edition.

In accordance with the general orientation of this volume as a reference source, no attempt has been made here to construct artificial linkages of disparate time series. Instead, the nature of breaks in series has been indicated as clearly as possible. In the case of the major break in the Financial Management series in 1970, although a considerable effort has been made to provide a five-year overlap on both the old and the new basis, the reader is left to do what he will with regard to constructing a linked time series. In particular, readers are warned that the data on municipal finance is particularly unsuitable for use in time series analysis.

The enormous changes that have taken place in federal-provincial fiscal arrangements since 1960 have considerably complicated the task of presenting recent data in a form comparable to that for earlier years. Although there have been transfers of funds since Confederation amongst the different levels of government in Canada, the size and nature of these arrangements have changed more radically in the last 15 years than ever in the country's history, thus complicating substantially the task of the historical statistician. Although series H466-485 in this section contain the best available post-war data on federal-provincial transfers, the changing nature of these arrangements has affected many of the revenue and expenditure figures presented throughout this section and some introductory comment is therefore required.

There have, for example, been three completely different types of arrangements with regard to the sharing of the income tax base (and, in earlier years, the estate tax base) between the federal and provincial governments. Beginning in World War II, tax agreements were made between the federal and provincial governments under which the provinces gave up for the war's duration the levying of personal income and corporation taxes, in return for payments by the federal government to the provinces. Subsequently, these temporary tax rental agreements were renewed every five years until 1961. The statistical result of this arrangement is that federal tax revenues were increased and provincial tax revenues reduced, with the offsetting payment by the federal government to the provinces taking the form of an unconditional grant.

In 1962, however, this tax rental system was replaced by a system of tax collection agreements, under which the federal government abated tax points and agreed to collect provincial taxes at rates chosen by the provinces. All provinces except Quebec participated in these arrangements. The former unconditional payment to the provinces was thus abolished and replaced by, in effect, a procedure under which the federal government turned over a certain proportion of revenue to the provinces in the form of a tax abatement.

In 1972, this system was, in its turn, discontinued, and provincial taxes were thereafter expressed as a direct percentage of reduced federal 'basic' income taxes rather than as a percentage of federal taxes with an offsetting federal abatement. The effect of this change on provincial revenue was nil, although provincial rates (expressed as a percentage of the federal tax) rose, and the federal rate structure was lowered. The provincial taxes were still collected by the federal government to a substantial extent. Quebec, however, has imposed its own personal income tax since 1954 using its own definitions of taxable income and rate schedule. The Quebec provincial tax now takes up, approximately, the room vacated by the federal government for all provinces plus an additional abatement as compensation in lieu of participating in certain joint programs. A cash adjusting payment is provided to make up the difference between the federal share of the cost of the programs and the value of the tax points transferred.

Neither this brief summary nor the later notes to series H466-485 can do justice to the complex and changing nature of these federal-provincial fiscal arrangements in the post-war period. Readers are referred to the study of Moore, Perry and Beach, *The Financing of Canadian Federation,* (Canadian Tax Foundation, 1966) for a thorough account of events up to 1966. Since that time, additional useful material may be found in occasional articles in the *Canadian Tax Journal* and other foundation publications.

Readers interested in updating the data in this edition are further warned that a further massive change in federal-provincial arrangements in 1977 will make it even more difficult to construct meaningful fiscal time series with Canadian data. The new Established Program Financing arrangements have basically put all provinces on the system mentioned above with respect to Quebec (although the basis of calculation is different). The former 'conditional grants' will now be replaced by a cash transfer called a 'specific purpose transfer' instead of a 'conditional grant' and by the transfer of tax points to the province.

A final point of considerable importance in this introduction concerns the relationship between the data appearing in this section and that appearing in, on the one hand, the national income accounts and on the other hand, in the original data sources, the provincial and federal public accounts and the provincial reports on municipal financial information. These three sets of data are each designed to serve a different purpose. The public accounts and the annual financial reports of municipal governments are intended to account for the money taken in and spent by these governments. These sources usually cover only direct

spending by the government in question plus payments to (or profits remitted by) enterprises. They also include adjustments relating to prior years and the current year's results. Most important for present purposes, the treatment of a number of items, such as capital expenditures, federal grants, and the sale of goods and services, is not at all uniform across the country. Owing to this basic lack of comparability, no direct consolidation or comparison of data appearing in these sources is advisable.

To overcome this problem, Statistics Canada has developed the Financial Management series, which is the primary source of most of the recent data in this section. This data source includes not only the departments of government but also various administrative, regulatory and special funds performing functions similar to departments at different levels of government. In the most recent years this system includes even the social insurance systems such as Workmen's Compensation Boards and Canada and Quebec Pension Plans, as well as such special items as local government waterworks. The purpose of this uniform system is to permit the consolidation of various levels of government and to permit comparability across governmental jurisdictions. Owing to frequent definitional changes, however, comparability over time, particularly at the municipal level, is more suspect, as noted earlier. The accounting system used in the Financial Management series is basically a modified cash system, as in the basic source documents of the public accounts.

In contrast, the national accounts analysis of government, which has the purpose of measuring the impact of government transactions on the economy, is constructed quite differently. Three of the most important differences are: first, the accounting system is on an accrual rather than a cash basis; second, capital transactions relating to existing assets are eliminated, as are all government sales and service operations conducted on a commercial basis; and third, all grants are considered to be expenditures of the recipient governments.

The importance of these various adjustments may be perhaps best indicated by presenting a brief table showing the reconciliation of the three analyses, for the federal level only.

Beginning with the ordinary budgetary revenues given in the public accounts, to arrive at 'gross general revenue' as now shown in the Financial Management series, one must make the additions and deductions shown in the table. Similarly, to convert gross general revenue into revenue on a national accounts basis, another series of additions and deductions are required. The same has to be done with respect to expenditures. In general, the results of these changes are that the Financial Management series totals for both revenue and expenditure tend to be larger than those shown in the public accounts, while those in the national accounts tend to be smaller than those shown in the Financial Management series but still larger than those in the public accounts. Readers are cautioned to use considerable care in going from one to the other of these data sources. This caution is particularly advisable since the precise differences amongst these concepts have changed considerably in recent years with the major revisions of both the national accounts series and of the Financial Management series. (The most complete account of the scope and significance of the public finance series used in this section may be found in Statistics Canada's publication, *The Canadian System of Government Financial Management Statistics,* (Catalogue 68-508). Briefer discussions of this question may

Reconciliation of Federal Government Finance Data

(Fiscal Year ended March 31, 1975)

Revenue	$'000,000
Budgetary revenue per Public Accounts	24,908.8
plus:	
Revenue of special funds	11,242.2
Revenue deducted from expenditure in the public accounts	577.3
Expenditure deducted from revenue in the public accounts	125.7
less:	
Refunds of current year's expenditure	-.3
Refunds of previous year's expenditures	-95.1
Advances	-.0
Amounts to adjust government enterprises to a "net" basis	-.2
Other deductions	-3.0
Budgetary revenue derived from special fund expenditure	-530.1
Special fund revenue derived from other special fund expenditure	-251.1
Special fund revenue derived from budgetary expenditure	-3,781.7
Gross General Revenue	
on a Financial Management basis	*32,192.5*
plus:	
Corporate tax accruals	4,639.0
Oil export tax accruals	1,509.8
Adjustment to reflect investment income within National Accounts concepts	390.4
Contributions of government as an employer to non-trusteed pension plans and social insurance funds	2,462.0
Capital consumption allowances	362.0
less:	
Corporation income tax collections	-4,068.4
Oil export tax collections	-1,669.4
Revenue of special funds not included in National Accounts	-4,030.7
Revenue of Post Office	-488.8
Other deductions (net)	-1,108.4
Revenue on a national accounts basis	**30,190.0**

Expenditure	
Budgetary expenditure as per public accounts	26,054.9
plus:	
Expenditure of special funds	8,712.9
Expenditure deducted from revenue in the public accounts	125.7
Revenue deducted from expenditure in the public accounts	577.3
less:	
Refunds of prior year's revenue	-.3
Amount to adjust government enterprises to a "net" basis	-.2
Advances	-14.3
Other	-1.9
Expenditure of special funds contributing to budgetary revenue	-530.1
Expenditure of special funds contributing to revenue of other special funds	-251.1
Budgetary expenditure contributing to revenue of special funds	-3,781.7
Gross general expenditure	
on a Financial Management basis	*30,891.2*
plus:	
Capital consumption allowances	362.0
Contributions of government as employer to non-trusteed pension plans and social insurance funds	349.6
Other additions	828.7
less:	
Purchases of land and used assets	-44.0
Proceeds from sale of goods and services	-847.3
Expenditure of the Post Office and the Bank of Canada	-733.0
Expenditure of the Canada Pension Plan	-399.0
Other non-relevant expenditures per National Accounts	-378.5
Expenditure on a national accounts basis	**30,693.0**

also be found in the Canadian Tax Foundation publications mentioned earlier.)

Federal Government Finance (Series H1-51)

General note

Although the data in this section are not in the most useful form for most analytical purposes, they are included here as providing the longest available continuous series on Canadian government finance. The original source of these data, which were prepared by the Department of Finance, is the *Public Accounts of Canada*. The data from 1867 to 1960 inclusive are taken unchanged from the first edition of

Historical Statistics of Canada. However, the data for 1951 and later years found in that source have been revised to reflect the current (and more meaningful) budgetary treatment of the old age security payments.

H1-18. Federal government budgetary revenue, by major source, 1867 to 1975

The data in this table include tax receipts that were credited to the Old Age Security Fund from 1951 to 1975 inclusive (although the taxes earmarked for this purpose were no longer recorded separately as non-budgetary revenue after 1970). This treatment has been followed both to make this table consistent with data for subsequent years and because the Old Age Security Fund was never more than a bookkeeping device in any case. The table excludes cash flows relating to new debt or the redemption of existing debt.

H1. 'Personal income tax' includes various special taxes on income levied at different times, for example, national defence tax and social development tax. For the fiscal years 1942-1943 to 1946-1947 this series excludes revenues equal to the estimated refundable (forced saving) portion of the tax.

H2. 'Corporate income tax' excludes excess profits taxes (H3 which were levied during and after World War I and World War II. It also excludes some small amounts of refundable corporation income tax which were levied from May 1966 to March 1967.

H4. 'Non-resident taxes' are those withheld on certain interest, dividends and other payments going abroad.

H5. 'Estates tax' includes duties levied under the Dominion Succession Duty Act. The estate tax was abolished in 1971; revenues for subsequent years reflect payments on estates of persons deceased in 1971 or earlier.

H6. 'Sales tax' includes amounts formerly earmarked for Old Age Security.

H8. 'Excise duties' are levied solely on liquor and tobacco products.

H10. 'Miscellaneous taxes' include for 1975 a special excise tax on gasoline ($425 million) and the oil export tax ($1,063 million); the latter is also included in 1974 ($1,669 million) and in 1973 ($287 million). This series also includes such minor items as Chinese head tax levied prior to World War I, taxes on insurance premiums and on export of electricity as well as revenue from a group of taxes on commodities which has varied greatly over the period (for example, automobiles, radios, jewellery, cigarettes).

H12. Post office revenues are gross receipts from services provided by the Post Office Department less certain amounts charged directly against revenue for salaries and rent allowances at semi-staff and revenue offices, commissions at sub-offices, and transit charges on Canadian mail forwarded through or delivered in foreign countries.

H13. Return on investment in Crown corporations is a special compilation to show separately this item as distinct from that of series H14 with which it is grouped in the public accounts. Series H13 is mainly profits from or interest on loans to the Bank of Canada, Canadian National Railways, Central Mortgage and Housing Corporation, Polymer Corporation, and other entities defined as Crown corporations under the Financial Administration Act.

H14. Other return on investments is profits from and interest on all loans, advances and investments other than those made to or in Crown corporations. For example, it includes return on loans to foreign governments.

H15. Miscellaneous non-tax revenue includes revenue from bullion and coinage, from privileges, licences and permits, from proceeds from sales, from receipts for services or service fees, from refunds of expenditure, and sundry small items.

H17. Special receipts and credits are non-recurring revenue items. Included are capital refunds, special receipts under war appropriation acts and other such items. Since 1955 they are not shown separately.

H19-34. Federal government budgetary expenditure, classified by function, 1867 to 1975

The data in this table include expenditures for old age security pensions and from the National Defence Equipment Account, although these items were not treated as budgetary in the years they were made. The data include, however, such continuing extra-budgetary expenditures as those from the unemployment insurance fund (other than the government contribution) and the Canada Pension Plan. These figures include both current and capital expenditures but not debt retirement. The functional classification was prepared by the Department of Finance and is not identical to the Statistics Canada classification used later in this chapter.

H19. 'Defence' includes Department of National Defence, Defence Production, and defence aid to other countries. It also includes for some years in the 1950s expenditures out of the National Defence Equipment Account. This account was credited with the value of defence materials and supplies transferred to members of the North Atlantic Treaty Organization, which credits could be used in subsequent years to purchase equipment and supplies for the Canadian forces. For a more detailed statement see *Public Accounts of Canada.* The amounts thus spent were as follows: (in millions of dollars) 1958, 211.7; 1957, 24.3; 1956, 45.9; 1955, 51.3; 1954, 74.3; 1953, 32.9; 1952, -14.2.

H20. 'Veterans' benefits' include payments for veterans' pensions and assistance, and hospitalization.

H21. Health expenditures are mainly grants to provinces to assist provincial health services, for capital outlays on hospitals and, beginning in July 1958, the federal contribution to hospital insurance. Beginning in 1968, the federal contribution to medicare is included. The decrease which took place in 1965 compared to 1964 was due mainly to the province of Quebec opting out of the hospital insurance program. For 1965 onward the payments to Quebec are recorded as payments to provincial and municipal governments. See also the discussion of intergovernmental fiscal transfers in the general introduction to this section.

H22. Family allowances are monthly allowances paid for each child under the age of 16, beginning in July 1945. Effective 1 January 1974, family allowance payments became taxable. The monthly allowance in January 1973 averaged $7.00 per child compared to $20.00 in January 1974.

H24. Welfare includes payments under the Canada Assistance Plan and for unemployment assistance and relief projects as well as old age assistance, blind and disabled persons' allowances. Since 1964 most payments under this heading have been made under the Canada Assistance Plan.

H25. Other welfare and social security are mainly the federal government's budgetary expenditures for unemployment insurance as well as welfare expenditures for native people and under the Annuities Act. The large increase in 1973 reflects the first payment of the government's contribution to the Unemployment Insurance Account subsequent to the major revision of the Unemployment Insurance Act.

H28. 'Economic development' (formerly 'resource development') includes a wide range of expenditures. The major year-over-year increase in 1974 reflects the introduction of the Oil Price Stabilization Program.

H29. Public debt charges are gross interest and carrying charges on public debt.

H30. General government includes general administration, law and order and justice.

H31. 'Foreign affairs' includes contributions to international agencies and foreign aid.

H32. Payments to provincial and municipal governments are discussed in more detail in the introductory notes to this section. The decrease in direct payments in 1962 as compared to 1961 resulted from the termination of the 1957 tax rental agreements. Prior to 1962 provinces abstained from imposing personal and corporate income taxes and in return received a direct budgetary payment from the federal government. Commencing in 1962 the federal government collected the provincial taxes for certain provinces, the remission of these taxes to the provinces being treated as non-budgetary transactions. The increase in payments in 1974 as compared to 1973 reflects mainly the payments resulting from the Revenue Guarantee Arrangements.

H35-51. Federal government, total direct and indirect debt less sinking funds, by type, 1867 to 1975

The debt shown in this table is in a sense gross debt (except for the sinking fund allowance). Considerable amounts of this debt may be held by public entities such as the Bank of Canada. In addition the federal government has substantial investments in foreign exchange balances, in cash balances, in loans to other countries, in Crown companies and agencies and the like. In particular, since 1966, substantial debt has been created under the financing arrangements of the Canada Pension Plan.

H35. Bonded debt given in this series is a direct liability of the federal government and includes Canada Savings Bonds. It is the total of bonds outstanding regardless of whether part is held by government corporations, agencies or funds.

H36. Sinking fund includes only assets (bonds) held specifically to meet retirements of maturing issues.

H38. Treasury bills include one month to one year maturities.

H39. Notes are the liability for the Dominion of Canada note issue. With the establishment of the Bank of Canada this liability was transferred to the bank in March 1935.

H40. Species reserves were transferred to the Bank of Canada in March 1935.

H43. Savings deposits and certificates were mainly deposits with the Post Office Savings Branch.

H44. Annuity, insurance, pension accounts are federal government liabilities under annuity contracts issued by the Annuities Branch, Department of Labour, under insurance issued to veterans, civil servants and others and for pensions to public servants and others. The Canada Pension Plan is included here, beginning in 1966. Since 1976 the Public Accounts show only *net* debt on account of the Canada Pension Plan, with the federal debt to the CPP being offset by the provincial bonds which the CPP holds. The CPP debt (thus treated) has also been separated from the general 'annuities' item in the public accounts presentation.

H45. Other direct debt is mainly outstanding cheques and accounts payable.

H47. Guaranteed bonds and debentures are mainly bonds of the Canadian National Railways and its predecessors. Small amounts at times for the National Harbours Board, Canadian National Steamships Ltd. and the like are included. The decline in guaranteed bonds and debentures reflects the Refunding Act, 1955 and various financing and guarantee acts by which advances were made to the Canadian National Railways for debt redemption and capital expenditures.

H48. Other guarantees are largely loans to students, farmers, fishermen, small business, and other groups including export credits insurance. Bank loans to Crown corporations, especially Central Mortgage and Housing Corporation and the Canadian Wheat Board are also important.

H51. Security investment account is given for information only, since it is an asset comprised of government bonds held directly by the government. It is used for temporary transactions in government bond issues.

All Government Finances (Series H52-381)

General note

The series in this section are taken from data originally compiled by the Public Finance Division of Statistics Canada. From 1970 on, the Statistics Canada series have been compiled on such a different basis than in earlier years that it has been decided to present two completely separate sets of tables in this section. The first group of tables updates to 1969 the series appearing in the original *Historical Statistics of Canada* volume. The second group of tables contains the new Statistics Canada series pushed back, for major aggregates, to 1965. The reader is thus provided with a five-year overlap on both bases.

A full account of the nature and origin of the net general revenue and net general expenditure series up to 1969 is contained in the notes to the original volume. The reader is cautioned, in particular, that the data for years before 1945 (originally prepared for the 1945 Dominion-Provincial Conference on Reconstruction) are in some respect *not* directly comparable with those for subsequent years. These data are included, however, as the only functional information on general government expenditure and revenue available in Canada for the pre-war period. (More aggregative data since 1926 may be found in the National Accounts Section of this volume, and a few series for earlier years may be found under 'Miscellaneous statistics' in this section.)

The data since 1946 are in general in quite good condition and directly comparable at least up to 1965. From 1966 to 1969, however, there were a considerable number of changes in the published Statistics Canada series on government finance as the Public Finance Division gradually moved from the old 'net general' concept to the new 'gross' concept (see below). The data for the late 1960s are thus not as firm and detailed as one would like, whether approached through the old or the new concept.

A particular feature of the old net general concept which should be noted is its treatment of intergovernmental transfers. Federal grants in aid and shared-cost program payments to provinces were left in federal expenditures by function and were therefore removed from provincial receipts and provincial expenditures by function. Similarly, provincial payments to municipalities were shown as a provincial outlay by function and not as a municipal outlay. In contrast, unconditional transfers were shown both as an expenditure of the paying government and as a receipt of the receiving government, though they were of course removed in the consolidation.

In addition to the detailed notes on the pre-1960 data in the original volume, several points should be made here about the 'net general' tables. Since 1960, liquor control board profits have been separated from other government enterprise profits on the grounds that for the most part they are more akin to excise taxes than to profits. Similarly, grants in lieu of taxes have been separated from other grants on related grounds. Data for the Yukon Territory and the Northwest Territories have been shown separately from 1961. From 1954 to 1957 these territories were included with the provinces, and from 1957 to 1959 with the municipalities in these tables. It should be noted that both federal and provincial expenditures subsequent to 1965 in these tables are substantially affected by the opting-out path taken by Quebec in that year.

As noted earlier, it has been necessary to provide two complete sets of series overlapping the 1965 to 1969 period. The only historically consistent series between the earlier net general series and the later gross general series are the following: for all levels, revenues from general sales taxes, motive fuel taxes, customs duties and natural resources; for the federal level only, personal and corporate income tax; and for the provincial level only, property tax and general purpose (unconditional) transfers. With respect to expenditures, the only continuous series that can be constructed are for local government general government expenditures and provincial general purpose transfer expenditures.

Data in the gross general series since 1970 have been taken from published Statistics Canada data. The new government universe in the Financial Management series since 1970 contains the Canada Pension Plan, Quebec Pension Plan, Unemployment Insurance Fund, Workmen's Compensation Funds, and certain items in the civil service superannuation accounts. In addition to expanding the universe and changing the treatment of transfers, there were various changes in the classification of expenditure by major and minor functions and of revenue. Most of these are spelled out in the publication *The Canadian System of Government Financial Management Statistics* (Catalogue 68-506), which users of these data are urged to consult carefully.

The 1965 to 1969 series have been constructed in order to provide a general feeling for the magnitude of government statistics on a gross basis in this period. These data were prepared in Statistics Canada and the Department of Finance by regrouping the published totals on a reasonably consistent basis to correspond to the current classification. Considerable care must be taken in using these data since the changes made are considered to be reliable only with respect to magnitude rather than the absolute value. In particular, the figures for particular functions and particular provinces were considered too misleading to release. The data included here, undetailed as they are, are thus all that there are.

It is also important to note that the present gross general system is *not* simply the sum of the three separate parts with respect to consolidation (as was the old net general series). There is both a three-level consolidation and a two-level consolidation, but it is not possible to subtract the two-level consolidation to arrive at the federal part. The reason for this difficulty arises because of the treatment of

intergovernmental transfers in the new series. Further details appear in the notes to the 'gross general' tables.

Those who wish to compare the data appearing in this section to that published by Statistics Canada for years after 1975 should also note that there will be a considerable discontinuity in the municipal revenue series from 1975 onward. Statistics Canada figures henceforth will gross up charges on debt issued on behalf of the municipal government enterprises. These charges will be included under debt charges on the expenditures side and classified as debt charges recoverable on the revenue side, thus constituting a reversal of the 1960 to 1974 practice (reflected in this section), which was to include enterprise liabilities in the category of indirect debt.

H52-74. All governments, net general revenue by major source, selected years, 1933 to 1969

All the tables in this section on the 'net general' basis reproduce the data from the original volume for the years 1933 to 1960 inclusive. Readers are referred to pp. 190-191 of the original volume for a detailed explanation of the sources and limitations of these data. The updating of the tables to 1965 was done on the same basis. From 1966 to 1969, however, the degree of comparability with the data for earlier years declined as Statistics Canada gradually shifted to the new 'gross' concept (see later tables). The problems here are *not* due to the widening of the universe to include, for example, the unemployment insurance fund which took place in 1970, but rather to the grossing up which occurred on items such as interest revenue (no longer offset against debt charges) and the inclusion in revenue of proceeds from sales of institutional services. The major problem encountered in extending the 'net general' series, however, came in 1966 when for the first time the source documents presented the concept 'cost of services provided' at the provincial and municipal levels, whether or not financed through federal transfers, in contrast to the previous treatment under which conditional (specific-purpose) grants and shared-cost payments were treated as functional expenditures of the paying rather than the receiving government, while unconditional transfers appeared as both an expenditure of the paying government and a receipt of the receiving government (but were of course removed in the consolidations). One result of the new treatment, which stresses 'who spends' rather than 'who pays', is that it is no longer possible to subtract the two-level consolidation (provincial-municipal) from the three-level consolidation to arrive at the federal share. In other words, the new system, unlike the old net general system, is not the simple sum of its three separate parts.

Readers should refer to notes in tables on individual levels of government for details on items included in the 'all governments' tables.

The consolidated net general revenues and expenditures shown in this and the following table are after elimination of all government transfers, as explained above.

'Other' revenue contains revenue from sales and services and fines and penalties up to 1961, but thereafter these two items are shown separately. In addition, it contains postal revenue, revenue from sales of bullion and coinage and non-revenue and surplus receipts.

Revenue from liquor control boards has been separated for 1961 and later on the grounds that in many ways revenue from this source is more akin to excise taxes than to other enterprise revenue.

H75-91. Federal government, net general revenue by major source, selected years, 1933 to 1969

H75. Corporate income tax includes revenue from the excess profits tax and part of the corporate income tax formerly earmarked for the old age security fund.

H76. Individual income tax includes the portion formerly earmarked for the old age security fund.

H79. General sales tax includes the portion formerly earmarked for the old age security fund. It is commonly referred to as the 'manufacturers' sales tax'.

H80. Motor fuel tax was a gasoline tax levied by the federal government during and immediately after World War II.

H81. Excise duties are levied solely on liquor and tobacco products. Excise taxes include revenue from a group of taxes on sales of commodities which has varied greatly over the period. Typical subjects taxed have been automobiles, radios, television sets, jewellery, cigarettes (in addition to excise duties) and miscellaneous luxury goods. (See special War Revenue Act and Excise Tax Act.)

H90. Other revenue includes post office gross receipts and miscellaneous revenues from sales and services. Interest on investments is not included in the former 'net general' concept, since it is netted against debt charges.

H92-112. Provincial governments, net general revenue by major source, selected years, 1933 to 1969

Readers are reminded that revenues received through conditional grants or cost-sharing arrangements are *excluded* from both revenues and expenditures of receiving governments in these 'net' tables.

H92. Corporate income tax for years from 1947 to 1975 was levied by Quebec, which did not participate in tax-rental and tax-sharing agreements after the wartime tax agreements expired. Ontario also levied corporate income tax from 1947 to 1951 and after 1957; in 1952 to 1956 Ontario had tax-rental agreements on corporation income taxes with the federal government. The figures for 1949 to 1951 also include the 5 per cent provincial corporation tax levied by the eight other provinces under terms of the 1947 tax-rental agreements.

H93. Individual income tax since 1954 is revenue from a tax levied only by Quebec.

H96. Motor fuel tax is the tax on petroleum products used for transportation purposes. It is net of rebates for motor fuel sold for uses which are tax-exempt.

H97. Other sales taxes include those on amusements and admission in all provinces, tobacco and alcoholic beverages in some provinces, hospital tax on meals in Quebec and long-distance telephone tax in Nova Scotia.

H98. Real and personal property tax has been levied by only a few of the provinces in the period covered.

H99. Succession duties were levied only by Ontario and Quebec in the period 1947 to 1969, and by British Columbia from 1963 to 1969; for other provinces in this period, succession duties were rented to the federal government from 1 April 1947 under the tax-rental and tax-sharing agreements.

H100. Other taxes include hospital insurance premiums, taxes on fire insurance premiums, fire prevention taxes, public utilities taxes, property and security transfers taxes and corporation taxes other than on income.

H102. Liquor control privileges, licences and permits include the sale of individual liquor permits to buy liquor, and sale of licences for premises, banquet licences and the like.

H104. Natural resources privileges, licences and permits include: fish and game royalties; fishing, hunting and trapping licences; timber royalties, grazing fees, hay and wood cutting privileges; mining (including oil and gas) royalties, dues or bonuses, beach, sand and water lot leases and water power or storage leases, licences or permit fees; income taxes on mining and logging operations.

H109. Other revenue includes sales and services, fines and penalties and a small amount of miscellaneous other revenue.

H111. 'Unconditional transfers' from other governments include revenues received from statutory subsidies and payments under federal-provincial tax agreements. A more detailed breakdown may be found in the notes to series H474-493 below.

H113-123. Municipal governments, net general revenue by major source, selected years, 1933 to 1969

The statistics of municipal governments cover revenue and expenditure of incorporated municipalities, other unincorporated local government areas and some joint boards set up separately but which carry on through ordinary municipal account in most areas. They exclude, except where it is impossible to separate items, the revenue and expenditure of municipal enterprises, of hospitals, of libraries and of certain special areas except for surpluses, deficits or levies of these bodies actually taken into the accounts. For education, only the local school taxes (which are in turn spent by school boards, or used for capital expenditures on schools and servicing of school debt) are included. Owing to differences among provinces and within them and the complexity of types of arrangement, the notes given below can cover only the main features of the data.

H113. General sales tax is principally a retail sales tax levied by Quebec municipalities.

H115. Real and personal property tax includes special assessments as well as the general municipal tax, business tax, and tax for education. It is mainly a tax on real property but some personal property has been taxed in the Maritime provinces over the years and vestiges remain in the Prairie provinces and British Columbia.

H116. 'Other taxes' include minor income taxes levied by municipalities in the early period ($4 million in each of 1933, 1937, 1939 and 1941) as well as poll taxes and other minor revenues.

H119. Government enterprises include profits of the municipalities' own enterprises and payments in lieu of taxes by federal and provincial enterprises.

H120. Other revenue includes income from tax penalties and miscellaneous other revenue.

H122. Subsidies from other governments include unconditional subsidies only and grants in lieu of municipal taxes from other governments. Municipal grants for specific purposes are included in the relevant expenditures for those purposes by the granting government.

H124-135. Provincial governments, total net general revenue, by province, selected years, 1933 to 1969

See the general introduction with regard to fiscal years and inclusion of unconditional transfers.

H136-147. Municipal governments, total net general revenue, by province, selected years, 1933 to 1969

See the general introduction with regard to fiscal years and inclusion of unconditional transfers.

H148-160. All governments, net general expenditure by major function, selected years, 1933 to 1969

This table is the sum of the federal, provincial and municipal tables which follow. See the general introduction for discussion of treatment of transfers in this and the next three tables.

H161-175. Federal government, net general expenditure by major function, selected years, 1933 to 1969

Figures in body of table include federal conditional transfers to other levels. There was a discontinuity in 1965 when Quebec opted out of certain health and other programs, taking tax points instead of federal transfers. Winter works programs were added under the welfare heading in 1964. See the special table on federal transfers in the miscellaneous tables at the end of this section.

H161. Defence and mutual aid includes the national defence equipment account.

H163. Health is made up in large part of grants to provinces.

H164. Social welfare includes payments of old age pensions from the old age security fund to all persons aged 65 and over, family allowances, unemployment insurance, contributions to provincial governments toward old age assistance to persons aged 65 to 69 years, toward blind persons' allowances and toward aid to unemployed and unemployables and relatively small other payments.

H165. Education includes grants to universities, grants for vocational training and outlays for Indian and Inuit schools.

H166. Transportation and communication include highways, roads and bridges, air services, canal services, maritime services, railway and steamship services, Board of Transport Commissioners, harbours and rivers, Trans-Canada Highway and the like. Freight subsidies on other than agricultural products are included. The post office which appears under this heading in series H27 is not included here but appears in series H172. The Canadian Broadcasting Corporation and payments of deficits of the Canadian National Railways appear in series H172, 'other'.

H167. Natural resources and primary industries include fish and game, forests, minerals and mines, water resources, land settlement and agriculture. Included in the latter with

other expenditures are the various payments made directly or indirectly to farmers and the like. Expenditures on such entities as the National Research Council and Atomic Energy of Canada Limited are not included here but appear in series H172, 'other'.

H168. Debt charges are net after subtraction of revenue from interest on government investments from gross debt charges.

H169. General government in this series differs from series H30 in that the latter includes protection of persons and property, shown separately in this table in series H160, and also includes recreational and cultural services and trade and industrial development, both of which are given in 'other', series H172, in this table.

H170. Protection of persons and property includes expenditures of the Royal Canadian Mounted Police, judges' salaries and travelling allowances, and cost of penitentiaries.

H171. International co-operation and assistance include assistance to other countries, contributions to international organizations and costs of representation abroad of the Department of External Affairs. General administration of the Department of External Affairs is included in series H172.

H172. 'Other' includes payments to own government enterprise (for example, the deficit of the Canadian National Railways and the payments to the Canadian Broadcasting Corporation), recreational and cultural services, post office, trade and industrial development, local planning and development, civil defence, immigration, external affairs, and sundry other items.

H174. Unconditional transfers include payments under the dominion-provincial tax-rental or tax-sharing agreements, provincial share of income tax on power utilities, statutory subsidies and special grants to Newfoundland and grants in lieu of taxes on federal property. These are all unconditional payments. Grants-in-aid and shared-cost contributions (conditional transfers) are included in the appropriate federal government functional expenditures.

H176-187. Provincial governments, net general expenditure by major function, selected years, 1933 to 1969

In each case provincial expenditure on a specific function excludes any grants received from another government specifically for that function but includes grants made to another government in aid of that function. Thus Trans-Canada Highway grants from the federal government are not included under provincial expenditure on transportation and communication, whereas provincial road and street grants to municipalities are included under this provincial heading.

H176. Health includes provincial expenditures under the federal-provincial hospital insurance plans (which in the main relate to general hospitals), mental care hospitals, tuberculosis sanitaria, public health, and other health expenditures.

H177. Social welfare includes aid to aged and blind persons, unemployment assistance, mothers' allowances, child welfare and sundry other social welfare.

H178. Education is grants to schools operated by local authorities, grants to universities, colleges and other schools, expenditures on technical schools and teachers' colleges, education of the handicapped, superannuation and pensions and small other educational expenses.

H179. Transportation and communication are mainly expenditure on highways, roads and bridges (including grants for this purpose to municipalities). Small amounts for railways, waterways, telephone, telegraph and wireless are included.

H180. Natural resources and primary industries include fish and game, forest, land settlement and agriculture, minerals and mines, water resources and sundry other.

H181. Debt charges are mainly net interest payments (gross payments less interest earned on loans and investments), amortization of premium or discount and certain management charges.

H182. General government includes expenditure on executive, administrative and legislative functions and small amounts for research, planning and statistics.

H183. Protection of persons and property includes law enforcement, provincial jails and reformatories, police protection and sundry other.

H184. 'Other' includes archives, art galleries, libraries, museums, parks, beaches and other recreational areas, trade and industrial development, local planning and development, contributions to government enterprises, housing, rural electrification, aid to municipal waterworks and the like.

H186. Unconditional transfers to municipalities are subsidies not tied to any specific function.

H188-196. Municipal governments, net general expenditure by major function, selected years, 1933 to 1969

From 1933 to 1959, school debenture debt charges are included in the debt charges column, and thereafter they are in education.

H188. Health includes hospital care, public health, medical, dental and allied services and small other general health expenditures.

H189. Social welfare includes aid to unemployed and unemployables, child care and sundry other items.

H190. Education is mainly expenditures of local school boards or boards of education from school taxes collected by the municipality. It includes the direct cost to municipality only and includes capital expenditure financed from borrowed funds.

H191. Transportation and communication includes expenditures for roads, streets and bridges.

H192. Debt charges do not include those on debentures issued by, or on behalf of, municipal enterprise. The item is net of interest earned on sinking funds.

H195. Other includes sanitation and waste removal, recreation and community services, payments to own government enterprise and sundry other.

H197-208. Provincial governments, total net general expenditure, by province, selected years, 1933 to 1969

Previous explanations of concepts of revenue and expenditure are applicable to these data by provinces.

H209-220. Municipal governments, net general expenditure, by province, selected years, 1933 to 1969

Previous explanations of concepts of revenue and expenditure are applicable to these data also.

Notes to series H221-381

The following 12 tables on the 'gross' basis are derived for 1970 to 1975 from the Financial Management series data published annually by Statistics Canada. The 1965 to 1969 series have been included to provide an overlapping period with the earlier 'net general' data and to give a general feeling of the magnitude of these gross concepts over time. Although every effort has been made to assemble these data on a reasonably consistent basis to correspond to the current classification, no formal reconciliation with the preceding 'net general' data is possible. Further, readers are cautioned that the data on individual functions by province were considered too liable to distortion to be used, although the total error in relation to the broader aggregates included here is considered to be slight.

H221-233. All governments, gross general revenue by source, 1965 to 1975

SOURCE: *Consolidated Government Finance,* 1974, (Catalogue 68-202), table 5.

H228. 'Other taxes' include hospital and medical care premiums, social insurance and universal pension plan levies, oil export tax (since 1973) and other. The latter contains minor items such as payroll tax, tax on insurance premiums, miscellaneous taxes on corporations and businesses, tax on certain payments and credits to non-residents, tax on amusements and admissions to places of entertainment, etc.

H232. Includes privileges, licences and permits, sales of goods and services and other revenue from own sources.

H234-248. Federal government, gross general revenue by major source, 1965 to 1975

SOURCE: *Federal Government Finance,* (Catalogue 68-211), from 1970 to 1975.

The series from 1965 to 1969 were prepared jointly by the Government Finance Division at Statistics Canada and the Department of Finance. Details as to the content of the various classifications may be found in the above publications and in tabular footnotes.

H249-266. Provincial governments, gross general revenue by major source, 1965 to 1975

SOURCE: *Provincial Government Finance,* (Catalogue 68-207), from 1970 to 1975.

Earlier estimates for the period 1965 to 1969 were prepared jointly by Statistics Canada and the Department of Finance. Additional detail on the content of classes is given in the above publications and in tabular footnotes.

H267-279. Local governments, gross general revenue by major source, 1965 to 1975

SOURCE: *Local Government Finance,* (Catalogue 68-204), for the period 1970 to 1974.

The year 1975 is estimated. The period 1965 to 1969 was estimated jointly by Statistics Canada and the Department of Finance. Additional detail as to classification and content is given in the above publications.

H280-291. Provincial governments, gross general revenue by province, 1965 to 1975

SOURCE: same as series H249-266.

The source publications provide a cross-classification of revenue items by provinces, and other details.

H292-303. Local governments, gross general revenue by province, 1965 to 1975

SOURCE: same as series H267-279.

H304-316. All governments, gross general expenditure by function, 1965 to 1975

SOURCE: same as series H221-233.

H317-331. Federal government, gross general expenditure by function, 1965 to 1975

SOURCE: same as series H234-248.

H332-344. Provincial governments, gross general expenditure by function, 1965 to 1975

SOURCE: same as series H249-266.

H345-357. Local governments, gross general expenditure by function, 1965 to 1975

SOURCE: same as series H267-279.

H358-369. Provincial governments, gross general expenditure by province, 1965 to 1975

SOURCE: same as series H280-291.

H370-381. Local governments, gross general expenditure by province, 1965 to 1975

SOURCE: same as series H292-303.

Miscellaneous Statistics (Series H382-493)

General note

The last part of this section contains some miscellaneous data needed to round off the general picture of the Canadian public finances. Three brief tables from the older edition which have been discontinued but which are of historical interest are repeated.

In addition, brief tables showing the detailed revenues and expenditures of the Canada and Quebec Pension Plans and of the Unemployment Insurance Fund have been included here for several reasons, even though similar information may be found in other sections in this volume. As was noted earlier, the new gross general revenue series includes both these funds. On the other hand, the earlier data on government expenditures and revenues exclude these funds (except for certain government contributions). Those who may wish to construct continuous series of government finance data will therefore need these tables also.

Another important table, included for the first time, in this compilation contains a good deal of information on federal transfers to provinces in the post-war period. Despite some problems (see detailed notes), this table presents the most complete and accurate picture of the changing nature of these transfers on a statistical basis that is available at this time.

Four tables on provincial and municipal debt by type and by province, are included in this part of the Section. Despite various efforts, it was not possible to consolidate all debt statistics and produce a general public debt table for purposes of this volume. Federal government debt was presented earlier in the section, on a somewhat different basis. The provincial and municipal debt tables presented here have been constructed to be consistent over time as far as possible despite various problems noted in the detailed notes to the tables. Although a considerable amount of other useful information on provincial and, to a lesser extent, municipal debt was assembled, it was not possible to push it back beyond 1968, which is really too short a period for a volume on historical statistics. Students of public debt in Canada are fairly well served for recent years by various government and Bank of Canada publications (although even these do not always distinguish adequately government-guaranteed debt, government enterprise debt, and debt held by public agencies), but the problems of assembling analytically meaningful historical series for the provincial and municipal levels are very great.

H382-397. Provincial governments, direct and indirect debt, selected years, 1933 to 1975

SOURCE: for 1961 to 1975, Public Finance Division, Statistics Canada; for 1933 to 1960, first edition of *Historical Statistics of Canada*.

Full source notes and definitions are provided in *Provincial Government Finance, Assets, Liabilities, Sources and Uses of Funds*, (Catalogue 68-209). Additional explanatory background is provided in *The Canadian System of Government Financial Management Statistics*, (Catalogue 68-506), Part VII, pages 39-44. The series from 1968 onward are fully consistent with the latter publication, in terms of the universe covered and the classification of transactions. However, for purposes of historical continuity, the gross funded debt (H382) has been shown net of sinking funds (H383) in order to arrive at net funded debt (H384). The total direct and indirect debt (H397) is therefore net of sinking funds. The series shown are believed to be reasonably continuous from 1933 to 1975.

H398-403. Local governments, total liabilities, by type, selected years, 1933 to 1975

SOURCE: *Local Government Finance, Revenue and Expenditures, Assets and Liabilities*, (Catalogue 68-204).

The series from the former volume from 1933 to 1960 were overlapped with the newer series given in the above source and are believed to constitute a reasonably continuous series in terms of the net debt concept used in the former volume.

A major change occurred in 1965, when debt of school boards and municipal enterprises was included in municipal government debt. Prior to that time, they had been shown separately, as indirect debt. Only the total of direct and indirect (net) debt can therefore be shown in the above table. Full information on the amount of municipal debt held by the provincial governments and their agencies is not available. For this reason the reader is cautioned against attempting to consolidate municipal and provincial debt. Further details are given in the source publication cited above.

H404-415. Provincial governments, direct and indirect debt, by province, selected years, 1933 to 1975

SOURCE: same as series H382-397.

See the notes to series H382-397.

H416-427. Local governments, total liabilities, by province, selected years, 1933 to 1975

SOURCE: same as series H398-403.

H428-435. Provincial current revenues, selected years, 1913 to 1937

SOURCE: same as series G310-317 in original volume.

This and the next two tables are repeated from the original edition of this volume. See page 195 of that volume for a general description and detailed notes. These series were prepared for the Royal Commission on Dominion-Provincial Relations, following much the same practices regarding netting of revenue against expenditure as those used by the Dominion Bureau of Statistics at the time, and reflected in preceding tables covering the years 1933 to 1969.

H436-447. Provincial current expenditures, selected years, 1933 to 1937

See the source and notes to series H428-435 above.

H448-457. Provincial current revenues, by province, selected years, 1913 to 1937

See the source and notes to series H428-435 above.

H458-465. Unemployment insurance account, 1942 to 1976

SOURCE: Unemployment Insurance and Manpower Section, Labour Division, Statistics Canada.

There were major changes in the Unemployment Insurance Act in 1971, involving almost universal coverage and extended benefit periods. As can be seen from the table, the government's contribution increased rapidly after that date, a result of both the 1974-1975 recession and the increased benefits. There were changes in 1971 also in the accounting system, from a fiscal year to a calendar year, in the name of the account, which was no longer termed a 'fund', and in the statistical detail on disbursements. Additional detail on coverage, claimants, beneficiaries and so forth is available in *Statistical Report on the Operation of the Unemployment Insurance Act*, (Catalogue 73-001), particularly in the January 1976 issue. Historical tables are given at the end of each publication. Claimants and beneficiaries data are also given in Section E of this volume.

H466-473. Revenue and expenditure of Canada and Quebec Pension Plans, 1965 to 1975

SOURCE: data for Canada Pension Plan provided by the Department of Finance; for Quebec Pension Plan, *System of National Accounts, National Income and Expenditure Accounts*, (Catalogue 13-201).

The Canada Pension Plan data are on a fiscal year basis for purposes of comparison with other aspects of federal government revenue and expenditure. The Quebec Pension Plan revenue and expenditure data from the national accounts, particularly the most recent revision covering the years 1962 to 1976, are also on a fiscal year basis.

H468. Total revenue consists of employer and employee contributions plus interest revenue from funds loaned to provinces.

H470-473. The revenues and expenditures of the Quebec Pension Plan have the same content as those described above.

H474-493. Federal government transfers to provinces and territories, 1947 to 1975

SOURCE: this table was provided by the Fiscal Policy Division, Department of Finance, in response to a request from the author.

The detailed notes accompanying the table are provided in the form of footnotes and are therefore not repeated here.

Readers should be alerted that the major 'tax sharing' arrangements, broadly defined, are reflected in several different columns in this table: from 1947 to 1962 under 'compensation for occupancy', from 1962 to 1972 under 'tax abatements' and since 1972 under 'provincial taxes collected'. Quebec was not included under the two latter arrangements. In addition, the value of tax abatements for post-secondary education is included under abatements rather than education, while the tax points turned over to Quebec for the established programs are not reflected in this table, except indirectly in the form of the adjustment payments shown under 'established programs'. As noted above, provincial taxes have been levied *directly* by the provinces since 1972-1973, with the federal government acting only as a collection agency. The figures shown in this column do not, of course, include the Quebec personal income tax which is collected directly by that province. For all provinces (including Quebec) the yield of provincial taxes at the standard rates (30.5 per cent of basic federal tax plus 10 per cent of corporate taxable income) would have been (in millions of dollars): 1972-1973, $3,528; 1973-1974, $4,411; 1974-1975, $5,372; and 1975-1976, $6,544.

Series H1-18. Federal government, budgetary revenue, by major source, 1867 to 1975
(millions of dollars)

Year[1]	Personal income tax	Corporate income tax	Excess profits tax	Non-resident tax	Estate tax[2]	Sales tax	Other excise taxes	Excise duties	Customs duties
	1	2	3	4	5	6	7	8	9
1975	12,709	5,748	–	481	11	3,515	438	816	1,887
1974	11,710	4,836	–	427	7	3,866	413	748	1,809
1973	9,226	3,710	–	324	15	3,590	408	686	1,385
1972	8,378	2,920	–	292	61	3,052	401	638	1,182
1971	7,227	2,396	–	288	132	2,653	388	607	989
1970	6,395	2,426	–	258	120	2,281	403	561	815
1969	5,588	2,839	–	249	101	2,294	378	519	818
1968	4,334	2,213	–	206	113	2,098	378	509	762
1967	3,650	1,821	–	221	103	2,146	337	489	747
1966	3,050	1,743	–	204	101	2,073	316	461	778
1965	2,637	1,759	–	170	109	1,917	296	446	686
1964	2,535	1,669	–	144	89	1,588	269	411	622
1963	2,168	1,375	–	125	91	1,278	273	393	581
1962	2,018	1,298	–	129	87	1,108	260	382	645
1961	2,052	1,302	–	112	85	1,045	263	363	535
1960	1,941	1,380	–	88	85	991	291	345	499
1959	1,752	1,234	–	73	88	1,003	287	335	526
1958	1,500	1,076	–	61	73	868	241	317	487
1957	1,635	1,296	–	64	72	879	249	300	498
1956	1,526	1,336	–	76	80	896	267	271	549
1955	1,288	1,081	–	66	67	802	261	249	481
1954	1,284	1,067	–	61	45	715	252	227	397
1953	1,278	1,247	–	54	39	734	296	227	407
1952	1,225	1,277	–	54	38	708	276	241	389
1951	976	1,133	2	55	38	598	312	218	346
1950	652	799	10	62	34	460	227	241	296
1949	622	603	-2	48	30	403	168	221	226
1948	763	492	45	43	26	377	259	205	223
1947	670	364	227	36	31	372	269	197	293
1946	671	239	443	30	24	298	281	196	237
1945	687	218	427	28	22	212	285	187	129
1944	673	276	341	29	17	209	334	152	115
1943	698	311	429	27	15	305	334	142	168
1942	484	348	435	28	13	233	256	139	119
1941	296	186	135	28	7	236	217	110	142
1940	104	132	24	13	–	180	104	89	131
1939	45	78	–	11	–	137	29	61	104
1938	47	85	–	10	–	122	40	51	79
1937	40	70	–	10	–	138	43	52	94
1936	36	58	–	9	–	113	40	46	84
1935	33	43	–	7	–	78	35	44	74
1934	25	36	–	6	–	72	40	43	77
1933	29	27	–	5	–	61	45	36	66
1932	26	36	–	–	–	57	25	38	70
1931	25	37	–	–	–	42	18	49	104
1930	27	44	–	–	–	20	15	58	131
1929	27	42	–	–	–	44	19	65	179
1928	25	35	1	–	–	63	20	64	187
1927	23	33	1	–	–	71	20	57	157
1926	18	29	1	–	–	81	24	49	142
1925	24	32	1	–	–	73	25	43	127
1924	25	31	3	–	–	63	23	39	108
1923	26	29	5	–	–	98	23	38	122
1922	32	28	13	–	–	90	17	36	118
1921	40	39	23	–	–	61	12	37	106
1920	33	14	41	–	–	38	41	37	163
1919	13	7	44	–	–	–	16	43	169
1918	8	1	33	–	–	–	12	30	147
1917	–	–	21	–	–	–	2	27	144
1916	–	–	13	–	–	–	2	24	134
1915	–	–	–	–	–	–	2	22	99
1914	–	–	–	–	–	–	–	22	76
1913	–	–	–	–	–	–	–	21	105
1912	–	–	–	–	–	–	–	21	112
1911	–	–	–	–	–	–	–	19	85
1910	–	–	–	–	–	–	–	17	72
1909	–	–	–	–	–	–	–	15	60
1908	–	–	–	–	–	–	–	15	47
1907	–	–	–	–	–	–	–	16	57
1906[1]	–	–	–	–	–	–	–	12	40

Series H1-18. Federal government, budgetary revenue, by major source, 1867 to 1975 (continued)
(millions of dollars)

Year[1]	Personal income tax	Corporate income tax	Excess profits tax	Non-resident tax	Estate tax[2]	Sales tax	Other excise taxes	Excise duties	Customs duties
	1	2	3	4	5	6	7	8	9
1905	—	—	—	—	—	—	—	14	46
1904	—	—	—	—	—	—	—	13	42
1903	—	—	—	—	—	—	—	13	41
1902	—	—	—	—	—	—	—	12	37
1901	—	—	—	—	—	—	—	11	32
1900	—	—	—	—	—	—	—	10	28
1899	—	—	—	—	—	—	—	10	28
1898	—	—	—	—	—	—	—	10	25
1897	—	—	—	—	—	—	—	8	22
1896	—	—	—	—	—	—	—	9	19
1895	—	—	—	—	—	—	—	8	20
1894	—	—	—	—	—	—	—	8	18
1893	—	—	—	—	—	—	—	8	19
1892	—	—	—	—	—	—	—	8	21
1891	—	—	—	—	—	—	—	8	21
1890	—	—	—	—	—	—	—	7	23
1889	—	—	—	—	—	—	—	8	24
1888	—	—	—	—	—	—	—	7	24
1887	—	—	—	—	—	—	—	6	22
1886	—	—	—	—	—	—	—	6	22
1885	—	—	—	—	—	—	—	6	19
1884	—	—	—	—	—	—	—	7	19
1883	—	—	—	—	—	—	—	6	20
1882	—	—	—	—	—	—	—	6	23
1881	—	—	—	—	—	—	—	6	22
1880	—	—	—	—	—	—	—	5	18
1879	—	—	—	—	—	—	—	4	14
1878	—	—	—	—	—	—	—	5	13
1877	—	—	—	—	—	—	—	5	13
1876	—	—	—	—	—	—	—	5	13
1875	—	—	—	—	—	—	—	6	13
1874	—	—	—	—	—	—	—	5	15
1873	—	—	—	—	—	—	—	6	14
1872	—	—	—	—	—	—	—	5	13
1871	—	—	—	—	—	—	—	5	13
1870	—	—	—	—	—	—	—	4	12
1869	—	—	—	—	—	—	—	4	9
1868	—	—	—	—	—	—	—	3	8
1867	—	—	—	—	—	—	—	3	9

Series H1-18. Federal government, budgetary revenue, by major source, 1867 to 1975 (continued)
(millions of dollars)

Year[1]	Miscellaneous taxes[3]	Total tax revenue	Post office	Return on investments		Other non-tax revenue	Total non-tax revenue	Special receipts and credits	Total budgetary revenue
				Crown corporations	Other				
	10	11	12	13	14	15	16	17	18
1975	1,488	27,093	444	1,495	601	322	2,863	—	29,956
1974	1,669	25,487	486	1,279	553	264	2,581	—	28,067
1973	287	19,630	480	1,029	460	264	2,233	—	21,863
1972	—	16,923	470	907	357	163	1,898	—	18,821
1971	—	14,680	404	790	343	128	1,665	—	13,345
1970	—	13,260	338	705	295	119	1,457	—	14,717
1969	—	12,786	355	621	239	154	1,369	—	14,155
1968	—	10,612	311	529	166	199	1,205	—	11,817
1967	—	9,511	282	448	164	166	1,060	—	10,571
1966	—	8,725	253	372	148	164	937	—	9,662
1965	—	8,020	238	320	118	170	846	—	8,865
1964	—	7,327	230	311	112	161	814	—	8,141
1963	—	6,284	201	247	119	153	720	—	7,003
1962	—	5,928	193	208	104	137	642	—	6,570
1961	—	5,755	184	209	99	127	619	—	6,374
1960	—	5,619	174	195	89	145	602	—	6,221
1959	1	5,299	168	153	87	130	538	—	5,837
1958	1	4,623	158	147	75	129	507	—	5,130
1957	2	4,994	153	115	55	104	426	—	5,420
1956	18	5,020	146	153	53	106	459	—	5,478
1955	17	4,312	137	85	64	118	404	—	4,716
1954	16	4,064	131	78	56	56	321	29	4,414
1953	15	4,297	111	104	48	55	318	75	4,689
1952	13	4,221	112	72	45	51	280	83	4,585
1951	6	3,684	105	73	44	60	282	41	4,007
1950	5	2,785	91	68	22	53	233	94	3,113
1949	4	2,323	85	65	27	30	206	51	2,580
1948	4	2,436	81	57	51	25	213	122	2,771
1947	4	2,452	78	58	18	24	178	242	2,872
1946	10	2,428	73	58	11	19	161	419	3,008
1945	9	2,202	69	56	15	21	161	650	3,013
1944	8	2,155	66	50	11	19	146	387	2,687
1943	8	2,437	61	42	7	24	133	195	2,765
1942	12	2,067	49	31	10	26	116	67	2,250
1941	3	1,361	46	16	6	35	103	25	1,489
1940	3	778	40	9	6	26	82	12	872
1939	2	468	37	5	8	23	73	21	562
1938	2	436	36	5	8	13	62	4	502
1937	3	449	36	5	8	12	61	6	517
1936	2	387	34	3	8	13	58	9	454
1935	4	317	33	4	7	12	55	—	373
1934	6	305	31	3	8	12	54	3	362
1933	2	272	31	4	7	10	52	1	325
1932	2	255	31	4	8	10	52	5	312
1931	2	275	32	4	6	10	51	8	335
1930	2	297	30	5	6	12	53	8	358
1929	2	379	33	4	9	16	63	12	453
1928	2	396	31	4	8	16	59	6	462
1927	3	365	32	4	7	15	58	8	431
1926	3	347	29	2	7	14	52	2	401
1925	3	328	30	2	6	14	53	3	383
1924	3	294	29	2	10	13	53	6	353
1923	2	342	29	2	10	14	55	11	408
1922	2	335	29	2	15	14	59	15	410
1921	2	320	26	2	20	14	62	13	395
1920	2	369	27	2	23	14	66	3	437
1919	2	294	25	3	14	15	56	—	350
1918	2	234	22	3	5	51	79	—	313
1917	2	197	21	3	2	38	64	—	261
1916	2	175	21	2	1	34	58	—	233

Series H1-18. Federal government, budgetary revenue, by major source, 1867 to 1975 (concluded)
(millions of dollars)

Year[1]	Miscellaneous taxes[3]	Total tax revenue	Post office	Return on investments		Other non-tax revenue	Total non-tax revenue	Special receipts and credits	Total budgetary revenue
				Crown corporations	Other				
	10	11	12	13	14	15	16	17	18
1915	2	125	19	3	1	25	47	—	172
1914	—	98	13	2	1	20	36	—	133
1913	—	126	13	1	1	22	37	—	163
1912	—	133	12	1	1	22	36	—	169
1911	—	104	11	1	1	20	32	—	136
1910	—	89	9	1	1	18	29	—	118
1909	—	75	8	1	2	16	27	—	102
1908	—	62	7	—	2	14	23	—	86
1907	—	73	7	—	2	14	23	—	96
1906[1]	—	52	5	—	1	10	17	—	68
1905	—	60	6	—	2	12	20	—	80
1904	—	54	5	—	2	10	17	—	71
1903	—	53	5	—	2	10	17	—	71
1902	—	49	4	—	2	11	17	3	69
1901	—	43	4	—	2	9	15	—	58
1900	—	39	3	—	2	9	14	—	53
1899	—	38	3	—	2	8	13	—	51
1898	—	35	3	—	2	7	12	—	47
1897	—	30	4	—	1	6	11	—	41
1896	—	29	3	—	1	5	9	—	38
1895	—	28	3	—	1	5	9	—	37
1894	—	25	3	—	1	5	9	—	34
1893	—	28	3	—	1	5	9	—	36
1892	—	29	3	—	1	5	9	—	38
1891	—	28	3	—	1	5	9	—	37
1890	—	30	3	—	1	5	8	—	39
1889	—	32	2	—	1	5	8	—	40
1888	—	31	2	—	1	5	8	—	39
1887	—	28	2	—	1	4	8	—	36
1886	—	29	2	—	1	4	7	—	36
1885	—	25	2	—	2	4	8	—	34
1884	—	25	2	—	2	4	7	1	33
1883	—	26	2	—	1	4	6	1	33
1882	—	29	2	—	1	4	7	1	37
1881	—	28	2	—	1	3	6	1	35
1880	—	24	1	—	1	4	6	—	30
1879	—	18	1	—	1	3	5	—	23
1878	—	18	1	—	1	2	4	5	27
1877	—	18	1	—	1	3	5	—	22
1876	—	18	1	—	1	3	5	1	23
1875	—	18	1	—	1	2	4	—	23
1874	—	20	1	—	1	2	4	—	25
1873	—	20	1	—	1	3	4	—	25
1872	—	17	1	—	—	2	3	—	21
1871	—	18	1	—	1	2	3	—	21
1870	—	16	1	—	1	2	3	—	19
1869	—	13	1	—	—	2	3	—	16
1868	—	11	1	—	1	1	3	—	14
1867	—	12	1	—	—	1	2	—	14

[1] Figures are for fiscal year ending nearest to 31 December of year named. Federal fiscal year end was changed from 30 June to 31 March in 1907 so 1906 figures are for nine months only.

[2] Includes duties levied under the Dominion Succession Duty Act, plus small amounts (under $500,000 in 1975 and nil in 1965 and earlier years) of miscellaneous receipts which are not specifically described in Public Accounts of Canada.

[3] Includes oil export tax from 1973 to 1975 and special excise tax on gasoline in 1975.

Series H19-34. Federal government budgetary expenditure, classified by function, 1867 to 1975
(millions of dollars)

Year[1]	Defence[2]	Veterans benefits	Health	Family allowances	Old age security payments	Welfare[3]	Other welfare and social security	Education assistance[4]	Transportation and communication	Economic development[5]	Public debt charges	General government	Foreign affairs[6]	Payments to provincial and municipal governments	Unclassified	Total budgetary expenditure
	19	20	21	22	23	24	25	26	27	28	29	30	31	32	33	34
1975	2,980	684	2,544	1,958	3,934	888	2,122	701	2,222	5,467	3,955	2,492	675	2,666	692	33,979
1974	2,512	621	2,121	1,824	3,445	663	1,879	641	2,205	4,284	3,208	2,092	546	2,639	567	29,245
1973	2,236	538	1,798	996	3,035	510	1,613	617	1,556	2,870	2,592	1,700	439	1,874	467	22,839
1972	1,908	452	1,643	610	2,524	480	604	588	1,163	2,419	2,321	1,612	384	1,501	435	18,645
1971	1,840	423	1,476	616	2,205	460	657	561	1,023	2,167	2,138	1,391	314	1,426	348	17,046
1970	1,773	410	1,193	619	1,907	397	573	463	940	1,857	1,920	1,264	282	1,229	263	15,089
1969	1,791	422	922	620	1,731	301	469	315	893	1,776	1,717	1,144	243	932	386	13,662
1968	1,763	428	674	616	1,541	270	390	287	910	1,527	1,480	1,055	227	867	273	12,309
1967	1,760	401	549	612	1,388	250	336	114	951	1,473	1,301	816	217	738	354	11,260
1966	1,651	391	447	607	1,073	192	350	90	887	1,205	1,191	744	230	515	298	9,871
1965	1,555	370	373	601	927	147	251	29	790	944	1,111	707	153	466	237	8,662
1964	1,582	352	498	575	885	182	309	138	818	599	1,051	509	104	399	103	8,104
1963	1,730	333	452	538	808	172	248	175	786	602	994	446	72	290	34	7,681
1962	1,606	335	393	532	734	159	233	246	751	564	918	447	63	308	16	7,305
1961	1,652	332	367	521	625	143	193	58	757	582	839	424	76	567	9	7,145
1960	1,538	292	270	506	592	103	166	29	681	532	798	387	85	563	7	6,551
1959	1,537	288	227	491	575	91	138	36	633	478	784	368	83	543	7	6,278
1958	1,654	289	132	475	559	74	123	34	608	421	648	378	61	490	6	5,951
1957	1,712	277	65	438	474	48	108	72	499	314	567	406	48	401	54	5,482
1956	1,830	252	62	398	379	38	96	21	408	283	534	411	47	406	54	5,218
1955	1,838	249	56	383	366	30	87	10	341	244	514	292	33	359	5	4,787
1954	1,762	240	53	367	353	24	84	10	359	213	502	287	35	363	5	4,657
1953	1,891	239	50	350	339	23	83	10	299	228	496	279	37	345	56	4,722
1952	1,959	241	45	334	323	22	85	11	260	214	465	237	32	342	77	4,646
1951	1,447	216	41	321	76	83	78	12	244	172	531	300	29	130	80	3,759
1950	787	217	33	310	—	106	86	5	219	245	439	222	15	126	93	2,901
1949	387	247	30	298	—	97	67	4	243	191	451	170	11	105	149	2,449
1948	269	277	19	271	—	67	68	5	200	180	475	150	15	102	79	2,175
1947	196	341	8	263	—	59	89	10	159	137	467	156	26	156	128	2,196
1946	388	605	6	245	—	45	89	16	133	132	477	165	4	109	220	2,634
1945	2,942	402	2	173	—	43	68	14	129	138	438	130	4	113	543	5,136
1944	4,000	114	1	—	—	41	48	3	143	132	340	139	1	108	175	5,246
1943	4,242	70	1	—	—	34	41	6	190	148	262	67	2	110	152	5,322
1942	2,563	62	1	—	—	31	36	7	116	81	203	70	3	109	1,107	4,387
1941	1,268	58	1	—	—	32	19	7	71	98	172	90	1	36	33	1,885
1940	730	60	1	—	—	50	10	1	86	48	146	67	1	19	33	1,250
1939	126	60	1	—	—	70	8	1	120	79	135	38	1	19	24	681
1938	35	57	1	—	—	72	6	1	123	54	133	45	2	21	3	553
1937	33	56	—	—	—	97	6	—	105	29	132	42	2	21	11	534
1936	23	57	—	—	—	99	7	—	108	26	138	37	1	17	19	532
1935	17	55	1	—	—	96	6	—	98	36	135	37	1	18	33	533
1934	14	55	1	—	—	76	5	—	102	30	139	26	2	15	15	478
1933	13	55	1	—	—	48	5	—	111	22	140	30	1	15	17	458
1932	14	56	1	—	—	48	5	—	161	57	135	33	1	15	7	532
1931	18	61	1	—	—	48	6	—	81	38	121	34	1	14	26	449
1930	23	57	1	—	—	10	7	—	115	35	121	29	1	19	22	442
1929	22	50	1	—	—	2	6	—	108	35	122	29	1	14	15	405
1928	20	63	1	—	—	1	6	1	86	39	125	28	1	14	9	394
1927	18	62	1	—	—	2	6	1	82	32	129	23	1	14	10	380
1926	15	46	1	—	—	—	5	1	80	32	130	21	—	13	17	359
1925	14	46	1	—	—	—	5	1	74	36	131	20	—	13	15	356
1924	13	45	1	—	—	—	5	1	74	37	135	17	—	13	12	352
1923	13	45	1	—	—	—	6	1	84	39	136	19	1	13	14	372
1922	14	48	1	—	—	1	6	1	150	35	138	20	—	12	17	441
1921	18	56	1	—	—	1	6	1	161	46	135	23	—	12	18	476
1920	30	76	1	—	—	—	5	1	164	59	140	20	1	12	22	529
1919	347	75	1	—	—	2	3	—	61	62	125	23	—	12	29	740
1918	439	30	—	—	—	—	4	—	86	24	77	8	—	11	16	696
1917	344	8	—	—	—	—	4	—	94	32	48	16	—	11	16	574
1916	312	3	—	—	—	—	3	—	69	30	36	14	—	12	18	497
1915	173	1	—	—	—	—	3	—	85	26	21	10	—	12	8	338
1914	72	1	—	—	—	—	3	—	79	43	16	13	—	12	8	246
1913	14	—	—	—	—	—	4	—	91	35	13	15	—	11	3	185
1912	11	—	—	—	—	—	5	—	69	18	13	10	—	13	4	143
1911	10	—	—	—	—	—	3	—	63	19	12	8	—	10	11	136

Series H19-34. Federal government budgetary expenditure, classified by function, 1867 to 1975 (concluded)
(millions of dollars)

Year[1]	Defence[2]	Veterans benefits	Health	Family allowances	Old age security payments	Welfare[3]	Other welfare and social security	Education assistance[4]	Transportation and communication	Economic development[5]	Public debt charges	General government	Foreign affairs[6]	Payments to provincial and municipal governments	Unclassified	Total budgetary expenditure
	19	20	21	22	23	24	25	26	27	28	29	30	31	32	33	34
1910	9	–	–	–	–	–	2	–	61	16	13	8	–	9	4	122
1909	6	–	–	–	–	–	2	–	54	18	13	8	–	9	4	114
1908	7	–	–	–	–	–	2	–	73	19	12	7	–	9	4	132
1907	7	–	–	–	–	–	2	–	58	14	11	6	–	9	3	110
1906[1]	4	–	–	–	–	–	2	–	30	9	7	4	–	7	3	65
1905	6	–	1	–	–	–	2	–	36	12	11	5	–	7	2	81
1904	4	–	1	–	–	–	2	–	34	12	11	6	–	5	4	77
1903	4	–	1	–	–	–	2	–	26	9	11	5	–	10	4	70
1902	3	–	1	–	–	–	2	–	23	8	11	4	–	4	4	59
1901	3	–	1	–	–	–	2	–	25	9	11	4	–	4	3	61
1900	3	–	1	–	–	–	2	–	24	5	11	4	–	4	3	56
1899	4	–	1	–	–	–	2	–	19	5	11	4	–	4	2	50
1898	3	–	1	–	–	–	1	–	20	5	11	4	–	4	2	49
1897	2	–	1	–	–	–	1	–	16	3	11	4	–	4	2	43
1896	3	–	1	–	–	–	1	–	14	2	11	4	–	4	2	41
1895	2	–	1	–	–	–	1	–	16	2	11	4	–	4	1	42
1894	2	–	1	–	–	–	1	–	14	3	11	5	–	4	2	41
1893	1	–	–	–	–	–	1	–	15	3	10	4	–	4	1	41
1892	2	–	–	–	–	–	1	–	14	3	10	4	–	4	1	39
1891	1	–	–	–	–	–	1	–	14	3	10	4	–	4	4	40
1890	1	–	–	–	–	–	1	–	15	3	10	4	–	4	1	39
1889	1	–	–	–	–	–	1	–	16	3	10	4	–	4	2	40
1888	1	–	–	–	–	–	1	–	15	4	10	4	–	4	3	42
1887	2	–	–	–	–	–	1	–	14	5	10	4	–	4	4	43
1886	2	–	–	–	–	–	2	–	15	4	10	2	–	4	1	40
1885	5	–	–	–	–	–	2	–	19	7	10	4	–	4	9	60
1884	3	–	–	–	–	–	2	–	22	3	9	3	–	4	2	48
1883	1	–	–	–	–	–	2	–	23	5	8	3	–	4	11	57
1882	1	–	–	–	–	–	2	–	20	4	8	3	–	4	1	42
1881	1	–	–	–	–	–	2	–	12	4	8	3	–	4	1	33
1880	1	–	–	–	–	–	1	–	14	2	8	3	–	4	1	33
1879	1	–	–	–	–	–	1	–	14	1	8	2	–	3	2	33
1878	1	–	–	–	–	–	1	–	12	1	7	2	–	3	2	30
1877	1	–	–	–	–	–	1	–	12	1	7	3	–	4	1	30
1876	1	–	–	–	–	–	1	–	14	2	7	2	–	4	2	32
1875	1	–	–	–	–	–	1	–	13	2	6	2	–	4	2	31
1874	1	–	–	–	–	–	1	–	11	4	7	3	–	4	3	32
1873	1	–	–	–	–	–	1	–	10	3	6	3	–	4	6	33
1872	1	–	–	–	–	–	1	–	9	2	5	3	–	3	15	39
1871	1	–	–	–	–	–	–	–	9	2	5	2	–	3	3	25
1870	1	–	–	–	–	–	–	–	6	2	5	1	–	3	1	19
1869	1	–	–	–	–	–	–	–	4	3	5	1	–	3	1	18
1868	1	–	–	–	–	–	–	–	2	2	5	2	–	3	1	15
1867	1	–	–	–	–	–	–	–	2	2	4	2	–	3	1	14

[1] Figures are for fiscal year ending nearest to 31 December of year named. Federal fiscal year was changed from 30 June to 31 March in 1907 so 1906 figures are for nine months only.

[2] Formerly Defence and Mutual Aid. Includes national defence equipment replacement account, from 1952 to 1958.

[3] Canada Assistance Plan (formerly Unemployment Assistance and Relief Projects), plus old age assistance, blind and disabled persons allowances.

[4] Consists mainly of grants to universities. Vocational training was moved to 'Economic development' after 1965.

[5] Formerly 'Resources and development'.

[6] Formerly 'International co-operation'.

Series H35-51. Federal government, total direct and indirect debt, less sinking funds, by type, 1867 to 1975

(millions of dollars)

Year[1]	Direct debt												Indirect debt			Total direct and indirect debt	Security investment account
	Unmatured debt less sinking fund			Treasury bills	Dominion of Canada notes				Savings deposits and certificates	Annuity, insurance, pension accounts[2]	Other direct debt	Total net direct debt	Guaranteed bonds and debentures[3]	Other guarantees	Total indirect debt		
	Bonded debt	Sinking fund	Net		Notes	Less specie reserve	Less loans to chartered banks	Net									
	35	36	37	38	39	40	41	42	43	44	45	46	47	48	49	50	51
1975	31,202	4	31,197	6,495	—	—	—	—	3	25,570	7,782	71,048	583	16,541	17,124	88,172	83
1974	27,456	—	27,456	5,630	—	—	—	—	3	22,328	6,597	62,014	596	15,035	15,631	77,645	81
1973	24,266	—	24,266	4,905	—	—	—	—	3	19,229	6,470	54,874	603	13,254	13,857	68,731	68
1972	24,749	—	24,749	4,290	—	—	—	—	3	16,793	4,931	50,766	815	11,919	12,734	63,500	64
1971	23,429	15	23,413	3,830	—	—	—	—	4	14,898	4,284	46,429	822	10,828	11,649	58,078	56
1970	21,466	7	21,459	3,735	—	—	—	—	4	13,047	3,362	41,607	1,005	9,532	10,537	52,144	57
1969	19,742	14	19,728	2,895	—	—	—	—	4	11,463	2,745	36,835	1,051	8,710	9,761	46,595	97
1968	19,261	6	19,255	2,840	—	—	—	—	8	9,899	2,770	34,771	1,131	7,896	9,027	43,799	44
1967	18,100	8	18,092	2,480	—	—	—	—	19	8,517	2,939	32,046	1,197	7,367	8,564	40,610	44
1966	17,630	3	17,627	2,310	—	—	—	—	21	7,486	2,169	29,613	1,276	7,004	8,279	37,892	198
1965	16,960	—	16,960	2,150	—	—	—	—	22	6,175	1,658	26,965	1,332	6,290	7,621	34,586	82
1964	16,838	—	16,838	2,140	—	—	—	—	23	5,676	1,634	26,311	1,368	5,701	7,069	33,380	63
1963	16,510	—	16,510	2,230	—	—	—	—	25	5,131	1,758	25,654	1,378	5,111	6,488	32,142	100
1962	15,797	22	15,775	2,165	—	—	—	—	26	4,747	1,811	24,523	1,381	4,611	5,992	30,516	34
1961	15,061	19	15,041	1,885	—	—	—	—	27	4,244	1,453	22,651	1,636	4,112	5,748	28,399	95
1960	14,133	17	14,116	1,935	—	—	—	—	29	3,956	1,337	21,372	1,673	3,344	5,016	26,389	102
1959	13,765	85	13,680	2,125	—	—	—	—	29	3,565	1,290	20,690	1,430	2,945	4,375	25,065	78
1958	13,979	83	13,896	1,595	—	—	—	—	34	3,302	1,151	19,978	988	2,254	3,242	23,220	98
1957	12,720	212	12,508	1,525	—	—	—	—	35	2,713	1,041	17,822	1,028	1,632	2,661	20,483	80
1956	12,743	211	12,533	1,625	—	—	—	—	36	2,427	1,149	17,769	793	1,253	2,046	19,815	204
1955	13,308	211	13,097	2,100	—	—	—	—	36	2,186	1,121	18,540	793	711	1,504	20,044	722
1954	12,906	191	12,716	1,590	—	—	—	—	37	1,977	1,098	17,417	908	353	1,262	18,679	46
1953	13,176	102	13,074	1,400	—	—	—	—	38	1,773	1,212	17,497	671	120	791	18,288	18
1952	13,261	28	13,233	1,550	—	—	—	—	39	1,567	1,218	17,608	528	46	574	18,182	60
1951	13,295	26	13,270	1,400	—	—	—	—	38	1,416	859	16,983	529	69	598	17,580	59
1950	13,602	23	13,580	1,400	—	—	—	—	38	979	694	16,690	577	38	615	17,305	10
1949	13,773	8	13,765	1,300	—	—	—	—	39	811	801	16,715	571	70	641	17,356	19
1948	14,115	—	14,115	1,300	—	—	—	—	38	718	766	16,937	555	29	583	17,520	456
1947	14,198	—	14,198	1,300	—	—	—	—	36	611	1,045	17,190	522	21	542	17,732	686
1946	14,718	—	14,718	1,280	—	—	—	—	36	527	1,134	17,695	567	15	582	18,277	276
1945	14,596	—	14,596	1,696	—	—	—	—	36	458	1,108	17,893	541	9	550	18,443	152
1944	11,654	—	11,654	1,886	—	—	—	—	34	407	934	14,913	607	85	691	15,605	336
1943	9,312	—	9,312	1,400	—	—	—	—	28	307	696	11,803	699	54	753	12,556	185
1942	6,524	—	6,524	1,370	—	—	—	—	24	425	473	8,815	717	90	807	9,622	34
1941	5,345	—	5,345	520	—	—	—	—	22	331	413	6,630	819	136	955	7,585	42

Series H35-51. Federal government, total direct and indirect debt, less sinking funds, by type, 1867 to 1975 (continued)

(millions of dollars)

Year[1]	Direct debt												Indirect debt			Total direct and indirect debt	Security investment account
	Unmatured debt less sinking fund			Treasury bills	Dominion of Canada notes				Savings deposits and certificates	Annuity, insurance, pension accounts[2]	Other direct debt	Total net direct debt	Guaranteed bonds and debentures[3]	Other guarantees	Total indirect debt		
	Bonded debt	Sinking fund	Net		Notes	Less specie reserve	Less loans to chartered banks	Net									
	35	36	37	38	39	40	41	42	43	44	45	46	47	48	49	50	51
1940	3,892	5	3,887	480	—	—	—	—	22	264	350	5,003	984	122	1,106	6,109	30
1939	3,541	67	3,474	155	—	—	—	—	23	243	67	3,962	1,085	68	1,153	5,114	7
1938	3,231	70	3,161	155	—	—	—	—	23	221	56	3,616	1,086	88	1,173	4,789	—
1937	3,165	66	3,099	150	—	—	—	—	23	201	67	3,540	1,051	18	1,069	4,609	—
1936	3,187	62	3,126	150	—	—	—	—	22	177	68	3,543	1,003	15	1,018	4,561	—
1935	3,145	58	3,087	120	—	—	—	—	22	151	52	3,432	995	96	1,091	4,523	1
1934	2,869	55	2,815	193	—	—	—	—	23	126	50	3,206	987	104	1,092	4,298	4
1933	2,734	69	2,664	125	173	71	40	61	23	110	47	3,030	993	93	1,086	4,116	—
1932	2,606	66	2,540	110	181	70	48	63	24	99	43	2,878	996	28	1,024	3,902	10
1931	2,564	62	2,502	15	157	65	32	61	24	90	43	2,735	1,001	—	1,001	3,736	4
1930	2,379	60	2,319	—	141	82	7	53	25	80	45	2,522	955	—	955	3,477	1
1929	2,284	56	2,227	—	174	66	50	58	26	70	46	2,429	837	—	837	3,266	—
1928	2,358	53	2,305	—	205	61	84	60	28	61	48	2,503	714	—	714	3,217	—
1927	2,409	49	2,360	—	189	95	36	57	31	52	46	2,546	667	—	667	3,213	—
1926	2,481	46	2,435	—	172	101	13	59	32	43	44	2,613	618	—	618	3,237	—
1925	2,444	42	2,402	70	183	99	10	74	33	36	45	2,660	581	—	581	3,240	—
1924	2,416	39	2,377	122	207	124	15	68	34	30	49	2,679	582	—	582	3,262	—
1923	2,444	36	2,408	91	217	103	23	90	34	26	44	2,693	526	—	526	3,219	—
1922	2,487	33	2,453	95	243	130	14	99	32	21	46	2,745	454	—	454	3,199	—
1921	2,452	30	2,422	144	242	86	47	109	35	17	44	2,769	249	—	249	3,018	—
1920	2,477	27	2,450	76	278	84	87	107	39	14	46	2,732	223	—	223	2,955	—
1919	2,554	22	2,532	74	312	105	110	97	42	12	47	2,804	174	—	174	2,978	—
1918	2,204	19	2,185	74	289	122	72	95	53	11	46	2,464	174	—	174	2,638	—
1917	1,428	17	1,411	75	251	120	29	102	53	10	46	1,697	174	—	174	1,871	—
1916	979	14	965	100	183	119	13	52	56	9	55	1,236	174	—	174	1,410	—
1915	621	13	608	25	178	121	1	56	54	7	52	802	172	—	172	974	—
1914	401	11	390	20	157	95	5	57	54	6	63	589	160	—	160	750	—
1913	304	9	294	8	118	101	—	17	56	5	54	434	116	—	116	550	—
1912	261	14	247	—	112	99	—	13	57	4	49	371	89	—	89	460	—
1911	287	12	274	—	113	99	—	14	58	3	47	397	66	—	66	463	—
1910	276	11	265	—	90	75	—	16	58	3	48	389	—	—	—	389	—
1909	262	15	248	17	87	70	—	17	58	2	44	386	—	—	—	386	—
1908	283	39	244	14	79	62	—	18	60	1	42	378	—	—	—	378	7
1907	229	42	187	9	61	42	—	19	63	1	46	324	—	—	—	324	7
1906	215	46	169	1	55	38	—	17	63	1	46	296	—	—	—	296	1

Series H35-51. Federal government, total direct and indirect debt and indirect debt less sinking fund, by type, 1867 to 1975 (concluded)

(millions of dollars)

| Year[1] | Direct debt | | | | | | | | | | | | Indirect debt | | | Total direct and indirect debt | Security investment account |
| | Unmatured debt less sinking fund | | | Treasury bills | Dominion of Canada notes | | | | Savings deposits and certificates | Annuity, insurance, pension accounts[2] | Other direct debt | Total net direct debt | Guaranteed bonds and debentures[3] | Other guarantees | Total indirect debt | | |
	Bonded debt	Sinking fund	Net		Notes	Less specie reserve	Less loans to chartered banks	Net									
	35	36	37	38	39	40	41	42	43	44	45	46	47	48	49	50	51
1905	213	48	165	3	50	35	—	15	62	1	64	309	—	—	—	309	2
1904	217	47	170	3	47	35	—	12	62	1	48	295	—	—	—	295	3
1903	217	45	172	5	42	29	—	12	62	—	39	291	—	—	—	291	5
1902	237	54	183	—	39	26	—	13	61	—	25	282	—	—	—	282	—
1901	237	51	186	—	33	19	—	14	58	—	38	297	—	—	—	297	—
1900	237	48	188	—	28	15	—	13	56	—	34	292	—	—	—	292	—
1899	237	46	191	—	26	13	—	14	53	—	30	288	—	—	—	288	—
1898	237	43	193	4	24	13	—	11	50	—	30	289	—	—	—	289	—
1897	237	41	196	—	22	11	—	11	50	—	29	287	—	—	—	287	—
1896	227	39	189	5	22	11	—	12	49	—	29	283	—	—	—	283	—
1895	228	36	192	2	20	9	—	12	47	—	29	281	—	—	—	281	1
1894	225	34	191	—	20	8	—	12	45	—	29	276	—	—	—	276	1
1893	215	32	182	2	20	8	—	12	43	—	28	268	—	—	—	268	1
1892	210	31	179	2	19	6	—	12	42	—	28	263	—	—	—	263	1
1891	209	29	181	—	17	5	—	12	40	—	29	262	—	—	—	262	1
1890	200	27	173	8	16	4	—	12	39	—	27	260	—	—	—	260	1
1889	201	25	177	2	15	3	—	12	41	—	27	258	—	—	—	258	1
1888	204	23	181	—	16	3	—	12	43	—	26	262	—	—	—	262	1
1887	194	21	173	6	16	4	—	12	41	—	27	260	—	—	—	260	1
1886	191	19	171	1	15	3	—	12	41	—	26	251	—	—	—	251	1
1885	193	18	175	1	16	4	—	12	37	—	26	252	—	—	—	252	1
1884	174	16	158	19	16	3	—	13	33	—	23	246	—	—	—	246	1
1883	175	14	161	—	15	2	—	13	29	—	23	226	—	—	—	226	1
1882	139	13	126	—	16	2	—	13	26	—	21	187	—	—	—	187	1
1881	146	13	133	—	16	4	—	12	22	—	22	190	—	—	—	190	1
1880	147	11	136	—	15	3	—	12	16	—	22	186	—	—	—	186	1
1879	149	10	139	—	14	3	—	11	11	—	21	182	—	—	—	182	1
1878	138	9	130	—	11	3	—	8	9	—	21	168	—	—	—	168	1
1877	130	7	123	—	11	3	—	8	9	—	26	165	—	—	—	165	1
1876	131	6	124	—	11	3	—	8	8	—	26	166	—	—	—	166	1
1875	120	6	115	—	12	3	—	9	7	—	22	153	—	—	—	153	1
1874	108	6	103	—	11	3	—	8	7	—	25	143	—	—	—	143	2
1873	95	4	91	—	12	3	—	9	7	—	27	134	—	—	—	134	2
1872	84	4	81	—	11	3	—	9	6	—	28	124	—	—	—	124	2
1871	85	4	81	—	11	3	—	8	5	—	22	116	—	—	—	116	2
1870	84	3	81	—	8	2	—	6	5	—	20	111	—	—	—	111	3
1869	86	2	84	—	8	2	—	6	3	—	19	112	—	—	—	112	1
1868	89	2	87	—	5	1	—	4	3	—	15	109	—	—	—	109	1
1867	73	2	71	—	4	1	—	4	2	—	18	94	—	—	—	94	1

1 Figures are for close of fiscal year ending nearest to 31 December of year named.
2 Including the Canada Pension Plan with effect from 1 January 1966.
3 Reflects the Refunding Act, 1955 and various financing and guarantee acts by which advances were made to the Canadian National Railways for debt redemption and capital expenditures.

Series H52-74. All governments, net general revenue by major source,[1] selected years, 1933 to 1969
(millions of dollars)

Year[2]	Taxes												
	Income tax				General sales	Motor fuel	Other sales	Excise duties and taxes	Customs duties	Real and personal property[3]	Succession duties	Other[4]	Total taxes
	Corporate	Individual	Non-resident	Total									
	52	53	54	55	56	57	58	59	60	61	62	63	64
1969	3,701	7,731	249	11,681	3,970	1,020	293	894	818	3,326	241	843	23,085
1968	2,873	6,099	206	9,178	3,494	944	258	885	762	2,999	234	520	19,273
1967	2,417	5,112	220	7,749	3,405	793	194	860	746	2,681	211	358	16,998
1966	2,307	4,159	204	6,670	3,083	744	163	775	778	2,314	219	298	15,042
1965	2,282	3,472	170	5,924	2,731	680	114	740	686	1,792	216	290	13,172
1964	2,124	3,043	144	5,311	2,318	616	78	679	622	1,771	181	326	11,902
1963	1,787	2,557	125	4,469	1,898	540	74	666	581	1,683	176	215	10,301
1962	1,693	2,378	129	4,200	1,666	484	69	641	645	1,587	159	201	9,654
1961	1,570	2,137	112	3,819	1,485	450	64	624	535	1,445	150	205	8,777
1960	1,649	2,002	88	3,739	1,283	403	60	633	499	1,340	145	188	8,290
1959	1,483	1,807	73	3,363	1,285	383	57	621	526	1,205	145	163	7,748
1958	1,302	1,548	61	2,911	1,113	364	57	557	487	1,069	128	78	6,764
1957	1,510	1,676	64	3,250	1,115	347	52	549	498	982	124	69	6,986
1956	1,398	1,562	76	3,036	1,125	301	48	538	549	868	144	67	6,676
1955	1,135	1,318	66	2,519	994	270	46	510	481	771	139	75	5,805
1954	1,116	1,309	61	2,486	881	241	45	478	397	716	85	64	5,393
1953	1,296	1,278	54	2,628	875	224	46	524	407	657	70	72	5,503
1952	1,342	1,225	54	2,621	836	200	41	508	390	607	71	80	5,354
1951	1,304	977	55	2,336	716	182	38	517	347	538	72	81	4,827
1950	961	652	62	1,675	561	157	34	455	296	407	65	116	3,766
1949	707	622	48	1,377	481	139	35	378	226	375	59	104	3,174
1948	625	763	43	1,431	440	125	31	448	223	343	55	96	3,192
1947	653	660	36	1,349	416	114	19	446	293	311	62	80	3,090
1946	682	671	30	1,383	335	110	18	423	237	282	58	62	2,908
1945	645	687	28	1,360	242	89	17	425	129	284	46	33	2,625
1943	741	700	27	1,468	331	71	8	331	288	266	39	36	2,838
1941	353	311	28	692	259	85	6	201	245	256	34	48	1,826
1939	89	61	11	161	145	53	3	87	107	249	28	49	882
1937	79	55	10	144	144	39	3	76	113	241	37	47	844
1933	31	38	5	74	61	26	3	67	81	235	13	39	599

Series H52-74. All governments, net general revenue by major source,[1] selected years, 1933 to 1969 (concluded)
(millions of dollars)

Year[2]	Privileges, licences and permits					Liquor control boards	Other government enterprises	Grants in lieu of taxes	Other revenue[7]	Total net revenue
	Liquor control	Motor vehicles	Natural resources	Other	Total					
	65	66	67	68	69	70	71	72	73	74
1969	89	363	638	155	1,245	416	285	36	1,672	26,740
1968	85	325	609	141	1,159	388	250	21	1,431	22,522
1967	69	325	508	110	1,012	363	231	26	1,169	19,798
1966	63	254	522	130	970	327	225	24	744	17,332
1965	62	244	520	104	931	298	220	23	748	15,393
1964	60	222	446	95	823	251	194	6	721	13,896
1963	56	211	372	92	730	233	164	24	644	12,096
1962	53	187	319	86	645	217	142	21	570	11,248
1961	51	182	300	80	613	197	155	11	529	10,282
1960	47	172	281	72	572	—	342	—	511	9,715
1959	45	165	309	72	591	—	321	—	478	9,138
1958	38	146	270	66	520	—	325	—	460	8,069
1957	41	140	282	59	522	—	283	—	426	8,217
1956	33	128	293	56	510	—	318	—	391	7,895
1955	33	114	261	52	460	—	235	—	373	6,873
1954	31	94	188	47	360	—	218	—	324	6,295
1953	32	88	198	43	361	—	222	—	368	6,454
1952	31	81	—[6]	201	313	—	207	—	362	6,236
1951	28	73	—[6]	168	269	—	187	—	262	5,545
1950	27	67	101	42	237	—	183	—	254	4,440
1949	26	58	83	39	206	—	163	—	247	3,790
1948	25	50	62	33	170	—	155	—	303	3,820
1947	24	46	44	30	144	—	149	—	410	3,793
1946	21	38	44	28	131	—	168	—	542	3,749
1945	20	32	—[6]	64	116	—	187	—	696	3,624
1943	—[5]	30	34	22	—	—	—[5]	—	249	3,173
1941	—[5]	32	35	20	—	—	—[5]	—	160	2,073
1939	—[5]	28	25	18	—	—	—[5]	—	124	1,077
1937	—[5]	26	26	18	—	—	—[5]	—	113	1,027
1933	—[5]	21	13	16	—	—	—[5]	—	93	742

[1] After elimination of intergovernmental transfers. Yukon and Northwest Territories are included from 1954 in provincial portion and from 1957 in municipal portion.
[2] Figures are for fiscal year ending nearest 31 December of year named.
[3] Includes business property tax, poll tax and special assessments.
[4] Includes hospital insurance premiums.
[5] Included in 'other revenue'.
[6] Included in 'other privileges, licences and permits'.
[7] Includes sales and services, fines and penalties, postal revenue, revenue from bullion and coinage and non-revenue and surplus receipts.

Series H75-91. Federal government, net general revenue by major source, selected years, 1933 to 1969
(millions of dollars)

Year[1]	Taxes								
	Income tax				General sales	Motor fuel	Excise duties and taxes	Customs duties	Succession duties
	Corporate	Individual	Non-resident	Total					
	75	76	77	78	79	80	81	82	83
1969	2,839	5,588	249	8,676	2,294	—	894	818	101
1968	2,213	4,334	206	6,753	2,098	—	885	762	112
1967	1,821	3,650	220	5,691	2,146	—	860	746	102
1966	1,743	3,050	204	4,997	2,073	—	775	778	101
1965	1,759	2,637	170	4,566	1,917	—	740	686	108
1964	1,669	2,535	144	4,348	1,588	—	679	622	89
1963	1,375	2,168	125	3,668	1,278	—	666	581	91
1962	1,298	2,018	129	3,445	1,108	—	641	645	87
1961	1,302	2,052	112	3,466	1,045	—	624	535	85
1960	1,380	1,941	88	3,409	991	—	633	499	85
1959	1,234	1,752	74	3,060	1,003	—	621	526	88
1958	1,076	1,500	61	2,637	868	—	557	487	72
1957	1,296	1,635	64	2,995	879	—	549	498	71
1956	1,336	1,526	76	2,938	896	—	538	549	80
1955	1,081	1,288	66	2,435	802	—	510	481	67
1954	1,067	1,284	61	2,412	715	—	478	397	45
1953	1,247	1,278	54	2,579	733	—	524	407	39
1952	1,277	1,225	54	2,556	705	—	508	390	38
1951	1,141[2]	977	55	2,173	598	—	517	347	38
1950	834[2]	652	62	1,548	460	—	455	296	34
1949	601[2]	622	48	1,271	403	—	378	226	30
1948	537[2]	763	43	1,343	377	—	448	223	26
1947	591[2]	660	36	1,287	372	2	446	293	31
1946	681[2]	671	30	1,382	298	36	423	237	24
1945	645[2]	687	28	1,360	212	30	425	129	21
1943	740[2]	698	27	1,465	305	25	331	288	15
1941	321[2]	296	28	645	236	25	201	245	7
1939	78	46	11	135	137	—	87	107	—
1937	70	40	10	120	138	—	76	113	—
1933	27	29	5	61	61	—	67	81	—

Year[1]	Taxes		Privileges, licences and permits			Government enterprises	Other revenue	Total net revenue
	Other	Total tax revenue	Natural resources	Other	Total			
	84	85	86	87	88	89	90	91
1969	6	12,789	7	21	27	247	470	13,914
1968	9	10,619	13	16	29	200	447	11,536
1967	12	9,557	4	12	16	190	353	10,327
1966	—	8,723	8	31	39	164	322	9,372
1965	—	8,018	12	27	39	157	371	8,695
1964	—	7,326	6	22	28	139	335	7,940
1963	—	6,283	5	24	29	125	350	6,855
1962	—	5,928	4	23	26	107	302	6,427
1961	1	5,754	4	21	24	122	284	6,249
1960	1	5,618	4	19	23	108	354	6,102
1959	1	5,299	6	20	26	88	323	5,736
1958	1	4,622	11	19	30	100	314	5,066
1957	2	4,994	4	17	21	78	302	5,395
1956	18	5,019	5	16	21	125	276	5,441
1955	17	4,312	4	15	19	60	277	4,668
1954	16	4,063	3	13	16	51	234	4,364
1953	15	4,297	3	11	14	61	278	4,650
1952	24	4,221	—[3]	17	17	47	290	4,575
1951	18	3,691	—[3]	16	16	40	189	3,936
1950	17	2,810	2	14	16	44	182	3,052
1949	15	2,323	1	14	15	28	179	2,545
1948	19	2,436	3	10	13	28	238	2,715
1947	21	2,452	2	9	11	27	350	2,840
1946	27	2,427	2	9	11	48	487	2,973
1945	25	2,202	—[3]	11	11	90	654	2,957
1943	7	2,436	1	5	6	50	91	2,583
1941	2	1,361	1	3	4	8	68	1,441
1939	2	468	1	2	3	1	52	524
1937	2	449	—	3	3	1	49	502
1933	2	272	—	3	3	—	40	315

[1] Figures are for fiscal year ending nearest 31 December of year named.
[2] Includes excess profits tax.
[3] Included in 'other privileges, licences and permits'.

Series H92-112. Provincial governments, net general revenue by major source, selected years, 1933 to 1969
(millions of dollars)

Year[1]	Taxes									
	Income tax			General sales	Motor fuel	Other sales	Real and personal property	Succession duties	Other	Total taxes
	Corporate	Individual	Total							
	92	93	94	95	96	97	98	99	100	101
1969	862	2,142	3,004	1,675	1,020	282	42	141	816	6,979
1968	660	1,764	2,425	1,396	944	247	36	122	500	5,670
1967	596	1,462	2,058	1,260	792	182	35	109	338	4,774
1966	565	1,109	1,673	1,010	744	163	23	118	281	4,010
1965	523	834	1,357	813	680	114	11	108	271	3,354
1964	455	508	963	726	616	78	10	92	215	2,700
1963	412	389	801	562	539	70	9	86	198	2,265
1962	395	360	755	516	484	65	9	72	187	2,088
1961	268	85	353	355	450	61	9	66	189	1,482
1960	269	61	330	212	402	57	8	60	177	1,246
1959	249	54	303	209	382	55	8	56	155	1,168
1958	226	48	274	187	364	53	9	56	67	1,010
1957	214	41	255	183	347	49	8	53	60	955
1956	62	36	98	178	300	45	8	64	39	732
1955	54	30	84	149	269	43	7	72	40	664
1954	49	25	74	129	240	43	7	40	33	566
1953	49	—	49	108	224	44	6	31	44	506
1952	65	—	65	101	200	39	7	33	42	487
1951	163	—	163	91	182	36	7	34	53	566
1950	127	—	127	76	157	34	7	31	46	478
1949	106	—	106	62	139	35	6	29	41	418
1948	88	—	88	48	125	31	6	29	36	363
1947	62	—	62	31	112	19	7	31	25	287
1946	1	—	1	25	74	18	7	34	6	165
1945	—	—	—	21	59	16	6	25	4	131
1943	—	1	1	18	46	8	7	24	4	108
1941	31	11	42	16	60	6	5	27	22	178
1939	11	12	23	3	53	3	6	28	23	139
1937	9	12	21	2	39	3	4	37	23	129
1933	3	5	8	—	26	3	4	13	19	73

Year[1]	Privileges, licences and permits					Own enterprises		Other revenue	Net general revenue	Transfers from other governments (unconditional)	Total net general revenue
	Liquor control	Motor vehicles	Natural resources	Other	Total	Liquor boards	Other own enterprises				
	102	103	104	105	106	107	108	109	110	111	112
1969	89	363	631	55	1,139	416	10	14	8,923	970	9,893
1968	85	325	596	57	1,062	388	12	9	7,442	863	8,305
1967	69	325	503	37	934	363	9	8	6,256	786	7,042
1966	63	254	514	45	876	327	28	8	5,380	522	5,902
1965	62	244	508	42	856	298	26	6	4,629	471	5,101
1964	60	222	440	39	761	251	26	17	3,833	374	4,208
1963	56	211	367	36	669	233	13	15	3,260	259	3,519
1962	53	187	316	34	589	217	8	9	2,977	279	3,256
1961	51	182	296	32	561	197	7	18	2,315	542	2,857
1960	47	172	277	28	524	191		53	2,014	538	2,552
1959	45	164	303	27	539	186		52	1,945	518	2,463
1958	38	146	259	23	466	180		53	1,709	467	2,176
1957	40	140	278	20	478	167		40	1,640	382	2,022
1956	33	128	288	20	469	157		37	1,395	395	1,790
1955	33	114	257	18	422	141		32	1,259	352	1,611
1954	31	94	185	17	327	130		30	1,053	359	1,412
1953	32	88	195	16	331	128		28	993	341	1,334
1952	31	81	—[2]	170	282	130		25	924	334	1,258
1951	28	73	—[2]	139	240	118		25	949	127	1,070
1950	27	67	99	14	207	115		28	828	123	951
1949	26	58	82	12	178	111		26	733	108	841
1948	25	50	59	11	145	107		27	642	103	745
1947	24	46	42	11	123	103		27	540	150	690
1946	21	38	42	10	111	104		21	401	101	502
1945	20	32	—[2]	47	9	80		12	322	107	429
1943	—[3]	30	33	10	—	—[3]		70	251	110	361
1941	—[3]	32	34	9	—	—[3]		49	302	37	339
1939	—[3]	28	24	9	—	—[3]		36	236	22	258
1937	—[3]	26	25	9	—	—[3]		32	221	24	245
1933	—[3]	20	13	8	—	—[3]		19	133	19	152

[1] Figures are for fiscal year ending nearest 31 December of year named.
[2] Included in 'other privileges, licences and permits'.
[3] Included in 'other revenue'.

Series H113-123. Municipal governments, net general revenue by major source, selected years, 1933 to 1969
(millions of dollars)

Year[1]	Taxes					Non-tax revenue			Total tax and non-tax revenue	Subsidies from other governments[3]	Total net revenue
	General sales	Other sales	Real and personal property	Other	Total taxes	Privileges, licences and permits	Government enterprises	Other revenue[2]			
	113	**114**	**115**	**116**	**117**	**118**	**119**	**120**	**121**	**122**	**123**
1969	–	11	3,284	22	3,317	79	64	444	3,903	337[2]	4,240
1968	–	11	2,962	11	2,984	68	59	434	3,544	321[2]	3,865
1967	–	11	2,646	8	2,667	62	58	429	3,215	283[2]	3,498
1966	–	–	2,291	17	2,308	55	57	158	2,579	280[2]	2,859
1965	–	–	1,781	19	1,800	36	62	171	2,069	222	2,291
1964	5	–	1,760	111	1,876	34	35	178	2,123	190	2,312
1963	58	3	1,674	17	1,753	32	50	146	1,981	112	2,093
1962	42	3	1,578	14	1,639	29	48	129	1,844	110	1,942
1961	85	3	1,437	15	1,540	28	37	113	1,718	106	1,824
1960	82	4	1,331	7	1,424	25	41	104	1,594	99	1,693
1959	74	3	1,196	8	1,281	25	45	103	1,454	91	1,545
1958	58	4	1,060	10	1,132	24	45	93	1,294	85	1,379
1957	53	3	974	7	1,037	22	37	84	1,180	74	1,254
1956	51	3	860	10	924	20	35	78	1,057	52	1,109
1955	43	3	764	18	828	19	32	64	943	45	988
1954	37	2	709	15	763	17	36	60	876	42	918
1953	34	2	651	13	700	16	33	62	811	30	841
1952	30	2	600	14	646	14	30	47	737	29	766
1951	27	2	531	10	570	13	29	48	660	24	684
1950	25	–	400	53	478	14	24	44	560	15	575
1949	16	–	369	48	433	13	24	42	512	9	521
1948	15	–	337	41	393	12	20	38	463	8	471
1947	13	–	304	34	351	10	19	33	413	6	419
1946	12	–	275	29	316	9	16	34	375	7	382
1945	9	1	278	4	292	6	17	30	345	6	351
1943	8	–	260	25	293	8	14	26	341	7	348
1941	7	–	251	24	286	8	12	25	331	3	334
1939	5	–	243	23	275	7	10	25	317	5	322
1937	4	–	237	21	266	6	9	23	304	3	307
1933	–	–	231	18	253	5	6	30	294	–	294

[1] Figures are for fiscal year ending nearest 31 December of year named.
[2] Includes sales and services, fines and penalties.
[3] Includes grants in lieu of taxes on federal and provincial enterprises.

Series H124-135. Provincial governments, total net general revenue, by province, selected years, 1933 to 1969
(millions of dollars)

Year[1]	Newfound-land	Prince Edward Island	Nova Scotia	New Brunswick	Quebec	Ontario	Manitoba	Saskat-chewan	Alberta	British Columbia	Yukon Territory and Northwest Territories	Total[2]
	124	125	126	127	128	129	130	131	132	133	134	135
1969	221	46	302	287	2,962	3,525	408	346	742	1,025	30	9,893
1968	195	39	233	239	2,636	2,777	336	343	651	833	21	8,305
1967	167	34	213	213	2,291	2,304	293	313	503	696	16	7,042
1966	128	28	167	153	1,820	1,977	222	293	469	634	12	5,902
1965	112	25	150	128	1,600	1,603	199	266	453	554	10	5,101
1964	94	21	129	109	1,240	1,358	162	236	383	464	9	4,208
1963	81	19	114	95	948	1,182	136	217	320	398	8	3,519
1962	76	19	114	90	865	1,095	131	201	294	364	7	3,256
1961	69	18	102	84	758	927	118	157	273	346	4	2,857
1960	64	16	92	87	641	833	104	149	246	320	—	2,552
1959	60	14	90	77	605	778	100	146	279	314	—	2,463
1958	62	13	76	71	557	647	77	141	236	296	—	2,176
1957	39	9	64	62	515	595	74	136	246	282	—	2,022
1956	37	8	58	57	446	482	66	122	241	273	—	1,790
1955	33	8	54	53	413	432	59	103	225	231	—	1,611
1954	33	8	51	51	339	399	57	99	175	200	—	1,412
1953	32	8	49	49	299	371	56	98	186	186	—	1,334
1952	32	7	47	47	285	365	55	91	144	185	—	1,258
1951	25	6	39	41	277	304	46	75	106	157	—	1,076
1950	21	5	36	32	239	266	41	67	105	139	—	951
1949	18	5	34	30	207	236	38	61	88	124	—	841
1948	—	5	33	28	203	220	36	56	63	101	—	745
1947	—	5	32	29	194	223	34	53	48	72	—	690
1946	—	4	22	20	151	151	23	37	36	58	—	502
1945	—	3	19	16	119	134	22	35	34	47	—	429
1943	—	2	17	12	97	117	19	31	27	39	—	361
1941	—	2	14	11	94	111	19	25	25	38	—	339
1939	—	2	12	8	60	87	16	21	20	32	—	258
1937	—	2	10	7	57	87	15	17	19	31	—	245
1933	—	1	7	5	31	52	13	12	12	19	—	152

[1] Figures are for fiscal year ending nearest 31 December of year named.   [2] Includes unconditional transfers from Government of Canada.

Series H136-147. Municipal governments, total net general revenue, by province, selected years, 1933 to 1969
(millions of dollars)

Year[1]	Newfound-land	Prince Edward Island	Nova Scotia	New Brunswick	Quebec	Ontario	Manitoba	Saskat-chewan	Alberta	British Columbia	Yukon Territory and Northwest Territories	Total[2]
	136	**137**	**138**	**139**	**140**	**141**	**142**	**143**	**144**	**145**	**146**	**147**
1969	18	9	95	35	1,135	1,760	192	202	370	420	3	4,240
1968	21	8	85	35	1,064	1,590	173	186	338	364	3	3,865
1967	15	7	77	30	957	1,462	151	176	294	327	2	3,498
1966	12	5	66	56	774	1,142	130	141	243	288	1	2,859
1965	10	5	61	55	402	1,027	120	129	225	256	1	2,291
1964	10	5	57	53	584	942	111	122	205	223	1	2,312
1963	8	4	54	48	485	874	104	113	196	205	1	2,093
1962	7	4	51	45	443	809	97	107	185	193	1	1,942
1961	7	4	46	41	438	749	90	102	170	177	1	1,824
1960	6	3	43	40	412	694	79	96	153	167	—	1,693
1959	6	3	39	36	383	628	73	88	138	151	—	1,545
1958	5	3	36	33	326	562	68	83	127	136	—	1,379
1957	4	2	34	30	293	519	64	78	112	118	—	1,254
1956	4	2	30	26	267	453	59	71	97	100	—	1,109
1955	3	2	27	24	239	400	53	66	87	87	—	988
1954	3	2	25	22	226	360	49	62	85	84	—	918
1953	2	2	24	21	217	319	46	57	76	77	—	841
1952	2	2	23	19	193	293	45	51	68	70	—	766
1951	2	1	20	16	182	254	42	46	58	63	—	684
1950	—	—	—	—	—	—	—	—	—	—	—	575
1949	—	—	—	—	—	—	—	—	—	—	—	521
1948	—	—	—	—	—	—	—	—	—	—	—	471
1947	—	—	—	—	—	—	—	—	—	—	—	419
1946	—	—	—	—	—	—	—	—	—	—	—	382
1945	—	1	12	9	100	125	23	27	26	28	—	351
1943	—	1	11	8	94	128	22	30	27	27	—	348
1941	—	—	10	8	92	133	21	22	23	25	—	334
1939	—	—	10	7	84	131	21	22	23	24	—	322
1937	—	—	9	6	81	133	20	15	21	22	—	307
1933	—	—	9	5	73	128	19	17	20	23	—	294

[1] Figures are for fiscal year ending nearest 31 December of year named.　　[2] Includes unconditional transfers from provincial governments.

Series H148-160. All governments, net general expenditure by major function,[1] selected years, 1933 to 1969
(millions of dollars)

Year[2]	Defence and mutual aid	Veterans pensions and benefits	Health	Social welfare	Education	Transportation and communication	Natural resources and primary industries	Debt charges	General government	Protection of persons and property	International co-operation and assistance	Other	Net general expenditure[4]
	148	149	150	151	152	153	154	155	156	157	158	159	160
1969	1,815	424	3,386	4,015	5,554	2,462	1,348	1,845	1,443	1,227	181	2,818	26,822
1968	1,797	428	2,591	3,677	4,807	2,341	1,084	1,779	1,335	1,089	149	2,729	23,805
1967	1,784	401	2,276	3,244	4,201	2,210	1,040	1,535	1,043	972	167	2,150	21,487
1966	1,664	392	1,903	2,641	3,481	2,261	901	1,355	946	841	212	2,130	18,727
1965	1,572	372	1,570	2,385	2,615	2,035	731	1,258	771	744	126	1,731	15,909
1964	1,562	356	1,414	2,246	2,450	1,772	624	1,147	643	648	108	1,466	14,435
1963	1,717	336	1,239	2,023	2,184	1,645	629	1,146	641	570	75	1,281	13,485
1962	1,595	338	1,153	1,904	2,141	1,525	549	1,035	600	537	57	1,268	12,701
1961	1,647	337	1,032	1,741	1,820	1,435	605	880	571	487	67	1,137	11,760
1960	1,534	296	841	1,629	1,579	1,452	567	817	532	448	82	1,007	10,784
1959	1,542	293	732	1,506	1,330	1,402	460	830	492	414	80	895	9,976
1958	1,664	295	535	1,427	1,108	1,259	421	702	478	380	63	827	9,159
1957	1,706	288	445	1,247	1,043	1,166	330	640	491	345	53	783	8,537
1956	1,819	261	394	1,073	841	1,004	288	593	487	309	35	705	7,809
1955	1,759	245	369	1,020	746	843	281	543	362	282	33	543	7,026
1954	1,724	233	354	970	680	711	275	539	334	261	27	572	6,680
1953	1,817	232	310	912	632	675	276	520	333	235	29	506	6,477
1952	1,917	234	290	869	571	657	259	497	277	215	12	483	6,281
1951	1,417	209	256	662	498	544	204	526	340	204	30	469	5,359
1950	607	210	232	638	442	474	192	464	236	83	17	544	4,139
1949	385	229	209	596	392	461	186	472	156	73	11	612	3,782
1948	269	270	154	506	342	429	173	475	138	60	9	514	3,339
1947	195	335	113	466	273	345	163	499	110	50	25	523	3,097
1946	466	602	84	416	225	255	174	512	95	42	2	484	3,357
1945	2,517	406	68	307	186	172	176	489	124	98	159	981	5,683
1943	4,016	65	52	125	151	293	118	323	—[3]	—[3]	—	429	5,572
1941	1,253	56	47	104	138	128	139	256	—[3]	—[3]	—	255	2,376
1939	127	55	47	161	129	163	98	266	—[3]	—[3]	—	231	1,277
1937	33	53	42	194	117	160	63	273	—[3]	—[3]	—	208	1,143
1933	15	51	35	133	107	89	34	299	—[3]	—[3]	—	187	950

[1] After elimination of intergovernmental transfers. The Yukon Territory and the Northwest Territories are included from 1954 in provincial portion and from 1957 in municipal portion.
[2] Figures are for fiscal year ending nearest 31 December of year named.
[3] Included in 'other' expenditure.
[4] This is the sum of net general expenditures in the federal, provincial and municipal tables which follow.

Series H161-175. Federal government, net general expenditure by major function, selected years, 1933 to 1969
(millions of dollars)

Year[1]	Defence and mutual aid	Veterans pensions and benefits	Health	Social welfare	Education	Trans- portation and communi- cation	Natural re- sources and primary indus- tries	Debt charges	General govern- ment	Pro- tection of persons and property	Inter- national co-oper- ation assis- tance	Other	Net general expen- diture	Uncondi- tional trans- fers	Total net expendi- ture
	161	**162**	**163**	**164**	**165**	**166**	**167**	**168**	**169**	**170**	**171**	**172**	**173**	**174**	**175**
1969	1,815	424	1,026	3,165	638	575	909	1,115	736	274	181	1,613	12,472	1,000	13,472
1968	1,797	428	737	2,852	589	593	690	1,074	688	245	149	1,458	11,300	928	12,228
1967	1,784	401	618	2,580	453	657	682	940	475	219	167	1,304	10,281	792	11,073
1966	1,664	392	510	2,096	431	669	543	903	428	189	212	1,133	9,169	563	9,732
1965	1,572	372	426[2]	1,872[2]	289[2]	598	444	897	340	163	126	922	8,022	511	8,533
1964	1,562	356	536	1,843[3]	216	531	381	791	267	138	108	796	7,524	392	7,916
1963	1,717	336	492	1,666	206	450	421	823	299	99	75	676	7,260	292	7,552
1962	1,595	338	425	1,565	275	435	357	755	290	95	57	672	6,858	310	7,168
1961	1,647	337	366	1,424	94	430	403	689	287	88	67	620	6,454	568	7,022
1960	1,534	296	267	1,328	65	377	366	654	266	79	82	556	5,870	565	6,435
1959	1,542	293	227	1,262	69	376	286	657	252	76	80	524	5,644	544	6,188
1958	1,665	295	130	1,202	65	329	263	546	262	73	63	509	5,402	490	5,892
1957	1,706	288	62	1,047	97	282	183	500	299	65	53	475	5,057	401	5,458
1956	1,820	261	62	896	39	216	156	471	316	61	35	430	4,763	406	5,169
1955	1,760	245	57	853	25	174	159	438	208	52	33	311	4,315	359	4,674
1954	1,724	233	54	817	22	164	168	432	200	55	27	313	4,209	363	4,572
1953	1,817	232	49	782	20	153	172	422	208	47	29	306	4,237	345	4,582
1952	1,917	234	46	747	19	141	162	400	167	45	12	301	4,191	341	4,532
1951	1,417	209	42	545	19	120	117	432	240	41	30	308	3,520	129	3,649
1950	607	210	34	477	13	114	120	377	199	32	17	332	2,532	125	2,657
1949	385	229	29	445	12	105	126	388	123	27	11	421	2,301	104	2,405
1948	269	270	19	386	12	84	98	395	104	25	9	338	2,009	102	2,111
1947	195	335	9	365	14	66	103	420	82	21	25	367	2,002	156	2,158
1946	466	602	6	333	19	53	128	429	74	18	2	358	2,488	109	2,597
1945	2,517	406	5	250	8	46	139	404	62	34	159	933	4,963	113	5,076
1943	4,016	65	2	67	7	205	88	222	217	14	—	67	4,970	110	5,080
1941	1,253	56	1	47	9	27	107	146	57	13	—	56	1,772	35	1,807
1939	127	55	1	58	4	46	68	153	46	11	—	48	617	19	636
1937	33	53	1	73	3	31	34	166	38	10	—	45	487	21	508
1933	15	51	1	45	2	28	17	189	31	10	—	40	429	15	444

[1] Figures are for fiscal year ending nearest 31 December of year named. Figures in body of table include federal conditional transfers to other levels.

[2] Quebec opted out of certain programs, beginning in 1965, taking tax points instead of federal transfers.

[3] Includes $59 million representing expenditure on winter works projects.

Series H176-187. Provincial governments, net general expenditure by major function, selected years, 1933 to 1969

(millions of dollars)

Year[1]	Health	Social welfare	Education	Transportation and communication	Natural resources and primary industries	Debt charges	General	Protection of persons and property	Other	Net general expenditure	Unconditional transfers to municipalities	Total net expenditure
	176	177	178	179	180	181	182	183	184	185	186	187
1969	2,272	761	3,158	1,295	439	238	394	459	539	9,555	324	9,879
1968	1,830	741	2,677	1,232	393	221	332	382	374	8,182	290	8,472
1967	1,625	605	2,371	1,214	358	152	302	313	254	7,194	259	7,453
1966	1,342	489	1,867	1,140	358	128	286	268	254	6,132	219	6,351
1965	1,070	456	1,483	1,001	287	128	212	226	214	5,087	200	5,289
1964	820	353	1,243	855	243	135	178	189	176	4,192	165	4,357
1963	692	310	1,089	790	208	123	154	172	133	3,671	79	3,750
1962	655	292	988	711	192	103	142	158	117	3,358	77	3,435
1961	600	275	841	659	202	84	135	141	100	3,037	71	3,108
1960	508	257	698	713	201	67	125	136	93	2,798	70	2,868
1959	436	206	602	680	174	57	110	126	86	2,477	66	2,543
1958	330	191	521	622	158	55	95	116	76	2,164	61	2,225
1957	301	168	452	587	147	55	83	108	78	1,979	54	2,033
1956	261	143	362	561	132	55	70	92	54	1,730	41	1,771
1955	246	134	333	447	122	55	65	82	53	1,537	36	1,573
1954	234	124	274	371	107	57	55	78	47	1,347	37	1,384
1953	209	103	234	353	102	53	52	77	44	1,227	30	1,257
1952	192	95	221	367	94	57	48	67	39	1,180	27	1,207
1951	174	92	196	299	85	57	45	61	41	1,050	23	1,073
1950	158	87	183	250	72	52	37	51	35	925	16	941
1949	143	80	160	254	60	53	33	46	33	862	14	876
1948	102	62	142	255	75	52	34	35	28	785	13	798
1947	78	54	124	207	60	49	28	29	19	648	8	656
1946	57	44	88	135	46	51	21	24	12	478	9	487
1945	42	41	70	78	37	56	22	21	9	376	9	385
1943	35	33	50	55	30	60	—[2]	—[2]	38	301	3	304
1941	30	34	43	71	32	63	—[2]	—[2]	38	311	3	314
1939	30	68	38	89	30	61	—[2]	—[2]	39	355	5	360
1937	26	82	33	101	29	54	—[2]	—[2]	35	360	3	363
1933	19	46	28	34	17	50	—[2]	—[2]	25	219	—	219

[1] Figures are for fiscal year ending nearest 31 December of year named. Figures in body of table include provincial conditional transfers to municipalities.

[2] Included in 'other expenditure'.

Series H188-196. Municipal governments, net general expenditure by major function, selected years, 1933 to 1969

(millions of dollars)

Year[1]	Health	Social welfare	Education	Transportation and communication	Debt charges[2]	General government	Protection of persons and property	Other	Net general expenditure
	188	**189**	**190**	**191**	**192**	**193**	**194**	**195**	**196**
1969	88	89	1,758	592	492	313	494	969	4,795
1968	24	84	1,540	516	483	315	462	900	4,324
1967	33	59	1,377	339	442	267	440	1,034	4,011
1966	51	56	1,183	452	325	232	384	743	3,426
1965	73	56	843	436	223	219	355	594	2,799
1964	58	50	991	387	220	198	321	514	2,739
1963	55	46	888	404	201	189	299	471	2,553
1962	73	47	878	380	177	169	283	478	2,485
1961	66	42	826	346	166	149	258	417	2,270
1960	66	44	765	361	145	141	232	357	2,111
1959	68	38	658	346	118	129	212	284	1,853
1958	75	34	522	309	101	121	191	241	1,594
1957	81	32	494	296	85	109	172	229	1,498
1956	70	34	440	226	67	101	156	221	1,315
1955	65	33	388	221	50	89	148	179	1,173
1954	65	29	384	176	50	78	128	212	1,122
1953	52	27	378	167	45	73	111	157	1,010
1952	52	27	331	147	39	62	103	146	907
1951	41	25	283	123	36	55	102	122	787
1950	40	74	246	110	35	—[3]	—[3]	177	682
1949	37	71	220	102	31	—[3]	—[3]	158	619
1948	33	58	188	90	28	—[3]	—[3]	148	545
1947	26	47	135	72	30	—[3]	—[3]	137	447
1946	21	39	118	67	32	—[3]	—[3]	114	391
1945	21	16	108	48	29	40	43	39	344
1943	15	25	94	33	41	—[3]	—[3]	94	302
1941	16	23	86	30	47	—[3]	—[3]	92	294
1939	16	35	87	28	52	—[3]	—[3]	88	306
1937	15	39	81	28	53	—[3]	—[3]	82	298
1933	15	42	77	27	60	—[3]	—[3]	82	303

[1] Figures are for fiscal year ending nearest 31 December of year named.
[2] Includes school debenture debt charges in all years.
[3] Included in 'other expenditure'.

Series H197-208. Provincial governments, total net general expenditure, by province, selected years, 1933 to 1969
(millions of dollars)

Year[1]	Newfoundland	Prince Edward Island	Nova Scotia	New Brunswick	Quebec	Ontario	Manitoba	Saskatchewan	Alberta	British Columbia	Yukon Territory and Northwest Territories	Total[2]
	197	198	199	200	201	202	203	204	205	206	207	208
1969	245	47	323	288	3,154	3,368	379	340	761	933	39	9,879
1968	242	39	274	273	2,684	2,887	325	331	655	736	29	8,472
1967	237	36	224	250	2,448	2,390	280	306	597	663	21	7,453
1966	221	38	182	171	2,116	1,936	237	297	548	590	17	6,353
1965	131	30	155	131	1,853	1,593	215	251	380	539	13	5,289
1964	126	24	132	117	1,437	1,381	185	226	311	407	10	4,357
1963	105	22	125	112	1,097	1,240	162	209	276	392	9	3,750
1962	101	23	113	101	952	1,172	146	179	282	357	9	3,435
1961	84	19	108	95	848	1,037	137	159	279	339	5	3,108
1960	75	15	112	95	749	937	137	150	266	332	—	2,868
1959	65	20	92	80	601	898	128	142	234	283	—	2,543
1958	62	14	86	71	533	742	98	137	215	267	—	2,225
1957	48	11	74	63	493	657	76	124	199	288	—	2,033
1956	44	10	71	59	434	552	63	110	170	258	—	1,771
1955	42	10	58	54	400	489	52	101	159	208	—	1,573
1954	39	9	53	51	350	421	49	96	138	178	—	1,384
1953	33	7	51	48	311	384	47	86	118	172	—	1,257
1952	29	7	46	45	313	372	42	80	104	169	—	1,207
1951	30	8	49	40	261	336	43	72	82	152	—	1,073
1950	27	7	52	41	224	279	35	62	73	141	—	941
1949	26	6	51	37	193	261	35	58	58	151	—	876
1948	—	6	43	40	230	235	33	55	55	101	—	798
1947	—	6	34	33	186	198	25	52	42	80	—	656
1946	—	4	24	25	140	156	18	35	31	54	—	487
1945	—	4	19	17	111	127	16	28	23	40	—	385
1943	—	2	13	10	91	102	14	20	22	30	—	304
1941	—	2	13	10	88	113	15	21	20	32	—	314
1939	—	3	15	17	108	116	17	29	22	33	—	360
1937	—	2	19	17	88	120	17	45	21	34	—	363
1933	—	1	11	6	50	73	16	22	18	22	—	219

[1] Figures are for fiscal year ended nearest 31 December of year named.   [2] Includes unconditional transfers paid to municipalities.

Series H209-220. Municipal governments, net general expenditure, by province, selected years, 1933 to 1969
(millions of dollars)

Year[1]	Newfoundland	Prince Edward Island	Nova Scotia	New Brunswick	Quebec	Ontario	Manitoba	Saskatchewan	Alberta	British Columbia	Yukon Territory and Northwest Territories	Total
	209	210	211	212	213	214	215	216	217	218	219	220
1969	19	11	114	43	1,269	2,019	194	211	453	460	3	4,795
1968	27	8	96	40	1,163	1,789	175	203	412	407	3	4,324
1967	18	8	93	35	1,126	1,638	153	191	364	381	3	4,011
1966	13	6	75	66	823	1,510	147	172	303	308	2	3,426
1965	16	5	71	62	452	1,304	146	161	268	313	1	2,799
1964	11	8	61	57	652	1,172	129	147	233	267	1	2,740
1963	8	8	61	53	579	1,103	130	138	234	239	1	2,553
1962	7	8	60	49	590	1,043	134	130	225	236	1	2,485
1961	9	6	55	45	535	956	133	119	198	213	1	2,270
1960	7	5	53	41	469	930	102	114	191	199	—	2,110
1959	6	3	47	41	377[2]	820	85	108	180	186	—	1,853
1958	6	4	43	39	278[3]	727	76	96	158	167	—	1,594
1957	7	3	39	34	248[3]	699	71	89	155	153	—	1,498
1956	5	3	33	33	229[3]	602	66	82	138	124	—	1,315
1955	3	3	28	29	202[3]	540	64	74	120	110	—	1,173
1954	3	3	29	27	197[3]	505	58	69	114	117	—	1,122
1953	3	2	27	26	251	379	53	61	113	95	—	1,010
1952	2	2	27	24	237	339	48	54	91	83	—	907
1951	1	2	25	20	201	294	46	47	76	75	—	787
1950	—	—	—	—	—	—	—	—	—	—	—	682
1949	—	—	—	—	—	—	—	—	—	—	—	619
1948	—	—	—	—	—	—	—	—	—	—	—	545
1947	—	—	—	—	—	—	—	—	—	—	—	447
1946	—	—	—	—	—	—	—	—	—	—	—	391
1945	—	1	11	9	92	126	24	27	26	28	—	344
1943	—	1	10	7	83	110	20	24	23	24	—	302
1941	—	1	10	6	86	106	20	21	21	23	—	294
1939	—	1	10	7	91	112	21	20	21	23	—	306
1937	—	1	10	7	85	114	21	18	20	22	—	298
1933	—	1	9	6	85	123	20	18	19	22	—	303

[1] After elimination of intergovernmental transfers.
[2] Includes $56 million capital expenditures for schools; does not include other capital expenditures out of capital fund.
[3] Does not include capital expenditures out of capital fund.

Series H221-233. All governments, gross general revenue by source, 1965 to 1975
(millions of dollars)

Year[1]	Income tax Personal	Income tax Corporation	Real and personal property	General sales	Motive fuel	Alcoholic beverages and tobacco	Customs duties	Other taxes[2]	Total taxes	Natural resource revenues	Return on investments	Other non-tax revenue[3]	Consolidated government revenue
	221	222	223	224	225	226	227	228	229	230	231	232	233
1975	19,193	7,921	4,990	7,206	1,962	1,474	1,887	8,653	53,286	2,695	4,959	4,952	65,891
1974	17,326	6,723	4,354	7,465	1,444	1,395	1,809	8,145	48,661	2,398	4,411	4,590	60,060
1973	13,616	4,914	3,909	6,599	1,419	1,322	1,385	5,397	38,561	1,252	3,546	4,354	47,713
1972	12,007	3,897	3,708	5,385	1,271	1,230	1,182	4,471	33,151	800	3,016	3,625	40,591
1971	10,194	3,181	3,424	4,664	1,168	1,157	989	4,187	28,965	649	2,697	3,064	35,374
1970	9,148	3,189	3,211	4,072	1,094	1,081	815	3,981	26,590	610	2,264	2,711	32,174
1969	7,731	3,701	2,974	3,974	1,021	994	818	3,594	24,806	638	1,873	2,503	29,819
1968	6,099	2,873	2,674	3,494	944	957	762	3,045	20,848	611	1,518	2,192	25,170
1967	5,112	2,417	2,388	3,405	793	837	746	2,725	18,423	511	1,226	1,926	22,085
1966	4,188	2,279	2,157	3,083	744	793	778	2,414	16,434	522	1,055	1,593	19,604
1965	3,472	2,282	2,006	2,731	680	742	686	1,519	14,117	520	889	1,479	17,005

1 Fiscal years ending nearest 31 December of year named.
2 'Other taxes' includes hospital and medical care premiums, social insurance and universal pension plan levies, oil export tax (since 1973) and other.
3 'Other non-tax revenue' consists of privileges, licences and permits, sales of goods and services and other revenue from own sources.

Series H234-248. Federal government, gross general revenue by major source, 1965 to 1975
(millions of dollars)

Year[1]	Income Personal	Income Corporation	General sales	Alcoholic beverages and tobacco	Customs duties	Social insurance levies[2]	Universal pension plan	Other taxes[3]	Total tax revenue	Natural sources revenue	Return on investments	Transfers specific purposes	Other non-tax revenue	Total non-tax revenue	Grand total of revenue
	234	235	236	237	238	239	240	241	242	243	244	245	246	247	248
1975	12,709	5,748	3,515	1,196	1,887	1,949	1,457	2,065	30,526	28	2,177	—	1,972	4,177	34,703
1974	11,710	4,836	3,866	1,127	1,809	1,670	1,213	2,135	28,367	21	1,904	—	1,900	3,825	32,193
1973	9,226	3,710	3,590	1,071	1,385	1,017	998	648	21,642	14	1,568	—	1,878	3,460	25,102
1972	8,378	2,920	3,052	991	1,182	742	879	398	18,541	11	1,329	—	1,545	2,885	21,426
1971	7,227	2,396	2,653	945	989	571	826	471	16,077	8	1,166	8	1,291	2,473	18,550
1970	6,395	2,426	2,281	887	815	495	813	458	14,571	8	949	5	1,110	2,071	16,642
1969	5,588	2,839	2,294	821	818	492	746	428	14,027	7	786	3	1,002	1,798	15,825
1968	4,334	2,213	2,098	819	762	433	698	394	11,750	15	613	6	813	1,447	13,197
1967	3,650	1,821	2,146	761	746	348	640	435	10,545	7	495	2	675	1,179	11,724
1966	3,050	1,743	2,073	717	778	344	587	362	9,654	8	388	1	555	952	10,607
1965	2,638	1,759	1,917	688	686	328	95	331	8,441	12	304	1	544	861	9,302

1 Fiscal year ended nearest 31 December of year named.
2 'Social insurance levies' refers to Unemployment Insurance premiums.
3 Includes oil export charges from 1973 to 1975 and motive fuel tax in 1975.

The amounts in 1975 were: oil export charge, $1,063 million and motive fuel tax, $425 million.

Series H249-266. Provincial governments, gross general revenue by major source, 1965 to 1975
(millions of dollars)

Year[1]	Taxes									
	Income		Real and personal property	General sales	Motive fuel	Alcoholic beverages and tobacco	Social insurance levies	Universal pension plan	Other taxes	Total tax revenue
	Personal	Corporation								
	249	250	251	252	253	254	255	256	257	258
1975	6,429	2,091	85	3,664	1,518	281	864	526	1,712	17,170
1974	5,616	1,888	77	3,596	1,444	268	674	400	1,601	15,564
1973	4,390	1,204	64	3,006	1,419	250	508	358	1,475	12,674
1972	3,629	978	60	2,331	1,271	239	401	331	1,358	10,597
1971	2,967	786	50	2,009	1,168	212	340	300	1,327	9,159
1970	2,753	763	50	1,787	1,094	194	320	273	1,275	8,506
1969	2,142	862	42	1,675	1,020	173	310	260	1,065	7,549
1968	1,764	660	36	1,395	943	139	285	245	730	6,197
1967	1,462	596	35	1,260	792	77	287	227	553	5,288
1966	1,137	536	23	1,010	743	75	259	202	487	4,472
1965	834	523	11	813	680	54	217	30	439	3,601

Year[1]	Non-tax revenue						Grand total of revenue	Revenue from own sources
	Natural resources revenue	Return on investments	Transfers		Other non-tax revenue	Total non-tax revenue		
			Specific purposes	General purposes				
	259	260	261	262	263	264	265	266
1975	2,603	2,946	5,176	2,717	1,953	15,395	32,565	24,672
1974	2,376	2,351	4,230	2,252	1,646	12,856	28,419	21,937
1973	1,238	1,888	3,251	1,827	1,562	9,767	22,442	17,363
1972	789	1,610	3,067	1,494	1,343	8,303	18,900	14,339
1971	641	1,470	2,850	1,509	1,145	7,617	16,776	12,416
1970	602	1,241	2,417	1,240	1,008	6,508	15,015	11,357
1969	631	1,021	1,796	970	968	5,386	12,936	10,170
1968	608	841	1,514	863	836	4,661	10,858	8,482
1967	512	670	1,348	786	670	3,986	9,274	7,141
1966	514	599	1,090	522	551	3,276	7,747	6,136
1965	508	525	881	471	521	2,907	6,508	5,155

[1] Fiscal year ended nearest to 31 December of year named.

Series H267-279. Local governments, gross general revenue by major source, 1965 to 1975
(millions of dollars)

| Year[1] | Taxes | | | | | Non-tax revenue | | | | | Total non-tax revenue | Grand total of revenue | Revenue from own sources |
| | Real and personal property[2] | General sales | Motive fuel | Other taxes[3] | Total taxes | Natural resources revenue | Return on investment | Transfers | | Other non-tax revenue | | | |
								Specific purpose	General purpose				
	267	**268**	**269**	**270**	**271**	**272**	**273**	**274**	**275**	**276**	**277**	**278**	**279**
1975	4,990	—	—	537	5,527	—	118	5,873	943	1,647	8,580	14,722	7,292
1974	4,277	—	—	453	4,730	—	130	5,222	729	1,476	7,557	12,287	6,337
1973	3,846	3	—	397	4,245	—	90	4,298	699	1,168	6,255	10,500	5,503
1972	3,648	2	—	362	4,012	—	77	4,076	457	955	5,566	9,578	5,045
1971	3,374	2	—	352	3,729	—	61	3,807	381	854	5,103	8,832	4,644
1970	3,161	4	—	348	3,513	—	74	3,189	321	757	4,341	7,854	4,344
1969	2,932	4	1	292	3,230	—	66	2,694	298	678	3,736	6,966	3,974
1968	2,638	1	1	261	2,901	—	64	2,300	290	637	3,292	6,193	3,603
1967	2,353	—	1	235	2,589	—	62	2,007	269	603	2,940	5,530	3,254
1966	2,134	—	1	173	2,308	—	68	1,567	247	502	2,384	4,692	2,879
1965	1,995	—	—	80	2,075	—	61	1,165	222	429	1,877	3,952	2,565

[1] Fiscal years ending nearest 31 December of year named.
[2] Includes real property, special assessments and personal property.
[3] Includes corporations and businesses, and other taxes.

Series H280-291. Provincial governments, gross general revenue by province, 1965 to 1975
(millions of dollars)

Year[1]	Newfoundland	Prince Edward Island	Nova Scotia	New Brunswick	Quebec	Ontario	Manitoba	Saskatchewan	Alberta	British Columbia	Yukon Territory and Northwest Territories	Total
	280	**281**	**282**	**283**	**284**	**285**	**286**	**287**	**288**	**289**	**290**	**291**
1975	815	189	1,050	925	9,389	9,898	1,278	1,483	3,531	3,316	204	32,565
1974	700	161	904	794	8,238	8,925	1,118	1,268	3,223	2,930	158	28,419
1973	561	140	779	679	6,554	7,395	954	896	1,988	2,353	143	22,442
1972	472	114	629	563	5,734	6,360	838	729	1,454	1,879	129	18,900
1971	439	98	555	506	5,121	5,656	710	640	1,285	1,665	102	16,776
1970	360	85	468	436	4,476	5,281	661	566	1,139	1,464	80	15,015
1969	318	69	439	386	3,600	4,604	562	517	1,060	1,327	54	12,936
1968	273	56	349	327	3,233	3,661	450	487	902	1,095	26	10,858
1967	241	50	322	293	2,839	3,066	404	443	705	888	22	9,274
1966	185	40	256	213	2,296	2,589	328	399	633	793	15	7,747
1965	172	35	211	187	1,859	2,107	274	358	593	699	13	6,508

[1] Fiscal year ending nearest 31 December of year named.

Series H292-303. Local governments, gross general revenue by province, 1965 to 1975
(millions of dollars)

Year[1]	Newfound-land	Prince Edward Island	Nova Scotia	New Brunswick	Quebec	Ontario	Manitoba	Saskat-chewan	Alberta	British Columbia	Yukon Territory and Northwest Territories	Total
	292	293	294	295	296	297	298	299	300	301	302	303
1975	77	45	422		3,772	5,981	668	604	1,450	1,575	25	14,722
1974	55	34	349	84	3,206	5,040	556	502	1,156	1,287	17	12,287
1973	37	32	304	58	2,612	4,461	463	437	953	1,131	11	10,500
1972	37	28	263	51	2,431	4,123	413	420	846	958	8	9,578
1971	36	23	242	46	2,295	3,725	401	392	806	860	7	8,832
1970	22	20	202	41	2,023	3,198	340	312	645	750	5	7,557
1969	20	19	187	38	1,778	2,940	329	330	622	700	4	6,966
1968	24	18	156	36	1,617	2,599	284	307	564	584	3	6,193
1967	17	15	136	32	1,413	2,348	247	295	507	517	3	5,530
1966	15	11	115	87	1,259	1,837	199	262	443	462	2	4,692
1965	13	9	102	71	1,063	1,554	173	223	375	367	2	3,952

[1] Fiscal year ending nearest 31 December of year named.

Series H304-316. All governments, gross general expenditure by function, 1965 to 1975
(millions of dollars)

Year[1]	General govern-ment	Protection of persons and property[2]	Transpor-tation and communi-cations	Health	Social welfare	Education	Natural resources	Recreation and culture	Housing	Foreign affairs	Debt charges	Other expen-diture[3]	Total consol-idated expen-diture
	304	305	306	307	308	309	310	311	312	313	314	315	316
1975	4,447	5,717	6,784	8,961	16,156	10,654	2,757	1,797	929	748	5,730	7,132	71,810
1974	4,088	4,809	6,013	7,358	13,299	8,792	2,077	1,432	544	584	4,695	5,605	59,298
1973	2,916	4,178	4,792	6,069	10,540	7,303	879	1,153	450	439	3,935	4,359	47,013
1972	2,506	3,650	4,084	5,478	8,666	6,953	720	911	428	385	3,375	3,853	41,009
1971	2,284	3,374	3,683	4,886	6,968	6,539	629	760	510	312	3,069	3,314	36,327
1970	1,973	3,123	3,202	4,262	5,808	5,994	538	584	296	289	2,618	2,796	31,484
1969	1,607	2,860	3,030	3,474	4,893	5,537	519	494	254	252	2,293	2,783	27,995
1968	1,457	2,682	2,898	2,713	4,463	4,826	484	433	176	210	2,058	2,404	24,802
1967	1,175	2,605	2,680	2,325	3,944	4,201	511	411	94	218	1,678	2,245	22,086
1966	1,043	2,381	2,633	1,995	3,330	3,296	433	337	98	251	1,511	2,013	19,319
1965	872	2,228	2,254	1,790	3,050	2,545	334	244	50	159	1,404	1,727	16,657

[1] Fiscal year ending nearest 31 December of year named.
[2] Including national defence and services.
[3] Includes agriculture, trade and industry and tourism; environment; labour, employment and immigration; supervision and development of regions and localities; research establishments; transfers to own enterprises; and other.

Series H317-331. Federal government, gross general expenditure by function, 1965 to 1975
(millions of dollars)

Year[1]	General government	Protection of persons and property[2]	Transportation and communication	Health	Social welfare	Education	Natural resources	Recreation and culture	Housing	Foreign affairs[3]	Debt charges	General purpose transfers	National defence and services[4]	Other expenditure[5]	Total gross general expenditure
	317	318	319	320	321	322	323	324	325	326	327	328	329	330	331
1975	1,873	763	2,479	2,782	12,385	1,178	1,981	346	338	748	2,832	2,688	2,634	3,820	36,845
1974	1,710	600	2,194	2,297	10,079	1,039	1,582	274	212	584	2,271	2,696	2,290	3,063	30,891
1973	1,382	479	1,765	1,951	8,109	919	570	253	138	439	1,735	1,883	2,123	2,530	24,277
1972	1,257	387	1,370	1,789	6,858	847	334	215	100	385	1,502	1,640	1,912	2,316	20,912
1971	1,110	342	1,207	1,603	5,418	864	277	164	71	312	1,423	1,546	1,872	2,011	18,218
1970	991	310	1,032	1,308	4,496	872	272	113	41	289	1,233	1,319	1,725	1,727	15,728
1969	749	280	1,058	1,037	3,818	773	279	103	38	252	1,151	1,001	1,634	1,686	13,858
1968	693	241	1,023	751	3,487	307	270	86	30	210	1,054	928	1,624	1,350	12,450
1967	493	244	1,032	622	3,144	566	308	109	16	218	893	792	1,630	1,180	11,243
1966	433	223	1,004	516	2,686	431	239	87	12	251	836	563	1,519	1,002	9,801
1965	358	196	900	486	2,469	296	178	58	14	159	818	430	1,469	807	8,637

[1] Fiscal year ending nearest 31 December of year named.
[2] Does not include national defence and services which is in H329.
[3] Includes international assistance.
[4] National defence and services does not include the expenditures of the Canadian Armed Forces Superannuation Account, the Defense Production Revolving Fund, an armed forces accommodation program now operated by Department of Public Works, and certain international military assistance now classified under foreign affairs.
[5] Other expenditure consists of agriculture, trade and industry and tourism; environment; labour, employment and immigration; supervision and development of regions and localities; research establishments; transfers to own enterprises; and other.

Series H332-344. Provincial[1] governments, gross general expenditure by function, 1965 to 1975
(millions of dollars)

Year[2]	General government	Protection of persons and property	Transportation and communication	Health	Social welfare	Education	Natural resources	Recreation and culture	Housing	Debt charges	General purpose transfers[3]	Other expenditure[4]	Total gross general expenditure
	332	333	334	335	336	337	338	339	340	341	342	343	344
1975	1,851	1,214	3,109	8,646	4,799	7,985	828	454	581	1,742	958	2,281	34,447
1974	1,810	1,077	2,616	7,054	3,734	6,573	561	359	237	1,592	732	1,695	28,038
1973	1,080	757	2,092	5,792	2,801	5,497	424	273	239	1,374	608	1,107	22,043
1972	890	654	1,846	5,200	2,138	5,040	355	195	282	1,146	415	903	19,064
1971	839	583	1,723	4,623	1,950	4,639	368	192	383	946	350	716	17,310
1970	698	514	1,511	3,979	1,624	4,052	292	149	301	815	326	590	14,849
1969	543	465	1,369	3,243	1,321	3,501	265	135	250	657	324	411	12,485
1968	450	392	1,305	2,558	1,234	2,997	259	108	167	554	290	333	10,646
1967	413	326	1,298	2,192	1,066	2,672	240	105	91	377	259	295	9,334
1966	376	280	1,258	1,840	872	2,016	224	95	93	319	219	315	7,906
1965	296	241	1,111	1,529	798	1,575	184	46	43	276	200	291	6,589

[1] Including the Yukon Territory and the Northwest Territories.
[2] Fiscal year ending nearest 31 December of year named.
[3] Includes only transfers to other levels of government.
[4] Includes agriculture, trade and industry and tourism; environment; labour and employment; immigration; supervision and development of regions and localities; research establishments; transfers to own enterprises; and other.

Series H345-357. Local governments, gross general expenditure by function, 1965 to 1975
(millions of dollars)

Year[1]	General govern- ment	Protec- tion of persons and property	Transpor- tation and communi- cation	Health	Social welfare	Education	Natural resources	Recreation and culture	Housing	Debt charges	General purpose trans- fers	Other expen- diture[2]	Total gross general expen- diture
	345	346	347	348	349	350	351	352	353	354	355	356	357
1975	715	1,224	1,926	735	521	6,753	60	1,012	255	945	—	1,837	15,982
1974	575	1,002	1,718	590	500	5,616	63	859	138	833	—	1,413	13,307
1973	456	902	1,346	538	453	4,726	55	671	121	826	—	1,155	11,248
1972	363	763	1,236	503	432	4,605	49	512	101	726	—	977	10,267
1971	337	634	1,117	466	360	4,417	10	422	102	701	—	876	9,440
1970	335	628	937	455	298	4,038	—	334	—	570	—	736	8,331
1969	314	525	868	399	206	3,685	—	263	—	493	—	771	7,524
1968	314	464	832	319	183	3,200	—	247	—	453	—	768	6,780
1967	269	449	637	261	141	2,798	—	216	—	411	—	854	6,036
1966	234	388	680	259	133	2,316	—	179	—	359	—	807	5,354
1965	220	353	613	235	131	1,819	—	146	—	313	—	694	4,524

[1] Fiscal year ending nearest 31 December of year named.
[2] Includes environment; agriculture, trade and industry, and tourism; transfers to reserves and allowances and to own enterprises; and other services.

Series H358-369. Provincial governments, gross general expenditure by province, 1965 to 1975
(millions of dollars)

Year[1]	Newfound- land	Prince Edward Island	Nova Scotia	New Brunswick	Quebec	Ontario	Manitoba	Saskat- chewan	Alberta	British Columbia	Yukon Territory and Northwest Territories	Total
	358	359	360	361	362	363	364	365	366	367	368	369
1975	929	198	1,098	1,011	10,104	11,371	1,331	1,336	3,071	3,783	215	34,447
1974	792	166	912	843	7,967	9,655	1,154	1,078	2,363	2,913	195	28,038
1973	617	139	785	673	6,344	7,716	947	801	1,743	2,114	164	22,043
1972	530	112	638	585	5,611	6,704	804	698	1,478	1,751	152	19,064
1971	547	99	566	515	5,034	6,162	714	620	1,416	1,520	117	17,310
1970	394	85	504	485	4,229	5,308	633	557	1,233	1,324	96	14,849
1969	335	69	455	381	3,466	4,387	525	509	1,070	1,226	63	12,485
1968	319	57	386	355	2,991	3,710	433	476	903	985	33	10,646
1967	310	54	331	327	2,744	3,087	386	436	799	835	26	9,334
1966	278	50	271	227	2,373	2,499	339	402	710	740	20	7,906
1965	191	40	211	187	2,075	2,050	286	342	515	679	15	6,589

[1] Fiscal year ending nearest 31 December of year named.

Series H370-381. Local governments, gross general expenditure by province, 1965 to 1975
(millions of dollars)

Year[1]	Newfound- land	Prince Edward Island	Nova Scotia	New Brunswick	Quebec	Ontario	Manitoba	Saskat- chewan	Alberta	British Columbia	Yukon Territory and Northwest Territories	Total
	370	371	372	373	374	375	376	377	378	379	380	381
1975	85	47	474	152	4,026	6,376	701	643	1,686	1,760	32	15,982
1974	60	33	395	110	3,468	5,368	568	515	1,312	1,458	20	13,307
1973	44	35	328	77	2,797	4,722	454	425	1,015	1,340	12	11,248
1972	50	30	275	66	2,646	4,363	429	407	913	1,078	11	10,267
1971	48	26	255	58	2,444	4,002	403	375	864	956	9	9,440
1970	23	22	221	49	2,127	3,420	336	305	719	805	6	8,033
1969	21	20	207	46	1,911	3,194	335	340	708	740	4	7,524
1968	31	19	168	42	1,781	2,858	287	325	639	628	4	6,780
1967	20	16	152	38	1,582	2,518	249	309	577	571	4	6,036
1966	16	12	129	100	1,318	2,240	229	300	522	486	3	5,354
1965	20	6	96	76	1,579	1,627	184	216	349	369	2	4,524

[1] Fiscal year ending nearest 31 December of year named.

Series H382-397. Provincial governments, direct and indirect debt, selected years, 1933 to 1975
(millions of dollars)

Year[1]	Direct debt								Indirect debt							Total direct and indirect debt
	Funded debt	Less sinking funds	Net funded debt	Short-term treasury bills	Savings deposits and certificates	Temporary loans and over-drafts	Other liabilities	Total direct debt	Guaranteed bonds and debentures	Less sinking funds	Net debt	Guaranteed bank loans	M.I.A.[2] act loans	Other	Total indirect debt	
	382	383	384	385	386	387	388	389	390	391	392	393	394	395	396	397
1975	23,721	916	22,805	667	621	2,322	3,633	30,048	20,971	980	19,991	1,002	—	2,015	23,008	53,056
1974	19,893	828	19,065	376	359	1,943	2,453	24,196	16,419	876	15,543	858	—	1,536	17,937	42,133
1973	17,518	773	16,745	350	386	1,767	1,919	21,167	14,098	751	13,347	568	—	1,060	14,975	36,142
1972	15,722	532	15,190	428	410	1,400	1,578	19,006	12,932	637	12,295	476	—	516	13,287	32,293
1971	13,843	469	13,374	358	338	1,122	1,490	16,682	11,675	581	11,094	451	—	658	12,203	28,885
1970	12,218	446	11,772	85	222	757	1,314	14,150	10,481	507	9,974	283	—	647	10,904	25,054
1969	10,941	516	10,425	128	190	575	1,550	12,868	9,565	443	9,122	240	—	670	10,032	22,900
1968	9,562	625	8,937	191	233	531	1,420	11,312	8,920	411	8,509	208	—	690	9,407	20,719
1967	7,558	870	6,688	139	366	187	1,004	8,384	8,109	376	7,733	489	—	417	8,639	17,023
1966	6,363	799	5,564	306	334	168	865	7,237	7,349	340	7,009	299	1	465	7,774	15,011
1965	5,579	755	4,824	144	288	104	669	6,029	6,424	289	6,135	352	1	65	6,553	12,582
1964	5,105	719	4,386	150	252	67	532	5,387	6,117	221	5,896	57	1	14	5,968	11,355
1963	4,730	699	4,031	68	208	76	475	4,858	5,516	214	5,302	65	1	100	5,469	10,327
1962	4,424	696	3,728	63	233	40	440	4,504	4,647	137	4,510	52	1	117	4,680	9,184
1961	4,126	661	3,465	68	165	20	347	4,065	4,259	114	4,145	36	1	139	4,321	8,386
1960	3,806	671	3,135	62	—[3]	32	437	3,666	3,362	83	3,279	26	2	129	3,436	7,102
1959	3,514	634	2,880	47	—[3]	26	370	3,323	2,996	67	2,929	25	2	126	3,082	6,405
1958	3,454	668	2,786	27	—[3]	26	336	3,175	2,577	50	2,527	21	2	131	2,681	5,856
1957	3,029	619	2,410	40	2	25	304	2,781	2,344	39	2,305	70	2	49	2,426	5,207
1956	2,939	550	2,389	29	3	21	270	2,712	1,840	25	1,815	103	3	32	1,953	4,665
1955	2,714	470	2,244	15	2	17	240	2,518	1,589	16	1,573	49	3	29	1,654	4,172
1954	2,629	429	2,200	5	2	30	219	2,456	1,459	11	1,448	32	3	28	1,511	3,967
1953	2,638	446	2,192	13	2	1	205	2,413	1,201	8	1,193	21	3	27	1,244	3,657
1952	2,451	423	2,028	43	2	9	199	2,281	1,049	5	1,044	19	3	26	1,092	3,373
1951	2,297	365	1,932	68	1	1	196	2,198	901	5	896	22	3	25	946	3,144
1950	2,036	308	1,728	63	2	5	207	2,005	787	5	782	23	4	—	809	2,814
1949	2,049	344	1,705	39	69	10	119	1,942	682	4	678	16	4	1	699	2,641
1948	1,864	264	1,600	40	67	7	106	1,820	502	3	499	16	5	1	521	2,341
1947	1,744	231	1,513	40	66	20	108	1,747	424	3	421	11	5	—	437	2,184
1946	1,848	223	1,625	35	64	3	91	1,818	179	3	176	8	5	—	189	2,007
1945	1,832	203	1,629	24	2	24	123	1,802	134	4	130	6	5	—	141	1,943
1943	—	—	1,502	62[4]	42	1	94	1,701	—	—	134	6	—[5]	12	152	1,853[6]
1941	—	—	1,557	111	38	8	84	1,798	—	—	135	14	—[5]	18	167	1,965[6]
1939	—	—	1,569	108	43	11	87	1,818	—	—	145	10	—[5]	20	175	1,993[6]
1937	—	—	1,385	103	47	14	76	1,625	—	—	139	12	—	18	169	1,794[6]
1933	—	—	1,177	89	31	10	47	1,354	—	—	102	17	—	17	136	1,490[6]

[1] Figures are as at fiscal year end nearest 31 December of year named.
[2] Municipal Improvements Assistance Act.
[3] Included in other liabilities.
[4] Deposit certificates included for years 1943 and prior.
[5] Included in other guaranteed debt.

[6] These totals differ from those on the table showing provincial debt by province. The breakdown of debt by type was only available after elimination of intergovernment debt as follows: 1933, 83; 1937, 172; 1939, 202; 1941, 203; 1943, 198.

Series H398-403. Local governments, total liabilities[1] by type, selected years, 1933 to 1975
(millions of dollars)

Year[2]	Funded debt	Less sinking funds	Net funded debt	Temporary loans and over-drafts	Other liabil-ities	Total direct and indirect debt	Year[2]	Funded debt	Less sinking funds	Net funded debt	Temporary loans and over-drafts	Other liabil-ities	Total direct and indirect debt
	398	399	400	401	402	403		398	399	400	401	402	403
1975P	12,922	843	12,079	1,461	2,455	15,995	1955	2,423	93	2,330	128	204	2,662
1974	11,545	807	10,738	1,262	1,611	13,611	1954	2,129	90	2,039	117	200	2,356
1973	10,251	734	9,517	832	1,465	11,814	1953	1,862	93	1,769	97	192	2,058
1972	9,722	674	9,048	737	1,020	10,805	1952	1,630	104	1,526	100	158	1,784
1971	9,101	580	8,521	608	900	10,029	1951	1,450	118	1,332	88	164	1,584
1970	8,671	587	8,084	598	722	9,404	1950	1,247	146	1,101	84	138	1,323
1969	8,252	491	7,761	582	702	9,045	1949	1,126	151	975	78	122	1,175
1968	7,718	438	7,280	546	595	8,421	1948	1,019	146	873	64	119	1,056
1967	7,223	378	6,845	511	727	8,083	1947	964	150	814	48	114	976
1966	6,553	346	6,207	487	652	7,346	1946	1,006	161	845	27	111	983
1965	5,891	298	5,593	407	597	6,597	1945	1,026	177	849	27	116	992
1964	5,451	260	5,191	307	552	6,050	1943	—	—	892	65	78	1,035[3]
1963	5,538	229	5,309	323	568	6,200	1941	—	—	990	102	75	1,167[3]
1962	5,088	190	4,898	251	507	5,656	1939	—	—	1,067	145	92	1,304[3]
1961	4,746	167	4,579	278	412	5,269	1937	—	—	1,147	118	91	1,356[3]
1960	4,351	154	4,197	264	381	4,842	1933	—	—	1,232	143	60	1,435[3]
1959	3,883	134	3,749	246	338	4,333							
1958	3,413	118	3,295	185	343	3,823							
1957	3,009	106	2,903	207	277	3,387							
1956	2,659	98	2,561	167	327	3,055							

[1] Includes debt issued by municipalities, school boards and municipal enterprises (formerly called direct and indirect debt). The source publication (Catalogue 68-204) contains only direct debt figures from 1966 on. Up to 1965, direct and indirect debt were available separately. Amounts in 1965 and 1964 were $9 and $10 million respectively. Montreal transit debt of $60 million was classified as direct debt beginning in 1961.

[2] Figures are as at 31 December of year named.

[3] These totals differ from those on table showing municipal debt by province (series H416-427). The breakdown of debt by type was only available after elimination of intergovernment debt as follows: 1933, 26; 1937, 30; 1939, 37; 1941, 47; 1943, 41.

Series H404-415. Provincial governments, direct and indirect debt, by province, selected years, 1933 to 1975
(millions of dollars)

Year[1]	Newfound-land	Prince Edward Island	Nova Scotia	New Brunswick	Quebec	Ontario	Manitoba	Saskat-chewan	Alberta	British Columbia	Yukon Territory and Northwest Territories	Total
	404	405	406	407	408	409	410	411	412	413	414	415
1975	2,135	183	1,810	1,554	13,947	17,734	3,290	1,062	5,236	5,889	216	53,056
1974	1,778	166	1,553	1,290	10,391	13,956	2,733	913	4,427	4,731	195	42,133
1973	1,413	144	1,412	1,142	8,942	12,102	2,214	793	3,778	4,059	143	36,142
1972	1,262	140	1,304	987	8,115	10,845	1,901	901	3,079	3,634	125	32,293
1971	1,130	136	1,131	924	7,152	9,464	1,696	904	2,916	3,342	90	28,885
1970	908	129	972	799	6,292	7,988	1,495	816	2,586	2,999	70	25,054
1969	772	124	841	735	5,795	7,426	1,339	891	2,198	2,729	50	22,900
1968	670	123	730	733	5,340	6,570	1,197	908	1,906	2,506	36	20,719
1967	585	112	557	682	5,005	5,560	914	659	888	2,034	27	17,023
1966	456	99	457	564	4,532	4,914	861	640	681	1,788	19	15,011
1965	329	81	383	405	3,761	4,253	775	597	550	1,492	16	12,582
1964	250	72	331	365	3,146	3,982	736	574	457	1,430	12	11,355
1963	211	60	312	326	2,594	3,798	663	552	391	1,410	10	10,327
1962	180	50	295	309	1,889	3,599	606	533	336	1,379	8	9,184
1961	109	41	291	292	1,501	3,463	547	490	272	1,376	4	8,386
1960	122	36	281	263	1,308	3,281	488	450	222	651	—	7,102
1959	109	35	260	241	1,101	3,128	401	372	173	585	—	6,405
1958	103	28	251	229	990	2,943	312	355	71	574	—	5,856
1957	99	26	233	229	930	2,585	250	290	47	518	—	5,207
1956	86	23	220	217	880	2,283	214	243	96	403	—	4,665
1955	83	21	202	194	816	2,014	192	231	96	323	—	4,172
1954	68	19	194	183	793	1,939	186	192	100	293	—	3,967
1953	51	18	190	182	727	1,755	167	184	103	280	—	3,657
1952	48	18	185	181	676	1,565	155	175	106	264	—	3,373
1951	37	18	180	176	660	1,376	141	165	111	280	—	3,144
1950	10	16	166	164	627	1,177	118	163	120	253	—	2,814
1949	10	15	143	151	636	1,076	98	152	138	222	—	2,641
1948	—	14	121	136	628	884	82	152	136	188	—	2,341
1947	—	12	112	115	596	810	77	157	139	166	—	2,184
1946	—	11	99	105	416	763	95	202	158	158	—	2,007
1945	—	11	96	95	377	757	92	196	164	155	—	1,943
1943	—	9	92	96	401	789	110	213	179	162	—	2,051
1941	—	10	102	100	419	848	115	229	176	169	—	2,168
1939	—	9	101	100	405	869	124	234	174	179	—	2,195
1937	—	6	93	82	286	806	122	216	175	180	—	1,966
1933	—	4	67	62	171	692	118	153	158	148	—	1,573

[1] Figures are as at fiscal year end nearest 31 December of year named.

Series H416-427. Local governments, total liabilities, by province, selected years, 1933 to 1975
(millions of dollars)

Year[1]	Newfound-land	Prince Edward Island	Nova Scotia	New Brunswick	Quebec	Ontario	Manitoba	Saskat-chewan	Alberta	British Columbia	Yukon Territory and Northwest Territories	Total
	416	417	418	419	420	421	422	423	424	425	426	427
1975P	164	38	420	196	6,011	4,626	562	272	1,909	1,771	26	15,995
1974	128	35	325	150	4,990	4,175	538	248	1,527	1,476	19	13,611
1973	113	33	291	131	3,696	4,114	501	253	1,356	1,313	13	11,814
1972	95	36	268	111	3,161	3,941	495	290	1,226	1,171	11	10,805
1971	95	15	257	96	2,915	3,782	452	303	1,161	945	8	10,029
1970	74	15	238	87	2,789	3,606	423	277	1,038	851	6	9,404
1969	73	16	221	81	2,739	3,490	407	286	945	783	4	9,045
1968	73	14	208	77	2,714	3,091	369	291	836	745	3	8,421
1967	66	14	187	70	2,582	3,052	340	290	758	721	3	8,083
1966	65	14	165	114	2,306	2,721	320	281	702	656	2	7,346
1965	55	12	153	112	1,986	2,502	284	261	631	599	2	6,597
1964	42	11	141	109	1,785	2,336	263	231	577	554	1	6,050
1963	34	12	137	107	2,185	2,195	233	211	552	533	1	6,200
1962	25	12	130	101	1,928	2,026	206	197	524	506	1	5,656
1961	22	10	120	106	1,771	1,885	193	178	512	471	1	5,269
1960	20	8	109	101	1,592	1,750	175	165	482	439	1	4,842
1959	19	7	100	94	1,422	1,570	148	144	445	383	1	4,333
1958	16	6	88	89	1,198	1,440	125	124	393	344	—	3,823
1957	17	7	78	82	1,028	1,266	118	111	364	316	—	3,387
1956	14	6	73	74	969	1,110	105	99	317	288	—	3,055
1955	11	6	62	69	855	945	94	86	261	273	—	2,662
1954	7	5	61	64	772	854	84	73	227	209	—	2,356
1953	6	4	56	58	681	746	73	57	181	196	—	2,058
1952	5	4	52	54	602	623	69	49	145	181	—	1,784
1951	4	4	45	47	549	546	66	47	125	151	—	1,584
1950	—	—	—	—	—	—	—	—	—	—	—	1,323
1949	—	—	—	—	—	—	—	—	—	—	—	1,175
1948	—	—	—	—	—	—	—	—	—	—	—	1,056
1947	—	—	—	—	—	—	—	—	—	—	—	976
1946	—	—	—	—	—	—	—	—	—	—	—	983
1945	—	—	—	—	—	—	—	—	—	—	—	992
1943	—	2	22	19	472	282	60	76	50	93	—	1,076
1941	—	3	25	22	503	342	72	87	57	103	—	1,214
1939	—	3	27	22	523	413	82	98	62	111	—	1,341
1937	—	3	27	23	507	464	96	87	67	112	—	1,386
1933	—	2	29	22	508	540	100	68	74	118	—	1,461

[1] Figures are as at 31 December of year named.

Series H428-435. Provincial current revenues, selected years, 1913 to 1937
(millions of dollars)

Year[1]	Total current revenues	Federal subsidies	Taxes	Licences, permits and fees	Public domain	Liquor control	All other current revenues	Federal subventions and grants-in-aid[2]
	428	429	430	431	432	433	434	435
1937	247.0	21.2	134.2	34.2	21.1	29.8	6.6	82.4
1936	221.6	16.9	113.6	35.3	18.7	26.7	10.3	72.6
1935	194.7	17.1	97.8	30.5	17.6	22.8	9.0	57.7
1934	164.9	16.1	79.2	29.1	14.4	17.5	8.7	57.5
1933	154.3	15.3	76.8	27.8	11.3	14.8	8.1	40.4
1932	158.4	15.4	75.0	27.6	12.2	19.8	8.4	45.2
1931	162.0	15.0	70.0	26.3	15.6	26.4	8.8	42.6
1930	178.3	14.3	77.7	28.7	17.0	31.0	9.7	9.2
1929	180.3	14.1	71.4	32.0	19.0	36.1	7.8	2.6
1928	164.2	14.2	57.5	30.0	20.0	32.9	9.5	2.3
1927	152.5	14.5	58.5	27.4	20.3	24.7	7.2	1.5
1926	136.2	12.5	55.3	23.8	19.7	17.6	7.2	1.4
1925	122.8	12.4	47.5	21.7	18.2	15.8	7.2	1.7
1921	91.1	11.9	35.3	15.4	14.8	7.9	5.9	1.5
1913	46.4	12.9	9.3	6.9	11.0	2.2	4.1	.1

[1] Fiscal years ending nearest the end of the year given: for fiscal years and fiscal year changes of the provinces see the general note to this section.

[2] Not included in total current revenues.

Series H436-447. Provincial current expenditures, selected years, 1913 to 1937
(millions of dollars)

Year[1]	Total current expenditures	Debt charges[2]	Public welfare Relief	Public welfare Other	Education	Administration of justice	Legislation	General government	Agriculture	Public domain	Highways, bridges and ferries	All other
	436	437	438	439	440	441	442	443	444	445	446	447
1937	261.1	50.9	42.9	45.8	32.5	11.7	3.2	19.3	6.2	14.5	25.3	8.7
1936	237.5	50.4	41.9	41.1	29.3	10.1	2.6	16.4	5.4	16.6	19.9	4.8
1935	243.3	54.4	52.7	36.1	28.0	10.5	2.4	15.6	5.0	15.4	20.8	2.6
1934	235.4	52.9	55.4	34.7	28.2	10.2	3.0	14.9	5.0	11.2	17.6	2.3
1933	202.9	50.2	33.3	31.0	28.8	9.6	2.4	14.4	4.9	9.9	15.9	2.8
1932	207.0	49.0	25.1	32.5	30.3	10.3	2.4	14.8	6.0	13.1	17.8	5.6
1931	210.5	39.2	25.8	34.3	34.2	11.5	2.4	15.4	6.4	14.2	22.7	4.4
1930	187.9	29.5	4.1	33.4	33.8	11.6	3.2	15.6	6.3	15.3	28.7	6.5
1929	163.2	27.8	.9	26.2	31.2	10.2	2.6	14.7	5.5	12.3	25.6	6.1
1928	150.1	25.9	.1	23.5	29.3	9.9	2.6	14.1	4.9	10.7	23.3	5.8
1927	142.2	26.2	.1	20.8	27.8	9.1	3.2	13.0	4.6	9.8	20.7	6.9
1926	127.0	25.0	.1	18.5	25.7	8.5	2.4	12.1	4.2	8.9	15.8	5.8
1925	120.9	23.1	.2	17.6	25.6	8.7	2.7	12.1	3.9	7.5	13.5	6.1
1921	91.4	14.4	.4	12.1	20.9	7.5	2.5	12.0	3.8	5.5	8.3	4.0
1913	48.9	3.3	—	4.3	9.6	4.9	1.9	6.5	2.3	5.3	8.7	2.2

[1] Fiscal years ending nearest the end of the year given: for fiscal years and fiscal year changes of the provinces see the general note to this section.

[2] Excluding sinking funds.

Series H448-457. Provincial current revenues, by province, selected years, 1913 to 1937
(millions of dollars)

Year[1]	Total current revenues	Prince Edward Island	Nova Scotia	New Brunswick	Quebec	Ontario	Manitoba	Saskat- chewan	Alberta	British Columbia
	448	449	450	451	452	453	454	455	456	457
1937	247.0	1.6	10.1	7.5	57.5	87.6	15.3	17.1	18.9	31.3
1936	221.6	1.5	9.5	6.6	43.5	87.0	14.0	14.0	17.0	28.4
1935	194.7	1.3	9.3[2]	6.0	41.5	70.0	12.9			
1934	164.9	1.2	7.0	5.3	35.8	54.6	12.6	11.4	13.9	23.1
1933	154.3	1.2	6.2	5.0	30.7	54.8	12.1	11.7	12.6	19.8
1932	158.4	1.2	7.1	5.4	33.4	55.1	10.6	12.0	12.9	20.7
1931	162.0	1.1	7.6	5.8	36.8	57.2	9.6	10.1	11.7	22.1
1930	178.3	1.2	6.9	6.3	43.1	58.4	11.2	13.3	13.8	24.1
1929	180.3	1.1	6.3	6.4	46.1	54.8	11.8	14.0	14.5	25.4
1928	164.2	1.0	5.8	5.7	41.1	47.5	10.3	15.7	14.1	23.1
1927	152.5	.9	5.6	5.2	35.8	45.0	9.4	13.3	14.6[3]	22.8
1926	136.2	.9	4.0	4.1	31.3	39.9	10.3	12.8	11.1	21.9
1925	122.8	.8	3.5	3.4	26.8	34.5	9.6	12.4	10.7	21.2
1921	91.1	.8	3.3	2.7	21.0	21.9	7.4	9.5	8.0	16.6
1913	46.4	.5	1.7	1.4	8.7	9.4	4.1	6.1[2]	4.4	10.2

[1] Fiscal years ending nearest the end of the year given: for fiscal years and fiscal year changes of the provinces see the general note to this section.

[2] Fourteen-month period.

[3] Fifteen-month period.

Series H458-465. Unemployment Insurance account, 1942 to 1976
(millions of dollars)

Year[1]	Receipts				Disbursements			
	Employer and employee premiums	Government share	Other[2]	Total	Net benefit paid	Interest paid	Administration expenses	Total
	458	459	460	461	462	463	464	465
1976	2,476	1,327	2	3,805	3,342	8	207	3,557
1975	1,953	1,683	1	3,638	3,144	14	192	3,350
1974	1,545	852	1	2,398	2,119	27	163	2,310
1973	928	897	2	1,826	2,004	17	141	2,162
1972	711	892	3	1,606	1,872	4	122	1,998
1971[3]	407	81	14	502	590	—[4]	—[4]	590
1971	495	99	29	624	758	—	—	758
1970	492	98	28	618	542	—	—	542
1969	433	87	19	539	459	—	—	459
1968	347	69	16	433	389	—	—	389
1967	344	69	11	424	307	—	—	307
1966	328	66	5	399	298	—	—	298
1965	311	62	2	375	335	—	—	335
1964	297	59	1	357	366	—	—	366
1963	286	57	3	346	403	—	—	403
1962	278	56	3	337	455	—	—	455
1961	275	55	2	333	514	—	—	514
1960	229	46	7	281	415	—	—	415
1959	185	37	12	234	479	—	—	479
1958	192	38	24	255	385	—	—	385
1957	188	38	26	252	231	—	—	231
1956	170	34	25	229	215	—	—	215
1955	159	32	26	217	258	—	—	258
1954	159	32	26	217	187	—	—	187
1953	155	31	23	209	136	—	—	136
1952	154	31	19	204	90	—	—	90
1951	129	28	16	172	90	—	—	90
1950	104	20	14	139	86	—	—	86
1949	99	21	12	132	50	—	—	50
1948	84	16	10	110	35	—	—	35
1947	76	15	8	99	43	—	—	43
1946	63	13	6	81	32	—	—	32
1945	64	13	6	83	5	—	—	5
1944	62	12	4	78	2	—	—	2
1943	57	11	2	71	1	—	—	1
1942	36	7	—	44	—	—	—	—

[1] Calendar year from 1976 to 1972, fiscal year ended nearest 31 December 1971 to 1942.

[2] Includes interest on investments, profit or loss on sale of securities less interest paid on loans.

[3] April to December, 1971.

[4] Data on interest paid and administration expenses not available prior to 1972.

Series H466-473. Revenue and expenditure of Canada and Quebec pension plans, 1965 to 1975
(millions of dollars)

Year[1]	Canada Pension Plan				Quebec Pension Plan			
	Revenue			Total expenditure[2]	Revenue			Total expenditure[2]
	Contributions	Interest	Total		Contributions	Interest	Total	
	466	**467**	**468**	**469**	**470**	**471**	**472**	**473**
1975	1,489	640	2,129	622	535	272	807	232
1974	1,239	519	1,758	429	407	219	626	163
1973	1,019	424	1,443	303	370	171	541	134
1972	897	346	1,243	229	336	141	477	79
1971	826	275	1,101	166	301	110	411	55
1970	813	211	1,024	112	275	86	361	39
1969	746	144	890	65	265	61	326	26
1968	698	87	785	30	248	39	287	14
1967	641	44	685	13	232	22	254	8
1966	588	12	600	8	205	8	213	5
1965	95	—	95	5	—	—	—	—

[1] Fiscal year nearest calendar year shown.

[2] Benefit payments plus expenses, net of small refunds.

Series H474–493. Federal government transfers to provinces and territories, 1947 to 1975
(millions of dollars)

Year[1]	Unconditional transfers							Conditional transfers									Total cash transfers	Tax abatements		
	Compensation for occupancy of tax fields[2]	Transfer of tax revenues[3]	Equalization and stabilization	Established programs[4]	Statutory subsidies[5]	Other unconditional transfers[6]	Total unconditional transfers	Agriculture	Health	Medicare	Welfare	Transportation and communication	Education	Resources development	Other	Total conditional transfers[7]	Total cash transfers	General[8]	Post-secondary education	Quebec contracting out
	474	475	476	477	478	479	480	481	482	483	484	485	486	487	488	489	490	491	492	493
1975	—	46	1,956	204	34	574	2,814	136	1,736	796	1,027	68	663	32	282	4,740	7,554	—[9]	855	914
1974	—	155	1,795	176	34	577	2,737	119	1,354	763	739	40	607	14	192	3,828	6,566	—[9]	708	743
1973	—	172	1,500	154	34	102	1,962	108	1,107	678	529	47	584	21	120	3,194	5,155	—[9]	581	620
1972	—	92	1,177	198	34	118	1,619	90	1,006	631	493	40	559	14	87	2,920	4,539	—[9]	445	498
1971	—	90	1,050	249	34	97	1,520	76	893	576	473	34	610	10	90	2,762	4,282	3,119	398	404
1970	—	84	899	185	32	33	1,237	58	789	401	409	45	568	24	161	2,455	3,692	2,678	341	379
1969	—	84	682	142	32	42	982	54	742	181	309	51	401	17	13	1,768	2,750	2,439	307	330
1968	—	80	565	170	32	30	877	30	640	33	298	60	388	16	6	1,471	2,348	2,016	247	273
1967	—	62	548	134	32	30	806	23	547	—	284	93	315	26	19	1,307	2,113	1,723	228	252
1966	—	54	335	54	32	47	522	28	450	—	232	105	239	12	40	1,106	1,628	1,340	—	201
1965	—	49	274	77	32	42	474	21	421	—	210	99	161	21	10	943	1,417	1,137	—	157
1964	—	51	227	10	32	40	360	10	491	—	183	87	107	30	39	947	1,307	909	—	—
1963	—	20	167	—	32	40	259	6	446	—	173	52	137	23	26	863	1,122	783	—	—
1962	9	27	173	—	32	40	279	5	388	—	160	44	208	16	28	849	1,128	676	—	—
1961	313	6	168	—	32	25	544	5	332	—	144	41	36	22	26	606	1,150	327	—	—
1960	289	4	192	—	29	25	539	4	237	—	103	54	9	18	11	436	975	—	—	—
1959	280	5	181	—	29	25	520	7	197	—	91	56	8	15	9	383	903	—	—	—
1958	249	9	149	—	35	26	468	2	101	—	74	54	8	9	—	248	716	—	—	—
1957	214	7	140	—	22	1	384	1	35	—	48	51	5	5	1	145	529	—	—	—
1956	366	7	—	—	23	—	396	1	36	—	38	27	5	3	1	111	507	—	—	—
1955	320	8	—	—	23	1	352	1	34	—	30	17	4	3	—	89	441	—	—	—
1954	327	7	—	—	24	1	359	1	32	—	24	19	4	2	1	83	442	—	—	—
1953	309	7	—	—	25	—	341	1	30	—	23	14	4	3	—	75	416	—	—	—
1952	309	4	—	—	26	—	339	1	27	—	22	13	5	2	1	71	410	—	—	—
1951	97	4	—	—	26	—	127	—	25	—	85	14	4	—	1	130	257	—	—	—
1950	94	5	—	—	25	—	124	2	19	—	104	7	4	—	14	150	274	—	—	—
1949	77	1	—	—	26	—	104	3	13	—	91	—	5	4	—	116	220	—	—	—
1948	85	—	—	—	17	—	102	—	—	—	67	—	—	—	22	89	191	—	—	—
1947	60	—	—	—	17	—	77	—	—	—	59	—	—	—	11	70	147	—	—	—

1 Fiscal year nearest 31 December of year shown.
2 Compensation to provinces under Tax Rental Agreements Act.
3 Comprised of provincial share of income tax on power utilities, federal estate tax, oil export tax and tax on 1971 undistributed income on hand.
4 Beginning in 1965, Quebec accepted the federal offer to assume financial responsibility for certain tax joint programs (hospital insurance and diagnostic services, special welfare programs and youth allowances) in exchange for personal income tax points. Those cash transfers represent adjustment payments which are the difference between the federal share of the costs of these programs and the value of the tax points. The value of the tax points are given under tax abatements.
5 Includes subsidies under the British North America Act and Newfoundland additional grants.
6 Includes Atlantic provinces adjustment grant, tax revenue guarantee payments, payments to the territories and other.

7 Excludes value of tax points and cash compensation payments to Quebec for established programs and also excludes value of tax abatements to provinces for financing of post-secondary education. Total federal conditional transfers can be calculated by adding established programs, conditional transfers and the tax abatements for post-secondary education and Quebec opting-out.
8 In 1962 tax rentals were replaced by a system of tax collections agreements in which the federal government abated tax points and agreed to collect provincial taxes at rates specified by the provinces. All provinces but Quebec participated.
9 In 1972 the abatement system was discontinued and now provincial taxes are expressed as a direct percentage of federal basic tax. Provincial taxes at the new standard rate of 30.5 per cent of federal basic tax and 10 per cent of corporate taxable income would amount to: (millions of dollars) 1975, $6,544; 1974, $5,372; 1973, $4,411; 1972, $3,528. This general abatement includes the post-secondary tax abatement in the adjoining column.

Section J: Banking and Finance

John Chant, *Carleton University*

The data of this section are presented in six groups as follows: the supply of money, series J1-54; central banking, series J55-74; chartered banking, series J75-272; other financial institutions, series J273-470; issues of stocks and bonds, yields and exchange rates, series J471-567; and year-end financial assets and liabilities according to the financial flow accounts, series J568-875.

The main sources of data, in addition to those mentioned in the first edition of this volume, are as follows. *Bank of Canada Review,* monthly, December 1971 to September 1978. (All table numbers cited below are those appearing in the September 1978 issue of the *Review.*) Bank of Canada, *Statistical Summary* (last issue November, 1971) and its annual *Supplement.* Statistics Canada, *Financial Institutions,* (Catalogue 61-006), Statistics Canada, *Financial Flow Accounts, Volume* II, *Annual Flows and Year-end Financial Assets and Liabilities, 1961-1976,* (Catalogue 13-563); Toronto Stock Exchange, *Review,* December, 1977 and earlier issues; Master of the Mint, *Annual Reports of the Royal Canadian Mint.*

Additional sources are mentioned in the notes to individual tables below. Most important of these is a large number of special tabulations provided by the Bank of Canada, Department of Banking and Financial Analysis, and by Statistics Canada, Business Finance Division and Financial Flows and Multinational Enterprises Division.

The main purpose of the present volume, like its predecessor, is to provide long annual series for purposes of historical and trend analysis as opposed to analysis of current events. As a result, annual averages of month-end series are typically used rather than the weekly series (average of Wednesdays) presented by the Bank of Canada. However, both weekly and month-end series are given in certain cases such as money supply and chartered bank assets and liabilities, because the classifications available differ between weekly and monthly data and it was felt useful to present both.

This volume contains a number of new series which have become available since 1960, the close-off date of the first edition. For the area of banking, the 1967 revision of the Bank Act was responsible for a number of improvements in availability of data. Nevertheless, some of the newer classifications are too detailed to put into the present volume, for reasons of space. Thus neither the chartered banks' general loans by class of borrower, by size and by industry nor the more recent loan data on a provincial basis have been included. On the liability side, deposits by size and other, newer classifications also have not been included. Most important, an annual set of data such as the present one cannot hope to do justice to the data on various reserve ratios. Much of the central bank's work is conducted on a daily and weekly basis and is reflected in weekly statistics. Annual averages of such data would not be very useful and they are accordingly omitted below. Users of such data are better served by the weekly and monthly publications of the Bank of Canada in any case.

The Supply of Money (Series J1-54)

General note

The first edition included a number of series in an attempt to compile information on the supply of money and on Canada's coinage. Since that time, much more attention has been directed to various concepts of money supply for analytical purposes. Any definition of money necessarily involves a degree of arbitrary judgment. For purposes of continuity, it has been decided to present, as in the first edition, a series of money defined as chartered bank deposits and notes and coin held outside the chartered banks. In addition, rather than presenting just a single concept of the money supply, it seemed useful to present a variety of different money supply series over recent years, according to their availability. See series J21-26 below.

J1-10. Currency and chartered bank deposits, 1913 to 1977

SOURCE: this table is an update of series H1-10 in the first edition. The data since 1960 are from the *Bank of Canada Review,* tables 3, 8 and 14.

Footnote 2 to series J4-7 refers to changes in definition of chartered bank deposits between 1935 and 1945 and in 1957. The original text, page 233, explains that the series contained foreign currency deposits in certain years and that 'other deposits' were obtained residually, by subtracting personal savings and Government of Canada deposits from total deposits less float. The original text states that 'further statistical refinements in the treatment of float and in reporting foreign currency deposits were made in 1954. Series H4-7 and series H10 for the years 1945 to 1960 reflect these changes and, as far as the estimates permit, are consistent over those years. The exception to this is series H4 which was revised in 1957 to exclude certain business and institutional deposits which, amounting to $140 million, were transferred to series H6 at that time'.

J11-20. Notes and coin held by banks and general public and chartered bank Canadian deposit liabilities, 1913 to 1977

SOURCE: see the first edition, page 223. The updates of the series described in the first edition were provided by the Department of Banking and Financial Analysis, Bank of Canada.

The first edition stated that these series were of inferior quality, but were included because they extended back to 1867. In the present edition, the series have been cut off at 1913 in order to save space. Series J20 differs from series J7 only in that the former includes float.

J21-26. Monetary aggregates, 1946 to 1977

SOURCE: *Bank of Canada Review,* table 14. The table includes the set of measures provided at the present time by the Bank of Canada. Measures which may be viewed by some to be useful undoubtedly have beem omitted. Moreover prevailing views may change over time with respect to the most useful measures of the money supply. Nevertheless the variety of measures presented by the bank provides a good representation of the different measures that may be used.

In describing these series, the Bank of Canada states that currency and chartered bank deposits have been combined in this table to show alternative measures of the monetary aggregates. All the series are net of float. Government of Canada deposits with the chartered banks are excluded from all the series. The data relate to averages of Wednesdays and to Wednesdays except for the series on coin held outside banks, which relates to the end of month figure for the previous month. Data for 'M1' and for currency and total Canadian dollar privately held bank deposits of residents are available on a weekly basis from January 1953, for 'M1B' from January 1967, for 'M2' from January 1968 and for 'M3' from January 1970.

'Currency outside banks' comprises Bank of Canada notes and coin in circulation. Holdings of notes are calculated by subtracting the amount held by the chartered banks from the total amount of notes outstanding. The amount of coin in circulation outside banks is obtained by subtracting coin held by the chartered banks and the Bank of Canada from the total amount outstanding as reported by the Royal Canadian Mint.

'Demand deposits' and the demand deposit component in each of the series are Canadian dollar deposits at chartered banks, net of estimated private sector float.

'M1' includes currency outside banks and demand deposits.

'M1B' includes currency outside banks, demand deposits, personal and non-personal chequable Canadian dollar deposits at chartered banks.

'M2' includes in addition to 'M1B', Canadian dollar personal non-chequable and fixed term deposits, and non-personal non-chequable notice deposits at chartered banks.

'M3' includes in addition to 'M2', Canadian dollar non-personal fixed term deposits and bearer term notes plus all foreign currency deposits of Canadian residents booked at chartered banks in Canada.

'Currency plus total Canadian dollar privately held bank deposits' corresponds to the series previously defined as currency and privately held deposits. It differs from 'M3' by the exclusion of foreign currency deposits of Canadian residents booked at chartered banks in Canada.

J27-32. Canadian coin minted, 1913 to 1976

SOURCE: Royal Canadian Mint, *Annual Reports*.

The first edition (series H21-26) contains the same series back to 1870. These series have simply been updated in the present edition.

J33-41. Gold received and coinage issued by the mint, 1913 to 1976

SOURCE: same as series J27-32.

See notes to series H27-35 in the first edition, where these series were extended back to 1901. The original series have simply been updated in the present edition.

J42-54. Canadian coin in circulation, coin withdrawn and net increase in circulation, 1960 to 1976

SOURCE: same as series J27-32.

This is a new table, designed to show the coin in circulation, coin withdrawn and net increase in circulation. There is of course a substantial disappearance of coinage due to destruction, loss or other causes, in addition to that which is withdrawn officially.

Central Banking (Series J55-74)

Data on the Bank of Canada are available on a month-end basis from the commencement of operations in March 1935 and on a weekly basis from 1954. In keeping with the purpose as stated in the introduction, only the month-end data are presented here. The month-end data, in addition, have the advantage of a more useful breakdown of the maturities of governement securities held by the bank. Bank of Canada profits are published in the *Annual Report of the Governor to the Minister of Finance*.

J55-74. Bank of Canada, assets and liabilities, 1935 to 1977

SOURCE: *Bank of Canada Review*, table 3. These are month-end series as at the end of December each year from 1935, the first year of the bank's operation, to 1977. The definitions of the individual series are given in the notes to table 3, at page S-139 of the *Review* (September, 1978).

For those wishing to use the weekly series (average of Wednesdays), which commenced in 1954, these data are available in table 4 of the *Review*.

Chartered Banking (Series J75-272)

The initial volume of *Historical Statistics of Canada* introduces chartered banking as follows:

"The statistical record of chartered banking in Canada has been shaped materially by the decennial revision of the Bank Act. This periodic revision permitted the authorities to request statistical information of the banks on specific areas of interest at various times in banking history; it permitted the trend toward more detailed banking statistics to proceed relatively smoothly; and it permitted banking statistics to be classified in a way which improved their usefulness in economic analysis. But as a consequence of these frequent changes it is difficult to construct consistent series of banking statistics over a long period of time. This is particularly the case with statistics of bank assets, and somewhat less so with those of bank liabilities and explains the decision made to show bank assets in a number of tables, each table reflecting changes in certain asset components from the table which preceded it.

Most of the statistics for the period preceding 1929 were compiled from C.A. Curtis, *Statistical Contribution to Canadian Economic History*, vol. I, 'Statistics of Banking', which volume remains the most comprehensive and convenient source of detailed banking statistics for that period. Readers are also referred to that volume for detailed discussion of historical banking statistics in general, and of particular series as well, full details of which cannot be given here. In addition the monthly return of the banks to the Department of Finance, appearing in the *Canada Gazette*, was frequently resorted to; it constitutes the primary source of statistics for the Curtis volume. Since 1935 the Bank of Canada, *Statistical Summary* and *Supplements*, have proved most helpful for this study; in addition, they show weekly and monthly statistics of chartered bank assets and liabilities."

The data supplied in the *Statistical Summary*, together with many new series, are mentioned in the *Bank of Canada Review*.

We show both (a) the monthly series back to 1913 and (b) the weekly series back to 1953. Both series are included primarily because of differences in the categories presented.

J75-106. Chartered bank assets, 1945 to 1977

SOURCE: *Bank of Canada Review*, table 7 and first edition of this volume, p. 225.

This is the month-end series for December of each year. Definitions of individual series are given in the notes to tables 5 to 8 in the *Review* (p. S-139). These notes cover both weekly and monthly classifications of the data which appear in the following group of tables on chartered bank assets and liabilities.

Following the 1967 revision of the Bank Act, the chartered banks began recording, as at the end of each financial year, accumulated appropriation for losses on the liability side of the balance sheet rather than on the asset side as deductions from loans and other assets. This change affected the series from 31 October 1967. In January 1970 a change was made in the classification of chartered banks holdings of short-term paper. Previously, a bank's holding of short-term paper issued by customers with established lines of credit were classified as loans. Short-term paper is now classified as a loan only if it is purchased directly from an issuer at time of issue. Paper purchased from third parties subsequent to issue is now classified as a security. In December 1970 foreign assets were redefined to include chartered banks holdings of foreign pay securities issued by Canadian borrowers; previously these securities had been included with Canadian securities. In addition, investments by the banks in controlled corporations abroad were included with foreign assets. The items affected have been revised back to August 1967. Thus a break in series occurs here.

J107-132, J133-156 and J157-180. Chartered bank assets, 1913 to 1944

It was necessary to divide the time period 1913 to 1944 into three parts because the classification of assets changed from period to period. In contrast, the liabilities which follow have a classification which is continuous from 1913 to 1977.

J181-201. Chartered bank liabilities and cash ratio, 1913 to 1977

SOURCE: *Bank of Canada Review*, table 8, and first edition of this volume, p. 226.

As noted above, this is the chartered bank monthly series. The weekly series are given below.

J202-208. Chartered bank assets, weekly series, 1953 to 1977

SOURCE: *Bank of Canada Review*, table 5.

These data are averages of Wednesdays in December of each year. The classifications are identical to those given in the *Review*.

J229-250. Chartered bank liabilities, weekly series, 1946 to 1977

SOURCE: *Bank of Canada Review*, table 6.

See notes above.

J251-260. Chartered banks, total foreign currency assets and liabilities, 1946 to 1977

SOURCE: *Bank of Canada Review*, table 15.

These are month-end series for December of each year. They are required to complement the above tables on the monthly series on money supply and chartered bank assets and liabilities.

J261-272. Chartered banks earnings, net income, taxes and dividends, 1929 to 1977

SOURCE: *Bank of Canada Review*, table A4, published annually in February issue of the *Review*.

Other Financial Institutions (Series J273-470)

J273-309. Trust companies, 1961 to 1976

SOURCE: Statistics Canada, *Financial Institutions*, (Catalogue 61-006), quarterly, and special tabulations provided by the Business Finance Division, Statistics Canada.

Complete notes on definitions, sources and methods are provided in the introduction to the above publication. These are new series beginning in 1961. The older data from 1914 to 1959 are given in series H503-648 in the first edition of this volume. The classifications used in the older series are quite different from those now in use.

J310-350. Mortgage companies, 1963 to 1976

SOURCE: same as series J273-309.

J351-368. Local credit unions, 1967 to 1976

SOURCE: same as series J273-309.

J369-384. Central credit unions, 1967 to 1976

SOURCE: same as series J273-309.

J385-408. Sales finance and consumer loan companies, 1960 to 1976

SOURCE: same as series J273-309.

J409-427. Investment funds, 1963 to 1976

SOURCE: same as series J273-309.

J428-446.   Life insurance, 1959 to 1976

SOURCE: special tabulations prepared in Business Finance Division, Statistics Canada.

These series were assembled from the annual reports of the federal Department of Insurance which covered all federally registered companies and societies and from the annual reports of the Superintendent of Insurance for Ontario which provided data for all large provincial companies and societies. This approach means that some provincial companies and societies which do not operate in Ontario were missed, but this omission should not have a significant impact on the figures. In the case of the federal companies, *Financial Flow Accounts, Volume* II, was used. While this book splits out the out-of-Canada asset data, it does not provide any out-of-Canada data on liabilities; however, reference to the quarterly survey for 1976 and 1977 shows that out-of-Canada liabilities are just under 90 per cent of out-of-Canada assets. The out-of-Canada business of provincial companies is small and since it was not readily available, it was ignored.

In respect of share capital and contributed surplus, the share capital only was available from federal companies, contributed surplus was not shown. In the summary reports on provincial companies no share capital and contributed surplus data were available. Consequently, share capital, contributed surplus, retained earnings and head office accounts (of British and foreign companies and societies) have been combined under the term 'Equity'.

A number of series on Canadian, British and foreign life insurance companies, from 1888 to 1959, are given in the first edition of this volume (series H373-408).

J447-470.   Property and casualty insurance companies, 1966 to 1976

SOURCE: same as series J273-309.

Bond and Stock Yields, Net New Issues of Securities and Foreign Exchange Rates (Series J471-567)

J471-480.   Bond and stock yields, annual averages, 1934 to 1977

SOURCE: *Bank of Canada Review,* table 20 (for bond yields), table 37 (for stock dividend yields).

See also the footnotes to series J471-480.

J481-494.   Indexes of common stock prices, 1914 to 1977

SOURCE: Toronto Stock Exchange, *Monthly Reports,* December, 1935 to December 1977, and TSE *300 Index of Stock Prices and Supplements.*

The classification from 1956 to 1977 contains more groups than that from 1914 to 1956. Hence the table is shown in two parts. The data in the older part are simply reproduced from the first edition of this volume. See also the footnotes to series J481-494.

J495-518.   Gross and net new issues of securities, 1936 to 1976

SOURCE: *Bank of Canada Review,* tables 29 and 30, from 1970 to 1978. Earlier data from Bank of Canada *Statistical Summary* and its former annual *Supplement.*

J519-534.   Summary of total bonds outstanding, 1935 to 1976

SOURCE: Bank of Canada, Department of Banking and Financial Analysis.

J535-551.   Net new security issues by type of security, 1936 to 1977

SOURCE: same as series J519-534.

J552-559.   Net new security issues payable in foreign currencies, 1936 to 1977

SOURCE: same as series J519-534.

J560-567.   Foreign exchange rates, 1913 to 1977

SOURCE: *Bank of Canada Review,* table 65.

These are annual averages of daily noon spot rates on the inter-bank market. British currency exchange rate is based on nominal quotations in terms of U.S. dollars converted to Canadian dollars.

Year-end Financial Assets and Liabilities According to the Financial Flow Accounts (Series J568-875)

The tables which follow are taken from Statistics Canada, *Financial Flow Accounts, Volume* II, *1961-1976,* (Catalogue 13-563). There are two tables for each sector, the year-end outstandings and the financial flows during the year. The flows are not the exact difference between any two adjacent year-end outstandings because of revaluations of assets, adjustments of liabilities, changes in corporate structure and other causes. However, both sets of data come from the same basic questionnaires of the Financial Flows Division. Explanatory notes may be found in the introduction to the above publication, and in an article in the *Canadian Statistical Review,* July 1976.

Both the sectors and the categories have been condensed herein to show the main headings only. The sectors are as follows: I and II: Persons and unincorporated business; III: Non-financial private corporations; IV: Non-financial government enterprises; V: The monetary authorities; VI: Banks and near-banks; VII: Insurance companies and pension funds; VIII: Other private financial institutions; IX: Public financial institutions; X: Federal government; XI: Provincial and local governments and hospitals; XII: Social security funds; and XIII: Rest of the world.

The main categories of assets and liabilities will be found in the column headings of the tables and are broadly similar from sector to sector.

The relationship between the national accounts figures on saving and non-financial investment and the flow-of-funds data on changes in financial assets and liabilities is shown in the first four columns of each flow table. The 'statistical discrepancy' between the above two sets of data is shown in the fifth column of each flow table.

Series J1-10. Currency and chartered bank deposits, 1913 to 1977
(millions of dollars)

Year[1] end	Currency outside banks			Chartered bank deposits (less float)				Total		Float
	Notes	Coin	Total	Personal savings	Government of Canada	Other (less float)	Total (less float)	Including Government of Canada	Excluding Government of Canada	
	1	2	3	4	5	6	7	8	9	10
1977	7,268	826	8,094	44,948	4,733	36,579	86,259	94,353	89,618	2,411
1976	6,573	760	7,333	40,478	3,103	31,880	75,461	82,794	79,691	1,350
1975	6,079	708	6,787	33,237	3,663	27,359	64,259	71,046	67,383	2,614
1974	5,213	656	5,868	29,789	4,682	21,784	56,255	62,124	57,442	2,542
1973	4,620	589	5,209	24,604	2,361	19,220	46,186	51,395	49,034	2,379
1972	4,056	518	4,574	19,949	2,407	16,892	39,248	43,822	41,415	1,480
1971	3,506	488	3,993	17,783	2,239	14,572	34,594	38,587	36,348	1,017
1970	3,106	461	3,568	16,615	1,257	10,972	28,845	32,412	31,155	1,044
1969	2,903	434	3,337	15,030	1,308	9,540	25,877	29,214	27,906	1,459
1968	2,660	399	3,060	13,622	669	10,507	24,798	27,858	27,188	1,582
1967	2,494	335	2,829	11,760	618	9,096	21,473	24,302	23,685	1,190
1966	2,296	293	2,589	10,248	919	7,741	18,908	21,497	20,578	1,108
1965	2,153	266	2,419	9,725	797	7,201	17,723	20,142	19,345	871
1964	2,025	229	2,254	8,935	696	6,164	15,795	18,049	17,353	902
1963	1,886	198	2,084	8,443	914	5,623	14,980	17,064	16,150	1,119
1962	1,817	177	1,994	7,932	564	5,193	13,689	15,683	15,119	1,010
1961	1,800	158	1,959	7,618	588	4,998	13,205	15,163	14,575	981
1960	1,732	144	1,876	7,215	510	4,313	12,037	13,914	13,404	884
1959	1,705	128	1,832	6,900	404	4,057	11,360	13,193	12,789	919
1958	1,660	121	1,781	6,844	319	4,303	11,466	13,247	12,927	1,224
1957	1,555	112	1,667	6,108[2]	423	3,725[2]	10,256	11,923	11,500	1,151
1956	1,498	108	1,605	6,007	246	3,580	9,833	11,438	11,192	1,330
1955	1,449	101	1,550	5,633	517	3,697	9,847	11,397	10,880	1,002
1954	1,362	96	1,458	5,218	176	3,462	8,856	10,314	10,137	827
1953	1,335	94	1,430	4,756	473	3,130	8,359	9,789	9,316	752
1952	1,289	88	1,377	4,600	49	3,281	7,930	9,307	9,258	706
1951	1,191	84	1,275	4,296	88	3,100	7,484	8,759	8,671	489
1950	1,136	78	1,214	4,176	257	3,116	7,549	8,763	8,506	430
1949	1,110	74	1,184	4,086	164	2,776	7,026	8,210	8,046	291
1948	1,115	70	1,185	3,752	236	2,725	6,713	7,898	7,662	359
1947	1,046	66	1,112	3,453	216	2,455	6,124	7,236	7,020	322
1946	1,031	65	1,096	3,179	281	2,482	5,942	7,038	6,757	298
1945	992	63	1,055	2,635	846[2]	2,186[2]	5,667[2]	6,722[2]	5,878[2]	275[2]
1944	930	60	990	2,173	707	2,022	4,902	5,892	5,185	243
1943	794	55	849	1,698	577	1,815	4,090	4,939	4,362	266
1942	633	49	681	1,423	314	1,660	3,397	4,078	3,764	210
1941	450	42	492	1,474	74	1,362	2,910	3,402	3,328	198
1940	341	38	379	1,451	21	1,161	2,633	3,012	2,991	172
1939	247	34	281	1,551	99	1,064	2,714	2,995	2,896	136
1938	207	31	238	1,660	64	658	2,382	2,620	2,556	116
1937	207	30	237	1,583[2]	13[2]	661[2]	2,257[2]	2,494[2]	2,481[2]	130
1936	191	29	220	1,548	25	622	2,195	2,415	2,390	128
1935	170	28	198	1,486	12	591[2]	2,089[2]	2,287[2]	2,275[2]	120
1934	157	27	184	1,407	24	517	1,948	2,132	2,108	102
1933	151	26	177	1,357	33	457	1,847	2,024	1,991	86
1932	144	27	171	1,378	53	417	1,848	2,019	1,966	80
1931	160	27	187	1,360	111	496	1,967	2,154	2,043	102
1930	163	25	188	1,426	27	548	2,001	2,189	2,162	127
1929	187	26	213	1,434	60	624	2,118	2,331	2,271	152
1928	193	25	218	1,520	46	582	2,148	2,366	2,320	167
1927	192	24	216	1,445	43	581	2,068	2,284	2,241	136
1926	190	23	213	1,373	16	512	1,901	2,114	2,098	124
1925	176	23	199	1,319	22	502	1,843	2,042	2,020	130
1924	177	23	200	1,238	25	498	1,761	1,961	1,936	151
1923	187	23	210	1,180	38	484	1,702	1,912	1,874	133
1922	184	23	207	1,185	19	464	1,668	1,875	1,856	117
1921	191	23	214	1,241	34	471	1,746	1,960	1,926	109
1920	235	23	258	1,293	10	540	1,843	2,101	2,091	150
1919	237	22	259	1,138	121	590	1,849	2,108	1,987	146
1918	229	21	250	958	148	620	1,726	1,976	1,828	116
1917	200	19	219	996	18	501	1,515	1,734	1,716	96
1916	157	17	174	845	18	408	1,271	1,445	1,427	77
1915	131	16	147	721	26	397	1,144	1,291	1,265	64
1914	113	16	129	663	11	329	1,003	1,132	1,121	49
1913	117	15	132	625	9	351	985	1,117	1,108	61

[1] Monthly series for end of December each year.   [2] Change in definition. See text.

Series J11-20. Notes and coin held by banks and general public and chartered bank Canadian deposit liabilities, 1913 to 1977

(millions of dollars)

Year[1] end	Subsidiary coin issue			Dominion or Bank of Canada note issue			Chartered bank note issue			Canadian deposits of the chartered banks
	Held by banks	Held by others	Total	Held by banks	Held by others	Total	Held by banks	Held by others	Total	
	11	12	13	14	15	16	17	18	19	20
1977	53	826	879	1,371	7,268	8,639	–	–	–	88,670
1976	66	760	826	1,240	6,573	7,813	–	–	–	76,773
1975	69	708	778	1,204	6,079	7,283	–	–	–	66,873
1974	54	656	709	1,078	5,213	6,290	–	–	–	58,797
1973	34	589	623	931	4,620	5,551	–	–	–	48,565
1972	42	518	560	750	4,056	4,806	–	–	–	40,728
1971	42	488	529	598	3,506	4,103	–	–	–	35,611
1970	43	461	505	526	3,106	3,632	–	–	–	29,888
1969	47	434	481	543	2,903	3,446	–	–	–	27,336
1968	36	399	436	569	2,660	3,229	–	–	–	26,379
1967	26	335	361	485	2,494	2,979	–	–	–	22,663
1966	34	293	328	438	2,296	2,734	–	–	–	20,016
1965	35	266	301	383	2,153	2,536	–	–	–	18,594
1964	32	229	261	355	2,025	2,381	–	–	–	16,697
1963	28	198	227	418	1,886	2,305	–	–	–	16,099
1962	27	177	204	417	1,817	2,234	–	–	–	14,699
1961	25	158	183	347	1,800	2,147	–	–	–	14,186
1960	25	144	169	330	1,732	2,062	–	–	–	12,921
1959	26	128	153	316	1,705	2,021	–	–	–	12,279
1958	23	121	144	338	1,660	1,998	–	–	–	12,690
1957	23	112	135	349	1,555	1,904	–	–	–	11,407
1956	19	108	127	371	1,498	1,869	–	–	–	11,162
1955	19	101	121	289	1,449	1,738	–	–	–	10,848
1954	19	96	116	262	1,362	1,624	–	–	–	9,683
1953	18	94	113	264	1,335	1,599	–	–	–	9,111
1952	18	88	106	273	1,289	1,561	–	–	–	8,636
1951	15	84	100	273	1,191	1,464	–	–	–	7,973
1950	14	78	93	231	1,136	1,367	–	–	–	7,979
1949	12	74	86	212	1,096	1,307	–	14	14	7,317
1948	11	70	81	191	1,098	1,289	–	16	16	7,072
1947	11	66	77	184	1,028	1,211	–	18	18	6,446
1946	11	65	76	177	1,009	1,186	–	21	21	6,240
1945	11	63	74	163	966	1,129	1	25	26	5,942
1944	9	60	69	139	897	1,036	1	33	34	5,145
1943	9	55	64	123	752	874	1	42	43	4,356
1942	5	49	54	121	573	694	2	60	62	3,608
1941	7	42	49	116	380	496	3	71	73	3,108
1940	7	38	45	98	262	360	4	80	84	2,805
1939	5	34	39	71	162	233	5	85	90	2,850
1938	5	31	36	57	118	175	6	88	95	2,498
1937	5	30	34	54	111	165	6	96	102	2,387
1936	5	29	34	48	88	136	6	103	109	2,323
1935	5	28	34	41	59	100	8	111	119	2,208
1934	7	27	34	183	33	217	13	123	136	2,050
1933	7	26	33	152	30	183	11	121	132	1,933
1932	7	27	33	162	29	191	12	115	127	1,928
1931	6	27	33	144	31	174	12	129	141	2,069
1930	7	25	32	146	30	175	15	133	148	2,128
1929	6	26	32	172	32	204	20	156	176	2,270
1928	6[2]	25[2]	31	192	30	222	23	163	186	2,315
1927	6[2]	24[2]	30	192	29	221	20	163	183	2,204
1926	7[2]	23[3]	30	180	31	210	16	159	175	2,025
1925	–	–	30	209	18	227	16	158	174	1,973
1924	–	–	30	233	28	262	17	149	166	1,912
1923	–	–	30	221	28	249	21	159	180	1,835
1922	–	–	30	230	27	257	–	–	176	1,784
1921	–	–	30	254	27	281	–	–	185	1,855
1920	–	–	30	279	32	312	–	–	229	1,993
1919	–	–	29	288	30	319	–	–	233	1,995
1918	–	–	26	298	29	327	–	–	225	1,842
1917	–	–	23	245	28	273	–	–	193	1,611
1916	–	–	21	157	25	181	–	–	149	1,348
1915	–	–	20	157	22	179	–	–	122	1,208
1914	–	–	20	143	19	162	–	–	106	1,052
1913	–	–	19	111	20	131	–	–	109	1,046

[1] Monthly series for end of December each year. [2] Estimated.

Series J21-26. Monetary aggregates, 1946 to 1977
(millions of dollars)

Year[1]	Currency outside banks	Currency and demand deposits (M1)	Currency and all chequable deposits (M1B)	Currency and all chequable notice and personal term deposits (M2)	Currency plus total privately held chartered bank deposits (M3)	Currency plus total Canadian dollar privately held chartered bank deposits
	21	22	23	24	25	26
1977	7,970	21,505	29,078	67,816	96,022	88,632
1976	7,241	19,266	26,344	60,794	84,853	78,169
1975	6,748	18,913	26,023	53,266	70,786	66,409
1974	5,791	15,376	21,834	45,819	61,634	56,591
1973	5,140	14,526	21,493	39,724	51,394	48,490
1972	4,438	13,053	19,695	33,769	42,524	41,049
1971	3,889	11,497	17,567	30,078	37,161	35,405
1970	3,483	9,797	15,394	26,990	34,043	30,835
1969	3,279	9,274	15,275	24,841	..	27,788
1968	2,988	8,961	15,950	23,048	..	26,819
1967	2,736	8,420	16,464	..	..	23,700
1966	2,491	7,783	..	..	..	20,403
1965	2,351	7,130	..	..	..	19,075
1964	2,183	6,693	..	..	..	17,033
1963	2,055	6,296	..	..	..	15,867
1962	1,981	6,077	..	..	..	14,908
1961	1,892	5,851	..	..	..	14,365
1960	1,816	5,499	..	..	..	13,218
1959	1,789	5,233	..	..	..	12,639
1958	1,756	5,420	..	..	..	12,834
1957	1,649	4,788	..	..	..	11,376
1956	1,589	4,761	..	..	..	11,164
1955	1,497	4,772	..	..	..	10,846
1954	1,424	4,439	..	..	..	9,990
1953	1,402	4,188	..	..	..	9,210
1952	1,381	..	..	..	..	9,224
1951	1,286	..	..	..	..	8,683
1950	1,206	..	..	..	..	8,507
1949	1,177	..	..	..	..	8,052
1948	1,178	..	..	..	..	7,680
1947	1,115	..	..	..	..	6,970
1946	1,102	..	..	..	..	6,739

[1] Weekly series, average of Wednesdays in December each year.

Series J27-32. Canadian coin minted, 1913 to 1976

(thousands)

Year	One cent pieces	Five cent pieces	Ten cent pieces	Twenty-five cent pieces	Fifty cent pieces	Silver dollars
	27	**28**	**29**	**30**	**31**	**32**
1976	701,122	55,140	95,018	86,898	2,940	2,498
1975	642,693	139,220	208,018	1,611,486	4,048	3,685
1974	692,058	94,704	201,566	192,360	3,436	2,799
1973	456,652	53,140	167,348	134,590	2,179	2,658
1972	451,304	62,417	60,169	43,743	2,515	2,676
1971	298,228	27,312	41,016	48,170	2,166	4,260
1970	311,145	5,726	5,249	10,302	2,429	4,140
1969	335,240	27,830	121,293[1]	133,037	2,139	5,007
1968	329,976	99,534	183,413[2]	160,431	4,247	6,245
1967	343,763	35,502	61,905	47,762	3,118	5,816
1966	182,970	27,004	33,657	24,716	7,010	9,239
1965	304,446	84,876	56,965	44,708	12,629	10,768
1964	484,655	78,075	49,518	36,479	9,377	7,296
1963	279,076	43,970	41,916	21,180	8,348	4,179
1962	227,244	46,307	41,864	29,559	5,208	1,884
1961	139,598	47,809	26,850	18,164	3,584	1,262
1960	75,772	37,157	45,446	22,835	3,488	1,420
1959	83,615	11,552	19,691	13,503	3,095	1,443
1958	59,385	7,607	10,621	9,336	2,957	3,039
1957	100,601	7,387	16,110	12,770	2,171	496
1956	78,685	9,399	16,732	11,209	1,379	209
1955	56,403	5,355	12,237	9,552	753	268
1954	21,891	6,998	4,493	2,318	506	246
1953	67,806	16,635	17,706	10,456	1,630	1,074
1952	67,631	10,891	10,474	8,864	2,597	411
1951	80,430	12,642	15,079	8,285	2,421	411
1950	60,444	12,669	17,823	9,673	2,384	301
1949	33,128	13,037	11,336	7,988	858	631
1948	69,623	11,405	10,061	6,958	76	39
1947	31,093	7,603	4,431	1,524	424	65
1946	56,662	6,952	6,300	2,210	950	93
1945	77,268	18,893	10,979	5,296	1,959	38
1944	44,131	11,532	9,383	7,216	2,460	—
1943	89,111	24,760	21,143	13,559	3,109	—
1942	76,113	10,243	10,214	6,935	1,974	—
1941	56,336	8,681	8,716	6,654	1,714	—
1940	85,740	13,920	16,526	9,583	1,996	—
1939	21,600	5,661	5,501	3,532	287	1,363
1938	18,365	3,898	4,197	3,149	192	90
1937	10,719	4,593	2,691	2,843	192	241
1936	8,768	4,400	2,460	972	38	306
1935	7,529	3,891	384	537	—	428
1934	7,062	3,832	384	384	38	—
1933	12,079	2,597	672	421	—	—
1932	21,316	3,198	1,154	537	19	—
1931	3,842	5,100	2,067	537	57	—
1930	2,513	3,685	1,827	961	—	—
1929	12,164	5,562	3,259	2,691	228	—
1928	9,121	4,558	2,451	2,089	—	—
1927	3,553	5,285	—	468	—	—
1926	2,145	933	—	—	—	—
1925	1,000	200	—	—	—	—
1924	1,596	3,066	—	—	—	—
1923	1,019	2,475	—	—	—	—
1922	1,243	4,763	—	—	—	—
1921	7,555	2,501	2,458	575	176	—
1920	22,373	10,660	6,295	1,937	559	—
1919	11,201	8,105	7,868	5,844	1,085	—
1918	12,905	5,790	5,109	4,167	832	—
1917	11,917	5,625	4,995	3,202	739	—
1916	11,110	2,404	4,231	1,454	454	—
1915	4,836	1,153	672	238	—	—
1914	3,403	4,190	2,543	1,202	157	—
1913	5,733	5,581	3,591	2,186	263	—

[1] Included are 35,000,000 pieces produced by the U.S. mint.   [2] Included are 50,170,000 pieces produced by the U.S. mint.

Series J33-41. Gold received and coinage issued by the mint, 1913 to 1976

(series J33 and 34 in thousands of troy ounces; series J35-41 in thousands of dollars)

| Year | Gold received | Gold bullion issued | Coinage issued | | | | | | |
			Gold	Silver	Nickel	Steel	Tombac	Bronze	Total issued
	33	34	35	36	37	38	39	40	41
1976	1,633	1,665	1,000	64,134	41,404	–	–	6,437	1,111,975
1975	1,079	1,056	–	58,204	60,938	–	–	6,295	674,437
1974	1,280	1,337	–	60,382	78,208	–	–	6,941	125,437
1973	1,476	1,483	–	8,804	58,128	–	–	4,768	71,699
1972	1,931	1,895	–	350	26,006	–	–	4,199	30,555
1971	2,010	2,009	–	556	20,702	–	–	3,207	24,464
1970	2,114	2,150	–	–	41,741	–	–	3,089	23,791
1969	2,147	2,089	–	–	45,472	–	–	3,301	48,773
1968	2,237	2,222	2,867	26,167	2,944	–	–	3,150	35,128
1967	2,439	2,288	3,887	27,322	656	–	–	3,451	35,318
1966	2,676	2,631	–	23,722	26,460	–	–	2,141	52,323
1965	2,991	3,027	–	33,479	3,878	–	–	2,961	40,318
1964	3,189	3,174	–	26,153	3,896	–	–	4,627	34,676
1963	3,457	3,468	–	17,689	2,196	–	–	2,791	22,676
1962	3,489	3,520	–	16,114	2,324	–	–	2,285	20,723
1961	3,800	3,812	–	10,300	2,512	–	–	1,418	14,230
1960	4,025	4,015	–	13,432	1,736	–	–	748	15,916
1959	3,909	3,837	–	8,274	577	–	–	829	9,679
1958	3,958	4,089	–	8,045	380	–	–	578	9,003
1957	3,896	3,777	–	6,236	366	–	–	1,004	7,607
1956	3,802	3,775	–	5,389	470	–	–	787	6,646
1955	3,948	3,953	–	4,269	268	–	–	567	5,104
1954	3,829	3,999	–	1,865	–	350	–	264	2,479
1953	3,684	3,626	–	6,139	1	832	–	655	7,626
1952	3,953	4,031	–	4,870	1	577	–	684	6,131
1951	4,169	4,167	–	5,214	423	183	–	783	6,603
1950	4,423	4,348	–	5,642	641	–	–	607	6,889
1949	3,926	3,865	–	4,149	638	–	–	322	5,108
1948	3,402	3,405	–	2,830	616	–	–	708	4,154
1947	2,869	2,859	–	1,186	391	–	–	360	1,937
1946	2,652	2,666	–	1,701	292	–	–	529	2,521
1945	2,503	2,499	–	3,416	–	950	–	749	5,115
1944	2,862	2,830	–	4,006	–	571	–	455	5,032
1943	3,617	3,646	–	7,044	–	–	1,238	881	9,163
1942	4,612	4,612	–	3,764	362	–	169	784	5,079
1941	5,093	5,134	–	3,534	454	–	–	575	4,563
1940	4,991	5,027	–	4,845	661	–	–	823	6,328
1939	4,869	4,834	–	2,794	321	–	–	215	3,330
1938	4,398	4,308	–	1,376	154	–	–	184	1,714
1937	3,933	3,938	–	1,322	251	–	–	105	1,679
1936	3,603	3,626	–	809	203	–	–	87	1,099
1935	3,159	3,177	–	601	194	–	–	75	870
1934	3,009	3,038	–	172	193	–	–	70	435
1933	2,569	2,590	–	155	125	–	–	121	401
1932	2,830	2,873	–	287	165	–	–	213	665
1931	1,721	1,735	–	475	281	–	–	51	808
1930	862	722	–	326	165	–	–	13	504
1929	438	468	–	1,081	267	–	–	123	1,471
1928	1,325	1,305	–	867	250	–	–	92	1,209
1927	1,448	1,452	–	574	249	–	–	38	861
1926	1,376	1,348	–	50	169	–	–	28	247
1925	121	122	–	14	126	–	–	22	162
1924	111	108	–	–	75	–	–	12	86
1923	614	640	–	28	127	–	–	19	174
1922	1,087	1,086	–	24	69	–	–	12	105
1921	818	803	–	128	–	–	–	61	189
1920	558	567	–	1,356	–	–	–	209	1,565
1919	520	492	661	3,258	–	–	–	115	4,034
1918	239	167	518	2,402	–	–	–	132	3,052
1917	40	89	286	1,862	–	–	–	117	2,265
1916	–	–	30	1,180	–	–	–	111	1,320
1915	–	–	–	61	–	–	–	50	112
1914	–	–	1,572	626	–	–	–	35	2,233
1913	–	–	1,909	927	–	–	–	56	2,891

Series J42-54. Canadian coin in circulation, coin withdrawn and net increase in circulation, 1960 to 1976
(thousands of dollars)

Year	Coin in circulation					Coin withdrawn					Net increase in circulation		
	Silver	Nickel	Tombac	Steel	Bronze	Silver	Nickel	Tombac	Steel	Bronze	Silver	Nickel	Bronze
	42	43	44	45	46	47	48	49	50	51	52	53	54
1976	508,680	423,711	549	3,439	77,926	..	..	..	..	..	..	..	..
1975	444,548	382,334	549	3,439	71,490	5	38	—	1	3	58,199	60,900	6,297
1974	386,350	321,434	549	3,440	65,199	13	20	—	1	1	60,369	78,187	6,939
1973	325,981	243,246	549	3,441	58,259	93	23	—	2	2	8,711	58,105	4,765
1972	317,269	185,141	549	3,442	53,494	114	15	—	1	2	236	25,991	4,197
1971	317,033	159,151	549	3,443	49,297	132	16	—	1	1	423	21,261	3,206
1970	316,610	137,890	549	3,444	46,092	105	10	—	1	2	—	20,691	3,087
1969	316,715	117,199	549	3,444	43,004	122	6	—	1	1	—	41,735	3,299
1968	316,837	75,464	549	3,445	39,705	98	3	—	1	2	26,069	45,469	3,148
1967	290,767	29,994	549	3,446	36,557	112	2	—	1	1	27,210	2,942	345
1966	263,557	27,052	549	3,447	33,107	93	2	—	1	2	23,630	654	2,139
1965	239,927	26,398	549	3,448	30,968	104	2	—	1	2	33,375	3,876	2,959
1964	206,552	22,522	549	3,449	28,009	94	1	—	1	1	26,059	3,894	4,626
1963	180,493	18,628	549	3,449	23,384	124	2	—	1	2	17,564	2,195	2,788
1962	162,929	16,433	549	3,451	20,596	88	1	—	1	1	16,026	2,323	2,284
1961	146,902	14,110	549	3,452	18,312	108	1	—	1	2	10,191	2,511	1,416
1960	136,711	11,599	549	3,453	16,896	65	1	—	1	2	13,367	1,734	746

Series J55-74. Bank of Canada, assets and liabilities, 1935 to 1977
(millions of dollars)

Year end[1]	Government of Canada direct and guaranteed securities					Bankers' acceptances	Amount of foregoing held under purchase and resale agreements	Advances	Foreign currency assets[4]	Investment in I.D.B.[5]	All other accounts[6]	Total assets or liabilities
	Treasury bills[2]	Other maturities			Total							
		3 years and under[3]	Over 3 years[3]	Total								
	55	56	57	58	59	60	61	62	63	64	65	66
1977	2,418	3,468	4,339	7,807	10,225	14	—	41[9]	1,261	687	1,189	13,416
1976	2,086	2,917	3,383	6,300	8,386	105	89	23[9]	1,431	858	1,041	11,843
1975	2,081	2,804	2,923	5,727	7,809	44	14	—	1,093	1,030	521	10,496
1974	1,590	2,529	2,860	5,388	6,979	140	—	8[9]	578	965	515	9,184
1973	1,081	2,282	2,613	4,895	5,976	39	9	—	809	721	455	7,999
1972	932	2,053	2,422	4,475	5,407	—	—	2[9]	468	586	593	7,056
1971	885	1,770	2,161	3,930	4,816	1	—	2[9]	258	514	429	6,019
1970	621	1,703	1,918	3,620	4,241	—	7	—	195	470	500	5,405
1969	478	1,930	1,651	3,580	4,058	3	39	1[9]	161	403	263	4,888
1968	453	1,541	1,890	3,431	3,885	—	—	5[9]	107	354	285	4,636
1967	538	1,270	1,940	3,210	3,748	—	—	3[9]	102	315	244	4,412
1966	409	1,143	1,867	3,010	3,419	—	—	—	227	282	279	4,207
1965	608	816	1,993	2,809	3,417	—	—	—	42	240	257	3,956
1964	479	531	2,055	2,586	3,064	—	100	—	111	213	254	3,642
1963	466	754	1,815	2,570	3,035	—	45	—	64	184	162	3,445
1962	455	809	1,619	2,427	2,883	3	—	—	73	158	114	3,231
1961	312	749	1,764	2,514	2,826	—	2	—	70	115	232	3,243
1960	404	595	1,690	2,285	2,690	—	—	—	79	89	187	3,044
1959	306	515	1,800	2,315	2,621	—	—	—	60	84	204	2,968
1958	36	749	1,837	2,586	2,622	—	—	2[9]	94	78	149	2,944
1957	467	779	1,181	1,960	2,428	—	—	—	80	61	90	2,659
1956	505	520[3]	1,369[3]	1,889	2,394	—	—	—	78	48	28	2,548
1955	263	1,021	1,084	2,105	2,368	—	—	2[9]	115	35	101	2,620
1954	169	1,193	861	2,054	2,222	—	—	—	66	36	77	2,401
1953	375	1,002	894	1,896	2,270	—	19	—	67	36	64	2,437
1952	283	1,177	767	1,944	2,227	—	—	—	85	31	39	2,381
1951	186	955	1,049	2,005	2,191	—	—	—	204	28	21	2,444
1950	263	967	713	1,679	1,942	—	—	—	360	25	24	2,350
1949	244	1,538	228	1,766	2,009	—	—	—	80	25	12	2,126
1948	250	984	779	1,763	2,013	—	—	—	1	25	20	2,059
1947	254	768	859	1,627	1,881	—	—	—	2	25	19	1,926
1946	233	962	708	1,670	1,904	—	—	—	1	15	29	1,949
1945	181	973	688	1,662	1,842	—	—	—	157	10	23	2,032
1944	96	809	573	1,385	1,477	—	—	—	172	10	28	1,687
1943	84	699	473	1,176	1,256	—	—	—	1	—	51	1,308
1942	112	692	209	905	1,012	—	—	1[9]	1	—	34	1,048
1941	61	327	217	548	605	—	—	—	201	—	37	843
1940	110	335	127	466	572	—	—	—	38	—	16	627
1939	89	89	50	143	228	—	—	—	290	—	9	527
1938	65	76	41	120	182	—	—	—	214	—	9	405
1937	67	12	91	107	171	—	—	—	210	—	10	390
1936	44	15	99	117	157	—	—	—	191	—	9	357
1935	3	28	83	86	114	—	—	4[10]	186	—	4	308

Series J55-74. Bank of Canada, assets and liabilities, 1935 to 1977 (concluded)
(millions of dollars)

Year end[1]	Liabilities							
	Notes in circulation			Canadian dollar deposits			Foreign currency liabilities	All other accounts[7,8]
	Held by		Total	Government of Canada	Chartered banks	Other		
	Chartered banks	Others						
	67	68	69	70	71	72	73	74
1977	1,371	7,268	8,639	26	3,705	131	100	817
1976	1,240	6,573	7,813	33	3,169	124	56	649
1975	1,204	6,079	7,283	27	2,749	63	8	367
1974	1,078	5,213	6,291	17	2,361	101	2	413
1973	931	4,620	5,551	6	2,007	54	25	356
1972	751	4,056	4,806	27	1,698	52	58	415
1971	598	3,506	4,103	68	1,473	44	39	291
1970	526	3,106	3,632	228	1,176	38	33	298
1969	544	2,903	3,446	81	1,109	42	24	187
1968	569	2,660	3,229	47	1,114	38	28	178
1967	485	2,494	2,979	42	1,062	38	35	256
1966	438	2,296	2,734	34	1,111	30	37	261
1965	383	2,153	2,536	116	1,034	35	31	204
1964	355	2,026	2,381	69	882	36	45	230
1963	418	1,886	2,305	49	811	39	53	188
1962	417	1,817	2,234	43	746	38	61	110
1961	347	1,800	2,147	41	749	33	59	213
1960	330	1,732	2,062	36	663	33	69	183
1959	316	1,705	2,021	46	637	35	50	180
1958	338	1,660	1,998	35	663	25	84	140
1957	349	1,555	1,904	35	518	31	70	101
1956	371	1,498	1,869	39	512	31	62	35
1955	289	1,449	1,739	89	551	34	98	110
1954	262	1,362	1,624	56	530	31	63	98
1953	264	1,335	1,599	52	624	30	64	69
1952	273	1,289	1,561	16	627	45	83	50
1951	273	1,191	1,464	95	619	66	156	44
1950	231	1,136	1,367	25	579	207	134	39
1949	212	1,096	1,307	31	542	127	80	40
1948	191	1,098	1,289	98	547	81	—	43
1947	184	1,028	1,211	69	536	68	1	40
1946	177	1,009	1,186	61	566	94	1	42
1945	163	966	1,129	153	521	30	157	42
1944	139	897	1,036	13	402	28	172	37
1943	123	752	874	21	340	18	—	55
1942	121	573	694	52	260	19	—	24
1941	116	380	496	74	232	6	—	35
1940	98	262	360	11	218	10	—	29
1939	71	162	233	46	217	18	—	13
1938	57	118	175	17	201	3	—	9
1937	54	111	165	11	196	4	—	14
1936	48	88	136	19	187	2	—	13
1935	41	59	100	18	182	1	—	8

[1] Monthly series for end of December each year.
[2] From 31 December 1956 on, the basis for the valuation of securities held by the Bank of Canada was changed to amortized values, whereas previously the basis was 'not exceeding market values'; for this reason, dates prior to 1956 are not directly comparable with those after.
[3] Before 1967, 'other maturities' broken down into; i) 2 years and under; ii) over 2 years. After 1967, composed of: i) 3 years and under; ii) over 3 years. An attempt has been made to update the sheet from 1958 under the post-1967 accounting categories.

[4] Foreign exchange and foreign securities. Includes gold for following year ends: 1939, 225.7; 1938, 185.9; 1937, 179.7; 1936, 179.4; 1935, 180.5.
[5] Industrial Development Bank capital stock, bonds and debentures.
[6] Bank premises and all other assets.
[7] For all year end dates prior to 31 December 1956, Government of Canada deposits are shown before the transfer of Bank of Canada profits for these years from 'All other accounts' to Government of Canada deposits.
[8] Capital, rest fund and all other liabilities.
[9] Advances to chartered and savings banks.
[10] Advances to Government of Canada.

Series J75-106. Chartered bank assets, 1945 to 1977

(millions of dollars)

Year end[1]	Notes of and deposits with Bank of Canada	Canadian day-to-day loans	Deposits with government against notes[2]	Treasury bills	Other Government of Canada direct and guaranteed securities[3]			Other Canadian securities			
					3 years and under	Over 3 years	Total	Provincial[3]	Municipal	Corporate	Total[3]
	75	**76**	**77**	**78**	**79**	**80**	**81**	**82**	**83**	**84**	**85**
1977	5,075	331	—	4,858	2,088	2,564	4,652	425	427	4,180	5,033
1976	4,410	176	—	4,141	2,187	2,256	4,444	606	439	2,877	3,922
1975	3,953	285	—	3,434	2,485	1,812	4,297	648	484	2,155	3,287
1974	3,439	343	—	3,703	2,161	2,197	4,358	471	462	2,024	2,957
1973	2,937	266	—	3,433	1,731	2,078	3,809	469	482	1,460	2,411
1972	2,448	319	—	2,964	2,113	2,048	4,161	492	474	1,577	2,543
1971	2,070	258	—	2,700	2,052	2,578	4,630	567	451	1,269	2,287
1970	1,703	310	—	2,689	1,956	1,954	3,909	449	357	843	1,649
1969	1,652	183	—	2,087	1,327	1,651	2,977	351	348	677	1,376
1968	1,683	193	—	2,124	1,680	1,758	3,438	349	345	675	1,369
1967	1,547	306	—	1,725	1,399	1,505	2,904	315	331	554	1,200
1966	1,549	278	—	1,548	1,130	1,208	2,337	280	327	560	1,167
1965	1,417	251	—	1,357	1,282	1,095	2,377	338	338	529	1,205
1964	1,237	253	—	1,257	1,376	1,087	2,462	372	307	487	1,166
1963	1,230	253	—	1,282	1,728	933	2,660	386	287	462	1,134
1962	1,162	293	—	1,127	1,394	847	2,241	407	250	457	1,114
1961	1,096	215	—	1,157	1,543	1,096	2,639	352	231	470	1,054
1960	992	172	—	967	1,086	1,001	2,088	324	208	473	1,005
1959	953	101	—	974	667	1,160	1,827	346	204	512	1,063
1958	1,001	123	—	950	1,405	1,157	2,562	415	195	554	1,164
1957	866	210	—	805	761	1,074	1,835	285	168	509	962
1956	882	74	—	740	530	1,145	1,675	269	185	510	964
1955	840	81	—	427	475	2,157	2,632	322	218	482	1,022
1954	791	68	—	360	636	2,318	2,953	264	177	353	794
1953	888	—	—	244	482	2,034	2,516	280	152	341	773
1952	899	—	—	138	869	1,777	2,646	304	159	370	834
1951	892	—	—	236	499	2,019	2,518	321	167	393	881
1950	810	—	—	129	694	2,256	2,950	385	194	402	981
1949	754	—	1	126	763	2,224	2,986	408	161	382	951
1948	738	—	1	129	656	2,173	2,830	408	140	450	998
1947	720	—	1	139	482	2,028	2,509	448	133	352	933
1946	743	—	1	147	1,052	2,118	3,170	312	115	205	632
1945	684	—	2	170	1,119	1,983	3,102	297	91	117	505

Series J75-106. Chartered bank assets, 1945 to 1977 (continued)
(millions of dollars)

Year end[1]	Loans in Canadian currency									Residential mortgages	Canadian dollar items in transit (net)	Customers' liabilities under acceptances, guarantees and letters of credit	All other Canadian assets
	Call and short		Provincial	Municipal	Grain dealers	Canada Savings Bonds	Instalment finance companies	General loans[4,5]	Total loans				
	Special call loans	Other call and short loans											
	86	87	88	89	90	91	92	93	94	95	96	97	98
1977	968	503	247	1,546	599	547	484	55,429	6,323	11,649	2,411	6,019	2,468
1976	903	492	77	1,924	748	525	428	49,214	54,311	9,020	1,350	5,076	1,940
1975	719	369	111	1,795	655	495	743	40,463	45,350	7,674	2,614	4,646	1,629
1974	744	285	62	1,456	546	490	699	35,002	39,284	6,023	2,542	4,288	1,545
1973	391	390	108	1,133	654	322	504	29,396	32,898	4,564	2,379	2,527	1,230
1972	457	306	65	830	631	314	303	23,435	26,341	3,394	1,480	1,945	1,056
1971	660		37	737	505	291	358	19,327	21,915	2,308	1,017	1,763	1,010
1970	593		91	792	705	246	397	15,726	18,550	1,457	1,044	1,484	822
1969	318		124	797	1,099	238	498	14,886	17,960	1,325	1,459	1,263	716
1968	516		144	694	835	231	429	13,252	16,101	1,043	1,582	866	541
1967	336		205	604	540	222	432	11,847	14,186	840	1,190	819	484
1966	291		101	627	272	228	435	10,455	12,409	783	1,108	848	479
1965	213		59	532	253	200	541	9,751	11,549	815	871	900	453
1964	150		30	363	148	198	299	8,222	9,410	851	902	722	431
1963	145		48	301	219	198	302	7,119	8,332	891	1,119	559	397
1962	189		29	244	311	200	284	6,445	7,702	921	1,010	457	371
1961	129		45	247	348	189	273	5,647	6,878	953	981	323	346
1960	65	73	128	217	463	186	371	5,032	6,535	971	884	257	321
1959	72	67	39	231	434	188	409	4,701	6,142	968	919	207	290
1958	54	62	69	217	351	169	352	4,138	5,411	790	1,224	197	253
1957	58	133	89	193	412	176	281	4,063	5,405	586	1,151	224	230
1956	89	68[3]	95	177	372	169	394	3,998	5,363[3]	493	1,330	210	211
1955	112	67	83	124	361	163	310	3,671	4,891	294	1,002	203	183
1954	68	75	61	103	404	147	181	3,056	4,096[4]	74	827[4]	155	172
1953	61	93	65	96	391	165	256	3,235	4,105	—	751	155	160
1952	73	82	79	97	257	146	236	2,786	3,519	—	752	199	160
1951	78	30	68	94	177	137	83	2,587	3,171	—	512	225	154
1950	134		72	84	160	124	127	2,368	2,941	—	431	258	135
1949	133		62	72	170	116	91	1,889	2,442	—	306	164	124
1948	101		83	56	179	97	74	1,802	2,317	—	374	206	113
1947	105		57	41	138	92	76	1,692	2,125	—	336	201	104
1946	135		33	25	113	92	1,250		1,649	—	273	213	96
1945	251		44	21	105	—	1,124		1,546	—	272	141	95

Series J75-106. Chartered bank assets, 1945 to 1977 (concluded)
(millions of dollars)

Year end[1]	Total Canadian assets	Foreign currency assets					Total assets	Total foreign and Canadian securities
		Cash item[6]	Foreign securities	Call loans	Current loans	Total foreign assets		
	99	**100**	**101**	**102**	**103**	**104**	**105**	**106**
1977	102,819	22,783	2,164	883	21,828	47,658	150,477	7,197
1976	88,790	20,033	618	454	16,508	37,652	126,403	4,540
1975	77,169	15,749	604	427	14,430	31,210	108,378	3,890
1974	68,481	15,590	726	526	11,692	28,534	97,015	3,683
1973	56,455	15,133	546	537	7,082	23,298	79,754	2,957
1972	46,650	9,476	613	973	5,510	16,572	63,222	3,156
1971	39,958	7,923	516	715	5,315	14,469	54,428	2,803
1970	33,616	7,664	733	623	4,671	13,691	47,307	2,382
1969	31,000	6,243	860	676	3,853	11,632	42,632	2,236
1968	28,940	3,338	814	712	2,943	7,806	36,746	2,183
1967	25,199	2,280	788	744	2,658	6,470	31,669	1,988
1966	22,505	1,507	621	892	2,622	5,643	28,148	1,788
1965	21,196	1,376	642	732	2,287	5,037	26,233	1,847
1964	18,692	1,564	587	1,017	2,011	5,179	23,871	1,753
1963	17,857	1,119	538	1,013	1,566	4,236	22,093	1,672
1962	16,398	1,121	705	684	1,366	3,876	20,274	1,819
1961	15,642	924	673	844	1,069	3,510	19,152	1,727
1960	14,192	541	557	814	814	2,725	16,917	1,562
1959	13,443	361	526	711	794	2,393	15,836	1,589
1958	13,676	393	494	613	666	2,165	15,841	1,658
1957	12,274	443	431	576	520	1,970[2]	14,244	1,393
1956	11,941	356	375	347[3]	408[3]	1,486	13,427	1,339
1955	11,575	327	282	177	341	1,127	12,702	1,304
1954	10,289	332	322	196	293	1,142	11,431	1,116
1953	9,592	280	244	272	268	1,064	10,656	3,777
1952	9,148	283	262	170	264	979	10,128	3,881
1951	8,589	254	206	131	278	869	9,458	3,841
1950	8,636	264	196	100	247	807	9,443	4,256
1949	7,853	276	244	70	211	801	8,653	4,307
1948	7,705	250	244	78	240	812	8,517	4,201
1947	7,067	281	273	56	234	844	7,911	3,854
1946	6,924	251	278	77	178	784	7,708	4,227
1945	6,517	282	244	120	151	797	7,311	4,021

[1] Monthly series for end of December each year.
[2] More fully 'Deposits with the government for the security of note circulation'.
[3] Figures for Government of Canada and provincial security holdings for 1957 and after are based on 'amortized values'. Before that year they are based on 'not exceeding market value'. The reallocation of inner reserves which this change in valuation entailed was applied against other asset items, mainly general loans, foreign currency loans and corporate securities. Therefore 1957 and later figures for these asset items are not strictly comparable with those for earlier years.

[4] From 1956 foreign currency loans made by Canadian branches were all excluded from the categories 'loans in Canadian currency' and included in the 'Foreign currency assets' category.
[5] Figures for 1954 and later are not adjusted for items in transit. This transit item amounted to +37 at the end of June 1954.
[6] Includes 'Gold and coin outside of Canada'. 'Government and bank notes other than Canadian', 'Deposits with other banks in currencies other than Canadian', and 'Foreign currency items in transit (net)'.

Series J107-132. Chartered bank assets, 1934 to 1944
(millions of dollars)

Year end	Notes of and deposits with Bank of Canada	Gold and coin in Canada	Deposits with government against notes	Balance with other chartered banks in Canada	Holdings of securities						
					Government of Canada and provincial securities			Canadian municipal securities	Other Canadian and non-government foreign securities	Foreign government securities	Total
					2 years and under	Over 2 years	Total				
	107	108	109	110	111	112	113	114	115	116	117
1944	541	8	2	2	1,941	1,288	3,229	77	96	210	3,611
1943	463	8	3	2	1,664	963	2,627	63	72	177	2,940
1942	381	6	4	3	1,262	739	2,001	69	83	140	2,293
1941	348	7	4	3	793	723	1,516	79	89	75	1,759
1940	316	7	5	3	691	597	1,288	92	99	51	1,530
1939	288	4	5	4	671	682	1,353	99	122	72	1,646
1938	257	5	5	4	469	693	1,162	101	127	73	1,463
1937	250	5	6	5	427	684	1,111	112	130	59	1,411
1936	235	5	7	3	469	647	1,116	110	112	47	1,384
1935	222	5	7	5	431	525	956	99	53	46	1,155
1934	189	39	7	5	404	376	781	93	40	54	966

Year end	Loans in Canada						Notes of other chartered banks	Cheques on other banks	Customers' liabilities under acceptances and letters of credit	Certain foreign assets					All other assets	Total assets
	Call	Provincial	Municipal	Other banks in Canada	Other current loans	Total loans in Canada				Balances due from banks and agencies abroad	Other cash items[1]	Call loans	Current loans		
	118	119	120	121	122	123	124	125	126	127	128	129	130	131	132
1944	92	12	17	—	1,182	1,303	243		121	213	104	96	130	85	6,459
1943	48	8	45	—	1,104	1,205	1	266	112	237	89	96	100	87	5,609
1942	31	6	62	—	1,100	1,199	2	210	113	225	51	74	113	93	4,767
1941	32	15	71	—	1,084	1,202	3	198	124	174	34	48	136	97	4,137
1940	40	17	92	—	999	1,148	4	172	68	171	33	42	131	101	3,731
1939	53	16	112	—	960	1,141	5	136	53	199	40	49	147	105	3,822
1938	65	22	112	—	806	1,005	6	116	53	170	37	51	152	107	3,431
1937	76	23	90	—	749	938	6	130	64	102	30	60	166	108	3,281
1936	114	20	96	—	675	905	6	128	67	125	30	75	162	110	3,242
1935	83	19	106	—	820	1,028	8	119	58	112	35	65	145	115	3,079
1934	103	30	108	—	839	1,080	13	102	51	86	31	99	134	78	2,919

[1] Includes 'Gold and subsidiary coin held elsewhere than in Canada', and 'Government and bank notes other than Canadian'.

Series J133-156. Chartered bank assets, 1923 to 1933
(millions of dollars)

Year end	Gold and subsidiary coin in Canada	Dominion notes	Central gold reserve deposits	Deposits with government against notes	Balances with other banks in Canada	Holdings of securities			Loans in Canada							
						Government of Canada and provincial securities	Other Canadian and foreign securities	Total	Call	Government of Canada	Provincial	Municipal	Other banks in Canada	Other current loans	Total loans in Canada
	133	134	135	136	137	138	139	140	141	142	143	144	145	146	147
1933	39	140	18	7	3	651	210	861	106	—	29	109	—	898	1,142
1932	38	153	20	7	4	562	216	778	103	—	28	112	—	964	1,207
1931	46	129	26	7	4	478	216	694	135	—	46	126	—	1,082	1,389
1930	47	127	33	7	5	409	196	604	205	—	30	96	—	1,149	1,480
1929	47	131	56	6	6	297	151	448	262	—	25	97	—	1,403	1,787
1928	47	134	79	6	5	371	154	525	266	—	23	73	—	1,231	1,593
1927	48	139	74	6	6	326	204	529	242	—	25	55	—	1,083	1,405
1926	45	138	69	6	6	304	180	484	151	—	25	61	—	970	1,206
1925	50	157	71	6	6	352	198	550	136	—	24	53	—	903	1,116
1924	44	182	61	8	11	324	211	536	128	—	22	50	—	939	1,139
1923	44	164	66	11	4	259	168	427	116	—	23	66	—	1,012	1,277

Year end	Notes of other chartered banks	Cheques on other banks	Customers' liabilities under letters of credit	Certain foreign assets				All other assets	Total assets
				Balances due from banks and agencies abroad	Other cash items[1]	Call loans	Current loans		
	148	149	150	151	152	153	154	155	156
1933	11	86	49	83	29	90	138	120	2,816
1932	12	80	43	113	33	91	152	121	2,852
1931	12	102	55	110	35	83	188	118	2,998
1930	15	127	78	90	59	146	214	111	3,144
1929	20	152	113	102	50	245	251	107	3,521
1928	23	167	99	78	56	293	262	103	3,470
1927	20	136	83	74	58	291	265	97	3,232
1926	16	124	75	76	54	273	270	98	2,940
1925	16	130	70	74	50	259	238	103	2,896
1924	17	151	61	79	42	187	185	104	2,807
1923	21	133	51	64	42	176	171	109	2,700

[1] Includes 'Gold and subsidiary coin held elsewhere than in Canada' and 'United States and other foreign currencies'. The latter item was previously included in the item 'Notes of other banks'.

Series J157-180. Chartered bank assets, 1913 to 1922
(millions of dollars)

Year end	Gold and subsidiary coin in Canada	Dominion notes	Central gold reserve deposits	Deposits with government against notes	Balances with other banks in Canada	Holdings of securities			Loans in Canada							
						Government of Canada and provincial securities	Other Canadian and foreign securities	Total	Call	Government of Canada	Provincial	Municipal	Other banks in Canada	Other current loans	Total
	157	158	159	160	161	162	163	164	165	166	167	168	169	170	171
1922	79	183	61	6	5	202	139	341	98	—	19	57	—	1,065	1,240
1921	60	196	68	7	6	214	153	368	113	—	8	65	—	1,174	1,360
1920	63	177	113	6	7	120	238	358	115	—	13	56	—	1,302	1,485
1919	63	173	126	6	6	150	310	460	126	—	15	43	—	1,207	1,391
1918	61	176	131	6	6	207	307	514	89	—	8	31	—	1,076	1,204
1917	55	167	97	6	7	189	280	468	72	—	10	36	—	859	976
1916	45	125	44	7	6	31	232	263	83	4	2	24	—	820	933
1915	43	146	17	7	15	16	107	122	84	14	5	31	—	776	910
1914	39	138	10	7	8	11	94	106	69	5	14	38	—	786	912
1913	26	105	8	7	5	11	93	104	73	—	4	31	—	822	930

Year end	Notes of other banks[1]	Cheques on other banks	Liabilities of customers under letters of credit	Certain foreign assets				All other assets	Total assets
				Balances due from banks and agencies abroad	Gold and subsidiary coin abroad	Call loan	Current loans		
	172	173	174	175	176	177	178	179	180
1922	44	117	20	71	15	186	158	94	2,619
1921	51	109	23	76	19	170	145	89	2,747
1920	54	150	44	106	20	211	185	76	3,057
1919	36	146	51	79	18	172	169	71	2,967
1918	31	116	34	57	18	150	119	67	2,690
1917	24	96	22	65	27	134	112	66	2,323
1916	20	77	9	76	27	174	76	102	1,984
1915	15	64	9	103	25	137	58	67	1,738
1914	13	49	12	46	24	85	43	64	1,556
1913	15	61	9	35	19	116	58	53	1,551

[1] Prior to 1923 includes notes of foreign banks.

Series J181-201. Chartered bank liabilities and cash ratio, 1913 to 1977
(millions of dollars)

Year end	Notes in circulation	Advances from Bank of Canada[2]	Canadian deposits[1] Government of Canada	Provincial governments	Personal savings[3]	Other notice[3]	Public demand[4] Personal chequing account	Other	Other banks	Total	Canadian and foreign interbank deposits	Foreign deposits[5]
	181	182	183	184	185	186	187	188	189	190	191	192
1977	—	41	4,733	1,234	44,948	20,911	3,140	12,473	1,231	88,670	—	45,483
1976	—	23	3,103	1,052	40,478	17,658	2,700	10,674	1,109	76,773	—	38,303
1975	—	—	3,663	1,077	33,237	13,357	2,539	11,715	1,285	66,873	—	31,461
1974	—	8	4,682	622	29,789	11,210	2,015	9,555	925	58,797	—	29,313
1973	—	—	2,361	724	24,604	9,283	1,819	9,281	493	48,565	—	24,577
1972	—	2	2,407	592	19,949	7,644	1,420	8,302	414	40,728	—	17,018
1971	—	2	2,239	587	17,783	6,215	1,112	7,325	351	35,611	—	14,162
1970	—	—	1,257	214	16,615	4,450	878	6,204	270	29,888	—	13,533
1969	—	1	1,308	209	15,030	3,392	721	6,316	360	27,336	—	11,630
1968	—	5	669	391	13,622	4,050	568	6,819	260	26,379	—	7,378
1967	—	3	618	309	11,760	3,255	366	6,120	235	22,663	—	6,309
1966	—	—	919	303	10,248	2,346	5,994		207	20,016	—	5,568
1965	—	—	797	344	9,725	2,044	5,486		198	18,594	—	5,083
1964	—	—	696	202	8,935	1,505	5,176		183	16,697	—	5,211
1963	—	—	914	183	8,443	1,191	5,182		187	16,099	—	4,214
1962	—	—	564	155	7,932	997	4,879		171	14,699	—	3,958
1961	—	—	588	134	7,618	929	4,701		216	14,186	—	3,488
1960	—	—	510	119	7,215	576	4,301		201	12,921	—	2,654
1959	—	—	404	136	6,900	558	4,144		138	12,279	—	2,372
1958	—	2	319	136	6,844	618	4,636		137	12,690	—	2,077
1957	—	—	423	125	6,108	548	4,095		108	11,407	—	1,827
1956	—	—	246	169	6,007	444	4,180		116	11,162	—	1,369
1955	—	2	517	181	5,633	464	3,915		139	10,848	—	1,056
1954	—	—	176	190	5,218	397	3,597		104	9,683	—	1,030
1953	—	—	473	166	4,756	278	3,368		69	9,111	—	963
1952	—	—	49	214	4,600	325	3,373		75	8,636	—	905
1951	—	—	88	185	4,296	316	2,993		95	7,973	—	878
1950	—	—	257	158	4,176	383	2,874		132	7,979	—	835
1949	14	—	367	167	4,086	347	2,483		70	7,317	—	795
1948	16	—	426	149	3,752	305	2,550		80	7,072	—	868
1947	18	—	376	113	3,453	287	2,295		81	6,446	—	898
1946	21	—	492	119	3,179	290	2,293		78	6,240	—	892
1945	26	—	846	86	2,635	230	2,084		60	5,942	—	901
1944	34	—	763	88	2,423		1,862		—	5,136	114	746
1943	43	—	662	88	1,948		1,697		—	4,395	100	655
1942	62	—	417	68	1,673		1,499		—	3,657	85	545
1941	73	—	114	53	1,669		1,268		—	3,104	68	462
1940	84	—	66	67	1,641		1,031		—	2,805	67	405
1939	90	—	130	50	1,741		853		—	2,774	129	474
1938	95	—	64	43	1,660		734		—	2,501	67	420
1937	102	—	13	39	1,583		699		—	2,334	76	409
1936	109	—	25	47	1,548		682		—	2,302	53	418
1935	119	—	12	41	1,486		641		—	2,180	50	379
1934	136	35	24	28	1,407		575		—	2,034	45	325
1933	132	50	33	28	1,357		502		—	1,920	51	322
1932	127	57	53	19	1,378		466		—	1,916	61	329
1931	141	47	111	20	1,360		567		—	2,058	59	310
1930	148	21	27	21	1,426		642		—	2,116	78	372
1929	175	82	60	32	1,434		729		—	2,255	123	442
1928	186	73	46	17	1,520		715		—	2,298	135	383
1927	183	33	43	19	1,445		684		—	2,191	87	374
1926	175	12	16	16	1,373		609		—	2,014	62	334
1925	174	15	22	22	1,319		597		—	1,960	51	354
1924	166	30	25	31	1,238		595		—	1,889	58	334
1923	180	31	38	44	1,180		560		—	1,822	47	300
1922	176	29	19	31	1,185		538		—	1,773	51	288
1921	185	87	34	29	1,241		541		—	1,845	49	271
1920	229	109	10	19	1,293		657		—	1,979	47	357
1919	232	104	121	19	1,138		703		—	1,981	53	275
1918	225	107	148	15	958		711		—	1,832	38	207
1917	193	48	18	17	996		569		—	1,600	33	175
1916	149	7	18	18	845		458		—	1,339	30	163
1915	122	2	26	19	721		424		—	1,190	33	135
1914	106	11	11	20	663		350		—	1,044	33	99
1913	109	—	9	23	625		381		—	1,038	29	103

Series J181-201. Chartered bank liabilities and cash ratio, 1913 to 1977 (continued)
(millions of dollars)

Year end	Acceptances, guarantees and letters of credit[6]	Capital and rest fund			Total Canadian liabilities	Total liabilities	Daily average data (annual)[7]		
		Capital paid up	Rest fund	Total			Chartered bank cash in Canada	Canadian deposits of the chartered banks	Per cent of cash to Canadian deposits
	193	194	195	196	197	198	199	200	201
1977	6,019	416	3,419	3,835	101,813	150,477	4,861	85,614	5.6
1976	5,076	411	2,926	3,337	88,100	126,403	4,063	69,642	5.8
1975	4,646	379	2,522	2,901	76,917	108,378	3,638	60,225	6.0
1974	4,288	355	2,103	2,458	67,662	97,015	2,993	49,814	6.0
1973	2,527	343	1,862	2,205	55,176	79,754	2,670	42,246	6.3
1972	1,945	321	1,663	1,984	46,204	63,222	2,301	36,951	6.2
1971	1,763	308	1,415	1,723	40,266	54,428	1,966	31,329	6.3
1970	1,484	306	1,278	1,584	33,774	47,307	1,699	27,066	6.3
1969	1,263	304	1,189	1,493	31,002	42,578	1,650	25,916	6.4
1968	866	293	1,062	1,355	29,368	36,699	1,490	23,314	6.4
1967	819	288	1,010	1,298	25,361	31,649	1,597	20,668	7.7
1966	848	286	964	1,250	22,582	27,773	1,506	18,607	8.1
1965	900	286	936	1,222	21,150	25,875	1,392	17,186	8.1
1964	722	282	881	1,163	18,661	23,872	1,263	15,598	8.1
1963	559	282	863	1,145	17,880	22,094	1,169	14,400	8.1
1962	457	277	812	1,089	16,315	20,273	1,124	13,812	8.1
1961	323	375	787	1,162	15,665	19,154	1,040	12,804	8.1
1960	257	266	730	996	14,263	16,917	985	12,052	8.2
1959	207	254	661	915	13,463	15,835	999	12,187	8.2
1958	197	226	581	807	13,764	15,840	943	11,452	8.2
1957	224	212	512	724	12,417	14,244	870	10,601	8.2
1956	210	195	452	647	12,059	13,428	873	10,528	8.3
1955	203	181	374	555	11,646	12,702	834	9,915	8.4
1954	155	168	344	512	10,403	11,433	853	8,959	9.5
1953	155	153	260	413	9,693	10,716	883	8,624	10.2
1952	199	149	220	369	9,223	10,145	844	8,110	10.4
1951	225	148	209	357	8,580	9,326	792	7,759	10.2
1950	258	146	198	344	8,608	9,478	755	7,487	10.1
1949	164	146	191	337	7,858	8,701	746	7,178	10.4
1948	206	146	186	332	7,649	8,565	711	6,547	10.9
1947	201	146	182	328	7,013	7,961	670	6,209	10.8
1946	213	146	177	323	—	7,788	672	5,916	11.4
1945	141	146	137	283	—	7,337	592	5,284	11.4
1944	121	146	137	283	—	6,441	527	4,575	11.8
1943	112	146	137	283	—	5,594	412	3,895	10.9
1942	113	146	137	283	—	4,752	340	3,263	10.5
1941	124	146	135	281	—	4,121	308	2,975	10.5

Series J181-201. Chartered bank liabilities and cash ratio, 1913 to 1977 (concluded)
(millions of dollars)

Year end	Acceptances, guarantees and letters of credit[6]	Capital and rest fund			Total Canadian liabilities	Total liabilities	Daily average data (annual)[7]		
		Capital paid up	Rest fund	Total			Chartered bank cash in Canada	Canadian deposits of the chartered banks	Per cent of cash to Canadian deposits
	193	194	195	196	197	198	199	200	201
1940	68	146	134	280	—	3,715	287	2,722	10.6
1939	53	146	134	280	—	3,807	268	2,582	10.4
1938	53	146	134	280	—	3,419	252	2,412	10.5
1937	64	146	134	280	—	3,269	257	2,350	10.7
1936	67	146	134	280	—	3,233	238	2,284	10.4
1935	58	146	133	279	—	3,070	222	2,164	10.3
1934	51	146	133	279	—	2,910	230	2,050	11.2
1933	49	145	133	278	—	2,806	186	1,933	9.6
1932	43	145	162	307	—	2,843	194	1,928	10.1
1931	55	145	162	307	—	2,983	174	2,128	9.3
1930	78	145	162	307	—	3,129	197	2,141	8.2
1929	113	143	158	301	—	3,504	197	2,270	8.7
1928	99	124	137	261	—	3,456	213	2,315	9.2
1927	83	123	134	257	—	3,217	221	2,204	10.0
1926	75	117	125	242	—	2,926	217	2,025	10.7
1925	70	116	125	241	—	2,884	—	—	—
1924	61	122	123	245	—	2,795	—	—	—
1923	51	123	124	247	—	2,686	—	—	—
1922	20	125	131	256	—	2,347	—	—	—
1921	23	129	128	257	—	2,472	—	—	—
1920	44	128	133	261	—	2,778	—	—	—
1919	51	119	125	244	—	2,707	—	—	—
1918	34	109	116	225	—	2,448	—	—	—
1917	22	112	114	226	—	2,082	—	—	—
1916	9	113	113	226	—	1,707	—	—	—
1915	9	114	112	226	—	1,499	—	—	—
1914	12	114	113	227	—	1,315	—	—	—
1913	9	115	112	227	—	1,309	—	—	—

[1] Figures for 1945 to 1960 are on a new basis and therefore are not strictly comparable with those of earlier years. See explanatory notes.
[2] From 1914 to 1934. 'Advances under the Finance Act'.
[3] Prior to 1944 'Public notice deposits'.
[4] 1867 to 1870 'Cash deposits not bearing interest'.
[5] Includes foreign interbank deposits from 1945 to 1960.
[6] From 1923 to 1934 'Letters of credit outstanding'; from 1913 to 1922. 'Acceptances under letters of credit'.

[7] Averages of juridical days except that from July 1954 in accordance with section 71 of the Bank Act of 1954, Bank of Canada notes and Canadian dollar deposit liabilities are averages of the four consecutive Wednesdays ending the second last Wednesday in the previous month. Prior to 1935 bank cash is composed of gold and coin in Canada, Dominion notes, and 'free' central gold reserve deposits; from 1935 to 1959 it is composed of chartered bank holdings of Bank of Canada notes, and chartered bank deposits with the Bank of Canada.

Series J202-228. Chartered bank assets, weekly series, 1953 to 1977
(millions of dollars)

Year end[1]	Canadian liquid assets								
	Bank of Canada deposits	Bank of Canada notes	Day-to-day loans	Treasury bills (par value)	Government of Canada direct and guaranteed bonds		Call and short loans		Total
					3 years and under	Over 3 years	Special call loans	Other call and short loans	
	202	203	204	205	206	207	208	209	210
1977	3,715	1,276	335	4,683	2,146	2,453	832	484	15,924
1976	3,109	1,139	159	4,198	2,189	2,177	608	477	14,056
1975	2,765	1,065	251	3,506	2,480	1,818	515	338	12,736
1974	2,366	947	335	3,839	2,154	2,172	586	329	12,729
1973	2,009	833	253	3,444	1,744	2,062	341	445	11,130
1972	1,728	770	309	2,956	2,073	2,098	565	315	10,814
1971	1,478	640	248	2,777	2,113	2,523	361	280	10,420
1970	1,153	577	233	2,752	1,959	1,872	397	236	9,179
1969	1,106	551	209	2,144	1,355	1,643	118	220	7,347
1968	1,053	552	212	2,200	1,592	1,831	171	319	7,930
1967	1,022	535	274	1,812	1,341	1,566	..	..	6,890
1966	1,112	499	247	1,556	..	..	..	..	6,004
1965	1,026	442	217	1,342	..	..	..	..	5,603
1964	878	407	216	1,218	..	..	..	..	5,340
1963	816	405	207	1,320	..	..	..	..	5,527
1962	751	399	204	1,165	..	..	..	..	4,818
1961	720	388	218	1,195	..	..	..	..	5,259
1960	650	385	119	955	..	..	..	..	4,335
1959	627	350	63	947	..	..	..	..	3,953
1958	661	343	105	931	..	..	..	..	4,836
1957	543	338	165	799	..	..	..	..	3,783
1956	549	357	70	747	..	..	..	..	3,567
1955	552	327	57	375	..	..	..	..	4,194
1954	527	286	81	350	..	..	..	..	4,370
1953	625	278	..	..	..	..	..	..	..

Year end[1]	Less liquid Canadian assets									
	Loans in Canadian dollars						Mortgages insured under National Housing Act	Other residential mortgages	Canadian securities	
	Provinces	Municipalities	Grain dealers	Canada Savings Bonds	Sales finance and consumer loan companies	General loans			Provincial	Municipal
	211	212	213	214	215	216	217	218	219	220
1977	262	1,540	624	572	390	55,060	6,988	4,639	444	419
1976	89	1,728	822	549	364	48,879	5,109	3,842	601	453
1975	125	1,686	670	524	623	40,278	4,096	3,507	666	494
1974	89	1,323	633	532	611	34,762	3,272	2,669	476	464
1973	171	1,023	647	327	452	29,283	2,868	1,593	475	483
1972	126	781	623	322	244	23,163	2,391	935	490	471
1971	78	690	521	304	278	18,839	1,655	613	543	443
1970	124	720	708	253	305	15,737	1,093	357	422	357
1969	122	763	1,110	248	401	14,962	984	326	356	349
1968	154	690	823	242	324	13,186	826	208	348	349
1967	210	582	552	225	302	11,888	747	88	314	334
1966	91	604	279	232	374	10,457	782	..	278	333
1965	56	524	242	208	481	9,721	823	..	333	340
1964	33	349	143	208	274	8,204	850	..	369	310
1963	44	304	186	206	249	7,086	891	..	391	287
1962	43	248	318	209	264	6,477	906	..	399	254
1961	47	238	335	193	247	5,656	950	..	354	233
1960	128	208	441	193	343	5,066	969	..	320	212
1959	48	232	429	195	390	4,810	958	..	347	206
1958	69	216	340	177	304	4,142	780	..	415	192
1957	96	186	402	187	256	4,149	579	..	284	163
1956	124	159	361	178	379	4,099	493	..	267	186
1955	94	121	359	174	297	3,691	281	..	329	217
1954	68	103	382	157	163	3,114	63	..	263	166
1953	65	103	365	..	250	3,013	..	..	..	..

Series J202-228. Chartered bank assets, weekly series, 1953 to 1977 (concluded)
(millions of dollars)

Year end[1]	Canadian securities		Total	Total Canadian dollar major assets	Net foreign currency assets	Holdings of selected short-term Canadian dollar assets		
	Corporate	Total				Short-term paper[2]	Chartered bank instruments[3]	Total
	221	222	223	224	225	226	227	228
1977	4,147	5,010	75,085	91,009	-1,274	626	447	1,074
1976	2,851	3,906	65,288	79,345	-893	795	438	1,232
1975	2,140	3,300	54,808	67,545	-205	697	376	1,073
1974	2,017	2,957	46,848	59,577	-1,030	652	348	1,000
1973	1,442	2,400	38,764	49,894	-1,585	185	205	390
1972	1,530	2,491	31,075	41,889	-512	378	187	564
1971	1,285	2,271	25,249	35,669	226	..	..	..
1970	816	1,595	20,891	30,070	89	..	..	..
1969	695	1,400	20,317	27,664	-82	..	..	..
1968	707	1,404	17,857	25,787	424	..	..	..
1967	567	1,215	15,809	22,699	244	..	..	..
1966	556	1,166	13,984	19,988	66	..	..	..
1965	527	1,200	13,253	18,856	-26	..	..	..
1964	478	1,157	11,217	16,557	-84	..	..	..
1963	461	1,140	10,106	15,633	14	..	..	..
1962	451	1,105	9,569	14,387	-85	..	..	..
1961	464	1,052	8,718	13,977	-31	..	..	..
1960	476	1,007	8,357	12,692	88	..	..	..
1959	517	1,070	8,132	12,085	-26	..	..	..
1958	548	1,155	7,183	12,019	66	..	..	..
1957	502	950	6,804	10,587	131	..	..	..
1956	510	964	6,757	10,324	98	..	..	..
1955	482	1,028	6,044	10,238	69	..	..	..
1954	347	776	4,826	9,196	117	..	..	..
1953	..	..	4,765	..	..	..	..	..

[1] Average of Wednesdays in December.
[2] Included in 'Less liquid Canadian assets'.

[3] Not included in 'Total Canadian dollar major assets'.

Series J229-250. Chartered bank liabilities, weekly series, 1946 to 1977
(millions of dollars)

Year	Canadian dollar deposit liabilities									Demand[1]	Total held by general public	Government of Canada	Total
	Personal savings				Non-personal term and notice								
	Chequable	Non-chequable	Fixed term	Total	Chequable	Non-chequable	Bearer term notes	Fixed term	Total				
	229	230	231	232	233	234	235	236	237	238	239	240	241
1977	7,026	21,427	16,133	44,586	547	1,178	4,134	16,682	22,541	13,535	80,662	4,747	85,409
1976	6,570	18,580	14,867	40,016	508	1,003	2,375	15,001	18,887	12,025	70,928	3,595	74,523
1975	6,687	15,333	10,960	32,980	424	949	1,942	11,204	14,517	12,164	59,661	4,065	63,726
1974	6,053	11,249	12,145	29,445	405	592	1,369	9,404	11,770	9,585	50,801	4,834	55,634
1973	6,572	9,127	8,579	24,277	394	526	1,759	7,008	9,686	9,386	43,350	2,200	45,550
1972	6,216	8,324	5,191	19,731	426	559	1,203	6,077	8,265	8,615	36,611	2,528	39,139
1971	5,674	7,732	4,127	17,533	396	651	351	4,977	6,375	7,608	31,516	2,571	34,087
1970	5,203	6,784	4,481	16,468	393	331	226	3,619	4,570	6,314	27,352	1,330	28,682
1969	5,634	5,663	3,594	14,892	366	309	65	2,881	3,622	5,995	24,509	1,437	25,946
1968	6,583	4,340	2,539	13,463	406	218	141	3,630	4,395	5,973	23,831	886	24,717
1967	7,592	2,775	1,261	11,628	..	..	..	..	3,652	5,684	20,964	683	21,647
1966	..	..	..	10,140	..	..	..	..	2,480	5,292	17,912	986	18,898
1965	..	..	..	9,642	..	..	..	..	2,303	4,779	16,724	893	17,617
1964	..	..	..	8,846	..	..	..	..	1,494	4,510	14,849	806	15,655
1963	..	..	..	8,357	..	..	..	..	1,215	4,241	13,812	994	14,806
1962	..	..	..	7,837	..	..	..	..	994	4,096	12,926	573	13,499
1961	..	..	..	7,543	..	..	..	..	970	3,959	12,473	670	13,143
1960	..	..	..	7,145	..	..	..	..	573	3,683	11,401	612	12,013
1959	..	..	..	6,849	..	..	..	..	556	3,444	10,850	510	11,360
1958	..	..	..	6,798	..	..	..	..	615	3,664	11,078	398	11,476
1957	..	..	..	6,043	..	..	..	..	545	3,139	9,727	445	10,172
1956	..	..	..	5,960	..	..	..	..	441	3,172	9,574	341	9,915
1955	..	..	..	5,603	..	..	..	..	470	3,275	9,349	541	9,890
1954	..	..	..	5,170	..	..	..	..	381	3,015	8,566	347	8,913
1953	..	..	..	4,744	..	..	..	..	278	2,786	7,808	525	8,333
1952	..	..	..	4,585	..	..	..	..	335	2,923	7,843	64	7,907
1951	..	..	..	4,281	..	..	..	..	333	2,783	7,397	67	7,464
1950	..	..	..	4,165	..	..	..	..	386	2,751	7,301	230	7,531
1949	..	..	..	4,088	..	..	..	..	352	2,436	6,875	198	7,073
1948	..	..	..	3,757	..	..	..	..	315	2,431	6,502	213	6,715
1947	..	..	..	3,441	..	..	..	..	284	2,130	5,855	238	6,093
1946	..	..	..	3,169	..	..	..	..	296	2,173	5,637	395	6,032

Series J229-250. Chartered bank liabilities, weekly series, 1946 to 1977 (concluded)
(millions of dollars)

Year	Canadian dollar deposit liabilities								
	Estimated net private sector float NG deposits	Total	Estimated total Canadian dollar float	Bankers' accep- tances out- standing	Debentures issued and out- standing	Foreign currency business with Canadian residents (booked in Canada)			Loans
							Deposits		
						Swapped	Other	Total	
	242	243	244	245	246	247	248	249	250
1977	1,566	86,975	1,750	1,197	1,293	1,545	5,845	7,390	4,190
1976	1,505	76,028	1,687	1,174	1,169	1,281	5,403	6,683	3,151
1975	1,972	65,698	2,107	1,133	952	848	3,528	4,376	2,641
1974	1,663	57,298	1,734	895	780	1,787	3,255	5,042	1,945
1973	1,256	46,805	1,334	361	657	880	2,002	2,903	1,099
1972	975	40,113	1,114	396	461	270	1,206	1,476	941
1971	781	34,869	873	414	190	758	998	1,755	1,009
1970	780	29,461	878	406	40	1,771	1,437	3,208	1,164
1969	996	26,942	1,066	171	40	1,592	1,606	3,197	915
1968	844	25,561	948	118	40	845	..	..	..
1967	645	22,292	757	151	40	894	..	..	..
1966	685	19,582	778	168	..	797	..	..	..
1965	..	18,378	761	149	..	543	..	..	..
1964	..	16,350	694	11	..	735	..	..	..
1963	..	15,432	626	10	..	473	..	..	..
1962	..	14,069	570	8	..	414	..	..	..
1961	..	13,761	619	..	..	..	..	..	..
1960	..	12,603	590	..	..	..	..	..	..
1959	..	12,075	715	..	..	..	..	..	..
1958	..	12,341	865	..	..	..	..	..	..
1957	..	10,917	745	..	..	..	..	..	..
1956	..	10,655	740	..	..	..	..	..	..
1955	..	10,495	605	..	..	..	..	..	..
1954	..	9,481	568	..	..	..	..	..	..
1953	..	8,842	509	..	..	..	..	..	..
1952	..	..	..	..	..	..	..	..	..
1951	..	..	..	..	..	..	..	..	..
1950	..	..	..	..	..	..	..	..	..
1949	..	..	..	..	..	..	..	..	..
1948	..	..	..	..	..	..	..	..	..
1947	..	..	..	..	..	..	..	..	..
1946	..	..	..	..	..	..	..	..	..

[1] Less private sector float.

Series J251-260. Chartered banks, total foreign currency assets and liabilities, 1946 to 1977
(millions of Canadian dollars)

Year end	Assets						Liabilities			Net foreign assets
	Call loans	Other loans	Securities	Deposits with banks	Other assets	Total	Deposits of banks	Other deposits	Total	
	251	252	253	254	255	256	257	258	259	260
1977	883	21,828	2,164	21,774	1,009	47,658	27,353	21,311	48,664	-1,006
1976	454	16,508	618	19,330	703	37,614	20,751	17,552	38,303	-689
1975	427	14,430	603	15,468	281	31,209	16,268	15,193	31,461	-253
1974	526	11,692	726	14,885	705	28,534	15,197	14,117	29,313	-804
1973	537	7,082	546	14,759	375	23,298	13,323	11,255	24,577	-1,279
1972	973	5,510	613	9,524	-48	16,572	8,411	8,607	17,018	-446
1971	715	5,315	516	7,669	254	14,469	6,419	7,743	14,162	307
1970	623	4,671	733	7,526	138	13,691	4,915	8,618	13,533	158
1969	676	3,853	860	6,381	-138	11,632	3,240	8,390	11,630	2
1968	712	2,943	814	3,263	75	7,806	2,134	5,243	7,378	429
1967	744	2,658	788	2,326	-46	6,470	1,529	4,780	6,309	162
1966	892	2,622	621	1,516	-9	5,643	1,271	4,297	5,568	75
1965	732	2,287	642	1,384	-8	5,037	1,260	3,822	5,083	-46
1964	1,017	2,011	587	1,597	-33	5,179	931	4,281	5,211	-33
1963	1,013	1,566	538	1,110	9	4,236	816	3,398	4,214	22
1962	684	1,366	705	1,204	-83	3,876	694	3,264	3,958	-82
1961	844	1,069	673	1,007	-83	3,510	703	2,786	3,488	21
1960	814	814	557	532	9	2,725	647	2,007	2,654	71
1959	711	794	526	361	..	2,393	530	1,842	2,372	21
1958	613	666	494	345	48	2,165	427	1,649	2,077	88
1957	576	520	431	378	65	1,970	270	1,557	1,827	143
1956	347	408	375	316	40	1,486	234	1,135	1,369	117
1955	177	341	282	284	43	1,127	106	950	1,056	71
1954	196	293	322	313	19	1,142	83	948	1,030	112
1953	..	..	..	..	..	..	..	..	..	101
1952	..	..	..	..	..	..	..	..	..	75
1951	..	..	..	..	..	..	..	..	..	-9
1950	..	..	..	..	..	..	..	..	..	-28
1949	..	..	..	..	..	..	..	..	..	5
1948	..	..	..	..	..	..	..	..	..	-56
1947	..	..	..	..	..	..	..	..	..	-54
1946	..	..	..	..	..	..	..	..	..	-108

Series J261-272. Chartered banks, earnings, net income, taxes and dividends, 1929 to 1977
(millions of dollars)

Financial years ending in	Current operating earnings				Current operating expenses					Net income	Income taxes	Dividends
	Interest and discount on loans	Interest, dividends and trading profits on securities	Exchange, commission, service charges and other current operating earnings	Total	Interest on deposits	Remuneration to employees[1]	Provision for depreciation of bank premises	Other current operating expenses	Total			
	261	262	263	264	265	266	267	268	269	270	271	272
1977	9,682	1,043	844	11,569	6,923	1,946	539	915	10,323	1,246	513	—
1976	8,606	947	757	10,310	6,198	1,700	452	759	9,110	1,200	536	209
1975	7,664	840	693	9,198	5,519	1,431	377	637	7,964	1,234	591	—
1974	6,758	749	540	8,047	5,232	1,139	312	491	7,173	873	429	169
1973	4,140	589	448	5,177	2,848	913	257	382	4,399	778	376	—
1972	2,924	561	385	3,869	1,929	740	218	313	3,200	670	231	130
1971	2,653	547	339	3,540	1,859	671	197	256	2,983	557	208	116
1970	2,758	500	334	3,592	2,043	620	176	224	3,063	528	211	108
1969	2,181	451	312	2,943	1,542	562	152	202	2,458	486	242	98
1968	1,541	396	272	2,209	1,032	487	132	178	1,828	381	129	84
1967	1,173	306	237	1,716	742	426	117	156	1,440	276	111	75
1966	1,043	265	188	1,496	631	380	107	135	1,253	243	103	71
1965	886	238	161	1,285	525	336	95	127	1,082	203	92	67
1964	779	241	154	1,174	456	317	90	115	978	196	92	65
1963	663	232	170	1,065	399	290	24	146	859	207	..	..
1962	612	211	154	977	355	275	22	135	788	189	..	..
1961	541	197	143	880	291	257	20	123	690	190	..	..
1960	526	182	135	842	271	243	18	114	646	197	..	..
1959	455	169	122	747	241	225	16	103	585	162	..	..
1958	387	161	126	673	203	210	14	92	520	154	..	..
1957	381	118	110	609	183	202	13	86	484	124	..	..
1956	314	103	97	514	129	182	11	78	400	114	..	..
1955	236	128	89	454	105	167	10	70	352	102	..	..
1954	219	124	82	426	92	158	9	64	321	104	..	..
1953	197	111	76	379	66	146	7	57	276	103	..	..
1952	166	101	70	337	62	138	7	53	260	77	..	..
1951	156	92	69	316	58	129	8	51	247	69	..	..
1950	125	101	56	282	58	114	7	45	223	59	..	..
1949	116	100	53	268	55	106	4	43	209	59	..	..
1948	107	90	47	243	51	98	4	41	193	51	..	..
1947	90	93	46	229	47	90	4	35	174	55	..	..
1946	71	89	44	203	41	73	3	30	148	56	..	..
1945	60	71	41	172	35	60	3	27	125	47	..	..
1944	57	60	37	154	29	56	2	26	113	41	..	..
1943	60	51	35	146	25	51	3[2]	23[2]	101[2]	46[2]	..	..
1942	64	45	30	139	22	50	2	20	95	44	..	..
1941	64	42	29	134	22	47	2	19	90	44	..	..
1940	62	41	26	129	22	44	2	19	87	42	..	..
1939	57	38	27	122	24	42	2	18	85	37	..	..
1938	58	39	22	120	24	41	2	18	84	36	..	..
1937	58	40	23	121	24	41	2	19	85	36	..	..
1936	58	43	22	123	28	40	2	18	86	36	..	..
1935	67	39	30	136	33	39	1	19	92	44	..	..
1934	76	37	22	134	40	39	1	19	99	35	..	..
1933	80	38	30	147	45	40	1	20	106	41	..	..
1932	98	33	28	159	51	43	1	20	115	44	..	..
1931	108	29	26	163	55	46	2	22	125	39	..	..
1930	132	22	27	180	59	49	3	26	137	43	..	..
1929	151	23	31	204	65	48	3	28	144	60	..	..

[1] Includes contributions to pension funds.
[2] For years 1929 to 1943 excludes taxes; for years 1944 to 1959 includes taxes other than income taxes.

Series J273-309. Trust companies, 1961 to 1976
(millions of dollars)

Year	Cash and demand deposits	Assets							Investments outside Canada
		Investments in Canada							
		Term deposits	Short-term bills and notes	Long-term bonds, debentures and notes	Corporation shares	Investment in subsidiaries	Other investments in Canada		
	273	**274**	**275**	**276**	**277**	**278**	**279**		**280**
1976	248	1,388	338	1,300	338	233	—		30
1975	163	1,123	277	1,265	280	100	—		32
1974	155	858	311	1,236	227	82	—		24
1973	87	850	277	1,323	170	77	—		27
1972	134	582	367	1,377	143	51	—		27
1971	257	299	441	1,407	120	67	—		26
1970	327	207	382	1,288	108	50	—		29
1969	231	104	307	1,293	107	82	—		63
1968	121	218	237	1,233	98	56	—		22
1967	93	185	159	1,132	86	32	—		23
1966	88	90	211	1,018	83	30	—		14
1965	99	—	220	915	75	19	—		5
1964	83	—	199	873	67	18	—		6
1963	71	—	162	729	65	10	—		4
1962	53	—	140	646	63	9	—		6
1961	54	—	121	617	53	7	—		6

Year	Assets									Total assets
	Loans						Accounts receivable and accruals	Land, buildings, etc.	Other assets	
	Mortgages			Personal	Collateral	Other loans				
	National Housing Act	Conventional								
		Residential	Non-residential							
	281	**282**	**283**	**284**	**285**	**286**	**287**	**288**	**289**	**290**
1976	1,943	9,640	1,587	202	462	192	233	179	30	18,335
1975	1,717	7,492	1,333	124	267	110	180	117	25	14,604
1974	1,617	6,039	1,190	93	278	34	166	106	25	12,443
1973	1,468	4,774	951	53	222	5	129	80	16	10,509
1972	1,216	3,585	661	30	236	10	99	67	16	8,601
1971	924	3,556		—	187	—	73	60	53	7,470
1970	723	3,106		—	169	—	63	57	57	6,564
1969	594	2,670		—	163	—	55	66	35	5,771
1968	546	2,181		—	142	—	42	53	30	4,980
1967	506	1,908		—	115	—	38	51	26	4,353
1966	493	1,677		—	120	—	25	46	29	3,924
1965		1,926		—	108	—	—	46	26	3,439
1964		1,449		—	102	—	—	44	19	2,860
1963		1,103		—	123	—	—	36	17	2,320
1962		831		—	82	—	—	33	13	1,876
1961		627		—	63	—	—	26	12	1,586

Series J273-309. Trust companies, 1961 to 1976 (concluded)
(millions of dollars)

Year	Liabilities											
	Demand deposits		Term deposits			Bank loans	Accounts payable	Income taxes payable	Owing to parent and affiliated companies	Deferred income	Deferred income taxes	Other liabilities
	Chequing	Non-chequing	Less than 1 year	1–5 years	Over 5 years							
	291	**292**	**293**	**294**	**295**	**296**	**297**	**298**	**299**	**300**	**301**	**302**
1976	629	2,527	1,468	11,786	149	33	435	3	103	10	128	120
1975	603	2,254	1,341	9,004	105	16	312	34	24	9	88	57
1974	492	1,722	1,740	7,366	63	15	270	8	26	6	86	11
1973	554	1,494	1,419	6,131	27	14	188	13	22	5	55	7
1972	530	1,450	1,158	4,664	26	8	157	11	16	6	27	10
1971	455	1,229	1,000	4,104	23	12	140	–	14	4	14	–
1970	404	1,068	960	3,453	29	8	119	–	64	4	4	11
1969	438	901	1,041	2,772	20	3	38	–	41	4	2	95
1968	575	650	799	2,386	30	5	20	–	38	–	–	88
1967	572	591	623	2,085	32	7	–	–	10	–	–	81
1966	557	539	612	1,784	30	6	–	–	8	–	–	51
1965	551	564		2,006		4	–	–	3	–	–	37
1964	505	543		1,551		2	–	–	4	–	–	5
1963	451	368		1,279		2	–	–	–	–	–	28
1962	656			1,026		2	–	–	–	–	–	8[1]
1961	558			848		9	–	–	–	–	–	9[1]

Year	Equity						Total liabilities and shareholder's equity
	Share capital		Contributed surplus	Mortgage and investment reserves	Reserve funds	Retained earnings	
	Preferred	Common					
	303	**304**	**305**	**306**	**307**	**308**	**309**
1976	36	244	194	23	198	250	18,335
1975	33	187	146	38	226	127	14,604
1974	23	159	126	35	212	98	12,443
1973	9	134	84	37	227	89	10,509
1972	10	127	75	40	216	70	8,601
1971	11		123	68	249	24	7,470
1970	15		111	94	202	17	6,564
1969	16		106	90	192	12	5,771
1968	116		–	85	177	12	4,980
1967	119		–	76	148	9	4,353
1966	114		–	69	142	12	3,924
1965	101		–	157		16	3,439
1964	93		–	135		22	2,860
1963	68		–	105		19	2,320
1962	65		–	102		17	1,876
1961	59		–	87		16	1,586

[1] For 1961 and 1962, other liabilities consists mainly of long-term debentures and notes.

Series J310-350. Mortgage companies, 1963 to 1976
(millions of dollars)

Year	Cash and demand deposits	Investments in Canada							Investments outside Canada
		Term deposits	Short-term bills and notes	Long-term bonds, debentures and notes	Corporation shares	Investments in subsidiaries	Other investments in Canada	
	310	311	312	313	314	315	316	317
1976	72	288	75	253	151	469	—	8
1975	33	229	41	224	142	416	—	7
1974	40	215	32	212	112	346	—	5
1973	31	176	23	249	110	291	—	3
1972	31	55	25	274	105	286	1	8
1971	43	56	62	292	79	295	—	9
1970	45	30	53	206	70	350	—	10
1969	34	13	19	216	73	285	—	8
1968	61	35	12	208	71	214	—	5
1967	38	22	19	211	68	208	—	5
1966	32	10	8	196	58	195	—	4
1965	54	—	2	197	55	201	—	4
1964	63	—	11	196	56	50	—	4
1963	20	—	7	172	52	43	—	4

Year	Loans						Accounts receivable and accruals	Land, buildings, etc.	Other assets	Total assets
	Mortgages			Personal	Collateral	Other loans				
	National Housing Act	Conventional								
		Residential	Non-residential							
	318	319	320	321	322	323	324	325	326	327
1976	914	5,769	865	85	85	94	115	62	26	9,332
1975	767	5,072	721	75	39	83	88	60	22	8,017
1974	688	4,217	605	52	36	21	81	62	20	6,743
1973	673	3,563	517	29	41	53	61	56	37	5,913
1972	530	2,773	446	16	54	42	48	57	25	4,778
1971	405	2,747		—	34	—	40	56	42	4,159
1970	330	2,538		—	32	—	32	53	30	3,778
1969	210	2,298		—	28	—	27	52	29	3,292
1968	152	2,083		—	25	—	25	61	24	2,978
1967	130	1,943		—	21	—	24	62	21	2,772
1966	128	1,820		—	22	—	22	59	16	2,570
1965		1,827		—	22	—	—	49	15	2,426
1964		1,492		—	13	—	—	41	10	1,936
1963		1,188		—	13	—	—	36	8	1,543

Series J310-350. Mortgage companies, 1963 to 1976 (concluded)
(millions of dollars)

Year	Liabilities											
	Savings deposits		Term deposits with original term of:			Bank loans	Short-term notes			Accounts payable	Income taxes	Owing to parent and affiliated companies
	Chequing	Non-chequing	Less than 1 year	1-5 years	Over 5 years		Mortgage company notes		Other			
							Less than 1 year	1 year or more				
	328	329	330	331	332	333	334	335	336	337	338	339
1976	184	621	223	4,741	561	51	236	224	13	242	5	437
1975	191	581	157	4,284	534	83	151	189	43	198	11	225
1974	166	494	188	3,473	492	65	233	100	28	165	1	135
1973	179	467	153	2,804	495	128	134	87	39	138	7	211
1972	177	429	78	2,109	526	62	107	53	30	102	9	169
1971	159	387	63	1,860	681	83	96	–	–	135	–	166
1970	150	333	34	1,644	629	30	181	–	–	107	–	173
1969	162	279	46	1,295	615	72		111		..	–	181
1968	157	293	41	1,092	645	45		82		–	–	180
1967	152	246	36	966	649	64		79		–	–	179
1966	165	219	27	834	625	69		95		–	–	176
1965	162	203		1,372		63		125		–	–	206
1964	155	166		1,182		25		108		–	–	46
1963	139	121		848		23		183		–	–	–

Year	Liabilities				Shareholder's equity						Total liabilities and shareholder's equity
	Debentures issued under trust	Deferred income	Deferred income taxes	Other liabilities	Share capital		Contributed surplus	Mortgage and investment reserves	General reserve	Retained earnings	
					Preferred	Common					
	340	341	342	343	344	345	346	347	348	349	350
1976	929	10	67	33	157	159	126	32	126	155	9,332
1975	591	–	53	26	137	152	99	26	129	158	8,017
1974	562	9	42	24	82	132	103	21	113	114	6,743
1973	452	7	35	20	73	130	68	26	168	88	5,913
1972	355	14	19	23	63	118	66	31	163	76	4,778
1971	–	8	18	–	75		177	34	151	64	4,159
1970	–	7	13	–	64	180		45	128	62	3,778
1969	–	5	12	86	58	158	–	42	117	51	3,292
1968	–	–	–	87	137		–	43	123	54	2,978
1967	–	–	–	65	133		–	37	112	54	2,772
1966	–	–	–	59	123		–	30	95	53	2,570
1965	–	–	–	–	123		–		111	61	2,426
1964	–	–	–	–	107		–		93	54	1,936
1963	–	–	–	15	80		–		87	47	1,543

Series J351-368. Local credit unions, 1967 to 1976
(millions of dollars)

Year	Cash and demand deposits	Invest-ments	Loans Cash	Loans Mortgage	Other assets	Total assets
	351	352	353	354	355	356
1976	1,739	2,354	4,404	6,668	526	15,692
1975	1,502	2,115	3,650	5,072	452	12,791
1974	1,217	1,627	3,075	4,035	361	10,315
1973	1,201	1,393	2,655	3,260	304	8,814
1972	935	1,347	2,183	2,321	253	7,040
1971	638	1,170	1,891	1,631	202	5,532
1970	537	854	1,673	1,327	178	4,570
1969	449	712	1,574	1,202	166	4,103
1968	397	679	1,428	1,105	149	3,758
1967	358	658	1,261	975	129	3,382

Year	Deposits Demand Chequing	Deposits Demand Non-chequing	Deposits Term	Loans payable Centrals	Loans payable Other	Accounts payable	Other	Share capital Ordinary	Share capital Other	Reserves	Undivided surplus	Total liabilities and share-holder's equity
	357	358	359	360	361	362	363	364	365	366	367	368
1976	3,111	3,508	5,303	297	41	203	67	2,574	17	320	251	15,692
1975	2,859	2,778	3,893	243	30	169	48	2,268	17	296	189	12,791
1974	4,021		3,486	240	26	102	35	1,921	13	289	182	10,315
1973	3,769		2,440	172	38	94	6	1,824	17	284	169	8,814
1972	3,202		1,639	124	18	52	3	1,581	17	249	153	7,040
1971	2,424		1,258	71	12	34	3	1,390		223	119	5,532
1970	2,374		421	98	15	16	6	1,333		205	102	4,570
1969	1,951		413	110	27	11	6	1,299		189	96	4,103
1968	1,769		262	116	17	8	2	1,326		161	96	3,758
1967	1,592		194	93	14	7	2	1,252		142	86	3,382

Series J369-384. Central credit unions, 1967 to 1976
(millions of dollars)

Year	Cash and demand deposits	Invest-ments	Loans Cash	Loans Mort-gage	Accounts receiv-able	Fixed assets	Other assets	Total assets	Deposits	Accounts payable	Notes and loans payable	Other liabil-ities	Share capital	Reserve funds	Undi-vided earnings	Total liabil-ities and equity
	369	370	371	372	373	374	375	376	377	378	379	380	381	382	383	384
1976	289	2,070	556	153	54	20	14	3,155	2,817	51	64	21	151	36	15	3,155
1975	203	1,753	444	133	37	21	11	2,602	2,342	45	41	1	130	29	14	2,602
1974	216	1,076	430	140	11	18	28	1,920	1,690	37	59	4	93	27	10	1,920
1973	93	1,026	339	100	21	14	19	1,611	1,404	21	71	4	79	25	7	1,611
1972	186	791	239	71	15	13	9	1,324	1,147	15	57	4	72	23	5	1,324
1971	120	520	151	29	..[1]	14	16	849	735	9	18	2	60	21	4	849
1970	161	290	159	29	..	10	9	658	556	6	19	3	52	19	4	658
1969	103	240	167	41	..	8	3	562	438	4	47	1	52	16	4	562
1968	102	206	165	37	..	7	3	520	405	4	41	3	50	14	3	520
1967	68	202	144	38	..	5	2	459	349	4	41	1	49	13	3	459

[1] Included in other assets in 1971 and earlier years.

Series J385-407. Sales finance and consumer loan companies, 1960 to 1976
(millions of dollars)

Year	Assets													
	Cash	Retail sales financing	Whole-sale financing	Business loans	Personal loans	Resident-ial mort-gages	Lease receiv-ables	Other receiv-ables	Allowance for doubtful accounts	Invest-ments in sub-sidiaries	Other invest-ments in Canada	Invest-ments outside Canada	Other assets	Total assets
	385	386	387	388	389	390	391	392	393	394	395	396	397	398
1976	139	4,590	1,778	272	1,805	806	929	95	-222	571	77	120	112	11,073
1975	153	4,244	1,649	246	1,821	666	729	95	-202	502	53	23	100	10,323
1974	130	4,067	1,486	224	1,847	613	659	89	-187	427	50	19	98	9,521
1973	101	3,537	1,047	235	1,782	453	509	66	-163	367	87	18	108	8,147
1972	105	3,266	878	186	1,924	332	432	60	-141	275	75	—	77	7,470
1971	143	1,990	647	170	1,727	271	250	64	-95	244	90	13	77	5,595
1970	108	2,076	442	158	1,715	249	207	67	-89	285	206	1	77	5,502
1969	128	2,271	628	166[1]	1,660	185[1]	153[1]	46[1]	-83	305	128	1	66	5,652
1968	96	1,843	503	—	1,464	—	576	—	-72	248	106	—	56	4,927
1967	107	1,737	446	—	1,303	—	447	—	-69	274	118	—	52	4,501
1966	109	1,852	424	—	1,163	—	324	—	-70	389	60	5	68	4,374
1965	57	1,796	452	—	1,043	—	512	—	-65	277	88	2	66	4,228
1964	58	1,623	268	—	904	—	455	—	-50	264	102	1	59	3,686
1963	39	1,394	301	—	810	—	288	—	-42	252	106	4	38	3,191
1962	29	1,241	240	—	714	—	208	—	-38	195	104	—	34	2,726
1961	29	1,151	184	—	594	—	142	—	-34	160	68	19	27	2,340
1960	29	1,221	229	—	549	—	77	—	-31	109	103	8	25	2,317

Year	Liabilities and equity								
	Bank loans	Short-term notes	Accounts payable	Owing to parent and affiliated company	Long-term notes, bonds and deben-tures and mortgages	Other liabil-ities	Share capital and contrib-uted surplus	Retained earnings	Total liabil-ities and equity
	399	400	401	402	403	404	405	406	407
1976	262	3,174	516	1,368	3,949	227	635	941	11,073
1975	711	3,031	490	1,248	3,218	187	607	820	10,323
1974	698	3,057	435	1,178	2,759	137	540	718	9,521
1973	452	2,556	356	1,027	2,603	106	423	626	8,147
1972	234	1,822	346	950	2,437	718	407	555	7,470
1971	256	1,310	321	790	1,608	578	356	376	5,595
1970	269	1,409	218	779	1,629	553	388	256	5,502
1969	403	1,540	227	856	1,510	533	376	207	5,652
1968	312	1,311	245	715	1,419	400	360	166	4,927
1967	359	983	238	699	1,384	334	363	142	4,501
1966	403	992	235	736	1,270	268	349	122	4,374
1965	534	911	230	621	1,179	246	331	176	4,228
1964	310	1,062	139	452	1,031	218	288	186	3,686
1963	308	803	110	493	869	185	261	163	3,191
1962	247	636	94	464	760	160	223	140	2,726
1961	195	493	90	415	689	139	192	127	2,340
1960	281	544	88	361	621	140	166	113	2,317

[1] Prior to 1969, less data was available due to the type of questionnaire used.

Series J409-427. Investment funds, 1963 to 1976
(millions of dollars)

Year	Cash and demand deposits	Investments in Canada: Term deposits	Investments in Canada: Short-term bills and notes	Investments in Canada: Long-term bonds, debentures and notes	Investments in Canada: Corporation shares	Other	Investments outside Canada	Accounts receivable and accruals	Land, buildings, etc.	Other assets	Total assets at cost	Unrealized appreciation	Total assets at market value
	409	410	411	412	413	414	415	416	417	418	419	420	421
1976	51	78	65	868	1,173	1	486	39	1	—	2,762	112	2,874
1975	44	72	122	756	1,265	—	506	36	—	—	2,801	-35	2,767
1974	47	78	159	570	1,309	2	532	30	—	1	2,729	-363	2,366
1973	58	116	54	537	1,312	—	661	42	—	1	2,781	201	2,982
1972	75	64	31	411	1,295	5	900	55	2		2,838	664	3,502
1971	99	50	27	317	1,339	5	1,013	49	1		2,901	358	3,259
1970	111	72	40	118	1,267	6	1,043	47	1		2,704	142	2,846
1969	159	27	107	151	1,208	3	1,233	84	6		2,980	262	3,242
1968	145	—	85	142	1,005	—	1,303	74	1		2,755	667	3,423
1967	67	—	99	154	1,008	—	858	43	1		2,229	467	2,696
1966	61	—	56	203	1,009	—	565	20	1		1,914	—	—
1965	46	—	34	208	918	25	320	21	—	—	1,572	—	—
1964	24	—	44	186	709	9	190	14	—	—	1,176	—	—
1963	12	—	9	135	582	11	161	11	—	—	921	—	—

Year	Liabilities: Bank loans	Liabilities: Accounts payable	Liabilities: Other liabilities	Shareholder's equity: Share capital and contributed surplus	Shareholder's equity: Retained earnings	Total liabilities and shareholders equity
	422	423	424	425	426	427
1976	1	35	—	2,325	400	2,762
1975	3	30	2	2,427	340	2,801
1974	2	28	2	2,324	373	2,729
1973	1	36	4	2,279	461	2,781
1972	—	46	2	2,387	402	2,838
1971	2	41	2	2,591	266	2,901
1970	—	55	2	2,415	232	2,704
1969	1	49	2	2,444	484	2,980
1968	7	92	6	2,186	465	2,755
1967	1	35	5	1,893	296	2,229
1966	1	15	3	1,724	171	1,914
1965	—	9	2	1,422	139	1,572
1964	1	10	2	1,071	92	1,176
1963	2	6	2	845	66	921

Series J428–444. Life insurance companies and fraternal benefit societies, 1959 to 1976
(millions of dollars)

Year	Assets								
	Cash	Bonds, debentures and notes	Corporation shares	Mortgages	Policy-holder loans	Real estate and ground rents	Other assets	Out-of-Canada assets	Total assets
	428	**429**	**430**	**431**	**432**	**433**	**434**	**435**	**436**
1976	202	8,731	1,321	9,896	1,294	1,332	824	7,028	30,628
1975	177	7,732	1,233	9,058	1,206	1,213	804	6,566	27,988
1974	97	6,968	1,146	8,375	1,117	1,134	675	6,248	25,760
1973	138	6,668	1,191	7,696	928	1,015	633	6,023	24,291
1972	184	6,277	1,092	7,141	855	925	526	5,690	22,689
1971	124	5,807	925	6,892	833	817	513	5,449	21,360
1970	126	5,318	801	6,802	806	673	428	5,193	20,147
1969	71	5,108	775	6,661	699	606	360	4,918	19,198
1968	74	5,292	640	6,361	587	544	310	4,651	18,460
1967	66	5,279	491	6,003	515	509	290	4,399	17,552
1966	59	5,057	427	5,703	477	461	260	4,124	16,568
1965	71	5,054	400	5,188	436	420	240	3,881	15,688
1964	54	4,986	342	4,668	422	375	234	3,655	14,736
1963	65	4,844	267	4,204	407	344	225	3,415	13,771
1962	51	4,595	233	3,782	392	333	212	3,228	12,826
1961	52	4,275	231	3,416	377	322	195	3,073	11,940
1960	49	4,059	188	3,119	362	310	205	2,929	11,221
1959	48	3,732	182	2,879	340	297	191	2,787	10,455

Year	Liabilities and equity							
	Actual liability	Outstanding claims	Amounts left on deposit	Provision for policy-holder dividends	Other liabilities	Reserves	Equity	Total liabilities and equity
	437	**438**	**439**	**440**	**441**	**442**	**443**	**444**
1976	24,164	371	1,716	656	894	736	2,091	30,628
1975	22,112	362	1,592	602	803	728	1,788	27,988
1974	20,340	305	1,475	570	700	589	1,780	25,760
1973	19,011	286	1,422	518	711	499	1,844	24,291
1972	17,716	265	1,323	473	610	465	1,837	22,689
1971	16,690	251	1,258	440	570	486	1,666	21,360
1970	15,703	247	1,263	406	570	446	1,512	20,147
1969	14,884	239	1,296	388	563	404	1,379	19,153
1968	14,320	215	1,270	374	490	366	1,424	18,460
1967	13,702	195	1,213	351	478	335	1,279	17,552
1966	13,000	175	1,118	328	457	306	1,184	16,568
1965	12,322	159	1,049	295	425	284	1,154	15,688
1964	11,553	141	985	270	405	273	1,111	14,736
1963	10,818	131	895	245	369	245	1,069	13,771
1962	10,127	109	819	224	335	240	974	12,826
1961	9,504	102	762	202	305	225	840	11,940
1960	8,914	94	707	184	302	215	806	11,221
1959	8,379	85	670	164	279	189	688	10,455

Series J447-470. Property and casualty insurance companies, 1966 to 1976
(millions of dollars)

Year	Cash and demand deposits	Investments in Canada						Investments outside Canada	Real estate	Accounts receivable	Deposits with reinsurers	Out-of-Canada net assets	Other assets	Total assets
		Term deposit	Short-term bills and notes	Long-term bonds, debentures and notes	Mortgages	Corporation shares	Investment in subsidiaries							
	447	448	449	450	451	452	453	454	455	456	457	458	459	460
1976	173	330	286	3,586	197	892	50	128	101	735	13	9	178	6,679
1975	179	271	199	3,020	127	739	49	94	79	585	19	8	187	5,556
1974	148	202	143	2,684	87	687	40	109	70	468	21	5	159	4,823
1973	115	159	97	2,470	70	660	29	94	65	398	17	1	172	4,347
1972	162	131	66	2,258	52	570	25	87	55	392	19	5	100	3,923
1971	126	80	55	1,928	57	506	8	92	47	381	14	—	76	3,370
1970	132	63	68	1,782	43	434	6	81	47	354	15	—	64	3,088
1969	118	39	81	1,570	34	385	13	73	43	316	12	—	73	2,758
1968	110	38	36	1,464	32	350	9	75	44	288	8	—	60	2,516
1967	112	38	33	1,366	26	292	3	82	38	254	2	—	58	2,304
1966	114	—	37	1,223	21	244	—	86	36	—	8	—	272	2,041

Year	Liabilities					Equity and retained earnings				Total liabilities and shareholders' equity
	Unearned premiums	Provision for unpaid claims	Accounts payable	Deposits by reinsurers	Other liabilities	Share capital and contributed surplus	Reserves	Retained earnings	Head office	
	461	462	463	464	465	466	467	468	469	470
1976	1,766	2,325	289	85	175	520	115	638	767	6,679
1975	1,474	1,906	171	115	142	428	106	501	714	5,556
1974	1,236	1,675	126	100	118	290	101	441	737	4,823
1973	1,122	1,437	111	91	111	267	70	451	688	4,347
1972	1,030	1,245	105	71	80	206	64	432	690	3,923
1971	923	1,075	86	51	71	120	65	388	591	3,370
1970	869	968	80	60	60	113	68	342	527	3,088
1969	808	877	67	45	60	99	68	316	419	2,758
1968	749	751	73	45	55	88	57	313	384	2,516
1967	710	667	82	33	53	90	52	267	350	2,304
1966	..	..	..	..	..	..	..	..	..	..

Series J471-480. Bond and stock yields, annual averages, 1934 to 1977
(yield in per cent)

Year	3 month treasury bills[1]	Government of Canada Average bond yields[2]				Other bond yield averages[3] Provincials	Municipals	Industrials	Public utilities	Stock dividend yields[4] (composite)
		1-3 years	3-5 years	5-10 years	10 years and over					
	471	**472**	**473**	**474**	**475**	**476**	**477**	**478**	**479**	**480**
1977	7.33	7.33	7.79	8.13	8.70	9.53	9.71	9.71	9.59	4.82
1976	8.87	8.11	8.31	8.72	9.18	10.11	10.40	10.48	10.42	4.48
1975	7.39	7.40	7.68	8.01	9.03	10.16	10.70	10.76	10.74	4.75
1974	7.82	8.03	8.12	8.27	8.90	9.90	10.22	10.16	10.21	4.25
1973	5.47	6.54	6.98	7.16	7.56	8.36	8.54	8.47	8.52	2.79
1972	3.56	5.54	6.26	6.74	7.23	8.13	8.35	8.30	8.36	2.77
1971	3.56	4.93	5.55	6.15	6.95	8.03	8.30	8.35	8.38	3.32
1970	5.99	6.57	7.10	7.58	7.91	9.04	9.44	9.18	9.27	3.68
1969	7.19	7.49	7.66	7.76	7.58	8.40	8.84	8.75	8.62	3.18
1968	6.27	6.37	6.68	6.85	6.75	7.60	7.80	7.92	7.77	3.45
1967	4.64	5.29	5.64	5.94	5.94	6.70	6.95	7.09	6.94	3.54
1966	4.99	5.38	5.55	5.74	5.69	6.29	6.46	6.50	6.39	3.61
1965	3.98	4.52	4.90	5.09	5.21	5.59	5.75	5.68	5.66	3.15
1964	3.75	4.41	4.72	4.92	5.18	5.53	5.67	5.50	5.52	3.11
1963	3.56	4.21	4.48	4.77	5.09	5.43	5.59	5.37	5.47	3.38
1962	4.05	4.28	4.60	4.76	5.11	5.50	5.70	5.45	5.41	3.29
1961	2.81	3.59	4.37	4.61	5.05	5.49	5.71	5.48	5.41	2.97
1960	3.20	3.96	4.52	4.85	5.18	5.65	6.00	5.70	5.68	3.53
1959	4.81	5.03	4.94	5.10	5.07	5.64	5.99	5.62	6.02	3.00
1958	2.25	3.28	3.47	3.69	4.11	4.75	5.15	5.00	4.90	3.67
1957	3.76	4.46	4.56	4.39	4.11	4.98	5.49	5.36	5.21	3.67
1956	2.92	3.60	3.76	3.75	3.62	4.26	4.69	4.61	3.94	3.29
1955	1.62	2.19	2.79	2.86	3.14	3.42	3.74	3.99	3.73	4.09
1954	1.43	2.18	2.67	2.90	3.18	3.49	3.92	4.10	3.94	4.99
1953	1.71	3.25	3.55	3.69	3.68	4.15	4.66	4.49	4.36	5.41
1952	1.06	2.68	3.22	3.58	3.59	4.13	4.65	4.29	4.24	5.35
1951	0.79	2.37	2.69	3.18	3.24	3.65	4.07	3.89	3.82	5.22
1950	0.55	1.81	2.22	2.67	2.78	3.12	3.46	3.50	3.30	5.96
1949	0.49	1.66	2.24	2.64	2.83	3.16	3.56	3.57	3.39	6.54
1948	0.41	1.44	2.27	2.72	2.93	3.13	3.43	3.51	3.44	5.84
1947	0.41	1.43	1.75	2.25	2.57	–	–	–	–	5.04
1946	0.39	1.39	1.69	2.32	2.61	–	–	–	–	4.06
1945	0.37	1.39	1.92	2.54	2.93	–	–	–	–	4.62
1944	0.39	1.46	2.13	2.68	2.99	–	–	–	–	5.33
1943	0.48	1.52	2.23	2.81	3.01	–	–	–	–	5.82
1942	0.54	1.48	2.18	3.03	3.06	–	–	–	–	7.19
1941	0.58	1.40	2.11	2.92	3.10	–	–	–	–	6.42
1940	0.70	1.48	2.16	2.96	3.28	–	–	–	–	5.88
1939	0.71	1.51	2.11	2.88	3.16	–	–	–	–	5.57
1938	0.59	1.14	1.93	2.76	3.09	–	–	–	–	5.82
1937	0.72	1.37	2.07	2.93	3.17	–	–	–	–	4.72
1936	0.85	1.28	1.72	2.46	2.97	–	–	–	–	4.28
1935	1.50	–	–	–	–	–	–	–	–	4.66
1934	2.50	–	–	–	–	–	–	–	–	4.84

[1] Twelve-month average of last Thursday in each month, from 1954 to 1977. Prior to 1954, average of weekly tenders.
[2] Twelve-month average of last Wednesday in each month, from 1954 to 1977. Prior to 1954, generally mid-month quotations. Also, prior to 1954, the yields are on theoretical 2-year, 5-year, 10-year and 15-year bonds.

[3] These are the McLeod, Young, Weir bond yield averages and they relate to the last business day in each month. 12-month averages were calculated.
[4] Stock dividend yields are averages of 12 monthly yields; source: Bank of Canada, *Review*, *Table 37*, series B4245, from 1956 to 1977. Prior to 1956, common stock prices from the first edition have been reproduced above.

Series J481-494. Indexes of common stock prices, 1914 to 1977
(1975=1,000 from 1956 to 1977; 1935-39=100 from 1914 to 1956)

Year[1]	Mines	Industrials	Utilities	Banks	Financial services	Oil and gas	Consumer products	Merchandising	TSE 300 composite
	481	**482**	**483**	**484**	**485**	**486**	**487**	**488**	**489**
1977	1,000	892	1,190	892	839	1,198	872	817	1,010
1976	1,191	1,031	1,061	951	944	1,069	916	933	1,039
1975	1,000	998	1,001	1,006	1,003	1,005	1,058	1,003	1,000
1974	1,070	967	970	934	856	1,069	1,134	924	1,018
1973	1,271	1,057	1,014	1,049	1,082	1,461	1,370	1,269	1,213
1972	1,088	989	1,096	1,038	1,066	1,267	1,287	1,258	1,136
1971	1,109	771	1,160	789	809	1,085	1,026	950	969
1970	1,280	706	1,041	684	685	857	986	774	911
1969	1,370	820	1,139	709	720	1,090	1,057	956	1,036
1968	1,286	755	1,120	585	586	905	927	1,001	931
1967	1,275	802	1,137	473	499	752	846	761	885
1966	1,233	805	1,171	439	479	571	782	669	835
1965	1,211	901	1,274	476	495	536	884	659	955
1964	1,076	759	1,184	476	533	493	801	568	797
1963	862	591	1,124	466	518	419	704	452	674
1962	824	505	1,066	455	503	423	639	410	625
1961	902	515	1,096	481	528	425	620	471	646
1960	684	431	910	396	415	342	466	365	514
1959	697	496	874	450	465	460	503	450	562
1958	616	395	837	363	377	499	405	353	495
1957	749	388	834	352	358	607	356	257	532
1956	829	359	886	373	374	586	399	251	568

Year	Mines	Industrials	Utilities	Banks	Total[2]
	490	**491**	**492**	**493**	**494**
1956	134.4	282.7	206.3	275.8	269.0
1955	116.9	239.6	197.0	246.3	232.7
1954	91.3	182.3	165.0	208.0	181.2
1953	92.1	160.1	157.2	168.9	160.3
1952	103.6	176.6	168.3	148.4	173.1
1951	99.2	172.0	162.3	144.6	168.3
1950	89.9	127.6	132.5	147.4	131.6
1949	87.4	103.1	117.4	134.4	109.4
1948	82.0	107.2	120.2	129.3	112.5
1947	86.7	99.3	117.3	130.8	106.0
1946	97.8	108.6	132.5	130.0	115.7
1945	95.2	93.7	120.2	95.7	99.6
1944	81.3	78.8	100.8	82.0	83.8
1943	70.1	78.6	101.3	80.5	83.5
1942	52.3	60.4	70.4	81.2	64.2
1941	72.4	63.9	70.7	90.5	67.5
1940	81.2	74.2	80.9	95.6	77.4
1939	104.5	91.2	86.1	102.5	91.5
1938	103.1	94.6	90.4	101.6	94.9
1937	102.1	113.6	122.4	109.3	115.8
1936	107.7	109.6	110.7	98.0	108.8
1935	85.9	79.9	92.7	89.6	83.6
1934	—	68.1	104.9	92.1	78.1
1933	—	51.8	97.3	84.7	62.5
1932	—	34.8	97.6	92.0	50.6
1931	—	53.7	167.8	123.1	77.7
1930	—	94.5	248.2	141.1	124.1
1929	—	146.8	293.4	164.8	173.8
1928	—	102.3	281.3	170.9	145.4
1927	—	72.4	243.7	140.7	112.5
1926	—	53.9	200.6	122.2	90.7
1925	—	41.7	173.0	115.0	73.5
1924	—	33.6	169.1	105.4	64.3
1923	—	33.0	158.6	107.6	62.4
1922	—	29.6	142.5	103.5	57.1
1921	—	26.8	130.2	103.9	52.7
1920	—	34.2	137.2	105.7	60.9
1919	—	29.7	157.6	110.6	59.8
1918	—	24.0	151.6	104.9	53.1
1917	—	23.9	166.6	106.6	55.2
1916	—	26.1	171.2	111.0	58.3
1915	—	20.4	160.8	114.0	51.6
1914	—	20.1	191.8	115.7	55.7

[1] Average of twelve month-end closing prices during year.

[2] Excluding mining stock index, 1914 to 1956.

Series J495-518. Gross and net new issues of securities[1], 1936 to 1976
(millions of dollars)

Year	Government of Canada						Provincial					
	Gross			Net			Gross			Net		
	Canadian dollars	Other currency	Total	Canadian dollars	Other currency	Total	Canadian dollars	Other currency	Total	Canadian dollars	Other currency	Total
	495	**496**	**497**	**498**	**499**	**500**	**501**	**502**	**503**	**504**	**505**	**506**
1976	6,137	—	6,137	2,590	-2	2,588	4,546	4,676	9,222	3,809	4,386	8,195
1975	6,129	—	6,129	3,434	-37	3,397	4,658	3,302	7,960	3,864	2,921	6,785
1974	9,057	—	9,057	3,317	-45	3,272	3,192	1,669	4,860	2,297	1,487	3,785
1973	3,138	—	3,138	-588	-90	-677	2,742	830	3,572	2,088	526	2,614
1972	3,470	—	3,470	1,270	-2	1,269	2,717	1,099	3,816	2,143	847	2,990
1971	5,208	—	5,208	2,344	-2	2,342	2,616	750	3,366	2,258	400	2,658
1970	4,359	—	4,359	1,224	-110	1,114	2,230	574	2,804	1,694	385	2,079
1969	6,424	16	6,440	255	14	269	1,619	1,074	2,693	977	977	1,953
1968	6,329	268	6,597	909	266	1,175	1,730	892	2,623	1,114	830	1,944
1967	3,694	—	3,694	820	-205	615	1,994	748	2,742	1,359	690	2,049
1966	4,159	—	4,159	415	-5	410	1,666	416	2,082	1,211	355	1,566
1965	2,874	—	2,874	-57	-5	-62	1,097	272	1,369	516	246	762
1964	3,383	—	3,383	557	—	557	977	416	1,393	582	356	938
1963	3,301	135	3,436	634	119	752	1,002	330	1,332	613	285	898
1962	3,307	135	3,442	425	96	521	1,118	113	1,231	591	96	687
1961	3,429	—	3,429	1,044	-55	990	1,137	33	1,170	940	5	946
1960	2,665	—	2,665	705	-1	704	675	93	768	455	25	480
1959	2,893	—	2,893	289	-149	141	556	336	889	313	249	562
1958	9,200	—	9,200	1,383	-2	1,382	559	166	725	469	144	613
1957	2,602	—	2,602	-52	-68	-120	632	133	765	504	44	547
1956	1,527	—	1,527	-500	-116	-616	420	214	635	348	191	540
1955	1,370	—	1,370	399	-60	340	371	—	371	260	-50	210
1954	3,400	—	3,400	-298	-3	-301	380	116	496	246	47	293
1953	2,033	—	2,033	457	-6	451	251	140	391	160	111	272
1952	827	—	827	-122	-2	-124	355	93	448	248	58	306
1951	578	—	578	-315	-53	-368	149	270	419	28	221	250
1950	2,108	62	2,170	-28	-73	-101	316	93	409	168	-9	159
1949	721	100	821	-406	12	-393	464	—	464	361	-30	331
1948	1,085	290	1,375	-392	148	-243	344	—	344	232	-33	199
1947	366	—	366	-257	-30	-288	442	7	449	324	-61	263
1946	914	—	914	220	-153	67	133	—	133	30	-32	-2
1945	3,636	—	3,636	3,536	-46	3,491	109	70	178	-6	-10	-16
1944	3,129	—	3,129	2,686	-65	2,621	69	32	101	-23	-21	-44
1943	2,950	99	3,050	2,634	-139	2,494	131	18	148	22	-24	-2
1942	2,069	—	2,069	1,820	-172	1,648	121	23	143	15	-70	-54
1941	925	11	936	743	-206	537	81	1	82	10	-31	-21
1940	609	—	609	457	-128	329	169	—	169	83	-10	73
1939	185	20	205	70	-56	14	106	48	154	56	-1	55
1938	190	89	278	84	-9	75	120	—	120	65	-13	52
1937	249	85	334	5	-10	-5	168	10	177	88	-22	66
1936	315	88	403	175	-26	150	118	—	118	76	-23	53

Series J495-518. Gross and net new issues of securities[1], 1936 to 1976 (concluded)
(millions of dollars)

Year	Municipal						Corporate					
	Gross			Net			Gross			Net		
	Canadian dollars	Other currency	Total	Canadian dollars	Other currency	Total	Canadian dollars	Other currency	Total	Canadian dollars	Other currency	Total
	507	**508**	**509**	**510**	**511**	**512**	**513**	**514**	**515**	**516**	**517**	**518**
1976	776	826	1,602	536	717	1,253	2,048	3,110	5,158	1,239	3,004	4,242
1975	882	535	1,417	642	479	1,121	3,227	795	4,022	2,293	621	2,915
1974	633	237	870	393	160	553	2,423	392	2,815	1,551	226	1,778
1973	627	111	738	370	29	399	2,135	162	2,297	1,578	-23	1,555
1972	632	147	779	374	72	445	2,215	254	2,468	1,551	71	1,623
1971	613	33	646	308	-50	259	2,345	286	2,631	1,786	49	1,834
1970	558	56	614	202	-26	176	1,650	546	2,196	1,131	362	1,494
1969	461	131	592	194	45	239	1,004	543	1,547	451	382	833
1968	411	124	535	214	73	288	936	508	1,444	436	298	734
1967	616	156	773	358	108	466	1,196	283	1,479	700	154	854
1966	519	158	678	280	69	349	917	684	1,601	404	566	970
1965	469	67	536	226	21	248	1,321	601	1,922	927	422	1,349
1964	553	151	704	285	115	401	1,006	314	1,320	573	214	787
1963	584	42	626	372	3	374	709	354	1,063	389	278	667
1962	451	58	509	223	21	244	591	273	864	226	178	404
1961	488	29	517	353	-20	333	602	268	870	196	149	345
1960	461	126	588	277	89	366	610	107	717	302	9	311
1959	395	120	514	218	84	302	418	57	475	86	13	99
1958	355	176	530	199	149	348	743	210	953	464	192	656
1957	287	127	414	176	103	279	787	410	1,197	555	387	942
1956	246	109	355	135	89	224	812	229	1,041	581	209	790
1955	302	43	344	214	19	234	689	9	698	369	-40	329
1954	298	46	344	211	30	241	588	88	676	367	54	422
1953	200	76	276	124	58	182	432	66	498	281	53	334
1952	183	48	231	111	40	151	434	148	582	239	135	374
1951	—	—	—	—	—	—	430	11	441	306	-9	296
1950	—	—	—	—	—	—	491	25	516	350	—	350
1949	—	—	—	—	—	—	314	—	314	184	-12	172
1948	—	—	—	—	—	—	354	—	354	268	-11	257
1947	—	—	—	—	—	—	507	6	513	320	-165	155
1946	—	—	—	—	—	—	410	176	586	131	-134	-3
1945	—	—	—	—	—	—	131	57	189	53	-55	-2
1944	—	—	—	—	—	—	76	67	143	-22	-21	-43
1943	—	—	—	—	—	—	34	27	61	-30	-36	-66
1942	—	—	—	—	—	—	43	13	55	-17	-149	-167
1941	—	—	—	—	—	—	20	2	22	-39	-30	-70
1940	—	—	—	—	—	—	45	5	50	-34	-38	-72
1939	—	—	—	—	—	—	193	65	257	112	-138	-26
1938	—	—	—	—	—	—	77	13	90	48	-36	12
1937	—	—	—	—	—	—	123	25	148	92	-90	2
1936	—	—	—	—	—	—	221	36	257	182	-164	18

[1] Excluding treasury bills.

Series J519-534. Summary of total bonds outstanding, 1935 to 1976
(millions of dollars)

Year	Government of Canada[1]			Provincial			Municipal			Corporate			Other institutions	Total currency		
	Canadian dollars	Other currency	Total	Canadian dollars	Other currency	Total	Canadian dollars	Other currency	Total	Canadian dollars	Other currency	Total	All currency	Canadian dollars	Other currency	Total
	519	**520**	**521**	**522**	**523**	**524**	**525**	**526**	**527**	**528**	**529**	**530**	**531**	**532**	**533**	**534**
1976	34,145	162	34,307	31,951	16,972	48,923	8,047	2,869	10,916	20,370	8,204	28,574	1,137	95,627	28,230	123,857
1975	31,555	165	31,720	28,162	12,453	40,615	7,510	2,113	9,623	19,136	5,211	24,347	1,100	87,439	19,966	107,405
1974	28,121	196	28,317	24,303	9,397	33,700	6,868	1,614	8,482	16,848	4,497	21,345	981	77,096	15,729	92,825
1973	24,803	244	25,047	22,022	7,780	29,802	6,476	1,392	7,868	15,301	4,283	19,584	905	69,478	13,728	83,206
1972	25,392	322	25,714	19,875	6,998	26,873	6,106	1,330	7,436	13,782	4,361	18,143	849	65,950	13,065	79,015
1971	24,121	326	24,447	17,752	6,189	23,941	5,733	1,266	6,999	12,264	4,333	16,597	781	60,596	12,169	72,765
1970	21,777	344	22,121	15,504	5,757	21,261	5,424	1,318	6,742	10,451	4,367	14,818	704	53,815	11,831	65,646
1969	20,553	454	21,007	13,810	5,751	19,562	5,222	1,436	6,658	9,319	4,286	13,605	593	49,450	11,974	61,424
1968	20,298	433	20,731	12,827	4,733	17,560	5,030	1,386	6,415	8,910	3,868	12,778	531	47,594	10,422	58,016
1967	19,389	167	19,556	11,706	3,901	15,608	4,816	1,312	6,128	8,484	3,569	12,053	457	44,850	8,951	53,801
1966	18,569	372	18,941	10,299	3,209	13,509	4,514	1,204	5,718	7,779	3,438	11,217	411	41,550	8,225	49,775
1965	18,153	378	18,531	9,069	2,853	11,921	4,234	1,134	5,369	7,387	2,842	10,229	379	39,220	7,210	46,430
1964	18,210	383	18,593	8,548	2,606	11,154	4,008	1,113	5,121	6,459	2,407	8,867	343	37,566	6,511	44,078
1963	17,653	383	18,036	7,965	2,249	10,214	3,724	997	4,720	5,871	2,193	8,065	332	35,543	5,824	41,367
1962	17,019	264	17,283	7,189	1,873	9,062	3,353	993	4,346	5,665	2,005	7,670	302	33,526	5,137	38,663
1961	16,594	157	16,751	6,598	1,643	8,241	3,135	899	4,034	5,433	1,691	7,124	292	32,052	4,390	36,442
1960	15,550	212	15,762	5,252	1,592	6,845	2,793	947	3,740	5,627	1,562	7,189	264	29,486	4,313	33,799
1959	14,845	213	15,058	4,796	1,563	6,362	2,516	854	3,370	5,304	1,548	6,852	239	27,700	4,178	31,878
1958	14,556	365	14,921	4,485	1,301	5,786	2,298	766	3,063	5,213	1,529	6,742	218	26,770	3,961	30,731
1957	13,173	367	13,540	4,016	1,153	5,168	2,098	612	2,710	4,752	1,332	6,084	213	24,252	3,464	27,716
1956	13,224	435	13,659	3,512	1,104	4,616	1,923	504	2,427	4,197	929	5,126	203	23,059	2,972	26,031
1955	13,724	551	14,275	3,164	910	4,073	1,788	415	2,203	3,620	716	4,336	195	22,491	2,592	25,083
1954	13,325	611	13,936	2,903	960	3,863	1,573	395	1,969	3,250	756	4,006	164	21,215	2,722	23,937
1953	13,623	614	14,237	2,657	911	3,568	1,358	371	1,729	2,884	700	3,584	131	20,653	2,596	23,249
1952	13,167	620	13,787	2,497	797	3,294	1,234	313	1,547	2,566	646	3,212	133	19,597	2,376	21,973
1951	13,289	622	13,911	2,248	738	2,986	1,123	272	1,395	2,318	509	2,827	105	19,083	2,141	21,224
1950	13,604	675	14,279	2,224	524	2,748	1,015	204	1,219	2,017	517	2,534	—	18,860	1,920	20,780
1949	13,632	818	14,450	2,056	587	2,643	875	230	1,105	1,667	568	2,234	—	18,230	2,203	20,433
1948	14,038	684	14,722	1,697	569	2,266	764	195	959	1,481	605	2,086	—	17,980	2,053	20,033
1947	14,429	536	14,965	1,464	603	2,067	677	204	881	1,214	615	1,829	—	17,784	1,958	19,742
1946	14,687	567	15,254	1,145	659	1,804	636	276	912	910	781	1,691	—	17,378	2,283	19,661
1945	14,466	778	15,244	1,115	760	1,875	633	313	946	780	969	1,749	—	16,994	2,820	19,814
1944	10,930	825	11,755	1,123	771	1,893	668	291	959	726	1,024	1,751	—	13,447	2,911	16,358
1943	8,244	890	9,134	1,152	786	1,937	690	296	986	748	1,047	1,795	—	10,834	3,019	13,853
1942	5,610	1,030	6,640	1,132	807	1,940	732	307	1,039	778	1,085	1,863	—	8,252	3,229	11,481
1941	3,789	1,202	4,991	1,136	858	1,994	781	319	1,100	797	1,243	2,040	—	6,503	3,622	10,125
1940	3,046	1,408	4,454	1,127	888	2,015	813	333	1,146	837	1,277	2,114	—	5,823	3,906	9,729
1939	2,589	1,536	4,125	1,044	898	1,943	827	349	1,176	868	1,321	2,189	—	5,328	4,104	9,432
1938	2,519	1,546	4,065	988	834	1,822	853	331	1,184	747	1,424	2,172	—	5,107	4,135	9,242
1937	2,435	1,555	3,990	923	848	1,771	866	352	1,218	708	1,450	2,158	—	4,932	4,205	9,137
1936	2,430	1,565	3,995	836	869	1,704	875	368	1,243	624	1,542	2,166	—	4,765	4,344	9,109
1935	2,255	1,590	3,845	760	891	1,651	888	382	1,270	430	1,716	2,146	—	4,333	4,579	8,912

[1] Excludes Canada Savings Bonds.

Series J535-551. Net new security issues, by type of security, 1936 to 1977

(par values in millions of Canadian dollars)

Year	Government of Canada[1]					Provinces[1,2]			Municipalities[1,3]	Corporations[4]		Other institutions and foreign debtors	Total	Short-term paper[5]		Bankers' acceptances	Total
	Canada Savings Bonds	Other bonds	Total bonds	Treasury bills	Total	Canada pension plan	Other	Total		Bonds	Stocks			Finance and loan corporations	Other commercial paper		
	535	536	537	538	539	540	541	542	543	544	545	546	547	548	549	550	551
1977	1,657	3,878	5,535	2,470	8,005	1,644	2,301	3,945	887	2,652	2,197	63	17,748	139	558	31	18,476
1976	754	1,835	2,590	1,645	4,235	1,508	2,299	3,807	541	1,034	1,127	37	10,780	99	638	88	11,605
1975	2,664	770	3,434	570	4,004	1,390	2,469	3,859	642	2,279	1,211	120	12,115	-91	-8	144	12,161
1974	2,444	873	3,317	940	4,257	1,232	1,066	2,297	393	1,553	724	81	9,306	405	1,740	561	12,013
1973	-384	-203	-588	530	-58	1,039	1,049	2,088	370	1,557	561	81	4,598	644	188	-48	5,382
1972	1,195	76	1,270	330	1,600	954	1,189	2,143	374	1,513	607	68	6,305	365	-133	-13	6,523
1971	2,519	-175	2,344	205	2,549	915	1,343	2,258	308	1,785	330	68	7,299	2	276	8	7,585
1970	714	510	1,224	730	1,954	863	831	1,694	202	1,133	328	113	5,424	-105	209	221	5,748
1969	325	-70	255	70	325	805	172	977	194	384	789	23	2,692	199	292	58	3,241
1968	40	869	909	370	1,279	704	410	1,114	214	432	519	79	3,638	342	133	-30	4,083
1967	229	591	820	285	1,105	669	690	1,359	358	694	443	46	4,005	-6	83	-24	4,058
1966	223	192	415	20	435	462	749	1,211	280	425	557	32	2,940	158	39	20	3,158
1965	253	-310	-57	10	-47	—	516	516	226	922	429	39	2,086	-156	-110	139	1,958
1964	480	77	557	-100	457	—	582	582	285	573	301	11	2,209	125	47	2	2,383
1963	514	120	634	75	709	—	613	613	372	389	-51	30	2,062	153	-34	2	2,183
1962	540	-115	425	280	705	—	591	591	223	226	316	8	2,069	115	40	7	2,231
1961	486	559	1,044	-100	944	—	940	940	353	196	219	28	2,680	-28	64	—	2,716
1960	383	323	705	-92	613	—	455	455	277	302	208	26	1,881	34	70	—	1,985
1959	317	-28	289	582	871	—	313	313	218	86	402	21	1,911	180	-6	—	2,085
1958	246	1,137	1,383	-130	1,253	—	469	469	199	464	310	5	2,700	-98	75	—	2,677
1957	108	-159	-52	50	-2	—	504	504	176	555	548	10	1,791	65	-5	—	1,851
1956	—	—	-616	-150	-766	—	—	540	224	794	689	—	1,575[6]	—	—	—	1,581
1955	—	—	340	195	535	—	—	210	234	324	462	—	1,843[6]	—	—	—	—
1954	—	—	-301	130	-171	—	—	293	240	417	173	—	914[6]	—	—	—	—
1953	—	—	451	—	451	—	—	272	182	494	237	—	1,591[6]	—	—	—	—
1952	—	—	-148	—	-148	—	—	306	152	378	245	—	952[6]	—	—	—	—
1951	—	—	-458	-100	-558	—	—	250	176	293	192	—	430	—	—	—	—
1950	—	—	-157	300	143	—	—	159	136	345	116	—	962	—	—	—	—
1949	—	—	-680	-100	-780	—	—	331	105	170	56	—	-116	—	—	—	—
1948	—	—	-329	100	-229	—	—	199	78	260	51	—	359	—	—	—	—
1947	—	—	-260	-346	-606	—	—	263	-31	151	-2	—	-214	—	—	—	—
1946	—	—	137	-250	-113	—	—	-2	-5	-8	67	—	-58	—	—	—	—
1945	—	—	3,710	-695	3,015	—	—	-16	-43	-1	25	—	2,980	—	—	—	—
1944	—	—	2,776	248	3,024	—	—	-44	-27	-43	—	—	2,910	—	—	—	—
1943	—	—	2,564	535	3,099	—	—	-2	-53	-66	—	—	2,978	—	—	—	—
1942	—	—	1,648	633	2,281	—	—	-54	-61	-166	-3	—	1,997	—	—	—	—
1941	—	—	537	290	827	—	—	-21	-46	-70	—	—	690	—	—	—	—
1940	—	—	329	315	644	—	—	73	-30	-71	19	—	635	—	—	—	—
1939	—	—	14	200	214	—	—	55	-41	-25	14	—	217	—	—	—	—
1938	—	—	75	5	80	—	—	52	-34	13	9	—	120	—	—	—	—
1937	—	—	-5	—	-5	—	—	66	-25	2	32	—	70	—	—	—	—
1936	—	—	150	12	162	—	—	53	-27	18	44	—	250	—	—	—	—

1 Data for all levels of government include guaranteed issues in the level of government that guarantees them.

2 Provincial bonds include issues purchased by provincial accounts and with Quebec pension plan funds. Retirements of provincial bonds do not include payment into sinking funds.

3 Municipal bonds do not include issues guaranteed by the provinces. Retirements of municipal bonds do not include payments into sinking funds.

4 Corporate bonds include all issues of Canadian corporations payable in Canadian dollars or in other currencies with the exception of finance company and commercial paper with an original term to maturity of one year or less, and issues sold to a parent company, whether the parent is incorporated in Canada or abroad. New preferred and common stock issues are shown at offering prices, and retirements at the actual amount paid by the corporation. Canadian stocks payable in foreign currencies include stocks issued in foreign currencies or with dividends payable in foreign currencies. Common stock retirements do not include purchases by life insurance companies of their own stock.

5 Figures for short-term finance and loan company paper are based on a Bank of Canada survey covering companies known to account for a very large share of the industry.

6 Excludes small amounts of 'other bonds'.

Series J552-559. Net new security issues payable in foreign currencies, 1936 to 1977
(par values in millions of Canadian dollars)

Year	Government of Canada bonds	Provinces	Municipalities	Corporations		Short-term paper		Total
				Bonds	Preferred and common stock	Finance and loan corporations	Other commercial	
	552	553	554	555	556	557	558	559
1977	-2	2,612	280	2,144	—	8	58	5,100
1976	-2	4,384	717	2,931	65	50	281	8,424
1975	-37	2,921	479	615	16	150	101	4,244
1974	-45	1,487	160	241	17	68	1	1,921
1973	-90	526	29	-24	51	27	28	509
1972	-2	847	72	69	12	8	-15	990
1971	-2	400	-51	30	11	-10	-13	370
1970	-110	385	-26	362	23	-20	28	642
1969	14	977	45	391	205	32	13	1,719
1968	266	830	73	303	39	-14	-12	1,486
1967	-205	690	108	158	6	9	7	772
1966	-5	355	69	569	7	-68	7	935
1965	-5	246	21	418	9	-59	1	632
1964	—	356	115	214	6	134	-1	824
1963	119	285	3	278	5	13	-9	693
1962	96	96	21	178	6	28	18	443
1961	-55	5	-20	149	10	-24	1	68
1960	-1	25	93	9	5	-10	1	122
1959	-149	249	84	13	2	—	2	201
1958	-2	144	149	192	2	—	-2	483
1957	-68	44	103	387	-31	—	-1	435
1956	-116	191	84	208	3	—	—	370
1955	-60	-50	19	-37	41	—	—	-89
1954	-3	47	30	55	1	—	—	129
1953	-6	111	58	53	28	—	—	216
1952	-2	58	41	135	—	—	—	232
1951	-53	221	68	-9	—	—	—	227
1950	-73	-9	4	39	—	—	—	-78
1949	12	-30	-6	-11	—	—	—	-35
1948	148	-33	-9	-9	—	—	—	97
1947	-30	-61	-72	-165	-13	—	—	-341
1946	-153	-32	-8	-134	-8	—	—	-335
1945	-46	-10	-8	-54	—	—	—	-118
1944	-65	-21	-5	-21	—	—	—	-112
1943	-139	-24	-11	-36	—	—	—	-210
1942	-172	-70	-12	-149	—	—	—	-403
1941	-206	-31	-14	-30	—	—	—	281
1940	-128	-10	-16	-37	—	—	—	-191
1939	-56	-1	-15	-138	—	—	—	-210
1938	-9	-13	-21	-36	—	—	—	-79
1937	-10	-22	-16	-90	—	—	—	-138
1936	-29	-23	-14	-164	—	—	—	-230

Series J560-567. Foreign exchange rates, 1913 to 1977
(Canadian dollars per unit of foreign currency)

Year[1]	U.S. dollar			British pound	French franc	German mark	Swiss franc	Japanese yen
	High	Low	Average					
	560	**561**	**562**	**563**	**564**	**565**	**566**	**567**
1977	1.1157	1.0015	1.0635	1.8571	0.2165	0.4586	0.4444	.00398
1976	1.0430	0.9638	0.9861	1.7811	0.2067	0.3920	0.3947	.00333
1975	1.0400	0.9906	1.0173	2.2594	0.2377	0.4144	0.3942	.00343
1974	0.9956	0.9576	0.9780	2.2884	0.2035	0.3785	0.3295	.00335
1973	1.0116	0.9875	1.0000	2.4533	0.2257	0.3782	0.3175	.00370
1972	1.0094	0.9741	0.9903	2.4788	0.1965	0.3108	0.2594	.00327
1971	1.0253	0.9931	1.0097	2.4688	0.1833	0.2900	0.2456	.00291
1970	1.0822	1.0725	1.0769	2.5019	0.1889	0.2863	0.2422	.00292
1969	1.0825	1.0725	1.0768	2.5739	0.2078	0.2746	0.2497	.00301
1968	1.0900	1.0725	1.0728	2.5794	0.2176	0.2699	0.2496	.00299
1967	1.0834	1.0725	1.0787	2.9658	0.2193	0.2706	0.2493	.00298
1966	1.0841	1.0734	1.0773	3.0090	0.2193	0.2694	0.2490	.00298
1965	1.0850	1.0731	1.0780	3.0143	0.2200	0.2699	0.2491	.00300
1964	1.0825	1.0725	1.0786	3.0118	0.2201	0.2714	0.2497	.00300
1963	1.0856	1.0759	1.0785	3.0201	0.2201	0.2706	0.2496	.00300
1962	1.0900	1.0469	1.0689	3.0015	0.2181	0.2674	0.2472	.00297
1961	1.0438	0.9825	1.0132	2.8395	0.2065	0.2522	0.2345	.00281
1960	0.9981	0.9494	0.9697	2.7228	0.1978	0.2325	0.2245	.00269
1959	0.9819	0.9456	0.9590	2.6939	..	..	..	..
1958	0.9916	0.9575	0.9706	2.7276	..	..	..	..
1957	0.9863	0.9422	0.9588	2.6788	..	..	..	..
1956	0.9997	0.9566	0.9841	2.7516	..	..	..	..
1955	1.0006	0.9647	0.9863	2.7535	..	..	..	..
1954	0.9875	0.9634	0.9732	2.7339	..	..	..	..
1953	0.9978	0.9675	0.9834	2.7666	..	..	..	..
1952	1.0113	0.9588	0.9789	2.7340	..	..	..	..
1951	1.0731	1.0119	1.0528	2.9468	..	..	..	..
1950	1.1050	1.0325	1.0892	3.0444	..	..	..	..
1949	1.1050	1.0000	1.0308	3.7613	..	..	..	..
1948	1.0050	1.0000	1.0025	4.0300	..	..	..	..
1947	1.0050	1.0000	1.0025	4.0300	..	..	..	..
1946	1.0050	1.0000	1.0025	4.2554	..	..	..	..
1945	1.1050	1.1000	1.1045	4.4478	..	..	..	..
1944	1.1100	1.1000	1.1050	4.4500	..	..	..	..
1943	1.1100	1.1000	1.1050	4.4500	..	..	..	..
1942	1.1100	1.1000	1.1050	4.4500	..	..	..	..
1941	1.1100	1.1000	1.1050	4.4500	..	..	..	..
1940	1.1100	1.1000	1.1050	4.4500	..	..	..	..
1939	1.1100	1.1000	1.0370	4.6105	..	..	..	..
1938	1.0350	0.9992	1.0056	4.9162	..	..	..	..
1937	1.0031	0.9973	0.9999	4.9432	..	..	..	..
1936	1.0069	0.9950	1.0006	4.9745	..	..	..	..
1935	1.0263	0.9900	1.0051	492.68	..	..	..	..
1934	1.0163	0.9688	0.9900	4.9891	..	..	..	..
1933	1.2300	0.9550	1.0874	4.6073	..	..	..	..
1932	1.1950	1.0663	1.1352	3.9801	..	..	..	..
1931	1.2488	0.9997	1.0381	4.7078	..	..	..	..
1930	1.0128	0.9984	1.0016	4.8698	..	..	..	..
1929	1.0300	1.0013	1.0076	4.8938	..	..	..	..
1928	1.0044	0.9975	1.0009	4.8706	..	..	..	..
1927	1.0019	0.9981	1.0000	4.8573	..	..	..	..
1926	1.0063	0.9980	0.9998	4.8550	..	..	..	..
1925	1.0047	0.9991	1.0002	4.8305	..	..	..	..
1924	1.0359	0.9994	1.0127	4.4671	..	..	..	..
1923	1.0300	1.0034	1.0196	4.6596	..	..	..	..
1922	1.0663	0.9986	1.0154	4.5254	..	..	..	..
1921	1.1775	1.0488	1.1164	4.2904	..	..	..	..
1920	1.1900	1.0800	1.1247	4.0836	..	..	..	..
1919	1.0525	1.0188	1.0357	4.5480	..	..	..	..
1918	1.0244	1.0047	1.0159	4.8224	..	..	..	..
1917	1.0094	0.9900	1.0018	4.7534	..	..	..	..
1916	1.0081	0.9992	1.0018	4.7586	..	..	..	..
1915	1.0100	0.9992	1.0039	4.7493	..	..	..	..
1914	0.9998	0.9800	0.9992	4.9019	..	..	..	..
1913	1.0000	0.9992	1.0001	4.8639	..	..	..	..

[1] Annual averages of daily noon spot rates on inter-bank market.

Series J568-579. Year-end outstandings, sectors I and II, persons and unincorporated business, 1961 to 1976
(millions of dollars)

Year		Total financial assets and liabilities	Currency and deposits	Receivables and payables	Loans	Government of Canada treasury bills	Finance and other short-term paper	Mortgages	Bonds	Life insurance and pensions	Stocks	Foreign investments	Other
		568	569	570	571	572	573	574	575	576	577	578	579
1976	Assets	267,907	103,921	455	—	36	644	8,435	30,368	51,667	49,212	2,368	20,801
	Liabilities	114,886		33,068	16,698	—	22	64,626	472	—	—	—	—
1975	Assets	234,659	87,702	439	—	19	525	7,660	30,313	46,097	44,519	2,239	15,146
	Liabilities	98,688		29,349	14,269	—	16	54,586	468	—	—	—	—
1974	Assets	205,399	75,117	402	—	—	990	7,689	27,243	40,895	39,470	2,064	11,529
	Liabilities	84,361		24,555	13,169	—	7	46,270	360	—	—	—	—
1973	Assets	177,735	64,347	368	—	—	70	7,208	23,400	37,187	33,452	1,770	9,933
	Liabilities	73,059		22,638	10,158	—	1	39,903	359	—	—	—	—
1972	Assets	156,162	52,633	331	—	—	—	6,286	22,803	33,420	30,681	1,042	8,966
	Liabilities	62,139		20,337	8,049	—	3	33,445	305	—	—	—	—
1971	Assets	140,760	47,017	302	—	—	273	5,278	21,515	30,290	29,093	611	6,381
	Liabilities	54,393		18,345	7,524	—	1	28,266	257	—	—	—	—
1970	Assets	126,341	41,358	300	—	6	254	5,125	19,169	27,993	27,455	531	4,150
	Liabilities	48,327		16,831	6,462	—	—	24,823	211	—	—	—	—
1969	Assets	117,856	37,435	296	—	—	756	4,765	17,511	26,102	26,437	253	4,301
	Liabilities	45,225		15,889	5,778	—	—	22,867	691	—	—	—	—
1968	Assets	109,366	34,294	287	—	11	594	4,345	16,691	24,415	24,981	406	3,342
	Liabilities	40,681		14,339	5,646	—	—	20,205	491	—	—	—	—
1967	Assets	100,480	30,299	276	—	—	—	4,859	16,477	22,659	23,196	790	1,924
	Liabilities	36,122		12,538	4,078	—	—	19,202	304	—	—	—	—
1966	Assets	91,316	26,260	267	—	—	—	4,098	15,713	21,051	21,980	843	1,104
	Liabilities	31,764		10,890	3,792	—	—	16,880	202	—	—	—	—
1965	Assets	83,932	23,735	264	—	—	—	3,744	14,978	19,593	20,090	970	558
	Liabilities	29,903		9,918	4,136	—	—	15,723	126	—	—	—	—
1964	Assets	76,978	21,006	256	—	111	—	3,472	14,276	18,058	18,442	1,063	294
	Liabilities	26,105		8,962	3,355	—	—	13,723	65	—	—	—	—
1963	Assets	70,963	18,698	252	—	31	—	3,390	13,703	16,647	16,823	1,078	341
	Liabilities	23,046		7,840	2,722	—	—	12,460	24	—	—	—	—
1962	Assets	66,280	17,093	251	—	79	—	3,443	13,182	15,257	15,828	1,093	54
	Liabilities	21,031		7,116	2,338	—	—	11,577	—	—	—	—	—
1961	Assets	60,923	15,972	236	—	—	9	2,683	11,862	14,070	14,905	990	196
	Liabilities	18,229		6,284	1,992	—	—	9,953	—	—	—	—	—

Series J580-595. Financial flows, sectors I and II, persons and unincorporated business, 1962 to 1976

(millions of dollars)

Year		580 Gross saving	581 Non-financial capital acquisition	582 Net lending or borrowing	583 Net financial investment	584 Discrepancy	585 Currency and deposits	586 Receivables and payables	587 Loans	588 Government of Canada treasury bills	589 Financial and other short-term paper	590 Mortgages	591 Bonds	592 Life insurance and pensions	593 Stocks	594 Foreign investments	595 Other
1976	National accounts	19,484	9,418	10,066	9,598	468											
	Change in assets				27,165		16,316	16		73	-3	775	274	5,667	-356	-255	4,658
	Change in liabilities				17,567			5,174	2,636		6	9,747	4				
1975	National accounts	17,516	7,700	9,816	8,383	1,433											
	Change in assets				22,414		12,460	37		98	-305	452	2,832	5,098	-575	23	2,294
	Change in liabilities				14,031			4,342	1,102		9	8,509	69				
1974	National accounts	14,632	6,010	8,622	7,043	1,579											
	Change in assets				20,306		10,909	33		81	878	481	3,739	4,154	-1,291	-50	1,372
	Change in liabilities				13,263			2,389	3,231		6	7,599	38				
1973	National accounts	11,256	5,435	5,821	4,771	1,050											
	Change in assets				18,246		12,101	38		-65	587	922	263	3,675	-921	62	1,584
	Change in liabilities				13,475			3,341	2,521		-3	7,576	40				
1972	National accounts	8,368	3,989	4,379	3,606	773											
	Change in assets				11,883		6,328	30		2	-320	1,008	1,710	2,919	-1,977	66	2,117
	Change in liabilities				8,277			1,577	1,375		2	5,260	63				
1971	National accounts	6,660	3,621	3,039	4,266	-1,227											
	Change in assets				10,131		5,822	9		-81	115	153	2,462	2,283	-1,546	-249	1,163
	Change in liabilities				5,865			1,864	1,054		1	2,909	37				
1970	National accounts	5,855	2,764	3,091	3,718	-627											
	Change in assets				7,117		4,316	5		110	-950	360	823	1,817	-675	61	1,250
	Change in liabilities				3,399			1,292	-53		—	2,082	78				
1969	National accounts	5,535	3,919	1,616	990	626											
	Change in assets				4,708		3,186	9		-94	96	420	385	1,741	-631	-326	-78
	Change in liabilities				3,718			1,390	522		—	1,762	44				
1968	National accounts	5,010	3,537	1,473	2,081	-608											
	Change in assets				5,516		4,011	11		40	221	-514	-605	1,668	140	-74	618
	Change in liabilities				3,435			1,839	810		—	730	56				
1967	National accounts	5,115	3,156	1,959	2,829	-870											
	Change in assets				7,340		4,164	8		-40	-86	761	450	1,614	-359	120	708
	Change in liabilities				4,511			1,551	860		—	2,102	-2				
1966	National accounts	5,164	3,340	1,824	2,430	-606											
	Change in assets				4,586		2,380	3		-8	209	354	268	1,474	-114	-67	87
	Change in liabilities				2,156			749	4		—	1,419	-16				
1965	National accounts	4,087	2,976	1,111	1,615	-504											
	Change in assets				4,824		2,792	8		-97	-51	272	333	1,488	43	-121	157
	Change in liabilities				3,209			735	564		—	1,917	-7				
1964	National accounts	3,459	2,643	816	922	-106											
	Change in assets				4,237		2,235	4		69	-181	82	784	1,427	-70	-83	-30
	Change in liabilities				3,315			1,130	778		—	1,406	1				
1963	National accounts	3,596	2,715	881	1,384	-503											
	Change in assets				3,109		1,653	1		-51	21	-53	506	1,309	-85	-145	-47
	Change in liabilities				1,725			653	108		—	939	25				
1962	National accounts	3,311	2,562	749	1,142	-393											
	Change in assets				4,113		875	16		110	1	760	1,135	1,167	45	14	-10
	Change in liabilities				2,971			831	502		—	1,638	—				

Series J596-607. Year-end outstandings, sector III, non-financial private corporations, 1961 to 1976
(millions of dollars)

Year		Total financial assets and liabilities	Currency and deposits	Receivables and payables	Loans	Government of Canada treasury bills	Finance and other short-term paper	Mortgages	Bonds	Claims on associated enterprises	Stocks	Foreign investments	Other assets and liabilities
		596	597	598	599	600	601	602	603	604	605	606	607
1976	Assets	75,196	7,892	34,595	1,231	75	1,548	2,182	417	17,884	1,446	335	7,591
	Liabilities	212,583	—	26,360	30,297	—	2,956	13,138	20,085	12,960	92,757	—	14,030
1975	Assets	70,474	6,415	32,794	1,352	34	1,745	2,102	478	16,559	1,305	322	7,368
	Liabilities	195,260	—	24,248	26,429	—	2,563	12,374	18,196	12,138	85,817	—	13,495
1974	Assets	64,997	6,292	29,430	1,229	9	1,336	2,083	490	15,374	1,371	386	6,997
	Liabilities	178,669	—	22,671	22,957	—	2,326	11,986	16,414	11,095	78,356	—	12,864
1973	Assets	54,909	5,685	24,433	940	11	1,334	1,770	585	12,774	1,169	338	5,870
	Liabilities	151,647	—	17,505	18,810	—	858	9,982	15,612	10,034	68,768	—	10,078
1972	Assets	47,634	4,729	21,307	483	5	523	1,500	1,065	11,086	1,265	366	5,305
	Liabilities	133,518	—	14,224	15,381	—	1,040	8,245	15,337	9,589	61,353	—	8,349
1971	Assets	43,225	4,304	19,342	393	29	693	1,107	738	9,739	1,463	398	5,019
	Liabilities	122,812	—	11,609	12,439	—	1,379	7,356	15,583	9,119	57,216	—	8,111
1970	Assets	39,376	3,604	17,676	329	8	706	1,049	724	8,759	1,372	398	4,751
	Liabilities	111,932	—	10,473	10,931	—	1,052	6,817	13,721	8,856	53,003	—	7,079
1969	Assets	36,410	3,504	16,583	350	10	631	1,128	879	7,592	1,616	500	3,617
	Liabilities	104,719	—	9,946	10,462	—	574	6,229	12,261	9,014	48,923	—	7,310
1968	Assets	33,878	3,334	15,299	288	7	697	1,032	927	7,214	1,476	292	3,312
	Liabilities	95,985	—	9,073	9,105	—	439	5,225	11,412	8,623	45,025	—	7,083
1967	Assets	31,428	3,060	14,188	227	10	519	896	1,199	6,717	1,361	291	2,960
	Liabilities	89,298	—	8,554	8,600	—	394	4,602	10,863	7,743	42,037	—	6,505
1966	Assets	29,337	2,790	13,368	195	63	399	766	1,219	6,309	1,320	364	2,544
	Liabilities	83,106	—	8,176	7,355	—	380	4,176	9,879	7,230	39,393	—	6,517
1965	Assets	26,838	2,798	11,859	—	37	223	725	1,474	6,002	1,161	252	2,307
	Liabilities	74,818	—	7,267	6,268	—	306	3,289	9,093	6,393	36,454	—	5,748
1964	Assets	24,205	2,668	10,337	—	63	365	584	1,398	5,718	1,005	260	1,807
	Liabilities	68,071	—	6,206	5,460	—	287	2,833	8,163	5,956	33,841	—	5,325
1963	Assets	22,194	2,497	9,380	—	103	479	562	1,336	5,071	891	231	1,644
	Liabilities	63,135	—	5,657	5,037	—	244	2,423	7,680	5,510	31,572	—	5,012
1962	Assets	20,565	2,339	8,615	—	139	462	499	1,207	4,650	829	234	1,591
	Liabilities	59,697	—	5,082	4,678	—	297	2,147	7,468	5,130	30,033	—	4,862
1961	Assets	18,653	2,256	7,758	—	97	436	459	1,140	4,260	667	210	1,370
	Liabilities	55,548	—	4,675	4,212	—	257	1,922	7,061	4,756	28,165	—	4,500

J608-623. Financial flows, sector III, non-financial private corporations, 1962 to 1976

(millions of dollars)

Year		Gross saving 608	Non-financial capital acquisition 609	Net lending or borrowing 610	Net financial investment 611	Discrepancy 612	Currency and deposits 613	Receivables and payables 614	Loans 615	Government of Canada treasury bills 616	Finance and other short-term paper 617	Mortgages 618	Bonds 619	Claims on associated enterprises 620	Stocks 621	Foreign investments 622	Other assets and liabilities 623
1976	National accounts	14,389	21,615	-7,226	-5,498	-1,728											
	Change in assets				5,610	—	1,503	2,238	-130	37	-239	79	-55	1,452	23	1	701
	Change in liabilities				11,108	—	—	1,177	3,690	—	393	757	2,132	1,103	1,170	—	686
1975	National accounts	12,555	17,082	-4,527	-4,049	-478											
	Change in assets				6,559	—	377	3,855	204	16	353	7	126	1,194	-29	-69	525
	Change in liabilities				10,608	—	—	2,523	3,345	—	212	332	2,112	661	960	—	463
1974	National accounts	11,917	19,919	-8,002	-7,067	-935											
	Change in assets				8,994	—	442	5,175	97	-79	-84	44	-125	1,967	214	40	1,303
	Change in liabilities				16,061	—	—	4,857	3,613	—	1,463	500	1,457	871	856	—	2,444
1973	National accounts	10,723	15,517	-4,794	-2,933	-1,861											
	Change in assets				6,366	—	534	3,210	79	73	488	19	-43	1,169	68	28	741
	Change in liabilities				9,299	—	—	2,315	3,335	—	-177	320	750	377	1,172	—	1,207
1972	National accounts	8,472	12,368	-3,896	-2,232	-1,664											
	Change in assets				3,390	—	216	1,413	8	-23	165	102	4	973	312	-127	347
	Change in liabilities				5,622	—	—	1,660	1,975	—	-238	336	863	302	376	—	348
1971	National accounts	7,608	10,734	-3,126	-2,951	-175											
	Change in assets				3,883	—	509	1,739	-4	61	-109	69	4	647	70	48	849
	Change in liabilities				6,834	—	—	1,232	1,450	—	320	530	1,698	357	692	—	555
1970	National accounts	7,163	9,444	-2,281	-2,154	-127											
	Change in assets				1,940	—	8	1,098	-98	-76	79	-22	-30	976	-69	-3	77
	Change in liabilities				4,094	—	—	288	272	—	60	499	1,369	682	812	—	112
1969	National accounts	6,799	8,988	-2,189	-2,628	439											
	Change in assets				2,348	—	51	851	-109	68	113	29	-17	614	118	176	454
	Change in liabilities				4,976	—	—	597	1,008	—	292	914	740	107	1,378	—	-60
1968	National accounts	6,491	7,521	-1,030	-1,261	231											
	Change in assets				2,900	—	175	938	-82	—	392	36	113	632	72	7	617
	Change in liabilities				4,161	—	—	237	347	—	160	596	667	700	862	—	592
1967	National accounts	5,991	7,048	-1,057	-1,542	485											
	Change in assets				2,515	—	209	1,004	706	-53	295	8	6	534	82	-65	389
	Change in liabilities				4,057	—	—	403	840	—	137	467	927	483	633	—	167
1966	National accounts	5,702	8,037	-2,335	-2,530	195											
	Change in assets				2,876	—	103	1,252	134	30	-19	197	-44	534	143	115	431
	Change in liabilities				5,406	—	—	900	919	—	131	806	873	778	656	—	343
1965	National accounts	5,317	7,204	-1,887	-2,053	166											
	Change in assets				2,893	—	57	1,487	—	-38	-34	354	95	583	134	-1	256
	Change in liabilities				4,946	—	—	1,181	878	—	35	654	944	311	703	—	240
1964	National accounts	5,015	5,852	-837	-858	21											
	Change in assets				2,468	—	205	1,035	—	-37	61	164	-144	798	113	52	221
	Change in liabilities				3,326	—	—	614	315	—	38	422	662	392	638	—	245
1963	National accounts	4,259	4,577	-318	-807	489											
	Change in assets				1,847	—	111	814	—	-34	9	137	109	668	79	-21	-25
	Change in liabilities				2,654	—	—	696	223	—	-41	278	406	360	597	—	135
1962	National accounts	3,933	4,078	-145	-828	683											
	Change in assets				1,912	—	83	857	—	42	40	40	53	390	162	24	221
	Change in liabilities				2,740	—	—	407	512	—	40	225	374	363	559	—	260

Series J624-635. Year-end outstandings, sector IV, non-financial government enterprises, 1961 to 1976
(millions of dollars)

Year		Total financial assets and liabilities	Currency and deposits	Receiv-ables and payables	Loans	Govern-ment of Canada treasury bills	Finance and other short-term paper	Mortgages	Bonds	Claims on asso-ciated enter-prises	Stocks	Foreign invest-ments	Other assets and liabilities
		624	625	626	627	628	629	630	631	632	633	634	635
1976	Assets	8,090	2,605	1,801	589	51	48	32	677	948	266	28	1,045
	Liabilities	46,332	—	2,834	4,113	—	137	1,123	22,539	13,855	256	—	1,475
1975	Assets	5,954	1,162	1,470	802	12	24	21	717	891	10	24	821
	Liabilities	39,011	—	2,713	2,724	—	182	1,042	17,742	13,001	169	—	1,438
1974	Assets	5,353	833	1,625	703	12	22	22	728	678	10	21	699
	Liabilities	33,056	—	2,965	1,863	—	269	920	14,666	11,103	89	—	1,181
1973	Assets	4,099	669	1,020	456	8	20	23	682	618	43	10	550
	Liabilities	27,820	—	1,703	1,724	—	186	780	12,632	9,758	34	—	1,003
1972	Assets	3,741	643	774	320	34	58	19	710	689	41	10	443
	Liabilities	25,062	—	1,289	1,288	—	170	677	11,352	9,330	34	—	922
1971	Assets	3,261	447	705	229	32	55	18	745	585	37	11	397
	Liabilities	23,302	—	1,128	1,113	—	263	585	10,242	9,005	4	—	962
1970	Assets	2,962	411	620	146	23	25	18	699	602	35	11	372
	Liabilities	21,636	—	1,114	1,043	—	327	441	9,547	8,330	4	—	830
1969	Assets	2,572	349	526	160	20	13	21	646	495	34	8	300
	Liabilities	19,766	—	984	1,128	—	351	344	8,902	7,323	4	—	730
1968	Assets	2,450	353	524	172	13	10	36	556	481	27	—	278
	Liabilities	18,239	—	930	876	—	347	263	8,431	6,710	4	—	678
1967	Assets	2,274	322	433	231	7	11	27	551	409	10	—	273
	Liabilities	16,812	—	844	870	—	—	185	8,104	6,179	4	—	626
1966	Assets	2,164	275	394	281	16	14	27	560	342	4	—	251
	Liabilities	15,482	—	937	703	—	—	130	7,588	5,506	4	—	614
1965	Assets	1,942	291	380	211	14	15	27	442	335	4	—	223
	Liabilities	14,102	—	797	583	—	—	104	6,958	5,140	4	—	516
1964	Assets	1,706	248	320	116	16	15	18	425	336	4	—	208
	Liabilities	12,968	—	503	360	—	—	67	6,725	4,851	4	—	458
1963	Assets	1,405	116	325	86	21	11	19	285	337	3	—	202
	Liabilities	12,379	—	523	596	—	—	59	6,176	4,838	5	—	182
1962	Assets	1,416	163	286	108	31	11	20	255	327	—	—	215
	Liabilities	11,610	—	520	467	—	—	58	5,677	4,703	5	—	180
1961	Assets	1,389	164	273	100	26	11	17	262	303	—	—	233
	Liabilities	11,263	—	491	527	—	—	58	5,481	4,532	5	—	169

Series J636-651. Financial flows, sector IV, non-financial government enterprises, 1962 to 1976
(millions of dollars)

Year		Gross saving	Non-financial capital acquisition	Net lending or borrowing	Net financial investment	Discrepancy	Currency and deposits	Receivables and payables	Loans	Government of Canada treasury bills	Finance and other short-term paper	Mortgages	Bonds	Claims on associated enterprises	Stocks	Foreign investments	Other assets and liabilities
		636	637	638	639	640	641	642	643	644	645	646	647	648	649	650	651
1976	National accounts	1,453	7,176	-5,723	-5,151	-572											
	Change in assets				2,528		1,428	292	-147	17	22	8	-19	499	244	-6	190
	Change in liabilities				7,679			96	1,363		-45	81	4,879	1,252	52		1
1975	National accounts	1,053	6,699	-5,646	-5,342	-304											
	Change in assets				614		335	-156	99	-6	2	1	-3	41	176	3	122
	Change in liabilities				5,956			-251	861		-87	123	3,075	1,898	80		257
1974	National accounts	1,295	4,417	-3,122	-3,143	21											
	Change in assets				1,239		176	564	246	5	1	-2	50	19	53	12	168
	Change in liabilities				4,382			1,212	167		84	78	1,330	1,280			178
1973	National accounts	1,050	3,376	-2,326	-2,477	151											
	Change in assets				253		10	177	134	2	-37	5	-31	-68	-1		62
	Change in liabilities				2,730			370	462		17	106	1,198	456			121
1972	National accounts	973	2,441	-1,468	-1,431	-37											
	Change in assets				506		196	67	92	2	3	1	-36	133	4	-1	45
	Change in liabilities				1,937			161	174		-92	92	1,109	503	30		-40
1971	National accounts	887	2,187	-1,300	-1,325	25											
	Change in assets				325		36	85	83	8	30	1	45	11	2	-1	25
	Change in liabilities				1,650			14	70		-64	144	695	659			132
1970	National accounts	879	2,063	-1,184	-1,091	-93											
	Change in assets				188		38	44	-15	4	12	-3	53	17	1	3	34
	Change in liabilities				1,279			52	-97		-24	97	611	606			34
1969	National accounts	807	2,133	-1,326	-1,403	77											
	Change in assets				118		-4	1	-13	7	3	-15	93	11	7	8	20
	Change in liabilities				1,521			50	256		4	81	471	607			52
1968	National accounts	736	1,864	-1,128	-1,232	104											
	Change in assets				184		32	91	-58	2	-1	9	9	78	17		5
	Change in liabilities				1,416			86	353			78	330	526			43
1967	National accounts	683	2,275	-1,592	-1,234	-358											
	Change in assets				98		46	39	-49	-11	-3		-7	55	6		22
	Change in liabilities				1,332			-89	151			55	532	671			12
1966	National accounts	610	2,113	-1,503	-1,167	-336											
	Change in assets				213		-19	16	69	-4	-1		123	-2			31
	Change in liabilities				1,380			140	115			26	629	369			101
1965	National accounts	616	1,644	-1,028	-914	-114											
	Change in assets				248		51	63	95	9		9	3	4			14
	Change in liabilities				1,162			302	223			37	233	307			60
1964	National accounts	543	1,203	-660	-246	-414											
	Change in assets				305		136	-3	31	-4	4	-1	135	-2	1		8
	Change in liabilities				551			-14	-233			8	549	-34			275
1963	National accounts	493	880	-387	-238	-149											
	Change in assets				295		-47	39	-22	-10		-1	33	15	302	-1	-13
	Change in liabilities				533			3	132			1	255	138			4
1962	National accounts	465	914	-449	-291	-158											
	Change in assets				79		2	15	8	-7		3	46	28			-16
	Change in liabilities				370			34	-53				196	181			12

Series J652-661. Year-end outstandings, sector V, the monetary authorities, 1961 to 1976
(millions of dollars)

Year		Total financial assets and liabilities	Official international reserves	Currency and deposits	Loans	Government of Canada treasury bills	Finance and other short-term paper	Bonds	Claims on associated enterprises	Other assets and liabilities	Official monetary reserve offsets
		652	653	654	655	656	657	658	659	660	661
1976	Assets	16,196	5,894		880	2,120	105	6,300		897	
	Liabilities	16,223		11,069					4,531	623	
1975	Assets	14,620	5,410		1,028	2,114	44	5,727		297	
	Liabilities	14,643		9,956					4,346	341	
1974	Assets	14,196	5,770		8	1,615	140	5,388	965	310	
	Liabilities	14,216		8,611					5,219	386	
1973	Assets	12,730	5,745			1,093	39	4,895	721	237	
	Liabilities	12,746		7,426					4,981	339	
1972	Assets	12,507	6,018		2	940		4,475	586	486	
	Liabilities	12,525		6,495					5,632	398	
1971	Assets	11,305	5,582		2	894	1	3,930	514	382	
	Liabilities	11,322		5,667					5,394	261	
1970	Assets	9,859	4,731			630		3,620	470	408	
	Liabilities	9,877		5,010					4,599	268	
1969	Assets	7,958	3,333		1	486	3	3,580	403	152	
	Liabilities	7,972		4,589					3,225	157	1
1968	Assets	7,727	3,268		5	459		3,435	354	206	
	Liabilities	7,743		4,374					3,220	148	1
1967	Assets	7,165	2,936		3	544		3,212	315	155	
	Liabilities	7,176		4,050					2,898	226	2
1966	Assets	6,830	2,927			412		3,010	282	199	
	Liabilities	6,839		3,839					2,763	232	5
1965	Assets	7,124	3,264			612		2,808	240	200	
	Liabilities	7,129		3,672					3,277	174	6
1964	Assets	6,615	3,103			482		2,586	213	231	
	Liabilities	6,624		3,356					3,062	200	6
1963	Assets	6,196	2,823			469		2,570	184	150	
	Liabilities	6,256		3,218					2,832	134	72
1962	Assets	5,873	2,759			458	3	2,427	158	68	
	Liabilities	6,017		3,012					2,764	80	161
1961	Assets	5,556	2,391			314		2,513	115	223	
	Liabilities	5,550		2,960					2,398	179	13

Series J662-675. Financial flows, sector V, the monetary authorities, 1962 to 1976

(millions of dollars)

Year		662 Gross saving	663 Non-financial capital acquisition	664 Net lending or borrowing	665 Net financial investment	666 Official international reserves	667 Discrepancy	668 Currency and deposits	669 Loans	670 Government of Canada treasury bills	671 Finance and other short-term paper	672 Bonds	673 Claims on associated enterprises	674 Other assets and liabilities	675 Official monetary reserve offsets
1976	National accounts	1	9	-8	-8										
	Change in assets					522			-149	4	61	572	225	601	
	Change in liabilities							1,111						283	
1975	National accounts	1	11	-10	-10										
	Change in assets					-404			13	492	-96	339	45	-17	
	Change in liabilities							1,345					-898	-65	
1974	National accounts	1	17	-16	-16										
	Change in assets					24			7	509	100	494	244	77	
	Change in liabilities							1,185					238	48	
1973	National accounts	1	8	-7	-7										
	Change in assets					-467			-2	149	39	420	135	-249	
	Change in liabilities							931					-844	-55	-1
1972	National accounts	1	3	-2			-2								
	Change in assets					336				46	-1	545	72	108	
	Change in liabilities							840					141	125	
1971	National accounts	1	2	-1	3		-4								
	Change in assets					896			3	263	1	311	44	-19	
	Change in liabilities							658					846	-8	
1970	National accounts	1	5	-4	4		-8								
	Change in assets					1,662			-1	144	-3	40	66	270	
	Change in liabilities							420					1,644	111	1
1969	National accounts	1	3	-2	1		-3								
	Change in assets					65			-4	25	3	145	50	-55	
	Change in liabilities							216					4	8	
1968	National accounts	1	1	1	-1		1								
	Change in assets					350			2	-86		223	39	52	
	Change in liabilities							321					337	-78	1
1967	National accounts	1	2	-1	-4		3								
	Change in assets					17			3	125		194	33	-44	
	Change in liabilities							201					141	-7	-3
1966	National accounts	1	1	1	1		-1								
	Change in assets					-360				-199		205	42	-2	
	Change in liabilities							169					-540	57	-1
1965	National accounts	1	3	-2			-2								
	Change in assets					158				129		226	27	-30	
	Change in liabilities							326					209	-25	
1964	National accounts	1	2	-1			-1								
	Change in assets					361				13		16	29	82	
	Change in liabilities							131					307	66	-3
1963	National accounts	1	2	-1	1		-2								
	Change in assets					142				10		142	26	83	
	Change in liabilities							206					142	54	-3
1962	National accounts	1		1	13		-12								
	Change in assets					157				143	3	-84	43	-153	
	Change in liabilities							50					143	-100	3

Series J676-687. Year-end outstandings, sector VI, banks and near-banks, 1961 to 1976
(millions of dollars)

Year		Total financial assets and liabilities	Currency and deposits	Receivables and payables	Loans	Government of Canada treasury bills	Finance and other short-term paper	Mortgages	Bonds	Claims on associated enterprises	Stocks	Foreign investments	Other assets and liabilities
		676	677	678	679	680	681	682	683	684	685	686	687
1976	Assets	145,170	21,687	20,416	45,907	4,271	1,594	37,171	11,762	1,098	553	152	559
	Liabilities	146,617	134,961		291		236		2,342	540	6,374		1,873
1975	Assets	121,275	17,853	16,675	38,325	3,543	1,224	30,509	10,961	995	457	152	581
	Liabilities	122,466	113,072		217		151		1,732	234	5,496		1,564
1974	Assets	106,382	17,232	13,768	33,055	3,760	1,428	25,003	10,078	988	339	127	604
	Liabilities	107,432	99,549		225		236		1,441	153	4,673		1,155
1973	Assets	89,789	15,549	11,416	26,996	3,476	789	20,258	9,535	785	267	113	605
	Liabilities	90,669	83,656		295		134		1,196	233	4,291		864
1972	Assets	72,688	11,270	9,220	21,796	2,984	874	15,339	9,805	679	224	92	405
	Liabilities	73,498	67,582		177		107		906	185	3,870		671
1971	Assets	62,456	9,593	7,492	18,597	2,717	590	11,919	10,069	677	200	124	478
	Liabilities	63,195	58,563		228				190	176	3,474		564
1970	Assets	54,768	9,952	6,178	16,314	2,720	460	9,815	8,139	646	179	111	254
	Liabilities	55,414	51,301		271				40	233	3,163		406
1969	Assets	49,264	8,649	5,582	15,878	2,139	325	8,608	6,888	538	180	141	336
	Liabilities	49,845	45,820		301				40	222	2,983		479
1968	Assets	43,564	6,487	4,940	14,188	2,155	240	7,400	7,254	398	170	111	221
	Liabilities	44,121	40,593		217				40	218	2,706		347
1967	Assets	38,342	5,477	4,091	13,034	1,760	160	6,581	6,438	350	153	104	194
	Liabilities	38,845	35,686		228				40	189	2,457		245
1966	Assets	33,875	4,656	3,411	11,852	1,590	196	5,974	5,552	324	141	203	-24
	Liabilities	34,390	31,475		224					184	2,299		208
1965	Assets	31,563	4,286	3,070	11,055	1,381	210	5,561	5,498	307	130	113	-48
	Liabilities	32,066	29,239		278					8	2,216		325
1964	Assets	28,051	4,679	2,513	9,170	1,284	191	4,567	5,437	138	123	68	-119
	Liabilities	28,538	26,532		172						1,695		139
1963	Assets	25,088	3,983	2,060	8,176	1,321	139	3,841	5,356	108	117	80	-93
	Liabilities	25,541	23,753		92						1,584		112
1962	Assets	19,682	1,434	1,719	6,988	1,157	126	3,319	4,749	99	101	12	-22
	Liabilities	20,072	18,439		69						1,470		94
1961	Assets	18,510	1,366	1,490	6,186	1,177	116	2,898	5,025	94	86	9	63
	Liabilities	18,866	17,229		28						1,415		194

Series J688-703. Financial flows, sector VI, banks and near-banks, 1962 to 1976
(millions of dollars)

Year		Gross saving 688	Non-financial capital acquisition 689	Net lending or borrowing 690	Net financial investment 691	Discrepancy 692	Currency and deposits 693	Receivables and payables 694	Loans 695	Government of Canada treasury bills 696	Finance and other short-term paper 697	Mortgages 698	Bonds 699	Claims on associated enterprises 700	Stocks 701	Foreign investments 702	Other assets and liabilities 703
1976	National accounts	705	310	395	394	1											
	Change in assets				23,426		3,660	3,739	7,547	710	335	6,378	845	102	95	14	1
	Change in liabilities				23,032		21,670		138		54		554	139	268		209
1975	National accounts	678	255	423	445	-22											
	Change in assets				14,421		351	2,903	5,070	-252	-171	5,430	901	3	83	27	76
	Change in liabilities				13,976		13,148		4		-85		301	48	307		253
1974	National accounts	421	227	194	79	115											
	Change in assets				16,659		1,762	2,361	6,072	271	648	4,743	369	366	71	16	-20
	Change in liabilities				16,580		15,858		-70		82		263	4	181		262
1973	National accounts	417	144	273	256	17											
	Change in assets				17,083		4,342	2,235	5,217	470	-107	4,850	-237	98	38	23	154
	Change in liabilities				16,827		16,008		100		65		344	42	78		190
1972	National accounts	342	97	245	261	-16											
	Change in assets				10,230		1,713	1,679	3,164	263	-81	3,370	43	22	18	-8	47
	Change in liabilities				9,969		9,439		46		—		308	10	99		67
1971	National accounts	265	98	167	207	-40											
	Change in assets				7,789		-297	1,314	2,301	5	130	2,111	1,895	39	16	13	262
	Change in liabilities				7,582		7,340		-41		—		150	-56	37		152
1970	National accounts	207	90	117	90	27											
	Change in assets				6,030		1,660	597	525	585	135	1,171	1,283	142	-3	-26	-39
	Change in liabilities				5,940		5,971		-58		—		—	11	87		-71
1969	National accounts	207	101	106	71	35											
	Change in assets				5,780		2,241	640	1,697	-21	63	1,244	-343	126	39	-33	127
	Change in liabilities				5,709		5,315		79		—		—	5	169		141
1968	National accounts	225	67	158	113	45											
	Change in assets				5,363		1,138	848	1,163	391	80	821	817	52	13	9	31
	Change in liabilities				5,250		5,036		-9		—		—	29	94		100
1967	National accounts	150	77	73	78	-5											
	Change in assets				4,476		844	712	1,209	173	-31	605	928	25	11	-97	97
	Change in liabilities				4,398		4,288		2		—		40	6	33		29
1966	National accounts	122	69	53	47	6											
	Change in assets				2,255		324	341	790	202	27	425	59	16	11	88	-28
	Change in liabilities				2,208		2,206		-42		—		—	—	13		31
1965	National accounts	113	74	39	78	-39											
	Change in assets				2,913		-401	501	1,670	94	19	933	51	9	9	45	-17
	Change in liabilities				2,835		2,689		110		—		—	—	24		12
1964	National accounts	110	73	37	21	16											
	Change in assets				2,991		713	453	997	-38	52	728	81	31	6	-11	-18
	Change in liabilities				2,973		2,815		79		—		—	—	51		28
1963	National accounts	88	63	25	33	-8											
	Change in assets				2,231		100	340	389	164	13	524	559	11	16	-4	119
	Change in liabilities				2,198		2,110		35		—		—	—	38		15
1962	National accounts	73	73	—	-1	1											
	Change in assets				1,172		70	230	803	-25	9	421	-276	7	14	3	-84
	Change in liabilities				1,173		1,107		22		—		—	—	18		26

Series J704-715. Year-end outstandings, sector VII, insurance companies and pension funds, 1961 to 1976
(millions of dollars)

Year		Total financial assets and liabilities	Currency and deposits	Receiv-ables and payables	Loans	Govern-ment of Canada treasury bills	Finance and other short-term paper	Mortgages	Bonds	Life insur-ance and pensions	Stocks	Foreign invest-ments	Other assets and liabilities
		704	705	706	707	708	709	710	711	712	713	714	715
1976	Assets Liabilities	48,986 50,494	1,210	1,386	62	34	918	14,097	21,315	50,494	8,167	1,081	716
1975	Assets Liabilities	43,487 44,900	1,160	1,327	19	22	960	12,512	18,720	44,900	7,207	873	687
1974	Assets Liabilities	38,395 39,677	1,038	1,247	28	8	801	11,125	16,296	39,677	6,462	724	666
1973	Assets Liabilities	34,773 35,949	798	1,059	31	5	501	9,930	14,840	35,949	6,289	731	589
1972	Assets Liabilities	31,257 32,155	656	1,003	23	5	443	8,996	13,393	32,155	5,556	708	474
1971	Assets Liabilities	28,157 29,024	482	941	24	4	335	8,478	12,424	29,024	4,371	698	400
1970	Assets Liabilities	25,872 26,716	517	876	18	4	310	8,201	11,430	26,716	3,454	679	383
1969	Assets Liabilities	24,093 24,819	383	810	19	4	190	7,881	10,731	24,819	2,999	730	346
1968	Assets Liabilities	22,511 23,130	380	698	12	16	8	7,459	10,598	23,130	2,403	603	334
1967	Assets Liabilities	20,837 21,375	286	627	11	10	12	7,010	10,239	21,375	1,892	398	352
1966	Assets Liabilities	19,282 19,771	251	511	11	12	31	6,624	9,640	19,771	1,579	278	345
1965	Assets Liabilities	17,869 18,321	231	465	11	14	32	6,003	9,241	18,321	1,366	199	307
1964	Assets Liabilities	16,390 16,800	134	449	12	15	18	5,333	8,855	16,800	1,130	155	289
1963	Assets Liabilities	15,026 15,407	125	429	11	33	11	4,765	8,380	15,407	891	112	269
1962	Assets Liabilities	13,676 14,038	100	411	11	18	11	4,230	7,802	14,038	751	91	251
1961	Assets Liabilities	12,532 12,882	95	394	11	18	11	3,768	7,297	12,882	645	65	228

Series J716-730. Financial flows, sector VII, insurance companies and pension funds, 1962 to 1976

(million of dollars)

Year		716 Gross saving	717 Non-financial capital acquisition	718 Net lending or borrowing	719 Net financial investment	720 Currency and deposits	721 Receivables and payables	722 Loans	723 Government of Canada treasury bills	724 Finance and other short-term paper	725 Mortgages	726 Bonds	727 Life insurance and pensions	728 Stocks	729 Foreign investments	730 Other assets and liabilities
1976	National accounts	35	157	-122	-122											
	Change in assets				5,569	56	58	41	16	-31	1,571	2,650		973	207	28
	Change in liabilities				5,691								5,691			
1975	National accounts	32	125	-93	-93											
	Change in assets				5,027	-7	86	-15	14	157	1,308	2,656		655	150	23
	Change in liabilities				5,120								5,120			
1974	National accounts	29	121	-92	-92											
	Change in assets				4,082	266	177	26	3	299	1,202	1,530		511	-8	76
	Change in liabilities				4,174								4,174			
1973	National accounts	25	109	-84	-84											
	Change in assets				3,617	196	56	13	—	58	948	1,453		753	23	117
	Change in liabilities				3,701								3,701			
1972	National accounts	24	83	-59	-59											
	Change in assets				2,862	151	51	-8	1	110	446	1,036		990	9	76
	Change in liabilities				2,921								2,921			
1971	National accounts	22	143	-121	-121											
	Change in assets				2,173	-65	65	14	—	24	287	1,010		804	20	14
	Change in liabilities				2,294								2,294			
1970	National accounts	20	73	-53	-53											
	Change in assets				1,770	107	62	-3	—	117	298	744		458	-51	38
	Change in liabilities				1,823								1,823			
1969	National accounts	18	82	-64	-64											
	Change in assets				1,679	154	105	7	-12	48	387	301		549	128	12
	Change in liabilities				1,743								1,743			
1968	National accounts	16	33	-17	-17											
	Change in assets				1,651	85	66	3	6	-4	463	427		418	205	-18
	Change in liabilities				1,668								1,668			
1967	National accounts	14	52	-38	-38											
	Change in assets				1,572	33	109	—	-2	-19	401	614		309	120	7
	Change in liabilities				1,610								1,610			
1966	National accounts	15	44	-29	-29											
	Change in assets				1,437	34	43	4	-2	-1	618	395		229	79	38
	Change in liabilities				1,466								1,466			
1965	National accounts	10	37	-27	-27											
	Change in assets				1,446	97	11	-1	-1	13	637	409		219	44	18
	Change in liabilities				1,473								1,473			
1964	National accounts	10	23	-13	-13											
	Change in assets				1,397	10	19	3	-18	8	567	527		216	43	22
	Change in liabilities				1,410								1,410			
1963	National accounts	8	13	-5	-5											
	Change in assets				1,282	33	20	1	15	—	483	554		137	21	18
	Change in liabilities				1,287								1,287			
1962	National accounts	9	24	-15	-15											
	Change in assets				1,121	5	17	—	—	—	475	452		126	24	22
	Change in liabilities				1,136								1,136			

Series J731-742. Year-end outstandings, sector VIII, other private financial institutions, 1961 to 1976
(millions of dollars)

Year		Total financial assets and liabilities	Currency and deposits	Receivables and payables	Loans	Government of Canada treasury bills	Finance and other short-term paper	Mortgages	Bonds	Claims on associated enterprises	Stocks	Foreign investments	Other assets and liabilities
		731	732	733	734	735	736	737	738	739	740	741	742
1976	Assets	43,914	2,183	4,726	7,164	396	2,635	3,269	4,500	12,652	3,320	923	2,146
	Liabilities	44,159		247	4,249	—	5,436	33	5,791	4,385	17,715		6,303
1975	Assets	37,468	1,725	4,602	6,462	309	2,234	2,756	3,760	10,136	3,123	843	1,518
	Liabilities	37,652		119	4,078	—	4,594	38	4,479	3,725	15,342		5,277
1974	Assets	31,189	1,209	4,409	5,742	130	1,910	2,165	3,346	6,649	2,963	774	1,892
	Liabilities	31,397		100	3,685	1	4,482	26	3,680	3,215	11,435		4,773
1973	Assets	27,285	1,331	4,173	3,654	75	1,281	1,596	3,153	6,478	3,091	890	1,563
	Liabilities	27,410		73	2,791	1	3,088	23	3,290	2,443	11,586		4,115
1972	Assets	23,801	1,100	3,797	3,254	133	1,294	1,030	2,999	4,607	3,078	1,229	1,280
	Liabilities	23,927		69	2,613	—	2,050	38	2,793	1,931	10,074		4,359
1971	Assets	19,307	898	2,832	2,677	116	917	812	2,637	3,066	3,024	1,284	1,044
	Liabilities	19,393		57	2,064	—	1,650	18	1,993	1,606	8,254		3,751
1970	Assets	18,061	780	3,283	1,962	197	861	578	2,371	2,961	2,908	1,195	965
	Liabilities	18,181		48	1,598	—	1,778	14	1,990	1,645	7,808		3,300
1969	Assets	17,550	712	3,412	1,938	135	631	475	2,081	2,962	2,764	1,452	988
	Liabilities	17,655		44	1,379	—	1,917	15	1,793	1,610	7,883		3,014
1968	Assets	15,727	607	2,979	2,082	82	506	364	1,980	2,654	2,574	1,587	312
	Liabilities	15,880		48	1,314	—	1,459	12	1,654	1,518	7,366		2,509
1967	Assets	13,627	515	2,662	1,528	85	434	122	2,121	2,193	2,293	1,030	644
	Liabilities	14,165		48	1,409	—	1,063	87	1,737	1,257	6,339		2,225
1966	Assets	12,612	399	2,347	1,417	49	372	85	1,920	2,153	2,197	740	933
	Liabilities	13,228		36	1,341	—	1,001	126	1,584	1,352	5,768		2,020
1965	Assets	11,195	379	2,174	1,629	51	373	65	1,589	1,523	2,008	504	900
	Liabilities	11,801		36	1,355	—	908	103	1,434	1,178	4,934		1,853
1964	Assets	9,547	320	1,939	1,311	139	278	35	1,570	1,338	1,622	323	672
	Liabilities	10,050		36	1,151	—	1,071	94	1,157	960	4,102		1,479
1963	Assets	8,296	252	1,684	1,109	207	117	38	1,464	1,278	1,327	304	516
	Liabilities	8,712		36	1,057	—	807	81	969	984	3,536		1,242
1962	Assets	7,358	239	1,515	888	198	95	28	1,467	1,133	1,116	247	432
	Liabilities	7,682		36	998	—	634	48	860	934	3,099		1,073
1961	Assets	6,692	221	1,350	721	171	36	18	1,443	1,076	1,001	250	405
	Liabilities	7,018		36	943	—	465	48	790	892	2,838		1,006

Series J743-758. Financial flows, sector VIII, other private financial institutions, 1962 to 1976

Year		Gross saving	Non-financial capital acquisition	Net lending or borrowing	Net financial investment	Discrepancy	Currency and deposits	Receivables and payables	Loans	Government of Canada treasury bills	Finance and other short-term paper	Mortgages	Bonds	Claims on associated enterprises	Stocks	Foreign investments	Other assets and liabilities
		743	744	745	746	747	748	749	750	751	752	753	754	755	756	757	758
1976	National accounts	657	31	626	626	—											
	Change in assets				4,414		399	111	640	74	336	523	738	1,127	-4	-38	508
	Change in liabilities				3,788			17	104		612	3	1,179	258	397		1,218
1975	National accounts	643	57	586	586	—											
	Change in assets				2,670		353	205	702	160	266	409	329	668	-88	-26	-308
	Change in liabilities				2,084			29	416		202	6	660	75	302		394
1974	National accounts	231	27	204	204	—											
	Change in assets				3,820		-219	229	1,715	68	583	514	214	672	-163	-50	257
	Change in liabilities				3,616			33	778		1,255	21	381	550	18		580
1973	National accounts	268	65	203	203	—											
	Change in assets				2,098		66	378	732	-62	-325	545	301	337	16	-178	288
	Change in liabilities				1,895			29	-152		859	-48	485	234	24		464
1972	National accounts	290	23	267	267	—											
	Change in assets				1,500		138	288	465	13	391	153	203	189	-314	-215	189
	Change in liabilities				1,233			23	384		342	13	304	-34	-226		427
1971	National accounts	294	20	274	275	-1											
	Change in assets				880		135	-98	429	-57	52	40	236	113	49	-16	-3
	Change in liabilities				605			-2	499		-127	3	87	-128	-123		396
1970	National accounts	238	25	213	213	—											
	Change in assets				682		-29	-40	-169	40	244	80	315	-3	181	-25	88
	Change in liabilities				469			16	212		-148	-1	195	-17	-66		278
1969	National accounts	159	21	138	135	3											
	Change in assets				1,444		99	431	301	78	119	4	50	258	149	-95	50
	Change in liabilities				1,309			-8	292		398	4	138	21	318		146
1968	National accounts	212	20	192	195	-3											
	Change in assets				1,546		80	260	245	-33	-1	24	102	151	185	401	132
	Change in liabilities				1,351			8	30		396	6	68	162	499		182
1967	National accounts	112	-5	117	129	-12											
	Change in assets				894		85	40	112	82	91	6	156	124	-20	215	3
	Change in liabilities				765			12	103		62	-1	120	-8	300		177
1966	National accounts	105	30	75	57	18											
	Change in assets				1,039		4	174	-102	18	19	21	325	227	149	221	-17
	Change in liabilities				982			—	-19		94	7	100	161	450		189
1965	National accounts	92	38	54	53	1											
	Change in assets				1,398		66	235	318	-90	55	27	21	69	330	169	198
	Change in liabilities				1,345			—	233		-162	10	204	248	482		330
1964	National accounts	61	26	35	38	-3											
	Change in assets				1,171		70	255	196	-64	161	-3	104	62	236	29	125
	Change in liabilities				1,133			—	100		263	1	190	-36	405		210
1963	National accounts	22	8	14	14	—											
	Change in assets				955		25	170	220	10	20	10	-8	142	205	54	107
	Change in liabilities				941			—	67		173	—	111	31	396		163
1962	National accounts	40	14	26	27	-1											
	Change in assets				658		17	165	162	23	-47	11	30	57	120	-1	27
	Change in liabilities				631			—	36		180	—	71	42	231		71

Series J759-770. Year-end outstandings, sector IX, public financial institutions, 1961 to 1976
(millions of dollars)

Year		Total financial assets and liabilities	Currency and deposits	Receivables and payables	Loans	Government of Canada treasury bills	Finance and other short-term paper	Mortgages	Bonds	Claims on associated enterprises	Stocks	Foreign investments	Other assets and liabilities
		759	760	761	762	763	764	765	766	767	768	769	770
1976	Assets	21,717	874	90	4,515	42	42	10,131	3,966	827	822	—	408
	Liabilities	22,750	1,253	121	1,103		64	92	146	18,245	567		1,159
1975	Assets	18,905	602	69	3,768	24	88	9,220	3,224	801	781	—	328
	Liabilities	19,976	1,093	102	1,236		27	59	76	15,817	564		1,002
1974	Assets	16,220	473	63	3,043	12	49	8,222	2,754	627	743	—	234
	Liabilities	16,944	815	84	172		45	54	70	14,395	427		882
1973	Assets	13,826	425	44	2,261	14	6	7,304	2,396	559	630	—	187
	Liabilities	14,380	672	74	169		63	41	77	12,371	267		646
1972	Assets	12,006	194	33	1,882	15	37	6,874	2,124	213	448	—	186
	Liabilities	12,453	460	48	81		45	35	52	11,050	137		545
1971	Assets	10,459	143	26	1,550	19	—	6,370	1,724	192	287	—	148
	Liabilities	10,812	385	30	81		—	30	52	9,789	—		445
1970	Assets	9,063	88	41	1,668	11	—	5,379	1,389	154	216	—	117
	Liabilities	9,331	322	26	26		—	25	47	8,508	—		377
1969	Assets	7,962	109	24	1,429	3	—	4,907	1,095	154	160	—	81
	Liabilities	8,186	326	14	16		—	11	47	7,416	—		356
1968	Assets	6,840	71	16	1,170	1	—	4,451	832	138	102	—	59
	Liabilities	7,023	279	10	15		—	5	31	6,381	—		302
1967	Assets	5,907	59	19	986	1	—	4,017	597	131	51	—	46
	Liabilities	6,052	242	8	25		—	3	28	5,493	—		253
1966	Assets	4,642	39	10	842	—	—	3,220	372	122	3	—	34
	Liabilities	4,778	217	12	14		—	3	28	4,292	—		212
1965	Assets	3,679	43	8	683	—	—	2,627	173	119	—	—	26
	Liabilities	3,793	201	8	17		—	—	5	3,375	—		187
1964	Assets	3,119	42	9	512	1	—	2,281	163	91	—	—	20
	Liabilities	3,238	189	7	10		—	—	3	2,863	—		166
1963	Assets	2,711	41	8	397	7	—	2,010	155	76	—	—	17
	Liabilities	2,800	173	7	6		—	—	3	2,461	—		150
1962	Assets	2,505	48	7	294	8	—	1,916	144	73	—	—	15
	Liabilities	2,580	153	6	3		—	—	3	2,280	—		135
1961	Assets	2,256	36	7	184	1	—	1,780	160	73	—	1	14
	Liabilities	2,307	168	5	—		—	—	3	2,014	—		117

Series J771-786. Financial flows, sector IX, public financial institutions, 1962 to 1976

(millions of dollars)

Year		Gross saving	Non-financial capital acquisition	Net lending or borrowing	Net financial investment	Discrepancy	Currency and deposits	Receivables and payables	Loans	Government of Canada treasury bills	Finance and other short-term paper	Mortgages	Bonds	Claims on associated enterprises	Stocks	Foreign investments	Other assets and liabilities
		771	772	773	774	775	776	777	778	779	780	781	782	783	784	785	786
1976	National accounts	67	54	13	37	-24											
	Change in assets				2,807		274	22	746	16	-52	911	745	26	39	–	80
	Change in liabilities				2,770		160	18	-134		36	33	70	2,428	2		157
1975	National accounts	-121	251	-372	-325	-47											
	Change in assets				2,713		130	5	726	11	40	997	471	202	38	–	93
	Change in liabilities				3,038		278	16	61		-18	5	6	2,430	143		117
1974	National accounts	-46	163	-209	-164	-45											
	Change in assets				2,357		33	9	774	5	50	917	352	59	121	–	37
	Change in liabilities				2,521		143	7	-27		-17	9	8	2,034	160		204
1973	National accounts	1	111	-110	-111	1											
	Change in assets				1,830		227	11	411	-3	-31	429	276	321	182	–	7
	Change in liabilities				1,941		213	28	90		18	6	20	1,342	130		94
1972	National accounts	13	76	-63	-93	30											
	Change in assets				1,548		52	6	332	1	37	504	395	21	161	–	39
	Change in liabilities				1,641		75	18	–		45	5	–	1,261	137		100
1971	National accounts	13	93	-80	-85	5											
	Change in assets				1,396		55	-14	243	6	–	630	336	38	71	–	31
	Change in liabilities				1,481		63	4	55		–	5	5	1,281	–		68
1970	National accounts	17	52	-35	-47	12											
	Change in assets				1,133		-8	25	179	–	3	542	299	–	52	–	41
	Change in liabilities				1,180		5	8	14		–	9	3	1,092	–		49
1969	National accounts	4	55	-51	-30	-21											
	Change in assets				1,133		38	8	197	2	–	527	266	16	58	–	21
	Change in liabilities				1,163		47	4	1		–	6	16	1,035	–		54
1968	National accounts	5	19	-14	-33	19											
	Change in assets				934		12	-3	125	–	–	494	235	7	51	–	13
	Change in liabilities				967		37	2	-15		–	2	3	888	–		50
1967	National accounts	11	1	10	-6	16											
	Change in assets				1,268		24	9	143	–	–	797	226	9	48	–	12
	Change in liabilities				1,274		25	-3	12		–	–	–	1,201	–		39
1966	National accounts	4	21	-17	-22	5											
	Change in assets				964		-4	2	159	–	–	593	199	3	3	–	9
	Change in liabilities				986		16	4	-1		–	3	23	917	–		24
1965	National accounts	4	9	-5	4	-9											
	Change in assets				560		1	-1	172	-1	–	346	9	28	3	–	6
	Change in liabilities				556		12	1	8		–	–	2	512	–		21
1964	National accounts	-1	16	-17	-28	11											
	Change in assets				409		1	–	117	-7	–	271	8	15	–	–	4
	Change in liabilities				437		16	-1	3		–	–	–	402	–		17
1963	National accounts	–	13	-13	-16	3											
	Change in assets				205		-5	1	102	-1	–	93	10	3	–	–	2
	Change in liabilities				221		20	2	3		–	–	–	181	–		15
1962	National accounts	-2	19	-21	-24	3											
	Change in assets				249		12	–	110	7	–	136	-16	–	–	-1	1
	Change in liabilities				273		-15	1	3		–	–	–	266	–		18

Series J787-799. Year-end outstandings, sector X, federal government, 1961 to 1976
(millions of dollars)

Year		Total financial assets and liabilities	Currency and deposits	Receivables and payables	Loans	Government of Canada treasury bills	Finance and other short-term paper	Mortgages	Bonds	Life insurance and pensions	Claims on associated enterprises	Stocks	Foreign investments	Other assets and liabilities
		787	788	789	790	791	792	793	794	795	796	797	798	799
1976	Assets	35,073	2,671	55	5,552	—	18	519	81		23,709	528	5	1,935
	Liabilities	48,176	821	68	250	7,845			33,623	1,173	331			4,065
1975	Assets	33,943	3,494	52	5,179	—	18	554	73		21,460	572	6	2,535
	Liabilities	43,797	773	92	262	6,200			31,080	1,197	313			3,880
1974	Assets	33,114	4,246	30	4,599	—	12	569	70		20,338	467	13	2,770
	Liabilities	39,189	704	81	207	5,630			27,664	1,218	243			3,442
1973	Assets	27,201	1,687	20	4,063	2	12	552	64		18,503	389	5	1,904
	Liabilities	33,912	618	50	147	4,690			24,225	1,238	184			2,760
1972	Assets	26,474	2,163	19	3,414	7	13	553	74		18,382	237	5	1,607
	Liabilities	33,733	554	57	85	4,160			24,861	1,265	167			2,584
1971	Assets	24,583	1,905	10	3,078	7	8	556	69		17,437	76	3	1,434
	Liabilities	31,388	529	65	59	3,830			23,601	1,266	147			1,891
1970	Assets	21,585	1,143	9	2,648	9	6	548	548		15,385	53	28	1,208
	Liabilities	28,222	504	62	11	3,625			21,030	1,277	132			1,581
1969	Assets	19,334	1,057	8	2,445	2	11	525	596		13,171	26	60	1,433
	Liabilities	25,966	480	50	65	2,895			19,902	1,283	118			1,173
1968	Assets	17,882	336	6	2,270	6	10	457	573		12,350	19	92	1,763
	Liabilities	25,586	446	34	209	2,825			19,406	1,285	100			1,281
1967	Assets	16,219	335	6	2,053	4	12	404	442		11,247	15	168	1,533
	Liabilities	23,825	380	32	271	2,445			18,334	1,284	73			1,006
1966	Assets	15,056	671	6	1,880	6	7	343	510		9,870	10	180	1,573
	Liabilities	22,518	344	41	164	2,170			17,558	1,280	96			865
1965	Assets	14,067	654	7	1,658	4	5	293	228		9,505	7	198	1,508
	Liabilities	21,763	319	30	27	2,150			17,136	1,272	33			796
1964	Assets	13,351	576	8	1,591	5	—	272	437		8,709	6	225	1,522
	Liabilities	21,636	282	21	19	2,140			17,205	1,258	26			685
1963	Assets	12,541	840	4	1,588	8	—	255	176		8,139	7	—	1,524
	Liabilities	21,058	253	22	25	2,240			16,623	1,240	15			640
1962	Assets	11,817	409	3	1,601	9	—	238	322		7,779	8	5	1,443
	Liabilities	19,888	230	18	26	2,170			15,619	1,219	10			596
1961	Assets	11,188	425	3	1,690	12	—	223	313		7,103	8	5	1,406
	Liabilities	19,011	230	13	30	1,885			15,072	1,188	9			584

Series J800–815. Financial flows, sector X, federal government, 1962 to 1976

(millions of dollars)

Year	Item	800 Gross saving	801 Non-financial capital acquisition	802 Net lending or borrowing	803 Net financial investment	804 Discrepancy	805 Currency and deposits	806 Receivables and payables	807 Loans	808 Government of Canada treasury bills	809 Finance and other short-term paper	810 Mortgages	811 Bonds	812 Claims on associated enterprises	813 Stocks	814 Foreign investments	815 Other assets and liabilities
1976	National accounts	-1,608	1,331	-2,939	-2,478	-461											
	Change in assets				1,909		-823	3	384	—	—	-35	8	2,289	-44	-1	128
	Change in liabilities				4,387		47	-24	-12	1,645			2,543	18			194
1975	National accounts	-2,430	1,232	-3,662	-3,336	-326											
	Change in assets				1,298		-752	22	518	—	6	-15	4	1,094	105	-7	323
	Change in liabilities				4,634		69	11	56	570			3,416	70			464
1974	National accounts	2,053	1,029	1,024	598	426											
	Change in assets				5,895		2,559	9	489	-1	1	17	6	1,838	78	8	891
	Change in liabilities				5,297		86	31	60	940			3,439	59			702
1973	National accounts	1,106	491	615	349	266											
	Change in assets				530		-474	1	645	-5	-1	-1	-10	-73	152	—	296
	Change in liabilities				181		65	-7	62	530			-636	17			176
1972	National accounts	55	610	-555	-611	56											
	Change in assets				1,840		281	9	326	—	5	-3	5	847	160	2	208
	Change in liabilities				2,451		26	59	26	330			1,260	20			732
1971	National accounts	369	510	-141	-108	-33											
	Change in assets				3,021		761	1	437	4	2	8	-479	2,102	24	-25	186
	Change in liabilities				3,129		25	2	48	205			2,571	14			275
1970	National accounts	731	455	276	218	58											
	Change in assets				2,504		89	—	195	2	-5	23	-48	2,489	26	-32	-235
	Change in liabilities				2,286		24	12	-54	730			1,129	14			437
1969	National accounts	1,507	488	1,019	1,050	-31											
	Change in assets				1,451		721	2	183	-4	—	69	23	811	7	-31	-330
	Change in liabilities				401		34	15	-144	70			495	18			-85
1968	National accounts	489	622	-133	-142	9											
	Change in assets				1,650		5	—	192	2	-2	51	131	1,112	5	-76	230
	Change in liabilities				1,792		66	2	-61	380			1,073	27			305
1967	National accounts	380	464	-84	-164	80											
	Change in assets				1,171		-336	1	167	-1	5	61	-68	1,390	4	-12	-40
	Change in liabilities				1,335		36	-9	107	275			776	-23			169
1966	National accounts	661	427	234	207	27											
	Change in assets				961		17	-1	210	1	2	50	281	340	3	-7	65
	Change in liabilities				754		25	11	136	20			421	63			70
1965	National accounts	895	347	548	607	-59											
	Change in assets				714		76	-1	72	—	5	21	-209	790	1	-27	-14
	Change in liabilities				107		36	9	8	10			-69	7			91
1964	National accounts	554	200	354	359	-5											
	Change in assets				909		-262	4	23	-3	-1	17	261	647	—	225	-2
	Change in liabilities				550		30	-1	-6	-100			582	11			17
1963	National accounts	-50	232	-282	-299	17											
	Change in assets				819		433	1	-3	-1	1	18	-146	435	—	—	81
	Change in liabilities				1,118		2	4	—	70			1,004	5			11
1962	National accounts	-237	269	-506	-471	-35											
	Change in assets				406		-16	—	-89	-3	—	15	9	453	—	—	37
	Change in liabilities				877		—	5	-4	285			547	1			12

Series J816-826. Year-end outstandings, sector XI, provincial and local governments and hospitals, 1961 to 1976

(millions of dollars)

Year		Total financial assets and liabilities	Currency and deposits	Receivables and payables	Loans	Government of Canada treasury bills	Finance and other short-term paper	Mortgages	Bonds	Claims on associated enterprises	Stocks	Other assets and liabilities
		816	817	818	819	820	821	822	823	824	825	826
1976	Assets	30,096	3,222	631	2,774	—	89	2,234	8,643	8,206	292	4,005
	Liabilities	53,725		1,457	5,308		459	186	42,828	553		2,934
1975	Assets	28,520	2,783	530	2,673	1	86	1,890	7,900	7,691	269	4,697
	Liabilities	48,055		1,335	4,798		633	177	37,762	487		2,863
1974	Assets	24,687	2,497	431	2,439	—	83	1,551	6,867	6,075	141	4,603
	Liabilities	41,059		949	4,236		204	168	32,551	400		2,551
1973	Assets	21,195	2,361	301	2,183	—	79	1,291	6,377	5,054	124	3,425
	Liabilities	36,601		791	3,437		343	158	29,133	353		2,386
1972	Assets	18,683	2,123	295	1,950	6	66	1,103	6,055	4,639	159	2,287
	Liabilities	32,998		755	2,728		435	177	26,801	385		1,717
1971	Assets	17,191	1,422	240	1,746	3	45	924	5,678	4,188	173	2,772
	Liabilities	29,737		656	2,377		313	157	24,003	232		1,999
1970	Assets	15,747	1,529	224	1,458	4	34	660	5,261	3,845	168	2,564
	Liabilities	27,084		653	2,198		174	159	21,817	191		1,892
1969	Assets	13,742	1,256	188	631	4	21	462	5,640	2,961	45	2,534
	Liabilities	24,334		502	1,987		118	143	19,822	77		1,685
1968	Assets	11,696	791	160	555	3	17	356	4,865	2,490	31	2,428
	Liabilities	22,090		475	1,761		—	190	17,929	80		1,655
1967	Assets	10,295	647	145	472	—	14	284	4,223	2,224	16	2,270
	Liabilities	19,819		423	1,592		—	121	15,967	73		1,643
1966	Assets	9,324	690	121	334	2	16	277	3,702	1,930	13	2,229
	Liabilities	17,307		343	1,383		—	99	13,811	68		1,603
1965	Assets	8,203	677	82	143	2	13	260	3,149	1,759	15	2,103
	Liabilities	15,111		253	980		—	86	12,186	67		1,539
1964	Assets	7,497	741	73	88	1	11	235	2,770	1,560	10	2,008
	Liabilities	13,784		169	729		—	80	11,284	39		1,483
1963	Assets	6,934	631	66	61	1	10	214	2,502	1,515	11	1,923
	Liabilities	12,647		123	585		—	71	10,394	36		1,438
1962	Assets	6,576	502	70	44	7	9	200	2,335	1,521	10	1,878
	Liabilities	11,689		99	487		—	63	9,578	36		1,426
1961	Assets	6,090	420	74	15	7	8	190	2,219	1,445	10	1,702
	Liabilities	10,790		81	466		—	55	8,818	37		1,333

Series J827–842. Financial flows, sector XI, provincial and local governments and hospitals, 1962 to 1976

(millions of dollars)

Year	Item	Gross saving (827)	Non-financial capital acquisition (828)	Net lending or borrowing (829)	Net financial investment (830)	Discrepancy (831)	Currency and deposits (832)	Receivables and payables (833)	Loans (834)	Government of Canada treasury bills (835)	Finance and other short-term paper (836)	Mortgages (837)	Bonds (838)	Claims on associated enterprises (839)	Stocks (840)	Foreign investments (841)	Other assets and liabilities (842)
1976	National accounts	2,592	5,774	-3,182	-3,760	578				—						—	
	Change in assets				2,054		505	101	100		3	344	757	913	23		-692
	Change in liabilities				5,814			122	422		-175	9	5,289	66			81
1975	National accounts	3,017	5,966	-2,949	-3,037	88				—						—	
	Change in assets				3,834		271	99	235		3	339	1,033	1,792	-48		110
	Change in liabilities				6,871			386	510		429	9	5,124	89			324
1974	National accounts	4,354	4,843	-489	-730	241				1						—	
	Change in assets				3,565		136	130	257		3	260	487	1,008	225		1,058
	Change in liabilities				4,295			158	740		-140	9	3,306	47			175
1973	National accounts	2,964	3,830	-866	-1,331	465				-5						—	
	Change in assets				1,423		189	6	201		14	188	309	487	-35		69
	Change in liabilities				2,754			36	695		-92	-19	2,124	-32			42
1972	National accounts	2,635	3,624	-989	-1,469	480				3						—	
	Change in assets				2,062		640	54	203		21	179	377	601	-14		-2
	Change in liabilities				3,531			99	349		122	21	2,710	153			77
1971	National accounts	2,197	3,537	-1,340	-1,008	-332				-1						—	
	Change in assets				1,563		-58	16	289		10	264	417	300	5		321
	Change in liabilities				2,571			3	148		139	2	2,150	41			88
1970	National accounts	2,042	2,959	-917	-985	68				—						—	
	Change in assets				1,602		273	28	64		14	198	509	464	32		20
	Change in liabilities				2,587			151	109		56	15	2,042	10			204
1969	National accounts	2,356	2,747	-391	-152	-239				1						—	
	Change in assets				2,051		465	28	76		4	106	777	474	14		106
	Change in liabilities				2,203			27	184		—	4	2,010	-2			-20
1968	National accounts	2,023	2,598	-575	-747	172				10						—	
	Change in assets				1,466		196	15	83		3	72	644	261	23		159
	Change in liabilities				2,213			52	109		—	44	1,962	8			38
1967	National accounts	1,863	2,690	-827	-1,422	595				-2						—	
	Change in assets				980		-42	23	128		-2	7	521	296	11		40
	Change in liabilities				2,402			80	100		—	23	2,156	4			39
1966	National accounts	1,897	2,434	-537	-865	328				-3						1	
	Change in assets				1,176		13	64	201		2	17	577	176	1		127
	Change in liabilities				2,041			90	257		—	14	1,630	-4			54
1965	National accounts	1,742	2,086	-344	-493	149				-7						—	
	Change in assets				709		-64	9	55		3	25	377	213	3		95
	Change in liabilities				1,202			84	191		—	6	896	29			-4
1964	National accounts	1,513	1,752	-239	-619	380				5						—	
	Change in assets				526		110	7	27		1	21	271	—	-1		85
	Change in liabilities				1,145			46	151		—	9	890	5			44
1963	National accounts	1,399	1,756	-357	-588	231				-5						—	
	Change in assets				374		129	-4	17		1	14	173	—	4		45
	Change in liabilities				962			24	93		—	7	816	9			13
1962	National accounts	1,431	1,650	-219	-382	163				-9						—	
	Change in assets				506		97	-4	33		1	10	116	87	—		175
	Change in liabilities				888			18	5		—	8	760	4			93

Series J843-845. Year-end outstandings, sector XII, social security funds, 1966 to 1976
(millions of dollars)

Year		Bonds	Claims on associated enterprises	Other financial assets
		843	**844**	**845**
1976	Assets	10,607	4,326	53
1975	Assets	9,088	3,683	40
1974	Assets	7,688	3,101	23
1973	Assets	6,447	2,567	18
1972	Assets	5,402	2,144	14
1971	Assets	4,442	1,730	13
1970	Assets	3,520	1,385	2
1969	Assets	2,653	1,058	3
1968	Assets	1,844	750	7
1967	Assets	1,135	461	2
1966	Assets	463	248	—

Series J846-851. Financial flows, sector XII, social security funds, 1966 to 1976
(millions of dollars)

Year		Gross saving	Net lending or borrowing	Net financial investment	Bonds	Claims on associated enterprises	Other assets
		846	**847**	**848**	**849**	**850**	**851**
1976	National accounts / Change in assets / Change in liabilities	2,175	2,175	2,175	1,519	643	13
1975	National accounts / Change in assets / Change in liabilities	1,999	1,999	1,999	1,400	582	17
1974	National accounts / Change in assets / Change in liabilities	1,775	1,775	1,775	1,241	529	5
1973	National accounts / Change in assets / Change in liabilities	1,472	1,472	1,472	1,045	423	4
1972	National accounts / Change in assets / Change in liabilities	1,375	1,375	1,375	960	414	1
1971	National accounts / Change in assets / Change in liabilities	1,278	1,278	1,278	922	345	11
1970	National accounts / Change in assets / Change in liabilities	1,193	1,193	1,193	867	327	-1
1969	National accounts / Change in assets / Change in liabilities	1,113	1,113	1,113	809	308	-4
1968	National accounts / Change in assets / Change in liabilities	1,003	1,003	1,003	709	289	5
1967	National accounts / Change in assets / Change in liabilities	887	887	887	672	213	2
1966	National accounts / Change in assets / Change in liabilities	709	709	709	463	248	-2

Series J852-862. Year-end outstandings, sector XIII, rest of the world, 1961 to 1976
(millions of dollars)

Year		Total financial assets and liabilities	Currency and deposits	Loans	Government of Canada treasury bills	Finance and other short-term paper	Mortgages	Bonds	Claims on associated enterprises	Stocks	Foreign investments	Other assets and liabilities
		852	853	854	855	856	857	858	859	860	861	862
1976	Assets	96,001	16,646	3,103	820	1,669	1,128	29,190	46,561	3,752		-6,868
	Liabilities	47,387	14,807	9,468					11,500		4,892	826
1975	Assets	83,456	14,264	2,417	122	1,218	1,052	20,574	44,012	3,480		-3,683
	Liabilities	41,124	12,266	8,012					10,502		4,459	475
1974	Assets	73,979	13,187	2,263	85	798	995	15,898	40,393	3,089		-2,729
	Liabilities	38,723	12,445	6,595					9,440		4,109	364
1973	Assets	67,624	12,694	2,032	7	542	955	14,150	36,676	3,069		-2,501
	Liabilities	36,005	13,174	5,085					7,955		3,857	189
1972	Assets	59,578	9,026	1,581	31	542	917	13,502	32,990	2,827		-1,838
	Liabilities	30,083	9,446	4,303					6,794		3,452	70
1971	Assets	55,688	7,131	1,232	9	689	950	11,950	31,649	2,520		-442
	Liabilities	27,199	8,198	3,643					6,605		3,129	42
1970	Assets	53,604	6,269	996	13	675	906	11,533	29,896	2,723		593
	Liabilities	25,425	8,514	2,999					6,194		2,953	34
1969	Assets	50,123	5,401	986	92	379	837	11,158	27,585	2,829		855
	Liabilities	22,091	7,640	2,721					5,211		3,144	42
1968	Assets	44,347	3,635	940	72	163	—	9,839	25,289	2,667		1,741
	Liabilities	18,111	4,596	2,539					4,617		3,091	—
1967	Assets	41,301	3,183	940	24	295	—	8,743	23,221	2,517		2,376
	Liabilities	15,984	3,825	2,412					4,030		2,781	—
1966	Assets	38,920	2,932	706	20	346	—	7,989	21,312	2,527		3,083
	Liabilities	14,886	3,088	2,552					3,711		2,608	—
1965	Assets	36,679	3,160	746	35	343	—	7,358	19,532	2,445		3,054
	Liabilities	14,284	2,823	2,492					3,469		2,236	—
1964	Assets	34,609	3,356	830	23	480	—	6,685	17,789	2,437		3,003
	Liabilities	14,254	3,411	2,374					3,272		2,094	—
1963	Assets	32,129	2,920	778	39	284	—	5,942	17,189	2,488		2,417
	Liabilities	12,502	2,706	2,086					3,082		1,805	—
1962	Assets	28,434	479	768	66	214	—	5,315	16,216	2,649		2,566
	Liabilities	9,878	972	1,636					2,784		1,682	45
1961	Assets	26,831	504	936	62	95	—	4,991	15,188	2,678		2,364
	Liabilities	9,156	872	1,645					2,596		1,530	122

Series J863-875. Financial flows, sector XIII, rest of the world, 1962 to 1976

(millions of dollars)

Year		Gross saving	Non-financial capital acquisition	Net lending or borrowing	Net financial investment	Currency and deposits	Loans	Government of Canada treasury bills	Finance and other short-term paper	Mortgages	Bonds	Claims on associated enterprises	Stocks	Other assets and liabilities
		863	864	865	866	867	868	869	870	871	872	873	874	875
1976	National accounts	4,733	546	4,187	4,187									
	Change in assets				9,432	2,352	630	698	449	76	8,616	-326	-28	-3,035
	Change in liabilities				5,245	2,682	1,455					312		352
1975	National accounts	5,274	495	4,779	4,779									
	Change in assets				5,964	843	198	37	407	56	4,675	597	91	-940
	Change in liabilities				1,185	-479	1,395					461		111
1974	National accounts	2,052	539	1,513	1,513									
	Change in assets				3,173	443	302	77	254	40	1,865	785	-139	-454
	Change in liabilities				1,660	-765	1,493					763		177
1973	National accounts	242	350	-108	-108									
	Change in assets				4,755	3,675	447	-24	2	36	579	743	13	-716
	Change in liabilities				4,863	3,649	764					841		118
1972	National accounts	667	281	386	386									
	Change in assets				2,809	1,971	353	22	-149	-33	1,375	604	-23	-1,311
	Change in liabilities				2,423	1,306	606					421		28
1971	National accounts	-184	247	-431	-431									
	Change in assets				1,034	918	238	-3	14	30	234	903	-126	-1,174
	Change in liabilities				1,465	-270	750					291		8
1970	National accounts	-916	190	-1,106	-1,106									
	Change in assets				2,463	1,266	5	-79	298	54	572	824	-79	-397
	Change in liabilities				3,569	1,300	337					351		-8
1969	National accounts	1,079	162	917	917									
	Change in assets				4,446	1,745	46	20	245	—	1,425	789	263	-87
	Change in liabilities				3,529	3,084	183					370		—
1968	National accounts	258	217	41	41									
	Change in assets				1,952	477	4	48	-132	—	1,354	636	176	-612
	Change in liabilities				1,911	751	113					225		—
1967	National accounts	615	128	487	487									
	Change in assets				1,549	288	230	4	-51	—	857	747	48	-571
	Change in liabilities				1,062	765	-126					125		—
1966	National accounts	1,232	70	1,162	1,162									
	Change in assets				1,479	-250	-40	-15	-13	—	809	942	-83	130
	Change in liabilities				317	186	56					5		—
1965	National accounts	1,135	5	1,130	1,130									
	Change in assets				1,040	-191	-69	12	-137	—	888	752	-257	42
	Change in liabilities				-90	-579	97					125		—
1964	National accounts	392	-32	424	424									
	Change in assets				2,088	456	64	-16	196	—	831	289	-134	405
	Change in liabilities				1,664	682	271					95		—
1963	National accounts	487	-34	521	521									
	Change in assets				1,089	43	11	-27	70	—	685	310	-236	236
	Change in liabilities				568	137	54					135		196
1962	National accounts	779	-51	830	830									
	Change in assets				1,007	-10	-62	4	119	—	483	505	-124	89
	Change in liabilities				177	-7	-58					105		-83

Section K: Price Indexes

A.D. Holmes, *Prices Division, Statistics Canada, (Retired)*

The price indexes presented herein have been grouped into seven subsections, namely: (1) consumer price indexes, series K1-32, (2) wholesale price indexes, series K33-55, (3) export and import price indexes, series K56-67, (4) industry selling price indexes, series K68-107, (5) construction price statistics, series K108-159, (6) fixed capital stocks implicit price indexes, series K160-171, and (7) implicit price indexes of gross national expenditures, series K172-183.

Group (1) indexes relate to purchase-for-consumption of specific population groups, whereas groups (2) to (5) relate to the production and distribution of goods and services. Group (6) reflects prices of the stock of fixed capital in Canada available for future production or consumption, and group (7) provides price indexes for broad summary aggregates of economic activity within the national accounting framework.

In the current edition of this publication, series which were published in the previous edition (1965) and which were terminated prior to 1961 have not been repeated. Discontinued series not repeated herein, continued series, and new series added in the current edition are summarized in tabular format in the descriptive text provided below for each group. For data, descriptive text and source references relating to series not reproduced in the current edition, users should consult Section J: Price Indexes, 1965 edition, pp. 281-305. For series continued in the current edition and for new series introduced herein, source references are included directly in the description of each series provided below. Publications in which current continuing indexes are released are also listed.

Only annual data are presented. With some exceptions, however, subannual figures are available apart from the very early periods, generally monthly. Also, indexes for only broad aggregates and their major components are presented here. Indexes for subcomponents and lower levels of detail are published currently and historical series of them over fairly long periods are available on request from Statistics Canada, Ottawa, Ont. Classification changes and other difficulties affecting comparability of series over longer periods tend to be more acute at less aggregative levels, however, and users are urged to consult Statistics Canada on questions of consistency, comparability and relevance of specific, detailed series in particular uses.

Particular attention is drawn to the fact that the indexes in this current edition, with only a few exceptions, have been placed on a 1971 price reference base, that is, 1971 = 100. While this does not change the year-to-year movements of previously published series (1965 edition), it does change the index number figures. The price reference base is simply the period for which an index is set equal to 100. An index can be arithmetically converted to any other reference base by multiplying each index number in the series by '100 ÷ the index number of the preferred reference period'.

General note

As stated in the 1965 edition, 'a price index number is a device for measuring price change in a group of commodities and services with reference to a base period for which the index is made equal to 100'. The notion of a price index may be considered in two ways. It may be viewed as measuring the changing aggregate value between two periods of a given set or basket of goods and services, where the basket is valued in each period in terms of prices of that period. The index then is the value in one period expressed as a percentage of the value in the other period, the price reference base period. Because the basket is identical between the two periods, the index measures price change only. Alternately, a price index may be viewed as an average of the price relatives between two periods of a given set of goods and services, in which a price relative is the ratio of the price of a commodity in a current period to its price in a price reference (base) period. In this view, it is seen more directly that a price index measures price change. In practice, most price indexes are weighted averages of the price relatives of the goods and services included in them. In either case, prices of individual items within price indexes should be comparable from period to period, that is, prices should relate to identical or equivalent quantity and quality of goods or services.

There are a variety of types of index numbers reflecting variation in the types of averages involved and the weight base periods employed. The most commonly used type for the series presented in this edition is the Laspeyres price index which is a base-period fixed-basket index or, alternately, a weighted arithmetic average index. It is the type employed for all series in the first five subsections listed above, that is for series K1-159, with the exception of series K146 which is an unweighted geometric mean. The indexes for the remaining series K160-183 are a quasi Paasche type, termed 'implicit' price indexes, computed as a byproduct of the derivation of constant dollar value series. The latter are described more fully in the texts below relating to series K160-171 and series K172-183.

The Laspeyres index formula may be written algebraically as

$$I = \frac{\Sigma p_n q_o}{\Sigma p_o q_o} \times 100$$

where the p's designate prices, the q's quantities, and the subscripts n and o the given current and base periods respectively. The Σ sign indicates summation over all the individual items of goods and services included in the index basket. The p's and q's relate to the individual detailed items. This 'basket' formula may be rewritten without changing the value of the index (I) as

$$I = \Sigma \frac{p_n}{p_o} \left(\frac{p_o q_o}{\Sigma p_o q_o} \times 100 \right)$$

In this formulation, the index is seen to be a weighted arithmetic average of the price relatives (p_n/p_o) of the individual detailed items included in the index. Here the weights attached to the price relatives are shown as the values in the base period of the base-period quantities expressed as a percentage or relative value of the base-period aggregate value of the index basket. In formula (1), of course, the q's in effect are weights attached to absolute prices. In practice, formula (1) tended to be employed for indexes in earlier periods, whereas formula (2) was and is used generally in latter and current periods. It should be noted that the two formulations yield identical indexes, the choice between them being dictated by practical problems of actual computation.

In the basic Laspeyres index the price reference base and the weight base period are identical, namely period '₀'. In practice the two periods can be different with the basket quantities relating to a period other than the price reference period. However, when this occurs, for example, if the q's relate to an earlier period, say "0-2", it is essential for weights in formula (2) above to value those quantities in terms of prices of the price reference period. In the example suggested the value weights attached to the price relatives (p_n/p_o) would become

$$W_o = (p_o q_{o-2}/\Sigma p_o q_{o-2})100$$

If this is not done, the index based on formula (1) will differ from that based on formula (2).

A final technical point concerns the fact that the longer term historical price index series are composed of chronologically successive but separate Laspeyres-type indexes, each separate index being based on an index basket and price reference base appropriate to the shorter segment of years to which the separate index relates. The successive indexes are 'linked' at selected overlapping periods to provide a longer term historical series. For example, the Consumer Price Index for Canada, 1913-1975 is a linked Laspeyres-type index derived by linking six separate but closely related indexes covering six distinct periods within the longer term of the linked series.

The necessity for linking arises because price index baskets of goods and services appropriate to a given period of time become less and less relevant to actual patterns of production, distribution and consumption in the economy in later time periods, and indexes in which such earlier weighting systems are used tend to become less reliable measures of current price movements. Accordingly, weighting systems for indexes are updated periodically to maintain the relevance of indexes to current conditions. Also periodically, price reference base periods are updated to facilitate percentage change comparisons among current time intervals and among indexes. To maintain a longer term index series the old index and the updated index are linked and the combined series placed on the most recent official price reference base.

Linking may be accomplished mechanically in a variety of ways. Given a new index with updated basket and a new price reference base, a standard practice is to link the old index to the new by multiplying the old index numbers by the ratio of the *new to the old* index at a selected period where both old and new index numbers overlap. In effect, then, the old index measures price change up to the link period and the new index measures price change forward from the link period. At the same time, both the adjusted old index numbers and the new index numbers express prices in any given year as a percentage of prices in the new price reference period. If the price reference year is not updated, then the new index is linked to the old using the ratio of the *old to the new* at the link period (rather than the new to the old). It should be emphasized that in linking indexes to form longer series, separate linking must be carried out at each level of detail of an index for which the linked series is wanted, using the ratio between the two indexes at the particular level of index detail being linked.

The choice of the link period is important. For linking, the old and new indexes must overlap, that is, there must be a common period in which both indexes are available. Accordingly, the minimum overlap period must be one year for annual indexes and one subannual period (month) for subannual indexes (monthly). The overlap period often is longer than the minimum required and a choice must be made of a particular year (month) or a sequence of years (months) and the link ratio between the two indexes calculated for that link period. Because index movements are unlikely to be the same for the two indexes throughout the overlap period link ratios based on different periods will not be identical. While there is no unique answer to the question of which, then, is the best link period, the problem of choice among them is minimized if prices are fairly stable over the overlap period or changing uniformly among commodities included in the two indexes. In this case, differences among alternative link ratios are slight. Where price movements are not fairly uniform among items in indexes to be linked, a link ratio based on a longer period averages out the differences among ratios of shorter link periods.

In the following descriptions of the specific price indexes presented in this volume information is provided in the following sequence: (a) an introductory general note, (b) basic source or sources for historical series of the particular price index presented and current publications in which current statistics on the price indexes are released, and (c) the objectives, scope and concepts of the indexes and the essentials of the methodology employed in their construction, including the primary sources of information on their nature and the detail of their construction. The summaries of necessity tend to be brief. Users requiring fuller accounts of the indexes may wish to consult the source documents and/or consult with the producers of the indexes. The price indexes presented here are produced at Statistics Canada with responsibility for the various series being vested in particular divisions of the bureau as follows: Prices Division: series K1-55 and K68-159; External Trade Division: series K56—67; Construction Division: series K160—171; and Gross National Product Division: series K172-183.

An important source reference for historical and current series of price indexes (and other series) has been developed by Statistics Canada since publication of the 1965 edition of this volume. The new source is the Canadian Socio-economic Information System (CANSIM) which is a fully computerized data bank. A *Summary Reference Index* is available, free on request, which provides a key to the contents of CANSIM. A *Users' Manual for Data Retrieval and Manipulation*, (Catalogue 12-531), and a *Series Directory* containing titles and descriptive detail of series in CANSIM are available from Statistics Canada, Ottawa, K1A 0Z8. In the description of indexes below, the matrix numbers for the series stored in CANSIM are provided as a source reference for historical data.

Retail Price Indexes (Series K1-32)

General note

Retail price indexes measure the changing cost to consumers of selected goods and services. The indexes are based on changing prices paid by consumers in retail outlets, including private and government stores, offices and other consumer service establishments. Prices in the indexes include sales and excise taxes insofar as they enter into the cost required to be paid by the consumer for acquisition of the goods or services from such retail outlets.

Retail price indexes presented in this edition and those presented in the 1965 edition are listed in the table below, including the periods covered in each edition and the price reference base periods. The dash (-) in columns (1) and (2) indicates the series is not included in the edition specified in the column heading.

For series J128-131 and series J132-138, see the 1965 edition of this volume (Section J) for index figures and their concept, scope and methodology.

Users should note also that the 1965 edition, series J147-152, which has been continued and extended in this edition as series K8-18, have been converted to a new price reference base 1971 = 100.

K1-7. Cost-of-living index, 1913 to 1952

SOURCE: *Historical Statistics of Canada*, (1965 edition) p. 304, series J139-146.

For a more detailed description of methods than is given here, see pp. 288-289 of the 1965 edition, and additional sources cited therein.

The cost-of-living index numbers presented here are reproduced from the 1965 edition because the indexes for the period 1913 to January 1949 are incorporated, through linking, in the longer term series K8-18 (Consumer Price Index for Canada) presented below. An understanding of the latter longer term series is therefore dependent on the description of these index series K1-7.

The cost-of-living index from 1913 to 1952 is a linked series of three separate indexes, namely, (a) an index for the period 1913 to 1926 (1913 = 100), (b) one for the period 1926 to January 1935 (1926 = 100) and (c) an index for the period January 1935 to 1952 (1935-39 = 100). The (b) index is linked to the (c) index using the ratio of the two indexes

	Series No.		Period covered		Price reference period = 100	
Current edition	1965 edition	Title	Current edition	1965 edition	Current edition	1965 edition
—	J128-131	Price index numbers of a family budget (Dept. of Labour)	—	1900-39	—	1913
—	J132-138	Price indexes of selected retail services	—	1900-38	—	1913
K1-7	J139-146	Cost-of-living index	1913-52	1913-52	1935-39	1935-39
K8-18	J147-152	Consumer price index	1913-75	1913-60	1971	1961
New series						
K19-22	—	Consumer price index for Canada, classified by goods and services	1961-75	—	1971	—
K23-32	—	Consumer price indexes for regional cities	1940-75	—	1971	—

for January 1935. The (a) index is then linked to that combined series using the ratio of the linked (b) index and the (a) index for the year 1926. Monthly indexes were linked first and then averaged to obtain the annual indexes.

The concept for the (a) index covering the period 1913 to 1926 (1913 = 100) was 'the measurement of the general movement of retail prices and living costs in the country as a whole'. A Laspeyres base-weighted index formula was used with weights based on the total consumption of each commodity in 1913. Prices used were obtained from the Department of Labour's collection for the earlier years and from direct surveys of retailers. The Department of Labour prices were collected by local correspondents of the *Labour Gazette* in approximately 60 cities, with Canada prices being simple averages of city prices.

In the (b) index in the linked series 1926 to January 1935, the concept of the previous period was continued. Weights were updated to 1926 and again based on aggregate consumption in Canada. The number of commodities included in the index was greatly increased, however.

For the (c) index from 1935 to 1952, a modification in concept and scope of the index was introduced. Weights for commodities, subgroups and groups were based on a 1938 family budget survey of urban wage-earner families with annual earnings ranging from $450 to $2,500. The index thus was specifically oriented to reflecting changes in the cost of living of a particular, but still broad, consumer group rather than consumers as a whole.

K8-18. Consumer Price Index for Canada, classified by main components, 1913 to 1975

SOURCE: CANSIM, Matrix No. 429(A) for series K8, 1913 to 1975; K9-18, 1949 to 1975. Retail Price Section files, Prices Division, Statistics Canada for series K9-14 and combined series 15-18, 1926 to 1948. Current indexes are published in *Consumer Price Movements*, (Catalogue 62-001) and *Prices and Price Indexes*, (Catalogue 62-002), both published monthly.

The Consumer Price Index for Canada, from 1913 to 1975 is a linked Laspeyres-type index derived by linking six separate but related indexes covering six distinct periods within the longer term. The six period indexes may be summarized as follows:

Index designation	Period covered	Weight base period	Price reference period	Link ratio period
(a)	1913-25	1913	1913	
(b)	1926-34	1926	1926	1926
(c)	1935-48	1938	1935-39	Jan. 1935
(d)	1949-60	1947-48	1949	Jan. 1949
(e)	1961-72	1957	1957	Jan. 1961
(f)	1973-75	1967	1967	Apr. 1973

Indexes designated (a), (b) and (c) are those described above under series K1-7. Note that the link ratio period (last column) is the period for which the ratio of the designated index to that of the immediately preceding index is used to link that particular pair of indexes. For example, the ratio between the (b) and (a) indexes in 1926 is used to link that specific pair of indexes. Also, with the exception of the (e) and (f) indexes, the link ratio period corresponds with the starting point of the designated index, either the price reference period or the beginning month of it. The reason for and the effect of the recent departures from this practice are outlined below in the descriptions of the (e) and (f) indexes.

The (d) index above represented a major updating of the item content and weighting system of the preceding cost-of-living index (see *The Consumer Price Index, January 1949 - August 1952*, Catalogue 62-502). The title was changed to Consumer Price Index to avoid the implication that the index measured all changes in living costs. The index was defined as measuring "the percentage change through time in the cost of purchasing a constant 'basket' of goods and services representing the consumption of a particular population group during a given period of time". The 'target group' for the index was modified to include families (1) living in cities of 30,000 population or more, (2) ranging in size from two adults to two adults with four children, and (3) with incomes ranging from $1,650 to $4,050. Index weighting was based on data from a family budget survey, (*Canadian Non-farm Family Expenditures, 1947-1948*, Catalogue 62-513) and the item content and price samples were expanded to reflect the buying habits and outlet sources of that period. The price reference base was changed to 1949 = 100 and the previous linked indexes were linked to the new index using the link ratio for January 1949.

Prices in the index from 1949 onward were collected from retail outlets at frequencies ranging from monthly to only annually depending on the volatility and sensitivity of prices. Where changes through time in qualities of items to be priced created an adjustment problem to ensure comparability of prices from period to period, collection was restricted to eight cities across Canada where full-time pricing agents were located. Where prices could be satisfactorily collected by mail, pricing was extended to 33 cities. Within each city judgment samples of typical retail outlets, by outlet type, were selected for pricing of index items characteristically sold therein, and prices were collected for narrowly specified qualities of items in those outlets. For each item, city average prices and then Canada average prices were derived from reported prices, using a system of internal weighting reflecting the relative importance of qualities, outlets and cities. Indexes were then computed for each item and weighted in a Laspeyres-type formula to derive indexes for successively larger and larger groupings of items and the 'total' index.

The index was again updated, effective January 1961, respecting item content, outlet sources and weights (*The Consumer Price Index for Canada (1949 = 100), Revision Based on 1957 Expenditures*, Catalogue 62-518), resulting in the (e) index indicated in the summary table above. The income criterion for the targeted population group for the index was revised upward to the range $2,500 to $7,000, in keeping with the general upward shift in incomes of urban families. The weighting system was revised based on family expenditure patterns of 1957 (*Urban Family Food Expenditure, 1957*, Catalogue 62-516 and *City Family Expenditure, 1957*, Catalogue 62-517). With the advent of government-sponsored hospital care plans direct payments by consumers

for this service became negligible and premiums paid did not reflect the price of the service. Accordingly, this item was dropped from the index. The bulk of pricing continued to be carried on by full-time pricing officers in eight major cities across Canada covering the full range of goods and services in the index. In seven other cities, part-time agents undertook pricing for a limited but significant range of items, including foods. Pricing by mail in smaller centres for less complex items was continued. Rents paid and data on the qualities of corresponding rental accommodation were obtained from monthly surveys of some 10,000 rented households in urban areas through the continuing Labour Force Survey.

The 1957-weighted index was linked to the 'official' Consumer Price Index series at January 1961 using the link ratio of that month. Even though the newly weighted index was available from 1957, the 1947-1948 weighted index was retained as the 'official' index for the period 1957 to 1960, to avoid very difficult revision problems of users where the official index was employed in escalation clauses of wage and other income contracts. For the total and most main component indexes, the 1957-weighted index rose insignificantly less than the official indexes. For the transportation and the recreation and reading components, the upward movement of the 1957-weighted indexes was appreciably less.

The latest periodic updating of the Consumer Price Index (the (f) index, above) incorporated a revised weighting system based on family spending patterns in 1967 (*Urban Family Expenditure, 1967*, Catalogue 62-530) and within the food component, patterns of food purchases in 1969 (*Family Food Expenditure in Canada, 1969*, Catalogue 62-531). The target population group for the index was widened to include urban families ranging in size from two to six persons of any adult-child composition, and the income range was updated and broadened to $4,000 to $12,000. The item content and price samples were extended and improved. However, doctors' services, optical care and prepaid medical care were deleted from the index because the introduction of federal-provincial medical care plans rendered realistic pricing through time highly improbable. The 1967-weighted index was linked to the previous linked series at April 1973, using the link ratio between the official linked series and the 1967-weighted index for that month.

Full details of the 1967 weight revision and an extended discussion of linking procedures and the rebasing of historical series to various price reference periods is given in *The Consumer Price Index for Canada (1961 = 100) Revision Based on 1967 Expenditures*, (Catalogue 62-539).

The long-term linked series from 1913 to 1975 on the 1961 = 100 price reference base was rebased to 1971 = 100 by arithmetic conversion. Current indexes are published monthly on the 1971 reference base.

K19-22. Consumer Price Index for Canada, classified by goods and services, 1961 to 1975

SOURCE: CANSIM, Matrix No. 429(A) for series K19 and K21, Matrix No. 431(A) for K20 and K22. Current indexes are published in the *Consumer Price Index*, (Catalogue 62-001) and *Prices and Price Indexes*, (Catalogue 62-002), published monthly.

The series K19 is identical to the series K8 described above. Series K20-22 result from a reclassification of the items in the Consumer Price Index for Canada into two broad categories, namely goods and services, according to 'their most characteristic or dominant attribute'. Indexes for sub-groups within 'Goods' classified by categories of expected useful life of the item are published in the above sources, as are indexes for sub-groups within 'Services' classified in broad functional categories. This classification system is a detailed reordering of items in the index. It is not just a merging of the traditional purpose classifications of the parent index.

The item content of the goods and services classifications and sub-groups within them is detailed in Appendix II(a) of *The Consumer Price Index for Canada, Revision Based on 1967 Expenditures*, (Catalogue 62-539). Appendix II(b) on page 41 of that publication provides a graphic outline of the system.

K23-32. Consumer Price Indexes for regional cities, 1940 to 1975

SOURCE: CANSIM, Matrix No. 7116 for K23 (1952 to 1975), K24-29 and K32 (1949 to 1975). Retail Prices Section files, Prices Division, Statistics Canada, K24-29 and K32 (1940 to 1948) and K30-31 (1940 to 1975). Current indexes are published monthly in *Consumer Price Indexes for Regional Cities*, (Catalogue 62-009), Statistics Canada.

The Consumer Price Indexes for regional cities are similar in concept and methodology to the Consumer Price Index for Canada (series K8-18), with the population group to which a given city index relates being a specified range of families living in the given city. Generally, the city population groups are similar to the Canada index group respecting range of income and family size and composition. The index for a regional city measures the effect of price change in that city on the cost of purchasing a constant (or equivalent) basket of goods and services representative of the expenditure-for-consumption patterns of the specified population group in the particular city. The indexes thus reflect the average movement of consumer prices in the respective cities. The indexes, however, *cannot* be used to compare levels of prices among cities, levels having been arbitrarily set equal to 100 in all cities in the price reference year (1971 = 100). The historical series are linked Laspeyres-type indexes.

Indexes for regional cities were first introduced in 1941 for eight cities, namely Halifax, Saint John, Montreal, Toronto, Winnipeg, Saskatoon, Edmonton and Vancouver (see *Regional changes in living costs, Canada, August 1939 to April 1941*, Catalogue 62-D-91). The item content and weights in each city were based on a 1938 family budget survey of urban wage-earner families with annual earnings ranging from $450 to $2,500. The price reference base was August 1939 = 100. Prices used in the indexes were the city prices collected in the price samples of the Canada index.

The indexes were converted to the reference base 1949 = 100 and new indexes with updated content and weights based on a 1947-1948 family budget survey (*Canadian Non-farm Family Expenditures*, Catalogue 62-513) were linked to the former indexes at September, 1953 using the link ratio of that month (see *Prices and Price Indexes*, October 1953, pp. 4-5, Catalogue 62-002). For the 1947-1948 weighted indexes, the index population group was revised, as in the Canada index, to include families ranging in size from two adults to two adults with four children, and income of $1,650 to $4,050. The index title was changed to 'Consumer Price Index'. Calculation of the city indexes from September 1953 was similar to that for the Canada index except for the shelter component. In city indexes the weight for home ownership was imputed to rent, that is, the price movements of home ownership were measured by changes in rents, whereas in the Canada index the home ownership component of the shelter index was measured directly by price and cost elements of ownership and maintenance. The effect of this difference in pricing was of little importance until fairly recent years.

Indexes for two additional cities also were introduced in the early 1950s, for Ottawa and for St. John's, Newfoundland. The Ottawa index was released in October 1953. It was originally developed on a reference base August 1939 = 100 and then converted to 1949 = 100. Weights used were those of the Canada index rather than the Ottawa city weights. Ottawa prices were used for food, fuel and lighting, rent, household supplies and services and miscellaneous items, whereas Toronto price indexes were employed for clothing and home furnishings (*Prices and Price Indexes*, October 1953 p. 5). A 1947-1948 weighted index based on Ottawa family budget patterns and Ottawa prices was linked to the former index at September 1953, as in the other city indexes.

The St. John's index was constructed on the reference base June 1951 = 100 and released in 1951 (*St. John's, Newfoundland, Cost-of-Living Index, June 1951 = 100*, Reference Paper No. 28, Catalogue 62-D-94, 1951). The item content and weights in the index were based on a range of data on production, imports and consumption from several sources and reflected a consumption pattern typical of average families in St. John's of the 1948 to 1950 period. Prices used in the index were collected by pricing agents located in St. John's. In the September 1953 revision of other city indexes, only a change in titles and a merging of some component classes were made for the St. John's index.

The city indexes were again updated for content, weight and price samples, effective February 1962. In this revision, weights were based on family expenditure patterns of 1957 (*Urban Family Food Expenditure, 1957*, Catalogue 62-516, and *City Family Expenditure, 1957*, Catalogue 62-517) in the respective cities. In regions where government sponsored hospital care programs made direct pricing of such services unrealistic, hospital care was deleted from the city indexes. As with the Canada index, the income range for the city target population group was revised upward to range from $2,500 to $7,000, and the price reference base year was retained as 1949 = 100. The 1957-weighted index was linked to the preceding linked series at February 1962 using the link ratio of that month.

The latest updating of index contents and weights was introduced in April 1973. Prior to that, city indexes had been arithmetically converted to a 1961 = 100 price reference year. Weights for the new indexes were based on city spending patterns in 1967 (*Urban Family Expenditure, 1967*, Catalogue 62-530) and within the food component 1969 patterns (*Family Food Expenditure in Canada, 1969*, Catalogue 62-531). The target population group was changed to include urban families of two to six persons of any adult-child composition, with income of $4,000 to $12,000. Because of growth in federal-provincial medical care programs and attendant direct pricing difficulties, doctor's services, optical care and prepared medical care were deleted as items in city indexes. The 1967-weighted indexes were linked to the previous 1961 = 100 linked historical series for each city at April 1973 using the link ratio of that month. The entire historical series were then arithmetically converted to the new price reference year 1971 = 100, for each city. Some 300 items are included in Consumer Price Indexes for Canada and regional cities.

Current indexes are published monthly and are available for other cities in Canada. Historical series of shorter duration also are available on request for other cities and separately for Saskatoon, Regina, Edmonton and Calgary. Indexes for major components of each city index are published currently and these as well as more detailed component indexes over varying historical periods are available on request from the Prices Division, Statistics Canada, Ottawa.

Wholesale Price Indexes (Series K33-55)

General note

The term wholesale price indexes may be ambiguous. The indexes include prices at various stages in the production and distribution of raw and processed materials, semi-finished goods and fully manufactured products. The prices relate to larger scale or bulk transactions. The indexes should not be interpreted therefore as relating to prices of 'wholesalers' or the 'wholesale trade'. Rather, the indexes measure movements of prices of a very broad but ill-defined mix of materials and products below the retail level.

The wholesale price indexes presented in this edition and those presented in the 1965 edition are listed in the table below, including the periods covered in each edition and the price reference base periods. The dash (-) in columns (1) and (2) indicates the series is not included in the edition specified in the column heading.

For index numbers in the 1965 edition not repeated herein, namely J1-14, J15-33, J45-61 and J62-69 and descriptions of them, readers are referred to Section J: Price Indexes (beginning page 281) in the 1965 edition. Note also that old series J73-74 have been continued in this edition as series K137 and 140, a later subsection (Construction Price Indexes).

| Series No. | | | Period covered | | Price reference period = 100 | |
Current edition	1965 edition	Series title	Current edition	1965 edition	Current edition	1965 edition
—	J1-14	Wholesale price indexes, by commodity groups (Mitchell)	—	1868-1925	—	1900
—	J15-33	Wholesale price indexes by commodity groups (Dept. of Labour)	—	1890-1924	—	1890-99
K33-43	J34-44	Wholesale price indexes, chief component material classification	1867-1975	1867-1960	1935-39	1935-39
—	J45-61	Wholesale price indexes, classified according to origin and degree of manufacture	—	1890-1948	—	1926
—	J62-69	Wholesale price indexes, classified according to purpose	—	1890-1948	—	1926
K44-46	J70-72	Wholesale price indexes, classified according to degree of manufacture, industrial materials	1890-1975	1890-1960	1935-39	1935-39
K137 140	J73-74	Wholesale price indexes, classified by residential, non-residential building materials	1926-75	1926-60	1971	1935-39, 1949
K47-55	J75-83	Wholesale price indexes of Canadian farm products	1890-1974	1890-1960	1935-39, 1913	1935-39, 1913

K33-43. General Wholesale Price Index, classified by chief component material, 1867 to 1975

SOURCE: *Historical Statistics of Canada*, (1965 edition), pp. 293-294 for period 1867 to 1960; *Prices and Price Indexes* (Catalogue 62-002), successive issues, for period 1961 to 1975; CANSIM, Matrix No. 262. Current indexes are published in the monthly *Industry Price Indexes*, (Catalogue 62-011).

The general wholesale price index is a linked series of five separate indexes, each covering a specific period within the longer term, and each having a unique weighting diagram representing an updating of weights to reflect the changed mix of materials and products of the successive index periods. The five period-indexes may be summarized as follows:

Index designation	Period covered	Weight base per	Price reference period = 100	Link ratio period	
(a)	1867-1889	none	1890		
(b)	1890-1912	around 1900	1890	1890	Net weights
(c)	1913-1925	1913	1913	1913	
(d)	1926-1934	1926	1926	1926	
(e)	1935-1975	1935-39	1935-39	Dec. 1934	

The description of the indexes and methods in constructing them given below have been condensed for the period 1867 to 1960 from the more detailed account provided in the 1965 edition of this publication (pp. 281-284).

The index numbers designated (a) in the above summary covering the period 1867 to 1889 were computed as unweighted geometric means of price relatives of 89 commodities. Prices were obtained from newspapers and trade journals. Indexes for components within the general (total) index were at best only approximate indicators of price movements for each group because of the small numbers of quotations, which were chiefly in the vegetable and animal product groups. The indexes were calculated retroactively on the price reference base 1890 = 100 and were linked to the (b) index using the link ratio between items for the year 1890.

For the (b) index of the period 1890 to 1912, a weighted Laspeyres index formula was introduced. Weights were 'net' quantities marketed in a period not later than 1900, that is, around 1900. The concept of 'net' marketings required that the quantities marketed of a commodity, for example wheat, be exclusive of quantities which were later used in domestic processing or production of another product, for example flour. This avoided over-weighting of the price of commodities at earlier stages of production which would be duplicated otherwise through prices of commodities at later stages. Prices were obtained from newspapers and trade journals, a major source being the Department of Labour's collection mainly from trade journals. The number of price series ranged between 203 and 247. As stated above, the (a) and (b) indexes were linked using the link ratio of 1890.

In the (c) index, for 1913 to 1925, a weighted Laspeyres-type index was continued with commodity weights updated to net marketings of the year 1913. The number of price series used in the index was 236. Lesser use was made of newspapers and trade journals for prices, with business firms and government agencies becoming an alternative source. This index was linked to the preceding (b) index using the link ratio for 1913.

The (d) index, for 1926 to 1934, was based on an updated weighting diagram, using net marketings of commodities in 1926. The number of price series was almost doubled to 502 and more use was made of mail surveys of business firms in price collection. The (d) index produced on the price reference base 1926 = 100, was linked with the linked series using the link ratio for 1926.

The (e) index, for 1935 to 1975 (1935-39 = 100), incorporates the last official updating of the weighting system for the general wholesale price index. The concept of the weights was changed to 'gross' marketings, that is, no adjustments were made to earlier-stage full marketings of a commodity for quantities used in domestic production of other products. Weights were based on marketings of the period 1935 to 1939. The weighting system included commodity, sub-group and group weights. The number of price series in the index was increased to 604. Specifications of transactions for pricing were improved and the principal source of prices were industrial firms and government agencies with direct market contacts. The majority of prices were collected by mail monthly, as of the 15th of the month. The (e) index was linked to the preceding linked series (1867 to 1934) using the ratio of the new to former series at December 1934. This automatically placed the entire series 1867 to 1975 on the 1935-39 = 100 price reference base.

Since 1960 index content and weighting has remained largely unchanged from that described in the 1965 edition of this volume. No changes have been made in the relative weights of major groups (K35-39, K41-43) in the index. Within major groups some changes were effected directly or implicitly. In the non-ferrous metals group, series K41, the relative weight for gold was reduced substantially in the early 1970s based on changes in production of minerals since 1961. Also, with development of the Industry Selling Price Indexes for manufacturing indexes (see below, series K68-107) commodity price series based on expanded price samples in that system of indexes became available. Where such new commodity series were appropriate in terms of item content and internal weighting, they were introduced into the General Wholesale Price Index by linking at the commodity level. This was done within the major group 'Iron and its products' in the earlier 1970s and implicitly altered the relative weightings of commodity content within the major group. By weight, only about 10 per cent of the General Wholesale Price Index was affected by such substitution of industry indexes. Most substitutions of this type have occurred in more recent years so that by the end of 1977 perhaps up to one-third of the General Wholesale Index, by weight, was represented by Industry Selling Price Indexes.

The General Wholesale Price Index is a commodity classified index. It is 'general', covering a heterogeneous mix of transactions rendering it incapable of association with any well-defined value aggregate. Its principal characteristic is its long historical continuity, an attribute useful for long-term cycle analyses. Its usefulness for shorter-term current analyses is doubtful and for this purpose it is being superseded by other specifically-defined indexes, for example, Industry Selling Price Indexes and Construction Price Indexes.

K44-46. General Wholesale Index, classified by degree of manufacture, 1890 to 1975

SOURCE: same as series K33-43.

These two series are merely regroupings of the major group indexes (K35-43) of the general wholesale price indexes described above, with grouping according to the two degrees of manufacturing specified in the column headings. Weights used in regrouping the indexes are those attached to component indexes in the general index, K34.

K46. Thirty industrial materials (price index), 1926 to 1975

SOURCE: CANSIM, Matrix No. 131. Current indexes are published monthly in the monthly *Industry Price Indexes*, (Catalogue 62-011).

This index was included in the 1965 edition of this volume as series J72 (p. 285), for the period 1926 to 1960.

The series was introduced in a reference paper published in 1939 (*Canadian Index Numbers of Industrial Material Prices*, Catalogue 62-D-71). Its purpose is to provide early and frequent (week-by-week) statistical measurement of price behavior in markets for basic materials required as inputs by industry. It was and still is an unweighted geometric mean of the price relatives of 30 selected commodities. The original selection, based on intensive testing of volatility, sensitivity to changing economic conditions and importance to industries, included 18 commodities sensitive to economic changes and 12 which exhibited a more stable price behavior. The commodities selected are listed on page 21 of the above reference paper (Catalogue 62-D-71). Of the 30, five are food and 25 are manufacturing materials.

No change has been made in the commodities included since the original selection, though Industry Selling Price Indexes have been substituted for some individual commodity price series in recent years. Materials which have become important as industry inputs since World War II are not represented in the index, such as plastics and other modern synthetics.

The index is currently published on a monthly basis. Component commodity index series are available on request from Statistics Canada.

K47-55. Wholesale Price Indexes of Canadian farm products, 1890 to 1974

SOURCE: *Historical Statistics of Canada*, (1965 edition) for period 1890 to 1958 (except for noted revisions footnoted 'r'). CANSIM, Matrix No. 953, for period 1959 to 1974 and footnoted revisions in period 1926 to 1958. *Industry Price Indexes*, (Catalogue 62-011) for period 1971 to 1974 (1971 = 100). Current monthly indexes are published in the monthly *Industry Price Indexes*. (Note: current indexes are subject to revisions based on delayed declarations of interim and final payments on some products.)

These indexes measure price movements of Canadian farm products at 'Terminal' markets such as stockyards, creameries and processing plants. Prices may include transportation, storage and some handling and processing costs, depending on the terminal market at which a price transaction is recorded. These indexes differ from indexes of prices received by farmers 'at the farm gate', (see series M88, this edition, Section M, Agriculture) which reflect prices at the farm for more broadly defined commodities.

The indexes are presented here in three time segments, namely for (1) the period 1890 to 1934 (1913 = 100), (2) the period 1926 to 1974 (1935-39 = 100) and the period 1971 to 1974 (1971 = 100). Indexes for the first two periods are a repeat of those included in the 1965 edition, with extension of the 1935-39 = 100 index to 1974 in this edition. The new series on the new reference base 1971 = 100 is presented here for the first time.

The indexes for the time segment 1890 to 1934 (1913 = 100) are identical to those presented and described in the 1965 edition. They are composed of three linked period series covering the successive periods 1890 to 1913, 1913 to 1926 and 1926 to 1934, each period index being a weighted Laspeyres-type index with weights relating to the respective periods. Weights for the 1890 to 1913 period were quantities based on the average production of index commodities as reported in the decennial censuses of production for the years 1890, 1900 and 1910. For the 1913 to 1926 period indexes, commodity weights were based on total quantities marketed in 1913, and for the 1926 to 1934 period indexes, weights were quantities marketed in 1926. The three period-indexes were linked at 1913 and 1926 using link ratios of those years. A full description of the series 1890 to 1934 including construction methods was published in *Wholesale Price Index Numbers of Canadian Farm Products*, 1890 to 1933, (Catalogue 62-504). Prices in the indexes were for specified grades at specified markets. The number of price series employed increased from 24 in the 1890 to 1913 period to 33 in 1913 to 1926 and to 36 in the 1926 to 1934 period, representing price movements for 10 field and nine animal commodity items.

Indexes for the time segment 1926 to 1974 (1935-39 = 100) incorporate some footnoted revisions, mostly minor, of the figures published in the 1965 edition for 1926 to 1960. These series also are linked Laspeyres-type indexes, the above-described 1926 to 1934 period index being linked to updated 1935-39 = 100 based indexes covering the period 1935 to 1974 (*Wholesale Price Index Numbers of Canadian Farm Products*, (Catalogue 62-504, 1947). Weights in the new index were the average value of index quantities marketed over the five-year period 1935 to 1939, with regional weighting at the commodity and group levels within the total index. Seasonal fruits and vegetables were not included because of difficulties in obtaining prices which would be comparable through time. Price series used in the index numbered 86 of which 46 were for Eastern markets (17 field, 29 animal) and 40 for Western markets (14 field, 26 animal). This version of the series continued to 1974.

In 1975, the indexes were revised to a 1971 price reference and weight base. New weights were based on farm cash receipts of 1971, using data produced by the Agriculture Division, Statistics Canada, with regional and commodity group weighting being employed in calculation of the indexes. Over 90 per cent of farm cash receipts are represented in the new index. Major exclusions are sugar beets, seasonal fruits and vegetables, and maple and forest products. No reference source is yet available.

Export and Import Price Indexes (Series K56-67)

General note

Price indexes of exports and of imports are designed to measure the movements of prices of commodities in Canada's external merchandise trade. In addition to price indexes for total exports and total imports, indexes are produced for major classifications of commodity groups within the totals. Up to 1964, commodity groupings were in accord with tariff classifications of exports and imports. The classification system was then changed to the *Trade of Canada Commodity Classification*, (TCCC). Indexes based on the tariff classifications were terminated in 1964. Indexes classified according to the TCCC system have been extended back in time to 1960. Indexes for commodity classes within total exports and total imports presented in this edition cover the period 1960 to 1975 only and are those based on the TCCC system of classification.

A feature of export and import price indexes is the widespread use of 'unit value' series rather than 'specification price' series for individual commodities included in the indexes. A specification price series is a sequence of prices through time of a narrowly specified quantity and quality of a commodity, in which the quantity-quality dimension of the commodity is kept constant or equivalent throughout the series period. A unit value series is a sequence of unit values through time of a more broadly defined commodity, in which the mix of quantities and qualities of implicit specifications within it may vary from period to period. The movement of unit value series thus may reflect both price and quantity-quality changes, the quantity change effect being dependent on the homogeneity through time in the internal mix within the commodity class.

Until fairly recently, Canadian export and import indexes were based primarily on unit value series obtained from trade statistics of quantities and values for commodity classes. Progressive efforts were made to minimize the quantity changes implicit in such series, including the use of specification price series where these became available and were appropriate. In more recent years, the availability of computers has made more detailed examination of class content feasible with attendant improvement in unit values as proxies for specification prices.

The Export and Import Price Indexes presented in this edition and those presented in the 1965 edition are listed in the table below, including the periods covered in each edition and the price reference base periods. The dash (-) in columns (1) and (2) indicates the series is not included in the edition specified in the column heading.

For index number series of the 1965 edition not repeated herein, namely, J84-127 (except J108 and J118) and descriptions of them, readers are referred to Section J: Price Indexes (beginning page 281) in the 1965 edition.

Series no.			Period covered		Price reference period = 100	
Current edition	1965 edition	Series title	Current edition	1965 edition	Current edition	1965 edition
–	J84-95	Export price indexes (Taylor)	–	1869-1915	–	1900
–	J96-107	Import price indexes (Taylor)	–	1869-1915	–	1900
		Export price indexes, 1913-1960				
K56	J108-117	Panel A	1926-70	1926-60	1948	1948
–	J108-117	Panel B	–	1913-34	–	1913
		Import price indexes, 1913-1960				
K62	J118-127	Panel A	1926-70	1926-60	1948	1948
–	J118-127	Panel B	–	1913-34	–	1913
New series						
		Export price indexes, 1926-75				
K56-61	–	Panel A	1968-75	–	1971	–
K57-61	–	Panel B	1960-70	–	1948	–
		Import price indexes, 1926-75				
K62-67	–	Panel A	1968-75	–	1971	–
K61-67	–	Panel B	1960-70	–	1948	–

K56-61.   Export price indexes, Trade of Canada commodity classification, 1926 to 1975

K62-67.   Import price indexes, Trade of Canada commodity classification, 1926 to 1975

SOURCE: *Panel B:* for series K56 and K62, for 1926 to 1959, Macmillan, *Historical Statistics of Canada,* 1965 edition, pp. 301-302; for series K56-61 and K62-67, for 1960 to 1970, files of External Trade Division, Statistics Canada.
Panel A: for series K56-61 and K62-67 for 1971 to 1975, Statistics Canada, *The 1971-based price and volume indexes of Canada's external trade,* (Catalogue 65-001, supplement, December 1976); for 1968 to 1970, files of External Trade Division, Statistics Canada. Current indexes are published in the monthly *Summary of Foreign Trade,* (Catalogue 65-001). See also CANSIM, Matrix No. 3716 for exports and Matrix No. 3681 for imports. Price indexes of the Paasche type also are available from 1971 onward (1971 = 100) and are published in current issues of the *Summary of Foreign Trade.* Readers please note that the Paasche indexes differ from the Laspeyres-type indexes included in this edition of *Historical Statistics of Canada.*

Panel B. The historical series, for 1926 to 1970 (1948 = 100), in *Panel B,* for total exports, series K56, and total imports, series K62, results from the linking of two period indexes,

one for the period 1926 to 1945 (1935-39 = 100), the second covering the period 1946 to 1970 (1948 = 100). Each of the indexes is a fixed-weight index, with weights relating to the value of exports (imports for import indexes) in the 1935-39 and the 1948 periods respectively. Price relative series for selected tariff-classified commodities were based primarily on unit value series, although some were from price series of wholesale and retail price records in Canada and the United States. Individual price relatives were weighted by the percentage of their value, in the respective fixed-weight periods, to the total value of broader tariff groups to which they belonged. The group indexes were in turn weighted by their percentage value shares in total exports (imports). The 1926 to 1945 indexes were linked to the 1946 to 1970 indexes using the link ratio of the latter to the former in 1946. Series K57-61 and K63-67 were constructed for the five one-digit levels of the TCCC commodity classification system, by regrouping and reweighting (1948 percentage value weights) the price relative series of tariff-classified commodities. Users of the indexes should note the doubtful validity of series K56-61 for the war years 1941 to 1945, during which period the commodities entering Canada's actual external trade were not similar in pattern to those of the 1948 peace-time weight base period.

Panel A. New index numbers of prices in merchandise trade were first published in the *Summary of External Trade,* July 1975, with weighting diagrams relating to 1971 trade values and the price reference base 1971 = 100. The indexes have been extended back to 1968 and are classified by the TCCC system of commodity classification. A detailed outline of the nature of the indexes and methods underlying their construction is provided in *The 1971-based price and volume indexes of Canada's external trade.* Both Paasche (variable current year weights) and Laspeyres (fixed 1971 base year weights) indexes were developed. The Paasche price indexes, *not* presented herein, are published currently in the monthly *Summary of Foreign Trade.* The Laspeyres price indexes presented herein are available currently from the External Trade Division on request. In the new indexes, an updated and larger selection of elementary price relatives at the five-digit TCCC commodity class level were incorporated. For export indexes, unit value series were used for 57 per cent of the commodity classes (by value weight), specification price series for 29 per cent, while 14 per cent of the classes were not covered directly by price relative. For import indexes, unit value and specification price series were employed for 23 and 50 per cent, by weight, of the classes, with 27 per cent not directly covered. Most of the specification price series for exports were from the Industry Selling Price Indexes and were for 'end products, inedible', series K61. Those for imports were mostly from the U.S. Bureau of Labor Statistics wholesale price indexes and were mostly in 'end products, inedible', series K67. All non-Canadian indexes were adjusted for changes in exchange rates through time.

Short-term price indexes, with 1968 as the weight and price reference bases, were produced and published for the period 1967 to March 1975. The weighting reflects marked changes in trading patterns resulting from the 1965 automotive pact with the United States. These have not been included in this addition because of the short period covered and because the 1971-based indexes, with coverage from 1968, are the current continuing indexes. The 1968-based indexes are available on request from the External Trade Division, Statistics Canada.

A longer term price index series for 1956 to 1975 (1971 = 100) for total exports, series K56, and total imports, series K62, is presented in this edition in Section G: Balance of Payments. For advice on linking of series on export and import price indexes, to obtain longer term series, users may consult the External Trade Division.

Industry Selling Price Indexes (Series K68-107)

General note

A new system of industry-classified price indexes was introduced in January 1961 by Statistics Canada through publication of a set of indexes entitled *Industry Selling Price Indexes, 1956-59,* (Catalogue 62-515). For each of some 100 manufacturing industries, the indexes measure the movement of selling prices of shipments of commodities produced by the industry.

In the new system, each index relates uniquely to an individual industry as classified in the Standard Industrial Classification (S.I.C.) of industries. In the S.I.C., each business establishment in Canada is classified to one, and only one, industry at the finest level of classification of industries.

The S.I.C. classification system is hierarchical, providing mutually exclusive groupings of lower level industry classes, at progressively higher levels. At the most aggregative level, manufacturing industries is one of 12 divisions of industries (in 1970). Within manufacturing, industries are divided into 20 major groups (two-digit level) each of which is subdivided again into three-digit and further for some into four-digit level classes of industry. Accordingly, at any given level of classification each manufacturing establishment is classified to one, and only one, industry.

Through use of the framework of the S.I.C., industry-classified price indexes can be specifically defined in scope and content. Further, they relate directly to important value aggregates of individual industry classes, for example, value of shipments, and are compatible in analytical uses with other major statistical series such as production, employment, man-hours and hourly earnings which also are classified by industry. Examples of analytical uses are studies of growth, productivity and employment. These indexes do not displace the previously available longer term series of commodity-classified wholesale price indexes. Rather, they provide differently classified price indexes for uses for which the commodity-classified indexes were not appropriate.

Industry-classified price indexes were not included in the 1965 edition. A table of indexes presented in this and the earlier edition, therefore, is omitted.

K68-107. Industry Selling Price Indexes, by industry class, Standard Industrial Classification (S.I.C.), 1956 to 1975

SOURCE: *Prices and Price Indexes,* (Catalogue 62-002), various monthly issues, 1961 to 1975. CANSIM: Matrix No. 675 to 693, corresponding to S.I.C. major group industries 01 to 20, excluding S.I.C. group 11 (see *Panel A* of data table for series K69-87); Matrix No. 694 for series K68. Current indexes are published monthly in *Industry Price Indexes,* (Catalogue 62-011). Detailed accounts of concepts, scope, content and methods are given in: *Industry Selling Price Indexes, 1956-59,* (Catalogue 62-515), and *Industry Selling Price Indexes, 1956-68,* (Catalogue 62-528).

The indexes introduced in 1961 have been continued with periodic updating of weights and classifications. The historical series presented in this edition of this publication for the first time, are linked series of Laspeyres base-weighted price indexes relating to three successive time segments within the historical period of the linked series. The three time-segment indexes are the 1956-based indexes for the period 1956 to 1960, the 1961-based indexes for 1960 to 1970 and 1971-based indexes covering the period from 1971 forward. Weights used in the successive indexes were values of shipments of specific commodities of the industry: namely, shipments in 1958 for the 1956-based indexes, 1961 shipments for the 1961-based indexes, and 1971 shipment values for the 1971-based indexes. Pricing and calculation methods common to the indexes are discussed below, following an outline of the selection of industry indexes presented in the data tables as series K68-87 (*Panel A*) and series K88-107 (*Panel B*).

In *Panel A,* composite indexes are presented for major groups (two-digit level of industry classification) and for manufacturing industries (one-digit level). These are gross-weighted averages of industry indexes produced at the three-digit, and in some cases four-digit, level of industry classes. They are gross weighted in the sense that intra-industry shipments of commodities among industries within the class are included in the industry weights used in averaging. Gross weights thus overweigh the effect in major group indexes (K69-87), and in the composite for manufacturing industries (K68), of price movements of commodities shipped to other industries in the same group for use as inputs in production of their shipments. For example, price movements of raw sugar are reflected initially in selling prices of refiners and again in prices of shipments of confectionery manufacturers, soft drink producers and biscuit manufacturers, which are all classed to the major group 'food and beverage industries' (K69). Despite the seriousness of this duplication effect on composite gross-weighted price indexes, which is variable among industries, the advantages to users in having composites for higher level industry groups are deemed to outweigh it. It has not been possible yet to obtain preferable net weights for this purpose.

It will be noted that *Panel A* includes columns for major groups in which no composite indexes or indexes for only very short periods are presented. For these, indexes at lower levels of classification are presented in *Panel B*. As part of the column headings for major groups in *Panel A* the official group S.I.C. number is included. In *Panel B*, the first two digits in the S.I.C. number designate the major group to which the industry belongs, the next three, the three-digit industry class, and the final digit indicates the four-digit level of classification. If the final digit is '0', the industry is a three-digit level industry. Indexes have been shown at the highest level of aggregation for which they are available. They are available for some 100 industries at the third or fourth digit classification stage, by months, with annual indexes being simple averages of the monthly indexes.

The industry indexes are constructed initially for three-digit or four-digit industry classes, using gross shipment values as commodity weights within the index. At this level, establishments in the class are sufficiently homogeneous that gross weighting causes insignificant duplication of commodity price movements. Prices are selected for each industry by a multi-stage sampling process in which selection is made of commodities, then establishments and finally detailed specifications of transactions for which price quotations are collected monthly as of the 15th of the month. Sampling is by purposive rather than random selection at each stage. Prices are prices for new orders, free on board manufacturing plant, net of quantity or trade discounts, subsidies, federal sales and excise taxes applicable at the manufacturers level. The specification price relative series developed from the prices so collected are averaged to successively higher composite price indexes through reverse stages of the sampling process, using relative shipment values as weights at each stage. The resulting commodity indexes are then averaged to yield the industry indexes. Weights are obtained from the censuses of manufacturers for the base-weight periods specified above.

Particular attention is given to the comparability of prices through time for each specification priced. Where a specification must be changed because quotations no longer can be obtained for it or because a substitute specification has become more important in current shipments, a range of techniques is employed to adjust the new price to maintain a constant or equivalent quantity- quality dimension for the price relative series.

A reference paper detailing scope and methods in the 1971-based updating of the indexes is in preparation for early publication.

Construction Price Indexes (Series K108-159)

General note

A number of price indexes relating to construction and capital expenditures in Canada have been developed since 1960 and are presented in this publication for the first time. In the 1965 edition, only three indexes relating to construction were included, namely a building and construction materials index (J68), a residential building materials price index (J73) and a non-residential building materials price index (J74). Indexes J73 and J74 are continued and extended to 1975 in the current edition as series K137 and K140 respectively. Index J68 is not repeated herein.

The delayed development of price indexes for capital goods is the result of serious difficulty in obtaining comparable prices through time. Capital goods tend to be unique, custom-designed products and capital entities are in turn unique combinations of structures and installed machinery and equipment. Seldom are identical facilities constructed in successive time periods and, correspondingly, it is seldom possible to observe prices in successive time periods for even closely similar capital facilities. The pricing difficulty persists for the components of such facilities insofar as they are not standard, repetitively produced components. Accordingly, price indexes of construction and capital expenditures so far developed are primarily composite-weighted averages of market prices of specified inputs into construction of buildings and structures, market prices of standard items of machinery and equipment, and 'model prices' of non-standard machinery and equipment. A major exception to this generality is the highway construction price indexes series (K150-159) in which 'in-place prices' of components are employed.

'In-place prices' are prices of identifiable units of work completed and in place. For such units of work, (for example, a specified quantity of gravel of specified size put in place on a highway of specified type), costs of all inputs such as materials, labour, construction machinery used, and contractors overheads and profits, and the effects of productivity changes through time on the total cost are included in the in-place price. This contrasts with composite prices of inputs *per se* in which profit margins and productivity-change effects are excluded.

'Model prices' are prices of specified models of machinery and equipment. In this technique of pricing, detailed specifications of models are drawn up after consultation with purchasers and manufacturers. Manufacturers then price the models annually as though they were tendering bid prices on contracts, having regard for changing input costs, profit margins and productivity in their manufacturing operations.

Construction price indexes presented in this edition and those presented in the 1965 edition are listed in the table below, including the periods covered in each edition and the price reference base periods. The dash (-) in columns (1) and (2) indicates the series is not included in the edition specified in the column heading.

K108-135. Union Wage Rate Indexes, for major construction trades, in major cities, by trade and by city, 1950 to 1975

SOURCE: 'Construction Union Wage Rates and Indexes, 1971 = 100', insert in *Construction Price Statistics*, October 1976, (Catalogue 62-007), for period 1971 to 1975. Files of

| Series no. | | | Period covered | | Price reference period = 100 | |
Current edition	1965 edition	Title	Current edition	1965 edition	Current edition	1965 edition
—	J68	Wholesale price indexes, classified according to purpose	—	1890-1948	—	1926
K137	J73	Wholesale price indexes, classified by	1926-75	1926-60	1971	1935-39
K140	J74	residential and non-residential building materials	1935-75	1935-60	1971	1949
New series						
K108-135	—	Union wage rate indexes for major construction trades in major cities	1950-75	—	1971	—
K136-141	—	Building construction input price indexes	1926-75	—	1971	—
K142-144	—	Construction machinery and equipment price indexes	1951-75	—	1968	
K145-149	—	Electric utility construction price indexes	1956-75	—	1971	
K150-159	—	Highway construction price indexes	1956-75	—	1971	

Capital Expenditure Section, Prices Division, for period 1950 to 1970. CANSIM: Matrix No. 961. Current indexes are published in *Construction Price Statistics*, monthly bulletin, (Catalogue 62-007) and quarterly report, (Catalogue 62-008).

The indexes of union wage rates are designed to measure the effect of collective labour agreements and changes in them on union basic wage rates and selected pay supplements of major construction tradesmen in major metropolitan areas in Canada. The indexes do *not* reflect changes in non-union wage rates, nor the effects of union rate changes in non-metropolitan areas. For basic union wage rates, composite indexes are presented here for each trade (K110-121) for each city (K122-135) and for the overall trade and city aggregate (K109) for the period 1950 to 1975. In addition, a composite for the trade-city aggregate is provided including combined wage rates and selected pay supplements (K108). The indexes measure changes through time. They do *not* measure differences in levels of wage rates among trades or among locations.

The historical series is composed of linked Laspeyres-type indexes in which the indexes for the period 1961 to 1970 (1961 = 100) with 1961 weights have been linked to 1971-weighted indexes covering the period 1971 to 1975 (1971 = 100). Weights for each trade in each city in the two period indexes were based on census of population data on occupations in 1961 and 1971 respectively, namely, numbers employed by trade and average earnings for construction by province. The indexes were extended backward to cover the period 1950 to 1960 in a special study for the Economic Council of Canada based on data in files of the Prices Division, Statistics Canada.

Rates in the indexes are mainly for the journeyman class for each construction trade and in later periods were derived primarily from the Canadian Construction Association (CCA) publication *Construction Collective Agreement Survey Service*, an assembly of collective agreements. In earlier periods, the CCA records were supplemented by rate collections of the federal Department of Labour and information from local unions and contractors. Basic union rates used are straight-time hourly compensation. The selected pay supplements included in K108 are payments explicitly stated in contracts as cents-per-hour items or as a percentage of the basic wage rates. They cover vacation pay, statu-

tory holiday pay, pension contributions (employer's contribution to private plans), health and welfare (employer's contribution) and employer's contribution to the industry promotion fund and training fund. In 1971, the number of trades included was expanded to 16 and the numbers of metropolitan areas to 22.

Indexes and rates in dollar terms, with and without pay supplements are available and are published for each trade in each metropolitan area, as well as composites (averages) for the total trades, the total cities and the combined trades and cities in the indexes.

Full descriptions of the indexes are provided in the following source documents: *Construction Price Statistics*, service bulletin, (Catalogue 62-006), vol. 1, No. 2, 'Basic Union Wage Rates and Indexes for Major Construction Trades and Selected Canadian Cities, 1961 = 100'; vol. 1, No. 5, 'Basic Union Wage Rate Indexes and Indexes Including Selected Pay Supplements, for Major Construction Trades and Specified Cities, 1961 to 1971 Annually, 1961 = 100'; and *Construction Price Statistics*, monthly bulletin, (Catalogue 62-007), October 1976, 'Construction Union Wage Rates, 1971 = 100'.

K136-141.   Building Construction Input Price Indexes, 1926 to 1975

SOURCE: CANSIM: Matrix No. 3781 for series K136-138 (residential) for period 1926 to 1975; Matrix No. 967 for series K139-141 (non-residential) for period 1935 to 1975. Current indexes are published in *Construction Price Statistics*, monthly bulletin, (Catalogue 62-007) and *Construction Price Statistics*, quarterly report, (Catalogue 62-008).

In this set of price indexes, the series for building materials, K137 (residential) and K140 (non-residential), are a continuation of the series J73 and J74 respectively presented previously in the 1965 edition of this publication for the period 1926 to 1960. In the current edition, these have been updated and extended to 1975 and placed on a 1971 = 100 price reference period. The materials indexes are presented here alongside corresponding labour wage rate series (K138 and K141) in the framework of inputs into residential and non-residential building construction, and composites of the labour and materials indexes are provided for each of the two categories of construction. Annual indexes for earlier periods are available back to 1890 on request to the Prices Division, Statistics Canada.

The indexes measure the effect of changes in materials prices and labour wage rates on the cost of specified baskets of inputs in building construction. The historical series are linked series of component and composite Laspeyres-type indexes covering separate but successive periods in the longer run series. The nature of the successive period-indexes are described below separately for the residential series (K136-138) and the non-residential series (K139-141).

It should be stressed that the indexes do *not* measure the effect of price changes on the costs of construction of completed buildings. Some input costs are not covered by the indexes, for example, capital inputs of machinery and equipment used in construction. Further, no account is taken of changes in productivity in construction or of changes in profit margins of contractors.

K136-138. Residential building construction input price indexes, 1926 to 1975. The price index series for residential materials (K137) is composed of three period-indexes covering the time periods 1926 to 1960, 1961 to 1970 and 1971 to 1975. Each period-index is of the Laspeyres-type employing fixed weights over the index period. In the 1926 to 1960 index, the item content and weights are based on 'units of material requirements valued at 1946 prices for the national housing target of that year'. Prices for materials in the index are, where possible, selling prices to large contractors, free on board site, but wholesale prices are used in many cases. The 90 commodity price series are weighted into nine commodity group indexes, with regional weights and prices used within groups where feasible. A full description is given in *Price Index Numbers of Residential Building Materials,* 1926 to 1948 (1935-39 = 100), (Catalogue 62-505). For the 1961 to 1970 period-index the nine commodity group weights are unchanged from those of the preceding index. Within groups, however, the commodity content is updated to reflect building materials in use since 1961. Also, price series from the industry selling price indexes, with addition of federal sales taxes where applicable, are substituted extensively for previously used wholesale prices (*Prices and Price Indexes,* May 1970, Catalogue 62-002).

The index for the period 1971 to 1975 incorporates major revisions of the target group, that is, the type of residential construction represented in the index, the commodity content and weighting and the classification structure within it ("Residential Building Construction Input Price Indexes, 1971 = 100', *Construction Price Statistics,* service bulletin, Catalogue 62-006, vol. 1, No. 7). The target group is restricted to single-detached units of residential construction. New weights are based on a 1969 survey by Central Mortgage and Housing Corporation of materials used in residential construction in Canada and a 1971 cost study, yielding unit material requirements valued at 1971 costs for each construction trade activity in each major city. Prices from the industry selling price indexes collection are employed with adjustment for federal sales tax. Price indexes are calculated for a variety of composites as weighted averages of detailed materials price series, for example, regional indexes, indexes for major construction activities, as well as for total materials.

The wage rate index series for residential construction labour inputs (K138) results from the linking of two period-indexes, one for the period 1926 to 1970, the other covering the period 1971 to 1975. The 1935 to 1970 index is based on wage rates data collected by the federal Department of Labour in annual surveys of fair wage rates from employers of construction trades in selected cities across Canada.

Rates incorporated in the index are base rates excluding fringe benefits, representing minimum rates in federal government contracts, for eight construction trades. The composite wage rate index is computed as an average of the trades indexes, using relative weights provided by the Department of Labour, based on materials and labour requirements in some 100 buildings, surveyed after World War II. Two trades, namely, labourers and carpenters, constitute 76 per cent, by weight, of the index. The second period-index for 1971 to 1975, incorporates a major revision of content, weights, and wage rate series, along with internal classification by trade and location as for the materials index (above). Rates used in the new index are basic union wage rates (see outline for series K108-135 above) for specific trades in residential building construction in major cities. Weights are labour requirements in 1969 valued at 1971 costs for each of specified construction activities in each major city, based on Central Mortgage and Housing Corporation studies. The weighted average of the city-trade indexes are linked to the 1926 to 1970 index at January 1971 to form the linked historical series.

The total (or composite) price index of residential building construction inputs (K136) was published as an official series for the first time in *Prices and Price Indexes,* May 1970, (Catalogue 62-002). Weights used to combine the 1926 to 1970 period materials and labour components are 62.5 and 37.5 per cent respectively and are based on the previously indicated surveys of residential construction conducted after the World War II. The materials and labour weights in the 1971 to 1975 index are 64.1 and 35.9 per cent.

Because of the major change in the classifications used in the indexes from 1971 forward, the longer term historical series is currently being continued for only total materials, total labour and their composite.

K139-141. Non-residential building construction input price indexes, 1935 to 1975. The series for non-residential materials (K140) is a linked series of three period-indexes covering the successive periods 1935 to 1960, 1961 to 1970 and 1971 to 1975. The materials item content and weights in the 1935 to 1960 index are based on cost data for a sample of 99 buildings constructed during the 1948 to 1950 period. Prices in the index are on-site prices paid by contractors or, where these were not available, manufacturers' or wholesale distributors' prices. A Laspeyres formula employing relative value weights is used to combine relative price series (1949 = 100) into weighted average indexes for 12 materials groups which in turn are averaged in calculating the total materials index (*Non-Residential Building Materials Price Index, 1935-1952,* Catalogue 62-506). Group weights are retained unchanged in the 1961 to 1970 index. Within groups, however, the item content and weights are modified to reflect materials important in non-residential building in the 1960s. Producers selling prices with adjustment for federal sales taxes as applicable are incorporated extensively as replacements for previously used wholesale and distributor prices (*Prices and Price Indexes,* Catalogue 62-002, May 1970). In the 1971 to 1975 index, item content and weights have been updated, based on analysis of three typical classes of non-residential buildings in four major cities valued at 1971 costs, and a major restructuring of material detail and sub-indexes is incorporated with classification by construction trade activity within metropolitan areas across Canada. The price series used are selling prices of building material producers and manufacturers from the industry selling price collection. The historical series is continued for total materials only by linking at January 1971, with 1971 = 100 as the reference base. No reference paper on the 1971 to 1975 index has been published as yet.

The index for labour wage rates in non-residential building construction is a linked series of two period-indexes, one for the period 1935 to 1970, the other for 1971 to 1975. The 1935 to 1970 index is the index used for the residential building inputs as outlined above (see the relevant paragraph under K136-138). In the 1971 to 1975 index, a major restructuring of index content with labour input classification by trade within construction trade activity, within metropolitan areas, is introduced. Previously used fair wage rates are replaced by basic union wage rates (see K108-135 above, paragraph 2). Base weights by trade within cities are derived from the above mentioned analysis of typical non-residential buildings in terms of 1971 costs. The index is a weighted average of trade-city rates, calculated at successive stages of aggregation of the rate series.

The total non-residential building input price index (K139) was first published in the May 1970 issue of *Prices and Price Indexes*, as a weighted average of the materials and labour indexes. Weights in the 1935 to 1970 period index were 65 and 35 per cent for materials and labour respectively. These were modified for the 1971 to 1975 period based on materials/labour statistics from *Construction in Canada*, (Catalogue 64-201). The indexes do not relate to engineering construction nor do they represent prices of completed buildings.

The historical series is being continued currently for only total materials, total labour and their composite.

K142-144. Construction Machinery and Equipment Price Indexes, 1961 to 1975

SOURCE: CANSIM: Matrix No. 84 for annual indexes, Matrix No. 1787 for monthly indexes. *Prices and Price Indexes*, June 1971, (Catalogue 62-002) for annual indexes from 1961 to 1970. *Construction Price Statistics*, quarterly report, (Catalogue 62-008), various issues for annual indexes from 1970 to 1975. Current indexes are published in *Construction Price Statistics*, quarterly report, (Catalogue 62-008).

The indexes measure the movements of prices in Canada of a fixed basket of machinery and equipment used in construction, representing annual expenditures for such capital goods of contractors classified to the construction industry. The index is the first in a planned program of development of industry-classified price indexes relating to gross capital additions of machinery and equipment. Prices used in the index are primarily manufacturers' selling prices, both Canadian and United States, with adjustment for import duties and federal sales tax as applicable. These are employed as proxies for theoretically preferred purchase prices of contractors, and their movements are expected to approximate movements of purchase prices with reasonable validity.

Prices are for specified quantities and qualities including terms of sale, and adjustments are incorporated for changed specifications when they, of necessity, are introduced. Indexes of manufacturers' selling prices produced by the U.S. Bureau of Labor Statistics for machinery and equipment of a kind related to Canadian imports are incorporated in the import component of the Canadian index where appropriate, with adjustments for duties and sales tax.

Fifteen types of machinery and equipment are priced for the index. Two types, namely, crawler tractors and front end loaders (wheeled), constitute 50.1 per cent by weight, the former being entirely imports, the latter of both domestic and import origin (U.S.). Relative value weights for each type are based on data from Census of Merchandising surveys of 1967 and 1969 supplemented by statistics on imports in those years. The item content and weighting diagrams are recorded in *Prices and Price Indexes*, June 1971, (Catalogue 62-002). The indexes are calculated using the base-weighted Laspeyres formula with relative value weights.

K145-149. Electric Utility Construction Price Indexes, 1956 to 1975

SOURCE: CANSIM: Matrix No. 118 for annual indexes for series K145-149. *Construction Price Statistics*, quarterly report, (Catalogue 62-008), third quarter, 1977 for period 1971 to 1975 for K145-148 and for the period 1966 to 1975 for K149. Current indexes are published in detail in the above quarterly report (Catalogue 62-008) and in summary form in *Construction Price Statistics*, monthly bulletin, (Catalogue 62-007).

The price indexes of electric utility construction are designed to measure the effect of price change on the cost of constructing and equipping electric generating, transforming, transmission and distribution facilities. Indexes for distribution systems, transmission lines, and for transformation and switching stations were the first to be developed. A full description of them respecting concept, scope, methods, uses and limitations accompanied the release of annual indexes of each (K145, 146 and 147) for the period 1956 to 1965 in *Price Indexes of Electric Utility Construction, 1956-1965*, (Catalogue 62-526). Indexes for hydroelectric generating stations (K148) were published initially for the period 1961 to 1970 with similar full description in *Construction Price Indexes for Hydro-Electric Generating Stations, 1961-1970*, 1961 = 100, (Catalogue 62-533). The series for fossil fuel fired steam generating stations (K149), the most recent development in the set was released with full description in June 1976 in *Construction Price Index for Steam-Electric Generating Stations (Fossil Fuel Fired) 1971 = 100*, as an insert in *Construction Price Statistics*, monthly bulletin, May 1976, (Catalogue 62-007).

Electric utility facilities are unique, custom-designed combinations of structures, machinery and equipment. The price indexes for them are, of necessity, base-weighted Laspeyres-type composites of price series for machinery and equipment components installed in them and for inputs employed in construction of the structures and in installation of the equipment. Through surveys undertaken by Statistics Canada in collaboration with the Canadian Electrical Association covering major electric utility capital projects over a number of years, the item content and weights of items in each of the five categories of indexes (K145-149) are established at the level of detail at which price series comparable through time are obtainable.

A wide range of price series sources are tapped, through utilizing existing collections as well as initiating new series. For standard, repetitively produced items of materials, machinery and equipment, price series are drawn from existing industry selling prices and wholesale price series, with adjustment for applicable sales taxes, and new series are collected from manufacturers where existing ones are not sufficiently appropriate. Price series for selected models of non-standard more complex equipment such as generators, turbines, feedwater heaters and pumps and condensers, supplement the standard item coverage of equipment. For labour inputs, sub-indexes from the union wage rate series (K108-135, above) are used for contract construction work, and wage rates reported by utilities for own-account construction items. Salary series from the federal Pay Research Bureau are employed for overhead inputs, and average hourly earnings series from Statistics Canada, where wage rate series are not available, for labour in-shop fabrication, field erection and construction camp operation. A number of in-place price series from the highway construction price indexes (K150-159, below) are employed, namely, the clearing, excavation and grading sub-indexes. Price indexes from foreign countries also have been incorporated in the indexes where imports of standard goods are appreciable, with adjustment for exchange, duty and federal sales tax changes. This broad outline does not exhaust the sources or the price series.

The item content and weights and the type and source of price series for items are detailed in the above-cited descriptive publications for each of the five series. Since introduction of the indexes, improvements in the price series have been introduced. Also, for the series K145-147, for the period 1971 to 1975, the content of the indexes is revised to include construction indirects (engineering, head office and administrative expenses), interest cost during construction, for K146 and K147, and initial grading and clearing costs for series K146. Weights also are updated, and more in-place pricing has been introduced in K146 and K147. A published account of this updating has not been issued. The historical series for K145-147 are linked Laspeyres-type indexes, the indexes to 1970 being linked to the indexes of the period 1971 to 1975. The series K148 is the original base-weighted index converted arithmetically to 1971 = 100. Series K149 is the base-weighted series produced originally on the reference base 1971 = 100.

Users should realize that the indexes are not indexes of either purchase prices or selling prices of electric utility capital plant and equipment. Indexes for many items of equipment within the indexes are purchase price indexes, or close to it, while those for structures are basically input price indexes which do not reflect changes in profit margins or productivity in construction.

K150-159. Highway Construction Price Indexes, 1956 to 1975

SOURCE: CANSIM: Matrix No. 120. Also, *Construction Price Statistics*, quarterly report, third quarter, 1977, (Catalogue 62-008). Current indexes are published in *Construction Price Statistics*, monthly bulletin, (Catalogue 62-007), in summary form and in *Construction Price Statistics*, quarterly report, (Catalogue 62-008) in full detail.

These price indexes measure the movements of prices paid by provincial governments for a constant or equivalent program of highway construction represented by contracts awarded by the respective governments in a specified period for new construction, reconstruction and betterment work of arterial and secondary highways. Excluded from the program (basket) are bridge work and routine maintenance and repair. Prices used in the indexes are contractors' bid prices for units of completed-work-in-place, for example, an acre of clearing, a cubic yard of excavation, a ton of gravel put in place, a ton of hot mix bituminous paving in place, and

prices paid by provincial governments for materials supplied by them to the contractor. Accordingly, the indexes may be described as contractors' selling price indexes. The historical series are linked Laspeyres-type indexes, with indexes for the period up to 1970 linked to those for the period 1971 to 1975.

Indexes for seven provinces were introduced initially in 1961 and a full description of them was published in *Price Indexes of Highway Construction in Canada, base-weighted and current-weighted, 1956 = 100*, (Catalogue 62-520), September 1962. Items and their weights in the indexes were derived from highway construction contracts valued at $50,000 or more awarded by the respective provincial governments over the 1956 to 1959 fiscal years. In such contracts, detailed units of construction work to be completed on an in-place basis are listed by the provincial government, and for each such unit the quantity, bid price and total cost is required to be recorded by the contractor in tendering for the contract. The quantities, prices and values of materials supplied by the governments to contractors for each unit of work in each contract are included. Bid prices for each of the in-place units so established were calculated as averages of bid prices in finely stratified classes of contracts. Factors such as size of contract, the location of the road, the type of material to be graded (earth, rock) or placed, cause prices to vary among contracts within a period and between periods, representing a difference in the quantity-quality of the units of work to which the prices relate. To minimize such quantity effects, contracts are stratified to ensure average prices within classes relate through time to basically constant quantity-quality unit of in-place work.

The indexes were revised for the entire period 1956 to 1966 as described in *Prices and Price Indexes*, December 1967, (Catalogue 62-002). The revision introduced additional refinements in the stratification of contracts to improve the comparability of bid price averages through time at the item level. Weights in the indexes for Ontario and British Columbia were updated to 1964 (valued in 1956 prices) but were unchanged for the other five provinces. The short-term index for contracted federal government highways was dropped, and the composite index correspondingly was modified. The price reference base 1956 = 100 was retained.

An annual index for the province of Quebec for the period 1964 to 1969 (1964 = 100) was introduced and described in *Prices and Price Indexes*, March 1971. Concepts, scope and methods were essentially the same as in the other provincial indexes. The item content and weights were based on contracts awarded over the fiscal years 1964 to 1967 with revaluation in terms of 1964 prices.

Indexes for the period 1971 to 1975 are based on updated item content and weights derived from highway construction contracts valued at $25,000 or more awarded by provincial governments during the fiscal years 1970 to 1972. Annual indexes for the province of Alberta also are presented for this period. Weights for combining provincial indexes into the composite average are based on expenditure data on contract highway construction in the censuses of construction, 1970 to 1972. A description of the indexes for this period, including detailed weighting diagrams, is provided in *Highway Construction Price Indexes, 1971 = 100*, as an insert in *Construction Price Statistics*, monthly bulletin, March 1977, (Catalogue 62-007). Up to two dozen items of units of in-place work and supplies are shown in the weighting diagrams. These are grouped into three major components of highway construction, namely, grading, granular base course, and paving. Indexes are published currently at the all-item, major component and item levels.

Implicit Price Indexes of Gross Fixed Capital Stocks (Series K160-171)

General note

Price indexes of fixed capital stocks are presented in this publication for the first time in the current edition. No price indexes of capital stock were included in the 1965 edition.

The price indexes are termed implicit because they are derived indirectly as the percentage ratio of two value series, namely, the time series of annual current-dollar value of fixed stocks and the corresponding annual constant-dollar value series. Movements through time in the current-dollar series ($\geqq p_n q_n$) result from both price and quantity changes, whereas movements in the constant-dollar series ($\geqq p_o q_n$) result *theoretically* from quantity change only. The annual ratios between the two series thus implicitly reflect the price movements embedded in the current-dollar value series.

Algebraically, the implicit price indexes may be written

$$I^p = \frac{\Sigma p_n q_n}{\Sigma p_o q_n} \times 100$$

in which the p's and q's denote prices and quantities respectively and the subscripts '$_o$' and '$_n$', the price reference base year and any given year respectively. The symbol $\geqq$ indicates summation over the items included in the aggregate. The index (I^p) is a Paasche price index, the superscript denoting Paasche. In this current-weighted index, the weights (q_n) are the quantities of the given year and these are different for different given years. Thus, while the movement of this index between the base reference year '$_o$' and any given year results from price change only, index movements between any other years in the series result from price change and some quantity changes. This contrasts with the Laspeyres base-weighted price index (described earlier in this section) in which price index movements throughout the series arise from price change only because quantities (the basket) are kept constant.

A principal favourable attribute of the Paasche price index is that its use in deflation of value indexes yields Laspeyres quantity indexes. Again algebraically, in ratio form,

$$\frac{\Sigma p_n q_n}{\Sigma p_o q_o} \div \frac{\Sigma p_n q_n}{\Sigma p_o q_o} = \frac{\Sigma p_o q_n}{\Sigma p_o q_o}$$

in which the first ratio (index) is the value series, the second is the Paasche price index and the term on the right is the Laspeyres quantity index. For many uses, it is the Laspeyres quantity index that is appropriate, for example, in studies of productivity and growth. In these uses, however, it is often the constant-dollar series itself ($\geqq p_o q_n$) which is most useful and it can be derived directly by deflating (dividing) the current-dollar series by the price index, thus

$$\Sigma p_n q_n \div \frac{\Sigma p_n q_n}{\Sigma p_o q_n} = \Sigma p_o q_n$$

from this it is obvious that the price index is implicitly derivable given the current- and constant-dollar series.

Unfortunately, in practice, Paasche price indexes are seldom available and Laspeyres base-weighted price indexes are used. However, the deflation is carried out at as low a level of components of an aggregate as possible. The resulting constant-dollar values of the components are then summed in each period (a year, say) to higher levels of aggregations. The implicit price indexes derived by dividing the current-dollar series by the resultant constant-dollar series are (1) Laspeyres price indexes at the component level at which the initial deflation was carried out and (2) quasi Paasche-type price indexes at the higher levels of aggregation. In the higher level indexes, the components are weighted implicitly by the relative current values of the components. In this sense they are partly base-weighted and partly current-weighted and, therefore, termed quasi Paasche price indexes.

K160-171. Fixed Capital Stocks Price Indexes (implicit), by industry and type of stock, 1926 to 1975

SOURCE: for 1926 to 1975, *Fixed Capital Flows and Stocks, 1926-1978,* (Catalogue 13-568). In addition to the implicit price indexes, this occasional publication includes the current- and constant-dollar capital stock series and the basic price indexes used in their derivation. Current indexes are available from the Construction Division, Statistics Canada, on request.

Price indexes of gross fixed capital stocks are presented for major classes of stocks, namely, building construction, engineering construction, and machinery and equipment, and for total stocks, within each of manufacturing industries, non-manufacturing industries and total industries categories in the Standard Industrial Classification. They are implicit price indexes calculated as percentage ratios of the current-dollar value to the constant-dollar value, annually, of gross fixed capital stocks at mid-year.

The current- and constant-dollar value series cover fixed tangible capital stocks produced by human effort. They exclude natural resources. The constant-dollar gross stock value series is derived on the basis of the 'perpetual inventory' method. In this method, the annual gross additions to stock (gross capital formation) for each detailed type of stock are revalued in prices of a selected price-base year. The revalued annual additions are then cumulated annually over time with deduction from the cumulative total in each year of previous additions whose estimated lifespans have expired. In the gross stock series no deductions are made for gradual depreciation, only the deduction for complete discard at the end of the expected life of the asset. The series by type of stock within industry groups are then summed to higher levels of aggregation.

The current-dollar series is derived from the constant-dollar series by inflating the latter to prices of the respective current years, using price indexes at the lowest component level possible within the series. The resulting annual current-dollar series for detailed components may then be summed to desired higher classes of aggregates.

The price indexes employed in deflation are primarily period price indexes of the Laspeyres base-weighted type. For construction, these deflators are primarily input indexes of materials and labour with weighting appropriate to types of structures, and deflation is undertaken at the level of type of structure. No adjustment is made for changes in profit margins (including the return to capital used in construction) or productivity in construction. In more recent periods, available in-place price indexes have been incorporated in the deflators. For machinery and equipment the deflators tend more to be output price indexes, particularly in more recent years. The historical series of constant-dollar values is a linked series, each segment of which is deflated by price indexes with price reference bases appropriate to the respective time segments.

The basic source document on methods used in fixed capital stock estimating is *Fixed Capital Flows and Stocks, Manufacturing, Canada, 1926-1960: Methodology*, (Catalogue 13-522). Historical series of both current- and constant-dollar values, annually, may be obtained from CANSIM, by industry and industry groups. The Matrix numbers for each industry and group are specified in table 3, page XV of *Fixed Capital Flows and Stocks*, (Catalogue 13-211). See also the descriptive text and historical series F183-224 in this publication.

Implicit Price Indexes of Gross National Expenditures (Series K172-183)

General note

For a discussion of the concept, interpretation and methods in principle for 'implicit' price indexes, see the general note for series K160-171 above.

The series K172-183 presented in this edition correspond precisely to series J153-164 in the 1965 edition. They have been extended in time to cover the period 1926 to 1975 and have been placed on a 1971 = 100 price reference base. In the 1965 edition the reference base is 1949 = 100. Also, for series K176 and K177, the series is extended back from 1949 to 1926 in the current edition.

K172-183. Implicit Price Indexes of Gross National Expenditures, 1926 to 1975

SOURCE: CANSIM: Matrix No. 529, except for K173 and K175 (the latter two from files of National Income and Expenditure Division, Statistics Canada). Current indexes are published in *National Income and Expenditure Accounts*, (Catalogue 13-001), quarterly and (Catalogue 13-201) annually.

These indexes are derived as percentage ratios of annual current-dollar values and constant-dollar values (1971 dollars) of the respective categories of gross national expenditures in Canada. The concepts, scope and content of these two value series and the methods employed in constructing them are outlined elsewhere in this publication (see the descriptive text and tables for series E14-32 and E33-35).

The constant-dollar series (E33-35) is based on deflation of the current-dollar series using primarily Laspeyres base-weighted price indexes at detailed disaggregated component levels of expenditure. Deflation is done separately for five successive time segments of the historical series, the deflators and the resulting constant-dollar series for each segment having different price reference bases appropriate to the respective periods. These are arithmetically linked to form the historical constant-dollar value series. The implicit price indexes are then computed for each year by dividing the current-dollar series by the constant-dollar series (and multiplying by 100) at each level of aggregation for which a price index is required. The resulting historical series of price indexes may be said to be composed of the following time-segment price indexes: 1920 to 1946, 1947 to 1955, 1956 to 1960, 1961 to 1970 and 1971 to 1975.

A feature of the deflators used for non-residential construction (K180) since 1949 is an annual adjustment of the price indexes of material and labour inputs for estimated rates of change in labour productivity in construction. Similar adjustment is made to the input deflators for residential construction (K179) for the period 1949 to 1970, while for the period 1971 forward direct valuations in terms of 1971 dollars are employed. The implicit indexes for these two series can be expected to move differently from the building construction input price indexes recorded previously (above) as series K136 and K139.

Series K1-7. Cost-of-living Index, 1913 to 1952
(1935–39 = 100)

Year	Total	Food	Fuel and light	Rent	Clothing	Home furnishings	Miscellaneous
	1	2	3	4	5	6	7
1952	188.4	237.4	151.1	147.4	209.4	197.8	151.5
1951	185.4	241.4	147.1	140.0	203.1	194.4	145.0
1950	167.3	210.9	138.3	132.9	182.3	169.2	136.0
1949	161.6	203.0	131.1	123.0	183.1	167.6	132.2
1948	155.7	195.5	124.8	120.7	174.4	162.6	126.8
1947	136.3	159.5	115.9	116.7	143.9	141.6	120.4
1946	124.5	140.4	107.4	112.7	126.3	124.5	116.5
1945	120.4	133.0	107.0	112.1	122.1	119.0	113.5
1944	119.8	131.3	110.6	111.9	121.5	118.4	113.1
1943	119.2	130.7	112.9	111.5	120.5	118.0	111.5
1942	117.2	127.2	112.8	111.3	120.0	117.9	107.8
1941	111.7	116.1	110.3	109.4	116.1	113.8	105.1
1940	105.6	105.6	107.1	106.3	109.2	107.2	102.3
1939	101.5	100.6	101.2	103.8	100.7	101.4	101.4
1938	102.2	103.8	97.7	103.1	100.9	102.4	101.2
1937	101.2	103.2	98.9	99.7	101.4	101.5	100.1
1936	98.1	97.8	101.5	96.1	99.3	97.2	99.1
1935	96.2	94.6	100.9	94.0	97.6	95.4	98.7
1934	95.6	93.0	101.8	93.4	97.2		97.9
1933	94.3	85.3	101.7	99.3	93.6		98.4
1932	98.9	86.2	106.2	110.6	100.9		100.6
1931	109.0	103.7	109.2	120.2	114.6		103.5
1930	120.8	132.3	111.0	123.6	131.0		105.8
1929	121.6	135.4	111.8	120.5	135.2		105.3
1928	120.2	132.2	112.4	118.1	135.8		104.9
1927	119.7	131.6	113.6	115.3	135.9		105.4
1926	121.7	134.2	116.0	116.7	139.7		106.3
1925	120.4	126.9	115.7	118.2	141.7		107.7
1924	119.3	121.1	118.0	118.2	142.1		109.8
1923	121.5	123.7	121.3	117.8	145.2		112.0
1922	121.1	122.8	121.5	114.8	147.1		112.7
1921	132.3	145.0	127.0	110.1	173.7		112.7
1920	150.4	188.8	119.0	100.7	213.8		110.6
1919	129.8	164.1	99.6	87.9	175.2		101.2
1918	118.1	153.6	91.8	80.6	152.5		91.3
1917	104.3	133.7	83.1	76.3	130.3		81.6
1916	88.1	103.5	74.7	71.1	110.8		74.9
1915	81.4	93.3	73.3	70.4	97.4		70.8
1914	80.0	92.0	74.5	72.6	89.2		70.4
1913	79.5	88.7	76.3	74.8	88.3		70.4

Series K8-18. Consumer Price Index for Canada, classified by main components, 1913 to 1975
(1971 = 100)

Year	Total	Food	Total, excluding food	Housing Total	Shelter	Household operation	Clothing	Transportation	Health and personal care	Recreation, education and reading	Tobacco and alcoholic beverages
	8	9	10	11	12	13	14	15	16	17	18
1975	138.5	161.9	130.5	133.2	130.9	136.4	125.1	129.4	133.0	128.5	125.3
1974	125.0	143.4	118.6	121.1	120.7	121.4	118.0	115.8	119.4	116.4	111.8
1973	112.7	123.3	108.9	111.4	112.7	109.1	107.7	105.3	109.8	107.1	106.0
1972	104.8	107.6	103.7	104.7	105.5	103.2	102.6	102.6	104.8	102.8	102.7
1971	100.0	100.0	100.0	100.0	100.0	100.0	100.0	100.0	100.0	100.0	100.0
1970	97.2	98.9	96.6	95.7	94.7	97.1	98.5	96.1	98.0	96.8	98.4
1969	94.1	96.7	93.1	91.2	88.9	94.9	96.7	92.4	93.8	93.5	97.2
1968	90.0	92.8	89.0	86.7	83.2	92.5	94.1	88.3	89.5	88.3	93.6
1967	86.5	89.9	85.3	82.9	78.5	90.1	91.4	86.1	86.0	84.1	85.8
1966	83.5	88.7	81.7	79.5	74.9	86.7	87.0	82.6	81.8	80.1	83.7
1965	80.5	83.4	79.5	77.3	72.7	85.0	83.8	80.7	79.4	77.9	81.7
1964	78.6	81.3	77.6	76.0	70.8	84.4	82.4	77.8	75.8	76.6	80.4
1963	77.2	80.0	76.2	74.8	69.1	84.2	80.3	76.9	73.5	75.4	78.9
1962	75.9	77.5	75.3	74.0	67.9	84.0	78.4	76.9	71.6	74.3	78.8
1961	75.0	76.1	74.6	73.1	66.8	83.6	77.7	77.0	70.2	73.7	77.8
1960	74.3	75.0	74.1	72.8	66.2	83.8	76.6	76.8	69.9	72.9	77.4
1959	73.4	74.4	73.2	72.1	65.1	83.4	75.9	75.8	67.9	71.5	76.2
1958	72.6	75.0	71.7	70.8	63.7	82.3	75.8	73.3	65.7	69.8	74.0
1957	70.7	72.8	69.9	69.5	62.1	81.3	74.9	71.1	62.5	65.5	73.2
1956	68.5	69.6	68.2	68.1	61.0	79.6	75.0	67.5	58.8	63.3	72.0
1955	67.5	68.8	67.2	67.2	59.6	79.1	74.6	64.9	57.3	61.9	71.8
1954	67.4	68.9	66.9	66.7	58.2	79.8	75.5	65.7	56.3	60.3	71.8
1953	67.0	69.1	66.2	65.9	56.9	79.5	76.1	65.3	54.3	58.9	72.2
1952	67.6	71.7	65.9	64.8	55.3	79.0	77.2	64.3	53.3	58.4	75.7
1951	66.0	71.8	63.7	62.4	52.7	76.8	75.8	61.9	50.2	55.4	74.6
1950	59.7	62.9	58.4	57.2	48.9	69.6	68.8	57.7	46.1	51.5	68.7
1949	58.0	61.3	56.7	54.9	46.0	68.0	69.1	54.7	45.2	50.4	66.9
1948	56.3	59.8	54.8	53.6	45.3	65.8	66.0			52.3	
1947	49.2	48.8	50.2	49.8	43.8	58.6	54.5			49.7	
1946	45.0	43.0	46.8	46.4	42.3	52.5	47.8			48.1	
1945	43.5	40.7	45.7	45.6	42.1	50.9	46.2			46.9	
1944	43.3	40.2	45.7	45.8	42.0	51.5	46.0			46.7	
1943	43.0	40.0	45.5	45.8	41.8	51.7	45.7			46.0	
1942	42.3	38.9	44.9	45.7	41.8	51.7	45.4			44.5	
1941	40.4	35.5	43.8	44.7	41.1	50.2	43.9			43.4	
1940	38.2	32.3	42.2	43.1	39.9	47.8	41.4			42.2	
1939	36.7	30.8	40.7	41.4	38.9	45.2	37.9			41.9	
1938	37.0	31.7	40.6	41.2	38.7	44.9	38.3			41.8	
1937	36.6	31.5	41.2	40.4	37.4	44.8	38.3			41.3	
1936	35.5	30.0	39.0	39.3	36.0	44.1	37.4			40.9	
1935	34.8	29.0	38.7	38.6	35.3	43.6	37.0			40.8	
1934	34.6	28.4	38.6	38.5	35.1	43.6	36.7			40.7	
1933	34.0	26.1	39.1	39.9	37.3	43.4	35.4			41.2	
1932	35.8	26.4	41.5	43.2	41.5	45.0	38.2			42.0	
1931	39.4	31.7	44.3	46.1	45.1	46.4	43.4			43.1	
1930	43.6	40.4	46.6	47.4	46.4	47.7	49.6			43.8	
1929	43.9	41.4	46.6	46.8	45.2	48.1	51.2			43.4	
1928	43.4	40.4	46.3	46.2	44.3	48.3	51.4			43.3	
1927	43.3	40.3	46.0	45.7	43.3	48.7	51.5			43.4	
1926	44.0	41.1	46.8	46.2	43.8	49.1	52.9			43.9	
1925	43.5	—	—	—	—	—	—			—	
1924	43.1	—	—	—	—	—	—			—	
1923	43.9	—	—	—	—	—	—			—	
1922	43.8	—	—	—	—	—	—			—	
1921	47.8	—	—	—	—	—	—			—	
1920	54.3	—	—	—	—	—	—			—	
1919	46.9	—	—	—	—	—	—			—	
1918	42.7	—	—	—	—	—	—			—	
1917	37.7	—	—	—	—	—	—			—	
1916	31.9	—	—	—	—	—	—			—	
1915	29.4	—	—	—	—	—	—			—	
1914	28.9	—	—	—	—	—	—			—	
1913	28.7	—	—	—	—	—	—			—	

Series K19-22. Consumer Price Index for Canada, classified by goods and services, 1961 to 1975
(1971 = 100)

Year	Total	Goods		Services	Year	Total	Goods		Services
		Total	Excluding food				Total	Excluding food	
	19	20	21	22		19	20	21	22
1975	138.5	142.0	127.7	133.4	1965	80.5	84.6	85.4	73.6
1974	125.0	128.1	116.7	120.5	1964	78.6	83.1	84.4	70.8
1973	112.7	113.7	106.4	111.7	1963	77.2	82.1	83.6	68.9
1972	104.8	104.6	102.3	105.2	1962	75.9	80.7	83.0	67.8
1971	100.0	100.0	100.0	100.0	1961	75.0	79.9	82.7	66.6
1970	97.2	98.2	97.8	95.3					
1969	94.1	96.3	96.1	90.0					
1968	90.0	93.4	93.7	84.4					
1967	86.5	90.0	90.4	80.2					
1966	83.5	87.8	87.3	76.1					

Series K23-32. Consumer Price Indexes for regional cities, 1940 to 1975
(1971 = 100)

Year	St. John's (Nfld.)	Halifax	Saint John (N.B.)	Montreal	Ottawa[1]	Toronto	Winnipeg	Saskatoon–Regina[2]	Edmonton–Calgary[3]	Vancouver
	23	24	25	26	27	28	29	30	31	32
1975	143.0	133.9	138.1	136.4	135.8	136.1	137.4	133.5	135.2	137.7
1974	128.3	121.6	123.7	123.0	123.9	123.0	122.2	120.4	121.7	123.9
1973	113.7	110.9	112.2	110.7	111.9	111.3	110.4	110.1	110.6	111.0
1972	105.0	103.7	104.5	103.8	104.1	104.1	103.8	104.0	103.9	104.0
1971	100.0	100.0	100.0	100.0	100.0	100.0	100.0	100.0	100.0	100.0
1970	98.5	98.5	98.6	98.2	97.5	98.4	98.8	99.0	97.6	96.9
1969	96.6	94.6	95.7	96.2	94.2	95.9	95.7	97.0	94.8	93.7
1968	93.8	90.4	91.9	93.3	90.6	92.2	91.9	93.9	91.1	90.6
1967	89.8	87.0	88.7	90.2	86.5	88.8	88.1	90.2	87.2	87.4
1966	87.4	85.0	86.1	86.8	84.5	86.2	85.0	87.8	83.9	84.3
1965	85.4	82.8	83.9	84.3	81.3	82.6	82.5	85.2	81.2	82.3
1964	84.1	81.3	82.7	82.5	80.0	80.6	80.7	83.9	80.0	80.8
1963	83.2	81.0	81.9	81.3	78.7	79.3	79.5	83.1	79.6	80.2
1962	81.6	80.2	80.6	79.9	77.4	78.0	78.8	82.4	78.7	79.0
1961	81.0	79.2	79.9	79.0	76.5	77.3	77.8	81.1	78.0	78.7
1960	80.1	78.4	79.2	78.2	75.6	76.8	76.6	80.4	77.5	78.5
1959	79.3	77.6	78.3	77.6	74.6	76.0	75.4	79.6	76.8	77.9
1958	77.7	75.7	76.8	76.7	73.7	75.7	75.0	78.8	75.8	76.5
1957	75.9	73.8	75.2	74.5	72.4	73.7	73.1	77.0	74.2	74.6
1956	74.1	71.5	72.8	72.4	70.0	71.1	71.4	74.9	72.2	72.8
1955	72.3	70.7	72.1	71.4	68.9	70.0	70.6	74.1	71.5	71,8
1954	71.3	70.3	71.5	71.4	68.3	69.7	70.3	73.8	71.7	71.4
1953	70.9	69.8	70.7	71.1	67.6	68.8	69.7	73.1	71.2	70.6
1952	71.8	71.0	72.0	71.9	68.6	69.2	70.8	72.9	71.6	71.5
1951	—	69.0	69.9	71.0	67.8	68.0	69.8	72.2	70.9	69.5
1950	—	62.9	63.3	63.4	60.6	61.3	63.3	66.1	64.9	63.0
1949	—	61.6	61.3	61.1	58.8	58.9	60.9	64.7	62.4	60.9
1948	—	59.6	59.4	59.1	56.7	57.1	58.4	62.6	60.0	58.4
1947	—	53.1	51.9	51.5	49.6	50.4	51.4	54.6	52.8	50.7
1946	—	49.1	47.8	47.0	44.9	45.9	47.2	49.5	48.5	46.2
1945	—	47.8	46.5	45.5	43.4	44.3	45.8	47.8	47.0	44.8
1944	—	47.4	46.2	45.0	43.1	44.1	45.4	47.5	46.5	44.3
1943	—	46.8	45.8	44.9	43.0	43.8	45.1	47.0	46.1	44.0
1942	—	45.7	45.0	44.0	42.3	43.4	44.5	46.2	44.9	42.7
1941	—	43.9	42.8	41.9	40.3	41.2	42.6	44.3	43.1	40.7
1940	—	42.2	40.7	39.6	38.4	38.9	40.6	41.8	41.4	38.7

[1] Data from 1940 to September 1953 are based on Toronto prices.
[2] Data from 1940 to September 1953 are based on Saskatoon prices.
[3] Data from 1940 to September 1953 are based on Edmonton prices.

Series K33-43. General Wholesale Price Index, classified by chief component material, 1867 to 1975
(1935-39 = 100)

Year	General index		Vegetable products	Animals and their products	Fibres, textiles, textile products	Wood, wood products, paper	Iron and its products	Non-ferrous metals and their products		Non-metallic minerals and their products	Chemicals and allied products
	Excluding gold	Including gold						Excluding gold	Including gold		
	33	34	35	36	37	38	39	40	41	42	43
1975	510.2	491.6	469.6	537.5	404.9	641.7	519.9	606.2	417.4	392.1	383.9
1974	480.2	461.3	485.6	493.0	423.1	563.1	447.7	607.5	417.7	331.2	325.3
1973	392.1	376.9	354.9	455.3	337.7	504.1	354.3	478.5	326.5	254.1	263.3
1972	322.9	310.3	249.2	371.8	278.3	436.0	325.0	388.4	262.9	233.6	245.5
1971	302.7	289.9	237.1	326.0	261.9	394.4	316.4	387.6	260.1	225.8	237.8
1970	300.6	286.4	238.4	326.0	257.0	377.5	305.1	422.9	281.0	215.8	225.7
1969	295.0	282.4	237.9	322.4	256.7	389.4	285.8	389.6	264.0	210.0	219.7
1968	281.4	269.9	230.8	294.6	256.5	367.9	276.8	365.8	250.8	206.0	213.7
1967	274.7	264.1	230.9	293.1	252.7	346.3	274.4	346.6	240.2	199.2	212.6
1966	269.4	259.5	225.9	296.2	251.5	337.8	268.0	328.2	229.9	193.7	207.1
1965	259.3	250.4	218.4	270.7	246.6	334.0	264.5	306.1	217.6	191.6	200.2
1964	253.3	245.4	223.3	250.8	248.4	330.9	256.4	284.9	205.9	190.9	191.2
1963	251.8	244.6	227.8	255.6	248.0	323.4	253.6	270.0	197.5	189.5	189.3
1962	246.9	240.0	211.6	262.5	241.2	315.9	256.2	260.8	192.1	189.1	190.5
1961	239.8	233.3	203.1	254.7	234.5	305.1	258.1	246.5	181.6	185.2	188.7
1960	237.4	230.9	203.0	247.6	229.8	303.8	256.2	242.9	177.8	185.6	188.2
1959	237.0	230.6	199.5	254.3	228.0	304.0	255.7	238.0	174.6	186.5	187.0
1958	233.5	227.8	198.1	250.7	229.0	298.5	252.6	224.1	167.3	188.5	183.0
1957	233.8	227.4	197.0	238.4	236.0	299.4	252.7	240.7	176.0	189.3	182.3
1956	233.7	225.6	197.3	227.7	230.2	303.7	239.8	280.2	199.2	180.8	180.1
1955	226.0	218.9	195.1	226.0	226.2	295.7	221.4	259.3	187.6	175.2	177.0
1954	222.7	217.0	196.8	236.0	231.1	286.8	213.4	224.1	167.5	177.0	176.4
1953	226.3	220.7	199.0	241.7	239.0	288.6	221.4	225.3	168.6	176.9	175.7
1952	232.0	226.0	210.3	248.2	251.5	291.0	219.0	233.5	172.9	173.9	180.1
1951	246.3	240.2	218.6	297.7	295.9	295.5	208.7	241.6	180.6	169.8	187.3
1950	215.4	211.2	202.0	251.3	246.7	258.3	183.6	200.8	159.5	164.8	157.8
1949	201.7	198.3	190.5	237.5	222.5	241.6	175.5	179.9	145.2	158.3	155.2
1948	197.2	193.4	185.7	236.7	216.3	238.3	161.4	185.1	146.9	150.8	152.2
1947	165.8	163.3	157.3	183.0	179.5	208.8	140.7	155.1	130.2	129.1	136.7
1946	139.2	138.9	134.2	160.2	137.9	172.1	127.4	111.1	108.0	114.5	120.3
1945	132.0	132.1	131.6	150.0	130.8	154.9	117.9	106.4	107.6	113.5	124.0
1944	130.5	130.6	129.1	146.6	130.7	151.6	117.8	106.8	107.8	114.3	124.9
1943	127.8	127.9	123.5	146.9	130.8	142.2	116.8	106.8	107.8	115.6	125.3
1942	122.8	123.0	114.9	137.1	131.2	132.3	116.0	105.8	107.2	114.5	127.9
1941	116.2	116.4	106.1	123.8	128.4	127.0	112.8	105.7	107.2	111.1	118.6
1940	107.8	108.0	98.1	106.1	118.1	119.0	108.7	105.2	106.9	106.7	108.5
1939	99.0	99.2	89.1	100.6	98.9	107.5	104.8	98.1	100.0	99.7	100.3
1938	101.9	102.0	100.5	102.6	95.5	106.9	105.8	98.3	98.9	101.5	100.4
1937	108.4	107.7	118.6	105.6	105.4	102.5	105.4	114.6	107.7	100.6	101.1
1936	96.7	96.8	98.8	96.0	101.4	93.6	92.6	96.3	97.6	98.2	98.4
1935	94.1	94.4	92.9	94.9	99.6	89.9	91.7	92.5	95.7	99.7	99.9
1934	93.4	92.0	91.5	89.5	102.2	90.7	91.2	87.5	92.1	100.9	102.3
1933	87.4	87.4	81.4	79.1	97.8	87.2	89.5	87.5	85.7	99.1	102.4
1932	86.9	85.7	75.3	79.5	97.8	95.9	90.5	80.2	75.7	100.3	105.7
1931	94.0	93.2	78.1	98.4	103.0	109.7	91.6	87.9	77.1	101.5	109.2
1930	112.9	111.5	106.6	132.0	114.8	123.1	95.5	109.7	91.0	107.2	116.9
1929	124.6	122.8	125.7	145.2	128.1	130.3	98.2	134.9	106.8	109.0	120.2
1928	125.6	123.9	127.6	144.0	132.6	137.0	97.7	125.1	100.7	108.6	120.1
1927	127.3	125.5	135.0	135.8	131.5	136.7	100.9	124.4	100.3	113.2	123.9
1926	130.3	128.5	137.3	133.2	140.3	138.7	104.8	136.0	107.5	117.3	126.0
1925	133.8	131.1	138.1	133.6	157.8	141.0	109.6	141.3	108.7	117.7	125.5
1924	129.5	126.9	122.5	122.3	165.4	147.0	116.4	129.0	104.4	122.2	129.2
1923	127.7	125.3	114.9	126.6	164.0	156.8	121.4	129.6	104.6	122.5	131.6
1922	126.8	124.5	118.4	127.8	127.8	147.5	109.7	132.4	105.6	125.6	132.8
1921	143.4	140.4	142.1	146.0	134.6	179.5	134.2	132.0	105.5	136.8	147.4
1920	203.2	198.2	229.2	193.2	247.6	214.2	176.5	184.3	123.5	131.6	178.3
1919	174.7	170.6	186.8	187.5	229.8	152.0	145.8	181.6	122.6	109.9	148.0
1918	166.0	162.3	175.6	169.3	220.4	123.7	164.5	193.0	126.5	96.6	149.5
1917	148.9	145.8	171.0	147.1	160.8	110.8	159.2	195.7	127.5	84.1	123.6
1916	109.8	108.1	119.5	113.2	108.9	88.8	109.7	183.8	123.3	68.0	98.3
1915	91.8	90.6	103.8	98.6	81.8	78.4	77.4	145.4	110.0	61.9	85.9
1914	85.4	84.5	88.9	96.7	79.8	83.7	70.6	128.8	104.3	63.0	82.2
1913	83.4	82.6	79.8	94.4	81.6	88.7	72.3	133.9	106.1	66.7	79.8
1912	85.2	84.5	93.4	90.1	73.6	86.3	67.1	136.0	107.1	66.6	78.0
1911	81.1	80.3	85.8	81.2	76.2	86.1	66.3	118.4	99.4	62.5	74.4

Series K33-43. General Wholesale Price Index, classified by chief component material, 1867 to 1975 (concluded)

(1935-39 = 100)

Year	General index		Vegetable products	Animals and their products	Fibres, textiles, textile products	Wood, wood products, paper	Iron and its products	Non-ferrous metals and their products		Non-metallic minerals and their products	Chemicals and allied products
	Excluding gold	Including gold						Excluding gold	Including gold		
	33	34	35	36	37	38	39	40	41	42	43
1910	78.5	77.8	81.0	84.0	78.3	81.2	65.3	119.5	100.0	63.5	69.0
1909	77.6	76.9	85.1	80.3	73.6	73.9	66.4	115.1	106.4	64.2	67.3
1908	76.3	75.6	84.7	75.2	71.3	75.5	69.9	118.2	99.4	65.2	72.4
1907	76.4	75.8	81.1	76.0	78.7	76.7	72.3	156.8	115.9	63.6	73.4
1906	70.7	70.2	71.7	70.9	76.3	73.0	69.0	147.4	111.9	61.2	64.0
1905	70.4	70.0	75.9	69.8	71.1	68.4	65.0	127.6	103.5	62.4	65.5
1904	68.3	67.8	75.0	64.2	71.6	66.6	66.0	115.8	98.4	64.2	65.1
1903	67.5	67.1	70.9	65.9	65.9	66.4	70.6	112.5	97.0	65.1	63.3
1902	66.6	66.2	68.7	68.2	65.4	59.1	71.0	114.7	97.8	62.9	62.9
1901	63.7	63.5	64.6	64.3	65.1	55.9	71.2	136.3	107.2	60.7	64.4
1900	62.4	62.1	58.9	64.6	67.9	56.3	78.7	139.3	108.5	57.0	61.8
1899	60.6	60.4	63.7	61.1	60.9	51.5	67.5	129.6	104.3	53.7	58.4
1898	59.4	59.3	66.6	58.1	60.3	50.0	58.9	99.2	91.3	53.5	58.7
1897	56.8	56.7	59.7	56.2	61.3	49.6	59.1	95.7	89.8	54.0	59.0
1896	55.9	55.9	58.0	53.1	62.5	49.8	64.6	102.6	92.7	55.0	60.4
1895	57.9	57.8	60.8	56.4	61.3	51.8	64.0	97.9	90.8	55.1	60.0
1894	59.1	58.9	60.7	58.1	61.6	54.9	66.3	99.4	91.4	56.2	60.8
1893	63.2	63.0	66.3	63.4	65.5	53.6	71.2	117.0	98.9	57.5	61.3
1892	62.3	62.1	65.7	60.3	65.7	53.8	72.9	126.2	102.8	58.0	61.6
1891	67.1	66.8	80.7	60.3	69.0	53.0	75.0	138.6	108.1	57.2	62.8
1890	67.1	66.8	76.2	60.6	75.5	53.4	81.6	148.9	112.5	58.7	62.5
1889	66.1	65.8	77.0	64.7	73.3	52.2	76.8	144.6	109.7	55.5	62.6
1888	66.2	65.7	79.8	63.3	70.7	50.8	76.5	156.6	117.6	53.5	63.4
1887	63.7	63.6	71.4	63.6	75.3	49.7	74.3	131.3	101.0	53.4	62.4
1886	62.3	62.2	70.3	62.5	68.6	47.1	73.0	128.2	99.0	55.1	62.5
1885	63.3	63.1	72.2	62.8	67.0	48.1	75.2	131.2	100.9	57.2	62.7
1884	67.0	66.8	74.6	71.5	68.3	48.9	79.6	141.5	107.7	62.1	66.1
1883	70.2	69.8	82.0	73.5	72.2	51.1	80.5	152.8	115.0	66.3	65.8
1882	72.5	72.0	90.6	74.5	79.6	48.4	83.3	160.8	120.2	63.9	68.4
1881	72.4	71.9	91.8	72.5	85.6	43.0	83.6	161.3	120.5	63.8	71.9
1880	71.8	71.3	88.5	68.1	95.1	34.7	99.1	167.4	124.4	57.1	75.8
1879	65.5	65.2	79.3	60.0	74.2	37.8	84.2	154.9	116.4	54.0	73.4
1878	68.0	67.6	81.0	60.4	78.5	41.2	83.9	163.6	121.3	57.4	74.6
1877	73.4	72.9	90.5	67.4	90.8	42.7	90.7	169.2	125.2	62.3	75.6
1876	77.6	76.9	86.6	71.9	91.1	44.0	100.4	177.5	129.5	75.7	78.6
1875	82.8	82.0	91.7	73.8	104.9	48.1	113.2	183.3	134.0	77.1	81.4
1874	86.4	85.4	96.6	74.5	116.0	49.0	128.3	189.9	137.9	76.2	82.9
1873	90.9	89.6	91.4	74.7	129.9	46.8	147.0	205.9	147.6	88.5	83.9
1872	90.6	89.3	92.6	72.7	155.7	41.1	142.1	207.1	148.3	87.9	81.9
1871	81.3	80.3	92.4	71.8	112.5	40.6	104.6	195.8	141.5	81.3	76.7
1870	79.8	78.7	88.2	74.8	105.0	35.5	105.8	203.1	145.9	79.9	78.4
1869	80.7	79.6	89.1	73.7	117.4	33.9	106.7	203.8	146.9	81.0	78.6
1868	80.0	79.0	96.4	70.8	108.4	31.7	106.8	197.6	143.2	87.3	78.4
1867	80.2	79.1	94.0	71.2	107.7	30.5	114.8	—	—	—	—

Series K44-46. Wholesale Price Indexes, classified by degree of manufacture, 1890 to 1975
(1935-39 = 100)

Year	General wholesale index		Thirty industrial materials	Year	General wholesale index		Thirty industrial materials
	Raw and partly manufactured[1]	Fully and chiefly manufactured			Raw and partly manufactured[1]	Fully and chiefly manufactured	
	44	**45**	**46**		**44**	**45**	**46**
1975	469.6	503.8	484.4	1930	106.5	113.4	110.3
1974	468.3	457.4	494.7	1929	124.7	120.8	132.8
1973	367.5	382.1	390.9	1928	124.6	123.4	134.4
1972	272.4	331.8	299.5	1927	127.5	125.3	139.6
1971	255.6	309.2	266.9	1926	127.7	129.9	144.3
1970	265.0	298.4	268.8	1925	128.8	134.8	—
1969	260.0	294.9	267.7	1924	121.3	132.4	—
1968	249.1	281.6	254.0	1923	116.7	133.9	—
1967	246.1	274.2	253.1	1922	121.2	130.4	—
1966	242.7	268.6	261.4	1921	136.7	150.8	—
1965	231.2	261.3	258.7	1920	194.7	203.3	—
1964	225.7	256.4	258.3	1919	165.2	171.6	—
1963	226.9	254.2	253.5	1918	153.4	165.9	—
1962	223.8	249.0	248.0	1917	144.5	147.4	—
1961	212.6	244.5	243.2	1916	110.0	109.9	—
1960	209.6	242.2	240.4	1915	93.7	92.4	—
1959	210.9	241.6	240.2	1914	86.0	85.2	—
1958	209.3	238.3	229.8	1913	83.0	84.2	—
1957	209.4	237.9	240.3	1912	86.5	83.8	—
1956	215.8	231.5	248.2	1911	80.7	80.8	—
1955	209.7	224.5	236.0	1910	78.5	80.9	—
1954	204.8	224.2	223.7	1909	79.9	81.2	—
1953	207.0	228.8	232.3	1908	76.9	82.9	—
1952	218.7	230.7	252.6	1907	76.3	82.6	—
1951	237.9	242.4	296.1	1906	73.2	78.2	—
1950	212.8	211.0	244.6	1905	69.9	79.2	—
1949	197.1	199.2	218.0	1904	69.0	77.2	—
1948	196.3	192.4	222.7	1903	68.4	76.8	—
1947	164.3	162.4	187.0	1902	66.3	76.1	—
1946	140.1	138.0	148.6	1901	63.8	74.9	—
1945	136.2	129.8	143.2	1900	61.9	76.4	—
1944	134.4	129.1	143.1	1899	59.3	73.0	—
1943	131.1	126.9	140.0	1898	59.7	72.2	—
1942	123.0	123.7	135.1	1897	55.7	70.1	—
1941	114.4	118.8	125.2	1896	53.4	70.7	—
1940	103.1	109.9	113.3	1895	55.5	72.3	—
1939	94.9	101.9	99.0	1894	55.4	74.4	—
1938	99.4	103.5	95.8	1893	59.7	78.3	—
1937	113.7	104.4	116.3	1892	59.0	78.8	—
1936	98.2	96.1	96.9	1891	64.6	83.5	—
1935	93.8	94.7	90.3	1890	63.3	86.1	—
1934	90.0	95.3	86.3				
1933	79.3	91.2	78.3				
1932	75.3	90.7	74.2				
1931	82.7	97.2	86.8				

[1] Includes gold prices.

Series K47-55. Wholesale Price Indexes of Canadian farm products, 1890 to 1974[1]

Year	Canada			Eastern			Western		
	Field	Animal	Total	Field	Animal	Total	Field	Animal	Total
	47	48	49	50	51	52	53	54	55
				1971 = 100					
1974	265.3	157.7	196.5	–	–	161.5	–	–	226.3
1973	194.3	152.8	167.8	–	–	151.0	–	–	182.0
1972	111.2	115.7	114.1	–	–	112.7	–	–	115.2
1971	100.0	100.0	100.0	–	–	100.0	–	–	100.0
				1935-39 = 100					
1974	438.2	557.7	499.8	393.6	524.5	481.3	489.3	626.2	534.4
1973	332.2	503.5	417.8	329.6	468.0	422.3	333.4	575.8	413.4
1972	200.6	395.6	298.1	217.7	371.1	320.5	192.1	445.4	269.9
1971	183.2	352.0	267.6	210.8	332.8	292.6	169.6	391.0	242.6
1970	185.0	352.1	270.4	220.6	330.6	294.6	173.1	395.7	246.5
1969	183.3	357.9	270.6	200.7	335.8	291.2	174.8	402.9	250.1
1968	191.6	329.3	260.4	206.9	310.4	276.2	184.1	367.7	244.7
1967	202.5	325.3	263.9	209.7	307.7	275.3	199.0	361.0	252.5
1966	209.7	321.5	265.6	217.6	304.1	275.5	205.8	356.8	255.6
1965	210.3	289.3	249.8	227.1	273.4	258.1	202.0	321.7	241.5
1964	198.2	267.3	232.7	194.3	253.7	234.1	200.1	294.9	231.4
1963	197.2	275.4	236.3	197.7	259.6	239.2	197.0	307.5	233.4
1962	195.5	286.0	240.8	190.7	268.5	242.9	197.9	321.7	238.7
1961	191.7	270.0	230.9	191.5	257.2	235.5	191.8	296.1	226.2
1960	189.1	264.1	226.6	217.8	251.5	240.4	175.0	289.6	212.8
1959	176.1	271.6	223.9	195.4	257.3	236.8	166.7	300.8	210.9
1958	171.4	274.5	222.9	181.3	260.9	234.6ʳ	166.5ʳ	302.1	211.2
1957	169.2	258.0	213.6	179.2	247.6	225.0ʳ	164.3ʳ	279.0	202.2ʳ
1956	181.6	246.9	214.2	210.1ʳ	237.5	228.5	167.6	265.9	200.0
1955	180.1	245.1	212.6	199.3	235.6	223.6	170.7	264.3ʳ	201.6
1954	170.9	256.3ʳ	213.6	179.6	247.1ʳ	224.8	166.6	274.7	202.2
1953	179.4	263.8	221.6	182.0	255.4	231.2	178.2	280.9	212.1
1952	223.0	277.5	250.2	281.2	262.6	268.8	194.3	307.7	231.7
1951	200.4	336.9	268.6	210.0	315.1	280.4	195.6	381.1	256.8
1950	191.9	281.4	236.7	186.7	263.6	238.2	194.5	317.5	235.1
1949	191.9	265.4	228.7	190.5	252.7	232.2	192.6	291.2	225.1
1948	200.6	263.7	232.1	211.0	253.5	239.5	195.5	284.2	224.8
1947	184.1	200.2	192.2	169.6	194.3	186.2	191.3	212.3	198.1
1946	177.9	181.2	179.5	159.6	176.7	171.0	186.9	190.5	187.9
1945	162.5	170.3ʳ	166.4	160.9	165.1	163.7	163.3	180.7	169.0
1944	144.5	166.1	155.3	145.8	161.1	156.1	143.9	176.3	154.6
1943	129.0	161.8	145.4	149.6	157.3	154.8	118.9	170.9	136.1
1942	109.7	144.6	127.1	136.2	141.8	140.0	96.6	150.2	114.3
1941	88.9	124.4	106.6	101.0	123.0	115.7	82.9	127.2	97.5
1940	85.4	106.7	96.1	94.6	105.8	102.1	80.9	108.6	90.0
1939	83.7	101.5	92.6	95.2	100.6	98.8	78.0	103.2	86.3
1938	100.9	104.8	102.9	90.7	104.7	100.1	105.9	105.1	105.6
1937	128.8ʳ	106.0	117.4	117.8	105.8	109.8	134.3	106.3	125.1
1936	102.2	93.7	97.9	110.3	94.4	99.6	98.2	92.2	96.2
1935	84.4	94.1	89.2	85.6	94.5	91.6	83.8	93.2	86.9
1934	80.5	86.5	83.5	89.1	87.8	88.2	76.3	83.8	78.8
1933	69.3	69.2	69.3	82.8	70.1	74.3	62.6	67.5	64.2
1932	60.4	70.5	65.5	68.6	71.2	70.3	56.4	69.2	60.6
1931	65.0	92.7	78.9	78.4	93.3	88.4	58.4	91.5	69.3
1930	105.8	133.3	119.5	126.0	131.7	129.8	95.8	136.6	109.3
1929	137.2	144.4	140.8	136.5	142.4	140.5	137.5	148.6	141.2
1928	134.3	138.2	136.3	131.4	136.5	134.8	135.8	141.6	137.7
1927	149.4	127.8	138.6	152.7	127.9	136.1	147.8	127.7	141.2
1926	158.5	130.2	144.4	180.9	131.4	147.7	147.4	127.9	141.0

Year	Canada		
	Field	Animal	Total
	47	48	49
		1913 = 100	
1934	95.4	87.9	92.6
1933	81.2	77.5	79.8
1932	72.9	78.8	75.1
1931	77.3	100.7	86.1
1930	124.2	133.6	127.7
1929	166.4	146.0	158.8
1928	164.3	148.4	158.4
1927	177.2	137.2	162.2
1926	177.4	129.8	159.6
1925	174.1	137.2	160.5
1924	146.6	126.2	139.1
1923	130.0	123.5	127.6
1922	144.3	128.6	138.5
1921	177.8	142.2	164.8
1920	295.3	195.8	258.8
1919	252.8	199.3	233.1
1918	234.0	173.5	211.9
1917	238.4	153.8	207.5
1916	157.4	118.7	143.3
1915	136.4	103.2	124.3
1914	116.0	101.7	110.8
1913	100.0	100.0	100.0
1912	123.7	92.9	116.0
1911	105.8	84.6	100.5
1910	98.9	89.2	96.5
1909	119.4	86.2	111.1
1908	108.0	79.9	101.0
1907	105.3	79.0	98.7
1906	85.0	74.3	82.3
1905	88.1	72.4	84.2
1904	91.4	69.8	86.0
1903	87.7	69.4	83.1
1902	83.3	71.4	80.3
1901	79.7	69.3	77.1
1900	73.2	67.8	71.9
1899	72.2	61.8	69.6
1898	81.0	61.6	76.2
1897	67.6	59.6	65.6
1896	70.0	56.3	66.6
1895	73.0	59.2	69.6
1894	67.2	58.8	65.1
1893	77.8	64.8	74.6
1892	78.3	62.2	74.3
1891	90.4	62.3	83.4
1890	84.9	63.3	79.5

[1] The index numbers of farm prices of agricultural products and prices paid by farmers for commodities and services used in farm production are shown in Section M, Agriculture.

Series K56-61. Export Price Indexes, Trade of Canada commodity classification, 1926 to 1975

Year	Total	Live animals	Food, feed, beverages and tobacco	Crude materials, inedible	Fabricated materials, inedible	End products, inedible	Year	Total	Live animals	Food, feed, beverages and tobacco	Crude materials, inedible	Fabricated materials, inedible	End products, inedible
	56	57	58	59	60	61		56	57	58	59	60	61
			Panel A:	*1971 = 100*[1]									
1975	180.9	151.4	229.0	251.2	182.6	126.7	1950	108.3	..	..	..	..	..
1974	161.5	161.4	232.8	210.9	159.4	114.0	1949	103.3	..	..	..	..	..
1973	119.0	156.9	149.1	122.5	121.7	104.2	1948	100.0	..	..	..	..	..
1972	103.3	123.7	106.9	101.5	104.4	101.9	1947	91.6	..	..	..	..	..
1971	100.0	100.0	100.0	100.0	100.0	100.0	1946	79.9	..	..	..	..	..
1970	99.3	101.8	97.3	99.9	100.8	98.1	1945	70.9	..	..	..	..	..
1969	96.9	98.4	100.8	96.2	97.9	95.0	1944	67.6	..	..	..	..	..
1968	95.0	89.3	104.8	94.1	93.7	93.5	1943	61.0	..	..	..	..	..
							1942	55.0	..	..	..	..	..
			Panel B:	*1948 = 100*			1941	51.9	..	..	..	..	..
1970	155.6	188.7	115.0	204.2	156.6	198.7	1940	49.9	..	..	..	..	..
1969	152.0	180.7	120.2	186.6	150.7	194.6	1939	45.1	..	..	..	..	..
1968	145.6	158.4	117.9	178.4	142.4	189.5	1938	47.1	..	..	..	..	..
1967	140.6	147.3	118.7	171.5	135.1	182.8	1937	53.4	..	..	..	..	..
1966	137.9	131.4	117.6	169.0	132.7	178.1	1936	45.8	..	..	..	..	..
1965	132.4	115.5	111.4	161.7	128.5	173.7	1935	43.4	..	..	..	..	..
1964	130.7	128.1	109.5	155.7	126.9	170.9	1934	42.6	..	..	..	..	..
1963	128.9	128.0	108.6	154.6	124.7	168.1	1933	39.9	..	..	..	..	..
1962	128.1	130.6	108.9	152.1	123.7	166.2	1932	40.3	..	..	..	..	..
1961	124.0	118.8	103.3	145.3	122.0	161.9	1931	44.8	..	..	..	..	..
1960	123.0	123.5	99.0	143.8	123.3	156.6	1930	54.0	..	..	..	..	..
1959	122.8	..	..	..	..	..	1929	64.4	..	..	..	..	..
1958	120.6	..	..	..	..	..	1928	65.4	..	..	..	..	..
1957	121.3	..	..	..	..	..	1927	67.6	..	..	..	..	..
1956	121.4	..	..	..	..	..	1926	70.2	..	..	..	..	..
1955	117.7	..	..	..	..	..							
1954	115.1	..	..	..	..	..							
1953	118.3	..	..	..	..	..							
1952	121.8	..	..	..	..	..							
1951	123.0	..	..	..	..	..							

[1] For extension of Series K56 back to 1961 (1971 = 100), see Section G.

Series K62-67. Import Price Indexes, Trade of Canada commodity classification, 1926 to 1975

Year	Total	Live animals	Food, feed, beverages and tobacco	Crude materials, inedible	Fabricated materials, inedible	End products, inedible	Year	Total	Live animals	Food, feed, beverages and tobacco	Crude materials, inedible	Fabricated materials, inedible	End products, inedible
	62	63	64	65	66	67		62	63	64	65	66	67
Panel A:				*1971 = 100*[1]									
1975	165.7	136.8	183.3	342.6	177.4	136.3	1950	110.3	..	..	..	..	..
1974	142.9	129.3	172.1	281.0	158.1	116.2	1949	102.6	..	..	..	..	..
1973	111.3	144.5	132.5	130.6	112.1	105.9	1948	100.0	..	..	..	..	..
1972	102.6	109.2	109.2	106.5	99.8	102.1	1947	88.0	..	..	..	..	..
1971	100.0	100.0	100.0	100.0	100.0	100.0	1946	76.9	..	..	..	..	..
1970	98.1	94.9	97.5	96.4	100.8	97.6	1945	73.5	..	..	..	..	..
1969	97.2	95.4	92.0	94.3	100.3	97.1	1944	73.1	..	..	..	..	..
1968	95.5	90.3	91.1	90.0	100.8	95.0	1943	70.0	..	..	..	..	..
							1942	63.6	..	..	..	..	..
Panel B:				*1948 = 100*			1941	57.8	..	..	..	..	..
1970	141.9	82.2	124.6	113.8	150.9	171.4	1940	53.2	..	..	..	..	..
1969	140.6	85.5	112.8	116.6	147.6	171.0	1939	47.3	..	..	..	..	..
1968	135.7	80.0	109.6	112.1	141.3	166.6	1938	47.3	..	..	..	..	..
1967	133.5	75.7	105.9	110.4	140.4	163.0	1937	50.9	..	..	..	..	..
1966	132.5	75.7	109.0	111.1	139.4	158.8	1936	46.4	..	..	..	..	..
1965	130.8	67.1	111.2	108.2	139.1	155.6	1935	45.5	..	..	..	..	..
1964	130.8	62.9	132.9	105.1	136.2	153.8	1934	45.3	..	..	..	..	..
1963	129.4	69.6	134.3	103.9	133.7	152.0	1933	42.5	..	..	..	..	..
1962	124.5	69.6	106.8	101.8	131.0	150.5	1932	44.4	..	..	..	..	..
1961	119.1	62.3	103.1	97.6	126.3	142.4	1931	45.4	..	..	..	..	..
1960	115.5	57.1	100.4	97.9	120.8	136.0	1930	54.0	..	..	..	..	..
1959	114.4	..	..	..	..	..	1929	61.9	..	..	..	..	..
1958	116.5	..	..	..	..	..	1928	63.4	..	..	..	..	..
1957	116.4	..	..	..	..	..	1927	64.6	..	..	..	..	..
1956	113.0	..	..	..	..	..	1926	67.9	..	..	..	..	..
1955	110.5	..	..	..	..	..							
1954	109.5	..	..	..	..	..							
1953	109.4	..	..	..	..	..							
1952	110.4	..	..	..	..	..							
1951	126.2	..	..	..	..	..							

[1] For extension of Series K62 back to 1961 (1971 = 100), see Section G.

Series K68-107. Industry Selling Price Indexes, by industry class, Standard Industrial Classification (S.I.C.), 1956 to 1975

(1971 = 100)

Panel A: Industry groups, 2-digit level of classification[1]

S.I.C. No.	01	02	03	04	05	06	07	08	09
Year	Manufac-turing industries	Food and beverage industries	Tobacco products industries	Rubber and plastics products industries	Leather industries	Textile industries	Knitting mills	Clothing industries	Wood industries	Furniture and fixture industries
	68	69	70	71	72	73	74	75	76	77
1975	153.7	171.2	—[1]	136.8	146.0	132.5	119.6	—[1]	151.3	153.2
1974	138.3	155.9	—[1]	124.3	137.7	131.1	118.9	—[1]	149.1	140.2
1973	116.2	131.9	—[1]	103.5	124.5	109.2	102.7	—[1]	151.9	116.2
1972	104.5	109.1	—[1]	100.9	111.8	99.3	97.7	—[1]	122.2	105.6
1971	100.0	100.0	—[1]	100.0	100.0	100.0	100.0	—[1]	100.0	100.0
1970	98.1	97.2	—[1]	—[1]	97.2	102.2	101.0	—[1]	89.6	97.3
1969	95.8	94.9	—[1]	—[1]	95.1	102.7	103.2	—[1]	99.7	94.1
1968	92.3	90.3	—[1]	—[1]	90.6	101.6	104.2	—[1]	92.8	90.5
1967	90.4	89.1	—[1]	—[1]	88.9	101.7	103.4	—[1]	82.9	88.8
1966	88.7	88.4	—[1]	—[1]	88.9	101.4	101.2	—[1]	79.8	85.9
1965	86.2	83.9	—[1]	—[1]	81.1	101.5	101.4	—[1]	76.8	83.6
1964	85.1	83.1	—[1]	—[1]	78.2	101.7	102.3	—[1]	74.7	83.1
1963	84.4	82.6	—[1]	—[1]	77.8	100.9	102.1	—[1]	72.9	81.5
1962	83.3	79.8	—[1]	—[1]	78.0	99.6	102.2	—[1]	70.5	80.7
1961	82.4	78.2	—[1]	—[1]	76.7	98.1	101.9	—[1]	68.3	80.7
1960	82.2	76.6	—[1]	—[1]	76.6	97.6	103.4	—[1]	70.0	—
1959	82.1	76.8	—[1]	—[1]	76.7	97.4	107.2	—[1]	71.8	—
1958	81.4	77.0	—[1]	—[1]	69.4	98.6	110.3	—[1]	69.1	—
1957	81.1	76.0	—[1]	—[1]	68.9	100.4	111.0	—[1]	69.9	—
1956	79.4	72.0	—[1]	—[1]	69.0	99.7	113.0	—[1]	71.8	—

S.I.C. No.	10	12	13	14	15	16	17	18	19	20
Year	Paper and allied industries	Primary metal industries	Metal fabricating industries[2]	Machinery industries (except electrical machinery)	Transpor-tation equipment industries	Electrical products industries	Non-metallic mineral products industries	Petroleum and coal products industries	Chemical and chemical products industries	Miscellaneous manufac-turing industries
	78	79	80	81	82	83	84	85	86	87
1975	178.4	160.7	152.3	142.7	—[1]	136.2	147.3	183.7	160.3	—[1]
1974	151.6	147.7	135.1	—[1]	—[1]	121.7	124.9	159.4	137.1	—[1]
1973	112.1	117.5	112.8	—[1]	—[1]	104.0	109.0	117.2	106.5	—[1]
1972	100.9	102.2	104.7	—[1]	—[1]	100.9	104.1	102.7	101.4	—[1]
1971	100.0	100.0	100.0	—[1]	—[1]	100.0	100.0	100.0	100.0	—[1]
1970	99.8	103.4	—[1]	—[1]	—[1]	—[1]	98.4	90.8	99.0	—[1]
1969	96.9	97.5	—[1]	—[1]	—[1]	—[1]	95.2	88.2	98.6	—[1]
1968	94.0	91.1	—[1]	—[1]	—[1]	—[1]	91.9	86.4	98.5	—[1]
1967	93.5	89.9	—[1]	—[1]	—[1]	—[1]	89.6	84.6	97.6	—[1]
1966	91.0	87.2	—[1]	—[1]	—[1]	—[1]	86.3	83.8	95.8	—[1]
1965	89.0	83.9	—[1]	—[1]	—[1]	—[1]	83.5	83.6	96.1	—[1]
1964	88.5	80.1	—[1]	—[1]	—[1]	—[1]	81.7	85.1	96.3	—[1]
1963	87.3	77.8	—[1]	—[1]	—[1]	—[1]	79.9	84.9	96.9	—[1]
1962	86.9	77.2	—[1]	—[1]	—[1]	—[1]	78.6	87.4	97.1	—[1]
1961	85.1	75.6	—[1]	—[1]	—[1]	—[1]	79.0	88.1	97.5	—[1]
1960	84.6	—	—[1]	—[1]	—[1]	—[1]	78.9	88.2	98.0	—[1]
1959	84.4	—	—[1]	—[1]	—[1]	—[1]	78.4	88.6	97.6	—[1]
1958	84.5	—	—[1]	—[1]	—[1]	—[1]	77.8	89.0	96.5	—[1]
1957	83.8	—	—[1]	—[1]	—[1]	—[1]	76.7	91.2	95.2	—[1]
1956	82.7	—	—[1]	—[1]	—[1]	—[1]	74.6	87.4	94.8	—[1]

Series K68-107. Industry Selling Price Indexes, by industry class, Standard Industrial Classification (S.I.C.), 1956 to 1975 (concluded)

(1971 = 100)

Panel B: Selected industries for which 2-digit level composites are not available

S.I.C. No.	02-1530	03-1623	03-1624	07-2431	13-3050	13-3060	13-3070	14-3110	15-3230	15-3250
Year	Tobacco products manufacturers	Tire and tube manufacturers	Rubber footware manufacturers	Men's clothing factories	Wire and wire products manufacturers	Hardware, tool and cutlery manufacturers	Heating equipment manufacturers	Agricultural implement industry	Motor vehicle manufacturers	Motor vehicle parts and accessories manufacturers
	88	89	90	91	92	93	94	95	96	97
1975	132.8	132.9	149.5	142.1	158.3	137.9	137.3	155.2	117.4	131.1
1974	113.5	121.2	134.3	128.6	136.6	122.2	121.9	128.1	108.9	114.9
1973	105.6	102.5	111.9	110.4	113.9	106.5	108.2	111.4	101.6	105.8
1972	100.6	101.5	104.7	102.6	104.4	102.5	104.0	105.0	101.8	102.4
1971	100.0	100.0	100.0	100.0	100.0	100.0	100.0	100.0	100.0	100.0
1970	95.8	97.8	96.1	96.8	96.7	96.9	97.7	97.3	97.6	98.3
1969	94.3	94.4	92.9	92.5	89.1	92.7	94.6	94.4	96.3	96.1
1968	90.6	90.4	92.2	89.4	85.8	88.6	91.9	91.1	95.6	94.1
1967	88.9	89.2	90.6	86.3	85.7	84.5	88.7	87.8	93.9	92.9
1966	81.9	87.5	87.1	83.8	84.9	81.4	86.7	86.2	93.9	91.5
1965	79.3	85.4	84.8	81.9	83.6	78.8	86.5	83.8	94.6	90.9
1964	76.7	82.8	82.1	80.1	81.0	77.8	87.3	82.8	95.1	89.9
1963	75.9	83.2	82.8	78.9	80.3	77.6	87.7	82.7	95.4	90.0
1962	75.8	82.3	82.4	77.1	80.6	76.6	86.8	81.2	95.0	87.8
1961	75.8	95.1	81.8	75.9	80.9	76.6	87.9	79.6	93.9	87.2
1960	75.3	..	..	75.4	..	..	..	78.2	93.5	86.0
1959	75.0	..	..	74.8	..	..	..	77.4	92.7	85.1
1958	74.2	..	..	74.5	..	..	..	76.0	89.3	85.1
1957	74.2	..	..	74.3	..	..	..	73.0	86.1	83.9
1956	74.2	..	..	73.1	..	..	..	70.3	80.4	82.2

S.I.C. No.	16-3310	16-3320	16-3340	16-3360	16-3380	16-3391	20-3912	20-3920	20-3996	20-3997
Year	Manufacturers of small electrical appliances	Manufacturers of major appliances[3]	Manufacturers of household radio and television receivers	Manufacturers of electrical industrial equipment	Manufacturers of electric wire and cable	Battery manufacturers	Clock and watch manufacturers	Jewellery and silverware industry	Pen and pencil manufacturers	Typewriter supplies manufacturers
	98	99	100	101	102	103	104	105	106	107
1975	124.3	134.6	107.7	149.2	140.8	150.7	136.0	234.1	140.8	148.8
1974	111.4	117.4	103.6	125.2	137.6	128.6	119.5	216.3	123.3	129.8
1973	101.6	102.3	99.2	103.8	109.8	106.7	109.9	149.4	100.0	106.3
1972	100.5	101.3	99.3	101.9	98.9	102.2	102.5	109.1	99.8	100.3
1971	100.0	100.0	100.0	100.0	100.0	100.0	100.0	100.0	100.0	100.0
1970	99.7	101.1	104.5	96.7	102.0	98.5	98.4	100.0	99.4	98.9
1969	97.1	99.8	107.9	91.0	93.4	94.5	96.7	96.9	93.7	98.8
1968	96.5	98.6	107.4	89.7	90.4	91.6	94.0	95.8	92.1	99.1
1967	96.3	97.8	107.1	92.0	93.1	91.3	92.2	86.7	91.1	99.7
1966	96.2	96.4	106.1	90.0	90.6	86.9	88.9	81.2	90.4	98.7
1965	96.4	95.8	107.2	88.2	80.4	84.6	87.0	78.8	89.9	98.2
1964	96.0	96.6	106.3	89.0	74.9	81.7	86.1	77.5	90.2	99.4
1963	96.4	98.5	105.8	89.6	71.1	79.0	85.6	75.7	90.9	99.4
1962	98.4	99.2	105.7	90.7	70.3	78.5	85.4	71.3	91.1	98.1
1961	100.3	99.7	108.5	89.2	69.8	80.1	81.4	67.3	89.5	97.4
1960	..	..	..	..	70.7	79.6	79.3	65.3	89.5	97.4
1959	..	..	..	..	70.2	80.4	79.5	64.7	89.5	97.4
1958	..	..	..	..	65.9	82.1	77.6	64.7	89.5	97.4
1957	..	..	..	..	71.4	82.4	77.4	65.2	92.2	96.1
1956	..	..	..	..	82.1	80.8	78.2	65.3	89.2	90.8

[1] Panel B contains selected industries for which 2-digit level composite not shown.

[2] Excludes machinery and transportation equipment industries.

[3] Includes electric and non-electric.

Series K108-135. Union Wage Rate Indexes, for major construction trades, in major cities, by trade and by city, 1950 to 1975

(1971 = 100)

Year	Composite index		Basic rate index for selected trades											
	Including selected supple-ments	Basic rate	Carpen-ter	Crane operator	Cement finisher	Electri-cian	Labourer	Plumber	Rein-forcing steel erector	Struc-tural steel erector	Sheet metal worker	Heavy equip-ment operator	Brick layer	Painter
	108	109	110	111	112	113	114	115	116	117	118	119	120	121
1975	156.3	151.4	150.7	157.9	153.1	147.9	159.7	146.6	153.3	151.8	149.2	163.5	145.8	152.5
1974	135.8	132.8	132.6	140.8	135.2	130.3	139.1	128.0	135.1	133.4	131.5	144.0	131.4	132.2
1973	122.9	121.2	120.2	128.4	122.0	120.2	125.3	117.9	124.3	123.0	120.3	129.5	120.5	120.8
1972	111.1	110.4	109.3	115.9	110.5	110.1	111.7	109.2	111.9	113.6	110.2	115.3	109.7	110.4
1971	100.0	100.0	100.0	100.0	100.0	100.0	100.0	100.0	100.0	100.0	100.0	100.0	100.0	100.0
1970	88.3	89.6	89.1	87.8	90.2	90.4	89.0	90.7	90.0	91.2	90.8	88.3	91.1	89.1
1969	77.6	79.4	79.5	77.0	79.3	79.7	79.0	80.8	79.9	81.9	79.5	78.7	80.7	77.9
1968	70.9	73.2	74.1	72.7	72.6	73.6	73.9	72.6	73.0	73.1	76.8	72.1	73.6	74.1	71.3
1967	64.6	66.8	67.4	66.5	65.9	67.0	65.9	68.4	65.0	69.3	65.0	67.0	67.8	64.9
1966	57.9	60.8	61.5	61.7	60.3	60.9	59.3	62.1	58.8	62.6	59.5	60.4	62.7	58.8
1965	53.6	56.7	57.8	57.5	55.9	57.5	54.0	57.8	54.2	59.4	55.9	54.8	59.0	55.3
1964	50.4	53.7	54.8	55.0	52.8	54.3	50.9	54.4	50.9	57.3	53.8	51.9	56.1	52.5
1963	48.5	51.9	52.9	52.8	51.1	52.3	48.9	52.5	49.5	55.7	52.4	50.3	54.6	51.1
1962	46.4	50.0	50.7	50.4	49.3	50.3	46.8	50.6	47.2	53.9	50.8	48.6	53.2	49.9
1961	44.6	48.1	48.9	48.5	47.3	48.4	44.4	49.1	45.0	51.7	48.8	46.7	51.3	48.0
1960	43.3	46.7	47.6	46.9	45.7	46.8	43.1	47.6	44.0	50.1	47.2	45.4	50.1	46.4
1959	40.8	43.9	45.1	44.7	42.8	44.2	39.6	44.9	40.9	47.3	44.0	42.9	47.6	43.7
1958	38.3	41.4	42.7	42.1	40.2	41.3	36.8	42.2	38.6	44.1	41.3	40.2	45.5	41.6
1957	35.8	38.8	40.2	40.2	38.2	38.8	33.8	39.4	35.9	41.7	38.6	38.2	43.4	38.9
1956	34.3	37.2	38.6	38.3	36.5	37.1	31.9	38.1	34.2	39.7	37.2	36.6	41.5	37.7
1955	33.0	36.0	37.5	36.2	35.1	35.9	30.3	37.1	33.3	38.5	36.1	35.4	40.2	36.2
1954	32.1	35.0	36.6	35.3	33.7	34.5	29.6	36.0	31.9	37.9	35.3	34.5	39.3	35.6
1953	31.0	33.8	35.5	33.3	32.4	33.3	28.2	34.7	30.8	36.5	34.0	33.2	38.3	34.2
1952	29.1	31.8	33.5	30.6	30.9	31.2	26.1	32.3	28.7	33.2	31.7	31.2	37.1	32.0
1951	26.5	28.9	30.4	28.1	27.6	28.2	23.9	29.5	26.8	30.3	28.5	29.1	34.7	28.7
1950	24.2	26.4	27.6	25.1	25.4	26.0	21.7	27.7	24.5	28.0	26.5	26.0	31.3	26.1

Year	Basic rate index for selected cities													
	St.John's (Nfld.)	Halifax	Saint John (N.B.)	Quebec	Montréal	Ottawa	Toronto	Hamilton	Windsor	Winnipeg	Regina	Calgary	Edmonton	Vancou-ver
	122	123	124	125	126	127	128	129	130	131	132	133	134	135
1975	192.4	152.1	169.1	169.6	147.8	153.4	146.6	141.2	132.7	153.3	173.5	159.6	161.0	154.8
1974	158.8	139.9	152.8	140.9	123.9	137.8	132.6	129.0	120.8	133.8	140.2	139.9	140.3	131.7
1973	133.7	125.6	131.6	125.9	113.6	127.0	122.5	119.9	114.7	122.5	122.0	125.1	126.3	116.3
1972	114.6	112.8	114.7	111.0	104.7	114.0	111.5	111.3	109.3	111.7	105.5	111.7	111.8	108.7
1971	100.0	100.0	100.0	100.0	100.0	100.0	100.0	100.0	100.0	100.0	100.0	100.0	100.0	100.0
1970	91.4	87.3	89.5	92.1	93.9	86.6	87.5	80.6	87.9	91.0	91.8	87.7	88.0	90.5
1969	85.2	79.8	80.0	79.3	86.1	73.1	76.0	68.6	73.2	80.8	81.1	77.9	77.6	81.2
1968	79.2	71.5	71.7	72.0	81.9	68.3	67.9	64.3	71.7	73.4	73.8	71.6	70.0	73.0
1967	73.8	64.3	62.0	67.3	73.2	62.3	63.7	59.2	63.6	66.4	66.8	65.1	64.3	66.8
1966	70.1	59.0	54.9	62.8	63.3	56.3	60.3	55.6	53.9	60.9	61.9	61.0	60.6	61.7
1965	68.0	55.8	51.5	59.0	57.7	51.0	57.2	52.4	52.4	56.9	56.8	57.4	57.3	58.4
1964	65.4	53.6	49.8	55.5	53.9	48.8	54.2	50.4	49.6	53.9	55.2	54.6	55.0	55.6
1963	63.7	51.7	48.2	52.6	52.1	46.7	52.6	47.4	47.6	53.3	53.1	53.5	53.6	53.1
1962	62.0	50.1	46.7	49.2	50.0	45.2	51.1	45.9	45.8	52.2	51.5	51.6	52.0	50.9
1961	60.2	47.7	44.3	46.4	46.7	43.4	49.4	44.5	43.9	51.7	50.5	50.6	51.1	50.1
1960	57.6	46.4	43.5	44.4	45.9	41.8	47.4	42.2	43.3	50.5	49.7	49.2	49.1	49.5
1959	55.2	44.7	41.6	41.2	42.8	39.7	44.4	39.6	40.2	48.1	48.1	46.4	46.2	47.4
1958	52.7	42.5	40.4	38.9	40.7	37.6	40.8	37.5	39.1	45.3	45.9	44.6	43.7	44.8
1957	50.2	41.8	37.7	37.7	38.1	35.3	38.9	34.0	36.3	42.1	44.1	41.3	41.0	40.8
1956	46.3	38.9	36.6	36.0	37.1	33.5	37.1	32.7	35.5	40.5	42.5	39.1	39.4	38.4
1955	43.4	37.6	35.5	35.2	35.6	32.4	35.5	31.4	35.1	38.9	41.8	37.8	38.7	37.9
1954	40.8	36.0	34.8	33.5	35.2	31.4	34.3	30.6	34.4	37.4	41.0	37.0	37.7	37.2
1953	38.7	34.8	33.9	32.3	34.0	30.0	33.1	29.0	31.5	36.6	38.7	35.7	36.3	36.2
1952	35.3	32.0	31.8	29.6	31.8	28.3	31.8	27.3	30.1	33.9	35.7	33.6	33.7	33.7
1951	—	29.4	29.4	26.5	28.9	25.5	29.5	24.7	28.2	30.6	32.5	30.0	30.6	30.3
1950	—	28.1	27.0	24.8	26.2	23.4	26.6	22.8	25.8	27.9	30.7	28.1	28.7	27.7

Series K136-141. Building Construction Input Price Indexes, 1926 to 1975
(1971 = 100)

Year	Residential building construction			Non-residential building construction			Year	Residential building construction			Non-residential building construction		
	Total	Materials	Labour	Total	Materials	Labour		Total	Materials	Labour	Total	Materials	Labour
	136	137	138	139	140	141		136	137	138	139	140	141
1975	144.0	139.7	151.6	150.4	147.0	154.1	1950	38.6	57.5	24.7	40.0	59.7	24.9
1974	134.7	135.2	133.9	136.1	137.3	134.7	1949	36.4	54.0	23.5	38.1	56.9	23.7
1973	123.2	124.0	121.8	117.5	113.1	122.3	1948	34.7	51.5	22.4	36.5	54.6	22.6
1972	110.1	109.8	110.6	107.8	104.9	111.0	1947	29.5	42.7	19.7	32.1	48.1	19.8
1971	100.0·	100.0	100.0	100.0	100.0	100.0	1946	26.1	36.6	18.3	29.0	42.7	18.4
1970	91.2	95.3	87.9	92.0	96.6	88.5	1945	24.5	35.1	16.7	27.2	40.6	16.8
1969	85.1	96.4	76.5	84.5	94.0	77.2	1944	24.3	34.7	16.5	26.9	40.3	16.7
1968	79.9	91.5	71.1	79.7	90.0	71.7	1943	23.4	33.0	16.2	26.6	39.9	16.4
1967	74.6	86.7	65.5	75.6	87.8	66.1	1942	21.8	31.0	15.1	25.7	39.4	15.2
1966	69.9	83.5	59.6	71.4	86.1	60.1	1941	20.5	29.0	14.2	24.5	37.6	14.3
1965	65.9	80.3	55.2	67.6	83.1	55.7	1940	18.7	26.1	13.3	23.0	35.3	13.4
1964	62.6	75.8	52.7	64.6	79.5	53.1	1939	17.6	24.2	12.8	22.2	34.3	12.9
1963	59.6	72.0	50.3	61.7	75.9	50.7	1938	17.5	24.0	12.7	22.4	34.9	12.8
1962	57.6	69.7	48.6	59.8	73.9	49.0	1937	17.8	25.3	12.3	22.6	35.9	12.4
1961	56.3	69.3	46.6	59.0	74.6	46.9	1936	16.6	22.9	12.0	21.3	33.2	12.1
1960	55.6	69.7	45.2	58.5	75.3	45.5	1935	16.2	22.0	11.9	21.1	33.0	12.0
1959	54.2	70.2	42.4	56.8	74.9	42.7	1934	16.2	22.6	11.5	–	–	–
1958	52.2	68.7	39.9	54.8	73.8	40.2	1933	15.8	21.1	11.8	–	–	–
1957	50.9	69.3	37.2	53.4	74.0	37.5	1932	16.5	20.7	13.3	–	–	–
1956	49.6	69.3	35.1	51.7	72.9	35.4	1931	18.0	22.5	14.6	–	–	–
1955	47.9	67.1	33.8	49.8	70.2	34.0	1930	19.2	24.8	15.1	–	–	–
1954	46.8	65.7	32.8	48.8	69.3	33.0	1929	19.8	26.6	14.7	–	–	–
1953	46.4	66.9	31.2	48.5	70.9	31.4	1928	18.9	25.8	13.8	–	–	–
1952	45.4	67.5	29.2	47.2	70.0	29.5	1927	18.5	25.4	13.3	–	–	–
1951	44.8	67.7	28.0	45.3	67.5	28.2	1926	18.4	26.0	12.8	–	–	–

Series K142-144. Construction Machinery and Equipment Price Indexes, 1961 to 1975
(1968 = 100)

Year	Total	Canadian made	Imported	Year	Total	Canadian made	Imported
	142	143	144		142	143	144
1975	160.7	152.4	164.9	1965	89.2	..	..
1974	130.1	127.8	131.2	1964	87.3	..	..
1973	114.9	114.3	115.2	1963	84.8	..	..
1972	110.8	112.2	110.2	1962	82.6	..	..
1971	108.4	109.2	108.1	1961	78.2	..	..
1970	106.4	105.8	106.6				
1969	104.4	103.6	104.8				
1968	100.0	100.0	100.0				
1967	94.7	..	..				
1966	92.1	..	..				

Series K145-149. Electric Utility Construction Price Indexes, 1956 to 1975
(1971 = 100)

Year	Distribution systems	Transmission lines	Transformer stations	Hydroelectric generating stations	Steam electric generating stations (fossil-fuel fired)	Year	Distribution systems	Transmission lines	Transformer stations	Hydroelectric generating stations	Steam electric generating stations (fossil-fuel fired)
	145	146	147	148	149		145	146	147	148	149
1975	154.2	161.9	159.0	157.6	158.4	1965	80.0	76.7	84.8	74.1	..
1974	137.5	137.7	136.2	137.9	139.6	1964	78.2	72.6	80.5	70.6	..
1973	114.1	115.3	111.1	116.1	115.9	1963	76.6	72.3	77.3	68.4	..
1972	104.4	106.1	104.1	106.3	106.1	1962	76.1	71.4	75.5	66.2	..
1971	100.0	100.0	100.0	100.0	100.0	1961	74.7	70.7	71.8	64.4	..
1970	96.6	96.5	95.2	95.6	94.3	1960	75.0	69.9	78.9	..	..
1969	89.9	90.2	86.5	89.9	87.8	1959	72.3	68.6	81.5	..	..
1968	86.4	86.2	84.2	84.8	82.2	1958	69.7	67.7	78.3	..	..
1967	86.8	83.9	87.1	81.5	80.0	1957	72.1	66.8	84.8	..	..
1966	84.0	79.9	87.9	78.7	79.1	1956	71.1	65.1	82.8	..	..

Series K150-159. Highway Construction Price Indexes, 1956 to 1975
(1971 = 100)

Year	Composite	Newfoundland	Nova Scotia	New Brunswick	Quebec	Ontario	Manitoba	Saskatchewan	Alberta	British Columbia
	150	151	152	153	154	155	156	157	158	159
1975	177.5	128.0	185.0	188.6	180.7	164.2	172.5	210.4	209.7	183.2
1974	158.7	129.0	164.1	191.8	154.0	149.5	166.8	175.8	184.7	170.2
1973	118.3	109.6	118.8	139.3	120.5	114.5	126.3	129.6	128.6	101.6
1972	105.1	101.1	107.2	123.9	106.6	106.3	111.3	104.4	99.5	95.7
1971	100.0	100.0	100.0	100.0	100.0	100.0	100.0	100.0	100.0	100.0
1970	92.7	82.6	90.4	105.7	87.2	96.8	100.9	98.5	..	96.7
1969	88.7	66.1	83.0	89.0	85.4	93.6	90.5	89.8	..	103.0
1968	84.8	68.6	80.8	88.7	80.5	92.1	88.2	84.9	..	91.1
1967	86.0	65.4	82.7	89.7	80.8	95.0	96.3	93.5	..	85.9
1966	89.4	73.6	78.3	90.2	82.6	95.7	95.7	114.3	..	93.3
1965	83.0	67.8	78.8	89.9	76.9	87.5	83.5	98.2	..	91.9
1964	76.2	61.5	65.0	90.3	79.6	75.2	77.5	79.4	..	76.3
1963	72.2	57.4	64.7	89.0	..	76.9	75.3	69.8	..	69.7
1962	67.6	61.9	66.2	86.5	..	67.0	67.6	66.9	..	68.5
1961	65.0	56.8	67.4	87.1	..	60.8	62.6	68.0	..	71.9
1960	72.1	70.8	79.8	84.3	..	65.2	72.9	71.6	..	81.8
1959	73.2	67.5	74.2	89.3	..	69.2	68.7	75.5	..	82.1
1958	73.0	74.0	69.9	89.9	..	66.4	69.8	82.6	..	80.3
1957	80.9	65.0	70.5	84.6	..	71.4	93.4	106.5	..	95.4
1956	87.1	77.3	77.6	87.0	..	81.6	83.3	103.7	..	102.4

Series K160-171. Implicit Price Indexes of Gross Fixed Capital Stocks, by industry group and type of stock, 1926 to 1975

(1971 = 100)

Year	Total industries				Manufacturing industries				Non-manufacturing industries			
	Total stocks	Building construction	Engineering construction	Machinery and equipment	Total stocks	Building construction	Engineering construction	Machinery and equipment	Total stocks	Building construction	Engineering construction	Machinery and equipment
	160	161	162	163	164	165	166	167	168	169	170	171
1975	143.8	135.0	155.1	140.9	144.2	133.3	144.2	146.6	143.8	135.2	155.9	139.1
1974	127.6	126.5	137.1	122.3	126.4	124.3	128.2	126.6	127.8	126.9	137.8	120.9
1973	111.0	112.5	116.4	107.1	109.5	109.5	115.0	108.7	111.4	113.0	116.5	106.5
1972	104.1	103.6	106.5	102.5	103.0	102.0	107.1	102.9	104.3	103.9	106.5	102.4
1971	100.0	100.0	100.0	100.0	100.0	100.0	100.0	100.0	100.0	100.0	100.0	100.0
1970	94.4	94.7	90.4	97.3	95.5	94.7	86.7	97.0	94.1	94.8	90.7	97.4
1969	90.3	90.3	85.9	93.4	91.6	89.1	82.7	93.6	89.9	90.5	86.1	93.4
1968	86.5	85.2	81.5	91.3	87.8	84.5	78.4	90.4	86.3	85.3	81.7	91.7
1967	86.3	85.1	80.8	91.2	89.0	84.9	77.9	91.2	85.7	85.1	80.9	91.1
1966	84.9	81.7	78.4	91.6	89.8	81.5	74.3	93.9	83.5	81.8	78.5	90.4
1965	80.9	76.5	74.2	89.1	86.7	76.3	70.6	91.4	79.4	76.5	74.3	87.9
1964	77.0	73.1	69.7	86.1	82.3	73.0	67.8	86.0	75.8	73.2	69.7	86.1
1963	74.9	71.8	68.3	83.3	78.0	72.0	67.0	80.8	74.2	71.8	68.3	84.3
1962	72.7	70.4	66.0	81.1	75.1	70.8	65.0	77.6	72.2	70.3	66.0	82.6
1961	71.3	70.7	64.8	78.7	73.5	71.2	64.5	75.0	70.8	70.7	64.8	80.2
1960	71.7	70.6	66.4	77.8	71.7	71.3	64.8	72.6	71.7	70.5	66.5	80.0
1959	71.0	69.8	66.0	77.1	69.6	70.5	64.2	70.2	71.3	69.7	66.1	79.8
1958	69.9	70.2	64.8	75.9	69.0	71.1	63.2	69.3	70.0	70.0	64.8	78.3
1957	69.6	69.9	65.4	74.1	67.6	70.6	63.2	67.2	70.1	69.7	65.5	77.4
1956	68.3	69.6	65.5	70.1	65.5	70.6	62.4	64.1	69.0	69.3	65.6	73.0
1955	65.0	67.7	61.0	66.7	62.2	69.0	59.4	60.5	65.7	67.4	61.2	69.2
1954	63.7	67.0	58.4	65.9	60.3	68.4	58.0	58.1	64.4	66.7	58.4	68.8
1953	63.4	67.9	58.5	64.6	60.4	69.6	58.8	57.8	64.1	67.5	58.4	67.4
1952	62.5	67.2	58.7	63.1	59.4	68.6	57.0	56.4	63.4	66.7	58.8	66.0
1951	61.0	64.2	56.1	62.6	58.0	65.9	53.5	55.3	61.8	63.7	56.2	65.5
1950	54.3	57.0	49.1	56.7	52.6	59.0	48.2	51.4	54.7	56.7	49.1	58.4
1949	51.3	54.6	46.8	52.8	49.3	57.0	45.8	47.6	51.8	54.1	46.8	54.7
1948	48.5	52.6	45.3	48.7	46.6	54.5	43.9	44.6	49.2	52.0	45.4	50.5
1947	43.6	46.3	40.4	44.2	42.2	48.5	38.8	40.5	44.2	45.4	40.6	45.9
1946	38.6	41.5	34.5	39.6	38.2	43.5	33.1	36.2	38.8	40.6	34.6	41.2
1945	38.3	39.9	32.4	40.5	37.7	41.2	31.5	37.3	38.5	39.4	32.5	41.5
1944	38.5	39.5	31.3	41.4	38.8	40.6	31.1	38.9	38.4	39.2	31.3	41.8
1943	37.7	39.2	30.7	42.8	38.6	40.1	30.3	38.6	37.5	39.0	30.7	44.1
1942	37.6	37.2	29.6	43.3	37.7	38.1	29.0	38.2	37.5	36.8	29.6	45.9
1941	36.0	34.6	28.4	41.3	36.0	36.2	27.2	36.6	35.9	34.0	28.4	44.0
1940	32.9	31.6	26.4	37.7	33.1	33.5	24.9	33.6	32.8	30.7	26.5	39.3
1939	31.1	29.8	26.6	35.7	31.7	33.2	24.7	31.7	31.0	29.0	26.7	36.8
1938	31.2	29.9	27.0	35.6	31.8	33.4	24.3	31.7	31.1	28.6	27.0	36.7
1937	31.1	30.7	27.2	34.9	31.8	33.6	25.0	31.5	30.9	29.0	27.2	36.0
1936	28.8	28.3	25.1	32.9	29.1	31.7	23.1	27.9	28.7	27.0	25.2	34.3
1935	27.6	27.2	24.4	31.8	27.9	31.5	22.9	27.0	27.5	26.2	24.4	33.7
1934	27.4	27.0	24.6	31.3	27.2	31.3	21.8	25.9	27.4	25.9	24.6	33.0
1933	26.4	27.2	23.3	29.9	26.5	31.4	21.3	24.3	26.3	26.0	23.4	31.9
1932	27.1	28.2	24.1	31.2	27.2	32.7	22.9	25.0	27.1	27.4	24.1	33.1
1931	27.9	30.8	24.6	31.4	27.4	34.2	23.4	24.6	28.0	30.0	24.6	33.9
1930	29.7	33.4	25.8	32.2	29.8	36.4	25.0	27.2	29.7	32.5	25.9	33.8
1929	31.3	34.7	26.6	33.6	32.4	37.4	26.2	29.2	31.0	33.4	26.6	34.7
1928	30.1	32.8	25.6	32.5	31.4	35.7	25.2	29.0	29.7	31.4	25.6	33.5
1927	30.1	32.0	25.6	32.7	31.2	35.4	25.2	29.1	29.8	30.4	25.6	33.9
1926	30.4	31.2	26.5	33.5	31.2	35.1	26.2	29.8	30.2	29.8	26.5	34.7

Series K172-183. Implicit Price Indexes of Gross National Expenditures, 1926 to 1975
(1971 = 100)

Year	Gross national expenditure at market prices		Personal expenditure on consumer goods and services	Government expenditure on goods and services			Business gross fixed capital formation				Exports of goods and services	Imports of goods and services
	Total	Excluding inventories		Total	Current expenditure	Gross fixed capital formation	Total	New residential construction	New non-residential construction	New machinery and equipment		
	172	**173**	**174**	**175**	**176**	**177**	**178**	**179**	**180**	**181**	**182**	**183**
1975	146.5	145.1	137.1	150.6	155.5	153.1	149.5	167.8	149.3	138.5	168.7	153.3
1974	131.7	131.2	123.9	133.1	134.6	138.0	132.3	147.7	133.1	121.4	152.2	134.7
1973	114.6	114.7	111.6	116.6	116.4	114.8	114.1	123.8	114.3	106.9	117.4	111.2
1972	105.0	105.0	104.0	107.2	107.2	105.2	104.9	107.1	105.7	102.6	103.9	103.1
1971	100.0	100.0	100.0	100.0	100.0	100.0	100.0	100.0	100.0	100.0	100.0	100.0
1970	96.9	96.9	97.7	94.4	94.2	95.3	95.3	94.1	94.2	97.4	99.7	98.2
1969	92.6	92.5	94.3	89.4	89.0	91.2	91.5	92.1	89.6	92.9	96.4	95.6
1968	88.7	88.6	90.8	83.1	82.2	87.0	87.9	87.9	84.9	90.8	94.3	93.0
1967	85.9	85.8	87.2	79.5	77.8	86.8	87.1	87.0	84.1	90.7	93.0	90.7
1966	82.6	82.5	84.3	75.4	72.8	85.9	85.1	82.2	80.8	91.2	91.1	89.2
1965	79.1	79.0	81.6	70.8	68.2	81.3	81.0	77.2	76.2	88.4	88.7	87.3
1964	76.6	76.6	80.0	67.3	65.2	76.3	77.2	73.0	72.2	85.1	87.1	86.6
1963	74.8	74.6	79.0	65.2	63.1	74.0	74.5	70.1	70.3	81.8	85.3	85.9
1962	73.4	73.2	77.8	62.7	60.6	71.4	72.5	68.6	68.4	79.6	84.5	84.0
1961	72.4	72.5	76.8	61.2	59.1	70.4	71.6	68.8	68.1	77.0	81.3	80.3
1960	72.1	72.0	76.3	60.2	57.3	72.8	71.4	68.2	68.3	76.5	80.3	78.2
1959	71.2	71.1	75.6	58.5	55.3	72.2	70.4	66.9	67.7	75.5	79.8	77.5
1958	69.8	70.0	74.7	56.7	53.5	71.9	69.7	67.0	67.3	73.8	78.7	78.0
1957	68.8	68.8	72.8	55.9	51.9	75.8	69.6	67.2	67.6	72.7	79.0	76.9
1956	67.4	66.9	70.6	53.7	49.4	80.3	67.8	65.3	67.7	69.0	79.4	75.0
1955	65.0	65.0	69.5	49.6	46.2	72.5	64.9	64.3	64.4	65.0	77.3	72.6
1954	64.6	64.7	69.5	47.7	44.7	67.4	63.6	63.1	62.9	63.9	74.3	71.4
1953	63.6	63.3	68.8	45.8	43.0	67.3	63.8	63.7	63.7	63.2	74.9	71.2
1952	63.7	63.2	69.0	45.3	42.0	71.5	63.0	63.1	63.2	62.1	76.7	71.3
1951	61.0	60.3	67.4	43.6	40.2	69.9	61.0	62.0	59.7	60.9	77.6	76.7
1950	54.8	54.4	61.2	39.2	35.9	58.9	53.8	53.8	52.8	54.0	69.8	69.4
1949	53.5	53.6	59.4	37.6	34.6	56.6	51.5	51.2	51.3	51.1	66.8	64.9
1948	51.3	51.2	57.3	35.5	32.3	54.4	49.1	49.1	49.7	48.0	63.6	62.8
1947	45.7	45.5	50.5	30.6	28.3	48.5	43.2	41.9	44.5	42.7	59.3	56.2
1946	42.0	41.9	46.2	27.7	26.3	44.1	39.1	37.2	39.9	38.2	52.9	56.2
1945	40.8	41.8	44.7	27.3	26.8	42.7	37.8	34.8	37.6	37.8	48.1	50.1
1944	39.8	40.2	44.2	25.6	25.4	43.5	37.7	34.5	37.4	38.7	46.6	47.1
1943	38.6	39.1	43.8	24.5	24.3	42.5	37.1	33.1	36.9	39.1	43.5	45.9
1942	37.3	36.8	42.6	23.7	23.5	40.2	35.2	31.2	35.2	36.9	41.4	44.3
1941	35.7	35.7	40.7	22.0	21.4	37.3	33.4	29.4	32.6	35.4	38.8	41.9
1940	33.1	32.7	38.1	21.3	20.6	35.0	31.0	26.6	30.9	32.8	37.3	38.4
1939	31.6	31.1	36.4	21.5	19.6	34.2	29.1	25.1	29.9	30.3	34.0	36.4
1938	31.9	31.8	36.6	21.9	19.6	35.0	29.3	24.9	30.3	30.5	35.0	32.9
1937	31.9	32.4	36.0	22.1	19.4	35.1	29.5	25.4	30.9	30.3	37.1	33.3
1936	31.1	31.6	35.0	20.6	18.8	33.3	27.4	23.5	28.7	28.2	34.0	35.0
1935	30.1	30.2	34.4	20.4	18.6	32.3	26.9	23.1	28.0	27.9	32.6	32.4
1934	30.0	29.9	34.2	20.0	18.3	32.1	26.6	23.0	27.5	27.5	32.0	31.5
1933	29.6	29.7	33.7	19.7	18.1	32.1	26.4	22.4	27.3	27.7	29.3	29.2
1932	30.1	30.2	35.1	20.3	18.4	33.1	27.1	23.5	27.8	28.4	28.9	30.1
1931	33.2	33.3	38.3	22.0	19.5	34.5	28.3	25.5	29.1	28.4	32.1	32.7
1930	35.4	35.4	42.0	23.3	20.0	36.1	29.9	27.5	31.5	29.3	38.3	37.2
1929	36.3	36.7	42.5	23.4	20.5	37.0	31.0	28.2	32.8	30.5	42.4	40.6
1928	35.9	35.8	42.1	23.0	20.3	36.0	30.1	26.9	31.8	29.9	43.3	41.1
1927	36.1	35.6	41.7	22.6	20.1	35.7	29.8	26.2	31.1	30.1	44.8	41.5
1926	36.5	36.6	42.3	22.4	20.3	36.1	30.2	26.2	31.0	31.1	45.8	42.8

Section L: Lands and Forests

Brian S. Osborne, *Queen's University*

This section is concerned with those statistics referring to the allocation of lands and the production of forests. To some extent, these two questions are compatible only in that they have fallen under the same administrative unit for the purposes of management and data collection. They continue together in this volume as a matter of convenience. The data relating to land refer to the allocation of lands for settlement, production and recreation, and are, wherever possible, reported at both the national and provincial level. Those data relating to forests are concerned with primary products, the manufacturing of lumber, pulp and paper, and exports. Sources, together with problems or qualifications associated with them, are identified in each table by footnotes.

The main concern of this volume has been to update the statistics to 1975 and, because of limitations of time or space, it is regretted that a more comprehensive review of the statistics could not be effected. In particular, the provision of statistics for earlier periods of land patenting for Ontario and Quebec and for the forest products in general was not attempted. Again, the reporting of some of the sets of data at the provincial level, particularly those referring to forest products, would have been desirable. Finally, the restructuring of certain themes to address new questions was not attempted. Such refinements remain as possible directions for future improvements of the work presented here.

It must be emphasized, therefore, that the revision attempted in this volume can only be advanced as an extension of the work performed by G.K. Goudrey in the original volume of the *Historical Statistics of Canada*. Structure, sources and research form the background of this section. Anyone wishing a fuller appreciation of the organization and collection of these data should, therefore, consult the extensive text which accompanies the earlier volume.

The data in this section are divided into two parts. Series L1-106 contain statistics on lands, including total areas, public parks, sales, grants and alienation of public lands, and receipts from sales and for the use of public lands. Series L107-210 contain statistics on forests, including data on production and exports of primary and secondary products, forest fires, and forestry revenues and expenditures of provinces.

The citations for sources of data up to and including the year 1959, are not repeated in the present edition. It is therefore necessary for the reader to consult the first edition of this volume. The original volume should be consulted also for detailed notes and comments on each table prior to 1959. The sources for the updates from 1959 to 1975 are given below.

Lands (Series L1-106)

L1-2. Area of Canada and provinces, 1867 to 1975

SOURCE: Statistics Canada, *Canada Year Book, 1976-77*, p. 32.

There have been no changes in land areas since Newfoundland entered Confederation in 1949. For convenience, the following table of land and water areas by province is provided. Primary sources are discussed in the original volume.

L3-4. Area of national and historic parks and provincial parks, selected years, 1885 to 1975

SOURCE: Statistics Canada, *Canada Year Book, 1975*, p. 43 and previous issues.

1.1 Approximate land and freshwater areas, by province

Province or territory	Land sq miles	Freshwater sq miles	Total sq miles	Percentage of total area
Newfoundland	143,045	13,140	156,185	4.1
Island of Newfoundland	*41,164*	*2,195*	*43,359*	*1.1*
Labrador	*101,881*	*10,945*	*112,826*	*3.0*
Prince Edward Island	2,184	–	2,184	0.1
Nova Scotia	20,402	1,023	21,425	0.6
New Brunswick	27,835	519	28,354	0.7
Quebec	523,860	71,000	594,860	15.4
Ontario	344,092	68,490	412,582	10.7
Manitoba	211,775	39,225	251,000	6.5
Saskatchewan	220,182	31,518	251,700	6.5
Alberta	248,800	6,485	255,285	6.6
British Columbia	359,279	6,976	366,255	9.5
Yukon Territory	205,346	1,730	207,076	5.4
Northwest Territories	1,253,438	51,465	1,304,903	33.9
Franklin	*541,753*	*7,500*	*549,253*	*14.3*
Keewatin	*218,460*	*9,700*	*228,160*	*5.9*
Mackenzie	*493,225*	*34,265*	*527,490*	*13.7*
Canada	3,560,238	291,571	3,851,809	100.0

L5-13.   Land acreage patented in Canada, by province, 1871 to 1975

SOURCE: *Annual Reports* of provincial departments of lands and forests; *A Statistical Reference of Lands and Forests Administration, 1966*, Operations Branch, Department of Lands and Forests, Ontario; Government of Canada, Indian and Northern Affairs, Northern Environment Branch.

The following definition is taken from the first edition of this volume. "The term 'patented' is used to mean that a deed bearing title to land has been drawn up by the Crown agency concerned, that is the federal or a provincial government, for Crown land that had not previously transferred into private hands and that this deed is then transferred to a private party. Acreage patented therefore is a measure of the amount of Crown land that is alienated from the Crown for the first time."

It should be noted that "Until 1936, the areas patented by the Dominion government have been distributed here among the provinces."

After 1936, the amounts sold by Canada became very small and diminished to zero by 1961. (See footnote 3 to series L13, and text of original edition.) Thus the sale of lands became entirely a provincial matter. For Indian lands however, see series L73-74. The federal government continues to have land sales in the Yukon Territory and the Northwest Territories.

L14-29.   Total acreage patented and average area patented by type of entry, by province, Western provinces, 1881 to 1975

SOURCE: *Annual Reports* of Alberta Department of Lands and Forests, 1960 to 1975, and original edition of this volume.

L30-33.   Land grants, entries and cancellations, number and acreage, by type of grant, Alberta, 1931 to 1975

SOURCE: same as series L14-29.

L34-41.   Land grants, number of entries and cancellations by province and type of grant, Western provinces, 1872 to 1931

These series terminate in 1931, but are repeated here for convenience. See notes in original edition.

L42-45.   Pre-emptions and purchased homesteads, number of entries and cancellations by province, Alberta and Saskatchewan, 1874 to 1931

See note to series L34-41.

L46-56.   Land sales and cancellations, school lands and other provincial lands, by province, Prairie provinces, 1931 to 1975

These series are a continuation, to 1975, of series L42-45, but with additional detail.

L57-64.   Land sales, school land and miscellaneous, by province, Prairie provinces, and school land cancellations, Alberta, 1905 to 1931

These series terminate in 1931, but are repeated here for convenience. See notes in original edition.

L65-72.   Land grants and sales, by province, Ontario and Quebec, 1867 to 1975

SOURCE: *Annual Reports*, 1960 to 1971, Ontario Department of Lands and Forests.

See also explanatory note in first edition.

L73-74.   Sales of Indian lands, acreage and value, Canada, 1874 to 1966

SOURCE: *Annual Reports*, Government of Canada, Indian and Northern Affairs, Ottawa.

The values shown here from 1957 to 1966 are fees and royalties for rights of way, leases, permits and mineral rights, for which the receipts were credited to the Indian bands, on capital accounts. There have been no such sales on behalf of the bands, by the department, since the policy was changed in the late sixties. See also note to series K73-74 in original volume.

L75-90.   Land sales by railway companies having Dominion land grants, and the Hudson's Bay Company, 1893 to 1930

These series terminate in 1930, but are repeated here for convenience. See notes in original edition.

L91-96.   Land sales by Hudson's Bay Company, Canadian Northern Land Department and Canadian Pacific Railway Company, 1925 to 1960

Correspondence with the above companies suggests that these should be regarded as terminated series. The Hudson's Bay Company had no land sales after 1960. The original table is reproduced here.

L97-106.   Government receipts on account of Dominion lands, 1873 to 1931

These series terminate in 1931, but are repeated here for convenience. See notes in original edition.

Forests (Series L107-210)

General note

The principal statistics of woods operations were affected by the 1961 revision of the Standard Industrial Classification, (S.I.C., including the new definition of establishments and the distinction between logging activity and total activity. For a complete description of these changes, see the general note to Section R, Manufactures. In the following tables of principal statistics, the historical series from the original volume have been updated to 1964, while the newer series have been shown in a separate table, from 1963 to 1975. Thus, a two-year overlap is provided between the old and new series.

The series on commodity production and exports were affected by changes in units of measure, such as the change from board feet to cubic feet in the case of logs and bolts and the change from thousand cubic feet to cunits (one hundred cubic feet) in the case of pulpwood. However, the former series were converted to the newer units in the following tables. The commodity series are regarded as being reasonably continuous, despite the above change in the S.I.C.

The main source of the following series is Statistics Canada, *Canadian Forestry Statistics Revised, 1974*, (Catalogue 25-505), which contains several historical tables on the new definitions. In addition, the annual publications of *Canadian Forestry Statistics*, (Catalogue 25-202), were used.

L107-118. Primary forest production and exports of primary products, by type of product (excluding fuel wood), selected years, 1922 to 1975

SOURCE: Statistics Canada, *Canadian Forestry Statistics*, (Catalogue 25-202).

A 'cunit' is defined as one hundred cubic feet. The other units of measurement used in the table are self explanatory. 'Pulpwood' in series L109 is distinguished from 'woodpulp' in series L168 in that it has not yet been processed into a pulp sulphite or sulphate. 'Pulpwood' is an earlier product of woods operations rather than pulp and paper mills.

L119-128. Principal statistics of woods operations, 1963 to 1975

L129-133. Principal statistics of woods operations, 1926 to 1964

The above two tables contain a two-year overlap, 1963 and 1964, between the former series and the newer ones, as explained in the General note to series L107-210.

L134-148. Lumber production by species, external trade and estimated consumption, 1908 to 1975

SOURCE: same as series L107-118.

L149-158. Principal statistics of the lumber industry, 1957 to 1975

L159-165. Principal statistics of the lumber industry, 1917 to 1959

The two tables above provide a three-year overlap for the period 1957 to 1959, to bridge the changes brought in by the 1961 revision of the S.I.C.

L166-175. Wood pulp, production and exports, 1908 to 1975

SOURCE: same as series L107-118.

L176-188. Manufactured paper, capacity, production and exports, 1916 to 1975

SOURCE: Statistics Canada, *Canadian Forestry Statistics*, (Catalogue 25-202), for production and exports; Canadian Pulp and Paper Association, for capacity.

L189-198. Principal statistics, pulp and paper mills, manufacturing activity and total activity, 1959 to 1975

L199-205. Principal statistics of the pulp and paper industry, 1919 to 1959

The two tables above constitute a unit, with a single year of overlap for the year 1959. The pulp and paper industry is a part of the larger group, paper and allied industries, which is shown in the Manufactures Section (Series R309-325).

L206-210. Forest fires, Canada, 1908 to 1975

SOURCE: Statistics Canada, *Canada Year Book, 1976-77*, and previous issues.

The remaining series in the first edition are terminated series and are not reproduced here for reasons of economy and space.

Series L1-2. Area of Canada and provinces, 1867 to 1975
(square miles)

Year	Total area of Canada	Area within provincial boundaries	
	1	2	
1949–75	3,851,809	2,339,830	Newfoundland entered Confederation, 1949
	3,560,238	2,101,454	Land
	291,571	238,376	Fresh water
1927–48	3,695,624	2,183,645	British Privy Council Award of Labrador to Newfoundland, 1927
1912–26	3,807,450	2,295,471	Quebec, Ontario and Manitoba enlarged, 1912
1905–11	3,807,450	1,563,403	Alberta and Saskatchewan formed, 1905
1898–1904	3,807,450	1,056,417	Quebec enlarged, 1898
1889–97	3,807,450	942,272	Ontario enlarged and defined; Manitoba enlarged, 1889
1880–88	3,807,450	899,692	Northern Islands to Canada, 1880
1874–79	3,357,348	840,300	Temporary Ontario boundary, 1874
1873	3,357,348	767,377	Prince Edward Island entered Confederation, 1873
1871–72	3,355,164	765,193	British Columbia entered Confederation, 1871
1870	2,988,909	398,938	Rupert's Land and Northwest Territories to Canada, Manitoba formed, 1870
1867–69	384,598	384,598	Original Confederation of Ontario, Quebec, Nova Scotia and New Brunswick, 1867

Series L3-4. Area of national and historic parks and provincial parks, selected years, 1885 to 1975
(square miles)

Year	National and historic parks	Provincial parks	Year	National and historic parks	Provincial parks
	3	4		3	4
1975	52,738	117,994	1930	29,360	12,159
1971	31,295	98,613	1925	26,245	11,196
1967	29,425	83,364	1921	9,092	11,076
1965	29,425	76,022	1918	8,878	11,076
1960	29,280	52,301	1913	4,016	11,076
1955	29,147	42,294	1911	4,028	8,413
1950	29,148	35,863	1907	10,573	7,585
1945	29,705	31,134	1895	353	7,585
1941	29,727	30,522	1893	299	2,741
1936	29,819	12,722	1885	10	—

Series L5-13. Land acreage patented in Canada, by province, 1871 to 1975
(thousands of acres)

Year[1]	British Columbia	Alberta	Saskatchewan	Manitoba	Ontario	Quebec	New Brunswick	Nova Scotia	Canada
	5	6	7	8	9	10	11	12	13
1975	..	196.3	137.3	..	..	..	11.6	.4	—
1974	..	218.0	..	..	..	..	3.8	.3	—
1973	42.5	192.1	139.8	..	..	..	..	6.4	—
1972	59.3	248.4	83.0	..	..	..	..	.3	—
1971	74.5	207.9	57.1	..	5.0	..	..	3.0	—
1970	38.4	310.5	237.8	..	5.1	..	..	11.9	—
1969	81.9	287.7	155.7	..	7.2	..	6.8	.3	—
1968	129.3	356.8	189.1	..	5.3	..	11.5	.4	—
1967	117.7	346.3	116.0	..	7.3	..	2.4	.1	—
1966	115.9	305.9	105.5	..	9.2	..	6.2	.2	—
1965	86.2	169.8	69.4	..	27.4	..	13.1	5.2	—
1964	93.6	173.0	73.8	..	19.0	..	8.1	.6	—
1963	77.4	273.0	74.1	..	19.8	..	8.0	.6	—
1962	68.0	245.5	..	25.0	22.9	..	6.9	4.3	—
1961	75.5	226.4	..	24.3	22.4	..	7.4	2.0	—
1960	79.8	369.1	..	22.9	29.2	..	3.7	2.1	—
1959	91.3	320.1	40.9	35.2	20.5	..	7.2	3.2	.1
1958	58.8	166.3	41.3	31.9	29.2	..	6.2	4.0	.1
1957	89.9	125.2	37.1	29.7	27.6	54.2	10.8	3.1	.2
1956	80.3	117.1	—	19.7	35.4	79.1	9.1	3.2	.6
1955	65.9	87.8	55.2	31.6	40.0	76.9	13.3	3.6	1.0
1954	73.4	70.9	55.5	34.7	55.2	93.4	10.6	4.5	.3
1953	99.0	58.5	69.8	43.3	54.7	95.5	15.8	3.1	.4
1952	98.6	41.6	223.7	36.1	58.6	86.5	24.3	4.1	.1
1951	77.5	157.8	40.4	13.1	55.8	87.7	3.2	2.9	—
1950	75.7	58.2	55.8	23.8	118.0	72.1	16.5	—	1.3
1949	219.7	136.6	88.7	21.3	56.0	82.3	16.6	2.0	2.4
1948	85.1	129.4	82.8	18.5	—	70.6	68.0[2]	2.0	1.6
1947	111.6	169.9	—	27.0	89.1	91.9	31.6	.2	3.0
1946	110.2	183.4	125.9	21.9	74.2	85.4	21.0	.4	1.0
1945	85.0	296.4	290.4	36.8	78.7	87.6	48.0[2]	.6	2.8
1944	65.3	249.4	265.4	35.2	77.0	65.8	13.7	.4	3.1
1943	65.5	229.7	256.3	21.6	41.7	57.1	11.8	.6	.9
1942	64.3	229.6	352.6	14.1	33.3	179.8	15.5	3.1	1.6
1941	64.5	295.6	454.9	4.5	36.9	107.9	23.2	.2	2.8
1940	59.6	301.4	505.0	9.8	36.3	148.1	11.9	.1	4.0
1939	59.9	517.4	204.1	15.1	40.8	95.2	7.8	1.5	5.5
1938	66.3	382.4	284.4	28.4	48.5	97.1	6.9	1.1	3.7
1937	93.7	325.6	335.2	39.9	27.5	41.4	4.9	.6	5.7[3]
1936	69.1	435.7	312.5	68.5	44.8	31.7	2.2	.9	—
1935	77.5	328.7	367.2	85.1	13.3	24.7	6.0	.7	—
1934	62.8	170.5	—[4]	42.3	42.8	135.7	3.6	.3	—
1933	59.2	191.8	291.9	23.4	36.4	19.3	5.2	1.3	—
1932	61.6	142.0	261.7	75.5	60.1	34.4	10.3	.7	—
1931	86.2	151.6	166.4	77.6	77.3	46.2	6.3	1.3	—
1930	87.4	349.2	376.8	81.9	84.8	44.2	12.7	2.8	—
1929	135.8	308.7	537.6	72.5	71.6	187.4	9.8	1.7	—
1928	101.2	461.7	382.6	66.5	67.3	47.1	12.8	2.2	—
1927	94.0	356.4	363.6	58.0	76.4	70.6	8.3	1.0	—
1926	106.8	243.6	402.0	135.3	94.8	57.9	11.7	7.0	—
1925	103.8	232.4	269.5	97.7	91.4	402.9[5]	12.9	.9	—
1924	195.6	257.8	389.8	112.2	102.0	87.6	12.3	2.8	—
1923	99.3	336.3	1,237.7	177.2	111.4	89.8	10.2	.8	—
1922	155.7	739.8	883.0	362.2	108.1	136.3	14.9	2.5	—
1921	201.1	979.7	1,338.3	397.4	91.8	306.1[6]	15.8	3.3	—
1920	238.7	903.1	1,541.7	317.0	101.3	388.9[6]	19.5	5.0	—
1919	548.5	1,176.8	1,616.0	233.8	104.8	227.8	39.1	9.1	—
1918	292.8	1,420.3	2,053.6	215.0	84.6	134.9	19.5	5.3	—
1917	218.8	1,157.0	1,636.6	192.7	111.0	139.6	12.2	5.3	—
1916	129.6	1,209.0	1,686.5	160.0	—	83.4	15.4	11.4	—
1915	106.1	1,554.0	2,205.6	204.2	—	74.4	10.6	7.0	—
1914	273.7	1,901.1	3,036.2	225.5	—	557.7[6]	17.9	14.5	—
1913	404.8	1,567.7	2,392.0	223.5	—	338.7[6]	12.8	6.4	—
1912	286.3[7]	1,189.5	1,786.5	143.8	—	739.1[6]	12.2	5.3	—
1911	543.7	1,253.9	2,268.6	163.6	—	145.7	15.7	9.9	—
1910	318.8	1,196.5	2,279.9	165.8	—		12.8	11.9	—
1909	342.8	1,315.1	2,499.3	382.1	—	395.3	16.3	13.2	—
1908	253.5[8]	—[8]	6,139.0[8]	—[8]	—		14.6	10.4	—
1907	599.4[9]	—	2,361.3[10]	—	—	126.2	19.3	9.9	—
1906	336.1	—	4,181.3	—	—	156.2	15.1	12.8	—

Series L5-13. Land acreage patented in Canada, by province, 1871 to 1975 (concluded)

(thousands of acres)

Year[1]	British Columbia	Alberta	Saskat-chewan	Manitoba	Ontario	Quebec	New Brunswick	Nova Scotia	Canada
	5	6	7	8	9	10	11	12	13
1905	133.2	—	6,196.3	—	—	128.0	15.3	24.3	—
1904	107.4	—	2,979.5	—	—		18.6	18.8	—
1903	83.7	—	3,263.8	—	—	287.7	21.5	32.6	—
1902	87.9	—	4,709.6	—	—		22.7	21.7	—
1901	4,632.8	—	6,846.3	—	—	100.6	17.7	31.4	—
1900	104.7	—	310.5 [10]	—	—	79.7	18.8	17.6	—
1899	672.1	—	714.7	—	—	75.1	18.1	40.8	—
1898	371.4 [9]	—	646.7	—	—	93.1	16.9	187.1 [11]	—
1897	609.6 [9]	—	499.9	—	—	79.9	15.2	42.9	—
1896	36.8 [9]	—	531.9	—	—	62.2	17.3	188.0	—
1895	95.5	—	349.0	—	—	70.6	11.5	62.6	—
1894	47.2	—	420.2 [12]	—	—	73.5	10.6	53.6	—
1893	124.6	—	502.6	—	—	108.5	16.2	27.4	—
1892	309.9 [9]	—	549.3	—	—	65.8	17.1	43.0	—
1891	143.5	—	411.1	—	—	159.4	23.5	35.9	—
1890	99.3	—	626.0	—	—	101.5	35.4	36.8	—
1889	134.2	—	661.6	—	—	81.1	30.2	42.4	—
1888	94.3	—	647.6	—	—	64.2	26.6	27.8	—
1887	74.0	—	1,071.4	—	—	146.2	26.7	26.0	—
1886	50.5	—	942.1	—	—		29.2	37.0	—
1885	128.8	—	898.5	—	—	83.6	40.6	25.5	—
1884	146.2	—	909.6	—	—	91.8	43.7	57.0	—
1883	54.6 [9]	—	831.3	—	—	61.9	59.7	48.5	—
1882	23.6	—	506.8	—	—	86.7	59.7	38.5	—
1881	23.1	—	400.9	—	—	44.7	56.7	66.4	—
1880	24.1	—	173.4	—	—	6,203.2 [13]	37.2	63.4	—
1879	46.8	—	426.1	—	—	—	35.9	45.1	—
1878	31.2	—	462.9	—	—	—	1,832.3 [14]	12.6	—
1877	10.0	—	478.8	—	—	—	—	25.8	—
1876	18.0	—	50.9	—	—	—	—	35.0	—
1875	18.0	—	74.2 [15]	—	—	—	—	46.5	—
1874	26.2	—	92.3 [15]	—	—	—	—	107.3	—
1873	—	—	67.2 [15]	—	—	—	—	116.0	—
1872	—	—	—	—	—	—	—	136.7	—
1871	—	—	—	—	—	—	—	134.7	—

[1] See the notes to series K5-13 for year endings, in the first edition.
[2] Includes grants to the Dominion of Canada, Acadian Forest Experimental Station, 1945, 22,500 acres and National Park, 1948, 50,880 acres.
[3] The acreage patented by the government of Canada prior to 1937 is distributed by the provinces.
[4] The government of Canada patented 8,585 acres; the provincial figure is not available.
[5] Includes a grant of 306,760 acres to Inter-provincial and James Bay Railroad Company.
[6] Includes railway grants: 1921, 64,500 acres; 1920, 48,400 acres; 1914, 424,300 acres; 1913, 147,400 acres; 1912, 547,100 acres.
[7] Area of 4,000,000 acres repurchased by the crown not included.

[8] For 1873 to 1908, series L7 includes land acreage patented for Alberta, Saskatchewan, Manitoba, the Yukon Territory and the Northwest Territories and Dominion lands in British Columbia.
[9] See note to series K5 for special grants not included (first edition).
[10] For 1907, 9 months ending 31 March 1907; for 1906, 6 months ending 30 June 1906.
[11] Includes 150,000 acre railway land grant.
[12] Year ended 31 October 1894: 66,102 acres patented in November and December 1894.
[13] Acreage patented for the period 1867 to 1880.
[14] Acreage patented for the period 1867 to 1878.
[15] For 1875, 1 January 1875 to 31 October 1875; for 1874, calendar year; for 1873, May 1873 to 31 December 1873.

Series L14-29. Total acreage patented and average area patented by type of entry, by province, Western provinces, 1881 to 1975

Year[1,2]	Homesteads							
	Total acreage patented (thousands of acres)				Average acreage patented per patent issued (acres)			
	British Columbia	Alberta	Saskatchewan	Manitoba	British Columbia	Alberta	Saskatchewan	Manitoba
	14	15	16	17	18	19	20	21
1975	–	42.4	–	–	–	261.7	–	–
1974	–	40.1	–	–	–	272.8	–	–
1973	–	33.9	–	–	–	251.1	–	–
1972	–	40.7	–	–	–	240.5	–	–
1971	–	32.3	–	–	–	241.0	–	–
1970	–	46.4	–	–	–	252.2	–	–
1969	–	59.6	–	–	–	248.3	–	–
1968	–	64.3	–	–	–	251.2	–	–
1967	–	59.9	–	–	–	250.6	–	–
1966	–	81.3	–	–	–	242.7	–	–
1965	–	59.7	–	–	–	239.8	–	–
1964	–	50.8	–	–	–	236.3	–	–
1963	–	78.8	–	–	–	264.4	–	–
1962	–	72.9	–	–	–	244.6	–	–
1961	–	65.9	–	–	–	236.2	–	–
1960	–	76.9	–	–	–	230.1	–	–
1959	–	76.7	–	–	–	231.1	–	–
1958	–	114.6	–	–	–	235.4	–	–
1957	–	61.1	–	–	–	227.2	–	–
1956	–	1.5	–	–	–	150.9	–	–
1955	–	1.1	–	–	–	158.4	–	–
1954	–	.8	–	–	–	159.2	34.3	–
1953	–	.6	3.5	–	–	157.8	159.8	–
1952	–	1.3	3.1	–	–	159.9	156.4	–
1951	–	5.9	3.5	–	–	144.8	159.3	–
1950	–	15.1	8.2	–	–	152.2	156.8	–
1949	–	42.4	14.5	–	–	155.4	157.1	–
1948	–	74.9	16.0	–	–	154.5	156.6	–
1947	–	111.3	–	–	–	154.4	–	–
1946	–	129.8	37.9	–	–	154.3	156.1	–
1945	–	160.4	49.2	.1	–	153.4	155.3	81.0
1944	–	184.3	95.6	–	–	154.1	157.2	–
1943	–	171.6	79.5	.3	–	153.8	156.8	160.0
1942	–	204.9	128.8	.3	–	154.8	157.1	136.5
1941	–	266.3	151.1	.2	–	151.1	156.9	158.3
1940	–	273.9	54.4	5.3	–	154.8	155.0	154.4
1939	–	443.6	175.7	10.0	–	195.1	155.4	150.9
1938	–	306.2	256.6	21.7	–	155.6	155.3	150.8
1937	–	292.1	296.6	33.4	–	156.7	156.1	152.6
1936	–	401.5	281.0	61.6	–	156.8	156.2	147.8
1935	–	261.8	–	76.0	–	157.6	–	151.3
1934	–	148.2	251.7	32.4	–	156.8	154.8	150.5
1933	–	159.8	–	17.3	–	157.6	–	148.9
1932	–	99.3	161.1	19.4	–	157.1	155.9	146.2
1931[2]	–	1.8	–	–	–	159.6	–	–
1931[4]	5.6	72.2	108.8	13.4	100.2	156.3	156.1	150.2
1930	10.2	109.5	180.5	30.3	104.0	155.6	155.8	149.1
1929	15.6	108.0	169.3	40.7	105.6	156.7	154.4	149.2
1928	20.0	120.9	141.1	45.5	116.1	156.0	154.9	149.8
1927	16.1	118.4	118.0	30.3	124.8	156.0	154.9	150.2
1926	13.8	102.2	124.7	43.4	119.7	155.4	156.2	152.3

Series L14-29. Total acreage patented and average area patented by type of entry, by province, Western provinces, 1881 to 1975 (continued)

Year[1,2]	Homesteads							
	Total acreage patented (thousands of acres)				Average acreage patented per patent issued (acres)			
	British Columbia	Alberta	Saskat-chewan	Manitoba	British Columbia	Alberta	Saskat-chewan	Manitoba
	14	15	16	17	18	19	20	21
1925	15.4	121.2	109.3	54.8	126.1	156.4	157.4	155.4
1924	16.1	174.8	166.3	76.4	123.2	155.6	157.0	153.5
1923	27.6	277.2	292.2	149.2	127.8	156.2	156.7	153.9
1922	35.8	572.4	570.9	321.3	123.8	156.3	156.9	155.7
1921	35.3	723.3	823.9	352.5	133.5	157.6	157.6	156.7
1920	22.3	610.6	740.8	264.1	125.4	161.6	157.1	156.9
1919	33.2	548.4	729.3	167.7	139.7	159.5	160.1	156.4
1918	31.8	866.4	1,251.7	183.2	141.4	160.9	160.6	161.0
1917	30.9	812.5	1,109.4	145.1	136.1	163.7	163.4	157.9
1916	22.0	1,023.7	1,346.1	109.0	131.9	168.4	165.7	157.5
1915	27.1	1,340.9	1,987.6	188.4	136.6	173.2	169.0	157.1
1914	26.5	1,753.1	2,791.7	198.5	141.1	173.9	170.6	155.4
1913	13.3	1,380.1	2,161.9	145.0	136.1	169.9	166.5	155.5
1912	15.1	961.5	1,611.8	106.4	142.1	158.6	158.7	153.7
1911	12.4	1,049.4	1,860.3	92.3	148.0	158.5	158.5	153.8
1910	14.8	1,066.1	2,049.4	90.2	142.2	159.0	158.4	153.1
1909	14.9	930.5	2,072.7	156.6	144.7	158.7	158.5	154.6
1908	14.8	—[5]	2,300.7[5]	—[5]	144.9	—[5]	158.6[5]	—[5]
1907	3.8	—	1,417.5	—	153.2	—	159.4	—
1906	8.4	—	1,366.5	—	147.3	—	158.8	—
1905	9.2	—	928.4	—	151.2	—	158.2	—
1904	8.1	—	647.4	—	139.6	—	158.5	—
1903	13.4	—	564.7	—	142.4	—	158.0	—
1902	32.2	—	687.9	—	147.8	—	158.2	—
1901	36.0	—	299.9	—	152.4	—	159.0	—
1900	1.8	—	183.1	—	137.8	—	155.7	—
1899	4.8	—	401.6	—	144.6	—	156.0	—
1898	3.9	—	282.4	—	133.9	—	158.3	—
1897	4.4	—	296.1	—	132.6	—	151.1	—
1896	6.8	—	273.4	—	170.7	—	164.4	—
1895	9.5	—	195.5	—	155.4	—	157.8	—
1894	15.3	—	223.1	—	157.8	—	156.6	—
1893	29.9	—	290.6	—	155.0	—	158.1	—
1892	22.1	—	260.7	—	146.1	—	159.5	—
1891	9.2	—	179.1	—	146.0	—	155.9	—
1890	6.5	—	212.4	—	157.8	—	153.4	—
1889	8.5	—	246.4	—	149.0	—	155.3	—
1888	—	—	269.5	—	—	—	155.7	—
1887	—	—	373.6	—	—	—	160.0	—
1886	—	—	466.9	—	—	—	160.3	—
1885	—	—	272.6	—	—	—	159.2	—
1884	—	—	288.4	—	—	—	159.1	—
1883	—	—	292.7	—	—	—	161.0	—
1882	—	—	64.0	—	—	—	158.4	—
1881	—	—	38.5	—	—	—	154.1	—

Series L14-29. Total acreage patented and average area patented by type of entry, by province, Western provinces, 1881 to 1975 (continued)

Year[1,2]	Pre-emptions				Purchased homesteads			
	Total acreage patented (thousands of acres)		Average area of pre-emptions patented (acres)		Total acreage patented (thousands of acres)		Average area of purchased homesteads patented (acres)	
	Alberta	Saskatchewan	Alberta	Saskatchewan	Alberta[3]	Saskatchewan	Alberta	Saskatchewan
	22	23	24	25	26	27	28	29
1975	–	–	–	–	111.1	–	249.1	–
1974	–	–	–	–	101.9	–	247.9	–
1973	–	–	–	–	96.3	–	250.2	–
1972	–	–	–	–	84.3	–	243.7	–
1971	–	–	–	–	64.7	–	242.4	–
1970	–	–	–	–	100.6	–	253.3	–
1969	–	–	–	–	125.5	–	251.9	–
1968	–	–	–	–	130.7	–	255.8	–
1967	–	–	–	–	99.7	–	251.7	–
1966	–	–	–	–	101.6	–	246.1	–
1965	–	–	–	–	14.0	–	241.6	–
1964	–	–	–	–	9.3	–	233.3	–
1963	–	–	–	–	81.3	–	229.2	–
1962	–	–	–	–	74.8	–	242.1	–
1961	–	–	–	–	67.3	–	237.1	–
1960	–	1.7	–	158.7	.2	.2	160.0	160.0
1959	–	1.0	–	160.0	.2	.2	160.0	161.0
1958	–	2.2	–	155.1	.3	–	326.0	–
1957	–	4.1	–	158.5	18.7	.3	242.6	159.5
1956	–	2.9	–	159.3	80.8	.3	231.4	160.0
1955	–	5.1	–	159.3	58.9	.2	211.7	161.0
1954	–	11.6	–	159.0	43.8	.6	216.7	154.5
1953	–	10.5	–	158.7	34.9	.3	215.3	160.5
1952	–	7.1	–	158.1	17.2	.5	186.6	160.3
1951	–	4.6	–	159.9	19.0	.3	191.7	159.5
1950	–	3.4	–	159.7	13.2	.3	191.4	160.0
1949	.2	13.1	160.0	159.2	.3	.6	160.0	158.5
1948	–	12.1	–	159.2	–	.9	–	151.3
1947	–	–	–	–	–	–	–	–
1946	–	10.0	–	158.9	–	.6	–	156.3
1945	.3	39.0	160.0	159.0	.2	1.8	157.6	152.4
1944	.3	31.7	160.0	159.3	–	1.7	–	156.8
1943	–	11.7	–	157.5	–	.8	–	159.4
1942	.3	4.5	159.0	156.8	–	.9	–	149.7
1941	–	4.4	–	158.0	.3	..6	159.5	160.0
1940	–	3.5	–	158.4	.2	.3	160.0	160.0
1939	.3	1.8	158.5	148.9	–	.2	–	161.0
1938	.5	.6	160.3	157.3	.1	.3	132.9	160.0
1937	.5	2.1	158.4	160.0	–	.2	–	160.0
1936	1.0	1.9	159.8	159.5	.2	.2	160.0	160.0
1935	.9	–	154.5	–	.5	–	152.6	–
1934	.5	.6	160.0	158.8	.1	.2	111.1	160.0
1933	1.1	–	160.0	–	.3	–	158.5	–
1932	.5	–	160.0	–	–	–	–	–
1931[2]	–	–	–	–	–	–	–	–
1931[4]	2.1	9.9	159.8	156.4	.2	.3	160.0	158.5
1930	10.6	58.2	159.8	158.9	1.4	3.9	158.8	146.1
1929	19.9	92.5	158.8	158.1	1.1	7.2	161.0	157.0
1928	16.3	90.6	158.4	158.7	2.1	8.7	159.6	157.9
1927	11.6	75.4	156.2	158.0	1.3	6.5	157.1	157.3
1926	12.0	61.7	157.7	157.9	1.6	7.7	158.0	154.4

Series L14-29. Total acreage patented and average area patented by type of entry, by province, Western provinces, 1881 to 1975 (concluded)

Year[1,2]	Pre-emptions				Purchased homesteads			
	Total acreage patented *(thousands of acres)*		Average area of pre-emptions patented *(acres)*		Total acreage patented *(thousands of acres)*		Average area of purchased homesteads patented *(acres)*	
	Alberta	Saskat-chewan	Alberta	Saskat-chewan	Alberta[3]	Saskat-chewan	Alberta	Saskat-chewan
	22	23	24	25	26	27	28	29
1925	10.8	56.3	158.1	158.5	1.8	6.5	159.6	155.0
1924	15.4	60.4	157.6	158.0	2.1	8.6	149.2	153.3
1923	16.3	71.9	156.7	157.6	3.2	10.7	145.6	151.3
1922	83.4	150.7	158.3	158.3	8.3	17.8	150.0	154.5
1921	169.1	361.6	158.4	158.6	18.1	44.2	154.7	155.6
1920	191.1	584.6	158.7	159.0	23.5	56.8	156.6	155.5
1919	215.4	452.3	158.3	158.8	27.0	64.8	154.5	155.1
1918	384.5	591.6	159.3	159.0	44.5	92.8	157.7	156.4
1917	207.8	359.1	159.0	159.0	39.7	78.0	159.3	156.3
1916	84.7	141.1	158.4	158.5	28.7	56.2	157.6	156.6
1915	43.6	85.0	159.7	158.4	21.4	56.1	158.6	156.7
1914	10.5	39.7	159.4	159.3	16.5	57.3	157.5	158.7
1913	—	—	—	—	—	—	—	—
1913	—	—	—	—	—	—	—	—
1912	—	—	—	—	—	—	—	—
1911	—	—	—	—	—	—	—	—
1910	—	—	—	—	—	—	—	—
1909	—	—	—	—	—	—	—	—
1908	—	—	—	—	—	—	—	—
1907	—	—	—	—	—	—	—	—
1906	—	—	—	—	—	—	—	—
1905	—	—	—	—	—	—	—	—
1904	—	—	—	—	—	—	—	—
1903	—	—	—	—	—	—	—	—
1902	—	—	—	—	—	—	—	—
1901	—	—	—	—	—	—	—	—
1900	—	—	—	—	—	—	—	—
1899	—	—	—	—	—	—	—	—
1898	—	—	—	—	—	—	—	—
1897	—	—	—	—	—	—	—	—
1896	—	—	—	—	—	—	—	—
1895	—	—	—	—	—	—	—	—
1894	—	—	—	—	—	—	—	—
1893	—	—	—	—	—	—	—	—
1892	—	—	—	—	—	—	—	—
1891	—	—	—	—	—	—	—	—
1890	—	—	—	—	—	—	—	—
1889	—	—	—	—	—	—	—	—
1888	—	—	—	—	—	—	—	—
1887	—	—	—	—	—	—	—	—
1886	—	—	—	—	—	—	—	—
1885	—	—	—	—	—	—	—	—
1884	—	—	—	—	—	—	—	—
1883	—	—	—	—	—	—	—	—
1882	—	—	—	—	—	—	—	—
1881	—	—	—	—	—	—	—	—

[1] For 1881 to 1894, departmental years ending 31 October of year given; for 1895 to 1899, calendar years; for 1900, 6 months ending 30 June; for 1901 to 1906, fiscal years ending 30 June of year given; for 1907, 9 months ending 31 March; for 1908 to 1931, fiscal years ending 31 March of year given; for Alberta, 1931 to 1960, fiscal years ending 31 March of year given; for Saskatchewan, 1931 to 1946, fiscal years ending 30 April of year given; for Saskatchewan, 1948 to 1954, fiscal years ending 31 March of year given; for Manitoba, 1932 to 1945, fiscal years ending 30 April of year given.

[2] For 1931 to 1960, data are from the provinces; see the notes.
[3] Notification of title at end of 10-year period. See also series L30-33.
[4] Data are for land patented by the Dominion for this and prior years. Data for 1931 are for 6 months, 1 April 1930 to 30 September 1930 for British Columbia, Alberta and Saskatchewan; for the period 1 April 1930 to 15 July 1930 for Manitoba.
[5] For 1881 to 1908, series L16 and L20 include Alberta, Saskatchewan, Manitoba and the Yukon Territory.

Series L30-33. Land grants, entries and cancellations, number and acreage, by type of grant, Alberta, 1931 to 1975

Year[1]	Entries		Cancellations		Year[1]	Entries		Cancellations	
	Number	Acres	Number	Acres		Number	Acres	Number	Acres
	30	**31**	**32**	**33**		**30**	**31**	**32**	**33**
	Panel A. Homestead and agricultural leases, civilian					*Panel B. Soldier grants and veterans' agricultural leases*			
1975	—	—	3	796	1975	—	—	—	—
1974	—	—	11	3,535	1974	—	—	3	959
1973	—	—	18	4,775	1973	—	—	—	—
1972	—	—	8	2,281	1972	—	—	2	481
1971	—	—	24	6,480	1971	—	—	2	634
1970	—	—	55	16,189	1970	—	—	1	160
1969	—	—	133	35,174	1969	—	—	7	1,762
1968	—	—	301	79,869	1968	—	—	23	5,886
1967	4	957	351	95,601	1967	—	—	34	9,869
1966	18	4,745	352	80,492	1966	1	318	19	5,691
1965	197	44,879	257	70,021	1965	47	12,746	20	5,529
1964	1,168	283,422	264	57,113	1964	103	29,219	25	7,380
1963	451	119,890	230	59,964	1963	50	14,524	30	8,006
1962	419	110,127	298	75,989	1962	38	11,013	54	15,862
1961	250	63,774	292	74,803	1961	13	3,091	40	10,672
1960	439	149,757	578	149,229	1960	23	6,405	88	24,632
1959	233	58,115	441	149,821	1959	20	6,335	57	16,521
1958	333	84,267	473	123,756	1958	33	9,054	127	38,930
1957	564	144,138	509	127,923	1957	50	14,035	87	23,973
1956	783	197,114	674	165,308	1956	91	24,987	119	35,597
1955	791	204,700	673	168,004	1955	111	30,201	88	24,476
1954	747	193,146	505	129,172	1954	112	32,271	101	28,083
1953	869	222,770	413	106,778	1953	130	37,505	105	29,950
1952	1,037	261,314	518	125,676	1952	194	54,943	100	27,438
1951	1,156	286,056	364[2]	83,633[3]	1951	334	93,712	211	59,311
1950	992	228,044	273[2]	54,041[3]	1950	252	71,147	100	24,686
1949	754	166,817	290[2]	49,276[3]	1949	202	54,037	85	21,147
1948	985	219,595	413[2]	53,965[3]	1948	561	138,473	114	26,021
1947	283	50,227	417[2]	29,691[3]	1947	906	242,615	35	8,278
1946	330	64,522	567[2]	22,344[3]	1946	40	9,144	2	480
1945	312	59,742	625[2]	14,284[3]	1945	—	—	—	—
1944	208	37,714	990[2]	17,435[3]	1944	—	—	—	—
1943	170	29,982	931[2]	9,568[3]	1943	—	—	—	—
1942	200	—	928[4]	—	1942	—	—	—	—
1941	224	—	1,119[4]	—	1941	—	—	—	—
1940	25[5]	—	1,648[4]	—	1940	—	—	—	—
1939	1,350	—	2,345[4]	—	1939	3	—	—	—
1938	1,590	—	2,663[4]	—	1938	10	—	—	—
1937	1,425	—	1,914[4]	—	1937	7	—	—	—
1936	1,515	—	1,816[4]	—	1936	13	—	—	—
1935	2,750	—	—	—	1935	30	—	—	—
1934	3,680	—	—	—	1934	26	—	—	—
1933	2,300	—	1,633[4]	—	1933	23	—	—	—
1932	2,547	—	1,302[4]	—	1932	19	—	—	—
1931	2,229	—	—	—	1931	81	—	—	—

[1] For fiscal year ending 31 March of the year given.
[2] For 1943 to 1951 includes homestead and soldier grant cancellations.
[3] Acreage for cancellation of agricultural leases only. The figures given are for 359 cancellations in 1951, 252 in 1950, 229 in 1949, 225 in 1948, 155 in 1947, 118 in 1946, 83 in 1945, 100 in 1944 and 58 in 1943.

[4] For 1932 to 1942 the data are for total entries cancelled.
[5] Includes some soldier grants. Homestead grants were discontinued in 1939. See the note to series K14-29 (first edition).

Series L34-41. Land grants, number of entries and cancellations by province and type of grant, Western provinces, 1872 to 1931

Year[1]	British Columbia		Alberta		Saskatchewan		Manitoba	
	Entries	Cancellations	Entries	Cancellations	Entries	Cancellations	Entries	Cancellations
	34	35	36	37	38	39	40	41

Panel A. Homesteads

Year[1]	Entries	Cancellations	Entries	Cancellations	Entries	Cancellations	Entries	Cancellations
1931	574	111	7,122	2,428	2,834	1,219	454	381
1930	893	202	9,795	3,823	6,089	2,261	727	552
1929	773	161	8,933	2,741	5,808	1,717	643	654
1928	173	262	3,411	2,203	2,961	1,522	688	1,034
1927	116	153	2,145	1,489	2,702	1,330	797	547
1926	150	131	1,556	1,211	2,363	1,312	616	746
1925	193	119	1,192	1,552	1,804	1,475	464	1,025
1924	186	207	1,326	1,722	1,699	1,499	632	759
1923	153	236	2,207	2,652	2,104	2,278	879	1,895
1922	200	207	2,928	3,383	2,733	2,370	1,488	1,846
1921	120	208	2,874	3,365	1,670	2,360	725	1,403
1920	134	166	3,448	3,673	1,918	2,389	1,232	1,663
1919	54	140	2,169	1,946	1,191	1,100	813	929
1918	177	180	3,808	2,813	2,741	2,193	1,593	1,128
1917	268	333	4,550	4,101	4,105	3,558	2,276	1,578
1916	413	267	6,410	5,149	6,247	5,722	3,960	1,593
1915	802	435	10,076	5,432	8,790	4,953	4,420	1,694
1914	1,931	350	12,208	6,615	14,504	7,662	3,186	1,370
1913	375	292	12,942	6,694	17,556	8,288	2,826	2,006
1912	325	—[2]	15,184	—[2]	20,484	—[2]	3,158	18,608 [2]
1911	206	—	15,964	—	25,227	—	3,082	22,122
1910	277	—	17,187	—	21,575	—	2,529	16,832
1909	429	—	13,771	—	21,120	—	3,761	14,677
1908	237	—	9,614	—	18,825	—	1,748	15,668
1907	72	—	6,843	—	13,501	—	1,231	14,110
1906	108	—	12,263	—	27,692	—	1,806	11,637
1905[3]	187	—	9,138	—	19,787	—	1,707	11,296
1904	208	—	8,201	—	15,659	—	2,005	8,702
1903	120	—	8,069	—	19,941	—	3,253	5,208
1902	117	—	5,681	—	6,612	—	2,263	3,296
1901	86	—	3,806	—	2,332	—	1,933	1,682
1900	80	—	2,470	—	2,703	—	2,154	1,096
1899	17	—	1,745	—	2,159	—	2,124	1,746
1898	41	—	1,049	—	960	—	1,426	1,546
1897	17	—	230	—	301	—	609	1,090
1896	91	—	411	—	362	—	993	1,165
1895	67	—	1,000	—	461	—	866	1,222
1894	—	—	—	—	—	—	3,209[4]	1,558
1893	119	—	1,513	—	1,159	—	1,276	—
1892	97	—	1,257	—	1,797	—	1,687	—
1891	160	—	784	—	930	—	1,651	—
1890	272	—	524	—	758	—	1,401	—
1889	431	—	504	—	1,242	—	2,225	1,337
1888	295	—	230	—	425	—	1,665	935
1887	356	—	271[5]	—	356[6]	—	1,053[7]	633
1886	—	—	—	—	—	—	2,657[4,8]	1,033
1885	—	—	—	—	—	—	1,858[4]	—
1884	—	—	—	—	—	—	3,753[4]	1,334
1883	—	—	—	—	—	—	6,063[4]	—
1882	—	—	—	—	1,121	—	6,262	—
1881	—	—	—	—	23	—	2,730	—
1880	—	—	—	—	—	—	2,074[4]	—
1879	—	—	—	—	—	—	4,068[4]	—
1878	—	—	—	—	—	—	1,788[4]	—
1877	—	—	—	—	—	—	845[4]	—
1876	—	—	—	—	—	—	347[4]	—
1875	—	—	—	—	—	—	499[4]	—
1874	—	—	—	—	—	—	1,376[4]	—
1873	—	—	—	—	—	—	878[9]	—
1872	—	—	—	—	—	—	283[9]	—

Series L34-41. Land grants, number of entries and cancellations by province and type of grant, Western provinces, 1872 to 1931 (concluded)

Year[1]	British Columbia		Alberta		Saskatchewan		Manitoba	
	Entries	Cancellations	Entries	Cancellations	Entries	Cancellations	Entries	Cancellations
	34	35	36	37	38	39	40	41
				Panel B. Soldier grants				
1931	49	23	339	203	108	106	10	173
1930	55	29	422	365	224	199	19	153
1929	52	11	413	285	249	204	28	124
1928	27	23	216	383	226	201	35	212
1927	21	16	184	190	217	238	46	130
1926	27	8	183	182	296	209	70	111
1925	29	7	195	253	280	220	80	135
1924	32	13	187	230	349	242	142	145
1923	46	—	328	—	370	—	468	—
1922	68	—	614	—	590	—	383	—
1921	58	—	1,171	—	1,188	—	475	—
1920	117	—	2,739	—	1,996	—	1,129	—
1919	—	—	501	—	—	—	—	—
			Panel C. South African veterans' grants				
1914	—	—	61	—	48	—	1	—
1913	—	—	97	—	79	—	—	—
1912	—	—	857	—	920	—	6	—
1911	—	—	778	—	1,185	—	10	—
1910	—	—	1,300	—	1,530	—	22	—
1909	—	—	179	—	166	—	—	—

[1] For 1872 to 1894, departmental years ending 31 October of year given; for 1895 to 1899, calendar years; for 1900, 6 months ending 30 June; for 1901 to 1906, fiscal years ending 30 June of year given; for 1907, 9 months ending 31 March; for 1908 to 1931, fiscal years ending 31 March of year given.

[2] Total homestead entries cancelled entered under Manitoba where available, 1884 to 1912.

[3] See note (in the first edition) for the division of entries by province prior to 1906.

[4] Total homestead entries for provinces and territories.

[5] Includes 2 military bounty warrants.

[6] Includes 22 military bounty warrants.

[7] Includes 21 military bounty warrants.

[8] Includes 561 military homesteads of 320 acres each.

[9] Includes certain entries from the territories.

Series L42-45. Pre-emptions and purchased homesteads, number of entries and cancellations by province, Alberta and Saskatchewan, 1874 to 1931

Panel A. Pre-emptions

Year[1]	Alberta Entries (42)	Alberta Cancellations (43)	Saskatchewan Entries (44)	Saskatchewan Cancellations (45)
1931	—	75	—	47
1930	—	177	—	177
1929	—	246	—	402
1928	—	546	—	740
1927	—	518	—	914
1926	—	613	—	863
1925	—	1,199	—	1,103
1924	—	301	—	823
1923	—	218	—	673
1922	—	149	—	490
1921	—	232	—	557
1920	—	297	—	521
1919	—	199	—	301
1918	220	482	547	708
1917	452	655	1,008	1,092
1916	578	775	1,662	1,313
1915	737	937	2,108	1,517
1914	1,604	1,440	4,560	2,509
1913	2,935	2,336	5,642	3,074
1912	3,682	—[2]	6,929	6,103[2]
1911	5,680	—	9,938	7,095
1910	7,759	—	9,533	3,463
1909	4,560	—	9,501	260
1908	—	—	—	32
1907	—	—	—	8
1906	—	—	—	38
1905	—	—	—	48
1904	—	—	—	96
1903	—	—	—	174
1902	—	—	—	242
1901	—	—	—	202
1900	—	—	—	155
1899	—	—	—	299
1898	—	—	—	382
1897	—	—	—	245
1896	—	—	—	255
1895	—	—	—	263
1894	—	—	—	411
1893	—	—	—	—
1892	—	—	—	—
1891	—	—	—	—
1890	—[3]	—	371[3]	—
1889	—	—	1,355	829
1888	—	—	454	1,892
1887	—	—	585	497
1886	—	—	1,046	637
1885	—	—	653	—
1884	—	—	2,762	972
1883	—	—	4,120	—
1882	—	—	5,654	—
1881	—	—	1,649	—
1880	—	—	1,004	—
1879	—	—	1,729	—
1878	—	—	1,580	—
1877	—	—	594	—
1876	—	—	263	—
1875	—	—	391	—
1874	—	—	643	—

Panel B. Purchased homesteads

Year[1]	Alberta Entries (42)	Alberta Cancellations (43)	Saskatchewan Entries (44)	Saskatchewan Cancellations (45)
1931	—	7	—	6
1930	—	10	—	19
1929	—	13	—	25
1928	—	27	—	49
1927	—	28	—	73
1926	—	24	—	56
1925	—	49	—	63
1924	—	18	—	75
1923	—	8	—	35
1922	—	9	—	29
1921	—	16	—	24
1920	—	11	—	4
1919	—	2	—	13
1918	67	12	124	46
1917	106	33	156	65
1916	92	31	210	50
1915	117	49	233	73
1914	239	61	517	97
1913	340	60	740	104
1912	365	—[4]	1,043	175[4]
1911	487	—	1,273	163
1910	359	—	897	49
1909	208	—	623	21

[1] For 1874 to 1894, year ending 31 October of year given; for 1895 to 1899, calendar year; for 1900, 6 months ending 30 June; for 1901 to 1906, fiscal year ending 30 June of year given; for 1907, 9 months ending 31 March; for 1908 to 1931, fiscal year ending 31 March of year given.

[2] Pre-emption cancellations 1874 to 1912, for Alberta and Saskatchewan included in series L45.

[3] Pre-emption entries 1874 to 1890, for Alberta and Saskatchewan included in series L44.

[4] Purchased homestead cancellations, 1909 to 1912, for Alberta and Saskatchewan included in series L45.

Series L46-56. Land sales and cancellations, school lands and other provincial lands, by province, Prairie provinces, 1931 to 1975
(series L48 and 55 in dollars; others in acres)

Year[1]	Alberta				Saskatchewan			Manitoba			
	Public land sales	School land sales		Total cancelled sales	Provincial land sales	School land sales	Total cancelled sales	Provincial land sales	School land sales		Total cancelled sales
		Number of acres	Value						Number of acres	Value	
	46	47	48	49	50	51	52	53	54	55	56
1975	3,148	—	—	1,682	369,099	—	—	—	—	—	—
1974	1,044	—	—	639	..	—	—	—	—	—	—
1973	1,389	—	—	561	527,293	—	—	—	—	—	—
1972	3,390	—	—	812	643,154	—	—	—	—	—	—
1971	2,987	—	—	484	709,722	—	—	—	—	—	—
1970	11,226	—	—	1,005	731,867	—	—	—	—	—	—
1969	24,693	—	—	1,520	761,889	—	—	—	—	—	—
1968	18,307	—	—	1,164	665,387	—	—	—	—	—	—
1967	25,620	—	—	1,735	626,715	—	—	—	—	—	—
1966	53,107	—	—	1,403	517,266	—	—	—	—	—	—
1965	42,440	—	—	1,324	284,064	—	17,316	—	—	—	—
1964	35,942	—	—	4,273	290,066	—	42,440	8,151	—	—	189,470
1963	11,933	—	—	2,125	255,846	—	58,042	16,459	—	—	41,359
1962	27,508	18,874	—	3,520	—	—	—	11,592	—	—	8,072
1961	30,133	31,173	—	2,075	—	—	—	3,140	—	—	—
1960	13,800	13,592	—	7,284	1,371	221	639	5,645	—	—	—
1959	7,765	22,423	97,296	9,609	2,150	196	1,120	9,319	—	—	—
1958	12,967	16,740	—	26,204	1,005	156	1,710	7,521	—	—	—
1957	14,288	18,177	—	8,416	1,246	555	3,186	7,121	—	—	2,840
1956	20,291	18,170	—	3,364	3,846[2]	2,483[2]	18,515[2]	6,008	165	1,651	1,963
1955	31,414	24,667	—	4,936	6,197	4,352	14,061	15,341	1,354	17,766	—
1954	38,017	28,759	—	1,620	19,552[3]	122,165[3]	46,596	37,298	13,574	97,483	—
1953	20,871	31,941	—	2,622	38,723[4]	2,228	11,434[2]	86,038	15,581	150,598	—
1952	85,339	98,664	—	937	9,903	4,664	7,015	98,347	53,521	451,797	—
1951	14,551	58,185	—	633	19,644	9,423	9,974	62,995	29,913	261,888	162
1950	32,619	61,456	—	—	30,588	29,625	6,211	93,629	14,359	119,878	320
1949	7,031	34,212	378,286	860	30,111	74,295[2]	7,353	52,562	7,863	60,123	1,235
1948	5,338	—	5,431	381[5]	164,641[2,6]	280	15,162	36,248	18,933	147,183	720
1947	8,816	—	16,275	622[5]	—	—	—	27,953	21,417	226,307	573
1946	7,088	—	17,692	216[5]	1,295	269	13,872	579	170	1,467	851
1945	8,970	—	31,357	127[5]	2,380	170	12,449	776	59	634	2,887
1944	—	—	2,985	—	2,371	73	—	2,197	3	6	3,316
1943	—	872	8,770	—	2,088	129	5,426	6,364	42	359	4,314
1942	—	845	—	—	3,071	84	15,219	17,963	29	293	5,672
1941	—	—	—	—	8,094	91	—	21,198	54	537	4,636
1940	—	2,604	—	—	19,389	118	31,298	27,182	657	5,323	4,573
1939	—	—	—	—	23,612	48	22,425	32,185	4,590	31,534	2,825
1938	—	120	—	—	20,081	38	22,907	32,885	11,065	92,726	3,791
1937	—	5,591	—	—	14,231	24	45,290	13,431	336	2,960	5,527
1936	—	338[7]	—	—	31,163	122	44,747	11,483	488	3,288	6,006
1935	—	—	—	—	—	—	—	37,810	2,029	12,908	14,619
1934	—	—	—	—	6,211	1,066	80,987	20,125	1,109	7,613	38,896
1933	—	—	—	—	—	—	—	14,738	21	211	16,309
1932	—	—	—	—	—	—	—[8]	17,558	135	1,544	18,595
1931	—	—	—	—	—	—	—	5,360	—	—	9,305

[1] For Alberta, 1931 to 1960, fiscal years ending 31 March of year given; for Saskatchewan, 1931 to 1946, fiscal years ending 30 April of year given; for Saskatchewan, 1948 to 1960, fiscal years ending 31 March of year given; for Manitoba, 1931 to 1946, fiscal years ending 30 April of year given; for Manitoba, 1947, 11 months ending 31 March; for Manitoba, 1948 to 1960, fiscal years ending 31 March of year given.
[2] For 1948 to 1956, series L50-51 include veterans' cultivation leases; for 1953 to 1956, series L52 includes terminations of such leases.

[3] Includes lands added to existing veterans' cultivation leases and changes in acreage from unbroken to cultivated lands.
[4] Includes 29,127 acres held in individual veterans' cultivation leases but farmed co-operatively, existing before fiscal 1953 but not accounted for in previous reports.
[5] Public land sales cancellations only.
[6] Includes veterans' cultivation leases of school lands.
[7] Total area sold since the transfer of resources, 30 September 1930.
[8] 545 sales cancelled, no acreage given.

Series L57-64. Land sales, school land and miscellaneous, by province, Prairie provinces, and school land cancellations, Alberta, 1905 to 1931

Year[1]	Alberta Cash, time, drainage, irrigation, etc. (acres)	Alberta School lands Number of acres	Value (dollars)	Cancelled sales (acres)	Saskatchewan School lands Number of acres	Value (dollars)	Manitoba School lands Number of acres	Value (dollars)
	57	58	59	60	61	62	63	64
1931[2]	7,056	14,674	166,887	5,804	293	2,241	6,318	75,147
1930	5,825	28,677	345,992	16,918	372,011	5,435,354	4,231	50,403
1929	11,221	299,393	4,266,713	26,052	357,412	4,608,151	12	97
1928	7,059	210,933	3,556,164	27,105	276,800	5,446,630	41	296
1927	6,600	69	877	33,583	482	6,611	451	3,444
1926	9,243	271	4,606	40,387	563	7,293	32	245
1925	6,204	50	1,129	38,378	222	2,951	117	753
1924	4,575	422	6,974	33,807	356	3,998	458	1,629
1923	4,727	145	2,391	28,285	4,155	54,601	332	4,274
1922	13,164	4,985	75,997	23,988	35,341	475,031	4,065	41,566
1921	5,897	122,536	2,165,850	19,381	84,405	1,234,058	10,463	130,975
1920	8,430	12	128	13,144	83	948	86	864
1919	84,533	90,310	1,570,557	6,888	535,066	12,060,096	132	1,212
1918	23,501	96,860	1,906,282	3,576	214,743	4,154,276	16,073	182,982
1917	38,502	144,993	2,039,037	4,568	116,695	1,664,234	37,370	352,539
1916	19,481	146	2,246	3,067	1,174	17,222	142	1,676
1915	26,227	73	2,153	3,820	359	5,802	14	190
1914	53,723	375	10,711	1,593	701	15,155	40	285
1913	106,591	2,375	111,240	320	103,593	2,003,528	64,539	711,147
1912	105,271	373	5,403	365	1,517	48,421	203	4,209
1911	295,306	182,384	2,216,912	366	304,581	4,568,722	670	15,438
1910	143,539	235,013	2,571,430	160	14,777	235,811	80,291	773,471
1909	79,901	723	10,381	160	540	6,320	121	1,545
1908	91,695	10,239	99,485	160	1,388	26,325	103,092	1,066,860
1907[1]	80,116	—	—	320	11,801	173,155	125,087	1,526,546
1906[1]	83,867	127,706	1,491,821	—	26,663	381,714	692	8,570
1905[3]	—	1,791	49,940	300	145,906	1,423,087	271,384	2,181,067

[1] Fiscal years ending 31 March of year given, 1908 to 1931, 9 months ending 31 March 1907, and fiscal year ending 30 June 1906.

[2] For 6 months, 1 April 1930 to 30 September 1930 for Alberta and Saskatchewan, series L57-62; for Manitoba, series L63-64, 1 April 1930 to 15 July 1930.

[3] Cumulative sales prior to 1 September 1905.

Series L65-72. Land grants and sales, by province, Ontario and Quebec, 1867 to 1975
(acres granted or sold)

Year[1]	Ontario Grants Acres located, free grant townships	Locations by returned soldiers	Ontario Sales Agricultural and townsite lands	University lands	School lands	Quebec Free grants	Crown and clergy lands sold	Cancellations of sales
	65	66	67	68	69	70	71	72
1975	—	—	..	—	—	—	—	—
1974	—	—	..	—	—	—	—	—
1973	—	—	..	—	—	—	—	—
1972	—	—	..	—	—	—	—	—
1971	—	—	3,641	—	—	—	—	—
1970	—	—	2,662	—	—	—	—	—
1969	—	—	4,966	—	—	—	—	—
1968	—	—	2,341	—	—	—	—	—
1967	—	—	1,585	—	—	—	—	—
1966	—	—	2,633	—	—	—	—	—
1965	—	—	2,838	—	—	—	—	—
1964	—	—	3,042	—	—	—	—	—
1963	—	—	3,911	—	—	—	—	—
1962	—	—	5,106	—	—	—	—	—
1961	—	—	14,530	—	—	—	—	—

Series L65-72. Land grants and sales, by province, Ontario and Quebec, 1867 to 1975 (continued)
(acres granted or sold)

Year[1]	Ontario					Quebec		
	Grants		Sales			Free grants	Crown and clergy lands sold	Cancellations of sales
	Acres located, free grant townships	Locations by returned soldiers	Agricultural and townsite lands	University lands	School lands			
	65	66	67	68	69	70	71	72
1960	386	156	12,341	—	—	—	—	—
1959	462	—	14,894	—	—	—	—	—
1958	—	797	16,772	—	—	—	—	—
1957	261	617	11,827	—	—	—	—	—
1956	2,709[2]	—[2]	21,341	—	—	—	—	—
1955	1,823	—	21,866	—	—	—	—	—
1954	2,757	—	20,918	—	—	—	—	—
1953	4,656	—	29,751	—	—	—	—	—
1952	3,411	—	32,809	—	—	—	—	—
1951	3,608	—	26,056	—	—	—	—	—
1950	6,193	—	58,903	—	—	—	—	—
1949	5,873	—	51,688	—	—	—	—	—
1948	—	—	—	—	—	—	—	—
1947	8,244	—	46,030	—	—	—	—	—
1946	5,737	—	45,173	—	—	—	—	—
1945	2,309[2]	—[2]	65,660	—	—	—	—	—
1944	2,694	—	38,812	—	—	—	—	—
1943	2,069	471	22,113	—	—	1,894	203,413	185,956
1942	5,921	501	17,570	—	—	607	216,849	186,253
1941	15,883	726	28,838	—	—	378	197,397	140,212
1940	22,640	1,158	38,009	396	—	1,529	290,976	206,797
1939	33,638	1,296	38,000	323	—	2,630	459,846	290,903
1938	36,763	2,846	38,811	355	—	664	390,359	369,527
1937	37,514	4,604	45,387	1,049	—	31	401,882	226,551
1936	58,965	5,449	61,070	719	—	1,352	275,593	358,827
1935	21,071	3,784	39,824	520	50	1,972	362,593	165,300
1934	48,152	10,897	82,857	1,746	—	4,202	556,606	253,679
1933	75,274	13,114	78,825	570	100	4,943	201,876	140,410
1932	70,269	11,586	83,029	1,261	375	3,387	211,981	153,661
1931	58,460	6,247	92,278	642	349	2,944	197,442	116,325
1930	62,891	—	113,129	—	573	1,882	162,814	121,461
1929	56,577	—	66,922	314	—	2,028	145,371	107,130
1928	43,279	—	83,772	499	—	1,451	156,897	97,278
1927	57,297	—	110,542	639	—	1,502	167,864	49,812
1926	65,733	—	86,220	657	—	3,781	175,511	100,360
1925	69,643	—	117,488	1,798	—	2,702	183,896	77,683
1924	98,487	—	173,643	3,710	—	3,289	174,291	89,751
1923	90,143	—	113,032	3,063	—	5,146	212,615	66,328
1922	135,656	—	132,188	2,155	369	5,229	216,133	65,818
1921	118,638	—	139,027	836	58	1,313	177,313	100,301
1920	88,814	—	72,591	721	297	184	197,226	207,977
1919	72,421	—	49,704	120	72	94	186,085	175,362
1918	54,183	—	51,401	1,288	339	59	297,409	75,646
1917	78,193	—	109,304	2,075	—	263	256,477	96,396
1916	85,139	—	98,209	2,968	50	150	207,380	103,658
1915	185,021	—	146,307	5,230	20	350	206,565	80,490
1914	258,371	—	137,666	6,047	25	689	202,587	97,466
1913	221,255	—	202,088	10,485	121	1,280	194,091	62,307
1912	237,152	—	349,319	11,891	3	1,205	179,130	68,095
1911	224,042	—	118,573	5,627	—	1,984	119,465	67,340
1910	194,760	—	92,560	4,020	37	775	124,849	91,315
1909	196,603	—	78,658	3,740	151	615	220,645	41,842
1908	297,543	—	74,912	3,110	157	650	292,479	86,431
1907	180,864	—	79,419	1,740	104	916	227,031	110,726
1906	126,085	—	69,861	1,412	107	322	195,736	112,053
1905	143,716	—	72,432	1,978	397	9,350	189,883	58,853
1904	152,699	—	72,781	2,731	624	11,038	135,752	43,481
1903	201,042	—	30,466	3,741	100	8,026	150,638	46,506
1902	193,070	—	66,868	5,722	421	10,200	190,231	40,779
1901	148,312	—	43,617	5,787	59	12,600	186,090	35,545
1900	132,665	—	65,996[3]	4,336	255	9,599	163,528	31,572
1899	85,194	—	69,279	3,953	273	11,450	149,971	72,053
1898	102,947	—	50,231	6,885	215	10,631	190,195	73,578
1897	91,910	—	60,148	6,010[4]	331	12,346	184,667	40,584
1896	95,476	—	49,471	793[4]	205	31,869	129,604	37,044
1895	100,040	—	35,209	969	1,119	26,814	167,708	39,912
1894	99,435	—	28,048	2,047	558	31,650	149,667	46,751
1893	57,440	—	28,136	889	413	37,646	156,925	40,534
1892	59,733	—	30,436	974	682	15,898	102,252	25,674
1891	79,948	—	71,855	7,740	356	2,117	137,829	38,203

Series L65-72. Land grants and sales, by province, Ontario and Quebec, 1867 to 1975 (concluded)
(acres granted or sold)

Year[1]	Ontario					Quebec		
	Grants		Sales			Free grants	Crown and clergy lands sold	Cancellations of sales
	Acres located, free grant townships	Locations by returned soldiers	Agricultural and townsite lands	University lands	School lands			
	65	**66**	**67**	**68**	**69**	**70**	**71**	**72**
1890	83,273	—	50,045	9,407	755	200	129,014	31,710
1889	114,050	—	53,640	2,874[4]	505	3,281	120,178	41,910
1888	109,002	—	52,962	—	737	2,093	107,260	27,779
1887	122,772	—	67,315	—	898	3,444	100,862	55,168
1886	162,734	—	55,641	—	940	3,474	101,788	25,504
1885	176,351	—	99,919	—	1,639	3,045	119,894	34,734
1884	161,964	—	61,189	—	1,067	6,099	135,241	77,365
1883	134,594	—	69,357	—	1,312	8,232	207,526	60,302
1882	129,535	—	98,814	—	2,514	7,901	219,368	36,226
1881	153,764	—	88,543	—	2,587	7,041	179,562	32,260
1880	—	—	621,162[5]	—	1,002[6]	9,027	129,768	69,761
1879	—	—	—	—	1,463	17,424	180,886	74,008
1878	—	—	—	—	2,300	7,962	139,134	63,766
1877	—	—	—	—	3,551	5,790	83,123	—
1876	—	—	—	—	2,238	3,606	73,185	—
1875	—	—	—	—	1,944	4,015	91,179	—
1874	—	—	—	—	3,584	4,271	109,609	—
1873	—	—	—	—	4,909	7,130	131,496	—
1872	—	—	—	—	2,068	11,212	174,592	—
1871	—	—	—	—	3,702[6]	21,302	169,155	—
1870	—	—	105,704[3,7]	—	3,256[8]	8,051[1]	159,849[1]	—
1869	—	—	—	—	6,183	—	—	—
1868	—	—	—	—	4,323	10,502[1]	220,687[1]	—
1867	—	—	—	—	5,581[8]	—	—	—

[1] For Ontario: for 1867 to 1908, calendar years; for 1909, 10 months ending 31 October; for 1910 to 1934, fiscal years ending 31 October of the year given; for 1935, 5 months ending 31 March; for 1936 to 1960, fiscal years ending 31 March of the year given. For Quebec: for 1868, 18 months ending 31 December 1868; for 1870, 18 months, 1 January 1869 to 30 June 1870; for 1871 to 1940, fiscal years ending 30 June of the year given; for 1941, 9 months ending 31 March 1941; for 1942 and 1943, fiscal years ending 31 March of the year given.

[2] For 1945 to 1956, 'Locations by returned soldiers' are included in series L65, 'Acres located, free grant townships'.

[3] For 1867 to 1900, series L67 includes mining lands.

[4] For 1897, includes 97 acres of railway lands. For 1889 to 1896, series L68 designated railway lands.

[5] Total for 1871 to 1880.

[6] For 1871 to 1880, common school lands only; total grammar school lands sold comprised 47,303 acres.

[7] Total for 1867 to 1870.

[8] For 1867 to 1870, common school lands only; total grammar school lands sold comprised 7,155 acres.

Series L73-74. Sales of Indian lands, acreage and value, Canada, 1874 to 1966
(series L73 in acres; series L74 in dollars)

Year[1]	Acreage	Value	Year[1]	Acreage	Value	Year[1]	Acreage	Value
	73	74		73	74		73	74
1966	—	165,018	1935	7,422	58,382	1900	52,455	51,115
			1934	6,535	37,790	1899	65,632	41,971
			1933	3,559	49,986	1898	14,168	27,318
			1932	2,948	54,594	1897	14,451	12,521
			1931	3,508	22,285	1896	17,759	21,052
1965	—	66,096	1930	29,222	452,664	1895	32,206	72,423
1964	—	50,269	1929	19,740	204,388	1894	41,297	76,419
1963	—	103,296	1928	11,480	113,957	1893	25,693	72,215
1962	—	41,003	1927	50,959	206,946	1892	22,817	45,185
1961	—	328,732	1926	24,571	224,713	1891	18,951	26,477
1960	—	1,408,334	1925	21,623	36,710	1890	6,731	22,951
1959	—	1,083,313	1924	16,480	72,651	1889	15,322	22,345
1958	—	255,704	1923	6,898	64,955	1888	21,345	30,345
1957	—	..	1922	5,804	58,207	1887	28,806	39,347
1956	—[2]	809,946	1921	32,492	127,592	1886	10,132	12,862
1955	—	211,032	1920	114,819	1,088,899	1885	9,629	13,183
1954	—	714,109	1919	19,010	104,657	1884	24,177	44,610
1953	—	42,576	1918	34,545	136,231	1883	32,412	31,557
1952	—	666,415	1917	35,121	76,387	1882	48,903	54,192
1951	—	49,597	1916	29,348	66,741	1881	33,294	52,787
1950	—	38,174	1915	15,268	142,969	1880	96,239	67,157
1949	—	—	1914	4,510	218,411	1879	61,997	45,115
1948	—	709,362	1913	7,835	132,513	1878	73,364	54,555
1947	—	249,001	1912	83,496	1,219,474	1877	43,813	75,244
1946	—	65,238	1911	52,331	678,568	1876	37,357	86,799
1945	—	172,812	1910	81,603	952,043	1875	33,650	38,065
1944	—	45,068	1909	64,924	462,682	1874	29,074	—
1943	—	72,028	1908	40,163	167,777			
1942	—[2]	45,441	1907	80,358	422,086			
1941	11,782	71,295	1906	38,033	365,684			
1940	5,472	39,934	1905	33,840	56,981			
1939	—	—	1904	67,965	62,943			
1938	—	44,611	1903	109,350	279,294			
1937	—	78,665	1902	103,461	160,520			
1936	14,650	134,233	1901	40,720	45,135			

[1] For 1874 to 1906, fiscal years ending 30 June of the year given; for 1907, 9 months ending 31 March 1907; for 1908 to 1956, fiscal years ending 31 March of the year given.

[2] For 1942 to 1956, acreage not given.

Series L75-90. Land sales by railway companies having Dominion land grants, and the Hudson's Bay Company, 1893 to 1930

(areas in thousands of acres, values in thousands of dollars)

Year[1]	Hudson's Bay Company		Canadian Pacific Railway Company		Manitoba South Western Colonization Railway Company		Calgary and Edmonton Railway Company		Great North West Central Railway Company		Canadian Northern Railway Company		Qu'Appelle, Long Lake and Saskatchewan Railroad and Steamboat Company		Total	
	Area	Value	Area	Value	Area	Value	Area	Value	Area	Value	Area	Value	Area	Value	Area	Value
	75	76	77	78	79	80	81	82	83	84	85	86	87	88	89	90
1930	216.0	2,090.5	255.2	3,145.5	6.9	49.5	6.0	68.4	3.8	39.0	67.5	934.9	7.7	32.9	563.1	6,360.6
1929	289.9	3,349.6	447.6	4,902.6	8.3	61.1	17.6	200.0	7.5	82.4	83.5	1,189.8	5.4	73.2	859.8	9,858.7
1928	289.7	3,546.6	387.0	4,349.8	4.9	46.3	17.2	205.7	9.2	93.6	67.7	924.0	7.9	93.8	783.6	9,259.8
1927	282.7	3,414.5	249.5	2,980.0	3.7	27.0	8.7	96.8	4.5	47.5	107.5	1,586.9	10.0	143.0	666.5	8,295.7
1926	184.6	2,276.1	169.0	2,263.9	3.7	31.0	10.1	93.6	3.7	45.9	79.1	1,128.0	7.6	115.6	457.8	5,954.2
1925	84.8	1,117.6	91.3	1,602.5	1.7	13.9	8.5	132.5	2.2	35.2	57.0	770.7	1.9	28.6	247.4	3,700.9
1924	33.4	456.4	45.9	775.2	.6	3.8	1.3	14.1	.8	14.9	71.5	1,103.4	6.2	92.1	159.8	2,460.1
1923	25.0	366.3	83.5	1,249.0	.4	5.1	1.0	15.6	1.1	21.6	11.2	190.1	1.1	17.0	123.3	1,864.6
1922	33.6	545.6	101.5	1,732.4	1.5	15.5	3.0	51.6	.2	4.0	14.2	263.2	1.3	22.3	155.2	2,633.6
1921	178.3	3,037.4	275.6	5,899.0	1.5	20.1	11.7	191.9	5.1	96.6	69.9	1,455.3	11.4	160.5	553.6	10,860.8
1920	276.6	4,724.9	571.6	11,356.1	4.6	56.8	27.0	425.7	28.0	464.6	86.3	1,685.2	32.1	474.9	1,026.2	19,188.2
1919	285.6	4,979.0	602.6	10,580.7	5.3	67.2	31.8	479.5	14.5	252.8	65.1	1,262.0	33.8	527.7	1,038.7	18,148.7
1918	386.4	6,914.9	545.3	11,044.9	25.9	321.0	53.3	815.6	16.0	275.7	39.5	732.4	49.7	783.1	1,116.2	20,887.6
1917	254.9	4,234.2	405.8	6,612.4	12.5	165.2	33.8	573.9	8.8	141.4	17.8	298.9	21.5	331.6	755.2	12,357.4
1916	79.3	1,273.1	242.2	3,670.4	4.8	58.8	11.7	172.0	4.6	81.2	—	—	12.2	180.4	354.9	5,435.9
1915	16.4	306.6	151.3	2,496.9	.5	5.5	23.0	444.0	.3	7.0	—	—	1.3	19.1	192.8	3,279.0
1914	26.3	572.8	264.0	4,242.1	7.6	91.9	19.6	460.1	—	—	182.5	2,009.6	1.6	21.5	501.6	7,398.2
1913	53.6	1,128.9	447.2	6,348.4	2.8	48.6	4.2	44.2	1.6	32.1	182.5	2,009.6	15.4	255.4	707.1	9,867.2
1912	42.6	808.9	855.3	12,420.5	18.9	117.5	10.9	154.4	.6	11.4	365.9	4,216.6	35.2	495.1	1,329.4	18,224.4
1911	267.0	3,747.8	715.1	10,372.7	20.3	284.9	11.8	116.2	1.4	27.4	277.4	3,336.8	113.5	1,237.2	1,406.7	19,122.9
1910	104.4	1,297.5	655.6	10,473.4	14.5	127.0	18.3	182.9	.6	6.9	285.4	2,783.0	106.0	964.6	1,184.8	15,835.2
1909	25.4	288.8	29.3	383.4	10.4	84.8	6.4	66.5	.2	7.9	—	—	27.7	380.4	99.4	1,211.9
1908	21.2	267.2	81.1	727.4	32.0	153.0	8.6	75.6	1.3	13.9	196.9	1,746.5	5.6	68.9	346.7	3,052.5
1907[1]	69.2	742.2	851.1	4,817.7	3.1	22.6	59.5	346.1	4.0	41.5	289.6	1,711.1	1.4	16.8	1,277.8	7,698.0
1906	236.2	1,863.4	1,012.3	6,015.1	83.4	360.9	85.8	480.1	20.0	137.5	205.0	1,014.4	—	—	1,642.7	9,871.2
1905	139.7	865.9	411.5	2,045.8	80.3	296.9	109.2	512.9	17.6	103.6	231.7	1,221.5	—	—	990.0	5,046.6
1904	144.9	879.9	857.5	3,516.9	29.5	113.3	129.0	563.5	41.9	177.1	64.5	313.6	—	—	1,267.2	5,564.2
1903	330.0	1,939.8	2,260.7	8,472.3	250.4	699.2	231.8	909.6	128.4	522.5	183.7	631.5	843.9	1,476.9	4,229.0	14,651.8
1902	269.6	1,412.3	1,362.5	4,440.5	206.4	713.4	323.5	1,033.4	—	—	—	—	39.8	147.4	2,201.8	7,747.0
1901	82.3	399.8	340.0	1,046.7	59.7	215.0	116.7	352.0	—	—	—	—	22.3	74.8	621.0	2,088.3
1900	70.2	352.6	379.1	1,152.8	133.5	437.4	46.7	128.3	—	—	—	—	18.9	54.0	648.4	2,125.1
1899	56.9	274.6	261.8	814.9	58.0	199.6	24.7	53.3	—	—	—	—	61.0	178.5	462.5	1,520.9
1898	62.0	310.0	242.1	757.8	106.5	364.0	15.5	—	—	—	—	—	22.5	—	448.6	—
1897	10.8	53.3	135.7	431.1	63.8	634.6	9.4	—	—	—	—	—	2.5	—	222.2	—
1896	9.3	52.4	66.6	220.4	21.3	88.6	10.6	—	—	—	—	—	.3	—	108.0	—
1895	4.3	23.2	55.5	177.0	5.6	22.3	46.8	—	—	—	—	—	2.4	—	114.6	—
1894	7.5	48.2	43.2	131.6	6.3	280.0	11.0	—	—	—	—	—	.6	—	68.7	—
1893	—	—	93.2	295.3	14.2	57.6	11.3	—	—	—	—	—	1.6	—	120.2	—

[1] For 1893 to 1899, calendar years; for 1900 to 1906, fiscal years ending 30 June of the year given; for 1907, 9 months ending 31 March 1907; for 1908 to 1930, fiscal years ending 31 March of the year given.

Series L91-96. Land sales by Hudson's Bay Company, Canadian Northern Land Department and Canadian Pacific Railway Company, 1925 to 1960

(series L91, 93, 95 in acres; series L92, 94, 96 in dollars)

Year[1]	Hudson's Bay Company		Canadian Northern Land Department		Canadian Pacific Railway Company	
	Acreage	Value	Acreage	Value	Acreage	Value[2]
	91	**92**	**93**	**94**	**95**	**96**
1960	2,244	9,856	–	–	–[3]	1,600,000[2]
1959	636	3,450	8,531	88,378	–[3]	3,400,000
1958	3,482	16,514	7,171	44,891	14,072	4,700,000
1957	5,218	35,015	10,857	64,488	57,876	7,600,000
1956	3,991	26,391	6,978	55,875	34,559	6,500,000
1955	10,500	43,260	7,689	43,061	42,950	5,000,000
1954	56,052	269,731	16,198	116,321	57,326	3,600,000
1953	131,425	511,629	43,321	267,296	25,629[4]	2,800,000
1952	81,370	376,965	21,818	202,478	23,945[5]	2,900,000
1951	96,344	356,478	10,439	66,655	104,417	6,600,000
1950	87,662	468,774	12,786	81,652	65,285	2,200,000
1949	120,847	494,249	39,044	259,195	87,748	3,000,000[2]
1948	120,412	654,572	28,050	226,015	178,469	3,336,041
1947	161,853	863,164	45,883	398,137	133,118	650,274
1946	241,135	1,413,693	85,036	935,413	212,170	1,141,102
1945	277,998	1,726,941	70,335	708,364	278,932	1,603,044
1944	159,914	993,307	70,661	742,366	232,371	1,373,018
1943	111,366	517,510	25,485	274,128	135,352	702,470
1942	86,568	431,621	9,664	72,205	94,233	488,239
1941	47,519	306,899	11,273	103,332	89,449	569,717
1940	51,596	395,817	14,553	125,137	99,933	807,678
1939	40,649	269,712	13,444	125,064	106,148	762,315
1938	47,663	331,358	12,577	129,266	116,085	996,214
1937	47,208	334,030	13,356	124,111	129,751	1,330,149
1936	32,913	245,855	16,869	176,680	92,210	955,520
1935	36,512	240,782	6,257	60,944	124,354	1,217,890
1934	21,931	107,336	6,712	71,991	120,355	1,334,343
1933	15,755	101,614	4,953	39,122	67,100	716,925
1932	11,659	92,245	8,121	68,646	59,581	803,664
1931	54,522	543,607	8,350	97,361	87,687	1,254,101
1930	235,773	2,334,760	30,402	398,883	199,312	3,137,109
1929	283,611	3,165,196	–	–	408,506	5,058,675
1928	263,646	3,229,903	–	–	664,411	7,743,847
1927	271,282	3,259,820	–	–	430,368	5,111,798
1926	163,966	2,031,291	–	–	–	–
1925	68,979	928,551	–	–	–	–

[1] For series L91-92, years ending 31 January of year given; for series L93-96, calendar years.

[2] For 1949 to 1960, values are rounded to nearest $100,000.

[3] No acreage given.

[4] Agricultural lands only, sold for $194,780.

[5] Agricultural lands only, sold for $177,193.

Series L97-106. Government receipts on account of Dominion lands, 1873 to 1931
(dollars)

Year[1]	Homestead fees	Pre-emption fees	Sales Cash	Sales Scrip	Timber dues	Grazing lands Cash	Grazing lands Scrip	Hay, coal-mining fees, stone quarries, export tax on gold, etc., cash	National parks	Gross revenue
	97	98	99	100	101	102	103	104	105	106
1931	109,890	—	84,288	—	486,424	67,495	—	640,082	218,844	1,832,173
1930	175,080	—	428,124	27	1,131,024	162,688	—	1,816,955	245,930	4,249,893
1929	161,890	—	785,661	—	1,395,726	171,012	—	1,197,890	234,613	4,152,279
1928	72,551	—	732,324	—	1,388,140	161,045	—	963,644[2]	275,343	3,763,409
1927	57,700	—	544,874	—	1,190,975	162,097	—	1,084,695	238,239	3,418,554
1926	46,900	—	467,601	—	1,098,692	166,388	—	793,358	180,886	2,880,197
1925	36,590	—	410,222	612	981,400	149,070	—	639,749	176,650	2,493,867
1924	38,640	—	404,952	160	847,773	141,871	—	723,763	115,163	2,353,847
1923	53,460	—	414,279	900	825,465	153,697	—	823,184	75,305	2,431,767
1922	73,540	—	761,850	—	683,491	144,345	—	1,071,396	74,303	2,918,530
1921	53,880	—	1,721,172	—	705,314	183,757	—	1,234,558	76,850	4,086,076
1920	67,460	—	2,799,605	80	589,780	183,662	—	896,413	76,742	4,738,921
1919	42,190	—	2,192,861	323	408,728	148,180	—	630,976	55,007	3,616,282
1918	83,180	7,870	3,046,092	131	482,006	125,301	240	630,428	52,161	4,557,810
1917	112,110	14,690	2,707,204	333	429,403	128,342	—	600,934	45,851	4,190,238
1916	170,350	22,760	1,090,842	—	378,961	118,955	160	476,409	37,494	2,443,640
1915	238,295	28,720	696,672	80	310,934	101,711	400	1,594,905	37,896	3,177,867
1914	317,412	61,660	1,303,587	240	378,365	84,926	320	865,499	48,800	3,313,820
1913	337,055	85,940	1,650,492	6,157	463,739	79,413	—	781,283[2]	37,449	3,655,202
1912	391,703	102,070	1,967,183	3,257	400,669	69,519	1,520	729,127	56,498	3,978,037
1911	445,135	156,485	1,193,756	1,438	387,055	60,703	2,356	774,569	69,055	3,306,073
1910	415,232	174,250	1,239,037	9,974	377,856	67,807	5,081	459,870	43,698	3,022,446
1909	389,039	141,550	951,442	20,136	269,837	53,313	3,258	253,339	31,321	2,277,678
1908	301,694	—	656,303	92,311	473,609	43,212	4,048	266,415	27,233	2,094,579
1907[1]	215,450	—	503,202	11,350	379,476	43,712	400	214,257	15,887[2]	1,490,503
1906	417,834	—	442,589	7,655	292,685	51,584	80	297,302	18,884	1,709,315
1905	304,806	—	154,128	19,645	266,951	36,145	5,237	364,928	14,060[2]	1,339,382
1904	255,772	—	196,750	189,705	397,344	19,790	13,921	495,583	9,498[2]	1,681,825
1903	320,410	—	155,537	158,453	470,917	13,912	15,041	607,724	5,064[2]	1,890,887
1902	144,425	—	66,950	169,767	207,791	7,292	8,409	737,882	2,861[2]	1,432,679
1901	79,910	—	40,361	326,270	209,399	4,726	14,672	1,102,147[2]	4,047	1,874,159
1900	72,690	—	103,248	88,756	126,346	8,383	4,083	1,038,383[2]	2,728	1,503,743
1899	58,235	—	116,594	21,308	155,361	5,246	—	1,130,706	2,994	1,584,328
1898	34,780	—	80,179	28,918	119,314	4,729	510	699,383	3,046	1,009,741
1897	21,179	—	49,336	16,929	68,993	4,715	2,500	8,634	2,132	198,676
1896	18,278	—	46,374	46,930	61,923	7,072	6,256	5,814	2,735	227,095
1895	29,665	—	37,294	23,270	74,079	5,354	8,628	5,230	2,322	202,983
1894	36,462	—	53,255	27,841	81,291	5,741	7,688	6,243	2,524	250,069
1893	37,690	—	96,171	77,231	105,865	6,381	11,542	6,266	4,983	394,826
1892	46,994	—	111,651	97,822	106,461	3,727	17,223	5,617	3,648	459,761
1891	29,164	—	91,665	171,425	102,903	3,080	16,194	8,788[2]	2,397	463,068
1890	35,920	8,580	54,897	228,744	84,643	1,306	9,022	9,242	1,094	464,019
1889	39,460	10,550	57,513	318,239	90,290	2,208	16,803	3,947	2,529	594,088
1888	23,691	4,830	52,238	313,523	94,965	5,922	23,023	2,354[2]	2,952	569,987
1887	19,614	6,888	48,176	337,640	65,112	14,243	39,488	1,650[2]	—	588,533
1886	26,110	14,371	76,140	214,658	64,820	29,563	3,131	1,285	—	457,974
1885	25,645	17,100	199,275	45,876	87,475	17,090	—	816	—	451,565
1884	41,580	28,810	424,863	40,920	147,983	11,371	—	641	—	1,001,777[3]
1883	73,015	54,725	516,092	33,638	90,066	22,844	—	914	—	1,051,404[3]
1882	54,155	39,844	1,240,328	50,591	58,753	2,245	—	40	—	1,805,735[3]
1881	20,450	10,802	71,170	70,828	32,028	—	—	—	—	206,991
1880	41,255	10,241	45,709	81,686	25,121	—	—	—	—	206,801
1879	17,690	—	4,998	210,905	325	—	—	—	—	234,733
1878	14,540	—	2,795	120,160	1,620	—	—	—	—	139,584
1877	2,250	—	1,086	136,955	320	—	—	—	—	140,755
1876	4,680	—	3,479	320	387	—	—	—	—	8,866
1875	11,510	—	13,667	—	2,335	—	—	—	—	27,641
1874	7,310	—	19,835	—	2,711	—	—	—	—	29,981
1873	6,960	—	19,170	—	109	—	—	—	—	26,239

[1] For 1873 to 1906, fiscal years ending 30 June of the year given; for 1907, 9 months ending 31 March 1907; for 1909 to 1931, fiscal years ending 31 March of the year given.

[2] Includes some scrip.

[3] Includes sales of colonization lands amounting to $354,036 in 1882, $248,492 in 1883 and $253,713 in 1884. These were the only years in which there were substantial sales of colonization lands.

Series L107-118. Primary forest production and exports of primary products, by type of product (excluding fuel wood), selected years, 1922 to 1975

(logs and bolts, volume in thousands of cubic feet; pulpwood, volume in cunits; all values in thousands of dollars)

Year	Production						Exports					
	Logs and bolts		Pulpwood		Other value[2]	Total value	Logs and bolts		Pulpwood		Other value	Total value
	Volume[1]	Value	Volume	Value			Volume[3]	Value	Volume[3]	Value		
	107	108	109	110	111	112	113	114	115	116	117	118
1975	2,597,160	1,139,306[4]	1,308,860	775,312[4]	−[1,4]	1,914,618	91,753	22,945	334,459	11,224	4,288	46,467
1974	3,012,170	1,387,540	1,696,300	791,225	12,454	2,191,249	165,695	24,443	424,368	12,690	4,371	48,990
1973	3,421,502	1,419,152	1,496,570	610,976	7,520	2,037,648	50,544	7,051	447,518	12,326	5,156	31,346
1972	2,867,942	1,006,562	1,357,066	528,456	9,518	1,544,536	72,976	7,804	493,560	13,979	5,333	33,734
1971	2,752,727	856,850	1,303,197	498,599	10,053	1,365,502	173,247	17,041	655,793	18,953	5,058	47,204
1970	2,673,720	802,924	1,424,418	543,161	9,696	1,355,781	285,409	27,917	929,900	26,806	5,464	67,163
1969	2,593,939r	866,484	1,512,369	533,848	10,244	1,410,576	115,906	11,916	880,600	24,489	5,965	49,606
1968	2,381,574	778,864	1,379,394	488,930	11,056	1,278,850	161,193	15,310	900,150	25,391	6,503	54,971
1967	2,237,537	696,091	1,329,048	487,463	12,661	1,196,215	184,892	15,935	984,300	27,489	6,080	55,711
1966	2,250,304	652,768	1,352,510	452,130	13,272	1,118,169	116,313	9,318	1,165,350	32,587	6,519	54,763
1965	2,211,299	648,525[4]	1,206,516	389,504[4]	8,632[4]	1,046,661[4]	64,467	6,262	1,149,200	33,827	7,064	52,338
1964	2,186,595	613,735	1,184,947	338,409	34,710	986,854	67,195	5,923	1,049,750	28,489	6,926	46,651
1963	2,118,600	548,513	1,129,605	324,095	35,881	908,489	93,392	6,359	946,900	25,903	7,071	45,340
1962	1,931,210	476,513	1,052,102	343,443	38,651	858,607	59,275	4,369	1,041,250	28,597	8,114	47,626
1961	1,730,433	404,016	1,150,086	369,633	36,137	809,786	88,762	6,198	978,350	27,157	7,021	45,992
1960	1,805,277	385,924	1,198,023	356,915	26,753	769,592	29,442	3,091	979,200	25,840	13,205	42,136
1959	1,650,176	344,424	1,241,089	320,244	24,528	689,196	21,281	2,250	940,950	25,706	12,733	40,688
1958	1,461,621	311,746	1,084,979	275,154	22,605	609,505	24,218	2,340	1,093,100	29,944	12,137	44,421
1957	1,553,715	409,227	1,272,246	340,235	36,937	786,398	34,939	3,167	1,530,000	42,332	15,226	60,725
1956	1,625,633	443,888	1,484,894	419,471	38,685	902,045	30,092	3,265	1,660,050	44,206	14,153	61,625
1955	1,563,135	393,861	1,367,476	369,476	31,874	795,211	39,102	3,532	1,600,550	43,274	13,561	60,367
1954	1,492,233	345,068	1,252,863	323,800	23,426	692,294	52,012	3,976	1,552,100	41,900	11,858	57,734
1953	1,513,972	331,296	1,151,340	309,011	25,674	665,981	51,399	4,539	1,516,400	42,704	14,211	61,455
1952	1,487,691	344,932	1,254,182	346,802	38,177	729,912	54,407	4,892	2,149,650	61,837	26,011	92,740
1951	1,433,900	339,423	1,542,908	416,196	24,795	780,415	46,250	4,831	2,459,900	66,077	10,066	80,974
1950	1,415,930	279,745	1,141,070	280,838	18,514	579,097	58,967	4,378	1,514,700	33,590	7,448	45,416
1949	1,277,860	229,450	876,246	202,544	24,418	456,412	72,540	4,094	1,397,400	30,384	12,915	47,394
1948	1,358,429	250,649	1,174,274	271,560	22,949	545,158	84,029	4,785	2,000,050	43,573	14,580	62,938
1947	1,356,630	251,990	1,160,856	249,912	22,566	524,469	55,240	3,055	1,700,850	34,529	14,348	51,932
1946	1,154,707	181,476	1,029,437	196,243	20,336	398,055	51,150	1,955	1,587,800	28,731	14,923	45,609
1945	1,080,522	152,312	932,713	159,270	13,903	325,485	58,649	2,238	1,431,400	23,882	8,315	34,436
1940	1,152,136	90,535	740,906	74,731	9,285	174,551	182,087	3,689	1,319,200	12,522	6,399	22,611
1935	625,533	34,078	518,076	41,196	8,323	83,597	334,410	3,351	943,500	7,041	1,884	12,275
1930	1,028,719	75,563	508,060	67,530	19,975	163,067	232,876	2,799	1,130,500	13,612	7,757	24,167
1925	850,450	76,633	432,860	62,182	30,946	169,761	291,509	4,778	1,210,400	14,168	9,884	28,830
1922	673,586	58,337	333,535	50,735	23,549	132,621	185,489	3,271	859,350	10,360	5,547	19,178

[1] Includes some pulpwood.
[2] Consists of poles and piling and other roundwood.
[3] A cunit is 100 cubic feet.
[4] Production values became shipments values in 1965 and later years.

Series L119-128. Principal statistics of woods operations, 1963 to 1975

(values in thousands of dollars)

Year	Estab- lishments	Logging activity						Total activity		Value added
		Production and related workers		Cost of fuel and electricity	Cost of materials and supplies	Value of shipments	Value added	Employees		
		Number	Wages					Number	Salaries and wages	
	119	120	121	122	123	124	125	126	127	128
1975	2,749	45,533	588,039	64,373	1,425,099	2,473,656	1,102,730	53,622	711,655	1,125,527
1974	3,253	50,733	601,102	68,145	1,585,159	2,732,598	1,220,836	59,491	717,410	1,244,490
1973	3,132	49,573	512,724	49,974	1,446,156	2,494,345	1,089,074	57,586	605,769	1,109,162
1972	2,798	40,363	382,071	36,754	995,676	1,872,572	814,264	47,553	457,586	829,421
1971	2,441	40,126	343,559	30,265	901,055	1,629,549	685,771	47,284	413,294	697,636
1970	2,653	44,814	344,788	29,103	898,981	1,619,622	682,953	52,230	411,734	694,004
1969	2,666	46,847	341,977	34,388	884,263	1,624,240	733,883	54,945	408,458	746,991
1968	2,376	45,187	302,343	30,809	762,529	1,449,580	644,108	52,605	360,009	655,548
1967	2,558	51,004	311,814	30,805	731,026	1,377,885	614,907	58,568	366,030	626,830
1966	2,609	54,317	303,266	29,559	669,600	1,268,206	596,464	61,791	351,471	611,524
1965	2,556	53,992	274,350	26,508	651,180	1,184,535	528,263	60,701	315,948	546,692
1964	2,758	55,882	262,797	24,845	532,666	1,020,075	480,058	62,419	300,252	507,740
1963	2,959	53,921	240,239	22,496	453,125	916,422	439,288	60,291	275,476	466,267

Series L129-133. Principal statistics of woods operations, 1926 to 1964
(values in thousands of dollars)

Year	Employees (number of man-years)[1]	Salaries and wages	Cost of materials	Net value of production	Gross value of production
	129	130	131	132	133
1964	95,894	442,374	157,763	857,983	1,015,746
1963	95,983	421,571	147,499	790,413	937,912
1962	85,280	398,575	140,900	746,914	887,814
1961	94,681	422,374	137,576	708,459	846,035
1960	86,539	374,731	72,923	733,566	806,488
1959	82,551	347,406	57,004	658,712	715,716
1958	67,327	338,284	68,595	570,016	638,611
1957	119,944	430,805	89,942	733,113	823,054
1956	132,015	472,035	97,808	841,334	939,143
1955	149,000	506,000	100,459	729,114	829,573
1954	127,000	428,000	84,396	643,974	728,370
1953	136,000	439,000	81,993	622,546	704,539
1952	150,000	466,000	91,815	671,373	763,189
1951	163,000	428,000	90,814	730,208	821,022
1950	141,000	343,000	72,884	540,162	613,046
1949	137,000	313,000	67,574	424,414	491,987
1948	156,000	360,000	68,760	510,255	579,015
1947	160,000	331,000	65,643	494,178	559,821
1946	149,000	248,000	44,443	391,263	435,706
1945	145,000	228,000	40,282	323,955	364,237
1944	140,000	208,000	37,039	293,781	330,820
1943	126,000	159,000	32,859	246,969	279,828
1942	140,000	151,000	31,445	218,064	249,510
1941	108,000	97,000	21,195	204,421	225,616
1940	126,000	109,000	33,243	168,840	202,083
1939	75,333	79,000	34,000	123,747	157,747
1938	71,000	74,000	32,000	116,266	148,266
1937	100,000	60,000	31,486	131,764	163,250
1936	90,000	54,000	26,000	108,804	134,804
1935	79,000	60,000	25,629	89,832	115,462
1934	74,000	47,000	23,427	82,113	105,540
1933	65,000	46,800	14,067	79,706	83,773
1932	60,000	43,200	13,817	78,289	92,106
1931	52,000	37,000	21,170	119,954	141,124
1930	90,000	67,000	31,030	175,823	206,853
1929	97,000	80,000	32,938	186,632	219,570
1928	103,000	80,000	31,945	181,006	212,951
1927	86,000	74,000	30,741	174,197	204,938
1926	81,000	72,000	30,668	173,769	204,436

[1] Man-year in British Columbia is 260 days; in other provinces 300 days.

Series L134-148. Lumber production by species, external trade and estimated consumption, 1908 to 1975
(volume in millions of feet board measure; value in thousands of dollars)

Year	Douglas fir volume	Spruce and balsam fir volume	Red and white pines volume	Total softwoods volume	Total hardwood production volume	Total production Volume	Total production Value	To United Kingdom volume	To United States volume	To other countries volume	Total exports Volume	Total exports Value	Imports volume	Stocks on hand[1]	Estimated consumption volume[2]
	134	135	136	137	138	139	140	141	142	143	144	145	146	147	148
1975	1,046	5,480	207	10,067	354	10,421	—	269	5,505	777	6,551	972,221	518	1,909	4,611
1974	1,353	6,535	287	12,453	520	12,973	—	638	6,499	1,147	8,284	1,289,201	476	2,127	4,865
1973	1,580	7,171	285	14,179	573	14,752	—	537	8,325	1,107	9,969	1,598,092	470	1,827	4,672
1972	1,667	6,445	278	12,799	480	13,279	—	373	8,558	861	9,792	1,173,990	383	1,246	4,342
1971	1,651	5,285	235	11,626	404	12,031	—	460	7,110	956	8,526	829,436	304	1,718	4,045
1970	1,575	4,488	245	10,270	441	10,712	—	638	5,506	1,322	7,466	663,775	253	1,954	3,378
1969	1,815	4,823	322	10,595	506	11,100	—	362	5,646	868	6,876	696,474	294	1,833	4,151
1968	1,930	4,256	302	10,222	532	10,755	—	587	5,550	1,045	7,182	652,696	305	1,466	3,664
1967	1,849	3,661	323	9,432	531	9,962	—	825	4,670	992	6,487	509,239	289	1,252	3,994
1966	1,920	3,781	331	9,469	539	10,008	—	788	4,580	765	6,133	478,034	290	1,482	3,991
1965	2,128	3,792	341	9,682	485	10,167	—	848	4,794	831	6,473	485,883	268	1,308	3,964
1964	2,175	3,745	374	9,577	483	10,060	—	1,010	4,741	703	6,454	473,305	272	1,310	3,716
1963	2,173	3,338	370	9,070	419	9,489	—	700	4,743	778	6,221	449,156	246	1,148	3,608
1962	2,142	3,076	344	8,190	384	8,575	—	631	4,299	516	5,446	394,491	228	1,242	3,358
1961	2,140	2,696	361	7,631	401	8,032	—	665	3,690	569	4,924	352,812	234	1,243	3,343
1960	2,091	2,737	368	7,569	443	8,012	512,262	671	3,486	417	4,574	346,300	243	1,244	3,496
1959	2,045	2,750	370	7,196	395	7,591	490,540	349	3,524	308	4,180	323,717	310	1,059	3,651
1958	2,110	2,376	347	6,800	379	7,179	459,901	437	3,125	380	3,942	293,600	268	989	3,631
1957	1,871	2,468	430	6,653	446	7,100	466,228	509	2,704	433	3,647	282,690	237	1,114	3,610
1956	2,085	2,695	468	7,279	460	7,740	539,262	486	3,067	399	3,951	328,099	285	1,034	3,905
1955	2,270	2,774	459	7,547	374	7,920	541,563	844	3,281	489	4,614	386,298	226	866	3,618
1954	2,124	2,398	462	6,817	427	7,244	482,912	870	2,796	383	4,049	326,027	172	951	3,429
1953	1,971	2,611	480	6,781	524	7,306	494,386	601	2,452	324	3,377	283,115	159	1,013	3,898
1952	1,743	2,511	483	6,298	510	6,808	483,195	857	2,252	231	3,340	297,205	152	823	3,613
1951	1,778	2,448	534	6,430	518	6,949	507,650	896	2,168	375	3,439	312,623	133	816	3,549
1950	1,782	2,231	520	6,107	447	6,554	422,481	276	3,024	279	3,579	291,121	86	723	3,083
1949	1,594	2,050	459	5,422	493	5,915	334,790	477	1,404	308	2,189	160,986	81	744	3,755
1948	1,514	2,120	445	5,399	509	5,909	340,851	566	1,615	287	2,468	196,575	43	693	3,294
1947	1,410	2,154	453	5,298	579	5,878	322,048	1,121	1,065	549	2,735	209,215	115	503	3,258
1946	1,128	1,912	414	4,565	517	5,083	230,190	710	965	409	2,083	126,193	59	—	3,059
1945	1,151	1,724	339	4,116	398	4,514	181,046	879	929	193	2,001	99,995	51	—	2,564
1944	1,141	1,685	364	4,091	421	4,512	170,351	852	879	152	1,883	90,950	36	—	2,666
1943	1,234	1,629	361	3,992	371	4,364	151,900	903	730	108	1,741	74,739	34	—	2,657
1942	1,534	1,759	387	4,526	404	4,935	149,855	647	1,432	100	2,180	80,692	41	—	2,796
1941	1,525	1,947	398	4,623	318	4,941	129,288	827	1,232	242	2,301	74,813	60	—	2,700
1940	1,692	1,557	410	4,339	291	4,629	105,991	1,617	651	280	2,549	69,803	82	—	2,162
1939	1,595	1,106	346	3,747	230	3,977	78,332	1,224	627	361	2,212	50,548	77	—	1,842
1938	1,402	1,132	319	3,521	247	3,768	72,633	985	450	318	1,753	37,412	80	—	2,096
1937	1,407	1,256	386	3,718	288	4,006	82,777	1,057	539	370	1,966	47,589	120	—	2,159
1936	1,422	908	299	3,197	215	3,412	61,966	958	531	369	1,858	38,669	89	—	1,644
1935	1,115	919	259	2,769	202	2,973	47,911	734	351	345	1,431	27,514	71	—	1,613
1934	1,032	774	229	2,426	151	2,578	40,510	861	234	396	1,491	27,842	57	—	1,144
1933	818	583	186	1,845	113	1,958	27,709	487	297	357	1,141	18,980	57	—	875
1932	642	592	180	1,684	124	1,810	26,882	195	327	269	791	14,159	43	—	1,062
1931	936	686	317	2,313	179	2,498	45,978	132	665	262	1,060	22,053	94	—	1,532
1930	1,254	1,313	500	3,711	275	3,989	87,711	194	1,121	327	1,642	39,689	135	—	2,482
1929	1,605	1,471	627	4,472	266	4,742	113,350	190	1,403	360	1,953	53,533	240	—	3,029
1928	1,517	1,277	593	4,081	255	4,337	103,590	208	1,358	336	1,902	51,471	263	—	2,699
1927	1,437	1,197	540	3,877	217	4,098	97,509	229	1,636	328	2,193	59,832	195	—	2,100
1926	1,294	1,318	609	3,967	217	4,185	101,071	177	1,777	295	2,249	64,586	171	—	2,107
1925	1,103	1,226	659	3,684	205	3,889	99,726	—	—	—	2,202	—	90	—	1,777
1924	1,000	1,331	739	3,679	198	3,879	104,445	—	—	—	2,087	—	132	—	1,924
1923	1,040	1,240	724	3,543	184	3,728	108,291	—	—	—	2,408	—	169	—	1,489
1922	821	1,116	643	2,992	143	3,139	84,554	—	—	—	2,007	—	148	—	1,279
1921	681	946	566	2,648	216	2,869	82,449	—	—	—	1,038	—	124	—	1,955

Series L134–148. Lumber production by species, external trade and estimated consumption, 1908 to 1975 (concluded)

(volume in millions of feet board measure; value in thousands of dollars)

Year	Softwood production				Total hardwood production volume	Total production		Exports					Imports volume	Stocks on hand[1]	Estimated consumption volume[2]
	Douglas fir volume	Spruce and balsam fir volume	Red and white pines volume	Total softwoods volume		Volume	Value	To United Kingdom volume	To United States volume	To other countries volume	Total exports				
											Volume	Value			
	134	135	136	137	138	139	140	141	142	143	144	145	146	147	148
1920	902	1,622	738	4,015	251	4,299	168,172	–	–	–	1,936	–	168	–	2,531
1919	818	1,475	569	3,294	186	3,820	122,031	–	–	–	–	–	–	–	–
1918	716	1,238	910	3,441	202	3,887	103,701	–	–	–	–	–	–	–	–
1917	704	1,572	894	3,792	147	4,152	83,655	–	–	–	–	–	–	–	–
1916	575	1,521	781	3,316	174	3,491	58,365	–	–	–	–	–	–	–	–
1915	454	1,798	972	3,633	210	3,843	61,920	–	–	–	–	–	–	–	–
1914	602	1,698	775	3,678	268	3,946	60,363	–	–	–	–	–	–	–	–
1913	793	1,339	823	3,553	264	3,817	65,796	–	–	–	–	–	–	–	–
1912	890	1,488	1,054	4,080	310	4,390	69,476	–	–	–	–	–	–	–	–
1911	846	1,680	1,189	4,628	291	4,918	75,831	–	–	–	–	–	–	–	–
1910	636	1,379	1,180	4,125	279	4,452	70,609	–	–	–	–	–	–	–	–
1909	470	1,216	1,213	3,514	220	3,815	62,819	–	–	–	–	–	–	–	–
1908	372	1,076	1,088	3,013	147	3,348	54,351	–	–	–	–	–	–	–	–

[1] Stocks on hand, 31 December.
[2] Estimated consumption = production – exports + imports + opening inventories – closing inventories.

Series L149–158. Principal statistics of the lumber industry, 1957 to 1975

(series L149, 150 and 156 in numbers; all other series in thousands of dollars)

Year	Establishments	Manufacturing activity						Total activity		
		Production and related workers		Cost of fuel and electricity	Cost of materials and supplies	Value of shipments of goods of own manufacture	Value added	Employees		Value added
		Number	Wages					Number	Salaries and wages	
	149	150	151	152	153	154	155	156	157	158
1975	1,368	40,788	462,430	51,179	1,113,447	1,996,856	849,323	49,156	577,555	850,833
1974	1,530	49,194	489,521	49,075	1,314,925	2,329,835	976,108	58,346	605,422	982,571
1973	1,519	53,643	454,797	43,326	1,359,529	2,558,546	1,274,620	62,476	553,569	1,279,633
1972	1,567	49,387	370,195	35,400	1,004,018	1,893,573	864,865	57,111	447,712	869,320
1971	1,631	44,107	304,528	28,369	788,768	1,395,507	571,594	50,963	366,440	574,247
1970	1,772	42,540	261,805	23,578	687,168	1,135,377	436,043	48,776	314,014	439,035
1969	1,896	44,425	252,474	24,667	723,888	1,267,194	554,505	49,837	294,436	557,810
1968	1,894	42,820	226,359	22,197	634,164	1,179,572	542,206	47,987	264,281	545,183
1967	2,136	42,431	206,452	20,139	529,723	959,782	406,362	47,463	240,460	412,272
1966	2,292	43,242	196,677	20,198	512,822	917,661	390,390	49,057	231,879	394,899
1965	2,559	44,477	188,346	20,159	501,559	896,240	384,484	50,848	223,921	389,127
1964	2,909	43,646	173,698	19,206	481,473	855,330	371,908	50,328	209,194	376,325
1963	3,094	41,475	159,262	17,218	425,931	782,628	342,306	49,438	196,490	348,934
1962	3,266	40,316	146,464	15,888	381,517	699,157	303,480	47,360	178,060	310,034
1961	3,467	38,636	131,780	13,190	358,479	619,515	249,928	46,688	165,100	256,057
1961	3,260	35,063	120,226	11,380	306,238	534,591	218,228	41,134	144,700	..
1960	3,719	36,714	119,648	9,501	295,824	530,187	224,855	43,886	145,449	..
1959	4,003	37,591	113,547	9,337	275,114	508,099	223,650	45,128	138,454	..
1958	4,004	35,675	110,428	8,763	262,456	480,675	209,453	43,484	134,346	..
1957	4,490	37,603	109,970	7,948	268,363	484,270	207,940	46,044	134,015	..

Series L159-165. Principal statistics of the lumber industry, 1917 to 1959

(series L159-160 in numbers; series L161-165 in thousands of dollars)

Year	Establishments	Employees	Salaries and wages	Cost of fuel and electricity	Cost of materials	Net value of production	Gross value of production
	159	160	161	162	163	164	165
1959	5,678	48,659	144,759	9,841	313,399	248,582	571,822
1958	5,769	47,763	142,700	9,204	300,343	236,753	546,299
1957	6,276	50,664	143,166	8,407	309,581	237,700	555,688
1956	6,629	57,078	153,809	8,958	350,746	279,711	639,414
1955	7,333	58,586	152,557	8,673	338,870	296,940	644,483
1954	7,696	57,010	139,572	7,439	301,118	263,629	572,186
1953	8,194	60,933	142,131	7,043	304,585	269,066	580,694
1952	8,283	60,931	135,541	7,191	299,507	261,326	568,023
1951	7,934	62,416	132,059	6,512	313,175	271,866	591,552
1950	7,551	58,722	111,492	5,402	252,322	239,225	496,948
1949	7,460	55,032	97,449	4,359	205,935	186,121	396,415
1948	7,035	56,756	95,066	3,763	208,568	196,936	409,267
1947	6,481	55,426	83,360	3,075	208,544	190,515	402,133
1946	6,001	49,352	63,811	2,394	156,108	129,408	287,910
1945	5,295	44,040	54,018	1,948	126,007	103,154	231,108
1944	5,506	43,516	51,516	1,861	118,167	96,529	216,557
1943	5,140	43,954	49,564	3,150	101,022	91,714	195,885
1942	5,277	47,765	49,562	2,938	98,774	91,207	192,919
1941	4,655	45,104	41,465	2,317	84,435	76,660	163,412
1940	4,675	39,501	34,022	1,257	70,949	61,700	133,905
1939	3,941	32,399	26,396	833	54,448	44,852	100,133
1938	3,873	31,182	25,345	803	52,788	39,265	92,856
1937	3,836	33,917	27,174	842	57,280	46,727	104,850
1936	3,638	28,760	21,357	762	43,599	35,983	80,343
1935	3,698	25,727	17,712	652	35,928	29,325	65,905
1934	3,572	22,605	14,118	560	29,487	24,772	54,819
1933	3,517	17,779	10,040	475	22,871	16,092	39,438
1932	3,595	18,285	10,761	411	23,406	14,691	38,507
1931	3,562	·22,361	16,410	568	37,379	24,822	62,769
1930	3,531	43,457	28,513	597	72,957	47,590	121,143
1929	3,161	46,466	36,158	734	83,744	62,511	146,990
1928	2,967	44,862	34,722	812	80,452	58,161	139,425
1927	2,720	44,598	34,422	842	77,439	55,340	133,621
1926	2,780	35,078	34,925	811	78,921	55,450	135,183
1925	2,700	35,457	34,097	815	78,220	55,379	134,414
1924	2,761	35,494	34,784	898	83,142	57,890	141,929
1923	2,883	35,070	33,491	—	73,326	—	139,895
1922	2,922	31,891	27,622	—	60,812	—	114,325
1921	3,126	30,336	26,708	—	57,243	—	116,891
1920	3,481	41,158	44,729	1,046	103,078	103,040	207,164
1919	3,410	39,121	35,494	1,203	72,691	70,506	144,401
1918	3,095	33,917	29,885	727	45,877	99,730	146,333
1917	2,879	32,078	24,582	—	40,725	—	115,885

Series L166-175. Wood pulp, production and exports, 1908 to 1975
(volumes in thousands of tons; values in thousands of dollars)

Year	Production				Exports					
	Groundwood		Total pulp		Groundwood		Total pulp		To United States	
	Volume	Value	Volume	Value	Volume	Value	Volume	Value	Volume	Value
	166	167	168	169	170	171	172	173	174	175
1975	6,622	—	16,659	—	209	30,276	5,471	1,817,998	2,926	991,879
1974	8,365	—	21,691	—	286	34,131	7,082	1,861,235	3,926	1,060,380
1973	7,932	—	20,462	—	279	19,890	6,517	1,054,166	3,716	617,217
1972	7,680	—	19,239	—	275	16,691	6,102	817,335	3,559	473,103
1971	7,405	—	18,234	—	232	14,784	5,666	796,334	3,372	480,725
1970	7,650	—	18,308	—	277	17,333	5,581	785,229	3,315	485,453
1969	7,680	—	18,590	—	255	15,943	5,795	753,488	3,833	516,879
1968	7,305	—	16,762	—	219	13,631	4,971	627,874	3,227	424,640
1967	7,249	—	15,857	—	221	14,613	4,269	543,433	2,903	382,390
1966	7,547	—	15,951	—	254	17,260	4,096	520,067	2,977	390,760
1965	6,989	—	14,573	—	313	20,743	3,852	493,501	2,816	371,428
1964	6,442	—	13,742	—	286	18,528	3,636	460,854	2,677	346,017
1963	5,850	—	12,474	—	248	16,833	3,340	405,292	2,506	309,915
1962	5,892	—	12,133	—	260	17,698	3,044	369,902	2,398	298,166
1961	5,878	—	11,779	—	236	15,982	2,868	346,661	2,176	268,949
1960	5,881	237,345	11,461	772,626	235	16,348	2,601	325,122	2,000	256,170
1959	5,656	229,656	10,832	744,940	240	16,661	2,450	311,253	1,966	254,049
1958	5,375	222,296	10,137	703,366	233	16,195	2,219	285,449	1,832	239,874
1957	5,574	227,668	10,425	706,195	248	17,567	2,283	292,406	1,847	235,258
1956	5,723	231,236	10,734	706,233	275	19,594	2,374	304,536	1,920	245,081
1955	5,467	218,558	10,151	693,403	262	18,188	2,366	297,304	1,869	233,797
1954	5,338	214,102	9,673	655,917	232	16,502	2,180	271,418	1,670	206,435
1953	5,123	209,900	9,077	624,866	228	15,828	1,950	248,675	1,599	202,248
1952	5,175	217,352	8,968	650,021	255	20,413	1,941	291,863	1,589	225,082
1951	5,172	213,953	9,315	727,880	323	26,742	2,243	365,133	1,831	276,761
1950	4,911	173,035	8,473	502,584	248	14,038	1,846	208,556	1,694	191,006
1949	4,719	166,592	7,853	445,138	207	11,921	1,557	171,504	1,305	141,641
1948	4,414	168,343	7,675	485,966	297	19,257	1,798	211,564	1,591	184,973
1947	4,275	147,424	7,254	403,853	319	19,099	1,699	177,803	1,499	156,122
1946	3,998	111,514	6,615	287,624	268	12,571	1,419	114,021	1,253	99,973
1945	3,342	86,375	5,601	231,873	274	12,101	1,435	106,055	1,094	79,589
1944	3,076	71,669	5,271	211,041	237	10,134	1,408	101,563	1,078	77,082
1943	2,999	63,427	5,273	194,519	273	10,069	1,556	100,013	1,269	80,970
1942	3,260	64,802	5,606	192,145	278	10,507	1,511	95,267	1,197	76,088
1941	3,495	61,327	5,721	175,440	271	8,836	1,412	85,898	1,109	68,161
1940	3,305	55,505	5,291	149,005	204	6,265	1,069	60,930	825	46,577
1939	2,738	43,062	4,166	97,132	169	4,090	706	31,001	607	26,837
1938	2,462	39,228	3,668	87,897	124	2,914	554	27,731	454	21,562
1937	3,309	46,144	5,142	116,729	167	4,146	871	41,816	698	32,765
1936	2,910	38,251	4,485	92,337	134	2,841	754	31,247	641	26,504
1935	2,505	32,035	3,868	79,722	124	2,632	662	27,626	531	22,290
1934	2,340	30,557	3,636	75,727	120	2,728	606	25,445	479	20,053
1933	1,825	25,151	2,980	64,114	132	2,688	609	23,355	487	18,815
1932	1,696	28,018	2,663	64,412	116	2,562	452	18,930	363	15,051
1931	2,016	37,097	3,168	84,781	165	4,606	623	30,057	492	23,646
1930	2,283	48,317	3,619	112,356	209	5,967	760	39,060	647	32,141
1929	2,421	51,617	4,021	129,033	209	5,907	831	43,368	711	36,285
1928	2,128	47,549	3,608	121,184	204	5,546	864	45,615	724	37,633
1927	1,922	44,175	3,279	114,443	261	7,761	879	46,996	711	37,942
1926	1,901	44,800	3,230	115,154	382	11,506	1,006	52,077	818	43,220
1925	1,622	39,130	2,773	100,216	360	10,573	961	47,932	824	41,587
1924	1,428	36,166	2,465	90,324	254	7,916	782	40,243	691	36,348
1923	1,420	37,587	2,476	99,073	341	11,599	875	47,027	678	38,797
1922	1,241	31,079	2,150	84,948	315	9,400	818	41,038	610	33,083
1921	932	32,314	1,549	78,338	223	9,272	527	33,134	391	23,762
1920	1,090	49,890	1,960	141,553	304	17,575	820	76,384	625	61,633
1919	991	23,317	1,716	73,320	312	7,182	709	37,185	493	27,970
1918	880	19,113	1,557	64,356	181	4,786	584	33,360	544	30,157
1917	924	25,919	1,464	65,515	250	7,082	512	26,193	474	23,049
1916	827	—	1,296	—	330	5,649	559	17,344	467	14,275
1915	744	—	1,075	—	—	—	364	9,279	—	—
1914	645	—	935	—	—	—	425	8,865	—	—
1913	600	—	855	—	—	—	298	5,914	—	—
1912	499	—	683	—	—	—	348	5,952	—	—
1911	362	—	497	—	—	—	260	4,903	—	—
1910	370	—	475	—	—	—	329	5,695	—	—
1909	326	—	445	—	—	—	281	4,899	—	—
1908	279	—	363	—	—	—	240	4,071	—	—

Series L176-188. Manufactured paper, capacity, production and exports, 1916 to 1975
(volumes are in thousands of tons; values in thousands of dollars)

Year	News-print capacity	Production				Exports							
		Newsprint production		Total paper products		Newsprint exports		Total exports of paper		Newsprint exports to U.S.		Total paper exports to U.S.	
		Volume	Value	Volume	Value	Volume	Value	Volume[1]	Value[1]	Volume	Value	Volume[1]	Value[1]
	176	177	178	179	180	181	182	183	184	185	186	187	188
1975	10,165	7,727	—	11,096	—	6,998	1,741,990	8,042	2,043,007	5,626	1,357,892	6,136	1,483,779
1974	10,038	9,667	—	14,570	—	8,699	1,721,768	10,268	2,141,511	7,057	1,352,758	7,798	1,542,010
1973	10,377	9,213	—	13,870	—	8,396	1,285,928	9,951	1,570,101	6,905	1,067,833	7,694	1,207,666
1972	10,300	8,906	—	13,097	—	8,102	1,157,509	9,529	1,382,244	6,390	933,761	7,124	1,039,294
1971	10,240	8,524	—	12,303	—	7,798	1,084,282	8,964	1,261,508	6,211	880,682	6,790	967,086
1970	9,845	8,814	—	12,403	—	8,090	1,110,393	9,112	1,278,137	6,212	872,544	6,667	950,774
1969	9,675	8,938	—	12,515	—	8,235	1,125,801	9,111	1,260,579	6,526	919,877	6,952	985,622
1968	9,655	8,193	—	11,461	—	7,479	989,831	8,247	1,101,511	6,138	826,809	6,452	871,043
1967	9,294	8,193	—	11,349	—	7,464	955,261	8,198	1,062,106	6,340	815,780	6,632	856,621
1966	8,878	8,530	—	11,611	—	7,821	968,224	8,527	1,068,039	6,652	823,664	6,964	863,645
1965	8,421	7,827	—	10,567	—	7,190	869,586	7,755	948,599	6,112	735,611	6,375	770,809
1964	8,274	7,380	—	9,944	—	6,816	834,646	7,331	909,071	5,676	689,406	5,889	714,650
1963	8,055	6,657	—	9,059	—	6,211	759,990	6,655	820,830	5,251	636,086	5,435	656,497
1962	7,844	6,663	—	8,879	—	6,148	753,060	6,520	804,243	5,227	633,037	5,384	650,197
1961	7,734	6,718	—	8,769	—	6,253	761,313	6,568	804,898	5,228	629,792	5,356	644,704
1960	7,611	6,689	783,364	8,923	1,167,040	6,190	757,930	6,490	798,702	5,230	631,230	5,360	647,412
1959	7,521	6,351	730,455	8,550	1,106,071	5,910	722,271	6,202	762,232	5,092	614,706	5,245	633,802
1958	7,239	6,031	699,906	8,081	1,044,640	5,683	690,209	5,929	724,699	4,881	590,167	5,009	606,361
1957	6,756	6,362	729,009	8,300	1,056,371	5,901	715,490	6,154	751,153	5,058	610,290	5,199	627,402
1956	6,243	6,445	735,644	8,467	1,070,492	5,967	708,385	6,203	741,292	5,219	615,942	5,359	632,804
1955	6,064	6,196	688,338	8,000	981,439	5,763	665,877	5,990	694,239	5,028	578,322	5,192	595,513
1954	5,920	6,001	657,487	7,650	925,591	5,522	635,670	5,675	655,938	4,867	558,634	4,976	570,823
1953	5,723	5,755	633,408	7,377	887,858	5,375	619,033	5,541	639,077	4,917	564,464	5,055	578,456
1952	5,510	5,707	600,516	7,202	838,105	5,327	591,790	5,526	622,136	4,851	534,373	4,990	549,318
1951	5,360	5,561	564,361	7,225	824,030	5,112	536,372	5,359	574,106	4,775	496,852	4,950	517,584
1950	5,227	5,319	506,968	6,812	710,154	4,938	485,746	5,118	505,314	4,725	463,156	4,878	477,089
1949	5,113	5,187	467,976	6,540	641,460	4,789	440,054	4,952	459,050	4,346	395,260	4,457	404,808
1948	4,883	4,640	402,100	6,064	582,347	4,328	383,123	4,588	416,682	3,917	340,334	4,068	354,177
1947	4,729	4,474	355,541	5,775	507,101	4,221	342,293	4,452	373,070	3,675	291,893	3,777	300,482
1946	4,641	4,162	280,810	5,347	396,956	3,858	265,865	4,046	287,438	3,323	224,782	3,396	229,644
1945	4,672	3,324	189,024	4,360	282,838	3,059	179,451	3,286	203,012	2,534	146,508	2,594	152,542
1944	4,726	3,040	165,655	4,044	255,546	2,806	157,191	3,013	177,290	2,409	133,399	2,471	138,729
1943	4,678	3,046	152,963	3,966	234,036	2,810	144,707	2,984	160,825	2,545	129,787	2,607	135,023
1942	4,763	3,257	147,074	4,232	230,269	3,005	141,066	3,242	157,838	2,792	130,519	2,897	137,952
1941	4,703	3,520	158,925	4,525	241,450	3,262	154,357	3,587	176,184	2,762	129,162	2,921	139,107
1940	4,716	3,504	158,447	4,319	225,837	3,243	151,360	3,490	170,880	2,586	119,362	2,609	121,312
1939	4,633	2,927	120,859	3,601	170,776	2,659	115,687	2,796	124,127	2,206	97,058	2,231	98,425
1938	4,535	2,669	107,051	3,249	151,650	2,425	104,615	2,545	112,873	1,938	85,191	1,959	86,161
1937	4,211	3,674	126,424	4,345	175,885	3,455	126,466	3,532	136,164	2,899	105,699	2,928	107,084
1936	4,218	3,225	105,215	3,807	146,355	2,993	103,640	3,061	110,861	2,399	83,546	2,430	84,832
1935	4,263	2,765	88,436	3,281	125,753	2,575	87,924	2,618	94,042	2,052	70,957	2,067	71,615
1934	4,182	2,605	86,811	3,070	120,892	2,414	82,504	2,454	87,634	1,960	68,092	1,972	68,676
1933	4,149	2,022	66,960	2,419	96,690	1,838	69,201	1,871	72,396	1,520	58,315	1,534	58,874
1932	4,142	1,919	85,540	2,291	113,873	1,777	82,966	1,805	86,324	1,520	72,007	1,530	72,605
1931	4,127	2,227	111,420	2,611	143,630	2,008	107,233	2,042	111,114	1,753	94,355	1,766	95,163
1930	3,902	2,498	136,182	2,927	173,306	2,333	133,371	2,373	138,530	2,008	115,259	2,024	116,664
1929	3,512	2,725	150,800	3,197	192,989	2,515	148,866	2,564	154,919	2,173	129,022	2,195	130,899
1928	3,262	2,414	144,147	2,849	184,305	2,207	141,104	2,253	147,157	1,935	123,507	1,954	125,199
1927	2,716	2,083	132,287	2,469	168,231	1,882	123,222	1,925	129,638	1,748	114,042	1,765	115,827
1926	2,121	1,889	121,065	2,266	158,182	1,732	114,091	1,770	121,414	1,628	106,759	1,643	108,799
1925	1,823	1,537	106,269	1,885	140,161	1,402	98,945	1,442	106,624	1,321	93,104	1,337	95,461
1924	1,638	1,388	100,277	1,719	133,319	1,219	90,991	1,263	99,248	1,193	88,994	1,213	91,707
1923	1,465	1,252	93,213	1,589	127,184	1,138	85,611	1,179	93,771	1,115	83,827	1,133	86,625
1922	1,277	1,081	75,971	1,367	106,260	959	68,363	995	74,826	888	62,860	905	65,000
1921	1,151	805	78,785	1,019	106,554	709	69,786	734	75,511	655	63,542	669	64,994
1920	1,016	876	80,865	1,215	132,023	762	72,920	781	86,744	—	—	—	—
1919	905	795	54,428	1,090	87,753	708	49,811	727	59,983	—	—	—	—
1918	837	735	46,231	968	73,124	636	37,301	650	42,951	—	—	—	—
1917	—	690	38,868	856	59,250	596	32,561	607	35,622	—	—	—	—
1916	—	—[2]	—	—	—	526	21,099	533	23,466	—	—	—	—

[1] Represents the weight of items of export classification for which tonnage figures are available: for example, exports of paper products are not recorded by weight, and exports of paper boards for 1927 to 1937 were not recorded by weight. Value of exports, however, covers all exports of paper and paper products.

[2] Annual average production: for 1913 to 1914, 436,000 tons; 1915 to 1919, 710,000 tons.

Series L189-198. Principal statistics, pulp and paper mills, manufacturing activity and total activity, 1959 to 1975
(series L189-190 in numbers; series L191-198 in thousands of dollars)

Year	Estab-lishments	Manufacturing activity						Total activity		
		Production and related workers		Cost of fuel and electricity	Cost of materials and supplies	Value of shipments of goods of own manufacture	Value added	Employees		Value added
		Number	Wages					Number	Salaries and wages	
	189	190	191	192	193	194	195	196	197	198
1975	147	64,329	754,892	398,692	2,191,527	5,122,093	2,569,050	84,046	1,091,675	2,601,472
1974	147	66,584	802,836	409,152	2,306,718	5,703,192	3,033,697	86,203	1,097,108	3,048,775
1973	146	61,783	645,084	270,637	1,700,933	3,790,939	1,803,889	80,085	884,242	1,812,569
1972	141	61,196	594,291	244,370	1,483,871	3,127,821	1,374,129	78,969	808,869	1,380,052
1971	142	61,426	546,239	232,985	1,363,567	2,832,267	1,272,551	79,397	745,608	1,276,837
1970	139	62,025	511,654	204,359	1,334,375	2,850,836	1,323,278	80,371	701,395	1,331,067
1969	138	62,307	488,854	198,541	1,314,262	2,771,276	1,259,411	75,427	611,591	1,268,022
1968	137	60,296	437,135	181,194	1,183,007	2,446,874	1,080,941	73,498	552,162	1,089,986
1967	136	61,237	413,537	172,329	1,097,505	2,301,044	1,052,085	73,983	516,724	1,059,268
1966	134	60,854	390,735	163,467	1,043,720	2,297,662	1,100,261	73,501	486,249	1,107,717
1965	132	58,074	339,363	151,237	924,406	2,104,425	1,033,532	69,897	423,732	1,042,399
1964	131	56,429	315,973	138,461	846,406	1,984,114	1,002,787	67,729	394,136	1,011,391
1963	126	53,982	290,107	126,126	750,188	1,793,231	914,258	65,040	364,513	922,431
1962	125	53,745	281,858	122,427	716,163	1,716,300	880,260	64,599	354,199	886,111
1961	125	53,428	271,234	117,084	680,168	1,632,834	840,647	63,789	338,968	847,834
1961	125	53,428	271,234	117,084	680,168	1,632,834	840,647	65,799	355,171	840,647
1960	126	53,313	260,199	111,259	657,865	1,583,107	814,798	65,772	345,093	814,798
1959	126	53,451	245,376	109,002	630,203	1,502,312	763,184	65,162	322,936	763,184

Series L199-205. Principal statistics of the pulp and paper industry, 1919 to 1959
(series L199-200 in numbers; series L201-205 in thousands of dollars)

Year	Establishments	Employees	Salaries and wages	Cost of fuel and electricity	Cost of materials	Net value of production	Gross value of production
	199	200	201	202	203	204	205
1959	127	65,028	322,311	108,859	628,269	761,036	1,498,164
1958	128	64,084	307,416	105,797	597,805	702,951	1,406,553
1957	128	69,940	307,628	108,637	617,176	693,476	1,419,288
1956	126	65,985	297,572	103,506	625,205	736,346	1,465,058
1955	125	62,205	265,298	91,041	546,079	689,818	1,326,938
1954	125	60,837	252,598	84,891	515,258	641,517	1,241,665
1953	127	58,194	235,742	80,380	499,351	599,935	1,179,665
1952	128	57,803	225,353	76,740	497,047	584,101	1,157,888
1951	126	57,291	213,170	75,626	483,014	679,258	1,237,897
1950	123	52,343	169,247	69,112	373,883	511,143	954,138
1949	123	52,050	157,704	64,110	348,663	423,376	836,148
1948	117	51,924	151,663	63,843	349,244	412,770	825,858
1947	115	49,946	129,478	55,442	295,444	356,085	706,972
1946	113	44,967	101,365	46,202	223,448	258,165	527,815
1945	109	39,996	80,463	39,033	179,369	180,402	398,805
1944	104	37,896	75,833	37,359	157,995	174,492	369,846
1943	106	37,020	71,199	36,211	143,956	164,244	344,412
1942	105	38,002	69,656	36,226	135,970	164,500	336,697
1941	106	37,154	63,678	34,437	125,437	174,852	334,726
1940	103	34,719	56,074	31,045	108,759	158,231	298,035
1939	100	31,016	44,737	25,095	79,934	103,124	208,152
1938	99	30,943	42,619	23,801	71,063	89,034	183,898
1937	98	33,205	48,758	29,121	91,122	106,002	226,245
1936	93	29,478	39,440	25,691	72,203	85,739	183,633

Series L199-205. Principal statistics of the pulp and paper industry, 1919 to 1959 (concluded)
(series L199-200 in numbers; series L201-205 in thousands of dollars)

Year	Establishments	Employees	Salaries and wages	Cost of fuel and electricity	Cost of materials	Net value of production	Gross value of production
	199	200	201	202	203	204	205
1935	95	27,836	35,893	22,683	57,995	78,648	159,326
1934	95	26,993	33,307	21,978	53,427	77,213	152,648
1933	95	24,037	26,658	18,902	47,633	56,881	123,415
1932	98	24,561	28,348	19,822	48,971	66,856	135,649
1931	103	26,669	34,792	22,928	63,948	87,858	174,734
1930	109	33,027	45,775	26,158	81,992	107,524	215,674
1929	108	34,202	50,214	25,356	96,875	121,740	243,971
1928	110	33,614	47,323	24,547	88,490	120,040	233,077
1927	114	32,876	45,674	24,024	84,813	110,492	219,330
1926	115	31,279	44,176	20,424	85,365	109,580	215,370
1925	114	28,031	38,561	17,507	76,515	99,071	193,093
1924	115	27,627	37,650	17,396	72,234	89,629	179,260
1923	110	29,234	38,383	18,422	71,323	95,077	184,822
1922	104	25,830	32,919	16,982	64,693	77,276	158,951
1921	100	24,619	34,199	14,962	62,276	73,765	151,003
1920	100	31,298	45,254	16,989	84,209	135,222	236,420
1919	99	26,647	32,264	12,503	54,085	71,325	137,913

Series L206-210. Forest fires, Canada,[1] 1908 to 1975

Year	Number of fires			Acres burned		Year	Number of fires			Acres burned	
	Under 10 acres	Over 10 acres	Total	Total	Merchant-able		Under 10 acres	Over 10 acres	Total	Total	Merchant-able
	206	207	208	209	210		206	207	208	209	210
1975	9,544	1,196	10,740	898,170	68,528	1945	3,681	1,080	4,761	741,531	159,909
1974	6,844	933	7,777	1,963,259	353,179	1944	3,943	1,877	5,820	2,403,061	503,764
1973	6,216	748	6,964	160,511	34,911	1943	2,355	1,015	3,370	827,830	87,809
1972	6,995	1,232	8,227	1,927,444	546,230	1942	3,437	1,354	4,791	1,838,471	318,435
1971	7,719	1,099	8,818	2,445,227	512,953	1941	3,833	2,118	5,951	4,252,651	1,498,128
1970	8,133	1,120	9,253	2,616,366	268,004	1940	4,477	1,807	6,284	2,691,135	462,454
1969	5,844	789	6,633	2,331,378	369,562	1939	3,990	1,623	5,613	1,115,179	199,288
1968	6,269	1,032	7,301	2,211,605	547,225	1938	4,476	2,171	6,647	3,125,768	722,199
1967	7,189	1,461	8,650	2,211,954	401,043	1937	3,886	2,063	5,949	4,271,431	662,792
1966	6,705	763	7,468	1,144,439	252,520	1936	4,031	1,915	5,946	3,026,646	919,764
1965	6,372	866	7,238	521,148	137,190	1935	3,277[2]	1,678[2]	4,955	856,183	172,592
1964	5,784	1,160	6,944	2,993,290	683,826	1934	4,014[2]	1,897[2]	5,911	1,475,117	321,414
1963	6,545	1,125	7,670	470,001	97,783	1933	3,999[2]	2,299[2]	6,298	1,008,558	204,405
1962	5,450	835	6,285	863,585	298,625	1932	3,777[2]	2,521[2]	6,298	2,463,923	708,085
1961	6,881	1,774	8,655	9,313,479	2,858,924	1931	—	—	6,965	2,093,922	394,824
1960	5,988	1,217	7,205	1,470,676	416,684	1930	—	—	6,805	2,670,188	746,129
1959	3,846	890	4,736	537,819	65,276	1929	—	—	6,712	6,028,551	663,574
1958	5,336	1,311	6,647	3,291,541	541,221	1928	—	—	4,243	1,346,026	217,350
1957	4,559	1,039	5,598	452,416	71,470	1927	2,838	767	3,605	471,878	114,708
1956	3,656	884	4,540	2,016,428	645,608	1926	4,154	1,536	5,690	1,824,015	575,732
1955	5,048	1,144	6,192	1,375,199	344,548	1925	3,876	1,614	5,490	1,316,321	217,293
1954	2,506	446	2,952	264,295	72,136	1924	3,995	1,629	5,624	1,984,786	377,146
1953	4,994	1,448	6,442	1,358,129	203,110	1923	3,705	2,484	6,189	6,196,817	1,853,079
1952	3,844	1,042	4,886	975,249	182,900	1922	5,425	2,774	8,199	3,323,401	609,132
1951	3,453	1,049	4,502	896,015	135,091	1921	3,905	2,168	6,073	2,142,446	408,455
1950	3,769	1,541	5,310	2,226,765	259,205	1920	3,315	1,943	5,258	1,708,368	363,142
1949	5,334	1,712	7,046	2,599,272	395,497	1919	3,438	1,785	5,223	7,589,669	2,159,995
1948	3,863	1,505	5,368	3,184,983	949,530	1918	3,064	1,079	4,143	562,752	75,527
1947	3,893	1,124	5,017	613,007	105,098	1917[3]	1,437	680	2,117	857,714[4]	135,382[4]
1946	4,372	1,531	5,903	1,016,706	109,478	1916[3]	1,324	444	1,768	277,598[4]	21,645[4]
						1915[3]	1,849	913	2,762	2,207,361[4]	705,039[4]
						1914[3]	2,898	939	3,837	1,023,431[4]	205,991[4]
						1909[3]	—	—	1,134	435,000	—
						1908[3]	—	—	835	188,390	—

[1] Excludes the Yukon Territory and the Northwest Territories.
[2] Estimated by the Forestry Branch from incomplete reports.
[3] See the notes to series K184-188 in original edition for the provinces covered by these data.
[4] Acres reported cover only fires over 10 acres in extent.

SECTION M: Agriculture

G.I. Trant, *Agriculture Canada*

The statistics of agriculture presented here are in five sections. Series M1-248 are the general statistics of the industry, covering such topics as farm population, area of farms, capital employed, cash income and prices of farm products. Series M249-309 are crop statistics, showing acreage, production and value of the various crops. Series M310-412 are livestock statistics, showing number and value of livestock on farms as well as production and disposition of various livestock products. Series M413-489 show exports and domestic disappearance of grains, animals and animal products, and food produced and consumed, per capita. Series M490-525 are miscellaneous statistics such as sales through marketing boards and purchases through co-operatives and farm implement and fertilizer sales.

It is regretted that space would not permit the inclusion of provincial breakdowns of crop and livestock statistics, for which a considerable amount of original research was carried out in the Agriculture Division of Statistics Canada. The voluminous tabulations on a provincial basis are available only in manuscript form in that division. However, provincial breakdowns have been given in the general statistics (Series M1-248) wherever possible.

The general note which appears in the first edition of this volume contains much useful background material which has not been repeated here, but which should be consulted by the interested reader. To a considerable extent, the following notes and tables constitute simply an updating of the previously published material. However, all previously published figures were checked and revised where necessary and several new series were added. A few series of mainly historical interest, which terminated prior to 1960, were not repeated in the present volume.

There are two general measures of the importance of agriculture in the total economy, which are given in Section F, National Income and the Capital Stock. These are series F56, gross domestic product in agriculture (current dollars) and series F226, real domestic product in agriculture (constant 1971 dollars, indexed). Both of these series show a long term decline in agriculture relative to the total economy. For example, the gross domestic product originating in agriculture was 17.2 per cent of the total economy in 1926 and 3.0 per cent in 1976. The real domestic product index for agriculture nearly doubled between 1935 and 1971, whereas that for the total economy grew six times. Further detail on the last mentioned series is given in series M239-248, 'Index numbers of physical volume of agricultural production, Canada and by province, 1935 to 1974.'

A third measure of the relative importance of agriculture, which excludes the rapidly growing service industries, is census value added in agriculture and other goods-producing industries, as published in *Survey of Production*, 1975, (Catalogue 61-202). Since this is the only source which cross-classifies industries by province, it is shown in tabular form below.

Census value added, 1975
(millions of dollars)

	Agriculture	All goods-producing industries	Per cent in agriculture
Newfoundland	—	1,037	—
Prince Edward Island	43	150	28.7
Nova Scotia	59	1,415	4.2
New Brunswick	51	1,323	3.9
Quebec	798	16,436	4.9
Ontario	1,535	28,505	5.4
Manitoba	639	2,547	25.1
Saskatchewan	1,885	3,717	50.7
Alberta	1,372	10,646	12.9
British Columbia	249	6,969	3.6
Yukon Territory and Northwest Territories	—	211	—
Canada	6,630	72,957	9.1

General Statistics (Series M1-248)

M1-11. Farm population, census data, Canada and by province, 1931 to 1971

SOURCE: for 1951 to 1971, Statistics Canada, *1971 Census of Canada: Agriculture,* vol. IV, parts 1 to 3, (Bulletins 4.1-1 to 4.3-4), Ottawa, 1973; for 1946, Canada, Dominion Bureau of Statistics, *Census of the Prairie Provinces, 1946: Agriculture,* vol. IV, Ottawa, 1949; for 1941, Canada, Dominion Bureau of Statistics, *Census of Canada, 1956: Agriculture,* vol. II, (Bulletins 2-2 and 2-11), Ottawa, 1957; for 1936, see source for 1946; for 1931, see source for 1941 (plus Bulletins 2.3 to 2.10).

There were no farm population data before the 1931 Census.

M12-22. Farm holdings, census data, Canada and by province, 1871 to 1971

SOURCE: for 1971, *Census of Canada*, vol. IV, parts 1 to 3; for 1951 to 1966, *1966 Census of Canada*, vols. III and V, (Bulletins 3-1 to 3-5, 4-1 to 4-2 and 5-1 to 5-4); for 1946, *Census of the Prairie Provinces, 1946*, vol. IV; for 1941, *Census of Canada, 1956*, vol. II, (Bulletins 2-2 and 2-11); for 1936, see source for 1946; for 1931, see source for 1941; for 1926, see source for 1946; for 1921, *Census of Canada, 1956*, vol. II, (Bulletins 2-2 to 2-11); for 1916, see source for 1926; for 1901 and 1911, Canada, Dominion Bureau of Statistics, *Ninth Census of Canada, 1951: Agriculture*, vol. VI, parts I and II; for 1881, *Eighth Census of Canada, 1941*, vol. VIII, parts I and II; for 1891, *Seventh Census of Canada, 1931*, vol. VIII; for 1871, see source for 1881.

For a discussion of the comparibility of the data see the first edition of this volume, page 342.

M23-33. Area of land in farm holdings, census data, Canada and by province, 1871 to 1971

SOURCE: for 1931 to 1971, same as series M1-11; for 1871 to 1926, same as series M12-22.

M34-44. Area of improved land in farm holdings, census data, Canada and by province, 1871 to 1971

SOURCE: same as Series M23-33.

M45-54. Current value of farm capital, Canada and by province, 1901 to 1974

SOURCE: for 1966 to 1975, Statistics Canada, *Quarterly Bulletin of Agricultural Statistics*, vols. 59 to 68, (Catalogue 21-003); for 1917 to 1965, Dominion Bureau of Statistics, *Monthly Bulletin of Agricultural Statistics*, vols. 12 to 58; for 1916, Department of Trade and Commerce, Census and Statistics Office, *Monthly Bulletin of Agricultural Statistics, 1918*, vol. II, and *1946 Census of the Prairie Provinces;* for 1911, *Ninth Census of Canada, 1951: Agriculture*, vol. VI, part I and II; for 1901, same as above, plus *Seventh Census of Canada, 1931: Agriculture*, vol. VIII.

The data for 1901 to 1929 are aggregates derived from the separate data on value of lands and buildings, implements and machinery and livestock and poultry.

M55-66. Male workers employed in agriculture, labour force estimates, Canada and by region and province, 1946 to 1974

SOURCE: for 1959 to 1974, Statistics Canada, *The Labour Force*, vols. 15 to 30, (Catalogue 71-001); for 1946 to 1958, Dominion Bureau of Statistics, *The Labour Force, November, 1945 - July, 1958.* Reference Paper No. 58, 1958 Revision, (Catalogue 71-502).

M67-77. Male workers employed in agricultural occupations, decennial census data, Canada and by province, 1891 to 1971

SOURCE: for 1971, Statistics Canada, *1971 Census of Canada: Occupations*, vol. III, part 2 (Bulletin 3.2-3), Ottawa, 1974; for 1961, Dominion Bureau of Statistics, *1961 Census of Canada: Labour Force-Occupations*, vol. III, part 1 (Bulletin 3.1-3), Ottawa, February 1963; for 1951, *Ninth Census of Canada, 1951: Labour Force Occupations and Industries*, vol. IV; for 1941, *Eighth Census of Canada, 1941: Gainfully Occupied by Occupations and Industries*, vol. VII; for 1931, *Seventh Census of Canada, 1931: Occupations and Industries*, vol. VII; for 1921, *Sixth Census of Canada, 1921: Occupations*, vol. IV; for 1911, Canada, Department of Trade and Commerce, *Fifth Census of Canada, 1911: Occupations of the People*, vol. VI; for 1891, Canada, Department of Agriculture and Statistics, *Census of Canada, 1890-91*, vol. II.

M78-88. Monthly wages without board for male farm labour, Canada and by region and province, 1909 to 1974

SOURCE: for 1941 to 1974, Statistics Canada, *Quarterly Bulletin of Agricultural Statistics, July- September* each year, vols. 35 to 65; for 1914 to 1940, *Monthly Bulletin of Agricultural Statistics*, vols. 15 to 33; for 1909 and 1910, *Monthly Bulletin of Agricultural Statistics*, vol. 13.

M89-98. Cash receipts from farming operations, Canada and by province, 1926 to 1974

SOURCE: for 1961 to 1974, Statistics Canada, *Farm Net Income, 1974*, (Catalogue 21-202); for 1960, Canada, Dominion Bureau of Statistics, *Quarterly Bulletin of Agricultural Statistics, 1969*, vol. 62, (Catalogue 21-003); for 1926 to 1959, Canada, Dominion Bureau of Statistics, *Handbook of Agricultural Statistics, Part II: Farm Income, 1926-1965*, (Catalogue 21-511).

M99-108. Realized farm gross income, Canada and by province, 1926 to 1974

SOURCE: same as series M89-98.

M109-118. Realized farm net income, Canada and by province, 1926 to 1974

SOURCE: same as series M89-98.

M119-128. Total farm net income, Canada and by province, 1926 to 1974

SOURCE: same as series M89-98.

M129-135. Reconciliation of net income from farm operations and accrued net income from farm production, Canada, 1926 to 1974

SOURCE: Statistics Canada, *National Income and Expenditure Accounts: The Annual Estimates, 1926 to 1974*, vol. 1, (Catalogue 13-531).

M136-145. Cash receipts from crops, Canada and by province, 1926 to 1974

SOURCE: for 1965 to 1974, Statistics Canada, *Farm Cash Receipts, 1974*, (Catalogue 21-201); for 1926 to 1964, Canada, Dominion Bureau of Statistics, *Handbook of Agricultural Statistics, Part II: Farm Income, 1926-1965*, (Catalogue 21-511).

M146-155. Cash receipts from livestock, Canada and by province, 1926 to 1974

SOURCE: same as series M136-145.

M156-165. Cash receipts from dairy products, Canada and by province, 1926 to 1974

SOURCE: same as series M136-145.

M166-175. Cash receipts from poultry and eggs, Canada and by province, 1926 to 1974

SOURCE: same as series M136-145.

M176-185. Miscellaneous cash receipts from farming operations, Canada and by province, 1926 to 1974

SOURCE: same as series M136-145.

M186-195. Composite index of farm prices of agricultural products, Canada and by province, 1935 to 1974

SOURCE: for 1960 to 1974, Statistics Canada, *Index Numbers of Farm Prices of Agricultural Products, 1975*, vol. 30, (Catalogue 62-003); for 1935 to 1959, Canada, Dominion Bureau of Statistics, *Index Numbers of Farm Prices of Agricultural Products: Revised to Time Base, 1961 = 100*, (Catalogue 62-529).

M196-205. Indexes of farm prices for groups of agricultural products, Canada, 1935 to 1974

SOURCE: files of Farm Income and Prices Section, Agriculture Division, Statistics Canada.

M206-220. Farm input prices indexes, Canada, 1961 to 1974

SOURCE: for 1970 to 1974, Statistics Canada, *Farm Input Price Indexes*, (Catalogue 62-004); for 1961 to 1969, Statistics Canada, *Farm Input Price Indexes*, (Catalogue 62-534).

M221-227. Price index numbers of commodities and services used by farmers, Canada, 1913 to 1961

SOURCE: Canada, Dominion Bureau of Statistics, *Prices and Price Indexes*, (Catalogue 62-002, previously 62-004 and 62-509).

M228-238. Wholesale market prices for selected agricultural products, 1867 to 1974

SOURCE: **M228-233.** for years 1918 to 1974, Statistics Canada, *Grain Trade of Canada*, (Catalogue 22-201); for 1915 to 1917, Canada, Department of Labour, *Annual Report, Wholesale Prices;* for 1890 to 1914, Canada, Department of Labour, *Wholesale Prices in Canada.*

M234-236. For 1890 to 1974, Statistics Canada, *Livestock and Animal Products Statistics*, (Catalogue 23-203); for 1870 to 1889, Michell, H., Statistics of Price, in Taylor and Michell, *Statistical Contributions to Canadian Economic History*, vol. II, Toronto, The MacMillan Company of Canada Limited, 1931.

M237-238. For 1913 to 1974, Statistics Canada, *Prices and Price Indexes*, vols. 21 to 53, (Catalogue 62-002 from 1955 to 1974 and Catalogue 62-501 from 1913 to 1954); for 1890 to 1913, Canada, Department of Labour, *Wholesale Prices, Canada,* various issues back to May, 1910; for 1867 to 1889, same as series M234.

Specifications

M228. Wheat. For 1971 to 1974, No. 1 Canadian Western Red Spring, 13.5 per cent; cents and eighths per bushel, basis in store Thunder Bay; average for crop year beginning 1 August of daily fixed price for export sales quoted by Canadian Wheat Board. This specification differed in prior years, as follows: in 1970, to No. 1 Manitoba Northern, daily fixed price for International Grains Arrangement sales, quoted by Canadian Wheat Board; in 1968, basis Fort William-Port Arthur; in 1967, average for International Wheat Agreement and domestic sales; in 1945, daily cash price at Winnipeg; in 1916, price on first market day of each week; in 1889, Ontario Winter No. 2 White, on last market day of each month at Toronto; and in 1867, Fall, ungraded, at Toronto.

M229. Oats. For 1974, No. 2 Canadian Western, cents and eighths per bushel, basis in store Thunder Bay, average for crop year beginning 1 August of daily fixed price for domestic sales quoted by Canadian Wheat Board. This specification differed in prior years as follows: in 1973, average of domestic and export prices; in 1948, prices quoted by Winnipeg Grain Exchange; in 1947, domestic price only, at Winnipeg; in 1923, crop year began 1 September, not 1 August; in 1916, first market day of each week; in 1911, No. 2 White Western; in 1910, first market day of each month; and in 1889, ungraded, at Toronto.

M230. Barley. In 1974, No. 2 Canadian Western, Six Row, cents and eighths per bushel, basis in store Thunder Bay, average for crop year beginning 1 August of daily fixed price for malting sales quoted by Canadian Wheat Board; in 1973, average of domestic and export prices; in 1968, No. 3 Canadian Western, Six Row; in 1948, at Winnipeg Grain Exchange; in 1947, domestic sales only; in 1946, at Winnipeg; in 1923, crop year beginning 1 September; in 1916, first market day of each week; in 1910, first market day of each month; and in 1889, ungraded, at Toronto.

M231. Flaxseed. From 1972 to 1974, No. 1 Canadian Western, cents and eighths per bushel, basis in store Thunder Bay, average for crop year beginning 1 August of daily closing cash prices for domestic and export sales at Winnipeg Commodity Exchange. This specification differed in prior years as follows: in 1971, at Winnipeg Grain Exchange; in 1947, domestic price on sales to crushers, at Winnipeg; in 1945, daily cash price at Winnipeg; in 1930, name changed to No. 1 North Western; in 1923, crop year beginning 1 September; in 1916, first market day of each week; and in 1910, first market day of each month.

M232. Rapeseed. No. 1 Canada, cents and eighths per bushel, basis in store Thunder Bay, average for crop year beginning 1 August of daily closing cash price at Winnipeg Commodity Exchange. The above specification differed in prior years as follows: in 1971, quoted by Winnipeg Grain Exchange; in 1969, basis in store Vancouver.

M233. Corn. For 1973 and 1974, No. 2 Canadian Eastern, cents and eighths per bushel, f.o.b. Chatham, average for crop year beginnning 1 August of daily buying price for carlots. This specification differed in prior years as follows: in 1972, No. 2 Ontario Yellow, 15.5 per cent moisture; in 1951, daily price for carlots delivered Toronto; and in 1947, Ontario Natural, carlots delivered Toronto.

M234. Steers. In 1974, Grade A1 and 2, cents per pound, weighted average price at Toronto; in 1972, good all weights; in 1957, good over 1,000 pounds; in 1948, good over

1,050 pounds; in 1935, good and choice, over 1,050 pounds; in 1929, good 1,000 to 1,200 pounds; in 1919, choice butcher; in 1918, first market day each week; in 1910, first market day each month; and in 1889, first quality export, last market day each month.

M235. Pigs. Index 100, cents per pound, dressed weight, weighted average price at Toronto. This specification differed in prior years as follows: in 1968, grade B; in 1959, grade B1; in 1942, bacon; in 1939, bacon live weight; in 1929, thick smooth; in 1922, select live weight; in 1918, first market day of each week; in 1912, choice select; in 1910, first market day of each month; and in 1889, first quality export, last market day of each month.

M236. Sheep. From 1949 to 1974, good sheep, cents per pound, weighted average price at Toronto. The above specification differed in prior years as follows: in 1948, good handyweight sheep; in 1921, choice sheep, average of monthly price; in 1912, light ewes, first market day of each week; in 1911, export ewes; in 1910, first market day of each month; and in 1889, last market day of each month.

M237. Eggs. From 1971 to 1974, grade A large, cents per dozen, at Toronto. The above specification differed in prior years as follows: in 1970, at Montreal; in 1952, fresh grade A large; in 1933, fresh extras; in 1925, new laid; in 1912, fresh; in 1910, storage, at Toronto; in 1889, new laid; and in 1867, ungraded.

M238. Butter. From 1953 to 1974, first grade prints, cents per pound, at Montreal. The above specification differed in prior years as follows: in 1952, first grade creamery prints; in 1935, No. 1 creamery; in 1925, creamery finest; in 1910, creamery prints at Toronto; in 1889, dairy prints; and in 1867, ungraded.

M239-248. Index numbers of physical volume of agricultural production, Canada and by province, 1935 to 1974

SOURCE: Statistics Canada, *Index of Farm Production*, (Catalogue 21-203).

Crop Statistics (Series M249-309)

M249-300. Seeded area, production and farm gross value of field crops, Canada, 1870, 1880, 1890, 1900 and 1908 to 1974

SOURCE: M249-293, for 1921 to 1974, Statistics Canada, *Handbook of Agricultural Statistics: Field Crops*, part I, (Catalogue 21-516); for 1908 to 1920, Canada, Dominion Bureau of Statistics, *Handbook of Agricultural Statistics: Field Crops*, part I, (Catalogue 21-507); for 1900, Canada, Dominion Bureau of Statistics, *Sixth Census of Canada, 1921: Agriculture*, vol. V; for 1890, same as for 1900; for 1880, Canada, Department of Agriculture, Census Branch, *Census of Canada, 1880-81*, vol. III; for 1870, Canada, Department of Agriculture, Census Branch, *Census of Canada, 1870-71*, vol. III.
M294-300, for 1916 to 1974, Statistics Canada, *Quarterly Bulletin of Agricultural Statistics*, (Catalogue 21-003); for 1911 to 1915, Canada, Department of Trade and Commerce, Census and Statistics Office, *Census and Statistics Monthly;* for 1890 to 1910, Canada, Department of Trade and Commerce, Census and Statistics Office, *Fifth Census of Canada, 1911: Agriculture*, vol. IV.

The Canada totals in this and the following three tables include Newfoundland, the Yukon Territory and the Northwest Territories.

M301-309. Crop statistics: production, imports, exports and domestic disappearance of wheat, Canada, 1868 to 1974

SOURCE: M301, for 1921 to 1974, Statistics Canada, *Handbook of Agricultural Statistics: Field Crops*, part I, (Catalogue 21-516); for 1908 to 1920, Canada, Dominion Bureau of Statistics, *Handbook of Agricultural Statistics: Field Crops*, part I, (Catalogue 21-507); for 1868 to 1907, Canada, Dominion Bureau of Statistics, *Monthly Bulletin of Agricultural Statistics*, vol. 30, (Catalogue 21-003).
M302, for 1960 to 1966, Canada, Dominion Bureau of Statistics, *Grain Trade of Canada*, (Catalogue 22-201); for 1868 to 1959, same as series M301.
M303-305, for 1962 to 1974, Statistics Canada, *Grain Trade of Canada*, (Catalogue 22-201); for 1868 to 1961, same as series M301.
M306-308, for 1917 to 1974, same as series M301 and M303-305.
M309, same as series M301 and M303-305.

Livestock Statistics (Series M310-412)

M310-320. Livestock statistics, number on farms and farm values at 1 June, Canada, 1871 to 1975

SOURCE: for 1907 to 1975, Statistics Canada, *Livestock and Animal Products Statistics*, (Catalogue 23-203), 1975. The above report is the 57th in an annual series covering livestock and animal products in Canada. The first volume, issued in 1920, covered the years 1909 to 1919 and subsequent volumes have maintained a continuous annual record of the operations of the livestock industry in Canada. Some historical and summary statements have been included to afford a long-time view of the industry. Newfoundland entered Confederation March 31, 1949, but, for the most part, current statistical data for Newfoundland are not available. Except for external trade statistics and estimates of meat production and consumption for the years 1964 to 1976, all data in this report refer to the other nine provinces only. However, a special section on Newfoundland is included on page 83 of the above report.

The survey date has been changed from 1 December to 1 January starting with 1 January 1974. In 1975 the 1 June semi-annual survey data was changed to 1 July.

Information has been assembled from various departmental sources. Commercial marketing and inspected slaughter of livestock are reported by the Food Production and Marketing Branch of Agriculture Canada; for years prior to 1907, see the first edition of this volume.

M321-330. Livestock product statistics, estimated number slaughtered and weight of meat produced, Canada, 1871, 1881, 1891 and 1920 to 1975

SOURCE: for 1961 to 1975, *Livestock and Animal Product Statistics*, (Catalogue 23-203), 1975; for years prior to 1961, see the first edition of this volume.

M331-342.   Utilization of total milk production, Canada, 1920 to 1975

SOURCE: CANSIM, Matrix No. 1330.

M343-356.   Dairy products and margarine: total domestic disappearance, Canada, 1920 to 1975

SOURCE: CANSIM, Matrix No. 1340.

M357-362.   Dairy products: domestic disappearance, in terms of milk, Canada, 1920 to 1975

SOURCE: CANSIM, Matrix No. 1342.

M363-368.   Dairy products: domestic disappearance in terms of milk, Canada, 1920 to 1975

SOURCE: CANSIM, Matrix No. 1342.

M369-376.   Number of poultry on farms, by class, Canada, 1916 to 1972

SOURCE: CANSIM, Matrix Nos. 1147 and 1148.

M377-384.   Total poultry meat: supply and disposition, Canada, 1926 to 1975

SOURCE: for 1970 to 1975, *Production of Poultry and Eggs*, (Catalogue 23-202), 1976; for 1926 to 1969, CANSIM, Matrix No. 1136.

M385-393.   Total poultry meat: production, disposition and farm value, Canada, 1941 to 1975

SOURCE: for 1970 to 1975, *Production of Poultry and Eggs*, (Catalogue 23-202), 1976; for 1941 to 1969, CANSIM, Matrix No. 1138.

M394-402.   Eggs, supply and disposition, Canada, 1920 to 1975

SOURCE: for 1970 to 1975, *Production of Poultry and Eggs*, (Catalogue 23-202), 1976; for 1920 to 1969, CANSIM, Matrix No. 1137.

M403-412.   Eggs, production and disposition, Canada, 1920 to 1975

SOURCE: for 1970 to 1975, *Production of Poultry and Eggs*, (Catalogue 23-202), 1976; for 1920 to 1969, CANSIM, Matrix No. 1144.

Exports and Domestic Disappearance (Series M413-489)

M413-416.   Exports of major agricultural products, grains (except wheat), quantity, Canada, crop years, 1868 to 1975

SOURCE: for 1961 to 1975, *Grain Trade of Canada, Export Clearances by Countries of Final Destination*, (Catalogue 22-201); for years prior to 1961, see the first edition of this volume.

M417-427.   Exports of major agricultural products, animals and animal products, quantity and value, Canada, 1868 to 1975

SOURCE: M417-424, *Livestock and Animal Product Statistics*, (Catalogue 23-203).
M425, for years 1974 and 1975, CANSIM, Matrix No. 1332; for years 1962 to 1973, *Handbook of Agricultural Statistics*, (Catalogue 21-515 Occasional).
M426, for years 1974 and 1975, *Grain Trade of Canada*, (Catalogue 23-201 Annual); for years 1961 to 1973, unpublished historical tables, Dairy Section, Agriculture Division.
M427, for 1976, *Production of Poultry and Eggs*, (Catalogue 23-202 Annual); for years 1970 to 1975, CANSIM, Matrix No. 1137.

M428-445.   Domestic disappearance of food products, per capita, Canada, 1919 to 1976

SOURCE: Statistics Canada, Agriculture Division.

The general procedure in this compilation was to start with an estimate of production at either the farm or processor level. Adjustments were made for beginning and year-end inventories and for imports and exports to obtain total supplies. To obtain an estimate of apparent domestic disappearance, the portion of total supplies used for livestock feed, seed, manufacturing inputs and waste was subtracted. Apparent domestic disappearance figures calculated in this way represent the amount of food moving into trade channels.

The data for the components of the food balance sheets are mainly derived from farm surveys and reports by firms engaged in producing and marketing in the food industry. The net food figure represents the supply of food leaving the wholesale level destined for retail distribution.

The per capita estimates of supplies of food are shown as retail or product weight with exceptions of meat and poultry which are calculated on a cold dressed carcass and eviscerated weight basis. The waste factors used for specific commodities attempt to account for waste up to the retail level but do not allow for losses in stores, households, private institutions or restaurants. Per capita values for meat also include features such as bone in and fat weight as well as the amounts of meat used in canned goods and pet foods.

Per capita values do not represent total food supplies actually consumed by an individual or by a specific group of individuals but provide data on what is available for consumption on the average each year by the total Canadian population.

M446-489.   Grain elevators, number and capacities, 1958 to 1977

SOURCE: *Grain Elevators in Canada*, compiled by Board of Grain Commissioners for Canada.

Miscellaneous Statistics (Series M490-525)

M490-505.   Marketing Boards in Canada

SOURCE: these statistics have been collected by the Marketing and Trade Division of the Canada Department of Agriculture, in co-operation with provincial governments, through a mail survey starting in the 1957-58 marketing (crop) year (12 months ending July 31). Farmers' receipts through marketing board agencies are shown as a percentage of total farm cash receipts for each group as estimated by the Agriculture Division of Statistics Canada. The data include all boards affecting agricultural products regardless of function, legal status or degree of producer control. The first broiler chicken marketing board was established in 1962-63 and the first egg board in 1967-68.

M506-522. Co-operatives in Canada, 1934 to 1975

SOURCE: these statistics have been collected by the Marketing and Trade Division of the Canada Department of Agriculture through a mail survey starting in the 1934 co-operative fiscal year.

M523-524. Farm implement and equipment sales and sales of repair parts, Canada, 1947 to 1976

SOURCE: Statistics Canada, *Farm Implement and Equipment Sales,* (Catalogue 63-203).

M525. Expenses for fertilizer, Canada, 1926 to 1976

SOURCE: these statistics were prepared in the Agriculture Division of Statistics Canada.

Series M1-11. Farm population, census data, Canada and by province, 1931 to 1971

Year	Canada[1]	Newfound-land	Prince Edward Island	Nova Scotia	New Brunswick	Quebec	Ontario	Manitoba	Saskat-chewan	Alberta	British Columbia
	1	2	3	4	5	6	7	8	9	10	11
1971	1,489,565	5,156	21,338	26,977	27,453	334,579	391,713	131,202	233,792	237,924	79,353
1966	1,960,365	9,236	31,041	46,283	52,042	507,869	498,025	161,662	281,089	281,583	91,443
1961	2,128,400	11,090	34,753	58,020	63,334	585,485	524,490	172,946	305,740	287,814	84,655
1956	2,746,755	13,055	43,296	98,944	128,978	765,459	683,148	206,729	362,231	332,191	112,668
1951	2,911,996	19,975	46,855	115,414	149,916	792,756	702,778	219,233	399,473	345,222	120,292
1946	–	–	–	–	–	–	–	224,919	434,019	335,610	–
1941	3,152,491	–	51,067	143,709	163,706	838,861	704,420	249,599	514,677	383,964	102,446
1936	–	–	–	–	–	–	–	261,167	573,894	400,390	–
1931	3,289,214	–	55,478	177,690	180,214	777,017	800,960	256,305	564,012	375,097	102,367

[1] Includes the Yukon Territory and Northwest Territories.

Series M12-22. Farm holdings, census data, Canada and by province, 1871 to 1971

Year	Canada	Newfound-land	Prince Edward Island	Nova Scotia	New Brunswick	Quebec	Ontario	Manitoba	Saskat-chewan	Alberta	British Columbia
	12	13	14	15	16	17	18	19	20	21	22
1971[1]	366,128	1,042	4,543	6,008	5,485	61,257	94,722	34,981	76,970	62,702	18,400
1966[1]	430,522	1,709	6,357	9,621	8,706	80,294	109,887	39,747	85,686	69,411	19,085
1961[1]	480,903	1,752	7,335	12,518	11,786	95,777	121,333	43,306	93,924	73,212	19,934
1956[1]	575,015	2,387	9,432	21,075	22,116	122,617	140,602	49,201	103,391	79,424	24,748
1951[1]	623,091	3,626	10,137	23,515	26,431	134,336	149,920	52,383	112,018	84,315	26,406
1946	–	–	–	–	–	–	–	54,448	125,612	89,541	–
1941[1]	732,858	–	12,230	32,977	31,889	154,669	178,204	58,024	138,713	99,732	26,394
1936	–	–	–	–	–	–	–	57,774	142,391	100,358	–
1931[1]	728,664	–	12,865	39,444	34,025	135,957	192,174	54,199	136,472	97,408	26,079
1926[2]	–	–	–	–	–	–	–	53,251	117,781	77,130	–
1921[2]	711,090	–	13,701	47,432	36,655	137,619	198,053	53,252	119,451	82,954	21,973
1916	–	–	–	–	–	–	–	46,580	104,006	67,977	–
1911[2,3]	682,329	–	14,113	52,491	37,755	149,701	212,108	43,631	95,013	60,559	16,958
1901[3]	511,073	–	13,748	54,478	37,006	140,110	204,054	32,252	13,445	9,479	6,501
1891[3,4]	542,181	–	14,549	60,122	38,577	174,996	216,195	22,008	9,244	–	6,490
1881[5]	464,025	–	13,629	55,873	36,837	137,863	206,989	9,077	1,014	–	2,743
1871	367,862	–	–	46,316	31,202	118,086	172,258	–	–	–	–

[1] Data for Canada include the Yukon Territory and Northwest Territories.
[2] Data for Manitoba, Saskatchewan and Alberta exclude farm holdings on Indian reserves.
[3] Excludes plots under one acre, to attain comparability with data for later years.
[4] Data for Saskatchewan comprise the districts of Assiniboia, Saskatchewan and Alberta.
[5] Data for Saskatchewan comprise the Northwest Territories, west of Manitoba.

Series M23-33. Area of land in farm holdings, census data, Canada and by province, 1871 to 1971
(thousands of acres)

Year	Canada	Newfound-land	Prince Edward Island	Nova Scotia	New Brunswick	Quebec	Ontario	Manitoba	Saskat-chewan	Alberta	British Columbia
	23	24	25	26	27	28	29	30	31	32	33
1971[1]	169,669	63	775	1,329	1,339	10,801	15,963	19,008	65,057	49,506	5,823
1966[1]	174,125	50	927	1,852	1,812	12,886	17,826	19,084	65,409	48,983	5,292
1961[1]	172,551	55	960	2,230	2,200	14,198	18,579	18,170	64,416	47,229	4,507
1956[1]	173,924	72	1,065	2,776	2,981	15,910	19,880	17,932	62,794	45,970	4,539
1951[1]	174,047	85	1,095	3,174	3,470	16,786	20,880	17,730	61,663	44,460	4,702
1946	—	—	—	—	—	—	—	16,671	59,416	41,452	—
1941[1]	173,566	—	1,169	3,817	3,964	18,063	22,388	16,891	59,961	43,277	4,034
1936	—	—	—	—	—	—	—	15,669	56,904	40,540	—
1931[1]	163,119	—	1,191	4,302	4,152	17,304	22,841	15,132	55,673	38,977	3,542
1926[2]	—	—	—	—	—	—	—	14,412	45,945	28,573	—
1921[2]	140,888	—	1,216	4,724	4,270	17,257	22,629	14,616	44,023	29,293	2,861
1916	—	—	—	—	—	—	—	13,437	36,801	23,063	—
1911[2]	108,969	—	1,202	5,260	4,538	15,613	22,172	12,184	28,099	17,359	2,540
1901	63,422	—	1,195	5,081	4,443	14,444	21,350	8,843	3,833	2,736	1,497
1891[3,4]	60,288	—	1,214	6,081	4,471	15,962	21,092	5,228	2,910	—	3,330
1881[5]	45,358	—	1,127	5,396	3,810	12,626	19,260	2,384	314	—	441
1871	36,047	—	—	5,031	3,828	11,026	16,162	—	—	—	—

[1] Data for Canada include the Yukon Territory and Northwest Territories.
[2] Data for Manitoba, Saskatchewan and Alberta include only improved land for farm holdings on Indian reserves.
[3] Data for Quebec include arpents that were not converted to acres.
[4] Data for Saskatchewan comprise the districts of Assiniboia, Saskatchewan and Alberta.
[5] Data for Saskatchewan comprise the Northwest Territories, west of Manitoba.

Series M34-44. Area of improved land in farm holdings, census data, Canada and by province, 1871 to 1971
(thousands of acres)

Year	Canada	Newfound-land	Prince Edward Island	Nova Scotia	New Brunswick	Quebec	Ontario	Manitoba	Saskat-chewan	Alberta	British Columbia
	34	35	36	37	38	39	40	41	42	43	44
1971[1]	108,149	19	494	386	487	6,450	10,865	12,804	46,427	28,460	1,755
1966[1]	108,154	21	570	486	639	7,629	12,004	12,446	45,469	27,276	1,614
1961[1]	103,403	20	580	498	734	7,864	12,033	11,964	43,118	25,289	1,303
1956[1]	100,326	24	645	630	951	8,630	12,572	11,454	40,506	23,746	1,167
1951[1]	96,853	29	646	662	1,006	8,829	12,693	10,762	38,807	22,271	1,148
1946	—	—	—	—	—	—	—	9,773	35,590	20,032	—
1941[1]	91,637	—	737	812	1,235	9,063	13,363	9,829	35,577	20,125	893
1936	—	—	—	—	—	—	—	8,855	33,632	18,363	—
1931[1]	85,733	—	766	845	1,330	8,994	13,273	8,522	33,549	17,749	705
1926[2]	—	—	—	—	—	—	—	8,346	27,714	13,204	—
1921[2]	70,770	—	767	992	1,368	9,065	13,169	8,058	25,037	11,768	544
1916	—	—	—	—	—	—	—	7,188	19,632	7,510	—
1911[2]	48,734	—	769	1,257	1,445	8,162	13,653	6,746	11,872	4,352	478
1901	30,166	—	726	1,257	1,410	7,440	13,266	3,995	1,123	475	474
1891[3,4]	28,603	—	718	1,994	1,510	8,671	14,158	1,232	197	—	123
1881[5]	21,866	—	597	1,847	1,253	6,410	11,294	250	29	—	185
1871	17,336	—	—	1,627	1,171	5,704	8,834	—	—	—	—

[1] Data for Canada include the Yukon Territory and Northwest Territories.
[2] Data for Manitoba, Saskatchewan and Alberta include improved land in farm holdings on Indian reserves.
[3] Data for Quebec include arpents that were not converted to acres.
[4] Data for Saskatchewan comprise districts of Assiniboia, Saskatchewan and Alberta.
[5] Data for Saskatchewan comprise the Northwest Territories, west of Manitoba.

Series M45-54. Current value of farm capital, Canada and by province, 1901 to 1974
(thousands of dollars)

Year	Canada[1]	Prince Edward Island	Nova Scotia	New Brunswick	Quebec	Ontario	Manitoba	Saskatchewan	Alberta	British Columbia
	45	46	47	48	49	50	51	52	53	54
1974	36,049,127	252,340	303,934	254,016	3,200,752	10,940,301	2,959,366	7,847,154	7,640,932	2,650,332
1973	29,522,164	204,796	246,665	209,998	2,779,457	8,824,189	2,436,014	6,502,496	6,344,473	1,974,076
1972	25,177,847	176,475	215,121	184,755	2,396,815	7,307,945	2,109,816	5,622,088	5,476,090	1,688,742
1971	23,886,381	161,452	205,263	171,976	2,167,891	6,869,964	2,048,397	5,465,483	5,201,634	1,594,321
1970	23,801,000	163,025	204,415	177,139	2,267,479	6,739,978	2,087,318	5,491,992	5,199,776	1,469,878
1969	23,507,468	159,009	196,029	169,975	2,175,554	6,678,735	2,083,161	5,527,031	5,167,704	1,350,270
1968	22,700,491	148,240	183,397	163,510	2,066,629	5,952,379	2,100,238	5,782,459	5,084,305	1,219,334
1967	21,069,186	139,689	173,121	154,437	1,966,530	5,409,992	1,959,484	5,508,084	4,706,933	1,050,916
1966	19,062,671	128,692	164,804	150,971	1,886,475	4,887,916	1,759,418	4,912,567	4,217,696	954,132
1965	17,217,847	114,596	153,507	147,438	1,788,049	4,453,250	1,595,254	4,343,586	3,805,820	816,347
1964	15,744,055	109,115	149,164	146,082	1,729,290	4,217,848	1,430,309	3,805,218	3,421,195	735,834
1963	14,508,524	104,886	145,269	145,119	1,700,155	3,967,097	1,279,104	3,369,700	3,094,810	702,384
1962	13,669,737	101,848	145,428	144,880	1,652,770	3,900,832	1,183,592	3,005,533	2,851,649	683,205
1961	13,159,169	96,314	146,157	145,414	1,625,810	3,745,307	1,155,354	2,865,086	2,719,163	660,564
1960	12,679,960	96,029	147,964	148,496	1,611,119	3,544,297	1,109,357	2,748,816	2,619,905	653,977
1959	12,308,287	95,794	148,943	150,874	1,587,119	3,574,816	1,046,676	2,597,417	2,473,227	633,421
1958	11,742,427	91,772	147,589	152,548	1,543,404	3,315,883	1,046,134	2,494,867	2,374,572	575,658
1957	10,842,372	86,906	148,032	151,165	1,459,350	3,005,946	979,253	2,347,577	2,132,335	531,808
1956	10,538,662	85,179	147,844	151,586	1,442,387	2,849,637	986,057	2,314,319	2,067,168	494,485
1955	10,313,420	83,997	150,176	152,987	1,400,752	2,783,580	966,365	2,256,571	2,035,413	483,579
1954	9,959,674	84,108	150,441	153,270	1,405,543	2,653,506	955,797	2,116,550	1,984,670	455,789
1953	10,110,116	84,985	152,250	155,737	1,397,969	2,610,014	1,012,522	2,173,392	2,082,286	440,961
1952	9,536,128	85,647	155,239	156,851	1,418,423	2,511,747	931,227	2,082,081	1,785,759	409,154
1951	9,450,890	87,198	152,665	157,808	1,397,856	2,546,839	917,286	1,992,441	1,789,753	409,044
1950	8,171,297	75,863	141,834	148,894	1,211,898	2,068,597	812,293	1,772,908	1,576,213	362,797
1949	7,503,161	71,659	131,860	135,077	1,103,061	1,927,344	733,806	1,612,596	1,453,849	333,909
1948	7,105,054	67,926	129,592	131,191	1,108,638	1,810,495	669,800	1,544,297	1,340,018	303,097
1947	6,389,548	63,410	125,565	129,503	1,056,477	1,685,814	556,895	1,370,403	1,125,859	275,622
1946	5,877,826	58,868	117,096	118,203	1,008,061	1,580,354	513,651	1,251,146	981,869	248,578
1945	5,580,407	59,346	113,332	119,572	954,420	1,514,654	453,367	1,194,744	942,177	228,795
1944	5,489,527	57,248	114,451	121,516	962,061	1,521,749	436,911	1,150,956	914,635	210,000
1943	5,274,723	53,966	103,654	108,253	956,651	1,510,293	422,817	1,049,536	876,760	192,793
1942	4,649,909	51,094	94,296	93,265	833,361	1,279,215	373,709	980,337	773,150	171,482
1941	4,247,196	47,158	88,630	81,181	741,481	1,190,142	339,917	896,274	712,057	150,356
1940	4,214,097	46,306	86,050	83,339	717,419	1,243,307	332,529	843,298	713,589	148,260
1939	4,298,763	50,896	98,885	97,393	730,854	1,261,183	343,002	875,916	691,678	148,956
1938	4,213,914	53,001	91,503	93,577	699,953	1,241,152	319,844	906,740	658,396	149,748
1937	4,383,894	51,977	101,036	93,214	723,403	1,281,126	330,833	967,643	689,087	145,575
1936	4,390,319	49,348	108,975	99,710	705,103	1,253,787	310,510	1,025,931	688,939	148,016
1935	4,523,308	50,072	100,331	92,798	767,606	1,216,397	327,904	1,130,558	695,270	142,372
1934	4,464,147	56,100	96,810	95,033	747,428	1,231,094	331,614	1,067,491	693,280	145,297
1933	4,443,159	53,960	95,570	95,818	781,678	1,167,065	327,181	1,072,625	698,051	151,211
1932	4,732,638	54,638	103,506	99,882	828,775	1,250,467	353,380	1,119,025	762,132	160,833
1931	5,220,660	58,392	107,154	104,929	879,323	1,394,104	383,836	1,256,381	859,643	176,898
1930	5,849,364	68,090	115,078	111,187	1,006,143	1,533,368	442,619	1,399,225	983,456	190,198
1929	6,304,476	67,015	134,725	141,130	1,131,745	1,776,278	569,841	1,413,120	875,110	195,510
1928	6,298,906	67,210	134,182	140,937	1,118,974	1,776,651	572,109	1,424,325	871,795	192,722
1927	6,228,657	65,628	131,742	138,684	1,098,038	1,755,749	566,226	1,417,808	869,070	185,713
1926	6,122,438	65,665	131,290	138,590	1,085,784	1,727,696	552,734	1,399,786	839,365	181,528
1925	6,125,175	65,897	130,290	137,600	1,081,876	1,719,283	554,495	1,410,827	846,641	178,266
1924	6,055,785	64,643	129,249	135,347	1,066,595	1,696,948	548,673	1,400,520	838,752	175,057
1923	6,023,247	63,521	128,164	135,921	1,061,350	1,697,265	545,934	1,383,876	832,050	175,167
1922[2]	5,353,128	54,874	141,005	107,484	961,758	1,443,359	536,791	1,233,151	647,347	227,358
1921	6,528,276	61,758	137,617	130,092	1,093,994	1,691,930	631,176	1,616,010	964,042	201,657
1920[2]	5,712,654	..	..	..	..	..	..	..	..	..
1919[3]	5,403,458	..	..	..	..	..	..	..	..	..
1917[3]	5,209,117	..	..	..	..	..	..	..	..	..
1916[4]	..	..	..	..	..	..	..	472,721	1,104,118	623,002	..
1911[5]	4,230,849	42,185	115,969	84,883	787,513	1,223,028	463,221	832,811	492,633	188,607
1901[5]	1,786,310	30,626	72,560	51,325	435,826	931,984	151,349	44,460	34,699	33,480

[1] Excludes Newfoundland, the Yukon Territory and Northwest Territories.
[2] Excludes value of machinery.
[3] Excludes value of machinery, poultry and fur animals.
[4] Excludes value of fur animals.
[5] Census data; excludes value of fur animals.

Series M55-66. Male workers[1] employed in agriculture, labour force estimates,[2] Canada and by region and province, 1946 to 1974
(thousands)

Year	Canada	Atlantic provinces	Prince Edward Island	Nova Scotia	New Brunswick	Quebec	Ontario	Prairie provinces	Manitoba	Saskat-chewan	Alberta	British Columbia
	55	**56**	**57**	**58**	**59**	**60**	**61**	**62**	**63**	**64**	**65**	**66**
1974	438	21	6	8	6	78	102	219	44	89	86	18
1973	430	18	5	6	6	84	115	197	31	83	83	16
1972	444	17	4	6	6	89	111	208	40	89	79	19
1971	469	21	6	8	6	89	121	215	43	88	84	23
1970	487	27	8	9	9	102	117	218	42	90	86	23
1969	493	25	8	9	7	91	119	239	50	109	80	19
1968	510	25	7	9	8	114	122	222	46	96	80	27
1967	518	29	7	12	9	107	130	232	45	99	88	20
1966	493	29	7	11	10	101	122	221	49	93	79	21
1965	557	31	9	9	12	112	144	250	47	119	84	20
1964	591	36	8	12	14	124	143	267	54	117	96	21
1963	609	31	8	11	10	125	164	271	56	118	97	18
1962	615	42	8	16	16	127	146	273	58	121	94	27
1961	644	55	11	18	25	136	150	279	61	118	100	24
1960	630	50	10	17	21	120	158	275	59	121	95	27
1959[3]	677	55	..	..	..	167	167	263	..	..	..	25
1958[3]	681	51	..	..	..	162	158	282	..	..	..	28
1957[3]	725	40	..	..	..	172	194	298	..	..	..	21
1956[3]	758	45	..	..	..	167	204	319	..	..	..	23
1955[3]	831	49	..	..	..	181	231	343	..	..	..	27
1954[3]	864	51	..	..	..	212	239	345	..	..	..	17
1953[3]	851	57	..	..	..	203	222	351	..	..	..	18
1952[3]	841	58	..	..	..	203	210	351	..	..	..	19
1951[3]	892	63	..	..	..	228	219	359	..	..	..	23
1950[3]	973	84	..	..	..	249	240	375	..	..	..	25
1949[3,4]	982	79	..	..	..	235	251	384	..	..	..	33
1948[3,4]	1,026	84	..	..	..	249	255	403	..	..	..	35
1947[3,4]	1,001	81	..	..	..	237	263	388	..	..	..	32
1946[3,4]	1,071	97	..	..	..	276	279	390	..	..	..	29

[1] Fourteen years of age and over, employed in June.
[2] Estimates under 10,000 suffer from a high level of sampling error.

[3] Data are unavailable for the separate provinces in the Atlantic and Prairie regions.
[4] Excludes Newfoundland.

Series M67-77. Male workers employed in agricultural occupations, decennial census data, Canada and by province, 1891 to 1971

Year	Canada[1]	Newfound-land	Prince Edward Island	Nova Scotia	New Brunswick	Quebec	Ontario	Manitoba	Saskat-chewan	Alberta	British Columbia
	67	68	69	70	71	72	73	74	75	76	77
Unadjusted data											
1971[2]	405,250	1,365	5,110	7,370	6,720	63,620	110,140	38,535	82,195	69,150	21,035
1961[2]	573,042	1,606	8,540	11,951	12,142	117,235	149,302	52,501	107,292	91,085	21,388
1951[3]	797,874	3,567	12,693	22,977	26,211	187,846	193,795	70,430	141,736	111,745	26,874
1941[4]	1,064,847	..	16,350	36,934	41,136	251,539	264,914	90,774	184,244	138,814	40,142
1931[5]	1,107,766	..	17,792	42,737	45,348	225,914	298,597	91,566	200,881	142,722	42,209
1921[5]	1,023,706	..	18,057	47,771	45,982	217,422	289,715	85,636	172,245	112,490	34,388
1911[5]	917,848	..	19,134	47,167	44,840	201,599	301,347	69,035	131,404	79,285	24,037
1901[6]	..	..	..	..	..	..	..	..	..	..	..
1891[5]	723,013	..	21,415	59,331	50,275	204,552	332,037	34,109	13,075	—[7]	8,219
Data adjusted to 1961 classification of occupations											
1961[2]	573,042	1,606	8,540	11,951	12,142	117,235	149,302	52,501	107,292	91,085	21,388
1951[2]	793,924	3,553	12,654	22,918	26,101	185,529	193,040	70,210	141,480	111,605	26,834
1941[8]	1,056,092	..	16,271	36,805	40,691	246,467	262,868	90,287	183,971	138,667	40,065
Data adjusted to 1951 classification of occupations											
1961[2]	573,042	1,606	8,540	11,951	12,142	117,235	149,302	52,501	107,292	91,085	21,388
1951[2]	793,924	3,553	12,654	22,918	26,101	185,529	193,040	70,210	141,480	111,605	26,834
1941[8]	1,056,092	..	16,271	36,805	40,691	246,467	262,868	90,287	183,971	138,667	40,065
1931[8]	1,094,396	..	17,629	42,429	44,570	218,094	296,256	90,761	200,236	142,328	42,093
1921[8]	1,007,498	..	17,844	47,316	45,272	209,351	286,585	84,725	170,089	112,086	34,230
1911[8]	912,471	..	19,090	46,961	44,671	200,428	298,678	68,654	130,983	79,067	23,939
1901[8,9]	709,345	..	..	..	..	..	..	..	..	..	..
Data adjusted to 1931 classification of occupations											
1951[3]	794,307	..	12,693	22,977	26,211	187,846	193,795	70,430	141,736	111,745	26,874
1941[4]	1,064,847	..	16,350	36,934	41,136	251,539	264,914	90,774	184,244	138,814	40,142
1931[4]	1,103,638	..	17,745	42,640	45,103	223,164	298,105	91,388	200,728	142,591	42,174
1921[4]	1,017,404	..	17,980	47,574	45,678	214,088	288,680	85,306	171,522	112,279	34,297
1911[4]	917,848	..	19,134	47,167	44,840	201,599	301,347	69,035	131,404	79,285	24,037
1901[4]	707,924	..	20,720	52,836	48,304	194,381	302,533	47,134	31,772	—[7]	10,244
Data adjusted to 1931 classification of occupations											
1941[4]	1,064,847	—	16,350	36,934	41,136	251,539	264,914	90,774	184,244	138,814	40,142
1931[5]	1,107,766	—	17,792	42,737	45,348	225,914	298,597	91,566	200,881	142,722	42,209
1921[5]	1,023,661	—	18,057	47,769	45,982	217,416	289,701	85,634	172,240	112,484	34,378
1911[5]	917,848	—	19,134	47,167	44,840	201,599	301,347	69,035	131,404	79,285	24,037
1901[5]	707,924	—	20,720	52,836	48,304	194,381	302,533	47,134	31,772	—[7]	10,244

[1] Excludes the Yukon Territory and Northwest Territories.
[2] Fifteen years of age and over; employment status based on labour force concept.
[3] Fourteen years of age and over; employment status based on labour force concept.
[4] Fourteen years of age and over; employment status based on gainfully employed concept.

[5] Ten years of age and over; employment based on gainfully employed concept.
[6] Data not available.
[7] Data for Alberta included with Saskatchewan; comprises the Northwest Territories, west of Manitoba.
[8] Fifteen years of age and over; employment status based on gainfully employed concept.
[9] Data not available for provinces.

Series M78-88. Monthly wages without board,[1] for male farm labour, Canada and by region and province, 1909 to 1974

(dollars)

Year	Canada[2]	Maritime provinces[3]	Prince Edward Island[4]	Nova Scotia[4]	New Brunswick[4]	Quebec	Ontario	Manitoba	Saskatchewan	Alberta	British Columbia
	78	79	80	81	82	83	84	85	86	87	88
1974	454	386	..	..	..	374	458	444	477	495	519
1973	397	349	..	..	..	315	422	394	404	416	418
1972	335	280	..	..	..	260	347	344	350	355	377
1971	311	270	..	..	..	257	314	317	312	338	358
1970	292	244	..	..	..	230	309	294	292	305	345
1969	285	232	..	..	..	235	300	287	292	292	331
1968	271	211	..	..	..	225	289	263	285	280	300
1967	251	185	..	..	..	213	256	244	274	263	293
1966	230	167	..	..	..	191	239	232	243	241	267
1965	208	149	..	..	..	183	216	203	218	220	256
1964	190	145	..	..	..	173	185	188	196	205	230
1963	183	140	..	..	..	172	172	175	190	196	223
1962	178	139	..	..	..	165	165	170	187	189	218
1961	172	136	..	..	..	161	164	167	185	182	209
1960	169	138	..	..	..	160	162	167	184	180	205
1959	167	138	..	..	..	156	156	161	178	183	195
1958	154	131	..	..	..	149	143	157	168	159	185
1957	153	126	..	..	..	145	141	146	168	164	178
1956	150	125	..	..	..	147	138	151	159	157	165
1955	136	123	..	..	..	131	125	128	151	151	160
1954	139	123	..	..	..	127	125	130	148	152	159
1953	140	118	..	..	..	131	128	141	152	156	146
1952	139	122	..	..	..	136	124	141	151	155	145
1951	135	..	98	109	134	134	124	141	141	147	140
1950	120	..	86	95	113	109	111	123	128	132	135
1949	115	..	83	100	118	114	107	121	122	122	118
1948	117	..	83	102	119	119	108	115	121	125	130
1947	109	..	75	101	108	110	99	103	116	114	118
1946	101	..	78	92	103	98	92	103	111	107	106
1945	97	..	76	91	103	92	87	98	102	111	103
1944	88	..	70	75	90	82	80	91	99	98	96
1943	85	..	54	66	86	84	90	80	78	89	87
1942	65	..	47	63	69	62	66	68	66	71	74
1941	51	..	38	51	52	47	54	51	50	57	57
1940	41	..	31	39	44	37	43	40	42	46	46
1939	40	..	30	40	39	39	41	37	38	42	49
1938	41	..	33	41	41	38	42	39	37	43	50
1937	40	..	36	40	44	40	43	37	35	40	49
1936	37	..	31	37	40	32	37	34	35	38	46
1935	35	..	31	37	35	31	36	32	33	37	45
1934	33	..	30	35	35	30	33	31	31	35	43
1933	32	..	30	34	31	28	32	29	31	34	42
1932	34	..	30	37	33	30	33	32	33	36	44
1931	43	..	39	44	43	41	43	39	42	44	58
1930	56	..	50	54	54	52	51	53	60	60	72
1929	63	..	52	57	60	61	57	61	69	68	76
1928	63	..	49	53	59	58	58	61	69	72	77
1927	62	..	46	55	57	58	59	60	67	70	78
1926	61	..	47	54	57	57	58	60	67	69	76
1925	63	..	47	56	54	56	54	60	66	68	72
1924	62	..	43	55	53	56	57	59	66	66	75
1923	61	..	43	56	59	59	59	62	65	70	76
1922	59	..	40	50	53	53	57	63	64	64	75
1921	67	..	45	56	54	58	60	79	80	78	79
1920	86	..	60	73	79	86	75	98	102	107	95
1919	78	..	51	69	79	76	70	89	94	95	96
1918	70	..	46	60	69	65	62	78	86	86	89
1917	64	..	40	54	57	59	59	68	73	76	78
1916	43	..	31	39	36	41	39	48	49	52	50
1915	37	..	27	33	34	33	31	45	42	44	49
1914	36	..	25	31	32	34	32	39	41	40	48
1910	35	..	27	34	34	36	31	40	40	40	57
1909	34	..	25	31	33	33	32	36	38	40	46

[1] 1940 to 1974, cash wages without board at August 15; 1909 to 1939, cash wages and value of board in summer season.

[2] Excludes Newfoundland.

[3] Not available for the years 1909 to 1951.

[4] Not available for the years 1952 to 1974.

Series M89-98. Cash receipts from farming operations,[1] Canada and by province, 1926 to 1974
(thousands of dollars)

Year	Canada[2]	Prince Edward Island	Nova Scotia	New Brunswick	Quebec	Ontario	Manitoba	Saskat- chewan	Alberta	British Columbia
	89	90	91	92	93	94	95	96	97	98
1974	8,836,528	84,418	104,311	103,571	1,159,932	2,413,583	842,437	2,054,638	1,702,630	371,008
1973	6,828,421	71,923	95,659	95,546	977,289	1,970,950	618,297	1,466,242	1,199,051	333,464
1972	5,439,712	44,758	73,734	64,953	776,398	1,623,173	487,883	1,202,870	917,464	248,479
1971	4,545,907	38,868	65,618	52,801	691,515	1,427,965	367,841	901,408	775,443	224,448
1970	4,192,643	44,613	67,644	58,486	667,414	1,410,863	335,731	686,057	705,073	216,762
1969	4,232,741	38,303	66,009	52,757	670,386	1,400,210	350,569	713,654	737,592	203,261
1968	4,369,412	34,999	56,960	49,559	638,245	1,327,911	364,707	884,055	803,127	209,849
1967	4,395,680	34,282	55,812	48,544	623,283	1,293,778	374,569	972,173	793,985	199,254
1966	4,272,215	37,281	55,292	52,443	592,431	1,256,350	377,213	949,242	762,580	189,383
1965	3,818,302	40,665	51,268	59,951	506,668	1,101,871	342,249	886,884	664,448	164,298
1964	3,495,646	31,469	45,896	47,484	457,403	1,020,203	299,313	842,221	597,712	153,945
1963	3,199,851	25,459	46,788	41,070	452,558	1,001,982	269,994	692,157	521,628	148,215
1962	3,111,936	24,146	46,163	40,878	442,223	931,126	250,952	673,321	554,006	149,121
1961	2,887,916	23,049	46,178	39,113	417,497	872,530	239,347	588,971	526,256	134,975
1960	2,734,498	28,114	43,682	45,057	402,505	850,334	223,113	542,684	471,362	127,647
1959	2,753,873	27,468	44,045	41,311	410,196	843,132	228,809	555,256	478,770	124,886
1958	2,754,229	27,075	43,128	42,197	414,406	837,192	222,153	565,937	480,677	121,464
1957	2,515,917	23,658	43,242	40,827	376,221	758,954	197,631	525,817	433,551	116,016
1956	2,529,300	25,153	43,759	43,479	363,530	718,654	208,685	584,509	426,599	114,932
1955	2,239,058	24,298	41,417	37,065	359,910	723,857	173,027	416,018	356,932	106,534
1954	2,292,708	23,198	43,474	40,591	352,488	693,741	187,716	463,169	378,012	110,319
1953	2,708,590	22,231	41,936	38,015	350,674	715,952	218,943	731,199	478,432	111,208
1952	2,798,534	31,836	41,863	50,018	379,626	739,254	243,706	701,606	502,765	107,860
1951	2,725,182	24,785	41,591	43,706	376,205	784,073	271,623	625,869	450,291	107,039
1950	2,121,978	21,415	35,314	41,348	321,160	649,960	198,644	410,043	354,033	90,061
1949	2,397,566	20,449	32,607	40,387	307,337	650,553	246,976	564,843	444,372	90,042
1948	2,381,327	21,351	34,053	42,352	319,367	650,256	245,771	533,906	440,534	93,737
1947	1,924,232	17,167	32,277	35,960	260,204	535,194	181,787	430,613	346,206	84,824
1946	1,681,851	15,803	33,507	33,968	222,931	461,733	166,465	388,909	283,270	75,265
1945	1,655,730	16,100	26,873	33,417	216,591	442,625	151,186	405,903	290,566	72,469
1944	1,805,838	13,694	28,604	32,106	205,154	410,710	172,752	533,960	341,270	67,588
1943	1,392,780	13,959	26,244	29,714	184,858	389,083	144,188	322,216	225,326	57,192
1942	1,101,070	11,372	22,250	23,588	165,783	357,848	104,580	197,523	173,100	45,026
1941	875,781	7,619	17,233	18,416	133,221	274,503	81,286	159,991	147,613	35,899
1940	731,120	7,155	14,761	16,016	110,165	215,774	62,807	149,624	124,061	30,757
1939	712,076	6,914	13,954	13,688	98,829	208,974	64,070	156,971	118,438	30,238
1938	649,658	5,636	18,361	12,188	91,397	201,156	64,273	92,507	134,470	29,670
1937	638,456	6,401	18,196	13,445	88,813	201,912	74,596	85,074	121,053	28,966
1936	587,282	6,684	15,578	12,562	80,388	176,532	47,401	127,546	95,401	25,190
1935	532,583	5,236	15,357	11,007	71,479	160,897	36,240	110,047	99,276	23,044
1934	503,234	4,877	13,411	9,569	67,508	149,922	43,217	95,708	97,014	22,008
1933	419,643	4,113	12,810	7,966	57,109	135,901	32,253	79,028	71,340	19,123
1932	409,045	3,619	10,365	7,416	58,651	131,472	28,861	79,675	70,912	18,074
1931	471,913	5,248	12,873	9,957	74,064	171,004	31,220	72,873	72,832	21,842
1930	641,925	8,482	16,445	13,599	91,622	213,471	47,327	123,986	96,759	30,234
1929	931,765	10,231	15,288	14,290	109,334	256,832	72,467	246,640	172,740	33,943
1928	1,064,246	9,666	16,394	14,389	110,574	259,610	82,062	323,115	215,262	33,174
1927	940,399	10,028	15,124	14,492	101,083	246,443	78,852	273,293	172,191	28,893
1926	961,194	9,645	13,940	16,574	101,324	245,868	89,221	293,127	164,889	26,606

[1] Comprises cash receipts from the sale of farm products at the farm level (including subsidies, bonuses and premiums, and excluding interfarm transfers), participation payments on previous years grain crops, and net cash advances on farm-stored crops.

[2] Excludes Newfoundland.

Series M99-108. Realized farm gross income,[1] Canada and by province, 1926 to 1974
(thousands of dollars)

Year	Canada[2]	Prince Edward Island	Nova Scotia	New Brunswick	Quebec	Ontario	Manitoba	Saskat- chewan	Alberta	British Columbia
	99	100	101	102	103	104	105	106	107	108
1974	9,710,578	92,663	113,440	110,810	1,257,262	2,716,579	903,460	2,184,244	1,863,534	468,586
1973	7,517,454	78,633	103,949	102,026	1,074,169	2,207,003	668,339	1,571,282	1,311,326	400,727
1972	6,012,892	50,388	80,488	70,367	860,169	1,817,290	529,270	1,291,636	1,009,684	303,600
1971	5,101,807	44,267	72,392	57,939	761,683	1,612,046	414,256	993,370	869,105	276,749·
1970	4,813,844	50,600	75,272	64,606	743,447	1,602,480	385,038	813,754	812,114	266,533
1969	4,823,258	44,608	74,263	59,116	747,484	1,600,237	397,027	814,979	836,508	249,036
1968	4,910,930	40,884	64,766	55,854	711,873	1,498,147	409,684	983,899	897,176	248,647
1967	4,887,282	39,873	63,790	54,658	697,144	1,446,515	415,216	1,061,626	877,132	231,328
1966	4,756,654	42,981	63,660	60,274	687,404	1,409,495	412,565	1,022,949	838,440	218,886
1965	4,243,009	45,719	59,300	67,603	578,528	1,231,940	375,388	961,711	733,362	189,458
1964	3,886,784	36,241	53,710	55,170	526,730	1,143,606	330,790	904,048	659,779	176,710
1963	3,580,329	30,180	54,389	48,871	521,509	1,119,694	299,004	754,376	582,316	169,990
1962	3,538,844	28,769	53,999	49,036	511,609	1,046,384	289,021	763,024	626,181	170,821
1961	3,277,634	28,087	54,187	47,496	488,857	984,764	269,587	664,809	583,768	156,079
1960	3,163,872	32,863	52,583	53,983	476,417	958,069	258,747	636,469	545,650	149,091
1959	3,122,418	32,288	53,414	50,673	483,590	950,523	255,887	618,138	532,150	145,755
1958	3,159,937	31,988	52,795	52,376	487,974	939,342	257,555	649,108	547,277	141,522
1957	2,848,316	28,341	53,183	51,398	449,132	855,452	223,392	575,366	477,553	134,499
1956	2,860,041	29,886	54,006	54,557	437,224	811,582	235,736	634,182	470,071	132,797
1955	2,593,718	28,893	51,634	48,413	431,755	817,102	202,677	486,026	404,137	123,081
1954	2,615,208	27,669	54,033	52,009	423,590	786,281	213,219	511,315	421,150	125,942
1953	3,040,061	26,930	52,702	49,876	423,523	807,925	246,125	781,473	524,625	126,882
1952	3,140,581	36,824	53,974	63,510	457,986	830,915	271,052	754,771	548,081	123,468
1951	3,070,138	29,694	53,174	56,876	450,908	876,700	299,500	682,361	498,716	122,209
1950	2,433,595	25,573	45,712	53,575	385,223	731,789	223,813	466,214	398,402	103,294
1949	2,713,544	24,831	43,545	52,520	370,201	733,345	271,839	627,160	486,997	103,106
1948	2,716,711	25,923	45,674	55,531	389,402	735,360	271,500	602,632	483,871	106,818
1947	2,220,474	21,165	43,085	48,447	327,846	611,489	203,349	485,918	382,641	96,534
1946	1,968,201	19,513	44,173	45,625	289,737	534,807	187,086	442,604	318,760	85,896
1945	1,920,381	19,816	37,048	44,577	281,469	513,614	169,860	448,057	323,217	82,723
1944	2,070,426	17,214	38,986	42,769	264,751	480,751	191,111	582,181	375,570	77,093
1943	1,666,485	17,441	36,457	40,480	244,026	458,187	166,595	374,757	262,298	66,244
1942	1,379,167	14,671	31,775	33,684	219,943	422,193	127,033	262,857	213,970	53,041
1941	1,096,584	10,461	25,754	26,861	178,030	329,776	99,013	207,176	176,901	42,612
1940	916,526	9,781	22,569	23,701	151,220	266,932	76,618	183,228	144,979	37,498
1939	890,754	9,529	21,832	21,646	140,533	263,526	76,187	184,175	136,431	36,895
1938	824,027	8,425	26,146	20,140	131,574	255,686	76,090	117,693	152,004	36,269
1937	815,679	9,238	26,359	21,420	128,685	258,415	86,809	110,310	138,940	35,503
1936	762,179	9,398	24,118	20,639	119,721	233,378	58,680	152,276	112,344	31,625
1935	698,692	7,789	23,118	18,623	109,471	213,388	47,169	134,830	115,225	29,079
1934	663,890	7,476	20,835	16,860	103,537	202,937	53,809	118,389	112,087	27,960
1933	573,276	6,619	20,152	15,233	92,368	185,776	42,066	100,546	85,412	25,104
1932	558,372	5,984	17,685	14,428	93,862	180,060	38,231	99,922	84,424	23,776
1931	654,273	8,063	21,374	18,497	116,111	233,358	42,162	97,412	88,748	28,548
1930	867,999	11,934	26,898	23,726	144,669	287,987	61,632	155,907	117,099	38,147
1929	1,177,834	13,824	26,638	25,650	164,988	338,610	89,562	281,743	194,514	42,305
1928	1,305,374	13,203	27,594	25,614	165,552	342,050	97,853	357,393	235,195	40,920
1927	1,180,809	13,463	26,887	25,927	156,443	330,235	94,366	305,628	191,105	36,755
1926	1,200,768	13,119	25,813	28,431	157,264	329,526	104,838	324,567	183,043	34,167

[1] Income from farming operations that is available immediately for farm expenses, family living expenses and investment.

[2] Excludes Newfoundland.

Series M109-118. Realized farm net income,[1] Canada and by province, 1926 to 1974
(thousands of dollars)

Year	Canada[2]	Prince Edward Island	Nova Scotia	New Brunswick	Quebec	Ontario	Manitoba	Saskat- chewan	Alberta	British Columbia
	109	**110**	**111**	**112**	**113**	**114**	**115**	**116**	**117**	**118**
1974	3,843,473	33,960	23,483	42,178	345,515	834,958	411,133	1,183,599	828,936	139,711
1973	2,746,432	32,309	30,476	46,318	333,088	609,610	291,311	768,471	497,102	137,747
1972	2,125,176	11,724	21,098	24,262	271,757	518,151	218,170	625,407	344,229	90,378
1971	1,469,377	7,839	16,416	14,538	215,748	389,573	125,267	370,202	249,968	79,826
1970	1,344,871	14,827	20,866	22,391	220,366	436,114	110,710	222,456	215,876	81,265
1969	1,414,779	10,614	21,628	17,136	244,172	467,726	125,229	207,463	245,547	75,264
1968	1,581,195	7,961	14,714	14,538	226,355	408,980	128,528	381,027	309,937	89,155
1967	1,670,109	8,350	14,935	14,120	210,285	376,966	149,087	488,888	329,632	77,846
1966	1,742,507	12,419	15,674	18,114	232,846	427,038	171,804	460,032	330,835	73,745
1965	1,515,931	17,836	15,009	27,206	166,999	336,724	161,829	455,088	272,942	62,298
1964	1,367,345	11,655	13,553	19,145	141,868	306,637	132,883	448,361	232,980	60,263
1963	1,213,554	7,192	15,517	13,443	151,898	339,264	115,642	319,816	189,554	61,228
1962	1,330,481	7,325	17,267	13,570	164,928	321,440	111,804	370,872	258,890	64,385
1961	1,199,349	6,875	19,582	12,497	162,138	279,234	110,402	309,419	241,973	57,229
1960	1,127,944	12,262	19,134	19,602	149,019	284,301	99,508	265,226	220,578	58,314
1959	1,161,402	11,893	20,913	16,387	164,289	290,676	105,320	273,641	219,616	58,667
1958	1,309,864	12,506	21,541	19,582	185,311	324,804	113,472	318,257	253,210	61,181
1957	1,112,086	10,047	23,214	20,062	176,481	280,723	84,997	255,488	201,572	59,502
1956	1,120,964	11,612	23,043	22,252	163,288	236,244	96,932	310,166	198,955	58,472
1955	971,663	10,806	22,663	17,891	181,179	293,509	70,592	175,244	145,339	54,440
1954	1,057,514	10,856	25,398	22,132	183,323	279,903	82,559	220,139	173,964	59,240
1953	1,485,450	10,189	24,906	19,901	199,790	320,104	111,322	466,843	269,121	63,274
1952	1,598,317	20,087	25,922	33,222	230,011	352,659	138,040	437,744	298,593	62,039
1951	1,603,944	15,334	25,964	28,325	235,664	413,933	170,539	391,335	260,346	62,504
1950	1,117,412	11,769	21,575	28,022	195,231	322,684	102,429	201,403	185,329	48,970
1949	1,480,734	11,288	18,787	27,162	190,408	349,860	157,004	381,315	294,189	50,721
1948	1,537,577	12,635	20,858	30,414	214,431	364,844	164,930	374,686	299,786	54,993
1947	1,154,600	9,376	19,179	25,013	158,667	281,084	111,201	281,510	219,238	49,332
1946	1,039,595	8,982	22,977	24,713	145,409	249,530	105,832	258,349	178,124	45,679
1945	1,091,007	10,221	17,506	25,081	154,071	262,545	95,460	279,902	198,628	47,593
1944	1,256,264	8,370	19,912	24,596	144,393	238,566	120,551	405,171	250,775	43,930
1943	895,656	8,825	18,192	23,008	124,317	217,323	101,355	219,382	146,314	36,940
1942	689,004	8,179	15,582	19,259	124,862	213,227	67,067	109,133	102,598	29,097
1941	531,547	4,570	11,358	14,267	98,852	158,599	48,448	87,759	85,160	22,534
1940	387,982	4,514	10,658	12,384	82,516	109,625	31,138	63,465	55,247	18,435
1939	377,206	4,458	9,781	10,568	73,870	111,298	31,427	65,809	51,790	18,205
1938	329,154	3,236	14,459	9,022	66,266	106,933	32,772	9,812	68,646	18,008
1937	317,844	4,005	14,340	10,178	60,373	104,247	42,295	7,916	56,989	17,501
1936	287,559	4,693	12,661	10,294	59,159	93,304	20,130	37,693	34,203	15,422
1935	233,910	3,222	12,631	8,964	49,828	79,621	9,426	19,244	37,460	13,514
1934	210,271	2,783	10,705	7,304	45,994	72,496	15,358	8,166	34,823	12,642
1933	142,364	2,299	10,547	5,946	38,173	61,557	6,146	−5,623	12,607	10,712
1932	109,833	1,587	7,558	5,019	37,157	52,756	1,087	−12,797	8,556	8,910
1931	155,359	2,349	9,573	7,053	51,295	84,588	2,119	−20,250	7,403	11,229
1930	277,233	5,491	13,955	10,213	69,251	115,149	10,290	11,673	22,934	18,277
1929	545,627	7,701	12,892	11,833	85,306	155,167	33,038	122,191	95,963	21,536
1928	665,638	7,444	14,657	12,594	87,557	159,809	39,417	188,685	134,918	20,557
1927	568,914	8,325	13,753	13,655	80,793	154,782	40,803	144,455	94,836	17,512
1926	615,926	7,965	12,934	16,256	84,632	160,479	48,879	170,483	98,192	16,106

[1] Measure of net returns from farming operations, excluding value of change in inventories, that are available immediately to farm operators and unpaid family workers for living expenses and investment.

[2] Excludes Newfoundland.

Series M119-128. Total farm net income,[1] Canada and by province, 1926 to 1974
(thousands of dollars)

Year	Canada[2]	Prince Edward Island	Nova Scotia	New Brunswick	Quebec	Ontario	Manitoba	Saskat-chewan	Alberta	British Columbia
	119	120	121	122	123	124	125	126	127	128
1974	3,783,024	45,932	25,652	56,204	376,462	792,366	337,054	1,202,961	802,655	143,738
1973	3,401,349	28,950	30,730	42,002	373,027	703,732	384,228	981,663	704,589	152,428
1972	1,872,831	12,187	21,847	18,552	265,487	523,756	185,064	408,429	345,789	91,720
1971	1,615,289	4,829	15,489	15,696	201,407	366,431	170,992	477,172	276,017	87,256
1970	1,407,868	15,188	21,027	22,293	232,689	445,159	95,525	241,781	248,023	86,183
1969	1,700,595	10,979	21,527	16,382	248,992	448,914	134,142	451,534	290,292	77,833
1968	1,813,080	9,942	15,015	15,730	226,733	417,017	179,045	484,806	371,909	92,883
1967	1,501,070	6,428	14,092	11,965	202,591	376,279	165,051	360,679	287,491	76,494
1966	1,915,899	17,609	14,974	22,152	243,295	467,275	144,695	565,915	366,685	73,299
1965	1,564,147	15,172	14,795	25,538	158,472	335,250	172,009	478,895	301,713	62,303
1964	1,281,645	12,598	13,208	19,298	139,169	290,568	161,868	339,481	240,875	64,580
1963	1,516,129	8,129	15,384	13,396	151,156	307,500	111,706	551,136	292,824	64,898
1962	1,524,427	7,171	16,329	12,516	168,291	343,441	164,318	466,320	280,064	65,977
1961	925,823	7,657	19,577	13,307	161,876	307,026	53,365	100,284	201,759	60,972
1960	1,195,848	13,510	18,923	20,420	150,044	292,449	107,904	332,984	199,388	60,226
1959	1,097,819	9,467	20,460	14,232	161,283	281,305	101,546	230,129	217,748	61,649
1958	1,262,940	11,444	20,599	17,090	179,437	356,665	129,020	241,391	246,778	60,516
1957	993,943	11,189	21,575	19,095	173,253	296,356	72,551	179,206	161,222	59,496
1956	1,315,931	11,854	21,797	22,597	169,964	258,417	128,607	402,147	242,999	57,549
1955	1,174,497	11,411	22,517	20,372	184,520	266,419	88,367	326,597	198,295	55,999
1954	980,363	10,073	25,615	19,823	183,745	293,078	70,079	135,947	179,828	62,175
1953	1,560,009	11,425	24,736	21,674	204,691	336,487	113,307	479,314	301,033	67,342
1952	1,880,482	24,405	27,588	33,957	233,613	371,684	161,513	607,571	354,591	65,560
1951	1,931,377	15,905	25,911	28,330	248,353	448,139	179,875	531,975	389,521	63,368
1950	1,249,254	11,243	21,340	26,784	197,288	370,620	117,759	265,466	192,791	45,963
1949	1,382,661	12,417	18,993	27,274	188,038	345,574	136,480	357,320	242,076	54,489
1948	1,524,959	12,440	19,820	28,998	211,153	361,235	175,384	371,355	293,112	51,462
1947	1,103,823	9,341	17,633	24,712	155,765	272,913	113,155	246,351	216,837	47,116
1946	1,053,097	8,177	22,389	24,016	148,558	252,111	104,694	253,806	193,916	45,430
1945	851,716	9,744	16,256	23,307	133,461	248,810	70,287	174,234	129,024	46,593
1944	1,127,881	8,541	20,110	24,073	153,263	251,450	99,788	331,401	194,646	44,609
1943	778,876	9,238	19,127	23,460	132,621	199,266	95,959	152,985	108,163	38,057
1942	1,016,257	8,321	15,534	19,446	123,092	225,633	96,130	293,393	205,515	29,193
1941	478,958	4,553	10,919	13,987	97,416	145,069	52,191	65,950	65,518	23,355
1940	465,635	4,383	10,673	12,224	84,689	113,837	39,985	93,117	87,036	19,691
1939	430,804	4,343	9,760	10,778	79,037	115,102	32,357	96,081	64,763	18,583
1938	364,201	3,296	14,563	9,021	68,046	109,496	32,207	28,868	81,029	17,675
1937	307,024	4,323	15,025	10,526	64,994	110,401	57,372	−36,336	63,360	17,359
1936	245,037	4,635	12,789	10,456	61,022	83,597	17,513	18,402	20,442	16,181
1935	237,636	3,268	12,220	8,497	49,943	84,488	8,989	27,708	28,202	14,321
1934	202,967	2,576	10,505	6,852	47,004	79,024	13,171	−1,821	33,319	12,337
1933	108,947	2,179	10,512	5,827	36,051	50,234	1,240	−14,483	4,798	12,589
1932	130,192	1,695	7,590	5,628	36,608	50,560	6,657	−1,473	13,832	9,095
1931	135,909	2,233	9,580	7,174	50,915	80,534	−5,821	−31,117	11,736	10,675
1930	361,061	5,690	13,756	10,640	69,708	128,459	23,778	38,202	53,931	16,897
1929	417,924	7,775	13,568	11,238	85,606	150,234	18,961	51,321	56,507	22,714
1928	641,526	7,520	14,175	12,516	90,480	155,579	51,654	184,665	102,366	22,571
1927	631,920	8,604	12,760	13,185	83,293	154,316	21,881	176,191	143,106	18,584
1926	618,058	7,765	13,385	16,892	86,860	148,513	58,117	168,648	99,721	18,157

[1] Measure of net returns from farming operations, including value of change in inventories, that are earned by farm operators and unpaid family workers as payment for labour, management services and equity in the farm capital investment.

[2] Excludes Newfoundland.

Series M129-135. Reconciliation of net income from farm operations and accrued net income from farm production, Canada, 1926 to 1974

(millions of dollars)

Year	Net income from farm operations[1]	Deduct: investment income[2]	Deduct: transfer payments[3]	Other adjustments[4]	Equals: net income from farm production	Adjustments on grain transactions[5]	Equals: accrued net income from farm production
	129	**130**	**131**	**132**	**133**	**134**	**135**
1974	3,783	210	5	−364	3,204	530	3,734
1973	3,401	187	12	−75	3,127	10	3,137
1972	1,873	156	14	21	1,724	−49	1,675
1971	1,615	133	8	35	1,509	65	1,574
1970	1,405	136	6	−144	1,119	92	1,211
1969	1,564	145	10	15	1,424	11	1,435
1968	1,710	149	8	28	1,581	−260	1,321
1967	1,475	142	4	5	1,334	−95	1,239
1966	1,949	127	8	−20	1,794	156	1,950
1965	1,567	115	11	−12	1,429	−40	1,389
1964	1,292	100	9	8	1,191	116	1,307
1963	1,521	93	15	14	1,427	135	1,562
1962	1,526	86	70	3	1,373	4	1,377
1961	922	83	36	−4	799	27	826
1960	1,196	78	77	−18	1,023	3	1,026
1959	1,098	76	22	20	1,020	−12	1,008
1958	1,263	75	60	−6	1,122	−6	1,116
1957	994	68	2	−7	917	−9	908
1956	1,316	64	5	8	1,255	28	1,283
1955	1,174	61	33	−10	1,070	50	1,120
1954	980	56	2	14	936	−18	918
1953	1,560	55	2	−8	1,495	−33	1,462
1952	1,880	49	5	7	1,833	45	1,878
1951	1,931	49	10	1	1,873	−5	1,868
1950	1,249	42	14	−28	1,165	136	1,301
1949	1,383	39	18	−5	1,321	−110	1,211
1948	1,525	39	21	−5	1,460	−100	1,360
1947	1,104	35	12	9	1,066	34	1,100
1946	1,053	27	17	−	1,009	22	1,031
1945	852	26	6	−	820	70	890
1944	1,128	25	8	−	1,095	−22	1,073
1943	779	22	−	−	757	−50	707
1942	1,016	20	32	−	964	−47	917
1941	479	18	7	−	454	−	454
1940	466	16	10	−	440	33	473
1939	431	17	2	−	412	−50	362
1938	364	16	−	−	348	5	353
1937	307	20	−	−	287	−7	280
1936	245	19	−	−	226	−27	199
1935	238	16	−	−	222	−4	218
1934	203	15	−	−	188	−21	167
1933	109	14	−	−	95	−29	66
1932	130	15	−	−	115	−11	104
1931	136	19	−	−	117	−23	94
1930	361	22	−	−	339	4	343
1929	418	26	−	−	392	1	393
1928	642	25	−	−	617	16	633
1927	632	25	−	−	607	−7	600
1926	618	23	−	−	595	12	607

[1] As published by the Agriculture Division of Statistics Canada.

[2] Includes corporation profits in agriculture and imputed net rent of owner-occupied houses.

[3] These items are deducted since transfer payments are excluded from net national income at factor cost. Includes payments under the provisions of the Prairie Farm Income Plan; the Prairie Farm Assistance Act; the Western Grain Producers' Acreage Payment Plan; the Federal-Provincial Emergency Unthreshed Grain Assistance Policy; payments to Prince Edward Island potato growers for losses to the 1960 potato crop; payments to eligible sugar beet growers following closure of the sugar beet refinery in southwestern Ontario.

[4] These adjustments consist of an estimate of net income of farm operators from farming operations in Newfoundland and an adjustment for the difference in the valuation of the physical change in inventories. The Agriculture Division values the change in the quantity of farm-held potato stocks

at average annual prices, whereas the national accounts estimates value this change each quarter in terms of average quarterly prices. A further inventory adjustment arises out of the national accounts valuation of the new grain crop at average annual prices. Statistical revisions for the years 1970 to 1975, not yet incorporated in the national accounts, are also included here.

[5] Since the national income measures earnings arising out of current production, rather than receipts of income, it is appropriate to include income accruing to farm operators from farm production rather than income received. Accordingly, an adjustment has been made to take account of the accrued earnings of farm operators arising out of the operations of the Canadian Wheat Board.

Series M136-145. Cash receipts from crops, Canada and by province, 1926 to 1974
(thousands of dollars)

Year	Canada[1]	Prince Edward Island	Nova Scotia	New Brunswick	Quebec	Ontario	Manitoba	Saskat-chewan	Alberta	British Columbia
	136	137	138	139	140	141	142	143	144	145
1974	4,150,462	49,345	21,779	53,965	137,521	818,791	503,121	1,597,359	836,378	132,203
1973	2,672,699	37,370	21,360	47,376	99,404	619,063	282,905	1,006,574	445,038	113,609
1972	2,137,468	16,130	16,652	24,102	66,569	505,800	233,132	828,776	368,435	77,872
1971	1,753,167	14,030	13,244	18,649	68,035	460,175	164,578	627,199	315,794	71,463
1970	1,468,224	18,372	13,699	23,537	66,348	449,057	128,703	448,834	245,981	73,693
1969	1,512,673	12,308	12,712	17,458	62,507	395,661	168,823	497,730	285,266	60,208
1968	1,765,111	11,436	9,726	16,426	65,115	379,292	187,754	655,899	368,275	71,188
1967	1,869,784	9,930	10,612	14,684	59,125	392,749	193,198	737,010	383,012	69,464
1966	1,791,469	14,421	10,370	21,039	57,485	342,304	200,084	724,202	359,829	61,735
1965	1,645,275	21,212	10,132	30,150	55,532	295,688	184,173	684,108	312,827	51,453
1964	1,600,437	14,991	8,335	19,083	51,616	304,957	170,174	671,790	305,196	54,295
1963	1,341,278	9,865	8,081	13,361	49,047	290,876	146,994	535,017	238,262	49,775
1962	1,247,543	7,568	7,128	11,176	46,986	258,941	136,175	497,720	235,917	45,932
1961	1,117,024	7,195	7,402	10,677	44,589	257,754	114,251	409,660	223,933	41,563
1960	1,072,083	13,177	6,400	16,849	46,303	248,946	113,551	394,281	193,843	38,733
1959	1,027,495	10,558	6,376	12,405	41,484	228,096	112,999	383,074	198,966	33,537
1958	1,007,462	9,877	5,875	11,874	43,294	232,756	100,752	383,211	186,139	33,684
1957	977,976	8,178	7,055	11,733	38,966	208,059	97,046	380,102	191,512	35,325
1956	1,066,483	10,811	6,405	14,465	38,869	175,688	114,421	458,753	215,918	31,153
1955	822,409	9,118	5,705	8,181	35,388	201,440	79,121	292,943	159,147	31,366
1954	887,661	7,045	6,741	8,755	35,270	183,427	93,497	341,880	176,326	34,720
1953	1,325,281	6,294	5,459	7,392	39,698	196,483	130,172	611,153	287,115	41,515
1952	1,384,095	15,387	7,795	18,096	47,705	196,049	152,255	584,605	321,905	40,298
1951	1,151,213	5,275	4,881	9,551	33,439	179,401	167,952	476,006	241,437	33,271
1950	765,205	4,836	4,241	9,343	26,940	145,029	103,755	274,837	164,126	32,098
1949	1,085,410	6,530	4,904	10,640	30,032	152,154	152,472	432,145	258,766	37,767
1948	1,033,084	7,175	4,667	12,479	32,688	156,135	149,888	382,132	248,364	39,556
1947	863,530	5,934	5,068	10,703	27,676	137,994	109,457	322,760	205,232	38,706
1946	729,024	5,334	8,262	10,567	29,434	118,602	94,354	276,777	148,772	36,922
1945	688,654	5,671	3,873	10,788	28,765	102,764	79,400	283,455	138,209	35,729
1944	851,568	4,151	7,377	10,847	28,417	96,526	97,453	396,542	175,768	34,487
1943	535,242	4,800	6,671	10,488	26,337	89,426	71,066	212,386	87,550	26,518
1942	364,229	3,745	6,397	6,972	24,525	87,462	42,631	113,651	59,311	19,535
1941	326,492	2,367	4,653	5,215	22,583	65,950	40,078	103,320	66,294	16,032
1940	303,121	2,648	4,062	4,714	19,652	50,631	29,763	111,187	67,226	13,238
1939	343,931	2,960	4,157	4,740	19,974	60,218	35,435	129,743	72,950	13,754
1938	296,540	1,474	7,884	2,950	15,242	58,770	37,252	69,335	90,686	12,947
1937	262,431	2,289	8,120	4,257	15,730	54,646	49,174	41,912	73,160	13,143
1936	255,832	2,560	6,563	4,165	15,070	43,160	26,162	94,275	53,133	10,744
1935	234,482	1,390	6,605	2,958	12,671	39,950	16,720	81,396	62,251	10,541
1934	231,658	1,944	6,001	3,513	12,695	34,421	26,596	72,108	64,331	10,049
1933	190,696	1,365	6,016	2,610	10,449	32,686	18,897	61,518	48,062	9,093
1932	186,115	1,000	3,275	2,079	10,045	31,617	15,833	63,626	50,533	8,107
1931	177,720	1,705	4,620	3,059	12,969	38,767	12,699	50,258	45,133	8,510
1930	271,119	3,375	6,071	4,952	16,264	47,333	25,891	96,009	58,508	12,716
1929	484,178	3,514	4,667	4,544	22,369	58,874	44,740	210,069	122,003	13,398
1928	618,412	2,925	5,388	4,206	21,292	57,903	55,126	289,267	169,122	13,183
1927	523,798	3,918	4,770	5,248	21,046	54,962	51,583	241,229	128,697	12,345
1926	555,731	4,552	4,729	8,206	26,722	55,695	65,808	260,894	116,547	12,578

[1] Excludes Newfoundland.

Series M146-155. Cash receipts from livestock,[1] Canada and by province, 1926 to 1974
(thousands of dollars)

Year	Canada[2]	Prince Edward Island	Nova Scotia	New Brunswick	Quebec	Ontario	Manitoba	Saskat-chewan	Alberta	British Columbia
	146	147	148	149	150	151	152	153	154	155
1974	2,481,174	20,942	21,225	13,886	285,938	814,733	221,800	372,149	681,235	49,266
1973	2,315,678	23,264	23,296	16,048	295,112	706,216	226,210	368,224	590,298	67,010
1972	1,784,441	18,079	18,592	14,536	217,218	583,217	170,338	291,491	417,945	53,025
1971	1,496,126	15,899	17,026	11,773	179,687	497,324	141,621	228,793	358,958	45,045
1970	1,468,345	17,524	17,306	12,795	184,034	504,978	139,473	190,290	360,415	41,530
1969	1,431,532	17,044	17,037	12,224	177,089	524,812	112,746	172,122	353,999	44,459
1968	1,374,598	14,052	14,368	11,031	166,788	484,698	112,552	186,430	341,081	43,598
1967	1,340,236	14,807	13,658	10,961	176,770	454,183	118,162	194,170	317,346	40,179
1966	1,337,909	14,493	12,975	10,387	167,993	479,625	113,756	183,912	315,094	39,674
1965	1,167,991	11,626	12,445	10,002	147,310	419,201	99,450	162,100	271,207	34,650
1964	971,500	9,294	11,480	9,605	137,128	359,826	74,456	123,520	218,351	27,840
1963	947,856	8,300	11,463	8,796	138,247	363,048	67,513	113,537	209,354	27,598
1962	980,302	9,445	12,369	10,001	135,804	337,587	64,095	133,347	245,533	32,121
1961	915,566	8,609	11,014	9,288	122,451	302,605	74,440	133,787	230,393	22,979
1960	822,622	7,514	10,262	8,847	118,657	288,055	58,647	103,179	205,587	21,874
1959	881,814	9,136	10,450	9,034	132,544	295,309	63,566	125,532	211,529	24,714
1958	897,382	9,325	9,280	9,323	131,355	286,468	67,541	134,127	226,643	23,320
1957	739,867	7,996	9,176	7,916	112,234	254,764	51,271	101,559	176,967	17,984
1956	668,282	6,404	9,400	7,671	103,562	246,618	43,758	82,199	147,181	21,489
1955	644,962	7,052	7,474	7,074	102,769	239,523	45,012	79,652	139,280	17,126
1954	653,935	8,233	8,908	8,080	104,837	236,207	46,898	80,084	143,877	16,811
1953	635,480	7,675	9,087	7,973	101,139	238,547	43,650	77,374	134,946	15,089
1952	702,158	9,121	10,313	9,639	129,172	268,584	50,098	76,623	130,331	18,277
1951	877,825	11,744	13,980	12,546	156,978	328,588	62,042	107,580	155,911	28,456
1950	787,378	10,040	11,504	12,167	132,984	288,635	60,276	102,615	146,777	22,380
1949	714,874	6,665	8,047	9,372	108,642	276,130	56,299	93,984	139,642	16,093
1948	710,252	7,131	8,865	10,117	107,448	258,709	53,943	103,128	142,206	18,705
1947	492,963	5,208	7,687	7,731	74,787	182,786	36,106	66,248	99,204	13,206
1946	463,590	4,711	7,401	7,280	62,758	156,004	39,650	74,315	99,009	12,462
1945	488,736	4,470	7,299	7,284	63,985	154,620	40,857	82,491	116,025	11,705
1944	498,597	4,051	6,647	6,499	56,986	144,744	44,957	95,076	129,208	10,429
1943	437,352	3,848	5,880	6,107	53,453	139,436	41,977	72,911	104,174	9,566
1942	374,031	3,301	5,063	5,480	46,698	129,123	36,503	53,942	85,531	8,390
1941	291,411	2,505	4,091	4,623	41,700	108,387	23,013	36,932	63,063	7,097
1940	220,912	2,294	3,440	3,820	34,348	84,297	19,745	23,862	43,483	5,623
1939	177,461	1,960	3,110	3,302	26,953	72,243	16,422	14,883	33,334	5,254
1938	155,290	1,768	2,830	3,030	24,183	65,119	13,625	10,492	28,850	5,393
1937	182,914	1,604	2,764	3,243	23,836	69,619	13,241	29,008	33,990	5,609
1936	146,252	1,659	2,613	2,671	18,886	57,126	9,976	19,956	29,349	4,016
1935	129,960	1,536	2,771	2,904	16,542	51,119	9,558	16,583	25,764	3,183
1934	110,613	832	1,411	1,236	13,754	48,872	7,724	12,389	21,760	2,635
1933	83,175	700	1,182	1,029	9,714	41,613	5,269	7,675	13,506	2,487
1932	79,275	711	1,309	1,223	10,598	39,491	5,150	7,038	11,439	2,316
1931	110,517	1,036	1,844	1,829	16,616	51,042	8,464	10,802	16,125	2,759
1930	156,172	1,837	2,847	2,428	21,650	75,423	9,598	13,772	24,762	3,855
1929	212,420	2,359	3,464	3,032	28,433	101,637	13,583	20,280	35,051	4,581
1928	208,639	2,268	3,836	3,360	29,440	99,838	14,477	19,211	31,990	4,219
1927	193,010	1,697	3,176	2,695	24,776	95,553	14,507	18,230	29,124	3,252
1926	191,609	1,453	2,522	2,525	22,145	96,882	11,757	17,413	34,197	2,715

[1] Comprises cattle, calves, hogs, sheep and lambs.

[2] Excludes Newfoundland.

Series M156-165. Cash receipts from dairy products, Canada and by province, 1926 to 1974
(thousands of dollars)

Year	Canada[1]	Prince Edward Island	Nova Scotia	New Brunswick	Quebec	Ontario	Manitoba	Saskat-chewan	Alberta	British Columbia
	156	157	158	159	160	161	162	163	164	165
1974	1,087,744	8,190	28,055	15,978	403,502	399,098	42,920	26,235	71,612	92,154
1973	849,455	6,696	22,183	13,113	311,264	317,101	31,503	21,306	57,605	68,684
1972	778,590	6,304	19,868	11,858	290,879	293,785	28,183	20,773	49,033	57,907
1971	705,697	5,822	18,386	10,921	262,297	264,074	24,171	19,920	46,843	53,263
1970	678,883	5,549	17,200	10,804	251,595	253,762	23,890	19,902	45,516	50,665
1969	677,030	5,437	16,052	10,808	256,012	255,847	23,551	19,263	43,345	46,715
1968	644,223	5,107	14,923	10,894	232,660	248,780	23,075	18,767	43,924	46,093
1967	624,416	5,330	14,184	11,201	225,133	241,106	22,665	18,974	41,821	44,002
1966	584,089	5,313	13,421	11,075	204,592	227,089	22,055	19,563	40,008	40,973
1965	559,424	5,445	12,596	11,285	190,010	219,234	23,255	20,908	40,324	36,367
1964	533,920	5,274	12,337	11,453	176,059	206,805	23,699	22,185	41,426	34,682
1963	509,803	4,831	11,745	11,075	168,747	193,454	23,984	22,550	39,709	33,708
1962	499,576	5,079	12,330	11,478	166,905	183,885	24,096	22,470	38,998	34,335
1961	495,852	4,984	12,763	11,757	166,263	178,333	24,084	23,435	39,398	34,835
1960	486,529	4,783	12,722	11,677	160,493	176,785	23,868	23,904	38,105	34,192
1959	490,037	5,187	13,089	11,898	161,767	179,019	24,144	24,443	36,318	34,172
1958	479,674	4,936	12,855	11,985	162,315	167,512	25,040	24,557	36,170	34,304
1957	448,736	4,527	12,779	11,776	150,267	158,652	22,834	21,639	33,214	33,048
1956	430,130	4,424	13,118	11,375	144,391	152,677	23,051	20,614	31,017	29,463
1955	421,737	4,337	12,718	11,446	141,054	147,655	22,806	21,687	30,870	29,164
1954	409,730	4,361	12,454	11,453	135,298	144,363	21,874	21,773	29,431	28,723
1953	398,162	4,101	12,155	11,102	129,914	140,956	21,379	22,384	28,928	27,243
1952	381,172	3,793	11,038	10,565	124,747	137,967	19,997	21,632	26,727	24,706
1951	371,702	4,068	10,555	10,822	117,421	136,869	19,785	22,603	26,955	22,624
1950	328,155	3,424	9,905	9,617	102,509	120,663	17,366	20,037	24,357	20,277
1949	350,253	3,749	10,199	10,268	109,586	128,314	19,599	22,637	25,371	20,530
1948	383,364	3,941	10,241	11,056	120,028	140,166	22,874	27,180	27,852	20,026
1947	323,681	2,706	9,348	8,507	99,222	123,081	18,972	23,106	22,318	16,421
1946	286,227	2,483	8,973	7,628	86,885	109,417	16,803	20,407	19,029	14,602
1945	270,612	2,410	8,676	7,793	80,307	104,496	15,139	19,427	18,615	13,749
1944	267,936	2,366	7,841	7,475	78,910	100,426	16,671	21,828	19,643	12,776
1943	247,760	2,294	7,388	6,646	70,941	94,643	16,767	20,134	18,158	10,789
1942	218,613	1,806	5,921	5,389	64,108	87,201	13,833	16,018	15,531	8,806
1941	155,018	1,075	4,699	4,108	45,101	61,805	10,204	11,364	10,240	6,422
1940	116,294	703	3,730	3,512	34,079	47,681	7,120	7,150	6,813	5,506
1939	113,384	670	3,099	2,859	34,560	47,437	6,660	5,788	7,091	5,220
1938	121,378	875	4,053	3,328	35,076	48,659	7,697	7,094	9,486	5,110
1937	112,820	760	3,652	3,036	32,598	46,134	7,061	7,014	8,138	4,427
1936	107,197	693	3,400	2,798	30,090	45,092	6,298	6,817	7,339	4,670
1935	98,690	604	3,144	2,388	27,262	41,657	5,747	6,479	6,755	4,654
1934	95,518	644	3,291	2,270	26,676	38,946	5,387	6,573	6,975	4,756
1933	89,506	704	3,219	2,143	24,809	37,386	5,010	6,068	6,407	3,760
1932	88,489	758	3,112	2,060	25,335	37,411	4,758	5,563	5,658	3,834
1931	107,346	822	3,518	2,604	29,867	45,885	6,088	6,735	6,930	4,897
1930	110,360	874	3,947	2,840	31,864	46,832	5,707	6,681	6,832	4,783
1929	118,190	1,115	4,017	2,873	33,744	49,151	7,108	7,918	7,664	4,600
1928	121,001	1,190	4,020	3,025	34,743	53,020	6,400	6,885	7,155	4,563
1927	118,998	1,118	4,184	2,890	33,199	52,498	6,416	6,694	7,357	4,642
1926	118,055	1,058	4,069	2,715	31,016	52,818	6,421	7,528	8,097	4,333

[1] Excludes Newfoundland.

Series M166-175. Cash receipts from poultry and eggs, Canada and by province, 1926 to 1974

(thousands of dollars)

Year	Canada[1]	Prince Edward Island	Nova Scotia	New Brunswick	Quebec	Ontario	Manitoba	Saskatchewan	Alberta	British Columbia
	166	167	168	169	170	171	172	173	174	175
1974	741,245	2,113	26,667	14,907	189,672	274,170	56,258	31,228	66,449	79,781
1973	681,724	1,792	23,787	15,034	167,748	258,486	54,342	28,013	61,129	71,393
1972	459,630	1,269	13,928	9,546	120,040	171,525	33,854	20,115	40,438	48,915
1971	414,295	1,192	13,158	8,292	108,277	153,223	28,873	18,614	36,895	45,771
1970	435,515	1,425	15,807	8,194	114,715	161,032	34,367	20,749	36,884	42,342
1969	440,092	1,453	16,287	8,122	113,354	171,738	34,743	17,409	35,041	41,945
1968	392,054	1,294	13,429	7,361	101,724	155,694	29,763	14,631	30,414	37,744
1967	371,252	1,351	13,011	6,745	96,951	146,706	27,445	13,506	30,739	34,798
1966	403,315	1,577	14,555	7,427	105,166	161,351	30,464	14,964	31,609	36,202
1965	344,573	1,487	12,205	6,283	87,226	138,846	26,233	14,946	26,535	30,812
1964	305,721	1,514	10,204	5,249	71,622	127,556	23,411	14,716	24,156	27,293
1963	317,243	1,680	12,054	5,479	72,311	128,594	23,903	16,988	26,305	29,929
1962	294,919	1,616	10,989	4,936	67,487	122,137	20,004	15,983	24,227	27,540
1961	286,128	1,744	11,232	4,938	60,353	115,612	21,408	17,813	27,127	25,901
1960	273,322	2,023	10,587	4,920	52,125	116,374	20,570	16,443	24,931	25,349
1959	277,708	2,008	10,359	4,835	49,595	121,331	21,574	18,642	24,632	24,732
1958	298,203	2,372	11,397	5,512	53,873	132,457	23,086	20,830	25,329	23,347
1957	275,624	2,388	10,448	5,390	48,964	119,656	20,677	19,278	25,822	23,001
1956	291,719	2,948	11,015	5,722	50,507	126,861	21,551	20,124	26,668	26,323
1955	275,652	3,216	11,573	5,721	52,707	119,161	20,007	18,886	21,560	22,821
1954	269,408	2,974	11,342	7,315	48,547	114,216	20,145	16,949	22,892	25,028
1953	282,167	3,599	11,196	6,261	53,912	124,982	19,270	17,767	22,146	23,034
1952	257,190	2,943	8,586	5,955	47,872	119,473	17,040	16,327	18,441	20,553
1951	248,199	3,022	7,791	4,504	40,378	120,203	16,943	16,686	19,995	18,677
1950	167,057	2,464	5,329	3,658	29,611	79,614	12,303	9,446	12,898	11,734
1949	181,997	3,157	5,472	3,910	33,270	82,687	13,930	11,386	14,918	13,267
1948	184,658	2,608	5,787	3,324	31,170	82,723	14,502	16,315	15,192	13,037
1947	168,609	2,532	5,210	3,323	28,146	76,776	12,208	13,382	13,122	13,910
1946	146,013	2,466	4,607	3,427	20,845	67,129	12,547	13,507	11,910	9,575
1945	152,781	2,570	3,701	3,292	22,675	69,598	12,257	16,488	12,714	9,486
1944	132,269	2,220	3,528	2,706	19,513	56,260	10,381	16,938	12,419	8,304
1943	120,138	2,015	3,097	2,331	15,128	53,270	11,043	13,351	11,323	8,580
1942	97,411	1,646	2,141	1,644	12,733	44,133	8,862	10,771	8,824	6,657
1941	63,632	1,055	1,354	1,110	8,344	29,732	5,768	6,162	5,146	4,961
1940	52,443	795	1,058	927	8,024	24,411	3,807	4,838	3,564	5,019
1939	48,311	644	774	873	7,254	22,574	3,534	4,606	3,006	5,046
1938	46,953	728	737	881	7,008	22,060	3,463	3,705	3,203	5,168
1937	48,358	693	742	793	6,894	24,354	3,004	3,949	3,209	4,720
1936	47,593	739	809	824	6,357	24,157	3,037	4,064	2,864	4,742
1935	43,429	748	773	800	5,776	21,658	2,839	4,265	2,789	3,781
1934	41,594	606	699	716	5,714	21,599	2,405	3,630	2,507	3,718
1933	35,789	632	651	672	4,807	18,686	2,174	2,989	2,141	3,037
1932	35,696	534	582	649	5,287	17,897	2,317	2,910	2,366	3,154
1931	51,613	789	779	738	5,904	28,075	3,035	4,119	3,182	4,992
1930	72,304	1,224	1,148	1,029	9,076	35,508	4,865	6,232	5,153	8,069
1929	79,373	1,282	1,198	1,033	9,074	38,467	5,611	6,482	5,941	10,285
1928	79,377	1,357	1,092	1,070	9,915	39,738	4,739	6,384	4,963	10,119
1927	71,245	1,357	1,030	1,061	9,166	34,891	4,636	6,158	5,248	7,698
1926	64,331	1,169	869	889	8,218	32,179	4,030	6,282	4,559	6,136

[1] Excludes Newfoundland.

Series M176-185. Miscellaneous cash receipts from farming operations,[1] Canada and by province, 1926 to 1974
(thousands of dollars)

Year	Canada[2]	Prince Edward Island	Nova Scotia	New Brunswick	Quebec	Ontario	Manitoba	Saskat-chewan	Alberta	British Columbia
	176	177	178	179	180	181	182	183	184	185
1974[3]	375,903	3,828	6,585	4,835	143,299	106,791	18,338	27,667	46,956	17,604
1973[4]	308,865	2,801	5,033	3,975	103,761	70,084	23,337	42,125	44,981	12,768
1972[5]	279,583	2,976	4,694	4,911	81,692	68,846	22,376	41,715	41,613	10,760
1971[6]	176,622	1,925	3,804	3,166	73,219	53,169	8,598	6,882	16,953	8,906
1970[7]	141,676	1,743	3,632	3,156	50,722	42,034	9,298	6,282	16,277	8,532
1969[7]	171,414	2,061	3,921	4,145	61,424	52,152	10,706	7,130	19,941	9,934
1968[7]	193,426	3,110	4,514	3,847	71,958	59,447	11,563	8,328	19,433	11,226
1967[7]	189,992	2,864	4,347	4,953	65,304	59,034	13,099	8,513	21,067	10,811
1966[8]	155,433	1,477	3,971	2,515	57,195	45,981	10,854	6,601	16,040	10,799
1965[8]	101,039	895	3,890	2,231	26,590	28,902	9,138	4,822	13,555	11,016
1964[9]	103,306	930	4,211	2,101	30,990	29,327	7,990	4,902	13,099	9,756
1963[7]	82,773	547	4,262	2,156	26,065	21,821	6,065	3,921	9,444	8,492
1962[7]	79,448	576	3,976	3,322	25,036	21,649	5,394	3,484	7,719	8,292
1961[10]	75,725	579	3,899	2,564	24,084	19,806	5,463	3,579	7,833	7,918
1960[8]	78,397	616	3,710	2,766	24,883	20,545	6,307	3,465	8,607	7,498
1959[6]	76,819	579	3,771	3,139	24,806	19,377	6,526	3,565	7,325	7,731
1958	71,508	565	3,721	3,503	23,569	17,999	5,734	3,212	6,396	6,809
1957	73,714	569	3,784	4,012	25,790	17,823	5,803	3,239	6,036	6,658
1956	72,686	566	3,821	4,246	26,201	16,810	5,904	2,819	5,815	6,504
1955	74,298	575	3,947	4,643	27,992	16,078	6,081	2,850	6,075	6,057
1954	71,974	585	4,029	4,988	28,536	15,528	5,302	2,483	5,486	5,037
1953	67,500	562	4,039	5,287	26,011	14,984	4,472	2,521	5,297	4,327
1952	73,919	592	4,131	5,763	30,130	17,181	4,316	2,419	5,361	4,026
1951	76,243	676	4,384	6,283	27,989	19,012	4,901	2,994	5,993	4,011
1950	74,183	651	4,335	6,563	29,116	16,019	4,944	3,108	5,875	3,572
1949	65,032	348	3,985	6,197	25,807	11,268	4,676	4,691	5,675	2,385
1948	69,969	496	4,493	5,376	28,033	12,523	4,564	5,151	6,920	2,413
1947	75,449	787	4,964	5,696	30,373	14,557	5,044	5,117	6,330	2,581
1946	56,997	809	4,264	5,066	23,009	10,581	3,111	3,903	4,550	1,704
1945	54,947	979	3,324	4,260	20,859	11,147	3,533	4,042	5,003	1,800
1944	55,468	906	3,211	4,579	21,328	12,754	3,290	3,576	4,232	1,592
1943	52,288	1,002	3,208	4,142	18,999	12,308	3,335	3,434	4,121	1,739
1942	46,786	874	2,728	4,103	17,719	9,929	2,751	3,141	3,903	1,638
1941	39,228	617	2,436	3,360	15,493	8,629	2,223	2,213	2,870	1,387
1940	38,350	715	2,471	3,043	14,062	8,754	2,372	2,587	2,975	1,371
1939	28,989	680	2,814	1,914	10,088	6,502	2,019	1,951	2,057	964
1938	29,497	791	2,857	1,999	9,888	6,548	2,236	1,881	2,245	1,052
1937	31,933	1,055	2,918	2,116	9,755	7,159	2,116	3,191	2,556	1,067
1936	30,408	1,033	2,193	2,104	9,985	6,997	1,928	2,434	2,716	1,018
1935	26,022	958	2,064	1,957	9,228	6,513	1,376	1,324	1,717	885
1934	23,851	851	2,009	1,834	8,669	6,084	1,105	1,008	1,441	850
1933	20,477	712	1,742	1,512	7,330	5,530	903	778	1,224	746
1932	19,470	616	2,087	1,405	7,386	5,056	803	538	916	663
1931	24,717	896	2,112	1,727	8,708	7,235	934	959	1,462	684
1930	31,970	1,172	2,432	2,350	12,768	8,375	1,266	1,292	1,504	811
1929	37,604	1,961	1,942	2,808	15,714	8,703	1,425	1,891	2,081	1,079
1928	36,817	1,926	2,058	2,728	15,184	9,111	1,320	1,368	2,032	1,090
1927	33,348	1,938	1,964	2,598	12,896	8,539	1,710	982	1,765	956
1926	31,468	1,413	1,751	2,239	13,223	8,294	1,205	1,010	1,489	844

[1] Includes cash receipts from furs, wool, honey, horses, wood products and maple products for 1926 to 1974; dairy supplementary payments for 1965 to 1974; and payments under the two price program for wheat during 1972 to 1974.
[2] Excludes Newfoundland.
[3] Includes payments under the Saskatchewan Hog Price Stabilization Program, the Alberta Hog and Lamb Price Stabilization Program and the Beef Subsidy Program; and price deficiency payments for fowl under the Agricultural Stabilization Act.
[4] Includes price deficiency payments for hogs and fowl.
[5] Includes price deficiency payments for potatoes, fruits, vegetables, hogs and fowl.
[6] Includes price deficiency payments for sugar beets, potatoes and wool.
[7] Includes price deficiency payments for eggs, sugar beets, potatoes and wool.
[8] Includes price deficiency payments for sugar beets and wool.
[9] Includes price deficiency payments for eggs and wool.
[10] Includes price deficiency payments for eggs, potatoes and wool.

Series M186-195. Composite index of farm prices of agricultural products, Canada and by province, 1935 to 1974

(1961 = 100)

Year	Canada[1]	Prince Edward Island	Nova Scotia	New Brunswick	Quebec	Ontario	Manitoba	Saskat-chewan	Alberta	British Columbia
	186	187	188	189	190	191	192	193	194	195
1974	229.1	297.7	209.9	261.2	229.0	209.5	235.3	250.1	234.2	202.5
1973	191.8	266.6	200.3	228.1	198.9	188.4	189.3	189.5	196.6	169.2
1972	132.9	153.3	132.9	140.9	154.7	143.4	119.7	112.0	129.6	134.9
1971	117.2	133.0	120.6	123.3	138.7	129.4	102.1	96.4	110.8	124.2
1970	116.0	149.2	123.4	135.5	129.0	128.4	103.0	97.3	110.8	121.6
1969	116.8	123.6	122.7	116.8	130.9	130.7	104.4	96.3	112.5	124.6
1968	114.0	123.2	114.0	116.9	125.9	124.0	105.2	99.1	109.6	118.7
1967	116.0	115.0	110.9	111.4	125.2	123.0	109.5	106.9	113.9	111.6
1966	117.0	134.0	113.9	122.5	125.2	122.0	110.9	108.1	115.9	115.1
1965	107.8	153.7	107.4	139.1	111.9	110.1	103.9	101.6	106.0	108.4
1964	101.3	118.9	98.3	111.6	101.4	100.5	99.8	101.7	102.0	99.1
1963	102.9	106.9	101.2	101.8	100.3	102.6	102.6	103.0	105.4	102.6
1962	104.3	100.2	101.8	97.8	100.9	102.6	105.6	105.8	108.2	103.0
1961	100.0	100.0	100.0	100.0	100.0	100.0	100.0	100.0	100.0	100.0
1960	96.1	128.3	100.0	120.8	100.8	100.3	92.8	89.0	91.8	99.7
1959	95.2	114.7	100.4	109.5	101.4	99.2	92.0	86.0	93.1	101.0
1958	95.2	102.1	102.7	102.6	103.2	101.0	91.5	84.2	91.9	102.7
1957	91.2	98.5	100.2	100.7	100.0	97.2	87.4	79.6	86.7	101.7
1956	90.9	119.2	96.5	107.3	97.0	94.7	87.9	82.1	87.1	99.5
1955	90.1	109.6	101.7	103.1	98.1	94.2	87.4	80.1	86.8	96.2
1954	91.7	97.4	106.4	96.6	99.1	95.6	88.1	82.2	90.4	96.7
1953	97.0	95.1	108.6	97.3	102.0	99.7	95.0	90.0	96.4	102.9
1952	106.3	174.6	127.2	157.2	108.8	108.1	103.4	96.8	103.2	112.8
1951	115.0	117.4	112.4	114.4	114.5	119.1	116.8	105.8	119.8	111.2
1950	101.0	94.2	95.5	98.9	97.8	100.2	106.3	99.0	107.4	94.6
1949	98.9	101.4	97.3	100.6	97.9	97.4	101.8	97.9	103.3	94.9
1948	99.1	117.5	99.0	114.2	99.5	97.7	100.6	97.3	102.2	93.0
1947	83.6	89.4	85.5	91.1	80.1	76.4	87.5	89.0	90.2	80.2
1946	79.1	96.5	88.4	94.8	73.8	71.0	81.1	85.5	85.5	77.1
1945	71.9	97.7	83.6	89.1	67.3	66.0	73.0	75.8	76.3	72.7
1944	66.8	85.8	80.1	78.4	64.4	63.9	67.1	67.5	68.8	69.5
1943	61.1	94.5	78.2	82.8	64.7	62.4	58.6	55.1	58.3	68.0
1942	51.6	77.6	66.6	73.2	57.5	55.6	47.3	43.5	47.3	54.4
1941	42.7	52.2	54.1	52.7	47.8	45.4	40.2	36.9	40.0	44.3
1940	37.5	50.4	46.0	50.2	38.9	39.4	36.0	34.1	35.2	40.1
1939	35.6	52.0	49.7	50.8	37.6	37.5	33.2	31.4	33.0	38.2
1938	40.7	45.9	46.9	44.5	40.1	39.3	40.6	42.4	41.1	38.8
1937	46.4	51.5	45.9	45.7	39.0	41.1	50.3	53.7	51.1	41.5
1936	37.5	58.6	47.8	50.3	37.0	37.3	36.4	36.8	36.5	38.9
1935	34.1	40.4	42.8	36.9	33.8	35.3	33.2	32.7	32.8	35.9

[1] Excludes Newfoundland.

Series M196-205. Indexes of farm prices for groups of agricultural products, Canada,[1] 1935 to 1974
(1961 = 100)

Year	Grains	Cattle	Hogs	Livestock[2]	Dairy products	Poultry	Eggs	Potatoes	Fruits	Vegetables
	196	**197**	**198**	**199**	**200**	**201**	**202**	**203**	**204**	**205**
1974	262.8	209.5	184.7	199.4	271.6	172.2	168.0	382.8	206.7	176.5
1973	188.2	210.0	193.3	205.4	201.1	154.8	150.5	319.1	176.0	158.3
1972	98.8	162.3	129.0	152.1	172.4	113.3	97.5	135.2	136.1	140.1
1971	84.4	146.7	89.2	127.9	165.3	103.3	86.1	117.1	125.0	122.1
1970	84.2	140.3	114.5	132.7	143.2	100.9	100.5	151.2	129.0	129.5
1969	83.5	—	—	133.9	142.8	107.1	117.8	101.0	140.2	125.1
1968	93.3	—	—	118.4	142.2	107.5	103.8	111.0	130.0	120.7
1967	104.1	—	—	118.4	140.2	104.6	96.6	89.3	115.5	127.2
1966	106.2	—	—	120.8	128.7	111.4	119.0	135.4	118.0	112.5
1965	102.0	—	—	107.5	112.8	105.9	100.2	196.6	113.4	104.2
1964	103.2	—	—	98.8	104.3	102.4	89.3	121.8	102.6	105.9
1963	102.5	—	—	104.3	101.4	107.0	106.9	97.4	99.2	105.3
1962	105.4	—	—	108.7	100.2	105.3	97.9	87.7	97.3	103.0
1961	100.0	—	—	100.0	100.0	100.0	100.0	100.0	100.0	100.0
1960	86.8	—	—	95.1	100.9	114.1	96.6	171.5	90.9	100.5
1959	82.5	—	—	100.4	102.1	109.7	95.8	126.8	78.5	101.9
1958	80.1	—	—	100.6	99.4	129.2	105.1	103.3	83.1	103.3
1957	78.0	—	—	91.8	96.1	132.7	102.0	98.2	93.5	100.8
1956	83.4	—	—	86.0	94.4	142.4	118.2	125.8	79.4	98.3
1955	81.5	—	—	86.1	93.8	141.0	116.4	125.4	82.9	95.2
1954	82.4	—	—	92.0	94.4	145.5	107.2	89.1	97.0	92.5
1953	91.8	—	—	95.8	95.0	154.8	130.0	93.6	94.1	97.3
1952	97.7	—	—	106.8	96.4	149.9	111.2	242.4	82.8	105.4
1951	98.5	—	—	138.4	96.9	178.0	142.3	91.4	74.6	91.6
1950	100.2	—	—	109.8	87.4	147.0	108.7	80.0	70.0	84.4
1949	101.1	—	—	97.8	91.8	150.9	123.6	87.1	79.7	88.5
1948	103.1	—	—	90.6	98.5	137.0	122.4	127.0	81.7	92.8
1947	99.5	—	—	67.1	79.1	117.0	101.5	96.3	82.2	82.9
1946	96.5	—	—	60.9	69.9	118.7	98.0	117.3	88.8	74.9
1945	84.7	—	—	56.2	64.5	114.8	91.9	109.2	82.9	74.3
1944	73.5	—	—	54.2	64.2	106.9	86.7	91.2	81.4	73.1
1943	56.4	—	—	54.3	60.6	109.0	95.5	108.2	70.7	68.6
1942	43.5	—	—	48.0	54.8	90.0	83.6	88.0	53.6	55.2
1941	37.3	—	—	39.0	47.1	78.0	68.6	51.8	42.6	46.2
1940	35.6	—	—	33.1	37.5	66.5	60.9	57.9	36.2	39.7
1939	32.9	—	—	31.2	34.3	66.6	61.0	61.4	40.6	37.5
1938	48.0	—	—	30.5	38.6	68.2	65.4	41.9	42.8	38.5
1937	66.0	—	—	30.4	37.4	64.9	63.7	52.9	45.4	41.2
1936	43.1	—	—	26.4	34.1	64.3	64.4	67.3	46.6	41.2
1935	37.3	—	—	26.4	31.9	59.8	59.2	34.3	44.9	40.3

[1] Excludes Newfoundland.   [2] Includes cattle and hogs.

Series M206-220. Farm input price indexes, Canada, 1961 to 1974
(1961 = 100)

Year	Total farm inputs	Land and farm build-ings[1]	Building replace-ment	Property taxes	Farm rent	Farm machine-ry and motor vehi-cles[1,2]	Machine-ry and motor vehicle replace-ment[2]	Machine-ry and motor vehicle opera-tion[2]	Hired farm labour[1]	Other materials and services[1]	Fertil-izer	Seed	Custom work	Feed	Feeder cattle
	206	207	208	209	210	211	212	213	214	215	216	217	218	219	220
1974	195.2	213.6	222.0	144.0	260.4	153.8	154.6	153.2	254.0	205.9	161.9	267.8	180.3	212.6	208.9
1973	166.7	190.7	201.2	135.0	232.8	137.7	139.0	136.7	216.1	166.9	115.5	147.6	157.6	168.8	236.9
1972	143.3	176.1	176.1	143.9	208.1	132.6	135.3	130.4	190.6	124.6	103.0	111.9	147.6	110.8	180.2
1971	135.9	158.1	157.8	140.9	168.6	128.8	131.4	126.8	178.2	120.2	99.6	115.7	141.6	110.3	158.0
1970	131.2	150.0	147.8	140.2	155.6	124.8	128.0	122.3	169.8	117.8	96.4	116.4	136.6	108.2	155.6
1969	129.1	151.4	146.3	149.5	161.0	121.8	124.6	119.5	161.8	116.2	98.9	120.1	132.6	108.1	145.3
1968	124.9	140.4	132.7	140.1	151.6	118.8	121.6	115.6	153.0	115.6	105.2	120.2	128.1	112.8	124.0
1967	121.5	135.0	126.9	132.6	151.7	114.8	118.0	111.2	142.6	115.1	102.1	115.2	123.0	114.8	124.6
1966	118.6	138.9	121.1	124.7	191.0	111.1	114.6	107.4	131.8	111.7	100.9	117.0	117.6	111.1	118.4
1965	112.0	127.4	114.0	118.0	164.8	107.6	110.9	104.1	118.5	106.6	102.8	116.0	111.6	106.6	98.4
1964	108.6	118.4	109.7	112.4	142.7	106.0	108.4	103.0	109.5	105.8	102.6	114.6	108.1	105.6	98.2
1963	108.0	119.6	104.4	108.4	163.4	103.4	105.7	100.8	105.3	106.8	102.6	112.2	104.8	106.8	109.8
1962	105.2	111.7	101.2	103.5	142.3	101.4	102.9	100.2	101.9	105.9	97.6	110.9	102.3	107.1	111.6
1961	100.0	100.0	100.0	100.0	100.0	100.0	100.0	100.0	100.0	100.0	100.0	100.0	100.0	100.0	100.0

[1] Major group of items.
[2] Farm share only.

Series M221-227. Price index numbers of commodities and services used by farmers, Canada, 1913 to 1961
(1935-39 = 100)

Year	Composite index inclusive of living costs	Composite index exclusive of living costs	Equip-ment and material	Farm machine-ry[1]	Taxes and interest rates[2]	Farm wage rates	Farm family living costs	Year	Composite index inclusive of living costs	Composite index exclusive of living costs	Equip-ment and material	Farm machine-ry[1]	Taxes and interest rates[2]	Farm wage rates	Farm family living costs
	221	222	223	224	225	226	227		221	222	223	224	225	226	227
1961	259.0	282.2	226.7	261.4	220.6	566.0	224.2								
1960	254.8	276.7	222.7	254.2	214.5	555.3	221.7	1935	96.4	95.4	95.6	95.5	101.0	87.6	97.9
1959	249.8	269.5	219.1	248.4	204.7	538.2	220.1	1934	96.5	95.5	96.8	94.6	102.3	82.3	97.9
1958	242.7	259.9	213.0	236.7	196.7	513.2	217.0	1933	92.2	89.8	88.8	92.1	102.9	77.7	95.8
1957	238.7	255.9	211.3	223.8	191.9	501.4	212.7	1932	95.1	93.3	89.3	94.1	113.2	83.4	97.8
1956	230.3	247.6	208.8	209.4	184.7	470.3	204.5	1931	102.1	100.9	92.2	94.9	119.5	110.7	103.9
1955	224.5	238.3	204.6	198.8	177.2	439.7	203.8	1930	115.7	117.0	105.6	97.0	128.4	145.6	113.7
1954	224.2	237.2	203.3	197.9	174.6	441.2	204.5	1929	123.7	127.9	117.6	97.5	130.3	163.8	117.3
1953	225.3	239.8	207.4	196.7	168.2	449.1	203.6	1928	125.0	129.3	118.3	97.6	130.8	168.3	118.5
1952	229.8	243.1	215.8	195.4	161.4	445.5	210.0	1927	126.7	131.2	119.9	97.5	134.7	169.5	119.8
1951	217.5	230.0	206.0	186.8	151.8	416.6	198.6	1926	126.8	130.6	119.9	97.6	135.5	164.5	121.1
1950	197.3	210.4	189.9	165.1	144.3	368.7	177.6	1925	128.6	131.8	123.2	97.9	135.2	159.4	123.9
1949	191.7	204.1	180.3	158.3	138.7	373.3	173.2	1924	129.3	131.9	122.3	102.4	137.3	160.9	125.5
1948	183.7	197.6	173.1	141.6	131.3	371.2	162.8	1923	129.6	130.6	118.3	92.9	138.6	166.5	128.3
1947	157.5	170.4	139.5	126.3	125.0	341.4	138.3	1922	131.7	134.1	124.6	89.9	141.1	161.0	127.9
1946	145.0	157.0	128.0	118.8	117.2	314.6	127.1	1921	147.4	152.5	147.4	111.4	143.2	184.4	139.9
1945	140.6	152.1	125.9	115.1	113.4	298.1	123.2	1920	180.3	186.5	190.1	92.2	136.7	238.6	171.3
1944	137.9	148.0	126.0	118.2	111.2	275.3	122.8	1919	157.5	167.9	169.1	86.9	127.2	216.4	143.0
1943	134.7	143.4	122.4	117.1	106.3	267.8	121.6	1918	148.2	160.2	164.1	82.1	125.9	190.8	131.1
1942	126.6	131.6	119.2	114.4	104.3	211.6	119.0	1917	128.6	140.5	140.7	62.0	116.5	171.4	111.5
1941	115.2	116.1	107.8	109.1	102.9	163.4	114.0	1916	97.8	100.5	101.7	55.1	102.5	97.6	93.7
1940	107.5	106.8	101.8	105.8	102.1	131.8	108.5	1915	89.6	91.6	96.9	54.4	86.0	82.7	86.5
1939	99.4	99.3	95.7	103.6	101.1	110.3	99.5	1914	84.1	85.3	90.2	55.0	79.7	78.0	82.3
1938	101.8	101.7	101.2	104.1	100.6	105.0	101.9	1913	—	—	85.4	54.6	—	—	80.1
1937	104.3	105.3	108.4	97.2	98.2	102.6	102.9								
1936	98.2	98.1	98.7	97.8	99.2	94.7	98.3								

[1] Includes motor trucks, beginning in 1935.

[2] Comprises taxes only for 1914 to 1916.

Series M228-238. Wholesale market prices for selected agricultural products, 1867 to 1974[1]
(series M228-233 in cents per bushel, series 237 in cents per dozen, all other series in cents per pound)

Year	Wheat	Oats	Barley	Flaxseed	Rapeseed	Corn	Steers	Pigs	Sheep	Eggs	Butter
	228	229	230	231	232	233	234	235	236	237	238
1974	526/3	188/0	354/7	954/2	723/2	301/2	49.37	50.29	23.45	75.0	83.0
1973	549/3	174/4	307/4	1,014/2	635/5	283/6	46.56	54.66	21.76	70.0	74.0
1972	262/5	109/2	176/5	482/6	364/0	175/1	35.61	37.39	14.17	45.0	71.0
1971	168/4	67/2	113/7	257/1	247/0	119/4	32.70	25.80	14.07	38.0	68.0
1970	179/2	83/2	130/7	253/5	277/3	141/0	30.40	32.20	14.40	53.0	68.0
1969	180/7	73/2	112/2	292/0	277/4	136/5	29.35	35.70	14.26	58.0	68.0
1968	194/7	85/4	119/6	330/6	221/7	130/3	26.90	29.80	11.37	50.0	67.0
1967	194/3	95/2	130/5	345/5	226/7	131/2	27.65	29.70	11.33	48.0	65.0
1966	211/6	92/5	137/1	300/2	278/3	153/0	25.85	34.90	10.60	58.0	62.0
1965	199/6	89/6	138/4	299/3	266/0	144/5	24.00	32.40	8.32	48.0	57.0
1964	198/3	83/0	133/2	320/3	287/0	139/7	22.70	26.30	8.80	44.0	55.0
1963	203/3	78/5	123/4	319/6	271/5	142/4	23.65	26.80	9.10	53.0	54.0
1962	196/1	81/6	130/6	335/0	—	137/0	25.75	28.60	9.44	48.0	57.0
1961	189/7	96/1	143/7	368/2	—	128/5	22.75	27.30	9.02	51.0	65.0
1960	167/4	81/2	107/5	311/4	—	122/6	22.65	23.75	9.12	49.0	65.0
1959	165/7	82/4	108/1	334/2	—	119/1	25.10	23.80	9.11	49.0	65.0
1958	166/2	77/6	109/7	302/0	—	125/2	22.90	28.13	8.36	53.0	64.0
1957	162/3	76/3	111/0	303/0	—	120/1	18.82	30.05	8.49	52.0	61.0
1956	168/1	80/6	116/0	298/4	—	132/0	19.07	26.50	8.62	57.8	58.6
1955	174/0	83/5	114/3	360/1	—	124/5	19.60	25.05	8.18	58.6	59.7
1954	173/0	90/4	122/4	309/1	—	144/0	19.34	30.90	9.03	52.1	59.9
1953	186/2	73/2	109/7	283/6	—	149/0	20.11	30.40	9.52	64.8	61.0
1952	185/6	80/3	136/5	329/0	—	—	25.85	25.70	14.80	54.2	62.4
1951	188/2	91/1	133/1	428/1	—	209/5	33.49	32.85	19.77	66.2	65.0
1950	191/2	96/1	149/6	441/4	—	197/7	26.72	28.98	14.32	51.5	58.0
1949	205/7	91/0	157/2	371/6	—	166/1	21.29	30.20	10.87	56.4	62.0
1948	205/0	78/1	119/3	403/1	—	164/4	19.40	29.96	9.33	56.0	69.8
1947	158/4	84/1	126/0	500/0	—	192/7	14.63	22.04	8.33	46.8	52.6
1946	138/4	56/4	75/2	300/0	—	241/0	13.05	19.85	8.55	44.3	40.8
1945	125/0	51/4	64/6	275/0	—	111/4	12.20	17.90	7.35	43.3	36.9
1944	125/0	51/4	64/6	275/0	—	121/1	11.99	17.25	5.06	40.6	36.5
1943	123/2	51/4	64/6	250/0	—	117/3	11.99	16.87	8.41	44.8	36.1
1942	94/4	49/2	61/1	225/0	—	108/0	10.39	15.69	8.14	40.6	36.5
1941	76/5	49/1	59/2	158/1	—	—	8.90	13.26	6.03	34.6	34.8
1940	74/0	34/6	44/3	144/3	—	—	7.83	11.42	5.33	31.9	27.5
1939	76/4	35/5	43/4	172/3	—	—	6.89	8.91	4.49	30.9	25.0
1938	62/0	29/0	36/0	143/4	—	—	6.27	9.45	4.16	33.5	28.4
1937	131/4	50/3	57/5	164/2	—	—	7.40	8.92	4.22	31.6	28.0
1936	122/5	53/0	70/6	171/3	—	—	5.41	8.43	3.98	34.0	25.3
1935	85/1	34/4	36/7	147/4	—	—	6.46	8.94	3.27	31.2	24.9
1934	81/7	42/6	48/1	138/6	—	—	5.54	8.60	2.87	31.5	24.3
1933	68.1	33.4	38.8	148.0	—	—	4.63	5.54	2.63	28.0	23.3
1932	54.3	26.4	32.2	90.4	—	—	5.56	4.66	2.48	30.4	22.6
1931	59.8	31.4	37.3	93.7	—	—	6.22	7.39	3.77	34.3	26.9
1930	64.2	29.9	28.4	114.1	—	—	8.78	12.32	5.38	45.5	34.2
1929	124.2	58.6	56.4	247.5	—	—	10.16	12.38	6.52	48.1	42.2
1928	124.0	58.8	71.4	202.2	—	—	10.48	10.51	6.51	49.2	40.6
1927	146.3	65.1	85.3	189.9	—	—	8.20	10.35	6.39	49.9	40.2
1926	146.2	58.8	72.7	195.0	—	—	7.33	13.32	6.82	46.5	39.0
1925	151.2	49.6	63.9	213.8	—	—	7.35	12.85	6.95	50.9	39.4
1924	168.5	59.6	88.5	241.1	—	—	6.75	9.10	6.88	48.1	37.2
1923	107.0	41.5	63.2	215.1	—	—	6.95	9.76	6.60	46.5	38.4
1922	110.5	47.3	54.3	227.3	—	—	7.36	12.63	6.30	47.0	36.0
1921	129.7	47.5	61.8	210.3	—	—	7.58	11.72	6.84	53.5	42.3
1920	199.4	53.6	90.0	209.6	—	—	12.89	18.98	9.36	69.7	58.3
1919	217.4	99.7	161.9	468.2	—	—	13.06	19.59	10.37	64.0	57.1
1918	224.2	78.4	108.4	403.4	—	—	12.89	18.17	13.71	56.9	47.3
1917	221.1	83.8	137.9	356.1	—	—	11.15	15.55	11.88	51.8	42.2
1916	205.5	63.3	109.4	270.0	—	—	8.42	10.54	8.36	39.5	35.1
1915	113.6	43.3	65.2	180.5	—	—	7.99	8.47	6.34	32.6	31.1
1914	132.4	57.5	69.2	148.2	—	—	8.29	8.29	6.14	33.8	27.1
1913	89.1	36.5	46.9	131.0	—	—	6.99	9.03	5.54	35.0	27.4
1912	90.1	34.8	48.4	120.6	—	—	6.76	7.69	4.89	32.4	29.4
1911	100.8	41.7	63.4	195.4	—	—	5.91	6.62	4.16	27.2	25.1
1910	94.2	34.3	55.0	226.6	—	—	6.15	8.48	4.74	22.6	26.6
1909	101.1	35.6	46.4	—	—	—	5.64	7.30	4.02	23.1	25.4
1908	109.0	41.9	53.0	—	—	—	4.95	5.95	4.22	19.9	27.0
1907	105.2	42.0	51.5	—	—	—	4.85	6.44	4.71	20.6	25.4
1906	78.8	36.1	43.8	—	—	—	4.52	6.81	4.63	17.0	23.6

Series M228-238. Wholesale market prices for selected agricultural products, 1867 to 1974[1] (concluded)

(series M228-233 in cents per bushel, series 237 in cents per dozen, all other series in cents per pound)

Year	Wheat	Oats	Barley	Flaxseed	Rapeseed	Corn	Steers	Pigs	Sheep	Eggs	Butter
	228	229	230	231	232	233	234	235	236	237	238
1905	77.2	34.0	39.2	–	–	–	4.57	6.22	3.89	17.3	22.7
1904	91.6	36.2	39.6	–	–	–	4.50	5.09	3.45	19.4	19.6
1903	78.8	31.4	31.9	–	–	–	4.47	5.83	3.33	14.9	21.1
1902	72.9	36.8	37.8	–	–	–	4.90	6.55	3.58	14.9	21.0
1901	75.2	40.3	39.5	–	–	–	4.36	6.69	3.34	13.1	21.1
1900	74.6	34.3	35.9	–	–	–	4.23	5.76	3.64	14.0	22.2
1899	70.9	32.2	32.6	–	–	–	3.88	4.62	3.44	14.5	20.4
1898	93.2	38.3	39.7	–	–	–	3.80	4.87	3.35	12.5	19.6
1897	78.7	27.1	28.0	–	–	–	3.39	5.05	3.19	10.4	19.0
1896	65.5	20.3	21.8	–	–	–	3.02	3.87	2.92	12.0	19.1
1895	71.8	27.2	30.8	–	–	–	3.71	4.28	3.33	12.8	19.9
1894	61.2	30.2	27.0	–	–	–	3.96	4.60	3.65	12.6	22.3
1893	73.3	27.8	29.5	–	–	–	4.45	6.21	4.93	14.7	24.0
1892	80.1	22.2	30.2	–	–	–	3.87	4.98	4.81	13.6	23.4
1891	93.1	34.6	33.0	–	–	–	3.96	4.82	4.99	15.3	23.3
1890	84.6	42.3	56.2	–	–	–	4.18	4.63	5.50	16.0	20.2
1889	99.3	32.5	56.2	–	–	–	3.95	4.74	4.85	15.8	17.2
1888	93.3	43.2	70.0	–	–	–	4.35	5.84	5.20	17.6	18.9
1887	83.4	33.5	64.1	–	–	–	4.30	5.54	5.35	17.0	18.7
1886	80.8	33.5	71.7	–	–	–	4.36	4.80	4.78	15.2	17.0
1885	88.7	34.8	74.4	–	–	–	4.75	4.75	4.33	16.5	16.3
1884	100.1	36.2	71.0	–	–	–	5.55	5.79	4.57	19.2	18.1
1883	111.4	42.0	73.1	–	–	–	5.75	5.95	5.34	20.2	19.4
1882	121.2	44.6	83.1	–	–	–	5.35	7.25	8.07	18.0	20.2
1881	126.3	39.3	89.4	–	–	–	5.02	6.73	6.50	17.4	18.9
1880	120.1	35.3	76.2	–	–	–	4.82	5.60	5.50	14.1	18.6
1879	107.3	36.1	76.8	–	–	–	4.61	4.98	6.00	15.0	15.0
1878	100.8	31.8	78.1	–	–	–	4.80	4.31	6.41	12.4	14.0
1877	137.2	42.2	72.6	–	–	–	5.17	5.71	5.46	15.8	19.2
1876	108.2	36.5	79.3	–	–	–	4.86	6.55	4.71	16.2	19.4
1875	120.6	43.4	90.4	–	–	–	5.16	7.33	5.30	17.2	19.6
1874	114.0	46.6	109.2	–	–	–	5.80	6.85	6.67	16.7	25.2
1873	122.8	41.1	84.5	–	–	–	7.21	5.26	5.88	17.8	19.0
1872	127.2	40.4	66.2	–	–	–	7.58	4.75	6.45	18.0	16.7
1871	126.5	46.7	65.5	–	–	–	7.48	5.35	5.75	16.4	18.2
1870	106.9	39.6	64.5	–	–	–	7.80	7.00	5.25	16.0	18.0
1869	87.9	46.8	82.2	–	–	–	–	–	6.10	15.8	19.3
1868	–	–	87.9	–	–	–	–	–	–	16.0	–
1867	180.0	47.0	67.0	–	–	–	–	–	–	14.0	15.0

[1] Specifications are given in text under each series number. Crop prices are in cents and eighths per bushel from 1934 to 1974.

Series M239-248. Index numbers of physical volume of agricultural production, Canada and by province, 1935 to 1974

(1961 = 100)

Year	Canada[1]	Prince Edward Island	Nova Scotia	New Brunswick	Quebec	Ontario	Manitoba	Saskat-chewan	Alberta	British Columbia
	239	240	241	242	243	244	245	246	247	248
1974	148.4	112.1	106.9	94.7	116.8	129.5	181.4	239.0	143.9	130.9
1973	153.3	102.9	101.4	88.9	111.3	122.4	218.8	267.2	150.5	140.1
1972	147.4	100.8	104.2	93.7	108.7	125.3	204.8	240.3	144.2	129.9
1971	159.7	107.7	105.8	96.3	116.9	127.9	231.5	295.0	144.4	135.1
1970	137.9	118.5	107.3	92.1	117.5	124.6	165.9	198.1	133.5	129.7
1969	149.8	120.9	108.9	99.9	117.0	117.7	182.0	279.7	144.2	117.0
1968	145.3	115.2	108.2	104.6	117.5	118.5	205.5	225.4	147.7	123.5
1967	134.7	113.3	106.4	98.5	112.8	114.6	192.2	199.7	128.0	125.9
1966	155.1	116.1	102.6	104.0	109.3	118.0	184.0	310.1	152.6	126.8
1965	137.1	107.0	98.7	96.8	103.7	108.6	192.4	242.7	132.7	109.2
1964	129.5	106.9	97.8	99.3	103.4	108.9	186.4	201.0	123.2	119.3
1963	139.9	101.6	101.4	97.8	105.4	106.4	151.6	291.2	128.2	112.9
1962	127.7	98.3	102.1	100.8	105.1	105.1	176.1	220.6	111.1	109.5
1961	100.0	100.0	100.0	100.0	100.0	100.0	100.0	100.0	100.0	100.0
1960	114.7	94.2	95.2	96.3	93.4	93.5	145.2	206.9	100.2	95.9
1959	107.9	96.2	95.0	92.5	93.6	90.6	139.6	165.0	104.2	90.8
1958	107.4	101.7	93.2	98.6	94.3	93.2	145.5	157.0	99.7	89.3
1957	99.2	105.6	94.9	102.3	90.6	84.7	119.7	152.3	88.0	88.8
1956	115.2	99.5	96.2	106.0	89.1	80.0	151.4	232.7	109.5	83.6
1955	107.3	101.1	97.4	104.6	89.8	78.9	119.8	210.4	99.0	81.1
1954	87.8	101.0	99.0	97.6	83.4	77.6	106.3	115.1	81.9	83.1
1953	109.9	103.7	90.7	105.8	82.4	77.5	127.1	224.8	107.3	82.6
1952	118.2	101.5	90.6	99.2	86.6	77.5	150.4	261.7	112.0	77.7
1951	103.2	80.6	80.1	92.2	81.5	75.8	132.6	198.8	100.4	68.9
1950	93.2	96.3	88.3	110.4	82.3	73.0	129.0	165.1	77.4	67.2
1949	84.4	105.1	85.4	115.5	76.2	73.5	115.4	127.7	67.0	73.9
1948	88.5	88.1	88.6	108.7	78.0	70.3	132.1	136.1	81.6	67.5
1947	84.9	84.8	88.0	104.4	74.1	66.6	118.2	129.7	82.8	68.6
1946	90.9	79.8	104.8	105.8	72.7	70.4	128.0	151.2	85.3	71.2
1945	78.2	81.8	85.8	95.3	69.1	64.4	104.1	128.1	65.8	61.0
1944	100.4	82.5	119.8	122.9	88.1	71.8	128.4	195.0	85.7	66.1
1943	80.3	72.0	102.9	120.7	80.3	58.4	132.2	130.3	66.2	54.4
1942	120.9	84.7	109.7	101.9	85.3	77.1	158.9	258.2	127.2	55.1
1941	76.7	65.6	92.7	87.8	72.2	65.6	117.5	110.1	68.9	47.5
1940	95.7	72.2	103.2	102.3	84.8	66.6	122.6	167.4	103.0	56.5
1939	95.0	72.8	109.1	92.1	82.1	70.6	117.2	179.8	88.8	53.8
1938	80.6	70.4	112.0	86.2	74.0	67.6	103.7	108.0	88.2	50.8
1937	63.4	68.7	116.4	96.0	78.6	67.3	107.1	33.2	56.1	49.4
1936	62.8	70.5	109.7	95.6	76.0	58.4	65.9	82.7	47.5	46.6
1935	71.2	62.5	110.8	85.4	72.2	65.0	66.2	113.1	59.8	44.6

[1] Excludes Newfoundland.

Series M249-300. Seeded area, production and farm gross value of field crops, Canada, 1870, 1880, 1890, 1900 and 1908 to 1974

Year	Wheat[1]			Oats for grain			Barley		
	Seeded area	Production	Farm gross value	Seeded area	Production	Farm gross value	Seeded area	Production	Farm gross value
	'000 acres	'000 bushels	$'000	'000 acres	'000 bushels	$'000	'000 acres	'000 bushels	$'000
	249	250	251	252	253	254	255	256	257
1974	22,077	488,513	2,055,608	6,106	254,745	398,120	11,800	404,286	892,447
1973	23,661	593,738	2,654,826	6,698	326,880	515,076	11,958	469,570	1,171,970
1972	21,350	533,288	993,349	6,104	300,208	266,733	12,509	518,316	646,184
1971	19,407	529,552	717,345	6,831	363,479	206,739	13,981	601,628	412,660
1970	12,483	331,579	476,614	6,882	353,073	211,438	9,894	408,287	307,415
1969	24,962	671,212	852,385	7,298	354,895	208,202	9,358	371,288	247,244
1968	29,426	649,950	872,754	7,431	356,700	211,569	8,854	326,045	265,822
1967	30,122	592,948	964,006	7,379	301,772	218,329	8,121	252,867	220,340
1966	29,693	827,338	1,457,123	7,896	370,678	275,108	7,461	296,235	310,690
1965	28,301	649,412	1,089,458	8,362	399,983	293,314	6,121	218,300	225,208
1964	29,698	600,726	957,696	7,984	347,006	239,328	5,495	168,463	167,944
1963	27,569	723,500	1,259,323	9,338	445,877	275,242	6,177	221,235	208,508
1962	26,818	565,585	941,488	10,568	492,610	328,658	5,287	165,872	156,024
1961	25,316	283,394	486,324	8,543	283,965	212,795	5,529	112,640	118,810
1960	24,538	518,379	812,838	9,620	398,505	269,885	6,857	193,473	155,161
1959	24,500	445,077	586,704	9,089	344,020	238,705	7,886	215,644	160,461
1958	22,149	398,077	527,076	9,234	345,731	222,077	9,286	237,811	182,294
1957	21,561	392,719	502,795	8,829	316,912	194,575	9,404	216,007	165,069
1956	22,781	573,040	714,053	10,471	467,517	272,184	8,390	269,065	211,336
1955	22,660	519,178	709,461	10,958	399,451	265,749	9,887	251,102	219,143
1954	25,539	331,981	411,781	10,053	306,401	206,537	7,842	175,196	155,278
1953	26,384	634,040	844,503	9,873	413,971	259,616	8,908	262,121	224,681
1952	26,164	701,973	1,112,865	11,057	471,117	313,487	8,478	291,572	308,008
1951	25,254	553,678	856,785	11,897	493,886	374,941	7,840	245,435	270,237
1950	27,311	466,490	717,449	11,184	401,768	313,875	6,510	167,495	188,518
1949	27,387	366,028	590,003	10,988	304,595	239,499	5,923	118,044	154,181
1948	23,705	381,413	630,774	10,855	345,305	243,256	6,401	152,281	146,735
1947	24,122	338,506	547,751	10,733	270,190	219,500	7,391	139,886	154,010
1946	24,376	411,601	660,108	11,782	360,860	207,429	6,186	146,852	112,963
1945	23,198	316,320	508,426	13,210	351,234	187,167	6,944	148,792	99,264
1944	22,677	414,859	514,052	13,412	474,044	254,424	7,008	187,326	140,874
1943	16,734	282,377	319,721	14,735	461,567	265,610	8,138	208,365	137,094
1942	21,560	556,067	427,441	13,532	641,488	249,339	6,879	256,037	117,695
1941	21,949	314,710	192,642	12,278	306,052	125,657	5,312	110,401	47,296
1940	28,726	540,190	309,553	12,298	380,526	106,771	4,342	104,256	33,350
1939	26,757	520,623	282,151	12,790	384,407	114,843	4,347	103,147	35,424
1938	25,931	360,010	211,265	13,010	371,382	89,335	4,454	102,242	28,446
1937	25,570	180,210	184,651	13,049	268,442	114,093	4,331	83,124	42,020
1936	25,605	219,218	205,327	13,288	271,778	116,267	4,438	71,922	49,512
1935	24,116	281,935	173,065	14,096	394,348	93,409	3,887	83,975	24,465
1934	23,985	275,849	169,631	13,731	321,120	103,124	3,613	63,742	29,975
1933	25,991	281,892	136,958	13,529	307,478	79,818	3,658	63,359	18,954
1932	27,182	443,061	154,760	13,148	391,561	75,988	3,758	80,773	18,855
1931	26,355	321,325	123,550	12,838	328,278	77,970	3,791	67,383	17,465
1930	24,898	420,672	204,693	13,259	423,148	102,919	5,559	135,160	27,254
1929	25,155	302,192	317,340	12,480	282,838	168,017	5,926	102,313	60,505
1928	24,119	566,726	451,235	13,137	452,153	210,956	4,881	136,391	76,112
1927	22,460	479,665	477,791	13,240	439,713	225,879	3,506	96,938	64,193
1926	22,896	407,136	442,221	12,741	383,416	184,098	3,648	99,987	52,059
1925	20,790	395,475	487,736	12,556	402,296	167,171	3,524	87,118	46,014
1924	22,056	262,097	320,362	14,491	405,976	200,688	3,407	88,807	61,760
1923	21,886	474,199	316,995	14,388	563,998	184,857	2,785	76,998	32,571
1922	22,423	399,786	339,419	14,541	491,239	185,455	2,600	71,865	33,335
1921	23,261	300,858	242,936	16,949	426,233	146,395	2,796	59,709	28,254
1920	18,232	263,189	427,357	15,850	530,710	280,115	2,552	63,311	52,821
1919	19,126	193,260	457,722	14,952	394,387	317,097	2,646	56,389	69,330
1918	17,354	189,075	381,678	14,790	426,312	331,357	3,154	77,287	77,379
1917	14,756	233,743	453,039	13,313	403,010	277,065	2,392	55,058	59,654
1916	15,370	262,781	344,096	10,997	410,211	210,958	1,803	42,770	35,024
1915	15,109	393,543	356,817	11,556	464,954	171,009	1,718	54,017	27,986
1914	10,294	161,280	158,236	10,062	313,078	151,811	1,496	36,201	21,557
1913	11,015	231,717	156,462	10,434	404,669	128,893	1,613	48,319	20,144
1912	10,997	224,159	139,090	9,966	391,629	126,304	1,581	49,398	22,354
1911	11,096	231,237	148,318	9,641	365,694	133,256	1,523	44,451	24,731
1910	8,865	132,078	104,817	8,656	245,393	86,796	1,283	28,848	14,654
1909	7,750	166,744	141,320	9,303	353,466	122,390	1,865	55,398	25,434
1908	6,610	112,434	91,228	7,911	250,377	96,489	1,746	46,762	21,353
1900	4,225	55,572	—	5,368	151,497	—	872	22,224	—
1890	2,701	42,223	—	3,961	83,428	—	869	17,223	—
1880	2,367	32,350	—	—	70,493	—	—	16,845	—
1870	1,647	16,724	—	—	42,489	—	—	11,496	—

Series M249-300. Seeded area, production and farm gross value of field crops, Canada, 1870, 1880, 1890, 1900 and 1908 to 1974 (continued)

Year	Mixed grains			Corn for grain			Flaxseed		
	Seeded area	Production	Farm gross value	Seeded area	Production	Farm gross value	Seeded area	Production	Farm gross value
	'000 acres	'000 bushels	$'000	'000 acres	'000 bushels	$'000	'000 acres	'000 bushels	$'000
	258	259	260	261	262	263	264	265	266
1974	1,811	80,754	168,909	1,460	101,910	313,705	1,450	13,800	130,940
1973	2,002	97,013	187,735	1,310	110,365	293,751	1,450	19,400	180,697
1972	2,065	104,285	107,437	1,327	99,538	164,100	1,321	17,617	70,863
1971	2,055	107,078	86,446	1,410	115,977	136,990	1,768	22,387	49,282
1970	1,959	99,271	83,286	1,234	103,684	142,297	3,313	47,966	105,963
1969	1,753	87,820	71,376	987	74,126	97,262	2,341	28,048	72,042
1968	1,689	86,820	74,264	964	81,744	101,666	1,524	19,666	56,594
1967	1,677	76,857	72,507	876	74,130	93,132	1,023	9,378	28,845
1966	1,767	81,443	76,112	807	66,363	97,588	1,918	22,520	61,252
1965	1,640	80,799	71,229	746	59,498	77,340	2,315	29,176	79,026
1964	1,535	71,151	61,461	655	52,840	68,680	1,977	20,305	59,745
1963	1,466	70,739	60,388	533	36,184	49,550	1,682	21,116	61,475
1962	1,524	72,278	63,443	439	33,399	42,734	1,446	16,065	49,156
1961	1,566	61,310	54,775	400	29,208	35,334	2,086	14,478	48,131
1960	1,366	58,935	48,930	456	26,099	32,075	2,513	22,571	62,173
1959	1,467	62,627	50,905	485	30,906	35,820	2,052	17,191	52,692
1958	1,398	63,835	52,072	494	29,785	36,031	2,551	22,342	58,594
1957	1,440	62,788	47,157	511	29,525	34,844	3,486	19,205	48,617
1956	1,561	66,618	56,008	509	27,814	33,377	3,041	34,991	89,631
1955	1,701	66,266	55,726	571	35,558	37,699	1,836	18,990	52,669
1954	1,670	63,649	53,216	460	24,891	36,011	1,178	10,998	27,963
1953	1,550	67,738	57,267	400	23,088	31,238	956	9,748	23,808
1952	1,572	64,054	62,027	364	21,192	30,535	1,110	11,660	36,856
1951	1,524	69,433	70,680	314	15,900	28,500	1,164	9,500	37,103
1950	1,421	62,838	63,069	311	14,103	22,585	587	4,975	17,274
1949	1,449	48,312	47,524	278	13,964	17,960	317	2,264	7,539
1948	1,327	53,678	51,825	258	12,697	16,739	1,969	18,488	70,447
1947	981	30,220	28,225	182	6,887	12,893	1,797	13,848	72,573
1946	1,164	47,629	31,475	260	11,007	11,635	887	6,828	20,552
1945	1,208	40,392	25,890	243	10,635	11,054	889	6,271	15,806
1944	1,274	48,948	29,015	276	11,976	11,830	1,245	8,967	22,717
1943	1,254	30,065	18,894	236	7,994	6,926	3,007	18,526	40,012
1942	1,481	61,565	32,309	364	14,689	11,646	1,564	15,584	31,118
1941	1,435	45,626	24,608	328	13,672	9,868	1,070	6,863	8,823
1940	1,220	43,133	16,994	186	6,956	3,826	393	3,095	3,459
1939	1,218	44,072	18,917	183	8,097	4,453	298	2,044	2,886
1938	1,160	39,161	15,126	180	7,690	3,614	210	1,259	1,420
1937	1,128	36,129	18,329	166	5,415	3,466	241	775	1,148
1936	1,172	33,639	18,751	164	6,083	4,258	477	1,795	2,588
1935	1,153	39,535	14,238	168	7,765	3,494	307	1,667	1,991
1934	1,159	37,926	15,634	161	6,798	4,419	227	910	1,049
1933	1,167	33,009	13,336	137	5,054	2,982	244	632	756
1932	1,184	39,036	13,063	130	5,057	2,276	462	2,719	1,682
1931	1,196	39,431	14,453	132	5,449	2,274	648	2,465	1,944
1930	1,201	44,276	18,435	161	5,826	5,054	582	5,069	4,741
1929	1,119	35,754	27,227	152	5,183	5,469	382	2,060	4,898
1928	1,107	39,130	27,672	139	5,241	5,860	378	3,614	5,758
1927	1,005	37,622	27,001	132	4,262	4,212	476	4,885	7,562
1926	956	33,875	22,385	210	7,813	7,780	738	5,995	9,688
1925	860	33,106	21,432	239	10,564	9,939	843	6,237	11,542
1924	848	31,995	22,626	295	11,998	14,227	1,277	9,695	18,849
1923	844	29,750	17,655	318	13,608	12,466	630	7,140	12,664
1922	780	27,708	16,501	318	13,798	11,510	566	5,008	8,639
1921	861	22,272	13,901	297	14,904	12,317	533	4,112	5,938
1920	812	32,421	29,236	292	14,335	16,593	1,428	7,998	15,502
1919	902	27,852	37,775	265	16,940	22,080	1,093	5,473	22,610
1918	922	35,662	40,726	250	14,205	24,903	1,068	6,055	18,951
1917	497	16,157	18,802	234	7,763	14,307	920	5,935	15,737
1916	413	10,585	9,301	173	6,282	6,747	658	8,260	16,890
1915	467	17,518	10,062	253	14,368	10,243	463	6,114	9,210
1914	463	16,382	10,759	256	13,924	9,808	1,084	7,175	7,368
1913	474	15,792	8,685	278	16,768	10,781	1,553	17,539	17,084
1912	497	17,198	10,194	298	16,942	10,534	2,022	26,130	23,608
1911	526	15,707	9,528	322	19,182	12,360	1,351	15,443	23,179
1910	427	13,086	6,308	294	14,318	7,664	582	4,245	8,870
1909	582	19,391	10,916	352	19,258	12,760	139	2,213	2,761
1908	582	19,049	10,140	366	22,868	11,834	139	1,499	1,457
1900	274	7,268	—	361	25,876	—	23	172	—
1890	—	—	—	195	10,711	—	16	139	—
1880	—	—	—	—	9,025	—	—	109	—
1870	—	—	—	—	3,803	—	—	118	—

Series M249-300. Seeded area, production and farm gross value of field crops, Canada, 1870, 1880, 1890, 1900 and 1908 to 1974 (continued)

Year	Rapeseed			Buckwheat			Dry peas		
	Seeded area	Production	Farm gross value	Seeded area	Production	Farm gross value	Seeded area	Production	Farm gross value
	'000 acres	'000 bushels	$'000	'000 acres	'000 bushels	$'000	'000 acres	'000 bushels	$'000
	267	268	269	270	271	272	273	274	275
1974	3,160	51,300	362,288	64	1,216	4,717	79	1,680	11,133
1973	3,150	53,200	304,078	89	1,379	4,459	66	1,591	7,140
1972	3,270	57,300	181,086	103	1,711	2,372	68	1,587	3,889
1971	5,306	95,000	205,530	122	2,525	3,662	81	1,927	3,838
1970	4,050	72,200	168,179	153	2,845	3,873	86	1,620	3,427
1969	2,012	33,400	76,494	101	1,715	2,605	73	1,271	2,733
1968	1,052	19,400	35,472	83	1,404	2,069	53	1,013	2,455
1967	1,620	24,700	47,506	76	1,305	2,001	47	1,111	2,680
1966	1,525	25,800	63,760	55	1,164	1,591	61	1,094	2,676
1965	1,435	22,600	54,360	55	888	1,003	59	1,327	2,710
1964	791	13,230	36,309	60	1,274	1,402	76	1,724	3,538
1963	478	8,360	21,042	51	1,197	1,516	53	1,045	2,456
1962	371	5,860	11,972	47	1,151	1,440	50	821	1,874
1961	710	11,220	20,179	58	1,217	1,390	66	1,040	2,313
1960	763	11,120	18,116	71	1,581	1,764	61	1,119	2,366
1959	214	3,560	7,120	69	1,431	1,520	69	1,016	2,203
1958	626	7,762	9,753	95	2,001	2,093	71	1,119	2,439
1957	618	8,661	13,720	108	2,212	2,363	82	1,351	2,747
1956	352	5,996	10,518	168	3,177	3,665	88	1,817	3,618
1955	138	1,559	2,759	131	2,418	2,908	73	1,019	2,598
1954	40	578	968	134	2,465	2,692	61	1,096	2,690
1953	30	491	876	151	3,572	3,747	65	1,313	2,682
1952	19	278	478	127	2,858	3,713	46	956	2,616
1951	7	120	210	123	3,022	4,077	37	752	2,116
1950	—	2	5	116	2,938	3,884	39	652	1,824
1949	20	340	850	126	2,646	3,265	45	772	1,967
1948	80	1,280	—	146	3,120	3,823	66	1,167	3,235
1947	58	438	—	233	4,180	4,857	110	1,558	4,319
1946	24	259	—	176	3,956	3,853	107	2,045	5,881
1945	13	168	—	215	4,310	3,680	86	1,335	3,655
1944	11	122	—	216	4,720	3,920	65	990	2,454
1943	3	44	—	243	5,339	4,251	87	1,341	2,908
1942	—	—	—	206	4,454	3,178	76	1,393	2,908
1941	—	—	—	205	4,139	2,819	70	1,182	2,354
1940	—	—	—	326	6,692	3,838	82	1,355	2,652
1939	—	—	—	335	6,848	4,103	76	1,307	2,350
1938	—	—	—	376	7,079	4,098	80	1,365	2,113
1937	—	—	—	396	7,745	5,592	84	1,200	2,012
1936	—	—	—	397	8,596	6,088	93	1,229	1,991
1935	—	—	—	380	7,949	4,017	95	1,616	1,767
1934	—	—	—	407	8,635	4,572	95	1,588	1,660
1933	—	—	—	398	8,483	4,233	85	1,377	1,371
1932	—	—	—	368	8,424	3,585	85	1,518	1,288
1931	—	—	—	336	6,917	3,454	81	1,369	1,160
1930	—	—	—	490	10,903	7,124	129	2,371	3,487
1929	—	—	—	516	10,470	9,867	125	1,980	4,079
1928	—	—	—	503	10,899	10,128	155	2,588	4,786
1927	—	—	—	471	10,890	9,727	151	2,795	4,959
1926	—	—	—	457	9,882	8,598	145	2,635	4,610
1925	—	—	—	474	10,546	8,965	183	3,411	5,616
1924	—	—	—	442	11,412	10,149	180	3,240	5,676
1923	—	—	—	440	9,744	8,192	169	2,898	4,987
1922	—	—	—	431	9,701	8,141	190	3,429	6,141
1921	—	—	—	361	8,230	7,285	193	2,770	5,439
1920	—	—	—	379	8,995	11,512	186	3,528	8,534
1919	—	—	—	445	10,551	15,831	230	3,406	9,739
1918	—	—	—	548	11,376	18,018	236	4,313	12,899
1917	—	—	—	396	7,149	10,443	199	3,026	10,724
1916	—	—	—	342	5,976	6,375	155	2,263	4,919
1915	—	—	—	344	7,866	5,913	200	3,537	5,724
1914	—	—	—	354	8,626	6,213	209	3,422	4,895
1913	—	—	—	381	8,372	5,320	223	4,038	4,382
1912	—	—	—	399	10,517	6,544	260	3,913	4,944
1911	—	—	—	373	8,466	5,443	295	4,669	4,770
1910	—	—	—	362	7,200	4,095	355	4,789	4,196
1909	—	—	—	282	7,806	4,554	393	8,145	7,124
1908	—	—	—	291	7,153	4,269	413	7,060	5,970
1900	—	—	—	262	4,547	—	670	12,349	—
1890	—	—	—	293	4,995	—	925	14,824	—
1880	—	—	—	—	4,901	—	—	13,750[10]	—
1870	—	—	—	—	3,726	—	—	9,906	—

Series M249-300. Seeded area, production and farm gross value of field crops, Canada, 1870, 1880, 1890, 1900 and 1908 to 1974 (continued)

Year	Dry beans			Soybeans			Potatoes		
	Seeded area	Production	Farm gross value	Seeded area	Production	Farm gross value	Seeded area	Production	Farm gross value
	'000 acres	'000 bushels	$'000	'000 acres	'000 bushels	$'000	'000 acres	'000 cwt[5]	$'000
	276	277	278	279	280	281	282	283	284
1974	172	3,548	28,568	445	11,040	70,057	283	54,783	158,321
1973	133	2,885	46,622	470	14,570	83,340	261	47,586	246,636
1972	134	3,233	17,736	405	13,770	53,703	244	43,886	149,443
1971	113	2,911	18,362	367	10,276	30,417	269	48,810	83,318
1970	82	1,859	10,589	335	10,385	28,870	316	55,123	109,370
1969	90	1,951	8,200	322	7,664	18,624	305	51,843	110,473
1968	91	1,621	8,092	295	9,027	22,026	303	52,871	82,011
1967	86	1,435	7,730	290	8,091	21,684	304	46,729	80,451
1966	118	2,932	12,019	279	9,012	27,036	319	54,679	78,513
1965	95	2,200	9,643	265	8,030	21,681	295	45,786	118,490
1964	83	2,057	8,721	231	6,976	20,021	277	47,333	136,772
1963	71	1,534	6,628	228	5,002	14,006	286	46,061	79,145
1962	66	1,425	5,989	221	6,608	16,388	287	46,878	73,407
1961	66	1,325	5,171	212	6,631	14,920	306	44,108	61,933
1960	66	995	3,832	227	5,001	10,153	292	42,696	85,023
1959	67	1,155	4,403	251	6,828	12,765	284	35,614	98,317
1958	67	1,223	4,476	263	6,649	12,511	305	39,610	68,221
1957	63	1,094	3,735	256	6,508	12,695	309	43,744	75,675
1956	66	1,146	4,383	243	5,301	11,400	313	42,325	74,274
1955	76	1,215	5,105	227	5,993	12,525	313	40,191	71,032
1954	71	1,012	5,060	245	4,778	11,467	304	32,163	77,951
1953	66	1,180	4,872	231	5,013	12,282	324	41,803	55,004
1952	60	1,296	5,714	172	4,128	10,526	296	36,959	103,795
1951	58	1,229	5,151	155	3,844	10,571	285	29,928	101,189
1950	66	1,185	5,685	142	3,323	8,474	370	43,825	54,329
1949	82	1,598	5,329	104	2,610	5,899	389	42,480	64,292
1948	80	1,434	5,906	94	1,824	4,195	401	44,395	72,749
1947	86	1,287	7,017	61	1,110	3,397	408	38,017	83,103
1946	79	1,364	4,082	59	1,072	2,369	446	41,756	71,133
1945	84	1,099	2,788	46	844	1,600	439	31,870	71,333
1944	86	1,211	3,067	36	681	1,354	471	44,187	67,198
1943	72	1,208	2,648	36	570	981	484	39,949	71,412
1942	66	1,316	2,072	42	872	1,509	467	39,711	60,143
1941	98	1,651	2,808	11	217	—	480	37,039	46,234
1940	97	1,477	2,721	—	—	—	545	42,300	35,394
1939	73	1,527	3,138	—	—	—	518	36,390	41,065
1938	71	1,557	1,725	—	—	—	522	35,938	33,093
1937	68	1,296	1,597	—	—	—	531	42,547	26,650
1936	64	876	1,790	—	—	—	502	39,614	45,125
1935	65	1,161	1,693	—	—	—	507	38,670	30,854
1934	57	814	1,079	—	—	—	569	48,095	23,822
1933	59	891	878	—	—	—	528	42,745	33,092
1932	67	1,141	629	—	—	—	522	39,416	24,920
1931	85	1,304	941	—	—	—	592	52,305	22,359
1930	99	1,439	3,261	—	—	—	571	48,241	39,858
1929	86	1,491	4,920	—	—	—	544	39,930	63,372
1928	70	1,170	4,184	—	—	—	599	50,195	40,874
1927	67	1,037	2,408	—	—	—	572	46,458	54,341
1926	72	1,160	3,060	—	—	—	523	46,937	69,204
1925	82	1,501	3,877	—	—	—	522	40,217	82,860
1924	72	1,194	3,307	—	—	—	562	56,648	47,956
1923	63	1,042	2,773	—	—	—	561	55,497	56,418
1922	80	1,303	3,714	—	—	—	684	55,745	50,320
1921	63	1,090	3,156	—	—	—	702	64,406	82,148
1920	72	1,265	4,918	—	—	—	785	80,299	129,803
1919	84	1,389	6,215	—	—	—	819	75,344	118,894
1918	229	3,563	19,284	—	—	—	735	62,610	102,235
1917	93	1,274	9,493	—	—	—	657	47,936	80,804
1916	33	413	2,228	—	—	—	473	37,978	50,982
1915	43	723	2,207	—	—	—	486	36,211	36,460
1914	44	798	1,844	—	—	—	476	51,404	41,598
1913	47	801	1,505	—	—	—	474	47,125	38,418
1912	53	920	2,008	—	—	—	484	50,931	37,329
1911	53	1,016	1,956	—	—	—	481	42,853	42,478
1910	46	826	1,417	—	—	—	465	33,277	27,427
1909	56	1,325	1,881	—	—	—	514	59,453	36,399
1908	60	1,245	1,988	—	—	—	504	44,273	34,819
1900	47	861	—	—	—	—	449	55,363	—
1890	43	800	—	—	—	—	450	53,491	—
1880	—	13,750[10]	—	—	—	—	464	55,369	—
1870	—	221	—	—	—	—	403	47,330	—

Series M249-300. Seeded area, production and farm gross value of field crops, Canada, 1870, 1880, 1890, 1900 and 1908 to 1974 (continued)

Year	Sugar beets			Tame hay			Fodder corn[2]		
	Seeded area	Production	Farm gross value	Seeded area	Production	Farm gross value	Seeded area	Production	Farm gross value
	acres	tons	$'000	'000 acres	'000 tons	$'000	'000 acres	'000 tons	$'000
	285	286	287	288	289	290	291	292	293
1974	67,538	829,092	41,690	13,033	25,402	1,104,256	1,048	11,070	144,051
1973	68,640	994,162	38,917	12,850	25,748	747,838	893	11,276	118,516
1972	77,610	1,069,744	21,193	12,459	23,229	537,446	812	10,042	79,129
1971	81,096	1,215,917	22,215	12,053	24,182	483,811	772	10,458	72,064
1970	68,771	916,906	14,789	12,978	26,958	512,731	726	9,822	65,289
1969	79,227	1,078,221	18,970	12,138	24,598	450,977	692	8,577	56,854
1968	79,666	1,098,221	18,923	12,117	22,400	415,748	636	7,975	53,065
1967	83,305	1,081,082	18,054	12,742	25,043	447,548	599	7,361	49,684
1966	81,272	1,166,554	19,126	13,154	26,049	469,284	578	6,643	44,044
1965	85,023	1,142,341	19,061	12,815	21,387	445,308	541	6,011	37,826
1964	101,312	1,297,912	19,091	12,613	21,570	400,982	497	5,864	34,556
1963	95,223	1,285,747	23,586	12,524	23,378	383,487	441	4,984	28,177
1962	84,677	1,105,704	21,004	12,429	22,640	361,009	398	4,784	26,180
1961	84,927	1,105,708	14,515	12,229	20,812	325,327	360	4,054	21,949
1960	86,128	1,098,673	15,778	12,106	21,595	318,695	366	3,323	15,616
1959	90,453	1,239,518	15,842	11,735	20,102	302,148	367	3,943	18,642
1958	97,800	1,324,870	19,177	11,471	17,924	281,041	379	3,753	17,598
1957	83,743	1,053,564	13,948	11,484	19,193	294,887	370	3,605	17,016
1956	78,786	892,872	15,470	10,922	19,655	302,698	394	3,450	16,519
1955	81,908	981,014	13,170	10,842	20,186	303,837	365	3,436	17,861
1954	90,453	1,003,869	12,108	10,737	20,118	281,156	354	3,046	14,692
1953	81,949	900,347	12,061	10,564	20,015	275,211	359	3,621	17,084
1952	92,588	1,022,884	15,493	10,629	19,720	279,418	367	3,881	17,738
1951	92,920	965,433	14,440	10,538	20,190	307,118	386	3,661	18,271
1950	101,496	1,115,854	18,299	10,228	14,834	269,319	463	4,717	25,381
1949	84,216	858,727	11,749	10,346	13,480	264,705	431	4,149	26,046
1948	60,065	629,206	9,202	10,405	17,598	280,784	419	3,933	22,147
1947	58,405	605,759	8,685	10,671	17,404	268,898	379	3,094	15,379
1946	66,619	735,850	9,196	10,500	15,879	204,653	388	3,323	13,777
1945	59,283	618,785	6,567	10,752	19,282	235,194	407	3,064	12,523
1944	55,021	566,294	6,283	10,787	16,921	214,654	399	3,801	14,755
1943	52,719	474,378	4,980	10,504	19,189	212,738	402	3,605	14,538
1942	62,381	715,524	6,053	10,474	18,327	194,940	409	3,930	15,116
1941	63,999	711,923	5,405	10,365	14,448	178,638	407	3,783	14,293
1940	77,532	825,345	5,612	9,843	16,658	142,969	496	4,155	12,235
1939	57,313	586,443	4,430	9,784	15,544	131,159	495	4,514	13,666
1938	45,131	498,102	3,286	9,679	15,859	120,778	460	4,413	12,422
1937	43,768	422,152	2,492	9,542	15,137	115,122	447	3,928	12,087
1936	50,445	555,976	3,233	9,638	15,769	123,780	402	3,128	10,572
1935	51,928	459,223	2,501	9,460	16,019	122,876	481	4,078	13,539
1934	38,485	412,672	2,328	9,560	12,502	148,117	497	3,815	15,729
1933	43,625	442,391	2,784	9,598	13,095	115,585	379	3,123	10,239
1932	44,814	505,671	3,097	9,478	15,323	111,785	366	2,858	7,868
1931	43,337	435,990	2,663	9,682	15,928	124,491	335	2,884	11,416
1930	51,610	467,108	3,209	11,362	18,037	180,999	426	3,476	17,142
1929	45,148	365,910	2,458	11,359	17,668	207,711	423	3,322	15,265
1928	50,475	417,608	3,018	11,175	18,525	194,363	441	3,666	17,204
1927	42,893	369,902	2,881	11,137	19,527	206,781	472	3,548	15,849
1926	46,697	508,249	3,350	10,353	16,119	197,887	511	4,490	21,926
1925	43,112	458,665	2,794	10,200	16,544	175,006	519	4,692	18,911
1924	36,080	334,000	2,268	10,348	16,217	180,292	719	5,741	29,380
1923	22,450	216,200	1,401	10,117	15,874	174,796	659	5,321	24,605
1922	20,725	190,400	1,500	10,308	15,294	205,245	655	5,879	29,198
1921	28,367	268,000	1,742	10,879	12,028	280,975	585	6,362	44,881
1920	36,288	412,400	5,279	10,618	13,923	362,054	589	5,642	43,701
1919	24,500	240,000	2,606	10,822	16,842	349,513	512	4,943	34,180
1918	18,000	180,000	1,845	10,740	15,217	249,224	502	4,788	29,439
1917	14,000	117,600	794	8,335	13,947	144,417	367	2,690	13,835
1916	15,000	71,000	440	7,921	14,814	171,612	293	1,908	9,396
1915	18,000	141,000	776	7,876	10,873	155,840	333	3,383	16,613
1914	12,100	108,600	651	8,087	10,477	149,091	317	3,251	15,950
1913	17,000	148,000	906	8,262	11,096	127,506	304	2,616	12,506
1912	18,900	201,000	1,005	8,376	12,402	137,761	299	3,038	14,977
1911	20,676	175,000	1,154	8,786	14,347	166,806	296	3,681	13,063
1910	17,045	188,000	1,096	8,344	10,521	91,289	294	2,705	8,775
1909	10,000	86,000	500	8,210	11,877	132,288	270	2,780	15,116
1908	10,800	109,000	578	8,211	11,450	121,884	260	2,938	11,812
1900	—	—	—	6,543	7,853	—	—	—	—
1890	—	—	—	5,932	7,694	—	—	—	—
1880	—	—	—	4,458	5,053	—	—	—	—
1870	—	—	—	3,650	3,819	—	—	—	—

Series M249-300. Seeded area, production and farm gross value of field crops, Canada, 1870, 1880, 1890, 1900 and 1908 to 1974 (concluded)

Year	Tobacco			Maple syrup		Maple sugar	
	Harvested area[3] acres	Production[4] '000 lb.	Farm gross value $'000	Production '000 gal	Farm gross value $'000	Production '000 lb.	Farm gross value $'000
	294	295	296	297	298	299	300
1974	122,846	256,787	230,594	1,751	12,629	646[6]	753[7]
1973	120,867	257,313	202,639	2,420	17,020	681[6]	696[7]
1972	103,283	186,836	142,893	1,986	13,706	640[6]	597[7]
1971	97,539	224,961	144,035	1,324	6,728	709[6]	485[7]
1970	108,213	221,863	142,915	1,631	8,189	844[6]	594[7]
1969	132,752	247,465	162,925	1,882	8,503	832[6]	544[7]
1968	134,871	218,807	153,807	2,612	11,443	901[6]	578[7]
1967	140,773	213,096	144,973	2,420	10,624	872[6]	556[7]
1966	130,198	234,182	164,029	3,129	13,954	997[6]	604[7]
1965	99,344	168,880	106,198	2,159	9,265	984[6]	569[7]
1964	85,316	153,414	83,118	1,722	7,319	478	271
1963	113,893	201,144	90,633	2,718	11,006	720	395
1962	131,056	203,027	95,904	2,746	10,580	750	374
1961	137,917	209,721	105,352	2,563	10,028	831	404
1960	135,962	214,167	114,699	2,516	10,692	405	206
1959	128,133	169,904	90,403	2,309	9,257	488	211
1958	134,126	197,302	89,603	2,403	8,064	815	376
1957	136,787	164,865	78,589	3,068	10,031	661	311
1956	127,722	161,940	72,059	2,618	9,676	586	260
1955	109,909	134,840	57,685	2,146	10,441	847	441
1954	131,755	184,763	77,788	2,304	10,513	1,175	525
1953	101,088	139,190	59,617	1,816	6,784	1,324	522
1952	91,639	139,719	56,797	3,254	11,256	2,161	919
1951	118,970	153,792	66,213	2,144	7,902	1,649	653
1950	101,839	120,298	51,292	2,801	9,954	1,824	682
1949	109,053	139,820	55,453	2,306	8,470	1,787	656
1948	110,590	126,629	50,272	2,159	7,721	2,350	820
1947	125,267	106,688	37,460	3,580	12,853	3,434	1,286
1946	110,358	141,384	49,472	1,889	5,582	2,543	700
1945	93,277	92,345	30,620	1,338	3,980	1,920	517
1944	88,495	105,416	31,002	2,870	8,466	2,207	591
1943	71,140	69,104	19,646	2,058	5,131	2,416	619
1942	78,730	89,699	21,539	2,877	5,966	3,737	750
1941	70,560	94,182	19,338	2,037	3,143	2,390	419
1940	67,880	61,136	10,470	2,755	3,679	3,438	531
1939	92,300	107,703	19,444	2,302	3,024	2,899	420
1938	83,575	101,395	20,270	2,955	3,479	3,454	370
1937	69,028	72,093	17,140	1,233	1,721	4,412	524
1936	54,993	46,116	9,374	2,022	2,656	9,233	1,058
1935	47,117	55,470	10,870	2,252	2,783	6,539	740
1934	40,962	38,735	7,218	1,838	2,464	4,941	576
1933	46,898	44,904	6,525	1,263	1,560	5,785	500
1932	53,966	53,987	6,178	1,710	2,004	7,260	702
1931	54,936	51,248	7,105	1,280	2,512	5,523	945
1930	41,444	36,716	7,163	2,186	3,870	8,208	1,381
1929	37,696	29,782	6,104	2,174	3,955	11,698	2,163
1928	43,138	41,956	6,812	1,687	3,315	13,798	2,269
1927	44,028	43,829	8,978	2,155	3,570	9,832	1,365
1926	33,356	28,824	7,379	1,747	3,577	7,137	1,321
1925	27,825	29,266	7,005	1,672	3,440	10,496	1,848
1924	21,317	18,711	4,359	1,972	4,083	9,385	1,908
1923	23,932	21,297	3,518	—	—	—	—
1922	25,762	25,948	4,548	—	—	—	—
1921	11,809	13,249	2,393	—	—	—	—
1920	53,114	48,088	5,893	1,510	4,395[8]	9,605	4,395[9]
1919	31,586	33,770	15,548	—	—	—	—
1918	13,403	14,232	—	—	—	—	—
1917	7,930	8,495	—	—	—	—	—
1916	5,891	5,943	—	—	—	—	—
1915	9,000	9,000	—	—	—	—	—
1914	9,750	10,000	—	—	—	—	—
1913	11,000	12,500	—	—	—	—	—
1912	—	13,000	—	—	—	—	—
1911	25,826	—	—	—	—	—	—
1910	18,928	17,632	—	1,803	2,587[8]	10,488	2,587[9]
1909	—	—	—	—	—	—	—
1908	—	—	—	—	—	—	—
1900	11,906	11,267	—	—	1,780[8]	17,805	1,780[9]
1890	4,765	4,278	—	—	—	25,088	—
1880	—	2,528	—	—	—	20,556	—
1870	—	1,596	—	—	—	17,276	—

[1] Comprises spring, winter (or fall) and durum wheats.
[2] Includes corn for silage.
[3] Planted area for 1945 and previous years.
[4] Estimated weight of green tobacco.
[5] Production in thousands of bushels for 1900 and previous years.
[6] Data include production of maple taffy.
[7] Data include value of maple taffy.
[8] Includes value of maple sugar.
[9] Includes value of maple syrup.
[10] Comprises peas and beans.

Series M301-309. Production, imports, exports and domestic disappearance of wheat,[1] Canada, 1868 to 1974
(thousands of bushels)

Year[2]	Production	Imports	Exports			Domestic disappearance			
			Wheat grain	Wheat flour[3]	Total	Human food	Animal feed[4]	Other uses[5]	Total[6]
	301	**302**	**303**	**304**	**305**	**306**	**307**	**308**	**309**
1974	488,513	—	375,853	18,741	394,594	69,945	62,440	36,909	169,294
1973	593,738	—	400,588	18,799	419,387	66,781	70,479	31,788	169,048
1972	533,288	—	553,242	23,354	576,596	64,685	75,721	34,644	175,050
1971	529,552	—	479,048	24,716	503,764	65,426	81,181	29,579	176,185
1970	331,579	—	410,410	24,846	435,257	64,361	79,203	27,294	170,858
1969	671,212	—	319,534	26,963	346,498	64,627	84,803	18,423	167,853
1968	649,950	—	281,216	24,623	305,838	61,397	64,197	39,199	164,794
1967	592,948	—	311,320	24,690	336,010	60,463	53,687	42,028	156,178
1966	827,338	4	483,456	31,851	515,307	59,006	57,445	43,957	160,407
1965	649,412	7	546,781	38,125	584,906	60,943	50,166	46,306	· 157,415
1964	600,726	10	368,052	31,542	399,594	57,507	46,879	43,172	147,558
1963	723,500	3	539,637	54,910	594,548	59,079	53,769	43,914	156,762
1962	565,585	13	304,102	27,265	331,367	53,038	44,204	40,800	138,042
1961	283,394	6	326,069	31,953	358,022	58,924	44,150	39,587	142,660
1960	518,379	7	317,568	35,682	353,249	56,265	62,293	37,825	156,384
1959	445,077	7	240,321	36,970	277,291	55,006	61,677	39,523	156,206
1958	398,077	4	257,421	37,125	294,546	53,662	74,095	36,231	163,988
1957	392,719	1	279,912	40,381	320,293	53,135	71,325	33,059	157,519
1956	573,040	148	230,856	33,540	264,396	53,786	70,628	30,406	154,820
1955	519,178	20	272,260	40,000	312,260	53,712	77,611	32,789	164,113
1954	331,981	178	211,288	40,622	251,909	53,672	75,768	32,736	162,176
1953	634,040	457	208,835	46,246	255,081	46,390	61,406	36,130	143,926
1952	701,973	17	329,026	56,501	385,527	52,303	60,398	37,755	150,456
1951	553,678	18	304,722	51,103	355,825	52,176	77,934	39,786	169,895
1950	466,490	12	185,039	55,921	240,961	51,106	59,808	37,624	148,538
1949	366,028	4	179,457	45,680	225,137	47,082	47,154	36,871	131,107
1948	381,413	289	184,235	48,094	232,329	42,617	44,024	38,031	124,672
1947	338,506	825	133,505	61,477	194,982	48,600	70,315	33,864	152,779
1946	411,601	16	163,388	76,033	239,421	53,300	70,957	35,398	159,655
1945	316,320	75	278,070	65,116	343,186	56,000	63,512	38,170	157,682
1944	414,859	405	280,288	62,657	342,946	49,900	83,498	37,378	170,776
1943	282,377	433	283,165	60,590	343,755	53,489	85,941	37,720	177,150
1942	556,067	3	158,112	56,588	214,701	49,525	93,908	27,062	170,495
1941	314,710	29	179,902	45,926	225,828	47,900	65,818	31,570	145,288
1940	540,190	123	184,907	46,300	231,206	49,499	48,100	31,852	129,451
1939	520,623	444	162,158	30,516	192,674	50,302	36,788	36,259	130,830
1938	360,010	1,891	139,315	20,719	160,034	48,043	41,215	34,506	123,492
1937	180,210	6,139	79,342	16,243	95,586	42,841	24,166	32,981	103,276
1936	219,218	403	189,407	20,365	209,773	43,549	20,809	34,112	100,163
1935	281,935	292	232,020	22,405	254,425	44,865	34,888	33,487	114,291
1934	275,849	897	144,375	21,376	165,751	42,843	26,024	32,345	100,044
1933	281,892	413	170,234	24,546	194,780	43,068	24,505	29,981	102,280
1932	443,061	173	240,137	24,168	264,304	43,261	32,304	32,277	97,214
1931	321,325	216	182,803	24,226	207,030	41,604	35,305	36,887	117,168
1930	420,672	244	228,536	30,157	258,694	41,916	52,940	39,172	150,207
1929	302,192	1,386	155,766	30,501	186,267	43,439	13,901	43,571	117,968
1928	566,726	1,346	354,425	53,139	407,564	44,086	42,449	44,196	124,425
1927	479,665	473	288,567	44,396	332,963	43,461	37,699	42,208	11,640
1926	407,136	407	251,266	41,615	292,881	42,836	31,411	39,305	99,180
1925	395,475	379	275,557	49,035	324,592	42,256	17,507	40,227	61,864
1924	262,097	630	146,958	45,764	192,722	42,139	21,987	38,452	87,381
1923	474,199	441	292,425	54,096	346,522	41,520	31,297	38,597	92,175
1922	399,786	398	229,849	49,516	279,365	40,865	18,794	39,782	130,794
1921	300,858	373	150,935	34,834	185,770	37,000	22,707	39,240	107,441
1920	263,189	455	136,969	30,247	167,215	39,479	18,423	40,707	59,747
1919[7]	193,260	202	63,450	29,049	92,500	28,951	10,733	31,907	100,962
1918[7]	189,075	322	55,921	41,039	96,960	37,961	14,171	33,497	92,436
1917[7]	233,743	281	118,580	50,661	169,240	35,339	21,370	30,369	64,784
1916	262,781	304	140,224	34,341	174,565	—	—	—	88,520
1915	393,543	305	235,739	33,419	269,158	—	—	—	124,690
1914	161,280	2,180	63,902	22,848	86,750	—	—	—	76,710
1913	231,717	358	114,902	20,685	135,587	—	—	—	96,487
1912	224,159	889	95,511	20,233	115,744	—	—	—	109,304
1911	231,237	375	78,787	18,814	97,601	—	—	—	134,012
1910	132,078	408	48,443	13,955	62,398	—	—	—	70,088
1909	166,744	209	52,624	15,184	67,808	—	—	—	99,145
1908	112,434	179	47,624	9,037	56,662	—	—	—	55,879
1907	93,131	303	40,078	7,506	47,584	—	—	—	45,851
1906	135,602	234	39,435	7,031	46,466	—	—	—	89,370

Series M301-309. Production, imports, exports and domestic disappearance of wheat,[1] Canada, 1868 to 1974 (concluded)
(thousands of bushels)

Year[2]	Production	Imports	Exports			Domestic disappearance			
			Wheat grain	Wheat flour[3]	Total	Human food	Animal feed[4]	Other uses[5]	Total[6]
	301	302	303	304	305	306	307	308	309
1905	107,033	254	40,399	6,894	47,293	–	–	–	59,993
1904	71,838	283	14,700	5,947	20,647	–	–	–	51,474
1903	81,888	221	16,799	7,144	23,943	–	–	–	58,186
1902	97,073	244	32,986	5,795	38,781	–	–	–	58,536
1901	88,337	360	26,118	4,889	31,007	–	–	–	57,690
1900	55,572	315	9,740	5,034	14,774	–	–	–	41,113
1899	59,912	255	16,845	3,456	20,301	–	–	–	39,866
1898	66,495	295	10,305	3,567	13,872	–	–	–	52,919
1897	54,418	218	18,963	5,623	24,586	–	–	–	30,051
1896	39,570	202	7,855	1,898	9,753	–	–	–	30,019
1895	55,703	329	9,920	840	10,760	–	–	–	45,272
1894	43,221	715	8,826	1,003	9,829	–	–	–	34,107
1893	41,347	207	9,272	1,929	11,201	–	–	–	30,353
1892	48,182	164	9,272	1,846	11,118	–	–	–	37,229
1891	60,721	231	8,714	1,715	10,429	–	–	–	50,523
1890	42,223	406	2,108	1,336	3,444	–	–	–	39,185
1889	30,792	953	422	518	940	–	–	–	30,805
1888	32,965	1,180	491	590	1,081	–	–	–	33,064
1887	38,954	293	2,164	1,575	3,739	–	–	–	35,508
1886	38,225	786	5,632	2,341	7,973	–	–	–	31,038
1885	42,736	972	3,419	1,738	5,157	–	–	–	38,551
1884	45,363	2,804	2,341	557	2,898	–	–	–	45,269
1883	30,481	2,689	746	888	1,634	–	–	–	31,896
1882	47,752	1,236	5,867	2,201	8,068	–	–	–	40,920
1881	38,000	1,122	3,845	2,114	5,959	–	–	–	33,163
1880	32,350	966	2,524	1,978	4,502	–	–	–	28,813
1879	34,276	468	5,091	2,450	7,541	–	–	–	27,203
1878	30,359	5,619	6,611	2,587	9,198	–	–	–	26,780
1877	25,903	7,051	4,394	2,143	6,537	–	–	–	26,416
1876	22,601	7,060	2,393	1,209	3,602	–	–	–	26,059
1875	26,093	7,548	6,070	1,870	7,940	–	–	–	25,701
1874	23,853	7,210	4,383	1,363	5,746	–	–	–	25,318
1873	24,180	9,702	6,581	2,432	9,013	–	–	–	24,869
1872	23,838	7,076	4,380	2,134	6,514	–	–	–	24,401
1871	23,149	5,862	2,993	2,039	5,032	–	–	–	23,979
1870	16,724	5,969	1,749	1,379	3,128	–	–	–	23,563
1869	22,578	5,872	3,557	1,720	5,277	–	–	–	23,173
1868	22,156	5,164	2,809	1,689	4,498	–	–	–	22,822

[1] Comprises spring, winter (or fall) and durum wheats.
[2] Year beginning 1 August for 1924 to 1974; 1 September for 1905 to 1923; and 1 July for 1868 to 1904.
[3] Converted to wheat grain equivalent.
[4] Includes waste and dockage.
[5] Comprises seed, industrial use and loss in handling.

[6] Total domestic disappearance is not equal to the aggregate of human food, animal feed, and other uses for 1917 to 1934. This discrepancy is attributed to an unexplained residual in the supply and disposition account for these years.
[7] Quantity of wheat used for human food is derived by subtracting exports of wheat flour from the total quantity of wheat used for milling.

Series M310-320. Livestock statistics, number on farms and farm values at 1 June, Canada, 1906 to 1975
(number of animals in thousands; value of animals in thousands of dollars)

Year	Milk cows Number	Milk cows Value	Other cattle Number	Other cattle Value	Total cattle Number	Total cattle Value	Hogs Number	Hogs Value	Sheep and lambs Number	Sheep and lambs Value	Hens and chickens Number
	310	311	312	313	314	315	316	317	318	319	320
1975[1]	2,132	867,743	13,128	2,590,643	15,260	3,458,386	5,284	357,039	703	21,759	—
1974	2,080	959,264	12,930	3,477,314	15,010	4,436,578	6,564	278,999	784	26,486	—
1973	2,117	891,385	12,010	3,313,015	14,128	4,204,400	7,022	356,972	832	25,174	—
1972	2,170	738,567	11,474	2,472,748	13,644	3,211,315	6,995	253,094	845	20,228	91,296
1971	2,255	634,948	11,016	2,015,214	13,271	2,650,162	7,624	177,318	851	18,871	90,240
1970	2,389	687,419	10,437	1,930,326	12,826	2,617,745	7,113	262,796	796	19,785	94,955
1969	2,442	678,787	9,924	1,803,330	12,366	2,482,117	5,809	217,173	796	18,101	86,680
1968	2,489	635,077	9,998	1,464,939	12,487	2,100,016	5,771	164,467	829	16,677	78,515
1967	2,569	631,786	10,128	1,477,860	12,697	2,109,646	6,070	196,231	922	17,306	78,887
1966	2,674	587,695	10,205	1,371,841	12,879	1,959,536	5,401	194,846	1,006	19,098	75,224
1965	2,795	544,537	10,465	1,247,369	13,260	1,791,906	5,147	143,415	1,132	18,389	70,691
1964	2,845	561,848	10,149	1,279,199	12,994	1,841,047	5,667	151,455	1,272	19,887	71,514
1963	2,873	578,853	9,492	1,202,803	12,365	1,781,656	5,211	148,224	1,346	21,147	67,645
1962	2,938	597,453	9,129	1,122,870	12,067	1,720,323	4,981	137,448	1,449	22,379	65,031
1961	2,987	595,021	8,947	1,049,850	11,934	1,644,871	5,331	143,443	1,548	23,714	69,962
1960	2,965	589,756	8,372	961,845	11,337	1,551,601	5,070	127,851	1,607	25,408	67,261
1959	2,955	594,822	8,103	991,241	11,058	1,586,063	6,519	169,661	1,608	26,075	71,611
1958	3,028	554,614	7,962	895,021	10,990	1,449,635	5,931	207,805	1,630	29,226	72,343
1957	3,098	445,326	8,167	719,649	11,265	1,164,975	4,758	154,515	1,628	27,133	71,636
1956	3,160	447,057	7,851	668,119	11,011	1,115,176	4,731	115,064	1,620	25,983	67,535
1955	3,151	460,980	7,452	674,436	10,603	1,135,416	4,800	132,915	1,634	27,726	65,019
1954	3,120	450,340	7,050	615,755	10,170	1,066,095	4,440	159,783	1,636	28,950	69,441
1953	3,084	521,130	6,722	697,576	9,806	1,218,706	3,970	124,425	1,592	31,202	64,918
1952	3,006	633,027	6,147	789,597	9,153	1,422,624	5,428	147,829	1,534	33,920	59,010
1951	2,973	741,356	5,390	852,585	8,363	1,593,941	4,914	185,773	1,461	38,439	64,541
1950	3,119	547,020	5,224	560,498	8,343	1,107,518	4,372	147,507	1,579	27,937	55,779
1949	3,237	502,139	5,404	476,588	8,641	978,727	4,452	152,648	1,773	25,594	63,628
1948	3,357	454,114	5,627	422,716	8,984	876,830	3,946	122,766	2,050	25,954	62,561
1947	3,411	397,021	5,674	351,058	9,085	748,079	4,957	119,636	2,465	27,250	78,143
1946	3,485	382,985	5,689	314,772	9,174	697,757	4,277	95,590	2,792	27,895	73,183
1945	3,631	354,615	6,001	304,898	9,632	659,513	4,964	98,996	3,032	28,711	74,477
1944	3,668	357,805	5,876	287,648	9,544	645,453	6,790	123,706	3,213	32,087	77,229
1943	3,623	368,976	5,499	281,758	9,122	650,734	7,413	121,943	3,107	34,059	68,824
1942	3,614	252,725	5,098	173,793	8,712	426,518	6,808	72,738	2,972	20,621	66,334
1941	3,626	191,128	4,891	138,389	8,517	329,517	6,081	54,912	2,840	17,039	58,994
1940	3,650	184,706	4,730	173,694	8,380	358,400	6,002	70,807	2,887	19,902	57,014
1939	3,681	170,804	4,693	154,961	8,374	325,765	4,364	60,104	2,911	19,458	55,749
1938	3,730	148,772	4,761	126,960	8,491	275,732	3,527	46,569	3,047	17,605	51,665
1937	3,844	152,161	5,071	128,029	8,915	280,190	4,016	49,382	3,071	17,172	52,235
1936	3,805	139,916	5,024	114,126	8,829	254,042	4,136	45,344	3,159	17,064	54,396
1935	3,841	132,994	5,132	110,676	8,973	243,670	3,651	42,843	3,224	16,145	52,538
1934	3,861	110,102	5,209	86,718	9,070	196,820	3,736	36,739	3,291	13,743	55,040
1933	3,690	112,704	5,264	89,841	8,954	202,545	3,854	34,213	3,307	13,221	54,710
1932	3,592	114,600	4,956	85,194	8,548	199,794	4,670	22,067	3,604	11,933	59,700
1931	3,372	160,655	4,601	94,952	7,973	255,607	4,700	33,288	3,627	19,680	61,277
1930	3,233	192,347	4,453	154,302	7,686	346,649	3,735	55,282	3,438	23,352	60,484
1929	3,213	239,553	4,305	200,749	7,518	440,302	4,048	65,867	3,350	33,283	59,778
1928	3,295	237,563	4,163	192,883	7,458	430,446	4,217	62,522	3,128	32,661	54,221
1927	3,366	205,647	4,238	165,593	7,604	371,240	4,302	59,777	2,968	29,177	50,862
1926	3,373	176,937	4,445	139,110	7,818	316,047	4,037	64,969	2,830	28,387	49,741
1925	3,273	166,503	4,703	145,241	7,977	311,744	4,009	63,285	2,628	25,652	48,678
1924	3,195	146,798	4,940	133,944	8,135	280,742	4,594	56,692	2,499	22,572	48,319
1923	3,179	151,028	4,796	124,058	7,975	275,086	3,986	47,227	2,601	20,180	47,092
1922	3,168	152,662	5,099	134,587	8,267	287,249	3,493	51,176	3,045	23,268	45,514
1921	3,087	188,518	5,283	146,567	8,370	335,085	3,324	35,869	3 200	20,675	41,125
1920	2,986	238,497	5,167	247,683	8,154	486,180	3,152	72,430	3,179	32,044	35,575
1919	2,997	278,876	5,488	323,989	8,485	602,865	3,623	91,866	2,949	43,618	37,629
1918	2,901	253,792	5,350	331,111	8,251	584,903	3,677	96,887	2,636	42,140	35,796
1917	2,927	250,236	4,862	282,293	7,790	532,529	3,292	84,330	2,422	36,940	34,936
1916	2,881	200,764	4,618	256,630	7,499	457,394	3,562	61,990	2,334	24,441	34,075
1915	2,834	174,985	4,387	199,089	7,221	374,074	3,464	48,343	2,359	18,910	—
1914	2,786	160,943	4,125	177,804	6,911	338,747	3,640	45,065	2,310	16,426	—
1913	2,766	—	4,089	—	6,855	—	3,683	—	2,333	—	—
1912	2,692	—	3,994	—	6,686	—	3,684	—	2,172	—	—
1911	2,645	111,833	3,881	84,021	6,526	195,854	3,635	26,987	2,174	10,702	29,773
1910	2,592	110,454	3,923	121,215	6,515	231,669	3,304	37,335	2,246	13,474	—
1909	2,593	94,212	4,058	116,905	6,651	211,117	3,287	38,782	2,327	13,460	—
1908	2,659	90,142	4,338	114,319	6,997	204,461	3,546	32,906	2,380	12,153	—
1907	2,686	—	4,467	—	7,153	—	3,701	—	2,350	—	—
1906	2,703	—	4,499	—	7,202	—	3,379	—	2,543	—	—

[1] Change in survey date to 1 July.

[2] Hens and chickens discontinued after 1972.

Series M321-330. Estimated number of livestock slaughtered and weight of meat produced, Canada, 1871, 1881, 1891 and 1920 to 1975

(animals slaughtered in thousands of head; meat produced in thousand of pounds)

Year	Number of cattle	Beef, cold dressed weight	Number of calves	Veal, cold dressed weight	Number of hogs	Pork, cold trimmed weight	Number of sheep and lambs	Mutton and lamb, cold dressed weight	Number of chickens	Fowl and chicken meat, eviscerated weight
	321	322	323	324	325	326	327	328	329	330
1975	4,070	2,190,873	1,009	122,273	8,803	1,148,497	424	18,090	231,665	707,363
1974	3,629	1,999,106	616	77,415	10,289	1,347,230	424	18,167	247,576	781,377
1973	3,412	1,910,575	482	65,857	10,399	1,360,418	501	21,893	256,201	801,170
1972	3,393	1,898,328	645	80,525	10,655	1,392,607	446	19,850	240,517	756,816
1971	3,373	1,877,575	838	98,516	11,904	1,557,254	423	18,189	229,265	720,761
1970	3,165	1,774,312	857	100,985	10,600	1,362,007	379	16,532	238,995	750,637
1969	3,177	1,758,340	894	107,619	8,636	1,122,150	391	17,133	215,686	686,786
1968	3,334	1,824,148	1,056	142,249	9,190	1,176,442	437	18,909	188,578	599,378
1967	3,195	1,719,352	1,152	145,618	9,268	1,195,012	494	21,452	187,079	598,752
1966	3,285	1,753,021	1,120	139,711	7,897	1,015,329	480	21,189	179,538	568,541
1965	3,368	1,749,949	1,302	162,505	7,932	1,006,533	578	25,091	162,538	515,129
1964	2,966	1,573,489	1,154	141,042	8,296	1,060,059	680	29,816	155,267	494,964
1963	2,679	1,423,049	1,049	126,761	7,622	980,998	722	31,548	144,128	462,737
1962	2,572	1,333,068	1,091	133,491	7,698	984,638	744	31,801	130,014	411,513
1961	2,554	1,320,307	1,058	124,441	7,589	975,366	803	34,552	131,992	416,387
1960	2,471	1,266,280	1,082	125,155	7,804	988,035	737	31,561	114,922	357,939
1959	2,261	1,153,037	1,094	120,505	9,662	1,237,682	726	31,784	116,948	365,198
1958	2,438	1,220,239	1,191	125,544	7,466	973,599	716	31,297	113,516	356,012
1957	2,514	1,244,584	1,358	148,058	6,295	818,403	763	33,180	96,763	315,336
1956	2,421	1,172,603	1,333	139,805	6,858	881,964	771	32,688	89,064	308,912
1955	2,271	1,102,619	1,295	134,551	6,932	887,708	755	32,385	80,362	225,093
1954	2,222	1,078,927	1,254	131,723	6,144	795,609	721	30,702	67,730	246,676
1953	2,005	994,081	1,165	123,765	6,198	796,482	693	29,708	66,831	238,232
1952	1,719	864,000	969	100,638	8,057	1,039,405	674	29,743	66,075	251,032
1951	1,592	785,553	1,040	108,004	6,753	876,513	584	26,581	60,914	218,863
1950	1,674	787,741	1,282	127,577	6,793	875,455	742	32,130	48,420	178,474
1949	1,843	863,364	1,285	133,729	6,466	845,268	877	38,828	51,865	189,034
1948	1,939	910,363	1,362	137,565	6,694	863,288	1,031	44,131	43,946	166,255
1947	1,944	926,321	1,287	129,626	7,394	976,728	1,326	59,653	52,563	196,974
1946	2,216	1,059,644	1,334	136,287	6,856	890,798	1,413	63,456	50,219	182,963
1945	2,401	1,142,540	1,419	146,992	8,709	1,130,388	1,477	64,228	50,175	192,073
1944	1,872	920,371	1,250	127,062	11,512	1,515,361	1,266	53,674	51,905	199,834
1943	1,586	789,605	1,199	128,400	10,426	1,407,557	1,226	52,550	46,375	178,544
1942	1,526	751,434	1,328	130,671	9,695	1,250,889	1,186	50,977	44,607	171,737
1941	1,516	723,739	1,308	123,985	9,116	1,114,758	1,170	50,850	39,766	151,897
1940	1,402	643,459	1,419	122,734	7,237	864,535	1,280	52,461	–	–
1939	1,337	615,620	1,348	116,775	5,122	624,965	1,477	60,304	–	–
1938	1,389	639,170	1,389	115,896	4,853	587,249	1,519	60,671	–	–
1937	1,398	623,122	1,478	129,639	5,745	678,686	1,534	60,289	–	–
1936	1,336	619,472	1,248	113,467	5,405	647,968	1,576	62,733	–	–
1935	1,275	595,395	1,206	106,083	4,700	563,745	1,610	63,087	–	–
1934	1,136	561,135	995	113,396	4,625	635,530	1,536	66,044	–	–
1933	997	498,300	910	97,370	4,694	626,649	1,547	63,431	–	–
1932	936	476,679	817	89,075	4,699	624,080	1,459	59,835	–	–
1931	970	497,661	799	87,080	4,181	561,522	1,511	61,951	–	–
1930	943	484,805	809	96,295	3,974	530,860	1,438	60,409	–	–
1929	1,065	534,429	774	82,829	4,376	595,587	1,387	56,871	–	–
1928	1,082	533,180	784	80,731	4,572	609,488	1,290	52,906	–	–
1927	1,124	573,342	776	73,797	4,471	601,336	1,260	54,171	–	–
1926	1,075	552,396	709	75,196	4,449	607,733	1,145	46,937	–	–
1925	1,051	542,264	705	76,162	4,611	608,612	1,139	48,977	–	–
1924	977	513,135	670	68,299	4,712	617,246	1,151	49,476	–	–
1923	979	529,855	609	62,098	3,973	518,529	1,217	65,707	–	–
1922	991	543,949	634	65,957	3,618	485,495	1,183	55,601	–	–
1921	933	476,814	511	56,243	3,157	420,801	1,293	55,612	–	–
1920	1,091	530,420	554	57,052	3,301	437,079	1,171	50,336	–	–
1891[1]	958	–	–	–	1,791	–	1,464	–	–	–
1881[1]	658	–	–	–	1,303	–	1,496	–	–	–
1871[1]	508	–	–	–	1,216	–	1,557	–	–	–

[1] Decennial census data: animals killed or sold.

Series M331-342. Utilization of total milk production, Canada,[1] 1920 to 1975
(thousands of pounds)

Year	Farm butter	Farm cheese	Creamery butter	Cheddar cheese	Cottage cheese	Other whole milk and cream cheese	Concentrated whole milk products	Ice cream mix[2]	Fluid sales[3]	Farm home consumed	Fed on farms	Total milk production
	331	332	333	334	335	336	337	338	339	340	341	342
1975	–	–	6,637,270	1,934,691	48,425	987,144	541,065	937,474	5,513,226	327,086	774,787	17,073,450
1974	–	–	5,431,421	2,138,015	48,580	1,009,903	590,861	902,147	5,611,587	374,760	704,313	16,811,587
1973	39,429	–	5,902,205	2,078,021	52,108	655,222	628,237	903,352	5,510,056	413,771	702,578	16,884,979
1972	52,814	–	6,799,993	2,113,166	48,034	626,915	640,915	889,173	5,394,419	448,121	662,653	17,676,203
1971	58,102	–	6,707,142	2,098,437	46,798	626,167	685,237	848,993	5,274,644	449,012	674,661	17,469,193
1970	65,052	–	7,670,356	1,822,799	41,734	541,644	660,573	834,879	5,200,302	504,449	682,970	18,024,758
1969	67,135	–	8,193,042	1,844,546	37,474	430,612	746,426	796,518	5,087,831	578,533	689,438	18,471,555
1968	71,159	–	7,859,966	1,830,433	33,684	360,565	802,077	742,864	5,129,388	633,044	689,356	18,152,536
1967	74,038	–	7,719,637	1,771,568	32,078	306,904	818,211	736,400	5,201,474	678,578	700,202	18,039,402
1966	77,477	–	7,813,400	1,849,606	31,000	288,507	869,605	636,504	5,247,898	742,211	709,287	18,265,495
1965	87,539	–	7,894,715	1,738,968	30,160	227,409	984,371	537,192	5,202,305	879,300	774,749	18,356,708
1964	114,847	–	8,230,763	1,591,084	28,544	186,849	999,821	489,917	5,114,869	925,240	823,437	18,505,371
1963	142,787	–	8,234,905	1,533,037	26,781	168,297	993,896	499,296	5,021,875	943,620	867,488	18,431,982
1962	173,628	–	8,464,248	1,290,080	24,994	144,952	953,093	536,047	4,972,281	936,060	883,777	18,382,160
1961	204,118	–	8,239,912	1,308,032	22,648	134,628	1,033,433	650,017	4,952,354	956,725	837,333	18,339,200
1960	233,906	–	7,497,430	1,214,092	15,008	133,232	1,169,725	696,320	5,018,391	1,007,134	761,237	17,746,475
1959	256,441	–	7,618,525	1,184,216	14,315	123,501	931,163	680,289	5,050,808	1,016,226	739,222	17,614,706
1958	282,649	–	7,862,166	1,004,531	14,091	111,792	924,432	621,622	5,111,397	1,055,025	685,277	17,672,982
1957	296,338	–	7,098,881	1,089,396	13,988	108,474	989,288	596,989	5,116,669	1,065,371	659,810	17,035,204
1956	326,218	–	7,097,548	932,217	13,207	96,663	944,618	564,961	5,175,222	1,112,333	644,478	16,907,465
1955	348,158	–	7,454,701	879,780	10,034	75,754	913,997	550,970	4,916,983	1,098,716	652,563	16,901,656
1954	388,020	–	7,329,582	938,828	9,213	74,645	863,710	486,965	4,680,887	1,068,449	654,790	16,495,089
1953	445,369	–	7,085,122	844,184	7,788	65,812	848,543	489,753	4,527,715	1,048,818	652,429	16,015,533
1952	528,409	–	6,569,456	745,998	6,471	65,793	897,123	477,085	4,316,793	1,051,372	640,558	15,299,058
1951	628,626	–	6,025,376	989,054	6,412	63,098	857,180	456,588	4,186,812	1,055,990	609,137	14,878,273
1950	640,839	–	6,126,102	1,087,866	4,892	54,905	741,771	428,796	4,130,743	1,090,114	601,575	14,907,603
1949	740,024	–	6,555,831	1,302,433	4,970	45,361	678,365	433,369	4,070,872	1,069,676	619,350	15,520,251
1948	816,801	–	6,692,287	991,738	4,050	53,097	781,446	360,194	4,022,558	1,032,552	642,400	15,397,123
1947	780,601	–	6,817,005	1,358,545	703	32,639	666,954	334,972	4,187,919	1,119,818	653,520	15,952,676
1946	775,101	–	6,361,034	1,627,543	726	31,740	624,546	226,196	4,293,329	1,132,062	669,140	15,741,417
1945	748,239	–	6,883,992	2,080,473	529	22,515	630,445	233,670	4,060,358	1,117,851	702,850	16,480,922
1944	814,882	–	7,000,345	2,006,102	649	20,283	607,802	252,461	3,975,167	1,117,452	706,430	16,501,573
1943	840,153	–	7,303,342	1,833,120	421	19,169	578,110	246,402	3,773,218	1,114,822	703,080	16,411,837
1942	1,459,762	–	6,667,967	2,297,235	318	13,533	554,210	217,580	3,441,665	1,085,736	705,220	16,443,226
1941	1,766,302	–	6,697,419	1,684,502	194	17,580	491,335	202,504	3,169,295	1,064,230	709,770	15,803,131
1940	1,853,303	–	6,202,483	1,611,791	191	13,056	388,900	157,747	3,077,876	1,185,829	711,940	15,203,116
1939	2,047,416	9,591	6,264,810	1,405,324	–	–	334,749	142,225	3,011,515	1,790,754	774,720	15,781,104
1938	2,130,545	10,455	6,258,600	1,388,479	–	–	311,598	140,529	3,013,270	1,789,911	776,320	15,819,707
1937	2,194,079	11,219	5,783,598	1,463,009	–	–	275,010	146,027	2,774,427	1,676,374	801,480	15,125,223
1936	2,233,432	11,885	5,874,313	1,334,183	–	–	200,254	129,642	2,828,751	1,697,646	812,320	15,122,426
1935	2,281,233	12,264	5,639,909	1,124,787	–	–	186,705	103,492	2,773,175	1,655,861	794,600	14,572,026
1934	2,315,837	11,606	5,497,908	1,112,682	–	–	165,822	94,067	2,786,248	1,646,452	821,640	14,452,262
1933	2,321,032	10,975	5,132,234	1,244,841	–	–	152,786	89,916	2,688,035	1,594,318	849,840	14,083,977
1932	2,313,495	10,276	5,009,790	1,349,872	–	–	146,864	97,008	2,699,411	1,569,252	801,360	13,997,328
1931	2,307,993	9,592	5,289,612	1,276,315	–	–	157,948	129,360	2,759,321	1,593,545	816,000	14,339,686
1930	2,283,157	9,106	4,348,432	1,333,978	–	–	201,406	152,516	2,524,288	1,444,538	774,000	13,071,421
1929	2,272,128	8,683	3,998,668	1,329,958	–	–	195,949	153,918	1,760,806	1,894,330	796,003	12,410,443
1928	2,326,954	8,213	3,933,513	1,619,348	–	–	197,003	133,922	1,814,454	1,910,517	764,234	12,708,158
1927	2,384,215	7,822	4,143,077	1,546,238	–	–	204,694	117,296	1,839,013	1,945,823	726,408	12,914,586
1926	2,430,379	7,521	4,148,469	1,923,394	–	–	180,703	108,365	1,896,115	2,044,898	735,770	13,475,614
1925	2,485,378	7,304	3,967,877	1,983,958	–	–	187,791	92,622	1,889,198	2,033,754	773,102	13,420,984
1924	2,540,804	7,164	4,187,907	1,676,724	–	–	176,895	86,324	1,860,444	1,855,362	792,090	13,183,714
1923	2,589,380	6,907	3,811,958	1,698,193	–	–	173,234	88,182	1,825,885	1,796,988	816,891	12,807,618
1922	2,510,067	6,673	3,570,070	1,521,196	–	–	130,968	75,273	1,728,274	1,697,101	868,061	12,107,683
1921	2,513,742	6,349	3,013,911	1,815,716	–	–	170,920	85,638	1,700,257	1,662,319	928,693	11,897,545
1920	2,422,643	5,976	2,614,703	1,671,061	–	–	203,412	90,739	1,565,035	1,539,213	863,454	10,976,236

[1] Excludes Newfoundland.
[2] Beginning in 1961, data are adjusted to exclude the milk equivalent of creamery butter used in the manufacture of ice cream mix.

[3] Represents milk and cream, in milk equivalent, sold off farms for fluid purposes.

Series M343-356. Dairy products and margarine, total domestic disappearance, Canada, 1920 to 1975
(thousands of pounds)

Year	Fluid products[1]	Creamery butter	Cheddar cheese	Process cheese	Other cheese	Cottage cheese	Skim milk cheese	Whey cheese	Evaporated whole milk	Condensed whole milk	Whole milk powder	Skim milk powder	Margarine	Ice cream
	343	344	345	346	347	348	349	350	351	352	353	354	355	356
1975	5,840,312	264,146	101,418	128,055	127,894	51,073	2,587	1,928	200,991	16,694	1,845	138,094	264,358	63,182
1974	5,986,347	290,647	101,736	128,055	127,375	51,081	3,179	1,780	217,364	18,923	1,461	127,474	240,945	61,095
1973	5,923,827	293,277	108,935	121,886	88,393	53,530	1,963	946	231,768	20,186	2,854	114,584	217,474	60,530
1972	5,842,540	316,759	91,836	113,798	82,378	49,332	2,063	1,182	244,546	17,093	1,720	103,373	211,678	60,913
1971	5,723,656	328,623	88,814	102,230	81,029	47,185	1,209	1,241	255,339	16,046	1,718	108,920	199,491	59,928
1970	5,704,751	327,873	88,280	95,707	69,730	43,419	729	980	258,547	16,653	1,016	133,002	198,672	59,996
1969	5,666,364	322,607	75,722	96,727	64,280	38,666	149	730	267,831	21,189	2,892	212,182	203,461	58,220
1968	5,762,432	333,110	69,192	90,164	55,402	34,218	384	764	285,649	25,619	3,108	161,806	195,696	55,851
1967	5,880,052	336,982	68,309	84,728	47,428	32,810	415	620	289,825	24,325	4,684	139,571	186,047	56,031
1966	5,990,109	347,819	58,785	84,450	40,909	31,967	448	574	299,970	22,352	1,298	163,640	178,511	53,561
1965	6,081,605	356,201	67,169	75,238	36,604	30,639	1,022	577	299,633	19,138	3,840	138,892	170,526	51,623
1964	6,040,109	357,323	65,625	68,824	32,117	29,517	1,004	567	302,546	17,587	2,976	153,406	171,458	49,489
1963	5,965,495	351,342	61,578	64,638	30,933	27,482	723	641	306,472	17,935	5,167	153,049	174,906	46,819
1962	5,908,341	320,752	61,003	61,109	27,358	25,567	1,102	562	307,542	16,082	2,820	132,977	183,535	44,133
1961	5,909,079	288,309	52,624	57,467	26,032	24,009	587	442	302,685	14,735	3,278	153,277	183,318	43,171
1960	6,025,525	289,889	50,597	55,176	22,750	22,331	286	503	312,831	14,253	4,899	122,749	167,058	41,228
1959	6,067,034	303,359	47,395	52,016	22,589	21,511	493	746	300,851	14,437	3,879	121,302	152,275	40,017
1958	6,166,422	312,255	47,162	50,214	19,615	19,145	850	232	302,212	14,562	3,320	109,673	144,928	36,566
1957	6,182,040	321,554	47,452	46,537	18,292	18,968	796	210	302,342	13,952	4,577	90,064	130,072	35,117
1956	6,287,555	313,606	41,318	45,506	16,577	17,841	1,033	—	299,715	14,982	5,024	81,736	124,304	33,181
1955	6,015,699	301,645	45,334	46,151	13,028	13,824	855	—	288,382	11,926	2,970	80,474	125,708	32,349
1954	5,749,336	293,292	39,943	46,184	11,601	12,420	786	—	275,955	12,348	5,211	71,768	115,591	28,571
1953	5,576,533	285,723	35,638	44,747	11,433	11,030	692	—	274,919	12,835	5,138	65,472	110,183	28,687
1952	5,368,165	274,911	31,778	41,024	11,327	9,459	1,954	—	265,079	11,017	5,041	50,727	111,328	27,219
1951	5,242,802	268,542	30,204	39,060	10,632	9,507	1,451	—	250,169	10,712	4,994	52,052	107,032	25,347
1950	5,220,857	276,671	31,697	36,178	8,648	8,051	185	—	239,408	10,976	6,038	46,817	93,602	23,620
1949	5,140,548	261,186	29,840	34,162	6,427	6,367	49	—	197,777	9,412	8,499	37,308	73,017	24,790
1948	5,055,110	305,553	22,288	33,913	5,907	5,414	—	7	198,431	13,309	8,983	31,898	—	25,206
1947	5,307,737	293,224	34,662	39,005	4,010	5,002	—	—	181,911	12,440	10,567	37,195	—	23,441
1946	5,425,391	259,150	24,232	33,611	4,224	5,572	12	4	145,706	12,208	9,948	35,658	—	15,829
1945	5,178,209	292,970	34,049	32,408	2,684	4,243	—	—	147,020	11,313	10,505	31,915	—	16,352
1944	5,092,619	299,404	27,683	33,062	2,355	3,837	—	—	130,950	10,251	13,394	27,538	—	17,667
1943	4,888,040	279,050	26,761	34,907	2,272	3,575	—	—	154,648	9,453	14,094	22,772	—	17,243
1942	4,527,401	304,721	24,134	25,429	2,036	3,297	—	—	142,659	8,978	7,954	25,620	—	15,226
1941	4,233,525	274,428	33,645	20,678	2,418	2,183	—	—	112,144	5,857	3,883	27,525	—	14,171
1940	4,263,705	271,227	26,865	16,553	2,201	1,857	—	—	102,017	7,049	1,774	25,769	—	11,039
1939	4,802,269	258,231	27,857	15,170	2,090	1,652	—	—	94,301	7,070	1,619	25,984	—	9,053
1938	4,803,181	252,427	29,718	13,708	1,387	2,149	—	—	74,152	5,860	2,325	19,092	—	8,945
1937	4,450,801	251,048	27,676	12,232	1,410	1,847	—	—	66,411	7,287	3,231	17,548	—	9,295
1936	4,526,397	241,931	28,482	12,024	1,240	1,362	—	—	56,108	6,604	3,082	13,789	—	8,252
1935	4,429,036	233,269	29,220	10,522	1,274	—	—	—	46,928	7,027	2,290	13,894	—	6,588
1934	4,432,700	227,096	28,700	11,256	946	—	—	—	38,715	6,798	2,010	11,643	—	5,988
1933	4,282,353	216,016	27,247	9,695	968	—	—	—	35,121	5,819	1,510	9,684	—	5,723
1932	4,268,663	213,274	24,930	9,734	1,167	—	—	—	33,111	7,791	1,740	8,457	—	6,175
1931	4,352,866	215,601	26,130	10,900	1,446	—	—	—	41,201	9,220	1,943	6,605	—	8,234
1930	3,968,826	214,933	25,140	13,006	1,788	—	—	—	45,681	10,282	2,060	8,317	—	9,708
1929	3,655,136	205,403	22,707	13,908	2,104	—	—	—	45,163	8,904	1,916	7,344	—	9,797
1928	3,724,971	190,537	24,697	13,062	1,779	—	—	—	42,423	6,924	2,196	7,782	—	8,525
1927	3,784,836	178,420	22,166	11,662	1,721	—	—	—	39,247	9,472	2,175	6,103	—	7,466
1926	3,941,013	172,305	31,834	9,425	1,219	—	—	—	36,518	2,940	2,520	3,323	—	6,898
1925	3,922,952	155,949	15,447	11,271	10,274	—	—	—	26,713	6,785	2,845	3,500	—	5,896
1924	3,715,806	151,159	15,359	16,894	909	—	—	—	27,268	6,674	1,659	3,834	—	5,495
1923	3,622,873	150,604	26,245	—	1,900	—	—	—	23,141	6,577	1,299	4,538	—	5,613
1922	3,425,375	134,127	26,005	—	687	—	—	—	25,411	6,511	1,476	3,633	—	4,791
1921	3,362,576	126,183	20,626	—	908	—	—	—	28,532	6,415	1,703	4,964	—	5,451
1920	3,104,248	100,293	22,409	—	480	—	—	—	25,934	6,246	1,732	5,843	—	5,776

[1] Includes fluid sales, plus milk and cream consumed in farm homes.

Series M357-362. Dairy products, domestic disappearance in terms of milk, Canada, 1920 to 1975

(thousands of pounds)

Year	Fluid products[1]	Butter	Cheese	Concentrated whole milk products	Ice Cream	Total
	357	358	359	360	361	362
1975	5,840,312	6,181,016	3,550,111	539,949	937,474	17,048,862
1974	5,986,347	6,801,140	3,548,135	577,959	902,147	17,815,728
1973	5,923,827	6,902,111	3,154,575	625,536	903,352	17,509,401
1972	5,842,540	7,464,975	2,834,422	639,145	889,173	17,670,255
1971	5,723,656	7,747,880	2,696,213	662,949	848,993	17,679,691
1970	5,704,751	7,737,280	2,511,600	665,539	834,879	17,454,049
1969	5,666,364	7,616,139	2,316,801	713,418	796,518	17,109,240
1968	5,762,432	7,865,933	2,092,573	769,454	742,864	17,233,256
1967	5,880,052	7,959,417	1,952,102	794,539	736,400	17,322,510
1966	5,990,109	8,216,442	1,771,033	795,876	636,504	17,409,964
1965	6,081,605	8,422,642	1,743,551	817,602	537,192	17,602,592
1964	6,040,109	8,476,205	1,626,761	819,240	489,917	17,452,232
1963	5,965,495	8,364,190	1,534,818	848,138	499,296	17,211,937
1962	5,908,341	7,679,225	1,461,542	823,770	536,047	16,408,925
1961	5,909,079	6,950,549	1,324,051	805,208	650,017	15,638,904
1960	6,025,505	7,017,309	1,241,093	832,927	696,320	15,813,174
1959	6,067,034	7,348,022	1,179,165	790,328	680,289	16,064,838
1958	6,166,422	7,589,416	1,129,882	787,745	621,622	16,295,087
1957	6,182,040	7,820,702	1,090,886	805,409	596,989	16,496,026
1956	6,287,555	7,664,553	996,626	803,706	564,077	16,316,517
1955	6,015,699	7,406,638	993,302	752,004	549,933	15,717,576
1954	5,749,336	7,251,052	922,908	741,831	485,707	15,150,834
1953	5,576,533	7,131,290	860,156	733,424	487,679	14,789,082
1952	5,368,165	6,961,383	823,957	702,987	476,332	14,332,824
1951	5,242,802	6,920,566	776,676	649,125	456,246	14,045,415
1950	5,220,857	7,123,259	759,427	619,011	425,160	14,147,714
1949	5,140,548	6,860,609	687,442	535,052	433,369	13,657,020
1948	5,055,110	7,977,119	573,046	548,088	360,194	14,513,557
1947	5,307,737	7,651,910	727,867	520,604	334,972	14,543,090
1946	5,425,391	6,849,175	579,680	436,439	226,196	13,516,881
1945	5,178,209	7,615,008	678,587	438,647	233,670	14,144,121
1944	5,092,619	7,830,822	606,357	421,913	252,461	14,204,172
1943	4,888,040	7,379,701	610,063	478,504	246,402	13,602,710
1942	4,527,401	8,601,668	505,436	401,801	217,580	14,253,886
1941	4,233,525	8,201,273	571,496	294,717	202,504	13,503,515
1940	4,263,705	8,207,272	461,376	260,174	157,747	13,350,274
1939	4,802,269	8,100,563	480,006	244,317	142,223	13,769,378
1938	4,803,181	8,031,901	475,344	200,305	140,526	13,651,257
1937	4,450,801	8,074,718	443,403	193,081	146,024	13,308,027
1936	4,526,397	7,895,374	449,378	166,942	129,639	13,167,730
1935	4,429,036	7,747,258	445,338	140,009	103,497	12,865,138
1934	4,432,700	7,627,633	438,188	121,402	94,071	12,713,994
1933	4,282,353	7,373,729	408,422	105,656	89,908	12,260,068
1932	4,268,663	7,309,889	384,322	105,749	97,009	12,165,632
1931	4,352,866	7,361,789	409,998	129,725	129,356	12,383,734
1930	3,968,826	7,309,188	419,950	143,111	152,513	11,993,588
1929	3,655,136	7,082,789	403,390	136,863	153,911	11,432,089
1928	3,724,971	6,788,783	414,462	128,383	133,928	11,190,527
1927	3,784,836	6,561,284	373,313	127,781	117,291	10,964,505
1926	3,941,013	6,457,250	456,879	106,360	108,368	11,069,870
1925	3,922,952	6,143,135	390,053	96,008	92,626	10,644,774
1924	3,715,806	6,076,557	331,280	88,235	86,326	10,298,204
1923	3,622,873	6,110,619	322,134	76,302	88,180	10,220,108
1922	3,425,375	5,655,856	305,625	82,361	75,267	9,544,484
1921	3,362,576	5,478,408	247,531	90,751	85,635	9,264,901
1920	3,104,248	4,769,764	262,338	85,327	90,741	8,312,418

[1] Includes fluid sales, plus milk and cream consumed in farm homes.

Series M363-368. Dairy products, domestic disappearance in terms of milk, Canada, 1920 to 1975
(pounds per capita)

Year	Fluid products[1]	Butter	Cheese	Concentrated whole milk products	Ice Cream	Total
	363	364	365	366	367	368
1975	255.81	270.73	155.49	23.65	41.28	746.96
1974	272.90	302.56	157.84	25.71	40.13	799.14
1973	274.45	311.96	142.58	28.27	40.83	798.09
1972	274.10	341.68	129.73	29.25	40.70	815.46
1971	271.62	358.78	124.85	30.70	39.31	825.26
1970	274.19	361.45	117.33	31.09	39.00	823.06
1969	276.23	361.14	109.86	33.83	37.77	818.83
1968	284.96	378.68	100.74	37.04	35.76	837.18
1967	295.30	389.38	95.50	38.87	36.03	855.08
1966	306.33	409.80	88.33	39.69	31.75	875.90
1965	316.92	428.02	88.60	41.55	27.30	902.39
1964	320.58	438.61	84.18	42.39	25.35	911.11
1963	322.69	441.06	80.93	44.72	26.33	915.73
1962	326.16	413.24	78.65	44.33	28.85	891.23
1961	332.34	381.10	72.60	44.15	35.64	865.83
1960	345.86	392.69	69.45	46.61	38.97	893.58
1959	356.00	420.30	67.45	45.21	38.91	927.87
1958	370.40	444.35	66.15	46.12	36.39	963.41
1957	381.94	470.84	65.68	48.49	35.94	1,002.89
1956	401.35	476.62	61.97	49.98	35.08	1,025.00
1955	393.39	471.82	63.28	47.90	35.03	1,011.42
1954	386.07	474.33	60.37	48.53	31.77	1,001.07
1953	385.60	480.38	57.94	49.41	32.85	1,006.18
1952	381.13	481.46	56.99	48.62	32.94	1,001.14
1951	384.14	494.01	55.44	46.34	32.57	1,012.50
1950	390.75	519.49	55.38	45.14	31.01	1,041.77
1949	392.35	513.48	51.45	40.06	32.44	1,029.78
1948	394.22	622.09	44.69	42.74	28.09	1,131.83
1947	422.89	609.67	58.00	41.49	26.69	1,158.74
1946	442.82	559.02	47.31	35.62	18.46	1,103.23
1945	444.48	653.65	58.25	37.64	20.06	1,214.08
1944	441.00	678.11	52.51	36.54	21.86	1,230.02
1943	425.31	642.10	53.08	41.63	21.44	1,183.56
1942	395.20	750.84	44.12	35.07	18.99	1,244.22
1941	370.87	718.46	50.07	25.82	17.74	1,182.96
1940	374.63	721.13	40.54	22.87	13.86	1,173.03
1939	426.22	718.96	42.60	21.68	12.62	1,222.08
1038	430.70	720.22	42.63	17.97	12.60	1,224.12
1937	402.97	731.08	40.15	17.48	13.22	1,204.90
1936	413.37	721.03	41.04	15.25	11.84	1,202.53
1935	408.39	714.36	41.06	12.92	9.54	1,186.27
1934	412.69	710.15	40.80	11.30	8.76	1,183.70
1933	402.74	693.48	38.41	9.95	8.46	1,153.04
1932	406.15	695.52	36.57	10.05	9.23	1,157.52
1931	419.51	709.50	39.51	12.51	12.47	1,193.50
1930	388.80	716.03	41.14	14.03	14.94	1,174.94
1929	364.46	706.23	40.23	13.64	15.35	1,139.91
1928	378.75	690.26	42.14	13.07	13.62	1,137.84
1927	392.74	680.84	38.74	13.25	12.17	1,137.74
1926	416.99	683.24	48.35	11.26	11.47	1,171.31
1925	422.10	660.97	41.97	10.32	9.97	1,145.33
1924	406.41	664.61	36.23	9.65	9.44	1,126.34
1923	402.09	678.20	35.76	8.46	9.79	1,134.30
1922	384.05	634.14	34.27	9.23	8.44	1,070.13
1921	382.63	623.39	28.16	10.32	9.74	1,054.24
1920	362.82	557.47	30.66	9.97	10.61	971.53

[1] Includes fluid sales, plus milk and cream consumed in farm homes.

Series M369-376. Number of poultry on farms, by class, Canada, 1916 to 1972
(in thousands)

Year	Hens and chickens	Turkeys	Geese	Ducks	Hens and chickens	Turkeys	Geese	Ducks
	369	370	371	372	373	374	375	376
	June				December[1]			
1972[2]	91,296.0	9,062.8	409.1	580.6	78.594.0	4,968.2	210.0	375.6
1971	90,239.5	9,540.8	415.5	553.9	75,298.0	4,481.0	214.7	376.7
1970	94,955.0	10,203.0	386.2	452.9	78,697.0	4,631.5	194.5	297.9
1969	86,680.0	9,098.0	377.0	439.9	74,212.0	3,887.0	164.5	263.7
1968	78,515.0	8,369.6	363.8	422.8	68.140.0	4,402.0	185.7	258.1
1967	78,887.0	8,757.5	347.6	407.7	62,400.0	3,907.0	183.1	237.1
1966	75,223.6	8,967.8	338.7	409.9	62,892.0	4,199.0	186.0	236.9
1965	70,691.0	7,942.0	330.7	403.0	57,120.0	4,134.0	203.0	259.5
1964	71,514.0	6,799.0	330.5	397.5	53,385.0	3,671.0	199.0	257.0
1963	67,645.0	6,653.0	331.8	391.3	51,840.0	3,354.0	224.0	263.0
1962	65,031.0	6,744.0	311.1	403.7	47,480.0	4,245.0	232.0	293.6
1961	69,962.0	7,668.5	314.2	397.5	48,273.0	3,722.0	247.3	321.0
1960	67,261.0	6,156.0	321.0	395.0	46,131.0	3,081.0	268.0	345.0
1959	71,611.0	7,542.0	329.0	413.0	46,454.0	3,384.0	279.0	343.0
1958	72,343.0	6,134.0	339.0	435.0	51,264.0	3,603.0	296.0	356.0
1957	71,636.0	5,232.0	322.0	401.0	45,609.0	3,396.0	295.0	344.0
1956	67,535.0	4,770.0	326.0	420.0	42,940.0	3,105.0	283.0	331.0
1955	65,019.0	3,793.0	368.0	522.0	41,230.0	2,458.0	316.0	366.0
1954	69,441.0	3,689.0	342.0	451.0	41,865.0	2,646.0	313.0	410.0
1953	64,918.0	2,885.0	374.0	474.0	40,625.0	2,446.0	338.0	407.0
1952	59,010.0	3,409.0	378.0	478.0	37,815.0	2,758.0	362.0	474.0
1951	64,541.0	2,527.0	353.0	437.0	39,110.0	2,048.0	335.0	425.0
1950	55,779.0	2,500.0	352.0	465.0	31,724.0	2,256.0	329.0	359.0
1949	63,628.0	2,620.0	417.0	479.0	36,938.0	2,294.0	348.0	378.0
1948	62,561.0	2,040.0	397.0	445.0	35,154.0	1,785.0	371.0	336.0
1947	78,143.0	3,063.0	515.0	603.0	45,734.0	2,298.0	434.0	411.0
1946	73,183.0	2,591.0	570.0	663.0	48,860.0	2,338.0	493.0	525.0
1945	74,477.0	3,205.0	615.0	742.0	47,361.0	2,392.0	506.0	548.0
1944	77,229.0	3,299.0	636.0	751.0	54,730.0	2,900.0	563.0	684.0
1943	68,824.0	2,937.0	585.0	658.0	52,191.0	2,765.0	546.0	638.0
1942	66,334.0	4,089.0	662.0	758.0	46,059.0	2,994.0	551.0	567.0
1941	58,994.0	3,135.0	650.0	621.0	44,194.0	2,768.0	575.0	551.0
1940	57,014.0	3,053.6	670.9	615.3	—	—	—	—
1939	55,749.0	2,935.7	679.9	612.8	—	—	—	—
1938	51,665.0	2,356.5	707.1	600.6	—	—	—	—
1937	52,235.0	2,223.4	791.6	639.6	—	—	—	—
1936	54,396.0	2,180.2	788.4	653.0	—	—	—	—
1935	52.538.0	1,965.0	805.2	647.1	—	—	—	—
1934	55,040.0	2,504.7	856.2	717.9	—	—	—	—
1933	54,710.0	2,488.3	904.0	791.8	—	—	—	—
1932	59,700.0	2,436.6	919.2	788.7	—	—	—	—
1931	61,277.0	2,223.2	902.3	749.9	—	—	—	—
1930	60,484.0	2,112.8	844.9	692.5	—	—	—	—
1929	59,778.0	2,164.0	836.8	793.3	—	—	—	—
1928	54,221.0	1,871.6	813.2	725.5	—	—	—	—
1927	50,862.0	1,713.7	808.1	703.0	—	—	—	—
1926	49,741.0	1,966.8	812.8	716.6	—	—	—	—
1925	48,678.0	1,969.7	825.7	750.2	—	—	—	—
1924	48,319.0	2,149.1	758.9	852.0	—	—	—	—
1923	47,092.0	1,926.0	670.6	718.8	—	—	—	—
1922	45,514.0	1,439.3	648.9	678.3	—	—	—	—
1921	41,125.0	1,084.8	588.5	548.9	—	—	—	—
1920	35,575.0	879.3	555.2	463.1	—	—	—	—
1919	37,628.8	906.1	619.0	595.7	—	—	—	—
1918	35,795.0	876.7	603.2	597.7	—	—	—	—
1917	34,935.6	874.8	607.0	587.6	—	—	—	—
1916	34,075.2	872.8	610.7	577.5	—	—	—	—

[1] Figures not available prior to 1941.   [2] No figures available after 1972.

Series M377-384. Total poultry meat, supply and disposition, Canada, 1926 to 1975
(eviscerated weight, series M384 in pounds, all other series in thousands of pounds)

Year	Supply				Disposition			
	Stocks at 1 January	Production[1]	Imports	Total	Exports	Stocks at 31 December	Domestic disappearance	
							Total	Per capita
	377	**378**	**379**	**380**	**381**	**382**	**383**	**384**
1975	90,110	907,465	28,383	1,025,958	6,861	48,620	970,477	42.6
1974	75,899	1,034,924	22,369	1,133,192	21,582	90,110	1,021,500	45.4
1973	56,454	1,043,373	17,572	1,117,399	4,931	75,899	1,036,569	46.9
1972	57,697	981,083	13,995	1,052,775	3,165	56,454	993,156	45.5
1971	71,671	957,065	3,240	1,031,976	12,910	57,697	961,369	44.5
1970	51,822	985,037	4,655	1,041,514	7,271	71,671	962,572	45.2
1969	54,810	897,219	7,627	959,656	1,403	51,822	906,431	43.1
1968	55,764	808,642	15,648	880,054	536	54,810	824,708	39.7
1967	55,432	815,084	17,995	888,511	509	55,764	832,238	40.8
1966	43,087	790,444	12,118	845,649	1,912	55,432	788,305	39.3
1965	41,419	710,081	12,988	764,488	1,922	43,087	719,479	36.6
1964	37,246	665,728	16,366	719,340	680	41,419	677,241	35.0
1963	38,464	616,368	7,696	662,528	1,021	37,246	624,261	33.0
1962	42,001	565,978	8,595	616,574	1,879	38,464	576,231	31.0
1961	25,805	567,203	16,214	609,222	257	42,001	566,964	31.1
1960	24,870	472,476	22,829	520,175	178	25,805	494,192	27.7
1959	44,223	502,249	8,233	554,705	717	24,870	529,118	30.3
1958	32,700	470,096	11,727	514,523	328	44,223	469,972	27.5
1957	37,495	411,955	13,236	462,686	249	32,700	429,733	25.9
1956	22,048	404,467	22,247	448,762	143	37,495	411,124	25.6
1955	22,251	365,558	14,830	402,639	233	22,048	380,358	24.3
1954	23,937	321,710	9,227	354,874	566	22,507	331,801	21.7
1953	18,765	291,867	9,633	320,265	368	23,937	295,960	19.8
1952	26,744	309,116	2,861	338,721	3,796	18,765	316,160	21.7
1951	15,182	261,245	5,258	281,685	1,327	26,744	253,614	18.0
1950	20,533	218,529	1,260	240,322	4,457	15,182	220,683	16.1
1949	13,312	230,658	296	244,266	13,844	20,533	209,889	15.8
1948	26,811	201,341	8	228,160	31,493	13,312	183,355	14.3
1947	23,672	238,084	1,816	263,572	8,193	26,811	228,568	18.2
1946	12,258	216,828	3,432	232,518	1,702	23,672	207,144	16.9
1945	18,492	229,521	139	248,152	8,624	12,258	227,270	19.8
1944	18,634	236,107	—	254,741	14,491	18,492	221,758	19.3
1943	11,212	212,537	—	223,749	658	18,634	204,457	18.3
1942	15,961	215,355	—	231,316	4,248	11,212	215,856	19.2
1941	9,537	190,042	—	199,579	1,497	15,961	182,121	16.1
1940	11,629	183,175	—	194,804	2,154	9,537	183,113	16.0
1939	9,855	177,579	—	187,434	2,796	11,629	173,009	15.4
1938	8,344	160,430	—	168,774	2,747	9,855	156,172	14.1
1937	12,831	161,157	—	173,988	8,638	8,344	157,006	14.3
1936	9,066	165,568	—	174,634	3,894	12,831	157,909	14.5
1935	8,939	160,060	—	168,999	2,360	9,066	157,573	14.5
1934	8,584	145,249	—	153,833	2,083	8,939	142,811	13.3
1933	5,617	120,948	—	126,565	1,137	8,584	116,844	10.8
1932	7,994	102,429	—	110,423	1,542	5,618	103,263	10.0
1931	—	88,962	—	88,962	816	—	88,146	8.5
1930	—	89,299	—	89,299	1,028	—	88,271	8.6
1929	—	88,926	—	88,926	3,484	—	85,442	8.6
1928	—	80,461	—	80,461	3,628	—	76,833	7.9
1927	—	76,019	—	76,019	3,580	—	72,439	7.6
1926	—	76,830	—	76,830	5,820	—	71,010	7.6

[1] Excludes Newfoundland.

Series M385-393. Total poultry meat: production, disposition and farm value, Canada, 1941 to 1975

Year	Total production			Consumed by producers			Sold		
	Birds '000	Weight '000 lb.	Value $'000	Birds '000	Weight '000 lb.	Value $'000	Birds '000	Weight '000 lb.	Value $'000
	385	386	387	388	389	390	391	392	393
1975	249,320	907,465	423,593	2,857	11,723	4,240	246,463	895,742	419,363
1974	268,549	1,034,924	476,292	2,668	11,494	4,147	265,881	1,023,430	472,150
1973	276,629	1,043,373	442,279	2,489	10,716	4,152	274,140	1,032,657	438,127
1972	259,308	981,083	298,573	2,223	10,163	2,720	257,085	970,920	295,853
1971	249,292	957,065	265,084	2,423	10,735	2,506	246,869	946,330	262,578
1970	258,663	985,037	265,972	3,047	13,664	3,261	255,616	971,373	262,711
1969	233,761	902,948	261,352	3,999	17,435	4,515	229,762	879,784	252,574
1968	206,292	813,901	238,369	4,504	19,403	4,813	201,788	789,239	230,037
1967	205,727	819,977	233,754	5,533	23,380	6,429	200,194	791,704	224,255
1966	198,256	795,691	242,170	5,187	23,025	6,354	193,069	767,419	232,833
1965	178,386	713,876	206,280	6,428	28,261	7,273	171,958	681,820	196,870
1964	169,415	669,790	185,030	6,575	28,928	6,681	162,840	636,800	176,909
1963	156,683	619,733	179,419	6,544	29,110	8,361	150,139	587,258	169,741
1962	142,558	568,739	164,065	7,412	31,422	9,126	135,146	534,556	153,848
1961	144,503	569,566	154,018	7,618	31,041	8,695	136,885	536,162	144,158
1960	124,696	473,971	146,257	7,590	30,979	9,830	117,106	441,497	135,548
1959	128,948	502,960	149,078	7,362	30,707	9,160	121,586	471,542	139,036
1958	123,022	470,335	162,813	8,234	32,668	11,521	114,788	437,428	150,404
1957	104,631	411,127	145,815	8,426	32,656	11,448	96,205	379,299	133,810
1956	96,472	403,263	157,035	8,206	32,404	12,092	88,266	372,064	144,830
1955	86,159	363,834	146,452	8,559	33,051	12,451	77,600	332,507	134,121
1954	73,621	409,216	158,156	10,011	49,887	17,316	63,610	355,767	140,840
1953	71,481	373,157	155,503	9,006	45,172	17,256	62,475	325,884	138,247
1952	71,114	395,030	161,963	10,638	53,535	19,931	60,476	339,234	142,032
1951	64,704	334,572	155,481	9,039	44,161	19,088	54,319	281,722	132,954
1950	52,068	279,426	96,368	9,124	45,104	14,088	41,849	226,252	80,062
1949	55,581	294,962	97,189	10,220	57,914	14,656	44,115	236,204	80,117
1948	47,176	257,663	81,178	10,391	52,525	15,063	35,467	196,326	63,731
1947	56,746	304,888	80,147	13,896	70,472	16,628	40,944	222,221	60,658
1946	53,758	278,155	75,532	12,830	63,683	16,030	38,863	201,747	56,596
1945	54,497	294,333	82,307	13,173	68,361	18,109	39,053	211,931	60,766
1944	56,008	302,926	69,524	13,443	70,146	15,446	40,238	218,497	51,222
1943	50,293	272,649	69,580	13,693	71,068	17,640	34,530	189,225	49,108
1942	49,515	275,191	53,785	14,167	74,679	13,863	33,356	188,304	37,771
1941	44,019	242,860	37,342	14,303	74,130	10,710	27,932	158,238	25,265

Series M394-402. Eggs, supply and disposition, Canada, 1920 to 1975
(thousands of dozens)

Year	Supply				Disposition				
	Stocks at 1 January[1]	Production[2]	Imports	Total	Exports	Stocks at 31 December[1]	Used for hatching	Domestic disappearance	
								Total	Per capita
	394	**395**	**396**	**397**	**398**	**399**	**400**	**401**	**402**
1975	5,086	448,069	12,092	465,247	10,681	4,291	24,061	426,214	18.7
1974	3,539	459,451	8,328	471,318	14,382	5,086	25,291	426,559	19.0
1973	6,307	461,720	4,084	472,111	12,014	3,393	26,575	430,129	19.4
1972	9,284	468,355	5,395	483,034	1,903	6,307	25,966	448,858	20.5
1971	5,801	489,663	4,112	499,576	3,597	9,284	25,688	461,007	21.3
1970	2,237	490,705	7,591	500,533	7,041	5,801	25,950	461,741	21.7
1969	4,138	464,023[2]	9,501	477,662	2,200	2,237	23,469	449,756	21.4
1968	8,340	444,603	9,338	462,281	724	6,420	21,537	433,600	20.9
1967	4,590	434,731	16,819	456,140	1,045	8,340	21,219	425,536	20.8
1966	5,490	416,689	17,083	439,262	1,040	4,590	23,295	410,307	20.5
1965	6,900	431,351	5,414	443,665	1,117	5,490	20,627	416,431	21.3
1964	4,260	435,698	2,232	442,190	2,374	6,900	20,186	412,730	21.5
1963	4,920	417,235	8,359	430,514	1,474	4,260	18,275	406,505	21.5
1962	3,750	433,762	3,256	440,768	1,536	4,920	16,504	417,808	22.5
1961	6,030	430,415	4,669	441,114	6,512	3,750	17,843	413,009	22.6
1960	6,030	435,606	1,772	443,408	10,911	6,030	15,111	411,356	23.0
1959	7,890	448,236	2,449	458,575	29,932	6,030	15,456	407,157	23.3
1958	13,200	441,438	2,434	457,072	19,386	7,890	15,976	413,820	24.2
1957	7,620	439,843	1,607	449,070	9,628	13,200	11,777	414,465	25.0
1956	6,240	399,758	4,118	410,116	3,939	7,620	12,377	386,180	24.0
1955	10,530	386,011	2,086	398,627	4,040	6,240	11,039	377,308	24.0
1954	5,250	385,819	2,187	393,256	7,274	10,530	10,394	365,058	23.9
1953	5,670	355,184	1,560	362,414	7,718	5,250	9,871	339,575	22.9
1952	5,310	342,527	1,550	349,387	13,420	5,670	9,626	320,671	22.2
1951	6,630	291,235	4,674	302,539	7,103	5,310	10,462	279,664	20.0
1950	4,800	293,727	897	299,424	14,792	6,630	7,988	270,014	19.7
1949	8,370	307,073	250	315,693	42,564	4,800	10,158	258,171	19.3
1948	12,703	352,699	27	365,429	81,238	8,370	9,384	266,437	20.8
1947	8,698	378,600	23	387,321	86,150	12,703	12,142	276,326	22.0
1946	10,066	338,813	44	348,923	61,347	8,698	11,776	267,102	21.8
1945	27,002	368,347	42	395,391	114,623	10,066	10,726	244,894	21.6
1944	7,095	357,501	17	364,613	62,201	27,002	12,303	247,276	22.0
1943	5,367	320,134	393	325,894	41,111	7,095	10,535	247,791	22.2
1942	5,010	288,985	27	294,022	28,489	5,367	8,312	242,264	21.7
1941	4,236	256,645	145	261,026	16,276	5,010	6,548	227,150	20.2
1940	4,388	229,725	286	234,399	10,980	4,236	8,583	210,600	18.5
1939	3,604	225,830	728	230,162	1,274	4,388	8,251	216,249	19.2
1938	4,475	210,997	505	215,977	1,843	3,604	7,646	202,884	18.2
1937	4,460	214,346	594	219,400	1,602	4,475	7,731	205,592	18.6
1936	3,599	224,064	870	228,533	1,204	4,460	8,051	214,818	19.6
1935	5,327	215,669	365	221,361	1,301	3,599	7,776	208,685	19.2
1934	3,116	225,216	137	228,469	2,001	5,327	8,146	212,995	19.8
1933	4,492	228,483	49	233,024	1,988	3,116	8,097	219,823	20.7
1932	6,661	248,875	118	255,654	273	4,492	8,836	242,053	23.0
1931	7,920	259,001	148	267,069	634	6,661	9,069	250,705	24.2
1930	2,946	220,519	4,081	227,546	189	7,920	8,952	210,485	20.6
1929	4,950	219,860	1,087	225,897	1,148	2,946	8,847	212,956	21.2
1928	3,773	197,637	3,017	204,427	988	4,950	8,025	190,464	19.4
1927	2,313	172,704	4,577	179,594	448	3,773	7,528	167,845	17.4
1926	4,439	160,460	4,480	169,379	1,777	2,313	7,362	157,927	16.7
1925	3,506	156,771	4,228	164,505	2,467	4,439	7,204	150,395	16.2
1924	2,357	150,606	5,722	158,685	2,717	3,506	7,151	145,311	15.9
1923	3,418	145,832	6,624	155,874	2,900	2,357	6,970	143,647	15.9
1922	2,104	141,314	8,140	151,558	3,620	3,418	6,736	137,784	15.4
1921	2,513	128,207	6,583	137,303	5,444	2,104	6,086	123,669	14.1
1920	3,574	112,148	—	—	—	2,513	5,265	—	—

[1] Includes fresh eggs in storage from 1 January 1966 to 31 December 1968.   [2] Starting in 1969, Newfoundland production is included.

Series M403-412. Eggs, production and disposition, Canada, 1920 to 1975

Year	Production				Disposition					
	Average number of layers	Eggs per 100 layers	Production	Value	Sold				Producers use	
					For consumption		For hatching		For consumption	
					Number '000 doz.	Value $'000	Number '000 doz.	Value $'000	Number '000 doz.	Value $'000
	'000	number	'000 doz.	$'000						
	403	404	405	406	407	408	409	410	411	412
1975	24,076	22,343	448,069	274,467	409,617	234,069	24,061	31,517	14,391	8,881
1974	25,283	21,811	459,451	283,871	420,140	248,906	25,291	26,553	14,020	8,412
1973	25,764	21,517	461,695	255,302	421,118	223,262	26,575	25,244	14,002	6,796
1972	26,315	21,378	468,355	173,882	426,460	147,446	25,966	20,517	15,931	5,919
1971	28,108	20,905	489,663	161,416	448,073	136,690	25,688	19,278	15,902	5,448
1970	28,212	20,872	490,705	183,715	446,864	158,160	25,950	18,942	17,891	6,613
1969	27,050	20,585	464,023	199,516	420,411	174,435	23,469	17,135	20,143	7,946
1968	26,181	20,378	444,603	168,181	404,733	147,056	21,537	14,961	18,333	6,164
1967	25,829	20,197	434,731	153,309	393,562	132,673	21,219	14,324	19,950	6,312
1966	25,165	19,870	416,689	178,489	374,896	156,487	20,772	13,995	21,021	8,007
1965	26,068	19,857	431,351	156,122	384,585	134,876	19,362	12,419	27,404	8,901
1964	26,273	19,900	435,698	142,272	385,648	120,981	19,300	12,515	30,750	8,967
1963	25,353	19,748	417,235	160,154	367,726	137,880	16,450	10,658	33,059	11,444
1962	26,368	19,740	433,762	152,774	380,898	130,559	15,783	9,845	37,081	11,847
1961	26,401	19,564	430,415	153,467	373,061	130,552	16,137	9,571	41,217	13,130
1960	27,058	19,319	435,606	149,341	381,573	128,312	14,480	8,662	39,431	12,298
1959	28,574	18,824	448,236	152,415	389,679	129,731	14,671	8,941	43,758	13,704
1958	28,561	18,547	441,438	163,125	381,219	138,353	15,144	9,446	44,956	15,285
1957	29,148	18,108	439,843	157,316	381,543	134,827	11,616	6,987	46,523	15,448
1956	27,106	17,698	399,758	165,986	338,656	139,767	12,138	7,122	48,723	18,997
1955	27,339	16,943	386,011	159,693	328,084	135,475	10,643	6,057	46,888	18,006
1954	27,456	16,863	385,819	145,646	327,493	122,929	9,939	5,639	47,932	16,913
1953	25,983	16,404	355,184	165,520	296,587	137,931	9,521	5,989	48,726	21,441
1952	25,602	16,055	342,527	134,630	279,845	110,042	9,023	5,116	53,056	19,256
1951	22,334	15,648	291,235	146,115	214,652	108,626	10,092	6,619	54,549	26,486
1950	23,556	14,963	293,727	111,426	218,988	83,110	7,349	3,885	57,989	20,714
1949	24,760	14,882	307,073	130,073	228,557	96,166	9,268	5,714	57,345	23,057
1948	28,487	14,857	352,699	152,237	269,846	116,105	8,234	4,822	57,870	24,105
1947	31,499	14,423	378,600	136,482	284,989	102,316	10,728	5,635	61,779	20,809
1946	27,696	14,680	338,813	119,811	241,260	84,603	9,941	4,814	65,434	22,596
1945	30,290	14,593	368,347	120,294	268,537	88,122	7,426	3,893	64,495	19,068
1944	30,059	14,272	357,501	107,484	255,634	77,232	8,829	3,815	65,491	18,104
1943	27,007	14,224	320,134	97,777	221,629	67,730	7,410	3,300	66,889	19,072
1942	24,570	14,114	288,985	84,721	193,528	57,477	5,474	2,162	68,084	18,450
1941	22,119	13,924	256,645	56,591	163,814	37,007	4,008	1,360	69,281	13,675
1940	20,691	13,323	229,725	50,058	—	—	—	—	—	—
1939	20,352	13,315	225,830	46,720	—	—	—	—	—	—
1938	18,947	13,363	210,997	44,103	—	—	—	—	—	—
1937	19,295	13,331	214,346	42,077	—	—	—	—	—	—
1936	20,118	13,365	224,064	46,548	—	—	—	—	—	—
1935	19,523	13,256	215,669	41,406	—	—	—	—	—	—
1934	20,563	13,143	225,216	39,538	—	—	—	—	—	—
1933	20,151	13,606	228,483	33,606	—	—	—	—	—	—
1932	22,545	13,247	248,875	35,149	—	—	—	—	—	—
1931	23,300	13,339	259,001	46,862	—	—	—	—	—	—
1930	22,424	11,801	220,519	65,710	—	—	—	—	—	—
1929	23,008	11,467	219,860	77,054	—	—	—	—	—	—
1928	20,995	11,353	198,637	70,715	—	—	—	—	—	—
1927	19,734	10,441	171,704	62,812	—	—	—	—	—	—
1926	19,357	9,947	160,460	51,751	—	—	—	—	—	—
1925	19,017	9,892	156,771	47,954	—	—	—	—	—	—
1924	18,953	9,536	150,606	42,577	—	—	—	—	—	—
1923	18,587	9,415	145,832	42,547	—	—	—	—	—	—
1922	18,038	9,401	141,314	41,518	—	—	—	—	—	—
1921	16,375	9,395	128,207	37,707	—	—	—	—	—	—
1920	14,229	9,458	112,148	33,960	—	—	—	—	—	—

Series M413-416. Exports of major agricultural products, grains (except wheat), quantity, Canada, crop years, 1868 to 1975

(thousands of bushels)

Year	Oats	Barley	Rye	Flaxseed	Year	Oats	Barley	Rye	Flaxseed
	413	414	415	416		413	414	415	416
1975	1,415	138,393	4,843	10,519	1920	19,077	10,891	2,504	861
1974	838	127,480	4,584	15,503	1919	13,679	8,272	940	1,198
1973	6,925	165,248	8,236	19,640	1918	32,548	6,553	1,037	3,855
1972	10,454	230,528	10,757	25,741	1917	68,204	7,873	1,022	6,451
1971	13,366	179,595	8,917	21,194	1916	56,286	8,855	818	3,447
1970	5,165	88,313	3,829	18,611	1915	13,651	2,886	280	4,633
1969	2,723	26,407	4,248	13,421	1914	36,521	12,299	127	18,052
1968	3,545	41,405	4,760	12,611	1913	15,066	9,431	26	13,632
1967	4,803	58,542	9,963	16,568	1912	11,541	2,643	1	3,714
1966	15,922	38,029	8,050	18,936	1911	7,819	1,155	83	2,106
1965	15,551	37,032	4,858	14,346	1910	7,820	2,080	53	2,365
1964	18,759	46,935	5,501	13,638	1909	7,294	2,933	264	760
1963	21,700	15,377	7,310	12,566	1908	—	1,990	—	11
1962	3,454	42,909	4,363	11,988	1907	—	1,198	—	122
1961	2,680	47,178	2,613	13,603	1906	—	880	—	3
1960	6,076	63,759	4,515	12,494	1904[2]	7,124	1,058	102	—
1959	7,513	70,444	3,222	14,276	1903	9,314	947	470	—
1958	26,184	80,298	5,446	13,650	1902	6,119	457	399	—
1957	18,681	81,537	5,448	21,582	1901	9,959	2,386	687	—
1956	4,142	68,700	12,918	11,583	1900	8,662	2,156	474	—
1955	22,247	80,876	9,311	6,345	1899	11,738	239	327	—
1954	70,700	93,742	16,835	5,172	1898	11,977	444	1,140	—
1953	65,371	122,077	8,993	4,060	1897	8,353	1,831	216	—
1952	70,646	73,472	6,820	2,882	1896	2,278	841	—	—
1951	35,397	27,403	9,367	4,131	1895	1,881	1,708	63	—
1950	20,547	20,848	9,954	3,034	1894	3,866	597	63	—
1949	23,220	24,605	10,239	4,413	1893	9,132	2,041	59	—
1948	10,202	4,327	10,226	1,788	1892	7,623	5,203	221	—
1947	29,759	7,658	5,274	61	1891	400	4,893	340	—
1946	43,861	5,088	3,003	346	1890	1,592	9,976	437	—
1945	85,798	39,968	6,340	4,327	1889	893	9,948	—	—
1944	74,735	37,200	8,175	10,050	1888	731	9,370	—	—
1943	63,323	34,862	2,114	5,202	1887	2,619	9,457	124	—
1942	11,861	3,009	2,845	865	1886	5,052	8,554	171	—
1941	13,651	4,594	2,043	76	1885	3,138	9,067	287	—
1940	23,591	12,829	2,824	18	1884	2,011	7,780	873	—
1939	12,934	16,811	788	14	1883	1,809	8,817	1,048	—
1938	8,228	16,166	650	16	1882	4,737	11,588	1,282	—
1937	9,501	19,617	3,634	178	1881	3,565	8,800	870	—
1936	15,515	10,115	2,459	19	1880	5,916	7,240	958	—
1935	17,863	17,443	1,189	12	1879	3,562	5,384	641	—
1934	9,141	5,470	2,582	187	1878	4,413	7,267	416	—
1933	14,419	7,470	2,868	794	1877	7,783	6,346	95	—
1932	18,010	15,369	9,048	251	1876	2,644	10,168	—	—
1931	11,477	19,976	2,090	1,998	1875	2,990	5,419	—	—
1930	4,169	2,653	348	415	1874	998	3,748	—	—
1929	16,310	40,191	5,751	1,935	1873	629	4,347	—	—
1928	14,865	26,517	11,265	2,386	1872	486	5,606	—	—
1927	8,701	38,927	8,303	3,278	1871	542	4,833	—	—
1926	36,827	34,181	6,223	2,953	1870	2,188	6,664	—	—
1925	38,460	27,772	6,338	4,966	1869	763	4,630	—	—
1924	43,302	15,396	7,579	3,482	1868	1,738	4,056	—	—
1923	25,883	13,842	10,177	2,322					
1922	30,117	12,422	4,525	2,631					
1921	32,015	10,816	3,226	2,834					

[1] For 1909 to 1960, the crop year for grains is from 1 August to 31 July of the year given; for 1908, the crop year was nine months ending 31 March; for 1867 to 1907, the year ending 30 June of the year given.

[2] No entries are available for 1905.

Series M417-427. Exports of major agricultural products, animals and animal products, quantity and value, Canada, 1868 to 1975

Year[1]	Cattle and calves[2]	Beef[2]	Hogs[2]	Pork[2]	Sheep and lambs[2]	Mutton and lamb[2]	Horses	Wool	Butter	Cheese	Eggs
	Number of head	'000 lb.	Number of head	'000 lb.	Number of head	'000 lb.	Number of head	'000 lb.	'000 lb.	'000 lb.	'000 doz.
	417	**418**	**419**	**420**	**421**	**422**	**423**	**424**	**425**	**426**	**427**
1975	223,603	44,808	30,673	89,687	4,375	187	1,906	2,173	50	4,877	10,681
1974	153,395	57,461	196,813	92,174	2,572	126	1,628	1,142	9	8,306	14,382
1973	426,350	88,241	90,191	125,614	9,456	156	2,314	1,568	6	11,852	12,014
1972	299,625	83,829	88,725	115,517	14,563	676	4,277	1,987	22	21,025	1,903
1971	245,221	114,062	88,671	98,929	5,780	93	5,521	1,540	4,473	32,813	3,597
1970	247,029	119,080	88,213	72,547	6,649	634	3,324	2,366	6	39,435	7,041
1969	242,490	68,802	16,958	58,203	22,509	691	2,320	2,509	4	35,958	2,200
1968	353,658	69,284	21,353	62,781	26,669	94	2,585	2,980	5	43,830	724
1967	261,873	41,725	19,785	61,496	13,383	184	1,959	3,402	55	27,683	1,045
1966	537,105	78,752	12,683 ·	50,981	10,530	622	1,849	3,021	681	35,949	1,070
1965	612,923	102,293	8,645	61,976	20,394	370	2,297	4,236	5,379	32,055	1,117
1964	222,192	42,770	4,184	59,467	14,505	757	2,624	3,223	113,666	31,658	2,374
1963	278,569	25,564	3,646	52,388	6,600	679	4,246	4,661	19,359	25,823	1,474
1962	492,236	27,656	4,617	52,307	25,656	556	7,360	3,972	4	27,252	1,536
1961	503,139	37,536	27,611	58,429	2,529	173	9,586	5,067	9	19,508	6,512
1960	272,800	25,942	6,781	73,090	3,154	109	10,214	3,679	3,014	18,780	10,911
1959	342,698	29,959	4,530	76,066	29,878	749	16,218	5,002	10,504	20,009	29,932
1958	670,484	63,924	8,069	69,405	41,318	1,377	21,821	4,002	5	15,701	19,386
1957	387,532	55,312	1,865	43,513	17,788	472	15,050	3,917	4	8,456	9,628
1956	56,517	18,634	1,655	67,870	5,090	45	8,698	3,594	2,115	12,217	3,939
1955	67,613	12,787	8,930	80,100	8,874	273	12,652	2,883	7,403	13,749	4,040
1954	89,194	22,580	26,508	76,136	2,402	53	17,775	2,865	143	5,006	7,274
1953	69,505	28,819	21,124	78,122	2,347	52	12,563	3,756	191	16,429	7,718
1952	15,446	68,054	703	32,095	661	46	6,996	3,639	866	2,095	13,420
1951	239,113	96,910	4,321	33,014	31,727	2,737	11,072	2,656	544	30,653	7,103
1950	458,756	90,740	1,646	85,099	87,658	2,761	26,858	4,328	1,629	63,110	14,792
1949	420,655	106,903	2,334	77,909	40,539	3,956	12,989	3,920	1,069	52,695	42,564
1948	457,352	133,822	7,363	229,046	51,909	5,056	21,599	4,929	882	39,827	81,238
1947	83,223	50,952	11,160	251,178	6,048	4,569	15,662	5,103	3,107	55,531	86,150
1946	104,618	138,191	7,590	300,777	4,653	11,268	40,120	6,409	4,509	106,495	61,347
1945	79,507	194,754	9,218	462,049	100,911	7,951	19,059	11,927	5,598	135,409	114,623
1944	59,173	107,411	9,739	717,714	137,808	1,589	22,196	15,520	4,727	131,429	62,201
1943	62,725	13,549	9,326	587,475	3,431	891	17,697	2,316	9,409	129,741	41,111
1942	215,778	15,961	5,999	537,431	6,049	628	4,764	384	1,601	141,504	28,489
1941	254,127	7,905	37,210	482,040	4,173	349	2,659	3,025	1,482	92,331	16,276
1940	233,781	—	7,203	353,015	3,991	183	5,416	2,681	1,338	106,631	10,980
1939	293,425	4,352	5,808	194,992	3,340	205	5,953	4,664	12,399	90,945	1,274
1938	179,224	5,692	5,500	178,494	3,073	202	5,914	4,260	3,893	80,989	1,842
1937	321,760	17,265	82,863	219,142	2,924	284	11,243	4,813	4,097	88,955	1,602
1936	285,414	12,416	76,488	174,493	3,533	232	18,107	9,103	5,129	81,890	1,204
1935	134,358	13,513	19,424	132,435	3,621	316	6,025	8,363	7,697	55,719	1,301
1934	64,975	15,092	4,602	123,750	2,090	370	4,479	4,260	428	61,168	2,001
1933	60,134	10,010	6,031	79,303	1,872	406	6,470	11,258	4,437	74,167	1,987
1932	33,285	4,466	5,593	46,061	1,633	348	5,077	3,712	3,506	86,940	273
1931	56,286	3,757	3,911	17,538	2,042	333	7,961	4,770	10,680	84,788	634
1930	63,322	8,087	2,324	20,475	2,876	242	4,429	4,382	1,180	80,164	189
1929	253,505	31,231	3,942	38,957	11,143	573	—	6,090	1,400	92,946	1,148
1928	245,428	—	23,263	52,354	11,506	—	—	—	1,995	—	988
1927	295,274	—	197,106	82,582	20,138	—	—	—	2,696	—	448
1926	241,968	—	85,972	109,983	21,754	—	—	—	9,814	—	1,777
1925	267,292	26,541	89,323	149,809	40,383	1,167	—	5,625	26,647	126,963	2,691
1924	218,601	20,557	28,197	128,171	20,719	1,716	—	6,009	22,344	116,777	2,890
1923	184,990	29,146	1,554	103,647	30,603	3,610	—	8,667	13,174	114,549	3,614
1922	240,327	28,405	2,338	100,822	91,864	7,897	—	1,034	21,505	133,850	4,400
1921	232,247	53,507	3,154	105,093	100,663	6,406	—	7,288	9,133	133,620	6,580
1920	315,179	—	1,399	109,364	184,002	—	—	9,085	13,361	126,396	6,000
1919	311,596	127,113	29,542	254,160	120,131	1,933	—	4,882	13,659	152,207	733
1918	191,356	86,565	8,184	157,425	134,705	856	—	10,577	4,926	169,531	4,897
1917	166,182	45,546	14,894	231,533	59,224	168	—	5,837	7,990	180,733	5,167
1916	241,560	47,422	1,527	211,388	94,478	100	—	4,546	3,441	168,692	7,898
1915	185,903	18,828	62,763	155,440	42,832	1,065	—	5,660	2,725	137,602	3,593
1914	219,729	13,133	214,989	78,531	20,543	65	—	2,841	1,229	144,478	124
1913	44,296	1,571	3,694	28,390	13,760	46	—	977	828	155,216	147
1912	61,517	949	689	43,949	21,418	49	—	747	8,844	163,451	203
1911	124,923	974	1,714	70,381	46,597	18	—	1,197	3,143	181,896	92

Series M417-427. Exports of major agricultural products, animals and animal products, quantity and value, Canada, 1868 to 1975 (concluded)

Year[1]	Cattle and calves[2]	Beef[2]	Hogs[2]	Pork[2]	Sheep and lambs[2]	Mutton and lamb[2]	Horses	Wool	Butter	Cheese	Eggs
	Number of head	'000 lb.	Number of head	'000 lb.	Number of head	'000 lb.	Number of head	'000 lb.	'000 lb.	'000 lb.	'000 doz.
	417	**418**	**419**	**420**	**421**	**422**	**423**	**424**	**425**	**426**	**427**
1910	157,386	1,318	3,011	51,247	111,107	70	2,762	2,321	4,615	180,960	160
1909	162,945	1,572	366	574	118,896	39	2,028	1,081	6,326	164,907	553
1908	150,993	2,253	942	770	227,001	342	2,270	1,848	4,787	189,710	1,366
1907	162,141	1,455	454	480	254,665	64	2,115	1,229	18,078	178,142	2,592
1906	176,030	2,888	783	776	244,262	105	2,794	1,425	34,032	215,834	2,922
1905	167,102	1,332	2,806	2,236	288,313	161	2,659	1,972	31,764	215,733	3,601
1904	157,417	2,963	1,351	4,289	364,053	90	2,395	1,775	24,568	233,981	5,780
1903	176,780	2,378	23,986	1,331	401,443	84	3,878	—	34,129	229,100	7,404
1902	184,473	4,327	5,778	623	348,443	83	12,687	—	27,856	200,946	11,635
1901	169,279	9,710	944	742	394,681	77	7,609	1,044	16,336	195,926	11,363
1900	205,524	2,847	1,634	1,110	459,944	43	10,053	2,181	25,260	185,984	10,188
1899	218,847	364	814	2,155	405,322	140	12,384	90	20,139	189,828	9,652
1898	213,010	898	814	1,602	351,789	138	14,349	1,014	11,254	196,703	10,370
1897	161,369	1,660	988	772	313,410	202	17,993	7,740	11,453	164,221	7,477
1896	104,451	411	8,333	1,343	391,490	150	21,852	3,916	5,889	164,689	6,521
1895	93,802	5,674	805	520	291,751	112	14,744	5,463	3,650	146,005	6,501
1894	86,057	2,277	1,009	756	233,361	82	8,734	80	5,535	154,977	5,142
1893	107,224	356	14,800	903	360,509	90	13,219	1,169	7,036	133,946	6,805
1892	107,179	146	284	142	329,427	383	11,063	916	5,737	118,270	7,931
1891	117,761	310	334	68	299,347	292	11,658	1,108	3,768	106,202	8,023
1890	81,454	252	670	239	315,931	62	16,550	1,048	1,951	94,260	12,840
1889	102,919	449	1,297	285	360,131	119	17,767	1,015	1,781	88,535	14,029
1888	100,747	551	1,583	294	395,074	493	20,397	995	4,415	84,173	14,171
1887	116,274	451	1,442	617	443,495	415	18,779	1,416	5,486	73,604	12,945
1886	91,866	533	2,994	346	359,407	422	16,525	1,524	4,669	78,113	12,758
1885	143,003	542	1,652	555	335,043	330	11,978	990	7,331	79,655	11,543
1884	89,263	424	3,883	631	304,403	177	11,595	1,501	8,076	69,755	11,491
1883	66,396	629	3,858	807	308,474	397	13,019	1,376	8,106	58,041	13,451
1882	62,106	750	3,263	1,225	311,669	334	20,920	1,053	15,162	50,807	10,499
1881	62,277	1,373	2,819	1,578	354,155	174	21,933	1,405	17,649	49,256	9,090
1880	54,944	693	6,229	1,281	398,746	101	21,393	3,619	18,535	40,369	6,452
1879	46,569	2,051	6,803	498	308,093	301	16,629	3,014	14,308	46,414	5,441
1878	29,925	5,134	3,201	914	242,989	411	14,179	2,446	13,007	38,054	5,263
1877	22,656	5,421[3]	2,063	2,976	209,899	—[3]	8,306	2,476	14,692	35,930	5,026
1876	25,357	1,762[3]	3,886	2,934	141,187	—[3]	4,299	2,907	12,250	35,024	3,881
1875	38,968	2,066[3]	16,779	3,041	242,438	—[3]	4,382	2,647	9,268	32,342	3,521
1874	39,623	6,610[3]	6,983	11,232	252,081	—[3]	5,339	2,765	12,233	24,051	4,408
1873	25,637	1,610[3]	5,335	4,988	315,832	—[3]	—	3,126	15,209	19,483	3,754
1872	22,438	2,130[3]	2,878	2,126	353,178	—[3]	—	3,196	19,068	16,424	3,725
1871	79,613	4,578[3]	11,187	6,215	313,619	—[3]	—	2,892	15,439	8,271	3,312
1870	107,731	3,106[3]	107,155	6,544	147,375	—[3]	—	2,444	12,261	5,828	2,461
1869	65,251	2,370[3]	32,271	2,677	195,682	—[3]	—	2,820	10,853	4,503	1,539
1868	44,442	3,491[3]	10,902	3,506	102,433	—[3]	—	1,606	10,650	6,142	1,893

[1] For most series, 1868 to 1906 data are for years ending 30 June of the year given; for 1907, nine months ending 31 March 1907; for 1908 to 1960, fiscal years ending 31 March of the year given; see footnote 2 for series given on a different basis.

[2] Calendar years, for cattle and calves, 1925 to 1960; for hogs, 1910 to 1960; for sheep and lambs, 1920 to 1960. Years ending 31 March of the year given, for cattle and calves, 1907 to 1924; for hogs, 1907 to 1909; for sheep and lambs, 1907 to 1919. Years ending 30 June of the year given, 1868 to 1906.

[3] Series M418 includes mutton for these years.

Series M428-445. Domestic disappearance of food products, per capita, Canada, 1919 to 1976
(series M432 in dozens; all other series in pounds)

Year	Wheat flour	Beef[1]	Pork[2]	Chicken and fowl[3]	Eggs	Fish[4]	Milk[5]	Whole milk evaporated[6]	Cheese	Ice cream	Total butter	Lard[7]	Margarine	Potatoes, white fresh[8]	Apples[9]	Refined sugar	Coffee green/beans equivalent	Tea
	428	429	430	431	432	433	434	435	436	437	438	439	440	441	442	443	444	445
1976	141.4	110.4	53.1	35.5	18.3	10.6	259.9	8.6	22.5	40.4	11.1	6.5	12.1	139.1	43.4	92.3	9.7	2.5
1975	135.7	102.1	50.9	32.5	18.7	8.4	255.8	8.8	21.6	41.1	11.6	6.1	11.6	154.4	44.4	87.3	9.5	2.4
1974	132.1	94.7	59.4	34.2	19.0	7.5	272.9	9.7	18.4	40.1	12.9	7.5	10.7	146.2	40.1	91.1	9.4	2.5
1973	129.8	91.8	57.6	46.9	19.4	7.0	274.4	10.5	17.0	40.8	13.3	6.7	9.8	150.4	36.8	104.4	9.3	2.5
1972	130.9	92.5	61.0	45.5	20.5	7.0	274.1	11.2	15.6	40.7	14.5	7.6	9.7	159.9	38.3	98.8	9.1	2.4
1971	124.0	89.1	68.3	44.5	21.3	7.0	271.6	11.8	14.9	39.3	15.2	8.2	9.2	159.0	40.0	101.1	9.0	2.4
1970	131.7	84.4	58.8	45.2	21.7	7.0	274.2	12.1	14.0	39.0	15.4	7.8	9.3	150.3	39.1	99.3	9.6	2.2
1969	133.8	86.3	51.4	43.1	21.4	7.5	276.2	12.7	13.1	37.8	15.3	7.6	9.7	166.3	41.0	100.3	9.0	2.1
1968	129.5	85.7	53.5	39.7	20.9	7.3	285.0	13.8	12.1	35.8	16.1	7.8	9.4	148.8	39.2	99.6	9.5	2.5
1967	129.2	83.4	54.5	29.9	20.8	7.3	295.3	14.2	11.5	36.0	16.5	7.8	9.1	170.5	39.2	98.0	8.7	2.4
1966	130.3	84.0	47.0	28.5	20.5	7.3	306.3	15.0	10.8	31.8	17.4	6.9	8.9	139.5	41.1	101.6	8.1	2.3
1965	141.2	83.6	47.9	26.7	21.3	7.5	316.9	15.2	10.7	27.4	18.1	7.4	8.7	136.6	41.3	97.1	8.7	2.4
1964	125.9	79.4	51.8	26.0	21.5	7.3	320.6	15.7	10.2	25.4	18.5	7.7	8.9	153.5	43.3	95.5	8.8	2.5
1963	137.9	74.3	50.7	24.3	21.5	7.7	322.7	16.2	9.8	26.3	18.5	7.5	9.2	149.5	43.2	93.1	9.0	2.6
1962	132.3	71.1	50.1	22.9	22.5	7.0	326.2	16.6	9.5	28.8	17.2	8.0	9.9	159.8	39.0	97.7	9.1	2.3
1961	133.8	70.6	50.3	23.0	22.6	7.3	332.3	16.6	8.8	35.6	15.8	8.4	10.0	144.6	32.3	94.9	8.7	2.5
1960	134.9	69.8	52.5	20.8	23.0	7.7	345.9	17.5	8.5	39.0	16.2	7.2	9.4	162.0	35.1	94.1	8.4	2.4
1959	134.4	65.4	56.5	22.0	23.3	7.5	356.0	17.2	8.3	38.9	17.3	10.3	8.7	151.7	37.9	95.8	8.7	2.6
1958	136.3	67.8	49.2	21.1	24.2	7.5	370.4	17.7	8.0	36.4	18.2	7.0	8.5	162.1	35.7	95.2	8.0	2.6
1957	137.2	71.8	44.3	19.4	25.0	6.8	381.9	18.2	8.0	35.9	19.3	7.4	7.8	164.1	33.9	92.2	7.6	2.8
1956	143.9	71.2	49.0	19.2	24.0	7.3	401.4	18.6	7.6	35.1	19.4	7.4	7.7	172.7	33.4	98.4	7.4	2.8
1955	142.2	69.0	49.1	18.9	24.0	7.3	393.4	18.4	7.6	35.0	19.2	8.7	8.0	158.5	42.4	97.6	7.0	2.7
1954	145.5	70.0	45.3	16.6	23.9	7.0	386.1	18.0	7.2	31.8	19.1	8.3	7.6	150.1	32.7	94.7	6.4	2.9
1953	143.8	64.9	48.5	15.9	22.9	6.9	385.6	18.5	7.0	32.9	19.2	8.4	7.4	178.4	30.3	95.4	7.4	3.1
1952	150.5	54.2	55.8	17.9	22.2	6.8	381.1	18.3	6.6	32.9	19.0	9.4	7.7	151.3	30.2	96.9	7.0	3.2
1951	151.3	49.2	58.4	15.0	20.0	6.8	384.1	17.9	6.5	32.6	19.1	8.1	7.6	159.6	37.5	96.8	6.4	3.0
1950	155.8	50.7	54.8	13.2	19.7	6.8	390.8	17.5	6.2	31.0	20.1	8.1	6.8	210.7	34.6	102.8	6.2	4.0
1949	149.4	56.3	54.5	12.9	19.3	6.2	392.4	14.8	5.8	32.4	19.4	9.9	5.5	170.3	31.5	101.6	7.3	0.4
1948	152.5	59.5	47.9	11.5	20.8	6.0	394.4	15.5	5.3	28.1	23.8	8.5	—	196.1	39.3	102.3	6.8	0.2
1947	164.1	64.8	52.4	15.0	22.0	5.4	422.9	14.5	6.6	26.7	26.2	9.9	—	142.1	47.5	90.6	4.1	3.6
1946	183.9	68.8	43.5	14.1	21.8	7.1	442.8	11.9	5.5	18.5	24.1	8.4	—	178.5	40.9	75.1	6.9	2.2
1945	197.2	67.0	52.7	16.4	21.6	6.8	444.5	12.6	6.3	20.1	28.1	11.3	—	156.8	25.6	74.3	4.5	4.2
1944	183.7	65.7	62.6	16.2	22.0	5.9	441.0	11.3	5.8	21.9	29.2	12.4	—	172.8	46.1	86.6	8.2	3.2
1943	183.2	62.8	62.3	15.3	22.2	6.7	425.3	13.5	5.9	21.4	27.6	13.8	—	189.2	39.4	77.5	4.9	3.1
1942	188.3	60.7	58.9	15.2	21.7	6.0	395.2	12.4	4.8	19.0	32.3	13.3	—	182.0	41.1	76.6	3.8	2.5
1941	165.5	58.5	51.6	13.0	20.2	6.6	370.9	9.8	5.2	17.7	30.9	10.8	—	194.4	34.3	101.0	4.7	3.2
1940	164.2	54.5	44.7	12.8	18.5	6.1	374.6	9.0	4.2	13.9	31.0	7.0	—	213.0	37.2	96.5	3.5	3.6
1939	191.1	53.2	38.4	12.3	19.2	—	426.2	8.4	4.2	12.6	30.9	4.8	—	166.1	40.1	99.3	4.1	3.8
1938	183.3	57.2	37.7	12.0	18.2	—	430.7	6.6	4.2	12.6	30.9	3.7	—	173.2	26.8	92.6	3.8	3.3
1937	168.0	54.6	42.5	12.2	18.6	—	403.0	6.0	3.9	13.2	31.4	3.5	—	211.7	30.2	91.4	3.4	3.6
1936	174.1	55.1	41.4	12.5	19.6	—	413.4	5.1	3.9	11.8	30.9	3.8	—	197.5	—	85.7	3.6	3.6

Series M428–445. Domestic disappearance of food products, per capita, Canada, 1919 to 1976 (concluded)
(series M432 in dozens; all other series in pounds)

Year	Wheat flour	Beef[1]	Pork[2]	Chicken and fowl[3]	Eggs	Fish[4]	Milk[5]	Whole milk evaporated[6]	Cheese	Ice cream	Total butter	Lard[7]	Margarine	Potatoes, white fresh[8]	Apples[9]	Refined sugar	Coffee green/beans equivalent	Tea
	428	429	430	431	432	433	434	435	436	437	438	439	440	441	442	443	444	445
1935	179.2	53.6	39.3	12.3	19.2	—	408.4	4.3	3.8	9.5	30.6	3.9	—	198.6	—	87.5	3.2	3.2
1934	173.6	50.6	47.4	10.8	19.8	—	412.7	3.6	3.8	8.8	30.5	6.4	—	265.4	—	83.2	3.2	3.5
1933	175.4	45.8	52.0	8.5	20.7	—	402.7	3.3	3.6	8.5	29.7	6.9	—	219.0	—	78.7	3.2	3.7
1932	179.5	45.5	55.3	7.7	23.0	—	406.2	3.2	3.4	9.2	29.8	8.2	—	210.8	—	87.2	2.9	3.8
1931	173.9	48.5	51.9	6.2	24.2	—	419.5	4.0	3.7	12.5	30.4	8.2	—	293.8	—	89.9	3.1	3.1
1930	175.9	49.1	52.8	5.9	20.6	—	388.8	4.5	3.9	14.9	30.7	8.4	—	235.9	—	92.9	3.0	4.9
1929	168.9	51.1	58.0	5.8	21.2	—	364.5	4.5	3.9	15.4	30.3	8.6	—	186.0	—	90.1	2.8	3.8
1928	180.4	50.5	58.4	5.3	19.4	—	378.8	4.3	4.0	13.7	29.7	8.3	—	284.2	—	92.6	2.8	3.9
1927	185.4	54.5	54.5	5.1	17.4	—	392.7	4.1	3.7	12.2	29.2	7.8	—	243.0	—	85.4	2.7	3.9
1926	177.1	55.2	53.5	5.0	16.7	—	417.0	3.9	4.5	11.5	29.4	7.9	—	239.7	—	92.4	2.6	3.9
1925	—	56.0	53.3	6.3	16.2	—	422.1	2.9	4.0	10.0	28.4	8.0	—	—	—	—	—	—
1924	—	53.0	54.8	6.4	15.9	—	406.4	3.0	3.6	9.4	28.5	8.2	—	—	—	—	—	—
1923	—	57.2	50.5	6.4	15.9	—	402.1	2.6	3.1	9.8	29.1	9.1	—	—	—	—	—	—
1922	—	58.2	48.6	6.2	15.4	—	384.1	2.8	3.0	8.4	27.2	8.2	—	—	—	—	—	—
1921	—	51.2	41.7	6.4	14.1	—	382.6	3.2	2.4	9.7	26.8	9.6	—	—	—	—	—	—
1920	—	57.4	42.1	—	—	—	362.8	3.0	2.7	10.6	24.0	9.3	—	—	—	—	—	—
1919	—	58.4	58.2	—	—	—	—	—	—	—	—	—	—	—	—	—	—	—

1 Data for beef are cold dressed carcass weight.
2 Data for pork are cold trimmed carcass weight.
3 Chicken and fowl for 1921 to 1955, data are for dressed weight; for 1956 to 1960, data are for eviscerated weight; the conversion factor is .77.
4 Fish and shellfish, fresh and frozen; edible weight 1948 and on.

5 Includes fluid sales, plus milk and cream consumed in farm homes.
6 Includes substantial quantities of powdered skim milk used in the feed industry.
7 Prior to 1949, includes certain quantities of lard used in manufacture of shortening.
8 For 1950 and prior years, potatoes includes the amount dumped or fed to livestock.
9 Data for apples are on a fresh equivalent basis.

Series M446-489. Grain elevators, number and capacities,[1] 1958 to 1977
(millions of bushels of wheat)

Year	Primary									
	Manitoba		Saskatchewan		Alberta		British Columbia		Total	
	Number	Capacity	Number	Capacity	Number	Capacity	Number	Capacity	Number	Capacity
	446	447	448	449	450	451	452	453	454	455
1977	454	43.1	2,032	173.0	1,232	113.7	21	2.9	3,739	332.7
1976	480	44.3	2,171	178.8	1,290	117.6	23	3.2	3,964	343.9
1975	502	44.9	2,309	186.9	1,330	120.4	24	3.2	4,165	355.5
1974	523	45.7	2,389	191.8	1,357	121.7	23	3.1	4,292	362.3
1973	540	46.4	2,431	195.0	1,390	123.7	22	2.9	4,383	368.0
1972	574	48.2	2,536	200.8	1,435	125.9	22	2.9	4,567	377.8
1971	616	51.0	2,667	208.1	1,543	131.9	23	3.0	4,849	394.0
1970	642	52.1	2,732	210.6	1,573	133.1	24	3.0	4,971	398.8[3]
1969	641	51.3	2,744	210.4	1,574	131.7	23	2.8	4,984	396.3[3]
1968	642	50.3	2,752	209.2	1,582	129.9	23	2.9	5,001	392.4[3]
1967	645	49.0	2,775	207.6	1,589	128.8	23	2.8	5,034	389.6[3]
1966	651	48.7	2,809	203.9	1,602	128.1	21	2.4	5,085	384.6[3]
1965	669	49.0	2,845	201.3	1,612	127.2	20	2.2	5,145	381.3[3]
1964	677	48.6	2,856	198.6	1,620	125.9	19	2.1	5,174	376.6[3]
1963	678	47.6	2,865	193.7	1,622	123.9	19	2.1	5,187	368.8[3]
1962	684	47.6	2,878	192.9	1,642	123.3	19	2.1	5,226	367.5[3]
1961	692	49.8	2,886	192.8	1,672	123.9	19	2.1	5,272	370.4[4]
1960	695	47.7	2,900	187.9	1,685	122.7	19	2.1	5,302	361.9[5]
1959[6]	698	48.9	2,911	195.6	1,693	127.0	18	2.0	5,322	373.6[7]
1958	701	48.3	2,922	193.7	1,708	125.6	15	1.7	5,348	369.5[8]

Year	Terminal											
	Manitoba		Saskatchewan		Alberta		British Columbia		Ontario		Total	
	Number	Capacity	Number	Capacity	Number	Capacity	Number	Capacity	Number	Capacity	Number	Capacity
	456	457	458	459	460	461	462	463	464	465	466	467
1977	1	5.0	2	11.0	3	6.1	5	25.8	14	82.6	25	130.5
1976	1	5.0	2	11.0	3	6.1	6	26.8	16	90.4	28	139.3
1975	1	5.0	2	11.0	3	6.1	7	28.3	17	90.4	30	140.8
1974	1	5.0	2	11.0	3	6.1	7	28.3	18	92.4	31	142.8
1973	1	5.0	2	11.0	3	6.1	7	28.3	20	101.1	33	151.5
1972	1	5.0	2	11.0	3	6.1	7	28.3	20	101.1	33	151.5
1971	1	5.0	2	11.0	3	6.1	7	28.3	22	102.6	35	153.0
1970	1	5.0	2	11.0	3	6.1	7	28.3	22	102.6	35	153.0
1969	1	5.0	2	11.0	3	6.1	8	29.1	23	104.3	37	155.5
1968	1	5.0	2	11.0	3	6.1	9	28.7	23	104.3	38	155.1
1967	1	5.0	2	11.0	3	6.1	9	24.8	23	104.3	38	151.3
1966	1	5.0	2	11.0	3	6.1	9	24.8	24	103.3	39	150.3
1965	2	6.0	2	11.0	3	6.1	9	24.8	24	103.3	40	151.3
1964	2	6.0	2	11.0	3	6.1	9	24.8	24	103.4	40	151.4
1963	2	6.0	2	11.0	3	6.1	9	24.8	24	103.4	40	151.4
1962	2	6.0	2	11.0	3	6.1	9	24.8	24	98.8	40	146.7
1961	2	6.0	2	11.0	3	6.1	9	24.9	24	95.1	40	143.2
1960	2	6.0	2	11.0	3	6.1	9	24.9	24	90.7	40	138.7
1959[6]	2	6.0	2	11.0	3	6.1	9	23.9	24	90.5	40	137.5
1958	2	6.0	2	11.0	3	6.1	9	23.9	24	90.5	40	137.5

Series M446-489. Grain elevators, number and capacities, 1958 to 1977 (concluded)
(millions of bushels of wheat)

Year	Process											
	Manitoba		Saskatchewan		Alberta		British Columbia		Ontario		Total	
	Number	Capacity	Number	Capacity	Number	Capacity	Number	Capacity	Number	Capacity	Number	Capacity
	468	**469**	**470**	**471**	**472**	**473**	**474**	**475**	**476**	**477**	**478**	**479**
1977	11	7.2	4	2.6	11	7.7	3	0.3	1	2.9	30	20.6
1976	12	7.3	5	2.7	8	7.0	5	0.8	1	2.9	31	20.6
1975	12	6.7	6	2.9	11	6.2	6	0.8	1	2.9	36	19.4
1974	10	6.1	6	2.9	10	5.6	1	—[2]	1	2.9	28	17.6
1973	7	5.7	5	2.7	10	5.1	1	—[2]	1	2.9	24	16.3
1972	8	5.8	4	2.3	9	4.3	1	—[2]	1	2.9	23	15.3
1971	9	6.0	4	3.2	9	4.3	1	—[2]	1	2.9	24	16.4
1970	8	5.9	4	3.2	8	4.2	1	—[2]	2	3.0	23	16.3
1969	7	5.7	4	3.2	9	4.3	1	—[2]	2	3.0	23	16.3
1968	7	5.7	4	3.2	10	5.5	1	—[2]	2	3.0	24	17.4
1967	7	5.7	4	3.2	10	5.5	1	—[2]	5	4.4	27	18.8
1966	8	5.7	5	5.0	10	5.5	1	—[2]	5	4.4	29	20.5
1965	8	5.7	5	4.9	11	5.6	1	—[2]	5	4.5	30	20.7
1964	8	5.7	5	4.9	10	5.6	2	0.2	5	4.5	30	20.9
1963	8	5.7	5	4.9	10	5.6	1	—[2]	5	4.5	29	20.7
1962	9	5.8	5	4.9	11	5.8	1	—[2]	5	4.5	31	21.0
1961	10	5.9	5	4.9	10	5.5	1	—[2]	5	3.9	31	20.2
1960	10	5.4	6	5.0	10	5.5	8	1.0	5	3.9	39	20.8
1959[6]	10	5.4	6	4.9	10	5.5	9	1.0	5	3.9	40	20.7
1958	10	5.4	6	4.9	11	5.6	9	1.0	5	3.9	41	20.7

Year	Transfer								All licensed	
	Ontario		Quebec		Manitoba		Total		Elevators	
	Number	Capacity	Number	Capacity	Number	Capacity	Number	Capacity	Number	Capacity
	480	**481**	**482**	**483**	**484**	**485**	**486**	**487**	**488**	**489**
1977	14	51.2	9	63.0	4	8.2	27	122.3	3,821	606.2
1976	14	51.2	9	63.0	3	7.7	26	121.8	4,049	625.6
1975	14	51.2	9	63.0	4	8.2	27	122.3	4,258	638.1
1974	14	51.2	10	65.6	4	8.2	28	125.0	4,379	647.7
1973	14	51.2	10	65.6	4	8.2	28	125.0	4,468	660.9
1972	14	51.2	10	69.1	4	8.2	28	128.5	4,651	673.1
1971	15	53.2	10	69.1	4	8.2	29	130.5	4,937	693.9
1970	16	54.4	10	69.1	4	8.2	30	131.8	5,060	700.0[3]
1969	16	54.4	10	69.1	4	8.2	30	131.8	5,074	700.0[3]
1968	16	54.4	11	69.9	4	8.2	31	132.6	5,094	697.5[3]
1967	17	55.7	10	59.5	4	7.2	31	122.4	4,130	682.2[3]
1966	17	55.7	10	59.5	4	7.2	31	122.4	5,184	677.8[3]
1965	18	56.7	10	58.4	4	7.2	32	122.3	5,247	675.7[3]
1964	18	56.7	10	56.4	4	7.2	32	120.3	5,276	669.2[3]
1963	18	56.7	10	55.7	4	7.2	32	119.6	5,288	660.5[3]
1962	17	55.7	9	45.7	4	7.2	30	108.6	5,327	643.8[3]
1961	19	58.0	9	45.7	4	7.2	32	111.0	5,375	644.7[4]
1960	19	58.0	9	45.1	4	7.2	32	110.4	5,413	631.8[5]
1959[6]	19	57.3	8	29.7	4	7.2	31	94.2	5,433	626.1[7]
1958	19	57.4	8	29.7	4	7.2	31	94.3	5,460	622.1[8]

[1] From 1970, primary: public country and private country; terminal: semi-public terminal; process: private terminal and mill; transfer: eastern.
[2] Capacity less than 50,000 bushels included in total.
[3] Includes primary in Ontario not shown prior to 1970.
[4] Total excluding primary supplementary storage of 4.6.
[5] Total excluding primary supplementary storage of 7.2.
[6] As of 1 December 1958.
[7] Total excluding primary supplementary storage of 13.0.
[8] Total excluding primary supplementary storage of 14.6.

Series M490-505. Marketing boards in Canada, 1957-58 to 1975-76

Year	Grains and oil seeds		Hogs		Dairy products		Poultry		Eggs		Fruits and vegetables		Canada total[1]		Total marketing boards	
	Value of receipts	Per cent of farm cash receipts	Value of receipts	Per cent of farm cash receipts	Value of receipts	Per cent of farm cash receipts	Value of receipts	Per cent of farm cash receipts	Value of receipts	Per cent of farm cash receipts	Value of receipts	Per cent of farm cash receipts	Value of receipts	Per cent of farm cash receipts	Number of reporting receipts	Number of producer members
	$'000		$'000		$'000		$'000		$'000		$'000		$'000			
	490	491	492	493	494	495	496	497	498	499	500	501	502	503	504	505
1975-76	3,064,466	82	583,363	66	1,608,181	100	372,123	90	204,519	77	185,609	39	6,309,013	64	103	384,934
1974-75	2,283,934	74	524,779	67	1,301,040	99	384,082	81	197,858	74	170,014	31	5,184,877	58	104	406,612
1973-74	1,353,474	75	550,118	67	871,757	89	357,621	82	196,608	81	138,783	30	3,689,903	54	101	428,372
1972-73	1,220,344	82	361,798	61	774,174	88	241,338	82	73,045	45	106,983	33	2,976,929	54	92	414,989
1971-72	901,293	77	239,842	54	675,276	84	202,514	78	52,044	34	99,467	39	2,355,333	52	86	422,129
1970-71	774,076	89	254,931	51	511,445	69	134,656	51	36,025	21	97,291	36	1,997,372	48	81	427,457
1969-70	686,931[2]	83	212,995	46	398,727	51	102,413	41	29,075	15	87,876	37	1,676,778	40	114	445,882
1968-69	1,106,920	98	168,977	41	329,250	51	88,317	39	17,851	11	96,610	40	2,004,162	46	110	405,465
1967-68	1,176,679	97	174,048	43	314,883	50	76,990	34	13,162	9	86,162	38	2,037,511	47	110	428,412
1966-67	1,117,821	97	165,941	39	174,129	30	49,706	21	—[4]	—[4]	85,264	36	1,794,935	42	91	427,707
1965-66	1,037,873[3]	97	142,532	38	167,091	30	8,344	4	—[4]	—[4]	64,350	26	1,558,950	41	81	405,195[3]
1964-65	22,463	3	112,230	35	156,219	29	6,500	4	—[4]	—[4]	59,304	27	488,771	14	75	211,344
1963-64	20,630	3	108,244	34	146,032	26	7,421	4	—[4]	—[4]	52,463	28	449,872	14	79	212,301
1962-63	15,381	2	106,149	32	141,943	26	5,382	4	—[4]	—[4]	51,654	30	450,669	14	77	223,886
1961-62	16,672	3	95,011	30	133,518	25	—[4]	—[4]	—[4]	—[4]	56,942	34	435,644	15	76	243,826
1960-61	13,038	2	95,948	35	126,039	24	—[4]	—[4]	—[4]	—[4]	48,263	26	403,545	15	76	221,074
1959-60	6,105	1	103,090	30	114,872	22	—[4]	—[4]	—[4]	—[4]	39,746	25	380,289	14	66	230,687
1958-59	15,954	3	93,993	29	107,578	22	—[4]	—[4]	—[4]	—[4]	43,034	27	366,688	13	66	222,184
1957-58	770[5]	3	89,078	31	72,808	16	—[4]	—[4]	—[4]	—[4]	40,306	27	298,619	12	47	165,562

1 Also included are marketing boards for tobacco, wood, honey, maple products, sheep and wool, and miscellaneous.
2 Prior to this year, only wheat, oats, barley and corn were included.
3 Prior to this year, the Canadian Wheat Board was not included.
4 No marketing boards were operating.
5 Includes only corn.

Series M506-522. Co-operatives in Canada, 1934 to 1975

(series M506-520 in millions of dollars; M521 in numbers and M522 in thousands)

Year	Supply and consumer goods								Product marketings						Total volume of business[1]	Total number of co-operatives reporting	Total membership of co-operatives reporting
	Food	Dry goods and hardware	Feed, fertilizer and chemicals	Miscellaneous farm supplies	Machinery	Petroleum	Building materials	Service revenue and other income	Dairy	Fruits and vegetables	Grain and seed	Livestock	Poultry and eggs	Fish			
	506	507	508	509	510	511	512	513	514	515	516	517	518	519	520	521	522
1975	526.5	220.8	555.2	109.3	138.3	272.7	98.6	174.4	916.3	76.8	1,924.9	315.7	107.5	46.9	5,542.0	2,391	2,109
1974	424.0	180.7	475.0	86.1	91.5	219.1	81.6	143.5	643.4	80.6	1,953.7	352.2	103.7	46.2	4,930.5	2,274	1,963
1973	358.6	138.0	326.1	58.3	78.3	168.6	59.6	112.3	514.0	58.6	1,107.8	394.9	98.6	42.2	3,564.5	2,255	1,869
1972	297.4	106.3	222.6	44.4	51.8	141.9	48.6	92.4	478.4	49.0	812.1	308.9	66.9	36.4	2,791.5	2,208	1,774
1971	272.6	89.5	209.5	40.2	39.9	128.2	45.1	84.4	412.8	49.1	628.1	258.7	61.5	30.4	2,381.3	2,389	1,772
1970	240.4	82.6	195.7	39.8	30.2	120.4	39.8	76.1	401.4	48.0	527.3	263.6	57.8	30.2	2,179.2	2,409	1,735
1969	224.2	84.2	196.7	32.2	37.7	112.5	39.5	81.8	378.2	52.4	501.1	243.4	55.0	28.0	2,092.1	2,373	1,690
1968	208.8	76.0	207.3	39.8	40.0	107.6	40.6	80.2	344.6	50.8	574.3	257.7	57.7	25.1	2,132.9	2,469	1,723
1967	190.3	71.9	208.8	37.3	40.6	99.9	37.3	75.1	333.3	48.0	673.2	257.4	57.6	26.8	2,179.4	2,518	1,688
1966	167.4	63.1	182.3	31.2	38.8	95.4	35.4	68.2	307.3	42.7	587.7	241.7	54.4	27.7	1,960.2	2,539	1,645
1965	153.5	56.0	162.0	26.9	36.1	91.1	30.8	54.9	296.8	47.2	574.7	224.1	51.6	25.9	1,851.8	2,615	1,615
1964	143.7	53.8	155.4	28.8	33.6	87.0	30.1	53.5	282.3	45.9	643.8	204.8	52.2	22.5	1,854.6	2,643	1,596
1963	132.7	50.5	149.2	25.7	31.4	82.9	25.7	57.3	257.6	43.1	525.8	215.7	48.6	20.2	1,681.5	2,705	1,648
1962	117.1	46.3	132.2	15.7	19.4	72.8	24.7	28.9	240.2	38.6	386.6	204.0	43.5	18.4	1,421.4	2,836	1,666
1961	108.0	39.1	122.4	15.7	16.0	70.7	24.3	24.5	228.6	33.4	427.2	270.4	44.3	17.4	1,470.5	2,868	1,627
1960	100.8	37.5	116.3	11.0	12.7	63.4	23.4	19.7	219.5	41.0	377.7	276.8	42.0	20.6	1,406.7	2,876	1,608
1959	94.5	33.1	109.6	12.2	10.8	57.9	20.0	23.2	216.4	41.7	366.6	287.2	38.8	21.0	1,363.8	2,905	1,565
1958	81.9	28.0	100.8	10.3	18.7	52.3	17.3	13.8	186.0	42.9	368.8	248.8	33.1	19.5	1,244.6	2,882	1,593
1957	75.0	9.4[2]	100.3	22.0[2]	10.4	47.4	22.4	15.8	166.1	29.7	377.0	199.8	31.9	17.4	1,152.4	2,876	1,628
1956	68.2	9.9	89.0	23.0	10.6	43.8	17.1	13.2	154.0	31.6	362.1	186.0	28.9	14.6	1,123.2	2,672	1,473
1955	61.5	9.3	75.1	20.4	8.3	38.5	17.9	11.4	143.6	32.0	316.5	104.6	24.9	11.9	967.2	2,522	1,410
1954	63.9	9.8	77.1	24.5	12.1	32.1	18.0	11.1	135.3	37.1	369.8	105.1	23.0	14.9	1,017.9	2,590	1,366
1953	70.1	9.0	86.4	26.3	15.3	30.0	12.8	8.9	131.9	38.6	510.5	103.9	23.7	17.2	1,176.9	2,767	1,364
1952	58.5	7.9	96.1	31.8	16.5	26.0	15.8	6.4	136.7	37.2	432.0	242.2	20.7	20.0	1,219.3	2,616	1,373
1951	57.8	7.6	76.5	23.8	7.5	25.5	14.6	9.3	117.1	32.5	336.3	192.9	25.6	15.4	1,016.6	2,768	1,416
1950	56.5	8.4	74.9	21.3	9.5	23.9	14.6	7.8	134.6	46.3	383.6	141.7	28.4	13.8	1,039.8	2,951	1,338
1949	49.6	8.6	77.6	17.0	8.4	21.9	11.3	9.6	141.9	39.6	371.8	135.4	35.2	14.9	1,001.4	2,637	1,220
1948	37.3	6.3	66.4	16.5	5.0	20.0	8.5	7.6	109.9	40.3	290.8	96.9	31.6	14.0	780.1	2,249	1,127
1947	27.9	3.9	53.4	18.9	1.7	14.7	8.0	7.8	83.2	44.2	283.3	91.6	26.0	10.6	712.6	2,095	983
1946	24.9	3.9	38.0	10.6	1.3	13.3	5.0	4.1	76.9	30.7	205.3	83.0	24.0	10.7	554.3	1,953	927
1945	19.1	2.9	32.1	9.4	0.9	12.2	4.7	3.8	60.9	32.1	268.9	88.1	17.8	5.2	585.7	1,824	740
1944	14.8	2.5	25.5	6.4	0.8	11.3	4.3	2.5	52.7	21.1	264.2	82.5	15.3	5.1	527.9	1,792	691
1943	12.6	2.2	19.3	6.3	0.5	9.9	4.9	1.6	44.3	19.5	134.2	62.8	10.9	2.6	352.8	1,650	586
1942	9.2	1.4	15.8	4.5	1.3	7.2	2.9	::	39.2	15.4	87.0	40.4	7.2	2.6	257.1	1,722	561
1941	::	::	::	::	::	::	::	1.3	24.2	11.4	139.3	26.0	4.6	2.6	242.2	1,395	452
1940	::	::	::	::	::	::	::	0.9	19.1	11.9	143.9	19.3	3.2	1.3	236.3	1,151	450
1939	::	::	::	::	::	::	::	0.6	19.9	11.1	113.0	16.8	4.4	1.0	201.7	1,332	446
1938	::	::	::	::	::	::	::	0.5	19.4	10.1	82.5	19.4	3.2	0.3	155.1	1,217	436
1937	::	::	::	::	::	::	::	0.5	16.6	9.7	110.8	15.7	3.3	::	173.9	1,024	397
1936	::	::	::	::	::	::	::	0.4	12.0	9.0	99.6	8.3	2.2	::	158.2	781	367
1935	::	::	::	::	::	::	::	0.3	8.8	7.2	94.9	5.6	1.8	::	130.4	697	341
1934	::	::	::	::	::	::	::	0.1	8.8	7.8	82.8	7.7	2.1	::	136.4	690	345

1 Amount greater than sum of items specified because of miscellaneous marketing and supply sales.
2 Years 1957 and earlier include hardware.

Series M523-524. Farm implement and equipment sales, and sales of repair parts, Canada, 1947 to 1976
(thousands of dollars)

Year	Farm implement and equipment sales	Sales of repair parts	Year	Farm implement and equipment sales	Sales of repair parts	Year	Farm implement and equipment sales	Sales of repair parts
	523	524		523	524		523	524
1976	1,134,086	154,711						
1975	966,299	144,042	1965	371,324	55,643	1955	153,124	28,452
1974	713,696	132,209	1964	326,976	53,156	1954	146,703	27,336
1973	573,866	107,326	1963	287,840	49,722	1953	238,050	31,819
1972	420,245	87,912	1962	238,797	43,879	1952	250,277	31,232
1971	326,165	76,813	1961	201,777	39,644	1951	235,620	28,773
1970	278,981	65,032	1960	217,465	41,313	1950	218,187	29,862
1969	344,309	65,751	1959	212,231	38,887	1949	217,090	28,105
1968	378,131	63,955	1958	172,014	33,979	1948	170,666	26,997
1967	432,300	61,999	1957	149,902	33,820	1947	122,395	23,276
1966	416,914	61,991	1956	170,767	31,825			

Series M525. Expenses for fertilizer, Canada, 1926 to 1976
(thousands of dollars)

Year	Fertilizer expenses	Year	Fertilizer expenses	Year	Fertilizer expenses	Year	Fertilizer expenses	Year	Fertilizer expenses
	525		525		525		525		525
1976	488,258								
1975	490,052	1965	133,279	1955	49,942	1945	21,622	1935	6,989
1974	319,028	1964	117,559	1954	52,883	1944	18,815	1934	6,410
1973	216,522	1963	97,197	1953	54,510	1943	17,728	1933	5,309
1972	172,535	1962	83,222	1952	47,505	1942	16,305	1932	5,657
1971	161,239	1961	77,040	1951	43,464	1941	12,348	1931	9,936
1970	135,472	1960	68,098	1950	38,529	1940	12,574	1930	12,050
1969	153,102	1959	64,920	1949	35,667	1939	11,141	1929	8,878
1968	207,261	1958	57,858	1948	29,741	1938	11,189	1928	6,849
1967	185,394	1957	53,332	1947	27,044	1937	10,157	1927	5,798
1966	159,422	1956	51,469	1946	23,608	1936	7,695	1926	6,182

Section N: Fisheries

N.H. Morse, *Dalhousie University*

Statistics of Canadian production and trade in fish are presented in four parts: primary operations (series N1-48), processing (series N49-82), value of exports and imports (series N83-113), and miscellaneous statistics (series N114-142).

The series included here contain the most generally useful data now being compiled. They are based on published sources or obtained directly from the Department of Fisheries and the Environment, Ottawa; the International Fisheries Commission, Seattle, Wash.; and the International Commission for the Northwest Atlantic Fisheries, Dartmouth, N.S. However, a great deal more information is currently available. Much of it can be found in the comprehensive annual volumes, *Fisheries Statistics of Canada*, issued by Statistics Canada. In addition the reader is referred to the following: three books on fisheries statistics issued by the federal Department of Fisheries and the Environment (hereafter called federal fisheries department): No. 1, *Landings in the Inshore Fishery of the Maritime Provinces, 1919-1950*, (Ottawa, mimeographed, 1953; No. 2, *The Canadian Commercial Fisheries of the Great Lakes*, (Ottawa, mimeographed, 1955); No. 3, *The Commercial Salmon Fisheries of British Columbia*, (Ottawa, mimeographed, 1958); and also periodic consolidations of fisheries statistics such as *Annual Statistical Review of Canadian Fisheries*, vols. I-IX, federal fisheries department, Ottawa; *British Columbia Catch Statistics*, federal fisheries department, (Ottawa, Queen's Printer); *Canadian Fisheries Statistics* published as a supplement to the *Acadian Fisheries Annual*, (Gardenvale, Que.); and Statistics Canada, *Monthly Review of Canadian Fisheries Statistics*, (Ottawa, Queen's Printer).

Reference should also be made to the monograph published by the Royal Commission on Canada's Economic Prospects, *The Commercial Fisheries of Canada*, (Ottawa, Queen's Printer, 1957).

Various statistics on fish landings, production, number of fishermen and other data can be found in reports of the provincial and federal royal commissions made since Confederation and in other official documents. However, examination of these statistics reveals they are almost invariably derived in the early years from the annual reports of the federal fisheries department.

General note

Under the power given to it by the British North America Act the federal government has full legislative jurisdiction over both the coastal and inland fisheries of Canada. Consequently, all regulations governing fishing are made by the federal government. Some regulations concerning the inland fisheries are made on the recommendation of the provinces. Initially, full administrative control also resided with the federal government. As a result of various court awards and agreements with the provinces through the years, administration of fisheries has become divided between the federal and provincial governments. The result is that the federal government administers all tidal and sea fisheries except those of Quebec, the inland fisheries of the Atlantic provinces, excepting possibly ponds and lakes in

Newfoundland, and fisheries of the Yukon Territory and Northwest Territories. Quebec administers all its fisheries including those in salt waters. Ontario, the Prairie provinces and British Columbia administer their freshwater species though the last does not collect any statistics.

Processing industries are under the legislative and administrative control of the provinces, though inspection for sanitary purposes, interprovincial trade and exports is under federal control.

Until the fiscal year ending 31 March 1917, statistics of the fisheries were assembled by the Fisheries Branch of the Department of Marine and Fisheries, established shortly after Confederation, through its widespread organization of fisheries officers. Starting with 1917 the data have been assembled at the Dominion Bureau of Statistics and its successor, Statistics Canada, though the fisheries officers of the Department of Fisheries and the Environment continue to play an important part in gathering the data (see below).

The quality of the data contained in the annual report for the period before 1917 is not high. Methods of reporting differed from area to area, and apparently supervisory procedures were not sufficiently well developed to permit early discovery and correction of errors in reporting and in methods of collection. On examination, the annual reports leave many questions unanswered concerning the basis on which the various compilations were made. The user will find it useful to refer to the comments of Ruth Fulton Grant in *Canadian Atlantic Fishery*, (Toronto, Ryerson Press, 1934), appendix A. Quality of the statistics is undoubtedly much higher for the period since 1917.

Primary Operations (Series N1-48)

General note

Primary operations include catching and landing of all products of the coastal and inland waters.

In most fisheries under federal administration, including all fisheries of the Atlantic provinces, the commercial waters of British Columbia, the Yukon Territory and Northwest Territories, the primary data on landings are obtained from purchase slips made out by the buyer at the time of landing and first sale, a procedure begun in the 1950s. These slips are sent to offices of the federal fisheries department where they are tabulated and the results forwarded to Statistics Canada for publication. They include data on species sold, quantity, prices, location of purchase and sometimes the size of fish and type of gear used. In Newfoundland, marketing facilities and practices are such that the foregoing procedures were not used until the mid-1960s. In the more remote parts, a considerable amount of processing on shore was done by fishermen themselves. In these areas the data were assembled by fisheries officers who obtained estimates of landings and stocks in storage. Supplementary purchase slips are prepared by fisheries officers, representing estimates of landed weight equivalents of fish processed by fishermen, direct sales to local users, bait used and fish consumed by fishermen's families.

In other areas of Canada, the data are collected through provincial administrative officers, tabulated in provincial offices and assembled by Statistics Canada. Quebec collects data from buyers who report weekly purchases or, in the remote areas, by the procedure formerly used in outlying areas of Newfoundland. In Ontario data are collected from fishermen who are required to report as a condition of obtaining licences. In Manitoba, Saskatchewan and Alberta, data come from the Freshwater Fish Marketing Corporation, fish buyers and fishermen.

Before recent procedures were introduced, heavy reliance was placed on working back from data on processed fish and fish products, with the use of conversion factors to estimate the landings in primary form from the processed form data. Information on processed forms was obtained from fish processing and handling plants and from fisheries inspectors for fish exported.

Prior to 1917 the data were obtained by officers of the Fisheries Branch of the Department of Marine and Fisheries, probably by visiting communities and estimating the annual catch and its disposition. A revision of procedures in the fiscal year 1910-11 improved the quality of data collected. Before that, reports covered marketings and included values of forms after processing on land. The department's annual reports suggest these might also have some duplication owing to the nature of the reporting forms provided to the officers. Beginning with 1910-11, two forms of improved design were used, one for recording data on landings and the other on the marketing of primary or processed products (excluding sales of primary products to processors) as they moved into channels of trade.

Fish are landed in primary forms varying from 'fresh round', that is, as taken from the water, to split and salted or even further processed forms. The value of landings is the actual value received on landing, whatever the form.

The basis of measuring weight on landings is the same as in Statistics Canada, *Fisheries Statistics of Canada, 1975*, (Catalogue 24-201), p. 7, as follows for the Atlantic Coast:

Fish and shellfish in the Atlantic provinces are reported as follows: cod, haddock, pollock, hake, cusk and catfish as 'gutted head on', halibut, swordfish and tuna as 'gutted head off', except in Newfoundland which reports halibut as 'gutted head on'. All other sea fish and freshwater fish are shown as 'round'. Molluscs and crustaceans are reported as 'in shell' except scallops which are 'shucked' and squid which are in the 'round'.

Some species of fish are landed in various forms and are converted to the forms mentioned above by multiplying the landed weight by appropriate factors.

The same source reports that in British Columbia no effort is made to convert fish, with the exception of salmon as landed, to a common landed form. In Ontario, landings are reported in the round form but it is possible that for the northern inland waters the figures include some dressed fish. For the Prairie provinces and the Northwest Territories, fish are landed in various forms and are converted to round weight by multiplying the landed weight by appropriate factors.

The method of reporting landed weight has been changed over time. For example, in *Fisheries Statistics of Canada, 1930*, it is stated that fresh fish (that is, weight landed) is gutted head on for cod, haddock, hake, cusk and pollock, that it is gutted head and tail off for albacore and that in all other cases it means fish as it comes from the water, in the round. It is probable that the reporting was on a reasonably uniform basis from year to year, at least for major species in the East, but West Coast measures may contain considerable variation in the mixture of different forms on landing.

N1-11. Value of fish landed, by province, 1911 to 1975

SOURCE: for 1917 to 1975, Statistics Canada, *Fisheries Statistics of Canada*, (Catalogue 24-201); for 1911 to 1917, Department of Marine and Fisheries, *Annual Report, Fisheries*.

Figures for Newfoundland in *Fisheries Statistics of Canada* begin in 1952. Prior to 1919 no landed values were reported in Ontario, Manitoba, Saskatchewan, Alberta and the Yukon Territory. Value of fish landed is value at the boat's side on landing, based on sale to the first buyer. Values given cover fish of all kinds, molluscs and crustaceans, livers, tongues, viscera and scales, seaweed, seal skins, bait worms and other aquatic life from both sea and inland fisheries.

For values landed by main species, see series N25-37 and also the general note to series N1-48.

N12-24. Quantities of fish landed, by region and by major species, 1869 to 1975

SOURCE: for 1917 to 1975, Statistics Canada, *Fisheries Statistics of Canada*, (Catalogue 24-201); for 1869 to 1917, Department of Marine and Fisheries, *Annual Report, Fisheries*, except as noted below.

N12. Cod, for 1869 to 1917, is from Oscar E. Sette, U.S. Department of Commerce, Bureau of Fisheries, *Statistics of the Catch of Cod off the East Coast of North America, to 1926*, appendix IX to the Report of the U.S. Commission of Fisheries for 1927 (Washington, U.S. Government Printing Office, 1928), table 7, p. 3. Sette's primary data prior to 1917 were drawn from the annual report of the Department of Marine and Fisheries. For 1910 to 1916 (fiscal years 1911 to 1917) Sette took the catch landed as reported. For years prior to 1910 he converted marketings, which were given in departmental reports and were solely for dried cod before 1903, to a landed basis, using conversion factors given in the document cited. These conversion factors were designed to give estimates on a fresh round basis. In an appended note to the document he states that he had mistakenly assumed landings were reported (presumably from 1910 onward) on a round basis but that they were in fact on a fresh gutted basis.

N12 and 16. East Coast cod and herring totals are aggregates of provincial data.

N13. Haddock, 1880 to 1910, is from A.W.H. Needler, U.S. Department of Commerce, *Statistics of the Haddock Fishery in North American Waters*, (Washington, U.S. Government Printing Office, 1930), table 2, pp. 30-31. Statistics given by Needler are calculated from the weights of products marketed as reported in the annual report of the Department of Marine and Fisheries with the use of conversion factors to yield weight on a fresh gutted basis as presented here. These factors are contained in Needler's document. He also makes the following comment (p. 31):

Doubt is cast on the accuracy of catches before 1888,

when 'hake and haddock' are given together in the detailed statistics, when the total for haddock is perhaps only an estimate, and when certain discrepancies occur in the compilation of the provincial totals to make the Canadian totals. The extreme catch in 1897 is due entirely to one county, Digby, which showed an increase of 400 per cent in the catch with no increase in the fishing equipment. This record is considered doubtful in the 1897 report itself, and we place no reliance on it here.

By using a figure for the Digby catch of the average in the two adjacent years, Needler arrives at an estimate for the total catch of 52.4 million pounds for 1897. There is a period of nine years from 1910-11 to 1918 during which haddock-landing statistics are available from the annual reports of the department. The statistics available from the source differ from Needler's by varying amounts. Needler's figures are invariably larger than those contained in the annual reports, in most years the difference being of the order of 5 to 7 million pounds. In two years, 1910-11 and 1918, the difference approached 15 million pounds.

N18. Scallop landings were reported in barrels for the period 1915-16 to 1934. These have been converted to pounds using the conversion factor 1 barrel equals 20 pounds shucked. For the period 1934 to 1950, landings were reported in gallons and have been converted to pounds using the conversion factor 1 gallon equals 10 pounds shucked. Subsequently, landings have been reported as shucked.

N24. West Coast halibut statistics are drawn exclusively from the records of Statistics Canada and the annual report of the federal fisheries department. Prior to 1934 total landings for British Columbia include landings by United States vessels at British Columbia ports.

The International Fisheries Commission constructed a revised series of Pacific halibut landings dating from 1888 in which they attempted to make corrections for duplications and errors in official statistics. The commission statistics of landings differ markedly from those recorded here for the period 1918 to 1933. Canadian West Coast halibut landings compiled by the commission are given in this volume as series N128. The reader is referred to the note on N128 and to F.H. Bell, H.A. Dunlop, and N.L. Freeman, *Pacific Coast Halibut Landings 1888 to 1950 and Catch According to Area of Origin*, (Seattle, Washington, International Fisheries Commission, 1952) for a full description of the commission's procedures in the construction of their series.

N25-37. Value of fish landed, by region and by major species, 1911 to 1975

SOURCE: for 1917 to 1975, Statistics Canada, *Fisheries Statistics of Canada*, (Catalogue 24-201); for 1911 to 1917, Department of Marine and Fisheries, *Annual Report, Fisheries*.

See the general note to series N1-48.

N38-48. Number of persons engaged in primary fishing operations, by province, 1878 to 1975

SOURCE: for 1917 to 1975, Statistics Canada, *Fisheries Statistics of Canada*, (Catalogue 24-201); for 1878 to 1917, Department of Marine and Fisheries, *Annual Report, Fisheries*.

The basis on which the number of fishermen is calculated differs from province to province.

N39. In Newfoundland the count represented the number of persons who were employed in the fishery for two weeks or more during the year, but in 1969 procedures were altered to conform to those adopted in the Maritime provinces and Quebec.

N40-43. In Nova Scotia, New Brunswick, Prince Edward Island and Quebec the data are based on one count for the year without reference to the amount of time the person was engaged in the fishery.

N44. In Ontario the count is based on the number of commercial fishing licences issued but adjustment is made to correct for the issuance of more than one licence to a person and for the fact that certain licensees may fail to engage in fishing.

N45-47. In Manitoba, Saskatchewan, Alberta and the Northwest Territories the data given are the total of all commercial licences issued with no adjustment for duplication or failure of licensees to engage in the fishery. Since different licences are necessary for different lakes and different seasons, data given for these provinces undoubtedly contain a substantial amount of duplication and must be regarded as a considerable overestimate of the number of persons engaged in the fishery.

N48. In British Columbia the count is based chiefly on the number of commercial licences issued with corrections for duplication. Estimates are made of the number of fishermen working as crews on fish packers and carrying smacks and these are included in the data given. Figures do not include persons employed to operate salmon traps.

Fish Processing (Series N49-82)

General note

Data on fish processing plants were obtained, like those of other sections, by questionnaire sent to the processing establishments. Fisheries officers of the federal fisheries department assist in obtaining accurate returns quickly.

Before collection of data by Statistics Canada, more limited data were collected by the fisheries officers of the old Department of Marine and Fisheries. These data were limited to the value of products marketed, the number of persons employed in processing and handling plants, and capital invested. They were obtained by fisheries officers going to the plants and obtaining the information directly.

In earlier years a considerable amount of processing was done by fishermen themselves after fish were landed. Data on the value of products thus prepared were estimated by fisheries officers from information obtained in much the same way as those on landings in remote areas of Newfoundland prior to the late 1960s (see the general note to series N1-48). A major part of the information is obtained from local merchants and in the warehouses where fish for export are inspected.

No information is collected on processing in Ontario and the Prairie provinces.

The data for series N49-82 cover fish processors, whose main business is cutting, freezing, drying, salting, smoking, pickling and canning; fish packers and handlers, who primarily buy and sell fresh fish only, or who buy processed fish and fish products and sell without further processing.

N49-58. Market value of fisheries products, by major process forms, Canada, 1870 to 1975

SOURCE: for 1917 to 1975, Statistics Canada, *Fisheries Statistics of Canada*, (Catalogue 24-201); for 1870 to 1917, Department of Marine and Fisheries, *Annual Reports, Fisheries;* for 1870 to 1960, the data were prepared by the Economics Service, Department of Fisheries and the Environment (the names of the service and of the department have changed over time).

Values given in the table represent sales value free on board the processing plant, except for items sold directly to consumers by fishermen or exported directly by fishermen, in which cases the values represent amounts received by fishermen.

The process categories listed in the table include the following specific product forms contained in the original statistics.

N50. Fresh whole includes fresh round or dressed fish, molluscs and crustaceans in the shell, and fresh roe, livers and caviar. Frozen whole (series N52), not given as a separate category prior to 1945, is included with series N50 before that year. Prior to the fiscal year ending 31 March 1910 the sources of information did not always list in detail the marketed form of the minor species. It is assumed that this fish was sold in the fresh state and therefore has been included under the category fresh whole.

N51. Fresh filleted includes fresh fillets, lobster meat, shucked scallops and shucked meats. Frozen filleted (series N53), not given as a separate category prior to 1945, is included with series N51 before that year.

N52. Frozen whole includes the same items as series N50, but the values of molluscs and crustaceans marketed in frozen form are small. This item is included in series N51 prior to 1945.

N53. Frozen filleted includes frozen fillets, frozen blocks and sticks, fresh and frozen steaks and frozen shucked molluscs or crustaceans. This item is included in series N51 prior to 1945.

N54. Canned includes all species canned and also canned and salted.

N55. Smoked includes smoked round or dressed and smoked fillets.

N56. Salted and pickled include salted, dried, boneless, mild cured, green salted, pickled, vinegar cured, dry salted, and salted and smoked.

N57. Oil includes all types of marine oils used for vitamin and industrial purposes.

N58. Meal includes fish meal, whale meal, liver meal and offal meal.

N59-64. Fish processing plant inputs, 1917 to 1975

SOURCE: Statistics Canada, *Fisheries Statistics of Canada*, (Catalogue 24-201).

N59 and 62. Wages and salaries include payments made for contract or piece work.

N60 and 63. Materials used include fish, by far the largest item, salt, containers, process supplies and other materials.

N61 and 64. Fuel and electricity includes coal, fuel oil, other petroleum products and wood, as well as electricity.

N65-68. Number of persons employed in fish processing plants, by area and by sex, 1895 to 1975

SOURCE: for 1960 to 1975, Statistics Canada, *Fish Products Industry*, (Catalogue 32-216); for earlier years prepared by the federal fisheries department from: for 1917 to 1960, Statistics Canada, *Fisheries Statistics of Canada*, (Catalogue 24-201); for 1895 to 1917, Department of Marine and Fisheries, *Annual Report, Fisheries.*

The number of persons employed in processing plants is calculated on the following basis: salaried employees are counted once for the year in question; the number of wage employees is calculated on the basis of the average number of workers employed. This average is calculated from counts of employees made monthly. Until 1953 this average was based on the number of months the plant in question actually operated. Since 1953 the average has been calculated on the basis of 12 months whether the plant operated for the whole of that period or not. The present method of calculation is therefore closer to a concept of person-years worked than to a count of the number of persons employed and would clearly be a considerable underestimate of the number of persons employed in fish processing plants for some period during the year.

Prior to 1917 the figures are total number of persons employed, the breakdown by sex not being available before that date.

N69-82. Number of fish processing establishments, by area and by value of output, 1919 to 1974

SOURCE: for 1960 to 1974, Statistics Canada, *Fish Products Industry*, (Catalogue 32-216); for 1939 to 1958, the statistics were provided directly by Statistics Canada; for 1959 and for 1919 to 1938, Statistics Canada, *Fisheries Statistics of Canada*, (Catalogue 24-201).

Value of Exports and Imports (Series N83-113)

N83-89. Value of exports of fish and fish products, by region, 1868 to 1975

SOURCE: for 1960 to 1975, Statistics Canada, *Exports by Commodities*, (Catalogue 65-004); for earlier years prepared by the federal fisheries department from: 1930 to 1959, Statistics Canada, *Fisheries Statistics of Canada*, (Catalogue 24-201); for 1914 to 1929, Department of Trade and Commerce, *Trade of Canada;* for 1911 to 1913, Department of Customs, *Report;* for 1867 to 1912, Department of Customs, *Trade and Navigation.*

N85. Other Europe includes Albania, Austria, Belgium and Luxembourg, Bulgaria, Czechoslovakia, Denmark, Finland, France, German Democratic Republic, Federal Republic of Germany, Gibraltar, Greece, Hungary, Iceland, Ireland, Italy, Malta, Netherlands, Norway, Poland, Portugal,

Romania, Spain, Sweden, Switzerland, Union of Soviet Socialist Republics and Yugoslavia.

N86. Continental South America includes Argentina, Bolivia, Brazil, Chile, Columbia, Ecuador, Falkland Islands, French Guiana, Guyana, Paraguay, Peru, Surinam, Uruguay and Venezuela.

N87. Central America and Caribbean include Bahamas, Barbados, Belize, Bermuda, Costa Rica, Cuba, Dominican Republic, El Salvador, French West Indies, Guatemala, Haiti, Honduras, Jamaica, Leeward and Windward Islands, Mexico, Netherlands Antilles, Nicaragua, Panama, and Trinidad and Tobago.

N88. United States and possessions include the 50 states, Puerto Rico and the U.S. Virgin Islands.

N89. Other includes Australia, Hong Kong, Japan, South Korea, Malaysia and all other countries not included in N84-88.

N90-100. Value of exports of fish and fish products, by major species, 1871 to 1973

SOURCE: for 1960 to 1973, Statistics Canada, *Exports by Commodities,* (Catalogue 65-004); for earlier years prepared by the federal fisheries department from: for 1917 to 1959, Statistics Canada, *Fisheries Statistics of Canada,* (Catalogue 24-201); for 1911 to 1917, Department of Trade and Commerce, *Trade of Canada;* for 1905 to 1910, Department of Trade and Commerce, *Canada Year Book;* (Catalogue 11-202); for 1871 to 1904, Department of Customs, *Trade and Navigation.*

The species classification includes all products derived from the species in question except reduction products which are included under series N99.

N90. Groundfish include the following sea fish: catfish, cod, cusk, flounders and soles, haddock, hake, lingcod, pollock, redfish, sablefish, turbot and small amounts of related species of sea fish. The distinction between groundfish and pelagic fish such as herring is that the former species are found on the bottom while the latter are found nearer the surface of the water. Halibut, which are groundfish, are shown separately in series N91.

N98. All other shellfish include clams, oysters, scallops, squid, crabs, shrimps and prawns.

N99. Oil and meal include these products from all species.

N100. All other include a large variety of sea fish and inland fish, not already covered, and seal skins.

N101-113. Value of imports of fish and fish products, by major species, 1873 to 1973

SOURCE: for 1960 to 1973, Statistics Canada, *Imports by Commodities,* (Catalogue 65-007); for earlier years prepared by the federal fisheries department from: for 1918 to 1959, Statistics Canada, *Fisheries Statistics of Canada,* (Catalogue 24-201); for 1914 to 1917, Department of Trade and Commerce, *Trade of Canada;* for 1873 to 1914, Department of Customs, *Trade and Navigation.*

The species classification includes all products derived from the species in question except reduction products which are included under series N112.

N102. Groundfish include cod, haddock, pollock and lingcod.

N111. All other shellfish include shrimps and prawns, and squid.

N112. Oil and meal include all oil and meal products from all species, including whales.

N113. All other include all other species of sea fish and inland fish, fur skins of marine animals, fish livers, sponges and turtles.

Miscellaneous Fisheries Statistics (Series N114-142)

N114-118. Index of prices received by fishermen and index of wholesale prices of fish products, 1913 to 1974

SOURCE: for 1961 to 1974, Statistics Canada, *Prices and Price Indexes,* (Catalogue 62-002); for earlier years, data for series N114-117, from 1913 to 1960, supplied by the federal fisheries department; series N118, from 1913 to 1950, is from Statistics Canada, *Wholesale Price Indexes, 1913-1950,* (Catalogue 62-D-102), and from 1950 to 1960, Statistics Canada, *Prices and Price Indexes,* (Catalogues 62-002 and 62-501).

N119-124. Expenditures of the federal fisheries department, 1932 to 1974

SOURCE: for 1961 to 1974 prepared by the Planning and Finance Service, Department of Fisheries and the Environment; for earlier years prepared by the Economics Service, Department of Fisheries from: for 1943 to 1960, *Public Accounts of Canada, Part II;* for 1932 to 1942, Auditor General's *Reports.*

The data in this table record expenditures for the fiscal year in which they were actually made. *Public Accounts of Canada* record amounts for the recouping of the working fund of the Prices Support Board and of the indemnity funds as of the year in which that fund was replenished by general vote. Consequently, totals shown in this table do not correspond in all cases with those published in the *Public Accounts of Canada.*

Only expenditures under the jurisdiction of the federal fisheries department are given here. Expenditures by other federal departments and agencies (for example, expenditures by the public works department on construction and maintenance of wharves and harbours) are not included.

Data on expenditures of the federal fisheries department are available for years prior to 1932 in the Auditor General's *Reports.*

N120. Administration includes all departmental administration expenditure that might be found in any government department.

N121. Resource development includes expenditures for the Fisheries Research Board, Protection Branch, Fish Culture Branch and for the development of the deep sea fisheries and the destruction of predators.

N122. Price support and deficiency payments include the fishing bounty, first instituted to encourage fishing in 1882, and payments under the Fisheries Prices Support Board.

N123. Other subsidies include payments through the Fishermen's Indemnity Plan and for the construction of vessels and bait facilities.

N124. Other expenditures include those for international commissions, branches for inspection and consumers, contributions to fishery exhibitions and wartime damage compensation.

N125-127. Catch in the areas covered by the International Convention for the Northwest Atlantic Fisheries (Sub-areas 1-5), 1951 to 1974

SOURCE: *Statistical Bulletins*, International Commission for the Northwest Atlantic Fisheries, (Dartmouth, N.S.), vols. I-XXIV.

In order to consider problems affecting the fisheries of the Northwest Atlantic, the United States convened a conference of 11 countries in Washington in January 1949, which resulted in the International Convention for the Northwest Atlantic Fisheries. Provision was made for the establishment and maintenance by the contracting governments of the International Commission for the Northwest Atlantic Fisheries (ICNAF) which was responsible for scientific investigation for maintaining fish stocks which supported international fisheries. The convention area and its five sub-areas were defined and a panel established for each sub-area. Membership in the commission expanded as additional countries entered ICNAF so that the commission eventually included: Bulgaria, Canada, Cuba, Denmark, France, German Democratic Republic, Federal Republic of Germany, Iceland, Italy, Japan, Norway, Poland, Portugal, Romania, Spain, Union of Soviet Socialist Republics, the United States and the United Kingdom. See ICNAF *Handbook*, (Dartmouth, N.S.) revised 1969, and subsequent updates.

N128. Pacific halibut landings, according to the International Fisheries Commission, Canada, 1890 to 1958

SOURCE: data for 1951 to 1958 were obtained directly from the International Fisheries Commission; for 1890 to 1950, F.H. Bell, H.A. Dunlop, N.L. Freeman, *Pacific Coast Halibut Landings 1888 to 1950 and Catch According to Area of Origin*, table 1, pp. 10 and 11.

Statistics are for fish landed head off and gutted. For 1929 to 1958 the data were collected by the International Fisheries Commission. Prior to 1929 estimates are based upon data for British Columbia obtained from annual reports of the Department of Marine and Fisheries and from the Dominion Bureau of Statistics, amended by information obtained from records of fish exchanges, by material from the *Pacific Fisherman*, a trade journal published in Seattle, and by logs and other records obtained from ship owners and captains.

Although it is stated that the data are for calendar years,

it appears that for 1907 to 1917 they are for fiscal years ending March 31 of the following year.

The figures are landings by Canadian registered vessels. Apparently landings by United States vessels in British Columbia were shipped in bond to the United States. There was little landing by Canadian vessels in United States ports. However, there may have been an error in recording the figure for 1907 and the figure given and reproduced here may be for the total of Canadian and United States landings in British Columbia.

N129. Exports of dried cod, Newfoundland, 1806 to 1948

SOURCE: for 1930 to 1948, *Report of the Newfoundland Fisheries Board;* for 1927 to 1929, *Newfoundland Fisheries Reports;* for 1806 to 1926, Oscar E. Sette, *Statistics of the Catch of Cod off the East Coast of North America to 1926*, table 2, pp. 738 and 739. Sette gave the source of his data as: for 1804 to 1904, William MacGregor, *Report on the Trade and Commerce of Newfoundland for the Four Years ending June 30, 1906;* for 1905 to 1924, annual reports of the Department of Marine and Fisheries in Newfoundland; for 1925 and 1926 the United States Consul, St. John's, Newfoundland.

The information appearing in this table was reported in quintals in the source. It has been converted to thousands of pounds using the conversion factor 1 quintal equals 112 pounds.

N130-131. Value of exports of fishery products in relation to total exports, Newfoundland, 1856 to 1949

SOURCE: Newfoundland customs returns.

N132-134. Number of male persons engaged in catching and curing fish in relation to persons occupied and total population, Newfoundland, census years, 1857 to 1945

SOURCE: for 1945, *Newfoundland Census, 1945;* for 1857 to 1935, *Census of Newfoundland and Labrador, 1935.*

N135-138. Production of salted codfish, by fishery, Newfoundland, 1930 to 1948

SOURCE: Newfoundland Fisheries Board.

The Newfoundland Fisheries Board was established in 1936 to introduce a group marketing procedure. This was followed by the establishment of the Newfoundland Associated Fish Exporters Limited in 1947 as selling agency for Newfoundland and Labrador salt cod.

N139-142. Number of fishermen employed in the salt cod fishery, by fishery, Newfoundland, 1937 to 1948

SOURCE: Newfoundland Fisheries Board.

Series N1-11. Value of fish landed, by province, 1911 to 1975
(thousands of dollars)

Year[1]	Canada[2]	Newfound-land	Nova Scotia	Prince Edward Island	New Brunswick	Quebec	Ontario	Manitoba	Saskat-chewan	Alberta	British Columbia[3]
	1	2	3	4	5	6	7	8	9	10	11
1975	290,692	45,728	91,010	12,410	25,515	15,433	11,052	5,961	2,238	975	79,681
1974	291,970	42,903	81,141	12,027	22,080	14,230	9,655	5,147	2,142	931	100,976
1973	317,439	47,297	74,956	11,243	22,217	12,627	10,376	5,041	1,625	802	130,409
1972	233,696	35,723	66,375	9,540	19,923	11,138	8,119	4,523	1,634	727	75,128
1971	201,078	35,693	57,660	9,426	16,251	10,594	6,948	2,403	1,802	729	58,588
1970	199,327	34,807	53,448	9,571	17,543	11,158	6,535	2,142	1,931	826	60,255
1969	178,434	29,455	54,021	7,566	15,853	9,145	7,389	3,354	2,294	935	47,387
1968	181,556	28,007	52,250	7,399	15,654	8,648	5,968	3,276	1,382	917	57,274
1967	159,286	28,116	45,401	6,967	10,877	7,743	5,988	2,527	1,163	758	48,971
1966	171,820	25,886	46,738	5,998	11,136	7,278	5,995	4,788	1,706	844	60,659
1965	157,395	23,176	48,193	6,825	10,651	6,938	6,402	4,370	1,734	677	47,435
1964	145,128	21,978	40,977	5,642	10,277	5,894	5,222	3,720	1,490	799	48,321
1963	127,973	20,086	35,145	4,462	9,320	5,868	5,498	4,356	1,300	676	40,466
1962	128,915	17,222	30,928	4,361	9,183	5,534	5,341	4,229	1,478	714	49,066
1961	110,233	14,922	27,741	4,489	7,730	4,710	5,746	3,174	1,385	883	38,778
1960	100,491	15,856	26,094	4,640	9,358	4,504	4,983	3,867	1,367	1,159	27,962
1959	105,534	14,529	27,112	4,287	8,763	4,316	4,866	3,757	1,190	1,016	34,995
1958	116,530	11,312	24,955	3,754	7,499	4,195	7,271	3,540	1,091	879	51,353
1957	94,247	13,672	23,084	3,550	7,014	4,068	7,047	3,279	939	854	30,021
1956	105,957	15,090	25,038	3,949	8,146	4,440	7,927	2,947	784	790	36,058
1955	91,390	14,161	23,582	3,279	6,753	3,453	6,783	3,477	763	688	27,711
1954	97,542	14,704	23,046	2,948	7,311	2,931	7,013	3,088	741	667	34,458
1953	89,832	12,015	21,928	2,870	6,910	3,395	7,027	2,717	553	667	31,281
1952[1]	92,746	12,928	22,679	2,660	7,825	3,572	7,407	3,439	679	654	30,158
1951	88,527	—	21,398	2,240	7,588	3,375	7,035	4,263	910	544	40,638
1950	82,187	—	21,400	2,556	6,792	3,200	6,252	3,880	718	437	36,345
1949	67,453	—	18,691	2,055	6,437	3,295	5,497	2,821	521	342	27,251
1948	75,375	—	19,071	2,201	7,885	3,435	5,683	3,181	513	375	32,644
1947	57,516	—	15,156	1,880	5,996	2,767	4,803	3,477	484	449	22,354
1946	67,162	—	20,560	3,086	7,145	4,475	5,597	3,304	729	600	21,372
1945	64,839	—	19,223	2,309	5,478	4,988	6,484	3,418	882	742	21,201
1944	52,078	—	14,851	1,797	5,404	3,974	4,389	2,830	1,032	465	17,334
1943	48,713	—	12,828	1,869	5,193	3,879	4,704	3,428	773	393	15,644
1942	41,735	—	8,875	1,148	3,649	2,747	3,574	2,727	384	213	18,415
1941	34,378	—	6,930	759	2,828	2,080	3,031	2,448	262	197	15,836
1940	23,630	—	5,800	554	2,028	1,611	2,560	1,555	228	222	9,068
1939	21,931	—	5,308	683	2,186	1,691	2,515	1,228	229	196	7,891
1938	22,830	—	5,324	649	1,800	1,714	2,851	1,307	250	262	8,669
1937	23,193	—	6,015	714	1,911	1,643	3,140	1,373	283	268	7,838
1936	22,084	—	5,492	725	2,100	1,878	2,714	1,262	183	214	7,504
1935	20,756	—	4,762	641	1,882	1,790	2,372	920	146	139	8,082
1934	19,715	—	4,619	695	1,916	2,071	1,833	966	116	155	7,330
1933	16,214	—	3,406	519	1,619	1,764	1,677	725	98	92	6,321
1932	15,061	—	3,856	714	1,505	1,452	1,708	858	113	103	4,732
1931	18,383	—	4,834	765	2,007	1,637	2,041	908	178	110	5,881
1930	29,763	—	6,843	844	2,520	2,199	2,693	1,377	125	266	12,873
1929	33,700	—	7,343	934	3,002	2,467	3,051	2,039	375	400	14,070
1928	33,749	—	7,396	849	2,618	2,320	3,477	1,621	371	422	14,634
1927	32,518	—	7,149	964	2,461	2,146	2,804	1,423	284	435	14,842
1926	35,327	—	8,670	924	2,877	2,470	2,522	1,745	268	506	15,333
1925	30,015	—	7,191	1,008	2,916	2,195	2,655	1,061	301	294	12,383
1924	27,365	—	6,270	879	3,315	1,726	2,803	886	299	218	10,954
1923	26,441	—	5,779	1,106	2,824	1,597	2,477	739	181	263	11,467
1922	27,593	—	7,443	905	2,706	1,551	2,212	658	150	159	11,802
1921	23,174	—	7,018	469	2,218	1,262	2,296	760	151	193	8,788
1920	31,266	—	9,277	954	2,480	1,882	2,727	879	176	232	12,625
1919	37,760	—	11,412	875	2,988	3,175	2,742	1,012	272	171	15,206
1918[4]	32,479	—	10,493	822	4,246	3,285	—	—	—	—	13,633
1917	31,303	—	9,834	963	3,896	2,169	—	—	—	—	12,546
1917[1,5]	20,857	—	7,412	820	3,754	1,873	—	—	—	—	6,997
1916[5]	19,572	—	6,664	497	3,245	1,468	—	—	—	—	7,698
1915[5]	19,016	—	6,011	801	3,443	1,114	—	—	—	—	7,625
1914[5]	21,385	—	6,585	1,017	2,946	1,191	—	—	—	—	9,647
1913[5]	16,766	—	5,248	895	2,909	857	—	—	—	—	6,857
1912[5]	17,810	—	6,303	706	3,307	945	—	—	—	—	6,550
1911[5]	15,753	—	7,133	744	3,193	923	—	—	—	—	3,761

[1] For 1911 to 1917, fiscal years ending 31 March of the year given; 1917 to 1975, calendar years. Newfoundland is included beginning in 1952.

[2] The figures shown under provinces do not add to those shown for Canada (series N1) owing to the inclusion of data for the Yukon Territory and the Northwest Territories in series N1 and to discrepancies in some years in the official statistics.

[3] Includes halibut landed in United States ports, 1961 to 1975, includes the Yukon Territory, 1961 to 1964.

[4] New Brunswick and Quebec figures include sea fish only. Inland fish landings not reported for this year.

[5] Figures apply to sea fisheries only.

Series N12-24. Quantities of fish landed, by region and by major species, 1869 to 1975
(thousands of pounds)

Year[1]	East coast[2]							Inland			West coast[3]		
	Cod	Haddock	Lobsters	Sword-fish	Herring and sardines	Redfish	Scallops	White-fish	Blue pickerel	Yellow pickerel	Salmon	Herring	Halibut[4]
	12	13	14	15	16	17	18	19	20	21	22	23	24
1975	264,253	35,146	38,554	35	533,314	226,890	18,423	17,026	8,303[5]		76,172	131,480	11,345
1974	287,878	27,151	31,388	3	497,360	193,331	14,044	14,163	7,309[5]		134,246	98,479	7,460
1973	324,533	33,452	35,599	23	498,953	349,300	11,143	16,052	7,294[5]		185,204	122,630	14,472
1972	402,611	31,610	33,185	—	670,313	242,322	12,044	18,175	7,429[5]		164,386	86,025	22,083
1971	449,168	53,601	38,159	—	924,361	248,624	11,171	19,379	6,063[5]		132,367	22,082	25,294
1970	483,240	49,483	36,588	8,016	1,055,898	239,227	12,980	19,675	7,157[5]		154,486	8,521	29,525
1969	540,318	81,287	40,167	7,108	1,073,815	213,194	13,809	20,553	7,676[5]		79,037	4,416	33,837
1968	593,543	91,113	37,310	7,337	1,555,165	214,822	15,648	18,300	8,534[5]		176,354	6,373	29,390
1967	520,891	102,750	34,924	8,007	761,139	189,295	13,321	18,529	—	8,965	133,175	116,741	26,221
1966	563,078	112,819	37,340	7,403	569,893	183,079	18,249	20,510	—	11,190	162,852	307,652	32,000
1965	575,446	92,933	40,522	7,805	405,757	130,370	19,704	24,236	1	9,717	90,190	444,061	32,973
1964	571,412	106,311	41,881	11,855	312,883	80,186	16,682	22,954	—	11,652	124,198	505,287	33,292
1963	609,722	90,981	44,373	12,589	252,703	83,274	16,217	25,279	—	16,115	119,324	572,202	37,274
1962	585,386	115,021	46,452	3,495	246,502	61,114	13,481	26,578	—	14,959	163,907	445,275	34,576
1961	516,861	118,395	47,547	3,196	193,369	56,216	13,145	27,184	2	13,346	121,633	448,433	29,481
1960	604,621	95,126	51,517	3,890	246,329	46,859	7,716	27,068	5	13,890	75,153	187,675	27,161
1959	639,138	111,997	45,714	6,703	238,916	40,618	4,909	24,796	50	12,996	105,680	444,032	23,799
1958	530,932	103,366	42,950	5,376	233,044	61,371	3,332	24,023	834	15,475	181,318	405,123	23,708
1957	641,834	131,638	44,438	5,180	222,314	46,361	3,329	24,444	6,398	19,215	131,897	295,376	22,542
1956	654,124	155,390	51,960	4,612	196,200	59,646	2,606	22,884	12,020	20,922	113,530	491,396	23,315
1955	579,562	135,573	48,569	4,546	201,090	43,980	1,684	21,990	12,070	19,739	131,008	305,692	19,679
1954	639,341	117,989	46,675	4,304	217,913	48,739	1,780	24,577	8,210	16,759	178,862	360,962	25,199
1953	530,599	72,969	46,397	3,324	224,719	46,543	1,780	25,571	10,399	15,974	186,914	298,241	24,882
1952[2]	622,009	63,975	47,857	3,158	292,905	38,561	1,261	27,895	7,447	16,599	146,965	189,497	23,488
1951	227,172	55,990	45,573	2,544	208,256	4,054	599	26,505	4,102	17,073	197,594	365,432	20,214
1950	250,080	47,319	44,685	2,156	230,761	2,070	784	24,776	8,665	13,877	184,699	397,566	18,882
1949	246,284	46,580	38,205	2,237	185,803	2,046	436	22,509	9,831	13,535	147,368	344,527	17,997
1948	256,075	56,789	35,647	2,363	226,173	1,139	871	19,909	5,868	15,980	145,168	416,967	18,753
1947	231,275	31,558	31,884	1,792	239,367	429	932	16,023	1,753	14,463	162,800	256,331	24,119
1946	323,123	34,738	38,309	2,776	249,853	301	879	19,200	1,972	13,754	149,676	212,365	17,991
1945	291,075	32,221	37,180	2,717	195,727	25	963	18,871	6,582	14,801	170,965	257,654	14,905
1944	235,104	25,965	33,350	1,989	213,565	28	603	17,700	9,413	14,984	107,572	187,104	13,167
1943	213,938	30,745	30,109	3,021	215,541	32	574	16,781	9,661	13,503	121,421	182,794	12,687
1942	193,557	26,206	28,025	1,934	189,781	127	700	16,706	4,438	12,804	162,198	232,483	11,028
1941	194,754	28,777	27,802	1,346	191,990	38	784	17,866	1,621	12,630	190,035	168,852	12,929
1940	191,633	35,557	26,799	2,290	169,566	281	665	16,818	2,118	10,580	143,190	339,501	12,694
1939	161,918	38,516	31,466	1,788	177,256	589	496	16,462	6,158	12,051	147,547	216,481	13,397
1938	168,338	39,359	31,438	1,093	151,796	478	957	15,424	7,317	12,881	173,466	132,891	12,025
1937	150,932	38,882	30,995	1,502	139,643	97	1,838	17,368	9,450	14,302	169,174	192,980	11,721
1936	169,188	40,301	28,327	1,785	167,531	211	1,708	14,460	6,900	14,564	199,550	162,062	10,592
1935	152,246	36,843	31,997	2,234	139,261	—	1,332	14,746	5,123	10,955	178,943	100,851	10,193
1934	170,125	35,607	36,199	1,409	142,662	—	899	14,462	2,432	12,251	165,990	82,036	9,768
1933	155,648	26,888	37,492	1,714	120,612	—	863	15,214	4,216	10,627	141,050	107,737	17,081
1932	142,619	36,018	48,349	1,036	95,630	—	468	13,848	4,061	8,950	129,149	100,320	16,885
1931	146,200	36,385	43,549	1,263	104,948	—	236	15,622	5,405	9,235	128,704	148,108	18,200
1930	166,147	48,634	40,726	1,193	116,262	—	373	16,975	5,928	10,315	229,621	122,196	25,480
1929	197,883	54,541	37,282	634	144,569	—	358	19,639	2,583	12,850	151,404	131,567	30,392
1928	214,982	48,171	32,244	809	137,292	—	526	18,070	2,150	14,261	225,746	153,512	30,282
1927	197,864	42,171	31,683	730	128,606	—	773	18,566	3,117	14,002	149,040	172,425	30,053
1926	269,476	49,680	33,958	1,294	141,591	—	464	19,064	3,038	12,609	212,556	130,127	31,510
1925	227,736	34,439	34,084	455	124,049	—	354	18,665	3,445	8,688	187,338	143,788	31,824
1924	184,779	33,786	27,221	558	138,459	—	207	16,771	3,060	10,161	196,516	115,762	33,138
1923	177,251	30,456	38,163	1,434	96,189	—	278	15,779	3,255	10,387	151,476	103,582	33,467
1922	232,021	30,773	36,392	1,116	125,996	—	216	15,878	6,358	8,315	150,908	100,252	29,318
1921	200,424	26,922	39,362	685	94,210	—	98	18,407	6,406	6,485	84,203	94,487	32,587
1920	194,860	44,174	39,998	335	132,842	—	84	18,176	3,380	6,188	126,286	100,136	23,877
1919	255,945	56,457	34,581	741	131,676	—	274	19,740	2,392	6,173	166,835	56,787	21,078
1918	216,239	55,437	26,410	364	171,884	—	250	20,504	—	—	149,350	63,692	18,623
1917	221,546	71,242	47,487	434	106,240	—	132	—	—	—	160,152	48,724	11,353
1917[1]	196,286	58,203	48,090	928	177,689	—	189	—	—	—	119,643	49,603	12,306
1916	211,689	58,252	44,528	1,853	198,354	—	137	—	—	—	136,939	46,745	19,490
1915	177,286	56,600	40,882	498	206,035	—	—	—	—	—	136,974	56,341	21,444
1914	163,538	40,563	51,465	1,332	198,631	—	—	—	—	—	150,935	64,906	22,346
1913	170,049	50,382	55,514	656	213,403	—	—	—	—	—	122,106	72,957	25,328
1912	207,220	53,022	58,914	794	240,067	—	—	—	—	—	110,367	54,544	19,649
1911	312,651	45,672	57,910	272	212,022	—	—	—	—	—	93,783	27,519	21,906

Series N12-24. Quantities of fish landed, by region and by major species, 1869 to 1975 (concluded)
(thousands of pounds)

Year[1]	East coast[2]							Inland			West coast[3]		
	Cod	Haddock	Lobsters	Sword-fish	Herring and sardines	Redfish	Scallops	White-fish	Blue pickerel	Yellow pickerel	Salmon	Herring	Halibut[4]
	12	13	14	15	16	17	18	19	20	21	22	23	24
1910	248,990	–	–	–	–	–	–	–	–	–	–	–	–
1909[1]	–	60,000	–	–	–	–	–	–	–	–	–	–	–
1908	217,170	49,000	–	–	–	–	–	–	–	–	–	–	–
1907	–	47,000	–	–	–	–	–	–	–	–	–	–	–
1906	203,364	48,100	–	–	–	–	–	–	–	–	–	–	–
1905	223,355	55,900	–	–	–	–	–	–	–	–	–	–	–
1904	238,610	46,900	–	–	–	–	–	–	–	–	–	–	–
1903	248,163	41,400	–	–	–	–	–	–	–	–	–	–	–
1902	299,173	45,200	–	–	–	–	–	–	–	–	–	–	–
1901	299,900	60,500	–	–	–	–	–	–	–	–	–	–	–
1900	267,684	50,200	–	–	–	–	–	–	–	–	–	–	–
1899	278,155	62,700	–	–	–	–	–	–	–	–	–	–	–
1898	212,837	59,200	–	–	–	–	–	–	–	–	–	–	–
1897	237,534	96,000[6]	–	–	–	–	–	–	–	–	–	–	–
1896	239,021	52,000	–	–	–	–	–	–	–	–	–	–	–
1895	241,078	48,700	–	–	–	–	–	–	–	–	–	–	–
1894	280,454	54,900	–	–	–	–	–	–	–	–	–	–	–
1893	266,507	53,300	–	–	–	–	–	–	–	–	–	–	–
1892	269,464	67,000	–	–	–	–	–	–	–	–	–	–	–
1891	254,691	60,000	–	–	–	–	–	–	–	–	–	–	–
1890	257,320	53,200	–	–	–	–	–	–	–	–	–	–	–
1889	271,368	50,300	–	–	–	–	–	–	–	–	–	–	–
1888	315,254	94,900	–	–	–	–	–	–	–	–	–	–	–
1887	323,476	86,400	–	–	–	–	–	–	–	–	–	–	–
1886	324,215	85,400	–	–	–	–	–	–	–	–	–	–	–
1885	323,218	74,400	–	–	–	–	–	–	–	–	–	–	–
1884	306,717	86,800	–	–	–	–	–	–	–	–	–	–	–
1883	322,536	69,200	–	–	–	–	–	–	–	–	–	–	–
1882	270,909	71,500	–	–	–	–	–	–	–	–	–	–	–
1881	322,675	47,100	–	–	–	–	–	–	–	–	–	–	–
1880	327,754	43,600	–	–	–	–	–	–	–	–	–	–	–
1879	320,245	–	–	–	–	–	–	–	–	–	–	–	–
1878	270,749	–	–	–	–	–	–	–	–	–	–	–	–
1877	244,520	–	–	–	–	–	–	–	–	–	–	–	–
1876	249,258	–	–	–	–	–	–	–	–	–	–	–	–
1875	224,636	–	–	–	–	–	–	–	–	–	–	–	–
1874	239,367	–	–	–	–	–	–	–	–	–	–	–	–
1873	264,253	–	–	–	–	–	–	–	–	–	–	–	–
1872	247,331	–	–	–	–	–	–	–	–	–	–	–	–
1871	202,381	–	–	–	–	–	–	–	–	–	–	–	–
1870	173,527	–	–	–	–	–	–	–	–	–	–	–	–
1869	154,007	–	–	–	–	–	–	–	–	–	–	–	–

[1] For 1869 to 1909 and for 1917 to 1975, calendar years; for 1910 to 1917, fiscal years ending 31 March of the year given.
[2] Newfoundland is included in series N12-18 beginning in 1952.
[3] No effort is made to convert fish to a common landed form, with the exception of salmon.

[4] Includes halibut landed in United States ports beginning in 1961.
[5] Breakdown not available since 1968.
[6] See note to series N13 for unusual size of this figure.

Series N25-37. Value of fish landed, by region and by major species, 1911 to 1975
(thousands of dollars)

Year[1]	East coast[2]							Inland			West coast[3]		
	Cod	Haddock	Lobsters	Sword-fish	Herring and sardines	Redfish	Scallops	White-fish	Blue pickerel	Yellow pickerel	Salmon	Herring	Halibut[4]
	25	26	27	28	29	30	31	32	33	34	35	36	37
1975	30,599	7,119	48,378	9	13,798	11,044	25,708	5,270	3,764[5]		46,913	13,267	10,125
1974	32,126	5,736	37,963	–	13,445	9,480	18,572	4,086	3,195[5]		73,998	12,043	5,440
1973	29,670	6,427	40,568	2	12,232	17,306	16,231	4,084	3,114[5]		99,998	10,951	10,698
1972	26,154	4,511	37,003	–	12,661	9,478	19,508	3,811	2,860[5]		50,341	2,726	13,684
1971	25,132	5,980	33,211	–	13,160	8,655	12,961	3,855	2,063[5]		44,479	556	8,135
1970	21,956	5,296	29,661	3,689	13,251	7,824	14,101	3,695	2,547[5]		45,076	290	10,588
1969	21,569	6,778	29,527	4,105	11,202	5,751	12,202	4,566	2,822[5]		27,810	221	14,400
1968	24,348	6,852	24,450	3,729	11,986	5,548	13,407	3,757	2,451[5]		44,889	231	7,348
1967	23,679	6,803	23,256	3,292	8,189	4,969	7,760	3,220	–	2,133	36,001	1,828	6,631
1966	25,099	8,036	22,038	3,214	6,217	5,083	7,446	3,507	–	3,965	38,654	5,107	11,471
1965	23,637	6,054	26,632	3,253	4,256	3,419	10,849	3,896	–	3,143	25,958	6,232	11,112
1964	22,055	6,228	24,244	3,561	3,210	2,170	7,278	3,459	–	2,916	30,244	6,167	8,309
1963	20,997	4,915	21,284	2,594	3,084	2,219	6,256	3,387	–	3,715	22,790	6,477	8,249
1962	18,904	4,869	19,781	1,580	3,430	1,585	4,524	3,817	–	3,226	30,559	4,752	10,912
1961	15,646	4,647	18,054	1,238	2,756	1,458	3,082	3,814	1	2,455	26,152	4,589	6,204
1960	16,538	3,685	18,031	1,342	3,682	1,172	2,021	3,494	2	3,020	18,401	2,178	4,379
1959	17,023	4,970	17,387	1,383	3,279	977	1,872	3,549	15	2,994	20,503	7,355	4,398
1958	13,228	4,092	15,376	1,439	2,826	1,488	1,269	3,496	216	3,387	37,129	6,712	4,902
1957	15,057	4,210	14,501	1,341	2,515	1,032	1,285	3,611	1,151	3,603	18,885	4,892	3,673
1956	16,396	4,882	18,023	1,295	2,391	1,274	1,118	3,636	1,802	3,161	21,356	7,077	5,067
1955	14,367	4,325	16,470	1,090	2,046	1,015	731	3,726	1,449	3,093	18,481	4,187	2,555
1954	15,990	4,244	15,558	1,139	2,731	1,106	633	4,425	1,231	2,667	23,579	4,565	3,984
1953	12,588	3,001	15,718	1,105	2,458	1,055	694	4,352	1,041	2,540	21,848	3,678	3,661
1952[2]	16,120	2,972	14,052	888	3,350	976	604	4,749	1,050	2,908	19,555	3,201	3,955
1951	6,817	2,669	12,206	998	2,889	120	227	4,530	817	3,281	28,396	5,654	3,429
1950	7,140	2,366	12,137	706	2,062	57	347	4,021	1,385	2,496	24,336	5,149	3,837
1949	7,399	2,123	10,201	726	2,560	62	171	3,510	887	1,852	15,656	4,174	2,785
1948	8,534	2,644	9,508	861	3,581	37	417	3,174	881	2,472	19,953	5,185	2,726
1947	6,415	1,369	8,275	702	3,035	12	441	2,319	346	2,521	12,577	2,462	3,885
1946	11,042	1,592	11,365	981	3,378	7	521	2,729	354	2,255	12,812	1,853	2,908
1945	10,590	1,452	9,783	1,030	2,554	–	509	3,088	1,316	2,185	11,268	1,939	2,601
1944	8,366	1,138	7,330	617	2,728	–	277	2,607	848	1,757	7,256	1,392	2,232
1943	7,517	1,282	5,844	820	2,571	–	279	2,663	1,257	1,654	7,202	1,371	2,398
1942	5,570	961	3,889	446	1,836	1	236	2,337	497	1,114	12,795	1,253	1,593
1941	4,037	746	2,912	218	1,502	–	169	1,909	169	973	11,425	656	1,242
1940	3,036	755	2,472	254	931	2	129	1,463	182	787	5,504	1,203	1,103
1939	2,027	659	2,934	186	1,128	2	62	1,213	369	640	5,828	508	970
1938	2,090	636	2,864	102	899	3	124	1,182	454	713	6,331	316	841
1937	2,044	637	3,750	170	701	1	279	1,422	718	796	5,276	440	927
1936	2,151	669	3,452	150	869	1	313	1,184	504	868	5,155	383	802
1935	1,822	575	3,171	148	798	–	207	1,069	256	617	6,172	287	657
1934	2,200	514	3,210	118	757	–	167	1,013	102	559	5,793	201	576
1933	1,695	331	2,296	118	548	–	161	817	224	437	4,464	469	868
1932	1,438	507	3,107	39	458	–	73	833	146	548	3,443	183	677
1931	2,041	603	3,255	140	582	–	39	1,035	141	607	3,291	633	1,156
1930	3,243	1,006	3,678	139	743	–	90	1,410	362	740	8,178	717	2,403
1929	4,038	1,053	3,847	70	1,103	–	105	1,785	155	1,148	7,310	962	3,556
1928	4,102	983	3,612	112	900	–	141	1,653	258	1,289	8,154	1,413	2,964
1927	3,448	727	3,962	88	889	–	207	1,485	125	1,066	8,195	1,342	3,343
1926	5,122	904	4,156	146	1,033	–	148	1,537	122	1,143	8,563	1,007	4,069
1925	4,517	657	3,813	68	902	–	94	1,426	207	833	7,142	992	3,122
1924	4,017	614	2,824	61	1,238	–	65	1,291	122	792	5,315	764	3,884
1923	2,744	501	4,378	95	903	–	81	1,227	130	701	5,471	903	4,235
1922	4,105	544	3,625	81	782	–	50	1,036	191	574	7,610	807	2,774
1921	3,526	474	3,068	74	635	–	30	1,364	128	502	4,483	636	3,170
1920	5,000	879	4,557	41	1,073	–	24	1,316	203	469	7,819	868	3,186
1919	8,100	1,363	3,307	96	1,094	–	71	1,355	144	490	10,603	696	2,640
1918	7,653	1,851	2,123	49	2,762	–	66	–	–	–	8,892	1,013	2,634
1917	5,994	1,610	3,285	23	1,930	–	27	–	–	–	9,678	677	1,290
1917[1]	4,042	1,220	3,477	45	1,925	–	38	–	–	–	4,827	580	943
1916	3,553	776	2,944	82	1,634	–	15	–	–	–	5,744	517	991
1915	2,727	908	2,990	23	1,910	–	–	–	–	–	5,308	609	1,070
1914	2,578	780	3,498	47	1,483	–	–	–	–	–	7,167	708	1,188
1913	1,744	772	3,308	33	1,332	–	–	–	–	–	3,648	823	953
1912	2,757	700	2,979	38	2,008	–	–	–	–	–	4,132	565	953
1911	4,328	695	2,690	18	1,605	–	–	–	–	–	2,109	363	708

1 For 1911 to 1917, fiscal years ending 31 March of the year given; 1917 to 1975, calendar years.
2 Newfoundland is included in series N25-31 beginning in 1952.
3 No effort is made to convert fish to a common landed form, with the exception of salmon.
4 Includes halibut landed in United States ports beginning in 1961.
5 Breakdown not available, included in pickerel.

Series N38-48. Number of persons engaged in primary fishing operations, by province, 1878 to 1975

Year[1]	Canada[2]	Newfound-land	Nova Scotia	Prince Edward Island	New Brunswick	Quebec	Ontario	Manitoba[3]	Saskat-chewan	Alberta	British Columbia[4]
	38	39	40	41	42	43	44	45	46	47	48
1975	–	–	–	–	–	7,164	2,220	1,688	1,651	1,279	12,578
1974	–	–	–	–	–	6,309	2,208	1,685	1,579	1,892	11,906
1973	–	15,313	–	–	–	6,083	2,215	1,827	992	370	11,117
1972	49,643	14,452	11,735	3,210	5,161	5,843	2,097	–	1,800	1,547	9,902
1971	58,845	15,961	10,688	2,677	5,269	5,823	1,999	1,394[5]	2,098	1,645	11,015
1970	61,521	17,765	11,018	2,801	5,215	5,741	1,836	1,204[5]	2,154	1,863	11,647
1969	64,983	17,770	11,717	2,965	5,511	5,856	1,959	3,835	2,100	1,966	10,942
1968	71,585	19,355	13,108	3,301	5,942	4,945	2,044	4,018	1,580	4,758	12,133
1967	71,250	19,814	12,589	3,369	5,665	4,594	2,197	4,019	1,724	4,750	12,117
1966	73,246	20,286	13,067	3,220	5,822	4,431	2,445	5,320	1,800	4,360	12,000
1965	78,157	21,701	14,049	3,566	6,241	4,664	2,544	5,440	2,000	4,507	13,000
1964	78,125	22,615	13,333	3,329	5,940	4,293	2,952	5,671	2,010	4,211	13,300
1963	81,682	21,407	13,467	3,372	5,977	4,332	3,271	5,837	1,827	5,117	16,624
1962	78,818	19,817	12,711	3,367	6,173	4,817	2,993	5,614	1,850	4,563	16,437
1961	78,360	18,756	12,578	3,464	6,228	4,944	3,059	5,018	1,750	5,422	16,805
1960	78,171	18,291	12,780	3,274	6,175	6,004	3,409	5,289	1,700	5,730	15,159
1959	80,045	18,430	13,012	3,260	6,382	6,424	3,527	5,312	1,650	6,089	15,456
1958	82,930	18,364	13,747	3,209	6,220	7,277	3,224	5,682	1,600	7,846	15,263
1957	79,044	16,469	15,265	3,000	8,167	6,712	3,066	5,395	1,500	5,941	12,999
1956[1]	74,623	14,956	14,379	2,967	9,785	6,312	3,135	5,389	997	4,277	11,851
1955	62,511	–	14,221	2,863	10,066	6,383	3,483	5,775	921	5,247	12,836
1954	63,262	–	14,864	2,794	9,703	6,272	3,567	5,970	1,066	5,324	13,038
1953	63,675	–	14,614	2,763	10,636	6,868	3,807	5,441	1,840	4,809	12,449
1952	64,342	–	15,248	2,665	10,536	6,054	3,878	6,410	2,368	5,105	13,066
1951	65,391	–	15,607	2,660	11,201	6,982	3,833	6,578	1,280	3,325	13,213
1950	65,037	–	15,723	2,895	11,621	8,031	3,886	5,904	1,322	2,825	12,159
1949	64,799	–	14,896	2,909	11,040	8,663	3,930	5,313	1,713	3,182	12,242
1948	66,115	–	14,915	3,046	10,973	9,042	3,736	6,700	1,370	3,659	12,226
1947	65,419	–	14,475	3,307	11,073	8,094	4,026	6,465	1,659	3,606	12,491
1946	73,514	–	15,860	2,960	11,074	9,980	4,244	7,293	2,173	5,588	13,665
1945	67,711	–	14,413	2,410	10,768	8,949	3,982	6,150	2,030	5,689	13,292
1944	64,208	–	13,863	2,269	10,392	8,820	3,809	6,169	2,381	4,004	12,463
1943	61,459	–	13,370	2,172	10,180	9,688	3,610	6,185	1,919	2,398	11,903
1942	61,367	–	13,452	2,267	10,481	10,566	3,336	5,557	1,581	1,897	12,199
1941	63,745	–	15,149	2,445	11,212	10,849	3,608	6,618	1,305	2,312	10,217
1940	68,817	–	17,590	2,874	12,425	13,270	4,020	4,205	1,284	2,676	10,444
1939	68,941	–	17,548	3,454	13,795	12,917	4,206	3,707	1,341	2,334	9,609
1938	71,510	–	18,548	3,309	14,130	12,684	4,170	3,819	1,547	2,954	10,314
1937	69,981	–	18,088	3,310	13,920	11,385	4,440	3,824	1,388	2,405	11,184
1936	71,735	–	18,359	3,093	14,207	13,778	4,280	3,586	973	2,035	11,393
1935	68,557	–	17,907	3,365	12,988	14,093	3,988	3,241	710	1,265	10,965
1934	68,634	–	18,448	2,973	13,062	13,981	4,125	3,031	530	767	11,700
1933	65,506	–	17,133	3,194	12,289	13,627	3,984	2,822	614	743	11,066
1932	64,484	–	16,258	3,018	13,411	13,618	3,816	2,868	686	676	10,116
1931	61,811	–	15,527	2,431	12,764	12,743	3,865	3,437	623	911	9,495
1930	63,836	–	15,265	2,281	12,047	11,226	4,074	4,781	945	1,179	12,000
1929	64,083	–	15,747	2,202	11,920	9,944	4,043	4,687	1,313	1,516	12,675
1928	62,785	–	15,857	2,396	11,040	10,847	4,128	4,172	1,084	1,401	11,818
1927	63,415	–	16,131	2,675	10,198	10,916	4,156	4,095	970	1,161	13,076
1926	61,371	–	16,315	2,916	9,024	10,892	4,145	3,809	864	1,212	12,162
1925	58,273	–	16,266	3,017	8,939	10,711	4,263	3,390	794	914	9,944
1924	53,914	–	15,805	2,537	8,743	8,824	4,267	2,828	908	675	9,274
1923	53,517	–	16,742	2,503	9,228	8,837	3,742	2,530	572	595	8,734
1922	57,880	–	19,495	2,201	9,394	10,089	4,003	2,113	423	615	9,495
1921	55,230	–	19,292	2,075	8,152	8,494	3,600	1,889	494	538	10,623
1920	57,197	–	18,965	2,793	8,218	8,894	3,693	1,688	577	631	11,669
1919	67,804	–	22,083	3,391	10,847	10,767	4,156	2,332	733	545	12,865
1918	68,516	–	21,598	3,684	13,212	10,876	3,918	2,235	846	733	11,239
1917	72,390	–	21,767	3,450	15,726	9,657	3,705	2,192	1,661	1,032	12,967
1917[1]	69,624	–	22,126	3,465	15,672	9,115	3,592	1,728	1,477	675	11,557
1916	74,862	–	22,765	3,093	16,702	8,851	4,114	1,165	927	5,711[6]	11,310
1915	69,954	–	22,606	3,360	15,945	9,194	4,076	1,555	813	947	11,232
1914	71,776	–	22,312	3,764	15,540	9,177	3,511	1,162	645	4,130	11,316
1913	65,081	–	21,443	3,308	14,944	9,417	3,604	1,420	484	1,589	8,747
1912	65,926	–	21,661	3,206	15,239	11,080	3,196	1,919	559	320	8,608
1911	68,610	–	21,580	4,466	16,158	10,998	3,611	1,909	717	464	8,583
1910	68,663	–	23,158	3,403	14,825	10,795	3,601	639	563	732	10,811[4]
1909	71,070	–	24,521	3,499	15,600	10,893	3,263	560	476	420	11,768
1908	71,254	–	23,543	3,594	14,319	11,235	3,180	854	425	1,270	12,834
1906[1]	76,104	–	24,206	3,577	14,477	11,893	3,085	1,460	813	1,658	15,535

Series N38-48. Number of persons engaged in primary fishing operations, by province, 1878 to 1975 (concluded)

Year[1]	Canada[2]	Newfound-land	Nova Scotia	Prince Edward Island	New Brunswick	Quebec	Ontario	Manitoba[3]	Saskat-chewan	Alberta	British Columbia[4]
	38	39	40	41	42	43	44	45	46	47	48
1905	82,871	—	25,362	3,437	14,273	13,367	3,185	2,659	1,098	1,270	18,220
1904	77,345	—	24,454	3,889	13,265	12,817	3,125	4,559[3]	—[3]	—[3]	15,236
1903	79,134	—	23,398	3,706	12,442	14,875	3,003	2,573	—	—	19,137
1902	77,801	—	23,327	4,324	13,067	12,123	2,885	3,512	—	—	18,563
1901	79,370	—	23,974	4,313	12,702	12,311	2,802	2,914	—	—	20,354
1900	81,064	—	25,212	4,994	12,639	13,097	2,502	1,326	—	—	21,294
1899	79,893	—	25,171	4,753	12,974	13,250	2,430	1,039	—	—	20,246
1898	81,534	—	26,235	4,404	12,273	12,332	2,847	1,329	—	—	22,114
1897	78,959	—	25,373	4,459	11,571	12,044	3,009	1,667	—	—	20,936
1896	75,237	—	24,975	4,754	11,270	13,415	3,298	1,600	—	—	15,925
1895	71,334	—	25,615	3,758	10,389	12,243	3,259	1,585	—	—	14,485
1894	70,719	—	25,478	3,329	11,650	12,081	4,155	1,376	—	—	12,650
1893	67,753	—	23,847	3,522	11,305	11,565	2,629	953	—	—	13,932
1892	63,678	—	24,070	5,020	12,265	10,694	2,709	750	—	—	8,170
1891	65,575	—	24,376	4,026	12,222	12,530	2,920	835	—	—	8,666
1890	66,256	—	27,684	4,798	11,139	11,367	3,045	—	—	—	8,223
1889	65,003	—	27,334	4,245	10,527	11,583	3,528	—	—	—	7,786
1888	62,683	—	28,107	4,379	9,840	11,114	3,303	—	—	—	5,940
1887	64,158	—	27,991	4,059	11,087	12,105	2,762	—	—	—	6,154
1886	62,000	—	27,485	3,496	9,359	12,652	2,797	—	—	—	6,211
1885	62,821	—	29,905	3,535	10,185	13,660	2,716	—	—	—	2,820
1884	61,822	—	29,997	4,020	8,676	12,983	2,865	—	—	—	3,281
1883[7]	62,225	—	—	—	—	—	—	—	—	—	—
1882	61,283	—	28,500	4,482	9,952	12,959	2,603	—	—	—	2,787
1881	59,056	—	27,526	3,635	8,737	13,657	2,608	—	—	—	2,893
1880	60,657	—	29,276	4,031	8,566	14,771	2,130	—	—	—	1,883
1879	61,395	—	27,610	5,198	8,053	15,055	3,358	—	—	—	2,121
1878	61,337	—	26,527	5,206	8,712	14,706	3,382	—	—	—	2,804

[1] For 1878 to 1906 and for 1917 to 1975, calendar years; for 1908 to 1917, fiscal years ending 31 March of the year given. Newfoundland is included beginning in 1956.

[2] The figures shown under the provinces do not add to that shown for Canada (series N38) owing to the inclusion of data for the Yukon Territory and the Northwest Territories in series N38 and to discrepancies in some years in the official statistics.

[3] From 1891 to 1904 data for Manitoba include the Northwest Territories (Alberta and Saskatchewan).

[4] For 1888 to 1910, a number of cannery employees are included.

[5] Reported by Freshwater Fish Marketing Corporation.

[6] Includes anglers.

[7] Breakdown by provinces not available.

Series N49-58. Market value of fisheries products, by major process forms, Canada, 1870 to 1975
(thousands of dollars)

Year[1]	Total all forms[2]	Fresh[3] Whole	Fresh[3] Filleted	Frozen[3] Whole	Frozen[3] Filleted	Canned	Cured Smoked	Cured Salted and pickled	Reduction products Oil	Reduction products Meal
	49	50	51	52	53	54	55	56	57	58
1975	598,470	82,411	44,382	72,905	243,534	83,281	5,388	49,765	4,048	12,756
1974	584,521	64,506	33,871	46,411	201,372	164,750	5,762	47,130	4,903	15,816
1973	669,222	75,340	34,848	80,885	235,519	169,244	6,266	41,162	3,722	22,236
1972	483,360	70,857	32,400	57,584	177,262	88,937	4,957	30,940	2,710	17,713
1971	422,166	63,885	21,889	33,845	153,181	93,068	4,203	30,660	4,852	16,583
1970	384,429	54,513	18,306	42,277	127,616	87,706	3,646	24,419	4,751	21,195
1969	343,965	51,420	26,229	35,433	119,882	55,958	4,186	23,956	4,615	22,286
1968	346,537	49,492	18,832	32,599	100,957	94,538	3,038	24,165	4,273	18,643
1967	311,010	55,396	17,909	24,998	85,525	77,377	4,598	27,400	3,626	14,181
1966	339,238	63,749	17,010	27,806	96,646	84,753	4,779	23,561	4,568	16,366
1965	298,337	65,273	18,096	22,823	93,641	52,763	3,463	22,815	5,159	14,304
1964	274,431	52,889	21,550	23,233	71,293	59,395	3,779	25,378	4,891	12,023
1963	248,764	49,323	21,625	18,265	61,487	50,841	2,133	28,387	4,745	11,958
1962	248,265	48,403	12,744	18,491	56,220	73,113	2,168	23,219	2,834	11,073
1961	197,844	47,067	11,724	15,080	46,853	40,099	2,007	22,798	3,416	8,800
1960	198,005	51,267	11,444	15,478	42,081	41,750	1,812	23,191	2,562	4,323
1959	203,040	46,513	12,536	12,479	40,667	50,513	1,896	20,037	5,120	9,573
1958	231,541	50,064	12,657	16,373	37,229	71,597	2,090	22,284	5,881	9,895
1957	188,018	43,813	12,396	10,291	32,872	49,695	2,081	22,772	3,989	7,355
1956	196,577	47,695	12,311	15,286	30,947	45,554	2,054	22,191	6,218	11,078
1955[4]	184,167	43,326	12,839	10,700	30,380	41,494	2,910	24,670	4,806	8,772
1954	162,508	42,745	10,626	11,221	16,790	51,119	3,276	12,495	3,862	7,490
1953	149,332	40,018	11,385	12,516	12,561	46,298	2,780	12,478	3,176	6,006
1952	149,821	42,699	10,649	12,064	14,668	40,580	4,429	14,261	2,585	5,653
1951	175,894	42,362	10,216	14,674	12,541	61,133	4,217	13,344	6,900	7,452
1950	153,119	43,708	9,457	15,714	8,529	43,063	3,946	13,620	5,496	6,534
1949	132,307	31,841	7,702	12,106	6,408	37,228	3,616	16,249	6,561	7,621
1948	139,826	34,093	7,593	12,905	7,380	42,269	3,366	16,068	7,891	5,493
1947	123,900	28,804	6,028	12,498	4,547	47,039	3,088	11,697	4,800	2,767
1946	121,125	30,895	7,810	8,862	8,972	39,129	4,556	12,632	3,935	1,447
1945	113,871	34,703	8,463	6,731	6,596	34,481	3,648	9,445	6,026	1,976
1944	89,440	29,585[3]	10,605[3]	—[3]	—[3]	26,050	2,409	10,018	7,419	1,921
1943	85,595	29,817	7,901	—	—	27,293	2,671	8,887	5,558	2,145
1942	75,117	21,368	5,543	—	—	31,949	1,918	6,630	4,326	2,286
1941	62,259	18,480	3,796	—	—	26,830	1,754	5,213	3,212	1,920
1940	45,119	15,686	3,238	—	—	17,873	1,279	3,021	1,199	1,981
1939	40,076	15,366	1,871	—	—	15,479	1,022	3,548	726	1,230
1938	40,493	14,971	1,983	—	—	16,298	1,038	3,376	850	1,151
1937	38,976	15,888	1,928	—	—	13,620	1,018	3,471	1,183	1,151
1936	39,165	14,787	1,897	—	—	15,565	998	3,451	817	1,026
1935	34,428	13,508	1,222	—	—	13,638	919	3,261	652	689
1934	34,022	11,756	1,135	—	—	14,208	883	4,234	504	663
1933	27,497	11,303	890	—	—	10,194	549	3,353	276	426
1932	25,957	11,021	779	—	—	9,789	633	2,448	260	566
1931	30,517	13,619	847	—	—	9,049	766	4,375	426	895
1930	47,804	18,107	1,256	—	—	18,444	1,241	5,848	1,108	1,094
1929	53,519	22,059	1,077	—	—	17,047	1,871	7,755	1,845	1,013
1928	55,051	21,193	894	—	—	18,445	1,709	8,689	2,121	1,237
1927	49,497	20,468	593	—	—	16,616	1,607	6,841	1,595	1,051
1926	56,361	21,402	221	—	—	21,642	2,280	8,188	1,215	607
1925	47,942	18,464	166	—	—	17,412	1,569	8,627	728	246
1924	44,534	19,908	84	—	—	14,154	1,243	7,987	471	92
1923	42,566	19,516	84	—	—	14,832	1,195	5,819	367	44
1922	41,800	16,718	61	—	—	15,418	1,079	7,629	236	49
1921	34,932	17,399	35	—	—	9,886	954	6,021	66	27
1920	49,241	17,725	29	—	—	19,755	1,902	8,504	646	15
1919	56,514	20,209	75	—	—	19,734	1,350	13,517	979	10
1918	60,251	22,074	67	—	—	18,780	1,556	15,424	1,699	25
1917	52,312	18,438	26	—	—	19,565	1,237	11,664	824	10
1917[1]	39,208	15,912	39	—	—	12,455	1,017	8,630	510	16
1916	35,861	15,222	18	—	—	11,380	847	7,515	371	6
1915	31,265	13,534	—	—	—	9,363	955	6,336	405	4
1914	33,208	13,386	—	—	—	11,587	748	6,351	445	16
1913	33,390	13,274	—	—	—	11,040	675	7,084	633	—
1912	34,668	12,446	—	—	—	11,502	933	8,120	789	—
1911	29,965	10,171	—	—	—	8,155	748	9,378	327	—
1910	29,629	10,412	—	—	—	9,356	511	7,855	200	—
1909	25,451	8,819	—	—	—	7,004	387	7,726	252	—
1908	25,499	9,526	—	—	—	6,764	432	7,347	539	—
1906[1]	26,280	10,208	—	—	—	6,464	611	7,589	254	—

Series N49-58. Market value of fisheries products, by major process forms, Canada, 1870 to 1975 (concluded)
(thousands of dollars)

Year[1]	Total all forms[2]	Fresh[3]		Frozen[3]		Canned	Cured		Reduction products	
		Whole	Filleted	Whole	Filleted		Smoked	Salted and pickled	Oil	Meal
	49	50	51	52	53	54	55	56	57	58
1905	29,480	10,317	–	–	–	9,432	589	7,684	260	–
1904	23,516	9,032	–	–	–	5,077	563	7,404	209	–
1903	23,102	8,691	–	–	–	5,163	448	7,269	226	–
1902	21,959	8,331	–	–	–	4,980	455	6,750	230	–
1901	25,737	8,132	–	–	–	8,100	513	7,405	227	–
1900	21,558	7,142	–	–	–	5,140	321	7,226	209	–
1899	21,892	7,375	–	–	–	5,809	417	6,705	235	–
1898	19,667	7,670	–	–	–	4,621	377	5,686	200	–
1897	22,784	7,369	–	–	–	7,196	266	6,689	163	–
1896	20,407	6,731	–	–	–	4,544	305	7,287	225	–
1895	20,199	6,395	–	–	–	4,599	234	7,263	248	–
1894	20,720	6,765	–	–	–	4,180	192	7,629	298	–
1893	20,687	6,838	–	–	–	4,854	120	7,025	322	–
1892	18,941	6,866	–	–	–	3,136	330	6,896	360	–
1891	18,978	5,618	–	–	–	3,542	623	7,392	359	–
1890	17,715	5,745	–	–	–	3,812	353	6,305	315	–
1889	17,655	5,817	–	–	–	3,718	673	6,006	408	–
1888	17,419	6,345	–	–	–	2,326	379	7,129	391	–
1887	18,386	6,303	–	–	–	2,663	405	7,777	405	–
1886	18,679	5,621	–	–	–	3,281	291	7,962	508	–
1885	17,723	4,522	–	–	–	3,078	411	8,499	492	–
1884	17,766	4,453	–	–	–	3,071	542	8,510	477	–
1883	16,958	4,338	–	–	–	3,072	376	7,904	666	–
1882	16,824	4,090	–	–	–	4,280	325	6,977	630	–
1881	15,817	2,743	–	–	–	4,064	297	7,463	670	–
1880	14,500	–	–	–	–	–	–	–	–	–
1879	13,529	–	–	–	–	–	–	–	–	–
1878	13,216	–	–	–	–	–	–	–	–	–
1877	12,006	–	–	–	–	–	–	–	–	–
1876	11,117	–	–	–	–	–	–	–	–	–
1875	10,350	–	–	–	–	–	–	–	–	–
1874	11,682	–	–	–	–	–	–	–	–	–
1873	10,755	–	–	–	–	–	–	–	–	–
1872	9,570	–	–	–	–	–	–	–	–	–
1871	7,573	–	–	–	–	–	–	–	–	–
1870	6,577	–	–	–	–	–	–	–	–	–

[1] For 1870 to 1906 and for 1917 to 1975, calendar years; for 1908 to 1917, fiscal years ending 31 March of the year given.
[2] Excludes animal foods, bones, fertilizer, glue, livers, roes, scales, fish skins, solubles, sounds, tongues and cheeks.
[3] For 1944 and previous years, frozen whole and frozen filleted, series N52 and N53 are included with fresh whole and fresh filleted, series N50 and N51 respectively.
[4] Newfoundland included beginning in 1955.

Series N59-64. Fish processing plant inputs, 1917 to 1975
(thousands of dollars)

Year[1]	East coast[1]			West coast		
	Salaries and wages paid	Materials used	Fuel and electricity used	Salaries and wages paid	Materials used	Fuel and electricity used
	59	60	61	62	63	64
1975	80,876	167,153	9,997	39,462	81,095	1,662
1974	83,144	204,302	8,897	33,985	124,518	1,262
1973	77,606	193,690	6,159	29,856	150,739	1,066
1972	62,362	158,347	5,449	25,702	93,963	951
1971	56,022	147,128	4,727	18,187	72,290	738
1970	53,203	148,543	4,735	18,198	68,938	712
1969	49,801	141,439	4,910	16,402	60,604	754
1968	44,795	129,415	4,114	19,377	78,292	912
1967	39,606	113,559	3,305	17,498	73,018	881
1966	37,309	108,986	3,022	18,783	83,170	1,185
1965	32,717	106,910	2,958	15,838	58,661	1,143
1964	27,419	92,011	2,543	15,235	56,597	1,195
1963	25,477	81,209	2,448	13,919	49,060	1,466
1962	22,973	73,213	2,126	14,677	62,715	1,335
1961	20,189	61,269	2,012	10,244	49,424	939
1960	22,226	85,757	2,212	9,620	38,341	706
1959	19,673	82,053	2,072	10,421	47,729	1,094
1958	18,879	73,695	1,942	11,407	68,282	1,124
1957	18,392	71,691	2,171	10,817	43,425	963
1956	18,476	70,955	2,054	10,458	49,535	960
1955	16,527	61,215	1,833	9,793	40,706	830
1954	15,139	52,969	1,669	10,862	42,663	936
1953	13,773	46,426	1,575	9,320	39,482	836
1952	14,360	51,295	1,697	10,066	35,163	836
1951[1]	13,396	49,975	1,792	11,349	51,646	932
1950	9,278	40,662	968	9,445	39,297	805
1949	8,685	36,490	969	8,285	32,600	762
1948	9,021	39,344	1,100	8,020	35,244	682
1947	7,949	32,088	823	7,912	30,693	588
1946	7,996	40,180	643	6,749	27,833	461

Year[1]	East coast[1]			West coast		
	Salaries and wages paid	Materials used	Fuel and electricity used	Salaries and wages paid	Materials used	Fuel and electricity used
	59	60	61	62	63	64
1945	6,332	34,443	538	5,635	27,621	436
1944	5,406	24,505	482	5,664	21,402	428
1943	4,605	22,367	404	5,435	21,000	446
1942	3,484	14,261	298	4,907	23,485	463
1941	2,729	10,176	262	4,008	19,936	378
1940	2,233	8,184	201	3,174	13,278	284
1939	1,916	7,092	168	2,431	11,023	222
1938	1,762	6,633	177	2,466	10,449	230
1937	1,774	6,859	158	2,268	9,460	239
1936	1,601	6,666	139	2,403	9,794	249
1935	1,464	5,832	155	2,090	8,941	190
1934	1,421	5,979	134	2,134	9,588	190
1933	1,199	4,252	121	1,826	6,708	144
1932	1,312	4,989	134	1,510	5,274	141
1931	1,608	6,387	164	1,575	5,533	150
1930	1,854	7,929	168	3,472	13,153	281
1929	1,923	8,676	201	3,489	12,821	270
1928	1,773	7,671	208	3,488	12,908	287
1927	1,649	6,996	187	3,725	11,369	278
1926	1,749	7,830	186	3,874	14,204	291
1925	1,620	7,044	173	3,352	11,636	239
1924	1,443	5,939	141	2,792	10,150	259
1923	1,448	6,560	169	2,322	8,771	198
1922	1,489	6,844	194	2,153	8,735	227
1921	1,331	5,280	198	1,639	6,410	214
1920	1,866	8,906	228	2,988	10,442	353
1919	1,658	8,424	185	2,597	10,896	299
1918	1,676	9,425	166	2,953	12,083	391
1917	1,876	—	177	1,747	—	202

[1] Newfoundland included beginning in 1951.

Series N65-68. Number of persons employed in fish processing plants, by area and by sex, 1895 to 1975

Year[1]	East coast[2]		West coast	
	Male	Female	Male	Female
	65	**66**	**67**	**68**
1975	7,121	4,125	1,701	1,250
1974	9,166	5,070	1,941	1,472
1973	11,224	5,766	2,067	1,635
1972	10,374	5,132	2,126	1,432
1971	10,285	4,710	1,635	964
1970	10,650	4,879	1,709	1,075
1969	10,564	4,948	1,743	982
1968	10,352	4,749	2,231	1,211
1967	9,815	4,094	2,115	1,037
1966	9,788	4,189	2,231	1,159
1965	9,155	3,814	2,329	990
1964	8,203	3,379	2,423	1,025
1963	7,998	3,314	2,451	918
1962	7,609	3,153	2,632	1,061
1961	7,441	3,065	2,630	1,000
1960	8,609	3,187	1,718	954
1959	8,183	2,965	2,007	1,006
1958	8,205	3,007	1,989	1,071
1957	8,006	2,943	2,194	1,064
1956	8,618	3,215	2,346	1,072
1955	7,926	3,285	2,357	1,058
1954	7,377	2,879	2,848	1,098
1953	7,560	2,779	2,275	1,127
1952	9,027	4,475	2,579	1,470
1951[2]	9,295	4,807	3,051	1,553
1950	7,010	3,944	2,812	1,095
1949	7,388	4,479	3,029	1,191
1948	7,511	4,806	2,818	1,362
1947	7,218	4,191	3,283	1,766
1946	8,191	5,126	3,263	2,816
1945	6,850	4,613	3,110	2,928
1944	6,366	4,756	3,462	2,688
1943	5,775	4,113	3,190	2,821
1942	5,183	3,578	3,410	3,546
1941	4,751	3,177	3,997	3,917
1940	4,450	3,151	4,332	3,111
1939	4,520	4,023	3,824	2,447
1938	4,451	3,930	3,445	2,658
1937	4,545	3,916	3,229	2,354
1936	4,714	3,928	3,859	2,737

Year[1]	East coast[2]		West coast	
	Male	Female	Male	Female
	65	**66**	**67**	**68**
1935	4,365	3,931	3,566	2,499
1934	4,634	3,942	3,714	2,512
1933	4,331	3,921	3,523	2,267
1932	4,644	4,374	2,789	1,917
1931	4,679	3,947	2,828	1,617
1930	4,584	3,791	4,729	2,618
1929	4,701	3,906	5,375	2,385
1928	4,540	3,718	5,090	2,086
1927	4,605	3,846	5,725	2,521
1926	4,854	4,118	5,908	2,528
1925	4,681	4,153	4,910	2,528
1924	4,579	4,051	4,956	1,950
1923	4,845	4,479	4,173	1,950
1922	5,621	4,638	4,194	2,124
1921	4,905	4,141	3,232	1,819
1920	6,637	4,645	5,073	2,139
1919	6,171	4,242	5,379	2,559
1918	5,717	3,857	6,149	2,769
1917	6,442	3,916	5,971	1,653
1917[1]	18,496		6,798	
1916	20,464		6,510	
1915	17,137		7,096	
1914	17,199		9,391	
1913	16,190		6,881	
1912	17,809		6,559	
1911	16,053		8,525	
1910	12,805		8,689	
1909	13,353		—	
1908	11,441[3]		—	
1906[1]	12,317		—	
1905	14,037		—	
1904	13,981		—	
1903	14,018		—	
1902	13,563		—	
1901	15,315		—	
1900	18,205		—	
1899	18,708		—	
1898	16,548		—	
1897	15,165		—	
1896	14,175		—	
1895	13,030		—	

[1] For 1895 to 1906 and for 1917 to 1975, calendar years; for 1908 to 1917, fiscal years ending 31 March of the year given.

[2] Newfoundland included in series N65 and N66 beginning in 1951.

[3] Only those employed in lobster canneries included from 1895 to 1908.

Series N69-82. Number of fish processing establishments by area and by value of output, 1919 to 1974

Year[1]	East coast Establishments having production valued at							West coast Establishments having production valued at						
	Under $10,000	$10,000–$19,999	$20,000–$49,999	$50,000–$199,999	$200,000–$999,999	$1,000,000 and under $5,000,000	$5,000,000 and over	Under $10,000	$10,000–$19,999	$20,000–$49,999	$50,000–$199,999	$200,000–$999,999	$1,000,000 and under $5,000,000	$5,000,000 and over
	69	**70**	**71**	**72**	**73**	**74**	**75**	**76**	**77**	**78**	**79**	**80**	**81**	**82**
1974	5		29[2]	52	108	63	15			22[3]			15	8
1973	8		27	42	91	68	17			20			16	10
1972	16		28	48	104	64	10			24			17	7
1971	7		35	48	112	62	8			20			15	6
1970	10		25	59	112	61	8			17			14	7
1969	13		38	64	103	61	4			21			14	6
1968	23		43	69	100	54	4			23			16	8
1967	20		53	77	99	48[4]				26			–	6
1966	21		48	84	83	52				26			17	7
1965	30		54	82	85	50				25			21	4
1964	27		68	83	76	43				26			16	5
1963	31		66	82	82	34				27			16	4
1962	37		63	83	74	31				22			18	5
1961	43		72	79	76	24				28			12	5
1960	60	45	77	161	111	24	–	1	3	5	7	24	12	3
1959	71	32	81	173	104	20	1	1	3	3	8	19	17	4[5]
1958	88	26	84	174	96	23	–	1	4	4	10	18	15	5
1957	86	27	66	172	95	21	–	2	2	6	8	21	15	2
1956	105	41	69	199	90	21	–	2	5	6	6	27	13	4
1955	107	53	89	157	66	20	–	8	5	9	9	21	18	2
1954	119	58	96	158	62	19	–	5	5	16	16	19	19	2
1953	111	68	102	155	70	12	–	3	6	17	13	22	14	3
1952	106	67	134	164	73	12	–	2	7	11	21	22	14	1
1951[1]	130	65	142	153	65	16	–	9	–	7	12	18	20	3
1950	118	58	129	161	45	11	–	3	2	7	13	23	17	3
1949	116	70	140	151	45	9	–	3	1	7	8	29	17	1
1948	114	67	150	151	45	10	–	1	2	5	9	28	16	1
1947	109	94	142	128	42	9	–	3	4	3	14	28	17	1
1946	86	75	145	149	50	8	–	2	2	7	19	31	11	1
1945	84	73	122	146	36	8	–	2	2	5	15	39	9	–
1944	104	81	140	112	18	7	–	2	–	4	20	37	9	–
1943	102	92	131	104	20	5	–	1	–	3	20	38	7	–
1942	146	93	105	69	10	4	–	1	1	5	15	33	9	1
1941	179	89	78	34	8	4	–	2	1	7	18	35	8	–
1940	225	64	56	25	8	2	–	6	–	–	24	34	3	–
1939	293	86	51	17	7	2	–	6	3	–	20	25	4	–
1938	326	92	45		23[6]			6	4	7		58[6]		
1937	347	81	61		23			9	12	10		54		
1936	363	91	53		26			9	9	16		57		
1935	377	95	48		19			12	7	14		58		
1934	392	99	55		20			14	6	17		62		
1933	399	68	41		16			19	6	18		53		
1932	360	102	57		21			14	9	17		49		
1931	372	105	53		33			7	10	29		53		
1930	344	118	69		40			10	10	20		88		
1929	339	128	79		45			9	6	31		93		
1928	350	116	74		37			6	10	17		103		
1927	396	109	81		38			11	10	24		104		
1926	431	138	65		39			25	6	31		96		
1925	457	151	64		29			27	9	22		87		
1924	519	108	44		31			23	13	21		73		
1923	550	161	71		27			23	21	12		73		
1922	513	160	79		32			38	21	21		60		
1921	552	90	61		33			21	8	14		60		
1920	515	161	116		39			11	14	10		72		
1919	509	162	98		53			9	5	11		70		

[1] Newfoundland plants included beginning in 1951.
[2] Establishments having production valued at $10,000 to $49,999.
[3] Establishments having production valued at $999,999 and under.
[4] Establishments having production valued at $1,000,000 and over.
[5] Includes one head office with no value.
[6] Establishments having production valued at $50,000 and over.

Series N83-89. Value of exports of fish and fish products, by region, 1868 to 1975
(thousands of dollars)

Year[1]	Total exports	United Kingdom	Other Europe	Continental South America	Central America and Caribbean	United States and possessions	Other
	83	84	85	86	87	88	89
1975	447,868	—	—	—	—	—	—
1974	408,500	—	—	—	—	—	—
1973	472,859	49,810	56,554	941	10,334	287,341	67,879
1972	346,171	26,782	37,523	563	10,070	224,673	46,560
1971	291,788	21,148	32,798	443	11,232	195,202	30,965
1970	278,425	13,954	25,126	916	12,774	186,645	39,010
1969	279,240	28,507	23,453	608	13,711	177,018	35,943
1968	257,951	29,079	19,615	1,093	12,984	164,372	30,808
1967	235,445	32,752	28,362	1,967	14,841	148,352	9,171
1966	221,172	22,204	20,811	1,697	15,283	154,395	6,782
1965	215,324	22,719	18,700	1,412	13,516	152,632	6,345
1964	205,651	28,607	20,653	2,011	15,811	132,725	5,844
1963	173,827	18,090	16,030	1,370	13,005	119,574	5,758
1962	156,616	14,125	8,584	1,312	12,277	117,285	3,033
1961	143,316	12,964	7,157	1,379	10,754	107,532	3,530
1960	138,130	11,525	6,482	1,295	12,215	102,472	4,123
1959	147,816	22,363	6,345	1,678	13,054	101,468	2,908
1958	154,469	25,453	6,171	1,419	11,425	106,826	3,175
1957	132,454	7,731	5,610	1,457	12,744	100,926	3,986
1956	133,707	8,800	6,501	1,003	13,309	99,991	4,103
1955	128,844	5,783	9,062	1,202	11,666	96,445	4,685
1954[2]	132,642	12,005	9,247	2,768	12,274	93,031	3,317
1953	114,376	5,249	8,443	791	11,086	87,141	1,666
1952	116,754	1,312	7,782	1,118	11,762	92,266	2,514
1951	123,045	8,078	10,828	1,602	10,127	89,530	2,880
1950	117,785	5,051	14,490	1,247	9,647	85,363	1,986
1949	99,530	8,081	8,185	2,051	9,951	69,048	2,213
1948	89,697	1,830	9,825	1,299	6,942	62,785	7,017
1947	83,811	6,760	10,719	1,518	6,187	46,692	11,936
1946	88,679	13,321	12,634	879	4,036	53,740	4,070
1945	84,801	13,794	4,538	575	3,670	54,098	8,126
1944	68,643	18,332	310	497	3,639	42,830	3,035
1943	60,313	17,678	199	365	2,544	37,467	2,061
1942	51,907	19,855	3	561	2,302	27,652	1,534
1941	42,964	15,349	47	622	2,727	21,655	2,563
1940	32,662	9,884	302	284	1,474	16,963	3,755
1939	29,641	8,718	1,524	267	1,387	13,964	3,780
1938	27,544	6,881	2,001	352	1,420	12,917	3,972
1937	28,902	6,722	1,962	337	1,463	14,229	4,189
1936	25,398	5,782	1,589	209	1,184	13,036	3,599
1935	24,860	6,760	1,726	217	1,389	10,657	4,112
1934	22,497	5,542	2,646	161	1,508	9,539	3,100
1933	20,224	4,384	2,878	166	1,088	9,038	2,671
1932	18,752	4,221	1,822	160	1,207	8,943	2,400
1931	25,849	5,708	2,754	259	1,710	11,920	3,498
1931[1]	29,695	5,181	3,805	516	2,368	14,250	3,574
1930	37,185	4,178	5,254	952	3,242	17,102	6,458
1929	37,963	3,781	5,832	1,037	3,012	17,845	6,457
1928	35,660	5,448	4,692	1,056	2,982	15,743	5,740
1927	36,366	5,613	4,428	894	2,993	16,386	6,051
1926	37,488	7,265	4,750	1,070	3,112	14,929	6,361
1925	33,967	6,710	4,497	832	2,875	14,542	4,512
1924	30,926	5,801	4,041	701	2,187	14,195	4,000
1923	27,817	3,757	4,154	965	2,287	14,169	2,485
1922	29,578	5,593	3,942	1,109	2,712	13,816	2,406
1921	33,615	7,703	1,614	1,783	3,123	16,929	2,463
1920	42,228	9,891	3,455	2,277	4,286	19,871	2,448
1919	37,137	8,634	1,790	1,009	3,890	19,572	2,242
1918	32,602	6,746	4,001	768	2,768	16,853	1,466
1917	24,889	7,317	1,671	970	2,289	11,401	1,242
1916	22,378	6,732	1,696	1,206	1,857	9,503	1,384
1915	19,687	5,449	1,600	605	1,579	8,994	1,460
1914	20,624	7,009	2,054	849	1,818	7,392	1,501
1913	16,337	3,947	1,809	1,041	1,876	6,326	1,339
1912	16,705	5,132	1,594	917	1,951	6,031	1,080
1911	15,676	4,436	1,526	1,171	2,048	5,484	1,011
1910	15,663	5,136	1,629	1,009	1,666	5,096	1,126
1909	13,320	3,580	1,513	798	1,657	4,740	1,032
1908	13,867	3,503	1,459	1,100	1,742	5,212	852
1907[1]	10,362	2,411	1,090	861	1,397	3,869	735
1906[1]	16,026	6,140	1,362	918	1,739	5,319	548
1905	11,114	2,525	1,031	607	1,408	4,955	589
1904	10,759	3,085	1,053	514	1,186	4,601	320
1903	11,800	3,905	1,194	880	1,334	4,164	323
1902	14,143	6,375	756	724	1,247	4,606	435
1901	10,720	3,113	860	666	1,263	4,498	320
1900	11,169	4,071	798	675	1,317	4,050	258
1899	9,910	3,611	734	557	1,705	3,184	118
1898	10,842	4,823	536	628	1,686	2,980	190
1897	10,314	4,366	462	518	1,887	2,999	82
1896	11,078	4,462	344	773	2,135	3,303	61
1895	10,692	4,144	210	796	2,424	3,027	92
1894	11,103	4,587	324	682	2,097	3,261	153
1893	8,743	2,347	279	569	1,997	3,504	47
1892	9,675	3,007	366	482	2,269	3,452	99
1891	9,715	2,748	285	543	2,082	3,809	250
1890	8,462	2,707	327	481	2,001	2,851	95
1889	7,212	1,250	353	488	2,093	2,840	188
1888	7,793	1,545	375	456	2,116	3,124	177
1887	6,876	1,704	302	539	1,527	2,718	86
1886	6,843	1,587	532	442	1,645	2,588	50
1885	7,960	1,543	300	393	2,040	3,561	123
1884	8,592	1,622	393	462	2,454	3,598	62
1883	8,809	2,337	297	547	2,362	3,190	76
1882	7,682	2,130	265	569	2,223	2,441	54
1881	6,868	1,563	218	577	2,257	2,242	11
1880	6,580	1,154	279	588	2,759	1,739	60
1879	6,929	1,495	302	515	2,645	1,899	73
1878	6,854	1,044	236	507	2,556	2,367	145
1877	5,874	808	311	507	2,827	1,318	104
1876	5,501	687	197	488	2,558	1,475	96
1875	5,381	653	196	210	2,615	1,645	61
1874	5,292	701	316	438	2,159	1,617	62
1873	4,779	483	—	—	—	—	—
1872	4,386	380	—	—	—	—	—
1871	3,994	349	—	—	—	—	—
1870	3,609	321	—	—	—	—	—
1869	3,243	236	—	—	—	—	—
1868	3,358	227	—	—	—	—	—

[1] For 1868 to 1906, fiscal years ending 30 June of the year given; nine months ending 31 March 1907; for 1908 to 1931, fiscal years ending 31 March of the year given; for 1931 to 1975, calendar years.

[2] Newfoundland exports included beginning in 1954.

Series N90-100. Value of exports of fish and fish products, by major species, 1871 to 1973
(thousands of dollars)

Year[1]	Groundfish	Halibut	Herring and pilchards	Sardines and anchovies	Salmon	Whitefish	Lobster Fresh	Lobster Canned	All other shellfish	Oil and meal[2]	All other
	90	91	92	93	94	95	96	97	98	99	100
1973	101,624	8,422	25,440	7,279	124,175	6,879	39,874	1,778	27,943	12,466	116,979
1972	81,736	8,941	20,477	2,386	69,696	6,950	36,954	1,417	23,448	7,953	86,213
1971	80,107	8,677	15,191	2,960	49,179	5,742	34,476	1,499	19,855	13,637	60,465
1970	74,264	8,931	11,579	5,766	38,384	5,727	29,614	1,837	20,705	17,947	63,671
1969	69,681	10,302	6,456	5,893	55,484	5,642	27,822	1,879	19,903	13,738	62,440
1968	66,323	6,978	6,443	5,972	51,427	5,566	24,166	1,704	18,956	10,357	60,059
1967	61,793	6,762	4,105	6,189	53,172	5,355	23,293	1,939	10,598	9,476	52,763
1966	68,477	8,734	4,983	5,502	36,475	5,953	22,160	2,591	9,722	10,224	46,351
1965	53,748	8,780	5,203	4,754	32,417	6,296	25,731	2,491	10,965	11,333	53,606
1964	53,348	6,771	4,555	4,961	39,843	5,842	22,659	2,702	9,279	12,195	43,483
1963	48,902	6,873	4,223	3,523	30,591	5,967	20,418	1,788	6,861	8,818	35,874
1962	42,866	8,202	4,200	2,613	25,626	6,963	19,727	2,539	5,186	7,146	31,553
1961	40,886	7,442	3,725	3,617	22,041	6,930	18,781	2,063	4,005	5,140	28,717
1960	45,190	6,536	4,050	3,523	20,348	7,083	17,702	2,453	3,112	5,847	22,286
1959	44,075	6,115	3,893	2,953	30,950	6,318	17,259	1,925	2,047	9,052	23,230
1958	45,849	6,254	3,662	2,798	41,323	6,472	15,590	1,822	1,808	5,168	23,725
1957	45,442	5,330	3,854	2,276	18,047	6,236	16,414	2,063	1,936	7,121	23,736
1956	42,420	4,595	3,634	2,117	21,444	5,928	16,846	2,073	1,630	9,834	23,187
1955	42,441	3,580	3,353	1,666	23,007	5,836	16,714	1,843	1,686	7,879	20,840
1954[3]	39,867	4,704	3,990	1,585	32,493	5,973	13,697	1,921	1,701	6,380	20,332
1953	35,361	3,886	3,937	1,405	23,178	6,209	13,769	1,967	1,850	4,284	18,531
1952	37,084	4,198	4,877	3,070	17,679	6,429	14,104	2,352	1,048	7,132	18,782
1951	38,515	4,228	5,304	1,767	20,802	6,357	11,798	2,214	1,196	11,085	19,777
1950	34,174	5,025	4,642	1,545	22,921	5,672	11,533	2,906	1,268	9,561	18,539
1949	26,414	2,995	4,696	1,959	18,314	4,985	10,116	2,353	1,001	10,916	15,781
1948	16,835	3,148	10,985	2,828	17,245	3,983	9,182	2,382	808	7,829	14,472
1947	12,965	3,464	17,194	3,870	16,835	2,904	7,627	2,438	907	1,452	14,155
1946	18,081	1,056	17,398	1,039	16,433	3,585	9,572	3,781	809	2,192	14,734
1945	18,196	1,607	12,304	362	13,640	3,587	9,518	2,690	804	4,653	17,440
1944	13,816	807	10,005	269	12,901	3,496	5,787	3,147	502	5,273	12,640
1943	8,954	1,585	9,574	51	13,924	3,404	4,331	2,243	350	3,192	12,706
1942	8,215	592	7,950	530	15,658	2,680	3,005	929	349	3,697	8,302
1941	5,848	730	6,267	1,114	13,378	2,216	2,463	739	273	3,115	6,820
1940	5,039	680	2,797	954	9,954	2,032	2,017	715	131	2,480	5,864
1939	3,289	1,203	1,917	725	10,772	1,444	2,011	1,431	100	1,543	5,206
1938	2,673	910	1,215	629	9,478	1,515	1,953	1,899	176	1,774	5,322
1937	2,865	680	1,168	694	9,946	1,606	2,438	1,984	308	1,730	5,484
1936	2,862	595	1,205	472	8,407	1,459	2,101	2,080	305	1,040	4,874
1935	2,835	486	1,261	448	9,461	1,260	1,641	2,275	238	601	4,353
1934	3,131	393	1,065	383	7,748	977	1,550	2,499	154	821	3,776
1933	2,720	339	1,072	227	6,871	988	1,606	2,451	167	444	3,340
1932	2,455	111	853	183	5,675	854	1,854	2,470	130	758	3,409
1931	3,743	392	1,834	292	7,995	1,004	1,876	3,113	159	1,075	4,367
1930	5,695	465	2,508	413	8,819	1,215	2,279	3,235	265	1,678	5,297
1929	6,519	668	3,059	578	10,849	1,519	2,266	3,114	345	2,295	6,335
1928	6,637	508	3,343	537	11,566	1,402	1,515	3,107	325	2,663	6,492
1927	5,627	445	3,640	396	10,805	1,332	1,485	3,236	320	938[2]	6,589
1926	6,715	581	3,776	—	11,568	1,456	1,350	3,607	316	1,053	6,668
1926[1]	6,844	431	3,973	—	12,809	1,375	1,256	4,037	248	609	5,906
1925	6,033	593	3,375	—	12,598	1,171	1,270	2,820	250	599	5,258
1924	5,002	520	3,335	—	9,500	1,147	1,321	4,468	190	320	5,124
1923	6,196	754	2,262	—	6,249	1,111	1,042	4,808	135	235	5,026
1922	7,247	855	2,222	—	7,887	1,151	1,403	3,756	120	141	4,796
1921	7,504	913	3,479	—	8,666	1,331	1,034	5,180	115	251	5,143
1920	11,502	476	3,748	—	13,770	1,060	848	4,084	110	1,240	5,389
1919	11,398	629	3,799	—	11,538	1,078	789	2,230	5	712	4,959
1918	9,266	628	2,974	—	9,685	—	856	3,325	10	800	5,058
1917	6,856	442	1,708	—	7,119	—	1,038	3,639	4	454	3,631
1916	6,122	550	1,381	—	7,137	—	935	2,672	3	376	3,202
1915	4,662	454	1,523	—	5,697	—	849	3,014	7	349	3,133
1914	4,742	282	1,028	—	7,417	—	708	2,984	4	448	3,010
1913	4,417	147	909	—	4,028	—	629	3,049	7	628	2,524
1912	4,271	130	858	—	4,313	—	567	3,081	6	1,076	2,404
1911	4,389	139	683	—	4,092	—	529	2,736	2	456	2,650
1910	3,620	84	1,074	—	4,888	—	528	2,619	3	386	2,461
1909	3,348	137	988	—	3,002	—	463	2,755	2	441	2,183
1908	3,715	107	653	—	3,438	—	481	2,652	4	259	2,559
1907[1]	3,102	58	624	—	2,551	—	164	1,369	4	153	2,339
1906[1]	3,548	35	616	—	5,707	—	498	3,010	2	112	2,498

Series N90-100. Value of exports of fish and fish products, by major species, 1871 to 1973 (concluded)
(thousands of dollars)

Year[1]	Groundfish	Halibut	Herring and pilchards	Sardines and anchovies	Salmon	Whitefish	Lobster		All other shellfish	Oil and meal[2]	All other
							Fresh	Canned			
	90	91	92	93	94	95	96	97	98	99	100
1905	2,955	75	572	—	2,111	—	376	2,755	2	43	2,225
1904	2,794	77	518	—	2,032	—	385	2,520	1	47	2,386
1903	3,390	33	446	—	2,985	—	398	2,592	2	54	1,902
1902	3,202	56	529	—	5,397	—	365	2,149	3	81	2,362
1901	2,807	34	412	—	3,151	—	301	2,284	4	50	1,677
1900	2,311	43	344	—	3,058	—	306	2,373	2	51	2,682
1899	2,724	39	312	—	2,584	—	368	2,320	2	47	1,514
1898	2,595	63	356	—	3,624	—	337	2,291	2	35	1,538
1897	2,707	104	366	—	3,108	—	331	2,075	2	50	1,572
1896	3,082	85	438	—	2,802	—	341	2,146	2	38	2,148
1895	3,333	103	475	—	2,182	—	307	1,829	2	41	2,422
1894	3,163	61	482	—	2,598	—	258	2,073	2	24	2,442
1893	3,025	33	503	—	1,038	—	291	1,780	2	66	2,006
1892	3,181	34	489	—	1,415	—	255	1,655	2	54	2,592
1891	3,131	23	548	—	1,920	—	179	1,751	1	18	2,145
1890	3,029	15	472	—	2,231	—	141	998	1	41	1,535
1889	3,105	14	541	—	931	—	111	1,099	1	55	1,357
1888	3,133	11	615	—	1,155	—	109	1,221	2	41	1,507
1887	2,551	11	441	—	793	—	81	1,379	2	27	1,592
1886	2,742	13	307	—	683	—	82	1,663	6	64	1,284
1885	3,159	8	630	—	809	—	53	1,653	2	117	1,530
1884	3,840	13	713	—	1,024	—	41	1,146	1	154	1,661
1883	3,789	12	702	—	1,422	—	31	1,479	1	157	1,216
1882	3,428	7	568	—	1,113	—	14	1,432	1	161	958
1881	3,180	4	464	—	471	—	1	1,348	1	121	1,279
1880	3,564	1	456	—	547	—	1	918	1	119	974
1879	3,197	—	447	—	927	—	1	1,104	3	131	1,120
1878	3,192	—	486	—	760	—	1	927	1	132	1,356
1877	3,390	1	607	—	271	—	—	670	1	121	814
1876	3,041	1	596	—	222	—	—	572	1	131	937
1875	2,725	1	532	—	383	—	2	593	—	89	1,056
1874	2,884	25	391	—	400	—	—	524	1	130	939
1873	2,755	—	381	—	215	—	6	278	47	127	972
1872	—	—	—	—	203	—	—	—	—	75	—
1871	—	—	—	—	258	—	—	—	—	80	—

[1] For years 1871 to 1906, fiscal years ending 30 June of the year given; nine months ending 31 March 1907; for 1908 to 1926, fiscal years ending 31 March of the year given; for 1926 to 1973, calendar years.

[2] Oil only is included for 1871 to 1927.
[3] Newfoundland exports included beginning in 1954.

Series N101-113. Value of imports of fish and fish products, by major species, 1873 to 1973
(thousands of dollars)

Year[1]	Total	Ground-fish[2]	Halibut	Herring and pilchards	Sardines and anchovies	Salmon	Tuna	Lobster Fresh	Lobster Canned	Oyster	All other shellfish	Oil and meal[3]	All other[4]
	101	102	103	104	105	106	107	108	109	110	111	112	113
1973	111,274	4,248	1,483	935	3,386	4,374	21,800	9,594	—	3,054	42,343	545	19,512
1972	81,574	2,021	2,822	693	2,474	3,602	11,900	7,373	—	3,115	33,411	655	13,508
1971	60,860	1,782	1,478	771	2,161	5,152	8,175	4,349	—	2,297	24,098	752	9,845
1970	54,458	—	1,561	979	1,816	4,515	7,398	3,449	—	2,099	21,852	628	10,161
1969	43,330	—	788	838	1,196	3,429	4,758	2,764	—	1,702	18,812	709	8,334
1968	35,027	—	495	840	1,080	831	5,747	2,423	—	1,544	15,712	586	5,769
1967	36,781	—	1,242	852	1,411	1,774	7,014	1,748	—	1,524	14,137	885	6,194
1966	31,305	—	1,220	864	1,405	3,471	4,453	1,980	—	1,125	10,765	1,004	5,018
1965	27,875	—	803	925	1,526	2,087	2,920	1,556	—	1,133	10,339	1,001	5,585
1964	23,184	—	808	879	1,319	930	2,497	1,223	—	1,013	7,847	941	5,727
1963	22,815	—	565	993	1,252	1,721	2,243	825	—	1,091	7,862	3,959	2,304
1962	21,914	—	280	939	1,322	702	2,561	215	—	1,052	6,893	4,529	3,421
1961	20,643	210	479	868	1,491	1,342	1,569	287	27	1,061	5,131	2,951	5,227
1960	17,213	166	270	871	1,217	1,215	1,472	217	22	961	5,164	1,251	4,387
1959	16,352	197	282	830	1,364	483	1,494	376	37	959	2,583	992	6,755
1958	17,482	120	220	998	1,389	2,574	1,028	156	31	933	2,482	1,745	5,809
1957	16,542	167	390	791	1,372	3,648	819	215	43	886	2,055	824	5,332
1956	17,490	196	394	765	1,189	5,207	815	218	73	841	2,423	902	4,470
1955	12,612	127	308	741	1,377	289	468	225	74	660	2,081	2,521	3,742
1954[5]	10,848	102	256	612	1,071	346	645	223	68	639	1,347	1,837	3,701
1953	9,115	67	181	481	1,101	150	123	196	125	669	1,560	1,204	3,256
1952	7,109	69	47	489	873	28	344	241	36	669	1,196	501	2,621
1951	7,485	61	236	481	1,282	190	269	188	61	617	828	779	2,494
1950	5,143	42	75	426	699	10	127	139	105	574	578	402	1,966
1949	6,398	306	93	287	760	519	94	62	42	681	1,038	761	1,754
1948	11,601	1,403	72	458	870	581	138	498	54	22	2	5,847	1,656
1947	12,952	874	30	350	720	500	248	412	41	356	225	7,418	1,778
1946	7,242	1,510	19	276	173	607	64	328	47	499	21	2,271	1,428
1945	5,696	1,227	21	135	21	313	—	290	4	437	1	2,208	1,038
1944	4,649	1,139	30	194	38	468	—	184	4	227	—	1,406	961
1943	4,262	917	37	148	38	368	—	188	20	3	—	1,742	801
1942	3,464	653	25	150	12	294	12	169	2	2	—	1,335	810
1941	3,444	423	32	85	38	457	121	43	10	49	58	1,215	914
1940	3,502	393	39	110	194	320	315	26	10	242	263	890	699
1939	3,439	95	17	142	358	333	377	67	38	239	392	673	708
1938	3,036	92	52	193	358	475	231	59	81	245	204	470	576
1937	2,877	55	39	176	319	200	172	137	69	275	225	628	584
1936	2,918	92	50	206	369	230	189	22	200	242	249	540	532
1935	2,598	61	63	182	360	119	116	2	91	212	147	734	511
1934	2,123	170	48	126	287	266	—	1	75	191	125	310	522
1933	1,694	35	21	146	251	138	—	1	80	183	137	232	471
1932	1,862	82	40	202	294	121	—	1	41	221	52	181	628
1931	2,654	178	78	224	453	161	—	1	95	302	38	241	883
1930	3,447	327	118	350	525	194	—	3	80	383	—	265	1,202
1929	4,234	404	164	402	789	233	—	6	108	482	—	243	1,404
1928	4,068	434	154	470	677	202	—	5	54	443	—	317	1,312
1927	3,769	564	195	415	650	170	—	2	2	385	—	288	1,097
1926	3,046	247	122	402	483	156	—	2	—	369	—	287	978
1926[1]	2,591	175	142	372	414	102	—	1	1	361	—	171	853
1925	3,061	459	103	324	547	112	—	3	6	341	—	284	884
1924	2,527	276	72	247	467	141	—	2	14	387	—	151	770
1923	2,966	437	226	376	428	297	—	3	41	375	—	109	675
1922	3,170	510	195	343	471	502	—	4	35	377	—	72	662
1921	4,293	964	248	462	709	239	—	9	104	455	—	278	825
1920	4,052	503	206	599	526	464	—	10	99	497	—	262	886
1919	3,184	601	74	713	70	211	—	3	75	321	—	542	575
1918	2,924[6]	524	52	560	150	271	—	2	40	260	—	525	539[6]
1917	2,476[6]	468	44	352	347	198	—	6	18	337	—	244	464[6]
1916	1,591[6]	153	39	339	225	55	—	5	38	285	—	154	299[6]
1915	1,856[6]	368	80	259	318	47	—	3	9	266	—	97[3]	410[4,6]
1914	2,332	442	127	239	418	113	—	3	23	390	—	100	476
1913	2,675	692	132	235	435	157	—	3	—	407	—	134	480
1912	2,410	786	116	249	289	62	—	7	39	406	—	137	320
1911	1,995	496	84	198	316	45	—	4	49	380	—	121	304
1910	1,773	558	58	183	231	58	—	1	30	364	—	84	206
1909	1,709	690	47	141	201	38	—	2	40	302	—	113	136
1908	1,942	852	54	243	172	37	—	1	5	350	—	86	143
1907[1]	1,659	685	37	179	116	91	—	—	30	326	—	72	124
1906[1]	2,049	893	54	244	137	62	—	—	59	351	—	85	165

Series N101-113. Value of imports of fish and fish products, by major species, 1873 to 1973 (concluded)
(thousands of dollars)

Year[1]	Total	Ground-fish[2]	Halibut	Herring and pilchards	Sardines and anchovies	Salmon	Tuna	Lobster		Oyster	All other shellfish	Oil and meal[3]	All other[4]
								Fresh	Canned				
	101	102	103	104	105	106	107	108	109	110	111	112	113
1905	1,504	384	41	184	135	56	–	–	86	359	–	127	132
1904	1,586	515	39	164	110	55	–	1	48	360	–	132	162
1903	1,403	397	39	201	90	89	–	2	53	315	–	92	127
1902	1,145	214	21	176	98	140	–	2	57	253	–	59	124
1901	982	130	19	138	95	85	–	2	85	242	–	58	127
1900	1,213	307	15	136	87	137	–	3	87	254	–	61	127
1899	955	236	20	84	86	58	–	4	106	231	–	50	81
1898	1,009	357	6	64	82	122	–	4	9	187	–	76	102
1897	1,037	359	4	35	61	160	–	3	3	192	–	114	106
1896	1,068	481	3	62	60	59	–	3	1	203	–	77	119
1895	1,243	550	2	112	53	40	–	3	65	211	–	58	151
1894	1,515	756	4	124	80	42	–	8	66	238	–	46	151
1893	1,225	402	5	161	77	33	–	8	53	262	–	106	119
1892	1,423	644	5	162	62	42	–	7	49	275	–	74	101
1891	1,415	551	4	218	64	42	–	6	8	284	–	131	107
1890	1,077	237	5	248	71	32	–	5	1	310	–	62	106
1889	1,076	249	4	281	66	36	–	5	–	286	–	68	82
1888	1,020	221	6	227	64	40	–	4	8	313	–	45	93
1887	982	195	4	195	70	40	–	4	1	301	–	85	87
1886	902	128	3	213	60	34	–	3	4	273	–	92	93
1885	1,118	225	2	19	–	12	–	2	2	284	–	162	410
1884	1,587	236	2	28	–	28	–	4	2	300	–	168	818
1883	1,653	264	2	23	–	36	–	4	3	310	–	239	771
1882	1,232	218	1	20	–	38	–	4	3	265	–	131	553
1881	1,267	180	1	38	–	47	–	4	3	214	–	274	507
1880	1,113	189	1	38	–	30	–	2	3	190	–	133	527
1879	1,193	215	1	18	–	34	–	3	9	191	–	138	585
1878	1,300	255	1	37	–	26	–	3	11	207	–	166	594
1877	1,371	291	1	52	–	18	–	2	15	237	–	108	647
1876	1,609	316	1	54	–	6	–	4	14	233	–	47	935
1875	1,600	207	1	46	–	22	–	5	15	284	–	110	912
1874	1,833	159	–	20	–	2	–	8	3	183	–	42	1,417
1873	1,002	93	1	5	–	–	–	5	–	167	–	14	716

[1] For 1873 to 1906, fiscal years ending 30 June of the year given; nine months ending 31 March 1907; for 1908 to 1926, fiscal years ending 31 March of the year given; for 1926 to 1973, calendar years.
[2] Groundfish include codfish, haddock, pollock and ling.
[3] Oil only is included 1873 to 1915.

[4] Fish meal not reported separately 1873 to 1915, presumably included in series N113 for those years.
[5] Newfoundland included beginning in 1954.
[6] Sponges of marine production not included 1915 to 1918.

Series N114-118. Index of prices received by fishermen and index of wholesale prices of fish products, 1913 to 1974[1]

Year	Index of prices received by fishermen				Fisheries wholesale price index	Year	Index of prices received by fishermen				Fisheries wholesale price index
	Canada[1]	British Columbia	Maritimes, Quebec	Fresh water fisheries			Canada[1]	British Columbia	Maritimes, Quebec	Fresh water fisheries	
	114	**115**	**116**	**117**	**118**		**114**	**115**	**116**	**117**	**118**
	Panel A: 1961=100				*1935-39 =100*		*Panel B: 1935-39=100*				
						1945	238	208	266	232	194.7
1974	317	356	304	217	939.1	1944	221	211	249	186	177.8
1973	288	320	279	204	806.1	1943	214	194	232	200	174.4
1972	218	184	247	186	654.1	1942	189	227	176	155	148.0
1971	185	162	198	174	579.2	1941	144	169	131	128	125.6
1970	173	160	188	160	555.8	1940	111	116	107	111	115.6
1969	174	196	167	153	497.1	1939	102	115	97	93	102.2
1968	142	131	154	132	459.8	1938	101	107	96	102	99.6
1967	139	125	147	121	447.9	1937	104	97	108	107	100.0
1966	134	124	135	136	435.5	1936	98	84	106	104	98.6
1965	138	135	141	131	424.4	1935	98	103	96	94	97.9
1964	121	113	127	120	395.2	1934	94	102	93	85	99.4
1963	106	93	115	102	385.6	1933	83	97	73	79	88.1
1962	107	107	108	101	368.4	1932	79	79	75	86	89.5
1961	99	98	98	99	352.8	1931	90	85	95	91	105.1
1960	98	105	93	101	339.6	1930	120	119	124	113	133.3
1959	96	96	98	100	326.4	1929	140	156	135	124	147.5
1958	97	100	94	115	312.0	1928	132	128	135	134	140.5
1957	84	78	85	99	302.6	1927	140	170	133	108	140.3
						1926	132	140	134	115	140.0
	Panel B: 1935-39=100					1925	126	128	132	112	137.7
1960	411	630	316	252	339.6	1924	117	104	136	101	129.6
1959	382	527	330	256	326.4	1923	122	131	129	99	117.2
1958	382	554	313	250	312.0	1922	128	159	125	86	128.8
1957	308	402	279	220	302.6	1921	132	163	126	93	128.3
1956	349	507	292	213	296.9	1920	162	195	163	109	156.5
1955	304	388	284	214	274.1	1919	168	205	170	110	160.1
1954	299	369	286	218	262.4	1918	–	206	189	–	155.6
1953	283	331	282	212	259.4	1917	–	–	–	–	123.4
1952	308	384	287	232	278.8	1916	–	–	–	–	96.6
1951	311	405	263	256	283.7	1915	–	–	–	–	90.5
1950	294	377	253	242	260.7	1914	–	–	–	–	89.1
1949	258	307	254	193	257.3	1913	–	–	–	–	90.2
1948	296	379	270	217	254.1						
1947	240	235	248	232	231.6						
1946	258	254	282	220	212.7						

[1] Excluding Newfoundland.

Series N119-124. Expenditures of the federal fisheries department, 1932 to 1974
(thousands of dollars)

Year[1,2]	Total expenditure	Administration	Resource development	Price support and deficiency payments	Other subsidies	Other expenditures	Year[1,2]	Total expenditure	Administration	Resource development	Price support and deficiency payments	Other subsidies	Other expenditures
	119	120	121	122	123	124		119	120	121	122	123	124
							1950[2]	7,917	768	4,810	1,029	79	1,231
1974	141,097	14,056	97,897	14,009	5,000	10,135	1949	5,864	406	3,868	697	83	810
1973	109,628	12,485	80,918	–	7,500	8,725	1948	4,315	255	2,978	160	98	825
1972	94,672	9,245	63,486	–	2,700	19,241	1947	3,839	196	2,585	160	88	810
1971	73,580	6,025	52,927	–	2,700	11,928	1946	3,628	187	2,078	160	123	1,080
1970[3]	51,706	4,044[4]	32,354	1,800	2,000	11,508	1945	2,621	180	1,423	158	177	683
1969	56,060	6,142	30,998	1,420	5,446	12,054	1944	1,978	164	1,251	159	145	259
1968	50,774	5,647	26,419	1,150	4,946	12,612	1943	1,913	151	1,221	160	62	320
1967	42,403	4,913	25,733	1,200	1,825	8,732	1942	1,704	147	1,211	160	–	187
1966	36,728	4,570	20,364	1,200	3,179	7,420	1941	2,005	149	1,170	160	–	527
1965	27,093	3,916	17,009	760	1,960	3,348	1940	3,024	125	1,453	160	–	1,286
1964	23,613	3,840	14,260	760	2,345	2,408	1939	2,568	128	1,683	160	–	598
1963	26,471	3,779	14,170	760	1,807	5,955	1938	2,151	141	1,471	160	–	379
1962	23,828	3,284	12,839	760	2,165	3,702	1937	2,033	135	1,370	160	–	368
1961	19,931	3,091	11,414	760	1,640	3,034	1936	1,710	120	1,385	160	–	46
1960	19,810	2,990	12,310	760	1,091	2,659	1935	1,641	110	1,334	160	–	36
1959	17,577	2,502	10,745	895	1,053	2,383	1934	1,597	111	1,288	159	–	38
1958	16,395	2,611	9,944	755	668	2,418	1933	1,787	143	1,400	160	–	84
1957	13,689	2,564	8,043	742	635	1,705	1932	2,046	177	1,647	159	–	62
1956	11,822	2,261	6,842	647	561	1,511							
1955	10,316	2,012	6,385	159	450	1,310							
1954	10,701	1,497	5,909	1,548	515	1,232							
1953	9,594	1,159	6,014	196	473	1,753							
1952	9,864	1,005	5,131	1,379	402	1,946							
1951	8,183	583	5,968	249	362	1,022							

[1] Fiscal years ending 31 March of the year given.
[2] Newfoundland included beginning in 1950.
[3] After 1970 change in method of setting up forecasts and main estimates.
[4] After 1970 'Administration' is for Minister's office only.

Series N125-127. Catch in the areas covered by the International Convention for the Northwest Atlantic Fisheries (Sub-areas 1-5) 1951 to 1974[1]
(thousands of metric tons)

Year	Total	Canada	Other countries	Year	Total	Canada	Other countries
	125	126	127		125	126	127
1974	3,045	845	2,200	1960	2,279	723	1,556
1973	3,461	885	2,576	1959	2,144	707	1,437
1972	3,167	923	2,244	1958	2,001	634	1,367
1971	3,280	1,105	2,175	1957	1,979	699	1,280
				1956	1,934	714	1,220
1970	3,274	1,171	2,103				
1969	3,719	1,202	2,517	1955	1,846	658	1,188
1968	3,922	1,263	2,659	1954	1,847	682	1,165
1967	3,352	1,041	2,311	1953	1,206	419	787
1966	3,189	997	2,192	1952	1,306	464	842
				1951	1,258	468	790
1965	3,199	862	2,337				
1964	2,952	829	2,123				
1963	2,783	801	1,982				
1962	2,604	745	1,859				
1961	2,401	655	1,746				

[1] Series N125-127 (catch in the area covered by the International Convention for the Northwest Atlantic Fisheries) are representative of catches in the area which extends along the Atlantic Coast from Greenland along the coasts of Labrador, Newfoundland, the Maritime provinces and south to New Jersey. The majority of the catches in the area attributed to Canada are made in the banks and waters adjacent to the Maritime provinces, Quebec and Newfoundland. In the early years represented by this series only ten countries were actively fishing northwest Atlantic waters; by the mid-1960s, 14 nations were involved; by 1973, 20 countries reported fishing operations in the area.

Series N128. Pacific halibut landings, according to the International Fisheries Commission, Canada, 1890 to 1958
(thousands of pounds)

Year	Quantity 128	Year	Quantity 128	Year	Quantity 128	Year	Quantity 128	Year	Quantity 128
		1945	15,121	1930	7,633	1915	18,609	1900	–
		1944	13,371	1929	9,040	1914	–	1899	–
1958	29,194	1943	12,940	1928	10,209	1913	–	1898	–
1957	24,754	1942	11,244	1927	8,466	1912	–	1897	1,968
1956	25,597	1941	13,109	1926	7,891	1911	–	1896	2,281
1955	22,148	1940	12,900	1925	7,353	1910	–	1895	2,537
1954	27,526	1939	13,688	1924	9,628	1909	–	1894	1,730
1953	25,853	1938	12,350	1923	9,121	1908	8,072	1893	1,369
1952	24,779	1937	11,917	1922	9,227	1907	12,915	1892	1,358
1951	21,045	1936	10,741	1921	10,157	1906	–	1891	1,136
1950	18,999	1935	10,208	1920	8,616	1905	–	1890	633
1949	18,921	1934	9,718	1919	7,466	1904	–		
1948	18,782	1933	8,286	1918	6,328	1903	–		
1947	24,159	1932	6,412	1917	9,901	1902	–		
1946	18,637	1931	7,783	1916	12,185	1901	–		

Series N129. Exports of dried cod, Newfoundland, 1806 to 1948
(thousands of pounds)

Year[1]	Quantity 129	Year[1]	Quantity 129	Year[1]	Quantity 129	Year[1]	Quantity 129	Year[1]	Quantity 129
		1920	152,745	1890	116,583	1860	149,879	1830	106,222
		1919	200,258	1889	120,569	1859	136,891	1829	103,515
1948	119,760	1918	188,358	1888	131,681	1858	116,266	1828	100,800
1947	84,502	1917	203,975	1887	120,963	1857	155,940	1827	100,800
1946	114,343	1916	175,618	1886	150,548	1856	142,053	1826	107,962
1945	111,845	1915	159,194	1885	143,888	1855	124,027	1825	109,028
1944	86,652	1914	122,555	1884	163,255	1854	86,701	1824	97,824
1943	85,737	1913	139,699	1883	171,587	1853	103,344	1823	96,851
1942	85,266	1912	157,761	1882	155,804	1852	108,971	1822	98,725
1941	76,735	1911	155,476	1881	171,984	1851	113,921	1821	100,503
1940	128,137	1910	132,465	1880	154,955	1850	121,988	1820	100,930
1939	102,104	1909	168,254	1879	155,430	1849	131,619	1819	103,515
1938	117,111	1908	194,027	1878	115,921	1848	103,081	1818	112,968
1937	102,651	1907	169,038	1877	115,819	1847	93,853	1817	114,628
1936	122,732	1906	159,314	1876	119,669	1846	98,449	1816	117,222
1935	116,453	1905	165,875	1875	128,150	1845	112,026	1815	121,662
1934	114,309	1904	134,043	1874	178,733	1844	95,442	1814	106,149
1933	125,597	1903	152,362	1873	147,480	1843	104,855	1813	99,832
1932	117,543	1902	160,079	1872	125,086	1842	112,894	1812	79,639
1931	114,936	1901	144,363	1871	130,759	1841	113,089	1811	103,436
1930	129,381	1900	138,108	1870	131,060	1840	102,569	1810	99,061
1929[1]	140,278	1899	145,670	1869	123,660	1839	96,922	1809	90,745
1928	144,872	1898	137,350	1868	99,463	1838	81,146	1808	64,527
1927	176,260	1897	128,300	1867	112,570	1837	88,138	1807	75,579
1926[1]	161,151	1896[1]	127,212	1866	99,309	1836	95,363	1806	86,555
1925	138,615	1895	147,012	1865	107,670	1835	79,810		
1924[1]	130,491	1894	124,062	1864	113,825	1834	90,302		
1923	141,643	1893	118,758	1863	111,898	1833	76,556		
1922	166,162	1892	117,523	1862	142,222	1832	69,348		
1921	178,309	1891	139,421	1861	138,698	1831	84,635		

[1] From 1896 to 1924 and from 1927 to 1929 data are for years ending 30 June of the following year. All other years are calendar years.

Series N130-131. Value of exports of fishery products in relation to total exports, Newfoundland, 1856 to 1949

Year[1]	Exports of fishery products (thousands of dollars)	Fishery products as a percentage of total value of exports[2]	Year[1]	Exports of fishery products (thousands of dollars)	Fishery products as a percentage of total value of exports[2]	Year[1]	Exports of fishery products (thousands of dollars)	Fishery products as a percentage of total value of exports[2]	Year[1]	Exports of fishery products (thousands of pounds)[3]	Fishery products as a percentage of total value of exports[2]
	130	131		130	131		130	131		130	131
			1920	27,823	79.8	1890	5,650	92.6	1860	1,247	98.0
1949[1]	28,901	31.2	1919	32,792	89.1	1889	6,371	93.0	1859	1,318	97.1
1948	29,000	36.0	1918	25,547	84.7	1888	6,527	99.2	1858	1,280	97.0
1947	31,000	42.8	1917	17,651	78.9	1887	4,906	94.8	1857	1,591	96.4
1946	29,697	47.4	1916	13,741	72.8	1886	4,562	93.8	1856	1,292	96.5
1945	21,869	44.9	1915	9,640	73.4	1885	4,447	94.1			
1944	18,486	41.6	1914	10,908	72.1	1884	6,409	97.6			
1943[1]	12,057	39.0	1913	10,243	69.8	1883	6,499	92.0			
1942[1]	12,656	32.1	1912	10,640	76.7	1882	6,428	91.8			
1941	9,735	26.1	1911	8,799	73.5	1881	7,160	91.6			
1940	8,100	24.3	1910	9,579	81.0	1880	5,070	90.0			
1939	7,439	23.3	1909	9,346	86.1	1879	5,243	88.6			
1938	7,453	21.3	1908	9,798	82.9	1878	4,733	84.1			
1937	6,890	24.6	1907	10,058	83.1	1877	6,439	94.1			
1936	7,338	25.4	1906	10,118	83.7	1876	5,808	88.5			
1935	8,288	30.4	1905	8,724	81.8	1875	5,710	88.8			
1934	7,664	28.6	1904	8,536	88.0	1874	7,042	96.0			
1933	6,597	27.0	1903	7,808	78.0	1873	6,224	80.8			
1932	6,394	24.0	1902	7,777	81.4	1872	5,461	95.7			
1931	10,470	31.2	1901	6,908	82.6	1871	6,166	98.0			
1930	14,963	37.4	1900	7,073	82.0	1870	5,916	95.4			
1929	16,032	43.6	1899	6,025	86.9	1869	5,807	95.9			
1928	15,135	45.0	1898	4,572	87.5	1868	4,176	97.9			
1927	15,150	49.0	1897	4,208	85.4	1867	4,969	98.0			
1926	14,549	52.9	1896[1]	5,851	88.1	1866	5,513	97.6			
1925	13,043	55.3	1895	5,853	94.1	1865	5,382	98.0			
1924	10,867	51.6	1894	5,145	88.5	1864	1,076	96.8			
1923	12,374	59.0	1893	5,467	87.0	1863	1,198	97.2			
1922	14,449	74.2	1892	4,562	80.7	1862	1,119	95.5			
1921	15,943	71.0	1891	6,680	89.8	1861	1,055	96.5			

[1] For 1856 to 1896, calendar years; for 1897 to 1942, years ending 30 June of year given; for 1943, nine months ending 31 March of that year; for 1944 to 1949, years ending 31 March of year given.

[2] Including re-exports.
[3] Value in Newfoundland monetary pounds.

Series N132-134. Number of male persons engaged in catching and curing fish in relation to persons occupied and total population, Newfoundland, census years 1857 to 1945

Year	Male persons engaged in catching and curing fish			Year	Male persons engaged in catching and curing fish		
	Number	As a percentage of persons occupied	As a percentage of total population		Number	As a percentage of persons occupied	As a percentage of total population
	132	133	134		132	133	134
1945	31,634	31.0	9.8	1891	36,694	64.6	18.1
1935	35,018[1]	39.5[1]	12.1[1]	1884	60,419	81.9	30.6
1921	40,511	50.4	15.4	1874	45,845	86.0	28.4
1911	43,795	53.1	18.1	1869	39,259	87.2	26.8
1901	41,231	61.2	18.7	1857	38,578	90.4	31.0

[1] Cod fishermen only.

Series N135-138. Production of salted codfish, by fishery, Newfoundland, 1930 to 1948
(quintals of 112 pounds dried weight)

Year[1]	Total	Inshore fishery	Deep-sea fishery	Labrador fishery	Year[1]	Total	Inshore fishery	Deep-sea fishery	Labrador fishery
	135	136	137	138		135	136	137	138
					1940	875,494	408,380	200,177	266,937
					1939	1,045,236	496,479	200,590	348,167
1948	940,000	610,000	144,000	186,000	1938	1,156,034	515,000	235,387	407,647
1947	1,166,929	835,000	164,860	167,059	1937	970,000	370,000	250,000	350,000
1946	987,538	649,231	136,166	202,141	1936	970,000	510,000	170,000	290,000
1945	955,217	641,502	127,630	186,085	1935	1,266,000	750,000	116,000	400,000
1944	988,768	590,034	116,727	282,007	1934	1,322,000	770,000	152,000	400,000
1943	940,000	551,324	112,939	275,737	1933	1,097,000	690,000	107,000	300,000
1942	703,456	431,645	62,000	209,811	1932	1,137,000	740,000	97,000	300,000
1941	830,758	493,862	159,877	177,019	1931	1,037,000	610,000	87,000	340,000
					1930	1,106,000	700,000	86,000	320,000

[1] Calendar year.

Series N139-142. Number of fishermen employed in the salt cod fishery, by fishery, Newfoundland, 1937 to 1948

Year[1]	Total	Inshore fishery	Deep-sea fishery	Labrador fishery	Year[1]	Total	Inshore fishery	Deep-sea fishery	Labrador fishery
	139	140	141	142		139	140	141	142
1948	28,000	23,145	1,265	3,590	1940	22,792	17,005	1,705	4,082
1947	28,081	22,456	1,550	4,075	1939	25,220	18,622	2,053	4,545
1946	26,162	20,638	1,304	4,220	1938	25,422	19,164	2,130	4,128
1945	24,836	19,650	1,039	4,147	1937	22,273	15,844	2,329	4,100
1944	22,387	17,220	1,151	4,016					
1943	20,019	15,554	974	3,491					
1942	17,645	13,955	822	2,868					
1941	18,643	13,724	1,680	3,239					

[1] Calendar year.

Section P: Mining

G. David Quirin, *University of Toronto*

This section includes production, exports and imports of metallic and non-metallic minerals, the latter category including structural materials but excluding fuels, which are reported in the Energy chapter, Section Q. The section contains three parts: metallic minerals, series P1-81; non-metallic minerals, series P82-150; and principal statistics, series P151-162. The first two parts contain quantities and value of production, exports and imports; the third part contains number of employees, salaries and wages, cost of fuel and electricity, cost of process supplies and containers, gross value of production and net value added by processing.

The basic sources used include the following Statistics Canada publications: *Canadian Mineral Statistics, 1866-1956*, (Reference Paper No. 68, 1957); *General Review of the Mineral Industries*, (Catalogue 26-201); *Canada Year Book*, (Catalogue 11-202); *Exports - Merchandise Trade*, formerly *Trade of Canada, Volume II, Exports*, (Catalogue 65-202); and *Imports - Merchandise Trade*, formerly *Trade of Canada, Volume III, Imports*, (Catalogue 65-203).

Use was made of the annual publications dealing with individual mineral industries, including *Asbestos Mines, Coal Mines, Contract Drilling for Petroleum and Other Contract Drilling*, (Catalogues 26-205 to 26-207); *Gold Quartz and Copper-Gold-Silver Mines, Iron Mines, Nickel — Copper Mines*, (Catalogues 26-209 to 26-211); *Crude Petroleum and Natural Gas Industry, Salt Mines, Sand and Gravel Pits, Silver-Cobalt and Silver-Lead-Zinc Mines, Stone Quarries*, (Catalogues 26-213 to 26-217), *Miscellaneous Metal Mines, Miscellaneous Non-metal Mines, Gypsum Mines, Potash Mines*, (Catalogues 26-219 to 26-222). Data was also extracted from the annual *Canadian Minerals Yearbook*, published by the Department of Energy, Mines and Resources. Finally, the compilations made from unpublished and other sources by John Davis, in the first edition of the *Historical Statistics of Canada (HSC I)* are repeated in this volume. The reader is referred to the additional references and explanatory notes beginning at page 408 of the first edition.

Attention should be drawn to the different conceptual bases used for reporting quantities and values for metallic and non-metallic minerals, respectively. For non-metallics, quantities are net shipments and values are free on board point of shipment. In the case of metals, unless otherwise stated, production is production of the metal from domestic smelters or refineries plus the estimated metal content (after deducting smelter loss) of ores and concentrate exported. A number of valuation bases have been used. Until 1926, prices in major U.S. markets, usually New York, were simply applied to the metal content figures without deduction of refining or transportation costs. Subsequent adjustments have brought values closer to actual producer receipts for shipments. As a consequence, data for earlier years in the series are not directly comparable with data for more recent years, and overstate the value of metallics in comparison with non-metallics. Data on other minerals of lesser economic importance may be found in the first two sources cited above.

Metallic Minerals (Series P1-81)

P1-26. Canadian production of principal metallic minerals, 1886 to 1975

SOURCE: for 1886 to 1956, Statistics Canada, *Canadian Mineral Statistics, 1886-1956*; for 1957 to 1975, *General Review of the Mineral Industries*, annuals, 1957 to 1975, and individual mining reports cited above. See notes on individual series in *HSC I*.

P3. Copper. Smelter losses in exported ores and concentrates are estimated at 10 pounds of copper per ton of concentrates. A deduction is made for refining costs.

P7. Iron. Until 1939, reported production is export tonnage.

P9. Lead. Smelter losses on exported ores and concentrates are estimated at 5 per cent. Montreal prices were used until 1926, London prices 1926 to 1946, New York prices 1947 to 1950.

P25. Zinc. A deduction of 160 pounds per ton of concentrates is made for smelter losses and exported concentrates.

P27-58. Canadian exports of principal metallic minerals, 1868 to 1977

SOURCE: for 1926 to 1977, Statistics Canada, *Exports - Merchandise Trade*, annual, 1926 to 1977; for 1868 to 1925, the files of the Department of Energy, Mines and Resources.

A new Export Commodity Classification was introduced in 1961 and a new Import Commodity Classification in 1964. Both differ greatly from the classifications which they replaced. As a result some of the export and import series in this chapter could not be continued on a basis comparable to that in the *HSC I*. In the present edition all series have been continued from 1960 according to the new classifications, but an attempt was made to achieve conformity with the commodity content of the old series. Where large parts of a commodity group, according to the new classification, had a reasonable degree of comparability with the old series, the appropriate parts of the new series were used to update the old series. However, where it was impossible to achieve reasonable continuity between the two classification systems, the commodity group according to the new system was used. The following notes to individual series indicate where substantital differences occur between the old classification (data to 1959) and the new classification (data from 1960 to 1975). In some cases quantity data have been lost for the years 1960 to 1963 in the conversion to the new classification.

P27. Aluminium, primary forms and scrap. Series is exactly comparable to pre-1960 data.

P29. Aluminium, semi-fabricated. Data from 1960 to 1977 is more comprehensive than data using the old classification.

P31. Copper blister ore, matte, etc. Series is exactly comparable to pre-1960 data.

P33. Copper ingots, bars, cakes, slabs, etc. Series is exactly comparable to pre-1960 data.

P35. Cobalt in ores. Data are no longer available.

P37. Cobalt, metals and alloys. Series is exactly comparable to pre-1960 data.

P39. Iron ore. Series is exactly comparable to pre-1960 data.

P41. Lead ore and scrap. Series is exactly comparable to pre-1960 data.

P43. Pig lead. Series is exactly comparable to pre-1960 data.

P45. Nickel matte, speiss, oxide. Series is exactly comparable to pre-1960 data.

P47. Nickel fine. Series is exactly comparable to pre-1960 data.

P49. Platinum. Series is exactly comparable to pre-1960 data.

P51. Silver in ores and concentrates. Series is exactly comparable to pre-1960 data.

P53. Silver bullion. Series is exactly comparable to pre-1960 data.

P55. Zinc in ores and scrap. Series is exactly comparable to pre-1960 data.

P57. Zinc spelter. Series is exactly comparable to pre-1960 data.

P59-81. Canadian imports of principal metallic minerals, 1880 to 1977

SOURCE: for 1926 to 1977, Statistics Canada, *Imports - Merchandise Trade,* annual, 1926 to 1977; for 1880 to 1925, the files of the Department of Energy, Mines and Resources.

P59. Alumina, bauxite, cryolite. Series is exactly comparable to pre-1960 data.

P61. Aluminium pigs, ingots, blocks and scrap. Series is exactly comparable to pre-1960 data.

P63. Cobalt. Data are no longer available.

P65. Copper. Data from 1960 on are more comprehensive than on the old basis. The series now includes: copper in ores, concentrates and scrap; copper refinery shapes; copper bars, rods, and shapes, n.e.s.; copper alloy refinery shapes, bars, rods and sections; copper and copper alloy fabricated materials, n.e.s.

P67. Iron ores. Series is exactly comparable to pre-1960 data.

P69. Lead. Data from 1960 to 1975 are less comprehensive than the pre-1960 data.

P71. Mangenese in ores. Series is exactly comparable to pre-1960 data.

P73. Nickel. Series is exactly comparable to pre-1960 data. Nickel in ores, concentrates, and scrap was added in 1966.

P75. Platinum. Series is exactly comparable to pre-1960 data.

P76. Silver. Series is exactly comparable to pre-1960 data.

P78. Tin. Series is exactly comparable to pre-1960 data.

P80. Zinc. Series is exactly comparable to pre-1960 data.

Non-metallic Minerals (Series P82-150)

P82-105. Canadian production of principal non-metallic minerals, 1886 to 1975

SOURCE: same as series P1-26.

P98. Sulphur. Until 1927, production is sulphur content of pyrites shipped, estimated at 40 per cent from 1886 to 1890 and 41 per cent from 1891 to 1910. From 1927, production includes content of smelter gases used for manufacture of sulphuric acid. Elemental sulphur is included from 1958 to 1975. Prior to 1958, elemental sulphur recovered from natural gas was treated as a manufacture and is excluded.

P106-127. Canadian exports of principal non-metallic minerals, 1886 to 1975

SOURCE: same as series P27-58.

P106. Asbestos, crude. Series is exactly comparable to pre-1960 data.

P108. Asbestos, milled fibres. Series is exactly comparable to pre-1960 data.

P110. Asbestos, waste refuse or shorts. Series is exactly comparable to pre-1960 data.

P112. Gypsum or plaster. Series is exactly comparable to pre-1960 data.

P114. Cement. Series is exactly comparable to pre-1960 data.

P116. Clay. Series is exactly comparable to pre-1960 data.

P118. Lime. Series is exactly comparable to pre-1960 data.

P120. Sand and Gravel. Series is exactly comparable to pre-1960 data.

P122. Salt. Data from 1962 to 1975 include part of a former miscellaneous class.

P124. Sulphur in ores. Series is exactly comparable to pre-1960 data.

P126. Sulphur, crude or refined, n.e.s. This is a new series beginning in 1960.

P128-150. Canadian imports of principal non-metallic minerals, 1886 to 1975.

SOURCE: same as series P59-81.

P128. Granite. Data from 1960 to 1975 are more comprehensive than data on the old basis. The value in 1960 is $735,000 compared to $427,000 on the old classification.

P129. Gypsum. Series is exactly comparable to pre-1960 data.

P131. Phosphate rock. Data from 1960 to 1975 are slightly more comprehensive than on old basis.

P133. Silex or crystallized quartz. Data from 1960 to 1975 are less comprehensive than data on the old basis. The value in 1960 is $126,000 compared to $161,000 on the old classification.

P135. Salt. Data from 1960 to 1975 are less comprehensive than data on the old basis. The value in 1960 is $785,000 compared to $841,000 on the old classification.

P137. Sulphur. Series is exactly comparable to pre-1960 data.

P139. Cement. Series is exactly comparable to pre-1960 data.

P141. Clay. Data from 1960 to 1975 are less comprehensive than data on the old basis. The value in 1960 is $2.8 million compared to $3.3 million on the old classification.

P143. Lime. Series is exactly comparable to pre-1960 data.

P145. Sand and Gravel. Series is exactly comparable to pre-1960 data.

P147. Sand Silica. Data from 1960 to 1975 are more comprehensive than data on the old basis. The value in 1960 is $2.6 million compared to $2.4 million on the old classification.

P149. Titanium oxide, white pigments and antimony oxide. Series is exactly comparable to pre-1960 data.

Principal Statistics (Series P151-162)

See the general introduction at the beginning of the Section, with regard to definition and content of the following principal statistics. The large change in the Standard Industrial Classification, which took place in 1960 and 1961, is described in detail in Section R: Manufacturing.

P151-156. Principal statistics of the Canadian metallic mineral industries, 1923 to 1975

SOURCE: for 1923 to 1944, the files of the Manufacturing and Primary Industries Division of Statistics Canada; for 1945 to 1975, Statistics Canada, *General Review of the Mineral Industries*, annual, 1945 to 1975.

P157-162. Principal statistics of the Canadian non-metallic mineral industries, 1925 to 1975.

SOURCE: same as series P151-156.

Series P1-26. Canadian production of principal metallic minerals, 1886 to 1975

Year	Cobalt		Copper		Gold		Iron ore	
	Quantity ('000 lb.)	Value ($'000)	Quantity ('000 lb.)	Value ($'000)	Quantity ('000 oz. t.)	Value ($'000)	Quantity ('000 tons)	Value ($'000)
	1	2	3	4	5	6	7	8
1975	2,986	12,548	1,617,809	1,030,502	1,654	270,830	49,486	918,065
1974	3,447	10,114	1,810,834	1,402,571	1,698	263,794	51,571	724,150
1973	3,334	8,899	1,816,482	1,157,507	1,954	190,376	52,358	606,106
1972	3,351	8,321	1,586,607	806,427	2,079	119,742	42,698	489,023
1971	4,323	9,430	1,442,860	760,016	2,261	79,903	47,352	555,136
1970	4,561	10,207	1,345,434	779,242	2,409	88,057	52,314	588,631
1969	3,256	6,851	1,146,491	588,281	2,545	95,925	40,054	454,076
1968	4,029	8,688	1,266,625	607,944	2,743	103,439	47,443	532,694
1967	3,604	7,352	1,226,628	582,585	2,986	112,732	42,318	470,122
1966	3,511	7,108	1,012,152	453,524	3,320	125,177	40,691	431,659
1965	3,648	7,529	1,015,753	380,952	3,603	136,052	39,959	413,065
1964	3,185	5,991	973,800	324,468	3,835	144,788	38,326	404,952
1963	3,025	6,122	905,118	284,404	4,003	151,118	30,144	313,183
1962	3,482	6,345	914,770	282,733	4,178	156,314	27,359	263,004
1961	3,183	4,752	878,175	255,158	4,474	168,637	20,357	137,950
1960	3,569	6,763	878,524	264,847	4,629	157,152	21,551	175,083
1959	3,150	5,955	790,539	233,103	4,483	150,508	24,488	192,666
1958	2,710	5,308	690,227	174,431	4,571	155,334	15,726	126,131
1957	3,923	7,784	718,219	206,898	4,434	148,757	22,272	167,221
1956	3,517	9,065	709,721	292,958	4,384	151,024	22,348	160,362
1955	3,319	8,564	651,987	239,756	4,542	156,789	16,283	110,436
1954	2,253	5,913	605,464	175,713	4,366	148,765	7,362	49,667
1953	1,603	4,013	506,504	150,954	4,056	139,598	6,510	44,103
1952	1,422	3,227	516,075	146,679	4,472	153,246	5,272	33,744
1951	952	2,000	539,942	149,026	4,393	161,873	4,681	31,141
1950	584	964	528,418	123,211	4,441	168,989	3,605	23,414
1949	619	952	526,914	104,719	4,124	148,447	3,675	21,204
1948	1,545	2,029	481,464	107,160	3,530	123,536	1,337	7,488
1947	573	876	451,723	91,542	3,070	107,458	1,919	9,313
1946	74	70	367,937	46,632	2,833	104,096	1,550	6,823
1945	109	90	474,914	59,322	2,697	103,824	1,135	3,635
1944	36	34	547,070	65,257	2,923	112,532	553	1,910
1943	176	191	575,190	67,171	3,651	140,575	641	2,032
1942	84	88	603,662	60,417	4,841	186,390	545	1,517
1941	263	256	643,317	64,407	5,345	205,789	516	1,426
1940	794	1,235	655,593	65,773	5,311	204,479	415	1,211
1939	733	1,213	608,826	60,935	5,094	184,116	124	342
1938	459	791	571,250	56,554	4,725	166,206	—	—
1937	507	848	530,029	68,917	4,096	143,326	—	—
1936	888	805	421,028	39,514	3,748	131,293	—	—
1935	681	513	418,998	32,312	3,285	115,595	—	—
1934	595	592	364,761	26,671	2,972	102,537	—	—
1933	467	598	299,982	21,635	2,949	84,350	—	—
1932	491	588	247,679	15,294	3,044	71,479	—	—
1931	521	651	292,304	24,114	2,694	58,093	—	—
1930	694	1,144	303,478	37,948	2,102	43,454	—	—
1929	929	1,802	248,121	43,415	1,928	39,862	—	—
1928	957	1,672	202,696	28,598	1,891	39,082	—	—
1927	881	1,765	140,147	17,195	1,853	38,300	—	—
1926	665	1,136	133,095	17,490	1,754	36,262	—	—
1925	1,116	2,329	111,451	15,650	1,736	35,881	—	—
1924	949	1,682	104,457	13,605	1,525	31,532	—	—
1923	888	2,531	86,882	12,529	1,233	25,495	31	115
1922	570	1,852	42,880	5,738	1,263	26,116	18	57
1921	252	756	47,621	5,954	926	19,149	60	230
1920	566	605	81,601	14,244	765	15,814	129	518
1919	596	1,019	75,054	14,028	767	15,850	197	693
1918	760	1,640	118,769	29,251	700	14,464	212	886
1917	674	1,138	109,227	29,688	739	15,273	215	759
1916	800	805	117,150	31,867	930	19,235	275	715
1915	412	383	100,785	17,411	918	18,978	398	774
1914	702	590	75,736	10,302	773	15,983	245	542
1913	1,642	420	76,977	11,754	803	16,599	308	630
1912	1,868	314	77,832	12,719	612	12,649	216	523
1911	1,704	171	55,648	6,887	473	9,781	210	522
1910	2,196	55	55,692	7,094	494	10,206	259	574
1909	3,066	95	52,494	6,815	454	9,382	268	659
1908	2,448	111	63,703	8,414	476	9,842	238	568
1907	1,478	104	56,979	11,398	406	8,383	313	667
1906	642	81	55,610	10,720	556	11,502	249	522

Series P1-26. Canadian production of principal metallic minerals, 1886 to 1975 (continued)

Year	Cobalt		Copper		Gold		Iron ore	
	Quantity ('000 lb.)	Value ($'000)	Quantity ('000 lb.)	Value ($'000)	Quantity ('000 oz. t.)	Value ($'000)	Quantity ('000 tons)	Value ($'000)
	1	2	3	4	5	6	7	8
1905	236	100	48,093	7,498	685	14,159	291	–
1904	32	20	41,384	5,307	796	14,463	219	–
1903	–	–	42,684	5,649	912	18,844	264	–
1902	–	–	38,804	4,511	1,032	21,337	404	–
1901	–	–	37,827	6,097	1,167	24,129	314	–
1900	–	–	18,937	3,066	1,350	27,908	122	–
1899	–	–	15,078	2,655	1,029	21,262	75	241
1898	–	–	17,747	2,135	666	13,775	58	153
1897	–	–	13,301	1,502	292	6,027	51	130
1896	–	–	9,393	1,022	133	2,755	92	192
1895	–	–	7,772	836	101	2,084	103	238
1894	–	–	7,709	737	55	1,129	110	227
1893	–	–	8,110	872	47	977	126	299
1892	–	–	7,087	819	44	908	103	269
1891	–	–	9,529	1,227	45	931	69	142
1890	–	–	6,014	947	56	1,150	77	155
1889	–	–	6,810	936	63	1,295	84	152
1888	–	–	5,563	927	53	1,099	79	152
1887	–	–	3,260	367	57	1,188	76	146
1886	–	–	3,505	386	71	1,463	64	–

Year	Lead		Magnesium		Molybdenum		Nickel	
	Quantity ('000 lb.)	Value ($'000)	Quantity ('000 lb.)	Value ($'000)	Quantity ('000 lb.)	Value ($'000)	Quantity ('000 lb.)	Value ($'000)
	9	10	11	12	13	14	15	16
1975	769,705	155,973	8,434	8,788	28,719	71,201	533,915	1,100,523
1974	648,750	134,330	13,133	9,260	30,736	61,778	593,199	974,594
1973	753,879	121,676	13,680	5,483	30,391	51,852	549,055	813,101
1972	738,849	113,990	11,848	4,537	28,493	44,068	517,975	717,485
1971	811,020	109,488	14,467	5,164	22,663	38,367	588,683	800,064
1970	778,370	123,138	20,707	7,141	33,772	57,141	611,762	830,167
1969	637,263	96,673	21,275	7,264	29,651	53,388	427,223	481,055
1968	680,351	91,439	19,857	6,182	22,464	37,318	528,716	528,236
1967	635,927	89,030	17,775	5,653	21,377	37,900	497,294	463,140
1966	601,244	89,827	13,446	4,176	20,596	34,671	447,220	337,479
1965	583,615	90,460	20,216	6,067	9,558	16,731	518,364	430,402
1964	407,434	54,759	18,706	5,588	1,225	2,057	456,993	379,321
1963	402,329	44,251	17,814	5,358	834	1,344	434,060	360,393
1962	430,659	42,721	17,631	4,822	818	1,261	464,484	383,785
1961	460,869	47,055	15,271	4,308	771	1,092	465,983	351,262
1960	411,300	43,927	14,577	4,314	769	1,015	429,013	295,640
1959	373,391	39,617	12,204	3,180	749	941	373,110	257,009
1958	373,361	42,414	13,592	4,065	888	1,153	279,117	194,142
1957	362,969	50,670	16,770	5,255	784	1,167	375,917	258,977
1956	377,709	58,583	19,212	6,080	842	956	357,030	222,205
1955	405,525	58,315	–	6,585[3]	834	824	349,857	215,866
1954	436,990	58,251	–	6,587[3]	451	458	322,558	180,173
1953	387,412	50,077	–	6,336[3]	194	216	287,386	160,430
1952	337,684	54,671	–	5,366[3]	506[5]	410	281,117	151,349
1951	316,463	58,229	–	3,907[3]	382	229	275,806	151,270
1950	331,394	47,886	–	1,545[3]	104	60	247,318	112,105
1949	319,550	50,489	–	1,041	–	–	257,379	99,173
1948	334,502	60,344	–	1,860	304	137	263,479	86,904
1947	323,337	44,200	–	725	760	309	237,251	70,651
1946	353,974	23,893	321	76	732	296	192,125	45,385
1945	346,994	17,350	7,359	1,607	978	412	245,131	61,982
1944	304,582	13,706	10,580	2,576	2,124	1,080	274,599	69,204
1943	444,061	16,670	7,154	2,075	684	550	288,019	71,675
1942	512,143	17,218	809	356	228	135	285,212	69,998
1941	460,167	15,471	11	3	196	88	282,258	68,657
1940	471,850	15,864	–	–	22	10	245,558	59,823
1939	388,570	12,314	–	–	2	1	226,106	50,920
1938	418,928	14,009	–	–	12	5	210,573	53,914
1937	411,999	21,053	–	–	16	8	244,905	59,505
1936	383,181	14,994	–	–	–	–	169,739	43,877

Series P1-26. Canadian production of principal metallic minerals, 1886 to 1975 (continued)

Year	Lead		Magnesium		Molybdenum		Nickel	
	Quantity ('000 lb.)	Value ($'000)	Quantity ('000 lb.)	Value ($'000)	Quantity ('000 lb.)	Value ($'000)	Quantity ('000 lb.)	Value ($'000)
	9	10	11	12	13	14	15	16
1935	339,105	10,625	—	—	—	—	138,516	35,345
1934	346,277	8,437	—	—	—	—	128,687	32,139
1933	266,475	6,373	—	—	—	—	83,265	20,130
1932	255,947	5,410	—	—	—	—	30,328	7,180
1931	267,342	7,260	—	—	2	—	65,666	15,267
1930	332,894	13,103	—	—	—	—	103,769	24,455
1929	326,523	16,544	—	—	18	6	110,276	27,115
1928	337,947	15,553	—	—	—	—	96,756	22,319
1927	311,423	16,477	—	—	—	—	66,799	15,262
1926	283,801	19,241	—	—	24	10	65,714	14,374
1925	253,591	23,127	—	—	30	11	73,857	15,947
1924	175,485	14,221	—	—	20	9	69,536	19,470
1923	111,234	7,986	—	—	—	—	62,454	18,332
1922	93,307	5,818	—	—	—	—	17,597	6,159
1921	66,680	3,829	—	—	—	—	19,293	6,753
1920	35,954	3,214	—	—	—	—	61,336	24,534
1919	43,828	3,053	—	—	80	69	44,545	17,818
1918	51,398	4,754	—	—	922	429	92,507	37,003
1917	32,576	3,628	—	—	3,100	320	84,330	33,732
1916	41,498	3,533	—	—	1,220	188	82,959	29,035
1915	46,316	2,594	—	—	78	29	68,309	20,493
1914	36,338	1,628	—	—	32	2	45,518	13,655
1913	37,663	1,755	—	—	—	—	49,677	14,903
1912	35,763	1,598	—	—	—	—	44,842	13,452
1911	23,785	828	—	—	—	—	34,099	10,230
1910	32,988	1,216	—	—	—	—	37,271	11,181
1909	45,857	1,692	—	—	—	—	26,283	9,462
1908	43,196	1,814	—	—	—	—	19,143	8,232
1907	47,739	2,542	—	—	—	—	21,190	9,535
1906	54,608	3,089	—	—	—	—	21,491	8,949
1905	56,865	2,677	—	—	—	—	18,876	7,551
1904	37,531	1,617	—	—	—	—	10,548	4,219
1903	18,139	769	—	—	170	1	12,506	5,002
1902	22,956	934	—	—	6	—	10,693	5,026
1901	51,901	2,249	—	—	—	—	9,189	4,595
1900	63,170	2,761	—	—	—	—	7,080	3,328
1899	21,862	977	—	—	—	—	5,744	2,068
1898	31,915	1,206	—	—	—	—	5,518	1,821
1897	39,018	1,397	—	—	—	—	3,998	1,399
1896	24,200	721	—	—	—	—	3,397	1,189
1895	16,462	532	—	—	—	—	3,889	1,361
1894	5,703	188	—	—	—	—	4,907	1,871
1893	2,135	80	—	—	—	—	3,983	2,071
1892	808	33	—	—	—	—	2,414	1,400
1891	89	4	—	—	—	—	4,035	2,421
1890	105	5	—	—	—	—	1,436	933
1889	165	6	—	—	—	—	830	498
1888	675	30	—	—	—	—	—	—
1887	205	9	—	—	—	—	—	—
1886	—	—	—	—	—	—	—	—

Series P1-26. Canadian production of principal metallic minerals, 1886 to 1975 (continued)

Year	Platinum group Quantity ('000 oz. t.)	Value ($'000)	Silver Quantity ('000 oz. t.)	Value ($'000)	Tungsten Quantity ('000 lb.)	Value ($'000)	Uranium Quantity ('000 lb.)	Value ($'000)	Zinc Quantity ('000 lb.)	Value ($'000)
	17	18	19	20	21	22	23	24	25	26
1975	399[1]	56,493	39,695	178,864	3,258	—	12,163	..	2,326,209	872,328
1974	385[1]	60,794	42,810	198,166	3,558	—	9,591	..	2,484,628	867,135
1973	354[1]	41,994	47,488	119,954	4,640	—	9,517	..	2,704,148	652,944
1972	406[1]	34,657	44,792	74,803	4,447	—	9,763	..	2,505,284	477,783
1971	475[1]	39,822	46,024	71,797	4,624	—	8,214	..	2,499,469	418,161
1970	482[1]	43,557	44,251	81,864	3,727	—	8,209	..	2,503,821	398,859
1969	310[1]	30,881	43,531	84,015	4,063	—	7,708	53,151	2,415,249	367,842
1968	486[1]	46,200	45,013	104,115	3,585	—	7,402	52,285	2,318,784	326,949
1967	401[1]	34,669	36,315	62,898	—[2]	—	7,476	53,022	2,222,906	322,099
1966	396[1]	32,370	33,418	46,752	—[2]	—	7,864	54,335	1,928,212	291,160
1965	463[1]	36,110	32,272	45,181	3,736	3,116	8,885	62,361	1,644,071	248,255
1964	376[1]	25,404	29,903	41,864	—[2]	—	14,570	83,509	1,369,025	193,991
1963	358[1]	22,585	29,933	41,426	—[2]	—	16,703	136,909	947,445	121,083
1962	471[1]	28,449	30,423	35,443	—[2]	—	16,859	158,184	926,289	112,081
1961	418[1]	24,534	31,382	29,581	—[2]	—	19,281	195,692	832,009	104,750
1960	484[1]	28,874[1]	34,017	30,244	—[2]	—[2]	25,495	269,938	813,745	108,635
1959	150	11,015	31,924	28,023	—[2]	—[2]	31,784	331,143	792,015	96,943
1958	146	9,481	31,163	27,053	691	1,898	26,805	279,538	850,198	92,501
1957	200	17,835	28,823	25,183	1,921	5,279	13,271	136,304	827,482	100,043
1956	151	15,726	28,432	25,498	2,271	6,351	4,581	45,732	845,265	125,437
1955	170	14,748	27,984	24,676	1,943	5,508	—[4]	26,032	866,714	118,306
1954	154	12,950	31,118	25,908	2,171	5,796	—[4]	26,373	752,982	90,207
1953	138	12,551	28,299	23,774	2,446	5,689	—[4]	—	803,523	96,101
1952	122	10,917	25,222	21,066	1,493	4,488	—[4]	—	743,604	129,833
1951	153	14,543	23,126	21,865	3	7	—[4]	—	682,224	135,763
1950	125	10,256	23,221	18,768	284	160	—[4]	—	626,455	98,040
1949	154	11,603	17,641	13,099	252	252	—[4]	—	576,524	76,372
1948	121	10,623	16,110	12,082	1,046	1,046	—[4]	—	468,327	65,238
1947	95	5,582	12,504	9,003	496	681	—[4]	—	415,726	46,686
1946	122	7,673	12,544	10,493	—	—	—[4]	—	470,620	36,755
1945	208	8,017	12,943	6,083	1	1	—[4]	—	517,214	33,309
1944	158	6,065	13,627	5,860	887	246	—[4]	—	550,823	23,685
1943	220	8,459	17,345	7,849	1,509	1,084	—[4]	—	610,754	24,430
1942	258	10,899	20,695	8,728	521	406	—[4]	—	580,257	19,793
1941	124	4,750	21,754	8,323	83	39	—	925	512,382	17,477
1940	108	4,240	23,834	9,116	12	7	—	410	424,029	14,464
1939	149	5,223	23,164	9,378	9	5	—	1,122	394,554	12,108
1938	161	5,197	22,219	9,660	—	—	—	1,045	381,507	11,724
1937	139	6,753	22,978	10,313	—	—	—	877	370,338	18,154
1936	132	5,321	18,334	8,274	—	—	—	606	333,183	11,045
1935	105	3,446	16,619	10,767	—	—	—	414	320,650	9,937
1934	116	4,491	16,415	7,761	—	—	—	159	298,580	9,088
1933	25	858	15,188	5,746	—	—	—	248	199,132	6,393
1932	27	1,099	18,348	5,811	—	—	—	—	172,284	4,144
1931	45	1,597	20,562	6,142	—	—	—	—	237,245	6,059
1930	34	1,543	26,444	10,089	—	—	—	—	267,644	9,635
1929	13	847	23,143	12,264	—	—	—	—	197,267	10,627
1928	11	709	21,936	12,762	—	—	—	—	184,647	10,143
1927	11	718	22,737	12,817	—	—	—	—	165,496	10,125
1926	10	924	22,372	13,895	—	—	—	—	149,938	11,110
1925	9	1,028	20,229	13,971	—	—	—	—	109,269	8,328
1924	9	1,091	19,736	13,180	—	—	—	—	98,909	6,275
1923	1	142	18,602	12,068	—	—	—	—	60,416	3,992
1922	—	46	18,626	12,577	—	—	—	—	56,290	3,218
1921	—	23	13,543	8,485	—	—	—	—	53,089	2,471
1920	1	28	13,330	13,450	—	—	—	—	39,864	3,058
1919	1	74	16,021	17,802	—	—	—	—	31,195	2,362
1918	1	71	21,384	20,694	27	12	—	—	35,083	2,862
1917	1	104	22,221	18,092	1	—	—	—	29,669	2,641
1916	1	85	25,460	16,717	—	—	—	—	23,365	2,992
1915	—	22	26,626	13,229	—	—	—	—	15[6]	555
1914	1	34	28,450	15,594	—	—	—	—	11	263
1913	—	9	31,846	19,041	—	—	—	—	8	187
1912	—	23	31,956	19,440	28	—	—	—	6	212
1911	1	29	32,559	17,355	—	—	—	—	3	101
1910	—	8	32,869	17,580	—	—	—	—	5	120
1909	1	14	27,529	14,179	—	—	—	—	18	243
1908	—	3	22,106	11,686	—	—	—	—	—	3
1907	—	7	12,780	8,349	—	—	—	—	2	49
1906	—	3	8,473	5,659	—	—	—	—	1	24

Series P1-26. Canadian production of principal metallic minerals, 1886 to 1975 (concluded)

Year	Platinum group		Silver		Tungsten		Uranium		Zinc	
	Quantity ('000 oz. t.)	Value ($'000)	Quantity ('000 oz. t.)	Value ($'000)	Quantity ('000 lb.)	Value ($'000)	Quantity ('000 lb.)	Value ($'000)	Quantity ('000 lb.)	Value ($'000)
	17	18	19	20	21	22	23	24	25	26
1905	1	12	6,000	3,621	—	—	—	—	9	139
1904	1	11	3,578	2,047	—	—	—	—	478[6]	24
1903	2	33	3,199	1,710	—	—	—	—	900	49
1902	2	47	4,291	2,238	—	—	—	—	142	7
1901	—	—	5,539	3,265	—	—	—	—	—	—
1900	—	—	4,468	2,740	—	—	—	—	213	9
1899	—	1	3,412	2,033	—	—	—	—	814	47
1898	—	2	4,452	2,594	—	—	—	—	788	36
1897	—	2	5,558	3,323	—	—	—	—	—	—
1896	—	1	3,205	2,150	—	—	—	—	—	—
1895	—	4	1,578	1,030	—	—	—	—	—	—
1894	—	1	848	534	—	—	—	—	—	—
1893	—	2	429	330	—	—	—	—	—	—
1892	—	4	311	272	—	—	—	—	—	—
1891	—	10	415	410	—	—	—	—	—	—
1890	—	5	401	419	—	—	—	—	—	—
1889	—	4	383	359	—	—	—	—	—	—
1888	—	6	437	411	—	—	—	—	—	—
1887	—	6	355	347	—	—	—	—	—	—
1886	..	..	..	..	..	..	..	..	..	..

[1] Palladium, iridium and other platinum group metals included from 1960 because of confidentiality requirements. Prior to 1960, platinum only.
[2] Intermittent transfer output due to accidents at mine, fire or mill etc.
[3] Includes value of calcium produced.
[4] Classified information.

[5] Molybdenum quantities for 1952 and earlier years are concentrates, principally molybdenite; for subsequent years, metal content is reported.
[6] Figures for 1898 to 1904, are zinc content of ores shipped; for 1905 to 1915, are ore concentrates, for 1916 to 1975, are recoverable zinc in ores exported, plus zinc refined in Canada.

Series P27-58. Canadian exports of principal metallic minerals, 1868 to 1977

Year	Aluminium				Copper			
	Primary forms and scrap		Semi-fabricated		Blister, ore matte and scrap, etc.		Ingots, bars, cakes, slabs, etc.	
	Quantity ('000 cwt)	Value ($'000)	Quantity ('000 cwt)	Value ($'000)	Quantity ('000 cwt)	Value ($'000)	Quantity ('000 cwt)	Value ($'000)
	27	28	29	30	31	32	33	34
1977	15,564	736,060	599	38,731	6,539	18,423	6,487	430,534
1976	12,330	454,822	393	18,231	7,006	18,847	7,015	451,461
1975	12,233	427,693	171	8,310	7,378	18,824	7,070	412,122
1974	16,260	493,155	675	22,690	7,935	26,185	6,303	513,174
1973	16,612	367,558	372	11,099	8,278	42,890	6,360	410,680
1972	16,610	370,519	414	13,159	6,375	17,160	6,811	333,742
1971	18,768	440,686	323	10,321	4,879	16,603	6,298	317,553
1970	17,718	454,251	252	9,198	4,190	24,248	5,848	385,030
1969	18,772	467,435	379	14,041	3,962	21,348	4,201	229,029
1968	18,294	430,973	591	24,238	4,590	21,234	5,532	288,598
1967	16,279	385,848	613	21,584	3,214	14,509	5,518	274,811
1966	15,243	353,534	683	22,827	2,494	12,042	3,814	192,762
1965	14,929	347,782	528	15,898	2,151	72,032	3,997	148,401
1964	13,216	308,405	361	10,753	2,361	61,102	4,485	148,809
1963	13,575	299,825	256	7,153	2,072	50,287	4,300	136,798
1962	12,129	275,162	453	12,585	1,953	45,211	4,461	139,701
1961	10,329	230,961	459	13,888	1,020	22,524	5,325	154,410
1960	11,594	252,083	602	16,071	1,183	31,616	5,561	170,153
1959	10,469	217,971	464	12,713	766	20,027	4,449	130,247
1958	9,941	212,780	318	9,662	828	17,927	4,493	109,904
1957	9,821	220,777	252	8,609	1,177	30,524	3,976	110,080
1956	10,360	230,021	142	4,786	1,112	42,483	3,497	141,767
1955	10,475	203,356	258	7,615	1,197	40,657	3,064	109,650
1954	9,648	173,351	349	9,041	1,167	30,719	3,123	91,356
1953	9,463	164,372	348	9,007	1,236	32,677	2,640	80,940
1952	8,322	143,395	472	11,710	723	15,963	2,274	71,406
1951	7,167	113,267	296	7,586	757	15,290	2,037	59,023
1950	6,807	97,713	229	5,493	771	15,814	2,685	59,666
1949	6,026	85,878	212	5,155	811	15,967	2,543	53,715
1948	6,999	89,333	123	3,404	676	11,020	2,323	50,683
1947	4,490	54,545	78	2,068	696	11,114	1,750	33,486
1946	3,876	50,083	49	1,307	377	2,651	2,028	27,463

Series P27-58. Canadian exports of principal metallic minerals, 1868 to 1977 (continued)

Year	Aluminium				Copper			
	Primary forms and scrap		Semi-fabricated		Blister, ore matte and scrap, etc.		Ingots, bars, cakes, slabs, etc.	
	Quantity ('000 cwt)	Value ($'000)	Quantity ('000 cwt)	Value ($'000)	Quantity ('000 cwt)	Value ($'000)	Quantity ('000 cwt)	Value ($'000)
	27	28	29	30	31	32	33	34
1945	7,776	122,540	38	1,070	415	2,933	2,587	32,098
1944	5,941	93,708	62	2,310	579	4,035	2,705	29,049
1943	7,510	124,479	–	–	821	5,965	1,287	12,731
1942	6,290	112,155	–	–	824	6,127	1,972	19,491
1941	3,855	75,798	–	–	1,225	9,334	2,528	25,352
1940	1,744	33,119	–	–	1,417	10,754	3,090	31,369
1939	1,433	25,950	–	–	1,595	12,164	3,316	33,730
1938	1,315	23,329	–	–	1,438	10,899	3,635	35,858
1937	997	17,968	–	–	903	9,292	2,961	38,705
1936	597	11,114	–	–	536	3,507	3,109	27,461
1935	626	10,370	–	–	1,184	7,820	2,435	18,061
1934	445	7,561	–	–	660	3,992	1,876	13,944
1933	354	6,156	–	–	554	3,239	1,533	10,347
1932	197	2,933	–	–	658	3,417	1,191 [3]	6,796 [3]
1931	253	3,987	–	–	916	7,786	–	–
1930	461	8,135	–	–	2,291	30,405	–	–
1929	764	13,665	–	–	2,468	37,232	–	–
1928	424	8,298	–	–	1,893	23,269	–	–
1927	524	10,611	–	–	1,330	14,641	–	–
1926	255	5,951	–	–	1,183	14,492	–	–
1925	273	6,559	–	–	1,147	14,176	–	–
1924	181	3,991	–	–	997	11,582	–	–
1923	176	3,380	–	–	761	9,351	–	–
1922	96	1,637	–	–	544	6,269	–	–
1921	54	1,260	–	–	452	6,359	–	–
1920	197	6,095	–	–	863	14,733	–	–
1919	146	4,455	–	–	639	9,601	–	–
1918	216	7,224	–	–	743	9,394	–	–
1917	223	7,621	–	–	1,024	18,480	–	–
1916	184	5,201	–	–	1,308	22,061	–	–
1915	187	3,334	–	–	856	9,288	–	–
1914	145	2,365	–	–	708	7,362	–	–
1913	130	1,762	–	–	844	9,804	–	–
1912	183	2,002	–	–	765	8,800	–	–
1911	50	748	–	–	552	5,460	–	–
1910	77	1,160	–	–	570	5,841	–	–
1909	61	918	–	–	544	5,832	–	–
1908	17	400	–	–	511	5,935	–	–
1907	55	1,109	–	–	547	8,742	–	–
1906	45	899	–	–	424	7,303	–	–
1905	25	508	–	–	407	5,444	–	–
1904	13	278	–	–	386	4,216	–	–
1903	–	–	–	–	384	3,874	–	–
1902	–	–	–	–	261	2,477	–	–
1901	–	–	–	–	325	3,405	–	–
1900	–	–	–	–	236	1,742	–	–
1899	–	–	–	–	114	1,200	–	–
1898	–	–	–	–	116	840	–	–
1897	–	–	–	–	140	850	–	–
1896	–	–	–	–	55	281	–	–
1895	–	–	–	–	37	237	–	–
1894	–	–	–	–	16	92	–	–
1893	–	–	–	–	48	269	–	–
1892	–	–	–	–	–	278	–	–
1891	–	–	–	–	–	348	–	–
1890	–	–	–	–	–	398	–	–
1889	–	–	–	–	–	168	–	–
1888	–	–	–	–	–	257	–	–
1887	–	–	–	–	26	138	–	–
1886	–	–	–	–	29	249	–	–
1885	–	–	–	–	26	263	–	–
1884	–	–	–	–	27	273	–	–
1883	–	–	–	–	14	149	–	–
1882	–	–	–	–	19	183	–	–
1881	–	–	–	–	12	126	–	–
1880	–	–	–	–	14	193	–	–
1879	–	–	–	–	4	48	–	–
1878	–	–	–	–	4	36	–	–
1877	–	–	–	–	19	245	–	–
1876	–	–	–	–	19	250	–	–

Series P27-58. Canadian exports of principal metallic minerals, 1868 to 1977 (continued)

Year	Aluminium				Copper			
	Primary forms and scrap		Semi-fabricated		Blister, ore matte and scrap, etc.		Ingots, bars, cakes, slabs, etc.	
	Quantity ('000 cwt)	Value ($'000)	Quantity ('000 cwt)	Value ($'000)	Quantity ('000 cwt)	Value ($'000)	Quantity ('000 cwt)	Value ($'000)
	27	28	29	30	31	32	33	34
1875	–	–	–	–	18	241	–	–
1874	–	–	–	–	9	112	–	–
1873	–	–	–	–	10	121	–	–

Year	Cobalt				Iron ore		Lead			
	Contained in ore		Metals and alloys				Ore and scrap[1]		Pig lead	
	Quantity ('000 lb.)	Value ($'000)	Quantity ('000 lb.)	Value ($'000)	Quantity ('000 tons)	Value ($'000)	Quantity ('000 cwt)	Value ($'000)	Quantity ('000 cwt)	Value ($'000)
	35	36	37	38	39	40	41	42	43	44
1977	–	–	1,508	9,241	49,586	1,064,055	3,390	53,435	2,884	79,521
1976	–	–	1,154	4,879	49,163	920,820	3,436	35,887	2,523	48,288
1975	–	–	950	4,068	39,293	678,646	4,934	56,064	2,445	46,049
1974	–	–	1,057	3,789	41,279	542,552	4,488	64,566	1,618	33,774
1973	–	–	1,214	3,720	41,521	461,996	4,928	52,208	2,506	39,294
1972	–	–	860	2,119	32,270	352,680	3,818	33,514	2,839	34,820
1971	–	–	748	2,066	37,659	413,332	4,404	36,952	2,738	30,664
1970	–	–	840	2,248	43,374	475,743	4,220	43,200	3,056	42,144
1969	–	–	2,445	2,283	31,255	333,131	2,930	26,179	2,142	27,002
1968	–	–	1,211	1,155	40,332	443,202	2,992	22,991	2,776	30,866
1967	–	–	887	1,855	35,175	383,063	2,645	20,440	2,646	28,969
1966	–	–	628	1,202	34,377	369,009	2,348	20,342	2,129	27,001
1965	–	–	292	571	34,495	360,819	2,320	22,946	2,581	40,666
1964	–	–	594	1,071	34,131	356,007	1,713	15,341	1,917	21,858
1963	–	–	739	1,215	26,718	270,949	1,155	7,686	1,943	15,546
1962	–	–	543	919	24,243	220,522	1,225	8,070	2,516	17,727
1961	–	–	604	1,039	16,652	142,566	1,469	9,404	2,353	18,190
1960	–	–	846	1,376	18,975	155,472	1,160	10,085	1,929	15,958
1959	–	–	684	1,220	20,779	157,814	1,135	10,286	1,845	15,183
1958	–	–	1,034	1,918	13,878	107,674	1,090	10,722	1,847	15,377
1957	15	16	2,168	4,156	20,130	152,281	890	10,534	1,691	18,862
1956	16	15	1,444	3,586	20,265	144,443	1,003	13,573	1,593	21,452
1955	–	–	1,555	3,518	14,569	99,814	1,176	15,115	1,854	22,078
1954	3	6	1,144	3,801	6,127	39,719	1,213	14,727	2,328	25,803
1953	37	60	781	2,487	4,820	30,843	1,244	14,859	2,058	22,976
1952	–	–	336	773	3,847	22,333	584	8,061	2,595	41,615
1951	35	47	193	383	3,226	18,596	421	7,167	2,115	38,123
1950	17	15	1[2]	10[2]	2,227	13,310	421	5,863	2,303	32,241
1949	49	37	46	230	2,550	14,117	436[1]	5,161[1]	2,271	36,725
1948	871	641	120	528	1,070	5,301	112	1,563	2,075	32,759
1947	89	69	100	389	1,750	6,023	135	1,602	2,499	29,099
1946	48	41	622	1,199	1,145	4,353	120	737	2,082	15,978
1945	65	57	904	2,202	771	2,553	157	574	2,146	8,603
1944	26	24	1,186	2,455	308	1,153	190	650	2,058	6,395
1943	163	189	1,125	2,529	375	1,451	115	425	3,087	9,222
1942	93	97	1,171	2,724	296	1,056	119	409	4,216	15,243
1941	280	281	1,187	2,388	282	1,040	132	441	3,686	13,085
1940	478	388	528	1,053	252	924	183	462	3,031	9,028
1939	204	178	136	268	11	43	82	400	3,615	9,450
1938	66	41	133	201	–	1	72	345	3,099	8,638
1937	92	59	60	95	5	14	165	863	3,531	16,978
1936	526	213	46	73	3	9	94	288	3,214	10,113
1935	419	125	28	47	3	10	113	290	2,829	6,871
1934	219	85	70	94	3	12	236	510	2,832	5,238
1933	54	19	76	103	2	2	76	268	2,843	4,923
1932	125	58	79	141	1	2	37	149	2,140	3,269
1931	273	166	75	152	2	5	44	177	2,164	4,483
1930	400	442	79	245	1	3	263	1,258	2,054	7,015
1929	379	484	372	851	4	19	160	1,047	2,284	10,053
1928	–	531	259	553	3	13	150	894	2,554	10,172
1927	1,366	243	368	767	2	12	130	845	2,394	11,981
1926	746	192	191	377	1	7	136	796	2,025	12,984

Series P27-58. Canadian exports of principal metallic minerals, 1868 to 1977 (continued)

Year	Cobalt				Iron ore		Lead			
	Contained in ore		Metals and alloys				Ore and scrap[1]		Pig lead	
	Quantity ('000 lb.)	Value ($'000)	Quantity ('000 lb.)	Value ($'000)	Quantity ('000 tons)	Value ($'000)	Quantity ('000 cwt)	Value ($'000)	Quantity ('000 cwt)	Value ($'000)
	35	36	37	38	39	40	41	42	43	44
1925	–	–	310	702	4	20	375	2,342	1,601	11,809
1924	–	–	173	394	5	22	132	785	1,087	6,866
1923	–	–	240	574	8	29	79	536	471	2,496
1922	–	–	116	310	2	14	109	550	415	1,877
1921	–	593	69	188	4	13	63	257	238	992
1920	–	537	315	537	20	99	75	386	–	2
1919	–	1,006	110	275	14	78	131	616	113	773
1918	–	1,901	366	1,047	130	651	227	1,322	75	669
1917	–	1,543	334	1,075	164	661	134	925	10	62
1916	–	–	–	–	161	542	90	558	1	8
1915	–	–	–	–	80	207	18	40	21	79
1914	–	–	–	–	135	361	2	3	5	20
1913	–	–	–	–	126	427	3	9	–	–
1912	–	–	–	–	118	382	3	8	–	–
1911	–	–	–	–	38	133	1	2	1	3
1910	–	–	–	–	114	324	–	1	77	248
1909	–	–	–	–	22	62	62	133	113	361
1908	–	–	–	–	4	72	45	153	139	469
1907	–	–	–	–	26	46	220	866	36	164
1906	–	–	–	–	75	149	181	622	33	114
1905	–	–	–	–	–	–	–	1,047	–	–
1904	–	–	–	–	–	–	–	559	–	–
1903	–	–	–	–	–	–	–	426	–	–
1902	–	–	–	–	–	–	–	457	–	–
1901	–	–	–	–	–	–	–	1,805	–	–
1900	–	–	–	–	6	14	–	1,918	–	–
1899	–	–	–	–	4	10	–	467	–	–
1898	–	–	–	–	–	–	–	885	–	–
1897	–	–	–	–	–	1	–	925	–	–
1896	–	–	–	–	1	2	–	462	–	–
1895	–	–	–	–	2	4	–	435	–	–
1894	–	–	–	–	–	21	–	145	–	–
1893	–	–	–	–	8	26	–	3	–	–
1892	–	–	–	–	8	37	–	3	–	–
1891	–	–	–	–	15	33	–	5	–	–
1890	–	–	–	–	14	31	–	–	–	–
1889	–	–	–	–	25	60	–	–	–	–
1888	–	–	–	–	14	40	–	–	–	–
1887	–	–	–	–	23	72	–	1	–	–
1886	–	–	–	–	8	23	–	–	–	–
1885	–	–	–	–	54	132	–	–	–	–
1884	–	–	–	–	25	67	–	–	–	–
1883	–	–	–	–	45	139	–	–	–	–
1882	–	–	–	–	44	135	–	–	–	–
1881	–	–	–	–	45	115	–	–	–	–
1880	–	–	–	–	31	76	–	–	–	–
1879	–	–	–	–	4	8	–	–	–	–
1878	–	–	–	–	5	13	–	–	–	–
1877	–	–	–	–	8	15	–	1	–	–
1876	–	–	–	–	14	31	–	–	–	–
1875	–	–	–	–	32	76	4	8	–	–
1874	–	–	–	–	44	98	–	–	–	–
1873	–	–	–	–	47	112	–	–	–	–
1872	–	–	–	–	26	65	–	–	–	–
1871	–	–	–	–	27	58	–	–	–	–
1870	–	–	–	–	15	35	–	–	–	–
1869	–	–	–	–	28	60	–	–	–	–
1868	–	–	–	–	25	55	–	–	–	–

Series P27-58. Canadian exports of principal metallic minerals, 1868 to 1977 (continued)

Year	Nickel				Platinum	
	Contained in matte speiss and oxide		Nickel fine		Including palladium, rhodium, iridium, etc.	
	Quantity ('000 cwt)	Value ($'000)	Quantity ('000 cwt)	Value ($'000)	Quantity ('000 oz. t.)	Value ($'000)
	45	46	47	48	49	50
1977	2,547	530,298	1,645	355,633	434	52,773
1976	2,660	516,621	1,939	389,897	494	45,319
1975	2,710	508,555	2,010	374,250	499	50,244
1974	3,006	431,816	2,632	405,784	551	62,233
1973	3,324	437,442	2,660	355,903	461	34,579
1972	3,029	380,889	2,402	297,515	430	33,370
1971	3,185	403,048	2,510	310,485	476	37,274
1970	2,836	356,947	3,064	417,981	294	28,377
1969	2,120	208,407	2,085	215,116	330	29,892
1968	2,752	253,619	2,542	234,828	587	38,304
1967	2,357	200,749	2,573	219,231	476	29,829
1966	2,344	185,715	2,654	204,681	442	25,800
1965	2,466	188,682	2,704	201,273	551	30,103
1964	2,211	165,474	2,567	192,294	409	20,812
1963	1,972	148,742	2,183	169,237	550	24,556
1962	1,771	131,835	2,434	185,518	571	24,341
1961	2,422	151,952	2,670	187,214	631	26,331
1960	1,743	115,781	2,167	142,549	403	16,069
1959	1,396	93,629	2,042	133,227	358	12,497
1958	1,381	93,794	1,703	118,786	—	15,014
1957	1,508	100,393	2,065	147,860	—	27,720
1956	1,450	87,864	2,087	135,045	—	35,386
1955	1,348	80,403	2,129	134,766	—	26,303
1954	1,346	74,326	1,828	107,829	—	27,630
1953	1,304	71,642	1,598	90,901	—	26,279
1952	1,299	71,310	1,541	79,672	—	30,529
1951	1,177	61,089	1,447	75,601	—	30,340
1950	1,095	47,731	1,338	57,569	—	21,201
1949	1,161	42,449	1,382	49,874	—	18,016
1948	1,212	29,341	1,425	44,461	—	16,777
1947	926	21,368	1,415	39,075	—	11,659
1946	623	11,255	1,616	43,949	—	15,409
1945	601	10,995	1,563	43,783	—	13,298
1944	702	12,760	1,950	55,640	—	6,769
1943	806	14,908	1,905	53,438	—	7,717
1942	1,010	19,113	1,766	49,295	—	9,831
1941	997	18,678	1,755	49,002	—	6,424
1940	847	15,650	1,643	45,513	—	5,899
1939	990	18,351	1,358	39,582	—	6,137
1938	923	17,156	1,054	35,340	—	9,320
1937	859	16,037	1,369	42,877	—	8,375
1936	669	12,694	1,067	31,900	—	6,842
1935	611	11,386	816	24,900	—	5,056
1934	634	12,555	547	16,358	133	5,186
1933	460	9,623	421	13,173	29	1,169
1932	169	3,261	152	4,023	15	1,156
1931	364	7,041	271	7,140	14	1,135
1930	486	9,243	431	11,263	20	1,611
1929	412	7,991	684	17,545	3	220
1928	460	8,462	512	13,320	1	78
1927	417	7,386	290	7,896	1	53
1926	392	6,074	247	6,386	1	55
1925	402	6,694	301	5,981	—	42
1924	367	5,177	260	5,090	—	48
1923	290	4,077	229	4,649	—	34
1922	168	2,536	144	4,288	—	4
1921	81	1,418	48	1,684	1	63
1920	517	9,006	85	2,983	—	54
1919	304	4,785	106	3,292	—	29
1918	858	10,556	17	707	—	1
1917	813	8,709	—	—	—	11
1916	804	8,662	—	—	1	42

Series P27-58. Canadian exports of principal metallic minerals, 1868 to 1977 (continued)

Year	Nickel				Platinum	
	Contained in matte speiss and oxide		Nickel fine		Including palladium, rhodium, iridium, etc.	
	Quantity ('000 cwt)	Value ($'000)	Quantity ('000 cwt)	Value ($'000)	Quantity ('000 oz. t.)	Value ($'000)
	45	46	47	48	49	50
1915	664	7,394	—	—	—	11
1914	465	5,149	—	—	—	2
1913	495	5,196	—	—	—	8
1912	442	4,662	—	—	—	4
1911	326	3,676	—	—	—	2
1910	360	4,039	—	—	2	63
1909	256	2,676	—	—	—	2
1908	194	1,867	—	—	—	1
1907	194	2,280	—	—	—	5
1906	207	2,043	—	—	—	15
1905	173	1,570	—	—	—	—
1904	112	1,091	—	—	—	—
1903	127	1,116	—	—	—	—
1902	—	1,007	—	—	—	—
1901	—	751	—	—	—	1
1900	—	1,031	—	—	—	—
1899	—	940	—	—	—	—
1898	—	1,019	—	—	—	—
1897	—	723	—	—	—	—
1896	—	658	—	—	—	—
1895	—	522	—	—	—	—
1894	—	559	—	—	—	—
1893	—	630	—	—	—	—
1892	—	293	—	—	—	—
1891	—	667	—	—	—	—
1890	—	90	—	—	—	—

Year	Silver				Zinc			
	Ore and concentrates		Bullion		Ore and scrap		Spelter	
	Quantity ('000 oz. t.)	Value ($'000)	Quantity ('000 oz. t.)	Value ($'000)	Quantity ('000 cwt)	Value ($'000)	Quantity ('000 cwt)	Value ($'000)
	51	52	53	54	55	56	57	58
1977	14,920	57,700	36,711	177,136	13,615	216,599	6,512	222,566
1976	14,011	50,047	30,460	130,136	14,764	244,891	7,762	267,164
1975	15,156	56,102	22,942	101,588	15,909	297,348	5,456	200,756
1974	19,378	61,541	21,339	98,625	19,580	318,601	6,529	217,573
1973	26,202	44,537	22,905	58,478	19,085	198,088	9,323	198,421
1972	22,144	28,395	19,825	32,280	15,517	128,740	8,201	125,415
1971	25,563	34,749	18,201	28,247	17,944	136,580	6,257	78,141
1970	21,820	33,927	24,199	45,354	17,989	125,364	7,029	87,881
1969	21,883	33,914	34,658	66,415	16,270	102,611	6,148	74,565
1968	21,502	41,027	28,105	64,934	17,242	99,593	6,374	75,411
1967	10,407	12,847	14,093	23,999	14,879	94,126	5,953	71,506
1966	11,850	13,927	12,221	17,028	12,026	77,745	5,123	66,814
1965	12,246	14,463	11,268	15,683	9,932	69,849	5,284	70,984
1964	9,478	10,760	10,583	14,723	8,218	54,776	4,762	61,726
1963	8,287	9,643	10,835	14,783	4,375	18,805	4,000	41,665
1962	8,862	9,170	9,445	10,942	4,959	19,782	4,214	40,776
1961	10,353	9,454	10,783	10,094	4,057	16,707	4,165	42,037
1960	8,897	8,255	12,761	11,315	3,505	17,179	4,142	46,355
1959	6,815	6,210	15,141	13,511	3,815	21,556	3,591	33,732
1958	5,099	4,274	16,027	14,280	4,468	21,957	3,914	33,428
1957	5,979	4,943	12,800	11,691	3,850	21,440	4,040	43,481
1956	6,924	5,871	14,342	12,821	4,096	26,997	3,675	47,013
1955	5,874	4,858	16,599	14,485	3,921	23,451	4,277	47,107
1954	8,672	6,961	14,467	11,992	3,706	19,204	4,121	39,188
1953	5,687	4,613	14,633	12,232	3,937	23,279	3,168	34,293
1952	3,546	2,830	14,929	12,618	3,708	34,973	3,337	61,310
1951	2,413	2,060	15,381	14,420	3,182	28,245	2,923	55,424
1950	3,494	2,743	8,355	6,679	2,693	18,116	2,938	40,594
1949	4,055	3,005	6,212	4,568	2,254	13,217	3,366	42,483
1948	3,295	2,434	5,434	4,026	1,229	5,651	2,898	36,686
1947	2,722	1,998	7,514	5,429	906	3,359	2,745	26,661
1946	1,864	1,429	2,317	2,061	1,239	3,485	2,898	24,175

Series P27-58. Canadian exports of principal metallic minerals, 1868 to 1977 (continued)

Year	Silver				Zinc			
	Ore and concentrates		Bullion		Ore and scrap		Spelter	
	Quantity ('000 oz. t.)	Value ($'000)	Quantity ('000 oz. t.)	Value ($'000)	Quantity ('000 cwt)	Value ($'000)	Quantity ('000 cwt)	Value ($'000)
	51	**52**	**53**	**54**	**55**	**56**	**57**	**58**
1945	2,232	1,153	2,724	1,444	1,973	6,118	2,439	14,123
1944	2,390	1,170	3,577	1,763	2,358	7,349	1,920	7,667
1943	2,253	1,040	9,199	4,518	2,268	6,256	2,586	10,260
1942	3,535	1,487	10,646	4,466	1,593	4,273	3,043	10,783
1941	4,069	1,513	13,166	5,072	1,166	2,402	2,822	9,877
1940	5,633	2,052	13,613	5,113	724	905	3,341	11,134
1939	6,828	2,801	14,203	5,724	452	579	3,120	9,344
1938	5,869	2,541	22,683	9,838	482	1,189	2,644	8,627
1937	5,769	2,567	14,620	6,556	721	2,752	2,684	12,739
1936	3,347	1,494	12,784	5,789	441	791	2,804	8,524
1935	1,364	882	16,963	10,953	259	401	2,709	7,810
1934	1,745	714	10,664	4,934	433	703	2,379	6,991
1933	3,362	1,093	10,739	3,759	146	182	1,735	4,991
1932	3,488	983	13,504	3,978	8[4]	10[4]	1,753	3,852
1931	4,017	1,168	14,649	4,231	11[4]	10[4]	2,380	5,555
1930	8,473	3,401	15,779	6,180	518	1,108	1,510	5,146
1929	7,058	3,736	14,880	8,023	334	1,678	1,351	7,032
1928	6,816	3,824	14,806	8,580	295	1,643	1,272	6,603
1927	5,445	2,894	15,971	8,995	563	1,041	1,124	6,827
1926	5,890	3,547	15,242	9,560	870	1,507	960	7,108
1925	4,755	3,021	14,317	9,861	967	1,778	498	3,781
1924	4,822	3,014	13,656	9,069	1,279	1,626	400	2,520
1923	4,861	3,091	12,324	8,046	11	5	385	2,514
1922	6,471	4,281	10,931	7,403	1	1	570	3,055
1921	2,782	1,655	10,385	6,544	1	1	257	1,336
1920	1,903	2,008	9,931	10,231	63	122	70	512
1919	2,855	2,851	12,550	13,560	133	296	77	701
1918	4,225	3,736	15,132	14,647	211	477	—	—
1917	21,719	17,621	—	—	—	—	—	—
1916	25,279	15,638	—	—	—	—	—	—
1915	27,672	13,812	—	—	—	—	—	—
1914	28,020	15,585	—	—	—	—	—	—
1913	37,372	21,441	—	—	—	—	—	—
1912	34,912	19,494	—	—	—	—	—	—
1911	31,217	15,807	—	—	—	—	—	—
1910	30,700	15,650	—	—	—	—	—	—
1909	31,127	15,720	—	—	—	—	—	—
1908	20,884	12,403	—	—	—	—	—	—
1907	14,814	9,942	—	—	—	—	—	—
1906	—	5,686	—	—	—	—	—	—

Series P27-58. Canadian exports of principal metallic minerals, 1868 to 1977 (concluded)

Year	Silver				Zinc			
	Ore and concentrates		Bullion		Ore and scrap		Spelter	
	Quantity ('000 oz. t.)	Value ($'000)	Quantity ('000 oz. t.)	Value ($'000)	Quantity ('000 cwt)	Value ($'000)	Quantity ('000 cwt)	Value ($'000)
	51	52	53	54	55	56	57	58
1905	—	2,777	—	—	—	—	—	—
1904	—	1,904	—	—	—	—	—	—
1903	—	1,989	—	—	—	—	—	—
1902	—	1,820	—	—	—	—	—	—
1901	—	2,027	—	—	—	—	—	—
1900	—	2,342	—	—	—	—	—	—
1899	—	1,624	—	—	—	—	—	—
1898	—	2,902	—	—	—	—	—	—
1897	—	3,576	—	—	—	—	—	—
1896	—	2,272	—	—	—	—	—	—
1895	—	994	—	—	—	—	—	—
1894	—	360	—	—	—	—	—	—
1893	—	214	—	—	—	—	—	—
1892	—	57	—	—	—	—	—	—
1891	—	225	—	—	—	—	—	—
1890	—	204	—	—	—	—	—	—
1889	—	212	—	—	—	—	—	—
1888	—	219	—	—	—	—	—	—
1887	—	206	—	—	—	—	—	—
1886	—	26	—	—	—	—	—	—
1885	—	29	—	—	—	—	—	—
1884	—	13	—	—	—	—	—	—
1883	—	9	—	—	—	—	—	—
1882	—	7	—	—	—	—	—	—
1881	—	15	—	—	—	—	—	—
1880	—	68	—	—	—	—	—	—
1879	—	154	—	—	—	—	—	—
1878	—	666	—	—	—	—	—	—
1877	—	43	—	—	—	—	—	—
1876	—	354	—	—	—	—	—	—
1875	—	473	—	—	—	—	—	—

[1] Lead scrap included for 1949 to 1960.
[2] Alloys only.

[3] Nine months, 1 April to 31 December 1932.
[4] Zinc in ore excluded in 1931 and 1932.

Series P59-81. Canadian imports of principal metallic minerals, 1880 to 1977[1]

Year	Alumina, bauxite and cryolite		Aluminium		Cobalt ore		Copper, ores and scrap	
	Quantity ('000 cwt)	Value ($'000)	Quantity ('000 cwt)	Value ($'000)	Quantity ('000 lb.)	Value ($'000)	Quantity ('000 cwt)	Value ($'000)
	59	**60**	**61**	**62**	**63**	**64**	**65**	**66**
1977	78,856	179,950	356	10,936	—	—	446	18,182
1976	47,137	151,240	197	4,260	—	—	414	19,521
1975	70,137	131,663	155	1,320	—	—	446	20,839
1974	79,348	114,314	129	2,484	—	—	1,197	65,824
1973	77,352	91,380	227	2,138	—	—	1,164	59,335
1972	72,659	75,481	164	1,082	—	—	433	14,194
1971	74,705	95,437	128	1,340	—	—	513	18,767
1970	76,473	97,907	115	1,683	—	—	222	3,649
1969	71,083	97,972	312	4,970	—	—	211	9,746
1968	67,218	81,914	326	1,754	—	—	374	61,345
1967	66,441	73,778	191	808	—	—	697	27,378
1966	66,648	75,370	468	1,253	—	—	51	2,639
1965	56,941	68,423	1,447	664	—	—	47	1,549
1964	52,445	69,577	888	402	—	—	48	1,475
1963	40,220	62,976	319	30	—	—	2	327
1962	40,360	56,583	299	26	—	—	2	75
1961	44,360	53,459	327	32	—	—	3	369
1960	59,824	46,428	30	645	—	—	94	2,878
1959	45,270	36,975	29	628	—	—	115	3,437
1958	46,482	35,088	230	5,440	—	—	85	2,358
1957	51,121	48,275	48	1,186	—	1	200	5,655
1956	52,159	33,393	54	1,401	2	1	229	9,047
1955	61,906	25,967	5	99	38	11	70	2,544
1954	59,331	21,216	4	74	10	1	71	1,896
1953	53,777	16,720	3	108	4,288	628	318	8,278
1952	49,149	13,417	11	147	14,943	2,318	321	9,431
1951	48,171	16,574	6	185	3,688	761	86	1,712
1950	37,312	10,569	10	133	3,913	436	45	1,035
1949	35,887	10,378	2	21	81	2	38	776
1948	40,307	10,962	5	32	848	65	42	844
1947	28,003	9,760	15	139	—	—	39	782
1946	25,724	9,074	17	193	1,170	450	28	472
1945	18,880	7,787	7	67	2,390	869	28	436
1944	26,613	10,272	6	60	3,676	1,328	8	132
1943	60,662	23,168	2	18	2,236	786	17	283
1942	26,680	13,310	—	1	4,336	1,485	11	184
1941	23,233	9,333	1	18	4,600	1,543	21	362
1940	13,963	6,410	4	148	3,921	1,165	17	311
1939	10,211	3,708	6	108	592	148	15	221
1938	7,495	2,920	12	140	—	—	14	189
1937	6,219	4,398	13	218	—	—	14	223
1936	3,489	2,937	7	132	—	—	11	146
1935	2,551	2,927	7	107	—	—	8	98
1934	1,643	2,211	4	64	—	—	8	91
1933	1,099	1,963	2	49	—	—	4	53
1932	1,035	2,060	3	40	—	—	9	96
1931	1,963	3,316	3	66	—	—	114	1,184
1930	2,185	3,284	2	41	—	—	418	5,870
1929	2,902	3,422	3	76	—	—	726	13,161
1928	3,344	4,634	14	416	—	—	501	7,602
1927	2,557	6,200	11	331	—	—	367	5,095
1926	1,515	3,488	10	271	—	—	294	4,343
1925	1,290	2,722	7	218	—	—	390	5,654
1924	1,298	2,446	7	183	—	—	290	3,965
1923	1,336	2,326	8	194	—	—	402	6,287
1922	426	938	12	251	—	—	265	3,781
1921	300	638	7	213	—	—	185	2,593
1920	1,148	1,889	19	623	—	—	456	8,597
1919	586	1,565	8	240	—	—	280	5,769
1918	1,864	2,071	3	109	—	—	223	5,879
1917	1,743	1,866	7	317	—	—	267	8,078
1916	538	1,114	14	524	—	—	220	5,988
1915	350	893	27	631	—	—	168	2,868
1914	286	571	38	746	—	—	221	3,213
1913	307	615	35	605	—	—	363[6]	6,034[6]
1912	224	448	24	410	—	—	325	4,258
1911	186	372	24	531	—	—	264	3,487
1910	195	403	32	675	—	—	198	2,670
1909	118	235	6[4]	167[4]	—	—	137	1,906
1908	15	30	4	132	—	—	120	2,400
1907	127	269	9[4]	218[4]	—	—	26[6]	52[6]
1906	90	239	7	168	—	—	139	2,364

Series P59-81. Canadian imports of principal metallic minerals, 1880 to 1977[1] (continued)

Year	Alumina, bauxite and cryolite		Aluminium		Cobalt ore		Copper, ores and scrap	
	Quantity ('000 cwt)	Value ($'000)	Quantity ('000 cwt)	Value ($'000)	Quantity ('000 lb.)	Value ($'000)	Quantity ('000 cwt)	Value ($'000)
	59	60	61	62	63	64	65	66
1905	54	139	6	155	—	—	106	1,498
1904	—	123	—	—	—	—	77	1,020
1903	—	45	—	—	—	—	83	1,066
1902	—	9	—	—	—	—	73	993
1901	—	2	—	—	—	—	41	674
1900	—	3	—	—	—	—	43	736
1899	—	2	—	—	—	—	37	525
1898	—	2	—	—	—	—	49	520
1897	—	2	—	—	—	—	18	166
1896	—	2	—	—	—	—	15	178
1895	—	—	—	—	—	—	14	147
1894	—	—	—	—	—	—	1	7
1893	—	—	—	—	—	—	2	16
1892	—	—	—	—	—	—	3	15
1891	—	—	—	—	—	—	1	10
1890	—	—	—	—	—	—	1	12
1889	—	—	—	—	—	—	—	3
1888	—	—	—	—	—	—	—	2
1887	—	—	—	—	—	—	—	3
1886	—	—	—	—	—	—	1	7
1885	—	—	—	—	—	—	—	—
1884	—	—	—	—	—	—	—	—
1883	—	—	—	—	—	—	—	—
1882	—	—	—	—	—	—	—	—
1881	—	—	—	—	—	—	—	—
1880	—	—	—	—	—	—	—	—

Year	Iron ore		Lead		Manganese ore[2]		Nickel[3]	
	Quantity ('000 tons)	Value ($'000)	Quantity ('000 lb.)	Value ($'000)	Quantity ('000 cwt)	Value ($'000)	Quantity ('000 lb.)	Value ($'000)
	67	68	69	70	71	72	73	74
1977	2,762	76,274	1,811	575	1,271	9,059	5,300	11,910
1976	3,329	81,514	4,280	928	2,626	15,988	37,100	84,238
1975	5,340	123,038	4,326	925	1,538	10,104	28,300	58,896
1974	2,572	38,108	25,037	6,169	2,758	11,590	35,600	59,537
1973	2,965	39,648	8,023	1,288	2,941	7,405	32,300	51,101
1972	1,932	22,291	23,377	2,980	1,964	5,074	36,000	51,149
1971	1,525	18,679	9,265	1,294	2,218	5,973	28,100	39,143
1970	2,381	28,228	4,400	668	2,536	6,244	23,700	32,552
1969	2,532	29,450	260	56	2,159	5,259	25,200	29,768
1968	3,080	34,611	304	54	1,384	3,942	22,800	23,871
1967	2,689	32,869	877	139	1,653	5,200	19,100	18,605
1966	4,842	56,024	1,252	188	3,682	10,866	57,800	47,653
1965	5,335	60,550	142	36	1,790	5,430	24,300	21,019
1964	5,861	67,287	147	26	1,256	3,945	20,900	17,986
1963	5,965	67,873	3,483	290	2,138	3,822	18,400	16,354
1962	5,157	56,324	1,155	83	1,815	4,038	14,988	—
1961	4,628	47,433	2,241	238	1,520	3,465	8,608	—
1960	5,056	48,370	1,635	175	1,127	2,544	3,524	3,951
1959	2,801	27,129	4,377	386	2,369	5,017	3,715	3,541
1958	3,413	28,932	3,678	325	841	1,723	4,309	3,894
1957	4,539	36,387	3,251	400	2,626	7,520	4,183	3,842
1956	5,069	38,722	483	74	4,160	9,137	5,108	4,804
1955	4,539	31,563	438	58	3,506	7,338	4,205	3,544
1954	3,035	20,416	381	51	979	2,277	3,167	2,673
1953	4,168	28,194	624	83	1,334	2,720	6,166	4,498
1952	4,268	26,519	974	175	3,888	8,274	3,298	2,741
1951	3,831	22,671	1,469	360	4,442	9,078	2,612	2,369
1950	3,071	16,802	3,014	350	2,714	4,994	2,674	2,082
1949	2,517	12,057	5,206	658	2,757	4,476	2,896	2,017
1948	4,300	15,507	161	25	4,666	6,450	2,727	1,570
1947	3,945	12,717	33	8	4,470	6,146	2,753	1,416
1946	2,282	6,467	95	6	2,880	2,485	3,204	1,581

Series P59-81. Canadian imports of principal metallic minerals, 1880 to 1977[1] (continued)

Year	Iron ore		Lead		Manganese ore[2]		Nickel[3]	
	Quantity ('000 tons)	Value ($'000)	Quantity ('000 lb.)	Value ($'000)	Quantity ('000 cwt)	Value ($'000)	Quantity ('000 lb.)	Value ($'000)
	67	**68**	**69**	**70**	**71**	**72**	**73**	**74**
1945	3,740	8,596	84	8	3,966	4,572	1,525	801
1944	3,127	7,394	36	5	1,716	2,370	849	461
1943	3,906	9,056	31	5	1,025	1,445	1,090	595
1942	2,702	6,230	31	3	1,148	860	997	473
1941	3,255	7,135	594	42	2,089	1,171	2,021	918
1940	2,418	5,513	347	19	1,409	777	1,188	525
1939	1,765	4,179	105	7	596	622	1,394	529
1938	1,302	2,830	111	6	421	464	981	401
1937	2,125	4,721	125	10	1,545	802	983	403
1936	1,317	2,634	97	6	1,285	684	933	382
1935	1,510	2,960	179	8	736	353	572	253
1934	977	1,827	162	6	619	234	691	257
1933	206	401	104	5	687	294	993	352
1932	68	184	187	8	30	88	539	234
1931	808	1,718	797	33	—	—	782	305
1930	1,485	3,324	2,286	128	1,976	992	1,382	471
1929	2,448	5,026	1,434	85	1,983	991	1,605	564
1928	2,223	4,325	693	42	2,129	1,059	1,167	429
1927	1,487	2,876	517	42	1,398	1,451	2,453	807
1926	1,466	2,854	884	80	767	779	1,118	243
1925	1,037	2,016	610	61	293[2]	428[2]	1,060	212
1924	913	2,345	809	64	30	65	875	180
1923	1,942	5,765	3,159	176	26	56	826	248
1922	887	2,259	2,266	123	6	20	1,367	258
1921	661	2,109	2,018	103	28	97	372	148
1920	1,984	5,716	27,771	2,274	26	73	736	257
1919	1,683	4,706	14,088	1,022	—	—	644[3]	225 [3]
1918	2,201	5,896	15,706	1,351	—	—	671	294
1917	2,251	5,125	16,980	1,732	—	—	1,020	403
1916	2,340	4,419	27,450	2,078	—	—	785	230
1915	1,504	2,332	43,528	2,066	—	—	675	172
1914	1,147	2,387	16,406	632	—	—	551	144
1913	1,942	3,878	12,694	527	—	—	713	194
1912	2,048[5]	3,932[5]	30,100	1,034	—	—	581	135
1911	—	—	23,062	551	—	—	557	137
1910	—	—	13,830	392	—	—	398	98
1909	—	—	6,386[4]	197[4]	—	—	249	67
1908	—	—	8,117	360	—	—	310	94
1907	—	—	9,329[4]	334[4]	—	—	—	—
1906	—	—	9,884	328	—	—	—	—
1905	—	—	7,487	186	—	—	—	—
1904	—	—	10,870	161	—	—	—	—
1903	—	—	11,007	103	—	—	—	—
1902	—	—	14,088	154	—	—	—	—
1901	—	—	10,162	175	—	—	—	—
1900	—	—	7,785	261	—	—	—	—
1899	—	—	15,946	323	—	—	—	—
1898	—	—	11,063	300	—	—	—	—
1897	—	—	7,580	188	—	—	—	—
1896	—	—	8,101	196	—	—	—	—
1895	—	—	7,400	156	—	—	—	—
1894	—	—	7,871	170	—	—	—	—
1893	—	—	10,689	248	—	—	—	—
1892	—	—	10,867	287	—	—	—	—
1891	—	—	10,203	291	—	—	—	—
1890	—	—	12,028	343	—	—	—	—
1889	—	—	8,840	257	—	—	—	—
1888	—	—	8,364	243	—	—	—	—
1887	—	—	7,531	215	—	—	—	—
1886	—	—	4,974	194	—	—	—	—
1885	—	—	4,547	111	—	—	—	—
1884	—	—	4,911	132	—	—	—	—
1883	—	—	5,737	178	—	—	—	—
1882	—	—	4,720	157	—	—	—	—
1881	—	—	3,446	128	—	—	—	—
1880	—	—	3,030	124	—	—	—	—

Series P59-81. Canadian imports of principal metallic minerals, 1880 to 1977[1] (continued)

Year	Platinum[4] Value ($'000)	Silver Quantity ('000 oz. t.)	Silver Value ($'000)	Tin[4] Quantity ('000 cwt)	Tin[4] Value ($'000)	Zinc Quantity ('000 cwt)	Zinc Value ($'000)
	75	76	77	78	79	80	81
1977	3,793	1,061	4,863	111	56,527	73	2,386
1976	3,570	19,013	8,047	93	31,709	276	9,856
1975	6,061	13,506	59,923	99	33,076	15	606
1974	6,847	29,246	123,642	123	43,243	155	5,604
1973	5,655	8,755	22,288	120	23,819	408	8,609
1972	2,858	1,218	2,143	130	21,545	250	4,410
1971	3,298	723	1,195	113	18,375	80	1,281
1970	3,123	4,319	8,052	113	20,148	7	115
1969	9,289	19,169	34,799	111	17,945	15	177
1968	17,077	14,061	32,959	96	14,892	30	315
1967	13,161	5,384	8,233	102	16,602	21	317
1966	14,930	14,478	20,213	95	16,884	3	36
1965	13,461	13,413	18,740	112	21,682	—	7
1964	17,369	5,198	7,271	109	17,568	—	8
1963	13,591	7,951	10,821	94	11,685	13	167
1962	12,925	15,182	17,658	51	6,204	14	187
1961	11,242	12,278	11,586	79	8,893	15	200
1960	12,951	3,849	3,473	84	8,258	1	22
1959	6,466	2,808	2,484	94	9,182	17	158
1958	8,641	3	2	78	7,060	12	122
1957	15,431	1,859	1,633	93	8,539	1	18
1956	19,580	1,010	902	85	8,194	2	43
1955	15,723	87	75	97	8,814	1	28
1954	17,784	60	50	86	7,442	2	32
1953	16,517	287	231	83	8,264	1	16
1952	17,373	146	128	88	10,595	10	194
1951	17,078	1,050	848	137	19,577	32	665
1950	21,340	342	274	108	10,337	1	21
1949	10,737	1,333	973	82	7,862	1	23
1948	10,738	718	528	81	7,898	—	7
1947	7,532	71	57	89	6,677	1	24
1946	8,613	1,928	1,586	84	5,977	—	6
1945	4,061	2	1	72	4,983	2	31
1944	62	—	—	27	1,768	90	822
1943	426	—	—	26	1,504	272	2,456
1942	628	31	13	72	4,167	118	1,064
1941	1,745	264	101	174	9,652	1	15
1940	5,560	1,355	519	118	6,235	—	5
1939	221	3,851	1,533	58	2,833	—	3
1938	238	2,011	850	53	2,205	—	1
1937	296	1,987	870	59	3,116	—	3
1936	141	—	2,390	48	2,182	—	1
1935	56	—	5,585	47	2,323	1	6
1934	52	—	2,193	40	2,054	—	1
1933	49	—	676	28	1,149	2	6
1932	30	—	586	31	809	2	5
1931	46	—	467	41	1,067	4	14
1930	87	—	611	53	1,757	44	214
1929	158	—	958	57	2,671	27	166
1928	139	—	985	54	2,822	18	108
1927	95	—	897	48	3,066	14	90
1926	138	—	1,011	51	3,264	12	95
1925	158	—	1,025	44	2,460	56	508
1924	167	—	665	40	1,971	43	344
1923	118	—	723	42	1,747	39	343
1922	91	—	658	37	1,166	50	368
1921	84	—	582	26	840	39	304
1920	106	—	2,453	48	3,030	50	534
1919	145	—	3,590	37	2,105	238	1,866
1918	31	—	437	35	2,492	313	2,804
1917	114	—	1,063	37	1,786	371	3,641
1916	89	—	875	35	1,372	148	2,141
1915	84	—	337	29	1,010	159	2,011
1914	80	—	629	34	1,191	140	741
1913	146	—	840	51	2,252	173	953
1912	232	—	1,100	49	2,134	218	1,304
1911	176	—	848	40	1,624	151	861

Series P59-81. Canadian imports of principal metallic minerals, 1880 to 1977[1] (concluded)

Year	Platinum[4] Value ($'000)	Silver Quantity ('000 oz. t.)	Silver Value ($'000)	Tin[4] Quantity ('000 cwt)	Tin[4] Value ($'000)	Zinc Quantity ('000 cwt)	Zinc Value ($'000)
	75	76	77	78	79	80	81
1910	102	—	975	32	1,059	141	752
1909	46[4]	—	—	34[4]	981[4]	82[4]	452[4]
1908	60	—	—	35	1,282	96	505
1907	113[4]	—	—	22[4]	892[4]	61[4]	395[4]
1906	54	—	—	33	1,172	75	449
1905	62	—	—	29	819	63	348
1904	28	—	—	27	720	60	303
1903	21	—	—	25	729	50	254
1902	19	—	—	32	599	53	222
1901	20	—	—	29	698	35	162
1900	58	—	—	22	581	35	186
1899	10	—	—	29	306	24	137
1898	10	—	—	25	292	38	126
1897	9	—	—	19	250	20	91
1896	6	—	—	21	210	31	121
1895	4	—	—	25	214	24	94
1894	7	—	—	—	—	29	126
1893	14	—	—	—	—	37	174
1892	2	—	—	—	—	36	190
1891	4	—	—	—	—	24	136
1890	5	—	—	—	—	33	164
1889	3	—	—	—	—	29	121
1888	13	—	—	—	—	24	96
1887	1	—	—	—	—	33	124
1886	1	—	—	—	—	29	104
1885	1	—	—	—	—	24	81
1884	..	..	..	..	..	..	..
1883	..	..	..	..	..	..	..
1882	..	..	..	..	..	..	..
1881	..	..	..	..	..	..	..
1880	..	..	..	..	..	..	..

[1] Content of the series is described in the text.
[2] Manganese data for 1920 to 1925 are for fiscal years ending 31 March.
[3] Nickel data for 1908 to 1919 are for fiscal years ending 31 March.
[4] For aluminium, lead, platinum, tin and zinc, 1908 and 1909 data are for fiscal years ending 31 March. For 1907, data are for nine months ending 31 March 1907. Earlier years are for fiscal years ending 30 June.

[5] Iron ore, nine months ending 31 December 1912.
[6] For copper, fiscal year ending 31 March used for the years 1908 to 1913. Nine months used for 1907; fiscal years ending 30 June for 1906 and earlier years were used.

Series P82-105. Canadian production of principal non-metallic minerals, 1886 to 1975

Year	Asbestos Quantity ('000 tons)	Asbestos Value ($'000)	Gypsum Quantity ('000 tons)	Gypsum Value ($'000)	Peat moss Quantity ('000 tons)	Peat moss Value ($'000)
	82	83	84	85	86	87
1975	1,164	267,246	6,305	20,304	398	22,273
1974	1,812	302,013	7,964	22,437	389	20,229
1973	1,863	234,323	8,389	21,067	371	15,458
1972	1,687	206,089	8,099	19,336	376	13,612
1971	1,634	203,999	6,702	15,083	337	11,803
1970	1,662	208,147	6,319	14,199	320	10,168
1969	1,611	195,211	6,374	14,995	330	9,562
1968	1,596	185,025	5,926	11,825	294	8,658
1967	1,452	165,119	5,175	11,348	281	8,006
1966	1,489	163,655	5,976	12,312	285	7,187
1965	1,388	146,188	6,306	12,533	288	8,983
1964	1,420	145,193	6,361	11,524	255	8,400
1963	1,276	136,956	5,955	11,238	243	8,680
1962	1,216	130,282	5,333	9,350	239	7,480
1961	1,174	128,956	4,940	7,751	224	7,295
1960	1,118	121,400	5,206	9,499	186	6,088
1959	1,050	107,433	5,879	8,394	184	6,227
1958	925	92,277	3,964	5,189	149	4,779
1957	1,046	104,489	4,577	7,745	138	4,735
1956	1,014	99,860	4,896	7,260	128	4,241

Series P82-105. Canadian production of principal non-metallic minerals, 1886 to 1975 (continued)

Year	Asbestos		Gypsum		Peat moss	
	Quantity ('000 tons)	Value ($'000)	Quantity ('000 tons)	Value ($'000)	Quantity ('000 tons)	Value ($'000)
	82	83	84	85	86	87
1955	1,064	96,191	4,668	8,037	118	3,485
1954	924	86,409	3,950	7,095	99	3,019
1953	911	86,053	3,841	7,400	82	2,643
1952	929	89,255	3,591	6,538	75	2,474
1951	973	81,584	3,803	5,881	77	2,433
1950	875	65,855	3,666	6,708	75	2,257
1949	575	39,746	3,014	5,424	80	2,377
1948	717	42,231	3,217	5,548	90	2,768
1947	662	33,006	2,497	4,735	80	2,280
1946	558	25,241	1,811	3,672	97	2,396
1945	467	22,805	840	1,783	84	2,011
1944	419	20,620	596	1,512	80	1,870
1943	467	23,170	447	1,381	64	1,461
1942	439	22,663	566	1,254	54	1,069
1941	478	21,469	1,593	2,248	28	644
1940	347	15,620	1,449	2,066	—	—
1939	364	15,859	1,422	1,935	—	—
1938	290	12,890	1,009	1,502	—	—
1937	410	14,506	1,047	1,540	—	—
1936	301	9,958	834	1,279	—	—
1935	210	7,055	542	932	—	—
1934	156	4,936	461	864	—	—
1933	158	5,211	383	676	—	—
1932	123	3,040	439	1,080	—	—
1931	164	4,813	864	2,112	—	—
1930	242	8,390	1,071	2,819	—	—
1929	306	13,173	1,212	3,346	—	—
1928	273	11,238	1,246	3,744	—	—
1927	275	10,621	1,063	3,251	—	—
1926	279	10,099	884	2,771	—	—
1925	274	8,978	740	2,390	—	—
1924	226	6,711	646	2,208	—	—
1923	231	7,523	578	2,243	—	—
1922	164	5,553	559	2,161	—	—
1921	93	4,906	387	1,786	—	—
1920	200	14,792	429	1,894	—	—
1919	159	10,975	299	1,215	—	—
1918	158	8,971	152	823	—	—
1917	154	7,230	336	882	—	—
1916	154	5,229	343	739	—	—
1915	137	3,575	475	855	—	—
1914	118	2,910	517	1,156	—	—
1913	161	3,850	636	1,448	—	—
1912	136	3,137	578	1,325	—	—
1911	127	2,943	518	993	—	—
1910	102	2,574	525	934	—	—
1909	87	2,302	473	810	—	—
1908	91	2,573	341	576	—	—
1907	90	2,505	486	647	—	—
1906	82	2,060	469	634	—	—
1905	68	1,503	442	536	—	—
1904	48	1,226	346	373	—	—
1903	42	930	314	388	—	—
1902	40	1,148	334	379	—	—
1901	40	1,260	294	340	—	—
1900	29	748	252	259	—	—
1899	26	486	245	257	—	—
1898	24	491	219	233	—	—
1897	30	445	240	245	—	—
1896	12	430	207	178	—	—
1895	9	368	226	203	—	—
1894	8	421	224	202	—	—
1893	6	310	193	196	—	—
1892	6	390	241	241	—	—
1891	9	1,000	204	206	—	—
1890	10	1,260	227	194	—	—
1889	6	427	213	205	—	—
1888	4	255	176	179	—	—
1887	5	227	154	157	—	—
1886	3	206	162	179	—	—

Series P82-105. Canadian production of principal non-metallic minerals, 1886 to 1975 (continued)

Year	Potash		Quartz[1]		Salt		Sodium sulphate		Titanium dioxide	
	Quantity ('000 tons)	Value ($'000)	Quantity ('000 tons)	Value ($'000)	Quantity ('000 tons)	Value ($'000)	Quantity ('000 tons)	Value ($'000)	Quantity ('000 tons)	Value ($'000)
	88	89	90	91	92	93	94	95	96	97
1975	5,152	358,570	2,747	13,112	5,647	59,714	521	22,049	–	55,812
1974	6,367	308,925	2,762	12,184	6,004	60,619	703	15,271	–	51,931
1973	4,909	176,876	2,766	11,051	5,565	49,631	543	7,165	–	46,619
1972	3,852	135,513	2,664	9,536	5,417	40,144	507	6,201	–	40,828
1971	4,000	134,955	2,554	7,411	5,542	40,111	482	7,064	–	39,064
1970	3,420	108,695	3,238	6,811	5,359	36,098	491	7,602	–	34,623
1969	3,492	69,383	2,300	6,280	4,658	30,406	518	8,052	–	30,364
1968	2,918	65,121	2,555	5,704	4,864	31,170	460	7,083	–	28,016
1967	2,383	67,395	2,611	5,530	4,996	27,808	428	6,359	–	23,737
1966	1,990	62,665	2,300	5,514	4,129	23,846	405	6,472	–	20,505
1965	1,491	55,971	2,434	5,124	4,584	23,986	345	5,527	–	22,425
1964	858	31,162	2,117	4,506	3,989	23,204	333	5,222	–	21,270
1963	627	22,500	1,837	3,688	3,722	22,317	257	4,121	–	13,807
1962	–	3,000	2,086	3,817	3,639	21,927	247	3,954	–	11,574
1961	–	–	2,194	3,153	3,247	19,552	251	4,037	–	16,724
1960	–	–	2,261	3,267	3,315	19,356	214	3,449	–	12,947
1959	–	–	2,164	3,437	3,290	18,035	180	2,882	–	8,507
1958	–	–	1,454	2,538	2,375	14,990	173	2,863	–	6,575
1957	–	–	2,139	3,185	1,772	13,990	158	2,569	186	9,741
1956	–	–	2,142	3,037	1,591	12,144	181	2,838	157	7,683
1955	–	–	1,870	2,040	1,245	10,122	179	2,800	117	5,193
1954	–	–	1,716	1,575	970	8,340	158	2,386	88	3,841
1953	–	–	1,786	2,071	955	6,975	116	1,681	101	4,206
1952	–	–	1,783	2,254	972	7,775	123	1,709	31	1,238
1951	–	–	1,905	2,258	965	7,906	192	2,384	14	739
1950	–	–	1,731	1,740	859	7,011	131	1,616	2	150
1949	–	–	1,722	1,589	749	5,567	120	1,615	–	–
1948	–	–	2,017	2,083	741	4,836	154	2,136	–	–
1947	–	–	1,836	1,797	729	4,437	163	1,793	–	–
1946	–	–	1,413	1,555	538	3,626	106	1,118	–	–
1945	–	–	1,514	1,535	673	4,055	93	884	–	–
1944	–	–	1,740	1,658	695	4,074	102	988	–	–
1943	–	–	1,777	1,608	688	4,379	107	1,025	–	–
1942	–	–	1,738	1,538	654	3,844	131	1,080	–	–
1941	–	–	2,053	1,366	561	3,196	116	932	–	–
1940	–	–	1,858	1,204	465	2,823	94	830	–	–
1939	–	–	1,583	1,100	425	2,487	71	628	–	–
1938	–	–	1,380	962	440	1,913	63	553	–	–
1937	–	–	1,377	1,129	459	1,799	80	618	–	–
1936	–	–	1,047[1]	598[1]	391	1,773	76	553	–	–
1935	..	..	233	425	360	1,881	45	344	–	–
1934	..	..	273	482	322	1,955	67	588	–	–
1933	..	..	186	298	280	1,940	50	485	–	–
1932	..	..	189	276	264	1,948	22	272	–	–
1931	..	..	196	303	259	1,904	45	421	–	–
1930	..	..	226	418	272	1,695	32	294	–	–
1929	..	..	266	562	330	1,578	5	64	–	–
1928	..	..	283	524	299	1,496	6	69	–	–
1927	..	..	234	496	269	1,615	6	11	–	–
1926	..	..	232	553	263	1,480	7	14	–	–
1925	..	..	197	364	234	1,411	4	19	–	–
1924	..	..	151	323	208	1,375	1	6	–	–
1923	..	..	264	599	202	1,714	1	10	–	–
1922	..	..	110	209	182	1,628	1	12	–	–
1921	..	..	100	313	165	1,674	1	19	–	–
1920	..	..	128	468	210	1,545	1	19	–	–
1919	..	..	95	528	148	1,398	–	–	–	–
1918	..	..	268	630	132	1,285	–	–	–	–
1917	..	..	216	496	139	1,048	–	–	–	–
1916	..	..	137	251	133	718	–	–	–	–
1915	..	..	127	205	120	600	–	–	–	–
1914	..	..	54	85	107	494	–	–	–	–
1913	..	..	78	170	101	491	–	–	–	–
1912	..	..	100	195	95	460	–	–	–	–
1911	..	..	61	84	92	443	–	–	–	–
1910	..	..	88	92	84	410	–	–	–	–
1909	..	..	57	71	84	415	–	–	–	–
1908	..	..	45	53	80	379	–	–	–	–
1907	..	..	57	124	73	342	–	–	–	–
1906	..	..	48	66	77	329	–	–	–	–

Series P82-105. Canadian production of principal non-metallic minerals, 1886 to 1975 (continued)

Year	Potash		Quartz[1]		Salt		Sodium sulphate		Titanium dioxide	
	Quantity ('000 tons)	Value ($'000)	Quantity ('000 tons)	Value ($'000)	Quantity ('000 tons)	Value ($'000)	Quantity ('000 tons)	Value ($'000)	Quantity ('000 tons)	Value ($'000)
	88	89	90	91	92	93	94	95	96	97
1905	..	..	—	—	67	321	—	—	—	—
1904	..	..	—	—	69	322	—	—	—	—
1903	..	..	—	—	62	298	—	—	—	—
1902	..	..	—	—	64	293	—	—	—	—
1901	..	..	—	—	59	262	—	—	—	—
1900	..	..	—	—	62	279	—	—	—	—
1899	..	..	1	1	59	254	—	—	—	—
1898	..	..	—	1	57	249	—	—	—	—
1897	..	..	—	—	51	226	—	—	—	—
1896	..	..	—	—	44	170	—	—	—	—
1895	..	..	—	—	52	160	—	—	—	—
1894	..	..	—	—	57	171	—	—	—	—
1893	..	..	—	1	62	196	—	—	—	—
1892	..	..	—	—	45	162	—	—	—	—
1891	..	..	—	—	45	161	—	—	—	—
1890	..	..	—	1	44	199	—	—	—	—
1889	..	..	—	—	33	130	—	—	—	—
1888	..	..	—	—	59	185	—	—	—	—
1887	..	..	—	—	60	166	—	—	—	—
1886	..	..	—	—	62	227	—	—	—	—

Year	Sulphur		Cement		Lime		Sand and gravel	
	Quantity ('000 tons)	Value ($'000)	Quantity ('000 tons)	Value ($'000)	Quantity ('000 tons)	Value ($'000)	Quantity ('000 tons)	Value ($'000)
	98	99	100	101	102	103	104	105
1975	5,262	101,488	11,237	331,524	1,608	41,131	272,442	305,181
1974	6,279	78,368	11,668	281,958	2,159	42,953	263,779	263,985
1973	5,351	33,886	11,271	241,945	1,973	32,533	233,461	213,437
1972	4,314	24,706	10,039	210,685	1,744	26,661	225,194	178,100
1971	3,768	25,932	9,076	183,374	1,644	24,435	213,291	152,628
1970	4,254	35,787	7,946	155,740	1,676	21,381	202,656	133,558
1969	3,650	68,679	8,250	162,091	1,635	19,239	201,581	122,159
1968	3,247	88,879	8,166	148,210	1,456	17,473	205,235	129,501
1967	3,091	75,796	7,995	143,150	1,423	16,567	215,213	146,698
1966	2,542	46,305	8,931	156,301	1,555	18,340	218,271	152,084
1965	2,513	30,712	8,428	142,523	1,620	20,134	205,260	133,820
1964	2,232	22,900	7,847	130,704	1,541	19,409	193,791	125,232
1963	1,603	16,868	7,014	118,615	1,451	18,504	189,571	123,854
1962	988	12,377	6,879	113,234	1,424	17,647	181,246	118,603
1961	672	9,996	6,206	103,924	1,415	19,217	170,751	104,654
1960	1,002	10,470	5,787	93,261	1,530	19,302	192,074	111,164
1959	888	8,770	6,284	95,148	1,686	21,304	185,124	104,651
1958	848	8,483	6,153	96,414	1,596	19,466	160,211	96,282
1957	750	7,130	6,049	93,167	1,379	16,679	159,830	91,939
1956	710	6,862	5,022	75,233	1,296	15,668	148,801	81,957
1955	628	5,985	4,404	65,650	1,331	15,811	127,524	67,775
1954	532	4,876	3,927	59,036	1,215	14,742	110,961	57,988
1953	359	3,173	3,892	58,842	1,229	14,484	101,034	53,485
1952	424	3,851	3,241	48,059	1,176	13,613	102,896	51,339
1951	372	3,121	2,976	40,446	1,241	14,083	92,973	44,628
1950	301	2,190	2,930	35,894	1,124	12,281	73,095	36,435
1949	262	2,039	2,785	32,902	1,019	11,310	63,356	31,182
1948	229	1,836	2,472	28,265	1,054	10,655	68,671	30,630
1947	222	1,823	2,089	21,969	977	8,543	56,790	23,114
1946	235	1,785	2,023	20,123	841	7,075	39,950	15,530
1945	250	1,881	1,483	14,246	832	6,525	29,751	10,568
1944	248	1,756	1,258	11,621	885	6,927	28,400	10,280
1943	258	1,753	1,278	11,599	908	6,833	25,744	9,006
1942	304	1,995	1,597	14,365	885	6,531	26,350	9,005
1941	260	1,703	1,465	13,064	861	6,358	31,605	10,376

Series P82-105. Canadian production of principal non-metallic minerals, 1886 to 1975 (concluded)

Year	Sulphur		Cement		Lime		Sand and gravel	
	Quantity ('000 tons)	Value ($'000)	Quantity ('000 tons)	Value ($'000)	Quantity ('000 tons)	Value ($'000)	Quantity ('000 tons)	Value ($'000)
	98	99	100	101	102	103	104	105
1940	171	1,298	1,323	11,775	717	5,195	31,375	11,759
1939	211	1,668	1,003	8,511	552	4,004	31,294	11,241
1938	112	1,045	966	8,241	487	3,543	32,224	12,003
1937	131	1,155	1,080	9,096	549	3,825	27,001	10,493
1936	122	1,033	789	6,908	468	3,336	22,124	6,921
1935	67	634	638	5,580	405	2,926	21,213	6,389
1934	52	516	662	5,668	368	2,746	14,854	4,035
1933	57	510	526	4,537	324	2,432	11,739	4,464
1932	53	470	787	6,931	321	2,395	14,470	4,481
1931	50	429	1,778	15,826	345	2,764	21,749	6,651
1930	38	315	1,931	17,713	491	4,039	28,548	8,345
1929	43	351	2,150	19,337	676	5,909	27,847	7,318
1928	39	321	1,929	16,739	507	4,535	28,103	5,809
1927	25	198	1,762	14,392	445	3,923	22,953	6,056
1926	9	64	1,524	13,013	414	3,781	17,113	4,941
1925	8	59	1,420	14,047	359	3,388	11,019	3,220
1924	10	96	1,312	13,398	320	3,179	11,604	3,181
1923	11	113	1,320	15,065	351	3,267	12,753	3,017
1922	7	74	1,215	15,438	314	3,165	11,666	3,503
1921	12	116	1,007	14,195	241	2,781	11,575	2,537
1920	68	719	1,164	14,798	330	3,019	11,531	4,201
1919	66	523	874	9,802	250	2,311	10,364	2,680
1918	154	1,705	629	7,077	223	1,876	11,262	2,367
1917	155	1,611	834	7,724	230	1,558	9,182	2,326
1916	117	1,084	940	6,548	192	1,091	8,156	1,838
1915	116	985	994	6,977	177	1,016	6,446	1,625
1914	94	745	1,255	9,188	246	1,361	—	2,505
1913	65	521	1,515	11,019	265	1,609	—	2,259
1912	33	314	1,248	9,107	297	1,345	—	1,512
1911	34	366	996	7,645	264	1,518	573	408
1910	22	187	832	6,412	205	1,137	625	408
1909	27	223	712	5,346	196	1,133	482	256
1908	19	225	467	3,710	126	713	299	161
1907	19	212	427	3,781	166	975	298	120
1906	18	170	372	3,171	183	1,009	337	139
1905	14	125	238	1,924	—	750	307	153
1904	15	134	169	1,338	—	780	400	190
1903	14	128	126	1,225	—	900	356	124
1902	15	139	126	1,128	—	892	160	119
1901	14	131	79	660	—	830	197	117
1900	16	155	73	663	—	800	198	102
1899	11	111	69	633	—	800	242	102
1898	13	129	44	398	—	650	166	90
1897	16	117	36	275	—	650	153	77
1896	14	101	26	202	—	650	225	80
1895	14	103	22	174	—	700	277	118
1894	17	122	19	145	—	900	325	87
1893	22	176	28	194	—	900	329	122
1892	26	179	21	148	—	411	298	85
1891	26	203	16	109	—	251	344	60
1890	20	123	18	92	—	412	342	66
1889	29	307	16	70	—	362	283	53
1888	25	286	9	36	—	340	261	38
1887	15	171	1	82	—	395	181	30
1886	17	193	—	—	—	285	125	24

[1] For 1936 to 1975, low grade fluxing sand figures are included.

Series P106-127. Canadian exports of principal non-metallic minerals, 1886 to 1975

Year	Asbestos[1]						Gypsum or plaster		Cement	
	Crude[2]		Milled fibres[2]		Waste, refuse or shorts					
	Quantity ('000 tons)	Value ($'000)	Quantity ('000 tons)	Value ($'000)	Quantity ('000 tons)	Value ($'000)	Quantity ('000 tons)	Value ($'000)	Quantity ('000 cwt)	Value ($'000)
	106	107	108	109	110	111	112	113	114	115
1975	—	45	623	231,774	562	70,316	4,069	11,381	21,971	23,902
1974	—	76	901	254,256	920	90,870	5,746	13,893	25,318	23,642
1973	—	39	929	205,333	955	75,498	6,343	14,115	28,192	24,438
1972	—	132	785	170,253	848	64,682	5,963	12,293	25,987	23,251
1971	—	113	780	167,037	795	59,635	5,035	9,685	17,757	15,731
1970	—	91	824	171,850	738	55,307	4,853	9,546	11,330	11,251
1969	—	104	779	160,104	786	56,067	4,871	9,108	9,729	9,196
1968	—	161	723	143,792	736	48,942	4,464	8,332	7,330	6,087
1967	—	189	653	127,570	688	44,639	3,896	7,323	6,560	5,208
1966	—	151	733	137,871	713	44,461	4,673	8,327	8,148	6,571
1965	—	116	630	115,885	688	42,655	4,747	8,335	6,698	5,214
1964	—	184	630	114,525	703	40,997	5,057	9,061	5,953	4,689
1963	—	165	555	101,707	651	37,575	4,703	7,674	5,456	4,202
1962	—	155	532	99,002	632	36,481	4,163	5,630	4,383	3,464
1961	—	164	528	97,790	589	33,387	3,819	5,554	4,988	3,866
1960	—	247	458	85,803	610	34,064	4,274	7,054	3,622	2,821
1959	—	426	402	76,376	612	33,629	4,849	9,845	6,063	5,003
1958	—	479	318	61,330	548	28,936	2,898	4,871	2,825	2,467
1957	1	568	393	73,949	637	32,542	3,411	5,905	6,766	6,052
1956	1	526	377	69,028	586	30,341	3,841	6,988	2,491	1,985
1955	1	481	366	63,435	635	30,888	3,039	4,931	3,378	3,139
1954	1	578	313	53,876	574	28,112	2,831	4,205	433	496
1953	1	720	317	55,183	561	28,070	2,770	3,794	52	78
1952	1	705	340	56,647	562	29,158	2,763	2,847	15	21
1951	1	548	325	48,855	617	30,930	3,028	3,128	9	12
1950	1	544	290	39,114	539	23,094	2,970	3,061	84	111
1949	1	416	182	22,769	353	13,749	2,545	2,637	67	52
1948	1	557	237	25,552	452	15,290	2,617	2,703	255	201
1947	1	445	224	20,276	412	11,571	1,937	2,043	308	198
1948	1	294	215	16,216	304	7,330	1,489	1,599	400	236
1945	1	367	210	15,858	230	5,618	559	582	987	535
1944	2	650	182	13,635	213	5,361	387	434	737	377
1943	2	860	211	15,674	230	5,848	185	213	604	344
1942	3	1,191	198	15,057	226	5,667	490	544	959	476
1941	3	935	217	13,616	234	4,860	1,166	1,186	1,088	518
1940	2	728	180	11,654	155	3,143	1,312	1,347	1,050	414
1939	186[2]	12,463[2]	—[2]	—[2]	160	2,902	1,260	1,390	548	160
1938	166	10,872	—	—	123	2,238	810	933	313	101
1937	197	10,973	—	—	195	3,242	841	961	254	83
1936	137	7,392	—	—	158	2,567	650	756	241	57
1935	100	5,300	—	—	100	1,585	439	508	195	44
1934	83	4,029	—	—	75	1,100	355	414	245	55
1933	79	3,998	—	—	70	991	287	344	184	47
1932	43	2,115	—	—	70	986	372	470	187	39
1931	71	3,929	—	—	89	1,245	619	741	399	124
1930	104	6,442	—	—	131	2,011	719	872	696	212
1929	144	10,127	—	—	148	2,507	893	1,087	819	253
1928	129	8,803	—	—	136	2,178	825	1,241	936	341
1927	133	8,697	—	—	130	2,038	589	960	874	308
1926	142	8,670	—	—	136	1,992	668	1,069	1,001	358
1925	137	8,090	—	—	121	1,592	534	861	3,493	1,498
1924	110	6,298	—	—	95	1,220	472	748	537	214
1923	138	7,629	—	—	78	931	397	579	1,728	825
1922	105	5,994	—	—	57	562	325	505	1,488	700
1921	63	5,465	—	—	22	216	230	418	848	651
1920	153	11,522	—	—	36	366	244	414	—	466
1919	119	9,626	—	—	25	261	148	200	—	2,194
1918	119	7,787	—	—	22	228	68	81	—	14
1917	94	4,903	—	—	52	431	224	245	—	17
1916	97[1]	3,872[1]	—	—	34[1]	241[1]	221	252	—	2
1915	85	2,735	—	—	25	157	292	336	—	5
1914	81	2,299	—	—	19	109	346	404	—	2
1913	104	2,848	—	—	25	139	418	504	—	2
1912	88	2,349	—	—	—	—	365	423	—	2
1911	75	2,067	—	—	—	—	362	425	—	4
1910	71	2,109	—	—	—	—	346	417	—	13
1909	57	1,730	—	—	—	—	315	372	—	113
1908	61	1,843	—	—	—	—	280	325	—	35
1907	57	1,669	—	—	—	—	375	425	—	10
1906	60	1,689	—	—	—	—	404	463	—	8

Series P106-127. Canadian exports of principal non-metallic minerals, 1886 to 1975 (continued)

Year	Asbestos[1]						Gypsum or plaster		Cement	
	Crude[2]		Milled fibres[2]		Waste, refuse or shorts					
	Quantity ('000 tons)	Value ($'000)	Quantity ('000 tons)	Value ($'000)	Quantity ('000 tons)	Value ($'000)	Quantity ('000 tons)	Value ($'000)	Quantity ('000 cwt)	Value ($'000)
	106	107	108	109	110	111	112	113	114	115
1905	47	1,386	–	–	–	–	–	–	–	3
1904	37	1,161	–	–	–	–	–	–	–	5
1903	32	891	–	–	–	–	–	–	–	3
1902	31	995	–	–	–	–	–	–	–	2
1901	32	1,070	–	–	–	–	–	–	–	2
1900	17	693	–	–	–	–	–	–	–	3
1899	18	473	–	–	–	–	–	–	–	3
1898	15	494	–	–	–	–	–	–	–	2
1897	16	473	–	–	–	–	–	–	–	1
1896	12	568	–	–	–	–	–	–	–	1
1895	7	422	–	–	–	–	–	–	–	1
1894	8	478	–	–	–	–	–	–	–	–
1893	6	339	–	–	–	–	–	–	–	1
1892	5	373	–	–	–	–	–	–	–	1
1891	8	562	–	–	–	–	–	–	–	3
1890	7	529	–	–	–	–	–	–	–	–
1889	6	360	–	–	–	–	–	–	–	–
1888	4	278	–	–	–	–	–	–	–	–
1887	3	159	–	–	–	–	–	–	–	–
1886	3	206	–	–	–	–	–	–	–	–

Year	Clay, ground or unground		Lime, quick and hydrated		Sand and gravel		Salt and brine		Sulphur, in ores		Sulphur, crude or refined	
	Quantity ('000 cwt)	Value ($'000)	Quantity ('000 cwt)	Value ($'000)	Quantity ('000 tons)	Value ($'000)	Quantity ('000 cwt)	Value ($'000)	Quantity ('000 tons)	Value ($'000)	Quantity ('000 tons)	Value ($'000)
	116	117	118	119	120	121	122	123	124	125	126	127
1975	62	91	5,160	6,344	153	365	–	5,183	–	170	3,620	113,036
1974	51	120	8,524	7,885	394	780	–	6,851	–	648	4,686	90,369
1973	113	327	7,462	5,543	881	953	–	6,051	–	659	3,850	44,348
1972	94	227	5,923	4,055	697	1,001	–	4,988	–	502	2,848	27,537
1971	88	103	5,675	3,937	775	1,094	–	7,029	–	1,074	2,648	27,132
1970	37	52	4,012	2,527	1,240	1,940	–	7,430	–	1,226	2,988	42,860
1969	17	32	3,903	2,302	458	640	–	5,107	–	1,104	2,264	62,742
1968	15	43	1,705	1,002	496	538	–	5,921	–	1,056	2,111	76,426
1967	6	27	1,802	1,043	601	861	–	5,926	–	1,067	1,774	58,699
1966	54	78	3,617	2,141	700	928	–	3,588	–	981	1,399	33,590
1965	26	51	4,787	2,672	688	875	–	4,996	–	979	1,498	26,491
1964	21	34	2,127	1,208	461	604	–	3,619	–	879	1,295	19,526
1963	22	30	1,962	1,141	356	454	–	3,701	–	938	821	11,972
1962	40	56	1,432	1,010	354	448	–	3,988	–	890	400	6,650
1961	13	18	624	538	389	510	–	2,829	–	899	217	3,968
1960	139	268	433	426	418	540	–	3,461	–	1,259	143	2,762
1959	110	243	493	430	486	537	25,482	4,640	–	1,019	–	–
1958	130	307	344	362	353	409	8,134	2,917	–	1,879	–	–
1957	105	280	724	742	321	392	9,158	3,241	–	2,853	–	–
1956	94	149	638	623	420	426	6,679	2,287	–	2,649	–	–
1955	147	95	581	538	336	380	2,929	1,001	–	2,002	–	–
1954	113	35	616	551	306	325	24	26	189	1,567	–	–
1953	84	25	666	543	368	348	47	32	130	1,034	–	–
1952	184	39	464	374	350	330	57	45	198	1,643	–	–
1951	162	35	710	534	370	359	91	63	178	1,177	–	–
1950	55	15	661	509	349	328	82	53	112	473	–	–
1949	97	18	604	499	337	315	69	63	91	382	–	–
1948	89	19	661	471	384	347	113	127	50	196	–	–
1947	81	17	572	298	377	295	224	244	56	282	–	–
1946	78	16	498	284	353	234	117	116	68	286	–	–
1945	23	6	420	237	317	193	106	105	75	315	–	–
1944	49	14	309	137	292	183	64	81	91	353	–	–
1943	2	4	308	133	382	213	161	118	105	410	–	–
1942	2	5	169	75	509	219	187	129	166	701	–	–
1941	1	2	260	114	454	159	251	122	130	585	–	–
1940	1	2	472	121	373	111	127	62	48	231	–	–
1939	1	2	184	75	242	79	213	76	110	793	–	–
1938	1	3	128	51	609	146	237	68	22	145	–	–

Series P106-127. Canadian exports of principal non-metallic minerals, 1875 to 1975 (concluded)

Year	Clay, ground or unground		Lime, quick and hydrated		Sand and gravel		Salt and brine		Sulphur, in ores		Sulphur, crude or refined	
	Quantity ('000 cwt)	Value ($'000)	Quantity ('000 cwt)	Value ($'000)	Quantity ('000 tons)	Value ($'000)	Quantity ('000 cwt)	Value ($'000)	Quantity ('000 tons)	Value ($'000)	Quantity ('000 tons)	Value ($'000)
	116	117	118	119	120	121	122	123	124	125	126	127
1937	1	3	203	85	364	78	187	62	46	252	—	—
1936	3	3	233	98	333	74	111	47	52	285	—	—
1935	6	3	105	50	100	21	181	51	8	48	—	—
1934	8	2	213	152	88	17	132	48	10	95	—	—
1933	10	2	208	192	102	16	107	43	15	121	—	—
1932	3	1	187	188	178	34	113	36	17	90	—	—
1931	8	4	289	283	486	146	123	55	27	140	—	—
1930	10	6	447	445	2,589	468	175	74	27	160	—	—
1929	16	7	485	428	1,903	442	187	71	32	247	—	—
1928	20	21	401	357	797	232	59	36	32	250	—	—
1927	15	3	421	368	638	178	24	23	14	106	—	—
1926	15	4	374	345	908	278	23	19	—	—	—	—
1925	7	8	326	312	865	198	46	27	—	—	—	—
1924	1	1	455	411	1,036	210	19	11	—	1	—	—
1923	—	—	487	428	765	183	17	10	10	47	—	—
1922	3	2	287	271	684	116	15	10	—	—	—	—
1921	2	1	254	247	1,397	202	7	·8	8	32	—	—
1920	5	2	460	382	1,492	194	6	9	119	458	—	—
1919	—	—	193	129	1,074	131	12	15	89	389	—	—
1918	—	—	150	71	903	230	18	17	240	949	—	—
1917	—	—	—	75	1,075	291	173	94	280	974	—	—
1916	—	—	—	66	1,115	388	3	2	157	557	—	—
1915	—	—	—	16	808	381	9	6	138	527	—	—
1914	—	—	—	17	952	802	10	5	90	378	—	—
1913	—	—	—	29	645	441	5	3	46	212	—	—
1912	—	—	—	35	660	460	3	4	6	12	—	—
1911	—	—	—	40	573	408	5	5	32	121	—	—
1910	—	—	—	45	625	408	3	3	31	110	—	—
1909	—	—	—	49	482	256	3	2	35	157	—	—
1908	—	—	—	43	299	161	5	4	17	97	—	—
1907	—	—	—	56	298	120	22	8	25	80	—	—
1906	—	—	—	57	337	140	6	3	26	65	—	—
1905	—	—	—	86	307	153	14	6	20	56	—	—
1904	—	—	—	74	400	130	10	4	18	50	—	—
1903	—	—	—	131	356	124	19	6	21	60	—	—
1902	—	—	—	116	160	119	7	4	19	50	—	—
1901	—	—	—	99	197	117	27	7	25	57	—	—
1900	—	—	—	81	198	102	26	9	18	41	—	—
1899	—	—	—	74	242	102	8	3	16	34	—	—
1898	—	—	—	50	166	90	4	1	10	26	—	—
1897	—	—	—	53	153	77	4	1	15	31	—	—
1896	—	—	—	71	225	80	3	1	15	34	—	—
1895	—	—	—	72	277	118	3	1	8	38	—	—
1894	—	—	—	84	325	87	3	1	9	33	—	—
1893	—	—	—	87	329	122	3	1	—	—	—	—
1892	—	—	—	122	298	85	1	1	—	—	—	—
1891	—	—	—	120	244	60	4	1	—	—	—	—
1890	—	—	—	—	342	66	5	1	—	—	—	—
1889	—	—	—	—	283	53	6	2	—	—	—	—
1888	—	—	—	—	261	38	11	4	—	—	—	—
1887	—	—	—	—	181	30	108	12	—	—	—	—
1886	—	—	—	—	125	24	157	17	—	—	—	—
1885	—	—	—	—	111	23	173	19	—	—	—	—
1884	—	—	—	—	74	20	117	15	—	—	—	—
1883	—	—	—	—	55	14	140	10	—	—	—	—
1882	—	—	—	—	60	16	127	18	—	—	—	—
1881	—	—	—	—	59	15	240	45	—	—	—	—
1880	—	—	—	—	54	11	327	46	—	—	—	—
1879	—	—	—	—	47	9	414	49	—	—	—	—
1878	—	—	—	—	50	8	285	37	—	—	—	—
1877	—	—	—	—	12	2	493	61	—	—	—	—
1876	—	—	—	—	—	—	637	84	—	—	—	—
1875	—	—	—	—	—	—	380	67	—	—	—	—

[1] For 1888 to 1916 the export figures were defined as 'The Produce of the Mine'.

[2] For 1939 and earlier years data for asbestos milled fibres are included with crude asbestos, series P106–107.

Series P128-150. Canadian imports of principal non-metallic minerals, 1886 to 1975

Year[1]	Granite[2] Value ($'000)	Gypsum, crude and ground		Phosphate rock		Silex or crystallized quartz	
		Quantity ('000 tons)	Value ($'000)	Quantity ('000 cwt)	Value ($'000)	Quantity ('000 cwt)	Value ($'000)
	128	129	130	131	132	133	134
1975	2,824	61	672	72,360	85,170	—	305
1974	2,679	62	513	74,220	40,368	—	282
1973	1,472	92	397	73,580	23,913	—	182
1972	1,463	62	267	39,700	17,986	—	64
1971	1,710	106	429	56,880	17,118	—	117
1970	975	39	143	49,400	14,870	—	128
1969	1,213	82	292	44,020	14,858	—	104
1968	809	69	281	47,000	18,799	—	218
1967	858	69	327	45,600	20,563	—	385
1966	678	86	309	43,620	19,601	—	395
1965	799	75	267	33,900	13,991	—	395
1964	785	81	289	28,120	11,719	—	327
1963	958	75	245	—	11,681	—	286
1962	1,076	70	301	—	10,291	—	222
1961	973	66	218	—	9,151	—	186
1960	735	60	195	—	8,426	—	126
1959	409	118	347	15,941	7,468	276	184
1958	467	108	609	14,883	6,854	240	151
1957	408	92	360	14,464	5,898	274	187
1956	356	70	303	12,553	5,186	538	327
1955	322	16	124	11,764	4,513	490	252
1954	313	5	51	12,897	4,578	568	275
1953	279	1	17	11,530	3,951	611	1,733
1952	188	1	19	9,418	3,130	523	1,980
1951	188	2	24	9,994	3,179	608	2,870
1950	186	1	24	9,821	3,296	495	408
1949	201	1	20	12,416	3,880	459	239
1948	197	1	22	9,640	2,911	349	169
1947	212	9	76	9,708	2,858	300	165
1946	203	4	23	7,474	2,165	214	114
1945	66	1	22	6,354	1,451	145	247
1944	69	1	17	7,765	1,710	175	530
1943	64	5	29	5,217	1,085	228	946
1942	62	1	23	5,427	1,053	196	442
1941	69	1	22	4,741	864	102	130
1940	57	1	16	3,317	664	83	57
1939	77	1	18	2,498	477	55	61
1938	73	—	14	2,568	456	61	78
1937	91	—	13	2,279	454	86	104
1936	78	—	10	1,669	298	81	84
1935	74	—	8	1,270	235	67	76
1934	71	—	5	635	165	46	53
1933	54	—	5	367	75	87	83
1932	56	—	5	1,311	347	124	168
1931	54	1	18	2,834	619	105	130
1930	87	1	31	944	298	101	111
1929	88[2]	1	24	364	115	80	80
1928	55	1	48	208	68	57	74
1927	5	1	46	350	95	64	75
1926	6	1	39	285	66	51	60
1925	2	5	70	280	62	44	39
1924	2	3	65	234	57	39	50
1923	13	4	43	317	86	46	58
1922	6	3	27	230	56	21	25
1921	5	3	34	274	87	24	36
1920	5	2	29	270	114	23	26
1919	5	1	25	—	30	13	14
1918	4	—	4	—	90	12	12
1917	3	—	6	—	63	17	13
1916	5	3	18	—	16	34	18
1915	2	2	10	—	14	8	6
1914	5	4	21	—	20	17	16
1913	15	7	34	—	14	14	16
1912	21	11	36	—	25	13	11
1911	4	4	15	—	46	8	8
1910	3	19	34	—	73	13	12
1909	2	15	29	—	39	11	9
1908	3	14	44	—	35	10	8
1907	9	12	40	—	32	26	22
1906	38	9	27	—	31	11	12

Series P128-150. Canadian imports of principal non-metallic minerals, 1886 to 1975 (continued)

Year[1]	Granite[2] Value ($'000)	Gypsum, crude and ground Quantity ('000 tons)	Value ($'000)	Phosphate rock Quantity ('000 cwt)	Value ($'000)	Silex or crystallized quartz Quantity ('000 cwt)	Value ($'000)
	128	129	130	131	132	133	134
1905	28	6	20	—	18	8	6
1904[1]	8	—	1	—	8	6	4
1903	1	1	2	—	19	4	3
1902	—	1	2	—	15	4	4
1901	1	—	2	—	20	4	2
1900	—	—	1	—	6	4	3
1899	—	—	1	—	6	4	3
1898	—	1	2	—	—	3	3
1897	—	—	1	—	—	3	3
1896	—	1	1	—	—	3	2
1895	—	1	1	—	—	3	2
1894	—	—	2	—	—	2	2
1893	—	1	1	—	—	2	1
1892	—	1	3	—	—	1	1
1891	—	—	1	—	—	4	2
1890	—	1	4	—	—	2	3
1889	—	1	3	—	—	5	1
1888	—	1	3	—	—	5	2
1887	—	2	3	—	—	15	5
1886	—	2	3	—	—	3	1

Year[1]	Salt Quantity ('000 cwt)	Value ($'000)	Sulphur Quantity ('000 cwt)	Value ($'000)	Cement Quantity ('000 cwt)	Value ($'000)	Clay Quantity ('000 cwt)	Value ($'000)
	135	136	137	138	139	140	141	142
1975	26,080	10,388	380	911	9,286	18,134	12,592	17,299
1974	16,240	4,423	700	1,246	5,540	8,565	13,030	15,330
1973	18,560	4,420	780	978	2,573	4,102	11,203	12,147
1972	20,480	5,192	560	670	868	2,149	11,913	10,875
1971	18,440	3,931	620	745	1,118	2,229	13,576	10,760
1970	12,360	2,840	1,060	1,468	1,944	3,485	14,204	10,416
1969	13,920	3,017	920	1,697	1,068	2,261	13,340	10,393
1968	12,880	3,119	1,580	3,057	1,031	2,039	11,944	8,885
1967	11,340	2,571	2,500	4,346	883	1,724	10,800	8,560
1966	10,180	2,118	2,900	4,160	1,012	1,978	10,490	8,125
1965	8,840	1,950	3,240	3,829	752	1,547	10,590	7,352
1964	8,120	1,931	3,000	3,475	658	1,278	8,974	6,298
1963	6,660	1,582	3,020	3,505	631	1,112	4,933	4,096
1962	4,900	1,023	3,900	4,638	530	908	4,545	3,610
1961	3,960	922	6,600	7,094	585	921	3,986	3,041
1960	3,820	785	6,560	6,629	450	728	3,865	2,790
1959	7,399	1,578	6,649	6,925	585	859	4,370	3,411
1958	6,818	1,503	7,507	8,324	831	1,003	4,095	3,215
1957	7,350	1,649	8,339	9,752	1,848	1,870	4,331	3,112
1956	6,382	1,606	9,482	11,858	11,992	8,078	4,639	3,141
1955	7,305	1,884	7,467	9,387	10,358	8,443	3,829	2,803
1954	7,408	2,151	6,203	7,816	8,023	6,317	3,322	2,370
1953	6,147	2,017	7,182	8,527	8,690	7,403	3,820	2,640
1952	5,762	2,060	8,304	8,377	10,199	9,068	3,571	2,310
1951	5,176	1,954	7,919	8,960	8,146	7,448	4,068	2,630
1950	4,765	1,734	7,807	7,730	4,852	3,789	3,428	2,273
1949	4,734	1,568	5,611	5,214	7,994	6,878	3,444	1,958
1948	3,721	1,079	7,092	5,529	3,922	3,995	3,672	2,090
1947	4,398	1,247	7,228	5,466	4,370	3,844	3,374	1,784
1946	4,566	1,367	5,470	4,271	1,225	1,099	2,769	1,286
1945	2,743	805	4,977	4,063	114	142	2,876	1,183
1944	2,946	847	4,719	3,876	49	77	2,774	1,111
1943	1,686	589	4,371	3,524	65	84	2,555	926
1942	1,387	441	5,802	4,681	92	116	3,026	1,074
1941	1,629	450	4,705	3,920	42	59	2,944	1,087
1940	2,250	558	4,312	3,628	46	70	2,630	974
1939	2,353	507	3,044	2,454	58	58	2,009	740
1938	2,163	454	1,874	1,472	170	105	1,842	718
1937	2,329	466	4,514	3,669	214	134	2,694	925
1936	2,178	461	3,375	2,802	140	107	2,233	776

Series P128-150. Canadian imports of principal non-metallic minerals, 1886 to 1975 (continued)

Year[1]	Salt		Sulphur		Cement		Clay	
	Quantity ('000 cwt)	Value ($'000)	Quantity ('000 cwt)	Value ($'000)	Quantity ('000 cwt)	Value ($'000)	Quantity ('000 cwt)	Value ($'000)
	135	136	137	138	139	140	141	142
1935	2,565	527	2,733	2,298	62	60	1,703	709
1934	2,776	586	3,154	2,589	50	46	1,565	586
1933	2,712	651	2,816	2,530	67	38	1,103	506
1932	2,041	596	2,100	2,023	75	58	732	456
1931	2,618	752	2,484	2,282	134	143	1,254	529
1930	2,568	661	3,595	3,177	502	570	1,610	684
1929	3,531	937	4,699	3,789	196	189	2,019	767
1928	3,781	1,123	3,655	2,963	119	146	1,682	623
1927	3,535	1,082	3,554	2,918	68	88	1,405	548
1926	3,768	1,037	3,683	2,946	74	78	1,298	477
1925	3,873	1,077	2,932	1,983	76	63	1,189	428
1924	3,658	1,134	2,631	1,777	97	69	1,277	494
1923	3,437	1,068	2,715	1,804	62	75	1,413	567
1922	3,917	1,274	2,463	1,701	108	83	874	381
1921	2,594	1,025	1,575	1,273	42	76	788	360
1920	3,113	1,435	2,895	2,114	115	112	1,281	651
1919	2,948	1,310	1,121	1,015	49	51	788	362
1918	3,310	1,267	1,841	2,059	21	20	211	554
1917	3,416	1,088	1,649	1,515	30	20	232	416
1916	3,024	695	1,469	1,187	72	32	381	325
1915	2,750	518	604	480	99	40	439	237
1914	2,853	541	839	871	343	147	—	288
1913	2,889	565	609	633	889	109	—	324
1912	2,693	468	773	807	5,020	1,970	—	288
1911	2,416	421	439	446	2,343	841	—	270
1910	2,528	448	457	475	1,223	468	—	293
1909	2,326	431	458	459	498	167	—	216
1908	2,529	444	425	411	1,644	532	—	197
1907	2,438	442	520	522	2,371	844	—	271
1906	2,322	422	420	435	2,038	690	—	226
1905	2,274	432	351	364	2,955	1,053	—	197
1904[1]	2,284	412	194	205	2,488	1,000	—	145
1903	2,473	403	244	259	2,331	874	—	176
1902	2,525	425	246	325	2,001	851	—	141
1901	2,279	374	239	271	1,630	661	—	141
1900	2,046	325	211	215	1,312	503	—	123
1899	1,948	300	245	266	1,302	469	—	—
1898	2,137	326	380	374	1,089	362	—	—
1897	2,278	346	87	88	747	257	—	—
1896	2,127	363	69	64	735	251	—	—
1895	2,102	363	49	57	706	250	—	—
1894	2,125	382	58	62	788	282	—	—
1893	2,130	361	64	77	820	324	—	—
1892	2,205	381	48	67	663	284	—	—
1891	2,106	381	36	46	655	311	—	—
1890	1,736	310	44	44	692	323	—	—
1889	1,920	292	24	34	448	187	—	—
1888	1,947	253	20	25	448	185	—	—
1887	2,135	321	31	39	381	157	—	—
1886	1,925	295	29	44	—	126	—	—

Series P128-150. Canadian imports of principal non-metallic minerals, 1886 to 1975 (continued)

Year[1]	Lime		Sand and gravel		Sand silica		Titanium oxide, white pigment and antimony oxide	
	Quantity ('000 cwt)	Value ($'000)	Quantity ('000 tons)	Value ($'000)	Quantity ('000 cwt)	Value ($'000)	Quantity ('000 lb.)	Value ($'000)
	143	**144**	**145**	**146**	**147**	**148**	**149**	**150**
1975	664	1,419	2,105	3,540	23,020	9,169	6,309	3,615
1974	463	770	1,734	2,485	21,080	7,562	10,705	4,973
1973	325	539	1,136	1,282	21,740	5,874	10,975	3,325
1972	574	761	1,068	1,049	27,380	5,893	12,817	3,244
1971	529	692	675	785	28,400	5,624	12,474	3,153
1970	676	778	503	538	25,940	5,337	6,408	2,150
1969	825	809	860	737	15,700	4,986	5,798	1,497
1968	495	526	683	642	22,140	4,263	5,569	1,394
1967	442	454	758	825	19,040	4,008	3,762	952
1966	585	568	567	741	20,260	3,863	3,997	1,090
1965	507	537	571	683	16,700	3,452	3,746	1,039
1964	416	480	593	741	15,440	3,060	4,387	1,174
1963	886	714	562	541	15,980	3,250	7,384	1,790
1962	722	554	839	557	15,480	3,138	25,869	5,899
1961	769	536	538	496	14,080	2,682	53,601	8,157
1960	676	430	886	444	14,620	2,566	54,230	7,745
1959	628	388	1,097	571	15,843	2,525	61,707	8,988
1958	313	203	234	247	12,067	2,115	59,201	8,535
1957	564	343	263	350	14,897	2,408	68,836	10,870
1956	946	551	319	370	16,807	2,597	76,007	12,661
1955	500	283	259	275	14,709	2,146	71,884	10,573
1954	531	289	284	287	13,117	1,884	64,492	9,198
1953	430	233	187	190	14,064	1,928	63,929	8,500
1952	334	170	183	175	12,858	1,772	48,584	6,514
1951	294	159	261	214	13,859	1,991	59,397	8,505
1950	281	160	201	209	11,467	1,565	54,250	7,054
1949	330	176	171	155	10,222	1,362	41,587	5,158
1948	478	219	135	113	11,680	1,447	39,293	4,610
1947	261	115	94	83	10,669	1,148	27,312	2,966
1946	152	50	71	71	7,800	914	23,931	2,194
1945	127	36	104	78	8,209	927	21,359	2,046
1944	134	35	84	58	9,152	914	20,175	1,871
1943	182	64	83	53	10,181	1,011	16,890	1,533
1942	125	44	132	90	10,818	1,011	14,643	1,423
1941	89	27	119	107	8,423	783	13,220	1,321
1940	83	23	160	98	5,575	557	8,770	783
1939	121	33	148	69	3,354	349	9,004	803
1938	133	36	87	62	3,441	339	4,710	512
1937	100	32	132	98	4,257	374	5,630	527
1936	19	12	122	78	2,872	271	4,198	424
1935	13	9	98	81	2,472	283	2,879	310
1934	7	5	61	57	1,923	226	984[3]	131[3]
1933	5	4	89	72	1,282	160	—	—
1932	6	6	36	49	1,184	163	—	—
1931	11	11	155	140	2,154	235	—	—
1930	42	28	185	168	3,287	353	—	—
1929	89	49	269	217	4,679	491	—	—
1928	108	65	588	275	3,088	332	—	—
1927	116	70	290	200	2,977	346	—	—
1926	77	43	255	212	3,102	372	—	—
1925	94	48	282	184	2,870	353	—	—
1924	88	47	151	118	2,636	324	—	—
1923	100	56	355	247	3,351	317	—	—
1922	51	28	351	176	2,157	224	—	—
1921	24	20	165	115	929	136	—	—
1920	55	49	219	268	2,267	332	—	—
1919	80	53	201	200	792	111	—	—
1918	100	54	311	436	—	—	—	—
1917	243	78	329	312	—	—	—	—
1916	424	96	234	184	—	—	—	—
1915	380	98	200	121	—	—	—	—
1914	682	211	274	225	—	—	—	—
1913	773	238	440	440	—	—	—	—
1912	660	207	533	446	—	—	—	—
1911	457	162	241	247	—	—	—	—
1910	425	139	196	197	—	—	—	—
1909	337	118	151	154	—	—	—	—
1908	287	99	134	135	—	—	—	—
1907	253	99	266	224	—	—	—	—
1906	294	108	196	226	—	—	—	—

Series P128-150. Canadian imports of principal non-metallic minerals, 1886 to 1975 (concluded)

Year[1]	Lime		Sand and gravel		Sand silica		Titanium oxide, white pigment and antimony oxide	
	Quantity ('000 cwt)	Value ($'000)	Quantity ('000 tons)	Value ($'000)	Quantity ('000 cwt)	Value ($'000)	Quantity ('000 lb.)	Value ($'000)
	143	144	145	146	147	148	149	150
1905	228	82	105	142	—	—	—	—
1904[1]	109	40	111	108	—	—	—	—
1903	62	22	92	96	—	—	—	—
1902	49	18	47	59	—	—	—	—
1901	39	15	36	43	—	—	—	—
1900	26	11	36	41	—	—	—	—
1899	31	11	30	42	—	—	—	—
1898	26	9	32	43	—	—	—	—
1897	32	11	21	25	—	—	—	—
1896	20	7	19	25	—	—	—	—
1895	24	6	20	25	—	—	—	—
1894	14	5	42	34	—	—	—	—
1893	14	5	26	32	—	—	—	—
1892	12	4	—	28	—	—	—	—
1891	13	4	—	24	—	—	—	—
1890	16	5	—	37	—	—	—	—
1889	26	9	—	34	—	—	—	—
1888	20	8	—	32	—	—	—	—
1887	22	9	—	31	—	—	—	—
1886	22	9	—	26	—	—	—	—

[1] For all series for 1904 and earlier years, data are for fiscal years ending 30 June of the year given.

[2] This series includes: for 1929 to 1975, sawn and rough granite; for 1928, sawn granite, 1 January to 31 December and rough granite, 1 April to 31 December; for **1898** to 1927, sawn granite only.

[3] For nine months ending 31 December 1934.

Series P151-156. Principal statistics of the Canadian metallic mineral industries, 1923 to 1975

(all values in thousands of dollars)

Year	Number of employees	Salaries and wages	Cost of fuel and electricity	Cost of process supplies and containers	Gross value of production	Net value added by processing
	151	152	153	154	155	156
1975	69,161	1,006,435	192,871	1,794,491	4,552,638	2,563,938
1974	70,038	862,533	168,265	1,656,994	4,990,924	3,171,375
1973	66,134	733,085	122,519	1,294,335	4,124,522	2,711,307
1972	61,994	620,588	98,608	982,835	2,679,657	1,609,759
1971	66,012	612,862	96,744	1,018,873	2,597,916	1,494,451
1970	66,590	580,546	85,648	971,621	2,890,322	1,846,310
1969	60,550	479,251	73,094	780,268	2,377,339	1,530,053
1968	63,369	474,772	71,701	756,194	2,291,281	1,470,312
1967	61,728	429,383	64,483	680,311	2,079,191	1,352,425
1966	61,670	385,143	57,337	585,262	1,820,698	1,191,194
1965	60,942	356,855	54,428	541,491	1,772,602	1,197,436
1964	57,648	321,605	44,115	460,688	1,598,477	1,110,455
1963	57,119	310,108	39,179	409,054	1,387,889	956,085
1962	58,243	306,004	34,327	391,371	1,342,654	926,209
1961	58,591	298,984	31,750	359,432	1,279,482	894,754
1960	61,882	308,043	38,161	129,545	1,003,696	706,059
1959	63,871	306,931	34,551	123,941	1,023,962	726,631
1958	61,999	289,630	32,110	114,352	864,084	601,244
1957	62,554	278,533	31,588	99,380	791,257	532,031
1956	57,564	242,947	28,410	79,309	743,722	509,210
1955	53,364	211,249	22,525	72,523	669,762	465,927
1954	51,599	195,197	20,651	67,571	555,989	389,227
1953	51,711	191,395	19,470	62,075	486,048	333,413
1952	55,338	197,683	19,201	63,415	535,126	377,127
1951	52,271	170,853	16,567	58,064	549,498	406,829
1950	47,697	142,030	15,144	51,140	473,291	344,925
1949	46,181	132,275		111,271	414,629	303,358
1948	41,890	114,744		84,118	394,360	310,242
1947	39,314	96,768		75,871	311,445	235,574
1946	35,445	77,464		57,118	340,726	183,608
1945	32,913	68,817		54,072	231,671	177,600
1944	34,559	71,891		59,000	248,680	189,680
1943	37,575	79,992		67,809	292,497	224,688
1942	43,013	89,545		78,417	327,063	248,646
1941	48,277	93,305		80,387	325,301	244,914
1940	46,885	83,759		69,687	300,824	231,137
1939	45,594	79,198		66,908	273,746	206,838
1938	43,703	74,917		60,213	251,489	191,276
1937	43,476	72,808		52,044	227,121	175,077
1936	36,440	57,671		29,911	170,079	140,168
1935	29,659	46,841		—	—	114,147
1934	25,845	39,759		—	115,175	—
1933	19,083	29,535		—	92,827	—
1932	16,588	26,205		—	81,068	—
1931	17,574	28,584		—	82,153	—
1930	21,997	35,055		—	81,359	—
1929	23,006	36,507		—	94,612	—
1928	21,056	32,458		—	79,690	—
1927	18,672	28,165		—	75,583	—
1926	17,516	26,449		—	82,323	—
1925	15,560	24,164		—	76,396	—
1924	14,288	21,557		—	65,065	—
1923	11,504	17,864		—	48,198	—

Series P157-162. Principal statistics of the Canadian non-metallic mineral industries, 1925 to 1975
(all values in thousands of dollars)

Year	Number of employees	Salaries and wages	Cost of fuel and electricity	Cost of process supplies and containers	Gross value of production	Net value added by processing
	157	158	159	160	161	162
1975	13,703	178,913	48,798	137,635	832,405	650,805
1974	16,198	173,879	46,551	137,493	777,264	595,994
1973	15,391	146,115	34,868	98,713	532,091	400,809
1972	14,866	131,746	31,006	86,774	471,893	355,863
1971	15,105	122,855	28,753	79,944	454,562	345,605
1970	15,150	115,425	26,535	77,896	418,954	315,575
1969	14,322	106,241	24,611	65,551	361,672	270,577
1968	13,673	92,667	21,258	60,903	336,012	254,004
1967	13,202	81,330	18,691	53,753	318,007	246,394
1966	12,422	70,941	16,849	48,075	299,793	235,091
1965	12,116	65,332	16,253	46,428	281,156	222,104
1964	11,727	60,950	13,910	39,233	251,179	201,093
1963	11,661	56,425	12,776	36,360	227,485	180,755
1962	11,408	53,937	11,302	32,835	199,950	158,001
1961	11,003	50,887	10,116	30,148	184,960	146,747
1960	11,206	49,546	10,256	22,321	182,022	148,972
1959	11,719	48,879	10,214	21,993	168,929	136,428
1958	11,660	46,895	9,542	19,651	141,827	112,405
1957	12,310	48,361	10,148	22,057	159,092	126,561
1956	12,548	47,128	9,631	20,295	152,572	122,414
1955	11,722	42,391	8,616	18,422	140,368	112,872
1954	10,892	37,878	7,075	16,247	122,102	98,627
1953	11,099	36,892	6,811	16,187	119,980	96,772
1952	11,247	36,002	6,414	16,237	121,840	98,920
1951	10,611	31,035	6,326	15,560	113,712	91,493
1950	10,116	25,334	5,307	12,022	94,198	76,700
1949	8,606	19,745		12,621	64,342	51,722
1948	9,604	21,297		15,347	67,190	51,844
1947	9,593	17,342		12,901	54,471	41,570
1946	9,108	14,308		10,012	43,416	33,404
1945	8,318	12,712		8,962	40,341	31,379
1944	8,233	12,164		8,105	37,737	29,632
1943	7,989	11,056		8,410	39,243	30,833
1942	8,117	10,793		7,822	35,678	27,856
1941	7,370	9,088		7,056	33,342	26,286
1940	6,471	7,618		5,906	25,217	19,312
1939	6,175	6,850		5,170	23,870	18,699
1938	5,933	6,322		4,365	19,025	14,660
1937	6,294	6,729		5,393	21,343	15,950
1936	4,723	4,652		3,594	15,714	12,121
1935	3,898	3,576		2,829	11,876	9,046
1934	3,737	3,238		—	9,994	—
1933	3,072	2,360		—	9,819	—
1932	2,688	2,506		—	7,748	—
1931	3,314	3,522		—	10,900	—
1930	5,373	5,723		—	15,229	—
1929	6,167	7,202		—	21,087	—
1928	6,052	6,746		—	18,827	—
1927	6,054	6,662		—	17,560	—
1926	5,910	6,800		—	16,496	—
1925	5,210	5,308		—	14,506	—

Section Q: Energy and Electric Power

G. David Quirin, *University of Toronto*

This section contains the major statistics pertaining to the energy-producing and energy-distributing industries in Canada. These statistics are collected and maintained by Statistics Canada using a classification based on nature of the resource base and level of activity, rather than the end-use classification that has been adopted here. In the previous edition, portions of the material which appears here appeared in Section N, Minerals and Fuel, others appeared in Section P, Electric Power.

Major published sources used include the following Statistics Canada publications: *Canada Year Book,* (Catalogue 11-202); *Trade of Canada: Imports,* (Catalogue 65-203); *Trade of Canada: Exports,* (Catalogue 65-202); *Electric Power Statistics,* annual, various issues, (Catalogue 57-001); *Central Electric Stations,* annual 1917 to 1955, (Catalogues 57-202 and 57-204); *Crude Petroleum and Natural Gas Industry,* annual, (Catalogue 26-213); *The Coal Mining Industry,* annual 1969 and prior years, (Catalogue 26-206); *Coal Mines,* annual from 1970, (Catalogue 26-206); *Petroleum Refineries,* annual, (Catalogue 45-205); *General Review of the Mining Industry,* annual, 1951 to 1960, (Catalogue 26-201); *Canadian Mineral Statistics, 1886-1956,* (Catalogue 26-501).

In addition, certain series collected and tabulated by the Canadian Petroleum Association and appearing in its *Statistical Handbook* have been included. For early years, compilations made from the files of the Water Resources Branch, the Mineral Statistics and Public Utilities sections of Statistics Canada and from industry sources by John Davis and published in the first edition of this work remain invaluable.

Q1-5. Canadian production of coal, 1867 to 1976
Q6-12. Canadian utilization of coal, 1867 to 1976

SOURCE: *Trade of Canada* ; *Canadian Mineral Statistics, 1886 to 1956; General Review of the Mining Industry* ; *The Coal Mining Industry* and its successor, *Coal Mines,* plus compilations made by J. Davis for the previous edition.

Production data prior to 1919 include sales, colliery consumption and coal used by operators. Since 1919, all production including stockpiles of coal, waste, etc. is included. Values are based on average sales realization. 'Other' in series Q1-5 includes New Brunswick and the Yukon Territory.

Q13-18. Production of crude petroleum by province, 1943 to 1975
Q19-25. Production and trade of crude petroleum, 1868 to 1976

SOURCE: *Trade of Canada; Canadian Mineral Statistics, 1886 to 1956; General Review of the Mining Industry* and the annual *Crude Petroleum and Natural Gas Industry,* together with compilations made for the previous edition by J. Davis.

Values are at wellhead except for the Northwest Territories where realization from sales at the refinery is used. Imports for 1880 to 1898 include petroleum products as well as crude. It is unknown whether exports prior to 1900 include products as well as crude. 'Other' in series Q13-18 includes the Northwest Territories and small amounts from New Brunswick in earlier years. Production since 1967 includes synthetic crude from tar sands. Small amounts of oil produced from oil shales in New Brunswick are included in production as applicable. Details of production prior to 1943 in the major provinces are obtainable from Energy or Oil and Gas Conservation Boards.

Q26-30. Production of natural gas by province, 1941 to 1975
Q31-37. Production and trade in natural gas, 1892 to 1976

SOURCE: *Trade of Canada; Canadian Mineral Statistics, 1886 to 1956; General Review of the Mining Industry* and the annual *Crude Petroleum and Natural Gas Industry,* as well as compilations made from unpublished sources by J. Davis.

Imports shown in series Q31-37 include unknown quantities of mixed natural and manufactured gas. Data on exports prior to 1901 to Buffalo and Detroit are no longer available. The permit authorizing operation of the relevant pipeline was rescinded in 1901. Output for the period prior to 1960 is output minus flared or wasted gas. For 1961 on, series Q31-37 reports marketable production and values, after deduction of processing shrinkage and line loss. Provincial figures in series Q26-30 are 'net production withdrawal'. Those exclude flared or wasted gas but not processing shrinkage or line loss. Values, prior to 1950, include value of condensate and 'pentanes plus'. Values are at wellhead or field gate, except in Ontario where an imputed wholesale price is used.

Details of prior years production in the major producing provinces may be obtained from the Energy Resources Conservation Board (Alberta) and the Ontario Energy Board.

Q38-45. Production of natural gas liquids, 1961 to 1975
Q46-54. Production and trade in natural gas liquids, 1961 to 1976

Output is that from natural gas field processing plants only, propane and butane is also produced in oil refineries in which case they are referred to as 'liquified refinery gases or LRG' (see series Q149-159). Condensate and 'pentanes plus' are also known as 'natural gasoline' and are usually used as feedstock or blending stock in refinery operations. Certain proportions of condensate output in earlier years, particularly those from the Turner Valley field in Alberta, are included in the crude petroleum statistics shown in series Q13-18 and Q19-25. This field was the only source of these products prior to the 1950s. Volumes were insignificant until large- scale gas exports from Alberta and British Columbia developed in the late 1950s. Some data on prior years output can be found in *Petroleum Refineries*, (Catalogue 45-205). Trade figures include propane and butane from refineries as well as field processing plants. Apparent consumption in series Q46-54 is thus apparent consumption net of LRG, which is reported in series Q149-159. The latter source derives from the apparent crude consumption shown in series Q19-25, and is thus a secondary, not a primary, source of energy.

Q55-58. Exploratory and development drilling in Western Canada, 1947 to 1976

SOURCE: a compilation, from provincial sources, made by the Canadian Petroleum Association and reported in its *Statistical Handbook*.

Exploratory wells include new field wildcats, new pool wildcats, deeper pool tests, shallower pool tests and outpost wells, following the classification developed by F.H. Lahee (Bulletin A.A.P.G., 1938). The same source reports some data for other provinces in recent years, the provinces and territories covered by this series account for the vast bulk of exploratory effort and discoveries.

Q59-63. Proven crude oil reserves, 1950 to 1975

Q64-69. Proven natural gas reserves, 1955 to 1977

Q70-74. Proven natural gas liquids reserves, 1951 to 1977

SOURCE: the Canadian Petroleum Association; the natural gas series is compiled by a joint Canadian Petroleum Association-Canadian Gas Association committees. They are based on estimates developed by engineering committees with access, as necessary, to confidential technical information, and represent the most authoritative estimate of proven reserves publicly available. The definitions used restrict proven reserves to those actually drilled or whose existence can be inferred from nearby wells. They do not include 'probable' reserves which might be inferred to exist within existing reservoirs on the basis of geophysical or geological interpretation and are thus deliberately conservative.

'Discoveries' include the initial reserve credited to pools discovered during the year, as indicated by the discovery well, successful follow-up wells and such limited surrounding area as appears justified on engineering evidence. 'Extensions and revisions' includes adjustments made to prior years' discoveries as the results of further drilling during the year or adjustments made on the basis of production experience. Though adjustments may be negative, for example, if recovery factor estimates have to be adjusted on the basis of production experience, most of the oil or gas discovered in a field will be reported in the extensions and revision column.

In series Q64-69, it should be noted that volumes are measured at the industry standard pressure of 14.65 psia (pounds per square inch absolute) and not the 14.73 psia used by Statistics Canada and forming the basis of series Q26-30 and Q31-37. Production reported in series Q64-69 is the amount removed from the reservoir, and thus includes flared or wasted gas, processing losses, etc., which are excluded from reported production in series Q26-30 and Q31-37. Volumes at 14.65 psia are approximately 1.0055 times

volumes at 14.73 psia. A temperature base of 60° F is used throughout.

Q75-80. Electrical generating capacity and output by type of ownership, 1919 to 1975

Q81-84. Electrical generating capacity by type of prime mover, 1917 to 1976

Q85-91. Electrical generation by type of prime mover, 1919 to 1976

Q92-96. Production and trade in electrical energy, 1919 to 1975

SOURCE: *Trade of Canada*, the annual *Electric Power Statistics* (since 1956) and its predecessor, *General Electric Stations* (for prior years) and compilations made from a variety of sources by J. Davis for the preceding edition. There is a distinct break in certain of the series in 1956, when a number of industrial producers which did not sell to the public were added to the coverage base, while a number of industrial producers having limited public sales, for example, to employees or to a nearby municipality were moved from the 'privately operated utilities' class to the 'industrial establishments' class. Series Q75-80 reports two sets of numbers for 1956 which give some indication of the magnitudes involved. Capacity figures for the pre-1956 series reflect horsepower of the prime movers; those for 1956 and subsequent years reflect name plate capacity of the generating equipment installed.

Q97-101. Electric utilities - number of customers by class, 1920 to 1975

Q102-106. Electric utility sales by class of customer, selected years, 1930 to 1975

Q107-113. Electric utility revenues by class of customer, 1919 to 1975

SOURCE: same as series Q75-80, Q81-84, Q85-91 and Q92-96.

Series Q97-101 indicates numbers of customers during December. Series Q102-106 indicates volumes sold, series Q107-113 revenues from power sales. Export sales values shown in series Q67-113 relate to the volumes shown in series Q92-96. The categorization of customers as commercial or industrial is that used by the utility providing the service and reflects choice by the customer of a particular rate schedule considered to be industrial or commercial; these differ from one utility to another and there is thus some ambiguity in these series. In the more recent years the classifications have been merged. It should be noted that many apartment residences are served under commercial rates and that 'residential' totals are thus understated to an unknown degree.

Q114-117. Gas utilities, number of customers by class, 1958 to 1976

Q118-125. Gas utilities sales by class of customer, 1958 to 1976

SOURCE: the annual publication *Gas Utilities (Distribution Systems)* which has been published since 1959.

In earlier years natural gas was available only in Alberta and certain portions of Southwestern Ontario; other areas were served with manufactured gas which was lower in caloritic value and (relatively) higher in effective costs. Statistics for earlier years were reported in *Gas Pipeline Transport* which incorporated both natural and manufactured gas statistics.

Q126-130.   Miscellaneous statistics of the electric power industry, selected years, 1891 to 1976

Q131-136.   Principal statistics of the petroleum and natural gas industry, 1929 to 1976

Q137-142.   Principal statistics of the Canadian coal mining industry, 1918 to 1976

Q143-148.   Miscellaneous statistics of natural gas utilities, 1959 to 1976

SOURCE: *Electric Power Statistics*; *General Review of the Mining Industry*; *The Petroleum and Natural Gas Industry* and *Coal Mines* and their predecessor publications.

These tables give employment and payroll statistics and other data used for value-added calculations, along with certain other series of interest.

Q149-159.   Canadian refinery shipments of petroleum products, 1949 to 1976

SOURCE: *Petroleum Refineries*.

Series Q19-25 gives apparent consumption of crude petroleum, series Q46-54 that of condensate and pentanes plus. These are not end products but inputs to the refining process. Series Q149-159 is intended to indicate the end product form in which apparent consumption was utilized.

Series Q1-5. Canadian production of coal, 1867 to 1976
(thousands of tons)

Year	British Columbia	Alberta	Saskatchewan	Nova Scotia	Other[1]
	1	2	3	4	5
1976	8,278	12,117	5,156	2,205	337
1975	10,560	11,084	3,912	1,826	487
1974	8,532	9,246	3,842	1,410	432
1973	7,773	9,196	4,028	1,176	414
1972	6,547	9,024	3,283	1,425	448
1971	4,637	8,012	3,300	1,965	538
1970	3,483	6,784	3,819	2,122	407
1969	902	4,426	2,020	2,621	708
1968	890	3,920	2,250	3,132	797
1967	961	3,596	1,997	3,748	839
1966	866	3,461	2,084	3,866	903
1965	815	3,413	2,113	4,154	1,004
1964	905	2,975	2,020	4,309	1,009
1963	828	2,293	1,860	4,576	894
1962	821	2,121	2,247	4,205	824
1961	879	1,991	2,262	4,304	900
1960	784	2,224	2,158	4,572	1,038
1959	684	2,486	1,925	4,405	1,013
1958	771	2,493	2,302	5,267	792
1957	996	3,078	2,216	5,686	983
1956	1,318	4,116	2,274	5,798	997
1955	1,454	4,455	2,294	5,731	889
1954	1,300	4,859	2,117	5,843	795
1953	1,443	5,917	2,021	5,787	732
1952	1,644	7,195	2,083	5,905	751
1951	1,739	7,659	2,223	6,308	657
1950	1,730	8,116	2,203	6,478	611
1949	1,907	8,617	1,870	6,182	544
1948	1,780	8,123	1,589	6,431	525
1947	1,764	8,070	1,571	4,118	—
1946	1,638	8,826	1,523	5,453	—
1945	1,700	7,800	1,533	5,113	—
1944	2,134	7,429	1,373	5,746	—
1943	2,039	7,677	1,666	6,103	—
1942	2,169	7,754	1,301	7,205	—
1941	2,021	6,970	1,323	7,388	—
1940	1,868	6,204	1,098	7,849	—
1939	1,693	5,519	960	7,051	—
1938	1,440	5,251	1,022	6,236	—
1937	1,599	5,563	1,049	7,259	—
1936	1,489	5,697	1,021	6,649	—
1935	1,331	5,463	922	5,822	—
1934	1,486	4,754	909	6,342	—
1933	1,382	4,719	928	4,558	—
1932	1,681	4,871	887	4,085	1
1931	1,876	4,564	663	4,956	1
1930	2,084	5,756	579	6,254	1
1929	2,490	7,151	580	7,056	—
1928	2,805	7,336	472	6,744	—
1927	2,746	6,934	470	7,072	—
1926	2,614	6,504	440	6,747	—
1925	2,742	5,869	472	3,843	1
1924	2,194	5,190	479	4,447	1
1923	2,823	6,854	438	6,598	—
1922	2,927	5,991	382	5,569	—
1921	2,890	5,909	336	5,735	—
1920	3,095	6,908	335	6,437	—
1919	2,650	4,934	379	5,790	—
1918	2,569	5,973	347	5,819	3
1917	2,434	4,736	355	6,327	5
1916	2,584	4,559	281	6,912	3
1915	2,066	3,361	240	7,463	10
1914	2,240	3,683	232	7,371	13
1913	2,714	4,015	213	7,980	20
1912	3,209	3,241	225	7,784	9
1911	2,543	1,511	207	7,004	3
1910	3,331	2,894	181	6,431	16
1909	2,606	1,995	192	5,652	7
1908	2,334	1,686	151	6,653	4
1907	2,365	1,592	151	6,354	15
1906	2,146	1,246	108	6,221	7

Series Q1-5. Canadian production of coal, 1867 to 1976 (concluded)
(thousands of tons)

Year	British Columbia	Alberta	Saskatchewan	Nova Scotia	Other[1]
	1	2	3	4	5
1905	1,945	932	108	5,647	7
1904	1,863	662	125	5,596	—
1903	1,677	496	117	5,633	2
1902	1,808	403	70	5,161	5
1901	1,919	340	45	4,158	6
1900	1,792	311	41	3,624	6
1899	1,431	310	25	3,149	..
1898	1,264	315	25	2,563	..
1897	1,019	242	25	2,494	..
1896	1,004	209	17	2,509	..
1895	1,058	170	16	2,225	..
1894	1,113	185	15	2,528	..
1893	1,094	230	8	2,445	..
1892	937	179	5	2,159	..
1891	1,130	174	—	2,268	..
1890	768	129	200	2,181	..
1889	636	97	—	1,919	..
1888	539	115	—	1,942	..
1887	486	74	—	1,859	..
1886	375	..	..	1,698	..
1885	373	..	..	1,548	..
1884	441	..	..	1,544	..
1883	240	..	..	1,579	..
1882	323	..	..	1,525	..
1881	257	..	..	1,280	..
1880	305	..	..	1,178	..
1879	260	..	..	866	..
1878	214	..	..	876	..
1877	156	..	..	880	..
1876	157	..	..	838	..
1875	109	..	..	931	..
1874	91	..	..	973	..
1873	166	..	..	1,108	..
1872	166	..	..	1,004	..
1871	166	..	..	755	..
1870	33	..	..	719	..
1869	40	..	..	648	..
1868	49	..	..	574	..
1867	35	..	..	596	..

[1] Includes New Brunswick and the Yukon Territory.

Series Q6-12. Canadian utilization of coal, 1867 to 1976
(quantities in thousands of tons, values in thousands of dollars)

Year	Production		Imports		Exports		Apparent consumption
	Quantity	Value	Quantity	Value	Quantity	Value	Quantity
	6	**7**	**8**	**9**	**10**	**11**	**12**
1976	28,083	607,100	16,092	544,312	12,965	557,328	31,210
1975	27,843	586,423	16,833	576,311	12,891	477,899	31,785
1974	23,445	302,826	13,669	302,898	11,876	251,707	25,238
1973	22,567	179,731	16,489	167,081	12,023	165,064	27,033
1972	20,709	150,600	19,274	178,893	8,573	105,952	31,410
1971	18,432	121,727	18,136	151,014	7,734	86,563	28,834
1970	16,604	86,067	18,864	150,390	4,392	29,155	31,076
1969	10,672	50,578	17,347	113,603	1,378	9,451	26,641
1968	10,989	53,970	17,047	160,118	1,447	16,336	26,589
1967	11,141	56,500	16,114	145,158	1,338	15,092	25,917
1966	11,180	81,801[1]	16,437	140,810	1,229	13,202	26,388
1965	11,500	76,295	16,595	125,946	1,226	12,672	26,869
1964	11,219	73,013	14,989	86,241	1,292	11,972	24,916
1963	10,452	72,052	13,370	78,663	1,054	9,870	22,768
1962	10,217	69,200	12,614	71,171	893	8,207	21,938
1961	10,336	70,181	12,306	71,560	939	8,540	21,703
1960	10,776	74,879	13,565	76,961	853	6,789	23,488
1959	10,513	74,089	14,236	84,488	474	3,582	24,275
1958	11,627	80,058	14,491	88,016	339	2,908	25,779
1957	12,960	90,252	19,480	117,714	396	3,358	32,044
1956	14,501	95,650	22,613	128,737	594	4,710	36,520
1955	14,411	93,579	19,743	106,551	593	4,871	33,561
1954	14,559	96,600	18,580	104,795	219	1,716	33,561
1953	15,451	102,722	23,266	136,567	255	2,000	38,462
1952	16,935	111,026	24,933	150,670	389	3,204	41,479
1951	17,973	109,039	26,801	168,089	435	3,496	44,339
1950	18,529	110,140	26,955	174,674	395	3,198	45,089
1949	18,560	110,915	22,195	141,149	432	3,564	40,323
1948	17,438	106,684	30,874	186,388	1,273	11,556	47,039
1947	15,869	77,475	28,892	138,950	715	5,441	44,046
1946	17,812	75,820	26,107	120,354	862	5,946	43,056
1945	16,507	567,588	25,062	102,432	841	5,304	40,728
1944	17,026	70,433	28,724[2]	113,138[2]	1,010	5,985	44,740
1943	17,859	67,878	28,109	101,245	1,110	5,428	44,858
1942	18,865	58,060	24,937	81,851	816	4,278	42,987
1941	18,226	54,676	20,388	61,588	531	2,597	38,083
1940	17,567	48,677	17,437	49,630	505	2,362	34,489
1939	15,693	43,982	14,999	41,579	376	1,667	30,315
1938	14,295	48,752	13,012	35,826	353	1,541	26,954
1937	15,836	45,792	14,671	38,159	355	1,442	30,151
1936	15,229	41,963	13,123	34,955	412	1,793	27,941
1935	13,888	42,046	12,079	33,331	418	1,907	25,548
1934	13,810	35,924	12,975	35,065	306	1,401	26,470
1933	11,903	37,118	11,204	28,122	259	1,188	22,848
1932	11,739	37,118	11,959	31,338	285	1,433	23,412
1931	12,243	41,208	13,121	36,829	360	1,910	25,004
1930	14,881	52,850	18,773	56,694	625	3,346	33,030
1929	17,497	63,065	18,204	56,013	843	4,375	34,858
1928	17,564	63,758	17,206	54,333	864	4,470	33,906
1927	17,427	61,867	18,687	61,785	1,113	5,890	35,001
1926	16,478	59,875	16,579	59,760	1,028	5,739	32,029
1925	13,135	49,262	16,350	59,159	786	4,329	28,699
1924	13,638	53,594	16,725	67,028	773	4,837	29,590
1923	16,991	72,059	20,990	96,370	1,654	10,661	36,326
1922	15,157	65,518	13,024	61,182	1,819	11,159	26,362
1921	15,057	72,452	18,302	88,925	1,987	13,896	31,372
1920	16,947	82,497	18,844	98,034	2,558	18,015	33,232
1919	13,919[3]	55,623[3]	17,293	61,161	2,070	12,439	29,142
1918	14,978	55,193	21,679	71,651	1,817	9,405	34,839
1917	14,047	43,200	20,857	70,562	1,733	7,387	33,171
1916	14,483	38,817	17,581	38,290	2,135	7,099	29,929
1915	13,267	32,111	12,466	28,340	1,767	5,406	23,966
1914	13,638	33,472	14,721	39,801	1,423	3,880	26,935
1913	15,012	37,335	18,202	47,949	1,562	3,961	31,652
1912	14,513	36,019	14,596	39,478	2,127	5,822	26,982

Series Q6-12. Canadian utilization of coal, 1867 to 1976 (concluded)
(quantities in thousands of tons, values in thousands of dollars)

Year	Production		Imports		Exports		Apparent consumption
	Quantity	Value	Quantity	Value	Quantity	Value	Quantity
	6	7	8	9	10	11	12
1911	11,323	26,468	14,559	39,293	1,501	4,357	24,382
1910	12,909	30,910	10,598	28,450	2,377	6,077	21,130
1909	10,501	24,781	9,873	26,832	1,588	4,456	18,786
1908	10,886	25,195	10,297	28,351	1,730	4,661	19,454
1907	10,511	24,382	10,651	28,861	1,894	4,880	19,269
1906	9,763	19,732	7,444 [4]	19,154 [4]	1,835	4,738	15,372 [5]
1905	8,668	17,520	7,431	20,440	1,635	4,029	14,464
1904	8,255	16,592	6,937	20,113	1,557	4,036	13,635
1903	7,960	15,943	5,519	15,226.	1,955	5,220	11,524
1902	7,467	15,211	5,189	12,999	2,090	5,402	10,566
1901	6,486	12,699	4,864	13,156	1,574	4,829	9,776
1900	5,777	13,742	4,424	11,012	1,788	4,840	8,413
1899	4,925	10,283	4,193	10,227	1,293	3,864	7,825
1898	4,173	8,224	3,374	9,100	1,150	3,619	6,397
1897	3,786	7,304	3,226	9,009	986	2,964	6,026
1896	3,746	7,226	3,323	9,020	1,107	2,389	5,962
1895	3,478	6,739	3,031	8,724	1,011	3,318	5,498
1894	3,847	7,429	3,008	9,719	1,014	3,542	5,751
1893	3,783	7,359	3,213	10,638	960	3,270	6,036
1892	3,288	6,364	3,176	9,779	824	2,807	5,640
1891	3,578	7,019	3,058	9,321	971	3,394	5,665
1890	3,085	5,676	2,664	8,155	724	2,437	5,025
1889	2,659	4,894	2,580	8,502	665	2,335	4,553
1888	2,603	4,674	2,399	8,778	589	1,975	4,413
1887	2,429	4,388	2,281	7,582	581	1,696	4,199
1886	2,117	3,740	1,963	6,657	521	1,426	3,559
1885	1,921	3,418	1,942	7,128	480	1,468	3,383
1884	1,985	3,594	1,999	7,459	452	1,201	3,532
1883	1,819	3,110	1,675	6,351	444	1,159	3,050
1882	1,848	3,284	1,275	4,659	421	1,079	2,702
1881	1,537	2,689	1,159	4,068	420	1,123	2,276
1880	1,483	2,657	977	2,740	345	1,014	2,115
1879	1,126	2,051	..	..	316	937	..
1878	1,090	1,941	..	..	340	1,211	..
1877	1,037	1,794	..	..	250	856	..
1876	995	1,730	..	..	278	977	..
1875	1,030	1,747	..	..	288	938	..
1874	1,064	1,763	..	..	418	1,344	..
1873			..	..	405	952	..
1872	3,033	5,073	..	..	296	579	..
1871			..	..	318	662	..
1870	753	1,243	..	..	287	589	..
1869	688	1,155	..	..	440	763	..
1868	623	1,073	..	..	265	641	..
1867	631	1,057	..	..	..	..	..

[1] Values prior to 1967 include subvention payments where applicable.
[2] Imports for 1944 and earlier years include briquettes. Separate figures shown in *Trade of Canada* for 1945 to date are very small.
[3] Prior to 1919, production includes only sales, colliery consumption, and coal used by operators; from 1919 to present production is total output, including stockpiling, etc.
[4] 1906 and earlier years' imports for fiscal years ending 30 June of the year given.
[5] 1906 and earlier years computed using fiscal year import data.

Series Q13-18. Production of crude petroleum by province, 1943 to 1975
(thousands of barrels)

Year	British Columbia	Alberta	Saskatchewan	Manitoba	Ontario	Other
	13	14	15	16	17	18
1975	14,295	441,556	59,038	4,414	704	1,000
1974	18,873	514,149	73,868	4,751	734	980
1973	21,195	540,703	85,998	5,086	808	954
1972	23,838	443,176	86,544	5,256	878	922
1971	25,147	370,604	87,992	5,618	958	928
1970	25,371	337,460	89,295	5,918	1,048	901
1969	25,272	289,122	87,289	6,213	1,162	781
1968	22,150	256,337	91,839	6,210	1,151	458
1967	19,716	230,083	92,458	5,579	1,240	698
1966	16,638	202,526	93,227	5,240	1,324	728
1965	13,445	183,422	87,807	4,956	1,279	655
1964	11,513	175,292	81,321	4,400	1,246	625
1963	12,506	167,656	71,300	3,773	1,205	610
1962	8,908	164,320	64,557	3,960	1,135	539
1961	985	157,657	56,020	4,480	1,149	539
1960	867	130,507	51,908	4,764	1,005	483
1959	866	129,967	47,442	5,056	1,002	445
1958	512	113,278	44,626	5,829	778	573
1957	341	137,492	36,861	6,090	624	440
1956	148	143,910	21,077	5,786	593	467
1955	—	113,035	11,317	4,146	526	416
1954	—	87,714	5,423	2,148	412	385
1953	—	76,816	2,798	654	300	331
1952	—	58,916	1,697	105	192	327
1951	—	45,915	1,249	11	197	244
1950	—	27,548	1,041	—	251	204
1949	—	20,087	782	—	261	175
1948	—	10,889	849	—	177	372
1947	—	6,770	540	—	131	251
1946	—	7,138	119	—	123	206
1945	—	7,980	14	—	113	376
1944	—	8,727	—	—	123	1,247
1943	—	9,602	—	—	132	318

Series Q19-25. Production and trade in crude petroleum, 1868 to 1976
(quantities in thousands of barrels, values in thousands of dollars)

Year	Production		Imports		Exports		Apparent consumption
	Quantity	Value	Quantity	Value	Quantity	Value	Quantity
	19	20	21	22	23	24	25
1976	479,397[1]	4,042,124	265,743	3,280,086	174,291	2,286,675	570,859
1975	520,911[1]	3,755,740	301,235	3,301,924	256,930	3,051,511	565,216
1974	513,412[1]	3,513,899	299,239	2,646,203	330,583	3,406,785	482,068
1973	654,311[1]	2,241,708	314,056	942,490	414,429	1,482,117	553,938
1972	560,468[1]	1,564,780	288,781	680,743	348,431	1,007,505	500,818
1971	491,171[1]	1,352,715	244,243	541,114	272,783	787,399	462,631
1970	459,977[1]	1,154,430	208,363	415,161	244,466	649,075	423,874
1969	409,832[1]	1,011,693	190,507	393,453	202,718	525,780	397,621
1968	378,403[1]	934,527	178,415	372,586	169,230	446,413	387,588
1967	350,254[1]	664,148	162,095	355,416	151,356	397,875	360,993
1966	319,568	768,718	158,544	299,001	126,799	321,681	351,313
1965	291,512	716,899	144,204	312,359	107,696	279,956	328,020
1964	274,479	673,965	143,835	320,637	101,718	262,023	316,596
1963	257,120	622,574	146,645	334,761	90,630	233,867	313,135
1962	243,238	546,239	135,365	304,898	86,128	232,497	292,475
1961	220,762	504,281	133,265	291,170	67,265	154,267	286,762
1960	189,534	422,926	125,560	283,172	42,235	94,450	272,859
1959	184,778	422,093	115,289	277,495	33,362	74,541	266,705
1958	165,496	398,748	104,039	273,948	31,679	73,044	237,856
1957	181,848	453,594	111,905	305,557	55,674	140,975	238,079
1956	171,981	406,562	106,470	270,882	42,907	103,923	235,543
1955	129,440	305,640	86,678	229,480	14,834	36,253	201,285
1954	96,080	293,877	78,772	212,497	2,345	6,318	172,508
1953	80,810	200,582	79,478	207,987	2,507	6,228	157,869
1952	61,237	143,038	81,200	206,840	1,424	3,452	141,013
1951	47,616	116,655	83,284	231,039	342	807	130,558

Series Q19-25. Production and trade in crude petroleum, 1868 to 1976 (continued)
(quantities in thousands of barrels, values in thousands of dollars)

Year	Production		Imports		Exports		Apparent consumption
	Quantity	Value	Quantity	Value	Quantity	Value	Quantity
	19	**20**	**21**	**22**	**23**	**24**	**25**
1950	29,044	84,620	78,660	200,538	—	—	107,704
1949	21,305	61,118	73,947	189,396	—	—	95,252
1948	12,287	37,419	75,559	192,027	1	3	87,845
1947	7,692	19,576	68,447	127,472	—	1	76,139
1946	7,586	14,989	63,407	89,483	—	—	70,993
1945	8,438	13,632	56,806	72,321	—	—	65,289
1944	10,009	15,430	57,048	71,943	—	—	67,147
1943	10,052	16,470	49,754	66,384	—	—	59,806
1942	10,365	15,969	44,120	57,454	1	3	54,484
1941	10,134	14,415	46,791	56,442	1	2	56,924
1940	8,591	11,160	42,623	48,320	—	—	51,214
1939	7,826	9,846	37,095	39,650	—	—	44,921
1938	6,966	9,230	34,245	41,067	—	—	42,068
1937	2,944	5,399	38,915	46,678	—	—	41,858
1936	1,500	3,422	35,833	39,538	—	—	31,102
1935	1,447	3,492	33,052	33,818	—	—	34,529
1934	1,411	3,449	30,643	31,917	—	—	32,100
1933	1,145	3,139	27,270	20,294	305	395	28,111
1932	1,044	3,023	25,432	26,324	208	245	26,269
1931	1,543	4,212	29,070	22,673	456	677	30,148
1930	1,522	5,034	28,931	38,300	550	881	29,736
1929	1,117	3,732	30,291	46,174	805	1,548	25,144
1928	624	2,035	24,404	35,258	615	1,099	20,454
1927	477	1,516	19,562	31,073	537	924	16,787
1926	364	1,312	16,298	31,345	601	852	13,673
1925	332	1,251	12,584	33,642	211	347	12,705
1924	161	467	13,317	20,271	522	529	12,099
1923	170	522	11,219	17,488	68	138	11,397
1922	179	611	12,014	21,679	201	289	11,153
1921	188	642	10,158	20,029	154	376	9,030
1920	196	822	8,312	20,844	77	293	8,689
1919	240	736	11,585	19,831	17	11	7,694
1918	305	885	10,789	21,723	8	28	5,797
1917	214	542	9,328	14,436	—	—	4,086
1916	198	392	7,231	8,460	4	11	5,533
1915	215	301	5,503	3,678	1	2	5,821
1914	215	343	5,577	5,751	—	—	5,297
1913	228	406	4,630	5,251	—	—	4,858
1912	243	345	3,431	3,997	1	4	3,673
1911	291	357	2,047	2,189	—	—	2,338
1910	316	389	1,532	1,639	—	—	1,848
1909	421	560	903	1,322	—	—	1,324
1908	528	747	712	895	—	—	1,240
1907	789	1,057	379	471	—	—	1,168
1906	570	762	566	668	—	—	1,136
1905	634	856	643	901	—	—	1,277
1904	503	936	123	276	—	—	626
1903	487	1,049	61	136	—	—	548
1902	531	951	17	41	—	—	548
1901	622	1,008	10	27	—	1	631
1900	710	1,151	10	23	—	—	720
1899	809	1,202	8	12	—	—	817
1898	758	1,062	259	725	—	—	..
1897	710	1,012	240	697	—	—	..
1896	727	1,156	229	740	—	—	..
1895	726	1,087	217	525	1	1	..
1894	829	835	188	440	2	3	..
1893	798	874	171	446	3	4	..
1892	780	984	161	476	9	13	..
1891	755	1,010	145	498	13	18	..
1890	795	903	145	516	12	18	..
1889	705	654	133	484	7	11	..
1888	695	714	129	408	6	75	..
1887	714	557	123	467	14	14	..
1886	584	526	109	422	7	10	..
1885	588	..	108	415	10	11	686
1884	571	..	90	380	31	30	630
1883	473	..	88	359	—	1	561
1882	390	..	86	398	..	..	476
1881	369	..	41	262	..	..	410

Series Q19-25. Production and trade in crude petroleum, 1868 to 1976 (concluded)
(quantities in thousands of barrels, values in thousands of dollars)

Year	Production		Imports		Exports		Apparent consumption
	Quantity	Value	Quantity	Value	Quantity	Value	Quantity
	19	20	21	22	23	24	25
1880	350	..	20	131	..	..	370
1879	575	..	..	..	..	..	..
1878	312	..	..	..	..	..	..
1877	312	..	..	..	..	..	..
1876	312	..	..	..	..	..	..
1875	220	..	..	..	..	..	..
1874	169	..	..	..	..	..	..
1873	365	..	..	..	..	..	..
1872	308	..	..	..	..	..	..
1871	270	..	..	..	..	..	..
1870	250	..	..	..	..	..	..
1869	220	..	..	..	..	..	..
1868	190	..	..	..	..	..	..

[1] Includes synthetic crude from tar sands.

Series Q26-30. Production of natural gas by province, 1941 to 1975
(millions of cubic feet)

Year	British Columbia	Alberta	Saskatchewan	Ontario	Other
	26	27	28	29	30
1975	353,270	2,029,756	52,002	10,887	449
1974	366,082	1,993,935	51,467	7,404	1,250
1973	425,261	1,955,241	53,216	9,441	552
1972	377,964	1,853,976	54,034	12,375	632
1971	288,729	1,664,613	57,306	16,260	1,439
1970	271,062	1,508,879	53,713	17,064	378
1969	252,975	1,293,297	48,572	11,332	286
1968	223,092	1,102,291	46,132	12,066	291
1967	197,539	966,343	38,861	14,229	200
1966	160,447	891,305	39,211	15,537	142
1965	138,277	844,055	33,771	12,620	143
1964	118,485	790,635	31,284	13,739	137
1963	105,062	696,418	29,397	15,855	167
1962	108,134	623,686	28,060	15,842	165
1961	95,449	424,146	26,327	14,691	147
1960	85,592	383,683	36,572	16,987	138
1959	69,129	297,569	33,613	16,839	185
1958	63,638	239,050	18,820	16,148	148
1957	8,275	183,141	13,994	14,401	196
1956	188	146,134	9,808	12,812	211
1955	—	133,007	6,707	10,853	205
1954	—	107,174	3,333	10,016	212
1953	—	89,652	1,422	9,709	202
1952	—	79,150	1,007	8,302	227
1951	—	69,877	860	8,443	281
1950	—	58,604	814	8,009	395
1949	—	51,180	813	8,024	440
1948	—	48,965	477	8,590	571
1947	—	44,107	274	7,786	490
1946	—	40,097	210	7,051	542
1945	—	40,393	164	7,200	655
1944	—	37,162	119	7,083	703
1943	—	35,569	116	7,914	677
1942	—	34,482	117	10,477	621
1941	—	30,905	106	11,829	655

Series Q31-37. Production and trade in natural gas, 1892 to 1976
(quantities in millions of cubic feet, values in thousands of dollars)

Year	Production		Imports		Exports		Apparent consumption
	Quantity	Value	Quantity	Value	Quantity	Value	Quantity
	31	**32**	**33**	**34**	**35**	**36**	**37**
1976	2,458,668	2,440,385	9,855	7,830	954,051	1,616,490	1,513,572
1975	2,446,364	1,413,619	10,447	8,818	949,465	1,092,168	1,507,346
1974	2,420,138	677,644	9,228	5,777	960,713	493,640	1,468,653
1973	2,443,711	417,801	14,700	7,793	1,030,913	350,745	1,427,498
1972	2,298,981	369,882	15,759	7,629	1,007,054	306,843	1,307,686
1971	2,028,343	318,796	16,010	7,021	903,051	250,719	1,141,306
1970	1,851,095	293,779	11,878	5,124	768,113	205,988	1,094,860
1969	1,606,462	244,315	37,733	16,025	699,816	176,188	974,379
1968	1,383,872	210,289	88,228	35,393	598,144	153,752	873,956
1967	1,217,172	184,732	52,872	19,914	505,165	123,664	764,879
1966	1,106,643	164,642	43,551	17,592	426,224	108,750	723,969
1965	1,028,866	147,388	15,673	5,809	403,909	104,280	640,630
1964	944,280	134,551	8,046	2,871	404,144	97,609	548,182
1963	846,899	116,721	6,877	2,356	340,953	75,630	512,823
1962	775,887	98,096	5,575	1,802	319,566	72,423	461,896
1961	560,760	68,320	5,574	1,708	168,180	41,689	398,154
1960	522,972	52,197	5,571	1,634	91,043	18,051	437,497
1959	417,335	39,609	11,963	3,797	84,764	16,953	344,534
1958	337,804	32,058	34,716	7,775	86,972	17,984	288,548
1957	320,007	20,963	30,551	7,240	15,731	2,322	234,827
1956	169,153	16,850	15,695	3,480	9,642	1,118	175,205
1955	150,772	15,099	11,116	2,698	11,360	..	150,372
1954	120,775	12,482	6,236	2,029	7,148	..	119,823
1953	100,986	10,877	6,097	1,991	9,629	..	97,454
1952	88,686	9,518	5,982	1,901	8,145	..	86,253
1951	79,461	7,159	3,699	1,286	—	—	83,160
1950	67,822	6,433	3,254	1,163	—	—	71,076
1949	60,457	11,620	1,263	488	—	—	61,720
1948	58,603	15,633	404	239	—	—	59,007
1947	52,657	13,430	433	253	—	—	53,090
1946	47,900	12,165	368	239	—	—	48,268
1945	48,412	12,310	346	233	—	—	48,758
1944	45,067	11,423	271	182	—	—	45,338
1943	44,276	13,159	232	158	—	—	44,276
1942	45,697	13,302	197	135	—	—	45,508
1941	43,495	12,665	172	117	—	—	43,667
1940	41,232	13,001	130	92	—	—	41,362
1939	35,185	12,507	114	75	—	—	35,299
1938	33,445	11,587	133	87	—	—	33,578
1937	32,381	11,675	114	75	—	—	32,495
1936	28,113	10,762	118	76	—	—	28,231
1935	24,911	9,363	106	70	—	—	25,018
1934	23,162	8,760	107	70	—	—	23,269
1933	23,138	8,712	101	73	—	—	23,239
1932	23,420	8,899	121	91	—	—	23,541
1931	25,875	9,027	109	75	—	—	25,984
1930	29,377	10,290	152	97	—	—	29,528
1929	28,378	9,977	133	85	—	—	28,511
1928	22,583	8,614	128	83	—	—	22,711
1927	21,377	8,043	104	66	—	—	21,481
1926	19,208	7,557	110	75	—	—	19,327
1925	16,903	6,833	64	41	—	—	16,967
1924	14,881	5,709	—	—	—	—	14,881
1923	15,961	5,885	—	—	—	—	15,961
1922	14,683	5,487	—	—	—	—	14,683
1921	14,078	4,594	—	—	—	—	14,078
1920	16,846	4,233	—	—	—	—	16,846
1919	19,938	4,176	—	—	—	—	19,938
1918	20,140	4,351	—	—	—	—	20,140
1917	27,409	5,095	—	—	—	—	27,409
1916	25,467	3,958	—	—	—	—	25,467
1915	20,124	3,706	—	—	—	—	20,124
1914	21,693	3,485	—	—	—	—	21,693
1913	20,478	3,309	—	—	—	—	20,478
1912	15,278	2,363	—	—	—	—	15,278
1911	11,644	1,918	—	—	—	—	11,644
1910	—	1,346	—	—	—	—	—
1909	—	1,207	—	—	—	—	—
1908	—	1,013	—	—	—	—	—
1907	—	815	—	—	—	—	—
1906	—	584	—	—	—	—	—

Series Q31-37. Production and trade in natural gas, 1892 to 1976 (concluded)
(quantities in millions of cubic feet, values in thousands of dollars)

Year	Production		Imports		Exports		Apparent consumption
	Quantity	Value	Quantity	Value	Quantity	Value	Quantity
	31	**32**	**33**	**34**	**35**	**36**	**37**
1905	—	380	—	—	—	—	—
1904	—	328	—	—	—	—	—
1903	—	202	—	—	—	—	—
1902	—	196	—	—	—	—	—
1901	—	339	—	—	—	—	—
1901	—	417	—	—	—	—	—
1899	—	387	—	—	—	—	—
1898	—	322	—	—	—	—	—
1897	—	326	—	—	—	—	—
1896	—	276	—	—	—	—	—
1895	—	423	—	—	—	—	—
1894	—	314	—	—	—	—	—
1893	—	376	—	—	—	—	—
1892	—	150	—	—	—	—	—

Series Q38-45. Production of natural gas liquids, 1961 to 1975
(thousands of barrels)

Year	British Columbia		Alberta		Saskatchewan		Total	
	Propane and butane	Condensate and pentanes plus	Propane and butane	Condensate and pentanes plus	Propane and butane	Condensate and pentanes plus	Propane and butane	Condensate and pentanes plus
	38	**39**	**40**	**41**	**42**	**43**	**44**	**45**
1975	1,206	1,260	55,259	53,258	816	313	57,279	54,831
1974	1,154	1,141	52,104	57,427	915	346	65,173	58,914
1973	1,253	1,194	51,792	59,979	1,075	412	54,120	61,585
1972	793	1,236	45,648	58,976	1,118	364	47,559	60,576
1971	784	1,214	37,471	44,937	1,180	391	39,435	46,542
1970	688	1,052	32,528	42,031	1,144	407	34,360	43,490
1969	729	1,043	26,768	36,621	1,198	377	28,694	38,041
1968	681	1,051	23,250	31,631	1,347	316	23,277	32,999
1967	797	1,060	20,480	29,339	1,268	296	22,545	30,695
1966	675	1,019	18,643	28,055	1,084	248	20,401	29,322
1965	553	978	14,369	26,635	1,004	255	15,927	27,869
1964	544	950	9,363	24,039	1,002	286	10,910	25,275
1963	486	855	5,628	20,595	854	272	6,967	21,722
1962	468	847	4,647	16,490	703	266	5,819	17,602
1961	472	788	2,860	7,723	551	225	4,883	8,736

Series Q46-54. Production and trade in natural gas liquids, 1961 to 1976
(quantities in thousands of barrels, values in thousands of dollars)

Year	Production[1]		Imports[1]		Exports[1]		Apparent consumption[1]	Condensate and pentanes plus	
	Quantity	Value	Quantity	Value	Quantity	Value	Quantity	Production	Value
	46	47	48	49	50	51	52	53	54
1976	56,320	385,533	80	3,471	17,577	350,027	38,823	48,965	420,214
1975	57,511	377,983	64	2,254	14,833	300,831	42,742	54,851	405,500
1974	55,460	295,214	73	2,328	36,439	244,157	19,094	58,897	364,188
1973	55,711	122,119	274	2,313	36,201	93,116	19,784	61,620	229,861
1972	48,191	73,126	83	1,337	31,298	62,861	16,976	60,816	179,965
1971	39,429	58,692	59	993	23,485	46,027	16,003	46,601	135,793
1970	34,350	44,509	327	1,835	20,772	37,506	13,905	43,521	115,953
1969	28,747	37,053	772	2,603	15,884	27,213	13,635	38,046	101,269
1968	25,443	37,869	411	2,010	13,488	23,887	12,366	32,962	88,494
1967	23,135	36,275	281	1,618	12,403	21,722	11,013	30,737	78,818
1966	20,311	28,166	84	829	10,323	15,045	10,072	29,346	75,804
1965	16,275	20,911	100	791	7,855	10,832	8,520	27,868	71,084
1964	11,057	14,504	90	801	4,829	7,657	6,318	25,264	64,127
1963	7,058	9,805	—	—	1,792	3,223	5,266	21,740	54,400
1962	5,901	8,415	—	—	—	2,905	..	17,593	39,698
1961	4,827	6,502	—	—	—	2,944	..	8,765	20,250

[1] Propane and butane.

Series Q55-58. Exploratory and development drilling in Western Canada, 1947 to 1976

Year	Exploratory		Development		Year	Exploratory		Development	
	Wells	Footage	Wells	Footage		Wells	Footage	Wells	Footage
	55	56	57	58		55	56	57	58
1976	2,389	7,550,561	3,104	9,912,534	1960	818	4,382,076	1,718	9,363,637
					1959	939	4,586,413	1,629	8,125,265
1975	1,565	5,628,789	2,467	7,596,072	1958	849	4,183,228	1,667	8,211,301
1974	1,648	6,467,507	3,104	7,341,268	1957	1,058	4,974,340	1,942	9,034,403
1973	2,126	7,885,450	2,271	8,089,704	1956	899	4,405,607	2,383	11,056,911
1972	1,649	7,141,243	1,936	6,459,603					
1971	1,445	6,107,395	1,489	5,181,071	1955	885	3,978,114	2,050	8,737,680
					1954	828	3,991,813	1,365	5,167,489
1970	1,414	6,182,702	1,522	5,282,936	1953	905	3,796,741	1,334	5,343,211
1969	1,624	7,171,493	1,553	6,190,445	1952	900	3,556,723	1,282	5,156,110
1968	1,495	7,405,922	1,500	6,188,889	1951	487	2,141,737	933	3,724,505
1967	1,341	6,277,720	1,537	6,428,760					
1966	1,447	6,726,248	1,605	7,032,859	1950	311	1,345,703	859	3,103,940
					1949	275	1,155,270	580	2,196,603
1965	1,470	6,818,998	2,163	9,497,826	1948	179	683,423	281	1,115,598
1964	1,293	6,016,234	2,007	9,547,966	1947	129	413,232	202	527,191
1963	1,011	5,181,969	1,850	9,028,332					
1962	869	4,584,100	1,640	8,409,737					
1961	769	4,273,836	1,743	9,476,975					

Series Q59-63. Proven crude oil reserves, 1950 to 1975
(millions of barrels)

Year	Discoveries	Extensions and revisions	Total added	Production	Remaining reserve at 31 December
	59	60	61	62	63
1975	1.7	-17.1	-15.4	502.8	6,653.0
1974	6.7	91.5	98.2	601.2	7,171.2
1973	8.9	270.8	279.7	625.7	7,674.2
1972	25.5	179.6	205.1	518.0	8,020.1
1971	17.8	236.4	204.2	480.1	8,333.1
1970	32.5	344.7	377.2	438.0	8,559.0
1969	79.9	551.7	631.6	393.4	8,619.8
1968	125.3	458.9	584.2	371.5	8,381.6
1967	190.8	530.5	721.3	344.2	8,168.9
1966	381.6	1,015.0	1,396.0	316.0	7,791.8
1965	196.2	629.0	825.2	291.6	6,711.2
1964	107.7	1,459.3	1,567.0	270.8	6,177.6
1963	28.2	629.0	657.3	256.5	4,881.5
1962	20.7	531.4	552.0	244.9	4,480.7
1961	21.4	694.7	716.1	221.0	4,173.6
1960	22.0	350.5	372.5	191.1	3,678.5
1959	93.9	421.1	515.0	183.7	3,497.1
1958	9.3	448.2	457.5	166.0	3,165.9
1957	39.8	167.0	206.8	181.8	2,874.5
1956	48.2	461.0	509.2	169.3	2,849.4
1955	63.6	365.9	429.4	127.5	2,509.5
1954	98.2	359.6	457.8	95.6	2,207.6
1953	94.9	151.9	246.8	80.9	1,845.4
1952	302.5	60.9	363.4	60.5	1,679.5
1951	137.2	83.1	220.3	47.3	1,376.6
1950	—	—	—	—	1,202.6

Series Q64-69. Proven natural gas reserves, 1955 to 1976
(billions of cubic feet)

Year	Discoveries	Extensions and revisions	Net change in storage	Total added	Production (reservoir withdrawal)	Remaining reserve at December 31
	64	65	66	67	68	69
1976	639.3	3,220.2	-11.0	3,859.5	2,541.2	58,281.9
1975	362.9	2,235.0	29.9	2,597.9	2,361.1	56,974.7
1974	284.4	6,349.3	10.4	6,633.7	2,393.5	56,708.1
1973	686.7	1,090.2	70.1	1,776.9	2,325.4	52,457.4
1972	487.5	-760.2	-5.6	-272.7	2,247.8	52,935.8
1971	775.5	3,263.8	0.1	4,039.3	1,953.1	55,461.9
1970	193.7	3,009.9	20.2	3,203.6	1,799.2	53,375.6
1969	1,104.4	4,734.5	2.2	5,838.9	1,556.5	51,951.0
1968	282.9	3,097.5	-1.3	3,380.4	1,394.9	47,666.5
1967	603.4	2,840.5	4.1	3,443.9	1,216.0	45,682.0
1966	512.1	3,690.8	17.9	4,202.9	1,125.3	43,405.1
1965	623.3	1,507.1	-7.8	2,130.4	1,087.6	40,354.5
1964	487.0	6,821.8	27.8	7,308.8	1,009.3	39,319.5
1963	1,159.5	1,493.6	25.6	2,653.1	903.6	32,992.3
1962	393.0	2,124.6	-0.4	2,517.6	836.0	31,217.2
1961	545.8	2,690.1	-0.3	3,235.9	693.7	29,536.0
1960	255.3	3,785.6	5.4	4,040.8	474.8	26,994.0
1959	659.8	2,662.8	34.3	3,358.5	438.3	23,422.6
1958	431.1	2,155.5	2.1	2,586.6	334.9	20,488.0
1957	699.2	515.2	2.8	1,214.4	243.5	18,234.2
1956	650.5	2,156.7	4.2	2,807.2	192.6	17,260.6
1955	514.1	1,641.2	3.6	2,155.3	145.9	14,641.8

Series Q70-74. Proven natural gas liquids reserves, 1951 to 1976
(millions of barrels)

Year	Discoveries	Extensions and revisions	Total added	Production	Remaining reserve at 31 December
	70	71	72	73	74
1976	0.9	65.1	66.0	106.0	1,456.1
1975	2.9	69.2	72.1	106.2	1,586.0
1974	—	134.0	134.0	108.6	1,620.2
1973	0.2	3.3	3.5	111.9	1,594.7
1972	1.7	-24.4	-22.7	103.6	1,703.0
1971	0.1	34.0	34.1	84.7	1,829.4
1970	1.0	62.0	63.0	78.9	1,880.0
1969	13.5	312.8	326.3	66.3	1,896.0
1968	5.9	312.5	318.4	61.3	1,636.0
1967	18.8	159.9	176.7	56.7	1,378.9
1966	25.4	284.2	309.6	49.6	1,258.9
1965	0.3	158.4	158.7	47.6	998.8
1964	—	181.1	181.1	41.1	887.8
1963	0.1	79.6	79.8	27.4	747.7
1962	3.7	139.5	143.2	23.5	695.4
1961	1.4	49.5	50.9	13.7	575.7
1960	10.9	34.0	44.9	8.6	538.5
1959	6.6	18.0	24.6	6.7	502.1
1958	35.4	59.0	94.4	4.9	484.2
1957	17.0	100.7	117.8	3.0	394.7
1956	15.0	20.5	35.5	2.7	279.9
1955	0.8	40.4	41.2	2.4	247.1
1954	21.3	(9.6)	11.7	1.4	208.3
1953	42.3	91.7	134.0	1.2	198.1
1952	15.0	39.7	54.6	0.6	65.4
1951	..	..	..	..	11.4

Series Q75-80. Electrical generating capacity and output by type of ownership, 1919 to 1975
(output in millions of kWh, capacity in thousand kWh 1956 to 70, in thousand HP 1919 to 56)

Year	Publicly operated utilities		Privately operated utilities		Industrial establishments	
	Output	Capacity	Output	Capacity	Output	Capacity
	75	76	77	78	79	80
1975	187,543	45,717.4	50,805	9,640.8	35,044	5,993.7
1974	197,680	42,164.5	43,737	9,495.3	38,839	5,869.9
1973	190,777	40,959.3	34,577	7,581.5	37,981	5,835.6
1972	176,806	38,118.8	29,497	6,443.6	33,910	5,381.2
1971	162,892	36,092.0	21,068	5,277.2	32,512	5,306.5
1970	151,407	33,215.8	20,504	430.8	32,793	5,301.0
1969	138,506	30,326.8	18,955	3,997.8	33,641	5,267.2
1968	126,074	23,961.8	17,809	3,759.0	32,495	5,244.6
1967	116,819	26,753.2	16,482	3,845.8	32,324	5,309.5
1966	109,185	22,461.2	16,814	3,293.8	32,137	5,010.0
1965	97,480	21,152.7	13,318	3,004.7	33,476	5,190.4
1964	90,254	19,299.9	12,635	2,591.1	32,098	5,136.4
1963	81,997	18,640.8	11,505	2,559.3	28,737	5,100.5
1962	66,716	15,430.5	25,380	5,042.5	25,373	4,584.0
1961	59,740	13,565.1	29,649	5,927.1	24,325	4,599.2
1960	57,850	12,532.7	31,306	5,899.8	25,301	4,616.3
1959	53,395	11,213.4	29,654	5,723.9	21,622	4,191.1
1958	46,829	,9,567.3	29,124	5,301.9	21,572	3,800.2
1957	45,117	8,019.6	26,406	5,020.0	19,592	3,688.6
1956	42,873	7,334.1	25,773	4,724.6	19,809	3,437.6
1956	42,868	..	35,136	..	10,400	..
1955	38,279	9,497.2	34,632	8,488.5	8,825	..
1954	32,553	8,710.3	33,383	8,011.5	8,040	..
1953	28,448	7,382.9	34,413	8,278.1	7,127	..
1952	26,526	6,542.3	32,883	7,679.5	6,695	..
1951	24,381	5,804.7	30,471	7,225.9	6,595	..
1950	20,061	5,171.7	28,432	6,804.5	6,544	..
1949	17,687	4,359.0	26,732	6,524.2	6,174	..
1948	16,692	4,085.1	25,697	6,134.5	4,872	..
1947	15,759	3,760.8	27,666	6,025.3	3,750	..
1946	14,739	3,612.5	26,998	6,389.2	2,926	..
1945	14,599	3,460.3	25,531	6,380.0	2,590	..
1944	14,910	3,424.7	25,689	6,474.2	2,972	..
1943	9,937	2,426.5	31,082	7,371.1	3,471	..
1942	9,178	2,408.3	28,177	6,400.3	3,652	..
1941	8,524	2,304.4	24,794	6,047.8	3,161	..
1940	7,822	2,291.1	22,287	5,839.7	2,953	..
1939	7,047	2,285.3	21,291	5,516.0	2,641	..
1938	6,666	2,240.9	19,488	5,431.7	2,449	..
1937	7,372	2,202.6	20,316	5,336.8	2,548	..
1936	6,887	2,173.0	18,515	5,146.9	1,696	..
1935	5,515	2,073.8	17,765	5,274.2	1,644	..
1934	5,136	1,964.0	16,061	5,097.6	1,552	..
1933	3,673	1,966.9	13,666	4,842.7	1,358	..
1932	3,714	1,824.0	12,338	4,704.5	1,401	..
1931	4,140	..	12,191	..	1,289	..
1930	5,157	..	12,937	..	1,374	..
1929	5,188	..	12,774	..	1,343	..
1928	4,877	..	11,461	..	1,173	..
1927	4,605	..	9,444	..	828	..
1926	4,296	..	7,797	..	—	..
1925	3,583	..	6,527	..	—	..
1924	3,291	..	6,024	..	—	..
1923	3,025	..	5,074	..	—	..
1922	1,621	..	5,120	..	—	..
1921	1,298	..	4,316	..	—	..
1920	1,438	..	4,456	..	—	..
1919	1,221	..	4,132	..	—	..

Series Q81-84. Electric generating capacity by type of prime mover, 1917 to 1976
(generating capacity in thousands of kilowatts 1956 to 1976, in thousand horsepower 1917 to 1955)

Year	Hydroelectric	Thermal	Nuclear	Total	Year	Hydroelectric	Thermal	Nuclear	Total
	81	82	83	84		81	82	83	84
1976	39,487.6	23,305.4	3,200	65,993.0					
1975	37,281.8	21,670.4	2,400	61,352.0	1945	9,216.6	623.7	—	9,840.3
1974	36,778.9	18,351.8	2,400	57,529.7	1944	9,268.0	630.9	—	9,898.9
1973	34,265.9	17,710.5	2,400	54,376.4	1943	9,205.2	592.4	—	9,797.6
1972	32,500.9	15,583.7	1,860	49,943.7	1942	8,234.3	574.4	—	8,808.7
1971	30,601.1	14,754.6	1,320	46,675.7	1941	7,784.4	567.8	—	8,352.2
1970	28,928.4	14,287.3	240	42,825.7	1940	7,567.1	563.7	—	8,130.8
1969	27,031.1	12,320.7	240	39,591.8	1939	7,241.0	560.3	—	7,801.3
1968	24,957.4	10,711.1	240	35,908.5	1938	7,155.6	517.0	—	7,672.6
1967	23,352.5	9,392.9	220	32,965.4	1937	7,023.2	516.2	—	7,539.4
1966	22,437.8	8,307.2	20	30,765.0	1936	6,810.7	509.2	—	7,319.9
1965	21,770.7	7,557.1	20	29,347.8	1935	6,808.0	503.0	—	7,311.0
1964	20,313.3	6,694.1	20	27,027.4	1934	6,560.7	500.9	—	7,061.6
1963	20,100.4	6,180.3	20	26,300.7	1933	6,306.0	503.6	—	6,809.6
1962	19,338.2	5,608.8	20	24,967.0	1932	6,036.3	492.3	—	6,528.5
1961	19,018.8	5,072.6	—	24,091.4	1931	5,422.3	468.5	—	5,890.8
1960	18,656.9	4,391.8	—	23,048.7	1930	5,144.1	428.3	—	5,572.6
1959	17,550.0	3,578.4	—	21,128.4	1929	4,718.9	378.5	—	5,097.4
1958	15,687.2	2,982.2	—	18,669.4	1928	4,445.5	341.4	—	4,786.9
1957	14,112.8	2,615.4	—	16,728.2	1927	3,975.0	343.4	—	4,318.4
1956[1]	13,070.0	2,426.1	—	15,496.2	1926	3,609.4	336.8	—	3,946.2
1955[2]	15,538.7	2,446.9	—	17,985.6	1925	3,416.0	326.7	—	3,742.7
1954	14,461.5	2,226.3	—	16,721.8	1924	2,708.0	309.6	—	3,017.6
1953	13,923.4	2,237.7	—	15,661.0	1923	2,282.5	290.9	—	2,573.4
1952	12,550.8	1,671.0	—	14,221.8	1922	2,112.3	296.4	—	2,408.7
1951	11,786.0	1,243.6	—	13,030.6	1921	1,826.4	285.1	—	2,111.4
1950	11,029.8	946.4	—	11,976.2	1920	1,754.1	279.5	—	2,033.6
1949	9,973.4	909.9	—	10,883.3	1919	1,737.0	287.9	—	2,024.9
1948	9,470.3	749.3	—	10,219.6	1918	1,682.2	276.5	—	1,958.6
1947	9,131.9	654.2	—	9,786.1	1917	1,652.7	191.9	—	1,844.6
1946	9,378.9	622.8	—	10,001.7					

[1] Includes main and auxiliary plant.
[2] Break in series in 1956. Pre-1956 figures in horsepower for central electrical stations.

Series Q85-91. Electrical generation by utilities and industrial establishments, by type of prime mover, 1919 to 1976

(millions of kWh)

Year	Hydroelectric		Thermal		Nuclear	Total	
	Utilities	Industrial	Utilities	Industrial	Utilities	Utilities	Industrial
	85	**86**	**87**	**88**	**89**	**90**	**91**
1976	188,804	23,988	58,505	6,317	16,430	263,739	30,304
1975	172,920	29,476	53,570	5,568	11,858	238,348	35,044
1974	178,207	32,730	49,345	6,109	13,865	241,417	38,839
1973	161,076	31,766	50,055	6,214	14,256	225,354	37,981
1972	151,528	28,417	48,658	5,493	6,117	206,303	33,910
1971	133,315	27,669	46,753	4,843	3,892	183,960	32,512
1970	128,856	27,853	42,105	4,940	969	171,930	32,793
1969	120,581	28,666	36,386	4,976	494	157,461	33,641
1968	107,313	27,660	36,570	4,835	—	143,883	32,495
1967	104,703	28,045	28,598	4,279	—	133,301	32,324
1966	101,868	27,966	24,130	4,171	—	125,998	32,137
1965	87,648	29,415	23,150	4,061	—	110,798	33,476
1964	84,871	28,472	18,018	3,625	—	102,889	32,098
1963	78,113	25,719	15,388	3,018	—	93,501	28,737
1962	81,334	22,707	10,762	2,665	—	92,096	25,373
1961	82,326	21,593	7,063	2,731	—	89,389	24,325
1960	83,202	22,680	5,954	2,621	—	89,156	25,301
1959	77,768	19,272	5,281	2,350	—	83,049	21,622
1958	71,171	19,338	4,782	2,235	—	75,953	21,572
1957	66,040	17,333	5,483	2,259	—	71,523	19,592
1956	64,742	17,614	4,404	2,195	—	68,646	19,809
1955	59,774[1]	16,964[1]	3,340[1]	2,143[1]	—	63,114[1]	19,107[1]
1954	53,010[1]	16,321[1]	3,282[1]	1,927[1]	—	56,292[1]	18,247[1]
1953	49,409[1]	15,113[1]	3,836[1]	1,943[1]	—	53,245[1]	17,056[1]
1952	49,578[1]	12,784[1]	2,293[1]	1,842[1]	—	51,871[1]	14,625[1]
1951	46,096[1]	12,158[1]	1,776[1]	1,746[1]	—	47,872[1]	13,904[1]
1950	39,713[1]	12,422[1]	1,693[1]	1,554[1]	—	41,406[1]	13,976[1]
1949	35,992[1]	12,000[1]	1,445[1]	1,454[1]	—	37,437[1]	13,454[1]
1948	34,712[1]	9,952[1]	1,177[1]	1,421[1]	—	35,889[1]	11,373[1]
1947	35,132[1]	9,711[1]	1,049[1]	1,283[1]	—	36,181[1]	10,994[1]
1946	40,692	—	1,045	—	—	41,737	2,926
1945	39,131	—	999	—	—	40,130	2,590
1944	39,553	—	1,045	—	—	40,599	2,972
1943	39,660	—	819	—	—	40,480	3,471
1942	36,583	—	772	—	—	37,355	3,652
1941	32,629	—	689	—	—	33,318	3,161
1940	29,524	—	585	—	—	30,109	2,953
1939	27,829	—	509	—	—	28,338	2,641
1938	25,688	—	467	—	—	26,154	2,449
1937	27,176	—	512	—	—	27,688	2,538
1936	24,933	—	470	—	—	25,402	1,696
1935	22,884	—	399	—	—	23,283	1,644
1934	20,817	—	380	—	—	21,197	1,552
1933	17,006	—	333	—	—	17,339	1,358
1932	15,724	—	328	—	—	16,052	1,401
1931	16,025	—	306	—	—	16,331	1,289
1930	17,749	—	345	—	—	18,094	1,374
1929	17,604	—	359	—	—	17,963	1,343
1928	16,106[2]	—	232[2]	—	—	16,338	1,173
1927	14,346	—	203	—	—	14,549	828
1926	11,911	—	182	—	—	12,093	..
1925	9,942	—	169	—	—	10,110	..
1924	9,159	—	156	—	—	9,315	..
1923	7,936	—	163	—	—	8,099	..
1922	6,570	—	171	—	—	6,741	..
1921	5,448	—	167	—	—	5,614	..
1920	5,730	—	165	—	—	5,895	..
1919	5,353	—	144	—	—	5,497	..

[1] As reclassified in 1956, 1949–56 output from central stations using former classification as follows: for Hydro utilities, 1956, 73,525; 1955, 69,478; 1954, 62,572; 1953, 58,926; 1952, 57,024; 1951, 52,955; 1950, 46,624; 1949, 42,779 and 1948, 41,070. For Thermal utilities, 1956, 4,480; 1955, 3,473; 1954, 3,364; 1953, 3,934; 1952, 2,386; 1951, 1,897; 1950, 1,870; 1949, 1,639 and 1948, 1,320. For Total industrial, 1956, 10,400; 1955, 8,825; 1954, 8,040; 1953, 7,127; 1952, 6,695; 1951, 6,595; 1950, 6,544; 1949, 6,174 and 1948, 4,872.

[2] Hydro, for the years 1919 to 1928, includes auxiliary thermal generation at hydro plants. Change probably accounts for only a small part of increased thermal output in 1929.

Series Q92-96. Production and trade in electrical energy, 1919 to 1975
(millions of kWh)

| Year | Net generation | Imports | Exports | | Apparent consumption |
			Firm (premium)	Surplus (secondary)	
	92	**93**	**94**	**95**	**96**
1975	273,392.4	3,971.6	2,375.1	9,034.1	265,954.8
1974	280,256.3	2,441.0	2,487.5	12,912.2	267,297.6
1973	263,334.9	2,249.2	2,637.1	13,649.0	249,298.0
1972	240,212.7	2,381.2	2,046.6	8,990.4	231,556.9
1971	216,472.2	3,378.4	1,860.2	5,460.8	212,530.1
1970	204,722.9	3,245.1	983.7	4,647.7	202,336.6
1969	191,102.2	3,740.2	837.9	3,482.2	189,521.3
1968	176,378.3	4,451.2	741.2	3,247.1	176,841.2
1967	165,624.8	4,181.0	705.0	3,288.8	165,812.0
1966	158,135.2	3,218.0	614.0	3,783.3	159,955.9
1965	144,273.8	3,575.0	634.8	3,049.3	144,164.7
1964	134,986.7	3,121.2	870.6	3,288.9	133,948.4
1963	122,238.2	2,884.3	882.4	2,730.4	121,509.7
1962	117,468.7	2,778.7	1,261.2	2,851.2	116,135.0
1961	113,713.3	1,394.0	1,192.3	2,964.9	110,950.1
1960	114,457.2	356.9	1,040.1	4,471.8	109,302.2
1959	104,670.6	512.0	1,075.7	3,517.3	100,589.5
1958	97,525.6	245.1	1,173.0	2,912.9	93,684.7
1957	91,114.8	833.0	1,311.3	3,521.2	87,115.2
1956	88,454.6	239.2	1,383.5	3,720.2	83,590.1
1955	82,221.3	158.6	1,516.3	2,917.2	77,946.4
1954	74,539.6	119.0	1,506.8	1,211.5	71,940.3
1953	70,300.0	180.6	1,701.8	722.2	68,057.5
1952	66,496.5	20.0	1,638.5	854.7	64,023.3
1951	61,775.7	9.0	1,618.1	757.5	59,409.1
1950	55,382.0	2.6	1,539.4	386.5	53,458.7
1949	50,890.2	31.2	1,378.6	378.2	49,164.6
1948	47,262.1	86.4	1,436.8	306.3	45,605.3
1947	47,174.4	53.0	1,429.0	637.5	45,160.9
1946	44,662.9	9.5	1,407.3	1,074.3	42,190.8
1945	42,720.4	15.9	1,426.3	1,426.3	40,089.9
1944	43,571.3	14.1	1,412.2	1,412.2	41,000.1
1943	43,950.2	0.6	1,429.5	1,115.6	41,405.8
1942	41,007.5	0.6	1,435.0	1,018.8	38,554.3
1941	36,479.1	0.7	1,443.9	915.6	34,120.3
1940	33,062.5	0.7	1,408.1	727.4	30,927.6
1939	30,978.6	0.7	1,424.7	487.9	29,066.7
1938	28,602.7	0.6		1,826.5	26,776.8
1937	30,225.4	1.3		1,578.1	25,521.3
1936	27,098.6	0.8		1,578.1	25,521.3
1935	24,926.7	0.7		1,364.6	23,562.7
1934	22,748.8	0.6		1,248.8	21,500.6
1933	18,696.9	0.6		989.4	17,708.1
1932	17,453.1	0.6		667.9	16,785.8
1931	17,620.3	5.4		1,235.3	16,390.5
1930	19,467.9	5.8		1,619.6	17,854.0
1929	19,305.7	6.1		1,444.5	17,867.3
1928	17,509.0	5.2		1,587.8	15,926.5
1927	15,377.5	5.0		1,632.6	13,749.9
1926	12,093 [1]	5.4		1,506.0	10,592.4 [1]
1925	10,110 [1]	..		1,285.5	8,824.5 [1]
1924	9,315 [1]	..		1,302.3	8,012.7 [1]
1923	8,099 [1]	..		1,343.5	6,755.5 [1]
1922	6,741 [1]	..		976.5	5,764.5 [1]
1921	5,614 [1]	..		885.3	4,728.7 [1]
1920	5,895 [1]	..		..	..
1919	5,497 [1]	..		..	..

[1] Utilities only, excludes industrial generation.

Series Q97-101. Electric utilities,[1] number of customers by class, 1920 to 1975

(thousands)

Year	Residential and farm	Commercial	Industrial	Street lighting	Total
	97	**98**	**99**	**100**	**101**
1975	6,988.5	921.7	—[2]	..	7,910.3
1974	6,798.4	900.6	—[2]	..	7,699.1
1973	6,612.1	801.3	83.4	..	7,496.9
1972	6,425.0	770.4	81.0	..	7,276.4
1971	6,215.1	750.1	76.1	..	7,042.1
1970	6,076.8	722.9	77.7	..	6,877.4
1969	5,818.4	691.9	88.0	9.9	6,708.2
1968	5,749.2	665.2	88.5	9.4	6,512.4
1967	5,590.7	638.5	90.0	8.7	6,327.9
1966	5,436.1	618.0	97.0	8.2	6,159.3
1965	5,282.5	608.6	91.6	7.1	5,989.9
1964	5,150.9	609.7	85.4	6.8	5,852.8
1963	4,975.1	575.9	96.8	7.1	5,654.9
1962	4,864.5	562.5	106.5	5.9	5,539.4
1961	4,716.8	548.1	104.3	6.2	5,375.4
1960	4,542.8	543.7	105.4	5.4	5,188.3
1959	4,381.6	528.6	103.5	5.0	5,018.7
1958	4,188.9	516.0	99.8	4.9	4,809.6
1957	4,004.2	506.5	95.7	4.7	4,611.2
1956	3,835.0	491.2	97.0	4.5	4,427.7
1955	3,645.3	481.9	93.3	4.4	4,424.9
1954	3,449.0	451.6	88.9[3]	4.2	4,001.6
1953	3,283.5	444.0	85.9	4.1	3,817.5
1952	3,112.3	422.4	82.0	3.9	3,620.6
1951	2,952.0	405.3	78.8	3.7	3,439.8
1950	2,797.4	392.4	76.4	3.5	3,269.8
1949	2,619.8	379.5	73.8	3.2	3,076.4
1948	2,398.8	349.7	70.4	3.1	2,822.0
1947	2,246.3	327.0	67.6	2.8	2,643.3
1946	2,104.5	306.6	63.0	2.7	2,476.8
1945	1,987.4	285.4	57.9	2.6	2,333.2
1944	1,906.5	273.5	55.7	2.5	2,238.0
1943	1,848.1	259.0	54.7	2.4	2,164.9
1942	1,803.7	264.7	54.5	2.4	2,125.3
1941	1,755.9	269.0	54.0	2.4	2,081.3
1940	1,686.4	265.2	52.6	2.3	2,006.5
1939	1,623.7	262.6	53.2	2.2	1,941.7
1938	1,559.4	259.9	52.2	2.2	1,873.6
1937	1,500.1	252.3	51.5	2.1	1,806.0
1936	1,443.1	245.1	50.6	2.0	1,740.8
1935	1,402.0	240.5	50.3	2.0	1,694.7
1934	1,379.2	229.2	49.8	2.0	1,660.1
1933	1,371.8	244.3	48.8	2.0	1,666.9
1932	1,357.5	248.5	49.5	2.0	1,657.5
1931	1,336.7	244.6	49.5	1.9	1,632.8
1930	1,317.3	238.8	50.0	1.7	1,607.9
1929	1,292.5	233.9[4]	28.0[4]	1.5	1,555.9
1928	1,207.5	215.7	40.8	—	1,464.0
1927	1,142.5	199.4	40.0	—	1,382.0
1926	1,110.6	188.6	38.4	—	1,337.6
1925	1,063.5	181.0	35.2	—	1,279.7
1924	988.5	176.4	36.0	—	1,201.0
1923	920.2	159.9	32.4	—	1,112.5
1922	889.3	164.2		—	1,053.5
1921	830.1	143.2		—	973.2
1920	764.9	129.3		—	894.2

[1] Includes customers of industrial establishments selling to the public.
[2] Included in commercial.
[3] Until 1954, customers buying electricity for resale were recorded as industrial customers. To eliminate double counting these were excluded from 1955 on. The number of such customers in 1955 was 624.

[4] In 1929, small industrial classified as commercial.

Series Q102-106. Electric utility sales[1] by class of customer, selected years, 1930 to 1975
(millions of kWh)

Year	Residential and farm	Commercial	Industrial	Street lighting	Total
	102	**103**	**104**	**105**	**106**
1975	64,128	128,472	—[2]	1,971	194,571
1974	59,295	132,218	—[2]	1,816	193,329
1973	54,020	37,676	84,293	1,735	177,724
1972	50,205	33,993	76,913	1,618	162,729
1971	46,541	30,252	68,879	1,540	147,203
1970	43,431	25,881	67,196	1,464	137,972
1969	40,446	22,642	62,967	1,396	127,451
1968	37,780	19,632	58,066	1,317	116,795
1967	35,005	17,148	54,403	1,206	107,762
1966	32,131	14,544	51,992	1,107	99,774
1965	29,738	13,280	46,808	1,021	90,847
1964	27,278	12,195	41,930	941	82,344
1963	25,322	10,887	52,129	871	89,209
1962	23,692	9,833	49,988	819	84,332
1961	21,980	8,667	48,500	727	79,874
1960	20,397	7,489	48,320	657	76,863
1959	19,007	8,058	44,220	603	71,888
1958	17,291	7,225	40,253	555	65,324
1957	15,858	6,113	38,062	511	60,544
1956[3]	14,339	5,323	36,247[3]	474	56,383[3]
1956[3]	14,332	5,322	46,003[3]	474	66,131[3]
1955	12,760	4,704	43,416	462	61,341
1954	11,281	5,210	40,640	407	56,537
1953	9,878	3,881	40,045	380	54,184
1952	8,741	3,489	38,348	348	50,927
1951	7,726	3,153	35,507	321	46,707
1950	6,750	2,809	31,707	303	41,570
1949	5,679	2,409	29,664	283	38,037
1948	4,984	2,155	28,804	264	36,207
1947	4,383	2,061	30,912	245	27,601
1946	3,882	1,840	29,449	223	35,394
1945	3,365	1,614	28,724	226	33,929
1944	3,047	1,418	29,783	198	34,446
1943	2,884	1,261	30,119	193	34,416
1942	2,717	1,313	27,112	199	31,341
1941	2,582	1,309	23,459	215	27,566
1940	2,437	1,207	21,042	206	24,891
1939	2,311	1,109	19,796	204	23,420
1938	2,173	1,032	17,934	197	21,336
1937	2,007	959	20,305	192	23,464
1936	1,887	871	18,347	196	21,295
1935	1,770	872	16,448	188	19,277
1934	1,717	808	14,462	188	17,175
1933	1,650	747	10,164	185	12,746
1931	1,564	763	..	..	..
1930	1,490	744	..	..	..

[1] Includes sales to the public by industrial establishments.
[2] Included with commercial.

[3] Series changed in 1956, a number of producers reclassified as industrial.

Series Q107-113. Electric utility revenues by class of customer, 1919 to 1975
(millions of dollars)

Year	Residential and farm	Commercial	Industrial	Street lighting	Total domestic	Exported to U.S. Final	Secondary
	107	108	109	110	111	112	113
1975	1,245.1	1,810.6	—[1]	57.9	3,113.6	20.4	84.5
1974	1,045.3	1,582.7	—[1]	48.8	2,676.8	20.9	147.9
1973	907.3	1,374.3	—[1]	44.0	2,325.6	19.9	95.0
1972	811.0	552.5	661.6	39.9	2,065.0	19.2	46.8
1971	748.8	493.8	597.8	37.9	1,878.3	13.3	43.0
1970	685.3	426.3	562.8	41.2	1,715.6	6.8	25.3
1969	607.3	372.8	512.6	37.7	1,530.4	5.7	9.3
1968	560.7	326.7	463.7	34.9	1,386.0	5.0	2.7
1967	507.1	291.3	417.8	32.0	1,248.2	4.7	3.1
1966	453.5	253.2	394.8	29.1	1,130.6	4.3	3.3
1965	424.9	234.2	358.0	26.2	1,043.3	5.6	4.4
1964	401.2	223.0	315.4	23.7	963.3	..	..
1963	384.0	200.9	359.6	21.7	966.2	4.6	2.0
1962	366.0	185.1	337.3	20.1	908.5	6.5	1.8
1961	346.8	166.7	327.5	17.9	858.9	5.8	3.8
1960	325.9	151.5	311.7	16.2	805.3	4.3	10.0
1959	305.7	141.5	293.8	14.8	755.8	5.0	8.9
1958	278.5	131.8	268.2	13.2	691.7	4.7	8.7
1957	257.0	119.5	250.3	11.9	638.7	4.7	13.1
1956	235.4	108.6	241.8	11.2	597.0	4.5	12.3
1955	211.5	97.1	229.7	10.4	548.7	11.7	
1954	190.7	88.9	216.2	9.7	505.5	2.7	
1953	168.3	80.7	211.1	8.9	469.0	2.4	
1952	144.7	71.5	191.4	7.9	415.5	2.5	
1951	127.7	64.4	175.2	7.3	374.6	2.4	
1950	109.0	57.4	150.6	6.8	323.8	1.9	
1949	90.3	49.0	134.9	6.1	280.3	1.8	
1948	79.9	42.9	128.9	5.7	257.4	1.7	
1947	70.3	40.8	122.4	5.4	238.9	2.1	
1946	62.8	37.2	120.8	5.3	226.1	2.5	
1945	55.8	32.9	121.4	5.0	215.1	2.7	
1944	43.3	30.5	126.9	4.6	215.3	2.6	
1943	51.3	28.1	120.7	4.7	204.8	..	
1942	50.7	29.4	118.7	5.0	203.8	..	
1941	48.7	29.4	102.9	5.1	186.1	..	
1940	46.4	27.5	87.3	5.0	166.2	..	
1939	43.8	25.7	76.7	4.9	151.1	1.9	
1938	44.3	24.3	73.8	4.9	144.3	..	
1937	39.3	23.1	76.3	4.8	143.5	..	
1936	38.4	22.2	70.5	4.8	135.9	..	
1935	36.8	21.0	64.6	4.8	127.2	..	
1934	36.5	20.1	63.2	4.7	124.5	..	
1933	36.0	19.5	57.3	4.7	117.5	..	
1932	36.4	20.4	59.5	4.9	121.2	..	
1931	35.3	20.7	61.5	4.8	122.3	..	
1930	34.1	20.6	66.7	4.6	126.0	..	
1929	33.6	23.3	61.6	4.4	122.9	..	
1928		50.3[2]	62.0[3]	..	112.3	..	
1927		45.8[2]	58.2[3]	..	104.0	..	
1926		42.0[2]	46.9[3]	..	88.9	..	
1925		38.8[2]	63.8[3]	..	102.6	..	
1924		36.0[2]	59.2[3]	..	95.2	..	
1923		33.2[2]	57.9[3]	..	91.1	..	
1922		31.7[2]	50.6[3]	..	82.3	..	
1921		28.8[2]	44.6[3]	..	73.4	..	
1920		25.4[2]	40.3[3]	..	65.7	..	
1919		20.2[2]	37.7[3]	..	57.9	..	

[1] Included with commercial.
[2] For lighting purposes.
[3] For all other purposes.

Series Q114-117. Gas utilities, number of customers by class, 1958 to 1976
(thousands)

Year	Residential	Commercial	Industrial	Total	Year	Residential	Commercial	Industrial	Total
	114	**115**	**116**	**117**		**114**	**115**	**116**	**117**
1976	2,153,597	229,051	17,176	2,399,824					
1975	2,065,333	218,391	16,316	2,300,039	1965	1,427,326	130,902	11,311	1,569,539
1974	1,992,897	211,446	15,206	2,219,549	1964	1,372,873	122,829	10,800	1,506,502
1973	1,915,566	200,673	14,851	2,131,090	1963	1,322,554	116,331	10,405	1,449,290
1972	1,835,786	190,117	13,192	2,039,095	1962	1,249,237	108,015	9,235	1,366,487
1971	1,763,745	180,892	13,397	1,958,034	1961	1,174,966	100,490	8,157	1,283,613
1970	1,704,028	172,898	12,882	1,889,808	1960	1,099,448	96,135	7,403	1,203,252
1969	1,658,273	165,820	12,588	1,836,681	1959	1,028,142	84,292	6,595	1,119,293
1968	1,599,197	156,002	11,811	1,767,010	1958	952,755	7,428	6,080	1,032,997
1967	1,521,819	145,649	11,075	1,678,543					
1966	1,476,408	138,944	11,431	1,626,783					

Series Q118-125. Gas utilities sales by class of customer, 1958 to 1976
(millions of cubic feet and thousands of dollars)

Year	Residential		Industrial		Commercial		Total[1]	
	Volume	Revenues	Volume	Revenues	Volume	Revenues	Volume	Revenues
	118	**119**	**120**	**121**	**122**	**123**	**124**	**125**
1976	312,846	558,712	763,179	894,808	294,885	442,023	1,370,910	1,895,543
1975	299,219	406,214	739,597	592,831	285,889	308,242	1,324,705	1,307,287
1974	292,961	326,705	745,929	422,228	275,431	231,462	1,314,321	980,395
1973	271,800	283,121	711,987	331,662	245,653	183,074	1,229,440	797,857
1972	280,811	286,762	623,405	278,047	241,581	175,574	1,145,795	740,383
1971	250,796	258,097	543,612	234,034	206,902	149,765	1,001,329	641,896
1970	241,793	246,786	489,503	202,563	186,145	132,969	917,441	582,317
1969	231,465	241,232	444,829	175,832	168,420	120,184	844,713	537,248
1968	214,662	226,359	407,287	158,292	144,056	105,461	766,006	490,112
1967	204,086	212,931	359,331	144,080	131,689	98,500	695,106	455,510
1966	195,261	202,327	324,532	129,474	115,722	84,411	635,515	416,212
1965	187,311	189,233	284,669	108,430	101,037	71,644	573,016	369,307
1964	163,626	170,553	257,403	97,201	83,475	60,229	504,503	327,983
1963	145,856	152,032	235,379	84,856	70,363	50,798	451,598	287,687
1962	134,919	138,439	213,468	73,657	63,675	45,564	412,062	257,660
1961	122,208	121,183	200,337	65,537	57,778	40,140	380,323	227,261
1960	110,132	106,983	164,234	52,851	51,122	34,656	325,730	194,584
1959	97,937	91,191	141,695	41,441	43,485	27,109	283,343	159,823
1958	77,224	67,573	94,134	26,723	36,261	20,166	207,807	115,000

[1] Totals for series Q124 and 125 may not add due to rounding.

Series Q126-130. Miscellaneous statistics of the electric power industry, selected years, 1891 to 1976
(all values in thousands of dollars)

Year	Capital invested	Number of employees	Salaries and wages	Cost of fuel	Pole line mileage
	126	**127**	**128**	**129**	**130**
1976	28,492.9	60,230	1,053,953	607,745	94,030 [1]
1975	24,666.0	57,937	886,400	402,833	90,074 [1]
1974	20,883.7	54,600	726,692	259,102	87,704 [1]
1973	18,527.9	52,629	621,396	201,204	89,358 [1]
1972	16,442.5	51,495	525,262	187,420	89,282 [1]
1971	15,073.1	50,626	497,825	175,331	85,417 [1]
1970	13,754.0	47,598	444,207	139,905	81,180 [1]
1969	12,488.4	46,308	391,265	119,597	81,920 [1]
1968	11,441.5	43,864	348,216	116,131	78,368 [1]
1967	10,401.6	43,866	314,898	97,112	72,766 [1]
1966	9,321.7	42,886	286,599	80,228	69,347 [1]
1965	8,479.8	43,794	265,582	77,564	66,931 [1]
1964	7,727.6	43,205	247,280	60,530	66,301 [1]
1963	7,300.5	41,344	226,302	42,422	63,817 [1]
1962	6,886.0	40,003	211,988	37,237	335,304
1961	6,456.9	39,389	198,416	24,673	330,313
1960	7,083.9	41,034	190,204	21,679	320,618
1959	6,570.7	39,440	182,789	19,285	310,840
1958	6,076.7	39,394	170,211	19,645	311,511
1957	5,595.8	37,817	153,952	23,733	285,306
1956	4,891.9	36,118 [2]	137,967 [2]	20,347 [2]	271,556 [2]
1955	..	35,178 [2]	128,370 [2]	17,078 [2]	243,773 [2]
1954	..	33,762	120,322	16,970	222,158
1953	..	..	115,652	19,727	213,176
1952	..	..	102,166	13,421	190,316
1951	..	..	89,130	11,000	170,582
1950	..	..	71,774	10,486	151,726
1949	..	..	70,552	10,185	135,329
1948	..	..	62,975	8,414	113,411
1947	..	..	54,111	6,684	98,530
1946	..	..	46,423	5,708	89,231
1945	..	21,283	39,251	5,099	83,178
1944	..	19,770	36,945	5,488	80,073
1943	1,778.2	19,120	35,786	3,968	70,063
1942	1,749.9	19,764	34,286	3,490	77,909
1941	1,641.5	19,880	31,648	2,934	77,253
1940	1,615.4	19,054	28,896	2,448	75,050
1939	1,564.6	18,848	28,223	2,017	72,132
1938	1,545.4	17,929	27,149	2,011	66,977
1937	1,497.3	17,018	25,624	2,583	63,035
1936	1,483.1	16,087	23,367	2,304	59,436
1935	1,459.8	15,342	22,520	2,055	59,436
1934	1,430.9	14,974	21,829	2,002	56,214
1933	1,386.5	14,717	21,432	1,846	56,570
1932	1,335.9	15,395	23,261	1,834	53,845
1931	1,230.0	17,014	26,307	1,892	52,399
1930	1,138.2	17,857	27,287	2,595	48,814
1929	1,055.7	16,184	24,832	3,016	42,913
1928	956.9	15,855	23,087	2,280	37,333
1927	866.8	14,708	22,946	2,303	33,573
1926	756.2	13,406	19,943	2,137	29,695
1925	726.7	13,263	18,756	2,266	27,653
1924	628.7	12,956	17,947	2,388	26,654
1923	581.8	11,094	14,784	2,639	23,560
1922	568.1	10,684	14,495	2,677	22,669
1921	484.7	10,714	15,235	3,025	21,714
1920	448.3	10,693	14,627	3,190	20,879
1919	416.5	9,656	11,487	2,621	18,911
1918	401.9	9,696	10,354	—	—
1917	356.0	8,847	7,778	—	—
1916	—	—	—	—	—
1915	248.6	—	—	—	—
1910	110.8	—	—	—	—
1905	80.4	—	—	—	—
1900	11.9	—	—	—	—
1891	4.1	—	—	—	—

[1] Distribution lines excluded from data available after 1962.   [2] Coverage changed in 1956.

Series Q131-136. Principal statistics of the Canadian petroleum and natural gas industry, 1929 to 1976

(all values in thousands of dollars)

Year	Number of employees	Salaries and wages	Cost of fuel and electricity[1]	Cost of materials and supplies[2]	Value of marketable production	Value added
	131	132	133	134	135	136
1976	19,096	341,032	60,300	159,697	7,238,022	7,050,003
1975	18,053	280,884	42,711	110,260	5,974,735	5,838,459
1974	18,155	257,969	44,452	81,688	4,836,328	4,724,990
1973	16,786	212,145	37,768	70,481	2,979,704	2,883,273
1972	16,604	195,920	27,394	59,813	2,162,661	2,083,466
1971	15,896	175,432	23,067	53,212	1,852,077	1,779,369
1970	14,970	152,845	20,502	51,141	1,612,224	1,551,637
1969	14,153	138,248	17,478	40,000	1,450,472	1,399,638
1968	13,611	123,412	14,973	37,284	1,360,252	1,312,414
1967	13,113	111,855	13,453	32,415	1,229,686	1,189,867
1966	12,378	95,997	12,952	29,159	1,092,535	1,059,395
1965	11,817	84,687	14,080	23,724	978,135	942,409
1964	11,243	77,306	13,531	22,171	909,573	880,828
1963	11,237	76,012	13,334	21,331	818,457	796,444
1962	11,232	75,325	11,237	18,180	707,837	690,075
1961	11,184	71,179	9,903	15,218	608,801	598,902
1960	5,371	27,981	6,355	10,958	470,699	453,386
1959	6,721	33,702	7,420	9,662	455,517	438,435
1958	7,064	33,316	6,404	10,267	423,776	407,106
1957	7,821	36,302	5,970	10,692	465,325	448,662
1956	8,092	36,353	4,807	9,087	417,566	403,672
1955	6,868	26,018	3,569	5,984	319,861	310,308
1954	6,757	24,621	3,135	4,171	256,141	248,841
1953	6,919	24,504	2,739	3,067	211,338	..
1952	6,275	21,907	2,007	2,743	145,451	..
1951	5,843	18,010	1,237	2,148	123,057	119,672
1950	5,035	13,552	791	1,109	91,040	89,140
1949	4,354	11,018	658	391	78,674	77,624
1948	3,472	6,511	2,002	117	52,079	..
1947	3,080	6,112	980	137	31,877	..
1946	3,218	5,752	1,142	131	25,313	24,041
1945	3,858	6,892	976	136	24,982	..
1944	4,357	8,700	1,188	255	25,591	24,146
1943	4,281	8,059	892	210	28,459	..
1942	3,912	6,476	1,064	248	28,232	..
1941	4,005	6,097	713	199	26,234	25,322
1940	3,930	5,584	1,020	542	22,689	..
1939	3,770	5,104	790	741	21,476	19,945
1938	..	..	..	..	..	..
1937	3,648	4,828	547	662	15,040	13,831
1936	..	..	..	..	..	..
1935	..	..	..	..	..	..
1934	..	..	..	..	..	..
1933	2,085	2,425	190	..	11,288	..
1932	..	..	..	..	..	..
1931	2,901	3,707	330	..	12,966	..
1930	..	..	..	..	..	..
1929	4,174	6,024	335	..	12,924	..

[1] Cost of fuel is excluded starting in 1961.   [2] Cost of fuel is included starting in 1961.

Series Q137-142. Principal statistics of the Canadian coal mining industry, 1918 to 1976
(all values in thousands of dollars)

Year	Number of employees	Salaries and wages	Cost of fuel and electricity	Cost of material and supplies	Value of production	Value added
	137	138	139	140	141	142
1976	8,995	128,461	19,790	124,525	619,801	474,338
1975	8,416	109,795	17,304	89,821	573,452	483,493
1974	8,142	91,622	10,776	63,968	309,272	239,148
1973	7,856	75,522	9,116	43,019	216,992	166,704
1972	8,704	77,874	9,203	46,029	185,376	130,614
1971	8,069	64,790	7,097	44,062	155,077	103,563
1970	7,874	56,745	5,891	42,693	122,619	73,210
1969	7,371	44,738	3,505	19,743	87,568	64,051
1968	8,427	46,583	3,367	19,856	89,291	66,181
1967	8,227	41,133	3,362	14,721	82,760	..
1966	8,564	39,091	3,559	15,244	81,560	..
1965	9,076	39,150	3,792	16,159	75,901	..
1964	9,087	37,535	3,821	13,950	72,735	..
1963	8,903	35,624	3,731	13,011	71,757	..
1962	9,470	34,385	3,818	10,445	69,160	..
1961	10,461	35,608	4,063	10,080	70,053	..
1960	11,587	38,735	3,314	11,720	74,676	..
1959	11,485	37,123	4,275	10,706	73,876	..
1958	13,162	42,250	4,967	10,787	79,963	..
1957	14,569	47,222	4,863	11,449	90,221	..
1956	16,095	49,478	5,141	11,176	95,350	..
1955	16,590	50,325	5,015	10,353	93,579	..
1954	18,050	53,650	4,933	10,699	96,600	..
1953	19,845	59,350	5,969	12,177	102,722	..
1952	21,753	66,028	5,404	13,554	111,026	..
1951	22,647	63,128	4,678	11,869	109,039	..
1950	23,418	60,939	4,362	10,103	110,140	..
1949	24,230	61,205	4,352	11,145	110,915	..
1948	24,318	58,565	5,845	10,374	106,684	..
1947	22,227	46,312	4,050	7,651	77,475	..
1946	25,487	51,344	4,100	8,537	75,820	..
1945	24,925	49,432	3,994	7,611	67,588	..
1944	25,234	55,021	4,066	8,647	70,433	..
1943	24,866	47,292	3,844	7,708	62,878	..
1942	24,763	42,091	3,710	7,256	62,898	..
1941	26,330	38,150	3,545	6,136	58,060	..
1940	26,434	34,043	3,310	5,686	54,676	..
1939	26,472	30,721	3,223	4,981	48,677	..
1938	27,074	28,700	3,147	4,804	43,982	..
1937	27,202	31,642	3,580	5,137	48,752	..
1936	26,918	28,873	3,507	4,720	45,792	..
1935	26,198	26,595	3,405	4,515	41,963	..
1934	25,961	25,663	3,449	4,921	42,045	..
1933	25,375	22,379	3,215	3,698	35,923	..
1932	26,960	25,043	3,067	4,027	37,118	..
1931	27,860	28,802	3,060	4,655	41,207	..
1930	29,172	36,442	3,494	5,526	52,850	..
1929	29,739	42,376	3,657	6,404	63,065	..
1928	30,256	43,321	3,680	5,087	63,758	..
1927	29,772	38,956	4,898	5,440	61,867	..
1926	28,368	35,842	1,737 [1]	4,786	59,875	..
1925	25,032	33,200	1,571	4,623	49,262	..
1924	27,183	35,123	1,386	5,137	53,594	..
1923	32,046	46,216	1,347	5,463	72,058	..
1922	31,838	39,551	..	4,745	65,518	..
1921	31,849	46,476	1,856	9,229	72,452	..
1920	—	—	—	—	82,497	..
1919	—	—	—	—	55,623	..
1918	—	—	—	—	55,193	..

[1] Electric power only, 1936 and prior years.

Series Q143-148. Miscellaneous statistics of natural gas utilities, 1959 to 1976
(all values in thousands of dollars)

| Year | Property account | Number of employees | Salaries and wages | Mileage of pipelines | | |
				Gathering	Transmission	Distribution
	143	144	145	146	147	148
1976	6,102,593	10,624	143,232	11,979	27,147	43,750
1975	5,718,398	11,062	144,264	9,635	25,962	41,410
1974	5,306,847	10,745	121,788	8,613	25,107	39,292
1973	4,913,160	10,232	104,060	8,064	24,505	38,088
1972	4,531,542	9,496	91,297	7,256	22,880	37,103
1971	4,003,299	9,466	84,789	7,175	20,601	35,116
1970	3,571,453	9,741	79,366	6,791	19,282	33,840
1969	3,271,554	9,906	76,166	6,517	17,872	31,980
1968	2,960,045	9,685	67,777	5,905	16,535	29,892
1967	2,688,390	9,561	62,938	5,376	15,613	27,305
1966	2,483,815	9,955	58,013	5,319	14,935	25,728
1965	2,334,239	11,172	65,529	5,206	14,206	24,661
1964	2,167,556	10,887	59,996	4,918	13,311	23,634
1963	1,961,850	10,916	57,727	4,692	12,388	22,540
1962	1,808,700	10,590	54,540	4,568	11,845	20,940
1961	1,709,365	10,725	52,502	4,877	11,217	19,545
1960	1,534,918	10,336	49,656	3,680	10,716	18,419
1959	1,391,317	9,889	44,610	3,308	9,941	17,162

Series Q149-159. Canadian refinery shipments of petroleum products, 1949 to 1976
(thousands of barrels)

Year	Gasoline and naphtha	Aviation turbo fuel	Kerosine and stove oil	Diesel fuel	Light fuel oils (nos. 2,3)	Heavy fuel oils (nos. 4,5,6)	Lubricants	Asphalt	Petroleum coke	Liquified refinery gas	Petro-chemical feed stocks
	149	150	151	152	153	154	155	156	157	158	159
1976	233,063	24,538	23,223	75,929	89,264	104,053	3,853	17,795	626	10,756	..
1975	223,876	23,763	22,231	75,685	90,988	110,709	3,717	18,727	1,020	8,734	..
1974	216,356	23,162	22,670	72,865	95,399	118,655	4,009	18,693	1,083	8,671	21,130
1973	210,131	20,625	24,706	68,654	90,208	114,836	4,179	18,265	1,016	9,334	19,022
1972	188,495	16,565	23,846	65,554	84,901	108,848	4,450	16,031	927	8,386	14,791
1971	171,711	14,853	22,284	60,544	73,710	78,645	4,202	15,117	645	7,701	16,415
1970	163,756	13,835	22,295	52,841	70,499	70,245	4,017	14,772	603	8,020	12,461
1969	157,513	10,861	21,116	49,971	65,938	65,318	3,636	13,423	675	6,546	11,648
1968	153,247	9,821	19,114	47,681	65,628	62,826	3,180	13,031	699	6,470	10,482
1967	143,605	8,799	18,515	45,629	62,062	54,329	3,239	12,584	1,094	6,384	10,255
1966	138,450	7,970	19,021	42,826	60,996	51,889	3,250	12,339	1,096	5,915	9,478
1965	131,106	6,734	18,681	39,470	58,657	48,093	3,273	11,161	1,156	5,018	8,298
1964	124,629	7,130	18,771	35,720	58,745	48,160	3,148	10,813	993	4,788	8,867
1963	118,841	7,479	18,716	32,531	59,000	46,076	2,815	9,964	958	4,409	6,662
1962	—	6,788	17,672	30,488	53,618	43,974	2,654	9,366	970	4,737	6,122
1961	107,223	6,378	17,140	28,707	52,197	41,320	2,373	9,257	964	4,247	5,114
1960[1]	104,144	4,879	14,611	28,192	48,621	38,043	1,754	9,557	178[2]	4,075	3,619
1959[1]	96,884	4,277	13,905	27,483	48,318	36,786	2,025	9,099	196[2]	2,998	6,237
1958[1]	90,910	4,302	11,514	23,264	41,619	34,374	1,888	9,162	177[2]	3,541	4,440
1957[1]	87,779	4,790	10,465	25,933	38,556	40,100	2,117	8,196	155[2]	2,834	1,930
1956[1]	87,264	4,013	11,565	21,102	38,511	42,136	2,116	8,441	156[2]	2,455	—
1955[1]	78,258	2,631	11,064	15,398	28,759	34,035	1,540[3]	7,201	154[2]	1,851	—
1954[1]	69,816	1,637	9,384	12,290	23,894	30,204	1,581[3]	5,834	157[2]	1,486	—
1953[1]	65,199	1,149	8,958	10,860	18,500	29,061	1,631[3]	5,579	147[2]	784	—
1952[1]	59,208	378	7,689	9,698	15,545	27,336	1,693[3]	5,395	151[2]	624	—
1951[1]	53,684	232	8,447	7,500	14,651	23,635	1,901[3]	4,913	121[2]	407	—
1950[1]	46,682	—	6,459	6,882	11,546	21,460	1,665[3]	4,165	88[2]	169	—
1949[1]	42,128	—	5,941	5,941	8,588	19,854	1,642[3]	3,944	84[2]	—	—

[1] 1960 and earlier output.
[2] Tons.
[3] Oil only.

Section R: Manufactures

John A. Sawyer, *University of Toronto*

This section updates the official statistics on manufactures for 1870 to 1959 presented in the first edition of *Historical Statistics of Canada*. Apart from minor revision to some series for the years 1952 to 1959, no revisions have been made to the statistics from 1870 to 1959. The descriptions of the statistics for this period have been reproduced without change from the description in the first edition written by Arthur J.R. Smith.

The principal changes in the concepts and definitions of statistics on manufactures since the publication of the first edition result from two revisions to the Standard Industrial Classification, the first in 1960 and the second in 1970. These changes are explained below. The 1960 revision resulted in a major discontinuity in some of the statistics. An overlap is provided to help users bridge the gap.

The statistics in the tables on manufactures fall into seven main groups: (1) series R1-161 contain selected principal statistics for manufacturing industries as a whole for Canada and the provinces; (2) series R162-489 contain the same principal statistics for each of the 20 major groups within manufacturing; (3) series R490-513 contain indexes of real domestic product for manufacturing by major groups; (4) series R514-620 contain statistics on gross fixed capital formation for manufacturing by major groups; (5) series R621-770 contain data on the quantity and value of shipments of selected manufactured commodities; (6) series R771-794 are on the number of manufacturing establishments and value of shipments by size of establishment, measured by value of shipments; and (7) series R795-825 are on the number of manufacturing establishments and number of employees by size of establishment, measured by number of employees.

Other series in this volume which relate to manufacturing activity are: (1) series F286-294: indexes of labour productivity and unit labour costs in manufacturing, 1946 to 1976. As yet these series are not available for major groups within manufacturing. (2) Series K68-107: industry selling price indexes by industry group, 1956 to 1975. Although not designed for this purpose, if the user wishes to express the gross value of production or shipments of manufacturers by industry in constant dollars, these price indexes are the best available deflators. (3) Although separate figures are not given for capital stocks, the reader interested in this statistic is referred to the description of series F183-220. Detail on stocks for manufacturing industries can be found in *Fixed Capital Flows and Stocks*, (Catalogue 13-211). (4) Series F222 and 224: year-end book value of inventories in total manufacturing, in current and constant dollars, 1925 to 1975.

The original edition of *Historical Statistics of Canada* included an appendix prepared by G.K. Bertram on selected general statistics for primary and secondary manufacturing by major groups, for 1870 to 1959. Resources were not available to update these series. Readers interested in this classification, which was originally introduced in D.H. Fullerton and H.A. Hampson, *Canadian Secondary Manufacturing Industry*, Royal Commission on Canada's Economic Prospects (Hull: Queen's Printer, 1957), might be

interested in knowing that two alternative classifications have been suggested. The first is in an unpublished note by Professor J.H. Dales, "A Suggested Definition of Primary Manufacturing" (1962). The second is in an unpublished note by the Central Classification Division of Statistics Canada, "Primary and Secondary Manufacturing in Canada" (1964).

The data on which all the series in this section are based were collected officially. For the most part, since 1917, the data were collected by Statistics Canada (formerly the Dominion Bureau of Statistics) in its annual census of manufactures; before 1917 they came from the census of manufactures taken with the decennial census or in special postal censuses. The data on fixed capital formation for 1926 to 1945 were obtained from tabulations prepared by the Department of National Revenue from income tax returns and those for 1946 to 1975 are based on returns to questionnaires obtained by Statistics Canada on capital formation. In general, since the inception of the annual census of manufactures in 1917, the quality of the basic material has improved as experience was gained in the formulation of questionnaires, as better coverage of establishments was obtained, and as the performance of respondents improved. The editing and tabulation of the data were also done officially, mostly by Statistics Canada and the earlier official bodies responsible for the censuses.

The statistics in this chapter from 1960 onward, and in many cases also for the earlier years, were prepared by personnel of Statistics Canada in the specific form they are presented here. For finer industry detail, the reader is referred to the individual industry publications of the census of manufactures.

The published sources of data given in this section are publications of Statistics Canada, decennial census offices, or the Department of Trade and Commerce. Publications of Statistics Canada used as sources are: *Manufacturing Industries of Canada: National and Provincial Areas*, (Catalogue 31-203), from 1972 onward; *General Review of the Manufacturing Industries of Canada, Vol. I, Industries by Province*, (Catalogue 31-203), from 1969 to 1971; *General Review of the Manufacturing Industries of Canada*, (Catalogue 31-201), from 1949 to 1961; *Manufacturing Industries of Canada*, Section A, (Catalogue 31-203), from 1949 to 1968; *Manufacturing Industries of Canada: Atlantic Provinces*, (Catalogue 31-204); *Quebec*, (Catalogue 31-205); *Ontario*, (Catalogue 31-206); *Prairie Provinces*, (Catalogue 31-207); *British Columbia, Yukon and Northwest Territories*, (Catalogue 31-208), from 1949 to 1971 (designated respectively as Sections B to F from 1949 to 1968); *The Manufacturing Industries of Canada*, from 1930 to 1948; *Canada Year Book*, (Catalogue 11-202), for statistics prior to 1930; *Manufacturing Industries of Canada: Type of Organization and Size of Establishment*, (Catalogue 31-210); *Products Shipped by Canadian Manufacturers*, (Catalogue 31-211); *The Quantity of Manufacturing Production in Canada, 1923-1929*, (1932); *Real Domestic Product by Industry, 1971-1976 (1971 = 100)*, (Catalogue 61-213), 1968 to 1970; *Real Domestic Product by Industry, 1974 Supplement*

(1961 = 100), (Catalogue 61-005), 1961 to 1967; *Indexes of Real Domestic Product by Industry, 1961-1969, (1961 = 100)*, (Catalogue 61-510), 1919 to 1960; *Indexes of Real Domestic Product by Industry - (1961 Base)*, (Catalogue 61-506); *Revised Index of Industrial Production, 1935-1957*, (Catalogue 61-502); *Indexes of Real Domestic Product by Industry of Origin, 1935-1961*, (Catalogue 61-505); *Canadian Statistical Review*, (Catalogue 11-003), monthly since January 1948, (formerly *Monthly Review of Business Statistics*,) 1926 to 1947; *Private and Public Investment in Canada, Outlook*, (Catalogue 61-205); *Private and Public Investment in Canada, 1946-1957*, (1959).

Publications of the census office are: Department of Agriculture, Census Branch, *Census of Canada, 1870-71, Vol. III*, (Ottawa, I.B. Taylor, 1875); Department of Agriculture, Census Branch, *Census of Canada, 1880-81, Vol. III*, (Ottawa, Maclean, Roger and Co., 1883); Department of Agriculture, Census Branch, *Census of Canada, 1890-91, Vol. III*, (Ottawa, Queen's Printer, 1894); The Census Office, *Fourth Census of Canada, 1901, Vol. III, Manufactures*, (Ottawa, King's Printer, 1905); Department of Agriculture, Census and Statistics Office, *Postal Census of Manufactures, 1906*, (Ottawa, King's Printer, 1907); Department of Trade and Commerce, The Census Office, *Fifth Census of Canada, Vol. III*, (Ottawa, King's Printer, 1913); Department of Trade and Commerce, Census and Statistics Office, *Postal Census of Manufacturers, 1916*, (Ottawa, King's Printer, 1917); Department of Trade and Commerce, *Private and Public Investment in Canada, 1926-1951*, (Ottawa, 1951).

General Statistics for Manufacturing Industries (Series R1-489)

The census of manufactures is an annual mail survey. The reporting unit for the census is designated as the establishment and a return is requested from every establishment classified to a manufacturing industry. Although respondents are required to submit reports covering the calendar year, financial year reports for other than the calendar year are accepted in instances where respondents find it impossible to supply calendar year data from accounting records. When an establishment is operated for only part of a year, a report is required covering the period of operation.

There are four different questionnaires used in the census: (a) short form, (b) long form, (c) head office questionnaire, and (d) commodity questionnaire. The short and long forms are used to obtain principal statistics and commodities shipped from establishments classified to manufacturing industries. The short form is a single-sheet questionnaire sent to small manufacturers and does not contain commodity questions. The cutoff for the short form varies according to the industry and the province. The head office questionnaire is generally used for company head offices and ancillary units separately located from manufacturing establishments. The commodity questionnaire is used to survey certain establishments which are coded (on the basis of their principal activity) to industries other than manufacturing in the Standard Industrial Classification, but which undertake some manufacturing as a subsidiary activity. This single-sheet questionnaire is designed to collect information on the quantity and value of goods of own manufacture shipped by such establishments in order to increase coverage of specified manufactured commodities.

The concepts and definitions used for statistics on manufactures have changed over time as concepts were clarified and as the requirement developed for statistics which cover the entire economy as evidenced, for example, by input-output tables. This evolution is reflected in the 1960 and 1970 revisions to the 1948 Standard Industrial Classification. The definitions and concepts in present use will first be discussed and then the earlier treatment compared to present practice. In this way the user can become aware of discontinuities in some of the series. It should be pointed out that in some cases the classification revisions made it impossible to construct continuous series even if resources had been available to do so. The reader is referred to Statistics Canada, *Standard Industrial Classification Manual, Revised 1970*, (Catalogue 12-501), pp. 7-14 for a general discussion of the principles of industrial classification.

A manufacturing establishment is typically a factory, mill, or plant principally engaged in manufacturing activities. The majority of such establishments are firms but many firms have more than one establishment. Such firms are requested to submit a separate census of manufactures report for each manufacturing establishment which can meet the reporting requirements embodied in the following definition. An establishment is:

The smallest unit which is a separate operating entity capable of reporting the following principal statistics:

materials and supplies used,

goods purchased for resale as such,

fuel and power consumed,

number of employees and salaries and wages,

man-hours worked and paid,

inventories,

shipments or sales.

Each establishment receiving a long form is required to report on the total economic activity (as indicated by the above items) carried out within its accounting boundaries and to report separately data on manufacturing, trading in goods not of own manufacture, construction by its own labour force for its own use, and revenue from services. It should be noted that the statistics for separate activities are not completely consistent since some respondents cannot distinguish in their records, materials, shipments and inventories relating solely to their own manufacturing activities. For example, inventory of goods purchased for resale may not be distinguishable from inventory of own manufactured goods. Complete consistency, therefore, can be obtained only at the "all operations" (total activity) level and for studies or statistical measures requiring accurate co-ordinated data, the 'total' statistics should be used.

All head offices and auxiliary units classified to the manufacturing industries, such as sales offices, adminsitrative offices, warehouses, and laboratories, are surveyed as part of the census of manufactures. These head offices and auxiliary units are either included in an establishment report or are surveyed by means of the head office questionnaire. The former is the most common case where a single establishment firm has its executive personnel, sales office, etc., located at the site of the manufacturing establishment. The special head office questionnaire is generally used where a firm, regardless of the number of establishments, has separately located offices or ancillary units. Such offices or units do not constitute establishments because they do not report the full range of industry statistics. They do not normally generate operational revenues, but give rise only to costs of operations (mainly salaries and wages). Although not considered as establishments, and hence not included in the 'establishment' count for an industry, their operational costs are reflected in the industry statistics for the industry accounting for the largest part of the company's value added by total activity or to the industry with which the head office, sales office or auxiliary unit has a definite association. Beginning with the 1960 census of manufactures three major changes took place, although it was not until the tabulation of the 1961 Census that the changes were fully implemented. The changes were: (1) the classification of establishments to industries according to the 1960 Standard Industrial Classification instead of the 1948 classification, (2) the use of the new definition of the establishment given above, and (3) the collection and tabulation of statistics relating to the total activity of manufacturing establishments instead of only their manufacturing activity. Thus, the use of the establishment as the basic reporting unit enabled two types of statistics to be tabulated from 1961 onward: (1) manufacturing activity of manufacturing establishments and (2) total activity of manufacturing establishments. Columns 2-7 of the tables containing series R1-489 refer to manufacturing activity while the last three columns refer to total activity conducted in such establishments.

The introduction of the new establishment concept also resulted in some changes in the data on the manufacturing activity of manufacturing establishments. It was possible to retabulate the data on manufacturing activity collected in the 1957 to 1959 censuses according to the new concept and according to the new classification of establishments. Hence for the three years 1957 to 1959 statistics for manufacturing activity exist on three bases: (1) the old definition of an establishment using the 1948 Standard Industrial Classification, (2) the old definition of an establishment using the 1960 S.I.C., and (3) the new definition of an establishment using the 1960 S.I.C. The figures for 1957 to 1971 shown in the upper part of the following tables for series R1-489 are on the third basis, while those for 1959 and earlier years shown in the lower part of the tables are on the first basis. (As is explained below, the most recent years are based on the 1970 S.I.C.)

The figures on census value added may help the reader to appreciate the magnitude of the changes at the total manufacturing level:

	1957	1958	1959	1960	1961	1962
			(millions of dollars)			
Census value added calculated according to:						
1) 1948 S.I.C., old establishment concept	9,822	9,793	10,321			
per cent change		*(-0.3)*				
2) 1960 S.I.C., old establishment concept	9,702	9,858	10,306	10,533		
3) 1960 S.I.C., new establishment concept		9,454	10,154	10,371	10,682	
per cent change			*(7.4)*	*(2.1)*	*(3.0)*	
4) 1960 S.I.C., new establishment concept						
a) manufacturing activity (revised data)					10,435	11,430
b) total activity					10,932	11,987
per cent change						*(9.6)*

A continuous index (1961 = 100) of total activity value added can be roughly estimated from the percentage changes shown above. For comparison an index of gross domestic product at factor cost is given below:

	1957	1958	1959	1960	1961	1962
5) Chained census value added	88.8	88.5	95.1	97.1	100.0	109.6
6) Gross domestic product at factor cost	85.0	87.9	92.8	96.6	100.0	108.4

Sources: Lines 1 and 2, *General Review of the Manufacturing Industries of Canada* (31-201), 1960, p. 29
           Line 3, *General Review of the Manufacturing Industries of Canada* (31-201), 1961, p. 14.
           Lines 4(a) and 4(b) *General Review of the Manufacturing Industries of Canada* (31-203), 1964, pp. 14-15.
           Line 6 *National Income and Expenditure Accounts* (13-531), Table 28.

A continuous index (1961 = 100) of total activity value added can be roughly estimated from the percentage changes shown above. For comparison an index of gross domestic product at factor cost is given below:

For summary statistics of manufacturing on the second basis for 1957 to 1961, the reader is referred to the lower part of Table 7, p. 29 in the 1960 issue of *General Review of the Manufacturing Industries of Canada*, (Catalogue 31-201). For a complete description of the procedures followed in establishing the revised series, reference should be made to the explanatory notes included in the 1960, 1961 and 1962 publications for individual industries.

The 1970 revision to the Standard Industrial Classification was not accompanied by changes in the definition of an establishment. It did, however, result in some establishments being classified to different industries. An overlap of two years is provided (1970 and 1971) for series R133-489 so that the user can see the effect of classifying establishments according to the 1960 and 1970 S.I.C. The change in the S.I.C. had no effect on total manufacturing statistics.

The following explanations refer to the items in the tables containing series R1-489.

The 'number of establishments' represents the number of operating units that are principally engaged in the activities of the manufacturing industries to which they have been classified. These units do not necessarily represent the total number engaged in the production of a commodity mainly produced in a certain industry. Some commodities are produced as secondary products in other manufacturing and non-manufacturing industries. It should be noted that head offices and ancillary units which are surveyed separately are not included in the establishment count. The number of establishments classified to manufacturing in 1959 fell from 36,193 to 32,075 with the revised definition of the establishment and the new classification of establishments according to the 1960 Standard Industrial Classification. In 1975, a large number of establishments which had no employees the previous year were excluded from the census, occasioning a sizable drop in establishment numbers. The omitted establishments, however, accounted for only 0.03 per cent of shipments in 1974. The 1975 data file still contained some establishments with no paid employees. (An establishment may have a work force consisting only of its owner or partners.)

'Production and related workers' in manufacturing activities include those engaged in production and assembling activities plus those employed in storing, inspecting, handling, packing, warehousing, etc. They also include employees engaged in maintenance, repair, janitorial and watchman services and line supervisors (working foremen) engaged in similar work to that of the employees they supervise. For those establishments reporting on the long form, the annual average of production and related workers engaged in manufacturing activity is requested. This procedure is followed even if the establishment did not operate in all months in order to arrive at equivalent annual full-time employment. The numbers are somewhat affected by turnover, in that employment is overstated when an employee changes employment during a pay period. Beginning in 1970, employment is imputed for establishments reporting on the short form. All such employment is classified as production and related workers.

"Wages" refer to gross earnings of employees before deductions for income tax and employees' contributions to social services, such as sickness, accident and unemployment insurance, and pensions. They include all wages,

bonuses, profits shared with employees, the value of room and board where provided, commissions (paid to regular employees only), as well as any other allowance forming part of the worker's earnings. Payments for overtime are included.

"Fuel and electricity" figures refer to amounts actually used (including fuel used in cars, trucks, locomotives, etc.), not to purchases unless the quantities are substantially the same. Any fuel and electricity produced by establishments for internal consumption are not included in the total cost. Values represent laid down cost at the establishment including freight, duty, etc. Although fuel and electricity used is considered part of manufacturing activity, it should be noted that it also includes relatively small amounts used in non-manufacturing activities since these cannot be reported separately.

'Materials and supplies' figures represent laid down cost values, at the establishment, of materials, supplies and purchased components owned and used during the year in manufacturing activities and related processes. These statistics represent only commodity items or physical goods (cost of services or overhead charges such as advertising, insurance, and depreciation are not included) whether purchased from others or received as transfers (in the form of materials, components or semi-processed goods) from other establishments of the reporting company. Included are maintenance and repair supplies not chargeable to fixed asset accounts and any amounts charged by other establishments for work done on materials owned by the reporting establishment. Cost of repairs or maintenance done by outside contractors and cost of returnable containers are not included.

'Value of shipments of goods of own manufacture' excludes goods purchased for resale and represents shipments of goods made from own materials either in the reporting establishments or by other manufacturers on the basis of a charge to the reporting establishments for work done. Included are revenue from repair and custom work, amounts received in payment for work done on materials owned by other establishments, and the cost (book value) of any goods shipped for the first time on a rental basis. Shipments are valued in Canadian dollars at the point at which the establishment relinquishes control.

All products and by-products of own manufacture shipped from the establishment are covered, including transfer shipments to sales outlets, distributing warehouses, or to other manufacturing plants of the reporting firm, when such units are treated as separate statistical units. The value of shipments is net of returned goods, discounts, returns, allowances, sales tax and excise taxes and duties, returnable containers, and charges for outward transportation by common or contract carriers. Transportation or delivery expense incurred by the reporting establishment's own carriers are included. In those industries where work on principal products extends over a relatively long period (Fabricated Structural Metal Industry, Aircraft and Parts Manufacturers, Railroad Rolling Stock Industry, and Shipbuilding and Repair Industry), up to 1973, the value of production rather than the value of shipments is recorded. Since then, shipments are adjusted by adding the net change in progress payments on the books not written off to sales, resulting in a measure closely related to production.

'Gross value of production' of goods of own manufacture is obtained by adding the change in the value of inventories of finished goods and goods in process to the value of shipments of goods of own manufacture. (The change in inventories is not explicitly shown in the tables.) The value of inventories relating to manufacturing activities represents the book value of manufacturing inventory owned in Canada. Inventories held for which progress payments have been received are not included. Where progress payment accounts are maintained, the change in these accounts is treated as a net adjustment to shipments. The inventory figures consist of inventory owned at the plant and at warehouses or selling outlets which are treated as extensions of establishments for the purpose of reporting shipments. Inventory owned in transit in Canada or on consignment in Canada is included. Goods shipped abroad and held in inventory are included in shipments. Opening inventories may differ from the closing inventories of the previous year because of changes in classification, the receipt of revised data, the inclusion of new establishments and the removal of establishments which did not operate during the survey year.

The gross value of shipments and production data contain considerable duplication, since the products of one establishment frequently become the materials used by, and thus eventually part of the gross value of production of, other establishments. The aggregate gross value figures therefore reflect an exaggerated picture of manufacturing output, and these are not always a satisfactory measure of the importance of individual industries. For the purpose of measuring an industry's contribution to total output, a more meaningful and useful indicator of the output of manufacturing industries is census value added by manufacture.

'Census value added by manufacturing activity' is compiled by deducting the cost of manufacturing materials, supplies, and fuel and electricity consumed from the gross value of production of goods of own manufacture. Census value added is calculated before the deduction of purchased services and therefore includes the value of such purchased services as well as the amount available for the payment of salaries and wages, depreciation, interest, rent, taxes, repairs, and all other overhead charges that must ordinarily be met, as well as profits. It is therefore a more inclusive measure than gross domestic product at factor cost which is the measure used in the real domestic product series (see the description of series R490-513 below).

The statistics relating to 'total activity' include, in addition to figures for manufacturing activity, figures for all non-manufacturing activities conducted by manufacturing establishments. Hence 'employees' on a total activity basis include, in addition to production and related workers engaged in manufacturing activity, production and related workers employed by manufacturing establishments who are engaged in non-manufacturing activities (for example, logging employees who are reported by a sawmilling establishment), administrative and office workers, and sales and distribution workers employed by manufacturing establishments. Beginning in 1961, working owners or partners are not included as employees. 'Wages and salaries' refers to payments to all employees of manufacturing establishments.

'Census value added: total activity' is obtained by first obtaining a generalized value of shipments figure which represents revenue from all production, sales, services and related activities of reporting establishments. This includes the net selling value at the establishment (net of discounts, returns, allowances, sales taxes and excise duties and taxes, and transportation charges by common or contract carriers) of all products or materials (including products transferred from other establishments of the reporting firm) sold as such in the same condition as purchased or received as transfers. All sales of consignment goods from other countries are included.

Also included is the book value of fixed assets (new construction and machinery and equipment including major repairs, alterations, additions, modifications, installation and assembly work) produced during the year for the use of reporting establishments by the establishment's own employees and for which depreciation accounts are maintained. Included also are any revenues from the sale of electricity and from any operations performed by the establishment's own employees, such as revenue from goods produced for rental (the book value of such goods are included as part of shipments of goods of own manufacture in the first year in which they are sold), servicing revenues, commissions on sales (when not included in value of sales), revenue for company-operated cafeterias and lunch counters, revenue from outside installation or construction work not related to the establishment's own products, sale of used materials (excluding sale of used fixed assets), research and development work. As mentioned previously, the figures do not include non-operating revenue such as dividends and interest.

To arrive at the gross production of the establishment, the value of shipments is adjusted for inventory change. Inventory change figures represent, in addition to the inventories relevant to manufacturing activity, the book value of inventory of goods purchased for resale as such without further processing which are owned by the reporting establishments and held at plants and at any warehouses or selling outlets which are treated as extensions of establishments. They also include other non-manufacturing inventory such as commodities for use by the establishment's labour force in new construction or in the production of machinery and equipment for the use of the establishment.

After the inventory adjustment is made, the cost of materials, fuel and electricity, etc., relevant to manufacturing activity and all other relevant costs, including the cost of purchases for resale and other materials and supplies used, is subtracted. Included in these costs is the cost of materials and supplies used in new construction and in the production of machinery and equipment (for the use of the reporting establishment) by the establishment's own employees and materials used for any capital repairs and alterations carried out by the establishment's employees. Amounts paid to outside contractors for construction and repair work are not included nor is the cost of purchased machinery and equipment. Also included is the cost of office supplies not chargeable to fixed asset accounts and the cost of such other items of materials and supplies used as food, beverages and supplies for establishment-operated cafeterias and lunch counters, first aid and medical supplies, laboratory supplies, etc.

The net figure so obtained is census value added on a total activity basis. This total value added figure may, in some cases, be less than value added by manufacturing activity as a result of expenditures associated with non-manufacturing exceeding revenues from such activities or because of a decrease in the book value of inventory of goods not of own manufacture exceeding the markup on the sale of such goods.

Prior to 1961, figures are not available for census value added on a total activity basis since prior to the introduction of the 1960 edition of the Standard Industrial Classification this concept was not used. Only figures for the manufacturing activity of manufacturing establishments are available, except where noted below. For these statistics, however, the revision to the Standard Industrial Classification introduced a discontinuity because of the adoption of a new set of major groupings of manufacturing establishments. These revisions of the classification reflect the changing structure of industry resulting from technological change and other factors.

The change in classification in 1960 which most affected the comparability of major groups of manufacturing industries was in the primary metal, metal fabricating, and machinery industries. Another change was in the treatment of establishments engaged principally in repair work. Classes were established for repair shops in a number of different divisions. For example, in retail trade separate classes were provided for motor vehicle repair shops; radio, television and electrical appliance repair shops; and watch and jewellery shops. The reader is referred to Statistics Canada publication, *Indexes of Real Domestic Product by Industry, 1961 Base*, (Catalogue 61-506), pp. 204-215 for a comparison of the 1948 and 1960 Standard Industrial Classifications. The changes in 1970 had effects in varying degrees on eight groups, with numbers 3 and 20 being particularly affected. A list of the changes introduced by the 1970 revision may be found in Statistics Canada publication, *Standard Industrial Classification Manual, Revised 1970*, (Catalogue 12-501).

In the course of preparation of the tables on general statistics for manufacturing for the first edition of *Historical Statistics of Canada*, efforts were made to review and revise earlier figures to make all data from 1870 to 1959 as conceptually consistent and comparable as feasible. Especially significant adjustments have been made in previously published census data for 1870 to 1910 and in the annual data from 1917 to 1925 to bring the conceptual content of these earlier figures as closely as possible in line with that in the latest annual census of manufactures used. Statistics Canada personnel reclassified the data for all years before 1949 on the basis of the 1948 Standard Industrial Classification and all the data in series R1-489 prior to 1961 (shown in the lower part of the tables) are based, therefore, on the 1948 classification. Consequently, much of the data for years preceding 1949 will not be found in published sources in the form presented herein.

In the reclassification of the data from the censuses before 1917 additional adjustments were also made. A number of categories of operations, included in the censuses, notably those connected with construction and some repair work, were omitted. In addition, the censuses of 1900 and 1910 did not cover very small manufacturing establishments and the data given in this section are based on estimates, prepared by Statistics Canada, of all manufacturing activity including small establishments. These estimates therefore provide data which are consistent with those for 1870, 1880, 1890 and 1905 and for 1917 to 1959 which are based on full coverage of establishments of all sizes.

Some rather small industries, such as motion picture making, production of flax fibre and the blueprinting industry, which had been dropped from the census of manufactures at various times between 1917 and 1948, have also been excluded for all years from the data given here.

The censuses of 1870, 1880, 1890, 1900 and 1910 were obtained by enumerators who called on the manufacturing concerns. The Postal Census of 1906 covering manufacturing in 1905 and the annual censuses of manufactures taken by Statistics Canada since 1917 have collected data by mailed questionnaire. Statistics Canada engages in a good deal of follow up after each census to clear up ambiguities in returns and to assure the material is on a consistent basis.

No data for the number of establishments are shown for 1900 and 1910, since the censuses of 1901 and 1911 enumerated only establishments employing "five hands and over".

However, full coverage estimates have been made for persons engaged in manufacturing, salaries and wages, and value of production data and these provide the data given in series R1-489. The exceptionally large figures for the number of establishments in 1870, 1880 and 1890 appear to be attributable in part to the inclusion of blacksmith shops as iron foundries, to the inclusion of a large number of repair establishments which cannot be satisfactorily eliminated from manufacturing establishments, and to the generally diffuse pattern of early manufacturing activity prior to spreading development of factory units. The 1906 Postal Census of Manufactures is strongly suspected of under-enumeration.

The Postal Census of Manufactures in 1916, covering the year 1915, involved limitations in its coverage of manufacturing establishments and their operations, and the data could not be satisfactorily converted to a full coverage basis. No manufacturing data for 1915 have therefore been included in series R1-489.

Regarding the number of persons engaged in manufacturing some conceptual differences exist between the statistics from 1949 onward and those for earlier years. The main differences in treatment in the earlier figures have been as follows:

(1) Prior to 1949 no special effort was made to survey head offices if these were located in a separate locality and not attached to any operating establishment. In 1949 such offices began to be covered with a separate questionnaire.

(2) For years prior to 1935, the number of working proprietors of establishments owned by unincorporated firms and their withdrawals were included with salaried personnel; before 1930 they were included with wage-earners. The increase in supervisory and office employees between 1930 and 1931 was probably due to the change in classification of working proprietors rather than an increase in employment. Data on working proprietors and their withdrawals were imputed for years prior to 1935, when they began to be collected, but it is not certain whether such imputations were made for all years back to 1917. In 1961 working proprietors were excluded from employees entirely and shown as a separate category, together with their withdrawals. Because of the increasingly uncertain quality of withdrawals, however, these data ceased to be published after 1973.

(3) From 1937, establishments were instructed to include travelling salesmen with salaried employees. There is little knowledge as to their treatment by reporting firms prior to this time. In 1930 firms were asked to exclude salesmen in reporting salaried employees. No specific mention was made of the appropriate treatment during the other years, although the instructions were changed in 1931 in such a way that firms may have begun to include salesmen at that time.

(4) Prior to 1925 the number of wage-earners was computed as the sum of the number recorded each month divided by 12, whether the establishment was operating 12 months or not. For 1925 to 1930 inclusive, in seasonal industries the averages were computed by dividing the sum of the wage-earners reported on the 15th of each month by the number of months in operation. This change of method increased the apparent number of employees in groups containing seasonal industries and in the overall total. In 1931 the old method of computing the average number of wage-earners was readopted.

Until 1952, gross value of production represents the total reported selling value of products produced by all manufacturing establishments, whether sold, transferred to other plants, or in stock. Since 1952, the figures on gross value of production are basically derived from the gross value of manufacturing shipments, adjusted for the difference between year-beginning and year-end inventories of finished products and goods in process. However, the changeover to the latter system took two years to implement and it was not until 1954 that the data could be provided on the new basis, as shown in series R17 and 18. In the first edition of *Historical Statistics of Canada* an incorrect adjustment was made to gross value of production and value added from 1952 onward. This resulted in the figures being inconsistent with those published in the industry reports. This error has been corrected in the present volume.

The cost of fuel and electricity was not collected in the censuses before 1917.

In the general statistics for manufacturing, data for Newfoundland are included beginning in 1949.

As a concluding comment on the general statistics, it should be emphasized that it is difficult to evaluate the earlier data, especially the census data prior to 1917, in the light of subsequent changes in concepts, reporting schedules, and so forth. Despite a careful review and revision of the figures, some questions still remain about the comparability of data. If coverage of manufacturing establishments has improved over the years, the more recent data may reflect this, but this may not be a significant factor. More important is the fact that as better information has been developed on industrial detail and the nature of activities in establishments, there has been an extended ability to eliminate data pertaining to establishments engaged in repair, merchandising, and other non-manufacturing activities.

General Statistics (Series R1-489)

R1-22. General statistics for all manufacturing industries

SOURCE: for 1957 to 1975, *Manufacturing Industries of Canada, National and Provincial Areas; General Review of the Manufacturing Industries of Canada;* for 1870, *Census of Canada, 1870-71, Vol. III;* for 1880, *Census of Canada, 1880-81, Vol. III;* for 1890, *Census of Canada, 1890-91, Vol. III;* for 1900, *Census of Canada, 1901, Vol. III;* for 1905, *Postal Census of Manufactures, 1906;* for 1910, *Census of Canada, 1911, Vol. III;* for 1917 to 1959, Annual Census of Manufactures as reported in various issues of the *Canada Year Book; The Manufacturing Industries of Canada* and *General Review of the Manufacturing Industries of Canada.* Data before 1949 were reclassified by Statistics Canada.

See the general note to series R1-489 for comments on these statistics.

R23-161. General statistics for all manufacturing industries, by province, 1957 to 1975

SOURCE: same as series R1-22.

General statistics for all manufacturing industries, by region, 1926 to 1959

SOURCE: annual census of manufactures, as reported in various issues of the *Canada Year Book* and *General Review of the Manufacturing Industries of Canada.* Data before 1949 were revised by Statistics Canada.

Regional manufacturing data do exist for the many years from 1927 to 1947 for which no data are shown as well as for the early census years and for 1917 to 1925. But these data are not consistent with the figures for total manufacturing shown in series R12-22, and have therefore not been included here.

R162-489. General statistics for manufacturing industries, by major group

SOURCE: same as series R1-22.

For 1957 to 1975, the 20 major groups are according to the 1960 and 1970 editions of the Standard Industrial Classification. See the general note on series R1-489 for a discussion of the effects of the changes in classification.

For 1870 to 1959, the 18 major industry groups covered represent the 17 major groups according to the Standard Industrial Classification of 1948, with the clothing and knitting mills group of that classification shown as two groups instead of one for the period 1917 to 1959. Details on classification are described in the *Standard Industrial Classification Manual, 1948.* Reporting establishments are classified or allotted to industries on the basis of the principal products produced or shipped.

Many types of adjustments have been involved in developing consistent figures for various industry groups. For example, previously published figures for the tobacco and tobacco products group included excise taxes in the gross value of production for the years 1917 to 1931; such taxes for these years have now been deducted from the gross value figures to provide for greater consistency. Another illustration is that in the non-ferrous metals groups, smelting was not classified as a manufacturing activity for the years 1920 to 1924 in previously published figures of this industry; the principal statistics for smelting have now been included for these years.

Indexes of Real Domestic Product for Manufacturing (Series R490-513)

These indexes of gross domestic product at factor cost originating in each industry provide a narrower measure of value added than that provided by the census value added measure. To obtain the gross domestic product measure, all purchased inputs from other industries (materials, fuel and electricity, services, etc.) except for payments for the services of labour and capital are subtracted from the value of output (valued before excise and sales taxes and duties). The residual value added figures therefore contain only wages and salaries and other payments to employees, interest and other payments for the use of capital, profits, and depreciation and other capital consumption allowances. The output and purchased inputs from other industries are estimated in constant (1971) dollars so that this value added is measured in constant (1971) dollars. It is therefore commonly known as real domestic product. It is converted to an index number by dividing by the 1971 figure. The indexes exist for all industries in the economy and are extensions of the Index of Industrial Production which existed only for goods-producing industries (excluding agriculture). The reader is referred to the general note for series F225-240 further discussion of the nature of these indexes.

R490. Index of real domestic product for total manufacturing, 1919 to 1976

SOURCE: for 1971 to 1976, *Real Domestic Product by Industry, 1971-1976, (1971 = 100)*, (Catalogue 61-213); for 1958 to 1970, *Real Domestic Product by Industry, 1974 Supplement (1961 = 100)*, released with the March 1974 issue, (Catalogue 61-005); for 1961 to 1967, *Indexes of Real Domestic Product by Industry, 1961-1969, (1961 = 100)*, (Catalogue 61-510) except for certain industries, for which revised data are given in the annual supplement in the previous references; for 1919 to 1960, *Indexes of Real Domestic Product by Industry (1961 Base)*, (Catalogue 61-506).

For the period prior to 1971, the data are not available on a 1971 base. To obtain a continuous record on a 1971 base, the indexes on a 1961 base were mechanically rebased to 1971 by multiplying by 100.0 and dividing by the 1971 index value on a 1961 base.

The conceptual basis of the real domestic product measure is the same as the index of industrial production. The concepts are described in *Revised Index of Industrial Production, 1935-1957*, (Catalogue 61-502) and in *Indexes of Real Domestic Product by Industry of Origin, 1935-1961*, (Catalogue 61-505). For technical notes concerning major changes in concepts, sources and methods in real domestic product (including the index of industrial production) resulting from the introduction of the 1960 Standard Industrial Classification and the adoption of the 1961 weight and reference base, see Catalogue 61-506. For technical notes concerning major changes in concepts, sources and methods in real domestic product (including the index of industrial production) resulting from the introduction of the 'Total activity' concept, the adoption of the final 1961 weighting system, the incorporation of up-to-date census-based annual production levels and the introduction of revised methodology, see Catalogue 61-510. For technical notes concerning changes in real domestic product resulting from the introduction of the 1970 S.I.C. and the adoption of the 1971 weights and reference base, see Catalogue 61-213.

R491-513. Indexes of real domestic product for manufacturing industries by major groups, 1935 to 1976

SOURCE: for 1971 to 1976, *Real Domestic Product by Industry, 1971-1976, (1971 = 100)*, (Catalogue 61-213); for 1958 to 1970, *Real Domestic Product by Industry, 1974 Supplement (1961 = 100)*, released with the March 1974 issue, (Catalogue 61-005); for 1961 to 1971, *Indexes of Real Domestic Product by Industry, 1961-1969, (1961 = 100)*, (Catalogue 61-510) except for certain industries, for which revised data are given in the annual supplement in the previous references; for 1919 to 1960, *Indexes of Real Domestic Product by Industry (1961 Base)*, (Catalogue 61-506).

The classification is for the 20 major groups in the 1960 and 1970 editions of the Standard Industrial Classification. The reader's attention is drawn to the footnotes to series R493 and R510 which explain two adjustments made to the series to achieve consistency in the series following the reclassification of industries. Readers will note that because of the introduction of the new S.I.C. and certain conceptual changes, the measures for some industries are no longer comparable between the 1949 and the 1961 weight-base periods and therefore are not shown in these tables prior to 1961. Those industries which were considered comparable are shown on a continuous basis as far back as data permit.

The effects of the introduction of the 1960 S.I.C. on the classification of industries are shown in detail in appendix I to *Indexes of Real Domestic Product by Industry, (1961 Base)*, (Catalogue 61-506).

Gross Fixed Capital Formation (Series R514-620)

Gross fixed capital formation in manufacturing comprises expenditures made by manufacturing establishments on new durable physical assets including structures, engineering works, land improvements, machinery and equipment created or acquired for the purpose of producing goods or services. These assets are considered to be durable when they are intended for use in their original form for more than one year. Included in the aggregates shown for total gross fixed capital formation and for total new machinery and equipment expenditures are expenditures on certain types of equipment which are considered as capital expenditures, but which are charged to current or operating account by respondent establishments. Such expenditures are shown separately in series R619-620. Only those assets erected in Canada or acquired for use within the country are included.

The value of new construction work includes both contract work and work done by the firm's own employees, and the expenditures shown for each year represent as far as possible the value of construction work put in place in that year irrespective of the time when payment is made.

New machinery and equipment investment includes the installed cost of machinery, motors, etc., and the delivered cost of office furniture and fixtures, motor vehicles, and other equipment. An item is classified to the machinery and equipment category if it is of such a nature that it can be moved from the structure in which it is housed without materially altering the structure. Expenditures on new machinery and equipment are included in the year in which such machinery and equipment is paid for by the end user; thus progress payments on heavy machinery are included in the year in which the payments are made. The estimates reflect gross expenditures including replacement costs before deduction for scrap or trade-in values. Machinery includes both that for use by the owner and that for rent to others.

For further details on concepts, definitions, sources and estimating techniques, see appendix B to *Private and Public Investment in Canada, 1946-1957*, and for a recent description of coverage, see *Private and Public Investment in Canada, Outlook, 1978*. For a description of the preparation of the data from 1926 to 1947, see *Private and Public Investment in Canada, 1926-1951*.

The estimates for 1926 to 1945 are based upon a sample of corporation returns to the Department of National Revenue. They appear to provide a reasonably accurate indication of gross fixed capital investment during these two decades. But the data from 1946 to date are of distinctly superior technical quality and are based on comprehensive reporting by all manufacturing industries.

Limitations in the sources of the industrial distribution figures for the years 1926 to 1945 made it necessary to combine some of the 17 major groups delineated in the Statistics Canada 1948 Standard Industrial Classification, and this practice was followed up to 1960 for the sake of consistency. Thus, tobacco and tobacco products, rubber products, and leather products are grouped; electrical apparatus and supplies are included in non-ferrous metal products, and products of petroleum and coal are shown in non-metallic mineral products.

Beginning in 1960, the 1960 Standard Industrial Classification is followed and 20 major groups are shown in the tables (figures for 1960 are presented on both bases). The reader is referred to the general notes in series R1-489 for a discussion of the implications of the classification change. There is a slight discontinuity because of the 1970 S.I.C. revision.

Quantity and Value of Shipments of Selected Manufactured Commodities (Series R621-770)

General note

Statistics are published by Statistics Canada on the quantity and value of shipments of several thousand manufactured commodities. Only a relatively small number of more important types of products are included in the series shown here, based on data derived from the annual census of manufactures. While a major part of the detail on which these series are based may be found in the annual census of manufactures reports on individual industries (see, for example, Table 7, 'Shipments of Selected Goods - All Industries' in the 1975 reports) and in *Products Shipped by Canadian Manufacturers*, (Catalogue 31-211), unpublished data were also used. The material was prepared by the Manufacturing and Primary Industries Division of Statistics Canada.

The quantities and values of commodities shown in series R621-770 relate to goods made from own materials either in reporting plants or made by other manufacturers on the basis of a charge to reporting plants for work done. These figures cover total shipments of goods of own manufacture, whether made for export or domestic use, including production for governments and institutions. Transfer shipments to sales outlets, distributing warehouses or to other manufacturing units of the reporting firms are included. Goods bought or received as transfers and resold without further processing are not included. For a few commodities, data are shown for production rather than shipments, since a large proportion of the output of certain commodities is used for processing in the same or other establishments of the reporting company. In such cases, values are not shown since they would be almost completely arbitrary. Where production rather than shipments is shown in the tables, it is clearly indicated as, for example, 'aluminum produced'.

For the purpose of calculating value of shipments correctly, manufacturers should ideally report the value of shipments on a standard basis. In practice, however, such standardization is impossible without resorting to difficult and arbitrary methods of valuation. Respondents are asked to specify whether they are reporting shipments (and transfers) at cost, book transfer value, final selling price or some other basis, but no attempt is made to relate these to the values of individual commodities. Comparability of values is also affected by differences in channels of distribution and in branch accounting procedures. Some firms sell direct to wholesalers while others sell direct to retailers or industrial users, and in some cases even sell direct to householders or ultimate consumers. As an example of different branch accounting procedures, a firm may ship through a central warehouse or sales branch which is charged only with the cost of production, the selling outlet being credited with all the profits made. In other cases, profits are credited to the manufacturing operations.

A further factor influencing the comparability of commodity series is the time period on which firms are allowed to report. Ideally, this should be the calendar year. However, in order to minimize the burden on those respondents whose fiscal year differs from the calendar year, reports are accepted for the company's fiscal year. Effective with the 1970 census, reports are accepted for fiscal years ending as early as 1 April of the reference year and as late as 31 March of the calendar year following the reference year. Prior to 1970, reports were accepted for fiscal years ending as late as 30 June of the calendar year following the reference year. In 1975, slightly over 70 per cent of commodity shipments were reported by firms with fiscal years ending in December; the next highest proportion, 5.8 per cent, with fiscal years ending in March. The lowest proportion, 1.2 per cent, was reported for both January and February.

Prior to 1952, the values shown relate to the value of products made. For most industries the change in concept does not materially affect the comparability of the production statistics, since in most cases inventory changes from year to year are only of a minor nature. But it should be noted that the shipments figures after 1952 are not strictly comparable with the earlier data.

At various times from 1970 to 1974, the collection of commodity data from small establishments was discontinued, in order to relieve the reporting burden on respondents. Previously, the commodity information had been collected on all forms, whether for large or small establishments. This has affected the continuity of several series (for example, bread) where smaller establishments previously accounted for a significant proportion of commodity output.

R621-770. Quantity and value of shipments of selected manufactured commodities, 1917 to 1975

COMMODITY	SERIES NUMBER
Aluminum produced	725
Automatic clothes driers	736
Automobile parts and accessories (except tires and auto fabrics)	722
Automobiles, passenger	708
Beer, ale, stout and porter	643
Beverage spirits sold	645
Boats	716
Book and writing paper	678
Boots and shoes with leather or fabric uppers (except felt)	655
Boxes, corrugated	686
Boxes, folding set-up	687
Boxes, paper	688
Bread	623

COMMODITY	SERIES NUMBER	COMMODITY	SERIES NUMBER
Canned fruits	631	Men's and youth's suits (excluding uniform suits)	668
Canned vegetables	633	Metal cans	706
Carbonated beverages	641	Mobile homes	712
Carpets	664	Newsprint paper	676
Cement	750	Outboard motors	718
Chlorine	765	Paints and enamels	759
Cigarettes	647	Paper, wrapping	680
Cigars	649	Paper bags	682
Clay bricks	748	Paper boards	689
Coke	756	Phonograph records	742
Commercial auto vehicles (including buses)	710	Pig iron	692
Confectionery	627	Plastic bags	684
Electric lamps and shades	673	Poultry, fresh and frozen	639
Electric wire and cable	746	Printed periodicals (gross revenue from advertising)	691
Fabrics, broad-woven cotton (unbleached or grey)	658	Radios, all types (except combinations)	738
Fabrics, broad-woven synthetic (including silk)	662	Railroad cars (freight and passenger)	725
Fabrics, broad-woven wool (all wool woven and worsted fabrics only)	660	Refrigeration, household	730
Farm implements and parts	707	Rubber tires	653
Fertilizer sold for consumption in Canada	769	Snowmobiles	720
Flour, wheat	621	Soaps and synthetic detergents	757
Freezers, home	732	Sodium hydroxide (caustic soda)	767
Frozen fruits and vegetables	635	Steel ingots and steel casting produced	693
Fuel oil	754	Steel pipes and tubing	702
Furniture, household	670	Steel plate, sheet and strip	700
Furniture, miscellaneous	672	Steel rails	698
Furniture, office	671	Steel wire, plain	704
Gasoline	752	Stove and ranges	728
Hot rolled iron and steel bars	694	Structural steel shapes	696
Jams, jellies and marmalades	629	Sugar, refined	625
Locomotives, steam and diesel	723	Sulphuric acid	763
Meats, fresh and frozen	637	Synthetic resins	761
Medicinal and pharmaceutical preparations	770	Tapes, pre-recorded	744

COMMODITY	SERIES NUMBER
Telephones and telephone equipment	747
Television sets	740
Tobacco, smoking	651
Trailers, travel and tent	714
Washing machines	734
Women's and misses' dresses (including house dresses)	666
Wood pulp	675
Yarns produced	657

SOURCE: published and unpublished data compiled by the Manufacturing and Primary Industries Division, Statistics Canada.

The commodities are listed in the tables in an order similar to that in the original volume so that related commodities appear adjacent to each other. Where possible both a quantity and a value figure are given and these (unlike in the original volume) are side by side. For convenience, an alphabetical list of the commodities included is given below with the series number. The series number refers to the first item (quantity or value) in the table.

Descriptions of the coverage and, in some cases, the basis of evaluation, of certain commodities are given below. Series numbers refer to the first series for the commodity.

R621. Wheat flour includes whole wheat and graham flour, as well as durum, semolina and other wheat flour.

R625. Refined sugar includes granulated, yellow or brown, pulverized icing and loaf sugar made from cane or beets.

R627. Confectionery includes all sugar and chocolate confectionery in bulk, bars or packages. Lozenges, toffee and chocolate or candy-coated nuts are also included, but not chewing gum.

R635. Frozen fruits and vegetables include frozen French-fried potatoes.

R637. Meats, fresh and frozen, include meats sold fresh or fresh-frozen. Excluded are fresh meats of animals slaughtered on a commission basis for firms or individuals not reporting under the slaughtering and meat processors industry (S.I.C. No. 1011).

R639. Poultry, fresh and frozen, includes shipments by all industries, beginning in 1960; prior to that, the shipments were only those from establishments classified to the slaughtering and meat packing industry.

R641. Carbonated beverages include beverages bottled, canned or sold in bulk but do not include natural or artificial mineral waters.

R645. Beverage spirits sold represent net sales outside the industry and do not include intercompany transfers. The values do not include excise taxes, sales taxes and duties.

R653. Rubber tires include pneumatic and solid tires for passenger cars, trucks, aircraft, tractors, implements, motorcycles and bicycles.

R655. The series for boots and shoes with leather or fabric uppers does not include felt footwear, slippers, moccasins or rubber footwear produced by the rubber products industries (S.I.C. No. 162).

R657. Yarns produced include all yarns produced for own use, for sale, or on a commission or custom basis. It includes yarns made of cotton, wool and synthetic fibres and their mixtures.

R658. Commencing with 1969, the series cotton broadwoven fabrics represents shipments of pure (95 per cent or more) cotton broad-woven fabrics including bleached and unbleached. Prior to 1969, it included unbleached or grey fabric only.

R660. Commencing with 1960, the series broad-woven wool fabrics includes pure wool and wool blends (worsted, woollen and mixtures). Prior to 1960 this series included pure wool fabrics only (worsted and woollen systems).

R666. Commencing with 1972, the series women's and misses' dresses does not include housedresses.

R670. Household furniture includes all wooden, metal and upholstered household furniture, furniture frames, seats and backs, excluding those for vehicles.

R671. Office furniture includes all wooden and metal office furniture and partitions.

R672. Miscellaneous furniture includes church, school, theatre, laboratory, hospital, hotel, motel and restaurant furniture but excludes fixtures, mattresses, springs and other related products.

R673. Electric lamps and shades include electric lamps and lamp shades shipped by all industries, and parts shipped by those establishments classified to electric lamp and shade manufacturers (S.I.C. No. 268) except for the 1961-1964 period when parts shipped by other industries were also included. Prior to 1961, electric lamps and shades were classified in miscellaneous industries and are not available as a separate commodity item.

R674. This is a total furniture series for the period prior to 1960. The disaggregation into series R670-673 is not available for the earlier years.

R675. Wood pulp includes both mechanical and chemical pulp, mechanical and chemical screenings, and defibrated and exploded wood, semi-chemical pulp, as well as other grades of pulp not specified as mechanical or chemical.

R682. Paper bags include self-opening square bags (grocery, check-stand and/or cash and carry, etc.), flat, wedge, satchel-bottom, multi-wall shipping, and shopping bags (with handles), as well as special bags of glassine, waxed or greased paper, etc.

R683. Plastic bags include cellulose film bags; polyethylene heavy duty shipping sacks, garbage bags, bakery bags, dry-cleaning and laundry bags (including shirt bags); other plastic film bags; plastic laminated and extrusion coated bags, and metal foil bags.

R688. This is a total paper box series for the period prior to 1960. The disaggregation into series R686-687 is not available for this period.

R689. Paperboards include container board, box board, building board and wet machine board.

R692. Pig iron produced includes basic, foundry and malleable pig iron made for sale and own use. Silvery pig iron has been included since 1950. Production values are not available.

R693. Steel ingots and castings produced include both carbon and alloy steels.

R696. Structural steel shapes made in primary mills include light structurals since 1951, (previously included with 'hot rolled iron and steel bars'), and sheet piling since 1949.

R701. Steel pipes and tubing include welded and seamless steel pipes and tubing, but exclude riveted pipes and sheet metal culverts.

R704. Plain steel wire includes the quantity made and used in subsequent processes in the same plant as in the manufacture of nails, galvanized wire, etc.

R706. Metal cans include metal cans made for foods as well as non-food products.

R708. Passenger automobiles include all types of cars, such as permanent closed cars, convertible cars and station wagons but do not include chassis sold without bodies. Selling values represent the wholesale value or the amount of money received by manufacturers from their dealers or distributors; taxes, dealers' commissions, etc., are not included.

R710. Commercial auto vehicles include all wheeled vehicles for military use. Not included are universal carriers and scout cars or chassis sold without bodies. Selling values represent the wholesale value of the amount of money received by manufacturers from dealers, distributors and government. Taxes, dealers' commissions, etc., are not included.

R716. Boats include canoes, rowboats, skiffs, dories, sailboats and outboard boats.

R723. Locomotives do not include railway electric cars.

R728. Stoves and ranges include stoves and ranges for cooking and heating. Stoves and ranges for wood, coal, gas, electricity, gasoline and fuel oil, as well as for some combination of fuels, are included.

R730. Household refrigerators include electric, gas, and all other types.

R734. Washing machines include only domestic washing machines powered by electricity or other power. Hand, automatic and conventional washing machines are included.

R752. Gasoline includes motor, aviation and tractor gasoline made for sale and own use.

R754. Fuel oil includes heavy and light fuel oil made for sale and own use. It does not include aviation or aviation turbine fuel oil.

R756. Coke includes beehive, byproduct and gas retort coke. Petroleum coke is not included.

R757. Soaps and synthetic detergents include laundry and household soaps, toilet soaps, soap powders, shaving and liquid soaps.

R759. Due to the introduction in 1973 of a new classification system for collecting data on paints and enamels, the former qualification 'ready-mixed' is no longer applicable. This series now includes oil-base paints (interior, exterior and combination); emulsion (water-borne) base paints (interior, exterior and combination); enamels (interior, exterior and special-purpose); and lacquers, stains and varnishes. It does not include such items as paint and enamel aerosol spray bombs; primers, sealers and undercoats; and shellac.

R761. Selected synthetic resins include polyvinyl chloride and polystyrene only for 1960 and 1961. Data for 1962 and subsequent years also include polyethylene.

R763. Sulphuric acid includes acid made for sale and own use.

R770. Medicinal and pharmaceutical preparations include patent medicines, antibiotics, vitamins, ethical specialities for human use as well as all other medicines for human and animal use.

Size of Manufacturing Establishments (Series R771-825)

R771-782. Number of establishments and value of shipments of goods of own manufacture, by size of establishment measured by the value of shipments of goods of own manufacture, 1960 to 1975

SOURCE: *Manufacturing Industries of Canada: Type of Organization and Size of Establishment*, (Catalogue 31-210).

Series R771-782 are comparable throughout the period 1960 to 1975, but are not entirely comparable with series R783-794 for the period prior to 1960 due to the change in coverage of manufacturing industries through the introduction of the 1960 Standard Industrial Classification and the new establishment concept. The size classes have also been changed to reflect the influence of increasing size of plants and rising price levels. In the lower range, the former three size classes have been replaced by two new ones: under $100,000 and $100,000-$499,999. In the upper range the size class $1,000,000 and over has been replaced by two new classes: $1,000,000-$4,999,999 and $5,000,000 and over.

R783-794. Number of establishments and gross value of production, by size of establishment, measured by gross value of production, selected years, 1900 to 1959.

SOURCE: *General Review of the Manufacturing Industries of Canada* (various issues); *The Manufacturing Industries of Canada*, the issues of 1945, 1941, 1936 and 1930 respectively, for the data for 1945, 1940, 1936 and 1930; *Canada Year Book*, the 1927 issue for 1925 data, 1925 issue for 1922 data, and 1906 issue for 1905 Postal Census data; *Postal Census of Manufactures, 1916*, for 1915 and 1910 data; *Census of Canada, 1901*, vol. III, for 1900 data.

The figures shown from 1900 to 1945 are not comparable with those in subsequent years because of differences in coverage and changes in the definition of 'manufacturing'. It should be noted that the data on the number of establishments and gross value of production from 1900 through 1945 in series R783 and R794 do not correspond with the figures shown earlier in series R12 and R17. As noted above, extensive revisions have been undertaken to develop more conceptually consistent and comparable figures for manufacturing in series R1-489. However, essential basic information is not available for similar revisions in the series relating to the size of manufacturing establishments.

The information collected for 1900 and 1910 pertains only to manufacturing establishments having five or more employees, whereas the postal censuses covered *all* of Canada's manufacturing establishments. In addition, electric light plants, gas plants, plumbing and tinsmithing, blacksmithing, dyeing and cleaning, bicycle repairing, and lock and gunsmithing, were included in the census of manufactures in 1900, 1905, 1910 and 1915; painting and glazing are covered in all these years except 1910; and housebuilding is in the 1910 and 1915 totals. The figures shown for 1922 to 1945 include some establishments in the public utilities and service categories that cannot be eliminated in these data on size of establishments.

R795-825. Number of establishments and number of employees, by size of establishment, measured by number of employees, selected years, 1915 to 1959

SOURCE: for 1960 to 1975, same as series R771-782; for 1915 to 1959, same as series R783-794.

These series are directly comparable throughout the period 1960 to 1975 with the exception that working owners and partners are included with employees in 1960 as in earlier years.

Comparability with series R812-825 is affected by the same qualifications as for series R783-794 with respect to coverage and industrial classification. Size classes in the original and updated series are identical with one exception: the size class 500 and over has been subdivided into two classes (500 to 999, and 1,000 and over) to reflect the increasing size of plants.

Data on the number of establishments and number of employees from 1915 to 1945 in series R812 and R813 do not correspond with the figures shown earlier in series R12 and R17. See the note to series R783-794.

There is also a small difference in the classification of manufacturing establishments by number of employees. The grouping given for the years prior to 1940 varies slightly from that available for subsequent years. In addition to the class for under 5 employees, the actual classes shown for these earlier years were 5 to 50 employees, 51 to 100 employees, 101 to 200 employees, 201 to 500 employees, and over 500 employees, instead of 5 to 49 employees, 50 to 99 employees, 100 to 199 employees, 200 to 499 employees, and 500 employees and over.

Series R1-22. Selected principal statistics on the manufacturing industries, Canada,¹ 1870 to 1975

Year	Number of establishments	Production and related workers		Cost of fuel and electricity ($'000)	Cost of materials and supplies used ($'000)	Gross value of production ($'000)	Value of shipments of goods of own manufacture ($'000)	Census value added: manufacturing activity ($'000)	Total employees		Census value added: total activity ($'000)
		Number	Salaries and wages ($'000)						Number	Salaries and wages ($'000)	
	1	2	3	4	5	6	7	8	9	10	11
1975	30,100	1,272,051	12,672,237	1,805,666	51,177,157	89,122,124	88,460,358	36,139,301	1,741,545	19,160,724	38,715,600
1974	31,535	1,300,792	11,637,073	1,623,617	47,499,791	84,208,159	82,455,109	35,084,752	1,785,977	17,556,982	37,654,465
1973	31,145	1,275,985	10,060,062	1,221,885	37,600,538	67,538,542	66,674,393	28,716,119	1,751,066	15,220,033	30,766,506
1972	31,553	1,213,106	8,763,104	1,078,916	31,137,946	56,481,691	56,190,740	24,264,829	1,676,130	13,414,609	25,981,742
1971	31,908	1,167,810	7,819,050	1,000,243	27,661,379	50,399,136	50,275,917	21,737,514	1,628,404	12,129,897	23,187,881
1970	31,928	1,167,063	7,232,256	903,264	25,699,999	46,651,064	46,380,935	20,047,801	1,637,001	11,363,712	21,417,748
1969	32,669	1,189,887	6,921,525	860,525	25,383,484	46,377,602	45,930,438	20,133,593	1,675,332	10,848,341	21,456,276
1968	32,643	1,160,226	6,278,429	808,764	23,090,970	42,231,938	42,061,555	18,332,204	1,642,352	9,905,504	19,483,614
1967	33,267	1,168,651	5,869,085	759,780	21,371,785	39,132,276	38,955,389	17,005,696	1,652,827	9,254,190	18,049,639
1966	33,377	1,172,943	5,575,206	731,726	20,642,695	37,718,848	37,303,455	16,351,740	1,646,024	8,695,890	17,260,256
1965	33,310	1,115,892	5,012,345	675,641	18,622,213	34,217,117	33,889,425	14,927,764	1,570,299	7,822,925	15,785,311
1964	33,630	1,057,502	4,513,633	615,108	16,928,476	31,076,667	30,856,099	13,535,991	1,491,257	7,080,939	14,247,184
1963	33,119	1,003,566	4,095,916	564,387	15,337,534	28,171,033	28,014,888	12,272,734	1,425,440	6,495,289	12,875,073
1962	33,414	974,376	3,834,514	540,447	13,974,877	25,949,283	25,790,087	11,429,644	1,389,516	6,096,174	11,986,666
1961	33,357	939,413	3,532,943	516,409	12,579,798	23,531,038	23,438,956	10,434,832	1,352,605	5,701,651	10,931,561
1960	32,852	971,610	3,565,124	503,978	12,451,637	23,326,899	23,279,804	10,371,284	1,275,476	5,150,503	..
1959	32,075	988,991	3,517,599	492,048	12,339,558	22,985,883	22,830,827	10,154,277	1,287,809	5,030,128	..
1958	32,446	972,468	3,305,975	470,608	11,630,825	21,556,387	21,434,815	9,454,954	1,272,686	4,758,614	..
1957	33,551	1,035,333	3,391,803	475,450	11,698,789	..	21,452,343	..	1,340,948	4,778,040	..

Year	Number of establishments	Production and related workers		Cost of fuel and electricity ($'000)	Cost of materials and supplies used ($'000)	Gross value of production² ($'000)	Census value added: manufacturing activity² ($'000)	Supervisory and office employees		Total employees	
		Number	Salaries and wages ($'000)					Number	Salaries and wages ($'000)	Number	Salaries and wages ($'000)
	12	13	14	15	16	17	18	19	20	21	22
1959	36,193	997,907	3,543,456	568,880	12,552,201	23,442,044	10,320,963	306,049	1,529,618	1,303,956	5,073,074
1958	36,741	981,735	3,333,172	549,307	11,821,567	22,163,380	9,792,506	307,867	1,469,324	1,289,602	4,802,496
1957	37,875	1,045,177	3,416,226	555,311	11,900,752	22,278,148	9,822,085	313,884	1,403,402	1,359,061	4,819,628
1956	37,428	1,051,723	3,298,666	523,941	11,721,537	21,850,903	9,605,425	301,297	1,272,026	1,353,020	4,570,692
1955	38,182	1,010,992	2,995,267	457,789	10,338,202	19,549,441	8,753,450	287,469	1,147,142	1,298,461	4,142,410
1954³	38,028	989,030	2,821,586	424,433	9,241,858	17,568,415	7,902,124	278,936	1,075,101	1,267,966	3,896,688
1953	38,107	1,053,226	2,940,339	411,788	9,380,559	17,785,416	7,993,069	274,225	1,016,679	1,327,451	3,957,018
1952	37,929	1,025,355	2,713,715	392,981	9,146,172	16,982,686	7,443,533	263,027	923,905	1,288,382	3,637,620
1951	37,021	1,010,588	2,459,566	376,714	9,074,526	16,392,187	6,940,947	247,787	816,715	1,258,375	3,276,281
1950	35,942	952,244	2,078,634	336,933	7,538,535	13,817,526	5,942,058	231,053	692,633	1,183,297	2,771,267
1949	35,792	949,656	1,963,463	305,796	6,843,231	12,479,593	5,330,566	221,551	628,428	1,171,207	2,591,891
1948	33,420	957,491	1,876,773	303,500	6,632,882	11,875,170	4,938,787	198,230	532,595	1,155,721	2,409,368
1947	32,673	940,153	1,610,583	254,627	5,534,011	10,078,452	4,289,814	190,972	474,401	1,131,125	2,084,985
1946	31,188	876,566	1,329,151	210,382	4,357,992	8,033,099	3,464,725	180,894	410,652	1,057,460	1,739,802
1945	28,979	927,772	1,426,934	212,289	4,472,362	8,245,186	3,560,533	190,243	416,948	1,118,015	1,843,883
1944	28,413	1,029,243	1,610,413	225,473	4,831,129	9,066,846	4,010,244	191,838	416,615	1,221,081	2,027,028
1943	27,581	1,046,748	1,597,374	225,879	4,689,345	8,725,350	3,810,129	192,579	387,624	1,239,327	1,984,998
1942	27,791	973,818	1,347,000	206,650	4,036,068	7,548,215	3,305,495	176,798	334,150	1,150,616	1,681,150
1941	26,241	801,531	977,906	174,599	3,295,629	6,072,067	2,601,840	158,764	285,915	960,295	1,263,821
1940	25,471	625,993	678,903	136,952	2,448,383	4,526,618	1,941,282	135,646	241,364	761,639	920,267
1939	24,772	533,012	519,691	107,548	1,835,069	3,472,828	1,530,210	124,661	217,625	657,673	737,316
1938	25,166	521,100	498,025	101,898	1,806,551	3,335,985	1,427,538	120,473	207,160	641,573	705,185
1937	24,800	544,240	525,422	109,588	2,005,990	3,623,426	1,507,846	115,712	195,803	659,952	721,225
1936	24,170	489,739	438,712	88,582	1,623,394	3,000,721	1,288,747	104,231	172,901	593,970	611,613
1935	24,000	458,597	398,949	81,266	1,418,447	2,652,520	1,152,806	97,766	160,197	556,363	559,146
1934	24,177	427,603	355,028	76,864	1,228,786	2,392,388	1,086,736	91,939	148,511	519,542	503,539
1933	23,747	381,913	296,868	66,671	967,312	1,952,904	918,923	86,453	139,040	468,366	435,908
1932	23,071	381,708	322,195	70,116	953,905	1,979,012	954,990	86,862	151,058	468,570	473,253
1931	23,049	437,041	415,197	81,181	1,221,375	2,516,057	1,213,500	91,266	171,949	528,307	587,148
1930	22,586	529,740	527,356	92,698	1,664,265	3,236,606	1,479,642	84,608	169,858	614,348	697,214
1929	22,184	577,424	601,515	98,373	2,029,173	3,840,871	1,713,326	88,757	175,408	666,181	776,925
1928	21,937	546,984	558,314	90,415	1,893,516	3,543,551	1,559,621	84,076	162,815	631,060	721,131
1927	21,464	515,901	511,067	88,423	1,740,646	3,223,012	1,393,943	78,730	151,260	594,631	662,327
1926	21,269	483,588	483,176	82,904	1,726,252	3,090,179	1,281,021	75,273	142,240	558,861	625,416
1925	20,956	451,406	436,418	77,799	1,584,991	2,808,485	1,145,695	71,255	133,373	522,661	569,791
1924	20,693	422,413	411,004	77,272	1,456,494	2,606,650	1,072,884	70,526	131,500	492,939	542,504
1923	21,077	437,259	420,222	71,077	1,483,108	2,690,344	1,136,159	73,849	137,173	511,108	557,395
1922	21,017	386,467	363,761	67,704	1,289,187	2,389,216	1,032,325	71,933	130,633	458,400	494,394
1921	20,836	371,253	370,934	71,121	1,373,498	2,491,280	1,046,661	70,535	130,786	441,788	501,720

Series R1-22. Selected principal statistics on the manufacturing industries, Canada,[1] 1870 to 1975 (concluded)

Year	Number of establishments	Production and related workers		Cost of fuel and electricity ($'000)	Cost of materials and supplies used ($'000)	Gross value of production[2] ($'000)	Census value added: manufacturing activity[2] ($'000)	Supervisory and office employees		Total employees	
		Number	Salaries and wages ($'000)					Number	Salaries and wages ($'000)	Number	Salaries and wages ($'000)
	12	13	14	15	16	17	18	19	20	21	22
1920	22,376	499,063	544,724	93,602	2,081,255	3,667,579	1,492,722	77,354	140,014	576,417	684,288
1919	22,578	496,308	456,895	75,902	1,788,958	3,152,237	1,287,377	75,558	113,091	571,866	569,986
1918	22,007	520,741	453,215	98,227	1,796,882	3,165,139	1,270,030	64,789	95,239	585,530	548,454
1917	22,043	523,491	397,750	72,584	1,524,674	2,768,046	1,170,788	62,454	82,248	585,945	479,998
1910	—	465,029	193,982	—	601,647	1,151,722	550,075	42,948	42,698	509,977	236,680
1905	15,197	347,672	130,351	—	—	698,594	—	35,030	29,618	382,702	159,969
1900	—	—	—	—	310,488	555,876	245,388	—	—	422,824	133,452
1890	69,716	—	—	—	245,993	449,982	203,989	—	—	351,139	94,382
1880	47,079	—	—	—	177,681	304,663	126,982	—	—	248,042	57,720
1870	38,898	—	—	—	123,272	217,176	93,904	—	—	181,679	39,547

[1] See the description in the text of these series for an explanation of the changes resulting from changes in the Standard Industrial Classification.

[2] From 1954 to 1959, most Statistics Canada reports on manufacturing show value of shipments (unadjusted for inventory change) and are therefore different from the figures shown here for gross value of production. The figures for value added by manufacture also differ from those shown in most Statistics Canada reports on manufacturing for the years 1954 to 1959 for the same reason. For the years 1952 and 1953, values of shipments have been shown because inventory data are incomplete.

[3] Because of a change in the method of valuation in the petroleum industry, a slight discontinuity exists from 1954 onwards. See footnote (1) to series R453 and R455.

Series R23-33. Selected principal statistics on the manufacturing industries, Newfoundland, 1957 to 1975

Year	Manufacturing activity								Total activity		
	Number of establishments	Production and related workers		Cost of fuel and electricity ($'000)	Cost of materials and supplies used ($'000)	Gross value of production ($'000)	Value of shipments of goods of own manufacture ($'000)	Census value added: manufacturing activity ($'000)	Total employees		Census value added: total activity ($'000)
		Number	Salaries and wages ($'000)						Number	Salaries and wages ($'000)	
	23	24	25	26	27	28	29	30	31	32	33
1975	270	10,164	97,085	26,149	418,747	652,916	650,008	208,020	13,000	132,261	224,139
1974	264	11,280	95,165	27,478	442,565	740,918	711,731	270,874	14,168	126,198	280,281
1973	245	11,492	78,190	17,075	186,843	386,672	382,610	182,754	13,924	101,270	196,779
1972	246	10,043	59,859	12,888	139,770	282,216	284,095	129,558	12,179	78,076	142,910
1971	245	10,399	55,284	12,320	130,987	264,326	261,931	121,019	12,580	72,757	135,496
1970	252	10,641	55,663	13,458	128,671	265,753	263,304	123,624	12,873	72,219	136,079
1969	259	9,941	48,892	11,580	116,353	240,455	242,386	112,522	12,302	65,325	120,537
1968	254	9,609	42,964	9,520	99,169	197,076	197,464	88,386	11,908	57,582	92,583
1967	263	9,389	40,627	9,265	93,980	189,933	186,056	86,689	11,620	54,246	90,632
1966	262	9,375	38,512	8,990	92,576	194,609	194,102	93,043	11,484	50,694	99,107
1965	287	8,577	31,724	8,701	84,490	175,598	174,532	82,407	10,463	42,516	86,543
1964	299	7,921	28,882	8,304	78,346	165,638	165,801	78,988	9,935	39,867	82,770
1963	307	8,001	27,613	7,626	72,050	153,653	155,208	73,977	10,021	38,093	76,964
1962	330	7,698	27,000	7,455	67,020	147,280	143,859	72,805	9,894	37,449	75,211
1961	338	7,809	26,671	7,035	60,177	136,485	135,893	69,273	9,854	36,310	70,644
1960	396	7,810	24,937	6,783	57,980	128,253	126,981	63,490	9,318	32,322	..
1959	468	7,499	23,077	6,509	52,985	115,622	116,664	56,128	9,095	29,992	..
1958	422	7,453	22,150	6,864	50,751	114,366	114,070	56,751	9,063	28,644	..
1957	465	7,954	25,375	7,268	52,148	..	113,730	..	9,677	32,087	..

Series R34-36. General statistics on the manufacturing industries, Atlantic provinces,[1] selected years, 1926 to 1959.

Year	Total employees	Salaries and wages ($'000)	Census value added by manufacture ($'000)	Year	Total employees	Salaries and wages ($'000)	Census value added by manufacture ($'000)
	34	35	36		34	35	36
1959	60,484	185,904	360,533	1950	60,810	119,862	244,981
1958	60,990	179,706	372,977	1949	61,438	116,527	230,738
1957	64,651	187,183	362,354	1948	56,432	98,546	191,396
1956	65,774	178,708	353,904	1945	57,775	85,789	150,913
				1942	54,759	68,661	119,497
1955	64,782	164,917	327,473				
1954	63,384	157,451	313,323	1939	33,214	30,927	64,167
1953	68,895	165,845	312,198	1936	30,649	26,192	52,623
1952	69,720	159,263	310,618	1933	24,535	19,439	39,275
1951	66,374	142,663	298,818	1929	40,009	32,757	63,740
				1926	35,525	27,096	55,458

[1] Newfoundland is included with the Atlantic provinces from 1949 onwards, except that figures for the Newfoundland fish processing industry are not available, and are not included for the years 1949 and 1950.

Series R37-47. Selected principal statistics on the manufacturing industries, Prince Edward Island, 1957 to 1975

Year	Number of establish-ments	Production and related workers		Cost of fuel and electricity ($'000)	Cost of materials and supplies used ($'000)	Gross value of production ($'000)	Value of shipments of goods of own manufacture ($'000)	Census value added: manufac-turing activity ($'000)	Total employees		Census value added: total activity ($'000)
		Number	Salaries and wages ($'000)						Number	Salaries and wages ($'000)	
	37	38	39	40	41	42	43	44	45	46	47
1975	117	1,817	13,090	2,234	74,173	110,539	108,562	34,132	2,353	18,107	36,741
1974	138	1,741	11,277	1,627	65,363	96,767	94,142	29,776	2,263	15,490	33,524
1973	131	1,898	9,365	1,118	54,646	82,426	81,619	26,662	2,400	12,844	29,090
1972	141	1,786	7,979	926	44,113	67,616	66,888	22,578	2,264	11,101	24,755
1971	153	1,795	7,527	1,010	38,748	59,911	58,024	20,153	2,290	10,464	22,384
1970	150	2,207	8,001	1,022	41,955	63,512	62,680	20,535	2,698	10,681	21,793
1969	148	2,070	7,075	1,018	37,884	57,371	56,859	18,468	2,606	9,746	19,726
1968	138	1,730	5,727	977	34,162	51,708	51,657	16,569	2,255	8,219	17,534
1967	145	1,751	5,352	867	34,764	51,134	51,083	15,504	2,253	7,671	16,935
1966	152	1,647	4,804	821	31,517	46,819	46,781	14,480	2,164	7,028	15,781
1965	155	1,629	4,397	757	30,045	43,526	43,076	12,724	2,197	6,617	13,885
1964	148	1,617	4,353	720	28,616	41,300	40,662	11,964	2,113	6,290	12,414
1963	147	1,455	3,488	605	24,798	36,010	35,599	10,608	1,863	5,019	11,314
1962	156	1,422	3,360	602	24,864	35,328	35,113	9,862	1,832	4,843	10,101
1961	161	1,307	2,949	472	21,483	30,441	30,598	8,486	1,681	4,195	8,764
1960	154	1,256	2,779	460	19,982	28,463	28,415	8,026	1,671	4,036	..
1959	154	1,243	2,526	439	18,465	25,901	25,792	6,997	1,672	3,701	..
1958	159	1,164	2,287	397	18,102	25,178	25,153	6,679	1,541	3,250	..
1957	167	1,161	2,217	388	16,815	..	22,896	..	1,537	3,110	..

Series R48-58. Selected principal statistics on the manufacturing industries, Nova Scotia, 1957 to 1975

Year	Number of establish-ments	Production and related workers		Cost of fuel and electricity ($'000)	Cost of materials and supplies used ($'000)	Gross value of production ($'000)	Value of shipments of goods of own manufacture ($'000)	Census value added: manufac-turing activity ($'000)	Total employees		Census value added: total activity ($'000)
		Number	Salaries and wages ($'000)						Number	Salaries and wages ($'000)	
	48	49	50	51	52	53	54	55	56	57	58
1975	689	27,895	247,063	51,332	1,139,514	1,866,551	1,819,094	675,705	37,365	362,252	700,019
1974	740	27,150	212,008	52,108	1,078,629	1,732,471	1,696,092	601,735	36,583	311,633	625,098
1973	746	27,557	180,184	31,527	772,840	1,270,842	1,250,695	466,475	36,788	267,868	492,461
1972	761	25,918	152,571	29,078	598,767	996,678	993,641	368,833	34,730	227,674	388,587
1971	795	24,253	129,170	26,348	481,528	805,630	798,152	297,754	31,958	188,792	311,757
1970	818	24,641	121,568	17,882	437,609	763,563	757,992	308,072	31,812	172,704	318,484
1969	846	25,741	116,142	18,347	419,168	736,048	731,475	298,533	33,229	165,640	315,736
1968	852	25,187	103,254	16,590	385,378	663,012	663,335	261,044	32,894	148,811	272,288
1967	904	25,463	99,011	14,749	357,738	613,521	610,299	240,783	33,025	141,729	251,812
1966	931	26,020	99,603	14,140	354,044	614,885	612,466	246,702	33,533	139,626	255,485
1965	944	24,763	91,076	13,728	328,887	565,276	563,155	222,662	32,100	127,558	231,510
1964	981	23,167	84,581	12,501	303,146	526,787	523,738	211,140	30,183	117,654	218,292
1963	1,009	21,949	76,626	11,046	261,974	460,926	458,915	187,905	28,648	106,956	193,235
1962	1,029	22,594	73,233	11,081	242,480	427,970	426,366	174,407	29,375	102,917	179,350
1961	1,029	21,247	66,386	10,050	211,094	382,326	381,415	161,183	27,822	94,263	165,408
1960	1,039	23,037	71,204	9,839	207,705	389,037	387,869	171,493	27,971	91,134	..
1959	1,054	22,718	67,449	8,795	205,910	369,428	370,947	154,723	27,491	86,570	..
1958	1,038	23,525	66,747	8,959	202,679	361,945	365,660	150,307	28,218	84,747	..
1957	1,084	25,735	71,917	10,146	221,051	..	377,465	..	30,611	89,398	..

Series R59-69. Selected principal statistics on the manufacturing industries, New Brunswick, 1957 to 1975

Year	Number of establishments	Production and related workers		Cost of fuel and electricity ($'000)	Cost of materials and supplies used ($'000)	Gross value of production ($'000)	Value of shipments of goods of own manufacture ($'000)	Census value added: manufacturing activity ($'000)	Total employees		Census value added: total activity ($'000)
		Number	Salaries and wages ($'000)						Number	Salaries and wages ($'000)	
	59	60	61	62	63	64	65	66	67	68	69
1975	559	22,348	211,698	77,788	1,041,867	1,702,817	1,669,422	583,162	29,300	295,087	610,085
1974	592	23,674	187,823	78,202	943,831	1,625,119	1,585,655	603,086	30,475	258,210	628,891
1973	585	23,400	155,057	46,795	698,436	1,180,051	1,175,511	434,820	29,940	213,995	457,239
1972	601	22,967	136,863	40,222	590,511	969,770	965,046	339,037	29,640	191,231	356,528
1971	609	22,053	123,853	34,843	497,389	812,648	806,806	280,416	28,565	173,118	296,802
1970	612	22,148	112,228	28,312	437,950	736,936	730,223	270,674	28,751	158,281	283,364
1969	628	22,146	104,217	26,494	413,997	710,350	708,939	269,859	28,984	148,206	283,782
1968	620	21,521	93,856	24,461	374,338	639,552	633,577	240,753	28,139	133,380	249,012
1967	676	20,252	85,495	23,516	342,586	576,197	573,897	210,129	26,770	121,406	221,440
1966	690	19,506	77,287	22,761	316,568	550,567	547,197	211,295	25,749	110,387	220,012
1965	704	18,793	69,321	21,370	294,293	511,900	512,705	196,237	25,153	99,771	205,534
1964	724	18,481	64,794	17,696	288,433	495,119	494,361	188,990	24,552	93,016	198,030
1963	715	18,262	62,666	16,508	275,519	459,694	456,249	167,667	24,039	88,288	175,719
1962	721	17,746	58,485	15,528	229,245	403,139	400,911	158,289	23,303	82,798	164,810
1961	733	17,284	53,337	15,229	221,582	391,726	390,573	154,915	22,932	76,796	161,104
1960	768	18,388	55,959	15,032	204,627	374,356	369,108	154,697	22,111	71,254	..
1959	779	17,113	49,568	13,856	170,525	314,347	314,220	129,966	20,520	63,271	..
1958	813	17,242	48,099	13,089	167,176	309,275	306,992	129,010	20,554	60,850	..
1957	858	17,421	48,031	14,036	170,922	..	306,026	..	20,665	60,061	..

Series R70-80. Selected principal statistics on the manufacturing industries, Quebec, 1957 to 1975

Year	Number of establishments	Production and related workers		Cost of fuel and electricity ($'000)	Cost of materials and supplies used ($'000)	Gross value of production ($'000)	Value of shipments of goods of own manufacture ($'000)	Census value added: manufacturing activity ($'000)	Total employees		Census value added: total activity ($'000)
		Number	Salaries and wages ($'000)						Number	Salaries and wages ($'000)	
	70	71	72	73	74	75	76	77	78	79	80
1975	9,375	394,333	3,520,808	537,647	13,662,494	24,158,157	23,966,501	9,958,016	532,932	5,382,265	10,458,512
1974	9,974	398,857	3,157,287	488,276	12,790,307	22,827,693	22,396,844	9,549,110	541,500	4,831,383	10,044,846
1973	9,947	391,518	2,684,885	348,090	9,772,414	17,716,474	17,464,942	7,595,970	533,759	4,166,825	8,025,855
1972	10,025	377,802	2,401,306	310,623	8,195,973	15,182,632	15,091,616	6,676,036	517,878	3,761,198	7,020,532
1971	10,135	366,198	2,171,882	289,628	7,513,331	13,857,816	13,833,179	6,054,856	508,591	3,459,043	6,406,236
1970	10,176	369,896	2,057,512	264,849	7,072,888	13,135,597	13,083,969	5,797,861	514,150	3,285,035	6,091,819
1969	10,466	379,869	1,991,387	255,434	6,975,374	12,905,245	12,810,214	5,674,438	529,027	3,166,701	5,967,988
1968	10,513	370,537	1,817,303	236,395	6,341,337	11,793,196	11,742,911	5,215,464	521,250	2,923,728	5,445,448
1967	10,772	372,408	1,696,769	222,829	5,935,243	11,011,510	10,966,429	4,855,896	524,688	2,739,520	5,088,243
1966	10,877	368,450	1,590,164	217,693	5,639,982	10,561,934	10,464,530	4,704,799	516,154	2,543,539	4,948,941
1965	10,952	356,780	1,433,816	199,392	5,083,140	9,583,451	9,492,182	4,305,379	499,177	2,298,750	4,516,700
1964	11,097	342,907	1,318,999	185,318	4,702,130	8,823,065	8,773,944	3,937,816	479,518	2,117,086	4,125,329
1963	10,980	328,495	1,208,471	167,762	4,354,652	8,087,833	8,072,507	3,568,875	462,014	1,956,758	3,724,337
1962	11,102	326,257	1,166,738	160,521	4,038,363	7,633,575	7,589,429	3,433,606	459,926	1,882,197	3,582,684
1961	11,217	319,231	1,087,610	156,722	3,707,062	7,051,841	7,022,199	3,188,058	452,543	1,775,710	3,313,604
1960	11,093	331,953	1,104,248	152,372	3,786,455	7,101,745	7,075,505	3,162,918	429,444	1,606,373	..
1959	10,671	331,850	1,064,579	149,423	3,691,667	6,827,765	6,802,195	2,986,675	427,016	1,536,945	..
1958	10,897	330,155	1,012,745	147,264	3,540,674	6,626,745	6,513,647	2,938,807	425,261	1,466,560	..
1957	11,295	348,105	1,036,007	149,420	3,514,510	..	6,422,702	..	444,962	1,468,063	..

Series R81-83. General statistics on the manufacturing industries, Quebec, selected years, 1926 to 1959

Year	Total employees	Salaries and wages ($'000)	Census value added by manufacture ($'000)	Year	Total employees	Salaries and wages ($'000)	Census value added by manufacture ($'000)
	81	82	83		81	82	83
				1950	390,163	851,335	1,798,320
				1949	390,275	809,579	1,651,630
				1948	383,835	756,079	1,533,798
1959	431,237	1,546,933	2,998,776	1945	383,314	606,586	1,146,941
1958	429,358	1,476,606	2,970,775	1942	398,336	535,582	1,057,448
1957	449,383	1,477,828	2,947,898				
1956	446,137	1,396,415	2,888,149				
1955	429,575	1,271,078	2,622,333	1939	220,024	223,422	469,908
1954	424,095	1,214,661	2,448,028	1936	194,685	182,098	376,995
1953	441,555	1,225,573	2,424,647	1933	157,345	134,525	287,999
1952	429,698	1,125,945	2,288,643	1929	206,468	225,081	500,426
1951	417,182	1,005,602	2,083,934	1926	174,931	182,809	378,447

Series R84-94. Selected principal statistics on the manufacturing industries, Ontario, 1957 to 1975

Year	Number of establish-ments	Production and related workers Number	Production and related workers Salaries and wages ($'000)	Cost of fuel and electricity ($'000)	Cost of materials and supplies used ($'000)	Gross value of production ($'000)	Value of shipments of goods of own manufacture ($'000)	Census value added: manufac-turing activity ($'000)	Total employees Number	Total employees Salaries and wages ($'000)	Census value added: total activity ($'000)
	84	85	86	87	88	89	90	91	92	93	94
1975	12,245	612,745	6,316,577	791,497	25,560,075	44,709,381	44,422,821	18,357,809	850,291	9,673,050	20,122,934
1974	12,662	632,850	5,914,093	692,739	23,577,721	42,399,295	41,404,361	18,128,835	883,730	9,074,122	19,920,508
1973	12,397	616,935	5,186,725	554,598	19,085,501	34,670,430	34,300,652	15,030,331	861,767	7,947,955	16,416,698
1972	12,589	583,932	4,507,383	491,741	16,020,243	29,331,884	29,181,103	12,819,900	821,614	6,989,621	14,000,176
1971	12,740	563,864	4,020,624	455,775	14,250,680	26,302,926	26,270,629	11,596,471	800,047	6,326,544	12,537,204
1970	12,736	562,858	3,711,437	417,851	13,226,000	24,168,606	24,009,636	10,524,756	806,638	5,942,507	11,459,488
1969	12,971	574,694	3,549,819	387,241	13,100,271	24,124,520	23,847,773	10,637,008	825,462	5,660,929	11,523,267
1968	12,932	563,777	3,238,023	372,847	11,932,954	22,020,690	21,942,620	9,714,889	810,724	5,171,178	10,516,406
1967	13,076	571,106	3,030,681	352,475	10,982,235	20,363,837	20,259,696	9,032,055	818,227	4,822,183	9,732,956
1966	12,986	578,559	2,912,675	339,748	10,712,883	19,694,311	19,452,570	8,648,180	820,387	4,571,684	9,209,568
1965	12,766	543,501	2,615,719	314,290	9,668,876	17,861,006	17,675,865	7,881,825	774,428	4,100,212	8,421,721
1964	12,781	509,758	2,320,944	283,965	8,627,975	15,978,380	15,842,949	7,066,985	728,936	3,666,810	7,489,116
1963	12,489	478,370	2,080,555	260,511	7,745,076	14,374,769	14,262,208	6,369,483	690,470	3,335,582	6,729,111
1962	12,585	456,026	1,908,474	249,459	6,944,729	13,012,586	12,919,454	5,815,088	662,533	3,078,549	6,149,611
1961	12,419	433,059	1,739,097	237,405	6,129,239	11,611,489	11,563,734	5,244,846	638,757	2,859,652	5,553,191
1960	12,090	441,856	1,733,838	235,718	6,036,929	11,487,876	11,479,327	5,215,229	594,317	2,557,397	..
1959	11,727	457,714	1,748,481	232,025	6,096,980	11,558,842	11,438,355	5,229,837	609,065	2,544,676	..
1958	11,858	445,315	1,620,462	215,498	5,624,613	10,580,923	10,579,486	4,740,812	598,969	2,391,435	..
1957	12,162	479,880	1,675,516	221,536	5,732,215	..	10,811,118	..	636,162	2,410,286	..

Series R95-97. General statistics on the manufacturing industries, Ontario, selected years, 1926 to 1959

Year	Total employees	Salaries and wages ($'000)	Census value added by manufacture ($'000)	Year	Total employees	Salaries and wages ($'000)	Census value added by manufacture ($'000)
	95	96	97		95	96	97
				1950	566,513	1,412,999	3,068,142
				1949	557,190	1,305,544	2,708,554
				1948	551,556	1,210,438	2,486,008
1959	615,746	2,564,684	5,332,082	1945	517,522	881,621	1,719,951
1958	606,362	2,412,655	4,914,074	1942	542,217	839,932	1,669,191
1957	644,245	2,430,676	5,047,711				
1956	641,190	2,310,634	4,868,570				
1955	613,872	2,088,906	4,426,655	1939	318,765	378,252	791,117
1954	598,914	1,954,767	3,930,730	1936	288,883	314,759	686,279
1953	634,554	2,017,982	4,130,126	1933	224,693	220,392	464,935
1952	609,696	1,844,186	3,811,107	1929	328,340	406,452	912,445
1951	599,433	1,669,387	3,569,400	1926	270,476	321,863	664,546

Series R98-108. Selected principal statistics on the manufacturing industries, Manitoba, 1957 to 1975

Year	Number of establish-ments	Production and related workers		Cost of fuel and electricity ($'000)	Cost of materials and supplies used ($'000)	Gross value of production ($'000)	Value of shipments of goods of own manufacture ($'000)	Census value added: manufac-turing activity ($'000)	Total employees		Census value added: total activity ($'000)
		Number	Salaries and wages ($'000)						Number	Salaries and wages ($'000)	
	98	99	100	101	102	103	104	105	106	107	108
1975	1,215	41,057	373,209	50,260	1,537,285	2,602,164	2,580,985	1,014,619	55,010	541,507	1,080,398
1974	1,291	40,642	325,581	38,216	1,386,579	2,331,230	2,279,697	906,434	54,309	471,038	962,611
1973	1,295	39,371	269,839	31,452	1,117,979	1,864,266	1,840,195	714,835	52,716	396,276	755,050
1972	1,322	37,683	235,681	28,602	894,262	1,522,732	1,509,334	599,867	50,602	347,465	629,514
1971	1,356	35,527	207,031	27,627	788,264	1,350,363	1,344,855	534,472	48,325	310,760	558,920
1970	1,350	35,553	194,259	26,335	745,381	1,268,937	1,260,416	497,221	48,707	294,625	522,667
1969	1,381	35,802	182,763	25,337	725,409	1,236,803	1,230,020	486,057	49,439	277,380	507,048
1968	1,393	34,153	161,942	23,860	657,609	1,124,471	1,118,813	443,002	48,100	251,869	463,577
1967	1,444	34,944	154,965	21,433	638,117	1,084,589	1,079,730	424,923	49,325	241,311	440,984
1966	1,456	34,406	141,077	20,017	606,600	1,029,381	1,019,000	402,954	48,523	220,051	416,884
1965	1,457	32,531	126,036	18,639	541,931	924,876	913,357	364,275	46,368	199,059	380,446
1964	1,471	31,506	116,586	16,616	506,648	863,992	861,356	340,824	44,850	184,809	357,272
1963	1,455	30,041	109,057	16,732	461,189	799,006	793,746	320,675	43,119	174,143	334,834
1962	1,458	29,054	104,108	16,440	434,814	753,902	753,240	302,835	41,943	167,229	314,452
1961	1,476	28,795	98,256	15,927	419,541	720,123	716,740	284,656	41,856	160,315	294,816
1960	1,414	31,834	108,530	12,107	411,598	713,131	711,219	289,426	41,288	151,438	..
1959	1,394	33,269	111,038	11,925	419,482	732,049	730,630	300,642	42,473	152,179	..
1958	1,392	32,549	102,260	10,832	395,048	674,361	673,914	268,481	41,508	140,314	..
1957	1,390	34,171	102,121	11,833	377,444	..	646,203	..	43,256	138,601	..

Series R109-111. General statistics on the manufacturing industries, Prairie provinces, selected years, 1926 to 1959

Year	Total employees	Salaries and wages ($'000)	Census value added by manufacture ($'000)	Year	Total employees	Salaries and wages ($'000)	Census value added by manufacture ($'000)
	109	110	111		109	110	111
				1950	78,313	170,128	350,439
1959	95,206	353,537	780,518	1949	79,222	163,478	329,373
1958	92,525	326,223	747,201	1948	77,162	150,005	309,604
1957	94,985	318,153	694,799	1945	71,426	109,427	234,492
1956	91,149	290,384	669,477	1942	65,697	88,123	186,234
1955	87,654	263,094	624,380	1939	43,083	50,758	101,692
1954	85,515	246,875	556,376	1936	40,035	42,824	85,189
1953	88,426	246,127	509,398	1933	33,399	33,103	67,722
1952	86,437	224,165	475,969	1929	43,217	54,893	123,704
1951	81,587	195,596	395,586	1926	33,024	41,976	89,861

Series R112-122. Selected principal statistics on the manufacturing industries, Saskatchewan, 1957 to 1975

Year	Number of establish-ments	Production and related workers		Cost of fuel and electricity ($'000)	Cost of materials and supplies used ($'000)	Gross value of production ($'000)	Value of shipments of goods of own manufacture ($'000)	Census value added: manufac-turing activity ($'000)	Total employees		Census value added: total activity ($'000)
		Number	Salaries and wages ($'000)						Number	Salaries and wages ($'000)	
	112	113	114	115	116	117	118	119	120	121	122
1975	653	13,995	143,740	22,622	719,195	1,178,969	1,176,473	437,152	19,213	208,281	455,185
1974	678	13,117	114,752	18,145	669,466	1,060,856	1,045,160	373,245	17,917	164,165	391,123
1973	675	12,246	95,376	15,201	494,861	830,035	809,648	319,973	16,753	136,307	330,995
1972	709	11,061	80,436	13,244	390,490	648,506	646,510	244,772	15,570	117,754	257,447
1971	723	10,177	69,461	12,166	356,713	578,843	578,039	209,965	14,578	103,147	217,941
1970	737	10,139	64,361	12,413	342,021	546,418	544,611	191,983	14,703	97,985	200,623
1969	748	9,889	58,686	12,160	332,722	531,773	530,443	186,891	15,267	95,082	194,956
1968	756	10,348	56,447	11,000	311,760	492,762	489,210	170,002	15,654	89,955	179,420
1967	779	10,222	51,491	10,130	305,487	481,546	479,582	165,986	15,611	83,558	174,505
1966	774	10,166	46,857	9,703	310,533	474,787	470,381	154,534	15,689	77,947	161,463
1965	754	9,491	41,074	9,255	275,818	423,735	421,452	138,692	14,960	69,840	146,543
1964	773	9,135	38,566	8,650	245,543	382,530	381,781	128,354	14,247	64,273	136,137
1963	749	8,768	35,906	8,201	237,720	372,393	370,512	126,495	13,744	59,841	133,475
1962	720	8,717	34,645	8,200	228,747	350,685	352,069	113,750	13,662	57,560	118,519
1961	710	8,648	33,029	7,792	213,881	334,952	331,863	113,279	13,555	54,787	117,320
1960	682	8,986	33,605	7,320	206,740	329,633	329,945	115,573	12,267	48,104	..
1959	673	8,828	32,242	7,103	210,481	340,100	337,658	122,516	12,035	45,798	..
1958	729	8,577	29,744	6,764	196,028	312,334	312,608	109,542	11,774	42,264	..
1957	700	8,537	28,363	6,345	186,844	..	286,847	..	11,670	40,171	..

Series R123-133. Selected principal statistics on the manufacturing industries, Alberta, 1957 to 1975

Year	Number of establish-ments	Production and related workers		Cost of fuel and electricity ($'000)	Cost of materials and supplies used ($'000)	Gross value of production ($'000)	Value of shipments of goods of own manufacture ($'000)	Census value added: manufac-turing activity ($'000)	Total employees		Census value added: total activity ($'000)
		Number	Salaries and wages ($'000)						Number	Salaries and wages ($'000)	
	123	124	125	126	127	128	129	130	131	132	133
1975	1,821	45,781	491,988	65,828	3,131,381	4,778,305	4,726,466	1,581,096	64,678	741,073	1,638,347
1974	1,864	43,030	400,522	47,978	2,525,293	3,891,546	3,821,306	1,318,276	60,827	603,881	1,371,080
1973	1,816	40,061	324,780	38,934	1,945,670	2,998,567	2,973,328	1,013,963	56,863	496,145	1,056,035
1972	1,818	38,138	282,246	33,947	1,550,492	2,433,954	2,425,341	849,515	54,194	433,327	885,500
1971	1,821	36,517	251,644	30,953	1,297,115	2,083,314	2,080,617	755,246	51,941	384,480	785,347
1970	1,813	35,902	230,190	29,036	1,194,894	1,916,816	1,900,206	692,885	51,331	356,653	716,885
1969	1,861	36,199	214,915	29,314	1,133,980	1,866,114	1,849,271	702,820	52,354	335,104	731,863
1968	1,822	33,962	183,747	26,490	1,041,058	1,672,077	1,667,034	604,529	49,759	292,983	629,197
1967	1,803	33,889	171,848	24,706	964,870	1,563,897	1,554,985	574,219	49,568	272,325	599,283
1966	1,784	32,506	152,607	24,277	892,825	1,444,212	1,429,020	527,197	47,611	242,988	549,970
1965	1,774	30,764	135,689	22,458	797,030	1,294,785	1,283,301	475,343	45,455	217,634	500,621
1964	1,746	29,225	123,694	21,007	743,949	1,198,142	1,193,780	433,187	43,517	200,062	454,935
1963	1,692	28,031	114,947	19,686	679,254	1,088,640	1,084,332	389,769	42,277	188,556	409,278
1962	1,679	27,667	110,597	18,025	625,958	1,015,989	1,015,527	372,006	41,506	179,559	389,302
1961	1,628	26,612	103,233	17,342	573,277	934,440	935,462	343,822	39,913	167,980	357,345
1960	1,586	28,625	108,312	16,307	511,159	866,843	859,966	339,377	38,034	153,272	..
1959	1,512	29,009	105,645	15,357	508,932	851,707	850,331	327,418	38,237	148,010	..
1958	1,436	27,719	97,238	14,054	481,517	791,426	788,083	295,855	36,678	136,358	..
1957	1,560	28,696	96,416	13,116	448,059	..	724,503	..	37,820	133,216	..

Series R134-144. Selected principal statistics on the manufacturing industries, British Columbia, 1957 to 1975

Year	Number of establish-ments	Production and related workers		Cost of fuel and electricity ($'000)	Cost of materials and supplies used ($'000)	Gross value of production ($'000)	Value of shipments of goods of own manufacture ($'000)	Census value added: manufac-turing activity ($'000)	Total employees		Census value added: total activity ($'000)
		Number	Salaries and wages ($'000)						Number	Salaries and wages ($'000)	
	134	135	136	137	138	139	140	141	142	143	144
1975	3,131	101,701	1,254,927	180,058	3,884,032	7,348,764	7,326,464	3,284,674	137,138	1,804,129	3,383,285
1974	3,309	108,257	1,216,812	178,661	4,013,277	7,492,241	7,411,103	3,300,302	143,964	1,698,586	3,392,543
1973	3,288	111,345	1,074,252	136,936	3,466,642	6,530,866	6,387,094	2,927,288	145,946	1,478,671	3,002,569
1972	3,315	103,597	897,391	117,451	2,709,384	5,038,885	5,020,254	2,212,050	137,237	1,255,357	2,272,210
1971	3,302	96,827	781,068	109,416	2,301,671	4,275,496	4,235,968	1,864,409	129,308	1,099,080	1,912,561
1970	3,253	92,853	675,556	92,024	2,067,782	3,777,197	3,760,567	1,617,392	125,088	971,301	1,663,113
1969	3,329	93,383	646,594	93,508	2,125,598	3,963,630	3,917,832	1,744,524	126,449	922,804	1,788,218
1968	3,331	89,268	574,288	86,547	1,910,838	3,550,399	3,550,399	1,575,436	121,490	826,671	1,615,580
1967	3,384	89,125	532,128	79,743	1,714,610	3,192,333	3,189,977	1,397,955	121,594	769,286	1,430,999
1966	3,444	92,197	510,926	73,496	1,682,834	3,103,443	3,063,675	1,347,065	124,571	731,013	1,381,175
1965	3,502	88,953	462,894	66,965	1,515,454	2,829,277	2,806,165	1,246,867	119,836	660,100	1,280,166
1964	3,597	83,676	411,681	60,275	1,401,893	2,597,896	2,573,832	1,135,779	113,250	590,306	1,170,556
1963	3,561	80,090	376,076	55,639	1,223,543	2,334,798	2,322,273	1,055,799	109,093	541,327	1,085,031
1962	3,618	77,085	347,333	53,063	1,136,238	2,165,130	2,150,532	975,790	105,389	502,348	1,001,394
1961	3,633	75,315	321,850	48,385	1,019,893	1,933,855	1,927,046	865,577	103,546	470,925	888,680
1960	3,616	77,772	321,244	47,992	1,007,018	1,904,740	1,908,543	849,730	98,931	434,557	..
1959	3,632	79,661	312,526	46,566	961,976	1,847,264	1,841,339	838,722	100,091	418,376	..
1958	3,688	78,659	303,727	46,856	951,518	1,756,244	1,751,607	757,870	98,979	403,521	..
1957	3,849	83,557	305,373	41,321	977,170	..	1,737,813	..	104,425	402,395	..

Series R145-147. General statistics on the manufacturing industries, British Columbia,[1] selected years, 1926 to 1959

Year	Total employees	Salaries and wages ($'000)	Census value added by manufacture ($'000)	Year	Total employees	Salaries and wages ($'000)	Census value added by manufacture ($'000)
	145	146	147		145	146	147
				1950	87,375	216,657	479,606
1959	101,168	421,405	848,404	1949	82,934	196,404	409,665
1958	100,222	406,628	786,620	1948	86,599	192,954	417,601
1957	105,631	405,130	767,914	1945	87,914	160,333	307,719
1956	108,595	393,869	824,249	1942	89,539	148,746	272,862
1955	102,408	353,811	750,878	1939	42,532	53,859	103,234
1954	95,867	319,803	651,813	1936	39,718	45,740	87,661
1953	93,844	300,921	615,686	1933	28,394	28,447	58,990
1952	92,667	283,531	556,172	1929	48,127	57,741	113,011
1951	93,647	262,626	592,449	1926	44,915	51,673	92,711

[1] Figures for the Yukon Territory and the Northwest Territories are included with British Columbia prior to 1939.

Series R148-158. Selected principal statistics on the manufacturing industries, the Yukon Territory and the Northwest Territories, 1957 to 1975

Year	Number of establish-ments	Production and related workers		Cost of fuel and electricity ($'000)	Cost of materials and supplies used ($'000)	Gross value of production ($'000)	Value of shipments of goods of own manufacture ($'000)	Census value added: manufac-turing activity ($'000)	Total employees		Census value added: total activity ($'000)
		Number	Salaries and wages ($'000)						Number	Salaries and wages ($'000)	
	148	149	150	151	152	153	154	155	156	157	158
1975	25	215	2,051	251	8,394	13,560	13,561	4,915	265	2,711	5,956
1974	23	194	1,753	186	6,759	10,024	9,020	3,079	241	2,277	3,959
1973	20	162	1,409	159	4,706	7,913	8,100	3,048	210	1,876	3,736
1972	26	179	1,390	195	3,942	6,818	6,911	2,681	222	1,806	3,582
1971	29	200	1,507	158	4,954	7,865	7,717	2,753	221	1,713	3,232
1970	31	225	1,481	82	4,849	7,730	7,332	2,798	250	1,719	3,433
1969	32	153	1,036	93	2,728	5,293	5,226	2,472	213	1,422	3,157
1968	32	134	879	76	2,367	4,573	4,535	2,130	179	1,127	2,569
1967	21	102	716	66	2,155	3,778	3,656	1,557	146	955	1,849
1966	21	111	693	80	2,331	3,900	3,734	1,489	159	933	1,870
1965	15	110	598	86	2,249	3,686	3,637	1,351	162	869	1,641
1964	13	109	554	56	1,795	3,818	3,893	1,967	156	766	2,333
1963	15	104	511	71	1,758	3,310	3,338	1,480	152	726	1,776
1962	16	110	540	73	2,420	3,700	3,588	1,206	153	725	1,232
1961	13	106	524	52	2,570	3,360	3,434	738	146	719	686
1960	14	93	468	49	1,445	2,819	2,928	1,325	124	616	..
1959	11	87	468	51	2,156	2,859	2,695	652	114	610	..
1958	14	110	517	31	2,720	3,591	3,595	840	141	672	..
1957	21	116	468	41	1,611	..	3,041	..	163	652	..

Series R159-161. General statistics on the manufacturing industries the Yukon Territory and the Northwest Territories,[1] selected years, 1926 to 1959

Year	Total employees	Salaries and wages ($'000)	Census value added by manufacture ($'000)	Year	Total employees	Salaries and wages ($'000)	Census value added by manufacture ($'000)
	159	160	161		159	160	161
				1950	123	286	569
1959	115	610	650	1949	148	359	605
1958	145	678	859	1948	137	346	380
1957	166	658	1,410	1945	64	127	518
1956	175	681	1,076	1942	68	106	263
1955	170	605	1,733	1939	55	98	92
1954	191	630	1,856	1936	–	–	–
1953	177	570	1,012	1933	–	–	–
1952	164	530	1,023	1929	–	–	–
1951	152	406	759	1926	–	–	–

[1] Figures for the Yukon Territory and the Northwest Territories are included with British Columbia prior to 1939.

Series R162-172. Selected principal statistics on the food and beverage industries, Canada, 1957 to 1975

Year	Number of establish-ments	Production and related workers		Cost of fuel and electricity ($'000)	Cost of materials and supplies used ($'000)	Gross value of production ($'000)	Value of shipments of goods of own manufacture ($'000)	Census value added: manufac-turing activity ($'000)	Total employees		Census value added: total activity ($'000)
		Number	Salaries and wages ($'000)						Number	Salaries and wages ($'000)	
	162	163	164	165	166	167	168	169	170	171	172
				Basis: 1970 Standard Industrial Classification and New Establishment Concept							
1975	4,740	145,357	1,396,422	193,841	11,325,767	16,549,644	16,492,290	5,030,036	220,415	2,312,018	5,375,417
1974	5,010	144,160	1,181,779	162,623	10,372,159	14,991,724	14,737,733	4,456,942	220,932	1,998,817	4,766,030
1973	5,129	146,676	1,033,417	127,739	8,417,406	12,515,416	12,375,344	3,970,271	222,512	1,756,091	4,222,899
1972	5,377	145,009	932,519	117,479	6,726,089	10,270,171	10,207,275	3,426,603	220,483	1,595,889	3,645,334
1971	5,599	142,427	852,873	109,336	5,899,753	9,169,148	9,111,176	3,160,060	218,315	1,471,184	3,361,324
1970	5,778	143,501	785,273	101,532	5,644,570	8,691,224	8,639,102	2,945,122	221,768	1,383,910	3,122,179
				Basis: 1960 Standard Industrial Classification and New Establishment Concept							
1971	5,599	142,427	852,873	109,336	5,889,753	9,169,148	9,111,176	3,160,060	218,315	1,471,184	3,361,324
1970	5,778	143,501	785,273	101,532	5,644,570	8,691,224	8,639,102	2,945,122	221,768	1,383,910	3,122,179
1969	6,082	140,553	718,760	102,871	5,337,505	8,273,289	8,223,767	2,832,912	224,111	1,293,546	2,992,330
1968	6,361	141,731	668,261	99,410	4,973,389	7,709,527	7,674,300	2,636,728	226,470	1,211,043	2,771,110
1967	6,737	142,172	625,884	95,189	4,850,398	7,462,418	7,429,270	2,516,832	228,748	1,140,377	2,644,474
1966	6,945	140,721	575,146	91,893	4,639,577	7,117,433	7,061,996	2,386,001	227,221	1,057,994	2,498,537
1965	7,150	135,110	522,768	87,681	4,182,451	6,459,576	6,428,799	2,189,443	220,700	971,700	2,295,474
1964	7,407	131,120	486,824	82,125	3,998,764	6,137,773	6,127,245	2,056,885	214,986	905,641	2,161,087
1963	7,528	128,082	455,475	77,455	3,764,887	5,741,712	5,714,198	1,899,370	210,119	848,348	1,986,128
1962	7,678	129,052	441,703	74,591	3,515,847	5,407,584	5,381,572	1,817,145	210,312	817,723	1,896,798
1961	7,734	129,977	425,211	71,226	3,273,280	5,057,680	5,039,544	1,713,173	210,762	783,737	1,782,701
1960	7,598	151,253	495,795	68,443	2,962,518	4,682,489	4,668,363	1,651,528	190,946	681,244	..
1959	7,520	150,454	480,813	67,467	2,949,210	4,604,998	4,622,536	1,588,321	189,180	655,115	..
1958	7,788	149,238	453,582	66,577	2,923,313	4,500,231	4,486,280	1,510,342	187,720	616,153	..
1957	7,931	150,473	431,183	66,405	2,691,887	4,142,396	4,134,738	..	189,104	583,265	..

Series R173-178. General statistics on the food and beverage industries, 1948 Standard Industrial Classification, Canada, selected years, 1870 to 1959

Year	Number of establishments	Number of employees	Salaries and wages ($'000)	Gross value of production ($'000)	Cost of materials ($'000)	Census value added by manufacture ($'000)
	173	174	175	176	177	178
1959	8,165	192,092	662,539	–	2,967,680	1,613,441
1958	8,417	190,445	623,290	4,542,573	2,939,312	1,536,379
1957	8,536	192,177	590,025	4,208,780	2,704,377	1,437,423
1956	8,023	183,008	531,634	3,832,198	2,474,174	1,299,493
1955	8,134	180,085	498,787	3,635,342	2,319,783	1,262,080
1954	8,090	177,883	477,059	3,578,626	2,334,167	1,193,266
1953	8,129	176,649	455,281	3,458,514	2,296,740	1,113,026
1952	8,263	175,552	429,650	3,457,272	2,333,089	1,076,699
1951	8,388	172,493	392,859	3,450,031	2,419,207	985,241
1950	8,401	167,664	346,715	3,029,811	2,102,438	885,322
1949	8,558	170,024	332,536	2,882,582	2,009,246	834,018
1948	8,686	168,893	311,236	2,839,531	2,034,844	766,435
1947	8,869	167,865	276,245	2,383,976	1,656,529	695,093
1946	8,862	160,821	241,770	2,040,709	1,408,819	604,120
1945	8,863	155,672	223,580	1,916,910	1,335,867	555,006
1944	8,979	152,823	212,092	1,880,304	1,328,807	526,450
1943	8,974	138,418	185,198	1,609,637	1,141,015	445,858
1942	9,063	135,085	168,365	1,436,012	976,822	437,892
1941	8,999	129,636	149,025	1,263,837	876,028	368,178
1940	8,958	118,630	128,896	1,007,846	676,765	314,671
1939	9,078	112,131	118,452	876,334	559,170	303,619
1938	9,314	109,264	114,034	870,977	571,669	286,274
1937	9,246	108,003	109,589	884,880	592,984	279,267
1936	9,127	99,814	97,562	787,540	507,836	267,644
1935	9,091	92,988	89,198	686,362	438,761	236,176
1934	9,393	89,551	84,049	641,097	404,636	225,346
1933	9,271	83,356	78,055	545,305	330,780	204,082
1932	9,045	81,006	80,610	555,473	321,798	223,142
1931	9,115	85,517	90,195	660,753	396,545	253,132
1930	8,837	95,613	95,584	846,727	537,575	297,492
1929	8,856	104,253	101,194	962,023	638,194	311,573
1928	8,683	99,060	95,963	944,791	643,480	289,284
1927	8,750	96,702	91,931	889,822	614,937	263,020
1926	8,699	93,845	86,856	846,885	603,931	230,896
1925	8,666	90,956	83,257	829,312	600,908	216,522
1924	8,412	80,681	81,152	753,262	536,995	205,133
1923	8,587	82,317	75,830	717,389	510,393	196,013
1922	8,584	70,108	73,669	709,069	503,610	194,537
1921	8,201	66,974	73,544	755,423	539,327	205,124
1920	8,627	77,158	83,186	1,035,877	775,911	246,521
1919	8,443	76,181	71,648	991,008	757,377	223,457
1918	8,375	70,021	58,559	875,389	655,013	210,180
1917	8,458	64,862	51,663	790,017	581,710	200,053
1910	–	65,459	23,503	280,749	187,260	93,489
1905	5,301	55,632	18,299	190,897	–	–
1900	–	59,231	15,811	153,854	116,975	36,879
1890	12,615	56,959	10,581	118,911	85,046	33,865
1880	5,383	25,802	5,803	82,409	63,516	18,893
1870	4,124	12,413	2,978	63,383	48,205	15,178

Series R179-189. Selected principal statistics on the tobacco products industries, Canada, 1957 to 1975

Year	Number of establish- ments	Production and related workers		Cost of fuel and electricity ($'000)	Cost of materials and supplies used ($'000)	Gross value of production ($'000)	Value of shipments of goods of own manufacture ($'000)	Census value added: manufac- turing activity ($'000)	Total employees		Census value added: total activity ($'000)
		Number	Salaries and wages ($'000)						Number	Salaries and wages ($'000)	
	179	180	181	182	183	184	185	186	187	188	189

Basis: 1970 Standard Industrial Classification and New Establishment Concept

1975	27	6,540	71,806	3,555	506,963	873,870	831,522	363,352	9,686	117,332	366,845
1974	24	6,974	64,200	2,936	417,455	723,087	704,948	302,697	9,596	98,528	306,559
1973	25	6,709	56,434	2,374	341,805	607,250	618,022	263,071	9,403	89,027	265,868
1972	27	6,885	53,246	2,225	326,352	580,668	596,236	252,091	9,525	82,540	254,645
1971	29	7,077	51,381	2,240	328,743	564,272	575,235	233,290	9,680	77,504	235,410
1970	29	7,331	49,522	2,042	346,750	555,936	527,228	207,144	9,992	74,054	208,088

Basis: 1960 Standard Industrial Classification and New Establishment Concept

1971	29	7,077	51,381	2,240	328,743	564,272	575,235	233,290	9,680	77,504	235,410
1970	29	7,331	49,522	2,042	346,750	555,936	527,228	207,144	9,992	74,054	208,088
1969	30	7,361	43,813	1,832	329,657	533,488	487,907	201,999	10,049	66,871	202,962
1968	30	7,505	42,252	1,702	320,785	492,295	508,814	169,808	10,179	63,901	170,751
1967	34	7,873	40,021	1,665	322,943	506,976	493,260	182,369	10,555	59,779	183,986
1966	34	7,819	36,929	1,540	265,336	436,745	429,816	169,869	10,177	53,489	171,022
1965	38	7,880	35,328	1,435	219,013	378,824	379,772	158,376	10,253	50,806	159,994
1964	39	8,219	34,288	1,309	218,876	356,048	348,811	135,863	10,867	49,634	139,166
1963	38	8,583	33,888	1,404	220,995	356,258	355,981	133,859	11,011	48,039	135,582
1962	39	8,413	31,963	1,289	212,294	339,416	346,517	125,833	11,137	47,586	126,755
1961	37	7,854	30,069	1,034	206,584	334,648	334,930	127,030	10,392	43,853	128,393
1960	39	8,159	29,414	975	218,139	335,075	334,370	115,961	9,731	38,354	..
1959	39	8,785	29,675	903	214,388	324,981	324,652	109,690	10,287	38,078	..
1958	39	8,895	29,266	901	207,506	305,530	305,124	97,123	10,319	37,144	..
1957	48	8,588	26,520	845	161,507	249,261	249,156	..	9,905	33,323	..

Series R190-195. General statistics on the tobacco products industries, 1948 Standard Industrial Classification, Canada, selected years, 1870 to 1959

Year	Number of establishments	Number of employees	Salaries and wages ($'000)	Gross value of production ($'000)	Cost of materials ($'000)	Census value added by manufacture ($'000)
	190	191	192	193	194	195
1959	40	10,287	38,078	—	212,771	111,694
1958	40	10,319	37,144	305,863	206,044	98,918
1957	49	9,905	33,323	249,839	160,710	88,284
1956	51	9,613	30,309	239,166	150,111	88,299
1955	56	9,529	29,447	251,973	163,027	88,214
1954	53	9,469	27,869	224,825	144,961	79,175
1953	55	9,494	26,766	213,322	138,491	74,191
1952	61	9,277	25,405	218,271	144,538	73,134
1951	62	9,826	24,438	179,177	119,590	59,033
1950	68	10,322	22,629	188,331	122,611	65,176
1949	72	10,686	21,897	172,420	113,357	58,529
1948	79	10,459	19,550	153,993	95,851	57,667
1947	91	10,880	16,235	146,793	97,121	49,221
1946	95	10,849	14,411	119,634	79,225	39,982
1945	86	12,164	15,738	122,544	79,177	42,986
1944	82	11,780	14,541	98,973	60,110	38,513
1943	85	12,475	13,981	88,419	52,500	35,582
1942	96	12,987	13,079	83,027	48,602	34,103
1941	100	11,374	10,739	68,243	37,216	30,745
1940	102	11,052	10,170	68,996	39,593	29,131
1939	99	10,794	9,761	69,593	41,235	28,111
1938	105	10,438	9,471	67,304	41,445	25,626
1937	109	9,840	8,813	57,745	33,994	23,540
1936	111	9,315	8,363	53,212	30,906	22,099
1935	137	9,634	8,163	47,340	26,509	20,630
1934	149	9,508	7,807	43,054	22,785	20,075
1933	149	9,967	7,750	43,894	23,435	20,269
1932	134	9,675	8,043	46,062	25,540	20,325
1931	105	9,091	8,097	37,126	21,449	15,529
1930	103	8,905	7,838	43,282	24,287	18,853
1929	109	9,333	8,355	43,788	25,656	17,977
1928	115	8,664	8,086	39,386	24,754	14,473
1927	115	8,165	7,604	38,146	24,040	13,948
1926	122	8,455	7,623	41,331	22,588	18,580
1925	128	8,223	7,405	38,776	23,532	15,091
1924	130	8,378	7,338	40,449	17,873	22,421
1923	148	8,689	7,565	40,648	17,951	22,529
1922	142	8,551	7,415	43,092	20,149	22,766
1921	119	9,806	7,599	45,785	23,439	22,159
1920	125	9,276	8,619	53,892	28,388	25,323
1919	144	10,683	7,740	46,931	27,652	18,588
1918	153	10,143	6,500	35,931	19,040	16,722
1917	176	10,236	5,992	33,759	19,093	14,496
1910	—	9,557	4,301	25,484	12,207	13,277
1905	155	7,633	2,844	15,275	—	—
1900	—	7,077	2,653	11,959	3,774	8,185
1890	149	5,325	1,461	5,743	2,502	3,241
1880	96	3,757	729	3,060	1,572	1,488
1870	77	2,216	407	2,435	1,198	1,237

Series R196-206. Selected principal statistics on the rubber and plastics products industries, Canada, 1957 to 1975

Year	Number of establish-ments	Production and related workers		Cost of fuel and electricity ($'000)	Cost of materials and supplies used ($'000)	Gross value of production ($'000)	Value of shipments of goods of own manufacture ($'000)	Census value added: manufac-turing activity ($'000)	Total employees		Census value added: total activity ($'000)
		Number	Salaries and wages ($'000)						Number	Salaries and wages ($'000)	
	196	197	198	199	200	201	202	203	204	205	206

Basis: 1970 Standard Industrial Classification and New Establishment Concept

Year	196	197	198	199	200	201	202	203	204	205	206
1975	771	39,473	355,806	34,722	972,106	1,970,910	1,955,825	964,082	52,963	531,854	1,030,971
1974	783	39,700	315,139	29,548	918,966	1,885,358	1,833,546	936,844	54,173	484,949	1,029,848
1973	740	40,135	295,314	23,998	733,269	1,583,019	1,577,303	825,752	54,377	442,123	885,409
1972	694	36,076	245,616	21,229	596,798	1,337,898	1,317,313	719,871	49,100	372,587	762,833
1971	664	32,593	204,821	17,133	529,032	1,161,996	1,163,894	615,831	44,672	313,461	649,369
1970	622	32,495	189,579	15,356	507,135	1,085,802	1,073,270	563,311	44,189	289,648	589,449

Basis: 1960 Standard Industrial Classification and New Establishment Concept

Year	196	197	198	199	200	201	202	203	204	205	206
1971	106	15,571	112,314	9,623	290,930	660,303	662,556	359,750	23,755	184,671	387,829
1970	107	16,064	107,369	8,882	298,005	641,796	634,959	334,909	24,032	174,925	354,286
1969	104	16,898	104,688	8,607	298,920	639,276	632,748	331,749	25,259	171,187	349,721
1968	104	16,364	93,116	7,948	256,192	567,423	565,339	303,283	24,833	154,959	318,300
1967	107	18,390	97,644	7,938	270,487	585,388	584,357	306,962	26,906	155,953	321,877
1966	104	19,579	95,870	7,523	260,339	552,710	540,540	284,848	27,821	148,753	299,171
1965	96	18,185	85,938	6,707	223,052	477,187	474,489	247,429	26,206	134,151	259,667
1964	95	17,575	79,354	6,315	208,955	433,673	426,624	218,403	24,972	122,530	228,333
1963	93	16,879	71,846	5,921	189,212	389,746	386,730	194,613	24,162	110,974	204,603
1962	90	15,664	66,331	5,550	170,771	356,849	353,962	180,528	22,788	104,203	187,712
1961	93	14,298	57,524	5,276	150,069	325,192	331,135	169,847	21,821	95,737	175,685
1960	89	15,113	57,766	5,223	153,840	332,874	328,459	173,811	20,298	84,531	..
1959	86	15,736	60,399	5,425	161,816	362,438	354,045	195,197	21,082	86,884	..
1958	87	14,746	52,139	5,034	129,641	312,486	314,792	177,811	19,948	76,497	..
1957	86	16,766	58,096	5,006	145,567	327,520	334,778	..	22,181	83,215	..

Series R207-212. General statistics on the rubber and plastics products industries, 1948 Standard Industrial Classification, Canada, selected years, 1870 to 1959

Year	Number of establishments	Number of employees	Salaries and wages ($'000)	Gross value of production ($'000)	Cost of materials ($'000)	Census value added by manufacture ($'000)
	207	208	209	210	211	212
1959	89	21,093	86,859	—	160,397	188,179
1958	89	19,943	76,445	308,430	128,573	174,828
1957	88	22,178	83,190	325,664	144,247	176,456
1956	91	23,136	82,155	364,173	160,687	198,602
1955	82	21,913	73,775	329,946	137,075	188,698
1954	73	20,894	67,477	259,937	106,502	149,435
1953	72	22,600	70,995	290,441	114,337	172,380
1952	70	21,582	65,477	285,650	120,799	161,488
1951	67	23,054	64,358	311,678	146,951	161,185
1950	61	21,812	54,263	239,185	101,774	134,062
1949	62	20,729	48,172	178,504	73,896	101,706
1948	56	21,703	48,273	194,112	84,223	107,000
1947	60	23,475	46,614	196,308	82,935	110,673
1946	60	22,055	37,813	159,408	62,136	93,451
1945	55	23,490	39,111	181,413	78,501	98,836
1944	56	21,421	35,979	169,511	81,188	82,813
1943	51	15,913	25,343	130,158	68,298	59,952
1942	49	15,497	23,413	122,231	61,576	58,896
1941	56	17,191	22,792	119,138	59,340	58,089
1940	52	14,297	16,835	83,021	38,228	43,404
1939	54	14,160	15,604	69,945	28,813	39,800
1938	53	12,879	14,062	61,031	24,301	35,492
1937	50	13,035	14,041	74,264	31,127	41,797
1936	50	11,881	11,954	62,055	23,599	37,199
1935	45	11,023	11,017	55,950	20,259	34,502
1934	51	11,079	10,859	55,230	18,440	35,598
1933	45	9,758	8,910	41,512	12,915	27,521
1932	47	10,325	9,341	40,747	11,907	27,756
1931	48	12,158	11,708	52,691	17,630	33,893
1930	47	15,163	15,895	73,753	28,822	43,608
1929	44	17,796	20,135	96,935	42,941	52,537
1928	45	17,095	18,944	97,209	45,119	50,791
1927	44	15,065	16,622	91,414	44,725	45,460
1926	39	13,587	14,708	86,508	49,902	35,408
1925	40	12,962	14,144	78,230	38,389	38,773
1924	38	10,778	11,413	57,412	24,468	31,861
1923	40	11,646	12,329	56,513	26,336	29,030
1922	62	10,369	10,623	46,487	19,295	26,080
1921	44	9,908	9,868	39,989	17,104	21,804
1920	35	15,238	16,199	80,717	41,838	37,500
1919	32	12,676	11,546	56,004	27,535	27,633
1918	30	10,842	8,501	46,280	21,508	23,778
1917	28	10,258	7,270	43,639	19,760	23,150
1910	—	1,869	937	7,046	3,608	3,438
1905	21	1,179	619	3,061	—	—
1900	—	762	336	1,589	977	612
1890	19	1,388	359	2,060	1,422	638
1880	4	525	177	771	478	293
1870	4	494	83	503	358	145

Series R213-223. Selected principal statistics on the leather industries, Canada, 1957 to 1975

Year	Number of establishments	Production and related workers		Cost of fuel and electricity ($'000)	Cost of materials and supplies used ($'000)	Gross value of production ($'000)	Value of shipments of goods of own manufacture ($'000)	Census value added: manufacturing activity ($'000)	Total employees		Census value added: total activity ($'000)
		Number	Salaries and wages ($'000)						Number	Salaries and wages ($'000)	
	213	214	215	216	217	218	219	220	221	222	223

Basis: 1970 Standard Industrial Classification and New Establishment Concept

Year	213	214	215	216	217	218	219	220	221	222	223
1975	415	23,440	158,242	4,659	308,751	622,657	619,191	309,247	26,834	200,819	316,474
1974	432	22,831	139,457	4,060	294,271	579,575	570,139	281,244	26,444	177,296	291,625
1973	417	23,561	122,444	3,456	271,578	514,661	508,813	239,627	27,251	158,581	248,174
1972	443	23,616	112,363	3,211	231,638	452,621	447,133	217,772	27,279	145,892	224,428
1971	470	24,273	108,682	3,025	205,483	421,576	420,208	213,067	27,930	140,015	219,153
1970	487	24,286	100,359	2,857	194,529	396,504	397,415	199,119	28,286	131,433	203,434

Basis: 1960 Standard Industrial Classification and New Establishment Concept

Year	213	214	215	216	217	218	219	220	221	222	223
1971	470	24,273	108,682	3,025	205,483	421,576	420,208	213,067	27,930	140,015	219,153
1970	487	24,286	100,359	2,857	194,529	396,504	397,415	199,119	28,286	131,433	203,434
1969	521	26,530	104,299	3,000	205,057	415,410	412,274	207,353	31,192	137,530	211,388
1968	513	27,017	100,033	2,927	192,767	397,612	396,242	201,918	31,741	131,879	204,455
1967	529	26,773	92,039	2,750	179,435	365,993	369,115	183,808	31,496	121,760	185,742
1966	537	27,847	90,329	2,587	192,696	377,044	370,910	181,760	32,589	117,671	183,474
1965	544	28,083	84,825	2,584	173,468	343,543	343,055	167,491	32,585	109,806	170,208
1964	543	27,994	82,075	2,488	165,445	331,746	328,055	163,812	32,404	105,673	164,970
1963	539	28,037	77,683	2,414	158,129	314,051	314,533	153,507	32,647	102,140	154,711
1962	547	28,009	75,708	2,355	161,979	310,294	309,178	145,960	32,960	100,425	147,065
1961	556	27,543	70,972	2,275	151,426	294,160	291,161	140,458	33,283	97,442	142,136
1960	580	26,312	64,628	2,251	133,299	264,891	265,667	129,341	30,266	83,448	..
1959	572	27,417	65,223	2,284	144,713	277,822	273,093	130,825	31,415	83,539	..
1958	591	26,811	62,619	2,319	126,236	250,152	250,886	121,597	30,784	80,311	..
1957	614	27,549	61,920	2,371	123,386	242,340	240,938	..	31,573	78,773	..

Series R224-229. General statistics on the leather industries, 1948 Standard Industrial Classification, Canada, selected years, 1870 to 1959

Year	Number of establishments	Number of employees	Salaries and wages ($'000)	Gross value of production ($'000)	Cost of materials ($'000)	Census value added by manufacture ($'000)
	224	225	226	227	228	229
1959	586	31,012	82,735	—	143,766	129,812
1958	598	30,151	78,684	246,027	124,664	119,088
1957	624	31,099	77,769	241,013	122,530	116,139
1956	646	31,384	74,970	238,946	123,791	112,857
1955	646	30,575	68,971	219,722	108,962	108,644
1954	673	30,748	67,161	202,511	101,251	99,194
1953	695	33,068	70,965	223,927	116,416	105,454
1952	701	32,103	66,153	215,846	115,714	98,156
1951	711	31,578	59,669	221,883	135,114	84,885
1950	747	32,990	57,810	210,563	121,218	87,419
1949	747	34,900	59,700	210,804	117,869	91,158
1948	757	34,291	55,123	203,759	114,819	86,948
1947	792	35,724	52,629	212,430	123,894	86,646
1946	776	37,290	49,713	192,749	108,703	82,319
1945	706	34,123	43,269	167,888	95,005	71,298
1944	650	31,925	40,050	155,424	88,757	65,172
1943	646	31,821	38,053	152,915	88,393	63,050
1942	645	32,698	35,323	140,954	85,068	54,529
1941	598	31,827	31,217	117,744	70,577	45,961
1940	591	27,898	24,692	93,825	53,880	38,884
1939	606	26,859	22,978	81,537	46,420	34,140
1938	598	25,160	20,946	69,961	38,011	31,056
1937	618	26,852	22,244	82,645	49,087	32,600
1936	610	25,477	19,937	72,462	41,691	29,824
1935	597	24,691	19,372	68,629	38,856	28,854
1934	604	23,000	17,451	61,367	33,611	26,890
1933	597	21,726	16,549	57,536	30,455	26,309
1932	556	20,428	17,230	54,516	27,653	26,099
1931	579	21,009	18,982	62,136	31,908	29,474
1930	562	21,041	20,098	72,807	40,001	31,987
1929	603	23,500	23,416	90,976	52,409	37,670
1928	636	24,518	24,332	103,624	62,688	39,960
1927	648	24,299	24,098	97,386	55,971	40,308
1926	661	23,520	23,490	90,191	51,933	37,143
1925	682	21,874	21,286	80,776	46,333	33,477
1924	700	22,361	22,219	81,515	45,652	34,758
1923	761	22,578	22,602	84,942	47,892	35,985
1922	748	21,824	21,964	84,034	44,722	38,237
1921	757	20,525	19,858	82,751	46,272	35,383
1920	471	21,807	23,448	129,788	84,039	44,605
1919	932	23,063	20,928	126,738	84,012	41,813
1918	922	20,714	15,420	93,118	58,293	33,854
1917	863	20,670	15,238	103,952	61,002	42,072
1910	—	25,108	11,908	64,068	35,045	29,023
1905	533	19,836	7,892	42,132	—	—
1900	—	35,135	12,056	52,435	32,808	19,627
1890	7,774	25,677	7,553	35,209	18,700	16,509
1880	6,809	27,457	6,701	36,456	21,871	14,585
1870	6,381	25,646	5,884	27,911	14,845	13,066

Series R230-240. Selected principal statistics on the textile industries, Canada, 1957 to 1975

Year	Number of establish-ments	Production and related workers		Cost of fuel and electricity ($'000)	Cost of materials and supplies used ($'000)	Gross value of production ($'000)	Value of shipments of goods of own manufacture ($'000)	Census value added: manufac-turing activity ($'000)	Total employees		Census value added: total activity ($'000)
		Number	Salaries and wages ($'000)						Number	Salaries and wages ($'000)	
	230	231	232	233	234	235	236	237	238	239	240

Basis: 1970 Standard Industrial Classification and New Establishment Concept

1975	923	56,450	435,869	51,515	1,344,492	2,463,884	2,439,005	1,067,877	71,050	614,644	1,099,789
1974	936	59,789	415,307	43,920	1,357,879	2,535,345	2,477,765	1,133,547	75,647	589,296	1,173,826
1973	914	61,255	381,971	33,641	1,188,967	2,192,676	2,183,210	970,068	76,863	537,423	1,001,922
1972	910	59,115	340,660	31,091	1,051,735	1,932,372	1,919,425	849,547	74,242	480,835	873,339
1971	915	55,150	297,265	26,361	939,239	1,691,425	1,697,932	725,825	69,350	422,780	751,116
1970	931	55,159	272,553	23,257	859,189	1,572,259	1,575,783	689,813	69,714	393,047	706,788

Basis: 1960 Standard Industrial Classification and New Establishment Concept

1971	935	57,263	310,816	27,853	989,396	1,781,176	1,786,591	763,927	72,547	446,137	789,255
1970	953	57,031	284,006	24,382	902,517	1,651,624	1,655,319	724,725	72,616	413,283	741,687
1969	973	59,582	281,177	23,900	946,744	1,718,608	1,688,357	747,964	75,351	399,543	759,714
1968	967	57,840	253,898	22,801	847,929	1,523,183	1,526,824	652,453	73,234	364,097	661,218
1967	990	60,161	243,351	21,673	795,599	1,418,853	1,404,939	601,581	77,360	359,553	612,500
1966	980	59,928	230,609	20,306	767,236	1,364,010	1,346,906	576,469	77,248	341,414	585,232
1965	960	60,522	217,054	19,348	709,835	1,287,586	1,276,657	558,403	76,676	315,082	569,574
1964	939	58,963	202,035	17,844	663,672	1,223,483	1,204,563	541,968	74,455	291,933	549,764
1963	922	55,193	178,984	16,298	601,691	1,107,392	1,099,838	489,403	70,276	263,380	497,383
1962	895	52,929	164,627	15,758	540,706	994,218	981,379	437,754	67,918	243,021	446,598
1961	884	50,274	150,532	15,114	470,792	875,063	874,487	389,157	64,969	224,645	397,120
1960	886	48,433	141,114	14,672	423,492	800,326	795,930	362,162	60,726	202,628	..
1959	854	49,518	137,237	14,806	423,705	791,680	785,623	353,169	62,304	198,640	..
1958	875	49,196	128,870	14,631	386,982	718,165	725,250	316,552	62,005	188,161	..
1957	902	54,026	139,934	15,217	407,063	736,034	736,147	..	67,046	197,664	..

Series R241-246. General statistics on the textile industries, 1948 Standard Industrial Classification, Canada,
selected years, 1870 to 1959

Year	Number of establishments	Number of employees	Salaries and wages ($'000)	Gross value of production ($'000)	Cost of materials ($'000)	Census value added by manufacture ($'000)
	241	242	243	244	245	246
1959	879	63,579	202,904	—	429,641	363,536
1958	903	63,472	193,328	732,095	394,621	322,533
1957	929	68,512	201,579	758,814	412,434	330,985
1956	965	70,873	199,328	769,250	430,420	323,821
1955	977	69,144	187,805	742,257	408,891	319,549
1954	975	64,581	170,196	631,529	350,114	269,169
1953	959	73,190	184,605	711,005	388,325	309,546
1952	918	72,739	178,689	737,155	418,523	305,640
1951	892	81,710	185,030	846,477	495,304	337,936
1950	846	80,328	169,175	741,263	412,683	315,557
1949	847	77,773	156,167	636,824	339,645	285,641
1948	722	75,816	141,002	604,946	331,943	261,775
1947	714	73,618	115,774	513,326	289,987	213,700
1946	684	66,889	95,074	401,231	215,853	177,176
1945	622	65,295	87,616	389,146	217,290	163,723
1944	593	64,017	84,666	387,470	217,165	162,040
1943	584	65,947	83,214	397,293	233,164	156,130
1942	577	69,032	81,471	409,171	230,430	170,826
1941	509	66,511	70,853	345,016	187,356	150,451
1940	488	58,585	59,685	283,971	150,816	126,419
1939	440	47,849	44,258	183,716	93,363	84,820
1938	433	45,640	40,237	155,050	80,344	69,984
1937	444	49,839	44,736	192,792	106,769	81,032
1936	443	47,669	40,791	175,412	93,695	76,938
1935	434	46,539	37,875	161,928	84,724	72,616
1934	428	44,631	36,410	156,644	80,458	71,739
1933	414	40,036	31,827	133,162	64,975	64,258
1932	384	36,979	30,854	110,820	52,790	54,516
1931	378	36,771	32,322	121,715	59,411	58,888
1930	347	36,479	31,464	137,340	75,371	58,596
1929	339	39,347	34,889	173,377	98,157	71,693
1928	335	40,045	35,229	171,041	100,923	66,562
1927	319	38,365	32,751	160,306	89,566	67,445
1926	289	35,922	29,233	157,126	94,888	59,207
1925	292	34,710	27,240	147,494	94,668	49,682
1924	295	32,818	25,233	140,948	88,593	49,667
1923	312	34,351	28,191	151,322	85,525	62,921
1922	288	32,883	26,422	135,016	69,231	62,769
1921	343	28,359	24,282	131,018	71,272	56,433
1920	335	33,743	29,593	197,191	120,264	73,543
1919	296	30,488	22,212	173,345	104,187	66,570
1918	280	29,684	18,840	155,195	93,798	58,901
1917	276	28,605	16,179	105,650	59,640	44,240
1910	—	25,919	9,721	51,674	29,454	22,220
1905	334	21,229	7,045	33,061	—	—
1900	—	27,392	7,919	33,010	17,644	15,366
1890	3,996	25,491	5,848	26,043	13,537	12,506
1880	1,835	13,418	2,595	15,376	9,077	6,299
1870	996	7,466	1,374	9,666	6,231	3,435

Series R247-257. Selected principal statistics on the knitting mills industries, Canada, 1957 to 1975

Year	Number of establish-ments	Production and related workers		Cost of fuel and electricity ($'000)	Cost of materials and supplies used ($'000)	Gross value of production ($'000)	Value of shipments of goods of own manufacture ($'000)	Census value added: manufacturing activity ($'000)	Total employees		Census value added: total activity ($'000)
		Number	Salaries and wages ($'000)						Number	Salaries and wages ($'000)	
	247	248	249	250	251	252	253	254	255	256	257

Basis: 1970 Standard Industrial Classification and New Establishment Concept

Year	247	248	249	250	251	252	253	254	255	256	257
1975	306	21,567	141,853	6,331	323,764	624,167	624,490	294,072	24,682	182,833	294,497
1974	320	22,421	126,855	5,668	330,581	613,464	600,631	277,215	25,540	163,883	277,340
1973	310	22,849	111,067	4,551	288,705	539,453	530,127	246,197	25,879	143,058	245,545
1972	311	21,752	99,292	4,018	248,939	471,907	470,083	218,950	24,732	127,626	218,299
1971	318	20,885	88,868	3,498	252,374	458,298	455,055	202,426	23,919	116,331	202,855
1970	318	20,658	81,779	3,217	232,900	414,423	414,690	178,306	23,735	106,985	178,881

Basis: 1960 Standard Industrial Classification and New Establishment Concept

Year	247	248	249	250	251	252	253	254	255	256	257
1971	318	20,885	88,868	3,498	252,374	458,298	455,055	202,426	23,919	116,331	202,855
1970	318	20,658	81,779	3,217	232,900	414,423	414,690	178,306	23,735	106,985	178,881
1969	333	21,578	80,886	2,974	227,137	410,551	402,637	180,440	24,704	104,850	181,088
1968	342	20,615	71,072	2,747	209,199	382,199	377,069	170,252	23,845	94,334	170,607
1967	339	19,720	63,915	2,549	179,461	325,043	325,543	143,033	22,814	85,434	143,805
1966	347	20,493	61,948	2,401	179,261	324,682	320,931	143,020	23,609	82,478	143,283
1965	361	20,911	59,701	2,329	174,335	311,536	308,890	134,871	24,070	78,661	134,907
1964	364	19,840	54,623	2,125	157,821	282,712	277,347	122,766	22,972	72,383	122,807
1963	359	19,457	49,856	1,994	144,125	256,289	254,611	110,170	22,573	66,551	110,219
1962	351	19,161	47,412	2,014	131,488	236,614	233,506	103,112	22,816	63,730	103,185
1961	358	18,667	44,990	1,927	117,069	220,312	219,378	101,316	22,691	62,189	101,206
1960	356	18,476	42,622	1,790	103,835	200,633	199,566	95,008	21,179	55,283	..
1959	313	19,005	42,384	1,943	98,360	192,686	190,522	92,383	21,376	53,338	..
1958	316	18,729	40,191	1,897	88,431	175,572	174,467	85,244	21,272	50,794	..
1957	306	19,587	41,406	2,014	88,908	176,364	173,617	..	22,110	51,484	..

Series R258-263. General statistics on the knitting mills industries, 1948 Standard Industrial Classification, Canada, selected years, 1870 to 1959

Year	Number of establishments	Number of employees	Salaries and wages ($'000)	Gross value of production ($'000)	Cost of materials ($'000)	Census value added by manufacture ($'000)
	258	259	260	261	262	263
1959	319	20,992	52,187	—	98,659	—
1958	321	20,936	49,829	174,448	88,610	83,975
1957	310	21,661	50,217	174,896	88,782	84,148
1956	286	21,913	49,638	166,998	83,926	81,159
1955	296	21,658	47,208	155,044	75,706	77,466
1954	297	21,622	47,578	147,723	70,119	75,755
1953	294	24,413	52,421	160,792	77,704	81,264
1952	288	23,234	48,961	162,821	80,374	80,619
1951	295	25,188	49,000	169,720	84,403	83,523
1950	293	25,255	44,141	146,226	68,718	75,853
1949	290	26,442	43,949	143,020	64,704	76,672
1948	271	27,634	42,807	148,556	69,115	77,807
1947	262	26,511	35,647	127,838	59,558	66,851
1946	247	24,941	30,211	105,209	47,272	56,681
1945	216	23,654	26,640	88,035	40,424	46,369
1944	200	22,939	25,535	84,218	39,133	43,882
1943	191	22,344	23,850	80,209	38,532	40,505
1942	186	23,462	23,423	80,134	38,550	40,485
1941	181	24,362	22,424	77,122	39,128	36,977
1940	172	23,225	20,696	69,427	35,755	32,755
1939	174	21,312	17,778	57,670	27,384	29,458
1938	174	20,031	16,154	49,505	23,049	25,713
1937	171	20,250	16,229	52,856	26,447	25,654
1936	168	19,429	15,120	49,469	24,361	24,338
1935	163	18,511	14,253	46,390	22,948	22,689
1934	167	17,978	13,566	44,957	21,831	22,377
1933	170	17,159	12,610	40,997	19,473	20,803
1932	169	17,655	13,475	43,253	19,350	23,198
1931	161	17,698	13,949	47,758	22,052	25,034

Series R258-263. General statistics on the knitting mills industries, 1948 Standard Industrial Classification, Canada, selected years, 1870 to 1959 (concluded)

Year	Number of establishments	Number of employees	Salaries and wages ($'000)	Gross value of production ($'000)	Cost of materials ($'000)	Census value added by manufacture ($'000)
	258	259	260	261	262	263
1930	167	18,570	15,057	54,118	25,510	27,949
1929	168	19,609	16,294	61,098	31,194	29,172
1928	165	17,974	15,057	58,552	31,252	26,608
1927	168	17,217	14,177	55,222	28,270	26,234
1926	167	16,474	13,312	53,676	29,213	23,770
1925	162	14,698	11,858	48,555	27,120	20,791
1924	158	13,917	11,090	44,506	24,758	19,140
1923	153	14,755	11,262	47,522	24,344	22,509
1922	141	14,179	10,572	44,963	22,544	21,719
1921	127	10,446	8,399	36,690	18,960	17,131
1920	128	14,024	11,072	56,737	34,238	21,729
1919	114	12,384	8,404	45,207	26,636	18,030
1918	108	12,627	7,231	45,755	26,527	18,616
1917	102	11,662	6,496	33,771	19,443	13,886
1910[1]	–	–	–	–	–	–
1905[1]	–	–	–	–	–	–
1900[1]	–	–	–	–	–	–
1890[1]	–	–	–	–	–	–
1880[1]	–	–	–	–	–	–
1870[1]	–	–	–	–	–	–

[1] Knitting mills included with clothing industries, series R275–280.

Series R264-274. Selected principal statistics on the clothing industries, Canada, 1957 to 1975

Year	Number of establishments	Production and related workers		Cost of fuel and electricity ($'000)	Cost of materials and supplies used ($'000)	Gross value of production ($'000)	Value of shipments of goods of own manufacture ($'000)	Census value added: manufacturing activity ($'000)	Total employees		Census value added: total activity ($'000)
		Number	Salaries and wages ($'000)						Number	Salaries and wages ($'000)	
	264	265	266	267	268	269	270	271	272	273	274
				Basis: 1970 Standard Industrial Classification and New Establishment Concept							
1975	2,094	89,347	573,274	7,856	1,201,314	2,314,844	2,306,619	1,105,674	100,528	722,130	1,143,188
1974	2,172	90,003	500,573	7,059	1,101,594	2,103,376	2,076,645	994,723	101,704	634,746	1,024,534
1973	2,120	92,673	448,593	6,112	981,813	1,870,256	1,837,587	882,331	104,300	569,612	903,143
1972	2,151	90,745	404,403	5,053	868,162	1,662,419	1,645,146	789,204	102,043	514,502	801,257
1971	2,164	87,495	362,021	4,560	776,852	1,490,498	1,487,773	709,806	98,457	461,021	716,175
1970	2,184	86,617	334,079	4,163	711,266	1,367,984	1,371,041	652,554	97,418	425,673	659,131
				Basis: 1960 Standard Industrial Classification and New Establishment Concept							
1971	2,164	87,495	362,021	4,560	776,852	1,490,498	1,487,773	709,086	98,457	461,021	716,175
1970	2,184	86,617	334,079	4,163	711,266	1,367,984	1,371,041	652,554	97,418	425,673	659,131
1969	2,289	87,214	321,035	4,186	698,687	1,339,477	1,331,832	636,603	99,091	412,543	642,872
1968	2,282	85,395	292,060	4,109	661,990	1,266,232	1,258,268	600,133	97,596	378,694	605,399
1967	2,311	85,422	270,432	4,069	614,267	1,176,065	1,176,755	557,730	98,263	356,027	564,732
1966	2,333	86,177	258,626	3,853	617,003	1,164,522	1,152,575	543,666	99,708	342,044	547,574
1965	2,315	84,668	240,286	3,584	572,833	1,071,828	1,063,401	495,411	98,659	321,730	498,694
1964	2,335	82,945	224,443	3,355	536,363	1,003,936	991,729	464,218	96,408	299,938	467,290
1963	2,294	78,736	204,124	3,167	501,017	932,017	924,223	427,834	92,305	277,089	431,297
1962	2,308	76,729	193,001	3,098	461,695	867,143	860,477	402,349	91,652	265,140	404,856
1961	2,307	76,741	180,880	3,018	427,256	808,917	802,719	378,644	93,306	256,123	381,368
1960	2,306	75,124	169,689	2,960	400,716	767,511	762,967	363,835	86,367	225,632	..
1959	2,258	74,805	168,089	2,908	397,650	757,587	751,806	357,029	86,181	222,595	..
1958	2,362	75,012	161,704	2,973	385,911	733,670	734,358	344,786	86,208	213,296	..
1957	2,445	77,717	162,598	3,168	394,501	735,260	735,264	..	89,425	213,478	..

Series R275-280. General statistics on the clothing industries, 1948 Standard Industrial Classification, Canada, selected years, 1870 to 1959

Year	Number of establishments	Number of employees	Salaries and wages ($'000)	Gross value of production ($'000)	Cost of materials ($'000)	Census value added by manufacture ($'000)
	275	276	277	278	279	280
1959	2,359	87,678	227,513	–	401,132	–
1958	2,460	87,740	217,973	747,460	389,244	355,057
1957	2,550	91,114	218,959	754,389	398,406	352,614
1956	2,525	89,799	208,216	739,733	399,249	337,266
1955	2,648	89,686	196,437	689,192	359,883	326,308
1954	2,733	89,693	191,495	648,351	339,959	305,510
1953	2,788	95,658	202,005	705,008	361,558	341,058
1952	2,753	94,434	191,579	684,415	363,583	318,557
1951	2,788	90,545	173,365	610,292	320,944	287,149
1950	2,758	90,993	167,082	587,988	308,833	277,037
1940	2,768	91,310	162,564	584,479	306,425	276,069
1948	2,829	87,471	149,060	561,133	292,102	267,222
1947	2,859	83,818	131,305	486,757	251,461	233,676
1946	2,741	80,927	116,055	446,123	238,298	206,337
1945	2,460	76,305	104,838	388,719	211,477	175,938
1944	2,190	71,975	95,020	357,533	196,596	159,690
1943	2,088	75,367	93,204	358,095	206,062	150,771
1942	2,078	78,396	88,753	340,857	198,087	141,519
1941	1,822	71,473	73,335	273,399	160,234	112,054
1940	1,690	62,422	59,403	220,312	127,934	91,421
1939	1,706	56,704	50,853	172,038	94,790	76,372
1938	1,705	54,468	47,848	159,700	87,149	71,716
1937	1,695	55,978	48,720	173,039	97,687	74,495
1936	1,620	51,916	43,394	157,922	89,039	68,055
1935	1,586	48,709	40,030	146,851	83,019	63,055
1934	1,566	46,433	36,639	139,344	79,195	59,410
1933	1,494	42,036	31,907	118,412	65,937	51,745
1932	1,327	39,585	33,003	115,372	62,516	52,234
1931	1,289	42,911	39,895	142,686	78,700	63,312
1930	1,220	45,981	44,381	164,936	91,208	73,115
1929	1,250	48,582	48,531	189,466	101,424	87,451
1928	1,251	48,643	48,165	188,340	103,421	84,221
1927	1,206	46,497	45,214	171,693	92,641	78,364
1926	1,111	42,728	42,094	159,490	89,029	69,834
1925	1,060	39,916	38,485	141,099	78,247	62,265
1924	1,026	38,266	37,288	133,606	71,454	61,597
1923	992	38,596	37,994	133,118	71,628	60,957
1922	894	36,824	36,141	127,584	67,266	59,667
1921	850	33,547	35,709	137,501	80,256	56,650
1920	980	41,222	45,228	182,615	105,617	76,390
1919	912	41,248	36,835	160,218	88,503	71,317
1918	834	38,509	27,970	125,328	68,171	56,595
1917	794	38,753	25,248	114,800	58,644	55,736
1910[1]	–	58,239	24,501	95,151	48,242	46,909
1905[1]	1,811	44,483	15,631	59,699	–	–
1900[1]	–	68,321	16,987	54,191	27,177	27,014
1890[1]	11,589	48,540	10,127	43,851	22,204	21,647
1880[1]	4,469	32,163	5,347	26,697	15,521	11,176
1870[1]	2,594	17,123	2,754	15,019	8,620	6,399

[1] Includes knitting mills.

Series R281-291. Selected principal statistics on the wood industries, Canada, 1957 to 1975

Year	Number of establishments	Production and related workers		Cost of fuel and electricity ($'000)	Cost of materials and supplies used ($'000)	Gross value of production ($'000)	Value of shipments of goods of own manufacture ($'000)	Census value added: manufacturing activity ($'000)	Total employees		Census value added: total activity ($'000)
		Number	Salaries and wages ($'000)						Number	Salaries and wages ($'000)	
	281	282	283	284	285	286	287	288	289	290	291

Basis: 1970 Standard Industrial Classification and New Establishment Concept

1975	2,920	81,588	846,138	79,405	2,098,283	3,732,230	3,802,635	1,554,542	97,717	1,070,932	1,689,596
1974	3,111	89,297	822,983	74,869	2,242,475	4,025,438	3,991,121	1,708,093	106,620	1,038,109	1,747,416
1973	3,063	94,818	755,805	64,497	2,181,369	4,192,738	4,055,996	1,946,872	111,600	938,843	1,976,683
1972	3,085	87,733	623,248	52,958	1,647,175	3,097,453	3,084,899	1,397,320	102,699	770,902	1,422,423
1971	3,164	78,420	517,425	43,500	1,295,814	2,342,253	2,346,945	1,002,939	91,846	638,202	1,016,958
1970	3,330	75,225	446,439	36,274	1,138,722	1,964,760	1,951,475	789,764	87,829	551,880	801,788

Basis: 1960 Standard Industrial Classification and New Establishment Concept

1971	3,164	78,420	517,425	43,500	1,295,814	2,342,253	2,346,945	1,002,939	91,846	638,202	1,016,958
1970	3,330	75,225	446,439	36,274	1,138,722	1,964,760	1,951,475	789,764	87,829	551,880	801,788
1969	3,503	79,646	439,285	37,414	1,209,892	2,198,522	2,149,584	951,215	92,524	541,323	963,911
1968	3,477	77,662	396,392	33,842	1,052,390	1,982,292	1,966,340	896,061	90,309	490,721	909,732
1967	3,793	77,428	364,575	31,307	912,692	1,677,283	1,675,642	733,283	89,873	451,192	750,956
1966	3,919	79,159	348,294	30,737	879,931	1,603,238	1,592,797	692,570	91,937	429,116	708,883
1965	4,206	78,389	322,232	29,564	818,177	1,502,918	1,487,600	655,177	91,589	398,939	668,894
1964	4,594	76,278	295,095	27,749	771,101	1,419,991	1,395,911	621,141	89,407	367,005	634,739
1963	4,779	72,836	269,759	25,176	685,784	1,282,877	1,276,848	571,917	86,888	340,750	586,681
1962	5,017	70,279	247,957	23,626	624,133	1,158,229	1,154,377	510,470	83,466	311,975	524,794
1961	5,243	67,532	226,212	20,460	581,239	1,038,201	1,036,179	436,501	82,085	292,700	451,583
1960	5,730	69,101	222,360	17,743	562,404	1,010,759	1,007,333	430,612	82,734	278,189	..
1959	6,002	72,190	216,818	17,174	552,701	1,017,562	1,015,657	447,687	86,181	271,219	..
1958	6,021	69,508	209,367	16,581	522,788	956,791	956,768	417,422	83,788	261,041	..
1957	6,808	72,941	208,818	15,666	529,836	945,698	944,710	..	88,163	259,610	..

Series R292-297. General statistics on the wood industries, 1948 Standard Industrial Classification, Canada, selected years, 1870 to 1959

Year	Number of establishments	Number of employees	Salaries and wages ($'000)	Gross value of production ($'000)	Cost of materials ($'000)	Census value added by manufacture ($'000)
	292	293	294	295	296	297
1959	9,808	123,791	387,862	—	761,354	644,856
1958	9,848	120,922	369,582	1,343,975	717,463	605,678
1957	10,796	126,839	368,660	1,336,016	730,076	585,783
1956	11,103	135,583	376,349	1,454,957	788,465	646,223
1955	11,804	133,673	354,440	1,376,128	723,815	633,395
1954	12,165	128,931	323,122	1,193,672	623,757	553,407
1953	12,462	134,310	325,620	1,248,022	649,731	583,389
1952	12,467	130,468	299,431	1,170,551	618,980	537,076
1951	11,975	131,278	283,062	1,153,377	610,808	529,300
1950	11,301	126,169	246,325	985,859	510,564	463,854
1949	11,191	121,632	224,903	840,356	436,638	393,929
1948	10,495	124,306	214,742	839,045	428,914	401,402
1947	9,744	120,434	186,468	771,403	398,879	365,050
1946	8,846	105,472	142,339	560,341	297,924	256,437
1945	7,710	96,048	124,435	474,298	251,592	217,538
1944	7,590	93,385	117,966	442,096	231,469	205,775
1943	7,118	90,860	109,493	395,295	202,195	186,947
1942	7,219	93,180	103,060	379,504	194,896	178,856
1941	6,505	88,794	88,503	327,011	169,172	153,113
1940	6,401	76,744	70,791	259,324	134,487	120,664
1939	5,681	65,794	57,433	198,899	102,561	93,749
1938	5,638	62,831	53,825	180,168	95,884	81,819
1937	5,526	66,511	55,712	200,028	104,479	93,088
1936	5,284	57,354	44,975	158,234	82,200	73,776
1935	5,296	52,185	38,578	133,106	69,057	61,980
1934	5,184	47,566	33,245	114,954	58,082	54,948
1933	5,197	41,118	27,550	94,103	48,478	43,857
1932	5,217	42,906	31,479	100,124	51,737	46,594
1931	5,193	51,529	45,104	150,835	78,995	69,725
1930	5,213	77,426	63,912	238,064	127,721	108,085
1929	4,823	83,778	76,806	289,931	154,095	133,359
1928	4,660	80,042	71,766	273,061	146,719	123,967
1927	4,281	76,341	67,759	252,073	134,819	114,907
1926	4,280	64,246	65,532	242,425	128,953	111,133
1925	4,258	63,165	62,734	233,502	126,920	104,191
1924	4,424	63,822	64,268	239,341	131,415	105,623
1923	4,542	63,484	63,476	244,258	124,369	117,697
1922	4,546	57,840	55,411	207,894	104,804	100,898
1921	4,716	53,205	53,514	208,093	98,910	106,999
1920	5,122	73,032	78,224	335,592	167,300	165,626
1919	4,923	102,325	87,058	322,211	121,876	198,154
1918	4,556	86,766	69,504	224,335	85,003	137,352
1917	4,427	93,187	63,532	202,138	80,760	119,473
1910	—	117,130	45,251	182,352	93,182	89,170
1905	3,054	84,595	33,724	109,721	—	—
1900	—	98,386	26,261	90,470	44,837	45,633
1890	11,553	79,982	21,405	84,544	42,661	41,883
1880	9,636	59,930	12,560	54,922	28,264	26,658
1870	9,751	50,551	9,191	40,862	21,380	19,482

Series R298-308. Selected principal statistics on the furniture and fixtures industries, Canada, 1957 to 1975

Year	Number of establish-ments	Production and related workers		Cost of fuel and electricity ($'000)	Cost of materials and supplies used ($'000)	Gross value of production ($'000)	Value of shipments of goods of own manufacture ($'000)	Census value added: manufac-turing activity ($'000)	Total employees		Census value added: total activity ($'000)
		Number	Salaries and wages ($'000)						Number	Salaries and wages ($'000)	
	298	299	300	301	302	303	304	305	306	307	308
Basis: 1970 Standard Industrial Classification and New Establishment Concept											
1975	1,959	41,460	329,384	11,848	642,136	1,361,848	1,363,703	707,864	49,688	431,897	724,645
1974	2,233	42,633	303,332	10,847	666,842	1,364,659	1,338,179	686,970	51,441	402,267	700,318
1973	2,137	40,507	255,891	8,848	545,423	1,135,823	1,118,534	581,552	49,051	340,706	595,718
1972	2,158	38,475	222,538	8,354	460,446	964,974	958,348	496,173	46,942	299,296	505,673
1971	2,165	35,011	187,115	7,287	375,291	790,591	786,564	408,013	43,021	253,530	414,999
1970	2,209	34,497	173,338	6,790	341,258	733,275	731,465	385,226	42,238	235,186	389,864
Basis: 1960 Standard Industrial Classification and New Establishment Concept											
1971	2,165	35,011	187,115	7,287	375,291	790,591	786,564	408,013	43,021	253,530	414,999
1970	2,209	34,497	173,338	6,790	341,258	733,275	731,465	385,226	42,238	235,186	389,864
1969	2,313	36,098	171,800	7,395	340,450	736,933	728,992	389,089	44,248	232,847	395,026
1968	2,300	35,117	154,488	6,525	312,168	665,498	660,281	346,805	43,171	211,140	351,880
1967	2,296	35,836	147,331	6,067	302,565	643,417	640,196	334,784	43,895	201,833	339,881
1966	2,282	35,735	139,956	5,626	288,113	607,760	602,711	314,021	43,598	189,781	319,054
1965	2,262	32,702	120,506	5,248	257,614	530,190	525,213	267,327	40,374	164,112	272,100
1964	2,216	30,598	107,961	4,561	232,607	474,939	470,312	237,771	37,986	148,201	242,077
1963	2,104	28,874	96,988	4,156	205,833	424,156	421,599	214,166	35,916	134,442	217,792
1962	2,144	27,601	90,282	4,085	187,748	390,489	386,569	198,655	34,362	125,172	201,416
1961	2,087	26,740	83,007	3,892	173,242	361,207	359,574	184,074	33,475	117,119	187,328
1960	2,070	27,211	82,061	3,800	164,162	342,523	341,989	174,561	33,738	111,006	..
1959	1,898	27,166	80,698	3,831	165,974	340,493	338,151	170,688	33,328	108,308	..
1958	1,835	26,457	74,580	3,670	153,700	317,260	316,878	159,890	32,411	99,685	..
1957	1,986	27,421	75,281	3,774	155,817	318,677	314,802	..	33,594	99,758	..

Series R309-319. Selected principal statistics on the paper and allied industries, Canada, 1957 to 1975

Year	Number of establish-ments	Production and related workers		Cost of fuel and electricity ($'000)	Cost of materials and supplies used ($'000)	Gross value of production ($'000)	Value of shipments of goods of own manufacture ($'000)	Census value added: manufac-turing activity ($'000)	Total employees		Census value added: total activity ($'000)
		Number	Salaries and wages ($'000)						Number	Salaries and wages ($'000)	
	309	310	311	312	313	314	315	316	317	318	319
Basis: 1970 Standard Industrial Classification and New Establishment Concept											
1975	665	95,794	1,054,795	418,836	3,346,680	7,163,043	7,131,614	3,397,527	127,342	1,553,080	3,469,803
1974	650	99,696	1,086,609	426,636	3,455,927	7,770,997	7,667,438	3,888,434	131,275	1,525,816	3,945,031
1973	649	93,123	885,584	284,067	2,535,690	5,258,409	5,271,027	2,438,652	123,138	1,248,340	2,476,434
1972	654	91,188	804,920	256,760	2,211,344	4,396,539	4,414,017	1,928,434	120,758	1,135,298	1,961,576
1971	642	90,086	731,326	243,687	2,023,370	4,039,445	4,000,851	1,772,389	119,709	1,039,306	1,803,683
1970	635	90,679	684,092	213,991	1,952,698	3,948,091	3,930,522	1,781,402	121,080	978,114	1,816,987
Basis: 1960 Standard Industrial Classification and New Establishment Concept											
1971	645	90,533	734,837	244,242	2,034,289	4,065,107	4,028,239	1,786,576	120,435	1,045,416	1,820,071
1970	638	91,174	687,755	214,544	1,963,911	3,972,455	3,955,435	1,794,000	121,883	984,453	1,830,971
1969	640	91,617	651,268	208,196	1,920,638	3,841,408	3,833,814	1,712,574	121,877	926,270	1,748,172
1968	635	88,568	584,041	189,853	1,753,820	3,422,902	3,422,015	1,479,229	117,959	836,084	1,505,910
1967	633	89,491	549,486	180,879	1,642,593	3,257,884	3,231,176	1,434,412	118,609	781,885	1,458,212
1966	623	88,414	514,675	171,482	1,559,415	3,185,480	3,165,664	1,454,583	116,840	727,120	1,477,123
1965	601	83,994	450,434	158,338	1,385,512	2,891,276	2,881,996	1,347,426	110,180	634,425	1,364,618
1964	605	81,397	418,590	144,998	1,274,800	2,715,887	2,707,345	1,296,089	106,309	588,358	1,313,675
1963	591	77,719	383,217	132,166	1,140,388	2,453,695	2,452,437	1,181,141	101,556	541,195	1,193,397
1962	580	77,141	369,715	127,953	1,080,364	2,338,969	2,333,578	1,130,652	100,075	518,784	1,146,972
1961	567	76,058	352,948	122,271	1,020,320	2,212,890	2,203,517	1,070,299	98,292	493,444	1,082,526
1960	565	76,040	338,844	116,088	978,958	2,129,476	2,125,895	1,034,430	95,281	458,223	..
1959	544	76,194	321,372	113,780	938,249	2,033,551	2,030,093	981,522	94,435	431,801	..
1958	546	75,140	305,542	110,532	885,869	1,909,493	1,894,559	913,092	93,227	410,855	..
1957	571	76,960	306,273	113,321	891,628	1,877,683	1,877,712	..	95,067	406,021	..

Series R320-325. General statistics on the paper and allied industries, 1948 Standard Industrial Classification, Canada, selected years, 1870 to 1959

Year	Number of establishments	Number of employees	Salaries and wages ($'000)	Gross value of production ($'000)	Cost of materials ($'000)	Census value added by manufacture ($'000)
	320	321	322	323	324	325
1959	559	94,231	430,365	—	935,329	980,578
1958	562	92,935	409,578	1,904,217	883,156	910,693
1957	582	94,283	403,286	1,874,483	883,395	877,986
1956	568	93,705	386,887	1,901,271	885,056	908,727
1955	580	89,750	349,777	1,754,932	793,008	867,149
1954	569	87,370	331,556	1,633,725	742,032	803,412
1953	555	84,436	310,107	1,566,543	717,460	765,566
1952	543	82,965	292,682	1,516,240	694,190	742,308
1951	547	82,889	276,521	1,589,842	683,488	827,925
1950	528	77,519	225,197	1,251,144	541,261	638,111
1949	524	76,471	208,349	1,093,060	494,300	532,289
1948	522	75,980	197,398	1,061,360	485,238	509,993
1947	502	73,445	168,632	911,239	410,457	443,374
1946	486	67,442	134,320	695,086	313,411	333,820
1945	475	60,819	109,627	536,860	255,266	241,121
1944	456	56,823	101,618	495,189	226,018	230,482
1943	452	54,995	94,847	461,403	207,420	216,494
1942	446	55,199	92,150	448,577	197,423	213,670
1941	432	53,186	83,830	437,382	183,775	217,991
1940	419	47,954	71,978	375,797	151,882	191,868
1939	405	42,707	58,092	269,632	114,698	129,022
1938	405	42,604	55,853	242,077	103,029	114,436
1937	393	44,757	61,717	286,690	123,696	133,044
1936	369	40,101	50,862	233,221	97,500	109,271
1935	362	36,949	45,612	205,142	79,996	101,868
1934	360	35,830	42,517	192,585	73,375	96,672
1933	339	32,287	34,925	157,509	64,895	73,226
1932	329	32,256	36,560	169,368	65,500	83,570
1931	351	35,913	45,292	217,250	85,053	108,783
1930	346	42,626	55,918	261,621	104,975	129,991
1929	324	43,530	60,622	290,950	121,401	143,720
1928	322	42,218	56,732	277,346	111,373	140,999
1927	308	40,978	54,489	259,205	105,275	129,485
1926	290	38,610	51,994	248,831	102,066	125,973
1925	283	34,889	45,431	222,615	91,815	112,624
1924	276	34,388	44,772	207,790	86,861	103,153
1923	262	36,104	45,825	216,176	86,795	110,727
1922	249	32,253	39,736	188,074	78,055	93,846
1921	236	30,751	40,746	179,167	75,382	88,421
1920	277	39,163	53,559	278,728	106,074	155,840
1919	306	34,408	38,841	169,840	68,412	89,052
1918	302	32,903	32,079	143,880	56,920	74,574
1917	290	30,485	25,450	120,370	45,707	66,011
1910	—	15,180	7,626	32,999	15,477	17,522
1905	136	11,099	4,685	18,761	—	—
1900	—	9,221	3,347	12,420	5,416	7,004
1890	155	4,689	1,455	6,206	3,160	3,046
1880	83	2,186	576	2,976	1,628	1,348
1870	29	1,464	295	1,725	874	851

Series R326-336. Selected principal statistics on the printing, publishing and allied industries, Canada, 1957 to 1975

Year	Number of establish-ments	Production and related workers — Number	Production and related workers — Salaries and wages ($'000)	Cost of fuel and electricity ($'000)	Cost of materials and supplies used ($'000)	Gross value of production ($'000)	Value of shipments of goods of own manufacture ($'000)	Census value added: manufac-turing activity ($'000)	Total employees — Number	Total employees — Salaries and wages ($'000)	Census value added: total activity ($'000)
	326	327	328	329	330	331	332	333	334	335	336

Basis: 1970 Standard Industrial Classification and New Establishment Concept

Year	326	327	328	329	330	331	332	333	334	335	336
1975	3,618	55,044	587,431	15,980	1,016,868	2,904,178	2,897,471	1,871,330	92,912	1,042,556	1,899,375
1974	3,812	52,764	505,481	14,785	882,885	2,572,878	2,550,516	1,675,208	92,425	929,939	1,700,326
1973	3,773	51,479	439,258	12,235	700,262	2,171,793	2,160,309	1,459,296	90,593	811,834	1,484,626
1972	3,725	49,877	393,902	11,113	608,559	1,859,089	1,853,532	1,239,417	86,071	712,463	1,263,749
1971	3,649	49,026	357,770	10,166	543,026	1,655,331	1,653,839	1,102,138	84,110	649,508	1,125,285
1970	3,600	49,671	337,788	9,169	510,291	1,544,666	1,545,320	1,025,206	84,045	606,958	1,039,238

Basis: 1960 Standard Industrial Classification and New Establishment Concept

Year	326	327	328	329	330	331	332	333	334	335	336
1971	3,649	49,026	357,770	10,166	543,026	1,655,331	1,653,839	1,102,138	84,110	649,508	1,125,285
1970	3,600	49,671	337,788	9,169	510,291	1,544,666	1,545,320	1,005,206	84,045	606,958	1,039,238
1969	3,650	47,804	309,843	9,935	487,131	1,493,471	1,488,302	996,404	84,654	576,928	1,010,503
1968	3,600	48,145	289,379	9,440	448,168	1,374,004	1,370,351	916,397	84,143	535,237	931,213
1967	3,568	47,877	269,501	8,572	428,418	1,299,072	1,297,275	862,082	83,594	497,916	877,722
1966	3,507	46,837	251,918	8,199	394,917	1,211,820	1,204,664	808,704	81,996	463,662	820,512
1965	3,465	44,746	230,592	7,560	346,677	1,088,967	1,085,229	734,730	78,737	422,225	748,200
1964	3,439	43,132	213,007	7,159	315,504	987,729	983,921	665,065	75,448	385,687	676,013
1963	3,452	43,419	203,922	6,886	298,383	930,667	927,922	625,397	75,166	371,074	635,861
1962	3,485	42,849	196,312	6,828	284,078	895,367	893,722	604,461	74,544	356,096	614,113
1961	3,450	43,448	187,394	6,534	271,522	856,264	854,832	578,207	75,193	343,620	589,584
1960	3,410	44,139	185,781	6,329	268,632	847,243	845,828	572,282	73,049	320,281	..
1959	3,300	43,794	178,677	5,941	256,237	809,283	804,769	547,105	71,622	304,828	..
1958	3,258	43,058	169,228	5,780	236,905	743,667	742,625	500,982	69,738	284,158	..
1957	3,340	43,663	160,029	5,833	228,514	704,300	704,298	..	70,944	269,169	..

Series R337-342. General statistics on the printing, publishing and allied industries, 1948 Standard Industrial Classification, Canada, selected years, 1870 to 1959

Year	Number of establishments	Number of employees	Salaries and wages ($'000)	Gross value of production ($'000)	Cost of materials ($'000)	Census value added by manufacture ($'000)
	337	338	339	340	341	342
1959	4,359	73,926	308,264	–	267,305	552,888
1958	4,433	72,221	287,971	763,128	248,244	509,065
1957	4,584	74,559	274,455	732,684	245,024	481,737
1956	4,585	72,361	254,373	689,954	225,202	459,224
1955	4,494	69,602	234,580	620,464	199,162	416,305
1954	4,227	68,614	220,276	579,283	188,726	385,944
1953	4,157	66,530	205,626	545,415	175,222	366,027
1952	4,124	64,485	186,251	489,073	160,394	324,800
1951	4,019	64,694	170,829	452,143	152,753	295,643
1950	3,869	63,125	154,370	413,012	135,510	274,099
1949	3,866	61,834	141,490	377,908	124,684	250,163
1948	2,496	54,541	119,088	307,346	96,385	208,208
1947	2,430	51,832	101,185	262,577	82,317	177,895
1946	2,379	48,731	86,113	221,689	65,258	154,349
1945	2,288	43,374	73,994	186,204	52,455	131,858
1944	2,272	40,389	66,594	167,155	47,151	118,220
1943	2,281	39,097	62,497	155,727	44,655	109,309
1942	2,349	39,083	59,150	145,541	43,384	100,416
1941	2,338	39,716	57,929	141,198	42,526	96,952
1940	2,297	37,737	53,049	125,815	36,019	88,194
1939	2,291	37,594	51,377	119,543	33,922	84,127
1938	2,273	37,459	50,565	117,593	32,768	83,354
1937	2,198	36,789	49,249	117,546	32,753	83,331
1936	2,184	35,346	46,354	110,345	29,325	79,592
1935	2,140	34,207	44,159	105,133	27,857	75,894
1934	2,126	32,980	41,846	99,010	25,741	71,924
1933	2,057	31,951	40,382	92,589	23,319	67,974
1932	1,966	32,515	44,525	101,316	26,402	73,611
1931	1,881	33,826	49,919	117,400	29,992	86,113

Series R337-342. General statistics on the printing, publishing and allied industries, 1948 Standard Industrial Classification, Canada, selected years, 1870 to 1959 (concluded)

Year	Number of establishments	Number of employees	Salaries and wages ($'000)	Gross value of production ($'000)	Cost of materials ($'000)	Census value added by manufacture ($'000)
	337	338	339	340	341	342
1930	1,831	34,877	52,722	133,040	34,975	96,746
1929	1,828	35,417	52,788	140,471	36,901	102,256
1928	1,811	33,633	48,882	129,285	35,009	93,070
1927	1,720	31,397	44,154	115,903	31,502	83,232
1926	1,647	29,415	41,501	105,756	29,302	75,359
1925	1,575	28,541	39,124	100,428	28,428	70,977
1924	1,625	27,707	38,177	98,483	27,868	69,449
1923	1,491	27,550	37,149	96,355	26,471	68,780
1922	1,520	26,853	35,610	93,780	24,560	68,196
1921	1,556	25,739	35,245	97,393	29,194	67,229
1920	1,779	29,088	37,337	104,521	33,415	70,064
1919	1,591	26,063	28,151	75,633	22,813	52,028
1918	1,556	24,000	21,922	60,258	19,454	40,000
1917	1,617	24,267	20,403	57,355	15,616	41,077
1910	—	17,939	10,957	26,486	7,813	18,673
1905	812	15,736	8,660	20,041	—	—
1900	—	13,359	6,243	14,200	3,990	10,210
1890	719	9,814	3,853	10,456	3,721	6,735
1880	489	6,915	2,256	6,785	2,605	4,180
1870	372	4,298	1,405	4,128	1,492	2,636

Series R343-353. Selected principal statistics on the primary metals industries, Canada, 1957 to 1975

Year	Number of establishments	Production and related workers		Cost of fuel and electricity ($'000)	Cost of materials and supplies used ($'000)	Gross value of production ($'000)	Value of shipments of goods of own manufacture ($'000)	Census value added: manufacturing activity ($'000)	Total employees		Census value added: total activity ($'000)
		Number	Salaries and wages ($'000)						Number	Salaries and wages ($'000)	
	343	344	345	346	347	348	349	350	351	352	353
				Basis: 1970 Standard Industrial Classification and New Establishment Concept							
1975	380	90,169	1,119,159	317,595	3,641,157	6,838,656	6,682,356	2,879,904	120,335	1,612,991	2,948,174
1974	397	94,538	1,052,519	276,034	3,535,568	6,657,991	6,535,413	2,846,389	122,219	1,455,671	2,911,812
1973	403	89,853	897,352	211,895	2,464,532	4,927,338	4,917,993	2,250,911	116,462	1,237,900	2,308,876
1972	413	86,335	781,209	186,299	2,102,098	4,205,714	4,193,421	1,917,318	113,958	1,108,809	1,960,592
1971	405	86,452	714,600	183,414	1,967,763	3,963,336	3,948,458	1,812,159	114,314	1,017,713	1,841,779
1970	407	88,839	680,780	170,690	2,025,371	3,965,148	3,918,548	1,769,087	116,545	958,507	1,808,878
				Basis: 1960 Standard Industrial Classification and New Establishment Concept							
1971	405	86,452	714,600	183,414	1,967,763	3,963,336	3,948,458	1,812,159	114,314	1,017,713	1,841,779
1970	407	88,839	680,780	170,690	2,025,371	3,965,148	3,918,548	1,769,087	116,545	958,507	1,808,878
1969	417	83,564	583,498	142,501	1,817,165	3,581,015	3,574,422	1,621,348	110,953	839,046	1,667,477
1968	405	86,237	570,183	142,944	1,733,408	3,391,220	3,384,248	1,514,867	113,023	803,456	1,534,444
1967	415	86,784	541,970	131,955	1,544,684	3,060,249	3,052,537	1,383,609	112,945	754,681	1,408,728
1966	408	87,748	518,347	128,229	1,593,497	3,108,928	3,085,130	1,387,202	113,645	716,557	1,414,996
1965	401	83,443	478,482	119,893	1,436,349	2,889,165	2,854,069	1,332,922	107,504	651,267	1,365,613
1964	398	77,770	427,710	106,304	1,312,594	2,555,392	2,546,923	1,136,495	100,407	583,191	1,163,390
1963	394	72,352	383,355	93,346	1,147,133	2,234,274	2,220,977	993,795	94,107	528,422	1,015,942
1962	398	71,127	363,650	88,719	1,057,236	2,076,053	2,069,840	930,098	91,713	496,878	946,538
1961	407	69,655	348,088	88,754	967,869	1,940,111	1,936,996	883,488	89,956	475,320	898,608
1960	404	71,704	345,886	88,096	1,555,515	2,734,473	2,728,774	1,090,862	89,258	451,057	..
1959	397	71,730	336,117	82,914	1,457,394	2,588,572	2,565,093	1,048,264	88,385	434,180	..
1958	403	65,906	289,332	73,666	1,212,041	2,305,335	2,199,318	1,019,628	82,468	385,777	..
1957	418	75,447	324,176	78,934	1,387,616	2,472,903	2,472,248	..	92,293	414,524	..

Series R354-359. General statistics on the iron and steel products industries, 1948 Standard Industrial Classification, Canada, selected years, 1870 to 1959

Year	Number of establishments	Number of employees	Salaries and wages ($'000)	Gross value of production ($'000)	Cost of materials ($'000)	Census value added by manufacture ($'000)
	354	355	356	357	358	359
1959	3,246	192,969	861,446	—	1,486,322	—
1958	3,254	179,440	757,173	2,670,092	1,270,710	1,342,827
1957	3,073	198,555	807,093	2,924,476	1,386,921	1,472,278
1956	2,963	196,918	766,376	2,825,690	1,315,814	1,444,536
1955	2,895	181,700	667,657	2,258,717	1,005,247	1,198,726
1954	2,801	173,698	605,526	1,962,256	829,238	1,087,283
1953	2,698	188,236	643,474	2,116,534	906,165	1,158,915
1952	2,625	189,191	617,011	2,188,026	947,993	1,187,037
1951	2,435	183,323	547,315	1,904,650	860,565	991,335
1950	2,390	164,528	438,245	1,524,384	662,332	817,060
1949	2,347	163,622	413,228	1,419,146	619,500	760,934
1948	2,263	170,071	400,878	1,320,527	570,290	709,347
1947	2,200	162,399	334,044	1,064,654	451,267	580,342
1946	2,086	151,373	279,568	824,766	337,982	461,502
1945	1,921	169,653	314,534	953,782	396,102	528,280
1944	1,913	192,145	363,713	1,130,769	467,437	631,753
1943	1,778	213,601	394,657	1,264,947	525,441	705,833
1942	1,674	188,291	321,063	1,051,647	432,030	588,404
1941	1,530	138,737	218,306	767,653	315,022	428,708
1940	1,230	95,224	134,125	483,141	211,142	255,320
1939	1,199	73,560	93,117	321,282	130,797	179,017
1938	1,201	73,722	90,291	295,083	122,881	161,532
1937	1,166	77,975	96,203	336,183	147,799	175,927
1936	1,141	65,350	74,459	249,043	105,092	133,509
1935	1,115	58,594	65,186	208,802	88,586	110,674
1934	1,118	50,701	53,952	172,688	71,506	92,974
1933	1,153	42,778	42,631	125,968	49,213	70,570
1932	1,099	45,914	49,489	137,102	54,004	77,061
1931	1,112	62,585	75,994	234,362	92,300	133,799
1930	1,093	77,694	103,513	343,788	142,824	190,223
1929	1,069	90,334	123,601	435,291	185,354	236,857
1928	1,051	80,273	108,128	378,194	159,031	207,323
1927	1,038	74,003	95,788	326,224	135,869	179,769
1926	1,034	69,285	87,966	300,546	131,014	160,027
1925	966	59,185	73,921	245,176	104,867	131,285
1924	915	57,388	70,604	230,133	100,515	119,298
1923	914	62,460	78,987	283,207	133,031	140,903
1922	941	55,115	64,847	206,519	93,007	105,324
1921	1,048	61,858	77,761	267,405	121,802	135,986
1920	1,347	85,365	115,374	449,221	205,706	225,598
1919	1,269	78,589	92,740	351,103	143,959	182,456
1918	1,214	90,085	104,460	496,305	247,970	212,430
1917	1,184	91,915	92,057	448,576	226,982	197,996
1910	—	66,816	38,761	143,240	66,750	76,490
1905	972	43,475	22,018	69,514	—	—
1900	—	41,802	17,697	51,983	22,181	29,802
1890	12,727	45,600	16,186	55,871	23,543	32,328
1880	10,478	35,206	10,238	34,183	14,446	19,737
1870	8,091	28,260	7,883	24,914	9,217	15,697

Series R360-370. Selected principal statistics on the metal fabricating industries,[1] Canada, 1957 to 1975

Year	Manufacturing activity							Total activity		
	Number of establishments	Production and related workers		Cost of fuel and electricity ($'000)	Cost of materials and supplies used ($'000)	Gross value of production ($'000)	Value of shipments of goods of own manufacture ($'000)	Census value added: manufacturing activity ($'000)	Total employees		Census value added: total activity ($'000)
		Number	Salaries and wages ($'000)						Number	Salaries and wages ($'000)	
	360	361	362	363	364	365	366	367	368	369	370

Basis: 1970 Standard Industrial Classification and New Establishment Concept

1975	3,882	117,106	1,241,513	61,289	3,056,957	6,267,877	6,216,654	3,149,631	150,899	1,727,946	3,278,286
1974	4,021	117,605	1,119,803	55,475	2,897,111	5,985,739	5,833,972	3,033,153	153,745	1,568,346	3,190,913
1973	3,932	111,043	940,437	44,188	2,239,851	4,605,599	4,539,418	2,321,560	144,921	1,313,501	2,437,659
1972	4,020	105,219	817,383	39,334	1,847,256	3,848,935	3,821,990	1,962,345	138,309	1,150,517	2,049,396
1971	4,143	103,890	749,349	36,870	1,697,565	3,548,171	3,535,379	1,813,736	137,015	1,060,181	1,889,307
1970	4,067	107,156	724,514	34,419	1,630,684	3,382,830	3,357,086	1,717,726	140,701	1,020,409	1,788,556

Basis: 1960 Standard Industrial Classification and New Establishment Concept

1971	4,109	102,937	741,954	36,637	1,684,723	3,519,170	3,506,877	1,797,810	135,839	1,050,858	1,873,196
1970	4,031	106,160	717,029	34,189	1,618,750	3,353,488	3,327,639	1,700,549	139,471	1,011,060	1,771,304
1969	3,991	105,409	662,245	34,671	1,520,883	3,187,685	3,162,039	1,632,131	141,417	957,930	1,705,444
1968	3,983	101,319	587,170	32,256	1,392,189	2,917,966	2,899,875	1,493,521	137,559	864,199	1,562,217
1967	3,956	103,116	559,680	30,712	1,310,830	2,745,903	2,732,066	1,404,551	139,232	817,639	1,463,965
1966	3,811	107,187	552,362	29,974	1,370,407	2,788,145	2,763,696	1,387,936	143,311	794,770	1,446,240
1965	3,581	99,839	478,655	27,457	1,246,332	2,502,345	2,466,811	1,228,592	133,992	691,525	1,295,719
1964	3,455	89,873	413,120	24,479	1,071,812	2,149,736	2,137,178	1,053,596	121,021	602,707	1,101,784
1963	3,116	83,185	368,172	22,505	946,412	1,887,659	1,877,234	918,635	113,278	543,982	962,909
1962	3,069	79,441	341,502	21,463	861,867	1,738,922	1,725,984	855,500	109,575	509,582	896,432
1961	2,964	72,156	300,215	19,718	735,817	1,510,083	1,510,625	754,549	101,054	457,886	788,347
1960	2,756	71,547	290,938	18,675	666,231	1,412,061	1,412,485	727,155	96,877	423,818	..
1959	2,576	73,758	291,845	18,727	683,512	1,435,229	1,420,315	732,990	99,049	419,920	..
1958	2,591	70,349	264,771	17,445	614,569	1,299,424	1,302,787	667,410	94,261	382,430	..
1957	2,425	76,978	281,777	18,406	640,090	1,331,292	1,330,034	..	101,013	395,247	..

[1] Excludes machinery and transportation equipment.

Series R371-376. General statistics on the non-ferrous metals products industries, 1948 Standard Industrial Classification, Canada, selected years, 1870 to 1959

Year	Number of establishments	Number of employees	Salaries and wages ($'000)	Gross value of production ($'000)	Cost of materials ($'000)	Census value added by manufacture ($'000)
	371	372	373	374	375	376
1959	580	52,025	236,728	–	1,076,051	–
1958	593	51,301	226,614	1,527,623	930,931	526,932
1957	592	54,581	228,268	1,691,622	1,014,416	611,975
1956	581	56,071	220,370	1,871,846	1,128,962	672,097
1955	581	53,311	201,110	1,634,631	974,792	597,439
1954	573	50,494	182,191	1,263,124	717,966	484,867
1953	551	52,058	178,710	1,241,712	726,128	457,881
1952	552	50,938	167,045	1,218,686	744,596	418,488
1951	536	50,114	150,734	1,253,599	797,412	406,617
1950	536	44,680	119,536	960,752	606,692	311,539
1949	532	44,698	114,591	867,043	537,218	289,125
1948	503	46,048	108,779	844,598	556,238	248,226
1947	503	43,344	91,047	668,075	434,518	201,163
1946	474	40,855	75,856	484,619	311,084	148,492
1945	436	44,221	81,890	548,853	337,872	180,653
1944	401	55,480	100,605	709,275	428,904	239,329
1943	374	62,594	109,967	788,620	506,003	234,957
1942	371	51,261	84,891	692,697	412,325	241,181
1941	368	40,364	61,684	548,445	328,666	190,390
1940	351	29,197	42,409	410,780	249,437	140,344
1939	336	24,302	33,974	327,000	202,731	107,347
1938	333	24,087	33,033	344,571	216,709	111,679
1937	335	22,908	31,431	383,599	240,837	127,153
1936	326	19,898	25,589	278,876	182,299	91,808

Series R371-376. General statistics on the non-ferrous metals products industries, 1948 Standard Industrial Classification, Canada, selected years, 1870 to 1959 (concluded)

Year	Number of establishments	Number of employees	Salaries and wages ($'000)	Gross value of production ($'000)	Cost of materials ($'000)	Census value added by manufacture ($'000)
	371	372	373	374	375	376
1935	323	18,064	22,721	227,370	149,497	73,226
1934	314	16,520	19,878	186,999	98,405	84,215
1933	304	13,506	15,671	127,753	57,487	66,771
1932	283	12,399	16,493	98,846	47,519	46,278
1931	292	16,207	23,637	130,284	62,959	60,539
1930	280	18,188	26,059	145,881	68,627	69,937
1929	269	18,996	27,778	169,749	75,276	87,341
1928	269	17,375	24,742	144,295	59,961	78,284
1927	271	16,630	23,542	121,811	54,879	59,719
1926	271	14,849	20,575	113,734	60,417	46,487
1925	256	13,623	19,242	99,611	48,633	44,233
1924	239	13,521	18,165	78,888	38,279	34,923
1923	233	13,109	17,955	72,093	31,362	34,592
1922	232	10,976	14,332	53,285	20,487	30,326
1921	249	10,310	13,255	49,371	20,058	24,927
1920	240	14,699	21,962	97,548	43,766	45,086
1919	956	15,493	18,745	93,503	47,628	40,533
1918	642	15,770	18,627	114,924	64,084	42,113
1917	621	16,827	17,251	125,702	66,962	52,737
1910	—	12,810	8,471	59,845	26,811	33,034
1905	151	14,896	9,144	37,893	—	—
1900	—	6,202	3,200	12,785	4,136	8,649
1890	741	4,771	2,027	7,400	3,357	4,043
1880	524	3,276	1,170	4,000	1,770	2,230
1870	274	1,618	476	1,594	673	921

Series R377-387. Selected principal statistics on the machinery industries,[1] Canada, 1957 to 1975

Year	Manufacturing activity								Total activity		
	Number of establishments	Production and related workers		Cost of fuel and electricity ($'000)	Cost of materials and supplies used ($'000)	Gross value of production ($'000)	Value of shipments of goods of own manufacture ($'000)	Census value added: manufacturing activity ($'000)	Total employees		Census value added: total activity ($'000)
		Number	Salaries and wages ($'000)						Number	Salaries and wages ($'000)	
	377	378	379	380	381	382	383	384	385	386	387
		Basis: 1970 Standard Industrial Classification and New Establishment Concept									
1975	1,098	63,699	698,998	27,411	1,999,276	3,792,397	3,731,625	1,765,710	92,290	1,073,613	2,046,762
1974	1,074	59,708	594,785	23,404	1,663,113	3,248,318	3,137,820	1,561,801	89,155	943,565	1,785,522
1973	1,005	54,216	481,318	19,104	1,324,196	2,508,925	2,431,899	1,165,625	81,640	772,468	1,337,275
1972	961	49,975	409,701	17,084	1,137,144	2,151,004	2,134,648	996,776	77,437	676,016	1,144,875
1971	913	45,712	350,173	14,357	968,026	1,855,595	1,865,818	873,212	71,062	584,534	1,010,465
1970	851	47,457	334,123	13,037	899,851	1,796,431	1,776,686	883,543	80,534	640,960	1,222,695
		Basis: 1960 Standard Industrial Classification and New Establishment Concept									
1971	910	45,279	348,102	14,311	958,352	1,842,660	1,851,282	869,997	70,434	580,807	1,001,138
1970	848	46,912	331,892	13,004	887,004	1,778,985	1,759,766	878,977	79,725	636,243	1,216,093
1969	830	48,749	322,398	12,768	883,235	1,774,175	1,734,673	878,173	81,747	602,881	1,162,465
1968	795	44,357	269,355	11,470	735,139	1,484,008	1,480,375	737,399	76,360	520,131	1,006,918
1967	752	47,506	273,220	11,232	779,260	1,527,470	1,516,875	736,978	79,171	505,095	967,909
1966	726	46,839	258,016	10,527	767,127	1,500,417	1,464,217	722,764	75,451	455,083	925,008
1965	684	43,007	224,124	9,286	648,831	1,290,219	1,235,388	632,101	70,683	399,342	802,204
1964	650	38,275	189,959	8,441	542,735	1,091,678	1,077,662	540,502	63,912	346,553	691,004
1963	599	34,489	161,482	7,416	431,900	888,044	884,052	448,729	58,912	305,715	575,358
1962	572	31,015	140,067	7,119	359,712	769,701	749,648	402,871	54,439	271,661	515,936
1961	544	28,179	121,473	6,931	308,487	669,576	658,319	354,158	50,639	243,436	444,144
1960	519	29,459	124,290	6,846	297,538	631,371	637,674	326,987	43,369	198,502	..
1959	508	31,556	131,928	7,096	300,150	634,921	614,035	327,675	45,023	199,876	..
1958	511	28,252	110,750	6,214	257,900	540,956	544,748	276,842	41,131	172,493	..
1957	483	32,418	120,640	6,058	265,370	602,829	596,554	..	45,876	180,246	..

[1] Excludes electrical machinery.

Series R388-398. Selected principal statistics on the transportation equipment industries, Canada, 1957 to 1975

Year	Number of establish-ments	Manufacturing activity							Total activity		
		Production and related workers		Cost of fuel and electricity ($'000)	Cost of materials and supplies used ($'000)	Gross value of production ($'000)	Value of shipments of goods of own manufacture ($'000)	Census value added: manufac-turing activity ($'000)	Total employees		Census value added: total activity ($'000)
		Number	Salaries and wages ($'000)						Number	Salaries and wages ($'000)	
	388	389	390	391	392	393	394	395	396	397	398

Basis: 1970 Standard Industrial Classification and New Establishment Concept

1975	991	120,833	1,446,395	80,239	7,636,055	11,232,644	11,193,031	3,516,350	159,642	2,033,079	4,208,537
1974	1,003	130,407	1,397,988	68,994	6,693,771	10,284,053	10,173,886	3,521,288	171,970	1,975,402	4,275,971
1973	987	131,715	1,278,429	58,151	6,056,058	9,185,857	9,056,704	3,071,648	173,358	1,800,378	3,663,988
1972	958	118,384	1,059,535	51,699	5,100,797	7,783,958	7,747,271	2,631,462	158,105	1,517,008	3,150,950
1971	963	111,338	912,231	46,012	4,528,011	6,935,622	6,931,367	2,361,599	150,155	1,337,495	2,756,558
1970	905	105,164	787,781	39,338	3,804,026	5,789,664	5,757,285	1,946,300	146,979	1,208,545	2,194,927

Basis: 1960 Standard Industrial Classification and New Establishment Concept

1971	963	111,338	912,231	46,012	4,528,011	6,935,622	6,931,367	2,361,599	150,155	1,337,495	2,756,558
1970	905	105,164	787,781	39,338	3,804,026	5,789,664	5,757,285	1,946,300	146,979	1,208,545	2,194,927
1969	881	115,737	837,408	39,467	4,148,804	6,514,459	6,484,568	2,326,189	157,755	1,228,156	2,597,875
1968	871	108,595	747,765	36,408	3,552,894	5,634,854	5,597,442	2,045,552	149,379	1,102,226	2,306,454
1967	852	109,440	666,422	32,709	2,875,703	4,736,450	4,720,876	1,832,835	150,215	997,333	2,051,904
1966	805	108,461	635,866	29,791	2,637,656	4,271,978	4,238,414	1,611,634	146,932	922,729	1,747,178
1965	770	99,705	576,180	26,081	2,416,857	3,890,383	3,864,971	1,455,911	135,481	830,251	1,606,153
1964	744	90,123	483,049	22,336	2,002,734	3,240,810	3,197,689	1,218,498	123,767	708,833	1,297,404
1963	703	80,706	421,953	21,027	1,716,958	2,855,388	2,817,747	1,121,134	111,822	619,685	1,183,332
1962	682	75,601	373,086	19,773	1,392,697	2,352,063	2,343,690	935,370	104,931	550,155	994,273
1961	659	70,320	321,271	18,087	1,075,697	1,864,363	1,845,785	770,579	99,280	494,028	840,763
1960	677	82,046	362,754	20,768	1,098,159	1,985,181	1,999,758	866,355	109,160	519,732	..
1959	630	86,277	373,579	20,458	1,127,180	2,042,128	2,011,433	894,490	113,706	532,266	..
1958	611	93,863	381,755	21,060	1,167,125	2,056,567	2,076,430	868,382	126,209	554,565	..
1957	610	110,771	422,372	22,560	1,299,229	2,268,744	2,269,076	..	144,824	592,253	..

Series R399-404. General statistics on the transportation equipment industries, 1948 Standard Industrial Classification, Canada, selected years, 1870 to 1959

Year	Number of establishments	Number of employees	Salaries and wages ($'000)	Gross value of production ($'000)	Cost of materials ($'000)	Census value added by manufacture ($'000)
	399	400	401	402	403	404
1959	645	113,606	531,588	—	1,120,283	910,947
1958	626	125,976	553,426	2,057,826	1,153,569	883,507
1957	623	144,639	591,461	2,266,600	1,288,243	956,076
1956	591	141,257	553,572	2,213,798	1,286,297	906,155
1955	594	131,789	490,435	1,971,630	1,117,769	834,785
1954	602	133,432	479,080	1,681,292	986,721	677,116
1953	621	156,059	555,411	2,098,469	1,110,954	969,736
1952	617	146,360	473,118	1,785,773	1,009,471	760,421
1951	599	122,517	368,106	1,541,590	870,179	657,424
1950	601	104,176	290,436	1,239,580	674,834	552,171
1949	596	104,750	270,852	1,063,211	584,064	466,529
1948	578	101,816	255,505	941,484	509,911	419,134
1947	550	103,558	229,584	798,285	423,897	363,537
1946	530	100,163	199,202	587,237	299,870	277,804
1945	495	154,221	325,831	1,029,226	494,541	522,194
1944	461	221,549	457,143	1,416,543	639,309	762,517
1943	435	223,688	440,743	1,317,039	609,180	694,086
1942	452	173,986	319,938	1,065,832	556,052	498,479
1941	416	116,439	191,297	719,760	402,350	309,198
1940	404	70,292	109,770	426,147	244,576	176,029
1939	407	48,632	66,481	234,856	132,605	98,265
1938	413	48,710	65,233	256,555	150,800	101,750
1937	414	50,522	68,208	291,648	181,575	105,908
1936	486	43,109	53,029	206,764	123,690	79,532
1935	501	41,308	49,757	191,838	118,595	69,842
1934	526	35,278	39,285	144,961	84,996	56,968
1933	521	31,712	30,458	92,731	50,157	39,855
1932	533	32,447	37,350	97,984	51,071	44,072
1931	545	40,020	51,659	156,739	83,735	69,820
1930	607	50,770	72,890	254,358	148,331	101,814
1929	623	56,118	84,385	369,592	227,277	137,776
1928	694	51,497	77,399	282,848	170,945	108,164
1927	691	43,531	62,793	245,197	144,654	96,959
1926	727	45,072	63,676	244,185	144,049	96,279
1925	724	40,737	54,642	196,366	113,694	79,220
1924	746	30,323	40,706	169,672	106,676	60,485
1923	772	34,051	46,574	207,310	131,850	71,502
1922	853	26,602	33,949	144,706	82,028	59,991
1921	827	26,318	36,034	158,050	89,605	65,521
1920	1,055	55,084	77,289	285,230	152,142	128,076
1919	922	51,344	65,605	251,739	129,413	120,251
1918	985	48,521	55,746	240,871	120,987	116,640
1917	1,046	49,395	47,734	197,795	100,675	92,870
1910	—	43,213	25,119	78,400	37,553	40,847
1905	538	26,193	13,108	40,305	—	—
1900	—	24,825	9,937	27,164	13,894	13,270
1890	4,009	18,529	6,561	23,345	10,157	13,188
1880	3,603	16,742	4,797	14,267	6,408	7,859
1870	3,039	14,316	3,455	9,889	3,480	6,409

Series R405-415. Selected principal statistics on the electrical products industries, Canada, 1957 to 1975

Year	Number of establish-ments	Production and related workers		Cost of fuel and electricity ($'000)	Cost of materials and supplies used ($'000)	Gross value of production ($'000)	Value of shipments of goods of own manufacture ($'000)	Census value added: manufac-turing activity ($'000)	Total employees		Census value added: total activity ($'000)
		Number	Salaries and wages ($'000)						Number	Salaries and wages ($'000)	
	405	406	407	408	409	410	411	412	413	414	415

Basis: 1970 Standard Industrial Classification and New Establishment Concept

1975	805	82,711	776,409	34,312	2,189,898	4,542,095	4,599,292	2,317,885	125,868	1,364,138	2,631,778
1974	784	88,311	728,866	29,787	2,296,434	4,542,266	4,344,902	2,216,045	133,204	1,273,787	2,520,030
1973	738	82,023	592,838	25,052	1,813,445	3,631,893	3,537,898	1,793,396	127,928	1,087,096	2,086,408
1972	753	76,149	511,058	22,954	1,541,178	3,117,479	3,062,536	1,553,347	121,135	965,915	1,787,865
1971	764	74,322	468,991	21,120	1,388,382	2,798,534	2,794,629	1,389,032	123,181	920,010	1,578,238
1970	736	75,551	451,711	19,592	1,355,751	2,654,557	2,671,736	1,279,214	121,054	850,241	1,422,442

Basis: 1960 Standard Industrial Classification and New Establishment Concept

1971	763	74,192	467,197	21,019	1,390,617	2,790,104	2,785,486	1,378,468	122,380	911,598	1,571,550
1970	735	75,382	449,473	19,494	1,360,847	2,648,669	2,664,368	1,268,328	120,112	840,938	1,411,615
1969	720	80,690	445,505	19,397	1,394,999	2,686,896	2,607,481	1,272,500	126,986	813,227	1,430,108
1968	689	76,410	401,171	18,189	1,220,287	2,412,276	2,407,472	1,173,800	124,215	747,909	1,298,389
1967	667	78,309	377,416	17,389	1,186,291	2,310,488	2,312,519	1,106,808	127,561	718,584	1,217,877
1966	639	77,753	363,433	15,886	1,149,149	2,266,934	2,186,554	1,101,899	124,498	670,340	1,215,149
1965	595	69,923	312,667	14,939	969,754	1,947,349	1,902,539	962,655	113,463	584,665	1,060,757
1964	578	64,079	277,019	13,918	835,388	1,723,362	1,703,964	874,056	105,414	527,084	959,657
1963	545	61,241	254,017	13,171	750,834	1,548,886	1,545,046	784,881	101,235	487,770	863,490
1962	531	58,029	233,250	12,145	670,945	1,419,117	1,389,683	736,027	96,595	453,357	811,119
1961	533	51,904	203,006	11,338	585,060	1,215,863	1,208,298	619,465	89,360	409,559	679,529
1960	536	51,895	200,658	11,695	552,102	1,163,403	1,165,737	599,606	78,827	349,172	..
1959	510	54,811	204,285	11,525	568,951	1,189,354	1,161,677	608,878	81,729	347,239	..
1958	501	53,846	197,195	10,494	535,278	1,090,129	1,094,891	544,357	82,290	343,221	..
1957	503	60,476	211,880	11,022	555,848	1,187,537	1,180,854	..	89,962	351,528	..

Series R416-421. General statistics on the electrical products industries, 1948 Standard Industrial Classification, Canada, selected years, 1870 to 1959

Year	Number of establishments	Number of employees	Salaries and wages ($'000)	Gross value of production ($'000)	Cost of materials ($'000)	Census value added by manufacture ($'000)
	416	**417**	**418**	**419**	**420**	**421**
1959	496	73,883	316,857	–	501,800	566,293
1958	492	74,944	316,358	1,006,922	473,903	523,827
1957	486	81,432	320,417	1,076,355	498,243	568,587
1956	473	83,296	310,523	1,144,826	558,250	577,412
1955	468	76,244	264,031	981,932	477,656	496,401
1954	457	75,075	258,510	872,183	396,583	468,176
1953	422	76,856	250,647	892,153	383,744	501,453
1952	401	69,200	217,565	731,398	313,713	411,459
1951	373	67,626	194,749	676,009	316,561	353,603
1950	382	60,262	155,334	580,578	260,305	315,137
1949	365	55,916	137,279	486,286	212,460	269,342
1948	314	53,873	122,114	425,725	180,345	241,334
1947	296	52,736	103,891	366,506	162,131	200,859
1946	266	43,998	74,510	234,573	101,940	129,969
1945	247	44,129	76,469	230,532	92,041	135,920
1944	234	48,834	82,305	283,071	120,413	160,170
1943	223	46,928	76,907	245,771	109,282	134,049
1942	225	39,676	61,799	208,873	92,799	113,824
1941	211	33,086	47,211	177,904	77,467	98,433
1940	194	25,120	33,247	130,001	58,371	70,009
1939	190	20,261	25,711	89,061	39,333	48,462
1938	188	20,353	24,978	90,129	35,916	53,014
1937	191	21,706	26,291	98,842	41,696	55,815
1936	186	17,037	19,502	72,289	30,435	40,616
1935	182	15,549	17,595	61,153	25,410	34,672
1934	174	13,657	15,220	50,235	21,308	27,940
1933	174	11,767	12,429	37,013	14,504	21,657
1932	169	14,305	16,262	53,265	20,415	31,874
1931	163	18,207	22,474	81,579	32,386	48,242
1930	149	20,568	26,260	104,578	43,112	60,383
1929	139	20,871	26,725	113,796	49,623	63,074
1928	137	18,193	22,756	93,672	38,784	53,929
1927	130	16,813	20,614	78,559	32,735	44,927
1926	132	15,246	18,627	69,767	30,196	38,506
1925	122	14,112	16,472	60,159	25,435	33,770
1924	109	13,670	16,090	56,490	24,371	31,235
1923	108	13,268	14,991	51,360	26,257	24,238
1922	101	10,630	12,162	41,208	17,547	22,790
1921	100	10,640	13,556	45,093	19,439	24,777
1920	99	14,115	16,587	55,966	27,221	27,748
1919	111	9,709	9,865	35,552	16,067	18,896
1918	83	8,994	8,599	31,416	14,686	16,063
1917	90	9,896	8,163	41,165	20,752	20,034
1910	–	6,427	3,548	15,235	6,384	8,851
1905	34	4,806	2,499	8,997	–	–
1900	–	2,120	1,009	3,275	1,222	2,053
1890	24	428	168	866	336	530
1880	–[1]	–[1]	–[1]	–[1]	–[1]	–[1]
1870	–[1]	–[1]	–[1]	–[1]	–[1]	–[1]

[1] Industry non-existent.

Series R422-432. Selected principal statistics on the non-metallic mineral products industries, Canada, 1957 to 1975

Year	Number of establish-ments	Manufacturing activity							Total activity		
		Production and related workers		Cost of fuel and electricity ($'000)	Cost of materials and supplies used ($'000)	Gross value of production ($'000)	Value of shipments of goods of own manufacture ($'000)	Census value added: manufac-turing activity ($'000)	Total employees		Census value added: total activity ($'000)
		Number	Salaries and wages ($'000)						Number	Salaries and wages ($'000)	
	422	423	424	425	426	427	428	429	430	431	432
Basis: 1970 Standard Industrial Classification and New Establishment Concept											
1975	1,199	42,149	471,466	174,274	974,686	2,595,095	2,569,385	1,446,135	55,932	669,350	1,502,408
1974	1,206	42,884	424,096	151,200	869,855	2,317,121	2,282,508	1,296,066	57,566	604,898	1,346,563
1973	1,241	41,502	366,030	109,769	707,009	1,926,154	1,922,982	1,109,376	55,949	522,112	1,149,843
1972	1,268	39,149	316,033	94,533	610,137	1,677,888	1,665,455	973,218	53,087	458,227	1,010,146
1971	1,307	38,035	281,047	83,180	549,770	1,488,636	1,489,174	855,686	51,291	405,131	889,282
1970	1,280	36,045	244,200	73,955	476,694	1,274,389	1,264,629	723,741	49,428	361,364	750,869
Basis: 1960 Standard Industrial Classification and New Establishment Concept											
1971	1,323	38,390	283,101	83,340	558,680	1,502,817	1,503,418	860,797	51,786	408,346	894,637
1970	1,298	36,422	246,297	74,112	485,178	1,288,602	1,278,895	729,312	49,963	364,661	756,544
1969	1,286	38,107	246,196	71,837	486,705	1,297,480	1,286,857	738,938	51,888	357,764	765,035
1968	1,260	37,795	223,174	67,968	456,870	1,210,879	1,204,177	686,041	51,670	326,042	710,614
1967	1,291	37,467	207,204	64,868	413,257	1,093,433	1,082,213	615,308	51,276	301,482	640,501
1966	1,370	39,561	206,120	67,391	427,208	1,130,221	1,121,442	635,622	53,189	294,931	663,685
1965	1,351	38,246	188,351	62,425	403,493	1,046,073	1,037,982	580,154	51,218	268,819	604,689
1964	1,336	35,598	164,303	55,685	350,358	918,974	918,237	512,931	48,501	240,129	537,333
1963	1,329	33,740	148,303	51,706	305,698	809,154	807,145	451,750	46,043	218,356	470,567
1962	1,327	33,680	143,593	50,815	290,357	776,839	771,771	435,667	45,471	210,094	453,841
1961	1,293	31,777	129,638	46,566	251,449	679,047	676,025	381,031	43,320	191,818	394,800
1960	1,296	32,368	127,614	47,092	229,450	643,186	639,090	366,644	41,308	172,425	..
1959	1,176	33,466	130,722	48,921	235,259	661,586	655,619	377,406	41,886	172,643	..
1958	1,172	31,481	117,946	49,007	217,985	612,324	600,614	345,332	39,466	156,467	..
1957	1,153	31,242	110,991	48,997	203,515	574,434	571,165	..	38,879	145,709	..

Series R433-438. General statistics on the non-metallic mineral products industries, 1948 Standard Industrial Classification, Canada, selected years, 1870 to 1959

Year	Number of establishments	Number of employees	Salaries and wages ($'000)	Gross value of production ($'000)	Cost of materials ($'000)	Census value added by manufacture ($'000)
	433	434	435	436	437	438
1959	1,251	43,349	178,654	–	240,923	405,957
1958	1,248	40,858	161,812	640,731	218,684	369,873
1957	1,231	40,120	150,313	602,573	209,982	340,621
1956	1,183	40,165	143,223	575,993	206,872	322,821
1955	1,171	38,949	131,007	517,555	174,489	302,996
1954	1,160	35,229	114,849	437,931	145,121	256,572
1953	1,094	34,352	107,275	411,109	134,119	242,016
1952	1,057	31,422	92,819	352,454	115,218	206,095
1951	1,042	31,522	86,079	334,875	109,011	195,349
1950	1,045	29,603	72,380	286,541	91,168	168,378
1949	1,020	28,139	64,594	246,458	78,401	143,873
1948	934	27,278	58,816	232,148	72,577	134,898
1947	863	26,443	50,456	201,787	66,267	115,278
1946	833	24,387	39,651	160,475	49,957	94,591
1945	709	20,993	34,289	135,569	42,441	79,560
1944	666	20,034	32,872	136,146	43,347	79,251
1943	662	20,528	32,578	140,707	44,544	82,368
1942	699	20,386	29,914	138,570	41,925	82,883
1941	693	19,133	25,518	116,836	33,251	71,692
1940	724	16,164	19,712	86,738	23,415	54,425
1939	723	14,197	16,326	64,558	16,786	41,105
1938	764	14,194	16,103	60,896	15,551	38,791
1937	733	14,673	16,433	68,048	18,319	42,486
1936	698	12,839	13,378	52,097	13,393	32,888
1935	685	11,509	11,738	43,908	10,970	28,010
1934	683	10,370	10,387	40,588	9,303	26,523
1933	681	8,821	8,534	31,120	7,160	20,273
1932	711	10,285	10,920	35,189	7,120	23,277
1931	797	14,327	17,380	60,959	11,133	42,084
1930	780	18,324	22,142	74,882	14,656	50,507
1929	775	20,377	24,866	90,455	17,193	61,510
1928	761	18,450	22,198	77,574	14,430	53,250
1927	778	16,858	19,848	68,460	13,177	45,772
1926	820	16,308	18,318	62,028	12,098	40,952
1925	807	12,714	16,326	57,715	10,650	38,988
1924	724	14,796	16,269	55,269	9,013	38,256
1923	726	15,378	17,143	57,781	9,353	45,442
1922	743	13,740	15,219	51,230	7,548	35,895
1921	683	14,777	15,230	47,852	7,086	32,372
1920	696	16,656	19,788	57,430	8,956	39,576
1919	594	12,105	12,900	38,782	9,210	24,656
1918	831	11,781	10,874	36,417	9,857	21,991
1917	942	13,261	11,199	33,593	5,986	23,601
1910	–	20,838	9,643	28,155	4,420	23,735
1905	788	16,873	6,668	16,272	–	–
1900	–	14,019	3,684	9,460	1,491	7,969
1890	2,160	12,695	3,041	8,198	2,011	6,187
1880	2,364	11,016	2,216	6,179	1,913	4,266
1870	1,809	8,532	1,506	3,874	858	3,016

Series R439-449. Selected principal statistics on the petroleum and coal products industries, Canada, 1957 to 1975

Year	Manufacturing activity								Total activity		
	Number of establishments	Production and related workers		Cost of fuel and electricity ($'000)	Cost of materials and supplies used ($'000)	Gross value of production ($'000)	Value of shipments of goods of own manufacture ($'000)	Census value added: manufacturing activity ($'000)	Total employees		Census value added: total activity ($'000)
		Number	Salaries and wages ($'000)						Number	Salaries and wages ($'000)	
	439	**440**	**441**	**442**	**443**	**444**	**445**	**446**	**447**	**448**	**449**
				Basis: 1970 Standard Industrial Classification and New Establishment Concept							
1975	101	7,877	122,267	49,786	5,108,677	6,016,130	5,953,330	857,667	17,264	298,040	865,952
1974	105	7,787	105,398	36,160	4,404,161	5,407,983	5,185,318	967,662	17,435	254,539	978,252
1973	105	6,822	84,538	27,856	2,563,984	3,165,768	3,073,197	573,928	16,087	210,443	580,695
1972	102	6,583	75,735	23,875	1,955,581	2,442,021	2,441,065	462,565	15,409	186,037	465,518
1971	101	6,557	68,215	21,421	1,675,011	2,125,588	2,114,324	429,156	15,517	172,593	435,285
1970	94	6,686	64,745	19,178	1,452,565	1,827,971	1,819,127	356,228	15,647	160,653	360,634
				Basis: 1960 Standard Industrial Classification and New Establishment Concept							
1971	101	6,557	68,215	21,421	1,675,011	2,125,588	2,114,324	429,156	15,517	172,593	435,285
1970	94	6,686	64,745	19,178	1,452,565	1,827,971	1,819,127	356,228	15,647	160,653	360,634
1969	99	6,590	61,218	18,522	1,385,467	1,721,158	1,720,340	317,168	15,633	151,653	324,540
1968	95	6,876	56,703	16,768	1,347,420	1,693,605	1,675,999	329,417	15,631	138,470	335,134
1967	91	6,839	52,462	13,695	1,253,774	1,560,259	1,558,207	292,791	15,662	128,781	295,920
1966	89	6,832	48,780	13,399	1,222,187	1,512,054	1,495,308	276,468	15,403	119,653	283,917
1965	90	6,825	43,387	12,576	1,155,311	1,433,175	1,430,572	265,288	14,330	102,825	269,854
1964	89	7,168	44,784	12,579	1,114,090	1,413,392	1,418,528	286,722	15,009	102,598	289,568
1963	84	7,281	43,369	11,337	1,080,171	1,376,304	1,365,647	284,797	15,398	101,042	286,746
1962	89	7,494	43,571	10,850	1,003,806	1,297,948	1,294,070	283,292	16,277	104,410	284,619
1961	91	7,769	43,092	11,351	920,680	1,221,664	1,219,178	289,633	16,392	100,310	287,960
1960	91	7,895	43,061	9,556	866,018	1,157,829	1,150,422	282,255	14,315	84,246	..
1959	84	7,854	41,304	9,950	864,765	1,116,516	1,114,603	241,801	14,252	81,544	..
1958	92	8,459	41,301	8,672	832,282	1,041,650	1,038,922	200,696	14,860	77,820	..
1957	82	8,906	42,522	8,445	832,240	1,041,727	1,042,270	..	15,131	76,800	..

Series R450-455. General statistics on the petroleum and coal products industries, 1948 Standard Industrial Classification, Canada, selected years, 1870 to 1959

Year	Number of establishments	Number of employees	Salaries and wages ($'000)	Gross value of production ($'000)	Cost of materials ($'000)	Census value added by manufacture ($'000)
	450	451	452	453	454	455
1959	112	16,775	93,896	–	936,188	–
1958	115	17,427	89,491	1,465,619	894,458	514,760
1957	106	17,757	88,688	1,492,072	898,830	534,157
1956	107	17,685	81,680	1,377,485	837,827	489,298
1955	106	17,486	72,436	1,161,198	704,385	417,821
1954	104	17,559	69,682	1,024,437 [1]	625,411	361,631 [1]
1953	100	17,112	66,565	823,927	576,311	212,390
1952	101	16,905	63,573	780,855	519,629	226,245
1951	82	15,598	51,948	709,550	497,982	179,873
1950	76	15,177	44,425	616,126	442,418	144,489
1949	77	14,552	39,784	533,731	391,036	117,819
1948	75	13,678	34,766	491,962	369,035	97,064
1947	80	12,769	28,690	361,333	257,421	84,074
1946	77	12,106	24,198	286,008	190,528	79,047
1945	80	11,532	22,905	270,167	188,900	65,637
1944	82	11,556	23,259	280,123	191,368	73,274
1943	85	10,466	20,704	248,007	170,594	64,093
1942	83	10,321	18,789	219,505	149,219	58,334
1941	80	9,696	16,859	207,454	149,890	45,734
1940	80	9,251	15,185	168,886	115,898	43,268
1939	86	8,829	13,742	143,609	91,193	44,407
1938	92	8,605	13,673	136,725	93,023	36,176
1937	90	9,164	13,956	140,157	97,620	35,181
1936	105	9,135	13,024	125,674	83,141	35,819
1935	102	8,963	12,781	118,425	74,103	38,043
1934	95	9,235	12,028	114,610	72,206	36,396
1933	89	8,154	10,748	100,205	61,917	32,544
1932	73	7,755	10,879	101,510	64,479	31,462
1931	73	8,128	11,832	107,408	64,512	37,555
1930	69	9,104	14,055	128,380	88,883	33,244
1929	68	8,880	14,093	139,319	95,378	37,557
1928	70	8,233	12,532	117,831	74,548	37,761
1927	71	8,002	12,057	98,574	69,675	23,293
1926	73	8,046	11,790	104,723	67,143	32,343
1925	86	10,260	11,993	82,279	52,971	23,548
1924	89	8,055	11,764	79,589	51,883	20,284
1923	84	8,115	10,628	82,953	58,660	19,834
1922	76	7,254	10,262	84,255	53,392	26,148
1921	75	7,567	11,516	87,309	57,507	25,245
1920	82	8,286	12,146	94,623	60,788	28,464
1919	74	7,609	9,926	77,514	51,167	23,081
1918	83	6,790	7,676	67,483	42,846	20,264
1917	92	6,657	6,460	59,057	30,485	24,553
1910	–	3,473	2,156	13,608	6,212	7,396
1905	70	2,211	1,153	8,204	–	–
1900	–	1,811	944	6,589	3,612	2,977
1890	74	1,495	656	4,952	2,254	2,698
1880	80	1,002	433	5,223	2,560	2,663
1870	73	793	333	3,845	1,706	2,139

[1] The method of valuation of the petroleum refining industry products was changed in 1954. Had the old method been used in 1954, it is estimated that the gross value of production for the petroleum and coal products industries in that year would have been $885 million, instead of $1,024 million.

Series R456-466. Selected principal statistics on the chemical and chemical products industries, Canada, 1957 to 1975

Year	Number of establishments	Production and related workers		Cost of fuel and electricity ($'000)	Cost of materials and supplies used ($'000)	Gross value of production ($'000)	Value of shipments of goods of own manufacture ($'000)	Census value added: manufacturing activity ($'000)	Total employees		Census value added: total activity ($'000)
		Number	Salaries and wages ($'000)						Number	Salaries and wages ($'000)	
	456	457	458	459	460	461	462	463	464	465	466

Basis: 1970 Standard Industrial Classification and New Establishment Concept

Year	456	457	458	459	460	461	462	463	464	465	466
1975	1,046	42,643	463,522	216,601	2,566,268	5,205,384	5,107,353	2,422,515	80,251	1,003,909	2,663,040
1974	1,068	40,924	401,850	185,409	2,233,126	4,752,893	4,607,691	2,334,358	79,795	893,309	2,578,974
1973	1,111	39,447	344,508	142,295	1,575,079	3,519,428	3,503,823	1,802,054	77,328	775,242	1,975,645
1972	1,125	37,578	303,613	117,690	1,303,279	2,945,033	2,943,118	1,524,064	74,731	697,117	1,676,041
1971	1,139	38,621	288,640	112,038	1,224,549	2,779,134	2,781,997	1,442,547	77,377	669,314	1,582,467
1970	1,128	40,086	279,854	104,708	1,157,262	2,639,593	2,620,835	1,377,623	79,070	637,157	1,493,749

Basis: 1960 Standard Industrial Classification and New Establishment Concept

Year	456	457	458	459	460	461	462	463	464	465	466
1971	1,139	38,621	288,640	112,038	1,224,549	2,779,134	2,781,997	1,442,547	77,377	669,314	1,582,467
1970	1,128	40,086	279,854	104,708	1,157,262	2,639,593	2,620,835	1,377,623	79,070	637,157	1,493,749
1969	1,136	39,751	259,022	96,929	1,126,614	2,604,871	2,581,824	1,381,328	78,441	592,574	1,492,512
1968	1,124	38,848	232,389	88,946	1,060,692	2,434,656	2,428,595	1,285,018	77,027	537,992	1,367,680
1967	1,142	37,955	211,854	83,698	1,012,819	2,290,078	2,268,769	1,193,561	75,245	488,652	1,273,292
1966	1,152	37,125	195,042	80,559	984,601	2,194,741	2,174,198	1,129,581	73,317	451,833	1,213,859
1965	1,118	35,057	173,350	69,941	888,211	1,993,635	1,973,320	1,035,483	70,975	412,402	1,109,232
1964	1,140	33,555	160,879	63,677	797,816	1,811,142	1,798,065	949,649	67,433	377,408	1,019,544
1963	1,093	32,511	150,881	59,901	719,705	1,650,252	1,644,786	870,646	65,494	355,064	929,346
1962	1,080	31,602	141,629	56,047	666,323	1,546,962	1,543,081	824,592	63,905	332,577	874,701
1961	1,067	31,694	137,070	54,660	623,024	1,441,431	1,435,752	763,747	63,357	318,709	808,526
1960	1,063	32,902	137,712	55,702	585,692	1,369,856	1,357,688	728,462	53,840	251,909	..
1959	1,042	32,909	131,374	50,870	584,260	1,312,122	1,310,154	676,992	53,630	239,126	..
1958	1,045	33,248	128,349	48,276	550,373	1,242,235	1,233,469	643,586	53,571	231,082	..
1957	1,049	32,966	120,853	42,525	519,789	1,136,882	1,134,398	..	53,536	218,136	..

Series R467-472. General statistics on the chemical and chemical products industries, 1948 Standard Industrial Classification, Canada, selected years, 1870 to 1959

Year	Number of establishments	Number of employees	Salaries and wages ($'000)	Gross value of production ($'000)	Cost of materials ($'000)	Census value added by manufacture ($'000)
	467	468	469	470	471	472
1959	1,137	54,782	243,218	—	627,366	701,480
1958	1,143	54,570	233,819	1,302,006	589,316	664,853
1957	1,137	54,708	222,045	1,213,122	565,746	605,274
1956	1,131	52,821	200,743	1,120,444	527,564	556,241
1955	1,126	51,856	185,268	1,038,837	480,104	525,648
1954	1,116	51,603	177,312	950,518	437,051	481,253
1953	1,105	50,207	164,591	898,139	403,686	464,912
1952	1,075	47,694	148,076	798,419	357,819	415,945
1951	1,037	45,664	131,310	776,489	366,957	384,026
1950	1,033	41,475	106,794	646,871	307,706	317,167
1949	1,037	41,328	100,690	587,398	280,008	288,172
1948	1,026	39,548	89,326	579,828	293,042	268,818
1947	1,046	39,237	78,994	488,307	238,307	234,057
1946	1,031	38,012	67,842	401,742	179,750	208,399
1945	992	61,366	107,074	498,739	228,922	252,985
1944	997	82,347	138,204	746,935	371,146	357,756
1943	961	92,736	147,327	774,876	375,812	381,295
1942	943	93,445	134,870	511,353	241,113	254,251
1941	866	54,388	76,091	312,654	141,165	159,216
1940	820	27,983	38,990	199,686	87,179	105,200
1939	817	22,834	31,841	163,694	68,332	90,041
1938	996	22,346	29,860	149,921	63,578	81,372
1937	960	22,425	28,953	154,124	68,546	80,292
1936	823	20,222	25,513	131,035	55,791	70,649
1935	813	19,221	23,973	121,694	50,707	66,677
1934	819	17,425	21,181	110,744	44,018	62,835
1933	706	15,598	18,962	94,907	35,813	55,885
1932	648	15,268	19,995	96,850	36,703	56,586
1931	604	15,206	20,901	108,020	42,967	61,375
1930	575	15,498	21,057	125,836	53,749	68,023
1929	539	16,606	22,531	143,237	59,749	78,859
1928	580	16,365	20,613	129,959	56,449	69,574
1927	569	14,798	18,965	117,287	52,605	61,203
1926	564	14,576	18,592	129,076	65,488	59,777
1925	503	13,974	17,475	116,290	59,757	53,277
1924	451	13,805	17,027	111,491	58,025	50,082
1923	469	15,159	18,399	113,840	57,953	52,410
1922	464	13,593	16,257	96,567	49,388	43,830
1921	446	12,138	15,667	89,755	44,953	41,363
1920	437	16,414	21,520	130,425	66,618	58,743
1919	403	14,750	15,428	94,095	44,167	46,205
1918	498	54,907	66,120	334,952	177,760	148,043
1917	523	55,422	50,934	227,512	98,602	122,406
1910	—	10,726	5,471	30,987	14,750	16,237
1905	245	4,988	2,303	14,855	—	—
1900	—	5,971	2,539	12,591	7,029	5,562
1890	761	4,615	1,400	10,135	5,703	4,432
1880	633	3,768	989	7,058	4,145	2,913
1870	919	3,555	625	5,022	3,049	1,973

Series R473-483. Selected principal statistics on the miscellaneous manufacturing industries, Canada, 1957 to 1975

Year	Number of establish- ments	Production and related workers		Cost of fuel and electricity ($'000)	Cost of materials and supplies used ($'000)	Gross value of production ($'000)	Value of shipments of goods of own manufacture ($'000)	Census value added: manufac- turing activity ($'000)	Total employees		Census value added: total activity ($'000)
		Number	Salaries and wages ($'000)						Number	Salaries and wages ($'000)	
	473	474	475	476	477	478	479	480	481	482	483

Basis: 1970 Standard Industrial Classification and New Establishment Concept

Year	473	474	475	476	477	478	479	480	481	482	483
1975	2,160	48,804	381,486	15,611	917,059	1,950,572	1,942,966	1,017,902	65,247	597,561	1,160,062
1974	2,394	48,360	350,052	14,201	865,618	1,845,895	1,794,937	966,076	65,091	543,820	1,103,575
1973	2,346	45,579	288,835	12,058	670,093	1,486,083	1,454,206	803,932	62,426	465,254	919,694
1972	2,418	43,263	256,132	11,960	563,238	1,283,550	1,267,828	708,352	60,085	417,134	802,803
1971	2,394	40,440	226,257	11,038	493,326	1,119,688	1,115,299	615,324	57,483	380,085	708,172
1970	2,337	39,960	209,747	9,698	458,487	1,045,557	1,037,691	577,372	56,749	348,987	659,172

Basis: 1960 Standard Industrial Classification and New Establishment Concept

Year	473	474	475	476	477	478	479	480	481	482	483
1971	2,951	56,063	310,908	16,721	681,721	1,542,152	1,538,529	843,710	76,587	497,654	941,956
1970	2,849	55,357	286,699	14,697	624,276	1,424,295	1,411,022	785,322	75,647	457,208	874,457
1969	2,871	56,409	277,182	14,122	617,794	1,409,430	1,398,021	777,514	77,452	441,672	853,133
1968	2,810	53,830	245,526	12,511	563,272	1,269,305	1,257,529	693,522	74,018	392,990	761,188
1967	2,764	50,092	214,678	10,865	496,312	1,089,554	1,083,797	582,378	69,407	348,236	645,657
1966	2,766	48,728	192,938	9,822	447,041	999,986	984,986	543,123	67,534	316,473	596,360
1965	2,722	44,657	167,486	8,664	394,106	881,342	868,672	478,572	62,624	280,194	528,759
1964	2,664	43,000	154,515	7,661	357,043	804,264	795,993	439,560	59,579	255,453	487,578
1963	2,557	40,246	138,644	6,943	328,280	732,212	723,334	396,989	56,532	231,272	433,730
1962	2,532	38,560	129,156	6,368	300,831	676,505	667,483	369,306	54,580	213,606	408,944
1961	2,483	36,827	119,353	5,977	268,915	604,368	600,523	329,475	52,978	199,974	369,256
1960	1,881	32,433	102,137	5,275	231,039	515,742	511,810	279,428	44,207	160,823	..
1959	1,766	31,566	95,060	5,125	215,084	492,374	486,950	272,165	42,758	148,989	..
1958	1,802	30,274	87,490	4,877	195,989	444,746	441,651	243,880	41,010	136,663	..
1957	1,791	30,438	84,535	4,882	176,476	409,874	409,583	..	40,322	127,836	..

Series R484-489. General statistics on the miscellaneous manufacturing industries, 1948 Standard Industrial Classification, Canada, selected years, 1870 to 1959

Year	Number of establishments	Number of employees	Salaries and wages ($'000)	Gross value of production ($'000)	Cost of materials ($'000)	Census value added by manufacture ($'000)
	484	485	486	487	488	489
1959	1,563	37,886	131,382	—	185,235	246,239
1958	1,599	36,002	119,981	395,234	170,066	220,598
1957	1,579	34,942	109,881	359,621	148,660	206,433
1956	1,556	33,432	100,348	330,968	138,870	187,989
1955	1,524	31,511	89,240	286,223	114,448	168,109
1954	1,360	31,071	85,479	254,356	102,179	148,822
1953	1,350	32,223	85,954	268,129	103,468	171,609
1952	1,313	29,833	74,134	223,790	87,550	133,372
1951	1,173	28,756	66,909	210,805	87,292	120,900
1950	1,007	27,219	56,410	169,313	67,469	99,629
1949	893	26,401	51,147	156,363	59,778	94,600
1948	814	22,315	40,906	125,116	48,007	75,511
1947	812	23,037	37,606	116,859	47,068	68,323
1946	715	21,149	31,158	111,498	49,955	60,247
1945	618	20,956	32,043	126,299	74,489	50,631
1944	591	21,659	34,868	126,112	51,812	73,157
1943	593	21,549	32,436	116,233	66,253	48,850
1942	576	18,631	21,697	73,730	35,769	36,947
1941	537	14,382	16,210	51,271	22,465	27,958
1940	498	9,864	10,636	32,901	13,002	19,276
1939	480	9,154	9,537	29,862	10,938	18,348
1938	481	8,782	9,019	28,740	10,443	17,754
1937	461	8,725	8,697	28,341	10,578	17,236
1936	439	8,078	7,808	25,072	9,350	15,190
1935	428	7,719	7,138	22,502	8,597	13,398
1934	420	7,800	7,223	23,321	8,892	13,906
1933	386	6,636	6,011	18,186	6,395	11,324
1932	381	6,867	6,748	21,216	7,403	13,335
1931	363	7,204	7,808	26,355	9,648	16,203
1930	360	7,521	8,369	33,215	13,638	19,089
1929	358	8,854	9,917	40,418	16,950	22,944
1928	352	8,782	9,607	36,542	14,626	21,401
1927	357	8,970	9,921	35,731	15,307	19,898
1926	343	8,677	9,529	33,901	14,045	19,346
1925	346	8,122	8,756	30,102	12,624	16,981
1924	336	8,265	8,929	27,806	11,795	15,519
1923	483	9,498	10,495	33,557	12,938	20,090
1922	433	8,806	9,803	31,453	11,554	19,306
1921	459	8,920	9,937	32,635	12,932	19,137
1920	541	12,047	13,157	43,296	18,974	23,625
1919	556	12,748	11,511	43,354	18,344	24,657
1918	555	12,473	8,826	37,302	14,965	21,914
1917	514	9,587	8,729	29,195	12,855	15,947
1910	—	9,274	4,804	16,242	6,481	9,761
1905	242	7,838	3,478	10,087	—	—
1900	—	7,190	2,830	7,902	3,325	4,577
1890	651	5,141	1,699	6,191	2,679	3,512
1880	593	4,879	1,143	4,301	1,907	2,394
1870	365	2,934	629	2,408	1,088	1,320

Series R490-513. Index numbers of real domestic product for manufacturing industries, by major groups, 1919 to 1976

S.I.C. No.		5:01	5:02	5:03	5:04	5:05	5:06	5:07	5:08	5:09	5:10	5:11
Year	Manufac-turing industries[1]	Food and beverage industries	Tobacco products industries	Rubber and plastics products industries[1]	Leather industries	Textile industries	Knitting mills	Clothing industries	Wood industries	Furniture and fixtures industries	Paper and allied industries	Printing, publishing and allied industries
	490	**491**	**492**	**493**	**494**	**495**	**496**	**497**	**498**	**499**	**500**	**501**
1976	120.0	111.6	115.3	145.6	101.8	110.5	99.8	113.0	129.5	116.3	113.3	115.1
1975	114.2	108.6	109.1	125.9	101.3	109.5	106.0	110.7	105.0	110.7	99.0	115.6
1974	120.1	106.8	112.8	131.8	104.5	119.9	109.8	111.6	114.7	124.8	122.3	114.3
1973	116.1	106.0	106.6	130.6	103.2	121.8	114.4	111.8	119.0	123.4	115.6	111.6
1972	106.9	103.2	102.9	113.7	100.9	113.4	106.8	105.5	108.7	115.5	108.7	105.6
1971	100.0	100.0	100.0	100.0	100.0	100.0	100.0	100.0	100.0	100.0	100.0	100.0
1970	94.5	95.8	99.3	94.2	96.5	91.4	91.0	94.2	90.1	96.0	99.9	95.6
1969	95.8	92.8	93.6	92.8	102.3	95.2	86.1	94.3	93.6	102.6	100.1	94.3
1968	89.1	89.6	90.5	84.1	102.3	83.9	78.9	92.7	89.0	97.2	90.1	90.0
1967	83.9	87.3	92.7	77.9	96.6	75.3	67.5	89.5	86.4	94.4	86.2	88.1
1966	81.5	82.4	87.6	70.8	99.4	73.4	68.1	91.0	85.0	92.5	86.9	85.2
1965	75.8	77.7	84.6	62.2	98.4	72.4	67.2	88.4	82.9	82.1	80.5	79.4
1964	69.5	75.2	81.2	58.2	96.9	69.5	64.3	85.5	80.4	72.1	76.3	74.3
1963	63.4	70.7	78.3	52.8	93.5	63.1	60.3	81.5	74.2	66.9	69.1	73.1
1962	59.4	67.7	75.5	50.3	93.0	57.8	53.6	77.7	69.2	62.5	65.6	71.6
1961	54.4	64.3	73.0	38.9	90.0	51.9	49.4	74.1	64.2	58.4	63.4	69.8
1960	52.3	61.8	70.1	39.8	81.4	47.5	45.1	70.9	62.7	54.8	62.9	68.0
1959	51.4	60.6	65.7	46.1	85.3	46.1	42.9	70.1	61.1	55.4	60.2	66.6
1958	47.9	57.7	62.1	39.8	81.2	40.8	37.6	68.8	58.3	51.2	56.1	61.7
1957	48.8	55.1	57.1	39.5	80.4	42.2	37.5	69.5	57.4	51.9	56.4	62.8
1956	48.9	53.0	52.4	41.7	81.5	41.9	37.5	69.2	62.2	52.3	57.5	61.8
1955	44.7	50.0	48.4	36.6	74.9	40.4	33.4	65.2	61.6	48.0	53.5	55.9
1954	40.8	48.1	43.7	30.9	69.0	33.7	30.9	62.2	55.0	43.7	51.4	53.2
1953	41.7	46.4	41.5	35.4	74.4	37.4	32.0	65.1	55.8	43.0	49.7	49.4
1952	38.9	45.1	38.2	30.8	70.0	35.2	29.3	64.5	52.2	38.7	47.2	45.0
1951	37.5	42.4	33.0	32.8	63.6	38.7	29.5	57.0	51.5	37.1	49.1	44.3
1950	34.5	41.0	35.3	30.9	67.1	37.9	28.3	58.0	48.0	36.5	45.5	43.1
1949	32.4	39.8	34.4	26.3	70.2	33.7	28.1	57.2	44.3	34.1	42.0	39.2
1948	31.5	39.2	32.1	30.6	67.1	32.8	28.0	55.4	44.8	33.4	39.9	36.4
1947	30.2	38.6	32.1	33.5	76.6	31.6	24.4	53.5	43.3	34.0	37.4	32.8
1946	27.6	39.0	31.2	23.6	87.0	29.9	23.2	56.6	37.6	31.7	34.1	30.2
1945	30.0	36.5	35.5	26.9	80.4	29.5	20.7	55.2	34.1	26.5	29.0	26.4
1944	34.3	35.6	30.8	22.2	77.6	29.6	20.9	55.3	34.1	24.9	26.8	24.1
1943	33.6	32.2	28.3	21.9	78.4	31.6	21.3	59.6	32.8	24.4	25.2	23.5
1942	31.1	30.9	26.2	22.4	77.8	34.3	22.6	61.2	35.6	22.8	25.9	24.0
1941	25.5	28.7	21.1	23.0	73.2	30.9	22.8	51.5	33.6	23.8	25.9	23.8
1940	19.5	24.8	18.3	17.4	60.1	27.3	23.0	43.7	29.7	20.5	22.8	21.4
1939	15.8	22.4	16.9	15.9	56.3	20.1	22.1	36.0	24.4	16.9	19.0	21.4
1938	14.6	21.2	15.8	14.5	48.3	16.2	18.6	33.8	22.8	16.4	16.5	20.7
1937	15.9	21.2	14.2	16.7	54.8	20.2	18.9	36.6	24.0	17.5	20.5	22.2
1936	13.9	19.8	12.3	14.3	50.0	18.7	16.9	34.3	21.2	15.8	17.8	20.9
1935	12.6	17.7	10.7	13.1	49.7	16.7	15.2	33.1	19.0	13.7	16.2	19.7
1934[5]	11.7	—	—	—	—	—	—	—	—	—	—	—
1971 G.D.P. % weight	22.862	3.254	0.212	0.650	0.206	0.756	0.205	0.742	0.968	0.420	1.878	1.123

Series R490-513. Index numbers of real domestic product for manufacturing industries, by major groups, 1919 to 1976 (concluded)

S.I.C. No.	5:12	5:13	5:14	5:15	5:16	5:17	5:18	5:19	5:20	5:01-07; 10; 11; 18-20	5:08; 5:09; 12-17	5:12-14
Year	Primary metals industries	Metal fabricating industries (excluding machinery and trans-portation equipment industries)	Machinery industries (excluding electrical machinery)	Transpor-tation equipment industries	Electrical products industries	Non-metallic mineral products industries	Petroleum and coal products industries	Chemical and chemical products industries	Miscel-laneous manufac-turing industries	Non-durable manufac-turing industries	Durable manufac-turing industries	Primary metal industries; metal fabricating industries; machinery industries
	502	503	504	505	506	507	508	509	510	511	512	513
1976	105.4	128.2	137.0	131.2	113.7	121.3	127.1	133.1	117.8[3]	117.3	122.7	120.8
1975	108.6	121.2	137.7	119.3	112.1	118.3	124.1	125.4	116.9	111.8	116.8	119.5
1974	111.8	125.0	137.4	120.9	126.3	123.3	127.4	125.0	124.9	116.7	123.4	125.5
1973	111.2	116.2	121.6	123.6	119.8	118.3	123.6	119.7	112.8	113.7	118.7	115.3
1972	103.5	104.2	108.7	110.3	108.2	106.7	108.3	106.7	104.0	106.4	107.4	104.8
1971	100.0	100.0	100.0	100.0	100.0	100.0	100.0	100.0	100.0	100.0	100.0	100.0
1970	100.9	97.7	97.2	85.6	95.3	86.6	94.4	95.0	94.4	95.7	93.2	98.9
1969	94.9	97.8	97.8	97.5	99.5	90.5	92.1	93.8	95.3	94.8	96.8	96.6
1968	92.9	90.5	85.8	87.4	92.1	87.1	88.7	85.2	89.8	88.4	89.7	90.3
1967	84.5	89.8	85.6	75.8	88.3	80.7	79.9	79.1	85.3	81.0	83.9	86.7
1966	87.9	89.9	83.6	65.2	87.4	86.0	79.2	76.8	82.5	81.6	81.5	87.6
1965	84.4	81.2	73.3	60.1	77.4	83.3	75.7	70.3	75.2	76.5	75.1	80.6
1964	76.8	71.1	65.5	48.4	69.0	76.0	73.0	64.0	70.5	72.6	66.2	72.0
1963	68.4	64.3	55.5	44.0	61.8	68.4	72.4	55.8	64.7	67.3	59.5	63.8
1962	63.7	59.7	51.1	38.1	56.9	68.0	67.1	52.3	61.8	64.0	54.8	59.3
1961	59.2	54.2	45.7	32.0	47.9	59.3	62.0	48.8	57.6	60.2	48.6	54.1
1960	..[4]	..[4]	..[4]	32.4	45.0	56.8	58.4	45.8	52.5	57.4	47.1	52.2
1959	..	..	..	33.5	43.4	58.7	56.0	43.6	50.9	55.9	46.9	51.5
1958	..	..	..	33.8	40.9	54.4	51.1	42.3	46.4	52.3	43.5	45.3
1957	..	..	..	38.5	41.8	52.4	50.6	39.8	45.1	51.4	46.2	49.5
1956	..	..	..	39.3	45.0	51.4	49.4	36.7	42.3	50.2	47.6	50.3
1955	..	..	..	36.5	39.8	45.3	42.2	33.4	38.1	46.5	43.1	44.1
1954	..	..	..	34.1	34.5	39.7	36.7	30.8	36.9	43.3	38.2	38.2
1953	..	..	..	41.6	34.3	38.1	34.1	28.3	36.5	42.6	40.8	40.1
1952	..	..	..	36.9	28.4	34.6	31.1	25.4	29.5	39.8	37.9	40.0
1951	..	..	..	32.2	27.5	33.0	28.5	23.6	28.3	38.7	36.2	39.6
1950	..	..	..	26.7	25.6	30.0	24.9	20.8	26.5	36.9	32.1	34.7
1949	..	..	..	24.7	22.7	27.0	22.2	19.1	22.8	34.5	30.1	33.7
1948	..	..	..	24.0	20.8	24.9	20.0	18.2	18.7	33.3	29.6	34.1
1947	..	..	..	23.5	20.4	23.3	17.7	17.3	18.7	32.2	28.1	31.3
1946	..	..	..	19.9	15.4	19.4	16.5	16.6	18.3	31.0	24.1	27.3
1945	..	..	..	38.8	16.1	17.2	15.9	20.4	20.4	30.4	30.1	33.0
1944	..	..	..	58.2	19.4	18.0	16.4	27.2	22.2	30.9	38.7	41.9
1943	..	..	..	49.0	19.3	18.6	14.5	25.8	22.0	29.7	38.6	46.6
1942	..	..	..	38.8	17.0	18.4	13.2	24.4	18.4	29.1	33.8	41.0
1941	..	..	..	26.2	14.1	16.2	13.6	14.7	14.0	25.5	25.9	30.7
1940	..	..	..	15.1	9.5	12.2	11.9	9.5	10.2	21.3	17.9	21.3
1939	..	..	..	9.3	6.5	9.7	10.7	7.8	8.9	18.5	12.9	15.4
1938	..	..	..	9.4	6.4	9.2	9.9	7.2	8.5	16.9	12.3	14.5
1937	..	..	..	10.7	7.4	10.3	10.0	7.5	8.6	18.2	13.6	15.8
1936	..	..	..	8.8	5.7	8.1	9.1	6.4	7.9	16.6	11.1	12.9
1935	..	..	..	8.4	5.2	6.6	8.4	6.0	7.3	15.2	9.9	11.0
1934[5]	..	..	..	—	—	—	—	—	—	—	—	—
1971 G.D.P. % weight	1.976	1.887	1.008	2.571	1.631	0.905	0.394	1.363	0.713	11.496	11.366	4.871

[1] For comparability with the 1970 Standard Industrial Classification, plastic fabricators have been transferred to major group 5:03 from major group 5:20.

[2] For comparability with the 1960 Standard Industrial Classification and the 1970 Standard Industrial Classification, the major groups primary metals industries; metal fabricating industries (excluding machinery and transportation equipment industries), and machinery industries (excluding electrical machinery), have been aggregated.

[3] For comparability with the 1960 Standard Industrial Classification and the 1970 Standard Industrial Classification, jewellery has been included with major group 5:20.

[4] For this series, non-availability of data is due to a break in historical continuity.

[5] The figures for series R490, for the years 1919 to 1934, are as follows: 1934, 11.7; 1933, 9.9; 1932, 9.2; 1931, 10.5; 1930, 12.3; 1929, 14.6; 1928, 14.1; 1927, 12.6; 1926, 12.4; 1925, 11.5; 1924, 10.6; 1923, 10.6; 1922, 9.3; 1921, 7.4; 1920, 8.5; 1919, 9.1.

Series R514-620. Gross fixed capital formation in manufacturing, by major groups, 1926 to 1975
(millions of dollars)

Year	Manufacturing industries			Food and beverage industries			Tobacco products industries			Rubber and plastics products industries			Leather industries		
	Total	Construction	Machinery and equipment	Capital formation	Construction	Machinery and equipment	Capital formation	Construction	Machinery and equipment	Capital formation	Construction	Machinery and equipment	Capital formation	Construction	Machinery and equipment
	514	515	516	520	521	522	526	527	528	529	530	531	532	533	534
1975	5,425.0	1,536.9	3,888.1	391.7	117.1	274.6	24.2	6.0	18.2	106.4	25.2	81.2	13.2	3.7	9.5
1974	4,949.9	1,425.3	3,524.6	418.1	139.3	278.8	25.7	7.1	18.6	136.4	36.1	100.3	12.3	3.3	9.0
1973	3,668.0	985.8	2,682.2	360.3	113.1	247.2	11.7	1.1	10.6	125.2	28.0	97.2	9.8	2.6	7.2
1972	2,948.0	829.0	2,119.0	282.0	82.2	199.8	12.2	1.8	10.4	90.6	23.0	67.6	14.0	6.0	8.0
1971	2,994.0	873.0	2,121.0	287.4	95.1	192.3	12.6	2.9	9.7	92.9	23.8	69.1	8.0	2.8	5.2
1970	3,223.0	997.0	2,226.0	304.5	96.8	207.7	11.3	2.9	8.4	56.1	22.3	33.8	5.8	1.3	4.5
1969	2,600.0	772.0	1,828.0	258.1	87.9	170.2	10.9	1.1	9.8	50.4	11.3	39.1	8.3	2.3	6.0
1968	2,199.0	657.0	1,542.0	241.2	77.2	164.0	13.0	3.8	9.2	34.7	9.3	25.4	8.1	2.2	5.9
1967	2,534.0	677.0	1,857.0	254.4	73.7	180.7	14.4	4.1	10.3	29.1	5.5	23.6	6.5	1.8	4.7
1966	2,914.0	788.0	2,126.0	241.3	79.3	162.0	14.4	5.4	9.0	48.8	14.9	33.9	8.1	2.6	5.5
1965	2,340.0	604.0	1,736.0	199.3	60.0	139.3	12.2	2.3	9.9	26.1	6.1	20.0	4.7	1.0	3.7
1964	1,831.0	443.0	1,388.0	176.4	53.6	122.8	8.4	2.4	6.0	23.8	5.7	18.1	5.2	1.4	3.8
1963	1,358.0	355.0	1,003.0	160.7	52.9	107.8	8.2	1.5	6.7	15.9	3.0	12.9	5.4	1.7	3.7
1962	1,269.0	353.0	916.0	168.7	57.3	111.4	6.3	0.9	5.4	17.0	2.9	14.1	4.5	0.9	3.6
1961	1,085.0	279.0	806.0	165.0	58.1	106.9	8.1	1.7	6.4	16.4	2.6	13.8	3.8	0.6	3.2
1960	1,177.4	334.7	842.7	151.9	52.7	99.2	6.9	1.7	5.2	23.9	6.9	17.0	3.9	1.3	2.6

1948 Standard Industrial Classification

Year	517	518	519	523	524	525	Rubber, leather and tobacco and their products		
							535	536	537
1960	1,200.7	354.6	846.1	150.4	52.2	98.2	34.7	9.8	24.9
1959	1,143.8	373.9	769.9	132.8	45.4	87.4	24.4	7.6	16.8
1958	1,095.0	397.6	697.4	126.2	40.5	85.7	22.4	6.6	15.8
1957	1,478.9	519.9	959.0	117.1	36.3	80.8	29.7	9.3	20.4
1956	1,393.8	487.7	906.1	109.1	32.6	76.5	26.4	8.2	18.2
1955	946.5	344.7	601.8	103.7	38.5	65.2	21.8	5.1	16.7
1954	822.1	287.6	534.5	104.3	38.6	65.7	21.1	5.7	15.4
1953	969.0	324.7	644.3	85.0	26.0	59.0	21.5	6.0	15.5
1952	972.6	343.6	629.0	77.3	26.6	50.7	14.6	3.8	10.8
1951	793.0	267.8	525.2	79.1	28.0	51.1	12.9	3.4	9.5
1950	502.5	135.4	367.1	75.2	26.0	49.2	9.8	2.3	7.5
1949	535.8	156.6	379.2	78.7	27.7	51.0	11.1	2.6	8.5
1948	573.0	180.8	392.2	88.4	31.9	56.5	12.1	3.5	8.6
1947	528.0	184.8	343.2	82.8	33.0	49.8	16.5	4.6	11.9
1946	337.2	132.2	205.0	53.1	24.7	28.4	12.8	6.7	6.1
1945	280.1	75.9	204.2	34.4	18.2	16.2	10.3	5.9	4.4
1944	211.4	61.3	150.1	22.1	10.7	11.4	5.0	2.3	2.7
1943	244.3[1]	84.6	159.7	14.1	6.1	8.0	3.9	2.2	1.7
1942	386.5[1]	137.3	249.2	19.4	8.5	10.9	4.2	2.4	1.8
1941	347.5[1]	95.2	252.3	23.7	9.7	14.0	5.1	2.4	2.7
1940	247.1[1]	66.7	180.4	23.1	10.7	12.4	5.0	2.7	2.3
1939	98.4	33.4	65.0	18.5	7.5	11.0	3.1	1.1	2.0
1938	115.2	44.8	70.4	19.6	7.8	11.8	3.3	.8	2.5
1937	140.4	64.1	76.3	19.0	8.5	10.5	4.2	1.8	2.4
1936	83.0	37.6	45.4	10.8	5.3	5.5	21.7	16.4	5.3
1935	66.6	21.1	45.5	8.9	3.5	5.4	2.0	.1	1.9
1934	49.9	19.5	30.4	5.3	1.6	3.7	1.9	.4	1.5
1933	42.0	18.1	23.9	2.8	.8	2.0	4.4	2.9	1.5
1932	47.2	19.3	27.9	8.0	4.9	3.1	1.5	.4	1.1
1931	95.3	40.9	54.4	12.6	7.2	5.4	2.2	.9	1.3
1930	163.0	75.5	87.5	17.4	7.4	10.0	4.3	2.1	2.2
1929	224.5	131.0	93.5	26.6	13.5	13.1	6.1	2.5	3.6
1928	214.5	121.7	92.8	19.3	9.6	9.7	5.8	2.9	2.9
1927	179.0	86.9	92.1	13.4	4.4	9.0	4.5	1.1	3.4
1926	129.3	55.7	73.6	10.8	2.7	8.1	2.2	.8	1.4

Series R514-620. Gross fixed capital formation in manufacturing, by major groups, 1926 to 1975 (continued)
(millions of dollars)

Year	Textiles industries			Knitting mills			Clothing industries			Wood industries			Furniture and fixtures industries		
	Capital formation	Construction	Machinery and equipment	Capital formation	Construction	Machinery and equipment	Capital formation	Construction	Machinery and equipment	Capital formation	Construction	Machinery and equipment	Capital formation	Construction	Machinery and equipment
	538	539	540	544	545	546	547	548	549	553	554	555	556	557	558
1975	158.9	34.1	124.8	10.2	0.8	9.4	15.6	4.7	10.9	257.9	69.4	188.5	26.2	8.0	18.2
1974	141.2	38.6	102.6	16.8	1.2	15.6	20.3	5.5	14.8	287.5	85.5	202.0	42.6	17.1	25.5
1973	113.3	26.0	87.3	21.7	3.3	18.4	24.9	9.6	15.3	276.7	76.3	200.4	32.5	11.5	21.0
1972	93.7	20.7	73.0	17.9	1.1	16.8	18.6	5.2	13.4	172.9	41.0	131.9	19.0	5.3	13.7
1971	74.8	14.0	60.8	15.7	1.5	14.2	11.8	2.0	9.8	153.5	37.2	116.3	13.6	3.9	9.7
1970	81.1	20.3	60.8	15.7	2.1	13.6	8.8	1.1	7.7	143.9	42.4	101.5	15.7	7.1	8.6
1969	77.1	20.5	56.6	17.2	2.9	14.3	12.8	3.8	9.0	150.4	42.5	107.9	12.2	2.9	9.3
1968	57.9	11.7	46.2	11.1	2.2	8.9	10.0	2.4	7.6	71.0	18.4	52.6	19.0	8.4	10.6
1967	74.2	17.8	56.4	7.7	0.8	6.9	9.4	2.0	7.4	61.5	15.6	45.9	19.8	10.2	9.6
1966	108.7	35.1	73.6	12.3	2.8	9.5	11.6	2.2	9.4	72.4	23.5	48.9	19.8	10.5	9.3
1965	108.8	32.8	76.0	8.2	1.3	6.9	10.7	2.6	8.1	76.5	22.9	53.6	15.6	6.7	8.9
1964	91.6	23.7	67.9	8.2	1.3	6.9	9.7	1.7	8.0	61.0	15.5	45.5	12.4	4.4	8.0
1963	49.7	10.9	38.8	7.1	0.9	6.2	8.9	1.4	7.5	50.5	12.5	38.0	10.4	4.7	5.7
1962	36.5	6.8	29.7	7.8	0.8	7.0	6.0	0.6	5.4	40.6	11.8	28.8	7.0	2.4	4.6
1961	27.5	5.5	22.0	6.1	1.1	5.0	7.1	1.9	5.2	44.6	13.6	31.0	4.7	1.2	3.5
1960	27.1	6.0	21.1	—	—	—	—	—	—	41.2	12.6	28.6	7.6	3.0	4.6

1948 Standard Industrial Classification

	Primary textiles and their products			Clothing and knitting mills				Wood and its products		
	541	542	543	550	551	552		559	560	561
1960	27.1	6.0	21.1	12.2	2.3	9.9		49.5	16.1	33.4
1959	22.8	4.7	18.1	12.5	1.6	10.9		50.7	15.3	35.4
1958	23.3	2.6	20.7	8.2	.7	7.5		30.9	8.8	22.1
1957	39.3	7.9	31.4	10.8	1.2	9.6		39.0	10.3	28.7
1956	38.3	10.3	28.0	9.7	1.3	8.4		50.8	14.0	36.8
1955	28.0	7.6	20.4	9.2	1.4	7.8		43.0	12.1	30.9
1954	28.5	7.5	21.0	9.8	2.2	7.6		32.9	8.4	24.5
1953	27.9	7.9	20.0	14.4	3.8	10.6		34.6	10.4	24.2
1952	31.5	7.0	24.5	12.7	1.6	11.1		31.8	9.3	22.5
1951	39.1	9.9	29.2	13.2	4.1	9.1		38.6	11.2	27.4
1950	27.4	6.6	20.8	11.9	2.5	9.4		29.4	8.1	21.3
1949	32.1	7.0	25.1	13.7	3.0	10.7		26.7	7.5	19.2
1948	35.6	6.5	29.1	12.3	2.1	10.2		26.4	7.9	18.5
1947	36.6	10.9	25.7	14.0	3.7	10.3		32.1	11.4	20.7
1946	24.6	8.4	16.2	8.4	2.6	5.8		20.4	10.9	9.5
1945	9.0	1.3	7.7	13.6	9.2	4.4		5.2	1.6	3.6
1944	6.7	1.8	4.9	3.9	2.8	1.1		5.3	2.9	2.4
1943	2.6	.8	1.8	2.8	1.6	1.2		20.4	16.8	3.6
1942	6.4	1.5	4.9	4.1	3.0	1.1		15.4	11.3	4.1
1941	11.7	3.1	8.6	13.0	10.9	2.1		17.1	10.8	6.3
1940	13.6	3.4	10.2	4.1	2.4	1.7		11.1	8.0	3.1
1939	5.6	.6	5.0	3.3	1.4	1.9		6.7	4.9	1.8
1938	6.4	1.4	5.0	1.4	.4	1.0		3.8	1.2	2.6
1937	8.8	2.6	6.2	3.4	1.8	1.6		17.7	14.1	3.6
1936	6.6	1.3	5.3	1.9	.8	1.1		4.3	2.8	1.5
1935	9.9	2.8	7.1	.8	.1	.7		3.2	1.0	2.2
1934	5.4	.6	4.8	1.2	.4	.8		5.6	4.4	1.2
1933	4.5	.9	3.6	1.7	1.1	.6		8.5	7.0	1.5
1932	3.7	1.0	2.7	1.8	1.3	.5		5.9	4.4	1.5
1931	12.3	1.7	10.6	2.2	1.6	.6		3.2	1.0	2.2
1930	9.9	6.8	3.1	1.8	.8	1.0		10.1	5.9	4.2
1929	6.0	1.4	4.6	15.5	13.3	2.2		13.0	10.2	2.8
1928	8.5	.6	7.9	12.3	10.8	1.5		11.1	7.4	3.7
1927	13.5	6.2	7.3	9.2	7.5	1.7		27.7	21.5	6.2
1926	7.2	4.7	2.5	3.5	2.0	1.5		7.7	3.3	4.4

Series R514-620. Gross fixed capital formation in manufacturing, by major groups, 1926 to 1975 (continued)
(millions of dollars)

Year	Paper and allied industries			Printing, publishing and allied industries			Primary metals industries			Metal fabricating industries			Machinery industries		
	Capital formation	Construction	Machinery and equipment	Capital formation	Construction	Machinery and equipment	Capital formation	Construction	Machinery and equipment	Capital formation	Construction	Machinery and equipment	Capital formation	Construction	Machinery and equipment
	562	563	564	568	569	570	574	575	576	577	578	579	580	581	582
1975	607.7	112.9	494.8	93.7	19.7	74.0	805.9	170.6	635.3	198.6	44.7	153.9	123.0	37.2	85.8
1974	554.3	120.5	433.8	85.6	16.7	68.9	697.7	148.0	549.7	207.6	59.7	147.9	125.3	42.8	82.5
1973	402.4	89.4	313.0	77.4	15.0	62.4	404.3	75.8	328.5	163.7	43.4	120.3	90.1	30.3	59.8
1972	448.0	116.5	331.5	65.6	15.3	50.3	371.9	95.3	276.6	118.6	20.4	98.2	57.8	14.6	43.2
1971	536.0	133.6	402.4	72.3	15.6	56.7	401.4	91.1	310.3	110.9	20.4	90.5	51.0	13.1	37.9
1970	532.0	132.6	399.4	65.0	13.8	51.2	425.2	118.2	307.0	136.9	32.5	104.4	72.9	26.1	46.8
1969	376.7	109.9	266.8	56.1	12.5	43.6	292.9	71.5	221.4	132.4	29.0	103.4	59.0	17.1	41.9
1968	291.3	70.3	221.0	49.8	10.4	39.4	235.4	81.3	154.1	109.9	21.7	88.2	49.5	11.8	37.7
1967	468.3	111.2	357.1	46.0	9.9	36.1	284.8	82.0	202.8	112.7	28.2	84.5	59.2	18.9	40.3
1966	550.0	137.1	412.9	57.4	12.6	44.8	385.9	85.3	300.6	134.1	36.8	97.3	61.3	23.6	37.7
1965	417.9	111.5	306.4	50.2	17.6	32.6	264.6	61.7	202.9	108.3	32.9	75.4	47.8	13.8	34.0
1964	318.8	69.4	249.4	55.6	17.1	38.5	272.8	58.3	214.5	72.6	17.9	54.7	54.6	19.2	35.4
1963	205.1	40.3	164.8	45.8	15.5	30.3	181.2	44.4	136.8	52.5	14.6	37.9	37.5	14.2	23.3
1962	173.4	40.5	132.9	36.5	10.8	25.7	217.5	58.4	159.1	51.1	12.4	38.7	24.1	5.4	18.7
1961	161.0	37.1	123.9	30.7	6.4	24.3	126.5	32.9	93.6	37.7	8.4	29.3	22.2	5.5	16.7
1960	166.3	35.1	131.2	29.1	7.4	21.7	194.2	51.3	142.9	46.7	12.2	34.5	23.0	8.4	14.6

1948 Standard Industrial Classification

Year	565	566	567	571	572	573		Iron and steel and their products[1]			Non-ferrous metals and products including electrical apparatus[2]		
								586	587	588	589	590	591
1960	164.3	34.1	130.2	29.2	7.4	21.8		196.8	47.2	149.6	101.1	32.5	68.6
1959	126.6	24.2	102.4	40.2	11.8	28.4		165.7	40.9	124.8	90.7	36.3	54.4
1958	127.2	25.5	101.7	33.5	13.4	20.1		126.4	35.7	90.7	125.0	51.0	74.0
1957	266.3	66.3	200.0	40.1	17.3	22.8		179.6	54.5	125.1	188.7	105.0	83.7
1956	257.4	85.1	172.3	25.5	5.3	20.2		162.5	40.3	122.2	158.9	77.1	81.8
1955	138.9	33.1	105.8	24.1	6.4	17.7		95.2	27.0	68.2	112.2	45.4	66.8
1954	87.3	21.6	65.7	31.4	11.7	19.7		88.4	22.0	66.4	85.3	32.0	53.3
1953	104.1	22.5	81.6	16.4	3.8	12.6		114.0	35.6	78.4	115.3	53.4	61.9
1952	129.5	33.6	95.9	14.3	3.3	11.0		135.9	46.2	89.7	111.1	56.9	54.2
1951	125.3	41.9	83.4	24.3	6.3	18.0		97.2	47.1	50.1	80.3	38.7	41.6
1950	78.5	21.1	57.4	19.4	5.0	14.4		44.2	13.5	30.7	36.1	12.0	24.1
1949	81.5	26.8	54.7	20.1	6.3	13.8		52.3	14.6	37.7	45.5	15.2	30.3
1948	89.5	29.1	60.4	19.4	7.0	12.4		56.3	19.6	36.7	36.4	9.7	26.7
1947	81.0	31.2	49.8	13.8	5.4	8.4		54.9	16.0	38.9	31.1	12.0	19.1
1946	55.0	27.2	27.8	7.3	2.9	4.4		36.9	14.9	22.0	19.3	5.3	14.0
1945	16.6	5.8	10.8	6.0	3.9	2.1		31.3	12.8	18.5	10.7	1.5	9.2
1944	14.7	8.0	6.7	2.4	.2	2.2		32.3	10.1	22.2	21.0	14.7	6.3
1943	6.8	1.7	5.1	1.4	.2	1.2		28.3	4.3	24.0	42.7	36.2	6.5
1942	13.4	3.8	9.6	2.3	.3	2.0		44.7	7.2	37.5	76.0	59.2	16.8
1941	14.4	8.8	5.6	2.6	—	2.6		41.9	9.9	32.0	46.6	26.0	20.6
1940	14.9	5.1	9.8	4.8	.6	4.2		20.0	4.9	15.1	24.3	15.7	8.6
1939	6.1	3.9	2.2	6.0	.3	5.7		9.4	4.3	5.1	7.6	.4	7.2
1938	7.2	2.6	4.6	3.8	.6	3.2		10.2	5.0	5.2	9.1	1.3	7.8
1937	10.6	4.2	6.4	3.9	1.2	2.7		18.3	10.0	8.3	10.1	.8	9.3
1936	5.1	1.5	3.6	1.7	—	1.7		5.9	3.1	2.8	3.6	.7	2.9
1935	4.6	2.2	2.4	6.1	.6	5.5		5.0	2.4	2.6	2.6	.8	1.8
1934	3.5	.8	2.7	.9	—	.9		4.9	2.5	2.4	2.1	.6	1.5
1933	.8	.1	.7	1.2	.3	.9		1.8	.6	1.2	1.4	.4	1.0
1932	3.3	2.1	1.2	2.8	.7	2.1		2.1	.5	1.6	3.8	.6	3.2
1931	13.2	11.3	1.9	3.1	.3	2.8		9.7	4.7	5.0	5.7	1.0	4.7
1930	25.2	4.4	20.8	4.7	.2	4.5		17.5	12.5	5.0	9.3	1.8	7.5
1929	25.6	16.0	9.6	15.7	7.5	8.2		18.1	8.3	9.8	8.4	3.5	4.9
1928	49.0	31.8	17.2	16.2	9.4	6.8		12.1	4.8	7.3	5.5	1.5	4.0
1927	47.4	23.7	23.7	3.8	.5	3.3		9.5	5.0	4.5	5.8	1.9	3.9
1926	43.9	21.4	22.5	4.9	.8	4.1		8.4	4.3	4.1	7.4	2.6	4.8

Series R514-620. Gross fixed capital formation in manufacturing, by major groups, 1926 to 1975 (continued)
(millions of dollars)

Year	Electrical products industries — Capital formation	Construction	Machinery and equipment	Transportation equipment industries — Capital formation	Construction	Machinery and equipment	Non-metallic mineral products industries — Capital formation	Construction	Machinery and equipment	Petroleum and coal products industries — Capital formation	Construction	Machinery and equipment	Chemical and chemical products industries — Capital formation	Construction	Machinery and equipment
	583	584	585	592	593	594	598	599	600	601	602	603	607	608	609
1975	136.7	34.0	102.7	263.2	69.2	194.0	193.3	38.4	154.9	455.9	350.1	105.8	976.3	382.9	593.4
1974	139.2	31.0	108.2	302.3	102.4	199.9	174.2	29.5	144.7	429.5	321.7	107.8	579.8	198.7	381.1
1973	127.0	32.2	94.8	190.6	47.7	142.9	188.7	37.6	151.1	318.8	229.7	89.1	293.3	100.7	192.6
1972	89.6	18.6	71.0	132.4	30.2	102.2	129.9	30.7	99.2	243.8	214.0	29.8	218.5	78.1	140.4
1971	106.3	28.6	77.7	138.6	30.2	108.4	80.3	22.5	57.8	231.4	211.3	20.1	227.9	107.6	120.3
1970	96.7	26.7	70.0	253.5	49.6	203.9	135.0	32.7	102.3	231.1	213.7	17.4	261.5	132.2	129.3
1969	87.9	22.4	65.5	178.1	43.6	134.5	121.1	37.1	84.0	129.8	116.9	12.9	235.5	119.4	116.1
1968	69.0	17.1	51.9	132.2	37.6	94.6	85.9	19.9	66.0	127.6	98.9	28.7	291.9	134.1	157.8
1967	96.5	26.4	70.1	192.7	56.4	136.3	119.8	40.9	78.9	100.2	78.8	21.4	270.3	78.7	191.6
1966	105.9	30.7	75.2	242.7	87.8	154.9	159.5	51.0	108.5	65.1	55.5	9.6	284.9	76.0	208.9
1965	66.5	17.6	48.9	221.6	64.5	157.1	108.3	30.0	78.3	40.6	30.3	10.3	279.5	76.2	203.3
1964	49.0	12.0	37.0	135.0	44.4	90.6	82.0	20.2	61.8	24.4	20.2	4.2	143.3	42.9	100.4
1963	42.1	9.5	32.6	79.4	27.1	52.3	52.6	13.7	38.9	46.5	37.9	8.6	118.0	39.5	78.5
1962	40.3	10.9	29.4	47.9	11.6	36.3	52.2	13.7	38.5	65.6	56.8	8.8	100.0	40.1	59.9
1961	30.2	7.8	22.4	47.1	13.9	33.2	44.7	11.9	32.8	31.9	27.9	4.0	125.7	35.4	90.3
1960	31.8	7.6	24.2	48.4	16.5	31.9	49.2	15.7	33.5	59.7	51.9	7.8	107.0	34.9	72.1

1948 Standard Industrial Classification

Year	595	596	597	Non-metallic minerals and products including products of petroleum and coal — 604	605	606	610	611	612
1960	48.7	16.4	32.3	130.9	88.0	42.9	110.3	36.2	74.1
1959	65.7	20.5	45.2	195.4	135.1	60.3	81.0	24.5	56.5
1958	54.3	16.6	37.7	183.6	150.4	33.2	116.6	43.1	73.5
1957	62.4	18.1	44.3	208.6	142.8	65.8	149.7	65.6	84.1
1956	60.3	16.7	43.6	213.0	135.3	77.7	144.9	57.9	87.0
1955	54.3	20.2	34.1	156.7	122.6	34.1	56.3	21.6	34.7
1954	65.2	20.9	44.3	136.8	99.2	37.6	39.8	15.1	24.7
1953	97.3	46.9	50.4	113.9	72.7	41.2	122.3	32.0	90.3
1952	62.1	37.1	25.0	111.8	52.3	59.5	141.0	61.2	79.8
1951	48.9	21.8	27.1	89.4	33.2	56.2	57.7	19.2	38.5
1950	27.3	9.9	17.4	49.2	18.7	30.5	26.3	7.3	19.0
1949	22.0	6.7	15.3	47.5	25.0	22.5	37.8	11.9	25.9
1948	15.4	5.4	10.0	70.8	40.4	30.4	41.9	15.0	26.9
1947	14.1	5.2	8.9	55.7	34.7	21.0	33.7	14.4	19.3
1946	15.7	5.4	10.3	17.5	8.7	8.8	19.6	11.6	8.0
1945	10.8	2.2	8.6	12.2	7.8	4.4	7.6	4.0	3.6
1944	6.3	1.6	4.7	6.0	3.5	2.5	3.0	1.4	1.6
1943	20.1	6.6	13.5	7.1	3.7	3.4	5.6	2.5	3.1
1942	45.5	27.9	17.6	7.1	3.9	3.2	10.0	5.3	4.7
1941	11.9	3.0	8.9	8.5	5.3	3.2	12.1	3.2	8.9
1940	11.4	3.4	8.0	9.1	6.4	2.7	6.4	1.9	4.5
1939	7.4	2.9	4.5	6.7	4.4	2.3	3.4	1.0	2.4
1938	20.8	14.5	6.3	7.3	5.3	2.0	6.3	2.9	3.4
1937	10.4	5.2	5.2	8.8	7.0	1.8	7.5	5.5	2.0
1936	3.3	.9	2.4	4.9	3.6	1.3	2.7	.4	2.3
1935	5.2	2.4	2.8	5.0	3.6	1.4	3.1	1.1	2.0
1934	3.4	2.1	1.3	4.8	3.3	1.5	4.0	2.4	1.6
1933	2.2	.6	1.6	3.3	2.0	1.3	3.9	1.0	2.9
1932	2.3	.2	2.1	3.8	2.1	1.7	1.8	.7	1.1
1931	2.8	.3	2.5	11.7	8.2	3.5	4.1	1.8	2.3
1930	5.1	1.8	3.3	30.9	27.2	3.7	6.4	2.9	3.5
1929	13.9	8.3	5.6	36.7	32.7	4.0	16.1	10.9	5.2
1928	13.2	7.0	6.2	35.2	32.0	3.2	3.8	1.2	2.6
1927	7.6	4.8	2.8	9.2	6.0	3.2	5.9	2.4	3.5
1926	1.9	.8	1.1	8.7	6.7	2.0	5.8	4.4	1.4

Series R514-620. Gross fixed capital formation in manufacturing, by major groups, 1926 to 1975 (concluded)
(millions of dollars)

Year	Miscellaneous manufacturing industries			Capital items charged to operating expenses
	Capital formation	Construction	Machinery and equipment	
	613	614	615	619
1975	36.0	8.2	27.8	530.4
1974	54.4	20.6	33.8	499.1
1973	42.4	12.5	29.9	393.2
1972	30.8	9.1	21.7	320.5
1971	59.3	16.1	43.2	308.8
1970	58.9	22.7	36.2	311.8
1969	67.3	17.8	49.5	266.2
1968	55.7	18.2	37.5	234.6
1967	48.5	14.1	34.4	257.5
1966	52.1	15.4	36.7	277.7
1965	39.9	12.4	27.5	232.6
1964	31.5	11.4	20.1	194.3
1963	28.7	8.5	20.2	151.2
1962	27.2	8.2	19.0	139.4
1961	19.8	5.6	14.2	124.0
1960	20.8	7.2	13.6	126.4

1948 Standard Industrial Classification

Year	616	617	618	620
1960	18.6	6.4	12.2	126.9
1959	16.5	6.0	10.5	118.8
1958	12.0	2.7	9.3	105.4
1957	15.1	6.6	8.5	132.5
1956	12.3	3.6	8.7	124.7
1955	10.8	3.7	7.1	92.3
1954	7.2	2.7	4.5	84.1
1953	8.7	3.6	5.0	93.6
1952	8.8	4.7	4.1	90.2
1951	7.4	3.0	4.4	79.6
1950	6.0	2.4	3.6	61.8
1949	5.9	2.3	3.6	60.9
1948	6.5	2.7	3.8	62.0
1947	5.7	2.3	3.4	56.0
1946	5.6	2.9	2.7	41.0
1945	3.3	1.7	1.6	109.1
1944	2.5	1.3	1.2	80.2
1943	3.1	1.9	1.2	85.4
1942	4.9	3.0	1.9	133.1
1941	4.0	2.1	1.9	134.9
1940	2.9	1.5	1.4	96.4
1939	1.6	.7	.9	13.0
1938	1.9	1.0	.9	14.1
1937	2.4	1.4	1.0	15.3
1936	1.4	.8	.6	9.1
1935	1.1	.5	.6	9.1
1934	.8	.4	.4	6.1
1933	.7	.4	.3	4.8
1932	.8	.4	.4	5.6
1931	1.6	.9	.7	10.9
1930	2.9	1.7	1.2	17.5
1929	4.1	2.9	1.2	18.7
1928	3.9	2.7	1.2	18.6
1927	3.1	1.9	1.2	18.4
1926	2.2	1.2	1.0	14.7

[1] Excluding outlay by the United Kingdom government for wartime plant expansion, amounting to $28 million in 1943; $84 million in 1942; $61 million in 1941 and $28 million in 1940.

[2] The two former groups of iron and steel and non-ferrous metal products, were expanded to the four groups shown at the top of this and the following page (that is including electrical apparatus).

Series R621-770. Quantity and value of shipments of selected manufactured commodities,[1] 1917 to 1975

Year	Wheat flour Quantity ('000 cwt)	Value ($'000)	Bread Quantity ('000,000 lb.)	Value ($'000)	Refined sugar Quantity ('000,000 lb.)	Value ($'000)	Confectionery Quantity ('000 lb.)	Value ($'000)	Jams, jellies and marmalades Quantity ('000 lb.)	Value ($'000)	Canned fruits Quantity ('000 lb.)	Value ($'000)	Canned vegetables Quantity ('000 lb.)	Value ($'000)
	621	622	623	624	625	626	627	628	629	630	631	632	633	634
1975	40,289	347,354	1,485	405,773	2,204	733,080	290,314	335,684	48,745	28,934	114,229	41,616	559,331	157,820
1974	39,749	299,707	1,499	366,036	2,254	642,203	316,008	295,984	56,736	27,221	123,378	36,040	631,714	152,550
1973	38,222	218,928	1,490	301,266	2,501	333,849	356,512	251,714	58,608	18,361	129,172	28,789	591,761	124,681
1972	39,391	200,866	1,641	302,380	2,290	265,929	327,073	210,846	54,956	16,350	138,805	27,054	604,117	119,408
1971	38,979	191,889	1,633	288,513	2,306	227,001	337,553	194,847	62,550	16,442	131,082	24,999	610,287	109,269
1970	39,990	202,658	1,748	283,085	2,257	203,902	394,798	185,454	75,554	19,102	134,900	25,438	583,909	102,422
1969	39,118	197,895	1,742	274,576	2,131	173,914	335,766	181,026	78,806	18,473	142,365	26,992	612,228	102,502
1968	37,090	183,287	1,770	272,599	2,154	150,302	340,400	179,941	82,820	19,340	150,402	28,453	653,049	112,572
1967	39,115	199,545	1,779	269,142	2,065	141,193	324,778	167,292	93,275	21,330	151,887	28,707	644,746	100,622
1966	42,336	210,146	1,747	253,770	2,065	140,179	313,215	155,743	106,704	23,337	144,410	26,573	635,839	97,561
1965	40,565	196,170	1,743	245,326	1,981	147,089	295,268	147,047	105,041	23,538	143,169	26,236	661,756	92,130
1964	48,965	240,132	1,741	244,982	1,872	222,840	271,114	132,436	101,185	24,410	159,900	29,281	621,568	84,031
1963	38,347	185,745	1,660	229,881	1,813	218,776	258,014	129,613	99,381	23,101	156,540	27,507	575,872	77,191
1962	39,468	181,638	1,668	225,124	1,775	131,907	243,025	105,898	95,684	19,736	164,775	26,502	560,207	74,348
1961	39,185	168,138	1,668	220,295	1,684	126,282	237,792	102,557	99,913	20,293	150,513	23,267	550,050	73,067
1960	40,897	176,581	1,652	215,287	1,675	124,144	232,809	100,730	106,180	22,071	147,238	23,807	540,352	70,109
1959	40,627	171,427	1,653	206,588	1,658	120,061	226,423	96,057	113,012	23,325	147,846	23,968	486,185	62,227
1958	41,146	169,642	1,650	203,659	1,645	133,374	214,805	97,818	104,085	21,716	140,785	22,216	477,509	60,178
1957	37,359	157,493	1,653	198,515	1,533	151,025	224,078	93,690	102,481	20,930	148,851	23,335	489,804	61,245
1956	40,053	167,911	1,607	186,061	1,553	121,727	199,089	81,226	105,850	19,985	141,976	23,290	474,924	59,605
1955	40,295	168,304	1,530	175,097	1,578	120,727	150,570	74,110	104,987	18,532	149,585	22,175	489,597	57,047
1954	41,354	180,178	1,526	173,166	1,441	111,362	147,544	75,543	107,688	19,301	147,596	23,482	434,515	51,578
1953	46,196	208,609	1,558	171,795	1,349	110,386	146,528	72,132	99,827	18,118	122,188	19,016	436,717	50,467
1952[18,19]	46,046	209,448	1,524	161,553	1,421	128,638	145,058	71,618	92,531	16,432	100,468	14,676	508,543	60,110
1951	45,821	213,638	1,418	149,482	1,310	133,896	134,487	65,223	84,832	15,275	134,322	20,916	439,421	53,010
1950	40,331	189,721	1,383	130,883	1,528	140,117	156,393	78,509	98,939	16,647	125,403	18,546	368,227	39,273
1949	39,792	188,615	1,350	121,716	1,386	113,238	157,008	76,031	86,344	13,515	127,165	18,451	401,822	39,521
1948	45,292	188,908	1,371	110,960	1,358	110,031	142,315	74,002	105,110	16,394	101,288	14,886	497,909	48,088
1947	56,093	211,156	1,385	92,140	1,085	77,429	121,449	56,621	120,224	18,000	127,976	17,213	359,727	35,160
1946	53,218	164,264	1,376	79,751	960	58,913	92,922	40,349	93,830	12,348	108,354	12,000	410,371	31,178
1945	49,230	139,811	1,292	73,769	981	59,991	97,412	41,276	87,132	11,018	56,650	5,709	320,363	22,643
1944	47,962	132,607	1,249	70,259	1,018	62,061	113,157	43,380	104,707	12,931	70,003	6,549	393,115	26,939
1943	47,014	112,345	1,244	68,904	871	49,830	105,640	40,203	92,613	10,678	42,217	4,226	226,484	15,288
1942	39,435	86,043	1,154	63,349	801	44,031	113,527	39,022	78,477	8,889	60,696	6,057	331,453	22,980
1941	40,904	79,270	1,068	58,322	1,227	60,757	134,698	38,233	75,196	8,114	85,432	7,501	369,530	23,331
1940	34,136	66,925	1,033	54,805	1,157	56,035	114,500	29,950	52,585	5,044	102,431	6,739	284,638	16,755
1939	30,873	54,322	999	51,665	1,157	49,016	108,309	26,725	52,977	4,975	116,500	7,769	250,422	14,446
1938	26,173	75,420	1,010	55,502	1,043	40,726	102,254	25,193	46,171	4,513	64,373	4,556	287,160	14,481
1937	27,849	80,597	963	55,253	1,026	40,254	102,097	24,861	48,081	4,822	69,142	5,252	324,794	17,084
1936	29,268	66,000	909	47,659	1,093	39,449	96,791	22,405	49,791	4,934	65,620	5,319	253,166	14,044
1935	27,710	57,169	904	44,491	969	35,816	91,100	20,420	44,141	4,231	58,441	4,757	221,215	12,058
1934	29,023	57,120	911	42,826	889	35,452	88,856	20,126	44,889	4,448	41,179	3,509	213,125	10,841
1933	29,845	49,284	878	39,125	872	36,794	87,958	16,895	45,943	4,598	38,578	2,895	159,323	8,221
1932	29,138	49,373	890	40,376	944	40,544	96,701	18,448	44,380	4,171	44,273	3,445	159,054	8,296
1931	29,180	56,597	943	46,930	998	43,339	104,891	23,545	53,043	5,357	22,298	2,445	160,584	10,943
1930	30,624	90,714	941	55,379	943	42,150	122,124	28,708	48,633	5,406	30,450	3,520	234,860	19,503
1929	38,723	114,553	936	59,635	932	46,160	126,013	32,514	61,944	7,069	31,467	3,827	150,947	15,224
1928	39,964	124,774	879	55,305	928	51,303	119,163	31,313	–	–	29,156	3,284	147,747	13,780
1927	36,823	125,111	786	54,386	979	59,718	111,091	29,765	–	–	17,083	2,256	119,461	11,635
1926	37,350	131,188	792	50,767	1,139	63,207	105,145	27,594	–	–	23,950	3,059	130,853	12,663
1925	34,827	131,858	760	49,268	1,171	66,983	103,743	27,072	–	–	–	–	–	–
1924	41,310	121,787	714	43,770	872	65,922	95,921	26,079	–	–	–	–	–	–
1923	37,389	102,571	670	41,319	842	76,145	97,769	27,448	–	–	–	–	–	–
1922	35,388	112,446	664	39,165	1,148	69,667	103,879	25,957	–	–	–	–	–	–
1921	30,031	136,257	619	42,662	784	68,627	89,486	27,142	–	–	–	–	–	–
1920	26,771	157,807	635	52,194	782	117,346	101,413	33,350	–	–	–	–	–	–
1919	34,972	185,982	596	42,948	1,017	100,712	111,755	33,263	–	–	–	–	–	–
1918	35,047	189,096	648	40,159	652	57,080	70,315	21,280	–	–	–	–	–	–
1917	34,667	170,382	707	42,452	778	60,223	43,257	12,977	–	–	–	–	–	–

Series R621-770. Quantity and value of shipments of selected manufactured commodities,[1] 1917 to 1975 (continued)

Year	Frozen fruits and vegetables		Meats, fresh and frozen		Poultry, fresh and frozen		Carbonated beverages		Beer, ale, stout and porter		Beverage spirits sold		Cigarettes	
	Quantity	Value	Quantity	Value	Quantity	Value	Quantity	Value	Quantity	Value	Quantity	Value	Quantity	Value
	('000 lb.)	($'000)	(tons)	($'000)	(tons)	($'000)	('000 gal)	($'000)	('000 gal)	($'000)	('000 proof gal)	($'000)	('000,000)	($'000)
	635	636	637	638	639	640	641	642	643	644	645	646	647	648
1975	59,592	138,038	1,528,030	2,436,689	400,340	539,573	322,009	655,099	442,930	699,029	43,611	415,705	58,885	507,650
1974	544,053	127,852	1,488,809	2,269,091	417,639	504,800	306,180	506,976	428,941	615,863	46,443	409,418	58,825	445,324
1973	527,003	104,530	1,433,992	2,134,369	451,648	486,200	304,439	409,814	417,690	534,829	42,503	365,756	55,959	399,707
1972	463,366	87,783	1,440,179	1,680,360	442,649	357,645	281,699	360,631	394,308	486,552	39,595	325,148	53,242	369,539 [12]
1971	413,376	73,811	1,379,996	1,374,078	389,412	287,507	277,900	339,928	375,588	440,500	39,450	324,772	51,446	935,395
1970	433,420	75,011	1,288,147	1,300,385	399,533	285,288	266,878	310,325	348,648	399,968	35,802	290,861	50,479	896,266
1969	424,389	74,810	1,225,050	1,236,810	385,791	286,973	269,871	304,151	329,487	374,171	35,410	289,567	46,681	819,917
1968	350,173	59,443	1,241,057	1,132,545	278,084	207,754	260,145	275,527	312,675	351,049	31,526	258,749	46,855	808,522
1967	378,937	62,020	1,195,213	1,078,589	287,911	214,102	250,772	260,884	306,685	335,583	28,847	236,877	47,595	773,099
1966	—	—	1,106,421	976,084	313,840	235,985	232,682	230,961	298,164	321,971 [16]	26,501	227,099	46,095	711,784
1965	—	—	1,076,921	845,943	299,405	212,972	206,861	205,934	281,622	476,432	23,490	197,541	43,621	657,698
1964	—	—	982,733	737,583	281,949	193,395	183,611	196,397	274,851	463,469	22,662	182,810	40,784	602,841
1963	—	—	884,426	696,917	246,441	178,758	178,168	180,113	265,631	443,413	20,009	161,816	40,102	588,604
1962	—	—	859,714	682,155	236,137	168,727	171,629	163,261	255,951	425,396	18,409	152,047	39,160	574,649
1961	—	—	878,396	650,869	224,392	154,085	165,396	156,359	244,409	412,973	16,979	143,475	36,900	540,979
1960	—	—	826,971	605,553	185,773	140,618	159,576	145,745	238,732	399,226	16,501	136,472	34,699	509,689
1959	—	—	828,943	627,108	34,541	26,920	157,463	142,736	235,184	388,131	16,173	132,958	34,273	493,911
1958	—	—	874,316	593,092	31,497	27,923	147,196	133,879	219,848	361,610	15,777	125,563	32,778	439,367
1957	—	—	831,109	549,017	22,344	19,617	137,151	123,272	224,783	364,993	13,830	110,532	30,395	407,237
1956	—	—	798,677	500,242	28,672	27,493	123,192	107,715	214,979	339,474	13,733	107,076	27,344	366,114
1955	—	—	749,604	474,037	22,222	21,260	118,442	103,652	211,102	331,117	11,848	91,212	24,864	332,012
1954	—	—	700,111	457,065	19,397	17,215	105,931	92,771	200,459	317,726	11,946	91,408	22,426	303,682
1953	—	—	655,647	465,571	16,692	16,940	110,175	94,077	206,908	324,204	12,445	97,716	21,156	289,425
1952	—	—	591,113	474,180	15,484	13,636	103,473	89,810	193,830	300,475	11,172	86,142	18,037	290,948
1951	—	—	514,571	495,838	12,207	13,141	94,803	77,286	177,658	271,555	10,801	84,454	15,816	261,910
1950	—	—	516,690	405,078	12,163	10,982	102,709	74,115	171,056	238,704	9,132	68,968	17,311	266,821
1949	—	—	550,407	370,908	10,321	9,180	101,188	73,144	173,294	228,334	8,842	60,761	17,053	255,714
1948	—	—	553,394	336,912	11,514	9,884	85,669	57,349	169,703	213,316	8,259	54,400	16,072	240,838
1947	—	—	446,617	203,545	10,553	7,640	69,413	48,116	160,875	194,312	8,854	50,671	15,687	220,649
1946	—	—	537,440	223,339	9,961	6,482	55,729	37,057	151,310	182,641	11,125	59,133	15,264	208,028
1945	—	—	597,455	231,875	12,366	7,757	51,335	34,598	128,910	157,568	9,151	46,863	17,685	207,613
1944	—	—	541,482	207,998	16,776	10,667	64,226	40,738	113,396	136,673	5,237	30,620	15,485	171,002
1943	—	—	443,716	168,593	10,067	6,333	58,020	36,785	95,691	114,759	4,738	25,207	13,591	155,931
1942	—	—	435,195	144,622	12,269	7,001	58,274	36,646	109,018	120,212	5,692	26,660	11,966	115,125
1941	—	—	427,601	118,721	8,424	4,369	59,804	37,155	90,247	96,421	4,994	18,636	9,548	86,653
1940	—	—	389,636	92,730	9,009	4,902	52,938	30,881	72,388	74,116	4,300	15,481	7,831	70,472
1939	—	—	366,190	81,972	7,488	3,162	43,956	26,278	62,780	59,130	5,151	17,918	7,163	57,277
1938	—	—	366,697	76,867	6,391	2,819	39,499	24,115	62,468	56,841	5,422	20,927	6,900	53,225
1937	—	—	390,621	76,961	7,342	2,972	31,699	20,576	63,467	57,438	7,482	27,360	6,724	52,138
1936	—	—	378,030	67,088	6,390	2,654	27,596	15,793	56,917	43,345	6,757	24,009	5,607	43,763
1935	—	—	324,243	59,046	5,341	2,100	22,432	12,782	54,657	40,071	4,356	18,213	5,325	41,526
1934	—	—	326,671	54,477	5,964	1,936	20,050	10,978	46,390	35,501	3,414	12,506	4,843	38,183
1933	—	—	289,035	43,610	4,791	1,472	16,970	9,900	37,910	30,099	3,061	10,399	4,310	34,878
1932	—	—	284,089	48,158	4,399	1,554	16,150	10,496	43,318	37,415	3,783	12,391	3,885	36,074
1931	—	—	290,198	62,330	3,774	1,851	17,487	12,533	52,089	47,965	3,504	12,958	4,432	42,865
1930	—	—	275,385	84,322	4,097	2,184	13,550	12,899	58,384	56,176	8,425	23,258	5,086	49,835
1929	—	—	289,662	94,196	3,132	2,102	12,249	11,827	62,087	60,834	15,712	41,437	4,967	49,259
1928	—	—	287,875	86,656	2,965	1,891	10,678	9,730	61,766	59,592	12,256	36,046	4,226	41,706
1927	—	—	291,707	77,547	3,410	2,204	8,712	7,676	54,912	50,511	9,025	23,963	3,613	36,282
1926	—	—	270,291	68,706	2,947	1,921	7,407	7,205	48,943	42,734	4,179	10,160	3,097	31,456
1925	—	—	278,757	64,354	—	—	6,878	6,714	48,399	38,058	3,945	8,488	2,705	27,869
1924	—	—	254,536	56,610	—	—	6,354	5,974	42,989	32,685	4,631	9,288	2,450	26,456
1923	—	—	234,056	53,561	—	—	6,409	6,240	39,200	28,490	2,029	3,080	2,079	23,964
1922	—	—	225,448	55,206	—	—	6,595	6,316	35,607	25,227	2,732	2,334	2,171	25,989
1921	—	—	200,387	62,672	—	—	9,177	8,906	41,796	30,020	2,680	2,626	2,604	31,114
1920	—	—	226,530	93,896	—	—	9,355	9,046	38,366	28,589	3,800	4,218	2,936	31,625
1919	—	—	207,421	81,455	—	—	10,322	4,537	34,891	19,123	4,803	4,467	2,964	25,457
1918	—	—	215,231	88,204	—	—	—	—	28,010	14,915	3,702	2,782	2,854	19,941
1917	—	—	245,635	79,576	—	—	—	—	26,792	15,426	3,535	2,658	—	12,474

Series R621-770. Quantity and value of shipments of selected manufactured commodities,[1] 1917 to 1975 (continued)

Year	Cigars Quantity ('000)	Cigars Value[10] ($'000)	Smoking tobacco Quantity ('000 lb.)	Smoking tobacco Value[10] ($'000)	Rubber tires Quantity ('000)	Rubber tires Value ($'000)	Boots and shoes with leather or fabric uppers (except felt)[2] Quantity ('000 pairs)	Boots and shoes Value ($'000)	Yarns produced Quantity ('000 lb.)	Broad-woven cotton fabrics Quantity ('000 sq yd)	Broad-woven cotton fabrics Value ($'000)	Broad-woven wool fabrics Quantity ('000 sq yd)	Broad-woven wool fabrics Value ($'000)
	649	650	651	652	653	654	655	656	657	658	659	660	661
1975	178,352	17,232	16,070	38,098	x	x	29,031	299,446	412,276	x	x	37,653	75,954
1974	219,009	18,005	15,649	34,052	x	x	33,347	290,301	484,441	x	x	34,139	66,038
1973	229,817	18,024	17,332	34,028	x	x	32,443	251,262	498,586	189,354	91,237	37,513	61,351
1972	229,211	16,849[13]	17,185	33,047[14]	21,853	372,723	32,843	222,985	477,011	218,185	87,319	32,187	47,508
1971	258,161	23,487	18,087	59,094	21,373	347,228	34,758	214,207	454,094	209,108	76,869	27,604	43,020
1970	x	x	17,604	56,066	20,418	333,983	33,816	201,206	425,522	216,202	77,508	34,047	51,787
1969	x	x	17,679	55,769	21,008	322,940	39,736	215,645	464,620	271,563	88,582	35,759	55,075
1968	x	x	17,828	55,569	18,602	271,405	41,242	209,181	408,909	288,326	63,355	34,304	55,346
1967	445,627	31,885	16,671	49,515	17,596	281,897	39,858	192,119	391,493	316,089	64,410	32,791	54,570
1966	444,683	25,819	17,434	49,343	16,073	246,956	41,233	188,718	376,375	265,717	63,169	37,778	59,881
1965	500,723	31,541	17,804	50,195	15,103	209,627	39,633	173,906	441,358	347,940	71,534	35,482	57,149
1964	476,949	31,272	x	x	13,423	187,982	39,258	167,314	421,836	322,276	68,184	38,374	56,854
1963	393,004	26,068	x	x	12,748	170,003	39,398	161,228	371,624	302,703	67,190	35,832	54,023
1962	354,038	24,287	x	x	11,212	156,456	39,584	160,406	332,053	280,754	61,432	34,007	49,944
1961	335,129	23,183	22,431	62,784	9,685	149,605	38,442	154,261	283,458	271,182	57,180	32,679	46,141
1960	328,688	22,662	22,089	59,308	8,603	148,568	36,550	144,311	272,459	229,179	49,354	30,405	45,216
1959	313,472	23,014	22,134	58,733	9,408	172,466	36,790	143,460	293,472	194,957	48,941	22,014	33,778
1958	319,595	22,518	21,609	55,771	8,415	153,463	36,374	136,073	252,338	191,880	47,023	16,044	27,295
1957	283,706	20,442	20,737	51,790	8,321	157,802	35,086	130,334	287,477	200,079	49,910	19,378	34,350
1956	260,900	19,723	21,588	53,655	8,596	175,569	34,390	124,536	307,106	214,923	56,059	21,862	36,920
1955	257,233	19,360	24,150	59,999	7,845	164,444	31,067	114,135	276,084	229,168	54,145	25,973	39,794
1954	240,520	17,926	25,125	62,604	6,596	130,771	30,684	112,210	238,706	182,362	45,379	19,296	34,527
1953	236,248	18,233	26,659	65,716	6,664	143,232	32,265	119,755	261,093	195,519	53,082	22,905	41,279
1952	201,517	15,487	31,635	77,789	5,582	143,020	31,203	117,420	262,667	158,521	54,095	20,370	49,890
1951	169,408	13,897	28,095	65,327	6,050	162,297	27,480	109,401	313,630	207,079	68,796	24,709	64,038
1950	198,987	14,467	26,795	50,864	6,038	122,402	27,361	100,277	316,915	224,055	60,657	18,071	49,901
1949	207,213	15,539	26,203	47,313	5,033	86,342	29,564	106,656	276,293	182,631	47,963	20,097	51,121
1948	210,335	14,453	26,337	46,607	5,606	96,074	27,178	96,660	277,399	161,485	46,421	22,127	55,229
1947	214,745	14,082	25,404	42,968	6,191	101,730	29,400	94,870	265,580	152,945	36,122	23,768	50,550
1946	219,985	14,691	25,983	40,912	4,007	64,945	34,113	84,543	255,036	157,717	25,385	23,291	43,198
1945	207,861	11,715	26,235	39,123	3,490	76,674	30,979	75,512	251,669	167,070	26,637	22,056	39,220
1944	198,512	10,471	24,263	36,098	2,680	64,210	29,278	70,505	254,113	182,515	29,341	20,062	35,253
1943	200,370	9,666	24,809	35,536	1,988	59,147	28,506	70,298	—	189,409	33,371	21,339	40,950
1942	206,486	7,906	25,743	31,702	1,962	60,462	27,828	62,775	—	230,958	35,307	22,174	42,560
1941	196,724	7,300	26,020	29,251	3,831	57,336	26,708	52,975	—	239,331	30,928	18,135	29,150
1940	165,455	6,276	26,156	27,984	3,275	37,288	21,818	42,383	—	204,628	24,518	13,804	22,111
1939	135,825	5,411	24,710	24,498	3,039	27,889	21,342	38,233	—	171,130	15,647	11,655	14,239
1938	132,715	5,690	22,535	22,844	2,759	25,596	19,005	34,800	—	139,672	12,698	10,258	11,829
1937	129,873	5,857	22,439	22,608	3,353	31,887	20,748	38,120	—	166,294	17,178	12,554	15,373
1936	119,827	5,283	20,080	20,582	2,913	25,516	18,675	33,039	—	150,218	15,842	12,044	13,955
1935	120,508	5,159	19,128	19,546	2,788	24,101	19,274	35,720	—	132,899	13,406	11,443	12,752
1934	116,858	4,558	19,240	19,814	3,016	23,993	17,183	30,309	—	135,621	13,419	10,313	12,095
1933	112,030	4,731	19,921	20,834	2,223	15,962	17,019	30,281	—	145,588	13,496	10,604	11,838
1932	131,392	5,976	18,607	19,968	1,960	14,099	16,029	30,556	—	115,398	9,586	7,607	8,423
1931	155,412	7,247	17,756	19,951	2,896	22,900	16,214	34,905	—	108,039	10,503	5,347	7,579
1930	197,398	10,024	17,426	20,238	3,720	31,577	15,635	38,284	—	81,179	8,672	3,674	5,958
1929	191,041	9,997	15,931	18,521	4,766	44,393	17,975	45,613	—	90,988	12,073	—	—
1928	184,284	9,322	15,830	18,193	4,579	42,053	18,008	46,628	—	112,570	14,889	—	—
1927	171,161	9,415	15,313	17,463	4,076	42,004	18,212	44,579	—	157,429	20,268	—	—
1926	166,770	8,959	14,543	16,933	3,251	39,718	17,564	43,259	—	106,996	15,985	—	—
1925	148,811	8,717	14,675	16,547	3,242	34,887	15,332	37,511	—	132,125	21,228	—	—
1924	159,875	9,740	14,097	16,341	2,391	23,966	15,222	38,236	—	—	—	—	—
1923	174,286	10,442	14,395	17,008	2,425	24,600	15,551	41,915	—	—	—	—	—
1922	152,958	10,130	14,533	18,021	1,692	20,367	15,099	42,139	—	—	—	—	—
1921	163,075	11,365	12,528	16,188	963	16,067	12,229	39,722	—	—	—	—	—
1920	194,361	14,110	14,205	19,517	1,840	36,489	14,566	60,474	—	—	—	—	—
1919	206,517	12,811	14,762	16,298	—	—	16,635	58,599	—	—	—	—	—
1918	203,016	11,694	11,699	12,382	—	—	12,379	39,003	—	—	—	—	—
1917	—	10,148	—	8,200	—	—	—	—	—	—	—	—	—

Series R621-770. Quantity and value of shipments of selected manufactured commodities,[1] 1917 to 1975 (continued)

Year	Broad-woven synthetic fabrics (including silk)		Carpets in rolls		Women's and misses' dresses (including house dresses)		Men's and youth's suits (excluding uniform suits)		House-hold furniture	Office furniture	Miscel-laneous furniture	Electric lamps and shades[3]	Total furniture	Wood pulp[4]
	Quantity ('000 sq yd)	Value ($'000)	Quantity ('000 sq yd)	Value ($'000)	Quantity ('000)	Value ($'000)	Quantity ('000)	Value ($'000)	Value ($'000)	Value ($'000)	Value ($'000)	Value ($'000)	Value ($'000)	Value ($'000)
	662	663	664	665	666	667	668	669	670	671	672	673	674	675
1975	405,677	223,325	73,666	327,379	12,476	206,086	2,434	146,781	613,829	177,156	70,297	41,483	—	1,982,617
1974	467,386	237,138	70,943	315,740	13,952	190,467	2,222	130,025	660,430	170,562	69,881	43,387	—	2,205,290
1973	392,524	192,621	65,263	265,202	15,025	194,506	2,090	115,583	555,845	133,060	67,440	36,919	—	1,301,486
1972	346,500	174,224	54,572	208,200	15,166	191,252	1,955	98,848	456,468	109,813	63,931	30,155	—	976,147
1971	316,022	158,074	40,405	157,265	16,753	180,796	1,831	90,030	364,949	87,980	58,573	23,216	—	878,132
1970	287,525	159,480	32,778	132,249	17,258	178,028	1,938	95,245	324,018	85,644	56,965	19,233	—	913,287
1969	277,609	165,274	33,403	137,686	18,045	177,407	1,944	96,705	331,059	88,444	56,625	20,398	—	862,098
1968	278,330	161,596	26,976	109,937	15,372	162,841	1,911	91,219	308,354	72,118	52,873	18,241	—	719,397
1967	219,643	143,464	x	x	15,118	147,040	1,960	86,692	303,318	70,227	48,529	18,406	—	630,604
1966	216,750	146,525	x	x	13,991	135,415	2,009	81,928	288,160	65,637	43,358	18,144	—	630,154
1965	205,410	138,001	x	x	14,191	124,323	2,062	80,244	255,328	54,177	36,368	16,897	—	592,238
1964	187,911	135,751	12,325	54,902	13,989	115,579	1,830	70,543	231,708	47,102	26,138	16,764	—	548,505
1963	175,588	117,122	9,747	44,121	13,727	106,784	1,792	65,688	212,140	38,506	27,830	15,240	—	479,040
1962	154,579	98,051	9,312	39,414	13,406	103,311	1,767	62,802	193,862	34,206	22,552	13,491	—	436,920
1961	145,659	87,021	8,009	33,168	12,337	95,497	1,719	60,782	187,146	27,546	23,004	12,631	—	392,655
1960	132,887	74,341	5,994	25,908	12,351	90,930	1,611	57,057	182,679	25,290	18,682	11,357	—	368,598
1959	94,875	71,903	..	..	12,633	90,929	1,676	57,212	—	—	—	—	237,506	744,940
1958	85,243	57,122	..	..	12,217	85,084	1,675	58,316	—	—	—	—	220,237	703,366
1957	84,079	58,587	..	..	12,194	84,211	1,693	59,109	—	—	—	—	220,817	706,195
1956	95,986	62,757	..	..	11,704	80,926	1,891	61,768	—	—	—	—	223,469	706,233
1955	97,512	64,079	..	..	12,688	76,715	1,710	57,616	—	—	—	—	181,589	693,403
1954	83,184	58,032	..	..	12,725	73,781	1,647	57,637	—	—	—	—	166,814	655,917
1953	99,648	72,507	..	..	12,652	75,600	1,827	63,997	—	—	—	—	165,656	624,866
1952	102,702	80,644	..	..	13,822	75,069	1,584	55,376	—	—	—	—	147,158	650,021
1951	117,171	92,551	..	..	12,684	69,497	1,560	55,628	—	—	—	—	138,302	727,880
1950	120,060	87,757	..	..	12,992	67,352	1,682	55,587	—	—	—	—	124,880	502,584
1949	116,034	83,805	..	..	13,461	70,892	1,721	53,990	—	—	—	—	113,441	445,138
1948	99,220	69,358	..	..	12,252	68,399	1,877	56,760	—	—	—	—	100,623	485,966
1947	82,941	52,522	..	..	10,486	57,362	1,752	46,489	—	—	—	—	87,059	403,853
1946	78,946	42,980	..	..	12,377	55,675	1,598	35,103	—	—	—	—	73,726	287,624
1945	82,116	38,534	..	..	12,005	47,578	1,344	28,221	—	—	—	—	51,964	231,873
1944	80,124	36,459	..	..	12,043	43,375	1,268	25,542	—	—	—	—	42,576	211,041
1943	83,301	37,051	..	..	12,813	39,851	1,192	23,128	—	—	—	—	40,528	194,434
1942	92,107	39,040	..	..	14,318	39,849	1,433	27,008	—	—	—	—	46,319	192,145
1941	92,548	37,006	..	..	12,682	32,789	1,429	25,093	—	—	—	—	44,260	175,440
1940	65,589	25,434	..	..	11,013	24,466	1,201	20,632	—	—	—	—	32,346	149,005
1939	57,210	21,354	..	..	10,020	22,215	1,306	21,352	—	—	—	—	24,688	97,132
1938	49,628	19,622	..	..	10,240	22,455	1,309	19,783	—	—	—	—	22,321	87,897
1937	53,990	20,865	..	..	10,160	24,440	1,433	22,324	—	—	—	—	24,616	116,729
1936	53,094	21,200	..	..	10,342	22,620	1,318	19,802	—	—	—	—	20,302	92,337
1935	54,112	21,996	..	..	7,448	21,946	1,281	18,169	—	—	—	—	17,158	79,722
1934	48,919	20,856	..	..	8,978	22,749	1,107	16,074	—	—	—	—	15,123	75,727
1933	30,623	16,127	..	..	8,294	20,069	902	12,499	—	—	—	—	13,377	64,114
1932	23,642	13,816	..	..	6,987	18,600	928	13,536	—	—	—	—	15,791	64,412
1931	16,478	11,949	..	..	8,849	25,903	988	16,243	—	—	—	—	25,377	84,781
1930	11,288	11,538	..	..	—	—	—	22,429	—	—	—	—	34,779	..
1929	5,966	7,309	..	..	—	—	—	27,675	—	—	—	—	33,506	..
1928	3,314	4,089	..	..	—	—	—	26,303	—	—	—	—	32,085	155,195
1927	2,050	2,746	..	..	—	—	—	23,229	—	—	—	—	27,699	115,462
1926	1,206	1,961	..	..	—	—	—	—	—	—	—	—	—	..
1925	792	1,466	..	..	—	—	—	—	—	—	—	—	—	101,173
1924	—	—	..	..	—	—	—	—	—	—	—	—	—	..
1923	—	—	..	..	—	—	—	—	—	—	—	—	—	
1922	—	—	..	..	—	—	—	—	—	—	—	—	—	74,948
1921	—	—	..	..	—	—	—	—	—	—	—	—	—	78,338
1920	—	—	..	..	—	—	—	—	—	—	—	—	—	141,553
1919	—	—	..	..	—	—	—	—	—	—	—	—	—	73,365
1918	—	—	..	..	—	—	—	—	—	—	—	—	—	..
1917	—	—	..	..	—	—	—	—	—	—	—	—	—	..

Series R621-770. Quantity and value of shipments of selected manufactured commodities,[1] 1917 to 1975 (continued)

Year	Newsprint paper Quantity ('000 tons)	Value ($'000)	Book and writing paper Quantity (tons)	Value ($'000)	Wrapping paper Quantity (tons)	Value ($'000)	Paper bags Quantity ('000 lb.)	Value ($'000)	Plastic bags Quantity ('000 lb.)	Value ($'000)	Corru-gated boxes Value ($'000)	Folding set-up boxes Value ($'000)	Paper boxes Value ($'000)
	676	677	678	679	680	681	682	683	684	685	686	687	688
1975	7,767	1,847,343	749,550	346,490	465,384	179,572	458,091	144,454	210,093	162,828	484,359	252,822	..
1974	9,657	1,854,917	1,138,016	495,976	701,627	241,631	606,751	166,305	226,857	173,270	515,038	251,901	..
1973	9,230	1,339,411	981,626	321,394	679,301	158,294	474,568	111,052	189,620	109,735	411,412	203,009	..
1972	8,962	1,177,178	950,882	261,656	591,992	123,868	452,899	100,974	156,183	91,331	343,658	180,297	..
1971	8,420	1,083,225	906,166	241,810	542,169	115,391	444,419	95,731	138,938	80,999	303,091	162,005	..
1970	8,764	1,106,688	879,700	238,232	484,159	102,231	434,155	93,790	118,527	73,265	281,225	150,785	..
1969	8,863	1,114,707	730,718	206,686	497,124	104,303	419,803	88,149	101,590	70,688	275,955	152,330	..
1968	8,205	1,015,794	663,063	187,145	459,199	92,219	394,439	81,011	81,386	62,501	243,957	145,842	..
1967	8,108	998,020	627,303	184,943	458,878	93,314	403,957	80,417	67,590	52,999	225,886	139,217	..
1966	8,493	1,025,048	620,975	176,278	412,977	89,685	387,044	76,854	..	49,429	208,340	134,241	..
1965	7,841	927,832	535,085	150,289	360,220	80,240	371,852	72,666	..	40,536	188,523	124,786	..
1964	7,378	887,612	490,838	138,157	342,155	76,432	353,941	71,292	..	37,001	172,565	120,408	..
1963	6,639	809,248	459,930	126,650	333,967	72,458	333,996	68,176	..	28,212	156,925	113,062	..
1962	6,648	819,079	434,022	119,405	323,078	69,891	336,537	67,751	..	28,027	148,089	109,680	..
1961	6,675	804,641	417,000	112,283	309,000	66,781	315,520	64,009	..	23,362	135,080	102,022	..
1960	6,774	793,470	400,000	105,915	301,000	65,917	313,784	63,320	..	20,815	127,670	100,615	..
1959	6,351	730,455	382,000	101,928	330,000	71,318	—	62,351	..	—	—	—	221,544
1958	6,031	699,906	344,622	91,079	292,727	64,650	—	57,876	..	—	—	—	197,940
1957	6,362	729,009	335,037	86,990	277,208	60,402	—	52,641	..	—	—	—	188,921
1956	6,445	735,644	341,580	86,524	288,146	61,098	—	52,238	..	—	—	—	180,213
1955	6,196	688,338	301,352	74,904	263,915	53,999	—	48,588	..	—	—	—	161,008
1954	6,001	657,487	269,353	68,614	250,408	51,341	—	45,274	..	—	—	—	147,624
1953	5,755	633,408	246,513	61,451	238,111	49,029	—	49,104	..	—	—	—	143,506
1952	5,707	600,516	224,683	57,464	222,529	45,357	—	41,298	..	—	—	—	127,934
1951	5,561	564,361	253,081	63,790	257,332	49,664	—	43,166	..	—	—	—	126,067
1950	5,319	506,968	214,097	47,356	222,840	37,776	—	30,881	..	—	—	—	105,965
1949	5,187	467,976	199,317	40,599	195,585	30,033	—	25,898	..	—	—	—	91,056
1948	4,640	402,100	231,608	45,179	207,128	31,037	—	23,607	..	—	—	—	80,474
1947	4,474	355,541	210,762	39,727	188,742	26,010	—	19,603	..	—	—	—	70,518
1946	4,162	280,810	189,318	29,995	175,369	20,797	—	15,182	..	—	—	—	57,957
1945	3,324	189,024	162,198	24,468	162,175	17,559	—	12,268	..	—	—	—	46,268
1944	3,040	165,655	155,498	23,700	156,721	16,700	—	11,251	..	—	—	—	42,908
1943	3,046	152,963	122,174	19,047	145,545	15,614	—	9,820	..	—	—	—	39,871
1942	3,257	147,074	121,419	19,182	165,991	17,222	—	9,141	..	—	—	—	38,770
1941	3,520	158,925	117,444	18,476	162,581	16,745	—	7,884	..	—	—	—	37,370
1940	3,504	158,447	102,696	15,519	139,716	14,457	—	6,088	..	—	—	—	28,493
1939	2,927	120,859	90,135	12,774	109,907	10,712	—	5,276	..	—	—	—	23,524
1938	2,669	107,051	73,834	11,099	90,879	9,069	—	4,714	..	—	—	—	23,008
1937	3,674	126,424	84,168	12,620	108,734	10,238	—	4,610	..	—	—	—	24,217
1936	3,225	105,215	74,940	10,866	95,916	8,761	—	3,840	..	—	—	—	20,729
1935	2,765	88,436	70,350	10,441	82,517	7,957	—	3,266	..	—	—	—	18,283
1934	2,605	86,811	64,991	9,682	79,779	7,741	—	3,183	..	—	—	—	16,876
1933	2,022	66,960	60,683	8,927	67,780	6,442	—	2,685	..	—	—	—	14,237
1932	1,919	85,540	56,781	8,688	69,018	6,289	—	2,740	..	—	—	—	13,853
1931	2,227	111,420	73,572	10,154	79,403	7,480	—	3,226	..	—	—	—	14,182
1930	2,498	136,182	90,287	12,262	79,720	7,880	—	3,491	..	—	—	—	15,066
1929	2,725	150,800	70,213	13,637	92,014	9,726	—	—	..	—	—	—	17,039
1928	2,414	144,147	65,077	14,008	50,791	10,424	—	—	..	—	—	—	16,059
1927	2,083	132,287	60,696	12,916	51,269	9,608	—	—	..	—	—	—	13,941
1926	1,889	121,065	—	14,766	—	8,552	—	—	..	—	—	—	12,341
1925	1,536	106,269	—	13,145	—	8,130	—	—	..	—	—	—	10,588
1924	1,388	100,277	—	12,606	—	8,028	—	—	..	—	—	—	10,043
1923	1,251	93,213	—	13,582	—	7,666	—	—	..	—	—	—	10,166
1922	1,081	75,971	—	12,561	—	8,220	—	—	..	—	—	—	9,051
1921	805	78,785	—	12,551	—	6,634	—	—	..	—	—	—	8,079
1920	876	80,865	—	21,869	—	12,161	—	—	..	—	—	—	14,442
1919	795	54,428	—	12,571	—	7,979	—	—	..	—	—	—	—
1918	735	46,231	—	10,733	—	7,341	—	—	..	—	—	—	—
1917	690	38,868	—	9,333	—	5,892	—	—	..	—	—	—	—

Series R621-770. Quantity and value of shipments of selected manufactured commodities,[1] 1917 to 1975 (continued)

Year	Paper boards Quantity (tons)	Paper boards Value ($'000)	Printed periodicals (gross revenue from advertising)[5] Value ($'000)	Pig iron produced[6] Quantity (short tons)	Steel ingots and steel castings produced Quantity (short tons)	Hot rolled iron and steel bars Quantity (short tons)	Hot rolled iron and steel bars Value ($'000)	Structural steel shapes Quantity (short tons)	Structural steel shapes Value ($'000)	Steel rails Quantity (short tons)	Steel rails Value ($'000)	Steel plate, sheet and strip Quantity (short tons)	Steel plate, sheet and strip Value ($'000)
	689	690	691	692	693	694	695	696	697	698	699	700	701
1975	1,657,417	412,442	860,633	10,808,607	14,268,166	1,352,775	378,008	771,042	189,182	387,322	109,088	6,531,678	1,685,311
1974	2,361,428	550,271	786,773	10,418,978	14,956,250	1,616,705	404,519	875,724	191,433	312,798	62,476	6,846,403	1,549,249
1973	2,273,349	378,355	699,414	10,524,319	14,664,886	1,622,538	299,680	836,276	142,096	300,882	43,583	6,724,517	1,267,963
1972	2,042,232	313,095	611,901	9,355,805	13,066,723	1,426,706	242,101	796,445	123,014	169,384	23,710	5,949,347	1,044,583
1971	1,814,816	268,280	535,278	8,635,231	12,177,269	1,504,905	244,465	698,077	104,905	288,395	38,621	5,418,040	892,508
1970	1,763,826	268,618	493,323	9,069,425	12,249,708	1,424,433	221,313	786,694	111,873	344,682	43,809	5,088,124	839,576
1969	1,756,593	265,356	481,053	7,430,687	10,047,557	1,374,925	201,687	631,257	85,904	302,881	36,667	4,658,297	746,583
1968	1,645,472	244,319	431,710	8,321,546	11,198,447	1,351,903	194,146	601,120	78,954	226,569	27,025	4,853,238	740,815
1967	1,582,298	232,112	405,736	6,950,803	9,700,832	1,147,551	176,105	582,686	67,064	271,768	31,906	4,114,931	638,549
1966	1,533,214	220,586	384,733	7,216,610	10,020,131	1,195,348	167,271	547,027	73,766	274,138	33,436	4,070,376	617,106
1965	1,421,244	202,174	360,781	7,079,439	10,068,342	1,233,152	175,914	565,883	74,809	220,611	26,458	4,021,521	604,837
1964	1,296,691	187,772	327,580	6,550,835	9,128,459	1,146,878	160,869	577,608	72,927	270,807	30,856	3,687,821	535,757
1963	1,213,735	175,183	313,307	5,933,270	8,197,070	936,734	132,304	496,334	62,370	334,422	35,707	3,185,858	445,957
1962	1,091,866	156,995	308,912	5,276,753	7,173,534	890,885	115,815	450,309	56,659	225,683	25,404	2,801,112	405,237
1961	1,017,000	149,768	298,678	4,946,021	6,488,307	839,795	107,439	318,664	40,413	190,760	21,556	2,550,491	376,311
1960	974,000	141,321	294,883	4,298,849	5,809,108	807,775	105,904	234,530	30,076	223,033	25,385	2,238,931	334,091
1959	1,256,000	163,152	282,953	4,182,775	5,901,487	949,865	139,735	268,573	34,968	286,989	31,700	—	—
1958	1,188,650	152,811	261,023	3,059,579	4,359,466	705,073	103,907	217,137	28,087	365,429	41,586	—	—
1957	1,114,726	143,079	249,575	3,718,350	5,068,149	865,533	129,302	347,693	43,538	393,926	39,979	—	—
1956	1,173,087	147,967	240,097	3,568,203	5,301,202	947,979	133,769	316,000	36,413	336,662	33,027	—	—
1955	1,027,441	130,366	212,474	3,215,367	4,534,672	742,494	95,336	241,698	25,833	228,991	22,353	—	—
1954	940,196	117,173	194,622	2,211,029	3,195,030	528,521	67,053	193,673	20,591	241,922	21,422	—	—
1953	948,955	114,978	180,824	2,681,585	4,116,068	732,275	92,779	283,203	29,733	303,318	26,466	—	—
1952	874,582	106,067	157,049	2,681,585	3,703,111	786,972	106,351	231,091	24,084	253,675	21,224	—	—
1951	960,493	113,470	140,733	2,552,893	3,568,720	763,005	94,994	250,362	24,300	257,244	19,911	—	—
1950	876,894	92,532	127,491	2,317,121	3,383,575	684,934	70,350	153,144	13,504	286,672	21,305	—	—
1949	797,023	80,632	117,853	2,154,485	3,190,377	662,488	61,525	191,018	15,331	329,749	24,581	—	—
1948	817,432	80,865	100,035	2,125,739	3,200,480	634,315	59,860	175,031	12,910	337,244	21,887	—	—
1947	744,377	66,126	71,443	1,962,848	2,945,952	609,763	50,165	180,226	11,298	250,049	13,237	—	—
1946	683,643	50,214	56,277	1,406,252	2,327,285	492,853	37,166	131,894	7,697	206,374	10,716	—	—
1945	595,131	40,101	47,360	1,777,949	2,877,927	574,446	41,492	191,907	10,490	291,651	14,230	—	—
1944	588,348	39,092	43,379	1,852,628	3,016,162	534,196	37,479	155,908	9,185	325,486	15,922	—	—
1943	568,101	37,528	38,974	1,758,269	3,004,124	598,113	52,783	146,965	8,528	263,920	12,310	—	—
1942	609,175	38,642	35,526	1,975,014	3,109,851	592,016	46,734	184,701	10,175	183,430	8,216	—	—
1941	649,840	40,215	36,164	1,528,053	2,712,151	542,575	36,347	189,783	9,428	137,298	5,575	—	—
1940	500,094	31,079	34,261	1,309,099	2,253,769	453,788	28,656	183,728	8,834	199,998	7,840	—	—
1939	413,687	21,360	33,480	755,731	1,551,054	314,050	17,785	90,810	4,499	123,023	5,182	—	—
1938	356,891	19,288	34,353	705,427	1,293,812	277,783	15,825	65,633	3,479	126,479	5,003	—	—
1937	422,710	21,720	34,964	898,855	1,571,227	388,662	21,839	93,279	4,548	86,932	3,423	—	—
1936	363,778	17,531	32,869	678,231	1,249,672	283,146	13,571	41,537	1,869	130,135	4,885	—	—
1935	314,849	15,052	31,471	599,875	1,054,509	243,574	12,242	42,529	1,883	122,302	4,485	—	—
1934	280,724	13,351	29,975	404,995	848,716	185,212	9,246	25,838	1,095	108,292	3,660	—	—
1933	232,190	10,598	28,638	227,317	459,176	94,088	4,646	18,091	799	75,975	2,900	—	—
1932	209,938	9,621	32,059	144,130	380,067	100,662	4,698	16,005	744	50,501	2,123	—	—
1931	202,854	10,226	39,639	420,038	752,762	234,978	10,865	37,931	1,722	156,962	—	—	—
1930	233,217	12,194	44,633	747,178	1,130,808	184,286	8,713	35,997	1,631	261,444	—	—	—
1929	250,061	13,540	49,047	1,080,160	1,543,427	273,944	12,930	35,060	1,563	428,962	—	—	—
1928	193,061	10,656	43,075	1,037,727	1,382,976	302,923	—	—	—	391,092	—	—	—
1927	161,497	8,986	38,743	709,697	1,016,898	220,866	—	—	—	263,965	—	—	—
1926	155,469	8,826	34,857	757,317	869,413	218,344	—	—	—	186,838	—	—	—
1925	144,646	8,379	32,244	570,766	842,803	244,029	—	—	—	216,695	—	—	—
1924	135,252	8,229	32,335	593,049	738,939	191,055	—	—	—	224,795	—	—	—
1923	130,582	8,480	28,219	879,822	987,306	239,468	—	—	—	231,684	—	—	—
1922	113,200	7,000	28,864	382,967	537,742	152,768	—	—	—	140,970	—	—	—
1921	89,120	6,226	29,993	593,829	747,582	134,079	—	—	—	298,110	—	—	—
1920	158,041	12,905	30,729	973,568	1,232,717	386,740	—	—	—	255,323	—	—	—
1919	137,678	8,892	21,364	819,447	1,030,342	—	—	—	—	316,305	—	—	—
1918	87,749	5,551	—	1,067,456	1,873,749	—	—	—	—	162,746	—	—	—
1917	54,080	3,543	—	1,045,071	1,745,744	—	—	—	—	46,311	—	—	—

Series R621-770. Quantity and value of shipments of selected manufactured commodities,[1] 1917 to 1975 (continued)

Year	Steel pipes and tubing		Plain steel wire		Metal cans	Farm implements and parts produced	Passenger automobiles		Commercial auto vehicles (including buses)		Mobile homes		Travel and tent trailers	
	Quantity (short tons)	Value ($'000)	Quantity (short tons)	Value ($'000)	Value ($'000)	Value ($'000)	Quantity (number)	Value ($'000)	Quantity (number)	Value ($'000)	Quantity (number)	Value ($'000)	Quantity (number)	Value ($'000)
	702	703	704	705	706	707	708	709	710	711	712	713	714	715
1975	1,423,000	634,837	294,004	119,541	340,743	762,106	1,028,674	4,088,430	347,902	1,690,061	21,713	260,374	40,030	98,990
1974	1,420,000	505,987	395,233	138,792	310,397	571,912	1,168,079	3,724,275	344,064	1,504,032	27,825	287,048	42,334	91,969
1973	1,272,000	352,613	363,349	97,859	268,590	423,380	1,220,133	3,358,383	331,678	1,197,629	23,727	216,283	41,719	87,455
1972	1,274,000	328,729	303,663	74,658	228,424	317,163	1,135,872	2,976,988	293,584	956,081	19,844	153,120	43,419	72,307
1971	1,072,000	267,016	286,549	68,592	213,803	239,714	1,083,351	2,810,759	263,967	786,613	15,284	113,640	40,861	60,841
1970	1,020,000	244,952	264,259	62,660	194,581	226,724	922,659	2,125,493	236,199	656,751	9,239	66,229	36,307	45,452
1969	1,018,000	230,870	240,733	55,434	186,631	289,734	1,032,571	2,474,040	301,261	787,791	9,151	60,352	45,630	47,809
1968	1,059,000	240,460	238,756	51,490	194,057	270,057	885,191	2,102,881	260,141	656,691	6,302	38,376	32,147	30,659
1967	800,000	181,587	221,028	46,468	168,183	323,433	711,883	1,644,635	211,911	537,654	4,362	23,388	25,235	27,893
1966	775,000	177,834	224,637	43,665	148,178	328,332	683,374	1,481,732	187,070	463,973	3,215	17,840	20,245	17,911
1965	786,000	181,103	220,635	41,875	144,503	285,099	705,620	1,561,154	138,225	358,814	3,395	15,461	..	13,677
1964	776,000	170,697	214,980	42,491	130,565	243,963	558,210	1,233,762	112,096	296,354	2,152	10,529	9,111	10,839
1963	610,000	132,308	175,112	32,544	123,734	182,767	530,160	1,148,706	98,427	238,813	1,562	6,471	..	..
1962	498,000	107,282	162,336	30,448	122,680	140,820	426,085	894,868	82,049	204,381	..	..	..	..
1961	678,000	142,446	152,913	28,508	109,578	138,045	321,927	656,155	63,799	153,354	..	..	..	..
1960	518,000	110,196	150,371	29,355	108,520	152,127	326,273	650,307	70,670	170,684	..	..	..	..
1959	488,900	106,004	360,874	..	114,450	151,974	296,943	611,318	67,262	170,506	—	—	—	—
1958	537,900	117,805	305,733	..	107,270	129,088	293,633	582,489	61,299	135,491	—	—	—	—
1957	612,400	132,178	290,881	..	97,844	117,896	334,112	638,063	71,798	149,522	—	—	—	—
1956	434,800	85,570	366,486	..	90,576	117,656	364,387	643,286	93,429	190,088	—	—	—	—
1955	331,300	57,573	316,593	..	88,559	109,701	361,683	605,760	78,345	143,070	—	—	—	—
1954	219,500	36,260	254,922	..	77,842	113,089	274,901	431,993	69,681	121,926	—	—	—	—
1953	220,800	41,943	252,026	..	74,309	159,851	344,281	531,848	120,312	198,625	—	—	—	—
1952	258,700	56,040	286,761	..	78,991	194,688	269,017	409,071	150,094	253,074	—	—	—	—
1951	239,100	47,925	294,373	..	73,394	162,349	267,768	428,855	132,645	212,667	—	—	—	—
1950	233,100	33,405	262,966	..	63,162	141,674	268,720	436,850	105,997	163,881	—	—	—	—
1949	197,400	30,185	251,553	..	56,592	169,617	183,999	271,392	99,028	146,697	—	—	—	—
1948	138,900	19,785	246,461	..	53,159	139,079	150,671	201,024	96,931	137,222	—	—	—	—
1947	141,400	19,930	238,301	..	47,742	83,930	153,334	174,213	90,758	116,357	—	—	—	—
1946	120,900	15,931	184,392	..	47,348	53,991	83,709	79,041	79,657	81,204	—	—	—	—
1945	160,200	17,971	214,475	..	36,325	38,701	1,866	1,637	130,777	167,103	—	—	—	—
1944	138,200	15,819	200,203	..	33,078	26,297	—	—	158,038	213,260	—	—	—	—
1943	132,600	15,573	191,210	..	22,557	18,930	—	—	178,064	222,393	—	—	—	—
1942	153,800	18,118	202,116	..	34,678	19,638	11,966	10,217	216,057	229,103	—	—	—	—
1941	175,200	19,737	220,285	..	34,878	22,411	91,331	79,306	173,588	163,414	—	—	—	—
1940	143,000	13,217	222,727	..	25,673	18,285	102,664	81,316	113,102	91,192	—	—	—	—
1939	90,000	7,918	176,262	..	23,277	16,035	90,148	66,030	47,057	28,073	—	—	—	—
1938	73,500	6,861	144,513	..	20,578	21,299	105,392	76,587	42,325	26,497	—	—	—	—
1937	99,100	8,754	171,230	..	20,842	18,961	132,835	88,002	54,417	30,389	—	—	—	—
1936	79,300	6,448	151,106	..	18,049	15,957	108,340	72,108	33,790	19,141	—	—	—	—
1935	70,100	6,247	146,434	..	15,133	13,692	111,782	73,273	37,315	19,804	—	—	—	—
1934	59,700	5,233	117,708	..	14,706	8,818	80,118	53,930	24,205	12,770	—	—	—	—
1933	37,700	3,341	87,225	..	11,602	5,326	47,510	30,606	12,003	6,062	—	—	—	—
1932	45,300	4,025	86,931	..	10,134	5,510	48,332	31,533	10,095	6,071	—	—	—	—
1931	71,200	6,655	110,866	..	11,747	11,175	64,629	42,312	17,487	10,331	—	—	—	—
1930	110,800	10,066	148,505	..	15,367	26,902	115,535	73,335	16,742	10,212	—	—	—	—
1929	140,100	12,803	155,680	..	14,121	40,659	188,721	128,496	50,293	25,762	—	—	—	—
1928	118,000	10,593	148,815	..	13,216	41,200	176,096	119,022	17,527	11,058	—	—	—	—
1927	79,300	6,577	118,784	..	—	42,996	137,290	97,255	29,603	13,712	—	—	—	—
1926	72,300	5,950	123,542	..	—	38,269	154,061	101,870	30,440	14,247	—	—	—	—
1925	—	—	94,018	..	—	24,770	120,205	81,248	26,397	12,234	—	—	—	—
1924	—	—	84,731	..	—	26,447	98,365	65,508	18,043	8,125	—	—	—	—
1923	—	—	123,148	..	—	26,026	106,226	69,904	19,226	8,941	—	—	—	—
1922	—	—	136,900	..	—	18,240	79,094	60,464	8,169	5,232	—	—	—	—
1921	—	—	72,722	..	—	38,948	57,401	51,995	5,148	3,843	—	—	—	—
1920	—	—	107,129	..	—	50,301	79,369	78,151	10,174	8,154	—	—	—	—
1919	—	—	—	..	—	41,063	68,408	58,756	7,899	5,120	—	—	—	—
1918	—	—	—	..	—	38,305	69,801	54,111	7,319	5,855	—	—	—	—
1917	—	—	—	..	—	36,568	—	—	—	—	—	—	—	—

Series R621-770. Quantity and value of shipments of selected manufactured commodities,[1] 1917 to 1975 (continued)

Year	Boats		Outboard motors		Snowmobiles		Automobile parts and accessories (except tires & auto fabrics)[7]	Locomotives, steam and diesel		Railroad cars (freight and passenger)		Aluminum produced	Stoves and ranges	
	Quantity	Value	Quantity	Value	Quantity	Value	Value	Quantity	Value	Quantity	Value	Quantity	Quantity	Value
	(number)	($'000)	(number)	($'000)	(number)	($'000)	($'000)	(number)	($'000)	(number)	($'000)	(short tons)	(number)	($'000)
	716	717	718	719	720	721	722	723	724	725	726	727	728	729
1975	..	76,186	x	x	86,581	78,743	2,325,802	x	x	..	245,075	967,891	476,439	91,454
1974	..	90,648	90,885	41,022	116,912	103,970	2,281,103	x	x	..	203,573	1,109,892	663,428	108,872
1973	..	66,119	81,462	33,671	165,437	128,176	2,304,562	x	x	..	127,196	1,025,381	623,253	91,203
1972	..	58,367	77,149	29,591	233,611	163,145	1,903,161	x	x	..	125,478	999,940	792,772	81,681
1971	..	45,054	73,654	26,992	320,256	191,884	1,660,665	x	x	..	103,056	1,104,644	577,279	72,461
1970	..	39,258	65,199	24,443	363,119	217,252	1,272,154	x	x	..	110,522	1,061,020	519,398	60,867
1969	..	40,039	69,246	23,957	324,508	196,363	1,340,376	x	x	..	99,090	1,078,717	450,902	63,202
1968	..	33,862	86,554	23,346	186,845	107,690	1,193,805	x	x	..	74,798	979,172	579,641	64,135
1967	..	28,738	76,537	19,232	116,665	63,682	912,422	x	x	..	109,987	963,343	520,919	58,123
1966	..	25,095	71,299	19,194	78,659	44,871	860,500	x	x	..	126,972	889,915	533,851	53,648
1965	..	22,957	61,530	16,657	..	..	755,608	x	x	6,057	110,962	830,505	519,529	50,842
1964	..	20,335	..	..	..	..	627,966	169	31,964	..	48,075	842,640	490,683	51,620
1963	35,049	18,943	..	..	..	..	544,869	159	28,668	2,156	30,135	719,390	448,546	50,612
1962	31,669	14,994	..	..	..	..	436,260	29	5,518	3,449	36,669	690,297	509,700	49,748
1961	28,431	12,695	..	..	..	..	352,613	43	4,353	1,762	19,754	663,173	507,711	48,414
1960	29,763	12,245	..	..	..	..	288,080	172	29,189	2,510	25,397	762,012	563,059	61,270
1959	—	—	—	—	—	—	360,066	380	66,824	3,585	40,370	593,630	537,011	52,857
1958	—	—	—	—	—	—	334,389	417	75,230	5,313	64,126	634,102	499,103	49,755
1957	—	—	—	—	—	—	355,121	530	94,830	10,475	98,666	556,715	484,719	47,280
1956	—	—	—	—	—	—	390,534	488	78,220	9,221	70,981	620,321	522,151	50,935
1955	—	—	—	—	—	—	350,702	362	59,693	3,736	27,822	612,543	482,375	47,186
1954	—	—	—	—	—	—	275,927	244	41,105	8,287	88,395	557,897	391,428	39,953
1953	—	—	—	—	—	—	382,317	260	42,259	8,464	85,879	548,445	437,945	45,198
1952	—	—	—	—	—	—	348,577	226	38,306	11,954	92,259	499,758	457,017	41,609
1951	—	—	—	—	—	—	334,222	267	41,893	10,613	75,429	447,095	525,061	40,581
1950	—	—	—	—	—	—	272,864	146	22,285	4,762	33,214	396,882	533,682	45,092
1949	—	—	—	—	—	—	216,595	319	38,144	10,798	60,685	369,466	643,786	43,359
1948	—	—	—	—	—	—	177,560	176	20,048	11,524	71,208	367,079	610,624	37,291
1947	—	—	—	—	—	—	162,992	125	14,431	5,765	30,838	299,066	600,331	27,814
1946	—	—	—	—	—	—	113,533	271	25,966	10,092	31,832	194,117	438,291	18,537
1945	—	—	—	—	—	—	159,284	378	29,499	13,480	47,571	215,712	443,484	12,457
1944	—	—	—	—	—	—	210,341	190	18,916	9,251	35,935	462,065	331,582	9,460
1943	—	—	—	—	—	—	222,203	99	10,803	6,248	24,706	495,749	287,274	8,486
1942	—	—	—	—	—	—	198,018	71	8,604	1,501	11,001	340,596	346,100	10,147
1941	—	—	—	—	—	—	131,761	3	163	2,711	9,751	213,873	408,470	13,737
1940	—	—	—	—	—	—	74,055	55	6,616	5,328	18,525	109,144	379,362	12,638
1939	—	—	—	—	—	—	47,054	1	17	2,423	9,746	82,840	329,635	10,343
1938	—	—	—	—	—	—	52,167	49	5,635	5,385	25,593	71,204	276,789	9,262
1937	—	—	—	—	—	—	59,949	46	4,863	7,504	28,827	46,906	330,262	10,896
1936	—	—	—	—	—	—	43,268	23	2,367	2,116	9,530	29,640	302,475	9,457
1935	—	—	—	—	—	—	—	4	112	550	2,018	23,171	217,982	7,492
1934	—	—	—	—	—	—	—	—	—	31	150	17,433	184,232	6,469
1933	—	—	—	—	—	—	—	—	—	589	1,726	17,766	127,351	4,543
1932	—	—	—	—	—	—	—	3	61	282	358	19,793	120,998	4,525
1931	—	—	—	—	—	—	—	26	1,897	5,288	19,783	34,052	176,062	6,879
1930	—	—	—	—	—	—	—	108	6,773	8,348	34,533	38,109	239,035	8,884
1929	—	—	—	—	—	—	—	98	8,390	13,242	53,934	31,715	309,184	11,603
1928	—	—	—	—	—	—	—	48	3,086	3,058	11,286	41,399	319,571	11,007
1927	—	—	—	—	—	—	—	57	4,418	5,005	14,640	41,368	278,183	9,853
1926	—	—	—	—	—	—	—	57	3,316	3,335	17,438	19,455	—	—
1925	—	—	—	—	—	—	—	8	342	1,435	3,415	15,553	—	—
1924	—	—	—	—	—	—	—	84	5,679	4,544	15,944	13,622	—	—
1923	—	—	—	—	—	—	—	138	7,667	7,856	29,967	12,128	—	—
1922	—	—	—	—	—	—	—	46	1,987	847	4,843	6,439	—	—
1921	—	—	—	—	—	—	—	81	4,069	6,099	23,151	3,168	—	—
1920	—	—	—	—	—	—	—	21	1,384	5,084	21,804	11,192	—	—
1919	—	—	—	—	—	—	—	—	1,800	—	32,984	10,791	—	—
1918	—	—	—	—	—	—	—	—	7,312	—	34,933	11,768	—	—
1917	—	—	—	—	—	—	—	—	296	—	24,823	11,044	—	—

Series R621-770. Quantity and value of shipments of selected manufactured commodities,[1] 1917 to 1975 (continued)

Year	Household refrigerators		Home freezers		Washing machines		Automatic clothes driers		Radios, all types (except combinations)		Television sets		Phonograph records	
	Quantity (number)	Value ($'000)	Quantity (number)	Value ($'000)	Quantity (number)	Value ($'000)	Quantity (number)	Value ($'000)	Quantity (number)	Value ($'000)	Quantity (number)	Value ($'000)	Quantity (number)	Value ($'000)
	730	731	732	733	734	735	736	737	738	739	740	741	742	743
1975	505,343	140,643	484,826	81,715	439,562	91,726	281,245	40,512	1,284,079	44,758	492,831	176,297	53,755,618	42,126
1974	589,701	139,249	367,698	48,086	487,526	88,339	314,839	41,053	x	x	624,247	214,204	44,348,368	32,049
1973	606,380	124,262	314,243	37,460	536,472	88,305	353,305	41,424	2,556,077	50,268	784,894	239,883	39,927,158	22,815
1972	485,704	91,303	308,336	42,591	500,752	73,735	319,478	37,351	x	x	751,049	217,410	42,704,300	22,067
1971	457,532	91,956	220,256	27,683	397,187	65,639	251,639	29,664	x	x	584,607	161,550	42,398,612	18,570
1970	374,918	72,174	165,764	21,049	344,427	54,371	198,994	24,157	1,627,093	37,114	545,782	126,141	45,318,698	18,810
1969	417,111	82,832	183,538	24,210	431,658	63,193	228,792	26,871	1,811,798	43,055	630,944	141,668	47,122,882	21,659
1968	430,300	81,757	175,847	23,505	429,631	60,047	214,539	24,926	1,937,484	41,028	519,176	105,070	43,811,000	22,377
1967	384,269	70,562	213,005	29,361	417,268	56,424	197,547	22,673	1,445,984	31,892	540,949	98,814	43,775,549	23,940
1966	403,447	65,898	197,807	27,585	421,308	55,070	203,783	22,593	1,011,090	23,581	639,841	109,665	38,606,390	23,115
1965	362,983	59,109	165,746	23,067	420,309	51,898	187,158	20,590	956,537	22,926	514,043	77,748	37,245,454	16,924
1964	330,872	55,583	157,150	23,304	379,292	46,347	153,360	17,318	759,827	18,026	564,634	81,659	29,067,084	15,524
1963	293,236	50,016	137,937	22,404	347,172	40,351	145,954	17,646	698,924	17,221	455,272	69,198	25,782,462	16,033
1962	247,693	41,444	127,683	20,545	315,857	36,045	131,862	16,568	591,531	14,345	427,167	70,023	25,014,247	15,959
1961	234,662	39,801	91,797	15,972	294,622	34,819	117,521	15,298	496,978	11,754	345,815	57,381	23,194,486	13,174
1960	239,436	40,212	73,606	13,531	289,766	33,926	110,511	14,997	471,947	10,181	342,488	53,726	20,692,789	12,245
1959	256,778	44,549	–	–	326,883	36,565	–	–	713,309	24,485	–	–	–	–
1958	226,523	39,749	–	–	300,068	34,418	–	–	745,318	25,511	–	–	–	–
1957	235,539	42,430	–	–	276,747	31,011	–	–	732,827	25,642	–	–	–	–
1956	269,213	47,443	–	–	305,922	33,481	–	–	740,656	23,878	–	–	–	–
1955	271,582	49,558	–	–	279,802	30,525	–	–	621,957	19,177	–	–	–	–
1954	230,092	44,064	–	–	226,238	24,942	–	–	487,620	16,509	–	–	–	–
1953	275,415	50,944	–	–	247,824	28,062	–	–	737,457	28,021	–	–	–	–
1952	244,433	46,047	–	–	253,538	27,547	–	–	567,738	22,179	–	–	–	–
1951	277,836	54,525	–	–	236,730	26,446	–	–	628,395	29,635	–	–	–	–
1950	341,596	66,226	–	–	301,110	29,162	–	–	820,772	33,498	–	–	–	–
1949	206,185	36,736	–	–	346,254	32,501	–	–	791,051	29,412	–	–	–	–
1948	138,714	25,164	–	–	334,473	31,254	–	–	639,493	25,411	–	–	–	–
1947	108,106	18,585	–	–	220,039	19,108	–	–	984,276	33,063	–	–	–	–
1946	56,786	8,597	–	–	115,190	8,247	–	–	603,199	15,760	–	–	–	–
1945	2,418	355	–	–	59,908	3,537	–	–	50,317	979	–	–	–	–
1944	237	71	–	–	33,858	1,679	–	–	–	–	–	–	–	–
1943	358	33	–	–	13,200	438	–	–	979	18	–	–	–	–
1942	37,792	4,586	–	–	67,251	3,718	–	–	177,149	4,682	–	–	–	–
1941	64,093	7,627	–	–	128,262	6,457	–	–	386,372	9,215	–	–	–	–
1940	53,165	6,249	–	–	117,511	5,841	–	–	485,010	11,268	–	–	–	–
1939	57,460	6,810	–	–	103,882	4,986	–	–	348,507	8,678	–	–	–	–
1938	52,934	6,341	–	–	105,850	5,059	–	–	242,721	8,802	–	–	–	–
1937	52,068	5,794	–	–	133,475	5,956	–	–	289,247	11,697	–	–	–	–
1936	40,688	5,055	–	–	102,638	5,601	–	–	253,896	11,388	–	–	–	–
1935	22,452	2,835	–	–	84,676	3,849	–	–	191,293	9,493	–	–	–	–
1934	27,897	3,502	–	–	84,079	3,821	–	–	188,710	8,196	–	–	–	–
1933	15,059	1,896	–	–	58,931	2,844	–	–	112,272	4,401	–	–	–	–
1932	19,454	2,219	–	–	58,486	3,317	–	–	121,468	6,809	–	–	–	–
1931	9,879	1,708	–	–	76,693	6,918	–	–	291,711	18,556	–	–	–	–
1930	6,302	1,608	–	–	86,058	9,392	–	–	170,082	19,197	–	–	–	–
1929	4,252	1,548	–	–	100,224	10,076	–	–	150,050	15,604	–	–	–	–
1928	3,158	781	–	–	86,397	8,311	–	–	81,032	7,486	–	–	–	–
1927	1,590	227	–	–	62,136	5,096	–	–	47,500	3,749	–	–	–	–
1926	–	–	–	–	51,109	3,371	–	–	42,430	2,253	–	–	–	–
1925	–	–	–	–	48,060	3,056	–	–	48,531	2,278	–	–	–	–
1924	–	–	–	–	36,925	2,113	–	–	–	–	–	–	–	–
1923	–	–	–	–	28,937	1,725	–	–	–	–	–	–	–	–
1922	–	–	–	–	28,758	1,222	–	–	–	–	–	–	–	–
1921	–	–	–	–	24,892	965	–	–	–	–	–	–	–	–
1920	–	–	–	–	–	–	–	–	–	–	–	–	–	–
1919	–	–	–	–	–	–	–	–	–	–	–	–	–	–
1918	–	–	–	–	–	–	–	–	–	–	–	–	–	–
1917	–	–	–	–	–	–	–	–	–	–	–	–	–	–

Series R621-770. Quantity and value of shipments of selected manufactured commodities,[1] 1917 to 1975 (continued)

Year	Pre-recorded tapes		Electric wire and cable	Telephone and telephone equipment	Clay bricks		Cement		Gasoline[8]		Fuel oil[8]		Coke produced
	Quantity (number)	Value ($'000)	Value ($'000)	Value ($'000)	Quantity (thousands)	Value ($'000)	Quantity ('000 bbl)	Value ($'000)	Quantity ('000 gal)	Value ($'000)	Quantity ('000 gal)	Value ($'000)	Quantity (short tons)
	744	745	746	747	748	749	750	751	752	753	754	755	756
1975	12,779,012	22,635	623,920	725,753	584,677	54,410	66,043	342,380	7,929,355	2,344,033	7,059,381	1,657,735	6,621,929
1974	9,584,171	11,905	667,754	400,996	559,719	48,854	66,675	281,958	7,473,340	1,941,819	7,491,890	1,611,617	6,916,052
1973	6,447,854	7,456	506,206	289,705	541,104	42,877	64,937	242,505	7,161,420	1,181,638	7,176,575	859,286	6,750,257
1972	5,381,225	6,243	418,503	231,551	556,747	37,227	57,592	210,685	6,395,550	940,383	6,781,245	683,098	5,743,698
1971	2,294,130	4,673	430,996	171,248	543,379	34,105	51,862	183,368	5,959,485	870,391	5,374,460	519,003	5,382,953
1970	1,890,074	4,984	452,114	216,982	564,355	35,363	45,405	155,737	5,676,860	769,396	4,926,040	422,868	5,636,528
1969	2,324,474	5,374	349,855	215,162	574,326	32,449	47,143	162,091	5,468,680	731,861	4,593,995	385,042	5,066,369
1968	..	..	302,755	216,924	559,889	29,936	46,662	148,210	5,325,390	738,318	4,495,890	391,785	5,674,910
1967	..	..	300,615	222,097	540,729	27,315	45,685	143,150	5,000,590	686,298	4,073,685	359,932	5,511,025
1966	..	..	320,445	160,223	516,940	25,972	51,032	156,301	4,817,960	657,811	3,950,975	347,814	5,493,854
1965	..	..	259,656	134,017	511,847	26,213	48,158	142,523	4,911,550	628,429	3,736,250	335,022	5,500,813
1964	..	..	212,330	125,014	511,366	24,799	44,842	130,704	4,345,915	614,246	3,741,675	347,202	5,296,422
1963	..	..	181,583	115,733	467,728	22,796	40,078	118,615	4,135,215	597,610	3,677,695	339,920	5,222,232
1962	..	..	167,043	100,915	477,756	23,207	39,307	113,234	3,979,430	577,805	3,415,720	314,056	5,029,309
1961	..	..	149,602	87,822	464,942	22,008	35,463	103,924	3,716,595	552,180	3,273,095	300,591	4,860,527
1960	..	..	148,608	87,164	465,171	22,994	33,070	93,261	3,593,730	531,698	3,368,855	304,649	3,969,634
1959	—	—	150,574	78,116	551,114	27,618	35,910	95,148	3,436,195	512,300	3,259,658	302,950	4,089,833
1958	—	—	136,812	74,102	547,673	27,482	35,161	94,158	3,215,554	635,420	2,923,172	324,879	3,483,105
1957	—	—	153,846	85,408	473,728	22,590	34,565	93,167	3,061,716	610,611	3,004,082	356,577	4,119,200
1956	—	—	186,519	70,725	510,101	24,006	28,694	75,233	3,063,284	561,464	3,062,815	341,299	4,331,216
1955	—	—	150,732	55,447	489,240	22,158	25,168	65,650	2,761,318	506,622	2,406,707	256,309	4,004,624
1954	—	—	122,660	53,854	467,738	20,752	22,437	59,036	2,438,654	446,869[8]	2,097,550	218,374[8]	3,424,218
1953	—	—	123,299	43,975	426,446	18,353	22,238	58,842	2,260,426	355,808	1,848,142	156,504	4,252,833
1952[8]	—	—	121,828	40,229	369,605	14,851	18,521	48,059	2,063,057	329,532	1,672,155	155,592	4,056,655
1951	—	—	123,769	40,255	379,434	14,042	17,008	40,446	1,845,847	300,360	1,505,830	140,948	3,931,626
1950	—	—	90,858	29,721	375,247	12,714	16,742	35,894	1,600,096	269,252	1,300,224	111,563	3,964,676
1949	—	—	85,775	33,154	330,867	10,524	15,917	32,902	1,440,467	234,153	1,126,485	91,993	3,864,603
1948	—	—	85,234	32,256	320,693	9,597	14,127	28,265	1,219,291	192,763	998,918	89,116	3,945,776
1947	—	—	78,127	22,157	295,446	7,931	11,936	21,969	1,074,550	143,342	916,016	66,821	3,514,151
1946	—	—	39,975	10,746	272,389	6,628	11,560	20,123	1,017,621	117,837	835,135	44,671	3,363,109
1945	—	—	36,681	6,411	200,241	4,566	8,472	14,246	953,017	110,786	771,188	38,904	3,912,320
1944	—	—	32,150	9,782	154,785	3,155	7,191	11,621	970,941	122,793	780,685	38,414	4,017,696
1943	—	—	35,475	8,915	138,678	2,809	7,302	11,599	869,288	110,044	752,304	37,741	3,551,773
1942	—	—	34,790	8,436	169,317	3,018	9,126	14,365	749,365	91,958	755,964	34,667	3,265,549
1941	—	—	34,827	9,634	208,871	3,765	8,369	13,064	857,924	90,281	732,494	33,442	3,145,715
1940	—	—	26,784	5,981	191,213	3,277	7,560	11,775	780,819	71,336	516,006	25,240	3,015,394
1939	—	—	15,958	4,717	165,024	2,677	5,731	8,511	740,564	64,491	510,467	18,235	2,410,095
1938	—	—	14,267	5,830	148,807	2,341	5,519	8,241	654,029	58,649	475,669	17,769	2,352,003
1937	—	—	15,654	6,260	153,770	2,375	6,169	9,096	640,300	58,568	484,592	18,820	2,570,385
1936	—	—	10,638	3,022	115,732	1,749	4,509	6,908	567,659	50,587	498,318	18,704	2,404,793
1935	—	—	9,125	2,552	100,538	1,555	3,648	5,580	513,717	45,183	469,968	17,578	2,257,604
1934	—	—	8,467	2,057	86,072	1,384	3,783	5,668	461,753	42,458	455,995	17,833	2,243,420
1933	—	—	5,908	1,811	67,700	1,125	3,007	4,537	422,937	39,853	430,314	15,968	1,772,164
1932	—	—	7,965	4,416	100,477	1,779	4,499	6,931	399,937	45,113	366,278	13,050	1,637,701
1931	—	—	11,299	7,397	237,143	4,289	10,162	15,826	469,925	50,109	428,753	14,040	1,832,700
1930	—	—	17,605	11,034	319,838	5,582	11,033	17,713	445,599	60,790	434,564	16,429	2,385,994
1929	—	—	27,674	8,785	458,630	8,003	12,284	19,337	436,621	63,502	448,700	17,895	2,677,581
1928	—	—	19,777	7,162	421,301	7,282	11,024	16,739	344,130	52,229	361,392	14,451	2,314,127
1927	—	—	15,598	7,926	398,439	6,941	10,066	14,392	258,550	35,173	286,526	13,584	2,026,438
1926	—	—	12,933	7,509	358,348	6,526	8,707	13,013	222,147	40,468	228,474	12,007	2,027,058
1925	—	—	10,963	7,772	351,186	5,944	8,117	14,047	164,850	27,639	172,387	9,652	1,546,739
1924	—	—	9,850	6,463	317,473	5,723	7,499	13,398	160,046	—	177,123	9,077	1,436,912
1923	—	—	12,413	4,648	323,965	5,346	7,544	15,065	124,156	—	139,683	7,974	1,668,298
1922	—	—	9,040	3,149	385,497	6,554	6,944	15,438	143,960	—	106,976	6,143	1,232,646
1921	—	—	6,677	2,270	301,385	5,306	5,753	14,195	119,888	—	129,716	6,611	1,463,999
1920	—	—	9,976	2,424	388,480	6,841	6,652	14,798	86,194	—	96,463	10,342	1,708,203
1919	—	—	8,536	1,836	365,894	5,154	4,995	9,802	—	—	—	—	1,675,032
1918	—	—	5,155	1,449	205,117	2,519	3,591	7,077	72,170	—	—	—	1,250,744
1917	—	—	8,506	1,675	257,040	2,652	4,768	7,724	—	—	—	—	1,245,862

Series R621-770. Quantity and value of shipments of selected manufactured commodities,[1] 1917 to 1975 (continued)

Year	Soaps and synthetic detergents		Paints and enamels		Selected synthetic resins		Sulphuric acid		Chlorine		Sodium hydroxide (caustic soda)		Fertilizer sold for consumption in Canada	Medicinal and pharmaceutical preparations
	Quantity	Value	Quantity	Value	Quantity	Value	Quantity (short tons of 100 per cent acid)	Value	Quantity	Value	Quantity	Value	Quantity	Value
	(short tons)	($'000)	('000 gal)	($'000)	('000 lb.)	($'000)		($'000)	(tons)	($'000)	(tons)	($'000)	(short tons)	($'000)
	757	758	759	760	761	762	763	764	765	766	767	768	769	770
1975	323,632	221,716	51,154	322,965	710,274	236,816	1,080,281	25,725	638,835	50,322	983,939	78,416	2,950,243	577,554
1974	316,620	225,127	58,002	307,914	880,687	251,306	1,167,925	23,229	709,288	43,237	965,529	63,328	2,875,518	534,741
1973	305,136	182,091	51,386[11]	242,585[11]	973,994	160,331	1,042,077	18,621	656,825	35,951	890,855	54,848	2,492,084	500,638
1972	284,172	160,424	29,856[15]	144,162[15]	863,612	130,653	1,074,047	18,001	596,938	31,440	895,060	48,763	2,173,893	442,068
1971	268,583	154,729	28,981[15]	138,355[15]	717,240	112,497	1,328,515	20,201	548,791	30,135	776,504	42,333	2,110,978	405,289
1970	274,650	146,998	27,960[15]	130,544[15]	625,617	96,818	1,265,829	19,224	514,967	28,387	738,416	40,406	1,867,522	368,760
1969	275,879	148,734	29,288	131,156	543,686	90,254	988,109	16,375	510,677	28,218	679,867	36,347	1,897,622	346,058
1968	277,981	145,427	31,964	136,968	472,533	76,968	1,315,693	22,224	435,010	24,617	613,078	33,682	2,292,723	313,785
1967	265,079	138,545	30,763	127,333	425,949	76,591	1,065,157	19,237	378,862	21,802	547,308	30,989	2,183,444	290,678
1966	254,923	132,234	29,727	122,214	399,761	74,599	1,044,199	17,883	383,171	22,049	538,000	29,890	1,917,864	264,192
1965	240,603	120,947	29,013	118,595	362,117	68,577	1,006,143	15,522	283,349	16,853	453,711	26,766	1,593,593	233,933
1964	228,167	115,779	26,241	110,294	357,025	70,362	983,389	15,500	246,121	15,303	356,012	21,872	1,454,332	203,588
1963	210,475	108,841	24,906	107,442	289,132	58,868	827,401	13,628	209,934	13,814	308,883	19,180	1,256,841	192,520
1962	197,498	106,848	22,345	98,051	245,699	44,092	729,276	13,706	193,544	12,839	287,673	17,647	1,144,000	176,562
1961	185,903	100,585	21,389	95,251	111,206[17]	23,070[17]	668,266	12,719	168,464	11,220	246,819	15,641	1,077,412	165,551
1960	170,192	97,910	21,998	94,527	94,701[17]	20,274[17]	833,050	17,631	176,126	10,758	264,082	14,597	935,428	159,390
1959	174,528	97,931	21,987	95,787	−	−	1,739,000	..	−	−	−	−	908,214	154,334
1958	167,500	91,062	21,270	92,447	−	−	1,586,000	..	−	−	−	−	870,539	139,621
1957	159,329	82,947	20,585	85,768	−	−	1,290,000	..	−	−	−	−	808,251	126,297
1956	154,866	77,098	20,134	81,701	−	−	1,052,000	..	−	−	−	−	800,680	110,002
1955	147,448	70,633	19,809	77,457	−	−	950,277	..	−	−	−	−	790,774	100,878
1954	143,515	68,312	17,301	69,073	−	−	923,800	..	−	−	−	−	811,641	90,799
1953	148,156	65,333	18,070	72,757	−	−	822,608	..	−	−	−	−	819,803	87,098
1952	141,417	61,057	16,856	67,852	−	−	816,270	..	−	−	−	−	768,545	81,432
1951	133,576	50,991	17,423	69,853	−	−	820,867	..	−	−	−	−	770,507	82,131
1950	141,824	47,757	16,212	61,557	−	−	756,110	..	−	−	−	−	764,581	69,325
1949	125,929	46,021	14,735	55,648	−	−	707,717	..	−	−	−	−	741,726	64,817
1948	137,671	51,783	15,114	55,528	−	−	679,448	..	−	−	−	−	672,171	55,942
1947	122,646	39,772	14,455	47,986	−	−	668,802	..	−	−	−	−	660,721	55,754
1946	117,332	28,203	13,500	37,330	−	−	593,577	..	−	−	−	−	632,943	54,324
1945	136,646	29,337	12,593	31,750	−	−	664,302	..	−	−	−	−	575,107	46,249
1944	120,548	26,963	11,929	29,081	−	−	639,884	..	−	−	−	−	535,108	43,359
1943	118,512	25,289	10,086	25,008	−	−	522,607	..	−	−	−	−	489,861	39,250
1942	116,921	25,632	10,490	25,494	−	−	464,503	..	−	−	−	−	419,547	33,200
1941	112,087	20,609	9,105	22,321	−	−	334,566	..	−	−	−	−	324,201	28,104

Series R621-770. Quantity and value of shipments of selected manufactured commodities,[1] 1917 to 1975 (concluded)

Year	Soaps and synthetic detergents		Paints and enamels		Selected synthetic resins		Sulphuric acid		Chlorine		Sodium hydroxide (caustic soda)		Fertilizer sold for consumption in Canada	Medicinal and pharmaceutical preparations
	Quantity	Value	Quantity	Value	Quantity	Value	Quantity (short tons of 100 per cent acid)	Value	Quantity	Value	Quantity	Value	Quantity	Value
	(short tons)	($'000)	('000 gal)	($'000)	('000 lb.)	($'000)		($'000)	(tons)	($'000)	(tons)	($'000)	(short tons)	($'000)
	757	758	759	760	761	762	763	764	765	766	767	768	769	770
1940	102,394	16,827	6,912	16,809	–	–	301,444	··	–	–	–	–	346,721	21,119
1939	100,815	16,405	6,112	14,657	–	–	237,927	··	–	–	–	–	334,003	19,132
1938	88,009	14,715	5,914	13,914	–	–	250,065	··	–	–	–	–	323,376	17,315
1937	94,518	16,149	5,126	11,674	–	–	263,463	··	–	–	–	–	298,276	17,946
1936	91,294	13,538	5,150	12,255	–	–	224,658	··	–	–	–	–	233,840	16,134
1935	90,674	13,446	4,461	10,731	–	–	209,128	··	–	–	–	–	212,479	15,494
1934	91,872	11,520	3,885	9,544	–	–	191,342	··	–	–	–	–	194,851	14,413
1933	83,132	12,328	3,032	7,358	–	–	138,054	··	–	–	–	–	166,407	12,891
1932	87,200	12,318	2,907	7,267	–	–	127,527	··	–	–	–	–	179,983	12,853
1931	85,049	14,151	3,889	9,686	–	–	111,401	··	–	–	–	–	284,217	13,677
1930	82,211	15,063	4,474	11,771	–	–	100,020	··	–	–	–	–	321,207	7,291
1929	79,192	15,232	5,490	13,826	–	–	103,207	··	–	–	–	–	323,750	7,853
1928	72,464	14,034	4,761	11,440	–	–	89,721	··	–	–	–	–	–	7,355
1927	69,390	12,337	4,252	10,692	–	–	91,764	··	–	–	–	–	169,564	6,990
1926	–	–	–	–	–	–	100,860	··	–	–	–	–	–	–
1925	–	–	–	–	–	–	77,700	··	–	–	–	–	–	–
1924	–	–	–	–	–	–	67,088	··	–	–	–	–	–	–
1923	–	–	–	–	–	–	81,215	··	–	–	–	–	–	–
1922	–	–	–	–	–	–	57,148	··	–	–	–	–	–	–
1921	–	–	–	–	–	–	43,981	··	–	–	–	–	–	–
1920	–	–	–	–	–	–	67,901	··	–	–	–	–	–	–
1919	–	–	–	–	–	–	45,485	··	–	–	–	–	–	–
1918	–	–	–	–	–	–	–	··	–	–	–	–	–	–
1917	–	–	–	–	–	–	–	··	–	–	–	–	–	–

1 See text regarding partial coverage of many commodity series, beginning in 1970 or later years, owing to exclusion of small establishments.
2 Excludes slippers, moccasins and athletic footwear.
3 Electric lamps and shades in miscellaneous group prior to 1960.
4 Wood pulp in thousand tons from 1917 to 1959; in thousands of dollars from 1960 to 1975.
5 Composition of the printing and publishing industry was changed in 1948 by including publishers of periodicals who did no printing.
6 Pig iron produced is in short tons from 1961 to 1975, in long tons prior to 1960.
7 Includes batteries.
8 A change in the method of valuation of the petroleum refining industry products for 1954 and subsequent years resulted in a larger increase, compared with 1953 and earlier years, for gross value of production and value added, than would have occurred had the 1953 method been continued.

9 Includes excise taxes and duties prior to 1966, except 1917, 1918 and 1919; excludes these for 1966 and subsequent years.
10 Includes excise taxes and duties prior to 1972, except 1917, 1918 and 1919; excludes these for 1972 and subsequent years.
11 Not comparable with previous years; see explanatory notes.
12 Value, including excise taxes and duties: $965,953,000.
13 Value, including excise taxes and duties: $22,264,000.
14 Value, including excise taxes and duties: $58,253,000.
15 Comparable data for the 1970 to 1972 period, on the 1973 base are as follows: 1972, 53,445,000 gallons, $241,866,000; 1971, 48,762,000 gallons, $218,456,000; 1970, 46,407,000 gallons, $206,014,000.
16 Value, including excise taxes and duties: $516,666,000.
17 Polyvinyl chloride and polystyrene only; data for 1962 and subsequent years also include polyethylene.
18 Does not include excise taxes and duties.
19 Beginning in 1952, data are for shipments.

Series R771-782. Number of establishments and value of shipments of goods of own manufacture, by size of establishment, measured by value of shipments of goods of own manufacture, 1960 to 1975
(establishments in numbers; value of shipments in millions of dollars)

Year	Total number of establishments	Under $100,000		$100,000 to $499,999		$500,000 to $999,999		$1,000,000 to $4,999,999		$5,000,000 and over		Total value of shipments of goods of own manufacture
		Establishments	Shipments of goods of own manufacture	Establishments	Shipments of goods of own manufacture	Establishments	Shipments of goods of own manufacture	Establishments	Shipments of goods of own manufacture	Establishments	Shipments of goods of own manufacture	
	771	772	773	774	775	776	777	778	779	780	781	782
1975	30,100 [1]	7,276	369.7	9,459	2,353.0	3,774	2,706.7	6,482	14,603.8	3,109	68,427.2	88,460.4
1974	31,535	9,467	435.4	9,349	2,308.2	3,790	2,719.2	5,965	13,573.6	2,964	63,418.7	82,455.1
1973	31,145	10,340	448.7	9,207	2,277.6	3,566	2,558.7	5,552	12,598.3	2,480	48,791.1	66,674.4
1972	31,553	11,455	476.9	9,413	2,313.6	3,417	2,439.6	5,154	11,551.9	2,114	39,408.8	56,190.7
1971	31,908	12,245	498.8	9,589	2,336.2	3,388	2,393.7	4,845	10,813.9	1,841	34,233.3	50,275.9
1970	31,928	12,682	511.1	9,547	2,322.8	3,337	2,370.1	4,673	10,297.9	1,689	30,879.0	46,380.9
1969	32,669	13,545	530.7	9,591	2,349.6	3,296	2,366.1	4,574	10,068.9	1,663	30,615.2	45,930.4
1968	32,643	13,979	533.6	9,628	2,344.5	3,202	2,285.3	4,303	9,415.5	1,531	27,482.7	42,061.6
1967	33,267	14,925	533.5	9,685	2,362.7	3,125	2,231.1	4,135	8,997.8	1,397	24,830.2	38,955.4
1966	33,377	15,417	565.1	9,617	2,324.4	3,033	2,158.2	3,962	8,621.4	1,348	23,634.4	37,303.5
1965	33,310	16,103	578.3	9,462	2,276.1	2,847	2,008.5	3,687	7,910.4	1,211	21,116.1	33,889.4
1964	33,630	16,941	587.4	9,441	2,248.8	2,692	1,894.0	3,464	7,393.3	1,092	18,732.7	30,856.1
1963	33,119	17,065	585.6	9,208	2,172.7	2,639	1,850.6	3,224	6,854.6	983	16,551.4	28,014.9
1962	33,414	17,900	597.8	9,078	2,143.3	2,485	1,750.2	3,062	6,495.9	889	14,802.8	25,790.1
1961	33,357	18,484	603.2	8,815	2,072.7	2,400	1,689.5	2,875	6,124.0	783	12,949.7	23,439.0
1960	36,682	21,645	658.3	9,162	2,120.0	2,377	1,683.6	2,723	5,771.3	775	13,514.3	23,747.5

[1] Reflects in part the deletion of some 1,400 establishments with no employees in 1974.

Series R783-794. Number of establishments and gross value of production by size of establishment measured by gross value of production, selected years, 1900 to 1959
(establishments in thousands; total value of production in thousands of dollars)

Year	Under $25,000		$25,000 to $199,999		$200,000 to $499,999		$500,000 to $999,999		$1,000,000 and over		Total number of establishments	Total production
	Establishments	Total value of production	Establishments	Total value of production	Establishments	Total value of production	Establishments	Total value of production	Establishments	Total value of production		
	783	784	785	786	787	788	789	790	791	792	793	794
1959 [1]	12.0	118,492	14.1	1,150,005	4.5	1,424,683	2.3	1,645,987	3.4	18,972,435	36.2	23,311,601
1958 [1]	12.5	124,234	14.4	1,163,412	4.4	1,393,009	2.2	1,570,427	3.2	17,912,104	36.7	22,163,186
1957 [1]	13.8	132,484	14.5	1,168,597	4.3	1,375,175	2.2	1,555,091	3.1	17,952,247	37.9	22,183,594
1955 [1]	15.3	143,481	14.2	1,136,774	4.0	1,261,917	2.0	1,411,585	2.7	15,560,177	38.2	19,513,934
1950	16.1	145,592	12.9	1,007,383	3.3	1,029,829	1.6	1,112,819	2.0	10,521,903	35.9	13,817,526
1945	13.7	128,803	10.6	795,194	2.4	742,817	1.0	709,213	1.4	5,874,341	29.1	8,250,368
1940	15.5	130,757	7.0	516,017	1.5	473,213	.7	484,350	.8	2,924,836	25.5	4,529,173
1936	15.8	119,767	6.1	436,722	1.3	391,284	.5	358,346	.5	1,696,284	24.5	3,002,403
1930 [2]	14.9	96,355	6.5	481,874	1.4	451,251	.6	392,124	.6	2,046,162	22.5	3,467,766
1925 [2]	13.8	128,137	6.3	460,597	1.2	381,157	.5	344,834	.5	1,633,820	22.6	2,948,545
1922 [2]	15.0	111,053	5.5	397,882	1.1	325,015	.5	355,702	.4	1,250,191	22.2	2,439,846
1915 [3]	—	—	20.2 [5]	383,652 [5]	.6	198,835	.3	201,054	.2	623,596	21.3	1,407,137
1910 [4]	—	—	18.1 [5]	431,337 [5]	.7	219,099	.2	156,519	.1	359,020	19.2	1,165,974
1905 [3]	—	—	15.1 [5]	—	.5	—	.1	—	.1	—	15.8	718,353
1900 [4]	—	—	14.2 [5]	—	.3	—	.1	—	.04	—	14.6	481,053

[1] Figures for 1955, 1957 to 1959 are for 'Value of factory shipments' and not 'Value of production'.
[2] Includes 'Central electric stations' and 'Dyeing, cleaning and laundry work' establishments.
[3] Postal census; incomplete coverage.
[4] Decennial census of establishments with five employees and over.
[5] Includes all establishments with value of production under $200,000.

Series R795-811. Number of establishments and number of employees by size of establishment, measured by number employed,[1] 1960 to 1975
(establishments and employees in numbers)

Year	Total number of establishments	Under 5 employed		5 to 49		50 to 99		100 to 199		200 to 499		500 to 999		1,000 and over		Separately located head offices and ancillary units	Total employees
		Establishments	Employees	Establishments	Employees	Establishments	Employees	Establishments	Employees	Establishments	Employees	Establishments	Employees	Establishments	Employees	Employees	
	795	796	797	798	799	800	801	802	803	804	805	806	807	808	809	810	811
1975	30,100[2]	8,054	15,189	15,574	284,498	2,839	198,907	1,962	274,642	1,207	362,824	311	211,088	153	305,716	88,681[3]	1,741,545
1974	31,535	9,516	14,929	15,493	274,130	2,779	196,004	1,940	272,196	1,297	393,739	349	238,443	161	320,276	76,260	1,785,977
1973	31,145	9,214	13,779	15,445	269,558	2,800	196,521	1,923	270,842	1,275	386,014	343	234,654	145	304,273	75,425	1,751,066
1972	31,553	9,753	14,268	15,514	266,493	2,781	194,087	1,854	259,440	1,190	358,844	319	217,196	142	291,718	74,084	1,676,130
1971	31,908	10,159	14,788	15,673	266,728	2,738	191,194	1,801	253,101	1,091	329,101	313	213,683	133	283,010	76,799	1,628,404
1970	31,928	9,985	14,166	15,929	270,388	2,726	189,849	1,780	253,073	1,069	325,179	302	212,916	137	293,449	77,981	1,637,001
1969	32,669	10,150	15,472	16,453	276,692	2,722	191,101	1,751	244,433	1,135	343,430	305	209,293	153	318,729	76,182	1,675,332
1968	32,643	10,302	15,422	16,401	273,987	2,724	190,333	1,693	238,020	1,081	329,762	289	198,723	153	322,210	73,895	1,642,352
1967	33,267	10,955	15,612	16,422	273,641	2,686	188,094	1,681	235,875	1,064	323,385	303	207,710	156	334,223	74,287	1,652,827
1966	33,377	11,062	15,740	16,444	270,005	2,708	189,750	1,644	229,605	1,066	326,014	300	208,498	153	336,259	70,153	1,646,024
1965	33,310	11,387	15,931	16,311	267,932	2,592	180,562	1,573	219,288	1,009	305,697	296	204,030	142	311,501	65,358	1,570,299
1964	33,630	12,075	16,614	16,145	263,508	2,527	175,552	1,515	211,016	966	293,256	275	191,468	127	278,630	61,213	1,491,257
1963	33,119	11,929	15,970	15,946	258,861	2,508	173,247	1,431	199,634	936	285,378	250	175,264	119	257,831	59,255	1,425,440
1962	33,414	12,270	16,154	16,017	257,050	2,462	170,033	1,396	193,418	902	273,534	256	178,696	111	242,598	58,033	1,389,516
1961	33,357	12,352	16,846	15,963	255,757	2,445	169,319	1,377	190,540	869	261,628	243	169,392	108	234,320	54,733	1,352,535
1960	36,682[4]	14,469	32,235	16,564	262,146	2,319	161,365	1,266	176,163	785	238,109	238	165,129	112	242,592	16,890[5]	1,294,629

1 The number employed includes working owners and partners and is the criterion used for defining size classes. The statistic, 'employees', tabulated for establishments in particular size classes, excludes working owners and partners, except for 1960 (and for earlier years not shown here).
2 Reflects in part the deletion of some 1,400 establishments with no employees in 1974.

3 Not entirely comparable with previous years due to a change in recording some employees in ancillary units formerly included as part of the parent establishment.
4 Includes 929 'not classifiable' establishments.
5 Not comparable with subsequent years.

Series R812-825. Number of establishments and number of employees by size of establishment measured by number of employees, selected years, 1915 to 1960

(establishments in thousands, employees in actual numbers)

Year	Total number of establishments	Under 5 employees		5 to 49		50 to 99		100 to 199		200 to 499		500 and over		Total employees
		Establishments	Employees	Establishments	Employees	Establishments	Employees	Establishments	Employees	Establishments	Employees	Establishments	Employees	
	812	813	814	815	816	817	818	819	820	821	822	823	824	825
1960	36.7	14.5	32,235	16.6	262,146	2.3	161.365	1.3	176,163	.8	238,109	.4	407,721	1,294,629[2]
1959	36.2[1]	14.6	31,710	16.2	255,064	2.3	156,127	1.3	173,220	.8	241,597	.4	429,551	1,289,602[2]
1958	36.7[1]	15.2	33,747	16.2	254,259	2.1	149,195	1.2	168,145	.7	238,246	.4	428,296	1,303,956[2]
1957	37.9[1]	16.0	35,020	16.5	257,445	2.1	148,329	1.2	168,810	.7	233,636	.4	498,196	1,289,602[2]
1955	38.2[1]	16.3	36,340	16.2	251,046	2.1	144,411	1.2	163,091	.7	227,667	.4	459,973	1,298,461[2]
1950	35.9[1]	16.7	34,719	15.1	235,546	1.9	133,374	1.1	156,489	.7	216,593	.3	395,304	1,183,297[2]
1945	29.1	12.9	30,052	12.5	195,796	1.7	116,422	1.0	136,961	.6	193,122	.4	447,019	1,119,372
1940	25.5	13.1	31,788	9.7	150,497	1.2	87,028	.8	105,607	.5	157,021	.2	230,303	762,244
1936	24.2	13.4	26,659	8.6	131,315	1.0	72,902	.7	91,966	.4	126,368	.1	145,149	594,359
1930[3]	24.0	12.6	24,186	8.9	144,700	1.2	86,077	.7	102,626	.4	124,548	.2	167,075	649,212
1925[3]	22.3	12.3	25,025	7.8	127,934	1.1	75,866	.6	86,287	.4	112,315	.1	133,405	560,832
1922[3]	22.3	14.8	26,407	5.6	101,076	.9	67,619	.5	71,338	.4	103,232	.1	91,714	461,386
1915[4]	21.3	8.3	—	5.2	—	.7	—	.4	—	.2	—	.1	—	462,200

[1] Includes 'Not classifiable' establishments numbering approximately 725 in 1959, 1,000 in 1957 and 1958, 800 in 1955, and 200 in 1950.

[2] Includes employees in head offices located away from the plant, not counted in the size breakdowns.

[3] Includes 'Central electric stations' and 'Dyeing, cleaning and laundry work' establishments.

[4] Based on wage-earners only.

Section S: Construction and Housing

Marion Steele, *University of Guelph*

The statistics in this section are arranged in five subsections. The first subsection (series S1-64) contains summary statistics for construction by type and by region. It also contains general statistics of the construction industry. The second subsection (series S65-166) contains statistics for non-residential construction by the sector 'purchasing' the construction. The third subsection (series S167-219) covers residential construction, the fourth (series S220-246) the housing stock and the fifth (series S247-335) mortgage funding. A major difference between this section and the similar section in the first edition of *Historical Statistics of Canada* is the elimination of most of the series on repair construction detail. On the other hand, a large number of series have been added. These include the series on mortgage funding and housing unit costs.

A substantial amount of the data in this section was obtained directly from the producing agency. In some cases the series do not appear in any publication. In other cases the series available in published sources are obsolete because of data revision and reclassification. The sources of the data in this section are given below.

Statistics Canada publications: *Private and Public Investment in Canada, Outlook,* (Catalogue 61-205); *Private and Public Investment in Canada, Outlook, Mid-Year Review,* (Catalogue 61-206); *Construction in Canada,* (Catalogue 64-201); *Building Permits,* (Catalogue 64-203); *National Income and Expenditure Accounts, 1926-1974,* (Catalogue 13-531) and subsequent annual issues, (Catalogue 13-201); *Housing Starts and Completions,* (Catalogue 64-002); *Fixed Capital Flows and Stocks in Manufacturing,* (Catalogue 13-522); *Fixed Capital Flows and Stocks,* (Catalogue 13-211).

Summary Statistics of Construction (Series S1-64)

General note

Virtually every series in this section and the next has to do with non-residential construction. There are three major sources of these data. One of these, the building permits survey, gives the value of building construction and some engineering construction at a point in time usually slightly before construction starts. Currently its geographic coverage is very good because almost all municipalities require building permits. A second source, the industry censuses, survey producers of construction output and have varied greatly in coverage. Further information on these two sources is given in notes to individual tables.

The most important of the three major sources used in this section is the capital expenditure survey. Information about this survey was obtained from *Private and Public Investment, Mid-Year Review, 1977, Construction in Canada, Private and Public Investment in Canada,* a xeroxed paper written in 1973 and from the staff of the Capital Expenditure Section, Construction Division, Statistics Canada. Unless otherwise indicated, references to estimation procedures used by this survey refer to those used in 1973.

The capital expenditure survey gathers information on investment in machinery and equipment and in construction, and information on repair expenditure. It is a survey of the purchasers of construction and other capital goods rather than of suppliers and its values relate to a later point in time than building permit values. Currently over 24,000 establishments are surveyed, compared with about 16,000 in the 1950s; these include institutions and governments as well as businesses. This survey is not a random sample survey. Instead, generally the aim is to get complete coverage of all establishments with sales greater than a certain cut-off amount. This cut off varies by industry, by province and over time. It was typically $500,000 in the mid-1970s and $200,000 in the early years of the survey.

Estimation of total construction for an industry is typically done in two stages. First, construction from the survey is divided into two categories. For manufacturing, for instance, the first category is construction purchased by ongoing establishments. The second category, called 'net additions', is roughly construction creating a new establishment. The first category is then grossed up to get an estimate for the universe of ongoing establishments. Grossing thus accomplishes coverage of non-surveyed and non-responding establishments; it is done using related series.

It can be seen that a problem for this survey is capturing construction which creates a new establishment, especially if the new establishment is also a new firm. A new firm may not be noticed until construction is well under way or has been completed. This is a problem of identifying the universe, not a sampling problem. Another problem for the survey is the grossing factor. An alternative grossing factor might be the ratio of the change in shipments in the industry, exclusive of 'net additions' establishments, to the change in shipments in the sample used for grossing. These difficulties should not be exaggerated, however, since it is estimated that survey coverage (the total in both categories before grossing) is about 90 per cent.

Construction is divided into new and repair. Conceptually new construction is construction having a life of more than one year. Thus, additions are included as well as entirely new buildings and engineering structures. Construction cost encompasses all overhead costs such as administrative, architectural, legal and engineering costs. It includes land improvement costs, so that land servicing as well as site preparation costs are covered. It also includes the cost of installed equipment such as elevators, heating systems and air conditioning. The construction may be carried out under contract or by the 'purchaser's' own labour force.

Construction does not include the purchase of existing buildings or land. Because land is excluded, 'new construction' understates substantially the non-equipment portion of investment by particular industries. Of course, industry investment will also be further understated when a firm purchases existing buildings from a firm in another industry. The use of rented buildings is attributed to the firm owning the building, not the firm renting the building. Thus a large part of all retail and office space and a small amount of industrial space is classified under 'other finance'. An exception to this is stores built under leaseback for some food chains; this construction is included under retail trade.

Repair construction is construction undertaken to maintain the operating efficiency of existing structures for the original life intended. Routine maintenance such as char service, sanding and snow removal is excluded.

There is some possibility that reported new construction excludes some activity which is conceptually included. Establishments report new construction under the heading 'capital' construction expenditure, and some may on occasion report only the construction costs they capitalize. This implies that the repair expenditure category contains some renovations and improvements which conceptually belong in the 'new' category. Accounting problems make it difficult to identify and report properly new construction, especially where the distinction between engineering work and machinery is a problem (e.g. petroleum refineries), and where categories of account, (as in government departments and institutions), are arranged in a format which does not allow an easy adaptation to the reporting categories of the survey.

Conceptually, the time basis for the capital expenditure survey construction data is work put in place. Because costs are often recorded on a cash flow basis, however, the reported data may lag behind the work put in place. The length of this lag is unknown. Respondents report expenditures, so that the lags may be very short if progress payments are frequent. It is also true that respondents are explicitly asked to report the value of holdbacks attributable to construction work done in the period concerned. Some holdbacks, however, are improperly reported for the period the payment is made, not for the period the work takes place. It is not known how important this problem is. Obviously it is potentially more important the longer the construction time of a project.

The capital expenditure survey was not started until 1941, and was carried out only in a limited way until 1946. Estimates of construction from 1926 to 1941 were first published in *Public Investment and Capital Formation, A Study of Public and Private Investment Outlay, Canada, 1926-1941*, Ottawa, 1945, (referred to as PICF). Total building construction was estimated by estimating the flow of building materials and then applying to this a ratio of the value of building construction to materials used. Ratios were available for several years in this period from censuses of construction. The breakdown into new and repair employed ratios from the same source. Building construction for some user categories was estimated directly. The residual included such categories as manufacturing, finance, universities. Virtually all engineering construction was covered by direct estimation.

The estimates in PICF, prepared under the direction of O. J. Firestone and M. C. Urquhart, were later replaced by estimates prepared under the direction of O. J. Firestone and appearing in *Private and Public Investment in Canada, 1926-1951*, Ottawa, 1951, (referred to as PPI). A major change was direct estimation for the manufacturing, construction, trade, finance (excluding banks) and commercial services sectors, using a sample of income tax returns of corporations. Further information on the PICF and PPI, including an assessment of the differences, is available in

Kenneth Buckley's note for this section in the previous edition of *Historical Statistics of Canada*. Information here on PICF and PPI is drawn from that note.

For the years 1956 to 1976, the figures for non-residential construction by purchasing category are taken directly from CANSIM. Many of the figures in earlier years are different from those in any publication. When the series were prepared for CANSIM, in 1976 and 1977, great effort was spent on regrouping, etc. to get series continued back to 1956 on a consistent format. (The basic documentation exists allowing this to be continued back to 1952, but no earlier.) A major problem for this work was the change in the SIC about 1960. It is important to note that while the series are consistent back to 1956 in the sense of the sectors each series conceptually contains, they are not statistically consistent. The new SIC used a more all-inclusive definition of the establishment (see the general note to Section R, Manufactures).

For the period 1946 to 1955, the series are taken from *Private and Public Investment in Canada, 1946-1957*, PPI, 1946-57. Estimates in this source are given at the Canada level only. It must be pointed out that when series were being prepared for CANSIM by province, it was not found possible to generate series which aggregated to the Canada totals given in this publication. Consequently, the Construction Division no longer uses PPI, 1946-57. The disaggregation problems encountered by the Construction Division arose from the use for PPI, 1946-57 of adjustment procedures applied directly to Canada-level numbers rather than to disaggregates. Unfortunately, the unavailability of documentation does not allow this hypothesis to be checked. In view of the fact that PPI, 1946-57 incorporates numerous revisions to the original series and was used for the previous edition of *Historical Statistics of Canada*, it was decided to use it rather than the annual outlook publications published for those years.

S1-7. New and repair construction expenditures, in current and constant dollars, 1926 to 1976

SOURCE: Series S1-3, for 1926 to 1955, the previous edition of *Historical Statistics of Canada*, series R1-3; series S1-3, for 1956 to 1976, CANSIM Matrix No. 001190; series S4-7, see text following.

For concepts and procedures see the general note.

S1 is the series as produced by the Construction Division plus (S180 - S179 + S181 - S9); this adjustment was done to make series S1 consistent with residential construction as it appears in the National Accounts.

Unfortunately, constant dollar series corresponding to series S1-3 are not available for the entire period 1926 to 1976, because of revisions to series S1-3. Constant dollar series corresponding to recent current dollar values for series S1 are available in *Private and Public Investment in Canada, Mid-Year Review, 1977*, table 21, and earlier editions of the same publication. Series S4-7 was produced especially for this volume as follows. Series S4 is residential construction (S180 - S179 + S181) deflated using the GNP residential construction deflator plus non-residential construction (S1 - (S180 - S179 + S181)) deflated using the GNP non-residential construction deflator. The deflators are from *National Income and Expenditure Accounts*, (Catalogues 13-531 and 13-201). Series S7 is S1 divided by S4. Series S5 is S2 divided by S7. Series S6 is S4 plus S5.

S8. Estimates of total new and repair construction, 1896 to 1930

SOURCE: Buckley, *Capital Formation in Canada*, 1896 to 1930, p. 128. The basic estimation procedure used for these estimates was similar to that used in PICF. First the annual flow of construction materials to construction uses was estimated. From this the total value of construction was estimated on the basis of data on the relation of the material component to the labour component and overhead and profit. The relation of material component to labour was the subject of substantial investigation. For 1896 to 1920 it was assumed that the ratio of materials to labour was constant, but for 1921 to 1930 this ratio of real inputs was varied. For the whole period it was assumed that overhead and profit was 14.3 per cent of the total value of construction.

S9-22. Total value of new construction work performed, by principle type of construction, 1926 to 1976

SOURCE: for 1926 to 1950, the previous edition of *Historical Statistics of Canada*, for 1951 to 1976, *Construction in Canada*, table 6.

See the general note to this section for a description of concepts and procedures. Much more detail on type of structure than is given here is available in the source document. For instance under commercial are listed eight categories: office buildings; stores, retail and wholesale; theatres, arenas, amusement and recreational buildings; hotels, clubs, restaurants, cafeterias, tourist cabins; warehouses, storehouses, refrigerated storage, etc.; garages and service stations; laundries and dry cleaning establishments.

Conceptually, series S1 and S22 are the same. They are in fact different because statistical revisions in the residential and agriculture components made for the years 1961 and earlier are incorporated in series S1 but not in S18 (or the relevant component series in this table).

S23-28. Total value of new construction work performed, by region and by major type, 1951 to 1976

SOURCE: *Construction in Canada*.

See the general note to this section for a description of concepts and procedures.

S29-58. Building permits issued, by region and major type, 1951 to 1976

SOURCE: Mr. J. P. Delisle, Housing and Building Permits Section, Construction Division. Current data are published in *Building Permits, Annual Summary*.

Almost all municipalities require a building permit to be taken out for a new building or for alterations and additions to an existing building. Statistics Canada has been collecting data on permits issued for many years and detail is available on a variable basis in bulletins beginning in 1922. Over the last two decades great efforts have been put forth to expand coverage, so that 1,900 municipalities were covered in 1977. Unfortunately, however, series on a consistent coverage basis, and with the region and type of detail shown here, are not available. There are, however, just two instances where substantial breaks occur because of coverage increases: 1957-58 and 1962-63. Coverage in some census years is given in the following table.

Building permits, geographic coverage

Year	Canada	Atlantic provinces	Quebec	Ontario	Prairie provinces	British Columbia[1]
			(Per cent of population covered)			
1976	86	74	82	94	74	93
1971	82	52	79	93	73	91
1961	68	37	67	81	61	77
1951	57	34	51	72	45	73
			(Number of municipalities covered)			
1976	1,875	302	562	497	402	112
1971	1,445	102	325	527	381	110
1961	1,003	71	217	324	271	120
1951	439	35	70	177	75	82

[1] Includes Yukon Territory and Northwest Territories.

The percentage coverage of buildings erected in the intended universe is probably much greater than the percentage population coverage, because municipalities with substantial building activity are more apt to have well-organized building departments than those where building is quiescent.

Not all types of construction are covered by building permits. The biggest gap is non-building (i.e. engineering) construction. Some types of buildings also frequently do not require building permits, most notably municipal and local school buildings. Some types of construction may legally require a permit but may often - perhaps even ordinarily - proceed without a permit. This is the case with alterations and additions. According to a survey of Kenneth Buckley, in Saskatoon for 1941 to 1951 only 20 to 25 per cent of residential conversions were covered by a permit, (see *Historical Statistics of Canada*, previous edition, p. 500). It is the writer's impression that even in the city of Toronto, where enforcement of building regulations might be expected to be better than in smaller cities, a very large percentage of alteration jobs are not covered by a permit.

The values of buildings for which permits are taken out are understated. An incentive for understatement exists because the cost of a building permit generally depends on the estimated cost of the work. Comparisons by Mr. J. P. Delisle of the Construction Division of costs given in National Housing Act applications in the early 1970s with permit costs of the same buildings indicated that the permit values of single detached dwellings averaged 87 per cent of the actual value of construction and for multiple unit residential buildings, just 80 per cent.

The building permit series make no adjustment for permits which are allowed to lapse. The importance of lapses is not known but is generally thought to be unimportant. A very large number of apartment buildings covered by permits in the Toronto area in late 1973, however, had no visible work started as late as early 1975. The permits for many of these buildings were probably renewed and the buildings ultimately started, but permits as an indicator of starts were obviously very defective in 1973. This particular problem was presumably caused by the tightness in financial markets in early 1974 and the escalation of construction costs in 1973 and 1974, so that it is plausible that permits are only defective indicators on rare occasions. The views of some Toronto area building officials substantiate this.

The building permit series provide quite similar information to the Canadata (formerly Southam, and earlier, Maclean) contract award series. Some contract award series were given in the previous edition of *Historical Statistics of Canada;* unfortunately, however contract award data are no longer available free of charge. The timing of the contract award series is generally somewhat different from that of the permit series, because contracts are awarded before permits are taken out. In some cases, however, the Canadata series is apparently essentially a permit series. This is probably the case for most residential building. For apartments the Canadata contract series reflects the problem in 1973 referred to above in the discussion of the permit series, i.e. a very large proportion of apartment 'contracts' apparently were cancelled.

The permit series constitute a useful check of the construction series from the capital expenditure survey. Remembering that the permits lead construction by many months, and that values in the permit series probably represent understatements of over 20 per cent, the detail in the building permit and construction publications suggests that the capital expenditure survey substantially understates the construction of retail and wholesale stores and hotels, clubs, restaurants, cafeterias and tourist cabins.

S59. Value of building permits issued, 1910 to 1960

SOURCE: previous edition of *Historical Statistics of Canada*, series R177.

This series like series S25-54, was produced by Statistics Canada and provides some indication of the effects of changes in geographic coverage, 1951 to 1960.

S60-64. Principal statistics of the construction industry (construction contractors), 1934 to 1976

SOURCE: for 1951 to 1975, *Construction in Canada* (Catalogue 64-201); for 1934 to 1950, *Construction Industry in Canada*, (Catalogue 64-D-21).

A construction census was first carried out by Statistics Canada in 1917. It was not carried out for the years 1923 to 1933 nor for the years 1951 to 1974, although partial censuses were carried out providing data for 1967 to 1974. These gaps arose because of dissatisfaction with the quality of the census. It is very difficult to take a census of this

industry. There are a very large number of small, widely dispersed establishments, and because of substantial fluctuations in demand the average life of establishments is short.

The data before 1951 are estimated very differently from those of the later period. For 1934 to 1950, all data come directly from the Census of Construction. Because of the intrinsic problems of identifying the universe, the coverage probably varied quite considerably from year to year, and in no year was coverage very good. Coverage of non-residential construction was much better than coverage of residential: for 1938, new residential construction reported in the construction census was just 37 per cent of all new residential construction expenditure as estimated in the national accounts (see series S180); for new non-residential construction the proportion was 66 per cent.

Note that these coverage figures are for all construction reported to the construction census, while series S60-64 relate only to construction carried out by contractors, i.e. series S60-64 do not cover construction carried out by industries other than the construction industry. The 1950 construction census report shows the value of work by contractors and builders to be 65 per cent of all work reported, while owner-builders, 'industrial organizations', steam and electric railways, utilities and governments account respectively for 5, 6, 2, 14 and 7 per cent.

Despite the incomplete coverage of this census, there seems no obvious reason why indexes and ratios constructed from it should be seriously biased and a number of investigators, including Buckley and this writer, have used the census in this way. Contained in the reports are 'capital invested', construction by detailed category (office buildings, stores, theatres, apartment houses, dwellings, etc.), and other useful information.

For 1951, a construction census was carried out, but after the results were compared with the capital expenditure survey, it was decided to discontinue the census. Starting in 1951 the value of work performed is taken from the response of 'purchasers' of construction to the capital expenditure survey. In that survey respondents are asked the amount of their construction expenditure carried out by contractors. Salaries and wages are estimated as follows. For each of the residential, non-residential building and engineering construction sectors, reports from the contract construction industry are used to compute the ratio of salaries and wages to value of work performed; this ratio times the value of work from the capital expenditure survey yields the estimate of salaries and wages for each sector and thus total salaries and wages. The remaining series are estimated similarly.

From 1951 to 1966, the contract construction industry data were obtained from all firms with sales over $100,000. These firms were identified by using sources such as the Business Register and Dun and Bradstreet. Starting with 1967, census data were used as well as the large-firm data. The census data available for 1967 were those for electrical contractors. Starting with 1975 the census covered all parts of the construction industry. Also starting in that year census procedures changed. Firms with revenue over $500,000 in 1975 reported on the census long form. Financial data for all firms between $50,000 and $500,000 and for a sample of firms under $50,000 were obtained from Revenue Canada. Non-financial data for a subsample of this group (numbering 10,000 in 1975) were obtained by a short-form survey. The sample results were appropriately weighted to obtain the universe estimates.

Non-residential Construction (Series S65-166)

Note: see the general note to the previous section.

S65-71. New construction in primary industries, 1946 to 1976

SOURCE: for 1946 to 1955, PPI, 1946 to 1957; for 1956 to 1976, CANSIM Matrix No. 001190 and 001194.

Agriculture and fishing are not included in the capital expenditure survey, essentially because both industries contain many small establishments which are difficult to survey. The agriculture estimation uses a benchmark obtained from a 1958 sample survey; this benchmark is then projected on the basis of farm income and sales of building materials. The fishing estimates are obtained from the Department of Fisheries and are estimated from their regional contacts. Construction in fishing industries includes items like docks, but boats are classified as machines. Fishing is dwarfed in importance by agriculture. For instance, in 1976 agriculture was $520.5 million while fishing was just $6.5 million. As described here, the agriculture and fishing series is probably of lower quality than the estimates based on direct surveys.

The forestry estimates are obtained by the capital expenditure survey. All establishments with sales over $500,000 are covered; in some provinces the cut-off is lower than this. It is likely that some forestry construction is incorrectly included in manufacturing with sawmills and with pulp and paper mills.

The mining and petroleum and gas estimates are probably of very high quality starting in 1967 (mining) and 1965 (petroleum and gas). These are the first years reflecting the use of a questionnaire especially designed for the industry. The mining survey is a census, i.e. there is no cut-off point - and indeed some exploration establishments which are captured do not report in the Census of Primary Industry. The petroleum and gas survey is also a census and uses the MAPID (Manufacturing and Primary Industries Division) form. The results of the survey are reviewed with industry representatives before publication.

Starting at the break-point, 1965, petroleum and gas includes exploratory and development drilling, including contract drilling. It also includes extraction from oil sands. Geological and geophysical exploration is excluded. Before 1965 the items included had varied to an unknown extent from establishment to establishment, depending on the establishment's interpretation of the definition of capital expenditure on the survey form. In 1960 also there was a conceptual change so that from 1960 gas processing plants are included; before this year gas processing is classified as manufacturing.

Starting at the break-point, 1967, mining includes on-property exploration and development but excludes outside and general exploration. As with petroleum and gas, the mining series before its break year contains some inconsistencies.

Estimates for the construction industry since 1975 are obtained using data from the Census of Construction (see notes to series S60-64). Prior to 1975, the data were obtained from both the partial census and the large-firm sample survey. The grossing variable was sales, with universe sales taken as total contract construction reported in the capital expenditure survey of all industries.

S72-93. New construction in manufacturing by major groups, 1926 to 1976

SOURCE: for 1926 to 1955, previous edition of *Historical Statistics of Canada*; for 1956 to 1976, CANSIM Matrix No. 001198; for 1946 to 1976, the estimates are taken from the capital expenditure survey. The estimate has two components, as indicated in the general note to this section. 'Net additions' is partly expenditure creating new establishments. New enterprises are identified by regularly searching trade papers and through personal contacts in industry and government. Net additions also includes expenditure by ongoing establishments when that expenditure is judged to be irregular.

For the second component, the expenditure of ongoing establishments, the expenditure of the sample is blown up by the ratio of universe to sample shipments. Where expenditure by a sample establishment is regarded as irregular it is removed and placed instead in the 'net additions' component. For the 'final' expenditure estimate for year t, the blow-up or 'grossing' ratio uses shipments for year (t-2). Normally (for 1973) sample establishments include all those with $500,000 or more of shipments; where industries or provinces have relatively few establishments of this size, the cut-off is lowered to $200,000.

As can be seen, failure to discover all new projects which should be included in net additions is an important source of possible error. Problems in editing may also create errors. The activity of an establishment may change, indicating its industry classification should change. Ancillary activities of some organizations may be inadequately covered.

Respondents may find it difficult to separate machinery from construction and new from repair.

For the period 1926 to 1945, the estimates are based on the tax records of 358 corporations engaged in manufacturing throughout the entire 20-year period. The sales of these corporations amounted in 1946 to 38 per cent of the manufacturing industry total. The sample was stratified by industrial classification and size group. Sample investment in each year was blown up by the 1945 or 1946 ratio of universe to sample sales within each stratum (Buckley, 1957, p. 111).

It is not clear how much the estimates are distorted by the choice of sample or the use of a constant blow-up factor. The selection criterion for the sample ensures that it excludes both companies which did not weather the depression of the thirties, and companies which were started to take advantage of opportunities in the late thirties and during World War II. A comparison of contracts awarded data for business and industrial building (series R170, R171, previous edition of *Historical Statistics of Canada*) with total non-residential building (series S14-S9) suggests that the estimation procedure has resulted in a level of the non-residential building estimates which is possibly too low for this whole period; and estimates for 1929 to 1939 may be too high relative to 1926 and 1946.

S94. New construction in manufacturing, 1871 to 1925

S95-106. New construction in manufacturing, by major groups, 1918 to 1925

SOURCE: *Fixed Capital Flows and Stocks in Manufacturing, 1926-1960.*

These series were estimated by Professor T.K. Rymes not for use as a stand-alone series, but for use as components in the estimation of capital stocks and flows for later years. As a consequence he regards them as more appropriate as indicators of trends than as indicators of turning points.

The basic source data used for these series are the data on the value of capital invested, given in the first five decennial censuses of Canada, the two postal censuses of manufactures (reporting data for 1905 and 1906) and the DBS *Annual Census of Industry,* 1917 to 1943. Rymes' estimation assumes that the 'value of capital invested' is in fact the book value of fixed assets, i.e. the original cost minus accumulated depreciation. For an instructive and detailed account of problems encountered in the estimation, and their solutions, see *Fixed Capital Flows and Stocks,* pp. 64-71.

The construction expenditure series estimated by Rymes was used to extrapolate back the existing PPI series (S72). Thus series S94 reflects any defects in the level of that series. Rymes' raw gross fixed capital formation was estimated to 1943 and it is interesting to note that the differences between that series and the PPI series in the case of the example displayed (food and beverages) are akin to the differences between the contracts awarded series and the PPI series for total manufacturing. It is quite possible that Rymes' series is much more accurate than the official PPI series for the period 1926 to 1943. This would not be surprising in view of the fact that Rymes used universe data while the PPI estimates used data from an unrepresentative sample. Unfortunately, *Fixed Capital Flows and Stocks* does not display any of the original gross fixed capital formation series except that for food and beverages.

Prior to 1918, decennial rather than annual data for the book value of capital invested are available. Annual estimates for machinery and equipment by major groups were obtained by using an interpolator based on the estimated annual aggregate flow (domestic appearance) of industrial and electrical machinery and equipment. The same interpolator was used for all major groups. This series was then used to produce a construction series by using ratios of construction to machinery and equipment expenditure for 1926 to 1930. The resulting series were checked against buildings and fixtures data in the 1890 and 1900 censuses (the earliest censuses giving these components of capital invested separately). In some instances, as a result of this check, the series was adjusted. Further details of the estimation are given in *Fixed Capital Flows and Stocks,* 1926-60, esp. pp. 70, 71, 75).

S107-121. New construction in transportation, communication, electric power, gas and water utilities, 1956 to 1976

SOURCE: for 1926 to 1955, previous edition of *Historical Statistics of Canada;* for 1956 to 1976, CANSIM Matrix No. 001202.

Details of the estimation of these series for the period 1926 to 1941 are given in PICF and in PPI, with a summary in the previous edition of *Historical Statistics of Canada.* Estimation procedures in recent years are generally similar to those used earlier. One difference is the usual current practice-as for manufacturing-of dividing the estimate into two components: 'net additions' and expenditure by ongoing establishments. It is convenient to give details of current estimation procedures by separate categories. It is worth noting that each transportation category includes relevant services to transport but coverage of these services is spotty.

For air transport, the expenditure of dominant airlines is included in net additions. The sample of ongoing establishments includes all those with revenue of $100,000 or more, with revenue the grossing variable. Coverage is good.

A sample is not used for rail transport because of the ease of covering the universe, which consists mainly of the Canadian National Railways and the Canadian Pacific Railways. The series includes actual annual outlays of the CNR for the whole period, but for 1941 and earlier CPR actual outlays are used only for 1926, 1929, 1930, 1933, 1937, 1941, with other years interpolated using related series.

The water transport sample currently (1973) includes all firms with revenues of $100,000 or more. Revenue is the grossing variable. Services to water transport does not use the two-component estimation procedure; instead all expenditures are classed as net additions. Two major service organizations are the St. Lawrence Seaway and the National Harbours Board.

The motor transport sector sample currently includes all establishments with over $100,000 revenue in smaller provinces, and $400,000 of revenue in larger provinces, with revenue the grossing variable. Included in this sector are interurban trucking and bussing. Where a trucking and warehousing operation has less than half its revenue attributable to warehousing, the whole operation is classified as motor transport. Surveying this sector is difficult because of instability of ownership (especially in trucking) and because of the methods used to finance fixed assets, as well as because of other practices.

The urban transport sector follows the same estimation procedure as the transport sector. Included are the two subway systems. Not included is taxicab service.

For the pipeline sector, data are obtained from all units in the universe. This is possible because of the financial census carried out by the National Energy Board and by the Energy Statistics section of MAPID. There is some problem in converting reported figures to the required conceptual basis because of industry accounting practice. Included under pipelines are transmission and gathering lines; excluded are field lines which are included elsewhere (under petroleum and gas, series S70).

The telephone sample currently includes all firms with $100,000 or more revenue, except that some large corporations are included in net additions. Because of the dominance of the industry by large enterprises, the sample expenditure plus net additions accounts for almost all the total. A problem in this sector is the frequent use of used materials.

All telegraph expenditure is included in net additions. Included in this sector are railway telegraphs, microwave systems, cable companies and Canadian Overseas Telecommunications Corporation.

All terminal grain elevators are surveyed, but for country grain elevators only firms operating 10 or more are surveyed. The grossing variable for the latter group is number of elevators.

The electric power sector includes both establishments generating power for sale to the public and the small number of establishments whose major activity is distributing power. The large provincial utilities are included in net additions, while other enterprises with $100,000 or more of revenue make up the sample. Revenue is the grossing variable. The amount added by grossing is only about 3 per cent of the total. A special questionnaire has been used for this sector in the 1970s because of various reporting problems for this industry. One relates to own account construction. Another problem is the distinction between construction and machinery. The wording of the question on hydraulic production plant expenditure conveys the nature of the problem. Under this heading, the description of the construction element is 'water conveying, control and other hydraulic structures'; the description of the machinery element is 'turbines and generators and other installations consisting predominantly of recognizable machine components'. For nuclear plants the machinery item is just 'other installations consisting predominantly of recognizable machinery components'.

In the gas distribution sector all firms are surveyed, with estimation required only to account for the few non-respondents.

Starting in 1969 water systems was divided into two parts. The first, represented by private or provincially owned operations, was grouped as a separate category and placed in 'other utilities'. The second category, represented by municipal systems, was added to municipal government expenditure.

For broadcasting, the CBC is included in net additions and all units in the television and cable sector are surveyed. The radio sample currently includes all stations with revenue of $100,000 or more and the grossing variable is revenue.

Other utilities currently include warehousing, some water systems (see above), toll highways and bridges and taxicab service. For 1955 and earlier, also included are air, motor and water transport and services pipelines, grain elevators and broadcasting.

S122. Net capital formation in railway transport and telegraphs, 1850 to 1930

SOURCE: previous edition of *Historical Statistics of Canada*.

As indicated by the title, this series is conceptually different from preceding series because it excludes that new construction and equipment expenditure which the railway companies regarded as replacement. This series was estimated by Kenneth Buckley using annual reports of both private and government-owned railways. He used information on a sample of roads to estimate both new construction and improvements. Details of his estimation are given in the previous edition of *Historical Statistics of Canada* and in the original source.

S123-127. New construction and repair, non-railway transport structures, 1901 to 1930

SOURCE: previous edition of *Historical Statistics of Canada*.

These series include only government expenditures. Currently these types of expenditures are classified as government department expenditures. These series were estimated by Kenneth Buckley using the federal Auditor General's Reports and the Public Accounts of the provinces. Details are available in his *Capital Formation in Canada, 1896-1930*.

S128-140. New construction in trade, finance and commercial services, 1946 to 1976

The trade series are of lower quality than most others. Trade, especially retail trade, is characterized by many small units and large numbers of firms entering and leaving the industry each year. In addition, much of the construction for retail trade is classified under 'other financial' because real estate developers are the enterprises owning and building shopping plazas and office developments. Stores built under leaseback arrangements, especially common among some food chains, are included here rather than in the owner's industry group. This is one of the rare instances where expenditure is assigned to the user where the user is not the owner.

In all but the independent group, all existing establishments above about $1,000,000 in sales are included in the sample, with grossing by sales. New stores are included in net additions. Until 1976, the independent group was estimated using a benchmark obtained in the 1950s and the department and chain series as projector. Starting in 1976 the independents were sampled. The sample was 1,300 in 1976. Automotive trade includes service stations, garages and car dealers.

In the banking sector, all units in the universe are surveyed. The universe includes the Bank of Canada, but not the caisses populaires (which are not covered anywhere). Credit unions are included although the sample was not updated until 1978; most credit union expenditure, however, is in the net additions category. Currently (1973) insurance companies with fixed assets over $200,000 are sampled, with fixed assets the grossing variable. The sample is chosen from information in the *Annual Report of the Superintendent of Insurance*. Trust and loan companies are covered in the same fashion, with the sample chosen using data from the Financial Corporations Section of the Business Finance Division of Statistics Canada.

The 'other financial' sector includes land developers, building lessors, real estate firms and insurance agents. From some points of view the 'other financial' series represents a serious conceptual problem. It includes commercial and, in a few cases, industrial buildings built for rent, or speculatively built for sale by developers and others. Users of these buildings may be in many different industries. As can be seen this series has become of increasingly great importance in recent years, representing 20 per cent or more of non-residential building (and a much higher proportion of private sector non-residential building), as compared with less than 5 per cent in 1956. The shopping centres, multi-purpose projects such as the Manulife Centre and Toronto Dominion Centre in Toronto, and other construction included in this series represent a very substantial part of all new construction intended for use by commercial and financial industries. Some of the new head office space rented by various industries is therefore included in this series. It is noteworthy that the conceptual basis of much of these items is inconsistent with that of housing. In this latter case, construction is classified as housing whether it is owned by occupiers or by real estate developers or other landlords.

Estimation of the 'other financial' series is difficult. It is not possible to identify all units in this universe and the series is thus of somewhat questionable quality. The series is derived by first attempting to discover as many medium- and large-sized projects and operations as possible; the reported data are then adjusted using building permit and contract award data for the current and preceding years.

Commercial services includes laundries and dry cleaners, theatres, hotels, restaurants, racetracks, ski developments, lessors of machinery and equipment, and any other organization providing services to persons or business, where that organization is not elsewhere classified. Hotels, the largest single component, is estimated partly by using a sample consisting currently of all those with rental revenue over $200,000, with rental revenue used as the grossing variable. The larger part of the hotel total, however, is net additions, i.e. construction of new hotels and motels. It is likely that many new motels are missed because their small size and remote location make them unlikely to be reported in trade journals or picked up by the Building Permits Section. Part of the expenditure in covered projects may be missed because the leaseholder may make the expenditure, not the owner. A laundries and dry cleaners series and a theatres series are also available separately; the amounts are very small. For other commercial, the universe is not easily identified. All expenditure is placed in the net additions category and information is gathered by a continuing search of trade publications and by other intelligence operations. Estimates for the non-covered portions are added, using information on motor vehicles, scientific and professional equipment and on building permits. The resulting series by its nature is downward biased and of lower quality than most other series.

S141-147. New construction in institutions and government departments, 1926 to 1976

SOURCE: for 1926 to 1960, previous edition of *Historical Statistics of Canada;* for 1961 to 1976, CANSIM Matrix Nos. 001218, 001222.

Churches include all dioceses of the Anglican and Roman Catholic churches, and some parishes of the United Church. The grossing variable for the United Church sample is its membership, as indicated in its annual reports. New construction by other denominations is placed in net additions. The coverage for the various denominations could be low, to the extent that new construction is not covered by building permits. For 1934 to 1946, the 1947 estimate was projected back according to an index based on church construction as reported in the construction censuses; for 1926 to 1933 the projector was based on reported church contracts awarded.

For universities, all degree-granting institutions are surveyed, with enrolment the grossing variable (necessary only for non-response). Some new construction may be missed because university accounting systems classify it as current, rather than capital, as a consequence of government funding procedures. Before 1947, the estimate was projected back using an index based on the net change in the value of university plant and equipment and an estimated annual depreciation rate.

Local schools, provincial schools and private schools are each dealt with separately. Estimates for local schools are from the survey of school boards by the Public Finance Division, Statistics Canada. A problem is the possibility that some new construction is missed because school accounting classifies it as repair. Estimates for provincial schools (including community colleges and other non-degree-granting provincially supported post-secondary institutions) are from the survey of provincial departments by the Census of Construction Section. Accounting is also a problem here. For private schools, a universe became available recently for direct surveys with enrolment as a basis for imputations for non-response and non-coverage. For 1926 to 1946, the 1947 estimate was projected back using public finance data of varying coverage.

Estimates for provincial hospitals are from the survey of provincial departments by the Census of Construction Section. Estimation for municipal and private hospitals (including religious hospitals) uses a sample of all hospitals above a certain number of beds (the cut off varying by province), with this also the grossing variable. Accounting is a problem. For 1926 to 1946, the 1947 estimate was projected back using data on outlays on new construction of municipal hospitals in 1933, 1937, 1941, 1943, and data on total municipal new construction in these and the remaining years of the period.

Other institutions are surveyed directly with grossing by beds, where applicable. This group does not include government-owned institutions. It does include profit-making and non-profit homes for the aged, homes for the blind and deaf, orphanages, day nurseries and non-profit recreational organizations such as YM-YWCA's.

Government departments include departmental Crown corporations (for example, the Agricultural Stabilization Board) and part or all of a few agency Crown corporations. (The remaining agency Crown corporations, and all proprietary Crown corporations, are classified with the relevant industry group.) The Post Office is included here. Federal government new construction currently consists largely of passenger terminals, landing fields, docks, highways and other transportation-related construction and office and educational buildings. Estimates of expenditure are obtained from the Census of Construction. Before 1949, estimates for selected years (1926, 1929, 1930, 1933, 1937 and 1941 to 1948) were obtained by classifying individual items of expenditure as given in various government accounts into new and repair categories. The remaining years plus 1933 were interpolated using a variety of data; the likely error is indicated to be less than 10 per cent. Buckley's correction (previous edition of *Historical Statistics of Canada,* p. 495) for 1946 to 1949 is retained.

Provincial government new construction currently consists largely of highway, street and associated construction, with these items overshadowing the next largest items, sewage systems, disposal plants, water mains and office and other institutional buildings. Estimates are obtained from the survey by the Census of Construction. Before 1947, estimates were obtained in a similar fashion to the federal early estimates. The likely error for interpolated years in this early period is indicated to be less than 4 per cent.

Municipal government new construction currently consists mostly of waterworks and sewage systems, and road and other transportation construction. Estimates are from the Public Finance Division which surveys all provinces except Quebec. In some cases the data are actually collected by the department of municipal affairs. Quebec data are from a survey carried out by that province. Before 1947, estimates were obtained in a fashion similar to the early federal estimates. Data from 16 municipalities were important in the construction of the interpolation index used for various years prior to 1940. For later interpolations data on municipal expenditure from the Bank of Canada were used.

S148-160. New construction by governments and government enterprises, by level of government and by category, 1946 to 1976

SOURCE: for 1946 to 1955, PPI, 1946-57 and previous edition of *Historical Statistics of Canada,* (series R16); for 1956 to 1976, CANSIM Matrix No. 001230.

The estimation procedures for government departments and for institutions are described in the previous section.

The only government institutions included in the 'institutions' category are provincial hospitals, schools and universities and municipal hospitals and schools. All other government-owned institutions, for example homes for the aged and federal hospitals, are included under government departments.

Government business enterprises are generally government enterprises whose principal source of revenue is derived from the provision of goods and services to the public. They include all proprietary Crown corporations as well as an occasional agency Crown corporation in whole or part, and some other corporations. Departmental Crown corporations are classified with government departments. Part of the agency Crown corporation Atomic Energy of Canada Limited is included here. Examples of federal Crown corporations included are Air Canada, the Bank of Canada, the Canadian Broadcasting Corporation, Eldorado Nuclear Ltd., Canadian Wheat Board. Among the provincial corporations included are the liquor commissions and electric power companies. Among the municipal corporations included are electric power distributing companies, transit authorities, parking authorities. A complete list of federal and provincial corporations and a partial list of municipal corporations included are available from the Construction Division; also the *Canada Year Book* lists all federal corporations, by type (departmental, agency, Crown, other).

Under federal housing is included housing expenditure by federal government departments (expenditure for non-rental government-owned housing built for federal employees) and expenditure by federal government enterprises. The latter is generally rental housing and its inclusion is regarded by the Construction Division as a mistake so that this series may be revised to eliminate it. For 1960, federal government department expenditure is: Department of National Defence, $7.7 million; other, $5.4 million. For 1960, government enterprise expenditure is: federal-provincial agreements, $14.3 million; other, $0.8 million. All other housing, including housing expenditure by provincial authorities such as the Ontario Housing Corporation, is excluded from aggregate new construction built by governments and government departments. It can thus be seen that the treatment here of housing is different from the treatment of non-residential construction.

S161-166. New construction, federal government 1868 to 1930, provincial governments 1901 to 1930

SOURCE: previous edition of *Historical Statistics of Canada*, series R120-125.

These series were estimated by Kenneth Buckley using the federal Auditor General's reports and the public accounts of the provinces. The railway series includes rolling stock purchased for federally owned railways. The provincial series in the 1920s is predominantly highway expenditure. Details of the estimation are given in Buckley's *Capital Formation in Canada, 1896-1930*.

Residential Construction (Series S167-219)

S167. Value of residential construction, constant (1971) dollars, 1926 to 1976

The price index used to deflate residential construction 1926 to 1950 is a weighted average of indexes of construction material prices and wage rates. The price index used

for 1951 to 1970 is substantially changed from the one used before the revision of the National Accounts published in 1975. Like the previous index, it is an input index. Starting with 1957, however, instead of union wage rates it uses average hourly earnings and in addition to the indexes of the 'price' of labour and the price of materials, it incorporates an index of the 'price' of gross profit. The latter is the ratio of gross profit to the total value of new residential construction. For 1951 to 1956, because of data unavailability, the index uses union wage rates and excludes the gross profit component.

The most important aspect of the index used for 1951 to 1970 is the productivity adjustment it incorporates. This productivity adjustment is based on the assumption that real residential construction is proxied by the volume of materials used. Specifically, the labour weight is deflated by the ratio of an index of the real value of materials to an index of labour input. Because of erratic year-to-year movements in this ratio, for each of the 1951 to 1960 and 1961 to 1970 periods a ratio assuming a constant annual increase is used. This constant annual increase is 2.9 per cent for 1961 to 1970. It will be seen that the effect of this is to reduce the size of the labour weight by 1/1.029 each year, and the sum of the weights becomes increasingly below one.

This productivity improvement adjustment implies that when productivity improves, the same materials but less labour are used. The productivity adjustment thus overstates actual productivity if the real value of materials increases as a ratio of (on-site) labour merely because of the use of off-site labour to produce prefabricated components. The productivity adjustment is also upward biased if the residential construction mix shifts toward types of structures which are less labour intensive. In fact, in 1974 the price index used here for 1951 to 1970 broke down. That is, the increase it showed was absurdly small. As a consequence the GNP Division shifted to a different and clearly better index, which is used for 1971 to date. This index is the outcome of the assumption that the real value per dwelling unit for each of four types of structure (single detached, duplex and double, row, apartment) is constant. The evidence shows that this is a somewhat faulty assumption; for instance it is likely that the real value of the average single detached dwelling fell in 1974. The GNP Division is now in the process of producing an index which allows for varying real value per dwelling unit.

S168-180. New residential construction, by component, 1926 to 1976

SOURCE: files of the Gross National Product Division

Residential construction is not easy to estimate and is subject to substantial error because of the large number of builders at scattered locations and because of the vast number of owners. In fact neither sellers nor purchasers of residential construction are the prime source of information for estimation. Rather, the fundamental source is municipal building permits. Since the late forties this has been importantly supplemented by National Housing Act data. Central Mortgage and Housing Corporation field offices have recorded the progress of construction of non-NHA as well as NHA houses for many years. An additional important source, especially for 1951 and earlier, is the census.

The estimates given here represent very substantial revisions from the estimates given in the previous edition of *Historical Statistics of Canada*. The revisions for 1926 to

1968 are part of the major revision of the National Accounts, published in 1975. These estimates are unlikely to be revised again soon. By the time this is published, however, the estimates for 1970 to 1976 will almost certainly have been further revised, especially the alterations and additions series. It is unlikely, however, that the estimators will have changed in any fundamental way from those used for 1970 to 1976. In the following it will be noted that the estimation is quite distinctly different for each of the periods 1926 to 1940, 1941 to 1950, 1951 to 1968 and 1969 to 1976. The estimates for the last two periods are discussed first and then the estimates for 1926 to 1950.

The discussion below draws heavily on information from the unpublished notes of Mr. J.P. Delisle of the Construction Division, including his *Appendix D: Gross Capital Formation in Residential Construction, Quarterly Methodology* (written about 1972); of Mr. D.H. Jones of the Input-Output Division (dated 25 January 1972, 23 March 1972, 12 January 1973 and 14 March 1977 respectively); and information from Mr. Hans Messinger and Miss Ellen Buckley of Gross National Product Division. The responsibility for opinions and errors remains with the author of this section.

For 1951 and later the major components of residential construction, work put in place in new buildings, by type (series S168, S169, S170 and S171) are estimated using three elements: data on dwelling unit starts, completions and units under construction; an estimator converting these data into dwelling units put in place; and unit values converting dwelling units put in place into values put in place. The starts survey is the source of the dwelling unit data and is discussed in the note to series S181-194.

For 1951 to 1968, units put in place are estimated for year t by province, by type, as

$$C(t) - k_1\, U(t-1,t) + k_2\, U(t)$$

where $C(t)$ is the number of dwellings started and completed during year t, $U(t-1,t)$ is the number under construction at the end of $(t-1)$ and completed during t, and $U(t)$ is the number under construction at the end of t. On the basis of work put in place in NHA houses, 1964-70, and the distribution of construction times of all houses, 1951-64, k_1 and k_2 are both taken as about .5. The parameters of this estimator are the same for all types of dwelling, despite the fact that large apartment buildings take much longer to complete than single detached dwellings. The understatement of the lag from start to expenditure because of this is probably not great, especially before the mid-sixties, because during this period few apartment buildings were large and apartments did not make up a large proportion of total starts.

It is worth noting that this work-put-in-place estimator is the equivalent of one-half starts plus one-half completions. The formula previously used was one-third starts plus two-thirds completions.

For 1969 to 1976, the estimator explicitly incorporates estimates of the lagged effect of starts on the value of work put in place. More precisely, the estimator for month t is

$$\sum_{i=t}^{t-20} av_i \sum_{j=i}^{i+20} w_{ijt}\, s_{ij}$$

where av_i is the estimated unit value of dwellings started in month i, s_{ij} is the number of dwellings started in i and completed in j (except that $s_{i,i+20}$ includes all dwellings completed in month $i+20$ or later) and w_{ijt} is for a sample of NHA dwellings a three-year average proportion of work in dwellings started in month i and completed in month j which is put in place in month t. The annual estimate cumulates the monthly totals.

For 1951 to 1968 the estimated unit value for each type of dwelling and province is the average construction cost of relevant NHA dwellings as of the date of loan approval. (Prior to the 1975 revision, the 1951 to 1959 unit values, disaggregated by type but not by province, were estimated using the relevant NHA construction costs and for 1960 and later years the 1959 values were extrapolated on the basis of the residential construction input price index.) Unfortunately, data from contract awards, building permits and conventional loan approvals show that NHA singles, doubles and duplexes were much higher in value than all houses before about 1954 (perhaps more than 25 per cent higher in 1959), of roughly the same value 1955-58, and of substantially lower value after this date, with the differential narrowing markedly after 1963. Thus the NHA series very much understates the rise in the unit value of houses 1951-63, with the distortion of change especially severe 1958-61. The same kind of evidence suggests, however, that NHA unit costs are not so seriously flawed as estimators of universe values in the case of apartment and row dwellings. NHA costs are apparently substantially greater than universe costs over the period 1951 to 1968 but the differential is generally not far from 10 per cent. The evidence for these statements is given in Steele, M., *The Current Dollar Average Unit Cost of New Dwelling Units by Type, 1947-1966* (Ottawa; processed, Statistics Canada, 1968).

For 1969 to 1976, the estimated unit value for each type of dwelling is the building permit value, adjusted for undervaluation. No adjustment is made to link these estimates to the ones for 1951 to 1968 because the unlinked estimates yield little break between 1968 and 1969 in the aggregate, residential construction. This arises because while for singles the permit-based value is substantially above the NHA-based value, offsetting this is the fact that for apartments it is substantially below. The undervaluation adjustment to permit values is estimated by comparing the permit value with the estimated construction cost for a sample of NHA dwellings. For recent years the upward adjustment is 15 per cent for singles and 25 per cent for multiples.

Conceptually, part of the work put in place on new dwellings but given as a separate series, S174, is supplementary costs. This includes legal fees, architects' fees, surveyors' fees and interest charges during construction, NHA mortgage insurance fees. The mortgage insurance fees of private insurers such as the Mortgage Insurance Corporation of Canada are not included. The supplementary costs estimator is the ratio of supplementary costs to construction costs of NHA dwellings times the construction costs of dwellings completed.

The estimator for conversions is the number of conversions reported in the building permit survey, adjusted for missing municipalities, times the value per conversion, adjusted for understatement. The missing municipalities factor (about 1.11 in 1971) is the ratio of total population to the population in reporting municipalities. The value adjustment factor (about 1.22 in 1971) is the ratio of the average value per start to the average permit value. The resulting estimates probably represent only a small proportion of the actual value of conversions, because they do not account for conversions done illegally and because the value of work is probably much more understated for conversions than for new buildings. Among the evidence on the first point are the results of the Census of the Prairie Census, 1946 as given in Statistics Canada, *Supplementary Report on Housing Characteristics in Urban Centres of 5,000 and over* (mimeographed, probably written in the late forties by Mabel Waddell). Far more conversions were reported than had been indicated by building permits. See also the discussion by Kenneth Buckley in the previous edition of *Historical Statistics of Canada*, p. 500.

The estimator for alterations and additions, 1951 to 1970, is the ratio of the value of alterations, improvements and repair reported in the permit survey to the value of new dwellings from that survey, times the value of starts. This estimator thus does not account for improvements effected without a permit. In about 1973 the accounts for 1946 and later were revised to partially remove this deficiency. 'Hardware', an item included in personal expenditure on consumer goods and services, was redefined to include building materials, supplies and miscellaneous hardware not accounted for in the rent and capital formation components of GNE. The adjustment was made to hardware, rather than to residential construction, for two reasons. First, it was a less disruptive change. Secondly, the amounts included repair as well as improvements. If the adjustment had not been made to hardware, the amount accounted for by repairs would have had to have been split off and added to the existing residential repair estimate. This would not have affected GNE, because repairs are only implicitly included (in gross rents). It would have affected the GNP side of the accounts, however, via a reduction in net paid and, especially, imputed rent. Yet imputed rent was regarded as too low already.

The hardware adjustment is estimated as follows. First benchmarks for 1961 and 1969 are estimated as: repairs and improvements by homeowners and tenants, as conservatively estimated using Family Expenditure survey data ($1.3 billion in 1969), minus residential repair and improvement already included in the accounts ($1.1 billion in 1969), itself reduced by an amount attributable to landlord repairs (conservatively estimated as $.3 billion in 1969). The resulting benchmark ($.5 billion in 1969) is regarded as an understatement both because of the conservative nature of the component estimates and because improvements made by landlords are omitted. Coincidentally, the benchmark in 1961 is almost identical to retail sales of hardware and building materials given by the 1961 Census of Merchandising. The benchmarks are interpolated and projected to other years on the basis of indexes of sales of retail hardware stores and retail building material outlets.

In 1976 the upward adjustment for improvements included in hardware was judged much too low and alterations and additions for 1971 to 1976 were revised as: (a) permit-based alterations and additions (see the description above for 1951 to 1970) plus (b) the sales of wholesale building material outlets to householders, adjusted by deducting from (b) (i) 10 per cent of (a), (ii) do-it-yourself repairs as estimated for the purpose of computing net rents, (iii) tool sales, (iv) materials for hobby use, (v) materials for owner-builders of new dwellings. The new total for alterations and additions plus hardware (adjusted to remove tools) equals about 140 per cent of improvements estimated using FAMEX data, unadjusted for understatement by respondents. S.A. Goldberg in 'Non-sampling Error in Household Surveys', *International Statistical Institute Bulletin*, vol. 36, part 2 cites evidence suggesting that, for repair, respondents reported $65 per family in an annual survey

while the cumulated annual total from monthly surveys was $171. This writer, assuming no under-reporting by FAMEX respondents and assuming landlords spend only 10 per cent per dwelling unit of the amount owner-occupiers spend, estimated improvements at $1.4 billion for 1974, 21 per cent of which was cottage improvements. See *A Report on Estimation of Residential Construction* (processed, Statistics Canada, Gross National Product Division, 1976, p. 38).

Mobiles, even those on footings, in practise apparently are not regarded as dwelling starts in the starts survey although the printed instructions for starts survey reporters exclude a mobile only when it is 'towable on its own chassis'. The estimator is domestic shipments (number) times the average value of mobiles reported in building permits, plus the value of imported mobiles. About 15 per cent of mobiles are reported in building permits. There is no deduction for mobile homes used as offices, on the grounds that this use is unlikely to be important in view of the fact that a criterion for inclusion in the shipments series is the existence of a kitchen.

Cottages are seasonal dwellings. They are estimated as the value in building permits times the undervaluation adjustment used for singles. To help ensure that dwellings labelled 'cottages' in permit reports are seasonal dwellings, all high-valued 'cottages' are excluded.

Prior to the revision of the National Accounts published in 1975 residential construction did not include real estate commissions on existing property. It is not clear what the basis of the estimates for early years is. For the later sixties the estimates assume that real estate commissions on (existing) residential property is a constant proportion of new construction. For 1971 and later the estimate is projected by using real estate commissions paid under the Multiple Listing Service system. Probably MLS sales are a higher proportion of sales in slow markets than in hot markets, so that the error in this series is variable.

Series S180, defence housing, is expenditure on non-rental housing such as military barracks built by the Department of National Defence for its employees. This housing is not conceptually part of capital formation and so it is deducted from the total of series S172 to S178 to arrive at series S180, residential construction, National Accounts basis.

The estimates for real estate commissions and defence are described above in the note for 1951 to 1968. The remaining series were estimated by the author of this section. The description below is relatively terse; for a detailed rationale and for component series, see the sources listed for series S198-202.

For 1926 to 1950, work put in place in new buildings is estimated as a linear function of the current and lagged value of starts. The value of starts for each type of dwelling is estimated as the value per unit times the number of starts, plus supplementary costs. The estimation of the number of starts is described in the note to series S198-202.

For 1926 to 1942, the value per unit for urban dwelling units in one-to-three-unit buildings is the average value of units in the McLean (later Southam) contract award series labelled 'residences' times 1.05. The 1.05 factor is the ratio for 1959-62 of the adjusted average permit value of singles, doubles plus duplexes to the average value of 'residences'. The adjustment to permit values assumes they understate actual values by 10 per cent; this compares with the estimate given above of understatement in the 1970s of 15 per cent. The average value of residences is calculated after making an adjustment for 1921 to 1928 to the number of residences reported for Quebec, because of evidence that in those years the Quebec count referred to buildings not dwelling units.

This estimation yields a current dollar value of $4,205 in 1926, rising to $4,724 in 1928, a peak not attained again until the late 1940s. In constant dollars, the unit value is 38 per cent less in 1938 than it is at the 1928 peak. The pattern shown by this series is roughly corroborated by data from the 1941 Census on value of dwelling by length of occupancy (see Steele, 1972, table 7.2). It is strongly at variance with the assumption of O.J. Firestone, *Residential Real Estate in Canada*, (Toronto: University of Toronto Press, 1951, p. 422), that constant dollar unit values of non-farm singles did not vary over this period. This assumption-made also for apartments and farm singles-underlies the residential construction series appearing in the previous edition of *Historical Statistics of Canada*.

For 1943 to 1950, in order to link these estimates to the 1951 to 1968 estimates, the value per unit for one-and-two-unit buildings is 1.27 times the value given by the estimator just described. As is pointed out in the note to the 1951 to 1968 estimates, the 1951 value on which this link is based is quite clearly much too high, so that the linking process yields a too-high level for the whole period 1943 to 1950 and later. The initial year of the linking series, 1943, was chosen because of the very low level of residential construction in that year.

For the whole period 1926 to 1950 the value per unit for rural dwelling units in one-to-three-unit (for 1943 to 1950, one-and-two-unit) buildings is taken as .531, the comparable urban value. This ratio is based on evidence from the 1941 and 1931 censuses.

For 1926 to 1942, the value per unit of 'other' dwellings is the average permit value of Montreal apartments times .91, the ratio of Canada to Montreal apartment values in 1946. The 1946 Canada value is .865, the average value of NHA apartments. This estimator is not as unsatisfactory as it might appear at first sight: in this period a substantial proportion of all new apartments in Canada were built in Toronto and Montreal-in many years over one-third - and the pattern of Toronto unit value for years it is available is consistent with the Montreal pattern (see Steele, 1972, tables 7.5, 7.6). In addition, because apartment starts are derived using this unit value (see note to series S201), problems in this estimator affect the starts series, but not the value of work put in place.

This estimation yields a pattern quite like the pattern for the values of one-to-three-unit buildings. The peak value is in 1929, at $4,164; and while the constant dollar value is 32 per cent less in 1938 than in 1929, it is substantially below the 1938 value both in 1933-34 and in the early war years.

For 1943 to 1950, in order to link these estimates to the 1951 to 1968 estimates (see the discussion for units in smaller buildings), the value per unit is 1.16 times the estimator just described.

To the above-described structure value per unit is added an estimate of supplementary costs (the costs of land improvements, and of architectural, legal and financial services). This is taken as 3.11 per cent of structure value for small buildings and 2.81 per cent for other dwellings. These ratios are from data on NHA loans approved in 1948 (O.J. Firestone, 1951, table XXII, p. 419).

The value of starts is converted into work put in place by assuming that 15 per cent of work started in any year is put in place in the following year; except that the carryover from both 1943 and 1944 is assumed at 20 per cent, from 1945 and 1946, 25 per cent, and 1947, 1948, 1949, 20 per cent. The higher ratios for 1943 to 1949 are used because of

the long completion times (Central Mortgage and Housing Corporation, *Housing in Canada*, January, 1949) observed during this period of material and labour shortages.

The estimator for alterations and additions is the value of starts times the estimated ratio of alterations and additions to starts. For 1940, 1944 to 1950 the ratio is just the ratio of alterations, additions and repairs to new, from residential permit reports of 204 municipalities. Because the presumed effect of war restrictions on new building was greater in these municipalities than elsewhere, the 1941 to 1943 ratio is estimated from Census of Construction data, except that the census of construction-based ratio is reduced by 25 per cent in order to link it with the permit-based ratio. The census of construction-based ratio is also used for 1934 to 1939, because permit alterations and additions are not available for those years. For 1926 to 1933, the ratio is estimated using parameters obtained by regressing the census of construction-based ratio on the value of starts (see Steele, 1972, p. 170 for details).

As can be seen, the estimator for additions and alterations 1926 to 1950 is essentially the same as the estimator used for 1951 to 1970. And as noted above the latter is clearly seriously downward biased. It may therefore be concluded that the estimator for 1926 to 1950 is also downward biased. It is worth noting, however, that the ratio of alterations and additions to work in new buildings 1926 to 1929 is over 12 per cent while the analogous ratio (alterations, additions and conversions to work in new buildings plus supplementary cost) in the late 1960s is only about 8 per cent. In view of the much greater average age of the stock in the late 1960s than in the earlier period, this suggests that alterations are much less understated in the earlier period than later.

S181-189. Dwelling starts by region, 1948 to 1976

S190-194. Dwelling starts by type, 1949 to 1976

SOURCE: Central Mortgage and Housing Corporation, *Canadian Housing Statistics*.

The precursor of the starts and completions survey was a survey of completions partially based on a sample designed by the young Nathan Keyfitz at Statistics Canada. This survey used reports from municipalities to estimate completions; it was carried out for 1945, 1946, 1947. In 1948 the starts survey was initiated. It was carried out by Statistics Canada with the help of CMHC, and was a complete survey of metropolitan and urban areas of 5,000 population and over. Outside these areas, about 400 sample areas were enumerated. Starting in 1963, the population cut-off for the complete survey was raised to 10,000 from 5,000. Some time before that date complete responsibility for the starts and completions survey was transferred to CMHC.

In late 1954 a redesigned sample was implemented; this indicated that the previous sample had deteriorated badly (CMHC, *Canadian Housing Statistics*, 1955, 4th Quarter, p. 5n) so that starts of singles in 1954 was understated by perhaps as much as 20 per cent. In view of this, a plausible adjustment to the published single starts series would add 14,000 units to the 1954 figure, 12,000 to 1953 and 7,000 to 1952. It seems reasonable to suppose that since 1954 there have not been substantial sampling problems. There has, however, certainly been at least one occasion when the starts have been substantially understated: in early 1959, 8,000 starts were missed. Because it is CMHC policy never to revise its published starts estimates, neither the estimates for 1949 to 1954 nor the estimate for 1959 were ever changed to correct the indicated errors. Series S181-194 are thus unrevised series.

In recent years, at least, and probably from the start of the survey, the major sources of information for starts survey enumerators have been CMHC inspection reports, in the case of NHA dwellings, and building permits, in the case of non-NHA dwellings. Because of the ease of discovering NHA starts as compared with the difficulties for non-NHA, especially in areas with lax or nonexistent permit systems, the starts survey is apt to be more accurate when NHA building is relatively important. Missed starts, when they do occur, are likely to be singles, doubles or duplexes in rural (sample) areas, because such areas are relatively time-consuming for CMHC field office staff to survey. More than likely missed starts are mistimed starts. Starts are attributed to

the month they are reported, not the month the start actually occurred. A problem for enumerators is the fact that occasionally the type of dwelling, or the number of dwellings in a building, changes after the building has been started.

The completions series analogous to series S190-193 are not used in the estimation of residential construction 1951 to 1960. Instead revised series are used. These revised series are estimated assuming that the completions undercount between the 1951 and 1956 censuses and between the 1956 and 1961 censuses is given in each case by the change in census dwellings (occupied plus vacant) plus estimated demolitions minus mobiles minus reported completions. The undercount is distributed within each five-year period assuming that the pattern of actual completions is the same as the pattern of reported completions. The revised series and the amounts of the revision are given below:

Completions estimates underlying residential construction estimates, 1951 to 1960

	Singles		Multiples	
Year	Revised completions	Revised minus reported completions[1]	Revised completions	Revised minus reported completions[1]
1951[2]	39,148	1,969	18,642	6,596
1952	58,939	2,972	26,509	9,389
1953	72,564	3,648	43,287	15,364
1954	75,563	3,803	46,810	16,605
1955	95,359	4,806	57,861	20,485
1956	99,471	3,815	54,909	14,865
1957	83,590	2,494	44,990	8,803
1958	99,816	2,986	61,968	12,112
1959	98,387	2,932	62,436	12,220
1960	80,514	2,401	56,742	11,098
1961[3]	24,727	743	17,460	3,415

[1] Reported completions are from CMHC, **Canadian Housing Statistics, 1968,** table 7.
[2] 1 June to 31 December 1951.
[3] 1 January to 1 June 1961.

It is apparent that the revised series presented here are probably greatly in error. The very small upward revision of singles is inconsistent with the evidence of understatement in the starts survey in the early 1950s. The very large upward revision of multiples is likely the outcome of the assumption that conversions net of mergers were zero. This assumption is prima facie implausible, especially for the early 1950s when there was still excess demand for housing. If indeed there were a substantial number of net conversions this would tend to increase the stock of multiple units and reduce the stock of single units, because conversion often is associated with the transformation of a single house into two or three apartments. It seems fair to conclude then that the large upward revision of multiples shown here is mainly the result of attributing to new building the increase in multiples brought about by conversion.

The net effect on the residential construction estimates of the error in these completions series and the error in the unit value series (see the note on series S168-180) is likely not very great. This is the fortunate outcome for the early 1950s of the fact that the overstatement of the volume of multiples (which are low in true unit value) and the understatement of the volume of singles (which are substantially higher in true unit value) tend to be offset by the overall overstatement of unit values.

S195-197.   Mobile home shipments, 1967 to 1976

SOURCE: Statistics Canada, *Truck Body and Trailer Manufacturers,* (Catalogue 42-217); Statistics Canada, *Merchandise Trade,* (Catalogue 65-203).

These series are included because the starts and completions surveys do not include mobile homes. An unknown number of mobile homes are in fact used as offices.

S198-202.   Dwelling starts by type, 1921 to 1950

SOURCE: Steele, M. L., *Dwelling Starts in Canada, 1921 to 1940,* (Toronto: unpublished Ph.D dissertation, University of Toronto); Steele, M. L., *Estimates of New Residential Construction, 1941-1950,* (Ottawa: processed, Statistics Canada, 1969).

These series are used to estimate residential construction, 1926 to 1950 (S179). They replace the completions series, R138, in the previous edition of *Historical Statistics of Canada* for 1921 to 1944. Series R138 was estimated by O. J. Firestone (1951). It should be noted that the completions underlying the residential construction estimates in the previous volume, for the years 1941 to 1950, are substantial upward revisions of this Firestone series (previous edition of *Historical Statistics of Canada,* p. 499).

O.J. Firestone completions 1921 to 1940 are estimated in two stages. First, completions for each decade 1921 to 1931 and 1931 to 1941 are estimated as equal to the increase in stock as given by census data plus demolitions and other dwelling losses minus dwellings added by conversion of existing buildings. Secondly, decade completions are allocated to years using a building materials index.

The use of a building materials index to yield the year-to-year pattern of new residential building is obviously objectionable. Because building materials are used for non-residential building, for repair work and for non-building purposes, it cannot be assumed that the pattern of their use will follow closely the pattern of new residential building. A second, less obvious problem in O. J. Firestone's estimation is his very low estimate of conversions. Essentially only those conversions authorized by municipal authorities are covered, yielding an estimate of 47,600 for 1921 to 1940 (previous edition of *Historical Statistics of Canada*, S139). Among the evidence that this estimate is a gross understatement is the fact that in the 1961 Census respondents reported 585,000 multiple dwellings built before 1920 (1961 Census, vol. II, 2, table 78) while the stock standing in 1921 was only about 335,000 (Steele, 1972, table 6.8), implying at least 250,000 conversions. (For Buckley's comments on O.J. Firestone's conversion estimates, and on the use of the building materials index, see previous edition of *Historical Statistics of Canada*, p. 500). Because the conversion process typically results in a loss to single detached stock and an addition to multiple stock, as a single house is converted into two or three apartments, an understatement of conversions implies an estimate of single completions which is somewhat too low and an estimate of multiples completions which is much too high. Thus it is not surprising that O.J. Firestone's estimates for urban areas in the 1930s show multiple completions nearly three times as great as singles completions despite the evidence of building permits, contract awards and the census of construction that apartment building was much weaker than other residential building in this period.

Like the O.J. Firestone estimates, series S198-202 have as their underpinning decade estimates derived using census and other data. The major difference from the O.J. Firestone results is the much lower estimate for the decade between the 1931 and 1941 censuses. The source of this difference is the much higher estimate of conversions. This is derived as an implication of the low ratio of multiple to single new construction as indicated by contract awards, censuses of construction and other data, at the same time as the much higher ratio of multiple to single gross flow given by the census reconciliations. (For details of the derivation see Steele, 1972, pp. 134-5 and Appendix VI).

Instead of the building materials index distributor used by O.J. Firestone to get annual estimates, series S198-202 essentially use the volume of residential building indicated by contract awards. This is accomplished as follows. First, the estimator for starts in urban one-to-three unit buildings is the number of contract awards 'residences' (corrected for a building-dwelling unit anomoly in Quebec, 1921 to 1928). The estimator for starts in other types of residential building is the value of apartment contract awards divided by the estimate of apartment unit value described in the note to series S168-180. The estimator for starts in commercial buildings is the ratio of such starts to all other starts in Montreal, times all other units in Canada. This ratio is 6 to slightly under 9 per cent in the early years of the period and well under 4 per cent in the last five years.

The remaining starts, those in one-to-three-unit buildings in rural areas, are estimated under two assumptions. First, it is assumed that the ratio of these starts to urban starts in one-to- three-unit buildings is the same in all years. Secondly, the difference in two-decade totals between the census-based estimate of all starts and the three components estimated as indicated above is assumed to equal rural starts in one-to-three-unit buildings. It will be noted that this estimating procedure means that while annual starts estimates summed over the two decades equal the sum of the census-based decade estimates, annual starts summed over a single decade are not constrained to equal the census-based decade estimate. This two-decade rather than one- decade constraint is used because (a) many of the component estimates used to derive the census- based decade estimates are subject to rather large error and the use of two-decade totals reduces the sensitivity to this error, and (b) there is evidence from the Quebec *Municipal Statistics* series, 'dwelling houses built', that the contract awards coverage of units in one-to-three-unit buildings did not change appreciably over 1921 to 1940.

For 1941 to 1950, the estimating procedure differs substantially from that used for earlier years, partly because the contract awards coverage changed substantially and partly because of the increased availability of alternative indicators. The estimating procedure is patchy, reflecting the varying quality of these indicators. Much of this variability is the result of disruptions caused by World War II and its aftermath. The estimation was carried out using two constraints. First, the decade total of starts had to be within the range 641,000 to 738,000, a range indicated as plausible by census-based decade estimates. In fact the total is 716,000. This compares with 594,000 completions for 1941 to 1950 shown by the unrevised series, (R-138) in the previous edition of *Historical Statistics of Canada;* and with 761,000 completions for June 1941 to June 1951 estimated for the purpose of preparing the residential construction estimates given in the previous edition of *Historical Statistics of Canada*. The second constraint is the requirement that the estimation procedure carried forward to 1951 had to yield an estimate of starts greater than the number yielded by the starts survey, but not more than 20 per cent greater.

For starts in one-and-two-unit buildings, the estimator for 1941 to 1945 is the 1940 estimate for units in one-to-three-unit buildings extrapolated on the basis of an index of starts of such units derived from Census of Construction data. This index is used because on the one hand, the coverage of this census appears stable for this period, and because permit and contract awards data both appear substantially affected by wartime regulations. For 1946 to 1950 the 1945 estimate is extrapolated using an index weighting equally data for this type of dwelling from the starts survey, from building permits; the Census of Construction data are not used because of evidence that its coverage of owner-builders increased and its editing practices changed. The ratio of rural to urban units is assumed to be .6.

For starts in apartment and other buildings, the 1941 estimate uses the 1921 to 1940 estimator. For 1942 to 1944, the 1941 estimate is extrapolated on the basis of an index in which Census of Construction data are weighted heavily. The 1945 to 1950 estimates are those given by the starts survey, and by starts derived from the predecessor completions survey.

The resulting estimates are much higher for the war years, especially 1942 and 1945, than the previous estimates

(Canadian Housing Statistics, 1968, table 1). Evidently while war regulation dampened building considerably in urban areas, it was not so strong an influence in rural areas. The estimates show little change from 1945 to 1947 and then a very large increase in 1948 followed by additional growth albeit at a lower rate in 1949 and 1950. The previous estimates show a much smaller rise in 1948 and then virtually no growth in 1949 and 1950.

S203-205. Dwelling starts by area, 1868 to 1920

SOURCE: Steele, M., *Housing Starts in Canada, 1868-1920*, (Guelph: processed, University of Guelph, 1977).

The estimation procedure used for these series is an adaptation of that used for later years. It has two major elements. First, decade starts are estimated using the identity that decade starts equals the change in occupied plus vacant permanent dwelling stock as given by the census, plus demolitions and other losses occurring during the decade minus dwellings added by conversions. This estimation is done for farm and non-farm components; farm units are defined for this purpose as dwellings on farms of 11 acres or more. The second element of the estimation is the construction of several annual distributor series. The Buckley urban distributor is Helen and Kenneth Buckley's index of urban building activity (1955, Appendix, table 0). The residential distributor incorporates data on residential building. It is essentially the same as the Buckley urban distributor, reflecting only Montreal residential building, until 1883. Starting in 1915 it reflects rural plus urban Quebec building. The urban mortgage distributor is based on the change in mortgage assets of insurance companies. The Pickett glass distributor is essentially James Pickett's window glass index.

Four separate non-farm series are produced using these distributor series as follows: the annual percentage change in the ratio of starts to the distributor is assumed to change smoothly; the estimation using this assumption is iterated until the decade sum of the results is within 5 per cent of the census-based estimate of decade starts. The non-farm estimates, S204, are weighted averages of the four series produced in this way, with the weights varying according to the quality of the basic distributor series. Specifically, for 1868 to 1870, S204 is simply the residential distributor-based estimates; for 1871 to 1877, these estimates and the estimates produced using the Pickett glass index are averaged; for 1878 to 1882, the mortgage distributor estimate replaces the Pickett glass estimate; for 1883 to 1900 the mortgage distributor estimates are weighted .25, the residential distributor estimates .75; for 1901 to 1914 these each have a weight of .25 and the Buckley urban estimates .5; for 1915 to 1920 the Buckley urban and the residential each have a weight of .5.

The farm estimates are produced using as distributor a series for 1868 to 1891 based on the change in mortgage assets of building societies and loan companies, and for 1892 to 1920, Buckley's annual farm series.

The results of this estimation are clearly subject to quite substantial error, especially in the case of the farm series, and especially for the period prior to 1883. At census years, however, the estimates are nicely consistent with the under-construction counts and scattered other data support them. The estimates are strikingly different from those of Pickett (previous edition of *Historical Statistics of Canada*, R149), especially for the early 1870s, when the high level shown by the Pickett series is essentially just the result of an arithmetic error, exacerbated by the annual distributor procedure used; and for 1915 to 1920, when wartime events damaged the usefulness of the glass index.

S206-219. Dwelling starts by principal source of financing and structural type, 1960 to 1976

SOURCE: Central Mortgage and Housing Corporation, *Canadian Housing Statistics*.

The number of starts under the NHA in any year is not the same as the number of loans in that year because of the typical lag of about a month between approval and start. NHA loans under sections 58 and 59 (numbered sections 40 and 40A before July 1971) include loans made to borrowers 'unable to obtain insured loans from private lenders'. These are almost all home-ownership loans. Loans made by CMHC under the Assisted Home Ownership Plan and the Assisted Rental Plan are included under 'Federal funds, other'. Also included in this category are: other CMHC loans under NHA, including those loans under sections 58 and 59 which are for low income housing; loans under the Veterans' Land Act, the Farm Credit Act, loans for Urban Military Housing; government expenditure for housing built for federal government employees. Under 'institutional funds' are included loans made by life insurance companies, loan and trust companies, chartered banks, Quebec savings banks, mutual benefit and fraternal societies. Under 'other' are starts of dwellings financed from sources such as provincial governments, caisses populaires, credit unions, guarantees under the Farm Improvement Loans Act and individual lenders, as well as starts of dwellings financed without mortgage loans.

S220-224. Housing stock at census dates, 1871 to 1951

SOURCE: 1871 to 1921: Steele, M., *Housing Starts in Canada, 1868-1920*, (Guelph: processed, University of Guelph, 1977); 1931, 1941: Steele, M., *Dwelling Starts in Canada, 1921-1940*, (Toronto: unpublished Ph.D dissertation, University of Toronto, 1972); 1951: 1951 Census vol. III, tables 2, 3.

The occupied figures for 1881, 1891, 1901, 1931, 1941, 1951 are taken directly from the census volumes. For 1871, the occupied total is that given in the census, vol. I plus the estimate for Prince Edward Island and the West by James Pickett *Residential Capital Formation in Canada, 1871-1921*, (Glasgow: processed, Royal College of Science and Technology, 1961, Appendix, table 1). For 1911 and 1921 the census dwelling count is not used because of confusion between building and dwelling unit in the instructions; the estimate here is the number of dwellings in the Yukon Territories and the Northwest Territories (plus the number of households elsewhere divided by the assumed ratio of households to dwelling units). This ratio is assumed 1.041 for 1911 and 1.054 for 1921. These numbers, and the assumed vacancy rate in 1921, were chosen after examination of contemporary data on crowding and vacancies. They yield a substantially smaller size of stock in 1921 and a slightly smaller stock in 1911 than Pickett's estimates, which are based largely on linear interpolation between census years.

Vacancies for 1871 to 1911 exclude prairies. For 1871 to 1901, the source is the same as for occupied dwellings. For

1911 the source is Pickett (1961, Appendix, table 1). For 1921, vacancies are assumed 2.24 per cent of stock. For 1931, urban vacancies are assumed 3.96 per cent of urban stock; this is the average rate observed in several cities in 1931 (O.J. Firestone, 1951, pp. 380, 381). In 1941 and 1951 vacancy data were once more collected in the census, and so figures for these years are from census volumes.

Temporary units, called 'vessels and shanties', are taken directly from census volumes for 1871 to 1891; for 1901 to 1921 temporary units are estimated using information on the number of prairie units of 'other' material of construction and the decline in the number of one-and-two-room dwellings. For 1931, the source is 1931 Census, V, table 85; for 1941 the source is a letter dated 1953 from F.G. Boardman of the Census Division, Statistics Canada.

S225-231. Dwelling units completed, urban structural conversions, urban demolitions and stock of dwellings at year end occupied by tenure, and vacant, 1956 to 1976

SOURCE: Mr. Paul Delisle, Construction Division, Statistics Canada.

The number of completions is taken from the starts and completions survey of CMHC. The number of structural conversions is the number for which building permits are issued inflated by the ratio of the population in all areas to the population in reporting municipalities; the number of demolitions is estimated in the same fashion. The number of vacant dwellings at census dates (1 June 1956 and every five years after that) is taken from the census; the number of vacancies in intervening years is estimated assuming the compound growth rate is constant. The tenure of the stock at census dates is taken from the census; the tenure in other years is estimated by linear interpolation.

The change in stock from one census to the next is identically equal to completions minus all conversions (structural and nonstructural) plus all losses from stock. Thus

$$(S231_t - S231_{t-5}) = \sum_{i=t-4}^{t} (S225_5 + S226_i - S227_i)$$

measures the net effect of errors and omissions in estimates of components of the change in stock, as long as the census stock count is correct. The residual is positive for each of the three earlier quinquennia (62,000 for 1956 to 1961, 16,000 for 1961 to 1966, 90,000 for 1966 to 1971) with Quebec and, to a lesser extent, Ontario accounting for most of these amounts; this pattern is consistent with the evidence of some under-reporting of completions in the late fifties and with the suspicion that unreported conversions were substantial in the late sixties. The residual is -31,000 for 1971 to 1976, suggesting there may have been a substantial number of two and three apartment houses changed back into single family use especially in Ontario and the western provinces.

S232-245. Apartment vacancy rates, by area and newly completed but unoccupied dwellings by type, 1957 to 1976

SOURCE: CMHC, *Canadian Housing Statistics* and CMHC files.

The vacancy rates are derived from a sample survey. The universe excludes apartment buildings financed by CMHC and buildings completed within six months of the survey date. It also excludes condominium buildings, even when many more than six units in such a building are occupied under rental tenure. The information is obtained by interviews with building owners and superintendents.

The count of newly completed but unoccupied dwellings is obtained by a survey of all units completed within six months of the survey; unoccupied units are dropped from the survey after six months. An NHA house or duplex is called occupied if it is either occupied or sold. Other units are called unoccupied even if they are already sold or rented. An apartment building is not called completed until 90 per cent of all units are completed, so that completed but unoccupied units in an apartment building called incomplete by this criterion will not be counted. If the practice of leaving some floors of an apartment building incomplete until other units are completed is widespread, the CMHC completion criterion implies that it substantially understates the completed but unoccupied count.

S246. Non-farm vacancy rates, 1921 to 1949

SOURCE: O.J. Firestone, *Residential Real Estate,* (Toronto: University of Toronto Press, 1951), table 69.

For 1921 to 1939, urban vacancies are estimated assuming the rate is the same as the geometric average of rates given in municipal reports of Toronto, Montreal, Winnipeg, Ottawa. Rural non-farm vacancies are estimated by extrapolating the 1941 Census vacancy rate using the urban vacancy rate series. For 1941 urban vacancies are estimated using the census urban rate; for 1940 and 1942 to 1946, urban vacancies are estimated for small cities using the 1941 Census rate, and for larger cities are estimated 'using the sample trend available for larger cities', (O.J. Firestone, 1951, p. 396). For 1947 to 1949, the rate used is extrapolated on the basis of data from 21 cities. For rural non-farm vacancies, the estimation is similar and uses the 1941 Census rate and 'the urban trend'.

S247-253. Net mortgage loans approved for new housing under the Dominion Housing Act and the National Housing Acts, by lender and type of loan, 1935 to 1976

S254-259. Net mortgage loans approved for existing housing under the NHA (1954), 1961-64 to 1976

SOURCE: CMHC, *Canadian Housing Statistics.*

Net mortgage loans approved take into account cancellations and alterations (such as a change in the number of dwelling units in an apartment building). Sections 58 and 59 loans include loans made to borrowers 'unable to obtain insured loans from private lenders'. Section 34.15 loans are Assisted Home Ownership Loans; AHOP loans not made by CMHC are made under a different section. Section 15 loans include loans made to entrepreneurs for low-rental housing projects. Approved lenders are lenders approved on an individual company basis for the purpose of making NHA loans. The majority of these are chartered banks and life, loan or trust companies; some pension funds are also approved lenders.

The source publication gives dollar values for these loans.

S260-271. Mortgage loans on new residential property approved by lending institutions, by type of lender, by type of loan, 1948 to 1976

S272-283. Mortgage loans on existing residential property approved, by type of lender, by type of loan, 1948 to 1976

S284-289. Mortgage loans on non-residential property approved, by type of lender, 1948 to 1976

SOURCE: CMHC, *Canadian Housing Statistics.*

Mortgage loans reported here are gross of cancellations and alterations; for NHA loans these are probably usually much less than 3 or 4 per cent. The possibility exists that they are occasionally much higher than this (see the comments above in the discussion of permit data). The data for these series are collected by a CMHC monthly survey; the life companies and the chartered banks report in summary form via their respective national organizations. The survey covers about 95 per cent of the universe. An NHA loan is called residential if at least 80 per cent of building it finances is for residential use.

The source publication gives S260-283 in terms of dwelling units and by structural type of dwelling unit as well as in millions of dollars.

S290-297. National Housing Act Mortgage Insurance Fund, 1955 to 1976

SOURCE: CMHC, *Canadian Housing Statistics.*

Starting in June, 1969, the mortgage insurance fee is, if insured progress instalments are made, one per cent for home-ownership loans and one and one-quarter per cent for rental loans. Prior to that the fee was double these amounts. The application fee is $35. If default occurs, the lender receives the principal amount owing on the mortgage; approved borrowers' charges; interest on the principal owing at the mortgage interest rate for the period during which the loan was in default, or for 12 months, whichever is shorter; interest at the mortgage rate less 2 per cent for a maximum of six months, in addition to the 12-month period; any reasonable amount (effective June 1973) approved by CMHC for the legal costs of acquisition when making a claim.

S298-310. Sales and purchases of insured National Housing Act mortgages, 1957 to 1976

SOURCE: CMHC, 1957 to 1976 *Canadian Housing Statistics.*

NHA-approved lenders must retain the servicing of mortgages they sell. Hatch has commented on S298-310 as follows: "The data in these tables must be interpreted with caution. They are intended to identify arms-length trading between non-affiliated firms; however, in some cases parent-subsidiary trades have been included in the data. There is also reason to believe that the data are incomplete due to a failure to report transactions properly." (Hatch, J.E., *The Canadian Mortgage Market,* (Toronto: Queen's Printer for Ontario), 1975.)

S311-322. Selected housing unit cost series, 1951 to 1976

SOURCE: CMHC, *Canadian Housing Statistics,* (S312, S317, S320); Section C of CMHC book of tables (S311, S313, S314, S315); The Canadian Real Estate Association, *Annual Report 1977* and *The Canadian Realtor* (S319); Smith, L.B., *The Postwar Canadian Housing and Residential Mortgage*

Markets and the Role of Government, (Toronto: University of Toronto Press, 1974), table V, p. 23 (S322).

The average cost of dwelling units by type is the average value from building permits times an inflation factor. This factor is 1.15 for singles and duplexes, for 1957 to 1971; 1.17 for 1972 to 1976. The factors for apartments and rows are 1.25 and 1.28 for 1957 to 1971 and 1972 to 1976 respectively. These factors are the ratio of actual to permit value estimated for a sample of NHA dwellings. It is possible that there is some non-trivial overstatement of costs per unit of singles in the early period here because of the deficient coverage in these years of building in smaller centres where, there is reason to believe (see discussion of S168-180), new houses may be of relatively low quality.

The average cost of NHA dwellings is the average of costs as estimated by loan applicants at the time of approval. Average estimated (total) cost differs little from the average selling price of the same units. The average land cost varies with the proportion of fully serviced, partially serviced and unserviced lots. NHA houses use a variety of construction materials and are built under a variety of programs (e.g. AHOP). NHA apartments include highrises and walkups, buildings of wood and of steel, and are built under low income and other programs. The difference between the average costs of all dwellings and NHA dwellings is affected by NHA loan maximum. This maximum changes over time; e.g. it was $25,000 for home-ownership loans in early 1972, $30,000 for these loans in late 1972 and varied on a regional basis starting in June 1974. Changes in the maximum affect the geographic composition of NHA houses. None of the NHA series (S312, S316, S320, S321 and S326) are reweighted in order to eliminate distortions caused by the changing geographic condition. This point is especially important for the interpretation of the cost-per-square-foot index as a price index.

Multiple Listing Service properties in the MLS average include single detached and condominium dwellings, and probably some small apartment buildings. The average is computed as the total value of sales for Canada divided by the total number of sales. Thus the average in any year is affected by the geographic composition of sales. In 1961, Ontario accounted for 60 per cent of the number of all sales. British Columbia for 16 per cent, Manitoba for 8 per cent, Alberta for 8 per cent, Saskatchewan for 4 per cent, the Atlantic provinces for only 0.3 per cent and Quebec for 5 per cent; the respective numbers for 1977 are 49, 15, 5, 13, 4, 3 and 11. Weighting the provincial averages in 1976 by their 1961 weights, however, yields an average value of $51,847, almost precisely the same as the current weighted average value. It is possible that year-to-year changes are distorted by the practice of increasing the use of 'exclusive' listings in hot markets. The remarkable similarity of the movement of this series and the average of S329-334 suggests that this is not a problem of consequence.

Average urban cash rent is for 1961 and 1971 average urban cash rent as reported in the census. The estimates for other years are extrapolations based on the percentage changes computed by Lawrence Smith (1974, p. 23) using average rents reported in the Labour Force Survey. It is worth noting that average gross rent (which includes an allowance for utilities where these are not included in cash rent) increased by just 53.8 per cent between the censuses of 1961 and 1971, as compared with 63.2 per cent for cash rent. Rent increases by quarter, computed from the Labour Force Survey data, are shown in Loyns, R.M.A., *An Examination of the Consumer Price Index and Implicit Price*

Index as Measures of Recent Price Change in the Canadian Economy, (Ottawa: Prices and Incomes Commission, 1972), p. 65. Average rents are currently computed quarterly by the Prices Division for use in GNP estimation, but are not available for publication.

S323-325. Average construction cost of new dwelling units, by type of dwelling, 1921 to 1950

SOURCE: See source for S168-180.

For description of estimation see the note to S168-180.

S326-335. Selected housing price series (1971 = 100), 1952 to 1976

SOURCE: CMHC, *Canadian Housing Statistics,* (S326); Statistics Canada, *Prices and Price Indexes,* (Catalogue 62-010), (S327, S335); CANSIM, Matrix No. D40680, (S328); Statistics Canada, *Construction Price Statistics,* Monthly Bulletin, (Catalogue 62-007), (S329-334).

For comment on S326, see the note to S311-322. The residential construction input price index starting in 1971 weights wages .359 and materials .641. For comments on S328 see the note to S167.

The new housing price indexes (S329-334) are based on prices provided by builders of single family housing who build 100 or more housing units a year. Smaller builders are included if they are able to provide prices for comparable models over a period of time. The price index is corrected for quality change in two ways. First, a cost-based correction is made where the change is a minor one; for example, if the quality of carpets installed in a given model is improved, the contractor is asked to estimate the cost change and this amount is removed from the amount of the price change. Secondly, a market-price-based correction is made when the quality change arises because of the introduction of a new model; that is, the relative prices of the new model and an existing model are taken to represent their relative quality. It can be seen that if builders are in the habit of pricing new models high relative to their equilibrium market value, and then letting the differential decline

over the time the model remains on the market, the new model correction will overstate quality improvement and lead to a downward bias in the index. There is no sign that this is a problem of importance here, however.

These price indexes are for the value of the house and its associated lot. Separate price indexes are also calculated for lots and for house value excluding lot. These indexes are not published because of some doubts about the validity of the split.

The rental component of the Consumer Price Index is computed from rent changes reported for units in the Labour Force Survey in the preceding as well as current month. It is widely agreed that this index is severely downward biased. Some evidence on this is provided by the fact it shows an increase of only 21.4 per cent between 1961 and 1971 while the Canada average gross rent as reported by the censuses increased by 55.8 per cent for the same period, and the urban Canada average gross rent by 53.8 per cent. Only a quality improvement in the stock of about 2.5 per cent per year would explain the difference. It has been plausible to suppose (e.g. see Loyns, 1972) that the apparent bias in the rental component of the CPI is the result of the 'new unit' problem discussed above in connection with the new housing price indexes. Evidence from a recent CMHC survey, however, suggests that this may be just a minor part of the problem. In 1975 CMHC did a special follow-up of its 1974 Survey of Housing Units. The average increase in gross rent of the same units, November 1974 to November 1975, it found, with the percentage increase shown by the CPI rental component shown in brackets were: St. John's, 12.8 (5.4); Halifax, 11.2 (2.6); Saint John, 15.8 (8.0); Montreal, 8.7 (5.2); Ottawa, 10.0 (4.4); Toronto, 13.2 (6.8); Winnipeg, 15.1 (9.8); Edmonton, 18.6 (10.6); Vancouver, 10.3 (7.6) (CMHC, *Analysis of Rental Market Focusing on the Impact of Removing Controls in 1977;* Ottawa: processed, 1976). It is important to emphasize that the CMHC estimates are not estimates of the change in average universe rents, but rather are estimates of the price change using basically the same procedure as used in computation of the CPI rental component. The differences in results has yet to be explained.

Series S1-7. New and repair construction expenditures, in current and constant dollars, 1926 to 1976
(millions of dollars)

Year	Current dollar estimates			Constant dollar estimates			Implicit deflator for new construction 1971=100
	New construction	Repair construction	New and repair construction	New construction	Repair construction	New and repair construction	
	1	2	3	4	5	6	7
1976	27,914	4,985	32,899	16,236	2,899	19,135	171.9
1975	24,757	4,320	29,077	16,008	2,793	18,801	154.7
1974	21,519	3,919	25,438	15,584	2,838	18,422	138.1
1973	17,598	3,217	20,815	14,952	2,733	17,685	117.7
1972	14,923	2,818	17,741	14,053	2,654	16,707	106.2
1971	13,600	2,588	16,188	13,600	2,588	16,188	100.0
1970	11,319	2,461	13,780	12,019	2,613	14,632	94.2
1969	10,824	2,380	13,204	11,978	2,634	14,612	90.4
1968	9,909	2,305	12,214	11,559	2,689	14,248	85.7
1967	9,474	2,145	11,619	11,171	2,529	13,700	84.8
1966	9,282	1,954	11,236	11,442	2,409	13,851	81.1
1965	8,174	1,755	9,929	10,689	2,295	12,984	76.5
1964	7,032	1,629	8,661	9,709	2,249	11,958	72.4
1963	6,156	1,559	7,715	8,763	2,219	10,982	70.2
1962	5,834	1,508	7,343	8,523	2,203	10,726	68.5
1961	5,630	1,455	7,085	8,245	2,131	10,376	68.3
1960	5,579	1,419	6,998	8,172	2,078	10,250	68.3
1959	5,849	1,353	7,202	8,672	2,006	10,678	67.4
1958	6,002	1,247	7,249	8,931	1,856	10,787	67.2
1957	5,921	1,223	7,144	8,772	1,812	10,584	67.5
1956	5,484	1,068	6,552	8,193	1,596	9,789	66.9
1955	4,352	1,141	5,493	6,762	1,773	8,535	64.4
1954	3,878	1,105	4,983	6,159	1,755	7,914	63.0
1953	3,853	1,070	4,923	6,049	1,679	7,728	63.7
1952	3,512	1,010	4,522	5,559	1,599	7,158	63.2
1951	2,859	987	3,846	4,739	1,636	6,375	60.3
1950	2,450	827	3,277	4,608	1,555	6,163	53.2
1949	2,110	765	2,875	4,116	1,492	5,608	51.3
1948	1,823	714	2,537	3,684	1,442	5,126	49.5
1947	1,311	613	1,924	3,007	1,407	4,414	43.6
1946	1,043	555	1,598	2,688	1,430	4,118	38.8
1945	752	513	1,265	2,072	1,414	3,486	36.3
1944	697	474	1,171	1,916	1,302	3,218	36.4
1943	931	397	1,328	2,573	1,097	3,670	36.2
1942	841	357	1,198	2,441	1,036	3,477	34.5
1941	711	330	1,041	2,232	1,036	3,268	31.9
1940	490	293	783	1,645	983	2,628	29.8
1939	405	283	688	1,426	997	2,423	28.4
1938	406	277	683	1,411	962	2,373	28.8
1937	439	269	708	1,489	913	2,402	29.5
1936	320	251	571	1,172	919	2,091	27.3
1935	287	238	525	1,075	891	1,966	26.7
1934	242	233	475	922	888	1,810	26.2
1933	197	215	412	758	827	1,585	26.0
1932	295	241	536	1,104	902	2,006	26.7
1931	567	287	854	2,017	1,021	3,038	28.1
1930	752	305	1,057	2,465	1,000	3,465	30.5
1929	868	328	1,196	2,755	1,041	3,796	31.5
1928	771	319	1,090	2,552	1,055	3,607	30.2
1927	621	296	917	2,120	1,011	3,131	29.3
1926	516	272	788	1,773	935	2,708	29.1

Series S8. Estimates of total new and repair construction, 1896 to 1930

(millions of dollars)

Year	Total construction	Year	Total construction	Year	Total construction
	8		**8**		**8**
1930	928	1915	341	1900	119
1929	1,046	1914	480	1899	87
1928	940	1913	583	1898	75
1927	783	1912	597	1897	67
1926	703	1911	535	1896	78
1925	697	1910	453		
1924	692	1909	396		
1923	697	1908	322		
1922	624	1907	360		
1921	631	1906	316		
1920	986	1905	253		
1919	618	1904	220		
1918	558	1903	194		
1917	464	1902	150		
1916	336	1901	118		

Series S9-22. Total value of new construction work performed, by principal type of construction, 1926 to 1976
(millions of dollars)

Year	Building						Engineering							Total building and engineering
	Residential[1]	Industrial	Commercial	Institutional	Other building construction	Total[2]	Road, highway and aerodrome construction	Water works and sewage systems	Electric power construction	Railway, telephone and telegraph construction	Gas and oil facilities	Other engineering construction[3]	Total	
	9	10	11	12	13	14	15	16	17	18	19	20	21	22
1976	10,853	1,042	3,182	1,379	991	17,347	1,966	1,344	2,694	859	1,753	2,183	10,799	28,145
1975	7,114	1,146	3,379	1,376	909	13,924	1,964	1,123	2,640	740	1,529	2,137	10,132	24,056
1974	7,010	1,201	2,612	1,199	704	12,726	1,789	974	1,693	720	1,451	1,418	8,045	20,771
1973	5,977	888	1,947	1,035	521	10,369	1,521	700	1,385	555	1,275	1,150	6,585	16,954
1972	4,820	706	1,467	1,094	437	8,524	1,410	625	1,123	446	1,209	1,133	5,945	14,469
1971	4,025	831	1,187	1,317	398	7,757	1,316	514	1,093	415	1,128	1,051	5,518	13,275
1970	3,138	804	1,066	1,205	362	6,575	1,012	412	1,125	376	939	882	4,745	11,320
1969	3,384	680	954	1,212	361	6,592	972	329	910	345	822	856	4,234	10,826
1968	2,806	549	961	1,274	303	5,894	854	325	747	338	774	976	4,015	9,909
1967	2,378	685	1,036	1,160	310	5,569	955	314	790	336	654	858	3,906	9,475
1966	2,180	830	1,089	1,080	297	5,476	946	339	675	315	615	915	3,805	9,281
1965	2,218	625	876	941	255	4,915	840	306	515	247	541	811	3,259	8,174
1964	1,990	522	716	693	212	4,133	770	235	482	254	544	615	2,900	7,033
1963	1,652	399	617	780	225	3,673	647	219	431	254	503	430	2,482	6,155
1962	1,555	364	603	753	309	3,584	603	187	396	223	442	400	2,250	5,834
1961	1,467	294	637	570	289	3,258	557	186	354	232	472	459	2,261	5,519
1960	1,456	331	621	543	234	3,185	631	193	299	299	409	437	2,268	5,453
1959	1,752	297	640	511	214	3,414	611	195	346	299	414	431	2,297	5,711
1958	1,782	287	589	493	186	3,336	543	170	457	250	611	463	2,494	5,830
1957	1,430	494	560	465	203	3,150	550	172	463	245	700	503	2,634	5,784
1956	1,575	487	480	396	265	3,204	458	159	415	215	499	350	2,096	5,300
1955	1,499	293	427	408	183	2,811	359	127	301	144	311	215	1,458	4,269
1954	1,178	262	463	331	144	2,378	309	158	290	119	245	201	1,322	3,700
1953	1,084	294	421	297	189	2,285	339	116	303	134	235	253	1,381	3,666
1952	826	389	337	273	93	1,919	432	116	357	114	199	144	1,363	3,282
1951	821	351	283	243	72	1,769	311	65	318	98	88	86	965	2,734
1950	923		770			1,693	..	..	..	..	..	..	760	2,453
1940	822		703			1,525	..	..	..	..	..	..	641	2,166
1948	635		612			1,247	..	..	..	..	..	..	577	1,824
1947	526		469			995	..	..	..	..	..	..	402	1,397
1946	407		332			739	..	..	..	..	..	..	305	1,044
1945	330		246			576	..	..	..	..	..	..	169	745
1944	279		251			530	..	..	..	..	..	..	215	745
1943	250		405			655	..	..	..	..	..	..	366	1,021
1942	244		471			715	..	..	..	..	..	..	228	943
1941	251		357			608	..	..	..	..	..	..	201	809
1940	186		232			418	..	..	..	..	..	..	145	563
1939	174		130			304	..	..	..	..	..	..	163	467
1938	148		128			276	..	..	..	..	..	..	179	455
1937	164		140			304	..	..	..	..	..	..	201	505
1936	131		103			234	..	..	..	..	..	..	143	377
1935	107		72			179	..	..	..	..	..	..	149	328
1934	92		65			159	..	..	..	..	..	..	118	275
1933	72		57			129	..	..	..	..	..	..	95	224
1932	90		87			177	..	..	..	..	..	..	143	320
1931	158		169			327	..	..	..	..	..	..	256	583
1930	191		260			451	..	..	..	..	..	..	324	775
1929	230		342			572	..	..	..	..	..	..	308	880
1928	220		295			515	..	..	..	..	..	..	254	769
1927	204		220			424	..	..	..	..	..	..	196	620
1926	201		165			366	..	..	..	..	..	..	167	533

[1] Unrevised; not consistent with National Accounts estimates before 1962 and 1971-1976.

[2] Estimates for types of structure in agriculture have been compiled for 1963 to 1968 on the basis of more recent related information and are therefore not comparable with data for types of structure in the years prior to 1963.

[3] Includes marine, and dams and irrigation.

Series S23-28. Total value of new construction work performed, by region and by major type, 1951 to 1976
(millions of dollars)

Year		Atlantic provinces	Quebec	Ontario	Prairie provinces	British Columbia[1]	Canada
		23	24	25	26	27	28
1976	Residential	703	2,220	3,189	2,221	1,431	9,764
	Non-residential	460	1,789	1,962	1,316	766	6,293
	Engineering	919	2,375	2,999	3,141	1,570	11,004
1975	Residential	574	1,574	2,553	1,300	1,112	7,113
	Non-residential	508	2,207	2,151	1,167	778	6,811
	Engineering	893	2,339	2,789	2,675	1,437	10,133
1974	Residential	566	1,470	2,872	1,068	1,034	7,010
	Non-residential	455	1,642	2,027	918	674	5,716
	Engineering	820	1,635	2,188	2,009	1,393	8,045
1973	Residential	493	1,169	2,577	850	889	5,977
	Non-residential	319	1,138	1,646	734	554	4,391
	Engineering	673	1,407	1,759	1,617	1,130	6,585
1972	Residential	343	969	2,037	737	734	4,820
	Non-residential	238	912	1,480	607	467	3,704
	Engineering	581	1,260	1,736	1,370	997	5,945
1971	Residential	299	861	1,642	635	588	4,025
	Non-residential	320	854	1,459	557	542	3,732
	Engineering	597	1,121	1,561	1,287	952	5,518
1970	Residential	229	678	1,287	470	474	3,138
	Non-residential	255	722	1,539	558	363	3,437
	Engineering	595	793	1,300	1,324	732	4,745
1969	Residential	226	677	1,425	579	476	3,384
	Non-residential	233	696	1,244	608	426	3,208
	Engineering	479	709	1,156	1,260	630	4,234
1968	Residential	173	597	1,184	453	399	2,806
	Non-residential	229	688	1,248	582	339	3,087
	Engineering	413	682	1,052	1,261	606	4,015
1967	Residential	130	559	981	362	346	2,378
	Non-residential	246	695	1,294	608	348	3,190
	Engineering	388	725	957	1,142	694	3,906
1966	Residential	125	541	903	313	298	2,180
	Non-residential	280	809	1,265	606	336	3,297
	Engineering	337	831	947	1,080	610	3,805
1965	Residential	133	581	884	330	291	2,218
	Non-residential	204	742	1,008	444	300	2,697
	Engineering	258	892	720	894	495	3,259
1964	Residential	123	560	760	311	237	1,990
	Non-residential	173	603	778	387	203	2,143
	Engineering	209	834	697	794	365	2,900
1963	Residential	101	476	600	276	200	1,652
	Non-residential	174	516	796	363	172	2,021
	Engineering	181	572	695	746	289	2,482
1962	Residential	103	445	540	297	170	1,555
	Non-residential	201	538	738	387	165	2,029
	Engineering	174	522	637	631	286	2,250
1961	Residential	116	379	577	279	146	1,497
	Non-residential	158	511	629	346	146	1,791
	Engineering	169	490	623	750	310	2,342
1960	Residential	122	377	573	266	184	1,522
	Non-residential	132	441	649	356	151	1,729
	Engineering	179	539	627	639	284	2,268
1959	Residential	112	463	689	342	229	1,835
	Non-residential	108	463	605	325	161	1,662
	Engineering	192	572	637	607	288	2,297
1958	Residential	99	498	748	335	226	1,906
	Non-residential	103	400	599	313	141	1,556
	Engineering	157	589	827	610	311	2,494
1957	Housing	96	402	590	245	193	1,526
	Non-residential	98	412	695	297	218	1,721
	Engineering	131	576	812	599	515	2,634
1956	Housing	106	490	638	274	201	1,709
	Non-residential	102	360	637	318	213	1,630
	Engineering	155	429	550	600	362	2,096

Series S23-28. Total value of new construction work performed, by region and by major type, 1951 to 1976 (concluded)

(millions of dollars)

Year		Atlantic provinces	Quebec	Ontario	Prairie provinces	British Columbia[1]	Canada
		23	24	25	26	27	28
1955	Housing	95	475	660	258	196	1,684
	Non-residential	92	319	507	266	129	1,312
	Engineering	127	345	375	440	172	1,458
1954	Housing	71	347	533	244	124	1,319
	Non-residential	76	298	478	239	109	1,200
	Engineering	99	350	355	385	134	1,322
1953	Housing	68	346	437	232	98	1,181
	Non-residential	85	284	469	244	119	1,201
	Engineering	82	294	399	372	234	1,381
1952	Housing	59	280	328	157	80	904
	Non-residential	81	259	422	220	110	1,093
	Engineering	72	341	405	318	228	1,363
1951	Housing	53	249	318	125	65	809
	Non-residential	67	213	383	169	115	948
	Engineering	63	234	307	218	144	965

[1] Includes the Yukon Territory and the Northwest Territories.

Series S29-58. Building permits issued, by region and major type, 1951 to 1976[1]

(millions of dollars)

Year	Residential						Industrial					
	Canada	Atlantic provinces	Quebec	Ontario	Prairie provinces	British Columbia[2]	Canada	Atlantic provinces	Quebec	Ontario	Prairie provinces	British Columbia[2]
	29	30	31	32	33	34	35	36	37	38	39	40
1976	7,476	433	1,565	2,563	1,791	1,123	1,010	57	218	473	128	134
1975	6,129	377	1,129	2,462	1,180	981	876	41	208	435	114	78
1974	4,576	283	805	2,002	720	766	1,316	58	396	534	239	89
1973	4,763	215	815	2,366	628	740	854	31	208	428	103	85
1972	3,638	171	676	1,714	546	531	520	13	116	279	54	58
1971	3,203	126	686	1,456	480	455	461	48	133	197	38	45
1970	2,312	98	468	1,079	329	338	498	20	113	231	45	89
1969	2,434	106	423	1,119	401	384	569	16	129	299	61	63
1968	2,412	88	467	1,130	388	339	531	15	214	183	60	59
1967	1,927	63	412	892	276	284	400	10	89	201	61	39
1966	1,592	55	379	728	215	215	474	15	80	282	54	43
1965	1,757	66	444	773	248	226	430	46	77	212	41	54
1964	1,615	59	400	707	244	206	381	31	76	183	56	35
1963	1,462	54	391	608	239	170	281	23	50	152	41	15
1962	1,209	39	331	475	228	137	218	8	62	109	25	14
1961	1,176	37	293	495	236	115	198	7	34	96	42	19
1960	944	21	205	439	181	99	184	3	35	107	25	14
1959	1,255	32	251	552	262	158	193	4	48	94	32	15
1958	1,381	27	281	649	247	178	180	3	32	90	44	11
1957	952	18	198	445	160	132	219	5	62	96	24	32
1956	974	25	204	455	161	129	222	5	53	101	27	36
1955	1,030	22	207	499	171	131	196	4	38	79	44	31
1954	884	19	178	443	142	101	176	4	32	94	30	16
1953	810	23	173	375	155	84	201	7	42	112	26	14
1952	610	18	134	285	111	61	101	1	19	70	6	5
1951	445	13	93	226	67	45	114	1	20	82	6	6

Series S29-58. Building permits issued, by region and major type, 1951 to 1976[1] (concluded)
(millions of dollars)

Year	Commercial						Institutional and government					
	Canada	Atlantic provinces	Quebec	Ontario	Prairie provinces	British Columbia[2]	Canada	Atlantic provinces	Quebec	Ontario	Prairie provinces	British Columbia[2]
	41	**42**	**43**	**44**	**45**	**46**	**47**	**48**	**49**	**50**	**51**	**52**
1976	2,546	133	703	686	618	406	1,168	94	318	352	243	162
1975	2,251	152	432	919	436	313	1,342	138	262	493	262	186
1974	2,293	108	532	905	448	299	1,096	130	288	385	174	118
1973	1,970	115	380	849	328	297	972	69	295	378	112	118
1972	1,412	101	305	564	235	205	893	54	188	431	132	88
1971	1,070	44	184	489	162	191	996	30	220	459	192	94
1970	807	40	130	415	110	113	1,084	27	218	578	196	64
1969	839	37	148	383	167	104	1,066	106	222	513	128	97
1968	696	40	121	294	154	87	1,144	76	265	552	189	63
1967	702	55	129	281	134	103	1,046	80	145	519	209	93
1966	737	40	177	330	114	75	913	56	105	453	214	85
1965	783	32	250	276	148	77	840	62	128	401	182	67
1964	598	31	157	240	108	62	674	43	156	304	114	57
1963	460	21	116	183	92	48	620	34	166	264	115	41
1962	469	20	137	177	91	45	620	27	118	304	131	40
1961	439	27	104	197	72	38	431	31	89	200	76	34
1960	436	15	116	173	84	48	460	31	109	187	99	34
1959	512	18	164	189	85	57	419	21	84	186	102	26
1958	370	13	87	155	82	33	425	24	91	203	64	43
1957	347	11	54	162	70	51	309	17	77	126	59	30
1956	336	12	71	126	71	55	296	13	71	128	58	27
1955	267	10	51	126	49	32	311	18	88	96	72	37
1954	197	9	30	93	44	20	265	11	62	101	63	28
1953	199	7	32	101	32	26	213	11	54	81	42	26
1952	188	8	29	87	47	18	164	8	61	61	23	11
1951	154	7	23	75	31	17	148	11	35	61	22	19

Year	Total					
	Canada	Atlantic provinces	Quebec	Ontario	Prairie provinces	British Columbia[2]
	53	**54**	**55**	**56**	**57**	**58**
1976	12,199	716	2,803	4,074	2,780	1,825
1975	10,598	708	2,031	4,309	1,993	1,557
1974	9,280	579	2,021	3,827	1,582	1,273
1973	8,559	429	1,699	4,021	1,171	1,239
1972	6,464	340	1,287	2,988	967	882
1971	5,730	248	1,224	2,600	872	786
1970	4,700	185	929	2,302	680	604
1969	4,907	266	921	2,314	756	650
1968	4,783	219	1,067	2,159	791	548
1967	4,074	208	774	1,892	681	518
1966	3,715	166	742	1,793	596	418
1965	3,810	206	899	1,661	620	423
1964	3,268	163	788	1,434	523	359
1963	2,823	132	722	1,207	488	274
1962	2,517	93	647	1,065	474	237
1961	2,244	102	521	988	426	207
1960	2,025	71	465	906	389	194
1959	2,379	75	547	1,021	482	255
1958	2,357	67	491	1,098	437	264
1957	1,827	50	391	829	313	245
1956	1,828	55	398	810	317	247
1955	1,805	54	384	801	335	231
1954	1,521	43	302	731	279	165
1953	1,422	48	301	668	256	150
1952	1,062	35	243	503	187	94
1951	861	32	171	444	125	87

[1] The number of municipalities reporting increases over time.
[2] Starting in 1972 includes the Yukon Territory and the Northwest Territories.

Series S59. Value of building permits issued, 1910 to 1960
(millions of dollars)

Year	Building permits issued	Year	Building permits issued	Year	Building permits issued
	59		**59**		**59**
	204 cities		58 cities		35 cities
1960	1,382	1940	80	1920	106
1959	1,637	1939	60	1919	77
1958	1,622	1938	61	1918	37
1957	1,307	1937	56	1917	34
1956	1,319	1936	41	1916	40
1955	1,309	1935	47	1915	34
1954	1,151	1934	27	1914	97
1953	1,089	1933	22	1913	154
1952	803	1932	42	1912	185
1951	681	1931	112	1911	138
1950	802	1930	166	1910	100
1949	616	1929	235		
1948	536	1928	219		
1947	373	1927	185		
1946	384	1926	156		
1945	197	1925	125		
1944	129	1924	127		
1943	80	1923	134		
1942	104	1922	148		
1941	135	1921	117		
1940	133	1920	117		

Series S60-64. Principal statistics of the construction industry (construction contractors), 1934 to 1976
(values in millions of dollars)

Year	Number of employees	Salaries and wages	Cost of materials	Value of work	Value added	Year	Number of employees	Salaries and wages	Cost of materials	Value of work	Value added
	60	**61**	**62**	**63**	**64**		**60**	**61**	**62**	**63**	**64**
1976	580,049	9,493	9,831	27,101	17,270	1955	359,661	1,271	1,956	4,060	2,104
						1954	334,923	1,147	1,666	3,523	1,856
1975	525,722	7,979	8,874	22,592	13,718	1953	332,233	1,143	1,634	3,456	1,822
1974	530,593	6,899	7,768	19,618	11,850	1952	303,598	994	1,659	3,105	1,446
1973	514,587	5,847	6,209	15,904	9,695	1951	279,691	767	1,279	2,479	1,200
1972	440,161	4,824	5,500	13,744	8,244						
1971	461,979	4,528	5,122	12,703	7,581	1950	213,078	523	809	1,619	811
						1949	210,568	489	669	1,348	679
1970	437,155	3,814	4,684	10,827	6,143	1948	284,000	605	836	1,666	830
1969	458,112	3,605	4,727	10,521	5,794	1947	204,954	403	599	1,097	498
1968	456,121	3,296	4,666	9,935	5,269	1946	165,518	295	427	775	349
1967	433,374	2,974	4,108	9,271	5,163						
1966	449,785	2,837	4,279	9,121	4,843	1945	110,405	185	249	459	210
						1944	92,912	158	181	381	200
1965	430,930	2,430	3,912	7,930	4,018	1943	121,482	215	262	511	249
1964	398,928	2,083	3,456	6,862	3,406	1942	141,234	227	308	575	267
1963	376,953	1,876	2,967	6,032	3,065	1941	139,587	195	342	564	222
1962	384,670	1,818	2,833	5,757	2,924						
1961	365,564	1,690	2,606	5,459	2,853	1940	103,898	131	227	380	152
						1939	91,147	104	161	287	126
1960	364,276	1,632	2,535	5,249	2,713	1938	96,010	107	153	281	129
1959	389,897	1,676	2,571	5,353	2,782	1937	96,865	107	152	278	126
1958	402,798	1,693	2,665	5,565	2,900	1936	76,834	75	105	197	92
1957	404,771	1,664	2,569	5,417	2,848						
1956	406,048	1,540	2,432	4,973	2,541	1935	63,349	59	76	148	71
						1934	46,479	39	52	99	48

Series S65-71. New construction in primary industries, 1946 to 1976 *(millions of dollars)*

Year	Agriculture and fishing[1]	Forestry	Total mining, quarrying and oil wells	Total metal mines	Total non-metal mines	Petroleum and gas[2]	Construction industry
	65	66	67	68	69	70	71
1976	527.0	89.0	2,356.9	597.6	161.3	1,598.0	121.3
1975	479.6	90.9	1,968.1	499.6	112.8	1,355.7	80.2
1974	433.1	98.2	1,586.5	409.6	116.0	1,060.9	66.0
1973	346.3	76.4	1,276.3	357.1	67.5	851.7	57.1
1972	292.0	52.0	1,105.4	345.7	50.5	709.2	49.0
1971	228.0	45.0	1,314.8	590.8	84.6	639.4	17.0
1970	225.0	48.0	996.1	335.6	107.9	552.6	15.0
1969	249.0	52.0	888.5	295.1	128.1	465.3	14.0
1968	253.0	37.0	782.4	264.8	110.2	407.4	14.0
1967	255.0	38.0	762.2	238.1	121.1	403.0	14.0
1966	243.0	43.0	766.6	209.9	107.3	449.4	13.0
1965	210.0	43.0	573.7	121.5	58.9	393.3	17.0
1964	195.0	39.0	520.6	147.0	40.6	333.0	14.0
1963	189.0	28.0	431.5	118.3	19.1	294.1	11.0
1962	185.0	29.0	418.7	137.8	25.2	255.7	14.0
1961	168.0	28.0	443.5	107.6	16.4	319.5	14.0
1960	167.3	27.0	303.2	88.8	14.8	199.6	14.0
1959	165.5	21.0	249.7	71.1	11.7	166.9	16.0
1958	148.5	19.0	241.5	62.5	18.8	160.2	16.0
1957	134.0	28.0	406.6	187.0	24.9	194.8	16.0
1956	148.3	41.0	378.2	144.8	20.2	213.2	16.0
1955	134.6	36.0	248.0	..	..	..	16.0
1954	140.8	26.0	184.0	..	..	..	9.0
1953	154.2	19.0	162.0	..	..	..	10.0
1952	130.3	19.0	133.0	..	..	..	5.0
1951	134.1	22.0	101.0	..	..	..	7.0
1950	74.0	17.0	68.0	..	..	..	14.0
1949	74.0	16.0	57.0	..	..	..	12.0
1948	58.0	14.0	47.0	..	..	..	8.0
1947	46.0	15.0	23.0	..	..	..	3.0
1946	39.0	6.0	13.0	..	..	..	5.0

[1] The estimation procedure used for agriculture, 1951 and later is different from that used for earlier years.

[2] Gas processing plants are included with manufacturing prior to 1960.

Series S72–93. New construction in manufacturing by major groups, 1926 to 1976
(millions of dollars)

Year	Total manufacturing			Food and beverages	Tobacco	Rubber	Leather	Textiles	Knitting mills	Clothing	Wood	Furniture and fixtures
	New	Repair	New plus repair									
	72	**73**	**74**	**75**	**76**	**77**	**78**	**79**	**80**	**81**	**82**	**82a**
1976	1,439.7	438.2	1,877.9	110.4	1.1	16.9	3.4	19.1	1.5	3.7	61.2	8.0
1975	1,568.5	381.0	1,949.5	118.2	5.7	23.0	2.7	31.6	0.3	8.5	73.6	9.2
1974	1,425.3	344.4	1,769.7	139.3	7.1	36.1	3.3	38.6	1.2	5.5	85.5	17.1
1973	985.8	275.8	1,261.6	113.1	1.1	28.0	2.6	26.0	3.3	9.6	76.3	11.5
1972	829.0	252.0	1,081.0	82.2	1.8	23.0	6.0	20.7	1.1	5.2	41.0	5.3
1971	873.0	207.0	1,080.0	95.1	2.9	23.8	2.8	14.0	1.5	2.0	37.2	3.9
1970	997.0	213.0	1,210.0	96.8	2.9	22.3	1.3	20.3	2.1	1.1	42.4	7.1
1969	772.0	205.0	977.0	87.9	1.1	11.3	2.3	20.5	2.9	3.8	42.5	2.9
1968	657.0	193.0	850.0	77.2	3.8	9.3	2.2	11.7	2.2	2.4	18.4	8.4
1967	677.0	180.0	857.0	73.7	4.1	5.5	1.8	17.8	0.8	2.0	15.6	10.2
1966	788.0	167.0	955.0	79.3	5.4	14.9	2.6	35.1	2.8	2.2	23.5	10.5
1965	604.0	151.0	755.0	60.0	2.3	6.1	1.0	32.8	1.3	2.6	22.9	6.7
1964	443.0	147.0	590.0	53.6	2.4	5.7	1.4	23.7	1.3	1.7	15.5	4.4
1963	355.0	140.0	495.0	52.9	1.5	3.0	1.7	10.9	0.9	1.4	12.5	4.7
1962	353.0	133.0	386.0	57.3	0.9	2.9	0.9	6.8	0.8	0.6	11.8	2.4
1961	279.0	124.0	403.0	58.1	1.7	2.6	0.6	5.5	1.1	1.9	13.6	1.2
1960	335.0	124.0	459.0	52.7	1.7	6.9	1.3	6.0	—	2.3	12.6	3.0
1959	374.0	125.0	499.0	45.4	3.3	3.5	0.8	4.7	—	1.6	15.3	—
1958	398.0	110.0	508.0	40.5	4.1	2.0	0.5	2.6	—	0.7	8.8	—
1957	520.0	115.0	635.0	36.3	1.9	6.1	1.3	7.9	—	1.2	10.3	—
1956	488.0	112.0	600.0	32.6	3.5	2.9	1.8	10.3	—	1.3	14.0	—
1956[1]	493.3	—	—	32.6		8.2			10.3	1.3	14.0	
1955	344.7	—	—	38.5		5.1			7.0	1.4	12.1	
1954	287.6	—	—	38.6		5.7			7.5	2.2	8.4	
1953	349.3	—	—	26.0		6.0			7.9	3.8	10.4	
1952	343.6	—	—	26.6		3.8			7.0	1.6	9.3	
1951	268.5	—	—	28.0		3.4			9.9	4.1	11.2	
1950	135.4	—	—	26.0		2.3			6.6	2.5	8.1	
1949	156.6	—	—	27.7		2.6			7.0	3.0	7.5	
1948	180.8	—	—	31.9		3.5			6.5	2.1	7.9	
1947	184.8	—	—	33.0		4.6			10.9	3.7	11.4	
1946	132.2	—	—	24.7		6.7			8.4	2.6	10.9	
1945	75.9	—	—	18.2		5.9			1.3	9.2	1.6	
1944	61.3	—	—	10.7		2.3			1.8	2.8	2.9	
1943	84.6	—	—	6.1		2.2			0.8	1.6	16.8	
1942	137.3	—	—	8.5		2.4			1.5	3.0	11.3	
1941	95.2	—	—	9.7		2.4			3.1	10.9	10.8	
1940	66.7	—	—	10.7		2.7			3.4	2.4	8.0	
1939	33.4	—	—	7.5		1.1			0.6	1.4	4.9	
1938	44.8	—	—	7.8		0.8			1.4	0.4	1.2	
1937	64.1	—	—	8.5		1.8			2.6	1.8	14.1	
1936	37.6	—	—	5.3		16.4			1.3	0.8	2.8	
1935	21.1	—	—	3.5		0.1			2.8	0.1	1.0	
1934	19.5	—	—	1.6		0.4			0.6	0.4	4.4	
1933	17.8	—	—	0.8		2.9			0.9	1.1	7.0	
1932	19.3	—	—	4.9		0.4			1.0	1.3	4.4	
1931	40.9	—	—	7.2		0.9			1.7	1.6	1.0	
1930	75.5	—	—	7.4		2.1			6.8	0.8	5.9	
1929	131.0	—	—	13.5		2.5			1.4	13.3	10.2	
1928	124.7	—	—	9.6		2.9			0.6	10.8	7.4	
1927	86.9	—	—	4.4		1.1			6.2	7.5	21.5	
1926	55.7	—	—	2.7		0.8			4.7	2.0	3.3	

Series S72-93. New construction in manufacturing by major groups, 1926 to 1976 (concluded)
(millions of dollars)

Year	Paper and allied	Printing and publishing	Primary metals	Metal fabrication	Machinery	Transportation equipment	Electrical products	Non-metallic mineral products	Petroleum and coal products	Chemical	Miscellaneous
	83	84	85	86	87	88	89	90	91	92	93
1976	128.6	15.0	144.8	43.1	36.9	63.7	35.6	46.6	255.9	430.7	13.5
1975	110.1	18.4	200.5	50.3	49.1	76.5	28.3	41.1	337.5	374.7	9.2
1974	120.5	16.7	148.0	59.7	42.8	102.4	31.0	29.5	321.7	198.7	20.6
1973	89.4	15.0	75.8	43.4	30.3	47.7	32.2	37.6	229.7	100.7	12.5
1972	116.5	15.3	95.3	20.4	14.6	30.2	18.6	30.7	214.0	78.1	9.1
1971	133.6	15.6	91.1	20.4	13.1	30.2	28.6	22.5	211.3	107.6	16.1
1970	132.6	13.8	118.2	32.5	26.1	49.6	26.7	32.7	213.7	132.2	22.7
1969	109.9	12.5	71.5	29.0	17.1	43.6	22.4	37.1	116.9	119.4	17.8
1968	70.3	10.4	81.3	21.7	11.8	37.6	17.1	19.9	98.9	134.1	18.2
1967	111.2	9.9	82.0	28.2	18.9	56.4	26.4	40.9	78.8	78.7	14.1
1966	137.1	12.6	85.3	36.8	23.6	87.8	30.7	51.0	55.5	76.0	15.4
1965	111.5	17.6	61.7	32.9	13.8	64.5	17.6	30.0	30.3	76.2	12.4
1964	69.4	17.1	58.3	17.9	19.2	44.4	12.0	20.2	20.2	42.9	11.4
1963	40.3	15.5	44.4	14.6	14.2	27.1	9.5	13.7	37.9	39.5	8.5
1962	40.5	10.8	58.4	12.4	5.4	11.6	10.9	13.7	56.8	40.1	8.2
1961	37.1	6.4	32.9	8.4	5.5	13.9	7.8	11.9	27.9	35.4	5.6
1960	35.1	7.4	51.3	12.2	8.4	16.5	7.6	15.7	51.9	34.9	7.2
1959	24.2	11.8		40.9		20.5	8.5	25.9	109.2	24.5	6.0
1958	25.5	13.4		35.7		16.6	7.3	14.4	136.0	43.1	2.7
1957	66.3	17.3		54.5		18.1	13.8	29.4	113.4	65.6	6.6
1956	85.1	5.3		40.3		16.7	14.7	51.4	83.9	57.9	3.6
1956[1]	85.1	5.3		40.3		16.7		218.0		57.9	3.6
1955	33.1	6.4		27.0		20.2		168.0		21.6	3.7
1954	21.6	11.7		22.0		20.9		131.2		15.1	2.7
1953	22.5	3.8		35.6		46.9		120.5		32.0	3.7
1952	33.6	3.3		46.2		37.1		109.2		61.2	4.7
1951	41.9	6.3		47.1		21.8		71.9		19.2	3.7
1950	21.1	5.0		13.5		9.9		30.7		7.3	2.4
1949	26.8	6.3		14.6		6.7		40.2		11.9	2.3
1948	29.1	7.0		19.6		5.4		50.1		15.0	2.7
1947	31.2	5.4		16.0		5.2		46.7		14.4	2.3
1946	27.2	2.9		14.9		5.4		14.0		11.6	2.9
1945	5.8	3.9		12.8		2.2		9.3		4.0	1.7
1944	8.0	0.2		10.1		1.6		18.2		1.4	1.3
1943	1.7	0.2		4.3		6.6		39.9		2.5	1.9
1942	3.8	0.3		7.2		27.9		63.1		5.3	3.0
1941	8.8	—		9.9		3.0		31.3		3.2	2.1
1940	5.1	0.6		4.9		3.4		22.1		1.9	1.5
1939	3.9	0.3		4.3		2.9		4.8		1.0	0.7
1938	2.6	0.6		5.0		14.5		6.6		2.9	1.0
1937	4.2	1.2		10.0		5.2		7.8		5.5	1.4
1936	1.5	—		3.1		0.9		4.3		0.4	0.8
1935	2.2	0.6		2.4		2.4		4.4		1.1	0.5
1934	0.8	—		2.5		2.1		3.9		2.4	0.4
1933	0.1	0.3		0.6		0.6		2.4		1.0	0.4
1932	2.1	0.7		0.5		0.2		2.7		0.7	0.4
1931	11.3	0.3		4.7		0.3		9.2		1.8	0.9
1930	4.4	0.2		12.5		1.8		29.0		2.9	1.7
1929	16.0	7.5		8.3		8.3		36.2		10.9	2.9
1928	34.8	9.4		4.8		7.0		33.5		1.2	2.7
1927	23.7	0.5		5.0		4.8		7.9		2.4	1.9
1926	21.4	0.8		4.3		0.8		9.3		4.4	1.2

[1] 1956 and prior years on basis of 1948 Standard Industrial Classification, breakdown of repair and new plus repair not available.

Series S94. New construction in manufacturing, 1871 to 1925
(millions of dollars)

Year	Total manufacturing	Year	Total manufacturing	Year	Total manufacturing
	94		**94**		**94**
1925	49.0	1905	25.3	1885	4.8
1924	55.4	1904	24.7	1884	5.5
1923	58.7	1903	24.1	1883	7.3
1922	37.4	1902	18.6	1882	7.6
1921	37.2	1901	15.0	1881	5.7
1920	62.4	1900	11.8	1880	3.6
1919	45.8	1899	9.4	1879	2.3
1918	43.1	1898	7.3	1878	2.2
1917	62.8	1897	5.6	1877	2.3
1916	60.5	1896	5.3	1876	2.4
1915	39.9	1895	4.1	1875	2.6
1914	53.3	1894	4.1	1874	2.6
1913	79.5	1893	4.4	1873	2.6
1912	77.4	1892	4.6	1872	2.4
1911	58.9	1891	4.7	1871	2.0
1910	45.6	1890	5.4		
1909	33.3	1889	5.6		
1908	32.1	1888	5.5		
1907	31.3	1887	5.3		
1906	27.2	1886	4.9		

Series S95-106. New construction in manufacturing, by major groups, 1918 to 1925
(millions of dollars)

Year	Food and beverages	Tobacco, rubber and leather products	Textile products	Clothing	Wood products	Paper products	Printing, publishing and allied industries	Iron and steel products	Transportation equipment	Non-ferrous metal products and electrical apparatus and supplies	Non-metallic mineral products and products of petroleum and coal	Chemical products
	95	**96**	**97**	**98**	**99**	**100**	**101**	**102**	**103**	**104**	**105**	**106**
1925	3.5	0.6	2.9	1.2	5.0	22.4	2.1	2.4	4.1	0.4	1.8	2.0
1924	6.0	0.4	3.6	1.3	9.9	20.3	1.5	1.6	2.5	1.2	5.3	0.8
1923	8.6	0.8	2.5	1.4	1.7	17.2	4.3	1.5	1.9	1.2	12.4	4.4
1922	7.8	0.6	2.8	1.9	1.8	13.1	2.4	2.0	1.4	0.4	0.3	2.1
1921	10.9	0.8	1.6	1.4	3.8	7.8	1.0	2.3	0.7	2.4	1.2	2.8
1920	9.9	1.0	3.7	2.1	1.7	25.3	2.6	3.3	3.9	2.0	3.8	2.9
1919	3.4	0.8	2.7	0.8	2.6	12.8	1.5	1.6	0.9	1.8	3.8	12.5
1918	4.5	0.9	1.2	1.1	2.3	3.0	1.0	3.4	8.9	1.5	3.7	11.3

Series S107-121. New construction in transportation, communication, electric power, gas and water utilities, 1956 to 1976
(millions of dollars)

Year	Total transportation	Air	Railway transportation	Water transportation and services	Motor	Urban transit	Pipelines	Total communication, electric power, gas and water utilities	Telephone and telegraph	Grain elevators	Electric power	Gas distribution	Water systems	Broadcasting	Other utilities
	107	108	109	110	111	112	113	114	115	116	117	118	119	120	121
1976	920.3	26.1	370.2	25.9	31.2	177.3	289.6	3,505.5	598.3	20.2	2,654.2	141.1	[1]	62.4	29.3
1975	966.9	29.8	370.9	59.0	25.5	160.5	321.2	3,436.0	533.9	18.2	2,660.8	150.2	[1]	51.4	21.5
1974	714.2	20.7	284.6	67.7	31.6	73.2	236.4	2,439.6	508.7	10.4	1,699.5	147.9	[1]	51.7	21.4
1973	702.9	16.1	228.4	47.2	17.9	54.0	339.3	1,969.7	371.0	10.6	1,416.7	108.4	[1]	39.2	23.8
1972	758.9	19.3	191.3	73.3	15.8	49.8	409.4	1,598.1	308.8	6.8	1,135.2	107.5	[1]	26.5	13.3
1971	674.7	33.2	187.7	76.8	14.9	23.9	338.2	1,553.1	285.5	3.2	1,079.1	86.4	[1]	32.7	66.2
1970	560.1	59.1	185.5	73.2	13.5	23.3	205.5	1,484.4	254.4	4.4	1,057.4	70.9	[1]	42.1	55.2
1969	470.2	21.0	167.5	62.0	10.8	19.1	189.8	1,249.0	233.0	17.6	856.1	85.4	[1]	29.9	27.0
1968	441.2	22.1	146.7	40.4	11.3	16.0	204.7	1,332.6	222.6	19.0	888.6	87.0	91.0	5.1	19.3
1967	433.9	4.8	181.9	43.2	8.9	44.4	150.7	1,313.8	194.2	34.9	875.3	58.5	100.4	7.1	43.4
1966	405.2	1.4	145.7	50.4	7.4	61.3	139.0	1,260.4	196.0	23.4	786.5	72.7	113.4	7.6	60.8
1965	319.0	1.0	107.5	35.6	5.9	72.7	96.3	1,124.4	158.6	9.8	727.3	54.2	109.9	7.5	57.1
1964	410.1	0.7	162.6	15.0	7.0	78.4	146.4	922.1	146.0	8.8	588.0	54.5	64.6	5.4	54.8
1963	326.7	0.6	173.3	15.6	7.3	30.6	99.3	783.9	148.3	10.3	459.1	70.4	59.8	5.3	30.7
1962	250.4	2.3	139.4	26.2	4.5	17.1	60.9	731.6	135.7	16.7	440.7	60.0	61.3	3.9	13.3
1961	380.5	4.2	161.5	42.5	6.6	18.1	147.6	707.9	122.7	17.3	413.0	52.0	71.2	4.8	26.9
1960	365.0	6.4	202.7	38.4	6.3	19.8	91.4	..	161.3	12.9	371.5	56.5	79.1	7.9	20.0
1959	364.0	17.3	225.6	56.0	4.8	4.9	55.4	..	136.1	17.2	387.3	77.0	87.4	4.0	45.4
1958	556.8	2.4	182.4	132.5	1.9	3.4	234.2	..	126.9	10.0	496.3	74.1	75.9	2.2	62.5
1957	626.2	3.5	188.2	114.4	6.8	9.3	304.0	..	112.9	7.0	559.8	64.8	62.2	4.6	37.9
1956	398.6	2.0	153.0	60.2	3.1	7.4	172.9	..	100.9	10.7	450.9	42.0	66.4	3.9	12.5

[1] Included in government departments from 1969 to 1976.

Series S122. Net capital formation in railway transport and telegraphs, 1850 to 1930
(millions of dollars)

Year	Net capital formation	Year	Net capital formation	Year	Net capital formation
	122		122		122
1930	93.6	1900	18.4	1870	9.1
1929	143.4	1899	15.0	1869	5.0
1928	71.7	1898	17.9	1868	5.3
1927	75.4	1897	9.9	1867	3.7
1926	49.3	1896	5.5	1866	2.0
1925	31.0	1895	7.5	1865	1.5
1924	58.7	1894	10.5	1864	1.9
1923	73.6	1893	14.2	1863	0.9
1922	25.7	1892	12.9	1862	1.5
1921	75.3	1891	20.6	1861	1.8
1920	86.1	1890	23.7	1860	5.2
1919	66.1	1889	25.9	1859	4.5
1918	66.1	1888	20.4	1858	10.3
1917	60.5	1887	19.8	1857	7.3
1916	42.0	1886	22.6	1856	9.2
1915	91.1	1885	32.6	1855	16.7
1914	126.5	1884	40.2	1854	13.3
1913	176.6	1883	35.6	1853	13.7
1912	153.5	1882	29.8	1852	6.2
1911	121.7	1881	13.4	1851	2.5
1910	105.1	1880	13.0	1850	1.3
1909	89.3	1879	12.2		
1908	97.2	1878	12.7		
1907	103.6	1877	14.8		
1906	57.6	1876	18.0		
1905	43.9	1875	13.2		
1904	33.8	1874	14.4		
1903	32.0	1873	23.7		
1902	20.7	1872	21.0		
1901	19.0	1871	15.8		

Series S123-127. New construction and repair, non-railway transport structures, 1901 to 1930
(millions of dollars)

Year	Gross investment			Repair	Gross investment and repair	Year	Gross investment			Repair	Gross investment and repair
	Provincial highways and bridges	Canals	Harbour and river work				Provincial highways and bridges	Canals	Harbour and river work		
	123	124	125	126	127		123	124	125	126	127
1930	54.3	—	51.7[1]	—	106.0	1915	6.9	6.2	13.7	4.9	31.7
1929	40.8	—	56.5[1]	—	97.3	1914	8.8	5.4	18.6	6.3	39.1
1928	—	—	—	—	—	1913	9.9	2.6	18.2	6.7	37.4
1927	—	—	—	—	—	1912	8.1	2.4	12.7	5.3	28.5
1926	19.1	13.5	9.3	13.8	55.7	1911	4.8	2.7	11.2	4.9	23.6
1925	18.7	12.3	14.6	14.0	59.6	1910	3.8	2.4	9.2	4.4	19.8
1924	15.6	10.2	15.9	12.8	54.5	1909	2.7	1.8	7.6	3.8	15.9
1923	24.6	8.0	14.9	12.3	59.8	1908	2.6	2.1	9.1	4.5	18.3
1922	21.2	7.2	10.7	10.1	49.2	1907	1.8	1.9	8.1	3.7	15.5
1921	20.3	6.2	9.8	8.9	45.2	1906	0.8	1.0	4.8	2.6	9.2
1920	16.5	6.1	9.8	8.7	41.1	1905	0.4	1.7	6.1	2.6	10.8
1919	10.0	4.9	6.9	6.8	28.6	1904	0.4	2.2	5.3	2.3	10.2
1918	4.5	2.4	4.4	4.9	16.2	1903	0.9	2.0	4.6	2.0	9.5
1917	4.2	1.9	8.3	4.4	18.8	1902	1.0	2.0	3.5	1.8	8.3
1916	4.2	4.5	10.5	4.7	23.9	1901	0.6	2.2	2.5	1.6	6.9

[1] These totals include canals, harbour and river work, new and repair, and highway repair.

Series S128-140. New construction in trade, finance and commercial services, 1946 to 1976
(millions of dollars)

Year	Total trade	Whole-sale	Chain	Independent	Depart-ment	Auto-motive	Total finance	Banks	Insurance trust and loan	Other	Total commercial services	Hotels	Other
	128	129	130	131	132	133	134	135	136	137	138	139	140
1976	385.9	109.0	70.4	36.0	77.0	93.5	1,734.3	127.2	60.0	1,547.1	604.1	129.1	475.0
1975	350.9	109.0	70.4	29.0	76.8	83.3	1,559.9	97.0	49.0	1,413.9	857.2	162.9	694.3
1974	391.6	99.4	91.2	43.5	73.1	84.4	1,337.0	82.3	45.6	1,209.1	455.4	225.3	230.1
1973	286.7	79.7	50.9	34.4	44.7	77.0	1,093.5	48.9	30.8	1,013.8	305.0	175.5	129.5
1972	203.8	38.9	45.5	26.3	24.3	68.8	776.9	33.1	34.0	709.8	231.0	125.9	105.1
1971	181.2	31.3	45.2	23.9	20.8	60.0	498.5	26.1	25.0	447.4	220.7	131.3	89.4
1970	210.0	36.5	43.5	28.7	36.1	65.2	418.9	28.0	40.0	350.9	130.5	63.3	67.2
1969	196.9	44.5	37.5	35.2	11.7	68.0	403.6	28.0	25.7	349.9	103.6	40.5	63.1
1968	198.5	50.3	44.4	33.0	15.2	55.6	399.2	25.7	16.8	356.7	111.6	37.9	73.7
1967	205.5	49.6	30.8	46.3	22.2	56.6	416.8	22.9	36.2	357.7	142.1	37.3	104.8
1966	196.2	43.5	29.9	46.0	36.6	40.2	406.0	21.6	18.1	366.3	258.0	63.2	194.8
1965	153.5	29.3	26.9	41.0	19.3	37.0	367.4	26.8	14.8	325.8	183.7	57.9	125.8
1964	146.2	36.3	25.3	38.5	17.5	28.6	289.5	30.3	16.8	242.4	112.3	41.3	71.0
1963	135.9	28.0	22.9	35.9	15.9	33.2	230.6	24.2	15.5	190.9	101.4	35.3	66.1
1962	120.4	21.2	18.7	30.6	20.4	29.5	248.8	28.6	25.4	194.8	69.0	24.0	45.0
1961	127.2	27.7	18.5	29.6	16.4	35.0	268.0	32.1	24.2	211.7	56.1	22.4	33.7
1960	164.9	34.0	29.4	43.2	16.2	42.1	243.0	32.5	21.4	189.1	58.3	24.2	34.1
1959	166.8	24.8	33.0	46.1	13.9	49.0	224.8	25.1	19.7	180.0	69.5	26.6	42.9
1958	194.9	23.4	43.1	75.4	13.2	39.8	150.3	20.0	16.3	114.0	51.3	22.8	28.5
1957	205.2	30.2	39.2	68.5	14.7	52.6	109.6	19.9	14.1	75.6	67.5	34.3	33.2
1956	177.2	35.5	26.4	53.0	13.0	49.3	99.3	16.9	9.4	73.0	51.1	22.8	28.3
1955	181.3	21.3	30.2	72.7	19.4	37.7	82.0	15.3	9.3	57.4	33.4	11.9	21.5
1954	204.1	33.4	32.3	79.1	27.9	31.4	90.4	14.4	18.0	58.0	25.3	9.3	16.0
1953	191.3	38.0	28.0	77.7	21.9	25.7	63.1	9.8	15.0	38.3	29.2	12.3	16.9
1952	95.4	20.0	17.1	38.8	3.9	15.6	36.5	9.3	8.9	18.3	28.7	11.8	16.9
1951	109.4	15.5	24.0	52.5	5.1	12.3	52.4	18.0	7.1	27.3	39.7	17.0	22.7
1950	121.7	15.3	31.0	63.6	2.6	9.2	48.6	15.1	4.1	29.4	35.5	11.1	24.4
1949	102.8	10.8	19.1	56.5	9.1	7.3	23.5	10.0	2.5	11.0	14.8	4.6	10.2
1948	95.1	12.4	16.1	45.8	5.6	15.2	26.1	7.9	1.5	16.7	37.9	9.4	28.5
1947	67.8	8.9	11.3	30.0	5.0	12.6	15.5	6.1	0.4	9.0	28.5	11.2	17.3
1946	47.3	5.9	7.9	20.7	3.9	8.9	11.2	4.3	0.7	6.2	18.0	7.2	10.8

Series S141-147. New construction in institutions and government departments, 1926 to 1976
(millions of dollars)

Year	Total institutions	Churches	Universities	Schools	Hospitals	Other	Total government departments
	141	142	143	144	145	146	147
1976	1,167.8	44.6	131.0	585.4	328.3	78.5	4,440
1975	1,190.6	36.2	124.8	649.0	311.5	69.2	4,392
1974	1,063.5	18.2	102.9	591.2	302.1	49.1	3,751
1973	913.6	12.8	119.8	498.0	239.2	43.8	2,962
1972	993.2	14.1	193.7	544.7	201.2	39.5	2,731
1971	1,199.3	13.2	276.9	625.4	228.2	55.6	2,443
1970	1,094.8	22.1	241.6	606.1	186.4	38.6	2,001
1969	1,134.2	23.3	290.0	606.3	188.3	26.3	1,908
1968	1,196.8	35.7	288.5	653.9	196.4	22.3	1,679
1967	1,107.1	42.1	259.3	607.1	179.5	19.1	1,732
1966	1,020.5	46.8	253.6	515.6	180.1	24.4	1,703
1965	867.4	45.4	222.5	423.4	152.5	23.6	1,494
1964	648.3	40.4	150.2	289.3	145.0	23.4	1,303
1963	756.9	46.8	117.8	425.1	148.8	18.4	1,154
1962	729.4	52.8	97.0	402.4	165.0	12.2	1,130
1961	535.8	58.6	97.2	223.1	146.6	10.3	1,125
1960	500.1	59.3	74.7	229.6	125.2	11.3	1,171
1959	478.9	54.6	73.2	213.5	128.1	9.5	1,128
1958	457.3	55.0	55.7	201.9	136.1	8.6	1,014
1957	407.4	52.8	38.0	197.6	111.7	7.3	1,025
1956	358.8	43.8	22.3	173.1	110.0	9.6	932
1955	366.9	33.9	22.0	171.4	130.0	9.6	728
1954	297.3	30.6	16.6	136.1	106.4	7.6	676
1953	269.6	24.8	14.5	122.2	103.1	5.0	710
1952	251.8	25.2	9.4	130.7	81.4	5.1	758
1951	211.7	28.3	11.5	102.3	65.5	4.1	534
1950	187.2	28.0	12.4	80.6	62.3	3.9	391
1949	172.4	30.2	9.8	67.2	61.3	3.9	344
1948	126.4	21.0	11.0	47.6	44.0	2.8	320
1947	78.0	9.8	11.9	27.6	27.0	1.7	240
1946	66.2	5.6	10.8	24.5	23.8	1.5	173
1945	40.1	2.2	6.1	12.9	18.9	—	146
1944	24.5	1.6	1.4	7.3	14.2	—	177
1943	16.7	1.0	1.8	6.9	7.0	—	312
1942	13.9	1.3	0.9	5.6	6.1	—	342
1941	14.8	1.9	2.8	5.0	5.1	—	300
1940	15.9	2.1	2.0	6.4	5.4	—	179
1939	26.3	2.6	4.2	11.2	8.3	—	114
1938	23.6	3.2	1.4	7.2	11.8	—	123
1937	19.4	2.7	2.6	7.4	6.7	—	142
1936	16.5	1.8	1.4	8.4	4.9	—	89
1935	12.2	1.5	0.9	6.0	3.8	—	98
1934	11.0	1.6	1.2	5.2	3.0	—	87
1933	12.9	2.0	0.9	6.7	3.3	—	65
1932	28.4	4.4	1.8	15.8	6.4	—	91
1931	45.5	6.3	7.4	21.5	10.3	—	134
1930	56.1	6.8	8.2	31.3	9.8	—	164
1929	47.7	7.2	3.9	26.4	10.2	—	128
1928	41.8	8.6	1.8	24.8	6.6	—	109
1927	40.1	9.3	3.0	22.7	5.1	—	93
1926	33.3	7.9	3.1	17.6	4.7	—	73

Series S148-160. New construction by governments and government enterprises, by level of government and by category, 1946 to 1976
(millions of dollars)

Year	Federal government				Provincial governments				Municipal governments				Total new
	Enterprises	Housing	Government departments	Total	Enterprises	Institutions	Government departments	Total	Enterprises	Institutions	Government departments	Total	
	148	149	150	151	152	153	154	155	156	157	158	159	160
1976	421.4	100.9	655.4	1,177.7	3,223.3	282.5	1,826.2	5,332.0	313.3	479.5	1,958.1	2,750.9	9,260.6
1975	442.0	80.9	649.7	1,172.6	3,043.0	339.8	1,954.7	5,337.5	636.7	496.5	1,787.4	2,920.6	9,430.7
1974	348.3	56.6	602.1	1,007.0	1,915.1	271.8	1,654.8	3,841.7	301.9	473.6	1,493.7	2,269.2	7,117.9
1973	247.6	49.9	452.5	750.0	1,375.5	206.1	1,381.0	2,962.6	171.8	418.1	1,128.3	1,718.2	5,430.8
1972	218.0	46.4	400.1	664.5	1,085.7	255.4	1,319.0	2,660.1	123.7	439.0	1,011.9	1,574.6	4,899.2
1971	285.4	43.5	359.1	688.0	965.7	286.0	1,187.2	2,438.9	99.7	547.6	896.5	1,543.8	4,670.7
1970	321.9	40.6	323.3	685.8	908.5	173.8	920.8	2,003.1	97.8	566.9	757.1	1,421.8	4,110.7
1969	198.7	35.3	364.2	598.2	750.3	200.3	875.2	1,825.8	86.0	577.6	668.4	1,332.0	3,756.0
1968	135.2	32.9	339.3	507.4	827.2	220.7	784.5	1,832.4	155.0	623.7	555.3	1,334.0	3,673.9
1967	168.6	25.6	331.9	525.7	915.7	243.9	864.8	2,024.4	185.5	551.6	534.9	1,272.0	3,822.1
1966	254.5	31.8	311.9	598.5	859.2	200.1	826.7	1,885.3	223.6	475.5	563.9	1,263.0	3,746.8
1965	150.3	13.3	267.1	431.3	770.7	177.2	725.2	1,673.2	231.3	363.8	501.5	1,096.6	3,201.1
1964	173.1	15.3	204.4	387.9	619.3	123.9	657.8	1,401.0	191.5	254.9	441.0	887.4	2,676.3
1963	170.1	19.5	197.3	387.3	454.4	115.3	532.5	1,102.2	126.8	394.1	424.1	945.0	2,434.5
1962	138.2	20.9	264.3	423.4	387.1	130.0	478.4	995.5	110.3	350.2	386.8	847.3	2,226.2
1961	159.6	19.7	308.3	487.6	384.0	67.8	463.0	914.8	113.0	220.2	353.7	686.9	2,089.3
1960	188.3	28.2	303.0	519.5	330.9	78.4	530.2	939.5	121.3	218.5	337.5	677.3	2,136.3
1959	226.6	31.9	330.3	588.8	318.3	81.3	485.6	885.2	119.2	201.8	312.5	633.5	2,107.5
1958	317.6	40.0	289.2	646.8	433.3	68.3	437.7	939.3	117.0	185.9	287.4	590.3	2,176.4
1957	282.8	39.1	305.6	627.5	459.0	58.8	460.6	978.4	98.5	184.5	258.4	541.4	2,147.3
1956	163.2	27.6	319.9	510.7	369.8	47.3	391.4	808.5	99.2	170.6	220.6	490.4	1,809.6
1955	89.0	24.0	243.0	356.0	244.0	44.0	289.0	577.0	76.0	168.0	196.0	440.0	1,373.0
1954	52.0	18.0	236.0	306.0	226.0	28.0	258.0	512.0	87.0	141.0	182.0	410.0	1,228.0
1953	50.0	40.0	315.0	405.0	228.0	25.0	228.0	481.0	74.0	133.0	167.0	374.0	1,260.0
1952	52.0	52.0	335.0	439.0	189.0	26.0	252.0	467.0	63.0	134.0	171.0	368.0	1,274.0
1951	31.0	57.0	204.0	292.0	166.0	26.0	189.0	381.0	50.0	105.0	141.0	296.0	969.0

Series S148-160. New construction by governments and government enterprises, by level of government and by category, 1946 to 1976 (concluded)
(millions of dollars)

Year	Federal government				Provincial governments				Municipal governments				Total new
	Enter-prises	Housing	Govern-ment depart-ments	Total	Enter-prises	Insti-tutions	Govern-ment depart-ments	Total	Enter-prises	Insti-tutions	Govern-ment depart-ments	Total	
	148	149	150	151	152	153	154	155	156	157	158	159	160
1950	21.0	56.0	111.0	188.0	192.0	25.0	160.0	377.0	40.0	84.0	120.0	244.0	809.0
1949	41.0	71.0	118.0	224.0	159.0	15.0	141.0	315.0	38.0	73.0	85.0	196.0	735.0
1948	31.0	67.0	76.0	168.0	93.0	5.0	171.0	269.0	30.0	51.0	73.0	154.0	591.0
1947	25.0	32.0	39.0	91.0	50.0	3.0	134.0	187.0	17.0	32.0	67.0	116.0	394.0
1946	22.0	39.0	28.0	83.0	29.0	2.0	81.0	112.0	13.0	30.0	64.0	107.0	302.0

Series S161-166. New construction, federal government, 1868 to 1930, provincial governments, 1901 to 1930
(millions of dollars)

Year[1]	Federal government				Pro-vincial govern-ment	Total federal and pro-vincial	Year[1]	Federal government				Pro-vincial govern-ment	Total federal and pro-vincial
	Railway	Other trans-portation	Buildings and other	Total				Railway	Other trans-portation	Buildings and other	Total		
	161	162	163	164	165	166		161	162	163	164	165	166
1930	—	—	—	63.2	67.7	130.9	1900	—	—	—	—	—	—
1929	—	—	—	45.9	51.5	97.4	1899	1.1	4.9	0.3	6.3	—	—
1928	—	—	—	40.2	41.2	81.4	1898	0.3	4.1	0.4	4.8	—	—
1927	—	—	—	36.9	31.6	68.5	1897	0.2	3.1	0.2	3.5	—	—
1926	2.7	22.8	3.1	28.6	24.1	52.7	1896	0.3	2.9	0.2	3.3	—	—
1925	—	26.9	4.9	31.7	26.6	58.3	1895	0.3	5.2	0.2	3.7	—	—
1924	—	26.1	5.0	31.1	24.8	55.9	1894	0.5	3.7	0.4	4.6	—	—
1923	—	22.9	2.5	25.4	34.8	60.2	1893	0.2	2.8	0.3	3.3	—	—
1922	1.0	17.9	2.0	20.8	30.2	51.0	1892	0.4	2.2	0.2	2.8	—	—
1921	1.5	16.0	3.8	21.3	32.3	53.6	1891	1.2	2.4	0.4	3.9	—	—
1920	1.7	15.9	5.4	23.0	25.0	48.0	1890	2.1	2.2	0.5	4.8	—	—
1919	3.8	11.8	9.6	25.3	15.8	41.1	1889	2.6	2.5	0.6	5.7	—	—
1918	6.4	6.8	8.1	21.3	8.6	29.9	1888	1.8	1.8	0.6	4.1	—	—
1917	9.1	10.2	3.4	22.7	6.9	29.6	1887	1.4	3.2	0.6	5.2	—	—
1916	15.3	15.0	3.8	34.1	9.4	43.5	1886	1.4	2.7	0.6	4.7	—	—
1915	17.6	19.9	5.7	43.1	14.5	57.6	1885	4.1	2.3	0.6	6.9	—	—
1914	19.6	24.0	10.4	54.0	17.3	71.3	1884	5.0	2.8	0.7	8.4	—	—
1913	20.7	20.8	9.2	50.6	19.5	70.1	1883	6.2	2.8	0.4	9.3	—	—
1912	17.6	15.1	4.8	37.5	15.7	53.2	1882	4.0	2.2	0.3	6.6	—	—
1911	22.4	13.9	3.1	39.3	11.2	50.5	1881	5.4	2.6	0.5	8.6	—	—
1910	23.6	11.6	2.1	37.3	9.1	46.4	1880	4.0	2.7	0.3	7.0	—	—
1909	21.0	9.4	2.7	33.2	5.8	39.0	1879	2.3	3.7	0.2	6.2	—	—
1908	27.5	11.2	4.6	43.3	5.0	48.3	1878	2.6	4.3	0.3	7.2	—	—
1907	21.0	10.0	3.3	34.4	3.0	37.4	1877	3.1	4.6	0.5	8.3	—	—
1906	6.2	5.8	2.1	14.1	1.3	15.4	1876	4.8	3.2	0.8	8.8	—	—
1905	3.9	7.8	3.5	15.2	0.6	15.8	1875	5.3	2.5	0.7	8.5	—	—
1904	3.6	7.5	2.5	13.6	0.7	14.3	1874	4.4	2.7	0.8	7.9	—	—
1903	1.8	6.6	1.4	9.7	1.1	10.8	1873	7.3	0.8	0.5	8.6	—	—
1902	2.7	5.5	1.3	9.4	1.2	10.6	1872	6.6	0.5	0.7	7.8	—	—
1901	3.2	4.7	1.7	9.6	0.8	10.4	1871	3.0	0.2	0.4	3.6	—	—
							1870	0.8	0.1	0.2	1.1	—	—
							1869	0.3	0.1	0.1	0.5	—	—
							1868	0.4	0.1	0.1	0.7	—	—

[1] For 1901 to 1930, calendar years; for 1868 to 1899, fiscal year ending 30 June of year given.

Series S167. Value of residential construction, constant (1971) dollars, 1926 to 1976
(millions of dollars)

Year	Total	Year	Total	Year	Total
	167		**167**		**167**
1976	6,537	1955	2,779	1935	320
		1954	2,240	1934	291
1975	5,562	1953	1,970	1933	237
1974	5,958	1952	1,502	1932	324
1973	5,986	1951	1,349	1931	627
1972	5,455				
1971	4,834	1950	1,776	1930	681
		1949	1,556	1929	868
1970	3,735	1948	1,345	1928	922
1969	4,189	1947	1,088	1927	873
1968	3,720	1946	1,121	1926	783
1967	3,243				
1966	3,184	1945	1,036		
		1944	716		
1965	3,424	1943	450		
1964	3,275	1942	416		
1963	2,805	1941	534		
1962	2,718				
1961	2,615	1940	463		
		1939	483		
1960	2,639	1938	442		
1959	3,199	1937	426		
1958	3,123	1936	361		
1957	2,488				
1956	2,797				

S168-180. New residential construction, by component, 1926 to 1976
(millions of dollars)

Year	Singles	Doubles and duplexes	Rows	Apartments	Sub-total	Supplementary costs	Cottages	Conversions	Additions and alterations	Mobile homes	Real estate commissions	Total, national accounts basis[1]	Defence
	168	**169**	**170**	**171**	**172**	**173**	**174**	**175**	**176**	**177**	**178**	**179**	**180**
1976	4,986	474	862	1,902	8,224	345	60	15	1,620	358	1,661	12,283	—
1975	3,741	355	487	1,313	5,896	267	53	11	1,292	296	1,518	9,333	—
1974	3,610	268	350	1,631	5,859	227	54	13	1,261	344	1,041	8,799	—
1973	3,016	244	313	1,529	5,102	187	42	11	1,030	250	789	7,411	—
1972	2,330	233	258	1,389	4,210	165	—	9	764	125	572	5,844	1
1971	1,796	204	227	1,387	3,614	140	—	10	587	—	483	4,834	—
1970	1,367	141	164	1,088	2,760	116	—	11	251	—	377	3,515	—
1969	1,532	154	107	1,224	3,017	124	—	13	230	—	475	3,859	—
1968	1,337	130	93	937	2,497	103	—	13	193	—	465	3,268	3
1967	1,175	127	75	739	2,116	85	—	11	166	—	446	2,822	2
1966	1,095	99	57	676	1,927	90	—	11	151	—	440	2,618	1
1965	1,036	98	58	781	1,973	70	—	7	168	—	426	2,642	2
1964	988	91	36	672	1,787	62	—	9	132	—	401	2,389	2
1963	911	78	37	452	1,478	46	—	11	117	—	314	1,966	—
1962	921	116	23	327	1,387	47	—	11	110	—	311	1,863	3
1961	929	114	16	271	1,330	43	—	10	114	—	304	1,798	3
1960	909	92		347	1,348	49	—	9	116	—	285	1,799	8
1959	1,159	102		373	1,634	78	—	13	110	—	316	2,139	12
1958	1,211	100		375	1,686	100	—	16	104	—	202	2,091	17
1957	999	84		240	1,323	71	—	13	119	—	164	1,671	19
1956	1,092	105		289	1,486	89	—	10	124	—	137	1,827	19
1955	1,071	92		316	1,479	87	—	12	106	—	120	1,788	16
1954	826	61		277	2,952	61	—	12	82	—	104	1,414	9
1953	739	70		232	1,041	51	—	10	79	—	94	1,254	21
1952	595	52		141	788	32	—	9	75	—	80	948	36
1951	537	54		109	700	28	—	9	72	—	77	836	50
1950	—	—	—	—	843				77	—	73	955	38
1949	—	—	—	—	708				58	—	57	798	25
1948	—	—	—	—	581				53	—	51	661	24
1947	—	—	—	—	402				38	—	47	457	30
1946	—	—	—	—	369				37	—	49	418	37
1945	—	—	—	—	297				40	—	35	362	10
1944	—	—	—	—	195				36	—	27	248	10
1943	—	—	—	—	137				23	—	18	150	28
1942	—	—	—	—	126				16	—	13	127	28
1941	—	—	—	—	136				17	—	13	157	9

S168-180. New residential construction, by component, 1926 to 1976 (concluded)
(millions of dollars)

Year	Singles	Doubles and duplexes	Rows	Apart-ments	Sub-total	Supple-mentary costs	Cottages	Conver-sions	Additions and alter-ations	Mobile homes	Real estate com-missions	Total, national accounts basis[1]	Defence
	168	169	170	171	172	173	174	175	176	177	178	179	180
1940	–	–	–	–		99			15	–	10	123	–
1939	–	–	–	–		96			16	–	9	121	–
1938	–	–	–	–		83			16	–	11	110	–
1937	–	–	–	–		81			17	–	10	108	–
1936	–	–	–	–		63			12	–	11	85	–
1935	–	–	–	–		54			12	–	8	74	–
1934	–	–	–	–		46			13	–	8	67	–
1933	–	–	–	–		37			8	–	8	53	–
1932	–	–	–	–		56			9	–	11	76	–
1931	–	–	–	–		123			19	–	18	160	–
1930	–	–	–	–		146			22	–	19	187	–
1929	–	–	–	–		194			24	–	27	245	–
1928	–	–	–	–		199			23	–	26	248	–
1927	–	–	–	–		182			23	–	24	229	–
1926	–	–	–	–		162			22	–	21	205	–

[1] Excludes defence residential construction.

Series S181-189. Dwelling[1] starts by region, 1948 to 1976
(in number)

Year	Atlantic provinces	Quebec	Ontario	Prairie provinces	British Columbia	Canada	Centres of 5,000 and over	Centres of 10,000 and over	Other areas
	181	182	183	184	185	186	187	188	189
1976[2]	20,793	68,748	84,682	61,253	37,727	273,203	–	209,762	63,441
1975	19,538	54,741	79,968	43,057	34,152	231,456	–	181,846	49,610
1974	18,114	51,642	85,503	35,444	31,420	222,123	–	169,437	52,686
1973	21,922	59,550	110,536	38,894	37,627	268,529	–	211,543	56,986
1972	16,502	55,746	102,933	39,416	35,317	249,914	–	206,954	42,960
1971	17,259	51,782	89,980	39,867	34,765	233,653	–	180,948	52,705
1970	12,480	47,118	76,675	26,939	27,316	190,528	–	150,999	39,529
1969	13,780	43,413	81,446	39,956	31,820	210,415	–	169,739	40,676
1968	11,039	46,477	80,375	32,792	26,195	196,878	–	162,267	34,611
1967	8,380	37,718	68,121	25,804	24,100	164,123	–	131,858	32,265
1966	8,016	35,911	52,355	20,439	17,753	134,474	–	108,329	26,145
1965	8,944	44,437	66,767	25,019	21,398	166,565	–	135,218	31,347
1964	9,387	43,194	65,617	25,795	21,665	165,658	–	133,562	32,096
1963	6,962	43,391	55,957	24,985	17,329	148,624	–	118,512	30,112
1962	7,443	40,152	44,306	24,302	13,892	130,095	96,598	102,008	28,087
1961	8,523	34,215	48,144	23,525	11,170	125,577	92,741	–	32,836
1960	8,125	28,589	42,282	17,858	12,004	108,858	76,687	–	32,171
1959	8,127	36,265	54,158	26,104	16,691	141,345	105,991	–	35,354
1958	7,000	46,324	63,753	28,256	19,299	164,632	121,695	–	42,937
1957	6,471	34,533	47,739	19,477	14,120	122,340	84,875	–	37,465
1956	8,018	35,999	48,712	19,645	14,937	127,311	87,309	–	40,002
1955	7,759	39,852	53,456	21,595	15,614	138,276	97,386	–	40,890
1954	6,082	29,958	46,382	21,502	9,603	113,527	89,755	–	23,772
1953	5,921	30,249	38,873	18,776	8,590	102,409	80,313	–	22,096
1952	4,720	26,355	30,016	15,044	7,111	83,246	63,443	–	19,803
1951	3,562	21,193	27,349	10,779	5,696	68,579	47,374	–	21,205
1950	7,451	28,515	33,430	15,599	7,536	92,531	68,599	–	23,932
1949	6,023	24,196	34,023	16,565	9,702	90,509	58,370	–	32,139
1948	5,712	24,192	29,976	17,891	11,633	90,194	57,671	–	32,523

[1] Excludes mobile homes.   [2] Unrevised.

Series S190-194. Dwelling starts[1,2] by type, 1949 to 1976

Year	Single detached	Semi-detached	Row	Apartment and other	Total
	190	**191**	**192**	**193**	**194**
1976	134,313	15,890	33,676	89,324	273,203
1975	123,929	15,403	21,763	70,361	231,456
1974	122,143	11,023	14,932	74,025	222,123
1973	131,552	13,235	17,291	106,451	268,529
1972	115,570	13,649	16,980	103,715	249,914
1971	98,056	13,751	15,659	106,187	233,653
1970	70,749	10,826	17,055	91,898	190,528
1969	78,404	10,373	10,721	110,917	210,415
1968	75,339	10,114	8,042	103,383	196,878
1967	72,534	9,939	7,392	74,258	164,123
1966	70,642	7,281	5,000	51,551	134,474
1965	75,441	7,924	5,306	77,894	166,565
1964	77,079	8,706	4,755	75,118	165,658
1963	77,158	7,891	3,895	59,680	148,624
1962	74,443	10,975	3,742	40,935	130,095
1961	76,430	11,650	1,864	35,633	125,577
1960	67,171	9,699	2,301	29,687	108,858
1959	92,178	10,468	1,908	36,791	141,345
1958	104,508	10,713	2,457	46,954	164,632
1957	82,955	9,272	2,214	27,899	122,340
1956	90,620	9,441	2,263	24,987	127,311
1955	99,003	10,606	1,909	26,758	138,276
1954	78,574	6,498	1,000	27,455	113,527
1953	70,782	7,202	553	23,872	102,409
1952	60,696	5,360	299	16,891	83,246
1951	53,002	5,658	54	9,865	68,579
1950	68,675	8,664	631	14,561	92,531
1949	71,425	7,536	—	11,548	90,509

[1] Excludes mobile homes.   [2] Unrevised.

Series S195-197. Mobile home shipments, 1967 to 1976
(in units)

Year	Domestic production	Imports	Total units	Year	Domestic production	Imports	Total units
	195	**196**	**197**		**195**	**196**	**197**
1976	19,149	2,878	22,027				
1975	21,713	3,476	25,189	1970	9,239	2,948[1]	12,187
1974	27,825	4,400	32,225	1969	9,151	3,602[1]	12,753
1973	23,727	3,835	27,562	1968	6,302	2,848[1]	9,150
1972	19,844	4,695	24,539	1967	4,362	2,284[1]	6,646
1971	15,284	3,886	19,170				

[1] Estimated.

Series S198-202. Dwelling starts by type, 1921 to 1950
(thousands of units)

Year	Dwellings in one to three unit buildings[1]			Other	Total	Year	Dwellings in one to three unit buildings[1]			Other	Total
	Urban	Rural	Total				Urban	Rural	Total		
	198	**199**	**200**	**201**	**202**		**198**	**199**	**200**	**201**	**202**
1950	—	—	91.6	15.2	106.8	1935	11.4	8.3	19.7	2.5	22.2
1949	—	—	87.0	11.5	98.6	1934	10.0	7.3	17.2	2.1	19.4
1948	—	—	86.4	9.3	95.7	1933	8.4	6.1	14.6	1.5	16.1
1947	—	—	59.4	8.3	67.7	1932	8.8	6.4	15.1	1.7	16.8
1946	—	—	60.5	6.4	66.9	1931	17.2	12.5	29.7	8.3	38.0
1945	—	—	64.6	6.8	71.5	1930	20.1	14.6	34.7	6.6	41.3
1944	—	—	42.2	7.6	49.8	1929	24.9	18.1	43.1	8.4	51.4
1943	—	—	42.6	3.3	45.9	1928	22.8	16.6	39.3	14.9	54.2
1942	—	—	51.4	3.2	54.6	1927	23.5	17.1	40.6	15.0	55.6
1941	—	—	55.1	3.7	58.8	1926	22.1	16.1	38.2	11.1	49.4
1940	20.5	15.0	35.5	4.4	39.9	1925	21.2	15.4	36.7	6.8	43.4
1939	21.6	15.7	37.3	5.0	42.2	1924	21.2	15.4	36.6	5.6	42.3
1938	18.3	13.3	31.7	5.0	36.6	1923	20.5	14.9	35.4	5.4	40.8
1937	18.0	13.1	31.0	3.5	34.6	1922	22.6	16.5	39.1	4.3	43.5
1936	13.4	9.8	23.2	2.5	25.7	1921	17.4	12.7	30.1	3.8	33.9

[1] For 1941 to 1950, dwellings in one and two unit buildings.

Series S203-205. Dwelling starts by area, 1868 to 1920
(thousands of dwelling units)

Year	Farm	Non-farm	Total	Year	Farm	Non-farm	Total
	203	**204**	**205**		**203**	**204**	**205**
1920	7.9	23.2	31.1	1895	3.0	7.6	10.7
1919	7.7	22.8	30.6	1894	2.7	8.4	11.0
1918	11.3	12.3	23.6	1893	3.8	12.0	15.8
1917	10.5	13.0	23.5	1892	3.5	17.5	21.0
1916	8.0	14.8	22.8	1891	2.5	19.5	22.0
1915	5.6	15.6	21.3	1890	4.1	16.1	20.2
1914	6.2	37.7	44.0	1889	4.5	17.6	22.1
1913	6.7	57.1	63.7	1888	5.2	16.2	21.4
1912	7.7	68.6	76.3	1887	4.2	13.8	18.0
1911	13.8	57.7	71.5	1886	5.9	9.6	15.6
1910	30.9	48.9	79.8	1885	6.3	6.6	12.9
1909	23.6	37.4	61.0	1884	6.1	5.0	11.1
1908	17.0	25.9	42.9	1883	5.0	3.2	8.2
1907	19.3	32.0	51.3	1882	7.8	3.6	11.4
1906	18.0	33.7	51.7	1881	9.1	5.8	14.9
1905	24.4	27.7	52.2	1880	11.4	7.9	19.3
1904	19.7	21.3	40.9	1879	9.7	6.3	16.0
1903	15.9	17.1	33.0	1878	9.5	5.8	15.3
1902	11.9	13.2	25.1	1877	11.0	5.7	16.7
1901	7.7	11.8	19.4	1876	9.9	8.1	18.0
1900	6.2	10.1	16.4	1875	8.1	12.1	20.2
1899	6.6	13.0	19.7	1874	10.7	14.1	24.8
1898	4.9	13.1	18.0	1873	5.7	12.9	18.5
1897	3.4	11.8	15.2	1872	3.7	12.3	15.9
1896	2.7	9.0	11.7	1871	7.4	15.4	22.7
				1870	6.2	11.6	17.8
				1869	4.2	9.0	13.2
				1868	2.3	11.2	13.5

Series S206-219. Dwelling starts by principal source of financing and structural type, 1960 to 1976
(dwelling units)

Year	Single detached							Other structural types						
	Federal funds		Institutional funds			Other	Total	Federal funds		Institutional funds			Other	Total
	NHA loans under sections 58 and 59[1]	Other	Loans under NHA	Conventional loans	Total			NHA loans under sections 58 and 59[1]	Other	Loans under NHA	Conventional loans	Total		
	206	207	208	209	210	211	212	213	214	215	216	217	218	219
1976	145	6,202	29,008	50,523	79,531	48,435	134,313	122	20,793	64,875	21,253	86,128	31,847	138,890
1975	125	14,394	18,683	46,831	65,514	43,896	123,929	2	30,363	28,449	20,074	48,523	28,639	107,527
1974	662	12,129	10,903	49,900	60,803	48,549	122,143	91	20,806	20,143	25,100	45,243	33,840	99,980
1973	635	8,168	24,762	51,355	76,117	46,632	131,552	153	23,314	50,707	42,286	92,993	20,517	136,977
1972	1,964	10,355	39,022	30,339	69,361	33,890	115,570	1,461	26,430	57,011	33,911	90,922	15,531	134,344
1971	2,776	7,751	34,891	20,615	55,506	32,023	98,056	2,132	31,707	52,911	35,010	87,921	13,837	135,597
1970	6,423	5,588	20,570	14,786	35,356	23,382	70,749	3,499	44,141	29,042	25,469	54,511	17,628	119,779
1969	8,335	3,645	16,597	25,504	42,101	24,323	78,404	1,388	16,509	39,048	60,176	99,224	14,890	132,011
1968	9,231	3,015	14,013	21,668	35,681	27,412	75,339	2,076	12,379	34,529	59,258	93,787	13,297	121,539
1967	24,313	2,902	4,532	17,912	22,444	22,875	72,534	9,549	8,561	16,297	46,771	63,068	10,411	91,589
1966	27,839	2,409	4,195	16,392	20,587	19,807	70,642	5,488	5,213	8,243	38,816	47,059	6,072	63,832
1965	23,276	1,990	8,397	22,115	30,512	19,663	75,441	4,672	2,722	15,775	66,554	82,329	1,401	91,124
1964	22,234	1,672	11,954	18,597	30,551	22,622	77,079	4,485	2,893	14,164	66,493	80,657	544	88,579
1963	17,146	2,739	19,459	17,170	36,629	20,644	77,158	2,238	3,146	9,046	54,813	63,859	2,223	71,466
1962	12,590	2,772	22,074	13,892	35,966	23,115	74,443	1,100	3,366	9,716	40,322	..	1,148	55,652
1961	18,383	2,583	21,440	12,907	34,347	21,117	76,430	1,918	4,730	13,894	25,409	..	3,196	49,147
1960	11,685	1,250	13,150	13,344	26,494	27,742	67,171	723	3,066	5,773	26,772	..	5,353	41,687

[1] Excludes low income housing.

Series S220-224. Housing stock at census dates, 1871 to 1951
(thousands of dwelling units)

Year	Occupied dwelling units				Vacant	Year	Occupied dwelling units				Vacant
	Temporary	Institutions and hotels	Other	Total			Temporary	Institutions and hotels	Other	Total	
	220	221	222	223	224		220	221	222	223	224
1951[1]	..	11.5[2]	3,409.3	3,420.8	112.9	1901	29.5	2.0	998.4	1,029.9	27.6[5]
1941[3]	23.7	8.9	2,565.4	2,598.0	62.0	1891	22.1	1.7	853.8	877.6	50.6[5]
1931[3]	11.9	8.8	2,206.3	2,227.0	50.0[4]	1881	14.7	1.4	736.9	753.0	45.8[5]
1921	23.7	3.8	1,777.8	1,805.3	40.9	1871	12.4	1.1	592.8	606.3	27.4[5]
1911	35.7	3.2	1,393.6	1,432.5	52.2[5]						

[1] Includes Newfoundland but excludes the Yukon Territory and the Northwest Territories.
[2] Includes military and industrial camps.
[3] Excludes the Yukon Territory and the Northwest Territories.
[4] Urban only.
[5] Excludes prairie vacancies.

Series S225-231. Dwelling units completed, urban structural conversions, urban demolitions and stock of dwellings at year end occupied by tenure, and vacant,[1] 1956 to 1976
(thousands of dwelling units)

Year	Completions	Structural conversions	Demolitions	Stock of dwellings at year end			
				Vacant	Owned	Rented	Total
	225	226	227	228	229	230	231
1976	236.2	1.9	11.9	400.3	4,361.8	2,749.5	7,488.6
1975	217.0	2.1	11.7	377.5	4,210.0	2,698.3	7,267.1
1974	257.2	3.4	14.6	356.0	4,063.6	2,659.9	7,065.0
1973	246.6	2.4	16.0	336.0	3,922.5	2,576.3	6,824.3
1972	232.2	2.3	15.3	317.3	3,786.4	2,499.4	6,596.8
1971	132.4	1.6	8.3	299.9	3,655.2	2,430.2	6,383.1
1970	175.8	2.6	11.8	283.6	3,552.5	2,352.6	6,188.7
1969	195.8	2.8	14.4	268.5	3,485.6	2,249.4	6,003.4
1968	171.0	2.9	14.7	254.3	3,418.6	2,127.5	5,800.5
1967	149.2	2.7	16.4	241.2	3,351.7	2,029.8	5,622.7
1966	91.4	1.5	9.4	228.9	3,284.8	1,955.0	5,468.7
1965	153.0	1.9	19.6	219.1	3,224.3	1,864.4	5,307.7
1964	151.0	2.4	19.7	212.2	3,172.6	1,784.1	5,168.9
1963	128.2	2.6	20.2	205.6	3,121.0	1,705.2	5,031.7
1962	126.6	3.0	15.0	199.4	3,069.3	1,649.0	4,917.6
1961	77.7	1.8	6.5	193.4	3,017.7	1,588.4	4,799.4
1960	123.8	2.5	8.7	184.4	2,969.8	1,521.7	4,676.0
1959	145.7	3.2	9.8	140.8	2,923.9	1,481.3	4,546.0
1958	146.7	4.5	10.6	138.2	2,833.4	1,423.0	4,394.6
1957	117.3	4.0	9.9	129.7	2,747.0	1,364.8	4,241.5
1956	91.3	2.1	5.8	121.1	2,267.7	1,319.9	4,117.8
1956[2]	—	—	—	116.8	2,615.3	1,290.9	4,023.0

[1] All series exclude mobile homes, and before 1961 exclude the Yukon Territory and the Northwest Territories.   [2] Stock at census date (June 1).

Series S232-245. Apartment vacancy rates, by area and newly completed but unoccupied dwellings by type, 1957 to 1977

Year	Vacancy rates in privately-initiated apartment buildings of six units and over by selected metropolitan area										Newly completed but unoccupied dwellings by type			
	Halifax	Quebec	Montreal	Ottawa-Hull	Toronto	Winnipeg	Calgary	Edmonton	Van-couver	Average[3]	Single detached, semi-detached and duplex dwellings[1]		Apartment and row dwellings[2]	
											Number[4]	As percentage of year's newly occupied	Number[4]	As percentage of year's completions
	232	233	234	235	236	237	238	239	240	241	242	243	244	245
1977[5]	1.5	1.9	3.6	2.2	1.0	1.9	0.1	0.1	2.5	2.3	10,494	..	15,735	..
1976[5]	1.4	0.7	1.3	3.4	1.2	1.4	0.1	—	0.7	1.3	8,229[6]	10.4[6]	9,766[6]	14.4[6]
1975[5]	1.8	1.4	0.7	2.7	1.8	2.1	0.4	0.3	0.1	1.2	5,222[6]	6.1[6]	9,825[6]	14.1[6]
1974[4]	2.3	1.6	1.2	2.8	1.1	1.7	1.1	0.8	0.1	1.2	6,182[6]	8.1[6]	10,789[6]	11.6[6]
1974[7]	2.7	4.7	2.6	3.6	1.0	2.9	5.7	5.5	0.3	2.5	—	—	—	—
1973[7]	2.5	5.3	3.8	2.4	2.1	4.1	8.6	8.3	1.0	3.4	2,659[6]	3.2[6]	8,666[6]	9.5[6]
1972[7]	4.8	6.5	5.7	2.6	3.3	5.4	8.9	7.6	2.4	4.5	4,974[6]	6.8[6]	10,272[6]	10.9[6]
1971[7]	4.1	4.8	7.2	2.1	3.0	3.5	10.7	6.3	4.1	5.0	4,440[8]	8.2[8]	9,316[8]	11.2[8]
1970[7]	2.6	3.8	8.2	2.2	2.8	2.6	5.8	5.7	2.7	5.0	6,571[8]	17.0[8]	10,613[8]	12.8[8]
1969[7]	0.5	2.8	7.6	1.7	2.7	1.6	1.7	3.7	1.2	4.0	5,256[8]	10.4[8]	13,739[8]	15.0[8]
1968[7]	0.5	2.2	5.0	1.5	1.5	1.6	1.3	2.8	1.3	2.7	4,414[8]	9.0[8]	12,245[8]	16.6[8]
1967[7]	2.8	2.2	1.2	2.1	1.2	1.7	1.6	2.8	1.0	1.4	4,502[8]	9.1[8]	6,960[8]	12.2[8]
1966[7]	3.8	4.8	4.5	7.6	1.0	4.1	5.8	2.8	1.5	3.2	2,928[9]	5.9[9]	8,123[9]	11.5[9]
1965[7]	5.4	—	—	9.1	1.6	4.9	8.0	6.5	4.0	4.5	3,551[9]	7.0[9]	7,777[9]	13.9[9]
1964[7]	4.4	—	—	8.2	2.8	5.6	11.6	13.0	4.7	5.5	3,446[9]	6.7[9]	8,795[9]	15.3[9]
1963[7]	4.9	—	—	—	4.4	3.7	14.4	9.2	4.2	6.1	4,066[9]	8.5[9]	6,196[9]	14.6[9]
1962	—	—	—	—	—	—	—	—	—	—	5,330[9]	10.0[9]	—	—
1961	—	—	—	—	—	—	—	—	—	—	4,223	8.7	—	—

Series S232-245. Apartment vacancy rates, by area and newly completed but unoccupied dwellings by type, 1957 to 1977 (concluded)

Year	Vacancy rates in privately-initiated apartment buildings of six units and over by selected metropolitan area										Newly completed but unoccupied dwellings by type			
	Halifax	Quebec	Montreal	Ottawa-Hull	Toronto	Winnipeg	Calgary	Edmonton	Van-couver	Average[3]	Single detached, semi-detached and duplex dwellings[1]		Apartment and row dwellings[2]	
											Number[4]	As percentage of year's newly occupied	Number[4]	As percentage of year's completions
	232	233	234	235	236	237	238	239	240	241	242	243	244	245
1960	–	–	–	–	–	–	–	–	–	–	4,473	9.1	–	–
1959	–	–	–	–	–	–	–	–	–	–	3,491	5.7	–	–
1958	–	–	–	–	–	–	–	–	–	–	3,213	5.1	–	–
1957	–	–	–	–	–	–	–	–	–	–	2,764	5.5	–	–

[1] Census metropolitan area rates weighted by units. Coverage increases over time.
[2] Census metropolitan areas.
[3] Census metropolitan areas, large urban centres and census agglomerations of 50,000 and over.
[4] Data relate to the month of December.

[5] Apartment vacancy rate data relate to the month of October.
[6] Data based on 1971 Census area definition.
[7] Apartment vacancy rate data relate to the month of June.
[8] Data based on 1966 Census area definition.
[9] Data based on 1961 Census area definition.

Series S246. Non-farm vacancy rates, 1921 to 1949

Year	Vacancy rate	Year	Vacancy rate	Year	Vacancy rate
	246		246		246
1949	1.6	1940	1.8	1930	4.1
1948	1.6	1939	2.6	1929	4.4
1947	1.6	1938	2.6	1928	4.7
1946	1.6	1937	2.7	1927	5.1
		1936	3.3	1926	5.2
1945	1.6				
1944	1.6	1935	3.7	1925	5.7
1943	1.6	1934	4.9	1924	6.3
1942	1.7	1933	6.7	1923	5.6
1941	1.8	1932	6.7	1922	2.7
		1931	4.7	1921	2.7

Series S247-253. Net mortgage loans approved for new housing under the Dominion Housing Act and National Housing Acts, by lender and type of loan, 1935 to 1976
(series S247-252 in dwelling units; series S253 in number)

Year	Approved lenders	Central Mortgage and Housing Corporation				Total	Hostel beds
		Market housing		Other	Total		
		Sections 34.15, 58 and 59	Section 15				
	247	248	249	250	251	252	253
1976	93,665	2,799	—	19,065	21,864	115,529	4,244
1975	74,937	16,717	10,150	16,841	43,708	118,645	6,836
1974	20,098	10,856	2,015	14,765	27,636	47,734	6,088
1973	68,530	6,342	4,311	12,035	22,688	91,218	5,142
1972	98,524	6,045	8,470	16,855	31,370	129,894	9,184
1971	97,647	13,261	11,059	23,075	47,395	145,042	11,700
1970	50,936	24,170	19,440	21,543	65,153	116,089	12,610
1969	45,581	7,795	7,364	19,128	34,287	79,868	17,235
1968	59,205	14,343	1,956	11,137	27,436	86,641	14,119
1967	25,913	33,132	—	9,912	43,044	68,957	12,628
1966	10,291	30,672	—	5,403	36,075	46,366	5,871
1965	24,936	29,793	70	2,451	32,314	57,250	6,965
1964	26,959	26,820	1,717	144	28,681	55,640	8,522
1963	30,085	22,515	2,094	—	24,609	54,694	5,197
1962	32,437	13,223	1,328	—	14,551	46,988	5,120
1961	36,810	20,302	3,326	—	23,628	60,438	2,231
1960	21,156	13,863	1,591	—	15,454	36,610	30
1959	25,082	27,792	4,518	-82	32,228	57,310	92
1958	45,716	30,246	6,282	-75	36,453	82,169	—
1957	23,987	20,409	4,124	416	24,949	48,936	464
1956	38,611	745	1,620	290	2,655	41,266	—
1955	63,238	721	1,423	56	2,200	65,438	—
1954	47,362	212	2,291	454	2,957	42,716	—
1953	30,873	3,373	1,295	3,073	7,741	38,614	—
1952	27,488	2,395	841	3,599	6,835	34,323	—
1951	17,742	376	174	991	1,541	19,283	—
1950	37,478	476	94	4,232	4,802	42,280	—
1949	19,847	289	144	4,886	5,319	25,166	—
1948	18,428	127	—	220	347	18,775	—
1947	10,681	72	—	180	252	10,933	—
1946	8,378	—	—	3,449	3,449	11,827	—
1945	4,980	—	—	—	—	5,387	—
1944	1,393	—	—	—	—	—	—
1943	1,721	—	—	—	—	—	—
1942	1,093	—	—	—	—	—	—
1941	4,323	—	—	—	—	—	—
1940	5,621	—	—	—	—	—	—
1939	5,973	—	—	—	—	—	—
1938	3,894	—	—	—	—	—	—
1937	1,817	—	—	—	—	—	—
1936	788	—	—	—	—	—	—
1935	97	—	—	—	—	—	—

Series S254-259. Net mortgage loans approved for existing housing under the National Housing Act (1954), 1961-64 to 1976
(dwelling units)

Year	Approved lenders	CMHC			Total	Hostel beds
		Sections 34.15, 58, 59	Other	Total		
	254	255	256	257	258	259
1976	35,454	194	1,464	1,658	37,112	773
1975	43,675	282	1,660	1,942	45,617	1,002
1974	23,803	9,101	1,735	10,836	34,639	1,112
1973	22,449	2,658	445	3,103	25,552	345
1972	20,874	1,694	866	2,560	23,434	729
1971	14,267	1,987	745	2,732	16,999	1,062
1970	5,344	2,049	544	2,593	7,937	329
1969	685	3,789	1,548	5,337	6,022	1,976
1968	5	3,660	634	4,294	4,299	1,802
1967	5	3,746	416	4,162	4,167	523
1966	—	8	1,337	1,345	1,345	369
1965	2	—	1,602	1,602	1,604	—
1964[1]	—	—	154	154	154	220

[1] Covers period 1961 to 1964.

Series S260-271. Mortgage loans on new residential property approved by lending institutions, by type of lender, by type of loan, 1948 to 1976
(millions of dollars)

Year	NHA financed Chartered banks	Life insurance companies	Trust companies	Loan companies	Other companies	Total	Conventionally financed Chartered banks	Life insurance companies	Trust companies	Loan companies	Other companies	Total
	260	261	262	263	264	265	266	267	268	269	270	271
1976	1,074.2	420.9	1,014.4	508.8	227.4	3,245.7	561.9	560.5	896.2	451.5	44.9	2,515.1
1975	772.9	270.5	749.3	402.1	102.7	2,297.6	799.3	291.9	737.2	501.0	54.1	2,383.5
1974	339.8	88.2	245.7	66.7	26.4	766.9	667.9	314.3	623.0	480.7	34.5	2,120.3
1973	573.0	216.3	520.8	123.3	67.4	1,500.8	650.5	372.0	723.8	432.7	33.5	2,212.5
1972	799.4	193.8	481.3	238.1	97.2	1,809.8	226.1	220.3	426.2	290.2	32.9	1,195.6
1971	696.5	185.8	429.6	245.7	88.4	1,646.1	154.6	166.7	312.4	156.2	34.5	824.4
1970	338.2	74.7	299.5	84.6	60.8	857.8	40.9	102.5	245.0	115.5	35.0	538.9
1969	234.2	118.2	236.4	66.7	45.2	700.6	50.2	260.3	413.9	200.8	64.2	989.5
1968	250.0	251.4	238.8	55.6	36.3	832.2	82.5	362.4	289.4	166.1	62.1	962.5
1967	85.0	88.1	161.7	6.1	14.9	355.8	42.5	405.5	140.8	131.1	25.2	745.1
1966	—	85.2	101.7	4.0	0.4	191.3	—	373.8	42.4	116.2	41.8	574.2
1965	6.2	113.5	194.3	6.0	0.2	320.2	—	576.8	121.4	150.4	53.5	902.1
1964	9.3	162.7	171.2	9.1	0.4	352.7	—	484.4	101.9	184.1	42.0	812.3
1963	—	217.9	145.3	21.2	0.8	385.2	—	398.4	104.3	130.2	19.3	652.2
1962	—	234.5	147.5	29.0	0.8	411.7	—	298.1	51.2	77.8	23.4	450.6
1961	0.2	257.5	175.3	19.9	0.3	453.2	—	237.5	15.0	62.5	17.6	332.6
1960	1.1	177.0	56.7	5.0	1.8	241.7	—	201.5	31.2	67.9	6.7	307.3
1959	175.4	113.1	11.9	6.8	0.7	307.8	—	238.8	52.5	46.0	5.7	343.0
1958	300.4	171.3	37.6	7.1	2.6	519.0	—	181.2	29.2	66.5	13.6	290.5
1957	173.4	95.8	4.8	3.0	1.0	278.0	—	155.3	32.5	40.8	10.8	239.3
1956	158.4	227.0	24.3	15.8		425.4	—	189.7		65.1		254.9
1955	326.2	271.1	28.4	13.6		639.4	—	157.2		77.8		235.0
1954	158.5	281.8	7.5	16.5		464.3	—	113.1		67.2		180.3
1953	—	246.7	—	9.1		255.7	—	73.1		45.8		118.8
1952	—	210.2	—	8.3		218.6	—	51.7		32.3		84.0
1951	—	134.6		6.4		141.0	—	..		..		95.3
1950	—	259.8		20.2		280.0	—	..		..		30.1
1949	—	115.4		7.3		122.7	—	..		..		89.6
1948	—	101.0		5.7		106.7	—	..		..		..

Series S272-283. Mortgage loans on existing residential property approved, by type of lender, by type of loan, 1948 to 1976
(millions of dollars)

Year	NHA financed Chartered banks	Life insurance companies	Trust companies	Loan companies	Other companies	Total	Conventionally financed Chartered banks	Life insurance companies	Trust companies	Loan companies	Other companies	Total
	272	273	274	275	276	277	278	279	280	281	282	283
1976	542.5	5.8	323.3	331.3	15.8	1,218.5	634.6	196.6	1,725.6	577.9	91.5	3,226.2
1975	543.6	6.5	289.5	417.0	26.6	1,283.3	672.5	183.6	1,518.3	605.5	66.2	3,046.0
1974	302.7	7.3	113.9	170.0	16.5	610.3	596.5	153.8	1,169.9	493.5	50.3	2,464.0
1973	166.6	5.7	122.8	111.0	24.6	430.7	798.9	148.5	1,382.2	455.7	42.6	2,827.9
1972	94.1	4.2	92.8	138.8	10.9	340.7	366.8	105.2	651.3	388.7	42.5	1,554.5
1971	23.1	2.6	59.2	130.3	5.1	220.3	229.8	71.1	552.5	254.5	30.7	1,138.6
1970	3.9	0.8	25.1	49.0	0.5	79.2	110.2	37.9	321.9	136.5	37.4	643.9
1969	0.9	0.1	3.5	5.9	—	10.4	80.1	54.0	350.7	147.0	30.2	662.0
1968	0.1	—	—	—	—	—	96.5	72.8	256.1	131.6	14.8	571.7
1967	—	—	—	—	—	—	101.6	134.9	250.6	150.7	17.0	654.9
1966	—	—	—	—	—	—	—	125.7	191.2	132.5	21.4	470.7
1965	—	—	—	—	—	—	—	198.1	295.6	210.7	44.6	749.0
1964	—	—	—	—	—	—	—	164.0	242.8	189.3	43.5	639.6
1963	—	—	—	—	—	—	—	126.5	155.6	122.8	25.1	430.0
1962	—	—	—	—	—	—	—	117.9	106.3	108.6	25.4	358.2
1961	—	—	—	—	—	—	—	103.4	85.5	88.7	22.6	300.2
1960	—	—	—	—	—	—	—	79.2	58.0	70.1	13.8	221.1
1959	—	—	—	—	—	—	—	95.2	55.4	56.9	8.8	216.3
1958	—	—	—	—	—	—	—	79.0	55.1	62.7	11.0	207.8
1957	—	—	—	—	—	—	—	56.6	37.4	46.0	9.5	149.5
1956	—	—	—	—	—	—	—	..	..	..	..	176.3

Series S272-283. Mortgage loans on existing residential property approved, by type of lender, by type of loan, 1948 to 1976 (concluded)
(millions of dollars)

Year	NHA financed						Conventionally financed					
	Chartered banks	Life insurance companies	Trust companies	Loan companies	Other companies	Total	Chartered banks	Life insurance companies	Trust companies	Loan companies	Other companies	Total
	272	273	274	275	276	277	278	279	280	281	282	283
1955	–	–	–	–	–	–	–	..	..	..	..	182.4
1954	–	–	–	–	–	–	–	..	..	..	..	144.3
1953	–	–	–	–	–	–	–	..	..	..	..	116.8
1952	–	–	–	–	–	–	–	..	..	..	..	118.0
1951	–	–	–	–	–	–	–	..	..	..	..	114.2
1950	–	–	–	–	–	–	–	..	..	..	..	115.2
1949	–	–	–	–	–	–	–	..	..	..	..	97.1
1948	–	–	–	–	–	–	–	..	..	..	..	98.9

Series S284-289. Mortgage loans on non-residential property approved, by type of lender, 1948 to 1976
(millions of dollars)

Year	Chartered banks	Life insurance companies	Trust companies	Loan companies	Other companies	Total
	284	285	286	287	288	289
1976	34.5	984.6	204.7	209.6	–	1,433.5
1975	66.4	758.1	211.5	252.3	1.2	1,289.5
1974	131.3	610.6	251.0	177.6	0.5	1,171.0
1973	205.7	728.6	383.1	200.2	0.2	1,517.7
1972	148.0	519.4	213.7	222.8	0.2	1,104.2
1971	60.7	423.4	249.1	113.6	0.2	847.1
1970	16.5	240.0	188.8	62.3	0.3	507.9
1969	15.8	188.7	172.1	54.1	0.9	431.6
1968	17.4	158.2	114.3	43.9	0.9	334.7
1967	23.7	171.3	109.3	62.7	2.1	369.1
1966	–	219.2	87.7	74.5	0.7	382.1
1965	–	269.4	196.7	113.6	1.5	581.1
1964	–	200.0	180.1	124.4	2.5	507.1
1963	–	160.1	115.0	94.8	2.8	372.7
1962	–	135.0	97.7	76.9	1.1	310.8
1961	–	140.0	59.8	95.8	2.7	297.9
1960	–	130.8	46.2	84.7	1.7	263.3
1959	–	130.1	28.0	57.6	0.3	216.0
1958	–	98.6	20.1	55.1	0.7	174.5
1957	–	70.2	8.1	24.8	0.8	103.9
1956	–	–	–	–	–	141.1
1955	–	–	–	–	–	138.3
1954	–	–	–	–	–	114.9
1953	–	–	–	–	–	89.4
1952	–	–	–	–	–	82.5
1951	–	–	–	–	–	84.0
1950	–	–	–	–	–	98.0
1949	–	–	–	–	–	84.4
1948	–	–	–	–	–	87.6

Series S290-297. National Housing Act Mortgage Insurance Fund, 1955 to 1976
(millions of dollars)

Year	Fees and premiums received	Other income (net)	Total	Claims paid and legal expenses	Other expenses	Total	Total reserves	Insurance in force[1]
	290	291	292	293	294	295	296	297
1976	35.4	43.0	78.4	13.1	2.7	15.8	521.8	15,130
1975	26.6	36.8	63.4	16.9	2.8	19.7	459.3	13,864
1974	20.3	39.9	60.2	19.8	2.7	22.5	415.6	11,915
1973	20.4	57.2	77.5	40.0	1.9	41.9	377.9	11,089
1972	20.2	41.1	61.3	29.3	1.1	30.4	342.3	10,056
1971	16.4	24.1	40.5	7.4	0.6	8.0	311.4	9,225
1970	10.7	18.5	29.2	2.7	0.5	3.2	278.9	8,051
1969	15.0	16.4	31.3	2.4	0.5	2.9	252.8	7,412
1968	14.6	13.9	28.6	2.1	0.6	2.7	224.4	6,732
1967	16.5	14.8	31.3	4.6	0.7	5.3	198.5	6,311
1966	14.3	18.8	33.1	10.4	—	10.4	172.6	5,789
1965	13.5	21.1	34.6	15.4	—	15.4	149.8	5,321
1964	12.1	17.4	29.5	14.7	—	14.7	130.6	4,934
1963	9.9	17.9	27.8	13.9	—	13.9	115.9	4,499
1962	11.6	12.3	23.8	8.6	—	8.6	102.0	4,123
1961	11.0	13.0	24.0	9.8	—	9.8	86.8	3,640
1960	8.5	4.6	13.0	1.5	—	1.5	72.6	3,090
1959	13.1	2.5	15.7	0.3	—	0.3	61.1	2,733
1958	13.8	1.6	15.4	0.1	—	0.1	45.7	2,100
1957	7.3	1.0	8.3	—	—	—	30.4	1,425
1956	9.8	0.5	10.4	—	—	—	22.1	1,083
1955	9.2	0.2	9.4	—	—	—	11.8	529

[1] As at 31 December.

Series S298-310. Sales and purchases of insured National Housing Act mortgages,[1] 1957 to 1976
(millions of dollars)

Year	Chartered banks		Life insurance companies		Trust companies		Loan and other companies		CMHC		Pension funds	Other firms and institutions	
	Sales	Purchases	Sales	Purchases	Sales	Purchases	Sales	Purchases	Sales	Purchases	Purchases	Corporate purchases	Unincorporated purchases
	298	299	300	301	302	303	304	305	306	307	308	309	310
1976	347.0	59.0	0.2	128.5	389.0	62.2	101.2	38.1	—	—	319.5	151.6	78.5
1975	168.0	76.8	0.5	31.2	159.6	40.0	73.5	2.1	—	—	127.4	100.9	23.2
1974	180.2	253.7	1.0	55.4	146.5	33.6	261.7	6.2	—	—	101.1	125.1	14.3
1973	190.0	120.0	—	27.8	71.3	33.3	141.3	48.1	—	2.0	50.9	105.3	15.2
1972	182.7	427.2	—	11.2	38.7	20.2	422.0	14.8	—	—	48.7	115.1	6.2
1971	33.8	28.0	2.1	7.4	22.8	4.4	4.0	0.5	21.4	—	24.3	14.5	5.0
1970	47.9	0.2	4.3	66.3	74.9	1.1	2.8	0.8	—	—	30.5	30.9	0.1
1969	39.9	0.1	17.8	50.3	65.8	—	4.1	3.0	—	—	59.3	14.8	0.1
1968	16.8	2.2	2.9	9.9	23.3	4.3	—	2.0	—	—	8.5	16.0	0.1
1967	1.6	4.9	—	56.3	65.8	1.7	0.6	2.2	—	—	2.1	0.8	—
1966	15.1	19.7	—	33.2	70.0	3.1	3.2	7.7	—	—	23.6	0.2	0.8
1965	0.7	31.6	0.5	25.3	52.2	30.2	2.2	7.5	80.8	—	5.7	35.5	0.6
1964	3.1	46.8	5.0	21.4	58.2	25.8	8.4	10.9	75.3	3.1	17.1	24.9	—
1963	0.2	49.1	1.0	15.6	58.9	24.8	7.9	3.6	61.1	—	23.3	12.3	0.4
1962	0.7	30.6	—	22.1	47.1	21.4	5.9	—	47.9	—	19.6	7.8	0.1
1961	—	18.3	—	11.5	19.3	14.7	2.6	—	40.0	—	4.6	12.8	—
1960	6.3	—	9.0	0.4	4.3	0.8	7.3	6.5	0.4	—	12.9	6.7	—
1959	36.8	—	1.9	3.4	3.4	0.1	0.1	—	0.4	—	38.1	1.0	—
1958	32.5	—	7.8	4.6	4.4	2.3	1.5	—	1.5	—	31.2	9.6	—
1957	41.2	—	8.6	10.3	9.7	0.8	2.1	—	0.6	—	31.2	19.9	—

[1] Data for initial sales and purchases only.

Series S311-322. Selected housing unit cost series, 1951 to 1976
(dollars)

Year	Average cost of new housing excluding land						Average land cost per dwelling unit, NHA		Average value, MLS[1]	Construction cost per square foot, NHA		Average urban cash rent
	Single detached		Doubles	Row	Apartments		Single detached[2]	Apartment[3]		Bungalow[2]	Apartment[3]	
	All	NHA	All	All	All	NHA[2]						
	311	312	313	314	315	316	317	318	319	320	321	322
1976	37,982	30,655	31,523	30,828	23,885	22,739	9,226	3,397	51,252	27.57	22.50	..
1975	33,691	28,246	27,278	27,808	21,770	20,955	7,246	2,464	45,886	25.37	21.62	..
1974	29,631	24,943	23,821	26,011	19,995	16,395	4,867	2,439	41,057	22.62	16.30	..
1973	24,630	20,844	19,922	20,246	16,240	14,752	4,673	2,403	32,306	18.64	14.21	..
1972	21,298	18,588	16,939	16,669	13,800	13,416	4,887	2,001	26,595	16.38	13.17	..
1971	19,700	17,506	15,360	13,140		12,237	4,588	2,000	24,581	15.30	11.28	111
1970	19,984	17,155	14,644	12,322		11,746	4,191	2,064	23,376	14.90	11.93	109
1969	19,357	17,659	14,230	11,368		11,847	4,201	2,466	23,234	14.62	11.65	102
1968	18,246	16,152	13,392	10,663		12,002	3,746	2,196	21,272	13.68	11.42	94
1967	17,475	16,031	12,871	10,188		11,670	3,580	1,853	19,111	13.04	12.09	90
1966	16,680	15,813	12,106	9,913		10,952	3,480	1,901	17,536	12.56	11.59	84
1965	15,477	14,307	11,184	9,115		11,149	3,095	1,590	15,918	11.62	10.71	79
1964	14,598	13,396	10,894	8,421		10,565	3,082	1,650	15,075	11.01	10.77	75
1963	14,131	12,709	10,111	8,528		8,794	2,973	1,277	14,427	10.68	9.33	72
1962	14,098	12,450	9,985	8,006		8,595	2,783	1,125	14,302	10.56	9.58	71
1961	13,615	12,286	9,938	8,286		8,511	2,602	1,259	14,203	10.61	9.44	68
1960	13,519	12,166	9,567	8,060		8,415	2,473	1,346	14,194	10.65	9.16	66
1959	13,002	12,196	9,621	7,503		8,356	2,533	990	14,208	10.78	9.58	65
1958	12,257	12,008	9,075	7,595		8,022	2,471	978	13,822	10.56	8.63	61
1957	12,018	12,018	8,648	7,595		7,501	2,260	992	12,781	10.41	8.43	58
1956	–	11,829	–	–	–	7,373	2,025	879	11,993	10.22	8.22	55
1955	–	11,022	–	–	–	7,591	1,819	793	–	9.81	8.07	53
1954	–	10,731	–	–	–	7,295	1,687	699	–	9.61	8.21	49
1953	–	10,541	–	–	–	–	1,197	–	–	–	–	45
1952	–	10,118	–	–	–	–	1,182	–	–	–	–	42
1951	–	–	–	–	–	–	–	–	–	–	–	37

[1] Average dollar value per multiple Listing Service Transaction.
[2] Includes loans approved on freehold tenure only. Costs are those estimated by owner and builder applicants at time of approval. Land costs reflect the prices paid for lots regardless of the extent of servicing or method of financing.

[3] Subsequent to 1967 includes loans approved on freehold tenure only. Includes low income housing financed under sections 58 and 59. Costs are those estimated by loan applicants.

Series S323-325. Average construction cost of new dwelling units, by type of dwelling, 1921 to 1950
(dollars)

Year	Dwellings in one- and two-unit dwellings[1]		Dwellings in apartment and row buildings	Year	Dwellings in one- and two-unit dwellings[1]		Dwellings in apartment and row buildings
	Urban	All areas			Urban	All areas	
	323	324	325		323	324	325
1950	–	6,464	5,356	1935	3,054	–	2,146
1949	–	5,734	5,420	1934	3,051	–	1,841
1948	–	5,072	5,086	1933	2,868	–	928
1947	–	4,358	4,648	1932	3,281	–	2,112
1946	–	4,421	3,783	1931	3,994	–	2,540
1945	–	3,680	3,623	1930	4,074	–	3,101
1944	–	3,323	2,687	1929	4,482	–	3,783
1943	–	2,393	2,204	1928	4,724	–	3,087
1942	–	2,197	1,954	1927	4,421	–	2,383
1941	3,107	2,359	2,282	1926	4,205	–	2,742
1940	3,023	–	2,232	1925	4,146	–	3,131
1939	2,806	–	2,231	1924	4,031	–	3,194
1938	2,705	–	2,290	1923	4,549	–	3,269
1937	2,946	–	2,355	1922	4,635	–	3,181
1936	3,046	–	2,093	1921	4,407	–	3,497

[1] One- to three-unit buildings, 1921 to 1940.

Series S326-335. Selected housing price series (1971 = 100), 1952 to 1976

Year	Average cost per square foot NHA single detached[1]	Residential building construction input price index[2]	Implicit price index residential construction	New housing price indexes, selected cities[3]						Rental component CPI
				Montreal	Toronto	Ottawa–Hull	Winnipeg	Calgary	Edmonton	
	326	327	328	329	330	331	332	333	334	335
1976	180.6	160.5	187.9	200.9	180.7	192.5	199.8	243.1	245.8	118.9
1975	167.1	144.0	167.7	190.3	171.0	178.3	177.5	195.0	205.3	111.1
1974	149.5	134.7	147.9	177.7	171.6	171.2	163.5	162.3	172.8	105.4
1973	122.2	123.2	123.8	125.8	137.6	138.2	128.4	126.4	132.6	102.6
1972	106.7	110.1	107.7	107.6	110.2	112.7	105.2	110.0	109.1	101.2
1971	100.0	100.0	100.0	100.0	100.0	100.0	100.0	100.0	100.0	100.0
1970	97.4	91.1	94.1	..	98.2	94.7	98.4	93.2	95.8	98.4
1969	95.5	85.1	92.1	..	..	..	94.8	89.5	90.9	95.3
1968	89.1	79.8	87.9	..	..	..	..	..	..	91.7
1967	84.0	74.6	87.0	..	..	..	..	..	..	87.9
1966	80.4	70.0	82.2	..	..	..	..	..	..	85.1
1965	74.7	65.9	77.2	..	..	..	..	..	..	83.7
1964	70.4	62.6	73.0	..	..	..	..	..	..	83.2
1963	67.7	59.6	70.1	..	..	..	..	..	..	82.9
1962	67.1	57.6	68.6	..	..	..	..	..	..	82.6
1961	68.3	56.2	68.8	..	..	..	..	..	..	82.4
1960	69.4	55.9	68.2	..	..	..	..	..	..	82.1
1959	70.6	54.4	66.9	..	..	..	..	..	..	81.7
1958	68.9	52.5	67.0	..	..	..	..	..	..	80.8
1957	67.7	51.2	67.2	..	..	..	..	..	..	79.4
1956	66.6	49.8	65.3	..	..	..	..	..	..	78.0
1955	64.0	48.1	64.3	..	..	..	..	..	..	76.6
1954	62.2	46.8	63.1	..	..	..	..	..	..	74.6
1953	60.4	46.7	63.7	..	..	..	..	..	..	72.1
1952	59.5	45.9	63.1	..	..	..	..	..	..	69.5

[1] Costs are those estimated by loan applicants at time of approval. Includes only approvals for freehold tenure.
[2] Materials and equipment prices are manufacturers new order selling prices. Wage rates are basic rates taken from union contracts.

[3] Selling prices of new houses built by large residential general contractors. Ottawa–Hull and Toronto series refers to single detached, semi-detached and row condominium houses. Other series refer to single detached only.

Section T: Transportation and Communication

Statistics Canada

There was no section chief for this chapter. The work of preparing text and tables was done in the Transportation and Communications Division of Statistics Canada, under the Director, G.E. Clarey. The officers principally responsible for both text and tables were Miss June Forgie and Mr. Murray McRae of that division. Advice in the early stages of the work was given by John Baldwin, Department of Economics, Queen's Univeristy.

The data of this section are in nine subsections as follows: rail transport, (series T1-82); water transport and canal statistics, (series T83-141); roads and road transport, (series T142-194); civil aviation, (series T195-246); oil and gas pipelines, (series T247-250); transportation accident victims (series T251-292); post office statistics, (series T293-314); telecommunications carrier industry, (series T315-352) and radio and television, (series T353-359).

Published sources of data are mainly Statistics Canada publications (formerly Dominion Bureau of Statistics). The following publications are given in the order in which they appear. For rail transport: Statistics Canada, *Railway Transport: Parts I to VI*, (Catalogues 52-207 to 52-212), issues for 1952 to 1975; and its predecessor, *Steam Railways*, for 1946 to 1951; *Canada Year Book*, (Catalogue 11-202), various issues, 1946 to 1975. For water transport: *Shipping seagoing and inland vessels arrived at and departed from Canadian ports*, Water Transport Section, Transportation and Communication Division, Statistics Canada, for 1960 to 1975; for 1971 to 1975, the Saint Lawrence Seaway Development Corporation, *Traffic Report for the St. Lawrence Seaway*, annual issues for 1946 to 1970; Statistics Canada, *Canal Statistics*, (Catalogue 54-201) annual issues, for 1960 to 1969; Saint Lawrence Seaway Development Corporation, 1959 to 1969 *Annual Reports*; Statistics Canada, *Shipping Report, Parts I to V*, (Catalogues 54-202 to 54-207). For road transport: Statistics Canada, *Road and Street Mileage and Expenditure*, (Catalogue 53-201), and its predecessors, *Highway and the Motor Vehicle in Canada* and *Highway Statistics*; *The Motor Vehicle: Parts I to IV*, (Catalogues 53-217 to 53-220); Statistics Canada, *Passenger Bus and Urban Transit*, and its predecessors, (Catalogue 53-215); Statistics Canada, *Motor Carriers - Freight and Household Goods Movers*, (Catalogue 53-222); Statistics Canada, *For-hire Trucking Survey*, (Catalogue 53-224). For Canadian commercial aviation: for 1970 to 1975, Statistics Canada, *Air Carrier Operations in Canada*, (Catalogue 51-002), October-December issues; for 1960 to 1969, *Civil Aviation*, (Catalogue 51-202), annual issues; *Canadian Civil Aircraft Register*, for 1961 to 1975, annual March 31 issues; 'Licensed Civil Airports' from the *Canada Year Book*, various issues 1961 to 1974; *Arriving and Departing Civil Flights at Selected International Airports*, Transport Canada, annual issues from 1960 to 1975; Statistics Canada, *Aircraft Activity Statistics*, formerly *Aircraft Movement Statistics*, (Catalogue 51-203), annual issues. For oil and gas pipelines, for 1969 to 1975, Statistics Canada, *Oil Pipe Line Transport*, (Catalogue 55-201), annual issues; for 1958 to 1968, Statistics Canada, Manufacturing and Primary Industries Division; for 1969 to 1975, Statistics Canada, *Gas Utilities*, (Catalogue 55-002), December issue each year; Statistics Canada, *Gas Utilities: Transport and Distribution Systems*, (Catalogue 57-205), annual issues; for 1960 to 1968, Statistics Canada, Manufacturing and Primary Industries Division; for 1938 to 1967, Statistics Canada, *Railway Transport, Part IV: Operating and Traffic Statistics*, for 1950 to 1967, Statistics Canada, special release of April 1969, "Pipeline Statistics"; for 1938 to 1967, Statistics Canada, *Railway Transport: Part IV, Operating and Traffic Statistics*, (Catalogue 52-210). For transportation accident victims: for 1973 to 1975, *Water Transport Accident Victims*, from Transport Canada, Marine Casualty Investigations, Canadian Coast Guard; for 1946 to 1972, Statistics Canada, *Water Transportation*, (Catalogue 54-205), annual issues; Statistics Canada, *Motor Vehicle Traffic Accidents*, (Catalogue 53-306), annual issues; Statistics Canada, *Civil Aviation*, (Catalogue 51-202), annual issues; for 1970 to 1975, Transport Canada, *Aviation Safety Investigation*; for 1946 to 1947, the publication, *Transport Canada*. The Post Office series: for 1961 to 1975, were provided by R.W. Jones, Comptroller, Post Office Department, and are based upon the material collected in the department and presented in the *Annual Report* of the Canada Post Office. For telecommunications carrier industry: Statistics Canada, *Telephone Statistics*, (Catalogue 56-203), issues for the years 1961 to 1975; long distance rates based on records of Bell Canada; Statistics Canada, *Telecommunications Statistics*, formerly *Telegraph and Cable Statistics*, (Catalogue 56-201), annual, from 1961 to 1975. For radio and television: Statistics Canada, *Radio and Television Broadcasting*, (Catalogue 56-204), annual issues.

Rail Transport (Series T1-82)

General note

The systematic collection of railway statistics began in Canada for the year ending 30 June 1875, following the enactment of the Railway Statistics Act in 1875 which required all railways to furnish annual statements to the Department of Railways and Canals. Annual collection of data has continued to the present.

J.L. McDougall, the author of the chapter on Transportation and Communication in the first edition of *Historical Statistics of Canada*, (*HSC I*) provided a superlative treatment of the statistics for the earlier years of rail transport and the reader is referred to page 516-7 of the first edition.

Since World War II, rail transport has lost its absolute dominance of internal transport in Canada, with the development of other modes of transport and the infrastructures necessary to support them.

There have been great changes in the railway industry itself. Steam engines have gone and unit trains have arrived. Piggyback, containers and all manner of specialized equipment for the transport of freight have been developed, whereas intercity passenger traffic has undergone a steady decline.

These new trends in rail transport began around 1946 and the following statistical series in general cover the period 1946 to 1975. The exception is the series Railway Accident Victims, T251-260, which begins in 1907 and is included in the new section on Transportation Accidents T251-292. For earlier years, as noted above, the reader is referred to *HSC I*.

T1-4. Railways, capital liability, 1946 to 1975

SOURCE: for 1948 to 1975, Statistics Canada, *Railway Transport: Part I*, issues from 1952 to 1975; for 1946 to 1947, *Steam Railways: Part III*, 1951 issue, page 143.

Statistics show railway capital at 31 December.

Under the terms of the Canadian National Railways Capital Revision Act the 'Government of Canada - Shareholders' Account' formerly called 'Dominion Government - Proprietors' Equity' was increased by $736,385,405 of the Canadian National Railways (CN) 4 per cent non-cumulative preferred stock and the 'Government of Canada - Loans and Debentures' account was reduced by a similar amount. These changes took effect 1 January 1952.

During 1963 there was a decrease in capital stock and in the funded debt of Canadian railways. Capital stock declined 0.8 per cent to $4,975 million while funded debt guaranteed by the federal government dropped $252 million.

T5-18. Railways, miles of line in operation, rolling stock, locomotives, cars in passenger and company service, 1946 to 1975

T19-27. Railways, rolling stock, freight cars in service, 1946 to 1975

SOURCE: for 1948 to 1975, Statistics Canada, *Railway Transport: Part I*, issues from 1952 to 1975; for 1946 to 1947, *Statistics of Steam Railways*, annual issues for 1946 and 1947.

In series T11, the 1948 figure includes 84 diesel locomotives formerly included in switching, and therefore under steam (series T10) in 1947. By 1956, when diesels were first differentiated by purpose, there were 850 road-switcher units and 516 yard-switcher units included in the diesel total of 1,895.

The CN completed their dieselization program during 1960, retiring all remaining steam locomotives from service, while the Canadian Pacific Limited (CP) had only 364 steam units to retire at the end of the year. Steam locomotives in Canadian service at the close of 1960 numbered 403 units, down from 1,514 units in 1959 and 2,849 units in 1956. Diesel units, on the other hand, totalled 3,308 in 1960, up from 3,155 a year previous and 1,895 in 1956.

By 1961, steam locomotives declined to 197 units; diesels remained virtually unchanged at 3,309.

A year later, the conversion from steam locomotives to diesel locomotives in the transportation service of Canadian railways was completed. Some steam locomotives remained in existence but were used only in work train or yard service with the last remaining coal burning steam locomotive retired in 1965.

In 1952 freight cars were reclassified, the number of classes was enlarged, and the new classification was extended back to 1948. The old classes 'flat', 'stock', 'tank'

and 'refrigerator' remained unchanged. 'Box' cars were separated into 'automobile' and 'box'. 'Coal' cars were separated into 'ballast', 'gondola', 'hopper' and 'ore' cars, and most of the 'other' cars were distributed over the same four classes.

To economize in space here, the old classes were continued after 1948, though there remain few cars in the 'other' group; but the numbers in the new classes are shown below. From the data of the new classification, series T21 was obtained by adding box and automobile cars together and series T24 by adding ballast, gondola, hopper and ore cars. The new figure published for box cars can be found by subtracting the number of automobile cars from the box car total as shown in series T21.

Number of freight cars in service in new classes, on 31 December, 1948 to 1975

	Ballast	Gondola	Hopper	Ore	Automobile (Rack)
1975	2,199	21,370	29,287	7,731	2,776
1974	2,296	20,414	27,398	7,151	2,617
1973	2,363	20,464	26,365	7,371	2,579
1972	2,383	20,450	25,539	7,241	2,607
1971	2,408	20,354	25,175	6,819	2,280
1970	2,639	20,975	24,496	6,735	2,178
1969	2,856	20,721	22,480	6,684	4,737
1968	2,863	20,438	21,660	6,722	4,551
1967	2,862	20,633	21,077	6,742	4,462
1966	2,877	19,997	19,787	6,605	4,367
1965	2,906	19,335	18,161	6,459	3,696
1964	2,977	19,049	16,989	6,477	6,907
1963	3,009	19,323	16,031	6,337	7,113
1962	3,054	19,729	16,089	6,379	7,204
1961	3,113	20,168	15,571	5,892	7,225
1960	3,128	20,310	15,578	5,930	7,249
1959	3,140	20,428	15,601	5,964	7,270
1958	2,708	20,522	15,493	6,004	6,722
1957	2,646	19,904	13,788	5,967	6,733
1956	2,156	19,052	12,840	5,465	6,370
1955	2,378	18,592	12,247	2,559	7,406
1954	2,245	18,469	12,129	2,555	7,439
1953	1,940	17,603	11,598	1,969	7,560
1952	1,847	16,552	10,083	1,878	7,330
1951	1,803	14,098	8,897	1,902	6,396
1950	1,862	13,922	8,903	1,954	6,087
1949	1,772	14,135	9,100	1,902	6,075
1948	1,705	13,114	7,996	1,923	5,057

SOURCE:
Railway Transport part I, 1960-1975 annual issues and similar tables in **Railway Transport** for earlier years.

T28-38. Railways, revenue train mileage, engine mileage and freight car mileage, 1946 to 1975

SOURCE: for 1957 to 1975, Statistics Canada, *Railway Transport: Part I*, issues for 1960 to 1975; for 1952 to 1956, *Railway Transport: Part I* and *Part II*, issues for 1952 to 1956; for 1946 to 1951, *Statistics of Steam Railways*, each annual issue.

T28-32 and T36-38. Revenue train mileage and freight car mileage do not include work train service. Motor unit cars are those cars which have space for the carrying of any one or all of passengers, baggage, express and mail and which also carry their own power unit.

With the 1971 issues of *Railway Transport*, the results of an extensive review of the railway surveys affected many of the series. In particular, a new concept, 'locomotive unit-miles' replaced the 'locomotive' or 'engine' mileage data of previous years. Series T33 and T35 therefore terminate in 1970. The table below shows the new series, which counts mileage for each locomotive, rather than that of the first engine only.

Locomotive unit-miles 1971-1975
(millions of miles)

	Total	Freight	Passenger	Switching
1975	248.1	170.8	44.7	32.6
1974	263.2	177.3	50.5	35.4
1973	246.8	169.8	43.5	33.5
1972	246.2	168.1	43.3	34.8
1971	232.1	159.1	38.7	34.3

T39-46. Railways, freight tonnage and mileage, passenger traffic and passenger mileage, 1946 to 1975

SOURCE: for 1956 to 1975, Statistics Canada, *Railway Transport: Part I*, issues for 1956 to 1975; for 1952 to 1955, *Railway Transport: Part I* and *Part II*, individual issues for each year; for 1946 to 1951, *Statistics of Steam Railways*, each annual issue.

T40. Revenue freight ton-miles is the mathematical product of tons carried times distance hauled; for example, 1,000 tons hauled 1,000 miles or 10,000 tons hauled 100 miles each produce 1,000,000 ton-miles.

T41. Revenue and non-revenue freight ton-miles differs from series T40 only in that it includes freight hauled on company service as well as revenue freight.

T42. Average load per loaded car-mile shows increasing values over the years partly because of a rise in the carrying capacity of the equipment, partly because of a change in the nature of the traffic handled. A loss of less than carload freight or a gain in ore traffic would tend to raise it even if there were no change in uniformly weighted series.

T43. Average length of freight haul is affected by changes in the nature of the traffic carried (see the note to series T42). It is calculated by taking the ratio of series T40, 'Revenue freight ton-miles', divided by the sum of series T47, 'Freight originating in Canada' and T48, 'Freight received from U.S. roads'. As it does not include the U.S. portion of an international freight haul, the series is biased downward by this omission.

T44. In 1970, the passenger details of 'GO Transit' were added to the series. 'GO Transit' is an expanded rail commuter service inaugurated 23 May 1967 by the province of Ontario and operating between Hamilton and Pickering under an agreement with Canadian National. There were 4.8 million passengers in 1969, 4.7 million in 1968 and 2.2 million in 1967.

T46. The average revenue passenger journey is the ratio of T45, 'Revenue passenger-miles', divided by T44, 'Revenue passengers'. The decline in the average passenger journey since 1969 is largely due to the addition of 'GO Transit' passenger detail to the series since 1970 (see the note to series T44).

T47-58. Railways, freight carried by origin and by commodity group, 1946 to 1975

SOURCE: for 1956 to 1975, Statistics Canada, *Railway Transport: Part I* individual issues; for 1952 to 1955, *Railway Transport: Part I* and *Part II* individual issues for each year; for 1946 to 1951, *Statistics of Steam Railways*, each annual issue.

During the period from 1946 to 1975, a number of changes have occurred in the reporting of freight traffic statistics which have directly affected the commodity series. Until 1969, it was possible to provide series which were consistent, albeit with some perturbations. The break came in 1970 and since that time, the commodity series have been structured on Statistics Canada's Standard Commodity Classification (S.C.C.) requiring a somewhat different presentation.

The major changes in this period begin with 1 January 1954 when freight traffic statistics were reported on a 90-code Freight Commodity Statistics Classification, a change from the previous 78-code system. As of 1 January 1957 freight traffic statistics were reported on the 262-class Freight Commodity Statistics Classification of the Association of American Railroads. Minor modifications for the purposes of its application within Canada resulted in a 266-code classification.

This classification was used from 1957 through 1969. Then, as noted above, revenue freight traffic was compiled on the basis of a new 320-commodity breakdown based on Statistics Canada's S.C.C.

Express-rated traffic was included under non-carload freight.

A bridge between the old 266-commodity series and the new 320-commodity series provides the 1969 data in both series. The difference in total carload traffic is due to a switch from a 'received' to a 'forward' basis of reporting by certain railways. The total is, however, over a million tons higher because of the inclusion of the aforementioned express-rated traffic in the non-carload category.

T47-48. Freight originating in Canada and freight received from U.S. roads are not homogeneous series. The heading of T48 in the source is 'received from U.S. roads' in 1956 to 1975. It is 'received from foreign connections' in 1946 to 1955. The result is that traffic received at Canadian ports for furtherance by rail appears in series T47 from 1956 to 1975; it is in series T48 in the years 1946 to 1955 inclusive.

T59-73. Railways, gross earnings by source and operating expenses by function, 1946 to 1975

SOURCE: for 1956 to 1975, Statistics Canada, *Railway Transport*, issues from 1956 to 1975; for 1952 to 1955, *Railway Transport: Part I* and *Part II*, individual issues for each year; for 1946 to 1951, *Statistics of Steam Railways*, each annual issue.

On 1 January 1956 CN and CP commenced reporting on the basis of the Uniform Classification of Accounts for Class I, Common Carriers by Railway. This method of reporting was also adopted by six other railways and was effective for all railways 1 January 1957.

T59. Total gross earnings include all rail line, water line and incidental earnings. (The last year for inclusion of the water line was 1956. See the previous edition of *HSC I* for details.)

T60. Total rail revenue includes, in addition to the items in series T61-65, revenue from baggage, sleeping parlour and chair cars, milk hauling, switching and water transfers.

T61. Freight receipts are for road haul service. They do not include switching or water transfers.

Railway freight operating revenues in 1961 were augmented by $50.0 million in interim payments from the federal government following recommendations of the MacPherson Royal Commission on Transportation.

Included in freight revenue for 1963 was federal government compensatory payments of approximately $22.0 million related to the Freight Rates Reduction Act and $50.0 million related to recommendations of the MacPherson Royal Commission on Transportation. Of these amounts some $6.0 million was referable to 1962.

T62. Passenger revenue is revenue from road transportation of passengers only. It does not include revenue from the sale of space or any other auxiliary activity.

T64. Express revenue is not a homogeneous series. From 1946 to 1955 the series includes the gross express revenues from CN; other roads reported only the rail portion of express revenues. In and after 1956, all roads conformed to the latter practice.

T65. Under the National Transportation Act of 1967 a number of specific subsidies for services provided in the national interest were replaced by payments to the railways of transitional subsidies or 'normal payments' beginning in 1967. Such payments in 1967 aggregated $108.9 million while in 1968 they were reduced to $95.1 million, in 1969 to $81.3 million and in 1970 to $67.4 million.

T66. Incidental revenue is a sum of a number of minor items such as revenue from dining and buffet cars, news and restaurant service, demurrage, grain elevators, rent of buildings and sundry other. The drop in this item after 1955 is the result of a reclassification in the source of 'telegraphs and telephones', later described as 'commercial communications', from series T66, 'incidental', to 'other income, rail, and not rail'. The latter is, in the main, income from outside interests of railways and is not included in series T59.

T67-73. Operating expenses are given by the familiar functional groups. The growth in general expenses, series T73, is due largely to the rise of the custom of paying pensions to all retired employees and to the custom of funding the accrued liability by annual charges to expense during the working life of the employee. In 1926 the charge to expenses for pensions was $1.5 million; in 1938, $6.6 million; in 1948, $18.9 million; in 1959, $59.5 million.

T71. For the period 1946 to 1956 inclusive, Water Line expenses have been included with the series. (For further information see *HSC I*.)

T74-78. Railways, freight and passenger receipts per unit of traffic, 1946 to 1975

SOURCE: For series T74 and T76-78, for 1959 to 1975, Statistics Canada, *Railway Transport; Part I* annual issues 1960 to 1975; for 1955 to 1958, *Canada Year Book, 1960*, pp. 814-15; for 1946 to 1954, *Canada Year Book, 1948-49*, pp. 689-90. For series T75, freight revenue per revenue freight ton-mile is available for the CPR back to 1885 (see *HSC I*) and this series is provided for purposes of continuation.

T79-82. Railways, number of employees, hours worked and compensation paid, 1946 to 1975

SOURCE: for 1960 to 1975, Statistics Canada, *Railway Transport: Part VI*, annual issues 1960 to 1975; for years before 1960, *Railway Transport*, and its predecessor, *Statistics of Steam Railways in Canada*, annual issues.

The employment statistics effective 1 January 1964 report in accordance with the Uniform Canadian Classification of Railway Employees. From 1956 to 1963 inclusive, the Canadian Classification of Railway Employees was used.

The Canada Labour Standards Code which became effective 1 July 1965 set minimum wages, working hours, vacations and general holidays for employees. The code provides for: a minimum wage of $1.25 per hour for all employees; two weeks vacation after one year; and eight hours work per day, 40 hours per week, with overtime for service beyond these hours.

In 1966, labour negotiations involving unions representing non-operating and train service employees and the railways reached an impasse and a seven-day suspension of railway operations resulted from 26 August to 2 September. On 1 September, Parliament met in an emergency session to deal with the situation and enacted legislation (Maintenance of Railway Operation Act, 1966) which called for a return to work by employees and provided for an 18 per cent wage increase phased over a two-year period.

Negotiations which followed the 1966 railway strike resulted in agreements signed early in 1967 with most of the non-operating unions. These agreements provided for basic wage increases totalling 24 per cent spread over a three-year period from 1 January 1966 to 31 December 1968 plus fringe benefits.

In 1969, the major railways concluded settlements with the United Transportation Union, which represents trainmen, providing for a 13 per cent increase over two years plus fringe benefits.

Series T79 shows the average number of railway employees. It does not include express, communications and other outside operations employees. Two methods of counting are permissable under the Uniform Canadian Classification of Railway Employees. These are based on (a) mid-month count of employees on payroll, or (b) a more complicated calculation described as follows: to one-half of the sum of the total number of employees who work a specified number of days in the first semi-monthly pay period and the total number of employees working the same number of days in the second semi-monthly pay period, add the total number of employees paid once a month.

Since 1963, CN has used the second method. The CP uses both methods. Prior to 1964, the count was taken at a fixed date each month.

Monthly and annual comparisons of CN counts, taken both ways, have indicated that method (b) tends to reduce the average number of employees by about 3 per cent.

T80 and 81. Hours worked and total compensation exclude express, communications and outside operations employees.

Where figures of days worked are given in the source for daily rated employees they are converted on the basis of one day equals eight hours.

In series T81, 'Total compensation' is the gross amount paid to employees and charged to operating, capital and other company accounts as well as to 'outside parties'. This includes pay for vacations, holidays and leaves of absence; it is calculated before deductions for income tax, unemployment insurance contributions and other purposes; it excludes fringe benefits and retroactive wage payments.

Water Transport and Canal Statistics (Series T83-141)

General note

The movements through each of the canals of the St. Lawrence River system are so various that the published aggregate data can be taken as indicative only of broad trends. The limitations are still greater for totals through all the canals. A further difficulty is that the classifications in the canal statistics are not the same as in the railway statistics so that only occasionally can one make meaningful cross comparisons.

The major water movements have always been of bulk cargo carrying the freight of one consignor to one destination, with mechanical loading and unloading. The contract of carriage may be for a single cargo or for the movement of an agreed tonnage within the navigation season at the convenience of the carrier. The freight to be paid is negotiated as between shipper and the carrier.

The carriage of general merchandise upon the Great Lakes, in which the carrier holds itself out to accept the goods of many shippers, is usually done at differentials under the rails rates. This has normally been a minor part of the total tonnage handled, but a more important part of the total revenue earned.

The rise of import and export traffic through the lake ports from 1959 onward with the opening of the St. Lawrence Seaway has added a new dimension to what had been, until then, a relatively simple operation.

The basic source of data on canals and canal traffic is *Canal Statistics*, which appeared as a supplement to the report of the Department of Railways and Canals from 1886 to 1918 and which was published by Statistics Canada until 1970. The Statistics Canada *Shipping Report*, which begins with 1938, continues statistics of foreign shipping formerly published by the Department of National Revenue. In this form it was of limited value; but beginning with the year 1952 the report was greatly expanded to cover a wider list of countries of origin and destination in foreign trade, and the coasting trade was reported fully for the first time. The list of commodities was also revised to follow more closely the S.I.C. of 1948.

The publication *Canal Statistics* terminated in 1970 as the principal data were a duplication of the series available from the Saint Lawrence Seaway Development Corporation.

T83-89. Shipping, seagoing and inland vessels arrived at and departed from Canadian ports, 1946 to 1975

SOURCE: Statistics Canada: for 1960 to 1975, data supplied by the Water Transport Section, Transportation and Communications Division; for 1946 to 1959, data supplied by the Transportation Section, Public Finance and Transportation Division as recorded in *HSC I*.

T90-96. Canals, total traffic through Canadian canals by nationality of vessel and origin of freight, navigation seasons, 1946 to 1970

SOURCE: Statistics Canada: for 1959 to 1970, *Canal Statistics*, annual issues from 1960 to 1970; for 1949 to 1958 *Canada Year Book, 1960*, p. 849; for 1946 to 1948, *Canada Year Book, 1951*, p. 760.

These series terminate with the final issue of *Canal Statistics* in 1970.

T90-91. Number and registered tonnage of Canadian and British vessels are mainly Canadian registered vessels. The British vessels were unimportant until the opening of the St. Lawrence Seaway in 1959. In 1960 there were transits of 1,303 British vessels with net registered tonnage of 3,971,587 tons. By 1969, there were 1,170 transits with 4,962,991 net registered tonnage.

T92-93. Number and registered tonnage of United States and other foreign vessels were mainly United States vessels to 1950. Thereafter other foreign shipping increased steadily though still much less than United States shipping until 1959. From 1959 onward other foreign tonnage was much greater than United States tonnage.

T97-106. Canals, cargo tonnage through St. Lawrence canals, 1946 to 1975 and associated toll revenues, 1959 to 1975

SOURCE: For series T97-105: for 1971 to 1975, Saint Lawrence Seaway Development Corporation, *Traffic Report of the St. Lawrence Seaway*, annual issues; for 1946 to 1970, Statistics Canada *Canal Statistics*, each issue from 1946 to 1970. For series T106: for 1970 to 1975, Saint Lawrence Seaway Development Corporation, *Annual Report*, each issue from 1970 to 1975; for 1960 to 1969, Saint Lawrence Seaway Development Corporation, *1969 Annual Report, Tenth Anniversary*, p. 18; for 1959, Saint Lawrence Seaway Development Corporation, *Annual Report*, French edition, p. 19.

Series T97-103 cover tonnage of the named class in both directions.

T106. The administration of the canals at Cornwall and Lachine as well as the Welland and Sault Ste Marie canals was turned over to the Saint Lawrence Seaway Development Corporation on 1 April 1959. The St. Lawrence Seaway was opened to commercial traffic on 25 April 1959. The toll revenues in the series are those collected in Canada and do not include United States tolls.

T107-116. Canals, tonnage through Welland Canal, 1946 to 1975, and associated toll or lockage revenue, 1959 to 1975

SOURCE: For series T107-115: for 1971 to 1975, Saint Lawrence Seaway Development Corporation, *Traffic Report of the St. Lawrence Seaway*, annual issues; for 1946 to 1970, Statistics Canada, *Canal Statistics*, each issue from 1946 to 1970. For series T116: for 1970 to 1975, Saint Lawrence Seaway Development Corporation, *Annual Report*, each issue from 1970 to 1975; for 1960 to 1969, Saint Lawrence Seaway Development Corporation, *1969 Annual Report, Tenth Anniversary* p. 18; for 1959, Saint Lawrence Seaway Development Corporation, *Annual Report*, French edition, p. 19.

The Welland and the Sault canals are both parts of an international waterway and therefore movements between U.S. ports will be contained in their figures. T116 - (see notes for series T106 and footnote for series T116).

T117-122. Water freight charges for wheat, Great Lakes system, 1946 to 1970

SOURCE: for 1946 to 1970, Statistics Canada, *Canal Statistics*, various years.

Water freights on grain from Thunder Bay are the result of a bargain between the shipper and the vessel owner for each movement. The series given herein are weighted annual averages of such bargains. These prices include all costs of loading, unloading, handling and other charges. At mid-summer 1955, these charges for movement from the Head of the Lakes to the Georgian Bay ports and Goderich totalled $11.15 per 1,000 bushels, which equalled 37.2 cents per ton, or about 28 per cent of the nominal charge of 4 cents per bushel. This gives a net revenue to the ship of 0.178 cents per ton-mile for a weighted average distance of 537 miles.

At May 1955, the rate on grain from the St. Lawrence to U.K. ports was reported as 74 shillings and sixpence per long ton. Out of this amount the ship was reported as bearing a cost of $2.10 per long ton. This left a net revenue to the ship of 0.211 cents per short ton on an average distance of 3,450 miles.

Until 1959 the freight to Montreal normally included a transfer from a large vessel at Port Colborne up to 1932, and at some port between Port Colborne and Prescott thereafter, to a canal-sized vessel.

These series terminate in 1970 with the final publication of *Canal Statistics*.

T123-125. Number and registered net tonnage and tons of cargo loaded, vessels departed from Canadian ports in coastwise shipping, 1946 to 1975

SOURCE: Statistics Canada, *Shipping Report: Part III, Coastwise Shipping, 1976.* Appendix A, p. 69. For purposes of economy, only the departure data is presented here. The data provided in the source also provides the complementary arrival information which, after the inclusion of data for non-custom ports in 1957, varies less than 1.5 per cent from the departure data.

T125. Prior to 1952, coastwise cargo data is not available.

T126-141. Cargoes loaded and unloaded at selected ports for and from foreign countries, 1946 to 1975

SOURCE: Statistics Canada, for 1961 to 1975, *Shipping Report: Part IV*, annual issues; for 1946 to 1960, *Shipping Report*, each annual issue.

Roads and Road Transport (Series T142-194)

General note

While road transport has had the most vigorous growth of all modes of transportation, the quality of its statistics has been variable to an extreme. The development of this mode has long been in the hands of a large number of entrepreneurs who have been able to start business with a limited initial capital and to grow without large appeals to the capital market. Problems of definition as well as maintaining records of 'births' and 'deaths' of trucking undertakings have been a formidable constraint on the provision of consistent statistical series. In the early 1970s, all surveys in this area were reassessed and reformulated. Those who are interested in recent statistics should consult Statistics Canada reports: *Passenger Bus and Urban Transit, Motor Carriers - Freight and Household Goods Movers, For-hire Trucking Survey.*

T142-146. Road and street mileage, by type of surface, 1946 to 1975

SOURCE: Statistics Canada: for 1974 and 1975, *Road and Street Length and Financing*, each issue; for 1958 to 1973, *Road and Street Mileage and Expenditure*, annual issues; for 1946 to 1957, *Highway Statistics*, annual issues.

The classification used here are too coarse to permit a classification of road mileage other than to give a broad indication of the development of roads. The former breakdown of rural and urban mileage was abandoned in 1969 when it became impossible to apply consistent definitions across Canada. For presentation purposes here, the series includes both rural and urban, federal, provincial and municipal mileage.

While most highways in Canada are two-lane, by 1974, there were 3,332 miles of non-municipal road with four or more lanes, of which 976 miles were reported by Ontario and 1,037 miles were reported by Quebec.

T147-194. Motor vehicle registrations, by province, 1903 to 1975

SOURCE: Statistics Canada: for 1975: *Road Motor Vehicles, Registrations*; for 1960 to 1974, *The Motor Vehicle: Part III, Registrations*, annual issues 1960 to 1974; for 1948 to 1959, *The Motor Vehicle*, each annual issue; for 1945 to 1947, *The Motor Vehicle in Canada*, annual issues; for 1935 to 1946, *The Highway and Motor Vehicle in Canada*, annual issues; for 1904 to 1934, *The Highway and the Motor Vehicle in Canada, 1934*, table 6, pp. 12-17; for 1903, Ontario Ministry of Transportation and Communications.

Motor vehicles were registered for the first time in 1903 by the province of Ontario. New Brunswick followed in 1905, Quebec, Saskatchewan and Alberta in 1906, British Columbia in 1907, Manitoba in 1908, Nova Scotia in 1909 and Prince Edward Island in 1913.

Before reciprocal arrangements were made in regard to the operation of motor vehicles registered in other provinces and in the United States, a large proportion of the cars registered in Ontario were owned outside the province, largely in the United States. In 1906, the first year they were recorded, 659 of these cars, or 56 per cent of the total registered, were outside cars. In 1908 they numbered 1,165 cars or 67 per cent and in 1914, 6,415 cars, or 20 per cent, and by 1917 were reduced to 386 cars, the reciprocal arrangement having become effective in 1916.

Total registrations showed a continuous and rapid growth to 1931 when a decline was recorded. Growth in registrations resumed in 1934, continuing until 1941. A decline in registrations from 1942 to 1945 coincided with the war years. Beginning in 1946, when passenger cars were again produced, registrations have continued to increase each year.

Commercial vehicles include buses and trucks both large and small. In recent years, the use of the term 'commercial' to cover many of the smaller trucks is misleading. These are often used for personal transportation instead of a passenger car.

Motorcycle registrations, which suffered a decline in the 1950s, rose sharply in 1965 with the advent of large importations of motorcycles from Japan. Although for most of Canada the use of a motorcycle for transportation is extremely seasonal, an aggressive sales policy has been a major factor behind a ten-fold increase in registrations from 1962 to 1975. It should be recognized that for most provinces off-road motorcycles do not require registration.

In the 1970s, the use of 'mopeds' became popular particularly in Quebec. For 1975, the total registrations for Canada and for Prince Edward Island, Nova Scotia and Quebec include registered 'mopeds'. The total 1975 registrations for Canada and these three provinces therefore are each larger than the corresponding sums of passenger automobile, commercial vehicle and motorcycle registrations.

The series of registrations of motor vehicles over the years contain a number of individual provincial changes in concept and often reflect a change in the provincial administration procedures. While attempts have been made to avoid duplicate registrations of the same vehicle within each province, it has not been possible to remove duplicate registrations between provinces. Such duplication will occur when a commercial vehicle is registered in more than one province or when an owner changes his province of residence and re-registers his vehicle(s). Occasionally, with the development of computer systems, it has required heroic efforts to provide an annual breakdown of registrations and ensure that registrations for vehicles no longer registered are removed from the total counts. While some station wagons prior to 1960 were included with commercial vehicles for British Columbia, the distinction between passenger and commercial vehicles is based more on the nature of the vehicle than the uses to which it is put. Taxi cabs are therefore included with passenger vehicles and small trucks used principally for personal transport are included under 'commercial vehicles'. In addition to trucks, 'commercial vehicles' includes buses, road tractors, ambulances, etc. but generally excludes non-powered vehicles such as trailers.

Registrations for the Northwest Territories were included with those of the Yukon Territory from 1947 onward. Beginning in 1972, they were published separately. For economies of space, their registrations are combined in series T191-194. Shown here separately, their registrations are as follows:

Registrations of motor vehicles

Northwest Territories

Year	Total	Passenger automobiles	Commercial vehicles	Motorcycles
1975	12,482	5,850ʳ	5,835	797
1974	13,048	5,658	6,591	799
1973	12,845	5,504	6,546	795
1972	11,158	4,874	5,749	535
1971	9,111	4,340	4,223	548

Yukon Territory

Year	Total	Passenger automobiles	Commercial vehicles	Motorcycles
1975	13,947	7,136ʳ	6,328	483
1974	13,620	6,785	6,283	572
1973	10,663	5,466	4,717	480
1972	11,232	5,942	4,859	431
1971	11,796	6,212	5,190	394

The drop in the 1975 commercial vehicle registrations for the Northwest Territories is due to the removal of 1,048 registered vehicles largely involved in construction.

T167 and 169. In Quebec, the practice in registration has been to register every motor vehicle in the province. The drop in commercial vehicles in 1972 reflects the removal of farm tractors, construction vehicles and snowmobiles from the count.

Civil Aviation (Series T195-246)

General note

The term 'civil aviation' is often used to refer to that part of civil aviation which more properly should be called 'commercial aviation'. While the commercial aspects of civil aviation are of great interest, there are data available concerning non-commercial aviation as well. In the following series, therefore, the term 'civil aviation' is reserved for those cases where the data refers to both commercial and private aircraft or activity, otherwise the term 'commercial aviation' is used.

With the immense changes in aviation since 1946, there have been parallel changes in the collecting of statistics. In 1960, a major revision of the statistical program was required to reflect the revised licence classification of the former Air Transport Board (now the Air Transport Committee of the Canadian Transportation Commission). In 1970, a major revision of the operating and financial statistics was related to the development of computer programs designed to handle the statistical reports of the air transport industry. Each of these changes has had a profound effect on the statistics gathered as some information has been dropped and other items added. In several cases, revisions have been made to the civil aviation data presented in the previous edition of *HSC I*. Such revisions are indicated in the individual notes on each series.

In the following tables, the term 'goods' encompasses freight, express and excess baggage. From 1947 onwards, transoceanic services are included in all applicable tables. Data for Canadian carriers such as hours and ton-miles are computed to cover their entire route, while that for foreign carriers are computed on an 'in Canada only' basis.

From 1951 onward, transborder traffic has been traffic between Canada and the United States, although services to Florida and Hawaii were not included under this designation until 1970. Until 1949, Canada-Newfoundland traffic was also included under transborder traffic.

From 1947 to 1950, series T206-208 include a small volume of transoceanic traffic, not reported separately until 1951. From 1951 only scheduled (unit toll) traffic is included.

T195-198. Canadian commercial aviation activity, 1946 to 1975

SOURCE: Statistics Canada: for 1970 to 1975: *Air Carrier Operations in Canada,* October - December annual issues; for 1960 to 1969, *Civil Aviation,* annual issues; for 1946 to 1959, *HSC I.*

Data for 1960, as included in *HSC I,* were revised to include the activity of group V carriers (gross annual flying revenues of less than $60,000). Series T195 and T196 include revenue and non-revenue passengers and goods until 1959. From 1960 onward, non-revenue passengers and goods are excluded. Series T198, hours flown, includes both revenue and non-revenue hours flown.

T199-205.   Canadian commercial aviation, domestic revenue traffic, scheduled services, 1946 to 1975

ιSOURCE: Statistics Canada: for 1970 to 1975, *Air Carrier Operations in Canada,* October - December annual issues; for 1961 to 1969, *Civil Aviation,* annual issues; for 1946 to 1960, *HSC I.* See the general note to series T195-246 for the interpretation of the series headings.

T206-208.   Commercial aviation, transborder traffic, 1946 to 1975

SOURCE: Statistics Canada: for 1970 to 1975, *Air Carrier Operations in Canada,* annual October - December issues; for 1960 to 1969, unavailable; for 1946 to 1959, *HSC I.*

Transborder traffic is traffic between Canada and the United States. See the general note to series T195-246 for the interpretation of the series headings.

T209-215.   Commercial aviation, transborder traffic via Canadian carriers, scheduled revenue traffic, 1946 to 1975

SOURCE: Statistics Canada: for 1970 to 1975, *Air Carrier Operations in Canada,* October - December annual issues; for 1961 to 1969, *Civil Aviation,* annual issues; for 1946 to 1960, *HSC I.*

See the note to series T206-208 and the general note to series T195-246.

T216-222.   Commercial aviation, Atlantic and Pacific scheduled revenue traffic via Air Canada (Trans-Canada Air Lines) and CP Air (Canadian Pacific Air Lines), 1947 to 1975

SOURCE: same as for series T209-215.

Starting in 1970, flights to and from Hawaii are classified as transborder. Prior to 1970, these flights were included in the totals for 'Pacific services'. See the general note to series T195-246 for the interpretation of series headings.

T223-225.   Commercial aviation, contract and charter traffic, Canadian carriers, 1946 to 1975

SOURCE: Statistics Canada: for 1970 to 1975, *Air Carrier Operations in Canada,* October - December annual issues; for 1960 to 1969, *Civil Aviation,* annual issues; for 1946 to 1959, *HSC I.*

Data for 1960 series T223 and T224, as included in *HSC I,* were revised to include the activity of group V of carriers (gross annual flying revenues of less than $60,000). Series T225, revenue miles flown, excluded group V carriers for the years 1960 to 1969.

T226-235.   Commercial aviation, operating revenues, passenger fares per unit of traffic and employment, Canadian carriers, 1946 to 1975

SOURCE: Statistics Canada: for 1970 to 1975, *Air Carrier Operations in Canada,* October - December annual issues; for 1960 to 1969, *Civil Aviation,* annual issues; for 1946 to 1959, *HSC I.*

Series T226 has required complete revision to include the data for series T232, Non-flying services. In addition revisions have been made to the 1960 data as published in *HSC I* for series T230, Charter services, and series T231, Other flying revenues.

T233 and T234. Scheduled passenger revenue per passenger-miles is strictly not comparable before and after 1960, when reporting concepts were revised. For 1946 to 1960, series T279 refers to Air Canada (TCA) only. For 1946 to 1959, series T234 refers to the large independents (see *HSC I*).

T236-239.   Civil aviation, number of aircraft and airports, 1946 to 1975

SOURCE: For series T236-238: for 1961 to 1975, Transport Canada, *Civil Aircraft Register,* annual March 31st issues; for 1946 to 1960, *HSC I.* For series T239: for 1961 to 1973, *Canada Year Book,* various issues 1961-1974; for 1946 to 1960, *HSC I.*

T240-246.   Arriving and departing civil flights at selected Canadian international airports, 1960 to 1975

SOURCE: for 1960 to 1975, Transport Canada, *Aircraft Movement Statistics,* each annual issue.

These series generally exclude military arriving and departing flights and all flights designated local such as flying training flights which remain at all times under airport tower control.

During the period 1960 to 1970, the mix of private and commercial aircraft has changed considerably at most of these airports. The development of satellite airports at some cities has removed a major portion of private aircraft activity from the international airports. While Toronto International airport in 1975 was the busiest airport for itinerant movements, the total activity at such airports as St. Hubert, Pitt Meadows and Edmonton Municipal was actually greater than that of Toronto. Each of these airports has a large component of activity involving local movements of small private aircraft.

Oil and Gas Pipelines (Series T247-250)

General note

The transportation implications of oil and gas pipelines are sometimes overlooked in the presentation of statistical series. The four series presented here refer to transportation only and the user should refer to the source material for broader and more detailed information on pipelines.

T247-250.   Oil and gas pipeline transport revenues and ton-miles, 1950 to 1975

SOURCE: For series T247: for 1969 to 1975, Statistics Canada, *Oil Pipe Line Transport,* annual issues; for 1958 to 1968, Statistics Canada, Manufacturing and Primary Industries Division. For series T248: for 1969 to 1975, Statistics Canada, *Gas Utilities, Transport and Distribution Systems,* annual issues; for 1960 to 1968, Statistics Canada, Manufacturing and Primary Industries Division. For series T249:

Statistics Canada, for 1968 to 1975, *Oil Transport,* annual issues 1969 to 1975; for 1950 to 1967, DBS Special Release, April 1969, *Freight Ton-Miles in Canada, 1938-1967.* For series T250: Statistics Canada, for 1968 to 1975, *Gas Utilities, Transport and Distribution Systems,* annual issues 1969 to 1975; for 1957 to 1967, DBS Special Release, April 1969, *Freight Ton-Miles in Canada, 1938 to 1967.*

T248. This series is an approximation to the transport revenue as it is derived from the total operating revenues of the natural gas transport systems less the value of the total gas supply (gas purchases, exchange gas, gas delivered to or withdrawn from underground storage and gas used) for the same gas transport systems.

Transportation Accident Victims (Series T251-292)

General note

The series presented here for railway transport, water transport, motor vehicle traffic and civil aviation accidents are not strictly comparable because of differing concepts and differing reporting procedures. Nevertheless, they provide important guides to the relative levels of accidents among the several modes of transportation as well as useful trend information.

Of the nearly 13,000 deaths which were due to accidents in Canada during 1975, 6,061 or 47 per cent were due to motor vehicle traffic accidents. While household accidents as well as accidents in the work place or during recreation account for the vast majority of injury accidents, transportation related accidents alone make up more than half of all accidental fatalities. Transportation has indeed left a distressing record.

T251-260. Railway accident victims, 1907 to 1975

SOURCE: Statistics Canada: for 1956 to 1975, *Railway Transport: Part I,* annual issues 1960 to 1975; for 1952 to 1955, *Railway Transport: Part I,* individual issues for each year; for 1922 to 1951, *Statistics of Steam Railways,* each annual issue; for 1919 to 1921, *Railway Statistics of Canada,* each issue; for 1907 to 1918, *Annual Report* of the Department of Railways and Canals, each issue on railway statistics.

The number of fatal victims is probably a homogeneous series, but the number injured is affected by institutional factors. With the advent of workmen's compensation there was a stronger pressure to report employee injuries. Series T254 and T258, Others, include postal, express and pullman employees, and trespassers and automobile accident victims at level crossings.

T261-270. Water transport accident victims, 1946 to 1975

SOURCE: for 1973 to 1975, Transport Canada, Marine Casualty Investigations, Canadian Coast Guard; for 1946 to 1972, Statistics Canada: *Water Transportation,* individual annual issues.

The number of fatal victims is probably a homogeneous series, but a change in reporting procedure in 1973 has reduced the number of injured victims to those seriously injured victims as reported to Transport Canada.

The water transport accident series exclude small pleasure craft accidents and all accidents involving commercial fishing.

T271-284. Motor vehicle traffic accidents, 1921 to 1975

SOURCE: Statistics Canada: for 1954 to 1975, *Motor Vehicle Traffic Accidents,* annual issues; for 1952 to 1954, *Motor Vehicle Accidents,* each issue; prior to 1952, *The Motor Vehicle,* annual issues.

Motor vehicle traffic accidents have been obtained by several differing methods, over the years, and with 13 different reporting jurisdictions (the 10 provinces, the two territories and the city of Montreal) there are a number of inconsistencies in concepts and collection procedures. While every attempt has been made to provide usable figures for the earlier years of the series, it is not possible to separate all the totals into their component parts. For careful interpretation, therefore, it is important to use the various footnotes to the series.

T285-292. Civil aviation flying accident victims, 1931 to 1975

SOURCE: for 1970 to 1975, Transport Canada, Aviation Safety Investigation; for 1948 to 1969, Statistics Canada, *Civil Aviation,* annual issues 1952 to 1969; for 1946 and 1947, Transport Canada; for 1931 to 1945, *Transportation Accidents, 1946: A Summary of Railway, Motor Vehicle and Aircraft Accidents 1931-1945.*

Without a doubt, civil aviation accident data are the most homogeneous and consistent of the several modes. It should be noted, however, that the number of injured victims refers to seriously injured victims only, and does not include more minor injuries which have been reported in the above sources for some of these years. While accidents involving commercial aircraft are included in these series, most of the accidents relate to small private aircraft. It is suggested, therefore, that those persons wishing to obtain information on those accidents involving commercial aircraft only consult the above sources.

Post Office Statistics (Series T293-314)

General note

The Post Office is both a means of communication and a user of transportation services. During the period covered, it has turned from rail to air for the carriage of most first-class mail. Its dependence on rail, although still substantial, has been supplemented by extensive use of motor vehicles.

T293-305. Post Office, number of post offices in Canada, by province, 1946 to 1975

SOURCE: for 1961 to 1975, provided by R.W. Jones, Comptroller, Post Office Department, based upon material collected in the department and presented in the *Annual Report* of the Canada Post Office; for 1946 to 1960, HSC I.

These data include sub post offices as well as post offices. In the fiscal year ending 31 March 1975, there were 2,257 such sub post offices.

T306-308. Post Office, transportation statistics, operations, 1946 to 1975

SOURCE: same as for series T293-305 and *Canada Year Book,* various issues.

T306. Total number of land mail services is a total of the number of non-rail land services. It is a sum of the number of rural routes, series T307, and of other land mail services, series T308.

T307. Number of rural routes is the number of separate routes.

T308. Number of other land services includes stage services (post office to post office by land), side services (railway or ship depot to post office), parcel post delivery in cities, street letter-box pick-up service, conveyance of letter carriers, local services (general post office to postal stations) and the like. This series does not include rail services.

T309-312. Post Office, transportation statistics, cost of services, 1946 to 1975

SOURCE: same as for series T293-305.

T312. Non-rail land services include rural route services and other land services. See the note to series T308.

T313-314. Post Office, gross postal revenues and pieces of first-class mail, 1946 to 1975

SOURCE: same as for series T293-305.

T313. Gross postal revenues are total receipts for post office services before any charges are made against them. Receipts include postage stamps and other postage revenue (by far the largest item), commissions on money orders and postal notes, transit charges on mail from other countries and the like. The figures here exceed those in series G14 in *HSC I* since there was some netting of expenditure against receipts in obtaining that series. The data in these series are dependable since they are based on a complete accounting as a part of the administrative control of operations.

T314. Prices of first-class mail handled are based on estimates.

Telecommunications Carrier Industry (Series 315-352)

General note

At the beginning of the period covered, the telephone industry and the telegraph and cable industry were considered distinct. However, developments in transmission technology have been such that large systems in both industries have the capability of providing a wide range of similar services. Depending on the terminal instruments, both can transmit voice, print, electronic data and images in colour. They made possible radio and television networks, cablevision and remote computer terminals. For both, microwave, satellites and cables are transmission alternatives. Because their business reporting systems have developed on diverse lines, their statistics remain separate.

In the statistics for the telephone industry, the revenue from telephone services is not fully identifiable. For the other telecommunications carriers, the revenue from 'commercial telegraph tolls' was $12,709,881 or 53 per cent of total operating revenue in 1950; by 1960 'public and government messages' accounted for revenues of $17,149,202 or 29 per cent; the equivalent figures for 1975 were $11,211,839 and 4 per cent of total operating revenue.

The series updated from those in *HSC I* reflect the extent of technological and other changes. They are only superficially comparable.

T315-323. Telecommunications carrier industry, telephones and telephone calls, 1946 to 1975

SOURCE: for 1961 to 1975, Statistics Canada, *Telephone Statistics,* issues for all years; for 1946 to 1960, *HSC I.*

Series T315-323 cover Canadian telephone systems including those of CN Telecommunications, which provides telephone services in the Yukon Territory and Northwest Territories, and in parts of British Columbia and Newfoundland. Thus from 1962, when CN Telecommunications began to operate telephone services in the Yukon Territory, these series are not fully comparable with the statistics provided in series T327-336.

T316. Business telephones include public pay telephones.

T318. Residence extensions are additional telephones which are or can be connected to the same circuit as the main residence telephone.

T319. Of the telephones connected to automatic central offices in 1975, 87.8 per cent had direct distance dialing capability.

T321-323. Statistics cover completed telephone calls only. Estimates of number of local calls are provided by the larger telephone systems; for each province and territory, Statistics Canada makes estimates for the remaining systems, on the assumption that telephones operated by these systems are used to the same extent as those of the reporting systems.

Long distance calls over the CN Telecommunications system are excluded.

T324-326. Telecommunications carrier industry, gross capital expenditures on new construction and machinery and equipment, 1946 to 1975

SOURCE: for 1960 to 1975, Statistics Canada and/or Department of Industry, Trade and Commerce, *Private and Public Investment in Canada, Outlook,* individual years; for 1946 to 1959, *HSC I.*

Series T324-326 show capitalized costs associated with the procurement, construction and installation of new durable plant and equipment, and include items such as architectural, legal and engineering fees, as well as value of work undertaken by firms with their own labour force. Construction includes not only buildings but also transmission lines and towers. In 1960, coverage was extended to telecommunications carriers other than telephone systems.

T327-335. Telephone industry, property, revenues, expenses, taxes, interest, employees and wages, 1946 to 1975

SOURCE: same as for series T315-323.

Series T327-335 give selected financial and operational statistics for the telephone industry. Excluded are other telecommunications carriers covered in series T343-352. See also introductory explanatory notes.

T327. Cost of property and equipment is gross property in use valued at cost. It includes land, buildings and other structures considered as outside plant, as well as equipment.

T328-329. Total revenues include revenues from all carriers, including local and toll service revenue for a wide variety of communications services, directory advertising and sales, plant and building rents and investment income.

T331. Comparability of the series has been maintained, although detail available from 1971 onward indicates that some non-operating expenses are included. For 1975 these amounted to $9,468,000.

T336-341. Telephone industry, long-distance rates between Montreal and selected cities, 1918 to 1975

SOURCE: records of Bell Canada and *HSC I*

From 1965 onward the rates shown are for customer-dialed calls.

T342-351. Other telecommunications carriers, financial and operating statistics, 1946 to 1975

SOURCE: Statistics Canada: for 1961 to 1975, *Telecommunications Statistics*, 1972 and later years, and *Telegraph and Cable Statistics*, various years; for 1946 to 1960, *HSC I*.

T342. Operating revenue includes both transmission and non-transmission revenue.

T343. Operating expenses are after deduction of expenses applicable to the carriers' rail operations and other departments.

T344. Non-transmission revenues are part of operating revenues, series T343. For 1960 and 1975 these non-transmission revenues were:

	1975	1960
Leased circuit	$ 70,214,651	$18,264,955
Other leased plant	44,801,666	6,104,495
Money order charges	692,811	230,060
Other non-transmission	39,109,386	3,922,995
	$154,818,514	$28,522,505

T345. Cost of property and equipment is the cost of the fixed assets in use before the deduction of accrued depreciation.

T346. Total telegrams transmitted is the sum of series T348 and T349.

T349. Total cablegrams is not the sum of series T351 and T352. Duplications have been removed, but transatlantic telex messages, numbering 4,484,501 in 1975, are included.

T352-359. Number of private radio and television stations, with operating revenues and expenses, for private stations and Canadian Broadcasting Corporation (CBC), 1959 to 1975

SOURCE: for 1959 to 1975, Statistics Canada, *Radio and Television Broadcasting*, annual issues from 1960 to 1975.

For additional information on broadcasting, the reader is also referred to the annual Statistics Canada publication, *Cable Television*.

T352 and T353. Number of radio and television stations, excluding the CBC, refer to the number of private stations for which the operating revenue and expenses are given. Stations operating on a non-commercial basis such as those operated by religious and educational institutes are not included.

T356 and T359. For several reasons, the data in this series for the CBC, while comparable with the data for the private stations, will not coincide with the annual report of the corporation. Since 1968, these series are based on a fiscal year ending 31 August rather than the annual report which covers a fiscal year ending 31 March. Additionally, some conceptual differences will affect the strict comparability. Major changes in reporting occurred in the period 1960-1961 making it impossible to provide comparable data before 1961.

Series T1-4. Railways, capital liability, 1946 to 1975
(millions of dollars)

Year	Total[1]	Stocks	Debenture stock	Funded debt[1]	Year	Total[1]	Stocks	Debenture stock	Funded debt[1]
	1	2	3	4		1	2	3	4
1975	6,629.7	3,037.3	292.5	3,299.8	1960	4,970.4	2,433.3	292.5	2,244.6
1974	6,141.8	2,965.7	292.5	2,833.6	1959	4,791.7	2,376.4	292.6	2,122.7
1973	5,853.7	2,815.3	292.5	2,745.9	1958	4,599.8	2,354.0	292.6	1,953.1
1972	5,718.7	2,811.7	292.5	2,614.5	1957	4,330.2	2,272.9	292.6	1,764.7
1971	5,640.7	2,785.9	292.5	2,562.3	1956	4,185.2	2,279.8	292.6	1,612.7
1970	5,544.0	2,774.1	292.5	2,477.3	1955	4,108.6	2,250.7	292.7	1,565.1
1969	5,388.0	2,670.5	292.5	2,424.9	1954	3,975.6	2,207.0	292.8	1,475.8
1968	5,301.1	2,604.7	292.5	2,403.9	1953	3,861.8	2,122.2	300.4	1,439.1
1967	5,223.5	2,574.8	292.5	2,356.1	1952	3,715.2	2,101.1	305.2	1,308.9
1966	5,102.2	2,604.1	292.5	2,205.6	1951	3,571.7	1,341.0	305.2	1,925.5
1965	5,030.7	2,550.6	292.5	2,187.6	1950	3,475.8	1,341.4	308.1	1,826.3
1964	4,996.6	2,522.6	292.5	2,181.5	1949	3,269.6	1,268.7	308.1	1,629.9
1963	4,974.6	2,498.5	292.5	2,183.6	1948	3,250.3	1,270.0	308.1	1,672.3
1962	5,014.3	2,476.6	292.5	2,245.2	1947	3,308.6	1,314.2	309.4	1,685.0
1961	4,982.9	2,456.0	292.5	2,234.3	1946	3,290.6	1,315.4	309.4	1,665.8

[1] Includes government loans.

Series T5-18. Railways, miles of line in operation, rolling stock, locomotives, cars in passenger and company service, 1946 to 1975

Year	Miles in operation				Number of locomotives[1]				Number of passenger train cars[1]					
	All tracks[2]	Single track[2]	Second track	Yark track, industrial track and sidings	Total	Steam	Diesel electric	Electric	Total[3]	Dining parlour and sleeping[3]	Passenger carrying cars[4]	Baggage, express postal[4]	Passenger cars with power units	Number of cars in company service
	5	6	7	8	9	10	11	12	13	14	15	16	17	18
1975	60,045	43,941	2,035	14,069	3,977	–	3,963	14	1,936	553	765	495	123	15,831
1974	60,247	44,266	2,019	13,962	3,884	–	3,870	14	2,056	589	788	557	122	15,320
1973	60,246	44,232	2,019	13,995	3,762	–	3,748	14	2,175	619	758	668	130	15,394
1972	60,037	44,025	2,018	13,994	3,612	–	3,598	14	2,383	675	772	808	128	15,576
1971	59,710	44,153	2,015	13,542	3,463	–	3,449	14	2,516	702	822	870	122	16,124
1970	59,629	43,983	2,018	13,628	3,417	–	3,399	18	2,801	729	913	1,037	122	16,053
1969	59,114	43,613	2,021	13,480	3,316	–	3,297	19	2,942	784	938	1,105	115	15,981
1968	58,658	43,168	2,049	13,441	3,294	–	3,275	19	2,999	796	963	1,125	115	15,876
1967	58,530	43,168	2,055	13,307	3,311	–	3,292	19	3,444	938	1,045	1,346	115	16,391
1966	58,300	43,193	2,056	13,051	3,346	–	3,327	19	3,669	967	1,161	1,426	115	16,243
1965	58,402	43,347	2,060	12,995	3,340	–	3,318	22	3,647	929	1,171	1,434	113	16,713
1964	58,443	43,545	2,066	12,832	3,321	1	3,298	22	3,994	922	1,249	1,723	100	17,367
1963	58,511	43,623	2,072	12,816	3,385	7	3,347	31	4,172	936	1,272	1,866	98	17,867
1962	58,759	43,654	2,129	12,976	3,497	138	3,320	39	4,378	969	1,377	1,933	99	18,508
1961	58,782	43,689	2,198	12,895	3,547	197	3,309	41	4,737	1,065	1,508	2,061	103	18,676
1960	59,193	44,029	2,288	12,876	3,752	403	3,308	41	5,119	1,147	1,643[4]	2,218[4]	111	19,165
1959	59,394	44,209	2,350	12,835	4,720	1,514	3,155	51	5,456	1,221	1,687	2,420	128	19,421
1958	59,319	44,125	2,444	12,750	4,823	1,960	2,799	64	5,733	1,236	1,938	2,420	139	19,547
1957	59,097	43,890	2,471	12,736	4,821	2,394	2,372	55	5,942	1,229	2,076	2,508	129	19,586
1956[4]	59,830	43,652	2,476	13,702	4,790	2,849	1,895	46	6,220	1,284	2,323	2,516	97	19,389
1955	59,315	43,444	2,486	13,385	4,714	3,225	1,455	33	6,574	1,342	2,609	2,548	75	19,194
1954	58,760	43,132	2,485	13,143	4,771	3,586	1,152	33	6,648	1,326	2,710	2,549	63	19,023
1953	58,695	43,163	2,485	13,047	4,818	3,829	956	33	6,456	1,142	2,686	2,569	59	18,725
1952	58,291	42,953	2,488	12,850	4,810	4,014	763	33	6,328	1,150	2,729	2,394	55	18,170
1951	58,150	42,956	2,487	12,707	4,715	4,108	574	33	6,366	1,152	2,823	2,342	49	17,643
1950	57,997	42,979	2,498	12,520	4,655	4,272	350	33	6,338	1,167	2,881	2,238	52	17,274
1949[5]	57,834	42,978	2,494	12,362	4,627	4,351	246	30	6,224	1,145	2,857	2,168	54	17,080
1948	57,005	42,248	2,495	12,262	4,521	4,340	148[6]	33	6,099	1,122	2,822	2,095	60	16,700
1947	57,051	42,322	2,489	12,240	4,451	4,364	54	33	6,030	1,120	2,822	2,024	64	16,654
1946	57,005	42,335	2,486	12,184	4,450	4,387	29	34	6,141	1,127	2,909	2,041	64	16,386

[1] Leased locomotives and passenger cars are included.
[2] Small mileages in the United States, operated as part of the Canadian systems, are included.
[3] Includes pullman cars in Canadian service.
[4] Multi-purpose cars included in passenger cars from 1960 onward.
[5] Newfoundland equipment included from 1949 onward.
[6] Includes 84 diesel locomotives formerly listed as switching and included under steam in 1947.

Series T19-27. Railways, rolling stock, freight cars in service, 1946 to 1975

Year	Number	Capacity (thousands of tons)	Box[1] (number)	Flat (number)	Stock (number)	Hopper, gondola, ballast, ore and coal[2] (number)	Tank (number)	Refrigerator (number)	Wood pulp and other[2] (number)
	19	20	21	22	23	24	25	26	27
1975	193,197	12,253	95,445	25,722	2,359	60,587	379	5,016	3,689
1974	190,892	11,855	98,155	24,898	2,463	57,259	494	4,772	2,851
1973	186,653	11,413	97,818	22,010	2,503	56,563	484	4,955	2,320
1972	186,541	11,179	99,769	20,414	2,583	55,613	424	5,292	2,396
1971	187,306	11,062	102,184	19,728	2,687	54,756	468	5,403	2,080
1970	188,737	10,989	103,924	18,043	2,827	54,845	487	6,673	1,938
1969	188,268	10,684	106,556	16,430	2,945	52,741	511	7,549	1,536
1968	188,254	10,566	108,454	15,087	2,987	51,683	538	8,074	1,421
1967	188,770	10,523	109,583	14,765	3,094	51,314	532	8,030	1,452
1966	186,560	10,256	109,929	14,412	3,124	49,766	526	8,024	1,281
1965	182,686	9,844	109,541	13,520	3,150	46,861	524	7,937	1,153
1964	180,457	9,633	110,036	12,800	3,281	45,492	552	7,555	741
1963	181,719	9,526	111,706	12,430	3,952	44,700	546	7,806	579
1962	185,169	9,652	114,192	12,261	4,352	45,251	544	8,207	362
1961	186,387	9,627	115,464	12,164	4,589	44,744	479	8,635	312
1960	191,553	9,841	118,466	12,645	4,917	44,946	472	10,076	31
1959	194,512	9,935	121,451	12,270	5,025	45,133	455	10,155	23
1958	196,893	9,998	124,326	12,058	5,195	44,727	382	10,184	21
1957	197,907	9,947	128,079	11,975	5,141	42,305	384	10,022	1
1956[2]	191,974	9,531	124,727	11,877	5,501	39,557	389	9,906	17
1955	185,956	9,031	122,220	12,037	5,776	35,776	378	9,735	34
1954	189,351	9,106	126,209	11,782	5,972	35,398	363	9,583	44
1953	187,980	8,934	127,313	11,690	6,057	33,110	328	9,438	44
1952	186,557	8,735	129,158	11,748	6,284	30,360	268	8,691	48
1951	180,725	8,315	127,714	11,062	6,509	26,700	460	8,231	49
1950	175,597	8,000	122,419	11,263	6,655	26,641	469	8,050	100
1949[3]	177,614	8,052	124,651	10,951	6,648	26,909	454	7,921	80
1948	172,406	7,755	123,539	10,326	6,115	24,738[4]	353	7,240	95[4]
1947	166,451	7,389	119,589	10,453	6,277	21,618	354	6,673	1,487
1946	163,345	7,194	116,809	10,868	6,382	20,938	358	6,467	1,523

[1] Includes automobile box and rack-type cars from 1971.
[2] London and Port Stanley railway cars allocated in 1956. For 1957 onward these cars are included as reported.
[3] Newfoundland equipment included from 1949 onward.

[4] Due to a revision in the system of classification, some ballast and gondola cars included in series T27 prior to 1948 have been included in series T24 from 1948 onward.

Series T28-38. Railways, revenue train mileage, engine mileage and freight car mileage, 1946 to 1975
(millions of miles)

Year	Revenue train mileage					Engine mileage			Freight car mileage		
	Total		Passenger		Freight locomotive drawn train[1]	Gross total[2]	Revenue road		Loaded	Empty	Caboose
	Grand total	Locomotive drawn train	Locomotive drawn train	Motor unit train			Steam	Diesel			
	28	29	30	31	32	33	34	35	36	37	38
1975	88.7	83.7	19.9	4.9	63.8	–	–	–	2,391.0	1,855.5	66.7
1974	97.0	92.1	22.6	4.8	69.5	–	–	–	2,510.8	1,838.5	71.5
1973	88.7	84.3	19.0	4.4	65.3	–	–	–	2,450.9	1,765.7	67.5
1972	90.9	86.2	19.2	4.7	67.0	–	–	–	2,473.4	1,762.9	69.3
1971	87.3	82.6	17.9	4.7	64.7	–	–	–	2,434.2	1,732.0	67.1
1970	87.8	82.9	19.9	4.9	63.0	110.7	–	83.1	2,336.3	1,690.1	65.1
1969	87.0	81.7	21.1	5.3	60.6	111.0	–	83.2	2,219.6	1,473.9	63.1
1968	87.8	82.3	22.1	5.5	60.2	111.5	–	84.1	2,190.5	1,455.0	62.1
1967	94.8	89.1	23.9	5.7	65.2	119.8	–	90.5	2,263.7	1,497.8	67.4
1966	96.4	90.8	22.0	5.6	68.8	122.8	–	92.2	2,396.8	1,541.1	70.8
1965	97.7	92.3	24.0	5.4	68.3	124.0	–	93.9	2,315.9	1,459.1	70.4
1964	95.8	90.5	23.4	5.3	67.1	121.8	–	92.2	2,296.7	1,422.3	69.0
1963	90.9	85.1	22.4	5.8	62.7	115.2	–	86.7	2,103.2	1,297.2	64.7
1962	89.5	83.7	23.4	5.8	60.3	113.6	–	85.1	2,003.3	1,190.7	62.1
1961	91.7	85.6	25.0	6.1	60.6	117.8	–	86.5	1,996.8	1,176.0	61.7
1960	98.4	91.8	27.9	6.6	63.9	126.6	1.0	92.3	2,028.1	1,156.6	64.4
1959	106.6	99.8	31.5	6.7	68.4	138.1	9.6	92.8	2,105.3	1,148.3	68.5
1958	109.2	102.7	34.0	6.5	68.7	142.7	21.6	84.7	2,127.1	1,128.3	69.1
1957	119.6	115.2	37.2	4.5	78.0	159.6	45.8	73.9	2,261.8	1,200.7	77.6
1956	130.9	127.7	40.6	3.2	87.1	178.6	74.1	61.4	2,505.9	1,297.4	87.5
1955	123.6	121.7	42.6	2.0	79.1	168.0	76.8	52.1	2,222.4	1,113.4	79.1
1954	121.1	119.6	44.2	1.5	75.3	163.6	91.2	34.8	2,020.0	993.6	75.0
1953	132.0	130.8	45.8	1.2	85.0	181.1	112.9	27.4	2,258.0	1,105.9	84.6
1952	136.9	135.7	46.5	1.2	89.2	189.3	127.5	18.6	2,334.5	1,128.8	88.5
1951	133.4	132.2	45.0	1.2	87.2	185.8	131.0	11.8	2,276.5	1,021.2	86.6
1950[2]	125.1	123.9	42.5	1.3	81.4	172.8	127.5	5.4	2,102.5	910.6	80.8
1949	127.3	126.0	44.3	1.3	81.6	174.4	132.4	–	2,076.1	934.2	81.3
1948	129.5	128.0	44.6	1.5	83.4	179.4	136.3	–	2,136.3	901.3	83.2
1947	127.7	126.3	43.9	1.4	82.4	176.9	135.1	–	2,158.3	936.4	82.0
1946	123.5	122.0	44.2	1.5	77.8	168.8	130.4	–	2,006.6	889.3	77.5

[1] Includes mixed train mileage.

[2] Newfoundland traffic included from 1950 onward.

Series T39-46. Railways, freight tonnage and mileage, passenger traffic and passenger mileage, 1946 to 1975

Year	Tons carried revenue freight[1] (millions of tons)	Revenue freight ton miles (millions of tons)	Revenue and non-revenue freight ton miles (millions of tons)	Average load per loaded car mile (tons)	Average length of freight haul[2] (miles)	Revenue passengers carried (millions)	Revenue passenger mile (millions)	Average revenue passenger journey[3] (miles)
	39	40	41	42	43	44	45	46
1975	279.5	135,081.9	138,576.6	51.44	542	23.6	1,821	77
1974	311.2	138,655.3	141,403.2	49.14	511	24.1	1,878	78
1973	304.3	130,760.2	133,197.0	48.47	492	19.8	1,599	81
1972	274.5	123,657.1	126,513.4	46.45	521	23.0	2,043	89
1971	274.9	118,559.8	121,291.3	46.73	502	24.1	2,186	91
1970	272.9	110,104.5	112,872.3	45.48	472	23.8[4]	2,272[4]	95[4]
1969	241.4	96,460.9	98,936.2	42.27	465	18.9	2,336	124
1968	254.2	95,100.3	97,291.8	42.48	439	20.0	2,554	128
1967	247.8	94,100.7	96,086.6	41.62	447	24.6	3,135	127
1966	248.5	96,828.1	98,680.5	40.67	451	23.2	2,589	112
1965	236.1	89,020.3	90,837.4	39.00	432	24.6	2,666	108
1964	221.2	86,974.2	88,709.6	38.44	435	22.9	2,683	117
1963	193.4	75,796.0	77,620.1	36.81	441	20.6	2,070	100
1962	182.8	67,937.1	69,686.4	34.71	422	19.3	2,019	105
1961	174.5	65,828.4	67,630.3	33.79	430	18.8	1,961	104
1960	178.8	65,444.8	67,325.8	33.11	413	19.5	2,264	116
1959	186.2	67,956.5	70,259.6	33.31	409	20.9	2,446	117
1958	174.2	66,356.8	68,914.3	32.35	432	21.4	2,486	116
1957	196.9	71,047.2	74,452.5	32.86	408	23.0	2,925	127
1956	214.1	78,820.0	83,105.0	33.12	416	26.1	2,908	112
1955	188.5	66,176.1	69,664.8	31.30	394	27.2	2,892	106
1954	162.5	57,547.3	61,397.0	30.34	402	28.4	2,863	101
1953	176.8	65,267.0	70,350.4	31.16	418	28.7	2,986	104
1952	185.1	68,430.4	73,961.1	31.68	422	30.2	3,151	104
1951	184.4	64,300.4	69,690.7	30.61	399	31.0	3,110	100
1950[5]	164.4	55,537.9	60,789.1	28.91	385	31.1	2,816	90
1949	162.3	56,338.2	61,660.2	29.65	395	34.9	3,913	92
1948	176.7	59,080.3	64,427.8	30.16	381	38.3	3,477	91
1947	175.6	60,143.0	65,234.6	30.23	393	40.9	3,733	91
1946	160.6	55,310.3	60,096.5	29.95	397	43.4	4,649	107

[1] See series T47, T48 and T49 for component values.
[2] Series is ratio of T40 divided by sum of T47 and T48.
[3] Ratio of series T45 divided by series T44.

[4] Go Transit passenger operations were shown for the first time in 1970.
[5] Newfoundland included from 1950 onward.

Series T47-58. Railways, freight carried, by origin and by commodity group, 1946 to 1975
(thousands of tons)

Year	Originating in Canada	Received from U.S. roads[2]	Received from connecting roads in Canada	Total[2]	Live animals	Food, feed beverages and tobacco	Crude materials inedible	Fabricated materials inedible	End products inedible	Special types of traffic	Total carload traffic	Non-carload
	47	48	49	50	51	52	53	54	55	56	57	58
1975	227,669	21,433	30,423	249,102	240	34,309	129,354	64,270	10,714	8,734	247,620	1,482
1974	243,565	27,950	39,701	271,516	219	34,999	137,590	75,899	10,864	9,522	269,094	2,422
1973	239,968	25,978	38,337	265,946	147	36,042	138,217	70,538	10,244	9,104	264,292	1,654
1972	213,405	24,505	36,564	237,910	173	40,550	111,575	66,993	9,254	7,932	236,477	1,432
1971	212,605	23,805	38,466	236,410	162	37,978	118,096	63,864	8,627	6,347	235,075	1,334
1970	207,177	25,987	39,706	233,163	214	35,117	119,271	65,150	7,658	4,512	231,923	1,241
1969[1]	—	—	—	208,992	265	28,408	103,319	62,908	8,454	4,164	207,517	1,475

Year	Originating in Canada	Received from U.S. roads[2]	Received from connecting roads in Canada	Total[2]	Animals and products	Products of agriculture	Products of mines	Products of forest	Manufactures and miscellaneous			
1969[1]	183,451	24,144	33,802	207,595	1,110	24,450	85,875	22,865	73,135			
1968	192,691	23,706	37,849	216,396	1,306	24,220	97,892	21,622	70,987			
1967	186,325	24,150	37,364	209,794	1,378	29,426	91,954	21,037	65,998			
1966	188,802	25,815	33,841	214,618	1,361	35,166	91,199	20,019	65,907			
1965	180,461	25,988	29,675	206,448	1,466	30,370	92,006	18,445	62,929			
1964	174,590	24,909	21,349	199,860	1,664	35,686	85,324	17,732	58,493			
1963	148,834	22,901	21,618	171,736	1,529	29,304	71,829	15,927	52,062			
1962	138,435	22,495	21,909	160,930	1,508	25,177	68,237	15,441	49,343			
1961	131,128	21,953	21,438	153,080	1,619	28,012	61,389	14,492	46,378			
1960	133,855	24,607	20,375	158,462	1,695	26,666	65,541	14,960	48,286			
1959	140,505	25,591	20,107	166,095	1,571	27,989	71,178	14,736	49,163			
1958	129,238	24,203	20,758	153,442	1,635	29,309	59,896	14,557	46,535			
1957[2]	143,349	30,695	22,847	174,044	1,940	28,376	73,323	16,646	51,690			
1956	156,518	33,090	24,470	189,608	2,085	34,771	78,397	18,958	53,113			
1955	131,409	36,453	20,668	167,862	2,066	27,275	69,996	17,717	48,581			
1954[2]	109,855	33,340	19,275	143,195	1,992	28,494	51,808	16,029	42,656			
1953	119,986	36,263	20,502	156,249	1,868	36,306	53,082	16,194	48,799			
1952	125,336	36,839	22,882	162,175	1,694	37,403	54,822	19,330	48,927			
1951	121,836	39,425	23,103	161,261	2,196	31,739	56,055	20,836	50,434			
1950	108,147	36,071	20,141	144,218	2,302	24,376	55,748	15,830	45,961			
1949	108,560	34,159	19,573	142,719	2,539	28,290	51,741	15,596	44,552			
1948	112,768	42,165	21,807	154,933	2,889	27,656	56,733	19,442	48,212			
1947	108,931	43,925	22,710	152,856	2,894	32,080	51,225	18,837	47,820			
1946	98,777	40,479	21,361	139,256	3,257	30,872	45,732	16,850	42,546			

[1] The new classification introduced in 1970 was structured on Statistics Canada's Standard Commodity Classification. To provide a bridge, 1969 data are shown in both systems. The small differences in total carload traffic between the two sets of data resulted from a change from a 'received' to a 'forwarded' system of reporting by certain railways. Less than carload traffic included for the first time small parcel freight moving at express rates.

[2] Changes in classification adopted in 1954 and 1957 account for irregularities in the series.

Series T59-73. Railways, gross earnings by source and operating expenses by function, 1946 to 1975
(millions of dollars)

Year	Total gross[1]	Gross earnings						Incidental	Total	Ways and structures	Equipment	Traffic	Rail line[3]	Miscellaneous operations	General expenses
		Rail line													
		Total (including other)[2]	Freight revenue	Passenger revenue	Mail revenue	Express revenue	Payments under the National Transportation Act, 1967								
	59	60	61	62	63	64	65	66	67	68	69	70	71	72	73
1975	2,733.8	2,651.6	2,263.2	83.8	12.0	27.9	237.4	82.2	2,577.9	501.9	544.9	65.4	1,119.3	28.3	318.1
1974	2,569.0	2,499.6	2,141.7	83.2	12.9	18.5	216.6	69.4	2,313.6	449.2	494.1	58.4	1,009.0	26.6	276.4
1973	2,123.0	2,071.5	1,822.7	57.2	10.2	14.6	144.4	51.5	1,864.3	354.8	420.1	49.7	784.8	18.0	237.0
1972	1,940.6	1,887.4	1,688.1	69.8	10.5	23.6	71.6	53.2	1,686.2	326.5	395.0	46.5	717.9	20.1	180.3
1971	1,805.7	1,757.8	1,579.7	64.4	10.8	23.9	53.5	47.8	1,572.6	301.3	381.9	45.0	660.8	20.1	163.5
1970	1,679.8	1,631.1	1,436.0	63.7	12.7	26.6	67.4	48.7	1,456.7	285.1	347.9	43.2	611.2	20.9	148.4
1969	1,583.8	1,534.9	1,331.3	63.0	14.3	20.2	81.3	48.9	1,393.2	275.3	326.6	41.8	582.6	22.4	144.5
1968	1,529.0	1,482.2	1,267.4	64.0	14.6	15.8	95.1	46.8	1,328.4	266.4	314.8	38.6	546.3	23.0	139.2
1967	1,519.4	1,470.4	1,222.2	78.7	16.6	17.5	108.9	48.9	1,341.1	271.9	316.0	40.2	556.0	25.1	131.8
1966	1,480.8	1,436.4	1,322.0	62.8	15.2	12.7	..	44.4	1,264.1	260.1	295.9	37.9	522.7	19.6	127.9
1965	1,372.3	1,329.6	1,210.7	65.7	15.7	15.4	..	42.7	1,202.2	251.1	284.9	34.4	493.4	20.4	117.9
1964	1,324.4	1,283.6	1,169.5	63.7	16.2	14.9	..	40.8	1,156.3	249.0	277.2	32.4	467.9	19.4	110.4
1963	1,210.2	1,175.4	1,067.3	59.5	15.9	14.8	..	34.9	1,081.4	242.9	259.7	30.6	427.7	14.7	105.8
1962	1,165.3	1,132.8	1,019.5	60.6	16.3	17.6	..	32.6	1,059.0	239.7	250.2	29.0	424.9	13.5	101.8
1961	1,156.5	1,125.3	1,013.0	61.2	16.9	16.1	..	31.2	1,053.7	243.4	249.4	29.0	423.4	13.6	95.0
1960	1,151.7	1,121.5	992.7	69.2	17.4	21.8	..	30.0	1,050.6	244.0	249.5	28.9	424.9	14.5	88.9
1959	1,224.6	1,193.8	1,058.0	73.6	17.7	23.1	..	30.6	1,103.1	260.0	256.8	29.1	443.3	14.8	99.2
1958	1,163.7	1,131.5	995.9	77.3	15.2	22.3	..	32.0	1,080.3	248.6	253.7	27.2	440.1	14.8	95.9
1957[3]	1,263.1	1,228.2	1,080.1	86.9	15.4	22.4	..	34.9	1,136.9	265.1	256.7	27.3	478.4	16.6	92.8
1956[3]	1,300.6	1,260.3	1,110.1	85.3	14.0	26.1	..	36.6	1,127.9	249.6	251.3	25.3	494.2	18.8	88.6
1955	1,198.4	1,137.1	965.9	83.0	14.5	50.1	..	56.6	1,048.6	212.4	227.9	23.8	485.5	17.7	81.3
1954	1,095.4	1,039.4	872.4	82.1	14.9	47.9	..	51.7	1,019.5	206.7	227.2	22.8	477.1	16.2	69.5
1953	1,205.9	1,148.6	971.8	86.0	15.3	51.8	..	52.2	1,100.4	227.1	254.0	22.8	516.1	16.4	64.0
1952	1,172.2	1,120.3	941.9	90.7	13.4	49.7	..	47.2	1,057.2	215.4	243.3	21.3	504.2	16.0	57.1
1951	1,088.6	1,040.6	876.0	89.0	12.5	42.0	..	43.7	977.6	202.5	224.2	20.0	468.7	15.6	46.7
1950[4]	959.0	916.7	769.2	78.6	14.7	36.0	..	37.8	833.7	164.0	189.5	18.6	404.0	14.3	43.3
1949	894.4	856.5	707.4	85.1	9.4	35.9	..	33.2	831.5	164.9	186.1	17.6	406.1	15.0	41.8
1948	875.8	840.5	698.7	83.5	9.2	32.5	..	31.0	808.1	160.0	174.5	16.8	403.8	14.6	38.5
1947	785.2	750.9	607.8	87.8	8.9	30.2	..	30.3	690.8	134.1	145.6	15.1	347.6	13.1	35.3
1946	718.5	684.6	531.8	100.0	8.6	27.7	..	30.4	623.5	122.1	135.9	13.8	304.6	14.0	33.2

[1] Includes water line revenues and receipts from joint facilities.
[2] Series T60 is not the sum of series T61-64. Small additional earnings from passenger train service and freight service are included.
[3] Series T71 includes water line expenses for 1956 and prior years. For details, see the first edition of Historical Statistics of Canada. From 1957, water line data were considered non-rail and excluded. In 1956, reporting under the new Uniform System of Accounts began. Equipment rents, joint facility rental and railway tax accruals were included under "operating expense" from 1956 onward. In previous years, the treatment of these items varied among the railways.
[4] Newfoundland is included beginning in 1950.

Series T74-78. Railways, freight and passenger receipts per unit of traffic, 1946 to 1975

Year	Freight receipts per ton mile (cents)	Freight revenue per ton mile Canadian Pacific Railway[1] (cents)	Freight receipts per ton originated (dollars)	Average receipts per passenger mile (cents)	Average receipts per passenger (dollars)	Year	Freight receipts per ton mile (cents)	Freight revenue per ton mile Canadian Pacific Railway[1] (cents)	Freight receipts per ton originated (dollars)	Average receipts per passenger mile (cents)	Average receipts per passenger (dollars)
	74	75	76	77	78		74	75	76	77	78
1975	1.695	1.73	9.41	4.60	3.56	1960	1.517	1.52	6.26	3.05	3.55
1974	1.565	1.52	8.16	4.44	3.45	1959	1.557	1.57	6.37	3.01	3.51
1973	1.415	1.35	7.12	3.57	2.88	1958	1.501	1.47	6.49	3.11	3.62
1972	1.380	1.30	7.32	3.39	3.01	1957	1.520	1.50	6.21	2.97	3.78
1971	1.353	1.30	6.96	2.95	2.67	1956	1.489	1.39	5.85	2.93	3.27
1970	1.327	1.30	6.74	2.81	2.67	1955	1.460	1.43	5.75	2.87	3.05
1969	1.405	1.39	6.70	2.70	3.34	1954	1.516	1.46	6.09	2.87	2.89
1968	1.359	1.39	6.13	2.51	3.21	1953	1.489	1.42	6.22	2.88	2.99
1967	1.324	1.32	6.08	2.51	3.20	1952	1.377	1.30	5.81	2.88	3.01
1966	1.365	1.34	6.16	2.43	2.71	1951	1.362	1.31	5.43	2.86	2.87
1965	1.360	1.37	5.86	2.47	2.67	1950	1.385	1.33	5.33	2.79	2.52
1964	1.345	1.32	5.85	2.38	2.78	1949	1.256	1.20	4.96	2.66	2.44
1963	1.408	1.44	6.21	2.88	2.89	1948	1.183	1.13	4.51	2.40	2.18
1962	1.501	1.51	6.34	3.00	3.15	1947	1.009	.95	3.98	2.35	2.14
1961	1.539	1.54	6.62	3.12	3.26	1946	.961	.93	3.82	2.15	2.30

[1] Series T75 continues a series begun in 1885.

Series T79-82. Railways, number of employees, hours worked and compensation paid, 1946 to 1975
(series T79 in thousands; series T80 in millions and series T81 and 82 in millions of dollars)

Year	Average number of railway employees[1]	Hours worked	Total compensation	Total compensation charged to operating expenses	Year	Average number of railway employees[1]	Hours worked	Total compensation	Total compensation charged to operating expenses
	79	80	81	82		79	80	81	82
1975	114.5	216.5	1,554.2	1,511.2	1960	145.1	290.1	632.3	659.3
1974	118.4	261.4	1,442.7	1,381.2	1959	156.3	315.6	668.8	689.2
1973	110.3	241.1	1,165.2	1,127.4	1958	159.9	323.8	646.4	669.6
1972	113.8	251.7	1,079.3	1,055.3	1957	177.2	357.1	678.0	702.2
1971	114.9	252.9	1,003.2	985.8	1956	181.6	375.1	677.4	707.3
1970	116.5	256.7	931.2	921.7	1955	171.8	369.3	595.9	601.7
1969	118.6	260.2	882.2	874.5	1954	172.9	366.6	594.3	594.8
1968	120.1	263.5	830.8	826.0	1953	188.6	404.6	655.5	644.5
1967	130.2	285.2	831.9	827.6	1952	191.9	421.2	609.7	610.2
1966	130.2	284.7	759.0	804.6	1951	183.5	425.9	570.7	566.6
1965	133.2	294.1	732.3	744.6	1950	171.2	410.8	477.3	477.2
1964	133.4	293.4	695.6	713.9	1949	173.1	419.6	478.2	473.3
1963	128.7	260.8	641.6	674.6	1948	170.9	424.1	468.6	464.5
1962	134.0	266.6	634.1	665.4	1947	166.3	409.7	393.5	391.6
1961	137.2	272.7	636.9	673.5	1946	162.7	403.7	364.1	360.4

[1] Refer to note to series T79 in text.

Series T83-89. Shipping, seagoing and inland vessels[1] arrived at and departed from Canadian ports, 1946 to 1975

(tonnage figures in thousands of tons)

Year	Registered tonnage total	British		Canadian		Foreign	
		Number	Tons register	Number	Tons register	Number	Tons register
	83	84	85	86	87	88	89
1975	231,354	2,720	23,525	13,963	53,325	23,839	154,504
1974	227,175	3,090	26,254	13,225	44,009	25,957	156,912
1973	244,466	3,512	25,416	15,031	52,183	28,548	166,867
1972	243,375	3,570	24,448	15,124	47,625	31,046	171,302
1971	228,561	3,880	23,509	14,738	44,589	31,621	160,463
1970	217,620	3,832	19,365	16,309	48,841	31,124	149,414
1969	197,390	4,321	20,195	16,921	45,873	29,319	131,322
1968	204,776	4,735	22,529	18,336	43,964	30,927	138,283
1967	197,441	4,362	22,672	18,046	40,679	32,313	134,090
1966	202,170	4,571	22,342	19,298	42,778	34,667	137,050
1965	199,454	5,174	25,045	17,896	35,820	35,456	138,589
1964	188,810	5,131	23,872	19,382	32,280	35,981	132,658
1963	175,589	4,884	22,532	18,729	31,227	35,403	121,830
1962	165,986	5,245	24,264	19,407	28,961	37,038	112,761
1961	156,987	4,797	22,720	24,465	28,565	35,615	105,702
1960	152,480	5,063	23,783	26,261	28,159	36,849	100,538
1959	138,110	5,287	23,643	25,792	27,201	36,900	87,266
1958	117,816	5,355	22,125	27,407	27,930	30,093	67,761
1957	134,994	5,242	21,524	34,377	40,505	33,016	72,964
1956	130,520	4,752	19,775	34,599	37,813	33,237	72,933
1955	118,325	4,665	18,841	33,734	34,398	31,459	65,086
1954	114,346	4,605	19,050	35,162	32,280	30,539	63,016
1953	118,552	4,603	18,876	37,258	38,347	29,685	61,329
1952	105,180	4,490	18,241	35,173	31,454	28,028	55,485
1951	105,954	5,258	20,793	37,389	35,343	26,112	49,818
1950	95,659	4,843	18,762	37,606	35,297	24,270	41,600
1949[2]	88,533	4,230	16,724	36,665	33,032	23,655	38,777
1948	83,772	8,639	13,574	36,987	37,595	19,023	32,603
1947	76,711	7,566	13,528	34,007	35,138	16,071	28,045
1946	64,512	7,741	12,781	32,983	31,246	13,741	20,485

[1] Exclusive of coastal vessels and ferriage.

[2] Newfoundland included with Canada from 1 April, 1949.

Series T90-96. Canals,[1] total traffic through Canadian canals by nationality of vessel and origin of freight, navigation seasons, 1946 to 1970

(tonnage figures in thousands of tons)

Year	Canadian and British vessels		United States and other foreign vessels		Tons of freight carried[2]		
	Number	Registered tonnage	Number	Registered tonnage	Total	Originating in Canada	Originating in United States
	90	**91**	**92**	**93**	**94**	**95**	**96**
1970[3]	13,869	63,335	5,965	18,072	116,998	48,028	68,970
1969	13,503	55,688	6,207	18,913	97,357	43,378	53,979
1968	14,254	57,789	6,124	21,595	108,274	57,953	50,321
1967	14,244	54,599	6,802	20,076	98,773	50,191	48,582
1966	16,621	59,289	6,845	20,847	110,702	49,498	61,204
1965	15,358	53,557	7,998	18,930	99,395	43,485	55,910
1964	16,299	49,519	6,856	18,638	93,276	38,139	55,137
1963	15,458	44,972	6,353	14,264	74,585	27,854	46,731
1962	15,774	38,357	7,062	15,063	63,568	26,052	37,516
1961	19,177	38,825	6,803	12,581	57,222	16,946	40,276
1960	21,119	32,935	8,510	13,117	52,947	—	—
1959	22,488	31,837	8,071	11,555	51,076	30,830	20,246
1958	22,065	26,834	5,386	4,823	35,097	21,833	13,264
1957	24,523	27,948	4,913	5,167	37,230	21,460	15,771
1956	27,740	31,206	5,125	4,817	40,017	24,698	15,319
1955	22,958	27,842	5,214	4,843	34,874	20,003	14,872
1954	21,066	25,303	4,226	4,139	30,071	17,238	12,833
1953	23,378	27,845	4,185	4,697	33,373	18,464	14,909
1952	22,565	25,608	3,757	4,201	31,354	17,245	14,109
1951	22,141	22,951	3,407	4,298	29,325	16,004	13,321
1950	21,179	21,989	3,241	3,514	27,439	15,138	12,301
1949	21,724	20,774	2,495	3,260	24,374	14,801	9,573
1948	19,859	19,724	2,784	4,220	23,559	11,170	12,390
1947	18,542	18,614	2,332	3,796	21,514	10,288	11,225
1946	17,199	16,206	1,794	3,221	18,655	8,905	9,750

[1] Figures include duplications where two or more canals are used.
[2] From 1961 to 1970, heading for series T95 should read: Tons of freight carried by direction "upbound", and series T96: "downbound".
[3] Comparable data not available from 1971 onward.

Series T97-106. Canals, cargo tonnage through St. Lawrence canals, 1946 to 1975 and associated toll revenues,[1] 1959 to 1975

(series T97-105 in thousands of short tons; series T106 in millions of dollars)

Year	Wheat	Total agricultural products[2]	Manufactures and miscellaneous[3]	Forest products	Total coal	Total mine	Total all freight	Total up	Total down	Toll revenue
	97	**98**	**99**	**100**	**101**	**102**	**103**	**104**	**105**	**106**
1975	12,414	9,169	8,085	121	439	17,782	48,010	21,935	26,074	16.5
1974	8,602	7,825	8,516	103	193	18,907	44,146	23,005	21,140	15.6
1973	11,417	13,201	13,153	187	277	19,399	57,634	27,630	30,003	20.4
1972	10,666	13,179	14,031	310	269	15,124	53,579	25,485	28,094	20.0
1971	9,411	13,607	13,782	362	330	15,456	52,948	26,026	26,921	20.0
1970	8,144	17,624	11,659	321	328	21,590	51,196	25,247	25,949	18.6
1969	4,881	11,586	11,021	403	394	18,056	41,066	22,464	18,602	15.6
1968	6,548	12,728	11,173	438	416	23,606	47,945	30,406	17,539	18.1
1967	6,811	13,214	8,775	559	359	21,453	44,001	26,705	17,295	16.4
1966	11,191	19,113	8,944	634	427	20,403	49,094	25,609	23,485	17.3
1965	8,641	16,964	8,422	613	564	17,379	43,378	22,174	21,203	15.5
1964	9,199	16,450	6,043	479	822	16,381	39,353	18,575	20,778	13.5
1963	7,254	13,866	4,919	415	454	11,882	31,082	17,447	13,636	10.7
1962	4,909	10,877	4,508	411	1,188	9,855	25,561	10,930	14,721	8.9
1961	6,509	10,503	4,043	352	1,129	8,483	23,381	8,223	15,158	8.1
1960	3,874	8,039	5,644	306	1,021	6,349	20,338	8,810	11,538	7.2
1959	3,587	7,512	4,597	357	1,137	8,516	21,221	11,155	10,066	7.1
1958	2,784	4,868	3,012	488	1,039	3,378	11,762	4,670	7,092	—
1957	2,085	3,523	3,237	523	1,643	4,893	12,191	5,089	7,103	—
1956	2,587	4,524	3,132	524	1,774	5,299	13,500	5,778	7,721	—
1955	2,027	3,763	2,934	474	1,602	4,253	11,447	4,782	6,665	—
1954	2,372	4,176	2,815	525	1,474	2,116	9,367	2,794	6,663	—
1953	2,081	4,366	3,152	530	1,567	2,032	10,082	2,997	7,085	—
1952	1,942	3,840	2,941	606	1,973	2,449	9,386	3,238	6,599	—
1951	1,847	2,693	3,392	794	2,379	3,036	9,917	4,047	5,870	—
1950	1,892	2,798	3,433	710	2,315	3,023	9,969	4,158	5,811	—
1949	2,223	3,129	2,481	455	1,333	1,890	1,960	2,832	5,128	—
1948	888	1,343	2,232	627	2,671	3,171	7,378	2,727	4,651	—
1947	940	1,199	1,964	591	2,956	3,420	7,180	2,329	4,851	—
1946	666	1,068	1,391	440	2,462	2,847	5,751	1,644	4,106	—

[1] Toll revenue for 1975 covers the 15-month period ending 31 March, 1976.
[2] Excludes animal products which are small in number.
[3] Includes animal products.

Series T107-116. Canals, tonnage through Welland Canal, 1946 to 1975 and associated toll or lockage revenue,[1] 1959 to 1975

(series T107-115 in thousands of short tons; series T116 in millions of dollars)

Year	Wheat	Total agricultural products[2]	Manufactures and miscellaneous[3]	Forest products	Total coal	Total mine	Total all freight	Total up	Total down	Toll or lockage revenue
	107	108	109	110	111	112	113	114	115	116
1975	13,087	9,958	7,074	75	8,488	21,167	59,849	18,890	40,958	3.7
1974	9,243	8,570	7,585	69	6,483	20,409	52,359	20,150	32,209	3.2
1973	11,892	13,906	10,950	135	8,139	22,172	67,194	23,714	43,480	4.2
1972	11,030	13,695	11,223	219	9,929	17,999	64,095	21,125	42,969	4.3
1971	9,772	14,431	11,682	244	9,198	17,582	62,909	21,585	41,323	4.3
1970	8,681	18,412	9,364	380	10,772	34,809	62,965	21,161	41,804	3.5
1969	11,516	12,165	9,083	419	10,774	31,906	53,573	19,361	34,211	2.5
1968	6,809	13,081	9,921	477	9,803	34,625	58,104	26,224	31,880	1.8
1967	7,290	13,909	7,425	588	8,678	30,928	52,850	22,372	30,478	0.9
1966	11,822	19,932	7,487	688	7,691	31,030	59,137	22,444	36,692	—
1965	12,499	17,206	7,065	671	7,152	28,494	53,436	19,974	33,462	—
1964	9,815	17,319	5,307	550	6,333	28,240	51,416	18,555	32,861	—
1963	7,709	14,655	4,432	525	4,978	21,713	41,325	13,178	28,147	—
1962	5,305	19,145	4,240	605	4,669	11,520	35,510	10,916	24,594	0.6
1961	7,172	11,456	4,009	547	4,233	15,392	31,404	7,644	23,759	1.5
1960	4,524	9,526	5,464	315	4,362	13,976	29,281	8,400	20,881	1.3
1959	3,956	8,706	5,078	364	4,785	13,357	27,506	9,597	17,909	1.2
1958	3,630	6,653	4,183	524	4,411	9,915	21,274	5,006	16,269	—
1957	2,764	5,054	4,296	561	5,503	12,462	22,373	5,141	17,232	—
1956	3,195	6,085	3,880	530	5,626	12,572	23,060	5,069	17,997	—
1955	2,733	5,336	3,470	510	5,422	9,515	20,894	4,260	16,634	—
1954	2,858	5,339	3,172	516	4,988	7,618	17,514	2,396	15,118	—
1953	2,795	5,607	4,138	500	5,966	9,297	19,542	2,582	16,960	—
1952	2,598	4,960	4,316	580	5,364	8,054	17,911	2,289	15,622	—
1951	2,808	4,118	4,076	614	4,842	7,390	16,198	2,752	13,445	—
1950	2,025	3,672	3,588	532	4,687	6,949	14,741	2,732	12,009	—
1949	2,890	4,476	3,501	504	3,391	5,211	13,692	2,141	11,552	—
1948	1,536	2,470	3,233	523	4,724	7,148	13,373	2,135	11,239	—
1947	1,528	2,405	3,228	501	3,877	5,671	11,806	1,945	9,861	—
1946	1,263	2,084	3,038	376	3,584	5,082	10,580	1,416	9,164	—

[1] Welland Canal tolls were suspended on 18 July, 1962. A lockage charge was introduced in 1967. Revenue for 1975 covers the 15-month period ending 31 March, 1976.

[2] Excludes animal products, which are small in number.
[3] Includes animal products.

Series T117-122. Water freight charges for wheat, Great Lakes system, 1946 to 1970

Year	Fort William to Georgian Bay ports			Fort William to Montreal		
	Average charge per bushel (cents)	Average charge per ton (dollars)	Average charge per ton mile (cents)	Average charge per bushel (cents)	Average charge per ton (dollars)	Average charge per ton mile (cents)
	117	118	119	120	121	122
1970[1]	4.69	1.56	.290	8.99	2.99	.243
1969	4.66	1.55	.288	8.00	2.66	.217
1968	4.55	1.52	.283	8.35	2.78	.226
1967	4.56	1.52	.283	10.01	3.33	.271
1966	4.57	1.52	.283	10.97	3.66	.298
1965	4.59	1.53	.284	10.41	3.47	.283
1964	4.55	1.52	.283	11.02	3.67	.299
1963	4.26	1.42	.264	9.45	3.15	.257
1962	3.83	1.28	.238	11.56	3.85	.314
1961	5.06	1.69	.314	13.02	4.34	.353
1960	5.05	1.68	.312	13.00	4.33	.353
1959	4.72	1.57	.292	13.32	4.44	.361
1958	6.04	2.01	.374	16.00	5.33	.434
1957	5.90	1.97	.367	16.00	5.33	.434
1956	5.51	1.83	.341	16.00	5.33	.434
1955	4.21	1.40	.261	13.50	4.50	.366
1954	4.26	1.42	.264	14.17	4.72	.384
1953	5.51	1.84	.343	15.90	5.30	.432
1952	5.53	1.84	.343	16.00	5.33	.434
1951	5.53	1.84	.343	16.00	5.33	.434
1950	4.50	1.50	.279	12.50	4.17	.340
1949	4.50	1.50	.279	12.50	4.17	.340
1948	4.27	1.42	.264	11.17	3.72	.303
1947	4.02	1.34	.250	10.00	3.33	.271
1946	3.57	1.19	.222	8.00	2.67	.217

[1] Comparable data from 1971 onward not available.

Series T123-125. Number and registered net tonnage and tons of cargo loaded, vessels departed from Canadian ports in coastwise shipping, 1946 to 1975

Year	Number of vessels departed	Registered net tons	Cargo loaded[1] (tons)	Year	Number of vessels departed	Registered net tons	Cargo loaded[1] (tons)
	123	124	125		123	124	125
1975	46,875	83,664,949	59,935,600	1960	118,852	85,279,786	40,849,804
1974	53,161	85,428,053	59,120,637	1959	109,358	82,359,631	40,228,176
1973	58,054	89,282,852	60,973,294	1958	99,364	74,012,136	38,569,541
1972	63,067	91,685,940	60,986,594	1957[2]	101,879	73,565,370	37,869,188
1971	68,237	96,202,069	60,767,761	1956	89,669	76,857,713	34,505,161
1970	79,884	100,368,093	63,154,162	1955	85,190	64,889,982	27,612,854
1969	87,851	93,284,500	57,199,373	1954	85,581	60,247,848	25,796,418
1968	88,592	89,918,028	56,130,716	1953	86,000	62,022,657	28,573,792
1967	95,633	86,405,639	54,868,302	1952	81,639	57,876,563	27,574,359
1966	102,035	93,931,833	60,761,594	1951	84,591	55,609,082	..
1965	97,906	83,137,405	53,131,205	1950	82,224	51,615,568	..
1964	104,134	87,662,780	51,997,367	1949[3]	80,762	52,203,784	..
1963	106,400	85,257,490	45,831,181	1948	73,000	47,680,583	..
1962	111,099	85,231,511	43,831,540	1947	71,678	47,018,417	..
1961	113,632	87,868,807	46,143,599	1946	65,880	41,218,108	..

[1] Cargo data not available prior to 1952.
[2] Data for non-customs ports included for the first time in 1957.
[3] Data for Newfoundland included from 1 April, 1949.

Series T126-141. Cargoes loaded and unloaded at selected ports for and from foreign countries,[1] 1946 to 1975
(thousands of tons)

Year	Halifax Loaded	Halifax Unloaded	Saint John Loaded	Saint John Unloaded	Montreal Loaded	Montreal Unloaded	Quebec Loaded	Quebec Unloaded	Hamilton Loaded	Hamilton Unloaded	Thunder Bay Loaded	Thunder Bay Unloaded	Toronto Loaded	Toronto Unloaded	Vancouver Loaded	Vancouver Unloaded
	126	127	128	129	130	131	132	133	134	135	136	137	138	139	140	141
1975	3,284	5,496	2,101	6,766	4,804	3,755	3,064	4,011	188	8,850	3,100	147	291	1,158	26,523	3,106
1974	3,848	5,846	1,919	5,699	5,224	4,357	3,829	4,526	194	5,648	4,155	317	158	1,132	25,594	3,266
1973	3,992	6,182	2,768	7,236	6,105	5,199	5,307	6,307	190	7,333	4,026	263	197	1,492	27,184	3,038
1972	3,685	5,434	2,347	6,019	4,739	5,579	4,323	5,773	351	7,620	4,534	148	268	2,298	24,364	2,918
1971	3,230	5,349	1,655	4,776	5,588	5,417	3,241	3,343	215	5,794	3,858	311	209	2,243	22,211	2,774
1970	3,044	5,476	1,784	3,367	5,786	5,434	2,689	2,306	361	6,610	3,968	97	269	2,799	15,358	1,910
1969	2,529	5,124	1,308	3,189	3,429	5,800	1,988	2,058	316	6,800	3,295	189	273	3,912	10,598	2,535
1968	2,192	4,934	1,068	3,077	3,418	5,778	2,004	1,546	258	7,151	3,726	241	206	3,333	12,956	2,400
1967	1,983	4,555	1,228	2,928	3,916	6,123	2,104	1,536	306	6,549	3,846	369	256	3,395	11,562	1,995
1966	2,846	4,228	1,571	2,947	5,548	6,475	1,614	1,191	191	7,320	3,431	420	223	3,159	10,409	1,859
1965	2,913	4,032	1,475	2,745	4,896	7,690	1,723	1,404	204	7,842	3,799	307	252	3,828	9,291	2,067
1964	2,829	3,800	1,464	2,743	5,548	6,432	1,689	841	201	7,776	4,284	180	421	3,289	10,212	1,377
1963	2,411	3,446	1,467	2,488	4,866	6,696	1,351	1,158	208	7,665	3,729	409	364	3,793	8,850	1,176
1962	2,545	3,301	1,113	2,224	3,403	7,481	943	766	235	6,959	3,641	410	298	2,781	7,240	1,124
1961	2,308	3,088	1,241	2,586	4,202	6,722	984	594	108	6,101	3,255	491	346	1,919	7,555	967
1960	2,408	3,226	1,096	2,249	3,800	5,868	859	772	229	7,003	3,600	443	291	2,096	5,987	915
1959	2,506	3,084	1,048	829	3,602	5,690	853	749	65	5,393	3,850	307	258	2,171	5,601	966
1958	1,912	2,863	1,081	699	4,232	4,436	880	463	12	5,322	1,972	480	123	2,027	5,617	760
1957	2,077	2,794	1,354	747	3,827	4,445	796	417	17	6,595	3,740	785	107	2,749	6,830	1,105
1956	2,221	2,636	1,558	816	7,292	5,469	987	699	20	6,358	4,966	1,279	91	2,672	6,071	1,464
1955	1,629	2,147	1,492	794	4,846	4,571	768	498	34	6,077	3,625	1,177	63	1,859	4,070	1,119
1954	613	1,804	893	682	3,862	4,810	655	298	35	4,489	2,987	976	74	2,309	4,659	1,482
1953	693	1,915	1,309	577	5,078	4,412	980	375	34	6,007	4,133	1,129	80	2,604	4,349	2,623
1952	758	1,980	1,585	541	5,655	3,979	1,061	472	15	4,936	4,363	1,741	33	2,511	4,480	2,677
1951	548	1,535	1,207	611	4,378	5,029	834	493	15	4,076	3,745	1,661	14	2,604	3,535	2,607
1950	512	1,613	881	678	3,323	6,454	423	596	5	3,547	2,674	1,378	8	2,460	2,565	2,510
1949	813	1,609	1,308	574	3,962	4,294	329	238	4	2,745	2,859	1,284	8	1,981	2,676	2,055
1948	987	1,689	1,528	559	3,735	4,656	185	457	5	3,654	2,198	3,162	13	2,550	2,098	2,240
1947	1,166	1,368	1,813	479	4,339	4,209	203	456	4	2,611	2,601	2,359	6	2,248	2,245	2,065
1946	1,207	1,208	1,617	495	4,275	3,031	247	300	8	2,216	2,136	2,308	36	1,966	2,445	1,640

[1] These series will differ in some cases from National Harbours Board information; for example, Montreal does not include the activity at Contrecoeur, Varennes and Lanoraie, while Vancouver does not include New Westminster. However, Vancouver includes Roberts Bank from 1970 onward.

Series T142-146. Road and street mileage, by type of surface, 1946 to 1975[1]
(thousands of miles)

Year	Grand total	Surfaced Total	Surfaced Concrete, bituminous pavement and bituminous surface	Surfaced Gravel, crushed stone and other surfaces	Earth	Year	Grand total	Surfaced Total	Surfaced Concrete, bituminous pavement and bituminous surface	Surfaced Gravel, crushed stone and other surfaces	Earth
	142	143	144	145	146		142	143	144	145	146
1975	541.6	434.6	149.4	285.2	107.0	1960[3]	459.2	310.8	70.5	240.3	148.5
1974	534.8	425.9	143.3	282.1	109.0	1959[4]	460.6	303.1	65.2	237.9	157.5
1973	526.1	420.0	134.8	285.2	106.1	1958	423.0	271.4	56.2	215.2	151.6
1972	520.9	412.8	129.5	283.3	108.0	1957[5]	448.8	254.0	52.5	201.5	194.8
1971	518.3	404.9	118.6	286.3	113.4	1956[6]	479.5	233.1	48.6	184.6	246.4
1970	515.9	400.9	113.4	287.4	115.1	1955[6]	480.2	222.6	45.0	177.6	257.6
1969[2]	518.2	396.1	109.2	286.9	122.1	1954	540.0	205.7	42.7	163.0	334.2
1968	513.7	386.0	104.5	281.4	127.7	1953	533.7	203.8	39.4	164.4	329.8
1967	495.5	372.5	96.6	275.9	123.0	1952	528.0	193.5	36.8	156.7	334.5
1966	485.3	359.7	93.1	266.6	125.6	1951[7]	526.7	186.7	34.0	152.6	340.0
1965	492.7	364.6	99.7	264.9	128.1	1950	581.6	177.8	32.2	145.6	403.8
1964	481.0	350.5	87.7	262.8	130.5	1949[8]	576.4	172.5	29.8	142.7	403.9
1963	484.5	344.1	85.6	258.6	140.4	1948	571.1	161.0	27.5	133.4	410.1
1962	478.4	330.5	82.1	248.5	147.8	1947	569.2	156.1	25.6	130.5	413.1
1961	467.1	318.5	78.0	240.4	148.6	1946	567.3	150.1	24.4	125.6	417.2

[1] In 1946, the mileages exclude towns under 2,000 population in Nova Scotia and New Brunswick, under 4,000 in Quebec and Ontario, and under 1,000 in the Western provinces.
[2] A revision in the survey includes all municipalities in Canada.
[3] Decrease is due in part to exclusion of certain mining roads in British Columbia not open to the public.
[4] Increase is mainly due to the inclusion of rural urban municipalities not previously reporting.
[5] Decrease is mainly due to deletions of duplications of parts of Alaska highway.
[6] Manitoba excluded approximately 72,000 miles of road allowance.
[7] Some 56,896 miles of improved road allowances, not in use, are excluded.
[8] Newfoundland was included.

Series T147-194. Motor vehicle registrations, by province, 1903 to 1975

Year	Canada[1]				Newfoundland				Prince Edward Island				Nova Scotia			
	Total	Passenger automobiles[2]	Commercial vehicles[3]	Motorcycles	Total	Passenger automobiles[2]	Commercial vehicles[3]	Motorcycles	Total	Passenger automobiles[2]	Commercial vehicles[3]	Motorcycles	Total	Passenger automobiles[2]	Commercial vehicles[3]	Motorcycles
	147	148	149	150	151	152	153	154	155	156	157	158	159	160	161	162
1975[4]	11,278,513	8,692,821	2,229,570	326,595	170,612	127,300	40,445	2,867	55,459	40,661	13,104	1,662	345,453	262,187	74,716	8,463
1974	10,854,558	8,328,393	2,206,242	319,923	163,975	121,859	39,553	2,563	53,332	39,430	12,460	1,442	346,392	253,521	85,949	6,922
1973	10,158,440	7,866,084	2,004,536	287,820	153,585	115,444	35,776	2,365	49,141	37,014	11,052	1,075	325,871	242,538	78,601	4,732
1972	9,481,432	7,407,275	1,825,656	248,501	140,650	113,300	25,600	1,750	45,430	34,231	10,393	806	304,028	229,034	70,066	4,928
1971	9,022,136	6,967,247	1,856,022	198,867	129,200	104,500	23,500	1,200	42,691	32,251	9,737	703	310,383	234,011	71,731	4,641
1970	8,497,339	6,602,176	1,737,761	157,402	118,641	89,568	27,673	1,400	40,233	30,376	9,164	693	271,573	201,954	65,363	4,256
1969	8,254,160	6,433,283	1,682,515	138,362	112,027	85,667	25,204	1,156	38,812	29,229	8,931	652	314,547	232,940	77,012	4,595
1968	7,887,077	6,159,573	1,587,217	140,287	108,220	81,459	25,776	985	37,152	27,752	8,721	679	276,609	207,477	64,799	4,333
1967	7,481,960	5,865,738	1,490,572	125,650	100,322	75,138	24,217	967	36,844	27,634	8,579	631	246,384	187,765	54,358	4,261
1966	7,035,261	5,480,724	1,446,603	107,934	95,704	71,839	23,120	745	35,299	26,689	8,150	460	234,532	174,380	56,484	3,668
1965	6,698,778	5,279,373	1,345,438	73,967	92,885	69,900	22,535	450	33,849	25,796	7,853	200	233,653	178,389	53,115	2,149
1964	6,382,033	5,037,861	1,297,033	47,133	87,990	65,384	22,366	240	35,062	24,323	10,597	142	222,827	169,490	52,441	896
1963	6,074,655	4,788,896	1,248,573	37,186	79,422	58,912	20,284	226	35,314	23,328	11,869	117	212,034	160,482	50,776	776
1962	5,774,810	4,531,384	1,210,325	33,101	74,119	54,373	19,444	302	33,888	22,092	11,659	137	206,370	153,595	51,962	813
1961	5,517,023	4,325,682	1,156,979	34,362	65,270	48,200	16,790	280	32,166	20,440	11,615	111	206,691	156,663	49,137	891
1960	5,256,341	4,104,415	1,117,450	34,476	61,952	45,586	16,095	271	30,147	19,170	10,850	127	187,065	140,151	46,022	892
1959	5,017,686	3,886,436	1,097,083	34,167	51,145	38,189	12,956	..	27,502	17,408	9,975	119	189,435	140,196	48,237	1,002
1958	4,723,825	3,631,381	1,058,571	33,873	51,575	37,014	14,281	280	25,504	15,860	9,527	117	164,954	119,569	44,382	1,003
1957	4,497,091	3,429,390	1,032,791	34,910	47,982	34,361	13,333	288	23,725	14,595	9,004	126	164,286	118,216	45,031	1,039
1956	4,265,437	3,222,484	1,007,373	35,580	45,997	32,555	13,144	298	23,373	14,163	9,062	148	157,544	111,141	45,231	1,172
1955	3,948,652	2,960,874	951,525	36,253	39,766	27,474	12,006	286	22,145	13,436	8,576	133	149,841	106,763	41,945	1,133
1954	3,644,589	2,706,025	900,899	37,665	34,423	24,000	10,108	315	20,848	12,551	8,157	140	133,087	90,068	41,468	1,201
1953	3,430,672	2,527,461	863,034	40,177	29,576	20,509	8,769	298	20,286	12,218	7,947	121	129,564	88,985	39,231	1,348
1952	3,155,824	2,306,374	807,365	42,085	23,630	15,936	7,354	340	18,717	11,667	6,950	100	114,982	74,831	38,639	1,512
1951	2,872,420	2,105,869	723,362	43,189	20,058	13,483	6,183	392	16,896	11,176	5,636	84	105,262	69,786	33,789	1,687
1950	2,600,269	1,913,355	643,244	43,670	16,375	10,907	5,149	319	15,383	10,392	4,910	81	94,743	62,417	30,679	1,647
1949	2,290,628	1,673,387	577,247	39,994	13,981	9,022	4,707	252	13,211	9,086	4,074	51	83,443	54,419	27,741	1,283
1948	2,034,943	1,497,983	503,021	33,939	–	–	–	–	11,290	8,297	2,945	48	76,319	50,198	25,105	1,016
1947	1,835,959	1,371,467	438,363	26,129	–	–	–	–	9,948	7,559	2,352	37	70,300	47,109	22,387	804
1946	1,622,463	1,235,309	369,991	17,163	–	–	–	–	9,192	7,134	2,013	45	62,660	42,791	19,284	585
1945	1,497,081	1,161,337	321,550	14,194	–	–	–	–	8,835	6,744	2,051	40	56,699	40,314	15,799	586
1944	1,502,567	1,178,879	308,643	15,045	–	–	–	–	8,412	6,833	1,539	40	57,933	41,756	15,483	694
1943	1,511,845	1,195,294	300,155	16,396	–	–	–	–	8,032	6,670	1,334	28	59,194	42,509	15,612	1,073
1942	1,524,153	1,218,493	289,842	15,818	–	–	–	–	7,537	6,268	1,236	33	58,872	42,844	15,225	803
1941	1,572,784	1,281,190	277,117	14,477	–	–	–	–	8,015	6,773	1,226	16	62,805	47,208	14,928	669
1940	1,500,829	1,236,492	250,958	13,379	–	–	–	–	8,070	6,824	1,223	23	57,873	45,120	12,285	468
1939	1,439,245	1,191,914	235,009	12,322	–	–	–	–	8,040	6,804	1,218	18	53,008	41,919	10,798	291
1938	1,394,853	1,161,480	221,300	12,073	–	–	–	–	7,992	6,840	1,130	22	51,214	40,876	10,066	272
1937	1,319,702	1,104,859	203,741	11,102	–	–	–	–	8,011	6,993	997	21	50,048	39,900	9,845	303
1936	1,240,124	1,041,529	187,770	10,825	–	–	–	–	7,632	6,746	865	21	46,179	37,478	8,405	296
1935	1,176,116	992,114	173,518	10,484	–	–	–	–	8,231	7,420	795	16	43,952	35,820	7,820	312
1934	1,129,532	955,151	164,075	10,306	–	–	–	–	7,206	6,409	774	23	41,932	34,443	7,160	329
1933	1,083,178	919,917	153,261	10,000	–	–	–	–	6,940	6,155	760	25	40,648	33,133	7,201	314
1932	1,113,533	948,312	155,802	9,419	–	–	–	–	6,982	6,181	772	29	41,013	33,798	6,880	335
1931	1,200,668	1,028,100	162,920	9,648	–	–	–	–	7,744	6,917	802	25	43,758	36,431	6,941	386
1930	1,232,489	1,061,500	161,562	9,427	–	–	–	–	7,376	6,611	739	26	43,029	36,078	6,632	319
1929	1,187,331	1,030,880	147,594	8,857	–	–	–	–	6,116	5,537	568	11	39,972	33,748	5,924	300
1928	1,069,343	930,619	130,827	7,897	–	–	–	–	5,404	4,952	444	8	35,194	30,327	4,663	204
1927	939,651	830,001	102,088	7,562	–	–	–	–	4,371	4,115	245	11	29,914	26,084	3,640	190
1926	832,268	736,729	88,019	7,520	–	–	–	–	3,448	3,289	153	6	25,746	22,551	3,018	177
1925	724,048	641,186	74,938	7,924	–	–	–	–	2,947	2,815	125	7	22,745	20,012	2,598	135
1924	645,263	573,204	64,003	8,056	–	–	–	–	2,571	2,462	103	6	20,606	18,199	2,270	137
1923	575,985	513,075	54,564	8,346	–	–	–	–	2,440	2,330	102	8	18,232	16,084	2,019	129
1922	509,382	368,510	37,643	9,375	–	–	–	–	2,154	2,059	87	8	16,029	14,177	1,707	145
1921	464,805	333,621	29,294	7,806	–	–	–	–	1,750	1,673	70	7	14,050	12,550	1,500	–
1920	408,790	251,945	22,310	8,195	–	–	–	–	1,418	1,354	54	10	12,450	11,150	1,300	–
1919	342,433	196,367	14,444	8,017	–	–	–	–	1,250	911	33	6	10,030	–	–	–
1918	276,893	157,079	9,611	6,902	–	–	–	–	620	594	21	5	8,150	–	–	–
1917	203,502	115,596	6,053	6,787	–	–	–	–	303	–	–	–	5,100	–	–	–
1916	128,328	77,963	3,519	5,696	–	–	–	–	50	–	–	–	3,050	–	–	–

Series T147-194. Motor vehicle registrations, by province, 1903 to 1975 (continued)

Year	Canada[1]				Newfoundland				Prince Edward Island				Nova Scotia			
	Total	Passenger automobiles[2]	Commercial vehicles[3]	Motorcycles	Total	Passenger automobiles[2]	Commercial vehicles[3]	Motorcycles	Total	Passenger automobiles[2]	Commercial vehicles[3]	Motorcycles	Total	Passenger automobiles[2]	Commercial vehicles[3]	Motorcycles
	147	148	149	150	151	152	153	154	155	156	157	158	159	160	161	162
1915	95,284	60,688	533	5,412	–	–	–	–	34	–	–	–	2,300	–	–	–
1914	74,246	45,716	384	4,769	–	–	–	–	31	–	–	–	1,710	–	–	–
1913	54,380	29,295	–	3,702	–	–	–	–	26	–	–	–	511	–	–	–
1912	36,429	20,367	–	2,291	–	–	–	–	–	–	–	–	456	–	–	–
1911	21,783	13,775	–	264	–	–	–	–	–	–	–	–	228	–	–	–
1910	9,158	5,890	–	55	–	–	–	–	–	–	–	–	148	–	–	–
1909	4,809	3,160	–	–	–	–	–	–	–	–	–	–	69	–	–	–
1908	3,054	2,172	–	–	–	–	–	–	–	–	–	–	–	–	–	–
1907	2,148	1,530	–	–	–	–	–	–	–	–	–	–	–	–	–	–
1906	1,447	1,176	–	–	–	–	–	–	–	–	–	–	–	–	–	–
1905	565	553	–	–	–	–	–	–	–	–	–	–	–	–	–	–
1904	535	535	–	–	–	–	–	–	–	–	–	–	–	–	–	–
1903	178	178	–	–	–	–	–	–	–	–	–	–	–	–	–	–

Year	New Brunswick				Quebec				Ontario				Manitoba			
	Total	Passenger automobiles[2]	Commercial vehicles[3]	Motorcycles	Total	Passenger automobiles[2]	Commercial vehicles[3]	Motorcycles	Total	Passenger automobiles[2]	Commercial vehicles[3]	Motorcycles	Total	Passenger automobiles[2]	Commercial vehicles[3]	Motorcycles
	163	164	165	166	167	168	169	170	171	172	173	174	175	176	177	178
1975[4]	288,658	218,919	60,083	9,656	2,702,272	2,188,895	328,508	155,461	3,913,452	3,225,243	615,659	72,550	535,808	395,098	131,396	9,314
1974	274,173	208,229	58,291	7,653	2,799,352	2,186,808	461,972	150,572	3,744,158	3,111,667	565,315	67,176	508,751	378,194	121,972	8,585
1973	256,042	198,671	51,361	6,010	2,556,260	2,009,868	410,847	135,545	3,583,379	3,002,091	519,088	62,200	471,507	355,175	108,854	7,478
1972	235,108	185,183	45,257	4,668	2,370,405	1,871,802	386,734	111,869	3,382,497	2,848,907	475,863	57,727	428,360	332,861	95,499	6,013
1971	216,710	171,567	41,325	3,818	2,279,722	1,690,802	513,408	75,512	3,209,862	2,713,054	443,982	52,826	419,314	318,821	94,524	5,969
1970	201,274	159,307	38,536	3,431	2,115,126	1,602,129	463,239	49,758	3,047,599	2,576,041	426,307	45,251	403,187	306,559	90,888	5,740
1969	199,980	156,102	40,448	3,430	1,998,001	1,534,682	421,799	41,520	2,953,789	2,501,718	412,196	39,875	394,975	299,695	90,128	5,152
1968	198,406	157,444	37,408	3,554	1,888,934	1,448,120	400,191	40,623	2,869,588	2,424,916	396,846	47,826	380,488	288,750	86,785	4,953
1967	188,617	149,723	35,013	3,881	1,769,154	1,370,514	365,369	33,271	2,736,366	2,312,344	381,081	42,941	371,077	280,480	85,461	5,136
1966	183,676	144,900	35,301	3,475	1,556,342	1,168,073	363,284	24,985	2,643,474	2,235,489	370,026	37,959	356,693	270,175	81,696	4,822
1965	174,428	137,137	35,227	2,064	1,480,743	1,145,785	318,372	16,586	2,516,680	2,139,696	352,914	24,070	342,335	260,339	78,720	3,276
1964	165,311	130,463	33,959	889	1,441,201	1,115,023	311,587	14,591	2,381,219	2,028,528	342,357	10,334	339,509	258,076	79,404	2,029
1963	156,768	123,035	32,934	799	1,381,801	1,068,291	299,336	14,174	2,268,320	1,926,878	333,701	7,741	324,806	247,105	76,197	1,504
1962	151,360	118,483	32,065	812	1,281,180	986,457	282,495	12,228	2,177,148	1,840,119	329,706	7,323	312,272	236,737	74,167	1,368
1961	145,951	112,764	32,351	836	1,183,978	909,322	261,722	12,934	2,126,270	1,794,444	322,882	8,944	299,998	226,376	72,288	1,334
1960	138,469	106,167	31,485	817	1,096,053	843,731	239,169	13,153	2,062,484	1,732,933	320,190	9,361	285,689	213,263	70,987	1,439
1959	129,629	98,523	30,227	879	1,040,366	798,935	228,603	12,828	1,973,737	1,647,379	316,272	10,086	269,974	199,467	68,971	1,536
1958	121,715	91,428	29,394	893	968,058	734,403	220,762	12,893	1,868,922	1,550,457	308,317	10,148	256,064	190,964	63,601	1,499
1957	116,712	86,518	29,277	917	901,065	677,336	210,689	13,040	1,793,499	1,477,409	304,568	11,522	246,188	182,555	62,031	1,602
1956	111,315	81,390	29,018	907	844,827	627,993	203,420	13,414	1,710,240	1,401,259	297,329	11,652	240,008	173,035	65,226	1,747
1955	106,648	74,602	31,084	962	743,682	549,129	180,598	13,955	1,617,853	1,317,590	287,942	12,321	222,474	162,362	58,750	1,362
1954	99,058	67,624	30,413	1,021	674,114	490,819	168,592	14,703	1,489,980	1,205,285	272,241	12,454	210,471	151,915	56,979	1,577
1953	93,914	63,041	29,680	1,193	617,855	440,720	162,059	15,076	1,406,119	1,130,882	261,923	13,314	203,652	145,052	56,838	1,762
1952	89,839	58,991	29,535	1,313	574,974	402,864	156,094	16,016	1,291,753	1,034,755	243,591	13,407	187,881	131,992	53,889	2,000
1951	83,023	54,327	27,310	1,386	500,729	350,435	133,862	16,432	1,205,090	966,357	225,271	13,470	171,265	119,775	49,535	1,955
1950	74,415	48,890	24,061	1,464	433,701	302,811	114,768	16,122	1,104,080	887,571	202,800	13,709	157,546	110,998	44,554	1,994
1949	67,280	43,989	21,982	1,309	384,733	267,097	103,623	14,013	970,137	772,744	184,331	13,062	139,836	99,974	38,105	1,757
1948	62,366	40,795	20,440	1,131	335,953	237,942	86,570	11,441	874,933	699,583	164,138	11,212	128,000	91,860	34,598	1,542
1947	51,589	34,611	16,247	731	296,547	215,322	74,263	6,962	800,058	646,546	143,943	9,569	112,149	80,201	30,830	1,118
1946	44,654	30,670	13,656	328	255,172	187,726	63,922	3,524	711,106	586,907	117,217	6,982	101,090	73,976	26,258	856
1945	41,577	28,794	12,524	259	228,681	171,240	54,607	2,834	662,719	556,740	100,234	5,745	92,758	69,268	22,796	694
1944	39,570	29,177	10,087	306	224,042	171,385	49,923	2,734	675,057	569,544	99,612	5,901	93,297	70,643	21,916	738
1943	40,205	30,083	9,745	377	222,676	171,369	48,493	2,814	691,615	587,483	97,717	6,415	93,494	71,603	21,143	748
1942	37,758	27,623	9,751	384	222,622	173,036	46,736	2,850	715,380	613,440	95,836	6,104	93,147	71,673	20,708	766
1941	41,450	31,945	9,144	361	232,149	184,167	45,107	2,875	739,194	638,278	95,022	5,894	96,573	75,962	19,885	726
1940	39,000	30,560	8,173	267	225,152	180,556	41,785	2,811	703,872	612,431	86,038	5,403	90,932	73,404	16,758	770
1939	38,116	30,457	7,472	187	213,148	171,766	38,503	2,879	682,891	595,586	82,206	5,099	88,864	70,506	17,691	667
1938	37,110	30,257	6,657	196	205,463	166,447	36,349	2,667	669,088	582,240	81,642	5,206	88,219	71,450	16,055	714
1937	36,780	29,937	6,669	174	197,917	161,317	34,074	2,526	623,918	543,649	75,687	4,582	80,860	65,747	14,473	640
1936	33,402	27,731	5,495	176	181,628	148,374	30,756	2,498	590,226	514,211	71,462	4,553	74,940	61,730	12,550	660
1935	31,217	26,185	4,859	173	170,644	139,497	28,658	2,489	564,076	491,980	67,590	4,506	70,660	59,470	10,600	590
1934	29,094	24,614	4,332	148	165,526	135,441	27,671	2,414	542,245	473,341	64,436	4,468	70,430	59,285	10,555	590
1933	26,867	22,890	3,831	146	160,012	130,658	27,089	2,265	520,353	456,223	59,760	4,370	68,590	58,254	9,726	610
1932	28,041	24,030	3,876	135	165,730	135,594	27,911	2,225	531,597	466,162	61,347	4,088	70,840	61,026	9,284	530
1931	33,627	29,223	4,226	178	177,485	146,266	28,901	2,318	562,216	493,890	64,256	4,070	75,210	64,852	9,818	540

Series T147-194. Motor vehicle registrations, by province, 1903 to 1975 (continued)

Year	New Brunswick				Quebec				Ontario				Manitoba			
	Total	Passenger automobiles[2]	Commercial vehicles[3]	Motorcycles	Total	Passenger automobiles[2]	Commercial vehicles[3]	Motorcycles	Total	Passenger automobiles[2]	Commercial vehicles[3]	Motorcycles	Total	Passenger automobiles[2]	Commercial vehicles[3]	Motorcycles
	163	164	165	166	167	168	169	170	171	172	173	174	175	176	177	178
1930	34,699	30,318	4,209	172	178,548	147,821	28,344	2,383	562,506	496,892	61,690	3,924	78,850	68,464	9,866	520
1929	31,736	27,962	3,612	162	169,105	140,229	26,496	2,380	540,207	481,448	55,218	3,541	77,259	68,372	8,315	572
1928	27,970	25,064	2,760	146	148,090	123,641	22,186	2,263	487,337	429,426	54,714	3,197	70,578	63,336	6,739	503
1927	24,457	22,289	2,075	93	128,104	107,204	18,684	2,216	433,504	386,903	43,442	3,159	63,412	57,671	5,257	484
1926	21,421	19,412	1,906	103	107,994	90,519	15,391	2,084	386,349	343,992	39,012	3,345	58,292	53,069	4,709	514
1925	18,863	17,420	1,358	85	97,418	80,854	14,481	2,083	342,174	303,736	34,690	3,748	50,884	46,703	3,639	542
1924	19,840	18,310	1,448	82	84,949	70,736	12,195	2,018	306,770	271,341	31,488	3,941	43,875	40,843	2,475	557
1923	16,662	15,405	1,183	74	71,320	60,363	9,256	1,701	278,752	245,815	28,612	4,325	42,083	39,192	2,249	642
1922	13,611	12,609	904	98	60,940	52,144	6,910	1,886	239,296	210,333	24,164	4,799	41,870	38,913	2,102	855
1921	13,460	12,585	875	—	54,670	47,365	5,596	1,709	206,521	181,978	19,554	4,989	40,336	39,240	—	1,096
1920	11,121	10,442	679	—	41,562	35,965	4,069	1,528	177,561	155,861	16,204	5,496	38,257	37,103	—	1,154
1919	8,252	7,840	412	—	33,525	29,456	2,565	1,504	144,804	127,860	11,428	5,516	31,208	30,223	—	985
1918	6,511	6,259	252	—	26,931	24,187	1,804	940	114,376	101,845	7,529	5,002	25,062	24,114	—	948
1917	4,889	—	—	—	21,213	19,448	1,121	644	88,970	78,861	4,929	5,180	18,169	17,220	—	949
1916	2,936	—	—	—	15,348	14,159	729	460	58,662	51,589	2,786	4,287	13,111	12,170	—	941
1915	1,900	—	—	—	10,112	9,288	528	296	46,520	42,346	—	4,174	9,937	9,010	—	927
1914	1,260	—	—	—	7,413	6,824	384	205	35,357	31,724	—	3,633	8,056	7,131	—	925
1913	824	—	—	—	5,452	—	—	—	26,600	23,700	—	2,900	6,397	5,596	—	802
1912	700	—	—	—	3,535	—	—	—	18,022	16,268	—	1,754	4,636	4,099	—	537
1911	48	—	—	—	1,878	—	—	—	11,339	11,339	—	—	2,700	2,436	—	264
1910	297	—	—	—	786	—	—	—	4,230	4,230	—	—	1,715	1,660	—	55
1909	167	—	—	—	485	—	—	—	2,452	2,452	—	—	708	708	—	—
1908	104	—	—	—	396	—	—	—	1,754	1,754	—	—	418	418	—	—
1907	79	—	—	—	254	—	—	—	1,530	1,530	—	—	—	—	—	—
1906	41	—	—	—	167	—	—	—	1,176	1,176	—	—	—	—	—	—
1905	12	—	—	—	—	—	—	—	553	553	—	—	—	—	—	—
1904	—	—	—	—	—	—	—	—	535	535	—	—	—	—	—	—
1903	—	—	—	—	—	—	—	—	178	178	—	—	—	—	—	—

Year	Saskatchewan				Alberta				British Columbia				Yukon and Northwest Territories[1]			
	Total	Passenger automobiles[2]	Commercial vehicles[3]	Motorcycles	Total	Passenger automobiles[2]	Commercial vehicles[3]	Motorcycles	Total	Passenger automobiles[2]	Commercial vehicles[3]	Motorcycles	Total	Passenger automobiles[2]	Commercial vehicles[3]	Motorcycles
	179	180	181	182	183	184	185	186	187	188	189	190	191	192	193	194
1975[4]	613,269	348,855	254,949	9,465	1,073,020	715,713	327,589	29,718	1,554,081	1,156,964	370,958	26,159	26,429	12,986	12,163	1,280
1974	568,918	328,940	231,795	8,183	1,035,562	687,345	317,743	30,474	1,333,277	999,957	298,338	34,982	26,668	12,443	12,854	1,371
1973	523,557	304,885	212,055	6,617	933,673	627,931	278,714	27,028	1,281,917	961,497	286,925	33,495	23,508	10,970	11,263	1,275
1972	496,214	292,487	197,853	5,874	864,397	588,399	251,470	24,528	1,191,953	906,268	256,313	29,372	22,290	10,816	10,608	966
1971	464,924	277,690	182,910	4,324	813,395	557,913	231,889	23,593	1,115,028	856,086	233,603	25,339	20,907	10,552	9,413	942
1970	464,405	284,251	175,897	4,257	768,759	530,420	218,946	19,393	1,046,697	811,590	212,607	22,500	19,845	9,981	9,141	723
1969	472,363	284,356	184,147	3,860	735,729	508,835	210,524	16,370	1,014,301	790,493	202,903	20,905	19,636	9,566	9,223	847
1968	464,017	287,611	172,541	3,865	703,151	486,401	202,542	14,208	941,935	740,979	182,492	18,464	18,577	8,664	9,116	797
1967	454,252	282,374	168,044	3,834	676,270	470,143	193,228	12,899	887,736	702,003	168,504	17,229	14,938	7,620	6,718	600
1966	438,558	272,749	161,459	4,350	638,852	445,195	182,042	11,615	838,992	664,791	158,814	15,387	13,139	6,444	6,227	468
1965	418,606	267,771	148,295	2,540	606,754	424,217	173,567	8,970	786,310	623,742	149,192	13,376	12,535	6,601	5,648	286
1964	396,742	259,919	135,781	1,042	583,713	408,382	167,507	7,824	716,644	571,807	135,825	9,012	11,815	6,466	5,215	134
1963	382,190	250,183	131,191	816	560,490	393,422	161,356	5,712	662,453	531,116	126,058	5,279	11,057	6,144	4,871	42
1962	372,219	242,271	129,128	820	535,459	376,095	154,485	4,879	620,426	495,308	120,729	4,389	10,369	5,854	4,485	30
1961	349,817	228,269	120,788	760	509,298	356,721	148,572	4,005	588,280	467,370	116,671	4,239	9,304	5,113	4,163	28
1960	335,148	213,147	121,215	786	486,370	339,512	143,324	3,534	564,351	446,050	114,221	4,080	8,613	4,705	3,892	16
1959	326,690	207,612	118,311	767	456,458	315,057	138,596	2,805	545,491	419,422	121,941	4,128	7,259	4,248	2,994	17
1958	314,423	199,495	114,212	716	430,081	294,910	132,897	2,274	515,244	393,337	117,866	4,041	7,285	3,944	3,332	9
1957	300,326	186,543	113,120	663	405,229	276,679	126,558	1,992	491,884	371,727	116,443	3,714	6,195	3,451	2,737	7
1956	291,265	179,986	110,628	651	381,153	256,177	123,127	1,849	454,217	341,650	108,843	3,724	5,498	3,135	2,345	18
1955	274,950	166,864	107,409	677	356,839	236,395	118,795	1,649	409,343	303,481	102,097	3,765	5,111	2,778	2,323	10
1954	267,373	162,980	103,751	642	338,541	222,305	114,383	1,853	371,711	276,161	91,806	3,744	4,983	2,317	2,651	15
1953	257,504	157,942	98,637	925	318,812	207,402	109,104	2,306	348,830	258,940	86,065	3,825	4,560	1,770	2,781	9
1952	237,014	147,824	88,119	1,071	291,469	189,287	99,813	2,369	321,482	236,711	80,842	3,929	4,083	1,516	2,539	28
1951	215,450	137,038	77,310	1,102	259,841	168,482	88,851	2,508	291,417	213,770	73,503	4,144	3,381	1,240	2,112	29
1950	199,866	129,302	69,340	1,224	230,624	150,546	77,605	2,473	270,312	198,397	67,306	4,609	3,224	1,124	2,072	28
1949	185,027	120,291	63,438	1,298	200,428	130,945	67,218	2,265	230,008	165,106	60,221	4,681	2,544	714	1,807	23
1948	167,515	109,718	56,618	1,179	173,950	115,350	56,786	1,814	202,126	143,675	53,915	4,536	2,491	565	1,906	20
1947	158,512	105,329	52,183	1,000	155,386	105,132	48,720	1,534	179,684	128,611	46,709	4,364	1,786	..	..	10
1946	148,206	100,905	46,506	795	138,868	95,764	42,110	994	150,234	109,077	38,119	3,038	1,281	359	906	16

Series T147-194. Motor vehicle registrations, by province, 1903 to 1975 (concluded)

Year	Saskatchewan				Alberta				British Columbia				Yukon and Northwest Territories[1]			
	Total	Passenger automobiles[2]	Commercial vehicles[3]	Motorcycles	Total	Passenger automobiles[2]	Commercial vehicles[3]	Motorcycles	Total	Passenger automobiles[2]	Commercial vehicles[3]	Motorcycles	Total	Passenger automobiles[2]	Commercial vehicles[3]	Motorcycles
	179	180	181	182	183	184	185	186	187	188	189	190	191	192	193	194
1945	140,257	96,268	43,217	772	130,153	92,334	37,077	742	134,788	99,421	32,861	2,506	614	214	384	16
1944	140,992	98,412	41,803	777	127,416	91,828	34,883	705	135,090	99,063	32,893	3,134	758	238	504	16
1943	133,839	93,895	39,222	722	127,559	92,551	34,119	889	134,691	98,920	32,465	3,306	540	211	305	24
1942	130,040	89,742	39,556	742	125,482	93,103	31,489	890	132,893	100,582	29,084	3,227	422	182	221	19
1941	131,545	94,973	35,828	744	126,127	96,303	29,083	741	134,499	105,410	26,668	2,421	427	171	226	30
1940	126,970	93,176	33,151	643	120,514	92,814	26,985	715	128,044	101,452	24,338	2,254	402	155	222	25
1939	119,018	89,471	28,994	553	113,702	88,516	24,512	674	122,087	96,737	23,412	1,938	371	152	203	16
1938	109,014	83,635	24,869	510	107,191	85,244	21,342	605	119,220	94,346	23,005	1,869	342	145	185	12
1937	105,064	83,905	20,672	487	100,434	81,713	18,174	547	116,341	91,549	22,979	1,813	329	149	171	9
1936	102,270	81,519	20,307	444	97,468	79,538	17,401	529	106,079	84,062	20,382	1,635	300	140	147	13
1935	94,792	75,727	18,700	365	93,870	76,882	16,508	480	98,411	78,999	17,868	1,544	263	134	120	9
1934	91,461	74,050	17,053	358	89,369	73,444	15,456	469	92,021	73,997	16,529	1,495	248	127	109	12
1933	84,944	69,713	14,884	347	86,041	71,331	14,243	467	88,554	71,439	15,669	1,446	229	121	98	10
1932	91,275	75,685	15,318	272	86,781	71,982	14,390	409	91,042	73,725	15,933	1,384	232	129	91	12
1931	107,830	91,805	15,719	306	94,642	79,140	15,119	383	97,932	79,451	17,047	1,434	224	125	91	8
1930	127,193	108,812	18,106	275	101,119	85,604	15,068	447	98,938	80,766	16,820	1,352	231	134	88	9
1929	128,426	109,537	18,671	218	98,720	85,848	12,482	390	95,571	78,065	16,234	1,272	219	134	74	11
1928	119,972	103,796	16,002	174	88,398	79,133	8,919	346	86,203	70,828	14,329	1,046	197	116	71	10
1927	105,088	93,563	11,346	179	73,306	68,347	4,699	260	77,327	63,715	12,650	962	168	110	50	8
1926	95,967	87,118	8,688	161	65,101	60,413	4,362	326	67,810	56,272	10,740	798	140	94	40	6
1925	77,940	72,196	5,560	184	54,538	51,038	3,138	362	56,427	46,336	9,321	770	112	76	28	8
1924	69,895	65,928	3,780	187	48,238	45,871	2,036	331	48,407	39,438	8,177	792	112	76	31	5
1923	63,224	60,931	2,086	207	42,323	39,742	2,191	390	40,854	33,144	6,842	868	95	69	24	2
1922	60,645	—	—	296	40,366	38,214	1,749	403	34,385	—	—	880	86	61	20	5
1921	61,184	—	—	—	39,852	38,163	1,689	—	32,900	—	—	—	82	67	10	5
1920	60,325	—	—	—	38,015	—	—	—	28,000	—	—	—	81	70	4	7
1919	56,855	—	—	—	34,000	—	—	—	22,420	—	—	—	89	77	6	6
1918	50,531	—	—	—	29,250	—	—	—	15,370	—	—	—	92	80	5	7
1917	32,505	—	—	—	20,624	—	—	—	11,645	—	—	—	84	67	3	14
1916	15,900	—	—	—	9,707	—	—	—	9,457	—	—	—	57	45	4	8
1915	10,225	—	—	—	5,832	—	—	—	8,360	—	—	—	64	44	5	15
1914	8,020	—	—	—	4,728	—	—	—	7,628	—	—	—	43	37	—	6
1913	4,659	—	—	—	3,773	—	—	—	6,138	—	—	—	—	—	—	—
1912	2,286	—	—	—	2,505	—	—	—	4,289	—	—	—	—	—	—	—
1911	1,304	—	—	—	1,631	—	—	—	2,220	—	—	—	—	—	—	—
1910	531	—	—	—	423	—	—	—	1,026	—	—	—	—	—	—	—
1909	149	—	—	—	275	—	—	—	504	—	—	—	—	—	—	—
1908	74	—	—	—	45	—	—	—	263	—	—	—	—	—	—	—
1907	55	—	—	—	55	—	—	—	175	—	—	—	—	—	—	—
1906	22	—	—	—	41	—	—	—	—	—	—	—	—	—	—	—
1905	—	—	—	—	—	—	—	—	—	—	—	—	—	—	—	—
1904	—	—	—	—	—	—	—	—	—	—	—	—	—	—	—	—
1903	—	—	—	—	—	—	—	—	—	—	—	—	—	—	—	—

[1] The Northwest Territories registrations are added to the Yukon Territory and Canada totals from 1947 onward.
[2] Passenger automobiles include taxi cabs.
[3] Commercial vehicles include buses, trucks, truck tractors, ambulances and in a few cases, other vehicles. (See notes at the beginning of this chapter).
[4] The Canada, Prince Edward Island, Nova Scotia and Quebec totals include registered mopeds for 1975 only.

Series T195-198. Canadian commercial aviation activity,[1] 1946 to 1975
(series T195 and 198 in number; series T196 and 197 in pounds)

Year	Passengers carried	Goods carried[2]	Mail carried	Hours flown[3]	Year	Passengers carried	Goods carried[2]	Mail carried	Hours flown[3]
	195	196	197	198		195	196	197	198
1975	25,626,253	987,751,516	118,521,390	2,501,015	1960	5,554,100	224,190,764	37,472,154	896,052
1974	24,621,116	945,337,199	126,066,036	2,332,596	1959	5,348,032	223,532,796	35,558,226	830,238
1973	22,094,309	935,007,118	113,955,915	2,180,411	1958	4,578,568	206,850,920	33,628,013	744,795
1972	18,079,859	816,741,563	99,733,908	1,955,014	1957	4,355,474	271,891,417	31,413,504	782,816
1971	16,128,712	739,384,212	93,024,472	1,844,157	1956	3,923,539	326,899,918	27,914,288	772,389
1970	15,040,414	678,299,789	80,217,671	1,717,218	1955	3,303,175	240,683,662	26,616,505	637,219
1969	13,505,085	603,496,332	76,978,315	1,702,916	1954	2,865,547	115,013,477	24,228,571	494,333
1968	12,073,627	486,969,327	68,294,540	1,677,046	1953	2,795,837	182,719,719	20,319,952	524,935
1967	11,813,762	389,599,228	61,666,351	1,596,769	1952	2,360,847	140,734,542	18,328,310	491,722
1966	9,248,298	375,988,640	53,929,067	1,397,286	1951	1,947,980	63,786,417	16,824,652	582,707
1965	8,061,671	315,746,104	54,677,855	1,147,837	1950	1,553,346	48,486,243	14,501,110	329,514
1964	6,987,883	267,329,868	50,705,488	966,144	1949	1,308,297	38,760,812	13,752,434	300,416
1963	6,450,884	241,648,677	45,210,723	883,094	1948	1,136,208	38,385,146	10,340,024	322,987
1962	6,220,578	228,715,071	41,596,384	858,670	1947	956,701	34,832,307	7,118,074	294,934
1961	5,892,075	221,442,327	39,024,564	882,889	1946	836,548	25,226,986	5,930,338	211,588

[1] Includes the activity of Canadian air carriers in domestic and international services and the activity of foreign scheduled air carriers in Canada.

[2] Freight, express and excess baggage.
[3] Includes revenue and non-revenue hours flown.

Series T199-205. Canadian commercial aviation, domestic revenue traffic, scheduled[1] services, 1946 to 1975[2]
(series T199, 200 and 205 in thousands; series T201 and 203 in thousands of pounds; series T202 and 204 in thousands of ton miles)

Year	Passengers carried	Passenger miles	Mail carried	Mail carried	Goods carried[3]	Goods[3]	Miles flown
	199	200	201	202	203	204	205
1975	13,841.4	8,768,414	78,945	35,295.9	285,194	172,304.1	142,225
1974	13,376.3	8,464,621	85,955	37,792.8	262,466	151,533.7	135,402
1973	11,928.6	7,534,957	76,184	35,156.8	248,270	144,919.5	121,008
1972	9,430.9	6,009,498	67,470	30,433.6	233,363	136,659.8	105,486
1971	8,255.5	5,178,504	64,544	30,287.6	216,226	131,285.2	99,973
1970	7,833.5	5,124,616	57,686	25,457.2	202,136	120,312.7	99,683
1969	6,849.5	4,416,557	55,307	24,903.8	159,018	94,966.2	91,864
1968	6,009.3	3,947,119	51,412	20,820.8	152,647	85,496.2	85,443
1967	5,787.5	3,814,373	47,537	19,529.2	127,422	68,671.3	78,577
1966	4,735.1	3,067,957	42,407	17,596.0	119,724	63,192.7	64,124
1965	4,137.3	2,622,336	44,728	15,708.9	100,108	51,804.8	56,174
1964	3,594.1	2,233,596	41,854	14,268.1	80,993	42,119.1	51,111
1963	3,421.2	2,102,748	38,212	12,997.9	68,230	32,869.4	50,061
1962	3,406.5	2,094,015	34,311	11,805.0	66,939	30,101.3	51,377
1961	3,304.3	1,968,429	35,749	10,919.1	64,889	25,935.6	51,583
1960	3,098.7	1,649,894	34,633 [4]	10,418.5	65,687	23,295.5	54,704
1959	3,098.3	1,449,151	29,422	9,844.1	59,392	19,393.1	52,234
1958	2,651.1	1,224,057	27,868	9,186.4	48,453	17,775.1	46,335
1957	2,393.9	1,073,192	26,114	8,770.9	46,457	15,091.4	44,689
1956	2,115.6	946,463	23,414	7,950.3	47,977	13,102.4	39,795
1955	1,797.2	794,797	22,669	7,293.3	35,603	11,071.5	36,384
1954	1,559.6	707,404	20,647	6,604.3	27,454	8,358.4	32,394
1953	1,419.6	628,098	15,971	5,265.3	23,889	6,373.4	31,146
1952	1,248.8	542,162	14,320	4,689.0	22,396	5,393.4	28,838
1951	1,053.7	451,051	13,408	4,369.3	19,278	4,547.9	30,933
1950	864.8	374,781	12,630	4,043.6	16,520	4,122.9	22,674
1949	709.3	313,265	11,788	3,783.4	13,322	3,021.0	20,090
1948	600.8	253,721	8,535	2,603.3	12,244	2,357.3	18,429
1947	462.3	179,383	5,587	1,527.5	10,035	1,607.5	17,122
1946	445.8	156,389	4,652	1,428.4	9,270	1,108.0	16,520

[1] "Scheduled" services in this context refers to "unit toll" services.
[2] Excludes the activity of foreign scheduled carriers in Canada.

[3] Goods include cargo, express and excess baggage.
[4] Includes international service by Canadian carriers from 1960 onward.

Series T206-208. Commercial aviation, transborder[1] traffic, 1946 to 1975
(series T206 in thousands; series T207 and 208 in thousands of pounds)

Year	Passengers	Mail	Goods[2]	Year	Passengers	Mail	Goods[2]
	206	207	208		206	207	208
1975	6,543.8	19,707.7	151,251.9	1960	..	..	..
1974	6,148.7	21,371.7	147,325.1	1959	1,366.3	3,541	20,200
1973	5,468.2	20,573.5	139,824.6	1958	1,193.8	3,463	18,127
1972	4,515.0	17,375.1	116,222.7	1957	1,179.3	3,323	18,677
1971	4,310.8	16,084.4	104,059.7	1956	1,040.6	2,844	19,569
1970	4,098.1	12,892.1	93,475.8	1955	915.8	2,521	18,273
1969	..	..	..	1954	780.6	2,269	15,083
1968	..	..	..	1953	718.9	1,925	14,091
1967	..	..	..	1952	579.2	1,743	11,582
1966	..	..	..	1951	536.9	1,830	7,995
1965	..	..	..	1950	421.1	1,318	5,780
1964	..	..	..	1949	364.1	1,293	3,963
1963	..	..	..	1948	310.7	1,228	3,220
1962	..	..	..	1947	311.4	1,108	2,214
1961	..	..	..	1946	319.8	1,063	1,341

[1] A change in the definition of the term "transborder" took place in 1970. After 1970, services to Hawaii and Florida were included under "transborder". Prior to 1970, such services were included under "Pacific" and "Southern" services respectively.

[2] Goods include freight, express and excess baggage.

Series T209-215. Commercial aviation, transborder[1] traffic via Canadian carriers, scheduled[2] revenue traffic, 1946 to 1975
(series T209, 210 and 215 in thousands; series T211 and 213 in thousands of pounds; series T212 and 214 in thousands of ton miles)

Year	Passengers	Passenger miles	Mail	Mail	Goods[3]	Goods[3]	Miles flown
	209	210	211	212	213	214	215
1975	2,496.2	2,261,931	7,090	3,504.5	60,180	33,043.1	23,918
1974	2,348.8	1,987,569	7,865	3,237.5	60,233	32,844.8	20,545
1973	1,773.7	1,697,851	7,441	3,241.3	52,548	27,011.0	19,740
1972	1,734.4	1,498,389	5,867	2,544.8	52,142	26,187.7	18,696
1971	1,879.3	1,387,112	5,502	1,944.8	51,563	22,747.0	19,523
1970	1,812.1	1,410,057	2,849	999.0	48,480	21,648.7	21,369
1969	..	736,755	..	740.6	..	10,921.2	13,352
1968	..	629,178	..	656.2	..	9,575.4	12,362
1967	..	563,403	..	644.6	..	6,747.4	10,215
1966	..	452,180	..	622.6	..	6,800.2	8,351
1965	..	421,158	..	519.9	..	5,457.6	7,753
1964	..	397,952	..	499.1	..	4,527.2	7,009
1963	..	360,098	..	471.2	..	3,882.2	6,952
1962	..	351,084	..	431.1	..	3,535.7	7,883
1961	..	313,402	..	400.0	..	2,347.4	8,352
1960	..	340,545	..	401.2	..	2,415.7	11,349
1959	848.0	284,278	1,917	348.9	12,553	2,130.2	9,220
1958	750.4	250,020	2,069	376.1	11,707	2,034.7	8,303
1957	665.0	225,938	1,864	342.3	11,821	1,875.5	7,387
1956	556.5	189,331	1,182	219.5	11,965	2,140.8	6,721
1955	429.7	144,263	746	141.2	11,315	2,014.7	5,542
1954	351.3	118,201	698	128.6	10,334	1,898.4	4,324
1953	340.7	116,416	550	99.9	9,820	1,768.3	4,328
1952	286.3	96,687	551	97.8	8,311	1,466.4	3,814
1951	254.1	80,826	532	85.4	4,725	768.9	3,293
1950	202.6	67,001	483	78.1	3,096	507.4	3,056
1949	151.1	47,767	350	59.1	1,748	287.0	2,365
1948	136.4	42,170	359	57.0	1,532	241.4	2,713
1947	122.0	35,215	322	53.0	659	99.2	3,290
1946	81.6	30,299	264	57.5	344	69.3	2,873

[1] A change in the definition of the term "transborder" took place in 1970. Starting in 1970 services to Hawaii and Florida were classified as "transborder". Prior to 1970, flights to Florida were counted in "Southern" services and flights to Hawaii were counted in the totals for "Pacific" services.

[2] "Scheduled" in this context refers to "unit toll" traffic.

[3] Goods include freight, express and excess baggage.

Series T216-222. Commercial aviation, Atlantic and Pacific scheduled[1] revenue traffic via Air Canada (Trans-Canada Air Lines) and CP Air (Canadian Pacific Air Lines), 1947 to 1975

(series T216, 217 and 222 in thousands; series T218 and 220 in thousands of pounds; series T219 and 221 in thousands of ton miles)

Year	Passengers	Passenger miles	Mail	Mail	Goods[2]	Goods[2]	Miles flown
	216	**217**	**218**	**219**	**220**	**221**	**222**
1975	975.8	3,711,932	11,424	23,404.3	74,212	144,084.5	32,696
1974	1,070.2	4,034,945	10,177	20,877.4	77,062	151,865.3	35,386
1973	976.5	3,609,837	9,013	18,756.9	72,641	145,595.4	35,028
1972	866.6	3,243,777	8,397	17,805.9	68,143	131,545.8	31,230
1971	633.4	2,315,893	6,524	14,235.6	57,699	114,543.8	31,211
1970[3]	610.0	2,441,672	4,110	9,826.0	57,176	100,409.0	30,789
1969	..	2,100,895	..	7,650.2	..	92,678.0	29,792
1968	..	2,085,558	..	7,061.9	..	70,079.6	28,674
1967	..	1,893,592	..	6,907.3	..	43,064.2	24,975
1966	..	1,530,394	..	5,681.0	..	33,492.4	19,634
1965	..	1,218,577	..	4,684.6	..	24,935.3	15,835
1964	..	914,950	..	3,432.0	..	17,667.6	12,240
1963	..	824,886	..	3,452.4	..	13,701.6	13,569
1962	..	735,510	..	2,637.0	..	10,140.1	12,147
1961	..	660,427	..	2,462.9	..	8,484.4	11,849
1960	..	565,744	..	2,634.8	..	8,593.7	10,652
1959	230.2	623,958	1,556	2,922.5	4,520	7,982.0	15,952
1958	197.8	562,086	1,450	2,663.1	3,601	6,605.4	14,800
1957	158.3	438,452	1,285	2,300.3	3,415	6,431.6	12,396
1956	124.7	344,846	975	1,724.3	3,176	6,089.4	9,551
1955	84.2	236,283	852	1,503.0	2,588	4,409.8	6,667
1954	75.2	197,530	816	1,405.2	2,247	3,356.7	5,846
1953	62.4	151,084	564	942.3	1,918	2,587.1	5,410
1952	56.2	126,506	451	771.9	1,876	2,412.8	4,849
1951	54.4	156,053	339	569.6	1,618	1,987.2	6,325
1950	37.5	99,904	260	439.2	1,345	1,687.0	4,568
1949	37.4	100,913	250	415.8	1,256	1,581.3	4,578
1948	32.8	100,536	230	369.6	750	984.2	4,597
1947	15.8	50,370	152	251.6	408	531.0	2,387

[1] "Scheduled" in this context refers to "unit toll" traffic.
[2] Goods include freight, express and excess baggage.
[3] Starting in 1970, flights to and from Hawaii are classified as "transborder".

Prior to 1970, these flights were included in the totals for "Pacific" services.

Series T223-225. Commercial aviation, contract and charter traffic, Canadian carriers, 1946 to 1975

(series T223 and 225 in thousands; series T224 in thousands of pounds)

Year	Passengers carried	Goods carried	Revenue miles flown[1]	Year	Passengers carried	Goods carried	Revenue miles flown[1]
	223	**224**	**225**		**223**	**224**	**225**
1975	2,742	362,972	79,034	1960	611	130,170	23,939
1974	2,345	340,412	74,692	1959	505	126,524	28,702
1973	2,149	357,150	70,657	1958	424	128,006	26,372
1972	1,849	306,391	63,801	1957	509	194,456	36,743
1971	1,761	280,918	58,698	1956	524	246,886	42,370
1970	1,478	254,468	55,517	1955	406	175,789	32,266
1969	1,341	260,821	50,983	1954	320	63,141	15,456
1968	1,093	168,731	42,138	1953	379	132,730	19,532
1967	1,009	136,019	36,654	1952	295	94,694	17,447
1966	949	143,096	34,900	1951	193	26,269	9,986
1965	854	133,195	30,904	1950	165	19,813	8,286
1964	798	122,665	27,047	1949	137	15,565	7,166
1963	734	122,115	26,818	1948	143	18,169	7,905
1962	632	115,309	23,277	1947	109	19,384	6,616
1961	559	121,902	21,569	1946	83	13,046	5,399

[1] Excludes carriers with gross annual flying revenues of less than $60,000 (Group V) for the years 1960 to 1969.

Series T226-235. Commercial aviation, operating revenues, passenger fares per unit of traffic and employment, Canadian carriers, 1946 to 1975

(series T226-232 in thousands of dollars; series T233 and 234 in cents per unit)

Year	Operating revenues, Canadian commercial air services							Scheduled[1] passenger revenue per passenger mile		Number of employees
	Total operating revenues	Scheduled[1] services			Charter services	Other flying revenues	Non-flying services	Trans-continental air carriers	Regional air carriers	
		Passenger	Mail	Goods						
	226	227	228	229	230	231	232	233	234	235
1975	1,891,307.4	1,230,123.1	37,112.6	150,004.7	357,311.7	48,993.5	67,761.8	7.42	11.93	40,321
1974	1,597,785.4	1,085,013.4	36,320.5	125,579.4	253,018.7	41,348.7	56,504.7	6.57	10.22	38,874
1973	1,253,743.7	826,692.2	31,702.2	106,496.2	208,580.6	36,781.0	43,491.5	5.77	9.31	34,071
1972	1,055,763.7	696,617.1	29,171.3	92,634.9	177,710.8	25,972.6	33,657.0	5.79	9.29	31,480
1971	918,389.5	607,869.3	29,338.0	81,040.9	150,088.8	23,446.9	26,605.6	6.10	9.18	29,622
1970	841,808.2	560,395.3	27,935.7	77,291.7	131,727.1	23,731.2	20,727.2	5.62	8.88	30,698
1969	721,112.5	480,256.1	27,180.3	61,655.6	108,800.9	23,155.7	20,063.9	5.69	8.84	28,625
1968	634,467.4	442,999.0	24,421.6	52,623.8	78,385.9	21,238.9	14,798.1	5.74	9.16	26,550
1967	560,814.4	398,645.8	23,586.7	40,564.7	65,173.2	20,057.4	12,786.6	5.60	9.15	24,686
1966	478,509.2	331,115.5	20,578.0	36,706.8	60,986.6	15,857.8	13,264.5	5.77	8.94	21,440
1965	407,688.2	283,495.9	18,755.5	30,346.5	54,201.8	13,459.1	7,429.4	5.86	9.03	19,007
1964	347,126.7	240,189.1	17,179.2	24,340.6	48,682.5	9,936.8	6,798.5	5.96	8.87	17,795
1963	318,633.8	225,678.7	15,812.3	20,375.8	41,119.9	8,111.7	7,535.4	6.09	9.33	17,577
1962	292,674.9	211,140.0	14,414.9	18,242.4	31,800.5	10,027.4	7,049.7	5.96	8.74	17,810
1961	263,644.9	186,890.4	13,867.9	15,887.1	31,003.7	7,697.1	8,298.7	5.80	8.72	17,700
1960	243,126.2	168,718.9	13,794.1	16,177.7	30,317.1	7,273.4	6,845.0	6.25	..	17,106
1959	220,423.6	152,317.2	13,437.8	14,549.2	29,003.3	6,491.2	4,624.9	6.31	6.75	16,565
1958	201,713.9	131,167.0	12,981.6	12,440.9	29,896.6	10,129.8	5,098.2	6.28	6.89	15,990
1957	190,043.1	112,295.3	12,661.8	11,594.9	40,719.2	7,867.4	4,904.4	6.26	7.05	16,014
1956	182,168.8	96,180.5	11,532.9	10,296.7	53,435.6	7,124.1	3,599.1	6.27	7.30	14,848
1955	152,739.0	77,598.1	10,904.7	8,815.2	44,543.3	6,722.0	4,155.7	6.34	7.59	13,271
1954	108,864.3	66,748.5	10,873.2	6,705.7	15,149.5	5,984.9	3,402.5	6.26	7.56	11,690
1953	104,255.5	59,566.0	10,089.1	5,985.6	19,664.1	5,716.7	3,234.0	6.37	7.98	10,703
1952	90,519.3	51,681.7	9,830.7	5,370.4	16,952.0	4,298.4	2,386.1	6.44	8.41	9,398
1951	73,051.5	46,059.5	9,186.1	4,235.3	10,202.7	1,599.7	1,768.2	6.78[2]	5.98[2]	6,942
1950	57,408.4	37,255.9	8,405.4	3,595.7	5,231.3	1,447.6	1,472.5	6.69	7.40	6,337
1949	49,803.4	31,600.8	8,261.2	2,915.0	4,286.0	1,289.8	1,450.6	6.77	8.36	6,513
1948	44,594.6	25,604.4	7,384.2	2,335.9	5,826.5	1,853.0	1,590.6	6.68	7.70	5,983
1947	31,900.2	17,483.1	6,097.4	1,799.7	3,848.4	1,292.5	1,379.1	6.41	8.38	5,725
1946	21,988.1	11,385.4	5,278.5	1,157.4	2,442.2	662.3	1,062.3	5.18	9.75	5,413

[1] "Scheduled" in this context refers to "unit toll" traffic.   [2] This figure is distorted by specially priced defence transportation.

Series T236-239. Civil aviation, number of aircraft and airports, 1946 to 1975
(in units)

Year	Number of aircraft			Licensed civil airports[1]	Year	Number of aircraft			Licensed civil airports[1]
	Total all aircraft	Commercial and state aircraft	Private aircraft			Total all aircraft	Commercial and state aircraft	Private aircraft	
	236	237	238	239		236	237	238	239
1975	16,435	4,686	11,749	—	1960	4,914	2,045	2,869	460
1974	14,764	4,291	10,473	—	1959	4,547	2,034	2,513	483
1973	13,365	3,981	9,384	772	1958	4,509	2,071	2,438	452
1972	12,230	3,704	8,526	—	1957	4,005	2,001	2,004	550
1971	11,403	3,493	7,910	796	1956	3,330	1,764	1,566	519
1970	10,840	3,364	7,476	791	1955	3,148	1,682	1,466	495
1969	10,062	3,172	6,890	—	1954	2,800	1,513	1,287	430
1968	9,296	2,825	6,471	761	1953	2,654	1,503	1,151	433
1967	8,454	2,549	5,905	721	1952	2,411	1,425	986	415
1966	7,674	2,367	5,307	692	1951	2,306	1,454	852	403
1965	7,016	2,217	4,799	675	1950	1,960	1,222	738	415
1964	6,563	2,174	4,389	672	1949	2,001	1,334	667	361
1963	6,270	2,161	4,109	593	1948	2,021	1,477	544	354
1962	5,915	2,176	3,739	541	1947	1,873	1,574	299	273
1961	5,429	2,071	3,358	493	1946	911	866	45	161

[1] Includes helicopters and sea plane bases.

Series T240-246. Arriving and departing civil flights at selected Canadian international airports, 1960 to 1975

Year	Calgary	Edmonton international	Montreal (Dorval)	Ottawa	Toronto	Vancouver	Winnipeg
	240	241	242	243	244	245	246
1975	117,750	58,862	187,860	76,932	228,688	198,416	114,459
1974	110,266	49,890	186,097	79,258	226,921	180,759	112,942
1973	93,280	45,244	180,029	98,534	208,775	167,837	104,472
1972	81,310	38,807	158,123	90,422	183,025	132,110	102,257
1971	80,925	31,699	152,578	90,729	176,984	122,244	111,151
1970	73,456	26,737	152,342	89,169	176,611	132,606	117,949
1969	70,060	23,538	148,027	93,194	165,426	142,120	114,161
1968	64,849	21,929	140,511	87,359	153,336	129,730	109,268
1967	57,197	20,250	151,502	82,705	141,477	124,748	106,776
1966	62,588	17,206	125,756	76,121	119,493	106,930	96,619
1965	66,948	15,524	107,255	62,845	99,958	84,879	74,787
1964	59,012	14,796	95,186	57,538	89,205	73,763	68,724
1963	57,674	14,262	80,821	61,555	86,012	72,881	64,763
1962	51,915	14,560	82,541	58,469	89,376	67,237	61,740
1961	49,823	14,662	84,364	55,515	91,764	60,252	66,213
1960	46,841	1,032[1]	87,104	60,035	95,388	59,671	69,186

[1] Edmonton international airport opened November 1960, December data only.

Series T247-250. Oil and gas pipeline transport revenues and ton-miles, 1950 to 1975
(series T247 and 248 in millions of dollars; series T249 and 250 in billions of ton-miles)

Year	Oil pipeline transport revenue	Gas pipeline transport revenue	Oil pipeline ton-miles	Gas pipeline ton-miles	Year	Oil pipeline transport revenue	Gas pipeline transport revenue	Oil pipeline ton-miles	Gas pipeline ton-miles
	247	248	249	250		247	248	249	250
1975	255.2	668.1	66.4	44.9	1960	73.6	64.1	17.2	6.4
1974	276.3	571.9	79.1	43.7	1959	67.6	—	16.7	3.6
1973	267.7	495.4	82.5	42.0	1958	59.1	—	14.3	1.6
1972	247.7	342.9	70.5	36.4	1957	—	—	16.5	0.2
1971	214.8	277.7	59.4	31.7	1956	—	—	16.2	—
1970	203.3	241.4	54.3	28.9	1955	—	—	12.3	—
1969	185.1	203.2	47.1	24.1	1954	—	—	9.1	—
1968	159.8	163.3	41.6	21.2	1953	—	—	6.8	—
1967	150.6	150.9	37.0	19.2	1952	—	—	4.7	—
1966	125.9	137.6	33.1	17.9	1951	—	—	3.5	—
1965	122.2	133.4	29.9	17.0	1950	—	—	0.6	—
1964	108.7	129.8	28.0	15.3					
1963	104.0	119.3	26.7	13.2					
1962	94.9	114.6	24.3	11.7					
1961	83.4	96.7	21.5	9.3					

Series T251-260. Railway accident victims, 1907 to 1975[1]
(in number)

Year[2]	Resulting from movement of trains								Other causes	
	Fatal victims				Injured victims				Killed total	Injured total
	Total	Passengers	Employees[3]	Others[3]	Total	Passengers	Employees	Others		
	251	252	253	254	255	256	257	258	259	260
1975	176	2	20	154	1,926	240	1,281	405	8	3,607
1974	188	1	22	165	2,045	244	1,393	408	11	3,833
1973	196	1	17	178	1,903	169	1,245	489	9	3,237
1972	226	5	17	204	2,122	194	1,387	541	15	3,295
1971	211	2	24	185	1,885	114	1,225	546	6	2,570
1970	180	1	17	162	1,835	157	1,223	455	8	2,870
1969	195	4	21	170	1,852	165	1,182	505	19	2,714
1968	215	6	25	184	1,910	235	1,168	507	10	2,509
1967	271	—	23	248	2,008	209	1,265	534	11	2,750
1966	305	4	20	281	2,114	216	1,307	591	8	2,688
1965	229	2	20	207	2,082	273	1,185	624	16	2,462
1964	251	8	23	220	1,776	138	1,085	553	12	2,239
1963	226	2	23	201	1,587	157	853	577	11	2,006
1962	253	—	19	234	1,465	106	877	482	20	2,116
1961	228	1	22	205	1,451	73	881	497	21	2,053
1960	262	2	24	236	1,586	151	895	540	10	1,903
1959	303	9	30	264	1,818	151	1,092	575	13	2,258
1958	304	1	33	270	1,462	83	1,016	363	23	2,422
1957	310	2	27	281	2,018	143	1,343	527	15	2,837
1956	359	7	55	297	2,311	84	1,637	590	20	2,842
1955	292	1	39	252	2,262	188	1,582	492	15	2,992
1954	281	4	37	240	2,359	215	1,646	498	16	3,132
1953	290	3	30	257	2,781	133	2,017	631	15	4,044
1952	375	2	61	312	3,156	125	2,430	601	18	4,753
1951	362	4	69	289	3,127	191	2,341	595	28	5,468
1950	299	18	54	227	3,098	262	2,244	592	18	6,051
1949	302	1	52	249	3,325	268	2,418	639	27	6,609
1948	352	15	76	261	3,841	284	2,906	651	33	7,315
1947	369	34	77	258	3,984	355	2,963	666	31	7,855
1946	304	2	90	212	3,780	349	2,844	587	23	8,858
1945	312	10	71	231	3,610	360	2,665	585	42	10,741
1944	320	8	81	231	3,548	416	2,637	495	33	10,831
1943	318	9	112	197	3,945	417	2,942	586	23	9,974
1942	411	43	103	265	3,430	639	2,163	628	32	8,100
1941	376	10	88	278	2,756	485	1,556	715	27	6,790
1940	275	5	49	221	2,070	277	1,278	515	25	5,145
1939	283	1	43	239	1,742	322	879	541	16	4,373
1938	284	4	45	235	1,741	314	898	529	11	4,139
1937	327	5	59	263	2,119	378	1,082	659	20	4,810
1936	362	6	83	273	2,572	657	1,293	622	19	5,160
1935	322	10	43	269	2,063	432	1,026	605	29	4,223
1934	295	16	43	236	2,106	417	1,119	570	20	4,094
1933	260	8	41	211	1,851	306	985	560	20	3,522
1932	304	7	57	240	1,855	339	957	559	22	3,716
1931	246	3	42	201	2,243	369	1,131	743	14	4,952
1930	425	15	81	329	2,692	488	1,477	727	38	8,371
1929	412	20	104	288	3,144	406	2,028	710	19	10,699
1928	479	15	114	350	3,257	326	2,214	717	28	10,548
1927	368	14	106	248	2,942	438	1,915	589	34	9,379
1926	424	20	102	302	3,068	375	2,141	552	35	8,638
1925	285	5	82	198	3,095	374	2,158	563	24	6,204
1924	334	19	105	210	3,197	401	2,350	446	28	6,611
1923	321	15	144	162	3,645	406	2,763	476	26	6,713
1922	323	11	107	205	3,256	336	2,440	480	18	5,991
1921	322	5	127	191	2,592	227	2,024	341	31	4,644

Series T251-260. Railway accident victims, 1907 to 1975[1] (concluded)
(in number)

Year[2]	Resulting from movement of trains								Other causes	
	Fatal victims				Injured victims				Killed total	Injured total
	Total	Passengers	Employees[3]	Others[3]	Total	Passengers	Employees	Others		
	251	252	253	254	255	256	257	258	259	260
1920	360	28	145	187	3,402	456	2,513	433	33	5,278
1919[2]	399	33	162	204	2,712	372	1,904	436	41	4,505
1919[2]	359	34	151	174	2,546	296	1,860	390	27	3,616
1918	383	32	154	197	2,549	322	1,868	359	27	3,540
1917	419	24	177	218	2,682	410	1,909	363	33	2,747
1916	437	20	149	268	2,058	291	1,468	299	31	2,920
1915	366	17	108	241	1,578	304	1,578	328	19	1,583
1914	565	25	200	340	2,287	402	1,475	410	35	1,752
1913	710	38	298	374	2,966	650	1,834	482	32	1,606
1912	545	47	215	283	2,437	485	1,606	346	23	1,343
1911	465	28	202	235	1,906	288	1,314	304	28	1,423
1910	524	60	214	250	1,441	270	926	245	91	698
1909	478	36	182	260	1,404	281	897	226	27	782
1908	449	28	202	197	2,347	345	1,111	209	22	682
1907	598	70	249	268	2,152	352	1,126	220	11	454

[1] Excludes electric railway accidents prior to 1956.
[2] From 1907 to 1919, the data are for the year ending 30 June of the year given. The year 1919 is also given on a calendar year basis as are all subsequent years.
[3] Newfoundland included from 1 April 1949.

Series T261-270. Water transport accident victims,[1] 1946 to 1975
(in number)

Year	Fatal victims					Injured victims				
	Total killed	Crew	Passengers	Other employees	Others	Total injured	Crew	Passengers	Other employees	Others
	261	262	263	264	265	266	267	268	269	270
1975	32	23	2	—	7	32	30	—	—	2
1974	15	14	—	—	1	42	40	1	—	—
1973[2]	13	8	—	5	—	17	15	2	—	—
1972	15	14	—	—	1	1,163	981	62	118	2
1971	7	7	—	—	—	1,534	1,165	77	284	8
1970	27	19	3	1	4	1,745	1,302	92	325	26
1969	14	10	1	3	—	1,602	1,136	86	372	8
1968	7	7	—	—	—	1,585	1,143	67	355	20
1967	10	9	—	—	1	1,651	1,145	80	404	22
1966	23	18	—	4	1	1,864	1,316	38	492	18
1965	19	17	—	1	1	1,826	1,235	66	503	22
1964	14	11	—	—	3	1,661	1,043	64	522	32
1963	16	12	—	2	2	1,679	1,137	69	451	22
1962	12	9	—	2	1	1,797	1,141	85	549	22
1961	18	16	—	2	—	1,886	1,229	50	553	54
1960	10	7	1	2	—	1,746	1,156	59	513	18
1959	13	11	2	—	—	1,744	1,160	66	515	3
1958	16	14	—	1	1	1,997	1,416	44	536	1
1957	14	13	—	1	—	1,946	1,446	39	458	3
1956	23	20	1	1	1	2,091	1,516	29	545	1
1955	19	17	2	—	—	1,879	1,414	20	441	4
1954	26	23	—	3	—	1,875	1,375	43	438	19
1953	23	23	—	—	—	1,790	1,323	50	412	5
1952	26	26	—	—	—	1,809	1,363	38	390	18
1951	12	10	—	1	1	1,700	1,270	28	402	—
1950	28	20	7	—	1	1,763	1,336	33	392	2
1949[3]	137	16	119[4]	2	—	1,995	1,402	115	476	2
1948	38	36	—	2	—	2,166	1,665	83	401	17
1947	89	79	5	4	1	2,350	1,845	32	465	8
1946	26	24	1	—	1	1,761	1,655	31	73	2

[1] Excludes small pleasure craft accidents and all accidents involving commercial fishing.
[2] From 1973 onward, data are given only for those accidents reported to Transport Canada.
[3] Newfoundland is included.
[4] Noronic disaster.

Series T271-284. Motor vehicle traffic accident victims, 1921 to 1975
(in number)

Year	Total killed	Drivers	Passengers	Pedestrians	Bicyclists	Motorcyclists	Others	Total injured	Drivers	Passengers	Pedestrians	Bicyclists	Motorcyclists	Others
	Fatal victims							Injured victims						
	271	272	273	274	275	276	277	278	279	280	281	282	283	284
1975	6,061	2,480	1,770	1,045	185	378	203	220,941	94,883	83,456	19,271	8,913	10,922	3,496
1974	6,290	2,529	1,854	1,115	182	360	250	229,641	98,673	86,993	19,871	8,546	12,045	3,513
1973	6,706	2,536	2,040	1,304	187	415	224	223,777	95,570	86,424	20,085	6,819	11,416	3,463
1972	6,221	2,508	1,799	1,203	179	314	218	215,705	90,010	84,708	20,640	6,561	10,051	3,735
1971	5,573	2,257	1,736	1,147	170	216	47	192,599	79,663	78,414	19,540	6,268	8,166	548
1970	5,080	1,990	1,540	1,181	132	201	36	178,501	72,295	73,350	20,041	4,901	7,338	576
1969	5,425	2,113	1,696	1,223	150	184	59	180,829	72,773	75,335	20,565	4,772	6,775	609
1968	5,318	2,012	1,705	1,198	156	202	45	173,901	67,681	72,778	20,489	4,877	7,586	490
1967	5,429	2,098	1,743	1,285	114	141	48	168,142[1]	63,525	72,669	21,430	4,567	5,370	581
1966	5,281	1,988	1,671	1,318	147	128	29	161,197	60,981	68,969	20,631	4,436	5,849	331
1965	4,902	1,765	1,655	1,254	138	70	20	150,612	56,769	65,151	19,862	4,541	3,979	310
1964	4,652	1,762	1,515	1,195	116	34[2]	30	139,632	52,878	61,579	19,056	3,966	1,807[2]	346
1963	4,210	1,607	1,302	1,132	131	25	13	126,086	46,711	55,996	18,080	3,664	1,332	303
1962	3,883	1,105[3]	1,675[3]	967	62[3]	12	62[3]	111,115	32,406[3]	57,636[3]	16,444	2,155[3]	898	1,576[3]
1961	3,426	956[3]	1,432[3]	931	50[3]	21	36[3]	99,263	28,129[3]	52,502[3]	15,484	2,187[3]	816	145[3]
1960	3,283	860[3]	1,394[3]	917	69[3]	24	19[3]	90,186	24,831[3]	47,355[3]	14,690	2,237[3]	851	222[3]
1959	3,231	829[3]	1,358[3]	918	63[3]	31	32[3]	84,751	23,221[3]	43,679[3]	14,576	2,036[3]	870	369[3]
1958	3,118	815[3]	1,276[3]	920	52[3]	25	30[3]	80,061	20,100[3]	42,394[3]	14,456	2,015[3]	930	166[3]
1957	3,260[4]	794	764	692	69	31	31	78,426[4]	19,508	27,012	9,246	1,988	986	184
1956	3,184[4]	836	781	658	52	37	17	72,884[4]	18,109	25,534	8,973	1,898	1,087	120
1955	2,084[4]	691	699	601	41	31	21	49,828[4]	15,586	22,798	8,611	1,775	924	134
1954	2,715[4]	616	643	618	73[5]	—[5]	10	47,020[4]	14,246	21,042	8,806	2,737[5]	—[5]	189
1953	2,921[4]	598[6]	713[6]	602	49	40	18	56,749[4]	14,297[6]	21,624[6]	8,788	1,859	1,054	204
1952	2,701[4]	545	638	558	51	38	12	57,738[4]	13,182	20,654	8,099	1,842	1,081	174
1951	2,412[4]	485	561	614	55	34	18	54,755[4]	11,933	18,640	7,602	1,673	1,185	232
1950	2,161[4]	382	474	498	55	60	8	50,032[4]	10,249	16,701	7,090	1,656	1,281	54
1949[7]	2,276	554	692	830	98	93	9	43,883	10,049	19,933	9,683	2,302	1,866	50
1948	1,976	464	581	738	79	77	30	38,098	8,532	16,515	8,832	2,067	1,409	520
1947	1,760	428	506	678	75	65	8	32,685	7,738	13,639	8,260	1,776	1,188	84
1946	1,663	387	440	678	95	55	8	30,679	7,208	12,302	8,247	1,920	900	102
1945[8]	1,556	283	362	624	87	27	16	24,422	5,025	9,712	7,327	1,690	603	65
1944	1,374	223	300	490	60	37	7	20,228	3,439	7,365	6,720	1,775	443	64
1943	1,437	234	284	544	68	28	3	20,390	3,555	7,383	7,165	1,830	376	81
1942	1,409	246	297	508	64	30	5	22,809	4,237	7,722	7,133	2,278	474	14
1941	1,852	306	492	658	123	32	3	30,984	5,368	11,983	8,689	3,262	706	19
1940	1,723	333	426	688	91	31	5	29,504	6,862	8,808	8,214	2,976	659	46
1939	1,584	347	306	589	111	20	7	25,104	7,348	6,308	7,177	2,516	541	94
1938	1,545	334	257	579	87	22	10	24,585	6,287	6,277	7,466	2,497	526	40
1937	1,642	409	289	661	121	37	9	25,703	7,162	6,249	8,129	2,520	588	111
1936	1,316	345	247	510	45	23	49	23,207	7,414	4,258	6,973	2,233	444	597
1935	1,224	353	215	460	53	10	73	20,989	6,665	4,483	7,205	1,322	333	981
1934	1,115	470		437	38	12	26	17,998	9,793		6,066	1,059	287	499
1933	955	322		321	28	11	36	14,947	6,780		5,232	718	228	909
1932	1,120	..	..	..	..	..	..	11,113	..	..	..	..	..	..
1931	1,316	..	..	..	..	..	..	..	..	..	..	..	..	..
1930	1,290	..	..	..	..	..	..	..	..	..	..	..	..	..
1929	1,300	..	..	..	..	..	..	..	..	..	..	..	..	..
1928	1,082	..	..	..	..	..	..	..	..	..	..	..	..	..
1927	865	..	..	..	..	..	..	..	..	..	..	..	..	..
1926	606	..	..	..	..	..	..	..	..	..	..	..	..	..
1925	425	..	..	..	..	..	..	..	..	..	..	..	..	..
1924	340	..	..	..	..	..	..	..	..	..	..	..	..	..
1923	355	..	..	..	..	..	..	..	..	..	..	..	..	..
1922	237	..	..	..	..	..	..	..	..	..	..	..	..	..
1921	197	..	..	..	..	..	..	..	..	..	..	..	..	..

[1] Total number injured in 1967 includes 9,325 persons injured in the city of Montreal between June and December for which no breakdown is available. These injuries have been distributed to the various categories on the basis of 1966 proportions of the province of Quebec.

[2] Prior to 1965, motorcyclists are included with bicyclists for New Brunswick.

[3] For 1958 to 1962, Quebec passengers included drivers, bicyclists and others.

[4] For 1950 to 1957, Quebec totals only included, no breakdown available.

Vital statistics used for some years. Some Manitoba figures estimated for 1950.

[5] Bicyclists include motorcyclists for 1954.

[6] In Manitoba for 1953, drivers killed were included with passengers killed.

[7] Newfoundland is included.

[8] Prior to 1946, total killed data come from Vital Statistics. Other details come from provincial reports. Series T271 will not be the sum of series T272-277.

Series T285-292. Civil aviation flying accident victims, 1931 to 1975
(in number)

Year	Fatal victims				Injured victims			
	Total killed	Crew	Passengers	Others	Total injured	Crew	Passengers	Others
	285	286	287	288	289	290	291	292
1975	175	80	91	4	92	47	43	2
1974	167	66	99	2	95	45	48	2
1973	154	73	77	4	77	37	34	6
1972	160	70	85	5	83	45	34	4
1971	169	78	91	—	104	54	47	3
1970	223	55	164	4	88	51	35	2
1969	136	64	71	1	85	51	34	—
1968	115	59	55	1	66	33	31	2
1967	157	83	73	1	77	37	39	1
1966	171	67	103	1	74	28	45	1
1965	130	53	75	2	67	35	31	1
1964	78	39	38	1	66	38	27	1
1963	211	53	157	1	49	25	24	—
1962	103	38	65	—	53	30	23	—
1961	74	38	36	—	43	23	19	1
1960	57	34	21	2	43	23	20	—
1959	91	41	49	1	39	18	20	1
1958	51	30	21	—	48	20	27	1
1957	180	45	135	—	48	30	13	5
1956	130	33	97	—	32	14	18	—
1955	86	42	42	2	44	17	26	1
1954	70	20	47	3	27	10	17	—
1953	74	31	43	—	21	8	11	2
1952	57	31	26	—	28	14	13	1
1951	109	32	77	—	18	10	7	1
1950	99	32	66	1	13	5	8	—
1949	82	27	55	—	14	7	6	1
1948	91	32	59	—	31	21	9	1
1947	49	19	30	—	67	30	37	—
1946	20	13	7	—	21	10	11	—
1945	4	2	2	—	13	4	9	—
1944	2	2	—	—	6	1	5	—
1943	8	3	2	3	4	1	3	—
1942	20	8	12	—	10	4	6	—
1941	24	10	14	—	15	5	10	—
1940	13	4	9	—	9	3	6	—
1939	14	6	8	—	9	3	6	—
1938	17	10	7	—	13	5	8	—
1937	7	4	3	—	8	3	4	1
1936	16	8	8	—	21	11	10	—
1935	12	6	5	1	15	6	9	—
1934	12	7	3	2	9	7	2	—
1933	25	10	12	3	13	8	5	—
1932	12	8	3	1	13	8	5	—
1931	27	10	16	1	20	11	7	2

Series T293-305. Post office, number of post offices in Canada, by province, 1946 to 1975

Year[1]	Total for Canada	Newfound-land	Prince Edward Island	Nova Scotia	New Brunswick	Quebec	Ontario	Manitoba	Saskat-chewan	Alberta	British Columbia	Yukon Territory	Northwest Terri-tories
	293	294	295	296	297	298	299	300	301	302	303	304	305
1975	8,665	..	..	..	..	..	..	..	..	..	..	..	..
1974	8,710	..	..	..	..	..	..	..	..	..	..	..	..
1973	8,684	..	..	..	..	..	..	..	..	..	..	..	..
1972	8,564	..	..	..	..	..	..	..	..	..	..	..	..
1971	9,023	..	..	..	..	..	..	..	..	..	..	..	..
1970	9,575	..	..	..	..	..	..	..	..	..	..	..	..
1969	10,450	..	..	..	..	..	..	..	..	..	..	..	..
1968	10,838	..	..	..	..	..	..	..	..	..	..	..	..
1967	11,059	..	..	..	..	..	..	..	..	..	..	..	..
1966	11,172	..	..	..	..	..	..	..	..	..	..	..	..
1965	11,255	690	106	782	513	2,461	2,722	800	1,166	1,042	909	20	44
1964	11,260	673	106	803	530	2,423	2,709	801	1,205	1,048	901	19	42
1963	11,336	661	107	830	536	2,414	2,704	805	1,248	1,062	906	20	43
1962	11,401	660	107	869	555	2,414	2,680	804	1,266	1,070	916	20	40
1961	11,421	654	106	901	568	2,408	2,651	809	1,276	1,071	916	20	41
1960	11,497	649	104	964	597	2,403	2,629	809	1,279	1,082	922	20	39
1959	11,634	647	104	1,031	634	2,405	2,624	814	1,298	1,089	932	19	37
1958	11,768	641	105	1,096	676	2,413	2,616	810	1,310	1,112	937	16	36
1957	11,879	640	105	1,117	703	2,435	2,627	817	1,318	1,124	940	16	37
1956	11,996	636	105	1,124	736	2,463	2,644	815	1,332	1,141	947	16	37
1955	12,138	626	105	1,148	789	2,487	2,654	822	1,347	1,156	955	16	33
1954	12,202	613	106	1,179	817	2,507	2,630	824	1,364	1,152	963	15	32
1953	12,259	606	105	1,215	834	2,516	2,613	831	1,384	1,156	955	13	31
1952	12,305	592	105	1,245	837	2,530	2,598	823	1,397	1,179	955	13	31
1951	12,390	573	105	1,278	874	2,545	2,602	823	1,407	1,179	958	15	31
1950	12,415	550	105	1,315	909	2,560	2,586	809	1,404	1,184	952	15	26
1949	11,930	—	105	1,362	922	2,567	2,590	806	1,418	1,186	933	15	26
1948	11,982	—	108	1,396	949	2,582	2,578	802	1,420	1,188	920	15	24
1947	12,033	—	109	1,441	968	2,577	2,562	791	1,429	1,195	923	15	23
1946	12,105	—	115	1,465	983	2,586	2,557	794	1,443	1,209	914	16	23

[1] Data are as of 31 March of the year given.

Series T306-308. Post office, transportation statistics, operations, 1946 to 1975

Year[1]	Total number of land mail services	Number of rural routes	Number of other land mail services	Year[1]	Total number of land mail services	Number of rural routes	Number of other land mail services
	306	307	308		306	307	308
1975	7,639	5,001	2,638	1960	11,262	5,516	5,746
1974	7,735	5,030	2,705	1959	11,674	5,464	6,210
1973	7,781	5,062	2,719	1958	12,083	5,424	7,379
1972	7,541	5,093	2,448	1957	12,489	5,396	7,093
1971	8,107	5,161	2,946	1956	—	5,356	—
1970	8,048	5,220	2,828	1955	12,908	5,319	7,589
1969	—	5,449	—	1954	13,282	5,278	8,004
1968	9,364	5,561	3,803	1953	13,353	5,236	8,117
1967	9,771	5,595	4,176	1952	13,442	5,199	8,243
1966	9,934	5,625	4,309	1951	13,485	5,170	8,315
1965	10,180	5,643	4,537	1950	13,402	5,087	8,315
1964	10,284	5,639	4,645	1949	12,858	4,976	7,882
1963	10,598	5,640	4,958	1948	12,903	4,912	7,991
1962	10,757	5,637	5,120	1947	12,899	4,887	8,012
1961	10,901	5,600	5,301	1946	12,913	4,850	8,063

[1] Data are as of 31 March of the year given.

Series T309-312. Post office, transportation statistics, cost of services, 1946 to 1975
(thousands of dollars)

Year[1]	Railway mail services	Water services	Air mail services	Non-rail land services	Year[1]	Railway mail services	Water services	Air mail services	Non-rail land services
	309	310	311	312		309	310	311	312
1975	16,204	1,308	36,854	53,409	1960	16,635	2,790	13,276	26,579
1974	12,302	1,058	32,386	46,968	1959	15,057	2,515	13,056	24,960
1973	11,363	1,087	30,580	47,047	1958	14,958	2,399	12,700	23,316
1972	10,785	1,334	28,241	51,965	1957	13,902	2,311	11,635	21,085
1971	11,650	1,461	27,103	51,171	1956	14,255	2,207	11,052	18,518
1970	13,218	1,624	27,813	53,959	1955	14,487	2,318	10,882	17,783
1969	13,621	1,934	24,544	48,403	1954	15,111	2,406	10,070	16,975
1968	14,890	2,419	23,631	45,664	1953	12,944	2,559	9,835	15,589
1967	14,061	2,325	21,206	40,889	1952	11,831	2,377	9,356	14,476
1966	13,725	2,444	18,968	37,052	1951	13,986	2,181	8,491	13,673
1965	14,442	2,389	17,427	34,391	1950	8,867	2,117	8,298	12,903
1964	14,698	2,313	15,842	32,676	1949	8,682	2,512	7,772	11,859
1963	15,043	2,561	14,405	31,303	1948	8,545	2,915	6,497	10,599
1962	15,591	2,667	13,709	30,120	1947	8,324	2,362	7,147	9,592
1961	16,080	2,781	13,755	29,045	1946	8,113	2,320	8,657	8,905

[1] Data are as of 31 March of the year given.

Series T313-314. Post office, gross postal revenues and pieces of first-class mail, 1946 to 1975

Year[1]	Gross postal revenues ($'000)	Pieces of first-class mail (millions)	Year[1]	Gross postal revenues ($'000)	Pieces of first-class mail (millions)	Year[1]	Gross postal revenues ($'000)	Pieces of first-class mail (millions)
	313	314		313	314		313	314
1975	617,743	3,504.0	1965	268,073	2,180.4	1955	151,682	1,849.7
1974	591,133	3,347.4	1964	239,725	—	1954	129,735	1,582.0
1973	563,159	3,141.3	1963	222,359	2,255.4	1953	129,267	1,576.4
1972	504,211	2,699.0	1962	213,579	2,138.2	1952	122,267	1,462.2
1971	432,911	2,723.0	1961	201,952	2,190.6	1951	105,534	1,453.2
1970	444,069	2,708.2	1960	193,593	2,096.2	1950	101,277	1,362.3
1969	374,902	2,531.7	1959	183,291	1,983.9	1949	95,957	1,333.3
1968	337,023	2,586.4	1958	177,433	1,956.5	1948	91,614	1,210.3
1967	305,473	2,489.7	1957	167,829	1,828.7	1947	86,401	1,151.8
1966	285,190	2,384.4	1956	158,286	1,727.0	1946	83,763	—

[1] Data are for fiscal years ending 31 March of the year given.

Series T315-323. Telecommunications carrier industry, telephones and telephone calls, 1946 to 1975
(series T315-320 in thousands, series T321-323 in millions)

Year	Number of telephones at 31 December						Number of telephone calls		
	Total[2]	Business	Residence[3]	Residence extension[3]	Connected to automatic central offices	Connected to manual central office units	Total	Local	Long distance
	315	**316**	**317**	**318**	**319**	**320**	**321**	**322**	**323**
1975	13,165	3,928	9,237	2,194	13,139	26	21,194.1	20,340.6	853.5
1974	12,454	3,691	8,763	2,011	12,420	34	20,701.0	19,936.8	764.2
1973	11,677	3,428	8,249	1,812	11,624	53	19,054.9	18,396.6	658.3
1972	10,987	3,183	7,804	1,667	10,920	67	18,348.9	17,777.0	571.9
1971	10,269	2,996	7,273	1,423	10,184	85	16,934.8	16,439.4	495.4
1970	9,750	2,854	6,896	1,293	9,646	104	15,895.2	15,436.8	458.4
1969	9,296	2,719	6,577	1,188	9,156	140	15,030.9	14,596.6	434.3
1968	8,818	2,557	6,261	1,084	8,658	160	14,381.6	13,993.6	388.0
1967	8,358	2,423	5,935	967	8,129	229	13,410.5	13,053.1	357.4
1966	7,893	2,290	5,603	875	7,620	273	13,169.5	12,846.2	323.3
1965	7,445	2,142	5,303	794	7,123	322	12,439.8	12,138.2	301.6
1964	7,019	2,016	5,003	711	6,651	368	11,939.3	11,658.1	281.2
1963	6,657	1,910	4,746	642	6,214	443	11,299.8	11,039.6	260.2
1962	6,329	1,817	4,512	580	5,824	505	10,808.3[1]	10,558.1[1]	250.2[1]
1961	6,014	1,730	4,284	521	5,357	657	10,468.9	10,242.6	226.3
1960	5,728	1,674	4,054	462	5,018	710	9,579.9	9,364.6	215.3
1959	5,439	1,569	3,870	409	4,598	841	9,250.2	9,044.8	205.4
1958	5,118	1,486	3,632	348	4,192	926	8,707.6	8,513.4	194.2
1957	4,827	1,409	3,418	308	3,855	972	8,255.7	8,077.1	178.6
1956	4,499	1,334	3,165	266	3,478	1,021	7,764.8	7,593.5	171.3
1955	4,152	1,237	2,915	224	3,070	1,082	6,961.5	6,808.4	153.1
1954	3,860	1,154	2,706	188	2,764	1,096	6,347.5	6,209.8	137.7
1953	3,606	1,085	2,521	170	2,486	1,120	6,084.7	5,952.8	131.9
1952	3,352	1,017	2,335	155	2,240	1,112	5,609.7	5,483.0	126.7
1951	3,114	957	2,157	141	2,005	1,109	5,273.6	5,146.2	127.4
1950	2,917	902	2,015	128	1,811	1,106	5,012.6	4,894.7	117.9
1949	2,700	846	1,854	115	1,627	1,073	4,559.3	4,454.0	105.3
1948	2,452	778	1,674	95	1,399	1,053	4,117.2	4,025.3	91.9
1947	2,231	712	1,519	81	1,256	975	3,843.3	3,760.6	82.7
1946	2,026	647	1,379	62	1,123	903	3,559.0	3,484.2	74.8

[1] See introduction note for series T321-323 in text.
[2] Series T315 is the sum of series T316 and T317; it is also the sum of series T319 and T320.
[3] Series T318 is included in series T317.

Series T324-326. Telecommunications carrier industry, gross capital expenditures on new construction and machinery and equipment, 1946 to 1975[1]
(millions of dollars)

Year	Total expenditure	Construction	Machinery and equipment	Year	Total expenditure	Construction	Machinery and equipment
	324	**325**	**326**		**324**	**325**	**326**
1975	1,692.4	533.9	1,158.5	1960	356.5[1]	161.3[1]	195.2[1]
1974	1,490.1	508.7	981.4	1959	314.1	126.9	187.2
1973	1,071.1	371.0	700.1	1958	329.6	126.7	202.9
1972	903.5	308.8	594.7	1957	305.2	112.7	192.5
1971	828.4	285.5	542.9	1956	248.2	98.7	149.5
1970	732.1	254.4	477.7	1955	211.9	90.8	121.1
1969	685.7	233.0	452.7	1954	181.0	76.0	105.0
1968	630.4	222.6	407.8	1953	161.7	70.9	90.8
1967	592.2	194.2	398.0	1952	141.3	58.3	83.0
1966	542.2	196.0	346.2	1951	125.4	53.2	72.2
1965	442.9	158.6	284.3	1950	113.0	47.3	65.7
1964	409.3	146.0	263.3	1949	114.7	51.3	63.4
1963	420.3	148.3	272.0	1948	103.6	46.0	57.6
1962	371.3	135.7	235.6	1947	81.3	35.3	46.0
1961	321.1	122.7	198.4	1946	44.6	25.8	18.8

[1] For the year 1960 and onward, series T324-326 are for all telecommunications carriers; for 1959 and previous years, only the telephone industry is covered.

Series T327-335. Telephone industry, property, revenues, expenses, taxes, interest, employees and wages, 1946 to 1975

(thousands of dollars, except series T334)

Year[1]	Cost of property and equipment	Total	Long distance	Total	Operating expenses[2]	Taxes	Interest	Number[3]	Salaries and wages[4]
	327	328	329	330	331	332	333	334	335
1975	11,426,333	3,054,705	1,435,202	2,650,396	1,938,305	364,724	347,367	82,866	1,091,350
1974	10,039,662	2,514,907	1,195,118	2,234,221	1,633,305	322,171	278,745	81,225	921,007
1973	8,791,434	2,200,702	1,012,751	1,920,423	1,390,447	298,452	231,524	75,407	775,700
1972	7,960,368	1,924,840	860,390	1,673,433	1,227,769	244,590	201,074	72,671	681,187
1971	7,255,227	1,725,302	748,757	1,504,854	1,092,794	230,653	181,407	69,995	600,949
1970	6,571,028	1,568,726	675,945	1,366,645	977,415	225,839	163,391	68,334	536,071
1969	5,988,211	1,404,325	586,861	1,227,420	884,547	197,587	145,286	66,578	479,068
1968	5,467,326	1,268,387	509,456	1,095,763	782,964	185,577	127,122	66,699	436,543
1967	5,010,999	1,163,856	460,692	1,006,494	727,240	169,553	109,701	68,431	408,066
1966	4,544,522	1,043,837	413,490	912,453	672,077	150,106	90,270	68,233	375,279
1965	4,127,387	948,177	363,046	821,205	605,375	137,657	78,173	63,467	335,365
1964	3,808,675	860,207	316,535	746,504	551,424	123,567	71,513	60,829	306,454
1963	3,510,479	787,375	276,656	687,273	512,116	110,437	64,720	58,416	286,068
1962	3,192,230	733,294	258,790	636,542	474,306	104,144	58,092	58,091	269,285
1961	2,926,527	679,306	238,129	590,428	444,072	94,452	51,904	56,322	254,208
1960	2,692,484	627,983	216,963	549,043	419,764	83,721	45,558	57,670	247,128
1959	2,444,577	582,263	200,080	509,727	396,720	75,528	37,479	58,826	240,691
1958	2,202,747	507,690	172,828	451,673	367,689	52,965	31,019	61,400	234,298
1957	1,941,592	467,702	159,542	412,158	334,427	51,262	26,469	64,074	219,693
1956	1,672,364	422,370	145,285	366,118	296,633	47,682	21,803	60,121	193,993
1955	1,470,679	376,717	127,228	328,881	265,200	43,902	19,779	55,673	173,923
1954	1,301,546	340,623	110,955	296,384	236,222	40,664	19,498	51,929	159,329
1953	1,152,310	310,834	100,694	269,818	214,498	38,172	17,148	50,540	145,110
1952	1,027,528	279,002	91,316	244,506	193,248	37,069	14,189	48,207	131,371
1951	909,581	240,763	81,275	213,824	173,069	28,130	12,625	47,387	117,678
1950	806,826	198,823	69,583	178,194	151,158	15,542	11,494	45,396	102,093
1949	716,520	169,113	58,700	153,066	131,672	11,358	10,036	42,326	90,634
1948	615,942	150,533	51,676	131,570	111,272	11,667	8,631	38,851	77,498
1947	521,184	134,667	46,021	116,623	96,763	12,417	7,443	35,578	66,624
1946	454,215	120,675	41,487	105,751	83,638	14,770	7,343	33,170	54,147

[1] Data as of 31 December or for years ending 31 December.
[2] Includes other expenses.
[3] Number of full-time employees only.
[4] For both full-time and part-time employees.

Series T336-341. Telephone industry, long-distance rates between Montreal and selected cities, 1918 to 1975
(rate for station-to-station, daytime, 3-minute call, in dollars)

Effective date	Between Montreal and					
	Ottawa	Toronto	Windsor	Halifax	Winnipeg	Vancouver
	336	337	338	339	340	341
1 July 1975	.93	1.38	1.58	2.10	2.67	3.15
1 July 1970	.80	1.30	1.50	1.75	2.35	3.00
1 July 1965	.80	1.30	1.65	1.75	2.35	3.65
6 November 1960	.80	1.70	2.10	2.00	2.75	3.50
1 June 1959	.80	1.70	2.10	2.00	2.85	3.65
1 December 1958	.80	1.70	2.10	2.00	2.95	4.40
15 May 1953	.80	1.75	2.30	2.00	2.95	4.40
22 July 1950	.80	1.75	2.30	1.75	3.00	4.70
1 September 1945	.65	1.75	2.30	1.75	3.00	4.70
10 July 1941	.65	1.75	2.30	1.75	3.25	5.75
1 April 1937	.65	1.75	2.30	1.80	3.75	6.75
1 September 1936	.65	1.90	2.85	1.80	3.75	6.75
1 January 1930	.65	1.90	2.85	2.05	4.00	8.00
1 February 1929	.70	1.95	3.05	2.05	4.00	8.00
21 April 1921	.70	2.05	3.25	3.20	7.05	14.50
20 November 1918	.70	2.05	3.25	3.20	7.10	14.60

Series T342-351. Other telecommunications carriers, financial and operating statistics, 1946 to 1975
(series T342 in thousands of dollars; series T346-351 in thousands of units)

Year[1]	Operating revenue	Operating expense	Non-transmission revenues	Cost of property and equipment	Total telegrams transmitted	Telegrams sent	Telegrams received from United States	Total cablegrams excluding duplication[2]	Cablegrams sent	Cablegrams received
	342	343	344	345	346	347	348	349	350	351
1975	259,059	193,811	154,819	939,560	4,431	4,115	316	8,016	1,558	1,246
1974	230,078	172,554	139,115	855,966	4,085	3,743	342	7,292	1,504	1,297
1973	190,703	140,114	120,308	789,269	3,830	3,454	376	7,412	1,463	1,278
1972	163,190	115,308	93,029	644,242	5,596	5,052	544	6,457	1,566	1,234
1971	146,413	107,567	91,449	606,744	6,389	5,888	501	5,347	1,497	1,290
1970	136,948	100,068	86,801	570,556	7,678	6,906	772	4,729	1,436	1,216
1969	126,568	92,770	80,460	545,695	8,498	7,618	880	4,235	1,459	1,242
1968	116,666	86,426	70,404	519,950	9,673	8,830	843	4,057	1,583	1,291
1967	104,505	78,716	65,981	494,486	10,474	9,383	1,091	3,576	1,466	1,266
1966	95,478	74,684	60,464	474,826	11,456	10,328	1,128	3,232	1,427	1,164
1965	86,087	68,869	52,117	447,295	12,789	11,534	1,255	3,038	1,479	1,094
1964	78,743	63,865	47,805	425,324	12,946	11,708	1,238	3,529	1,362	996
1963	73,611	60,257	45,320	391,173	13,339	11,931	1,408	2,940	1,280	935
1962	71,379	56,452	41,280	336,374	14,451	12,834	1,617	2,920	1,257	933
1961	64,054	51,735	33,938	299,568	15,139	13,441	1,698	2,810	1,271	975
1960	58,546	45,538	28,523	267,379	16,257	13,726	1,820	2,663	1,199	933
1959	52,963	43,512	24,036	226,914	16,391	14,437	1,954	2,603	1,203	909
1958	47,634	39,909	19,445	199,289	17,296	15,375	1,921	2,500	1,154	909
1957	44,797	39,272	17,408	169,258	19,164	17,037	2,127	2,581	1,232	964
1956	40,720	33,689	14,067	149,954	20,381	18,150	2,231	2,430	1,151	939
1955	39,321	32,502	16,627	124,301	20,068	17,887	2,181	2,238	1,086	873
1954	38,204	33,204	6,453	118,272	19,806	17,763	2,143	2,106	1,000	831
1953	36,920	33,953	14,308	110,831	21,222	19,041	2,181	2,043	955	813
1952	33,094	31,617	11,462	100,221	21,614	19,513	2,101	1,934	887	777
1951	29,128	27,808	9,749	90,506	21,816	19,693	2,123	1,786	816	722
1950	23,922	22,546	7,722	82,296	20,478	18,520	1,958	1,688	748	663
1949	22,257	22,063	6,692	76,249	20,063	18,100	1,963	1,642	742	678
1948	19,423	20,292	5,627	71,121	19,013	16,970	2,043	1,580	743	702
1947	18,515	17,360	5,032	67,111	17,988	15,596	2,392	1,614	745	710
1946	17,998	16,029	4,826	63,910	18,442	16,222	2,220	1,846	845	812

[1] Data are for the calendar year.

[2] Includes wireless messages and transatlantic telex messages.

Series T352-359. Number of private radio and television stations, with operating revenues and expenses, for private stations and Canadian Broadcasting Corporation (CBC), 1959 to 1975
(millions of dollars)

Year	Number of radio stations (excluding CBC)	Number of television stations[1] (excluding CBC)	Operating revenue Private stations Radio	Operating revenue Private stations Television	Operating revenue CBC	Operating expenses Private stations Radio	Operating expenses Private stations Television	Operating expenses CBC
	352	353	354	355	356	357	358	359
1975	392	59	208.2	233.6	64.0	168.3	183.4	314.1
1974	385	59	182.5	194.0	50.1	145.5	161.2	279.1
1973	348	60	159.9	170.7	46.1	127.9	129.2	244.3
1972	343	56	145.4	132.1	38.7	113.8	98.3	210.5
1971	341	64	125.7	115.8	36.3	109.0	102.4	221.8
1970	338	66	114.5	111.2	37.6	101.3	93.5	202.2
1969	329	67	108.1	106.6	37.8	93.4	84.6	203.9
1968[2]	319	68	95.7	100.0	29.9	83.3	82.5	175.5
1967	305	66	88.8	95.2	30.3	77.1	79.3	176.0
1966	291	65	79.6	85.8	27.0	69.9	70.0	145.1
1965	281	65	70.5	75.3	25.8	63.4	60.9	124.9
1964	265	66	65.0	63.6	25.0	58.9	54.4	115.4
1963	239	63	58.2	53.6	24.4	53.5	49.5	106.9
1962	198	58	53.6	47.6	23.2	49.3	46.5	100.2
1961	194	55	49.4	37.7	23.4	46.4	40.5	94.1
1960	193	47	47.0	28.5	..	42.3	21.0	..
1959	181	43	45.1	23.7	..	38.0	18.5	..

[1] Originating stations for years 1972 to 1975.

[2] From 1968 onward, the reported data are for a uniform fiscal period ending 31 August, each year. The 1968 reporting period includes adjustments to actually reported data.

Section V: Internal Trade

Mel. S. Moyer, *York University*

The data of this section are in three parts. Series V1-331 contain statistics on retail trade, series V332-409 on wholesale trade and series V410-448 on service establishments.

The published sources of data in this section are all publications of Statistics Canada. Accordingly, in the following list of published sources the name of the author, Statistics Canada or its predecessor, the Dominion Bureau of Statistics, is not repeated with each publication. The name of the printer is also omitted except on decennial census publications.

General historical note on Internal Trade

The collection of data on internal merchandising and services in Canada, in common with many countries, began at a relatively late date. A first attempt at obtaining such data was made by the Dominion Bureau of Statistics in 1924 to cover retail and wholesale trade in 1923. The list of establishments to whom questionnaires were mailed was based upon information collected in the decennial census of 1921 and enlarged from other sources (see the note for the decennial census of merchandising and services below). The number of returns received, however, was not large enough to provide reliable results for the whole of retail and wholesale trade. No further attempt was made to collect internal trade data until the decennial census of 1931, though estimates of retail trade were later made for the period back to 1923.

Regular collection of data on wholesale and retail trade and on some services began for 1930.

In the past, the decennial census of merchandising and services was taken in two parts. At the time of the decennial population census enumeration, at the beginning of June in the census year, the census enumerators compiled lists of wholesale, retail and service establishments in their census areas with relevant information for a later questionnaire survey. The lists prepared by census enumerators were supplemented by information from trade associations, trade directories, and other such sources. When the lists were complete, questionnaires were mailed to the businesses listed. The usual procedure of checking with delinquents by correspondence and, if necessary, through regional offices of Statistics Canada was followed in order to obtain as complete a coverage as possible. The tabulations based on the returned questionnaires formed benchmark data for the annual and monthly series. The years covered by the complete censuses are 1930, 1941, 1951, 1961, 1966 and 1971.

Annual figures on wholesale and retail sales have been prepared from data collected annually and/or monthly from samples, in the main, of wholesalers, independent retailers, most of the large department stores and chain stores. For chain stores the annual survey has been based on complete coverage from the beginning.

The annual surveys were first taken for wholesale and retail trade and retail chain stores for 1933. At the same time, data for 1931 and 1932 were obtained from the same respondents. Thereafter until 1939 such surveys were taken yearly.

Monthly surveys on a sample basis of retail trade began in the early 1930s. Their coverage included department stores, chain stores and some independents.

For wholesale trade, the monthly sample survey of wholesalers began in late 1934. The annual survey was distinct from the monthly survey, covered a larger sample, and in the case of retail trade obtained more information than gathered in the monthly reports, which were confined to sales.

With the outbreak of war the annual surveys of both wholesale and retail trade were discontinued (except the complete annual survey of retail chain stores, which was continued). Annual data were compiled from the monthly trade reports. Special efforts were made after the end of each year to complete the returns of all businesses in the monthly sample for that year, checking being done by correspondence and through the regional offices.

The system of obtaining annual intercensal sales data from monthly returns for both wholesale and retail trade was continued until 1957 for retail trade and until 1960 for wholesale trade.

In 1957, an annual survey of retail trade, as distinct from the monthly surveys, was begun again.

The size of the sample of independent retail stores was 3,000 for the monthly in 1935, 7,200 in 1945, 9,000 in 1955, 10,000 in 1960 and 16,000 in 1975. The sample of department stores has always included the larger department stores. It has always had a high proportion of coverage, and in recent years that coverage has been 100 per cent of known department stores. Annual retail chain store sales are based on complete annual coverage though monthly sales are obtained for a sample. The total number of retail stores in 1930 was 125,000; in 1941 it was 137,000; in 1951 it was 152,000; in 1961 it was 153,000; in 1966 it was 154,000; and in 1971 it was 157,000.

For retail trade, the data obtained in the annual and monthly surveys have been used to estimate total retail sales by the application of the annual results to the data of census benchmark years. The method used was to 'chain' from year to year using a link-relative approach. During the later 1940s, 1950s and 1960s, adjustments were made to the annual sales to take account of births and deaths of retail stores. The deaths were obtained from a continuing group carried through from sample surveys in particular areas taken in connection with the Labour Force Survey.

In 1958, a complete census of wholesale trade proper was taken based on lists in the employers' index of the Unemployment Insurance Commission.

The total number of wholesale locations in 1930 was 13,000; in 1941 it was 25,000; in 1951 it was 26,000; and in 1961 it was 31,000. The total number of wholesale establishments in 1966 was 31,000.

The wholesale series were not adjusted for births and deaths before 1951. However, the sample was adjusted at times to take account of changes in the size of wholesalers' scale of operations. An estimate of total annual wholesale sales, apart from the complete census, has been available only for 1930 to 1939 and from 1951 onward. For 1939 to 1951 the annual series on wholesale sales are in the form of indexes. These indexes cover only some categories of whole-sale trade. They are formed by linking each year to the preceding year. These indexes are available back to 1935. Revisions have been made in intercensal data, based on new data of the latest census.

The foregoing data relate mainly to sales. In addition, since 1938, Statistics Canada has collected periodically on a sample basis data on operating statistics and financial structure of retail concerns. The 1938 survey was taken with the regular annual census of retail trade. Since the end of the war these surveys have generally been taken biennially. This program was discontinued in the mid-1960s and begun again in the mid-1970s. The surveys have dealt with employment, payrolls, costs of materials, trade margins, inventories, and the like. The sample sizes are given in the reports.

Retail sales include, in addition to the sales of retailers proper, sales of retail units, if a distinct entity, of businesses engaged in other activities. Thus retail sales branches of manufacturers are included, as are sales units of electrical utilities selling electrical appliances. The statistics do not include: door-to-door sales of any kind; retail sales of wholesalers and service establishments; retail sales by manufacturing bakeries, manufacturing dairies and purchasing co-operatives; sales of meals, beverages and tobacco by hotels; line elevator sales; retail sales of manufacturers other than through separate retail units; nor sales of businesses with more than 50 per cent of their receipts coming from repair work.

Trading concerns engaged in both wholesale and retail trade are classified to the sector which makes the greatest contribution to total gross profit. For example, a hardware store may sell $50,000 of merchandise, 60 per cent wholesale and 40 per cent retail. Assume the gross margin in selling hardware at wholesale is 18.1 per cent and at retail 28.9 per cent. The hardware store would be classified as a retail establishment even though more than half of its total sales were made at wholesale.

Annual wholesale sales are, in the main, for wholesalers proper. However, sales of petroleum products bulk tank stations and packing houses were included in the annual survey for 1930 to 1939. Beginning in the census year 1961, trade by commission agents, brokers, assemblers, manufacturers' sales branches and the like are excluded.

In 1947, Statistics Canada began a series showing operating statistics and financial structure of wholesale concerns. Its history has parallelled that of the retail trade series.

Descriptions of the collection of data on service trades are given in the notes on individual tables in the remainder of the text, since methods differ somewhat among the service trades.

Retail Trade (Series V1-331)

V1-24. Retail sales, by kind of business, 1930 to 1975

SOURCE: for 1969 to 1971, 1972 to 1974, and 1975, *Retail Trade*, January 1972, June 1975, and March 1976, respectively, (Catalogue 63-005); for 1966 to 1968, *Retail Trade, Revisions to 1966-1970 Postcensal Estimates*, (Catalogue 63-519); for 1961 to 1965, *Retail Trade, Revisions to 1961-1966 Intercensal Estimates*, (Catalogue 63-517); for 1931 to 1960 (excluding census years), *Retail Trade, 1930-1961*,

Revisions to 1951-61 Intercensal Estimates, (Catalogue 63-510); for 1951, *Census of Canada, 1952*, vol. VII, *Distribution, Retail Trade*; for 1941, *Census of Canada, 1941*, vol. X, *Merchandising and Services, part 1*; for 1930, *Census of Canada, 1931*, vol. X, *Merchandising and Services, part 1*. For alcoholic beverage data, *Retail Chain Stores*, (Catalogue 63-210), various issues; for 1931 to 1950, excluding census years, estimates derived from *Retail Trade*, for series V3, 4, 5 and 23.

For the general method of obtaining these data see the general note to Section V.

'Retail Trade', is currently defined as 'the aggregate sales made through retail locations (outlets)'.

A 'retail location', as defined by Statistics Canada, is a 'business location (usually a store) in which the principal activity is the sale of merchandise and related services to the general public, for household or personal consumption'.

Retail trade estimates do not include any form of direct selling which bypasses the retail store. Excluded, therefore, are direct door-to-door selling; sales made through automatic vending machines; sales of newspapers or magazines sold directly by printers or publishers; and sales made by book and record clubs. The only exception is the mail-order and catalogue sales activities of department store businesses; they have been classified to the 'general merchandise store' category. In addition, retail trade excludes: retail sales through ancillary units, e.g., warehouses, head offices, etc.; sales of contractors whose major activity is not retailing; and retail transactions between individuals.

'Total net sales' include sales of merchandise and receipts from related services, such as repairs, equipment rental, and food serving, less returns, adjustments and discounts. Total net sales also include: trade-in allowances; withdrawals of goods for personal use (at retail); and commissions earned from sales of goods owned by others. Non-trading revenues, bad debts recovered and sales taxes are excluded. For further information on this subject, see the general historical note on Internal Trade.

Classification

Kind of Business[1]

Estimates of retail trade are stratified by geographical area and by kind of business. These groupings are based on the Standard Industrial Classifications and the retail kind-of-business categories employed in the 1971 Census of Merchandising and Services.

The monthly retail trade survey is a 'location' survey. Therefore, each individual retail location of a firm is assigned a kind-of-business code based on its major activity or on the type of commodities sold.

For 1931 to 1940, sales of meat markets (series V4), garages and filling stations (series V10) and all other retail (series V24) were not given in *Retail Trade, 1930-1961*, (Catalogue 63-510). Further, alcoholic beverage outlets (series V3) and other food stores (series V5) were included in all other retail (series V24). They were estimated as follows:

To obtain meat market sales, 1931 to 1940, the ratio of meat store sales to sales of grocery and combination stores was calculated for each of the complete census years 1930 and 1941 and the arithmetic average taken. This average was then applied to the annual sales of grocery and combination stores, 1931 to 1940, to estimate meat store sales.

For garages and filling stations, the ratios of their sales to new motor vehicle sales were calculated for each of 1930 and 1941, and the arithmetic average taken. This average was then applied to new motor vehicle sales 1931 to 1940 to estimate garage and filling station sales for these years.

With calculation of the above two series for 1931 to 1941, and with the total of retail sales being given, the figures for all other retail were calculated as a residual to fill in these years in the source table.

Sales of alcoholic beverage outlets were estimated by taking the ratio of sales of these outlets, as shown in the complete censuses, to the sales of outlets reporting annually to the bureau in these census years. Intercensal estimates were made by applying the average ratio of the terminal years in each of the intercensal periods to the annual sales of alcoholic beverage outlets reporting to the bureau. (These outlets do not include taverns, lounges and bars.)

Sales of other food stores (series V5) were calculated in two parts. The sales of other food chains were taken from the annual survey of chain stores. For other independent food stores the ratio of their sales to the entire all other retail item was calculated for the census years. The average of these ratios is applied to the entire all other retail group.

The estimates in series V1-24 cover sales of independent stores, retail chain stores and department stores. For retail sales not included see the general note to Section V.

Beginning in 1951, scientific and medical instrument dealers, milk dealers, and optometrists are excluded from retail trade.

Beginning in 1961, caterers, bars and night clubs, cocktail lounges, taverns, beverage rooms and public houses, and refreshment booths and stands are excluded from retail trade. Beverage stores were reclassified to the all other stores category.

Beginning in 1961, TV sales and service shops and TV, radio, piano and music stores are excluded from furniture, TV and appliance stores, but are included in the all other category.

Beginning in 1961, other building material dealers, farm implement dealers, feed stores, farm supply stores, harness shops, and heating and plumbing equipment dealers are excluded from retail trade.

Beginning in 1961, bicycle repair shops, previously contained in the service sector, are included with sporting goods stores, in the all other category of retail trade.

Beginning in 1961, garages, previously contained in the service sector, are included in the garages kind of business in the retail sector.

Beginning in 1961, paint and body shops, car washes, other specialty (auto) repair shops, auto establishments n.e.s., previously contained in the service sector, are included in the all other category in the retail sector.

Beginning in 1961, lumber and building material dealers and restaurants were transferred from retail trade to wholesale trade.

Beginning in 1961, restaurants were transferred from retail trade to the service trades.

Beginning in 1966, only sales of actual department store locations are included in the department store kind of business. Excluded from the department store kind of business are sales data on the other kinds of businesses which may be operated by department store organizations. These ancillary businesses, such as general stores, appliance stores, etc., have been classified to the kind of business category that is most appropriate in view of their respective commodity mixes. The mail-order and catalogue sales offices of department stores are included with general merchandise stores,

which in table V1-24 are included under all other category. Sales of concessions are generally included in the total business of department stores in which they are located.

Beginning in 1972, confectionery stores are excluded from other food stores and are included with grocery, confectionery and sundries stores, which are included in column 2 of table V1-24.

Beginning in 1972, electrical supply stores, which were previously classified to the all other category, are included in the furniture, TV, radio and appliance stores kind of business.

Beginning in 1972, patent medicine, cosmetic and perfume stores and proprietary stores, which were previously classified to the all other category, are included in the drug stores kind of business.

Beginning with 1971, fuel dealers were transferred from retail trade to wholesale trade.

For a comparison of the new retail trade survey kinds of business for 1972 and later years, with the old retail trade survey kinds of business for years prior to 1972, consult *Retail Trade*, June 1975, monthly, (Catalogue 63-005), pages x and xi.

For kind of business composition, refer to the above mentioned publication pages 54 and 55.

V25-34.   Retail sales, by kind of business, 1923 to 1933

SOURCE: for 1931 to 1933, *Retail Trade, 1930-1961 Revisions to 1951-1961 Intercensal Estimates*, occasional, (Catalogue 63-510); for 1930, *Census of Canada, 1941*, vol. X, *Merchandising and Services, part 1;* for 1923 to 1929, *A Decade of Retail Trade, 1923 to 1933* (Catalogue 63-D-54).

The data of these series were calculated in Statistics Canada in 1934 and 1935. The figures for 1930 were taken from the complete census for that year. Those for 1931 to 1933 were estimated from the survey of a sample of retail stores for 1933 which also covered sales of these stores for 1931 and 1932 (see the general historical note to Section V) and which was the first of the annual censuses of retail trade. Data for the period 1923 to 1929 were estimated in a variety of ways which are described in the first edition of *The Historical Statistics of Canada*. See that source for the description methods on which the following notes are based.

The kinds of retail trade covered are the same as for series V1-24 though the classifications differ (see the notes to series V1-24 and the general historical note to Section V).

V35-52.   Retail sales, by kind of business, and number of chains and stores, chain stores, 1930 to 1975

SOURCE: same as series V1-24. Also, for number of chains and average number of stores and kind of business data, for 1931 to 1960, excluding census years, *Retail Chain Stores*, annual, (Catalogue 63-210), various issues.

Beginning in 1966, series V48 excludes all other home furnishing stores.

The average number of chains are not available by province for any year.

A chain organization is currently defined as an organization operating four or more retail outlets in the same kind of business under the same legal ownership. Exceptions to this definition are department stores, which are treated statistically as chains even though they may fail to meet the criteria of operating four retail outlets. By implication, this definition excludes franchise operations. On the other hand, because of the use of the term 'legal ownership', this definition of a chain organization has tended to include as more than one chain those organizations which operate retail outlets in two or more provinces, are provincially incorporated and meet the chain definition in each province in which they operate stores.

The classifications are the same as those used for total retail trade, series V1-24.

In addition to sales figures given here the source reports include data on numbers employed (in earlier years), salaries and wages, inventories and accounts outstanding at year end. These data are given for various classes of chain stores.

V53-88.   Retail sales and number of chains and stores, chain stores, by province, 1930 to 1975

SOURCE: *Retail Chain Stores*, annual, (Catalogue 63-210), various issues; for 1951, *Census of Canada, 1951*, vol. VII, *Distribution, Retail Trade*; for 1941, *Census of Canada, 1941*, vol. X, *Merchandising and Services, part 1*; for 1930, *Census of Canada, 1931*, vol. X, *Merchandising and Services, part 1*.

V89-99.   Retail sales, by province, 1923 to 1975

SOURCE: same as V1-24. Also, for 1923 to 1933, *A Decade of Retail Trade, 1923 to 1933*, (Catalogue 63-D-54).

Movements of sales within provinces are based upon data in the decennial censuses and the annual sample returns from each province. Adjustments to intercensal and postcensal estimates were made whenever a new census appeared. However, this was not done for the 1967 to 1970 period using the 1971 Census data. Sales of mail-order houses in 1930 were attributed to the province in which the store was located. In 1941, 1961, 1966 and 1971, mail-order sales made through local ordering offices were attributed to the province in which the office was located, but mail-order sales arising from orders sent in directly by customers were attributed to the province in which the store was located. In 1951 all mail-order sales were allocated to the province of the customer. In the revision of intercensal data from 1941 to 1951 adjustments were made to put the data on the 1951 basis (see, *Retail Trade, 1930-1951*, p. 11) but apparently no adjustment was made for 1930 to 1941. The provincial data are carried forward from 1951 on the 1951 Census basis.

For methods of allocating sales to provinces in 1923 to 1929 see, *A Decade of Retail Trade, 1923-1933*. The division of sales among provinces in 1930 provided the main basis for the division in earlier years.

See the general note to series V1-24 for kinds of retail sales included and excluded.

V100-129.   Retail trade, gross profit margins by kind of business, 1938 to 1960

SOURCE: series V100-104, for 1954 to 1960, *Operating Results and Financial Structure, Retail Food Stores, 1960*, tables 1, 6, 11, 16 and 21; for 1938 to 1952, same title but for the year 1952, p. K-8; series V105-112, for 1954 to 1960, *Operating Results and Financial Structure, Retail Clothing Stores, 1960*, tables 1, 9, 16 and 23; for 1941 to 1950, same

title but for the year 1952, p. L-8; for 1938, *Operating Results of Independent Clothing and Shoe Stores in Canada, 1938*, pp. 2-3; series V113-118, for 1952 to 1959, *Operating Results and Financial Structure, Retail Hardware, Furniture, Appliance, Radio and Television Stores, 1959*, tables 1, 9 and 15; for 1948 and 1950, same title (word 'television' omitted), but for year 1950, pp. M10, M15 and M17; for 1938 to 1948, same title but for 1948, p. 11, series V119-120, for 1952 to 1959, *Operating Results and Financial Structure of Filling Stations and Garages, 1959*, tables 1 and 6; for 1938 to 1950, individual reports of the same title but for the particular year for which the data apply; series V121, for 1954 to 1960, *Operating Results and Financial Structure, Independent General Stores, 1960*, table 1, p. 4; for 1950 to 1952, same title but for 1952, pp. 1-9; for 1945 to 1948, *Operating Results and Financial Structure, Miscellaneous Retail Stores, 1948*, table 1, p. 12; for earlier years, *Operating Results of Country General and Dry Goods Stores*; series V122-129, for 1952 and later years, separately published reports for each category under the general title *Operating Results and Financial Structure*, with the following subtitles: *Independent Restaurants, 1959*; *Independent Fuel Dealers, 1959*; *Independent Drug Stores, 1959*; *Independent Jewellery Stores, 1959*; and *Independent Tobacco Stores, 1956*; for 1938 to 1950, *Operating Results and Financial Structure, Miscellaneous Retail Stores*, reports for the years to which the data apply, for chain stores, series V100-102, *Operating Results of Chain Food Stores, 1959*, table 3, p. 7, table 5, p. 9; same title for 1957, table 8, p. H-14; same title for 1947, table 1, p. 12; series V106-112, *Operating Results of Chain Clothing Stores, 1959*; series V116, *Operating Results of Chain Furniture Stores, 1959*, table 1, p. 4; series V126, *Operating Results of Chain Drug Stores, 1959*, table 1, p. 4.

See the general historical note to Section V for a description of the manner in which these data are obtained.

In 1952 a sample of 17,000 independent stores (originally selected in 1944) was canvassed and about 10,000 usable returns were obtained (see DBS, *History, Function, Organization, 1952*, pp. 76-7, (Catalogue 12-D-52)). The numbers reporting in the various categories are given in the reports.

The data on retail chain stores, for the years covered, were obtained at the same time that the annual survey was taken.

Gross profit margin is the ratio of the difference between net sales and cost of goods sold to net sales. Cost of goods sold is obtained by adding the beginning inventory to net purchases of goods and deducting the ending inventory.

The gross profit margins of chain variety stores (which did not fit in with any cateogry of independent stores) as a percentage of net sales from 1947 to 1959 were as follows: 1947 (37.7), 1949 (37.5), 1951 (37.8), 1953 (37.8), 1955 (38.3), 1957 (38.6) and 1959 (38.7). See *Operating Results of Chain Variety Stores, 1959*, table 1, p. 4.

The reports also give details of operating costs and balance sheet data by size classes for the various categories of stores.

V130-131.   Retail sales, by commodity, 1968 and 1974

SOURCE: for 1974, *Retail Commodity Survey, 1974*, (Catalogue 63-526); for 1968, *Retail Commodity Survey, 1968*, (Catalogue 63-518).

It will be noted that the total retail commodity figure

from this table does not always match the total retail trade figure in series V1-24. It is important to realize that the survey from which data for table V130-131 was obtained, represents an activity study of the businesses surveyed. As such, it raised the problem for most businesses of reporting data not readily available under normal accounting practices. Many businesses reviewed purchase invoices or examined inventory movements for the information required; others used their best estimates. Despite these problems of reporting, the overall response rate exceeded 73 per cent of business surveyed. For known chains and department stores which were all surveyed, the response rate was 100 per cent.

A stratified simple random sample of 43,000 retail establishments was selected without replacement from among 115,000 establishments classified to the retail sector on a central file of employers maintained by Statistics Canada.

Statistics on merchandising and services businesses are presented under two concepts, 'location' and 'establishment'. Location statistics show every separate place of business in its own kind of business classification, while establishment statistics comprise the accounting entity, which measures the sales activities in one or more business locations, not necessarily all in the same industrial sector (i.e. retail trade) or kind of business. A retail establishment is classified in total to the kind of business which comprises its major activity. The data reported by establishments having more than one trading location may therefore include business activities in more than one kind of business, possibly in more than one province and in other economic activities as well. Liquor, wine and beer stores were excluded from the retail commodity survey. They accounted for $1.765 billion in 1974. For these reasons, the results of the 1968 and 1974 Retail Commodity Surveys, which are based on the establishment, will not necessarily be comparable, at the kind of business level nor at the provincial level, with the results by location-based surveys of retail trade.

V132-142. Number and sales of shopping centres, by province, 1956 to 1973

SOURCE: number of shopping centres: for 1966 to 1973, *Shopping Centres in Canada*, 1973, annual, (Catalogue 63-214); for 1961 to 1965, *Shopping Centres in Canada*, 1972, annual, (Catalogue 63-214); for 1959 and 1960, *Retail Trade*, 1960, annual, (Catalogue 63-209); for 1958, *Retail Trade*, 1959, annual, (Catalogue 63-209); for 1957, *Retail Trade*, 1958, annual, (Catalogue 63-209); for 1956, *Shopping Centres in Canada, 1951-1973, Research Paper No. 1*, (Catalogue 63-527), Retail Sales in Shopping Centres: for 1972 and 1973, *Shopping Centres in Canada*, 1973, annual, (Catalogue 63-214); for 1969 and 1970, *Shopping Centres in Canada*, 1970, annual, (Catalogue 63-214); for 1961 and 1968, *Shopping Centres in Canada*, 1968, annual, (Catalogue 63-214); for 1967, *Shopping Centres in Canada*, 1966-67, annual, (Catalogue 63-214); for 1956, 1959 and 1964, *Shopping Centres in Canada, 1951-1973, Research Paper No. 1*, (Catalogue 63-527); sales for Canada: for 1956 to 1968, *Shopping Centres in Canada*, 1968, annual, (Catalogue 63-214).

It is important to note that the addition of a shopping centre in a specific year does not necessarily mean that the centre was newly constructed and began operating during that year. The shopping complex may have been in operation in earlier years but did not meet all the requirements of the definition of a 'shopping centre'. For the purpose of this table a shopping centre is defined as:

"A group of stores which are planned, developed and designed as a unit, containing a minimum of five retail establishments (or four retail establishments and a restaurant) in operation during any part of the current year. The centre must have a minimum of 20,000 square feet of usable parking area adjacent to it, and the parking facilities must be free of charge to customers. For shopping centres with paved parking areas of 20,000-50,000 square feet, the ratio of parking area to gross floor area must be 1.5 to one, or better. The merchandising development must contain either a grocery and combination store (i.e. a grocery store with sales of fresh meat accounting for 20 to 40 per cent of total sales), a department store, or a chain variety store. While a shopping centre is usually designed as a single project, all establishments do not necessarily have to be leased from a single (private or collective) ownership. A retail establishment may own the building and the land on which it is situated and still be fully integrated with the centre. A shopping centre usually bears a name and, as a rule, matters of common interest to the tenants, such as children's playgrounds, community activities, parking, etc., originate from one authority."

This definition excludes most downtown malls and a number of multi-store, multi-level shopping plazas because they do not provide free parking, or fail to meet the requirements of the foregoing definition in some other way.

V143-146. Shopping centres in Canada, by type, 1956 to 1973

SOURCE: number of shopping centres: for 1973, *Shopping Centres in Canada*, 1973, annual, (Catalogue 63-214); for 1961 to 1972, *Shopping Centres in Canada*, 1972, annual, (Catalogue 63-214); for 1960, *Retail Trade*, 1960, annual, (Catalogue 63-209); for 1956 and 1959, *Shopping Centres in Canada, 1951-1973, Research Paper No. 1*, (Catalogue 63-527); for 1957 and 1958, *Retail Trade*, 1958, annual, (Catalogue 63-209). Retail sales in shopping centres: for 1964, 1968, 1969, 1970, 1972 and 1973, *Shopping Centres in Canada*, annual, (Catalogue 63-214), 1965, 1968, 1969, 1970, 1972 and 1973 respectively; for 1966 and 1967, *Shopping Centres in Canada*, 1966-67, annual, (Catalogue 63-214); for 1961 to 1963, *Shopping Centres in Canada*, 1961-63, annual, (Catalogue 63-214); for 1959 and 1960, *Retail Trade*, annual, (Catalogue 63-209), 1959 and 1960 respectively; for 1957 and 1958, *Retail Trade*, 1958, annual, (Catalogue 63-209); for 1956, *Shopping Centres in Canada, 1956, Reference Paper 87*, (Catalogue 63-504). Total sales, for 1956 to 1968, *Shopping Centres in Canada*, 1968, annual, (Catalogue 63-214).

Regular shopping centres are stratified on the basis of the number of retail outlets and/or restaurants (see definition above) operating within the centre: type A, 5 to 15 outlets; type B, 16 to 30 outlets; type C, over 30 outlets.

The number of outlets operating within certain shopping centres may change slightly from year to year. These centres, therefore, may be reclassified to a different type in any one year.

Total retail sales in shopping centres for the years 1956 to 1967 are revised figures which exclude the receipts of restaurants located in shopping centres (see *Shopping Centres in Canada*, 1968, annual).

For the years 1956 to 1967, retail sales, excluding restaurant receipts, in shopping centres, by type A, B and C have been prorated using the distribution of sales including restaurants, by type A, B and C, given in various annual publications (see sources) 1956 to 1967.

V147-162. Shopping centre sales, by kind of business, 1956 to 1973

SOURCE: for 1973, *Shopping Centres in Canada, 1973*, annual, (Catalogue 63-214); for 1967 to 1972, *Shopping Centres in Canada, 1972*, annual, (Catalogue 63-214); for 1964, 1965 and 1966, *Shopping Centres in Canada*, annual, (Catalogue 63-214), 1964, 1965 and 1966 respectively; for 1961 to 1963, *Shopping Centres in Canada, 1961-63*, annual, (Catalogue 63-214); for 1956, 1957, 1958, 1959 and 1960, *Retail Trade*, annual, (Catalogue 63-209), 1956, 1958, 1959 and 1960 respectively.

See V1-24 for changes in retail trade kinds of business (these changes also apply to shopping centre kinds of business) and for a description of the old Retail Trade Survey kind-of-business categories shown in this table.

V163-177. Receipts of service trades in shopping centres, 1967 to 1973

SOURCE: for 1970 to 1973, *Shopping Centres in Canada, 1973*, annual, (Catalogue 63-214); for 1967, 1968 and 1969, *Shopping Centres in Canada*, annual, (Catalogue 63-214), 1966-67, 1969 and 1970 respectively.

For additional data on service outlets located in shopping centres, see source publications.

V178-190. Number and sales of vending machines, by province, 1958 to 1975

SOURCE: number of machines: for 1973, 1974 and 1975, *Vending Machine Operators*, annual, (Catalogue 63-213), 1973, 1974 and 1975 respectively; for 1960 to 1972, *Vending Machine Operators, 1974*, annual, (Catalogue 63-213); for 1958 and 1959, *Vending Machine Operators, 1959*, annual, (Catalogue 63-213). Sales: for 1958 and 1959, 1960, 1961 to 1969, 1970 to 1974 and 1975, *Vending Machine Operators*, annual, (Catalogue 63-213), 1959, 1961, 1972, 1974 and 1975 respectively.

Up to and including 1971 the statistics cover those vending machine operators who operated one or more vending machines on premises other than their own. From 1972 only vending machine operators operating a minimum of 10 full-size vending machines or 200 bulk confectionery machines or reporting total sales of at least $20,000 were included in the survey. At the same time the clause concerning the necessity of operating on other than their own (operators) premises was eliminated .

For the purposes of this table a vending machine is defined as a device which automatically dispenses merchandise after a requisite amount of money is inserted into the device. The merchandise vended includes tobacco products, beverages and food products as well as non-food products such as pens, hosiery, batteries, toiletry goods, books, etc. Excluded are gasoline and newspapers as well as services such as music, amusements, laundry and dry cleaning, photographs and photocopies, shoeshines, etc.

V191-214. Sales through vending machines, by commodity, 1958 to 1975

SOURCE: for all years, *Vending Machine Operators*, annual, (Catalogue 63-213), 1959, 1961, 1972, 1973, 1974 and 1975 respectively.

Beginning in 1973, sales through vending machines were reported by type of machine; prior to 1973 sales through vending machines were reported by product. Table V191-214 was completed making the best possible matching of the two sets of data (1958 to 1972 and 1973 to 1975). The user is advised to utilize the table with extreme caution as the two sets of data are not strictly comparable.

V215-218. Retail sales, by type of store, 1930 to 1975

SOURCE: same as V1-24. Also, *Retail Chain Stores*, annual, (Catalogue 63-210), various issues.

For 1931 to 1960 (excluding census years), the data were derived as follows: Total all stores (series V1-24) *minus* chain stores (series V35-52) *minus* department stores *equals* independant stores. For department stores, see *Retail Trade, 1930-1961, Revisions to 1951-61 Intercensal Estimates*, (Catalogue 63-510), occasional.

V219-229. Retail sales, by type of store, by province, selected years, 1930 to 1971.

SOURCE: for 1971, *Retail Trade*, January 1972, (Catalogue 63-005); for 1966, *Retail Trade, Revisions to 1966-1970 Postcensal Estimates*, (Catalogue 63-519); for 1961, *Retail Trade, Revisions to 1961-1966 Intercensal Estimates*, (Catalogue 63-517); for 1951, *Census of Canada, 1951*, vol. VII, *Distribution, Retail Trade*; for 1941, *Census of Canada, 1941*, vol. X, *Merchandising and Services, part 1*; for 1930, *Census of Canada, 1931*, vol. X, (Merchandising and Services, Part 1.)

In the case of chain stores for 1966, the provincial data will not add to the Canada total because the sales of department stores are included with chain store sales for three provinces.

In the case of independent stores for 1930 and 1941, the sales of department stores must be added to the appropriate sales of independent stores for each of Quebec, Ontario and British Columbia, before the provincial data will add to the Canada total.

V230-248. Sales of retail chain stores, by kind of business, selected years, 1930 to 1971

SOURCE: same as series V219-229.

For a description of the kind of business categories shown in this table please refer to the source publications. Changes in the composition of various kinds of business have occurred from one census year to the next.

V249-267. Sales of independent retail stores, by kind of business, selected years, 1930 to 1971

SOURCE: same as series V219-229.

For a description of the kind of business categories shown in this table please refer to the source publications. Changes in the composition of various kinds of business have occurred from one census year to the next.

V268-290. Direct selling, by commodity, 1969 to 1975.

SOURCE: for 1975, *Direct Selling in Canada*, 1975, annual, (Catalogue 63-218); for 1969 to 1974, *Direct Selling in Canada*, 1974, annual, (Catalogue 63-218).

Direct selling refers to the substantial volume of consumer goods sold to the household consumer for his personal use by other than the regular retail store outlet: department store, chain store or independent retail dealer. This occurs at all levels in the movement of goods from the primary producer or importer to the consumer: at the agricultural level by greenhouse and nursery operators and some market gardeners; at the manufacturing stage through sales exclusively to employees at company-operated on-premises stores, or through integrated sales divisions using mail-order or door-to-door canvassers; by some wholesalers and importers, by specialized direct sellers and through vending machine operators.

Statistics on these non-store retail sales supplement the regular retail trade statistics which are also compiled and published in the monthly retail trade report to form the principal basis of the 'personal expenditure on consumer goods and services' component of the National Accounts of Canada.

This table, however, covers only the direct sales made by some primary producers (greenhouses and nurseries, etc.), manufacturers and specialized direct sellers. It does not include foreign mail-order sales to Canadians, direct sales made by Canadian department stores' mail-order divisions, or direct sales made by wholesalers, vending machine operators and service establishments. Estimates of the value of some of these latter categories appear in the special table on the value of 'total known retail trade' published as part of the *1971 Census of Merchandising and Services*, vol. VII, (Catalogue 97-702).

V291-313. Direct selling, by commodity, by province, 1971

SOURCE: *Direct Selling in Canada*, 1971, (Catalogue 63-218).

V314-319. Retail trade, by legal form of organization, selected years, 1930 to 1966

SOURCE: for 1966, *Census of Canada, 1966*, vol. VI, *Retail Trade, Locations*, (Catalogue 97-606); for 1961, *Census of Canada, 1961*, vol. VI, Part 1, (Catalogue 97-504); for 1951, *Census of Canada, 1951*, vol. VII, *Distribution, Retail Trade*; for 1941, *Census of Canada, 1941*, vol. X, *Merchandising and Services, Part 1*; for 1930, *Census of Canada, 1931*, vol. X, *Merchandising and Services, Part 1*.

V320-331. Summary statistics, census of retail trade, by province, selected years, 1930 to 1971.

SOURCE: for 1971, *Census of Canada, 1971, Retail Trade*, (Catalogue 97-702); for 1966, *Census of Canada, 1966*, vol. VI, *Retail Trade, Locations*, (Catalogue 97-602); for 1961, *Census of Canada, 1961*, vol. VI, *Part 1*, (Catalogue 97-501); for 1951, *Census of Canada, 1951*, vol. VII, *Distribution Retail Trade*; for 1930 and 1941, *Census of Canada, 1941*, vol. X, *Merchandising and Services, Part 1*.

Wholesale Trade (Series V332-409)

V332-350. Estimated annual sales of wholesalers proper, by kind of business, 1951 to 1975

SOURCE: for 1972, 1973, 1974 and 1975, *Wholesale Trade*, monthly, December 1973, 1974 and 1975 respectively (Catalogue 63-008); for 1961 to 1971, *Wholesale Trade, 1961-1971*, (Catalogue 63-521); for 1951 to 1960, *Wholesale Trade, 1951-1968*, (Catalogue 63-515).

The surveys cover wholesalers proper who are described as middlemen between the producer and retailer or producer and business, industrial or institutional user. They hold inventories and buy and sell on their own account. Not included are agents and brokers, manufacturers' sales branches, assemblers of primary products, petroleum bulk stations and certain other types of operations not included in the survey but usually considered to perform wholesale functions.

It is important to note that in 1960 a major revision took place in the Standard Industrial Classification which affected wholesale trade in 1961. The composition of the wholesale merchant universe was affected by the addition of lumber and building material dealers, other building material dealers, farm implement dealers, feed and seed stores, farm supply stores and harness shops. These trades were formerly included in the retail trade sector of merchandising.

For example, as a result of the change, approximately $651,000,000 was added to the trade group 'Other construction materials and supplies, including lumber'. Similar adjustments were made to the other trade groups affected.

In addition to the S.I.C. revisions of 1960, a number of changes in coding and concepts were implemented in the 1961 Census. For example, a 'value added' approach was used for the first time in determining the correct classification of retail and wholesale businesses. The 'location' and 'establishment' concepts also appeared at that time.

The implementation of the establishment concept is noticeable in comparing the 1961 figures with the amounts for the same trades in 1960. This concept has a tendency to increase the sales totals in some trades and decrease the sales totals in others. The establishment is the smallest accounting entity which can provide a full range of statistics.

The implementation of the 'value added concept' in classifying businesses between wholesale and retail accounts for a loss of an unknown amount of wholesale sales. For example, a hardware business with 51 per cent sales at wholesale would be included in prior censuses as wholesale. For 1961, the value added in retailing being larger than in wholesaling, this same business would be classed as retail.

For further details on these points, the user of these statistics is referred to the *Standard Industrial Classification Manual*, Revised 1960, (Catalogue 12-501), pp. 7-9.

The statistics in this table measure the net sales (gross sales less returns and allowances), including sales taxes collected and other trading revenues of all wholesaler merchants operating in Canada, whether Canadian or foreign and whether sales are domestic or abroad. Some duplication may exist where wholesalers sell to other wholesalers. Excluded from the table are statistics on manufacturers' sales branches, assemblers of primary products, agents and brokers, and petroleum bulk tank plants and truck distributors.

For a detailed description of the kind of business categories shown in the table please refer to *Wholesale Trade*, December 1975, (Catalogue 63-008).

Beginning in 1961, heating and plumbing equipment dealers, previously in the retail trade sector, are included in series V347 in this table.

V351-360.   Index numbers of sales of wholesalers proper, by selected kind of business, 1930 to 1975

SOURCE: for 1954 to 1975, same as V332-350; for 1950 to 1953, the index was calculated as the arithmetic average of the monthly indexes given in *Wholesale Trade*, (Catalogue 63-008), monthly issues to the end of 1954; for 1941 to 1949, *Wholesale Trade, 1949 Revised Indexes*, table 2, p. B-9, (Catalogue 63-D-32); for 1935 to 1940, *Summary Monthly Indexes of Wholesale Sales in Canada, 1935-1943*, (Catalogue 63-D-32); for 1930 to 1937 (basis 1930 = 100), *Wholesale Trade in Canada and the Provinces, 1939*, tables 1 and 2, pp. 5-7, (Catalogue 63-D-33). The method noted above of obtaining the indexes for 1950 to 1953 was that used by the bureau from 1935 to 1949.

The indexes for 1935 to 1953 were obtained as averages of monthly indexes based on the monthly surveys of a sample of wholesalers. The sample size was 200 from 1935 to 1939, became 300 in 1940, and 400 from 1944 to the end of the period covered. These indexes are for wholesalers proper (see the note to series V332-350 and the general note to Section V). Only nine trades are covered and the index of total sales is based on these nine trades only. The index of trade for each month was obtained by linking with the same month a year earlier on the basis of reported sales for each of the two months.

These estimates provide the only data on annual sales available for 1940 to 1950. They have been revised on the basis of information in the decennial censuses of 1941 and 1951.

The indexes for 1930 to 1937 (basis 1930 = 100) are from the annual survey of wholesale trade, which was conducted from 1933 to 1939, and from the decennial census of 1930. The annual survey was based on a larger sample than the monthly survey. It covered all branches of wholesale trade proper and in addition petroleum bulk tank stations and meat packing plant wholesale outlets. A classification similar to that of the 1930 Census but somewhat different from that of the monthly survey was used. For this table, items were selected to correspond as closely as possible to the categories of the monthly survey. The index for all kinds of business, series V351, has a considerably wider coverage than that obtained from the monthly survey.

The types of business covered in the monthly survey are best described by reference to the classification of wholesale trade by kinds of business, given in the 1930 Census of Wholesale Trade *Census of Canada*, 1931, vol. XI, Merchandising and Services, part 2, p. 483. A statement of what is included in the monthly indexes is given in *Current Trends in Wholesale Trade*, mimeographed, 1936 and in the indexes based on annual surveys in *Wholesale Trade in Canada and the Provinces*, 1933.

Because comparable annual data for sales of wholesalers proper are no longer available for the entire period 1930 to 1975, it has been necessary to establish new base years in 1935 and 1954.

V361-373.   Wholesale sales, by kind of business and type of operation, selected years, 1930 to 1966

SOURCE: for 1966, *Census of Canada, 1966, Wholesale Trade: Establishments*, (Catalogue 97-627); for 1961, *Census of Canada, 1961*, Bulletin 6.2-1, vol. VI, Part 2, (Catalogue 97-511) and Bulletin 6.2-4, vol. VI, Part 2, (Catalogue 97-514); for 1951, *Census of Canada, 1951*, vol. VIII, *Distribution, Wholesale Trade and Services*; for 1930 and 1941, *Census of Canada, 1941*, vol. XI, *Merchandising and Services, Part 2*.

Sales of wholesalers proper, within kinds of business, will differ from sales in V332-350 because of different kind of business composition. The reader should refer to source publications for the kind of business composition in each census year.

The data in this table include only the categories in which the largest values of sales were found. There were smaller amounts in a number of other categories. For total sales by the various categories of outlets and for sales of petroleum bulk tank stations see series V374-387.

The content of the various kinds of business and the nature of type of operation in the 1951 Census may be found in *Census of Canada, 1951*, vol. VIII, *Distribution, Wholesale Trade, Services*, appendix B and appendix A respectively. See also table 3 in the same volume.

Beginning in 1961, lumber and building material dealers, previously in the retail sector, are included in series V369 of this table.

A number of manufacturers' sales branches which reported sales, or for which sales were estimated, were included in wholesale trade in 1951 but were excluded in 1961 if they were not accounting entities able to report a full range of statistics. It is estimated that the sales through these 3,478 locations in 1961 exceeded $4 billion.

The figures for 1930 include certain sales offices situated at the same location as the manufacturing plant which are omitted from the results for 1941.

Series V370 in 1961 reflects a lack of accounting entities able to report a full range of statistics.

Due to differences in scope and coverage, direct comparisons between the results for 1941 and 1930 in series V370 should be made with caution.

V374-387.   Wholesale trade, by major type of operation, by province, selected years, 1930 to 1966

SOURCE: for 1966, *Census of Canada, 1966, Wholesale Trade: Establishments*, (Catalogue 97-627); for 1961, *Census of Canada, 1961*, Bulletin 6.2-1, vol. VI, Part 2, (Catalogue 97-511); for 1941 and 1951, *Census of Canada, 1951*, vol. VII, *Distribution, Wholesale Trade and Services*; for 1930 *Census of Canada, 1941*, vol. XI, *Merchandising and Services, Part 2*.

According to certain common characteristics, each wholesale establishment is assigned to one of the following types of operations:

1. *Primary Product Dealers.* Establishments mainly engaged in purchasing primary products, such as grain, livestock, raw furs, fish, leaf tobacco, pulpwood, etc., directly from Canadian farmers, loggers, fishermen and trappers or acting as agents in such transactions. Co-operative marketing associations marketing primary products of their members are considered as primary product dealers.

2. *Wholesale Merchants.* Establishments primarily engaged in buying and selling goods on own account. Such a business may be described as export and/or import merchant, cash-and-carry wholesaler, drop shipper or desk jobber, mail-order wholesaler, truck distributor, rack jobber, etc.

3. *Agents and Brokers.* Establishments primarily engaged in buying and/or selling products for others on a commission basis. They may be known as auction companies, commission merchants, export and/or import agents or brokers, manufacturer's agents, purchasing agents or resident buyers, selling agents, etc. Not every agent or broker is classified to this type of operation. An agent dealing in primary products by buying directly from Canadian farmers is classified as a primary product dealer (type 1); agency-type wholesale operations by manufacturers as a manufacturers' sales branch (type 4); and agents dealing primarily in petroleum products as a petroleum bulk tank plant and truck distributors (type 5).

4. *Manufacturers' Sales Branches.* Businesses owned by manufacturing firms for marketing their own products. These may or may not be separately incorporated, and goods produced by others may also be sold. There are two exceptions to this rule: (a) manufacturers' sales branches which are owned by a firm that has a manufacturing plant(s) outside Canada only and (b) manufacturers' sales branches which are incorporated and sell less than 50 per cent of their parent manufacturers' products. These are classified not as manufacturers' sales branches but as wholesale merchants. It should be noted that exception (a) was not applied in the 1961 Wholesale Trade Census. Those manufacturers' sales branches which are not separate accounting entities but mere extensions of the manufacturing plant(s) and thus do not mark up their goods received from the parent plant nor are remunerated on a commission basis by the parent company are part of the manufacturing establishments and as such were considered to be out of scope for the census of wholesale trade.

5. *Petroleum Bulk Tank Plants and Truck Distributors.* Businesses primarily engaged in the wholesale distribution of petroleum products, such as salaried, independent or agency operated bulk tank plants and independent or agency-type truck distributors.

Where a wholesale establishment is engaged in more than one type of operation, it is classified to the primary type accounting for the largest part of its gross margin. In case of an agency or brokerage operation, the total amount of commission received represents the gross margin. For example, if a certain establishment is partly a wholesale merchant and partly an agent and earns $20,000 gross margin on own account business and receives a revenue of $30,000 from commissions, then as the commission income exceeds the margin earned on own account transactions, the establishment is classified to the Agents and Brokers type.

The 'establishment' concept is based primarily on the system of accounting used in business. The establishment is defined as the smallest unit which is a separate operating entity capable of reporting those elements of input and output necessary to the calculation of gross margin, as well as employment, wages and salaries. The only proviso imposed on this definition is that wholesale trade establishments were not to cross the boundaries of the five Canadian regions. (The Atlantic region comprises Newfoundland, Prince Edward Island, Nova Scotia and New Brunswick. Quebec

and Ontario are independent regions. Manitoba, Saskatchewan and Alberta make up the Prairie region; British Columbia, the Yukon Territory and the Northwest Territories belong to the British Columbia region.) For multi-unit wholesale firms with business locations in more than one region, artificial establishments were created. The establishments for such firms were based on regional boundaries, regardless of their accounting entities.

The 'location' is defined as the physical outlet in which business activity takes place. The location is not necessarily dependent upon the availability of accounting-based data but has to be capable of providing a limited range of statistics even though these may have to be estimated. Where the accounting records are designed to measure the detailed business activity of a single location, the establishment and location coincide; otherwise two or more locations belong to a certain establishment.

Beginning in 1961, country grain elevators under contract to the Canadian Wheat Board are excluded from wholesale trade and from column V384 and are included in the storage industry.

The procedure followed in dealing with line elevator companies differed between 1930 and 1941. In the 1930 Census the selling function of these companies was stressed. Each company was considered as one unit and one report covering the activities of the head office and sales organization alone was filed. In the 1941 Census the assembling rather than the selling function of these elevators has been reflected in the table. The head office was omitted altogether but each local elevator was considered as a unit. The volume of business shown for line elevators represents payments to farmers at the local elevator points. This difference in procedure results in the showing of a greatly increased number of establishments for this classification in 1941 compared with 1930.

V388-397. Wholesale trade, gross profit margins by kind of business biennially, 1947 to 1957

SOURCE: *Operating Results of Food Wholesalers*, biennial, 1947 to 1957, each issue, table on summary of results, (Catalogue 63-419); *Operating Results of Automotive Parts and Accessories Wholesalers*, issues for 1953, 1955 and 1957, table 1, (Catalogue 63-416); *Operating Results of Hardware Wholesalers*, issues for 1953, 1955 and 1957, table 1, (Catalogue 63-421); *Operating Results of Plumbing and Heating Supplies Wholesalers*, issues for 1953, 1955 and 1957, table 1, (Catalogue 63-423); *Operating Results of Drug Wholesalers*, issues for 1953, 1955 and 1957, table 1, (Catalogue 63-417); *Operating Results of Miscellaneous Wholesalers*, issues for 1947, table 1, p. 9, issue for 1949, p. E-7 and issue for 1951, p. 7, (Catalogue 63-D-42). The last-named publication contained data for wholesalers in automotive parts and accessories, hardware, plumbing and heating supplies and drugs, which became separate publications in 1953.

See the general note to Section V concerning the collection of data on operating results of retail and wholesale firms and the note to series V100-129 for a definition of gross profit margins.

The surveys were made of all wholesalers proper in 10 trades which, in 1941, accounted for 35 per cent of sales of all wholesalers proper. The 10 trades covered were selected for their importance in the distribution of consumer goods to retailers and in most cases a very high proportion of sales was made to retailers. The piece goods trade was a notable exception, with the dominant sales being to other wholesalers and large users, and plumbing and heating supplies were sold predominantly to contractors. The companies covered for each trade included only those with a high proportion of their trade in the designated kind of business.

The operating ratios given in this table are for all wholesalers for whom tabulations were made. In addition, in each report, profit margins were given for identical firms in the year being covered and in the previous survey two years earlier. However, the number of identical firms changed between each pair of years for which comparisons were given, and for this reason their profit margins are not given here.

Descriptions of the detailed content of the various trades are not given in the sources. The descriptions of the trades covered in series V351-360 given in the notes to those series probably indicate the nature of the trades covered.

A good deal of additional information is given in the source. In general it is similar to that provided in kindred reports for retail trades (see the note to series V100-129). Some separate data are provided for incorporated companies only.

In 1953, 1955 and 1957, an additional trade *Household Appliance and Electrical Supply*, (Catalogue 63-422) was added. The gross profit margins were 19.67 per cent in 1953, 18.67 per cent in 1955 and 18.93 per cent in 1957.

V398-409. Summary statistics, census of wholesale trade, by province, selected years, 1930 to 1966

SOURCE: for 1966, *Census of Canada, 1966, Wholesale Trade: Establishments*, (Catalogue 97-627); for 1961, *Census of Canada, 1961*, vol. VI, Part 2, (Catalogue 97-511); for 1951, *Census of Canada, 1951*, vol. VIII, *Distribution, Wholesale Trade and Services*; for 1941, *Census of Canada, 1941*, vol. XI, *Merchandising and Services, Part 2*.

Service Establishments (Series V410-448)

V410-413. Power laundries, cleaning and dyeing plants, selected operating statistics, 1917 to 1974

SOURCE: for 1973 and 1974, *Power Laundries, Dry Cleaning and Dyeing Plants*, 1974, annual, (Catalogue 63-205); for 1961 to 1972, *Power Laundries, Dry Cleaning and Dyeing Plants*, 1972, annual, (Catalogue 63-205); for 1930 to 1960, *Laundries, Cleaners and Dyers*, 1960, tables 5 and 13, (Catalogue 63-205); for 1917 to 1929, *Power Laundries and Cleaning and Dyeing Establishments in Canada*, 1939, table 7, p. 12 and table 20, p. 32, (Catalogue 63-205); for 1917 to 1926, *Report on the Dyeing, Cleaning and Laundry Industry in Canada*, 1928, p. 3, (Catalogue 63-205).

This table deals with the business activities of power operated laundries and dry cleaning and dyeing plants. Plants are classified as power laundries if the greater part of their revenue is derived from laundry work or if the greater part of their revenue is derived from rental services, where it is evidenced that the plant does its own laundry of the items rented. Plants are classified as dry cleaners and dyers if the greater part of their revenue is derived from cleaning and dyeing. This table does not include dyeing plants doing work on a commercial or industrial scale for textile plants, etc. There are inconsistent variations from year to year for power laundries and dry cleaning and dyeing plants due to

the method of classification; however, the combined data for the two classifications do show consistent annual changes.

These data were collected as a part of the annual census of manufacturers from 1917 to 1936; thereafter they were collected annually by the Internal Trade Branch of the Industry and Merchandising Division later the Merchandising and Services Division of Statistics Canada.

The data for 1917 to 1926 are not strictly comparable with those for later years. They were not given separately for laundries and dyeing and cleaning establishments. Dyeing and finishing of textile goods was included in those years but excluded in the data for 1927 to 1960: in 1927 the value of work done on dyeing and finishing textiles was $2,871,000; in 1928 it was $3,074,000. Finally in 1921 to 1924 considerable numbers of hand laundries were included, affecting mainly the number of establishments.

Historically, the annual report covering this industry has been based upon a 100 per cent survey of all firms. In 1969, however, it was decided to attempt a sample survey, thus the number of plants data were not published. A full-coverage survey was reinstated for the 1970 survey and all data are completely comparable with previous years. The source provides other data not reported here.

V414-416. Selected statistics of hotels, 1930, 1941 and 1949 to 1973

SOURCE: for 1969 to 1973, *Traveller Accommodation Statistics*, annual, 1969 to 1973, (Catalogue 63-204); for 1961 to 1968, *Hotels*, annual, 1961 to 1968, (Catalogue 63-204); for 1949 to 1960, series V200 and V201 from *Hotels*, 1960, p. 7, for series V202 from each individual issue of *Hotels* for the year concerned, various tables, (Catalogue 63-204); for 1941, all data from *Hotel Statistics*, 1941, table 1, p. 4, (Catalogue 63-D-63); for 1930, all data from *Census of Canada, 1931*, vol. XI, pp. 1237-9.

The statistics in this table refer to all hotels in Canada: (1) full-year licensed, (2) full-year non-licensed, (3) seasonal licensed, (4) and seasonal non-licensed.

A hotel-type room is defined as a room contained in a main lodge or hotel, having access from a main lobby but with no direct access from the exterior of the building. A hotel-motel-type room is defined as a main lodge or hotel, having access from a main lobby as well as direct access from the exterior of the building. This type of room is equated to a hotel-type room for the purpose of our establishment classification.

The definition of 'full-year licensed' hotels includes establishments: (1) operating six or more hotel or hotel-motel-type rooms; (2) operating for at least 10 or more months during the year; (3) licensed to serve alcoholic beverages provided that receipts from room rentals are equal to or greater than 1 per cent of alcohol sales; (4) reporting that the sum of rooms, meals and alcohol receipts are equal to or greater than 2/3 of merchandise sales; (5) reporting that room receipts are primarily derived from catering to transient guests.

'Full-year, non-licensed'. Same as 'full-year licensed' above, except for criterion (3) which should read: not licensed to serve alcoholic beverages.

'Seasonal, licensed'. Same as 'full-year licensed' above, except for criterion (2) which should read: operating for less than 10 months during the year.

'Seasonal, non-licensed'. Same as 'full-year licensed' above, except for criteria (2) and (3) which should read: (2)

operating for less than 10 months during the year; (3) not licensed to serve alcoholic beverages.

Above definitions as of 1973; consult source publications for possible changes in concepts or definitions.

Data on hotels have been collected in the decennial census, 1931 and 1941, and annually since 1949. All hotels are covered in each year. For the way in which lists of such establishments are obtained in decennial census years see the general note to Section V. The lists collected in the decennial census are supplemented by lists of licensed hotels provided by provincial governments.

The source provides other data not reported here.

V417-419. Selected statistics of advertising agencies in Canada, 1941 and 1946 to 1974

SOURCE: for 1965 to 1974, *Advertising Agencies*, 1974, annual, (Catalogue 63-201); for 1961 to 1964, *Advertising Agencies*, 1967, annual, (Catalogue 63-201); for 1941 and 1946 to 1963, *Advertising Agencies*, 1960, table 1, p. 2, (Catalogue 63-201).

The decennial census survey of advertising agencies in 1941 and the annual surveys since 1944 cover all businesses in this particular field.

The data are collected on the basis of business units and not by establishments.

These data pertain to businesses whose main activity is placing advertising in various media, principally publications, television or radio, on a commission or fee basis. Some market surveys and research and production work may be done. Business concerns whose activities are confined to preparing advertising copy, commercial art, printing or other production work are not included.

Due to a change in the questionnaire design commencing with the 1968 survey year, the gross revenue data for the years 1968 to 1974 are not comparable to those shown for the years prior to 1968.

The source provides other data not reported here.

Other data on advertising may be found in *Advertising Expenditures in Canada*, 1954, Reference Paper No. 67, 1956, in which data collected largely from various advertising media are given. It contains considerable detail on revenue of different advertising media, internal cost of advertisers, advertising costs in various industries and the like.

V420-423. Selected statistics of motion picture and drive-in theatres, 1930 to 1974

SOURCE: for 1965 to 1974, *Motion Picture Theatres and Film Distributors*, 1974, annual, (Catalogue 63-207); for 1961 to 1964, *Motion Picture Theatres and Film Distributors*, 1966, annual, (Catalogue 63-207); for 1940 to 1960, *Motion Picture Theatres and Film Distributors*, 1960, table 1, p. 7 and table 9, p. 12, (Catalogue 63-207); for 1930 to 1939, *Motion Picture Theatres, Exhibitors and Distributors*, 1955, table 1, p. R-7, (Catalogue 63-207).

V420 and V421. Series deal only with regular motion picture theatres and includes those using 16 mm. as well as theatres using 35 mm. projection equipment. For purposes of this table, establishments having more than one auditorium at one location were shown as single establishments.

V422 and V423. Series refer to drive-in theatres only.

A census of all motion picture theatres was first taken with the decennial census of 1931 for the year 1930. An annual census covering all such theatres has been taken

regularly since 1933. The original list of motion picture theatres was obtained by the population census enumerators in 1931 (see the general note to Section V). Since then lists of licensed operators have been obtained each year from the various provincial licensing authorities.

The data for 1948 to 1960 are for regular motion picture theatres and drive-in theatres. They do not cover itinerant operators who show pictures in halls or community enterprises, such as churches, lodges, boards of trade and the like which show pictures in community halls on a non-profit basis. Prior to 1948, data for community enterprises are included. Information for itinerant operators and community enterprises has not been collected since 1957.

The data are collected on an establishment basis.

V421 and V423. Receipts from admissions are what the theatres receive and do not include amusement taxes. Revenue from sales of candy, drinks, cigarettes and the like, from rental revenue of vending machines, from revenue for showing commercial films and from other sources, provide additional receipts. Such revenue amounted to $29,355,000 in 1974.

The source provides other data which are not reported here.

Material in other sections of this volume related to trade and service may be found in Section D on the labour force in distribution and services, in Section E on total wages and salaries by industry, in Section F on distribution of national product by industry, in Section G on external trade, in Section K on prices, in Section M on domestic disappearance of certain agricultural foodstuffs, in Section Q on sales of electricity and in Section T on expenditure for transportation.

V424-436. Receipts of selected kinds of service establishments, 1961 to 1975

SOURCE: Restaurant receipts: for 1970 to 1975, *Restaurant Statistics*, (Catalogue 63-011), December 1970 to 1975, respectively; for 1961 to 1969, *Restaurant Statistics*, February 1970, (Catalogue 63-011). Motels: for 1969, 1970, 1972, 1973 and 1974, *Traveller Accommodation Statistics*, annual, (Catalogue 63-204), 1969, 1970, 1972, 1973 and 1974 respectively. Power laundries, dry cleaning and dyeing plants: for 1961 to 1974, *Power Laundries, Dry Cleaning and Dyeing Plants*, annual, (Catalogue 63-205). Funeral directors: for 1972, *Funeral Directors*, 1972, (Catalogue 63-523); for 1968, *Funeral Directors*, 1968, (Catalogue 63-520); for 1964, *Funeral Directors*, 1964, (Catalogue 65-511); for 1966, *Census of Canada, 1966*, vol. VIII, *Services: Establishments*, (Catalogue 97-647). Hotels: for 1969 to 1974, *Traveller Accommodation Statistics*, annual, (Catalogue 63-204), 1969 to 1974 respectively; for 1961 to 1969, *Hotels*, annual, (Catalogue 63-204); 1961 to 1968. See also sources for series V414-416. Motion picture theatres: for 1968 to 1974, *Motion Picture Theatres and Film Distributors*, 1974, annual, (Catalogue 63-207); for 1961 to 1967, *Motion Picture Theatres and Film Distributors*, 1967, annual, (Catalogue 63-207). Computer services: for 1974, *Computer Service Industry*, 1974, annual, (Catalogue 63-222).

Data on restaurants include receipts from: (1) regular restaurants, (2) restaurants with merchandise, and (3) restaurants with alcoholic beverages. Both independent and chain restaurant locations are included as well as restaurants that operate under a franchise.

The statistics on motels refer to all motels in Canada both full-year and seasonal. As of 1973, definitions were as follows: 'A motel-type room is a room in a building sharing a common roof which has direct access from the exterior of the building but no access from a central lobby and which has adjacent parking.'

'Full-year' includes establishments: (1) operating three or more motel-type rooms and less than six hotel and/or motel-type rooms; (2) operating for at least 10 or more months during the year; (3) licensed or not licensed to serve alcoholic beverages; however, room rentals for licensed motels must be equal to or greater than 1 per cent of alcohol sales; (4) reporting that the sum of rooms, meals and alcohol receipts are equal to or greater than 2/3 of merchandise sales; (5) reporting that room receipts are primarily derived from catering to transient guests.

V437-448. Summary statistics, census of service trades, by province, selected years, 1930 to 1971

SOURCE: for 1971, *Census of Canada, 1971*, Services, unpublished worksheets, subject to revision; for 1966, *Census of Canada, 1966*, vol. VIII, *Services: Locations*, (Catalogue 97-643); for 1961, *Census of Canada, 1961*, vol. VI, *Part 2*, (Catalogue 97-517); for 1951, *Census of Canada, 1951*, vol. VIII, *Distribution, Wholesale Trade and Services*; for 1941, *Census of Canada, 1941*, vol. XI, *Merchandising and Services, Part 2*; for 1930, *Census of Canada, 1931*, vol. XI, *Merchandising and Services, Part 2*.

'Seasonal' is the same as 'full-year' above, except for criterion (2) which should read: (2) operating for less than 10 months during the year. Receipts of funeral directors include payments for funeral services, sale of vaults, and extra charges (cemetery and shipping charges, extra cars, newspaper notices, clothing, etc.).

Computer services refer to establishments in Canada primarily engaged in providing computer services as a major activity. 'Computer services' are defined to include processing services, input preparation, software and systems services, systems development and maintenance, other software and systems services, equipment maintenance services and other computer services (including computer-related education services, computer facility management, feasibility studies, etc.).

Series V1-24. Retail sales, by kind of business, 1930 to 1975
(millions of dollars)

Year[1]	Total sales	Grocery and combination stores	Alcoholic beverage outlets	Meat markets	Other food stores	General stores	Department stores	Variety stores	Motor vehicle outlets	Garages and filling stations	Men's clothing stores	Family clothing stores
	1	2	3	4	5	6	7	8	9	10	11	12
1975	51,200	11,984	..		897	995	5,786	819	10,184	3,857	664	740
1974	44,569	10,263	2,058		870	887	5,055	772	8,303	3,595	606	643
1973	38,335	8,595	1,870		787	736	4,316	711	7,422	2,978	557	563
1972	34,107	7,721	1,717		719	673	3,714	673	6,240	2,687	516	469
1971	30,646	7,260	1,540		654	617	3,184	571	4,925	2,695	476	424
1970	28,034	6,849	1,352		640	575	2,852	553	4,197	2,531	446	398
1969	27,401	6,401	1,236		620	567	2,737	542	4,796	2,318	424	385
1968	25,711	5,986	1,117		581	572	2,445	513	4,714	2,180	398	381
1967	24,155	5,686	1,053		579	573	2,158	532	4,433	2,004	372	371
1966	22,686	5,352	931		554	558	1,974	494	4,338	1,874	357	338
1965	21,155	4,825	848		669	510	2,010	521	4,175	1,778	363	357
1964	19,493	4,481	759		647	530	1,892	442	3,612	1,695	336	320
1963	18,207	4,176	717		626	557	1,730	405	3,312	1,624	306	290
1962	17,137	3,914	684		612	580	1,629	389	2,957	1,582	278	263
1961	16,073	3,704	660		594	607	1,551	374	2,599	1,492	247	251
1960	17,390	3,581	612		728	598	1,495	353	2,650	1,211	247	242
1959	17,087	3,378	588		678	593	1,456	333	2,701	1,160	241	231
1958	16,139	3,201	556		646	592	1,375	317	2,485	1,083	230	232
1957	15,423	2,955	530		619	569	1,306	297	2,547	976	229	223
1956	14,774	2,685	528		571	547	1,262	277	2,598	851	225	219
1955	13,473	2,464	466		524	514	1,166	251	2,415	738	210	203
1954	12,317	2,303	433		520	503	1,072	234	2,055	646	205	194
1953	12,189	2,148	436		499	514	1,034	215	2,303	565	213	210
1952	11,567	2,047	420		503	537	994	214	2,105	511	212	210
1951	10,653	1,899	390	182	308	520	910	196	1,885	474	202	193
1950	9,617	1,615	396	165	243	480	880	175	1,505	459	175	174
1949[1]	8,532	1,474	381	162	229	483	860	168	994	451	175	168
1948	7,835	1,368	364	156	232	455	796	159	803	415	167	165
1947	6,963	1,176	352	152	221	424	699	139	725	362	156	153
1946	5,787	999	327	129	205	377	606	127	475	240	138	135
1945	4,573	849	277	110	179	324	510	113	240	109	115	111
1944	4,093	768	217	102	104	298	460	104	201	94	105	100
1943	3,786	707	191	96	164	274	420	99	180	89	98	94
1942	3,619	663	177	92	155	245	419	98	217	116	96	88
1941	3,441	567	145	83	136	215	378	85	371	205	80	74
1940	2,935	469	119	68	124	194	327	70	340	189	68	61
1939	2,578	404	103	60	120	183	291	59	294	160	60	51
1938	2,530	396	97	60	122	187	280	54	302	153	59	47
1937	2,593	398	94	62	120	189	289	53	326	170	64	51
1936	2,289	352	83	57	115	173	274	47	254	130	59	47
1935	2,105	327	73	54	116	161	259	43	212	106	55	43
1934	1,984	317	74	54	117	155	254	40	175	85	51	39
1933	1,773	317	70	56	107	137	242	37	127	61	44	32
1932	1,908	316	85	57	128	144	254	40	133	63	47	32
1931	2,305	361	109	67	171	168	313	44	184	85	59	37
1930	2,756	405	127	83	127	208	355	44	254	114	72	42

Series V1-24. Retail sales, by kind of business, 1930 to 1975 (concluded)
(millions of dollars)

Year[1]	Women's clothing stores	Shoe stores	Hardware stores	Lumber and building material dealers	Furniture stores	Appliance and radio stores	Restaurants	Fuel dealers	Drug stores	Jewellery stores	Tobacco stores	All other retail
	13	14	15	16	17	18	19	20	21	22	23	24
1975	863	474	581	—	694	678	—	—	1,488	427		10,069[2]
1974	745	425	529	—	590	620	—	—	1,304	385		6,919
1973	643	395	452	—	499	573	—	—	1,107	313		5,818
1972	639	367	433	—	450	503	—	—	1,027	261		5,296
1971	622	346	409	—	942		—	523	907	236		4,317
1970	561	328	383	—	847		—	473	840	219		3,990
1969	545	318	391	—	868		—	466	792	225		3,771
1968	502	306	392	—	816		—	471	737	214		3,386
1967	485	285	366	—	784		—	461	703	208		3,102
1966	435	252	356	—	740		—	475	650	192		2,816
1965	392	248	332	—	678		—	448	610	186		2,204
1964	369	230	320	—	627		—	421	555	174		2,083
1963	345	217	310	—	601		—	425	517	160		1,888
1962	334	211	301	—	587		—	412	487	152		1,764
1961	315	195	300	—	572		—	347	467	145		1,653
1960	305	192	299	644	620		767	349	450	144		1,905
1959	298	173	302	708	653		741	366	433	146		1,908
1958	286	162	297	666	628		689	348	408	141		1,797
1957	275	149	286	609	621		650	339	394	137		1,714
1956	262	139	278	616	632		606	326	345	136		1,671
1955	236	131	248	548	576		540	278	312	128		1,526
1954	229	126	241	470	510		505	257	290	119		1,406
1953	224	126	244	460	496		510	228	288	123		1,354
1952	212	120	230	389	453		486	237	269	116		1,301
1951	192	111	227	357	356		453[3]	232	248	105	78	1,135
1950	166	103	221	348	142	193	390	220	223	99	71	1,175
1949[1]	186	104	213	277	134	169	364	201	212	91	76	961
1948	171	97	199	251	135	139	330	196	197	84	74	880
1947	143	91	180	206	131	120	298	171	179	81	71	737
1946	129	82	156	143	112	80	270	144	168	82	62	603
1945	111	69	104	100	79	37	232	137	148	71	65	482
1944	102	62	89	97	69	31	216	131	138	60	59	427
1943	94	57	85	84	62	33	196	138	128	52	56	393
1942	87	54	81	82	66	42	158	123	115	44	49	352
1941	71	44	73	80	64	46	131[3]	99	101	38	43	312
1940	55	34	65	66	57	43	87	87	84	32	36	260
1939	40	30	59	53	46	35	69	83	76	25	31	248
1938	35	30	59	49	44	35	71	77	74	23	30	246
1937	40	32	58	51	48	37	78	80	74	24	30	226
1936	34	30	53	45	38	32	66	77	67	21	26	210
1935	29	28	49	38	33	30	55	73	63	19	24	214
1934	29	27	47	36	29	26	49	72	61	17	23	207
1933	24	26	43	29	23	23	40	70	57	15	22	172
1932	28	27	47	35	26	28	46	71	64	16	24	197
1931	41	32	59	48	35	40	61	76	71	21	27	196
1930	49	36	71	66	41	52	76[3]	86	77	27	31	313

[1] Includes Newfoundland beginning in 1949.
[2] Includes alcoholic beverage outlets.
[3] Includes refreshment booths and stands.

Series V25-34. Retail sales, by kind of business, 1923 to 1933
(millions of dollars)

Year	Total sales	Food group	Country general stores	General merchandise group	Automotive group	Apparel group	Building materials group	Furniture and household group	Restaurants and eating places	Other retail stores
	25	26	27	28	29	30	31	32	33	34
1933	1,773	480	137	313	218	147	83	51	42	302
1932	1,908	501	144	331	235	156	96	59	48	338
1931	2,305	599	168	401	298	189	129	82	62	377
1930	2,756	615	208	473	381	220	164	100	76	519
1929	3,158	668	259	495	488	268	207	120	83	570
1928	3,036	640	261	482	420	266	220	105	79	561
1927	2,783	609	255	444	366	244	207	92	75	490
1926	2,568	560	242	410	333	228	192	83	69	449
1925	2,304	514	229	380	241	205	177	73	64	421
1924	2,139	492	210	354	205	196	158	69	61	395
1923	2,179	500	205	344	222	203	168	71	62	405

Series V35-52. Retail sales, by kind of business, and number of chains and stores, chain stores, 1930 to 1975
(series V35-36 in numbers; series V37-52 in millions of dollars)

Year[1]	Number of chains	Average number of stores	Sales of all chain stores	Grocery and combination stores	Meat markets	Variety stores	Men's and boys' clothing stores	Family clothing stores	Women's apparel and accessories stores
	35	36	37	38	39	40	41	42	43
1975	..	..	15,966	7,110	..	620	179	320	451
1974	874	18,500	13,732	6,135	22	585	148	260	347
1973	834	17,239	11,342	4,997	18	547	127	223	278
1972	895	16,542	10,077	4,410	15	518	104	148	294
1971	833	15,976	8,550	3,868	13	479	70	114	222
1970	661	14,330	7,747	3,522	11	466	62	101	183
1969	649	13,515	7,021	3,101	12	463	56	91	168
1968	666	13,062	6,384	2,806	12	440	47	90	152
1967	713	12,865	6,019	2,611	16	465	47	73	147
1966	721	12,695[2]	5,516	2,401	..	429	47	74[3]	115
1965	602	10,677	4,836	2,249	19	455	63	113	97
1964	579	10,209	4,291	2,068	14	378	50	93	91
1963	559	9,718	3,906	1,890	11	340	41	76	90
1962	559	9,443	3,654	1,770	10	323	38	58	95
1961	580	9,434	3,495	1,711	9	313	28	56	97
1960	537	9,954	3,468	1,603	10	298	29	65	84
1959	507	9,491	3,280	1,481	8	283	30	50	81
1958	509	9,122	3,073	1,369	8	264	29	45	78
1957	493	8,822	2,842	1,242	8	247	28	40	71
1956	499	8,559	2,647	1,096	8	229	29	36	67
1955	496	8,274	2,354	963	8	208	27	33	62
1954	491	8,136	2,147	863	7	194	25	32	55
1953	466	7,835	2,048	773	6	188	25	36	49
1952	476	7,766	1,925	702	7	180	25	36	46
1951[1]	..	8,094[2]	1,776	610	7	164	25	42	42
1950	423	7,155	1,560	505	6	148	20	36	39
1949	381	6,839	1,420	434	6	142	18	34	37
1948	403	6,821	1,336	387	7	134	18	34	35
1947	422	6,716	1,177	302	8	118	17	30	29
1946	422	6,559	1,015	238	7	108	13	24	23
1945	429	6,580	876	214	7	96	11	20	19
1944	431	6,560	770	199	6	86	10	18	17
1943	444	6,780	704	180	6	84	10	17	15
1942	455	7,010	687	188	5	84	8	15	14
1941	..	8,011[2]	643	173	5	74	10	14	13
1940	451	7,131	509	141	4	61	7	10	8
1939	446	7,215	432	124	4	51	6	9	6
1938	457	7,356	414	117	5	47	7	8	6
1937	447	7,346	414	116	5	46	7	9	6
1936	457	7,588	395	107	4	41	7	9	6
1935	445	7,666	364	101	4	38	7	8	5
1934	445	7,804	347	101	4	36	6	7	5
1933	461	7,900	329	99	5	33	5	7	4
1932	486	8,066	361	104	5	35	6	4	5
1931	506	8,188	434	117	6	39	8	4	7
1930	..	8,476[2]	504	124	8	41	10	5	9

Series V35-52. Retail sales, by kind of business, and number of chains and stores, chain stores, 1930 to 1975 (concluded)

(series V35-36 in numbers; series V37-52 in millions of dollars)

Year[1]	Shoe stores	Hardware stores	Lumber and building material dealers	Furniture stores	Household appliance, radio and music stores	Restaurants	Drug stores	Tobacco stores and stands	Other chain stores
	44	45	46	47	48	49	50	51	52
1975	266	91	–	144	206	–	333	..	6,246
1974	225	83	–	136	175	–	262	47	5,307
1973	210	71	–	101	168	–	197	40	4,365
1972	193	88	–	87	137	–	187	x	3,896
1971	168	74	–	164		–	139	x	3,239
1970	153	70	–	60	91	–	125	33	2,870
1969	142	68	–	65	92	–	112	33	2,618
1968	135	70	–	64	78	–	106	–	2,384
1967	130	63	–	63	77	–	96	33	2,198
1966	113	55	–	62	80	–	87	..	2,053
1965	119	50	–	57	73	–	91	32	1,418
1964	105	46	–	108		–	75	27	1,236
1963	99	42	–	103		–	69	23	1,122
1962	91	36	–	99		–	59	21	1,054
1961	82	28	–	36	67	–	56	19	993
1960	77	49	95	49	64	41	55	..	949
1959	70	49	103	54	73	41	53	..	904
1958	64	43	107	52	76	38	50	..	850
1957	58	39	97	53	74	36	45	..	804
1956	53	37	100	55	78	36	41	16	766
1955	48	20	92	48	69	35	37	15	689
1954	45	18	84	38	59	34	36	16	641
1953	43	14	91	44	53	34	35	17	640
1952	42	13	82	43	52	32	33	17	615
1951[1]	38	17	76	33	42	31	31	17	601
1950	33	11	67	36	36	23	29	16	555
1949	32	9	59	35	29	21	27	16	521
1948	31	8	56	36	27	22	27	16	498
1947	29	6	51	33	23	21	27	15	499
1946	26	6	44	22	17	21	26	14	426
1945	24	5	39	18	12	20	24	13	354
1944	21	5	37	16	9	20	23	11	292
1943	20	4	31	14	10	19	22	10	262
1942	19	4	25	14	13	16	20	8	254
1941	16	4	20	15	19	15	19	7	239
1940	12	5	17	10	15	8	16	7	188
1939	11	5	14	5	3[4]	7	14	6	167
1938	10	5	13	5	3[4]	7	14	6	161
1937	10	5	13	5	3[4]	7	14	6	162
1936	9	5	13	4	2[4]	7	13	6	162
1935	8	4	11	5	2[4]	7	12	6	146
1934	8	4	11	5	x	7	12	6	135
1933	7	3	10	4	1[4]	7	11	5	128
1932	7	3	11	5	9	8	13	6	140
1931	8	4	13	8	12	11	14	7	176
1930	8	4	19	9	17	14	14	8	214

[1] Includes Newfoundland beginning in 1951.
[2] Maximum number of stores.
[3] Reclassified a number of stores to "General merchandise".
[4] Includes radio and music stores only.

Series V53-88. Retail sales and number of chains and stores, chain stores, by province, 1930 to 1975
(all series in numbers except 'Sales of all chain stores', in millions of dollars)

Year	Canada			Newfoundland			Prince Edward Island			Nova Scotia		
	Number of chains[1]	Maximum number of stores	Sales of all chain stores	Number of chains	Maximum number of stores	Sales of all chain stores	Number of chains	Maximum number of stores	Sales of all chain stores	Number of chains	Maximum number of stores	Sales of all chain stores
	53	54	55	56	57	58	59	60	61	62	63	64
1975	..	..	15,966	..	..	293	..	..	60	..	..	552
1974	874	19,695	13,732	53	232	243	28	60	56	101	697	472
1973	834	18,555	11,342	48	211	196	27	49	41	99	635	386
1972	895	17,269	10,078	51	221	169	26	51	37	94	583	351
1971	833	16,317	8,550	46	203	131	25	50	28	90	563	299
1970	661	15,156	7,747	43	200	117	20	45	26	82	546	266
1969	649	14,153	7,021	39	186	111	20	45	..	82	523	..
1968	666	13,728	6,384	37	185	106	20	42	..	79	530	..
1967	713	13,395	6,019	42	215	95	20	38	..	88	534	..
1966	721	12,695	5,516	31	197	87	13	35	..	75	516	..
1965	602	11,240	4,836	26	159	62	13	27	11	68	415	178
1964	579	10,703	4,291	24	140	49	13	25	10	65	388	154
1963	559	10,300	3,906	23	131	45	11	23	9	58	383	141
1962	559	9,986	3,654	19	112	39	12	24	9	58	376	129
1961	580	9,683	3,495	22	125	38	15	26	9	57	358	126
1960	537	10,594	3,468	28	131	37	14	28	8	56	358	116
1959	507	10,047	3,280	25	126	36	14	24	6	51	331	106
1958	509	9,604	3,073	20	111	24	14	24	6	51	331	105
1957	493	9,257	2,842	21	111	24	13	24	5	50	330	98
1956	499	9,046	2,647	20	109	15	14	24	5	52	329	90
1955	496	8,734	2,354	18	100	13	12	22	5	46	298	83
1954	491	8,468	2,147	18	103	14	13	24	5	43	306	73
1953	466	8,153	2,048	18	106	14	11	19	5	43	302	71
1952	476	8,047	1,925	17	110	14	11	18	5	43	307	70
1951	..	8,094	1,776	..	99	11	..	17	4	..	291	64
1950	423	7,483	1,560	—	—	—	10	15	3	50	289	58
1949	381	7,123	1,420	—	—	—	8	9	1	47	283	57
1948	403	7,152	1,336	—	—	—	7	8	1	49	287	55
1947	422	6,962	1,177	—	—	—	8	13	1	49	283	51
1946	422	6,743	1,015	—	—	—	8	13	1	46	275	50
1945	429	6,705	876	—	—	—	..	..	..	..	..	..
1944	431	6,774	770	—	—	—	..	..	1	..	..	42
1943	444	7,021	704	—	—	—	..	..	..	..	..	..
1942	455	7,139	687	—	—	—	..	..	1	..	..	38
1941	..	8,011	643	—	—	—	..	17	1	..	323	32
1940	451	7,522	509	—	—	—	..	..	..	..	..	..
1939[2]	446	7,595	432	—	—	—	9	9	1	49	290	20
1938[2]	457	7,692	414	—	—	—	8	9	1	49	293	18
1937	447	7,815	414	—	—	—	7	7	1	49	295	17
1936	457	8,124	395	—	—	—	7	7	1	50	301	15
1935	445	8,022	364	—	—	—	8	8	1	47	283	14
1934	445	8,210	347	—	—	—	7	8	1	47	274	13
1933	461	8,230	329	—	—	—	5	8	1	50	283	12
1932	486	8,398	361	—	—	—	8	10	1	50	276	13
1931	506	8,557	434	—	—	—	7	8	1	50	262	16
1930	..	8,476	504	—	—	—	..	12	1	..	221	13

Series V53-88. Retail sales and number of chains and stores, chain stores, by province, 1930 to 1975 (continued)

(all series in numbers except 'Sales of all chain stores', in millions of dollars)

Year	New Brunswick			Quebec			Ontario			Manitoba		
	Number of chains	Maximum number of stores	Sales of all chain stores	Number of chains	Maximum number of stores	Sales of all chain stores	Number of chains	Maximum number of stores	Sales of all chain stores	Number of chains	Maximum number of stores	Sales of all chain stores
	65	66	67	68	69	70	71	72	73	74	75	76
1975	..	..	455	..	..	3,292	..	..	6,831	..	..	646
1974	99	487	382	312	4,277	2,821	447	8,771	5,934	122	695	548
1973	89	451	313	292	4,031	2,312	432	8,358	4,960	118	692	455
1972	81	426	296	296	3,761	2,023	435	7,606	4,427	123	687	408
1971	79	403	254	282	3,568	1,785	408	7,264	3,729	111	609	334
1970	77	401	218	227	3,195	1,612	325	6,751	3,389	99	558	313
1969	67	375	204	229	3,087	1,492	310	6,308	3,080	93	516	285
1968	59	361	201	226	2,949	1,293	319	6,083	2,826	85	480	250
1967	60	352	197	239	2,782	1,323	335	5,981	2,606	88	466	227
1966	49	327	168	230	2,622	1,149	333	5,660	2,407	81	475	212
1965	47	265	146	210	2,407	1,005	293	5,275	2,232	72	358	161
1964	42	257	123	199	2,324	890	291	5,051	2,001	71	339	150
1963	39	232	112	191	2,219	823	293	4,897	1,829	69	311	137
1962	39	226	106	189	2,135	790	288	4,712	1,695	69	323	130
1961	38	220	105	189	2,085	764	292	4,536	1,635	68	325	122
1960	42	228	94	174	2,124	713	264	4,566	1,579	72	469	142
1959	41	208	85	167	1,950	674	259	4,355	1,509	75	449	132
1958	40	202	80	163	1,795	620	266	4,228	1,451	74	427	121
1957	37	197	76	155	1,725	577	254	4,069	1,335	69	406	112
1956	39	201	75	162	1,698	541	247	3,919	1,230	68	399	101
1955	41	204	68	163	1,650	488	251	3,740	1,096	67	393	94
1954	44	213	63	159	1,615	447	247	3,611	1,000	69	387	87
1953	41	210	62	150	1,537	423	233	3,446	942	69	392	87
1952	39	198	60	151	1,523	398	227	3,404	875	68	367	85
1951	..	204	55	..	1,495	359	..	3,472	809	..	361	79
1950	39	179	44	138	1,396	318	223	3,176	723	76	361	73
1949	38	180	43	127	1,290	283	206	3,015	641	70	344	68
1948	39	181	43	129	1,286	271	212	3,008	596	70	343	63
1947	38	173	41	133	1,252	247	220	2,896	509	64	320	56
1946	38	176	37	136	1,185	202	220	2,839	435	62	290	50
1945	..	..	..	..	..	..	..	..	..	..	..	..
1944	..	..	24	..	..	156	..	..	335	..	..	37
1943	..	..	..	..	..	..	..	..	..	..	..	..
1942	..	..	21	..	..	135	..	..	314	..	..	31
1941	..	216	20	..	1,446	132	..	3,385	295	..	335	28
1940	..	..	..	..	..	..	..	..	..	..	..	..
1939	46	219	13	134	1,344	82	233	3,102	194	61	327	19
1938	46	216	13	135	1,416	83	235	3,114	186	62	323	18
1937	44	205	13	134	1,481	83	230	3,180	185	63	331	18
1936	46	211	11	138	1,628	80	227	3,277	182	66	355	17
1935	45	194	9	139	1,612	73	206	3,173	172	72	370	16
1934	42	195	8	142	1,680	73	213	3,223	162	70	364	15
1933	41	190	8	147	1,668	73	217	3,210	151	73	374	14
1932	41	181	9	163	1,764	86	230	3,287	164	77	393	16
1931	42	171	10	168	1,772	106	239	3,314	195	84	404	19
1930	..	165	12	..	1,698	120	..	3,269	223	..	433	23

Series V53-88. Retail sales and number of chains and stores, chain stores, by province, 1930 to 1975 (concluded)

(all series in numbers except 'Sales of all chain stores', in millions of dollars)

Year	Saskatchewan			Alberta			British Columbia[2]			Yukon Territory and Northwest Territories		
	Number of chains	Maximum number of stores	Sales of all chain stores	Number of chains	Maximum number of stores	Sales of all chain stores	Number of chains	Maximum number of stores	Sales of all chain stores	Number of chains	Maximum number of stores	Sales of all chain stores
	77	78	79	80	81	82	83	84	85	86	87	88
1975	..	..	588	..	..	1,319	..	..	..	..	..	..
1974	105	697	493	183	1,618	1,061	189	2,090	..	10	71	..
1973	103	654	389	172	1,449	860	179	1,963	..	9	62	..
1972	105	656	364	172	1,395	775	173	1,820	..	9	63	..
1971	97	628	304	154	1,212	633	166	1,817	1,054	..	..	..
1970	92	616	268	118	1,127	585	143	1,717	953	..	..	..
1969	84	581	253	113	974	523	131	1,558	815	..	..	..
1968	82	589	243	115	965	473	139	1,544	751	..	..	..
1967	84	587	232	114	923	436	145	1,517	678	..	..	..
1966	69	571	218	109	885	406	134	1,407	..	..	..	..
1965	60	456	167	90	721	350	111	1,157	524	..	..	..
1964	54	417	149	90	674	315	103	1,088	450	..	..	..
1963	57	414	134	90	647	284	104	1,043	393	..	..	..
1962	56	402	125	85	636	265	107	1,040	366	..	..	..
1961	56	386	117	85	613	244	111	1,009	337	..	..	..
1960	75	688	140	94	854	263	111	1,082	368	4	66	8
1959	76	699	137	93	812	246	105	1,030	342	4	63	8
1958	71	693	129	93	774	220	102	959	309	5	60	9
1957	67	682	119	88	714	198	99	943	289	4	56	8
1956	69	681	111	85	699	182	101	932	290	5	55	7
1955	66	685	102	79	678	161	98	910	238	4	54	6
1954	65	668	96	82	647	147	93	844	209	4	50	6
1953	66	657	95	75	626	144	87	808	200	4	50	5
1952	68	654	90	76	607	132	94	802	189	5	57	7
1951	..	670	83	..	605	121	..	821	183	..	59	8
1950	71	662	73	81	588	107	93	762	155	4	55	5
1949	64	655	72	72	543	97	84	745	152	4	59	5
1948	66	680	67	70	530	85	88	770	149	4	59	5
1947	64	663	63	72	539	73	90	769	131	4	54	5
1946	66	684	60	69	516	66	85	711	110	4	54	4
1945	..	..	..	..	..	..	..	..	..	..	..	..
1944	..	..	44	..	..	51	..	..	80	..	..	..
1943	..	..	..	..	..	..	..	..	..	..	..	..
1942	..	..	34	..	..	41	..	..	72	..	..	..
1941	..	883	33	..	577	36	..	767	64	..	62	..
1940	..	..	..	..	..	..	..	..	..	..	..	..
1939	83	979	26	82	572	29	73	692	47	..	..	..
1938	83	977	22	81	564	27	77	708	46	..	..	..
1937	82	983	23	79	565	26	77	696	46	4	72	1
1936	82	986	24	81	574	24	76	717	41	4	68	1
1935	88	1,009	23	87	594	20	76	704	37	5	75	1
1934	88	1,038	22	92	627	19	79	725	34	5	76	1
1933	90	1,046	21	93	637	17	81	740	32	4	74	1
1932	92	1,074	21	91	637	18	84	699	33	4	77	1
1931	100	1,176	24	98	662	20	91	704	41	5	84	2
1930	..	1,232	35	..	675	26	..	690	49	..	81	2

[1] The aggregate of chains (number) by province does not add to Canada total since many chains operate and are consequently counted in more than one province.

[2] Includes the Yukon Territory and the Northwest Territories from 1961 to 1971 inclusive.

Series V89-99. Retail sales, by province, 1923 to 1975
(millions of dollars)

Year	Total for Canada[1]	Newfound- land	Prince Edward Island	Nova Scotia	New Brunswick	Quebec	Ontario	Manitoba	Saskat- chewan	Alberta	British Columbia[2]
	89	90	91	92	93	94	95	96	97	98	99

From *Retail Trade*

Year	89	90	91	92	93	94	95	96	97	98	99
1975	51,200	972	241	1,619	1,338	12,812	19,156	2,192	2,243	4,557	6,070
1974	44,569	843	208	1,445	1,141	11,201	16,564	1,989	1,904	3,734	5,540
1973	38,335	717	176	1,227	977	9,697	14,505	1,699	1,533	3,070	4,735
1972	34,107	638	156	1,102	892	8,612	13,058	1,496	1,363	2,728	4,062
1971	30,646	533	141	1,023	835	7,681	11,877	1,318	1,139	2,467	3,632
1970	28,034	493	132	930	740	7,074	10,885	1,227	1,018	2,274	3,260
1969	27,401	481	123	884	703	6,962	10,588	1,188	1,052	2,255	3,165
1968	25,711	464	122	862	687	6,565	9,885	1,118	1,082	2,067	2,859
1967	24,155	438	113	793	635	6,379	9,091	1,073	1,081	1,903	2,648
1966	22,686	406	108	753	595	5,882	8,625	1,006	1,047	1,758	2,507
1965	21,155	377	103	711	570	5,534	8,043	918	984	1,607	2,307
1964	19,493	342	95	664	515	5,120	7,366	873	924	1,508	2,086
1963	18,207	315	90	632	474	4,770	6,948	827	845	1,426	1,880
1962	17,137	297	83	602	447	4,486	6,526	801	776	1,368	1,751
1961	16,073	286	79	580	436	4,108	6,207	767	734	1,272	1,604

Atlantic provinces[1]

Year	89	90	91	92	93	94	95	96	97	98	99
1960	17,390	..	1,421		..	4,213	6,751	907	919	1,424	1,755
1959	17,087	..	1,356		..	4,114	6,615	870	933	1,405	1,793
1958	16,139	..	1,287		..	3,854	6,271	801	902	1,318	1,705
1957	15,423	..	1,233		..	3,710	5,943	763	846	1,245	1,683
1956	14,774	..	1,209		..	3,463	5,734	732	807	1,188	1,640
1955	13,473	..	1,125		..	3,109	5,296	694	745	1,057	1,447
1954	12,317	..	1,024		..	2,868	4,762	655	756	980	1,274
1953	12,189	..	1,004		..	2,793	4,666	684	812	990	1,241
1952	11,567	..	971		..	2,658	4,409	653	746	941	1,190
1951	10,653	160	54	394	286	2,437	4,116	609	654	848	1,095
1950	9,617	..	822		..	2,183	3,715	567	571	777	982
1949	8,532	..	734		..	1,872	3,294	523	538	697	874
1948	7,835	..	607		..	1,792	3,067	466	473	611	818
1947	6,963	..	564		..	1,621	2,721	407	410	504	737
1946	5,787	..	491		..	1,342	2,265	338	341	416	594
1945	4,573	..	387		..	1,081	1,774	269	279	329	455
1944	4,093	..	351		..	976	1,574	243	249	296	404
1943	3,786	..	319		..	913	1,488	220	219	266	362
1942	3,619	..	301		..	876	1,447	206	201	243	346
1941	3,441	..	16	165	102	819	1,407	211	187	221	313
1940	2,935	..	235		..	683	1,191	182	174	198	273
1939	2,578	..	196		..	602	1,039	166	154	180	242
1938	2,530	..	188		..	598	1,026	164	136	177	240
1937	2,593	..	199		..	605	1,068	165	136	165	255
1936	2,289	..	170		..	518	941	150	138	147	225
1935	2,105	..	157		..	473	875	139	124	137	200
1934	1,984	..	147		..	454	833	131	115	125	179
1933	1,773	..	129		..	419	735	121	103	109	157
1932	1,908	..	140		..	462	783	131	112	115	165
1931	2,305	..	172		..	558	945	153	133	134	210
1930	2,756	..	14	100	84	651	1,100	189	189	177	252

From *A Decade of Retail Trade*

Year	89	90	91	92	93	94	95	96	97	98	99
1933	1,777	..	131		..	421	737	120	104	108	155
1932	1,917	..	141		..	465	787	131	113	116	164
1931	2,326	..	173		..	562	951	155	138	137	210
1930	2,756	..	198		..	651	1,100	189	189	177	252
1929	3,158	..	215		..	722	1,250	227	244	216	284
1928	3,036	..	199		..	674	1,186	229	265	215	267
1927	2,783	..	185		..	625	1,081	211	246	188	247
1926	2,568	..	174		..	576	998	196	227	168	229
1925	2,304	..	160		..	515	901	180	194	148	205
1924	2,139	..	153		..	485	850	163	160	135	191
1923	2,179	..	157		..	495	863	165	173	134	192

[1] Includes Newfoundland beginning in 1949.

[2] Includes the Yukon Territory and the Northwest Territories.

Series V100-129. Retail trade, gross profit margins by kind of business, 1938 to 1960
(per cent of net sales)

Year	Retail food stores					Retail clothing stores			
	Grocery stores	Combination stores	Meat markets	Fruit and vegetable stores	Confectionery stores	Men's clothing stores		Women's clothing stores	
						Unincorporated	Incorporated	Unincorporated	Incorporated
	100	101	102	103	104	105	106	107	108
					Independent stores				
1960	15.35	15.36	20.25	19.67	19.91	28.8	31.5	29.9	32.5
1959	–	–	–	–	–	–	–	–	–
1958	15.07	15.07	19.07	19.00	19.15	28.6	30.9	28.8	31.9
1956	14.76	15.40	19.61	19.39	18.98	28.2	30.8	28.3	31.8
1954	14.38	15.09	18.90	18.42	17.57	27.0	29.8	27.4	31.2
1952	13.88	14.50	17.78	17.74	18.93	26.4	29.2	26.8	29.8
1950	14.4	14.9	16.1	17.5	18.2	26.8	29.8	26.8	29.0
1948	14.0	14.6	16.6	17.5	19.1	25.9	28.6	25.8	28.5
1946	14.3	15.1	17.2	16.1	18.9	26.9	30.5	27.1	29.2
1945	14.1	14.9	16.9	16.0	20.7	27.5	31.5	27.7	30.5
1944	14.2	15.2	17.1	16.4	19.5	27.2	–	27.9	–
1941	15.2	16.9	–	–	–	27.7	–	27.5	–
1938	16.0	17.4	22.4	–	–	28.7	–	29.7	–
					Chain stores[1]				
1959	16.5	17.9	–	–	–	–	35.7	–	34.6
1957	15.5	17.4	20.2	–	–	–	32.1	–	34.4
1955	16.0	16.5	18.8	–	–	–	31.0	–	32.7
1953	15.0	–	–	–	–	–	30.9	–	31.5
1951	15.5	15.8	15.8	–	–	–	28.8	–	28.3
1949	16.0	15.6	17.6	–	–	–	29.1	–	29.4
1947	16.8	16.0	20.5	–	–	–	30.0	–	31.0

Year	Retail clothing stores				Hardware, furniture, appliance stores					
	Family clothing stores		Family shoe stores		Hardware stores		Furniture stores		Appliance, radio and television stores	
	Unincorporated	Incorporated	Unincorporated	Incorporated	Unincorporated	Incorporated	Unincorporated	Incorporated	Unincorporated	Incorporated
	109	110	111	112	113	114	115	116	117	118
					Independent stores					
1960	26.6	30.5	30.0	34.1	–	–	–	–	–	–
1959	–	–	–	–	27.0	27.9	27.2	26.3	29.7	25.3
1958	27.1	30.6	29.3	33.2	–	–	–	–	–	–
1956	26.5	30.3	29.4	33.5	25.8	26.9	26.1	28.0	25.6	25.5
1954	25.9	29.5	27.8	31.5	25.8	27.0	26.9	28.2	26.1	26.4
1952	24.5	29.7	27.2	30.1	25.9	27.3	27.8	–	26.4	–
1950	24.4	29.6	27.4	32.0	25.8	27.0	27.1	–	27.8	–
1948	23.4	28.8	26.6	32.1	24.7	26.2	26.7	–	27.4	–
1946	23.8	29.3	26.8	31.8	23.7	–	26.7	–	29.2	–
1945	24.8	29.1	27.3	31.9	24.6	–	28.0	–	36.4	–
1944	24.3	–	27.6	–	25.7	–	29.9	–	35.2	–
1941	–	–	26.3	–	25.7	–	–	–	–	–
1938	27.1	–	29.8	–	25.6	–	33.5	–	–	–
					Chain stores[1]					
1959	–	32.6	–	35.9	–	–	–	36.1	–	–
1957	–	33.0	–	34.0	–	–	–	36.7	–	–
1955	–	33.4	–	33.0	–	–	–	33.5	–	–
1953	–	31.0	–	31.6	–	–	–	31.8	–	–
1951	–	28.8	–	31.6	–	–	–	30.7	–	–
1949	–	30.2	–	30.8	–	–	–	35.1	–	–
1947	–	26.4	–	30.8	–	–	–	32.6	–	–

Series V100-129. Retail trade, gross profit margins by kind of business, 1938 to 1960 (concluded)
(per cent of net sales)

Year	Other retail outlets										
	Filling stations	Garages	General stores	Restaurants	Fuel dealers		Drug stores		Jewellery stores		Tobacco stores
					Unincorporated	Incorporated	Unincorporated	Incorporated	Unincorporated	Incorporated	
	119	**120**	**121**	**122**	**123**	**124**	**125**	**126**	**127**	**128**	**129**
Independent stores											
1960	—	—	15.4	—	—	—	—	—	—	—	—
1959	22.3	33.2	—	40.3	22.4	23.7	31.6	33.0	42.0	41.1	—
1958	—	—	14.8	—	—	—	—	—	—	—	—
1956	20.8	33.6	14.8	40.8	21.1	22.1	30.3	32.8	40.8	44.2	18.7
1954	20.8	30.6	15.2	37.7	23.0	22.4	29.8	32.1	40.2	43.5	18.3
1952	20.1	29.9	14.9	38.9	20.4	22.0	29.1	34.1	39.5	41.8	16.5
1950	18.7	27.8	14.5	38.7	20.6	20.2	28.9	33.4	38.8	41.7	17.6
1948	19.0	26.2	15.1	37.1	20.4	19.9	28.4	33.1	39.1	40.8	16.5
1946	18.2	27.7	15.5	37.2	21.1	—	27.0	32.2	37.1	—	15.6
1945	17.9	27.9	15.4	36.8	20.1	—	27.2	33.9	38.6	39.8	15.9
1944	16.5	26.7	14.7	—	20.7	—	25.9	—	41.3	—	17.3
1941	17.2	—	16.0	35.8	21.2	—	27.4	—	38.9	—	—
1938	21.6	33.1	16.1	40.2	21.1	—	29.8	—	40.2	—	21.5
Chain stores[1]											
1959	—	—	—	—	—	—	—	33.9	—	—	—
1957	—	—	—	—	—	—	—	34.4	—	—	—
1955	—	—	—	—	—	—	—	34.9	—	—	—
1953	—	—	—	—	—	—	—	33.8	—	—	—
1951	—	—	—	—	—	—	—	33.7	—	—	—
1949	—	—	—	—	—	—	—	33.3	—	—	—
1947	—	—	—	—	—	—	—	34.2	—	—	—

[1] See text for gross profit margins of chain variety stores.

Series V130-131. Retail sales, by commodity, 1968 and 1974
(millions of dollars)

Commodity	1974	1968
	130	**131**
Total, all commodities	46,409.2	23,911.9
Food	10,101.7	5,540.9
Meat, fish and poultry	2,505.9	1,515.1
Fresh fruits and vegetables	1,082.0	577.3
Fresh bakery products	536.7	338.3
Dairy products and eggs	1,121.6	506.9
Canned goods	1,548.9	805.2
Frozen foods	748.3	930.5
Candy and confectionery	355.5	252.1
Tea, coffee and cocoa	307.9	182.5
Baby foods, all kinds	90.8	—
Dietetic foods, all kinds	42.1	—
All other grocery products	1,752.8	375.6
Beverages	444.0	245.8
Soft drinks	369.2	183.8
Brewed, fermented and distilled	70.6	—
Apparel and dry goods	5,792.8	3,593.8
Men's and boys' clothing and furnishings	1,699.9	999.6
Women's, misses' and children's clothing and furnishings	2,773.8	1,691.6
Footwear	717.6	539.2
Dry goods and notions	599.6	363.4
Automotive and allied products	14,306.5	6,863.7
Motor vehicles, parts, accessories and supplies	10,234.5	5,324.0
Recreational vehicles, accessories and supplies	222.0	—
Mobile homes and trailers, new and used	389.7	—
Automotive fuels and additives	3,460.3	1,539.7
Hardware, home furnishings and supplies	6,093.2	2,774.6
Household furniture	1,686.6	620.9
Home furnishings	1,011.8	583.4
Household appliances	941.2	501.0
Radios, record-players and television sets	801.2	343.0
Housewares, equipment and supplies	749.0	316.1 [1]
Hardware and building supplies	613.5	223.2
Paints, varnishes, glass and wallpaper	287.9	187.0
Drugs, drug sundries and health appliances	1,625.2	954.0
Drugs and drug sundries	924.7	650.9
Toilet articles, cosmetics and preparations, men's and women's	580.7	291.0
Health appliances	119.8	—
Sporting and recreational equipment and supplies	1,166.8	316.4
Sporting equipment and supplies	413.5	128.0 [2]
Recreational equipment and supplies	534.8	157.2
Other sporting and recreational equipment and supplies	218.4	31.2
Miscellaneous merchandise	6,879.1	3,622.7 [3]
Cameras and photographic equipment	420.6	122.0
Jewellery, silverware, clocks and watches	547.2	233.0
Luggage, brief-cases and leather goods	79.6	25.1
Paper products and related supplies	783.9	402.8
Tobacco products and supplies	1,079.3	518.0
Musical instruments, records and accessories	303.7	101.0
Antiques, all kinds	19.0	—
Handicrafts	47.2	—
Paintings, sculptures, carvings and artists' supplies	75.7	—
Stamps, coins, medals and related supplies and accessories	9.4	—
Toys, games and hobby supplies	380.8	187.1
Garden and farm equipment and supplies	521.8	29.4
Pets, pet foods, supplies and accessories	188.0	—
Wigs and hair-pieces	8.0	—
Office and store equipment and supplies	50.3	—
Professional and scientific instruments, equipment and supplies	8.0	—
Second-hand merchandise	31.7	—
Fuels and fuel oil	7.2	484.6
All other merchandise	177.4	—
Receipts from repairs and other services	2,140.2	897.0
Miscellaneous merchandise	—	—

[1] Electrical equipment and supplies added to Housewares, equipment and supplies.

[2] Arrived at by deducting "Recreational equipment and supplies" and "Other sporting goods and recreational equipment and supplies" from total "Sporting and recreational equipment and supplies".

[3] Arrived at by deducting the seven groups from grand total.

Series V132-142. Number and sales of shopping centres, by province, 1956 to 1973

Year	Canada	Newfoundland	Prince Edward Island	Nova Scotia	New Brunswick	Quebec	Ontario	Manitoba	Saskatchewan	Alberta	British Columbia
	132	133	134	135	136	137	138	139	140	141	142
Number of shopping centres											
1973	664	5	2	13	16	154	266	25	20	72	91
1972	599	3	1	9	10	143	247	23	19	64	80
1971	..	..	..	..	..	..	..	..	..	..	..
1970	541	2	1	8	8	127	228	20	19	59	69
1969	499	2	—	8	5	109	219	16	17	62	61
1968	480	2	—	8	4	102	217	15	17	55	60
1967	461	2	—	8	4	93	213	14	15	54	58
1966	420	1	—	8	4	85	188	14	15	52	53
1965	386	1	—	8	3	74	175	11	13	47	54
1964	369	1	—	8	2	68	170	11	12	46	51
1963	346	1	—	6	2	66	168	9	10	38	46
1962	305	1	—	5	2	57	147	7	10	32	44
1961	281	1	—	4	2	55	136	6	9	26	42
1960	231	1	—	3	2	43	113	4	5	26	34
1959	193	1	—	2	1	32	100	1	2	29	25
1958	125	—	—	2	—	19	71	—	2	18	13
1957	95	—	—	2	—	15	57	—	2	12	7
1956	64	—	—	1	—	10	41	—	—	7	5
Retail sales in shopping centres *(millions of dollars)*											
1973	6,737	77		148	146	1,471	2,980	262	126	691	836
1972	5,467	46		100	96	1,172	2,489	211	143	573	636
1971	..	..	..	..	..	..	..	..	..	..	..
1970	3,866		168			832	1,772	156	87	401	450
1969	3,321		128			682	1,578	114	73	364	382
1968	2,873		106			574	1,399	94	65	304	332
1967	2,552	..	..	..	..	541	1,233	..	..	270	289
1966	2,100	..	..	..	..	..	..	..	..	..	..
1965	1,832	..	..	..	..	..	..	..	..	..	..
1964	1,560	..	..	..	..	303	799		72	158	173
1963	1,316	..	..	..	..	..	..	..	..	..	..
1962	1,150	..	..	..	..	..	..	..	..	..	..
1961	976	..	..	..	..	205	499	..	..	97	101
1960	782	..	..	..	..	..	..			..	..
1959	617	..	..	..	..	128	348		15	61	49
1958	461	..	..	..	..	..	..	..	..	..	..
1957	360	..	..	..	..	..	..	..	..	..	..
1956	234	..	..	..	..	45	154	..	..	..	..

Series V143-146. Shopping centres in Canada, by type, 1956 to 1973

Year	Total	Type A[1]	Type B[2]	Type C[3]	Year	Total	Type A[1]	Type B[2]	Type C[3]
	143	144	145	146		143	144	145	146
Number of shopping centres					**Retail sales in shopping centres** *(millions of dollars)*				
1973	664	417	146	101	1973	6,737	1,988	1,577	3,171
1972	599	390	125	84	1972	5,467	1,654	1,245	2,568
1971	..	..	..	..	1971	..	..	..	..
1970	541	371	107	63	1970	3,866	1,316	989	1,561
1969	499	343	107	49	1969	3,321	1,084	914	1,322
1968	480	335	99	46	1968	2,873	955	827	1,092
1967	461	323	95	43	1967	2,552	854	726	972
1966	420	301	84	35	1966	2,100	704	596	800
1965	386	281	73	32	1965	1,832	645	522	665
1964	369	270	70	29	1964	1,560	543	452	565
1963	346	250	72	24	1963	1,316	449	449	418
1962	305	212	67	26	1962	1,150	382	389	379
1961	281	191	67	23	1961	976	312	349	315
1960	231	158	54	19	1960	782	244	287	251
1959	193	142	36	15	1959	617	188	241	188
1958	125	84	32	9	1958	461	135	213	113
1957	95	62	27	6	1957	360	107	180	73
1956	64	37	21	6	1956	234	60	120	54

[1] 5 to 15 outlets.
[2] 16 to 30 outlets.
[3] Over 30 outlets.

Series V147-162. Shopping centre sales, by kind of business, 1956 to 1973
(millions of dollars)

Year	All stores	Grocery and combination stores	All other food stores	Department stores	General merchandise stores	Variety stores	Service stations and garages	Men's clothing stores	Women's clothing stores	Family clothing stores	Shoe stores	Hardware stores	Furniture, television, radio and appliance stores	Drug stores	Jewellery stores	All other stores
	147	148	149	150	151	152	153	154	155	156	157	158	159	160	161	162
1973	6,737	2,230	92	2,228	56	138	58	141	280	89	123	68	98	239	72	826
1972	5,467	1,793	76	1,844	54	121	52	110	243	69	108	68	69	204	52	605
1971[2]	..	..	..	..	..	..	..	..	..	..	..	..	..	..	..	..
1970	3,866	1,309	53	1,213	36[1]	113	40	78	160	48	76	56	54	153	33	444
1969	3,321	1,068	50	1,056	27[1]	112	37	66	132	42	68	53	47	132	30	401
1968	2,873	954	45	867	27[1]	110	33	56	113	37	60	51	43	117	27	333
1967	2,552	864	44	727[3]	4	128	28	49	99	32	61	47	36	107	23	307
1966	2,100	778	33	554[3]	4	111	20	43	71	38	46	40	29	88	18	231
1965	1,832	711	31	425	..	147	14	36	68	23	39	32	22	74	14	196
1964	1,560	635	95	345	..	87	11	29	59	18	34	27	22	65	11	120[5]
1963	1,316	570	75	248	..	76	9	25	53	15	31	25	18	55	9	107
1962	1,150	513	63	213	..	70	7	21	47	11	27	25	15	47	8	82
1961	976	444	50	173	..	64	5	19	41	9	24	21	14	41	6	66
1960	782	369	41	127	..	50	4	15	32	7	20	18	11	34	5	49
1959	617	282	32	114	..	40	3	12	26	4	14	13	12	26	4	36
1958	461	214	23	84	..	30	3	9	20	3	10	11	7	19	3	26
1957	360	169	16	69	..	22	2	7	16	1	8	8	7	14	2	20
1956	234	105	5	56	..	14	1	5	11	1	6	6	4	9	1	10

[1] Includes both general merchandise store sales and sales through mail order catalogue sales offices. Excludes sales through mail order catalogue counters in department stores; these are included with department store sales data.
[2] 1971 data will not be available until final results of the 1971 Census of Merchandising and Services are tabulated.
[3] Includes sales through mail order catalogue sales offices in shopping centres.
[4] Included in "all other stores".
[5] Includes discount department stores.

Series V163-177. Receipts of service trades in shopping centres, 1967 to 1973
(thousands of dollars)

Year	All trades	Amusement and recreational group				Personal services group						Miscellaneous services[1]	Restaurant group		
		Movie theatres	Billiard parlours	Bowling alleys	Other amusement and recreation services	Barber shops	Beauty salons	Dry cleaning and laundries		Shoe repair shops	Other personal services		Restaurants	Take-out food shops	Other eating and drinking places
								Plant and pick-up offices	Self-service laundromats and launderettes						
	163	164	165	166	167	168	169	170	171	172	173	174	175	176	177
1973	270,528	23,891	1,092	9,083	2,376	12,307	26,507	24,665	6,367	2,980	9,872	7,866	121,836	14,460	7,226
1972	226,468	13,019	1,466	8,011	2,120	10,405	23,310	21,729	4,881	3,378	6,590	3,586	107,704	10,252	10,018
1971	..	..	..	..	..	..	..	..	..	..	..	..	..	..	..
1970	162,927	10,199	1,091	5,810	1,539	8,743	18,963	19,176	4,149	2,085	3,522	1,564	75,063	5,600	5,422
1969	144,316	6,166	1,083	4,116	1,599	8,486	17,699	17,915	3,955	2,001	3,189	2,042	66,948	4,851	4,267
1968	126,264	5,007	972	3,654	1,502	7,298	15,981	16,747	3,743	1,905	2,651	4,288[2]	55,573	3,274	3,668
1967	111,824	3,495	1,156	3,227	1,049	7,286	15,210	15,654	3,204	1,614	1,196	3,834[2]	51,353	1,445	2,101

[1] Includes photographers, automobile and truck rentals, driving schools, etc.
[2] Includes business services (advertising, accounting), and repair services.

Series V178-190. Number and sales of vending machines, by province, 1958 to 1975

Year	Canada	Atlantic region	New-foundland	Prince Edward Island	Nova Scotia	New Brunswick	Quebec	Ontario	Prairie region	Manitoba	Saskatchewan	Alberta	British Columbia
	178	179	180	181	182	183	184	185	186	187	188	189	190
						Number of machines							
1975	110,287	9,221	686	714	4,951	2,870	29,932	46,957	15,043	5,207	1,825	8,011	9,134
1974	106,278	9,510	..	..	..	..	29,162	45,773	13,637	..	..	..	8,196
1973	104,253	9,489	..	..	..	..	29,076	46,791	11,819	..	..	..	7,078
1972	106,758	..	..	..	..	..	..	..	..	..	..	..	..
1971	97,965	..	..	..	..	..	..	..	..	..	..	..	..
1970	103,751	..	..	..	..	..	..	..	..	..	..	..	..
1969	100,948	..	..	..	..	..	..	..	..	..	..	..	..
1968	95,867	..	..	..	..	..	..	..	..	..	..	..	..
1967	91,289	..	..	..	..	..	..	..	..	..	..	..	..
1966	84,154	..	..	..	..	..	..	..	..	..	..	..	..
1965	85,091	..	..	..	..	..	..	..	..	..	..	..	..
1964	75,392	..	..	..	..	..	..	..	..	..	..	..	..
1963	78,477	..	..	..	..	..	..	..	..	..	..	..	..
1962	73,397	..	..	..	..	..	..	..	..	..	..	..	..
1961	65,028	..	..	..	..	..	..	..	..	..	..	..	..
1960	47,770	..	..	..	..	..	..	..	..	..	..	..	..
1959	40,237	2,457	..	..	..	..	13,088	18,987	3,364	..	..	..	2,341
1958	34,464	1,540	..	..	..	..	12,263	15,935	2,562	..	..	..	2,164
						Sales *(thousands of dollars)*							
1975	249,960	14,635	1,307	519	7,139	5,671	73,918	100,565	35,782	11,307	6,191	18,284	25,060
1974	227,445	13,908	1,128	458	6,812	5,510	67,854	91,730	30,614	9,754	4,328	16,532	23,340
1973	207,081	12,192	1,217	390	6,278	4,307	64,247	84,213	26,164	7,681	4,067	14,417	20,265
1972	178,909	10,896	1,208	262	5,217	4,209	54,929	72,645	22,275	6,299	4,081	11,895	18,165
1971	162,249	10,698	..	..	..	..	47,838	65,420	22,536	..	..	..	15,759
1970	156,822	9,494	..	..	..	..	51,659	62,146	19,620	..	..	..	13,904
1969	142,910	8,332	..	..	..	..	46,760	56,664	18,564	..	..	..	12,590
1968	127,059	8,028	..	..	..	..	43,416	48,176	16,615	..	..	..	10,823
1967	119,651	6,525	..	..	..	..	42,406	46,038	14,282	..	..	..	10,399
1966	107,540	5,332	..	..	..	..	37,006	43,435	11,712	..	..	..	10,054
1965	89,815	4,737	..	..	..	..	28,441	38,177	9,509	..	..	..	8,951
1964	78,562	3,795	..	..	..	..	26,119	33,069	7,922	..	..	..	7,657
1963	67,580	3,468	..	..	..	..	21,959	28,145	6,779	..	..	..	7,228
1962	57,799	3,099	..	..	..	..	18,704	24,210	5,461	..	..	..	6,326
1961	44,960	2,405	..	..	..	..	14,237	18,158	4,401	..	..	..	5,758
1960	38,711	1,514	..	..	..	..	11,929	16,900	3,582	..	..	..	4,786
1959	33,742	1,156	..	..	..	..	10,051	15,651	2,841	..	..	..	4,044
1958	26,331	769	..	..	..	..	7,481	13,266	1,930	..	..	..	2,885

Series V191-214. Sales through vending machines, by commodity, 1958 to 1975
(thousands of dollars)

Year	Total	Cigarettes	Beverage vending machines									
			Coffee machines		Soft drink machines					Packaged milk and flavoured milk products	Other vending machines for beverages
			Instant/ freeze dry	Fresh brew (single cups)	Bottled	Canned beverages (including juices)	Convertible can/bottle	Cup (post-mix)	Cup (pre-mix)		
	191	192	193	194	195	196	197	198	199	200	201
1975	249,960	112,212	24,757	16,899	3,375	14,165	791	15,738	4,322	8,552	377
1974	227,445	105,431	20,310	15,838	3,493	11,932	824	14,937	3,460	7,528	824
1973	207,081	99,731	17,167	14,863	3,677	9,259	470	14,397	3,442	6,524	302
1972	178,909	87,429	28,242			13,950		15,095		4,185	—
1971	162,249	82,090	24,108			12,390		13,794		4,236	—
1970	156,822	75,177	23,536			11,554		14,967		3,967	—
1969	142,910	68,236	21,138			10,351		14,324		3,438	—
1968	127,059	63,030	17,814			9,398		12,886		3,100	—
1967	119,651	58,103	17,666			8,769		13,522		2,907	—
1966	107,540	54,771	15,942			5,978		11,236		2,745	—
1965	89,815	47,685	13,551			4,728		8,197		2,594	—
1964	78,562	43,884	12,122			2,571		6,565		2,210	—
1963	67,580	39,148	9,792			2,076		6,216		1,769	—
1962	57,799	34,165	7,695			2,037		5,347		1,326	—
1961	44,960	27,014	5,902			1,809		4,376		761	—
1960	38,711	22,900	5,145			1,497		4,296		1,035	—
1959	33,742	19,948	4,102			1,225		4,653		699	—
1958	26,331	15,048	3,603			1,099		3,588		512	—

Year	Vending machines for confections and foods										All other vending machines		
	Bulk confectionery	Packaged confectionery (excluding pastries)	Pastry only	Snack foods	Hot canned foods and soups	Ice cream	Fresh foods			Other vending machines for foods	Combination food and non-food	Non-food (aspirins, combs, cosmetics, etc.)	All other (including amusement, laundry, etc.)
							Hot (casseroles, hot dogs, etc.)	Cold (sandwiches, salads, etc.)	Hot/cold combination				
	202	203	204	205	206	207	208	209	210	211	212	213	214
1975	2,430	13,949	7,906	2,482	4,208	892	1,241	7,781	6,414	793	167	273	238
1974	2,004	12,345	7,172	1,665	4,077	840	1,684	6,742	5,563	154	352	183	86
1973	2,545	10,193	6,250	1,537	3,384	684	3,224	5,876	3,040	136	187	148	45
1972	1,608	8,129	7,453	—	2,779	433		9,311			295		
1971	1,576	7,022	6,784	—	2,290	401		7,290			268		
1970	1,537	7,302	6,637	—	2,159	326		9,322			339		
1969	1,552	5,874	7,259	—	1,827	290		8,472			149		
1968	1,483	4,942	6,040	—	1,440	330		6,358			238		
1967	1,244	4,694	6,080	—	1,373	502		4,545			246		
1966	1,256	4,423	4,550	—	1,335	228		4,914			163		
1965	1,256	3,499	3,006	—	1,010	242		3,888			161		
1964	1,644	3,295	2,218	—	883	190		2,890			90		
1963	1,471	2,763	1,611	—	735	258		1,715			25		
1962	1,331	2,105	1,824	—	606	121		1,217			25		
1961	1,175	1,419	1,017	—	455	120		713			199		
1960	955	1,242	697	—	400	[1]		376			167		
1959	1,015	913	597	—	340	[1]		199			50		
1958	869	806	401	—	233	[1]		149			22		

[1] Included in "Packaged milk and flavoured milk products".

Series V215-218. Retail sales, by type of store, 1930 to 1975
(millions of dollars)

Year	Total, all stores	Chain stores	Department stores	Independent stores	Year	Total, all stores	Chain stores	Department stores	Independent stores
	215	**216**	**217**	**218**		**215**	**216**	**217**	**218**
1975	51,200	15,966	5,786	29,448	1950	9,617	1,560	880	7,177
1974	44,569	13,732	5,055	25,782	1949	8,532	1,420	860	6,252
1973	38,335	11,342	4,316	22,677	1948	7,835	1,336	796	5,703
1972	34,107	10,077	3,714	20,316	1947	6,963	1,177	699	5,087
1971	30,646	8,550	3,184	18,912	1946	5,787	1,015	606	4,166
1970	28,034	7,747	2,852	17,435	1945	4,573	876	510	3,187
1969	27,401	7,021	2,737	17,644	1944	4,093	770	460	2,863
1968	25,711	6,384	2,445	16,881	1943	3,786	704	420	2,662
1967	24,155	6,019	2,158	15,978	1942	3,619	687	419	2,513
1966	22,686	5,516	1,974	15,197	1941	3,441	643	378	2,420
1965	21,155	4,836	2,010	14,309	1940	2,935	509	327	2,099
1964	19,493	4,291	1,892	13,310	1939	2,578	432	291	1,855
1963	18,207	3,906	1,730	12,571	1938	2,530	414	280	1,836
1962	17,137	3,654	1,629	11,854	1937	2,593	414	289	1,890
1961	16,073	3,495	1,551	11,027	1936	2,289	395	274	1,620
1960	17,390	3,468	1,495	12,427	1935	2,105	364	259	1,482
1959	17,087	3,280	1,456	12,351	1934	1,984	347	254	1,383
1958	16,139	3,073	1,375	11,691	1933	1,773	329	242	1,202
1957	15,423	2,842	1,306	11,275	1932	1,908	361	254	1,293
1956	14,774	2,647	1,262	10,865	1931	2,305	434	313	1,558
1955	13,473	2,354	1,166	9,953	1930	2,756	504	355	1,897
1954	12,317	2,147	1,072	9,098					
1953	12,189	2,048	1,034	9,107					
1952	11,567	1,925	994	8,648					
1951	10,653	1,776	910	7,967					

Series V219-229. Retail sales, by type of store, by province, selected years, 1930 to 1971
(millions of dollars)

Year	Canada	Newfoundland	Prince Edward Island	Nova Scotia	New Brunswick	Quebec	Ontario	Manitoba	Saskatchewan	Alberta	British Columbia
	219	**220**	**221**	**222**	**223**	**224**	**225**	**226**	**227**	**228**	**229**
						Total, all stores					
1971	30,646	533	141	1,023	835	7,681	11,877	1,318	1,139	2,467	3,632[1]
1966	22,686	406	108	753	595	5,882	8,625	1,006	1,047	1,758	2,507[1]
1961	16,073	286	79	580	436	4,108	6,207	767	734	1,272	1,604[1]
1951	10,653	160	54	394	286	2,437	4,116	609	654	848	1,095[1]
1941	3,441	—	16	165	102	819	1,407	211	187	221	310
1930	2,756	—	14	100	84	651	1,100	189	189	177	249
						Chain stores					
1971	8,550	131	28	299	254	1,785	3,729	334	304	633	1,054
1966	5,516	86	21[2]	239[2]	168	1,149	2,407	211	218	406	994[2]
1961	3,495	38	9	126	105	765	1,636	121	117	243	337
1951	1,776	11	4	64	55	359	809	79	83	121	191
1941	643	—	1	32	20	132	295	28	33	36	64
1930	504	—	1	13	12	120	223	23	35	26	49
						Department stores					
1971	3,184	43	11	71	59	579	1,250	215	73	368	515
1966	1,974	22	—	—	26	377	745	155	53	212	—
1961	1,551	34	8	45	29	275	527	137	71	169	255
1951	910	17	5	30	19	165	309	93	51	86	135
1941	378	—		29		59	152		95		44
1930	355	—		24		55	140		97		38
						Independent stores					
1971	18,912	359	102	653	522	5,318	6,899	769	762	1,466	2,063
1966	15,197	297	86	514	401	4,356	5,473	640	776	1,140	1,513
1961	11,027	214	62	410	302	3,068	4,044	509	547	860	1,012
1951	7,967	132	45	300	211	1,913	2,998	438	520	642	769
1941	2,797[2]	—	15[2]	133[2]	82[2]	628	960	183[2]	154[2]	185[2]	202
1930	2,252[2]	—	13[2]	87[2]	72[2]	476	737	166[2]	154[2]	151[2]	162

[1] Includes the Yukon Territory and the Northwest Territories.

[2] Includes department stores.

Series V230-248. Sales of retail chain stores, by kind of business, selected years, 1930 to 1971

(millions of dollars)

Year	Total, all stores	Grocery and combination stores	All other food stores	Department stores	General merchandise stores	General stores	Variety stores	Motor vehicle dealers	Service stations and garages	Men's clothing stores	Women's clothing stores	Family clothing stores	Shoe stores	Hardware stores	Furniture, TV and appliance stores	Drug stores	Jewellery stores	Fuel dealers	All other stores
	230	231	232	233	234	235	236	237	238	239	240	241	242	243	244	245	246	247	248
1971	11,734	3,868	48	3,184	740	104	479	77	171	70	222	115	168	74	164	139	90	83	1,939
1966	7,490	2,951	48	1,974	482	90	429	67	64	47	115	74	113	55	142	87	65	76	1,161
1961	5,046	1,711	41	1,551	..	25	313	35	9	28	97	56	82	29	102	56	38	41	832
1951	1,776	610	15	—	22	38	165	23	4	26	42	42	38	17	80	31	31	5	586
1941	643	173	..	—	..	7	74	..	14	10	13	14	16	..	34	19	..	..	269
1930	504	123		—	..	4	41	..	16	10	..	..	8	..	..	14	..	..	288
							Percentage distribution of retail chain stores sales												
1971	100.0	33.0	0.4	27.1	6.3	0.9	4.1	0.7	1.5	0.6	1.9	1.0	1.4	0.6	1.4	1.2	0.8	0.7	16.5
1966	100.0	32.1	0.6	26.4	6.4	1.2	5.7	0.9	0.9	0.6	1.5	1.0	1.5	0.7	1.9	1.2	0.9	1.0	15.5
1961	100.0	33.9	0.8	30.7	—	0.5	6.2	0.7	0.2	0.6	1.9	1.1	1.6	0.6	2.0	1.1	0.8	0.8	16.5
1951	100.0	34.3	0.8	—	1.2	2.1	9.3	1.3	0.2	1.5	2.4	2.4	2.1	1.0	4.5	1.7	1.7	0.3	33.0
1941	100.0	26.9	—	—	—	1.1	11.5	—	2.2	1.6	2.0	2.2	2.5	—	5.3	3.0	—	—	41.8
1930	100.0	24.4	—	—	—	0.8	8.1	—	3.2	2.0	—	—	1.6	—	—	2.8	—	—	57.1

Series V249-267. Sales of independent retail stores, by kind of business, selected years, 1930 to 1971

(millions of dollars)

Year	Total, all stores	Grocery and combination stores	All other food stores	Department stores	General merchandise stores	General stores	Variety stores	Motor vehicle dealers	Service stations and garages	Men's clothing stores	Women's clothing stores	Family clothing stores	Shoe stores	Hardware stores	Furniture, TV and appliance stores	Drug stores	Jewellery stores	Fuel dealers	All other stores
	249	250	251	252	253	254	255	256	257	258	259	260	261	262	263	264	265	266	267
1971	18,912	3,392	607	—	199	513	92	4,847	2,524	405	400	309	178	335	778	768	146	440	2,979
1966	15,196	2,951	506	—	163	468	65	4,271	1,810	310	320	264	139	301	598	563	127	399	1,941
1961	11,027	1,993	553	910	..	582	61	2,564	1,484	219	218	195	113	271	470	411	107	306	1,481
1951	8,877	1,289	475	378	147	482	31	1,862	470	176	150	151	73	210	276	217	74	227	1,658
1941	2,798	394	..	..	..	208	11	..	191	70	58	60	28	..	76	82	..	..	1,242
1930	2,252	282	..	355	..	204	3	..	98	62	..	..	28	..	..	63	..	..	1,157
							Percentage distribution of independent retail stores sales												
1971	100.0	17.9	3.2	—	1.1	2.7	0.5	25.6	13.3	2.1	2.1	1.6	0.9	1.8	4.1	4.1	0.8	2.3	15.8
1966	100.0	19.4	3.3	—	1.1	3.1	0.4	28.1	11.9	2.0	2.1	1.7	0.9	2.0	3.9	3.7	0.8	2.6	12.8
1961	100.0	18.1	5.0	—	—	5.3	0.6	23.3	13.5	2.0	2.0	1.8	1.0	2.5	4.3	3.7	1.0	2.8	13.4
1951	100.0	14.5	5.4	10.3	1.7	5.4	0.3	21.0	5.3	2.0	1.7	1.7	0.8	3.1	3.1	2.4	0.8	2.6	18.7
1941	100.0	14.1	—	13.5	—	7.4	0.4	—	6.8	2.5	2.1	2.1	1.0	—	2.7	2.9	—	—	44.4
1930	100.0	12.5	—	15.8	—	9.1	0.1	—	4.4	2.8	—	—	1.2	—	—	2.8	—	—	51.4

Series V268-290. Direct selling, by commodity, 1969 to 1975
(thousands of dollars)

Year	All commod- ities	Meat, fish and poultry	Frozen food plans	Dairy products	Bakery products	All other foods and beverages[1]	Canvas, awnings, sails, tents, etc.	Clothing	Fur goods	Furniture re- upholstery and repairs	Books	News- papers
	268	269	270	271	272	273	274	275	276	277	278	279
1975	1,333,576	16,754	27,220	221,847	47,044	43,685	8,305	12,123	11,713	56,953	90,909	176,830
1974	1,227,047	15,658	30,701	203,716	46,763	42,584	6,967	11,362	9,818	47,733	82,889	164,800
1973	1,043,575	14,263	29,352	187,757	45,533	35,712	6,032	9,878	8,262	42,204	72,022	146,237
1972	934,660	12,571	23,568	184,075	42,082	34,362	5,549	9,244	7,067	35,980	63,287	136,670
1971	849,470	11,612	18,062	185,000	42,897	33,148	6,437	12,981	7,046	32,535	53,975	130,000
1970	817,873	10,672	19,282	184,000	42,471	34,308	5,314	13,284	6,115	31,000	51,197	120,005
1969	809,449	9,356	22,838	183,000	46,983	34,086	5,053	13,628	5,200	32,000	54,295	110,257

Year	Magazines	Aluminum windows, doors, screens and awnings	Dinnerware, kitchenware and utensils	Sailboats and pleasure crafts	Household electrical appliances	Pharma- ceuticals and medicines	Brushes, brooms mops and household soaps and cleaners	Cosmetics and costume jewellery	Phonograph records and tapes	Greenhouse flowers and nursery seeds	Miscel- laneous
	280	281	282	283	284	285	286	287	288	289	290
1975	22,452	27,220	67,981	15,718	120,929	2,809	38,510	124,925	18,845	50,937	129,867
1974	20,839	24,109	49,806	12,568	103,519	2,882	31,331	123,758	26,352	38,216	130,676
1973	20,135	21,354	38,731	12,528	84,750	3,455	26,099	102,972	23,190	36,027	77,082
1972	18,227	18,386	31,625	9,186	63,053	5,172	27,352	91,386	26,421	25,461	63,936
1971	16,348	16,944	25,535	8,799	46,582	4,897	23,471	77,744	14,260	19,688	61,509
1970	14,013	15,656	26,863	8,397	38,154	5,964	22,270	77,266	14,180	16,643	60,819
1969	12,030	17,910	24,657	8,388	39,341	5,250	20,679	71,995	12,617	19,060	60,826

[1] Includes sales of meals and alcoholic beverages on airlines and railways.

[2] Includes leather goods, textiles, stamps, coins and personal stationery and sales of merchandise to credit-card holders of gasoline oil companies, etc.

Series V291-313. Direct selling, by commodity, by province, 1971
(thousands of dollars)

	All commodities	Meat fish and poultry	Frozen food plans	Dairy products[1]	Bakery products[1]	All other foods and beverages[1]	Canvas, awnings, sails, tents, etc.	Clothing	Fur goods	Furniture re- upholstery and repairs	Books	News- papers[1]
	291	292	293	294	295	296	297	298	299	300	301	302
Canada	849,470	11,612	18,062	185,000	42,897	33,148	6,437	12,981	7,046	32,535	53,975	130,000
Newfoundland	6,967	–	–	925	515	30	–	–	–	60	227	910
Prince Edward Island	3,547	137	–	1,480	43	41	–	–	–	–	167	520
Nova Scotia	21,931	368	–	4,625	1,287	173	171	221	–	327	2,151	3,250
New Brunswick	18,603	94	–	3,145	1,373	1,414	8	183	–	231	1,510	2,180
Quebec	253,122	3,602	3,639	72,890	14,714	12,794	2,395	4,791	4,058	9,301	10,314	28,079
Ontario	346,583	2,190	12,081	65,305	16,258	15,689	2,326	5,519	2,645	11,889	21,152	64,420
Manitoba	35,532	1,437	49	6,105	1,544	1,428	370	513	222	1,325	2,979	6,890
Saskatchewan	24,752	874	–	5,180	1,115	316	146	181	–	387	2,082	3,561
Alberta	60,129	1,652	2,293	12,210	2,488	374	686	624	–	2,558	5,595	8,229
British Columbia	78,300	1,259	–	13,135	3,561	889	334	950	121	6,456	7,798	11,960

Series V291-313. Direct selling, by commodity, by province, 1971 (concluded)
(thousands of dollars)

	Magazines	Aluminum windows, doors, screens and awnings	Dinner- ware, kitchen- ware and utensils	Sailboats and pleasure crafts	Household electrical appliances	Pharma- ceuticals and medicines	Brushes, brooms, mops and household soaps and cleaners	Cosmetics and costume jewellery	Phonograph records and tapes	Greenhouse flowers and nursery seeds[1]	Miscel- laneous
	303	304	305	306	307	308	309	310	311	312	313
Canada	16,348	16,944	25,535	8,799	46,582	4,897	23,471	77,744	14,260	19,688	61,509
Newfoundland	159	–	226	–	742	–	117	2,149	88	452	367
Prince Edward Island	226	–	52	–	199	–	64	411	41	19	147
Nova Scotia	346	521	774	490	1,214	136	316	3,062	381	291	1,827
New Brunswick	563	314	523	144	1,103	118	692	2,359	316	166	2,167
Quebec	3,236	5,752	8,275	912	15,691	2,356	7,292	23,277	1,283	3,188	15,283
Ontario	7,391	7,307	7,560	4,202	15,282	986	8,591	28,407	9,600	11,098	26,685
Manitoba	755	283	1,556	199	1,698	782	1,593	2,782	395	316	2,311
Saskatchewan	515	1,212	895	–	1,649	201	1,397	2,619	210	122	2,090
Alberta	1,333	135	3,097	238	4,273	192	1,414	5,903	748	2,202	3,885
British Columbia	1,823	1,419	2,576	2,613	4,730	125	1,996	6,776	1,198	1,834	6,747

[1] Provincial data pro-rated, so their sum will equal a revised Canada total.

Series V314-319. Retail trade, by legal form of organization, selected years, 1930 to 1966
(millions of dollars)

Year	Total	Indi- vidual propri- etorship	Partner- ships	Corpora- tions	Co-oper- ative associ- ations	Other forms
	314	315	316	317	318	319
1966	22,686	5,703	1,198	14,738	251	796
1961	16,073	4,964	995	9,391	168	556
1951	10,653	4,081	1,292	4,805	134	341
1941	3,441	1,590	319	1,401	20	112
1930	2,756	1,142	271	1,324	16	2

Series V320-331. Summary statistics, census of retail trade, by province, selected years, 1930 to 1971

Year	Canada	Newfound-land	Prince Edward Island	Nova Scotia	New Brunswick	Quebec	Ontario	Manitoba	Saskat-chewan	Alberta	British Columbia	Yukon Territory and Northwest Territories
	320	321	322	323	324	325	326	327	328	329	330	331
					Total number of locations							
1971	156,518	4,467	841	6,056	4,823	48,204	53,229	6,209	6,797	10,364	15,264	264
1966	153,620	4,779	906	6,388	5,123	46,980	51,119	6,497	7,464	10,182	13,948	234
1961	152,620	4,747	867	6,523	5,215	45,273	52,157	6,575	7,591	9,902	13,558	212
1951	151,626	4,090	972	7,176	5,430	43,572	50,119	7,432	9,585	9,943	13,151	156
1941	137,331	—	863	6,790	4,988	39,712	47,055	7,219	10,088	9,222	11,253	141
1930	125,003	—	851	6,464	4,434	34,286	43,045	6,859	10,841	8,592	9,501	130
					Total sales (millions of dollars)							
1971	31,405	583	142	1,080	823	7,945	12,115	1,297	1,158	2,590	3,597	77
1966	22,686	406	108	753	595	5,882	8,625	1,007	1,047	1,758	2,463	44
1961	16,073	286	79	580	436	4,108	6,207	767	735	1,272	1,575	29
1951	10,653	160	54	394	286	2,437	4,116	609	654	848	1,083	12
1941	3,441	—	16	165	102	819	1,407	211	187	221	310	4
1930	2,756	—	14	100	84	651	1,100	189	189	177	249	3
					Number of working proprietors							
1971	116,459	3,710	684	4,473	3,648	39,292	39,971	4,557	4,809	6,202	8,982	131
1966	122,456	4,076	789	4,902	4,164	40,377	40,595	5,189	5,729	7,151	9,381	103
1961	130,414	4,270	778	5,384	4,500	40,661	44,339	5,761	6,553	7,932	10,124	112
1951	150,089	4,135	997	6,685	5,076	42,690	50,103	7,687	9,925	10,319	12,372	100
1941	131,823	—	859	6,250	4,629	38,574	44,891	7,058	9,644	9,186	10,658	74
1930	125,169	—	949	6,601	4,509	34,091	43,623	6,910	10,166	8,469	9,798	53
					Number of paid employees							
1971	624,688	11,847	3,076	21,752	16,565	153,906	243,859	26,771	22,879	51,418	71,285	1,330
1966	668,965	12,245	3,129	24,273	17,893	161,370	262,357	32,950	27,129	52,520	74,019	1,080
1961	587,378	10,609	2,697	22,402	15,551	143,188	233,563	29,815	24,087	45,815	58,918	733
1951	454,794	7,070	2,196	17,844	12,916	108,734	181,563	27,798	20,782	30,501	45,067	323
1941	392,608	—	1,733	17,295	11,062	96,749	165,842	25,456	19,252	21,399	33,569	251
1930	275,459	—	1,309	9,426	7,636	70,710	111,113	19,762	15,625	15,021	24,463	394

Series V332-350. Estimated annual sales of wholesalers proper, by kind of business, 1951 to 1975
(millions of dollars)

Year	Total, all trades	Fresh fruits and vegetables	Groceries and food specialties	Meat and dairy products	Clothing and furnishings	Footwear	Other textile and clothing accessories	Coal and coke	Drugs and drug sundries	Newsprint paper and paper products
	332	333	334	335	336	337	338	339	340	341
1975	45,377	795	6,693	1,091	416	93	832	84	983	729
1974	43,210	751	5,804	1,083	396	96	851	70	893	694
1973	34,081	653	4,800	1,061	358	83	705	43	755	519
1972	28,167	607	4,223	872	334	75	656	49	701	448
1971	24,896	559	3,830	757	308	78	588	65	654	421
1970	23,048	519	3,717	781	305	81	518	69	612	409
1969	22,475	517	3,526	717	284	97	491	92	522	426
1968	20,597	496	3,309	585	249	83	440	95	473	394
1967	19,422	439	3,123	643	231	73	430	105	437	366
1966	18,922	418	2,888	589	219	70	417	107	396	366
1965	17,005	395	2,619	502	207	62	394	116	351	324
1964	15,124	373	2,350	414	192	54	359	108	320	309
1963	13,336	335	2,143	340	178	49	309	96	291	264
1962	12,169	311	1,933	279	171	45	276	79	278	227
1961[1]	11,049ʳ	281	1,736	232	190	40	246	70	266	198
1960	9,527	284	1,661	232	182	39	242	90	245	289
1959	9,415	276	1,554	230	178	38	263	99	236	274
1958	8,466	260	1,393	226	174	34	243	113	215	251
1957	8,161	235	1,270	194	159	31	224	139	198	260
1956	8,053	236	1,163	181	148	32	219	152	185	260
1955	7,057	229	1,083	166	135	31	200	134	171	237
1954	6,244	219	1,014	171	117	28	186	138	157	221
1953	6,299	207	1,000	158	112	29	188	157	151	210
1952	6,039	213	952	147	101	30	187	185	141	203
1951	5,784ʳ	183	923	173	85	28	180	227	133	213

Year	Tobacco, confectionery, soft drinks	Auto parts and accessories	Commercial, institutional and service equipment and supplies	Other construction materials and supplies, including lumber	Farm machinery	Hardware	Household electrical appliances	Industrial and transportation equipment and supplies	All other kinds of businesses
	342	343	344	345	346	347	348	349	350
1975	1,556	2,809	995	5,368	2,006	956	993	4,497	14,481
1974	1,343	2,529	941	5,358	1,607	904	897	3,889	15,104
1973	1,182	2,060	789	4,720	1,259	755	802	3,169	10,368
1972	1,081	1,721	666	3,731	958	677	673	2,596	8,099
1971	1,000	1,519	593	3,115	793	638	600	2,223	7,155
1970	940	1,355	565	2,597	633	617	532	2,022	6,776
1969	863	1,190	628	2,867	901	577	532	2,141	6,104
1968	791	1,047	546	2,572	848	553	460	1,788	5,868
1967	734	917	495	2,304	952	543	414	1,787	5,429
1966	668	829	414	2,258	921	526	379	1,775	5,682
1965	610	734	338	2,005	787	487	323	1,555	5,196
1964	562	656	296	1,845	671	479	267	1,299	4,570
1963	542	605	255	1,638	532	442	252	1,049	4,016
1962	526	544	222	1,499	435	442	258	922	3,722
1961[1]	502	470	197	1,368	390	437	253	826	3,347
1960	746	466	186	885	83	399	232	806	2,461
1959	728	452	171	971	94	381	225	830	2,415
1958	683	401	144	831	76	364	204	752	2,104
1957	639	373	134	784	62	362	193	833	2,071
1956	588	363	128	803	74	358	190	833	2,141
1955	536	322	109	739	62	317	186	632	1,769
1954	508	284	97	605	54	286	164	503	1,493
1953	498	285	90	576	72	283	147	549	1,587
1952	500	271	80	523	73	266	130	536	1,501
1951	458	247	73	515	66	267	93	437	1,483

[1] As of 1961, estimates are based on establishments instead of locations.

Series V351-360. Index numbers of sales of wholesalers proper, by selected kind of business, 1930 to 1975

Year	All kinds of business	Groceries and food specialties	Fresh fruits and vegetables	Tobacco, confectionery, soft drinks	Clothing and furnishings	Dry goods[1]	Footwear	Auto parts and accessories	Hardware	Drugs and drug sundries
	351	352	353	354	355	356	357	358	359	360
				Census and monthly survey (1954 = 100)						
1975	726.7	660.3	362.6	306.1	355.5	445.8	328.3	990.0	334.1	625.3
1974	692.0	572.6	342.6	264.2	338.6	456.5	339.2	891.5	315.8	567.8
1973	545.8	473.5	297.8	232.7	306.2	378.2	294.3	726.3	263.7	480.1
1972	451.1	416.6	276.8	212.7	285.7	352.0	266.4	606.7	236.7	445.7
1971	398.7	377.8	254.8	196.7	262.9	315.5	274.2	535.4	223.0	415.8
1970	369.1	366.7	236.8	185.1	260.4	277.9	287.3	477.7	215.7	389.4
1969	359.9	347.9	235.8	169.8	242.7	263.2	341.0	419.6	201.6	331.8
1968	329.8	326.5	226.3	155.6	212.8	235.7	291.5	369.2	193.3	301.0
1967	311.0	308.1	200.3	144.5	197.0	230.5	258.7	323.1	189.7	278.2
1966	303.0	284.9	190.6	131.5	187.4	223.3	245.6	292.2	183.9	252.0
1965	272.3	258.4	180.3	120.0	176.8	211.2	217.7	258.6	170.1	223.1
1964	242.2	231.9	170.3	110.5	164.3	192.7	191.2	231.3	167.4	203.7
1963	213.6	211.4	152.8	106.6	152.0	165.5	174.2	213.1	154.3	185.0
1962	194.9	190.7	141.8	103.5	146.3	147.9	160.1	191.8	154.6	177.0
1961	176.9	171.2	128.3	98.8	162.6	132.0	140.6	165.5	152.7	169.0
1960	152.6	163.8	129.6	146.9	155.5	129.5	137.5	164.1	139.5	155.5
1959	150.8	153.7	125.8	143.3	152.2	141.0	133.9	159.1	133.1	150.2
1958	135.6	137.4	118.7	134.4	148.5	130.1	120.8	141.2	127.0	136.7
1957	130.7	125.3	107.0	125.8	135.7	120.2	111.0	131.3	126.3	126.1
1956	129.0	114.7	107.4	115.6	126.6	117.2	112.7	127.8	124.9	117.9
1955	113.0	106.9	104.3	105.5	115.7	107.3	110.2	113.4	110.7	108.8
1954	100.0	100.0	100.0	100.0	100.0	100.0	100.0	100.0	100.0	100.0
				Annual averages of monthly indexes[2] (1935-39 = 100)						
1953	362.2	318.9	305.3	419.9	260.2	238.0	335.6	592.4	452.3	381.5
1952	362.5	314.7	329.1	428.9	263.0	243.3	438.9	567.2	446.9	371.4
1951	338.9	305.1	292.6	412.3	252.6	249.4	328.5	510.9	455.6	348.8
1950	306.6	274.6	272.8	395.2	247.2	246.1	283.2	429.1	396.4	312.4
1949	291.3	257.0	263.0	372.8	248.2	240.4	281.9	397.6	374.9	305.5
1948	283.2	254.0	237.2	354.8	265.1	264.7	286.8	379.9	359.7	281.8
1947	272.0	244.2	274.7	317.1	255.4	244.5	300.8	369.8	325.0	254.6
1946	244.0	208.9	291.2	296.9	229.3	197.5	279.4	334.0	277.4	245.2
1945	205.4	180.2	262.4	258.1	186.3	161.9	224.0	242.8	212.0	222.1
1944	186.0	169.3	222.0	230.1	183.1	165.9	188.8	197.2	183.8	201.9
1943	168.3	150.3	206.1	207.3	177.5	150.9	173.1	158.1	173.1	184.2
1942	156.2	146.5	158.5	172.4	170.9	160.2	161.0	147.6	170.0	165.7
1941	142.0	134.7	131.2	150.6	142.8	141.8	141.6	157.8	165.2	145.2
1940	120.7	116.2	116.2	130.6	121.1	116.5	124.2	135.3	131.9	122.7
1939	109.1	108.6	107.7	113.4	106.1	105.8	111.5	112.8	110.6	111.0
1938	101.6	101.1	103.4	106.4	95.9	96.1	93.7	106.5	103.4	104.1
1937	105.3	104.1	105.2	102.5	106.3	107.9	107.4	101.7	109.6	104.2
1936	95.6	96.3	96.0	91.0	97.7	97.4	97.0	94.5	93.9	93.5
1935	88.5	90.0	87.7	76.7	94.0	92.8	90.4	84.5	82.5	87.3
				Annual survey[2] (1930 = 100)						
1937	98.7	105.2	92.7	102.8	91.9	82.6	—	99.2	100.3	105.7
1936	86.2	97.3	84.0	90.3	85.3	74.8	—	88.7	85.0	95.2
1935	78.9	90.8	76.2	84.1	80.5	71.6	—	78.7	74.7	88.7
1934	74.7	87.8	72.9	77.3	75.8	70.3	—	73.1	70.1	83.4
1933	65.7	82.4	63.7	70.1	68.3	61.2	—	62.8	57.7	79.1
1932	68.7	79.4	70.1	76.5	72.4	63.0	—	64.9	59.4	85.2
1931	81.6	87.7	83.5	89.1	83.5	77.7	—	83.9	76.5	96.3
1930	100.0	100.0	100.0	100.0	100.0	100.0	—	100.0	100.0	100.0

[1] For the years 1954 to 1975, "Dry goods" should read "Other textile and clothing accessories".

[2] See the notes for differences in content of the annual survey and the annual averages based on monthly series.

Series V361-373. Wholesale sales, by kind of business and type of operation, selected years, 1930 to 1966
(millions of dollars)

Year	Groceries and food specialties	Other food and tobacco	Farm products[1]	Chemicals, drugs and allied products	Dry goods and apparel	Furniture and house furnishings	Automotive	Electrical goods	Lumber and building materials[2]	Paper and paper products	Hardware	Machinery equipment and supplies	Metal and metalwork
	361	**362**	**363**	**364**	**365**	**366**	**367**	**368**	**369**	**370**	**371**	**372**	**373**
					All wholesalers 1961								
Establishment[3]	1,886	1,983	4,243	431	815	248	862	624	1,408	377	461	1,804	573
Location[3]	1,856	1,958	4,242	428	813	249	860	621	1,394	375	465	1,797	586
					Wholesalers proper								
1966	2,684	1,879	1,851	633	665	394	1,175	717	1,856	366	512	3,287	757
1961	1,555	1,296	1,226	403	455	204	716	426	1,161	200	423	1,501	356
1951	883	854	136	163	282	93	349	185	317	213	261	606	217
1941	347	405	150	94	126	28	69	44	118	140	111	208	111
1930	221	254	27	35	102	14	27	23	52	22	66	59	14
					Manufacturers' sales branches								
1966	312	254	x	70	48	—	402	235	194	399	3	230	159
1961	120	169	88	10	25	—	110	141	195	156	5	215	23
1951	307	274	x	259	274	30	316	408	303	327	16	465	581
1941	116	100	—	98	161	12	50	134	33	50	5	78	177
1930	97	25	x	36	56	11	75	112	34	25	6	57	51
					Agents and brokers								
1966	353	318	x	29	445	—	69	80	151	351	47	95	292
1961	211	246	1,507	18	335	—	36	57	52	21	33	88	194
1951	145	138	1,345	15	192	23	14	32	77	95	20	37	161
1941	102	83	364	20	117	—	4	8	29	5	12	43	38
1930	76	45	181	20	73	4	5	8	18	29	6	25	32
					Assemblers of primary products								
1966	—	331	2,239	—	—	—	—	—	—	—	—	—	—
1961	—	271	1,423	—	—	—	—	—	—	—	—	—	—
1951	—	302	1,160	—	—	—	—	—	—	—	—	—	—
1941	x	74	368	—	—	—	—	—	—	—	—	—	—
1930	2	41	328	—	—	—	—	—	—	—	—	—	—

[1] Raw materials.
[2] Other than metal.

[3] Includes co-operative marketing associations and other dealers of primary products and petroleum bulk tank plants and truck distributors which are not shown separately in the table.

Series V374-387. Wholesale trade, by major type of operation, by province, selected years, 1930 to 1966
(millions of dollars)

Year	All types		Wholesalers proper		Manufacturers' sales branches		Agents and brokers		Petroleum bulk tank stations		Assemblers of primary products		Other types	
	Number	Sales	Number	Sales	Number	Sales	Number	Sales	Number	Sales	Number	Sales	Number	Sales
	374	**375**	**376**	**377**	**378**	**379**	**380**	**381**	**382**	**383**	**384**	**385**	**386**	**387**
							Canada							
1966	30,900	31,172	24,124	18,922	499	2,638	2,216	3,731	2,787	3,193	1,274	2,687	—	—
1961	30,855	19,453	22,434	11,219	767	1,401	2,042	2,984	4,335	2,067	1,277	1,780	—	—
1951	26,167	14,401	10,493	5,494	2,703	3,795	1,741	2,494	3,886	1,021	7,179	1,518	165	79
1941	24,758	5,291	9,417	2,358	1,622	1,207	2,106	908	3,973	216	7,366	453	274	148
1930	13,140	3,325	5,108	1,111	1,546	755	1,798	572	3,602	185	767	374	319	329
							Newfoundland							
1966	..	..	..	..	..	´..	..	..	..	..	..	..	—	—
1961	447	240	308	139	10	—	53	32	68	44	8	x	—	—
1951	281	128	186	73	17	—	44	15	25	19	9	x	—	—
1941	—	—	—	—	—	—	—	—	—	—	—	—	—	—
1930	—	—	—	—	—	—	—	—	—	—	—	—	—	—
							Prince Edward Island							
1966	..	..	..	..	..	..	..	..	..	..	..	..	—	—
1961	208	67	112	34	1	—	4	—	42	13	49	15	—	—
1951	157	33	48	—	8	—	11	1	26	6	64	8	—	—
1941	100	13	33	5	2	—	6	—	19	1	40	5	—	—
1930	..	..	..	..	..	..	..	..	..	..	..	..	..	..
							Nova Scotia							
1966	..	..	..	..	..	..	..	..	..	..	..	..	—	—
1961	894	420	563	246	31	56	43	27	171	71	86	20	—	—
1951	740	308	364	137	125	110	29	13	138	34	84	15	—	—
1941	681	153	345	83	61	43	60	12	112	10	103	5	—	—
1930	..	..	..	..	..	..	..	..	..	..	..	..	..	..
							New Brunswick							
1966	..	..	..	..	..	..	..	..	..	..	..	..	—	—
1961	709	304	456	163	24	38	40	22	138	68	51	12	—	—
1951	568	252	252	110	113	72	30	7	101	33	72	30	—	—
1941	507	88	222	50	59	x	36	x	81	8	100	4	9	1
1930	..	..	..	..	..	..	..	..	..	..	..	..	..	..
							Quebec							
1966	8,336	7,792	7,152	5,337	122	769	570	769	269	760	223	157	—	—
1961	7,094	4,475	5,722	2,896	112	373	481	549	578	472	201	185	—	—
1951	5,165	4,033	3,304	1,756	583	1,320	445	559	341	218	422	160	70	21
1941	5,075	1,727	3,291	849	403	452	626	292	240	27	411	34	104	72
1930	2,932	905	1,479	356	365	247	526	167	235	29	214	18	113	89
							Ontario							
1966	10,394	10,066	8,420	6,291	167	1,095	703	955	701	1,066	403	659	—	—
1961	10,105	6,126	7,812	3,803	262	515	565	690	989	754	477	365	—	—
1951	6,512	4,384	3,669	1,955	907	1,304	486	354	676	390	686	323	88	57
1941	6,244	1,745	3,539	818	548	479	654	208	510	91	865	84	128	66
1930	3,938	1,014	2,004	388	477	288	617	152	476	59	292	32	72	95
							Manitoba							
1966	..	..	..	..	..	..	..	..	..	..	..	..	—	—
1961	2,166	3,499	1,347	1,378	57	x	273	1,128	404	x	85	806	—	—
1951	2,370	2,026	600	320	258	251	260	1,148	420	61	832	246	—	—
1941	2,206	580	540	188	181	74	232	247	530	15	712	50	11	6
1930	..	..	..	..	..	..	..	..	..	..	..	..	..	..
							Saskatchewan							
1966	..	..	..	..	..	..	..	..	..	..	..	..	—	—
1961	2,646	803	1,619	488	60	x	70	53	841	x	56	72	—	—
1951	4,526	799	338	199	157	123	50	31	984	—	2,996	372	1	x
1941	4,897	284	286	72	75	30	70	x	1,361	24	3,104	143	1	x
1930	..	..	..	..	..	..	..	..	..	..	..	..	..	..
							Alberta							
1966	..	..	..	..	..	..	..	..	..	..	..	..	—	—
1961	3,332	1,451	2,200	841	115	117	185	152	719	193	113	147	—	—
1951	3,695	1,099	646	393	243	202	130	102	802	x	1,872	310	2	x
1941	3,336	323	385	103	128	x	118	48	851	25	1,844	108	10	x
1930	..	..	..	..	..	..	..	..	..	..	..	..	..	..

Series V374-387. Wholesale trade, by major type of operation, by province, selected years, 1930 to 1966 (concluded)
(millions of dollars)

Year	All types		Wholesalers proper		Manufacturers' sales branches		Agents and brokers		Petroleum bulk tank stations		Assemblers of primary products		Other types	
	Number	Sales	Number	Sales	Number	Sales	Number	Sales	Number	Sales	Number	Sales	Number	Sales
	374	**375**	**376**	**377**	**378**	**379**	**380**	**381**	**382**	**383**	**384**	**385**	**386**	**387**
						British Columbia								
1966	3,451	3,584	2,580	2,297	75	183	360	669	299	345	137	91	—	—
1961	3,222	2,058	2,281	1,228	93	148	327	330	371	196	150	156	—	—
1951	2,137	1,334	1,079	534	291	392	256	263	367	95	140	50	4	1
1941	1,712	379	776	192	165	72	304	78	269	16	187	21	11	1
1930	1,129	253	440	97	183	49	223	44	194	19	55	9	34	35
					Yukon Territory and Northwest Territories									
1966	..	..	..	..	..	..	..	..	..	..	..	..	..	..
1961	32	11	14	4	2	x	1	x	14	5	1	x	—	—
1951	16	3	7	x	1	x	—	—	6	x	2	x	—	—
1941	—	—	—	—	—	—	—	—	—	—	—	—	—	—
1930	—	—	—	—	—	—	—	—	—	—	—	—	—	—

Series V388-397. Wholesale trade, gross profit margins by kind of business, biennially, 1947 to 1957
(per cent of net sales)

Year	Grocery	Fruits and vegetables	Tobacco and confectionery	Dry goods	Piece goods	Footwear	Automotive parts and accessories	Hardware	Plumbing and heating	Drugs
	388	**389**	**390**	**391**	**392**	**393**	**394**	**395**	**396**	**397**
1957	6.84	12.14	6.73	16.04	17.21	13.60	25.36	20.25	16.97	11.79
1955	7.20	11.50	7.33	16.43	16.44	16.40[1]	25.41	19.17	16.37	12.73
1953	7.66	11.79	7.63	16.01	16.10	13.51	24.91	19.45	16.99	12.36
1951	7.96	11.27	7.55	16.96	15.19	14.07	25.29	20.49	17.78	13.43
1949	7.73	10.57	7.14	15.73	15.93	12.78	25.18	19.26	19.07	12.48
1947	8.07	9.13	6.85	16.64	18.40	12.64	24.48	20.14	20.45	12.77

[1] This figure, for 25 businesses, seems high: the figure given in the 1955 report for 19 identical businesses in 1953 and 1955 is 13.32 per cent.

Series V398-409. Summary statistics, census of wholesale trade, by province, selected years, 1930 to 1966

Year	Canada	Newfound-land	Prince Edward Island	Nova Scotia	New Brunswick	Quebec	Ontario	Manitoba	Saskat-chewan	Alberta	British Columbia	Yukon Territory and Northwest Territories
	398	399	400	401	402	403	404	405	406	407	408	409
Total number of locations												
1966	30,900		1,995			8,336	10,394		6,724		3,451[1]	—
1961	30,855	447	208	894	709	7,094	10,105	2,166	2,646	3,332	3,222	32
1951	26,167	281	157	740	568	5,165	6,512	2,370	4,526	3,695	2,137	16
1941	24,758	—	100	681	507	5,075	6,244	2,206	4,897	3,336	1,712[1]	—
1930	13,140	—	61	420	388	2,932	3,938	1,307	1,659	1,306	1,129	—
Total sales (millions of dollars)												
1966	31,172		1,592			7,792	10,066		8,137		3,584[1]	—
1961	19,453	240	67	420	304	4,475	6,126	3,499	803	1,451	2,058	11
1951	14,401	129	33	308	252	4,034	4,384	2,027	799	1,099	1,334	3
1941	5,291	—	13	153	88	1,727	1,745	580	284	323	379[1]	—
1930	3,325	—	14	72	73	905	1,014	669	137	190	253	—
Number of working proprietors												
1966	13,059		781			3,236	4,690		3,433		919[1]	—
1961	15,165	190	128	377	303	3,565	5,160	1,186	1,535	1,632	1,071	18
1951	11,989	159	130	329	253	3,173	3,817	941	988	1,152	1,031	16
1941	13,656	—	78	359	281	3,668	4,276	1,151	1,597	1,280	966[1]	—
1930	2,735	—		161		1,004	994		334		242	—
Number of paid employees												
1966	316,373		22,007			87,066	116,372		57,123		33,805[1]	—
1961	240,033	3,876	1,298	7,444	5,249	60,698	90,346	16,161	10,547	19,876	24,414	124
1951	178,658	3,263	566	5,683	4,659	46,190	59,751	15,099	10,471	14,907	18,031	38
1941	117,471	—	441	4,013	3,084	32,634	40,450	9,566	8,141	8,147	10,995[1]	—
1930	90,564	—	313	2,522	2,825	26,171	31,155	9,362	5,441	5,756	7,019	—

[1] Includes the Yukon Territory and the Northwest Territories.

Series V410-413. Power laundries, cleaning and dyeing plants, selected operating statistics, 1917 to 1974

Year[1]	Power laundries		Cleaning and dyeing plants	
	Number of plants	Receipts	Number of plants	Receipts
	410	411	412	413
1974	348	151,032	2,295	170,768
1973	339	132,682	2,193	149,744
1972	336	113,951	2,114	144,038
1971	..	..	..	..
1970	359	107,773	2,197	152,323
1969	..	111,310	..	164,669
1968	378	108,715	2,176	161,914
1967	362	105,256	2,150	159,728
1966	363	99,421	2,107	153,890
1965	352	89,690	1,896	136,857
1964	362	85,249	1,826	122,750
1963	367	79,295	1,796	112,711
1962	367	75,840	1,756	106,656
1961	375	72,286	1,769	104,630
1960	329	69,251	1,514	94,214
1959	330	68,096	1,483	92,212
1958	322	65,350	1,417	87,195
1957	320	63,106	1,381	84,282
1956	308	58,874	1,338	78,527
1955	306	54,200	1,205	70,734
1954	299	50,513	1,107	67,223
1953	310	49,121	1,029	64,029
1952	307	46,853	991	58,478
1951	317	44,053	981	52,798
1950	323	40,587	919	46,250
1949[1]	332	38,660	905	42,574
1948	294	35,361	787	36,621
1947	244	30,459	530	28,584
1946	238	27,427	452	23,721
1945	217	25,463	385	18,618
1944	227	24,559	399	16,887
1943	225	23,436	362	15,218
1942	238	22,396	365	14,353
1941	237	19,817	363	12,678
1940	230	16,719	300	10,057
1939	234	14,268	268	8,659
1938	232	13,735	230	7,994
1937	225	13,164	193	7,179
1936	229	12,024	191	6,305
1935	237	10,983	179	5,328
1934	236	10,589	175	5,014
1933	239	10,374	172	4,866
1932	243	12,297	166	5,006
1931	250	14,380	157	6,145
1930	242	16,284	126	6,412
1929	230	16,353	127	6,689
1928	233	14,590	124	5,924
1927	223	13,088	115	4,340
Power laundries, cleaning and dyeing plants[2]				
1926	350	17,642	—	—
1925	343	15,578	—	—
1924	518	15,577	—	—
1923	605	15,552	—	—
1922	620	14,650	—	—
1921	535	13,879	—	—
1920	379	14,168	—	—
1919	366	11,841	—	—
1918	341	8,969	—	—
1917	333	8,319	—	—

[1] Includes Newfoundland beginning in 1949.

[2] Data for 1917 to 1926 include dyeing and finishing of textiles (see the note to series V196-199).

Series V414-416. Selected statistics of hotels, 1930, 1941 and 1949 to 1973

Year[1]	Number of hotels	Number of rooms	Bed capacity
	414	415	416
1973	4,984	179,294	249,260
1972	5,139	173,277	236,618
1971	..	..	..
1970	5,028	168,707	231,551
1969	4,922	163,913	231,306
1968	4,769	158,124	218,788
1967	4,621	154,679	213,742
1966	4,685	153,074	214,476
1965	4,846	154,959	220,876
1964	4,976	155,657	301,763
1963	4,787	150,687	288,793
1962	4,983	152,467	288,306
1961	5,128	154,674	288,901
1960	5,294	155,538	288,007
1959	5,269	154,725	282,686
1958	5,088	151,362	274,483
1957	5,151	151,517	278,513
1956[2]	5,067	149,625	271,182
1955[3]	5,081	147,812	266,846
1954	5,208	148,890	264,912
1953	5,209	149,653	261,455
1952	5,157	149,615	263,357
1951	5,092	146,441	257,657
1950[3]	5,169	146,353	237,735
1949	5,425	150,098	—
1941[4]	5,646	128,980[5]	—
1930[4]	4,953	129,462	—

[1] Newfoundland is included beginning in 1949.

[2] In 1956 two changes in tabulating the data were made: occupancy rates became rates for hotels with 11 or more rooms rather than for all hotels which was the practice for 1955 and earlier years; principal operating expenses as a percentage of total receipts became based on a panel of hotels with 11 to 99 rooms rather than on all hotels as in 1955 and earlier years.

[3] In both 1950 and 1955 some establishments formerly included were dropped either because it had become evident they had less than six rooms or were of the tourist home type.

[4] The decennial census data for 1941 and 1931 include public houses in Ontario which are not included for 1949 to 1960. There were 422 public houses, with 5,414 rooms in Ontario in 1949 with total receipts of $30.8 million of which $26.6 million was from beer, wine and liquor sales.

[5] In addition to the 128,980 rooms, it was stated there was accommodation in cabins, etc., for 13,937 persons. This ancillary accommodation is included in other years, though the number of rooms would be less than the number of persons that can be accommodated.

Series V417-419. Selected statistics of advertising agencies in Canada, 1941 and 1946 to 1974
(values in thousands of dollars)

Year[1]	Number of firms	Total amount of billings	Gross revenue on total billings	Year[1]	Number of firms	Total amount of billings	Gross revenue on total billings
	417	418	419		417	418	419
1974	220	175,800	115,421	1960	131	272,740	45,150
1973	211	586,162	103,667	1959	122	254,146	41,127
1972	189	535,066	92,064	1958	123	237,654	38,073
1971	..	..	..	1957	113	226,084	35,758
				1956	110	204,581	32,204
1970	194	470,352	82,896	1955	104	177,240	27,690
1969	163	456,143	78,874	1954	91	156,163	24,579
1968	171	426,145	72,476	1953	88	144,339	22,592
1967	176	429,595	72,835	1952	88	121,667	19,060
1966	165	402,176	66,915	1951	83	108,414	17,015
1965	159	362,559	60,995	1950	75	96,221	15,013
1964	149	318,140	53,592	1949	74	86,742	13,526
1963	143	302,852	50,465	1948	75	73,762	11,553
1962	143	298,585	59,348	1947	67	64,595	10,092
1961	134	282,561	46,090	1946	57	52,169	8,458
				1941	49	29,224	4,824

[1] The source does not indicate when Newfoundland was first included; presumably it was in 1949.

Series V420-423. Selected statistics of motion picture and drive-in theatres, 1930 to 1974
(values in thousands of dollars)

Year	Motion picture theatres		Drive-in theatres		Year	Motion picture theatres		Drive-in theatres	
	Number of establishments	Receipts from admissions	Number of establishments	Receipts from admissions		Number of establishments	Receipts from admissions	Number of establishments	Receipts from admissions
	420	421	422	423		420	421	422	423
1974	1,116	149,720	307	22,963	1950	1,801	82,708	62	2,291
1973	1,135	129,876	299	20,726	1949[1]	1,731	77,419	30	1,394
1972	1,128	122,493	284	17,881	1948	1,604	68,694	15	659
1971	..	..	..	..	1947	1,693	62,865	7	274
					1946	1,477	59,889	—	—
1970	1,156	111,692	279	17,047					
1969	1,157	102,363	271	15,658	1945	1,323	55,431	—	—
1968	1,148	99,041	261	14,656	1944	1,298	53,173	—	—
1967	1,156	90,804	253	12,759	1943	1,265	51,485	—	—
1966	1,149	83,005	245	11,362	1942	1,247	45,720	—	—
					1941	1,240	40,796	—	—
1965	1,171	75,372	247	9,790					
1964	1,209	69,325	242	9,023	1940	1,229	37,474	—	—
1963	1,245	63,817	241	7,825	1939	1,183	33,696	—	—
1962	1,278	60,941	240	6,807	1938	1,130	33,346	—	—
1961	1,341	62,229	238	6,653	1937	1,044	32,163	—	—
					1936	956	29,440	—	—
1960	1,427	65,505	232	6,790					
1959	1,515	68,370	234	7,144	1935	859	27,012	—	—
1958	1,622	75,139	232	6,254	1934	796	25,281	—	—
1957	1,716	76,486	229	5,725	1933	762	24,906	—	—
1956	1,849	80,666	237	5,394	1932	—	28,585	—	—
					1931	—	33,706	—	—
1955	1,950	86,374	242	5,755					
1954	1,938	97,012	230	6,317	1930	907	38,130	—	—
1953	1,906	100,889	174	5,863					
1952	1,843	98,851	104	4,409					
1951	1,808	90,986	82	3,348					

[1] Includes Newfoundland beginning in 1949.

Series V424-436. Receipts of selected kinds of service establishments, 1961 to 1975
(millions of dollars)

Year	Canada	Newfound-land	Prince Edward Island	Nova Scotia	New Brunswick	Quebec	Ontario	Manitoba	Saskat-chewan	Alberta	British Columbia	Yukon Territory	Northwest Territories
	424	**425**	**426**	**427**	**428**	**429**	**430**	**431**	**432**	**433**	**434**	**435**	**436**
					Total restaurant receipts								
1975	1,980.5	18.5	4.8	41.0	36.5	635.4	722.2	100.4	58.5	159.2	204.0	..	..
1974	1,771.5	16.9	4.0	37.9	32.5	574.6	648.9	87.1	52.3	135.0	182.3	..	..
1973	1,561.4	15.5	3.6	37.1	30.9	536.6	554.2	71.2	43.7	114.8	153.8	..	..
1972	1,386.6	13.1	3.2	34.0	28.0	481.1	483.2	63.4	38.5	107.8	134.4	..	..
1971	1,286.2	12.0	3.2	31.3	25.8	439.4	446.7	59.1	36.2	105.3	127.4	..	..
1970	1,218.9	10.8	3.2	30.2	24.4	411.6	423.2	57.3	35.3	102.9	120.1	..	..
1969	1,199.4	11.2	3.2	29.1	24.1	405.4	409.3	56.5	38.4	100.2	122.0	..	..
1968	1,166.1	10.5	3.4	28.3	22.6	395.2	405.9	53.6	42.0	92.9	111.6	..	..
1967	1,139.0	11.7	3.2	27.4	21.5	403.5	393.7	51.5	41.9	85.0	99.6	..	..
1966	1,078.4	11.7	3.2	25.5	20.8	364.6	380.3	49.7	42.2	77.8	102.6	..	..
1965	999.2	10.7	2.9	24.4	19.6	341.7	351.5	47.2	40.3	69.9	90.9	..	..
1964	933.5	9.4	2.9	22.4	18.2	317.8	333.6	45.9	39.7	65.1	78.6	..	..
1963	892.3	7.9	2.6	20.9	15.8	297.4	317.8	44.8	39.9	67.7	77.4	..	..
1962	853.0	7.0	2.6	19.9	15.4	284.5	302.9	43.1	38.1	64.5	74.9	..	..
1961	796.4	5.9	2.4	19.1	14.4	259.1	284.8	41.1	34.7	61.5	73.4	..	..
					Total receipts from motels								
1974	271.0	5.7	3.3	12.1	14.8	48.7	87.0	7.6	10.7	25.8	52.0	2.1	1.2
1973	235.2	4.3	3.9	11.9	13.6	42.9	75.7	6.9	8.7	21.1	43.4	1.8	1.0
1972	220.9	2.8	3.1	10.4	10.7	42.8	74.5	6.5	8.2	19.4	39.9	2.0	0.7
1971	..	..	..	..	..	..	..	..	..	..	..	..	..
1970	165.8	–	1.4	7.4	6.2	32.0	59.7	4.9	5.6	14.2	30.8	1.4	–
1969	141.9	2.5	0.9	4.5	5.6	25.4	53.8	3.9	5.4	11.6	27.0	1.2	0.1
					Power laundries, dry cleaning and dyeing plants								
1974	321.8	3.6		7.3	5.0	78.9	139.0	15.8	7.6	25.2	39.5[1]	..	..
1973	282.4	2.8		6.8	4.6	69.9	122.9	13.9	6.4	21.4	33.8[1]	..	..
1972	258.0	2.6		6.6	4.4	60.9	115.4	10.9	6.3	20.1	30.7[1]	..	..
1971	..	..		..	..	..	..	..	..	..	..	..	..
1970	260.1	2.8		6.5	4.4	61.8	115.1	11.3	6.5	21.2	30.5[1]	..	..
1969	276.0	..		..	..	..	..	..	..	..	..	..	..
1968	270.6	3.0		6.6	5.0	67.1	115.3	11.3	7.4	22.1	32.7[1]	..	..
1967	265.0	2.9		5.9	4.7	68.3	111.9	11.7	7.0	20.9	31.7[1]	..	..
1966	253.3	2.8		6.0	4.6	64.9	105.9	11.6	7.3	19.6	30.7[1]	..	..
1965	226.5	2.6		5.5	4.0	56.0	96.3	11.6	6.5	18.1	26.0[1]	..	..
1964	208.0	2.4		5.3	3.8	52.5	87.8	10.9	6.0	16.3	22.9[1]	..	..
1963	192.0	2.4		5.1	3.5	48.9	80.1	10.6	5.3	15.1	21.0[1]	..	..
1962	182.5	2.2		4.8	3.3	46.6	75.0	9.6	5.4	14.8	20.8[1]	..	..
1961	176.9	2.1		5.0	3.3	43.5	73.1	9.5	5.4	14.4	20.6[1]	..	..
					Receipts of funeral directors								
1972	119.5	1.2	0.6	4.6	3.3	32.8	51.9	5.1	4.8	6.8	8.3	..	..
1968	97.1	0.8	0.5	3.5	2.6	27.1	42.2	4.3	4.0	5.1	7.0	..	..
1966	85.9	0.6	..	3.2	2.1	25.4	35.6	3.7	3.5	5.0	6.3	..	..
1964	74.0	0.5	0.4	2.6	1.8	20.5	31.5	3.5	3.2	4.1	5.9	..	..
					Receipts of hotels								
1974	1,852.7	23.6	5.2	34.2	21.5	407.7	554.6	128.0	95.0	240.7	319.4	10.8	12.0
1973	1,566.2	20.4	3.5	25.3	17.6	357.6	472.6	108.8	85.6	197.6	258.8	8.4	10.1
1972	1,376.7	18.6	2.1	20.6	14.4	326.2	417.4	100.1	78.5	170.3	212.9	7.2	8.4
1971	..	..	..	..	..	..	..	..	..	..	..	..	..
1970	1,128.4	13.1	1.9	16.4	10.4	265.0	350.2	84.6	63.9	135.9	174.8	6.9	5.4
1969	1,044.3	11.2	1.7	14.0	9.3	254.0	324.4	76.7	62.2	119.2	162.5	5.1	4.1
1968	956.2	9.7	1.0	12.7	7.7	243.3	291.5	73.1	61.4	106.9	141.2	4.9	2.7
1967	888.2	8.7	0.9	11.1	7.2	238.5	267.0	66.4	58.3	94.1	129.7	3.8	2.4
1966	790.5	7.0	0.8	10.7	6.7	199.4	244.2	58.5	54.5	86.3	116.8	3.6	2.1
1965	740.0	6.8	0.8	9.8	6.3	187.1	229.7	55.3	51.9	79.2	113.1	–	–
1964	686.8	6.4	1.0	8.6	5.6	177.7	209.8	54.0	49.2	71.2	103.3	–	–
1963	622.6	6.0	0.8	7.4	5.2	153.6	192.0	50.2	46.6	67.2	93.7	–	–
1962	587.7	5.5	0.7	7.3	4.5	146.6	181.4	45.6	44.5	66.4	85.1	–	–
1961	567.8	4.3	0.8	7.0	4.2	144.8	176.6	45.4	43.6	61.7	79.3	–	–
					Motion picture theatres-receipts from admissions (excluding taxes)								
1974	149.7	1.6	0.7	4.1	2.9	37.8	56.1	6.2	5.0	14.6	20.0	0.6	
1973	129.9	1.3	0.3	3.8	2.3	35.0	48.5	5.1	3.9	12.8	16.3	0.6	
1972	122.5	1.4	0.3	3.7	2.2	32.6	46.0	5.1	3.8	12.4	14.3	0.6	
1971	..	..	..	..	..	..	..	..	..	..	..	..	

Series V424-436. Receipts of selected kinds of service establishments, 1961 to 1975 (concluded)
(millions of dollars)

Year	Canada	Newfound-land	Prince Edward Island	Nova Scotia	New Brunswick	Quebec	Ontario	Manitoba	Saskat-chewan	Alberta	British Columbia	Yukon Territory	Northwest Territories
	424	425	426	427	428	429	430	431	432	433	434	435	436
					Motion picture theatres-receipts from admissions (excluding taxes)								
1970	111.7	1.2	0.3	3.4	1.7	31.1	43.1	4.5	3.7	9.8	12.5	0.5	
1969	102.4	0.9	0.3	3.0	1.8	26.6	40.8	4.2	3.7	8.8	11.8	0.5	
1968	99.0	1.0	0.3	2.8	1.7	26.2	39.8	3.7	3.8	8.0	11.2	0.4	
1967	90.8	0.9	0.2	2.6	1.7	23.9	36.8	3.6	3.2	6.8	10.7	0.4	
1966	83.0	0.8	0.2	2.2	1.4	23.0	33.9	3.3	2.8	6.1	9.3	..	
1965	75.4	0.8	0.2	2.1	1.3	20.8	31.2	2.8	2.6	5.5	8.1	..	
1964	69.3	0.7	0.2	1.9	1.3	19.0	28.4	2.8	2.5	5.0	7.7	..	
1963	63.8	0.7	0.2	1.7	1.2	18.1	26.0	2.6	2.1	4.5	6.8	..	
1962	60.9	0.7	0.2	1.8	1.1	17.1	23.9	3.1	2.2	4.5	6.4	..	
1961	62.2	0.7	0.2	1.7	1.2	16.9	24.9	2.8	2.5	4.9	6.5	..	
					Computer services, total operating revenue								
1974	211.0		3.4			32.7	126.0	10.4		23.1	15.4	—	—

[1] Includes the Yukon Territory and the Northwest Territories

Series V437-448. Summary statistics, census of service trades, by province, selected years, 1930 to 1971

Year	Canada	Newfound-land	Prince Edward Island	Nova Scotia	New Brunswick	Quebec	Ontario	Manitoba	Saskat-chewan	Alberta	British Columbia	Yukon Territory and Northwest Territories
	437	438	439	440	441	442	443	444	445	446	447	448
					Total number of locations							
1971	117,861	1,445	798	3,450	2,903	33,633	43,883	4,724	4,872	8,533	13,331	289
1966	93,791	1,167	362	2,678	2,236	27,232	34,518	4,058	4,366	6,751	10,222	201
1961	84,765	834	360	2,538	2,066	23,803	32,014	3,853	4,263	5,921	8,957	156
1951	58,748	650	367	2,050	1,600	16,501	20,540	3,117	3,771	4,227	5,848	77
1941	49,271	—	325	1,860	1,484	13,807	17,612	2,977	3,704	3,341	4,147	14
1930	42,223	—	335	1,504	1,393	10,916	15,566	2,493	3,658	2,881	3,458	19
					Receipts *(millions of dollars)*							
1971	8,901	105	22	199	143	2,336	3,635	380	251	748	1,055	27
1966	4,587	47	10	92	77	1,253	1,839	217	165	351	523	13
1961	2,980	31	6	64	43	821	1,176	154	124	238	314	8
1951	1,086	7	3	23	19	280	415	67	57	94	119	3
1941	255	—	1	9	6	65	110	15	10	13	25[1]	—
1930	250[1]	—	1	6	4	64	109	16	10	13	25	—
					Number of working proprietors							
1971	104,690	1,146	735	2,779	2,397	30,985	40,625	4,115	4,333	6,659	10,691	225
1966	82,261	952	334	2,215	1,815	24,708	31,144	3,450	3,957	5,480	8,038	168
1961	78,880	764	353	2,313	1,879	22,636	30,372	3,477	4,065	5,182	7,698	141
1951	58,704	643	389	1,993	1,545	16,929	20,433	3,189	3,758	4,091	5,662	72
1941	50,224	—	327	1,869	1,519	14,074	18,058	2,999	3,740	3,438	4,187	13
1930	44,622	—	350	1,565	1,422	11,278	16,687	2,652	3,891	3,040	3,717	20
					Number of paid employees							
1971	545,734	6,418	2,004	14,110	10,253	144,348	216,308	24,002	15,109	46,148	65,514	1,520
1966	398,232	4,290	959	9,630	7,557	105,726	157,591	19,733	13,535	32,099	46,365	747
1961	308,465	2,629	758	7,803	4,777	81,963	125,263	16,380	11,141	23,952	33,265	534
1951	143,800[2]	1,099	559	4,151	2,896	37,369	56,782	8,669	6,432	10,580	15,065	198
1941	62,781	—	273	2,353	1,261	16,425	27,226	4,308	2,111	2,961	5,849	14
1930	55,257	—	146	1,426	1,058	15,663	22,467	3,976	1,936	2,799	5,752	34

[1] Includes the Yukon Territory and the Northwest Territories.   [2] Minimum number of employees.

Section W: Education

M. Wisenthal, *Statistics Canada*

This section is in three main parts as follows: Summary Statistics (series W1-66); Elementary and Secondary Education (series W67-306) and Post-secondary Education (series W307-532). Within each part there are series on enrolment, number and qualifications of teachers and financial data. Additional information on degrees awarded and libraries is given in the third part.

The main sources consist of the following publications of the Education, Science and Culture Division of Statistics Canada: *Salaries and Qualifications of Teachers in Public Elementary and Secondary Schools*, (Catalogue 81-202); *University and College Libraries in Canada*, (Catalogue 81-206); *Survey of Education Finance*, (Catalogue 81-208); *Elementary-Secondary School Enrolment*, (Catalogue 81-210); *Degrees, Diplomas, Certificates Awarded by Degree-granting Institutions*, (Catalogue 81-211); *Education in Canada*, (Catalogue 81-229) and *Historical Compendium of Education Statistics*, (Catalogue 81-568 Occasional).

Several of the above titles and catalogue numbers have been altered in recent years. Additional sources are given in *Statistics Canada Catalogue*, (Catalogue 11-204E). An important additional source is *Enrolment in Educational Institutions by Province, 1951-52 to 1980-81* by Z. Zsigmond and C. Wenaas, Staff Study Number 25, Economic Council of Canada, Ottawa, 1970. The book by Robin S. Harris, *A History of Higher Education in Canada, 1663 to 1960*, University of Toronto Press, 1976, was also used. A long list of sources for earlier years is given in the first edition of this volume. Many of those earlier data sources are now consolidated in the above Statistics Canada publications.

The 1960s were a period of unprecedented expansion and reorganization for Canadian education. For example, the Council of Ministers of Education was created to promote an exchange of views on educational policies among provinces, and to identify a common core of statistical information; a network of community colleges was established across the country; the structure of education in Quebec underwent a fundamental reorganization. These changes brought a demand for improved statistical information, including the development of new series, improvements in existing ones, and a limited examination and revision of data published in the past.

In general, data presented here are more inclusive than those in the previous edition, although some series have been discontinued or replaced by new ones. For example, elementary-secondary enrolment now covers not only public and private schools, but also federal schools for native people. Because the academic qualifications for teaching have been upgraded, classification of elementary and secondary teachers by type of certificate held is less relevant. Therefore, elementary and secondary teachers in this publication are not classified by type of certificate, but by the highest university degree obtained. New series include full-time enrolment in post-secondary non-university institutions, university undergraduate enrolment by field of specialization beginning with 1961, part-time university enrolment, information about centralized libraries in public elementary and secondary schools and university libraries.

Space limitations meant that some series had to be excluded. For example, enrolment in elementary and secondary schools by grade, sex and type (or control) of school proved too unwieldy for inclusion. However, this information and other detailed data may be found in a new Statistics Canada publication, *Historical Compendium of Education Statistics*. In most cases, if tables in this volume give data for Canada only, provincial breakdowns are in the above publication.

The form of presentation has also been altered. Fairly comprehensive information is now available for enrolment covering the period from 1951 to 1975, and for finance from 1950 to 1974. Therefore, it is possible to present trends for these two subjects over the last quarter century. Data on teachers, classified by level of instruction, are available only from 1960 to 1975.

In the following tables, data are given for school years beginning in the year shown, whereas in the first edition of *Historical Statistics of Canada*, data were given for school years ending in the year shown.

Statistical data reported for recent years are acceptably accurate and complete. However, the more remote the information is in time, the more likely it is to be inexact. The degree of accuracy varies considerably from province to province, and can be assessed only by comparison with other related variables, or by reference to original reports. Summary tables, covering the period from 1950 (or 1951) to 1975 are generally reliable. Data on teachers, classified by level of instruction, are given only from 1960, because it was not possible to obtain reliable information in such detail for earlier years from private and federal schools.

Summary Statistics (Series W1-66)

W1-9. Summary of total full-time enrolment, by level of study, Canada, selected years, 1951 to 1975

SOURCE: 1960 to 1975, *Education in Canada*; 1951 to 1959, *Economic Council of Canada, Staff Study No. 25*; and unpublished data.

W10-20. Summary of total full-time enrolment, by level of study, related to relevant population, Canada, selected years, 1951 to 1975

SOURCE: 1960 to 1975, *Education in Canada*; 1951 to 1959, *Economic Council of Canada, Staff Study No. 25.*

Changes in the levels of enrolment must be viewed in the light of two factors that affect education, namely: (i) demography - the steep decline in the birth rate and the somewhat more gradual decline in the number of live births beginning around 1960, and (ii) enrolment rates - generally increasing rates, particularly at the secondary and, even more so, at the post-secondary levels.

Total full-time enrolment, which stood at 2,715,900 in 1951, increased 61 per cent to 4,367,500 by 1960, then grew by almost another 2 million or 46 per cent to a peak of 6,363,900 in 1970. It then began a decline, to 6,186,000 by 1975.

These fluctuations reflect the decreasing number of children in the younger age groups, but also changing enrolment rates.

Because changes in population affect enrolment, especially at the lower rungs of the education ladder, it is necessary to examine the trends by level.

(i) Kindergarten

The decline in the birth rate and the number of live births has already affected the youngest age groups. The five-year-old population rose steadily from 301,200 in 1951 to a peak of 469,200 in 1966 (an increase of 168,000), then declined to a low of 359,400 in 1974 (a drop of 109,800). In 1975, it rose to 370,300, reflecting a temporary increase in the number of births in 1970. This rise in births is a random fluctuation and not a harbinger of future trends. It is, however, expected that in the second half of the 1970s the number of births will indeed increase due to the growing number of women in the child-bearing age born during the 'baby boom' era, and in spite of still decreasing birth rate.

But it is apparent that 'Pre-grade 1' enrolment has been increasing much faster than the five-year-old population. The picture is somewhat distorted by inclusion of private kindergartens and nursery schools in the Canada totals from 1965 to 1974. The number ranged from 38,000 in 1965 to a high of 52,200 in 1970, and then tapered off to 38,600 in 1974. In 1975, the survey of private kindergartens and nursery schools was discontinued. Thus, for an accurate time series, it is necessary to recast the figures.

The following tabulation contains the data as they appear in series W1-9 and series W10-20, the revised figures, and the index based on 1951. Each year in the seventies is shown since it was then that enrolment rates exceeded 100 per cent of the five-year-old population. This rapid growth in kindergarten enrolment occurred chiefly because of the creation of junior kindergartens in public schools enrolling four-year-old and even some younger children. In 1975, the four-year-old and younger children enrolled represented around 35 per cent of the four-year-old population.

Pre-grade one enrolment and enrolment rates

	Enrolment		Enrolment rates		Index of revised enrolment
	Including private kindergartens	Excluding private kindergartens	Including private kindergartens	Excluding private kindergartens	
	(thousands)		(%)	(%)	(1951 = 100)
1975	–	398.5	–	107.6	477.2
1974	423.5	384.9	117.8	107.1	461.0
1973	388.9	349.2	107.7	96.1	418.2
1972	386.2	341.3	99.9	88.3	408.7
1971	377.3	336.8	91.7	81.9	403.4
1970	402.4	350.2	91.0	79.2	419.4
1965	267.8	229.8	58.0	49.7	275.2
1960	–	145.6	–	34.4	174.4
1955	–	102.8	–	27.6	123.1
1951	–	83.5	–	27.7	100.0

These figures indicate the extent of the distortion caused by inclusion of private kindergartens and nursery schools (the latter enrolling even three-year-olds); the adjusted enrolment rates are lower by 8 per cent to 12 per cent.

Nonetheless, the recast numbers demonstrate the rapid increases in both enrolment and enrolment rates. By 1970, enrolment had grown more than fourfold from 1951, and enrolment rates rose from 28 per cent to 79 per cent. While the numbers fell in the early 1970s as a result of the declining birth rates in the 1960s, enrolment rates kept rising and exceeded 100 per cent in the last two years.

(ii) Grades 1 to 8

The 6 to 13-year-old population has also been affected by the demographic changes. It rose to a peak of 3,702,400 in 1971, and then declined to 3,410,300 in 1975.

Elementary enrolment increased throughout the 1950s and most of the 1960s, consistently exceeding the relevant population, due to overage students. However, the rate of increase diminished: from 1951 to 1955 it was 25 per cent, from 1955 to 1960, 22 per cent, and from 1960 to 1965, 13 per cent. Peak enrolment of 3,844,100 occurred in 1968, 5 per cent above the 1965 figure and 79 per cent over 1951, producing an enrolment rate of 106 per cent. The subsequent decline was due mainly to two factors: (1) a gradual phasing out of the Grade 7 in Quebec, and (2) a faster promotion of students not only in Quebec but in most other provinces. Consequently, the proportion of overaged students declined and so did the enrolment rate.

The seeming increase in 1975 'Grades 1-8' enrolment (series W1-9) and the decrease in 'Grades 9 and higher' are entirely due to a change in the classification of Quebec 'Secondary II' enrolment. Until 1974, this level was included in 'Grades 9 and higher', but in 1975 was transferred to 'Grades 1 to 8'. Elimination of the effect of this change would produce a further decline of 'elementary' and a continued increase in 'secondary' enrolment.

If, for the sake of comparability with previous years, enrolment in Quebec 'Secondary II' (121,200) is excluded, enrolment would be 3,359,900, resulting in an enrolment rate of 99 per cent (not 102 per cent). Using the adjusted figure, the drop in enrolment from 1968 would be 484,200, or 13 per cent over the seven-year period.

(iii) Grades 9 and above

The population in the secondary education age group (14-17) is still growing but at slower rates than in the 1950s and 1960s. Thus, most rapid increases in enrolment occurred in the late 1950s and early 1960s and then tapered off.

But during the entire period enrolment increased steadily, and even more quickly than the population, hence the rising enrolment rates. The apparent decline in 1975 was caused by transfer of Quebec 'Secondary II' enrolment to the 'Grades 1 to 8' category. If Quebec 'Secondary II' were included at this level, 1975 enrolment would be 1,831,900, and the enrolment rate 98 per cent (not 91 per cent as shown in table 2). The following tabulation shows percentage increases in enrolment and population at five-year intervals:

	Enrolment %	Population %
1951 to 1955	28.6	11.1
1955 to 1960	55.5	25.6
1960 to 1965	58.5	26.4
1965 to 1970	33.3	13.7
1970 to 1975[1]	9.9	10.1

1. Calculated using recast 1975 enrolment.

(iv) Post-secondary

The population aged 18-24, from which about 80 per cent of post-secondary students are drawn, is also still growing, and will continue to do so for several more years.

Total post-secondary enrolment increased more than six-fold between 1951 and 1975, from 91,100 to 592,100. The participation rate rose from 6 per cent of the 18 to 24-year-old population to 20 per cent. During the same period, non-university enrolment increased eight times, from 27,600 to 221,000, and university enrolment almost six times, from 63,500 to 371,100.

University education showed the fastest rate of expansion in the late 1950s and early 1960s, while non-university institutions experienced the greatest growth in the second half of the 1960s. This reflects the fact that in the early years, the non-university sector consisted mainly of teacher colleges, technical institutes and nursing schools. The most significant expansion occurred after community colleges were established across the country beginning in 1967 and 1968, in response to the need for broader post-secondary educational opportunities than those available at the time. The following tabulation of percentage increases in enrolment in five-year intervals demonstrates relative growth:

Percentage increases in post-secondary enrolment

	Non-university %	University %	Total %
1951-1955	20.7	14.5	16.4
1955-1960	48.3	56.4	52.0
1960-1965	40.5	79.6	69.8
1965-1970	139.3	51.6	73.8
1970-1975	33.1	19.9	24.5

As a result of the popularity and rapid expansion of non-university education, the ratio of university to non-university enrolment fell from 2.3 in 1951 to 1.7 in 1975.

W21-29.   Summary of total full-time teachers, by level of instruction, Canada, 1960 to 1975

SOURCE: *Education in Canada,* 1974 to 1976.

To keep up with escalating enrolment more teachers were needed, but the rate of increase in their number was even greater than was occasioned by enrolment growth. Since data on teachers by level of instruction are available only from 1960, the comparisons with enrolment can be made from that year on. While total enrolment increased by 42 per cent over the 15-year period, the number of teachers rose by 84 per cent.

A few corresponding percentages of teachers and enrolment illustrate the relative rates of growth. At the elementary-secondary level, the number of teachers increased by 68 per cent, enrolment by 33 per cent; at the post-secondary level the figures are 305 per cent and 263 per cent. The one exception is the sub-category of post-secondary non-university education, where enrolment grew at a faster rate than teachers; 347 per cent as opposed to 322 per cent.

W30-40.   Persons leaving full-time studies and potentially available to the labour force, by sex and educational attainment, Canada, 1971 to 1975

SOURCE: *Projected Potential Labour Force Entrants from the Canadian Educational System, 1971 to 1985,* a study by Z.E. Zsigmond and Edith Rechnitzer, Education Division, Statistics Canada.

W41-46.   Total expenditures on education, by level, Canada, selected years, 1950 to 1974

SOURCE: *Financial Statistics of Education, 1974-75.*

W47-60.   Total expenditures on education, by source of funds, and percentage distribution, Canada, selected years, 1950 to 1974

SOURCE: *Financial Statistics of Education, 1974-75.*

W61-66.   Total expenditures on education in relation to socio-economic and demographic variables, Canada, selected years, 1950 to 1974

SOURCE: *Financial Statistics of Education, 1974-75.*

In no other aspect of education was the recent 'explosion' more apparent than in the field of finance. Although figures are available from 1950, expenditures in the 1950s were so small relative to later years that comparisons presented here cover only the years from 1960 to 1974.

Figures in table 5 indicate a more than sixfold rise in expenditures, from $1,706 million in 1960 to an estimated $11,049 million in 1974. Applying this yardstick to various levels of education, expenditures for elementary-secondary education increased 5.4 times (from $1,328 to $7,191 million), and for post-secondary, almost 10 times (from $331 to $3,165 million). The largest percentage rise in spending was at the post-secondary non-university level, an almost fourteenfold increase (from $58 to $792 million). Expenditures on university education increased almost ninefold (from $273 to $2,372 million).

Huge as these sums are, there are indications of an effort in recent years to restrain this rapid growth. Series W61-66 show that, in relation to leading economic indicators, expenditures on education reached their peak in 1970, amounting to 9 per cent of the GNP and 12 per cent of personal income. Thereafter, percentages declined each year, to 8 per cent and 10 per cent respectively, by 1974. These declining percentages indicate that other social concerns, notably welfare, are making greater claims on the public purse. It has been calculated that in 1968 education accounted for 22 per cent of all public expenditures, the largest single item, compared with 16 per cent for social welfare. According to estimates, by 1973 the order of priorities had been reversed: 19 per cent for education and 21 per cent for welfare.

Nevertheless, as shown in series W61-66, expenditures on education per capita of population, labour force, and full-time student, have been growing without pause. Probably the most significant ratio is that of the labour force which, after all, carries the burden of all spending in one way or another. Expenditures on education increased fourfold, from $266 per labour force member in 1960 to $1,144 by 1974.

Obviously, expenditures of that magnitude, in excess of $11 billion in 1974, could not be financed by individuals. In recognition of the national importance of education, the money had to be collected in the form of various taxes and disbursed by government. As the needs increased so did the share of funds provided by the public sector. This is clearly reflected in series W47-60. From 1960 to 1974, public funding rose from 89 per cent of the total to 92 per cent, while private contributions (fees and other private sources) fell from 11 per cent to 8 per cent. All the same, the private sector still plays an important role - its contribution increased almost fivefold, from $191 to $901 million, in this period.

Elementary and Secondary Education (Series W67-306)

W67-93. Total enrolment and percentage of average daily attendance in public elementary and secondary schools, Canada and provinces, selected years, 1866 to 1975

SOURCE: for 1974 to 1975, Statistics Canada, unpublished data; for 1952 to 1973, *Enrolment in Elementary and Secondary Schools in Canada*, various issues, and unpublished data; for 1951, Economic Council of Canada, Staff Study No. 25, unpublished summaries; for 1920 to 1950 *Survey of Elementary and Secondary Education in Canada*; for 1915 and prior years, *Historical Statistics of Canada*, first edition.

Public school enrolment shown in Series W67-93 is a continuation of series V1-20 of the previous edition. In addition to provincial figures, those for the territories and Department of National Defence overseas schools have been added, where available. Thus the series is more complete. Since the late 1950s, more accurate information than previously available was assembled and published. As far as possible, irregular trends in the years before 1940 have been corrected, either by reference to original reports or by estimation and interpolation, so that the figures give a truer picture of the development of public schools.

Quebec's complex school system (public and private for both Roman Catholic and Protestant denominations) resulted in greatly varying figures for the period from Confederation to 1930. By reference to original annual reports in some years, and interpolation in others, figures have been revised or estimated to reflect more closely than before the development of the public school system in that province.

In other provinces, three estimates were made to fill gaps: in Prince Edward Island for 1870 and 1875, and in Manitoba for 1875.

W94-149. Total enrolment in elementary and secondary schools, by control, Canada and provinces, selected years, 1920 to 1975

SOURCE: for 1955 to 1975, *Education in Canada*, various issues, and *Elementary-secondary School Enrolment*, 1973-74; for 1940 to 1950, *Survey of Elementary and Secondary Education*, 1959-60; for 1920 to 1935, annual *Survey of Education*.

Series W94-149 show the trends of all elementary and secondary enrolment over the last 55 years. Enrolment by grade, sex and control of schools may be found in Statistics Canada's *Historical Compendium of Education Statistics*.

W150-191. Full-time teachers in public elementary and secondary schools, by sex, Canada and provinces, selected years, 1867 to 1975

SOURCE: for 1972 to 1975, *Education in Canada*, 1974, 1975 and 1976; for 1940 to 1971, *Salaries and Qualifications of Teachers in Public Elementary and Secondary Schools*, and *Education in Canada*, various issues; for 1920 to 1935, annual and biennial *Surveys of Education*; for 1867 to 1915 *Historical Statistical Survey of Education*, 1921, provincial annual reports, and *Historical Statistics of Canada*; for 1870 to 1950, Quebec data obtained from *Quebec Yearbook*, 1914 and 1954.

The number of teachers in public schools corresponds with series V68-78 of the previous edition. As with enrolment, teachers in the territories and in schools overseas are included. Previously published figures have been amended if more recent publications or new sources of information warranted a revision.

The figures for the early years of this series, mostly in the last century, are questionable for at least two provinces: Ontario and British Columbia.

The number of full-time teachers in Ontario from 1867 to 1900 appears to be under-reported, resulting in pupil-teacher ratios ranging from 77.7 in 1867 to 48.9 in 1900. Comparable ratios in three eastern provinces from 1870 to 1900 were: Nova Scotia, from 49.3 to 39.5; New Brunswick, from 35.2 to 36.8; and Quebec, from 39.2 to 26.9. Only in 1925 did Ontario's pupil-teacher ratio drop below the mid-or low-40s (37.5).

An even more striking case of teacher under-enumeration occurred in British Columbia for the years 1885 to 1910, producing obviously improbable ratios ranging from 550 in 1885 to 100.7 in 1905 and 61.4 in 1910.

Therefore, data on Ontario and British Columbia teachers are questionable up to 1920 for the former, and up to 1910 for the latter. If there are inaccuracies in other provinces, they are not apparent.

Alternatively, in Quebec the number of full-time teachers may have been overstated. This is suggested by a relatively low pupil-teacher ratio: as early as 1885 it was 28.4, and remained in the mid-20s up to modern times.

W192-247. Full-time teachers in elementary and secondary schools, by control, Canada and provinces, selected years, 1930 to 1975

SOURCE: for 1960 to 1975, *Education in Canada*, various issues (revised); for 1930 to 1959, annual and biennial *Surveys of Education*.

The total number of teachers in all elementary and secondary schools (including private and federal) is shown in the above table.

W248-259. Percentage of full-time teachers in public elementary and secondary schools, by highest university degree held and sex, provinces, selected years, 1952 to 1973

SOURCE: 1972 to 1973 *Education in Canada*, 1976; for 1952 to 1971, *Salaries and Qualifications of Teachers in Public Elementary and Secondary Schools*, various issues.

This table classifies public school teachers by sex and the highest university degree they hold. Data concerning qualifications of Quebec teachers are not available, therefore, with some exceptions (indicated in the footnotes), totals represent nine provinces.

To make the data easier to interpret, the numbers of teachers with various degrees are shown as percentages of the total, by sex and for both sexes combined. Hence, in 1952 only 22 per cent of all teachers had university degrees, while 78 per cent had none. By 1973, more than half had degrees (57 per cent).

Although there were fewer men teachers, a higher proportion of them had university degrees - at each level of degree and in all years. However, the women upgraded their educational credentials at a faster rate than men. For example, a comparison of 1952 with 1973 reveals that between those years at the 'Master and higher' level the rate of increase for men was 2.5, and 2.8 for women. At the bachelor's level, narrowing of the gap was even faster: a rate of increase of 1.6 for men and 3.7 for women. Even so, men teachers on the whole have higher educational standing. In 1973, 77 per cent of them had university degrees versus 41 per cent of the women. (The comparable percentages in 1952 were 46 per cent and 12 per cent.)

A provincial breakdown indicates that those provinces which started with the lowest percentages of teachers, men and women, with university degrees, showed the greatest rate of upgrading over the span of 21 years. The proportion of university-educated teachers in provinces where their percentages were relatively high in 1952 increased more slowly.

The following figures illustrate this point:

Teachers qualifications — public elementary and secondary schools

	Percentage of teachers with university degrees		Rate of increase
	1952	1973	
Newfoundland	4.4	51.6	11.73
Prince Edward Island	5.1	38.6[1]	7.57
Nova Scotia	19.4	49.9	2.57
New Brunswick	11.4	52.3	4.59
Ontario	24.6	52.5	2.13
Manitoba	19.4	59.4	3.06
Saskatchewan	13.3	52.5	3.95
Alberta	35.5	73.8	2.08
British Columbia	36.2	66.9	1.85
9 Provinces	21.8	57.0[2]	2.61[2]

1. 1972 data.
2. Excluding Prince Edward Island in 1973.

Thus, in Newfoundland and Prince Edward Island, where only 4 per cent and 5 per cent of the teachers had degrees in 1952, the rates of increase were about twelvefold and eightfold, respectively. At the other end of the scale, Alberta and British Columbia, 36 per cent of whose teachers were degree-holders in 1952, had growth rates of 2.1 and 1.9, although they did retain their high standing in the overall proportions of teachers with degrees.

Probably the most significant change in the composition of the teaching force over those 21 years was a fourfold increase in the number of male teachers (from 20,341 to 80,881) while female teachers only doubled their numbers (48,077 to 105,367). As a result, the percentage of male teachers went from 30 per cent in 1952 to 43 per cent in 1973. Considering public school teachers in all provinces and territories (series W150-191), between 1950 and 1975, the number of male teachers increased 4.6 times versus 2.3 times for females, and the proportion of male teachers increased from 27 per cent to 42 per cent. Thus, teaching at the elementary and secondary levels is no longer an overwhelmingly female occupation, as was the case in the first half of the century when the percentage of men hovered between 20 per cent and 25 per cent, and in 1920 was even as low as 17 per cent. The rapid growth of secondary education since 1951 has been one of several factors contributing to this development.

W260-274. Statistics of centralized public school libraries, Canada and provinces, 1958 to 1967 and 1972

SOURCE: for 1972, Statistics Canada, unpublished data; for 1958 to 1967, *Survey of Libraries*, part II: *Academic Libraries*, various issues.

A new table, summarizing the operations of centralized libraries in publicly operated elementary-secondary schools, has been added to demonstrate how quickly this essential aid to education expanded between 1958 and 1972. Similar data for each province are shown in *Historical Compendium of Education Statistics*.

W275-300. Operating and capital expenditures of public school boards on elementary and secondary education, Canada and provinces, selected years, 1900 to 1974

SOURCE: for 1959 to 1974, *Financial Statistics of Education*, various issues; for 1900 to 1955, *Historical Statistics of Education*, revised.

W301-306. Expenditures on elementary and secondary education, by source of funds, Canada, selected years, 1950 to 1974

SOURCE: for 1950 to 1974, *Financial Statistics of Education*, 1974-75.

These tables present expenditures on elementary and secondary education. Series W275-300 is comparable to the Series V158-170 in the original volume, except that school board expenditures are all-inclusive, i.e., they include not only provincial grants and local assessments but also income from fees and other sources. The trend in expenditures on education has already been discussed; it is sufficient to observe that while enrolment in publicly controlled schools grew by only 37 per cent, between 1960 and 1970, these expenditures increased almost fourfold, resulting in a large rise in the cost per pupil.

Series W301-306 show all expenditures on elementary and secondary education. In addition to public school boards, provincial administrative expenditures and federal funds spent on federal schools are included. School boards represent the largest part of these expenditures, amounting to almost 84 per cent in 1974. Classification by source permits a quick assessment of the importance of public funds at this level of education. In 1960, public sources provided 94 per cent of the total; by 1974, the share had increased to 96 per cent. A provincial breakdown is given in *Historical Compendium of Education Statistics.*

Post-secondary Education (Series W307-532)

W307-339. Full-time enrolment in post-secondary non-university institutions, by sex, Canada and provinces, 1955 and 1958 to 1975

SOURCE: for 1960 to 1975 *Education in Canada,* 1975 and 1976; for 1955 to 1959 Statistics Canada, unpublished data.

For the first time, enrolment in post-secondary non-university institutions from 1955 to 1975 is presented. It represents students in post-secondary courses only (i.e., excludes trade courses) in community colleges (e.g., CEGEP's in Quebec; CAAT's in Ontario); institutes of technology; teachers' colleges, and comparable institutions.

Expansion of this type of education began in the mid-1960s. Therefore, if 1960 is used as a base year, the rapid development can be demonstrated. In 15 years, from 1960 to 1975, enrolment increased more than four times. It is interesting to note that the percentage of women enrolled declined from 71 per cent to 51 per cent. The explanation is that in the early 1960s, enrolment in teachers' colleges and schools of nursing, both predominantly female, represented a majority of the enrolment at this level. In the 1970s, teachers' colleges have been practically eliminated and teacher training transferred to universities (where it contributed to the rise in the proportion of female students). At the same time, nursing diploma courses in most provinces have been shortened from three to two years. In addition, as new types of courses were introduced, particularly technology and business programs, the proportion of male students rose steadily.

W340-438. Full-time university enrolment, by sex, Canada and provinces, selected years, 1920 to 1975

SOURCE: for 1960 to 1975, *Education in Canada,* 1974, 1975 and 1976; for 1955 to 1959, Economic Council of Canada, Staff Study No. 25, unpublished summaries; for 1920 to 1950, *Historical Statistics of Canada,* series V184-195 and V196-206.

The above table combines series V184-195 and V196-206 of the previous edition, and extends them to 1975. Both Canada and provincial data are shown, and permit comparisons over a span of 55 years. Two features of the time series stand out: (1) total enrolment increased very rapidly after 1960 (3.3 times to 1975), and (2) the proportion of females went from 24 per cent to 44 per cent during those 15 years.

W439-455. Full-time university undergraduate enrolment, by field of specialization and sex, Canada, selected years, 1861 to 1975

SOURCE: for 1962 to 1975, *Education in Canada,* 1975 and 1976; for 1958 to 1961, Economic Council of Canada, Staff Study No. 25, unpublished summaries; for 1920 to 1955, *Historical Statistics of Canada,* series V184-195 for total Canada figures; breakdown by specialization: *Survey of Higher Education,* 1950 to 1955, and *Survey of Education,* 1919 to 1949; for 1861 to 1911, *A History of Higher Education in Canada, 1663-1960,* by Professor Robin S. Harris, University of Toronto Press, 1976.

Series W439-455 introduce a new series: undergraduate enrolment by field of specialization and sex. Although figures at the Canada level are presented from 1861 to 1975, developments in the 1960s and 1970s are most noteworthy. Again, the large increase in the proportion of women (from 25 per cent in 1960 to 42 per cent in 1975) is evident. In addition, this table shows the relative decline of certain professional courses, as enrolment in general arts and science increased. There were declines in the share of engineering, medicine, pharmacy and dentistry. On the other hand, certain professions underwent considerable enrolment growth, notably education and commerce.

The proportion in the general arts and science courses combined went from 51 per cent to 55 per cent.

Data in the above series appear reasonable throughout, and have been reliably reported since the 1950s. Special credit is due to Professor Robin S. Harris of the University of Toronto, from whose well-researched volume, *A History of Higher Education in Canada, 1663-1960,* information for the years 1861 to 1911 in this table was taken.

Provincial figures are given in *Historical Compendium of Education Statistics,.* However, these data are available only from 1962.

W456-465. Full-time graduate enrolment, by broad field of specialization and sex, Canada, 1970 to 1975

SOURCE: for 1970 to 1975, *Education in Canada,* 1973 to 1976.

A similar series has been prepared for graduate students classified by broad field of specialization (series 340-438), but at this level data are available for only six years: 1970 to 1975, and only for Canada as a whole.

W466-474. Part-time university enrolment, by sex, Canada, 1962 to 1975

SOURCE: for 1962 to 1975, *Education in Canada,* 1975 and 1976.

Another new series, shown in the above table, gives part-time university enrolment from 1962 to 1975. Part-time enrolment increased much faster than full-time: 32 per cent vs. 163 per cent. The proportion of females enrolled part-time also grew impressively, from 38 per cent to 51 per cent in 1975. These statistics suggest that education is increasingly becoming a continuous process throughout life.

W475-485. Full-time university teachers, Canada and provinces, selected years, 1920 to 1975

SOURCE: for 1960 to 1975, *Education in Canada*, 1973 to 1976, for 1958 to 1959, Statistics Canada, unpublished data; for 1955 to 1957, *Historical Statistics of Canada*; for 1920 to 1950, *Survey of Higher Education*, (Catalogue 81-211), various issues.

W486-503. Full-time university teachers, by highest degree held and sex, Canada, 1958 to 1974

SOURCE: for 1970 to 1974, *Education in Canada*, 1973 to 1976; for 1958 to 1969, Statistics Canada, unpublished data.

The above two tables deal with university teachers. Series W475-485 are a continuation to 1975 of series V215-225 in the former volume.

Series W486-503 are new series that classify university teachers according to the highest degree they hold and by sex. Since values are expressed as percentages, it is easy to observe a general trend.

Between 1960 and 1974 the percentage with doctorates increased from 44 per cent to 57 per cent, however, the proportion of women PhD's rose at a rate faster than that of men (1.5 compared with 1.3 for men). As the proportion of doctorates grew, the proportions holding lower degrees diminished in all categories and for both sexes. However, the rates of decline for men in the master's and bachelor's categories were much greater than for women. In fact, the proportion of female teachers with a master's degree declined only marginally in these 14 years, from 43 per cent to 41 per cent.

W504-512. Degrees awarded by Canadian universities and colleges, by sex, Canada, selected years, 1831 to 1973

SOURCE: for 1961 to 1973, *Education in Canada*, 1975 and 1976; for 1920 to 1960, *Survey of Higher Education*, part II; various issues; for 1831 to 1916, *A History of Higher Education in Canada, 1661-1960*, by Professor Robin S. Harris, University of Toronto Press, 1976.

Statistics Canada has reasonably complete and reliable data in this series from 1920. Information for 1831 to 1916 was, again, derived from Professor Harris's book.

With two significant changes, series W504-512 correspond to series V207-214 in the previous edition: bachelor's degrees have been extended from 1920 back to 1831, and honourary doctorates have been excluded.

Using 1960 as a base year, it is possible to assess the relative increase for various degrees granted. The great expansion of university education in the sixties meant that there was a concurrent demand for university teachers with higher degrees. Hence, it is not surprising that the number of doctorates and master's degrees grew at a faster rate than bachelor's degrees. From 1960 to 1973, doctorates increased 6.2 times, masters 4.6 times, and bachelors 3.8 times.

The proportion of women receiving all three types of degrees rose, but at varying rates. The proportion of masters increased most, by a factor of 1.7 (from 16 per cent to 27 per cent), and doctorates by 1.4 (from 9 per cent to 12 per cent). Thus females are approaching parity with males at the bachelor and master levels but lag considerably behind in doctorates.

W513-518. Statistics of university libraries, Canada, 1958 to 1972

SOURCE: for 1972, Statistics Canada, unpublished data; for 1970 to 1971, *University and College Libraries in Canada*; for 1958 to 1967, *Survey of Libraries*, part II: Academic Libraries, various issues.

Table 24 is a new time series showing data on university libraries from 1958 to 1972. During that period, coverage of the survey was expanded twice. Only since 1970 have all institutions classified as 'universities' been surveyed. Nevertheless, data from 1961 are roughly comparable, as in the 1960s those omitted were small colleges, mostly schools of theology, with enrolment of less than 100.

If 1961 is used as the base year, by 1972, the student population served increased threefold (total full-time enrolment grew 2.9 times). Library holdings (books, periodicals, etc.) increased almost four times; staff, nearly six times; and operating expenditures about elevenfold.

W519-532. Operating and capital expenditures of universities, by source of funds, Canada, selected years, 1920 to 1974

SOURCE: for 1950 to 1974, *Financial Statistics of Education*, 1974-75; for 1920 to 1945, Statistics Canada, unpublished data.

The following percentage distributions demonstrate important changes in sources of funds:

Expenditures of universities, 1960 and 1974
Sources of funds

	Operating		Capital	
	1960 (%)	1974 (%)	1960 (%)	1974 (%)
Governments:				
Federal	21.9	9.4	11.4	6.5
Provincial	41.9	69.7	45.2	40.4[1]
Municipal	0.2	–	0.4	–
Sub-total	64.0	79.0	57.0	46.9
Fees	25.2	13.8	–	–
Other	10.8	7.1	43.0	53.1[1]
Sub-total	36.0	20.9	43.0	53.1
Total	100.0	100.0	100.0	100.0
In $ millions	$182.6	$1,838.0	$79.8	$188.8
Add: capital	79.8	188.8		
Grand total	$262.4	$2,026.8		
% capital to grand total	30.4	9.3		

1. The apparent decline in provincial capital grants is due, in part, to the change in the classification of outlays of the Ontario Capital Aid Corporation. Previously, they were treated as grants, but in 1974 were included in "borrowings". Had this item ($17.3 million) been included in grants, the provincial share would have been 50 per cent and "other" sources 44 per cent. In 1973, provincial grants amounted to 65 per cent.

This table presents financial statistics (operating and capital) for universities, classified by source of funds, from 1920 to 1974. Expenditures in 1920 are so insignificant relative to the 1970s that any comparison is unrealistic. Therefore, as with other variables, 1960 is taken as the base year. Operating and capital expenditures are shown separately because the latter fluctuate widely, e.g., in 1960 they amounted to $78.9 million, reached a peak of $392.2 million in 1970 and declined to $188.9 million in 1974, with considerable ups and downs between. Moreover, the methods of financing operating and capital expenditures differ significantly, especially the former which have been greatly affected by the Federal-Provincial Fiscal Arrangements Act of 1967.

Several points are apparent. During these 14 years, operating expenditures grew tenfold, while capital outlays increased only 2.4 times, although 1974 was not the peak of capital spending.

Public financing has become more important, with a corresponding decline in the private sector. All the increase has been at the provincial level, while the federal share dropped significantly. However, federal transfers of funds to the provinces equalled 50 per cent of total operating expenditures. These federal transfers have been rising rapidly from $422 million in 1967-68 to an estimated $1.4 billion in 1975-76. However, since the transfers to provincial governments are made unconditionally, and expenditures are made at the discretion of the provincial governments, these sums are included in provincial grants and officially treated as such. Federal departments still make significant grants for research and research facilities, but the share has declined.

Whereas student fees represented 25 per cent of all operating expenditures in 1960, they fell to 14 per cent in 1974, despite a great increase in enrolment. Other private sources also declined in relative importance, from 11 per cent to 7 per cent. However, in absolute amounts, both rose: fees fivefold, other sources 6.6 times. These shifts in the relative importance of sources testify to the fact that university education requires large-scale government support.

Most provincial governments provide operating grants, based on formulae related to enrolment. Similar schemes or budgetary grants apply to capital expenditures. In the latter field, private funds still play an important role (44 per cent in 1974 and 43 per cent in 1960). These private contributions include private and corporate donations, income from endowments, fees for services rendered, profits from the sale of assets, and even borrowing when necessary.

Series W1-9. Summary of total full-time enrolment,[1] by level of study, Canada, selected years, 1951 to 1975
(thousands)

Year[2]	Total	Pre-grade 1 to end of secondary					Post-secondary[3]		
		Pre-grade 1[4]	Grades 1–8	Grade 9 and higher	Blind and deaf	Subtotal	Non-university	University	Subtotal
	1	2	3	4	5	6	7	8	9
1975	6,186	399	3,481[5]	1,711[6]	4	5,594	221	371	592
1974	6,232	424	3,432	1,814	4	5,674	211	347	558
1973	6,257	389	3,531	1,799	4	5,723	202	332	534
1972	6,330	386	3,670	1,757	4	5,817	191	322	513
1971	6,364	377	3,763	1,723	4	5,867	174	323	497
1970	6,364 r	402 r	3,816 r	1,666 r	4	5,888 r	166	310	476
1969	6,262 r	405 r	3,841 r	1,576 r	4	5,825 r	143	294	437
1968	6,093	374	3,844	1,476	4	5,698	130	266	395
1967	5,870	328	3,819	1,366	4	5,517	99	254	353
1966	5,667	295	3,754 r	1,304 r	4	5,356	80	230	311
1965	5,475	268	3,680 r	1,250 r	4	5,201	69	204	274
1964	5,241	204	3,619	1,171	4	4,997	66	178	244
1963	5,026	184	3,526	1,091	3	4,805	62	158	220
1962	4,809	169	3,438	1,002	3	4,613	56	141	197
1961	4,595	157	3,357	895	3	4,413	53	129	182
1960	4,368	146	3,267	789	3	4,204	49	114	163
1959	4,157	138	3,155	715	..	4,009	46	102	148
1958	3,964	132	3,033	662	..	3,827	42	95	137
1955	3,397	103	2,681	507	..	3,291	33	73	106
1951	2,716	84	2,147	395	..	2,625	28	64	91

[1] Does not include enrolment in trade schools, private business colleges and apprenticeship programs.
[2] School year beginning in the year shown.
[3] By type of institution.
[4] Includes private kindergartens and nursery schools from 1965 to 1974.
[5] Includes Quebec "Secondary II"; increase due to change in classification.
[6] Excludes Quebec "Secondary II"; decrease due to change in classification.

Series W10-20. Summary of total full-time enrolment, by level of study, related to relevant population, Canada, selected years, 1951 to 1975
(percentages)

Year[1]	Total enrolment		Pre-grade 1 to end of secondary					Post-secondary[2]			
			Pre-grade 1[3]	Grades 1–8	Grade 9 and higher	Blind and deaf	Subtotal	Non-university	Under-graduate	Graduate	Subtotal
	0–99 years	5–24 years	5 years	6–13 years	14–17 years	6–17 years	5–17 years	18–21 years	18–21 years	22–24 years	18–24 years
	10	11	12	13	14	15	16	17	18	19	20
1975	27.1	71.2	107.6	102.1[4]	91.1[5]	0.1	98.9	12.3	18.4	3.3	19.5
1974	27.8	72.1[3]	117.8	98.0	98.1	0.1	99.4	12.1	17.7	3.2	19.0
1973	28.3	72.8	107.7	98.3[5]	98.8[3]	0.1	99.1	12.0	17.6	3.3	18.9
1972	29.0	73.4	99.9	100.3	98.4	0.1	99.8	11.6	17.3	3.3	18.4
1971	29.5	74.3	91.7	101.6	97.6	0.1	99.8	11.2	18.5	3.2	18.5
1970	29.9	75.2	91.0 r	103.4 r	97.7 r	0.1	100.9[3]	10.6	17.6	3.1	18.1
1969	29.8 r	75.3 r	89.3 r	104.5 r	94.7 r	0.1	100.5 r	9.4	17.4	3.0	17.3
1968	29.4	74.8	80.9	105.6	90.8	0.1	99.5	8.9	16.4	2.7	16.4
1967	28.8	74.0	71.4	106.3	86.1	0.1	97.8	7.1	16.4	2.7	15.4
1966	28.3	73.7	62.9	106.1	87.3	0.1	97.4	5.9	15.6	2.4	14.2
1965	27.9	73.5	58.0	106.7	83.8	0.1	96.2	5.6	15.0	2.2	13.4
1964	27.2	72.6	44.6	107.4	80.8	0.1	94.7	5.6	13.9	1.8	12.5
1963	26.5	72.0	40.9	107.0	78.8	0.1	93.6	5.6	13.1	1.5	11.9
1962	25.9	71.2	38.8	106.3	76.1	0.1	92.5	5.2	12.5	1.2	11.1
1961	25.2	70.2	36.7	106.0	72.0	0.1	91.2	5.3	11.9	1.1	10.6
1960	24.4	68.7	34.4	106.7	66.4	0.1	90.0	5.0	10.8	0.9	9.7
1959	23.8	67.5	33.4	107.0	63.2	..	89.2	4.8	10.0	0.7	8.9
1958	24.3	66.3	32.4	106.8	61.2	..	88.4	4.5	9.5	0.7	8.3
1955	21.6	63.4	27.6	108.2	53.7	..	86.7	3.8	7.8	0.5	6.8
1951	19.4	58.1	27.7	106.7	46.4	..	82.9	3.2	7.0	0.6	6.0

[1] School year beginning in the year shown.
[2] Enrolments by institution (non-university and university) were used to calculate these ratios.
[3] Includes private kindergartens and nursery schools from 1965 to 1974 inclusive.
[4] Includes Quebec "Secondary II"; increase due to change in classification.
[5] Excludes Quebec "Secondary II"; decrease due to change in classification.

Series W21-29. Summary of total full-time teachers, by level of instruction, Canada, 1960 to 1975
(thousands)

Year[1]	Total	Pre-grade 1 to end of secondary					Post-secondary		
		Pre-grade 1[2]	Grades 1–8	Grade 9 and higher	Blind and deaf	Subtotal	Non-university	University	Subtotal
	21	22	23	24	25	26	27	28	29
1975	323	18	158	98	1	275	17	31	48
1974	324	20	154	103	1	278	16	30	46
1973	322	19	155	103	1	277	16	29	45
1972	322	18	158	102	1	278	16	29	44
1971	317	17	158	100	1	276	14	28	42
1970	313	18	160	97	1	276	12	25	37
1969	304	18	159	94	1	271	11	23	33
1968	287	16	155	86	1	258	9	20	29
1967	271	13	154	76	1	244	7	19	26
1966	249	12	146	68	1	226	6	17	23
1965	232	11	139	62	1	212	5	14	20
1964	222	8	139	58	1	205	5	12	17
1963	210	7	134	53	—	194	5	11	16
1962	200	7	130	49	—	186	4	10	14
1961	188	6	125	43	—	174	4	9	13
1960	176	6	121	37	—	164	4	8	12

[1] School year beginning in the year shown.   [2] Includes private kindergartens and nursery schools from 1965 to 1974.

Series W30-40. Persons leaving full-time studies and potentially available to the labour force, by sex and education attainment, Canada, 1966 and 1971 to 1975
(thousands)

Year and sex		Total	Elementary			Post-secondary						Total post-secondary
			Some	Completed	Total	Some	Certificate or diploma	Bachelor's or first professional degree	Master's degree or graduate diploma	Doctorate (earned)	Subtotal	
		30	31	32	33	34	35	36	37	38	39	40
1975	Male	288	138	45	183	59	15	26	5	1	46	105
	Female	255	106	63	169	40	22	22	2	—	47	86
	Total	543	244	108	352	98	37	49	7	1	93	191
1974	Male	299	140	46	185	67	16	26	4	1	47	114
	Female	265	118	65	183	39	22	20	2	—	44	83
	Total	565	257	111	368	106	37	46	6	1	91	197
1973	Male	286	150	41	191	49	15	26	4	1	46	96
	Female	250	113	64	176	33	22	18	2	—	41	74
	Total	537	263	105	367	82	37	43	6	1	88	170
1972	Male	282	146	40	187	50	14	27	5	1	46	95
	Female	237	105	65	170	26	21	18	2	—	41	67
	Total	519	251	105	357	75	35	45	7	1	87	162
1971	Male	271	146	40	186	44	12	24	5	1	41	85
	Female	247	119	64	182	27	21	16	2	—	38	65
	Total	518	264	103	368	71	33	39	6	1	80	150
1966	Male	187	102	49	151	13	7	14	2	—	23	36
	Female	174	88	55	143	8	15	8	1	—	23	31
	Total	361	190	104	294	21	21	22	3	—	46	67

Series W41-46. Total expenditures on education, by level, Canada, selected years, 1950 to 1974
(thousands of dollars)

Year	Total	Elementary and secondary	Post-secondary[1]			Vocational
			Non-university	University	Subtotal	
	41	**42**	**43**	**44**	**45**	**46**
1974	11,048,813	7,190,845	792,408	2,372,171	3,164,579	693,389
1973	9,635,215	6,312,881	656,527	2,029,910	2,686,437	635,897
1972	8,669,208	5,624,968	572,993	1,867,801	2,440,794	603,446
1971	8,349,705	5,389,256	530,023	1,864,517	2,394,540	565,909
1970	7,676,049	4,880,426	429,995	1,790,812	2,220,807	574,816
1969	6,624,045	4,281,421	346,573	1,603,781	1,950,354	392,270
1968	5,777,133	3,775,118	251,203	1,359,972	1,611,175	390,840
1967	5,025,457	3,230,038	200,077	1,243,411	1,443,488	351,931
1966	4,155,245	2,790,942	124,965	991,647	1,116,612	247,691
1965	3,399,505	2,410,798	98,763	736,583	835,346	153,361
1964	2,889,947	2,066,156	93,112	597,326	690,438	133,353
1963	2,540,807	1,879,077	82,108	461,397	543,505	118,225
1962	2,377,937	1,808,782	73,633	378,693	452,326	116,829
1961	1,930,671	1,499,459	58,428	310,629	369,057	62,155
1960	1,705,986	1,328,294	57,600	272,940	330,540	47,152
1959	1,474,784	1,162,397	46,716	229,077	275,793	36,594
1955	829,132	674,446	30,997	104,443	135,440	19,246
1950	438,751	359,124	11,600	55,247	66,847	12,780

[1] Includes operating and capital expenditures of institutions, federal and provincial departmental expenditures and student aid.

Series W47-60. Total expenditures on education, by source of funds, and percentage distribution, Canada, selected years, 1950 to 1974
(series W47-53 in thousands of dollars; series W54-60 in per cent)

Year	Governments				Fees	Other	Total	Governments				Fees	Other	Total
	Federal[1]	Provincial	Municipal	Subtotal				Federal[1]	Provincial	Municipal	Subtotal			
	47	**48**	**49**	**50**	**51**	**52**	**53**	**54**	**55**	**56**	**57**	**58**	**59**	**60**
1974	1,056,478	7,028,879	2,062,773	10,148,130	470,487	430,196	11,048,813	9.6	63.6	18.7	91.9	4.2	3.9	100.0
1973	984,773	5,847,196	1,940,013	8,771,982	436,581	426,652	9,635,215	10.2	60.7	20.2	91.1	4.5	4.4	100.0
1972	943,829	5,257,033	1,777,306	7,978,168	414,434	276,606	8,669,208	10.9	60.6	20.5	92.0	4.8	3.2	100.0
1971	923,993	4,966,741	1,713,572	7,604,306	386,806	358,593	8,349,705	11.1	595	20.5	91.1	4.6	4.3	100.0
1970	930,061	4,315,985	1,719,354	6,965,400	320,509	390,140	7,676,049	12.1	56.2	22.4	90.7	4.2	5.1	100.0
1969	756,522	3,656,000	1,626,038	6,038,560	269,709	315,776	6,624,045	11.4	55.2	24.5	91.1	4.1	4.8	100.0
1968	658,187	3,141,058	1,477,699	5,276,944	253,081	247,108	5,777,133	11.4	54.4	25.5	91.3	4.4	4.3	100.0
1967	626,607	2,596,882	1,312,003	4,535,492	223,673	266,292	5,025,457	12.5	51.7	26.1	90.3	4.4	5.3	100.0
1966	539,852	1,984,762	1,155,367	3,679,981	220,322	254,942	4,155,245	13.0	47.8	27.8	88.6	5.3	6.1	100.0
1965	368,606	1,588,303	1,036,126	2,993,035	198,937	207,533	3,399,505	10.8	46.7	30.5	88.0	5.9	6.1	100.0
1964	290,139	1,328,324	914,588	2,533,051	168,819	188,077	2,889,947	10.0	46.0	31.6	87.6	5.9	6.5	100.0
1963	297,677	1,122,363	826,067	2,246,107	148,634	146,066	2,540,807	11.7	44.2	32.5	88.4	5.8	5.8	100.0
1962	355,255	1,035,800	739,655	2,130,710	128,244	118,983	2,377,937	14.9	43.6	31.1	89.6	5.4	5.0	100.0
1961	161,023	852,456	691,336	1,704,815	116,111	109,745	1,930,671	8.3	44.2	35.8	88.3	6.0	5.7	100.0
1960	132,218	729,243	653,207	1,514,668	102,602	88,716	1,705,986	7.8	42.7	38.3	88.8	6.0	5.2	100.0
1959	119,489	612,521	582,734	1,314,744	94,552	65,488	1,474,784	8.1	41.5	39.5	89.1	6.4	4.5	100.0
1955	56,755	342,806	343,267	742,828	50,258	36,046	829,132	6.9	41.3	41.4	89.6	6.1	4.3	100.0
1950	20,717	172,864	199,303	392,884	35,363	10,504	438,751	4.7	39.4	45.4	89.5	8.1	2.4	100.0

[1] Excludes federal transfers to provinces for post-secondary education since 1967-1968 and for teaching in minority language since 1970-1971, which are included in provincial funds.

Series W61-66. Total expenditures on education in relation to socio-economic and demographic variables, Canada, selected years, 1950 to 1974

(series W61 in thousands of dollars; series W64-66 in dollars; series W62-63 in per cent)

Year	Total expenditures on education	Expenditures related to variables				Per full-time student[1]	Year	Total expenditures on education	Expenditures related to variables				Per full-time student[1]
		Per cent of GNP	Per cent of personal income	Per capita of					Per cent of GNP	Per cent of personal income	Per capita of		
				Population	Labour force						Population	Labour force	
61	**62**	**63**	**64**	**65**	**66**		**61**	**62**	**63**	**64**	**65**	**66**
1974	11,048,813	7.5	9.4	492	1,144	1,773	1965	3,399,505	6.1	8.3	173	476	622
1973	9,635,215	7.8	9.8	436	1,038	1,542	1964	2,889,947	5.7	7.8	150	417	548
1972	8,669,208	8.2	10.3	397	975	1,371	1963	2,540,807	5.5	7.3	134	377	503
1971	8,349,705	8.8	11.3	387	967	1,312	1962	2,377,937	5.5	7.3	128	359	492
							1961	1,930,671	4.9	6.4	106	296	419
1970	7,676,049	9.0	11.5	360	917	1,207							
1969	6,624,045	8.3	10.7	315	812	1,060	1960	1,705,986	4.4	5.8	95	266	389
1968	5,777,133	8.0	10.4	279	729	948	1959	1,474,784	4.0	5.2	84	236	355
1967	5,025,457	7.6	9.9	247	653	857	1955	829,132	2.9	3.9	53	148	244
1966	4,155,245	6.7	9.0	208	560	734	1950	438,751	2.4	3.1	32	..	166

[1] Excludes students in vocational training programs.

Series W67-93. Total enrolment and percentage of average daily attendance (ADA) in public elementary and secondary schools, Canada and by province, selected years, 1866 to 1975

Year[1]	Canada		Newfoundland		Prince Edward Island		Nova Scotia		New Brunswick		Quebec		Ontario	
	Enrolment[2] '000	ADA[3] %	Enrolment '000	ADA %	Enrolment '000	ADA %	Enrolment '000	ADA %	Enrolment '000	ADA %	Enrolment '000	ADA %	Enrolment '000	ADA %
	67	**68**	**69**	**70**	**71**	**72**	**73**	**74**	**75**	**76**	**77**	**78**	**79**	**80**
1975	5,376	..	158	..	28	..	203	..	165	..	1,375	..	1,995	..
1974	5,424	..	158	..	28	..	204	..	167	..	1,423	..	1,995	..
1973	5,489	..	160	..	29	..	208	..	170	..	1,465	..	2,009	..
1972	5,587	..	162	..	29	..	211	..	174	..	1,527	..	2,028	..
1971	5,654	..	163	..	31	..	215	..	176	..	1,577	..	2,031	..
1970	5,661	..	161	..	31	..	215	..	176	..	1,589	..	2,022	..
1969	5,587	..	160	..	30	..	213	..	174	..	1,581	..	1,987	..
1968	5,463	..	157	..	29	..	209	..	172	..	1,569	..	1,931	..
1967	5,274	..	152	..	29	..	205	..	170	..	1,505	..	1,869	..
1966	5,084	..	148	..	29	..	201	..	167	..	1,441	..	1,801	..
1965	4,918	..	147	..	28	..	200	..	165	..	1,384	..	1,739	..
1964	4,752	..	144	..	28	..	198	..	164	..	1,331	..	1,674	..
1963	4,562	..	141	..	27	..	194	..	161	..	1,275	..	1,597	..
1962	4,380	90.8	138	91.1	26	89.7	191	91.8	157	91.6	1,224	91.0	1,529	88.4
1961	4,192	94.0	134	90.1	26	87.5	186	90.9	155	90.8	1,158	93.9	1,462	95.5
1960	3,997	92.4	129	90.5	25	90.2	179	93.3	152	90.8	1,098	92.2	1,389	92.3
1959	3,810	91.4	125	91.5	24	89.7	177	91.1	148	90.8	1,043	91.2	1,319	90.9
1958	3,632	91.1	119	89.4	23	85.5	171	89.7	142	89.4	999	90.7	1,250	91.7
1955	3,118	90.7	103	87.8	21	83.7	157	89.5	127	89.5	862	88.0	1,038	94.6
1950	2,391	86.5	79	85.3	19	81.0	135	85.0	106	80.3	641	87.0	768	87.9
1945	2,039	85.4	71	73.9	18	79.0	121	82.4	95	78.3	557	84.7	667	88.6
1940	2,075	87.0	67	68.6	18	69.7	117	76.5	92	75.3	588	92.9	644	90.6
1935	2,132	85.9	59	66.3	18	70.8	117	79.0	93	76.5	587	92.0	674	89.3
1930	2,099	86.0	61	66.5	18	71.3	116	75.7	89	79.8	543[r]	93.4	668	89.4
1925	1,993	77.3	59	61.8	17	66.7	112	71.5	81	72.2	500[e]	84.3	671	76.4
1920	1,834	72.7	56	60.8	18	64.0	110	71.4	74	67.3	458[r]	81.5	638	70.7
1915	1,552	64.1	—	—	19	60.8	109	63.4	73	65.9	390[e]	..	564	65.1
1910	1,318	64.2	—	—	18	59.3	103	59.6	69	62.0	351[r]	77.5	519	58.9
1905	1,128	63.9	—	—	19	62.0	100	59.0	67	57.8	297[e]	79.1	493	57.9
1900[5]	1,055	61.2	—	—	21	58.6	98	54.5	67	56.2	277[r]	73.8	493	55.9
1895	1,011	59.8	—	—	22	59.8	101	53.5	62	60.8	256[e]	75.2	517	52.5
1890	943	62.2	—	—	23	57.3	86	57.6	60	57.2	228	89.7	514	52.2
1885	911	53.3	—	—	23	56.0	87	58.8	62	53.4	217	59.9	503	49.3
1880	852	57.9	—	—	22	55.1	80	54.2	50	62.7	204	88.4	489	45.5
1875	858	54.6	—	—	18[e]	..	82	55.4	48	57.6	206	89.3	499	39.8
1870	768	45.2	—	—	14[e]	..	77	56.5	32	55.3	201[r]	..	443	42.5
1867	723	40.7	—	—	13	..	72	55.2	31	47.1	195[r]	..	411	41.4
1866	682	44.8	—	—	..	..	70	52.6	28	52.1	194[r]	..	390	42.9

Series W67-93. Total enrolment and percentage of average daily attendance (ADA) in public elementary and secondary schools, Canada and by province, selected years, 1866 to 1975 (concluded)

Year[1]	Manitoba		Saskatchewan		Alberta		British Columbia		Yukon		Northwest Territories		Overseas[4]
	Enrol-ment '000	ADA %	Enrol-ment '000	ADA %	Enrol-ment '000	ADA %	Enrol-ment '000	ADA %	Enrol-ment '000	ADA %	Enrol-ment '000	ADA %	Enrol-ment '000
	81	82	83	84	85	86	87	88	89	90	91	92	93
1975	228	..	221	..	439	..	543	..	5	..	13	..	5
1974	230	..	224	..	432	..	542	..	5	..	13	..	5
1973	235	..	224	..	420	..	549	..	5	..	13	..	5
1972	239	..	234	..	425	..	537	..	5	..	11	..	5
1971	245	..	244	..	428	..	524	..	5	..	11	..	5
1970	247	..	247	..	426	..	527	..	5	..	10	..	6
1969	246	..	250	..	414	..	513	..	4	..	8	..	8
1968	240	..	250	..	402	..	491	..	4	..	1	..	9
1967	232	..	246	..	386	..	469	..	4	..	1	..	8
1966	225	..	242	..	373	..	446	..	3	..	1	..	8
1965	222	..	238	..	362	..	421	..	3	..	1	..	8
1964	219	..	233	..	351	..	400	..	3	..	1	..	7
1963	213	..	228	..	337	..	378	..	3	..	1	..	7
1962	204	93.5	220	92.4	322	96.2	359	92.5	3	..	1	..	7
1961	195	95.4	216	92.4	308	96.0	341	91.7	3	..	1	..	8
1960	190	92.7	209	92.8	294	95.2	321	92.4	3	..	1	..	7
1959	178	92.0	202	91.4	278	94.9	306	91.8	2	..	1	..	7
1958	167	90.4	199	91.0	262	94.2	292	91.3	2	..	..	..	6
1955	160	90.0	181	89.3	224	89.4	242	90.6	..	..	..	..	4
1950	129	87.4	168	82.1	174	86.2	173	88.9	..	..	..	..	—
1945	121	86.3	174	79.7	156	85.7	131	87.5	..	..	..	..	—
1940	132	84.2	201	77.4	163	82.9	120	86.3	..	..	—	—	—
1935	143	81.2	217	75.6	167	79.4	117	87.3	..	..	—	—	—
1930	154	78.6	231	76.7	169	79.5	114	87.3	..	..	—	—	—
1925	148	72.0	213	71.4	148	73.5	102	83.9	..	..	—	—	—
1920	129	66.7	185	61.4	138	71.9	86	79.8	..	..	—	—	—
1915	104	64.2	129	55.3	99	60.8	65	78.8	..	..	—	—	—
1910	81	56.1	72	53.0	62	52.8	45	72.4	..	..	—	—	—
1905	64	54.4	31	50.5	29	51.4	29	69.5	..	..	—	—	—
1900[5]	52	53.2	24	..	—	—	24	64.8	—	—	—	—	—
1895	38	53.2	—	—	—	—	15	64.1	—	—	—	—	—
1890	24	51.9	—	—	—	—	9	54.8	—	—	—	—	—
1885	16	54.1	—	—	—	—	5	55.6	—	—	—	—	—
1880	5	49.0	—	—	—	—	3	53.8	—	—	—	—	—
1875	3 e	..	—	—	—	—	2	58.8	—	—	—	—	—
1870	1	..	—	—	—	—	—	—	—	—	—	—	—
1867	—	—	—	—	—	—	—	—	—	—	—	—	—
1866	—	—	—	—	—	—	—	—	—	—	—	—	—

[1] School year beginning in the year shown.
[2] Excludes Newfoundland prior to 1950.
[3] Average daily attendance has not been reported from 1963 on; for 1940 to 1962, average daily attendance percentages were calculated using the data published in the *Survey of Elementary and Secondary Education, 1962-63;* for prior years data shown in the *Historical Statistics of Canada* were used.

[4] Average daily attendance not available overseas for 1955 to 1975 inclusive; not applicable in previous years.
[5] Average daily attendance for Canada in 1900 and prior years was calculated excluding provinces for which enrolment was available but average daily attendance was not.

Series W94-149. Total enrolment in elementary and secondary schools, by control,[1] Canada and by province, selected years, 1920 to 1975
(series W94-97 in thousands; series W98-149 in number)

Year[2]	Canada				Newfoundland				Prince Edward Island			
	Public[3]	Private	Federal	Total	Public	Private	Federal	Total	Public	Private	Federal	Total
	94	95	96	97	98	99	100	101	102	103	104	105
1975	5,376	182	33	5,590	157,768	280	–	158,048	27,850	–	57	27,907
1974	5,424	175	33	5,632	158,014	360	–	158,374	28,149	–	57	28,206
1973	5,489	158	33	5,680	159,831	872	–	160,703	29,056	–	53	29,109
1972	5,587	152	30	5,768	161,723	843	–	162,566	29,340	–	65	29,405
1971	5,654	140	29	5,823	162,818	746	–	163,564	30,570	–	66	30,636
1970	5,661	143	28	5,832	160,915	722	–	161,637	30,622	29	71	30,722
1969	5,587	156	29	5,771	160,097	553	–	160,650	29,553	70	65	29,688
1968	5,463	146	38	5,647	156,757	364	–	157,121	29,368	136	72	29,576
1967	5,274	158	39	5,471	151,976	230	–	152,206	29,174	140	53	29,367
1966	5,084	189	39	5,312	148,352[4]	1,175[4]	–	149,527	28,536	345	30	28,911
1965	4,918	204	38	5,160	146,503	1,024	–	147,527	27,787	511	50	28,348
1964	4,752	203	39	4,994	144,129	573	–	144,702	27,740	497	43	28,280
1963	4,562	201	39	4,802	140,735	602	–	141,337	27,212	502	43	27,757
1962	4,380	192	38	4,610	137,700	859	–	138,559	26,193	857	33	27,083
1961	4,192	180	38	4,410	133,747	570	–	134,317	25,664	639	40	26,343
1960	3,997	168	37	4,202	128,917	218	–	129,135	24,450	692	37	25,179
1959	3,810	164	35	4,009	124,867	24	–	124,891	24,070	708	37	24,815
1958	3,632	160	35	3,827	119,279	98	–	119,377	22,618	1,423	36	24,077
1955	3,118	145	32	3,295	102,633	100	–	102,733	21,346	1,131	39	22,516
1950	2,391	103	24	2,518	79,328	–[6]	–	79,328	18,863	969	51	19,883
1945[7]	2,039	108	19	2,165	70,460	–	–	70,460	18,085	804	28	18,917
1940	2,075	91	17	2,183	67,184	–	–	67,184	18,194	638	16	18,848
1935	2,132	89	18	2,239	59,310	–	–	59,310	18,183	547	20	18,750
1930	2,099	94	16	2,209	60,592	–	–	60,592	17,506	570	34	18,110
1925	1,993	86	15	2,094	59,088	–	–	59,088	17,324	580	26	17,930
1920	1,834	81	12	1,928	55,588	–	–	55,588	17,510	682	42	18,234

Year[2]	Nova Scotia				New Brunswick				Quebec			
	Public	Private	Federal	Total	Public	Private	Federal	Total	Public	Private	Federal	Total
	106	107	108	109	110	111	112	113	114	115	116	117
1975	202,606	1,418	665	204,689	164,999	421	838	166,258	1,374,765	87,987	4,751	1,467,503
1974	204,280	1,372	668	206,320	166,550	137	782	167,469	1,422,485	86,892	4,875	1,514,252
1973	207,651	1,286	645	209,582	170,179	467	728	171,374	1,464,599	72,785	5,059	1,542,443
1972	211,262	1,394	624	213,280	173,851	636	704	175,191	1,526,586	67,940	4,016	1,598,542
1971	214,780	1,405	565	216,750	175,997	398	671	177,066	1,577,079	57,067	4,658	1,638,804
1970	214,897	1,649	524	217,070	175,912	463	615	176,990	1,588,788	58,779	4,350	1,651,917
1969	213,131	2,125	506	215,762	173,808	353	620	174,781	1,581,020	71,728	4,402	1,657,150
1968	208,838	2,748	640	212,226	172,337	381	637	173,355	1,568,991	61,263	4,327	1,634,581
1967	204,607	3,255	649	208,511	169,703	468	682	170,853	1,505,289	68,900	4,395	1,578,593
1966	200,681	4,508	750	205,939	166,750	1,389	638	168,777	1,441,087	92,951	4,417	1,538,455
1965	199,856	5,362	744	205,962	165,228	1,654	644	167,526	1,383,962	104,138	4,192	1,492,292
1964	197,496	6,201	818	204,515	164,124	1,791	686	166,601	1,330,691	102,062	3,320	1,436,073
1963	194,410	6,212	842	201,464	160,801	1,993	654	163,448	1,274,856	104,537	3,029	1,382,422
1962	190,527	6,122	806	197,455	156,491	2,491	639	159,621	1,223,581	102,611	2,871	1,329,063
1961	186,326	6,470	804	193,600	155,216	2,574	640	158,430	1,158,398	96,478	2,895	1,257,771
1960	179,395	6,243	773	186,411	152,289	2,369	618	155,276	1,097,678	91,499	2,861	1,192,038
1959	177,092	6,244	769	184,105	147,836	2,618	498	150,952	1,043,059	91,413	2,179	1,136,651
1958	171,386	5,967	681	178,034	141,786	2,882	517	145,185	998,849	90,312	2,118	1,091,279
1955	156,847	5,503	651	163,001	127,134	1,677	467	129,278	861,789	88,245	2,621	952,655
1950	134,483	4,709	591	139,783	105,690	2,129	416	108,235	640,833	55,667	2,208	698,708
1945	120,655	3,362	533	124,550	95,227	2,903	357	98,487	557,341	67,751	1,548	626,640
1940	116,880	2,986	438	120,304	92,048	2,935	319	95,302	588,229	55,847	1,519	645,595
1935	116,888	3,044	429	120,361	92,959	3,079	330	96,368	586,689	55,775	1,645	644,109
1930	115,511	2,746	409	118,666	88,836	4,082	320	93,238	542,622ʳ	57,320	1,539	601,481
1925	112,391	2,956	318	115,665	81,330	3,528	274	85,132	500,000ᵉ	54,767	1,598	556,365
1920	109,483	3,047	246	112,776	73,771	2,607	264	76,642	457,980ʳ	54,671	1,334	513.985

Series W94-149. Total enrolment in elementary and secondary schools, by control,[1] Canada and by province, selected years, 1920 to 1975 (continued)

(in number)

Year[2]	Ontario				Manitoba				Saskatchewan			
	Public	Private	Federal	Total	Public	Private	Federal	Total	Public	Private	Federal	Total
	118	**119**	**120**	**121**	**122**	**123**	**124**	**125**	**126**	**127**	**128**	**129**
1975	1,994,638	54,598	7,391	2,056,627	228,127	7,122	7,254	242,503	220,973	1,453	5,530	227,956
1974	1,994,489	51,239	7,465	2,053,193	229,552	6,849	7,303	243,704	224,176	1,853	5,309	231,338
1973	2,008,610	47,500	7,149	2,063,259	234,620	6,912	6,830	248,362	223,798	1,309	5,290	230,397
1972	2,028,114	44,826	7,106	2,080,046	238,861	7,224	6,376	252,461	234,152	1,268	4,465	239,885
1971	2,031,360	43,949	7,157	2,082,466	244,452	7,438	6,064	257,954	243,579	1,710	3,358	248,647
1970	2,022,401	44,116	6,671	2,073,188	246,946	8,284	5,914	261,144	247,332	1,552	3,354	252,238
1969	1,986,796	43,007	6,605	2,036,408	245,564	8,178	5,938	259,680	249,915	1,854	3,430	255,199
1968	1,931,397	41,604	6,790	1,979,791	240,132	8,958	5,847	254,937	249,662	1,917	3,922	255,501
1967	1,868,788	42,986	6,752	1,918,526	231,650	9,708	6,225	247,583	245,526	1,987	5,025	252,538
1966	1,800,897	46,072	6,495	1,853,464	224,531	10,244	6,683	241,458	242,137	2,227	5,156	249,520
1965	1,738,781	45,554	6,572	1,790,907	222,249	10,576	6,317	239,142	238,320	2,439	4,802	245,561
1964	1,673,774	44,470	7,266	1,725,510	218,770	11,335	6,069	236,174	233,213	4,316	5,475	243,004
1963	1,597,374	41,721	7,427	1,646,522	212,644	11,175	5,943	229,762	227,641	4,665	5,434	237,740
1962	1,528,607	32,458	7,280	1,568,345	204,172	11,375	5,839	221,386	220,345	4,813	5,263	230,421
1961	1,462,230	27,826	7,619	1,497,675	194,854	11,150	5,734	211,738	215,625	4,823	5,228	225,676
1960	1,389,163	26,175	7,483	1,422,821	189,573	10,379	5,632	205,584	208,679	4,734	4,961	218,374
1959	1,319,225	25,316	7,145	1,351,686	178,116	10,399	5,422	193,937	202,310	4,566	4,553	211,429
1958	1,249,673	23,742	7,085	1,280,500	167,299	10,075	5,117	182,491	198,847	4,370	4,816	208,033
1955	1,038,176	20,155	6,792	1,065,123	160,171	7,601	4,494	172,266	181,152	3,488	4,066	188,706
1950	768,202	20,141	5,736	794,079	128,868	6,226	3,205	138,299	167,485	3,138	3,423	174,046
1945	666,451	16,336	4,426	687,213	121,272	4,643	2,650	128,565	173,559	3,682	2,652	179,893
1940	643,628	13,458	4,477	661,563	131,562	4,509	2,158	138,229	201,390	1,985	2,373	205,748
1935	673,706	11,809	4,664	690,179	142,482	5,131	2,468	150,081	217,247	2,003	2,266	221,516
1930	668,061	12,236	4,296	684,593	153,553	5,864	2,346	161,763	230,492	2,853	2,072	235,417
1925	670,640	10,126	3,830	684,596	148,279	4,534	2,263	155,076	213,357	2,358	1,892	217,607
1920	637,467	9,961	3,590	651,018	129,015	3,149	1,944	134,108	184,822	1,608	1,337	187,767

Year[2]	Alberta				British Columbia				Yukon Territory			
	Public	Private	Federal	Total	Public	Private	Federal	Total	Public	Private	Federal	Total
	130	**131**	**132**	**133**	**134**	**135**	**136**	**137**	**138**	**139**	**140**	**141**
1975	439,354	5,651	3,719	448,724	542,680	23,071	2,258	568,009	4,975	—	—	4,975
1974	432,177	5,541	3,418	441,136	541,575	21,055	3,013	565,643	4,903	—	—	4,903
1973	419,737	5,367	3,661	428,765	549,019	21,421	3,083	573,523	4,957	—	—	4,957
1972	425,251	5,403	3,409	434,063	537,067	22,061	3,036	562,164	4,749	—	—	4,749
1971	427,968	5,439	3,595	437,002	524,305	21,777	3,108	549,190	4,806	—	—	4,806
1970	425,987	5,688	3,564	435,239	526,991	21,319	3,360	551,670	4,634	—	—	4,634
1969	413,719	5,342	3,553	422,614	513,150	22,359	3,491	539,000	4,090	—	—	4,090
1968	401,587	5,231	3,635	410,453	490,930	23,172	4,267	518,369	3,617	—	82	3,699
1967	385,972	5,614	3,668	395,254	468,659	24,160	5,028	497,847	3,456	—	93	3,549
1966	372,894	5,324	3,625	381,843	445,633	24,762	5,194	475,589	3,365	—	79	3,444
1965	362,159	6,570	3,998	372,727	420,847	25,853	5,354	452,054	3,164	—	107	3,271
1964	350,906	6,292	3,836	361,034	399,944	25,469	5,934	431,347	3,001	—	141	3,142
1963	336,652	6,436	4,334	347,422	378,387	23,242	6,237	407,866	3,177	—	161	3,338
1962	322,227	6,486	4,527	333,240	359,320	23,395	5,953	388,668	2,992	—	112	3,104
1961	307,702	6,374	4,671	318,747	341,219	22,731	5,812	369,762	2,731	—	162	2,893
1960	294,435	6,121	4,650	305,206	321,312	19,733	5,988	347,033	2,607	—	148	2,755
1959	277,920	6,242	4,732	288,894	306,021	16,188	5,778	327,987	2,293	—	352	2,645
1958	261,554	5,471	4,612	271,637	292,403	15,811	5,967	314,181	2,027	—	247	2,274
1955	223,949	3,826	4,193	231,968	241,477	12,793	5,925	260,195	..	—	323	..
1950	173,969	3,527	3,141	180,637	173,354	6,170	5,094	184,618	..	—	317	..
1945	155,455	2,852	1,987	160,294	130,605	5,576	4,160	140,341	..	—	192	..
1940	163,425	3,813	2,029	169,267	119,634	5,003	3,714	128,351	..	—	121	..
1935	167,193	3,083	1,954	172,230	116,722	4,568	3,807	125,097	..	—	191	..
1930	168,730	2,944	1,582	173,256	113,914	5,276	3,438	122,628	..	—	144	..
1925	148,245	2,281	1,283	151,809	101,688	4,624	2,852	109,164	..	—	192	..
1920	138,220	2,274	1,033	141,527	85,950	3,159	2,393	91,502	..	—	146	..

Series W94-149. Total enrolment in elementary and secondary schools, by control,[1] Canada and by province, selected years, 1920 to 1975 (concluded)

(in number)

Year[2]	Northwest Territories				Overseas			
	Public	Private	Federal	Total	Public	Private	Federal	Total
	142	**143**	**144**	**145**	**146**	**147**	**148**	**149**
1975	12,496	–	–	12,496	4,624	–	–	4,624
1974	12,504	–	–	12,504	4,621	–	–	4,621
1973	12,627	–	–	12,627	4,566	–	–	4,566
1972	11,369	–	–	11,369	4,589	–	–	4,589
1971	11,209	–	–	11,209	4,569	–	–	4,569
1970	10,006	–	–	10,006	5,867	–	–	5,867
1969	8,192	–	–	8,192	7,916	–	–	7,916
1968	1,071	–	7,347	8,418	8,658	–	–	8,658
1967	1,056	–	6,774	7,830	8,303	–	–	8,303
1966	964	–	6,026	6,990	8,439	–	–	8,439
1965	932	–	5,487	6,419	7,800	–	–	7,800
1964	841	–	5,101	5,942	7,282	–	–	7,282
1963	895	–	4,647	5,542	7,376	–	–	7,376
1962	801	–	4,429	5,230	7,302	–	–	7,302
1961	610	–	4,330	4,940	7,937	–	–	7,937
1960	759	–	3,762	4,521	7,274	–	–	7,274
1959	488	–	3,709	4,197	6,624	–	–	6,624
1958	..	–	3,692	..	5,845	–	–	5,845
1955	..	–	2,841[5]	..	3,690	–	–	3,690
1950	..	–	..	..	–	–	–	–
1945	..	–	..	..	–	–	–	–
1940	..	–	..	..	–	–	–	–
1935	..	–	..	..	–	–	–	–
1930	..	–	..	..	–	–	–	–
1925	..	–	..	..	–	–	–	–
1920	..	–	..	..	–	–	–	–

[1] Public schools include Department of National Defence schools in various provinces.
[2] School year beginning in the year shown.
[3] From 1955, includes overseas schools of the Department of National Defence.
[4] Elementary grades of Labrador City Collegiate reported as private from 1960 to 1966; thereafter they became public.
[5] In 1955, the government of the Northwest Territories took under its control all parochial and mining companies' schools not reported previously.
[6] In 1950 and prior years, included with Nova Scotia.
[7] Canada totals in 1945 and prior years exclude Newfoundland.

Series W150-191. Full-time teachers in public elementary and secondary schools, by sex, Canada and by province, selected years, 1867 to 1975

Year[1]	Canada[2]			Newfoundland			Prince Edward Island			Nova Scotia		
	Male	Female	Total	Male	Female	Total	Male	Female	Total	Male	Female	Total
	150	**151**	**152**	**153**	**154**	**155**	**156**	**157**	**158**	**159**	**160**	**161**
1975	110,429	153,833	264,262	3,433	3,994	7,427	514	930	1,444	4,061	6,720	10,781
1974	110,834	153,083	263,917	3,316	4,042	7,358	483	925	1,408	3,869	6,700	10,569
1973	108,840	154,731	263,571	3,103	3,969	7,072	470 e	945 e	1,415 e	3,658	6,622	10,280
1972	108,395	156,590	264,985	2,946	3,949	6,895	440	1,021	1,461	3,434	6,586	10,020
1971	104,682	158,444	263,126	2,763	3,885	6,648	477	1,162	1,639	3,236	6,633	9,869
1970	100,820	161,637	262,457	2,554	3,883	6,437	437	1,169	1,606	3,061	6,938	9,999
1969	97,098	159,974	257,072	2,398	3,917	6,315	390	1,096	1,486	2,699	6,744	9,443
1968	89,512	155,619	245,131	2,277	3,929	6,206	341	1,117	1,458	2,399	6,513	8,912
1967	82,558	148,553	231,111	2,064	3,791	5,855	315	1,082	1,397	2,189	6,298	8,487
1966	74,122	137,055	211,177	1,986	3,658	5,644	272	1,046	1,318	1,926	6,107	8,033
1965	67,832	129,261	197,093	2,035	3,510	5,545	238	971	1,209	1,867	6,030	7,897
1964	64,632	127,123	191,755	2,010	3,341	5,351	228	938	1,166	1,749	5,889	7,638
1963	59,107	121,764	180,871	1,887	3,149	5,036	207	925	1,132	1,632	5,791	7,423
1962	54,618	118,920	173,538	1,791	2,998	4,789	189	883	1,072	1,467	5,709	7,176
1961	49,357	113,692	163,049	1,689	2,813	4,502	174	839	1,013	1,416	5,535	6,951
1960	44,593	108,447	153,040	1,592	2,725	4,317	145	824	969	1,258	5,406	6,664
1959	40,498	103,439	143,937	1,450	2,569	4,019	132	772	904	1,157	5,275	6,432
1958[3]	37,865	100,124	137,989	1,381	2,515	3,896	122	731	853	1,065	5,112	6,177
1955[4]	31,058	84,777	115,835	1,047	2,059	3,106	131	691	822	940	4,646	5,586
1950	24,064	65,618	89,682	847	1,652	2,499	118	601	719	710	3,726	4,436
1945[5]	17,415	60,064	77,479	694	1,537	2,231	105	563	668	409	3,297	3,706
1940	19,417	55,970	75,387	728	1,272	2,000	120	534	654	482	2,867	3,349
1935	18,492	54,593	73,085	625	1,101	1,726	195	462	657	532	3,127	3,659
1930	14,255	55,990	70,245	544	1,145	1,689	148	480	628	331	3,153	3,484
1925	12,069	51,771	63,840	463	1,066	1,529	142	474	616	276	3,044	3,320

Series W150-191. Full-time teachers in public elementary and secondary schools, by sex, Canada and by province, selected years, 1867 to 1975 (continued)

Year[1]	Canada[2]			Newfoundland			Prince Edward Island			Nova Scotia		
	Male	Female	Total	Male	Female	Total	Male	Female	Total	Male	Female	Total
	150	**151**	**152**	**153**	**154**	**155**	**156**	**157**	**158**	**159**	**160**	**161**
1920	9,600	48,178	57,778	302	1,121	1,423	100	483	583	203	2,886	3,089
1915	8,789	41,453	50,242	..	..	..	138	457	595	246	2,773	3,019
1910	7,849	32,627	40,476	..	..	..	178	413	591	331	2,468	2,799
1905	6,392	25,818	32,210	..	..	..	246	327	573	366	2,212	2,578
1900	6,205	21,164	27,369	..	..	..	298	291	589	540	1,952	2,492
1895	6,069	18,652	24,721	..	..	..	..	..	..	582	1,856	2,438
1890	5,797	16,753	22,550	..	..	..	278	253	531	572	1,568	2,140
1885	5,772	14,719	20,491	..	..	..	277	221	498	661	1,365	2,026
1880	6,181	11,411	17,592	..	..	..	263	196	459[6]	720	1,089	1,809[6]
1875	5,338	10,329	15,667	..	..	..	..	..	..	672	1,103	1,775[6]
1870	5,143	8,180	13,323	..	..	..	—	—	—	767	798	1,565[6]
1867	3,312	2,840	6,152	..	..	..	—	—	—	..	..	..

Year[2]	New Brunswick			Quebec			Ontario			Manitoba		
	Male	Female	Total	Male	Female	Total	Male	Female	Total	Male	Female	Total
	162	**163**	**164**	**165**	**166**	**167**	**168**	**169**	**170**	**171**	**172**	**173**
1975	2,967	4,902	7,869	25,700e	45,800e	71,500e	40,700e	53,900e	94,600e	5,256	6,220	11,476
1974	2,867	4,987	7,854	26,200e	46,600e	72,800e	41,965	52,191	94,156	5,097	6,223	11,320
1973	2,801	5,004	7,805	26,890e	47,810e	74,700e	41,100e	54,000e	95,100e	5,037	6,413	11,450
1972	2,795	5,166	7,961	27,760e	49,340e	77,100e	41,546	54,675	96,221	4,874	6,549	11,423
1971	2,664	5,292	7,956	27,540e	50,460e	78,000e	38,998e	53,800e	92,798	4,786	6,945	11,731
1970	2,510	5,387	7,897	27,508	50,470	77,978	37,200e	55,800e	93,000	4,428	7,106	11,534
1969	2,368	5,454	7,822	26,612	50,806	77,418	36,152e	53,777e	89,929	4,183	7,011	11,194
1968	2,114	5,423	7,537	24,452	50,436	74,888	33,300e	51,490e	84,790	3,950	6,869	10,819
1967	1,952	5,300	7,252	21,928	49,371	71,299	31,384	47,916	79,300	3,566	6,360	9,926
1966	1,741	5,186	6,927	17,925	43,013	60,938	28,939	45,004	73,943	3,408	6,024	9,432
1965	1,692	5,120	6,812	14,743	40,678	55,421	27,104	41,498	68,602	3,365	5,867	9,232
1964	1,586	4,991	6,577	14,909	42,844	57,753	25,014	39,115	64,129	3,324	5,651	8,975
1963	1,439	4,919	6,358	13,031	41,218	54,249	22,864	37,147	60,011	3,110	5,424	8,534
1962	1,365	4,903	6,268	12,412	41,473	53,885	20,507	35,280	55,787	2,925	5,328	8,253
1961	1,337	4,702	6,039	10,819	38,767	49,586	18,304	34,140	52,444	2,743	5,326	8,069
1960	1,261	4,605	5,866	9,618	36,076	45,694	16,336	32,956	49,292	2,489	4,971	7,460
1959	1,154	4,477	5,631	8,845	34,503	43,348	14,434	30,937	45,371	2,238	4,838	7,076
1958	1,017	4,320	5,337	8,248	32,836	41,084	13,482	30,104	43,586	2,089	4,830	6,919
1955	839	3,797	4,636	6,676	28,625	35,301	10,836	24,724	35,560	1,744	4,336	6,080
1950	619	3,288	3,907	5,543	21,108	26,651	7,919	18,283	26,202	1,405	3,585	4,990
1945	336	2,565	2,901	5,641	20,823	26,464	5,453	16,900	22,353	920	3,555	4,475
1940	417	2,339	2,756	5,065	20,244	25,309	6,460	15,369	21,829	1,094	3,061	4,155
1935	441	2,284	2,725	4,621	18,946	23,567	5,735	15,633	21,368	1,014	3,048	4,062
1930	272	2,436	2,708	3,751	17,220	20,971	3,777	15,989	19,766	881	3,546	4,427
1925	268	2,257	2,525	3,175	15,947	19,122	2,996	14,884	17,880	849	3,218	4,067
1920	155	1,987	2,142	2,631	14,570	17,201	2,191	13,266	15,457	796	2,912	3,708
1915	193	1,896	2,089	2,263	13,083	15,346	2,007	11,730	13,737	491	2,500	2,991
1910	220	1,715	1,935	1,786	11,104	12,890	2,145	9,871	12,016	651	2,217	2,868
1905	301	1,536	1,837	1,422	9,779	11,201	2,376	8,368	10,744	596	1,769	2,365
1900	351	1,460	1,811	1,265	8,927	10,192	2,948	7,125	10,073	618	1,051	1,669
1895	392	1,404	1,796	1,178	8,319	9,497[6]	3,198	6,364	9,562	570	523	1,093
1890	372	1,218	1,590	1,008	7,449	8,457[6]	3,039	5,781	8,820	451	389	840
1885	431	1,123	1,554	1,034	6,599	7,633[6]	3,080	5,123	8,203	231	245	476
1880	502	815	1,317	987	5,391	6,378[6]	3,709	3,920	7,629	..	..	..
1875	452	765	1,217	1,146	4,776	5,922	3,068	3,685	6,753	..	..	..
1870	402	507	909	1,115	4,005	5,120	2,859	2,870	5,729	..	..	..
1867	407	459	866	..	..	..	2,905	2,381	5,286	—	—	—

Series W150-191. Full-time teachers in public elementary and secondary schools, by sex, Canada and by province, selected years, 1867 to 1975 (continued)

Year[2]	Saskatchewan			Alberta			British Columbia			Yukon Territory		
	Male	Female	Total	Male	Female	Total	Male	Female	Total	Male	Female	Total
	174	**175**	**176**	**177**	**178**	**179**	**180**	**181**	**182**	**183**	**184**	**185**
1975	5,005	5,749	10,754	9,553	11,627	21,180	12,610	13,361	25,971	125 e	140 e	265 e
1974	5,019	5,894	10,913	9,352	11,815	21,167	12,041	13,076	25,117	125 e	140 e	265 e
1973	4,928	5,996	10,924	9,050	11,320	20,370	11,204	12,043	23,247	125 e	145 e	270 e
1972	4,731	6,013	10,744	8,842	11,426	20,268	10,466	11,278	21,744	120	138	258
1971	4,576	6,140	10,716	8,830	11,691	20,521	10,281	11,831	22,112	108	139	247
1970	4,487	6,490	10,977	8,334	12,024	20,358	9,810	11,765	21,575	89	134	223
1969	4,547	7,006	11,553	7,839	11,982	19,821	9,374	11,441	20,815	73	146	219
1968	4,406	7,083	11,489	7,307	11,463	18,770	8,666	10,820	19,486	62	128	190
1967	4,191	6,918	11,109	6,630	10,862	17,492	8,046	10,226	18,272	64	105	169
1966	4,088	6,835	10,923	6,115	10,243	16,358	7,447	9,519	16,966	51	110	161
1965	3,950 e	6,550 e	10,500 e	5,724	9,794	15,518	6,882	8,877	15,759	49	98	147
1964	3,742	6,254	9,996	5,307	9,395	14,702	6,543	8,336	14,879	42	100	142
1963	3,594	5,962	9,556	4,898	8,986	13,884	6,233	7,834	14,067	34	104	138
1962	3,378	5,868	9,246	4,510	8,626	13,136	5,862	7,449	13,311	29	100	129
1961	3,126	5,871	8,997	4,086	8,328	12,414	5,499	7,015	12,514	26	83	109
1960	2,940	5,698	8,638	3,654	8,108	11,762	5,146	6,722	11,868	20	83	103
1959	2,811	5,526	8,337	3,330	7,741	11,071	4,803	6,482	11,285	21 e	75 e	96
1958	2,704	5,536	8,240	3,186	7,669	10,855	4,461	6,206	10,667	15 e	70 e	85
1955	2,551	5,073	7,624	2,593	5,798	8,391	3,641	4,898	8,539	—	—	—
1950	2,230	4,988	7,218	2,216	4,572	6,788	2,457	3,815	6,272	—	—	—
1945	1,708	5,323	7,031	1,411	4,034	5,445	1,432	3,004	4,436	—	—	—
1940	2,261	5,092	7,353	1,946	3,851	5,797	1,572	2,613	4,185	—	—	—
1935	2,517	4,733	7,250	2,043	3,798	5,841	1,394	2,562	3,956	—	—	—
1930	2,394	6,021	8,415	1,520	4,324	5,844	1,181	2,821	4,002	—	—	—
1925	2,044	5,735	7,779	1,453	3,682	5,135	866	2,530	3,396	—	—	—
1920	1,583	5,961	7,544	1,346	3,974	5,320	595	2,139	2,734	—	—	—
1915	1,550	4,237	5,787	1,378	3,236	4,614	523	1,541	2,064	—	—	—
1910	1,348	2,199	3,547	867	1,784	2,651	323	856	1,179	—	—	—
1905	629	669	1,298	280	644	924	176	514	690	—	—	—
1900	..	..	..	..	..	..	185	358	543	—	—	—
1895	..	..	..	..	..	..	149	186	335	—	—	—
1890	..	..	..	..	..	..	77	95	172	—	—	—
1885	..	..	..	..	..	..	58	43	101	—	—	—
1880	..	..	..	..	..	..	..	..	..	—	—	—
1875	..	..	..	..	..	..	..	..	..	—	—	—
1870	..	..	..	..	..	..	..	..	..	—	—	—
1867	—	—	—	—	—	—	..	..	..	—	—	—

Series W150-191. Full-time teachers in public elementary and secondary schools, by sex, Canada and by province, selected years, 1867 to 1975 (concluded)

Year[2]	Northwest Territories			Overseas		
	Male	Female	Total	Male	Female	Total
	186	**187**	**188**	**189**	**190**	**191**
1975	345 e	340 e	685 e	160 e	150 e	310 e
1974	340 e	340 e	680 e	160 e	150 e	310 e
1973	313	314	627	161 e	150 e	311
1972	290	322	612	151	127	278
1971	277	310	587	146	156	302
1970	247	271	518	155	200	355
1969	256	300	556	207	294	501
1968	31	34	65	207	314	521
1967	32	31	63	197	293	490
1966	29	28	57	195	282	477
1965	27	29	56	156	239	395
1964	25	26	51	153	243	396
1963	24	29	53	154	276	430
1962	21	26	47	162	277	439
1961	14	19	33	124	254	378
1960	12 e	16 e	28	122	257	379
1959	11 e	14 e	25	112 e	230 e	342
1958	..	..	..	95 e	195 e	290 e
1955	–	–	–	60 e	130 e	190 e
1950	–	–	–	–	–	–
1945	–	–	–	–	–	–
1940	–	–	–	–	–	–
1935	–	–	–	–	–	–
1930	–	–	–	–	–	–
1925	–	–	–	–	–	–
1920	–	–	–	–	–	–
1915	–	–	–	–	–	–
1910	–	–	–	–	–	–
1905	–	–	–	–	–	–
1900	–	–	–	–	–	–
1895	–	–	–	–	–	–
1890	–	–	–	–	–	–
1885	–	–	–	–	–	–
1880	–	–	–	–	–	–
1875	–	–	–	–	–	–
1870	–	–	–	–	–	–
1867	–	–	–	–	–	–

[1] School year beginning in the year shown.
[2] Canada totals in 1905 and prior years include only those provinces which were at the time members of the Confederation, except where data were not available, namely: (a) Prince Edward Island in 1895 and 1875; (b) Nova Scotia in 1867; (c) Quebec in 1867; (d) Manitoba in 1880, 1875 and 1870 and (e) British Columbia in 1880 and 1875.
[3] In 1958 and prior years, excludes the Northwest Territories.

[4] In 1955 and prior years, excludes the Yukon Territory.
[5] Canada totals, for 1945 and prior years, exclude Newfoundland.
[6] In some cases, because of the nature of the source, data reported do not coincide exactly with the year indicated. These exceptions are: (a) Prince Edward Island, 1880 data for 1879; (b) Nova Scotia, 1880 data for 1879, 1875 data for 1874 and 1870 data for 1869; (c) Quebec, 1895 data for 1896, 1890 data for 1891, 1885 data for 1886 and 1880 data for 1881.

Series W192-247. Full-time teachers[1] in elementary and secondary schools, by control, Canada and by province, selected years, 1930 to 1975

Year[2]	Canada				Newfoundland				Prince Edward Island			
	Public[3]	Private[4]	Federal	Total	Public	Private	Federal	Total	Public	Private	Federal	Total
	192	193	194	195	196	197	198	199	200	201	202	203
1975	264,262	8,982	1,605	274,849	7,427	26	—	7,453	1,444	—	5	1,449
1974	263,917	8,780	1,610	274,307	7,358	27	—	7,385	1,408	—	5	1,413
1973	263,571	8,063	1,604	273,238	7,072	71	—	7,143	1,415 e	—	4	1,419
1972	264,985	7,862	1,428	274,275	6,895	62	—	6,957	1,461	—	4	1,465
1971	263,126	7,744	1,292	272,162	6,648	62	—	6,710	1,639	—	4	1,643
1970	262,457	7,920	1,215	271,592	6,437	59	—	6,496	1,606	—	5	1,611
1969	257,072	10,226	1,267	268,565	6,315	59	—	6,374	1,486	6	4	1,496
1968	245,131	9,233	1,699	256,063	6,206	48	—	6,254	1,458	9	3	1,470
1967	231,111	10,366	1,763	243,240	5,855	26	—	5,881	1,397	11	2	1,410
1966	211,177	12,067	1,708	224,952	5,644	82	—	5,726	1,318	20	2	1,340
1965	197,093	11,784	1,698	210,575	5,545	73	—	5,618	1,209	22	2	1,233
1964	191,755	12,335	1,676	205,766	5,351	39	—	5,390	1,166	22	2	1,190
1963	180,871	11,280	1,646	193,797	5,036	37	—	5,073	1,132	25	2	1,159
1962	173,538	10,128	1,573	185,239	4,789	56	—	4,845	1,072	40	2	1,114
1961	163,049	9,283	1,539	173,871	4,502	41	—	4,543	1,013	33	2	1,048
1960	153,040	9,015	1,523	163,578	4,317	—5	—	4,317	969	35	2	1,006
1959	143,937	8,818	1,411	154,166	4,019	—	—	4,019	904	36	2	942
1958	137,989 6	8,367	1,391	147,747	3,896	—	—	3,896	853	56	2	911
1955	115,835 7	6,712	1,281	123,828	3,106	—	—	3,106	822	39	2 e	863
1950	89,682	5,240	943 8	95,865	2,499	—	—	2,499	719	32	3	754
1945 9	77,479	5,909	726	84,114	2,231	—	—	2,231	668	27	2 e	697
1940	75,387	5,425	670	81,482	2,000	—	—	2,000	654	25 4	1 e	680
1935	73,085	5,099	685	78,869	1,726	—	—	1,726	657	22 e	1 e	680
1930	70,245	5,119	630	75,994	1,689	—	—	1,689	628	21 e	2 e	651

Year[2]	Nova Scotia				New Brunswick				Quebec			
	Public	Private	Federal	Total	Public	Private	Federal	Total	Public	Private	Federal	Total
	204	205	206	207	208	209	210	211	212	213	214	215
1975	10,781	113	30	10,924	7,869	45	40	7,954	71,500 e	4,640 e	225	76,365
1974	10,569	109	30	10,708	7,854	12	35	7,901	72,800 e	4,610 e	230	77,640
1973	10,280	105	30	10,415	7,805	32	33	7,870	74,700 e	3,900 e	235	78,835
1972	10,020	88	27	10,135	7,961	49	34	8,044	77,100 e	3,670 e	220	80,990
1971	9,869	100	26	9,995	7,956	46	27	8,029	78,000 e	3,500 e	205	81,705
1970	9,999	109	25	10,133	7,897	48	25	7,970	77,978	3,622	172	81,772
1969	9,443	159	24	9,626	7,822	40	26	7,888	77,418	4,396	188	82,002
1968	8,912	187	24	9,123	7,537	42	26	7,605	74,888	3,644	186	78,718
1967	8,487	199	24	8,710	7,252	60	28	7,340	71,299	4,377	189	75,865
1966	8,033	243	27	8,303	6,927	104	25	7,056	60,938	6,092	190	67,220
1965	7,897	254	29	8,180	6,812	119	25	6,956	55,421	5,988	188	61,597
1964	7,638	300	33	7,971	6,577	135	25	6,737	57,753	6,640	182	64,575
1963	7,423	289	31	7,743	6,358	154	24	6,536	54,249	6,000 e	144	60,393
1962	7,176	250	32	7,458	6,268	169	25	6,462	53,885	5,500 e	125	59,510
1961	6,951	282	34	7,267	6,039	163	24	6,226	49,586	4,980	125	54,691
1960	6,664	279	33	6,976	5,866	153	23	6,042	45,694	5,140	123 r	50,957
1959	6,432	274	30	6,736	5,631	172	21	5,824	43,348	5,125	101	48,574
1958	6,177	252	30	6,459	5,337	176	22	5,535	41,084	4,896	100	46,080
1955	5,586	213	29 e	5,828	4,636	91	20 e	4,747	35,301	3,825 e	125 e	39,251
1950	4,436	171	27 e	4,634	3,907	124	18 e	4,049	26,651	2,686	105 e	29,442
1945	3,706	155	24 e	3,885	2,901	143	15 e	3,059	26,464	3,611	75 e	30,150
1940	3,349	145 e	20 e	3,514	2,756	150 e	14 e	2,920	25,309	3,200	75 e	28,584
1935	3,659	152	20 e	3,831	2,725	148	14 e	2,887	23,567	3,100 e	75 e	26,742
1930	3,484	138	19 e	3,641	2,708	165	14 e	2,887	20,971	3,200 e	75 e	24,246

Series W192-247. Full-time teachers¹ in elementary and secondary schools, by control, Canada and by province, selected years, 1930 to 1975 (continued)

Year²	Ontario				Manitoba				Saskatchewan			
	Public	Private	Federal	Total	Public	Private	Federal	Total	Public	Private	Federal	Total
	216	217	218	219	220	221	222	223	224	225	226	227
1975	94,600e	2,214	340e	97,154	11,476	356	330	12,162	10,754	71	290	11,115
1974	94,156	2,211	335e	96,702	11,320	357	330	12,007	10,913	80	270	11,263
1973	95,100e	2,121	320e	97,541	11,450	365	314	12,129	10,924	65	266	11,255
1972	96,221	2,150	317	98,688	11,423	335	267	12,025	10,744	67	225	11,036
1971	92,798	2,220	302	95,320	11,731	353	247	12,331	10,716	93	165	10,974
1970	93,000	2,248	263	95,511	11,534	415	241	12,190	10,977	84	170	11,231
1969	89,929	3,316	278	93,523	11,194	532	240	11,966	11,553	141	174	11,868
1968	84,790	3,028	270	88,088	10,819	564	234	11,617	11,489	140	184	11,813
1967	79,300	3,365	278	82,943	9,926	583	254	10,763	11,109	159	225	11,493
1966	73,943	3,240	277	77,460	9,432	557	260	10,249	10,923	166	217	11,306
1965	68,602	2,984	294	71,880	9,232	542	248	10,022	10,500e	180	198	10,878
1964	64,129	2,817	272	67,218	8,975	580	232	9,787	9,996	267	219	10,482
1963	60,011	2,589	289	62,889	8,534	559	232	9,325	9,556	276	226	10,058
1962	55,787	1,991	280	58,058	8,253	531	230	9,014	9,246	282	213	9,741
1961	52,444	1,713	287	54,444	8,069	504	207	8,780	8,997	294	204	9,495
1960	49,292	1,584	275	51,151	7,460	430	211	8,101	8,638	273	223	9,134
1959	45,371	1,555	255r	47,181	7,076	424	216	7,716	8,337	268	193	8,798
1958	43,586	1,398	245	45,229	6,919	401	205	7,525	8,240	244	201	8,685
1955	35,560	1,234	240e	37,034	6,080	309	165e	6,554	7,624	205	170e	7,999
1950	26,202	1,232	205e	27,639	4,990	298	120e	5,408	7,218	159	140e	7,517
1945	22,353	1,064	160e	23,577	4,475	204	100e	4,779	7,031	178	110e	7,319
1940	21,829	1,000e	160e	22,989	4,155	205e	80e	4,440	7,353	140e	100e	7,593
1935	21,368	842	165e	22,375	4,062	208	90e	4,360	7,250	99	95e	7,444
1930	19,766	797	155e	20,718	4,427	186	85e	4,698	8,415	110	85e	8,610

Year²	Alberta				British Columbia				Yukon Territory			
	Public	Private	Federal	Total	Public	Private	Federal	Total	Public	Private	Federal	Total
	228	229	230	231	232	233	234	235	236	237	238	239
1975	21,180	294	220	21,694	25,971	1,223	125e	27,319	265e	—	—	265e
1974	21,167	288	210	21,665	25,117	1,086	165e	26,368	265e	—	—	265e
1973	20,370	273	236	20,879	23,247	1,131	166	24,544	270e	—	—	270e
1972	20,268	259	192	20,719	21,744	1,182	142	23,068	258	—	—	258
1971	20,521	266	171	20,958	22,112	1,104	145	23,361	247	—	—	247
1970	20,358	284	165	20,807	21,575	1,051	149	22,775	223	—	—	223
1969	19,821	317	174	20,312	20,815	1,260	159	22,234	219	—	—	219
1968	18,770	291	167	19,228	19,486	1,280	187	20,953	190	—	4	194
1967	17,492	313	179	17,984	18,272	1,273	205	19,750	169	—	4	173
1966	16,358	310	171	16,839	16,966	1,253	202	18,421	161	—	3	164
1965	15,518	365	195	16,078	15,759	1,257	207	17,223	147	—	4	151
1964	14,702	354	190	15,246	14,879	1,181	231	16,291	142	—	4	146
1963	13,884	333	201	14,418	14,067	1,018	236	15,321	138	—	5	143
1962	13,136	325	200	13,661	13,311	984	225	14,520	129	—	5	134
1961	12,414	340	211	12,965	12,514	933	229	13,676	109	—	5	114
1960	11,762	304	202	12,268	11,868	817	223	12,908	103	—	11r	114
1959	11,071	286	204	11,561	11,285	678	191	12,154	96	—	11	107
1958	10,855	281	202	11,338	10,667	663	205	11,535	85	—	10r	95
1955	8,391	192	180e	8,763	8,539	604	205e	9,348	..	—	15e	..
1950	6,788	193	135e	7,116	6,272	345	175e	6,792	..	—	15e	..
1945	5,445	158	85e	5,688	4,436	369	145e	4,950	..	—	10e	..
1940	5,797	190e	85e	6,072	4,185	370e	130e	4,685	..	—	5e	..
1935	5,841	183	85e	6,109	3,956	345	130e	4,431	..	—	10e	..
1930	5,844	182	70e	6,096	4,002	320	120e	4,442	..	—	5e	..

Series W192-247. Full-time teachers[1] in elementary and secondary schools, by control, Canada and by province, selected years, 1930 to 1975 (concluded)

Year[2]	Northwest Territories				Overseas			
	Public	Private	Federal	Total	Public	Private	Federal	Total
	240	241	242	243	244	245	246	247
1975	685 e	–	–	685 e	310 e	–	–	310 e
1974	680 e	–	–	680 e	310 e	–	–	310 e
1973	627	–	–	627	311	–	–	311
1972	612	–	–	612	278	–	–	278
1971	587	–	–	587	302	–	–	302
1970	518	–	–	518	355	–	–	355
1969	556	–	–	556	501	–	–	501
1968	65	–	414	479	521	–	–	521
1967	63	–	375	438	490	–	–	490
1966	57	–	334	391	477	–	–	477
1965	56	–	308	364	395	–	–	395
1964	51	–	286	337	396	–	–	396
1963	53	–	256	309	430	–	–	430
1962	47	–	236	283	439	–	–	439
1961	33	–	211	244	378	–	–	378
1960	28	–	197	225	379	–	–	379
1959	25	–	187	212	342	–	–	342
1958	..	–	169	..	290 e	–	–	290 e
1955	..	–	130 e	..	190 e	–	–	190 e
1950	..	–	..	..	–	–	–	–
1945	..	–	..	..	–	–	–	–
1940	..	–	..	..	–	–	–	–
1935	..	–	..	..	–	–	–	–
1930	..	–	..	..	–	–	–	–

[1] Includes principals, heads of departments and other teaching staff, but excludes inspectors and board administrators.
[2] School year beginning in the year shown.
[3] Canada totals include teachers in the Department of National Defence schools overseas from 1950 on.
[4] Includes part-time teachers prior to 1970.
[5] Newfoundland teachers included in Nova Scotia.

[6] In 1958 and prior years, teachers in the Northwest Territories are excluded.
[7] In 1955 and prior years, teachers in the Yukon Territory are excluded.
[8] In 1950 and prior years, teachers in the Northwest Territories are excluded.
[9] Canada totals in 1945 and prior years exclude Newfoundland teachers.

Series W248-259. Percentage of full-time teachers in public elementary and secondary schools, by highest university degree held and sex, by province, selected years, 1952 to 1973
(Series W248-256 in per cent; Series W257-259 in number)

Year[1]	Master and higher			Bachelor			No degree			Total		
	Male	Female	Total	Male	Female	Total	Male	Female	Total	Male	Female	Total
	248	249	250	251	252	253	254	255	256	257	258	259
	Nine provinces[2]											
1973	11.5	2.8	6.6	65.7	38.3	50.4	22.8	58.9	43.0	80,881	105,367	186,248
1972	10.1	2.4	5.7	62.2	33.5	45.8	27.7	64.1	48.5	80,074	106,663	186,737
1971	9.1	2.3	5.1	65.8	34.1	47.2	25.1	63.6	47.7	37,613	53,579	91,192
1970	8.5	2.1	4.6	63.0	29.9	43.0	28.5	68.0	52.4	35,621	54,762	90,383
1969	8.0	1.9	4.2	59.4	26.1	38.8	32.6	72.0	57.0	33,798	54,651	88,449
1968	7.6	1.7	3.9	57.2	23.2	35.9	35.2	75.1	60.2	31,460	53,217	84,677
1967	6.8	1.5	3.5	51.9	20.5	32.4	41.3	78.0	64.1	60,337	98,753	159,090
1966	6.5	1.4	3.3	49.8	18.9	30.4	43.7	79.7	66.3	55,922	93,622	149,544
1965	6.4	1.4	3.2	48.1	18.2	29.4	45.5	80.4	67.4	48,907	81,667	130,574
1964	6.0	1.3	3.0	46.3	16.7	27.7	47.7	82.0	69.3	49,503	83,910	133,413
1963	5.9	1.3	3.0	45.4	16.1	27.0	48.7	82.6	70.0	44,425	75,218	119,643
1962	4.8	1.2	2.4	44.7	14.7	25.3	50.5	84.1	72.3	41,994	77,044	119,038
1961	5.7	1.2	2.7	46.4	14.0	25.0	47.9	84.8	72.3	38,374	74,569	112,943
1960	4.7	1.1	2.3	43.0	13.0	22.8	52.3	85.9	74.9	34,821	72,015	106,836
1959	4.7	1.1	2.2	42.9	12.4	22.0	52.4	86.5	75.8	31,509	68,617	100,126
1958	4.7	1.0	2.2	40.7	11.6	20.5	54.6	87.4	77.3	29,507	67,023	96,530
1954	4.7	1.0	2.1	40.8	10.6	19.6	54.5	88.4	78.3	22,475	53,065	75,540
1952	4.7	1.0	2.1	41.2	10.5	19.7	54.1	88.5	78.2	20,341	48,077	68,418

Series W248-259. Percentage of full-time teachers in public elementary and secondary schools, by highest university degree held and sex, by province, selected years, 1952 to 1973 (continued)

Year[1]	Master and higher			Bachelor			No degree			Total		
	Male	Female	Total	Male	Female	Total	Male	Female	Total	Male	Female	Total
	248	249	250	251	252	253	254	255	256	257	258	259

Newfoundland

1973	6.8	1.8	3.9	59.7	38.2	47.7	33.5	60.0	48.4	3,103	3,969	7,072
1972	5.5	1.4	3.1	56.9	31.2	42.2	37.6	67.4	54.7	2,946	3,949	6,895
1971	4.7	1.5	2.8	52.4	24.7	36.2	42.9	73.8	61.0	2,763	3,885	6,648
1970	3.9	1.5	2.4	46.0	18.2	29.2	50.1	80.3	68.4	2,554	3,883	6,437
1969	3.2	1.2	2.0	40.6	14.4	24.3	56.2	84.4	73.7	2,398	3,917	6,315
1968	3.6	1.2	2.0	35.2	10.5	19.5	61.2	88.3	78.5	2,277	3,929	6,206
1967	3.3	0.8	1.7	31.1	8.5	16.4	65.6	90.7	81.9	2,064	3,791	5,855
1966	3.1	0.7	1.5	25.9	7.2	13.8	71.0	92.1	84.7	1,986	3,658	5,644
1965	3.1	0.9	1.7	23.2	5.9	12.3	73.7	93.2	86.0	2,035	3,510	5,545
1964	2.6	0.9	1.5	21.7	5.7	11.7	75.7	93.4	86.8	2,010	3,341	5,351
1963	2.8	0.6	1.4	20.4	5.6	11.2	76.8	93.8	87.4	1,887	3,149	5,036
1962	2.8	0.7	1.5	18.9	5.6	10.5	78.3	93.7	88.0	1,791	2,998	4,789
1961	2.0	0.9	1.3	18.4	5.0	10.0	79.6	94.1	88.7	1,689	2,813	4,502
1960	1.8	0.6	2.8	18.1	4.8	9.7	80.1	94.6	87.5	1,592	2,725	4,317
1959	1.4	0.6	0.9	16.3	4.0	8.5	82.3	95.4	90.6	1,450	2,569	4,019
1958	1.5	0.6	0.9	17.4	3.9	8.6	81.1	95.5	90.5	1,381	2,515	3,896
1957	1.0	0.3	0.6	12.3	2.2	5.5	86.7	97.5	93.9	1,018	2,031	3,049
1956	0.9	0.3	0.5	8.8	1.7	3.9	90.3	98.0	95.6	879	1.857	2,736

Prince Edward Island

1973	..	..	..	..	..	..	..	..	..	..	..	..
1972	7.0	1.6	3.2	62.2	23.4	35.4	30.8	75.0	61.4	440	1,021	1,461
1971	6.1	1.4	2.7	63.3	20.8	33.2	30.6	77.8	64.1	477	1,162	1,639
1970	5.3	1.4	2.4	59.0	15.0	27.0	35.7	83.6	70.6	437	1,169	1,606
1969	4.4	1.3	2.1	54.4	11.1	22.5	41.2	87.6	75.4	390	1,096	1,486
1968	5.0	0.8	1.8	46.6	9.1	17.9	48.4	90.1	80.3	341	1,117	1,458
1967	3.5	0.5	1.1	46.7	9.6	18.0	49.8	89.9	80.9	315	1,082	1,397
1966	1.8	0.6	0.8	42.6	6.9	14.3	55.6	92.5	84.9	272	1,046	1,318
1965	0.8	0.5	0.6	35.3	5.7	11.5	63.9	93.8	87.9	238	971	1,209
1964	0.9	0.5	0.6	34.6	4.9	10.7	64.5	94.6	88.7	228	938	1,166
1963	0.5	0.6	0.6	31.9	5.5	10.3	67.6	93.9	89.1	207	925	1,132
1962	–	0.2	0.2	25.4	4.5	8.2	74.6	95.3	91.6	189	883	1,072
1961	0.6	0.2	0.3	25.9	3.6	7.4	73.5	96.2	92.3	174	839	1,013
1960	1.4	0.1	0.3	24.8	3.8	6.9	73.8	96.1	92.8	145	824	969
1959	1.5	0.3	0.4	24.2	2.7	5.9	74.3	97.0	93.7	132	772	904
1958	3.3	0.3	0.7	19.7	2.5	4.9	77.0	97.2	94.4	122	731	853
1954	0.9	–	0.1	20.6	2.4	4.9	78.5	97.6	95.0	107	671	778
1952	0.8	–	0.1	18.6	2.4	5.0	80.6	97.6	94.9	118	623	741

Nova Scotia

1973	11.8	3.7	6.6	60.0	34.1	43.3	28.2	62.2	50.1	3,658	6,622	10,280
1972	11.9	3.5	6.3	58.6	31.7	40.9	29.5	64.8	52.8	3,434	6,586	10,020
1971	12.6	3.4	6.5	57.3	30.4	39.2	30.1	66.2	54.3	3,236	6,633	9,869
1970	12.5	3.3	6.1	56.9	28.0	36.9	30.6	68.7	57.0	3,061	6,938	9,999
1969	12.6	3.1	5.8	54.6	24.7	33.3	32.8	72.2	60.9	2,699	6,744	9,443
1968	13.4	2.9	5.7	54.4	23.4	31.8	32.2	73.7	62.5	2,399	6,513	8,912
1967	13.8	2.7	5.6	51.2	21.2	28.9	35.0	76.1	65.5	2,189	6,298	8,487
1966	14.4	2.7	5.5	48.0	19.6	26.5	37.6	77.7	68.0	1,926	6,107	8,033
1965	14.5	2.7	5.6	45.3	18.1	24.5	40.2	79.2	69.9	1,867	6,030	7,897
1964	12.9	2.5	4.9	43.5	17.4	23.3	43.6	80.1	71.8	1,749	5,889	7,638
1963	12.8	2.7	5.0	42.4	16.3	22.0	44.8	81.0	73.0	1,632	5,791	7,423
1962	12.7	2.7	4.7	43.6	15.2	21.0	43.7	82.1	74.3	1,467	5,709	7,176
1961	13.0	2.7	4.7	42.7	14.1	19.9	44.3	83.2	75.4	1,416	5,535	6,951
1960	14.1	2.5	4.7	42.6	13.7	19.1	43.3	83.8	76.2	1,258	5,406	6,664
1959	13.8	2.2	4.3	40.0	12.0	17.1	46.2	85.8	78.6	1,157	5,275	6,432
1958	14.2	2.7	4.6	43.2	12.5	17.8	42.6	84.8	77.6	1,065	5,112	6,177
1954	14.3	2.2	4.2	38.6	10.4	15.0	47.1	87.4	80.8	876	4,469	5,345
1952	16.2	2.0	4.3	42.2	10.0	15.1	41.6	88.0	80.6	789	4,236	5,025

Series W248-259. Percentage of full-time teachers in public elementary and secondary schools, by highest university degree held and sex, by province, selected years, 1952 to 1973 (continued)

Year[1]	Master and higher			Bachelor			No degree			Total		
	Male	Female	Total	Male	Female	Total	Male	Female	Total	Male	Female	Total
	248	249	250	251	252	253	254	255	256	257	258	259

New Brunswick												
1973	8.6	2.1	4.4	68.4	36.4	47.9	23.0	61.5	47.7	2,801	5,004	7,805
1972	8.3	2.0	4.2	65.1	32.0	43.7	26.6	66.0	52.1	2,795	5,166	7,961
1971	7.3	1.6	3.5	63.4	27.7	39.6	29.3	70.7	56.9	2,664	5,292	7,956
1970	6.8	1.3	3.0	59.1	23.2	34.6	34.1	75.5	62.4	2,510	5,387	7,897
1969	6.5	1.2	2.8	55.4	19.2	30.1	38.1	79.6	67.1	2,368	5,454	7,822
1968	5.5	1.0	2.2	49.5	15.3	24.9	45.0	83.7	72.9	2,114	5,423	7,537
1967	4.1	1.8	1.8	46.6	12.6	21.8	49.3	85.6	76.4	1,952	5,300	7,252
1966	4.3	0.8	1.7	45.8	11.0	19.7	49.9	88.2	78.6	1,741	5,186	6,927
1965	4.7	0.8	1.8	42.3	10.2	18.1	53.0	89.0	80.1	1,692	5,120	6,812
1964	5.0	0.8	1.8	40.6	9.3	16.8	54.4	89.9	81.4	1,586	4,991	6,577
1963	..	..	..	..	..	..	..	..	..	1,439	4,919	6,358
1962	5.4	0.8	1.8	33.1	6.9	12.6	61.5	92.3	85.6	1,365	4,903	6,268
1961	5.5	1.0	2.0	32.9	6.7	12.5	61.6	92.3	85.5	1,337	4,702	6,039
1960	5.5	0.9	1.9	33.0	6.3	12.0	61.5	92.8	86.1	1,261	4,605	5,866
1959	6.0	1.0	2.0	31.8	6.2	11.5	62.2	92.8	86.5	1,154	4,477	5,631
1958	6.9	1.0	2.1	32.3	6.0	11.0	60.8	93.0	86.9	1,017	4,320	5,337
1954	7.9	0.8	2.0	31.0	6.4	10.5	61.1	92.8	87.5	720	3,665	4,385
1952	8.6	0.9	2.1	29.1	5.6	9.3	62.3	93.5	88.6	642	3,361	4,003
Ontario												
1973	12.8	2.8	7.2	60.3	33.6	45.3	26.9	63.6	47.5	41,100 e	54,000 e	95,100 e
1972	10.6	2.4	6.0	56.8	29.3	41.2	32.6	68.3	52.8	41,546	54,675	96,221
1971	..	..	..	..	..	..	..	..	..	38,998 e	53,800 e	92,798
1970	..	..	..	..	..	..	..	..	..	37,200 e	55,800 e	93,000
1969	..	..	..	..	..	..	..	..	..	36,152 e	53,777 e	89,929
1968	..	..	..	..	..	..	..	..	..	33,300 e	51,490 e	84,790
1967	6.5	1.4	3.4	49.2	20.2	31.7	44.3	78.4	64.9	31,384	47,916	79,300
1966	6.2	1.4	3.3	48.5	19.4	30.9	45.3	79.2	65.8	28,939	45,004	73,943
1965	6.0	1.2	3.1	48.6	18.7	30.6	45.4	80.1	66.3	27,104	41,498	68,602
1964	5.9	1.2	3.0	47.7	18.0	29.6	46.4	80.8	67.4	25,014	39,115	64,129
1963	5.9	1.1	3.0	47.5	17.1	28.7	46.6	81.8	68.3	22,864	37,147	60,011
1962	4.0	0.9	2.0	48.6	16.2	28.1	47.4	82.9	69.9	20,507	35,280	55,787
1961	5.9	1.1	2.8	53.9	16.0	29.2	40.2	82.9	68.0	18,304	34,140	52,444
1960	4.0	0.9	1.9	46.3	13.9	24.6	49.7	85.2	73.5	16,336	32,956	49,292
1959	4.1	0.9	1.9	47.6	13.9	24.7	48.3	85.2	73.4	14,434	30,937	45,371
1958	4.4	0.8	1.9	44.0	12.9	22.5	51.6	86.3	75.6	13,482	30,104	43,586
1954	4.2	0.9	1.9	44.4	11.3	21.3	51.4	87.8	76.8	9,983	23,076	33,059
1952	4.2	0.9	1.9	46.5	12.2	22.7	49.3	86.9	75.4	8,898	20,218	29,116
Manitoba												
1973	8.9	3.0	5.6	73.7	38.4	53.9	17.4	58.6	40.5	5,037	6,413	11,450
1972	8.2	2.6	5.0	70.3	33.6	49.3	21.5	63.8	45.7	4,874	6,549	11,423
1971	7.4	1.9	4.1	65.8	29.6	44.4	26.8	68.5	51.5	4,786	6,945	11,731
1970	6.3	1.9	3.6	58.5	24.8	37.7	35.2	73.3	58.7	4,428	7,106	11,534
1969	5.5	1.5	2.9	56.3	21.9	34.8	38.2	76.6	62.3	4,183	7,011	11,194
1968	5.5	1.4	2.9	55.4	20.3	33.1	39.1	78.3	64.0	3,950	6,869	10,819
1967	5.1	1.2	2.7	51.8	19.0	30.8	43.1	79.8	66.5	3,566	6,360	9,926
1966	5.4	1.2	2.8	46.7	17.7	28.2	47.9	81.1	69.0	3,408	6,024	9,432
1965	5.2	1.4	2.9	43.1	17.0	26.5	51.7	81.6	70.6	3,365	5,867	9,232
1964	5.1	1.5	2.8	41.2	16.2	25.5	53.7	82.3	71.7	3,324	5,651	8,975
1963	5.5	1.3	2.9	39.7	15.3	24.2	54.8	83.4	72.9	3,110	5,424	8,534
1962	5.4	1.5	2.9	38.2	14.5	22.9	56.4	84.0	74.2	2,925	5,328	8,253
1961	5.4	1.4	2.8	37.4	13.7	21.8	57.2	84.9	75.4	2,743	5,326	8,069
1960	5.3	1.5	2.7	32.5	12.5	19.2	62.2	86.0	78.1	2,489	4,971	7,460
1859	5.5	1.5	2.7	34.0	11.9	18.9	60.5	86.6	78.4	2,238	4,838	7,076
1958	4.8	0.9	2.1	29.9	11.4	17.0	65.3	87.7	80.9	2,089	4,830	6,919
1954	5.8	1.1	2.4	32.1	11.6	17.4	62.1	87.3	80.2	1,668	4,169	5,837
1952	5.7	1.0	2.3	32.7	10.8	17.1	61.6	88.2	80.6	1,528	3,830	5,358

Series W248-259. Percentage of full-time teachers in public elementary and secondary schools, by highest university degree held and sex, by province, selected years, 1952 to 1973 (concluded)

Year[1]	Master and higher			Bachelor			No degree			Total		
	Male	Female	Total	Male	Female	Total	Male	Female	Total	Male	Female	Total
	248	249	250	251	252	253	254	255	256	257	258	259
Saskatchewan												
1973	4.6	1.1	2.7	75.4	28.9	49.8	20.0	70.1	47.5	4,928	5,996	10,924
1972	4.1	0.9	2.3	70.2	24.0	44.3	25.7	75.0	53.4	4,731	6,013	10,744
1971	4.5	1.1	2.5	66.9	20.9	40.6	28.6	78.0	56.9	4,576	6,140	10,716
1970	4.5	1.0	2.5	63.3	18.9	37.0	32.2	80.1	60.5	4,487	6,490	10,977
1969	4.6	0.9	2.4	55.8	16.0	31.6	39.6	83.1	66.0	4,547	7,006	11,553
1968	4.3	0.8	2.2	54.5	15.2	30.3	41.2	84.0	67.5	4,406	7,083	11,489
1967	3.8	0.9	1.9	52.3	13.8	28.3	43.9	85.3	69.8	4,191	6,918	11,109
1966	3.7	0.9	2.0	48.4	12.7	26.0	47.9	86.4	72.0	4,088	6,835	10,923
1965	..	..	..	..	..	..	..	..	..	3,950 e	6,550 e	10,500 e
1964	2.7	0.8	1.5	40.4	9.9	21.3	56.9	89.3	77.2	3,742	6,254	9,996
1963	2.4	0.7	1.4	37.2	9.2	19.7	60.4	90.1	78.9	3,594	5,962	9,556
1962	2.1	0.6	1.1	35.4	8.6	18.4	62.5	90.8	80.5	3,378	5,868	9,246
1961	2.0	0.6	1.1	33.6	8.0	16.9	64.4	91.4	82.0	3,126	5,871	8,997
1960	1.7	0.6	1.0	31.4	7.6	15.7	66.9	91.8	83.3	2,940	5,698	8,638
1959	2.0	0.6	1.0	29.9	7.2	14.8	68.1	92.2	84.2	2,811	5,526	8,337
1958	1.9	0.7	1.1	28.6	6.7	10.0	69.5	92.6	88.9	2,704	5,536	8,240
1954	1.7	0.5	0.9	28.7	6.0	13.3	69.6	93.5	85.8	2,369	4,976	7,345
1952	1.3	0.4	0.7	27.6	5.7	12.6	71.1	93.9	86.7	2,298	4,936	7,234
Alberta												
1973	11.5	3.2	6.9	78.9	57.3	66.9	9.6	39.5	26.2	9,050	11,320	20,370
1972	10.8	3.0	6.4	76.3	50.8	61.9	12.9	46.2	31.7	8,842	11,426	20,268
1971	9.9	2.9	5.9	73.3	45.3	57.3	16.8	51.8	36.8	8,830	11,691	20,521
1970	9.1	2.6	5.3	71.7	40.1	53.0	19.2	57.3	41.7	8,334	12,024	20,358
1969	9.0	2.3	5.0	68.0	34.7	47.8	23.0	63.0	47.2	7,839	11,982	19,821
1968	8.3	2.0	4.4	65.9	30.0	44.0	25.8	68.0	51.6	7,307	11,463	18,770
1967	8.0	1.7	4.2	62.7	26.3	40.1	29.3	72.0	55.7	6,630	10,862	17,492
1966	8.1	1.6	4.1	60.2	23.9	37.4	31.7	74.5	58.5	6,115	10,243	16,358
1965	7.9	1.3	3.8	57.2	21.5	34.7	34.9	77.2	61.5	5,724	9,794	15,518
1964	7.7	1.3	3.6	55.2	19.3	32.3	37.1	79.4	64.1	5,307	9,395	14,702
1963	7.5	1.2	3.5	53.3	17.4	30.1	39.2	81.4	66.4	4,898	8,986	13,884
1962	7.6	1.2	3.4	51.4	15.8	28.0	41.0	83.0	68.6	4,510	8,626	13,136
1961	7.7	1.1	3.3	50.2	14.5	26.2	42.1	84.4	70.5	4,086	8,328	12,414
1960	7.4	1.1	3.1	49.0	13.6	24.6	43.6	85.3	72.3	3,654	8,108	11,762
1959	7.1	1.0	2.7	46.2	12.6	22.7	46.7	86.4	74.6	3,330	7,741	11,071
1958	5.9	0.9	2.4	44.3	11.1	20.9	49.8	88.0	76.7	3,186	7,669	10,855
1954	6.0	1.1	2.6	44.0	11.6	21.7	50.0	87.3	75.7	2,409	5,305	7,714
1952	5.5	0.9	2.4	40.3	16.2	33.1	54.2	82.9	64.5	2,277	4,861	7,138
British Columbia												
1973	13.0	2.8	7.7	70.0	49.2	59.2	17.0	48.0	33.1	11,204	12,043	23,247
1972	12.4	2.6	7.3	66.2	44.1	54.7	21.4	53.3	38.0	10,466	11,278	21,744
1971	12.0	2.4	6.9	66.0	41.7	53.0	22.0	55.9	40.1	10,281	11,831	22,112
1970	11.1	2.4	6.4	65.1	38.4	50.5	23.8	59.2	43.1	9,810	11,765	21,575
1969	10.3	2.3	6.0	62.9	35.4	47.8	26.8	62.3	46.2	9,374	11,441	20,815
1968	9.6	2.0	5.4	61.0	33.0	45.4	29.4	65.0	49.2	8,666	10,820	19,486
1967	8.7	1.8	4.9	60.1	30.7	43.7	31.2	67.5	51.4	8,046	10,226	18,272
1966	8.0	1.7	4.5	58.1	29.1	41.8	33.9	69.2	53.7	7,447	9,519	16,966
1965	7.8	1.8	4.2	56.6	27.3	40.1	35.6	70.9	55.7	6,882	8,877	15,759
1964	7.2	1.7	4.1	54.6	25.3	38.2	38.2	73.0	57.7	6,543	8,336	14,879
1963	6.7	1.8	3.9	52.7	23.7	36.5	40.6	74.5	59.6	6,233	7,834	14,067
1962	5.9	1.8	3.7	51.5	22.5	35.3	42.6	75.7	61.0	5,862	7,449	13,311
1961	5.9	1.7	3.5	50.3	21.1	33.9	43.8	77.2	62.6	5,499	7,015	12,514
1960	5.2	1.6	3.2	50.8	20.9	33.9	44.0	77.5	62.9	5,146	6,722	11,868
1959	4.8	1.8	3.1	50.1	19.2	32.3	45.1	79.0	64.6	4,803	6,482	11,285
1958	4.9	1.6	3.0	49.4	18.5	31.5	45.7	79.9	65.5	4,461	6,206	10,667
1954	4.8	1.4	2.8	52.9	18.1	32.5	42.3	80.5	64.7	3,325	4,703	8,028
1952	4.6	1.5	2.8	54.0	19.0	33.4	41.4	79.5	63.8	2,912	4,155	7,067

[1] School year beginning in the year shown.
[2] Excludes Prince Edward Island in 1973; New Brunswick in 1963; Ontario from 1968 to 1971; Saskatchewan in 1965. Information for Quebec is not available.

Series W260-274. Statistics of centralized public school libraries, Canada, 1958 to 1967 and 1972

Year[1]	Schools			Enrolment				Books per		Full-time librarians			Per student expenditures		
	Total[2]	Reporting centralized libraries	Proportion of schools reporting libraries	Total[3]	In schools reporting libraries	Proportion of students in schools with libraries	Book holdings[4]	Student served	Library	Professional[5]	Other[6]	Total	Print[7,8]	Non-print	Total[7,8]
	number		%	'000		%	'000	average number[8]		number			dollars		
	260	**261**	**262**	**263**	**264**	**265**	**266**	**267**	**268**	**269**	**270**	**271**	**272**	**273**	**274**
1972	14.493	8,373	57.8	5,566.4	3,976.9	71.4	42,674.2	10.7	5,097	566	2,409[9]	2,975	..	..	5.73[9]
1967[10]	17,091	5,188	30.4	5,261.5	2,466.6	46.9	16,302.9	6.6	3,142	365[11]	1,124[11,12]	1,489[11,12]	5.45	..	..
1966	18,365	3,271[11]	18.4[11]	5,071.5	2,262.8	44.6	12,653.1	5.6	2,925	..	..	..	3.90[9]	..	..
1965	19,987	2,154[9]	14.0[9]	4,905.7	1,921.0	39.2	10,109.0	5.3	3,260[9]	..	..	..	3.46	..	..
1964	21,521	2,595	12.1	4,740.7	1,493.9	31.5	7,920.4	5.3	3,052	263	907	1,170	2.86	..	..
1963[13]	22,554	2,602	11.5	4,550.7	1,461.9	32.1	7,912.9	5.4	3,041	211	713	924	2.63	..	..
1962	23,706	2,067	8.7	4,369.1	1,213.2	27.8	6,084.7	5.0	2,944	179	490	669	2.45	..	..
1961	24,717	1,958	7.9	4,180.9	1,105.2	26.4	5,190.2	4.7	2,651	185	361	546	2.18	..	..
1960[14]	24,625	1,613	6.9	3,986.0	944.1	24.6	4,326.1	4.6	2,682	155	281	436	2.36	..	..
1959	26,169	1,472	5.6	3,800.5	857.9	22.6	3,713.7	4.3	2,523	125	255	380	..	..	..
1958	27,611	1,058	3.8	3,623.7	666.7	18.4	2,897.8	4.3	2,740	159	..	..	..	..	..

[1] School year beginning in the year shown.
[2] Total number of schools as shown in the *Survey of Libraries,* except for 1958 and 1959 where numbers were taken from the *Survey of Elementary and Secondary Education,* Catalogue 81-210.
[3] Enrolment as reported in series W94-149.
[4] Books, volumes of periodicals, current subscriptions and pamphlets, except for 1965 when pamphlets were excluded.
[5] Persons with a degree in library science.
[6] In most years trained teachers either with some library training or none; in 1972 persons with training in school librarianship.
[7] Expenditures per student based on enrolment in schools reporting expenditure.

[8] Median in 1972, averages in other years.
[9] Excludes Quebec. Most 1972 Quebec figures are incomplete.
[10] No surveys were carried out for the years 1968 to 1971.
[11] Excludes Ontario.
[12] Includes 249 librarians without either library or teacher training: Quebec, 179; Manitoba, 1; Alberta, 62 and British Columbia, 7.
[13] Up to 1962, survey covered school boards in municipalities having population of 10,000 or more. Beginning in 1963, all school boards were surveyed regardless of the size of the population, however, all did not report in some years.
[14] Excludes Newfoundland.

Series W275-300. Operating and capital expenditures of public school boards on elementary and secondary education, Canada and by province, selected years, 1900 to 1974
(thousands of dollars)

Year	Operating expenditures												
	Canada	Newfoundland	Prince Edward Island	Nova Scotia	New Brunswick	Quebec	Ontario	Manitoba	Saskatchewan	Alberta	British Columbia	Yukon Territory	Northwest Territories
	275	**276**	**277**	**278**	**279**	**280**	**281**	**282**	**283**	**284**	**285**	**286**	**287**
1974	5,379,876	100,453	21,558	163,535	123,149	1,553,430	1,997,267	223,116	202,797	434,556	529,358	7,294	23,363[1]
1973	4,695,729	83,125	18,032	138,602	105,857	1,354,921	1,775,230	192,496	180,724	379,124	442,815	6,196	18,607[1]
1972	4,194,338	66,624	16,920	125,350	96,258	1,091,401	1,709,057	174,643	160,985	348,949	385,215	5,267	13,669[1]
1971	3,919,082	59,737	15,506	113,044	83,514	1,075,793	1,576,738	160,214	147,128	320,017	351,689	4,454	11,248[1]
1970	3,597,125	48,614	13,099	101,393	73,035	1,006,008	1,457,203	145,147	143,130	289,323	315,665	3,633	875
1969	3,179,705	44,403	11,175	83,466	64,224	891,118	1,275,215	132,386	134,801	258,233	280,784	3,095	805
1968	2,730,794	38,144	10,571	72,416	55,743	771,276	1,066,243	119,145	121,999	226,443	245,392	2,688	734
1967	2,279,977	30,444	9,459	61,268	45,949	645,035	869,509	99,607	108,798	193,402	213,445	2,456	605
1966	1,930,132	25,948	6,912	52,140	40,637	553,780	725,791	78,238	96,948	163,764	183,366	2,112	496
1965	1,680,914	22,645	5,711	46,631	36,051	488,050	625,596	68,701	86,226	140,958	158,060	1,844	441
1964	1,460,009	20,707	5,125	43,290	32,096	400,000	550,072	62,937	76,616	127,107	140,168	1,511	380
1963	1,265,991	18,158	4,727	38,508	30,070	327,041	475,326	58,521	69,968	114,437	127,614	1,267	354
1962	1,125,821	16,036	3,899	35,104	27,418	274,792	425,879	54,434	64,931	105,509	116,323	1,130	366
1961	1,009,616	14,722	3,231	32,571	25,254	225,181	389,029	50,701	61,681	96,764	109,327	905	250
1960	902,206	13,497	3,008	29,425	23,357	185,937	353,875	46,282	57,053	86,304	102,539	737	192
1959	798,578	11,825	2,512	26,698	21,059	161,805	315,523	40,243	51,951	75,769	90,411	610	172
1955	474,830	7,186	1,604	15,838	13,405	95,039	187,161	25,182	33,230	44,146	51,525	389	125
1950	261,555	3,652	1,054	10,998[2]	9,632[2]	51,593	99,184	14,602	20,771	24,654	25,267	148	—
1945	138,971[3]	—[3]	559	5,578[2]	3,491[2]	28,884	54,148	9,489	12,748	12,560	11,458[2]	56	—
1940	99,727	—	437	3,812[2]	2,834[2]	19,164	40,927	6,709	8,185	8,760	8,863[2]	36	—
1935	85,903	—	426	3,520[2]	2,437[2]	15,529	36,465	5,848	6,962	7,596	7,084[2]	36	—
1930	101,004	—	429	3,268[2]	2,290[2]	18,222	40,179	7,668	12,207	9,252	7,442[2]	47	—
1925	88,892	—	396[r]	3,058[2]	2,050[2]	13,528	38,889	7,699	10,236	7,405	6,186[2]	45	—
1920	63,369	—	295	2,080	1,240[2]	8,691	24,367	7,032	9,141	6,326	4,156[2]	41	—
1915	33,714	—	201	1,332	986[2]	5,381	12,764	3,099	3,324	3,535	3,047[2]	45	—
1910	19,575	—	152	1,020	738[2]	3,151[2]	8,377	1,760	1,612	1,204	1,523[2]	38	—
1905	11,792	—	145	843	566[2]	1,829[2]	5,982	1,002	445	399	581[2]	—	—
1900	8,558	—	144	709	455[2]	1,180[2]	4,765	658	—[4]	—[4]	314[2]	—	333[4]

Series W275-300. Operating and capital expenditures of public school boards on elementary and secondary education, Canada and by province, selected years, 1900 to 1974 (concluded)
(thousands of dollars)

Year	Capital expenditures												
	Canada	Newfound-land	Prince Edward Island	Nova Scotia	New Brunswick	Quebec	Ontario	Manitoba	Saskat-chewan	Alberta	British Columbia	Yukon Territory	Northwest Terri-tories
	288	289	290	291	292	293	294	295	296	297	298	299	300
1974	648,116	22,142	2,608	15,154	—[5]	175,484	263,748	25,457	17,087	57,286	66,659	1,143	1,348
1973	665,371	21,745	3,038	14,663	—[5]	185,954	275,059	27,806	14,468	55,606	59,072	2,048	5,912[1]
1972	625,026	16,865	2,199	12,639	—[5]	189,551	246,143	22,579	18,195	51,610	53,079	2,812	9,354[1]
1971	526,962	13,274	1,998	11,151	—[5]	133,158	223,464	20,135	17,508	49,201	48,673	704	7,696[1]
1970	489,565	12,297	1,710	10,975	—[5]	127,112	211,556	16,519	16,300	46,664	45,104	1,275	53
1969	459,729	8,181	1,149	10,292	—[5]	139,482	184,182	15,807	15,485	41,216	41,547	2,326	62
1968	438,823	8,997	909	9,561	—[5]	120,724	193,764	14,939	14,373	34,627	39,714	1,135	80
1967	392,172	6,862	765	9,402	2,680	100,965	176,482	15,101	13,892	31,025	33,984	921	93
1966	344,359	3,667	849	8,991	5,594	89,710	150,797	13,655	12,893	27,060	30,399	670	74
1965	329,519	3,455	974	8,048	4,875	103,950	130,785	12,073	13,545	23,939	27,274	564	37
1964	312,443	3,209	952	7,852	6,044	100,000	122,238	11,302	12,185	23,799	24,547	304	11
1963	300,836	3,213	916	8,270	6,555	92,358	107,952	11,024	11,814	35,582	22,035	1,041	76
1962	284,683	3,090	713	9,306	5,477	86,759	98,064	10,125	9,900	40,387	19,107	1,655	100
1961	255,827	3,369	676	6,369	4,909	82,446	89,789	9,735	14,085	26,146	17,357	696	250
1960	230,156	3,667	468	6,111	4,725	71,591	80,536	8,458	12,997	25,803	14,995	658	147
1959	200,569	3,079	364	4,852	4,314	61,272	70,813	7,101	10,115	24,356	13,999	269	35
1955	101,050	1,769	215	1,573	2,140	31,634	35,534	3,401	6,242	7,686	10,374	468	14
1950	46,960	857	126	1,079[2]	1,832[2]	11,325	13,837	2,774	4,339	3,512	7,245	34	—
1945	22,656	—[3]	7	540[2]	650[2]	8,540	7,714	1,275	1,246	1,674	1,010[2]	—	—
1940	21,164	—	8	374[2]	369[2]	6,899	7,971	1,097	1,566	2,132	748[2]	—	—
1935	17,342	—	62	199[2]	170[2]	6,249	5,694	1,308	1,201	1,744	715[2]	—	—
1930	24,648	—	10	206[2]	778[2]	5,618	9,281	1,724	3,549	1,940	1,542[2]	—	—
1925	15,968	—	17	315[2]	1,316[2]	5,027	2,410	1,304	2,501	1,795	1,283[2]	—	—
1920	11,373	—	15	366	428[2]	2,950	2,406	994	1,681	1,668	865[2]	—	—
1915	11,937	—	33	142	87[2]	3,029	4,285	1,082	1,580	1,065	634[2]	—	—
1910	6,218	—	10	106	139[2]	767[2]	2,603	802	643	831	317[2]	—	—
1905	2,453	—	7	68	76[2]	607[2]	1,184	165[e]	108	117	121[2]	—	—
1900	1,734	—	6	121	152[2]	633[2]	541	160[e]	—[4]	—[4]	66[2]	—	55[4]

[1] In 1971, the public school system assumed responsibility for Indian and Eskimo schools.
[2] The sum of operating and capital expenditures is actual, but an estimate was necessary to separate them.
[3] Prior to 1950, Canada totals exclude Newfoundland.
[4] Saskatchewan and Alberta are included in the Northwest Territories.
[5] Included in provincial departmental expenditures.

Series W301-306. Expenditures on elementary and secondary education, by source of funds,[1] Canada,[2] selected years, 1950 to 1974
(thousands of dollars)

Year[3]	Government				Fees and other[4]	Total
	Federal	Provincial	Municipal	Subtotal		
	301	302	303	304	305	306
1974	211,349	4,618,426	2,061,597	6,891,372	299,473	7,190,845
1973	180,099	3,842,374	1,930,542	5,953,015	359,866	6,312,881
1972	153,780	3,478,696	1,772,317	5,404,793	220,175	5,624,968
1971	203,197	3,228,393	1,708,570	5,140,160	249,096	5,389,256
1970	275,754	2,686,779	1,714,820	4,677,353	203,073	4,880,426
1969	218,834	2,274,128	1,622,301	4,115,263	166,158	4,281,421
1968	194,802	1,929,197	1,475,221	3,599,220	175,898	3,775,118
1967	179,813	1,605,191	1,308,592	3,093,596	136,442	3,230,038
1966	182,255	1,296,527	1,151,122	2,629,904	161,038	2,790,942
1965	141,065	1,097,611	1,034,952	2,273,628	137,170	2,410,798
1964	99,155	938,783	913,407	1,951,345	114,811	2,066,156
1963	121,975	816,180	824,885	1,763,040	116,037	1,879,077
1962	188,802	772,295	738,735	1,699,832	108,950	1,808,782
1961	62,032	638,059	689,832	1,389,923	109,536	1,499,459
1960	51,448	541,882	652,503	1,245,833	82,461	1,328,294
1959	47,870	465,587	582,303	1,095,760	66,637	1,162,397
1955	25,219	261,312	342,572	629,103	45,343	674,446
1950	12,215	128,465	199,041	339,721	19,403	359,124

[1] Includes public, private and federal schools, special education, and related federal and provincial expenditures.
[2] Includes overseas programs and undistributed expenditures.
[3] Financial year beginning in the year shown.
[4] Includes surplus of revenues over expenditures as a deduction.

Series W307-339. Full-time enrolment in post-secondary non-university institutions, by sex, Canada and by province, 1955 and 1958 to 1975

Year[1]	Canada			Newfoundland			Prince Edward Island			Nova Scotia		
	Male	Female	Total	Male	Female	Total	Male	Female	Total	Male	Female	Total
	307	308	309	310	311	312	313	314	315	316	317	318
1975[2]	108,097	112,949[3]	221,046	766	1,198	1,964	307	401	708	904	1,573	2,477
1974	106,200	104,635[3]	210,835	743	1,118	1,861	376	466	842	841	1,479	2,320
1973	106,915	94,536[3]	201,451	683	955	1,638	312	548	860	994	1,515	2,509
1972	101,738	89,216[3]	190,954	598	893	1,491	145	345	490	924	1,553	2,477
1971	94,071	79,708	173,779	658	890	1,548	192	392	584	1,021	1,872	2,893
1970	88,217	77,862	166,079	566	854	1,420	113	237	350	1,006	1,849	2,855
1969	74,157	68,585	142,742	632	811	1,443	64	209	273	945	1,773	2,718
1968	64,494	65,034	129,528	596	766	1,362	—	186	186	915	1,811	2,726
1967	48,032	51,378	99,410	555	651	1,206	—	191	191	571	1,772	2,343
1966	35,872	44,331	80,203	495	609	1,104	—	195	195	418	1,779	2,197
1965	28,564	40,803	69,367	370	633	1,003	—	203	203	390	1,724	2,114
1964	24,346	41,666	66,012	178	616	794	19	245	264	365	1,615	1,980
1963	20,487	41,684	62,171	42	577	619	21	208	229	315	1,519	1,834
1962	16,819	38,785	55,604	—	528	528	24	237	261	273	1,546	1,819
1961	16,491	36,884	53,375	—	507	507	31	254	285	249	1,462	1,711
1960	14,498	34,916	49,414	—	509	509	15	227	242	254	1,524	1,778
1959	14,687	31,580	46,267	—	481	481	13	233	246	125	1,398	1,523
1958	..	..	42,431	—	438	438	6	207	213	..	..	1,396
1955	..	..	33,328	—	300	300	5	217	222	..	..	1,209

Year[1]	New Brunswick			Quebec			Ontario			Manitoba		
	Male	Female	Total	Male	Female	Total	Male	Female	Total	Male	Female	Total
	319	320	321	322	323	324	325	326	327	328	329	330
1975[2]	609	700	1,309	60,663	57,000[3]	117,663	29,617	30,023	59,640	1,286	1,760	3,046
1974	514	673	1,187	57,839	54,343[3]	112,182	28,110	28,532	56,642	1,151	1,641	2,792
1973	535	701	1,236	58,512	49,097	107,609	28,106	27,293	55,399	1,195	1,594	2,789
1972	687	1,282	1,969	54,331	45,896	100,227	27,392	25,129	52,521	1,548	1,822	3,370
1971	755	1,751	2,506	46,574	37,635	84,209	26,772	23,573	50,345	1,754	2,054	3,808
1970	730	1,968	2,698	40,873	33,503	74,376	28,422	25,977	54,399	1,538	1,839	3,377
1969	766	1,989	2,755	33,310	28,173	61,483	25,245	23,717	48,962	1,209	1,743	2,952
1968	730	2,051	2,781	27,723	27,074	54,797	22,788	22,240	45,028	920	1,613	2,533
1967	736	1,895	2,631	20,616	19,285	39,901	16,012	17,658	33,670	668	1,590	2,258
1966	818	1,850	2,668	17,138	16,617	33,755	9,866	15,091	24,957	586	1,495	2,081
1965	703	1,924	2,627	14,037	15,399	29,436	7,551	13,664	21,215	551	1,504	2,055
1964	595	1,922	2,517	12,570	16,886	29,456	6,704	13,310	20,014	582	1,839	2,421
1963	522	1,753	2,275	10,557	17,338	27,895	5,989	12,912	18,901	434	1,776	2,210
1962	322	1,294	1,616	8,966	16,154	25,120	5,072	11,812	16,884	171	1,620	1,791
1961	209	1,226	1,435	8,626	14,361	22,987	5,192	11,782	16,974	206	1,652	1,858
1960	191	1,147	1,338	7,671	12,648	20,319	4,614	11,982	16,596	205	1,559	1,764
1959	209	1,227	1,436	8,792	10,604	19,396	4,027	11,032	15,059	181	1,571	1,752
1958	132	1,072	1,204	7,739	10,334	18,073	..	..	13,766	..	..	1,831
1955	64	969	1,033	..	..	12,480	..	..	10,871	..	..	1,317

Series W307-339. Full-time enrolment in post-secondary non-university institutions, by sex, Canada and by province, 1955 and 1958 to 1975 (concluded)

Year[1]	Saskatchewan			Alberta			British Columbia		
	Male	Female	Total	Male	Female	Total	Male	Female	Total
	331	**332**	**333**	**334**	**335**	**336**	**337**	**338**	**339**
1975[2]	810	1,587	2,397	5,612	9,651	15,263	7,523	9,056	16,579
1974	806	1,541	2,347	7,455	6,636	14,091	8,365	8,206	16,571
1973	1,116	1,407	2,523	7,974	5,616	13,590	7,488	5,810[3]	13,298
1972	1,092	1,369	2,461	7,854	5,476	13,330	7,167	5,451[3]	12,618
1971	1,063	1,373	2,436	7,526	5,101	12,627	7,756	5,067	12,823
1970	876	1,275	2,151	6,316	5,127	11,443	7,777	5,233	13,010
1969	782	1,144	1,926	5,857	4,808	10,665	5,347	4,218	9,565
1968	648	1,273	1,921	5,714	4,413	10,127	4,460	3,607	8,067
1967	612	1,325	1,937	4,237	3,646	7,883	4,025	3,365	7,390
1966	564	1,346	1,910	3,455	2,756	6,211	2,532	2,593	5,125
1965	484	1,306	1,790	2,805	2,553	5,358	1,673	1,893	3,566
1964	436	1,265	1,701	2,225	2,424	4,649	672	1,544	2,216
1963	683	1,920	2,603	1,744	2,160	3,904	180	1,521	1,701
1962	564	2,032	2,596	1,223	2,036	3,259	204	1,526	1,730
1961	655	2,180	2,835	1,125	1,935	3,060	198	1,525	1,723
1960	460	2,112	2,572	947	1,704	2,651	141	1,504	1,645
1959	381	1,945	2,326	627	1,640	2,267	332	1,449	1,781
1958	286	1,894	2,180	..	..	2,026	..	..	1,304
1955	228	1,847	2,075	..	..	1,675	312	1,834	2,146

[1] Academic year beginning in the year shown.
[2] Preliminary.

[3] Includes estimates.

Series W340-438. Full-time university enrolment, by sex, Canada and by province, selected years, 1920 to 1975

Year[1]	Canada								
	Undergraduate			Graduate[2]			Total		
	Male	Female	Total	Male	Female	Total	Male	Female	Total
	340	341	342	343	344	345	346	347	348
1975	190,696	140,258[3]	330,954	28,461	11,647[3]	40,108	219,157	151,905[3]	371,062
1974	182,290	127,251[3]	309,541	27,481	10,334[3]	37,815	209,771	137,585[3]	347,356
1973	178,211	116,765	294,976	27,487	9,661	37,148	205,698	126,426	332,124
1972	175,161	109,736	284,897	28,387	9,120	37,507	203,548	118,856	322,404
1971	178,842	108,276	287,118	27,784	8,124	35,908	206,626	116,400	323,026
1970	174,945	101,352	276,297	25,765	7,407	33,172	200,710	108,759	309,469
1969	168,994	94,921	263,915	24,024	6,207	30,231	193,018	101,128	294,146
1968	155,940	83,783	239,723	21,259	4,861	26,120	177,199	88,644	265,843
1967	150,966	78,333	229,299	19,511	4,676	24,187	170,477	83,009	253,486
1966	139,571	71,047	210,618	16,176	3,543	19,719	155,747	74,590	230,337
1965	125,859	61,190	187,049	14,061	3,135	17,196	139,920	64,325	204,245
1964	113,378	50,424	163,802	11,477	2,320	13,797	124,855	52,744	177,599
1963	103,997	42,830	146,827	9,334	1,799	11,133	113,331	44,629	157,960
1962	95,827	36,854	132,681	7,160	1,276	8,436	102,987	38,130	141,117
1961	89,447	31,836	121,283	6,142	1,205	7,347	95,589	33,041	128,630
1960	80,582	26,629	107,211	5,532	986	6,518	86,114	27,615	113,729
1959	73,943	22,747	96,690	4,487	757	5,244	78,430	23,504	101,934
1958	69,771	20,673	90,444	3,984	566	4,550	73,755	21,239	94,994
1955	54,545	14,765	69,310	2,970	457	3,427	57,515	15,222	72,737
1950	50,170	13,866	64,036	3,857	702	4,559	54,027	14,568	68,595
1945	48,991	12,870	61,861	2,240	630	2,870	51,231	13,500	64,731
1940	26,710	8,107	34,817	1,243	326	1,569	27,953	8,433	26,386
1935	26,028	7,494	33,522	1,198	388	1,586	27,226	7,882	35,108
1930	24,148	7,428	31,576	998	352	1,350	25,146	7,780	32,926
1925	19,580	5,272	24,852	625	221	846	20,205	5,493	25,698
1920	19,075	3,716	22,791	315	108	423	19,390	3,824	23,214

Year[1]	Newfoundland								
	Undergraduate			Graduate[2]			Total		
	Male	Female	Total	Male	Female	Total	Male	Female	Total
	349	350	351	352	353	354	355	356	357
1975	3,311	2,425	5,736	304	141	445	3,615	2,566	6,181
1974	3,283	2,200	5,483	348	156	504	3,631	2,356	5,987
1973	3,681	2,404	6,085	237	96	333	3,918	2,500	6,418
1972	4,303	2,647	6,950	267	92	359	4,570	2,739	7,309
1971	4,165	2,560	6,725	264	88	352	4,429	2,648	7,077
1970	3,829	2,216	6,045	252	81	333	4,081	2,297	6,378
1969	3,148	1,761	4,909	202	46	248	3,350	1,807	5,157
1968	2,902	1,661	4,563	193	26	219	3,095	1,687	4,782
1967	2,765	1,559	4,324	127	22	149	2,892	1,581	4,473
1966	2,427	1,397	3,824	61	8	69	2,488	1,405	3,893
1965	1,970	1,136	3,106	55	7	62	2,025	1,143	3,168
1964	1,781	820	2,601	34	17	51	1,815	837	2,652
1963	1,467	730	2,197	37	10	47	1,504	740	2,244
1962	1,336	628	1,964	25	9	34	1,361	637	1,998
1961	1,109	631	1,740	13	4	17	1,122	635	1,757
1960	820	385	1,205	28	5	33	848	390	1,238
1959	675	364	1,039	17	4	21	692	368	1,060
1958	668	381	1,049	16	5	21	684	386	1,070
1955	376	197	573	3	1	4	379	198	577
1950	..	..	380	—	—	—	..	..	380
1945	—	—	—	—	—	—	—	—	—
1940	—	—	—	—	—	—	—	—	—
1935	—	—	—	—	—	—	—	—	—
1930	—	—	—	—	—	—	—	—	—
1925	—	—	—	—	—	—	—	—	—
1920	—	—	—	—	—	—	—	—	—

Series W340-438. Full-time university enrolment, by sex, Canada and by province, selected years, 1920 to 1975 (continued)

Year[1]	Prince Edward Island								
	Undergraduate			Graduate[2]			Total		
	Male	Female	Total	Male	Female	Total	Male	Female	Total
	358	359	360	361	362	363	364	365	366
1975	788	675	1,463	–	–	–	788	675	1,463
1974	733	610	1,343	–	–	–	733	610	1,343
1973	763	646	1,409	–	–	–	763	646	1,409
1972	888	693	1,581	–	–	–	888	693	1,581
1971	990	781	1,771	–	–	–	990	781	1,771
1970	1,018	737	1,755	–	–	–	1,018	737	1,755
1969	914	652	1,566	–	–	–	914	652	1,566
1968	884	671	1,555	–	–	–	884	671	1,555
1967	838	531	1,369	–	–	–	838	531	1,369
1966	688	451	1,139	–	–	–	688	451	1,139
1965	573	351	924	–	–	–	573	351	924
1964	549	253	802	–	–	–	549	253	802
1963	540	198	738	–	–	–	540	198	738
1962	462	243	705	–	–	–	462	243	705
1961	467	216	683	–	–	–	467	216	683
1960	387	176	563	–	–	–	387	176	563
1959	359	166	525	–	–	–	359	166	525
1958	315	98	413	–	–	–	315	98	413
1955	227	36	263	–	–	–	227	36	263
1950	..	..	270	–	–	–	..	..	270
1945	..	..	268	–	–	–	..	..	268
1940	..	..	128	–	–	–	..	..	128
1935	..	..	93	–	–	–	..	..	93
1930	..	..	102	–	–	–	..	..	102
1925	..	..	108	–	–	–	..	..	108
1920	..	..	107	–	–	–	..	..	107

Year[1]	Nova Scotia								
	Undergraduate			Graduate[2]			Total		
	Male	Female	Total	Male	Female	Total	Male	Female	Total
	367	368	369	370	371	372	373	374	375
1975	9,251	7,588	16,839	1,036	436	1,472	10,287	8,024	18,311
1974	8,895	6,994	15,889	972	388	1,360	9,867	7,382	17,249
1973	8,666	6,538	15,204	842	316	1,158	9,508	6,854	16,362
1972	8,723	6,211	14,934	854	308	1,162	9,577	6,519	16,096
1971	9,010	6,135	15,145	839	307	1,146	9,849	6,442	16,291
1970	8,763	5,731	14,494	852	280	1,132	9,615	6,011	15,626
1969	7,920	5,001	12,921	775	260	1,035	8,695	5,261	13,956
1968	7,165	3,841	11,006	595	146	741	7,760	3,987	11,747
1967	6,300	3,423	9,723	536	144	680	6,836	3,567	10,403
1966	6,052	3,137	9,189	413	109	522	6,465	3,246	9,711
1965	5,893	3,004	8,897	378	82	460	6,271	3,086	9,357
1964	5,447	2,544	7,991	329	71	400	5,776	2,615	8,391
1963	5,140	2,193	7,333	231	38	269	5,371	2,231	7,602
1962	4,841	1,826	6,667	207	35	242	5,048	1,861	6,909
1961	4,434	1,691	6,125	119	53	172	4,553	1,744	6,297
1960	4,108	1,455	5,563	113	34	147	4,221	1,489	5,710
1959	3,871	1,296	5,167	106	24	130	3,977	1,320	5,297
1958	3,675	1,189	4,864	101	15	116	3,776	1,204	4,980
1955	3,351	1,034	4,385	42	17	59	3,393	1,051	4,444
1950	..	..	3,879	..	..	119	..	..	3,998
1945	..	..	3,400	..	..	78	..	..	3,478
1940	..	..	1,964	..	..	60	..	..	2,024
1935	..	..	2,099	..	..	59	..	..	2,158
1930	..	..	1,968	..	..	40	..	..	2,008
1925	..	..	1,561	..	..	21	..	..	1,582
1920	..	..	1,660	..	..	18	..	..	1,678

Series W340-438. Full-time university enrolment, by sex, Canada and by province, selected years, 1920 to 1975 (continued)

Year[1]	New Brunswick								
	Undergraduate			Graduate[2]			Total		
	Male	Female	Total	Male	Female	Total	Male	Female	Total
	376	**377**	**378**	**379**	**380**	**381**	**382**	**383**	**384**
1975	5,989	4,670	10,659	375	133	508	6,364	4,803	11,167
1974	5,650	4,347	9,997	369	135	504	6,019	4,482	10,501
1973	5,778	4,192	9,970	385	120	505	6,163	4,312	10,475
1972	5,848	3,811	9,659	447	123	570	6,295	3,934	10,229
1971	6,401	3,900	10,301	492	159	651	6,893	4,059	10,952
1970	6,307	3,679	9,986	483	111	594	6,790	3,790	10,580
1969	5,921	3,087	9,008	503	97	600	6,424	3,184	9,608
1968	5,599	2,723	8,322	534	105	639	6,133	2,828	8,961
1967	5,076	2,307	7,383	468	76	544	5,544	2,383	7,927
1966	4,465	1,958	6,423	384	55	439	4,849	2,013	6,862
1965	4,242	1,746	5,988	335	48	383	4,577	1,794	6,371
1964	4,010	1,458	5,468	278	27	305	4,288	1,485	5,773
1963	3,698	1,256	4,954	186	13	199	3,884	1,269	5,153
1962	3,555	1,160	4,715	165	16	181	3,720	1,176	4,896
1961	3,395	989	4,384	136	13	149	3,531	1,002	4,533
1960	3,098	875	3,973	84	6	90	3,182	881	4,063
1959	2,844	724	3,568	82	5	87	2,926	729	3,655
1958	2,655	648	3,303	62	2	64	2,717	650	3,367
1955	1,995	502	2,497	37	10	47	2,032	512	2,544
1950	..	..	2,020	..	..	32	..	..	2,052
1945	..	..	2,137	..	..	22	..	..	2,159
1940	..	..	1,011	..	..	9	..	..	1,020
1935	..	..	863	..	..	26	..	..	889
1930	..	..	903	..	..	5	..	..	908
1925	..	..	560	..	..	6	..	..	566
1920	..	..	487	..	..	6	..	..	493

Year[1]	Quebec								
	Undergraduate			Graduate[2]			Total		
	Male	Female	Total	Male	Female	Total	Male	Female	Total
	385	**386**	**387**	**388**	**389**	**390**	**391**	**392**	**393**
1975	39,347	26,333[3]	65,680	7,680	3,414[3]	11,094	47,027	29,747[3]	76,774
1974	36,645	23,254[3]	59,899	7,368	2,873[3]	10,241	44,013	26,127[3]	70,140
1973	36,427	22,274	58,701	6,732	2,443	9,175	43,159	24,717	67,876
1972	35,838	20,803	56,641	7,169	2,434	9,603	43,007	23,237	66,244
1971	35,478	19,069	54,547	6,309	1,963	8,272	41,787	21,032	62,819
1970	36,725	18,110	54,835	5,421	1,857	7,278	42,146	19,967	62,113
1969	40,475	19,800	60,275	5,058	1,497	6,555	45,533	21,297	66,830
1968	40,396	18,028	58,424	4,739	1,238	5,977	45,135	19,266	64,401
1967	48,744	21,976	70,720	5,744	1,918	7,662	5,488	23,894	78,382
1966	47,092	21,478	68,570	5,161	1,339	6,500	52,253	22,817	75,070
1965	42,796	18,710	61,506	4,552	1,258	5,810	47,348	19,968	67,316
1964	39,149	15,610	54,759	3,789	852	4,641	42,938	16,462	59,400
1963	36,481	13,256	49,737	3,174	694	3,868	39,655	13,950	53,605
1962	33,480	11,031	44,511	2,290	523	2,813	35,770	11,554	47,324
1961	31,734	9,115	40,849	1,819	488	2,307	33,553	9,603	43,156
1960	28,552	7,310	35,862	1,645	336	1,981	30,197	7,646	37,843
1959	25,776	6,171	31,947	1,327	282	1,609	27,103	6,453	33,556
1958	24,431	5,577	30,008	1,227	180	1,407	25,658	5,757	31,415
1955	18,883	3,909	22,792	1,011	194	1,205	19,894	4,103	23,997
1950	..	..	19,819	..	..	1,465	..	..	21,284
1945	..	..	16,534	..	..	921	..	..	17,455
1940	..	..	10,930	..	..	419	..	..	11,349
1935	..	..	10,249	..	..	385	..	..	10,634
1930	..	..	9,090	..	..	369	..	..	9,459
1925	..	..	8,039	..	..	253	..	..	8,292
1920	..	..	7,157	..	..	113	..	..	7,270

Series W340-438. Full-time university enrolment, by sex, Canada and by province, selected years, 1920 to 1975 (continued)

Year[1]	Ontario								
	Undergraduate			Graduate[2]			Total		
	Male	Female	Total	Male	Female	Total	Male	Female	Total
	394	395	396	397	398	399	400	401	402
1975	81,387	60,454	141,841	12,647	5,213	17,860	94,034	65,667	159,701
1974	78,664	54,703	133,367	12,124	4,643	16,767	90,788	59,346	150,134
1973	75,952	48,635	124,587	12,629	4,337	16,966	88,581	52,972	141,553
1972	73,484	45,216	118,700	12,631	3,864	16,495	86,115	49,080	135,195
1971	74,039	44,000	118,039	12,735	3,645	16,380	86,774	47,645	134,419
1970	68,390	37,914	106,304	11,658	3,153	14,811	80,048	41,067	121,115
1969	62,340	33,027	95,367	10,772	2,686	13,458	73,112	35,713	108,825
1968	53,792	27,642	81,434	9,497	2,001	11,498	63,289	29,643	92,932
1967	46,582	23,069	69,651	8,195	1,587	9,782	54,777	24,656	79,433
1966	41,478	19,725	61,203	6,445	1,282	7,727	47,923	21,007	68,930
1965	36,063	16,352	52,415	5,696	1,163	6,859	41,759	17,515	59,274
1964	31,901	13,662	45,563	4,535	889	5,424	36,436	14,551	50,987
1963	28,514	11,652	40,166	3,536	665	4,201	32,050	12,317	44,367
1962	25,950	10,108	36,058	2,861	467	3,328	28,811	10,575	39,386
1961	24,312	8,761	33,073	2,501	402	2,903	26,813	9,163	35,976
1960	22,015	7,561	29,576	2,257	342	2,599	24,272	7,903	32,175
1959	20,821	6,373	27,194	1,900	311	2,211	22,721	6,684	29,405
1958	19,764	6,004	25,768	1,778	259	2,037	21,542	6,263	27,805
1955	16,302	4,786	21,088	1,373	181	1,554	17,675	4,967	22,642
1950	..	..	21,268	..	..	1,939	..	..	23,207
1945	..	..	20,278	..	..	1,463	..	..	21,741
1940	..	..	11,693	..	..	717	..	..	12,410
1935	..	..	12,066	..	..	751	..	..	12,817
1930	..	..	11,414	..	..	633	..	..	12,047
1925	..	..	8,785	..	..	385	..	..	9,170
1920	..	..	9,050	..	..	190	..	..	9,240

Year[1]	Manitoba								
	Undergraduate			Graduate[2]			Total		
	Male	Female	Total	Male	Female	Total	Male	Female	Total
	403	404	405	406	407	408	409	410	411
1975	9,962	7,282[3]	17,244	1,134	352	1,486	11,096	7,634	18,730
1974	9,429	6,817[3]	16,246	1,121	327	1,448	10,550	7,144	17,694
1973	9,229	6,433	15,662	1,082	281	1,363	10,311	6,714	17,025
1972	9,322	6,346	15,668	1,091	264	1,355	10,413	6,610	17,023
1971	9,655	6,288	15,943	1,126	282	1,408	10,781	6,570	17,351
1970	9,577	5,951	15,528	1,124	289	1,413	10,701	6,240	16,941
1969	9,366	5,767	15,133	1,176	288	1,464	10,542	6,055	16,597
1968	8,575	5,353	13,928	942	229	1,171	9,517	5,582	15,099
1967	7,839	4,792	12,631	685	110	795	8,524	4,902	13,426
1966	7,262	4,440	11,702	571	116	687	7,833	4,556	12,389
1965	6,612	3,857	10,469	493	107	600	7,105	3,964	11,069
1964	6,006	2,635	8,641	443	88	531	6,449	2,723	9,172
1963	5,759	2,479	8,238	482	82	564	6,241	2,561	8,802
1962	5,303	2,142	7,445	254	42	296	5,557	2,184	7,741
1961	4,726	1,927	6,653	258	36	294	4,984	1,963	6,947
1960	4,335	1,673	6,008	224	27	251	4,559	1,700	6,259
1959	4,089	1,554	5,643	171	33	204	4,260	1,587	5,847
1958	3,816	1,329	5,145	120	12	132	3,936	1,341	5,277
1955	3,181	1,034	4,215	84	10	94	3,265	1,044	4,309
1950	..	..	4,411	..	..	174	..	..	4,585
1945	..	..	5,427	..	..	59	..	..	5,486
1940	..	..	2,483	..	..	68	..	..	2,551
1935	..	..	2,670	..	..	73	..	..	2,743
1930	..	..	2,608	..	..	50	..	..	2,658
1925	..	..	2,239	..	..	40	..	..	2,279
1920	..	..	1,644	..	..	30	..	..	1,674

Series W340-438. Full-time university enrolment, by sex, Canada and by province, selected years, 1920 to 1975 (continued)

Year[1]	Saskatchewan								
	Undergraduate			Graduate[2]			Total		
	Male	Female	Total	Male	Female	Total	Male	Female	Total
	412	**413**	**414**	**415**	**416**	**417**	**418**	**419**	**420**
1975	7,876	5,798	13,674	529	147	676	8,405	5,945	14,350
1974	7,563	5,412	12,975	481	123	604	8,044	5,535	13,579
1973	7,758	5,146	12,904	495	134	629	8,253	5,280	13,533
1972	7,722	4,962	12,684	584	112	696	8,306	5,074	13,380
1971	8,579	5,453	14,032	670	99	769	9,249	5,552	14,801
1970	8,567	5,502	14,069	633	112	745	9,200	5,614	14,814
1969	8,693	5,540	14,233	580	106	686	9,273	5,646	14,919
1968	8,077	5,100	13,177	542	114	656	8,619	5,214	13,833
1967	7,363	4,656	12,019	526	120	646	7,889	4,776	12,665
1966	6,734	4,241	10,975	495	61	556	7,229	4,302	11,531
1965	6,545	3,721	10,266	368	39	407	6,913	3,760	10,673
1964	5,962	3,288	9,250	304	33	337	6,266	3,321	9,587
1963	5,160	2,312	7,472	285	30	315	5,445	2,342	7,787
1962	4,848	1,913	6,761	233	20	253	5,081	1,933	7,014
1961	4,453	1,644	6,097	209	17	226	4,662	1,661	6,323
1960	4,016	1,422	5,438	190	20	210	4,206	1,442	5,648
1959	3,605	1,117	4,722	154	14	168	3,759	1,131	4,890
1958	3,457	1,008	4,465	101	8	109	3,558	1,016	4,574
1955	2,362	645	3,007	82	6	88	2,444	651	3,095
1950	..	..	2,575	..	..	168	..	..	2,743
1945	..	..	3,997	..	..	46	..	..	4,043
1940	..	..	1,945	..	..	49	..	..	1,994
1935	..	..	1,776	..	..	58	..	..	1,834
1930	..	..	1,755	..	..	62	..	..	1,817
1925	..	..	878	..	..	21	..	..	899
1920	..	..	647	..	..	10	..	..	657

Year[1]	Alberta								
	Undergraduate			Graduate[2]			Total		
	Male	Female	Total	Male	Female	Total	Male	Female	Total
	421	**422**	**423**	**424**	**425**	**426**	**427**	**428**	**429**
1975	16,474	12,405	28,879	2,442	868	3,310	18,916	13,273	32,189
1974	15,618	11,360	26,978	2,294	792	3,086	17,912	12,152	30,064
1973	15,250	10,355	25,605	2,476	949	3,425	17,726	11,304	29,030
1972	14,735	9,522	24,257	2,586	921	3,507	17,321	10,443	27,764
1971	15,520	10,067	25,587	2,510	672	3,182	18,030	10,739	28,769
1970	15,621	10,693	26,314	2,534	676	3,210	18,155	11,369	29,524
1969	14,190	9,422	23,612	2,417	595	3,012	16,607	10,017	26,624
1968	12,478	8,268	20,746	2,006	461	2,467	14,484	8,729	23,213
1967	10,133	6,639	16,772	1,597	327	1,924	11,730	6,966	18,696
1966	8,877	5,604	14,481	1,338	265	1,603	10,215	5,869	16,084
1965	7,910	4,801	12,711	1,110	194	1,304	9,020	4,995	14,015
1964	7,317	4,012	11,329	890	158	1,048	8,207	4,170	12,377
1963	6,397	3,444	9,841	707	118	825	7,104	3,562	10,666
1962	5,933	2,995	8,928	590	66	656	6,523	3,061	9,584
1961	5,252	2,525	7,777	429	42	471	5,681	2,567	8,248
1960	4,706	2,107	6,813	312	38	350	5,018	2,145	7,163
1959	4,167	1,754	5,921	268	26	294	4,435	1,780	6,215
1958	3,781	1,472	5,253	223	23	246	4,004	1,495	5,499
1955	2,788	1,085	3,873	102	5	107	2,890	1,090	3,980
1950	..	..	3,015	..	..	239	..	..	3,254
1945	..	..	2,996	..	..	101	..	..	3,097
1940	..	..	1,939	..	..	84	..	..	2,023
1935	..	..	1,745	..	..	84	..	..	1,829
1930	..	..	1,490	..	..	84	..	..	1,574
1925	..	..	1,085	..	..	66	..	..	1,151
1920	..	..	989	..	..	41	..	..	1,030

Series W340-438. Full-time university enrolment, by sex, Canada and by province, selected years, 1920 to 1975 (concluded)

Year[1]	British Columbia								
	Undergraduate			Graduate[2]			Total		
	Male	Female	Total	Male	Female	Total	Male	Female	Total
	430	431	432	433	434	435	436	437	438
1975	16,311	12,628	28,939	2,314	943	3,257	18,625	13,571	32,196
1974	15,810	11,554	27,364	2,404	897	3,301	18,214	12,451	30,665
1973	14,707	10,142	24,849	2,609	985	3,594	17,316	11,127	28,443
1972	14,298	9,525	23,823	2,758	1,002	3,760	17,056	10,527	27,583
1971	15,005	10,023	25,028	2,839	909	3,748	17,844	10,932	28,776
1970	16,148	10,819	26,967	2,808	848	3,656	18,956	11,667	30,623
1969	16,027	10,864	26,891	2,541	632	3,173	18,568	11,496	30,064
1968	16,072	10,496	26,568	2,211	541	2,752	18,283	11,037	29,320
1967	15,326	9,381	24,707	1,633	372	2,005	16,959	9,753	26,712
1966	14,496	8,616	23,112	1,308	308	1,616	15,804	8,924	24,728
1965	13,255	7,512	20,767	1,074	237	1,311	14,329	7,749	22,078
1964	11,256	6,142	17,398	875	185	1,060	12,131	6,327	18,458
1963	10,841	5,310	16,151	696	149	845	11,537	5,459	16,996
1962	10,119	4,808	14,927	535	98	633	10,654	4,906	15,560
1961	9,565	4,337	13,902	658	150	808	10,223	4,487	14,710
1960	8,545	3,665	12,210	679	178	857	9,224	3,843	13,067
1959	7,736	3,228	10,964	462	58	520	8,198	3,286	11,484
1958	7,209	2,967	10,176	356	62	418	7,565	3,029	10,594
1955	5,080	1,537	6,617	236	33	269	5,316	1,570	6,886
1950	..	..	6,399	..	..	423	..	..	6,822
1945	..	..	6,824	..	..	180	..	..	7,004
1940	..	..	2,724	..	..	163	..	..	2,887
1935	..	..	1,961	..	..	150	..	..	2,111
1930	..	..	2,246	..	..	107	..	..	2,353
1925	..	..	1,597	..	..	54	..	..	1,651
1920	..	..	1,050	..	..	15	..	..	1,065

[1] Academic year beginning in the year shown.
[2] Prior to 1955, graduate enrolment includes part-time students.

[3] Includes estimates.

Series W439–455. Full-time university undergraduate enrolment, by field of specialization[1] and sex, Canada, selected years, 1861 to 1975

Year and sex[2]		Arts and science	Agriculture	Commerce and business administration	Education	Engineering and applied science	Fine and applied arts	Medical and health professions					Household science	Law	Religion and theology	Veterinary medicine	Unclassified	Total
								Dentistry	Medicine	Nursing	Pharmacy	Miscellaneous health professions						
		439	440	441	442	443	444	445	446	447	448	449	450	451	452	453	454	455
1975	Male	89,991	3,420	23,296	17,205	29,160	4,475	1,666	6,442	174	1,062	522	96	6,510	1,487	704	4,486	190,696
	Female	71,864	1,193	6,674	27,913	1,708	6,947	250	2,401	6,247	1,624	2,351	4,225	2,375	765	295	3,426	140,258
	Total	161,855	4,613	29,970	45,118	30,868	11,422	1,916	8,843	6,421	2,686	2,873	4,321	8,885	2,252	999	7,912	330,954
1974	Male	88,696	3,297	21,690	15,797	26,783	4,303	1,653	6,171	125	1,094	422	129	6,403	1,477	701	3,549	182,290
	Female	66,943	960	5,401	24,508	1,271	6,211	215	2,190	5,608	1,539	2,163	4,365	1,994	735	242	2,906	127,251
	Total	155,639	4,257	27,091	40,305	28,054	10,514	1,868	8,361	5,733	2,633	2,585	4,494	8,397	2,212	943	6,455	309,541
1973	Male	89,460	2,889	20,616	15,943	25,050	4,137	1,719	5,366	108	1,121	641	113	6,735	1,389	685	2,239	178,211
	Female	63,220	702	4,561	22,507	865	5,763	167	1,722	4,997	1,441	2,261	4,322	1,718	726	207	1,586	116,765
	Total	152,680	3,591	25,177	38,450	25,915	9,900	1,886	7,088	5,105	2,562	2,902	4,435	8,453	2,115	892	3,825	294,976
1972	Male	89,039	2,628	18,672	15,606	24,987	3,798	1,682	5,293	90	1,142	614	98	6,666	1,478	698	2,670	175,161
	Female	61,138	489	3,594	21,164	669	5,207	153	1,522	4,770	1,395	1,987	3,739	1,468	740	158	1,543	109,736
	Total	150,177	3,117	22,266	36,770	25,656	9,005	1,835	6,815	4,860	2,537	2,601	3,837	8,134	2,218	856	4,213	284,897
1971	Male	92,653	3,065	17,386	17,154	25,986	3,457	1,658	5,048	99	1,090	776	36	6,609	1,633	665	1,527	178,842
	Female	63,205	462	2,803	21,687	649	4,048	134	1,282	4,641	1,204	2,067	3,367	1,155	657	128	787	108,276
	Total	155,858	3,527	20,189	38,841	26,635	7,505	1,792	6,330	4,740	2,294	2,843	3,403	7,764	2,290	793	2,314	287,118
1970	Male	94,313	3,332	15,035	16,805	25,232	2,353	1,560	4,694	91	1,054	595	20	6,328	2,037	621	875	174,945
	Female	60,302	389	1,712	21,726	474	3,093	92	1,039	4,300	1,014	1,904	2,921	922	633	86	745	101,352
	Total	154,615	3,721	16,747	38,531	25,706	5,446	1,652	5,733	4,391	2,068	2,499	2,941	7,250	2,670	707	1,620	276,297
1969	Male	91,693	3,235	14,754	15,292	24,677	1,903	1,497	4,607	85	1,060	538	36	5,752	2,342	571	952	168,994
	Female	57,346	303	1,363	20,335	399	2,508	85	951	4,137	884	2,023	2,799	707	711	70	300	94,921
	Total	149,039	3,538	16,117	35,627	25,076	4,411	1,582	5,558	4,222	1,944	2,561	2,835	6,459	3,053	641	1,252	263,915
1968	Male	85,725	2,512	13,755	12,339	24,469	1,047	1,418	4,448	74	1,011	203	16	5,231	2,288	550	854	155,940
	Female	52,070	233	1,227	16,418	397	1,412	69	792	3,922	778	1,370	2,729	504	671	55	1,136	83,783
	Total	137,795	2,745	14,982	28,757	24,866	2,459	1,487	5,240	3,996	1,789	1,573	2,745	5,735	2,959	605	1,990	239,723
1967	Male	84,281	2,481	12,259	12,095	22,925	752	1,295	4,314	62	1,042	174	16	4,695	2,983	508	1,084	150,966
	Female	48,807	204	1,122	16,006	355	1,186	71	689	3,508	693	1,172	2,578	372	501	48	1,021	78,333
	Total	133,088	2,685	13,381	28,101	23,280	1,938	1,366	5,003	3,570	1,735	1,346	2,594	5,067	3,484	556	2,105	229,299
1966	Male	78,762	2,388	11,281	11,375	20,593	619	1,264	4,170	69	991	180	15	4,183	2,666	465	550	139,571
	Female	43,141	173	951	15,902	282	1,001	71	625	3,491	671	1,032	2,489	281	50	43	844	71,047
	Total	121,903	2,561	12,232	27,277	20,875	1,620	1,335	4,795	3,560	1,662	1,212	2,504	4,464	2,716	508	1,394	210,618
1965	Male	70,010	2,228	9,932	10,672	18,475	460	1,218	4,012	42	1,021	175	13	3,804	2,803	466	528	125,859
	Female	36,983	186	808	13,373	205	779	66	532	3,160	633	965	2,272	249	44	46	853	61,190
	Total	106,993	2,414	10,740	24,045	18,680	1,239	1,284	4,580	3,202	1,654	1,140	2,285	4,053	2,847	512	1,381	187,049
1964	Male	61,249	2,198	9,079	9,660	16,987	349	1,187	4,103	35	1,083	181	8	3,329	2,992	518	420	113,378
	Female	29,950	140	668	10,968	169	638	54	532	2,980	570	827	1,923	191	44	43	727	50,424
	Total	91,199	2,338	9,747	20,628	17,156	987	1,241	4,635	3,015	1,653	1,008	1,931	3,520	3,036	561	1,147	163,802
1963	Male	54,547	2,099	8,248	9,062	16,400	315	1,128	3,925	14	1,137	160	10	3,000	3,087	485	380	103,997
	Female	25,261	102	539	8,886	119	549	54	518	2,703	528	820	1,794	170	33	41	713	42,830
	Total	79,808	2,201	8,787	17,948	16,519	864	1,182	4,443	2,717	1,665	980	1,804	3,170	3,120	526	1,093	146,827
1962	Male	49,398	1,887	7,343	8,239	15,812	245	1,200	3,856	9	1,169	147	5	2,739	2,954	443	381	95,827
	Female	21,429	87	511	7,822	138	474	55	450	2,111	467	715	1,732	153	34	31	645	36,854
	Total	70,827	1,974	7,854	16,061	15,950	719	1,255	4,306	2,120	1,636	862	1,737	2,892	2,988	474	1,026	132,681
1961	Male	44,273	1,896	6,764	7,403	16,005	190	1,186	3,836	4	1,112	119	—	2,530	3,387	429	313	89,447
	Female	18,360	83	510	6,853	119	375	56	417	1,776	417	564	1,706	142	46	27	385	31,836
	Total	62,633	1,979	7,274	14,256	16,124	565	1,242	4,253	1,780	1,529	683	1,706	2,672	3,433	456	698	121,283
1960	Male	38,130	1,722	6,065	6,116	16,009	165	1,007	3,843	5	1,087	116	—	2,353	3,229	441	294	80,582
	Female	15,159	63	473	5,464	62	323	48	401	1,654	395	480	1,598	127	77	25	280	26,629
	Total	53,289	1,785	6,538	11,580	16,071	488	1,055	4,244	1,659	1,482	596	1,598	2,480	3,306	466	574	107,211

Series 439-455. Full-time university undergraduate enrolment, by field of specialization[1] and sex, Canada, selected years, 1861 to 1975 (continued)

Year and sex[2]	Arts and science	Agri-culture	Commerce and business admin-istration	Education	Engi-neering and applied science	Fine and applied arts	Medical and health professions						Law	Religion and theology	Veter-inary medicine	Unclas-sified	Total
							Dentistry	Medicine	Nursing	Pharmacy	Miscel-laneous health professions	House-hold science					
	439	**440**	**441**	**442**	**443**	**444**	**445**	**446**	**447**	**448**	**449**	**450**	**451**	**452**	**453**	**454**	**455**
1959 Male	33,948	1,636	5,408	4,966	15,498	100	959	3,891	—	974	93	—	2,595	3,153	415	307	73,943
Female	12,752	62	429	4,621	73	324	41	375	1,424	333	397	1,461	115	77	17	246	22,747
Total	46,700	1,698	5,837	9,587	15,571	424	1,000	4,266	1,424	1,307	490	1,461	2,710	3,230	432	553	96,690
1958 Male	31,554	1,512	4,744	3,851	15,812	87	888	4,015	—	942	90	—	2,590	3,075	392	217	69,771
Female	11,454	50	452	3,891	95	204	39	355	1,450	277	428	1,432	124	97	12	313	20,673
Total	43,008	1,562	5,196	7,742	15,907	291	927	4,370	1,452	1,219	518	1,432	2,714	3,172	404	530	90,444
1955 Male	23,453	1,234	3,501	1,849	12,329	87	818	4,094	5	985	81	—	2,507	3,009	375	218	54,545
Female	8,189	47	424	1,925	67	256	32	296	1,275	214	477	1,146	117	103	15	182	14,765
Total	31,642	1,281	3,925	3,774	12,396	343	850	4,390	1,280	1,199	558	1,146	2,624	3,112	390	400	69,310
1950 Male	22,190	1,592	3,091	1,626	9,588	144	941	4,135	—	1,288	133	—	2,325	2,632	485	—	50,170
Female	8,428	76	333	1,198	48	408	6	274	1,034	170	275	1,411	96	97	12	—	13,866
Total	30,618[r]	1,668	3,424	2,824	9,636	552	947	4,409	1,034	1,458	408	1,411	2,421	2,729	497	—	64,036
1945 Male	23,416	2,110	3,069	737	11,527	54	744	2,965	—	547	—	—	1,172	2,264	386	—	48,991
Female	8,483[r]	88	298	680[r]	64	225	9	235	974	191	395	1,110[r]	54	55	9	—	12,870
Total	31,899[r]	2,198	3,367	1,417	11,591	279	753	3,200	974	738	395	1,110[r]	1,226	2,319	395	—	61,861
1940 Male	12,410	1,347	1,015	302	4,677	33	462	2,780	510[r]	372	—	—	678	2,393	241	—	26,710
Female	5,682[r]	26	175	503	23	133[r]	6	160	510[r]	40	—	790	19	36[r]	4	—	8,107
Total	18,092[r]	1,373	1,190	805	4,700	166[r]	468	2,940	510[r]	412	—	790	697	2,429[r]	245	—	34,817
1935[3] Male	12,596	1,088	684	410	3,590	25	436	2,908	—	445	—	—	982	2,619	245	—	26,028
Female	5,489[r]	20	102	447	28	130[r]	3	129	372	39	—	688	23	24	—	—	7,494
Total	18,085[r]	1,108	786	857	3,618	155[r]	439[r]	3,037	372	484	—	688	1,005	2,643	245	—	33,522
1930[3] Male	11,623	889	757	247	3,820	3	375	2,798	—	481	—	—	816	2,217	122	—	24,148
Female	5,633[r]	10	126	447	7	33	5	123	301	31	—	639	29	44	—	—	7,428
Total	17,256[r]	899	883	694	3,827	36	380	2,921	301	512	—	639	845	2,261[r]	122	—	31,576
1925[3] Male	9,562	582	533	134	2,220	—	594	2,494	—	430	—	—	836	2,113	82	—	19,580
Female	4,303[r]	17	47	280	3	7[e]	10	113	188	29	—	197	21	56	1	—	5,272
Total	13,865[r]	599	580	414	2,223	7[e]	604	2,607	188	459	—	197	857	2,169	83	—	24,852

Series 439-455. Full-time university undergraduate enrolment, by field of specialization[1] and sex, Canada, selected years, 1861 to 1975 (concluded)

Year and sex[2]	Arts and science	Agri-culture	Commerce and business administration	Education	Engineering and applied science	Fine and applied arts	Medical and health professions — Dentistry	Medicine	Nursing	Pharmacy	Miscellaneous health professions	Household science	Law	Religion and theology	Veterinary medicine	Unclassified	Total
	439	440	441	442	443	444	445	446	447	448	449	450	451	452	453	454	455
1920[3]																	
Male	6,642	845	361	68	3,002	—	1,253	3,088	—	529	—	—	1,076	2,095	116	—	19,075
Female	3,072	11	11	110	4	—	23	148	122	33	—	100	41	41	—	—	3,716
Total	9,714	856	372	178	3,006	—	1,276	3,236	122	562	—	100	1,117	2,136	116	—	22,791
1911[4]																	
Male	4,121	821	—	157	2,157	—	330	1,617	—	206	—	—	686	..	116	118	10,329
Female	1,683	—	—	350	1	—	1	24	—	—	—	504	—	..	—	—	2,562
Total	5,804	821	—	507	2,157	—	331	1,641	—	206	—	504	686	..	116	118	12,891
1901[4]																	
Male	2,184	290	—	—	698	—	150	1,788	—	123	—	—	452	..	102	86	5,873
Female	740	—	—	—	—	—	—	25	—	3	—	—	—	..	—	—	768
Total	2,924	290	—	—	698	—	150	1,813	—	126	—	—	452	..	102	86	6,641
1891[4]																	
Male	1,973	159	—	—	268	—	66	1,239	—	102	—	—	505	..	153	56	4,521
Female	549	—	—	—	—	—	—	40	—	—	—	—	2	..	—	—	591
Total	2,522	159	—	—	268	—	66	1,279	—	102	—	—	507	..	153	56	5,112
1881[4]																	
Male	1,616	112	—	—	44	—	34	662	—	118	—	—	250	..	40	88	2,964
Female	40	—	—	—	—	—	—	2	—	—	—	—	—	..	—	—	42
Total	1,656	112	—	—	44	—	34	664	—	118	—	—	250	..	40	88	3,006
1871[4,5]																	
Male	..	..	—	—	..	—	—	..	—	..	—	—	..	..	..	—	..
Female	..	..	—	—	..	—	—	..	—	..	—	—	..	..	..	—	..
Total	1,012	3	—	—	1	—	—	452	—	6	—	—	87	..	29	—	1,590
1861[4,5]																	
Male	..	..	—	—	..	—	—	..	—	..	—	—	..	..	—	—	..
Female	..	..	—	—	..	—	—	..	—	..	—	—	..	..	—	—	..
Total	620	2	—	—	15	—	—	454	—	10	—	—	75	..	—	—	1,176

1 For the sake of comparability over the years, specialization indicated include other categories, as follows: (1) arts and science: letters, philosophy, environmental studies, journalism, library science and social work; (2) commerce and business administration: secretarial science; (3) education: physical and health education; (4) engineering and applied sciences: architecture and forestry; (5) fine and applied arts: music; (6) miscellaneous health professions: dental hygiene, optometry, physiotherapy and occupational therapy; (7) unclassified: fisheries.

2 Year shown denotes the beginning of the academic year.
3 In the years 1920 to 1935, students in universities in the Maritime provinces, preparing for teaching certificates, are reported as arts students.
4 In the years 1861 to 1911, students of theology are included, where identified.
5 Data for 1861 and 1871 include a few graduate students.

Series W456-465. Full-time graduate enrolment, by broad field of specialization and sex, Canada, 1970 to 1975

Year[1] and sex		Agriculture and biological sciences	Education	Engineering and applied sciences	Fine and applied arts	Health professions and occupations	Humanities and related	Mathematics and the physical sciences	Social sciences and related	Other	Total
		456	457	458	459	460	461	462	463	464	465
1975	Male	1,915	1,986	3,395	242	4,288	3,955	3,479	8,606	595	28,461
	Female	731	1,415	190	310	1,579	2,840	544	3,621	417	11,647
	Total	2,646	3,401	3,585	552	5,867	6,795	4,023	12,227	1,012	40,108
1974	Male	1,655	1,745	3,120	236	4,360	3,941	3,298	8,279	847	27,481
	Female	591	1,158	160	273	1,318	2,735	506	3,159	434	10,334
	Total	2,246	2,903	3,280	509	5,678	6,676	3,804	11,438	1,281	37,815
1973	Male	1,764	2,126	2,950	223	4,597	3,817	3,427	7,659	924	27,487
	Female	547	1,446	133	231	1,286	2,372	487	2,684	475	9,661
	Total	2,311	3,572	3,083	454	5,883	6,189	3,914	10,343	1,399	37,148
1972	Male	1,718	2,191	3,165	184	4,508	4,104	3,747	7,717	1,053	28,387
	Female	482	1,394	109	215	1,049	2,512	470	2,515	374	9,120
	Total	2,200	3,585	3,274	399	5,557	6,616	4,217	10,232	1,427	37,507
1971	Male	2,061	1,919	3,343	159	3,960[r]	3,925	4,079	7,574	764	27,784
	Female	510	988	79	156	970[r]	2,354	411	2,321	335	8,124
	Total	2,571	2,907	3,422	315	4,930[r]	6,279	4,490	9,895	1,099	35,908
1970	Male	2,091	1,966	3,569	161	1,713	3,712	4,360	7,265	928	25,765
	Female	515	948	91	144	563	2,162	419	2,210	355	7,407
	Total	2,606	2,914	3,660	305	2,276	5,874	4,779	9,475	1,283	33,172

[1] Academic year beginning in the year shown.

Series W466-474. Part-time university enrolment, by sex, Canada, 1962 to 1975

Year[1]	Undergraduate			Graduate			Total		
	Male	Female	Total	Male	Female	Total	Male	Female	Total
	466	467	468	469	470	471	472	473	474
1975	72,287[2]	86,007[2]	158,294	18,659[2]	8,072[2]	26,731	90,946[2]	94,079[2]	185,025
1974	65,997[2]	79,792[2]	145,789	17,424[2]	7,036[2]	24,460	83,421[2]	86,828	170,249
1973	63,360	74,294	137,654	17,094	6,416	23,510	80,454	80,710	161,164
1972	62,519	69,981	132,500	15,165	5,316	20,481	77,684	75,297	152,981
1971	72,516	64,842	137,358	13,693	4,336	18,029	86,209	69,178	155,387
1970	81,883	60,323	142,206	10,958	3,412	14,370	92,841	63,735	156,576
1969	61,404	46,883	108,287	10,454	3,265	13,719	71,858	50,148	122,006
1968	51,758	39,424	91,182	8,202	2,282	10,484	59,960	41,706	101,666
1967	50,245	36,923	87,168	8,126	2,570	10,696	58,371	39,493	97,864
1966	42,607	32,071	74,678	7,792	2,319	10,111	50,399	34,390	84,789
1965	38,386	26,913	65,299	6,192	1,532	7,724	44,578	28,445	73,023
1964	33,472	23,009	56,481	5,879	1,389	7,268	39,351	24,398	63,749
1963	30,798	19,629	50,427	5,367	1,131	6,498	36,165	20,760	56,925
1962	22,727	15,912	38,639	4,438	913	5,351	27,165	16,825	43,990

[1] Academic year beginning in the year shown.   [2] Includes estimates.

Series W475-485. Full-time university teachers, Canada and by province, selected years, 1920 to 1975

Year[1]	Canada	Newfound-land	Prince Edward Island	Nova Scotia	New Brunswick	Quebec	Ontario	Manitoba	Saskat-chewan	Alberta	British Columbia
	475	476	477	478	479	480	481	482	483	484	485
1975	30,858[2]	679	121	1,549	1,030	6,860 e	12,290	1,573	1,360	2,574	2,822
1974	29,959	747	117	1,471	1,011	6,441	12,115	1,520	1,355	2,486	2,696
1973	28,912	706	122	1,381	1,022	6,243	11,650	1,468	1,340	2,460	2,520
1972	28,482	662	129	1,376	928	6,176	11,581	1,440	1,332	2,358	2,500
1971	27,557	601	125	1,324	877	5,878	11,104	1,458	1,330	2,372	2,488
1970	24,733	500	123	1,184	785	5,700	9,335	1,352	1,268	2,108	2,378
1969	22,705	422	120	1,038	710	5,535	8,390	1,150	1,090	1,980	2,270
1968	20,065	340	120	925	665	4,955	7,390	1,040	970	1,620	2,040
1967	19,100	240	100	820	590	5,720	6,580	925	880	1,375	1,870
1966	16,675	210	80	715	490	5,250	5,580	820	760	1,140	1,630
1965	14,370	170	35	635	455	4,580	4,695	715	690	975	1,420
1964	12,360	145	25	580	410	3,930	4,070	580	610	860	1,150
1963	10,865	125	25	525	375	3,460	3,535	555	485	740	1,040
1962	9,640	110	25	470	345	3,035	3,130	490	440	645	950
1961	8,755	100	25	425	315	2,730	2,860	440	390	560	910
1960	7,760	70	20	390	285	2,350	2,555	410	360	490	830
1959	7,310 r	60	20	375	265	2,340 r	2,350	400	340	430	730
1958	7,005 r	60	15	350	240	2,300 r	2,310	390	330	380	630
1957	6,695 r	54	16	335	210	2,250 r	2,220 r	380	320	330	580
1956	6,355 r	50	15	310	200	2,220	2,050 r	370	300	300	540
1955	5,992 r	46	14	308	187	2,190 r	1,810 r	353	279	275	530
1950	5,539	26	12	262	186	2,185	1,757	275	199	242	395
1945	4,503	—	16	202	104	2,154	1,336	214	162	155	160
1940	3,169	—	14	192	87	1,121	1,179	149	157	139	131
1935	3,115	—	18	199	60	1,209	1,036	164	192	121	116
1930	2,882	—	10	175	86	1,021	992	159	172	106	161
1925	2,291	—	13	116	65	842	823	110	87	114	121
1920	2,225	—	14	155	71	701	805	198	80	84	117

[1] Academic year beginning in the year shown.

[2] Includes estimates.

Series W486-503. Full-time university teachers, by highest university degree held and by sex, Canada, 1958 to 1974

(series W486-500 in per cent; series W501-503, actual number)

Year[1]	Doctorate			Professional			Master's		
	Male	Female	Total	Male	Female	Total	Male	Female	Total
	486	**487**	**488**	**489**	**490**	**491**	**492**	**493**	**494**
1974	61.1	34.3	57.4	5.1	2.9	4.8	25.2	41.1	27.4
1973	60.3	34.6	57.0	5.8	2.8	5.4	26.0	42.6	28.2
1972	58.4	32.2	55.1	5.0	2.6	4.7	27.4	43.9	29.5
1971	56.6	30.5	53.2	4.6	2.7	4.4	28.4	43.4	30.3
1970	54.6	27.9	51.2	6.5	5.7	6.4	31.0	46.5	32.9
1969	53.7	27.1	50.2	6.2	4.8	6.0	31.2	46.6	33.2
1968	53.0	25.6	49.4	6.1	4.1	5.8	31.1	45.3	33.0
1967	50.4	24.2	46.9	7.1	6.4	7.0	30.1	42.4	31.7
1966	..	..	..	..	..	..	..	..	..
1965	47.5	23.2	44.4	6.8	5.4	6.6	33.1	44.5	34.6
1964	..	..	..	..	..	..	..	..	..
1963	46.2	22.6	43.4	6.7	5.3	6.6	32.8	42.3	33.9
1962	47.0	23.7	44.4	7.2	6.2	7.0	31.7	42.0	32.9
1961	..	..	..	..	..	..	..	..	..
1960	46.4	22.4	43.7	7.2	4.6	6.9	31.7	42.9	32.9
1959	..	..	..	..	..	..	..	..	..
1958	44.2	20.6	41.7	9.5	5.4	9.1	32.2	43.5	33.4

Year[1]	Bachelor's			Other			Total[2]		
	Male	Female	Total	Male	Female	Total	Male	Female	Total
	495	**496**	**497**	**498**	**499**	**500**	**501**	**502**	**503**
1974	6.3	17.6	7.9	2.3	4.1	2.5	25,802	4,157	29,959
1973	6.3	16.3	7.6	1.6	3.7	1.8	24,698	3,701	28,399
1972	7.5	17.5	8.8	1.7	3.8	1.9	24,169	3,562	27,731
1971	8.5	18.9	9.8	1.9	4.5	2.3	23,457	3,506	26,963
1970	7.2	17.4	8.5	0.7	2.5	1.0	21,465	3,139	24,604
1969	8.0	18.6	9.4	0.9	2.9	1.2	18,976	2,863	21,839
1968	8.2	19.9	9.6	1.6	5.1	2.2	16,371	2,493	18,864
1967	8.7	18.3	10.0	3.7	8.7	4.4	14,469	2,234	16,703
1966	..	..	..	..	..	..	..	..	..
1965	10.8	20.8	12.0	1.8	6.1	2.4	10,545	1,540	12,085
1964	..	..	..	..	..	..	..	..	..
1963	11.5	21.0	12.6	2.8	8.8	3.5	8,063	1,062	9,125
1962	12.4	21.6	13.5	1.7	6.5	2.2	6,997	893	7,890
1961	..	..	..	..	..	..	..	..	..
1960	13.5	24.1	14.7	1.2	6.0	1.8	5,718	736	6,454
1959	..	..	..	..	..	..	..	..	..
1958	12.6	23.7	13.8	1.5	6.8	2.0	4,752	573	5,325

[1] Academic year beginning in the year shown.

[2] Only those who reported.

Series W504-512. Degrees awarded by Canadian universities and colleges, by sex, Canada, selected years, 1831 to 1973

Year[1]	Bachelor and first professional[2]			Master's[3,4]			Doctorate (earned)[4]		
	Male	Female	Total	Male	Female	Total	Male	Female	Total
	504	505	506	507	508	509	510	511	512
1973	43,784	31,067	74,851	7,426	2,770	10,196	1,662	234	1,896
1972	42,592	28,104	70,696	7,778	2,852	10,630	1,712	217	1,929
1971	43,973	28,591	72,564	7,715	2,543	10,258	1,564	160	1,724
1970	41,596	25,504	67,100	7,516	2,122	9,638	1,474	151	1,625
1969	37,273	23,180	60,453	6,640	1,821	8,461	1,247	128	1,375
1968	34,494	20,201	54,695	5,486	1,549	7,035	1,021	87	1,108
1967	31,601	17,186	48,787	4,594	1,148	5,742	908	98	1,006
1966	28,498	14,729	43,227	4,214	1,051	5,265	716	63	779
1965	25,501	12,357	37,858	3,660	812	4,472	619	77	696
1964	23,013	10,042	33,055	2,894	687	3,581	512	54	566
1963	20,577	8,158	28,735	2,601	564	3,165	443	38	481
1962	18,017	6,922	24,939	2,256	499	2,755	387	34	421
1961	16,566	6,270	22,836	2,026	415	2,441	295	26	321
1960	14,689	5,108	19,797	1,874	353	2,227	279	27	306
1959	13,976	4,772	18,748	1,704	390	2,094	259	22	281
1958	12,997	4,063	17,060	1,344	366	1,710	254	30	284
1955	10,611	3,146	13,757	1,156	303	1,459	249	17	266
1950	13,411	3,774	17,185	1,344	220	1,564	191	11	202
1945	6,362	2,901	9,263	731	100	831	92	12	104
1940	5,960	2,193	8,153	520	67	587	70	5	75
1935	5,342	2,106	7,448	402	83	485	63	5	68
1930	4,411	1,820	6,231	358	100	458	39	7	46
1925	3,646	1,276	4,922	257	67	324	24	4	28
1920	3,306	701	4,007	170	48	218	23	1	24
1916	..	..	1,788	..	..	..	..	..	..
1911	..	..	1,775	..	..	..	..	..	..
1906	..	..	1,293	..	..	..	..	..	..
1901	..	..	1,214	..	..	..	..	..	..
1896	..	..	1,062	..	..	..	..	..	..
1891	..	..	822	..	..	..	..	..	..
1886	..	..	591	..	..	..	..	..	..
1881	..	..	494	..	..	..	..	..	..
1876	..	..	255	..	..	..	..	..	..
1871	..	..	235	..	..	..	..	..	..
1866	..	..	257	..	..	..	..	..	..
1861	..	..	184	..	..	..	..	..	..
1856	..	..	101	..	..	..	..	..	..
1851	..	..	40	..	..	..	..	..	..
1846	..	..	23	..	..	..	..	..	..
1841	..	..	11	..	..	..	..	..	..
1836	..	..	12	..	..	..	..	..	..
1831	..	..	4	..	..	..	..	..	..

[1] Academic year beginning in the year shown.
[2] From 1920 to 1959, undergraduate diplomas are included.

[3] From 1920 to 1959, licences are included.
[4] Prior to 1920, master's and doctorate degrees were not reported.

Series W513-518. Statistics of university libraries,[1] Canada, 1958 to 1972
(series W513-514 and 517, actual number; series W515, 516 and 518, in thousands)

Year[2]	Number of institutions[3] Parent university only	Number of institutions[3] Including affiliated colleges[4]	Full-time enrolment[5]	Volumes of books, periodicals and pamphlets	Volumes per Student	Volumes per Library	Year[2]	Number of institutions[3] Parent university only	Number of institutions[3] Including affiliated colleges[4]	Full-time enrolment[5]	Volumes of books, periodicals and pamphlets	Volumes per Student	Volumes per Library
	513	514	515	516	517	518		513	514	515	516	517	518
1972[6]	64	113	321.9	29,334.0	81.8	264.3	1962	52	73	121.8	9,039.8	74.2	123.8
1971	65	117	322.6	26,842.1	83.2	229.4	1961	48	67	108.6	8,107.8	74.7	121.0
1970	64	109	307.5	24,093.5	78.4	221.0	1960	26	34	..[9]	6,963.6	..[9]	204.8
							1959	27	35	..[9]	6,538.4	..[9]	186.8
1967[7,8]	61	86	230.4	18,556.2	80.5	213.3	1958	26	32	..[9]	6,030.5	..[9]	188.5
1966	58	80	195.9	15,778.2	80.5	197.2							
1965	54	79	171.0	13,244.4	77.5	167.7							
1964	55	81	158.4	10,955.3	69.2	135.3							
1963	55	81	136.2	10,068.6	73.9	124.3							

[1] For 1958 to 1960 data include universities and affiliated colleges with full-time enrolment of 500 students or more. From 1961 to 1967, data were collected from institutions with enrolment of 100 full-time students or less (mostly theological and affiliated).
[2] Academic year beginning in the year shown.
[3] Reporting institutions only.
[4] Includes constituent and affiliated colleges operating separate libraries under their administration.

[5] Enrolment as reported for the Survey of Libraries.
[6] In the 1970s, coverage represents enrolment on Canada level, ranging from 97 to almost 100 per cent.
[7] No surveys were conducted for the years 1968 and 1969.
[8] From 1961 to 1967, coverage represents institutions with a full-time enrolment ranging from 84 to 91 per cent.
[9] Because of the irregular pattern of enrolment reported for Quebec, Canada and Quebec enrolment figures and per student ratio have been omitted.

Series W519-532. Operating and capital expenditures of universities, by source of funds, Canada,[1] selected years, 1920 to 1974
(thousands of dollars)

Year[2]	Operating Government Federal[3]	Operating Government Provincial	Operating Government Municipal	Operating Government Subtotal	Operating Fees	Operating Other[4,5]	Operating Subtotal	Capital Government Federal	Capital Government Provincial	Capital Government Municipal	Capital Government Subtotal	Capital Other[5]	Capital Subtotal	Total
	519	520	521	522	523	524	525	526	527	528	529	530	531	532
1974	172,577	1,281,294	657	1,454,528	252,999	130,437	1,837,964	12,235	76,292	99	88,626	100,228	188,854	2,026,818
1973	153,962	1,090,072	4,549	1,248,583	238,105	94,268	1,580,956	9,191	145,888	112	155,191	68,628	223,819	1,804,775
1972	139,323	976,685	473	1,116,481	223,019	94,212	1,433,712	14,842	174,854	156	189,852	49,072	238,924	1,672,636
1971	132,245	934,557	934	1,067,736	225,838	72,153	1,365,727	16,668	182,015	118	198,801	116,393	315,194	1,680,921
1970	120,717	811,287	769	932,773	190,456	100,718	1,223,947	12,363	282,362	274	294,999	97,244	392,243	1,616,190
1969	114,579	698,057	2,724	815,360	178,782	90,055	1,084,197	15,867	229,042	393	245,302	111,003	356,305	1,440,502
1968	101,254	551,472	1,777	654,503	162,332	80,018	896,853	20,721	265,251	461	286,433	49,503	335,936	1,232,789
1967	83,759	445,361	1,812	530,932	144,490	73,446	748,868	17,564	248,928	1,334	267,826	110,275	378,101	1,126,969
1966	133,683	252,159	1,759	387,601	129,953	64,741	582,295	11,154	208,731	2,486	222,371	102,095	324,466	906,761
1965	73,125	183,613	577	257,315	110,624	64,793	432,732	6,997	163,386	597	170,980	80,832	251,812	684,544
1964	63,134	136,745	533	200,412	89,738	55,072	345,222	8,810	123,611	648	133,069	84,677	217,746	562,968
1963	57,133	110,825	668	168,626	75,573	45,732	289,931	11,180	88,617	514	100,311	45,789	146,100	436,031
1962	50,526	91,517	563	142,606	62,397	39,012	244,015	7,119	77,660	357	85,136	27,351	112,487	356,502
1961	41,922	78,912	627	121,461	56,249	33,620	211,330	6,208	60,369	877	67,454	17,554	85,008	296,338
1960	39,986	76,378	417	116,781	45,991	19,796	182,568	9,046	36,142	287	45,475	34,325	79,800	262,368
1959	38,492	50,092	380	88,964	40,789	20,007	149,760	7,690	36,575	51	44,316	25,049	69,365	219,125
1955	15,687	32,793	245	48,725	21,600	13,720	84,045	684	15,180	450	16,314	—	16,220	100,265
1950	2,412	16,765	262	19,439	14,025	8,034	41,498	—	12,144	—	12,144	—	12,144	53,642
1945[6]	2,714	7,691	81	10,486	9,779	5,093	25,358	..	..	..	..	..	5,173	30,531
1940	..	6,719	86	6,805	5,143	4,208	16,156	..	..	..	..	..	1,378	17,534
1935	..	5,314	45	5,359	4,457	3,923	13,739	..	..	..	..	..	1,686	15,425
1930	..	6,872	56	6,928	3,323	4,186	14,437	..	..	..	..	..	7,538	21,975
1925	..	5,471	—	5,471	2,380	3,443	11,294	..	..	..	..	..	4,043	15,337
1920	..	4,522	—	4,522	1,826	2,627	8,975	..	..	..	..	..	2,800 e	11,775

[1] Data on university income and expenditures in 1950 and prior years represent institutions accounting for 80 to 95 per cent of full-time enrolment.
[2] Financial year beginning in the year shown.
[3] Federal transfers to the provinces for post-secondary education (inaugurated in 1967) are included in provincial grants.

[4] Includes ancillary enterprises, net.
[5] Includes surplus of revenue as a deduction.
[6] Prior to 1950 Newfoundland is excluded.

Section Y: Politics and Government

Jean Louis Roy,[1] *McGill University*

The data in the tables of Section Y fall into two major divisions. Series Y1-296 concern the federal scene, series Y297-387 the 10 provincial scenes. Within the first major division, series Y1-40 contain data on executive and legislative posts and occupants; series Y41-210 on elections and parliamentary sessions; series Y211-263 on employees and representation abroad; and series Y264-296 on disallowance of provincial acts, reservation of provincial bills and on federal Royal Commissions. Within the second division, series Y297-801 present provincial data on Lieutenant-Governors and premiers; series Y302-387 the results of provincial elections.

The statistics of this section are obtained in a way that places them in two major categories: those for which there are official records, such as the data for the monarchy, for the Governor General and provincial Lieutenant-Governors, for parliamentary terms and for elections; and those for which only unofficial records exist, including all those involving election results by political parties, and political affiliation of ministers, electoral candidates and elected members of legislatures. This distinction arises from the nature of governmental and electoral processes.

Official data become available in several ways. First, official acts of the Government of Canada are published in the *Canada Gazette*, an official publication existing specifically for this purpose, and official acts of provinces are published in similar provincial publications. Thus notices of accession of Monarchs, of appointments of Governors General and Lieutenant-Governors, of establishment of portfolios or like posts and of the appointment of occupants, of the establishment of Royal Commissions and of the appointment of the commissioners, and of proclamation of elections and dissolution of parliament are published officially. Secondly, for the federal government, the *Debates of the House of Commons (Hansard)* and other parliamentary documents are published. Some provinces also publish the debates of their legislatures but the practice is not general and where followed is in most cases of recent origin. Thirdly, chief electoral officers of the federal government and of provincial governments publish results of elections giving numbers on electoral lists, votes polled by each candidate, spoiled ballots and the like. Finally, government departmental records are the sources of data such as the numbers of employees.

Unofficial data must be relied upon for those statistics which, for one reason or another, governments do not obtain or prepare. Except rarely, the political affiliation of candidates for election are not placed on ballots; the voter is presumed to vote for individuals. Consequently the results of voting by parties must be prepared by private individuals or bodies from information collected in various ways about party affiliation of the candidates who have been officially listed. Similarly, the designation of political affiliation of members of elected bodies, of ministries and the individual members thereof, is not given officially though it is fairly easy to obtain in most cases from the official or unofficial records of actions of legislating bodies. It nevertheless remains that the exercise of personal and private

judgment plays some part in the listing of matters of party affiliation. An exception to the above is the fact that beginning with the election of 1945 for the federal Parliament, a document was sent to those members of the armed forces voting under the provisions of the election act giving the party affiliation of each candidate as designated by the candidate himself. Some provincial governments in more recent periods also have given party affiliation on the ballot. Even in these cases problems may arise as more than one person in an electoral district may designate himself as a candidate for a given political party.

The reliability of the data, both official and unofficial, may vary depending on the process by which they are made known. Data obtained from official acts of governments are quite reliable. Official election results are also reliable though there is room for error. The counting of ballots is ordinarily done at each poll. Unless a recount is necessary there is no further counting. The results are sent from the polls to returning officers for electoral districts, and from returning officers to the Chief Electoral Officer of Canada or the provinces. Sources of error lie in the counting at polls, in the transmission of information from one person to another and in their final publication. The errors are apt to be small and may, to some extent, offset one another. The remaining official data, on employees in the Public Service of Canada, discussed more fully below, are subject to a lesser degree of accuracy owing to problems of classification of personnel, the dates at which a count is taken, and the inadequacy of departmental records in earlier years.

The unofficial data vary in accuracy depending on the nature of the material and the care exercised in handling it. In earlier years, when party affiliations were loose in any event, there is considerable room for error and even more recently the element of judgment involved in designating party affiliation allows some inaccuracies. Further, the assembly of electoral district data to obtain provincial and national aggregates requires careful handling. Owing to these factors, varying unofficial sources sometimes are in conflict. In such cases, that source which is believed to have the greatest accuracy is used.

The following list of sources used in assembling the data includes both official and unofficial publications. Official publications may give data coming from unofficial sources and unofficial publications may give data from official sources.

Government publications

Statistics Canada, *Canada Year Book*, (Catalogue 11-202), annual since 1905, various years, (Ottawa, Supply and Services Canada); Public Archives of Canada, *Guide to Canadian Ministries since Confederation July 1, 1867 - April 1, 1973*, (Ottawa, Supply and Services Canada, 1974); Dominion Bureau of Statistics, *Statement of Civil Service Personnel and Salaries in the Month of January, 1912-1924*, (Ottawa, King's Printer, 1925); Parliament of Canada, *Civil Service Employees: Number, Total Salaries and Bonus*, (Ottawa, King's Printer, 1923); Civil Service Commission, *Personnel Administration in the Public Service, A Review* of Civil Service Legislation, (Ottawa, Queen's Printer, 1959); G.V. LaForest, Department of Justice, Disallowances and Reservations of Provincial Legislation, (Ottawa, Queen's Printer, 1955); Debates of the House of Commons, (Ottawa, Queen's Printer), various years; Journals of the House of Commons of Canada, (Ottawa, Supply and Services Canada), various years; Chief Electoral Officer, Report of the Chief Electoral Officer, various years; A Statistical History of all the Electoral Districts of the Province of Ontario, (Toronto, undated); Province of Quebec, Bureau of Statistics, Annuaire du Québec, (Quebec, Queen's Printer), annual since 1913; Province of Saskatchewan, Who's Who; Great Britain, The Public General Acts and Church Assembly Measure, 1960, (London, Her Majesty's Stationery Office, 1961).

Non-government publications

J.M. Beck, The Government of Nova Scotia, (Toronto, University of Toronto Press, 1957); George Henderson, Federal Royal Commissions in Canada 1867-1966, a Checklist, (Toronto, University of Toronto Press, 1967); H. McD. Clokie, "Basic Problems of the Canadian Constitution", Canadian Journal of Economics and Political Science, vol. 8, no. 2, February 1942; R. Ares, Dossier sur le pact fédératif de 1867, (Montréal, Bellarmin, 1967); Canadian Parliamentary Companion, annual 1862 to 1897 (various editors and published at various places); Copp Clark Publishing, Canadian Almanac and Directory (Vancouver, Calgary, Toronto, Montreal), various years; R. MacGregor Dawson, The Government of Canada, 3rd edition (Toronto, University of Toronto Press, 1957); James G. Foley, Resume of General Elections, 1896-1911; Canadian Annual Review, beginning in 1960, (Toronto, University of Toronto Press); Paul Gérin-Lajoie, Constitutional Amendment in Canada, (Toronto, University of Toronto Press, 1950); J.E. Hodgetts, Royal Commissions of Inquiry in Canada, (University of Toronto, M.A. thesis, 1939); Cole Taylor, The Canadian Bureaucracy: a study of Canadian civil servants and other public employees, 1939-1947 Duke University Press, 1949; Pierre G. Normandin, editor, Canadian Parliamentary Guide, annual since 1898, apparently a successor of the Canadian Parliamentary Companion, (Ottawa); John Saywell, The Office of Lieutenant-Governor, (Toronto, University of Toronto Press, 1957); H.G. Skilling, Canadian Representation Abroad, from Agency to Embassy, (Toronto, University of Toronto Press, 1945); Norman Ward, The Canadian House of Commons: Representation, (Toronto, University of Toronto Press, 1950).

Important sources of information, which contain much material included in the above sources, are the federal and provincial sessional papers.

The British North America Act (BNA Act) 1867 and its Amendments are the main formal foundation of government in Canada. They are not complete statements, however, of even the formal part of the constitution. Other statutes of the United Kingdom, such as the Statute of Westminster 1931, statutes of the Parliament of Canada on such matters as the houses of Parliament themselves, on election procedures and the like, and statutes of provincial governments on matters such as their own electoral and legislative forms are examples of the more formal part of the constitutional structure. In addition the informal part of the constitution is very important. The system of Cabinet government, responsible to Parliament and particularly the House of Commons as developed in the United Kingdom, has been

adopted in Canada; and other usages have also been adopted from the British Parliament. The increasing numbers of conventions that have developed within the Parliament of Canada itself and within the provincial legislative bodies are also important parts of the constitution. (See the Canada Year Book, 1957-58, pp. 39-41, for the short but good statement on which this paragraph is based.)

The Federal Government, Executive and Legislative Posts and Occupants (Series Y1-40)

Y1-2.   The monarchy, 1867 to 1978

SOURCE: Canada Year Book, 1976-77, p. 85.

Y3-5.   Governors General, 1867 to 1978

SOURCE: Canada Year Book, 1976-77, p. 85.

The Governor General of Canada is now appointed by the Queen on the advice of the Prime Minister of Canada. Before 1890 the Governor General was appointed by the Monarch on the advice of British authorities alone, but thereafter the Government of Canada was usually (though not always) consulted. The present practice dates from the Imperial Conference of 1926 which agreed that a Governor General was not the representative or agent of the British government but of the Monarch. Until 1952, when a Canadian was first appointed Governor General of Canada, the incumbent was invariably a person of title from the United Kingdom. The term of appointment of the Governor General is not fixed, though six years is considered normal. No Governor General of Canada has been removed from office, though undoubtedly the government could advise the Monarch to remove her representative. The Governor General has two deputies (both are justices of the Supreme Court of Canada) who are empowered to act in his absence and in the event of a vacancy in the office the BNA Act recognizes an administrator who can carry on in the name of the Queen.

Y6-16.   Canadian ministries, dates, numbers of portfolios, turnover of personnel, and party affiliation, 1867 to 1976

SOURCE: Guide to Canadian Ministries since Confederation, July 1, 1867 - January 1, 1957; Canada Year Book, 1976-77, pp. 89-90; Canadian Parliamentary Guide, various issues.

The Canadian ministry at any one time consists of all those sworn to act as the Monarch's confidential advisers on affairs of state. The great majority of the ministers serve as heads of departments of government (for example, the Minister of Agriculture is said to hold the Agriculture portfolio), but it is common for the ministry to include one or more 'ministers without portfolio', who have the same responsibilities as any other minister except those of a department head. Usually in Canada the ministry and the Cabinet consist of the same people, but before 1926 it was customary for the incumbents of a few junior portfolios to be outside the Cabinet. The parliamentary secretaries (members of Parliament assigned to assist ministers) are not officially recognized as members of the ministry, although after some initial experimentation during World

War I they have been accepted as a permanent part of governmental machinery. The term of a ministry is not fixed, but coincides with the term of a prime minister, who serves as long as he has the confidence of a majority of the members of the House of Commons, and thus may continue through several general elections. During the life of one ministry, a single portfolio may be held in succession by several individuals, while a single individual may in succession hold several portfolios. It is not uncommon for a portfolio to be temporarily vacant, during which period an acting minister will serve, or for one individual to hold two portfolios coincidentally. Ordinarily all members of the Cabinet must have, or obtain, a seat in the House of Commons, except for the government leader in the Senate.

The following qualifications and definitions apply to series Y6-16.

Y7. Dates of ministry are opening and closing dates of the prime minister's term in office.

Y8. Party gives the affiliations of prime minister and cabinet members.

Y9. Number of portfolios gives the total number of separate portfolios in existence during the ministry (excludes the position of prime minister).

Y10. Number of occupants gives the total number of persons holding portfolios in series Y9, including acting ministers and the prime minister, if he held a portfolio.

Y11. Ministers without portfolio, number of posts, gives the maximum number of such posts in existence, at any one time in the ministry.

Y12. Ministers without portfolio, number of occupants, gives the total number of persons holding posts of series Y11 at any time in the ministry.

Y13. Non-cabinet posts are the total number of ministerial posts whose incumbents were not members of the Cabinet.

Y14. Number of occupants of non-cabinet ministers posts is the total number occupying such posts, at any time.

Y15. Parliamentary secretaries' posts (the term was first used in Borden's ministry of 1917-20) are non-cabinet posts held by Members of Parliament, and identified by the term. The figures give the maximum number of posts at any one time in the term of the ministry.

Y16. Number of occupants of parliamentary secretaries' posts gives the total number of persons holding such posts at any time in the ministry's life.

Y17-29. Growth of representation in the House of Commons and redistribution (general and partial), by province, 1867 to 1974

SOURCE: *Canada Year Book, 1976-77*, p. 97; Ward, *The Canadian House of Commons*, p. 56.

Representation in the Canadian House of Commons is based on the single-member constituency system (with two exceptions, each having two members) adapted to recognize the federal principle. Seats in the House of Commons were divided among the provinces after each decennial census, in accordance with a formula described in the BNA Act. At present, the House of Commons has a total of 264 seats divided among the provinces, primarily on a basis proportionate to population. No province can have fewer members

of Parliament in the House of Commons than it has senators. The allocation of seats among the provinces is prescribed by law, but the actual drawing of constituency boundaries within each province, from 1903 to 1962, was effected by legislation prepared by a committee of the House of Commons; prior to that, constituencies were created by legislation sponsored by the Cabinet. Since 1963, changes in representation are governed by the Electoral Boundaries Readjustment Act which is administered by the Office of the Representation Commissioner. The revised representation, which was given Royal Assent in December 1974, will go into effect in the General Election of 1979. Each province will have the following number of members: Ontario, 95; Quebec, 75; Nova Scotia, 11; New Brunswick, 10; Manitoba, 14; British Columbia, 28; Prince Edward Island, four; Saskatchewan, 14; Alberta, 21; Newfoundland, seven; the Northwest Territories, two; the Yukon Territory, one; for a total of 282.

Series Y17-29 show general redistributions (1872, 1882, 1892, 1903, 1914, 1924, 1933, 1947, 1952, 1968, 1974); partial redistributions occasioned by the admission of one or more new provinces (1871, 1873, 1887, 1907, 1949); or a constitutional amendment (1915).

Y25-26. Saskatchewan and Alberta, for the period prior to their creation in 1905, show the representation of the Northwest Territories from which they were formed.

Y28. The Yukon Territory was the only territory represented in the House of Commons after 1905, until the creation of the constituency of Mackenzie River in 1952. Since then, each territory has had one representative in the House of Commons.

Y30-40. Growth of representation in the Senate of Canada, 1867 to 1975

SOURCE: *Canada Year Book, 1976-77*, p. 152; supplemented by information in *Journals of the House of Commons*, various issues.

Representation in the Senate of Canada, as prescribed by the BNA Act, was originally intended to give equal representation of 24 senators each to the three main regions of Canada: the Maritimes, Quebec and Ontario, 72 in all. As the four western provinces developed, the same regional equality was ultimately extended to them by a constitutional amendment in 1915 and total Senate representation reached 96. The admission of Newfoundland in 1949 marred the symmetry of representation in the Senate but it had been agreed in 1915 that, in the event of Newfoundland's admission to Canada, the province was to be given the same number of seats as each of the last four provinces that were brought up to the basic principle of equality. As a result, the number of senators reached 102 in 1949. In 1975, an act of Parliament amended the Canadian Constitution to entitle the Yukon Territory and the Northwest Territories to be represented by one senator each. Total membership in the Senate is now 104.

The Federal Government, Elections and Parliamentary Sessions (Series Y41-210)

Y41-50. Dates of general elections and sessions of federal parliaments, 1867 to 1974

SOURCE: *Canada Year Book, 1976-77*, p. 151; supplemented

by information in *Journals of the House of Commons,* various issues.

The Parliament of Canada has no fixed term. The BNA Act sets a maximum life of five years to a Parliament, the time beginning from the day on which the writs certifying each member's election are returned. In 1916 the life of the 12th Parliament was extended one year by constitutional amendment. Within the five years prescribed by law, the actual choice of the date of a dissolution, a general election, and an opening and closing (or prorogation) of each parliamentary session, are within the discretion of the government, which formally advises the Governor General to make the appropriate announcement. A dissolution terminates the life of a Parliament, and is shortly followed by an election.

Y45. Days of session include some adjustments to source data to adjust for the fact that, for an unexplained reason, the official sources deduct numerous adjourned days, commonly in long sessions, from the length of the session. Where they can be detected, these omitted days have been added in obtaining series Y45.

Y46. Sitting days are not available before 1936 but could be computed from the *Journals of the House of Commons* for each year. There are minor discrepancies in the sources. For example, the *Canada Year Book, 1945,* p. 53, gives the length of the 18th Parliament as 4 years, 3 months, 13 days; the *Journals of the House of Commons, 1951,* p. 61, gives it as 4 years, 2 months, 16 days.

Y51-74. General elections, number of electors on lists and votes polled, by province and election, 1896 to 1974

SOURCE: *Canada Year Book,* various issues; Foley, *Resume of General Elections, 1896-1911.* No official compilations of numbers of electors on lists exists before 1911; the detailed reports of general elections, constituency by constituency, appear in the *Sessional Papers* following each general election, 1867 to 1908. The statistics compiled by Foley were accumulated by him while he was Clerk of the Crown in Chancery and thus are virtually official. For changes in the franchise see Ward, *The Canadian House of Commons.*

Lists of electors in Canada are compiled for each general election, by house to house enumeration; an urban elector must be on a list in order to vote, but rural electors can be sworn in on polling day. Since 1920, the franchise has been determined by the Parliament of Canada, but for two periods, 1867 to 1885 and 1898 to 1920, provincial franchises were used in federal elections; during most of these periods, provincial polling lists were also used. The columns entitled 'Polled' indicate the numbers of electors who cast ballots and include wasted ballots, which are now a negligible factor in elections.

Series Y55-58 from 1896 to 1965, and series Y59-60 and Y63-64 from 1896 to 1930, are skewed by the existence of two-member constituencies. In each instance each elector had two votes, but was counted only once as an elector; thus in Prince Edward Island in 1965, for instance, 24,250 electors cast 44,895 votes in one constituency. See *Canada Year Book,* various issues, and also for slight skewing of results caused by occasional acclamations. Series Y73-74 include the electoral districts of the Yukon Territory and Mackenzie River, 1953 to 1958; the Yukon Territory alone, 1908 to 1949; and the Northwest Territories alone, 1896 to

1900. (Alberta and Saskatchewan were formed from the Northwest Territories in 1905.)

Female suffrage in federal elections began on a partial basis in 1917, when female relatives of members of the armed forces voted, and was general for the election of 1921.

Y75-198. Votes polled in federal elections, by party and province, 1896 to 1974

SOURCE: Foley, *Resume of General Elections, 1896-1911; Canadian Annual Review, 1917,* p. 643; *1921,* p. 509; *1925-6,* p. 45; Chief Electoral Officer of Canada. The series for 1926 to 1940 were compiled by The Canadian Press and thereafter by the Chief Electoral Officer, who was required after 1944 to ascertain party affiliations for the convenience of electors in the armed forces.

Compilations of election results by parties are at best semi-official. The actual votes polled by individual candidates in each constituency are initially counted by the deputy returning officers in each polling division and reported to the constituency returning officer, who in turn reports to the Chief Electoral Officer. The party affiliations of candidates do not appear on the ballots or other official papers, except those used by members of the armed forces. The series for each general election show, in the left-hand column, the party polling the most votes but not necessarily (as in 1926 and 1957) winning the election.

Y80. 'Others' refers more often to independents from Quebec than to any other group of candidates. A multiplicity of parties began to appear after the general election of 1917, however, and the 'Others' columns altogether include votes polled by over twenty separate groups, all of which are identified in the compilations made by the Chief Electoral Officer after 1944, and The Canadian Press, 1926 to 1940.

Y199-210. Members elected in federal elections, by party and province, 1867 to 1974

SOURCE: *Canadian Parliamentary Companion; Canadian Parliamentary Guide; Canadian Annual Review; Canadian Almanac and Directory;* all throughout their years of publication.

The series depend primarily on newspaper compilations of election results, and each Member of Parliament's own statement of his party affiliation as listed in biographical works such as the *Canadian Parliamentary Guide.*

No official statistics on election results by parties are kept and there is room for disagreement over the classification of particular Members of Parliament, especially for the earlier years. There are discrepancies in the sources and the table has been corrected where possible by other evidence. Each general election result lists the winning party first.

The Liberal party has been popularly called by that name since shortly after Confederation; for earlier years, members frequently identified themselves as 'Reform' or 'Grit'. The party now called Progressive Conservative has changed its name several times: Progressive Conservative 1945 to date; National Government in 1940; Conservative and Liberal Conservative before 1935, except for 1917, when most Conservative candidates (and many Liberals) ran as Unionists. These various changes in name are not all shown in the series.

The Federal Government, Employees and Representation Abroad (Series Y211-263)

Y211-259. Federal government employment, by department, branch and service, 1900 to 1977

SOURCE: for 1968 to 1977, Statistics Canada, *Federal Government Employment*, (Catalogue 72-004) from 1968 to 1977; for 1924 to 1967, Statistics Canada, *Canada Year Book*, (Catalogue 11-202), various years; for 1912 to 1924, Statistics Canada, *Statement of Civil Personnel and Salaries in the Month of January, 1912-1924*; for 1900 to 1915, Parliamentary Returns, *Civil Service Employees*.

A continuously reliable series of statistics on government employees classified by department or agency does not exist. Changes in the names and internal organizations of departments; the transfer of branches from one department to another; changes in the ways in which civil servants are classified as permanent, casual, and temporary, and in records concerning them; all make a single consistent set of series impossible. Therefore, the statistics in this series must be used with great caution. A statement of the limitations on statistics from the *Canada Year Book* can be obtained from Statistics Canada. In order to enable the user to judge on the consistency of the series in the three sources, overlaps of the data are given for 1924 and for 1912 to 1915. The report on *Civil Service Employees* actually gave data running from 1900 to 1922.

For the years 1924 to 1958, the *Canada Year Book* gives tables for government employment under different headings for different years. The figures in the tables are subject to the qualifications and reservations given in the relevant years of the *Canada Year Book*, in addition to those given in these notes. The series from 1925 to 1952 was originally intended to list only employees covered by the Civil Service Act, but Statistics Canada is the authority for the statement that there was considerable diversity among departments in reporting on their employees, so that some lists do not include all civil servants covered by the act while others include employees not covered by the act. A new series (explained in the *Canada Year Book, 1954*, p. 98) was begun after 1954.

For 1912 to 1924, inclusive, the *Statement of Civil Service Personnel and Salaries in the Month of January, 1912-1924*, is now a scarce document. This second source is generally not comparable with the first, for it was compiled on a different basis than the tables in the *Canada Year Book* after 1924.

The source for figures prior to 1915, *Civil Service Employees*, printed by order of Parliament in 1923, is also a scarce document. Here a very different basis for these statistics was used, and the figures before 1915 from this source are generally not comparable with those for later years from the other sources. Each of the three sources employs a different time period as the basis of selection.

Further information on sizes of staffs from 1878 to 1900 (not given here because no complete figures could be compiled) can be found in the *Reports of the Auditor General of Canada* after 1878, and in the *Civil Lists* published annually from 1867.

All statistics in this table, according to the sources, show the total number of employees (permanent and temporary, casual and other, and inside and outside service which includes staff at Ottawa and elsewhere) who can properly be regarded from the records as members of the staff of the departments and services named. Admittedly this compilation of totals can be misleading, especially for departments employing large numbers of casual workers. Further, it seems apparent from a comparison of the two sets of overlapping data for the years 1912 to 1915 that the figures given in *Civil Service Employees* must have omitted at least substantial numbers of outside employees for certain departments such as the post office (series Y241), transport (series Y255) and others. In some instances the detailed notes in the last-mentioned source state that the figures are only for the inside service. The *Canada Year Book*, for the series for 1953 to 1955 and 1956 to 1958, breaks down totals into subtotals. The table does not list separately most temporary departments and branches such as Registrar General, Industry, Resources and Development, Mines and Resources, Reconstruction and Supply, and Munitions and Supply. Nor does it list Soldiers' Settlement Board (1918 to 1948, when its activities were absorbed into Veterans Affairs) and Soldiers' Civil Re-establishment (1918 to 1927), statistics of which can be found in all three sources given above. Where possible, temporary departments are tabulated with the newer departments into which they subsequently developed, and such tabulations are explained below. Other departments and services which were absorbed into new or reorganized departments are referred to below.

The series do not include the significant numbers of staff members (now around 130,000) employed by the non-departmental Crown corporations and other public enterprises. Tables of employment in these institutions, showing totals only for 22 enterprises, appeared first in the *Canada Year Book, 1955*, p. 112, and were published in the same source until 1972. Since then the data appears in *Federal Government Employment*. Detailed figures by enterprises can be calculated from the annual reports of most of the separate enterprises and from evidence which some of them have given to committees of the House of Commons.

In the following detailed notes for each series, the dates given for the establishment of departments are taken from the first annual report of the department itself.

Y211. 'Total', this is the grand total of series Y212-259. The totals for 1933 to 1936 given in the *Canada Year Book* have been adjusted to exclude employees of the Canadian Broadcasting Commission since they disappear from the figures from 1937 onward when the commission became a corporation and employees were no longer a part of the civil service. Similarly, employees of the National Capital Commission (and its predecessor, the Federal District Commission) have been removed from the total and from series Y242, Privy Council, for 1953 to 1955, since as far as could be determined they were not included before 1953 and again after 1955 when they are reported with Crown corporations. The totals for 1912 to 1924 from *Civil Service Personnel in the Month of January*, as given in the source, are the sums of the figures in series Y212-259.

For 1956 to 1959 the total combines the categories of 'Classified Prevailing Rate' and 'Casuals and Others' as given in the *Canada Year Book*; for 1953 to 1955 the totals, as adjusted, combine 'Classified' and 'Exempt'.

Y212. Agriculture, created in 1867, for 1900 to 1915, it includes the total of permanent and other employees. From 1912 to 1922, figures include a small number of employees from the Conservation Commission.

Y213. Auditor General's Office, created in 1878, has performed the same general functions throughout its life.

Y214. Chief Electoral Officer, created in 1920, contains statistics for prior years referring to the relevant staff in the office of Secretary of State. The statistics are for Ottawa staff only.

Y215. Citizenship and Immigration, created in 1949, includes employees of services previously in other departments. Citizenship and Immigration combined the Administrative Branch, Canadian Citizenship Branch and Canadian Citizenship Registration Branch previously under Secretary of State (series Y250) and those for Immigration and Indian Affairs previously under Mines and Resources.

For the years 1900 to 1936 this series includes statistics for the Department of Immigration and Colonization created in 1917. From 1867 to 1892 immigration was handled by the Department of Agriculture and from 1892 to 1917 by the Department of the Interior. This series, 1900 to 1915, from *Civil Service Employees* includes employees in the inside service only. See also the note to series Y219.

In 1966, Immigration was transferred to Manpower and Immigration (series Y234).

Y216. Communications, created in 1969, includes employees previously in other departments or agencies such as the National Research Council (series Y238) and Transport (series Y255). Data on employment became available in 1970. See also the note to series Y241, Post Office.

Y217. Consumer and Corporate Affairs, created in 1967, incorporated the former Department of the Registrar General of Canada which existed as a separate department only from 1966 to 1967. Before that date, the Registrar General was included with the Secretary of State (series Y250).

Y218. Defence Production, created in 1951, includes statistics for Reconstruction and Supply (1945 to 1949) and Munitions and Supply (1940 to 1945). Munitions and Supply was not organized until after the fiscal year 1939-40, hence there are no data for 1940. Defence Production was transferred to Supply and Services (series Y253) in 1970. See also the note to series Y244 which explains the jump in employees which occurs in 1965.

Y219. Energy, Mines and Resources was created in 1966. The department was known by various names throughout the period covered here. From 1907 to 1935, it was called Mines; from 1935 to 1949, Mines and Resources; and from 1949 to 1966, Mines and Technical Surveys. In 1936 the former departments of Immigration and Colonization, Indian Affairs, and Interior, were transferred to Mines and Resources. For the period prior to 1936 the last two departments are shown separately. The series for all departments from 1900 to 1915, from *Civil Service Employees*, show employees in the inside service only.

Y220. Environment, created in 1971, includes the former Department of Fisheries (series Y223); and Forestry (series Y224); as well as the Atmospheric Environment Service formerly with Transport (series Y255); Inland Waters, formerly with Energy, Mines and Resources (series Y219); Wildlife Service and Lands Service, formerly in Indian Affairs and Northern Development (series Y227).

Y221. External Affairs, created in 1909, included the staff of the Prime Minister's Office for the years prior to 1948. Since then, the latter has been included with the Privy Council. The Information Division of the department, created in 1947, integrated the former Canadian Information Service into the department. The employees of the Canadian Information Service for 1946-47 and its predecessor, the Wartime Information Board, 1943 to 1945, have been added to External Affairs. Data for the International Joint Commission has been included in External Affairs since 1912.

Y222. Finance, created in 1869, includes the staff of the Comptroller of the Treasury from 1934 to 1969; and, where necessary, the Government Contracts Supervision Commission, Wartime Prices and Trade Board and similar groups. The series includes civil servants in inside and outside services throughout.

Y223. Fisheries was created in 1930, from part of the former Department of Marine and Fisheries (see also the note on series Y255). In 1969, it was transferred to the new Department of Fisheries and Forestry and the data for Fisheries include Forestry (series Y224) for the years 1970 and 1971. Since 1972, the data for Fisheries are included with Environment (series Y220).

Y224. Forestry and Rural Development was created in 1960 from relevant branches of the departments of Agriculture, and Northern Affairs and National Resources. In 1969, the Forestry Branch of the department was merged with Fisheries (series Y223), and the data for 1970 and 1971 are included with Fisheries. Since 1972, the data are contained in Environment (series Y220).

Y225. Governor General and Lieutenant-Governors include figures for staff only, and exclude the Governor General or Lieutenant-Governors themselves; before 1953, the figures are for the Governor General's secretarial staff only.

Y226. Indian Affairs, created in 1880, disappears in 1936, when this department was transferred to Mines and Resources. This series for 1900 to 1915, from *Civil Service Employees*, includes employees in the inside service only. See also the note on series Y219. In 1949, Indian Affairs became part of Citizenship and Immigration (series Y215) and the data are included with that department from 1950 to 1966. Since 1967 the data appear under Indian Affairs and Northern Development (series Y227).

Y227. Indian Affairs and Northern Development was created in 1966, superseding the Department of Northern Affairs and National Resources. See also the note to series Y240.

Y228. Industry, Trade and Commerce was created in 1969 from the former departments of Industry and of Trade and Commerce. Industry had a short duration (from 1963 to 1969) and the data for those years are included with Trade and Commerce (series Y254).

Y229. Insurance, created in 1875 as a branch of Finance, is reported separately from Finance. It became a separate department of government in 1910.

Y230. Interior, created in 1873, disappears in 1936 when this department was transferred to Mines and Resources, later Mines and Technical Surveys and later still Energy, Mines and Resources. This series, for 1900 to 1915, from *Civil Service Employees*, gives employees in the inside service only. See also the note to series Y219.

Y231. Justice, created in 1868, includes the staff of the Commissioner of Penitentiaries and Solicitor General's office until 1966, when the new Department of the Solicitor General was formed (series Y251). From 1952 to 1956, approximately three hundred judges, then listed as salaried employees, were included in the data.

Y232. Labour, created in 1900, includes only full-time employees for 1900 to 1915, from *Civil Service Employees*, and thereafter as described in *Canada Year Book* for the various years.

Y233. Legislation, includes statistics for the House of Commons, Senate, and Library of Parliament; these three institutions are listed separately in the sources down to 1952, and together thereafter. The records of the House of Commons were destroyed by fire in 1916, and the series from 1912 to 1916 is for the Senate and Library only.

Y234. Manpower and Immigration was created in 1966, from the Immigration Branch of Citizenship and Immigration (series Y215) and certain components formerly included in Labour (series Y232). See also the note to series Y257.

Y235. National Defence, created in 1922, includes the former Department of Militia and Defence, the Naval Service and Air Board. The series shows permanent civilian employees only. From 1941 to 1947, the data include employees of National War Services.

Y236. National Film Board, created in 1939, is given separately though the board has been attached in turn to several departments, and statistics of its employees have had an erratic history. The board was not organized for the fiscal year 1939-40; statistics of its employees for 1941 were included with Trade and Commerce, and for 1945 to 1947 with National Health and Welfare.

Y237. National Health and Welfare, created in 1944 from part of the former Department of Pensions and National Health also includes predecessor bodies. The Department of Pensions and National Health was formed in 1928 from the Department of Soldiers' Civil Re-establishment, which had been created in 1918; the Department of Health, created in 1919; the Board of Pension Commissioners, established in 1917; and the Federal Appeal Board, established in 1926. The Military Hospitals Commission, 1916 to 1918, had in turn been incorporated in Soldiers' Civil Re-establishment. From 1919 to 1928, by far the larger part of the combined employment was in Soldiers' Civil Re-establishment which had 8,121 employees in 1920, 3,823 employees in 1923 and 1,890 employees in 1928. In 1945, many employees of the department were transferred to the new Department of Veterans Affairs. See also the note to series Y236.

Y238. National Research Council, created in 1917, and whose first laboratories were established in Ottawa in 1928, was included in Trade and Commerce before 1934. The Atomic Energy Control Board, created in 1946 and a separate body, has been included here.

Y239. National Revenue, created in 1927, covers also the predecessor departments of Customs and Excise (1921 to 1927) and of Customs and Inland Revenue (1918 to 1921). Before 1918 customs and inland revenue acts were administered by separate departments and the statistics before 1918 combine the data from these departments. The series for 1900 to 1915, from *Civil Service Employees*, include both inside and outside service employees. The figures for 1924 and 1925 include the Commissioner of Income Taxation, listed separately in the *Canada Year Book, 1925*, p. 986. From 1917 to 1924 the data from *Civil Service Personnel in the Month of January* also include the Commissioner of Income Taxation.

Y240. Northern Affairs and National Resources was created in 1953 from the former Department of Resources and Development. Before 1950 it was part of Mines and Resources. See also the notes to series Y219, Y220 and Y227.

Y241. Post Office, created in 1867, gives data for personnel in the inside service only for the period 1900 to 1915, from *Civil Service Employees*. From 1970 to 1972, the data for Post Office were included in the new Department of Communications. Figures were extracted from annual reports for the Post Office and this amount subtracted from the total to provide data for Communications. See also the note to series Y216.

Y242. The Privy Council was created in 1867 and for administration purposes has been regarded as a department of government since 1946. The series does not include employees of the Wartime Information Board (1943-44); the Canadian Information Service (1944 to 1946); the Federal District Commission and the National Capital Commission (throughout their existence). In 1958, 21 employees of the Royal Commission on Price Spreads in Food Products and the Royal Commission on Energy Policies were included with Privy Council. Data for the Prime Minister's Office, included with External Affairs before 1948, has been included with Privy Council from 1948 to 1977. See also the notes to series Y211 and Y221.

Y243. Public Archives and National Library, created in 1872 and 1953 respectively, are combined in official sources after 1953. Before that date the series is for archives only, except for 1951 and 1952, when six and eight members of the staff of the Bibliographic Centre were included. Before 1913, the archives statistics were included with Agriculture.

Y244. Public Printing and Stationery, created in 1886, was attached to Secretary of State until 1963. In that year, all the printing functions were transferred to the Department of Defence Production and became known as the Canadian Government Printing Bureau. The decrease in employees did not show in employment data until 1965. Public Printing and Stationery ceased to exist when its small remaining staff was transferred to Supply and Services in 1970.

Y245. Public Service Commission, created in 1967, replaced the Civil Service Commission which had existed from 1908 to 1966. The statistics on employees relate to a consistent function throughout.

Y246. Public Works was created in 1867. From 1900 to 1915, the data from *Civil Service Employees* are for inside service only. The statistics on employees relate to a roughly consistent function throughout.

Y247. Regional Economic Expansion was created in 1969 from the Rural Development Branch of the former Department of Forestry and Rural Development (series Y224). Statistics first became available in 1970.

Y248. Royal Canadian Mounted Police, created in 1873 as the North-West Mounted Police, includes only the administrative staff prior to 1953. Since 1953, the force itself is included in the official sources.

Y249. Science and Technology was created in 1971 but separate statistics on employees did not become available until 1973.

Y250. Secretary of State, created in 1867, contains roughly comparable statistics throughout. For 1920 to 1927, the staff of Patents and Copyrights (formerly in Agriculture), listed separately in official sources, has been added; for 1940 and 1941, the staff of Superintendent of Bankruptcy, also given separately, has been added; and for 1950 to 1955, the staff of the Custodian of Enemy Property, again listed separately, has been added. From 1950 to 1966, Citizenship was included with Citizenship and Immigration (series Y215). Since 1967, Citizenship has reverted to Secretary of State.

Y251. Solicitor General became a separate department of government in 1966 and includes the Canadian Penitentiary Service. Prior to 1966 data were included with Justice (series Y231).

Y252. Statistics Canada (formerly Dominion Bureau of Statistics) was created in 1918. Since 1967, data on employees have been available separately. Before that time the figures were included with Trade and Commerce (series Y254).

Y253. Supply and Services, created in 1969, includes the former Department of Defence Production (series Y218) and the Office of the Comptroller of the Treasury (formerly part of Finance, series Y222) as well as small segments of other departments.

Y254. Trade and Commerce, created in 1887, has rough comparability until 1966. Since 1967, data for Statistics Canada (series Y252) has been shown separately. The department was merged with Industry in 1969 to form the new Department of Industry, Trade and Commerce (series Y228). See also the notes to series Y236 and Y238.

Y255. Transport, created in 1936, covered various departments and agencies in earlier years. Transport was formed from the former departments of Marine and of Railways and Canals, and from the Civil Aviation Branch of National Defence.

For the years 1930 to 1936 the series include employees in the departments of Marine and of Railways and Canals and of the Board of Railway Commissioners. The Department of Marine had in turn been established in 1930, when the Department of Marine and Fisheries was separated into the departments of Marine and of Fisheries. Prior to 1930 the fisheries personnel are included in this series. See also the note to series Y223.

Y256. The Treasury Board, created in 1867, was an integral part of the Department of Finance (series Y222) until 1966 when it became a separate department of government. Since 1967, the data have been shown separately.

Y257. Unemployment Insurance Commission was created in 1940, and employee data are available since 1942. In 1977, the Unemployment Insurance Commission was merged with the Department of Manpower and Immigration (series Y234) to form Canada Employment and Immigration Commission. As the series in this table run only to 1977, no figures are provided for the new entity.

Y258. Urban Affairs was created in 1971 and data are available since 1972.

Y259. Veterans Affairs, created in 1944, includes for 1945 to 1948 the staff of the Soldier Settlement Board, and prior to 1945 consists exclusively of that staff. The series does not include the Department of Soldiers' Civil Re-establishment (1916 to 1927), which was merged into Pensions and National Health in 1928. See also the note to series Y237.

Y260-263. Representation of the Government of Canada abroad, 1867 to 1977

SOURCE: Statistics Canada, *Canada Year Book, 1976-77,* pp. 1095-1103; files of the Historical Division, Department of External Affairs. See also Skilling, *Canadian Representation Abroad, from Agency to Embassy.*

Prior to the Imperial Conference of 1926, Canada's sole formal representative abroad was the High Commissioner to the United Kingdom, an office created in 1880. Although Canada began to play an important role in the negotiation of commercial treaties with other countries early in its nationhood, the formal role of representatives of the British government, as co-signers of treaties, continued until World War I. In the negotiation of political treaties Canadian progress was slower and it was not until Dominion status was achieved in 1926 (and confirmed in the Statute of Westminster in 1931) that Canada and the other members of the Commonwealth assumed a role as fully independent nations in external affairs. Independence in internal affairs had been achieved much earlier. After 1926 Canadian representation abroad grew steadily, as is shown in series Y260-263. The status of representatives is hierarchical: high commissioner (in Commonwealth countries) and ambassador (in non-Commonwealth countries) rank highest; then come minister, chargé d'affaires, consul general and consul. Prior to World War II Canada had only six representatives ranked as ambassadors and four high commissioners to Commonwealth countries. This changed dramatically in the 1940s, 1950s and 1960s as Canada established diplomatic relations with the new emerging nations.

The Federal Government Disallowances of Provincial Acts, Reservations of Provincial Bills and Federal Royal Commissions (Series Y264-296)

Y264-266. Formal amendments to the British North America Act, 1867 to 1975

SOURCE: no official list of amendments to the BNA Act, 1867, exists, but there is general agreement among authorities that the amendments to the act include more than just the statutes subsequent to 1867, also entitled BNA Act. The list in series Y264-266 is from a standard monograph, Gérin-Lajoie, *Constitutional Amendment in Canada;* supplemented by data in Dawson, *The Government of Canada;* and Great Britain, *The Public General Acts and Church Assembly Measure, 1960.* There is disagreement, however, among authorities as to the number and classification of amendments to the BNA Act, 1867. For a list somewhat different from series Y264-266, see Clokie, "Basic Problems of the Canadian Constitution", in *Canadian Journal of Economics and Political Science,* vol. 8, no. 1, (February 1942), pp. 1-32. The formal citation of each statute refers to the year of the Monarch's reign (for example, 9 Elizabeth II is the ninth year of the reign of Elizabeth II). See also *A Consolidation of the British North America Acts, 1867 to 1975,* (consolidated as of June 1, 1976), Ottawa, Supply and Services Canada, 1976.

Until 1949 most relevant sections of the BNA Act could be amended formally only by the Parliament of the United

Kingdom, which passed the original statute. All the amendments before 1949 are statutes of the United Kingdom. In 1949, the Parliament of Canada assumed jurisdiction over those parts of the BNA Act which refer only to the federal government's part of the constitution.

Y267-270. Provinces and territories, dates and processes of admission and present areas, 1867 to 1976

SOURCE: *Canada Year Book, 1976-77*, pp. 33 and 72. The source should be consulted for more detailed information on changes in the areas of several of the provinces after their original establishment, and of the territories. See also series L1-2.

The provinces have become parts of Canada in three ways: by original creation as provinces in 1867; by subsequent creation out of territories that were themselves part of Canada; and by the admission as provinces of new areas that were not formerly part of Canada. The Canadian government's power to admit certain colonies as provinces was recognized in the BNA Act of 1867, and enlarged to include the creation of new provinces out of territories in 1871. Thus British Columbia, Prince Edward Island and Newfoundland were admitted as established entities. The Prairie provinces were created from the territories which had been purchased from the Hudson's Bay Company in 1870, and then annexed to Canada. Once a new province is established, the Canadian government is not competent to alter the act of creation except in regard to boundary changes, which can be made only with the province's consent.

Y271-281. Number of provincial statutes disallowed by the federal government, by province and decade, 1867 to 1976

SOURCE: LaForest, *Disallowance and Reservation of Provincial Legislation*, pp. 83-101. The source lists each statute by citation, title, reasons for disallowance, date of report of the Minister of Justice, and provides further references.

The Canadian government has the unqualified power to disallow any act of a provincial legislature within a year of its passage. The power was widely used in the four decades immediately following 1867, but its employment is now rare, as political, legal and economic developments have all enhanced the status of the provinces within Confederation. The power still exists in law, unrestricted, and attempts to persuade the federal government to use it against provincial legislation that is unpopular with various organized groups are not uncommon.

Some of the earlier statistics are in one sense misleading, for sometimes the federal government disallowed substantially the same provincial act several times; each separate disallowance is given in the series.

Y282-292. Number of provincial bills reserved by Lieutenant-Governors, by province and decade, 1867 to 1976

SOURCE: LaForest, *Disallowance and Reservation of Provincial Legislation*, pp. 102-115. The source includes a detailed examination and list of reserved bills, including the disposition made of each bill, and the reasons therefore; James R. Mallorey, "The Lieutenant-Governor's Discretionary Powers: The Reservation of Bill 56" *Canadian Journal of Economics and Political Science*, Toronto, vol. 27, 1961.

The Lieutenant-Governor of each province, who is appointed by the Governor General on the advice of the Prime Minister of Canada, has the power to reserve assent to any bill passed by the provincial legislature, and to refer it to the federal government for the signification of the latter's pleasure. If the federal government takes no action of any kind for one year, the bill dies; but the Canadian government may also instruct that assent to the bill be given, or give assent itself. Generally the federal authorities have held that Lieutenant-Governors should reserve a provincial bill only on instructions from Ottawa, but in fact most reserved bills have been reserved without instructions, and in most cases the federal government has taken no action. As with disallowance, the use of the reservation power has declined, but it was employed in 1961 when the Lieutenant-Governor of Saskatchewan reserved a bill without instructions, and in due course was instructed to give his assent.

Y293-295. Federal royal commissions, 1867 to 1976

SOURCE: Henderson, George F., *Federal Royal Commissions in Canada, 1867-1966*, supplemented by a list available on photostat in the Privy Council; J.C. Courtney and John Childs, *Canadian Royal Commissions of Inquiry; 1946 to 1962: An Investigation of an Executive Instrument of Inquiry*, Ph.D. thesis, Duke University.

The definition of 'Royal Commission' is not at all clear. Presumably all commissions issued under Part I of the Public Inquiries Act qualify; but these include many minor investigations into individual charges of political partisanship and the like. A number of these may have been omitted from the column headed 'minor commissions'. Commissions issued under Part II of the Inquiries Act do not bear the Great Seal and therefore technically fail to qualify; but again several important investigations set up as 'departmental inquiries' under Part II have been regarded as royal commissions. The compilation contains some of these. Several other statutes have provided for public inquiries, and commissioners appointed under these acts have often been designated royal commissioners, for example: 38 Victoria, chap. 53 (1875) to adjust claims to Manitoba lands; the Combines Act; the Judges Act (to study a case for dismissal of a judge). Pre-dating the Industrial Disputes Investigation Act there were also many commissions set up to study industrial unrest. These have been included, mainly in the column headed 'minor commissions'. The segregation into 'major' and 'minor' commissions has been based on the importance of the subject and/or the value of the report(s).

Y296. Subjects of major royal commissions, 1867 to 1976

SOURCE: see series Y293-295.

Series Y296 lists the major federal royal commissions designated in series Y293.

The Provincial Governments, Lieutenant-Governors and Premiers (Series Y297-301)

Y297-298. Lieutenant-Governors, by province, 1867 to 1976

SOURCE: Department of Provincial Affairs, Newfoundland; MacKinnon, *The Government of Prince Edward Island*;

Deputy Provincial Secretary, Nova Scotia; Beck, *The Government of Nova Scotia; Annuaire du Québec*, Quebec, various issues; Saskatchewan, *Who's Who*, various issues; *Canada Year Book*, various issues; *Canadian Parliamentary Guide*, various issues. See also Saywell, *The Office of Lieutenant-Governor.*

The Lieutenant-Governor is nominally the chief executive officer of each province. He is appointed and paid by the federal government, ordinarily for a term of five years though removable for cause, and was originally intended to be a federal official in each province. Judicial decision has added to his powers a status not unlike that of the Governor General, that is, he is Her Majesty's representative in each province. His functions are largely ceremonial, but Lieutenant-Governors have made more frequent use of their powers to reserve or withhold assent to bills than have Governors General of Canada or Monarchs in the United Kingdom. The powers and prestige of the Lieutenant-Governor vary from individual to individual and from place to place, but in general have declined throughout Canada since 1867. The Lieutenant-Governor is still nonetheless an integral part of each provincial legislature.

Y299-301. Ministries, by province and premier, 1867 to 1976

SOURCE: MacKinnon, *The Government of Prince Edward Island;* Deputy Provincial Secretary, Nova Scotia; Beck, *The Government of Nova Scotia; Annuaire du Québec,* Quebec, various issues; Saskatchewan Archives Board; Clerk of the Legislative Assembly, Alberta; Deputy Provincial Secretary, British Columbia; and various issues of the *Canadian Parliamentary Companion, Canadian Parliamentary Guide,* and *Canada Year Book.*

The office of premier, as leader of a government with a majority in the legislature, has been recognized in most provinces since their establishment, though Professor W.L. Morton has observed in *Encyclopedia Canadiana*, vol. 2, p. 45, that it is doubtful if the position of premier was recognized in Manitoba before 1874. Certainly the powers of the premier, and his views of his functions and his relations with the other parts of the provincial government, have not been identical in all the provinces since they entered Confederation.

The determination of party affiliations for earlier years is in several instances difficult, and in a few impossible. In any event, a provincial party label then, as now, did not always mean that a provincial premier of one party gave his whole-hearted support to the same party at the federal level, or paid much attention to the party of the same name in other provinces.

The Provincial Governments, Provincial Elections (Series Y302-387)

Y302-387. Provincial government elections, party standing and size of legislature, 1867 to 1977

SOURCE: Chief Electoral Officer, Newfoundland; MacKinnon, *The Government of Prince Edward Island;* Chief Electoral Officer, Prince Edward Island; Chief Electoral Officer, Nova Scotia; Department of the Provincial Secretary, New Brunswick; *Annuaire du Québec,* Quebec, various issues;

Chief Electoral Officer, Ontario; *A Statistical History of All the Electoral Districts of the Province of Ontario since 1867;* Saskatchewan Archives Board; Clerk of the Legislative Assembly, Alberta; Chief Electoral Officer, British Columbia; and various issues of the *Canadian Parliamentary Companion, Canadian Parliamentary Guide, Canadian Almanac and Directory,* and *Canada Year Book.*

Provincial election results, by parties, include some of the most elusive political statistics in Canada, and must be used with caution. The Deputy Provincial Secretary, Prince Edward Island, for example, has confirmed that information in the *Canadian Parliamentary Guide* may be considered official for P.E.I.; although it has included inconsistencies in its data, including different dates for the same election and different party affiliations for individuals. Other provinces appear to have kept official statistics of their elections since Confederation.

Several sections of series Y302-387 require special qualification.

First, multi-member constituencies are far less common than they were. In Nova Scotia, for example, all constituencies returned at least two members from 1876 to 1916; now only three two-member constituencies remain. See *Acts of Nova Scotia:* 1914, chap. 16; 1932, chap. 19; 1948, chap. 47; 1955, chap. 7.

Second, series Y327-335 excludes the former Legislative Council of Quebec. Quebec, in 1968, was the last province to divest itself of a bicameral legislature, though several of the older provinces formerly were bicameral. The series throughout Y302-387 refer only to the lower houses.

Third, party affiliations in Manitoba, series Y347-359, have not always been sufficiently clear to make tabulation easy, and in earlier years (especially 1870 and 1874) the number of members whose affiliation was not known (shown in 'Other' column) is formidable. Detailed study of party results in Manitoba requires more qualification than can be provided here. The main limitations on series Y347-359 are: (a) after 1932, the column 'Liberal and Liberal Progressive' represents a combination of Liberal and Progressive forces which cannot be separated; (b) the elections of 1941, 1945 and 1949 resulted in coalition governments of a type not suggested in the statistics, (see the *Canadian Parliamentary Guide* for relevant year); (c) the election of 1921 is shown in the *Canadian Parliamentary Guide* as returning 21 'Government' candidates who were Liberals according to the biographical sketches in the 1921 issue of that publication, although other Liberals opposed 'Government' candidates at the polls.

Fourth, the Province of British Columbia is authority for the statement that the election of 1903, in series Y379-387, was the first run on party lines, hence the gaps in the table before that date. The *Canadian Parliamentary Guide* for elections before 1903 identifies candidates as 'Government' and 'Opposition' only.

---

[1] The author of this section wishes to acknowledge that he has used the excellent text of Dr. Norman Ward, prepared for the 1965 edition of the *Historical Statistics of Canada.* The bibliography has been updated and minor changes to Dr. Ward's introduction were made.

Series Y1-2. The monarchy, 1867 to 1978

Year of reign	Monarch	Accession
	1	2
1952-[1]	Elizabeth II	6 February 1952
1936-1952	George VI	11 December 1936
1936	Edward VIII	20 January 1936[2]
1910-1936	George V	6 May 1910
1901-1910	Edward VII	22 January 1901
1837-1901	Victoria I	20 June 1837

[1] As of 31 December 1978.
[2] Abdicated before coronation.

Series Y3-5. Governors General, 1867 to 1978

Term of office	Number	Governor General	Appointed	Assumed office
		3	4	5
1973-[1]	21	The Right Honourable Jules Léger, C.C., C.M.M., C.D.	5 October 1973	14 January 1974
1967-1973	20	The Right Honourable Roland Michener, C.C., C.M.M., C.D.	29 March 1967	17 April 1967
1959-1967	19	Major-General Georges Philias Vanier, D.S.O., M.C., C.D.	1 August 1959	15 September 1959
1952-1959	18	The Right Honourable Vincent Massey, C.H.	24 January 1952	28 February 1952
1946-1952	17	Field Marshal Viscount Alexander of Tunis, K.G., G.C.B., G.C.M.G., C.S.I., D.S.O., M.C., A.D.C.	1 August 1945	12 April 1946
1940-1946	16	Major-General The Earl of Athlone, K.G., P.C., G.C.B., G.C.M.G., G.C.V.O., D.S.O.	3 April 1940	21 June 1940
1935-1940	15	Lord Tweedsmuir of Elsfield, G.C.M.G., G.C.V.O., C.H.	10 August 1935	2 November 1935
1931-1935	14	The Earl of Bessborough, G.C.M.G.	9 February 1931	4 April 1931
1926-1931	13	Viscount Willingdon of Ratton, G.C.S.I., G.C.I.E., G.B.E.	5 August 1926	2 October 1926
1921-1926	12	General The Lord Byng of Vimy, G.C.B., G.C.M.G., M.V.O.	2 August 1921	11 August 1921
1916-1921	11	The Duke of Devonshire, K.G., G.C.M.G., G.C.V.O.	19 August 1916	11 November 1916
1911-1916	10	Field Marshal, H.R.H. The Duke of Connaught, K.G.	21 March 1911	13 October 1911
1904-1911	9	Earl Grey, G.C.M.G.	26 September 1904	10 December 1904
1898-1904	8	The Earl of Minto, G.C.M.G.	30 July 1898	12 November 1898
1893-1898	7	The Earl of Aberdeen, K.T., G.C.M.G.	22 May 1893	18 September 1893
1888-1893	6	Lord Stanley of Preston, G.C.B.	1 May 1888	11 June 1888
1883-1888	5	The Marquis of Lansdowne, G.C.M.G.	18 August 1883	23 October 1883
1878-1883	4	The Marquis of Lorne, K.T., G.C.M.G.	5 October 1878	25 November 1878
1872-1878	3	The Earl of Dufferin, K.P., K.C.B., G.C.M.G.	22 May 1872	25 June 1872
1869-1872	2	Lord Lisgar, G.C.M.G.	29 December 1868	2 February 1869
1867-1869	1	Viscount Monck, G.C.M.G.	1 June 1867	1 July 1867

[1] As of 31 December 1978.

Series Y6-16. Canadian ministries, dates, numbers of portfolios, turnover of personnel and party affiliation, 1867 to 1976

Year	Number	Prime Minister	Dates of ministry	Party[1]	Portfolios		Ministers without portfolio		Non-cabinet ministers		Parliamentary secretaries	
					Number	Number of occupants	Number of posts	Number of occupants	Number of posts	Number of occupants	Number of posts	Number of occupants
	6		**7**	**8**	**9**	**10**	**11**	**12**	**13**	**14**	**15**	**16**
1968–	20	Rt. Hon. Pierre Elliot Trudeau	20 April 1968[2]	Lib.	34	120	7	18	—	—	32	140
1963–1968	19	Rt. Hon. Lester Bowles Pearson	22 April 1963–20 April 1968	Lib.	31	68	3	12	—	—	26	54
1957–1963	18	Rt. Hon. John George Diefenbaker	21 June 1957–22 April 1963	Cons.	22	37	3	4	—	—	19	29
1948–1957	17	Rt. Hon. Louis Stephen St. Laurent	15 November 1948–21 June 1957	Lib.	25	51	2	3	—	—	18	38
1935–1948	16	Rt. Hon. William Lyon Mackenzie King	23 October 1935–15 November 1948	Lib.	32	86	2	4	—	—	17	25
1930–1935	15	Rt. Hon. Richard Bedford Bennett	7 August 1930–23 October 1935	Cons.	21	34	4	5	—	—	—	—
1926–1930	14	Rt. Hon. William Lyon Mackenzie King	25 September 1926–7 August 1930	Lib.	24	31	2	2	—	—	—	—
1926	13	Rt. Hon. Arthur Meighen	29 June 1926–25 September 1926	Cons.	20	34	4	5	—	—	—	—
1921–1926	12	Rt. Hon. William Lyon Mackenzie King	29 December 1921–28 June 1926	Lib.	22	41	5	8	1	1	—	—
1920–1921	11	Rt. Hon. Arthur Meighen	10 July 1920–29 December 1921	Unionist	22	33	4	4	1	1	—	—
1917–1920	10	Rt. Hon. Sir Robert Laird Borden	12 October 1917–10 July 1920	Unionist	24	38	4	4	1	1	3	5
1911–1917	9	Rt. Hon. Sir Robert Laird Borden	10 October 1911–12 October 1917	Cons.	21	43	3	3	3	4	—	—
1896–1911	8	Rt. Hon. Sir Wilfrid Laurier	11 July 1896–6 October 1911	Lib.	18	46	2	5	3	6	—	—
1896	7	Hon. Sir Charles Tupper	1 May 1896–8 July 1896	Cons.	15	15	3	3	1	1	—	—
1894–1896	6	Hon. Sir Mackenzie Bowell	21 December 1894–27 April 1896	Cons.	15	31	3	4	3	4	—	—
1892–1894	5	Rt. Hon. Sir John Sparrow David Thompson	5 December 1892–12 December 1894	Cons.	13	13	2	2	3	3	—	—
1891–1892	4	Hon. Sir John Joseph Caldwell Abbott	16 June 1891–24 November 1892	Cons.	14	23	1	1	—	—	—	—
1878–1891	3	Rt. Hon. Sir John Alexander Macdonald	17 October 1878–6 June 1891	Cons.	16	50	2	4	—	—	—	—
1873–1878	2	Hon. Alexander Mackenzie	7 November 1873–8 October 1878	Lib.	14	35	2	2	—	—	—	—
1867–1873	1	Hon. Sir John Alexander Macdonald	1 July 1867–5 November 1873	Cons.	15	45	—	—	—	—	—	—

[1] See note to series W165–176 in previous edition for changes in official party names through the years.

[2] As of 31 December 1976.

Series Y17-29. Growth of representation in the House of Commons and redistribution (general and partial), by province, 1867 to 1974

Year	Total for Canada	Newfoundland	Prince Edward Island	Nova Scotia	New Brunswick	Quebec	Ontario	Manitoba	Saskatchewan	Alberta	British Columbia	Yukon Territory	Northwest Territories
	17	18	19	20	21	22	23	24	25	26	27	28	29
1974[1]	282	7	4	11	10	75	95	14	14	21	28	1	2
1968	264	7	4	11	10	74	88	13	13	19	23	1	1
1953	265	7	4	12	10	75	85	14	17	17	22	1	1
1952	265	7	4	12	10	75	85	14	17	17	22	2[2]	—
1949[3]	262	7	4	13	10	73	83	16	20	17	18	1	—
1947	255	—	4	13	10	73	83	16	20	17	18	1	—
1933	245	—	4	12	10	65	82	17	21	17	16	1	—
1924	245	—	4	14	11	65	82	17	21	16	14	1	—
1915[3]	235	—	4	16	11	65	82	15	16	12	13	1	—
1914	234	—	3	16	11	65	82	15	16	12	13	1	—
1907[3]	221	—	4	18	13	65	86	10	10	7	7	1	—
1903	214	—	4	18	13	65	86	10		10[4]	7	1	—
1892	213	—	5	20	14	65	92	7		4[4]	6	—	—
1887[3]	215	—	6	21	16	65	92	5		4[4]	6	—	—
1882	211	—	6	21	16	65	92	5	—		6	—	—
1873[3]	206	—	6	21	16	65	88	4	—		6	—	—
1872	200	—	—	21	16	65	88	4	—		6	—	—
1871[3]	185	—	—	19	15	65	82	4	—		—	—	—
1867	181	—	—	19	15	65	82	—	—		—	—	—

[1] New representation will take effect with the General Election of 1979.
[2] Includes one member for Mackenzie River.
[3] See note on series Y17-29.
[4] Northwest Territories.

Series Y30-40. Growth of representation in the Senate of Canada, 1867 to 1975

Year	Total for Canada	Atlantic provinces				Quebec	Ontario	Western provinces			
		Newfoundland	Prince Edward Island	Nova Scotia	New Brunswick			Manitoba	Saskatchewan	Alberta	British Columbia
	30	31	32	33	34	35	36	37	38	39	40
1975[1]	104	6	4	10	10	24	24	6	6	6	6
1949	102	6	4	10	10	24	24	6	6	6	6
1915	96	—	4	10	10	24	24	6	6	6	6
1905	87	—	4	10	10	24	24	4	4	4	3
1903	83	—	4	10	10	24	24	4		4[2]	3
1892	81	—	4	10	10	24	24	4		2[2]	3
1887	80	—	4	10	10	24	24	3		2[2]	3
1882	78	—	4	10	10	24	24	3	—		3
1873	77	—	4	10	10	24	24	2	—		3
1871	77	—	—	12	12	24	24	2	—		3
1870	74	—	—	12	12	24	24	2	—		—
1867	72	—	—	12	12	24	24	—	—		—

[1] In June 1975, the Yukon Territory and the Northwest Territories each had one member appointed to the Senate.
[2] Northwest Territories.

Series Y41-50. Dates of general elections and sessions of federal parliaments, 1867 to 1974[1]

Year of election	Parliament	Session	Date of opening	Date of prorogation	Days of session	Sitting days of House of Commons	Date of election	Writs returnable	Dissolution	Length of Parliament
41	42		43	44	45	46	47	48	49	50
1974	30	3	18 October 1977	—	—	—	—	—	—	—
		2	12 October 1976	17 October 1977	370	174	—	—	—	—
		1	30 September 1974	12 October 1976	743	343	—	—	—	—
1972	29	2	27 February 1974	8 May 1974	71	50	30 October 1972	20 November 1972	9 May 1974	1y, 5m, 20d
		1	4 January 1973	26 February 1974	418	206	8 July 1974	30 July 1974	—	—
1968	28	4	17 February 1972	1 September 1972	197	91	25 June 1968	25 July 1968	1 September 1972	4y, 1m, 8d
		3	8 October 1970	16 February 1972	497	244	—	—	—	—
		2	23 October 1969	7 October 1970	349	155	—	—	—	—
		1	12 September 1968	22 October 1969	386	199	—	—	—	—
1965	27	2	8 May 1967	23 April 1968	352	155	8 November 1965	9 December 1965	23 April 1968	2y, 4m, 15d
		1	18 January 1966	8 May 1967	476	250	—	—	—	—
1963	26	3	5 April 1965	8 September 1965	157	53	8 April 1963	8 May 1963	8 September 1965	2y, 4m, 1d
		2	18 February 1964	3 April 1964	411	248	—	—	—	—
		1	16 May 1963	21 December 1963	220	117	—	—	—	—
1962	25	1	27 September 1962	5 February 1963	131	72	18 June 1962	18 July 1962	6 February 1963	6m, 20d
1958	24	5	18 January 1962	18 April 1962	117	93	31 March 1958	30 April 1958	19 April 1962	3y, 11m, 20d
		4	17 November 1960	—	—	—	31 March 1958	30 April 1958	—	—
		3	14 January 1960	10 August 1960	210	146	—	—	—	—
		2	15 January 1959	18 July 1959	185	127	—	—	—	—
		1	12 May 1958	6 September 1958	117	93	—	—	—	—
1957	23	1	14 October 1957	1 February 1958	111	78	10 June 1957	8 August 1957	1 February 1958	5m, 25d
1953	22	5	8 January 1957	12 April 1957	95	71	10 August 1953	8 October 1953	12 April 1957	3y, 6m, 5d
		4	26 November 1956	8 January 1957	44	5	—	—	—	—
		3	10 January 1956	14 August 1956	218	152	—	—	—	—
		2	7 January 1955	28 July 1955	203	140	—	—	—	—
		1	12 November 1953	26 June 1954	227	139	—	—	—	—
1949	21	7	20 November 1952	14 May 1953	176	108	27 June 1949	25 August 1949	13 June 1953	3y, 9m, 20d
		6	28 February 1952	20 November 1952	267	87	—	—	—	—
		5	9 October 1951	29 December 1951	82	56	—	—	—	—
		4	30 January 1951	9 October 1951	253	105	—	—	—	—
		3	29 August 1950	29 January 1951	154	17	—	—	—	—
		2	16 February 1950	30 June 1950	135	90	—	—	—	—
		1	15 September 1949	10 December 1949	87	64	—	—	—	—
1945	20	5	26 January 1949	30 April 1949	95	59	11 June 1945	9 August 1945	30 April 1949	3y, 8m, 22d
		4	5 December 1947	30 June 1948	209	119	—	—	—	—
		3	30 January 1947	17 July 1947	169	115	—	—	—	—
		2	14 March 1946	31 August 1946	171	118	—	—	—	—
		1	6 September 1945	18 December 1945	104	76	—	—	—	—
1940	19	6	19 March 1945	16 April 1945	29	19	26 March 1940	17 April 1940	16 April 1945	5y
		5	27 January 1944	31 January 1945	371	136	—	—	—	—
		4	28 January 1943	26 January 1944	364	120	—	—	—	—
		3	22 January 1942	27 January 1943	371	124	—	—	—	—
		2	7 November 1940	21 January 1942	441	105	—	—	—	—
		1	16 May 1940	5 November 1940	174	61	—	—	—	—
1935	18	6	25 January 1940	25 January 1940	1	1	14 October 1935	9 November 1935	25 January 1940	4y, 2m, 16d
		5	7 September 1939	13 September 1939	7	6	—	—	—	—
		4	12 January 1939	3 June 1939	143	103	—	—	—	—
		3	27 January 1938	1 July 1938	156	102	—	—	—	—
		2	14 January 1937	10 April 1937	87	62	—	—	—	—
		1	6 February 1936	23 June 1936	139	91	—	—	—	—
1930	17	6	17 January 1935	5 July 1935	170	—	28 July 1930	18 August 1930	15 August 1935	4y, 11m, 29d
		5	25 January 1934	3 July 1934	160	—	—	—	—	—
		4	6 October 1932	27 May 1933	234	—	—	—	—	—
		3	4 February 1932	26 May 1932	113	—	—	—	—	—
		2	12 March 1931	3 August 1931	145	—	—	—	—	—
		1	8 September 1930	22 September 1930	15	—	—	—	—	—
1926	16	4	20 February 1930	30 May 1930	100	—	14 September 1926	2 November 1926	30 May 1930	3y, 7m
		3	7 February 1929	14 June 1929	128	—	—	—	—	—
		2	26 January 1928	11 June 1928	138	—	—	—	—	—
		1	9 December 1926	14 April 1927	127	—	—	—	—	—
1925	15	1	7 January 1926	2 July 1926	177	—	29 October 1925	7 December 1925	2 July 1926	6m, 26d
1921	14	4	5 February 1925	27 June 1925	143	—	6 December 1921	14 January 1922	5 September 1925	3y, 7m, 26d
		3	28 February 1924	19 July 1924	143	—	—	—	—	—
		2	31 January 1923	30 June 1923	151	—	—	—	—	—
		1	8 March 1922	28 June 1922	113	—	—	—	—	—

Series Y41-50. Dates of general elections and sessions of federal parliaments, 1867 to 1974[1] (concluded)

Year of election	Parliament	Session	Date of opening	Date of prorogation	Days of session	Sitting days of House of Commons	Date of election	Writs returnable	Dissolution	Length of Parliament
	41	42	43	44	45	46	47	48	49	50
1917	13	5	14 February 1921	4 June 1921	111	—	17 December 1917	27 February 1918	4 October 1921	3y, 7m, 6d
		4	26 February 1920	1 July 1920	127	—	—	—	—	—
		3	1 September 1919	10 November 1919	71	—	—	—	—	—
		2	20 February 1919	7 July 1919	138	—	—	—	—	—
		1	18 March 1918	24 May 1918	68	—	—	—	—	—
1911	12	7	18 January 1917	20 September 1917	246	—	21 September 1911	7 October 1911	6 October 1917	6y
		6	12 January 1916	18 May 1916	127	—	—	—	—	—
		5	4 February 1915	15 April 1915	71	—	—	—	—	—
		4	18 August 1914	22 August 1914	5	—	—	—	—	—
		3	15 January 1914	12 June 1914	148	—	—	—	—	—
		2	21 November 1912	6 June 1913	198	—	—	—	—	—
		1	15 November 1911	1 April 1912	139	—	—	—	—	—
1908	11	3	17 November 1910	29 July 1911	255	—	26 October 1908	3 December 1908	29 July 1911	2y, 7m, 28d
		2	11 November 1909	4 May 1910	175	—	—	—	—	—
		1	20 January 1909	19 May 1909	120	—	—	—	—	—
1904	10	4	28 November 1907	20 July 1908	236	—	3 November 1904	15 December 1904	17 September 1908	3y, 9m, 4d
		3	22 November 1906	27 April 1907	157	—	—	—	—	—
		2	8 March 1906	13 July 1906	128	—	—	—	—	—
		1	11 January 1905	20 July 1905	191	—	—	—	—	—
1900	9	4	10 March 1904	10 August 1904	154	—	7 November 1900	5 December 1900	29 September 1904	3y,9m, 26d
		3	12 March 1903	24 October 1903	227	—	—	—	—	—
		2	13 February 1902	15 May 1902	90	—	—	—	—	—
		1	6 February 1901	23 May 1901	107	—	—	—	—	—
1896	8	5	1 February 1900	18 July 1900	168	—	23 June 1896	13 July 1896	9 October 1900	4y, 2m, 26d
		4	16 March 1899	11 August 1899	149	—	—	—	—	—
		3	3 February 1898	13 June 1898	131	—	—	—	—	—
		2	25 March 1897	29 June 1897	97	—	—	—	—	—
		1	19 August 1896	5 October 1896	48	—	—	—	—	—
1891	7	6	2 January 1896	23 April 1896	111	—	5 March 1891	25 April 1891	24 April 1896	5y
		5	18 April 1895	22 July 1895	96	—	—	—	—	—
		4	15 March 1894	23 July 1894	131	—	—	—	—	—
		3	26 January 1893	1 April 1893	66	—	—	—	—	—
		2	25 February 1892	9 July 1892	136	—	—	—	—	—
		1	29 April 1891	30 September 1891	155	—	—	—	—	—
1887	6	4	16 January 1890	16 May 1890	121	—	22 February 1887	7 April 1887	3 February 1891	3y, 9m, 27d
		3	31 January 1889	2 May 1889	92	—	—	—	—	—
		2	23 February 1888	22 May 1888	90	—	—	—	—	—
		1	13 April 1887	23 June 1887	72	—	—	—	—	—
1882	5	4	25 February 1886	2 June 1886	98	—	20 June 1882	7 August 1882	15 January 1887	4y, 5m, 10d
		3	29 January 1885	20 July 1885	173	—	—	—	—	—
		2	17 January 1884	19 April 1884	94	—	—	—	—	—
		1	8 February 1883	25 May 1883	107	—	—	—	—	—
1878	4	4	9 February 1882	17 May 1882	98	—	17 September 1878	21 November 1878	18 May 1882	3y, 5m, 28d
		3	9 December 1880	21 March 1881	103	—	—	—	—	—
		2	12 February 1880	7 May 1880	86	—	—	—	—	—
		1	13 February 1879	15 May 1879	92	—	—	—	—	—
1874	3	5	7 February 1878	10 May 1878	93	—	22 January 1874	21 February 1874	17 August 1878	4y, 5m, 25d
		4	8 February 1877	28 April 1877	80	—	—	—	—	—
		3	10 February 1876	12 April 1876	63	—	—	—	—	—
		2	4 February 1875	8 April 1875	64	—	—	—	—	—
		1	26 March 1874	26 May 1874	62	—	—	—	—	—
1872	2	2	23 October 1873	7 November 1873	16	—	20 July 1872– 12 October 1872	3 September 1872	2 January 1874	1y, 4m
		1	5 March 1873	13 August 1873	161	—	—	—	—	—
1867	1	5	11 April 1872	14 June 1872	65	—	7 August 1867– 20 September 1867	24 September 1867	8 July 1872	4y, 9m, 15d
		4	15 February 1871	14 April 1871	59	—	—	—	—	—
		3	15 February 1870	12 May 1870	87	—	—	—	—	—
		2	15 April 1869	22 June 1869	69	—	—	—	—	—
		1	6 November 1867	22 May 1868	199	—	—	—	—	—

[1] As of 31 December 1977.

Series Y51-74. General elections, number of electors on lists and votes polled, by province and election, 1896 to 1974

Year of election	Total for Canada		Newfoundland		Prince Edward Island		Nova Scotia		New Brunswick		Quebec	
	Polling lists	Polled	Polling lists	Polled	Polling lists	Polled	Polling lists	Polled	Polling lists	Polled	Polling lists	Polled
	51	52	53	54	55	56	57	58	59	60	61	62
1974	13,620,353	9,671,002	304,370	175,534	73,069	58,649	524,767	388,830	406,518	289,492	3,848,426	2,592,801
1972	13,000,778	9,974,661	289,294	182,482	68,992	59,078	492,001	391,590	387,136	298,164	3,693,918	2,790,172
1968	10,860,888	8,217,916	237,594	161,570	58,216	51,225	412,791	339,600	317,912	254,716	3,083,260	2,229,345
1965	10,274,904	7,796,728	226,082	148,392	72,006	56,484	420,146	401,521	304,734	244,184	2,933,031	2,073,314
1963	9,910,757	7,958,636	221,321	152,175	69,486	57,029	419,352	401,874	304,732	245,557	2,807,634	2,143,246
1962	9,700,325	7,772,656	215,565	155,263	73,509	56,542	423,556	398,161	302,313	252,053	2,728,191	2,117,644
1958	9,131,200	7,357,139	204,778	160,928	54,200	69,302	390,196	418,479	294,387	249,706	2,576,682	2,045,199
1957	8,896,011	6,682,462	197,239	92,858	54,224	67,218	384,948	394,130	291,036	237,001	2,504,978	1,815,586
1953	8,401,691	5,701,963	194,715	111,768	55,469	66,562	380,836	334,855	287,657	225,390	2,352,619	1,565,400
1949	7,893,629	5,903,572	182,439	105,190	55,772	68,393	373,585	338,928	286,723	225,877	2,177,152	1,610,510
1945	6,952,445	5,305,193	—	—	54,794	63,807	362,754	312,954	262,261	204,273	1,956,225	1,433,591
1940	6,588,888	4,672,531	—	—	55,339	62,943	335,990	283,428	251,986	174,734	1,799,942	1,189,489
1935	5,918,207	4,452,675	—	—	53,284	61,641	304,313	275,523	229,266	177,485	1,575,159	1,162,862
1930	5,153,971	3,922,481	—	—	46,985	59,519	275,762	268,727	207,006	186,277	1,351,585	1,029,480
1926	4,665,381	3,273,062	—	—	46,208	55,569	273,712	229,846	210,028	162,777	1,133,633	809,295
1925	4,607,419	3,168,412	—	—	45,454	49,558	277,073	222,883	211,190	152,652	1,124,998	805,492
1921	4,435,310	3,119,306	—	—	46,879	52,556	294,473	260,860	204,575	156,263	1,056,792	779,591
1917	2,093,799	1,650,377 [1]	—	—	28,221	32,249	133,930	106,621	94,456	84,408	396,666	301,519
1911	1,820,742	1,307,528	—	—	—	28,636	136,994	113,022	101,112	79,072	455,288	324,039
1908	1,463,591	1,174,703	—	—	—	28,782	132,914	111,138	98,026	75,651	415,076	283,132
1904	1,385,440	1,030,788	—	—	—	29,427	124,086	103,651	95,487	72,799	372,198	257,064
1900	1,167,402	950,763	—	—	—	21,026	106,451	105,194	94,877	68,267	350,250	237,320
1896	1,358,328	899,046	—	—	25,245	18,672	111,125	100,685	91,697	64,100	351,275	224,690

Year of election	Ontario		Manitoba		Saskatchewan		Alberta		British Columbia		Yukon Territory and Northwest Territories	
	Polling lists	Polled	Polling lists	Polled	Polling lists	Polled	Polling lists	Polled	Polling lists	Polled	Polling lists	Polled
	63	64	65	66	67	68	69	70	71	72	73	74
1974	4,803,485	3,581,767	633,411	448,431	569,316	415,268	1,016,314	684,649	1,407,066	1,014,219	33,611	21,362
1972	4,601,282	3,650,542	610,568	453,642	558,876	442,246	955,531	722,338	1,312,832	961,441	30,348	22,966
1968	3,846,064	2,973,745	531,563	403,272	517,598	416,793	774,565	567,416	1,059,959	804,108	21,366	16,126
1965	3,609,895	2,770,222	517,928	382,362	508,733	404,631	725,447	534,870	972,063	731,438	18,986	15,163
1963	3,455,363	2,799,870	516,525	401,870	505,551	419,793	700,920	552,164	921,074	740,229	18,734	14,714
1962	3,397,647	2,719,020	508,920	393,023	502,495	426,426	680,253	505,752	891,696	691,930	18,552	14,480
1958	3,189,422	2,534,555	481,552	385,648	488,139	399,949	608,820	452,977	830,237	629,982	12,787	10,414
1957	3,100,456	2,295,033	473,802	351,827	484,318	392,266	591,043	431,184	802,017	596,424	11,950	8,935
1953	2,894,150	1,938,959	465,374	276,422	480,532	356,479	548,747	343,258	730,882	475,456	10,710	7,414
1949	2,718,118	2,042,294	451,882	324,079	472,884	375,471	492,228	341,222	673,782	464,785	9,064	6,823
1945	2,457,937	1,831,806	433,921	327,794	445,601	379,539	430,430	315,863	545,077	433,402	3,445	2,164
1940	2,340,344	1,625,439	425,066	320,860	481,931	373,376	423,609	272,418	472,584	368,103	2,097	1,741
1935	2,174,188	1,608,244	377,733	284,589	451,386	347,536	368,956	241,107	382,117	292,423	1,805	1,265
1930	1,894,624	1,364,960	328,089	235,192	410,400	331,652	304,475	201,635	333,326	243,631	1,719	1,408
1926	1,847,512	1,226,267	257,244	198,028	353,471	246,460	279,463	157,993	262,262	185,345	1,848	1,482
1925	1,821,906	1,223,027	250,505	171,124	346,791	197,246	283,529	161,423	244,352	183,748	1,621	1,259
1921	1,738,020	1,139,635	255,143	173,941	333,613	225,236	273,706	173,824	230,451	156,012	1,658	1,388
1917	904,075	710,077	138,029	109,542	133,806	99,253	140,757	107,272	122,071	97,994	1,788	1,442
1911	693,485	480,572	98,588	77,696	142,414	89,043	107,228	69,775	83,081	43,559	2,552	2,114
1908	660,340	462,280	84,537	68,047	—	59,868	—	45,972	69,827	37,368	2,871	2,465
1904	607,854	444,257	70,121	48,122	—	—	—	—	45,345	25,184	70,349	50,284
1900	482,003	427,173	64,027	41,714	—	—	—	—	38,448	26,451	31,346	23,618
1896	650,473	422,075	65,685	32,884	—	—	—	—	38,010	18,152	24,818	17,788

[1] An unusually large number of acclamations (31) affected the statistics for 1917, as did the Wartime Elections Act of that year.

Series Y75-198. Votes polled in federal elections, by party and province, 1896 to 1974

Province	Federal general election 1974						Federal general election 1972					
	Liberal	Progressive Conservative	New Democratic Party	Social Credit	Independent	Others	Liberal	Progressive-Conservative	New Democratic Party	Social Credit	Independent	Others
	75	76	77	78	79	80	81	82	83	84	85	86
Newfoundland	81,299	75,816	16,445	143	242	–	78,505	85,857	8,165	266	616	1,637
Prince Edward Island	26,932	28,578	2,666	–	–	77	22,950	29,419	4,229	55	–	–
Nova Scotia	157,582	183,897	43,470	1,457	–	458	129,738	204,460	47,072	1,316	–	501
New Brunswick	135,723	94,934	24,869	8,407	23,299	118	125,935	131,455	16,703	16,450	839	1,109
Quebec	1,330,337	520,632	162,080	420,018	6,712	18,896	1,289,139	457,418	168,910	639,207	43,495	26,867
Ontario	1,609,786	1,252,082	680,113	6,575	5,232	11,749	1,366,922	1,399,148	768,076	12,937	7,898	23,071
Manitoba	122,470	212,990	104,829	4,750	286	1,406	136,906	184,363	116,474	3,228	517	1,666
Saskatchewan	127,282	150,846	130,391	4,539	316	560	109,342	159,629	155,195	7,717	199	422
Alberta	168,973	417,422	63,310	22,909	1,524	8,431	177,599	409,857	89,811	31,689	302	1,694
British Columbia	336,435	423,954	232,547	12,433	1,134	4,378	274,468	313,253	332,345	25,107	1,483	1,633
Yukon Territory	2,784	3,913	1,618	–	–	–	2,633	4,332	951	–	252	–
Northwest Territories	3,173	4,271	5,410	–	–	–	4,121	4,339	5,597	–	–	–
Totals for Canada	4,102,776	3,369,335	1,467,748	481,231	38,745	46,073	3,718,258	3,383,530	1,713,528	737,972	55,601	58,600

Province	Federal general election 1968					Federal general election 1965					
	Liberal	Progressive Conservative	New Democratic Party	Ralliement créditiste	Others	Liberal	Progressive Conservative	New Democratic Party	Ralliement créditiste	Social Credit	Others
	87	88	89	90	91	92	93	94	95	96	97
Newfoundland	68,549	84,483	7,042	–	126	94,291	47,638	1,742	–	2,352	1,022
Prince Edward Island	22,854	26,276	1,636	–	–	31,352	38,566	1,463	–	–	–
Nova Scotia	127,962	186,026	22,676	–	293	175,415	203,123	38,043	–	–	1,249
New Brunswick	111,843	125,269	12,277	1,769	821	114,781	102,714	22,759	1,081	352	–
Quebec	1,170,417	466,492	164,466	358,327	24,590	928,530	432,901	244,339	357,153	–	74,389
Ontario	1,372,903	942,979	607,011	–	25,599	1,196,308	933,753	594,112	1,204	9,791	8,615
Manitoba	166,025	125,713	99,974	949	7,732	117,442	154,253	91,193	–	16,315	237
Saskatchewan	112,332	153,233	147,941	–	919	96,740	193,254	104,626	–	7,526	179
Alberta	201,045	283,987	52,720	–	26,083	119,014	247,734	43,818	–	119,586	1,275
British Columbia	333,949	155,101	260,989	–	48,703	217,726	139,226	239,132	–	126,532	3,368
Yukon Territory	3,048	3,110	325	–	–	2,546	3,136	–	–	–	–
Northwest Territories	6,018	2,211	1,203	–	–	5,194	3,615	431	–	–	–
Totals for Canada	3,696,945	2,554,880	1,378,260	361,045	134,866	3,098,339	2,499,913	1,381,658	359,438	282,454	90,334

Province	Federal general election 1963					Federal general election 1962				
	Liberal	Progressive Conservative	Social Credit	New Democratic Party	Others	Progressive Conservative	Liberal	New Democratic Party	Social Credit	Others
	98	99	100	101	102	103	104	105	106	107
Newfoundland	97,576	45,491	–	6,364	1,943	55,396	90,896	7,590	158	–
Prince Edward Island	32,073	35,965	–	1,140	–	37,388	31,603	3,802	153	–
Nova Scotia	195,007	195,711	401	26,617	–	198,902	178,520	39,689	3,764	–
New Brunswick	115,036	98,462	21,050	8,899	–	115,973	111,291	13,220	9,016	–
Quebec	966,172	413,562	578,347	151,061	8,903	620,475	830,250	91,795	542,433	4,970
Ontario	1,286,791	979,359	56,276	442,340	11,896	1,056,095	1,122,222	456,459	49,734	3,135
Manitoba	134,905	169,013	28,157	66,652	826	161,824	121,041	76,514	26,662	3,297
Saskatchewan	100,747	224,700	16,110	76,126	443	213,385	96,676	93,444	19,648	317
Alberta	121,473	249,067	141,956	35,775	1,255	214,699	97,633	42,305	146,662	686
British Columbia	237,896	172,501	97,846	222,883	4,846	187,389	187,438	212,035	97,396	1,931
Yukon Territory	2,455	2,969	560	–	–	3,250	2,664	–	–	–
Northwest Territories	3,659	4,814	–	–	–	3,519	3,842	–	948	–
Totals for Canada	3,293,790	2,591,614	940,703	1,037,857	30,112	2,868,295	2,874,076	1,036,853	896,574	14,336

Series Y75-198. Votes polled in federal elections, by party and province, 1896 to 1974 (continued)

Province	Federal general election 1958						Federal general election 1957					
	Progressive Conservative[1]	Liberal[2]	Cooperative Commonwealth Federation	Social Credit[3]	Labour Progressive Party	Others	Liberal[2]	Progressive Conservative[1]	Cooperative Commonwealth Federation	Social Credit[3]	Labour Progressive Party	Others
	108	109	110	111	112	113	114	115	116	117	118	119
Newfoundland	72,282	86,960	240	–	–	263	56,993	34,795	321	–	–	–
Prince Edward Island	42,911	25,847	215	–	–	–	31,162	34,965	680	–	–	–
Nova Scotia	237,422	160,026	18,911	–	–	–	176,891	197,676	17,117	473	–	–
New Brunswick	133,935	107,297	4,541	1,711	–	–	112,518	114,060	2,001	2,420	–	3,159
Quebec	1,005,120	935,881	45,594	12,858	1,162	23,634	1,116,028	562,133	31,780	3,877	2,377	73,865
Ontario	1,413,730	815,524	262,120	8,386	3,035	1,718	845,308	1,104,366	274,069	38,418	1,432	978
Manitoba	216,948	82,450	74,906	6,753	1,503	–	93,258	124,867	82,398	45,803	1,579	205
Saskatchewan	204,442	78,121	112,800	1,745	458	146	118,282	90,359	140,293	40,830	212	122
Alberta	269,942	61,583	19,666	97,502	1,196	–	119,190	118,225	27,127	162,083	815	212
British Columbia	308,971	100,889	153,405	59,762	2,515	–	121,301	192,988	131,873	143,145	1,345	887
Yukon Territory	3,069	2,340	–	–	–	–	2,422	2,358	–	–	–	–
Mackenzie River	2,080	2,782	–	–	–	–	2,686	1,253	–	–	–	–
Totals for Canada	3,910,852	2,459,700	692,398	188,717	9,869	25,761	2,796,039	2,578,045	707,659	437,049	7,760	79,428

Province	Federal general election 1953						Federal general election 1949						
	Liberal[2]	Progressive Conservative[1]	Cooperative Commonwealth Federation	Social Credit[3]	Labour Progressive Party	Others	Liberal[2]	Progressive Conservative[1]	Cooperative Commonwealth Federation	Social Credit[3]	Union des Électeurs	Labour Progressive Party	Others
	120	121	122	123	124	125	126	127	128	129	130	131	132
Newfoundland	74,357	31,060	707	–	–	4,459	75,235	29,203	197	–	–	–	–
Prince Edward Island	33,874	31,836	552	–	–	–	33,480	32,989	1,626	–	–	–	–
Nova Scotia	176,554	133,498	22,357	–	794	–	177,680	126,365	33,333	–	–	–	–
New Brunswick	121,936	93,450	6,769	931	–	–	123,453	88,049	9,450	–	2,172	–	533
Quebec	1,001,655	455,688	23,833	–	10,819	54,778	984,131	397,803	17,767	–	80,990	4,868	107,741
Ontario	898,692	772,691	212,224	5,427	18,414	7,972	930,719	757,987	306,551	3,225	2,036	13,613	8,043
Manitoba	110,843	73,644	64,402	17,260	6,194	434	153,857	70,689	83,176	–	–	6,523	6,666
Saskatchewan	133,493	41,538	156,406	18,810	3,906	–	161,887	53,624	152,399	3,474	–	1,531	–
Alberta	118,941	49,450	23,573	138,847	9,155	275	116,647	56,947	31,329	131,007	–	2,201	–
British Columbia	145,570	66,426	125,487	123,700	10,340	–	169,018	128,620	145,442	2,109	–	3,887	11,992
Yukon Territory	2,176	590	–	998	–	–	3,284	–	1,140	–	–	–	2,283
Mackenzie River	1,722	1,344	–	–	–	421	–	–	–	–	–	–	–
Totals for Canada	2,819,813	1,751,215	636,310	305,973	59,622	68,339	2,929,391	1,742,276	782,410	139,815	85,198	32,623	137,258

Province	Federal general election 1945							Federal general election 1940				
	Liberal[2]	Progressive Conservative[1]	Cooperative Commonwealth Federation[4]	Social Credit	Bloc Populaire	Labour Progressive Party	Others	Liberal[2]	Conservative[5]	Cooperative Commonwealth Federation	New Democrat[6]	Others
	133	134	135	136	137	138	139	140	141	142	143	144
Prince Edward Island	30,696	30,025	2,685	–	–	–	–	34,664	28,028	–	–	–
Nova Scotia	141,911	114,214	51,892	–	–	1,800	850	151,731	112,206	17,715	–	–
New Brunswick	100,939	77,225	14,999	2,300	–	–	6,423	97,062	74,970	761	–	–
Quebec	722,707	138,344	33,729	63,310	168,389	14,641	273,049	868,663	231,851	7,610	11,191	52,182
Ontario	745,571	757,057	260,502	3,906	5,038	36,333	6,560	834,146	687,816	61,166	786	25,480
Manitoba	111,863	80,303	101,892	10,322	–	15,984	2,451	151,480	82,240	61,448	5,831	15,884
Saskatchewan	124,191	70,830	167,233	11,449	–	3,183	–	159,530	52,496	106,267	12,106	40,735
Alberta	67,662	58,077	57,077	113,821	–	14,136	–	102,060	35,116	35,082	93,023	4,062
British Columbia	125,085	128,529	132,068	9,890	–	25,128	7,741	136,065	110,619	103,181	506	12,773
Yukon Territory	–	849	584	–	–	687	–	793	915	–	–	–
Totals for Canada	2,170,625	1,455,453	822,661	214,998	173,427	111,892	297,074	2,536,514	1,416,257	393,230	123,443	151,116

Series Y75-198. Votes polled in federal elections, by party and province, 1896 to 1974 (continued)

Province	Federal general election 1935								
	Liberal	Conservative	Reconstruction	Cooperative Commonwealth Federation	Social Credit	Independent Liberal	Communist	Others	Rejected Ballots
	145	146	147	148	149	150	151	152	153
Prince Edward Island	35,757	23,602	2,089	–	–	–	–	–	193
Nova Scotia	142,334	87,893	38,175	–	–	–	5,365	–	1,756
New Brunswick	100,537	56,145	18,408	–	–	672	–	–	1,723
Quebec	623,579	323,177	103,857	7,326	–	70,504	3,385	14,693	16,341
Ontario	675,803	562,513	181,981	129,457	–	14,459	8,945	21,089	13,997
Manitoba	100,535	75,574	16,439	54,491	5,751	18,973	9,229	–	3,597
Saskatchewan	134,914	71,285	2,273	73,505	63,593	–	–	–	1,966
Alberta	50,539	40,236	1,785	29,066	111,627	–	2,672	2,588	2,594
British Columbia	91,729	71,034	19,208	97,015	1,796	–	1,555	6,446	3,640
Yukon Territory	–	–	–	–	–	555	–	696	14
Totals for Canada	1,955,727	1,311,459	384,215	390,860	182,767	105,163	31,151	45,512	45,821

Province	Federal general election 1930								
	Conservative	Liberal	Progressive	Labour Progressive	Labour	Independent	United Farmers of Alberta	Farmer	Communist
	154	155	156	157	158	159	160	161	162
Prince Edward Island	29,692	29,698	–	–	–	–	–	–	–
Nova Scotia	140,513	127,189	–	–	–	–	–	–	–
New Brunswick	109,839	75,221	–	–	–	–	–	–	–
Quebec	456,037	542,135	–	–	–	21,776	–	–	313
Ontario	745,414	590,071	12,815	–	992	8,785	–	–	1,499
Manitoba	111,312	37,234	–	59,155	19,809	2,018	–	–	3,873
Saskatchewan	129,420	153,673	18,178	–	–	6,155	–	22,766	–
Alberta	67,808	60,148	–	–	8,769	2,727	60,924	–	–
British Columbia	119,074	98,933	–	–	15,732	7,894	–	–	–
Yukon Territory	846	558	–	–	–	–	–	–	–
Totals for Canada	1,909,955	1,714,860	30,993	59,155	45,302	49,355	60,924	22,766	5,685

Province	Federal general election 1926								Federal general election 1925				
	Conservative	Liberal	Progressive	Labour Progressive	Labour	Independent	United Farmers of Alberta	Rejected Ballots	Liberal	Conservative	Progressive	Labour	Independent
	163	164	165	166	167	168	169	170	171	172	173	174	175
Prince Edward Island	26,217	29,222	–	–	–	–	–	130	25,681	23,799	–	–	–
Nova Scotia	122,965	99,581	–	–	6,412	–	–	888	92,525	124,545	–	3,617	–
New Brunswick	87,080	74,465	–	–	–	–	–	1,232	61,161	90,405	–	–	84
Quebec	266,824	507,775	–	–	–	8,787	–	5,909	469,475	273,818	–	1,685	58,588
Ontario	680,742	441,254	50,360	38,112	6,282	5,356	–	4,161	392,039	691,365	108,051	9,552	19,104
Manitoba	83,100	36,242	22,092	38,379	17,194	–	–	1,021	34,538	70,264	45,859	18,335	–
Saskatchewan	67,524	125,849	38,324	13,413	–	–	–	1,350	82,810	51,512	62,268	–	1,914
Alberta	49,514	38,451	–	–	8,148	163	60,740	977	44,291	51,114	50,592	8,572	6,040
British Columbia	100,066	68,317	–	–	11,757	4,330	–	875	63,506	90,032	15,829	11,463	888
Yukon Territory	823	648	–	–	–	–	–	11	508	742	–	–	–
Totals for Canada	1,504,855	1,421,804	110,776	89,904	49,793	18,636	60,740	16,554	1,266,534	1,467,596	282,599	53,224	87,618

Series Y75-198. Votes polled in federal elections, by party and province, 1896 to 1974 (concluded)

Province	Federal general election 1921				Federal general election 1917				Federal general election 1911		
					Unionist		Laurier-Liberals		Conservative	Liberal	Other
	Liberal	Conservative	Progressive	Independent	Civilian	Soldiers	Civilian	Soldiers			
	176	177	178	179	180	181	182	183	184	185	186
Prince Edward Island	23,950	19,504	8,990	—	10,450	2,775	12,224	434	14,638	13,998	—
Nova Scotia	136,064	87,988	35,741	—	40,985	10,699	49,831	1,474	55,209	57,462	351
New Brunswick	76,653	61,172	17,447	—	35,871	9,934	32,397	919	38,880	40,192	—
Quebec	558,056	163,743	31,790	39,477	61,808	14,206	240,504	2,927	159,299	164,281	459
Ontario	351,717	445,150	329,502	9,003	419,928	95,212	263,300	5,793	269,930	207,078	3,564
Manitoba	29,525	46,486	83,350	13,361	83,469	23,698	26,073	1,157	40,356	34,781	2,559
Saskatchewan	46,447	37,345	136,486	3,610	68,424	12,996	30,829	2,672	34,700	52,924	1,419
Alberta	27,404	35,181	104,295	6,024	60,399	19,575	48,865	1,055	29,675	37,208	2,892
British Columbia	46,249	74,226	21,786	12,739	59,944	26,461	40,050	2,059	25,622	16,350	1,587
Yukon Territory	658	707	—	18	666	293	776	32	1,285	829	
Totals for Canada	1,296,723	971,502	769,387	84,232	841,944	215,849	744,849	18,522	669,594	625,103	12,831

Province	Federal general election 1908			Federal general election 1904			Federal general election 1900			Federal general election 1896		
	Liberal	Conservative	Other	Liberal	Conservative	Other	Liberal	Conservative	Other	Liberal	Conservative	Other
	187	188	189	190	191	192	193	194	195	196	197	198
Prince Edward Island	14,496	14,286	—	14,441	14,986	—	10,887	10,139	—	9,515	9,157	—
Nova Scotia	56,638	54,500	—	56,526	46,131	994	54,384	50,810	—	49,176	50,772	737
New Brunswick	40,716	34,935	—	37,158	35,503	138	35,401	32,638	228	28,383	31,399	4,318
Quebec	162,176	115,579	5,377	144,992	111,550	522	133,566	103,253	501	120,321	102,884	1,485
Ontario	217,963	237,548	6,769	219,871	223,627	759	212,595	212,413	2,165	169,480	189,927	62,668
Manitoba	30,892	35,078	2,077	26,713	20,119	1,290	21,597	20,177	—	11,519	15,459	5,906
Saskatchewan	33,885	22,007	3,976 ⎱	27,173[7]	19,367[7]	136[7]	13,012[7]	10,606[7]	—	8,191[7]	7,811[7]	1,786[7]
Alberta	23,100	20,433	2,439 ⎰									
British Columbia	13,412	17,503	6,453	12,458	9,781	2,945	12,985	10,814	2,652	8,921	9,231	—
Yukon Territory	992	265	1,208	1,495	2,113	—	—	—	—	—	—	—
Totals for Canada	594,270	552,134	28,299	540,827	483,177	6,784	494,427	450,790	5,546	405,506	416,640	76,900

[1] Includes Independent Progressive Conservative.
[2] Includes Independent Liberal.
[3] Includes Independent Social Credit.
[4] Includes Independent Cooperative Commonwealth Federation.

[5] Includes Independent Conservative and National Government.
[6] Includes Social Credit.
[7] Northwest Territories.

Series Y199-210. Members elected in federal elections, by party and province, 1867 to 1974

Year	Party	Totals for Canada	New-found-land	Prince Edward Island	Nova Scotia	New Bruns-wick	Quebec	Ontario	Mani-toba	Saskat-chewan	Alberta	British Columbia	Yukon Territory and Northwest Terri-tories
		199	200	201	202	203	204	205	206	207	208	209	210
1974	Liberal	141	4	1	2	6	60	55	2	3	–	8	–
	Progressive Conservative	95	3	3	8	3	3	25	9	8	19	13	1
	New Democratic Party	16	–	–	1	–	–	8	2	2	–	2	1
	Social Credit	11	–	–	–	–	11	–	–	–	–	–	–
	Independent	1	–	–	–	1	–	–	–	–	–	–	–
1972	Liberal	109	3	1	1	5	56	36	2	1	–	4	–
	Progressive Conservative	107	4	3	10	5	2	40	8	7	19	8	1
	New Democratic Party	31	–	–	–	–	–	11	3	5	–	11	1
	Social Credit	15	–	–	–	–	15	–	–	–	–	–	–
	Independent	2	–	–	–	–	1	1	–	–	–	–	–
1968	Liberal	154	1	–	1	5	56	63	5	2	4	16	1
	Progressive Conservative	72	6	4	10	5	4	17	5	5	15	–	1
	New Democratic Party	22	–	–	–	–	–	6	3	6	–	7	–
	Ralliement créditiste	14	–	–	–	–	14	–	–	–	–	–	–
	Liberal Labour	1	–	–	–	–	–	1	–	–	–	–	–
	Independent	1	–	–	–	–	–	1	–	–	–	–	–
1965	Liberal	131	7	–	2	6	56	51	1	–	–	7	1
	Progressive Conservative	97	–	4	10	4	8	25	10	17	15	3	1
	New Democratic Party	21	–	–	–	–	–	9	3	–	–	9	–
	Ralliement créditiste	9	–	–	–	–	9	–	–	–	–	–	–
	Social Credit	5	–	–	–	–	–	–	–	–	2	3	–
	Independent	1	–	–	–	–	1	–	–	–	–	–	–
	Independent Progressive Conservative	1	–	–	–	–	1	–	–	–	–	–	–
1963	Liberal	128	7	2	5	6	47	51	2	–	1	7	–
	Progressive Conservative	95	–	2	7	4	8	27	10	17	14	4	2
	New Democratic Party	17	–	–	–	–	–	6	2	–	–	9	–
	Social Credit	24	–	–	–	–	20	–	–	–	2	2	–
	Liberal Labour	1	–	–	–	–	–	1	–	–	–	–	–
1962	Progressive Conservative	116	1	4	9	4	14	35	11	16	15	6	1
	Liberal	99	6	–	2	6	35	43	1	1	–	4	1
	Social Credit	30	–	–	–	–	26	–	–	–	2	2	–
	New Democratic Party	19	–	–	1	–	–	6	2	–	–	10	–
	Liberal Labour	1	–	–	–	–	–	1	–	–	–	–	–
1958	Progressive Conservative	208	2	4	12	7	50	67	14	16	17	18	1
	Liberal	48	5	–	–	3	25	14	–	–	–	–	1
	Cooperative Commonwealth Federation	8	–	–	–	–	–	3	–	1	–	4	–
	Liberal Labour	1	–	–	–	–	–	1	–	–	–	–	–
1957	Progressive Conservative	112	2	4	10	5	9	61	8	3	3	7	–
	Liberal	105	5	–	2	5	63	20	1	4	1	2	2
	Independent Liberal	1	–	–	–	–	1	–	–	–	–	–	–
	Cooperative Commonwealth Federation	25	–	–	–	–	–	3	5	10	–	7	–
	Social Credit	19	–	–	–	–	–	–	–	–	13	6	–
	Liberal Labour	1	–	–	–	–	–	1	–	–	–	–	–
	Independent	2	–	–	–	–	2	–	–	–	–	–	–
1953	Liberal	170	7	3	10	7	66	50	8	5	4	8	2
	Independent Liberal	2	–	–	–	–	2	–	–	–	–	–	–
	Progressive Conservative	51	–	1	1	3	4	33	3	1	2	3	–
	Cooperative Commonwealth Federation	23	–	–	1	–	–	1	3	11	–	7	–
	Social Credit	15	–	–	–	–	–	–	–	–	11	4	–
	Independent	3	–	–	–	–	3	–	–	–	–	–	–
	Liberal Labour	1	–	–	–	–	–	1	–	–	–	–	–
1949	Liberal	190	5	3	10	7	66	56	12	14	5	11	1
	Independent Liberal	3	–	–	–	1	1	1	–	–	–	–	–
	Progressive Conservative	41	2	1	2	2	2	25	1	1	2	3	–
	Cooperative Commonwealth Federation	13	–	–	1	–	–	1	3	5	–	3	–
	Social Credit	10	–	–	–	–	–	–	–	–	10	–	–
	Independent	5	–	–	–	–	4	–	–	–	–	1	–

Series Y199-210. Members elected in federal elections, by party and province, 1867 to 1974 (continued)

Year	Party	Totals for Canada	New-found-land	Prince Edward Island	Nova Scotia	New Bruns-wick	Quebec	Ontario	Mani-toba	Saskat-chewan	Alberta	British Columbia	Yukon Territory and Northwest Territories
		199	200	201	202	203	204	205	206	207	208	209	210
1945	Liberal	125	–	3	8	7	54	34	10	2	2	5	–
	Independent Liberal	2	–	–	–	–	2	–	–	–	–	–	–
	Progressive Conservative	67	–	1	3	3	1	48	2	1	2	5	1
	Independent Conservative	1	–	–	–	–	1	–	–	–	–	–	–
	Cooperative Commonwealth Federation	28	–	–	1	–	–	–	5	18	–	4	–
	Independent Cooperative Commonwealth Federation	1	–	–	–	1	–	–	–	–	–	–	–
	Social Credit	13	–	–	–	–	–	–	–	–	13	–	–
	Independent	5	–	–	–	–	4	–	–	–	–	1	–
	Bloc Populaire	2	–	–	–	–	2	–	–	–	–	–	–
	Labour Progressive Party	1	–	–	–	–	1	–	–	–	–	–	–
1940	Liberal	178	–	4	10	5	61	55	14	12	7	10	–
	Independent Liberal	3	–	–	–	–	3	–	–	–	–	–	–
	Conservative	39	–	–	1	5	–	25	1	2	–	4	1
	Independent Conservative	1	–	–	–	–	1	–	–	–	–	–	–
	Social Credit	10	–	–	–	–	–	–	–	–	10	–	–
	Cooperative Commonwealth Federation	8	–	–	1	–	–	–	1	5	–	1	–
	Liberal Progressive	3	–	–	–	–	–	2	1	–	–	–	–
	Independent	1	–	–	–	–	–	–	–	–	–	1	–
	Unity	2	–	–	–	–	–	–	–	2	–	–	–
1935	Liberal	171	–	4	12	9	55	56	12	16	1	6	–
	Independent Liberal	5	–	–	–	–	5	–	–	–	–	–	–
	Conservative	39	–	–	–	1	5	25	1	1	1	5	1
	Independent Conservative	1	–	–	–	–	–	–	–	–	–	–	–
	Social Credit	17	–	–	–	–	–	–	–	2	15	–	–
	Cooperative Commonwealth Federation	7	–	–	–	–	–	–	2	2	–	3	–
	Liberal Progressive	2	–	–	–	–	–	–	2	–	–	–	–
	Reconstruction	1	–	–	–	–	–	–	–	–	–	1	–
	Independent	1	–	–	–	–	–	–	–	–	–	1	–
	United Farmers of Ontario— Labour	1	–	–	–	–	–	1	–	–	–	–	–
1930	Conservative	137	–	3	10	10	24	59	11	8	4	7	1
	Liberal	88	–	1	4	1	40	22	1	11	3	5	–
	United Farmers	10	–	–	–	–	–	1	–	–	9	–	–
	Progressive	2	–	–	–	–	–	–	–	2	–	–	–
	Liberal Progressive	3	–	–	–	–	–	–	3	–	–	–	–
	Labour	2	–	–	–	–	–	–	2	–	–	–	–
	Independent Labour	1	–	–	–	–	–	–	–	–	–	1	–
	Independent	2	–	–	–	–	1	–	–	–	–	1	–
1926	Liberal	116	–	3	2	4	60	23	4	16	3	1	–
	Conservative	91	–	1	12	7	4	53	–	–	1	12	1
	United Farmers of Alberta	11	–	–	–	–	–	–	–	–	11	–	–
	Progressive	13	–	–	–	–	–	4	4	5	–	–	–
	Liberal Progressive	9	–	–	–	–	–	2	7	–	–	–	–
	Labour	3	–	–	–	–	–	–	2	–	1	–	–
	Independent	2	–	–	–	–	1	–	–	–	–	1	–
1925	Liberal	101	–	2	3	1	60	12	1	15	4	3	–
	Conservative	116	–	2	11	10	4	68	7	–	3	10	1
	Progressive	24	–	–	–	–	–	2	7	6	9	–	–
	Labour	2	–	–	–	–	–	–	2	–	–	–	–
	Independent	2	–	–	–	–	1	–	–	–	–	1	–
1921	Liberal	117	–	4	16	5	65	21	2	1	–	3	–
	Conservative	50	–	–	–	5	–	37	–	–	–	7	1
	Progressive	64	–	–	–	1	–	24	12	15	10	2	–
	Labour	3	–	–	–	–	–	–	1	–	2	–	–
	Independent	1	–	–	–	–	–	–	–	–	–	1	–
1917	Unionist	153	–	2	12	7	3	74	14	16	11	13	1
	Liberal	82	–	2	4	4	62	8	1	–	1	–	–
1911	Conservative	133	–	2	9	5	27	72	8	1	1	7	1
	Liberal	86	–	2	9	8	37	13	2	9	6	–	–
	Independent	2	–	–	–	–	1	1	–	–	–	–	–

Series Y199-210. Members elected in federal elections, by party and province, 1867 to 1974 (concluded)

Year	Party	Totals for Canada	New-found-land	Prince Edward Island	Nova Scotia	New Bruns-wick	Quebec	Ontario	Mani-toba	Saskat-chewan	Alberta	British Columbia	Yukon Territory and Northwest Terri-tories
		199	200	201	202	203	204	205	206	207	208	209	210
1908	Liberal	133	—	3	12	11	53	36	2	9	4	2	1
	Conservative	85	—	1	6	2	11	48	8	1	3	5	—
	Independent	3	—	—	—	—	1	2	—	—	—	—	—
1904	Liberal	139	—	1	18	7	54	38	7	—	—	7	7
	Conservative	75	—	3	—	6	11	48	3	—	—	—	4
1900	Liberal	128	—	3	15	9	56	35	2	—	—	3	5
	Conservative	78	—	2	5	5	7	54	3	—	—	3	—
	Other (no details)	8	—	—	—	—	—	—	—	—	—	—	—
1896	Liberal	117	—	2	10	5	49	43	2	—	—	4	2
	Conservative	89	—	3	10	9	16	44	4	—	—	2	1
	Independent	7	—	—	—	—	—	5	1	—	—	—	1
1891	Conservative	123	—	2	16	13	30	48	4	—	—	6	4
	Liberal	92	—	4	5	3	35	44	1	—	—	—	—
1887	Conservative	123	—	—	14	10	33	52	4	—	—	6	4
	Liberal	92	—	6	7	6	32	40	1	—	—	—	—
1882	Conservative	139	—	4	15	10	48	54	2	—	—	6	—
	Liberal	71	—	2	6	6	17	37	3	—	—	—	—
1878	Conservative	137	—	5	14	5	45	59	3	—	—	6	—
	Liberal	69	—	1	7	11	20	29	1	—	—	—	—
1874	Liberal	133	—	6	17	11	33	64	2	—	—	—	—
	Conservative	73	—	—	4	5	32	24	2	—	—	6	—
1872	Conservative	103	—	—	11	7	38	38	3	—	—	6	—
	Liberal	97	—	—	10	9	27	50	1	—	—	—	—
1867	Conservative	101	—	—	3	7	45	46	—	—	—	—	—
	Liberal	80	—	—	16	8	20	36	—	—	—	—	—

Series Y211-259. Federal government employment, by department, branch and service, 1900 to 1977

Year[1]	Totals for Canada	Agri- culture	Auditor General	Chief Electoral Officer	Citizenship and Immi- gration	Communi- cation	Consumer and Corporate Affairs	Defence Production	Energy, Mines and Resources	Environ- ment	External Affairs	Finance	Fisheries
	211	212	213	214	215	216	217	218	219	220	221	222	223

Federal government employees — Statistics Canada

Year[1]	211	212	213	214	215	216	217	218	219	220	221	222	223
1977	338,114	11,419	407	37	—	2,756	2,667	—	4,487	12,652	6,629	1,493	—
1976	322,626	10,937	354	35	—	2,619	2,549	—	4,206	11,752	6,562	785	—
1975[2]	307,390	10,137	316	42	—	2,409	2,496	—	4,074	11,303	6,382	730	—
1974	300,342	10,528	286	30	—	2,173	2,231	—	3,947	11,508	6,148	654	—
1973[2]	287,055	10,566	291	45	—	1,737	2,161	—	3,727	10,936	5,771	605	—
1972	273,537	10,292	278	28	—	1,537	1,944	—	4,293	10,269	5,286	518	—
1971	250,672	9,587	238	37	—	1,242	1,660	—	5,538	—	3,885	476	—
1970	244,197	9,026	206	21	—	838	1,462	—	5,330	—	3,904	397	—
1969[2]	232,862	9,319	207	22	—	—	1,370	4,481	4,873	—	3,284	5,893	4,917
1968[2]	235,492	9,928	193	18	—	—	730	4,459	4,552	—	3,418	5,878	4,365
1967[2]	225,342	9,782	202	29	—	—	—	4,686	4,086	—	3,208	5,323	2,531
1966[2]	212,646	9,559	196	18	6,613	—	—	4,290	3,592	—	2,838	5,367	2,344
1965[2]	203,419	9,247	178	26	5,407	—	—	3,736	3,036	—	2,710	5,156	2,202
1964[2]	201,610	9,034	156	17	4,711	—	—	1,613	3,217	—	2,451	5,031	2,111
1963	198,821	9,089	154	19	5,009	—	—	1,506	2,861	—	2,322	5,113	2,219
1962	205,553	9,285	152	18	5,143	—	—	1,517	2,821	—	2,294	5,327	2,071
1961	202,807	8,712	135	19	5,058	—	—	1,432	2,671	—	2,121	5,301	2,094
1960	195,630	8,025	130	17	4,898	—	—	1,449	2,355	—	2,015	5,285	1,969
1959	197,909	8,135	133	16	4,407	—	—	1,432	2,734	—	1,963	5,291	1,989
1958	195,390	7,760	133	89	4,596	—	—	1,427	2,126	—	1,954	5,340	1,768
1957[3]	—	—	—	—	—	—	—	—	—	—	—	—	—
1956	182,835	7,444	129	17	3,899	—	—	1,456	2,349	—	1,594	4,874	1,925
1955	181,582	7,679	140	18	3,855	—	—	1,455	1,982	—	1,548	5,126	1,875
1954	171,065	7,544	141	20	3,462	—	—	1,522	1,919	—	1,474	5,176	1,847
1953	165,161	7,320	145	22	3,435	—	—	1,678	1,703	—	1,395	5,157	1,875
1952	131,646	6,888	158	21	3,095	—	—	1,488	1,746	—	1,339	4,959	1,031
1951	124,580	7,078	163	14	2,917	—	—	—	1,720	—	1,353	5,135	962
1950	127,196	6,667	169	13	2,657	—	—	—	1,661	—	1,311	5,874	883
1949	123,924	5,914	173	19	—	—	—	408	5,187	—	1,238	6,664	569
1948	118,370	5,381	173	10	—	—	—	329	4,211	—	1,058	6,774	533
1947	125,337	3,833	198	12	—	—	—	986	3,842	—	893	10,839	350
1946	120,557	3,535	247	12	—	—	—	1,925	4,361	—	764	14,860	361
1945	115,908	3,195	263	12	—	—	—	3,835	3,694	—	685	12,772	374
1944	112,658	3,326	262	9	—	—	—	4,027	3,601	—	576	12,707	364
1943	104,055	3,303	269	10	—	—	—	4,303	3,517	—	499	10,828	318
1942	83,781	3,202	359	38	—	—	—	3,219	3,307	—	376	6,673	332
1941	66,937	3,110	292	16	—	—	—	1,244	3,278	—	298	3,347	289
1940	49,656	3,362	280	38	—	—	—	—	3,177	—	225	2,103	312
1939	46,106	3,122	231	15	—	—	—	—	3,147	—	199	1,432	325
1938	44,143	2,926	226	5	—	—	—	—	3,106	—	191	1,475	301
1937	42,836	2,633	220	6	—	—	—	—	3,124	—	174	1,409	309
1936	41,001	2,344	233	14	615	—	—	—	456	—	178	1,399	320
1935	40,709	2,280	221	13	635	—	—	—	368	—	165	1,466	339
1934	40,401	2,176	212	3	647	—	—	—	354	—	165	1,466	310
1933	41,901	2,292	214	3	722	—	—	—	373	—	165	526	349
1932	44,002	2,385	220	4	781	—	—	—	394	—	165	536	362
1931	45,581	2,247	211	7	883	—	—	—	532	—	160	405	382
1930	44,175	2,113	205	10	955	—	—	—	383	—	159	419	381
1929	42,790	1,962	202	4	924	—	—	—	361	—	148	414	—
1928	41,243	1,846	202	5	887	—	—	—	343	—	134	421	—
1927	39,592	1,758	206	12	869	—	—	—	310	—	114	409	—
1926	39,154	1,698	214	12	884	—	—	—	317	—	107	416	—
1925	38,883	1,574	196	4	928	—	—	—	310	—	108	444	—
1924	40,068	1,538	211	4	1,119	—	—	—	298	—	114	503	—

Civil service personnel in the month of January — Statistics Canada

Year[1]	211	212	213	214	215	216	217	218	219	220	221	222	223
1924	38,062	1,597	209	4	840	—	—	—	296	—	104	546	—
1923	38,992	1,481	199	6	747	—	—	—	282	—	109	589	—
1922	41,094	1,370	205	39	713	—	—	—	276	—	110	479	—
1921	41,957	1,224	195	8	706	—	—	—	259	—	136	534	—
1920	47,133	1,171	158	—	607	—	—	—	275	—	144	656	—
1919	41,825	1,171	142	—	709	—	—	—	276	—	156	713	—
1918	38,369	1,230	150	—	824	—	—	—	267	—	87	803	—
1917	32,435	1,174	142	—	674	—	—	—	303	—	70	248	—
1916	29,219	1,080	111	—	728	—	—	—	260	—	58	176	—

Series Y211-259. Federal government employment, by department, branch and service, 1900 to 1977 (continued)

Year[1]	Totals for Canada	Agriculture	Auditor General	Chief Electoral Officer	Citizenship and Immigration	Communication	Consumer and Corporate Affairs	Defence Production	Energy, Mines and Resources	Environment	External Affairs	Finance	Fisheries
	211	212	213	214	215	216	217	218	219	220	221	222	223

Civil service personnel in the month of January – Statistics Canada (continued)

Year[1]	Totals for Canada	Agriculture	Auditor General	Chief Electoral Officer	Citizenship and Immigration	Communication	Consumer and Corporate Affairs	Defence Production	Energy, Mines and Resources	Environment	External Affairs	Finance	Fisheries
1915	28,010	1,027	95	—	718	—	—	—	224	—	46	138	—
1914	25,107	870	97	—	663	—	—	—	195	—	38	122	—
1913	22,621	851	96	—	564	—	—	—	182	—	36	113	—
1912	20,016	738	83	—	476	—	—	—	148	—	31	113	—

Civil service employees – Parliamentary return

1915	—	1,264	101	2	109	—	—	—	255	—	21	129	—
1914	—	1,181	102	3	100	—	—	—	221	—	18	120	—
1913	—	1,128	88	12	96	—	—	—	200	—	14	121	—
1912	—	1,326	92	23	82	—	—	—	170	—	11	121	—
1911	—	1,001	87	—	83	—	—	—	150	—	10	121	—
1910	—	949	85	—	74	—	—	—	115	—	9	110	—
1909	—	960	93	—	76	—	—	—	104	—	6	111	—
1908	—	799	72	—	61	—	—	—	108	—	—	114	—
1907	—	576	71	—	57	—	—	—	73	—	—	109	—
1906	—	548	72	—	47	—	—	—	57	—	—	110	—
1905	—	652	74	—	33	—	—	—	62	—	—	105	—
1904	—	646	58	—	33	—	—	—	59	—	—	98	—
1903	—	702	54	—	26	—	—	—	54	—	—	90	—
1902	—	713	48	—	21	—	—	—	54	—	—	80	—
1901	—	770	44	—	18	—	—	—	53	—	—	74	—
1900	—	471	42	—	14	—	—	—	51	—	—	—	—

Year[1]	Forestry	Governor General and Lieutenant-Governors	Indian Affairs	Indian Affairs and Northern Development	Industry, Trade and Commerce	Insurance	Interior	Justice	Labour	Legislation	Manpower and Immigration	National Defence	National Film Board
	224	225	226	227	228	229	230	231	232	233	234	235	236

Federal government employees – Statistics Canada

Year[1]	Forestry	Governor General and Lieutenant-Governors	Indian Affairs	Indian Affairs and Northern Development	Industry, Trade and Commerce	Insurance	Interior	Justice	Labour	Legislation	Manpower and Immigration	National Defence	National Film Board
1977	—	89	—	11,912	2,876	186	—	1,822	814	3,030	14,193	41,767	891
1976	—	88	—	11,029	2,840	185	—	1,755	823	3,155	14,005	38,653	842
1975[2]	—	78	—	10,610	2,834	183	—	1,678	1,518	2,850	13,248	37,290	842
1974	—	82	—	11,269	2,630	161	—	1,474	1,395	2,624	13,274	40,862	866
1973[2]	—	50	—	11,916	2,529	154	—	884	781	2,253	11,337	38,390	1,030
1972	—	97	—	10,290	2,286	153	—	770	778	1,894	10,048	42,484	969
1971	—	41	—	8,734	2,749	152	—	594	703	1,565	9,282	37,757	961
1970	—	34	—	8,779	2,588	133	—	488	849	1,454	9,046	39,027	1,120
1969[2]	2,094	59	—	6,975	2,539	124	—	426	751	1,379	8,534	39,308	1,086
1968[2]	1,848	57	—	6,138	—	122	—	372	654	1,356	8,811	44,353	1,060
1967[2]	1,715	60	—	6,826	—	116	—	328	670	1,318	7,624	42,791	983
1966[2]	1,255	29	—	—	—	104	—	4,206	859	1,260	—	44,049	908
1965[2]	1,194	19	—	—	—	103	—	3,452	710	1,074	—	44,462	867
1964[2]	1,175	17	—	—	—	100	—	3,395	663	1,016	—	47,690	785
1963	1,055	16	—	—	—	99	—	3,224	610	518	—	48,590	740
1962	1,146	16	—	—	—	102	—	2,880	637	961	—	52,139	777
1961	7	17	—	—	—	95	—	2,840	602	944	—	52,813	743
1960	—	15	—	—	—	91	—	2,527	598	955	—	52,117	761
1959	—	13	—	—	—	94	—	2,366	625	925	—	54,267	756
1958	—	13	—	—	—	89	—	2,183	625	521	—	55,223	732
1957[3]	—	—	—	—	—	—	—	—	—	—	—	—	—
1956	—	24	—	—	—	93	—	2,186	598	880	—	54,805	616
1955	—	24	—	—	—	92	—	2,286	602	873	—	53,909	591
1954	—	24	—	—	—	94	—	2,263	650	897	—	45,718	553
1953	—	28	—	—	—	94	—	2,148	633	877	—	42,820	558
1952	—	13	—	—	—	83	—	1,714	601	855	—	24,175	579
1951	—	10	—	—	—	82	—	1,713	635	857	—	17,757	565

Series Y211-259. Federal government employment, by department, branch and service, 1900 to 1977 (continued)

Year[1]	Forestry	Governor General and Lieutenant-Governors	Indian Affairs	Indian Affairs and Northern Development	Industry, Trade and Commerce	Insurance	Interior	Justice	Labour	Legislation	Man-power and Immigration	National Defence	National Film Board
	224	225	226	227	228	229	230	231	232	233	234	235	236

Federal government employees — Statistics Canada (continued)

Year[1]	Forestry	Governor General and Lieutenant-Governors	Indian Affairs	Indian Affairs and Northern Development	Industry, Trade and Commerce	Insurance	Interior	Justice	Labour	Legislation	Man-power and Immigration	National Defence	National Film Board
1950	—	10	—	—	—	72	—	1,556	645	843	—	16,847	596
1949	—	10	—	—	—	63	—	1,434	620	822	—	16,904	547
1948	—	12	—	—	—	59	—	1,326	620	720	—	15,039	598
1947	—	11	—	—	—	54	—	1,239	835	711	—	18,670	—
1946	—	10	—	—	—	53	—	1,113	1,359	741	—	19,273	—
1945	—	10	—	—	—	49	—	1,032	2,720	616	—	28,137	—
1944	—	10	—	—	—	47	—	996	2,637	646	—	30,801	476
1943	—	10	—	—	—	47	—	975	644	696	—	31,047	377
1942	—	12	—	—	—	49	—	1,048	356	687	—	22,921	49
1941	—	13	—	—	—	53	—	1,086	355	716	—	1,079	—
1940	—	11	—	—	—	53	—	1,115	303	328	—	3,592	—
1939	—	14	—	—	—	53	—	1,091	244	688	—	1,424	—
1938	—	12	—	—	—	54	—	1,044	244	736	—	1,306	—
1937	—	12	—	—	—	49	—	1,016	238	690	—	1,336	—
1936	—	12	1,029	—	—	50	945	1,049	200	649	—	1,143	—
1935	—	11	1,072	—	—	49	947	1,093	176	727	—	1,096	—
1934	—	10	1,020	—	—	47	969	1,064	164	701	—	1,103	—
1933	—	10	1,056	—	—	45	1,010	1,091	170	627	—	1,256	—
1932	—	10	1,077	—	—	43	1,125	874	197	605	—	1,352	—
1931	—	10	1,074	—	—	42	2,037	819	143	750	—	1,358	—
1930	—	10	1,035	—	—	40	2,415	707	141	602	—	1,244	—
1929	—	10	988	—	—	40	2,323	679	137	652	—	1,206	—
1928	—	11	934	—	—	38	2,229	675	125	657	—	1,163	—
1927	—	12	929	—	—	36	2,132	647	109	645	—	1,123	—
1926	—	12	912	—	—	34	2,068	621	102	639	—	1,113	—
1925	—	12	896	—	—	35	2,048	614	99	632	—	1,088	—
1924	—	12	858	—	—	35	2,092	600	96	626	—	1,110	—

Civil service personnel in the month of January — Statistics Canada

Year[1]	Forestry	Governor General and Lieutenant-Governors	Indian Affairs	Indian Affairs and Northern Development	Industry, Trade and Commerce	Insurance	Interior	Justice	Labour	Legislation	Man-power and Immigration	National Defence	National Film Board
1924	—	12	794	—	—	34	2,052	599	94	231	—	1,304	—
1923	—	13	784	—	—	35	2,153	592	123	228	—	1,538	—
1922	—	15	784	—	—	32	2,179	562	146	224	—	2,398	—
1921	—	13	775	—	—	31	2,008	499	139	218	—	2,685	—
1920	—	14	787	—	—	29	1,975	494	154	184	—	5,547	—
1919	—	13	788	—	—	27	1,904	454	238	136	—	7,392	—
1918	—	12	711	—	—	22	1,896	469	67	140	—	5,771	—
1917	—	11	847	—	—	21	1,861	504	45	227	—	4,143	—
1916	—	12	843	—	—	19	1,888	512	45	50	—	2,708	—
1915	—	12	803	—	—	18	1,765	504	44	52	—	1,747	—
1914	—	11	787	—	—	20	1,532	467	43	56	—	919	—
1913	—	11	731	—	—	18	1,386	443	35	54	—	841	—
1912	—	11	659	—	—	16	1,270	419	30	50	—	725	—

Civil service employees — Parliamentary return

Year[1]	Forestry	Governor General and Lieutenant-Governors	Indian Affairs	Indian Affairs and Northern Development	Industry, Trade and Commerce	Insurance	Interior	Justice	Labour	Legislation	Man-power and Immigration	National Defence	National Film Board
1915	—	—	90	—	—	25	976	540	44	—	—	128	—
1914	—	—	93	—	—	23	909	531	42	—	—	130	—
1913	—	—	78	—	—	19	806	507	33	—	—	125	—
1912	—	—	78	—	—	17	720	477	27	—	—	112	—
1911	—	—	78	—	—	17	701	414	24	—	—	103	—
1910	—	—	76	—	—	14	666	387	21	—	—	94	—
1909	—	—	72	—	—	12	663	387	17	—	—	96	—
1908	—	—	64	—	—	11	578	400	14	—	—	99	—
1907	—	—	63	—	—	10	468	385	13	—	—	44	—
1906	—	—	63	—	—	9	403	360	11	—	—	39	—
1905	—	—	56	—	—	9	360	347	11	—	—	39	—
1904	—	—	56	—	—	6	335	366	11	—	—	36	—
1903	—	—	56	—	—	6	274	341	11	—	—	34	—
1902	—	—	52	—	—	6	231	341	9	—	—	36	—
1901	—	—	52	—	—	8	206	338	10	—	—	32	—
1900	—	—	52	—	—	—	194	—	—	—	—	32	—

Series Y211-259. Federal government employment, by department, branch and service, 1900 to 1977 (continued)

Year[1]	National Health and Welfare	National Research Council	National Revenue	Northern Affairs and National Resources	Post Office	Privy Council	Public Archives and National Library	Public Printing and Stationery	Public Service Commission	Public Works	Regional Economic Expansion	Royal Canadian Mounted Police	Science and Technology
	237	238	239	240	241	242	243	244	245	246	247	248	249

Federal government employees — Statistics Canada

Year[1]	237	238	239	240	241	242	243	244	245	246	247	248	249
1977	11,112	3,049	27,374	—	65,907	923	1,197	—	3,984	9,694	1,840	19,525	207
1976	11,361	2,957	27,625	—	60,718	820	1,186	—	3,805	9,094	1,934	18,815	188
1975[2]	10,358	3,402	27,012	—	55,591	796	1,130	—	2,886	9,031	1,813	17,926	191
1974	9,853	3,402	25,856	—	51,832	744	944	—	2,901	8,287	1,576	16,419	204
1973[2]	9,623	3,649	24,627	—	47,996	666	970	—	2,433	7,911	1,822	15,236	157
1972	8,765	3,473	21,322	—	46,102	745	885	—	1,790	8,308	1,856	14,667	—
1971	8,495	3,428	19,848	—	43,891	616	639	—	1,391	8,169	1,652	13,600	—
1970	7,614	3,408	18,967	—	45,482	626	543	—	1,342	8,384	1,485	12,253	—
1969[2]	7,348	3,576	18,676	—	40,926	558	469	202	1,021	8,367	—	12,872	—
1968[2]	7,205	3,633	18,504	—	39,026	528	456	233	990	7,974	—	12,469	—
1967[2]	5,789	3,515	18,142	—	37,262	406	390	212	1,101	8,471	—	11,513	—
1966[2]	5,612	3,415	16,597	8,702	29,785	389	336	189	961	8,697	—	9,327	—
1965[2]	5,112	3,264	15,650	4,308	28,483	313	276	169	824	8,998	—	8,877	—
1964[2]	4,860	3,131	15,233	4,321	28,054	276	204	1,682	720	8,341	—	8,597	—
1963	4,861	3,128	14,421	4,350	27,411	273	183	1,717	680	8,215	—	8,491	—
1962	5,206	3,214	14,396	5,300	27,040	228	173	1,779	714	8,759	—	8,127	—
1961	4,834	3,086	14,220	5,923	26,322	196	155	1,873	678	8,517	—	7,804	—
1960	4,569	2,992	15,367	3,618	25,706	165	143	1,775	656	8,352	—	7,479	—
1959	4,567	2,905	14,967	5,164	24,739	135	141	1,776	647	8,494	—	7,281	—
1958	4,422	2,809	15,258	4,659	24,245	113	134	1,674	639	8,077	—	6,915	—
1957[3]	—	—	—	—	—	—	—	—	—	—	—	—	—
1956	4,077	2,577	14,657	2,548	21,827	91	99	1,453	585	7,718	—	6,232	—
1955	3,926	2,517	14,707	2,733	21,320	107	83	1,390	595	7,870	—	6,236	—
1954	3,737	2,415	14,058	2,335	19,789	103	78	1,295	570	7,797	—	6,112	—
1953	3,727	2,268	13,439	2,402	19,298	106	79	1,199	578	7,595	—	5,969	—
1952	3,239	2,052	12,540	1,671	19,510	90	67	1,132	544	7,183	—	828	—
1951	2,954	1,898	13,205	1,689	19,478	85	65	1,041	536	7,231	—	622	—
1950	2,801	1,701	16,715	1,570	19,096	87	61	991	580	6,954	—	568	—
1949	2,585	1,531	17,480	—	18,049	72	55	856	572	6,547	—	490	—
1948	2,346	1,550	16,030	—	17,105	68	54	786	532	6,574	—	463	—
1947	2,517	2,246	12,423	—	16,499	43	57	783	618	6,341	—	422	—
1946	1,830	1,379	11,771	—	15,256	43	52	771	684	6,184	—	459	—
1945	1,302	1,385	10,706	—	13,770	44	50	794	560	5,845	—	499	—
1944	4,998	1,232	9,285	—	13,105	51	50	824	591	5,694	—	425	—
1943	4,038	1,135	7,949	—	12,622	32	51	817	568	5,378	—	389	—
1942	3,371	792	6,657	—	12,809	23	53	766	453	4,858	—	323	—
1941	2,980	585	5,904	—	13,160	24	55	709	364	4,538	—	251	—
1940	2,578	310	5,700	—	12,857	23	69	665	277	4,250	—	127	—
1939	2,335	226	5,706	—	12,518	19	67	652	235	4,124	—	86	—
1938	2,288	185	5,784	—	12,122	18	74	635	230	4,027	—	100	—
1937	2,354	171	5,521	—	11,649	18	69	622	195	3,860	—	108	—
1936	2,290	144	5,454	—	10,847	17	77	617	147	3,682	—	114	—
1935	2,264	129	5,374	—	10,780	17	77	627	133	3,620	—	126	—
1934	2,266	126	5,360	—	10,842	19	76	601	124	3,594	—	161	—
1933	2,711	—	5,654	—	11,140	18	80	692	137	3,794	—	200	—
1932	2,750	—	6,260	—	11,676	18	81	709	155	3,950	—	88	—
1931	2,848	—	6,309	—	11,961	18	83	721	176	4,050	—	78	—
1930	2,518	—	6,131	—	11,739	20	83	715	173	4,030	—	70	—
1929	2,332	—	5,935	—	11,515	20	83	714	157	4,003	—	58	—
1928	2,289	—	5,771	—	10,871	21	83	696	144	3,933	—	48	—
1927	2,261	—	5,252	—	10,455	21	78	690	143	3,836	—	47	—
1926	2,452	—	5,137	—	10,240	21	79	689	138	3,897	—	47	—
1925	2,723	—	5,037	—	10,254	21	76	686	146	3,160	—	41	—
1924	3,156	—	5,101	—	10,259	20	84	715	155	3,326	—	40	—

Civil service personnel in the month of January — Statistics Canada

Year[1]	237	238	239	240	241	242	243	244	245	246	247	248	249
1924	3,408	—	5,136	—	10,213	19	81	688	172	3,004	—	41	—
1923	4,130	—	5,241	—	10,068	20	81	663	176	2,970	—	36	—
1922	5,194	—	5,308	—	10,007	18	79	729	219	3,020	—	35	—
1921	6,573	—	5,269	—	9,950	21	80	702	217	3,030	—	21	—
1920	9,466	—	4,719	—	9,740	25	80	1,142	118	3,103	—	15	—
1919	3,876	—	4,376	—	10,002	27	76	1,192	52	3,015	—	12	—
1918	3,852	—	4,525	—	9,084	29	78	1,260	13	2,189	—	10	—
1917	648	—	4,294	—	8,729	26	76	1,165	12	2,085	—	10	—
1916	47	—	4,225	—	8,057	27	76	1,150	14	2,007	—	10	—

Series Y211-259. Federal government employment, by department, branch and service, 1900 to 1977 (continued)

Year[1]	National Health and Welfare	National Research Council	National Revenue	Northern Affairs and National Resources	Post Office	Privy Council	Public Archives and National Library	Public Printing and Stationery	Public Service Commission	Public Works	Regional Economic Expansion	Royal Canadian Mounted Police	Science and Technology
	237	238	239	240	241	242	243	244	245	246	247	248	249

Civil service personnel in the month of January — Statistics Canada (continued)

Year[1]	237	238	239	240	241	242	243	244	245	246	247	248	249
1915	—	—	4,144	—	7,849	25	74	1,106	13	1,911	—	12	—
1914	—	—	4,037	—	7,171	21	62	989	14	1,708	—	12	—
1913	—	—	3,651	—	5,919	27	59	915	11	1,554	—	11	—
1912	—	—	3,214	—	5,082	20	—	862	11	1,481	—	11	—

Civil service employees — Parliamentary return

Year[1]	237	238	239	240	241	242	243	244	245	246	247	248	249
1915	—	—	4,274	—	694	30	—	42	16	326	—	11	—
1914	—	—	4,194	—	727	28	—	42	16	285	—	12	—
1913	—	—	3,884	—	638	22	—	48	16	251	—	10	—
1912	—	—	3,464	—	596	28	—	54	14	234	—	11	—
1911	—	—	3,051	—	504	24	—	58	13	232	—	11	—
1910	—	—	2,923	—	497	23	—	70	10	233	—	10	—
1909	—	—	2,827	—	475	29	—	70	9	208	—	7	—
1908	—	—	2,749	—	370	37	—	34	5	203	—	10	—
1907	—	—	2,560	—	347	30	—	30	—	178	—	10	—
1906	—	—	2,454	—	329	31	—	33	—	155	—	9	—
1905	—	—	2,382	—	310	30	—	32	—	146	—	9	—
1904	—	—	2,314	—	326	32	—	30	—	159	—	8	—
1903	—	—	2,214	—	283	30	—	27	—	137	—	6	—
1902	—	—	2,130	—	271	33	—	27	—	132	—	6	—
1901	—	—	2,140	—	246	31	—	27	—	108	—	6	—
1900	—	—	2,087	—	246	30	—	26	—	—	—	6	—

Year[1]	Secretary of State	Solicitor General	Statistics Canada	Supply and Services	Trade and Commerce	Transport	Treasury Board	Unemployment Insurance Commission	Urban Affairs	Veterans Affairs
	250	251	252	253	254	255	256	257	258	259

Federal government employees — Statistics Canada

Year[1]	250	251	252	253	254	255	256	257	258	259
1977	4,493	10,132	5,687	10,627	—	22,064	924	10,877	193	8,178
1976	4,550	9,333	5,365	10,402	—	21,086	820	10,891	304	8,198
1975[2]	4,399	8,172	5,746	10,135	—	20,306	764	10,251	295	8,132
1974	3,075	7,405	5,092	9,714	—	19,071	656	11,030	223	9,916
1973[2]	3,252	6,440	5,750	9,993	—	17,400	629	12,517	183	10,588
1972	2,437	5,524	5,119	9,569	—	17,416	557	9,740	77	10,971
1971	1,986	5,149	5,357	9,007	—	18,696	504	7,153	—	10,973
1970	1,570	4,832	4,886	9,268	—	17,556	435	5,361	—	11,118
1969[2]	1,260	4,625	3,790	—	—	16,645	467	5,218	—	11,277
1968[2]	1,086	4,478	3,971	—	3,359	17,062	432	5,584	—	11,876
1967[2]	1,699	4,228	2,860	—	2,860	16,426	211	5,931	—	12,010
1966[2]	1,221	—	—	—	5,191	15,471	—	5,883	—	13,353
1965[2]	985	—	—	—	4,585	14,832	—	10,249	—	12,884
1964[2]	748	—	—	—	3,973	14,617	—	10,657	—	12,984
1963	738	—	—	—	3,852	14,189	—	10,078	—	13,090
1962	745	—	—	—	3,791	14,622	—	10,737	—	13,436
1961	736	—	—	—	4,492	14,033	—	10,831	—	13,503
1960	731	—	—	—	4,262	12,939	—	10,343	—	13,326
1959	712	—	—	—	4,194	13,387	—	10,106	—	13,548
1958	671	—	—	—	4,014	13,607	—	10,058	—	13,516
1957[3]	—	—	—	—	—	—	—	—	—	—
1956	592	—	—	—	3,665	12,166	—	8,754	—	12,905
1955	628	—	—	—	3,685	11,482	—	8,766	—	13,483
1954	608	—	—	—	3,699	12,298	—	8,881	—	13,986
1953	594	—	—	—	3,924	11,546	—	8,330	—	14,218
1952	579	—	—	—	3,686	9,073	—	6,885	—	13,822
1951	588	—	—	—	3,720	9,301	—	7,051	—	14,155

Series Y211-259. Federal government employment, by department, branch and service, 1900 to 1977 (concluded)

Year[1]	Secretary of State	Solicitor General	Statistics Canada	Supply and Services	Trade and Commerce	Transport	Treasury Board	Unemployment Insurance Commission	Urban Affairs	Veterans Affairs
	250	251	252	253	254	255	256	257	258	259

Federal government employees – Statistics Canada (continued)

Year[1]	250	251	252	253	254	255	256	257	258	259
1950	608	–	–	–	3,748	9,682	–	7,148	–	15,082
1949	557	–	–	–	3,401	8,721	–	6,957	–	15,479
1948	528	–	–	–	3,500	8,000	–	7,140	–	16,851
1947	470	–	–	–	3,318	7,536	–	8,493	–	21,098
1946	457	–	–	–	2,907	7,432	–	8,477	–	14,241
1945	387	–	–	–	2,620	6,797	–	6,392	–	7,364
1944	361	–	–	–	2,657	6,833	–	5,728	–	339
1943	365	–	–	–	2,755	6,363	–	4,097	–	253
1942	426	–	–	–	3,302	5,705	–	1,360	–	255
1941	434	–	–	–	1,839	5,604	–	–	–	258
1940	421	–	–	–	1,801	5,414	–	–	–	265
1939	346	–	–	–	1,794	5,710	–	–	–	303
1938	324	–	–	–	1,607	4,816	–	–	–	307
1937	312	–	–	–	1,867	4,549	–	–	–	325
1936	294	–	–	–	1,685	4,662	–	–	–	335
1935	208	–	–	–	1,682	4,678	–	–	–	336
1934	196	–	–	–	1,756	4,526	–	–	–	343
1933	212	–	–	–	2,065	4,919	–	–	–	370
1932	214	–	–	–	2,632	4,970	–	–	–	369
1931	220	–	–	–	1,870	5,683	–	–	–	504
1930	216	–	–	–	1,675	5,458	–	–	–	528
1929	206	–	–	–	1,497	5,682	–	–	–	538
1928	197	–	–	–	1,363	5,611	–	–	–	546
1927	188	–	–	–	1,341	5,473	–	–	–	496
1926	188	–	–	–	1,112	5,516	–	–	–	489
1925	182	–	–	–	1,037	6,018	–	–	–	514
1924	195	–	–	–	1,236	5,956	–	–	–	609

Civil service personnel in the month of January – Statistics Canada

Year[1]	250	251	252	253	254	255	256	257	258	259
1924	236	–	–	–	1,403	4,327	–	–	–	618
1923	246	–	–	–	1,426	4,364	–	–	–	692
1922	247	–	–	–	1,487	4,449	–	–	–	770
1921	221	–	–	–	1,068	4,239	–	–	–	1,136
1920	177	–	–	–	1,021	4,157	–	–	–	1,175
1919	82	–	–	–	931	3,997	–	–	–	68
1918	77	–	–	–	695	4,106	–	–	–	2
1917	75	–	–	–	694	4,351	–	–	–	–
1916	68	–	–	–	499	4,549	–	–	–	–
1915	51	–	–	–	463	5,169	–	–	–	–
1914	52	–	–	–	437	4,784	–	–	–	–
1913	45	–	–	–	463	4,605	–	–	–	–
1912	38	–	–	–	293	4,235	–	–	–	–

Civil service employees – Parliamentary return

Year[1]	250	251	252	253	254	255	256	257	258	259
1915	55	–	–	–	249	341	–	–	–	–
1914	51	–	–	–	292	347	–	–	–	–
1913	47	–	–	–	338	334	–	–	–	–
1912	39	–	–	–	418	320	–	–	–	–
1911	34	–	–	–	147	301	–	–	–	–
1910	35	–	–	–	145	311	–	–	–	–
1909	34	–	–	–	121	251	–	–	–	–
1908	34	–	–	–	104	164	–	–	–	–
1907	34	–	–	–	101	153	–	–	–	–
1906	32	–	–	–	90	136	–	–	–	–
1905	30	–	–	–	71	135	–	–	–	–
1904	32	–	–	–	76	134	–	–	–	–
1903	32	–	–	–	66	119	–	–	–	–
1902	31	–	–	–	45	118	–	–	–	–
1901	31	–	–	–	17	119	–	–	–	–
1900	32	–	–	–	13	48	–	–	–	–

[1] Data for 1924 to 1977 are for 31 March.
[2] For some government organizations figures have been omitted as they are too small to be identified separately, but have been included in all totals.

These figures were: 1975, 34; 1973, 50; 1969, 26; 1968, 42; 1967, 38; 1966, 30; 1965, 31; 1964, 30.
[3] No separate tabulation available.

Series Y260-263. Representation of the Government of Canada abroad, 1867 to 1977

Year	Total number of places where represented	Place of representation	Year credentials presented	Status of representative at 30 June 1978
	260	261	262	263

Regular diplomatic representation

1977, 31 December	145	Bahamas	1972	High Commissioner[1]
		Bahrein	1974	Ambassador[1]
		Bangladesh	1972	High Commissioner
		Belize	1976	Commissioner[1]
		Bermuda	1976	Commissioner[1]
		Cape Verde Islands	1976	Ambassador[1]
		Comores (Islands)	1977	Ambassador[1]
		Djibouti	1977	Ambassador[1]
		German Democratic Republic	1977	Ambassador[1]
		Grenada	1974	High Commissioner[1]
		Guinea-Bissau	1974	Ambassador[1]
		Hong Kong	1971	Commissioner
		Liberia	1971	Ambassador[1]
		Malawi	1973	High Commissioner[1]
		Mauritius	1970	High Commissioner[1]
		Mongolia	1974	Ambassador
		Mozambique	1977	Ambassador[1]
		Oman	1974	Ambassador[1]
		Papua New Guinea	1975	High Commissioner[1]
		Philippines[2]	1973	Ambassador
		Qatar	1974	Ambassador[1]
		Saudi Arabia	1973	Ambassador
		Seychelles	1976	High Commissioner[1]
		Suriname, Republic of	1975	Ambassador[1]
		Tonga	1975	High Commissioner[1]
		United Arab Emirates	1974	Ambassador[1]
		Viet-Nam, Socialist Republic of[3]	1973	Ambassador[1]
		Western Samoa	1975	High Commissioner[1]
		Yemen Arab Republic	1975	Ambassador[1]
		Yemen, People's Democratic Republic of	1976	Ambassador[1]
1970, 31 December	115	Afghanistan	1964	Ambassador[1]
		Algeria	1965	Ambassador
		Barbados	1966	High Commissioner
		Benin, People's Republic of (formerly Dahomey)	1962	Ambassador[1]
		Bolivia	1961	Ambassador[1]
		Botswana	1968	High Commissioner[1]
		Bulgaria	1967	Ambassador[1]
		Burundi	1969	Ambassador[1]
		Cameroon	1962	Ambassador
		Central African Empire	1962	Ambassador[1]
		Chad	1962	Ambassador[1]
		China, People's Republic of[4]	1970	Ambassador
		Congo, People's Republic of the	1962	Ambassador[1]
		Costa Rica	1961	Ambassador
		Cyprus	1961	High Commissioner[1]
		Ecuador	1961	Ambassador[1]
		El Salvador	1962	Ambassador[1]
		Ethiopia	1966	Ambassador
		Fiji	1970	High Commissioner[1]
		Gabon	1962	Ambassador[1]
		Gambia	1967	High Commissioner[1]
		Guatemala	1961	Ambassador
		Guinea	1962	Ambassador[1]
		Guyana	1966	High Commissioner
		Holy See	1970	Ambassador[1]
		Honduras	1961	Ambassador[1]
		Hungary	1965	Ambassador
		Iraq	1961	Ambassador
		Ivory Coast	1963	Ambassador
		Jamaica	1962	High Commissioner
		Jordan	1965	Ambassador[1]
		Kenya	1965	High Commissioner
		Korea	1964	Ambassador
		Kuwait	1965	Ambassador[1]
		Lesotho	1968	High Commissioner[1]

Series Y260-263. Representation of the Government of Canada abroad, 1867 to 1977 (continued)

Year	Total number of places where represented	Place of representation	Year credentials presented	Status of representative at 30 June 1978
	260	261	262	263

Regular diplomatic representation (continued)

1970, 31 December		Libyan Arab Republic	1968	Ambassador[1]
		Madagascar, Democratic Republic of	1967	Ambassador[1]
		Mali	1970	Ambassador[1]
		Malta	1965	High Commissioner[1]
		Mauritania	1969	Ambassador[1]
		Morocco	1962	Ambassador
		Nepal	1965	Ambassador[1]
		Nicaragua	1961	Ambassador[1]
		Niger	1962	Ambassador[1]
		Panama	1961	Ambassador[1]
		Paraguay	1962	Ambassador[1]
		Romania	1967	Ambassador
		Rwanda	1967	Ambassador[1]
		Senegal	1962	Ambassador
		Sierra Leone	1961	High Commissioner[1]
		Singapore	1966	High Commissioner
		Somali Democratic Republic	1968	Ambassador[1]
		Sudan	1961	Ambassador[1]
		Swaziland	1969	High Commissioner[1]
		Syrian Arab Republic[5]	1965	Ambassador[1]
		Tanzania, United Republic of	1964	High Commissioner
		Thailand	1962	Ambassador
		Togo	1962	Ambassador[1]
		Trinidad and Tobago	1962	High Commissioner
		Tunisia	1961	Ambassador
		Uganda	1962	High Commissioner[1]
		Upper Volta	1962	Ambassador[1]
		Zaire, Republic of	1962	Ambassador
		Zambia	1966	High Commissioner
1960, 31 December	51	Austria	1952	Ambassador
		Burma	1958	Ambassador[1]
		Colombia	1953	Ambassador
		Dominican Republic	1954	Ambassador[1]
		Egypt, Arab Republic of[5]	1954	Ambassador
		Ghana	1957	High Commissioner
		Haiti	1954	Ambassador
		Indonesia	1953	Ambassador
		Iran	1958	Ambassador
		Israel	1954	Ambassador
		Lebanon	1954	Ambassador
		Malaysia	1958	High Commissioner
		Nigeria	1960	High Commissioner
		Portugal	1952	Ambassador
		Spain	1953	Ambassador
		Sri Lanka (formerly Ceylon)	1953	High Commissioner
		Uruguay	1952	Ambassador[1]
		Venezuela	1952	Ambassador
1950, 31 December	33	Argentina	1941	Ambassador
		Brazil	1941	Ambassador
		Chile	1942	Ambassador
		Cuba	1945	Ambassador
		Czechoslovakia	1943	Ambassador
		Denmark	1946	Ambassador
		Finland	1949	Ambassador
		Germany, Federal Republic of	1950	Ambassador
		Greece	1943	Ambassador
		Iceland	1949	Ambassador[1]
		India	1947	High Commissioner
		Italy	1947	Ambassador
		Luxembourg	1945	Ambassador[1]
		Mexico	1944	Ambassador
		Norway	1943	Ambassador

Series Y260-263. Representation of the Government of Canada abroad, 1867 to 1977 (continued)

Year	Total number of places where represented	Place of representation	Year credentials presented	Status of representative at 30 June 1978
	260	**261**	**262**	**263**

Regular diplomatic representation (continued)

Year	Total	Place	Year	Status
1950, 31 December		Pakistan	1950	Ambassador (formerly High Commissioner)
		Peru	1944	Ambassador
		Poland	1943	Ambassador
		Sweden	1947	Ambassador
		Switzerland	1947	Ambassador
		Turkey	1947	Ambassador
		Union of Soviet Socialist Republics	1943	Ambassador
		Yugoslavia	1943	Ambassador
1940, 31 December	10	Austria	1939	High Commissioner
		Belgium	1939	Ambassador
		Ireland	1940	Ambassador
		Netherlands	1939	Ambassador
		New Zealand	1940	High Commissioner
		South Africa, Republic of	1940	Ambassador (formerly High Commissioner)
1930, 31 December	4	France	1928	Ambassador
		Japan	1929	Ambassador
		United States of America	1927	Ambassador
1920, 31 December	1	Britain	1880	High Commissioner

Consulates[6]

Year	Total	Place	Year	Status
1977, 31 December	33	Australia, Melbourne	1973	Consul General
		Sydney	1973	Consul General
		Brazil, Rio de Janeiro	1974	Consul
		Britain, Belfast	1974	Consul
		Birmingham	1974	Consul
		Glasgow	1974	Consul
		Manchester	1974	Consul
		France, Strasbourg	1975	Consul General
		Germany, Federal Republic of, Stuttgart	1973	Consul
		Monaco (Marseille)	1971	Consul General
		South Africa, Republic of, Capetown	1975	Consul
		United States of America, Atlanta	1972	Consul General
1970, 31 December	21	France, Bordeaux	1965	Consul General
		Marseille	1965	Consul General
		Germany, Federal Republic of, Düsseldorf	1961	Consul General
		Italy, Milan	1963	Consul General
		San Marino (Rome)	1969	Consul
		United States of America, Buffalo	1970	Consul
		Cleveland	1964	Consul
		Dallas	1967	Consul
		Minneapolis	1970	Consul
		Philadelphia	1961	Consul
		San Juan, Territory of Puerto Rico	1968	Consul
1960, 31 December	10	Germany, Federal Republic of, Hamburg	1956	Consul General
		United States of America, Los Angeles	1953	Consul General
		New Orleans	1953	Consul General
		Seattle	1953	Consul General
1950, 31 December	6	Brazil, Sao Paulo	1947	Consul
		United States of America, Boston	1948	Consul General
		Chicago	1947	Consul General
		Detroit	1948	Consul
		New York	1943	Consul General
		San Francisco	1948	Consul General

Series Y260-263. Representation of the Government of Canada abroad, 1867 to 1977 (concluded)

Year	Total number of places where represented	Place of representation	Year credentials presented	Status of representative at 30 June 1978
	260	261	262	263

Special Missions

Year	Total number of places where represented	Place of representation	Year credentials presented	Status of representative at 30 June 1978
1977, 31 December	15	Geneva, Multilateral Trade Negotiations	1975	Head of Delegation (Ambassador)
		Nairobi, United Nations Environmental Program	1976	Permanent Representative
		Vienna, Mutual and Balanced Force Reduction Talks	1973	Head of Delegation (Ambassador)
		Washington, Organization of American States	1972	Permanent Observer (Ambassador)
1970, 31 December	11	Geneva, Conference of the Committee on Disarmament	1962	Permanent Representative (Ambassador)
		Vienna, United Nations Industrial Development Organization	1969	Permanent Representative
1960, 31 December	9	Brussels, European Communities (Atomic Energy, Coal and Steel, Economic)	1958	Head of Mission
		Vienna, International Atomic Energy Agency	1957	Permanent Representative
1950, 31 December	7	Berlin, Canadian Military Mission[7]	1946	Head of Mission
		Brussels, North Atlantic Council	1949	Permanent Representative (Ambassador)
		Geneva, United Nations[8]	1945	Permanent Representative (Ambassador)
		New York, United Nations[9]	1945	Permanent Representative (Ambassador)
		Paris, United Nations Educational, Scientific and Cultural Organization	1946	Permanent Delegate (Ambassador)
		Paris, Organization for Economic Co-operation and Development	1950	Permanent Representative (Ambassador)
		Rome, United Nations Food and Agriculture Organization	1945	Permanent Representative

[1] Multiple accreditation, representative not resident in country.
[2] A consul general was resident in Manila from 1947, an ambassador since 1973.
[3] Includes the former areas of North Viet-Nam and South Viet-Nam.
[4] From 1942 to 1970, representation was to Nationalist China; from 1970 to date, the representation is to the People's Republic of China.
[5] From 1954, representation was to the United Arab Republic; from 1965, the representation has been to the Arab Republic of Egypt and the Syrian Arab Republic.
[6] In addition to the consuls and consuls general listed, Canada has "Honorary Consuls" in the following locations: France, Saint Pierre; Mexico, Acapulco and Guadalajara; Spain, Malaga; and an "Honorary Consul General" in Iceland, Reykjavik.

[7] The Mission was suspended in 1970 and reinstated in 1973.
[8] The Permanent Mission in Geneva is accredited to the following United Nations specialized agencies: International Labour Organization, International Telecommunications Union, World Health Organization, World Meteorological Organization and World Intellectual Property Organization.
[9] Canada is also a member of the following United Nations specialized agencies to which there is no accredited permanent representative: Inter-governmental Maritime Consultative Organization, London; International Bank for Reconstruction and Development, Washington; International Development Agency, Washington; International Finance Corporation, Washington; International Monetary Fund, Washington; Universal Postal Union, Berne.

Series Y264-266. Formal amendments to the British North America Act, 1867 to 1975

Year of amendment	Citation	Title	Subject
	264	**265**	**266**
1975	23-24 Elizabeth II. ch. 53 (Can.)	The British North America Act, 1975	Representation in the Senate
1965	14 Elizabeth II, ch. 4 (Can.)	The British North America Act, 1965	Retirement for Senate members
1964	12-13 Elizabeth II, ch. 2 (U.K.)	The British North America Act, 1964	Old age pension
1960	9 Elizabeth II, ch. 2 (U.K.)	The British North America Act, 1960	Tenure of office of judges
1952	1 Elizabeth II, ch. 15 (Can.)	The British North America Act, 1952	Representation in the House of Commons
1951	14-15 George VI, ch. 32 (U.K.)	The British North America Act, 1951	Federal jurisdiction over old age pensions
1949	13 George VI, ch. 81 (U.K.)	The British North America (No. 2) Act, 1949	Amendment of the constitution
1949	12-13 George VI, ch. 22 (U.K.)	The British North America (No. 1) Act, 1949	Entry of Newfoundland
1946	10 George VI, ch. 63 (U.K.)	The British North America Act, 1946	Representation in the House of Commons
1943	6-7 George VI, ch. 30 (U.K.)	The British North America Act, 1943	Postponement of adjustment of representation in the House of Commons
1940	3-4 George VI, ch. 36 (U.K.)	The British North America Act, 1940	Transfer of jurisdiction over unemployment insurance to the federal government
1931	22 George V, ch. 4 (U.K.)	The Statute of Westminster	To give effect to certain resolutions passed by Imperial Conferences of 1926 and 1930
1930	20-21 George V, ch. 26 (U.K.)	The British North America Act, 1930	Transfer of natural resources to Prairie provinces
1916	6-7 George V, ch. 19 (U.K.)	The British North America Act, 1916	To extend life of House of Commons elected in 1911
1915	5-6 George V, ch. 45 (U.K.)	The British North America Act, 1915	Representation in Senate and House of Commons
1907	7 Edward VII, ch. 11 (U.K.)	The British North America Act, 1907	Dominion-provincial financial arrangements
1895	58 Victoria, Session 2, ch. 3 (U.K.)	The Canadian Speaker (Appointment of Deputy) Act	To remove doubts concerning Parliament's power re appointment of deputy for Speaker of Senate
1889	52-53 Victoria, ch. 28 (U.K.)	The Canada (Ontario Boundary) Act, 1889	Determination of boundaries of Ontario
1886	49-50 Victoria, ch. 35 (U.K.)	The British North America Act, 1886	Representation of territories in House of Commons and the Senate
1875	38-39 Victoria, ch. 38 (U.K.)	The Parliament of Canada Act, 1875	To remove doubts of privileges, etc., of Parliament and members
1871	34-35 Victoria, ch. 28 (U.K.)	The British North America Act, 1871	Federal government's power to establish new provinces from territories

Series Y267-270. Provinces and territories, dates and processes of admission and present areas, 1867 to 1976

Year	Province, territory or district	Date of admission or creation	Process of admission	Present area (square miles)
	267	**268**	**269**	**270**
1949	Newfoundland	31 March 1949	The British North America Act, 1949, 12-13 George VI, ch. 22 (U.K.)	156,185
1920	Mackenzie[1]	1 January 1920	Order in Council, 16 March 1918	527,490[1]
	Keewatin[1]			228,160[1]
	Franklin[1]			549,253[1]
1905	Alberta	1 September 1905	Alberta Act, 1905, 4-5 Edward VII. ch. 3 (Can.)	255,285
1905	Saskatchewan	1 September 1905	Saskatchewan Act, 1905, 4-5 Edward VII, ch. 42 (Can.)	251,700
1898	Yukon Territory	13 June 1898	Yukon Territory Act, 1898, 61 Victoria, ch. 6 (Can.)	207,076
1873	Prince Edward Island	1 July 1873	Imperial Order in Council, 26 June 1873	2,184
1871	British Columbia	20 July 1871	Imperial Order in Council, 16 May 1871	366,255
1870	Manitoba	15 July 1870	Manitoba Act, 1870, 33 Victoria, ch.3 (Can.) and Imperial Order in Council, 23 June 1870	251,000
1870	Northwest Territories[1]	15 July 1870	Rupert's Land Act, 1868, 31-32 Victoria, ch.105 (U.K.) and Imperial Order in Council, 23 June 1870	1,304,903[1]
1867	Ontario	1 July 1867	The British North America Act, 1867, 30-31 Victoria, ch. 3 (U.K.) and Imperial Order in Council, 22 May 1867	412,582
	Quebec			594,860
	New Brunswick			28,354
	Nova Scotia			21,425

[1] The districts of Mackenzie, Keewatin and Franklin are divisions of the present Northwest Territories.

Series Y271-281. Number of provincial statutes disallowed by the federal government, by province and decade, 1867 to 1976

Decade	Totals	Newfound-land	Prince Edward Island	Nova Scotia	New Brunswick	Quebec	Ontario	Manitoba	Saskat-chewan	Alberta	British Columbia
	271	272	273	274	275	276	277	278	279	280	281
1967-1976	–	–	–	–	–	–	–	–	–	–	–
1957-1966	–	–	–	–	–	–	–	–	–	–	–
1947-1956	–	–	–	–	–	–	–	–	–	–	–
1937-1946	11	–	–	–	–	–	–	–	–	11	–
1927-1936	–	–	–	–	–	–	–	–	–	–	–
1917-1926	6	–	–	3	–	–	–	–	–	1	2
1907-1916	8	–	–	–	–	1	2	1	3	–	1
1897-1906	22	–	–	–	–	–	–	2	–	–	20
1887-1896	13	–	–	–	–	2	–	10	–	–	1
1877-1886	32	–	–	1	1	1	5	9	–	–	15
1867-1876	20	–	–	5	–	2	3	6	–	–	4
Totals	112	–	–	9	1	6	10	28	3	12	43

Series Y282-292. Number of provincial bills reserved by Lieutenant-Governors, by province and decade, 1867 to 1976

Decade	Totals	Newfound-land	Prince Edward Island	Nova Scotia	New Brunswick	Quebec	Ontario	Manitoba	Saskat-chewan	Alberta	British Columbia
	282	283	284	285	286	287	288	289	290	291	292
1967-1976	–	–	–	–	–	–	–	–	–	–	–
1957-1966	–	–	–	–	–	–	–	–	–	–	–
1947-1956	–	–	–	–	–	–	–	–	–	–	–
1937-1946	3	–	–	–	–	–	–	–	–	3	–
1927-1936	–	–	–	–	–	–	–	–	–	–	–
1917-1926	2	–	–	–	–	–	–	–	–	–	2
1907-1916	2	–	–	–	–	–	–	–	–	–	2
1897-1906	5	–	1	–	1	1	–	–	–	–	2
1887-1896	12	–	2	–	3	4	–	3	–	–	–
1877-1886	8	–	3	1	–	1	–	2	–	–	1
1867-1876	37	–	4	2	7	1	2	16	–	–	5
Totals	69	–	10	3	11	7	2	21	–	3	12

Series Y293-295. Federal royal commissions, 1867 to 1976
(number)

Year appointed	Major commissions	Minor commissions	Total	Year appointed	Major commissions	Minor commissions	Total
	293	294	295		293	294	295
1976	2	—	2	1920	1	6	7
1975	2	—	2	1919	4	6	10
				1918	3	7	10
1973	1	—	1	1917	4	7	11
1970	—	1	1	1916	5	10	15
1969	1	—	1				
1967	1	1	2	1915	3	7	10
1966	1	4	5	1914	2	5	7
				1913	5	5	10
1965	1	3	4	1912	7	2	9
1964	2	4	6	1911	1	1	2
1963	1	1	2				
1962	1	1	2	1910	1	5	6
1961	3	—	3	1909	3	3	6
				1908	3	2	5
1960	3	1	4	1907	4	1	5
1959	2	2	4	1906	2	5	7
1958	1	1	2				
1957	4	—	4	1905	3	4	7
1956	—	—	—	1904	3	6	9
				1903	5	6	11
1955	3	—	3	1902	2	—	2
1954	3	3	6	1901	1	8	9
1953	—	1	1				
1952	—	1	1	1900	4	6	10
1951	1	3	4	1899	2	4	6
				1898	2	5	7
1950	—	4	4	1897	—	10	10
1949	1	—	1	1896	1	7	8
1948	2	1	3				
1947	—	2	2	1895	1	2	3
1946	3	—	3	1894	—	8	8
				1893	—	1	1
1945	2	4	6	1892	2	4	6
1944	3	2	5	1891	1	3	4
1943	2	1	3				
1942	1	2	3	1890	—	1	1
1941	—	1	1	1889	—	1	1
				1888	—	2	2
1940	—	2	2	1887	—	6	6
1939	—	2	2	1886	4	3	7
1938	2	2	4				
1937	1	2	3	1885	—	2	2
1936	6	1	7	1884	1	2	3
				1883	—	1	1
1935	2	4	6	1882	—	4	4
1934	3	4	7	1881	—	3	3
1933	2	2	4				
1932	2	7	9	1880	1	2	3
1931	3	2	5	1879	—	2	2
				1878	—	1	1
1930	1	8	9	1877	—	2	2
1929	1	1	2	1876	—	3	3
1928	2	4	6				
1927	3	4	7	1875	—	1	1
1926	3	2	5	1874	1	3	4
				1873	1	1	2
1925	—	2	2	1872	—	—	—
1924	1	1	2	1871	—	1	1
1923	3	5	8				
1922	2	—	2	1870	1	1	2
1921	1	3	4	1869	—	1	1
				1868	1	—	1
				1867	—	—	—

Series Y296. Subjects of major royal commissions, 1867 to 1976

Year appointed	Subjects	Year appointed	Subjects
296		**296**	
1976	Bilingual air traffic services in Quebec; Financial management and accountability.	1925	—
1975	Marketing of beef; Corporate concentration.	1924	Failure of Home Bank.
1973	Airport inquiry.	1923	Lake freight rates; Grain trade; Pulpwood export.
1969	Mail transport in Montreal.	1922	Pacific fisheries; Pensions and re-establishment.
1967	Status of women in Canada.	1921	Marketing of grain (no report).
1966	Canadian security methods and procedures.	1920	Uniformity in labour laws.
1965	Post Office department.	1919	Treatment of soldiers on "Northland"; Reindeer and musk ox in Arctic; Relations between capital and labour; Racing and betting.
1963	Bilingualism and biculturalism.		
1962	Taxation.	1918	Pilotage, Victoria, Vancouver, etc.; Pilotage, Halifax, etc.; Allegations re Chambly–Verchères election.
1961	Health services; Unemployment Insurance Act; Banking and finance.	1917	Newsprint industry; Export of electricity; Packers' profits; Findings of Mr. Justice Galt against Rogers.
1960	Automotive industry; Government organization publications.	1916	Fire in Parliament Buildings; Railway development in Canada; Cost of food; Sale of small arms ammunition; Grain, handling and marketing.
1959	Freight rates and transportation problems; Coal.		
1958	Boxcar allocation.		
1957	Diesel issue re CPR; Newfoundland terms of union; Energy; Price spreads.	1915	Supply of munitions and raw materials; Agricultural production; War contracts.
1956	—	1914	Georgian Bay Canal; Loss of *Empress of Ireland* .
		1913	Better terms for B.C.; Penitentiaries; Cost of living; Coal mining disputes in Vancouver; Sale and disposal of Dominion lands since 1896.
1955	Coasting trade; Long-term economic prospects; Broadcasting.		
1954	Operation of Patent Act, etc.; Criminal law re sexual psychopaths; Criminal law re defence of insanity.	1912	National Transcontinental Railway; Farmers Bank failure; Dominion's resources (Imperial Commission); Shell fisheries of Maritimes; State of departmental records; Indian lands in B.C.; Public departments.
1953	—		
1952	—		
1951	South Saskatchewan river projects.	1911	Public Service.
1950	—	1910	Industrial and technical education.
1949	Arts, letters and sciences.	1909	Fisheries of Manitoba and Saskatchewan; Swine industry; Trade with West Indies (Imperial Commission).
1948	Prices; Transportation.		
1947	—	1908	Civil Serivce of Canada; Losses to Chinese in Vancouver; Shad fisheries of Minas Basin.
1946	Espionage in government service; Administrative classifications in Public Service; Indian Act and administration.	1907	Civil Service of Canada; Quebec bridge collapse; Losses to Japanese in Vancouver; Methods of inducing oriental immigration.
1945	Veterans' qualifications; Loyalty of Japanese.	1906	Insurance; Grain trade.
1944	Coal; Co-operatives and Income Tax Act; Taxation of annuities.		
1943	Japanese welfare in B.C.; Wages, western coal mines.	1905	B.C. fisheries; Georgian Bay fisheries; Employment of aliens on Père Marquette Railway.
1942	Despatch of troops to Hong Kong.		
1941	—	1904	Salmon and lobster fishery; Employment of aliens on Grand Trunk Railway; Italian labourers in Montreal.
1940	—	1903	Defalcation in Militia department; Tread gold and other concessions in Yukon; Transportation; Herring and sardine fishery; Industrial disputes in B.C.
1939	—		
1938	Bren gun contract; Alaska highway.		
1937	Dominion-Provincial relations.	1902	Salmon fishing in B.C.; Tobacco trade.
1936	Textile industry; Penal system of Canada; National employment; Anthracite coal; Grain trade; Indian affairs.	1901	Alleged paper combine.
1935	Unemployment of ex-servicemen; Canadian Performing Rights Society.	1900	Chinese and Japanese immigration; North West rebellion—scouts claims (two commissions); Election frauds.
1934	Natural resources of Alberta; Price spreads and mass buying; Maritime claims.	1899	Manitoba grain trade; Mining disputes in British Columbia.
1933	Banking system of Canada; Natural resources of Saskatchewan.	1898	Lobster fishing industry; Charges against government officials in Yukon.
1932	Canadian Performing Rights Society; Ports of Canada.	1896	Manitoba school question.
1931	Grain futures; Chignecto Canal; Transportation.	1895	Sweating system.
1930	Compensation to provinces on return of natural resources.	1892	Liquor traffic; Charges against Sir A.P. Caron.
1929	Technical and professional officials of Civil Service.	1891	Civil Service of Canada.
1928	Transfer of natural resources Manitoba; Radio broadcasting.	1886	Railways; Labour relations; Rebellion losses; Lachine Canal leases.
1927	Reconveyance of land to B.C.; Political partisanship in Department of Soldiers' Civil Re-establishment; Fishing industry in Maritimes.	1884	Chinese immigration.
		1880	Civil Service of Canada.
1926	Maritime claims; Customs and Excise Department; Toronto Harbour Commissioners.	1874	Prohibition.
		1873	Charges re CPR.
		1870	Improvement inland navigation.
		1869	Obstruction to William McDougall in North West.
		1868	Civil Service of Canada.

Series Y297-298. Lieutenant-Governors, by province, 1867 to 1976

Term of commission	Number	Lieutenant-Governor	Date of commission	Term of commission	Number	Lieutenant-Governor	Date of commission
		297	**298**			**297**	**298**
		Newfoundland		1917–1923	15	William Pugsley	6 November 1917
1974–	6	Gordon A. Winter	4 July 1974	1916–1917	14	G.W. Ganong	29 June 1916
				1912–1916	13	Josiah Wood	6 March 1912
1969–1974	5	E. John A. Harnum	2 April 1969	1907–1912	12	L.J. Tweedie	2 March 1907
1963–1969	4	Fabian O'Dea	1 March 1963	1902–1907	11	Jabez B. Snowball	30 January 1902
1957–1963	3	Campbell Macpherson	16 December 1957				
1949–1957	2	Lt.-Col. Sir Leonard Outerbridge	5 September 1949	1896–1902	10	A.R. McClelan	9 December 1896
1949	1	Sir Albert Joseph Walsh	1 April 1949	1893–1896	9	John A. Fraser	20 December 1893
				1893	8	John Boyd	21 September 1893
		Prince Edward Island		1885–1893	7	Sir Samuel Leonard Tilley	31 October 1885
1974–	21	Gordon L. Bennett	24 October 1974	1880–1885	6	Robert Duncan Wilmot	11 February 1880
1969–1974	20	J. George MacKay	6 October 1969	1878–1880	5	E. Baron Chandler	16 July 1878
1963–1969	19	W.J. MacDonald	1 August 1963	1873–1878	4	Samuel Leonard Tilley	5 November 1873
1958–1963	18	F.W. Hyndman	31 March 1958	1868–1873	3	L.A. Wilmot	14 July 1868
1950–1958	17	T.W. Prowse	4 October 1950	1867–1868	2	Col. F.P. Harding	18 October 1867
1945–1950	16	J.A. Bernard	18 May 1945	1867	1	Maj.-Gen. Sir C. Hastings Doyle	1 July 1867
1939–1945	15	Bradford W. LePage	11 September 1939			*Quebec*	
1933–1939	14	George D. DeBlois	28 December 1933	1966–	23	Hugues Lapointe	22 February 1966
1930–1933	13	Charles Dalton	19 November 1930	1961–1966	22	Paul Comtois	6 October 1961
1924–1930	12	Frank R. Heartz	8 September 1924				
1919–1924	11	Murdoch McKinnon	2 September 1919	1958–1961	20	Onésime Gagnon	14 February 1958
				1950–1958	19	Gaspard Fauteux	3 October 1950
1915–1919	10	A.C. Macdonald	3 June 1915	1939–1950	18	Maj.-Gen. Sir Eugène Fiset[1]	30 December 1939
1910–1915	9	Benjamin Rogers	1 June 1910	1934–1939	17	E.L. Patenaude	29 April 1934
1904–1910	8	D.A. MacKinnon	3 October 1904	1929–1934	16	Henry George Carroll	2 April 1929
1899–1904	7	P.A. McIntyre	23 May 1899				
1894–1899	6	George W. Howlan	21 February 1894	1928–1929	15	Sir Lomer Gouin	31 December 1928
				1924–1928	14	Narcisse Pérodeau	8 January 1924
1889–1894	5	Jedediah S. Carvell	2 September 1889	1923–1924	13	Louis-Philippe Brodeur	31 October 1923
1884–1889	4	Andrew A. Macdonald	18 July 1884	1918–1923	12	Sir Charles Fitzpatrick	21 October 1918
1879–1884	3	Thomas H. Haviland	10 July 1879	1915–1918	11	Sir Pierre-Evariste Leblanc	9 February 1915
1874–1879	2	Sir Robert Hodgson	4 July 1874				
1873–1874	1	William Robinson	10 June 1873	1911–1915	10	Sir François Langelier	5 May 1911
				1908–1911	9	Sir Charles A.P. Pelletier	15 September 1908
		Nova Scotia		1898–1908	8	Sir Louis-Amable Jette[1]	20 January 1898
1973–	25	Clarence L. Gosse	1 October 1973	1892–1898	7	Sir Joseph-Adolphe Chapleau	5 December 1892
1968–1973	24	Victor de B. Oland	22 July 1968	1887–1892	6	Auguste-Réal Angers	24 October 1887
1963–1968	23	H.P. MacKeen	1 March 1963				
1958–1963	22	Maj.-Gen. E.C. Plow	15 January 1958	1884–1887	5	L.F.R. Masson	4 October 1884
1952–1958	21	Alistair Fraser	1 September 1952	1879–1884	4	Théodore Robitaille	26 July 1879
				1876–1879	3	Luc Letellier de Saint-Just	15 December 1876
1947–1952	20	J.A.D. McCurdy	12 August 1947	1873–1876	2	René-Edouard Caron	11 February 1873
1942–1947	19	Lt.-Col. H. Ernest Kendall	17 November 1942	1867–1873	1	Sir Narcisse F. Belleau[1]	1 July 1867
1940–1942	18	Frederick F. Mathers	31 May 1940				
1937–1940	17	Robert Irwin	7 April 1937			*Ontario*	
1931–1937	16	Walter H. Covert	5 October 1931	1974–	22	Pauline McGibbon	17 January 1974
				1968–1974	21	W. Ross MacDonald	4 July 1968
1930–1931	15	Frank Stanfield	19 November 1930				
1925–1930	14	James C. Tory	24 September 1925	1963–1968	20	William Earl Rowe	1 May 1963
1925	13	J. Robson Douglas	12 January 1925	1957–1963	19	John Keiller Mackay	30 December 1957
1916–1925	12	MacCallum Grant[1]	29 November 1916	1952–1957	18	Louis O. Breithaupt	24 January 1952
1915–1916	11	David MacKeen	19 October 1915	1946–1952	17	Ray Lawson	26 December 1946
				1937–1946	16	Albert Matthews	23 November 1937
1910–1915	10	James D. McGregor	18 October 1910				
1906–1910	9	Duncan C. Fraser	27 March 1906	1932–1937	15	Col. Herbert Alexander Bruce	25 October 1932
1900–1906	8	Alfred G. Jones	26 July 1900	1926–1932	14	William Donald Ross	20 December 1926
1890–1900	7	Sir Malachy Bowes Daly[1]	11 July 1890	1921–1926	13	Col. Henry Cockshutt	10 September 1921
1888–1890	6	A.W. McLelan	9 July 1888	1919–1921	12	Lionel Clarke	27 November 1919
				1914–1919	11	Lt.-Col. Sir John S. Hendrie	26 September 1914
1883–1888	5	Matthew Henry Richey	4 July 1883				
1873–1883	4	Sir A.G. Archibald[1]	4 July 1873	1908–1914	10	Sir John M. Gibson	22 September 1908
1873	3	Joseph Howe	1 May 1873	1903–1908	9	Sir William Mortimer Clark	20 April 1903
1867–1873	2	Lt.-Gen. Sir C. Hastings Doyle[1]	18 October 1867	1897–1903	8	Sir Oliver Mowat	18 November 1897
1867	1	Lt.-Gen. Sir W.F. Williams	1 July 1867	1892–1897	7	Sir George A. Kirkpatrick	28 May 1892
				1887–1892	6	Sir Alexander Campbell	8 February 1887
		New Brunswick					
1971–	24	Hédard J. Robichaud	8 October 1971	1880–1887	5	John Beverly Robinson	30 June 1880
1968–1971	23	Wallace S. Bird	1 February 1968	1875–1880	4	D.A. MacDonald	18 May 1875
1965–1968	22	John B. McNair	9 June 1965	1873–1875	3	John W. Crawford	5 November 1873
1958–1965	21	J. Leonard O'Brien	6 June 1958	1868–1873	2	W.P. Howland	14 July 1868
				1867–1868	1	Maj.-Gen. H.W. Stisted	1 July 1867
1945–1958	20	David Laurence MacLaren	1 November 1945				
1940–1945	19	W.G. Clark	5 March 1940			*Manitoba*	
1935–1940	18	Col. Murray MacLaren	5 February 1935	1976–	19	Francis L. Jobin	15 March 1976
1928–1935	17	Maj.-Gen. Hugh H. McLean	11 December 1928	1970–1976	18	William John McKeag	2 September 1970
1923–1928	16	William F. Todd	24 February 1923	1965–1970	17	Richard S. Bowles	1 September 1965
				1960–1965	16	Errick F. Willis	15 January 1960

Series Y297-298. Lieutenant-Governors, by province, 1867 to 1976 (concluded)

Term of commission	Number	Lieutenant-Governor	Date of commission	Term of commission	Number	Lieutenant-Governor	Date of commission
		297	**298**			**297**	**298**
		Manitoba (continued)				*Alberta*	
1953–1960	15	John Stewart McDiarmid	1 August 1953	1974–	10	Ralph G. Steinhauer	2 July 1974
1940–1953	14	Roland Fairbairn McWilliams	1 November 1940	1966–1974	9	John W.G. MacEwan	6 January 1966
1934–1940	13	William J. Tupper	1 December 1934	1959–1966	8	J. Percy Page	19 December 1959
1929–1934	12	J.D. McGregor	25 January 1929	1950–1959	7	John J. Bowlen	1 February 1950
1926–1929	11	Theodore A. Burrows	9 October 1926	1937–1950	6	J.C. Bowen	20 March 1937
1916–1926	10	Sir James A.M. Aikins[1]	3 August 1916	1936–1937	5	Philip C.H. Primrose	10 September 1936
1911–1916	9	Sir Douglas C. Cameron	1 August 1911	1931–1936	4	William L. Walsh	24 April 1931
1900–1911	8	Sir Daniel H. McMillan[1]	10 October 1900	1925–1931	3	William Egbert	20 October 1925
1895–1900	7	J.C. Patterson	2 September 1895	1915–1925	2	Robert George Brett[1]	6 October 1915
1888–1895	6	J.C. Schultz	1 July 1888	1905–1915	1	George H.V. Bulyea[1]	24 August 1905
1882–1888	5	James C. Aikins	29 September 1882				
1877–1882	4	Joseph E. Cauchon	8 October 1877			*British Columbia*	
1872–1877	3	Alexander Morris	2 December 1872	1973–	22	Walter Stewart Owen	19 March 1973
1872	2	Francis G. Johnson	9 April 1872	1968–1973	21	Col. John R. Nicholson	2 July 1968
1870–1872	1	A.G. Archibald	20 May 1870	1960–1968	20	Maj.-Gen. George R. Pearkes	12 October 1960
				1955–1960	19	Frank Mackenzie Ross	3 October 1955
		Saskatchewan		1950–1955	18	Col. Clarence Wallace	1 October 1950
1976–	13	George Porteous	3 March 1976	1946–1950	17	Col. Charles Arthur Banks	1 October 1946
1963–1976	12	Robert L. Hanbidge	1 March 1963	1941–1946	16	Lt.-Col. William C. Woodward	29 August 1941
1958–1963	11	F.L. Bastedo	1 September 1958	1936–1941	15	Eric W. Hamber	29 April 1936
1951–1958	10	W.J. Patterson	4 July 1951	1931–1936	14	J.W. Fordham Johnson	18 July 1931
1948–1951	9	J.W. Uhrich	24 March 1948	1926–1931	13	R. Randolph Bruce	21 January 1926
1945–1948	8	Reginald J.M. Parker	22 June 1945	1920–1926	12	Walter C. Nichol	24 December 1920
1945	7	Thomas Miller	27 February 1945	1919–1920	11	Col. Edward G. Prior	9 December 1919
1936–1945	6	A.P. McNab	10 September 1936	1914–1919	10	Sir Frank S. Barnard	5 December 1914
1931–1936	5	Lt.-Col. H.E. Munroe	31 March 1931	1909–1914	9	T.W. Paterson	3 December 1909
1921–1931	4	H.W. Newlands[1]	17 February 1921	1906–1909	8	James Dunsmuir	11 May 1906
1915–1921	3	Sir Richard S. Lake	6 October 1915	1900–1906	7	Sir Henri G. Joly de Lotbinière	21 June 1900
1910–1915	2	George W. Brown	5 October 1910	1897–1900	6	Thomas Robert McInnes	18 November 1897
1905–1910	1	A.E. Forget	24 August 1905	1892–1897	5	Edgar Dewdney	1 November 1892
				1887–1892	4	Hugh Nelson	8 February 1887
				1881–1887	3	Clement F. Cornwall	21 June 1881
				1876–1881	2	Albert Norton Richards	27 June 1876
				1871–1876	1	Sir J.W. Trutch	5 July 1871

[1] Appointed for second term.

Series Y299-301. Ministries, by province and premier, 1867 to 1976

Years of ministry	Number of ministry	Premier	Date of appointment	Party
	299		**300**	**301**

Newfoundland

| 1972– | 2 | Frank D. Moores | 18 January 1972 | Conservative |
| 1949–1972 | 1 | Joseph R. Smallwood | 1 April 1949 | Liberal |

Prince Edward Island

1966–	25	Alexander B. Campbell	28 July 1966	Liberal
1959–1966	24	Walter Shaw	1 September 1959	Conservative
1953–1959	23	A.W. Matheson	25 May 1953	Liberal
1943–1953	22	J. Walter Jones	11 May 1943	Liberal
1936–1943	21	Thane A. Campbell	14 January 1936	Liberal
1935–1936	20	Walter M. Lea	15 August 1935	Liberal
1933–1935	19	William J.P. MacMillan	14 October 1933	Conservative
1931–1933	18	James D. Stewart	29 August 1931	Conservative
1930–1931	17	Walter M. Lea	20 May 1930	Liberal
1927–1930	16	Albert C. Saunders	12 August 1927	Liberal
1923–1927	15	James D. Stewart	5 September 1923	Conservative
1919–1923	14	J.H. Bell	9 September 1919	Liberal
1917–1919	13	Aubin Arsenault	21 June 1917	Conservative
1911–1917	12	John A. Mathieson	2 December 1911	Conservative
1911	11	H. James Palmer	16 May 1911	Liberal
1908–1911	10	F.L. Haszard	1 February 1908	Liberal
1901–1908	9	A. Peters	29 December 1901	Liberal
1898–1901	8	D. Farquharson	August 1898	Liberal
1897–1898	7	A.B. Warburton	October 1897	Liberal
1891–1897	6	F. Peters	27 April 1891	Liberal
1889–1891	5	N. McLeod	November 1889	Conservative
1879–1889	4	W.W. Sullivan	25 April 1879	Conservative
1876–1879	3	L.H. Davies	August 1876	Liberal (Coalition)
1873–1876	2	L.C. Owen	September 1873	Conservative
1873	1	J.C. Pope	April 1873	Conservative

Nova Scotia

1970–	19	Gerald A. Reagan	28 October 1970	Liberal
1967–1970	18	George L. Smith	13 September 1967	Conservative
1956–1967	17	Robert L. Stanfield	20 November 1956	Conservative
1954–1956	16	Henry D. Hicks	30 September 1954	Liberal
1954	15	Harold Connolly	13 April 1954	Liberal
1945–1954	14	Angus L. Macdonald	8 September 1945	Liberal
1940–1945	13	A.S. MacMillan	10 July 1940	Liberal
1933–1940	12	Angus L. Macdonald	5 September 1933	Liberal
1930–1933	11	Col. Gordon S. Harrington	11 August 1930	Conservative
1925–1930	10	E.N. Rhodes	16 July 1925	Conservative
1923–1925	9	E.H. Armstrong	24 January 1923	Liberal
1896–1923	8	George H. Murray	20 July 1896	Liberal
1884–1896	7	W.S. Fielding	28 July 1884	Liberal
1882–1884	6	W.T. Pipes	3 August 1882	Liberal
1882	5	J.S.D. Thompson	25 May 1882	Conservative
1878–1882	4	S.H. Holmes	22 October 1878	Conservative
1875–1878	3	P.C. Hill	11 May 1875	Liberal
1867–1875	2	William Annand	7 November 1867	Liberal
1867	1	H. Blanchard	4 July 1867	Conservative

New Brunswick

1970–	24	Richard Hatfield	12 November 1970	Conservative
1960–1970	23	L.J. Robichaud	12 July 1960	Liberal
1952–1960	22	H.J. Flemming	8 October 1952	Conservative
1940–1952	21	J.B. McNair	13 March 1940	Liberal
1935–1940	20	A. Allison Dysart	16 July 1935	Liberal
1933–1935	19	L.P.D. Tilley	1 June 1933	Conservative
1931–1933	18	Charles D. Richards	19 May 1931	Conservative
1925–1931	17	John B.M. Baxter	14 September 1925	Conservative
1923–1925	16	Peter Veniot	28 February 1923	Liberal
1917–1923	15	Walter E. Foster	4 April 1917	Liberal
1917	14	James Murray	1 February 1917	Conservative
1914–1917	13	George G. Clarke	17 December 1914	Conservative
1911–1914	12	James K. Flemming	16 October 1911	Conservative
1908–1911	11	J.D. Hazen	24 March 1908	Conservative
1907–1908	10	C.W. Robinson	31 May 1907	Liberal
1907	9	William Pugsley	6 March 1907	Liberal
1900–1907	8	L.J. Tweedie	31 August 1900	Conservative
1897–1900	7	H.R. Emmerson	29 October 1897	Liberal
1896–1897	6	James Mitchell	July 1896	Conservative

Series Y299-301. Ministries, by province and premier, 1867 to 1976 (continued)

Year of ministry	Number of ministry	Premier	Date of appointment	Party
	299		**300**	**301**
New Brunswick (continued)				
1883–1896	5	A.G. Blair	1883	Liberal
1882–1883	4	D.L. Hannington	1882	Conservative
1878–1882	3	J.J. Fraser	1878	Conservative
1872–1878	2	G.E. King	1872	Liberal
1867–1872	1	A.R. Wetmore	1867	—
Quebec				
1976–	27	René Lévesque	25 November 1976	Parti Québécois
1970–1976	26	Robert Bourassa	29 April 1970	Liberal
1968–1970	25	Jean-Jacques Bertrand	2 October 1968	Union Nationale
1966–1968	24	Daniel Johnson	5 June 1966	Union Nationale
1960–1966	23	Jean Lesage	5 July 1960	Liberal
1960	22	Antonio Barrette	7 January 1960	Union Nationale
1959–1960	21	Paul Sauvé	10 September 1959	Union Nationale
1944–1959	20	Maurice Duplessis	30 August 1944	Union Nationale
1939–1944	19	Adélard Godbout	8 November 1939	Liberal
1936–1939	18	Maurice Duplessis	24 August 1936	Union Nationale
1936	17	Adélard Godbout	11 June 1936	Liberal
1920–1936	16	L. Alexandre Taschereau	9 July 1920	Liberal
1905–1920	15	Sir Lomer Gouin	23 March 1905	Liberal
1900–1905	14	S. Napoléon Parent	3 October 1900	Liberal
1897–1900	13	F. Gabriel Marchand	24 May 1897	Liberal
1896–1897	12	Edmund J. Flynn	11 May 1896	Conservative
1892–1896	11	L. Olivier Taillon	16 December 1892	Conservative
1891–1892	10	Charles E.B. deBoucherville	21 December 1891	Conservative
1887–1891	9	Honoré Mercier	29 January 1887	Liberal
1887	8	L. Olivier Taillon	13 January 1887	Conservative
1884–1887	7	John J. Ross	23 January 1884	Conservative
1882–1884	6	J. Alfred Mousseau	1 August 1882	Conservative
1879–1882	5	J. Adolphe Chapleau	31 October 1879	Conservative
1878–1879	4	Henri C. Joly	8 March 1878	Liberal
1874–1878	3	Charles E.B. deBoucherville	22 September 1874	Conservative
1873–1874	2	Gédéon Ouimet	27 February 1873	Conservative
1867–1873	1	Pierre J. Chauveau	15 July 1867	Conservative
Ontario				
1971–	18	William G. Davis	1 March 1971	Conservative
1961–1971	17	John P. Robarts	8 November 1961	Conservative
1949–1961	16	Leslie M. Frost	4 May 1949	Conservative
1948	15	T.L. Kennedy	19 October 1948	Conservative
1943–1948	14	George Drew	17 August 1943	Conservative
1943	13	H.C. Nixon	18 May 1943	Liberal
1942–1943	12	G.D. Conant	21 October 1942	Liberal
1934–1942	11	M.F. Hepburn	10 July 1934	Liberal
1930–1934	10	G.S. Henry	15 December 1930	Conservative
1923–1930	9	G.H. Ferguson	16 July 1923	Conservative
1919–1923	8	E.G. Drury	14 November 1919	United Farmers of Ontario
1914–1919	7	Sir William Hearst	2 October 1914	Conservative
1905–1914	6	Sir J.P. Whitney	8 February 1905	Conservative
1899–1905	5	G.W. Ross	21 October 1899	Liberal
1896–1899	4	A.S. Hardy	25 July 1896	Liberal
1872–1896	3	Oliver Mowat	25 October 1872	Liberal
1871–1872	2	Edward Blake	20 December 1871	Liberal
1867–1871	1	J.S. Macdonald	16 July 1867	Conservative
Manitoba				
1969–	17	Edward Schreyer	15 July 1969	N.D.P.[1]
1967–1969	16	Walter Weir	25 November 1967	Conservative
1958–1967	15	Dufferin Roblin	16 June 1958	Conservative
1948–1958	14	D.L. Campbell	7 November 1948	Liberal
1943–1948	13	S.S. Garson	8 January 1943	Coalition
1922–1943	12	John Bracken	8 August 1922	Coalition[2]
1915–1922	11	T.C. Norris	12 May 1915	Conservative
1900–1915	10	Sir R.P. Roblin	29 October 1900	Conservative
1900	9	H.J. Macdonald	8 January 1900	Conservative
1888–1900	8	T. Greenway	19 January 1888	Liberal
1887–1888	7	D.H. Harrison	26 December 1887	Conservative
1878–1887	6	John Norquay	16 October 1878	Conservative

Series Y299-301. Ministries, by province and by premier, 1867 to 1976 (concluded)

Years of ministry	Number of ministry	Premier	Date of appointment	Party
	299		**300**	**301**

		Manitoba (continued)		
1874–1878	5	R.A. Davis	3 December 1874	—[3]
1874	4	N.A. Girard	8 July 1874	Conservative
1872–1874	3	J.H. Clarke	14 March 1872	—[4]
1871–1872	2	N.A. Girard	14 December 1871	Conservative[4]
1870–1871	1	A. Boyd	16 September 1870	—[4]

		Saskatchewan		
1971–	11	R.E. Blakeney	30 June 1971	N.D.P.
1964–1971	10	W. Ross Thatcher	22 May 1964	Liberal
1961–1964	9	W.S. Lloyd	7 November 1961	N.D.P.–C.C.F.[5]
1944–1961	8	T.C. Douglas	10 July 1944	C.C.F.
1935–1944	7	W.J. Patterson	1 November 1935	Liberal
1934–1935	6	J.G. Gardiner	19 July 1934	Liberal
1929–1934	5	J.T.M. Anderson	9 September 1929	Conservative
1926–1929	4	J.G. Gardiner	26 February 1926	Liberal
1922–1926	3	C.A. Dunning	5 April 1922	Liberal
1916–1922	2	W.M. Martin	20 October 1916	Liberal
1905–1916	1	Walter Scott	12 September 1905	Liberal

		Alberta		
1971–	10	P. Lougheed	10 September 1971	Conservative
1968–1971	9	H.E. Strom	12 December 1968	Liberal
1943–1968	8	E.C. Manning	31 May 1943	Social Credit
1935–1943	7	William Aberhart	3 September 1935	Social Credit
1934–1935	6	Richard G. Reid	10 July 1934	United Farmers of Alberta
1925–1934	5	John E. Brownlee	November 1925	United Farmers of Alberta
1921–1925	4	Herbert Greenfield	13 August 1921	United Farmers of Alberta
1917–1921	3	Charles Stewart	30 October 1917	Liberal
1910–1917	2	A.L. Sifton	26 May 1910	Liberal
1905–1910	1	Alex Rutherford	2 September 1905	Liberal

		British Columbia		
1975–	29	W.R. Bennett	11 December 1975	Social Credit
1972–1975	28	David Barrett	30 August 1972	N.D.P.
1952–1972	26 – 27	W.A.C. Bennett	1 August 1952	Social Credit
1947–1952	25	Byron Johnson	18 January 1947	Coalition
1947	24	Byron Johnson/Herbert Anscomb	29 December 1947	Coalition
1941–1947	23	John Hart	9 December 1941	Coalition
1933–1941	22	T.D. Pattullo	15 November 1933	Liberal
1928–1933	21	Simon F. Tolmie	21 August 1928	Conservative
1927–1928	20	John D. Maclean	20 August 1927	Liberal
1918–1927	19	John Oliver	6 March 1918	Liberal
1916–1918	18	Harlan C. Brewster	23 November 1916	Liberal
1915–1916	17	William J. Bowser	15 December 1915	Conservative
1903–1905	16	Richard McBride	1 June 1903	Conservative
1902–1903	15	E.G. Prior	21 November 1902	—
1900–1902	14	J. Dunsmuir	15 June 1900	—
1900	13	Joseph Martin	28 February 1900	—
1898–1900	12	C.A. Semlin	12 August 1898	—
1895–1898	11	J.H. Turner	4 March 1895	—
1892–1895	10	T. Davie	2 July 1892	—
1889–1892	9	J. Robson	2 August 1889	—
1887–1889	8	A.E.B. Davie	15 May 1887	—
1883–1887	7	W. Smythe	29 January 1883	—
1882–1883	6	R. Beaven	13 June 1882	—
1878–1882	5	G.A. Walkem	25 June 1878	—
1876–1878	4	A.C. Elliott	1 February 1876	—
1874–1876	3	G.A. Walkem	11 February 1874	—
1872–1874	2	A. De Cosmos	23 December 1872	—
1871–1872	1	J.F. McCreight	13 November 1871	—

[1] New Democratic Party.
[2] Successively United Farmers, Progressive, and then Coalition.
[3] Elected as candidate of Grangers.

[4] See notes on series W253–255, in first edition of this volume.
[5] Cooperative Commonwealth Federation.

Series Y302-387. Provincial government elections, party standing and size of legislature, 1867 to 1977

Newfoundland

Year of election	Number of legis- lature	Date of election	Liberal	Progres- sive Conser- vative	Other	Size of legis- lature
	302	303	304	305	306	307
1975	9	16 September 1975	16	30	5	51
1972	8	24 March 1972	9	33	—	42
1971	7	28 October 1971	20	21	1	42
1966	6	8 September 1966	38	4	—	42
1962	5	19 November 1962	34	7	1	42
1959	4	20 August 1959	31	3	2	36
1956	3	2 October 1956	32	4	—	36
1951	2	26 November 1951	24	4	—	28
1949	1	27 May 1949	22	5	1	28

Prince Edward Island

Year of election	Number of legis- lature	Date of election	Liberal	Progres- sive Conser- vative	Other	Size of legis- lature[2]
	308	309	310	311	312	313
1974	28	29 April 1974	26	6	—	32
1970	27	11 May 1970	27	5[1]	—	32
1966	26	30 May and 11 July 1966	17	15	—	32
1962	25	10 December 1962	11	19	—	30
1959	24	1 September 1959	8	22	—	30
1955	23	25 May 1955	27	3	—	30
1951	22	26 April 1951	24	6	—	30
1947	21	11 December 1947	24	6	—	30
1943	20	15 September 1943	20	10	—	30
1939	19	18 May 1939	27	3	—	30
1935	18	23 July 1935	30	—	—	30
1931	17	6 August 1931	12	18	—	30
1927	16	25 June 1927	24	6	—	30
1923	15	24 July 1923	5	25	—	30
1919	14	24 July 1919	25	4	1	30
1915	13	16 September 1915	13	16	1	30
1912	12	3 January 1912	2	27	1	30
1908	11	18 November 1908	16	14	—	30
1904	10	7 December 1904	22	8	—	30
1900	9	12 December 1900	21	9	—	30
1897	8	28 July 1897	20	10	—	30
1893	7	13 December 1893	23	7	—	30[2]
1890	6	30 January 1890	15	15	—	30
1886	5	30 June 1886	11	19	—	30
1882	4	8 May 1882	11	19	—	30
1879	3	2 April 1879	3	25	2[3]	30
1876	2'	17 August 1876	9	14	7[3]	30
1873	1	2 April 1873	11	17	—	28

Series Y302-387. Provincial government elections, party standing, and size of legislature, 1867 to 1977 (continued)

Nova Scotia

Year of election	Number of legis- lature	Date of election	Liberal	New Demo- cratic Party[4]	Progres- sive Conser- vative[5]	Other	Size of legis- lature[6]
	314	**315**	**316**	**317**	**318**	**319**	**320**
1974	28	2 April 1974	31	3	12	—	46
1970	27	13 October 1970	23	2	21	—	46
1967	26	30 May 1967	6	—	40	—	46
1963	25	8 October 1963	4	—	39	—	43
1960	24	7 June 1960	15	1[4]	27	—	43
1956	23	30 October 1956	18	1	24	—	43
1953	22	26 May 1953	22	2	13	—	37
1949	21	9 June 1949	28	2	7	—	37
1945	20	23 October 1945	28	2	—[5]	—	30
1941	19	28 October 1941	23	3	4	—	30
1937	18	29 June 1937	25	—	5	—	30
1933	17	22 August 1933	22	—	8	—	30
1928	16	1 October 1928	20	—	23	—	43
1925	15	25 June 1925	3	—	40	—	43[6]
1920	14	27 July 1920	29	—	3	11	43
1916	13	20 June 1916	30	—	13	—	43
1911	12	14 June 1911	27	—	11	—	38
1906	11	20 June 1906	32	—	5	1	38
1901	10	2 October 1901	36	—	2	—	38
1897	9	20 April 1897	35	—	3	—	38
1894	8	15 March 1894	25	—	13	—	38
1890	7	21 May 1890	28	—	10	—	38
1886	6	15 June 1886	29	—	8	1	38
1882	5	20 June 1882	24	—	14	—	—
1878	4	17 September 1878	8	—	30	—	38
1874	3	17 December 1874	24	—	14	—	38
1871	2	16 May 1871	25	—	13	—	38
1867	1	18 September 1867	36	—	2	—	38

New Brunswick

Year of election	Number of legis- lature	Date of election	Liberal	Progres- sive Conser- vative[7]	Other	Size of legis- lature[8]
	321	**322**	**323**	**324**	**325**	**326**
1974	27	18 November 1974	25	33	—	58
1970	26	26 October 1970	26	32	—	58
1967	25	23 October 1967	32	26	—	58
1963	24	22 April 1963	32	20	—	52
1960	23	27 June 1960	31	21	—	52
1956	22	18 June 1956	15	37	—	52
1952	21	22 September 1952	16	36	—	52
1948	20	28 June 1948	47	5	—	52
1944	19	28 August 1944	36	12	—	48
1939	18	20 November 1939	29	19[7]	—	48
1935	17	27 June 1935	43	5	—	48
1930	16	19 June 1930	17	31	—	48
1925	15	10 August 1925	11	37	—	48
1920	14	9 October 1920	28	13	7[9]	48
1917	13	24 February 1917	27	21	—	48
1912	12	20 June 1912	2	44	2	48
1908	11	3 March 1908	10	31	5	46
1903	10	28 February 1903	27	15	4	46
1899	9	18 February 1899	41	5	—	46
1895	8	16 October 1895	34	10	2	46
1892	7	22 October 1892	27	13	1	41[8]
1890	6	21 January 1890	7	34	—	41
1886	5	26 April 1886	18	19	4	41
1882	4	15 June 1882	20	15	6	41
1878	3	June 1878	24	13	4	41
1874	2	June 1874	35	4	2	41
1870	1	June–July 1870	25	16	—	41

Series Y302-387. Provincial government elections, party standing, and size of legislature, 1867 to 1977 (continued)

Quebec

Year of election	Number of legislature	Date of election	Conservative	Crédit social	Liberal	Parti québécois[10]	Union nationale[11]	Other	Size of legislature[12]
327	328		329	330	331	332	333	334	335
1976	31	15 November 1976	–	1	26	71	11	1	110
1973	30	29 October 1973	–	2	102	6	–	–	110
1970	29	29 April 1970	–	12	72	7[10]	17	–	108
1966	28	5 June 1966	–	–	50	–	56	2	108[12]
1962	27	15 November 1962	–	–	63	–	31	1	95
1960	26	22 June 1960	–	–	51	–	43	1	95
1956	25	20 June 1956	–	–	20	–	72	1	93
1952	24	16 July 1952	–	–	23	–	68	1	92
1948	23	28 July 1948	–	–	8	–	82	2	92
1944	22	8 August 1944	–	–	37	–	48	6	91
1939	21	25 October 1939	–	–	70	–	15	1	86
1936	20	17 August 1936	–	–	14	–	76[11]	–	90
1935	19	25 November 1935	16	–	48	–	–	26	90
1931	18	24 August 1931	11	–	79	–	–	–	90
1927	17	16 May 1927	9	–	75	–	–	1	85
1923	16	5 February 1923	19	–	64	–	–	2	85
1919	15	23 June 1919	5	–	74	–	–	2	81
1916	14	22 May 1916	6	–	75	–	–	–	81
1912	13	15 May 1912	15	–	64	–	–	2	81
1908	12	8 June 1908	13	–	58	–	–	3	74
1904	11	25 November 1904	6	–	68	–	–	–	74
1900	10	7 December 1900	7	–	67	–	–	–	74
1897	9	11 May 1897	23	–	51	–	–	–	74
1892	8	8 March 1892	51	–	21	–	–	1	73
1890	7	17 June 1890	24	–	42	–	–	7	73
1886	6	14 October 1886	28	–	31	–	–	6	65
1881	5	2 December 1881	49	–	15	–	–	1	65
1878	4	1 May 1878	33	–	30	–	–	2	65
1875	3	7 July 1875	43	–	19	–	–	3	65
1871	2	June–July 1871	45	–	20	–	–	–	65
1867	1	August–September 1867	50	–	14	–	–	1[13]	65

Ontario

Year of election	Number of legislature	Date of election	Labour and Liberal-Labour	Labour Progressive (Communist)	Liberal	New Democratic Party[14]	Progressive	Progressive Conservative[7]	United Farmers of Ontario	Other	Size of legislature
336		337	338	339	340	341	342	343	344	345	346
1977	31	9 June 1977	–	–	34	33	–	58	–	–	125
1975	30	18 September 1975	–	–	36	38	–	51	–	–	125
1971	29	21 October 1971	–	–	20	19	–	78	–	–	117
1967	28	17 October 1967	–	–	28	20	–	69	–	–	117
1963	27	25 September 1963	–	–	24	7	–	77	–	–	108
1959	26	11 June 1959	–	–	22	5[14]	–	71	–	–	98
1955	25	9 June 1955	–	–	11	3	–	84	–	–	98
1951	24	22 November 1951	1	1	7	2	–	79	–	–	90
1948	23	7 June 1948	1	2	13	21	–	53	–	–	90
1945	22	4 June 1945	3	2	11	8	–	66	–	–	90
1943	21	4 August 1943	–	2	15	34	–	38[7]	–	1	90
1937	20	6 October 1937	–	–	63	–	–	23	1	3	90
1934	19	19 June 1934	–	–	66	1	–	17	1	5	90
1929	18	30 October 1929	1	–	14	–	5	91	1	–	112
1926	17	1 December 1926	1	–	17	–	13	74	3	4	112
1923	16	25 June 1923	3	–	14	–	–	77	17	–	111
1919	15	20 October 1919	11	–	29	–	–	25	44	3	112
1914	14	29 June 1914	1	–	25	–	–	84	–	1	111
1911	13	11 December 1911	1	–	21	–	–	83	–	–	105
1908	12	8 June 1908	1	–	19	–	–	86	–	–	106
1905	11	25 January 1905	–	–	28	–	–	69	–	1	98

Series Y302-387. Provincial government elections, party standing, and size of legislature, 1867 to 1977 (continued)

Ontario (continued)

Year of election	Number of legislature	Date of election	Labour and Liberal-Labour	Labour Progressive (Communist)	Liberal	New Democratic Party[14]	Progressive	Progressive Conservative[7]	United Farmers of Ontario	Other	Size of legislature
	336	337	338	339	340	341	342	343	344	345	346
1902	10	29 May 1902	–	–	51	–	–	46	–	–	97
1898	9	1 March 1898	–	–	49	–	–	43	–	1	93
1894	8	26 June 1894	–	–	49	–	–	27	–	16[15]	92
1890	7	5 June 1890	–	–	54	–	–	36	–	–	90
1886	6	28 December 1886	–	–	64	–	–	26	–	–	90
1883	5	27 February 1883	–	–	48	–	–	36	–	2	86
1879	4	5 June 1879	–	–	58	–	–	29	–	1	88
1875	3	18 January 1875	–	–	51	–	–	33	–	4	88
1871	2	21 March 1871	–	–	41[16]	–	–	32[16]	–	7	80
1867	1	August–September 1867	–	–	23[16]	–	–	56[16]	–	5	84

Manitoba

Year of election	Number of legislature	Date of election	Labour	Labour Progressive (Communist)	Liberal	Liberal and Liberal Progressive	New Democratic Party[14]	Progressive	Progressive Conservative[17]	Social Credit	United Farmer	Other	Size of legislature[18]
	347	348	349	350	351	352	353	354	355	356	357	358	359
1977	31	11 October 1977	–	–	1	–	23	–	33	–	–	–	57
1973	30	28 June 1973	–	–	5	–	31	–	21	–	–	–	57
1969	29	25 June 1969	–	–	4	–	28	–	22	1	–	2	57
1966	28	23 June 1966	–	–	14	–	11	–	31	1	–	–	57
1962	27	14 December 1962	–	–	13	–	7	–	36	1	–	–	57
1959	26	14 May 1959	–	–	–	1	10[14]	–	36	–	–	–	57
1958	25	16 June 1958	–	–	–	19	11	–	26	–	–	1	57
1953	24	8 June 1953	–	1	–	35	5	–	12	2	–	2	57
1949	23	10 November 1949	–	–	–	29	7	–	10	–	–	11	57
1945	22	15 October 1945	–	1	–	26	10	–	13	2	–	3	55
1941	21	22 April 1941	–	–	–	25	3	–	14[17]	3	–	10	55
1936	20	27 July 1936	–	1	–	23	7	–	16	5	–	3	55
1932	19	16 June 1932	5	–	–	–	–	38	10	–	–	2	55
1927	18	28 June 1927	3	–	7	–	–	29	15	–	–	1	55
1922	17	18 July 1922	6	–	7	–	–	1	6	–	27	8	55
1920	16	29 June 1920	11	–	21	–	–	–	7	–	12	4	55
1915	15	16 September 1915	–	–	40	–	–	–	5	–	–	4	49
1914	14	10 July 1914	–	–	21	–	–	–	28	–	–	–	49
1910	13	11 June 1910	–	–	13	–	–	–	28	–	–	–	41
1907	12	7 March 1907	–	–	13	–	–	–	28	–	–	–	41
1903	11	20 July 1903	–	–	9	–	–	–	31	–	–	–	40
1899	10	7 December 1899	–	–	14	–	–	–	26	–	–	–	40
1896	9	15 January 1896	–	–	32	–	–	–	5	–	–	3	40
1892	8	23 July 1892	–	–	25	–	–	–	14	–	–	1	40
1888	7	11 July 1888	–	–	28	–	–	–	5	–	–	5	38
1886	6	9 December 1886	–	–	13	–	–	–	19	–	–	3	35
1883	5	23 January 1883	–	–	7	–	–	–	22	–	–	2	31
1879	4	16 December 1879	–	–	4	–	–	–	18	–	–	2	24
1878	3	18 December 1878	–	–	4	–	–	–	13	–	–	7	24
1874	2	23 December 1874	–	–	4	–	–	–	8	–	–	12	24[18]
1870	1	27 December 1870	–	–	1	–	–	–	8	–	–	15	24

Series Y302-387. Provincial government elections, party standing, and size of legislature, 1867 to 1977 (continued)

Saskatchewan

Year of election	Number of legis-lature	Date of election	Liberal	New Demo-cratic Party[18]	Progres-sive	Progres-sive Conser-vative[20]	Social Credit	Other	Size of legis-lature
	360	361	362	363	364	365	366	367	368
1975	18	11 June 1975	15	39	—	7	—	—	61
1971	17	23 June 1971	15	45	—	—	—	—	60
1967	16	11 October 1967	35	24[19]	—	—	—	—	59
1964	15	22 April 1964	33	25	—	1	—	—	59
1960	14	8 June 1960	17	38	—	—	—	—	55
1956	13	20 June 1956	14	36	—	—	3	—	53
1952	12	11 June 1952	11	42	—	—	—	—	53
1948	11	24 June 1948	19	31	—	—	—	2	52
1944	10	15 June 1944	5	47	—	—[20]	—	—	52[21]
1938	9	8 June 1938	38	10	—	—	2	2	52
1934	8	19 June 1934	50	5[22]	—	—	—	—	55
1929	7	6 June 1929	28	—	5	24	—	6	63
1925	6	2 June 1925	50	—	6	3	—	4	63
1921	5	9 June 1921	45	—	6	2	—	10	63
1917	4	26 June 1917	51	—	—	7	—	1	59[21]
1912	3	11 July 1912	46	—	—	8	—	—	54
1908	2	14 August 1908	27	—	—	14[23]	—	—	41
1905	1	13 December 1905	16	—	—	9[23]	—	—	25

Alberta

Year of election	Number of legis-ature	Date of election	Labour	Liberal	New Demo-cratic Party[4]	Progres-sive Conser-vative[17]	Social credit	United Farmers of Alberta	Other	Size of legis-lature
	369	370	371	372	373	374	375	376	377	378
1975	18	26 March 1975	—	—	1	69	4	—	1	75
1971	17	30 August 1971	—	—	1	49	24	—	1	75
1967	16	23 May 1967	—	3	—	6	55	—	1	65
1963	15	17 June 1963	—	2	—	—	60	—	1	63
1959	14	18 June 1959	—	1	—[4]	1	62	—	1	65
1955	13	29 June 1955	—	15	2	3	37	—	4	61
1952	12	5 August 1952	—	4	2	2	52	—	1	61
1948	11	17 August 1948	—	3	2	—	50	—	2	57
1944	10	8 August 1944	—	—	2	—[17]	51	—	4	57
1940	9	21 March 1940	1	1	—	—	36	—	19	57
1935	8	22 August 1935	—	5	—	2	56	—	—	63
1930	7	19 June 1930	4	11	—	5	—	39	4	63
1926	6	28 June 1926	6	7	—	4	—	43	—	60
1921	5	18 July 1921	4	13	—	1	—	39	2	59
1917	4	7 June 1917	1	33	—	19	—	1	4	58
1913	3	17 April 1913	—	39	—	17	—	—	—	56
1909	2	22 March 1909	—	36	—	2	—	—	3	41
1905	1	9 November 1905	—	23	—	2	—	—	—	25

Series Y302-387. Provincial government elections, party standing, and size of legislature, 1867 to 1977 (concluded)

Year of election	Number of legis- lature	Date of election	Labour	Liberal	New Demo- cratic Party[14]	Progres- sive Conser- vative[7]	Social Credit	Other[24]	Size of legis- lature
					British Columbia				
	379	380	381	382	383	384	385	386	387
1975	31	11 December 1975	–	1	18	1	35	–	55
1972	30	30 August 1972	–	5	38	2	10	–	55
1969	29	27 August 1969	–	5	12	–	38	–	55
1966	28	12 September 1966	–	6	16	–	33	–	55
1963	27	30 September 1963	–	5	14	–	33	–	52
1960	26	12 September 1960	–	4	16 [14]	–	32	–	52
1956	25	19 September 1956	1	2	10	–	39	–	52
1953	24	9 June 1953	1	4	14	1	28	–	48
1952	23	12 June 1952	1	6	18	4	19	–	48
1949	22	15 June 1949	2	39 [25]	7	– [25]	–	–	48
1945	21	25 October 1945	1	37 [25]	10	– [25]	–	–	48
1941	20	21 October 1941	1	21 [26]	14	12 [7,26]	–	–	48
1937	19	1 June 1937	1	31	7	8	–	1	48
1933	18	2 November 1933	1	34	7	–	–	5	47
1928	17	18 July 1928	1	12	–	35	–	–	48
1924	16	20 June 1924	3	27	–	16	–	2	48
1920	15	1 December 1920	–	26	–	14	–	7 [24]	47
1916	14	14 September 1916	–	37	–	9	–	1	47
1912	13	28 March 1912	–	–	–	40	–	2	42
1909	12	25 November 1909	–	3	–	36	–	3	42
1907	11	2 February 1907	–	13	–	26	–	3	42
1903	10	3 October 1903	1	17	–	21	–	3	42
1900	9	9 June 1900	–	–	–	–	–	–	38
1898	8	9 July 1898	–	–	–	–	–	–	38
1894	7	7 July 1894	–	–	–	–	–	–	33
1890	6	13 June 1890	–	–	–	–	–	–	33
1886	5	7 July 1886	–	–	–	–	–	–	26
1882	4	24 July 1882	–	–	–	–	–	–	26
1878	3	22 May 1878	–	–	–	–	–	–	26
1875	2	11 September 1875	–	–	–	–	–	–	25
1871	1	October-December 1871	–	–	–	–	–	–	25

[1] The Conservative Party became the Progressive Conservative Party in 1971.

[2] The legislature was bicameral until 1894. The series shows the assembly only, before that date.

[3] Includes several members whose affiliation is not known.

[4] The Cooperative Commonweath Federation became the New Democratic Party in 1962.

[5] The Conservative Party became the Progressive Conservative Party in 1946.

[6] The legislature was bicameral until 1928. The series shows the assembly only, before that date.

[7] The Conservative Party became the Progressive Conservative Party in 1943.

[8] The legislature was bicameral until 1893. The series shows the assembly only, before that date.

[9] United Farmers of New Brunswick.

[10] In 1968, the Rassemblement pour l'indépendance nationale and Mouvement souveraineté association amalgamated to form the Parti québécois.

[11] Union nationale formed in 1936 from Conservative and Action libérale nationale sources.

[12] The legislature was bicameral until 1968. The series shows the assembly only, before that date.

[13] One election (Kamouraska) annulled; seat vacant until 1871.

[14] The Cooperative Commonwealth Federation became the New Democratic Party in 1961.

[15] Includes 14 Patrons of Industry.

[16] Counts Unionists as Conservatives, and Reformers as Liberals.

[17] The Conservative Party became the Progressive Conservative Party in 1944.

[18] The legislature was bicameral until 1876. The series shows the assembly only, before that date.

[19] The Cooperative Commonwealth Federation became the New Democratic Party in 1967.

[20] The Conservative Party became the Progressive Conservative Party in 1945.

[21] Plus three armed services representatives.

[22] Farmer–Labour.

[23] Known as Provincial Rights party.

[24] Includes Socialist Party before 1924.

[25] Coalition of Liberal and Conservative parties.

[26] The Liberals and Conservatives formed a coalition to carry on as the government.

Section Z: Justice

Paul Reed, *Statistics Canada*

This section on crime and justice contains 328 series, arranged in four main sub-sections: crime and law enforcement, (series Z1-65); court proceedings, (series Z66-172); penal institutions, (series Z173-226); and juvenile delinquency, (series Z227-291). Population statistics are appended to facilitate use of the series, (series Z292-328). These series have been selected and arranged not only to provide usable quantitative information covering the field of criminal justice but also to indicate something of the historical development of justice statistics in Canada over the past century.

Although we have endeavoured to maintain essential continuity with series from the Justice Section in the first edition, numerous changes have been made for this second edition. Beyond the normal updating and revising of series, there have been additions and deletions reflecting developments in Canadian law and in justice statistics over the past 15 years. Extensive statistics from police forces, for example, have been included for the first time while series on suicide, bankruptcy and commercial failure have been omitted. Certain series (e.g. some on murder) have been included but drawn from different sources than in the first edition. In addition, the sequence of presentation of the series has been altered to accomodate these and other changes.

Endemic to extended time series is the question of their accuracy and consistency. For this section, potentially relevant figures which were known with certainty to be variably incomplete from year to year (such as police statistics on crime from 1920 to 1961) have been omitted.

The series pertain almost exclusively to criminal matters because there are so few data on other aspects of the justice system. In this respect, the organization and content of these statistics are naturally determined to a great degree by the organization of the criminal justice system itself. Criminal law is embodied principally in the Criminal Code of Canada, a federal statute which first came into force on 1 July 1893 and was founded on the English draft code of 1878. The Criminal Code was last revised in 1954 and came into effect on 1 April, 1955; the latest consolidated revisions were printed in 1970.

The British North America Act (BNA Act) of 1867 specifies in Section 91 that criminal law and procedures in criminal matters are under the exclusive authority of the Parliament of Canada; Section 92 states that the organization and maintenance of all provincial courts, both of civil and criminal jurisdiction, and of procedures in civil matters in these courts are under the legislative authority of the provinces. Under Section 92 of the BNA Act the provincial power to enforce provincial legislation by imposing penalties has resulted in the creation of an important body of law which is criminal in all but name but violation of which does not constitute an indictable offence under existing legislation (examples of this may be found in series Z60-61).

The provisions of the Criminal Code apply throughout Canada except (a) in the Northwest Territories, wherever they are inconsistent with the Northwest Territories Act, and (b) in the Yukon Territory, wherever they are inconsistent with the Yukon Act. In addition, Parliament may declare offences defined in other statutes to be criminal acts (i.e., the Narcotic Control Act) and to put such declarations into force throughout Canada; this fact increases the comparability of data in time series of criminal offences.

By the very nature of law breaking and law enforcement in our society, statistics pertaining to crime and justice are not, by and large, simple measures of simple phenomena. Measuring crime and justice activities has long been one of the more intractable problems of social statistics for a variety of reasons. Because a significant proportion of crime is not reported or known to the police, it is not investigated, prosecuted, punished - or statistically enumerated. It has been observed that criminal statistics are facts (more or less faithfully recorded) about the amount of business that officially comes to the attention of the criminal justice system, and how it is dealt with; but these are only partial and selective facts about actual crime and criminals. As well, there are alternative, different, and sometimes incommensurate units of count, which may be used to measure the same phenomenon. The series which follow, for example, variously give counts of incidents, persons, occurrences, offences, offenders, appearances, victims, convictions, etc. The locus and mode of measurement or enumeration may seriously affect the statistics - crime as measured by the police is not likely to coincide with a measure taken from the courts; unduplicated counts of persons are notoriously more difficult to prepare accurately than duplicated counts. Of course, because criminal acts are defined by law, statistical measures of crime may change whenever the law is changed.

Since the measure of crime is a function of the level and nature of law enforcement and judicial activity, it is not possible, using official statistics, to measure the extent or the nature of crime in Canada independently of measuring the behaviour of the justice system.

The 1970s have witnessed several new trends in the field of justice statistics. Considerable criticism has been levelled against official statistics on crime and justice in Canada and other countries in recent years for both technical and conceptual shortcomings. With the computerization of administrative record systems and statistical data processing, some technical improvements have been made such as evaluating and reducing the non-reporting of data. The problem of interdependency between statistical measures of crime and law enforcement is being addressed through special direct surveys of the population to ascertain the extent of criminal victimizations.

Computerization has also resulted in improved statistical coverage or detail in some programs. However, the very large increases in the workload of the entire justice system has made the derivation of statistical data from administrative record-keeping systems much more complex and costly.

Statistics On Crime And Law Enforcement (Series Z1-65)

General note

Police statistics on crime were first published in Canada in 1921 as a section of *Criminal-Statistics,-1920*. These statistics were provided in the early years by only a small and incomplete number of municipal police forces. Over the ensuing four decades, there was a gradual increase in the number of police forces reporting and in the detail of the figures they reported. These statistics did not at all provide a full picture of crime or law enforcement in Canada, and were not comparable from year to year until 1 January 1962, when the Uniform Crime Reporting (UCR) System commenced. This system was developed by the Dominion Bureau of Statistics in concert with the Canadian Association of Chiefs of Police, Commitee on the Uniform Recording of Police Statistics. The UCR system was designed to provide more complete, accurate, and standardized (comparable) statistics on crime and police activity in Canada than had previously been possible.

Initially, the system required police departments to send monthly crime statistics reports to Statistics Canada covering 19 Criminal Code offence categories, the Narcotic Control Act, the Food and Drug Act, other federal statutes, and municipal by-laws. Standardized offence definitions and rules for counting were established. In the reporting of offences, police included the number reported or known to the police, offences adjudged by police to be unfounded, the actual number (calculated by substracting the number of unfounded offences from reported or known offences), offences cleared (or solved), and persons charged. Separate figures were compiled for both adults and juveniles who were charged. The upper age limit for juveniles was specified by each province under the Juvenile Delinquents Act.

These rules of compilation continue to the present with the same person being counted for each separate incident or occasion where he or she is charged with the commission of an offence. (An incident is the alleged occurrence of at least one offence in one single, distinct, place and time.) Where several charges are laid against a person for offences in one incident, only the most serious offence is counted by police for statistical purposes. The most serious offence is defined as the one having the greatest maximum penalty by law, or the offence that is considered the most serious by police when the penalties are the same, or the offence which appears first in the offence classification.

Since commencement of the UCR system in 1962 there have been minor changes to increase the number of offence categories and (in 1974) to report the number of juveniles dealt with informally as well as formally, but there have been no fundamental changes in the basic rules of the reporting system.

Under the UUCR system, crime reports are expected from all police forces in communities with a population of 750 and over, including urban areas policed under contract by the Royal Canadian Mounted Police (RCMP), the Ontario Provincial Police, and the Quebec Provincial Police (now the Quebec Police Force). Also included are communities of less than 750 population, townships, districts and rural municipalities policed under contract by the RCMP, QPP, or OPP. Excluded from the reporting system are communities of less than 750 population, and communities of more than 750 which do not have police forces or contracted police protection. In 1962, there were 698 urban communities in Canada with a population of over 750 operating their own police forces, and reports were received from 91.4 percent of these communities (although some respondents submitted reports for only part of the year as it was the inaugural year of the Uniform Crime Reporting System). In addition, of course, reports were submitted by the RCMP, the OPP and the QPP. Because nearly all of the non-reporting communities were small in size, it is estimated that | this non-reporting and part-year reporting resulted in a national statistical under-enumeration less than 2 per cent of crime recorded by police.

In 1975, there were 503 urban communities having populations of over 750 operating their own police forces. (The process of amalgamation and merging of smaller forces and new agreements between municipalities and contracted police forces accounts for the continuing decline in the number of potential reporting points.) In 1975, reports were received from 96.2 per cent of these communities.

While statistics were tabulated manually and mechanically from police reports for publication in 1962, by 1973 all statistics were created by computer, with a substantial portion of the total volume of statistical data on crimes being submitted to Statistics Canada on magnetic tape.

Commencing in 1974, police-reported crime statistics have been presented in broad groupings: (i) crimes of violence, (ii) property crimes, (iii) other Criminal Code offences, (iv) federal statute drug offences, (v) other federal statute offences, (vi) provincial statute offences, and (vii) municipal by-law offences. By agreement of the Uniform Crime Reporting Committee of the Canadian Association of Chiefs of Police, only selected Criminal Code offences were to be reported by police forces in sufficient detail to permit those offences to be included in the first two groups - crimes of violence and property crimes. For this reason, these two general categories do not include all the appropriate offences; not included in the category, 'crimes of violence', is kidnapping, for example, while both arson and wilful damage are omitted from the category of 'property crimes'. These and other such offences are included in the category, 'other Criminal Code offences'. There is one exception to this which should be noted, however; robbery, although classified in the Criminal Code as an offence "against the right of property", is counted in these crime statistics as a crime of violence.

Statistics produced by the UCR system constitute official crime statistics in Canada. Questions have been raised in recent years as to the reliability of these statistics as accurate measures of the extent and nature of crime in Canada. It is now recognized, for example, that a significant portion of criminal occurrences are not reported to or known by the police; it is also known that changes in law enforcement policies or programs may have a marked effect on crime statistics, making comparisons over time and among jurisdictions highly problematic. These statistics, then, are a mixed measure of both law-breaking and law enforcement behaviour together. Insofar as they are a measure of crime or law-breaking, they are a measure only of publicly known and recorded crime and are probably more indicative of the distribution or nature of this law breaking than of its magnitude.

Z1-14.   Actual and cleared offences reported by police, by type of offence, Canada, 1962 to 1975

SOURCE: 1972 to 1975, Statistics Canada, *Crime and Traffic Enforcement Statistics*, (Catalogue 85-205); for 1961 to

1971, Dominion Bureau of Statistics, *Crime Statistics (Police)*, (Catalogue 85-205).

Statistics derived from reports by police forces and published by Statistics Canada prior to 1962 were incomplete and therefore could not be compared from year to year. The two categories, 'crimes of violence' and 'crimes against property', correspond to categories conventionally used in UCR publications; they do not correspond to the distinction in the Criminal Code between offences against the person and offences against property. In crime statistics, robbery is classified as a crime of violence while the Criminal Code classifies it as an offence against property. In similar fashion, the Criminal Code classifies kidnapping and abduction as offences against the person, yet they are excluded from the category of 'crimes of violence' in crime statistics and listed instead as 'other criminal code'.

In the Uniform Crime Report statistics, 'crimes of violence' comprises murder, manslaughter, infanticide (for 1974 and 1975 only), rape, indecent assault, assault, and robbery. 'Property crimes' is a category encompassing breaking and entering, theft, possession of stolen goods, and fraud. Up to 1971, the Criminal Code distinguished between 'theft of $50 and under' and 'theft over $50'. This was changed in 1972 to 'theft of $200 and under' and 'theft over $200' respectively. This is one of many statutory changes which inevitably have had an effect on the statistics and must be taken into account when making year-to-year comparisons using the subcategories of theft.

Federal drug offences are those specified by the Narcotic Control Act and the Food and Drugs Act. Other federal statute offences are those specified by such federal statutes as the Post Office Act, Bankruptcy Act, Customs Act, Excise Act, and others.

Z15-20. Murder, actual offences and persons charged, Canada, 1961 to 1975

Source: for 1972 to 1975, Statistics Canada, *Crime and Traffic Enforcement Statistics*, (Catalogue 85-205); for 1962 to 1971, Statistics Canada *Crime Statistics (Police)*, (Catalogue 85-205); for 1961, Statistics Canada Judicial Division, unpublished figures.

Since 1961, a Homicide Statistics program has been operated by Statistics Canada in conjunction with police forces across the country. Whenever an unusual death is reported to or found by police, it is investigated and designated as either accidental or a homicide of some kind - either a murder, manslaughter, or infanticide. All cases of homicide are statistically recorded through the Uniform Crime Reporting program; as well, more detailed information is transmitted on a special form to the Homicide Statistics program of Statistics Canada. Because figures are prepared more rigorously in the Homicide Statistics program and are continuously being updated, they do not always coincide perfectly with figures in published crime reports. Series Z15-20 are drawn from annual crime reports; series Z21-27 are derived from the Homicide Statistics program.

In Canadian law, murder is the most serious form of culpable homicide (the others being manslaughter and infanticide). Broadly stated, it is the act of unlawfully causing the death of another person intentionally, or recklessly with intent to cause bodily harm. The legal definition of murder and its several specific forms has undergone numerous changes since 1961. (For a summary of these changes, see the Appendix, *Homicide in Canada*.)

Z15. One murder offence is counted for every victim. In incidents having more than one victim, as many offences would be counted as there were victims. All such reported offences are those believed or alleged by police to have been murder; subsequent investigation in some cases reveals that it was not, in fact, a murder. Furthermore, a significant proportion of cases designated as murder by police are ultimately found by courts not to be murder. Thus, the count of actual murder offences is, to an unknown degree, higher than the true number.

Z16. When police, in each case, establish the identity of the person or persons believed to have committed the murder, they lay a charge of murder against that person. (Only in a few rare exceptions is no charge laid - when the suspect is in a mental institution or has left the country, for example.) Although a person may have more than one murder charge laid against him in an incident where there are several victims, that person would be counted only once for statistical purposes.

Z21. Number of criminal homicide deaths, Canada, 1926 to 1975

SOURCE: for 1975, Statistics Canada, *Murder Statistics*, (Catalogue 85-209); for 1961 to 1974, Statistics Canada, *Homicide in Canada*, (Catalogue 85-505); for 1926 to 1960, *Historical Statistics of Canada*, first edition, Section Y: Justice, series Y67.

The number of murder offences (series Z15) does not provide a valid measure of the total number of criminal homicide deaths. In Canada, there are two separate and quite different national statistical programs within Statistics Canada to enumerate the number of criminal homicide deaths: the Homicide Statistics program of the Justice Statistics Division, and the Vital Statistics Section of the Health Division. These two systems draw data from different sources and according to different definitions and rules of counting; naturally, the figures they produce are not identical. While the basic data in the Homicide Statistics program is provided by police forces throughout the country, Vital Statistics figures are based on reports from death certificates provided by provincial registrars, which are usually issued by coroners following a post-mortem inquiry, investigation, or inquest. In the Homicide Statistics program, homicide is defined to include all suspected cases of criminal homicide (murder, manslaughter, and infanticide) occurring in Canada, regardless of whether a suspect has been identified in the killing; it does not include Canadian residents killed in other countries as does the Vital Statistics program.

Figures in Series Z21 have been drawn from both sources - for the years 1961 to 1975, from the Homicide Statistics program; for the years 1926 to 1960, from *Historical Statistics of Canada* which in turn drew its figures from both Vital Statistics reports (with some adjustment) and from annual reports of the Joint Committee of the Senate and the House of Commons on Capital Punishment, Corporal Punishment and Lotteries. Excluded from figures for all years are cases of criminal negligence causing death, deaths due to legal intervention by the police, deaths by legal execution, and deaths due to the late effects of some criminal act.

Z22-27. Murder incidents, distribution by type of suspect-victim relationship, Canada, 1961 to 1975

SOURCE: for 1975, Statistics Canada, *Murder Statistics*, (Catalogue 85-209); for 1961 to 1974, Statistics Canada, *Homicide in Canada*, (Catalogue 85-505).

The phenomenon of murder may be enumerated in terms of the number of victims (or offences), or the number of incidents. An incident is the occurrence of one or more criminal offences at one place and time in what is essentially a single event. For every incident designated as murder, police record it as being unsolved, or if solved, the nature of the incident in terms of the relationship between suspect(s) and victim(s).

Z28-33 Rape, actual offences and persons charged, Canada, 1962 to 1975

SOURCE: for 1972 to 1975, Statistics Canada, *Crime and Traffic Enforcement Statistics*, (Catalogue 85-205); for 1962 to 1971, Statistics Canada *Crime Statistics (Police)*, (Catalogue 85-205).

Rape is an offence whose statistical incidence is especially prone to being affected by social factors and law enforcement policies. It is a crime long known to be seriously underenumerated because of the unwillingness of many victims to report the event to police. There is believed to have been a relaxation in recent years in this reluctance to report, possibly creating the appearance of a greater increase in the number and rate of rape offences than may actually have taken place.

Rape is also notable for having an unusually high proportion of offences which are reported or known to the police ultimately designated by police as unfounded, resulting in a significantly lower count of 'actual' offences. The unreliability of statistics on rape offences is further exacerbated by variations in law enforcement policy pertaining to whether an incident is statistically classified as rape, attempted rape, or indecent assault on a female. Careful examination of figures since 1974 (when the last offence was designated for the first time in published crime statistics) shows great variation among the provinces in the extent and proportion of rape and attempted rape, and indecent assault on a female.

Although the Criminal Code defines rape as an offence committed by males, females are charged with the offence as well by virtue of being parties to the offence under Section 21 of the Criminal Code of Canada.

Z34-39. Assault (not indecent), actual offences and persons charged, Canada, 1962 to 1975

SOURCE: for 1972 to 1975, Statistics Canada, *Crime and Traffic Enforcement Statistics*, (Catalogue 85-205); for 1962 to 1971, Statistics Canada *Crime Statistics (Police)*, (Catalogue 85-205).

The Criminal Code states that "a person commits an assault when (a) without the consent of another person or with consent, where it is obtained by fraud, he applies force intentionally to the person of the other, directly or indirectly; (b) he attempts or threatens, by an act or gesture, to apply force to the person of the other, if he has or causes the other to believe upon reasonable grounds that he has present ability to effect his purpose; or (c) while openly wearing or carrying a weapon or an imitation thereof, he accosts or impedes another person and begs."

Figures on assault reported by police currently (1973 onward) include wounding, assault causing bodily harm, assault on a police officer, assault on a public officer or peace officer, and other assaults. The latter category comprises common assault, assault with intent to resist arrest, and assault to rescue goods seized. Indecent assaults are classified as sexual offences and excluded from the statistical category of assaults. From 1962 to 1973, figures for only two categories of assault were published: wounding and assault - not indecent. (From 1951, when assaults were first reported by police, until 1961, figures were published for aggravated assault or assault causing bodily harm, and assault on a police, public, or peace officer.) Depending on the seriousness and circumstances of an assault, law enforcement officials may lay a charge of either common assault (the least serious), assault causing bodily harm, wounding, or attempted murder (the most serious, but statistically recorded in regular publications in the category of homicide).

Z40-45. Robbery, actual offences and persons charged, Canada, 1962 to 1975

SOURCE: for 1972 to 1975, Statistics Canada, *Crime and Traffic Enforcement Statistics*, (Catalogue 85-205); for 1962 to 1971, Statistics Canada, *Crime Statistics (Police)*, (Catalogue 85-205).

Robbery is defined in the Criminal Code to be stealing or unlawful taking with violence, the threat of violence, or while armed. Notwithstanding this, the Criminal Code designates robbery to be an offence against the rights of property. It is therefore a criminal act both against property and against the person. In police-reported crime statistics, it is classified as a crime of violence; in court-reported statistics, it is classified as an offence against property.

Z46-51. Breaking and entering, actual offences and persons charged, Canada, 1962 to 1975

SOURCE: for 1972 to 1975, Statistics Canada, *Crime and Traffic Enforcement Statistics*, (Catalogue 85-205); for 1962 to 1971, Statistics Canada, *Crime Statistics, (Police)* (Catalogue 85-205).

Breaking and entering includes any unlawful entry of a place with intent to commit or the commission of an indictable offence, whether or not force was used to gain entry. A 'place' may be a dwelling house, a building or other such structure, or a vehicle, vessel, aircraft, or trailer. Where it is a dwelling house that is unlawfully entered, the maximum penalty is life imprisonment; the maximum penalty for unlawful entry into any other place is fourteen years.

Prior to 1974, published crime statistics provided only an aggregate count of breaking and entering offences; since 1974, published statistics have indicated separately the number of offences of breaking and entering of business premises, of residences, and of other places.

Z52-57. Theft, actual offences and persons charged, Canada, 1962 to 1975

SOURCE: for 1972 to 1975, Statistics Canada, *Crime and Traffic Enforcement Statistics*, (Catalogue 85-205); for 1962 to 1971, Statistics Canada *Crime Statistics (Police)*, (Catalogue 85-205).

From the commencement of the UCR system in 1962 until 1971, figures for three categories of theft were published:

theft - motor vehicle, theft over $50, and theft of $50 and under. In 1972, the latter two categories were changed to theft over $200, and theft of $200 and under, respectively, directly as a result of amendments to the Criminal Code.

In 1974 and in subsequent years, figures have been published not only for these three main categories of theft but for more specific types of theft within each; for theft - motor vehicle, separate statistics are shown for thefts of automobiles, of trucks, of motorcycles, and of other motor vehicles. For the other two main categories of theft, separate statistics are shown for thefts of bicycles, thefts from motor vehicles, shoplifting, and other thefts. Figures given in Series Z52-57 are aggregate counts covering all categories and types of theft as reported by police.

Z58-62. Serious traffic incidents with persons charged, and minor traffic charges, Canada, 1962 to 1975

SOURCE: for 1972 to 1975, Statistics Canada, *Crime and Traffic Enforcement Statistics*, (Catalogue 85-205); for 1962 to 1971, Statistics Canada, *Traffic Enforcement Statistics*, (Catalogue 85-206).

One of the major responsibilities of police is to enforce traffic laws and to investigate motor vehicle accidents. Statistics are provided in series Z58-62 as a measure of police activity in the latter areas. Traffic incidents are those in which one or more motor vehicles are involved, with motor vehicles comprising automobiles, trucks, motorcycles, and other mechanically or otherwise propelled road vehicles except those which operate on rails.

Although traffic statistics were published by Statistics Canada for many years prior to 1962, the figures were incomplete and incomparable for the same reasons as were crime statistics. With the advent of the UCR system (which covered traffic as well as crime statistics), 1962 was the first year of relatively reliable traffic statistics, which are reported by exactly the same police forces as report crime statistics.

Since 1962, up to eight Criminal Code traffic offence categories have been separately reported, along with traffic offences under three provincial statutes. The Criminal Code offences are criminal negligence causing death, criminal negligence causing bodily harm, criminal negligence in operating a motor vehicle, failing to stop or remain at the scene of an accident, dangerous driving, failing or refusing to provide a sample of breath, driving while impaired, and driving while disqualified or while license suspended or cancelled. The provincial statute offences are failing to stop or remain at the scene of an accident, dangerous driving or without due care and attention, and driving while disqualified or while license suspended or cancelled. For these Criminal Code and provincial statute offences, the actual numbers of offences and the numbers of persons charged have been provided by police since 1962. For minor traffic offences under all other federal and provincial statutes and municipal by-laws, only the total number of charges laid is reported each year. (The numbers of charges, shown in series Z62, cannot be compared with the numbers of persons charged, shown in series Z59 and Z61.)

Because of the fact that the three selected provincial statute offences closely parallel certain Criminal Code offences, police have the discretionary authority to lay a charge under either the Criminal Code or under the respective provincial Highway Traffic Act. Law enforcement policy varies from province to province and among police forces in which statute is used.

In the chronology of traffic statistics in Canada, several interesting items may be cited. In 1876, the first year of nationally published judicial statistics, there is no reference to offences of a traffic nature. In 1900, there was a statistical record of convictions and sentences for offences relating to highways. Figures for 1920 provided more specific details as to breaches of various street and traffic regulations - by motor vehicles, by bicycles, by cabs and drays, and by obstructing street and sidewalk. Further included in 1922 figures were breaches of street and traffic regulations by vehicles exceeding the speed limit, and in 1923, by vehicles overloading, and in 1924, by driving a motor vehicle while drunk. In 1938, driving while drunk was statistically recorded as an indictable offence.

Z63-65. Police strength in Canada, 1920 to 1975

SOURCE: for 1960 to 1975, Statistics Canada, *Police Administration Statistics*, (Catalogue 85-204); for 1950 to 1959, Statistics Canada, *Police Statistics* (Catalogue 85-203); for 1926 to 1949, Statistics Canada, *Statistics of Criminal and Other Offences*, Police Statistics Section; for 1921 to 1925, Statistics Canada, *Criminal Statistics*, Police Statistics Section.

In their annual reports to Statistics Canada which commenced in 1921, municipal police forces recorded the number of policemen employed as of 31 December of the preceding year. Until standardization and full reporting by all police forces was implemented in the Uniform Crime Reporting system in 1962, the published figures did not provide complete or accurate totals. From 1920 until 1946 figures were given only for a partial and changing number of municipal police forces, and the ratio of policemen per 1,000 population (Series Z64) for those years and until 1956 applied only as an average to reporting municipalities.

In 1947 figures were added for the RCMP, the British Columbia Provincial Police, the Canadian Pacific Railway Police, and the Canadian National Railway Police, followed in 1948 by the further addition of the OPP. (In 1950, law enforcement in British Columbia was taken over by the RCMP under contract to the provincial government.) The QPP first provided figures in 1960, but only for certain municipal areas in which they had jurisdiction. Prior to 1960, reports were received from municipal police forces only in urban areas having populations of 4,000 or more. In 1960, this was changed to urban areas having populations of 750 or more.

With implementation of the UCR system in 1962, the final major changes in police reporting of administrative information took place providing complete and standardized statistics; the QPP provided figures for the entire force, and the National Harbours Board Police commenced reporting. There has in subsequent years been some improvement in the level of detail of reported figures.

Statistics On Court Proceedings (Series Z66-172)

General note

Statistics on criminal judicial proceedings in Canada have been collected from courts and published on a nationwide basis since 1876. The Criminal Statistics Act of that year made specific provisions for the furnishing of information by the various trial courts of general jurisdiction on their criminal proceedings and by wardens of penal institutions on their inmates to the Minister of Agriculture who published until 1911 an annual report based on these returns. The first reports, entitled *Criminal Statistics*, showed the number of persons charged, acquitted and convicted, with sentences for the latter, by judicial district, and by types of offences, together with the major social characteristics of convicted persons. For the years 1912 to 1916, the annual reports were published under the aegis of the Minister of Trade and Commerce; since 1917, they have been published by Statistics Canada. The first Statistics Act of 1918, which provided for the establishment of the Bureau, consolidated the stipulations of the Criminal Statistics Act concerning the centralized collection of statistics by requiring that information pertaining to court proceedings be transmitted to the Dominion Statistician. Thus, The Dominion Bureau of Statistics collected and Statistics Canada continues to collect data on criminal proceedings from registrars of the Assize and General Sessions of the Peace and Supreme Courts,, and from clerks of provincial, county and district courts, officials of the Magistrate's and Family Courts, and from Justices of the Peace.

In 1926, the title of the published annual statistical reports was changed from *Criminal Statistics* to *Statistics of Criminal and Other Offences*, and this latter title has continued to the latest year of publication, 1972. These publications constitute a continuous statistical record covering nearly an entire century; few of the constituent series, however, have continued without change of some kind over this period. For example, in 1876 the basic and initial unit of count was 'persons charged'; in 1895 the figures were given as 'charges' until 1923, when the primary unit of count reverted to 'persons charged'. In 1926 the figures changed once again to 'charges' which remained in effect through 1948. The figures for 1949 and all subsequent years have been for 'persons charged'. These two units of statistical tabulation differ significantly and cannot be used interchangeably.

The comparibility of these judicial statistics is further restricted by changes in the method of counting. A person may be charged with one or more offences occurring in the same single incident, and may be convicted of more than one offence at the same trial. Prior to 1893, there was partial unduplicated counting of identical charges and convictions for the same incident and heard at the same trial; that is, if a person was charged and convicted for two offences of robbery, only one was recorded, but if the same person was charged and convicted at the same trial of both assault and robbery, both offences were recorded. From 1893 through 1948, all charges and convictions were counted, including duplicate ones. During this period, for every accused person charged and (or) convicted for more than one offence at the same trial, each one of the offences was recorded.

A Dominion-Provincial conference on Criminal Statistics, held in Ottawa in 1949, proposed that the basic unit of compilation become the person. Consequently figures for 1949 and all subsequent years provide a fully unduplicated count of persons with each different individual being counted once, for only one selected offence for which he or she was charged or convicted, regardless of the total number of charges or convictions that may have been registered against him or her during the calendar year. This offence is selected according to the following criteria: (i) if the person was tried on several charges, the offence selected is that for

which proceedings were carried to the furthest stage - conviction and sentence; (ii) if there were several convictions, the offence selected is that for which the heaviest punishment was imposed; (iii) if the final result of proceedings on two or more charges was the same, the offence selected is the more serious one as measured by the maximum penalty allowed by law; (iv) if a person was prosecuted for one offence and convicted of another - for example, charged with murder and convicted of manslaughter - the offence selected is the one of which the person was convicted.

Although the figures published since 1949 based on an unduplicated count of persons are not directly comparable with figures for earlier years, in order to make some historical comparisons possible, Statistics Canada continued to published a limited number of tables showing figures based on offences. Comparisons of figures for extended historical periods should be made only with careful reading both of footnotes to the series presented in this chapter and of explanatory notes in the annual publications, *Criminal Statistics* and *Statistics of Criminal and Other Proceedings*. (For a detailed study of the continuities and discontinuities in these published series, see the Justice Statistics Division's research report, *Judicial Statistics as History: A Case Study,* prepared in 1974.)

For the preceeding reasons generally, and because the extent of non-reporting and under-reporting by courts is unknown but believed to have been significant, the figures must be used with extreme caution. Also making difficult the comparison of figures between years were such factors as changes in the legal definition of offences and sometimes in the meaning attached even to common terms, as well as changes in police and court procedures. An offence is any violation of the law; if the law changes, or if it is not enforced in the same way by the group whose function it is to do so, the comparability of the statistics is affected. There are always new laws which accompany social changes and new laws 'create' new offences.

Changes and improvements in collecting and processing source data as well as changes in the number and sizes of reporting units also affect the comparability of these judicial statistics. In 1876, there were 85 judicial districts reporting and by 1972 the number had risen to about 1200 counts, from which about 40,000 forms were received (exclusive of Alberta and Québec). No data were provided from the Yukon Territory until 1899; from Alberta and Saskatchewan until 1906; and from Newfoundland until 1951. Likewise, no data from Quebec and Alberta have been included in published statistics after 1968 as a result of the development of different court statistics systems in those provinces. (Statistics for Quebec for 1968, 1969, and 1970 will become available from Statistics Canada in September, 1978; figures for Quebec for other years, and for Alberta, may be released at an unspecified later date.) These variations in the number of reporting jurisdictions must be taken into account when analysing the figures, especially for trend analysis.

Criminal offences consist of an array of prohibited acts, ranging from the relatively minor offence of a traffic violation to murder, the most serious crime. Generally, the more serious crimes are by far the least numerous, but socially and legally the most important. Canada's legal system recognizes two broad types of offence: indictable offences, which include all serious crimes covered by the Criminal Code as well as by such other federal statutes as the Combines Investigation Act, the Food and Drugs Act, the Narcotic Control Act, the Customs Act, and the Post Office

Act, and summary or non-indictable offences which comprise all breaches of municipal by-laws and provincial statutes, and certain federal statutes, including less serious Criminal Code offences. Indictable offences are serious offences by virtue of being considered to be offences not only against a person but against the state and the entire social order. Indictable offences are specifically designated as such in the statutes creating them and providing for their punishment. Indictable offences differ from summary offences as well by having in many instances more formal and more varied modes of trial and appeal procedure and by carrying more severe maximum penalties. Summary or ordinary offences are those which are not expressly made indictable; they are, as a rule, minor misdemeanours and are at most considered wronging the person only and not society. The distinction between indictable and other offences is not based entirely on the nature of the act itself because in some cases the same act may be qualified as indictable or not according to the circumstances or severity of the act or according to the mode of trial which is elected by the Crown (prosecutor). Offences have been classified under these two headings since the inception of published court statistics in 1876. Only figures relating to indictable offences are presented in the time series in this section; statistics relating to the other offences can be found in the annual reports, *Criminal Statistics* and *Statistics of Criminal and Other Offences*.

In the published annual reports of court statistics, the distinction has traditionally been made among a number of broad, general classes of indictable offences: (i) offences against the person, (ii) offences against property with violence, (iii) offences against property without violence, (iv) malicious offences against property, (v) forgery and offences relating to currency, and (vi) other offences. It should be noted that these general classes do not fully correspond either to offence groupings in the Criminal Code or, in recent years, to the general categories used in police-reported crime statistics - crimes of violence, property crimes, other Criminal Code offences, federal statute offences, provincial statute offences, and municipal by-law offences. The six offence groupings in published court statistics may not, therefore, be compared with those in UCR crime statistics. However, the offences contained in the groupings in court statistics have remained consistent since the series began in 1876 (with the exception of enactment and repeal of statutes specifying offences within these groupings) and may, other things being equal, be compared over time.

It should be noted that all figures given in this section on court proceedings are almost exclusively for adults; statistics on court proceedings involving juveniles will be presented separately in a later sub-section, due to the significantly different ways in which these proceedings involving juveniles must, by law, be conducted. This caveat also covers juveniles whose cases were elevated to adult court, except in Series Z109-123.

The figures presented in these series concerning court proceedings do not by any means represent the total number of offences, nor do they reliably represent the total number of offenders. They provide a measure of those offences which were prosecuted and statistically reported as such. Only an unmeasured portion of all committed offences are known to law enforcement officials, and not all of those

which are known are prosecuted. Thus, these statistics are principally a measure of court proceedings and decisions. Because of the unknown magnitude of non-reporting and under- reporting by courts, and because of the changing method of enumeration, these figures probably should not be taken singly nor literally as reliable counts of the units given (persons, convictions, etc.); rather, they ought to be viewed at best as measures of relative distributions, on the untested assumption that the rate of non-reporting and under-reporting does not vary sufficiently from year to year, from sex to sex, and from region to region, to distort their representativeness.

Z66-78. Convictions for indictable offences of persons aged 16 years and older, Canada, and the provinces, 1886 to 1972

SOURCE: for 1961 to 1972, Statistics Canada, *Statistics of Criminal and Other Offences*, (Catalogue 85-201); for 1886 to 1960, *Historical Statistics of Canada*, first edition, Section Y: Justice, series Y1-13.

Although national court-reported statistics were first published in 1876, figures for years prior to 1886 are not comparable with those for later years. Until 1884, no distinction was made between indictable and other offences, and in 1885 the indictable offences which were tried summarily were counted with the summary offences. Several other features make difficult the comparison of figures from year to year. Up to and including 1950, figures are given for the 12 months ending 30 September; later figures are for the calendar year. Until 1948, statistics on indictable crime were compiled on the basis of offences and figures for the number of persons convicted are not available on a satisfactory basis (see introductory note to this section for a fuller explanation). Even after 1949, some duplications existed in the data based on the number of persons convicted; in 1953, revised processing methods eliminated some duplication.

Allowance must also be made for the fact that not all provinces and territories are included in every year's figures (see footnotes to the table), and after 1967 the figures were prepared according to the various provincial upper age limits for juveniles (see footnote (2) of series Z19-20 for details) instead of the uniform upper age limit of 16 years. Figures pertaining to juveniles under age 16 (or the respective provincial age limit in 1968 and subsequent years) are given in series Z227-248.

The convictions enumerated in these and other following series derived from *Statistics of Criminal and Other Offences* are from trial courts and are not necessarily the final disposition, some of the verdicts (both convictions and acquittals) of lower courts are disallowed or overturned by appellate courts. Separate figures on appeals are provided in series Z168-172.

Z79-84. Convictions for indictable offences by type of offence, Canada, 1886 to 1972

SOURCE: for 1961 to 1972, Statistics Canada, *Statistics of Criminal and Other Offences*, (Catalogue 85-201); for 1886 to 1960, *Historical Statistics of Canada*, first edition Section Y: Justice, series Y27-32.

Figures prior to 1886 have been omitted as not comparable (see comments for Series Z66-78). A set of historical figures for the period 1876 through 1936, in which no distinction is made between indictable and other offences, can be found in the annual report for 1936, Statistics of Criminal and Other Offences, Historical Appendix, table I.

Figures for 1886 to 1921 include both adults and juveniles under 16 years of age; these figures are not comparable with those for 1922 and later years which relate only to persons aged 16 years and over.

Offences are grouped in classes which correspond only approximately to major divisions of the Criminal Code. These classes have remained in use in judicial statistics since 1876; while they may have closely approximated major divisions of the law in those early years, they do so only imperfectly today as a result of the evolution of the criminal law in Canada over the past century.

Offences against federal statutes other than the Criminal Code are included and classified under the heading 'other offences', series Z84. Figures in this residual category are strongly influenced by the inclusion of new offences and of existing summary offences made indictable by new provisions in the law, as well as by changes in judicial practices relating to offences which may be tried either as indictable or as non-indictable, according to the circumstances or the severity of the case.

Z79. Since 1876 'offences against the person' have included not only murder, rape, assaults of various kinds, kidnapping and abduction, but also such varied offences as bigamy and polygamy, seduction, procuration, carnally knowing a girl of tender years, incest and other sexual offences, abandoning child, wife desertion, neglecting to provide for family, abortion, infanticide, libel, dangerous operation of a vessel, intimidation, endangering safety of passengers on a railway, threatening letters, criminal negligence causing no death or harm, and numerous others.

Z80. 'Offences against property with violence' include robbery, highway robbery, extortion, burglary, having burglars tools, breaking and entering, possession of explosives and damages by, forcible entry and detainer, and others.

Z81. 'Offences against property without violence' have comprised theft, theft of stray cattle, receiving or having in possession stolen goods, false pretenses, fraud, embezzlement, sacrilege, bringing stolen property into Canada, stealing post letters, theft by conversion, and others.

Z82. 'Malicious offences against property' is a category consisting almost exclusively of arson and attempted arson, killing and maiming cattle; also included are other unspecified malicious injuries to or interference with property.

Z83. 'Forgery and offences against currency' include counterfeiting, forgery, uttering forged documents, and other offences against currency.

Z84. 'Other offences' includes a large number of other offences specified by the Criminal Code, other federal statutes, provincial statutes, and municipal by-laws. Among those specifically cited in Criminal Statistics and Statistics of Criminal and Other Offences are counselling or aiding suicide, gambling, having an illicit still, riot, indecent exposure, threatening or insulting or profane language, keeping or frequenting a bawdy house, escaping prison, smuggling, vagrancy, sedition and usury. Offences defined by other federal statutes which may be included in this category in some years are the Post Office Act, the Excise Act and Customs Act, the Combines Investigation Act, the Bank Act,

the Trade Mark Act, the Election Act, and the Bankruptcy Act. Among the Provincial statute offences included are breaches of liquor laws and traffic laws such as dangerous driving and failing to stop at the scene of an accident.

Z85-93.   Sentences for indictable offences, Canada, 1886 to 1951

SOURCE: Historical Statistics of Canada, first edition, Section Y: Justice, series Y33-41.

These series are presented unchanged from the first edition of Historical Statistics of Canada. The publication of figures in series Z85-93 tabulated on the basis of convictions was discontinued in 1951, two years after the changing of the basic counting unit from offence to person. For similar figures covering the period 1952 to 1972, see series Z94-102,

Figures for 1886 through 1921 include both adults and juveniles under 16 years of age and are not comparable with those for later years relating only to adult persons aged 16 years and over.

Courts impose sentences which are authorized and in some cases required by law. Thus, changes between years in each of these series may reflect not only an increase or decrease in the number of offences for which the sentence indicated in the heading was imposed, but also changes in the provisions of the law with respect to minimum or mandatory sentences, changes in judicial practices (greater leniency or severity), and changes in available penal facilities and institutions required to carry out a specific type of sentence. Figures in series Z88 and Z93 are especially affected by this last factor.

Only offenders sentenced to two years of imprisonment or more could be sent to a penitentiary (Z89-91). Under the Criminal Code in force before 1955, treason, piracy, murder, and rape were the offences for which capital punishment was prescribed (Z92). A sentence could be suspended (Z93) only in the case of a first offender convicted of an offence punishable with not more than two years' imprisonment. If the offence was punishable with more than two years' imprisonment, a suspended sentence could not be authorized unless the Crown Counsel concurred.

Z94-102.   Sentences of persons convicted for indictable offences, Canada, 1952 to 1972

SOURCE: Statistics Canada, Statistics of Criminal and Other Offences, (Catalogue 85-201).

These are substantially modified continuations of series Z85-93; they are not comparable with those in the preceding set for two reasons: series Z94-102 are based on unduplicated counts of persons whereas series Z85-93 are based on counts of offences, and the categories of sentence are incomparably different. These categories were changed as a result of changes in law as well as shifts in the convention of statistical reporting.

The exclusion of figures for Quebec and Alberta from 1969 to 1972 makes difficult the comparison of series in these years with earlier figures.

These series cover adults only. From 1952 to 1967, the upper age limit of juveniles was less than 16 years; in 1968 this convention was discontinued and the upper age limit established by each of the provinces was used.

Z103-108.   Murder, charges, dispositions, commutations, and executions, Canada, 1879 to 1960.

SOURCE: *Historical Statistics of Canada,* first edition, Section Y: Justice, series Y61-66.

Series Z103-108 are presented without change from the first edition of *Historical Statistics of Canada.* The figures relate both to adults as well as to juveniles.

These figures provide a measure of how murder incidents and suspects were dealt with; they are not indicative of the incidence of murder (see series Z15-20 and Z22). If a murder is unsolved, or if the suspect(s) disappears, or is adjudged mentally incapacitated, or commits suicide, no charge is laid. It is quite common for suspects to be charged with murder but convicted of manslaughter or some other lesser offence. Prior to 1953, figures on convictions for reduced offences are not available; therefore they have not been included for later years in order to ensure comparability.

Z109-113. Murder, persons charged, acquitted, and convicted, Canada, 1961 to 1975

SOURCE: Statistics Canada, *Murder Statistics,* (Catalogue 85-209).

With commencement of the Homicide Statistics program by the Judicial Section of Statistics Canada in 1961, statistics on murder cases were greatly improved in detail and accuracy. Although statistics on murder as routinely reported by the courts have continued to be published annually in *Statistics of Criminal and Other Offences,* they are not as reliable nor as extensive as those produced in the Homicide Statistics program. The figures comprising series Z109-113 and Z114-123 are derived from the Homicide Statistics Branch and are a modified extension of the preceding series Z103-108.

Since a person charged with more than one murder would be counted once for each charge, these figures are not unduplicated counts of persons.

Figures for the years 1961-1966 include both adults and juveniles, whether tried in adult courts or in juvenile courts. For the years 1967-1975, the figures include only adults and juveniles tried in adult courts. For these series in all years, the upper age limit of juveniles has been taken as that established by each province under the Juvenile Delinquents Act (see footnote (2) to series Z19-20 for details).

Z111. These figures show the numbers of persons originally charged with murder and acquitted either of murder or of some lesser offence (to which the original charge was reduced prior to, or during, trial) such as manslaughter, wounding, or assault causing bodily harm.

The number of persons charged is tabulated according to the year in which the murder incident was reported or discovered, not necessarily the year in which the charge was laid (this is accomplished by continual updating and revision of figures in the Homicide Statistics program) whereas the numbers of acquittals and convictions are tabulated according to the years in which they were rendered. For example, if police in 1970 discovered an apparent murder which took place in 1968 and charged a suspect in 1971 with that murder, the existing 1970 count of persons would have one more added. When that person was tried in, say, 1972, the acquittal or conviction would be counted in the 1972 figures. Since murder cases are often lengthy, judicial dispositions may not have been made in a considerable number of cases for which charges were reported for 1974 and 1975. For these reasons as well as the fact that there are other possible dispositions in addition to those shown in

series Z110-113, the totals of acquittals and convictions in each year do not equal the number of charges.

The verdicts indicated by these series are final verdicts from appellate courts in cases where the verdict of the trial court was appealed. In cases where the initial verdict was not appealed, or where the appeal had not been heard, or the results of the appeal had not yet been reported for statistical purposes, the verdicts are those rendered by the trial court and may have been changed later.

For numbers of actual offences and duplicated counts of the numbers of persons charged as reported by police, see series Z15-20; for numbers of murder incidents and their distribution by type, see series Z22-27.

Z114-123. Sentences of persons charged with murder and convicted for murder or manslaughter, Canada, 1961 to 1975

SOURCE: Statistics Canada, Justice Statistics Division, Homicide Statistics program, unpublished figures.

Since 1961 there have been a number of major changes in the statutory definition of murder and its penalty; these changes must be taken into account when comparing the figures from year to year.

During the period covered by the series, the minimum mandatory penalty for murder has been life imprisonment and the maximum sentence, death. For the offence of manslaughter, life imprisonment is the maximum but not a mandatory sentence. For this reason, and because the majority of convictions resulting from charges of murder are for manslaughter, there are numerous sentences of less than life imprisonment shown for each year.

Z121. Although courts have sentenced persons convicted of murder to death in some years since 1961, all but two of these death sentences have been commuted to life imprisonment. The last in which death sentences were carried out in Canada was 1962 when two men were hanged. A *de facto* moratorium on the death penalty was in force in Canada from 1967 onward, and the death penalty for murder was finally abolished by Parliament in 1976.

The sentences shown in these series are final sentences in cases where the verdict or sentence of the trial court was appealed. In cases where the initial verdict or sentence were not appealed, or where the appeal had not been heard, or the results of the appeal had not yet been reported for statistical purposes, the sentences are those imposed by the trial court. It should be noted that figures in series Z103-108 pertain only to trial court decisions and do not include any changes of these decisions by appellate courts.

For all years in these series, figures include sentences for all convicted adults and juveniles tried in adult courts; excluded are juveniles tried in juvenile court.

Z124-134. Rape, persons convicted and sentences, Canada, 1952 to 1972

SOURCE: Statistics Canada, *Statistics of Criminal and Other Offences,* (Catalogue 85-201).

Figures in series Z124-134 are based on unduplicated counts of adult persons; only one offence (of any kind) per individual is counted within any one calendar year. Details of the rules by which one offence is selected in cases where the same person is charged with more than one offence during a year are given in the General note to this section on

Court Proceedings. These figures, therefore, do not represent a complete count of all rape convictions in Canada, and are not directly comparable with figures for earlier years.

The maximum sentence permitted by law upon conviction for rape is life imprisonment. The penalty for attempted rape is up to ten years' imprisonment.

Although the figures are generally comparable among the years shown, it should be noted that Quebec and Alberta are excluded for 1969 and subsequent years, and that from 1968 on the upper age limit for juveniles (who are excluded from these figures) was changed from under 16 years to the various age limits specified by individual provinces.

See series Z28-33 for figures reported by police on actual offences of rape and the numbers of persons charged (a duplicated count) for the years 1962 to 1975.

The category 'Extra sentence' (series Z134 in this table, and also series Z145, Z156, and Z166 in the following tables) has included over the years such varied designations as 'Strap', 'Lash', 'Penal institution and fine', 'Probation and fine', 'Jail and bound over to keep the peace', 'Order prohibiting driving', 'Order prohibiting navigating', 'Deportation', and occasionally 'Preventive detention'. This last category, although quite rare, has been imposed in cases where a person has been adjudged to be an habitual criminal or a dangerous sexual offender.

Z135-145. Robbery, persons convicted and sentences, Canada, 1952 to 1972

SOURCE: Statistics Canada, *Statistics of Criminal and Other Offences*, (Catalogue 85-201).

Series Z135-145 constitute unduplicated counts of adult persons, with only one offence of any kind counted for any individual within a calendar year. The figures are therefore an incomplete count of all convictions for robbery. Although the figures are generally comparable among the years shown, it should be noted that Quebec and Alberta are not included in the figures for 1969 to 1972, and that for the years 1968 to 1972 the provincial upper age limits for juveniles were used instead of a universal upper age limit of under 16 years.

Robbery is a completed theft accomplished through the use or threat of violence. The Criminal Code of Canada specifies a maximum penalty of life imprisonment for robbery and fourteen years for extortion (which is included with robbery for statistical purposes).

The reader is referred to the first edition of *Historical Statistics of Canada* which presented statistics on 'Convictions for robbery, by sentence, Canada, 1879 to 1951', Series Y51-60. These statistics were taken from an Historical Appendix to *Statistics of Criminal and Other Offences* discontinued in 1952. Because of changes in the rules of compilation and because of changes in the statistical categories of sentence, figures for the earlier period (1879 to 1951) are not comparable with those for the latter period (1952 to 1972).

See series Z40-45 for police-reported numbers of actual offences of robbery and a (duplicated) count of persons charged, yearly since 1962.

Z146-156. Breaking and entering, persons convicted and sentences, Canada, 1952 to 1972

SOURCE: Statistics Canada *Statistics of Criminal and Other Offences,* (Catalogue 85-201).

Being any unlawful entry of a place or vehicle to commit an offence, breaking and entering is punishable by imprisonment up to life if the place is a residence and for a term of up to fourteen years for other places or a vehicle.

Series Z146-156 provide unduplicated counts of adult persons convicted for breaking and entering and their sentences, with only one offence of any kind counted for any individual within the calendar year. These figures are therefore an incomplete count of all convictions for breaking and entering offences. Series for the years 1969-1972 differ from those for other years in that they do not include figures for Quebec or Alberta; for 1968 to 1972, they differ as well by virtue of the upper age limit of juveniles being that prescribed by each province rather than, as in years prior to 1968, a universal age limit of less than 16 years.

See series Z46-51 for numbers of actual breaking and entering offences and persons charged (a duplicated count) as reported by police since 1962.

Although the first edition of *Historical Statistics of Canada* contained statistics on 'Convictions for Breaking and Entering, By Sentence, Canada, 1879 to 1951' in series Y42-50 (taken from an Historical Appendix to *Statistics of Criminal and other Offences*) discontinued after 1951, those figures are not comparable with figures in series Z146-156 because of differences in rules of compilation and in the categories of sentence used in publications.

Z157-166. Theft, persons convicted and sentences, Canada, 1952 to 1972

SOURCE: Statistics Canada, *Statistics of Criminal and Other Offences*, (Catalogue 85-201).

Upon conviction, theft over $200 is punishable by a term of imprisonment of up to ten years, and theft of $200 or less is punishable by a term of up to two years if proceeded with by indictment. The amount of $200 came into effect in 1972; in earlier years the amount was $50. Figures in series Z157-166 are based on unduplicated counts of convicted adult persons; conviction for only one offence of any kind per individual is counted within any calendar year. (For details concerning the rules by which one offence is selected for persons who are charged with more than one offence during a year, see the introductory notes to this section on court proceedings.) These figures, for this reason, do not provide a complete count of all convictions for theft.

Figures for 1968 to 1972 do not include Quebec or Alberta, and were tabulated using different upper age limits for juveniles than were used for earlier years.

See series Z52-57 for figures reported by police relating to actual offences and persons charged (not an unduplicated count).

Z167. Convictions for drug-related offences, Canada, 1921 to 1974

SOURCE: for 1961 to 1974, Department of National Health and Welfare, Bureau of Dangerous Drugs, annual reports; for 1921 to 1960, *Historical Statistics of Canada*, First edition, Section Y: Justice, series Y68.

The first law prohibiting the importation, manufacture, and sale of opium in Canada was enacted in 1908: in 1911, the law was extended to other drugs as defined by the Governor General-in-Council, and was known as the Opium and Narcotic Drug Act. This was a federal statute and according to an amendment of 1921, any person who committed an offence could be proceeded against under the Act either by indictment or upon summary conviction with the exception of the offence of selling, giving away, or distributing any drug to a minor; in the latter case, the law required the proceeding to be by indictment. This Act was repealed on September 15, 1961, and replaced by the federal Narcotic Control Act. The RCMP have been responsible since 1920 for enforcing this Act and the related Food and Drugs Act.

Figures are based on offences; a person is counted as many times as he or she is convicted in a year.

Z168-172. Dispositions of appeals of convictions for indictable offences, Canada, 1937 to 1972

SOURCE: for 1961 to 1972, Statistics Canada, *Statistics of Criminal and Other Offences*, (Catalogue 85-201); for 1937 to 1960, *Historical Statistics of Canada*, first edition, Section Y: Justice, series Y69-73.

Either the verdict or the sentence rendered by a trial court, or both, may be appealed by the accused, the Crown, or the informant. Appeals are heard by the Appeal Division of the provincial Supreme Courts and the Supreme Court of Canada.

Statistics On Penal Institutions, Pardons, and Parole (Series Z173-226)

General note

There have been several distinct types of penal and detentive institutions in Canada: penitentiaries; provincial prisons; other provincial institutions such as reformatories, industrial farms, and training schools for juveniles; and municipal jails. With the evolution of penal and correctional philosophy, nearly all reformatories and industrial farms and training schools have gradually been phased out in recent .years. Since municipal jails serve mainly as temporary detention centres rather than as places where convicted persons serve their sentences, the principal penal institutions are penitentiaries and prisons.

Under the BNA Act, the federal Government of Canada has exclusive responsibility for establishing, maintaining, and managing penitentiaries. Penitentiaries are the penal institutions where convicted persons sentenced to two years' imprisonment or more serve their terms. Provincial prisons are under the jurisdiction of their provincial governments; persons sentenced to less than two years' imprisonment serve their terms in these institutions. (Since 1972, however, there have been federal-provincial transfer agreements under which persons with sentences of less than two years may in certain circumstances serve their term in a penitentiary and some persons with sentences of two years or more may serve their terms in provincial prisons.)

In 1867, the first year for which statistics are available, there were three penitentiaries - in Halifax, St. John, and Kingston. By 1975, there were 50 penitentiaries and related federal institutions, including psychiatric and reception centres and minimum, medium, and maximum security penitentiaries.

Three types of information pertaining to penitentiaries are available (not necessarily for all years): the number of prisoners in penitentiaries on a specified date, the movement of population in penitentiaries (admissions, transfers, and releases throughout the year), and selected social characteristics of penitentiary inmates. Since 1867, statistics concerning penitentiaries have been provided in annual reports of penitentiary officials and of the federal Department of Justice and the Ministry of the Solicitor General. In 1918 Statistics Canada commenced publication of statistics on the number of prisoners in custody at the beginning and end of the reporting year, along with the number of admissions and releases, for penitentiaries and provincial penal institutions. These statistics were first published in the annual reports, *Statistics of Criminal and Other Offences* and later in *Correctional Statistics* and *Penitentiary Statistics*. And in 1937, Statistics Canada began collecting statistics on legal and social characteristics of convicted persons admitted to penitentiaries which was first published in 1938. Penitentiary statistics published by Statistics Canada are now based on data derived from administrative records by the Canadian Penitentiary Service.

Statistics on provincial prisons (or jails) and other penal institutions have been published since 1918 by Statistics Canada in the annual reports, *Statistics of Criminal and Other Offences* until 1955, and in *Correctional Statistics* thereafter. A program for uniform reporting of statistical data specifically on training schools was inaugurated in 1963, with 1964 being the first complete year for which data were available. Publication of statistics continued until 1974; data were accumulated for several years following without being published, and the program was ultimately terminated.

Details on the various sources of statistical information concerning penal institutions for the years 1867 to 1960 will be found in the first edition of *Historical Statistics of Canada*, p. 640.

Z173-174. Number of prisoners in penitentiaries, by sex, Canada, 1867 to 1975

SOURCE: for 1975, Statistics Canada, *Penitentiary Statistics*, (Catalogue 85-210); for 1961 to 1974, Statistics Canada, *Correctional Institution Statistics* (Catalogue 85-207); for 1867 to 1960, *Historical Statistics of Canada*, first edition, Section Y: Justice, series Y156-157.

The figures given show the penitentiary population 'on register' as of the last day of the reporting year; they are not a measure of the average or maximum population during that year. These figures do not include the small numbers of persons not convicted but being held in temporary detention in penitentiaries, nor persons who were on register but released on temporary absence on the day of count. Included are prisoners transferred from provincial prisons under federal-provincial transfer agreements; not included are penitentiary inmates who have been transferred to a provincial prison to serve their sentences.

The number of penitentiary inmates in each year and any trends over periods of time are affected by a great many factors including the rates of commission, apprehension, and conviction for serious crimes, the prisoner capacity of penitentiaries, and judicial policy regarding sentences of two years and longer.

Z175-182. Admissions of males to penitentiaries by age, Canada, 1938 to 1960

SOURCE: *Historical Statistics of Canada*, first edition, Section Y: Justice, series Y158-165.

In 1956 a change was made in the definition of the 'admitted convict' used as the basic statistical unit; this change was adjudged by the author of the Justice Section of the first edition of *Historical Statistics of Canada* not to have affected significantly the comparability of figures in each series. Presumably it is because of the very small numbers of females who are admitted to or in penitentiaries that statistics are given only for males at time of admission (see series Z173-174).

It should be noted that the age distribution of males as recorded at time of admission is not necessarily equivalent to the age distribution of the male penitentiary population at any other time - the latter distribution would be relatively skewed, to an unknown degree, toward the higher ages.

Z183-197. Admissions of males to penitentiaries, by age, Canada, 1961 to 1975

SOURCE: for 1975, Statistics Canada, *Penitentiary Statistics* (Catalogue 85-210); for 1965 to 1974, Statistics Canada, *Correctional Institution Statistics*, (Catalogue 85-207); for 1961 to 1964, Annual Report of the Commissioner of Penitentiaries.

These series are an extension in modified and more detailed form of series Z175-182. These figures do not include admissions due to transfers between penitentiaries.

Z198-201. Number of prisoners in reformatories and training schools, by sex, in jails, and in all penal institutions, Canada, 1916 to 1956

SOURCE: for 1956, Statistics Canada, *Correctional Institutions Statistics*, (Catalogue 85-207); for 1916 to 1955, *Historical Statistics of Canada*, first edition, Section Y: Justice, series Y170-173.

Figures show the population on the last day of the reporting year. The term 'jails', caption for Z200, has been replaced since 1957 by the terms 'prisons' or 'provincial adult institutions'. Jails or prisons contain a relatively larger proportion of persons being held in detention (awaiting arraignment or trial, or whose probation or parole have been suspended or forfeited) than do other provincial institutions and penitentiaries. They also experience a much higher rate of turnover of prisoners due to the considerable numbers of prisoners serving short sentences. Thus, the year-end figures are not at all indicative of the total number of persons who were incarcerated (whether for detention only or for punishment) in those institutions during the year.

Z202-208. Number of prisoners in training schools, reformatories, and industrial farms, by sex, and in provincial adult institutions and all penal institutions, Canada, 1957 to 1975

SOURCE: Statistics Canada, *Correctional Institution Statistics*, (Catalogue 85-207).

As a result of changes in the categories of penal institution in the published statistics, series Z198-201 could not be updated; those series are extended in modified form in series Z202-208. For example, over the two decades prior to 1975, reformatories shifted over time from being penal institutions for young persons to being institutions mainly for adults, and statistics for them were no longer published in a category by themselves.

The caption of series Z206, 'Provincial Adult Institutions', was changed in 1957 from 'Jails', used previously.

The figures for 'Training Schools' for the mid-1960s and later years are of questionable validity; the publication *Correctional Institution Statistics* gives the total number of juveniles in training schools in 1973 as 2,053 while the publication *Training Schools* gives the total as 3,561.

Z209-212. Tickets of leave and pardons, Canada, 1876 to 1955

SOURCE: *Historical Statistics of Canada*, first edition, Section Y: Justice, series Y174-177.

According to the Ticket of Leave Act of 1899 (which was repealed in 1958), the Governor General was empowered to grant to any convicted person under sentence of imprisonment in any penal institution the right to be at large in Canada during such portion of his term of imprisonment and according to such conditions as he deemed appropriate. All releases granted under this Act are classified in series Z210, 'Released Under Ticket of Leave'. Figures in series Z210 become more meaningful if related for each year to the population in penal institutions during that year. Comparability of figures across years is affected by such changes as the inclusion in figures from 1929 to 1950 of releases on temporary tickets of leave. Fluctuations in this series are due partly to changes in policy (re: the portion of term of imprisonment that must be served before the release is granted), as well as to changes in practices as to what legal disposition under which the prerogative of mercy of the Crown is exercised.

'Other conditional or unconditional pardons', series Z211, include commutations of death sentences, also presented separately in series Z107, remission of corporal punishment, granting of free pardons on the ground of innocence established and admitted by the prosecution, granting of free pardons on the ground of special considerations of an unusual character, remission of sentences of imprisonment (not to be confused with the benefit of parole under the Ticket of Leave Act), and remission in whole or in part of fines, pecuniary penalties, forfeitures and costs. As with the other series, these figures are better understood when related to the population of persons who may benefit from conditional and unconditional pardons. Fluctuations in this series are due to changes in policy as well as to special proclamations of clemency which would affect a great number of convicted persons.

Z213-222. Parole granted, violations, and pardons, Canada, 1957 to 1975

SOURCE: National Parole Board, Annual Reports.

The Ticket of Leave Act was repealed in 1958 and replaced by the Parole Act. The first annual report of the Parole Board, published for the calendar year 1959, gave figures pertinent to these series for 1957 and 1958. These statistics continued to be given in the annual reports of the National Parole Board until 1969. The federal Ministry of the Solicitor General was established in October, 1966 with jurisdiction over the National Parole Board, and these statistics were published in 1970 and subsequent years in the annual report of the Ministry of the Solicitor General. These annual reports of the Solicitor General cover fiscal years ending 31 March, but for the years 1970 and 1971 calendar year figures were also presented.

Z215. Mandatory supervision means that an inmate who is not on parole but is released before the end of his sentence, through remission, will be subject to mandatory supervision if the period of his remission exceeds 60 days.

Z216. Under day parole, an inmate may be released from prison to enter a community for such purposes as education or employment or some similar purpose. He or she must continually return to the institution but not necessarily every night. Day parole is regarded as an effective way of finding how an inmate may act on an ordinary parole.

Z217. Day parole (temporary) relates to release for special work projects or educational programs of more limited and specified duration.

Z223-226.　Penitentiaries operating costs, Canada, 1895 to 1975

SOURCE: for 1961 to 1975, Canadian Penitentiary Service, annual reports and unpublished figures. for 1895 to 1960, *Historical Statistics of Canada*, first edition Section Y: Justice, series Y166-169.

For each year before 1936, the average operating cost per capita (that is, per prisoner) shown in series Z225, and the average operating cost per capita per diem in series Z226 were calculated on the net cost - the actual cost less the value of supplies on hand at the end of the fiscal year, and less the estimated value of labour on production of capital and revenue. The actual cost was computed by adding the net expenditures (gross expenditures less revenues) and the value of supplies on hand at the beginning of the fiscal year. For 1936 and later years, the operating costs for services rendered and goods consumed during the fiscal year have been used as a basis for computing the average costs per capita. This item does not include capital expenditures; on the other hand, revenues are not deducted. Therefore, figures for 1936 onward are not strictly comparable with those for previous years. From 1944 to 1949, the average cost given in the annual reports for these years was computed on the basis of operating costs including disbursement on capital. In order to make the figures comparable, the basis of computation was revised and the equivalent average costs calculated accordingly.

These figures have not been adjusted to take account of transfers of prisoners between federal penitentiaries and provincial prisons, under federal-provincial transfer agreements.

Because capital costs are not included in these figures, these series are not indicative of the total penitentiary costs.

Statistics On Juvenile Delinquency (Series Z227-291)

General note

Juveniles in Canada are dealt with differently, and under a different law, as compared to adults.

Many judicial statistics pertaining to juveniles are therefore different from, and not comparable with, those for adults and are presented separately in this section. All of series Z227-291 are based on data provided by courts. For the numbers of juveniles charged as reported by police

since 1962, refer to series Z32-33, Z38-39, Z44-45, Z50-51, and Z56-57. Statistics on juveniles in penal institutions will be found in series Z176-178, Z184-186, Z198-199, and Z202-203. In order to facilitate the use and interpretation of juvenile delinquency statistics, census and estimated population figures for persons aged 7-15 years are presented in series Z305-328.

The necessity for treating children who commit offences differently from adult offenders was formally recognized in Canada in 1894. A law was passed in that year which amended the Criminal Code and provided for separate trials of 'young persons apparently under the age of sixteen years' and for 'their incarceration, prior to sentence, separately from older persons'. But it was only the Juvenile Delinquents Act of 1908 that provided for special courts under provincial statutes to deal with young offenders.

The Juvenile Delinquents Act approximately as we know it today came into force on 14 June, 1929, and was revised in 1952. This Act states that a 'juvenile delinquent' is "any child who violates any provision of the Criminal Code or of any federal or provincial statute, or of any by-law or ordinance of any municipality, or who is guilty of sexual immorality or any similar form of vice, or who is liable by reason of any other act to be committed to an industrial school or juvenile reformatory under any federal or provincial statute". A commission of any of these acts constitutes an offence known as a delinquency.

The Juvenile Delinquents Act further defines a child as a boy or a girl apparently or actually under the age of sixteen years, with a provision empowering the Governor in Council to raise the age limit in any province up to 18 years. The upper age limit was set at under 16 in Prince Edward Island, Nova Scotia, New Brunswick, Ontario, and Saskatchewan; at under 17 in Newfoundland, and at under 18 in Quebec, Manitoba, and British Columbia. In Alberta, the provision for the older age in effect from 1935 to 1950 was repealed in 1951 and the age limit of under 16 years, as stated in the Juvenile Delinquents Act of 1929, was put into effect. Subsequently, during the same year, the definition was changed again with the upper limit of under 18 years re-established for girls only; in 1956, the age limit was set at under 18 for both girls and boys. In 1970 the upper age limit in British Columbia was changed to under 17 years. In Newfoundland, for offences committed by young persons under 17 years of age, proceedings which would have been under the Criminal Code and the Juvenile Delinquents Act of Canada in other provinces are under a provincial statute, the Welfare of Children Act, which operates by virtue of the terms of agreement between Canada and Newfoundland. Until 1968, figures relating to juvenile delinquents aged 16 years and over in those provinces where the upper limit was higher than 16 were included in the statistics for court proceedings pertaining to adults (series Z66-172); for the years 1953 to 1958, for example, their numbers were 1,176, 1,283, 1,212, 1,526, 2,202 and 2,311 respectively (as reported in Statistics Canada *Juvenile Delinquents*, report for each year). And juveniles, regardless of age, whose cases, because of their seriousness or other circumstances, were heard in adult court, would be counted in the court statistics on adults.

Statistics on juveniles have been published in Canada beginning in 1886 and presented as part of *Criminal Statistics* until 1926. During the decade following the enactment of the Juvenile Delinquent Act in 1908 many courts for juveniles were established but data on juvenile delinquents continued to be reported and tabulated together with figures on adult offenders until 1922. By that year a sufficient number of juvenile courts had been established to warrant Statistics Canada commencing the separate statistical handling of juvenile delinquency cases. From 1922 to 1926 inclusive, juvenile delinquency figures were tabulated on the basis of offences; it was only in 1927 that 'appearance at court' became the unit of counting. Since 1927, Statistics Canada has published an annual report entitled *Juvenile Delinquents*, which until 1969 was based on this method of compilation. For 1970 and following years, the procedure was revised to produce two different kinds of figures; an unduplicated count of juveniles appearing before the court; and a count of delinquencies, consisting of all delinquencies recorded during that year but excluding the most serious delinquency committed by each juvenile in the particular year, which is recorded in the unduplicated count of juveniles. Figures for 1970 and later years are therefore not commensurate with those prior to 1970 and have not been included. Their comparability has been impaired as well by the fact that a number of provinces since 1970 have reorganized their systems of statistical reporting of juveniles; these reorganizations resulted in very marked increases in the number of forms submitted from certain provinces in some years, indicating a significant rate of non-reporting in earlier years. (The problem of non-reporting and under-reporting inherent in adult court statistics, mentioned in the General note to series Z66-172, also afflicts statistics from juvenile courts.) Note that series Z270-281 cover the period 1886 to 1926 while all the other series start with 1927; they are not comparable.

Several reasons may be cited as to why court statistics on juveniles are not comparable with court statistics on adults. Juvenile delinquency statistics are tabulated (with the exception of series Z270-281) on the basis of appearances at court. The figures therefore do not provide an unduplicated count of the number of children brought before the court, for a child referred to a court two or more times during the year is counted as a separate case each time. Neither do they represent the number of offences committed by the boys and girls brought before a court for more than one offence because, for a juvenile charged with two or more offences at the same hearing, only the most serious offence would be recorded. To illustrate: for the years from 1953 to 1957, the number of court apppearances per hundred of the unduplicated number of boys was 109, 108, 107, 105 and 109 respectively (from Statistics Canada *Juvenile Delinquents*, yearly reports).

There is and has been extensive variation among the provinces in judicial policy regarding procedures for juvenile cases. At one extreme, a formal charge is laid in every instance where a delinquent act is alleged to have occurred; at the other extreme, cases which are not deemed serious by law enforcement and court officials may be dealt with informally without any charge being laid, or formal charges may be withdrawn if it is thought that no benefit would accrue or where the appearance of the juvenile in court might prove damaging to him or to his family. Therefore figures would be smaller in jurisdictions where there was a policy of more informal handling of juvenile delinquents. It is a known fact that the number of juvenile cases dealt with informally and not statistically recorded exceeds the number of cases formally heard and recorded, and that the proportion of informally heard cases is on the increase.

Finally, the dispositions for juveniles brought before a court for some reason are not the same as the potential dispositions for adults. While adults are found guilty or not guilty at trial, there is not so strong an element of responsibility attributed to juveniles and thus a diminished attribution of guilt or innocence in juvenile cases. Juveniles are charged in the same way as adults, but if found by the court to have committed some prohibited act, they are 'adjudged delinquent' rather than found guilty. The Juvenile Delinquents Act states that "where a child is adjudged to have committed a delinquency he shall be dealt with, not as an offender, but as one in a condition of delinquency and therefore requiring help and guidance and proper supervision."

There are also several caveats which apply to the comparability of Juvenile delinquency figures across years. Because juvenile delinquency encompasses, by law, not only offences under the Criminal Code and all other statutes but morality and other unspecified offences as well, this makes the figures vulnerable both to changes in the laws (especially provincial statutes and municipal by laws) and shifts in norms of behaviour and morality.

From 1927 to 1949 offences committed by juveniles were divided into major and minor offences which corresponded roughly to indictable and non-indictable offences for adults in the Criminal Code. Some offences, however, punishable on summary conviction if committed by an adult, were considered serious enough to be classified as major offences when committed by a juvenile; this division was somewhat arbitrary and was therefore eliminated in 1950.

There have been numerous changes in the structure of juvenile justice since its formal inception around the turn of the century, and these have resulted in changes over the years in the agencies which reported data on juvenile delinquency. Up to 1973, statistical returns were submitted directly to Statistics Canada by Juvenile Courts and by those magistrates and justices of the peace who heard children's cases where no juvenile court was established. In three provinces, however - Saskatchewan, Alberta, and British Columbia - court returns were collected by a provincial agency and forwarded to the Bureau. Since 1973, forms have been submitted directly by the courts in all provinces.

Although figures from adult courts in Quebec and Alberta have not been included in published national statistics since 1969, figures on juvenile cases in these two provinces have been included in *Juvenile Delinquents* for 1969. In that same report, figures for Manitoba were presented separately from those of the other provinces because of a new, different method used to tabulate statistics on juvenile delinquents in that province.

Z227-248. Delinquency cases, by sex and by province, 1927 to 1969

SOURCE: for 1961 to 1969, Statistics Canada, *Juvenile Delinquents*, (Catalogue 85-202); for 1927 to 1960, *Historical Statistics of Canada*, first edition, Section Y: Justice, series Y119- 140.

Figures include only cases formally heard by a court which resulted in a finding of delinquency. Not enumerated are cases heard informally and cases where the juvenile was not adjudged delinquent. Figures which were presented separately for major and minor offences in the original publications up to 1949 have been combined in these series (see General note to these series on juvenile delinquency). Figures for years prior to 1927 and subsequent to 1969 are not comparable with the figures presented here (see note for series Z270-281). Figures for 1969 do not include cases from Manitoba; figures for 1968 and 1969 are based on the provincial age limits, as compared with the standard upper limit of under 16 years used for all preceding years.

Z249-260. Delinquency cases, by nature of the offence, Canada, 1927 to 1969

SOURCE: for 1961 to 1969, Statistics Canada, *Juvenile Delinquents*, (Catalogue 85-202); for 1927 to 1960, *Historical Statistics of Canada*, first edition, Section Y: Justice, series Y141-146.

When a girl or a boy is charged with more than one offence at the same hearing (reportedly a rare practice), only the most serious offence was to be recorded for statistical purposes. This compilation procedure provided a duplicated count of juvenile persons.

In an Historical Appendix to the report for 1950, figures for 1926 through 1950, which had been compiled separately for major and minor offences, were revised and minor offences were redistributed among the categories established for major offences (see note for series Z261-269). This method of presentation was instituted in the 1950 report and continues. Figures prior to 1927 are not comparable (see note for series Z270-281) nor are figures for 1970 and later years (see General note to this sub-section).

Figures for 1968 and 1969 are based on the upper age limits in force in each province; for all earlier years, the upper age limit used was under 16 years. Figures for 1969 do not include cases from Manitoba, which adopted a different and incompatible statistical system for juvenile delinquents in that year.

Z261-269. Appearances of juveniles before the court and results, by sex, Canada, 1927 to 1969

SOURCE: for 1961 to 1969, Statistics Canada *Juvenile Delinquents*, (Catalogue 85-202); for 1927 to 1960, *Historical Statistics of Canada*, first edition, Section Y: Justice, series Y110-118.

From 1927 to 1949, figures on appearances before the court and results were compiled separately for major and for minor offences (see General note to this sub-section). In the annual reports for 1950 and later the two classes of offences are grouped together and in the Historical Appendix to the 1950 report the figures for the major and minor offences were also grouped together for the years 1926 through 1949.

Figures prior to 1927 are not comparable with those in these series (see note for series Z270-281). The comparability of figures for 1927 through 1949 with those for later years is affected by the fact that appearances in court for minor offences which resulted in dismissal were not recorded prior to 1950 but have been from 1950 onward.

There have been variations among courts in their policy concerning the definition of juvenile delinquent for statistical purposes. Some courts considered adjournment *sine die* equivalent to a suspended sentence and treated these cases as tentative dismissals and therefore did not report these cases as being delinquent, while other courts did. Further, there have been changes over the years in the number of courts espousing each policy.

Figures for 1969 do not include cases from Manitoba, and figures for 1968 and 1969 are based on provincial age limits in place of the upper age limit of under 16 years which had

been used since the inception of national statistics on juvenile delinquency.

Z270-281. Convictions for major offences of juveniles under 16 years, Canada and the provinces, 1886 to 1926

SOURCE: *Historical Statistics of Canada*, first edition, Section Y: Justice, series Y74-85.

Convictions of juveniles were tabulated together with convictions of adults until 1921 (see series Z66-78). From 1922 to 1926 they were compiled separately and offences which would have been indictable if committed by adults were called 'major offences' (see General note to series Z227-291). In 1927 the basic statistical unit became the 'appearance at court'. Therefore, figures in series Z270-281 are not comparable with those in series Z227-269 and Z283-291.

Z282. Juveniles adjudged delinquent, Canada, 1927 to 1973

SOURCE: Statistics Canada *Juvenile Delinquents*, (Catalogue 85-202).

While figures based on cases have been provided in detail in the annual reports, *Juvenile Delinquents*, a simple, aggregate count of the number of delinquents has been given each year since 1927. Because of the change in 1953 from the duplicated count of juveniles, in use from 1927 to 1953, to an unduplicated count from 1953 to the present, figures from these two periods are not comparable. The upper age limit used in tabulating the series changed in 1968 from the standard, 'under 16 years' to the age limit in force in each province.

Z283-291. Delinquency cases, by disposition, Canada, 1927 to 1969

SOURCE: for 1961 to 1969, Statistics Canada, *Juvenile Delinquents*, (Catalogue 85-202); for 1927 to 1960, *Historical Statistics of Canada*, first edition, Section Y: Justice, series Z147-155.

In the 1950 annual report, figures for 1926 to 1949, tabulated separately for minor and major offences, were revised and the two classes of offences were grouped together. Figures prior to 1927 are not comparable (see General note and note for series Z270-281). 'Indefinite detention', series Z284, refers to a short period of detention, from a few days to about a month, during which the child was under observation or awaiting a hearing. This practice of detaining children has declined, due partly to better community facilities and more extensive use of them. Under 'supervision of the court', series Z285, are listed those children who have been placed in foster homes by Children's Aid Societies and provincial or municipal welfare departments or who have been placed under the care of a probation officer.

Some figures in series Z283-291 are inter-related in that upward trends in some series are accompanied by downward trends in others.

Figures for 1969 do not include cases from Manitoba (see General note to this sub-section).

Population Statistics, (Series Z291-328)

Z292-304.   Census and estimated population aged 7-15 years by sex, Canada and the provinces, 1881 to 1975

Z305-328.   Census and estimated population aged 7-15 years, by sex, Canada and the provinces, 1927 to 1975

SOURCE: for 1956 to 1975, Statistics Canada, *Census of* *Canada* for 1956, 1961, 1966, and 1971; *Population Estimates* for all other years; for 1881 to 1955, *Historical Statistics of Canada,* first edition, Section Y: Justice, series Y14-26.

Census figures are those for the years 1881 to 1921 inclusive and for 1931, 1941, 1951 and 1956. In the intercensal years, Statistics Canada prepares estimates of population by sex and age groups; these estimates are adjusted at the next census. Revised estimates have been used in all years where available (up to 1970).

Series Z1-14. Actual[1] and cleared[2] offences[3] reported by police, by type of offence, Canada, 1962 to 1975

Year	Crimes of violence		Property crimes		Other Criminal Code offences		Federal drug offences		Other federal statute offences		Provincial statute offences		Municipal bylaw offences	
	Actual	Cleared	Actual	Cleared	Actual	Cleared	Actual	Cleared	Actual	Cleared	Actual	Cleared	Actual	Cleared
	1	2	3	4	5	6	7	8	9	10	11	12	13	14
1975	135,424	92,414	1,041,036	277,003	409,345	169,222	55,542	48,280	44,972	39,303	381,388	366,243	64,800	47,492
1974	126,053	89,953	946,793	256,959	384,039	158,729	58,585	52,071	44,394	40,341	368,716	355,655	81,306	59,978
1973	117,760	87,240	833,148	235,724	347,643	148,315	52,772	46,077	42,786	36,729	339,119	329,218	75,907	61,918
1972	110,468	80,873	807,468	221,794	271,869	123,392	28,816	23,474	39,779	35,626	318,250	305,342	73,580	61,967
1971	108,095	79,288	801,379	220,749	254,231	113,811	24,007	16,608	39,667	34,091	344,771	333,584	73,915	63,295
1970	102,358	74,244	748,519	209,529	256,572	113,479	18,789	13,392	36,494	33,033	335,788	323,327	73,086	63,301
1969	95,084	68,403	655,304	184,799	242,273	106,322	10,520	6,324	47,070	42,503	346,541	335,270	71,839	61,761
1968	87,544	62,735	584,996	161,994	223,443	100,035	5,443	2,965	40,058	36,214	317,912	305,303	74,501	65,061
1967	77,614	54,322	506,151	137,817	200,803	90,875	2,874	1,475	35,226	31,310	296,504	284,935	69,532	62,531
1966	69,386	50,013	451,980	127,914	181,443	86,717	1,425	657	34,569	30,889	290,096	275,016	65,990	58,070
1965	58,780	41,906	410,688	115,414	158,950	77,578	768	484	29,614	25,843	271,857	259,745	58,794	51,997
1964	54,769	38,251	414,048	117,353	157,221	80,660	623	463	33,168	27,994	248,772	234,223	52,316	42,888
1963	47,229	30,792	387,517	106,125	137,359	64,664	902	484	25,775	22,553	219,288	207,532	56,502	49,986
1962	44,026	27,164	351,483	99,098	122,477	61,919	1,003	520	30,135	26,027	195,853	185,668	54,698	48,486

[1] Actual offences are those known to the police which are adjudged to have happened or to have been attempted. Not included are offences reported to police but adjudged by police to be unfounded.
[2] Cleared offences are those for which at least one charge has been laid or for which there is enough information to support the laying of a charge but the police are unable to do so for some reason (e.g., death of the suspect).
[3] Excluding traffic and parking offences.

Series Z15-20. Murder, actual offences and persons charged, Canada, 1961 to 1975

Year	Actual[1] offences	Persons charged				
		Total persons charged	Adults		Juveniles[2]	
			Male	Female	Boys	Girls
	15	16	17	18	19	20
1975	633	494	405	61	21	7
1974	545	466	370	62	34	—
1973	479	405	333	49	23	—
1972	479	395	315	54	21	5
1971	426	368	313	38	14	3
1970	433	314	265	31	16	2
1969	347	277	218	42	16	1
1968	315	261	208	27	24	2
1967	282	197	173	15	9	—
1966	222	201	158	26	17	—
1965	243	171	143	16	11	1
1964	218	167	146	18	3	—
1963	215	186	162	14	10	—
1962	217	150	129	16	4	1
1961	185	146	-3	-3	-4	-4

[1] Actual offences are those known to the police which are adjudged to have happened; offences reported to police but adjudged to be unfounded are not counted. Attempted murders are excluded from these figures.
[2] The Juvenile Delinquents Act defines a child as any boy or girl apparently or actually under the age of 16 years or such other age as may be directed in any province. In Prince Edward Island, Nova Scotia, New Brunswick, Ontario, Saskatchewan, Yukon and Northwest Territories, the official age limit for a juvenile is under 16 years; in Newfoundland and British Columbia, under 17 years; in Quebec and Manitoba, under 18 years; and in Alberta under 16 years for boys and under 18 years for girls. The figure for 1975 (21 boys, 7 girls) does not include 2 juveniles dealt with "informally"; i.e., not charged but given an informal hearing in Juvenile Court and/or handed over to their parents or a guardian, or to a social agency or an appropriate department. This provision was introduced in 1974. (In 1974, there were no juveniles reported by police as having been dealth with informally subsequent to incidents of murder.)
[3] A total of 140 adults were charged with murder in 1961.
[4] In 1961, a total of 6 juveniles were charged.

Series Z21. Number of criminal homicide deaths, Canada, 1926 to 1975

Year	Number of deaths	Year	Number of deaths	Year	Number of deaths
	21		21		21
1975[1]	701	1955	157	1935	153
1974[1]	599	1954	157	1934	142
1973	546	1953	149	1933	147
1972	520	1952	135	1932	158
1971	473	1951	137	1931	172
1970	467	1950	112	1930	214
1969	391	1949[4]	172	1929	182
1968	375	1948	155	1928	150
1967	338	1947	146	1927	124
1966	250	1946	146	1926	120
1965	277	1945	152		
1964	253	1944	106		
1963	249	1943	125		
1962	265	1942	113		
1961[2]	211	1941	130		
1960	244	1940	148		
1959	167	1939	124		
1958	198	1938	127		
1957	165	1937	138		
1956[3]	171	1936	137		

[1] Figures for 1974 and 1975 include infanticides, which were not reported during 1961–1973.
[2] The numbers of criminal homicide deaths shown for the years 1961 to 1975 were derived from special homicide reports provided by police forces across Canada. Figures shown for years prior to 1961 were derived from other sources and are not comparable with the police figures. (See text for explanation.)
[3] Statistics relating to the Yukon Territory and the Northwest Territories have been included since 1956.
[4] Statistics for Newfoundland have been included since 1949.

Series Z22-27. Murder incidents, distribution by type of suspect-victim relationship, Canada, 1961 to 1975

Year	Canada	Suspect–victim relationship types				
		Domestic[1]	Social or business[2]	During commission of another criminal act[3]	No known relationship	Unsolved
	22	23	24	25	26	27
1975	570	183	—[4]	45	—[4]	139
1974	499	186	136	47	43	87
1973	447	169	132	53	31	62
1972	412	151	130	42	28	61
1971	395	141	129	41	29	55
1970	354	121	108	45	25	55
1969	320	125	91	27	25	52
1968	292	121	80	34	18	39
1967	239	99	83	24	8	25
1966	206	94	63	22	17	10
1965	216	88	75	23	18	12
1964	199	80	70	23	13	13
1963	192	81	52	27	13	19
1962	196	86	48	22	17	23
1961	173	87	49	14	11	12

[1] "Domestic" includes immediate family, other kinship, and common-law family relationships.
[2] "Social or business" type of relationship comprises "Lovers' quarrel and love triangle", "Close acquaintance", "Casual acquaintance", and "Business relationship".
[3] Incidents which occur during commission of another crime and in which suspect and victim were domestically related are classified as "domestic", but where there was a social or business relationship or no known relationship in such incidents, they are classified as "during commission" cases.
[4] These figures are not available separately. The combined total number of incidents in both categories was 203 in 1975.

Series Z28-33. Rape, actual offences and persons charged, Canada, 1962 to 1975

Year	Actual[1] offences	Persons charged					
		Total persons charged	Adults		Juveniles[2]	
			Male	Female	Boys	Girls
	28	29	30	31	32	33
1975	1,848	1,006	935	3	65	3
1974	1,823	1,016	918	3	84	11
1973	1,593	917	852	2	62	1
1972	1,285	750	674	8	66	2
1971	1,230	718	683	5	29	1
1970	1,079	715	634	3	76	2
1969	1,019	760	726	2	32	—
1968	892	634	598	—	34	2
1967	773	555	528	—	27	—
1966	652	486	463	—	23	—
1965	641	424	400	—	23	1
1964	745	491	474	1	16	—
1963	549	333	292	—	41	—
1962	579	393	364	—	29	—

[1] Actual offences include attempts. See footnote (1) of series Z15 for the meaning of "actual offences".

[2] See footnote (2) of series Z20 for the legal definition of juveniles. The figures for 1974 (84 boys, 11 girls) do not include 7 juveniles dealt with "informally"; i.e., not charged but given an informal hearing in Juvenile Court and/or handed over to their parents or a guardian, or to a social agency or an appropriate department. This provision was introduced in 1974. The corresponding number for 1975 was 13.

Series Z34-39. Assault (not indecent), actual offences and persons charged, Canada, 1962 to 1975

Year	Actual[1] offences	Persons charged					
		Total persons charged	Adults		Juveniles[2]	
			Male	Female	Boys	Girls
	34	35	36	37	38	39
1975	101,886	34,276	29,570	2,889	1,458	359
1974	96,864	34,099	29,644	2,700	1,429	326
1973	91,577	32,894	28,555	2,644	1,410	285
1972	86,838	30,302	26,681	2,145	1,240	236
1971	84,867	29,489	25,931	1,885	1,438	235
1970	78,979	27,951	24,629	1,645	1,462	215
1969	73,718	25,800	22,740	1,386	1,440	234
1968	67,983	24,484	21,457	1,309	1,505	213
1967	60,179	22,603	20,153	1,076	1,225	149
1966	54,505	21,755	19,396	1,213	997	149
1965	45,373	19,420	17,440	999	900	81
1964	41,297	17,764	16,111	863	741	49
1963	34,027	16,042	14,502	816	671	53
1962	29,076	14,692	13,449	719	466	58

[1] Actual offences include attempts. See footnote (1) of series Z15 for the meaning of "actual offences".

[2] See footnote (2) of series Z20 for the legal definition of juveniles. The figures for 1974 (1,429 boys, 326 girls) do not include 2,985 juveniles dealt with "informally"; i.e., not charged but given an informal hearing in Juvenile Court and/or handed over to their parents or a guardian, or to a social agency or an appropriate department. This provision was introduced in 1974. For 1975, a total of 2,931 juveniles were reported by police to have been dealt with informally subsequent to incidents of assault.

Series Z40-45. Robbery, actual offences and persons charged, Canada, 1962 to 1975

Year	Actual[1] offences	Persons charged					
		Total persons charged	Adults		Juveniles[2]	
			Male	Female	Boys	Girls
	40	**41**	**42**	**43**	**44**	**45**
1975	21,299	7,422	5,549	398	1,384	91
1974	16,955	6,152	4,674	302	1,063	113
1973	13,166	5,203	3,923	285	903	92
1972	11,832	4,576	3,509	198	828	41
1971	11,239	4,408	3,401	217	727	63
1970	11,630	4,443	3,399	206	774	64
1969	10,028	3,724	2,885	153	645	41
1968	8,382	3,464	2,765	165	521	13
1967	7,212	2,929	2,392	124	398	15
1966	5,710	2,616	2,082	78	437	19
1965	5,576	2,395	1,901	125	349	20
1964	5,666	2,588	2,097	95	387	9
1963	5,885	2,133	1,693	95	333	12
1962	4,951	2,069	1,651	56	349	13

[1] Actual offences include attempts. See footnote (1) of series Z15 for the meaning of "actual offences".

[2] See footnote (2) of series Z20 for the legal definition of juveniles. The figures for 1974 (1,384 boys, 91 girls) do not include 182 juveniles dealt with "informally"; i.e., not charged but given an informal hearing in Juvenile Court and/or handed over to their parents or a guardian, or to a social agency or an appropriate department. This provision was introduced in 1974. For 1975, 189 juveniles were reported by police to have been dealt with informally subsequent to incidents of robbery.

Series Z46-51. Breaking and entering, actual offences and persons charged, Canada, 1962 to 1975

Year	Actual[1] offences	Persons charged					
		Total persons charged	Adults		Juveniles[2]	
			Male	Female	Boys	Girls
	46	**47**	**48**	**49**	**50**	**51**
1975	260,652	54,235	30,381	1,098	21,695	1,061
1974	233,362	46,157	25,978	923	18,351	905
1973	198,040	40,601	22,141	865	16,793	802
1972	190,939	36,858	20,834	710	14,784	530
1971	188,462	36,512	20,884	639	14,443	546
1970	177,712	34,777	19,872	545	13,855	505
1969	161,677	33,283	17,968	409	14,440	466
1968	144,895	29,534	16,402	353	12,420	359
1967	119,394	24,419	13,747	316	10,035	321
1966	102,132	21,738	12,777	261	8,350	350
1965	96,530	21,474	12,592	303	8,375	204
1964	97,224	21,884	12,914	244	8,507	219
1963	94,249	21,341	13,051	238	7,863	189
1962	82,104	18,796	11,764	209	6,674	149

[1] Actual offences include attempts. See footnote (1) of series Z15 for the meaning of "actual offences".

[2] See footnote (2) of series Z20 for the legal definition of juveniles. The figures for 1974 (18,351 boys, 905 girls) do not include 7,227 juveniles dealt with "informally"; i.e., not charged but given an informal hearing and/or handed over to their parents or a guardian, or to a social agency or an appropriate department. This provision was introduced in 1974. For 1975, 7,490 juveniles were reported by police to have been dealt with informally subsequent to incidents of breaking and entering.

Series Z52-57. Theft, actual offences and persons charged, Canada, 1962 to 1975

Year	Actual[1] offences	Persons charged					
		Total persons charged	Adults		Juveniles[2]		
			Male	Female	Boys	Girls	
	52	53	54	55	56	57	
1975	678,120	107,981	57,260	18,831	26,468	5,422	
1974	622,246	97,790	52,296	16,453	24,209	4,832	
1973	549,546	89,487	48,622	14,367	22,198	4,300	
1972	533,944	84,828	47,503	12,927	20,464	3,934	
1971	532,383	83,920	46,108	11,920	21,889	4,003	
1970	491,580	78,569	44,152	9,923	21,206	3,288	
1969	425,485	68,416	37,633	7,434	20,564	2,785	
1968	383,820	64,050	34,299	6,163	20,892	2,696	
1967	338,602	56,862	30,420	6,158	18,009	2,275	
1966	306,336	53,781	29,609	5,416	16,453	2,303	
1965	276,018	50,407	27,884	4,751	15,934	1,838	
1964	277,549	49,355	27,652	4,373	15,916	1,414	
1963	257,305	46,006	27,940	3,546	13,491	1,029	
1962	234,722	42,829	27,628	2,708	11,680	813	

[1] Actual offences include attempts. See footnote (1) of series Z15 for the meaning of "actual offences".

[2] See footnote (2) of series Z20 for the legal definition of juveniles. The figures for 1974 (24,209 boys, 4,832 girls) do not include 29,857 juveniles dealt with "informally"; i.e., not charged but given an informal hearing and/or handed over to their parents or a guardian, or to a social agency or an appropriate department. This provision was introduced in 1974. For 1975, a total of 29,141 juveniles were reported by police to have been dealt with informally as a result of incidents of theft.

Series Z58-62. Serious traffic incidents with persons charged, and minor traffic charges, Canada, 1962 to 1975

Year	Traffic offences under the Criminal Code[1]		Serious traffic offences under selected provincial statutes[2]		Charges for minor traffic offences[3] under other federal and provincial statutes and municipal bylaws
	Number of actual incidents	Number of persons charged	Number of actual incidents	Number of persons charged	
	58	59	60	61	62
1975	252,734	182,545	115,341	64,678	2,708,176
1974	239,737	174,559	113,402	67,853	2,598,675
1973	192,914	139,063	90,837	61,673	2,372,983
1972	185,013	132,920	82,364	58,093	2,450,232
1971	163,921	117,114	69,379	48,789	2,326,828
1970	142,486	100,154	66,044	49,419	2,238,748
1969	110,734	70,208	68,988	56,306	2,363,922
1968	101,360	66,309	61,155	51,557	2,327,463
1967	93,235	61,940	52,204	44,682	1,968,795
1966	89,751	59,430	46,404	38,843	1,892,514
1965	84,726	56,130	—	—	1,786,136
1964	75,837	52,684	—	—	1,635,164
1963	67,133	48,584	—	—	1,786,136
1962	63,086	47,517	—	—	1,330,708

[1] Eight major traffic offences under the Criminal Code of Canada constitute the basis of the count of incidents and persons charged: criminal negligence causing death, criminal negligence causing bodily harm, criminal negligence in operating a motor vehicle, failing to stop or remain at the scene of an accident, dangerous driving, failing or refusing to provide a breath sample, driving while impaired, and driving while disqualified or while licence suspended or cancelled.

[2] The count of incidents and of persons charged is based on the following selected provincial traffic offences which are parallel to Criminal Code offences: failing to stop or remain at the scene of an accident, dangerous driving without due care and attention, and driving while disqualified or while licence suspended or cancelled.

[3] Exclusive of parking infractions.

Series Z63-65. Police strength[1] in Canada,[2] 1920 to 1975

Year[3]	Number of police officers	Rate of police officers per 1,000 population[4]	Other full-time personnel[5]	Year[3]	Number of police officers	Rate of police officers per 1,000 population[4]	Other full-time personnel[5]
	63	64	65		63	64	65
1975	50,667	2.2	11,458	1945	6,086	1.2	—
1974	48,051	2.2	10,052	1944	5,729	1.1	—
1973	45,809	2.1	10,214	1943	5,904	1.1	—
1972	43,762	2.0	9,770	1942	5,932	1.2	—
1971	41,940	1.9	8,652	1941	5,945	1.3	—
1970	40,295	1.9	8,253	1940	5,778	1.3	—
1969	38,589	1.8	7,445	1939	5,665	1.3	—
1968	37,044	1.8	6,937	1938	5,596	1.3	—
1967	35,881	1.7	6,660	1937	5,502	1.2	—
1966	34,069	1.7	6,299	1936	5,435	1.2	—
1965	32,010	1.6	5,925	1935	5,231	1.2	—
1964	30,605	1.6	5,528	1934	5,157	1.2	—
1963	29,023	1.5	4,930	1933	5,087	1.1	—
1962	27,744	1.5	4,734	1932	5,192	1.2	—
1961	26,189	1.4	4,597	1931	5,321	1.2	—
1960	16,412	1.5	1,759	1930	5,301	1.6	—
1959	24,173	1.5	3,806	1929	5,004	1.5	—
1958	23,041	1.4	3,759	1928	4,720	1.4	—
1957	19,647	1.5	3,109	1927	4,460	1.3	—
1956	19,100	1.4	3,235	1926	4,331	1.3	—
1955	19,358	1.6	3,869	1925	4,259	1.3	—
1954	18,029	1.5	2,961	1924	4,172	1.3	—
1953	16,961	1.5	2,687	1923	4,074	1.2	—
1952	16,494	1.5	2,462	1922	3,948	1.2	—
1951	19,293	1.7	3,807	1921	3,889	1.2	—
1950	12,538	1.2	531	1920	3,614	—	—
1949	14,063	2.6	—				
1948	13,225	2.5	—				
1947	11,714	2.3	·				
1946	6,954	1.4	—				

[1] Police strength is the number of peace officers employed full-time for the preservation and maintenance of the public peace. Cadets and other full-time employees of police departments are excluded but are classified as "other full-time personnel". The totals cover four types of police force: federal, provincial, municipal, and certain specialized departments; i.e., Canadian National Railway, Canadian Pacific Railway, and the National Harbours Board Police.

[2] From 1920 to 1956, statistics were provided for only those municipalities of 4,000 population and up having a police force. In 1947 the coverage was extended to include the RCMP, the British Columbia Provincial Police, and the Canadian National and Canadian Pacific Railways police. The British Columbia Provincial Police was included only for 1947, 1948 and 1949. In 1948, the Ontario Provincial Police participated for the first time and, like the other non-municipal forces, has continued — with the exception of 1957 — to the present day. In 1960, the Quebec Provincial Police also joined the program. It changed its name in 1969 to the Quebec Police Force. Newfoundland police were included for the first time in 1950. In 1957, the scope of participation was further widened by including all municipalities with a population size of 750 and over which had a police force. The current method of collecting and reporting police statistics, known as the "Uniform Crime Reporting System", commenced on January 1, 1962.

[3] For the calendar year ending 31 December.

[4] For 1920 to 1956: population estimated for cities and towns of 4,000 and over, having a police force. For 1957 to 1975: population based on Canada census figures.

[5] Until 1950, no data were available for other full-time personnel (i.e., clerical, civilian, cadets or other non-uniformed officers).

Series Z66-78. Convictions for indictable offences of persons aged 16 years and over, Canada and the provinces, 1886 to 1972

Year[1]	Canada	New-found-land[2]	Prince Edward Island	Nova Scotia	New Brunswick	Quebec	Ontario	Manitoba	Saskat-chewan	Alberta	British Columbia	Northwest Terri-tories[3]	Yukon Territory[4]
	66	67	68	69	70	71	72	73	74	75	76	77	78
1972	77,650[7]	1,596	22	2,998	2,547	—	39,097	6,904	5,758	—	18,096	—	632
1971	79,437[7]	1,968	60	3,093	3,207	—	42,660	5,259	6,493	—	16,011	—	686
1970	75,334[7]	1,946	96	3,136	3,113	—	39,325	7,180	5,808	—	14,306	—	424
1969	62,550[7]	1,759	187	2,386	2,645	—	33,334	5,081	4,846	—	11,938	—	374
1968[5]	82,312[5,8]	1,314	202	2,101	2,255	16,536	30,149	5,154	4,393	9,375	10,510	—	323
1967	76,681	792	187	2,047	1,882	14,922	26,962	5,259	3,856	8,516	11,933	—	325
1966	79,865	1,347	154	2,056	1,877	17,775	28,359	5,065	3,888	7,746	11,077	—	521
1965	75,300	1,282	201	2,310	1,405	16,876	25,756	5,418	3,631	8,095	10,014	—	312
1964	76,310	1,402	54	2,086	1,582	15,503	25,903	5,414	4,345	9,323	10,470	—	228
1963	78,518	1,634	86	2,126	1,779	17,170	27,722	5,015	3,497	8,868	10,256	—	365
1962	71,507	1,412	99	1,940	1,632	14,239	26,201	5,060	3,289	8,257	8,982	—	396
1961	71,262	1,146	45	1,888	1,681	14,510	25,927	5,345	3,512	8,004	8,816	—	388
1960	64,707	717	34	1,956	1,350	13,548	25,010	4,317	2,755	7,135	7,605	—	280
1959	56,204	806	98	1,771	1,122	12,361	21,695	1,770	2,054	7,080	7,280	—	167
1958	62,839	848	154	1,656	1,295	12,644	21,795	3,462	3,052	11,048	6,797	—	88
1957	54,900	1,013	119	1,504	1,051	12,304	19,227	4,272	2,027	6,727	6,569	—	87
1956	45,913	838	78	1,317	953	10,248	16,750	3,692	2,409	4,237	5,325	—	66
1955	46,239	788	142	1,802	937	10,809	18,118	3,300	1,804	3,733	4,804	—	2
1954	47,981	838	175	1,744	965	11,215	18,795	2,803	2,096	3,784	5,492	—	74
1953	45,071	584	291	1,699	820	9,932	17,771	2,734	1,993	4,170	4,994	—	83
1952	41,591	628	94	1,323	902	8,528	17,096	2,570	1,647	3,895	4,811	—	97
1951	40,289	553	11	1,359	876	8,042	16,399	2,566	1,795	3,902	4,602	—	84
1950[1]	10,772	—	25	336	277	2,085	4,366	677	444	1,251	1,288	—	23
1950	42,624	—	125	1,557	1,056	8,907	17,594	2,756	1,676	3,649	5,138	—	166
1949	41,661	—	130	1,590	899	9,232	17,303	2,553	1,710	3,573	4,552	—	119
1948	41,632	—	127	1,550	1,170	8,176	17,705	3,207	1,737	3,462	4,369	45	84
1947	44,056	—	177	1,843	1,468	7,279	20,178	2,808	2,172	3,850	4,125	54	102
1946	46,939	—	320	2,261	1,492	8,578	21,379	2,834	2,503	3,526	3,916	49	81
1945	41,965	—	231	2,116	1,248	9,592	17,287	2,517	2,204	3,201	3,480	5	84
1944	42,511	—	262	1,782	1,310	10,386	17,613	2,420	2,074	3,164	3,418	11	71
1943	41,752	—	174	1,725	1,211	11,669	16,779	2,060	2,213	2,787	3,092	20	22
1942	39,309	—	205	1,646	1,063	10,269	15,070	2,419	2,621	3,193	2,792	26	5
1941	42,646	—	207	1,675	1,185	11,514	15,861	2,811	3,106	3,263	2,996	22	6
1940	46,723	—	251	1,573	1,131	12,152	17,558	3,353	2,886	4,411	3,392	13	3
1939	48,107	—	268	1,635	1,107	10,804	19,804	3,220	3,450	4,087	3,701	24	7
1938	43,599	—	225	1,269	912	10,277	17,248	3,041	2,555	3,619	4,443	3	7
1937	37,148	—	98	1,081	759	7,781	14,569	2,830	3,083	3,589	3,331	10	8
1936	36,059	—	75	1,147	744	9,497	13,594	2,631	2,194	3,138	3,021	10	8
1935	33,531	—	59	1,002	576	9,354	12,653	2,382	1,976	2,424	3,088	14	3
1934	31,684	—	88	992	525	7,687	11,761	2,571	2,396	2,708	2,946	7	3
1933	32,942	—	70	1,160	479	7,713	13,152	2,667	2,049	2,544	3,094	7	7
1932	31,383	—	78	1,072	514	7,086	12,428	2,982	1,893	2,241	3,072	—	17
1931	31,542	—	57	1,184	461	5,737	12,000	3,102	2,716	2,887	3,385	5	8
1930	28,457	—	59	875	354	5,540	11,774	2,272	2,355	2,525	2,694	3	6
1929	24,097	—	55	869	358	4,780	9,489	1,988	1,918	2,201	2,425	6	8
1928	21,720	—	43	891	365	4,299	9,052	1,672	1,761	1,701	1,931	—	5
1927	18,836	—	14	680	287	3,621	7,962	1,457	1,492	1,483	1,833	4	3
1926	17,448	—	14	752	222	3,053	7,248	1,383	2,052	1,463	1,252	6	3

Series Z66-78. Convictions for indictable offences of persons aged 16 years and over, Canada and the provinces, 1886 to 1972 (concluded)

Year[1]	Canada	New-found-land[2]	Prince Edward Island	Nova Scotia	New Brunswick	Quebec	Ontario	Manitoba	Saskat-chewan	Alberta	British Columbia	Northwest Terri-tories[3]	Yukon Territory[4]
	66	67	68	69	70	71	72	73	74	75	76	77	78
1925	17,219	—	3	624	244	3,084	7,751	1,215	1,654	1,254	1,385	3	2
1924	16,258	—	25	595	224	2,729	7,180	1,160	1,647	1,423	1,265	1	9
1923	15,188	—	13	400	148	2,655	6,886	1,094	1,446	1,424	1,116	5	1
1922	15,720	—	27	701	322	2,885	7,021	1,188	1,391	1,171	1,004	—	10
1921	16,169	—	15	712	313	2,654	7,548	1,159	1,220	1,263	1,282	—	3
1920	15,088	—	4	580	375	2,517	6,707	987	1,467	1,233	1,212	—	6
1919	14,520	—	14	663	241	2,960	6,605	919	1,134	1,028	951	—	5
1918	13,266	—	12	563	230	2,916	6,111	811	1,067	886	659	—	11
1917	11,953	—	21	427	228	2,667	4,824	755	1,057	894	1,058	—	22
1916	16,003	—	11	519	241	3,166	6,023	914	1,711	1,895	1,503	—	20
1915	17,575	—	12	840	206	2,427	7,112	1,362	1,993	2,082	1,517	—	24
1914	18,810	—	18	669	179	2,918	7,479	1,284	1,889	2,235	2,112	—	27
1913	16,007	—	8	598	140	2,336	6,272	1,331	1,594	1,908	1,794	—	26
1912	13,685	—	11	657	107	2,052	5,456	1,120	1,204	1,513	1,532	7	26
1911	11,188	—	19	356	123	1,865	5,067	888	957	870	1,015	4	24
1910	10,327	—	31	684	164	1,810	4,539	744	896	709	727	—	23
1909	10,299	—	18	463	156	2,136	4,524	784	737	645	799	—	37
1908	10,130	—	10	535	202	2,194	4,371	715	637	591	849	—	26
1907	8,106	—	9	402	147	1,827	3,392	773	587	395	532	—	42
1906	7,310	—	21	269	118	1,819	3,145	668	359	334	533	—	44
1905	6,824	—	35	342	110	1,861	2,805	534	—	—	574	524	39
1904	6,057	—	26	368	108	1,614	2,645	408	—	—	365	472	51
1903	5,483	—	32	393	131	1,397	2,344	318	—	—	443	369	56
1902	4,801	—	38	368	125	1,222	2,078	185	—	—	470	268	47
1901	4,621	—	14	287	100	1,222	2,169	185	—	—	401	203	40
1900	4,853	—	21	257	109	1,279	2,260	221	—	—	447	161	95
1899	4,777	—	14	210	103	1,495	2,176	185	—	—	341	253	—
1898	4,951	—	21	205	87	1,364	2,457	186	—	—	443	188	—
1897	4,998	—	29	223	87	1,528	2,451	216	—	—	294	170	—
1896	4,544	—	23	250	103	1,277	2,338	168	—	—	243	142	—
1895	4,648	—	28	226	101	1,389	2,349	133	—	—	307	151	—
1894	4,571	—	28	159	90	1,420	2,310	169	—	—	227	168	—
1893[6]	3,962	—	22	164	101	1,205	1,889	163	—	—	283	135	—
1892	3,316	—	28	110	74	1,156	1,599	78	—	—	186	85	—
1891	3,349	—	27	108	80	1,167	1,664	86	—	—	144	73	—
1890	3,340	—	16	111	68	1,038	1,759	77	—	—	179	92	—
1889	3,521	—	18	100	76	1,123	1,927	78	—	—	142	57	—
1888	3,145	—	13	72	62	1,042	1,734	54	—	—	119	49	—
1887	2,835	—	15	150	52	945	1,500	64	—	—	96	13	—
1886	3,123	—	39	85	60	911	1,734	75	—	—	168	51	—

[1] Figures for the years 1886 to 1950 are the 12 months ending 30 September; later figures are for the calendar year. Cases not entirely disposed of within a year (i.e., tried but sentence postponed) are included in the next year's figures.

[2] The Canadian Criminal Code came into force in Newfoundland on 1 August 1950.

[3] Figures for the years 1886 to 1905 include statistics relating to that part of the Northwest Territories which became in 1905 the provinces of Alberta and Saskatchewan. Figures for the years 1886 to 1899 include statistics relating to the Yukon Territory.

[4] For the years 1906 to 1910, 1913 to 1922, 1932 and 1949 to 1960 figures include statistics relating to the Northwest Territories.

[5] The Integrated Court Reporting Programme, province of Quebec, commenced in 1968. Refer to supplement in Statistics of Criminal and Other Offences 1968 (Catalogue 85-201).

[6] Prior to 1893, only one charge was recorded for a person charged with more than one offence of the same kind at the same trial.

[7] Quebec and Alberta not included. See Introduction, Statistics of Criminal and Other Offences, 1969 (Catalogue 85-201).

[8] From 1968 on, the upper age limit for juveniles established by the province was used in this series.

Series Z79-84. Convictions for indictable offences, by type of offence, Canada, 1886 to 1972[1]

Year[1]	Offences against the person	Offences against property with violence	Offences against property without violence	Malicious offences against property	Forgery and offences against currency	Other offences
	79	80	81	82	83	84
Persons aged 16 years and over						
1972[2]	6,246	13,100	41,333	2,075	4,628	10,268
1971[2]	7,265	14,547	43,729	1,894	5,043	6,959
1970[2]	7,130	13,304	41,530	1,686	4,517	7,167
1969[2]	6,289	11,542	33,186	1,552	4,075	5,906
1968[3]	9,987	20,121	49,909	2,443	5,849	8,929
1967	7,863	15,821	40,758	2,051	4,007	6,181
1966	8,401	16,487	42,341	1,905	4,651	6,080
1965	7,933	15,859	39,077	1,682	5,387	5,362
1964	7,945	16,366	40,476	1,535	4,789	5,199
1963	7,486	17,189	41,797	1,496	4,945	5,605
1962	7,252	14,806	37,948	1,275	5,490	4,736
1961	6,808	15,750	37,591	1,131	5,502	4,480
1960	6,145	14,776	35,040	1,078	4,036	3,632
1959	5,451	12,590	29,984	914	3,633	3,632
1958	5,857	12,320	32,172	941	3,420	8,129
1957	6,165	10,298	27,752	866	3,309	6,510
1956	5,684	8,525	22,067	808	2,906	5,923
1955	5,743	8,466	20,115	652	3,255	8,008
1954	6,460	8,450	20,117	425	2,911	9,618
1953	6,485	7,661	19,988	452	2,139	8,346
1952	6,015	6,550	18,672	710	2,232	7,412
1951[5]	5,554	6,427	18,450	686	1,980	7,192
1950[4]	1,450	1,509	5,044	210	508	2,051
1950	6,405	6,734	18,878	903	1,985	7,719
1949	6,408	5,999	18,610	993	2,024	7,627
1948	6,814	5,541	17,115	1,050	1,988	9,124
1947	7,925	5,304	17,111	1,036	1,780	10,900
1946	7,784	5,783	16,586	1,167	1,607	14,012
1945	6,197	5,297	15,552	944	985	12,990
1944	5,549	5,291	15,902	843	934	13,992
1943	5,610	4,223	15,419	863	1,044	14,593
1942	5,465	3,920	14,721	830	1,225	13,148
1941	5,142	4,217	15,779	805	1,089	15,614
1940	5,268	5,416	19,112	812	1,603	14,512
1939	5,478	6,147	21,358	755	2,126	12,243
1938	5,624	5,509	19,683	584	1,319	10,880
1937	4,824	4,604	18,494	591	1,242	7,393
1936	4,757	4,841	17,022	492	1,094	8,153
1935	3,985	4,147	16,161	439	910	7,889
1934	3,588	4,238	15,853	484	690	6,831
1933	4,019	4,347	16,349	519	825	6,883
1932	4,091	4,267	15,585	518	902	6,020
1931	4,483	4,327	16,143	568	899	5,122
1930	4,314	3,696	14,766	432	1,009	4,240
1929	4,015	2,553	12,138	381	724	4,286
1928	3,678	2,167	11,016	315	554	3,990
1927	3,209	1,910	9,928	278	477	3,034
1926	3,368	1,625	8,958	239	385	2,873
1925	2,904	1,934	8,796	195	408	2,982
1924	2,923	1,718	8,147	234	328	2,908
1923	2,574	1,325	7,303	275	311	3,400
1922	2,804	1,977	7,598	218	465	2,658
Persons of all ages						
1921	3,007	2,611	10,438	297	542	2,501
1920	2,901	2,313	10,022	328	430	2,449
1919	2,605	2,608	9,911	370	377	2,525
1918	2,526	2,051	9,602	249	256	2,686
1917	2,526	1,322	8,393	301	238	2,779
1916	3,443	1,484	9,541	264	315	4,113
1915	3,975	2,242	12,626	256	347	1,179
1914	4,428	1,810	13,000	248	519	1,433
1913	4,256	1,478	10,608	260	541	1,177
1912	3,486	1,196	9,073	273	415	1,124
1911	2,442	978	7,803	211	328	865
1910	2,632	945	6,780	214	237	892
1909	2,441	852	6,638	190	279	1,049
1908	2,413	914	6,796	164	262	786
1907	1,849	684	5,509	163	190	715
1906	1,618	649	4,570	81	220	954
1905	1,609	670	4,222	94	173	856
1904	1,603	565	3,960	100	152	374
1903	1,602	562	3,725	128	120	384
1902	1,329	419	3,443	98	70	301
1901	1,189	493	3,462	106	92	296
1900	1,235	431	3,622	80	91	309
1899	1,168	456	3,666	77	108	236
1898	1,154	555	3,654	90	85	249
1897	1,204	489	3,549	74	82	323
1896	1,099	419	3,305	76	87	218
1895	1,108	483	3,449	57	61	316
1894	1,163	467	3,270	56	37	265
1893	1,124	366	2,800	68	46	226
1892[6]	1,026	262	2,454	51	41	206
1891	905	292	2,493	59	36	189
1890	876	288	2,417	73	46	234
1889	992	307	2,617	50	41	201
1888	817	234	2,276	95	45	284
1887	737	227	1,967	59	43	220
1886	735	268	2,055	56	43	352

[1] For total number of convictions, see series Z66 and Z270.
[2] Quebec and Alberta not included. See footnote (7) in series Z66-78.
[3] Does not include federal statutes in Quebec. See also footnote (6) in series Z66-78.
[4] Figures for the years 1886 to 1950 are for the 12-month period ending 30 September; later figures are for the calendar year. Cases not entirely disposed of within a year (i.e., tried but sentence postponed) are included in the next year's figures.
[5] Statistics relating to Newfoundland included since 1951.
[6] Prior to 1893 only one charge is recorded for a person who is charged with more than one offence of the same kind at the same trial.

Series Z85-93. Sentences for indictable offences, Canada, 1886 to 1951[1]

Year[2]	Jail			Committed to reformatories	Penitentiary			Death	Suspended sentence and other disposition
	With option of a fine	Without option			2 years and under 5	5 years and over	Life		
		Under 1 year	1 year and over						
	85	86	87	88	89	90	91	92	93

Persons aged 16 years and over

1951[2,3]	9,376	12,744	2,565	3,244	4,030	812	6	15	7,497
1950	9,974	13,460	2,719	4,016	3,767	760	5	19	7,904
1949	10,397	13,454	2,754	3,672	3,482	539	4	26	7,333
1948	12,680	12,926	2,460	3,233	3,134	725	3	19	6,452
1947	15,077	13,004	2,157	3,349	2,763	417	5	18	7,266
1946	18,789	12,747	1,976	3,138	2,874	708	8	32	6,667
1945	16,900	11,189	1,664	2,912	2,389	559	2	17	6,333
1944	17,367	11,134	1,569	3,041	2,594	426	6	11	6,363
1943	17,789	10,735	1,587	2,614	2,532	356	3	9	6,127
1942	15,573	11,139	1,516	2,241	2,173	347	1	15	6,304
1941	16,828	12,354	1,578	2,596	2,119	459	7	13	6,692
1940	14,873	14,766	1,784	2,738	3,103	500	7	17	8,935
1939	13,047	16,246	1,904	3,629	3,558	497	3	14	9,209
1938	11,368	15,115	1,740	3,122	2,804	608	7	22	8,813
1937	9,310	12,224	1,506	2,519	2,434	644	2	13	8,496
1936	9,593	11,319	1,651	2,572	2,371	528	6	22	7,997
1935	9,374	10,631	2,357	467	2,191	462	3	15	8,031
1934	8,614	10,492	2,391	297	1,902	353	5	19	7,611
1933	8,973	10,132	2,656	168	2,018	451	15	24	8,505
1932	8,143	9,314	2,760	376	2,347	536	9	23	7,875
1931	8,036	8,801	2,728	597	2,551	568	10	25	8,226
1930	7,472	7,589	2,502	224	2,502	508	4	17	7,639
1929	7,050	6,423	1,715	319	1,781	374	9	26	6,400
1928	6,719	5,737	1,668	227	1,622	362	7	19	5,359
1927	5,606	5,016	1,456	195	1,370	364	5	12	4,812
1926	5,469	4,612	1,309	172	1,198	351	4	15	4,318
1925	4,712	4,385	1,336	370	1,244	278	14	18	4,862
1924	5,142	3,702	1,461	149	1,054	330	5	22	4,393
1923	4,916	3,601	1,057	105	949	223	2	15	4,320
1922	4,430	3,982	1,531	89	1,153	435	11	19	4,070

Persons of all ages

1921	5,059	3,932	1,262	502	1,124	481	9	17	7,010
1920	5,447	3,750	886	615	873	245	7	26	6,594
1919	5,053	3,455	921	678	978	229	7	28	7,047
1918	5,106	3,284	783	678	701	185	4	20	6,609
1917	4,845	2,890	462	584	540	145	1	15	6,077
1916	6,786	3,816	666	568	799	178	5	21	6,321
1915	5,344	5,774	893	517	1,074	241	7	34	6,741
1914	5,518	6,306	946	592	967	241	8	27	6,833
1913	4,655	5,263	798	551	1,007	293	3	23	5,727
1912	4,144	4,779	738	433	931	308	9	25	4,200
1911	3,071	3,994	568	315	821	259	5	17	3,577
1910	3,088	3,621	444	433	729	151	2	21	3,211
1909	2,916	3,579	470	300	844	275	2	18	3,045
1908	3,126	3,794	497	327	779	202	6	15	2,589
1907	2,260	3,062	426	305	533	204	5	8	2,307
1906	1,878	2,685	384	253	622	180	5	2	2,083
1905	1,796	2,697	368	305	519	153	2	12	1,772
1904	1,302	2,454	367	232	501	156	—	14	1,728
1903	1,261	2,260	268	325	431	172	1	6	1,797
1902	1,130	2,149	214	245	358	116	1	11	1,436
1901	953	2,064	251	248	383	140	—	6	1,593
1900	1,067	2,170	286	256	378	157	5	10	1,439
1899	870	2,332	245	252	428	162	2	11	1,400
1898	864	2,501	323	231	369	189	1	13	1,296
1897	930	2,461	328	177	426	178	5	4	1,212
1896	723	2,384	267	205	371	162	2	6	1,084
1895	884	2,414	286	236	354	145	—	5	1,150
1894	798	2,428	263	190	388	173	9	11	998
1893	817	2,114	234	168	274	137	1	6	879
1892[4]	646	1,889	203	187	249	111	4	5	746
1891	572	1,925	184	201	299	119	2	7	665

Series Z85-93. Sentences for indictable offences, Canada, 1886 to 1951[1] (concluded)

Year[2]	Jail			Committed to reformatories	Penitentiary			Death	Suspended sentence and other disposition
	With option of a fine	Without option			2 years and under 5	5 years and over	Life		
		Under 1 year	1 year and over						
	85	86	87	88	89	90	91	92	93

Persons of all ages

Year	85	86	87	88	89	90	91	92	93
1890	568	1,927	215	204	284	124	2	8	602
1889	592	2,109	196	271	300	138	5	8	589
1888	596	1,887	182	216	231	117	5	9	508
1887	543	1,717	201	167	249	91	3	4	278
1886	622	1,731	203	153	316	136	13	14	321

[1] For the total number of indictable offences, see series Z66 and Z270.

[2] Figures for the years 1886 to 1950 are for the 12-month period ending 30 September; figures for 1951 are for the calendar year; statistics for the intervening months (October–December 1950) not available. Cases not entirely disposed of within a year (i.e., tried, but sentence postponed) are included in next year's figures.

[3] Includes statistics relating to Newfoundland.

[4] Prior to 1893 only one charge was recorded for a person charged with more than one offence of the same kind at the same trial.

Series Z94-102. Sentences of persons[1] convicted for indictable offences, Canada, 1952 to 1972

Year	Sentence suspended		Fine	Prison or jail	Reformatory and/or training school	Penitentiary			Death
	Without probation	With probation				2 years and over	Preventive detention	Life	
	94	95	96	97	98	99	100	101	102
1972[2,3]	3,449	11,147	15,162	13,016	1,041	1,726	4	68	1
1971[2,3]	3,370	11,779	15,634	13,653	1,446	1,962	2	28	–
1970[2,3]	3,559	11,290	14,487	12,179	2,241	2,076	5	40	3
1969[2,3]	3,890	8,216	10,822	10,916	1,920	2,227	4	22	–
1968[2]	4,860	6,847	10,558	11,875	2,052	2,383	8	25	1
1967	5,809	8,577	12,636	13,568	2,125	2,933	12	36	7
1966	5,729	8,538	12,778	13,550	2,163	2,853	12	38	9
1965	4,318	8,293	11,045	13,097	1,903	3,100	22	35	19
1964	4,903	7,827	10,124	13,857	2,072	3,244	30	35	5
1963	4,854	7,698	10,098	14,735	2,077	3,398	8	35	11
1962	4,665	6,789	8,503	13,441	1,917	3,310	4	21	13
1961	4,482	6,541	8,508	13,993	2,064	3,059	2	18	12
1960[4]	4,358	5,820	7,703	12,497	2,125	2,923	–	7	10
1959[4]	3,631	4,911	6,839	10,943	2,074	2,674	–	4	16
1958[4]	4,493	4,325	8,934	11,732	2,165	2,873	–	8	16
1957[4]	3,734	4,496	8,967	10,284	1,941	2,334	–	1	8
1956[4]	3,117	3,476	8,050	9,030	1,697	2,028	–	5	10
1955[4]	3,271	2,467	9,312	9,434	1,689	2,080	–	4	16
1954	3,177	2,426	10,571	10,814	1,484	2,342	6	13	15
1953	2,393	3,099	10,371	10,155	1,478	2,051	5	5	10
1952	3,825	1,822	9,489	10,782	1,904	1,909	5	8	17

[1] These series are modified continuations of series Z85-90 (ending in 1951). The above series are not comparable with those prior to 1952 because the unit of count in series Z91-99 is persons while in series Z82-90 the unit of count is offences. The categories used are similar to those given in the 1972 issue of *Statistics of Criminal and Other Offences*. Note that the caption, "Penitentiary — 2 years and over" contains several variations introduced since 1953 including the current category, "Penitentiary — 1 day to 14 years and over" which is used for composite sentencing.

[2] Does not include Quebec.

[3] Does not include Alberta.

[4] For the years 1955 to 1960, preventive detention was not enumerated and it is likely that any such sentences would be included in "Penitentiary — 2 years and over".

Series Z103-108. Murder, charges, dispositions, commutations and executions, Canada, 1879 to 1960

Year[1]	Charges	Acquittals[2]	Detained for insanity	Death sentences	Commu-tations[3]	Execu-tions[3]
	103	104	105	106	107	108
1960	32	13	9	10	..	..
1959	57	34	7	16	..	..
1958	35	13	3	19	15	2
1957	42	25	9	8	6	4
1956	24	8	6	10	8	4
1955	34	14	4	16	5	8
1954	35	16	4	15	1	4
1953	36	18	8	10	10	11
1952	50	32	—	18	3	12
1951[1,4]	52	30	7	15	2	6
1950	29	9	1	19	6	13
1949	55	27	2	26	4	13
1948	56	33	4	19	4	12
1947	61	30	13	18	6	10
1946	66	29	5	32	8	14
1945	35	10	8	17	3	6
1944	33	20	2	11	3	6
1943	23	10	4	9	—	7
1942	41	17	9	15	4	6
1941	40	19	8	13	6	9
1940	40	18	5	17	6	8
1939	37	20	3	14	5	7
1938	45	19	4	22	7	7
1937	35	16	6	13	4	12
1936	48	18	8	22	3	8
1935	46	22	9	15	5	17
1934	46	24	3	19	1	12
1933	43	11	8	24	4	16
1932	47	18	6	23	6	16
1931	49	14	10	25	2	22
1930	54	30	7	17	5	10
1929	50	17	7	26	8	11
1928	42	18	5	19	8	7
1927	45	23	11	11	1	9
1926	51	31	5	15	5	9
1925	54	32	4	18	10	6
1924	61	34	5	22	6	13
1923	47	27	5	15	6	13
1922	56	34	3	19	7	9
1921	77	55	5	17	10	8

Year[1]	Charges	Acquittals[2]	Detained for insanity	Death sentences	Commu-tations[3]	Execu-tions[3]
	103	104	105	106	107	108
1920	57	28	3	26	14	7
1919	79	44	7	28	7	19
1918	50	23	7	20	10	6
1917	48	28	3[5]	17	8	7
1916	56	32	3	21	13	8
1915	86	48	4	34	13	14
1914	62	31	4	27	16	13
1913	55	27	5	23	15	9
1912	52	24	3	25	11	8
1911	53	34	2	17	8	7
1910	55	31	3	21	2	13
1909	42	23	1	18	4	13
1908	42	24	3	15	8	7
1907	37	28	1	8	4	7
1906	30	26	2	2	2	2
1905	38	24	2	12	5	5
1904	27	11	2	14	6	6
1903	26	20	—	6	5	5
1902	28	17	—	11	3	9
1901	22	14	1	7	3	4
1900	18	7	1	10	3	6
1899	23	9	3	11	6	9
1898	25	11	1	13	4	8
1897	17	13	—	4	3	3
1896	28	20	2	6	2	—
1895	16	10	1	5	1	3
1894	27	16	—	11	7	4
1893	20	13	1	6	1	1
1892	23	18	—	5	5	4
1891	18	10	1	7	2	2
1890	26	17	1	8	1	10
1889	26	17	1	8	3	1
1888	25	12	4	9	3	7
1887	13	9	—	4	5	3
1886	26	10	2	14	6	2
1885	20	10	—	10	4	12
1884	26	13	2	11	3	6
1883	25	14	—	11	4	5
1882	28	16	1	11	4	4
1881	40	23	1	16	2	3
1880	25	20	—	5	2	6
1879	36	22	—	14	6	5

[1] Figures for the years 1879 to 1950 are for the 12 months ending 30 September; all other figures are for the calendar year. Figures for the intervening months (October–December 1950) not available. Cases not entirely disposed of within a year (i.e., tried but sentence postponed) are included in the next year's figures.

[2] Includes acquittals, jury disagreements, stay of proceedings, no bill and *nolli prosequi*.

[3] Figures represent commutations and executions that took place the year mentioned regardless of the year sentences of death were imposed. Figures are not included in the totals.

[4] Statistics relating to Newfoundland included since 1951.

[5] Figures include two Eskimos convicted of murder and exiled in the north.

Series Z109-113. Murder,[1] persons[2] charged, acquitted, and convicted, Canada, 1961 to 1975

Year	Number of persons charged[2]	Persons acquitted for insanity	Persons acquitted of murder or lesser offence	Persons convicted of murder	Persons convicted of manslaughter
	109	110	111	112	113
1975[3]	512	10	17	40	96
1974[3]	457	20	47	99	134
1973	434	30	58	81	160
1972	412	29	50	74	167
1971	378	29	42	81	148
1970	333	21	49	55	134
1969	292	21	38	60	124
1968	279	22	34	36	109
1967	200	13	27	40	85
1966	204	3	32	43	64
1965	199	10	20	51	61
1964	177	8	25	50	55
1963	196	11	47	49	55
1962	147	10	28	43	44
1961	146	8	46	29	44

[1] These series (Z109-113) together with Z114-123 constitute a modified continuation of series Z103-108.
[2] For the years 1967 to 1975, the count of persons includes only adults and juveniles tried in adult court; for 1961 to 1966, the count includes, in addition, juveniles tried in juvenile court. Note also that a person charged with more than one murder would be counted once for each charge.

[3] Since murder cases are often lengthy, dispositions may not yet have been made in a considerable number of cases reported in 1974 and 1975.

Series Z114-123. Sentences[1] of persons[2] charged with murder[1] and convicted for murder or manslaughter, Canada, 1961 to 1975

Year	Total	Sentence suspended, probation, and/or fine	Under 2 years	2 years and under 5	5 years and under 10	10 years and over	Life imprisonment	Death[1]	Death commuted to life	Other[3]
	114	115	116	117	118	119	120	121	122	123
1975	138	5	22	20	30	16	41	—	—	4
1974	100	—	8	21	17	6	45	2	—	1
1973	230	9	18	25	64	35	77	2	—	—
1972	243	6	13	46	55	41	81	—	1	—
1971	232	2	25	35	46	42	81	1	—	—
1970	187	6	20	24	50	32	53	—	1	1
1969	182	1	14	31	42	35	57	—	2	—
1968	146	2	14	29	35	29	37	—	—	—
1967	126	1	12	15	35	21	40	—	2	—
1966	108	3	13	17	21	13	39	—	2	—
1965	115	1	11	17	22	8	41	—	15	—
1964	113	1	8	13	24	14	41	—	12	—
1963	104	1	8	9	19	21	39	—	7	—
1962	84	3	5	13	15	7	31	1	8	1
1961	71	2	1	12	12	14	22	1	7	—

[1] Over the period 1961 to 1975, there were changes in the legal definition and the penalty for murder. For a short summary of these changes, see *Homicide in Canada* (Appendix), (Catalogue 85-505).
[2] Includes all adults, and juveniles dealt with in adult court, but excludes juveniles alleged to have committed murder and dealt with in juvenile

court. The latter are subject to different judicial procedures and different sentences. Between 1961 and 1975, approximately half of the estimated 250 juveniles charged with murder were dealt with in juvenile court.
[3] Includes pardons, intermittent sentences, sentences pending, and conditional and absolute discharges.

Series Z124-134. Rape,[1] Persons convicted and sentences, Canada, 1952 to 1972

Year	Persons convicted	Sentence suspended		Fine	Prison or jail	Reformatory and/or training school	Penitentiary			Institution[2]	Extra sentence[3]
		Without probation	With probation				Under 2 years	2 years and over	Life imprisonment		
	124	125	126	127	128	129	130	131	132	133	134
1972[4]	94	2	2	2	20	5	—	63	—	—	—
1971[4]	76	—	1	—	17	3	—	55	—	—	—
1970[4]	51	2	1	—	14	5	—	29	—	—	—
1969[4]	70	3	1	—	—	—	—	—	—	66	—
1968	80	—	—	—	—	9	—	—	—	80	4
1967	75	5	3	1	—	—	—	—	—	66	3
1966	65	1	—	—	—	6	—	—	—	64	7
1965	64	1	1	—	—	—	—	—	—	62	2
1964	78	1	1	1	—	7	—	—	—	75	9
1963	93	—	2	3	—	3	—	—	—	88	3
1962	70	1	1	2	—	2	—	—	—	66	3
1961	73	1	2	—	—	8	—	—	—	70	1
1960	65	1	—	—	15	10	—	39	—	—	—
1959	62	—	—	1	15	10	—	36	—	—	—
1958	62	—	—	—	16	4	—	42	—	—	—
1957	62	2	1	1	14	6	—	37	—	—	—
1956	62	—	—	2	13	2	—	45	—	—	5
1955	62	1	—	—	13	2	—	46	—	—	10
1954	44	1	—	2	12	5	—	24	—	—	2
1953	52	1	—	—	12	3	—	36	—	—	10
1952	52	2	—	—	13	2	—	33	2	—	5

1 Includes attempted rape.
2 Refers to unspecified incarceration in either a prison or penitentiary.
3 Extra sentences are punishments (e.g., whipping until abolition in 1972) or special requirements (e.g., restitution) imposed by the court in addition to the principal sentence.
4 Quebec and Alberta not included.

Series Z135-145. Robbery, persons convicted and sentences, Canada, 1952 to 1972

Year	Persons convicted	Sentence suspended		Fine	Prison or jail	Reformatory and/or training school	Penitentiary			Institution[1]	Extra sentence[2]
		Without probation	With probation				Under 2 years	2 years and over	Life imprisonment		
	135	136	137	138	139	140	141	142	143	144	145
1972[3]	792	13	80	6	304	55	4	329	1	—	6
1971[3]	889	14	100	8	313	90	—	364	—	—	8
1970[3]	814	15	71	5	271	118	—	332	2	—	6
1969[3]	763	8	88	2	—	111	—	—	—	554	17
1968	1,275	67	62	9	—	95	—	—	—	1,042	—
1967	998	57	114	18	—	93	—	—	—	716	28
1966	1,017	41	122	14	—	102	—	—	—	738	35
1965	1,053	38	100	8	—	67	—	—	—	840	31
1964	1,089	40	96	10	—	83	—	—	—	860	30
1963	1,007	37	90	15	—	75	—	—	—	790	28
1962	879	28	78	13	—	86	—	—	—	674	24
1961	933	34	63	9	—	73	—	—	—	754	8
1960	932	38	54	17	261	109	—	453	—	—	5
1959	843	33	60	9	254	82	1	404	—	—	13
1958	948	35	39	17	267	95	—	495	—	—	13
1957	714	37	48	13	223	110	—	283	—	—	11
1956	659	40	50	21	187	97	—	264	—	—	7
1955	615	15	42	7	205	88	—	258	—	—	10
1954	631	14	45	19	194	80	—	279	—	—	7
1953	634	12	38	15	205	74	—	290	—	—	14
1952	624	19	15	4	217	102	—	267	—	—	13

1 Refers to unspecified incarceration in either a prison or penitentiary.
2 See footnote (3) in series Z134.
3 Quebec and Alberta not included.

Series Z146-156. Breaking and entering, persons convicted and sentences, Canada, 1952 to 1972

| Year | Persons convicted | Sentence suspended | | Fine | Prison or jail | Reformatory and/or training school | Penitentiary | | | Institution[1] | Extra sentence[2] |
		Without probation	With probation				Under 2 years	2 years and over	Life imprisonment		
	146	**147**	**148**	**149**	**150**	**151**	**152**	**153**	**154**	**155**	**156**
1972[4]	6,035	370	2,406	92	2,393	352	4	417	1[3]	–	178
1971[4]	6,795	388	2,691	128	2,615	500	–	473	–	–	246
1970[4]	6,417	369	2,494	104	2,213	692	–	545	–	–	161
1969[4]	5,585	393	1,921	100	–	–	–	–	–	2,509	207
1968	7,776	1,100	1,890	135	–	–	–	–	–	3,943	4
1967	7,181	828	2,255	229	–	–	–	–	–	3,261	194
1966	6,948	792	2,107	170	–	–	–	–	–	3,320	208
1965	6,974	601	2,036	241	–	–	–	–	–	3,529	188
1964	7,310	679	1,881	192	–	–	–	–	–	3,952	176
1963	7,694	760	1,897	191	–	–	–	–	–	4,271	160
1962	6,897	680	1,521	145	–	–	–	–	–	3,986	133
1961	6,930	730	1,437	174	–	–	–	–	–	3,901	104
1960	6,710	690	1,313	168	2,676	854	3	1,006	–	–	63
1959	5,592	602	1,061	153	2,121	736	22	897	–	–	63
1958	5,948	729	932	184	2,313	771	–	1,019	–	–	46
1957	4,874	447	911	167	1,859	668	–	822	–	–	65
1956	3,921	415	598	136	1,548	546	–	678	–	–	46
1955	3,991	527	509	139	1,534	576	–	706	–	–	55
1954	4,112	411	404	139	1,775	497	–	886	–	–	53
1953	3,540	291	448	118	1,528	467	–	688	–	–	23
1952	3,416	476	258	90	1,432	572	–	588	–	–	19

[1] Refers to unspecified incarceration in either a prison or penitentiary.
[2] See footnote (3) in series Z134.
[3] This was a special sentence of preventive detention.
[4] Quebec and Alberta not included.

Series Z157-166. Theft, persons convicted and sentences, Canada, 1952 to 1972

| Year | Persons convicted | Sentence suspended | | Fine | Prison or jail | Reformatory and/or training school | Penitentiary | | Institution[1] | Extra sentence[2] |
		Without probation	With probation				Under 2 years	2 years and over		
	157	**158**	**159**	**160**	**161**	**162**	**163**	**164**	**165**	**166**
1972[4]	18,006	1,720	3,861	8,926	2,646	168	3	129	–	553
1971[4]	20,238	1,741	4,379	9,813	3,877	267	–	161	–	–
1970[4]	20,633	2,764	4,406	8,478	3,760	496	–	190	–	539
1969[4]	15,490	1,984	2,843	5,961	–	400	–	–	3,956	346
1968	15,878	2,314	2,508	5,865	–	450	–	–	4,445	296
1967	19,478	2,828	3,784	6,528	–	446	–	–	5,410	482
1966	19,961	2,891	3,967	6,292	–	531	–	–	5,681	599
1965	17,458	2,075	3,885	5,287	–	469	–	–	5,286	456
1964	17,365	2,363	3,761	4,592	–	510	–	–	5,834	305
1963	17,508	2,302	3,751	4,293	–	537	–	–	6,312	313
1962	15,590	2,119	3,376	3,679	–	468	–	–	5,731	217
1961	16,125	2,100	3,290	3,716	–	505	–	–	6,221	293
1960	14,502	2,118	3,054	3,413	4,727	615	–	413	–	162
1959	12,835	1,807	2,615	2,814	4,244	812	–	369	–	174
1958	12,837	2,339	2,111	2,889	4,252	699	–	415	–	132
1957	11,469	2,003	2,248	2,411	3,777	515	–	350	–	165
1956	9,271	1,343	1,852	1,858	3,193	553	–	320[3]	–	148
1955	8,303	1,310	1,073	1,562	3,343	477	–	394	–	144
1954	7,652	1,186	848	1,594	3,350	287	–	246	–	141
1953	7,757	968	1,236	1,656	3,373	212	–	219	–	93
1952	8,649	1,624	796	1,688	3,867	364	–	248	–	62

[1] Refers to unspecified incarceration in either a prison or penitentiary.
[2] See footnote (3) in series Z134.
[3] In 1956, an additional four persons were given a special sentence of preventive detention.
[4] Quebec and Alberta not included.

Series Z167. Convictions for drug-related[1] offences, Canada, 1921 to 1974

Year[2]	Number of convictions	Year[2]	Number of convictions	Year[2]	Number of convictions
	167		**167**		**167**
1974	30,485	1955	357	1935	184
1973	21,469	1954	391	1934	271[2]
1972	12,811	1953	381	1933	—[2]
1971	10,137	1952	411	1932	178
		1951[4]	364	1931	135
1970	6,745	1950	407	1930	236
1969	3,338	1949	343	1929	266
1968	1,779	1948	320	1928	161
1967	995	1947	238	1927	176
1966	447	1946	142	1926	280
1965	390	1945	193	1925	355
1964	337	1944	151	1924	218
1963	336	1943	95	1923	506
1962	331	1942	190	1922	800
1961	478	1941	176	1921	610
1960[3]	509	1940	173		
1960	580	1939	150		
1959	585	1938	155		
1958	473	1937	131		
1957	354	1936	102		
1956	453				

[1] From 1921 to 1961, convictions for offences under the Opium and Narcotic Drug Act (repealed 15 September 1961). From 1961 to 1974, convictions for offences under the Narcotic Control Act and the Food and Drug Act.

[2] Figures for the years 1921 to 1932 are for the 12-month period ending 30 September; figures for the years 1935 to 1960 are for the 12-month period ending 31 March; figures for the year 1934 are for the period 1 October 1932 to 31 March 1934 (18 months). For the years 1960 to 1974, figures are for the calendar year.

[3] Number of convictions are repeated for the calendar year 1960, and figures for ensuing years are based on the calendar year.

[4] Statistics on Newfoundland included since 1951.

Series Z168-172. Dispositions of appeal of convictions for indictable offences, Canada, 1937 to 1972

Year[1]	Number of appeals disposed of during the year	Appeal dismissed	Convictions quashed	Sentences varied	New trial directed
	168	169	170	171	172
1972[2]	3,123	2,338	130	585	70
1971[2]	3,735	2,332	459	852	92
1970[2]	1,910	1,033	105	681	91
1969	3,719	2,524	134	976	85
1968	4,118	2,904	210	896	108
1967	3,312	2,176	130	924	82
1966	3,273	2,198	132	847	96
1965	3,101	2,033	374	617	77
1964	2,536	1,815	103	548	70
1963	2,721	1,953	113	582	73
1962	2,301	1,684	105	431	81
1961	2,247	1,532	179	483	53
1960	2,036	1,396	79	501	60
1959	1,311	888	73	317	33
1958	1,313	876	95	290	52
1957	1,427	1,004	90	297	36
1956	1,093	751	86	198	58
1955	1,207	836	114	201	56
1954	976	646	83	205	42
1953	830	513	86	195	36
1952	847	526	87	168	66
1951[3]	839	511	115	166	47
1950	895	538	104	201	52
1949	721	429	89	164	39
1948	799	527	95	125	52
1947	662	450	80	93	39
1946	729	439	109	151	30
1945	557	351	80	100	26
1944	519	321	78	85	35
1943	354	214	48	66	26
1942	319	188	53	45	33
1941	421	257	65	74	25
1940	443[4]	245	72	89	37
1939	424[5]	233	70	84	37
1938	530	325	92	83	30
1937	428	255	85	67	21

[1] Appeals in a specific year include cases which were tried during that year as well as the years before; similarly, the results of new trials ordered by appeal courts in that specific year are included in later years depending on when the case is disposed of.

[2] Excludes Alberta.

[3] Statistics relating to Newfoundland included since 1951.

[4] Includes 27 cases held over from previous year.

[5] Includes 20 cases held over from previous year.

Series Z173-174. Number of prisoners in penitentiaries, by sex, Canada, 1867 to 1975

Year[1]	Males	Females	Year[1]	Males	Females	Year[1]	Males	Females
	173	174		173	174		173	174
1975[1]	8,441	139	1940	3,739	33	1905[1]	1,367	—
1974	9,075	164	1939	3,768	35	1904	1,328	—
1973	8,683	140	1938	3,541	39	1903	1,250	—
1972	7,671	108	1937	3,232	32	1902	1,214	—
1971	7,369	89	1936	3,098[3]	—[3]	1901	1,382	—
1970	7,274	101	1935	3,552	34	1900	1,424	—
1969	7,058	102	1934	4,220[3,4]	—[3]	1899	1,445	—
1968	6,946	111	1933	4,539[5]	48	1898	1,446	—
1967	7,072	113	1932	4,112	52	1897	1,383	—
1966	7,322	122	1931	3,670	44	1896	1,361	—
1965	7,403	115	1930	3,149	38	1895	1,277	—
1964	7,517	138	1929	2,737	32	1894	1,223	—
1963	7,092	127	1928	2,520	40	1893	1,194	—
1962	7,030	126	1927	2,441	39	1892	1,228	—
1961	6,614	124	1926	2,440	34	1891	1,249	—
1960	6,220	124	1925	2,318	27	1890	1,251	—
1959[1]	6,181	114	1924	2,194	31	1889	1,195	—
1958	5,682	88	1923	2,486[3]	—[3]	1888	1,094	—
1957	5,347	86	1922	2,640	—	1887	1,159	—
1956	5,426	82	1921	2,150	—	1886	1,200	—
1955	5,412	95	1920	1,931	—	1885	1,112	—
1954	5,025	95	1919	1,689	—	1884	1,039	—
1953	4,829	105	1918	1,468	—	1883	1,113	—
1952	4,561	125	1917	1,694	—	1882	1,127	—
1951	4,712	105	1916	2,118	—	1881	1,218	—
1950	4,650	90	1915	2,064	—	1880	1,213	—
1949[2]	4,173	87	1914	2,003	—	1879	1,200	—
1948	3,777	74	1913	1,970	—	1878	1,110[6]	—
1947	3,695	57	1912	1,895	—	1877	1,108	—
1946	3,313	49	1911	1,865	—	1876	1,069	—
1945	3,077	52	1910	1,859	—	1875	848	—
1944	3,035	43	1909	1,765	—	1874	679	—
1943	2,917	52	1908	1,476	—	1873	567	—
1942	3,193	39	1907	1,423	—	1872	605	—
1941	3,642	46	1906	1,439	—	1871	692	—
						1870	756	—
						1869	745[6]	—
						1868	861[6]	—
						1867	972	

[1] From 1867 to 1876 the reporting year ends on 31 December; from 1877 to 1905 on 30 June; from 1906 to 1959 on 31 March; and from 1960 to 1975 on 31 December.

[2] Figures include statistics relating to Newfoundland since 1949.

[3] Figures in series Z173 for the years 1936, 1934 and prior to 1924 include female prisoners.

[4] Figures include 531 Doukhobors in custody at Piers Island.

[5] Figures include 570 Doukhobors in custody at Piers Island.

[6] Does not include penitentiary at Halifax; see footnote (3).

Series Z175-182. Admissions of males to penitentiaries, by age, Canada, 1938 to 1960[1]

| Year[2] | Admissions | Age at admission in penitentiary | | | | | | |
| | | Under 16 | 16 | 17 | 18 | 19 | 20 | 21 and over |
	175	176	177	178	179	180	181	182
1960	3,332	30	59	115	166	189	217	2,556
1959	2,975	22	57	101	143	156	173	2,323
1958	2,929	37	67	98	138	197	159	2,233
1957	2,266	25	66	86	101	111	113	1,764
1956	2,363	26	51	78	104	121	113	1,870
1955	2,328	14	45	75	116	115	115	1,848
1954	2,418	24	46	78	114	89	123	1,944
1953	2,101	18	48	71	90	111	116	1,647
1952	1,806	9	23	43	71	96	82	1,482
1951	1,951	5	21	49	76	67	94	1,639
1950	1,996	6	20	59	85	92	109	1,625
1949	1,843	4	18	49	64	83	91	1,534
1948	1,547	2	15	42	75	100	67	1,246
1947	1,663	4	19	44	70	113	89	1,324
1946	1,635	4	15	51	69	93	101	1,302
1945	1,335	2	12	40	68	84	75	1,054
1944	1,476	4	20	56	87	93	94	1,122
1943	1,171	10	15	49	42	71	66	918
1942	1,143	1	6	33	41	68	52	942
1941	1,489	2	20	33	56	79	71	1,228
1940	1,685	1	12	30	77	72	73	1,420
1939	1,896	3	20	38	67	97	83	1,588
1938	1,447	1	17	27	61	64	69	1,208

[1] Persons admitted to and transferred to another penitentiary during the same year are counted only once.

[2] Figures are for the fiscal year ending 31 March.

Series Z183-197. Admissions of males to penitentiaries, by age, Canada, 1961 to 1975

| Year | Admissions | Age at admission to penitentiary | | | | | | | | | | | | | |
| | | Under 16 | 16 | 17 | 18 | 19 | 20-24 | 25-29 | 30-34 | 35-39 | 40-44 | 45-49 | 50-59 | 60 and over | Not specified |
	183	184	185	186	187	188	189	190	191	192	193	194	195	196	197
1975[1]	4,221	—	28	88	—	868	1,090	931	493	303	192	118	91	19	—
1974[1]	3,521	—	11	56	111	190	1,196	856	458	254	171	109	91	18	—
1973[1]	4,230	1	9	70	109	247	1,403	1,030	503	336	210	156	129	27	—
1972[1]	4,162	3	14	78	157	235	1,361	969	524	308	225	139	116	37	—
1971[1]	4,312	1	11	53	120	222	1,429	1,004	578	348	268	145	115	18	—
1970[1]	4,391	—	11	65	151	242	1,472	896	566	372	263	173	137	43	—
1969[1]	4,057	1	12	60	119	210	1,321	880	568	331	230	163	120	40	2
1968[2]	3,433	5	17	63	112	174	1,071	727	461	314	204	115	133	33	4
1967[2]	3,401	3	26	76	156	184	1,011	729	453	281	218	118	115	31	—
1966[2]	3,514	10	48	89	181	201	1,097	668	430	320	217	114	108	30	1
1965[2]	3,621	11	37	116	183	210	1,030	726	476	327	222	130	124	29	—
1964[2]	3,816	9	39	107	201	227	1,149	729	465	368	221	137	129	35	—
1963[2]	3,656	26	36	95	170	205	1,080	680	500	330	235	126	137	34	2
1962[2]	3,331	17	66	104	156	204	908	655	437	345	186	111	109	32	1
1961[2]	3,272	29	57	119	158	184	953	589	471	281	182	114	108	23	4

[1] Figures given are for calendar years.
[2] Figures given are for the fiscal year ending 31 March.

Series Z198-201. Number of prisoners in reformatories and training schools, by sex, in jails, and in all penal institutions, Canada, 1916 to 1956

Year	Reformatories and training schools[1]		Jails[2]	All penal institutions[3]	Year	Reformatories and training schools[1]		Jails[2]	All penal institutions[3]
	Male	Female				Male	Female		
	198	**199**	**200**	**201**		**198**	**199**	**200**	**201**
1956	4,862	1,079	5,903	17,352	1935	2,823	722	3,419	10,550
					1934	2,987	734	3,958	11,899
1955	5,058	1,086	6,397	18,048	1933	3,132	764	4,174	12,657
1954	4,883	1,083	6,283	17,369	1932	3,528	852	4,711	13,255
1953	4,651	1,019	5,779	16,383	1931	3,426	932	4,477	12,549
1952	4,630	931	5,599	15,846					
1951	4,222	834	5,422	15,295	1930	3,105	648	4,283	11,223
					1929	2,846	602	3,579	9,796
1950	4,390[4]	892	5,990[4]	16,012	1928	2,435	437	3,129	8,561
1949	4,545	804	4,964	14,573	1927	2,409	441	2,634	7,964
1948	4,304	780	4,519	13,454	1926	2,249	431	2,439	7,593
1947	3,887	682	4,160	12,481					
1946	3,319[5]	785	4,185	11,651	1925	2,193	403	2,602	7,543
					1924	2,187	387	2,327	7,126
1945	3,275	949	3,981	11,334	1923	1,922	383	2,058	6,849
1944	3,818	1,024	3,292	11,212	1922	1,878	405	2,678	7,601
1943	3,671	1,020	3,202	10,862	1921	2,023	344	2,674	7,191
1942	3,012	851	3,356	10,451					
1941	3,286	973	3,816	11,763	1920	1,636	281	2,156	6,004
					1919	1,319	298	2,136	5,442
1940	3,883	964	4,332	12,951	1918	1,195	311	2,052	5,026
1939	3,925	879	4,267	12,874	1917	1,188	309	1,977	5,168
1938	4,023	857	4,978	13,438	1916[6]	1,198	276	1,867	5,459
1937	3,740	792	4,412	12,208					
1936	3,420	688	3,948	11,154					

[1] Numbers are for the last day of the reporting year, which ended on 30 September.

[2] From 1916 to 1948 the reporting year ends on 30 September with the exception of Ontario (31 March), Nova Scotia (30 November) and Quebec (31 December). Since 1949 the reporting year ends on 31 March with the exception of Quebec where it ends on 31 December. Figures given are for the last day of the reporting year.

[3] Includes convicts detained in penitentiaries as shown in series Z173-174.

[4] Oakalla Prison Farm, B.C., previously classed as a reformatory for men, was changed to a jail.

[5] Figures prior to 1946 include a few women prisoners at Oakalla Prison Farm.

[6] Figures relate to the beginning of the reporting year 1917.

Series Z202-208. Number of prisoners in training schools, reformatories and industrial farms, by sex; and in provincial adult institutions and all penal institutions, Canada, 1957 to 1975

Year	Training schools		Reformatories and industrial farms		Provincial adult institutions	Penitentiaries	All penal institutions
	Boys	Girls	Male	Female			
	202	**203**	**204**	**205**	**206**	**207**	**208**
1975[1]	..	..	—	—	11,409	8,600	20,009[2]
1974	—	—	—	—	9,987	8,499	20,407[3]
1973	—	—	—	—	9,802	9,111	20,966[4]
1972[5]	1,269	608	—	—	10,006	8,253	20,136
1971	1,308	651	—	—	10,682	7,483	20,124
1970[6]	1,501	742	—	—	11,881	7,108	21,232
1970[7]	2,154	957	—	—	11,881	7,337	22,329
1969	2,686	1,107	—	—	12,538	7,117	23,448
1968	2,552	1,104	—	—	12,686	7,026	23,368
1967	2,478	1,127	—	—	12,339	7,167	23,111
1966[8]	2,545	1,215	—	—	12,257	7,438	23,455
1965	2,706	1,332	3,970	129	8,528	7,514	24,179
1964	2,662	1,416	4,117	150	8,292	7,651	24,288
1963	2,466	1,072	3,919	171	8,665	7,219	23,512
1962	2,435	1,090	3,670	171	8,225	7,156	22,747
1961	2,382	1,019	4,012	180	7,629	6,738	21,960
1960	2,423	965	3,769	144	6,983	6,344	20,628
1959	2,339	990	3,886	172	7,108	6,295	20,790
1958	2,334	1,086	3,887	164	7,141	5,770	20,382
1957	2,132	998	3,057	145	6,537	5,432	18,301

[1] Statistics on training schools no longer published.

[2] Does not include an unknown number of juveniles in training schools.

[3] Includes 1,921 juveniles reported in training schools.

[4] Includes 2,053 juveniles reported in training schools.

[5] All institutions now reporting number of prisoners on the last day of the calendar year, 31 December.

[6] Training schools, federal penitentiaries, and Quebec prisons/jails reporting on a calendar year basis.

[7] All figures except for Quebec prisons/jails are given for the fiscal year-end, 31 March, from 1957 to 1970.

[8] Reformatories and industrial farms no longer classified separately.

Series Z209-212. Tickets of leave and pardons, Canada, 1876 to 1955

Year[1]	Total	Released under ticket of leave	Other conditional or unconditional pardon	Ticket-of-leave man granted further clemency	Year[1]	Total	Released under ticket of leave	Other conditional or unconditional pardon	Ticket-of-leave man granted further clemency
	209	210	211	212		209	210	211	212
1955	1,672	1,342	284	46	1915	1,593	1,287	231	75
1954	1,236	906	313	17	1914	1,430	1,193	175	62
1953	1,139	857	250	32	1913	1,146	980	138	28
1952	1,070	792	235	43	1912	1,035	913	94	28
1951[2]	1,127	818	243	66	1911	927	782	114	31
1950[1]	422	263	137	22	1910	740	505	121	24
1950	1,820	1,287	475	58	1909	734	578	133	23
1949	1,464	942	468	54	1908	601	396	187	18
1948	1,437	972	418	47	1907	590	419	158	13
1947	1,368	980	357	31	1906	471	306	158	7
1946	1,155	809	300	46	1905	405	219	181	5
1945	1,399	844	505	50	1904	352	192	153	7
1944	1,326	663	604	59	1903	412	189	220	3
1943	1,155	604	519	32	1902	442	247	195	—
1942	1,101	705	364	32	1901	326	169	157	—
1941	971	457	459	55	1900	302	124	178	—
1940	1,441	663	691	87	1899	240	—	240	—
1939	1,651	733	897	21	1898	153	—	153	—
1938	1,548	644	890	14	1897	163	—	163	—
1937	1,268	588	668	12	1896	143	—	143	—
1936	1,492	716	758	18	1895	193	—	193	—
1935	1,652	770	851	31	1894	159	—	159	—
1934	2,448	1,160	1,256	32	1893	107	—	107	—
1933	2,863	1,982	862	19	1892	190	—	190	—
1932	1,449	944	487	18	1891	119	—	119	—
1931	1,423	982	429	12	1890	156	—	156	—
1930	1,472	778	668	26	1889	130	—	130	—
1929	1,457	1,105	320	32	1888	147	—	147	—
1928	1,669	645	1,001	23	1887	116	—	116	—
1927	1,681	761	838	82	1886	130	—	130	—
1926	1,113	763	299	51	1885	99	—	99	—
1925	1,197	747	380	70	1884	134	—	134	—
1924	1,670	1,137	460	73	1883	126	—	126	—
1923	1,640	1,154	425	61	1882	105	—	105	—
1922	1,473	1,182	264	27	1881	103	—	103	—
1921	1,012	847	143	22	1880	123	—	123	—
1920	1,241	751	466	24	1879	117	—	117	—
1919	1,495	840	613	42	1878	153	—	153	—
1918	1,183	703	453	27	1877	122	—	122	—
1917	1,389	1,143	200	46	1876	86	—	86	—
1916	1,321	1,098	146	77					

[1] Figures for the years 1876 to 1950 are for the 12 months ending 30 September; later figures are for the calendar year.

[2] Statistics relating to Newfoundland included since 1951.

Series Z213-222.   **Parole granted, violation, and pardons, Canada, 1957 to 1975**

Year		Parole granted					Violations				Pardons[6]
Calendar	Fiscal	All parole[1]	Full parole	Mandatory supervision[2]	Day parole[3]	Day parole (temporary)[4]	Full parole	Mandatory supervision	Revocation, forfeiture	Other decisions[5]	
		213	**214**	**215**	**216**	**217**	**218**	**219**	**220**	**221**	**222**
	1975	–	3,172	2,521	1,436	941	640	746	–	–	1,344
	1974	–	2,859	1,721	1,466	607	885	575	–	–	1,268
	1973	–	3,468	941	1,201	–	1,466	248	–	–	821
	1972	5,744	–	95	1,186	–	–	24	1,513	–	404
	1971	6,053	–	–	812	–	–	–	1,222	–	–
1971		6,278	–	–	–	–	–	–	1,509	–	–
	1970	5,851	–	–	–	–	–	–	–	–	139
1970		5,923	–	–	–	–	–	–	1,004	–	–
1969		4,782	–	–	–	–	–	–	551	–	120
1968		3,518	–	–	–	–	–	–	382	–	75
1967		3,086	–	–	–	–	–	–	375	–	–
1966		2,291	–	–	–	–	–	–	112	307	–
1965		1,992	–	–	–	–	–	–	104	271	–
1964		1,754	–	–	–	–	–	–	71	195	–
1963		1,789	–	–	–	–	–	–	123	178	–
1962		1,872	–	–	–	–	–	–	110	156	–
1961		2,297	–	–	–	–	–	–	210	94	–
1960		2,525	–	–	–	–	–	–	191	–	–
1959		2,038	–	–	–	–	–	–	110	–	–
1958		994	–	–	–	–	–	–	76	–	–
1957		1,093	–	–	–	–	–	–	108	–	–

[1] All parole includes full parole, day parole, short parole, ordinary, with gradual, short, temporary, parole for deportation, and voluntary departure.
[2] Mandatory supervision came into full effect late 1971.
[3] Day parole also commenced in 1971.
[4] Day parole (temporary) was introduced during fiscal year 1973–74.
[5] Other decisions re: violations include suspension alone or combined with revocation or forfeiture.

[6] Pardons may be granted in accordance with the Criminal Records Act which was implemented in June 1970. The figures given for 1968 and 1969 were for pardons granted under the elementary sections of the Parole Act. (The major difference in the two Acts is that in the Criminal Records Act the criminal record of a persons pardoned is erased.)

Series Z223-226. Penitentiaries operating costs, Canada, 1895 to 1975

(series Z223 in thousands of dollars; series Z224 in number; series Z225 and 226 in dollars)

Year[1]	Operating cost[2]	Average population	Average operating cost per capita per year	Average operating cost per capita per diem	Year[1]	Operating cost[2]	Average population	Average operating cost per capita per year	Average operating cost per capita per diem
	223	224	225	226		223	224	225	226
1975	121,688	8,823	13,792	37.79	1935	1,889	3,895	485	1.33
1974	97,254	9,316	10,439	28.60	1934	2,104	4,358	483	1.32
1973	78,386	8,691	9,019	24.71	1933	2,285	4,425	516	1.41
1972	65,678	7,477	8,784	24.07	1932	1,984	3,931	505	1.38
1971	56,477	7,253	7,787	21.33	1931	1,873	3,434	545	1.49
1970	51,122	7,219	7,081	19.40	1930	1,457	2,868	508	1.39
1969	47,402	7,123	6,654	18.23	1929	1,351	2,643	511	1.40
1968	40,151	7,554	5,315	14.56	1928	1,331	2,423	549	1.50
1967	37,115	7,574	4,900	13.42	1927	1,237	2,456	504	1.38
1966	26,601	7,755	3,430	9.40	1926	1,179	2,396	492	1.35
1965	23,792	7,739	3,074	8.42	1925	1,205	2,217	544	1.48
1964	20,419	7,444	2,743	7.52	1924	1,129	2,373	476	1.30
1963	19,524	7,091	2,753	7.54	1923	1,442	2,582	558	1.53
1962	17,351	7,156	2,425	6.64	1922	1,365	2,417	565	1.55
1961	15,224	6,738	2,259	6.19	1921	1,503	2,058	731	2.00
1960	12,787	6,141	2,082	5.70	1920	1,068	1,832	583	1.60
1959	11,714	5,935	1,974	5.41	1919	901	1,530	589	1.61
1958	10,965	5,312	2,064	5.66	1918	845	1,513	559	1.53
1957	10,033	5,257	1,908	5.23	1917	794	1,938	410	1.12
1956	8,833	5,237	1,687	4.62	1916	809	2,074	390	1.07
1955	8,253	5,204	1,586	4.34	1915	777	1,989	390	1.07
1954	7,624	4,722	1,615	4.42	1914	763	1,946	392	1.07
1953	7,364	4,708	1,564	4.29	1913	678	1,911	355	0.97
1952	6,956	4,721	1,474	4.04	1912	612	1,853	330	0.90
1951	6,121	4,700	1,302	3.57	1911	474	1,834	258	0.70
1950	5,271	4,390	1,201	3.29	1910	491	1,824	269	0.74
1949	4,709	3,989	1,181	3.23	1909	488	1,620	301	0.83
1948	3,914	3,769	1,039	2.84	1908	500	1,418	353	0.97
1947	3,394	3,541	958	2.63	1907[1]	327	1,433	228	0.63
1946	2,979	3,175	938	2.57	1906[1]	411	1,407	292	0.80
1945	2,747	3,063	897	2.46	1905	374	1,359	275	0.75
1944	2,614	3,000	871	2.39	1904	349	1,286	272	0.74
1943	2,541	3,028	839	2.29	1903	409	1,224	335	0.92
1942	2,539	3,439	738	2.02	1902	343	1,294	265	0.79
1941	2,449	3,685	665	1.82	1901	403	1,405	287	0.79
1940	2,508	3,736	671	1.84	1900	349	1,430	244	0.67
1939	2,429	3,618	671	1.84	1899	345	1,447	238	0.65
1938	2,265	3,371	672	1.85	1898	279	1,415	197	0.54
1937	2,150	3,103	693	1.89	1897	312	1,353	230	0.63
1936	2,243	3,148	712	1.95	1896	345	1,314	263	0.72
					1895	441	1,250	353	0.97

[1] For the years 1895 to 1906 the figures are for the fiscal year ending 30 June of the year given. Figures for 1907 are for nine months ending 31 March 1907. From 1908 to 1975 the figures are for the fiscal year ending 31 March of the year given.

[2] Exclusive of capital expenditure and revenue.

Series Z227-248. Delinquency cases, by sex and by province, 1927 to 1969[1,6]

Year[2]	Newfound-land[3]		Prince Edward Island		Nova Scotia		New Brunswick		Quebec		Ontario	
	Male	Female	Male	Female	Male	Female	Male	Female	Male	Female	Male	Female
	227	228	229	230	231	232	233	234	235	236	237	238
1969[5]	687	67	2	—	665	81	568	53	6,781	634	8,941	1,573
1968[7]	628	52	10	—	624	59	566	38	5,551	516	7,476	1,235
1967	436	22	20	3	633	59	423	33	3,665	392	7,617	1,214
1966[4]	641	52	38	5	689	51	375	33	3,281	415	7,588	1,277
1965	595	34	50	—	644	64	382	17	2,534	353	7,402	1,268
1964	510	34	30	—	630	63	494	35	2,564	215	8,045	1,226
1963	478	33	61	4	675	74	427	25	2,428	215	7,348	1,103
1962	452	32	53	3	768	55	412	23	2,636	213	6,637	1,010
1961	380	20	52	—	514	37	456	31	2,549	252	5,942	877
1960	383	26	34	1	612	70	406	54	2,430	262	4,650	714
1959	247	15	39	3	577	46	337	18	2,166	244	3,647	552
1958	322	21	25	—	624	52	381	50	1,989	240	3,574	534
1957	280	21	35	—	451	41	298	26	1,193	158	3,488	563
1956	329	7	47	1	381	31	287	24	1,058	126	3,441	504
1955	243	11	30	—	363	27	187	15	890	150	2,801	337
1954	213	5	43	—	404	36	212	12	583	95	2,637	308
1953	186	10	32	1	413	30	217	18	678	95	2,653	322
1952	197	18	29	—	326	30	243	24	591	37	2,597	292
1951	167	8	51	1	458	25	237	24	1,089	91	2,729	295
1950	—	—	10	—	320	31	249	9	1,201	168	2,753	303
1949[2]	—	—	10	—	130	10	49	6	285	34	573	81
1949	—	—	45	4	405	28	177	21	1,172	151	2,301	240
1948	—	—	27	1	388	33	238	30	1,607	257	2,538	261
1947	—	—	29	1	377	35	311	23	1,555	287	2,546	284
1946	—	—	52	3	360	24	329	53	1,765	390	2,751	353
1945	—	—	99	16	459	34	298	40	1,985	402	3,132	399
1944	—	—	98	11	442	33	444	30	1,920	339	3,984	444
1943	—	—	71	18	449	39	411	18	2,721	475	3,779	399
1942	—	—	89	12	321	32	323	27	3,523	521	4,063	331
1941	—	—	72	3	331	54	413	23	3,391	576	3,201	266
1940	—	—	41	4	281	32	299	18	2,561	505	2,732	200
1939	—	—	44	4	279	30	316	19	2,166	410	2,737	178
1938	—	—	22	1	341	46	250	7	1,980	335	2,576	190
1937	—	—	48	3	476	38	348	21	2,033	334	2,861	147
1936	—	—	19	1	391	26	255	11	1,911	270	2,761	164
1935	—	—	31	3	293	19	342	13	2,233	251	2,589	164
1934	—	—	8	2	411	32	258	19	2,234	299	2,287	140
1933	—	—	10	2	333	17	337	19	1,977	293	2,365	150
1932	—	—	4	2	236	26	257	16	1,742	231	2,415	176
1931	—	—	15	—	202	15	340	46	1,613	210	2,441	177
1930	—	—	8	2	301	24	272	29	1,427	154	2,927	181
1929	—	—	7	—	269	26	190	9	1,248	175	2,802	153
1928	—	—	11	—	302	18	208	13	1,283	176	2,516	184
1927	—	—	21	—	251	15	213	15	1,469	271	2,921	135

Series Z227-248. Delinquency cases, by sex and by province, 1927 to 1969[1,6] (concluded)

Year[2]	Manitoba[5]		Saskat-chewan		Alberta		British Columbia		Yukon Territory and the Northwest Territories	
	Male	Female	Male	Female	Male	Female	Male	Female	Male	Female
	239	**240**	**241**	**242**	**243**	**244**	**245**	**246**	**247**	**248**
1969[5]	–	–	154	17	2,131	410	3,859	548	18	8
1968[7]	2,852	390	209	33	1,968	332	4,104	496	2	1
1967	1,012	216	162	20	1,540	263	2,591	414	1	7
1966[4]	897	163	195	17	1,553	215	2,351	454	17	3
1965	727	129	234	14	1,214	229	2,148	314	–	–
1964	699	94	232	17	1,440	195	2,513	300	22	7
1963	671	78	227	10	1,124	140	2,155	274	–	–
1962	648	130	189	27	1,086	112	1,842	230	46	4
1961	607	116	245	15	1,062	168	1,695	195	2	–
1960	875	144	219	12	910	121	1,867	175	–	–
1959	556	73	171	11	804	107	1,841	197	35	–
1958	686	104	76	9	776	130	1,594	194	10	–
1957	605	103	26	–	678	88	1,433	188	3	1
1956	524	69	41	3	601	114	1,254	137	5	1
1955	307	94	54	3	467	68	844	134	–	–
1954	287	54	56	3	391	37	857	99	–	–
1953	297	63	48	1	313	44	852	100	3	1
1952	319	90	75	6	261	56	780	97	–	–
1951	280	67	61	3	223	19	736	79	1	–
1950	344	56	76	–	181	23	632	56	6	–
1949[2]	155	19	30	3	52	9	159	18	–	–
1949	360	43	168	3	237	9	744	89	1	–
1948	319	45	165	4	217	20	843	156	11	–
1947	373	51	203	9	265	12	1,040	127	17	–
1946	273	25	184	11	378	27	779	99	–	–
1945	316	26	324	10	507	24	747	91	–	–
1944	374	42	399	23	543	22	671	98	–	–
1943	393	45	402	19	428	19	550	60	–	–
1942	559	43	446	20	814	21	562	51	–	–
1941	351	27	293	23	676	40	528	42	–	–
1940	310	33	235	6	542	27	568	36	1	–
1939	305	23	221	8	423	21	395	34	–	–
1938	217	17	237	4	422	18	342	30	–	–
1937	199	19	320	11	429	19	380	30	–	–
1936	281	43	225	13	391	25	397	26	–	–
1935	532	50	270	12	367	13	464	33	–	–
1934	783	59	195	21	462	11	545	39	–	1
1933	950	87	151	9	279	17	442	15	–	–
1932	1,034	109	235	21	410	22	405	22	–	–
1931	1,175	100	327	26	577	12	463	29	–	–
1930	1,281	108	437	20	638	13	578	25	–	–
1929	1,444	132	323	23	508	11	485	21	–	–
1928	1,478	139	307	25	422	4	576	37	–	–
1927	1,597	152	263	20	343	8	472	19	–	–

[1] For totals for Canada, see series Z267-269.
[2] Figures for the years 1927 to 1949 are for the 12 months ending 30 September; later figures are for the calendar year. Cases not entirely disposed of within a year (i.e., tried but sentence postponed) are included in the next year's figures.
[3] The Canadian Criminal Code came in force in Newfoundland on 1 August 1950.

[4] Prior to 1966, figures for the Yukon Territory and the Northwest Territories were given jointly in publication 85-202.
[5] See footnote (6) in series Z261-269 re: Manitoba.
[6] See footnote (7) in series Z261-269.
[7] See footnote (8) in series Z261-269.

Series Z249-260. Delinquency cases, by nature of the offence, Canada, 1927 to 1969[1]

Year[2]	Against the person	Against property with violence	Against property without violence	Wilful offences against property	Forgery and uttering	Other offences	Year[2]	Against the person	Against property with violence	Against property without violence	Wilful offences against property	Forgery and uttering	Other offences
	249	250	251	252	253	254		255	256	257	258	259	260
1969[8,9]	883	6,834	11,122	1,866	106	6,386	1945	220	1,513	2,964	1,190	29	2,993
1968[6]	849	6,754	10,509	1,784	108	7,138	1944	216	1,739	3,393	1,269	22	3,278
1967	574	4,881	8,155	1,772	96	5,265	1943	260	1,550	3,658	1,140	21	3,667
1966[7]	559	4,403	8,557	1,691	77	5,023	1942	206	1,536	4,039	1,228	11	4,738
							1941	263	1,407	3,467	1,063	14	4,096
1965	539	4,130	7,722	1,490	93	4,378							
1964	525	4,361	8,364	1,654	51	4,410	1940	208	1,261	3,058	762	8	3,134
1963	490	3,864	7,386	1,630	48	4,138	1939	190	1,207	2,926	700	13	2,577
1962	460	3,563	7,129	1,420	49	3,987	1938	187	1,122	3,062	692	9	1,963
1961	382	3,511	6,435	1,248	33	3,606	1937	186	1,222	3,143	824	10	2,331
							1936	204	1,019	3,106	791	11	2,079
1960	369	2,953	5,694	1,272	36	3,641							
1959	265	2,408	4,748	952	27	3,286	1935	248	1,031	3,562	745	12	2,081
1958	346[3]	2,268	4,436	985	36	3,320	1934	227	1,072	3,114	1,013	11	2,369
1957	254	2,005	3,764	994	28	2,634	1933	247	972	3,164	1,016	4	2,650
1956	250	1,888	3,572	839	39	2,397	1932	232	927	3,104	978	11	2,111
							1931	256	961	3,150	1,041	10	2,350
1955	181	1,548	2,767	629	29	1,871							
1954	184	1,444	2,489	673	32	1,510	1930	199	951	3,686	972	17	2,600
1953	169	1,416	2,415	770	19	1,588	1929	219	976	3,096	1,049	12	2,474
1952	172	1,456	2,496	633	25	1,286	1928	184	824	3,265	883	13	2,530
1951[4]	188	1,542	2,563	765	20	1,566	1927	179	772	3,311	1,021	7	2,895
1950	151	1,337	2,394	667	16	1,853							
1949[2]	49	310	608	163	2	491							
1949	176	1,346	2,244	600	15	1,817							
1948	204	1,229	2,400	729	15	2,578							
1947	189	1,389	2,449	677	23	2,818							
1946	173[5]	1,353	2,594	887	23	2,826							

1 For total delinquency cases, see series Z267–269.
2 Figures for the years 1927 to 1949 are for the 12 months ending 30 September; later figures are for the calendar year. Cases not entirely disposed of within the year (i.e., tried but disposition postponed) are included in the next year's figures.
3 Beginning in 1958 this series includes criminal negligence and criminal negligence in operation of motor vehicles, previously listed under heading "other offences".
4 The Canadian Criminal Code came in force in Newfoundland on 1 August

1950. Statistics on juvenile delinquency in this province are reported since 1951.
5 Beginning in 1946 this series includes intimidation, sodomy and bestiality previously listed under heading "other offences".
6 Upper age limit changed from 16 to those used by the provinces.
7 Corporal punishment was removed from dispositions in 1966.
8 After 1969, the method of counting changed from appearances to unduplicated counts of juveniles. Refer to Introduction, page 8, Juvenile Delinquents, 1970.
9 Does not include Manitoba.

Series Z261-269. Appearances of juveniles before the court and results, by sex, Canada, 1927 to 1969[7]

Year[1]	Appeared before the court[2]		Dismissed[2]		Adjourned *sine die*		Found delinquent		
	Boys	Girls	Boys	Girls	Boys	Girls	Boys	Girls	Total
	261	**262**	**263**	**264**	**265**	**266**	**267**	**268**	**269**
1969[6]	30,755	4,699	1,043	160	5,906	1,148	23,806	3,391	27,197
1968[8]	28,919	4,179	867	115	4,062	912	23,990	3,152	27,142
1967	21,288	3,335	557	77	2,631	615	18,100	2,643	20,743
1966	20,248	3,151	474	54	2,149	412	17,625	2,685	20,310
1965	18,129	2,846	451	76	1,748	348	15,930	2,422	18,352
1964	18,968	2,492	547	65	1,242	241	17,179	2,186	19,365
1963	17,603	2,283	668	108	1,341	213	15,594	1,962	17,556
1962	16,578	2,129	730	113	1,079	177	14,769	1,839	16,608
1961	15,024	1,952	517	53	1,003	188	13,504	1,711	15,215
1960	14,137	1,872	455	62	1,296	231	12,386	1,579	13,965
1959	11,843	1,486	330	40	1,093	180	10,420[3]	1,266[4]	11,686
1958	11,568	1,566	360	56	1,151	176	10,057[3]	1,334[4]	11,391
1957	10,482	1,446	292	39	1,700	218	8,490	1,189	9,679
1956	9,120	1,195	200	21	952	157	7,968	1,017	8,985
1955	7,186	1,001	180	27	820	135	6,186	839	7,025
1954	6,956	795	216	21	1,057	125	5,683	649	6,332
1953	6,999	830	185	31	1,122	114	5,692	685	6,377
1952	6,465	748	168	10	879	88	5,418	650	6,068
1951[5]	6,805	716	185	10	588	94	6,032	612	6,644
1950	6,548	756	176	21	600	89	5,772	646	6,418
1949[1]	1,623	199	39	3	141	16	1,443	180	1,623
1949	6,362	676	146	20	606	68	5,610	588	6,198
1948	6,988	890	179	11	461	72	6,348	807	7,155
1947	7,363	902	191	6	456	67	6,716	829	7,545
1946	7,617	1,090	171	12	575	93	6,871	985	7,856
1945	8,599	1,157	150	12	582	103	7,867	1,042	8,909
1944	10,274	1,280	240	7	1,159	231	8,875	1,042	9,917
1943	10,795	1,430	246	21	1,345	317	9,204	1,092	10,296
1942	12,388	1,414	237	24	1,451	332	10,700	1,058	11,758
1941	10,812	1,325	226	4	1,330	267	9,256	1,054	10,310
1940	8,857	1,119	232	7	1,055	251	7,570	861	8,431
1939	8,514	983	224	11	1,404	245	6,886	727	7,613
1938	8,086	843	240	5	1,459	190	6,387	648	7,035
1937	8,886	789	280	5	1,512	162	7,094	622	7,716
1936	8,060	708	224	14	1,205	115	6,631	579	7,210
1935	8,645	752	180	7	1,344	187	7,121	558	7,679
1934	8,662	786	253	10	1,226	153	7,183	623	7,806
1933	8,154	708	274	9	1,036	90	6,844	609	7,453
1932	8,420	734	368	17	1,314	92	6,738	625	7,363
1931	9,183	767	345	15	1,685	137	7,153	615	7,768
1930	10,162	743	296	14	1,997	173	7,869	556	8,425
1929	9,812	697	218	19	2,318	128	7,276	550	7,826
1928	9,488	645	209	7	2,176	42	7,103	596	7,699
1927	9,520	699	237	11	1,733	53	7,550	635	8,185

[1] Figures for the years 1927 to 1949 are for the 12 months ending 30 September; later figures are for the calendar year. Cases not entirely disposed of within a year (i.e., tried but disposition postponed) are included in the next year's figures.

[2] From 1927 to 1949 figures in series Z263-264 refer to boys and girls brought to court for major offences only. In the same period series Z261-262 do not include boys and girls brought to court for minor offences whose cases were dismissed, although they do include those on minor charges whose cases were not dismissed. From 1950 onward those charged with minor offences whose cases were dismissed are included in all series Z261-264.

[3] In 1959 the figure includes 33 cases and in 1958, 892 cases "adjourned *sine die*" compiled for statistical purposes under the heading "found delinquent".

[4] In 1959 the figure includes two cases and in 1958, 64 cases "adjourned *sine die*" compiled for statistical purposes under the heading "found delinquent".

[5] The Canadian Criminal Code came in force in Newfoundland on 1 August 1950. Statistics on juvenile delinquency in this province are reported since 1951.

[6] Does not include Manitoba which initiated a new program reporting on juvenile delinquency. Captions on tables for appearances are disaggregated and, therefore, not comparable with captions on series Z261-269.

[7] After 1969, the system of counting changed from appearances to unduplicated counts of juveniles. Refer to Introduction, page 8, Juvenile Delinquents, 1970 (Catalogue 85-202).

[8] Upper age limit changed from under 16 to that prescribed by each province.

Series Z270-281. Convictions for major offences of juveniles under 16 years, Canada and the provinces, 1886 to 1926

Year[1]	Canada	Prince Edward Island	Nova Scotia	New Brunswick	Quebec	Ontario	Manitoba	Saskat- chewan	Alberta	British Columbia	Northwest Terri- tories[2]	Yukon Territory[3]
	270	271	272	273	274	275	276	277	278	279	280	281
Major offences												
1926	5,299	6	195	55	870	2,282	1,002	246	317	326	—	—
1925	5,246	18	263	77	971	2,230	915	280	277	215	—	—
1924	4,722	31	251	59	782	2,044	750	362	251	192	—	—
1923	4,165	10	253	60	864	1,633	581	249	268	246	—	1
1922	4,065	5	167	45	655	1,852	627	196	278	240	—	—
Indictable offences												
1921	3,227	9	149	77	821	1,597	333	27	201	13	—	—
1920	3,355	15	133	59	771	1,707	436	1	226	7	—	—
1919	3,876	17	104	92	960	2,023	467	1	200	12	—	—
1918	4,104	25	154	104	831	2,202	553	32	200	3	—	—
1917	3,606	12	155	104	709	2,100	335	8	176	7	—	—
1916	3,157	3	125	55	658	1,865	312	18	116	5	—	—
1915	3,050	4	110	72	626	1,822	215	29	163	6	—	3
1914	2,628	7	97	50	668	1,453	210	39	101	2	—	1
1913	2,313	4	87	48	653	1,131	251	23	110	5	—	1
1912	1,881	—	72	28	463	992	181	16	121	8	—	—
1911	1,439	2	27	23	179	844	159	20	134	49	—	2
1910	1,373	17	75	49	252	834	11	12	71	52	—	—
1909	1,150	7	69	32	228	689	30	8	34	52	—	1
1908	1,204	5	38	28	277	661	117	26	43	9	—	—
1907	1,004	5	48	16	230	499	148	3	54	1	—	—
1906	782	4	25	22	194	383	116	1	33	4	—	—
1905	800	2	42	16	204	431	75	—	24	—	3	3
1904	697	2	66	14	124	389	81	—	14	—	4	3
1903	1,038	6	51	24	279	540	63	—	73	—	1	1
1902	859	11	50	33	183	492	38	—	47	—	4	1
1901	1,017	3	42	27	268	600	17	—	56	—	4	—
1900	915	6	68	28	208	509	48	—	42	—	6	—
1899	936	2	40	22	284	517	39	—	29	—	3	—
1898	836	16	35	17	239	443	14	—	70	—	2	—
1897	723	13	32	8	209	404	29	—	28	—	—	—
1896	660	11	29	13	143	445	13	—	4	—	2	—
1895	790	11	13	18	226	480	27	—	10	—	5	—
1894	687	11	23	19	233	372	17	—	9	—	3	—
1893	668	2	35	20	169	426	5	—	11	—	—	—
1892[4]	714	3	40	19	182	465	4	—	1	—	—	—
1891	615	2	16	16	189	382	7	—	1	—	2	—
1890	594	4	15	11	182	364	14	—	4	—	—	—
1889	687	4	31	4	238	391	15	—	4	—	—	—
1888	602	—	8	9	159	410	13	—	3	—	—	—
1887	418	3	20	2	78	307	6	—	—	—	2	—
1886	386	—	16	5	78	282	2	—	1	—	2	—

[1] Figures are for 12 months ending 30 September of the year given. Cases not entirely disposed of within a year (i.e., tried but disposition postponed) are included in next year's figures.

[2] Figures for the years 1886 to 1905 include statistics relating to that part of the Northwest Territories which became the provinces of Alberta and Saskatchewan. Figures for the years 1886 to 1899 include statistics relating to the Yukon Territory.

[3] For the years 1906 to 1910 and 1913 to 1922 figures include data on the Northwest Territories.

[4] Prior to 1893 only one offence is recorded for a person who is charged with more than one offence of the same kind at the same trial.

Series Z282. Juveniles adjudged delinquent, Canada,[1] 1927 to 1973

Year	Number of convictions	Year	Number of convictions	Year	Number of convictions
	282		282		282
1973	44,151	1955	6,542	1935	5,514
1972	42,183	1954	6,015	1934	5,353
1971	38,798	1953[5]	5,990	1933	5,144
		1952	6,068	1932	5,096
1970	37,119	1951[7]	6,644	1931	5,311
1969	28,399				
1968[1]	22,984	1950[8]	6,418	1930	5,653
1968[3]	23,482	1950[9,10]	8,041	1929	5,106
1967[4]	22,583	1949[10]	4,544	1928	5,063
1967[6]	18,248	1948[11]	4,591	1927[2]	5,156
1966	17,844	1947	4,683		
		1946	4,949		
1965	16,107				
1964	17,005	1945	5,758		
1963	15,591	1944	6,529		
1962	14,519	1943	6,494		
1961	13,358	1942	6,920		
		1941	6,204		
1960	12,331				
1959	10,443	1940	5,298		
1958	10,307	1939	5,018		
1957	8,811	1938	5,055		
1956	8,238	1937	5,224		
		1936	4,970		

[1] The revised number shown for 1968 does not include Manitoba, as a new juvenile deliquents program was introduced during that year with a different method of enumerating juvenile delinquents. (This program included "nonjudicial" and "no contact" cases where the child does not appear before a judge.) Although new, separate provincial juvenile programs were introduced in Manitoba (1968). Alberta (1971), and Ontario (1972), the figures given for and since these years are comprehensive for Canada, including these provinces (excepting Manitoba in 1968).

[2] Prior to 1927, the disposition "adjourned sine die" was considered equivalent to "suspended sentence". Since 1927, these cases have been treated similarly to those "dismissed".

[3] From 1968 on, the figures are given for juveniles in accordance with the provincial age limits.

[4] 1967 figures have been provided in original and revised form to allow comparability with 1968 figures.

[5] From 1927 to 1949, the basic unit of counting was appearance at court, and this included repeated appearances of the same child within a prescribed year. In 1953, however, provision was made to determine an unduplicated count of juveniles found delinquent within a year and this method has continued to the present. By this method, a juvenile may be counted only once during the same year, regardless of how many additional times he or she may be adjudged delinquent. This series provides a duplicated count from 1927 to 1952 and an unduplicated count from 1953 to 1973.

[6] Up to 1967, figures are for juveniles under age 16 regardless of the provincial age limit.

[7] The 1951 total of 6,644 includes for the first time cases (175) from Newfoundland. In all subsequent years, figures from Newfoundland are included.

[8] In 1950, the prescribed year for statistical reporting changed from fiscal (1 October to 30 September) to calendar (1 January to 31 December). This figure is for the calendar year ending 31 December 1950.

[9] This figure is for the period 31 October 1949 to 31 December 1950.

[10] The categories "major" and "minor" offences were used from 1922 to 1949. In 1950, they were replaced with the designation, "delinquency". A major offence committed by a juvenile was regarded as corresponding to an indictable offence committed by an adult.

[11] The expression "conviction of juveniles" was last used in 1948. From then on, a juvenile is "adjudged" or "found" delinquent.

Series Z283-291. Delinquency cases, by disposition, Canada, 1927 to 1969[1]

Year[2]	Reprimand	Indefinite detention	Release on probation		Fine or restitution	Training school	Final disposition suspended	Corporal punishment	Mental hospitals[3]
			Supervision of court	Care of parents					
	283	284	285	286	287	288	289	290	291
1969	653	235	13,309	1,880	3,264	2,334	5,500	—	22
1968	983	298	13,563	1,296	3,728	2,167	5,081	—	26
1967	854	93	11,268	1,116	2,230	1,978	3,185	—	19
1966[5]	791	90	10,826	1,014	2,343	1,971	3,258	—	17
1965	773	80	10,021	550	2,133	1,925	2,845	—	25
1964	1,062	139	9,624	612	2,247	1,967	3,699	—	15
1963	977	99	8,292	462	2,460	2,043	3,180	—	43
1962	697	89	8,827	369	2,219	1,862	2,533	—	12
1961	544	89	7,341	644	2,148	1,974	2,466	—	9
1960	442	42	7,413	518	2,289	1,791	1,456	—	14
1959	236	9	6,151	412	2,810	1,678	1,381	—	9
1958	504	13	5,728	294	1,624	1,822	1,389	3	14
1957	460	63	3,822	300	2,261	1,563	1,202	1	7
1956	359	30	3,155	404	2,015	1,440	1,577	—	5
1955	181	50	3,067	365	1,064	1,172	1,118	—	8
1954	199	27	2,595	174	1,095	1,121	1,119	2	—
1953	227	28	2,620	186	1,147	1,107	1,062	—	—
1952	243	1	2,412	148	1,015	1,149	1,095	2	3
1951[4]	309	45	2,313	154	1,433	1,141	1,247	2	—
1950	354	26	2,392	94	1,148	1,144	1,257	3	—
1949[2]	139	13	533	25	341	300	272	—	—
1949	196	39	2,141	98	1,655	1,036	1,029	4	—
1948	248	47	2,201	55	1,850	1,120	1,622	12	—
1947	182	40	2,273	69	2,116	1,108	1,733	24	—
1946	233	53	2,291	67	1,854	1,180	2,150	28	—
1945	352	65	2,698	109	2,367	1,348	1,947	23	—
1944	395	92	2,780	112	2,547	1,376	2,551	64	—
1943	464	101	2,854	140	1,962	1,401	3,322	52	—
1942	432	118	3,069	83	2,302	1,454	4,249	51	—
1941	422	139	5,024	130	1,397	1,332	1,831	35	—
1940	296	163	3,448	33	823	1,194	2,433	41	—
1939	404	156	2,262	28	608	984	3,143	28	—
1938	383	45	2,705	38	472	847	2,497	48	—
1937	474	48	3,862	37	608	774	1,864	49	—
1936	470	27	3,660	36	528	779	1,653	57	—
1935	482	17	4,030	61	510	743	1,705	131	—
1934	821	22	3,928	30	337	670	1,965	33	—
1933	902	15	3,592	27	426	666	1,799	26	—
1932	845	15	3,294	81	544	780	1,772	32	—
1931	902	32	3,743	62	938	629	1,438	24	—
1930	758	70	3,522	58	1,268	719	2,008	22	—
1929	652	126	3,001	196	1,835	660	1,318	38	—
1928	1,093	200	2,698	137	1,327	631	1,549	64	—
1927	825	346	2,559	158	1,639	669	1,880	109	—

[1] For total delinquency cases, see series Z267-269.
[2] Figures for the years 1927 to 1949 are for the 12-month period ending 30 September; later figures are for the calendar year. Cases not entirely disposed of within the year (i.e., tried but disposition postponed) are included in next year's figures.

[3] Category added in 1952.
[4] The Canadian Criminal Code came in force in Newfoundland on 1 August 1950. Statistics on juvenile delinquency in this province are reported since 1951.
[5] Corporal punishment deleted.

Series Z292-304. Census and estimated population aged 16 years and over, Canada and the provinces, 1881 to 1975

(thousands)

Year[1]	Canada[2]	Newfoundland[3]	Prince Edward Island	Nova Scotia	New Brunswick	Quebec	Ontario	Manitoba	Saskatchewan	Alberta	British Columbia	Northwest Territories[4]	Yukon Territory[4]
	292	293	294	295	296	297	298	299	300	301	302	303	304
1975	16,316	348	82	578	466	4,481	5,933	727	651	1,227	1,790	21	13
1974	15,885	339	80	566	451	4,378	5,784	716	636	1,176	1,728	21	12
1973	15,449	334	78	554	439	4,275	5,614	700	629	1,141	1,653	21	13
1972	15,086	325	76	541	427	4,191	5,478	690	626	1,109	1,591	20	12
1971	14,742	315	74	531	417	4,113	5,345	682	625	1,079	1,532	19	12
1970	14,412	308	72	522	407	4,055	5,193	673	628	1,046	1,480	18	11
1969	14,070	304	72	513	402	3,988	5,033	665	633	1,012	1,422	17	10
1968	13,733	295	71	503	396	3,903	4,907	654	629	980	1,372	16	9
1967	13,389	288	70	493	388	3,815	4,776	643	621	948	1,323	16	9
1966	13,048	282	69	487	381	3,722	4,635	638	616	926	1,268	16	9
1965	12,705	277	68	482	376	3,625	4,490	635	608	910	1,210	15	9
1964	12,420	272	68	479	370	3,536	4,373	629	601	895	1,172	15	9
1963	12,157	268	67	475	367	3,453	4,267	623	595	879	1,138	15	9
1962	11,935	262	67	472	364	3,373	4,191	614	595	861	1,113	15	9
1961	11,727	256	65	466	358	3,294	4,130	606	594	841	1,095	13	9
1960	11,535	252	64	461	354	3,219	4,074	598	589	819	1,083	13	9
1959	11,335	249	63	457	351	3,148	4,004	591	586	797	1,068	12	8
1958	11,117	246	63	452	346	3,075	3,927	582	578	775	1,055	12	8
1957	10,890	242	62	449	342	3,005	3,841	577	574	754	1,025	12	8
1956	10,607	238	63	447	339	2,927	3,714	573	580	733	974	12	8
1955	10,419	234	64	441	336	2,872	3,643	570	581	717	943	11	7
1954	10,220	230	65	436	333	2,810	3,568	563	581	699	917	11	7
1953	9,992	225	66	432	330	2,747	3,475	558	577	676	891	10	6
1952	9,787	220	65	427	328	2,693	3,394	553	568	655	868	10	6
1951	9,546	214	64	422	323	2,622	3,296	542	562	638	847	10	6
1950	9,410	216	63	424	325	2,583	3,235	541	567	623	835	—	—
1949	9,277	216	62	421	325	2,538	3,180	536	569	606	823	—	—
1948	8,918	—	62	421	322	2,489	3,122	532	577	587	807	—	—
1947	8,784	—	64	420	318	2,452	3,072	530	577	569	783	—	—
1946	8,642	—	64	416	315	2,408	3,024	523	576	558	758	—	—
1945	8,511	—	63	425	309	2,365	2,959	527	579	565	720	—	—
1944	8,426	—	62	421	305	2,327	2,930	527	578	566	709	—	—
1943	8,313	—	62	419	306	2,294	2,896	523	577	548	688	—	—
1942	8,201	—	61	408	307	2,244	2,872	523	579	540	668	—	—
1941	8,083	—	65	398	302	2,197	2,796	524	609	552	630	7	4
1940	7,963	—	65	393	298	2,149	2,761	523	607	547	622	—	—
1939	7,842	—	64	386	293	2,101	2,720	518	606	542	611	—	—
1938	7,719	—	65	381	290	2,049	2,684	510	608	536	597	—	—
1937	7,592	—	64	374	284	2,003	2,644	502	608	530	583	—	—
1936	7,473	—	64	368	280	1,957	2,609	493	608	520	574	—	—
1935	7,347	—	63	360	274	1,929	2,562	487	601	513	558	—	—
1934	7,233	—	61	353	268	1,906	2,521	483	592	504	546	—	—
1933	7,117	—	60	346	264	1,873	2,483	478	585	495	534	—	—
1932	7,001	—	59	340	259	1,841	2,444	472	578	485	523	—	—
1931	6,883	—	58	335	255	1,791	2,409	466	574	477	511	6	3
1930	6,735	—	58	335	253	1,752	2,372	453	558	459	495	—	—
1929	6,589	—	58	335	252	1,712	2,331	440	541	439	481	—	—
1928	6,430	—	58	334	250	1,670	2,284	426	523	418	466	—	—
1927	6,265	—	57	333	248	1,626	2,234	412	505	398	451	—	—
1926	6,109	—	57	332	247	1,581	2,189	399	488	379	437	—	—
1925	5,990	—	56	332	244	1,547	2,144	393	477	375	422	—	—
1924	5,871	—	56	332	243	1,509	2,101	387	465	371	407	—	—
1923	5,767	—	57	332	241	1,474	2,063	382	457	368	394	—	—
1922	5,691	—	59	335	241	1,445	2,035	379	451	366	381	—	—
1921	5,596	—	58	335	240	1,409	1,996	374	443	364	367	5	3
1911	4,694	—	61	316	220	1,192	1,739	294	317	247	296	4	7
1901	3,411	—	64	294	206	975	1,452	152	54	43	132	15	25
1891	2,969	—	66	280	194	868	1,336	92	—	—	72	61[5]	—
1881	2,552	—	65	264	190	783	1,150	37	—	—	34	31[5]	—

[1] Figures for 1881 to 1921, 1931, 1941, 1951, 1956, 1961, 1966, and 1971 are census figures. Figures for 1972 to 1975 are subject to revision when 1976 Census figures become available.

[2] Owing to rounding, totals shown for Canada do not necessarily correspond to sums of data shown for provinces and territories. Estimated totals for intercensal years 1922 to 1950 do not include figures for the Northwest Territories and the Yukon Territory.

[3] Newfoundland became part of the Confederation in 1949.

[4] Estimates for the intercensal years prior to 1951 not available.

[5] Includes figures for Saskatchewan, Alberta and the Yukon Territory.

Series Z305-328. Census and estimated population aged 7-15 years, by sex, Canada and the provinces, 1927 to 1975

(thousands)

Year[1]	Canada[2]		Newfoundland[3]		Prince Edward Island		Nova Scotia		New Brunswick		Quebec	
	Male	Female	Male	Female	Male	Female	Male	Female	Male	Female	Male	Female
	305	**306**	**307**	**308**	**309**	**310**	**311**	**312**	**313**	**314**	**315**	**316**
1975	2,044	1,952	60	58	11	11	76	73	65	62	562	538
1974	2,083	1,989	61	58	12	11	78	74	66	63	581	556
1973	2,110	2,017	62	59	12	11	79	75	67	64	595	570
1972	2,127	2,030	61	59	12	11	80	76	68	64	606	580
1971	2,123	2,029	60	58	12	11	80	76	68	65	609	584
1970	2,100	2,009	60	58	12	11	80	75	68	65	611	586
1969	2,078	1,988	60	58	12	11	80	75	68	65	610	585
1968	2,047	1,961	60	57	11	11	78	74	68	65	606	581
1967	2,011	1,927	59	57	11	11	77	73	68	65	599	574
1966	1,957	1,878	58	57	11	11	76	73	68	65	589	565
1965	1,920	1,838	58	56	11	11	76	73	68	65	578	554
1964	1,876	1,796	57	56	11	11	76	73	67	65	566	544
1963	1,832	1,756	57	55	11	11	76	72	67	65	554	533
1962	1,787	1,713	56	54	11	11	75	72	67	65	542	522
1961	1,739	1,664	55	53	11	11	74	71	67	64	530	509
1960	1,673	1,603	52	51	11	10	72	69	65	62	514	495
1959	1,605	1,538	50	50	10	10	70	67	62	60	496	478
1958	1,538	1,477	48	47	10	10	68	65	60	58	480	463
1957	1,466	1,409	46	46	10	10	67	64	58	56	463	448
1956	1,390	1,338	44	44	10	9	65	63	56	54	444	429
1955	1,308	1,256	43	42	10	10	62	59	55	52	421	405
1954	1,248	1,199	41	39	10	9	61	58	53	50	399	385
1953	1,191	1,145	39	37	10	9	59	56	51	48	383	369
1952	1,140	1,098	37	36	9	9	57	55	49	47	368	355
1951	1,095	1,056	35	34	9	8	56	54	47	46	353	341
1950	1,063	1,029	33	33	9	8	54	52	46	45	344	334
1949	1,041	1,010	32	32	8	8	53	50	45	44	336	328
1948	988	962	—	—	8	8	52	50	44	43	329	322
1947	973	947	—	—	8	8	51	49	43	42	322	316
1946	960	938	—	—	8	8	51	49	43	42	317	312
1945	951	933	—	—	8	8	51	50	42	41	315	312
1944	966	941	—	—	9	8	52	50	42	42	319	314
1943	971	951	—	—	9	8	52	50	43	42	321	318
1942	981	960	—	—	9	8	51	50	44	43	323	319
1941	988	967	—	—	9	9	51	49	43	43	324	320
1940	994	973	—	—	9	8	50	48	44	43	327	322
1939	1,007	984	—	—	9	9	51	49	44	43	331	326
1938	1,015	991	—	—	8	8	51	49	44	43	334	329
1937	1,017	996	—	—	8	8	51	49	45	44	333	329
1936	1,019	999	—	—	8	8	51	50	44	43	332	327
1935	1,022	1,003	—	—	9	8	52	50	45	44	322	319
1934	1,022	1,003	—	—	9	9	53	51	45	44	312	310
1933	1,014	994	—	—	9	9	53	51	45	44	303	301
1932	1,001	979	—	—	9	9	52	51	45	43	294	293
1931	991	970	—	—	9	8	52	50	44	42	294	292
1930	976	957	—	—	9	8	52	50	43	42	288	288
1929	958	944	—	—	9	8	52	50	43	41	280	283
1928	942	929	—	—	9	8	52	50	42	41	272	279
1927	925	915	—	—	9	8	51	50	42	40	267	273

Series Z305-328. Census and estimated population aged 7-15 years, by sex, Canada and the provinces, 1927 to 1975 (concluded)

(thousands)

Year[1]	Ontario		Manitoba		Saskatchewan		Alberta		British Columbia		Yukon Territory and the Northwest Territories[4]	
	Male	Female	Male	Female	Male	Female	Male	Female	Male	Female	Male	Female
	317	318	319	320	321	322	323	324	325	326	327	328
1975[5]	717	682	89	85	84	81	166	159	207	197	7	6
1974[5]	727	692	90	87	87	83	167	160	208	199	7	6
1973[5]	733	697	92	88	89	86	169	162	207	199	7	6
1972[5]	734	699	93	89	92	88	169	162	206	197	6	6
1971	728	694	94	89	94	90	169	161	203	195	6	6
1970	714	680	93	89	96	92	165	157	198	190	5	5
1969	699	668	94	90	97	93	162	154	193	185	5	5
1968	685	655	93	89	97	93	158	151	187	180	5	5
1967	669	641	93	89	97	92	154	147	180	173	5	4
1966	647	619	92	88	96	92	148	141	171	164	4	4
1965	629	601	92	88	95	91	146	139	163	156	4	4
1964	611	583	91	87	93	90	142	135	157	150	4	4
1963	593	567	89	86	92	88	136	131	152	145	4	4
1962	577	550	88	84	91	87	131	125	147	140	4	4
1961	558	531	85	82	89	85	125	120	142	136	4	3
1960	533	508	82	79	87	83	119	114	136	130	3	3
1959[6]	507	483	79	75	85	80	113	107	129	124	3	3
1958[6]	482	460	76	73	81	78	107	102	123	119	3	3
1957[6]	452	432	74	70	78	75	101	96	115	111	3	2
1956	420	402	71	67	77	74	95	91	106	102	3	3
1955	386	371	68	65	75	73	89	85	97	93	2	2
1954	368	353	65	62	74	71	85	82	91	87	2	2
1953	348	335	62	60	71	69	81	78	86	82	2	2
1952	331	317	60	58	70	67	77	74	81	78	2	2
1951	317	304	58	56	69	66	74	71	76	74	2	2
1950	306	296	57	54	69	67	72	70	73	71	—	—
1949	301	289	56	54	69	68	70	69	70	69	—	—
1948	294	285	55	54	70	68	68	67	67	66	—	—
1947	290	281	55	53	71	69	67	65	66	64	—	—
1946	287	279	55	53	72	70	66	64	62	61	—	—
1945	282	275	55	53	74	71	67	65	58	58	—	—
1944	286	278	56	54	77	73	67	66	58	56	—	—
1943	288	281	57	55	78	75	67	66	57	56	—	—
1942	292	285	58	57	80	78	68	66	56	55	—	—
1941	292	284	61	59	85	83	70	69	54	53	—	—
1940	291	284	62	60	88	85	70	69	54	53	—	—
1939	295	287	63	61	90	88	71	70	55	53	—	—
1938	296	288	64	62	92	89	71	70	54	53	—	—
1937	297	289	65	63	94	91	71	70	54	53	—	—
1936	296	289	66	65	96	93	73	72	53	52	—	—
1935	301	293	68	67	98	96	73	72	56	54	—	—
1934	304	297	69	67	100	98	74	73	57	55	—	—
1933	303	295	70	68	101	98	74	73	56	55	—	—
1932	300	291	70	68	101	99	74	72	56	55	—	—
1931	296	286	70	68	100	98	73	71	55	53	—	—
1930	291	283	70	68	99	96	71	69	54	52	—	—
1929	285	280	70	68	97	94	70	68	52	51	—	—
1928	282	275	70	68	96	93	68	66	51	50	—	—
1927	276	273	70	68	94	91	67	65	50	48	—	—

[1] Figures for 1931, 1941, 1951, 1956, 1961, 1966, and 1971 are census figures. Figures for 1972 to 1975 are subject to revision when 1976 Census figures become available.

[2] Owing to rounding, totals shown for Canada do not necessarily correspond to sums of data shown for provinces and territories. Prior to 1951 estimated totals do not include figures for the Yukon Territory and the Northwest Territories.

[3] Newfoundland became part of the Confederation in 1949.

[4] Figures prior to 1951 not available.

[5] Subject to revision when the 1976 Census figures become available.

[6] Please note addition of these revised figures.

INDEX

INDEX